-9

TENNY.

Longmans' Annotated English Poets

GENERAL EDITOR: F. W. BATESON

*Plate 1* Tennyson aged about 31. By Samuel Laurence

# THE POEMS OF
# TENNYSON

EDITED BY

CHRISTOPHER
RICKS

LONGMANS

LONGMANS, GREEN AND CO LTD
London & Harlow
*Associated companies, branches and representatives throughout the world*



*First published 1969*

*Made and printed in Great Britain by William Clowes and Sons Ltd London and Beccles*

# Contents



POEMS

## IDYLLS OF THE KING



## APPENDICES

# List of Illustrations

# Note by the General Editor

This series has been planned to apply to the major English poets the requirements, critical and scholarly, that a serious reading of their poems entails today. Whereas editorial emphasis has recently been on what may be called textual refinements, sometimes carried to grotesque extremes, Longmans' Annotated English Poets concerns itself as a series primarily with the *meaning* of the various texts in their separate contexts. With the aids provided in the table of dates, the headnotes and the footnotes, the modern reader should have all, or almost all, that he requires both for aesthetic appreciation and for proper emotional response to the whole poetic corpus of each poet represented.

Our ideal of comprehension, for the reader, combined with comprehensiveness, for the poet, has three logical consequences:

1. Since an essential clue to an author's intentions at any point is provided, on the one hand, by what he has already written and, on the other hand, by what he will write later, an editor will print his poems as far as possible in the order in which they were composed.
2. A poet writing in a living language, such as English, requires elucidation of a different kind from that suitable to the poet of a dead language, such as Sanskrit, Latin or Old English: with minor exceptions vocabulary and syntax can be taken for granted, but sources, allusions, implications and stylistic devices need to be spelt out.
3. Since the reader in any English-speaking country will tend to pronounce an English poet of the past (at any rate to Chaucer) as if he was a contemporary, whatever impedes the reader's sympathetic identification with the poet that is implicit in that fact–whether of spelling, punctuation or the use of initial capitals–must be regarded as undesirable. A modern pronunciation demands a modern presentation, except occasionally for rhymes (e.g. *bind–wind*) or obsolete archaisms (*eremite*, hermit).

Some exceptions have had to be admitted to the principles summarized above, but they have been few and unimportant.

F. W. BATESON

# Preface

*Text*

The text is that of the Eversley edition of Tennyson's *Works* (nine volumes, Macmillan, 1907–8), which was carefully edited by Hallam Lord Tennyson. *Eversley* has been collated with the one-volume edition of 1894 (Macmillan), which includes Tennyson's late revisions, and the very few differences in wording between *1894* and *Eversley* are noted. When the text below departs in its wording from *Eversley*, this too is noted. But the punctuation has sometimes been silently corrected; *Eversley* omits punctuation, especially at the end of a line, and in such cases the punctuation has been supplied, usually from *1894*. Modern practice has been followed (in variants as well as text) in the spelling of such words as 'though' and 'through' (instead of 'tho'' and 'thro''); in supplying the *e* for such words as 'Heav'n' and 'th''; and in using ed/èd. But Tennyson's use of *-t* ('slipt') has been preserved.

The text for all the poems which were not included in Tennyson's final edition (such poems are marked*) is specified in each case. The present is the first collected edition to include all the poems which Tennyson published, together with those since published by his son Hallam and by his grandson Sir Charles Tennyson, and those surviving in MS. Quotations from Tennyson's notes expand his references (*Ael. Lamprid.* is given as *Aelius Lampridius*), and emend their system of reference to accord with the practice in the other notes. Not all of the notes in *Eversley* are reproduced, though most which still have much relevance, whether critical, historical or biographical. *Eversley* is the source of all statements by Tennyson, Hallam Tennyson or Edward FitzGerald for which no specific reference is given. Those poems such as *Locksley Hall* which use an exceptionally long line have been set in smaller print, to avoid what is usually an ugly and awkward breaking of the lines.

*Published variants*

The footnotes record all differences in wording between Tennyson's first published text of a poem and that of *Eversley/1894*. Readings from his errata slips are silently incorporated except when the change of wording is a genuine revision (in which case both readings are given), not a correction of a printer's error. But no record is given of changes in wording which Tennyson introduced later than his first published text and then withdrew before *Eversley/1894*–except when such variants are of especial interest (e.g. the close of *The Vision of Sin*, where Tennyson, in *1865* alone, added two lines). Variants in punctuation, capitalization, spelling, etc. are not recorded. The notes follow Tennyson's own practice in speaking of *Poems* (published December 1832, with the title-page dated 1833) as *1832*. In certain cases, an earlier reading survived inadvertently in some editions though definitively amended in others. Thus 'blowing' in *Maud* i 582 was changed to the final reading, 'glowing', in *A Selection* (1865)–but 'blowing' is still to be found in the 1867 reprint of *Maud*. Since there can be no doubt of Tennyson's intentions, the textual point is one which may be left to the bibliographer. The formula adopted in such cases ignores the inadvertent lingerers:

*glowing*] *1865 Selection*; blowing *1855–65*.

*MS variants*

One day there will be an edition of Tennyson which records all MS variants–in ten large volumes? But Longmans' Annotated English Poets do not aim to be textually all-inclusive, and in any case the crucial MSS at Trinity College, Cambridge, may not be copied or quoted *in perpetuity*. Nevertheless, information may be elicited from the Trinity MSS, and there are very important MSS elsewhere which are not under interdiction. So, despite a certain arbitrariness, it has seemed worth giving a selection of MS variants. Since the authenticity of the MSS is beyond question, no note is made of whose hand a particular MS is written in; most are in Tennyson's hand, and most of the rest are in those of his family. In selecting MS variants, the principles ordinarily were: that the poem for which such variants are given is important; or that the MS variant is important; or that many years elapsed between composition and publication. In the case of such poems as *Ulysses* or *In Memoriam*, it seemed right to quote all such MS variants as may be quoted. For certain of the poems, it is specifically noted that all MS variants are given, but this has not been noted throughout. When printing poems from MS, Hallam Tennyson and Sir Charles Tennyson sometimes provided titles not deriving, apparently, from the MS. The family tradition is itself worth retaining in such cases (and there may have been MSS not now extant). In some few cases, however, where the authority of a title might be of some importance, the headnote records that the title is not in the MS cited. When it is noted that all MS variants have been given, the footnotes do not explicitly state (though they implicitly provide) the readings of MSS or trial editions when such readings agree with those of the first published editions. It is to be understood in such cases that the MS readings are those of the earliest published text (or cited trial edition) unless specifically noted otherwise.

*MS 1st reading* usually implies that a subsequent correction to the MS brought it into the wording of the first published text. In accordance with the practice of Hallam Tennyson and of Sir Charles Tennyson, MS material (whether poems, fragments or variants) is not reproduced *literatim*; spelling and capitalization have been modified, and punctuation has been amended and added. This applies to all poems which Tennyson left in MS, including those which have since been published; wherever possible such poems have been newly edited from the MSS. In a sympathetic review (*Notes and Queries*, September 1966) of Kenneth Allott's *Arnold* in this series, J. C. Maxwell expressed doubts about such modifying of MS material. But in an edition which neither seeks to be nor (for external reasons) could be a definitive record of all MS variants, it seems best to give precedence to the reader's convenience. Tennyson used to write out whole stanzas without punctuation, but there is nothing sacred in the practice or in his occasional misspellings. Though he himself did not stumble through his draft, a modern reader probably would.

*The Trinity MSS*

These were presented to Trinity College, Cambridge, in 1924, by Hallam Tennyson, on conditions which the college interprets as forbidding copying or quotation in perpetuity. The present Lord Tennyson and Sir Charles Tennyson, the poet's grandson, wish these conditions to be relaxed. Tennyson permitted Hallam Tennyson to publish variants, and Hallam himself published poems from these MSS. Tennyson would probably have destroyed the MSS if he had dreaded quotation. True, Tennyson disliked variant readings, but he also said: 'I like those old Variorum Classics–all the Notes make the Text look precious' (*Tennyson and His Friends*, 1911, p. 147). By now Tennyson is himself a classic.

But the wishes of the poet's descendants have not been met. One consequence is that there can be no authoritative correction of Hallam Tennyson's own errors of transcription made in publishing poems from these MSS. It seems unlikely that Tennyson would really have preferred to see *Armageddon* printed in 1931, and below, from the damaged Harvard MS (with lacunae in the opening lines), rather than permit the supply of the missing words from the Trinity MS of the poem. The MSS include many unpublished poems and fragments, as well as fascinating drafts of Tennyson's best poems and a MS of *In Memoriam* (this latter presented by Lady Simeon in 1897). Not only do the restrictions make a definitive edition impossible, they also put great obstacles in the way of such an edition as the present one. A detailed scholarly examination of the MSS–which is *not* forbidden by the donor's conditions–is rendered almost impossible by the ban on copying anything from them, even though such material would not be released but would be used solely to investigate the MSS themselves. As it is, anyone studying the Trinity MSS has to hope to hold in his head all of Tennyson's published and unpublished poetry. Still, the headnotes and footnotes below make such use as they may of the MSS. (Abbreviation *T.MS.*)

*Other collections*

Fortunately there are no restrictions on the Commonplace Book kept by Tennyson's Cambridge friend, J. M. Heath, and now in the Fitzwilliam Museum. It was compiled from 1832 to 1834, and includes many of Tennyson's early poems. For a full description, see Sir Charles Tennyson, *Cornhill* cliii (1936) 426–49. The Allen Notebook at Trinity College is similar, though less important.

The notebooks and loose papers in the Houghton Library at Harvard were formerly in the possession of Sir Charles, and they comprise a collection which rivals even that at Trinity College. The Harvard MSS are described and indexed by E. F. Shannon and W. H. Bond in the *Harvard Library Bulletin* x (1956) 254–74. Not susceptible of description or indexing, but of great interest, are the innumerable stubs of the notebooks, which offer evidence not only of known poems but also of many poems which have not survived. (Abb. *H.MS*, *H.Nbk*, *H.Lpr.*)

The Tennyson Research Centre in the City Library, Lincoln, though it has valuable MS material (especially letters), is remarkable chiefly as the repository of not only Tennyson's library but also that of his father and his brother Charles. Lincoln also has a smaller but valuable Tennyson collection (including a MS of *In Memoriam*) at present housed in the Usher Gallery; since it is hoped that this collection will be incorporated as part of the Research Centre, the headnotes and footnotes do not differentiate these two collections but refer simply to *Lincoln*. Nor did there seem any need to differentiate two kinds of evidence showing that a particular book was in the library at Somersby: the presence now of the book itself in the Centre, and a copy of the Sale Inventory of George Clayton Tennyson's library, 8–9 June 1831, which is also now in the Centre.

Since the completion of this edition, George Moore has completed a study of Dr Tennyson's library (M.A. thesis, Nottingham, 1966).

*Publication*

T. J. Wise's *Bibliography of the Writings of Tennyson* (1908) is indispensable, but it is inaccurate and is corrupted by his forgeries. Mr W. H. Bond is now working on a bibliography of Tennyson's publications–a gigantic task. Until there exists a complete list of the myriad editions, no textual apparatus can hope to be impeccable. Even *Studies in Bibliography*–which comes armoured from the University of Virginia–committed four textual errors through not having come across two printings of the *Ode on the Death of the Duke of Wellington* in 1859 and 1864.

The headnotes, in citing the first publication of a poem or volume, make no attempt to list all Tennyson's privately printed editions. 'Publication' is taken in its simplest sense: 'issued for sale to the public'. But full details are given whenever a privately printed edition had real importance (e.g. *The Window*, p. 1196).

'In 1842 [before publishing *Poems*, 1842] he had eight of the blank verse poems printed for his private use, because he always liked to see his poems in print some months and sometimes some years before publication, "for", as he said, "poetry looks better, more convincing, in print". This little volume was entitled *Morte d'Arthur; Dora, and other Idyls*' (*Mem.* i 189–90*n*). These private volumes contain important textual evidence. Though Tennyson certainly used them as proofs, they had for him a function which goes beyond proof-correcting, and it therefore seemed best to refer to them as trial editions. A bibliographer of Tennyson may have to differentiate trial editions from proofs; for this edition no such differentiation seemed necessary. Hallam Tennyson speaks of 'the first unpublished edition' which included *Locksley Hall* (*Mem.* i 195), and the textual notes below likewise treat all such trial editions as essentially prepublication MS material, and so give only selected variants from them.

Hallam Tennyson had privately printed *Materials for a Life of A.T.*, a draft of his *Tennyson: A Memoir* (1897). The headnotes do not specify the first printing in *Materials* of poems and fragments which were first *published* in the *Memoir*.

*The order of the poems*

As is standard for this series, the poems are printed in their chronological order of composition. This removes many anomalies but it also creates some. Reviewing Kenneth Allott's *Arnold* in *Victorian Studies* ix (1966) 215–17, A. Dwight Culler conceded that there is no ideal order in which to print the poems, and he specified two problems. First, 'we simply do not know very precisely when many of Arnold's poems were written'. Second, 'Arnold seems to have kept a good many poems going simultaneously'. Yet Professor Culler on the whole approved: 'Having said all this, I am nonetheless glad that Professor Allott decided upon this arrangement; for, after all, we have the other in the Tinker and Lowry edition.'

All these considerations apply to Tennyson. The obstacles to a chronological ordering are that for many poems no precise date of composition exists (and this is particularly true of the extraordinarily fertile years till 1834), and that Tennyson kept many poems going simultaneously, often working on a poem for decades. Yet we do have the other arrangement, roughly by the original volumes, in other easily available editions–Macmillan's, or Oxford Standard Authors. Despite the anomalies, the advantages of a chronological ordering, even a tentative one, are considerable. With a poet whose active career was so long, no reader can avoid pondering the development of his art.

An attempt is made to mitigate the anomalies by inserting cross-references at points where the ordering might mislead. The major problem has been the poems which comprise a linked series written over several years. *In Memoriam* was begun in 1833, and published in 1850; it is printed under 1850, with a note under 1833. *The Epic* could not be separated from *Morte d'Arthur* which it introduces, and this meant either placing *Morte d'Arthur* misleadingly under 1837, or *The Epic* misleadingly under 1833. The latter seemed preferable, with a note under 1837. Some other cases, where it seemed that linked poems did not *have* to be printed together (so violating chronology), could invoke the precedent set by Hallam Tennyson himself. In *Tennyson and His Friends* (pp. 75–7), he saw nothing objectionable in printing *To Edward FitzGerald* without *Tiresias*, and *To Professor Jebb*, etc., without the poems to which they act as introductions. In all such cases, chronological ordering is at odds with keeping the poems together. Which of the two has been allowed to win is a matter of each particular case. 'How grave is the violation of chronology?' has had to contend with 'How grave is it to divorce these two linked poems?'

There is little precise evidence for dating the early poems, and so the poems in the three volumes of *1827*, *1830* and *1832* have been kept in the sequence in which they appeared in their respective volumes. The chronological ordering therefore begins with the four poems which antedate *1827*; then come the poems of *1827* in the order in which they were originally printed; then a few intermediate poems; then the poems of *1830*; again a few intermediate poems; and then the poems of *1832*. After which (with No. 123) all poems are given in a suggested chronological order (with subsequent volumes therefore broken up). In the absence of evidence it would have been merely bluff to reorder the poems in *1827*, *1830* and *1832*; what needs to be borne in mind is that the chronological ordering from 1824 to 1833 is decidedly more approximate than thereafter. Throughout, though, there are unavoidably tentative datings.

Since Tennyson would have wished it, *Crossing the Bar* has been placed at the end of the main chronology, with a cross-reference given in sequence.

The *Idylls of the King* were written over a large span of years, and yet clearly needed to be printed as one sequence; they are therefore printed together at the end of the volume (Nos. 463–76), followed by *Songs from the Plays* (No. 477), also out of the main sequence, and by three Appendices containing respectively Alternative Drafts, Fragments and Doubtful Poems.

*The plays*

Though it includes his early play, *The Devil and the Lady*, this edition omits the plays which Tennyson published from 1875. The decision was based only in part on a judgement of their quality; the fact that they are readily available not only in nineteenth-century but also in modern editions made it seem reasonable to omit them here. The size and price of the edition would otherwise have swollen considerably. Tennyson himself authorized collected editions which omitted the plays, retaining only–as in the present case–the songs from the plays.

*Parallel passages*

The footnotes cite many parallel passages. As in any annotated edition these illustrate a range of possible likenesses. At one end is conscious allusion to another poet; then unconscious reminiscence; then phrasing which is only an analogue and not a source. Some of the instances cited here are probably analogues, not sources, but they are cited because Tennyson's phrasing can be illuminated by the comparison. Though eighteenth-century diction has been well studied, nineteenth-century late romantic diction has remained relatively unexplored. Parallel passages from, say, Keats and Shelley point not always to a source but to a common fund of poetic materials. What precisely Tennyson made of such materials may best be seen when we invoke–for comparison and contrast–his predecessors. Certainly Tennyson himself disliked such source-hunters as John Churton Collins:

> There is, I fear, a prosaic set growing up among us, editors of booklets, book-worms, index-hunters, or men of great memories and no imagination, who *impute themselves* to the poet, and so believe that *he*,

> too, has no imagination, but is for ever poking his nose between the pages of some old volume to see what he can appropriate. They will not allow one to say "Ring the bell" without finding that we have taken it from Sir P. Sidney, or even to use such a simple expression as the ocean "roars", without finding out the precise verse in Homer or Horace from which we have plagiarised it (fact). (*Eversley* iv 239–40)

But he was prepared nevertheless to quote such parallels himself. His note at *Eversley* i 334 says: 'Many of the parallelisms here given are accidental. The same idea must often occur independently to two men looking on the same aspects of Nature.' Accidental parallels may, then, have their own interest, even if the major interest still belongs to what is not accidental but a source.

Translations of the classics are from the Loeb editions whenever possible. As to acknowledging the work of previous scholars on this and similar matters, the principle has been to provide specific acknowledgements when a scholarly point was made for the first time during the last thirty years or so. It did not seem necessary to acknowledge by name the earlier discoverers, except when a particular interest or authority attaches to them.

*Poems by Two Brothers (1827)*

The only major problem of attribution concerns *Poems by Two Brothers*, by Tennyson and his brother Charles, with a few poems by their brother Frederick. It was published in April 1827 (the persistent statement that it was published late in 1826 is certainly an error). Tennyson later said to Sir James Knowles: 'There were twenty-six misprints, but the publisher would not make a longer list of errata' than the seven which appear (*Nineteenth Century* xxxiii (1893) 181). The epigraph was *Haec nos novimus esse nihil* (Martial, XIII ii 8: *nos haec* . . . 'We know these efforts of ours are nothing worth'). The poems were prefaced by an Advertisement dated March 1827:

> The following Poems were written from the ages of fifteen to eighteen, not conjointly, but individually; which may account for their difference of style and matter. To light upon any novel combination of images, or to open any vein of sparkling thought untouched before, were no easy task: indeed the remark itself is as old as the truth is clear; and, no doubt, if submitted to the microscopic eye of periodical Criticism, a long list of inaccuracies and imitations would result from the investigation. But so it is: we have passed the Rubicon, and we leave the rest to fate; though its edict may create a fruitless regret that we ever emerged from "the shade," and courted notoriety.

It is to be noted that many of Tennyson's best youthful poems 'were omitted from the *Poems by Two Brothers*, being thought too much out of the common for the public taste' (*Mem.* i 23).

In 1893 Hallam Tennyson authorized a reprint of *1827*, and prefaced it by saying:

> It is requested that none of the poems in this volume said to be by my father and consequently signed A.T., be included in any future edition of his Works, as my uncle, Frederick Tennyson, cannot be certain of the authorship of every poem, and as the hand-writing of the manuscript is known not to be a sure guide.
>
> The Additional Poems at the end form part of the original manuscript of 1827, and were omitted for some forgotten reason.
>
> My father writes, "The Preface states 'written from 15 to 18.' I was between 15 and 17, Charles between 15 and 18."
>
> The following is from Frederick Tennyson, and explains itself: "I return you the Poems, with which I have been greatly interested, as I did not expect to find them so good as they really are. The initials are right as appended to my four poems, but *I cannot be sure of the others.*"

(The correspondence with Frederick is now at Yale.) Despite this Preface, Hallam Tennyson permitted W. J. Rolfe to include Tennyson's poems of *1827* in his edition of 1898; for this edition Hallam modified the attributions in some cases (the headnotes below indicate this where it is of importance).

Hallam Tennyson saw to the appending of initials (A.T., C.T. and F.T.) in 1893, some with queries. A letter from Robert Bowes to Hallam, 1 March 1893 (now at Lincoln), makes it clear that the main evidence was the handwriting of the MS of *1827* (watermarked 1823), despite the doubts expressed in the Preface. In addition to the memory of the aged Frederick, further evidence for the attributions exists in three surviving copies of *1827*.

Professor W. D. Paden has studied two of these copies in an article in *The Library* xix (1964) 147–61, and the present edition is much indebted to him. First: the Haddelsey copy, with attributions by Tennyson, now in the Brotherton Collection at Leeds: 'This copy was presented by Lord Tennyson to Mr Haddelsey the family Solicitor with the poems marked by him showing that Three Brothers were concerned in the book.' Second: Charles's own copy in which he marked attributions (in the possession of Mr Paden). The divergences between these three sources (*1893*, the Haddelsey copy, Charles's copy) are sufficient to suggest that the sources have independent authority, and this lends great weight to the fact that in most cases the attributions are identical. Mr Paden argues that the agreement of both the Haddelsey and Charles's copy should be considered to outweigh a dissenting attribution in *1893* (see Appendix C, Doubtful Poems, p. 1806). For full details, his article must be studied. Subsequent to it, a third copy of *1827* with attributions has turned up. This was given by Tennyson's Aunt Russell to a Mrs Robinson in 1827, and it includes Mrs Russell's attributions – only one of which (Frederick's *The Oak of the North*) is followed by a query. This, the Russell copy, now belongs to Mr Chilton Thomson, who has kindly allowed the use of it. As with the Haddelsey and Charles's copy, the divergences in the Russell copy are sufficient to suggest that it has independent authority, and this again lends important weight to the fact that most of its attributions concur with the three other sources.

When a headnote below quotes solely the *1893* attribution, it is to be understood that *1893* is supported by all three of the marked copies of *1827*. Whenever these four authorities do not agree, the headnote to a poem says so.

# Acknowledgements

My greatest debt is to Sir Charles Tennyson, the poet's grandson, for his published work on Tennyson, which is here drawn on throughout; for his personal assistance which has been most generous; and for his permission to make use of Tennyson MSS. My thanks are also due to the present Lord Tennyson for the interest he has shown in the edition and for permission to quote a great deal of copyright material including Tennyson MSS.

Macmillan and Co. have kindly given permission to quote from the Eversley edition of Tennyson's *Works; Alfred Tennyson: A Memoir* by Hallam Tennyson (1897); and *Works* (1913); and to reprint *The Devil and the Lady* (1930) and *Unpublished Early Poems* (1931). The *Twentieth Century* has also kindly given permission to reprint *The Christ of Ammergau*, which was first published in its pages in January 1955.

For help of many kinds, my gratitude is due to: John Barnard; W. Rayner Batty; Sir Benjamin C. Brodie; A. N. Bryan-Brown; Rowland L. Collins; Martin Dodsworth; Miss M. J. Donahue (Mrs Ellmann); Philip L. Elliott; David Fleeman; William E. Fredeman; Miss Joyce Green (Mrs Garnier); Miss Elaine Hasløv; David Jeffcock; Mrs Catherine Barham Johnson; John Killham; Cecil Y. Lang; W. S. G. Macmillan; George O. Marshall, Jr; J. C. Maxwell; Stephen Orgel; W. D. Paden; R. L. Purdy; Ralph Wilson Rader; Edgar F. Shannon, Jr; B. C. Southam; John Sparrow; John Spedding; Mrs Marguerite Sussman; Alfred Tennyson d'Eyncourt; Mrs Ruth Tennyson d'Eyncourt; Chilton Thomson. The General Editor of this series, F. W. Bateson, has been most generous with his time, his knowledge and his vigilance.

Of the libraries which have made possible this edition, my greatest debts are due to the Tennyson Research Centre housed in the City Library, Lincoln, and its director, Mr F. T. Baker; to the Houghton Library at Harvard; to the Bodleian Library, Oxford; and to Trinity College, Cambridge. Among other libraries which have been of great assistance are: the Bapst Library, Boston College; the British Museum; the Brotherton Library, Leeds; the University Library, Cambridge; the Fitzwilliam Museum, Cambridge; the University of Hawaii; the Huntington Library; the Lincolnshire Archives Committee; the University of London Library; the Mitchell Library, Sydney; the Pierpont

Morgan Library; the National Library of Australia; the New York Public Library, especially the Berg Collection; the Royal College of Music; the University of Texas; the Victoria and Albert Museum; the University of Virginia; Yale University Library.

# Chronological Table of Alfred Tennyson's Life and Chief Publications

1809 (*6 August*) Born at Somersby, Lincolnshire, fourth son of Rev. George Clayton Tennyson the younger, Rector of Somersby, and of Elizabeth Tennyson (*née* Fytche). T.'s father had been virtually disinherited by T.'s grandfather in favour of a younger brother, and T.'s youth was overshadowed by this family feud between the Tennysons of Somersby and the grandparents with their favoured son (later Charles Tennyson d'Eyncourt) of Bayons Manor.

1815 Pupil at Louth Grammar School, where his elder brothers Frederick (b. 1807) and Charles (b. 1808) had started in 1814.

1820 Leaves Louth, to be privately educated at home by his father.

1823–4 Writes *The Devil and the Lady*, in imitation of Elizabethan drama.

1824 Serious breakdown in the health, physical and mental, of his father.

1827 (*April*) Publishes *Poems by Two Brothers*, by T. and his brother Charles, with a few poems by Frederick. T.'s contributions were written 'between 15 and 17'.

(*November*) Enters Trinity College, Cambridge, together with Charles, joining Frederick there.

1828 (*October*) Arthur Henry Hallam (b. 1811) enters Trinity, meeting T. probably in April 1829.

1829 Friendship with Hallam.

(*May*) Elected a member of the 'Apostles', an undergraduate debating society to which most of his Cambridge friends belonged.

(*June*) Wins the Chancellor's Gold Medal with his prize poem, *Timbuctoo*.

(*December*) Hallam meets T.'s sister Emily (b. 1811), with whom he was to fall in love.

1830 (*June*) Publishes *Poems, Chiefly Lyrical*.

(*July–September*) Visits the Pyrenees with Hallam.

1831 (*March*) Death of his father.

Leaves Cambridge without taking a degree.

(*August*) Hallam's essay 'On Some of the Characteristics of

Modern Poetry and on the Lyrical Poems of Alfred Tennyson' in *Englishman's Magazine*.

1832 (*May*) Severe, though not indiscriminate, review of *1830* by 'Christopher North' (John Wilson) in *Blackwood's Magazine*.

(*July*) Visits the Rhine country with Hallam.

(*October*) Insanity, eventually incurable, of his brother Edward (b. 1813).

(*December*) Publishes *Poems* (title-page dated 1833).

1833 Hallam's engagement to Emily recognized by the Hallams. Begins revising many poems of *1830* and *1832*.

(*April*) Venomous review of *1832* by J. W. Croker in *Quarterly Review*.

(*September*) Death of Hallam from a haemorrhage, while visiting Vienna.

1834 Falls in love with Rosa Baring, with whom he seems to have become disillusioned by 1835–6. (She married Robert Shafto in 1838.)

1835 (*March*) His brother Charles inherits an estate and changes his name to Turner.

1836 (*May*) Marriage of Charles to Louisa Sellwood, and the beginning of T.'s love for her sister Emily Sellwood.

1837 (*May*) The Tennysons move from Somersby to High Beech, Epping.

(*September*) Persuaded by Richard Monckton Milnes to contribute to *The Tribute*, in which he publishes *Oh! that 'twere possible*.

1838 Engagement to Emily Sellwood recognized by her family.

1840 Engagement broken off, partly because of T.'s financial insecurity. The Tennysons move to Tunbridge Wells (and in 1841 to Boxley).

(*February*) Edward FitzGerald reports that T. is 'really ill in a nervous way', a condition which persists into the late 1840s.

1840–41 Invests his fortune (about £3,000) in a wood-carving scheme, which has collapsed by 1843.

1842 (*May*) Publishes *Poems*. The first volume selects poems from *1830* and *1832* together with a few written *c.* 1833; the second volume consists of new poems.

1843 Receives treatment in a hydropathic hospital near Cheltenham.

1845 (*September*) Is granted a Civil List pension of £200 p.a.

1846 (*August*) Visits Switzerland with his publisher Edward Moxon.

1847 (*December*) Publishes *The Princess*.

1848 Visits Ireland and Cornwall, taking up again a projected Arthurian epic.

1849 Renews correspondence with Emily Sellwood.

1850 (*May*) Publishes *In Memoriam* anonymously in the last week of May (the first commercial announcement, 1 June).
(*June*) Marries Emily.
(*November*) Appointed Poet Laureate, Wordsworth having died in April.

1851 (*April*) A still-born baby boy.
(*July*) Visits Italy with Emily, returning in October.

1852 (*August*) Birth of his son Hallam Tennyson.
(*November*) Publishes *Ode on the Death of the Duke of Wellington.*

1853 (*November*) Moves to Farringford, Isle of Wight, which he buys in 1856.

1854 (*March*) Birth of his son Lionel.

1855 (*June*) Hon. D.C.L. at Oxford.
(*July*) Publishes *Maud, and Other Poems.*

1859 (*July*) Publishes *Idylls of the King*, namely *Enid*, *Vivien*, *Elaine* and *Guinevere.*
(*August*) Visits Portugal with F. T. Palgrave.

1860 Assists Palgrave in selecting poems for *The Golden Treasury.*

1861 (*June*) Visits the Pyrenees with his family.

1862 (*January*) Writes Dedication for a new edition of the *Idylls of the King*, in memory of Albert, Prince Consort (d. December 1861).
(*April*) First audience with Queen Victoria, at Osborne, Isle of Wight.

1864 (*April*) Visit by Garibaldi to Farringford.
(*August*) Publishes *Enoch Arden* [etc.].

1865 (*January*) Publishes *A Selection from the Works of Alfred Tennyson.* Refuses offer of a baronetcy.
(*February*) Death of his mother.

1868 (*April*) Foundation stone laid of his second home, Aldworth, at Blackdown, Haslemere.

1869 (*April*) Attends the meeting to organize a 'Metaphysical Society', which he joins and which flourishes until 1879.
(*December*) Publishes *The Holy Grail and Other Poems* (title-page dated 1870).

1870 (*December*) Reluctantly publishes *The Window* (title-page dated 1871), with music by Arthur Sullivan.

1872 (*October*) Publishes *Gareth and Lynette* [etc.]. The Imperial Library edition of the *Works* (1872–3) brings together the *Idylls of the King* (with a new Epilogue: *To the Queen*), virtually complete except for *Balin and Balan* (written 1874).

1873 (*April*) Again refuses offer of baronetcy, as also in 1874.

1875 (*June*) Publishes *Queen Mary*, inaugurating his career as a playwright.

1876 (*April*) Production of *Queen Mary*.
(*December*) Publishes *Harold* (title-page dated 1877).

1878 (*February*) Marriage of his son Lionel to Eleanor Locker.

1879 (*April*) Death of his brother Charles Tennyson Turner.
(*May*) After repeated piracies, publishes *The Lover's Tale*, which had been omitted from *1832*.
(*December*) Production of *The Falcon*.

1880 (*December*) Publishes *Ballads and Other Poems*.

1881 (*July*) Henry Irving's production of *The Cup*, with Ellen Terry and Irving.

1882 (*November*) Production of *The Promise of May*, his only published work in prose.

1883 (*September*) Visits Denmark with Gladstone.
(*December*) Accepts the offer of a barony, taking his seat in the House of Lords in March 1884.

1884 (*February*) Publishes *The Cup and The Falcon*.
(*June*) Marriage of his son Hallam to Audrey Boyle.
(*December*) Publishes *Becket*.

1885 (*December*) Publishes *Tiresias and Other Poems*.

1886 (*April*) Death of his son Lionel, aged thirty-two, returning from India.
(*December*) Publishes *Locksley Hall Sixty Years After*, which includes *The Promise of May*.

1888 Severe rheumatic illness, from which he does not recover till May 1889.

1889 (*December*) Publishes *Demeter and Other Poems*.

1892 (*March*) Production of *The Foresters* in New York.
(*April*) Publishes *The Foresters*. Irving at last agrees to produce *Becket* (acted February 1893).
(*September*) His last illness.
(*6 October*) Dies at Aldworth.
(*28 October*) Posthumous publication of *The Death of Œnone, Akbar's Dream, and Other Poems*.

# Abbreviations

*CT* = Sir Charles Tennyson, *Alfred Tennyson* (1949)
*E. and S.* = *Essays and Studies*
*Eversley* = the Eversley edition of Tennyson's *Works* (nine volumes, Macmillan, 1907–8), edited by Hallam Lord Tennyson
*H.Lpr* = *Harvard Loosepaper*
*H.MS* = *Harvard Manuscript*
*H.Nbk* = *Harvard Notebook*
*HnMS* = *Huntington Manuscript*
H.T. = Hallam Tennyson
*JEGP* = *Journal of English and Germanic Philology*
*L.MS* = *Lincoln Manuscript*
*Mat.* = Hallam Lord Tennyson, *Materials for a Life of A.T.* (privately printed, no date)
*Mem.* = Hallam Lord Tennyson, *Alfred Lord Tennyson: A Memoir* (1897)
*MLN* = *Modern Language Notes*
*MLR* = *Modern Language Review*
*MP* = *Modern Philology*
*OED* = *Oxford English Dictionary*
*PL* = *Paradise Lost*
*PMLA* = *Publications of the Modern Language Association of America*
*QR* = *Quarterly Review*
*RES* = *Review of English Studies*
*SP* = *Studies in Philology*
T. = Tennyson
*TLS* = *Times Literary Supplement*
*T.Nbk* = *Trinity Notebook*
*VP* = *Victorian Poetry*
*VS* = *Victorian Studies*
*Y. MS* = *Yale MS*
* = poems not included by Tennyson in his final edition
*1913* = the one-volume edition of Tennyson's *Works* (1913), edited by Hallam Lord Tennyson, based upon but slightly modifying the Eversley edition
*1931* = *Unpublished Early Poems by Alfred Tennyson*, edited by Sir Charles Tennyson (1931)

The following studies, of recurring importance, have sometimes been abbreviated to the names of their authors:

Jerome Hamilton Buckley, *Tennyson: The Growth of a Poet* (1960)
T. H. Vail Motter, ed., *The Writings of Arthur Hallam* (1942)
W. D. Paden, *Tennyson in Egypt: A Study of the Imagery in His Earlier Work* (1942)
Ralph Wilson Rader, *Tennyson's 'Maud': The Biographical Genesis* (1963)
Edgar Finlay Shannon, Jr., *Tennyson and the Reviewers* (1952)
Sir Charles Tennyson, *Alfred Tennyson* (1949)

# THE POEMS

# 1 *Translation of Claudian's 'Rape of Proserpine'

Lines 1–44 were printed by Sir Charles Tennyson, *Nineteenth Century* cix (1931) 369–70. Printed in full *1931*, pp. 1–5: 'This is a free translation into 133 English lines of the first 93 lines of Claudian's *De Raptu Proserpinae*. The MS of this fragment is in the same notebook as that of the earliest version of *The Devil and the Lady*, which it precedes. The title-page of the notebook is inscribed "Translation of Claudian's Proserpine, by A. Tennyson", and bears no reference to *The Devil and the Lady*, so that the Claudian translation is evidently the earlier poem of the two, and the earliest extant poem by Tennyson. He himself said that he wrote "hundreds and hundreds of lines in the regular Popeian metre", after reading Pope's *Iliad*, which was a favourite book of his when he was about eleven or twelve. The first draft of *The Devil and the Lady* was written when he was fourteen . . ., and this translation, therefore, belongs to a period between the eleventh and fourteenth years of the poet.' T.'s schoolboy translations from some of the *Odes* of Horace are at *Lincoln*. Other poems in the heroic couplet are *The Ganges* (1826–7, p. 162), and T.'s poem on Napoleon's retreat from Moscow (*T.Nbk 19*). Claudian's mythological epic on Dis's (Pluto's) abduction of Proserpine is in three books and is incomplete. MS readings below are from *H.Nbk 1*, which is watermarked 1824, inscribed 'Somersby', and includes poems of *1827*.

The gloomy chariot of the God of night,
And the wan stars that sickened at the sight,
And the dark nuptials of the infernal King,
With senses rapt in holy thought, I sing.
Away! away! profane ones! ye whose days
Are spent in endless sin and error's maze,
Seraphic transports through my bosom roll,
All Phoebus fills my heart and fires my soul.
Lo! the shrines tremble and a heavenly light
Streams from their vaulted roofs serenely bright,
The God–the God appears! the yawning ground
Moans at the view, the temples quake around,

¶ 1.2. Cp. *Paradise Lost* x 412: 'the blasted Starrs lookt wan'. *stars that sickened*: cp. Pope, *Dunciad* iv 636: 'The sickening stars'.

5. *Procul, o procul este, profani* (*Aeneid* vi 258). A. T. Walker (quoted by Paden, p. 104) comments: 'He has not understood the meaning of *profani*, who are in both Vergil and Claudian the persons not directly concerned in the rites in progress.'

And high in air the Eleusinians raise
The sacred torch with undulating blaze;
Hiss the green snakes to sacred rapture given
And meekly lift their scaly necks to heaven,
With easy lapse they win their gentle way
And rear their rosy crests and listen to my lay.
See! see! where triform Hecate dimly stands,
And mild Iacchus leads the tuneful bands!
Immortal glories round his temples shine,
And flowering ivy-wreaths his brows entwine;
From Parthia's land he clasps beneath his chin
The speckled honours of the tiger's skin;
A vine-clad thyrsus with celestial grace
Sustains his reeling feet and props his falling pace.
Ye mighty Demons, whose tremendous sway
The shadowy tribes of airy Ghosts obey,
To whose insatiate portion ever fall
All things that perish on this earthly ball,
Whom livid Styx with lurid torrent bounds
And fiery Phlegethon for aye surrounds,
Dark, deep and whirling round his flaming caves
The braying vortex of his breathless waves,
Eternal Spirits! to your bard explain
The dread Arcana of the Stygian reign–
How that stern Deity, Infernal Jove,
First felt the power, and owned the force of love;
How Hell's fair Empress first was snatched away
From Earth's bright regions, and the face of day;
How anxious Ceres wandered far and near

13. *Eleusinians*: the mysteries in honour of Demeter and Persephone (Proserpine) were celebrated at Eleusis.
15. *snakes . . . rapture*] serpents once to Ceres *H.MS 1st reading.*
19. *triform Hecate*: as in *The Devil and the Lady* I i 31. Luna in heaven, Diana on earth, Hecate in hell.
20. *Iacchus*: a minor deity, variously said to be son of Demeter, of Persephone, or to be consort of Demeter. Often identified, as here, with Bacchus (Dionysus). Cp. *Semele* (p. 574).
24. *honours*: adornments, as in Pope's *Odyssey* xi 235: 'leafy honours', and (xviii 182): 'He shook the graceful honours of his head.'
34. T. quoted this line of Claudian as a note to *On Sublimity* 77 (*1827*, p. 118). Paden (p. 102) points out that T.'s 'breathless' for *anhelis*, on both occasions, is in Claudian 'panting', of a raging whirlpool.
39. *snatched*] torn *MS 1st reading*; rent *MS 2nd reading.*
40. Cp. Pope, *Windsor Forest* 388: 'To the bright Regions of the rising Day.'
41. *anxious Ceres*] her sad mother *MS 1st reading.*

Now torn by grief and tortured now by fear,
Whence laws to man are given, and acorns yield
To the rich produce of the golden field.
Hell's haughty Lord in times of old began
To rouse 'gainst Heaven the terrors of his clan;
Stern fury shook his soul–that he alone
Of every God upon his glittering throne,
Should lead a dull and melancholy life,
Without the fond endearments of a wife–
Wretch that he was, who knew not how to claim
A consort's or a father's dearer name!
Now Hell's misshapen monsters rush to arms
And fill the wide abyss with loud alarms;
The haggard train of midnight Furies meet
To shake the Thunderer from his starry seat,
And pale Tisiphone, with baleful breath
Calls the thin Ghosts within the camp of Death;
High in her hand amid the shades of Night
The gleaming Pine shoots forth a dismal light,
Around her head the snaky volumes rise
And dart their tongues of flame and roll their gory
eyes.
Now had all Nature gone to wrack again
And Earth's fell offspring burst their brazen chain,
And from the deep recesses where they lay
Uprisen in wrath to view the beam of day,
Now had the fierce Aegaeon thrown aside
The adamantine limits of his pride,
Upreared his hundred-handed form on high
And dared the forkèd terrors of the sky;

*46. rouse*] arm *MS 1st reading.*

*57. Tisiphone*: one of the Furies.

*61. volumes*: coils. Pope has 'shining Volumes', *Windsor Forest* 143, and 'dark volumes', *Dunciad* ii 364.

*63. PL* vi 669–70: 'And now all Heav'n / Had gon to wrack.'

*64. fell*] fierce *MS 1st reading.* *offspring*: the Titans, children of Heaven and Earth, who warred on Jove. *PL* x 697: 'Bursting thir brazen Dungeon.'

*67. Aegaeon*: so called by men, and called Briareus by the gods; a giant with a hundred hands and fifty heads, thrown under Mount Etna for his rebellion.

*68. adamantine limits*: Shelley, *The Devil's Walk* 135. Cp. *Revolt of Islam* II xx 6: 'The adamantine armour of their power.'

*69–70.* Cp. Shelley, *Prologue to Hellas* 145: 'the hundred-forkèd snake'. *forkèd*: cp. *Of old* 15: 'Who, God-like, grasps the triple forks', on which T. commented: 'Like Zeus with his *trisulca fulmina*, the thunderbolts.'

But the dire Parcae with a piercing yell
Before the throne of gloomy Pluto fell,
Around his knees their suppliant hands were thrown,
Those awful hands which make the world their own,
Whose dreadful power the shades of Hades fear
And men on earth, and Gods in Heaven revere—
Which mark the lot of fate's unerring page
And ply their iron tasks through every age.
First Lachesis began (while all around
Hell's hollow caverns shuddered at the sound),
'Dark Power of night and God of Hell, for whom
We draw the fated threads of human doom,
Thou end and origin of all on earth,
Redeeming death below by human birth!
Thou Lord of life and dissolution! King
Of all that live (for first from thee they spring
And to thee they return, and in thy reign
Take other shapes and seek the world again)!
Break not, ah! break not with unholy deed
That peace our laws have fixed, our threads decreed.
Oh, wake not thou the trumpet's impious swell
Nor raise thy standard in the gulph of Hell
Nor rouse the Titans from their dread abode,
The hideous Titans, foes to man and God.
Jove–Jove himself shall grant thine ardent wish
And some fond wife shall crown thy nuptial bliss.'
She spake–the God was struck with sudden shame
And his wild fury lost its former flame.
So when with whirlwinds in his icy train
Stern Boreas sweeps along the sounding plain,
Bright o'er his wings the glittering frost is spread
And deathless winters crown his hoary head,
Then bow the groves, the woods his breath obey,
The heaving Ocean tosses either way.
But lo! if chance on far Aeolia's shores

*71. Parcae*: The three Fates (Lachesis, who assigns the lot; Clotho, who spins the thread of life; and Atropos, who severs it). A. T. Walker (quoted by Paden, p. 104) comments on T.'s paraphrase: 'The worst change is probably that concerning the Parcae, who in Claudian come to make most humble supplication to Pluto; Tennyson said that they come *with piercing yell*, because he needed a rhyme for *fell*.'

*80. hollow*] echoing *MS 1st reading*.

*90. threads*] *MS*; threats *1931*.

*100. Boreas*: the north wind.

The God of winds should close his brazen doors,
With sudden pause the jarring tumults cease,
And Earth, Air, Ocean, find one common peace.
Then Maia's son he calls, in haste to bear
His fixed commands through all the deep of air;
Prompt at the word Cyllenius is at hand
Adorned with pinioned brow and magic wand,
Himself the God of terrors, reared on high,
Sits throned in shades of midnight majesty,
Dim wreaths of mist his mighty sceptre shroud,
He veils his horrors in a viewless cloud.
Then thus in haughty tone the God began
(Through Hell's wide halls the echoing accents ran,
The bellowing beast that guards the gates of Hell
Repressed the thunder of his triple yell,
And sad Cocytus at the sudden cry
Recalled his wailing stream of misery.
From Acheron's banks no sullen murmurs spread,
His hoarse waves slumbered on his noiseless bed,
'Gan Phlegethon in surly haste retire
And still his whirling waves and check his flood of fire),
'Grandson of Atlas, thou whose footsteps stray
Through Hell's deep shadows, and the realms of day,
To whom alone of all the Gods 'tis given
To tread the shores of Styx and halls of Heaven,
Chain of each world and link of either sphere,
Whom Tegea's sons in silent awe revere,
Go, cleave the winds and bear my will to Jove,
That haughty God who sways the realms above.

## 2 *The Devil and the Lady

Printed *1930*. In his Introduction, Sir Charles Tennyson says:

'My Uncle, Hallam, Lord Tennyson (who was the poet's son, and died in December 1928), when he gave the most complete MS of this play to

*106. God of winds*: Aeolus.

*109. Maia's son*: Mercury, messenger of the gods, born on Mt Cyllene (l.111). Maia was daughter of Atlas (l. 127).

*119. beast*: the three-headed dog Cerberus.

*121–6.* Cp. Milton's account of the rivers of Hell, *PL* ii 577–81: 'Abhorred *Styx* the flood of deadly hate, / Sad *Acheron* of sorrow, black and deep; / *Cocytus*, nam'd of lamentation loud / Heard on the ruful stream; fierce *Phlegeton* / Whose waves of torrent fire inflame with rage.'

*132. Tegea*: Greek city (*Tegeaee*, Arcadian-born).

Trinity College, Cambridge [*T.Nbk 19*, watermarked 1823], had a copy made of it, which he left to me with other manuscripts of his father's poems, giving me leave to publish at my discretion. With this copy [now *Lincoln*] he wrote the following preface:

'"I have published *The Devil and the Lady* because of the note in my Grandfather, Dr Tennyson's handwriting to the effect that the comedy was composed by my father at the early age of fourteen. [This note is on *T.MS.*] He thought that it showed evidence of a wide range of reading, a power of drawing character, and an extraordinary variety of knowledge on many subjects remarkable in a youth of that age. It has been thought that this work, as a literary curiosity, might well be given to the World, not only for the benefit of students of my father's poems, but also for a wider public."

'My Uncle did not, in fact, publish the play, although he included in his *Memoir* of the poet a short quotation from it. [*Mem.* i 25–6 quotes I v 229–47.]

'I know, however, that publication was often in his mind and that, in issuing this volume, I am not acting against his wishes.

'To anyone who reads the play it must seem an almost incredible achievement for a boy of fourteen. But though Dr Tennyson's statement is astonishing, I do not think that there can be any doubt of its substantial accuracy. It is confirmed by the poet himself in a statement quoted in the *Memoir* [i 12: "Somewhat later (at fourteen) I wrote a Drama in blank verse, which I have still."], and clearly referring to this play. Moreover, the manuscript evidence suggests that the first version of the play at least was composed by the poet at the age stated by his father, though it may have been revised and added to during the succeeding year or two years.

'The Trinity manuscript is not all in the poet's writing. the greater part of it being written in a hand which I cannot identify. There is, however, another manuscript (in my possession) [now *H.Nbk 1*] which is all in Tennyson's own hand. It is contained in a small, brown-covered notebook, measuring about 5½ inches by 3 inches, with a number of other early poems and fragments, and is clearly an earlier draft than the Cambridge manuscript, since many passages of importance are added in the latter, and some of them are written out roughly on isolated pages of the notebook, evidently as the result of a revision of the first draft, and (judging by the handwriting) immediately after its completion. Amongst other differences, the name of the Lady in the first draft is "Jessica", while in the later version it has been changed to the much less hackneyed and more suitable "Amoret"....

'This book contains another curious foretaste of the mature Tennyson in the Latin sentence written on the title-page–'*Spes alit juventutem et poesin, vituperatio premit et laedit*' (Hope nourishes youth and poesy, abuse represses and injures it). One sees here, already shadowing his boyish mind, that extravagant sensibility to criticism which he was never able to shake off even at the zenith of his fame....

'The Trinity manuscript, which is contained in a notebook of similar size and binding, is evidently a copy, made mostly by another hand, from this first draft, and the poet afterwards worked on the second draft, since many passages are added by his hand, some interpolated in the text and some written on the blank pages alongside of the text, while the last few pages (about one-fifth of the whole) are all in his writing. These added passages seem to be in a later hand than that of the first draft. The ink is blacker and the writing freer, more sloping and more like the poet's mature hand. I do not think, however, judging from the other contents of the Trinity volume and from a comparison with other early manuscripts, that any of these passages are likely to have been written after the poet was sixteen, and one or two are revisions of added passages in the earlier notebook. It is remarkable that many of the best passages occur in the first draft, though the later additions contain the more characteristically Tennysonian passages.'

The three MSS are therefore *H.MS* (early draft); *T.MS* (revised draft); and *L.MS* (copy made from *T.MS*). Variants given below as 'MS' are from the *H.MS*, which breaks off with II vi 77 (thereafter sheets are missing from the notebook). Variants from *T.MS* may not be quoted. The text below silently corrects a few misprints in *1930*, but notes all other divergences from *1930*. In *1930*, the numbering of scenes jumps from II iv to II vi; this has been amended. On T.'s source, see W. D. Paden, *Journal of American Folklore* lviii (1945) 35–47. Since there are copies of the *Quarterly Review* at *Lincoln*, Paden is certainly right in suggesting as T.'s source Francis Palgrave's article on 'Popular Mythology of the Middle Ages', *QR* (Jan. 1820). He quotes *QR* xxii (1820) 358:

'A native of Hildesheim, who distrusted the fidelity of his wife, said to him [Hödeken], when he was about to depart on a journey, – I pray thee have an eye upon my wife whilst I am abroad: I commend my honour to thy care: – Hoodekin accepted the trust without anticipating the nature of his labours. Paramour succeeded paramour – Hoodekin broke the shins of the first, led the second into the horse-pond, and thrust the third into the muck-heap; and yet the dame had well nigh evaded his vigilance. – "Friend," exclaimed the weary Devil to the husband, when he returned to Hildesheim, "take thy wife back; as thou left'st her, even so thou find'st her; but never set me such a task again: sooner would I tend all the swine in the woods of Westphalia, than undertake to keep one woman constant against her will."'

T.'s other debt was to Elizabethan and Jacobean comedy, especially Shakespeare; see Adolf Füting, *Tennyson's Jugenddrama* (Marburg, 1932). Füting suggests the influence of *Dr Faustus* (and its comic scenes), Ben Jonson's *The Devil is an Ass* and Dekker's *If This Be Not a Good Play*. T. created a brilliant pastiche of the dramatists' manner, but there are fewer specific borrowings than one would have expected; on such borrowings, see E. A. Mooney, *Shakespeare Association Bulletin* xv (1940) 118–24 and *Classical Journal* xxxvi (1940) 35–7.

Since even the revised draft breaks off uncompleted, we can only speculate as to the ending. In a note to *T.MS*, H.T. referred to *The Vision of Sin* (p. 718), and suggested that the play too would have ended with a chorus and dancing. Paden makes the valuable suggestion: 'We may only imagine the hurly-burly that was to follow; the devil's proud report to Magus of the chastisements and humiliations he has inflicted upon the six suitors; his own mortification when, having led Magus to Amoret's bed-chamber in order to exhibit her chaste slumbers, he discovers a seventh wooer nearing his goal; Amoret's voluble and tearful indignation (modelled upon that of Donna Julia in the first canto of *Don Juan*?) over her husband's misinterpretation of circumstantial evidence; Magus's lame and wavering apology; and the final rueful scene between the husband and the devil. But these developments seem clearly foreshadowed by the youthful playwright.'

*H.MS* and *T.MS* make clear that at one stage T. intended to include a further character, Pygmachus, 'a prime swell'. For a chorus see p. 1784.

## *DRAMATIS PERSONAE*

Magus *A Necromancer*
Amoret *His Wife*
Antonio *A Lawyer*
Pharmaceutus *An Apothecary*
Stephanio *A Sailor*
Angulo *An Astronomer and Mathematician*
Campano *A Soldier*
Benedict *A Monk*
Devil

## ACT I

### SCENE I

[*Scene, a wood near Magus's Cottage.*
*Storm.* Magus *solo*]

*Magus.* Now doth the vollied and rebellowing thunder
Rock the huge earth, and all the dizzy hills
Quake at his coming, while the arrowy bolt
With ravaging course athwart the dark immense
Comes rushing on its wings of fire; the North
With hoarse congratulation and wild threats
Gives answer to his brother winds that rave
From the three corners of the lurid sky.

¶ 2.I i *1.* Cp. *Paradise Lost* iv 928: 'The blasting volied Thunder.'
I i *4.* Cp. *PL* ii 829: 'the void immense'.
I i *8. sky*] heaven *H.MS 1st reading.*

The spirits of past time are on the blast,
They leave their misty halls to commune with
The airy-footed children of the storm;
Dimly they ride in gleaming steel upon
The vaultings of their cloudy chariots.
O thou omnipotent Love, whose boundless sway
And uncontrolled dominion boweth down
The Spirits of the Mighty, thou great Despot,
Who bindest in thy golden chains the strong
And the imbecile, thou immortal Pan-Arch,
Tyrant o' the earth and sea whose sunless depth
And desolate Abyss is vivified
And quickened at thy bidding. Thou vast link
Of the Creation, thou deep sentiment!
Thou only to be understood by those
Who feel thee and aid thy purpose, albeit I summon
Into thy presence Beings whose dark brows
Are furrowed with the care of pride, whose natures
Hold less congeniality with thine
Than the condensèd, cold compacted wave
To a consuming fire. But to my task!

[*He draws a cabalistic ring on the ground*]

'Tis well! Misshapen imp,
Last born of triform Hecate, hear my voice!
Stand forth and wait my summons, Spirit of Hell!

[Devil *starts up in the middle of the ring*]

All hail! All hail! thou solitary power
Whose habitation is the grisly flame
Which guards that gate of Hell that looks along
The measureless deep, whose inky waste divides
The Evil and the Blest. Now weave thy web
Of subtile machination, ply thy power

I i *9–29. . . . fire*] *Not MS.*

I i *18. Pan-Arch*: *OED* gives only Panarchic (all-ruling), from Jonson's *Alchemist*, and Panarchy, from 1839.

I i *20. desolate Abyss*: *PL* iv 936.

I i *29–30. But . . . imp*] *formed a pentameter in MS.* The Attendant Spirit in *Comus* 18 says, 'But to my task'.

I i *31. triform Hecate*: see T.'s translation of Claudian 19 and *n* (p. 4).

I i *33. solitary*] melancholy *MS 1st reading.*

I i *34.* Cp. *PL* vi 876: 'habitation fraught with fire'.

I i *35–7. that looks . . . Blest*] *Not MS.*

In such a delicate and important cause
As needs thy chief attention. Mark me well!
*Devil.* I come, O I come, at the sound of my name
From the depths and the caverns of Hell where I lie,
I can rush through the torrent and ride on the flame
Or mount on the whirlwind that sweeps through the
sky.
What wilt thou have me do for thee? Shall I weave
The sunbeams to a crown for thy bald brows?
Shall I ungarter the Pleiades for thee
And twist their glittering *periscelides*
To keep the hose up on thy 'minishing calves?
Shall I unchair Cassiopeia's brightness
And fetch her close-stool for thee? or pluck the
Nanny-goat
From off the back of that old blade whose haunches
Quiver beneath the feathered foot of Perseus?

I i *41–4.* For the rhythm, cp. Jonson, *The Devil is an Ass*, in whose first scene Iniquity is called up: 'Child of hell, this is nothing! I will fetch thee a leape / From the top of *Pauls*-steeple, to the Standard in *Cheepe*: / And lead thee a daunce, through the streets without faile, / Like a needle of *Spaine*, with a thred at my tayle.' E. A. Mooney, *Shakespeare Association Bulletin*, xv (1940) 118–24, suggests that the Devil's opening speech is based on Ariel's first speech to Prospero, *Tempest* I ii 189–93.
I i *45–60. Shall ... me*] MAGUS Good Devil / I will have none of these: but! prithee, hear me *MS*. But on separate sheets of the *MS* are drafts of ll. 45–60.
I i *46. thy bald brows*] thee, good Master *MS addition.*
I i *47. Pleiades*: 'Seven stars, in the neck of the constellation Taurus' (*English Encyclopaedia*, 1802, *Lincoln*).
I i *48. twist*] twine *MS addition.* *periscelides*: 'Greek word meaning "garters"' (*1930*). Mooney (*Classical Journal* xxxvi (1940) 35–7) suggests that T.'s source was Horace, *Epistles* I xvii 56.
I i *50. Cassiopeia*: 'mother of Andromeda [and] one of the constellations of the northern hemisphere' (*English Encyclopaedia*).
I i *51. fetch ... for*] *1930*; hand her night chair to *L.MS. close-stool*: 'a chamber utensil enclosed in a stool' (*OED*).
I i *51–3.* 'This refers to the constellation Auriga, which is shown on old astronomical maps as an old man seated with a goat on his left arm, the constellation Perseus, which is next to Auriga on the right, being shown as a standing figure of the hero facing towards Auriga with the right foot raised' (*1930*).
I i *53. foot*] heel *MS addition.*
I i *53 ∧ 4*] Shall I phlebotomise Andromeda / And bring a cupful of her starry blood? *MS addition.*

Shall I ungird Orion's strength, or bring thee
A grinder of that mighty snake, whose folds
Far stretching through the unconfinèd space
Involve seven worlds?
*Magus.* A truce with thine heroics!
A murrain take thine ill timed pleasantry!
If thou art not the most impertinent Devil
That ever smelt bitumen! prithee hear me.
Affairs of high importance call me hence,
Nor would I borrow of that usurer
Procrastination, whose vast interest
Is almost higher than his principal.
Procrastination, like the wayward tide,
With imperceptible and secret course
Gains hourly on us till that we are left
No landing-place whereon to set our feet,
So lost and tangled is the maze of cares
Protracted and put off from day to day.
*Devil.* What is the end and purport of thy words?
And wherewith can I serve thee?
*Magus.* Thou shalt hear:
For I forthwith upon the yeasty wave,
With hasty expedition of swift oars
Shall now embark, but to thee I commit
(Until such time as I retrace my way)
My loving wife, to guard her chaste and pure
As stainless snow, brushed by the windy wing
Of Eagle on the stormy mountain top,
Or like the virgin lily, whose rare sweets
Combining with the ambient atmosphere,
Do make a paradise of this fair earth,
So delicate are its odours.
*Devil.* Gentle master,
I would do aught but this; I'd dive i' the sea,
I'd ride the chariot of the rocking winds

I i *54. bring*] fetch *MS addition.*
I i *55. grinder*: originally specifically a molar tooth. *snake*: the constellation Serpentarius or Ophiuchus. *folds*] volumes *MS addition 1st reading.*
I i *57. worlds?*] worlds in their enormous spires? *MS addition 1st reading.*
I i *58. murrain*: plague.
I i *63.* Cp. Young's *Night Thoughts* i (1742): 'Procrastination is the Thief of Time.' T. copied out a long passage from *Night Thoughts* in *H.Nbk 2* (which contains fragments of this play).
I i *73. yeasty wave*: *Macbeth* IV i 53, 'yesty waves', as in *Timbuctoo* 15.
I i *84. I'd*] to *MS 1st reading*. Likewise ll. 85, 88, 89.

Alarumed by the thunder's awful knell,
Or from the hornèd corners of the Moon
I'd pluck the charmèd flowers that flourish there;
I'd visit far Arcturus, the bright length
Of the Ecliptic and the spangled Lyre,
Or that dim star which in Boötes' Wain
Shines nightly, or I'd bring thee gems from out
The stilly chambers of the mighty deep,
The boundless halls of porphyry, where sit
The ancient fathers of the sea with beards
That sweep the burnished chrysolite beneath 'em;
All this and more I'd do for thee, for these
Are trifles to that weighty task, to guard
A woman 'gainst her will.
*Magus.* This once, good Fiend,
Exert thy power; the task is short; eftsoones
I shall be here again. Till then farewell!
[*Exit* Magus.]

### SCENE II

*Devil.* A very decent, tolerable task:
Outwit a woman–that were difficult;
Place in one scale my graceless Devilship,
Her ladyship in t'other, weigh us both,
I do much fear me lest her ladyship

I i *87–8.* Mooney compares *1 Henry IV* I iii 201–5: 'By heaven, methinks it were an easy leap, / To pluck bright honour from the pale-faced moon, / Or dive into the bottom of the deep, / Where fathom-line could never touch the ground, / And pluck up drownéd honour by the locks.'

I i *89. Arcturus*: 'a fixed star . . . in the constellation of Arctophylax, or Boötes' (*English Encyclopaedia*).

I i *89–90. the . . . Ecliptic*] and the belt / That girds Orion *MS. Ecliptic*: 'a great circle of the sphere . . . that path or way among the fixed stars, that the earth appears to describe to an eye placed in the sun' (*English Encyclopaedia*).

I i *90,91. Lyre, Boötes*: constellations of the northern hemisphere.

I i *93. stilly*: *OED* dates this poeticism from 1776. Cp. Thomson, *Winter* 168: 'secret chambers of the deep'.

I i *94–6*] *Not MS. porphyry*: described by the *English Encyclopaedia* as harder than other marble.

I i *98–9.* Paden quotes Palgrave (*QR*): 'sooner would I tend all the swine in the woods of Westphalia, than undertake to keep one woman constant against her will'.

I i *99. Fiend*] *MS*; Friend *1930, L.MS.*

I ii. *This scene is not in MS.*

Untwist my meshes, foil my purposes
And by her subtile intricacy of wit
Mislead my choicest, noblest, nicest guile.
The very fuscous and embrownèd cheek
Of his Satanic Majesty might blanch
Before a woman's art. O Styx and Acheron!
What deprecations, amulets and charms,
What exorcisms, crossings and bead countings,
What Ave-Maries will be played against me!
I value not your amulets and charms
The twentieth part of half a rotten murphy
Or a split pea, albeit I do confess me
I'm apt to turn tail on an Ave-Mary,
And quail a little at a Pater-Noster,
Except when it's said backwards. I remember me
When I was summoned up by this same Magus
And unto this same office ('twas the dead
Of a most chilly winter) that I lit
I' the grey o' the morning on a blue nosed Monk
And plucked him by the beard, whereat he shrunk
In all his sinews like a sensitive plant
And chattered from the bottom of his cowl
'*Apage Sathanas iniquissime!*'
Whereat I tripped him up and laid him prone
Holding close conference with his Mother Earth
About the damage of his splintered nose,
And having punched him fundamentally
With my strong hooves, I left him bruised and battered
As a beefsteak.

SCENE III

*Magus.* There is nothing on all this earth that's precious
To him who owns it, but Anxiety,
With heavy Antithesis i' the other scale,
O'er-balances the pleasure on't: the rich ore
Is mixed with so much dross we cannot separate it.

I ii *9. fuscous*: swarthy.
I ii *11. Styx and Acheron*: two of the rivers of Hades.
I ii *12. deprecations*: 'prayers for averting evil' (*OED* 2).
I ii *16. murphy*: slang for a potato (*OED* from 1811).
I ii *28. Apage*: begone (Mooney suggests that T.'s source was Terence).

I iii. *This scene is not in MS.*
I iii *3. Antithesis*] *L.MS;* Anthesis *1930*.

There gleams no blue speck in the clouded waste
Of the charged atmosphere (not more perchance
Than is enough to make a butcher's surtout)
But minute after minute threatens us,
Lest in the misty wrappings of gray clouds
We lose that island space of narrowing blue–
The man who hoards a casket, shuddering
Will press it closer to his aching heart,
If the deep reed-bed should but tremble to
The wind that strays through its rustling depths, or wave
Its trembling shadows to the ambiguity
Of moonlight. So it fares with him who knows
The windings of the world and fain would cherish
All that he loves from its intrusion:
Distrust increases with increase of years,
She is the firstborn of Experience
And ye may know her by her stealthy shuffle
And the keen gray twinkle of her deep-sunk eye,
And the rejectings of her anxious front
To gaze at her own shadow. If ye greet her,
Or pass your hand in hers, she will respond
With an uncordial and relaxing grasp,
As though she did repent her courtesy
E'en in the doing o't; but from her counsel
We learn that many a gay flower, which disperses
Incense to every wandering air, fades off
And grows to a poisonous berry, which gives death
To all who taste it–that the broidered side
Of Life's fair tapestry, with its woven groups
Of gloomy imagery, and the inwrought splendour
Of flower and fruitage, showeth fair to the eyes
Of inexperienced immaturity,
But unto those whose rarity of locks
The hand of Time hath salted, she exhibits
The dark reverse of it,
The intertwinings and rough wanderings
Of random threads and wayward colourings–
A mêlée and confusion of all hues,
Disorder of a system which seemed Order.

I iii *8. surtout*: overall or overcoat.

I iii *12–17*. Based on Juvenal x 19–21. Cp. Johnson's *Vanity of Human Wishes* 40–2: 'Increase his riches and his peace destroy; / Now fears in dire vicissitude invade, / The rustling brake alarms, and quiv'ring shade.'

I iii *16. OED* quotes Kirke White, *c.* 1800: 'faint ambiguous shadows fall'.

Yet never, in my gayest hour of Being,
Was I so sanguine as to deem my fate
Would with each longing of impatient Hope,
Each gasp and indraw of the hasty breath,
Sparkle like Oroonoko in a tube,
Which even as it ignites and inflames
Doth change to bitter ashes.

SCENE IV

*Enter* Amoret

*Magus*. Here Amoret, a word with thee!
*Amoret*. Proceed.
*Magus*. I am called hence by strong necessity.
*Amoret*. Alas! and when shall Heaven's auspicious breath
Restore thee to these longing eyes?
*Magus*. Perhaps
Ere yet again the silver moon shall fill
The curvèd radiance of her glowing horns.
*Amoret*. How in thy tedious absence shall I chide
The lazy motion of the lagging hours?
Hours will seem days.
*Magus*. Sweet Amoret I would
Thy tongue were not at variance with thy heart.
*Amoret*. True as the handle of the horologe,
As ever movèd by the works within,
So move my lips responsive to my heart:
True as the many-chorded Harp returns
Harmonious answers to a master's touch–
So speaks this tongue congenial to my Soul.
*Magus*. It is not mine to draw aside the veil
Of dark deception, or unmask the thoughts
Of other minds. My Necromantic arts
Could never teach me this–sooner might I
Transmute this bodily form into some shape
Of wingèd bird or lazy quadruped
Or bloodless habitant of Ocean's wave.
*Amoret*. Alas! and why should false suspicion's breath,

I iii *49*. *Oroonoko*: 'a name once given to the commonest sort of tobacco in Virginia' (*1930*).

I iii *51*. *PL* x *566*: 'Chewd bitter Ashes.'

I iv. *Numbered I ii in MS*.

I iv *11*. *horologe*: 'instrument or machine for measuring the hours' (*English Encyclopaedia*).

I iv *24* ∧ *5*] Blasting the lustre [sunlight *1st reading*] of my character, *MS*.

With such ill-omened and pernicious words
Tarnish the lustre of my spotless fame?
*Magus.* I cannot trace the windings of a heart,
The searchless windings of a woman's mind,
For that Egyptian labyrinth famed of old
With all its maze of avenues and chambers
Were nothing to it–like a lightsome feather
When put in balance with a ton of lead.
*Amoret* (*weeping*).
What weighty cause, what reason have I given
That thou should'st treat me thus unkindly, Magus?
Have I not lent to thee my youth, my time,
And all that I possess? To thee o'er whom
Full eighty suns have rolled, while these young eyes
Have barely seen a score! Yet would I live
Embosomed in the fulness of content,
Did not thy temper, fretful and morose,
Still find new themes to harp upon and rail,
Making the shadow of a sound reality,
And the thin air solidity of substance,
For thou art jealousy personified.
*Magus.* Pass not too harsh a judgment on me, Amoret.
Causes however slight do oft give birth to
The same effects as spring from weightier reasons.
The little burning taper's tremulous ray
And the inexhaustible fount of fire which lives
And emanates from the great Sun, would move
The Dial's circling shadow equally.
And, if thy nature in itself be fickle,
Remember that the windy vane will veer
To the Heavens' lightest murmuring, as well as
To the strong tempest's chidings; one light word,
One thoughtless look, may lead frail spirits as far
As the vice premeditated.
Who shall know man, or freely explicate

I iv *26. lustre*] splendour *MS* (*which had* lustre *as 1st reading*).
I iv *28. woman's*] human *MS 1st reading.*
I iv *29.* The labyrinth near Alexandria is described in George Sandys's *Travels* (1658, *Lincoln*), p. 88.
I iv *45–86*] *Not MS.* But on a separate sheet of the *MS* are ll. 45–57 and 82–6.
I iv *51. shadow*] *MS addition and L.MS;* shadows *1930.*
I iv *54. Heavens'*] wind's *MS addition 1st reading.*
I iv *56. frail . . . far*] unstable minds *MS addition 1st reading.*
I iv *57*] *MS addition follows with*: Nay, my Jessica, / Turn not thy bright eyes from me–prithee hear me.

The many folds of character? or who
Shall bear the lamp of subtle scrutiny
Into the deep recesses of the heart?
Each Being is a world within himself,
A complicated Engine, whose main springs
Are circumstance and habit, and were this space
Of limited life a chain of centuries,
And each particular minute o't employed
In the developing another's nature,
'Twere all too short for the purpose.
I have lived long and shall live longer, I
Have mixed with life in all its variations,
I have visited the camp, the court, the mob,
The riotous tavern, the unruly Hell,
The penetrated hovel, the high palace,
I have had friends and they were steadfast, enemies
And they were bitter, I have wandered far
From the utmost Arctic to its opposite,
I have seen the thievish Russ, the crusty Spaniard,
The bold, brave Switzer, the freehearted Scot,
The musical Italian, the proud Angle,
The volatile, light-heelèd Frank, the sleepy Turk,
The money-loving and broad-based Mynheer–
*Amoret.* Illiberal innuendos and dark hints
Are gendered of suspicion–she who views
All objects through a mighty magnifier
And multiplies to her diseasèd vision
Accumulation of anxieties.
*Magus.* Well, Amoret, I will believe thee true
And faithful as the compass to the pole.
For in life's passage would I always look
Upon that side of things which showeth fairest,
Else were our days but one continued gloom,
A weary scene of surmise and mistrust.
The breath of life blows chillingly enow
To nip our sweetest hopes, and Heaven forfend
That we should waken bootless grievances–
When the keen Ether is condensed with frost
Who would not cleave to the sunny side o' the wall?
And hark ye, Amoret, one word of counsel!

I iv 73. *penetrated*: by wind and rain.
I iv 85. *to . . . vision*] unto her dark existence *MS addition 1st reading.*
I iv 93–8] *Not MS.*
I iv 97. J. H. Buckley (p. 13) compares *The Ancient Sage* 68: 'Cleave ever to the sunnier side of doubt.'

Close thou thy casement early, nor look down
At sound of querulous serenade or flute
Wooing the dewy wings o' the midnight air
To carry upwards on their whispering down
Unto the gaping portals of thine ears
Its soothing luxury of tender tone.
Regard not thou the glancing of the eye–
The pressure of the hand–the easy lapse
Of honeyed words from amatory lips–
All this regard not. Now farewell; may Heaven
And the good Saints protect thee!
[*Going*]
*Amoret.* The like wish
Attend thee on thy way!
*Magus* (*returning*). If I have said
Aught roughly or in anger–
*Amoret.* Think not of it!
Once more farewell–
*Magus.* Farewell, my own good Amoret,
And if my humour should sometimes show testy,
Impute it all unto the love I bear thee,
Which effervesceth of its own intensity,
And oftentimes mounts upward and boils over
Because of its own fervour.
[*Exit*]
*Amoret.* Go thy ways!
Thou yellowest leaf on Autumn's withered tree!
Thou sickliest ear of all the sheaf! thou clod!
Thou fireless mixture of Earth's coldest clay!
Thou crazy dotard, crusted o'er with age
As thick as ice upon a standing pool!
Thou shrunken, sapless, wizen Grasshopper,
Consuming the green promise of my youth!
Go, get thee gone, and evil winds attend thee,
Thou antidote to love! thou bane of Hope,

I iv *100. serenade . . . flute*] *transposed MS.*
I iv *101. dewy . . . air*] midnight air with gentle [its soft *1st reading*] note *MS.*
I iv *102–3*] *Not MS.*
I iv *104. Its*] And *MS.*
I iv *110. way*] journey *MS 1st reading.*
I iv *112–17. Farewell . . . fervour*] *Not MS.*
I iv *117.* Go] Begone and go *MS.*
I iv *120* ∧ *21*] Thou nincompoop, thou wizen-faced ninny! *MS deleted.*
I iv *123–4*] *Not MS.* Cp. the legend told in *Tithon* (*Tithonus*).
I iv *126–43*] *Not MS.*

Which like the float o' the fisher's rod buoys up
The sinking line and by its fluctuations
Shows when the pang of Disappointment gnaws
Beneath it! But to me are both unknown:
I never more can hope and therefore never
Can suffer Disappointment.
He bears a charmèd life and will outlast me
In mustiness of dry longevity,
Like some tough Mummy withered, not decayed–
His years are countless as the dusty race
That people an old Cheese and flourish only
In the unsoundest parts on't.
The big waves shatter thy frail skiff! the winds
Sing anything but lullabies unto thee!
The dark-haired Midnight grant no ray to thee,
But that of lightning, or the dreadful splendour
Of the conflicting wave! the red bolt scathe thee!
Why was I linked with such a frowzy mate,
With such a fusty partner of my days?

SCENE V *Enter* Devil

[Amoret *shrieks, covers her face with her hand and runs to the door.* Devil *brings her back and forces her into a chair.*]

*Devil.* Madam! What's this? What? Railing? Fie! for shame!
(Nay, sit you still and hear me.) Think you then
To play Xantippe with impunity,
Who gave her philosophical old spouse
So choice and delicate a water bath
To whet his appetite one frosty morning
Before his breakfast? Do you hearken to me?
*Amoret.* Ye saints defend me–I shall die with terror.
*Devil.* Now, now, my dainty one, my delicate ward,
My pretty piece of frail mortality,
Where think you is the rendezvous of Saints,
Where their celestial club-room, that you make
A fretwork argent of your snowy fingers,
And cast your jetty pupils up on high
Until the blank, unanimated white
Usurps the field of vision?

I iv *143. scathe*: *OED* notes this sense as deriving from *PL* i 613.

I v *3. Xantippe*: wife of Socrates.

I v *9. Now*] *L.MS*; How *1930*.

I v *9–38*] *Not MS.* But a separate sheet of the *MS* has ll. 26–9, 33–4.

A most unphilosophical conclusion!
Point thy hands downward, turn thine eyes to the floor!
There is a Heaven beneath this Earth as fair
As that which roofs it here.
Dost think that Heaven is local, and not rather
The omnipresence of the glorified
And liberated Spirit – the expansion
Of man's depressed and fettered faculties
Into omniscience?
*Amoret.* O ye Powers have mercy!
*Devil.* Have mercy, quoth'a! when had thy tongue
mercy
Upon thy betters, mistress? Curb it straightly,
'Tis the most dangerous member of the Body –
Unto the wise a blessing and a benefit,
A healing balm of mild Persuasion,
A sewer up of rents, sweet Pity's oracle,
A curber of dissension's contumely –
But in the mouth of the improvident
Worse than an Adder's fang.
It prompts the brain to hatch, the hand to execute,
The heart to shake off conscience and the back
To throw away the burden of restraint,
The saucy foot to spurn Authority.
Faith and troth, Madam, if my fates had bid me
To tread the thorny path of life with thee,
If the indissoluble, firm-knit chain
Of fixed alliance in its sacred bond
Had joined the fortune of thy stars with mine,
Would I become a target of your taunts?
The mark and butt of your unruly tongue?
Would I be baffled, like the idle wave
Fuming and fretting on a changeless rock,
Without the power to make impression
On the obdurate nature of the stone?
Would I be hurried like the dust of the earth
With every gale of passion to and fro,

I v *26–34. James* iii 5–8: 'Even so the tongue is a little member, and boasteth great things. Behold, how great a matter a little fire kindleth! And the tongue is a fire, a world of iniquity: so is the tongue among our members, that it defileth the whole body, and setteth on fire the course of nature; and it is set on fire of hell . . . But the tongue can no man tame; it is an unruly evil, full of deadly poison.'

I v *41. indíssolúble.*

I v *44–5*] *Not MS.*

Or be the plaything of your haughtiness
To gibe and sneer at?
*Amoret.* Hence! Avaunt, foul fiend!
Bear hence the terrors of thy crooked horns
And the long windings of thy sinuous tail!
Oh! that I could speak Latin, whose magic sounds
And Elfin syllables might drive thee far
To thy remotest Hell.
*Devil.* Ha! Ha! Ha! Ha!
Now by my Devilship 'tis wondrous plain,
Plain as the polish of a marble floor,
Plain as the surface of a bowling green,
Plain as the nose upon a Negro's face,
That husbands are the veriest dolts in nature.
Ye henpecked mates, who, like insensate drones,
Doze out your sleepy melancholy days,
Who twist and twine beneath the oppression
Of woman's will, did ever Nature leave
To man on earth a want unsatisfied?
Has she not planted in each towering hedge
That fronts the King's highway, in each green wood
That crowns the balmy summit of the hill
A sovereign remedy to curb the power
Of overbearing insolence and pride?
Ye are all wrapt in apathy, else where
Would ARGUMENTUM BACULINUM be?
'Tis a most delicate physic, suited to
All ages from the schoolboy to the wife.
It quickens business, makes the lazy blood,
Which heretofore was stagnant, circulate,
'Tis the primeval origin of virtue,
Moulding the mind to good, it checks the freaks
Of growing vice i' the heart; corrects the hardness
Of our ferocious natures like the iron
Which when most beaten is most ductile; thus
Men's natures are all malleable: should'st thou use
them
Mildly, they turn again and trample thee;
But should'st thou hold and rein them straitly in,

I v 75. *Argumentum Baculinum*: baculine, 'of punishment by caning' (Latin *baculum*, a rod). Paden notes Palgrave's reference to the baculine exorcism.

I v 80. *virtue*] good *MS 1st reading.*

I v 84. *;thus*] too: *MS 1st reading.*

I v 85. *Men's*] Our *MS 1st reading.*

And curb the mettled nature of their spirits,
When first they leave life's starting-post, they fear
thee,
And fearing honour, honouring obey thee,
Obeying, love thee. Honour, love and fear
All meet in a bamboo. Oh! Heaven and Earth!
Why wilt thou crouch and bow and lick the dust
Whereon thy consort treads? Beat back the stream
And to the violence of the ridgèd waves
Oppose the massy stonework of thy power,
Though for awhile it roar and bound above
The opposition of thy barrier–
Yet raise thy dam up higher–higher still–
Till the submissive stream with silent course
Seek its far fount. She'll never rave again,
Unless in negligence or flexibility
Of yielding nature thou should'st leave some avenue
To her insinuating and sapping force
(Which will not leave one stone unturned, until
She doth recover her dominion),
Some faithless fissure or uncemented hole,
Whence her ebullient spirit may leap forth,
At first in an attenuated stream,
Unto new contest, and enlarging straightly
May hurry thy frail mound down its rough bed,
And leave thee with one finger in thine eye
To wail the pliability which led thee
To trust thus far.
*Amoret.* I know not whence thou comest,
Nor who thou art, nor what thy message here,
Nor how I may exorcise thee, or drive
Thy troubled spirit to its biding-place.
If there be aught of pity in thy soul,
I do beseech thee leave me to my thoughts
And solitude.
*Devil.* Thoughts! Thoughts! what thoughts are
thine
But evil and dishonour?
*Amoret.* Nay, I'll kneel
And pray thee to depart.

I v *88. nature*] natures *MS.*

I v *93–4.* Cp. *PL* ix 526: 'Fawning, and lick'd the ground whereon she trod'.

I v *95.* Cp. *Song* [*The winds*] 2: 'the ridgèd sea'.

I v *101–14. She'll . . . far*] *Not MS.*

*Devil.* Out on thee, woman!
Devils are faithful to their trust.
*Amoret.* Alas!
Am I entrusted then to thee?
*Devil.* Dost weep?
Is that a tear which stains thy cheek? Nay–now
It quivers at the tip-end of thy nose
Which makes it somewhat dubious from which
feature
It first had issue.
*Amoret.* I conjure thee–
*Devil.* Tears!
The rain of sentiment, the dews of feeling,
The beads of sensibility!
They are the coinage of a single wish.
I know that ye can summon them at will.
They are a woman's weapons, sword and shield,
Wherewith she braves remonstrance and breaks
hearts–
Those faithful sluices never are drawn dry.
Even the withering heat of passion
But leads them forth in greater plenitude.
What! more! I know ye can command them, woman,
Even to the precise number, ten or twenty,
As suits occasion–
More yet? Methinks the cavity o' thy skull
Is brine i' the room o' brains. More yet? at this rate
You'd float a ship o' the line.
This is the cogent stream wherewith ye turn
The mill-wheel of men's love (whose motion
Guides all the inner workings o' the heart)
And grind what grist ye please.
*Amoret.* I prithee–
*Devil.* Begone!
Get thee to bed–yet stay–but one word more–
Let there be no somnambulations,
No colloquy of soft-tongued whisperings
Like the low hum of the delighted bee
I' the calyx of a lily–no kerchief-waving!
No footfalls i' the still night! Lie quietly,
Without the movement of one naughty muscle,

I v *124–47. Dost . . . thee*] Begone *MS.*
I v *133. Lear* II iv 273: 'women's weapons, water drops'.
I v *147. Begone!*] *L.MS; not 1930.*
I v *149–68*] *Not MS.*

Still as a kernel in its stone, and lifeless
As the dull yolk within its parent shell,
Ere yet the *punctum saliens* vivify it.
I know ye are perverse, and ever wish,
Maugre my wholesome admonitions,
To run obliquely like the bishop at chess,
But I'll cry 'check' to ye, I warrant ye
I'll prove a 'stalemate' to ye.
*Amoret* (*half aside*). In all conscience
My mate is stale enough.
*Devil.* Dost mutter? how?
Would you outface the devil, Insolence?
Or tweak me like St Dunstan by the nose,
Who scarified my smeller for a twelvemonth?
Who would cast seeds i' the ocean? who would graft
Good counsel's fruits upon a stock so sterile?
Oh! Amoret! there is no honour in thee;
Thou art the painted vision of a dream,
Whose colours fade to nothing, a fair rainbow
Mocking the tantalized sight, an airy bubble,
O'er whose bright surface fly the hues of light,
As if to hide the nothingness within.
Few will bear sounding; cast the plummet in
And it will draw up mud, vile, worthless mud.
Gaze on the mirror of the silver lake
In its clear picture deftly pencilling
The soft inversion of the tremulous woods,
But probe it not to the bottom: weeds, rank weeds,
Darkness and swarming reptiles harbour there.
Now go and ponder on my words. Begone.
[*Exit* Amoret]
I am in troth a moralizing devil,
Quite out o' my element; my element, fire.
Then come my spirit, with thy torch light up

I v *157*. *punctum saliens*: defined in *English Encyclopaedia* as 'the first rudiments of the heart in the formation of the foetus, where a throbbing motion is perceived. This is said to be easily observed with a microscope in a brood-egg, wherein, after conception, we see a little speck or cloud, in the middle whereof is a spot that appears to beat or leap, a considerable time before the foetus is formed for hatching.'

I v *159*. *Maugre*: despite.

I v *163*. Cp. *Taming of the Shrew* I i 58: 'To make a stale of me amongst these mates.'

I v *175*. *sounding*] searching *MS*.

The strongest flame of thine ability,
Use all thine efforts–work thy passage, as
The restless rushing of a fiery flood
Within the hollow and sonorous earth.
Now to my charge. I must be violent, fierce,
And put that ugly disposition on
Which is my portion by inheritance
From my great grandsire Lucifer. Good lack!
I'll make the scurvy-pated villains skip
As they were mad, e'en though they thronged about
me,
As thick as Beelzebub on Beelzebub,
Alias as thick as horseflies on horse-dung.
'Twill be a troublesome office. Nay, by Phlegethon,
I'd rather be the chilly watch, whose voice
Sounds midnight through the length o' the hazy streets
In some great city, by the misty light
O' the fumigated moon, than guard a woman.
When will the reign of feminine intrigues
Of female politics and folly cease?
It will be much about that time, methinks,
When this dark field of earth shall be sowed thick
With the gay stars of Heaven and the keen ploughshare
Shall trench deep furrows in the inverted sky;
When his triple-mitred Holiness shall become
An arrant Protestant, and all their Eminences
Shall be *unboiled* into the humility
Of black canonicals; when a second Becket
Shall thunder excommunication
From out his lordly see of Canterbury;
When Summer shall be Winter, and Spring Autumn;
When cold shall rarefy and heat condense;
When Almack's shall become the rendezvous

I v *188. fiery flood*: cp. *Measure for Measure* III i 121, and T.'s *Life of the Life* 9.
I v *191*. Cp. *Hamlet* I v 172: 'To put an antic disposition on.'
I v *195. e'n . . . me*] Ha! Ha! Ha! Ha! Ha! Ha! *MS.*
I v *196–247*] *Not MS.*
I v *196. Beelzebub*: 'lord of flies'.
I v *198. Phlegethon*: a river of Hades.
I v *202. OED fumigation* 1 refers to ceremonies of incantation, witchcraft.
I v *206–7. PL* vii 358: 'And sowd with Starrs the Heav'n thick as a field.'
I v *211. unboiled*: cp. II ii 50, 'flaming as a scarlet mailèd lobster'.
I v *217*. For Almack's Coffee House and Almack's Assembly Rooms, see B. Lillywhite, *London Coffee Houses* (1963), p. 670.

Of burly citizens and citizens' wives,
And Lady J—y wearied shall throw down
The reins of Fashion and–think better things;
When high souled man shall walk upon his head,
When Colonel B—y shall shake hands with Decency
And read or write a sermon.
So! So! methinks in good truth I have hemmed in
My proposition with a sweeping circle
Of insurmountable improbabilities.
Yon taper sinks i' the socket; Time wears quickly,
Yet treads in shoes of felt. What is't o'clock?
[*Going to the timepiece*]
Half after midnight! These mute moralizers,
Pointing to the unheeded lapse of hours,
Become a tacit eloquent reproach
Unto the dissipation of this Earth.
There is a clock in Pandemonium,
Hard by the burning throne of my Great Grandsire,
The slow vibrations of whose pendulum,
With click-clack alternation to and fro,
Sound 'EVER, NEVER!' through the courts of Hell,
Piercing the wrung ears of the damned that writhe
Upon their beds of flame, and, whensoe'er
There may be short cessation of their wailings,
Through all the boundless depth of fires is heard
The shrill and solemn warning 'EVER, NEVER'.
Then bitterly, I trow, they turn and toss
And shriek and shout, to drown the thrilling note–
[*Looking again at the timepiece*]
Half after midnight! Wherefore stand I here?
Methinks my tongue runs twenty knots an hour:
I must unto mine office.
[*Exit abruptly*]

## ACT II

### SCENE I

[Magus's *cottage with the wood and lake in the distance. Enter* Devil *and takes his station before the cottage door attired in a cap and gown.*]

*Devil.* The starry fires of yon Crystalline vault
Are waning, and the airy-footed Night

I v *228*. Cp. *Lear* IV vi 183–4: 'It were a delicate stratagem to shoe / A troop of horse with felt.'

I v *233*. *Pandemonium*: described in *PL* i 710–30.

Will soon withdraw the dismal solitude
Of her capacious pall, wherewith she clouds
Yon mighty and illimitable sky,
Placing a death-like colour in all things,
Monopolizing all the varied Earth
With her dim mantle.

[*A pause*]

Oh! ye eyes of Heaven,
Ye glorious inextinguishable lights,
High blazing mid the lone solemnity
Of night and silence, shall the poor worm, Man,
The creature of this solitary earth,
Presume to think his destiny enrolled
In your almighty everlasting fires?
Shall this poor thing of melancholy clay,
This lone ephemeris of one small hour,
Proudly suppose his little fate inscribed
In the magnificent stars? What have the worlds
Of yon o'er-arching Heaven–the ample spheres
Of never-ending space, to do with Man?
And some romantic visionaries have deemed
This petty clod the centre of all worlds.
Nay–even the Sun himself, the gorgeous Sun,
Pays homage to it. Ha! Ha! Ha! Poor Man,
Thou summer midge! Oh, ye shine bravely now
Through the deep purple of the summer sky,
I know that ye are Earths as fair and fairer
And mightier than this I tread upon–
For I have scaled your mountains, to whose cones
Of most insuperable altitude
This Earth's most glorious Eminences and heights
All piled and heaped upon each other's brows,
And massed and kneaded to one common substance,
Were but a molehill.
And I have swum your boundless seas, whose waves
Were each an ocean of this little orb,
Yet know I not your natures, or if that
Which we call palpable and visible
Is condensation of firm particles.

II i *7–8 . . . mantle*] Assimilating what is beautiful / To that which is not *MS.*

II i *16. ephemeris*: *OED* gives 'record of daily occurrences', and 'astronomical almanac'; also here *ephemera*, 'an insect that lives only for a day'.

II i *21. deemed*] made *MS 1st reading.*

II i *25–57. Oh . . . doubt*] *Not MS.*

O suns and spheres and stars and belts and systems,
Are ye or are ye not?
Are ye realities or semblances
Of that which men call real?
Are ye true substance? are ye anything
Except delusive shows and physical points
Endowed with some repulsive potency?
Could the Omnipotent fill all space, if ye
Or the least atom in ye or the least
Division of that atom (if least can dwell
In infinite divisibility) should be impenetrable?
I have some doubt if ye exist when none
Are by to view ye; if your Being alone
Be in the mind and the intelligence
Of the created, should some great decree
Annihilate the sentient principle
Would or would ye not be non-existent?
'Tis a shrewd doubt.

[*A sound of footsteps heard*]

But softly! who comes here?
What stealthy foot invades these secret woods?
'Tis some Alcinous or Eurymedon
Who haunts this wild and wanton Amoret!
Perchance some smooth-chinned Tyro just emerging
From Hobbledehoyhood's twilight, and elated
With the dark sproutings of incipient beard,
Or some sleek monk enveloping the bronze
Of his dark cheek beneath his rusty cowl.
Now will I cloak myself, and thus conceal
This grim, fantastic nose and these wide lips,
That staring shew the black and knotty teeth

II i *49–50*. Cp. *Mem.* i 319*n.*: 'He would point out the difficulties of materialism, and would propound to us, when we were boys, the old puzzle: "Look at the mystery of a grain of sand; you can divide it for ever and for ever. You cannot conceive anything material of which you cannot conceive the half."'

II i *51–2*. Cp. T.'s Berkeleyan speculations in *The Idealist* (p. 169).

II i *59*. Antinous and Eurymachus were the leading suitors of Penelope. T. may simply have got the names wrong, or he may be following the whimsical classical practice of using similar names which scan like the real ones.

II i *61–5*] *Not MS.* *Tyro*: beginner.

II i *62*. *Hobbledehoyhood*: adolescence (T. antedates *OED*'s first example, 1836). *twilight*: morning twilight.

That fence my jaws like hedge-stakes (I have lost
Much of original beauty since my fall),
Now will I smooth the harshness of my voice
Into a feminine croak, tuck up my tail,
And thus unsex myself.
[*Draws the hood over his face*]

SCENE II

*Enter* Antonio

*Antonio*. Ye gracious Heavens,
Is't Amoret, the rosebud of whose cheeks
Is preferable to a suit at Law
Successfully unravelled – the rich sound
Of whose harmonious and most silver voice
Steals sweeter on mine ear than does the chink
Of golden or of silver boys wrung out
From the hard client's gripe – whose delicate smile
Is worth a ten-days' fee? Lo! here I come
To pay my devoirs at the shrine of beauty.
For this, as soon as e'er the deep-mouthed voice
Of the most lonely tempest ceased to shake
Heaven's pillars and the solid earth, I paced
This wild and marshy wood; for this have burrs
Clung to me as thou seest, more in number
Than cases in the Court of Common Pleas;
For this the drizzly trees and dripping shrubs
Showered on me as I hurried past, more thickly
Than diamonds on a birthnight.
*Devil* (*speaking in an undertone*). Gentle Sir,
You overrate yourself. True love had scorned
The petty hindrances of wind and weather.
Gods! why a lover is all heat and fire,
A mustard pot, a very pepper-box,

II i *69–70*. *PL* i 591–2: 'His form had yet not lost / All her Original brightness'; and *Paradise Regained* i 377–8: 'I have lost / Much lustre of my native brightness.'

II i *73*. *Macbeth* I v 39–40: 'Come, you spirits / That tend on mortal thoughts, unsex me here.'

II ii *7*. '"Yellow Boys" – early slang for guineas' (*1930*).

II ii *9*. *Lo*] *MS*; So *1930*, *L.MS*.

II ii *10*. *devoirs*: dutiful respects (*OED* 4).

II ii *13*. *and*] *MS*; of *1930*, *L.MS*.

II ii *19*. *birthnight*: the court festival for a royal birthday.

II ii *23*] *Not MS*.

And his internal warmth of temperament
Might guard him from external cold. Ay! though
Thou hadst bolted through the very teeth o' the storm
Bareheaded, every gusty drop of Heaven
Had run off hissing from thy glowing surface,
As from a bar of red-hot iron. Believe me,
If thou wert a true lover, wind and rain
Would have no power on thee. 'Twas never known
That one who loved most ardently and truly
Was ever laid up for a single se'nnight
With a red nose.
*Antonio.* Now on mine honour–
*Devil.* Prithee,
If thou desirest aught of credit with me,
Most commendable and good Antonio,
Swear not upon thine honour! It is rare
With those of thy most honourable cut,
As is the desert fire-born biped sprung
From its own ashes. If thou swearest, swear
By that thou lovest best.
*Antonio.* Then by my fees–
*Devil.* Ay–there the right nail's struck upon the head.
*Antonio.* Or by thy dearer self–
*Devil.* Now, prithee, lie not,
Keep thy first oath–thy fees are dearer to thee.
*Antonio.* Well, by my fees (that I may humour thee
And put an end to dissertation)
I know a most true lover Leontio,
That hath a nose as red as a skinned eel
Or pickled cabbage steeped in vinegar,
And flaming as a scarlet mailèd lobster,
Although he hath a lady in his head.
*Devil.* Then it proceedeth from the warmth within,
Not from the cold without.
*Antonio.* How prove you that,
Fair Amoret? The case is clearly mine,
Let A be then the heart and B the nose,
True love is centred in the heart. What then?
It follows that the heat's in A the heart
And not in B the nose–PROBATUM EST.

II ii *25–9. Ay . . . iron*] *Not MS.*
II ii *33. se'nnight*: week (cp. fortnight).
II ii *39. biped*: Phoenix.
II ii *45. humour*] *MS*; honour *1930, L.MS.*
II ii *56. is centred in*] proceedeth from *MS 1st reading.*

*Devil.* Good Sir, the case is this–the lover's heart
Is so o'erchargèd with the secret flames
That do consume its melancholy core,
That all the superfluity of love,
And the redundant heat, escaping thence,
Take up their station in the lover's nose
Which thence doth show like beetroot.
*Antonio.* SATIS EST;
A truce to dissertation. Let us use
More soft discussion, gentle paramour.
Gaze all around thee–see yon canopy
Of the eternal boundless Heavens, yon host
Of all the congregated stars, this earth,
This fair green plain of the luxuriant earth,
Breathe, fair one, breathe the soul-inspiring air
Full of the all-heavenly incense wafted from
The groves, the fruits, the gaily-blooming flowers,
Which the rough tempest hath but waked to beauty
More fresh than heretofore. Is this a time
For disputation? Starlight, incense, flowers,
And two young loving hearts!
*Devil.* Talk not of love,
Thou need'st must wait cessation of the storm–
*Antonio.* What, harping on the old string again?
*Devil.* Ay, Sirrah,
Did not Leander swim the roaring main,
The boundless Hellespont (as Homer calls it),
On such a dark and dismal night as this was
Half one good hour ago?
*Antonio.* And perished too.
*Devil.* Go to–thou art no lover!
*Antonio.* Thou beliest me–
I am an honest, true and proper lover,
A gentle, comely, comfortable lover,
A well-proportioned and most gracious lover,
As ever woman set her eyes upon.
*Devil.* Thou knowest that my spouse did journey hence
At midnight, yet didst thou delay thy coming
Until the storm had swept above thine head.

II ii *70*. Cp. *PL* vii 308: 'congregated Waters'; and *The Mystic* 25: 'congregated hours' (p. 230).
II ii *80*. Cp. *Epigram on a Musician* (p. 127).
II ii *81*. Cp. T.'s *Hero to Leander* (p. 228).
II ii *82*] *Not MS.*

*Antonio.* Inimitable mistress of my heart,
I sat in judgment on my love and judged it,
I issued out a WRIT against my conscience,
And sent a MITTIMUS unto my soul,
I tried and proved it thoroughly and found
That it was free from blame–PROBATUM EST.
But come, unveil those eyes, whose dazzlingness
Shoots forth more deadly and more certain shafts
Than those the curly-headed Indian sends
By force of breath from out the echoing tube.
*Devil.* 'Tis a chill night. I fear the damp; I cannot
Uncloak myself in such wise.
*Antonio.* Will it please you
To enter in?
*Devil.* Proceed! I follow thee.
*Antonio.* Thy deeds do give the lie unto thy tongue,
Thou art as motionless as Lot's wife.
*Devil.* Begone,
On pain of my displeasure; hie thee hence;
I will attend thee in as many moments
As there are peas in a pod or teats upon
The gentle cow's most elegant dugs, or on
Old ALMA MATER, which are two or three–
Albeit she hath the credit for some dozens.

[*Exit* Antonio *into the Cottage.* Devil *throws up his hood and proceeds.*]

### SCENE III

*Devil.* Now, most sweet Sir, I have thee,
Thou shalt repent of thine audacity
Wherewith upheld, thus buoyantly and highly,
Thou spurrest thy desires to lawless deeds
Of bronze-browed arrogance, and darest thus

II ii *96. Mittimus*: 'command in writing, under the hand and seal of a justice of the peace . . . for the receiving and safe keeping of an offender charged with any crime, until he be delivered by due course of law' (*English Encyclopaedia*).

II ii *99. But come, unveil*] Ah! why conceal *MS 1st reading.*

II ii *111–3. or . . . dozens*] Hence, Sirrah! / Shall I bid twice? *MS.*

II ii *112. Alma Mater*: 'the Goddess Rhea or Cybele, wife of Saturn and mother of the Gods, often represented with a number of breasts as an emblem of fertility' (*1930*).

II iii *4. desires*] *MSS;* desire *1930.*

To climb into the solitary fold
Of thy good neighbour, and to cull the fleece
Which he esteemeth best. But I will prove
No tame, submissive, crouching sentinel:
But I will take such fearful hold on thee,
As doth the wayward irritable crab
On the poor traveller; thou art thoughtless, young,
Full of high-mettled hopes, hot-blooded, sanguine,
With haughty self-sufficiency of nature,
Which is the attribute of thy green years
That brook not sober meditation.
Visions of happiness do float before thee,
Gay-gilded figures and most eloquent shapes,
Moulded by Fancy's gentle fingering
To the appearance of reality,
With youthful expectations and fond dreams,
All rendered sunlike by the light of youth,
Which glances on them, flit before thine eyes:
But these shall be pinched out of thee – ere morn
There shall be no sound place within thy person;
Thou shalt be all the colours of the rainbow,
With bruises, pinches, weals, ET CETERA;
And various as the motley-coloured slime,
Which floats upon the standing pool, wherein
Do breed all kinds of reptiles – creeping things,
Vile jellies and white spawn and loathsome newts.
But come descend, thou penthouse:
[*Draws down his hood*]
Hither comes
One Pharmaceutus, an apothecary,
A mad, drug-dealing, vile apothecary,
A thing of gallipots and boluses,
Lean, lanthorn-jawed, splay-handed, pasty-faced,
Hard-favoured and loose-jointed, ill-proportioned,
Whose hips do roll on castors, and whose love
Is nauseous as his physic. Faugh! I know not
How I can keep my character. But here
He comes and brings his fetid atmosphere
About his person.

II iii *18. figures*] visions *MS 1st reading.*

II iii *29–31.* Suggesting *Lear* III iv 133, on the newts and reptiles of 'the standing pool', and III vii 82: 'vile jelly'.

II iii *35. gallipots*: small pots used for ointments and medicines. *boluses*: 'an extemporaneous form of medicine, soft, coherent, a little thicker than honey' (*English Encyclopaedia*).

SCENE IV

*Enter* Pharmaceutus.

Welcome, gentle Sir.
*Pharmaceutus.* Welcome, fair lady, may the bloom of joy
And the medicinal virtue of all health
Spread the fair carpet of thy roseate face
With its gay colouring.
*Devil* (*aside*). How cursedly
He stinks of assafœtida. Art cold?
Dost shake and shiver?
*Pharmaceutus.* Marry do I.
*Devil.* What?
Didst not escape the tempest?
*Pharmaceutus.* No, i' faith,
I am half palsied with frigidity,
I'm below zero, I am perfect ice
Congealed to all intents and purposes,
My nose, my ears, and each particular toe,
Will quit their station. Hark! my grinders chatter
Like castanets, or fulling mills. Let's in–
And hark ye, some of Magus's brown stout;
I'll smoke a pipe of comfortable shag-tail
By the fireside with thee. Wilt let us in?
*Devil.* Ay, presently.
*Pharmaceutus.* 'Sdeath, Madam, instantly!
Or thaw me with a look, a loving look
From the full lustre of thy melting eyes!
'Sblood! thou art hooded and pent up as tightly
As a sea-urchin.
*Devil.* Is't not fitting, prithee?
Didst thou not talk of nose dropping?
*Pharmaceutus.* Ay, Madam,
The storm hath left a chill i' the air, 'tis damp,
Rheumatic mists are whitening in the marshes,
And pale-faced Ague wanders all abroad.
But let us enter; eh?

II iv *5. assafœtida*: a strong-smelling gum used in medicine as an anti-spasmodic.

II iv *10*] *Not MS.*

II iv *13. fulling*: 'cleansing, scouring, and pressing cloths' (*English Encyclopaedia*).

II iv *14*] *Added to MS.*

II iv *24*] *Not MS.*

II iv *25*] *Added to MS.*

[*Here* Antonio *half opens the cottage door and exclaims*]

*Antonio.* Where art thou, fair one?
*Devil.* Here, sirrah, with this gentleman!
*Antonio* (*coming forward*). How now!
What! with this scurvy rascal, this poor drug,
This compound of all ugliness, this dog,
This Ipecacuanha, this emetic,
This wall-eyed monster, this anomaly,
This piece of speckled parchment, this vile patchwork,
Whose sallow and carbuncled face resembles
A red design upon a yellow ground?
*Pharmaceutus.* Pills! plasters! powders! poultices! what now!
*Antonio.* Sirrah! I'll knock thy grinders down thy throat.
*Pharmaceutus* (*staggering backwards*). Bole! Borax!
Blister! Balsam! Bark! What now?
*Antonio.* Thou hocus-pocus of deformity!
Thou scum! thou outcast of society!
*Pharmaceutus.* Galls! garlic! ginger! guiacum! what now?
*Antonio.* I'll punch thee into jelly, scatter thee
To the four winds of Heaven–thou scarecrow, thou!
*Devil.* Good words, sweet words, Antonio, prithee.
*Pharmaceutus.* Bless thee,
My honey of squills, my oil of almonds, bless thee!
Thou hast a good heart.
*Antonio.* How! you sorry rascal!
Do you make love to the lady?
*Pharmaceutus.* Mercy on us!
The man is mad–he must be blooded.

II iv *30*] *Added to MS. Ipecacuanha*: 'a West-Indian root . . . one of the mildest and safest of emetics' (*English Encyclopaedia*).
II iv *31*. *anomaly*] ungracious wretch *MS.*
II iv *32*] *Not MS.*
II iv *37*. '"Bole armeniac"–an astringent earth brought from Armenia and used as an astringent and styptic' (*1930*). *Borax*: 'a salt . . . in medicine it has been given as a narcotic' (*English Encyclopaedia*). *Bark*: 'There are a great many kinds of bark in use in the several arts: some in Medicine, as the Cinchona' (*ibid*).
II iv *40*. *guiacum*: a medicinal bark.
II iv *41*. *punch*] beat *MS 1st reading.*
II iv *44*. *squills*: 'The most remarkable species is the *maritima*, or sea-onion, whose roots are used in medicine' (*English Encyclopaedia*).

*Antonio.* How
Dost prate, thou vile anatomy? Bind up
Thy jaws or by the Devil and his dam
I'll make a gap within thy villainous throat
And pour libations of thy wretched blood
Unto this Goddess. What! thou fulsome scrag!
Wouldst thou make love with that untoward chin
Hooked and turned upwards like a Chinese shoe?
*Pharmaceutus.* Beshrew my heart but thou art wondrous mad,
Mad as a March hare, and as hot as Cowhage
Without molasses.
*Antonio.* Hang dog!
*Devil.* Peace, Antonio!
Why, thou art 80, man, by Réaumur's scale,
And more than twice as much by Fahrenheit,
And the unconquerable turbulence
And violent usage of your fiery temper,
Expanded by the heat of passion,
Will burst the tube of temperance. Methinks
I am afraid to look upon you, lest
Your head should part in twain, and thence should issue
The subtile fluid which distends you so.
*Antonio.* Thou fairest excellence of what is most
Excelling in all nature! loveliest mixture
Of all that is most lovely! is it tolerable
That this sad miscreant, this uncouth Behemoth,
Thus monstrous in his vanity of mind,
And loathsome in deformity of person,
Each rendered still more horrible by each,
When thus contrasted – is it tolerable
That he should raise the base and abject scum
Of his vile thoughts so high, and thus presume
To come within the rich and glorious sphere
Of thine attractions? Fie! it must not be.
*Devil.* Did I not say that thou wert hotly raised
By thine inexorable fire of anger
As high as 'WATER-BOIL'?
*Antonio.* No – by the Law!
It is but 'SUMMER-HEAT'.

II iv *56. Cowhage*: 'a tropical plant *Mucuna pruriens*, with stinging hairs on its pods, used medicinally' (*1930*).
II iv *70. Behemoth*: 'the hippopotamus, or river-horse' (*English Encyclopaedia*).

*Devil.* I prithee cloak not
Thy faults beneath the colouring of fair names,
Nor modify the wild unevenness
Of thy capricious disposition
With sounds of softest import: for i'faith
Thy Spirits boil at least!
*Antonio.* That fusty wretch
Hath roused them up to fermentation.
*Pharmaceutus.* Sir,
You are as bitter as Alum.
*Antonio.* You, as foul
As your own fetid pills.
*Pharmaceutus.* And you as brisk
As bottled beer.
*Antonio.* Do you chop logic with me,
You dunderhead?
*Pharmaceutus.* Who? I, Sir? No, Sir.
*Antonio.* Sirrah!
If thou presumest to give thy fool's tongue
The damning license of a repartee,
I'll have the substance of thy cursèd brains
Pounded and beat up in a red-hot mortar
And with a burning pestle; of thine hide
Will I make ass-skin breeches.
*Pharmaceutus.* Mercy on us!
The man is hypochondriac or hysterical.
Here! here! bring spirits of hartshorn and burnt
feathers
And clap hot bricks to 's feet!
*Antonio.* I'll knit thee up,
And thou shalt hang in the mid-air as prettily
As a vile cur that sucks hen's eggs, while I
Will sing thy parting elegy, and thou
Shalt beat the due observance of the time
With thy unwieldy toes! Thou shalt be balanced
As neatly as a difficult case between
Two able pleaders!
*Devil.* Fie, Antonio, fie!

II iv *90–91*. *brisk*: *OED* 4, 'of liquors: agreeably sharp; effervescent'.
II iv *92*. *dunderhead*] loggerhead *MS*.
II iv *93–4*] *Not MS*.
II iv *97*. Cp. *The Knight of the Burning Pestle*, by Francis Beaumont.
II iv *100*. *hartshorn*: ammonia solution. *burnt feathers*: stimulating nose and throat in the case of fainting.
II iv *101*. *hot bricks*: for vigorous stimulation.

Excess of violence becomes thee not,
It sits as ill upon thy shoulders as
Love on an old maid with a hump-back.
*Antonio.* Or
On this same Pharmaceutus. Ha! ha! ha!
*Pharmaceutus.* Now by Hippocrates, by Galen, Celsus
And the great Boerhaave, the dazzling sun
And star of Medical science, I do think
Thy wits are on the turn. Let's feel thy pulse,
Is't feverish or low? Give me a fleshbrush
That I may rub thee into sense.
*Antonio.* How now!
Thou most illiterate whelp, thou bristly cub,
Whom thy great Mother Bear hath never licked
To aught that may be called proportion!
Why! thou dead idiot, wouldst thou thus behave
As I were mad? In troth and faith I were so
If I should bear with thee. I should deserve
Commission of lunacy preferred against me
By the Lord Mayor.
*Pharmaceutus.* Fair Sir, I do presume
That you have heard the useful apothegm
That 'Anger is short madness'.
*Antonio.* Villainous wretch–
*Pharmaceutus.* Here! pills of aloes! rhubarb!
spanish soap!
*Antonio.* Wouldst thou not madden aught beneath the
sun
With thine accursèd clucking?
*Pharmaceutus.* Gentle Sir,
Be not enraged–the stormy voice of wrath,

II iv *113*. *Hippocrates*: 'the greatest physician of antiquity'. *Galen*: 'prince of the Greek physicians after Hippocrates'. *Celsus*: 'a celebrated physician of the first century'.

II iv *114*. *Boerhaave*: 'one of the greatest physicians, as well as best men, that this or perhaps any age has ever produced', 1668–1738 (all *English Encyclopaedia*).

II iv *117*. *fleshbrush*: used for rubbing, in order to excite the circulation.

II iv *121* ^ *2*] What! thou forsooth mak'st one o' the faculty / Without one faculty to make thee one! *MS deleted.*

II iv *128*. Tilley's *Proverbs* A246, from Horace. *Timon of Athens* I ii 28: 'They say, my lords, "ira furor brevis est".' Jonson, *The Staple of News* V vi 14: 'If your short madnesse, be not more than anger.'

II iv *129*. 'With Boerhaave soap was a general medicine' (*English Encyclopaedia*).

The lifting of the hand, the clenchèd fist,
And the wild glare of the tumultuous eye,
The broken interrupted words, which sound
Hollowly, like a bruised tin-kettle–
*Antonio.* Oaf!
*Pharmaceutus.* The inflation of the fiery cheeks,
blown up
With wind of idle passion, whence proceeds
The flushing of the face like the red clouds
Upon a blowy morning–
*Antonio.* Loon!
*Devil.* Be still,
Antonio, let us hear him out.
*Pharmaceutus.* All these
Betoken anger which is madness. These
Disorder all the animal functions, these
Puzzle the progress of the chyle and hurt
The process of digestion.
*Antonio.* Curses on thee!
When the next sessions sit, i' faith I'll have thee
Indicted for a public nuisance to
His Majesty's loving subjects.
*Pharmaceutus.* Now, by Galen,
Thou art as fine a subject for Phlebotomy
As ever came to my inspection.
I prithee let me breathe a vein, 'twill do thee
An ample service.

[*Here* Antonio *raises his fist to strike him.*]

No, no, not the hand!
I never bleed there, look ye, here's my instrument,
The neck, the nape o' the neck, Sir!
*Antonio.* The grimed Imps
Of Hell arrest thee at the Devil's suit!
The red fiend ride thee into Chancery,
Which is the worst curse I can vent upon thee!
*Devil.* A most ungentlemanly wish, Antonio,
Deserving objurgation–A propos,
The Devil is an ill thing to be jested with;
What if he should be standing by thee now,
Speaking as I do–dressed as I am? What

II iv *144. chyle*: 'intestinal fluid' (*1930*).
II iv *148–98. Now . . . hither*] but behold! /Who is't comes hither? *MS.*
II iv *149. Phlebotomy*: 'The opening of a vein with a proper sharp-edged and pointed instrument' (*English Encyclopaedia*).

If HIS TENEBRIOUS BITUMENSHIP
Should be in hearing o' thee?
*Antonio.* Why, my Amoret,
Thou art an angel and he dare not venture–
*Devil.* A fallen one, I grant ye.
*Antonio.* If a fallen one,
So many sparks of thine ethereal nature
Yet linger round thee as to make thy presence
A portion of the Heaven thou hadst fallen from.
*Devil.* Older and wiser, my good counsellor,
An hour may change thy humour.
*Antonio.* Ay, the section
Of one small minute (if 'twere spent with thee)
Nay, the minutest point of time in which
The inconceivable velocity
Of light can travel through one barley-corn
Of the blue Ether, were enough to raise me
(Providing always it were spent with thee)
From out my present humour, which is that
Of the strong sea when in its ridged advance
Bruised by the inroad of a vassal river,
Or an enchafèd plaintiff face to face
With the defendant.
*Devil.* In the mind of youth
And pertinacious inexperience
A hasty judgment showeth like green fruit!
The more unripe and immature it be,
The harder clings it to its parent bough.
*Antonio.* Thou art the first o' thy sex that e'er found fault with
The judgment of that man who called thee 'Angel'.
I am immutable in nothing, save
The love I bear thee. But behold who is't
Comes swaggering hither? Why, what wants he here?
Methinks he seems a sailor by his swing;
His hat is cocked obliquely on his brow,
One eye is null and void or shut in waggery,
The never-failing tokens of a rascal.
His arms are fixed akimbo, his left cheek
Protruded by a quid–what varlet's this?
Why wends he hither?

II iv *175*. *barley-corn*: 'in length the third part of an inch, and in breadth the eighth' (*English Encyclopaedia*).
II iv *197*. *quid*: chewing-tobacco.

SCENE V

*Enter* Stephanio

*Stephanio.* Blood and thunder, messmates,
It seems I've run aground here.
*Antonio.* True!
*Pharmaceutus.* Ay, true!
*Stephanio.* And anchored damnably in shelves and shallows
And ruinous sandbanks and unwholesome mists.
*Antonio.* How! dost thou stand in bodily fear of us?
*Stephanio.* No, by the Devil and his dam!
*Devil* (*aside*). That's I
And mother Hecate.
*Antonio.* How is then thy case
So ruinous and unwholesome?
*Stephanio.* Split my timbers!
Thou art a lawyer and thus ruinous,
And thou a nauseous apothecary,
And thus unwholesome. Why! we sailors call
Our sharks, sea-lawyers, and our lump fish, doctors.
Have I run foul of ye? how got ye first
Ahead o' me? Why! I came cutting hither
With a fresh breeze i' my stern.
*Antonio.* With what intent?
*Stephanio.* Bound from the cape of hope to the port of love,
To win the prize in yon rich galleon there.
*Antonio.* What! can the heavenly essence of high love
And all the little tendernesses which
Make up the catalogue of love, inhabit
Such tenement as that thy breast affords?
Why, art thou bona fide then in love?
*Stephanio.* I tell thee, fellow, I'm half drowned in love.
*Antonio.* I'faith! I see that thou art half seas over.
*Stephanio.* How! you landlubber, do you banter me?
My senses are all foundered in deep love,
My cables rotted and my timbers beaten
In by the force of love!
*Antonio.* And wilt thou place
Thy claim in opposition to mine?

II v *3–4*] *MSS*; *not 1930*. See ll. 7–8.

II v *12. lump fish*: 'Cyclopterus, the Sucker . . . It adheres with vast force to anything it pleases' (*English Encyclopaedia*).

II v *16*. Cp. Milton's pun on 'the Cape of Hope', *PL* iv 160.

Oyer and terminer! what misdemeanour
Wilt thou be guilty of?
*Stephanio.* And who art thou?
Thou cock-boat, thou poor cock-boat, thou mere shallop
Varnished and painted, whose weak delicate planks
Would shrink beneath a capful o' wind!
*Pharmaceutus.* But I–
*Stephanio.* And thou, sad, leaky, cracked and bulging hull,
Wilt thou too tow thy sluggishness within
Reach of my bomb-shot?
*Antonio.* Marry! here come more
To stretch the thread of my poor Patience
Into so thin and spidery a fibre
That it will crack, unless the vexing grasp
Of these uncomely interruptions
Relax the hold they've ta'en on't–
What man of points is this who cometh first,
In whose whole stature is no wavy line,
No flexure but what is abrupt and sudden?
His eyebrows have no arch, his hair is gathered
Conewise upon his squared and narrow brow,
His thin dry lips seem parallel straight lines,
His red and angular and shapeless nose
Shows like a Gyron gules in Heraldry,
And his sharp chin so narrowed to a point,
That if 'twere possible his neck could bend
'Twould perforate and pierce his collar bone.

### SCENE VI

*Enter* Angulo, Campano, Benedict

*Angulo.* Most glorious luminary, round whose light,
Attracted by thy Majesty of Grace
We make our lowly revolutions,
Exert not thy centrifugal force upon me
But gently lead me to thee, by the power
Of thy centripetal might, that so I may

II v *30*. 'The Anglo-French phrase *oyer et terminer* "to hear and determine" partly anglicized . . . The most comprehensive of the commissions granted to judges on circuit' (*OED*).
II v *43–53*] *Not MS.*
II v *50*. *Gyron*: 'an "ordinary" of triangular shape used in Heraldry' (*1930*). *gules*: red.

By due progression fall within thine arms!
*Campano.* 'Faith, 'tis a garrison well 'curtainèd'!
And it hath much of 'crown-work'!
*Stephanio.* So say I.
Ho! Madam, lower your colours!
*Angulo.* Prithee, heed us
Nor shroud thyself in envious eclipse!
Thou seest we encompass thee like satellites!
*Devil.* Right, Angulo! and, sooth, it gratifies
My woman's vanity to see ye stand thus,
Myself the centre of the circle which
My charms have bowed unto my vassalage!
But there be those among you upon whom
My looks fall distantly, and those on whom
The soft expression of mine eyes emits
A nearer and more partial ray.
*Angulo.* Nay, pardon me–
The radii of a circle are all equal
Unto each other, my good Amoret,
The centre of it equally removed
From any point in the periphery.
*Benedict.* Take heed not of the ungodly! I do come
To give thee ghostly consolation,
But find thee thus encircled with a crew
Of most ungracious sinners, led astray
By machinations of the evil one.
*Devil* (*aside*). True to a hair!
*Benedict.* Now, by our blessèd Lady,
Hearken not to these fleshly-minded men,
Vessels of wrath, the stumbling-blocks of life
(Whom God requite hereafter for their deeds!),
But let us go and count our beads together.
I have a piece of the true cross, inclosed
In crystal, which I'll show thee.
[*Pulling* Devil *after him*]
*Stephanio.* Avast! avast! hi!
Get under weigh, my lads! what all at anchor?

II vi *8. curtained*: 'part of the rampart . . . behind which the soldiers stand to fire'.

II vi *9. crown-work*: 'in fortification, is an outwork running into the field' (both *English Encyclopaedia*).

II vi *12–24*] *Not MS.*

II vi *31. Colossians* ii 18, 'vainly puffed up by his fleshly mind'.

II vi *32. vessels of wrath*: *Romans* ix 22. *stumbling blocks*: Biblical.

II vi *36–8. Avast . . . away*] *Not MS.*

Yare! yare! you see he's towing her away.
*Campano* (*to* Benedict). And so you think to carry it by sap;
We'll countermine you though. Halt, holy rascal!
*Benedict*. Ave Maria! what a speech was that!
Off, sinner! look ye! here's the blessèd Virgin!
[*Shewing her image*]
Wouldst thou impede the saving of a soul?
*Antonio*. Why, who art thou, who with thy raisèd forehead,
Curled lip, and archèd brow, wouldst beat us back,
Squinting through thy green leeky eyes, and shaking
Thy carroty locks, thus smoothly combed upon
Thine austere front–who treadest on this earth
As though thou wert not of it? who art thou?
*Benedict*. One that would hold no converse with thee.
Off!
My soul rejects thee, sinner, and my hair
Doth bristle at thy gross impiety, like
Some baited Boar when blown on by the breathings
Of the rude dog.
*Antonio*. Thou hog in a high wind!
Thou barrel-bellied sanctity!
*Benedict*. Avaunt!
You excommunicated heretic!
*Antonio*. Oh! you tithe pig, and you would worm your way
With that demurity of countenance,
That frozen simulation of innocence,
Into your neighbour's strongholds?
*Campano*. Not so fast, sir,
We'll stick a *cheval de frise* within the breach

II vi *38*. *Yare*: 'among sailors, implies ready or quick' (*English Encyclopaedia*); cp. *Tempest* I i 5–7.

II vi *39–40*] A rat! A rat! / Let us not be undermined thus! Stay, holy Rascal! *MS*. *sap*: 'in sieges, is a trench, or an approach made under cover' (*English Encyclopaedia*).

II vi *44*. *forehead*] front *MS 1st reading*.

II vi *46*. Mooney compares *Midsummer Night's Dream* V i 334: 'His eyes were green as leeks'.

II vi *47*. The tradition that Judas had red hair.

II vi *51–62*. . . . *backward*] CAMPANO Hear, Hear! he braves us.
STEPHANIO Board [Floor *1st reading*] him. *MS*.

II vi *61*. 'A large piece of timber pierced, and traversed with wooden spikes, armed or pointed with iron . . . Its use is to defend a passage, stop a breach' (*English Encyclopaedia*).

And beat him backward.
*Stephanio.* Board him!
*Angulo.* Warring planets!
Here's bullying Mars with front as red as fire,
Here's Mercury and he's the hottest o' ye
And also as they say, the prince of thieves,
With this old crafty Saturn who exceedeth
The rest in bulk, and all at variance
For Venus–why, who'll square the difference?
*Stephanio.* The ship yaws.
*Devil.* Gentlemen, this is not fitting
That ye with noisy and contentious brawls
And dissonance of tongues should thus disturb
The sober, drowsy, stealthy-footed night,
And rudely wake her echoes, shaking thus
These peaceful dewdrops from the boughs above us.
Rather come in and, if ye be inclined
To exalt your voices, send them forth in songs,
Glees, catches, merry madrigals, and such like
Till the roof totter o'er ye!
*Benedict.* Be it so.
'Tis good to be afflicted. I will enter.
*Antonio.* The Devil take the hindmost!
*Devil.* Well said, lawyer!
[*Exeunt into the Cottage. Manet* Devil]

SCENE VII

*Devil.* O Race of Vipers, what should hinder me
From crushing ye to nothing? O vile wasps,
That flying round the honeyed vase dispute
Who first shall dare immersion, could I take ye
And dashing ye upon the earth could bruise
Each impotent passion out o'ye, 'twere well;
But if I left one spark of life in ye,
The slightest glimmerings of existence, straightly
Your teeming and prolific brains would hatch
Conceptions of new vice, and, by and by,

II vi *62. Stephanio . . . him!*] *L.MS; not 1930.*
II vi *63–5. with . . . the*] and Mercury, *MS.*
II vi *66–7. who . . . and*] *Not MS.*
II vi *68–9. why . . . yaws*] *Not MS.* *yaws*: rolls off course.
II vi *71. tongues should*] voices *MS 1st reading.*
II vi *77*] *MS breaks off (missing sheets).*

II vii *1. Matthew* iii 7, 'O generation of vipers'.

When the strong hand of chastisement relaxed,
Ye would run down the steep ascent again
Into the sink from whence ye were exalted,
And would return to the forbidden thing
With renovated zest. In after-life
Were punishment the herald of reform
The infliction o't were good: but who shall fashion
Clay that is hard and untenacious?
Reform is rarer seen in after-life
Than a rose i' the brows of winter. Hark! I hear ye
Head over ears in controversy and strife,
I must unto ye and at any rate
I'll thwart your present schemings–
Bluebeard and Hickathrift! but I'll kick up
The Devil of a Row, or more correctly
The Row of a Devil.
Belial, Abaddon, Astaroth, Asmodeus,
Turn up your smoky eyes, ingrained with soot,
And envy me the pranks which I shall play.
Said I, Asmodeus? 'faith, he was a craven
and a ninny and scared with the fume of fish-liver, which I do much marvel, whether it were owned by Pike, Turbot, Salmon, or Sturgeon–or what fish liver ever possessed such puissant and devil-driving abilities. But, by Styx, they may broil half the fry that swims, before my Devilship would budge an inch.

[*Exit into the Cottage*]

## ACT III

### SCENE I

[*A room in the cottage, a table laid out with meats, wines, etc.* Devil, Antonio, Pharmaceutus, Stephanio, Angulo, Campano *and* Benedict *at table*.]

*Devil*. Here! push the bottle to Antonio,
He's a choice spirit, whose wit shows brightest when
Burnished by wine. Drink sippingly, but not
So as to surfeit the senses; only kindle
The combination of images

II vii *24*. Paden suggests that T. learnt of Tom Hickathrift from *QR* (1819).

II vii *27*. *PL* ii 109, i 422, iv 168; *PR* iv 624.

From whose collision leaps the brilliant spark
Of Heaven-born wit.
*Antonio.* Fair Amoret, I drink
Unto the absence of thy loving husband.
[*To* Stephanio]
Hark ye, Stephanio, ply the Monk with wine,
Mellow his austere nature.
*Stephanio.* Master Benedict,
The bottle is with you.
*Benedict.* With me! O Shame!
Take it away! it doth pollute mine eye-sight.
The simple mountain stream that gusheth down
The cavern doth suffice my natural wants
And the few roots that spring uncultivated.
*Antonio.* Tush! man, thy fair round juicy corporation
Doth give the lie unto thine utterance!
An thou wert buried underneath an oak
It were the goodliest tree in Christendom.
*Stephanio.* 'Tis a fine cargo of guts.
*Angulo.* That is as plain
As that two straight lines can't enclose a space,
The angles of his elbows and his knees
And all the other angles of his person
Are all obtuse. Good living hath worn down
Their natural acuteness. Both his haunches
Are as the segments of a circle.
*Benedict.* Faugh!
*Angulo.* And each particular hair upon his skull
Makes up the shortest distance 'tween two points.
*Benedict.* Avaunt! the upright shall not soil his speech
To answer to the ungodly.
*Stephanio.* Ay, is't so?
Then, Master Benedict, d'ye hear, bring to,
Unless thy weighty flanks desire bombardment,
Although, i' faith, good Nature gave thy carcase
*Broadside* enough. But, rot me, once for all
Drink or be d—d.
*Benedict.* The righteous were made
To suffer persecution.
*Stephanio.* Drink on–
*Benedict.* Hush!

III i *16*. *corporation*: prominent abdomen (*OED* from 1753).
III i *28*. '*i.e.* are combed exactly straight upon his forehead. This is the definition which Archimedes gives of a straight line' (T.'s note).

Blast not my hearing with thine obscene oaths.
Sooner than listen to them, I, by drinking,
Will do a violence unto my nature;
Not that I love the carnal taste of wine,
For the Lord knows I'll only wet my lips
That I may stop your execrations.
[*Drinks off the bumper*]
*Antonio.* Bravo! take heed, he only wets his lips!
*Pharmaceutus.* A little wine in moderation
Doth brace the nerves and lend the flagging
spirits
A healthful tonic and decent gaiety.
*Antonio.* Would it could brace thy person.
*Pharmaceutus.* Or mend thy temper.
*Antonio.* Make thy hips firmer.
*Pharmaceutus.* Or thy tongue less voluble.
*Devil.* Fie, Gentlemen, no brawls!
*Stephanio.* Fair Excellence,
Thou hast held out long enough. I prithee now
Capitulate on honourable terms,
Disclose the dazzling windows of thine eyes,
Display the rosy banners of thy cheeks,
And open the portcullis of thy lips,
Within whose crimson tenement are ranged
Thine ivory files of teeth. Consider, prithee,
How shall the airy ardent kiss make way
Through the thick folds of that dark veil, which bars
All access to the fortress of thy soul.
*Antonio.* Ay! Ay! unveil.
*Angulo.* Disperse thy 'nebulae.'
*Devil.* Ay and the *nebulones* that surround me.
*Antonio.* Thou wert not used to such reservedness.
Veil versus BEAUTY is a case which will
Admit of many pleadings.
*Devil.* 'Troth, I dare not
Unveil lest ye should quarrel for my nose
(*Aside*) (No fear of that methinks) and make partition
Of all the other features of my face.
*Angulo.* And think you that we would bisect your
visage?

III i *60*. *nebulae*: cloudlike clusters of stars.

III i *61*. *nebulones*: 'Latin word meaning idle rascals' (*1930*). Mooney suggests as T.'s source Horace, *Epistles* I ii 28. Sidney's *Arcadia* speaks of 'you brute Nebulons' (*OED*).

III i *68–86*] *MS separate sheet, omitting ll. 73–4.*

*Antonio.* Will you not face us?
*Devil.* Nay, I cannot countenance ye.
*Antonio.* Prithee unveil! why, only double-faces
Do lurk beneath a veil.
*Devil.* And said I not
You wished to halve my physiognomy?
You hint that I am double-faced and hence
'Tis plain you wish that half my face were off.
*Angulo.* Equals from equals taken remain equals.
*Devil.* Let me have no divisions on the point.
*Angulo.* A point hath neither parts nor magnitude,
Thy face hath both and therefore is no point.
*Devil.* From thine own wit I judge thy wit is
pointless,
For thou hast parts and therefore lackest point.
*Antonio.* How should his inability proceed
From his ability? If he hath parts
Then is he not without ability,
But if his language hath no point in it,
Then his ability is null and void.
*Angulo.* Which is absurd.
*Antonio.* Canst solve it?
*Angulo.* I say still
A point hath neither parts nor magnitude–
*Devil.* But this is size-point and hath parts and
magnitude.
*Antonio.* Thou art as full of point as a woolcard,
Amoret.
*Devil.* But you are 'contre-point' and meet me half-
way.
*Campano.* The devil take discussion–that bears
point-blank.
*Stephanio.* I wish the *point* were *doubled.*
*Antonio.* Nay, i' faith
We've had enough on't.
[*Here* Benedict *helps himself*]
What, old Confidence,
Thou top and Pink of all Morality,
Thy taste improves then. Marry, but I had
Some shrewd suspicion that that demi-circle
Of entrails was bowed out with better stuff
Than herb and biscuit.

III i *89. woolcard*: pointed instrument for combing wool.
III i *90. contre-point*: heraldic, with the points meeting.
III i *92. doubled*: *OED* 9, nautical: 'to sail or pass round or to the other side of (a cape or point)'.

*Benedict.* A–avaunt, I–I will not heed the unrighteous.
*Antonio.* Thou dost not like the *carnal* taste of wine?
*Angulo.* How the saint reels about his centre of gravity,
His spine subtends an arc of ninety degrees.
*Stephanio.* 'Faith he hath no small matter in his hold,
He'd keep both pumps at work, I warrant him.
*Devil.* I pray ye, Gentlemen, give ear to me,
It is my wish that ere I do unveil
The ineffable magic of my charms, that each
In turn should chaunt some love-lorn madrigal,
Some amorous ditty which may give him scope
To laud with Love's exaggeration
Unto the height of his ability
My loveliness of feature: after which
To him whose strains are sweetest and whose praise
Sounds softest to the ear of vanity
I purpose the unveiling of my beauty
And will admit him to snatch as many kisses
From lips, cheeks, eyebrows, forehead as he wish
*Ad libitum.* Doth it hit your fancies?
*Antonio.* Ay!
Certes, fair Amoret. Shall I begin?
My voice is sweeter than the chink of silver.
*Campano.* Mine louder than the bugle's clamour.
*Angulo.* And mine
Falls with more regular cadence than–
*Stephanio.* And mine's
Like any cannon.
*Devil.* What saith Benedict?
*Benedict.* My voice was ever yet employed in psalmody.
*Pharmaceutus.* But mine—
*Antonio.* What! thine! the clicking of thy tongue
Upon thy worn-out palate doth resemble
The livelong hammering of thy cursèd pestle
Upon the druggèd mortar and doth surfeit
Our hearing, as thy physics do our taste.
*Devil.* Antonio, prithee sing first.
*Antonio.* Why, then, here goes!
By Jove, I'll warble like the captive thrush.
Thou hast cast over me the golden net,

III i *109. amorous ditty*: cp. *PL* i 449.

The all-subduing trammels of strong love.
My soul is held in such sweet thrall by thee
Had I the power I would not grant it bail,
Therefore, sweet Excellence, my strains shall be
Most like the imprisoned linnet's.
*Devil.* Prithee, gaol-bird,
No prelude to thy warblings–quick–dispatch.
*Stephanio.* I can roar out a catch with the best o' ye.
*Antonio.* If thou presumest to exalt thy voice–
*Stephanio.* Avast! Avast there, messmate! Anchor
quietly.
What! do you bear against me? Put about ship
Or ere a hand can reef the mizzen top-sail,
I'll lend thy stern so warm a cannonading
As peradventure, man, may make thy bowsprit
Drip with salt water.
*Devil.* What, Stephanio,
Wouldst print the booted fury of thy five toes
Into his yielding carcase?
*Stephanio.* Marry, would I.
*Pharmaceutus* (*whispering* Stephanio)
Ay, do't, Stephanio, prithee, do it now.
He lacketh salutary chastisement.
*Antonio.* Thou wouldst not meddle sure with my
entailments.
*Campano.* How! wouldst thou violate his back
settlements?
*Stephanio.* What! do you *side* with him? do you
*back* him?
*Campano.* No,
Not his back-side.
*Antonio.* If thou but stirrest one finger
Or look'st upon me but commandingly, thus,
I'll let more light into thy skull than ever
Shone there of nature, with as rude a polt
As ever cudgel-swinging bumpkin lent
His blue and battered brother-labourer.
*Angulo.* There will be 'Vulgar Fractions' then,
methinks.
*Antonio.* So! So! you thrust your tongue into your
cheek

III i *151.* With a pun on the entailing of property.
III i *155. but*] *L.MS; not 1930.*
III i *157. polt*: 'meaning a hard blow, used by Miss Burney in *Cecilia*, and in Jervas's *Don Quixote*' (*1930*).

As if you doubt my prowess. Why, come on then!
Dost think a lawyer hath but legal weapons?
Canst toddle to the scratch? I'll sew your sees up!
I'll Chancery your upper tenements.
I'll file and bore you scientifically.
I'll make the patchwork peep, I warrant you,
Disorganise your victualling-office, uncork
The claret of your nob, and dim your daylights,
And make your ivories chatter in the tusk box.
*Stephanio.* I'll bring my guns to bear on ye enow,
I'm only gathering wind before I crowd sail.
*Antonio.* Ay, ay, for every mugger thou shalt give me,
I'll lend thee ten and ten and ten to that.
*Angulo.* Oh! a recurring decimal.
*Stephanio.* Come, unrig.
*Antonio.* I am your man.
*Devil.* (*coming behind*) And I your woman, Sir. (*Trips him up*)
*Angulo.* Quod erat demonstrandum!
*Stephanio.* Ha! Ha! foundered!
*Campano.* He hath received some damage in his rear,
And total rout unto his advanced guard.
*Antonio.* How now! the devil! Amoret!
*Devil.* The Devil's Amoret
Is a good part if done in character.
The Devil Amoret! the Devil, Sir!
I was an Angel twenty minutes since,
Did I not say that you would change your humour?
*Antonio.* Assault and battery!
*Devil.* Ha! Ha! Ha! Antonio,
And would you swear me in to keep the peace?
*Pharmaceutus.* It was a bad concussion. Shall I bleed you?
*Antonio.* I am bedevilled and bewizarded.
*Devil.* And have you not the grace to say 'bewitched'?
*Antonio.* Methought a Giant grappled me–What spells
Have put such thew and sinew in an arm
Whose rounded purity seemed only able
To string a necklace or to clasp a bracelet?
*Devil.* What! have I tickled you? your nose drops blood.

III i *164*. *scratch*: starting line.

*Stephanio.* How! hath he sprung a leak? hath he
bilged?
*Angulo.* He hath proved
The law of gravitation lustily–
And yet, methought, the vacuum in his skull
Might have buoyed up his carcase to some purpose.
*Stephanio.* He pitches bravely.
*Antonio.* Murrain take ye all!
Am I a shrovetide cock that ye should crack
Your jests upon me thus? but I'll not stand it.
*Devil.* No, 'faith, you measured all your length just
now.
*Antonio.* What do you take me for?
*Angulo.* A baffled lawyer
Diverging from the perpendicular
Which you have done before now–
*Benedict.* Yea, by'r Lady,
He hath swerved from rectitude.
*Antonio.* O chattering Apes,
Do ye make mouths at me? do ye snap your fingers
As ye esteemed me less than the heated air
Whose rarefied attenuated substance
Would scarce endure the thistle beard to sport
Upon its yielding subtlety? then, here's for ye,
I value not a single soul among ye
The interest which one poor farthing yields
I' the fraction of a second.
*Angulo.* How!
*Campano.* What!
*Stephanio.* Do you brave us all?
*Antonio.* Ay.
*Stephanio.* Split my–
*Devil.* Hist!
[*Knocking*]
*Antonio.* O Lord, the Necromancer!
*Benedict.* Holy Virgin
Defend us!
*Antonio.* We shall all be cats or foxes.
*Stephanio.* 'Twill blow a rough gale.
[*Knocking*]
*Benedict.* Saints deliver me!
I'll never do an evil thing again.

III i *200*. 'A cock tied up and pelted with sticks on Shrove Tuesday' (*OED*).

*Antonio*. I'll never nim a client of his due.
*Pharmaceutus*. I'll never kill a patient any more.
*Stephanio*. Would I were safe i' my hammock, out at sea!
*Pharmaceutus*. Would I were mixing draughts or rolling o' pills!
*Devil*. Wishes prove nothing but the vanity
Of him that wisheth: though, like telescopes,
They bring far things awhile beneath the view,
They cannot 'minish the long interval
And space between the object and the wish.
[*Knocking*]
Quick, quick, be expeditious, Gentlemen.
Look ere you leap but tarry not in looking,
Were a good proverb.
A quick decision i' the nick of time
Outruns mature deliberation
As the strong gush o' the tide in some strait river
Precurses the more sober ocean.
You mount the chimney, Benedict–what now!
Do you stick fast in't? doth its sooty breath
Offend thy proud olfactories? Up farther,
My ghostly chimney-sweep. I warrant this
Is not the first time you have made a chimney
The medium of intrigue. Up farther yet,
Work thy way inward. Hark ye! Pharmaceutus,
Stow your long body cheek by jowl with Angulo
Within the closet yonder. You, Campano,
Cower down beneath the heap o' musty sacks
There i' the corner with Stephanio.
You i' this chest, my worthy Counsellor,
Must with contracted stomach chafe your knees.
So! So! ye are all safe now.
[*Loud and continued knocking*]
I prithee, patience.

## SCENE II

*Outside of the cottage–early morning*

*Magus*. I do much fear my Devil hath played false
Or that the weeds of wanton Idleness
Have mantled his clear wit. Why comes he not?
There is no punishment too sharp for him

III i *220*. *nim*: 'used in seventeenth-century slang, meaning "steal"' (*1930*).

That doth forsake his trust, betray the station
Where we have set him in Authority.
If the frail reed we lean upon should break,
Where most we hope its succour, it were meet
That we should hew it from the wholesome Earth
Which nourisheth and perfects better things.
If he should answer my suspicions,
I'll pen him for some centuries in ice
Up to the neck, I'll rack his thumbs with screws;
I'll twitch his tail until the black blood spout
Forth at each end; I'll fill his jaws with tooth-ache;
I'll stick hot pins through's liver–Hark! he comes.
[*Enter* Devil, *still veiled*]
Ha! Amoret, awake, abroad so early
Blanching the roses of thy cheeks. What now!
The grey cock hath not crowed, the glow-worm still
Leads on unpaled his train of emerald light.
*Devil.* Good faith, most venerable necromancer,
The roses of my visage are not blanched
But rather have attained (be thou my judge)
Unto a depth of dusky colouring. [*Unveils*]
*Magus.* How now, my Hellish Minister, dark child
Of bottomless Hades; what rude waggery,
What jejune undigested joke is this?
To quilt thy fuscous haunches with the flounced,
Frilled, finical delicacy of female dress.
How hast thou dared to girdle thy brown sides
And prop thy monstrous vertebrae with stays?
Speak out, thou petticoated Solecism.
Thou hairy trifler! what mad pranks have sent
Thy diabolical wits a wool-gathering?
*Devil.* A linen-gathering I grant you, Master.
*Magus.* Certes, it seems your Devilship tonight
Is unaccountably facetious!
Speak and beware the magic of my spells!
Or I will rive yon mighty Cedar-Tree
Sheer from its topmost windiest branch unto
The lowest fang o' the root–between each half

III ii *15. each*] *L.MS; the 1930.*

III ii *20. unpaled*: T. antedates *OED*'s first example in this sense, 1831.

III ii *32. Solecism*: 'a false manner of speaking, contrary to the rules of grammar' (*English Encyclopaedia*).

III ii *39–42.* Cp. Prospero threatening Ariel, *Tempest* I ii 294–6: 'If thou more murmur'st, I will rend an oak, / And peg thee in his knotty entrails, till / Thou hast howled away twelve winters.'

I'll place thy sinful carcase and again
When the cleft stem shall close without a fissure
Thy bunching body shall be quashed as flat
As spider in a hinge.
*Devil.* Nay, prithee–
*Magus.* Speak, then,
And tell me why thy horny scalp is thus
Enveloped in the foldings of this veil?
*Devil.* Why lurks the Bravo's dagger in the sheath
Ere yet it glitter o'er his enemy?
Why is the curvèd fish-hook buried in
The length o' the twisting worm? My gudgeons play
Around the baited snare. My horny scalp
Is buried in the foldings of this veil
To save thy scalp from horns.
*Magus.* Ay? is it so?
Good Devil bear with me. My nature is
Most quickly moved to anger which as quickly
Is wasted like the flint o' the veiny Earth
Which underneath the hoof one moment flashes
A particle of intense fire which dies
As instantly. But wind and wave have chafed me,
The Anarchy of the impetuous blast
And the wet beatings of the step-dame surge
Have ruffled my smooth temper.
*Devil.* Gentle Master,
Unless thine oars had been swift wings, thy boat
Some pinioned steed of air, thine ocean-path
The limitless Abyss of Ether's space,
I know not how thou hast measured back thy way
So keenly.
*Magus.* Half the powers o' the other world
Were leagued against my journeying: but had not
The irresistible and lawless might
Of brazen-handed fixed Fatality
Opposed me, I had done it. The black storm–
From out whose mass of volumed vapour sprang
The lively curling thunderbolt–had ceased

III ii *48. Bravo*: desperado.
III ii *54. horns*: symbol of cuckoldry.
III ii *62. step-dame*: as in Campbell's *Lines on the Grave of a Suicide*: 'the stepdame buffetings of fate'.
III ii *73. volumed*: 'formed into a rolling, rounded, or dense mass', *OED* 2, citing Scott ('volumed flame'), and Byron ('volumed smoke').

Long ere from out the dewy depth of Pines
Emerging on the hollowed banks, that bound
The leapings of the saucy tide, I stood –
The mighty waste of moaning waters lay
So goldenly in moonlight, whose clear lamp
With its long line of vibratory lustre
Trembled on their dun surface, that my Spirit
Was buoyant with rejoicings. Each hoar wave
With crispèd undulation arching rose,
Thence falling in white ridge with sinuous slope
Dashed headlong to the shore and spread along
The sands its tender fringe of creamy spray.
Thereat my shallop lightly I unbound,
Spread my white sail and rode exulting on
The placid murmurings of each feathery wave
That hurried into sparkles round the cleaving
Of my dark Prow; but scarcely had I past
The third white line of breakers when a squall
Fell on me from the North, an inky Congress
O' the Republican clouds unto the zenith
Rushed from the horizon upwards with the speed
Of their own thunderbolts.
The seas divided and dim Phantasies
Came thronging thickly round me, with hot eyes
Unutterable things came flitting by me;
Semblance of palpability was in them,
Albeit the wavering lightnings glittered through
Their shadowed immaterialities.
Black shapes clung to my boat; a sullen owl
Perched on the Prow, and overhead the hum
As of infernal Spirits in mid Heaven
Holding aerial council caught mine ear.
Then came a band of melancholy sprites,
White as their shrouds and motionlessly pale
Like some young Ashwood when the argent Moon
Looks in upon its many silver stems.
And thrice my name was syllabled i' the air
And thrice upon the wave, like that loud voice

III ii *81. their*] *L.MS*; the *1930*.

III ii *97ff.* Cp. *Armageddon* i 47–54, 'Black, formless, unclean things came flitting by . . .' (p. 67). Cp. (noting l. 111) *Comus* 205–9: 'A thousand fantasies / Begin to throng into my memory / Of calling shapes, and beckning shadows dire, / And airy tongues, that syllable mens names / On Sands, and Shoars, and desert Wildernesses.'

III ii *112–4.* Plutarch, *De Defectu Oraculorum* 17: 'Suddenly from the island of Paxi was heard the voice of someone loudly calling Thamus, so that all

Which through the deep dark night i' the olden time
Came sounding o'er the lone Ionian.
Thereat I girded round my loins the scarf
Thy Mother Hecate gave me and withstood
The violent tempest: the insulting surge
Rode over me in glassy arch but dared not
Sprinkle one drop of its nefarious spray
Upon my charmèd person: the red heralds
O' the heavy-footed thunder glanced beside me,
Kissed my bared front and curled around my brow
In lambent wreaths of circling fire, but could not
Singe one loose lock of vagrant grey, that floated
To the wind's dalliance. But nor magic spells,
Vigour of heart or vigilance of hand,
Could back the Ocean's spumy menacings,
Which drove my leaky skiff upon the sands.
Soon as I touched firm Earth, each mounting billow
Fell laxly back into its windless bed,
And all the moon-lit Ocean slumbered still.
Thrice with bold prow I breasted the rough spume
But thrice a vitreous wall of waves up-sprung
Ridging the level sea–so fared it with me
Foiled of my purpose. Some unwholesome star,
Some spells of darker Gramarie than mine,
Ruled the dim night and would not grant me
passage.
*Devil.* Thou hast come fittingly.
*Magus.* How so?
*Devil.* My plans
Are growing to a head.
*Magus.* And hast thou guarded
With scrupulous exactness–
*Devil.* Grant me but
The tenth part of an hour and I will mesh
In the entanglement of stratagem
These lawless insolents; thyself shall take
That vengeance which thou wishest.
*Magus.* Who are within?
*Devil.* Water and oil.

were amazed. Thamus was an Egyptian pilot, not known by name even to many on board. Twice he was called and made no reply, but the third time he answered; and the caller, raising his voice, said, "When you come opposite to Palodes, announce that Great Pan is dead."'

III ii *136*. *Gramarie*: *OED* 2, 'occult learning, magic, necromancy. Revived [originally 1470] in literary use by Scott', *Lay of the Last Minstrel* (1805).

*Magus.* What mean you?
*Devil.* Salt and pepper.
*Magus.* Be less ambiguous.
*Devil.* A most warring compound
Of uncongenial elements, good Master.
'Faith, seldom doth thy dice box, Intercourse,
Turn up such rude unmated numbers.
*Magus.* Ha!
Where's Amoret?
*Devil.* Asleep.
*Magus.* Art sure?
*Devil.* Most certain.
*Magus.* 'Tis well. I wait without. What signal, prithee,
Shall summon my approach?
*Devil.* A beat o' the foot, or
The shrill collision of my palms–thus–thrice, or
A clearing of the throat–thus–meaningly.
*Magus.* I will be sure to mark it. Get thee gone
And do thy bidding, Devil.
[*Exit* Devil]
'Tis even thus–
And they would pluck from the casket the sole gem
Of mine affections, taint its innocent lustre,
And give it back dishonoured, they would canker
My brightest flower, would muddy the clear source
Whence flows my only stream of earthly bliss;
Would let the foul consuming worm into
The garner of my love. O Earthliness!
Man clambers over the high battlements
That part the principalities of good
And ill–perchance a few hot tears, and then
The seared heart yields to 't and Crime's signet stamps
Her burning image there. The summer fly
That skims the surface of the deep black pool
Knows not the gulf beneath its slippery path.
Man sees, but plunges madly into it.
We follow through a night of crime and care
The voice of soft Temptation, still it calls,
And still we follow onwards, till we find
She is a Phantom and–we follow still.
When couched in Boyhood's passionless tranquillity,
The natural mind of man is warm and yielding,
Fit to receive the best impressions,
But raise it to the atmosphere of Manhood
And the rude breath of Dissipation
Will harden it to stone. 'Tis like the seaplant

Which in its parent and unshaken depths
Is mouldable as clay, but when rude hands
Have plucked it from its billowless Abyss
Unto the breathings of Heaven's airs, each gust
Which blows upon 't will fix it into hardness.
I'll to the Northern casement which looks over
The shrubby banks o' the mountain Lake, for thence
The slightest whisper from within may reach me.

### SCENE III

*Interior of* Magus's *cottage. Enter* Devil

*Devil.* O ye puissant spirits whose tried powers
The issue of this night hath fully proved,
Though your undoubted prowess hath descended
In dearth of other merriment to play
At hide and seek–come forth!
*Stephanio* (*whispering from under his sacks*).
Is the coast clear?
Has he heeled offward?
*Antonio* (*half raising the lid of the chest*).
Is the sorcerer gone?
*Devil.* 'Awake, arise, or be for ever fallen.'
*Campano.* What! did he beat a parley with thee,
Amoret?
Or did ye sally forth, and nail his Ordnance
Ere it had vent?
*Benedict* (*up in the chimney*).
The Lord deliver me!
That ever Benedict should come to this!
*Devil.* Out of your holes, ye Rats! uncavern ye,
White-livered conies!
*Antonio.* Why, thou art a Shrew.
*Devil.* Nay, give the Devil his due, I am not shrewish.
*Antonio.* Beshrew me, if thou art not. Where is
Magus,
And his familiar?
*Devil.* Fear, like Drunkenness
Sees ever double: there was only one.
'Twas an old suitor whom I had discarded,
A miserly craving man, whose white hairs preach
Against his manners,
One who hath heaped up coin until the means

III iii *1. puissant*: three syllables.
III iii *7. PL* i 330.

Became the end of being; his hair was laced
With cobwebs, his sad calculating brows
Gathered into a hundred dusty wrinkles.
A rusty key with many less ones dangled
Beside him, his parched person showed most like
A disembowelled Mummy or dried Moth.
There was no moisture on his fissured lip.
He thrust his shrivelled fingers into mine,
And mumbled from his dry and corky tongue
Some sentences which intimated Love,
But sounded like chafed parchment or the whistle
Of tight and corded Inexpressibles.
Even such an one so sapless and so withered
I closed my door upon.
*Benedict* (*groaning in the chimney*).
Beate Martin!
*Antonio*. He calls for Betty Martin.
*Devil*. And he'll find her,
For she is marvellously fond of soot.
*Pharmaceutus* (*who has advanced into the stage with* Angulo).
Did you speak verity, my oil of Roses?
Who shook the door so keenly?
*Angulo*. Ay, good mistress,
Are we correct i' the data?
*Devil*. Know you not
Philargyrus, to whose roof the sparrow's nest
Owes not a straw that lines it?
*Pharmaceutus*. Know him? Ay,
A weak, old patient with a thready pulse,
And dry unfruitful palm, which lacketh ever
The wholesome dew of perspiration.
But I much marvel how he knocked so briskly.
*Devil*. He was enraged we did not open to him:

III iii *25. on*] *L.MS; in 1930.*

III iii *30. corky tongue*: as in *Memory* [*Ay me*] 39 (p. 264).

III iii *33.* 'I suggest, with some diffidence, that this line refers to the whistling sound which is caused by the rubbing together of the legs of corduroy trousers in walking' (*1930*). *OED* gives (for 'inexpressibles') breeches or trousers, from 1790.

III iii *36.* 'All my eye and Betty Martin' (*Oxford Dictionary of English Proverbs*, from 1785).

III iii *41.* 'Philargyrous', money-loving (*OED*, 1654).

III iii *43. thready*: *OED* 4 (from 1753) cites a definition in 1899: 'a small, scarcely perceptible pulse found in the terminal stages of fatal diseases'.

And irritation oftentimes doth nerve
The puny frame with artificial strength.
A child in wrath will cast a heavy stone,
Which in his tamer mood he scarce had moved.
But to the point! We tarry long in colloquy,
The cool and pearly grey of dawn hath crept
Into the sable bosom of the night.
It were fit time that I should call from ye
The man that hits my fancy.
*Pharmaceutus.* Wilt unveil then,
My liniment of Linseed, my Electuary,
My syrup of Poppies, eh? my flower of sulphur?
*Devil* (*aside*). That's a *home* touch, though but a random hit.
My flower of sulphur quotha! By the Cabbala
A pretty flower of sulphur shall ye find me.
My thoughts begin to burn: a Devil's heat
Glows through me to the core: have at ye, Sirs!

# 3 *Armageddon

Passages of the poem were printed by Sir Charles Tennyson, *Nineteenth Century* cix (1931) 371–3. Printed in full *1931*, pp. 6–16: 'When Tennyson was in his second year at Cambridge, his father pressed him to enter for the Prize Poem (the "Chancellor's Medal"). He consented, though much against his will. The subject of the composition was *Timbuctoo*, and Tennyson, apparently unwilling to devote much thought or labour to the task, sent home for this early poem on the somewhat incongruous theme of *Armageddon*, which he adapted to the subject in hand. The poem won the prize .... *Armageddon* is evidently very early work and this is probably an early draft, seeming from the handwriting to have been written when the poet was not more than fifteen.' The *1931* text of *Armageddon* is from *H.Nbk 2* (watermarked 1824), and from this text it appeared that less than fifty lines of *Armageddon* were incorporated in *Timbuctoo* (p. 170). But a different version of *Armageddon* in *T.Nbk 18* (which may not be quoted) makes it clear that about 120 lines, roughly half of *Timbuctoo*, were taken over almost verbatim from *Armageddon*. The whole central vision of *Timbuctoo* (ll. 62–190) was present, with a few trivial variants, in *Armageddon* in this

III iii *57*. *Electuary*: 'a medical paste made of some powder or other ingredient mixed with honey or syrup' (*1930*).

III iii *60*. *Cabbala*: 'using improperly certain passages of Scripture for magic operations, or forming magic characters or figures with stars or talismans' (*English Encyclopaedia*).

III iii *63*] *Here the MS ends abruptly* (*1930*).

notebook (which is dated 10 Jan. 1828). *Armageddon* includes some extra lines, so that there is not the uninterrupted sequence *Timbuctoo* 62–190. *T.MS* makes clear that H.T. did not exaggerate in saying that T. 'patched up an old poem on *The Battle of Armageddon*' (*Mem.* i 45–6), and that T. was right to speak of 'the turning of an old poem on *Armageddon* into *Timbuctoo* by a little alteration of the beginning and the end' (*Mem.* ii 355). There are two further links: that, as Sir Charles Tennyson remarks, *Armageddon* provided *Timbuctoo* with its opening line: and that *Timbuctoo* 28–40, on the city and the priestess, are a reworking of passages from the *T.MS* of *Armageddon*. See C. Ricks, *MLR* lxi (1966) 23–4.

The further differences between *T.MS* of *Armageddon* and *1931* are as follows. *T.MS* is divided into sections i–ix, of which i–vi correspond to *1931*'s 'I'. These six sections include about fifty extra lines. Sections vii–viii are *1931*'s 'II'. Section ix consists of what was to be *Timbuctoo* 184, followed by twenty-two lines (not in *Timbuctoo* or *1931*) that describe the pavilion; several of these lines were adopted in *Pierced through* 30–41 (p. 473), and there is a version of them in *The Coach of Death* 177–88 (p. 81). Here *T.MS* ends (thereafter leaves are missing from the notebook), which means that it does not contain the last ten lines of *1931*'s 'II' or any of 'III' and 'IV'. Though *T.MS* is somewhat fuller in the opening passages, it omits a good deal of *1931* but does include a great deal more of *Timbuctoo*.

Paden (p. 148) discovered that the source for the description of Cotopaxi's eruption was Ulloa's *Voyage to South America*, which is quoted in *1827* (p. 58); the 1772 edition is at *Lincoln*. Paden reproduces a plate from this edition: 'In the foreground rises Cotopaxi, in eruption. While the sun rises, a man looks west to see his own image, reflected from invisible Andean vapors; the apparition is surrounded by three concentric rainbows and a white outer arch. Behind the man stand a temporary shelter made from three tree-trunks and some leafy boughs, and a field tent .... There can be little doubt that [T.] remembered the collocation of Cotopaxi, the lurid sun, the enhaloed vision and the tents when he came to write *Armageddon*. In that poem the eery and oppressive atmosphere of the days preceding a volcanic eruption has become a symbol of the Day of Doom.' Armageddon (*Revelation* xvi 16) is the site of the last decisive battle at the Day of Judgment: 'And he gathered them together into a place called in the Hebrew tongue Armageddon. And the seventh angel poured out his vial into the air; and there came a great voice out of the temple of heaven, from the throne, saying, It is done. And there were voices, and thunders, and lightnings; and there was a great earthquake, such as was not since men were upon the earth, so mighty an earthquake, and so great. And the great city was divided into three parts, and the cities of the nations fell: and great Babylon came in remembrance before God, to give unto her the cup of the wine of the fierceness of his wrath. And every island fled away, and the mountains were not found.' George Townsend, like T. of Trinity College, Cambridge, had published a Miltonic blank verse poem *Armageddon* (1815).

I

........Prophecy whose mighty grasp
.......ings whose capacious soul
.......illimitable abyss
.......bottomless futurity
.....giant figures that shall pace
.....of its stage–whose subtle ken
.....the doubly darkened firmament
.....to come with all its burning stars
At awful intervals. I thank thy power,
Whose wondrous emanation hath poured
Bright light on what was darkest, and removed
The cloud that from my mortal faculties
Barred out the knowledge of the Latter Times.

I stood upon the mountain which o'erlooks
The valley of destruction and I saw
Things strange, surpassing wonder; but to give
Utterance to things inutterable, to paint
In dignity of language suitable
The majesty of what I then beheld,
Were past the power of man. No fabled Muse
Could breathe into my soul such influence
Of her seraphic nature, as to express
Deeds inexpressible by loftiest rhyme.

I stood upon the mountain which o'erlooks
The valley of Megiddo.–Broad before me
Lay a huge plain whereon the wandering eye,
Weary with gazing, found no resting-place,
Unbroken by the ridge of mound or hill

¶ 3.i *1–8. 'MS obliterated here': 1931. T.MS unfortunately may not be used to supply these words.*

i *6. subtle ken*] prescience *H.MS 1st reading.*

i *9. At awful*] *H.MS;* ... erful *1931.* *I ... power*] Pour on me now *H.MS 1st reading.*

i *10*] The influence of thy nature, as shall throw *H.MS 1st reading.*

i *11. was*] is *H.MS 1st reading.*

i *14.* Incorporated as *Timbuctoo* I, as Sir Charles Tennyson remarks.

i *16. give*] paint *H.MS 1st reading.*

i *17. inutterable*] *H.MS;* unutterable *1931.*

i *19 ^ 20*] *T.MS has three lines.*

i *23.* Miltonic: cp. *PL* viii 113: 'Distance inexpressible'; *Lycidas* 11: 'lofty rhyme'.

i *25. Megiddo*: Armageddon is the Hebrew *har megiddon*, the mountain district of Megiddo.

Or far-off cone of some aerial mount
Varying the horizon's sameness.
Eve came down
Upon the valleys and the sun was setting;
Never set sun with such portentous glare
Since he arose on that gay morn, when Earth
First drunk the light of his prolific ray.
Strange figures thickly thronged his burning orb,
Spirits of discord seemed to weave across
His fiery disk a web of bloody haze,
Through whose reticulations struggled forth
His ineffectual, intercepted beams,
Curtaining in one dark terrific pall
Of dun-red light heaven's azure and earth's green.

The beasts fled to their dens; the little birds
All winged their way home shrieking: fitful gusts
Of violent tempest shook the scanty palm
That clothed the mountain-ridge whereon I stood:
And in the red and murky Even light,
Black, formless, unclean things came flitting by;
Some seemed of bestial similitude
And some half human, yet so horrible,
So shadowy, indistinct and undefined,
It were a mockery to call them aught
Save unrealities, which took the form
And fashioning of such ill-omened things
That it were sin almost to look on them.

There was a mingling too of such strange sounds
(Which came at times upon my startled hearing)
Half wailing and half laughter; such a dissonance
Of jarring confused voices, part of which

i *36–7*. Cp. *In Memoriam* iii 5–8: '"The stars," she whispers, "blindly run; / A web is woven across the sky; / From out waste places comes a cry, / And murmurs from the dying sun.'

i *39*. *ineffectual*: cp. *Hamlet* I v 90, 'uneffectual fire'.

i *40–1*. *Macbeth* I v 49–50: 'Come, thick night, / And pall thee in the dunnest smoke of hell'. Cp. iii 14–15 and iv 3 below.

i *43*. *fitful gusts*: as in Keats, 'Keen fitful gusts'.

i *46–54*. Cp. *The Devil and the Lady* III ii 97–102: 'The seas divided and dim Phantasies / Came thronging thickly round me, with hot eyes / Unutterable things came flitting by me; / Semblance of palpability was in them, / Albeit the wavering lightnings glittered through / Their shadowed immaterialities.'

i *54*. *That . . . almost*] It were almost a sin *H.MS 1st reading*.

Seemed hellish and part heavenly, whisperings,
Low chauntings, strangled screams, and other notes
Which I may liken unto nothing which
I ever heard on Earth, but seemed most like
A mixture of the voice of man and beast;
And then again throughout the lurid waste
Of air, a breathless stillness reigned, so deep,
So deathlike, so appalling, that I shrunk
Into myself again, and almost wished
For the recurrence of those deadly sounds,
Which fixed my senses into stone, and drove
The buoyant life-drops back into my heart.

Nor did the glittering of white wings escape
My notice far within the East, which caught
Ruddy reflection from the ensanguined West;
Nor, ever and anon, the shrill clear sound
Of some aerial trumpet, solemnly
Pealing throughout the Empyrean void.

Thus to some wakeful hind who on the heights
Outwatches the wan planet, comes the sound
Of some far horn along the distant hills
Echoing, in some beleaguered country, where
The pitiless Enemy by night hath made
Sudden incursion and unsafe inroad.

The streams, whose imperceptible advance,
Lingering in slow meanders, once was wont
To fertilize the plain beneath–whose course
Was barely marked save by the lazy straws
That wandered down them–now, as instinct with life,
Ran like the lightning's wing, and dashed upon
The curvature of their green banks a wreath
Of lengthened foam; and yet, although they rushed
Incalculably swift and fringed with spray
The pointed crags, whose wave-worn slippery height
Parted their glassy channels, there awoke

i *63 ∧ 4*] *T.MS has sixteen lines.* They describe the noise of reptiles etc., like the clashing of two torrents in a valley.

i *73 ∧ 4*] *T.MS has four lines.* They are about a city in its evil day.

i *78. wan planet*: cp. *PL* x 412–13: 'the blasted Starrs lookt wan, / And Planets'.

i *84. slow meanders*: *Comus* 232, 'slow *Meander*'s'.

i *90. lengthened foam*: Keats, *Endymion* ii 348: 'lengthened wave'.

i *92. wave-worn*: *Tempest* II i 119.

i *93. channels, ∧ there*] *T.MS has two lines.*

No murmurs round them—but their sapphire depths
Of light were changed to crimson, as the sky
Glowed like a fiery furnace.
In the East
Broad rose the moon, first like a beacon-flame
Seen on the far horizon's utmost verge,
Or red eruption from the fissured cone
Of Cotopaxi's cloud-capt altitude;
Then with dilated orb and marked with lines
Of mazy red athwart her shadowy face,
Sickly, as though her secret eyes beheld
Witchcraft's abominations, and the spells
Of sorcerers, what time they summon up
From out the stilly chambers of the earth
Obscene, inutterable phantasies.

The sun went down; the hot and feverish night
Succeeded; but the parched, unwholesome air
Was unrecruited by the tears of heaven.
There was a windless calm, a dismal pause,
A dreary interval, wherein I held
My breath and heard the beatings of my heart.
The moon showed clearer yet, with deadlier gleam,
Her ridgèd and uneven surface stained
With crosses, fiery streaks, and wandering lines—

i *95 ∧ 6*] *T.MS has four lines on the heat.*
i *96–100*] *T.MS* has a different version, on temple priests.
i *97. first*] most *H.MS 1st reading.*
i *100. Cotopaxi*] Chimborazo *H.MS 1st reading*. The two mountains are juxtaposed in *On Sublimity* 87–8: 'Hoar Cotopaxi's cloud-capt majesty, / Enormous Chimborazo's naked pride.' Here too Cotopaxi is 'cloud-capt' (from *Tempest* IV i 152).
i *104. Witchcraft's*] *H.MS*; Witchcrafts, *1931.*
i *104, 107.* Cp. the monsters of Milton's Hell, 'Abominable, inutterable', *PL* ii 626.
i *106. stilly*: This poeticism is listed in *OED* from 1776 (Mickle, Coleridge, Shelley, Moore).
i *107 ∧ 8*] *T.MS has thirteen lines.* They include a description of the sea.
i *110.* Cp. *The Tears of Heaven* (p. 239). *unrecruited:* unrefreshed; cp. Wesley's *Psalm* civ 4, 'Thy Rains from Heaven parched Hills recruit'.
i *110 ∧ 11*] *T.MS has three lines*: on dew blighting plants.
i *111. windless calm: The Lover's Tale* ii 204; Shelley, *Scenes from Calderon* ii 97.
i *114. deadlier gleam*: cp. Shelley, *The Cenci* II i 189: 'deadlier gloom'.

Bloody impressions! and a star or two
Peered through the thick and smoky atmosphere.

Strange was that lunar light; the rock which stood
Fronting her sanguine ray seemed changed unto
A pillar of crimson, while the other half
Averted, and whatever else around
Stood not in opposition to her beams,
Was shrouded in the densest pall of night
And darkness almost palpable.
Deep fear
And trembling came upon me, when I saw
In the remotest chambers of the East
Ranges of silver tents beside the moon,
Clear, but at distance so ineffable,
That, save when keenly viewed, they else might seem
But little shining points or galaxies,
The blending of the beams of many stars.

Full opposite within the livid West,
In clear relief against the long rich vein
Of melancholy red that fringed the sky,
A suite of dark pavilions met mine eyes,
That covered half the western side of Heaven,
Far stretching, in the midst of which towered one
Pre-eminent, which bore aloft in air
A standard, round whose staff a mighty snake
Twined his black folds, the while his ardent crest
And glossy neck were swaying to and fro.

II

A rustling of white wings! The bright descent
Of a young seraph! and he stood beside me
In the wide foldings of his argent robes

i *118. thick*] dun *H.MS 1st reading.*

i *125.* Cp. *PL* xii 188 (the plagues of Egypt): 'palpable darkness'.

i *133. livid*] *H.MS* (?); lurid *1931.* The former reading is supported by Thomson, *Winter* 224: 'the livid east'.

i *137. side*] *H.MS*; tide *1931.*

ii *1*] *T.MS precedes this with Timbuctoo 62, beginning the major incorporation into the later poem.*

ii *1. A*] *H.MS*; The *1931.*

ii *2. beside*] before *H.MS 1st reading.*

ii *3*] *1931, H.MS; not T.MS.* (This line, unlike those around it, was not incorporated in *Timbuctoo*.)

There on the ridge, and looked into my face
With his inutterable shining eyes,
So that with hasty motion I did veil
My vision with both hands, and saw before me
Such coloured spots as dance athwart the eyes
Of those that gaze upon the noonday sun.

'O Son of Man, why stand you here alone
Upon the mountain, knowing not the things
Which will be, and the gathering of nations
Unto the mighty battle of the Lord?
Thy sense is clogged with dull Mortality,
Thy spirit fettered with the bond of clay–
Open thine eyes and see!'
I looked, but not
Upon his face, for it was wonderful
With its exceeding brightness, and the light
Of the great Angel Mind which looked from out
The starry glowing of his restless eyes.
I felt my soul grow godlike, and my spirit
With supernatural excitation bound
Within me, and my mental eye grew large
With such a vast circumference of thought,
That, in my vanity, I seemed to stand
Upon the outward verge and bound alone
Of God's omniscience. Each failing sense,
As with a momentary flash of light,
Grew thrillingly distinct and keen. I saw
The smallest grain that dappled the dark Earth,
The indistinctest atom in deep air,
The Moon's white cities, and the opal width
Of her small, glowing lakes, her silver heights
Unvisited with dew of vagrant cloud,
And the unsounded, undescended depth
Of her black hollows. Nay–the hum of men

ii *5. inutterable*] *H.MS*; unutterable *1931*.
ii *8. athwart*] *H.MS*; before *1931*.
ii *12. of*] *H.MS*; of the *1931*.
ii *14. dull Mortality*: Shelley, *Epipsychidion* 389; Keats, *Endymion* iii 907.
ii *16.* Cp. the Angel Michael's clearing of Adam's sight for the vision from the mountain in *PL* xi 411ff: '*Adam*, now ope thine eyes'.
ii *19. which*] *H.MS*; that *1931*.
ii *24.* Cp. Shelley, *Epipsychidion* 550: 'Within that calm circumference of bliss'.
ii *31. deep air*: Shelley, *Hellas* 629, and *Prometheus Unbound* IV 336.
ii *36. hollows.* ‸ *Nay*] *T.MS has Timbuctoo 103–9.* ('The . . . Sapphire').

Or other things talking in unknown tongues,
And notes of busy Life in distant worlds,
Beat, like a far wave, on my anxious ear.

I wondered with deep wonder at myself:
My mind seemed winged with knowledge and the strength
Of holy musings and immense Ideas,
Even to Infinitude. All sense of Time
And Being and Place was swallowed up and lost
Within a victory of boundless thought.
I was a part of the Unchangeable,
A scintillation of Eternal Mind,
Remixed and burning with its parent fire.
Yea! in that hour I could have fallen down
Before my own strong soul and worshipped it.

Highly and holily the Angel looked.
Immeasurable Solicitude and Awe,
And solemn Adoration and high Faith,
Were traced on his imperishable front–
Then with a mournful and ineffable smile,
Which but to look on for a moment filled
My eyes with irresistible sweet tears,
In accents of majestic melody,
Like a swollen river's gushings in still night
Mingled with floating music, thus he spoke.

### III

'O Everlasting God, and thou not less
The Everlasting Man (since that great spirit
Which permeates and informs thine inward sense,
Though limited in action, capable
Of the extreme of knowledge–whether joined
Unto thee in conception or confined
From former wanderings in other shapes
I know not–deathless as its God's own life,

ii *44. swallowed up and lost*: *PL* ix 642.
ii *48. burning*] glowing *H.MS 1st reading.*
ii *50* ‸ *51*] *T.MS has Timbuctoo 113–45.* The MS follows this with thirteen lines on history; then *Timbuctoo* 146–57; then (a new section) *Timbuctoo* 158–83; then (the beginning of a new section) *Timbuctoo* 184, followed by twenty-two lines describing the pavilion. *T.MS* then ends.
ii *53. solemn Adoration*: *PL* iii 351 (the angels praising God).
ii *55–60*] *These are the only lines to be found in both 1931 and Timbuctoo that are not in T.MS.*

Burns on with inextinguishable strength),
O Lords of Earth and Tyrannies of Hell,
And Thrones of Heaven, whose triple pride shall clash
In the annihilating anarchy
Of unimaginable war, a day
Of darkness riseth on ye, a thick day,
Palled with dun wreaths of dusky fight, a day
Of many thunders and confusèd noise,
Of bloody grapplings in the interval
Of the opposèd Battle, a great day
Of wonderful revealings and vast sights
And inconceivable visions, such as yet
Have never shone into the heart of Man–
THE DAY of the Lord God!'
His voice grew deep
With volumes of strong sound, which made the rock
To throb beneath me, and his parted locks
Of spiral light fell raylike, as he moved,
On each white shoulder: his ambrosial lip
Was beautifully curved, as in the pride
And power of his mid Prophecy: his nostril
Dilated with Expression; half upturned
The broad beneficence of his clear brow
Into the smoky sky; his sunlike eyes
With tenfold glory lit; his mighty arm
Outstretched described half-circles; small thin flashes
Of intense lustre followed it.

IV

I looked,
And lo! the vision of the night was changed.
The sooty mantle of infernal smoke
Whose blank, obliterating, dewless cloud
Had made the plain like some vast crater, rose
Distinct from Earth and gathered to itself
In one dense, dry, interminable mass

iii *13. war*] fight *H.MS 1st reading.*
iii *14–15. Macbeth* I v 49–50: 'Come, thick night, / And pall thee in the dunnest smoke of hell'. Cp. i 40–1 and iv 3.
iii *20. inconceivable*] unimaginable *H.MS 1st reading*; inexpressible *H.MS 2nd reading.*
iii *34. lustre* ^ *followed*] quickly *H.MS deleted.*
iv *1–2.* Cp. *PL* xi 712: 'He look'd, and saw the face of things quite chang'd'.
iv *4. dewless*: cp. Thomas Campbell, *Pleasures of Hope* I: 'When the sea-wind wafts the dewless day'.

Sailing far Northward, as it were the shadow
Of this round Planet cast upon the face
Of the bleak air. But this was wonderful,
To see how full it was of living things,
Strange shapings, and anomalies of Hell,
And dusky faces, and protruded arms
Of hairy strength, and white and garish eyes,
And silent intertwisted thunderbolts,
Wreathing and sparkling restlessly like snakes
Within their grassy depths. I watched it till
Its latest margin sank beneath the sweep
Of the horizon.
All the crimson streaks
And bloody dapplings faded from the disk
Of the immaculate Moon.
An icy veil
Of pale, weak, lifeless, thin, unnatural blue
Wrapt up the rich varieties of things
In grim and ghastly sameness.
The clear stars
Shone out with keen but fixed intensity,
All-silence, looking steadfast consciousness
Upon the dark and windy waste of Earth.
There was a beating in the atmosphere,
An indefinable pulsation
Inaudible to outward sense, but felt
Through the deep heart of every living thing,
As if the great soul of the Universe
Heaved with tumultuous throbbings on the vast
Suspense of some grand issue.

# 4 *The Coach of Death

## A Fragment

Printed *Mem.* i 28–32, as 'written at 14 or 15' ('about 16', *Mat.* i 43). Lines 133–92 are now first printed from *Y.MS.* The poem appears in *H.Nbk 2* (watermarked 1824), along with *Armageddon* and *The Devil and the Lady*. In *T.Nbk 19* (which may not be quoted), it is with *The Devil and*

iv *21. Moon*] *H.MS*; morn *1931*.
iv *23. things*] Earth *H.MS 1st reading.*
iv *27. windy . . . Earth*] windless waste below *H.MS 1st reading.*
iv *29.* Cp. *In Memoriam* xcv 40: 'The deep pulsations of the world'.
iv *31. heart*] soul *H.MS 1st reading.*

*the Lady*; this MS does not include ll. 105–32 (on 'the Paradise coach'), but it does have a few of the stanzas on Hell now first printed. T. probably worked on it at least until 1828. It uses some of the same material as *Armageddon* and *Timbuctoo* (1829), especially in its closing lines; ll. 177–88 are a reworking of some lines in *T.MS* of *Armageddon* (which may not be quoted). The legend is common, but T. may have been influenced by the poem on *The Death Coach* in T. C. Croker's *Fairy Legends* (ii, 1828, pp. 133–7), the source of *Walking to the Mail*; see ll. 91–2*n*. T. later owned a copy of Croker (1834, *Lincoln*). He used to recite the ballad of Clerk Saunders (*Mem.* i 48). The early part of the poem is tinged with *The Ancient Mariner*; the account of Hell draws heavily on Milton. Cp. *The Vision of Sin* (p. 718).

Far off in the dun, dark Occident,
  Behind the burning Sun:
Where his gilding ray is never sent,
  And his hot steeds never run:

There lies a land of chilling storms,
  A region void of light,
A land of thin faces and shadowy forms,
  Of vapours, and mist, and night.

There never green thing will gaily spring
  In that unwholesome air,
But the ricketty blast runs shrilly and fast
  Through the bony branches there.

When the shadow of night's eternal wings
  Envelops the gloomy whole,
And the mutter of deep-mouthed thunderings
  Shakes all the starless pole,

Thick sobs and short shrill screams arise
  Along the sunless waste,
And the things of past days with their horrible eyes
  Look out from the cloudy vast.

And the earth is dry, though the pall of the sky
  Leave never an inch of blue:
And the moaning wind before it drives
  Thick wreaths of cloudy dew.

¶ 4.*8. vapours*] vapour *Y.MS.*
*13. When*] Where *Y.MS.*
*17. screams*] shrieks *Y.MS.*
*23. drives*] drive *Y.MS.*
*24. Thick*] Vast *Y.MS.*

Whoever walks that bitter ground
His limbs beneath him fail;
His heart throbs thick, his brain reels sick:
His brow is clammy and pale.

But some have hearts that in them burn
With power and promise high,
To draw strange comfort from the earth,
Strange beauties from the sky.

---

Dark was the night, and loud the roar
Of wind and mingled shower,
When there stood a dark coach at an old Inn door
At the solemn midnight hour.

That Inn was built at the birth of Time:
The walls of lava rose,
Cemented with the burning slime
Which from Asphaltus flows.

No sound of joy, no revelling tones
Of carouse were heard within:
But the rusty sign of a skull and cross-bones
Swung creaking before the Inn.

No taper's light looked out on the night,
But ever and anon
Strange fiery eyes glared fiercely through
The windows of shaven bone.

And the host came forth, and stood alone
And still in the dark doorway:
There was not a tinge on each high cheek bone,
But his face was a yellow gray.

*25–32*] *Not T.MS.*

*29–31.* Cp. *The Ancient Mariner* 585–7: 'This heart within me burns . . . / I have strange power of speech'.

*35–6.* 'The time of its appearance is always midnight', according to Croker, who may have suggested the Inn in *The Vision of Sin*.

*37–40*] *Added in margin T.MS.* Presumably added when T. was working on the lines describing Hell's bridge, since ll. 39–40 recall Milton's bridge, 'Bound . . . with *Asphaltic* slime' (*PL* x 297–8). Milton mentions 'Asphaltus' in Hell, i 729.

*44. Swung*] Swang *Y.MS.*

*45. out*] *Not Y.MS.*

*47. glared*] gazed *Y.MS.*

The skin hung lax on his long thin hands;
  No jolly host was he;
For his shanks were shrunken to willow wands
  And his name was Atrophy!

Dimly the travellers looked through the glooms,
  Worn and wan was their gaze, I trow,
As the shrivelled forms of the shadowy grooms
  Yoked the skeleton horses to.

They lifted their eyes to the dead, pale skies,
  And above the barkless trees
They saw the green verge of the pleasant earth,
  And heard the roar of her seas.

They see the light of their blest firesides,
  They hear each household voice:
The whispered love of the fair young wives;
  And the laugh of their rose-lipped boys.

The summer plains with their shining leaves,
  The summer hills they see;
The dark vine leaves round the rustling eaves,
  And the forests, fair and free.

---

There came a gaunt man from the dark Inn door,
  A dreadnought coat had he:
His bones cracked loud, as he stept through the crowd,
  And his boots creaked heavily.

Before his eyes so grim and calm
  The tingling blood grew chill,
As each put a farthing into his palm,
  To drive them where he will.

*57–60*] *H.Nbk 2 has this stanza as a fragment, with variants: Dimly*] Keenly; *was their gaze*] were their looks; *shrivelled*] tall thin.
*59. the shadowy*] shadowy *Y.MS.*
*61–4*] *Added in margin T.MS.*
*65–72*] *Not T.MS. T.MS* does have (as a later separate jotting) two stanzas on their hearing the noise of other days; the lines may not be quoted.
*68. their*] the *Y.MS.*
*69. leaves*] sheaves *Y.MS.* Neither reading is quite satisfactory; 'leaves' recurs awkwardly in l. 71, and 'sheaves' fits ill with 'summer'.
*74*] In a dreadnought coat was he: *Y.MS.*
*79. into*] in *Y.MS.*

His sockets were eyeless, but in them slept
 A red infernal glow;
As the cockroach crept, and the white fly leapt
 About his hairless brow.

They mounted slow in their long black cloaks,
 The tears bedimmed their sight:
The grim old coachee strode to the box,
 And the guard gasped out 'All's right.'

The leaders bounded, the guard's horn sounded:
 Far away through the night ran the lengthened tones:
As the quick wheels brushed, and threw up the dust
 Of dead men's pulverised bones.

Whose blood in its liveliest course would not pause
 At the strife of the shadowy wheels,
The chattering of the fleshless jaws,
 And the beat of the horny heels?

Deep dells of snow sunk on each side below
 The highway, broad and flat,
As the coach ran on, and the sallow lights shone
 Dimly and blurly with simmering fat.

Vast wastes of starless glooms were spread
 Around in the chilling air,
And heads without bodies and shapes without heads
 Went leaping here and there.

---

*81–4] Added in T.MS.*

*83. the white fly*] white worm *Y.MS.*

*85–8]*
 The travellers sat in long black cloaks,
  The lamps shed a pale blue light;
 A grim old coachee mounted the box,
  And the guard shrieked out 'All's right.'

*H.Nbk 2 as a fragment.*

*91–2.* Cp. Croker: 'See the wheels! how they fly o'er the stones! / And whirl, as the whip it goes crack: / Their spokes are of dead men's thigh bones.'

*93–6.* Cp. *King Charles's Vision* 45–8: 'For a blue livid flame, round the hall where he came, / In fiery circles ran; / And sounds of death, and chattering teeth, / And gibbering tongues began.'

*97–104] Added in T.MS.*

*101. glooms*] gloom *Y.MS.* Shelley has 'a starless and a moonless gloom', *Revolt of Islam* X xliii 1.

*103.* Cp. Croker ii 146, *The Headless Horseman*: 'on they went–heads with bodies, and bodies without heads'.

O Coachee, Coachee, what lights approach
With heavenly melodies?
Oh! those are the lights of the Paradise coach,
That so gaily meet their eyes!

With pleasant hymns they soothe the air
Of death, with songs of pride:
With sackbut, and with dulcimer,
With psaltery they ride.

These fear not the mists of unwholesome damps
That through that region rove,
For all wreathed with green bays were the gorgeous lamps,
And a bright archangel drove.

They passed (an inner spirit fed
Their ever-burning fires),
With a solemn burst of thrilling light,
And a sound of stringèd lyres.

With a silver sound the wheels went round,
The wheels of burning flame;
Of beryl, and of amethyst
Was the spiritual frame.

Their steeds were strong exceedingly:
And rich was their attire:
Before them flowed a fiery stream;
They broke the ground with hoofs of fire.

They glittered with a steadfast light,
The happy spirits within;
As stars they shone, in raiment white,
And free from taint of sin.

In Heaven's gardens they shall walk
With Saints and Prophets old
And evermore on that blest shore
Feel neither heat nor cold.

*105–32*] *Not T.MS.*
*114. That*] Which *Y.MS.*
*119. thrilling light*: as in Shelley, *Rosalind* 616.
*122–4.* Cp. the Messiah's chariot: 'the wheels / Of Beril, and careering Fires between', *Paradise Lost* vi 755–6.
*128. broke*] brake *Y.MS.*
*133–92*] *Y.MS; not Mem., T.MS (but see ll. 137–44n).*
*134. Prophets old*: *PL* iii 36.

A gloomy shore the others reach,
 Hard by a gloomy sea
Where cinders for pebbles strewed the beach
 As far as the eye might see.

To the ashy strand in an inky van
 The mourning surges came,
In fuscous foam together ran
 And broke in tawny flame.

The bridge, the marvellous bridge, it spans
 The jet black gulph betwixt,
It takes the ocean at a leap
 And in its leap is fixed.

It riseth high and pierceth through
 The solid black of Night,
Ten thousand arcs of adamant
 Uprear its wondrous height.

The heavy base by the burning Mace
 Of loathly Sin was laid,
The arcs of during adamant
 Strong Death above it made.

Beneath its freight the bridge of death
 Did shake with fear and glee,
The black bitumen howled beneath
 In dreadful sympathy.

*137–44*] *T.MS includes these lines as a fragment.*
*137. gloomy shore*: cp. Shelley's *Lines among the Euganean Hills* 137–40, suggesting T.'s subject: 'Till he pass the gloomy shore, / Lest thy dead should, from their sleep / Bursting o'er the starlight deep, / Lead a rapid masque of death / O'er the waters of his path.'
*138. gloomy sea*: as in Shelley, *Rosalind* 645.
*141. inky van*: cp. Milton's 'cloudie Van', *PL* vi 107.
*143. fuscous*: dusky.
*145–60.* Based closely on the bridge built by Sin and Death, *PL* x 293–324.
*147.* Adapted in *Gareth and Lynette* 886–7: 'this a bridge of single arc / Took at a leap'.
*151. PL* x 318–19: 'With Pinns of Adamant / And Chains they made all fast'.
*152.* Milton twice uses the adjective 'wondrous' in connection with the bridge, *PL* x 312, 348.
*153. PL* x 293–5: 'The aggregated Soyle / Death with his Mace petrific, cold and dry, / As with a Trident smote.'
*155. during*: cp. *PL* iii 45, vii 206: 'ever-during'.
*159. bitumen*: cp. *PL* x 562: 'that bituminous Lake'.

Anon it rose and high upthrew
The smutty sparkling spray,
Those livid bowers of branching blue
O'erarched their upward way.

They reached the highest–what vivid rim
(Even here its heat is felt)
Doth skirt that ocean's yeasty brim
And gird it like a belt?

A vivid rim–a burning belt–
A range of pillars high,
That darken with excess of heat
And run from sky to sky.

Amid a waste of spiral fires
Lo! Bloodred Pyramid
And bloodred domes and bloodred spires
And obelisks bloodred.

And from amidst them all a great
Pavilion did arise

*162. smutty*: cp. Milton's description of gunpowder, 'The Smuttie graine / With sudden blaze diffus'd, inflames the Aire' (*PL* iv 817–8).
*163–4.* Combining Milton's 'livid flames' (*PL* i 182) and his Hell (i 303–4) when it is likened to 'where th'*Etrurian* shades / High overarch't imbowr.'
*167. yeasty*: cp. *Macbeth* IV i 53: 'yesty waves'. T. used the adjective in *Timbuctoo* 15, following 'pillars high' in l. 12–cp. l. 170 below.
*169. burning belt*: cp. *Chorus* 23: 'The burning belts, the mighty rings'.
*171. PL* iii 380: 'Dark with excessive bright thy skirts appear'.
*172. run from sky to sky*: adopted in *Ode to Memory* 104.
*173.* Cp. *PL* i 222–3: 'the flames / Drivn backward slope thir pointing spires'; and ii 1013, 'Springs upward like a Pyramid of fire'.
*174–6.* Cp. Keats, *Hyperion* i 176–80: 'His palace bright / Bastioned with pyramids of glowing gold, / And touched with shade of bronzed obelisks, / Glared a blood-red through all its thousand courts, / Arches, and domes, and fiery galleries.' T.'s lines are the germ of *The Holy Grail* 473–6: 'Blood-red, and sliding down the blackened marsh / Blood-red, and on the naked mountain top / Blood-red, and in the sleeping mere below / Blood-red.' The Pyramid, domes, spires, and obelisks, all appear in *Timbuctoo*.
*177–88.* A version, some of it verbatim, of the lines on the Pavilion in *T.MS* of *Armageddon* (which may not be quoted); adapted also in *Pierced through with knotted thorns* (p. 472).
*178–80.* The fearful pavilion, the contrast of black and red, and the 'imageries' suggest *Gareth and Lynette* 1329ff.

Of ebon black its stately height
With cunning imageries.

On the Eastern side, prime worship stood
Imperial Dionys,
And round about his brows was flung
The bunchy vine I wis.

Beneath the span of Heaven's bow
A wondrous keel there sailed
Behind him on a carvèd field
With peaky waves engrailed.

Beside him Chus and Chamon stood
And On and regal Oph,
Great Esta and the later brood
Of Saturn and of Jove.

## 5 *Memory [Memory! dear enchanter]

Published *1827*, not reprinted. *1893* quotes T. as saying that his poems of *1827* were written 'between 15 and 17', i.e. 1824–26. Cp. *Memory* [*Ay me*!]

*180*. Cp. Keats, *Eve of St Agnes* 208–216: 'carven imag'ries' which precedes the 'scutcheon blushed with blood'.
*181–8*. Cp. *Pierced through with knotted thorns* 36–41 (p. 473): 'On the Eastern wall in a clear light revealed / Stood kingly Dionys, prime worship hailed, / The bunchy vine down-dangled to his heel. / And close behind him on a carven field / With semblance of the peaky wave engrailed / Laboured an immeasurable keel.' The Rainbow and the Ark are from Jacob Bryant's *New System of Ancient Mythology*, of which there was a copy at Somersby (*Lincoln*). See *Pierced through* (p. 473), which also explains the link between Dionysus and Noah. Cp. the picture of Dionysus (Bacchus) in *Semele* (p. 574).
*188*. This line, after being experimented with here, in *Armageddon* (p. 65), and in *Pierced through*, finally became *The Palace of Art* 113: 'Or over hills with peaky tops engrailed'.
*189–91*. The deities are from Bryant. 'Chus was the father of all those nations, styled Ethiopians, who were more truly called Cuthites and Cuseans' (1807 edn, i 7). Bryant relates Ham or Cham and Ammon: 'Ham, as a Deity, was esteemed the Sun: and his priests were styled Chamin' (i 4). 'On . . . was another title of the Sun among the Amonians' (i 19). 'Oph signifies a serpent . . . It was an emblem of the Sun' (i 57–8). Cp. 'their crownèd brethren ON and OPH', *A Fragment* 21 (p. 290), which also uses Bryant. 'Esta signified fire; and also the Deity of that element' (i 77).
*191–2*. *PL* i 511–12: 'With his enormous brood, and birthright seis'd / By younger *Saturn*, he from mightier *Jove* . . .'

(p. 262), and *Ode to Memory* (p. 210). Paden (pp. 42–8) discusses the psychological significance of the imagery, especially in ll. 29–40, with its tone of reprobation and remorse; the imagery derives from Sir William Jones's *The Palace of Fortune*, and Byron: *Childe Harold* IV cxx, cxxvi, and *Love's Last Adieu*. Jones's works were at Somersby (*Lincoln*).

The Memory is perpetually looking back when we have nothing present to entertain us: it is like those repositories in animals that are filled with stores of food, on which they may ruminate when their present pasture fails.

ADDISON [*Spectator* 471]

Memory! dear enchanter!
Why bring back to view
Dreams of youth, which banter
All that e'er was true?

Why present before me
Thoughts of years gone by,
Which, like shadows o'er me,
Dim in distance fly?

Days of youth, now shaded
By twilight of long years,
Flowers of youth, now faded,
Though bathed in sorrow's tears:

Thoughts of youth, which waken
Mournful feelings now,
Fruits which time hath shaken
From off their parent bough:

Memory! why, oh why,
This fond heart consuming,
Show me years gone by,
When those hopes were blooming?

Hopes which now are parted,
Hopes which then I prized,
Which this world, cold-hearted,
Ne'er has realized?

I knew not then its strife,
I knew not then its rancour;
In every rose of life,
Alas! there lurks a canker.

Round every palm-tree, springing
With bright fruit in the waste,
A mournful asp is clinging,
Which sours it to our taste.

¶ 5.29–32. Cp. *Memory* [*Ay me!*] 35–6: 'As a hungry serpent coiled / Round a palm tree in the wild . . .'

O'er every fountain, pouring
  Its waters through the wild,
Which man imbibes, adoring,
  And deems it undefiled,

The poison-shrubs are dropping
  Their dark dews day by day;
And Care is hourly lopping
  Our greenest boughs away!

Ah! these are thoughts that grieve me
  Then, when others rest.
Memory! why deceive me
  By thy visions blest?

Why lift the veil, dividing
  The brilliant courts of spring–
Where gilded shapes are gliding
  In fairy colouring–

From age's frosty mansion,
  So cheerless and so chill?
Why bid the bleak expansion
  Of past life meet us still?

Where's now that peace of mind
  O'er youth's pure bosom stealing,
So sweet and so refined,
  So exquisite a feeling?

Where's now the heart exulting
  In pleasure's buoyant sense,
And gaiety, resulting
  From conscious innocence?

All, all have past and fled,
  And left me lorn and lonely;
All those dear hopes are dead,
  Remembrance wakes them only!

I stand like some lone tower
  Of former days remaining,
Within whose place of power
  The midnight owl is plaining;–

Like oak-tree old and grey,
  Whose trunk with age is failing,
Through whose dark boughs for aye
  The winter winds are wailing.

Thus, Memory, thus thy light
O'er this worn soul is gleaming,
Like some far fire at night
Along the dun deep streaming.

# 6 *The Exile's Harp

Published *1827*, not reprinted.

I will hang thee, my Harp, by the side of the fountain,
On the whispering branch of the lone-waving willow:
Above thee shall rush the hoarse gale of the mountain,
Below thee shall tumble the dark breaking billow.
The winds shall blow by thee, abandoned, forsaken,
The wild gales alone shall arouse thy sad strain;
For where is the heart or the hand to awaken
The sounds of thy soul-soothing sweetness again?
Oh! Harp of my fathers!
Thy chords shall decay,
One by one with the strings
Shall thy notes fade away;
Till the fiercest of tempests
Around thee may yell,
And not waken one sound
Of thy desolate shell!

Yet, oh! yet, ere I go, will I fling a wreath round thee,
With the richest of flowers in the green valley springing;
Those that see shall remember the hand that hath crowned thee,
When, withered and dead, to thee still they are clinging.
There! now I have wreathed thee–the roses are twining
Thy chords with their bright blossoms glowing and red:
Though the lapse of one day see their freshness declining,
Yet bloom for one day when thy minstrel has fled!
Oh! Harp of my fathers!
No more in the hall,
The souls of the chieftains
Thy strains shall enthral:
One sweep will I give thee,
And wake thy bold swell;
Then, thou friend of my bosom,
For ever farewell!

# 7 *'Why should we weep for those who die?'

Published *1827*, not reprinted. T. included it in a letter to his sisters' governess, as 'a review of death' (*Mem.* i 10). Cp. Byron's *Bright be the place of thy soul* (1815), which ends: 'For why should we mourn for the blest?' Byron's poem was, as Paden says (pp. 107, 138), a source of Charles's *A Sister* in *1827*. The epigraph is abbreviated from the pseudo-Ciceronian *Consolatio*. See the edition of Cicero which was at Somersby (ed. J. A. Ernesti, 1810) [vii] 969. ('Wherefore, if death brings an end of sorrows, if it brings the beginning of a serener and better life, if it averts future ills, ... why [do we wish] to inveigh so much against it ... when it would be right rather to draw from it consolation and gladness?')

*Quamobrem, si dolorum finem mors affert, si securioris et melioris initium vitæ: si futura mala avertit–cur eam tantopere accusare [velimus], ex qua potius consolationem et lætitiam haurire fas esset?*

CICERO

Why should we weep for those who die?
They fall–their dust returns to dust;
Their souls shall live eternally
Within the mansions of the just.

They die to live–they sink to rise,
They leave this wretched mortal shore;
But brighter suns and bluer skies
Shall smile on them for evermore.

Why should we sorrow for the dead?
Our life on earth is but a span;
They tread the path that all must tread,
They die the common death of man.

The noblest songster of the gale
Must cease, when Winter's frowns appear;
The reddest rose is wan and pale,
When Autumn tints the changing year.

The fairest flower on earth must fade,
The brightest hopes on earth must die:
Why should we mourn that man was made
To droop on earth, but dwell on high?

The soul, the eternal soul, must reign
In worlds devoid of pain and strife;
Then why should mortal man complain
Of death, which leads to happier life?

# 8 *Remorse

Published *1827*, not reprinted. Cp. *Supposed Confessions* (p. 197). In mood and theme it recalls Coleridge's *The Pains of Sleep* (published 1816). Epigraph: *Satires* i 167, *tacita sudant* ... ('he sweats with the secret consciousness of sin').

*sudant tacita praecordia culpa.*

JUVENAL

Oh! 'tis a fearful thing to glance
Back on the gloom of mis-spent years:
What shadowy forms of guilt advance,
And fill me with a thousand fears!
The vices of my life arise,
Portrayed in shapes, alas! too true;
And not one beam of hope breaks through,
To cheer my old and aching eyes,
T'illume my night of wretchedness,
My age of anguish and distress.
If I am damned, why find I not
Some comfort in this earthly spot?
But no! this world and that to come
Are both to me one scene of gloom!
Lest ought of solace I should see,
Or lose the thoughts of what I do,
Remorse, with soul-felt agony,
Holds up the mirror to my view.
And I was cursèd from my birth,
A reptile made to creep on earth,
An hopeless outcast, born to die
A living death eternally!
With too much conscience to have rest,
Too little to be ever blest,
To yon vast world of endless woe,
Unlighted by the cheerful day,
My soul shall wing her weary way;
To those dread depths where aye the same,
Throughout the waste of darkness, glow
The glimmerings of the boundless flame.

¶ 8.*21*. Cp. *The Outcast*, 1826 (p. 159).
*26*. *the cheerful day*: Gray's *Elegy* 87.
*27*. Cp. Gray's *Elegy* 3: 'plods his weary way'.
*30*. Cp. Milton's Hell: 'the glimmering of these livid flames', *Paradise Lost* i 182.

And yet I cannot here below
Take my full cup of guilt, as some,
And laugh away my doom to come.
I would I'd been all-heartless! then
I might have sinned like other men;
But all this side the grave is fear,
A wilderness so dank and drear,
That never wholesome plant would spring;
  And all behind–I dare not think!
I would not risk the imagining–
  From the full view my spirits shrink;
And starting backwards, yet I cling
To life, whose every hour to me
Hath been increase of misery.
But yet I cling to it, for well
  I know the pangs that rack me now
Are trifles, to the endless hell
  That waits me, when my burning brow
And my wrung eyes shall hope in vain
For one small drop to cool the pain,
The fury of that maddening flame
That then shall scorch my writhing frame!
Fiends! who have goaded me to ill!
Distracting fiends, who goad me still!
If e'er I worked a sinful deed,
  Ye know how bitter was the draught;
Ye know my inmost soul would bleed,
  And ye have looked at me and laughed,
Triumphing that I could not free
My spirit from your slavery!
Yet is there that in me which says,
  Should these old feet their course retread
From out the portal of my days,
  That I should lead the life I've led:
My agony, my torturing shame,
My guilt, my errors all the same!
Oh, God! that thou wouldst grant that ne'er
  My soul its clay-cold bed forsake,

*31–3.* Recalling *Macbeth* I vii 7–12: 'we'ld jump the life to come . . . our poisoned chalice to our own lips'.

*49–52.* Cp. *The Devil and the Lady* I v 238–9: 'piercing the wrung ears of the damned that writhe / Upon their beds of flame'.

*54. Distracting*: driving to madness.

*68. clay-cold*: traditionally used in ballads and in funeral contexts, as by Young and Shelley.

That I might sleep, and never wake
Unto the thrill of conscious fear;
For when the trumpet's piercing cry
Shall burst upon my slumbering ear,
And countless seraphs throng the sky,
How shall I cast my shroud away,
And come into the blaze of day?
How shall I brook to hear each crime,
Here veiled by secrecy and time,
Read out from thine eternal book?
How shall I stand before thy throne,
While earth shall like a furnace burn?
How shall I bear the withering look
Of men and angels, who will turn
Their dreadful gaze on me alone?

# 9 *The Dell of E—

Published *1827*, not reprinted. The *1893* attribution to T. is supported by *T.MS* and by Haddelsey and Russell, *1827*; Charles's copy makes no attribution. Epigraph, *Aeneid* iii 415: 'Such vast change can length of time effect.'

*Tantum aevi longinqua valet mutare vetustas!*
VIRGIL

There was a long, low, rushy dell, embossed
With knolls of grass and clumps of copsewood green;
Mid-way a wandering burn the valley crossed,
And streaked with silvery line the wood-land scene;
High hills on either side to heaven upsprung,
Y-clad with groves of undulating pine,
Upon whose heads the hoary vapours hung,
And far–far off the heights were seen to shine
In clear relief against the sapphire sky,
And many a blue stream wandered through the shade
Of those dark groves that clomb the mountains high,

70. *conscious*: having a guilty secret.

¶ 9.1. *embossed*: studded with; also the Miltonic meaning, 'imbosked'; cp. *Samson* 1700: 'In the *Arabian* woods embost'.

4–5. Cp. the 'Silvan Scene' in *Paradise Lost* iv 140–3, where 'The verdurous wall of paradise up sprung'.

And glistening 'neath each lone entangled glade,
At length with brawling accent loudly fell
Within the limpid brook that wound along the dell.

How pleasant was the ever-varying light
Beneath that emerald coverture of boughs!
How often, at the approach of dewy night,
Have those tall pine-trees heard the lover's vows!
How many a name was carved upon the trunk
Of each old hollow willow-tree, that stooped
To lave its branches in the brook, and drunk
Its freshening dew! How many a cypress drooped
From those fair banks, where bloomed the earliest flowers,
Which the young year from her abounding horn
Scatters profuse within her secret bowers!
What rapturous gales from that wild dell were borne!
And, floating on the rich spring breezes, flung
Their incense o'er that wave on whose bright banks they sprung!

Long years had past, and there again I came,
But man's rude hand had sorely scathed the dell;
And though the cloud-capt mountains, still the same,
Upreared each heaven-invading pinnacle;
Yet were the charms of that lone valley fled,
And the grey-winding of the stream was gone;
The brook, once murmuring o'er its pebbly bed,
Now deeply–straightly–noiselessly went on.
Slow turned the sluggish wheel beneath its force,
Where clattering mills disturbed the solitude:
Where was the prattling of its former course?
Its shelving, sedgy sides y-crowned with wood?
The willow trunks were felled, the names erased
From one broad shattered pine, which still its station graced.

Remnant of all its brethren, there it stood,
Braving the storms that swept the cliffs above,
Where once, throughout the impenetrable wood,
Were heard the plainings of the pensive dove.
But man had bid the eternal forests bow

*23–5*. Cp. *PL* viii 286: 'a green shadie Bank profuse of Flours'.
*26–8*. Cp. *PL* viii 515–7: 'fresh Gales . . . / . . . flung Odours from the spicie Shrub'.
*45*. 'Woods impenetrable', *PL* ix 1086.

That bloomed upon the earth-imbedded base
Of the strong mountain, and perchance they now
Upon the billows were the dwelling-place
Of their destroyers, and bore terror round
The trembling earth: –ah! lovelier, had they still
Whispered unto the breezes with low sound,
And greenly flourished on their native hill,
And flinging their proud arms in state on high,
Spread out beneath the sun their glorious canopy!

## 10 *Antony to Cleopatra

Published *1827*, not reprinted. It was probably influenced in a general way by Horace's *Odes* I xxxvii. For a similar subject, cp. *Mithridates Presenting Berenice with the Cup of Poison* (p. 125); for T.'s later treatment of Cleopatra, cp. *A Dream of Fair Women* 125–64 (p. 447).

O, Cleopatra! fare thee well,
We two can meet no more;
This breaking heart alone can tell
The love to thee I bore.
But wear not thou the conqueror's chain
Upon thy race and thee;
And though we ne'er can meet again,
Yet still be true to me:
For I for thee have lost a throne,
To wear the crown of love alone.

Fair daughter of a regal line!
To thraldom bow not tame;
My every wish on earth was thine,
My every hope the same.
And I have moved within thy sphere,
And lived within thy light;
And oh! thou wert to me so dear,
I breathed but in thy sight!
A subject world I lost for thee,
For thou wert all my world to me!

Then when the shriekings of the dying
Were heard along the wave,

¶ 10.5. Cp. *Antony and Cleopatra* IV xiv 61–2: 'She which by her death our Caesar tells / "I am conqueror of myself".'
*15*. Cp. *A and C* II vii 14–15: 'To be called into a huge sphere, and not to be seen to move in it'; and IV xv 9–10: 'O sun, / Burn the great sphere thou movest in'.

Soul of my soul! I saw thee flying;
    I followed thee, to save.
The thunder of the brazen prows
    O'er Actium's ocean rung;
Fame's garland faded from my brows,
    Her wreath away I flung.
I sought, I saw, I heard but thee:
For what to love was victory?

Thine on the earth, and on the throne,
    And in the grave, am I;
And, dying, still I am thine own,
    Thy bleeding Antony.
How shall my spirit joy to hear
    That thou art ever true!
Nay–weep not–dry that burning tear,
    That bathes thine eyes' dark hue.
Shades of my fathers! lo! I come;
I hear your voices from the tomb!

## 11 *'I wander in darkness and sorrow'

Published *1827*, not reprinted. Cp. *The Outcast* (1826, p. 159), with its hall, and its 'weedy, chinky floors', where 'the sere leaf rustles to and fro'. The idea of the storm as not the worst enemy seems to derive from *King Lear* III ii: 'I tax not you, you elements, with unkindness' (cp. l. 17ff); indeed, it is a kind of solace: 'This tempest will not give me leave to ponder / On things would hurt me more'. T.'s poem, too, turns on the idea of 'one minded like the weather, most unquietly', and the storm in *Lear* may have suggested l. 1 (cp. *Lear*: 'the very wanderers of the dark') and 'pitiless', 'hurricanes' (l. 38), as well as l. 43 (cp. *Lear*: 'the green mantle of the standing pool').

I wander in darkness and sorrow,
    Unfriended, and cold, and alone,
As dismally gurgles beside me
    The bleak river's desolate moan.

*25. brazen*: Horace's epithet *aerata* for the ships, *Odes* II xvi 21, III i 39. Keats has 'brazen prow', *Lamia* i 224.

*27*. Cp. Cleopatra on the death of Antony (IV xv 64): 'O, withered is the garland of the war.'

¶ 11.*2*. *Unfriended*: perhaps suggested by the opening line of Goldsmith's *The Traveller*, which has 'wandering' in l. 2.

The rise of the volleying thunder
The mountain's lone echoes repeat:
The roar of the wind is around me,
The leaves of the year at my feet.

I wander in darkness and sorrow,
Uncheered by the moon's placid ray;
Not a friend that I loved but is dead,
Not a hope but has faded away!
Oh! when shall I rest in the tomb,
Wrapt about with the chill winding sheet?
For the roar of the wind is around me,
The leaves of the year at my feet.

I heed not the blasts that sweep o'er me,
I blame not the tempests of night;
They are not the foes who have banished
The visions of youthful delight:
I hail the wild sound of their raving,
Their merciless presence I greet;
Though the roar of the wind be around me,
The leaves of the year at my feet.

In this waste of existence, for solace,
On whom shall my lone spirit call?
Shall I fly to the friends of my bosom?
My God! I have buried them all!
They are dead, they are gone, they are cold,
My embraces no longer they meet;
Let the roar of the wind be around me,
The leaves of the year at my feet!

Those eyes that glanced love unto mine,
With motionless slumbers are prest;
Those hearts which once throbbed but for me,
Are chill as the earth where they rest.
Then around on my wan withered form
Let the pitiless hurricanes beat;
Let the roar of the wind be around me,
The leaves of the year at my feet!

Like the voice of the owl in the hall,
Where the song and the banquet have ceased,
Where the green weeds have mantled the hearth,
Whence arose the proud flame of the feast;

5. *volleying*: a traditional epithet for thunder: cp. Milton, *Paradise Lost* vi 854: 'his Thunder in mid Volie'.
26. *lone spirit*: as in Keats and Shelley.

So I cry to the storm, whose dark wing
Scatters on me the wild-driving sleet–
'*Let the roar of the wind be around me*,
'*The fall of the leaves at my feet!*'

## 12 *The Old Sword

Published *1827*, not reprinted. It is missing from *T.MS.*

Old Sword! though dim and rusted
Be now thy sheeny blade,
Thy glittering edge encrusted
With cankers Time hath made;
Yet once around thee swelled the cry
Of triumph's fierce delight,
The shoutings of the victory,
The thunders of the fight!

Though age hath past upon thee
With still corroding breath,
Yet once streamed redly on thee
The purpling tide of death:
What time amid the war of foes
The dastard's cheek grew pale,
As through the feudal field arose
The ringing of the mail.

Old Sword! what arm hath wielded
Thy richly gleaming brand,
'Mid lordly forms who shielded
The maidens of their land?
And who hath cloven his foes in wrath
With thy puissant fire,
And scattered in his perilous path
The victims of his ire?

Old Sword! whose fingers clasped thee
Around thy carvèd hilt?
And with that hand which grasped thee
What heroes' blood was spilt;
When fearlessly, with open hearts,
And lance to lance opposed,
Beneath the shade of barbèd darts
The dark-eyed warriors closed?

¶ 12.22. *puissant*: trisyllabic, a less common pronunciation but one found in Shakespeare, Shenstone, etc.

Old Sword! I would not burnish
  Thy venerable rust,
Nor sweep away the tarnish
  Of darkness and of dust!
    Lie there, in slow and still decay,
      Unfamed in olden rhyme,
    The relic of a former day,
      A wreck of ancient time!

## 13 *'We meet no more'

Published *1827*, not reprinted. The attribution in *1893* is confirmed by *T.MS*, where it is in T.'s hand, and by Haddelsey and Russell, *1827*. Charles's copy makes no attribution. Nevertheless W. J. Rolfe's edn (1898) quoted H.T. as agreeing 'this is incorrectly assigned to T.'. It may have been suggested by Moore's *Lalla Rookh: The Fire-Worshippers*, where the man says 'We meet no more', and she says: 'Yet go–on peril's brink we meet; / Those frightful rocks–that treacherous sea.'

We meet no more–the die is cast,
  The chain is broke that tied us,
Our every hope on earth is past,
  And there's no helm to guide us:
We meet no more–the roaring blast
  And angry seas divide us!

And I stand on a distant shore,
  The breakers round me swelling;
And lonely thoughts of days gone o'er
  Have made this breast their dwelling:
We meet no more–We meet no more:
  Farewell for ever, Ellen!

## 14 *Written by an Exile of Bassorah, while sailing down the Euphrates

Published *1827*, not reprinted. *1893*'s attribution is supported by Haddelsey and Russell, *1827*; Charles's copy makes no attribution. Paden (p. 131) relates it to *Recollections of the Arabian Nights* (p. 205), based on the story of Noureddin and the Fair Persian: 'Noureddin is probably the exile of Bassorah. He was exiled from Balsora (as Galland spelled it–the modern form is Basra) for seducing the Fair Persian, who was destined for the harem of the king, while she was in the custody of his father; and in their subsequent adventures she did attempt to guide his "course on this earth thro' the storms of mischance" [ll. 27–8]. Being a forceful person, he took her with him to Bagdad. Her absence, like the hero's harp and his melancholy, must be charged to Tennyson. Egypt was the land of the lotus, "denominated by Herodotus the lilly of the Nile" (Savary's *Letters* I xviii); it was therefore [T.'s] "land of the Lily".'

Thou land of the Lily! thy gay flowers are blooming
In joy on thine hills, but they bloom not for me;
For a dark gulf of woe, all my fond hopes entombing,
Has rolled its black waves 'twixt this lone heart and thee.

The far-distant hills, and the groves of my childhood,
Now stream in the light of the sun's setting ray;
And the tall-waving palms of my own native wild-wood
In the blue haze of distance are melting away.

I see thee, Bassorah! in splendour retiring,
Where thy waves and thy walls in their majesty meet;
I see the bright glory thy pinnacles firing,
And the broad vassal river that rolls at thy feet.

I see thee but faintly–thy tall towers are beaming
On the dusky horizon so far and so blue;
And minaret and mosque in the distance are gleaming,
While the coast of the stranger expands on my view.

I see thee no more: for the deep waves have parted
The land of my birth from her desolate son;
And I am gone from thee, though half broken-hearted,
To wander through climes where thy name is unknown.

Farewell to my harp, which I hung in my anguish
On the lonely palmetto that nods to the gale;
For its sweet-breathing tones in forgetfulness languish,
And around it the ivy shall weave a green veil.

Farewell to the days which so smoothly have glided
With the maiden whose look was like Cama's young glance,

¶ 14.*21–22*. Cp. *The Exile's Harp*.
*26*. *Cama*: Indian god of love, of whom T. learnt from the works of Sir William Jones; cp. *Love* [*Almighty Love*] (p. 146).

And the sheen of whose eyes was the load-star which guided
My course on this earth through the storms of mischance!

## 15 *The Vale of Bones

Published *1827*, not reprinted. It was influenced by John Leyden's *Ode on Visiting Flodden*, which is in Scott's *Minstrelsy of the Scottish Border*: 'May whitening bones thy surface strew! / Soon as I tread thy rush-clad vale...' Cp. l. 25; note T.'s 'tartans', l. 59; and see ll. 77–8*n*. Paden (p. 151) compares Scott's *The Lady of the Lake* III v: '... a dreary glen, / Where scattered lay the bones of men, / In some forgotten battle slain, / And bleached by drifting wind and rain.' There was a copy of Scott's poem at Somersby (*Lincoln*). Epigraph: *Satires* I viii 16 ('ground ghastly with bleaching bones'). Cp. *Inverlee* (p. 160).

*Albis informem–ossibus agrum.*
HORACE

Along yon vapour-mantled sky
The dark-red moon is riding high;
At times her beams in beauty break
Upon the broad and silvery lake;
At times more bright they clearly fall
On some white castle's ruined wall;
At times her partial splendour shines
Upon the grove of deep-black pines,
Through which the dreary night-breeze moans,
Above this Vale of scattered bones.

The low, dull gale can scarcely stir
The branches of that blackening fir,
Which betwixt me and heaven flings wide
Its shadowy boughs on either side,
And o'er yon granite rock uprears
Its giant form of many years.
And the shrill owlet's desolate wail
Comes to mine ear along the gale,
As, listening to its lengthened tones,
I dimly pace the Vale of Bones.

Dark Valley! still the same art thou,
Unchanged thy mountain's cloudy brow;
Still from yon cliffs, that part asunder,

Falls down the torrent's echoing thunder;
Still from this mound of reeds and rushes
With bubbling sound the fountain gushes;
Thence, winding through the whispering ranks
Of sedges on the willowy banks,
Still brawling, chafes the rugged stones
That strew this dismal Vale of Bones.

Unchanged art thou! no storm hath rent
Thy rude and rocky battlement;
Thy rioting mountains sternly piled,
The screen of nature, wide and wild:
But who were they, whose bones bestrew
The heather, cold with midnight dew,
Upon whose slowly-rotting clay
The raven long hath ceased to prey,
But, mouldering in the moon-light air,
Their wan, white skulls show bleak and bare?
And, aye, the dreary night-breeze moans
Above them in this Vale of Bones!

I knew them all – a gallant band,
The glory of their native land,
And on each lordly brow elate
Sate valour and contempt of fate,
Fierceness of youth, and scorn of foe,
And pride to render blow for blow.
In the strong war's tumultuous crash,
How darkly did their keen eyes flash!
How fearlessly each arm was raised!
How dazzlingly each broad-sword blazed!
Though now the dreary night-breeze moans
Above them in this Vale of Bones.

What lapse of time shall sweep away
The memory of that gallant day,
When on to battle proudly going,
Your plumage to the wild winds blowing,
Your tartans far behind ye flowing,
Your pennons raised, your clarions sounding,
Fiercely your steeds beneath ye bounding,
Ye mixed the strife of warring foes
In fiery shock and deadly close?
What stampings in the maddening strife,
What thrusts, what stabs, with brand and knife,
What desperate strokes for death or life,

¶ 15.*57–61*. Adapted for *Oriana* 14–17 (p. 248).

Were there! What cries, what thrilling groans,
Re-echoed through the Vale of Bones!

Thou peaceful Vale, whose mountains lonely,
Sound to the torrent's chiding only,
Or wild-goat's cry from rocky ledge,
Or bull-frog from the rustling sedge,
Or eagle from her airy cairn,
Or screaming of the startled hern–
How did thy million echoes waken
Amid thy caverns deeply shaken!
How with the red dew o'er thee rained
Thine emerald turf was darkly stained!
How did each innocent flower, that sprung
Thy greenly-tangled glades among,
Blush with the big and purple drops
That dribbled from the leafy copse!
I paced the valley, when the yell
Of triumph's voice had ceased to swell;
When battle's brazen throat no more
Raised its annihilating roar.
There lay ye on each other piled,
Your brows with noble dust defiled;
There, by the loudly-gushing water,
Lay man and horse in mingled slaughter.
Then wept I not, thrice gallant band;
For though no more each dauntless hand
The thunder of the combat hurled,
Yet still with pride your lips were curled;
And e'en in death's o'erwhelming shade
Your fingers lingered round the blade!
I deemed, when gazing proudly there
Upon the fixed and haughty air
That marked each warrior's bloodless face,
Ye would not change the narrow space
Which each cold form of breathless clay
Then covered, as on earth ye lay,
For realms, for sceptres, or for thrones–
I dreamed not on this Vale of Bones!

*77–8.* A traditional metaphor, but cp. Leyden: 'Green Flodden! on thy blood-stained head / Descend no rain nor vernal dew . . . / Blood, blood alone, should dew the hero's tomb.' *The Oak of the North* (*1827*), by T.'s brother Frederick, speaks of blood as 'that deadly dew'.

*85–6.* Cp. Milton, *Paradise Lost* xi 713: 'The brazen Throat of Warr had ceast to roar'; Cowper had adopted 'brazen throat', *The Task* iv 104.

*88. 1827* note: '*Non indecoro pulvere sordidos.* Horace', *Odes* II i 22.

But years have thrown their veil between,
And altered is that lonely scene;
And dreadful emblems of thy might,
Stern Dissolution! meet my sight:
The eyeless socket, dark and dull,
The hideous grinning of the skull,
Are sights which Memory disowns,
Thou melancholy Vale of Bones!

# 16 *'Did not thy roseate lips outvie'

Published *1827*, not reprinted. Epigraph: Horace, *Odes* II viii 1–5, to a coquette ('Had ever any penalty for violated vows visited thee, Barine; didst thou ever grow uglier by a single blackened tooth or spotted nail, I'd trust thee now').

*Ulla si juris tibi pejerati*
*Poena, Barine, nocuisset unquam;*
*Dente si nigro fieres, vel uno*
*Turpior ungui*
*Crederem.*
HORACE

Did not thy roseate lips outvie
The gay Anana's spicy bloom;
Had not thy breath the luxury,
The richness of its deep perfume–

Were not the pearls it fans more clear
Than those which grace the valvèd shell;
Thy foot more airy than the deer,
When startled from his lonely dell–

Were not thy bosom's stainless whiteness,
Where angel loves their vigils keep,
More heavenly than the dazzling brightness
Of the cold crescent on the deep–

¶ 16.2. *1827* note: 'Ulloa says, that the blossom of the West-Indian Anana is of so elegant a crimson as even to dazzle the eye, and that the fragrancy of the fruit discovers the plant though concealed from sight. See *Ulloa's Voyages* i 72'. The 1772 edn of Ulloa's *Voyage to S. America* was at Somersby (*Lincoln*).

Were not thine eye a star might grace
Yon sapphire concave beaming clear,
Or fill the vanished Pleiad's place,
And shine for aye as brightly there–

Had not thy locks the golden glow
That robes the gay and early east,
Thus falling in luxuriant flow
Around thy fair but faithless breast:

I might have deemed that thou wert she
Of the Cumaean cave, who wrote
Each fate-involving mystery,
Upon the feathery leaves that float,

Borne through the boundless waste of air,
Wherever chance might drive along.
But she was wrinkled – thou art fair:
And she was old – but thou art young.

Her years were as the sands that strew
The fretted ocean-beach; but thou–
Triumphant in that eye of blue,
Beneath thy smoothly-marble brow;

Exulting in thy form thus moulded,
By nature's tenderest touch designed;
Proud of the fetters thou hast folded
Around this fond deluded mind–

Deceivest still with practised look,
With fickle vow, and well-feigned sigh.
I tell thee, that I will not brook
Reiterated perjury!

Alas! I feel thy deep control,
E'en now when I would break thy chain:
But while I seek to gain thy soul,
Ah! say – hast thou a soul to gain?

*15.* 'In the constellation of the Pleiades the star of Merope appears more dim and obscure than the rest, because she, as the poets observe, married a mortal, while her sisters married some of the gods or their descendants' (*English Encyclopaedia*, 1802, of which a copy was at Somersby, *Lincoln*).
*21–30.* The Sibyl, Ovid, *Metamorphoses* xiv 136–9. Phoebus granted her as many years as there were grains in a pile of sand, but she forgot to ask for youth and so withered away. Cp. the story of *Tithonus* (p. 1112).
*25. the waste of air*: as in Gray, *Couplet about Birds*. Gray's couplet did not appear in his *Works* till 1884, but it suggests that the phrase is eighteenth-century diction.

# 17 *Persia

Published *1827*, not reprinted. Paden (p. 29) suggests that it was influenced by Charles Rollin's *Ancient History* (1789 translation, *Lincoln*): 'Cyrus and Alexander, the one founder, the other destroyer, of the powerful empire of Persia'. The details are from Rollin, and from Xenophon's *Anabasis*–see ll. 43*n*, 61*n*. Cp. *The High-Priest to Alexander* (p. 138), and *Alexander* (p. 469); also *The Ganges* (p. 162).

*The flower and choice*
*Of many provinces from bound to bound.*

MILTON [*PR* iii 314–15]

Land of bright eye and lofty brow!
Whose every gale is balmy breath
Of incense from some sunny flower,
Which on tall hill or valley low,
In clustering maze or circling wreath,
Sheds perfume; or in blooming bower
Of Schiraz or of Ispahan,
In bower untrod by foot of man,
Clasps round the green and fragrant stem
Of lotos, fair and fresh and blue,
And crowns it with a diadem
Of blossoms, ever young and new;
Oh! lives there yet within thy soul
Ought of the fire of him who led
Thy troops, and bade thy thunder roll
O'er lone Assyria's crownless head?
I tell thee, had that conqueror red
From Thymbria's plain beheld thy fall,
When stormy Macedonia swept
Thine honours from thee one and all,
He would have wailed, he would have wept,
That thy proud spirit should have bowed
To Alexander, doubly proud.
Oh! Iran! Iran! had he known

¶ 17.*1–12*. Paden (p. 125) points out the influence of Collins's *Oriental Eclogues*, and of Sir William Jones, whose works were at Somersby (*Lincoln*).

*8*. Paden suggests that this 'may hint at a harem', since the blue lotus was commonly compared to the beloved, as in *Thou camest to thy bower* (p. 136).

*14*. *him*: Cyrus.

*24*. *Íran*.

The downfall of his mighty throne,
Or had he seen that fatal night,
  When the young king of Macedon
  In madness led his veterans on,
And Thais held the funeral light,
Around that noble pile which rose
  Irradiant with the pomp of gold,
  In high Persepolis of old,
Encompassed with its frenzied foes;
He would have groaned, he would have spread
The dust upon his laurelled head,
To view the setting of that star,
Which beamed so gorgeously and far
O'er Anatolia, and the fane
Of Belus, and Caïster's plain,
  And Sardis, and the glittering sands
  Of bright Pactolus, and the lands
Where Croesus held his rich domain:
On fair Diarbeck's land of spice,
Adiabene's plains of rice,
Where down the Euphrates, swift and strong,
The shield-like kuphars bound along;
And sad Cunaxa's field, where, mixing
  With host to adverse host opposed,
'Mid clashing shield and spear transfixing,
  The rival brothers sternly closed.
And further east, where, broadly rolled,
Old Indus pours his stream of gold;
And there, where tumbling deep and hoarse,

*29. Thais*: Alexander's mistress, said to have persuaded him to burn Persepolis. This is the theme of Dryden's *Alexander's Feast*, which mentions Alexander's 'madness'.

*38–9. fane of Belus*: the temple at Babylon.

*42. Croesus*: king of Lydia.

*43. 1827* note: 'Xenophon says, that every shrub in these wilds had an aromatic odour'.

*44. Paradise Regained* iii 319–20: 'The neighbouring plains / Of Adiabene', which follows T.'s epigraph.

*46. kuphars*: boats. *1827* note: 'Rennel on Herodotus'. Paden (p. 124) observes that James Rennell (1800) used the spelling 'kufah', which suggests that T. used an intermediate source.

*47–50.* The battle of Cunaxa, where Cyrus the Younger tried to seize the throne from his brother Artaxerxes. 'The Retreat of the Ten Thousand' (Cyrus's defeated army) is the subject of Xenophon's *Anabasis*, which supplied most of T.'s ensuing geography.

Blue Ganga leaves her vaccine source;
Loveliest of all the lovely streams
That meet immortal Titan's beams,
And smile upon their fruitful way
Beneath his golden orient ray:
And southward to Cilicia's shore,
Where Cydnus meets the billows' roar,
And where the Syrian gates divide
The meeting realms on either side;
E'en to the land of Nile, whose crops
  Bloom rich beneath his bounteous swell,
  To hot Syene's wondrous well,
Nigh to the long-lived Æthiops.
And northward far to Trebizonde,
  Renowned for kings of chivalry,
Near where old Hyssus, from the strand,
  Disgorges in the Euxine sea–
The Euxine, falsely named, which whelms
  The mariner in the heaving tide,
To high Sinope's distant realms,
  Whence cynics railed at human pride.

# 18 *The Druid's Prophecies

Published *1827*, not reprinted. *1827* note: '*Stabat pro littore diversa acies, densa armis virisque, intercursantibus feminis in modum Furiarum, quae veste ferali, crinibus dejectis, faces praeferebant. Druidaeque circum, preces diras, sublatis ad coelum manibus, fundentes, etc.*–Tacitus, *Annals* XIV xxx.' ('On the beach stood the adverse array, a serried mass of arms and men, with

54. *1827* note: 'The cavern in the ridge of Himmalah, whence the Ganges seems to derive its original springs, has been moulded, by the mind of Hindoo superstition, into the head of a cow'. Paden shows that this was from Rennell. There was a discussion of Rennell and the cow's-mouth in *QR* xvii (1817) 409. *QR* influenced other poems of *1827*, and there were copies at Somersby (*Lincoln*). Cp. *The Ganges* (p. 162).
61. *the Syrian gates*: the pass 'formed by the near approach of the foot of mount *Amanus* to the *Sinus Issicus*' (Rennell, *The Expedition of Cyrus*, 1816, p. 39). *1827* note: 'See Xenophon's *Expeditio Cyri*'. As in *Alexander* 3.
65. *Syene*: Aswan.
67–74. The army, as Xenophon relates, finally reached the Euxine and passed Trebizond and Sinope. Milton had associated Trebizond with chivalry, *Paradise Lost* i 584.
69. *Near . . . Hyssus,*] Where Hyssus, rolling *1827 corrected in Errata.*
71. The Black Sea, *euxinus* meaning hospitable in Greek.
74. Alexander's meeting with Diogenes of Sinope.

women flitting between the ranks. In the style of Furies, in robes of deathly black and with dishevelled hair, they brandished their torches; while a circle of Druids, lifting their hands to heaven and showering imprecations ...') For the Roman destruction of the Druids' groves in Anglesey (Mona), cp. *Boädicea* (p. 1118), which is based on the same chapter of Tacitus. These prophetic denunciations derive from Gray's *The Bard*; cp., all *1827*, *Lamentation of the Peruvians*, *The Fall of Jerusalem*, *God's Denunciations against Pharaoh-Hophra*, and *The High Priest to Alexander*. The Druids provide the choruses in William Mason's tragedy *Caractacus* (1759), which T. used for *Time*. Sources: in addition to Tacitus, Gibbon's *Decline and Fall of the Roman Empire*, Chapters iv–xii; and hence Suetonius's *The Twelve Caesars* (see *1827* notes).

Mona! with flame thine oaks are streaming,
  Those sacred oaks we reared on high:
Lo! Mona, Lo! the swords are gleaming
  Adown thine hills confusedly.

Hark! Mona, Hark! the chargers' neighing!
  The clang of arms and helmets bright!
The crash of steel, the dreadful braying
  Of trumpets through the maddening fight!

Exalt your torches, raise your voices;
  Your thread is spun–your day is brief;
Yea! Howl for sorrow! Rome rejoices,
  But Mona–Mona bends in grief!

But woe to Rome, though now she raises
  Yon eagles of her haughty power;
Though now her sun of conquest blazes,
  Yet soon shall come her darkening hour!

Woe, woe to him who sits in glory,
  Enthronèd on thine hills of pride!
Can he not see the poignard gory,
  With his best heart's-blood deeply dyed?

Ah! what avails his gilded palace,
  Whose wings the seven-hilled town enfold?
The costly bath, the crystal chalice?
  The pomp of gems–the glare of gold?

¶ 18.*6–8*. Cp. *Paradise Lost* vi 209–10: 'Arms on Armour clashing bray'd / Horrible discord, and the madding Wheeles . . .'
*10*. Gray's *Bard* 98: 'The thread is spun'.
*21*. Cp. Landor, *Rose Aylmer* (1806): 'Ah what avails the sceptred race'.
*22*. *1827* note: 'Pliny says, that the golden palace of Nero extended all round the city', *Natural History* XXXVI xxiv.

See where, by heartless anguish driven,
  Crownless he creeps 'mid circling thorns;
Around him flash the bolts of heaven,
  And angry earth before him yawns.

Then, from his pinnacle of splendour,
  The feeble king, with locks of grey,
Shall fall, and sovereign Rome shall render
  Her sceptre to the usurper's sway.

Who comes with sounds of mirth and gladness,
  Triumphing o'er the prostrate dead?
Ay, me! thy mirth shall change to sadness,
  When Vengeance strikes thy guilty head.

Above thy noon-day feast suspended,
  High hangs in air a naked sword:
Thy days are gone, thy joys are ended,
  The cup, the song, the festal board.

Then shall the eagle's shadowy pinion
  Be spread beneath the eastern skies;

*26. 1827* note: '*Ut ad diverticulum ventum est, dimissis equis inter fruticeta ac vepres, per arundineti semitam aegre, nec nisi strata sub pedibus veste, ad adversum villae parietem evasit.–Suetonius, Vit. Caesar.*' ('When they came to a by-path leading to the villa, they turned the horses loose and he made his way amid bushes and brambles and along a path through a thicket of reeds to the back wall of the house, with great difficulty and only when a robe was thrown down for him to walk on', VI xlviii.)

*28. 1827* note: '*Statimque tremore terrae, et fulgure adverso pavefactus, audiit ex proximis castris clamorem, etc.–Ibid.*' ('At once he was startled by a shock of earthquake and a flash of lightning full in his face, and he heard the shouts from the camp hard by.')

*30. 1827* note: 'Galba'.

*32. 1827* note: 'Otho'.

*34. 1827* note: '*Utque campos, in quibus pugnatum est, adiit (i.e. Vitellius) plurimum meri propalam hausit, etc.–Suetonius.*' ('When he came to the plains where the battle was fought . . . he openly drained a great draught of unmixed wine', VII x.)

*41–4.* The rhyme *pinion/dominion*, and the eagle are from Gray's *Progress of Poesy* 114–16. Later T. praised these lines of Gray's as 'among the most liquid lines in any language' (*Mem.* ii 288). But cp. also Thomas Moore, *Odes of Anacreon* xxxvi: 'That when Death came, with shadowy pinion, / To waft me to his bleak dominion.' Also Wordsworth's *The Green Linnet* 12, 16 (1807).

*42. 1827* note: 'At the siege of Jerusalem'.

And dazzling far with wide dominion,
Five brilliant stars shall brightly rise.

Then, coward king! the helpless agèd
Shall bow beneath thy dastard blow;
But reckless hands and hearts, enragèd,
By double fate shall lay thee low.

And two, with death-wounds deeply mangled,
Low on their parent-earth shall lie;
Fond wretches! ah! too soon entangled
Within the snares of royalty.

Then comes that mighty one victorious
In triumph o'er this earthly ball,
Exulting in his conquests glorious–
Ah! glorious to his country's fall!

But thou shalt see the Romans flying,
O Albyn! with yon dauntless ranks;
And thou shalt view the Romans dying,
Blue Carun! on thy mossy banks.

*44. 1827* note: 'The five good Emperors; Nerva, Trajan, Adrian, Antoninus Pius, and Marcus Aurelius, or Antoninus the Philosopher. Perhaps the best commentary on the life and virtues of the last, is his own volume of "Meditations".'

*45. 1827* note: '*Debiles pedibus, et eos, qui ambulare non possent, in gigantum modum, ita ut a genibus de pannis et linteis quasi dracones digererentur; eosdemque sagittis confecit.–Aelius Lampridius in Vita Comm.*–Such were the laudable amusements of Commodus!' ('Certain men who were lame in their feet and others who could not walk, he dressed up as giants, encasing their legs from the knee down in wrappings and bandages to make them look like serpents, and then despatched them with his arrows.') T.'s reference to the *Scriptores Historiae Augustae* (Commodus ix) is from Gibbon (Paden, p. 102).

*48. 1827* note: 'He was first poisoned; but the operation not fully answering the wishes of his beloved, he was afterwards strangled by a robust wrestler.'

*49. 1827* note: 'Pertinax and Didius Julian.' Cp. *PL* vi 368: 'Mangl'd with gastly wounds'.

*50. parent earth*: as in Gray's *Alliance of Education* 85.

*54. 1827* note: 'Severus, who was equally victorious in the Eastern and Western World: but those conquests, however glorious, were conducive to the ruin of the Roman Empire.–See Gibbon, vol. vi [*read* i] chap. v. p. 203.'

*58. 1827* note: 'In allusion to the real or feigned victory obtained by Fingal over Caracul or Caracalla.–See *Ossian*.' This is taken from Gibbon.

But lo! what dreadful visions o'er me
  Are bursting on this agèd eye!
What length of bloody train before me,
  In slow succession passes by!
Thy hapless monarchs fall together,
  Like leaves in winter's stormy ire;
Some by the sword, and some shall wither
  By lightning's flame and fever's fire.

They come! they leave their frozen regions,
  Where Scandinavia's wilds extend;
And Rome, though girt with dazzling legions,
  Beneath their blasting power shall bend.

Woe, woe to Rome! though tall and ample
  She rears her domes of high renown;
Yet fiery Goths shall fiercely trample
  The grandeur of her temples down!

She sinks to dust; and who shall pity
  Her dark despair and hopeless groans?
There is a wailing in her city–
  Her babes are dashed against the stones!
Then, Mona! then, though wan and blighted
  Thy hopes be now by Sorrow's dearth,
Then all thy wrongs shall be requited–
  The Queen of Nations bows to earth!

# 19 *The Expedition of Nadir Shah into Hindostan

Published *1827*, not reprinted. The Russell copy of *1827* is alone in attributing this to Charles. The source is Sir William Jones's *History of Nadir Shah* (l. 16*n*). Nadir Shah of Persia was the last of the great Mohammedan conquerors of India; he swept Hindustan in 1739 and sacked Delhi.

*61–4.* Cp. Gray's *Bard* 105–7: 'But oh! what solemn scenes on Snowdon's height / Descending slow their glitt'ring skirts unroll? / Visions of glory, spare my aching sight.' Both Gray and T. recall *Macbeth* IV i, the visionary procession of kings.

*64. 1827* note: 'Very few of the Emperors after Severus escaped assassination.'

*68. 1827* note: 'Macrinus, Heliogabalus, Alexander, Maximin Pupienus, Balbinus, Gordian, Philip, etc., were assassinated; Claudius died of a pestilential fever; and Carus was struck dead by lightning in his tent.'

Cp. Byron's *Destruction of Sennacherib.* The first epigraph is the opening of Racine's play, as Paden points out (p. 106). The second epigraph quotes *squalent populatibus agri, In Eutropium* i 244 ('The countryside was ravaged and brought to ruin').

*Quoi! vous allez combattre un roi, dont la puissance*
*Semble forcer le ciel de prendre sa defense,*
*Sous qui toute l'Asie a vu tomber ses rois*
*Et qui tient la fortune attachée a ses lois!*

RACINE, *Alexandre*

*Squallent populatibus agri.*

CLAUDIAN

As the host of the locusts in numbers, in might
As the flames of the forest that redden the night,
They approach: but the eye may not dwell on the glare
Of standard and sabre that sparkle in air.
Like the fiends of destruction they rush on their way,
The vulture behind them is wild for his prey;
And the spirits of death, and the demons of wrath,
Wave the gloom of their wings o'er their desolate path.

Earth trembles beneath them, the dauntless, the bold;
Oh! weep for thy children, thou region of gold;
For thy thousands are bowed to the dust of the plain,
And all Delhi runs red with the blood of her slain.

For thy glory is past, and thy splendour is dim,
And the cup of thy sorrow is full to the brim;
And where is the chief in thy realms to abide,
The 'Monarch of Nations', the strength of his pride?

Like a thousand dark streams from the mountain they
throng,
With the fife and the horn and the war-beating gong:

¶ 19.*10. 1827* note: 'This invader required as a ransom for Mohammed Shah no less than thirty millions, and amassed in the rich city of Delhi the enormous sum of two hundred and thirty-one millions sterling. Others, however, differ considerably in their account of this treasure.'

*16. 1827* note: 'Such pompous epithets the Oriental writers are accustomed to bestow on their monarchs; of which sufficient specimens may be seen in Sir William Jones's translation of the History of Nadir Shah. We can scarcely read one page of this work without meeting with such sentences as these: "Le roi de rois;" "Les etendards qui subjuguent le monde;" "L'ame rayonnante de sa majesté;" "Le rayonnant monarque du monde;" "Sa majesté conquerante du monde;" etc.'

The land like an Eden before them is fair,
But behind them a wilderness dreary and bare.

The shrieks of the orphan, the lone widow's wail,
The groans of the childless, are loud on the gale;
For the star of thy glory is blasted and wan,
And withered the flower of thy fame, Hindostan!

## 20 *The Maid of Savoy

Published *1827*, not reprinted. Paden (p. 134) suggests the influence of William Coxe's account of Switzerland (1776), which was quoted in *1827* (p. 177). Cp. *Switzerland* (p. 1810).

Down Savoy's hills of stainless white
A thousand currents run,
And sparkle bright in the early light
Of the slowly-rising sun:
But brighter far,
Like the glance of a star
From regions above,
Is the look of love
In the eye of the Maid of Savoy!

Down Savoy's hills of lucid snow
A thousand roebucks leap,
And headlong they go when the bugles blow,
And sound from steep to steep:
But lighter far,
Like the motion of air
On the smooth river's bed,
Is the noiseless tread
Of the foot of the Maid of Savoy!

*19–20. 1827* note: '"The land is as the garden of Eden before them, and behind them a desolate wilderness."–*Joel.*' The words which precede *Joel* ii 3 are also apt to T.'s poem: 'A great people and a strong, there hath not been ever the like, neither shall be any more after it, even to the years of many generations. A fire devoureth before them, and behind them a flame burneth.' With l. 9, cp. *Joel* ii 10: 'The earth shall quake before them, the heavens shall tremble'; with ll. 17–18, *Joel* ii 5: 'Like the noise of chariots on the tops of mountains shall they leap'; and l. 23 was perhaps suggested by *Joel* ii 10: 'the stars shall withdraw their shining'.

*23.* Cp. *Paradise Lost* x 412: 'the blasted Starrs lookt wan'.

In Savoy's vales, with green arrayed,
A thousand blossoms flower,
'Neath the odorous shade by the larches made,
In their own ambrosial bower:
But sweeter still,
Like the cedars which rise
On Lebanon's hill
To the pure blue skies,
Is the breath of the Maid of Savoy!

In Savoy's groves full merrily sing
A thousand songsters gay,
When the breath of spring calls them forth on the wing,
To sport in the sun's mild ray:
But softer far,
Like the holy song
Of angels in air,
When they sweep along,
Is the voice of the Maid of Savoy!

## 21 *Midnight

Published *1827*, not reprinted. Source: *1827* note to l. 19, 'The succeeding lines are a paraphrase of Ossian'. The passage is that from which T. quoted in *Oh! ye wild winds* (p. 141), from a Macpherson poem quoted with *Croma*. The 1809 edn of Macpherson's *Ossian* was at Somersby (*Lincoln*).

'Tis midnight o'er the dim mere's lonely bosom,
Dark, dusky, windy midnight: swift are driven
The swelling vapours onward: every blossom
Bathes its bright petals in the tears of heaven.
Imperfect, half-seen objects meet the sight,
The other half our fancy must portray;
A wan, dull, lengthened sheet of swimming light
Lies the broad lake: the moon conceals her ray,
Sketched faintly by a pale and lurid gleam
Shot through the glimmering clouds: the lovely planet
Is shrouded in obscurity; the scream
Of owl is silenced; and the rocks of granite
Rise tall and drearily, while damp and dank
Hang the thick willows on the reedy bank.

¶21.*10*. Cp. Milton, *Paradise Lost* ii 1036–7: 'Shoots farr into the bosom of dim Night / A glimmering dawn'; cp. l. 1 above.

Beneath, the gurgling eddies slowly creep,
    Blackened by foliage; and the glutting wave,
That saps eternally the cold grey steep,
    Sounds heavily within the hollow cave.
All earth is restless–from his glossy wing
    The heath-fowl lifts his head at intervals;
    Wet, driving, rainy, come the bursting squalls;
All nature wears her dun dead covering.
Tempest is gathered, and the brooding storm
Spreads its black mantle o'er the mountain's form;
And, mingled with the rising roar, is swelling,
From the far hunter's booth, the blood hound's yelling.
The water-falls in various cadence chiming,
    Or in one loud unbroken sheet descending,
        Salute each other through the night's dark womb;
    The moaning pine-trees to the wild blast bending,
        Are pictured faintly through the chequered gloom;
The forests, half-way up the mountain climbing,
    Resound with crash of falling branches; quiver
        Their agèd mossy trunks: the startled doe
    Leaps from her leafy lair: the swelling river
        Winds his broad stream majestic, deep, and slow.

## 22 *Scotch Song

Published *1827*, not reprinted. *1893* attribution was '(?)'; but it is attributed to T. in the Russell and Haddelsey copies of *1827* and in Charles's copy, and it is in T.'s hand in *T.MS.*

There are tears o' pity, an' tears o' wae,
An' tears for excess o' joy will fa';
*Yet the tears o' luve are sweeter than a'!*
There are sighs o' pity, an' sighs o' wae,
An' sighs o' regret frae the saul will gae;
*Yet the sighs o' luve are sweeter than a'!*

*16.* Cp. Keats, *On the Sea 2–3*: 'with its mighty swell / Gluts twice ten thousand caverns'.

*19–36.* Ossian (see headnote): 'The distant dog is howling from the hut of the hill . . . the heath-cock's head is beneath his wing . . . The old tree groans to the blast; the falling branch resounds . . . The hunter starts from sleep, in his lonely hut . . . Loud roar two mountain streams which meet beside his booth . . . the squalls of wind.'

There's the look o' pity, the look o' wae,
The look o' frien', an' the look o' fae;
*Yet the look o' luve is sweeter than a'!*

There's the smile o' friends when they come frae far,
There's the smile o' joy in the festive ha';
*Yet the smile o' luve is sweeter than a'!*

## 23 *Song
## [It is the solemn even-time]

Published *1827*, not reprinted. Cp. Thomas Moore's *National Airs* (1818): 'Hark! the vesper hymn is stealing / O'er the waters soft and clear; / Nearer yet and nearer pealing, / And now bursts upon the ear . . .'

It is the solemn even-time,
  And the holy organ's pealing:
And the vesper chime, oh! the vesper chime!
  O'er the clear blue wave is stealing.

It is the solemn mingled swell
  Of the monks in chorus singing:
And the vesper bell, oh! the vesper bell!
  To the gale is its soft note flinging.

'Tis the sound of the voices sweeping along,
  Like the wind through a grove of larches:
And the vesper song, oh! the vesper song!
  Echoes sad through the cloistered arches.

## 24 *Friendship

Published *1827*, not reprinted. Its theme, though not its tone, somewhat anticipates *In Memoriam*. The arguments as to the rarity of friendship are from J. Bigland's *Essays* (1805, *Lincoln*); see ll. 20–4*n*. Epigraph: Cicero's *De Amicitia* vi 22: 'I am not now speaking of the ordinary and common-place friendship–delightful and profitable as it is–but of that pure and faultless kind, such as was that of the few whose friendships are known to fame.' For T.'s use of the Spenserian stanza, cp. the opening of *The Lotos-Eaters* (p. 429).

*Neque ego nunc de vulgari aut de mediocri, quae tamen ipsa et delectat et prodest, se de vera et perfecta loquor (amicitia) qualis eorum qui pauci nominantur, fuit.*

CICERO

O thou most holy Friendship! wheresoe'er
  Thy dwelling be–for in the courts of man
But seldom thine all-heavenly voice we hear,
  Sweetening the moments of our narrow span;
And seldom thy bright foot-steps do we scan
  Along the weary waste of life unblest,
For faithless is its frail and wayward plan,
  And perfidy is man's eternal guest,
With dark suspicion linked and shameless interest!–

'Tis thine, when life has reached its final goal,
  Ere the last sigh that frees the mind be given,
To speak sweet solace to the parting soul,
  And pave the bitter path that leads to heaven:
'Tis thine, whene'er the heart is racked and riven
  By the hot shafts of baleful calumny,
When the dark spirit to despair is driven,
  To teach its lonely grief to lean on thee,
And pour within thine ear the tale of misery.

But where art thou, thou comet of an age,
  Thou phoenix of a century? Perchance
Thou art but of those fables which engage
  And hold the minds of men in giddy trance.
Yet, be it so, and be it all romance,
  The thought of thine existence is so bright
With beautiful imaginings–the glance
  Upon thy fancied being such delight,
That I will deem thee Truth, so lovely is thy might!

## 25 *'And ask ye why these sad tears stream?'

Published *1827*, not reprinted. Paden (p. 138) compares Byron's *On the Death of a Young Lady*. Epigraph: Ovid's *Heroides* xv 123, Sappho to the absent Phaon: 'You, my dreams bring back to me'.

*Te somnia nostra reducunt.*

OVID

¶*24.10–13*. The theme of *The Dying Man to His Friend* (p. 153).
*19–20*. Cp. *Come hither* 12: 'the star, the meteor of his century'.
*20–4*. Based on J. Bigland, ii 18 (see headnote): 'We must not expect to meet with that romantic friendship so much cried up, but so seldom experienced, and which is, indeed, so rare, that the man who should set out on the pursuit, would, in all probability, waste life in fruitless expectation, like the naturalist in search of the Phoenix.'

And ask ye why these sad tears stream?
Why these wan eyes are dim with weeping?
I had a dream–a lovely dream,
Of her that in the grave is sleeping.

I saw her as 'twas yesterday,
The bloom upon her cheek still glowing;
And round her played a golden ray,
And on her brows were gay flowers blowing.

With angel-hand she swept a lyre,
A garland red with roses bound it;
Its strings were wreathed with lambent fire,
And amaranth was woven round it.

I saw her mid the realms of light,
In everlasting radiance gleaming;
Co-equal with the seraphs bright,
Mid thousand thousand angels beaming.

I strove to reach her, when, behold,
Those fairy forms of bliss Elysian,
And all that rich scene wrapt in gold,
Faded in air–a lovely vision!

And I awoke, but oh! to me
That waking hour was doubly weary;
And yet I could not envy thee,
Although so blest, and I so dreary.

## 26 *On Sublimity

Published *1827*, not reprinted. Paden (pp. 24–7) points out that it is a general imitation of Collins's *Ode on the Popular Superstitions of the Highlands*; the raw material is from *The Hundred Wonders of the World*, by 'C. C. Clarke' (1818).

*The sublime always dwells on great objects and terrible.*
BURKE [*On the Sublime and the Beautiful*]

O tell me not of vales in tenderest green,
The poplar's shade, the plantane's graceful tree;

¶25.2. *wan eyes*: five times in Shelley, e.g. 'The tears which fell from her wan eyes', *Rosalind* 415.
11. *lambent*: licking like a tongue; a stock epithet for fire (*OED* from 1647).
12. *amaranth*: the unfading flower in Milton's Heaven.

Give me the wild cascade, the rugged scene,
  The loud surge bursting o'er the purple sea:
On such sad views my soul delights to pore,
  By Teneriffe's peak, or Kilda's giant height,
Or dark Loffoden's melancholy shore,
  What time grey eve is fading into night;
When by that twilight beam I scarce descry
The mingled shades of earth and sea and sky.

Give me to wander at midnight alone,
  Through some august cathedral, where, from high,
The cold, clear moon on the mosaic stone
  Comes glancing in gay colours gloriously,
Through windows rich with gorgeous blazonry,
  Gilding the niches dim, where, side by side,
Stand antique mitred prelates, whose bones lie
  Beneath the pavement, where their deeds of pride
Were graven, but long since are worn away
By constant feet of ages day by day.

Then, as Imagination aids, I hear
  Wild heavenly voices sounding from the choir,
And more than mortal music meets mine ear,
  Whose long, long notes among the tombs expire,
With solemn rustling of cherubic wings,
  Round those vast columns which the roof upbear;
While sad and undistinguishable things
  Do flit athwart the moonlit windows there;
And my blood curdles at the chilling sound
Of lone, unearthly steps, that pace the hallowed
    ground!

I love the starry spangled heaven, resembling
  A canopy with fiery gems o'erspread,
When the wide loch with silvery sheen is trembling,
  Far stretched beneath the mountain's hoary head.
But most I love that sky, when, dark with storms,
  It frowns terrific o'er this wildered earth,
While the black clouds, in strange and uncouth forms,
  Come hurrying onward in their ruinous wrath;
And shrouding in their deep and gloomy robe
The burning eyes of heaven and Dian's lucid globe!

¶ *26.6.* Collins's *Ode on Superstitions* has a stanza on St Kilda.
*15–26.* Paden shows the reminiscence of *Il Penseroso* 156–66 in the setting: windows, rich, dim, choir, roof.

I love your voice, ye echoing winds, that sweep
Through the wide womb of midnight, when the veil
Of darkness rests upon the mighty deep,
The labouring vessel, and the shattered sail–
Save when the forkèd bolts of lightning leap
On flashing pinions, and the mariner pale
Raises his eyes to heaven. Oh! who would sleep
What time the rushing of the angry gale
Is loud upon the waters?–Hail, all hail!
Tempest and clouds and night and thunder's rending peal!

All hail, Sublimity! thou lofty one,
For thou dost walk upon the blast, and gird
Thy majesty with terrors, and thy throne
Is on the whirlwind, and thy voicc is heard
In thunders and in shakings: thy delight
Is in the secret wood, the blasted heath,
The ruined fortress, and the dizzy height,
The grave, the ghastly charnel-house of death,
In vaults, in cloisters, and in gloomy piles,
Long corridors and towers and solitary aisles!

Thy joy is in obscurity, and plain
Is nought with thee; and on thy steps attend
Shadows but half-distinguished; the thin train
Of hovering spirits round thy pathway bend,
With their low tremulous voice and airy tread,
What time the tomb above them yawns and gapes:
For thou dost hold communion with the dead,
Phantoms and phantasies and grisly shapes;
And shades and headless spectres of St Mark,
Seen by a lurid light, formless and still and dark!

*56. the blasted heath*: *Paradise Lost* i 615, following 'thunder' (also *Macbeth* I iii 77).

*61–70.* In *T.MS* (which may not be quoted), T. deleted a note on Ossian and on Ann Radcliffe, author of *The Mysteries of Udolpho.*

*65. 1827* note: 'According to Burke, a low tremulous intermitted sound is conducive to the sublime.'

*69. 1827* note: 'It is a received opinion, that on St Mark's Eve all the persons who are to die on the following year make their appearances without their heads in the churches of their respective parishes.–See Dr. Langhorne's Notes to Collins.' Langhorne's edition (1765), p. 154, refers to Collins's *Ode to Fear.*

What joy to view the varied rainbow smile
On Niagara's flood of matchless might,
Where all around the melancholy isle
The billows sparkle with their hues of light!
While, as the restless surges roar and rave,
The arrowy stream descends with awful sound,
Wheeling and whirling with each breathless wave,
Immense, sublime, magnificent, profound!
If thou hast seen all this, and could'st not feel,
Then know, thine heart is framed of marble or of steel.

The hurricane fair earth to darkness changing,
Kentucky's chambers of eternal gloom,
The swift-paced columns of the desert ranging
The uneven waste, the violent Simoom,
Thy snow-clad peaks, stupendous Gungotree!
Whence springs the hallowed Jumna's echoing tide,
Hoar Cotopaxi's cloud-capt majesty,
Enormous Chimborazo's naked pride,
The dizzy cape of winds that cleaves the sky,
Whence we look down into eternity,

The pillared cave of Morven's giant king,
The Yanar, and the Geyser's boiling fountain,

*72. Níagára*, as in Goldsmith, *The Traveller* 412: 'And Niagara stuns with thund'ring sound'.

*73. 1827* note: 'This island, on both sides of which the waters rush with astonishing swiftness, is 900 or 800 feet long, and its lower edge is just at the perpendicular edge of the fall.'

*76. arrowy stream*: as in *Timbuctoo* 141.

*77. 1827* note: '"Undis Phlegethon perlustrat *anhelis*"–Claudian.' Paden (p. 102) observes that *undis* should be *gurgitibus* (*De raptu* i 24), and that T.'s *breathless* for *anhelis* is in Claudian 'panting', of a raging whirlpool. Paden is in error in saying that T.'s translation of Claudian gives 'steaming'; *The Rape of Proserpine* 32–4: 'And fiery Phlegethon for aye surrounds, / Dark, deep and whirling round his flaming caves / The braying vortex of his breathless waves.'

*82. 1827* note: 'See Dr. Nahum Ward's account of the great Kentucky Cavern, in the *Monthly Magazine*, October 1816.'

*85–6. Jumna*: should have been Ganges; T. took over the error from *The Hundred Wonders*, as Paden observes.

*89. 1827* note: 'In the Ukraine.'

*91. 1827* note: 'Fingal's Cave in the Island of Staffa. If the Colossus of Rhodes bestrid a harbour, Fingal's powers were certainly far from despicable:–

*A chos air Cromleach druim-ard*

The deep volcano's inward murmuring,
  The shadowy Colossus of the mountain;
Antiparos, where sun-beams never enter;
  Loud Stromboli, amid the quaking isles;
The terrible Maelstroom, around his centre
  Wheeling his circuit of unnumbered miles:
These, these are sights and sounds that freeze the blood,
Yet charm the awe-struck soul which doats on solitude.

Blest be the bard, whose willing feet rejoice
  To tread the emerald green of Fancy's vales,
Who hears the music of her heavenly voice,
  And breathes the rapture of her nectared gales!
Blest be the bard, whom golden Fancy loves,
  He strays for ever through her blooming bowers,
Amid the rich profusion of her groves,
  And wreathes his forehead with her spicy flowers
Of sunny radiance; but how blest is he
Who feels the genuine force of high Sublimity!

# 27 *Time: An Ode

Published *1827*, not reprinted. The large-paper edition of *1893* reproduces *T.MS.* T. acknowledged a borrowing from William Mason's *Caractacus* (1759); see l. 45*n*. T., writing in an eighteenth-century manner, expands other lines from Mason (pp. 26–7): 'The time will come, when Destiny and Death, / Thron'd in a burning car, the thund'ring wheels / Arm'd with gigantic scythes of adamant, / Shall scour this field of life, and in their rear / The fiend Oblivion: kingdoms, empires, worlds / Melt in the general blaze: when, lo, from high / Andraste darting, catches from the wreck / The roll of fame, claps her ascending plumes, / And stamps on orient stars each patriot name, / Round her eternal dome.'

---

*Chos eile air Crommeal dubh*
*Thoga Fion le lamh mhoir*
*An d'uisge o Lubhair na fruth.*

With one foot on Cromleach his brow,
The other on Crommeal the dark,
Fion took up with his large hand
The water from Lubhair of streams.

See the Dissertations prefixed to Ossian's *Poems.*'

*92. Yanar*: *1827* note: 'Or, perpetual fire.'

*94. 1827* note: 'Alias, the Spectre of the Broken.'

*96. Strómboli.*

I see the chariot, where,
Throughout the purple air,
The forelocked monarch rides:
Armed like some antique vehicle for war,
Time, hoary Time! I see thy scythèd car,
In voiceless majesty,
Cleaving the clouds of ages that float by,
And change their many-coloured sides,
Now dark, now dun, now richly bright,
In an ever-varying light.
The great, the lowly, and the brave
Bow down before the rushing force
Of thine unconquerable course;
Thy wheels are noiseless as the grave,
Yet fleet as Heaven's red bolt they hurry on,
They pass above us, and are gone!
Clear is the track which thou hast past;
Strewed with the wrecks of frail renown,
Robe, sceptre, banner, wreath, and crown,
The pathway that before thee lies,
An undistinguishable waste,
Invisible to human eyes,
Which fain would scan the various shapes which glide
In dusky cavalcade,
Imperfectly descried,
Through that intense, impenetrable shade.
Four grey steeds thy chariot draw;
In the obdurate, tameless jaw
Their rusted iron bits they sternly champ;
Ye may not hear the echoing tramp

¶ 27.2. *purple*: on this Augustan epithet, see A. Johnston, *RES*, n.s. xiv (1963) 389–93. On Pope's 'purple year', Warburton comments: 'used in the Latin sense of the brightest, most vivid colouring in general, not of that peculiar tint so called'. Cp. Dryden's 'Purple Spring', *Virgil's Pastorals* ii 62.
3. *forelocked*: the traditional representation of Time.
5. Cp. Thomas Warton, *Ode* xxi 11: 'Swept the pale legions with the scythed car.'
6. *voiceless*] noiseless *T.MS 1st reading.*
17. *track*] path *MS 1st reading.*
24. *dusky*] glittering *MS 1st reading.*
28. *obdúrate*: both pronunciations are common in the early nineteenth century. *tameless*: an archaism used by Shelley (*West Wind* 56), but one that survived as applied to horses (*OED*, 1890).
29. *sternly*] fiercely *MS 1st reading.*

Of their light-bounding, windy feet,
Upon that cloudy pavement beat.
Four wings have each, which, far outspread,
Receive the many blasts of heaven,
As with unwearied speed,
Throughout the long extent of ether driven,
Onward they rush for ever and for aye:
Thy voice, thou mighty Charioteer!
Always sounding in their ear,
Throughout the gloom of night and heat of day.
Fast behind thee follows Death,
Through the ranks of wan and weeping,
That yield their miserable breath,
On with his pallid courser proudly sweeping.
Armed is he in full mail,
Bright breast-plate and high crest,
Nor is the trenchant falchion wanting:
So fiercely does he ride the gale,
On Time's dark car, before him, rest
The dew-drops of his charger's panting.

On, on they go along the boundless skies,
All human grandeur fades away
Before their flashing, fiery, hollow eyes;
Beneath the terrible control
Of those vast armèd orbs, which roll
Oblivion on the creatures of a day.
Those splendid monuments alone he spares,
Which, to her deathless votaries,

*35*] As on with restless and unwearied speed *MS 1st reading.*
*39. Always*] Alway *MS.*
*44. courser*] charger *MS 1st reading.*
*45. 1827* note: 'I am indebted for the idea of Death's Armour to that famous Chorus in *Caractacus* beginning with–"Hark! heard ye not that footstep dread?"' *Caractacus*, pp. 68–9: 'Hark! heard ye not yon footstep dread / That shook the earth with thund'ring tread? / 'Twas Death.–In haste / The Warrior past; / High tower'd his helmed head: / I mark'd his mail, I mark'd his shield, / I 'spi'd the sparkling of his spear, / I saw his giant-arm the falchion wield; / Wide wav'd the bick'ring blade, and fir'd the angry air.'
*55. orbs*: the 'scythed' wheels; suggesting, as do the fiery eyes, the Messiah: 'the Orbes / Of his fierce Chariot rowld', *Paradise Lost* vi 828–9. This passage of Milton provided many of the details of the Ode from *Caractacus* which T. used.

Bright Fame, with glowing hand, uprears
Amid the waste of countless years.

'Live ye!' to these he crieth; 'live!
'To ye eternity I give–
'Ye, upon whose blessèd birth
'The noblest star of heaven hath shone;
'Live, when the ponderous pyramids of earth
'Are crumbling in oblivion!
'Live, when, wrapt in sullen shade,
'The golden hosts of heaven shall fade;
'Live, when yon gorgeous sun on high
'Shall veil the sparkling of his eye!
'Live, when imperial Time and Death himself shall die!'

## 28 *God's Denunciations against Pharaoh-Hophra, or Apries

Published *1827*, not reprinted. Based on *Ezekiel* xxix–xxx; influenced by Charles Rollin's *Ancient History* (see l. 2*n*). Cp. the many other prophecies of woe in *1827*, such as *Lamentation of the Peruvians* (p. 131).

Thou beast of the flood, who hast said in thy soul,
'I have made me a stream that for ever shall roll!'
Thy strength is the flower that shall last but a day,
And thy might is the snow in the sun's burning ray.

Arm, arm from the east, Babylonia's son!
Arm, arm for the battle–the Lord leads thee on!
With the shield of thy fame, and the power of thy
pride,
Arm, arm in thy glory–the Lord is thy guide.

*59. glowing hand*: as in Keats, *Eve of St Agnes* 271. T. used it, each time with personification as here, in *Mithridates* 10: 'The glowing hands of Honour'; and *Locksley Hall* 31: 'Love took up the glass of Time, and turned it in his glowing hands'.

*67. sullen*: cp. Scott, *Don Roderick* II i: 'All sleeps in sullen shade'.

¶ 28.*2*. *1827* note: 'Pliny's reproach to the Egyptians, for their vain and foolish pride with regard to the inundations of the Nile, points out one of their most distinguishing characteristics, and recalls to my mind a fine passage of Ezekiel, where God thus speaks to Pharaoh, one of their kings: "Behold, I am against thee, Pharaoh king of Egypt, the great dragon that lieth in the midst of his rivers, that hath said, My river is mine own, and I have made it for myself."–Rollin i 216.' Referring to *Ezekiel* xxix 3.

5. Nebuchadrezzar, king of Babylon.

Thou shalt come like a storm when the moonlight is dim,
And the lake's gloomy bosom is full to the brim;
Thou shalt come like the flash in the darkness of night,
When the wolves of the forest shall howl for affright.

Woe, woe to thee, Tanis! thy babes shall be thrown
By the barbarous hands on the cold marble-stone:
Woe, woe to thee, Nile! for thy stream shall be red
With the blood that shall gush o'er thy billowy bed!

Woe, woe to thee, Memphis! the war-cry is near,
And the child shall be tossed on the murderer's spear;
For fiercely he comes in the day of his ire,
With wheels like a whirlwind, and chariots of fire!

## 29 *The Grave of a Suicide

Published *1827*, not reprinted.

Hark! how the gale, in mournful notes and stern,
 Sighs through yon grove of agèd oaks, that wave
(While down these solitary walks I turn)
 Their mingled branches o'er yon lonely grave!

Poor soul! the dawning of thy life was dim;
 Frowned the dark clouds upon thy natal day;
Soon rose thy cup of sorrow to the brim,
 And hope itself but shed a doubtful ray.

That hope had fled, and all within was gloom;
 That hope had fled – thy woe to phrenzy grew;
For thou, wed to misery from the womb –
 Scarce one bright scene thy night of darkness knew!

Oft when the moon-beam on the cold bank sleeps,
 Where 'neath the dewy turf thy form is laid,

*13, 17. Tanis* and *Memphis*: *1827* note: 'The Scriptural appellations are "Zoan" and "Noph".' T. is in error (Paden, p. 126). For Noph and Zoan, see *Ezekiel* xxx 13–14.

*20.* Based on *Ezekiel* i, the whirlwind and the wheels of fire. T. would have remembered Milton's use of this chapter in his account of the Messiah's Chariot, *Paradise Lost* vi 749–51: 'forth rush'd with whirlwind sound / The Chariot of Paternal Deitie, / Flashing thick flames, Wheele within Wheele undrawn.'

¶ 29.*13. Merchant of Venice* V i 55: 'How sweet the moonlight sleeps upon this bank!'

In silent woe thy wretched mother weeps,
By this lone tomb, and by this oak-tree's shade.

'Oh! softly tread: in death he slumbers here;
''Tis here,' she cries, 'within his narrow cell!'–
The bitter sob, the wildly-starting tear,
The quivering lip, proclaim the rest too well!

# 30 *The Walk at Midnight

Published *1827*, not reprinted.

*Tremulo sub lumine.*
VIRGIL [*Aeneid* vii 9]

Soft, shadowy moon-beam! by thy light
Sleeps the wide meer serenely pale:
How various are the sounds of night,
Borne on the scarcely-rising gale!

The swell of distant brook is heard,
Whose far-off waters faintly roll;
And piping of the shrill small bird,
Arrested by the wandering owl.

Come hither! let us thread with care
The maze of this green path, which binds
The beauties of the broad parterre,
And through yon fragrant alley winds.

Or on this old bench will we sit,
Round which the clustering woodbine wreathes;
While birds of night around us flit;
And through each lavish wood-walk breathes,

Unto my ravished senses, brought
From yon thick-woven odorous bowers,
The still rich breeze, with incense fraught
Of glowing fruits and spangled flowers.

The whispering leaves, the gushing stream,
Where trembles the uncertain moon,
Suit more the poet's pensive dream,
Than all the jarring notes of noon.

*18. his narrow cell*: Gray's *Elegy* 15.
¶ 30.*18*. Cp. *Paradise Lost* ix 437: 'thick-wov'n Arborets and Flours'.

Then, to the thickly-crowded mart
The eager sons of interest press;
Then, shine the tinsel works of art–
Now, all is Nature's loneliness!

Then, wealth aloft in state displays
The glittering of her gilded cars;
Now, dimly stream the mingled rays
Of yon far-twinkling, silver stars.

Yon church, whose cold grey spire appears
In the black outline of the trees,
Conceals the object of my tears,
Whose form in dreams my spirit sees.

There in the chilling bed of earth,
The chancel's lettered stone above–
There sleepeth she who gave me birth,
Who taught my lips the hymn of love!

Yon mossy stems of ancient oak,
So widely crowned with sombre shade,
Those ne'er have heard the woodman's stroke
Their solemn, secret depths invade.

How oft the grassy way I've trod
That winds their knotty boles between,
And gathered from the blooming sod
The flowers that flourished there unseen!

Rise! let us trace that path once more,
While o'er our track the cold beams shine;
Down this low shingly vale, and o'er
Yon rude rough bridge of prostrate pine.

# 31 *Mithridates Presenting Berenice with the Cup of Poison

Published *1827*, not reprinted. The deaths of Mithridates VI of Pontus and of his concubine are from Charles Rollin's *Ancient History* (Paden, p. 126). There was a copy of the 1789 translation at Somersby (*Lincoln*). *1827* note: 'In reality Mithridates had no personal interview with Monima and Berenice before the deaths of those princesses, but only sent his eunuch Bacchidas to signify his intention that they should die. I have chosen

*30*. 'gilded car', *Comus* 95.
*48*. Recalling, as do the preceding lines, Gray's *Elegy*: 'Full many a flower is born to blush unseen.'

Berenice as the more general name, though Monima was his peculiar favourite.' Cp. *Antony to Cleopatra* (p. 91).

Oh! Berenice, lorn and lost,
This wretched soul with shame is bleeding:
Oh! Berenice, I am tost
By griefs, like wave to wave succeeding.

Fallen Pontus! all her fame is gone,
And dim the splendour of her glory;
Low in the west her evening sun,
And dark the lustre of her story.

Dead is the wreath that round her brow
The glowing hands of Honour braided;
What change of fate can wait her now,
Her sceptre spoiled, her throne degraded?

And wilt thou, wilt thou basely go,
My love, thy life, thy country shaming,
In all the agonies of woe,
Mid maddening shouts, and standards flaming?

And wilt thou, wilt thou basely go,
Proud Rome's triumphal car adorning?
Hark! hark! I hear thee answer 'No!'
The proffered life of thraldom scorning.

Lone, crownless, destitute, and poor,
My heart with bitter pain is burning;
So thick a cloud of night hangs o'er,
My daylight into darkness turning.

Yet though my spirit, bowed with ill,
Small hope from future fortune borrows;
One glorious thought shall cheer me still,
That thou art free from abject sorrows–

Art free for ever from the strife
Of slavery's pangs and tearful anguish;
For life is death, and death is life,
To those whose limbs in fetters languish.

Fill high the bowl! the draught is thine!
The Romans!–now thou need'st not heed them!
'Tis nobler than the noblest wine–
It gives thee back to fame and freedom!

The scalding tears my cheek bedew;
My life, my love, my all–we sever!
One last embrace, one long adieu,
And then farewell–farewell for ever!

# 32 *Epigram on a Musician, whose Harp-strings were Cracked from Want of Using

Published *1827*, not reprinted. *1893*: '(?)'; but it is in T.'s hand in the *T.MS* and is attributed to T. in the Russell and Haddelsey copies of *1827* and in Charles's copy. Cp. *The Devil and the Lady* II ii 79: 'What, harping on the old string again?' In the manner of Thomas Moore.

'Why dost thou not *string thine old Harp?*' says a friend:
'Thy complaints,' replied Dolce, 'I think never end;
'I've reason enough to remember the thing,
'For you always are *harping upon the old string*.'

# 33 *The Old Chieftain

Published *1827*, not reprinted. Epigraph: the opening line of *The Lay of the Last Minstrel* iii.

*And said I, that my limbs were old!*
SCOTT

Raise, raise the song of the hundred shells!
Though my hair is grey and my limbs are cold;
Yet in my bosom proudly dwells
The memory of the days of old;
When my voice was high, and my arm was strong,
And the foeman before my stroke would bow,
And I could have raised the sounding song
As loudly as I hear ye now.

For when I have chanted the bold song of death,
Not a page would have stayed in the hall,
Not a lance in the rest, not a sword in the sheath,
Not a shield on the dim grey wall.

And who might resist the united powers
Of battle and music that day,
When, all martialled in arms on the heaven-kissing towers,
Stood the chieftains in peerless array?

¶ 33.*15*. *heaven-kissing*: *Hamlet* III iv 59.

When our enemies sunk from our eyes as the snow
  Which falls down the stream in the dell,
When each word that I spake was the death of a foe,
  And each note of my harp was his knell?

So raise ye the song of the hundred shells;
  Though my hair is grey and my limbs are cold,
Yet in my bosom proudly dwells
  The memory of the days of old!

## 34 *The Fall of Jerusalem

Published *1827*, not reprinted. T.'s authorship is confirmed by *H.Nbk 1*, which has ll. 1–47, entitled *Ode*. *T.MS* was reproduced in the large-paper edition of *1893*. Joyce Green (*The Development of the Poetic Image in Tennyson*, Cambridge thesis, 1954) suggests the influence of Henry Milman's *Fall of Jerusalem*; the young T. mentioned Milman (*Mem.* i 10). The probability is increased by the fact that *QR* xxiii (1820) 198–225 had a review of Milman's poem with many extracts; *QR* was the source of two poems of *1827*, *Come hither* and *King Charles's Vision*, and there were copies of it at Somersby (*Lincoln*). T. was probably influenced by Byron's *On the Day of the Destruction of Jerusalem by Titus*; the details are from Rollin's *Ancient History*, as Paden points out (p. 126).

Jerusalem! Jerusalem!
  Thou art low! thou mighty one,
How is the brilliance of thy diadem,
  How is the lustre of thy throne
Rent from thee, and thy sun of fame
  Darkened by the shadowy pinion
    Of the Roman bird, whose sway
    All the tribes of earth obey,
  Crouching 'neath his dread dominion,
And the terrors of his name!

How is thy royal seat–whereon
    Sate in days of yore
Lowly Jesse's godlike son,
And the strength of Solomon,
  In those rich and happy times
    When the ships from Tarshish bore

¶ 34.*6*. Cp. *The Druid's Prophecies* 41–3: 'the eagle's shadowy pinion', again rhyming with 'dominion'; in both cases from Gray's *Progress of Poesy* 114–6. Also Thomas Moore, *Odes of Anacreon* xxxvi: 'That when Death came, with shadowy pinion, / To waft me to his bleak dominion.'

Incense, and from Ophir's land,
With silken sail and cedar oar,
Wafting to Judea's strand
All the wealth of foreign climes–
How is thy royal seat o'erthrown!
Gone is all thy majesty:
Salem! Salem! city of kings,
Thou sittest desolate and lone,
Where once the glory of the Most High
Dwelt visibly enshrined between the wings
Of Cherubims, within whose bright embrace
The golden mercy-seat remained:
Land of Jehovah! view that sacred place
Abandoned and profaned!

Wail! fallen Salem! Wail:
Mohammed's votaries pollute thy fane;
The dark division of thine holy veil
Is rent in twain!
Thrice hath Sion's crownèd rock
Seen thy temple's marble state,
Awfully, serenely great,
Towering on his sainted brow,
Rear its pinnacles of snow:
Thrice, with desolating shock,
Down to earth hath seen it driven
From his heights, which reach to heaven!

Wail, fallen Salem! Wail:
Though not one stone above another
There was left to tell the tale
Of the greatness of thy story,
Yet the long lapse of ages cannot smother
The blaze of thine abounding glory;
Which through the mist of rolling years,
O'er history's darkened page appears,
Like the morning star, whose gleam
Gazeth through the waste of night,
What time old ocean's purple stream

*25–8. Exodus* xxv 17–22: 'And I will commune with thee from above the mercy seat, from between the two cherubims which are upon the ark of the testimony.'
*31. fallen Salem!*] Io! Io! *H.Nbk 1* (*likewise in l. 43*).
*37*] Grand, magnificent and great *H.MS 1st reading.*
*44.* Jesus speaking of the Temple, *Matthew* xxiv 2, 'There shall not be left here one stone upon another, that shall not be thrown down.'

In his cold surge hath deeply laved
Its ardent front of dewy light.
Oh! who shall e'er forget thy bands, which braved
The terrors of the desert's barren reign,
And that strong arm which broke the chain
Wherein ye foully lay enslaved,
Or that sublime Theocracy which paved
Your way through ocean's vast domain,
And on, far on to Canaan's emerald plain
Led the Israelitish crowd
With a pillar and a cloud?
Signs on earth and signs on high
Prophesied thy destiny;
A trumpet's voice above thee rung,
A starry sabre o'er thee hung;
Visions of fiery armies, redly flashing
In the many-coloured glare
Of the setting orb of day;
And flaming chariots, fiercely dashing,
Swept along the peopled air,
In magnificent array:
The temple doors, on brazen hinges crashing,
Burst open with appalling sound,
A wondrous radiance streaming round!

'Our blood be on our heads!' ye said:
Such your awless imprecation:
Full bitterly at length 'twas paid
Upon your captive nation!
Arms of adverse legions bound thee,
Plague and pestilence stood round thee;
Seven weary suns had brightened Syria's sky,
Yet still was heard the unceasing cry–
From south, north, east, and west, a voice,
'Woe unto thy sons and daughters!

*54. cold surge*] blue depth *T.MS 1st reading.*

*69–73.* Cp. *Paradise Lost* ii 533–5: 'As when to warn proud Cities warr appears /Wag'd in the troubl'd Skie, and Armies rush / To Battel in the Clouds.'

*71. orb of day*: as in Gray's *Bard* 136.

*73. the peopled air*: Gray's *Ode on Spring* 23.

*76. Burst*] Flew *T.MS 1st reading.*

*78. Matthew* xxvii 25, 'Then answered all the people, and said, His blood be on us, and on our children.'

'Woe to Salem! thou art lost!'
A sound divine
Came from the sainted, secret, inmost shrine:
'Let us go hence!'–and then a noise–
The thunders of the parting Deity,
Like the rush of countless waters,
Like the murmur of a host!

Though now each glorious hope be blighted,
Yet an hour shall come, when ye,
Though scattered like the chaff, shall be
Beneath one standard once again united;
When your wandering race shall own,
Prostrate at the dazzling throne
Of your high Almighty Lord,
The wonders of his searchless word,
The unfading splendours of his Son!

# 35 *Lamentation of the Peruvians

Published *1827*, not reprinted. Francisco Pizarro, discoverer and conqueror of Peru, in 1532 treacherously seized his welcomer Ataliba, who was murdered in 1533. Ataliba and Pizarro are the main characters in Sheridan's *Pizarro*, a translation from the German of Kotzebue. There was a copy at Somersby (*Lincoln*). Paden (p. 123) suggests the influence of Thomas Campbell; e.g. *Lochiel's Warning*: 'Lochiel, Lochiel! beware of the day / When the Lowlands shall meet thee in battle array!' Cp. l. 1 with Byron, 'The Assyrian came down like a wolf on the fold'; and cp. the prophetic denunciation by Gray's *Bard* (see ll. 7–8*n*). T. had in *1827* many other prophecies of woe, e.g. *Babylon* (p. 142).

The foes of the east have come down on our shore,
And the state and the strength of Peru are no more:
Oh! cursed, doubly cursed, was that desolate hour,
When they spread o'er our land in the pride of their
power!
Lament for the Inca, the son of the Sun;
Ataliba's fallen–Peru is undone!

*89*] A sound as of some voice divine *T.MS 1st reading.*
*91. a noise*] a dreadful noise *T.MS 1st reading.*
¶ 35.5. The Incas being the 'people of the Sun'. Note the wording in *QR* xvi (1816) 264: 'Mango Capac was the son of the sun.' *QR* was a source for several poems of *1827*, and there were copies at Somersby (*Lincoln*).

Pizarro! Pizarro! though conquest may wing
  Her course round thy banners that wanton in air;
Yet remorse to thy grief-stricken conscience shall cling,
  And shriek o'er thy banquets in sounds of despair.
It shall tell thee, that he who beholds from his throne
  The blood thou hast spilt and the deeds thou hast done,
Shall mock at thy fear, and rejoice at thy groan,
  And arise in his wrath for the death of his son!

Why blew ye, ye gales, when the murderer came?
Why fanned ye the fire, and why fed ye the flame?
Why sped ye his sails o'er the ocean so blue?
Are ye also combined for the fall of Peru?
And thou, whom no prayers, no entreaties can bend,
Thy crimes and thy murders to heaven shall ascend:
For vengeance the ghosts of our forefathers call;
At thy threshold, Pizarro, in death shalt thou fall!
Ay there–even there in the halls of thy pride,
With the blood of thine heart shall thy portals be dyed!
Lo! dark as the tempests that frown from the north,
From the cloud of past time Manco Capac looks forth–
Great Inca! to whom the gay day-star gave birth,
Whose throne is the heaven, and whose foot-stool the earth–
His visage is sad as the vapours that rise
From the desolate mountain of fire to the skies;
But his eye flashes flame as the lightnings that streak
Those volumes that shroud the volcano's high peak.
Hark! he speaks–bids us fly to our mountains, and cherish
Bold freedom's last spark ere for ever it perish;
Bids us leave these wild condors to prey on each other,
Each to bathe his fierce beak in the gore of his brother!

*7–8.* Cp. the prophecy of Gray's *Bard* 1–4, the poem behind all such baneful prophecies: '"Ruin seize thee, ruthless King! / "Confusion on thy banners wait, / "Though fanned by Conquest's crimson wing / "They mock the air with idle state . . ."' T. has 'state', 'mock', 'fanned', ll. 2, 13, 16.
*22–4.* Pizarro was assassinated in 1541 at Lima, the city he founded.
*26.* Manco Capac was the son of the Great Inca Huayna Capac (with whom T. seems to confuse him), and was crowned after Pizarro's conquest; the Great Inca died the year before Pizarro arrived.
*28. Matthew* v 34: 'Swear not at all; neither by heaven; for it is God's throne: Nor by the earth; for it is his footstool.'
*32. volumes*: winding clouds.

This symbol we take of our godhead the Sun,
And curse thee and thine for the deeds thou hast done.
May the curses pursue thee of those thou hast slain,
Of those that have fallen in war on the plain,
When we went forth to greet ye–but foully ye threw
Your dark shots of death on the sons of Peru.
May the curse of the widow–the curse of the brave–
The curse of the fatherless, cleave to thy grave!
And the words which they spake with their last dying breath,
Embitter the pangs and the tortures of death!

May he that assists thee be childless and poor,
With famine behind him, and death at his door:
May his nights be all sleepless, his days spent alone,
And ne'er may he list to a voice but his own!
Or, if he shall sleep, in his dreams may he view
The ghost of our Inca, the fiends of Peru:
May the flames of destruction that here he has spread
Be tenfold returned on his murderous head!

## 36 *'The sun goes down in the dark blue main'

Published *1827*, not reprinted. T.'s authorship is confirmed by *H.Nbk 1*. Cp. *How gaily sinks* (p. 140).

*Irreparabile tempus.*
VIRGIL [*Aeneid* x 467]

The sun goes down in the dark blue main,
  To rise the brighter tomorrow;
But oh! what charm can restore again
  Those days now consigned to sorrow?

The moon goes down on the calm still night,
  To rise sweeter than when she parted;
But oh! what charm can restore the light
  Of joy to the broken-hearted?

*47. thee*] *1893*; *not 1827.*
¶ 36.*4. now*] *added to H.MS.*
*5. on*] in *MS.*
*6. sweeter*] brighter *MS.*

The blossoms depart in the wintry hour,
To rise in vernal glory;
But oh! what charm can restore the flower
Of youth to the old and hoary?

## 37 *On a Dead Enemy

Published *1827*, not reprinted. The Russell copy of *1827* makes no ascription. Paden (p. 126) suggests that it was probably inspired by Alexander's discovery of the body of Darius, as related in Charles Rollin's *Ancient History* (1789 translation, *Lincoln*).

*Non odi mortuum.*
CICERO [*De officiis* iii 73]

I came in haste with cursing breath,
And heart of hardest steel;
But when I saw thee cold in death,
I felt as man should feel.

For when I look upon that face,
That cold, unheeding, frigid brow,
Where neither rage nor fear has place,
By Heaven! I cannot hate thee now!

## 38 *The Duke of Alva's Observation on Kings

Published *1827*, not reprinted. *1827* note: 'See D'Israeli's *Curiosities of Literature*'. The 1807 edition was at Somersby (*Lincoln*). Under 'Monarchs', it has: 'There are two excellent observations on Kings made by the Duke of Alva, an experienced politician, to a courtier.–"Kings," (said he) "who affect to be familiar with their companions make use of *men* as they do of *oranges*: they take oranges to extract their juice; and when they are well sucked they throw them away. Take care the king does not do the same to you; be careful that he does not read all your thoughts; otherwise he will throw you aside to the back of his chest, as a book of which he has read enough."'

Kings, when to private audience they descend,
And make the baffled courtier their prey,
Do use an orange, as they treat a friend–
Extract the juice, and cast the rind away.

9. *the wintry*] winter's *MS*.
10. *in vernal*] again in their *MS*.

When thou art favoured by thy sovereign's eye,
Let not his glance thine inmost thoughts discover;
Or he will scan thee through, and lay thee by,
Like some old book which he has read all over.

# 39 *'Ah! yes, the lip may faintly smile'

Published *1827*, not reprinted. *1893*: 'A.T.(?)' But it is attributed to T. in the Russell copy, the Haddelsey copy and Charles Tennyson's copy, all *1827*. It is not in *T.MS* but some lines of it are in *H.Nbk 2*. On a faithless girl, cp. *A Contrast* (p. 139).

Ah! yes, the lip may faintly smile,
The eye may sparkle for a while;
But never from that withered heart
The consciousness of ill shall part!

That glance, that smile of passing light,
Are as the rainbow of the night;
But seldom seen, it dares to bloom
Upon the bosom of the gloom.

Its tints are sad and coldly pale,
Dim-glimmering through their misty veil;
Unlike the ardent hues which play
Along the flowery bow of day.

The moon-beams sink in dark-robed shades,
Too soon the airy vision fades;
And double night returns, to shroud
The volumes of the showery cloud.

¶ 39.*6*. T. would have read about lunar rainbows in the acknowledged source of *St Simeon Stylites*, William Hone's *Every-Day Book* (1827 edn), ii 1230–1; the account ends as does the poem: 'But by that time all was over, the moon was darkened by clouds, and the rainbow of course vanished.'
*8–10*. Suggesting *Paradise Lost* ii 1036–7: 'into the bosom of dim Night / A glimmering dawn'.
*13–15*. Cp. *Comus* 335: the 'double night of darknes, and of shades'.
*16*. *volumes*: coils. Cp. *The Devil and the Lady* III ii 73: 'volumed vapour.' For the cadence, cp. *PL* vi 759: 'colours of the showrie Arch', which will have come to mind because it invokes the rainbow.

# 40 *'Thou camest to thy bower, my love'

Published *1827*, not reprinted. Paden (pp. 31–2) points out that it is largely based on Sir William Jones's translation of the semi-dramatic erotic poem, the *Gítagóvinda*; see *1827* notes below. For T.'s similar use of Jones, see *Love* [*Almighty Love*] (p. 144). The epigraph combines *mulier egregia forma* (*Andria* I i 73), with *virgo facie egregia* (*Phormio* I i 100), as Paden points out (p. 101).

*Virgo egregia forma.*
TERENCE

Thou camest to thy bower, my love, across the musky grove,
To fan thy blooming charms within the coolness of the shade;
Thy locks were like a midnight cloud with silver moon-beams wove,
And o'er thy face the varying tints of youthful passion played.
Thy breath was like the sandal-wood that casts a rich perfume,
Thy blue eyes mocked the lotos in the noon-day of his bloom;
Thy cheeks were like the beamy flush that gilds the breaking day,
And in the ambrosia of thy smiles the god of rapture lay.
Fair as the cairba-stone art thou, that stone of dazzling white,
Ere yet unholy fingers changed its milk-white hue to night;
And lovelier than the loveliest glance from Even's placid star,

¶ 40. *3. 1827* note: 'A simile elicited from the songs of Jayadeva, the Horace of India.' *Gítagóvinda* [i 481]: 'His locks, interwoven with blossoms, were like a cloud variegated with moonbeams.'

*8. 1827* note: '*Vide* Horace's Ode–*Pulchris* excubat *in genis*'. (*Odes* IV xiii 8: 'he keeps his watch on the fair cheeks'.)

*9. 1827* note: '*Vide* Sale's *Koran*.' There was a copy of George Sale's translation of the *Koran* at Somersby (*Lincoln*; 1801 edn). The Caaba is the sacred building at Mecca which contains the venerated Black Stone. Sale says: 'They fable that it is one of the precious stones of paradise, and fell

And brighter than the sea of gold, the gorgeous
Himsagar.

In high Mohammed's boundless heaven Al Cawthor's
stream may play,
The fount of youth may sparkling gush beneath the
western ray;
And Tasnim's wave in chrystal cups may glow with
musk and wine,
But oh! their lustre could not match one beauteous
tear of thine!

# 41 *The Passions

Published *1827*, not reprinted. Epigraph: Ann Radcliffe's novel (1794), to which T. referred in a note on *On Sublimity* (p. 117).

You have passions in your heart–scorpions; they sleep now–beware how you awaken them! they will sting you even to death!
*Mysteries of Udolpho*, vol. iii

---

down to the earth with Adam, and being taken up again, or otherwise preserved at the deluge, the angel Gabriel afterwards brought it back to Abraham, when he was building the Caaba. It was at first whiter than milk, but grew black long since by the touch of a menstruous woman, or, as others tell us, by the sins of mankind' (i 156). T. would also have read of the stone ('being touched by an impure woman, it became black') in *QR* xv (1816) 326; *QR* was the source of other poems of *1827*, and there were copies at Somersby (*Lincoln*). See l. 14*n*. Paden (p. 127) observes that the spelling 'cairba' (like 'Al Cawthor', l. 13) is not from Sale.
*12. 1827* note: 'See Sir William Jones on Eastern Plants.' Paden (p. 127) suggests the influence of *Lalla Rookh*: *The Light of the Haram*, which quotes Jones in a footnote: 'Hemasagara, or the Sea of Gold'. Moore's lines have a similar setting: 'Beneath the moonlight's hallowing beams, / For this enchanted Wreath of Dreams. / Anemones and Seas of Gold . . .'
*13. Al Cawthor*: the river of paradise, Al Cawthar, is mentioned in Sale's *Koran* i 128.
*14. 1827* note: 'The fabled fountain of youth in the Bahamas, in search of which Juan Ponce de Leon discovered Florida.' *QR* xi (1814) 57 (see l. 9*n*): 'Juan Ponce de Leon, the discoverer of Florida, sent a ship in search of the island of Bimini, where the Spanish conquerors as well as the Indians firmly believed there was a fountain which possessed the virtue of Medea's kettle, and restored to youth whoever bathed in it.'
*15.* Sale's *Koran* ii 487: 'They shall be given to drink of pure wine, sealed; the seal whereof shall be musk: and to this let those aspire, who aspire to happiness: and the water mixed therewith shall be of Tasnim, a fountain whereof those shall drink who approach near unto the Divine Presence.'

Beware, beware, ere thou takest
The draught of misery!
Beware, beware, ere thou wakest
The scorpions that sleep in thee!

The woes which thou canst not number,
As yet are wrapt in sleep;
Yet oh! yet they slumber,
But their slumbers are not deep.

Yet oh! yet while the rancour
Of hate has no place in thee,
While thy buoyant soul has an anchor
In youth's bright tranquil sea:

Yet oh! yet while the blossom
Of hope is blooming fair,
While the beam of bliss lights thy bosom–
O! rouse not the serpent there!

For bitter thy tears will trickle
'Neath misery's heavy load,
When the world has put in its sickle
To the crop which fancy sowed.

When the world has rent the cable
That bound thee to the shore,
And launched thee weak and unable
To bear the billow's roar;

Then the slightest touch will waken
Those pangs that will always grieve thee,
And thy soul will be fiercely shaken
With storms that will never leave thee!

So beware, beware, ere thou takest
The draught of misery!
Beware, beware, ere thou wakest
The scorpions that sleep in thee!

# 42 *The High-Priest to Alexander

Published *1827*, not reprinted. Paden (p. 126) shows that the source was Charles Rollin's *Ancient History*, describing the day at Jerusalem when Alexander was shown that Daniel (Chapter 2) had predicted his destroying four empires. There was a copy of the 1789 translation at Somersby (*Lincoln*). Cp. *Persia* (p. 102) and *Alexander* (p. 469). Epigraph: Alonso de

Ercilla y Zúñiga's sixteenth-century Spanish epic ('Bloodshed in the whole globe of the earth, / Arms, fury, and new war'). There was a copy of this epic at Somersby (*Lincoln*).

*Derrame en todo el orbe de la tierra*
*Las armas, el furor, y nueva guerra.*
*La Araucana*, cant. xvi

Go forth, thou man of force!
The world is all thine own;
Before thy dreadful course
Shall totter every throne.
Let India's jewels glow
Upon thy diadem:
Go, forth to conquest go,
But spare Jerusalem.
For the God of gods, which liveth
Through all eternity,
'Tis he alone which giveth
And taketh victory:
'Tis he the bow that blasteth,
And breaketh the proud one's quiver;
And the Lord of armies resteth
In his Holy of Holies for ever!

For God is Salem's spear,
And God is Salem's sword;
What mortal man shall dare
To combat with the Lord?
Every knee shall bow
Before his awful sight;
Every thought sink low
Before the Lord of might.
For the God of gods, which liveth
Through all eternity,
'Tis he alone which giveth
And taketh victory:
'Tis he the bow that blasteth,
And breaketh the proud one's quiver;
And the Lord of armies resteth
In his Holy of Holies for ever!

## 43 *A Contrast

Published *1827*, not reprinted.

Dost ask why Laura's soul is riven
By pangs her prudence can't command?

To one who heeds not she has given
Her *heart*, alas! *without her hand.*

But Chloe claims our sympathy,
To wealth a martyr and a slave;
For when the knot she dared to tie,
*Her hand without her heart she gave.*

## 44 *'How gaily sinks the gorgeous sun within his golden bed'

Published *1827*, not reprinted. *1893*: 'A.T.(?)'; but it is clearly referred to by T. as his in a very early letter (*Mem.* i 10), and is in his hand in *T.MS.* The Russell and Haddelsey copies of *1827* and Charles's copy attribute it to T. Epigraph: Jean-Baptiste Rousseau's *Odes* i (Paden, p. 105). For the theme and detail, cp. *The sun goes down in the dark blue main* (p. 133).

*Tu fais naître la lumière*
*Du sein de l'obscurité.*
ROUSSEAU

How gaily sinks the gorgeous sun within his golden bed,
As heaven's immortal azure glows and deepens into red!
How gaily shines the burnished main beneath that living light,
And trembles with his million waves magnificently bright!
But ah! how soon that orb of day must close his burning eye,
And night, in sable pall arrayed, involve yon lovely sky!
E'en thus in life our fairest scenes are preludes to our woe;
For fleeting as that glorious beam is happiness below.
But what? though evil fates may frown upon our mortal birth,
Yet Hope shall be the star that lights our night of grief on earth:
And she shall point to sweeter morns, when brighter suns shall rise,
And spread the radiance of their rays o'er earth, and sea, and skies!

¶ 44.6. *involve*: enwreathe.

# 45 *'Oh! ye wild winds, that roar and rave'

Published *1827*, not reprinted. The epigraph is from a poem quoted with Macpherson's *Croma* in *Ossian*: 'It is the mighty army of the dead returning from the air'. This is, as Paden (p. 108) points out, the poem which T. paraphrased in *Midnight* (p. 111). T. took up details, and was clearly influenced by: 'Ghosts ride on the storm to-night. Sweet is their voice between the squalls of wind. Their songs are of other worlds'; cp. l. 6. The 1809 edition of *Ossian* was at Somersby (*Lincoln*). Paden (p. 138) compares Byron's *Lachin y Gair* 17–18: 'Shades of the dead! have I not heard your voices / Rise on the night-rolling breath of the gale?'

*It is the great army of the dead returning on the northern blast.*
*Song of the Five Bards in Ossian*

Oh! ye wild winds, that roar and rave
Around the headland's stormy brow,
That toss and heave the Baltic wave,
And bid the sounding forest bow,

Whence is your course? and do ye bear
The sighs of other worlds along,
When through the dark immense of air
Ye rush in tempests loud and strong?

Methinks, upon your moaning course
I hear the army of the dead;
Each on his own invisible horse,
Triumphing in his trackless tread.

For when the moon conceals her ray,
And midnight spreads her darkest veil,
Borne on the air, and far away,
Upon the eddying blasts they sail.

Then, then their thin and feeble bands
Along the echoing winds are rolled;
The bodyless tribes of other lands!
The formless, misty sons of old!

And then at times their wailings rise,
The shrilly wailings of the grave!
And mingle with the maddened skies,
The rush of wind, and roar of wave.

¶ 45.7. Cp. *Paradise Lost* ii 829: 'through the void immense'; and Shelley's *Queen Mab* ii 39: 'the immense of Heaven'.

Heard you that sound? It was the hum
Of the innumerable host,
As down the northern sky they come,
Lamenting o'er their glories lost.

Now for a space each shadowy king,
Who swayed of old some mighty realm,
Mounts on the tempest's squally wing,
And grimly frowns through barrèd helm.

Now each dim ghost, with awful yells,
Uprears on high his cloudy form;
And with his feeble accent swells
The hundred voices of the storm.

Why leave ye thus the narrow cell,
Ye lords of night and anarchy!
Your robes the vapours of the dell,
Your swords the meteors of the sky?

Your bones are whitening on the heath;
Your fame is in the minds of men:
And would ye break the sleep of death,
That ye might live to war again?

# 46 *Babylon

Published *1827*, not reprinted. Based on Isaiah's prophecy of the destruction of Babylon by Cyrus; suggested by Charles Rollin's *Ancient History*, which supplied T.'s eight biblical references (Paden, p. 126). There was a copy of the 1789 translation of Rollin at Somersby (*Lincoln*). For the theme and manner, cp. Byron's *The Destruction of Sennacherib*, and other *Hebrew Melodies* such as *Vision of Belshazzar* and *By the Waters of Babylon*.

*Come down, and sit in the dust, O virgin daughter of Babylon; sit on the ground: there is no throne.*

ISAIAH xvii 1

Bow, daughter of Babylon, bow thee to dust!
Thine heart shall be quelled, and thy pride shall be
crushed:
Weep, Babylon, weep! for thy splendour is past;
And they come like the storm in the day of the blast.

Howl, desolate Babylon, lost one and lone!
And bind thee in sack-cloth–for where is thy throne?
Like a wine-press in wrath will I trample thee down,
And rend from thy temples the pride of thy crown.

37. *narrow cell*: Gray's *Elegy* 15.

Though thy streets be a hundred, thy gates be all brass,
Yet thy proud ones of war shall be withered like grass;
Thy gates shall be broken, thy strength be laid low,
And thy streets shall resound to the shouts of the foe!

Though thy chariots of power on thy battlements bound,
And the grandeur of waters encompass thee round;
Yet thy walls shall be shaken, thy waters shall fail,
Thy matrons shall shriek, and thy king shall be pale.

The terrible day of thy fall is at hand,
When my rage shall descend on the face of thy land;
The lances are pointed, the keen sword is bared,
The shields are anointed, the helmets prepared.

I call upon Cyrus! He comes from afar,
And the armies of nations are gathered to war;
With the blood of thy children his path shall be red,
And the bright sun of conquest shall blaze o'er his head!

Thou glory of kingdoms! thy princes are drunk,
But their loins shall be loosed, and their hearts shall be sunk;
They shall crouch to the dust, and be counted as slaves,
At the roll of his wheels, like the rushing of waves!

For I am the Lord, who have mightily spanned
The breadth of the heavens, and the sea and the land;
And the mountains shall flow at my presence, and earth
Shall reel to and fro in the glance of my wrath!

Your proud domes of cedar on earth shall be thrown,
And the rank grass shall wave o'er the lonely hearth-stone;
And your sons and your sires and your daughters shall bleed
By the barbarous hands of the murdering Mede!

¶ *46.20. 1827* note: '"Arise, ye princes, and anoint the shield", *Isaiah* xxi 5.'
*25. 1827* note: '"I will make drunk her princes", *Jeremiah* li 57.'
*31. 1827* note: '"The mountains melted from before the Lord", *Judges* v 5. "Oh! that the mountains might flow down at thy presence!", *Isaiah* lxiv 1. And again, ver. 3, "The mountains flowed down at thy presence".'

I will sweep ye away in destruction and death,
As the whirlwind that scatters the chaff with its breath;
And the fanes of your gods shall be sprinkled with gore,
And the course of your stream shall be heard of no more!

There the wandering Arab shall ne'er pitch his tent,
But the beasts of the desert shall wail and lament;
In their desolate houses the dragons shall lie,
And the satyrs shall dance, and the bittern shall cry!

## 47 *Love [Almighty Love!]

Published *1827*, not reprinted. (The Russell copy of *1827* attributes this to Charles.) Paden (p. 128) shows that T. here versified Sir William Jones's translations of the *Hymns* to the amorous Hindu deities; section ii draws on Jones's *Hymn to Bhavani* (goddess of fecundity) and *Hymn to Camdeo* (see T.'s note to l. 45). Jones's *Works* (1799) were at Somersby (*Lincoln*). Cp. *Love* [*Thou, from the first*] (*1830*, p. 243).

I

Almighty Love! whose nameless power
  This glowing heart defines too well,
Whose presence cheers each fleeting hour,
  Whose silken bonds our souls compel,
  Diffusing such a sainted spell,

As gilds our being with the light
  Of transport and of rapturous bliss,
And almost seeming to unite
  The joys of other worlds to this,
  The heavenly smile, the rosy kiss; –

*40. 1827* note: "A drought is upon her waters", *Jeremiah* l 38.'
*44. 1827* note: 'Vide *Isaiah* xiii 20'. 'It shall never be inhabited, neither shall it be dwelt in from generation to generation: neither shall the Arabian pitch tent there; neither shall the shepherds make their fold there.

'But wild beasts of the desert shall lie there; and their houses shall be full of doleful creatures; and owls shall dwell there, and satyrs shall dance there.

'And the wild beasts of the islands shall cry in their desolate houses, and dragons in their pleasant palaces: and her time is near to come, and her days shall not be prolonged.'

Before whose blaze my spirits shrink,
  My senses all are wrapt in thee,
Thy force I own too much, to think
  (So full, so great thine ecstacy)
  That thou art less than deity!
Thy golden chains embrace the land,
  The starry sky, the dark blue main;
And at the voice of thy command,
  (So vast, so boundless is thy reign)
  All nature springs to life again!

II

The glittering fly, the wondrous things
  That microscopic art descries;
The lion of the waste, which springs,
  Bounding upon his enemies;
The mighty sea-snake of the storm,
The vorticella's viewless form,
The vast leviathan, which takes
  His pastime in the sounding floods;
The crafty elephant, which makes
  His haunts in Ceylon's spicy woods–
Alike confess thy magic sway,
Thy soul-enchanting voice obey!

O! whether thou, as bards have said,
  Of bliss or pain the partial giver,
Wingest thy shaft of pleasing dread
  From out thy well-stored golden quiver,

¶ 47.*26*. *1827* note: 'See Baker on Animalculæ'. Henry Baker's *Of Microscopes* (1785) was at Somersby (*Lincoln*). Paden (p. 128) remarks that 'the vorticella was supposed by some (not explicitly by Baker) to be bisexual'.

*27–8*. Suggested by Addison, *Tatler* 119: 'Your microscopes bring to sight shoals of living creatures in a spoonful of vinegar [cp. ll. 21–2]; but we who can distinguish them in their different magnitudes, see among them several huge leviathans, that terrify the little fry of animals about them, and take their pastime as in an ocean'. To take one's pastime had erotic connotations for T. Cp. *Love and Duty* 28.

*29*. The elephant decoyed by a tame female (Paden). Possibly influenced by *QR* xiv (1815) 29, on catching elephants in Ceylon; *QR* was a source for several poems of *1827*. There is a similar account in the *English Encyclopaedia* (1802), of which there was a copy at Somersby (*Lincoln*).

*30*. Cp. Dryden, *Annus Mirabilis* 12: 'And in hot Ceylon spicy forests grew', the stress *Céylon*.

O'er earth thy cherub wings extending,
Thy sea-born mother's side attending; –

Or else, as Indian fables say,
Upon thine emerald lory riding,
Through gardens, mid the restless play
Of fountains, in the moonbeam gliding,
Mid sylph-like shapes of maidens dancing,
Thy scarlet standard high advancing; –

Thy fragrant bow of cane thou bendest,
Twanging the string of honeyed bees,
And thence the flower-tipped arrow sendest,
Which gives or robs the heart of ease;
Camdeo, or Cupid, O be near,
To listen, and to grant my prayer!

## 48 *Exhortation to the Greeks

Published *1827*, not reprinted. Paden (p. 127) compares Byron's similar exhortation to the Greeks to shake off the Turks, *Childe Harold* II lxxiii–vi. Epigraph: Sallust's *Bellum Catilinae* xx 14: 'Lo, here, here is the freedom for which you have often longed.'

*En illa, illa quam saepe optastis, libertas!*

SALLUST

Arouse thee, O Greece! and remember the day,
When the millions of Xerxes were quelled on their
way!
Arouse thee, O Greece! let the pride of thy name
Awake in thy bosom the light of thy fame!
Why hast thou shone in the temple of glory?

*38. sea-born*: Venus. Jones identified Cama or Camdeo (l. 49) with Cupid.
*39–50.* The winged throne of Cama; see *Love* [*Thou, from the first*] ii 13, and *The Palace of Art* 113–16: 'The throne of Indian Cama slowly sailed'. *lory*: parrot-like bird. For Cama in early nineteenth-century verse, cp. Southey, *Curse of Kehama* (1810) X xix: ''Twas Camdeo riding on his lory, / 'Twas the immortal Youth of Love.'
*45. 1827* note: 'See Sir William Jones's *Works* vi 313. "He bends the luscious cane, and twists the string; / With bees how sweet, but ah! how keen the sting! / He with five flowrets tips thy ruthless darts, / Which through five senses pierce enraptured hearts."'

Why hast thou blazed in those annals of fame?
For know, that the former bright page of thy story
Proclaims but thy bondage and tells but thy shame:
Proclaims from how high thou art fallen!–how low
Thou art plunged in the dark gulf of thraldom and woe!
Arouse thee, O Greece! from the weight of thy slumbers!
The chains are upon thee!–arise from thy sleep!
Remember the time, when nor nations nor numbers
Could break thy thick phalanx embodied and deep.
Old Athens and Sparta remember the morning,
When the swords of the Grecians were red to the hilt:
And, the bright gem of conquest her chaplet adorning,
Platæa rejoiced at the blood that ye spilt!
Remember the night, when, in shrieks of affright,
The fleets of the East in your ocean were sunk:
Remember each day, when, in battle array,
From the fountain of glory how largely ye drunk!
For there is not ought that a freeman can fear,
As the fetters of insult, the name of a slave;
And there is not a voice to a nation so dear,
As the war-song of freedom that calls on the brave.

# 49 *King Charles's Vision

Published *1827*, not reprinted. Source: *QR* xv (1816) 525–7, a review of J. T. James, *Journal of Travels* (1816). *QR* was also the source of *Come hither*, and there were copies of it at Somersby (*Lincoln*). 'Such persons as are desirous of looking into what is to come, may be amused by the following narrative of an extraordinary vision of Charles XI [of Sweden]. . . . It is taken from an account written with the king's own hand'. T. either misunderstood or altered the prophecy, making it 'prophetic of the Northern Alexander' (see his headnote below), i.e. Charles XII. But this king was not 'the sixth' (l. 91) after Charles XI, and the *QR* prophecy refers not to Charles XII but to another. (The king's memorandum is misdated '1791' instead of '1691' in *QR*'s copying from James.) T. may have felt that the military exploits of Charles XII would make a better fulfilment of the prophecy.

¶ 48.*14*. *embodied*: in martial array, deriving from Milton, *Paradise Lost* i 574: 'such imbodied force'.
*18*. *Platæa*: a Greek city, the scene of the Greek rout of the Persians, 479 B.C.

A Vision somewhat resembling the following, and prophetic of the Northern Alexander, is said to have been witnessed by Charles XI of Sweden, the antagonist of Sigismund. The reader will exclaim, '*Credat Judæus Apella!*'

King Charles was sitting all alone,
In his lonely palace-tower,
When there came on his ears a heavy groan,
At the silent midnight hour.

He turned him round where he heard the sound,
But nothing might he see;
And he only heard the nightly bird
That shrieked right fearfully.

He turned him round where he heard the sound,
To his casement's archèd frame;
'And he was aware of a light that was there,'
But he wist not whence it came.

He lookèd forth into the night,
'Twas calm as night might be;
But broad and bright the flashing light
Streamed red and radiantly.

From ivory sheath his trusty brand
Of stalwart steel he drew;
And he raised the lamp in his better hand,
But its flame was dim and blue.

And he opened the door of that palace-tower,
But harsh turned the jarring key:
'By the virgin's might,' cried the king that night,
'All is not as it should be!'

Slow turned the door of the crazy tower,
And slowly again did it close;
And within and without, and all about,
A sound of voices rose.

¶ 49. *T.'s Headnote.* 'Northern Alexander', as in Gibbon. *Credat* . . . : 'Apella, the Jew, may believe it [not I]', Horace, *Satires* I v 100.

*1–11.* 'Charles XI, it seems, sitting in his chamber between the hours of eleven and twelve at night, was surprised at the appearance of a light in the window of the hall of the diet' (*QR*). The groan is added by T.

*11. 1827* note: '"And he was aware of a Grey-friar." *The Grey Brother.* "And he was aware of a knight that was there." *The Baron of Smalhome.*'

*20.* The blue flame is a sign of haunting.

*24.* 'He thought he observed a crowd of persons in the hall: upon this, said he, Sirs, all is not as it should be' (*QR*, in which the king goes down with a party of men).

The king he stood in dreamy mood,
For the voices his name did call;
Then on he past, till he came at last
To the pillared audience-hall.

Eight and forty columns wide,
Many and carved and tall,
(Four and twenty on each side)
Stand in that lordly hall.

The king had been pight in the mortal fight,
And struck the deadly blow;
The king he had strode in the red red blood,
Often, afore, and now:

Yet his heart had ne'er been so harrowed with fear
As it was this fearful hour;
For his eyes were not dry, and his hair stood on high,
And his soul had lost its power.

For a blue livid flame, round the hall where he came,
In fiery circles ran;
And sounds of death, and chattering teeth,
And gibbering tongues began.

He saw four and twenty statesmen old
Round a lofty table sit;
And each in his hand did a volume hold,
Wherein mighty things were writ.

In burning steel were their limbs all cased;
On their cheeks was the flush of ire:
Their armour was braced, and their helmets were laced,
And their hollow eyes darted fire.

With sceptre of might, and with gold crown bright,
And locks like the raven's wing,
And in regal state at that board there sate
The likeness of a king.

*30–48.* Not represented in *QR*.
*37. 1827* note: '"A hideous rock is *pight* / Of mighty magnes-stone" *Spenser*. "You vile abominable tents, / Thus proudly *pight* upon our Phrygian plains!" *Shakespeare*.' Paden (p. 107) points out that neither usage (*Faerie Queene* II xii st. 4; *Troilus and Cressida* V x 24) is like T.'s.
*45–8.* Cp. *The Coach of Death* (p. 74).
*49–52.* 'In the centre was a round table, where sat sixteen venerable men, each with large volumes lying open before them' (*QR*).
*53–70.* Not represented in *QR*.

With crimson tinged, and with ermine fringed,
And with jewels spangled o'er,
And rich as the beam of the sun on the stream,
A sparkling robe he wore.

Yet though fair shone the gem on his proud diadem,
Though his robe was jewelled o'er,
Though brilliant the vest on his mailèd breast,
Yet they all were stained with gore!

And his eye darted ire, and his glance shot fire,
And his look was high command;
And each, when he spoke, struck his mighty book,
And raised his shadowy hand.

And a headman stood by, with his axe on high,
And quick was his ceaseless stroke;
And loud was the shock on the echoing block,
As the steel shook the solid oak.

While short and thick came the mingled shriek
Of the wretches who died by his blow;

*64. 1827* note: 'This is, perhaps, an unpardonable falsehood, since it is well known that Charles was so great an enemy to finery as even to object to the appearance of the Duke of Marlborough on that account. Let those readers, therefore, whose critical nicety this passage offends, substitute the following stanza, which is "the whole truth, and nothing but the truth":

With buttons of brass that glittered like glass,
And brows that were crowned with bays,
With large blue coat, and with black jack-boot,
The theme of his constant praise.

'Nothing indeed could exceed Charles's affection for his boots: he eat, drank, and slept in them: nay, he never went on a bootless errand. When the dethroned monarch Augustus waited upon him with proposals of peace, Charles entertained him with a long dissertation on his unparalleled aforesaid jack-boots: he even went so far as to threaten (according to Voltaire), in an authoritative epistle to the senate at Stockholm, that unless they proved less refractory, he would send them one of his boots as regent! Now this, we must allow, was a step beyond Caligula's consul.'

*71–2.* 'A certain sign with his head, which as often as he did, the venerable men struck their hands on their books with violence' (*QR*).

*73.* The form 'headman' occurs in Byron's *Parisina* 446, in the 1819 edition of his *Works* which was at Somersby (*Lincoln*).

*73–80.* 'I beheld a scaffold and executioners, and men with their clothes tucked up, cutting off heads one after the other so fast, that the blood formed a deluge on the floor: those who suffered were all young men' (*QR*).

And fast fell each head on the pavement red,
 And warm did the life-blood flow.

Said the earthly king to the ghostly king,
 'What fearful sights are those?'
Said the ghostly king to the earthly king,
 'They are signs of future woes!'

Said the earthly king to the ghostly king,
 'By St Peter, who art thou?'
Said the ghostly king to the earthly king,
 'I shall be, but I am not now.'

Said the earthly king to the ghostly king,
 'But when will thy time draw nigh?'
'Oh! the sixth after thee will a warrior be,
 'And that warrior am I.

'And the lords of the earth shall be pale at my birth,
 'And conquest shall hover o'er me;
'And the kingdoms shall shake, and the nations shall quake,
 'And the thrones fall down before me.

'And Cracow shall bend to my majesty,
 'And the haughty Dane shall bow;
'And the Pole shall fly from my piercing eye,
 'And the scowl of my clouded brow.

'And around my way shall the hot balls play,
 'And the red-tongued flames arise;
'And my pathway shall be on the midnight sea,
 ''Neath the frown of the wintry skies.

'Through narrow pass, over dark morass,
 'And the waste of the weary plain,
'Over ice and snow, where the dark streams flow,
 'Through the woods of the wild Ukraine.

'And though sad be the close of my life and my woes,
 'And the hand that shall slay me unshown;
'Yet in every clime, through the lapse of all time,
 'Shall my glorious conquests be known.

*81–8.* Expanded from *QR*.
*89–92.* 'On my crying out a second time, the young king answered me, saying, This shall not happen in your time, but in the days of the sixth sovereign after you' (*QR*).
*93–116.* Not represented in *QR*, which is not concerned with Charles XII.
*110.* Voltaire in his life of Charles XII said that he was killed by a cannon-ball and not by his aide-de-camp, but the latter in fact confessed.

'And blood shall be shed, and the earth shall be red
'With the gore of misery;
'And swift as this flame shall the light of my fame
'O'er the world as brightly fly.'

As the monarch spoke, crew the morning cock,
When all that pageant bright,
And the glitter of gold, and the statesmen old,
Fled into the gloom of night!

## 50 *'Come hither, canst thou tell me if this skull'

Printed *1893* from the MS of *1827*, where it had been omitted 'for some forgotten reason'. T. said he was 'between 15 and 17' when he wrote his poems of *1827*. *H.Lpr 185* is a transcript of part of *T.MS* where the poem, in T.'s hand, is deleted. T.'s note says: 'See the very amusing account of the Catacombs in the *Quarterly Review*.' (Paden, *Journal of American Folklore* lviii (1945) 46, independently suggested *QR* xxi (1819) 373–4, as a possible source.) 'The National Convention, in the year 1793, passed a decree . . . that the graves and monuments of the kings in St Denis, and in all other places throughout France, should be destroyed' (*QR*). The article quotes a French poem by Mme de Vaunoz on the incident with Henry IV, which probably spurred T. into writing. Cp. James Shirley's *The glories of our blood and state* (Paden). The poem is a very early example of T.'s hatred and fear of the French Revolution; cp. *Aylmer's Field* (p. 1159) and *Beautiful City* (p. 1422). For the theme of the mocking crowd, cp. (especially for ll. 21–4) *The Dead Prophet* (p. 1322) and *To–, After Reading a Life and Letters* (p. 846).

1

Come hither, canst thou tell me if this skull
Which I thus handle was the bold Turenne?
Or is thine intellect so dense and dull
Thou dost not know it by its marks? What then?

2

Death levels all. The crown, the crimsoned flags,
The scutcheons of the mighty robed in black,

*117–20.* 'Having thus said, the whole vanished' (*QR*).

¶ 50.*2.* The Vicomte de Turenne (1611–75), a Marshal of France, was as a great honour buried with the kings at St Denis. 'The first vault which they opened was that of Turenne. . . . As Turenne did not happen to be an object of popular obloquy, some enthusiasm was felt or affected at the sight of his remains' (*QR*).

Are no more in Death's eye than those poor rags
Which the wind sports with on the beggar's back.

3

When the great Henri from his tomb was raised,
The jest of all the rabble that stood by,
He, whose bright fame so brilliantly had blazed,
The star, the meteor of his century,

4

That glorious monarch, at whose nod the throne
Of Empire tottered to its base, was brought
And reared before the people on a stone
To work them sport (Oh! souls without a thought

5

Save the blind impulse of the brutal zeal
Which urges the mad populace to vent
Upon the breathless dead that cannot feel,
The fury of their senseless chastisement).

6

There came a woman from the crowd and smote
The corpse upon the cheek: to earth it fell,
That eye was dim, that glorious tongue was mute,
The soul had fled its cold receptacle.

## 51 *The Dying Man to His Friend

Printed *1893*, as omitted from *1827* 'for some forgotten reason'. It is not deleted in *T.MS.* Cp. *The Dying Christian* (p. 1809), and *The Wanderer* (p. 845).

Fare thee well! for I am parting
  To the realms of endless bliss;
Why is thus thy full tear starting?
  There's a world more bright than this.

Fare thee well! my soul is fleeting
  To the radiant realms of day;

*9.* Henry IV of France (1553–1610). 'The body was placed upright upon a stone, for the rabble to divert themselves with it; and a woman, reproaching the dead Henri with the crime of having been a king, knocked down the corpse by giving it a blow in the face' (*QR*).
*17–20.* 'A savage spirit may sometimes impel men in a civilized age to vent their disgraceful anger upon the dead' (*QR*, which speaks too of 'senseless vengeance').

Hark! what airy tongues repeating,
'Why so long on earth delay?'

Though we part, 'tis not for ever,
Why that sad and rayless eye?
What though here in grief we sever,
'Tis to meet again on high;

When a few short years are over
Thou must lie as low as I.
Brother, parent, son, and lover,
Friend or foe alike must die.

When the pang of Death shall seize thee,
And the dying hour of pain,
This fond thought alone shall ease thee,
That in heaven we meet again.

Then my shade shall hover o'er thee,
Show thee visions of the blest,
Smooth the path to Heaven before thee,
Lead thee to eternal rest.

Other worlds are opening on me,
Now my course on earth is done;
Holy Jesus! look upon me,
Holy Father, take thy son.

# 52 *'Unhappy man, why wander there'

Printed *1893*, as omitted from *1827* 'for some forgotten reason'. The poem is in T.'s hand, not deleted, in *T.MS*, where it has as epigraph *Macbeth* III i 110–13: 'And I another / So weary with disasters, tugged with fortune, / That I would set my life on any chance, / To mend it, or be rid on't.' Cp. *The Outcast* (p. 159).

*Q*. Unhappy man, why wander there,
For bleak the northwinds blow,
And cold and bitter is the air,
And falls the driving snow?

*A*. Oh! murky, murky is the night,
And darksome is the Lea,
And there is not a ray of light,
But it's all the same to me.

¶ 51.7. *airy tongues*: *Comus* 208.

The sultry noon, the freezing night,
The storm-tost winter sea,
The halls of luxury, beaming bright,
Are all the same to me.

Whether in Afric's scorching clime,
Or Lapland's wilds I flee,
I heed not season, place, or time,
They're all the same to me.

For all my hopes on earth are crost
With baleful misery,
And all my goods on earth are lost,
So it's all the same to me.

I have no home where I may go,
Despair alone I see,
And grief on grief and woe on woe
Are all the same to me.

Then tell me not that from the storm
And whirlwind I should flee;
Beat on upon this shattered form,
'Tis all the same to me.

# 53 *Written During the Convulsions in Spain

Printed *1893*, as omitted from *1827* 'for some forgotten reason'. In the *T. MS* it is in T.'s hand, not deleted. Cp. the other poems praising revolt against tyranny, e.g. *Switzerland* (p. 1810). The liberal revolt against Ferdinand VII, which became revolution in 1820, was ended by the entry from France of the Duke of Angoulême, against which Britain protested vigorously. Epigraph: *Odes* II vi 2 ('to the Cantabrians not yet schooled to bear our yoke').

*Cantabrum indoctum juga ferre.*

HORACE

Roused is thy spirit now,
Spain of the lofty brow!
Streams o'er thy campaign the far-flashing glaive:
Sweetly may Freedom's rays
Smile on thy future days,
Smile on the hopes of the young and the brave!

¶ 53.*3*. *glaive*: sword.

Fresh be their tombs who fall,
Green be they one and all,
There may the red rose and wild laurel wave!
There may the sunbeams glance,
There may the maidens dance,
There may the olive bend over their grave!

Bright be their bays who live,
Bright as all Earth can give,
Fair be their deeds in the annals of fame!
Strong be their arm in war,
Brilliant their glory's star,
Fierce be their valour and fearful their name!

Hark! to the trumpet's bray!
Hark! to the charger's neigh,
Be your death-blows as keen as your bosoms are bold!
O'er your glorious array,
As ye rush on your way,
May the broad flag of liberty proudly unfold!

Wake, Pampeluna, wake!
Rouse thee for freedom's sake!
Rouse for the wail and the lone widow's sigh!
Rise, Saragossa, rise!
Hark to the battle-cries,
Pealing sonorous along thy blue sky!

Rouse thee, Valladolid;
Where are thine heroes hid?
Arm them for combat and shout, '*To the fight!*'
Shake the throne of thy Lord
To its base with their sword,
So, on to the combat, and God help the right!

## 54 *'I dare not write an Ode for fear Pimplæa'

Printed by C. Ricks, *Victorian Poetry* iii (1965) 55–7. From *H.Lpr 185*, which attributes it to T. and is a copy of some poems of *1827* that were omitted 'for some forgotten reason'. H.T. printed four such poems in *1893*. It is in T.'s hand in *T.MS*, where it is not deleted. It is, for all its traditional self-depreciation, the earliest example of T.'s lifelong contempt for reviewers, and one of the very few satirical pieces by the young T. Cp. the epigraph on the title-page of *The Devil and the Lady* (p. 8): *Spes alit juventutem et poesin, vituperatio premit et laedit* ('Hope nourishes youth and poetry, abuse represses and injures them'). The deftness of its classical allusions, especially to Horace, recalls T.'s later remarks on Horace as a school text: 'It was not till many years after boyhood that I could like Horace. Byron expressed what I felt, "Then farewell Horace whom I hated so." Indeed I was so over-dosed with Horace that I hardly do him justice even now that I am old' (*Mem.* i 16). Epigraph: Persius, *Prologue* 1–3: 'I never soused my lips in the Nag's Spring; never, that I can remember, did I dream on the two-topped Parnasus, that I should thus come forth suddenly as a poet.'

*Nec fonte labra prolui caballino*
*Nec in bicipiti somniasse Parnasso*
*Memini, ut repente sic poeta prodirem.*

PERSIUS, *Prologue*

I dare not write an Ode for fear Pimplæa
  Should fork me down the double-crested hill,
And sneering say that Fancy, like Astræa,
  Has left the world to ignorance and ill–
Should clip my wings, disgrace my wreath of laurel,
And crown me with a withered bunch of sorrel.

I dare not pen a Sonnet lest the scorner
  With eyes acute my glaring faults pursue,
And hem me in within the 'Poet's Corner',
  Tagged at the wrong end of the Month's Review,
Where I shall be cut up by those undoers
Of doggrel Bards, the pitiless Reviewers.

I dare not make an Essay without shrinking
  Lest in that same dread page I be enrolled:

¶ 54.*1*. *Pimplæa*: the Muse (Horace, *Odes* I xxvi 9), named from the hill of the Muses.

*2*. *double-crested hill*] hill like Mentula *H.MS 1st reading*. Alluding to Catullus cv: *Mentula conatur Pipleum scandere montem: / Musae furcillis praecipitem eiciunt.* ('Mentula strives to climb the Piplean mount: the Muses with pitchforks drive him out headlong.')

*3*. *Astræa*: goddess of justice; in the golden age she distributed blessings, but she left the earth in disgust.

*4*. *world . . . ill*] good-for-nothing world for aye *1st reading*.

*8*] Should place my glaring errors full in view, *1st reading*.

*13*. *an Essay*] a Satire *1st reading*.

*14*] At being in that same dread page enrolled: *1st reading*.

What shall I do? I cannot sleep for thinking
(Friend Flaccus made the same complaint of old),
And having but small store of nerve and fibre,
Though bathed in oil I could not swim the Tiber.

Nor have I yet in Epics made a sally
Since my misgiving conscience complains
I could not sing the 'pereuntes Galli'
In anything at all like decent strains.
I know my laboured lines would only just go
To wrap up sundries in the 'vico Tusco'.

Or should I boldly make a feint to stock a
Whole volume, like the Sketch-book, with a string
Of sentiments, there's Mr Knickerbocker
Would beat me out and out like anything,
And loath I should be to be deemed as weak as
The tribe of imitators 'Servum pecus'!

But ah! my hopes are all as dead as mutton,
As vain as Cath[oli]ck Em[anci]p[atio]n,
E'en now my conscience pulls me by the button
And bids me cease to prate of imitation.
What countless ills a minor bard environ–
'*You're imitating Whistlecraft and Byron*'.

*15–18.* Horace, *Satires* II i 7–8: '*verum nequeo dormire.*' '*Ter uncti / transnanto Tiberim, somno quibus est opus alto.*' ('But I cannot sleep.' 'Let those who need sound sleep oil themselves and swim across the Tiber thrice.')

*17.* Suggested by the complaint that Horace's work was *sine nervis*, *Satires* II i 2.

*21.* Horace, *Satires* II i 12–14: '*vires / deficiunt: neque enim quivis horrentia pilis / agmina nec fracta pereuntis cuspide Gallos . . .*' ('My strength fails me. Not everyone can paint ranks bristling with lances, or Gauls falling with spearheads shattered.')

*24.* Horace, *Satires* II iii 228: *Tusci turba impia vici.* ('The Tuscan Street's vile throng'.)

*26–7.* Washington Irving ('Diedrich Knickerbocker'), and his *The Sketch-Book* (1820).

*30.* Horace, *Epistles* I xix 19: *o imitatores, servum pecus* ('O you mimics, you slavish herd').

*32. Catholick Emancipation*: a recurring issue in the 1820s.

*35–6.* Byron, *Don Juan* III xxxvi: 'Ah! what is man? what perils still environ / The happiest mortals even after dinner! / A day of gold from out an age of iron . . .' Echoing *Hudibras* I iii 1–2: 'Ay me! what perils do environ / The Man that meddles with cold Iron!' *Whistlecraft*: J. H. Frere published his mock-heroic cantos (1817–18) as the work of the brothers Whistlecraft.

# 55 *The Outcast

Printed *1931*, pp. 28–9, from *Heath MS* where it has no title and is dated 1826. It is also on the stubs of *H.Nbk 7* (which is watermarked 1826, inscribed 'Trin. Coll.', and includes poems of *1830*). Cp. two poems of *1827*, *Unhappy man* (p. 154), and *I wander in darkness and sorrow* (p. 92) with its hall, weeds and leaves. Paden (p. 138) compares Byron, *On Leaving Newstead Abbey* 1–4: 'Through thy battlements, Newstead, the hollow winds whistle: / Thou, the hall of my Fathers, art gone to decay; / In thy once smiling garden, the hemlock and thistle / Have choaked up the rose which late bloomed in the way.'

I will not seek my Father's groves,
They murmur deeply o'er my head
Of sunless days and broken loves:
Their shade is dim and dark and dead.
There through the length of cool arcades
Where noonday leaves the midnight dews,
Unreal shapes of twilight shades
Along the sombre avenues,
To Memory's widowed eyes would spring
In dreamy, drowsy wandering.

I will not seek my Father's hills,
Their hue is fresh and clear and bright,
What time the early sunbeam fills
Their bush-clad depths with lonely light.
Each broken stile, each wavy path,
Each hollowed hawthorn, damp, and black,
Each brook that chatters noisy wrath
Among its knotted reeds, bring back
Lone images of varied pain
To this worn mind and fevered brain.

I will not seek my Father's Hall:
There peers the day's unhallowed glare,
The wet moss crusts the parting wall,
The wassail wind is reveller there.

¶ 55.7. Cp. Milton's *Nativity Ode* 188: 'in twilight shade of tangled thickets mourn'.

*14.* 'lonely lights', *The Two Voices* 83.

*16–18.* Suggesting the opening of Goldsmith's *Deserted Village*.

*20.* Cp. *The Bridal* 27–8 (1828): 'A dark form glances quick / Through her worn brain, hot and sick.'

*23.* Cp. the desolation in *Mariana* 1–2: 'With blackest moss the flower-plots / Were thickly crusted, one and all' (rhyming with 'wall').

Along the weedy, chinky floors
Wild knots of flowering rushes blow
And through the sounding corridors
The sere leaf rustles to and fro:
And O! what Memory might recall,
If once I paced that voiceless Hall!

# 56 *Inverlee

Printed by Sir Charles Tennyson, *Cornhill* cliii (1936) 448–9. In *Heath MS* and *Allen MS* it is dated 1826. Cp. *The Bridal* (*c.* 1828, p. 164), with its dance in the Scottish hall; and for the early part, cp. *The Vale of Bones* (p. 97). Some of the details (e.g. the oriel, l. 39) suggest Scott's *Lay of the Last Minstrel* II 1ff, of which there was a copy at Somersby (*Lincoln*).

The stars are out along the hills,
The cold blue hills of Inverlee,
And the low breeze of midnight fills
Mine ears with pleasant harmony.
The Moon is white along the fells,
The echoing fells of Inverlee,
And the far river sinks or swells
With varying mournful melody.
The wind is moaning through the vales,
The stony vales of Inverlee,
And through the crazy steeple wails,
And the deserted hawthorn tree.
Black nettles crowd the chancel tombs
Along the church of Inverlee,
Their hallowed depth of vaulted glooms
Thin streams of arrowy moonlight see:
For through the broken ceiling fall
Those pencilled rays at Inverlee,
And through the failing fissured wall
Shine into the obscurity,
Then pierce the subterranean dusk
In the brick walls at Inverlee,
Through the close coffin's mouldering husk,
Among the white bones gleamingly.

*29–30.* Cp. the fear of Memory, the hall at *Inverlee* 31–2: 'To them all life's uncounted ills / Hold no such curse as Memory.'

¶ *56.15. vaulted gloom*: *The Bridal* 7.

*16–24.* Cp. *On the Moon-Light Shining upon a Friend's Grave* (p. 1808).

When round the holy table prest
The old and young at Inverlee,
That race of buxom youth grown old
Are fading far beyond the sea.
Their eyes are fixed on foreign hills,
Their hearts are here at Inverlee,
To them all life's uncounted ills
Hold no such curse as Memory.
For aye recur the whitening towers
Of the old hall at Inverlee,
The merry, merry hall, whose bowers
Rang loud to midnight minstrelsy;
What time in gay and gorgeous light
Lay the long feast at Inverlee,
And the rich Oriel's blazoned height
Shone redly through the dark countrie;
What time the dancers beat the floor
With bright, white feet at Inverlee,
The arched roof trembling to the roar
Of song and shout at Inverlee.

## 57 *No More

Published Oct. 1830 in *The Gem* for 1831; not reprinted. Written 1826 (dated, *Allen MS*). 'Although my father considered the poem crude, it is remarkable for a boy of seventeen' (*Mem.* i 80). It is the germ of *Tears, idle tears* (p. 784): sad, sweet, strange, no more, eyes, tears, fathomdeep / depth. Cp. *Song* [*Who can say*] (p. 453). Shelley's *A Lament* (pub. 1824) has the refrain 'No more–Oh, never more!'

Oh sad *No More!* Oh sweet *No More!*
   Oh strange *No More!*
By a mossed brookbank on a stone
I smelt a wildweed-flower alone;
There was a ringing in my ears,
And both my eyes gushed out with tears.
Surely all pleasant things had gone before,
Lowburied fathomdeep beneath with thee, NO MORE!

*32.* Cp. *The Outcast* (p. 159, also 1826), with its hall and its awe of Memory (and its hawthorn, cp. l. 12).
*35. merry, merry*: part of the refrain of *The Bridal*.

# 58 *The Ganges

Unpublished. From a MS (*Lincolnshire Archives Committee*) formerly belonging to Mrs E. C. Tennyson-d'Eyncourt. It has the title 'Alfred's Verses. The Ganges', and the headnote: 'Early verses by A.T. copied by his first cousin, George H. Tennyson-d'Eyncourt'. The MS is in the hand of Tennyson-d'Eyncourt, whose own poem on the Ganges has thirty-three lines and ends: 'Thus sang the Maiden, when in turn the swain / Touching the strings, poured forth the following strain.' Then the note: 'To be finished with some of Alfred's'. There is also a concluding note by Tennyson-d'Eyncourt: 'It is to be recollected, that there was scarcely any time to write these lines, and that they were wrote off without a revisal.' Written 1826–7 (?). A later hand has suggested 'January 1827?'; Sir Charles Tennyson has noted: 'Probably about 1826 but possibly from Cambridge 1828.' Source: Sir William Jones's translation of the *Hymn to Ganga* (*Works*, 1799, vi 383–92; this edn was at Somersby). *Persia* 53–8 (*1827*, p. 104) refers to Ganga's 'vaccine source', and also has 'lotos', 'bower', 'incense', and 'flower'. *The Ganges* is of interest as one of the very few poems by T. in heroic couplets. *T.Nbk 19* has a heroic-couplet poem on Napoleon's retreat from Moscow, which may not be quoted; and see T.'s translation from Claudian (p. 1).

Most glorious Ganga! down whose golden tide,
In light canoes the tawny natives glide,
Prolific stream! what tongue thy praise may tell,
The lavish bounties of thine annual swell,
Laving in silent state the sunny plains
Where the rich light of endless summer reigns?
Thy blossomed woods, thy palm-trees' musky ranks?
The gilded Pagods glittering on thy banks?
The fragrant texture of thy Lotus-bowers,
And the full incense of thy fruits and flowers.
Brightest of floods that meet the orient day
When his red beams along thy bosom play,
Chain of far realms! within whose current shines
The scattered ore of Thibet's hidden mines.
If, as the Hebrews say, thy waves of spice
Bathed in old time the walls of Paradise,
What marvel that, in joyous musing, there
The enraptured Brahmin pour his soul in prayer,

¶ 58.*1*. *MS* note: 'The Hindoo appellation for the Ganges.'
*7–9*. 'Musky', 'Lotus' and 'bower' suggest *Thou camest to thy bower* (*1827*, p. 136).

Laud thine unrivalled flood, thy course adore,
And with raised hands invoke thy plenteous power?
But who may tell thy source, thy secret springs,
The beauty of thy matchless wanderings?
Or the gay streams that to thy sapphire tide
O'er sands of gold in mazy labyrinths glide,
Where Calinadi's flowery current smiles,
And Gandac views her countless crocodiles
Roll deeply o'er thy sands – thy fragrant reeds,
And the rich emerald of thy velvet meads.
What rapturous breezes from thy bosom blow,
How gaily bright thy crispèd surges flow.
Give me to trace thy course along the plain,
From distant Thibet to the Southern main,
To view the giant Burram faster join,
In murmurs hoarse, his kindred waves with thine.
Give me to wander by the hoary brow
Of Himola that frowns with endless snow,
Where down the rocks precipitously steep
In one broad sheet thy boiling waters leap,
Deafening the awe-struck ear with mingled clash
And thunder of thy thousand waves, which dash
From cliff to cliff with stern tumultuous hiss,
Down to their dark and fathomless abyss.
Hail! ample-sheeted Ganga! vast expanse!
O'er whose blue breast the bounding shallops dance,
How vain the lyre that would attempt thy praise.
How weak the hand! how worthless are the lays.

# 59 *Playfellow Winds

Printed by Sir Charles Tennyson, *Nineteenth Century* cix (1931) 373; then *1931*, p. 41: 'These lines are from a notebook inscribed 'A. Tennyson, Trin. Coll. Camb.' [*H.Nbk 7*]. A copy also exists, written in another hand and dated 1827 [*Heath MS*]. It was more probably written in 1828, in a mood of depression during the poet's first days at Cambridge.' Paden (p. 113) points out that T. was in residence in Cambridge from Nov. 1827. *H.Nbk 7* is watermarked 1826 and includes poems of *1830*.

*25–6. Calinadi* and *Gandac*: *MS* note, '2 tributary streams.' Cp. Jones: 'where *Calinadi* brings / To *Cányacuvja*, seat of kings, / On prostrate waves her tributary flow'rs / . . . Red *Gandac*, drawn by crocodiles'.
*36. Himola*: Jones notes that this derives 'from a *Sanscrit* word signifying *snow*'.

Playfellow winds and stars, my friends of old,
For sure your voice was friendly, your eyes bright
With sympathy, what time my spirit was cold
And frozen at the fountain, my cheek white
As my own hope's quenched ashes. As your memories
More than yourselves ye look; so overcast
With steam of this dull town your burning eyes:
Nay, surely even your memories wear more light
Than do your present selves. Ye sympathize
As ever with me, stars, from first to last.

## 60 *The Bridal

Printed *Mem.* i 26–8, as 'written at 14 or 15'. It is dated 1828 in *Heath MS* and *Allen MS*. It was written 'after reading the *Bride of Lammermoor*'; Chapter 34 provided this climax of the family feud. T. drew on Scott's novel for *Maud*, and alluded to it in *The Flight* 57: 'The dear, mad bride who stabbed her bridegroom on her bridal night'. Cp. *Inverlee* (p. 160).

The lamps were bright and gay
On the merry bridal-day,
When the merry bridegroom
Bore the bride away!
A merry, merry bridal,
A merry bridal-day!
And the chapel's vaulted gloom
Was misted with perfume.
'Now, tell me, mother, pray,
Why the bride is white as clay,
Although the merry bridegroom
Bears the bride away,
On a merry, merry bridal,
A merry bridal-day?
And why her black eyes burn
With a light so wild and stern?'

¶ 59.*6. ye*] *H.MS*, *Heath MS*; you *1931*.
*7.* Horace (*Odes* III xxix 12): *fumum et opes strepitumque Romae* ('the smoke, the riches, and the din of Rome'), as in *In Memoriam* lxxxix 8: 'The dust and din and steam of town'.
*8. Nay,*] *MSS*; Now *1931*.
¶ 60.*5.* For the refrain, cp. *Inverlee* 35: 'the merry, merry hall'.
*7. vaulted gloom*: *Inverlee* 15.
*11. Although*] Though *Heath MS*.

'They revel as they may,'
  That skinny witch did say,
'For–now the merry bridegroom
  Hath borne the bride away–
Her thoughts have found their wings
  In the dreaming of past things:
And though girt in glad array,
  Yet her own deep soul says nay:
For though the merry bridegroom
  Hath borne the bride away,
A dark form glances quick
  Through her worn brain, hot and sick.'
And so she said her say–
  This was her roundelay–
That though the merry bridegroom
  Might lead the bride away,
Dim grief did wait upon her,
  In glory and in honour.
In the hall, at close of day,
  Did the people dance and play,
For now the merry bridegroom
  Hath borne the bride away.
He from the dance hath gone
  But the revel still goes on.
Then a scream of wild dismay
  Through the deep hall forced its way,
Although the merry bridegroom
  Hath borne the bride away;
And, staring as in trance,
  They were shaken from the dance.
Then they found him where he lay
  Whom the wedded wife did slay,
Though he a merry bridegroom

*18 ∧ 19*]
But each hour the Kirk hears both
Death hymn and marriage oath;
The freshest bloom in May
Is knit to damp decay;
  And though now the &c.

*MS margin, and H.Nbk 7.*

*28.* Cp. *The Outcast* 20: 'worn mind and fevered brain'.

*31. though*] *Not MS.*

*34 ∧ 5*] *Mem. inserts asterisks, which might misleadingly suggest a lacuna.*

*45. trance*] *Mem., MS*; a trance *Eversley notes.*

*49. Though*] Although *MS.*

Had borne the bride away,
And they saw *her* standing by,
With a laughing crazèd eye,
On the bitter, bitter bridal,
The bitter bridal-day.

## 61 *Home

Printed by H.T., *Eversley* i 344, as written 1828 (a date confirmed by *Heath MS* and *Allen MS*). Presumably on leaving Somersby for Cambridge. Cp. *Love of Home: A Rejoinder* (1830), by T.'s brother Charles: 'My love of home no circumstance can shake'.

What shall sever me
From the love of home?
Shall the weary sea,
Leagues of sounding foam?
Shall extreme distress,
Shall unknown disgrace,
Make my love the less
For my sweet birth-place?
Though my brains grow dry,
Fancy mew her wings,
And my memory
Forget all other things,–
Though I could not tell
My left hand from my right,–
I should know thee well,
Home of my delight!

## 62 *'Among some Nations Fate hath placed too far'

Unpublished, except ll. 3–4 (*Mem.* i 20); dated 1828 in *Heath MS* (text below) and *Allen MS*. Cp. *Love* [*Thou, from the first*] i (p. 243). The sonnet form is extremely irregular, as with most of T.'s early sonnets.

*54. The*] A *MS*, which has the order 53–4, 51–2.
¶ 61.*3. weary sea*: as in Shelley, *Rosalind* 971.
*4.* Cp. *If I were loved* 13: 'leagues of roaring foam'.
*10. mew*: moult.

Among some Nations Fate hath placed too far
The lamps of song have never risen or set,
As rays of many a rolling central Star
Aye flashing earthward have not reached us yet.
Light in a moment from his chambers brought
Striking the dark of crannied caverns dim
Beats through the eyelids of the slumbering sea:
But nothing is so swift as liberty
Linked to the thunderbolt of ruining thought,
The subtle strength of an undying hymn.
One throne there is, round whose unshaken base
The myriad feet of all on Earth might move,
One King into whose everlasting face
All eyes might look and live, his name is Love.

# 63 *To Poesy [O God, make this age great]

Printed *Mem.* i 60. Written 1828 (dated, *Heath MS* and *Allen MS*). Cp. the very similar sonnet *To Poesy* [*Religion be thy sword*] (p. 168), written at this date by T. and Arthur Hallam. The large claims for poetry reflect the high-minded opinions current in Cambridge.

O God, make this age great that we may be
As giants in Thy praise! and raise up Mind,
Whose trumpet-tongued, aërial melody
May blow alarum loud to every wind,
And startle the dull ears of human kind!

¶ 62.*7*. Combining *Lycidas* 26: 'eyelids of the morn'; and Shelley, *Queen Mab* viii 24: 'That wakes the wavelets of the slumbering sea'.

*9*. Cp. *Paradise Lost* i 328: 'linked Thunderbolts'; 'ruining', with its suggestion of falling, is a Miltonic Latinism.

*11*. Cp. *PL* vi 833–4: 'The stedfast Empyrean shook throughout, / All but the Throne it self of God.'

¶ 63.*1*. *1 Chronicles* xxix 12: 'in thine hand it is to make great, and to give strength unto all'.

*3*. *trumpet-tongued*: from *Macbeth* I vii 19, supported by 'wind'.

*4*. *alarum*] alarums *H.Nbk 3*.

*5*. *ears*] *Mem.*, *Allen MS*; ear *H.MS*, *Heath MS*. *H.MS 1st reading* was 'dull hearing of mankind'.

Methinks I see the world's renewèd youth
A long day's dawn, when Poesy shall bind
Falsehood beneath the altar of great Truth:
The clouds are sundered toward the morning-rise;
Slumber not now, gird up thy loins for fight,
And get thee forth to conquer. I, even I,
Am large in hope that these expectant eyes
Shall drink the fulness of thy victory,
For thou art all unconscious of thy Might.

## 64 *The Lark

Printed *Mem.* i 58. It is dated 1828 in *Heath MS* and *Allen MS*, which–like the version in *H.Nbk 7*–employ more archaisms, e.g. the spelling i', o', chaunt, dronck.

Full light aloft doth the laverock spring
From under the deep, sweet corn,
And chants in the golden wakening
Athwart the bloomy morn.
What aileth thee, O bird divine,
That thou singest with main and with might?
Is thy mad brain drunk with the merry, red wine,
At the very break of light?
It is not good to drink strong wine
Ere the day be well-nigh done;
But thou hast drunk of the merry, sweet wine,
At the rising of the sun.

## 65 *To Poesy [Religion be thy sword]

Printed by T. H. Vail Motter, *The Writings of Arthur Hallam* (1943), p. 46, from *Allen MS*, where it is dated 1828. It is a joint composition of T. and

*6–7.* Cp. Milton's *Areopagitica*: 'Methinks I see her as an Eagle muing her mighty youth, and kindling her undazl'd eyes at the full midday beam.'
*7. long*] great *H.MS 1st reading.*
*9. sundered*] silvered *H.MS 1st reading.*
*14. For*] *H.MS, Heath MS, Allen MS*; Though *Mem.*
¶ 64.*1. aloft*] on loft *Heath MS.* Cp. *The Oak of the North (1827)*, by T.'s brother Frederick: 'Though now the lavrock pours at morn . . .'.
*3. wakening*] dawining *Heath MS.*
*4*] Above the blosmy lawn. *Heath MS.*

Hallam; the latter noted, 'I had some hand in the worst part of this.' The joint authorship is also specified in *Heath MS*. Cp. *To Poesy* [*O God*] (p. 167).

Religion be thy sword; the armoury
Of God shall yield it tempered; make thy stand
In this thy Canaan set apart for thee;
Go forth and in thy right possess the land.
Oh might I be an arrow in thine hand,
And not of viewless flight, but trailing flame,
Like the old King's on the Sicilian strand,
Accompanied with tumult of acclaim!
Not bearing my own triumph in conceit
Of eminence, but gathering all eyes
Because I seek to bless my native earth,
For this is the condition of our birth,
That we unto ourselves are only great
Doing the silent work of charities.

# 66 *The Idealist

Unpublished. It is dated 1829 in the *Allen MS* (text below) and in *Heath MS*.

A mighty matter I rehearse,
A mighty matter undescried;
Come listen all who can.
I am the spirit of a man,
I weave the universe,
And indivisible divide,
Creating all I hear and see.
All souls are centres: I am one,

¶ 65.*1–2*. Based on *Ephesians* vi 13ff: 'the whole armour of God . . . the sword of the Spirit which is the word of God'; the 'fiery darts of the wicked' suggested T.'s flaming arrow (l. 6). Cp. *Paradise Lost* vi 320–2: 'the sword / Of *Michael* from the Armorie of God / Was giv'n him temperd so.' 'The Armoury of God' recurs at vii 200.

*4*. *Deuteronomy* i 8, 'Go in, and possess the land'.

*7*. *Aeneid* v 519–28, where the arrow of Acestes mystically traced its path in flame, for which he was acclaimed.

*8*. *tumult of acclaim*: aptly used as praise of Hallam in *In Memoriam* lxxv 20; cp. *The Dying Swan* 33: 'the tumult of their acclaim'.

*11*] To work the welfare of my native earth, *Allen MS 1st reading*.

I am the earth, the stars, the sun,
I am the clouds, the sea.
I am the citadels and palaces
Of all great cities: I am Rome,
Tadmor, and Cairo: I am Place
And Time, yet is my home
Eternity: (let no man think it odd,
  For I am these,
And every other birth of every other race;)
I am all things save souls of fellow men and
  very God!

## 67 *Timbuctoo

Published in *Cambridge Chronicle and Journal*, 10 July 1829; in *Prolusiones Academicae* (1829, the text below). It was subsequently included in collections of *Cambridge Prize Poems*, but was not reprinted by T. H.T. included it in *1893*, and in an Appendix to *Eversley*. The subject 'Timbuctoo' was announced for the Chancellor's Gold Medal in Dec. 1828 (Paden, p. 139). 'On June 6th, 1829, the announcement was made that my father had won the prize medal for his poem in blank verse on *Timbuctoo*. To win the prize in anything but rhymed heroics was an innovation. My grandfather had desired him to compete, so unwillingly he patched up an old poem on *The Battle of Armageddon*, and came out prizeman over Milnes, Hallam and others' (*Mem.* i 45–6). A text of *Armageddon* (p. 64) was printed in *1931*, and from this (now *H. Nbk 2*) it appeared that less than fifty lines of *Armageddon* were incorporated in *Timbuctoo*. But a different version of *Armageddon* in *T.Nbk 18* (which may not be quoted) makes it clear that about 120 lines, roughly half of *Timbuctoo*, were taken over almost verbatim from *Armageddon*. The whole central vision of *Timbuctoo* (ll. 62–190) was present, with a few trivial variants, in *Armageddon* in this notebook (which is dated 10 Jan. 1828). For the few exceptions to this, see ll. 71–5*n*, 77–80*n*, and 185–190*n*. *Armageddon* however includes some extra lines, so that there is not the uninterrupted sequence *Timbuctoo* 62–190. There are two further links: that, as Sir Charles Tennyson says, the opening line of *Timbuctoo* is from *Armageddon*; and that *Timbuctoo* 28–40, on the city and the priestess, are a reworking of passages from the Trinity *Armageddon*. *T.MS*, described by

¶ 66.*10*] *Not Heath MS* (*slip*).
*13. and*] or *Heath MS. Tadmor*: 'Palmyra, or Tadmor, a noble city of ancient Syria, now in ruins', *English Encyclopaedia* (1802), which also had two plates of the ruins. There was a copy at Somersby (*Lincoln*).
*18*] *Heath MS* has 'And very God!' as a separate line, but that leaves 'men' without a rhyme. For the sentiment, cp. *The Higher Pantheism* (p. 1204).

C. Ricks, *MLR* lxi (1966) 23–4, makes clear what had been disguised by the *1931* text: that H.T. did not exaggerate in using the words 'patched up', and that T. was right to speak of 'the turning of an old poem on *Armageddon* into *Timbuctoo* by a little alteration of the beginning and the end' (*Mem.* ii 355).

*Sources.* These are discussed in great detail by Paden (pp. 69–71, 139–48). T.'s opinions on discovery suggest Hugh Murray's *Historical Account of Africa* (2nd edn, 1818, i 6–8): 'Thus we find these fairy spots successively retreating before the progress of discovery, yet finding still, in the farthest advance which ancient knowledge ever made, some remoter extremity to which they can fly.' This opinion, which is 'an orthodox doctrine of the early nineteenth century' (Paden), would have been reinforced by Washington Irving's *Life of Columbus* (1828), the source of *Anacaona.* A strong stylistic influence was Milton, naturally enough since the poem describes, in blank verse, an angelic vision.

*Epigraph.* If T. meant *George* Chapman, it would seem to be a hoax, since no one has ever found these lines there. Certainly they are very Tennysonian. Paden (p. 144) remarks that an article on Chapman happened to follow an article on the *Memoirs of Signor Gaudentio di Lucca* (1737, often reprinted) in the *Retrospective Review* (iv, 1821); Paden suggests that Gaudentio's elaborate account of the city Phor may have influenced T.'s city, as well as supplying the lion of the epigraph.

*Reception.* T.'s Cambridge contemporaries were much impressed by his success, the first public testimony to his gifts. They were also mystified by the poem. Charles Wordsworth wrote to his brother Christopher (who had won the Medal in 1827), on 4 Sept. 1829: 'If such an exercise had been sent up at Oxford, the author would have had a better chance of being rusticated, with the view of his passing a few months at a Lunatic Asylum, than of obtaining the prize. It is certainly a wonderful production; and if it had come out with Lord Byron's name, it would have been thought as fine as anything he ever wrote' (*Mem.* i 46). Arthur Hallam (*ibid.*), in an important letter to W. E. Gladstone, 14 Sept. 1829, spoke at first of his own entry, and went on: 'My friend Tennyson's poem, which got the prize, will be thought by the ten sober persons afore-mentioned twice as absurd as mine; and to say the truth, by striking out his prose argument, the Examiners have done all in their power to verify the concluding words, "All was night [dark]." The splendid imaginative power that pervades it will be seen through all hindrances. I consider Tennyson as promising fair to be the greatest poet of our generation, perhaps of our century.'

Hallam believed he had influenced the poem: Hallam 'is delighted that Tennyson is successful. He says that Tennyson deserved it, but that he borrowed the pervading idea from him, so that "he is entitled to the honours of a Sancho Panza in the memorable victory gained in the year 1829 over prosaicism and jingle jangle"' (J. M. Gaskell, 25 June 1829; *Records of an Eton Schoolboy*, 1883, p. 139). One of the Cambridge group, possibly Richard Monckton Milnes (*CT*, pp. 91–2), reviewed the poem in

*The Athenaeum*, 22 July 1829: 'These productions have often been ingenious and elegant, but we have never before seen one of them which indicated really first-rate poetical genius, and which would have done honour to any man that ever wrote. Such, we do not hesitate to affirm, is the little work before us; and the examiners seem to have felt about it like ourselves, for they have assigned the prize to its author, though the measure in which he writes was never before (we believe) thus selected for honour.' Milnes wrote in a letter, 22 Oct. 1829: 'Tennyson's poem has made quite a sensation; it is certainly equal to most parts of Milton' (T. W. Reid, *Life of Milnes*, 2nd edn, 1890, i 72). Because of his 'horror of publicity', T. did not recite the poem himself in July in the Senate House; that was done by his friend Charles Merivale, who had won the Latin prize in 1829 and this prize in 1828. T.'s letter of request went on: 'I hope you found my letter sufficiently clear relatively to corrections. The Vice-Chancellor observed to me, "We cannot do these things quite so well by proxy as with the person himself, to whom several of my objections might have been stated and answered immediately"' (*Mem.* i 47). But despite his success, T. was critical of the poem. In 1831 he replied to a request to include it in *Cambridge Prize Poems* (*Mem.* i 45):
'Sir, As you intend to reprint the Cambridge Prize Poems, it would seem odd to leave mine out, though for my own part I had much rather you had not thought of it. Prize Poems (without any exception even in favour of Mr Milman's *Belvedere*) are not properly speaking "Poems" at all, and ought to be forgotten as soon as recited. I could have wished that poor *Timbuctoo* might have been suffered to slide quietly off, with all its errors, into forgetfulness: however as I do not expect to turn you from your purpose of republishing the p^e^ p^s^, I suppose mine must be printed along with them: only for "cones of Pyramids," which is nonsense [l. 164], I will thank you to substitute "peaks of Pyramids".'

In 1834 T. persuaded Henry Hallam to omit the introductory note to Arthur's *Timbuctoo*, which praised T.'s poem. T. wrote that Arthur's 'poem is everyway so much better than that wild and unmethodized performance of my own, that even his praise on such a subject would be painful' (*Eversley* iii 258–9).

*Deep in that lion-haunted inland lies*
*A mystick city, goal of high emprise.*
CHAPMAN

I stood upon the Mountain which o'erlooks
The narrow seas, whose rapid interval
Parts Afric from green Europe, when the Sun
Had fallen below the Atlantick, and above
The silent Heavens were blenched with faery light,
Uncertain whether faery light or cloud,

¶ 67.*1*. This line is from *Armageddon* (see headnote).

Flowing Southward, and the chasms of deep,
deep blue
Slumbered unfathomable, and the stars
Were flooded over with clear glory and pale.
I gazed upon the sheeny coast beyond,
There where the Giant of old Time infixèd
The limits of his prowess, pillars high
Long time erased from Earth: even as the Sea
When weary of wild inroad buildeth up
Huge mounds whereby to stay his yeasty waves.
And much I mused on legends quaint and old
Which whilome won the hearts of all on Earth
Toward their brightness, even as flame draws air;
But had their being in the heart of Man
As air is the life of flame: and thou wert then
A centred glory-circled Memory,
Divinest Atalantis, whom the waves
Have buried deep, and thou of later name
Imperial Eldorado roofed with gold:
Shadows to which, despite all shocks of Change,
All on-set of capricious Accident,
Men clung with yearning Hope which would not die.
As when in some great City where the walls
Shake, and the streets with ghastly faces thronged
Do utter forth a subterranean voice,
Among the inner columns far retired
At midnight, in the lone Acropolis,
Before the awful Genius of the place
Kneels the pale Priestess in deep faith, the while

*11–12.* Calpe (Gibraltar) and Abyla (on the African coast) formed the Pillars of Hercules, the limits for the Mediterranean seafarer.

*15. yeasty waves*: *Macbeth* IV i 53. T. speaks of 'the yeasty wave' in *The Devil and the Lady* I i 73.

*21.* Incorporated as *The Lover's Tale* i 436.

*22. Atalantis*: the unusual spelling of the sunken island derives from Irving's *Columbus* (Paden, p. 141).

*24. Eldorado*: the golden city of the Amazon. By the confusion of Guinea and New Guinea, it was sometimes transferred to Africa. Paden (p. 141) quotes from Hugh Murray a collocation of Timbuctoo, El Dorado, and gold roofs. Pope, *Windsor Forest* 412: 'And other *Mexico's* be roof'd with Gold'. ('Roof'd with Gold' is from Dryden's *Aeneis* vi 17.)

*28–40.* These lines on the city and the priestess are a reworking of part of *Armageddon*. The earthquake suggests the volcanic eruption in *Armageddon* i 99–100.

*29. Paradise Lost* xii 644: 'With dreadful Faces throng'd'.

Above her head the weak lamp dips and winks
Unto the fearful summoning without:
Nathless she ever clasps the marble knees,
Bathes the cold hand with tears, and gazeth on
Those eyes which wear no light but that wherewith
Her phantasy informs them.
                                        Where are ye
Thrones of the Western wave, fair Islands green?
Where are your moonlight halls, your cedarn glooms,
The blossoming abysses of your hills?
Your flowering Capes, and your gold-sanded bays
Blown round with happy airs of odorous winds?
Where are the infinite ways, which, Seraph-trod,
Wound through your great Elysian solitudes,
Whose lowest deeps were, as with visible love,
Filled with Divine effulgence, circumfused,
Flowing between the clear and polished stems,
And ever circling round their emerald cones
In coronals and glories, such as gird
The unfading foreheads of the Saints in Heaven?
For nothing visible, they say, had birth
In that blest ground but it was played about
With its peculiar glory. Then I raised
My voice and cried, 'Wide Afric, doth thy Sun
Lighten, thy hills enfold a City as fair
As those which starred the night o' the elder World?
Or is the rumour of thy Timbuctoo
A dream as frail as those of ancient Time?'
  A curve of whitening, flashing, ebbing light!
A rustling of white wings! the bright descent
Of a young Seraph! and he stood beside me
There on the ridge, and looked into my face

*36–7.* In 1867 T. marked these lines and ll. 55–6, in a copy of the poem (*Virginia*) as 'the only good passages in the Poem'.

*38. hand*] *1829, Prolusiones;* hands *Eversley*.

*41.* Cp. the many other poems by T. on the Isles of the Blest, especially *The Hesperides* (p. 423), and *The Lotos-Eaters* (p. 429). Paden (pp. 142–3) discusses them.

*42. cedarn*: *Comus* 990 is the earliest *OED* example; then *Kubla Khan*. Keats has 'cedar gloom', *Endymion* iii 483.

*45. odorous winds*: conventional diction, found four times in Shelley.

*49. Divine effulgence*: *PL* v 458.

*55–6.* See ll. 36–7*n*.

*62–190.* Incorporated from *Armageddon*.

With his unutterable, shining orbs.
So that with hasty motion I did veil
My vision with both hands, and saw before me
Such coloured spots as dance athwart the eyes
Of those, that gaze upon the noonday Sun.
Girt with a Zone of flashing gold beneath
His breast, and compassed round about his brow
With triple arch of everchanging bows,
And circled with the glory of living light
And alternation of all hues, he stood.

'O child of man, why muse you here alone
Upon the Mountain, on the dreams of old
Which filled the Earth with passing loveliness,
Which flung strange music on the howling winds,
And odours rapt from remote Paradise?
Thy sense is clogged with dull mortality,
Thy spirit fettered with the bond of clay:
Open thine eyes and see.'

I looked, but not
Upon his face, for it was wonderful
With its exceeding brightness, and the light
Of the great Angel Mind which looked from out
The starry glowing of his restless eyes.
I felt my soul grow mighty, and my Spirit

*66. shining orbs*: *PL* iii 668 and 670, where however it means planets.
*71–5*] *Not Armageddon, T.MS, 1931*. The descent of the angel may owe something to a similar scene in Akenside's *Pleasures of Imagination* (1744) Book ii; there the spirit's opening words are 'Vain are thy thoughts, O child of mortal birth', and he is clad 'with a radiant zone of gold'. There was a copy of the poem at Somersby (*Lincoln*).
*73. triple arch*: suggesting Keats's 'triple-arch'd', *Eve of St Agnes* 208, the context of which includes: 'And on her hair a glory, like a saint: / She seem'd a splendid angel.'
*74.* Cp. *Sonnet* [*Me my own Fate*] 3: 'Thy spirit, circled with a living glory'.
*76. child*: F. Locker reported that 'This stood "son", professor Smyth made him alter it' (*Virginia* copy; see ll. 36–7*n*).
*77–80.* Altered from *T.MS* of *Armageddon*, where they had described the great battle, with which T. was no longer concerned.
*81. dull mortality*: Keats, *Endymion* iii 907; Shelley, *Epipsychidion* 389.
*83.* Cp. the angel Michael's clearing of Adam's sight for the visions from the mountain in *PL* xi 411ff: '*Adam*, now ope thine eyes'. This passage mentions Eldorado, as Paden observes.
*88–130.* Paden (p. 71): 'The passage is apparently the first of Tennyson's references to that mystical experience which, occurring throughout his

With supernatural excitation bound
Within me, and my mental eye grew large
With such a vast circumference of thought,
That in my vanity I seemed to stand
Upon the outward verge and bound alone
Of full beatitude. Each failing sense
As with a momentary flash of light
Grew thrillingly distinct and keen. I saw
The smallest grain that dappled the dark Earth,
The indistinctest atom in deep air,
The Moon's white cities, and the opal width
Of her small glowing lakes, her silver heights
Unvisited with dew of vagrant cloud,
And the unsounded, undescended depth
Of her black hollows. The clear Galaxy
Shorn of its hoary lustre, wonderful,
Distinct and vivid with sharp points of light,
Blaze within blaze, an unimagined depth
And harmony of planet-girded Suns
And moon-encircled planets, wheel in wheel,
Arched the wan Sapphire. Nay–the hum of men,
Or other things talking in unknown tongues,
And notes of busy life in distant worlds
Beat like a far wave on my anxious ear.

A maze of piercing, trackless, thrilling thoughts,
Involving and embracing each with each,
Rapid as fire, inextricably linked,
Expanding momently with every sight
And sound which struck the palpitating sense,
The issue of strong impulse, hurried through
The riven rapt brain; as when in some large lake
From pressure of descendant crags, which lapse
Disjointed, crumbling from their parent slope
At slender interval, the level calm
Is ridged with restless and increasing spheres
Which break upon each other, each the effect
Of separate impulse, but more fleet and strong

life, formed the personal basis of his faith'. Cp. *The Mystic* (p. 229), and *The Ancient Sage* (p. 1349). T. says of such an experience: 'It is no nebulous ecstasy, but a state of transcendent wonder, associated with absolute clearness of mind' (*Mem.* ii 473–4).

*104. PL* i 596: 'Shorn of his Beams'.

*112 ∧ 3*] *T.MS* of *Armageddon* has at this point *Armageddon* ii 40–50.

*113. trackless*: five times in Shelley.

Than its precursor, till the eye in vain
Amid the wild unrest of swimming shade
Dappled with hollow and alternate rise
Of interpenetrated arc, would scan
Definite round.
I know not if I shape
These things with accurate similitude
From visible objects, for but dimly now,
Less vivid than a half-forgotten dream,
The memory of that mental excellence
Comes o'er me, and it may be I entwine
The indecision of my present mind
With its past clearness, yet it seems to me
As even then the torrent of quick thought
Absorbed me from the nature of itself
With its own fleetness. Where is he that borne
Adown the sloping of an arrowy stream,
Could link his shallop to the fleeting edge,
And muse midway with philosophic calm
Upon the wondrous laws, which regulate
The fierceness of the bounding Element?

My thoughts which long had grovelled in the slime
Of this dull world, like dusky worms which house
Beneath unshaken waters, but at once
Upon some Earth-awakening day of Spring
Do pass from gloom to glory, and aloft
Winnow the purple, bearing on both sides
Double display of starlit wings which burn,
Fanlike and fibred, with intensest bloom;
Even so my thoughts, erewhile so low, now felt
Unutterable buoyancy and strength

*127. wild unrest*: *In Memoriam* xv 15.
*141.* Cp. Byron, *Childe Harold* III lxxi: 'arrowy Rhone'.
*145 ^ 6. T.MS* of *Armageddon* has thirteen lines on history.]
*146–54.* The simile anticipates the argument in *The Two Voices* 8–15; see p. 523 for the influence of Jacob Bryant.
*149. Earth-awakening*: from Shelley's *Ode to Liberty* 81, where the context includes 'river' and 'winged'.
*151. Winnow*: this sense derives from Milton, *PL* v 270: 'Winnows the buxom Air'. T. was probably influenced by Shelley's fondness for it; cp. 'Winnowing the crimson dawn', *Prometheus Unbound* II i 27.
*152–3.* Cp. Keats, *Endymion* iv 583–4: ''stead of feather'd wings, / Two fan-like fountains'.

To bear them upward through the trackless fields
Of undefined existence far and free.

Then first within the South methought I saw
A wilderness of spires, and chrystal pile
Of rampart upon rampart, dome on dome,
Illimitable range of battlement
On battlement, and the Imperial height
Of Canopy o'ercanopied.

Behind
In diamond light upsprung the dazzling peaks
Of Pyramids as far surpassing Earth's
As Heaven than Earth is fairer. Each aloft
Upon his narrowed Eminence bore globes
Of wheeling Suns, or Stars, or semblances
Of either, showering circular abyss
Of radiance. But the glory of the place
Stood out a pillared front of burnished gold,
Interminably high, if gold it were
Or metal more etherial, and beneath
Two doors of blinding brilliance, where no gaze
Might rest, stood open, and the eye could scan,
Through length of porch and valve and boundless hall,
Part of a throne of fiery flame, wherefrom
The snowy skirting of a garment hung,
And glimpse of multitudes of multitudes
That ministered around it–if I saw
These things distinctly, for my human brain
Staggered beneath the vision, and thick night
Came down upon my eyelids, and I fell.

With ministering hand he raised me up:
Then with a mournful and ineffable smile,

*156.* Wordsworth has 'trackless fields', *Excursion* iv 694.

*159–63.* Suggested by the view of the city from the mountain in *PL* iii 549–50; and by *Paradise Regained* iv 44–54: 'The Imperial Palace . . . / With gilded battlements, conspicuous far, / Turrets and Terrases, and glittering Spires.'

*164. peaks*] *Eversley*; cones *1829*. See headnote. Shelley liked 'upspring', 'upsprung'.

*176. valve*: door, as in Pope's *Odyssey* i 557.

*182. thick night*: *Macbeth* I v 49, and Keats, *Hyperion* ii 80.

*185–90.* These are the only lines in *Timbuctoo* which are to be found in the *1931* text of *Armageddon* but not in *T.MS.*

Which but to look on for a moment filled
My eyes with irresistible sweet tears,
In accents of majestic melody,
Like a swoln river's gushings in still night
Mingled with floating music, thus he spake:

'There is no mightier Spirit than I to sway
The heart of man: and teach him to attain
By shadowing forth the Unattainable;
And step by step to scale that mighty stair
Whose landing-place is wrapt about with clouds
Of glory' of Heaven. With earliest light of Spring,
And in the glow of sallow Summertide,
And in red Autumn when the winds are wild
With gambols, and when full-voiced Winter roofs
The headland with inviolate white snow,
I play about his heart a thousand ways,
Visit his eyes with visions, and his ears
With harmonies of wind and wave and wood,
–Of winds which tell of waters, and of waters
Betraying the close kisses of the wind–
And win him unto me: and few there be
So gross of heart who have not felt and known
A higher than they see: They with dim eyes
Behold me darkling. Lo! I have given *thee*
To understand my presence, and to feel
My fullness; I have filled thy lips with power.
I have raised thee nigher to the spheres of Heaven,
Man's first, last home: and thou with ravished sense
Listenest the lordly music flowing from
The illimitable years. I am the Spirit,
The permeating life which courseth through

*196. 1829* note: 'Be ye perfect even as your Father in Heaven is perfect', *Matthew* v 48. The apostrophe, 'glory' of Heaven', indicates elision; *Eversley* mistakenly sinks it to a comma.

*212–5.* Adapted for *Ode to Memory* 40–2: 'Sure she was nigher to heaven's spheres, / Listening the lordly music flowing from / The illimitable years.' Referring to the music of the spheres which man could hear before the Fall. *listening*: as a transitive verb, somewhat archaic, but cp. Wordsworth, *Evening Walk* 436 (1793 text): 'List'ning th'aëreal music'.

*215–24.* Paden (p. 152) points out that the high praise of mythology suggests the influence of Jacob Bryant's religious mythologizing in *A New System, or, An Analysis of Ancient Mythology* (1774–6), a greatly influential book which T. used for *A Fragment* (p. 289) and *Pierced through* (p. 472). There was a copy of Bryant at Somersby (*Lincoln*). Paden also cites Wordsworth's *Excursion* iv 630–940, on religion and imagination.

All the intricate and labyrinthine veins
Of the great vine of *Fable*, which, outspread
With growth of shadowing leaf and clusters rare,
Reacheth to every corner under Heaven,
Deep-rooted in the living soil of truth;
So that men's hopes and fears take refuge in
The fragrance of its complicated glooms,
And cool impleachèd twilights. Child of Man,
Seest thou yon river, whose translucent wave,
Forth issuing from the darkness, windeth through
The argent streets o' the city, imaging
The soft inversion of her tremulous Domes,
Her gardens frequent with the stately Palm,
Her Pagods hung with music of sweet bells,
Her obelisks of rangèd Chrysolite,
Minarets and towers? Lo! how he passeth by,
And gulphs himself in sands, as not enduring
To carry through the world those waves, which bore
The reflex of my City in their depths.
Oh City! oh latest Throne! where I was raised
To be a mystery of loveliness
Unto all eyes, the time is well-nigh come
When I must render up this glorious home
To keen *Discovery*: soon yon brilliant towers
Shall darken with the waving of her wand;
Darken, and shrink and shiver into huts,
Black specks amid a waste of dreary sand,
Low-built, mud-walled, Barbarian settlements.
How changed from this fair City!'

217. *labyrinthine veins*: Shelley, *Prometheus Unbound* I 490.
225. The Niger, on which Timbuctoo stood, was still thought by some to lose itself in the desert (l. 233). *translucent wave*: *Comus* 861, but T.'s use of 'imaging' (l. 227) suggests also Shelley, *Alastor* 457–9: 'A well, / Dark, gleaming, and of most translucent wave, / Images all the woven boughs above.'
229. *frequent*: crowded (Miltonic). Cp. *PL* ix 435: 'Stateliest Covert, Cedar, Pine, or Palme'.
240–45. A widespread feeling in the nineteenth century; see headnote. Paden (p. 140) cites Washington Irving's *Columbus* (1828), the Appendix on the Terrestrial Paradise: 'the mystery and conjectural charm that reigned over the greatest part of the world, and which have since been completely dispelled by modern discovery'. Cp. also Irving I iii: 'imagination went hand in hand with discovery, and as the latter groped its slow and cautious way, the former peopled all beyond with wonders'.

Thus far the Spirit:
Then parted Heaven-ward on the wing: and I
Was left alone on Calpe, and the Moon
Had fallen from the night, and all was dark!

## 68 Claribel

### A Melody

Published *1830*; from *1870* among 'Juvenilia'. 'All these ladies were evolved, like the camel, from my own consciousness' (T.). The name was possibly suggested by the innocent Claribel killed by her jealous lover, *Faerie Queene* II iv st. 29. Cp. the close of *My life is full of weary days* (p. 351).

I

Where Claribel low-lieth
The breezes pause and die,
Letting the rose-leaves fall:
But the solemn oak-tree sigheth,
Thick-leaved, ambrosial,
With an ancient melody
Of an inward agony,
Where Claribel low-lieth.

II

At eve the beetle boometh
Athwart the thicket lone:
At noon the wild bee hummeth
About the mossed headstone:
At midnight the moon cometh,
And looketh down alone.

*245. How changed*: an epic formula, Virgil's *quantum mutatus ab illo* (*Aeneid* ii 275–6). *PL* i 84–7: 'But O how fall'n! how chang'd / From him, who in the happy Realms of Light / Cloth'd with transcendent brightness didst outshine / Myriads though bright.' Cp. *Sense and Conscience* 79: 'How changed from that fair vision which, clad in light'. The application to a city may have been suggested by George Sandys's *Travels* (the 1658 edition was at Somersby, *Lincoln*; p. 89). Sandys says of Alexandria: 'Such was this Queen of Cities and *Metropolis* of *Africa*: but *Heu quantum* [*haec*] *Niobe, Niobe distabat ab illa!* "Ah how much different is that Niobe from this!", who now hath nothing left her but ruines . . ."'

¶ 68.*7. inward agony*: *To the Rev. W. H. Brookfield* 10, recalling T.'s Cambridge days.

*11. wild bee*] *1842*; bee low- *1830*.

Her song the lintwhite swelleth,
The clear-voiced mavis dwelleth,
The callow throstle lispeth,
The slumbrous wave outwelleth,
The babbling runnel crispeth,
The hollow grot replieth
Where Claribel low-lieth.

# 69 Lilian

Published *1830*; 'Juvenilia'. It is to Sophy Rawnsley, who was born 1818 (H. D. Rawnsley, *Memories of the Tennysons*, 1900, p. 64); for T.'s attraction to her, see Rader, pp. 60–6.

I

Airy, fairy Lilian,
Flitting, fairy Lilian,
When I ask her if she love me,
Claps her tiny hands above me,
Laughing all she can;
She'll not tell me if she love me,
Cruel little Lilian.

II

When my passion seeks
Pleasance in love-sighs,
She, looking through and through me
Thoroughly to undo me,
Smiling, never speaks:
So innocent-arch, so cunning-simple,
From beneath her gathered wimple
Glancing with black-beaded eyes,
Till the lightning laughters dimple
The baby-roses in her cheeks;
Then away she flies.

*15. lintwhite*: linnet.
*16. mavis*: songthrush.
*17. callow*] *1853*; fledgling *1830–51*.
*17–19.* Adapted by T. for *Mariana in the South* 42–3, *1832* text: 'She heard the callow nestling lisp, / And brimful meadow-runnels crisp'.
*19. crispeth*: curleth.
¶ *69.14. gathered*] *1842*; purfled *1830*. *wimple*: head-cloth.
*16–17.* In his review of *1842* in the *Church of England Quarterly Review* (Oct. 1842), Leigh Hunt gave these lines as 'an instance of that injudicious crowd-

III

Prythee weep, May Lilian!
Gaiety without eclipse
Wearieth me, May Lilian:
Through my very heart it thrilleth
When from crimson-threaded lips
Silver-treble laughter trilleth:
Prythee weep, May Lilian.

IV

Praying all I can,
If prayers will not hush thee,
Airy Lilian,
Like a rose-leaf I will crush thee,
Fairy Lilian.

# 70 Isabel

Published *1830*; 'Juvenilia'. 'The poet's mother was more or less described' (H.T.); the character of T.'s father is also touched on. Paden (pp. 157–8) connects the chastity of Isabel with the heroine of *Measure for Measure*. In his review of *1842* in the *Church of England Quarterly Review* (Oct. 1842), Leigh Hunt described *Isabel* as 'a panegyric of chastity in that ultra-super-exalting spirit of Beaumont and Fletcher, which renders the sincerity of it suspicious'. (The works of Beaumont and Fletcher were at Somersby, *Lincoln*.)

I

Eyes not down-dropt nor over-bright, but fed
With the clear-pointed flame of chastity,
Clear, without heat, undying, tended by
Pure vestal thoughts in the translucent fane
Of her still spirit; locks not wide-dispread,
Madonna-wise on either side her head;
Sweet lips whereon perpetually did reign
The summer calm of golden charity,
Were fixèd shadows of thy fixèd mood,
Reverèd Isabel, the crown and head,

ing of images which sometimes results from Mr Tennyson's desire to impress upon us the abundance of his thoughts'.
*23. Song of Solomon* iv 3, 'Thy lips are like a thread of scarlet'.
¶ 70. *5.* 'lockes ... wide dispred', *Faerie Queene* II iii 30, describing the chaste Belphoebe.

The stately flower of female fortitude,
Of perfect wifehood and pure lowlihead.

II

The intuitive decision of a bright
And thorough-edgèd intellect to part
Error from crime; a prudence to withhold;
The laws of marriage charactered in gold
Upon the blanchèd tablets of her heart;
A love still burning upward, giving light
To read those laws; an accent very low
In blandishment, but a most silver flow
Of subtle-pacèd counsel in distress,
Right to the heart and brain, though undescried,
Winning its way with extreme gentleness
Through all the outworks of suspicious pride;
A courage to endure and to obey;
A hate of gossip parlance, and of sway,
Crowned Isabel, through all her placid life,
The queen of marriage, a most perfect wife.

III

The mellowed reflex of a winter moon;
A clear stream flowing with a muddy one,
Till in its onward current it absorbs
With swifter movement and in purer light
The vexèd eddies of its wayward brother:
A leaning and upbearing parasite,
Clothing the stem, which else had fallen quite
With clustered flower-bells and ambrosial orbs
Of rich fruit-bunches leaning on each other–
Shadow forth thee:–the world hath not another
(Though all her fairest forms are types of thee,
And thou of God in thy great charity)
Of such a finished chastened purity.

*12. lowlihead*: *OED* has no example between Lydgate and T.

*16. marriage*] *1842*; wifehood *1830*.

*17. blanchèd*] *1842*; blenchèd *1830*. *2 Corinthians* iii 3, 'tables of the heart'. In his review of *1842*, Leigh Hunt compared Thomas Heywood's famous phrase in *A Woman Killed with Kindness*: 'The expression "*blanched* tablets of the heart," will not do at all after its beautiful original in the old poet, "the *red-leaved* tablets [tables] of the heart"'.

*26. gossip*: silly woman's.

# 71 Leonine Elegiacs

Published *1830* as *Elegiacs*; not reprinted till restored *1884*, 'Juvenilia'. Cp. *Elegiacs* (p. 262). *Leonine:* 'a kind of verse which rhyme at every hemistic, the middle always chiming to the end' (*English Encyclopaedia*, 1802, of which there was a copy at Somersby, *Lincoln*).

Low-flowing breezes are roaming the broad valley dimmed in the gloaming:
Thorough the black-stemmed pines only the far river shines.
Creeping through blossomy rushes and bowers of rose-blowing bushes,
Down by the poplar tall rivulets babble and fall.
Barketh the shepherd-dog cheerly; the grasshopper carolleth clearly;
Deeply the wood-dove coos; shrilly the owlet halloos;
Winds creep; dews fall chilly: in her first sleep earth breathes stilly:
Over the pools in the burn water-gnats murmur and mourn.
Sadly the far kine loweth: the glimmering water outfloweth:
Twin peaks shadowed with pine slope to the dark hyaline.
Low-throned Hesper is stayèd between the two peaks; but the Naiad
Throbbing in mild unrest holds him beneath in her breast.
The ancient poetess singeth, that Hesperus all things bringeth,
Smoothing the wearied mind: bring me my love, Rosalind.
Thou comest morning or even; she cometh not morning or even.
False-eyed Hesper, unkind, where is my sweet Rosalind?

¶ 71.*6. wood-dove*] *1884*; turtle *1830*.
*8.* Keats, *To Autumn* 27: 'Then in a wailful choir the small gnats mourn'. The natural history here had encouraged T. to suppress the poem: 'Some of the things don't seem to agree with the time spoken of . . . the water-gnats are not right: they would not be out so late' (1883; William Allingham's *Diary*, 1907, p. 319). Allingham's praise of the poem at this date will have encouraged T. to reprint it.
*10. shadowed with pine*: adapted for *Œnone* 96, *1832* text: 'Shadowed with singing pine'. *hyaline*: like glass; H.T. compares ὡς θάλασσα ὑαλίνη ('a sea of glass like unto crystal'), *Revelation* iv 6; probably via *PL* vii 619.
*11. Hesper*: the evening star.
*13.* T. compares Sappho, *Fragment 149*: ϝέσπερε, πάντα φέρεις, ὄσα φαίνολις ἐσκέδασ' αὔως, / φέρεις ὄϊν, φέρεις αἶγα, φέρεις ματέρι παῖδα. ('Evening Star that bringest back all that lightsome Dawn hath scattered afar, thou bringest the sheep, thou bringest the goat, thou bringest her child home to the mother'.) Cp. *The Hesperides* 96: 'All good things are in the west'; and *Locksley Hall Sixty Years After* 185: 'Hesper, whom the poet called the Bringer home of all good things'.
*14.* See *Rosalind* (p. 438).
*15. or*] [*the first*] *1884*; and *1830*.

# 72 *The 'How' and the 'Why'

?

Published *1830*, not reprinted. The poems not reprinted often had elaborate schemes of rhyme and metre, as here. Cp. *Song* [*Who can say*] (p. 453). In his review of *1830* in *The Tatler*, 24 Feb. 1831, Leigh Hunt spoke of 'a piece of perplexity called *The 'How' and the 'Why'*, which the uninitiated readers of Mr Wordsworth's "Moods" would think puerile, as they did some of those; but it is man's writing. We only hope that it is not sick writing, and that the author, in these mystifications of himself, only feels the pleasure of a healthy wonderment.'

I am any man's suitor,
If any will be my tutor:
Some say this life is pleasant,
  Some think it speedeth fast:
In time there is no present,
In eternity no future,
  In eternity no past.
We laugh, we cry, we are born, we die,
Who will riddle me the *how* and the *why*?

The bulrush nods unto its brother,
The wheatears whisper to each other:
What is it they say? What do they there?
Why two and two make four? Why round is not
  square?
Why the rock stands still, and the light clouds fly?
Why the heavy oak groans, and the white willows
  sigh?
Why deep is not high, and high is not deep?
Whether we wake, or whether we sleep?
Whether we sleep, or whether we die?
How you are you? Why I am I?
Who will riddle me the *how* and the *why*?

The world is somewhat; it goes on somehow;
But what is the meaning of *then* and *now*?
  I feel there is something; but how and what?
I know there is somewhat; but what and why?
I cannot tell if that somewhat be I.
  The little bird pipeth–'why? why?'
In the summerwoods when the sun falls low

¶ 72.23–4. Cp. *De Profundis* 62–3 (p. 1283): 'We feel we are nothing–for all is Thou and in Thee; / We feel we are something–*that* also has come from Thee.'

And the great bird sits on the opposite bough,
And stares in his face and shouts, 'how? how?'
And the black owl scuds down the mellow twilight,
And chaunts, 'how? how?' the whole of the night.

Why the life goes when the blood is spilt?
  What the life is? where the soul may lie?
Why a church is with a steeple built;
  And a house with a chimneypot?
Who will riddle me the how and the what?
  Who will riddle me the what and the why?

# 73 Mariana

Published *1830*; 'Juvenilia'. T. says: 'The *moated grange* was no particular grange, but one which rose to the music of Shakespeare's words.' The epigraph is from *Measure for Measure* III i 212ff: 'She should this Angelo have married: was affianced to her by oath, and the nuptial appointed. . . . Left her in her tears, and dried not one of them with his comfort. . . . What a merit were it in death to take this poor maid from the world! . . . There, at the moated grange, resides this dejected Mariana.' The poem was influenced by Keats's *Isabella* 233ff, where she waits in vain: 'She weeps alone for pleasures not to be; / Sorely she wept until the night came on . . . / And so she pined, and so she died forlorn.' Keats's 'aloof/roof' may have suggested the rhymes in ll. 73–5. Cp. Samuel Rogers, *Captivity* (1801): 'Caged in old woods, whose reverend echoes wake / When the hern screams along the distant lake, / Her little heart oft flutters to be free, / Oft sighs to turn the unrelenting key. / In vain! the nurse that rusted relic wears, / Nor moved by gold – nor to be moved by tears; / And terraced walls their black reflection throw / On the green-mantled moat that sleeps below.' These eight lines T. later praised to Palgrave 'for their delicate music' (*Mem.* ii 503). Rogers' *Poems* (1812) was at Somersby (*Lincoln*).

T. seems to have invented the stanza form; J. F. A. Pyre remarks that the best of the early poems are those that stay most strictly with a stanza, as here (*The Formation of Tennyson's Style*, 1921, p. 26). Cp. *Mariana in the South* (p. 361 below).

*Mariana in the moated grange*
(*Measure for Measure*)

With blackest moss the flower-plots
  Were thickly crusted, one and all:

¶ 73.*1–2*. Adapted from *The Outcast* 23 (1826): 'The wet moss crusts the parting wall', followed by 'knots'.

The rusted nails fell from the knots
That held the pear to the gable-wall.
The broken sheds looked sad and strange:
Unlifted was the clinking latch;
Weeded and worn the ancient thatch
Upon the lonely moated grange.
She only said, 'My life is dreary,
He cometh not,' she said;
She said, 'I am aweary, aweary,
I would that I were dead!'

Her tears fell with the dews at even;
Her tears fell ere the dews were dried;
She could not look on the sweet heaven,
Either at morn or eventide.
After the flitting of the bats,
When thickest dark did trance the sky,
She drew her casement-curtain by,
And glanced athwart the glooming flats.
She only said, 'The night is dreary,
He cometh not,' she said;
She said, 'I am aweary, aweary,
I would that I were dead!'

*4. pear*] *1862*; peach *1830–60*. T. says: '"peach" spoils the desolation of the picture. It is not a characteristic of the scenery I had in mind.' *gable-wall*] *1869*; garden-wall *1830–68*.

*13.* Cp. Horace, *Odes* II ix 10–12: *nec tibi Vespero / surgente decedunt amores / nec rapidum fugiente solem.* ('Nor do thy words of love cease either when Vesper comes out at evening, or when he flies before the swiftly coursing sun'.) Cp. also 'Her tears are mixed with the beaded dews', from *Song* [*I' the glooming light*] (p. 214), a poem comparable to *Mariana*: 'Death standeth by; / She will not die; / With glazèd eye / She looks at her grave: she cannot sleep; / Ever alone / She maketh her moan . . .'. John Churton Collins remarked that ll. 13–14 were evidently adapted from Cinna: *Te matutinus flentem conspexit Eous, / Te flentem paulo vidit post Hesperus idem.* Alongside this suggestion, T. wrote: 'I read this for the first time' (*Cornhill*, Jan. 1880, *Lincoln*).

*15.* Cp. the deserted Dido, *Aeneid* iv 451: *taedet caeli convexa tueri* ('she is weary of gazing on the arch of heaven').

*18. trance*: throw into a trance. T.'s is the earliest figurative use in *OED*.

*20.* Cp. *A Fragment* 17: 'Looking athwart the burning flats'; and *Fatima* 13: 'I looked athwart the burning drouth', where the suffering heroine awaits her lover. Keats has 'athwart the gloom', *Sleep and Poetry* 146.

Upon the middle of the night,
  Waking she heard the night-fowl crow:
The cock sung out an hour ere light:
  From the dark fen the oxen's low
Came to her: without hope of change,
  In sleep she seemed to walk forlorn,
  Till cold winds woke the gray-eyed morn
About the lonely moated grange.
    She only said, 'The day is dreary,
      He cometh not,' she said;
    She said, 'I am aweary, aweary,
      I would that I were dead!'

About a stone-cast from the wall
  A sluice with blackened waters slept,
And o'er it many, round and small,
  The clustered marish-mosses crept.
Hard by a poplar shook alway,
  All silver-green with gnarlèd bark:
  For leagues no other tree did mark
The level waste, the rounding gray.
    She only said, 'My life is dreary,
      He cometh not,' she said;
    She said, 'I am aweary, aweary,
      I would that I were dead!'

And ever when the moon was low,
  And the shrill winds were up and away,
In the white curtain, to and fro,
  She saw the gusty shadow sway.
But when the moon was very low,
  And wild winds bound within their cell,
  The shadow of the poplar fell
Upon her bed, across her brow.

25. *Measure for Measure* IV i 35: 'Upon the heavy middle of the night'; and Keats, *Eve of St Agnes* 49: 'Upon the honey'd middle of the night'.
25–6. T. compares the ballad of Clerk Saunders: 'O cocks are crowing of merry midnight'; and H.T. adds *Oriana* 12: 'At midnight the cock was crowing'.
31. *gray-eyed morn*: *Romeo and Juliet* II iii 1.
40. *marish-mosses*: 'the little marsh-moss lumps that float on the surface of water' (T.).
43. *mark*] *1845*; dark *1830–43*.
50. *and*] *1842*; an' *1830*.
54. The cave of Aeolus, mentioned in *Lycidas* 97– cp. l. 80*n*.

She only said, 'The night is dreary,
He cometh not,' she said;
She said, 'I am aweary, aweary,
I would that I were dead!'

All day within the dreamy house,
The doors upon their hinges creaked;
The blue fly sung in the pane; the mouse
Behind the mouldering wainscot shrieked,
Or from the crevice peered about.
Old faces glimmered through the doors,
Old footsteps trod the upper floors,
Old voices called her from without.
She only said, 'My life is dreary,
He cometh not,' she said;
She said, 'I am aweary, aweary,
I would that I were dead!'

The sparrow's chirrup on the roof,
The slow clock ticking, and the sound
Which to the wooing wind aloof
The poplar made, did all confound
Her sense; but most she loathed the hour
When the thick-moted sunbeam lay
Athwart the chambers, and the day
Was sloping toward his western bower.
Then, said she, 'I am very dreary,
He will not come,' she said;
She wept, 'I am aweary, aweary,
Oh God, that I were dead!'

# 74 To – [Clear-headed friend]

Published *1830*; 'Juvenilia'. T. says: 'The first lines were addressed to Blakesley . . . but the poem wandered off to describe an imaginary man'. J. W. Blakesley (1808–85) was a friend of T.'s at Cambridge, and later Dean of Lincoln. T. said: 'He ought to be Lord Chancellor, for he is a subtle and powerful reasoner, and an honest man' (*Mem.* i 38). Cp. T.'s other poems on his contemporaries, particularly *To J.M.K.* (p. 257).

*63. in*] *1850*; i' *1830–48*. Cp. the empty house in *Maud* i 257–60, with its 'shrieking rush of the wainscot mouse' (p. 1055).
*80*] *1842*; Downsloped was westering in his bower. *1830*. Echoing *Lycidas* 31: 'had slop'd his westering wheel'.

I

Clear-headed friend, whose joyful scorn,
Edged with sharp laughter, cuts atwain
The knots that tangle human creeds,
The wounding cords that bind and strain
The heart until it bleeds,
Ray-fringèd eyelids of the morn
Roof not a glance so keen as thine:
If aught of prophecy be mine,
Thou wilt not live in vain.

II

Low-cowering shall the Sophist sit;
Falsehood shall bare her plaited brow:
Fair-fronted Truth shall droop not now
With shrilling shafts of subtle wit.
Nor martyr-flames, nor trenchant swords
Can do away that ancient lie;
A gentler death shall Falsehood die,
Shot through and through with cunning words.

III

Weak Truth a-leaning on her crutch,
Wan, wasted Truth in her utmost need,
Thy kingly intellect shall feed,
Until she be an athlete bold,
And weary with a finger's touch
Those writhèd limbs of lightning speed;
Like that strange angel which of old,
Until the breaking of the light,

¶ 74.*3. knots that tangle*] *1842*; knotted lies of *1830*.
*4. that*] *1842*; which *1830*.
*6–7*. Cp. *To a Lady Sleeping* 1–3: 'fringèd lids . . . Unroof the shrines of clearest vision'. Keats, *Endymion* ii 563: 'fringed lids'. *eyelids of the morn*: *Lycidas* 26, as T. points out (deriving from *Job* xli 18).
*8*. Cp. Nathaniel Lee, *To the Prince and Princess of Orange*: 'If aught of Prophesie their Souls inspire' (Dryden's *Miscellany Poems* iii, 1693).
*11–12*. Cp. Keats, *Endymion* i 759–62: '"Why pierce high-fronted honour to the quick / For nothing but a dream?" Hereat the youth / Look'd up: a conflicting of shame and ruth / Was in his plaited brow.'
*13–14*. Cp. *Memory* [*Ay me*] 4: 'subtle shafts of pierceant flame'.
*14*. 'trenchant sword', *Timon of Athens* IV iii 116.
*23. limbs*: of Falsehood.
*24–9*. *Genesis* xxxii 22–31; Jacob 'passed over the ford Jabbok . . . And Jacob was left alone: and there wrestled a man with him, until the breaking of the day. And when he saw, that he prevailed not against him, he touched

Wrestled with wandering Israel,
Past Yabbok brook the livelong night,
And heaven's mazèd signs stood still
In the dim tract of Penuel.

# 75 Madeline

Published *1830*; 'Juvenilia'. The name was perhaps suggested by Keats's *Eve of St Agnes*. Arthur Hallam implied that it was to some extent a portrait (Rader, p. 138).

I

Thou art not steeped in golden languors,
No trancèd summer calm is thine,
Ever varying Madeline.
Through light and shadow thou dost range,
Sudden glances, sweet and strange,
Delicious spites and darling angers,
And airy forms of flitting change.

II

Smiling, frowning, evermore,
Thou art perfect in love-lore.
Revealings deep and clear are thine
Of wealthy smiles: but who may know
Whether smile or frown be fleeter?
Whether smile or frown be sweeter,
Who may know?
Frowns perfect-sweet along the brow

the hollow of his thigh: and the hollow of Jacob's thigh was out of joint, as he wrestled with him . . . And he said, Thy name shall be called no more Jacob, but Israel: for as a prince hast thou power with God, and with men, and hast prevailed . . . And Jacob called the name of the place Penuel: for I have seen God face to face, and my life is preserved. And as he passed over Penuel, the sun rose upon him, and he halted upon his thigh.'

*27.* T. remarks: 'Jabbock not so sweet as Yabbok . . . The Hebrew J is Y'.

*28.* Cp. Milton, *Nativity Ode* 69–70: 'The Stars with deep amaze / Stand fixt in stedfast gaze.'

*29.* Cp. Shelley, *Alastor* 556: 'dim tracts'.

¶ 75.*1.* Cp. Keats, *Ode on Indolence* 47: 'steep'd in honied indolence' (written 1819, but not published till 1848).

*2.* In contrast with the 'summer calm' of *Isabel* (p. 183). *trancèd summer*: Keats, *Hyperion* i 72.

*7. airy form*: Keats, *Endymion* ii 301.

Light-glooming over eyes divine,
Like little clouds sun-fringed, are thine,
Ever varying Madeline.
Thy smile and frown are not aloof
From one another,
Each to each is dearest brother;
Hues of the silken sheeny woof
Momently shot into each other.
All the mystery is thine;
Smiling, frowning, evermore,
Thou art perfect in love-lore,
Ever varying Madeline.

III

A subtle, sudden flame,
By veering passion fanned,
About thee breaks and dances:
When I would kiss thy hand,
The flush of angered shame
O'erflows thy calmer glances,
And o'er black brows drops down
A sudden-curvèd frown:
But when I turn away,
Thou, willing me to stay,
Wooest not, nor vainly wranglest;
But, looking fixedly the while,
All my bounding heart entanglest
In a golden-netted smile;
Then in madness and in bliss,
If my lips should dare to kiss
Thy taper fingers amorously,
Again thou blushest angerly;
And o'er black brows drops down
A sudden-curvèd frown.

# 76 The Merman

Published *1830*; 'Juvenilia'. See *The Mermaid* and headnote (p. 195).

I

Who would be
A merman bold,

*16–17*. Cp. Keats, *Endymion* iii 872: 'thunder-gloomings'. Keats's Madeline has 'maiden eyes divine', rhyming with her name, *Eve of St Agnes* 57.
*44. amorously*] three-times-three *1830 corrected in Errata*. It suggested she had nine fingers. *taper fingers*: Keats, *I stood tip-toe* 59.
*45*. Keats, *Hyperion* i 182: 'Flush'd angerly'.

Sitting alone,
Singing alone
Under the sea,
With a crown of gold,
On a throne?

II

I would be a merman bold,
I would sit and sing the whole of the day;
I would fill the sea-halls with a voice of power;
But at night I would roam abroad and play
With the mermaids in and out of the rocks,
Dressing their hair with the white sea-flower;
And holding them back by their flowing locks
I would kiss them often under the sea,
And kiss them again till they kissed me
Laughingly, laughingly;
And then we would wander away, away
To the pale-green sea-groves straight and high,
Chasing each other merrily.

III

There would be neither moon nor star;
But the wave would make music above us afar–
Low thunder and light in the magic night–
Neither moon nor star.
We would call aloud in the dreamy dells,
Call to each other and whoop and cry
All night, merrily, merrily;
They would pelt me with starry spangles and shells,
Laughing and clapping their hands between,
All night, merrily, merrily:
But I would throw to them back in mine
Turkis and agate and almondine:
Then leaping out upon them unseen
I would kiss them often under the sea,
And kiss them again till they kissed me
Laughingly, laughingly.
Oh! what a happy life were mine
Under the hollow-hung ocean green!
Soft are the moss-beds under the sea;
We would live merrily, merrily.

¶ *76.32. Turkis*: Miltonic (*Comus* 894), for turquoise, to avoid the 'ugly nasal sound' (T.). *almondine*: 'a small violet garnet' (T.).
*40.* The refrain was suggested by Ariel's, *The Tempest* V i 92–3: 'Merrily, merrily, shall I live now, / Under the blossom that hangs on the bough.'

# 77 The Mermaid

Published *1830*; 'Juvenilia'. Sources: Walter Scott's *Minstrelsy of the Scottish Border*, which included John Leyden's *The Mermaid*; T. C. Croker's *Fairy Legends* (1825–8), which included Grimm's amorous underworld, and which T. later owned (*Lincoln*); and possibly Thomas Keightley's *Fairy Mythology* (1828). On all of these, see Paden (pp. 156–7), who adds that mermen and mermaids were types of the great deities in G. S. Faber's religious mythologizing. Cp. *The Merman* (p. 193); also *The Sea-Fairies* (p. 254), and *The Kraken* (p. 246). T. quotes Walter Scott: 'No more misshapen from the waist, / But like a maid of mortal frame.' In a draft of *Eversley* (*Lincoln*), H.T. quotes T.: 'I never thought of Mermen and Mermaidens with tails.'

I

Who would be
A mermaid fair,
Singing alone,
Combing her hair
Under the sea,
In a golden curl
With a comb of pearl,
On a throne?

II

I would be a mermaid fair;
I would sing to myself the whole of the day;
With a comb of pearl I would comb my hair;
And still as I combed I would sing and say,
'Who is it loves me? who loves not me?'
I would comb my hair till my ringlets would fall
Low adown, low adown,
From under my starry sea-bud crown
Low adown and around,
And I should look like a fountain of gold
Springing alone
With a shrill inner sound,
Over the throne
In the midst of the hall;
Till that great sea-snake under the sea

¶ 77.*16*. Combining Shelley's 'crowns of sea-buds', *Rosalind* 1081, with his 'starry sea-flower crowns', *Prometheus Unbound* III ii 47, on the Nereids under the sea.

*23–7*. Paden points out that there is no obvious source for the sea-snake's

From his coilèd sleeps in the central deeps
Would slowly trail himself sevenfold
Round the hall where I sate, and look in at the gate
With his large calm eyes for the love of me.
And all the mermen under the sea
Would feel their immortality
Die in their hearts for the love of me.

III

But at night I would wander away, away,
I would fling on each side my low-flowing locks,
And lightly vault from the throne and play
With the mermen in and out of the rocks;
We would run to and fro, and hide and seek,
On the broad sea-wolds in the crimson shells,
Whose silvery spikes are nighest the sea.
But if any came near I would call, and shriek,
And adown the steep like a wave I would leap
From the diamond-ledges that jut from the dells;
For I would not be kissed by all who would list,
Of the bold merry mermen under the sea;
They would sue me, and woo me, and flatter me,
In the purple twilights under the sea;
But the king of them all would carry me,
Woo me, and win me, and marry me,
In the branching jaspers under the sea;
Then all the dry pied things that be
In the hueless mosses under the sea
Would curl round my silver feet silently,
All looking up for the love of me.
And if I should carol aloud, from aloft
All things that are forkèd, and hornèd, and soft
Would lean out from the hollow sphere of the sea,
All looking down for the love of me.

love of the mermaid, though Leyden mentions the snake; possibly T. was influenced by G. S. Faber on Vivien, 'beneath the waters of an inchanted lake, while she caresses a vast serpent into which form she had metamorphosed one of her lovers'. T. had written of the power of desire over 'the mighty sea-snake' in *Love* [*Almighty Love*] (p. 145).

*29–30.* As Paden says, this refers to the belief that true human love extinguishes the immortality of a merman.

*48. dry*: probably meaning crustaceous; contrast 'soft', l. 53.

*54.* 'An underworld of which the sea is the heaven' (T.).

# 78 Supposed Confessions of a Second-Rate Sensitive Mind

Published *1830*, with the longer title . . . *Mind Not In Unity With Itself*; not reprinted till restored *1884*, 'Juvenilia'. Cp. *Remorse* (p. 87); *Perdidi Diem* (p. 269); and *Pierced through* (p. 472). The doubts precede Arthur Hallam's death, and anticipate *The Two Voices* and *In Memoriam*. T. says: 'If some kind friend had taken him by the hand and said, "Come, work"–"Look not every man on his own things, but every man also on the things of others" (*Philippians* ii 4)–he might have been a happy man, though sensitive.' T. quarried it for *A Fragment* (p. 289).

O God! my God! have mercy now.
I faint, I fall. Men say that Thou
Didst die for me, for such as *me*,
Patient of ill, and death, and scorn,
And that my sin was as a thorn
Among the thorns that girt Thy brow,
Wounding Thy soul.–That even now,
In this extremest misery
Of ignorance, I should require
A sign! and if a bolt of fire
Would rive the slumbrous summer noon
While I do pray to Thee alone,
Think my belief would stronger grow!
Is not my human pride brought low?
The boastings of my spirit still?
The joy I had in my freewill
All cold, and dead, and corpse-like grown?
And what is left to me, but Thou,
And faith in Thee? Men pass me by;
Christians with happy countenances–
And children all seem full of Thee!
And women smile with saint-like glances
Like Thine own mother's when she bowed
Above Thee, on that happy morn
When angels spake to men aloud,
And Thou and peace to earth were born.

¶ 78.*2*. Cp. Shelley, *Indian Serenade* 18: 'I faint! I fail!'
*9–10*. *1 Corinthians* i 22, 'For the Jews require a sign'; *Matthew* xii 39, 'an evil and adulterous generation seeketh after a sign; and there shall no sign be given to it'.
*11*. *the slumbrous summer noon*: incorporated in *A Fragment* 11.

Goodwill to me as well as all–
I one of them: my brothers they:
Brothers in Christ–a world of peace
And confidence, day after day;
And trust and hope till things should cease,
And then one Heaven receive us all.

How sweet to have a common faith!
To hold a common scorn of death!
And at a burial to hear
The creaking cords which wound and eat
Into my human heart, whene'er
Earth goes to earth, with grief, not fear,
With hopeful grief, were passing sweet!

Thrice happy state again to be
The trustful infant on the knee!
Who lets his rosy fingers play
About his mother's neck, and knows
Nothing beyond his mother's eyes.
They comfort him by night and day;
They light his little life alway;
He hath no thought of coming woes;

*36.* Cp. *To–[Clear-headed friend]* 4: 'The wounding cords that bind and strain'.

*39 ∧ 40]*
A grief not uninformed, and dull,
Hearted with hope, of hope as full
As is the blood with life, or night
And a dark cloud with rich moonlight.
To stand beside a grave, and see
The red small atoms wherewith we
Are built, and smile in calm, and say–
'These little motes and grains shall be
'Clothed on with immortality
'More glorious than the noon of day.
'All that is passed into the flowers,
'And into beasts, and other men,
'And all the Norland whirlwind showers
'From open vaults, and all the sea
'O'erwashes with sharp salts, again
'Shall fleet together all, and be
'Indued with immortality.' *1830*

Cp. l. [9] with *2 Corinthians* v 4, 'not for that we would be unclothed, but clothed upon, that mortality might be swallowed up of life'. 'The Norland whirlwind' of l. [13] is in *Oriana* 6.

*42. rosy] 1884*; waxen *1830*.

He hath no care of life or death;
Scarce outward signs of joy arise,
Because the Spirit of happiness
And perfect rest so inward is;
And loveth so his innocent heart,
Her temple and her place of birth,
Where she would ever wish to dwell,
Life of the fountain there, beneath
Its salient springs, and far apart,
Hating to wander out on earth,
Or breathe into the hollow air,
Whose chillness would make visible
Her subtil, warm, and golden breath,
Which mixing with the infant's blood,
Fulfils him with beatitude.
Oh! sure it is a special care
Of God, to fortify from doubt,
To arm in proof, and guard about
With triple-mailèd trust, and clear
Delight, the infant's dawning year.

Would that my gloomèd fancy were
As thine, my mother, when with brows
Propt on thy knees, my hands upheld
In thine, I listened to thy vows,
For me outpoured in holiest prayer–
For me unworthy!–and beheld
Thy mild deep eyes upraised, that knew
The beauty and repose of faith,
And the clear spirit shining through.
Oh! wherefore do we grow awry
From roots which strike so deep? why dare
Paths in the desert? Could not I
Bow myself down, where thou hast knelt,
To the earth–until the ice would melt
Here, and I feel as thou hast felt?
What Devil had the heart to scathe
Flowers thou hadst reared–to brush the dew
From thine own lily, when thy grave
Was deep, my mother, in the clay?
Myself? Is is thus? Myself? Had I
So little love for thee? But why
Prevailed not thy pure prayers? Why pray

*56. salient springs*: *Adeline* 26; as in Wordsworth, *The Borderers* 1788. Cp. 'the salient blood' (i.e. leaping), *Sonnet* [*Shall the hag*] 5.

*65. proof*: armour.

To one who heeds not, who can save
But will not? Great in faith, and strong
Against the grief of circumstance
Wert thou, and yet unheard. What if
Thou pleadest still, and seest me drive
Through utter dark a full-sailed skiff,
Unpiloted i' the echoing dance
Of reboant whirlwinds, stooping low
Unto the death, not sunk! I know
At matins and at evensong,
That thou, if thou wert yet alive,
In deep and daily prayers wouldst strive
To reconcile me with thy God.
Albeit, my hope is gray, and cold
At heart, thou wouldest murmur still–
'Bring this lamb back into Thy fold,
My Lord, if so it be Thy will.'
Wouldst tell me I must brook the rod
And chastisement of human pride;
That pride, the sin of devils, stood
Betwixt me and the light of God!
That hitherto I had defied
And had rejected God–that grace
Would drop from his o'er-brimming love,
As manna on my wilderness,
If I would pray–that God would move
And strike the hard, hard rock, and thence,
Sweet in their utmost bitterness,
Would issue tears of penitence
Which would keep green hope's life. Alas!
I think that pride hath now no place
Nor sojourn in me. I am void,
Dark, formless, utterly destroyed.
Why not believe then? Why not yet
Anchor thy frailty there, where man
Hath moored and rested? Ask the sea
At midnight, when the crisp slope waves

97. *reboant*: re-bellowing; T.'s is the earliest example in *OED*.
116. *Numbers* xx 11.
121–2. *void, dark*: Coleridge's *Dejection* 21. Cp. *On Sublimity* 70: 'formless and still and dark'. Also several words are taken up from *Paradise Lost* iii 11–16: 'waters dark and deep, / Won from the void and formless infinite. / Thee I re-visit now with bolder wing, / Escap't the *Stygian* Pool, though long detain'd / In that obscure sojourn, while in my flight / Through utter and through middle darkness borne . . .'.
126. *slope*: sloping.

After a tempest, rib and fret
The broad-imbasèd beach, why he
Slumbers not like a mountain tarn?
Wherefore his ridges are not curls
And ripples of an inland mere?
Wherefore he moaneth thus, nor can
Draw down into his vexèd pools
All that blue heaven which hues and paves
The other? I am too forlorn,
Too shaken: my own weakness fools
My judgment, and my spirit whirls,
Moved from beneath with doubt and fear.

'Yet,' said I, in my morn of youth,
The unsunned freshness of my strength,
When I went forth in quest of truth,
'It is man's privilege to doubt,
If so be that from doubt at length,
Truth may stand forth unmoved of change,
An image with profulgent brows,
And perfect limbs, as from the storm
Of running fires and fluid range
Of lawless airs, at last stood out
This excellence and solid form
Of constant beauty. For the Ox
Feeds in the herb, and sleeps, or fills
The hornèd valleys all about,
And hollows of the fringèd hills
In summer heats, with placid lows
Unfearing, till his own blood flows
About his hoof. And in the flocks
The lamb rejoiceth in the year,

*126–9. A Fragment* 10–11 has 'broadbased . . . sloped . . . slumbrous' (cp. l. 11*n*).
*129.* Cp. *Ode: O Bosky Brook* 22: 'the mountain tarn's unbroken sleep'.
*145.* Adapted for *A Fragment* 3: 'A perfect Idol with profulgent brows'.
*147–8.* Cp. *The Princess* ii 101: 'This world was once a fluid haze of light'.
*150–71.* G. O. Marshall (*A Tennyson Handbook*, 1963, p. 32) notes the influence of Pope, *Essay on Man* i 77–86: 'Heav'n from all creatures hides the book of Fate, / All but the page prescrib'd, their present state; / From brutes what men, from men what spirits know: / Or who could suffer Being here below? / The lamb thy riot dooms to bleed to-day, / Had he thy Reason, would he skip and play? / Pleas'd to the last, he crops the flow'ry food, / And licks the hand just rais'd to shed his blood. / Oh blindness to the future! kindly giv'n, / That each may fill the circle mark'd by Heav'n.'

And raceth freely with his fere,
And answers to his mother's calls
From the flowered furrow. In a time,
Of which he wots not, run short pains
Through his warm heart; and then, from whence
He knows not, on his light there falls
A shadow; and his native slope,
Where he was wont to leap and climb,
Floats from his sick and filmèd eyes,
And something in the darkness draws
His forehead earthward, and he dies.
Shall man live thus, in joy and hope
As a young lamb, who cannot dream,
Living, but that he shall live on?
Shall we not look into the laws
Of life and death, and things that seem,
And things that be, and analyse
Our double nature, and compare
All creeds till we have found the one,
If one there be?' Ay me! I fear
All may not doubt, but everywhere
Some must clasp Idols. Yet, my God,
Whom call I Idol? Let Thy dove
Shadow me over, and my sins
Be unremembered, and Thy love
Enlighten me. Oh teach me yet
Somewhat before the heavy clod
Weighs on me, and the busy fret
Of that sharp-headed worm begins
In the gross blackness underneath.

O weary life! O weary death!
O spirit and heart made desolate!
O damnèd vacillating state!

# 79 *The Burial of Love

Published *1830*, not reprinted. The poems not reprinted often had elaborate rhyme schemes and stanza forms, as here. Cp. *Song* [*I' the glooming light*] for the mood and the personification (p. 214).

*158. fere*: companion.
*169. man*] *1884*; men *1830*.
*181. Shadow*: to protect with wings, a biblical sense.

His eyes in eclipse,
Palecold his lips,
The light of his hopes unfed,
Mute his tongue,
His bow unstrung
With the tears he hath shed,
Backward drooping his graceful head,
Love is dead:
His last arrow is sped;
He hath not another dart;
Go–carry him to his dark deathbed;
Bury him in the cold cold heart–
Love is dead.

Oh, truest love! art thou forlorn,
And unrevenged? thy pleasant wiles
Forgotten, and thine innocent joy?
Shall hollowhearted apathy,
The cruellest form of perfect scorn,
With languor of most hateful smiles,
For ever write,
In the withered light
Of the tearless eye,
An epitaph that all may spy?
No! sooner she herself shall die.

For her the showers shall not fall,
Nor the round sun shine that shineth to all;
Her light shall into darkness change;
For her the green grass shall not spring,
Nor the rivers flow, nor the sweet birds sing,
Till Love have his full revenge.

## 80 *To–[Sainted Juliet!]

Published *1830*, not reprinted. The poems not reprinted often had elaborate stanza forms, as here. A variation on Romeo's words, *Romeo and Juliet* I i 189–90: 'Love is a smoke made with the fume of sighs: / Being purged, a fire sparkling in lovers' eyes.'

¶ 79.*1*. Cupid blinded; for the metaphor, cp. Keats, *Endymion* ii 877: Argus's 'eclipsing eyes' (being eclipsed).
*5*. Horace, *Odes* III xxvii 67–8, where Cupid is with *remisso arcu* instead of *intento arcu*; adapted by T. in *Eleänore* 117: 'His bow-string slackened, languid Love'.

Sainted Juliet! dearest name!
If to love be life alone,
Divinest Juliet,
I love thee, and live; and yet
Love unreturned is like the fragrant flame
Folding the slaughter of the sacrifice
Offered to gods upon an altarthrone;
My heart is lighted at thine eyes,
Changed into fire, and blown about with sighs.

# 81 Song–The Owl

Published *1830*; 'Juvenilia'. Based on 'When icicles hang by the wall' in *Love's Labour's Lost* V ii: 'Then nightly sings the staring owl, / Tu-who ... / Tu-whit to-who.'

I

When cats run home and light is come,
And dew is cold upon the ground,
And the far-off stream is dumb,
And the whirring sail goes round,
And the whirring sail goes round;
Alone and warming his five wits,
The white owl in the belfry sits.

II

When merry milkmaids click the latch,
And rarely smells the new-mown hay,
And the cock hath sung beneath the thatch
Twice or thrice his roundelay,
Twice or thrice his roundelay;
Alone and warming his five wits,
The white owl in the belfry sits.

¶ 81.*1*] When dark is gone and gray light come, *H.Nbk 7*.
*4. whirring*] miller's *MS*.
*5*] *Not MS*.
*6*. T. quotes 'Bless thy five wits! Tom's a-cold', *Lear* III iv 56. *wits*: 'senses' (T.).
*8*] When Colin's hand is on the latch, *MS*.
*12*] *Not MS*.

# 82 Second Song

## To the Same

Published *1830*; 'Juvenilia'. See previous headnote. *H.Nbk 7* has stanza i only.

I

Thy tuwhits are lulled, I wot,
Thy tuwhoos of yesternight,
Which upon the dark afloat,
So took echo with delight,
So took echo with delight,
That her voice untuneful grown,
Wears all day a fainter tone.

II

I would mock thy chaunt anew;
But I cannot mimick it;
Not a whit of thy tuwhoo,
Thee to woo to thy tuwhit,
Thee to woo to thy tuwhit,
With a lengthened loud halloo,
Tuwhoo, tuwhit, tuwhit, tuwhoo-o-o.

# 83 Recollections of the Arabian Nights

Published *1830*; 'Juvenilia'. Based, according to T., on two of the *Arabian Nights* in the Galland translation: *Noureddin and the Fair Persian*, and the *History of Aboulhassen*. The 1805 edition was at Somersby (*Lincoln*). Paden (p. 131) argues that many details are from Savary's *Letters on Egypt*, which was the source of *Egypt*; cp. also Moore's *Lalla Rookh*. Killham summarizes the tale of the Fair Persian, who was seduced by Noureddin but finally won Haroun Alraschid when he was in disguise; Killham points out that it deals with 'the ill-usage suffered by women in their relations with men', comparing *A Dream of Fair Women* and *The Princess*: 'in her is to be found the type of the Princess . . . the exotic Near Eastern setting invented for the Persian girl is carried over' (*Tennyson and 'The Princess'*, 1958, pp. 181–4).

¶ 82.*3–4*. Miltonic; cp. *Comus* 249–52: 'float upon the wings / Of silence . . . smoothing the Raven doune / Of darknes till it smil'd'; and *At a Vacation Exercise* 20: 'takes . . . with delight'.
*5*] *Not MS* (*as in the first Song*).

When the breeze of a joyful dawn blew free
In the silken sail of infancy,
The tide of time flowed back with me,
  The forward-flowing tide of time;
And many a sheeny summer-morn,
Adown the Tigris I was borne,
By Bagdat's shrines of fretted gold,
High-wallèd gardens green and old;
True Mussulman was I and sworn,
  For it was in the golden prime
    Of good Haroun Alraschid.

Anight my shallop, rustling through
The low and bloomèd foliage, drove
The fragrant, glistening deeps, and clove
The citron-shadows in the blue:
By garden porches on the brim,
The costly doors flung open wide,
Gold glittering through lamplight dim,
And broidered sofas on each side:
  In sooth it was a goodly time,
  For it was in the golden prime
    Of good Haroun Alraschid.

Often where clear-stemmed platans guard
The outlet, did I turn away
The boat-head down a broad canal
From the main river sluiced, where all
The sloping of the moon-lit sward
Was damask-work, and deep inlay
Of braided blooms unmown, which crept
Adown to where the water slept.
  A goodly place, a goodly time,
  For it was in the golden prime
    Of good Haroun Alraschid.

¶ 83.*4.* Arthur Hallam's *A Farewell to the South* 589–90 speaks of 'the tide of time' (Motter, p. 24).

*10. the golden prime*: *Richard III* I ii 247. Cp. (noting l. 1) Shelley, *Epipsychidion* 192: 'In the clear golden prime of my youth's dawn'. T. was to say in 1869: 'I think I like his *Epipsychidion* as much as anything by him' (*Mem.* ii 70).

*13–14.* 'The deeps were driven before the prow' (T.).

*23. platans*: plane trees.

*29. braided blooms*] *1842*; breaded blosms *1830*.

*30. water*] *1853*; waters *1830–51*.

A motion from the river won
Ridged the smooth level, bearing on
My shallop through the star-strown calm,
Until another night in night
I entered, from the clearer light,
Imbowered vaults of pillared palm,
Imprisoning sweets, which, as they clomb
Heavenward, were stayed beneath the dome
  Of hollow boughs.–A goodly time,
  For it was in the golden prime
    Of good Haroun Alraschid.

Still onward; and the clear canal
Is rounded to as clear a lake.
From the green rivage many a fall
Of diamond rillets musical,
Through little crystal arches low
Down from the central fountain's flow
Fallen silver-chiming, seemed to shake
The sparkling flints beneath the prow.
  A goodly place, a goodly time,
  For it was in the golden prime
    Of good Haroun Alraschid.

Above through many a bowery turn
A walk with vary-coloured shells
Wandered engrained. On either side
All round about the fragrant marge
From fluted vase, and brazen urn
In order, eastern flowers large,
Some dropping low their crimson bells
Half-closed, and others studded wide
  With disks and tiars, fed the time
  With odour in the golden prime
    Of good Haroun Alraschid.

*47. rivage*: bank (Spenserian).

*48. rillets*: as in Keats, *Endymion* ii 945. A glossary made by the young T. (*H.Nbk 4*) attributes the word to Chaucer, though it does not occur in his works.

*58. engrained*: cp. Spenser, *Shepherd's Calendar: February* 131: 'With Leaves engrained in lusty greene', where it is already an archaism and is annotated, 'dyed in grain'.

*64. tiar*: poetic form of 'tiara', as in Milton, Pope and Keats.

Far off, and where the lemon grove
In closest coverture upsprung,
The living airs of middle night
Died round the bulbul as he sung;
Not he: but something which possessed
The darkness of the world, delight,
Life, anguish, death, immortal love,
Ceasing not, mingled, unrepressed,
Apart from place, withholding time,
But flattering the golden prime
Of good Haroun Alraschid.

Black the garden-bowers and grots
Slumbered: the solemn palms were ranged
Above, unwooed of summer wind:
A sudden splendour from behind
Flushed all the leaves with rich gold-green,
And, flowing rapidly between
Their interspaces, counterchanged
The level lake with diamond-plots
Of dark and bright. A lovely time,
For it was in the golden prime
Of good Haroun Alraschid.

Dark-blue the deep sphere overhead,
Distinct with vivid stars inlaid,
Grew darker from that under-flame:
So, leaping lightly from the boat,
With silver anchor left afloat,
In marvel whence that glory came

*68. coverture*: T. compares *Much Ado* III i 30. It is used also by Spenser and Keats.

*70. bulbul*: 'the Persian name for Nightingale' (T.).

*76. flattering*: making beautiful, as in Shakespeare's *Sonnet 33*, where 'golden' follows 'flatter'.

*78. Black*] *1842*; Blackgreen *1830*. Arthur Hallam (*Englishman's Magazine*, Aug. 1831) objected to 'Black-green', especially in the vicinity of 'gold-green'.

*84. counterchanged*: chequered (heraldic), as in H.T.'s gloss to *In Memoriam* lxxxix 1.

*86. dark and bright*] *1842*; saffron light *1830*.

*90. inlaid*] *1842*; unrayed *1830*. Arthur Hallam objected to 'unrayed', as not conveying 'a very precise notion'. Cp. *Cymbeline* V v 352: 'To inlay heaven with stars'. *Distinct*: adorned (Spenserian); cp. *Timbuctoo* 105: 'Distinct and vivid with sharp points of light'.

*93.* Paden (p. 131) comments: 'The silver anchor, the most absurd of the

Upon me, as in sleep I sank
In cool soft turf upon the bank,
Entrancèd with that place and time,
So worthy of the golden prime
Of good Haroun Alraschid.

Thence through the garden I was drawn –
A realm of pleasance, many a mound,
And many a shadow-chequered lawn
Full of the city's stilly sound,
And deep myrrh-thickets blowing round
The stately cedar, tamarisks,
Thick rosaries of scented thorn,
Tall orient shrubs, and obelisks
Graven with emblems of the time,
In honour of the golden prime
Of good Haroun Alraschid.

With dazèd vision unawares
From the long alley's latticed shade
Emerged, I came upon the great
Pavilion of the Caliphat.
Right to the carven cedarn doors,
Flung inward over spangled floors,
Broad-basèd flights of marble stairs
Ran up with golden balustrade,
After the fashion of the time,
And humour of the golden prime
Of good Haroun Alraschid.

The fourscore windows all alight
As with the quintessence of flame,
A million tapers flaring bright
From twisted silvers looked to shame
The hollow-vaulted dark, and streamed

overprecious images, may possibly have been a recollection of Tasso (*Jerusalem Delivered*, tr. Fairfax XII li); the context is of a tempting relevance: "Now, now, the fatal ship of conquest lands, / Her sails are struck, her silver anchors fall, / Our champion broken hath his worthless bands, / And looseth from the soil that held him thrall . . ."' T. knew Fairfax's *Tasso* (see *The Lotos-Eaters*, headnote, p. 429).

*100. drawn*] *1842*; borne *1830*.

*101. pleasance*: Spenserian.

*103. stilly sound*: 'stilly sounds', *Henry V* IV prologue.

*107–8.* Cp. *A Fragment* 12–13: 'obelisks / Graven with gorgeous emblems'.

*125. twisted*] *1842*; wreathèd *1830*. *silvers*: 'candelabra' (T.).

Upon the moonèd domes aloof
In inmost Bagdat, till there seemed
Hundreds of crescents on the roof
Of night new-risen, that marvellous time
To celebrate the golden prime
Of good Haroun Alraschid.

Then stole I up, and trancedly
Gazed on the Persian girl alone,
Serene with argent-lidded eyes
Amorous, and lashes like to rays
Of darkness, and a brow of pearl
Tressèd with redolent ebony,
In many a dark delicious curl,
Flowing beneath her rose-hued zone;
The sweetest lady of the time,
Well worthy of the golden prime
Of good Haroun Alraschid.

Six columns, three on either side,
Pure silver, underpropt a rich
Throne of the massive ore, from which
Down-drooped, in many a floating fold,
Engarlanded and diapered
With inwrought flowers, a cloth of gold.
Thereon, his deep eye laughter-stirred
With merriment of kingly pride,
Sole star of all that place and time,
I saw him–in his golden prime,
THE GOOD HAROUN ALRASCHID.

# 84 Ode to Memory

Addressed to ——

Published *1830*; 'Juvenilia'. Instead of the dedication (*1872*), *1830* has: 'Written very early in life'. T. says it was 'a very early poem; all except [ll. 119–21], which were addressed to Arthur Hallam and added'. 'My father considered this one of the best of his early and peculiarly concentrated Nature-poems' (H.T.). Cp. *Memory* [*Memory! dear enchanter*] (p. 82),

*127.* T. comments: 'crowned with the Mohammedan crescent moon. The crescent is Ottoman, not Arabian, an anachronism pardonable in a boy's vision.'
*140. beneath*] *1842*; below *1830*.
*148. diapered*: diversified like fretwork (heraldic and Spenserian).

and *Memory* [*Ay me!*] (p. 262). The versification recalls *Lycidas* (which influenced the wording), five-stress and three-stress iambics; and possibly Wordsworth's *Immortality Ode*. William Shenstone's *Ode to Memory* is suggested as an influence in Edmund Blunden's selection from T. (1960).

I

Thou who stealest fire,
From the fountains of the past,
To glorify the present; oh, haste,
Visit my low desire!
Strengthen me, enlighten me!
I faint in this obscurity,
Thou dewy dawn of memory.

II

Come not as thou camest of late,
Flinging the gloom of yesternight
On the white day; but robed in softened light
Of orient state.
Whilome thou camest with the morning mist,
Even as a maid, whose stately brow
The dew-impearlèd winds of dawn have kissed,
When, she, as thou,
Stays on her floating locks the lovely freight
Of overflowing blooms, and earliest shoots
Of orient green, giving safe pledge of fruits,
Which in wintertide shall star
The black earth with brilliance rare.

III

Whilome thou camest with the morning mist,
And with the evening cloud,
Showering thy gleanèd wealth into my open breast
(Those peerless flowers which in the rudest wind
Never grow sere,
When rooted in the garden of the mind,
Because they are the earliest of the year).
Nor was the night thy shroud.
In sweet dreams softer than unbroken rest
Thou leddest by the hand thine infant Hope.
The eddying of her garments caught from thee
The light of thy great presence; and the cope
Of the half-attained futurity,
Though deep not fathomless,

¶ 84.*14*. *dew-impearlèd*: possibly from Drayton's sonnet *Cleere Ankor*.
*25*. Cp. *Lycidas* 2: 'with Ivy never-sear.'
*29*. Daydreams.

Was cloven with the million stars which tremble
O'er the deep mind of dauntless infancy.
Small thought was there of life's distress;
For sure she deemed no mist of earth could dull
Those spirit-thrilling eyes so keen and beautiful:
Sure she was nigher to heaven's spheres,
Listening the lordly music flowing from
The illimitable years.
O strengthen me, enlighten me!
I faint in this obscurity,
Thou dewy dawn of memory.

IV

Come forth, I charge thee, arise,
Thou of the many tongues, the myriad eyes!
Thou comest not with shows of flaunting vines
Unto mine inner eye,
Divinest Memory!
Thou wert not nursèd by the waterfall
Which ever sounds and shines
A pillar of white light upon the wall
Of purple cliffs, aloof descried:
Come from the woods that belt the gray hill-side,
The seven elms, the poplars four
That stand beside my father's door,
And chiefly from the brook that loves
To purl o'er matted cress and ribbèd sand,
Or dimple in the dark of rushy coves,
Drawing into his narrow earthen urn,
In every elbow and turn,
The filtered tribute of the rough woodland,
O! hither lead thy feet!
Pour round mine ears the livelong bleat
Of the thick-fleecèd sheep from wattled folds,
Upon the ridgèd wolds,
When the first matin-song hath wakened loud
Over the dark dewy earth forlorn,

*40–2.* Adapted from *Timbuctoo* 212–15: 'I have raised thee nigher to the spheres of Heaven / Man's first, last home: and thou with ravished sense / Listenest the lordly music flowing from / The illimitable years.' *listen*: listen to. Cp. Wordsworth, *An Evening Walk* 436 (1793 edn): 'list'ning th' aëreal music'.

*48. flaunting*: Milton, *Comus* 545, 'flaunting Hony-suckle'.

*56–9.* 'The rectory at Somersby' (T.), like ll. 105–10.

*66. Comus* 344: 'The folded flocks pen'd in their watled cotes'.

*68. wakened*] *1842*; wakèd *1830*.

What time the amber morn
Forth gushes from beneath a low-hung cloud.

V

Large dowries doth the raptured eye
To the young spirit present
When first she is wed;
And like a bride of old
In triumph led,
With music and sweet showers
Of festal flowers,
Unto the dwelling she must sway.
Well hast thou done, great artist Memory,
In setting round thy first experiment
With royal frame-work of wrought gold;
Needs must thou dearly love thy first essay,
And foremost in thy various gallery
Place it, where sweetest sunlight falls
Upon the storied walls;
For the discovery
And newness of thine art so pleasèd thee,
That all which thou hast drawn of fairest
Or boldest since, but lightly weighs
With thee unto the love thou bearest
The first-born of thy genius. Artist-like,
Ever retiring thou dost gaze
On the prime labour of thine early days:
No matter what the sketch might be;
Whether the high field on the bushless Pike,
Or even a sand-built ridge
Of heapèd hills that mound the sea,
Overblown with murmurs harsh,
Or even a lowly cottage whence we see
Stretched wide and wild the waste enormous marsh,
Where from the frequent bridge,
Like emblems of infinity,
The trenchèd waters run from sky to sky;
Or a garden bowered close
With plaited alleys of the trailing rose,

*86.* Cp. *Il Penseroso* 159–60: 'storied Windows' (and 'light').
*96. Pike*: 'Cumberland word for Peak' (T.).
*100–4.* T. says these 'refer to Mablethorpe', where the Tennysons had a cottage; cp. *Lines* (p. 499).
*103*] *1842*; Emblems or glimpses of eternity, *1830*.
*104. run from sky to sky*: incorporated from *The Coach of Death* 172.
*106. plaited*] *1842*; pleachèd *1830*.

Long alleys falling down to twilight grots,
Or opening upon level plots
Of crownèd lilies, standing near
Purple-spikèd lavender:
Whither in after life retired
From brawling storms,
From weary wind,
With youthful fancy re-inspired,
We may hold converse with all forms
Of the many-sided mind,
And those whom passion hath not blinded,
Subtle-thoughted, myriad-minded.

My friend, with you to live alone,
Were how much better than to own
A crown, a sceptre, and a throne!

O strengthen me, enlighten me!
I faint in this obscurity,
Thou dewy dawn of memory.

## 85 *Song [I' the glooming light]

Published *1830*, not reprinted. The poems not reprinted were often, as here, complicated in metre and rhyme. Cp. the mode of personification in *The Burial of Love* (p. 202).

I

I' the glooming light
Of middle night
So cold and white,
Worn Sorrow sits by the moaning wave;
Beside her are laid
Her mattock and spade,
For she hath half delved her own deep grave.
Alone she is there:
The white clouds drizzle: her hair falls loose;
Her shoulders are bare;
Her tears are mixed with the beaded dews.

*113. weary wind*: *The Dying Swan* 9, as three times in Shelley.
*117. And those*] *1842*; The few *1830*.
*118. myriad-minded*: Coleridge's epithet for Shakespeare, *Biographia Literaria* xv. Cp. *Amy* 1: 'Highminded and pure-thoughted'.
*119. you*] *1843*; thee *1830–42*. Cp. *Il Penseroso* 176: 'And I with thee will choose to live'. The friend is Arthur Hallam (see headnote).
*120. Were how much*] *1850*; Methinks were *1830–48*.

II

Death standeth by;
She will not die;
With glazèd eye
She looks at her grave: she cannot sleep;
Ever alone
She maketh her moan:
She cannot speak: she can only weep,
For she will not hope.
The thick snow falls on her flake by flake,
The dull wave mourns down the slope,
The world will not change, and her heart will not break.

# 86 Song [A spirit haunts the year's last hours]

Published *1830*; 'Juvenilia'. 'Written at Somersby' (H.T.). Stanza I appears in *T.Nbk 18*, with poems of 1828.

I

A spirit haunts the year's last hours
Dwelling amid these yellowing bowers:
To himself he talks;
For at eventide, listening earnestly,
At his work you may hear him sob and sigh
In the walks;
Earthward he boweth the heavy stalks
Of the mouldering flowers:
Heavily hangs the broad sunflower
Over its grave i' the earth so chilly;
Heavily hangs the hollyhock,
Heavily hangs the tiger-lily.

II

The air is damp, and hushed, and close,
As a sick man's room when he taketh repose
An hour before death;
My very heart faints and my whole soul grieves
At the moist rich smell of the rotting leaves,

¶ 85.*20. thick*] swift *H.Nbk 4*.

¶ 86.*13. damp . . . hushed*] hushed . . . damp *H.Nbk 4*.

*16. very . . . whole*] whole . . . very *MS*. Cp. *The Lover's Tale* i 261–2: 'My whole soul languishes / And faints'. Also *Maud* ii 237–8: 'weep / My whole soul out to thee'.

And the breath
Of the fading edges of box beneath,
And the year's last rose.
Heavily hangs the broad sunflower
Over its grave i' the earth so chilly;
Heavily hangs the hollyhock,
Heavily hangs the tiger-lily.

# 87 Adeline

Published *1830*; 'Juvenilia'. The name may be from Byron's *Don Juan* xiii, where Adeline is 'not indifferent', but 'a hidden nectar under a cold presence'. A companion piece to *Margaret* (p. 454).

I

Mystery of mysteries,
Faintly smiling Adeline,
Scarce of earth nor all divine,
Nor unhappy, nor at rest,
But beyond expression fair
With thy floating flaxen hair;
Thy rose-lips and full blue eyes
Take the heart from out my breast.
Wherefore those dim looks of thine,
Shadowy, dreaming Adeline?

II

Whence that aery bloom of thine,
Like a lily which the sun
Looks through in his sad decline,
And a rose-bush leans upon,
Thou that faintly smilest still,
As a Naiad in a well,
Looking at the set of day,
Or a phantom two hours old
Of a maiden past away,
Ere the placid lips be cold?
Wherefore those faint smiles of thine,
Spiritual Adeline?

III

What hope or fear or joy is thine?
Who talketh with thee, Adeline?

¶ 87.*16*. *Naiad*: a nymph or deity of river or spring.

For sure thou art not all alone.
Do beating hearts of salient springs
Keep measure with thine own?
Hast thou heard the butterflies
What they say betwixt their wings?
Or in stillest evenings
With what voice the violet woos
To his heart the silver dews?
Or when little airs arise,
How the merry bluebell rings
To the mosses underneath?
Hast thou looked upon the breath
Of the lilies at sunrise?
Wherefore that faint smile of thine,
Shadowy, dreaming Adeline?

IV

Some honey-converse feeds thy mind,
Some spirit of a crimson rose
In love with thee forgets to close
His curtains, wasting odorous sighs
All night long on darkness blind.
What aileth thee? whom waitest thou
With thy softened, shadowed brow,
And those dew-lit eyes of thine,
Thou faint smiler, Adeline?

V

Lovest thou the doleful wind
When thou gazest at the skies?
Doth the low-tongued Orient
Wander from the side of the morn,
Dripping with Sabæan spice
On thy pillow, lowly bent
With melodious airs lovelorn,
Breathing Light against thy face,
While his locks a-drooping twined

*26. salient springs*: i.e. leaping, *Supposed Confessions* 56. Wordsworth has 'salient spring', *The Borderers* 1788 (written 1797, but not published till 1842).
*43. odorous sighs*: emitted by the flowers in Shelley, *Triumph of Life* 14.
*47.* Cp. William Collins, *Ode to Pity* 12: 'Eyes of dewy Light'.
*53. Sabæan*: Arabian. Cp. *Paradise Lost* iv 162: 'Sabean Odours from the spicie shoare'.
*57. a-drooping*] *1863*; a-dropping *1830–62*. In his review of *1842* in the *Church of England Quarterly Review* (Oct. 1842), Leigh Hunt italicized 'a-dropping', and asked: 'The meaning?'

Round thy neck in subtle ring
Make a carcanet of rays,
And ye talk together still,
In the language wherewith Spring
Letters cowslips on the hill?
Hence that look and smile of thine,
Spiritual Adeline.

# 88 A Character

Published *1830*; 'Juvenilia'. A 'character' after Theophrastus, epigrammatically combining a moral temperament and a personal sketch. It is on Thomas Sunderland (1808–67), who was at Trinity College with T. and was 'a very plausible, parliament-like, and self-satisfied speaker at the Union' (FitzGerald). He won the Trinity declamation prize in 1829. Written 1829 or early 1830, when T.'s friends Richard Monckton Milnes and J. W. Blakesley complained of Sunderland's zest for 'perfect solitude' and his 'direct contemplation of the absolute' (Joyce Green, *The Development of the Poetic Image in Tennyson*, Cambridge thesis, 1954). In his review of *1842* in the *Church of England Quarterly Review* (Oct. 1842), Leigh Hunt wrote: 'We look upon the above, after its kind, as a faultless composition; and its kind is no mean one. Considered as a poetical satire, it brings an atmosphere of imagination round the coldest matter of fact; and the delicate *blank* effect of the disposition of the rhymes completes the seemingly passionless exposure of its passionless object.'

With a half-glance upon the sky
At night he said, 'The wanderings
Of this most intricate Universe
Teach me the nothingness of things.'
Yet could not all creation pierce
Beyond the bottom of his eye.

He spake of beauty: that the dull
Saw no divinity in grass,
Life in dead stones, or spirit in air;
Then looking as 'twere in a glass,

*59. carcanet*: necklace.
*62.* T. comments: 'The red spots on the cowslip bell, as if . . . letters of a fairy alphabet; cp. *Cymbeline* II ii 39'. There too the context is erotic: 'On her left breast / A mole cinque-spotted, like the crimson drops / I' th' bottom of a cowslip.'

He smoothed his chin and sleeked his hair,
And said the earth was beautiful.

He spake of virtue: not the gods
More purely, when they wish to charm
Pallas and Juno sitting by:
And with a sweeping of the arm,
And a lack-lustre dead-blue eye,
Devolved his rounded periods.

Most delicately hour by hour
He canvassed human mysteries,
And trod on silk, as if the winds
Blew his own praises in his eyes,
And stood aloof from other minds
In impotence of fancied power.

With lips depressed as he were meek,
Himself unto himself he sold:
Upon himself himself did feed:
Quiet, dispassionate, and cold,
And other than his form of creed,
With chiselled features clear and sleek.

# 89 *Song
# [The lintwhite and the throstlecock]

Published *1830*, not reprinted. The poems suppressed often had complicated schemes of metre and rhyme, as here.

I

The lintwhite and the throstlecock
Have voices sweet and clear;
All in the bloomèd May.
They from the blosmy brere
Call to the fleeting year,

¶ 88.*11*. *sleeked*: smoothed, as in Milton, *Comus* 882: 'sleeking her soft alluring locks'.
*17*. The moralizing fool in *As You Like It* II vii 21 had a 'lack-lustre eye'.
*18*. Thomson, *Autumn* 16–17: 'Devolving through the maze of eloquence / A roll of periods'; from Horace's *verba devolvit* (*Odes* IV ii 11).
*27*. Cp. *Troilus and Cressida* II iii 153–4: 'He that is proud eats up himself: pride is his own glass'; see l. 10.
¶ 89.*1*. *lintwhite*: linnet, as in *Claribel* 15.
*4*. *blosmy*: Chaucerian, as is *brere*, briar.

If that he would them hear
And stay.
Alas! that one so beautiful
Should have so dull an ear.

II

Fair year, fair year, thy children call,
But thou art deaf as death;
All in the bloomèd May.
When thy light perisheth
That from thee issueth,
Our life evanisheth:
Oh! stay.
Alas! that lips so cruel-dumb
Should have so sweet a breath!

III

Fair year, with brows of royal love
Thou comest, as a king.
All in the bloomèd May.
Thy golden largess fling,
And longer hear us sing;
Though thou art fleet of wing,
Yet stay.
Alas! that eyes so full of light
Should be so wandering!

IV

Thy locks are all of sunny sheen
In rings of gold yronne,
All in the bloomèd May.
We prithee pass not on;
If thou dost leave the sun,
Delight is with thee gone,
Oh! stay.
Thou art the fairest of thy feres,
We prithee pass not on.

*17. lips*] one *H.Nbk 8 1st reading.*

*29. yronne*: clustered. *1830* note: '"His crispè hair in ringis was yronne." *Chaucer, Knight's Tale*'. Chaucer continues: 'And that was yelow, and glytered as the sonne' (2165–6); the description is of King Emetreus, so cp. ll. 19–22. T.'s archaisms were probably also influenced by the songs of Chatterton.

*35. fere*: companion.

# 90 *Song [Every day hath its night]

Published *1830*, not reprinted. The poems suppressed often had complicated schemes of metre and rhyme, as here.

I

Every day hath its night:
Every night its morn:
Thorough dark and bright
Wingèd hours are borne;
Ah! welaway!
Seasons flower and fade;
Golden calm and storm
Mingle day by day.
There is no bright form
Doth not cast a shade–
Ah! welaway!

II

When we laugh, and our mirth
Apes the happy vein,
We're so kin to earth,
Pleasaunce fathers pain–
Ah! welaway!
Madness laugheth loud:
Laughter bringeth tears:
Eyes are worn away
Till the end of fears
Cometh in the shroud,
Ah! welaway!

III

All is change, woe or weal;
Joy is Sorrow's brother;
Grief and gladness steal
Symbols of each other;
Ah! welaway!
Larks in heaven's cope
Sing: the culvers mourn
All the livelong day.
Be not all forlorn:
Let us weep in hope–
Ah! welaway!

¶ 90.*13. Apes*] Imps *H.Nbk 8.*
*29. culvers*: doves. Cp. Spenser, *Amoretti* 89: 'the culver on the bared bough, / Sits mourning'.

# 91 The Poet

Published *1830*; 'Juvenilia'. Influenced by the lofty opinions of poetry current at Cambridge, and especially those of F. D. Maurice, as Paden observes (pp. 149–50). The stanza form anticipates *The Palace of Art* and *The Dream of Fair Women*. Cp. *The Poet's Mind* (p. 224).

The poet in a golden clime was born,
With golden stars above;
Dowered with the hate of hate, the scorn of scorn,
The love of love.

He saw through life and death, through good and ill,
He saw through his own soul.
The marvel of the everlasting will,
An open scroll,

Before him lay: with echoing feet he threaded
The secretest walks of fame:
The viewless arrows of his thoughts were headed
And winged with flame,

Like Indian reeds blown from his silver tongue,
And of so fierce a flight,
From Calpè unto Caucasus they sung,
Filling with light

And vagrant melodies the winds which bore
Them earthward till they lit;
Then, like the arrow-seeds of the field flower,
The fruitful wit

Cleaving, took root, and springing forth anew
Where'er they fell, behold,
Like to the mother plant in semblance, grew
A flower all gold,

¶ 91.*1. golden clime*: Keats, *Endymion* iii 455.

*3.* 'The poet hates hate; and scorns scorn' (T.). F. D. Maurice wrote of the poet: 'He cannot be a scorner' (*Athenaeum*, 8 April 1828; quoted by Paden).

*10.* Cp *Macbeth* III iv 126: 'the secret'st man of blood'.

*11–12.* Cp. *To Poesy* [*Religion be thy sword*] 5–6, by T. and Arthur Hallam: 'Oh might I be an arrow in thy hand, / And not of viewless flight, but trailing flame.' Cp. Keats, *Ode to a Nightingale* 33: 'But on the viewless wings of Poesy'.

*15. Calpè*: Gibraltar, 'the western limit of the old world, as Caucasus was the eastern' (T.).

*19.* 'The dandelion' (T.).

And bravely furnished all abroad to fling
The wingèd shafts of truth,
To throng with stately blooms the breathing spring
Of Hope and Youth.

So many minds did gird their orbs with beams,
Though one did fling the fire.
Heaven flowed upon the soul in many dreams
Of high desire.

Thus truth was multiplied on truth, the world
Like one great garden showed,
And through the wreaths of floating dark upcurled,
Rare sunrise flowed.

And Freedom reared in that august sunrise
Her beautiful bold brow,
When rites and forms before his burning eyes
Melted like snow.

There was no blood upon her maiden robes
Sunned by those orient skies;
But round about the circles of the globes
Of her keen eyes

And in her raiment's hem was traced in flame
WISDOM, a name to shake
All evil dreams of power–a sacred name.
And when she spake,

Her words did gather thunder as they ran,
And as the lightning to the thunder
Which follows it, riving the spirit of man,
Making earth wonder,

27. *breathing spring*: as in Pope and Collins.
34. *one*] *1842*; a *1830*.
41–6. *Revelation* xix 12–16: 'His eyes were as a flame of fire, and on his head were many crowns; and he had a name written, that no man knew, but he himself. And he was clothed with a vesture dipped in blood . . . And out of his mouth goeth a sharp sword [cp. ll. 53–4] . . . And he hath on his vesture and on his thigh a name written, King of Kings.' But T.'s substitution of 'eyes' for 'thigh' confuses the meaning. T. O. Mabbott suggests that T. refers to the image of the word (Wisdom) on the garments of Freedom as it is reflected in the retina (*Explicator*, Oct. 1944).
45] *1842*; And in the bordure of her robe was writ *1830*.
47] *1842*; Hoar anarchies, as with a thunderfit. *1830*.

So was their meaning to her words. No sword
  Of wrath her right arm whirled,
But one poor poet's scroll, and with *his* word
    She shook the world.

# 92 The Poet's Mind

Published *1830*; 'Juvenilia'. It has been said to be a retort to the rationalism of T.'s friend J. W. Blakesley, according to his descendants (*Poetical Works of Tennyson*, Ward Lock, 1905). But it is very unlikely that T., even good-humouredly, would call Blakesley a 'sophist' when in *To–[Clear-headed friend]* (p. 190) T. tells how Blakesley makes the Sophist cower. The main influence, noted by G. H. Ford (*Keats and the Victorians*, 1944, p. 34), is the end of Keats's *Lamia*: 'Do not all charms fly / At the mere touch of cold philosophy? . . . / The stately music no more breathes; / The myrtle sickened in a thousand wreaths.' Lamia died after 'the sophist's eye' had been 'brow-beating her fair form'.

I

Vex not thou the poet's mind
  With thy shallow wit:
Vex not thou the poet's mind;
  For thou canst not fathom it.
Clear and bright it should be ever,
Flowing like a crystal river;
Bright as light, and clear as wind.

II

Dark-browed sophist, come not anear;
  All the place is holy ground;

54. *whirled*] *1842*; hurled *1830*.

¶ 92.7 ∧ II]
Clear as summer mountainstreams,
Bright as the inwoven beams,
Which beneath their crisping sapphire
In the midday, floating o'er
The golden sands, make evermore
To a blossomstarrèd shore.
Hence away, unhallowed laugher! *1830*

*8–9*. Wordsworth's *A Poet's Epitaph* opposes poetry to the philosopher, 'all eyes', and to the lawyer: 'draw not nigh!' Gray, *Ode for Music* 10–12, speaks of 'the Muse's walk': 'Hence, away, 'its holy Ground'. *Exodus* iii 5: 'Draw not nigh hither: put off thy shoes from off thy feet, for the place whereon thou standest, is holy ground'.

9. *All the place*] *1842*; The poet's mind *1830*.

Hollow smile and frozen sneer
Come not here.
Holy water will I pour
Into every spicy flower
Of the laurel-shrubs that hedge it around.
The flowers would faint at your cruel cheer.
In your eye there is death,
There is frost in your breath
Which would blight the plants.
Where you stand you cannot hear
From the groves within
The wild-bird's din.
In the heart of the garden the merry bird chants.
It would fall to the ground if you came in.
In the middle leaps a fountain
Like sheet lightning,
Ever brightening
With a low melodious thunder;
All day and all night it is ever drawn
From the brain of the purple mountain
Which stands in the distance yonder:
It springs on a level of bowery lawn,
And the mountain draws it from Heaven above,
And it sings a song of undying love;
And yet, though its voice be so clear and full,
You never would hear it; your ears are so dull;
So keep where you are: you are foul with sin;
It would shrink to the earth if you came in.

# 93 Nothing Will Die

Published *1830*; not reprinted until restored *1872*, 'Juvenilia'. 'All things are evolved' (T.). A companion to *All Things Will Die* (p. 227). In its review of *1830*, *The Spectator* (21 Aug.) said of these two poems that they were 'a pair of little metaphysical pieces: in reading them, we could almost imagine that we had before us some recently-recovered fragment of Cowley' (E. F. Shannon, *Tennyson and the Reviewers*, 1952, p. 4). Cowley's works were at Somersby (*Lincoln*).

*12.* As an exorcism.
*27. melodious thunder*: *Semele* 10; *The Princess* ii 452.
*35. never would*] *1842*; would never *1830*.

When will the stream be aweary of flowing
Under my eye?
When will the wind be aweary of blowing
Over the sky?
When will the clouds be aweary of fleeting?
When will the heart be aweary of beating?
And nature die?
Never, oh! never, nothing will die;
The stream flows,
The wind blows,
The cloud fleets,
The heart beats,
Nothing will die.

Nothing will die;
All things will change
Through eternity.
'Tis the world's winter;
Autumn and summer
Are gone long ago;
Earth is dry to the centre,
But spring, a new comer,
A spring rich and strange,
Shall make the winds blow
Round and round,
Through and through,
Here and there,
Till the air
And the ground
Shall be filled with life anew.

The world was never made;
It will change, but it will not fade.
So let the wind range;
For even and morn
Ever will be
Through eternity.
Nothing was born;
Nothing will die;
All things will change.

¶ 93.*14–15*. Cp. Shelley, *The Cloud* 76: 'I change, but I cannot die'. But alongside John Churton Collins's note of this (*Cornhill*, Jan. 1880), T. expostulated 'Oh!' (*Lincoln*).

*22. rich and strange*: *The Tempest* I ii 405.

# 94 All Things Will Die

Published *1830*; not reprinted until restored in *1872*, 'Juvenilia'. A companion to *Nothing Will Die* (p. 225). Cp *Οἱ ῥέοντες*, of which the refrain is 'And all things flow like a stream' (p. 227).

Clearly the blue river chimes in its flowing
Under my eye;
Warmly and broadly the south winds are blowing
Over the sky.
One after another the white clouds are fleeting;
Every heart this May morning in joyance is beating
Full merrily;
Yet all things must die.
The stream will cease to flow;
The wind will cease to blow;
The clouds will cease to fleet;
The heart will cease to beat;
For all things must die.
All things must die.
Spring will come never more.
Oh! vanity!
Death waits at the door.
See! our friends are all forsaking
The wine and the merrymaking.
We are called – we must go.
Laid low, very low,
In the dark we must lie.
The merry glees are still;
The voice of the bird
Shall no more be heard,
Nor the wind on the hill.
Oh! misery!
Hark! death is calling
While I speak to ye,
The jaw is falling,
The red cheek paling,
The strong limbs failing;
Ice with the warm blood mixing;
The eyeballs fixing.
Nine times goes the passing bell:
Ye merry souls, farewell.

¶ 94.*35*. 'Nine times for a man' (T.). Cp. *My Brother* (*1827*), by T.'s brother Charles: 'The tolling of thy funeral bell, / The nine low notes that spoke thy knell.'

The old earth
Had a birth,
As all men know,
Long ago.
And the old earth must die.
So let the warm winds range,
And the blue wave beat the shore;
For even and morn
Ye will never see
Through eternity.
All things were born.
Ye will come never more,
For all things must die.

## 95 *Hero to Leander

Published *1830*, not reprinted. The poems not reprinted often had over-elaborate schemes of rhyme and metre, as here. The famous story, which ends with Leander's drowning and Hero's suicide, had been told by Marlowe and Chapman, among others. D. Bush comments on the tradition of the aubade, the lovers' parting complaint at dawn, and suggests the influence of Hood's *Hero and Leander* (1827), which opens with the tearful parting (*Mythology and the Romantic Tradition*, 1937, p. 200). There is no apparent debt to Leigh Hunt's *Hero and Leander* (1819), though T. later drew on it in *Tears, idle tears*. Cp. *The Devil and the Lady* II ii 81: 'Did not Leander swim the roaring main . . .'

Oh go not yet, my love,
  The night is dark and vast;
The white moon is hid in her heaven above,
  And the waves climb high and fast.
Oh! kiss me, kiss me, once again,
  Lest thy kiss should be the last.
Oh kiss me ere we part;
Grow closer to my heart.
My heart is warmer surely than the bosom of the main.

O joy! O bliss of blisses!
  My heart of hearts art thou.
Come bathe me with thy kisses,
  My eyelids and my brow.
Hark how the wild rain hisses,
  And the loud sea roars below.

Thy heart beats through thy rosy limbs,
So gladly doth it stir;
Thine eye in drops of gladness swims.
I have bathed thee with the pleasant myrrh;
Thy locks are dripping balm;
Thou shalt not wander hence tonight,
I'll stay thee with my kisses.
Tonight the roaring brine
Will rend thy golden tresses;
The ocean with the morrow light
Will be both blue and calm;
And the billow will embrace thee with a kiss as soft as mine.

No western odours wander
On the black and moaning sea,
And when thou art dead, Leander,
My soul must follow thee!
Oh go not yet, my love,
Thy voice is sweet and low;
The deep salt wave breaks in above
Those marble steps below.
The turretstairs are wet
That lead into the sea.
Leander! go not yet.
The pleasant stars have set:
Oh! go not, go not yet,
Or I will follow thee.

# 96 *The Mystic

Published *1830*, not reprinted. It was the only blank verse poem of *1830*.

Angels have talked with him, and showed him thrones:
Ye knew him not: he was not one of ye,
Ye scorned him with an undiscerning scorn:
Ye could not read the marvel in his eye,

¶ 95.*33*. *Thy voice*: in contrast to the moaning sea. Possibly the germ of the sea-song in *The Princess* ii ^ iii: 'Sweet and low, sweet and low, / Wind of the western sea.'

¶ 96.*1*. Cp. *Revelation* xx 1–4: 'And I saw an angel come down from heaven . . . And I saw thrones'. Also Dante, *Paradiso* xxxii: 'St Bernard shows him, on their several thrones, the other blessed souls' (Cary's translation, which was at Somersby, *Lincoln*).

The still serene abstraction: he hath felt
The vanities of after and before;
Albeit, his spirit and his secret heart
The stern experiences of converse lives,
The linkèd woes of many a fiery change
Had purified, and chastened, and made free.
Always there stood before him, night and day,
Of wayward varycolored circumstance
The imperishable presences serene
Colossal, without form, or sense, or sound,
Dim shadows but unwaning presences
Fourfacèd to four corners of the sky:
And yet again, three shadows, fronting one,
One forward, one respectant, three but one;
And yet again, again and evermore,
For the two first were not, but only seemed,
One shadow in the midst of a great light,
One reflex from eternity on time,
One mighty countenance of perfect calm,
Awful with most invariable eyes.
For him the silent congregated hours,
Daughters of time, divinely tall, beneath
Severe and youthful brows, with shining eyes
Smiling a godlike smile (the innocent light
Of earliest youth pierced through and through with all
Keen knowledges of low-embowèd eld)
Upheld, and ever hold aloft the cloud
Which droops lowhung on either gate of life,
Both birth and death: he in the centre fixt,
Saw far on each side through the grated gates
Most pale and clear and lovely distances.
He often lying broad awake, and yet
Remaining from the body, and apart
In intellect and power and will, hath heard
Time flowing in the middle of the night,
And all things creeping to a day of doom.
How could ye know him? Ye were yet within
The narrower circle; he had wellnigh reached
The last, which with a region of white flame,

*18. respectant*: facing each other (heraldic). *OED* glosses T.'s usage 'looking backward'.

*25. congregated*: cp. *The Devil and the Lady* II ii 70: 'the congregated stars'. Also Milton, *Paradise Lost* vii 308: 'congregated Waters'; and Gray, 'congregated fires', in his translation of Propertius III v 36 (*Pleiadum spisso cur coit igne chorus*).

Pure without heat, into a larger air
Upburning, and an ether of black blue,
Investeth and ingirds all other lives.

# 97 The Dying Swan

Published *1830*; 'Juvenilia'. The widespread tradition of the swan's death-song was discussed in William Hone's *Every-Day Book* (1827 edn, ii 964–8), the acknowledged source of *St Simeon Stylites.*

I

The plain was grassy, wild and bare,
Wide, wild, and open to the air,
Which had built up everywhere
An under-roof of doleful gray.
With an inner voice the river ran,
Adown it floated a dying swan,
And loudly did lament.
It was the middle of the day.
Ever the weary wind went on,
And took the reed-tops as it went.

II

Some blue peaks in the distance rose,
And white against the cold-white sky,
Shone out their crowning snows.
One willow over the river wept,
And shook the wave as the wind did sigh;
Above in the wind was the swallow,
Chasing itself at its own wild will,
And far through the marish green and still
The tangled water-courses slept,
Shot over with purple, and green, and yellow.

III

The wild swan's death-hymn took the soul
Of that waste place with joy

*41–4.* Cp. the final canto of Dante's *Paradiso.*
*44. largior . . . aether, Aeneid* vi 640.
¶ 97.*7. And*] *1850*; Which *1830–48.*
*9. weary wind*: *Ode to Memory* 113, and also three times in Shelley.
*16. was*] *1842*; sung *1830.*
*17.* Cp. Wordsworth, *Westminster Bridge* 12: 'The river glideth at his own sweet will'.
*21. wild swan*: since the tradition excluded the domestic swan (a point made by Hone). *took*: enraptured.

Hidden in sorrow: at first to the ear
The warble was low, and full and clear;
And floating about the under-sky,
Prevailing in weakness, the coronach stole
Sometimes afar, and sometimes anear;
But anon her awful jubilant voice,
With a music strange and manifold,
Flowed forth on a carol free and bold;
As when a mighty people rejoice
With shawms, and with cymbals, and harps of gold,
And the tumult of their acclaim is rolled
Through the open gates of the city afar,
To the shepherd who watcheth the evening star.
And the creeping mosses and clambering weeds,
And the willow-branches hoar and dank,
And the wavy swell of the soughing reeds,
And the wave-worn horns of the echoing bank,
And the silvery marish-flowers that throng
The desolate creeks and pools among,
Were flooded over with eddying song.

# 98 A Dirge

Published *1830*; 'Juvenilia'. Cp. the dirge in *Cymbeline* IV ii 258, 'Fear no more the heat o' th' sun'; also William Collins, *Song from Shakespear's Cymbeline.*

I

Now is done thy long day's work;
Fold thy palms across thy breast,
Fold thine arms, turn to thy rest.
Let them rave.
Shadows of the silver birk

*26. coronach*: 'Gaelic funeral-song' (T.).
*30. free and bold*: cp. Hone, 'with the sentiment of entire liberty, it has also the tones'.
*31–4.* Based on *Iliad* iv 452–5. T. here anticipates *Ode on Wellington* 142–7 (p. 1012).
*33.* Cp. 'tumult of acclaim', *In Memoriam* lxxv 20, and *To Poesy* [*Religion*] 8.
*38. soughing*: 'Anglo-Saxon *sweg*, a sound. Modified into an onomatopœic word for the soft sound or the deep sighing of the wind' (T.).
*42.* Cp. *Timbuctoo* 9: 'were flooded over with clear glory'.
¶ 98.*1.* Cp. the dirge in *Cymbeline*: 'Thou thy worldly task hast done'.
*5. birk*: northern form for birch.

Sweep the green that folds thy grave.
Let them rave.

II

Thee nor carketh care nor slander;
Nothing but the small cold worm
Fretteth thine enshrouded form.
Let them rave.
Light and shadow ever wander
O'er the green that folds thy grave.
Let them rave.

III

Thou wilt not turn upon thy bed;
Chaunteth not the brooding bee
Sweeter tones than calumny?
Let them rave.
Thou wilt never raise thine head
From the green that folds thy grave.
Let them rave.

IV

Crocodiles wept tears for thee;
The woodbine and eglatere
Drip sweeter dews than traitor's tear.
Let them rave.
Rain makes music in the tree
O'er the green that folds thy grave.
Let them rave.

V

Round thee blow, self-pleachèd deep,
Bramble roses, faint and pale,
And long purples of the dale.
Let them rave.
These in every shower creep
Through the green that folds thy grave.
Let them rave.

8. *carketh*: 'vexeth' (T.).

23. *eglatere*: eglantine. T. compares the fifteenth-century *The Floure and the Leafe* 56. A later use there made of it (ll. 79–84) is similar to T.'s: '. . . so sweet an aire / Of the eglentere, that certainly / There is no heart, I deme, in such dispaire, / Ne with thoughts froward and contraire / So overlaid, but it should soone have bote, / If it had ones felt this savour soote.'

29. *pleachèd*: plaited, as in Shakespeare and Keats.

31. *long purples*: 'the purple vetch' (T.). *1830* had it in inverted commas, suggesting *Hamlet* IV vii 168, where the context is of death; T. subsequently disowned a debt to *Hamlet*, probably because the context is obscene.

VI

The gold-eyed kingcups fine;
The frail bluebell peereth over
Rare broidry of the purple clover,
Let them rave.
Kings have no such couch as thine,
As the green that folds thy grave.
Let them rave.

VII

Wild words wander here and there:
God's great gift of speech abused
Makes thy memory confused:
But let them rave.
The balm-cricket carols clear
In the green that folds thy grave.
Let them rave.

# 99 *The Grasshopper

Published *1830*, not reprinted. The poems not reprinted often had elaborate rhyme schemes and stanza forms, as here. Cp. Anacreon, *Ode* xxxiv (translated by Thomas Moore, 1800), in praise of the grasshopper and its exemption from 'every weak decay, / That withers vulgar frames away.' Cowley (whose poems were at Somersby, *Lincoln*) had translated this ode.

I

Voice of the summerwind,
Joy of the summerplain,
Life of the summerhours,
Carol clearly, bound along.
No Tithon thou as poets feign
(Shame fall 'em they are deaf and blind)
But an insect lithe and strong,
Bowing the seeded summerflowers.
Prove their falsehood and thy quarrel,

47. *balm-cricket*: T. says: 'cicala. There is an old school-book used by me when a boy (*Analecta Graeca Majora et Minora*). In the notes there to a poem of Theocritus I found τέττιξ translated "balm-cricket". "Balm" was evidently a corruption of *Baum*, tree (Baum-grille).' Cp. *Elegiacs* 3-4: 'balm-cricket / Under a full-leaved spray chirruped and carolled away'.

¶ 99.5. The legend in *Tithonus*, in its first version *Tithon*. He was mercifully turned into a grasshopper in his 'withered immortality'.

Vaulting on thine airy feet.
Clap thy shielded sides and carol,
Carol clearly, chirrup sweet.
Thou art a mailèd warrior in youth and strength
complete;
Armed cap-a-pie,
Full fair to see;
Unknowing fear,
Undreading loss,
A gallant cavalier,
*Sans peur et sans reproche*,
In sunlight and in shadow,
The Bayard of the meadow.

II

I would dwell with thee,
Merry grasshopper,
Thou art so glad and free,
And as light as air;
Thou hast no sorrow or tears,
Thou hast no compt of years,
No withered immortality,
But a short youth sunny and free.
Carol clearly, bound along,
Soon the joy is over,
A summer of loud song,
And slumbers in the clover.
What hast thou to do with evil
In thine hour of love and revel,
In thy heat of summerpride,
Pushing the thick roots aside
Of the singing flowerèd grasses,
That brush thee with their silken tresses?
What hast thou to do with evil,
Shooting, singing, ever springing
In and out the emerald glooms,
Ever leaping, ever singing,
Lighting on the golden blooms?

*13.* 'Christopher North' accused T. of plagiarizing Wordsworth's beetle, 'A mailèd angel on a battle-day', from *Stanzas on 'Castle of Indolence'* 61 (E. F. Shannon, *Tennyson and the Reviewers*, 1952, p. 195).

*18–21.* *Bayard*: T. would have read of Bayard (d. 1524) in *QR* xxxii (1825) 355–97–a review of *The History of the Chevalier Bayard, the Good Knight without Fear and without Reproach*. *QR* was the source of *Come hither* and *King Charles's Vision*, and there were copies of it at Somersby (*Lincoln*).

*34.* Cp. *Comus* 122: 'What hath night to do with sleep?'.

# 100 *Love, Pride, and Forgetfulness

Published *1830*, not reprinted. Cp. the use made of personification in *The Lover's Tale* (1827–32) i 808–10: 'At last she sought out Memory, and they trod / The same old paths where Love had walked with Hope, / And Memory fed the soul of Love with tears.'

Ere yet my heart was sweet Love's tomb,
Love laboured honey busily.
I was the hive, and Love the bee.
My heart the honeycomb.
One very dark and chilly night
Pride came beneath and held a light.

The cruel vapours went through all,
Sweet Love was withered in his cell;
Pride took Love's sweets, and by a spell
Did change them into gall;
And Memory though fed by Pride
Did wax so thin on gall,
Awhile she scarcely lived at all.
What marvel that she died?

# 101 *Chorus,

## IN AN UNPUBLISHED DRAMA, WRITTEN VERY EARLY

Published *1830*, not reprinted. At fourteen or fifteen, T. wrote *The Devil and the Lady* and another drama which has not survived; possibly it contained the scene printed in *Mem.* i 23–5, and possibly this *Chorus*. The poems which T. did not reprint often had complicated schemes of metre and rhyme, as here. T.'s refrain was suggested by Shelley, *On Death* 23–4: 'All that is great and all that is strange / In the boundless realm of unending change.'

The varied earth, the moving heaven,
 The rapid waste of roving sea,
The fountainpregnant mountains riven
 To shapes of wildest anarchy,

¶ 101.*1*. *The varied earth*: *The Devel and the Lady* II i 7. Shelley has 'the moving heavens', *Epipsychidion* 61. T. later praised Shelley to Frederick Locker-Lampson: 'I think I like his *Epipsychidion* as much as anything by him' (*Mem.* ii 70).

By secret fire and midnight storms
 That wander round their windy cones,
The subtle life, the countless forms
 Of living things, the wondrous tones
  Of man and beast are full of strange
  Astonishment and boundless change.

The day, the diamonded night,
 The echo, feeble child of sound,
The heavy thunder's griding might,
 The herald lightning's starry bound,
The vocal spring of bursting bloom,
 The naked summer's glowing birth,
The troublous autumn's sallow gloom,
 The hoarhead winter paving earth
  With sheeny white, are full of strange
  Astonishment and boundless change.

Each sun which from the centre flings
 Grand music and redundant fire,
The burning belts, the mighty rings,
 The murmurous planets' rolling choir,
The globefilled arch that, cleaving air,
 Lost in its own effulgence sleeps,
The lawless comets as they glare,
 And thunder through the sapphire deeps
  In wayward strength, are full of strange
  Astonishment and boundless change.

## 102 *Lost Hope

Published *1830*, not reprinted. The poems not reprinted often had irregular stanza forms, as here.

You cast to ground the hope which once was mine:
 But did the while your harsh decree deplore,
Embalming with sweet tears the vacant shrine,
 My heart, where Hope had been and was no more.

*13. griding*: originally piercing, here grating. Cp. Shelley, *Prometheus Unbound* III i 47–8: 'the thunder of the fiery wheels / Griding the winds'. The same sense is in *In Memoriam* cvii 11.

*22. redundant*: rolling in waves; cp. *Paradise Lost* ii 889: 'redounding smoak and ruddy flame'.

So on an oaken sprout
A goodly acorn grew;
But winds from heaven shook the acorn out,
And filled the cup with dew.

# 103 The Deserted House

Published *1830*; not reprinted till restored in *1848*; 'Juvenilia'.

I

Life and Thought have gone away
Side by side,
Leaving door and windows wide:
Careless tenants they!

II

All within is dark as night:
In the windows is no light;
And no murmur at the door,
So frequent on its hinge before.

III

Close the door, the shutters close,
Or through the windows we shall see
The nakedness and vacancy
Of the dark deserted house.

IV

Come away: no more of mirth
Is here or merry-making sound.
The house was builded of the earth,
And shall fall again to ground.

V

Come away: for Life and Thought
Here no longer dwell;
But in a city glorious–
A great and distant city–have bought
A mansion incorruptible.
Would they could have stayed with us!

¶ 103.*9–12*. These lines fall into something resembling the *In Memoriam* stanza, here too used elegiacally; cp. *In Memoriam* vii: 'Dark house . . .', which seems to be tinged with this ancient idea of the corpse as a deserted house (p. 870).

*15–22*. *2 Corinthians* v 1: 'For we know that if our earthly house of this tabernacle were dissolved, we have a building of God, an house not made with hands, eternal in the heavens.'

# 104 *The Tears of Heaven

Published *1830*, not reprinted. In his review of *1830* in *The Tatler* (26 Feb. 1831), Leigh Hunt spoke of this poem as 'a conceit, not founded in natural, and therefore not in poetical truth'.

Heaven weeps above the earth all night till morn,
In darkness weeps as all ashamed to weep,
Because the earth hath made her state forlorn
With selfwrought evils of unnumbered years,
And doth the fruit of her dishonour reap.
And all the day heaven gathers back her tears
Into her own blue eyes so clear and deep,
And showering down the glory of lightsome day,
Smiles on the earth's worn brow to win her if she may.

# 105 *Love and Sorrow

Published *1830*, not reprinted. Many of the poems not reprinted had irregular metres and rhyme scheme; T. may have come to dislike what resembles extreme experimentation with the sonnet form. In his review of *1830* in *The Tatler* (26 Feb. 1831), Leigh Hunt said of this poem: 'The author must have been reading Donne when he wrote it. It might pass for a leaf out of his book. . . . This is the very Analogical Doctor come back again.' Cp. *Almeida* (1826, p. 1784); the name was a favourite for tragic heroines in the late eighteenth century.

O maiden, fresher than the first green leaf
With which the fearful springtide flecks the lea,
Weep not, Almeida, that I said to thee
That thou hast half my heart, for bitter grief
Doth hold the other half in sovranty.
Thou art my heart's sun in love's crystalline:
Yet on both sides at once thou canst not shine:
Thine is the bright side of my heart, and thine
My heart's day, but the shadow of my heart,
Issue of its own substance, my heart's night
Thou canst not lighten even with *thy* light,
All powerful in beauty as thou art.

¶ 105.*6*. *crystalline*: sky (Miltonic).

Almeida, if my heart were substanceless,
Then might thy rays pass through to the other side,
So swiftly, that they nowhere would abide,
But lose themselves in utter emptiness.
Half-light, half-shadow, let my spirit sleep;
They never learned to love who never knew to weep.

## 106 *To a Lady Sleeping

Published *1830*, not reprinted. For the theme of this Keatsian fragment, cp. *O wake ere I grow jealous of sweet Sleep* (p. 291), which has the same rhyme scheme except that it lacks a concluding line. The poem is a variation of the lover's aubade or dawn-song.

O thou whose fringèd lids I gaze upon,
Through whose dim brain the wingèd dreams are borne,
Unroof the shrines of clearest vision,
In honour of the silverfleckèd morn:
Long hath the white wave of the virgin light
Driven back the billow of the dreamful dark.
Thou all unwittingly prolongest night,
Though long ago listening the poisèd lark,
With eyes dropt downward through the blue serene,
Over heaven's parapets the angels lean.

*15.* Cp. Coleridge's *Ancient Mariner* 264, where the moon 'no where did abide'.

¶ 106.*1–3.* Cp. *To–[Clear-headed friend]* 6–7: 'Ray-fringèd eyelids of the morn / Roof not a glance so keen as thine.' *fringèd lids*: Keats, *Endymion* ii 563.

*5.* Cp. *Endymion* ii 113: 'a virgin light to the deep'.

*8.* Cp. *Endymion* ii 720: 'And sing above this gentle pair, like lark'.

*9–10. blue serene*: traditional, twice in Shelley. Cp. Keats's 'pure serene', *On First Looking into Chapman's Homer* 7; and his *To one who has been long in city pent*: 'E'en like the passage of an angel's tear / That falls through the clear ether silently.' Also *Endymion* ii 526: 'Queen Venus leaning downward'. The transition from the dawn conflict of light and dark to Heaven's parapets suggests *Paradise Lost* ii 1034–42: 'But now at last the sacred influence / Of light appears, and from the walls of Heav'n / Shoots farr into the bosom of dim Night / A glimmering dawn.' T.'s 'wave' metaphor comes from the description here of Satan, who 'Wafts on the calmer wave by dubious light'.

## 107 *Sonnet [Could I outwear my present state of woe]

Published *1830*, not reprinted. An irregular sonnet, like most of T.'s early ones.

Could I outwear my present state of woe
With one brief winter, and indue i' the spring
Hues of fresh youth, and mightily outgrow
The wan dark coil of faded suffering–
Forth in the pride of beauty issuing
A sheeny snake, the light of vernal bowers,
Moving his crest to all sweet plots of flowers
And watered vallies where the young birds sing;
Could I thus hope my lost delight's renewing,
I straightly would command the tears to creep
From my charged lids; but inwardly I weep:
Some vital heat as yet my heart is wooing:
This to itself hath drawn the frozen rain
From my cold eyes and melted it again.

## 108 *Sonnet [Though Night hath climbed her peak of highest noon]

Published *1830*, not reprinted. An irregular sonnet, like most of T.'s early ones.

Though Night hath climbed her peak of highest noon,
And bitter blasts the screaming autumn whirl,
All night through archways of the bridgèd pearl,
And portals of pure silver walks the moon.
Walk on, my soul, nor crouch to agony,
Turn cloud to light, and bitterness to joy,

¶ 107.*4*. *coil*: suggesting also the meaning 'turmoil'; influenced by Hamlet's 'mortal coil'. Crabbe has 'sad coil', *Parish Register* iii 914.

*5–8*. Cp. the rebirth of the 'sable-sheeny' snake in *Love* [*Thou, from the first*] iii (p. 245).

¶ 108.*1*. Cp. *Il Penseroso* 67–8: 'the wandring Moon, / Riding neer her highest noon'–i.e. her place at midnight.

*6–7*. Cp. Shakespeare's *Sonnet 33*: 'Gilding pale streams with heavenly alchemy, / Anon permit the basest clouds to ride'.

And dross to gold with glorious alchemy,
Basing thy throne above the world's annoy.
Reign thou above the storms of sorrow and ruth
That roar beneath; unshaken peace hath won thee;
So shalt thou pierce the woven glooms of truth;
So shall the blessing of the meek be on thee;
So in thine hour of dawn, the body's youth,
An honourable eld shall come upon thee.

## 109 *Sonnet [Shall the hag Evil die with child of Good]

Published *1830*, not reprinted.

Shall the hag Evil die with child of Good,
Or propagate again her loathèd kind,
Thronging the cells of the diseasèd mind,
Hateful with hanging cheeks, a withered brood,
Though hourly pastured on the salient blood?
Oh! that the wind which bloweth cold or heat
Would shatter and o'erbear the brazen beat
Of their broad vans, and in the solitude
Of middle space confound them, and blow back
Their wild cries down their cavernthroats, and slake
With points of blastborne hail their heated eyne!
So their wan limbs no more might come between
The moon and the moon's reflex in the night,
Nor blot with floating shades the solar light.

*8. annoy*: vexation; cp. Keble's *Christian Year* (1827): 'earth's annoy'.
*11. glooms*: shaded places, as in Collins, *The Passions* 64. Cp. Sir William Jones, *A Persian Song*: 'Nor hope to pierce the woven gloom'. (Jones's *Works* were at Somersby, *Lincoln*.)
*14. eld*: old age; cp. Thomson, *Castle of Indolence* II xxxi: 'venerable eld'.
¶ 109.*5. salient*: leaping.
*8.* Milton's Satan has 'sail-broad vans' (wings), *Paradise Lost* ii 927.
*9–10.* Adam's 'cries' are 'Blown stifling back on him', *PL* xi 310–13.
*11. eyne*: eyes, archaic plural (pronounced 'een'). Cp. *The Lover's Tale* iii 27–8: 'I, too, was borne along and felt the blast / Beat on my heated eyelids.' Milton's fallen angels are punished by 'Sulphurous Hail' and 'dire Hail', *PL* i 171, ii 589.

# 110 *Sonnet [The pallid thunderstricken sigh for gain]

Published *1830*, not reprinted. An irregular sonnet, like most of T.'s early ones.

The pallid thunderstricken sigh for gain,
Down an ideal stream they ever float,
And sailing on Pactolus in a boat,
Drown soul and sense, while wistfully they strain
Weak eyes upon the glistering sands that robe
The understream. The wise, could he behold
Cathedralled caverns of thickribbèd gold
And branching silvers of the central globe,
Would marvel from so beautiful a sight
How scorn and ruin, pain and hate could flow:
But Hatred in a gold cave sits below:
Pleached with her hair, in mail of argent light
Shot into gold, a snake her forehead clips,
And skins the colour from her trembling lips.

# 111 *Love [Thou, from the first]

Published *1830*, not reprinted. Cp. *Love* [*Almighty Love!*] (1827, p. 144); and *Among some Nations* (1828, p. 166) which ends: 'One King into whose everlasting face / All eyes might look and live, his name is Love.' D. B. MacEachen (*Victorian Newsletter*, Fall 1958) observes that T. wrote no sonnet strictly on the Spenserian model, but that i has a Spenserian octave; ii and iii show, like most of the *1830* sonnets, T.'s extreme irregularity in structure and rhyme.

I

Thou, from the first, unborn, undying love,
Albeit we gaze not on thy glories near,

¶ 110.*1*. Cp. *What Thor Said* 5: 'the flock of the thunder-stricken'.
*3*. *Pactolus*: 'a river of Lydia, called *Chrysorboas*, from its rolling down golden sand, according to Herodotus, Plutarch, Pliny, and Strabo' (*English Encyclopaedia*, 1802, of which a copy was at Somersby, *Lincoln*). Cp. *Persia* 40–1: 'the glittering sands / Of bright Pactolus'.
*7*. Keats has 'cathedral cavern', *Hyperion* i 86.
*12*. *Pleached*: plaited (Keatsian).
¶ 111.i *1*. Cp. (noting 'brood', l. 13) *Paradise Lost* i 19–21: 'Thou from the first / Wast present, and with mighty wings outspread / Dove-like satst brooding'.

Before the face of God didst breathe and move,
Though night and pain and ruin and death reign here.
Thou foldest, like a golden atmosphere,
The very throne of the eternal God:
Passing through thee the edicts of his fear
Are mellowed into music, borne abroad
By the loud winds, though they uprend the sea,
Even from its central deeps: thine empery
Is over all: thou wilt not brook eclipse;
Thou goest and returnest to His lips
Like lightning: thou dost ever brood above
The silence of all hearts, unutterable Love.

II

To know thee is all wisdom, and old age
Is but to know thee: dimly we behold thee
Athwart the veils of evil which infold thee.
We beat upon our aching hearts in rage;
We cry for thee; we deem the world thy tomb.
As dwellers in lone planets look upon
The mighty disk of their majestic sun,
Hollowed in awful chasms of wheeling gloom,
Making their day dim, so we gaze on thee.
Come, thou of many crowns, whiterobèd love,
Oh! rend the veil in twain: all men adore thee;
Heaven crieth after thee; earth waiteth for thee:
Breathe on thy wingèd throne, and it shall move
In music and in light o'er land and sea.

III

And now – methinks I gaze upon thee now,
As on a serpent in his agonies
Awestricken Indians; what time laid low
And crushing the thick fragrant reeds he lies,

i *5. golden atmosphere*: Shelley's *Prometheus Unbound* II ii 75.

i *13.* Perhaps suggested by *Paradise Lost* v 730–2: 'To whom the Son with calm aspect and cleer / Light'ning Divine, ineffable, serene, / Made answer'.

ii *10.* Milton, *On the Death of a Fair Infant* 54: 'Or that crown'd Matron, sage white-robed Truth'.

ii *13–14.* The 'wingèd throne' of the Hindu god Cama or Camdeo; cp. *Love* [*Almighty Love*!] 39–50, and *The Palace of Art* 115. Cp. Shelley, *Adonais* 414: 'Assume thy wingéd throne'.

iii *1–3.* T. adapted this for *The Lover's Tale* ii 183–87: '. . each heart / Grew closer to the other, and the eye / Was riveted and charm-bound, gazing like / The Indian on a still-eyed snake, low-couched – / A beauty

When the new year warmbreathèd on the earth,
Waiting to light him with her purple skies,
Calls to him by the fountain to uprise.
Already with the pangs of a new birth
Strain the hot spheres of his convulsèd eyes,
And in his writhings awful hues begin
To wander down his sable-sheeny sides,
Like light on troubled waters: from within
Anon he rusheth forth with merry din,
And in him light and joy and strength abides;
And from his brows a crown of living light
Looks through the thickstemmed woods by day and night.

# 112 Love and Death

Published *1830*; 'Juvenilia'. Cp. Thomas Moore's *Love and Reason* (1806): 'No wonder Love, as on they passed, / Should find that sunny morning chill, / For still the shadow Reason cast / Fell on the boy, and cooled him still.'

What time the mighty moon was gathering light
Love paced the thymy plots of Paradise,
And all about him rolled his lustrous eyes;
When, turning round a cassia, full in view,
Death, walking all alone beneath a yew,
And talking to himself, first met his sight:
'You must begone,' said Death, 'these walks are mine.'
Love wept and spread his sheeny vans for flight;
Yet ere he parted said, 'This hour is thine:

which is death.' Note the context of love. Paden (p. 159) connects the serpent with G. S. Faber's religious mythologizing: 'casting its skin and appearing again in renovated youth'. Paden also compares *Sonnet* [*Could I outwear*] 5–6: 'Forth in the pride of beauty issuing / A sheeny snake'.

¶ 112.*1*. Virgil, *Georgics* i 427: *luna revertentis cum primum colligit ignis. mighty moon*: as in Wordsworth and Shelley.

*3*. Cp. Keats, *Ode to a Nightingale* 29–30: 'Where Beauty cannot keep her lustrous eyes / Or new Love ...'; here following the Keatsian 'moon' and 'plots'.

*4*. *cassia*: 'a kind of laurel' (T.).

*8*. *vans*: wings; T. compares *Paradise Lost* ii 927–8: 'his Sail-broad Vannes / He spreads for flight'. Cp. also *Par. Reg.* iv 583: 'plumy Vans'.

Thou art the shadow of life, and as the tree
Stands in the sun and shadows all beneath,
So in the light of great eternity
Life eminent creates the shade of death;
The shadow passeth when the tree shall fall,
But I shall reign for ever over all.'

# 113 The Kraken

Published *1830*, not reprinted until restored in *1872*, 'Juvenilia'. T. comments: 'See the account which Erik Pontoppidan, the Norwegian bishop, born 1698, gives of the fabulous sea-monster–the Kraken (*Biographie Universelle*)' [1823]. Pontoppidan's account was summarized in the *English Encyclopaedia* (1802), of which a copy was at Somersby (*Lincoln*). T. would also have read of the kraken in Scott's *Minstrelsy* (Leyden's *the Mermaid*), and in T. C. Croker's *Fairy Legends* ii (1828) 64, a book which he knew and later owned (*Lincoln*). Paden (p. 155) observes that T.'s monster has only its name in common with Pontoppidan's, and argues that T. associated it with G. S. Faber's religious mythologizing, where the serpent (the evil principle) leads to the deluge: hence the sea-snake, and hence the 'latter fire'. Two other of Faber's books were at Somersby (*Lincoln*): *Horae Mosaicae* (1818 edn), and *The Difficulties of Infidelity* (2nd edn, 1833). D. Bush, *Major British Writers* (1959) ii 380, cites *Revelation* xiii 1, 'And I stood upon the sand of the sea, and saw a beast rise up out of the sea.'

Below the thunders of the upper deep;
Far, far beneath in the abysmal sea,
His ancient, dreamless, uninvaded sleep
The Kraken sleepeth: faintest sunlights flee
About his shadowy sides: above him swell
Huge sponges of millennial growth and height;
And far away into the sickly light,
From many a wondrous grot and secret cell
Unnumbered and enormous polypi
Winnow with giant arms the slumbering green.

*13. eminent*: 'standing out like a tree' (T.). Milton's 'Tree of Life' was 'High eminent', *PL* iv 219.

¶ 113.*7. sickly light*: *OED* 6, 'of light, colour', from Prior, *An English Ballad* 135 (1695).

*9.* Pontoppidan: 'This Krake must be of the Polypus kind, notwithstanding its enormous size' (*Natural History of Norway* (tr. 1755) ii 217).

*10. arms*] *1872*; fins *1830*. Pontoppidan ii 210: 'full of arms'. *Winnow*: in this sense, influenced by Milton, *Paradise Lost* v 269–70: 'Then with quick

There hath he lain for ages and will lie
Battening upon huge seaworms in his sleep,
Until the latter fire shall heat the deep;
Then once by man and angels to be seen,
In roaring he shall rise and on the surface die.

## 114 The Ballad of Oriana

Published *1830*; 'Juvenilia'. FitzGerald, in his copy of *1842* (*Trinity College*), says that the poem was 'in some measure inspired' by the ballad of Helen of Kirkconnell. T. knew it by heart (*Mem.* i 48), presumably in the version given in Scott's *Minstrelsy*. The name Oriana is from the chivalric romance *Amadis de Gaula*; it is much used in Fletcher's plays (of which a set was at Somersby, *Lincoln*), and Scott mentions Oriana in *Marmion*, at the end of 'Introduction to Canto First' (*Marmion* was at Somersby).

My heart is wasted with my woe,
Oriana.
There is no rest for me below,
Oriana.

Fann / Winnows the buxom Air'. T. probably observed Shelley's fondness for *winnow*. For the context, cp. *Timbuctoo* 146–51: 'My thoughts which long had grovelled in the slime / Of this dull world, like dusky worms which house / Beneath unshaken waters, but at once / Upon some Earth-awakening day of Spring / Do pass from gloom to glory, and aloft / Winnow the purple.'

*12.* Shelley, *Prometheus Unbound* IV 542: 'The dull weed some sea-worm battens on'. The kraken's 'ability to feed while sleeping may have been suggested by [Pontoppidan's] account of a strong scent by which krakens attract fish into their clutches' (Paden, p. 155).

*13–15. Revelation* viii 8–9: 'And the second angel sounded, and as it were a great mountain burning with fire was cast into the sea; and the third part of the sea became blood; And the third part of the creatures which were in the sea, and had life, died.' In Faberian terms (see headnote), this was 'another in that series of dissolutions of which the mystae were taught' (Paden, p. 155).

*14. man*] *1830*, *1872*; men *correction in 1830 Errata*. Pontoppidan ii 211–12: 'Amongst the many great things which are in the ocean, and concealed from our eyes, or only presented to our view for a few minutes, is the Kraken', whose whole body 'in all likelihood no human eye ever beheld'.

¶ 114.*1. wasted*] hollow *H.Nbk 4 revision*.

*3. for me*] no sleep *MS revision*.

When the long dun wolds are ribbed with snow,
And loud the Norland whirlwinds blow,
Oriana,
Alone I wander to and fro,
Oriana.

Ere the light on dark was growing,
Oriana,
At midnight the cock was crowing,
Oriana:
Winds were blowing, waters flowing,
We heard the steeds to battle going,
Oriana;
Aloud the hollow bugle blowing,
Oriana.

In the yew-wood black as night,
Oriana,
Ere I rode into the fight,
Oriana,
While blissful tears blinded my sight
By star-shine and by moonlight,
Oriana,
I to thee my troth did plight,
Oriana.

She stood upon the castle wall,
Oriana:
She watched my crest among them all,
Oriana:
She saw me fight, she heard me call,
When forth there stept a foeman tall,
Oriana,
Atween me and the castle wall,
Oriana.

The bitter arrow went aside,
Oriana:

*6.* 'The Norland whirlwind' appears in *Supposed Confessions* 39 ^ 40, *1830* text.

*12.* Cp. 'O, cocks are crowing a merry midnight', in the ballad of Clerk Saunders which T. knew by heart (*Mem.* i 48) and which he would have known in the version given in Scott's *Minstrelsy*.

*14–17.* Adapted from *The Vale of Bones* 57–9: 'When on to battle proudly going, / Your plumage to the wild winds blowing, / Your tartans far behind ye flowing.'

*30. watched my crest*] saw my plume *MS 1st reading*.

The false, false arrow went aside,
Oriana:
The damnèd arrow glanced aside,
And pierced thy heart, my love, my bride,
Oriana!
Thy heart, my life, my love, my bride,
Oriana!

Oh! narrow, narrow was the space,
Oriana.
Loud, loud rung out the bugle's brays,
Oriana.
Oh! deathful stabs were dealt apace,
The battle deepened in its place,
Oriana;
But I was down upon my face,
Oriana.

They should have stabbed me where I lay,
Oriana!
How could I rise and come away,
Oriana?
How could I look upon the day?
They should have stabbed me where I lay,
Oriana–
They should have trod me into clay,
Oriana.

O breaking heart that will not break,
Oriana!
O pale, pale face so sweet and meek,
Oriana!
Thou smilest, but thou dost not speak,
And then the tears run down my cheek,
Oriana:
What wantest thou? whom dost thou seek,
Oriana?

I cry aloud: none hear my cries,
Oriana.
Thou comest atween me and the skies,
Oriana.

39] *MS 1st reading transposed with l. 41.*
54 ∧ 5] *MS had here ll. 82–90.*
55–63] *Added in MS.*

I feel the tears of blood arise
Up from my heart unto my eyes,
Oriana.
Within thy heart my arrow lies,
Oriana.

O cursèd hand! O cursèd blow!
Oriana!
O happy thou that liest low,
Oriana!
All night the silence seems to flow
Beside me in my utter woe,
Oriana.
A weary, weary way I go,
Oriana.

When Norland winds pipe down the sea,
Oriana,
I walk, I dare not think of thee,
Oriana.
Thou liest beneath the greenwood tree,
I dare not die and come to thee,
Oriana.
I hear the roaring of the sea,
Oriana.

## 115 Circumstance

Published *1830*; 'Juvenilia'. 'Circumstance' was an important word to T. in that it suggested an earlier usage as 'the totality of surrounding things', hence 'the heavens'. See his note to 'The hollow orb of moving Circumstance', *The Palace of Art* 255 (p. 416); also 'This ever-changing world of circumstance', *To the Duke of Argyll* 10.

Two children in two neighbour villages
Playing mad pranks along the heathy leas;
Two strangers meeting at a festival;
Two lovers whispering by an orchard wall;
Two lives bound fast in one with golden ease;

*80*] My heart is hollow with my sighs *MS 1st reading*.
*93*] I walk alone and think of thee *MS 1st reading*.
¶ 115.*1–2*. Cp. the opening of *Dualisms*, of which l. 14 is: 'Two children lovelier than Love adown the lea are singing'.

Two graves grass-green beside a gray church-tower,
Washed with still rains and daisy blossomèd;
Two children in one hamlet born and bred;
So runs the round of life from hour to hour.

## 116 *English Warsong

Published *1830*, not reprinted.

Who fears to die? Who fears to die?
Is there any here who fears to die?
He shall find what he fears; and none shall grieve
For the man who fears to die;
But the withering scorn of the many shall cleave
To the man who fears to die.
*Chorus*. Shout for England!
Ho! for England!
George for England!
Merry England!
England for aye!

The hollow at heart shall crouch forlorn,
He shall eat the bread of common scorn;
It shall be steeped in the salt, salt tear,
Shall be steeped in his own salt tear:
Far better, far better he never were born
Than to shame merry England here.
*Chorus*. Shout for England! &c.

There standeth our ancient enemy;
Hark! he shouteth–the ancient enemy!
On the ridge of the hill his banners rise;
They stream like fire in the skies;
Hold up the Lion of England on high
Till it dazzle and blind his eyes.
*Chorus*. Shout for England! &c.

Come along! we alone of the earth are free;
The child in our cradles is bolder than he;
For where is the heart and strength of slaves;
Oh! where is the strength of slaves?
He is weak! we are strong; he a slave, we are free;
Come along! we will dig their graves.
*Chorus*. Shout for England! &c.

9. *So runs*] *1842*; Fill up *1830*.

There standeth our ancient enemy;
Will he dare to battle with the free?
Spur along! spur amain! charge to the fight:
Charge! charge to the fight!
Hold up the Lion of England on high!
Shout for God and our right!
*Chorus*. Shout for England! &c.

## 117 *National Song

Published *1830*; not reprinted, but adapted for Act II of *The Foresters* which was completed in 1881, published 1892. Written 1828–9 (*Mem.* ii 390). In his review of *1830* in *The Tatler* (26 Feb. 1831), Leigh Hunt said: 'We hold the *National Song* to be naught.' It was perhaps influenced by Thomas Campbell's patriotic ballads, which T. recited (*Mem.* i 77), though it is more in the vein of Charles Dibdin. Cp. *Song* [*The winds, as at their hour*] (p. 254), with its boast 'We are free' (cp. l. 18); and *English Warsong* (p. 251).

There is no land like England
Where'er the light of day be;
There are no hearts like English hearts,
Such hearts of oak as they be.
There is no land like England
Where'er the light of day be;
There are no men like Englishmen,
So tall and bold as they be.

*Chorus*. For the French the pope may shrive 'em,
For the devil a whit we heed 'em:
As for the French, God speed 'em
Unto their heart's desire,
And the merry devil drive 'em
Through the water and the fire.

*Full Chorus*. Our glory is our freedom,
We lord it o'er the sea;
We are the sons of freedom,
We are free.

¶ 117.*9–14*] *Not The Foresters.*
*15–18*] And these will strike for England
And man and maid be free
To foil and spoil the tyrant
Beneath the greenwood tree. *The Foresters*

There is no land like England,
    Where'er the light of day be;
There are no wives like English wives,
    So fair and chaste as they be.
There is no land like England,
    Where'er the light of day be;
There are no maids like English maids,
    So beautiful as they be.

*Chorus.* For the French, &c.

[1830. *The Sleeping Beauty*–see p. 627]

# 118 *Dualisms

Published *1830*, not reprinted. The poems not reprinted often had over-elaborate schemes of rhyme and metre, as here; and T. was to admit doubt about some of his early unhyphenated compound words (*Mem.* i 50), of which this poem is full.

Two bees within a chrystal flowerbell rockèd
    Hum a lovelay to the westwind at noontide.
        Both alike, they buzz together,
        Both alike, they hum together
        Through and through the flowered heather.
Where in a creeping cove the wave unshockèd
            Lays itself calm and wide,
        Over a stream two birds of glancing feather
        Do woo each other, carolling together.
        Both alike, they glide together,
            Side by side;
        Both alike, they sing together,
Arching blueglossèd necks beneath the purple weather.

27] *The Foresters again omits the Chorus, and substitutes for the Full Chorus*:
And these shall wed with freemen,
    And all their sons be free
To sing the songs of England
    Beneath the greenwood tree.

¶ 118.*13*. *purple*: brightly coloured; it was used multifariously in eighteenth-century diction. Cp. Pope's 'purple year', *Spring* 28. See A. Johnston, *RES*, n.s. xiv (1963) 389–93.

Two children lovelier than Love adown the lea are singing,
As they gambol, lilygarlands ever stringing:
Both in blosmwhite silk are frockèd:
Like, unlike, they roam together
Under a summervault of golden weather;
Like, unlike, they sing together
Side by side,
MidMay's darling goldenlockèd,
Summer's tanling diamondeyed.

# 119 Song [The winds, as at their hour of birth]

Published *1830*, as *We Are Free*; not reprinted till restored in *1872*, 'Juvenilia'. Cp. the patriotic poems of *1830*, like *National Song* (p. 252).

The winds, as at their hour of birth,
Leaning upon the ridgèd sea,
Breathed low around the rolling earth
With mellow preludes, 'We are free.'

The streams through many a lilied row
Down-carolling to the crispèd sea,
Low-tinkled with a bell-like flow
Atween the blossoms, 'We are free.'

# 120 The Sea-Fairies

Published *1830*; not reprinted until restored, much revised, in *Poems*, 8th edn, 1853; 'Juvenilia'. The revision was undertaken in 1853, judging by *T.Nbk 24*. Cp. *The Merman* (p. 193) and *The Mermaid* (p. 195); also *The Lotos-Eaters* (p. 429), which is closer to the *1830* text. Paden (p. 157) points out that T. was influenced by T. C. Croker's *Fairy Legends* (1825–8), and by the Sirens in the *Odyssey* xii 184–205.

*21.* Cp. Keats, *Ode to a Nightingale* 48: 'mid-May's eldest child' (with 'summer', l. 50). T.'s progression to 'diamondeyed' may owe something to Keats, *Fancy* 52: 'Sapphire queen of the mid-May'.
*22.* *Cymbeline* IV iv 29–30: 'But to be still hot Summer's tanlings, and / The shrinking slaves of Winter' (the only *OED* example before T.).
¶ 119.*2.* Cp. *The Devil and the Lady* I v 95: 'the ridgèd waves'; from *Lear* IV vi 71: 'the enridgèd sea'.

Slow sailed the weary mariners and saw,
Betwixt the green brink and the running foam,
Sweet faces, rounded arms, and bosoms prest
To little harps of gold; and while they mused
Whispering to each other half in fear,
Shrill music reached them on the middle sea.

Whither away, whither away, whither away? fly no
    more.
Whither away from the high green field, and the
    happy blossoming shore?
Day and night to the billow the fountain calls:
Down shower the gambolling waterfalls
From wandering over the lea:
Out of the live-green heart of the dells
They freshen the silvery-crimson shells,
And thick with white bells the clover-hill swells
High over the full-toned sea:
O hither, come hither and furl your sails,
Come hither to me and to me:

¶ 120.*2. Betwixt*] *1853*; Between *1830*.
*2* ∧ *3*] White limbs unrobèd in a chrystal air, *1830*.
*6* ∧ *7*] SONG *1830*.
*7* ∧ *8*] Whither away wi' the singing sail? whither away wi' the oar? *1830*.
*8* ∧ *9*]
Weary mariners, hither away,
  One and all, one and all,
Weary mariners come and play;
We will sing to you all the day;
  Furl the sail and the foam will fall
  From the prow! One and all
  Furl the sail! drop the oar!
    Leap ashore!
Know danger and trouble and toil no more.
Whither away wi' the sail and the oar?
    Drop the oar,
    Leap ashore,
    Fly no more!
Whither away wi' the sail? whither away wi' the oar?
*1830*

*12*] *1853*; *not 1830*.
*16–31*] *1853*;
Merrily carol the revelling gales
  Over the islands free:
From the green seabanks the rose downtrails
  To the happy brimmèd sea. *1830*

Hither, come hither and frolic and play;
Here it is only the mew that wails;
We will sing to you all the day:
Mariner, mariner, furl your sails,
For here are the blissful downs and dales,
And merrily, merrily carol the gales,
And the spangle dances in bight and bay,
And the rainbow forms and flies on the land
Over the islands free;
And the rainbow lives in the curve of the sand;
Hither, come hither and see;
And the rainbow hangs on the poising wave,
And sweet is the colour of cove and cave,
And sweet shall your welcome be:
O hither, come hither, and be our lords,
For merry brides are we:
We will kiss sweet kisses, and speak sweet words:
O listen, listen, your eyes shall glisten
With pleasure and love and jubilee:
O listen, listen, your eyes shall glisten
When the sharp clear twang of the golden chords
Runs up the ridgèd sea.
Who can light on as happy a shore
All the world o'er, all the world o'er?
Whither away? listen and stay: mariner, mariner, fly
no more.

*32. O*] *1853*; Come *1830*.

*36. jubilee*] *1853*; revelry *1830*.

*39. the ridgèd sea*: *Song* [*The winds*] 2. Cp. *The Devil and the Lady* I v 95, 'the ridgèd waves'. From *Lear* IV vi 71: 'the enridgèd sea'.

*40. Who . . . as*] *1853*; Ye will not find so *1830*.

*41–2*] *1853*;
Weary mariners! all the world o'er.
Oh! fly no more.
Harken ye, harken ye, sorrow shall darken ye,
Danger and trouble and toil no more;
Whither away?
Drop the oar;
Hither away,
Leap ashore;
Oh fly no more–no more.
Whither away, whither away, whither away with the sail
and the oar? *1830*

# 121 To J.M.K.

Published *1830*; 'Juvenilia', 'Early Sonnets II'. Written 1829–30. 'To my old college friend, J. M. Kemble' (T.); 'he gave up his thought of taking Orders, and devoted himself to Anglo-Saxon history and literature' (H.T.). It is the only sonnet of *1830* which T. reprinted; on his sonnets, see D. B. MacEachen, *Victorian Newsletter*, Fall 1958.

My hope and heart is with thee–thou wilt be
A latter Luther, and a soldier-priest
To scare church-harpies from the master's feast;
Our dusted velvets have much need of thee:
Thou art no sabbath-drawler of old saws,
Distilled from some worm-cankered homily;
But spurred at heart with fieriest energy
To embattail and to wall about thy cause
With iron-worded proof, hating to hark
The humming of the drowsy pulpit-drone
Half God's good sabbath, while the worn-out clerk
Brow-beats his desk below. Thou from a throne
Mounted in heaven wilt shoot into the dark
Arrows of lightnings. I will stand and mark.

# 122 *Οἱ ῥέοντες [All thoughts, all creeds]

Published *1830*, not reprinted. The title was the nickname of the Heraclitean philosophers who held that all things were in a constant state of flux. T. ends with a bantering footnote. Contrast *The Higher Pantheism* 4: 'Dreams are true while they last, and do we not live in dreams?' Cp. *All Things Will Die* (p. 227).

I

All thoughts, all creeds, all dreams are true,
All visions wild and strange;
Man is the measure of all truth
Unto himself. All truth is change:

¶ 121.*3*. Cp. *Paradise Regained* ii 402–3 (after the tempting of Christ): 'Both Table and Provision vanish'd quite / With sound of Harpies wings, and Talons heard.'

*9*. *proof*: including the earlier sense of 'armour'.

*12–14*. *Zechariah* ix 14, 'And the Lord shall be seen over them, and his arrow shall go forth as the lightning.'

All men do walk in sleep, and all
Have faith in that they dream:
For all things are as they seem to all,
And all things flow like a stream.

II

There is no rest, no calm, no pause,
Nor good nor ill, nor light nor shade,
Nor essence nor eternal laws:
For nothing is, but all is made.
But if I dream that all these are,
They are to me for that I dream;
For all things are as they seem to all,
And all things flow like a stream.

Argal–this very opinion is only true relatively to the flowing philosophers.

# 123 *Ilion, Ilion

Printed by Sir Charles Tennyson, *Nineteenth Century* cix (1931) 502–3; then *1931*, pp. 47–8: 'This fragment is from a pocket-book [*H.Nbk 4*] which contains fragments of many of the poems published in the volume of 1830. It is therefore almost certainly of the Cambridge period. I have retained the compound words which the poet employed at this period but afterwards abandoned, as they seem almost essential to the rhythm.' *H.Nbk 4* is watermarked 1828, inscribed 'Trin: Coll.', and includes poems of *1830. 1931* gives T.'s scansion from the MS. Troy was built by the music of Apollo; cp. *Tithonus* 62–3: 'Like that strange song I heard Apollo sing, / While Ilion like a mist rose into towers.' Cp. Horace, *Odes* III iii 17–18: *gratum elocuta consiliantibus / Iunone divis: 'Ilion, Ilion . . .'* ('What time Juno, among the gods in council gathered, spake the welcome words: "Ilium, Ilium . . ."') T. translated this ode as a schoolboy (*Lincoln*).

Ilion, Ilion, dreamy Ilion, pillared Ilion, holy Ilion,
City of Ilion when wilt thou be melody born?
Blue Scamander, yellowing Simois from the heart of
piny Ida
Everwhirling from the molten snows upon the
mountainthrone,

¶ 122.*6–8*. Cp. Shelley, *The Sensitive Plant* iii 124–5: 'Where nothing is, but all things seem, / And we the shadows of the dream.'
¶ 123.*3*. *piny*: used five times by Shelley.

Roll Scamander, ripple Simois, ever onward to a melody
Manycircled, overflowing thorough and thorough the flowery level of unbuilt Ilion,
City of Ilion, pillared Ilion, shadowy Ilion, holy Ilion,
To a music merrily flowing, merrily echoing
When wilt thou be melody born?

Manygated, heavywallèd, manytowered city of Ilion,
From the silver, lilyflowering meadowlevel
When wilt thou be melody born?
Ripple onward, echoing Simois,
Ripple ever with a melancholy moaning,
In the rushes to the dark blue brimmèd Ocean, yellowing Simois,
To a music from the golden twanging harpwire heavily drawn.
Manygated, heavywallèd, manytowered city of Ilion,
To a music sadly flowing, slowly falling,
When wilt thou be melody born?

## 124 *Amy

Printed by Sir Charles Tennyson, *Nineteenth Century* cix (1931) 499–500, with omissions; then *1931*, pp. 54–5: 'These lines are from the same pocket-book [*H.Nbk 4*] as the *Ilion* fragment in what is apparently a hurried first draft of a poem which the poet intended to revise.' *H.Nbk 4* is watermarked 1828, inscribed 'Trin: Coll.', and includes poems of *1830*.

Highminded and pure-thoughted, chaste and simple,
In Life's broad river set
A lily, where the waters faintly dimple,
Leaving the flower unwet;

*6. flowery level*: as in Akenside's *Pleasures of Imagination* ii (*Lincoln*); *The Princess* iii 318 has 'flowery levels'.
*10. manytowered*: applied to Camelot, *The Lady of Shalott* 5.
*11*] *H.Nbk 4* has a fragment of the poem including: 'By the green brink lilybraided violetwoven'.
*14. with*] to *MS 1st reading.*
*15. dark blue brimmèd*] *added to MS.*
¶ 124.*1. Highminded and pure-thoughted,*] Growing alone I find the *H.MS 1st reading*. Cp. *Ode to Memory* 118: 'Subtle-thoughted, myriad-minded'.

The silver tongues of featherfooted rumour
Ne'er spake of thee to me,
Thou hast no range of wit, no wealth of humour,
But pure humility
Dwelling like moonlight in a silver vapour;
Not pale St Agatha
Bent o'er her missal by her waxen taper,
Not sweet Cecilia,
St Agnes on St Agnes' Eve, who leadeth
Over the snowy hill
Her snowwhite lambs and with hushed footstep treadeth,
Is not so chaste and still
In the cold moon, e'er yet the crocus flamy
Or snowdrop burst to life;
Yet with a human love I love thee, Amy,
And woo thee for my wife.
And thou from human love thy name dost borrow
But thou art Heaven's bride.
Speak to me, Amy, I am full of sorrow
And full of human pride,
And more and more my gladness from me stealeth
And pleasant visions flow
And there are moments when the proud man feeleth
The lowest of the low.
Dear sainted Amy, thou dost never tremble
To starts or thrills of love,
But rather in thy motion dost resemble
Hill-shaded streams, that move
Through the umber glebe and in brown deeps embosom
The tremulous Evenstar,
Fold within fold thou growest, a virgin blossom,
In dewy glades afar.

*13. leadeth*] leads *MS 1st reading*. Cp. *St Agnes' Eve* (p. 552).

*15. with . . . treadeth*] ever tells her beads *MS 1st reading*.

*17. In . . . yet*] Before the snowdrop or *MS 1st reading*. Pope, *Iliad* xiv 400: 'flamy crocus'.

*18*] Is warmed to second life; *MS 1st reading*.

*21–8*] *MS*; *not 1931*.

*32. Hill-shaded*] Deep, quiet, *MS 1st reading*.

*33*. Cp. Shelley, *Alastor* 422–3: 'whose brown magnificence / A narrow vale embosoms'.

*34*. Shelley, *Witch of Atlas* 434: 'tremulous stars'.

*35. Fold . . . growest,*] And thou unfoldest like *MS 1st reading*.

*36. dewy glades*] stilly woods *MS 1st reading*.

I never found a soul more mild or holier,
  A face more glassyfair,
Nor met a maiden lovelier or lowlier
  Than Amy anywhere.
Controlling all the haughty by the meekness
  Which is her natural dower,
And in her very lowliness and weakness
  Concentering her power.
So full of Heaven, so built upon one notion,
  Not scorning earthly things,
Passing with such an equal motion,
  A dove with balanced wings.
A maid with lips of love so tender-hearted
  I never knew till now,
With such black hair uncurled and straightly parted
  Upon her marble brow.
O shape more slender than the fabled fairy,
  Like streaks of cloud by night
That overlay the stars in January
  But cannot hide their light.
O long black hair! O pale thin hands! O splendour
  Of starry countenance
Wherein I lose myself from life, and wander
  In utter ignorance
As in some other world where strong desire
  Fulfils ideals and draws
Homeward to all things men of orders higher
  Subject to loftier laws.
Poring on thee my soul flows deep and stillier–
  You love me not as man,
You love me with that love which St Cecilia
  Did love Valerian,
When in a pure embrace he did enfold her,
  Saying 'My heavenly spouse',
And speaking low, she leaned upon his shoulder
  Her lilywreathèd brows.
Yet take blind Passion; give him eyes; and freeing
  His spirit from his frame,
Make double-natured love lose half his being
  In thy spiritual flame,

*37–72*] *MS*; *not 1931*.
*54–6*. Cp. *Œnone* 213–15: 'never see them overlaid / With narrow moon-lit slips of silver cloud, / Between the loud stream and the trembling stars.'
*62–4*] *MS illegible*. The readings are conjectual.
*75*. Cp. *Lucretius* 192–4 on the 'twy-natured' satyr (p. 1214).

Till like a rainbow in a rainbow folded
 And of a rainbow made,
My spirit within thy spirit may be moulded,
 My soul of thine the shade.

# 125 *Elegiacs

Printed by Sir Charles Tennyson, *Nineteenth Century* cix (1931) 503; then *1931*, p. 49: 'These lines come from a notebook [*H.Nbk 7*] inscribed "A. Tennyson, Trin. Coll., Cambridge." They are very roughly written and entirely without stops. There is a gap in the MS. between lines eight and nine, which suggests that the poet may have intended to add another couplet there. The lines may be compared with the *Leonine Elegiacs* in the 1830 volume' (p. 185). *H.Nbk 7* is watermarked 1826, and includes poems of *1830*.

Over an old gate leaning i' the mellow time of the gleaning
Pleasant it was to hark unto the merry woodlark,
Loudly he sang from the thicket, and nigher the shrilly balm-cricket
Under a full-leaved spray chirruped and carolled away.
Under a sky red-copèd the lights of the evening slopèd,
All with a roseate heat tipping the points of the wheat;
Every cloud over the dim sun was barred and bridgèd with crimson,
Only one great gold star burned through a cleft from afar.
Over a brook and two meadows beyond, up among the elm shadows,
Steeped in the sunlight calm glowed the white walls of the farm;
Three full wains had been thither with labour, three empty come hither;
Half of the gold stack stared over the pales in the yard.

# 126 *Memory [Ay me!]

Printed by Sir Charles Tennyson, *Nineteenth Century* cix (1931) 377–8; then *1931*, pp. 33–4: 'This fragment, which is very hastily written, occurs in the same notebook as the two preceding poems, *O Bosky Brook* and *In Deep and Solemn Dreams* [*H.Nbk 7*]. It, too, appears to belong to the Somersby-Cambridge transition period.' *H.Nbk 7* is watermarked 1826, inscribed 'Trin: Coll.', and includes poems of *1830*. Cp. *Memory! dear enchanter*

¶ 125.*3*. Cp. *A Dirge* 47 (*1830*): 'The balm-cricket carols clear'.
*4*. *full-leaved*: Keats, *Eve of St Mark* 45.
*7*. Cp. Keats, *To Autumn* 25–6: 'While barred clouds bloom the soft-dying day, / And touch the stubble-plains with rosy hue.' (Note the season of *Elegiacs*.)

(*1827*, p. 82). Paden (pp. 47–8) points out that the buffaloes are from C.-E. Savary's *Letters on Egypt* (the 1799 translation is at *Lincoln*), a passage which follows a description of the Egyptian maidens naked by the Nile: 'The buffaloes have replaced, in the dream, by the process of substitution, the naked girls who also swam in the shallows of the Nile. The image of dalliance has merged with those of fierce drouth and envenomed death.' Paden (p. 135) also compares Collins, *Persian Eclogues* ii 61–4: 'At that dead Hour the silent Asp shall creep, / If ought of rest I find, upon my Sleep: / Or some swoln Serpent twist his Scales around, / And wake to Anguish with a burning Wound.'

Ay me! those childish lispings roll
As thunder through my heart and soul,
Those fair eyes in my inmost frame
Are subtle shafts of pierceant flame.

Blessèd, cursèd, Memory,
Shadow, Spirit as thou mayst be,
Why hast thou become to me
A conscience dropping tears of fire
On the heart, which vain desire
Vexeth all too bitterly?
When the wand of circumstance
All at once hath bid thee glance,
From the body of the Past,
Like a wandering ghost aghast,
Why wearest thou, mad Memory,
Limb and lip and hair and eye,
Life–life without life or breath,
Death forth issuing from Death?

May goes not before dark December,
Nor doth the year change suddenly;
Wherefore do I so remember
That Hope is born of Memory
Nightly in the house of dreams?
But when I wake, at once she seems

¶ 126.*3*. *inmost frame*: *The Lover's Tale* i 584; Shelley, *Revolt of Islam* VIII xvii 2.

*3–4*. Cp. *Fatima* 17–18: 'A thousand little shafts of flame /Were shivered in my narrow frame.' Also *To*-[*Clear-headed friend*] 13: 'With shrilling shafts of subtle wit'. *pierceant*: Spenser's 'persant', *FQ* I x st. 47; Keats's 'perceant', *Lamia* ii 301.

*8*. Cp. *Sense and Conscience* 90, where Conscience weeps 'tears of fire'.

*16*. *Limb*] *MS*; Lip *1931 with note*: 'The first word of this line is very hard to decipher and I cannot guarantee the text'. T. wrote 'Lip' but corrected it to 'Limb'.

The faery changeling wan Despair,
Who laughs all day and never speaks–
O dark of bright! O foul of fair!
A frightful child with shrivelled cheeks.

Why at break of cheerful day
Doth my spirit faint away
Like a wanderer in the night?
Why in visions of the night
Am I shaken with delight
Like a lark at dawn of day?
As a hungry serpent coiled
Round a palm tree in the wild,
When his bakèd jaws are bare
Burning in the burning air,
And his corky tongue is black
With the raging famine-crack,
If perchance afar he sees
Winding up among the trees,
Lordly-headed buffaloes,
Or but hears their distant lows,
With the fierce remembrance drunk
He crushes all the stalwart trunk
Round which his fainting folds are prest,
With delirium-causing throes
Of anticipated zest.

# 127 *Ode: O Bosky Brook

Printed by Sir Charles Tennyson, *Nineteenth Century* cix (1931) 374–6; then *1931*, pp. 23–7: 'This fragment is evidently of early origin. A preliminary and less complete version exists in a notebook [*H.Nbk 2*] which contains some very early verses, apparently of about the date of *The Devil and the*

*35–6.* Cp. *Memory! dear enchanter* 29–32 (*1827*): 'Round every palm-tree, springing / With bright fruit in the waste, / A mournful asp is clinging, / Which sours it to our taste.'

*39.* Cp. *The Devil and the Lady* III iii 30: 'dry and corky tongue'. From 'corky arms', *Lear* III vii 29.

*40. famine-crack*: *OED* is of little help. 'Parched by hunger into cracking'?

*45. fierce remembrance*: *Samson Agonistes* 952, where the context is of physical violence.

*47.* Cp. Shelley, *The Sensitive Plant* i 31: 'Till, fold after fold, to the fainting air'.

*Lady* (written *aetat.* fourteen). The fragment is in three somewhat disconnected parts. The first is addressed to a brook, not the famous Holywell brook, though no doubt the description is, in parts, reminiscent of it, but to an imaginary mountain stream. The second is addressed to the moon, the last to darkness.' *H.Nbk 2* (*A* below) is watermarked 1824 and includes drafts of *Armageddon* and *Timbuctoo*. The *1931* text is from *H.Nbk 7* (*B* below), which is watermarked 1826, inscribed 'Trin: Coll.', and includes poems of *1830*. Paden (pp. 33–4) remarks that the third section is 'a panegyric to a goddess of the night. Its composition may have been originally suggested by the *Hymn to the Night* that Sir William Jones translated from one of the Vedas, but its goddess did not come from India, and it became a very personal poem. . . . Tennyson found his goddess in the *Letters on Egypt* of Savary, where he read that "One of the most antient of the Egyptian Deities was Athor; which, in the Coptic, signifies Night. The priests, by this word, did not mean that privation of light which succeeds sun-set; but the darkness of Chaos, before creation; of which, animating it by his breath, God made all creatures . . . Damasius, speaking of antient Egyptian Theology, says, "they held Darkness to be the first principle, which human reason might not comprehend, and which they thrice celebrated in their sacred hymns."""' The works of Jones (1799) and Savary's *Letters* (1799) were at Somersby (*Lincoln*).

I

O bosky brook, which I have loved to trace
Through all thy green and winding ways,
Wandering in the pure light of youthful days
    Along yon dusky windy hills,
Whose dark indent and wild variety
Curtails the Southern sky,
Following, through many a windy grove of pines,
White undergrowth of hemlocks and hoar lines
Of sallows, whitening to the fitful breeze,
    The voiceful influx of thy tangled rills–
How happy were the fresh and dewy years
    When by thy damp and rushy side,
    In the deep yellow Eventide,
I wept sweet tears,
Watching the red hour of the dying Sun,
And felt my mind dilate
With solemn uncontrollable pleasure, when

¶ 127.*7–10*] *Added on later page in A.*
*8. hemlocks*] *B*; hemlock *1931.*
*9.* Shelley, *Rosalind* 959: 'fitful breezes'.
*10.* Cp. *The Dying Swan* 19: 'tangled water-courses'. *voiceful*: *OED* 1 b, 'of a stream, the sea' (William Browne, Coleridge).

The sad curve of the hueless Moon,
Sole in her state,
Varied with steadfast shades the glimmering plain,
And full of lovely light
Appeared the mountain-tarn's unbroken sleep,
Which never felt the dewy sweep
Of oars, but blackly lay
Beneath the sunny living noon,
Most like an insulated part of night,
Though fair by night as day:
So deep, that when day's manhood wears his crown
Of hottest rays in Heaven's windy Hall,
To one who pryeth curiously down,
From underneath the infathomable pall
And pressure of the upright wave,
The abiding eyes of Space, from forth the grave
Of that black Element,
Shine out like wonderful gleams
Of thrilling and mysterious beauty, sent
From gay shapes sparkling through the gloom of
dreams.

II

Well have I known thee, whatsoe'er thy phase,
In every time and place,
Pale Priestess of grey Night,
Whether thy flood of mournful rays,
Parted by dewless point of conic hill,
Adown its richer side
Fell straying
Into the varied valley underneath;
Or where, within the eddying tide
Of some tumultuous mountain-rill,
Like some delusive charm
Thy mimic form,
Full opposite to thy reality,
Broken and flashing and playing
In tremulous darts of slender light,

*29.* Cp. *Lucretius* 136: 'the windy halls of heaven', and *The Lover's Tale* i 63, MS: 'Heaven's windy halls.'

*31. infathomable*] unfathomable *A*.

*38*] I have adored thee whatsoe'er thy phase, *A*, *B 1st reading*.

*43. side*] slope *A 1st reading*.

*45* ∧ *6*] *A has ll. 54–60.*

*48*] *Not A.*

*52*] *A breaks off here but has ll. 63–7 in a fragment.*

Beguiled the sight;
Or on the screaming waste of desolate heath
In midnight full of sound,
Or in close pastures soft as dewy sleep,
Or in the hollow deep
Of woods, whose counterchanged embroidery
Of light and darkness chequered the old moss
On the damp ground;
Or whether thou becamest the bright boss
  Of thine own Halo's dusky shield,
    Or when thou burnest beaconlike upon
  The margin of the dun and dappled field
    Of vagrant waves, or higher risen, dost link
    Thy reflex to the steadfast brink,
  With such a lustrous chord of solemn sheen,
That the heart vibrates with desire to pace
The palpitating track of buoyant rays;
  Or when the loud sea gambols and the spray
Of its confliction shoots and spreads and falls,
Blossoming round the everduring walls
      Which build up the giant cape,
      Whose massed and wonder-stirring shape
        And jutting head,
        Citadel-crowned and tempest-buffeted,
Runs far away,
(What time the white West glows with sickening ray)
And in the middle ocean meets the surging shock,
And plumes with snowy sheen each gathered crest,
The lighthouse glowing from the secret rock,
The seabird piping on the wild salt waste.

*56.* J. H. Buckley (p. 264) compares *The Palace of Art* 86–7: 'On dewy pastures, dewy trees, / Softer than sleep.' Virgil's *somno mollior herba* (*Eclogues* vii 45). *dewy sleep*: Shelley, *Adonais* 61, and his *Ginevra* 127.

*57. hollow deep*: *Paradise Lost* i 314.

*61–4.* Sir Charles Tennyson points out that these were adapted as *The Voyage* 29–32: 'Far ran the naked moon across / The houseless ocean's heaving field, / Or flying shone, the silver boss / Of her own halo's dusky shield.'

*65. waves . . . risen,*] waters and *B 1st reading.*

*66. steadfast*] Ocean *A, fragment.*

*76, 79.* Sir Charles Tennyson points out that these were adapted as *Will* 8–9: 'In middle ocean meets the surging shock, / Tempest-buffeted, citadel-crowned.'

*80. sheen*] light *B 1st reading.*

III

I savour of the Egyptian and adore
Thee, venerable dark! august obscure!
Sublimest Athor!
It is not that I doat upon
Thy glooms, because the weary mind is fraught
With fond comparison
Of thy deep shadow to its inward strife,
But rather,
That as thou wert the parent of all life,
Even so thou art the mother of all thought,
Which wells not freely from the mind's recess
When the sharp sunlight occupies the sense
With this fair world's exceeding comeliness,
The goodly show and varied excellence
Of lithe tall trees, the languor of sweet flowers
Into the universal herbage woven,
High hills and broad fair vallies river-cloven,
Part strown with lordly cities and with towers,
Part spotted with the gliding white of pregnant sails;
Add murmur, which the buxom gales
(As my glowing brows they fan)
Bear upward through the happy heights of air,
Chirp, bellow, bark and distant shout of man–
Not that the mind is edged,
Not that the spirit of thought is freshlier fledged
With stillness like the stillness of the tomb
And grossest gloom,
As it were of the inner sepulchre.
Rare sound, spare light will best address
The soul for awful muse and solemn watchfulness.

87. *fraught*] wrought *B 1st reading.*
88. *With*] Unto the *B 1st reading.*
89. *shadow*] shadows *B 1st reading.* *inward strife*: *Love thou* 53.
100. *Part*] And *B 1st reading.*
105. *shout*] voice *B 1st reading.*
105 ∧ 6] Or whistle and hum of large-eyed flies. *B deleted.*
109–10. Cp. *A Dream of Fair Women* 67–8: 'Gross darkness of the inner sepulchre / Is not so deadly still.' The sepulchre was probably suggested by C.-E. Savary's *Letters on Egypt* (1799 translation, *Lincoln*), who describes entering the great pyramid (Paden, pp. 136–7).
112. *watchfulness*] thoughtfulness *B 1st reading.*

# 128 *Perdidi Diem

Printed by Sir Charles Tennyson, *Nineteenth Century* cix (1931) 378–80; then *1931*, pp. 35–7: 'This fragment is from a notebook [*H.Nbk 7*, watermarked 1826 and including poems of *1830*] inscribed "A. Tennyson, Trin: Coll:, Cambridge." An earlier version of the first few lines also exists, suggesting that the lines were begun at Somersby.' The title alludes to the saying of the Emperor Titus (quoted in Suetonius) when he found at night that he had done no good action that day. Cp. *Remorse* (*1827*, p. 87); *Supposed Confessions* (*1830*, p. 197); and *Pierced through* (p. 472).

I

And thou hast lost a day! Oh mighty boast!
Dost thou miss one day only? I have lost
A life, perchance an immortality;
I never *lived* a day, but daily die,
I have no real breath;
My being is a vacant worthlessness,
A carcase in the coffin of this flesh,
Pierced through with loathly worms of utter Death.
My soul is but the eternal mystic lamp,
Lighting that charnel damp,
Wounding with dreadful rays that solid gloom,
And shadowing forth the unutterable tomb,
Making a 'darkness visible'
Of that which without thee we had not felt
As darkness, dark ourselves and loving night,

¶ 128.*5–12.* Forming part of *Pierced through* 15–24:

I lay with sobbing breath,
Walled round, shut up, imbarred, moaning for light,
A carcase in the coffin of this flesh,
Pierced through with loathly worms of utter death.
And in that spiritual charnel low and damp
All my past thoughts and actions I did mark
Thick-thronging to and fro amid the gloom.
My soul was but the eternal mystic lamp
Wounding with dreadful rays the solid dark
And shadowing out the unutterable tomb.

*6. worthlessness*] nothingness *H.MS 1st reading.*

*7.* Cp. *Vastness* 33: 'our own corpse-coffins at last'.

*8. loathly worms*: Shelley, *Prometheus Unbound* III iv 36. Cp. *The Vision of Sin* 209: 'pierced with worms'.

*11. Wounding*] Piercing *MS 1st reading.* *rays*] *MS*; days *1931.*

*13. 'darkness visible'*: *Paradise Lost* i 63.

Night-bats into the filtering crevices
Hooked, clinging, darkness-fed, at ease:
Night-owls whose organs were not made for light.
I must needs pore upon the mysteries
Of my own infinite Nature and torment
My spirits with a fruitless discontent:
As in the malignant light
Of a dim, dripping, moon-enfolding night,
Young ravens fallen from their cherishing nest
On the elm-summit, flutter in agony
With a continual cry
About its roots, and fluttering trail and spoil
Their new plumes on the misty soil,
But not the more for this
Shall the loved mother minister
Aerial food, and to their wonted rest
Win them upon the topmost branch in air
With sleep-compelling down of her most glossy breast.
In chill discomfort still they cry:
What is the death of life if this be not to die?

II

You tell me that to me a Power is given,
An effluence of serenest fire from Heaven,
Pure, vapourless, and white,
As God himself in kind, a spirit-guiding light,
Fed from each self-originating spring
Of most inviolate Godhead, issuing
From underneath the shuddering stairs which climb
The throne,
Where each intense pulsation
And going-on o' the heart of God's great life,
Out of the sphere of Time,
As from an actual centre is heard to beat,
And to the thrilling mass communicate,

*16.* Paden (pp. 136–7) compares the account of entering the great pyramid in C.-E. Savary's *Letters on Egypt* (1799 translation, *Lincoln*): 'thousands of bats, much larger than those of Europe, that, darting up and down, beat against our hands and faces and extinguished several of our lights'. Paden also compares the 'inner sepulchre' of *Ode: O Bosky Brook* 108–10.
*19. I must*] Men will *MS 1st reading.*
*20. my . . . Nature*] their . . . Natures *MS 1st reading.*
*21. My*] Their *MS 1st reading.* *spirits*] *MS, Nineteenth Century*; spirit *1931.* (Sir Charles Tennyson's text in *Nineteenth Century* cix (1931) 378).
*32. Win*] Warm *MS 1st reading.*
*40. each*] the ever *MS 1st reading.*

Goes through and through with musical fire and through
The spiritual nerves and arteries
Of those first spirits, which round the incorruptible base
Bow, with furled pinions veiling their immortal eyes,
As not enduring, face to face,
Eye-combat with the unutterable gaze.
These are the highest few:
Thence to the lower, broader circle runs
The sovran subtil impulse on and on,
Until all Heaven, an inconceivable cone
Of vision-shadowing vans and claspèd palms,
Of circle below circle, file below
File, one life, one heart, one glow,
Even to the latest range which tramples on the highest suns,
With every infinite pulsation
Brightens and darkens; downward, downward still
The mighty pulses thrill
With wreathèd light and sound,
Through the rare web-work woven round
The highest spheres,
Prompting the audible growth of great harmonious years.
Base of the cone,
Last of the link,
Each rolling sun and hornèd moon,
All the awful and surpassing lights
Which we from every zone
Of the orbed Earth survey on summer nights,
(When nights are deepest and most clear)
Are in their station cold;
The latest energies of light they drink:
The latest fiat of Divine Art,
Our Planets, slumbering in their swiftness, hear
The last beat of the thunder of God's heart.

*51.* Based on *PL* ii 138, describing God on his throne.

*53. face to face*: *1 Corinthians* xiii 12, 'For now we see through a glass, darkly; but then face to face.' See *Crossing the Bar* 13–16*n* (p. 1459).

*59. -shadowing vans*] shading plumes *MS 1st reading.*

*66. wreathèd light*: Keats, *Otho* V v 38.

*78–9. Fiat lux*; cp. Milton's Creation, when the sun can 'drink the liquid Light', *PL* vii 362.

*81*] *MS then has* 'III' *marked.*

# 129 *Sonnet [Conrad! why call thy life monotonous?]

Printed by Sir Charles Tennyson, *Nineteenth Century* cix (1931) 508; then *1931*, p. 66, from *H.Nbk 7* (watermarked 1826, inscribed 'Trin: Coll.', and including poems of *1830* and *1832*). 'Conrad' is probably an invention, perhaps from the pirate-chief in Byron's *The Corsair* III xxii: 'On Conrad's stricken soul Exhaustion prest, / And Stupor almost lulled it into rest . . . / There is no darkness like the cloud of mind, / On Grief's vain eye – the blindest of the blind! / Which may not – dare not see – but turns aside / To blackest shade – nor will endure a guide!' Also Thomas Campbell's *The Pleasures of Hope* ii 436, on Conrad and his 'tedious watch'.

Conrad! why call thy life monotonous?
   Why brood above thine anchor? The woven weed
   Calms not, but blackens, the slope water bed.
The shores of Life are fair and various,
   But thou dost ever by one beach abide.
Why hast thou drawn thine oars across the boat?
Thou canst not without impulse downward float,
   The wave of Life hath no propelling tide.
We live but by *resistance*, and the best
   Of Life is but the struggle of the will:
   Thine unresisting boat shall pause – not still
But beaten on both sides with swaying Unrest.
Oh! cleave this calm to living eddies, breast
   This sloth-sprung weed with progress sensible.

# 130 *Sense and Conscience

Printed *1931*, pp. 42–6: 'These lines are an unfinished allegory of the struggle between Sense and Conscience. The giant whose fate is here

¶ 129. *3*] Flattens the swaying waves which round thee spread. *H.MS 1st reading.* *slope*: sloping, as in *Paradise Lost* iv 261; Keats, *Lamia* ii 26.
*4*] Albeit the shores of Life are various, *MS 1st reading.* *shores of Life*: taken up and developed as in *Sonnet* [*When that rank heat*] 3 (p. 292), with which this sonnet argues.
*8*. Cp. Shelley, *Revolt of Islam* II xxiii 9: 'the wave of life's dark stream'.
*12*. *with*] *MS*; by *1931*.
*13*. *calm*] death *MS 1st reading.*
*14*. Cp. *In Memoriam* xxvii 11: 'But stagnates in the weeds of sloth'. *sensible*: the main sense is *OED* 4, 'appreciable, considerable'.

described is Conscience; he is drugged by the adherents of Sense and cast out into a remote forest. The poem is contained in a notebook inscribed: "A. Tennyson, Trin: Coll:, Cambridge." [*H.Nbk 7*, watermarked 1826 and including poems of *1830* and *1832*]'. *1931* omitted ll. 79–88: 'I have omitted one very involved and obviously imperfect passage of ten lines, the deletion of which causes no interruption of the sense'. Cp. the blank verse of *The Lover's Tale*, and see ll. 99–104*n* below. Paden (p. 56) discusses the imagery of the poem.

Working high treason toward thy sovranty,
A traitorous and unfaithful minister,
Have I been lavish of thy treasures, Time.
Thy stores were shallow enow, but on their briefness
Have I drawn largely and often, hoping they
Were deeper than I found them, ill-informed,
An ignorant vain steward: they lie so thin now
I cannot choose but see their shallowness.
When they are wasted I am out of place,
And that must needs come quickly: for I have not
(As the condition of mine office ran)
Used them to furnish necessary wars
With fitting front of opposition
And subtil temperament of hardened arms,
Wherewith to embattail *Spirit*, whose fair ranks,
Strong in their essence but undisciplined,
Were shocked and riven and shaken asunder wide,
And ridden over by the exulting *Sense*,
Their clamorous shrieks dust-stifled–
Rather, Time,
Unto the abuse of thy most precious ore,
Did I win over the Arch-Enemy *Sense*,
And set him in the chiefest offices
And heights o' the State, unto the infinite rack
Of those few faithful in the land, which still
Cried out against my stewardship. Then Sense
Grew large and prospered at the court of Time,
Say rather, took away all thought of Time
By his own imminent greatness, and then first
Made me his bondsman, and by violence
Wrenched from my grasp the golden keys which guard
The doors o' the Treasure-house. Great Conscience then,
The boldest of the warriors of Time,
Prime mover of those wars of Spirit and Sense,
The wisest of the councillors of Time,
Erewhile my bosom friend, whose voice till now

Was loudest in the Council-room against
The prevalent Ministry, was drugged to sleep
By a most stealthy potion given by Sense–
To *sleep!* for neither edge of finest steel
Nor barbèd firẹ of spears, nor deadliest draught
Could drive him to the death: such subtlety
Of revivescence in his spirit lay,
Infused by his immortal Parentage,
*Reason* and *Will!*
They drove him to deep shades,
A gloom monotonously musical
With hum of murmurous bees, which brooded deep
In ever-trembling flowers, and constant moan
Of waterfalls i' the distance, and low winds
Wandering close to Earth, and voice of doves,
Which ever bowing cooed and cooing bowed
Unto each other as they could not cease.
Long time he lay and slept: his awful brows
Pillowed on violet-woven mosses deep;
The irrepressible fire of his keen eyes
Burned through the shadow of their down-dropt lids;
One hand was flung to distance; the barred iron
Of battle-writhen sinews crushed and massed
The pleasurable flowers; the other grasped
The hilt of that great blade of puissant flame
Hight the *heart-cleaver*.
Alway in his sight
Delicious dreams floated unto the music
Of winds (whose fragrance and whose melodies
Made sweet contention which should sweeter be,
And through contention grew to perfectness
Of most inviolate communion),

¶ 130.*40. barbèd fire*: Shelley, *Adonais* 99.
*46–9.* Cp. *The Princess* vii 206–7: 'The moan of doves in immemorial elms, / And murmuring of innumerable bees.' Cp. Keats, *Ode to a Nightingale* 50: 'The murmurous haunt of flies'.
*49–51.* Adapted in *Heath MS* of *The Gardener's Daughter* 89–90: 'That ever bowing cooed and cooing bowed, / And to themselves were all in all.'
*52.* Reminiscent of Keats's *Endymion* and *Hyperion*.
*53. violet-woven*: as in *Ilion, Ilion* 11, MS.
*54. fire*] *H.MS*; power *1931*. Cp. *The Lover's Tale* ii 161–3, on eyes: 'Now the light / Which was their life, burst through the cloud of thought / Keen, irrepressible.'
*57–8.* Cp. *Fatima* 11–12 and *n* (p. 383): 'I rolled among the tender flowers: / I crushed them on my breast, my mouth.'

And witching fantasies which won the heart,
Lovely with bright black eyes and long black hair
And lips which moved in silence, shaping words
With meaning all too sweet for sound.
At last
Came Memory wandering from afar, with stern
Sad eyes and temples wan cinctured with yew;
Pain went before her alway half turned round
To meet her coming with drawn brows low-bent
Whetting a dart on which her tears fell ever,
Softening the stone that she might point the steel.
The Giant raised his eyes and saw and knew
The blackness of her shadow where she stood
Between him and the moonlight of his soul.
How changed from that fair vision which, clad in light,
(The woof of Earth Heaven-dipt, in orient hues
Storying the Past which charactered in fire
Burned from its inmost folds) whilome disdained
All shadow, heralded by Pleasure pure–
Say rather, from the centre of his heart
Filled the whole spirit with unquenchèd Noon
And flung beyond its orbit aught of shade
Thrown from unwelcome height, from whence the feet
Of pallid intellect reel.
Aghast with shame
He started to his feet, but lacking strength
From so long sleep fell prone, and tears of fire
Wept, filling all the joyous flower-cups
With burning blight and odour-quenching sighs,
So that their golden colours fell away

*71. cinctured*: *OED*'s first example is Gray, *Progress of Poesy* 62: 'feather-cinctured Chiefs'.

*77.* Cp. *Paradise Lost* ix 425: 'Veil'd in a Cloud of Fragrance, where she stood'; as in *Sonnet* [*She took*] 4: 'And like a master-painting where she stood'. The likeness is in cadence and positioning.

*79–88*] *MS; not 1931* (see headnote).

*79. How changed*: an epic formula, Virgil's *quantum mutatus ab illo* (*Aeneid* ii 274–6). *PL* i 84–7: 'But O how fall'n! how chang'd / From him, who in the happy Realms of Light / Cloth'd with transcendent brightness didst outshine / Myriads though bright.' Cp. *Timbuctoo* 245: 'How changed from this fair City!'

*80.* Cp. Michael, *PL* xi 244: '*Iris* had dipt the wooff'.

*90. tears of fire*: a close link with 'A conscience dropping tears of fire'. *Memory* [*Ay me*!] 8.

*93–4.* Cp. Shelley, *The Zucca* 63: 'O'erflowed with golden colours'.

O'erflown with pale. Rage seized upon him then
And grasping with both palms his wondrous blade,
Sheer through the summits of the tallest flowers
He drave it: the rose fell, the argent lily,
The dappled fox-glove with its poisoned leaves,
And the tall poppy fell, whose eminent flower,
Hued with the crimson of a fierce sunrise,
Like to the wild youth of an evil King
Is without sweetness, but who crowns himself
Above the secret poisons of his heart
In his old age. The ivy from the stem
Was torn, the vine made desolate; his feet
Were crimsoned with its blood, from which flows joy
And bitterness, first joy from bitterness,
And then again great bitterness from joy.
Soon shrouding with his hand his guilty eyes,
Into the heart o' the realm afar he fled
And lived on bitter roots which Memory
Dug for him round his cell.
One solemn night
He could not sleep, but on the bed of thorns,
Which Memory and Pain had strown for him,
Of brambles and wild thistles of the wood,
Lay tossing, hating light and loathing dark,
And in his agony his heart did seem
To send up to his eyes great drops of blood,
Which would not fall because his burning eyes
Did hiss them into drought. Aloud he wept,
Loud did he weep, for now the iron had come
Into his soul: the hollow-vaulted caverns
Bore out his heavy sobs to the waste night,
And some the low-browed arch returned unto
His ear; so sigh from sigh unceasing grew.

# 131 *Why to Blush is Better than to Paint

Unpublished, *H.Nbk 7* (which is watermarked 1826, inscribed 'Trin: Coll.', and includes poems of *1830*).

*96. summits*] *MS*; summit *1931*.
*99–104.* Incorporated, as Sir Charles Tennyson remarks, almost verbatim as *The Lover's Tale* i 344–9.
*111. bitter*] *MS*; little *1931*.
*120.* Cp. *In Memoriam* cxviii 23: 'baths of hissing tears'.

Lo! how, as in the early Summer days,
Crimson hath stolen away the pulseless white,
And all the Heaven of her cheek grows bright
With shame that is an honour to her face:
All consciously unconscious of her grace
She blushes still for that she blushed before
And wilfully did beautify the more
That which was beautiful: but who would place
This to her vanity, for here we see
The Soul was Artist: even as far as matter
Doth fall from spirit so the colours rare
With which the first doth glorify the latter
Than some coarse pencil's false emblazonry
Show in their nature more exceeding fair.

## 132 *'In deep and solemn dreams'

Printed *1931*, pp. 30–2: 'There are several extant versions of this poem, which seems to have been begun at Somersby and finished at Cambridge' From *H.Nbks 7 and 8* (*A* and *B* below). *H.Nbk 7* is watermarked 1826, inscribed 'Trin: Coll.', and includes poems of *1830*. *Notebook 8* is watermarked 1825, inscribed 'Trinity Coll.', and also includes poems of *1830*. Paden (pp. 145–7) relates the city to Alexandria as described in C.-E. Savary's *Letters on Egypt* (1799 translation, *Lincoln*). There are obvious affinities with *In Memoriam*; see ll. 47–8*n*.

In deep and solemn dreams I view
Great cities by an ocean blue,
Terrace upon terrace bright
Standing out in sunny light,

And sheeny spires and turrets mixt
With pomp of burnished domes betwixt,

¶ 131.*2. pulseless*: probably from Shelley, *Hellas* 142.
*13. emblazonry*: Miltonic. Perhaps suggested by Keats, *Eve of St Agnes* 215, 'emblazonings', where 'blushed' follows.
¶ 132.*1. view*] see *A*.
*2. an ocean blue*] a silent sea *A*.
*3–9*. Cp. the description of Rome in *Paradise Regained* iv 53–4: 'With gilded battlements, conspicuous far, / Turrets and Terrases, and glittering Spires.'

And pinnacles, and airy halls
With fairy fretwork on the walls,

And rows of pillars high and light,
That end in lines of streaky white,
Brooded o'er by dovelike rest,
Like a City of the Blest.

All adown the busy ways
Come sunny faces of lost days,
Long to mouldering dust consigned,
Forms which live but in the mind.

Then methinks they stop and stand,
And I take each by the hand,
And we speak as we have spoken
Ere our love by death was broken.

With tearless ageless eyes that glisten
In light and tranquil mirth, they listen,
And as sleep the brain beguiles
Smile their old familiar smiles.

But ere long that silent sea,
Rising wild and wrathfully,
Sweeps in all-embracing Night
Friends and city from my sight–
Then I lie and toss and mourn
Hopeless, heartless and forlorn.

Then I dream again, and lo!
Round me press a laughing row,
A careless, free and happy crowd,
With merry hearts and voices loud,

*8.* Cp. the MS alteration of *The Palace of Art* 189, *1832* text: 'Ranged on the fairy fretted woodwork round'.
*9. pillars*] columns *A*.
*11.* Milton, *Paradise Lost* i 21: 'Dove-like satst brooding'.
*17–20.* Suggesting *In Memoriam* (the earliest drafts of which rhymed *abab*).
*21–4*] *Not B.*
*21. ageless*] *1931*; changeless *A*.
*22. and*] *1931*; of *A*.
*25. that silent sea*: Coleridge, *Ancient Mariner* 106.
*27. Night*] *A–B*; might *1931*.
*29. Then*] And *A*.
*30*] *B ends.*
*33. , free and*] and a *A*.

On the level sungirt lawn
Ere the glorious sun be born.

And I gaze without a tear
On their countenances clear,
On their noble foreheads white,
And their eyes divine with light–

'Hark away! 'tis early morn,
The East is crimson to the dawn,
We have waked the matin bird
And the brooks may yet be heard.

Brothers, come! the twilight's tears
Are heavy on the barley spears,
And the sweet winds tremble o'er
The large leaves of the sycamore.

Hark away! we'll weave today
A garland of all flowers gay,
Where the freshest flowers be
To the far wood-walks will we.'

Yet a little, brothers, keep
The sacred charm of tearless sleep–
Oh unkind! what darkening change
Hath made your features dim and strange!

Dear lips, loved eyes, ye fade, ye fly,
Even in my fear ye die,
And the hollow dark I dread
Closes round my friendless head,

And far away, to left and right,
Whirlwinds waste the dizzy night,
And I lie and toss and mourn,
Hopeless, heartless and forlorn.

*35. sungirt*] flowergirt *A*. Cp. the 'Lawns, or level Downs' of Milton's Paradise, *PL* iv 252.

*45–8.* Sir Charles Tennyson observes that these were adapted as *In Memoriam* xcv 54–5: 'A breeze began to tremble o'er / The large leaves of the sycamore.'

*57.* Suggesting *In Memoriam* cxxix 6–7: 'Sweet human hand and lips and eye; / Dear heavenly friend that canst not die.'

*59. dark*] night *A 1st reading.* *hollow dark*: *A Dream of Fair Women* 18; Keats, *Fall of Hyperion* i 455 (which was not published, though, until 1856).

# 133 *Sonnet [She took the dappled partridge fleckt with blood]

Printed by Sir Charles Tennyson, *Nineteenth Century* cix (1931) 505; then *1931*, p. 58, from *H.Nbk 8* (watermarked 1825, inscribed 'Trinity Coll.', and including poems of *1830*).

She took the dappled partridge fleckt with blood,
And in her hand the drooping pheasant bare,
And by his feet she held the woolly hare,
And like a master-painting where she stood,
Lookt some new Goddess of an English wood.
Nor could I find an imperfection there,
Nor blame the wanton act that showed so fair–
To me whatever freak she plays is good.
*Hers* is the fairest Life that breathes with breath,
And *their* still plumes and azure eyelids closed
Made quiet Death so beautiful to see
That Death lent grace to Life and Life to Death
And in one image Life and Death reposed,
To make my love an Immortality.

# 134 *Sonnet: Salve Lux Renata!

Printed by Sir Charles Tennyson, *Nineteenth Century* cix (1931) 505–6; then *1931*, p. 60: 'This sonnet is obviously, and no doubt deliberately, reminiscent of the Invocation to Light at the beginning of Book iii of *Paradise Lost*.' From *H.Nbk 8* (watermarked 1825, inscribed 'Trinity Coll.', and including poems of *1830*).

Hail, Light, another time to mortal eyes
Issuing from behind the starry veil,
How gently morn steals from the misty skies
Touching dim heights with sheeted radiance pale.

¶ 133.*1*. *fleckt with blood*: Shelley, *Cenci* III i 13.
*4*. Cp. *Paradise Lost* ix 425: 'Veil'd in a Cloud of Fragrance, where she stood'; as in *Sense and Conscience* 77: 'The blackness of her shadow where she stood.'
*10*. Cp. Keats, *Eve of St Agnes* 262: 'azure-lidded sleep'.
¶ 134.*4*. *sheeted*: dispread, as in Shelley's 'sheeted spray', *Alastor* 335; 'sheeted lightning', Coleridge's *Cain* 345, and Keats's *Full Many* 6.

Pleased I behold, for to my inward sight
Within that dawn there dawns a mystery,
The shining marvel of another light,
On this auspicious day newborn to me.
Therefore, oh Lord, whose effluence increate
Was light from everlasting; who dost call
Each several morn 'Let there be light' and strait
For a day's space the light is over all,
Grant to my dawn of joy a dawnlike strength
To lead up into day of summer length.

## 135 *Milton's Mulberry

Printed by Sir Charles Tennyson, *Nineteenth Century* cix (1931) 380; then *1931*, p. 67: 'This poem, which is clearly of the Cambridge period, refers, of course, to the mulberry tree at Christ's College, reported to have been planted by the poet.' From *H.Nbk 10* (watermarked 1826 and including part of *In Memoriam*).

Look what love the puddle-pated squarecaps have for me!
I am Milton's mulberry, Milton's Milton's mulberry–
But they whipt and rusticated him that planted me,
Milton's Milton's mulberry, Milton's Milton's mulberry.
Old and hollow, somewhat crookèd in the shoulders as you see,
Full of summer foliage yet but propt and padded curiously,
I would sooner have been planted by the hand that planted me,
Than have grown in Paradise and dropped my fruit on Adam's knee–
Look what love the tiny-witted trenchers have for me.

*9. PL* iii 6: 'Bright effluence of bright essence increate'.
*13. dawnlike*] *H.MS, Nineteenth Century*; dawnlight *1931*.
¶ 135.*1. puddle-*] addle- *H.MS 1st reading*.
*3. that*] *MS*; who *1931*. Referring to the tradition of such an incident during Milton's college life.
*9. trenchers*: academic caps and so their wearers (the 'squarecaps' of l. 1).

# 136 *'Thy soul is like a landskip, friend'

Printed *Mem.* i 37–8. It is in *T.Nbk 23* (1830). Written at Cambridge between 1828 and 1830: 'Another verse-portrait my father quoted to me, which he remembered with pleasure that Hallam had praised.' Presumably it is not addressed to Hallam. Possibly it is to James Spedding; cp. *Dear friend* (p. 1786), to Spedding, which immediately follows *Thy soul* in *T.MS* and which makes a similar use of landscape. Cp. the sonnet *To J.M.K.* (p. 257); *To–* (J. W. Blakesley, p. 190); *To–*with *The Palace of Art* (R. C. Trench, p. 399); *To the Rev. W. H. Brookfield* (p. 1232); and *To–[Thou mayst remember]* (below).

Thy soul is like a landskip, friend,
   Steeple, and stream, and forest lawn,
   Most delicately overdrawn
With the first twilight of the even,
Clear-edged, and showing every bend
   Of each dark hill against the Heaven,
Nor wanting many a sombre mound,
   Stately and mild, and all between
Valleys full of solemn sound,
   And hoary holts on uplands green,
And somewhat loftier antient heights
Touched with Heaven's latest lights.

# 137 *To – [Thou mayst remember what I said]

Printed *Mem.* i 60. It is in *T.Nbk 23* (1830), where it has a third stanza comparing the speaker's joy to that of Mary at the resurrection of Lazarus; this stanza (which may not be quoted) was apparently deleted by H.T., possibly because of *In Memoriam* xxxi–xxxii (p. 891). Written at Cambridge between 1828 and 1830, it is another 'character-poem' (H.T., *1913*). Cp. *Thy soul is like a landskip* (above). Arthur Hallam had been disturbed by religious doubts, but the tone of the closing lines here differs considerably from that of *In Memoriam* xcvi (p. 948) and *The Philosopher* (p. 1773). Probably the person addressed was T.'s friend R. J. Tennant, who certainly suffered grave religious doubts which were assuaged by T. (*Mat.* i 160 1), and who had a mood of despondency in 1829 or 1830. Hallam wrote to him *Lines in Answer to a Desponding Letter*, which stressed the value of T.'s friendship.

Thou mayst remember what I said
When thine own spirit was at strife
With thine own spirit. 'From the tomb
And charnel-place of purpose dead,
Through spiritual death we come
Into the light of spiritual life.'

God walked the waters of thy soul,
And stilled them. When from change to change,
Led silently by power divine,
Thy thought did scale a purer range
Of prospect up to self-control,
My joy was only less than thine.

# 138 *The Doctor's Daughter

Printed *Mem.* i 248, as commemorating 'a Cambridge joke'. Presumably written *c.* 1830. Of the songs added to *The Princess* in 1850, T. says: 'Another old song of mine I intended to insert was that of *The Doctor's Daughter.*' Cp. *The Miller's Daughter* and *The Gardener's Daughter*; T. had contemplated writing *The Innkeeper's Daughter* (according to a letter from Arthur Hallam to R. Monteith, 22 June [1832], *Bodleian Library*).

Sweet Kitty Sandilands,
The daughter of the doctor,
We drest her in the Proctor's bands,
And past her for the Proctor.

All the men ran from her
That would have hastened to her,
All the men ran from her
That would have come to woo her.

Up the street we took her
As far as to the Castle,
Jauntily sat the Proctor's cap
And from it hung the tassel.

# 139 *Anacaona

Printed *Mem.* i 56–8; ll. 37–48 are now supplied from *Heath MS.* Probably written 1830; it was recited in Oct. (H. Alford, *Life*, 1873, p. 61), and was described by Arthur Hallam as 'lately written', in a letter at the end of 1830

¶ 137.*3–5*. Cp. *Pierced through* 19: 'that spiritual charnel'.
5. *death*] dark *Mem.*

enclosing the '2nd Version' (*Mat.* iv 457). An earlier version is in *Heath MS* (all variants are below), which differs in natural history and rhymes: 'My father liked this poem but did not publish it, because the natural history and the rhymes did not satisfy him. He evidently chose words which sounded well, and gave a tropical air to the whole, and he did not then care, as in his later poems, for absolute accuracy' (*Mem.* i 56). T. resisted Hallam's plea: 'Is it possible he will not publish it? If he has merely forgotten, let him write immediately' (to T.'s sister Emily, 20 Oct. 1832; *Wellesley College MS*). FitzGerald (in his copy of *1842*, *Trinity College*) reports T. as saying that it 'would be confuted by some Midshipman who had been in Hayti latitudes and knew better about Tropical Vegetable and Animal'. Paden (p. 140) suggested Ulloa's *Voyage to S. America* as the source of the natural history; the 1772 translation was at Somersby (*Lincoln*). Anacaona was the queen of Xaragua, a province of Hispaniola or Hayti. She welcomed the Spaniards but was later killed by them. T.'s source was Washington Irving's *Life of Columbus*, 1828 (Paden, p. 140), which he later used for *Columbus*. Cp. the island paradises in *The Lotos-Eaters*, *Locksley Hall*, and *The Islet*; also *Columbus* 177–80: 'Ah God, the harmless people whom we found / In Hispaniola's island-Paradise! / Who took us for the very Gods from Heaven, / And we have sent them very fiends from Hell.'

A dark Indian maiden,
  Warbling in the bloomed liana,
Stepping lightly flower-laden,
  By the crimson-eyed anana,
Wantoning in orange groves
  Naked, and dark-limbed, and gay,
Bathing in the slumbrous coves,
In the cocoa-shadowed coves,
  Of sunbright Xaraguay,
Who was so happy as Anacaona,
  The beauty of Espagnola,
  The golden flower of Hayti?

All her loving childhood
  Breezes from the palm and canna
Fanned this queen of the green wildwood,
  Lady of the green Savannah:

¶ 139.2. *liana*: twining plant.
4. *anana*: pineapple. Cp. Ulloa (see headnote) on the anana: 'so elegant a crimson, as even to dazzle the eye' – which T. quoted in *Did not thy roseate lips 2n* (p. 100).
12. This refrain was suggested by Irving on Anacaona: 'her name, in the Indian language, signified flower of gold' (ii 420). She was 'celebrated throughout the island for her beauty' (ii 225).
14. *and canna*] did fan her *Heath MS*. *canna*: exotic flower.
15. *Fanned this*] She was *MS*.

All day long with laughing eyes,
    Dancing by a palmy bay,
In the wooded paradise,
The cedar-wooded paradise
    Of still Xaraguay:
None were so happy as Anacaona,
    The beauty of Espagnola,
    The golden flower of Hayti!

In the purple island,
    Crowned with garlands of cinchona,
Lady over wood and highland,
    The Indian queen, Anacaona,
Dancing on the blossomy plain
    To a woodland melody:
Playing with the scarlet crane,
The dragon-fly and scarlet crane,
    Beneath the papao tree!
Happy happy was Anacaona,
    The beauty of Espagnola,
    The golden flower of Hayti!

Many an emerald flyer
    Through the snow-white thicket flitting
Glanced, and birds plume-flecked with fire
    In the lustrous woodland sitting
Looked with bright bright eyes across
    The glooming ebony tree:
Only came the Albatross,
The shadow of the Albatross

*18. palmy*] waveless *MS.*
*20. cedar-*] *MS 1st reading*; tamarind- *MS.*
*26*] The mild Indian did enthrone her *MS.* *cinchona*: a shrub.
*31.* 'Perhaps the scarlet ibis, *guara rubra*, not now known to visit Hayti' (H.T.). T.'s error is from Irving; the 'scarlet cranes' recur in *The Progress of Spring* 75 (Paden, p. 140).
*33. papao*: a fruit.
*37–48*] *MS*; *not Mem.* Probably missing because the second half of the stanza is cut away from *T.Nbk 16.* In *Nbk 23* the lines were at first out of sequence. Arthur Hallam's letter (*Mat.* iv 459) at first left them out inadvertently and then omitted ll. 43–5 (which are deleted in *H.Lpr 34*). T. presumably doubted that the albatross visits Hayti.
*40.* The germ of *Locksley Hall* 162: 'slides the bird o'er lustrous woodland'.
*41.* Cp. Coleridge, *The Nightingale* 67: 'Their bright, bright eyes, their eyes both bright and full'.

Floating down the sea.
Happy happy was Anacaona,
The beauty of Espagnola,
The golden flower of Hayti!

The white man's white sail, bringing
To happy Hayti the new-comer,
Over the dark sea-marge springing,
Floated in the silent summer:
Then she brought the guava fruit,
With her maidens to the bay;
She gave them the yuccaroot,
Maizebread and the yuccaroot,
Of sweet Xaraguay:
Happy, happy Anacaona,
The beauty of Espagnola,
The golden flower of Hayti!

Naked, without fear, moving
To her Areyto's mellow ditty,
Waving a palm branch, wondering, loving,
Carolling 'Happy, happy Hayti!'
She gave the white men welcome all,
With her damsels by the bay;
For they were fair-faced and tall,
They were more fair-faced and tall,
Than the men of Xaraguay,
And they smiled on Anacaona,
The beauty of Espagnola,
The golden flower of Hayti!

Following her wild carol
She led them down the pleasant places,
For they were kingly in apparel,
Loftily stepping with fair faces.
But never more upon the shore
Dancing at the break of day,
In the deep wood no more,–
By the deep sea no more,–
No more in Xaraguay
Wandered happy Anacaona,
The beauty of Espagnola,
The golden flower of Hayti!

*62*] To the Areytos full of beauty *Allen MS.* *her*] the *Heath MS.* Anacaona 'was said to excel in composing those little legendary ballads, or areytos' (Irving ii 420). Keats has 'mellow ditties', *Endymion* iv 160.
*77. upon*] along *MS.*

# 140 *Lines on Cambridge of 1830

Printed by R. H. Shepherd, *Tennysoniana* (1879), from a copy of *1832* in the Dyce Collection (*South Kensington*). Then reluctantly printed by H.T., *Notes and Queries* and *The Times*, 15 March 1884. It is dated 1830 in *Mem.* i 67, which provides T.'s revised text given below. The text in *T.Nbk 23* (1830) is that of *Heath MS.* T.'s note in the draft of *Eversley* (*Lincoln*) says that he could 'only regret that this spirit of undergraduate irritability against the Cambridge of that day ever found its way into print, but I place the lines here in deference to the wishes of my friends' – i.e. Aubrey de Vere (*Mem.* i 67).

Therefore your Halls, your ancient Colleges,
Your portals statued with old kings and queens,
Your gardens, myriad-volumed libraries,
Wax-lighted chapels, and rich carven screens,
Your doctors, and your proctors, and your deans,
Shall not avail you, when the Day-beam sports
New-risen o'er awakened Albion. No!
Nor yet your solemn organ-pipes that blow
Melodious thunders through your vacant courts
At noon and eve, because your manner sorts
Not with this age wherefrom ye stand apart,
Because the lips of little children preach
Against you, you that do profess to teach
And teach us nothing, feeding not the heart.

# 141 *Sonnet [Me my own Fate to lasting sorrow doometh]

Published Oct. 1831, *Friendship's Offering* for 1832; not reprinted. It is in *T.Nbk 23* (1830), and placed early in *Heath MS.* Probably it addresses Arthur Hallam. D. B. MacEachen (*Victorian Newsletter*, Fall 1958) shows that it combines a Shakespearean internal structure with a rhyme scheme

¶ 140.*3*] Your bridges and your busted libraries, *1879*, *Heath MS.*
*5. doctors*] Masters *Heath MS.*
*10. At noon and eve, because*] At morn and even; for *1879*, *Heath MS.*
*11. wherefrom . . . apart*] nor with the thoughts that [roll] *1879*; nor with our thought and speech *Heath MS.*
*14*] And have taught nothing, feeding not the soul. *1879*.

which is Italian until the final two lines; its form is unique among T.'s sonnets, which may explain his not reprinting it.

Me my own Fate to lasting sorrow doometh:
Thy woes are birds of passage, transitory:
Thy spirit, circled with a living glory,
In summer still a summer joy resumeth.
Alone my hopeless melancholy gloometh,
Like a lone cypress, through the twilight hoary,
From an old garden where no flower bloometh,
One cypress on an inland promontory.
But yet my lonely spirit follows thine,
As round the rolling earth night follows day:
But yet thy lights on my horizon shine
Into my night, when thou art far away.
I am so dark, alas! and thou so bright,
When we two meet there's never perfect light.

# 142 *Anacreontics

Published Oct. 1830, in *The Gem* for 1831; not reprinted. An amatory lyric in the manner of Anacreon, as often in seven-syllable lines. In Thomas Moore's *Odes of Anacreon* (1800), the first is on the effect of the lover's garland: 'I twined it round my thoughtless brow, / And ah! I feel it's magic now! / I feel that ev'n his garland's touch / Can make the bosom love too much.' The name 'Lenora' was possibly suggested by Bürger's famous ballad *Lenore*.

With roses muskybreathèd,
And drooping daffodilly,
And silverleavèd lily,
And ivy darkly-wreathèd,
I wove a crown before her
For her I love so dearly,
A garland for Lenora.
With a silken cord I bound it.
Lenora, laughing clearly
A light and thrilling laughter,
About her forehead wound it,
And loved me ever after.

¶ 142.*2–3*. Cp. *The Lady of Shalott* 6–7, *1832* text: 'The yellowleavèd waterlily, / The greensheathèd daffodilly.'

# 143 *A Fragment [Where is the Giant of the Sun]

Published Oct. 1830, in *The Gem* for 1831; not reprinted. The draft in *H.Nbk 4* (*c.* 1830; all variants are below) continues for another eleven lines; see l. 31*n*. T. quarried for it in *Supposed Confessions* (p. 197). Paden (p. 153) has a full account of the sources. Charles Rollin's *Ancient History* provided the Colossus of Rhodes; there was a copy of the 1789 translation at Somersby (*Lincoln*). C.-E. Savary's *Letters on Egypt* (1799 translation, *Lincoln*) provided the imagery. From Jacob Bryant's *New System of Ancient Mythology* came the details of the sons of Cush who invaded Mizraim (l. 5, the biblical name for Egypt) under the names of Anakim (l. 20); they built temples, colossi, tombs and pyramids, and a branch of this race settled in Rhodes as children of the Sun. They were skilled navigators who gave the name Canopus (associated with the holy dragon, ll. 5–6) to the brightest star in Argo. In Egypt they worshipped the sun as ON, and the image of a serpent as OPH (l. 21). There was a copy of Bryant at Somersby (*Lincoln*). Cp. *Egypt* (p. 1806), and *Cleopatra's Needle* (p. 1249); also *The Coach of Death* 190: 'And On and regal Oph'.

Where is the Giant of the Sun, which stood
In the midnoon the glory of old Rhodes,
A perfect Idol with profulgent brows
Farsheening down the purple seas to those
Who sailed from Mizraim underneath the star
Named of the dragon – and between whose limbs
Of brassy vastness broadblown Argosies
Drave into haven? Yet endure unscathed
Of changeful cycles the great Pyramids
Broadbased amid the fleeting sands, and sloped
Into the slumbrous summernoon; but where,
Mysterious Egypt, are thine obelisks

¶ 143.2. *midnoon*: not a common word, so perhaps T. recalls *Paradise Lost* v 311, where l. 309 has 'glorious'.

3. Adapted from *Supposed Confessions* 145: 'An image with profulgent brows'.

5. *Mizraim*] Egypt *H.MS.*

7. *broadblown*] full-blown *MS.*

8–9] . . . endure / Unscathed of changeful times the Pyramids *MS.*

10. *Broadbased amid*] Broadbasèd on *MS.*

11. Incorporated from 'the slumbrous summer noon', *Supposed Confessions* 11, of which ll. 126–9 include 'slope', 'broad-imbasèd', 'slumbers'.

12. Adapted from *Recollections of the Arabian Nights* 107–8: 'obelisks / Graven with emblems'.

Graven with gorgeous emblems undiscerned?
Thy placid Sphinxes brooding o'er the Nile?
Thy shadowing Idols in the solitudes,
Awful Memnonian countenances calm
Looking athwart the burning flats, far off
Seen by the highnecked camel on the verge
Journeying southward? where thy monuments
Piled by the strong and sunborn Anakim
Over their crownèd brethren ON and OPH?
Thy Memnon when his peaceful lips are kist
With earliest rays, that from his mother's eyes
Flow over the Arabian bay, no more
Breathes low into the charmèd ears of morn
Clear melody flattering the crispèd Nile
By columned Thebes. Old Memphis hath gone down:
The Pharaohs are no more: somewhere in death
They sleep with staring eyes and gilded lips,
Wrapped round with spicèd cerements in old grots
Rockhewn and sealed for ever.

15] *Added to MS.*
17. *athwart the burning*] across the desert *MS*. Cp. *Mariana* 20: 'And glanced athwart the glooming flats', and *Fatima* 13: 'I looked athwart the burning drouth'.
22. *Memnon*: the statue near Thebes that made music when struck by the rising sun. Cp. *The Palace of Art* 171.
23. *rays, that*] light which *MS*.
26] Clear [Low *1st reading*] melodies which stay the crispèd Nile *MS*.
27. Cp. George Sandys, *Travels* (the 1658 edn was at Somersby, *Lincoln*; p. 103): 'the regall City of *Memphis*; the strength and glory of old *Egypt* . . . some erroniously affirm old *Memphis* to have been the same with new *Cairo*.'
28–9. *in death / They sleep*] *Transposed MS.*
31] *MS continues:*

In one night
(For the day would not look on it), red fire
And thick-enfouldred smoke abolishèd
That fane of costliest roof which [leaning?]
[That stateliest temple builded to the breeze(?) *1st reading*]
Upon a thousand marble piles sustained
Diana of the Ephesians where she stood
A glorious mystery, most beautiful
Of sculptures new or old, with argent feet
Upon a crescent curve–though many an age
Far off unto the sea-worn Mariner

# 144 *'O wake ere I grow jealous of sweet Sleep'

Unpublished. Its placing in *Heath MS* suggests that it was written 1830. Cp. *To a Lady Sleeping* (p. 240), which has the same rhyme scheme but with an extra concluding line.

O wake ere I grow jealous of sweet Sleep;
All to himself he hath thine eyes in thrall,
And holdeth talk with thee in visions deep:
Wake ere I rend his poppy coronal.
What if she dreams of me, and now is seeing
My shadowed Memory! It were ill to level
A suicidal aim at my own Being
Though it were to gaze on Heaven, and to revel
In the new birth of those immortal eyes.

# 145 *'The constant spirit of the world exults'

Unpublished, except that there is a facsimile of a MS in A. G. Weld's *Glimpses of Tennyson* (1903, facing p. 32). Text from *Heath MS* (Weld MS has no variants). It is in *T.Nbk 23* (1830), where there is a very different early draft which may not be quoted. An irregular sonnet, like most of T.'s early ones. For its theme, cp. *Chorus* (p. 236).

The constant spirit of the world exults
  In fertile change and wide variety,

---

That temple in the entrance of the bay
Shone with its reflex, like a star.

These lines refer to the story of Eratostratus, 'an Ephesian who burnt the famous temple of Diana the same night that Alexander the Great was born. . . . Eratostratus did this villainy merely to eternize his name by so uncommon an action' (*English Encyclopaedia*, 1802, of which there was a copy at Somersby, *Lincoln*). Also in Rollin's *Ancient History* (1789 translation, *Lincoln*). *enfouldred*: with thunderbolts, from *Faerie Queene* I xi st. 40: 'With fowle enfouldred smoake and flashing fire.'

¶ 144.*4*. Cp. Keats, *Sleep and Poetry* 348: 'Sleep, quiet with his poppy coronet'; 'coronal' is Keatsian, probably from Wordsworth's *Immortality Ode* 40.

And this is my delight to live and see
Old principles still working new results.
Nothing is altogether old or new
Though all things in another form are cast,
And what in human thought is just and true
Though fashioned in a thousand forms will last.
But some high-thoughted moods and moulds of mind
Can never be remodelled or expressed
Again by any later century,
As in the oldest crusts of the Earth we find
Enormous fossilbones and shapes imprest
Of ancient races that have ceased to be.

## 146 *Sonnet [When that rank heat of evil's tropic day]

Printed by Sir Charles Tennyson, *Nineteenth Century* cix (1931) 507–8; *1931*, p. 65: 'This sonnet expresses a characteristic mood of depression and self-depreciation. Possibly the friend to whom it was addressed was Arthur Hallam.' From *Heath MS* (assembled 1833–4).

When that rank heat of evil's tropic day
Made floating cloud of flowing joy, and cleft
My shores of life (their freshness steamed away,
Nothing but salt and bitter crystals left),
When in my lonely walks I seemed to be
An image of the cursèd figtree, set
In the brown glens of this Mount Olivet,
Thy looks, thy words, were . . . and rain to me.
When all sin-sickened, loathing my disgrace,
Far on within the temple of the mind
I seemed to hear God speaking audibly,
'Let us go hence'–sometimes a little space,
Out of the sphere of God, I dared to find
A shadow and a resting place in thee.

¶ 146.*3. shores of life*: as in *Sonnet* [*Conrad!*] (p. 272).
*6. Matthew* xxi 17–20.
*8. . . . and rain*] *lacuna Heath MS, Allen MS*; [sun] and rain *H.Lpr 106* (*not in T.'s hand*); sun and rain *1931*. This suggested reading is not very appropriate, since sun and heat in the poem are described as the enemies of freshness, and it is 'a shadow' that the poet finds 'in thee'.
*12. John* xiv 31, 'But that the world may know that I love the Father; and as the Father gave me commandment, even so I do. Arise, let us go hence.'

# 147 *Marion

Printed *Mat.* i 69–71, described as 'Unfinished' and as one of 'Unpublished poems written (1828–31) at Cambridge'. Then *1931*, pp. 50–1: 'The last two lines [not in *Mat.*] do not fit into the rhyme scheme, so *Marion* cannot be regarded as a finished work.' From *Heath MS* (assembled 1833–4); it is also in the *Allen MS*. Sir Charles Tennyson's first thoughts when printing the poem, *Nineteenth Century* cix (1931) 496–7, were to prefer the *Heath* text, which is preferred below; all variants are noted. Cp. the other girls of *1830*.

Thou art not handsome, art not plain,
And thou dost own no graceful art,
Thou hast no little winning ways
Wherewith to buy our love or praise,
Yet holdest thou an ample reign
Within the human heart.
It is a sort of pride in thee
In every shade of joy or woe
Still with the general mind to flow,
Nor more nor less, but even so.
What is it oversteps this law
And overshowers the daily and the real
As with a fruitful rain of grace?
Let me die, Marion, if I ever saw
Such ideal unideal,
Such uncommon commonplace!
Though thought and act and speech in thee
Run parallel with thought and speech
In the universal mind,
My gentle Marion, couldst thou teach
That peculiar alchemy
To the rest of womankind,
Which evermore to precious ore
Changes common thought in thee,
That spiritual economy,
Which wasteth not itself in signs,

¶ 147.*1. art not plain*] *Heath MS, Nineteenth Century;* no, nor plain *Mat., 1931.*
*4. Wherewith to buy*] *MS, Nineteenth Century*; Whereby to win *Mat., 1931.*
*9. mind*] *MS, Mat., Nineteenth Century*; mood *1931.*
*10. even*] *MS*; ever *Mat., Nineteenth Century, 1931.*
*12. and the*] *MS, Nineteenth Century, 1931; not Mat.*
*17. act*] *MS, Nineteenth Century*; art *Mat., 1931.*
*19. universal mind*: Shelley, *Daemon* ii 248.

And yet with power intertwines
Thine image with the memory,
The world would build thee silver shrines.
From what far inward source
Is that rare influence drawn,
Enlightening all intercourse
With thee, my quiet Marion?
Which can illustrate every nameless act,
And from the eyelids of hardfeatured fact
Rain tender starlight on the heart?
That magically woven net
Thou threwest round me when we met,
Thin-threaded as the cobweb round
In a corner of the glass,
Wherewith the green-wingèd midge is bound
And seeth not and cannot pass.
It is the slow-increased delight
Of unperceivèd gentleness,
That touching with scarce visible ray
The barren life of every day,
Possesseth all its nakedness
With stealing shadow and with light.

Love is a vine, and in the hot
And southern slopes he takes delight;
He curls his tendrils in thy light,
But his grape-clusters ripen not;
But mild affection taketh root
And prospers in thy placid light.
Thou art the soul of commonplace,
The body all mankind divide.

34. *illústrate*: make illustrious. Cp. Wordsworth, *Tintern Abbey* 34: 'His little, nameless, unremembered acts'.
36. Shelley has 'tender light' four times.
40] *Not Mat.* (*slip*).
41. *midge*] *MS, Mat.*; moth *Nineteenth Century, 1931.*
43. *-increased delight*] *MS, Nineteenth Century, 1931*; increasèd might *Mat.*
45. *scarce*] *MS, Nineteenth Century, 1931;* some *Mat.*
46. *life*] *MS, Mat., Nineteenth Century*; light *1931.*
48. *shadow . . . light*] *MS, Nineteenth Century*; shadows dusk and bright *Mat., 1931.*
51. *curls*] *MS, Nineteenth Century, 1931*; casts *Mat.* *light*] *MS, Nineteenth Century, 1931*; sight *Mat.* (*an emendation, possibly correct, because of l.54*).
52. *But*] *MS, Nineteenth Century, 1931*; Yet *Mat.*
54 ∧ 5] *Allen MS leaves a gap.*
55–6] *MS, Nineteenth Century, 1931; not Mat.*

# 148 *Lisette

Printed by Sir Charles Tennyson, *Nineteenth Century* cix (1931) 497–8; then *1931*, pp. 52–3, from *Heath MS* (assembled 1833–4). Cp. the other girls of *1830*.

My light Lisette
Is grave and shrewd,
And half a prude,
And half coquette,
So staid and set,
So terse and trim,
So arch and prim
Is my Lisette.

A something settled and precise
Hath made a home in both the eyes
Of my Lisette,
Lives in the little wilful hands,
The little foot that glides and flits,
Braced with dark silken sandal-bands,
Even in the coxcomb parrokette
That on the drooping shoulder sits
Of trim Lisette.

The measured motion of the blood;
The words, where each one tells,
Too logical for womanhood,
Brief changes rung on silver bells;
The cheek with health's close kisses warm,
The finished form so light;
Such fullness in a little form
As satisfies the sight;
The bodice fitted so exact;
The nutbrown tress so crisply curled,
And the whole woman so compact,
Her match is nowhere in the world;
Such knowledge of the modes of life,
And household order such,
As might create a perfect wife,
Not careful overmuch;
All these so moved me
When we met,

¶ 148.*18. measured motion*: Shelley, *Stanzas Written in Dejection* 17.
*24–8.* Cp. Keats, *Hyperion* ii 209: 'In form and shape compact and beautiful'.

I would she loved me,
Trim Lisette.

What if tomorrow morn I go,
And in an accent clipt and clear
Say some three words within her ear,
I think she would not answer 'No.'
But by the ribbon in her hair,
And those untasted lips, I swear,
I keep some little doubt as yet;
With such an eye
So grave and sly,
Looks my Lisette.
What words may show
The 'Yes'–the 'No'–
Of trim Lisette?
The doubt is less,
Since last we met,
Let it be 'Yes'
My sweet Lisette.

# 149 *Life

Printed *Mem.* i 59, among poems of 1828–30. Its place in *H.Nbk 3* (all variants are below) would suggest at least the later date and conceivably towards 1832, though the extreme irregularity of the sonnet's rhyme scheme more resembles the sonnets of *1830* than of *1832.*

Why suffers human life so soon eclipse?
For I could burst into a psalm of praise,
Seeing the heart so wondrous in her ways,
E'en scorn looks beautiful on human lips!
Would I could pile fresh life on life, and dull
The sharp desire of knowledge still with knowing!

*46. grave and sly*: Johnson, *Short Song of Congratulation* 16, a poem which may have influenced *The Vision of Sin.*

¶ 149.*4. Twelfth Night* III i 147–8: 'What a deal of scorn looks beautiful / In the contempt and anger of his lip!'.

*5. Would . . . fresh*] Oh that I could pile *H.MS 1st reading.*

*5–6.* Adapted for *Ulysses* 22–31: 'How dull it is to pause . . . / . . . Life piled on life / Were all too little . . . / To follow knowledge'.

*6. The sharp desire*: *Paradise Lost* ix 584, possibly by association with *knowledge.*

Art, Science, Nature, everything is full,
As my own soul is full, to overflowing–
Millions of forms, and hues, and shades, that give
The difference of all things to the sense,
And all the likeness in the difference.
I thank thee, God, that thou hast made me live:
I reck not for the sorrow or the strife:
One only joy I know, the joy of life.

# 150 *Sonnet [Check every outflash, every ruder sally]

Published *Englishman's Magazine*, Aug. 1831 (punctuated as below); *Friendship's Offering* for 1833 (Oct. 1832); not reprinted. D. B. MacEachen (*Victorian Newsletter*, Fall 1958) demonstrates the Shakespearean sonnet structure with a rhyme scheme neither Italian nor Shakespearean, unique in T.– which may be why he did not reprint it.

Check every outflash, every ruder sally
Of thought and speech; speak low, and give up wholly
Thy spirit to mild-minded Melancholy;
This is the place. Through yonder poplar alley,
Below, the blue-green river windeth slowly,
But in the middle of the sombre valley,
The crispèd waters whisper musically,
And all the haunted place is dark and holy.
The nightingale, with long and low preamble,
Warbled from yonder knoll of solemn larches,
And in and out the woodbine's flowery arches
The summer midges wove their wanton gambol,
And all the white stemmed pinewood slept above–
When in this valley first I told my love.

7] Nature and Art are very beautiful *MS 1st reading.*
8. *As . . . full*] And everything is full *MS 1st reading*; As my own soul full even *MS.*
10. *things to*] unto *MS 1st reading.*
¶ 150.*2–3.* Adapted as *The Lotos-Eaters* 108–9: 'To lend our hearts and spirits wholly / To the influence of mild-minded melancholy.'

## 151 *Sonnet [There are three things which fill my heart with sighs]

Published Oct. 1831, in the *Yorkshire Literary Annual* for 1832, with the note 'London, September 20th, 1831'; not reprinted. T. was in the Pyrenees in summer 1830, so 'Bayona' (l. 11) is Bayonne (the form 'Bayona' presumably suggested by the Spanish stronghold of *Lycidas* 162). An irregular sonnet, like most of T.'s early ones.

There are three things which fill my heart with sighs,
And steep my soul in laughter (when I view
Fair maiden-forms moving like melodies)
Dimples, roselips, and eyes of any hue.
There are three things beneath the blessèd skies
For which I live, black eyes and brown and blue:
I hold them all most dear, but oh! black eyes,
I live and die, and only die for you.
Of late such eyes looked at me–while I mused,
At sunset, underneath a shadowy plane,
In old Bayona nigh the southern sea–
From an half-open lattice looked at *me.*
I saw no more–only those eyes–confused
And dazzled to the heart with glorious pain.

## 152 *St Lawrence

Printed by E. F. Shannon and W. H. Bond, *Harvard Library Bulletin* x (1956) 259–60. There are four versions, dating from *c.* 1825 to *c.* 1833; the text below is from *H.Nbk 3*, *c.* 1831. For the other versions, see Appendix A (p. 1767). There is a longer version than any of these in *T.Nbk 15* (which may not be quoted); it consists of forty-nine lines of blank verse, beginning as below, continuing with a passage on Abednego, and then resembling the more epigrammatic versions; it also includes *Sir John Oldcastle* 176–81 (1880), all but verbatim. St Lawrence was burned alive on a gridiron. His martyrdom is described in William Hone's *Every-Day Book* (1825, under 'August 10'), the acknowledged source of *St Simeon Stylites* (p. 542). Cp. *St Agnes' Eve* (p. 552).

No portion of my mind misgives.
Come, strip me: lay me on these bars!
Too slow–too slow: my spirits yearn
To float among the clear cold stars.

I know that my Redeemer lives.
I cannot argue, I can burn.
O Lord! I am not mine, but thine.
Christ is my life, my blood, my breath.
When he comes down to meet his Bride,
Hereafter I shall stand and shine
Clothed in white raiment at his side.
His arm hath plucked me forth from Hell,
He hath moved from me all my guilt.
This is his love ineffable,
He hath baptized me unto death
With fire. I am not mine but thine–
My Lord, do with me as thou wilt.

## 153 The Lover's Tale

Published May 1879; Part iv (*The Golden Supper*) had been published in *1869* ('*1870*'). *1879* headnote: 'The original Preface to *The Lover's Tale* states that it was composed in my nineteenth year. Two only of the three parts then written were printed, when, feeling the imperfection of the poem, I withdrew it from the press. One of my friends however who, boylike, admired the boy's work, distributed among our common associates of that hour some copies of these two parts, without my knowledge, without the omissions and amendments which I had in contemplation, and marred by the many misprints of the compositor. Seeing that these two parts have of late been mercilessly pirated, and that what I had deemed scarce worthy to live is not allowed to die, may I not be pardoned if I suffer the whole poem at last to come into the light–accompanied with a reprint of the sequel–a work of my mature life–*The Golden Supper*?' [*May 1879*]

T. had printed Parts i and ii in 1832, for inclusion in *1832*. On 20 Nov. *1832*, he withdrew them, writing to his publisher Moxon (*Mem.* i 90): 'After mature consideration, I have come to a resolution of not publishing the last poem in my little volume, entitled, *Lover's Tale*: it is too full of faults and though I think it might conduce towards making me popular, yet, to my eye, it spoils the completeness of the book, and is better away.' T. resisted Arthur Hallam's protest: 'You must be point-blank mad' (*CT*, p. 129). But he permitted a few copies to circulate, dated 1833 and subtitled *A Fragment*, with the following headnote (British Museum copy): 'The

¶ 152.5. *Job* xix 25: 'For I know that my Redeemer liveth, and that he shall stand at the latter day upon the earth.'
*11. Revelation* iii 4–5: 'They shall walk with me in white: for they are worthy. He that overcometh, the same shall be clothed in white raiment.'

Poem of the Lover's Tale (the lover is supposed to be himself a poet,) was written in my nineteenth year, and consequently contains nearly as many faults as words. That I deemed it not wholly unoriginal is my only apology for its publication – an apology, lame, and poor, and somewhat impertinent to boot; so that if its infirmities meet with more laughter than charity in the world, I shall not raise my voice in its defence. I am aware how deficient the Poem is in point of Art, and it is not without considerable misgivings that I have ventured to publish even this fragment of it. "Enough," says the old proverb, "is as good as a feast."' In Jan. 1868 he lent the MS to Mrs Marian Bradley: 'He said, "Oh I can't pick it to pieces and make it up again, it is not worth that; but I think it is very rich and full – but there are mistakes in it." I said I liked the page about the camel [i 132–6]. "That is an instance of a mistake", he replied, "In the middle moonlit nights there could have been no crimson colouring"' (*Diary*, British Museum; quoted *Mem.* ii 50). He thought of publishing it in 1868 (trial edition, quoted by T. J. Wise), but again withdrew, as he also did from including it in *1869* ('*1870*'). A trial edition of *1869* (*Lincoln*) introduces it with: 'This Poem, founded upon a story of Boccaccio, was begun in early youth, – afterwards partly altered and revised – and concluded in later years.' He was finally spurred by R. H. Shepherd's piracy; for details, see W. D. Paden, *Studies in Bibliography* xviii (1965) 111–45. T. says that it 'was written before I had ever seen Shelley, though it is called Shelleyan. . . . Allowance must be made for abundance of youth. . . . The poem is the breath of young Love' (to Mrs Bradley).

*Composition*: Parts i–iii were written in his 'nineteenth year', 1827–8. Paden (p. 160) assumed that the Part iii of 1832 is not that of 1868: 'He had at the time [1832] written a third Part; of this continuation nothing seems to be known.' *Mem.* i 48, ii 239, says that the poem was 'written 1827', and 'written when he was seventeen'. Since T. was manifestly dissatisfied, he must have worked at it until 1832; there are fragments in *H.Nbk 3*, which consists mainly of poems of *1832*. The fragmentary drafts in *T.Nbk 18* (1828), which may not be quoted, include many unadopted passages and lines; for example, the MS begins with fifteen lines of a night scene, and then has twenty lines expanding i 40–1 which describe the summerhouse. Part iv does not appear until the trial edition of 1868, and was presumably written then.

*Text*: for *1879*, T. greatly revised the text of *1832*. All variants from *1832* are below, from the B.M. copy which has corrections made by T. in 1835. T. began revising at least as early as this (T. J. Wise, *Bibliography* i 28). J. C. Thomson printed a thoroughly inaccurate text of *1832* in *The Suppressed Poems of Tennyson* (1904, 1910). The text of 1868 represents a halfway stage. From 1868 selected variants only are given (from Wise). Since there was no printed Part iii till 1868 (though a Part iii was written by 1832 – see T.'s headnote), revisions for this Part cannot be traced.

*Source*: the trial edition of *1869* (above) mentioned Boccaccio, and Part iv had the note in *1869*: 'This poem is founded upon a story in Boccaccio.' T.'s adaptation of *Decameron* (10th Day, 4th Tale) is discussed by H. G.

Wright, *Boccaccio in England* (1957), pp. 437–8, where the contemporary influence of Boccaccio is also discussed. T. added the explanation that her body was not in a coffin, and the moonlight which lit her face; he is responsible for 'the reverence with which Julian kisses her.... In his counterpart there is more of passion than reverence' (Wright). He expanded the Supper, and created the waste-land atmosphere (iv 124ff); moreover Julian does not, as he does in Boccaccio, settle down with the reunited husband and wife, but rides away. In his choice of source, T. may have been influenced by the adaptations by 'Barry Cornwall' (B. W. Procter), which are similar in style and tone. The influence of Keats combines with the adaptation of Boccaccio in Keats's *Isabella.* For the blank verse and mannerisms, cp. *The Gardener's Daughter* (p. 507).

See Clarice Short, *PMLA* lxxxii (1967) 78–84.

*Argument*

Julian, whose cousin and foster-sister, Camilla, has been wedded to his friend and rival, Lionel, endeavours to narrate the story of his own love for her, and the strange sequel. He speaks (in Parts II and III) of having been haunted by visions and the sound of bells, tolling for a funeral, and at last ringing for a marriage; but he breaks away, overcome, as he approaches the Event, and a witness to it completes the tale.

I

Here far away, seen from the topmost cliff,
Filling with purple gloom the vacancies
Between the tufted hills, the sloping seas
Hung in mid-heaven, and half-way down rare sails,
White as white clouds, floated from sky to sky.
Oh! pleasant breast of waters, quiet bay,
Like to a quiet mind in the loud world,
Where the chafed breakers of the outer sea
Sank powerless, as anger falls aside
And withers on the breast of peaceful love;
Thou didst receive the growth of pines that fledged
The hills that watched thee, as Love watcheth Love,
In thine own essence, and delight thyself
To make it wholly thine on sunny days.
Keep thou thy name of 'Lover's Bay'. See, sirs,
Even now the Goddess of the Past, that takes
The heart, and sometimes touches but one string
That quivers, and is silent, and sometimes
Sweeps suddenly all its half-mouldered chords

¶ 153.i *9. Sank*] Sunk *1832.* *as*] even as *1832 but corrected by T. in BM copy.*
i *11. the growth*] that belt *1832.*
i *17. touches*] toucheth *1832.*

To some old melody, begins to play
That air which pleased her first. I feel thy breath;
I come, great Mistress of the ear and eye:
Thy breath is of the pinewood; and though years
Have hollowed out a deep and stormy strait
Betwixt the native land of Love and me,
Breathe but a little on me, and the sail
Will draw me to the rising of the sun,
The lucid chambers of the morning star,
And East of Life.

Permit me, friend, I prythee,
To pass my hand across my brows, and muse
On those dear hills, that never more will meet
The sight that throbs and aches beneath my touch,
As though there beat a heart in either eye;
For when the outer lights are darkened thus,
The memory's vision hath a keener edge.
It grows upon me now–the semicircle
Of dark-blue waters and the narrow fringe
Of curving beach–its wreaths of dripping green–
Its pale pink shells–the summerhouse aloft
That opened on the pines with doors of glass,
A mountain nest–the pleasure-boat that rocked,
Light-green with its own shadow, keel to keel,
Upon the dappled dimplings of the wave,
That blanched upon its side.

O Love, O Hope!
They come, they crowd upon me all at once–
Moved from the cloud of unforgotten things,
That sometimes on the horizon of the mind
Lies folded, often sweeps athwart in storm–

*20. some*] an *1832.*
i *21*] On those firstmovèd fibres of the brain. *1832.*
i *23*] Oh! lead me tenderly, for fear the mind
Rain through my sight, and strangling sorrow weigh
Mine utterance with lameness. Though long years *1832*
i *24. deep and stormy strait*] valley and a gulf *1832.*
i *28.* Cp. Thomson, *Winter* 15–16: 'Till through the lucid chambers of the south / Looked out the joyous Spring, looked out, and smiled'.
i *43*] Upon the crispings of the dappled wave *1832.*
i *45*] My soul, that holds the light of other times,
Begins to brighten at the skirts. They come,
*Heath MS: 'A Fragment of The Lover's Tale'*

Flash upon flash they lighten through me–days
Of dewy dawning and the amber eves
When thou and I, Camilla, thou and I
Were borne about the bay or safely moored

i *49–50*] They flash across the darkness of my brain,
The many pleasant days, the moonlit nights,
The dewy dawnings and . . . *1832*;
Flash upon flash they lighten through my brain,
The days, the pleasant days–the moonlit nights, *Heath MS*

i *50 ∧ 51*] Those revelations of the eventide,
When air and ocean filled one hollow globe
With wild red light, that touched on amber streams
The waving snows of sea-gull plumes–what times
O'er long loud waters, like a sinking star,
Mixed with the gorgeous West the lighthouse shone. *Heath MS*

Cp. ll. 57–8. The fifth line suggests *Ulysses* 31: 'To follow knowledge like a sinking star'.

i *51. Camilla*] Cadrilla *1832 passim.*

i *52–61*] . . . or sitting gazed
Till gradually the powers of the night
That range above the region of the wind
Deepening the courts of twilight, broke them up
Through all the silent spaces of the worlds
Beyond all thought, into the Heaven of Heavens.
When thou and I, Cadrilla, thou and I
Were moored by some low cavern, while without
Through the long dark, with various voices poured
From all the horizon gathering half the deep,
The roaring ridges into cataracts
Clashed, calling to each other. Low in the East
The bickering Dog-star danced in sparkles–higher
Mars, glaring by the lonely sisters seven
Followed white Venus, whiter than all stars,
Down to the quiet limit of the world.
O look, she loiters in the balmy blue
Close by the deep grain of yon upland field;
She knows me, and I know her beams of old;
She listens to my tale–*Heath MS*

T. incorporated ll. [2–6] verbatim as *The Princess: Conclusion* 111–15. Sir Charles Tennyson (*Cornhill* cliii, 1936, 445) compares l. [11] with *Locksley Hall* 6: 'And the hollow ocean-ridges roaring into cataracts'. Cp. l. [16] with *Tithonus* 7: 'Here at the quiet limit of the world'; and ll. [14–15] with *From the East of life* 3–8: 'White Venus, whiter than all stars– / Then uprose trouble, red like Mars. // Joy set: he stayed: as Mars in heaven / Burns by the lonely sisters seven / When Venus having measured all / The arch in

Beneath a low-browed cavern, where the tide
Plashed, sapping its worn ribs; and all without
The slowly-ridging rollers on the cliffs
Clashed, calling to each other, and through the arch
Down those loud waters, like a setting star,
Mixt with the gorgeous west the lighthouse shone,
And silver-smiling Venus ere she fell
Would often loiter in her balmy blue,
To crown it with herself.
                                        Here, too, my love
Wavered at anchor with me, when day hung
From his mid-dome in Heaven's airy halls;
Gleams of the water-circles as they broke,
Flickered like doubtful smiles about her lips,
Quivered a flying glory on her hair,
Leapt like a passing thought across her eyes;
And mine with one that will not pass, till earth
And heaven pass too, dwelt on my heaven, a face
Most starry-fair, but kindled from within

western mist doth fall.' Cp. l. [13] with *The Princess* v 252–3: 'And as the fiery Sirius alters hue, / And bickers into red and emerald.'

i *53. a*] some *1832.* *tide*] wave *1832.* Cp. Milton, *L'Allegro* 8: 'low-brow'd Rocks'.

i *54–70*] . . . ribs; (the while without,
And close above us, sang the windtost pine,
And shook its earthy socket, for we heard,
In rising and in falling with the tide,
Close by our ears, the huge roots strain and creak,)
Eye feeding upon eye with deep intent;
And mine with love too high to be exprest,
Arrested in its sphere, and ceasing from
All contemplation of all forms, did pause
To worship mine own image, laved in light,
The centre of the splendours, all unworthy
Of such a shrine–mine image in her eyes
By diminution made most glorious,
Moved with their motions, as those eyes were moved
With motions of the soul, as my heart beat
Time to the melody of her's. Her face
Was starry-fair, not pale, tenderly flushed *1832*

Cp. l. [10] with *Armageddon* ii 49–50: 'Yea! in that hour I could have fallen down / Before my own strong soul and worshipped it.' Cp. l. [13] with *Samson Agonistes* 303: 'glory's diminution'.

i *58.* Cp. *Paradise Lost* ii 3: 'the gorgeous East'.

i *63. airy*] windy *Heath MS.* Cp. *Lucretius* 136: 'the windy halls of heaven'.

As 'twere with dawn. She was dark-haired, dark-eyed:
Oh, such dark eyes! a single glance of them
Will govern a whole life from birth to death,
Careless of all things else, led on with light
In trances and in visions: look at them,
You lose yourself in utter ignorance;
You cannot find their depth; for they go back,
And farther back, and still withdraw themselves
Quite into the deep soul, that evermore
Fresh springing from her fountains in the brain,
Still pouring through, floods with redundant life
Her narrow portals.

Trust me, long ago
I should have died, if it were possible
To die in gazing on that perfectness
Which I do bear within me: I had died,
But from my farthest lapse, my latest ebb,
Thine image, like a charm of light and strength
Upon the waters, pushed me back again
On these deserted sands of barren life.
Though from the deep vault where the heart of Hope
Fell into dust, and crumbled in the dark–
Forgetting how to render beautiful
Her countenance with quick and healthful blood–
Thou didst not sway me upward; could I perish
While thou, a meteor of the sepulchre,
Didst swathe thyself all round Hope's quiet urn
For ever? He, that saith it, hath o'erstept
The slippery footing of his narrow wit,
And fallen away from judgment. Thou art light,
To which my spirit leaneth all her flowers,
And length of days, and immortality
Of thought, and freshness ever self-renewed.
For Time and Grief abode too long with Life,

i *81. life*] light *1832.* *redundant*: rolling in waves; cp. *Chorus* 22: 'redundant fire'.

i *95–7*] With such a costly casket in the grasp / Of memory? . . . *1832 but corrected by T. in BM copy with* Hope's] *her*. Beckford's *Vathek* (1786, p. 176) refers to 'those phosphoric meteors that glimmer by night in places of interment' (*OED*).

i *98. slippery footing*: Keats, *Hyperion* ii 85.

i *101.* Cp. *Psalm* xxi 4: 'He asked life of thee, and thou gavest it him, even length of days for ever and ever.'

i *103–11.* This mode of personification is very characteristic of early T.;

And, like all other friends i' the world, at last
They grew aweary of her fellowship:
So Time and Grief did beckon unto Death,
And Death drew nigh and beat the doors of Life;
But thou didst sit alone in the inner house,
A wakeful portress, and didst parle with Death, –
'This is a charmèd dwelling which I hold;'
So Death gave back, and would no further come.
Yet is my life nor in the present time,
Nor in the present place. To me alone,
Pushed from his chair of regal heritage,
The Present is the vassal of the Past:
So that, in that I *have* lived, do I live,
And cannot die, and am, in having been –
A portion of the pleasant yesterday,
Thrust forward on today and out of place;
A body journeying onward, sick with toil,
The weight as if of age upon my limbs,
The grasp of hopeless grief about my heart,
And all the senses weakened, save in that,
Which long ago they had gleaned and garnered up
Into the granaries of memory –
The clear brow, bulwark of the precious brain,
Chinked as you see, and seamed – and all the while
The light soul twines and mingles with the growths
Of vigorous early days, attracted, won,
Married, made one with, molten into all
The beautiful in Past of act or place,
And like the all-enduring camel, driven
Far from the diamond fountain by the palms,
Who toils across the middle moonlit nights,

cp. i 803–10, and *The Burial of Love* (p. 202), *Song [I' the glooming light]* (p. 214), and *Love, Pride, and Forgetfulness* (p. 236).

i *118*. Contrast *The Lotos-Eaters* 92: 'Portions and parcels of the dreadful Past'.

i *121*] The lithe limbs bowed as with a heavy weight, *1832*.

i *122*] *Not 1832*.

i *122 ∧ 3*] The hand of naked time above my brow, *1868*.

i *123*. *save in that*] in all, save that *1832*.

i *124–6*. Cp. Keats, *When I have fears that I may cease to be*: gleaned, garnered, granaries, brain.

i *127*] Now seamed and chinked with years – and all the while *1832*.

i *132*. *And like*] Even as *1832*.

i *134*. *Who . . . across*] Toils onward through *1832*.

i *134 ∧ 5*] Shadowed and crimsoned with the drifting dust; *1832*.

Or when the white heats of the blinding noons
Beat from the concave sand; yet in him keeps
A draught of that sweet fountain that he loves,
To stay his feet from falling, and his spirit
From bitterness of death.

Ye ask me, friends,
When I began to love. How should I tell you?
Or from the after-fulness of my heart,
Flow back again unto my slender spring
And first of love, though every turn and depth
Between is clearer in my life than all
Its present flow. Ye know not what ye ask.
How should the broad and open flower tell
What sort of bud it was, when, prest together
In its green sheath, close-lapt in silken folds,
It seemed to keep its sweetness to itself,
Yet was not the less sweet for that it seemed?
For young Life knows not when young Life was born,
But takes it all for granted: neither Love,
Warm in the heart, his cradle, can remember
Love in the womb, but resteth satisfied,
Looking on her that brought him to the light:
Or as men know not when they fall asleep
Into delicious dreams, our other life,
So know I not when I began to love.
This is my sum of knowledge–that my love
Grew with myself–say rather, was my growth,
My inward sap, the hold I have on earth,
My outward circling air wherewith I breathe,
Which yet upholds my life, and evermore
Is to me daily life and daily death:
For how should I have lived and not have loved?
Can ye take off the sweetness from the flower,
The colour and the sweetness from the rose,
And place them by themselves; or set apart
Their motions and their brightness from the stars,
And then point out the flower or the star?
Or build a wall betwixt my life and love,
And tell me where I am? 'Tis even thus:

i *138–9. Psalm* lvi 13: 'For thou hast delivered my soul from death: wilt not thou deliver my feet from falling, that I may walk before God in the light of the living?' *bitterness of death*: *1 Samuel* xv 32.

i *140. you*] ye *1832*.

i *164. Is*] Was *1832*.

In that I live I love; because I love
I live: whate'er is fountain to the one
Is fountain to the other; and whene'er
Our God unknits the riddle of the one,
There is no shade or fold of mystery
Swathing the other.

Many, many years,
(For they seem many and my most of life,
And well I could have lingered in that porch,
So unproportioned to the dwelling-place,)
In the Maydews of childhood, opposite
The flush and dawn of youth, we lived together,
Apart, alone together on those hills.

Before he saw my day my father died,
And he was happy that he saw it not;
But I and the first daisy on his grave
From the same clay came into light at once.
As Love and I do number equal years,
So she, my love, is of an age with me.
How like each other was the birth of each!
On the same morning, almost the same hour,
Under the selfsame aspect of the stars,
(Oh falsehood of all starcraft!) we were born.
How like each other was the birth of each!
The sister of my mother–she that bore
Camilla close beneath her beating heart,
Which to the imprisoned spirit of the child,
With its true-touchèd pulses in the flow
And hourly visitation of the blood,
Sent notes of preparation manifold,
And mellowed echoes of the outer world–
My mother's sister, mother of my love,
Who had a twofold claim upon my heart,
One twofold mightier than the other was,
In giving so much beauty to the world,
And so much wealth as God had charged her with–
Loathing to put it from herself for ever,
Left her own life with it; and dying thus,
Crowned with her highest act the placid face
And breathless body of her good deeds past.

So were we born, so orphaned. She was motherless
And I without a father. So from each

i *185*. *John* viii 56, 'Your father Abraham rejoiced to see my day: and he saw it, and was glad'.

Of those two pillars which from earth uphold
Our childhood, one had fallen away, and all
The careful burthen of our tender years
Trembled upon the other. He that gave
Her life, to me delightedly fulfilled
All lovingkindnesses, all offices
Of watchful care and trembling tenderness.
He waked for both: he prayed for both: he slept
Dreaming of both: nor was his love the less
Because it was divided, and shot forth
Boughs on each side, laden with wholesome shade,
Wherein we nested sleeping or awake,
And sang aloud the matin-song of life.

She was my foster-sister: on one arm
The flaxen ringlets of our infancies
Wandered, the while we rested: one soft lap
Pillowed us both: a common light of eyes
Was on us as we lay: our baby lips,
Kissing one bosom, ever drew from thence
The stream of life, one stream, one life, one blood,
One sustenance, which, still as thought grew large,
Still larger moulding all the house of thought,
Made all our tastes and fancies like, perhaps–
All–all but one; and strange to me, and sweet,
Sweet through strange years to know that whatsoe'er
Our general mother meant for me alone,
Our mutual mother dealt to both of us:
So what was earliest mine in earliest life,
I shared with her in whom myself remains.

As was our childhood, so our infancy,
They tell me, was a very miracle
Of fellow-feeling and communion.
They tell me that we would not be alone,–
We cried when we were parted; when I wept,
Her smile lit up the rainbow on my tears,
Stayed on the cloud of sorrow; that we loved
The sound of one-another's voices more
Than the gray cuckoo loves his name, and learned
To lisp in tune together; that we slept

i *225. nested*] rested *1832 but corrected by T. in BM copy.*

i *230. a*] one *1832.*

i *236–8*] Perchance assimilated all our tastes
And future fancies. 'Tis a beautiful
And pleasant meditation, that whate'er *1832*

i *239. Our general mother*: *PL* iv 492.

In the same cradle always, face to face.
Heart beating time to heart, lip pressing lip,
Folding each other, breathing on each other,
Dreaming together (dreaming of each other
They should have added), till the morning light
Sloped through the pines, upon the dewy pane
Falling, unsealed our eyelids, and we woke
To gaze upon each other. If this be true,
At thought of which my whole soul languishes
And faints, and hath no pulse, no breath–as though
A man in some still garden should infuse
Rich atar in the bosom of the rose,
Till, drunk with its own wine, and overfull
Of sweetness, and in smelling of itself,
It fall on its own thorns–if this be true–
And that way my wish leads me evermore
Still to believe it–'tis so sweet a thought,
Why in the utter stillness of the soul
Doth questioned memory answer not, nor tell
Of this our earliest, our closest-drawn,
Most loveliest, earthly-heavenliest harmony?
O blossomed portal of the lonely house,
Green prelude, April promise, glad new-year
Of Being, which with earliest violets
And lavish carol of clear-throated larks
Filled all the March of life!–I will not speak of thee,
These have not seen thee, these can never know thee,
They cannot understand me. Pass we then
A term of eighteen years. Ye would but laugh,
If I should tell you how I hoard in thought
The faded rhymes and scraps of ancient crones,

i *261.* Cp. *Song* [*A spirit haunts*] 16: 'My very heart faints and my whole soul grieves'.
i *263. still garden*: *The Gardener's Daughter* 196; *In Memoriam* xliii 10.
i *268. leads me*] leaneth *1832*.
i *273*] Most loveliest, most delicious union? *1832*.
i *274*] Oh, happy, happy outset of my days! *1832*.
i *275. prelude*] springtide *1832*.
i *275–6.* Adapted in a MS of *The Gardener's Daughter*, *T.Nbk 17*.
i *280. we*] on *1832*.
i *282. you*] ye *1832*.
i *282 ∧ 3*] Those rhymes, 'The Lion and the Unicorn,'
'The Four-and-Twenty Blackbirds,' 'Banbury Cross,'
'The Gander,' and 'The Man of Mitylene,' *1832*
i *283. The . . . and*] And all the quaint old *1832*.

Gray relics of the nurseries of the world,
Which are as gems set in my memory,
Because she learnt them with me; or what use
To know her father left us just before
The daffodil was blown? or how we found
The dead man cast upon the shore? All this
Seems to the quiet daylight of your minds
But cloud and smoke, and in the dark of mine
Is traced with flame. Move with me to the event.
  There came a glorious morning, such a one
As dawns but once a season. Mercury
On such a morning would have flung himself
From cloud to cloud, and swum with balanced wings
To some tall mountain: when I said to her,
'A day for Gods to stoop,' she answered, 'Ay,
And men to soar:' for as that other gazed,
Shading his eyes till all the fiery cloud,
The prophet and the chariot and the steeds,
Sucked into oneness like a little star
Were drunk into the inmost blue, we stood,
When first we came from out the pines at noon,
With hands for eaves, uplooking and almost
Waiting to see some blessèd shape in heaven,
So bathed we were in brilliance. Never yet
Before or after have I known the spring
Pour with such sudden deluges of light
Into the middle summer; for that day
Love, rising, shook his wings, and charged the winds

i *284*] *Not 1832.*
i *286. use*] profits it *1832.*
i *287*] To tell ye that her father died, just ere *1832.*
i *289*] The drownèd seaman on the shore? These things *1832.*
i *290. Seems to*] Unto *1832.*
i *291. But*] Are *1832.* *and*] but *1832.*
i *292. Is*] Show *1832.* *the event.*] that hour, *1832.*
i *292* ∧ *3*] Which was the hinge on which the door of Hope
Once turning, opened far into the outward,
And never closed again.
I well remember, *1832*
i *293. There came*] It was *1832.*
i *297–310*] To some tall mountain. On that day the year
First felt his youth and strength, and from his spring
Moved smiling toward his summer. On that day, *1832*
i *299–301.* Elisha and Elijah, *2 Kings* ii 11.
i *311. rising*] waking *1832.* *and*] that *1832.*

With spiced May-sweets from bound to bound, and blew
Fresh fire into the sun, and from within
Burst through the heated buds, and sent his soul
Into the songs of birds, and touched far-off
His mountain-altars, his high hills, with flame
Milder and purer.

Through the rocks we wound:
The great pine shook with lonely sounds of joy
That came on the sea-wind. As mountain streams
Our bloods ran free: the sunshine seemed to brood
More warmly on the heart than on the brow.
We often paused, and, looking back, we saw
The clefts and openings in the mountains filled
With the blue valley and the glistening brooks,
And all the low dark groves, a land of love!
A land of promise, a land of memory,
A land of promise flowing with the milk
And honey of delicious memories!
And down to sea, and far as eye could ken,
Each way from verge to verge a Holy Land,
Still growing holier as you neared the bay,
For there the Temple stood.

When we had reached
The grassy platform on some hill, I stooped,
I gathered the wild herbs, and for her brows
And mine made garlands of the selfsame flower,
Which she took smiling, and with my work thus
Crowned her clear forehead. Once or twice she told me
(For I remember all things) to let grow
The flowers that run poison in their veins.
She said, 'The evil flourish in the world.'
Then playfully she gave herself the lie–

i *317. Through*] Up *1832.*
i *319. streams*] brooks *1832.*
i *323. mountains*] hills all *1832.*
i *325. all*] with *1832.*
i *326*] Where Love was worshipped upon every height,
Where Love was worshipped under every tree– *1832*
i *329. And . . . and*] Down to the sea, as *1832.*
i *330*] From verge to verge it was a Holy Land, *1832.*
i *335. made garlands*] wove chaplets *1832.*
i *336. thus*] there *1832.*

'Nothing in nature is unbeautiful;
So, brother, pluck and spare not.' So I wove
Even the dull-blooded poppy-stem, 'whose flower,
Hued with the scarlet of a fierce sunrise,
Like to the wild youth of an evil prince,
Is without sweetness, but who crowns himself
Above the naked poisons of his heart
In his old age.' A graceful thought of hers
Graven on my fancy! And oh, how like a nymph,
A stately mountain nymph she looked! how native
Unto the hills she trod on! While I gazed
My coronal slowly disentwined itself
And fell between us both; though while I gazed
My spirit leaped as with those thrills of bliss
That strike across the soul in prayer, and show us
That we are surely heard. Methought a light
Burst from the garland I had woven, and stood
A solid glory on her bright black hair;
A light methought broke from her dark, dark eyes,
And shot itself into the singing winds;
A mystic light flashed even from her white robe
As from a glass in the sun, and fell about
My footsteps on the mountains.

Last we came
To what our people call 'The Hill of Woe'.

i *342*. Cp. Coleridge, *The Nightingale* 15: 'In Nature there is nothing melancholy'.

i *344–9*. Incorporated almost verbatim, as Sir Charles Tennyson observes (*1931*, p. 46), from *Sense and Conscience* 99–104 (p. 276).

i *344*. *poppy-stem*, '*whose flower*] poppy, 'whose red flower *1832*.

i *346*. *prince*] king *1832*.

i *348*. *naked*] *1882*; secret *1832–81*. Corrected by T. in a copy of *Works*, 1881 (*Lincoln*).

i *350*] Graven on my fancy! As I said, with these
She crowned her forehead. O, how like a nymph, *1832*

i *352–4*] . . . on! What an angel!
How clothed with beams! My eyes, fixed upon hers,
Almost forgot ever to move again. *1832*

i *356*. *strike*] shoot *1832*.

i *362*. *mystic light*] light, methought, *1832*.

i *364*. *Last we came*] About sunset *1832*.

i *365–71*] We came unto the hill of woe, so called
Because the legend ran that, long time since,
One rainy night, when every wind blew loud,

A bridge is there, that, looked at from beneath
Seems but a cobweb filament to link
The yawning of an earthquake-cloven chasm.
And thence one night, when all the winds were loud,
A woful man (for so the story went)
Had thrust his wife and child and dashed himself
Into the dizzy depth below. Below,
Fierce in the strength of far descent, a stream
Flies with a shattered foam along the chasm.
The path was perilous, loosely strown with crags:
We mounted slowly; yet to both there came
The joy of life in steepness overcome,
And victories of ascent, and looking down
On all that had looked down on us; and joy
In breathing nearer heaven; and joy to me,
High over all the azure-circled earth,
To breathe with her as if in heaven itself;
And more than joy that I to her became
Her guardian and her angel, raising her
Still higher, past all peril, until she saw
Beneath her feet the region far away,
Beyond the nearest mountain's bosky brows,

A woeful man had thrust his wife and child
With shouts from off the bridge, and following plunged *1832*

i *372. depth*] chasm *1832.*

i *373–4*] Sheer through the blackwalled cliff the rapid brook
Shot down his inner thunders, built above
With matted bramble and the shining gloss
Of ivyleaves, whose lowhung tresses, dipped
In the fierce stream, bore downward with the wave. *1832*

i *375. perilous,*] steep and *1832.*

i *376. there came*] of us *1832.*

i *377–86*] It was delight, not hindrance: unto both
Delight from hardship to be overcome,
And scorn of perilous seeming: unto me
Intense delight and rapture, that I breathed,
As with a sense of nigher Deity,
With her to whom all outward fairest things
Were by the busy mind referred, compared,
As bearing no essential fruits of excellence
Save as they were the types and shadowings
Of hers–and then that I became to her
A tutelary angel as she rose,
And with a fearful self-impelling joy
Saw round her feet the country far away, *1832*

Arise in open prospect–heath and hill,
And hollow lined and wooded to the lips,
And steep-down walls of battlemented rock
Gilded with broom, or shattered into spires,
And glory of broad waters interfused,
Whence rose as it were breath and steam of gold,
And over all the great wood rioting
And climbing, streaked or starred at intervals
With falling brook or blossomed bush–and last,
Framing the mighty landscape to the west,
A purple range of mountain-cones, between
Whose interspaces gushed in blinding bursts
The incorporate blaze of sun and sea.

At length
Descending from the point and standing both,
There on the tremulous bridge, that from beneath
Had seemed a gossamer filament up in air,
We paused amid the splendour. All the west
And even unto the middle south was ribbed
And barred with bloom on bloom. The sun below,
Held for a space 'twixt cloud and wave, showered down
Rays of a mighty circle, weaving over
That various wilderness a tissue of light
Unparalleled. On the other side, the moon,
Half-melted into thin blue air, stood still,

*388. Arise in*] *1884*; Burst into *1832–83.*
i *391. shattered into spires*] shivered into peaks *1832.*
i *395. streaked or starred at*] starred at slender *1832.*
i *396*] With blossomtufts of purest white; and last, *1832.*
i *400. blaze*] light *1832 but corrected by T. in BM copy.*
i *401*] *Not 1832.*
i *402. There on*] Upon *1832.*
i *403–4*] Seemed with a cobweb filament to link
The earthquakeshattered chasm, hung with shrubs,
We paused with tears of rapture. All the West, *1832*
In *1868* the second line read: 'The yawning of that earthquake-shattered chasm'.
i *405–6.* Keats, *To Autumn* 25: 'While barred clouds bloom the soft-dying day'.
i *406. below*] beneath *1832.*
i *411.* Adapted from a fragment in *H.Nbk 2*:
Night drew her shadowy sketch of waving hill
Around me and the undefinèd Moon
Half-melting into starless cloud stood still.

And pale and fibrous as a withered leaf,
Nor yet endured in presence of His eyes
To indue his lustre; most unloverlike,
Since in his absence full of light and joy,
And giving light to others. But this most,
Next to her presence whom I loved so well,
Spoke loudly even into my inmost heart
As to my outward hearing: the loud stream,
Forth issuing from his portals in the crag
(A visible link unto the home of my heart),
Ran amber toward the west, and nigh the sea
Parting my own loved mountains was received,
Shorn of its strength, into the sympathy
Of that small bay, which out to open main
Glowed intermingling close beneath the sun.
Spirit of Love! that little hour was bound
Shut in from Time, and dedicate to thee:
Thy fires from heaven had touched it, and the earth
They fell on became hallowed evermore.

We turned: our eyes met: hers were bright, and mine
Were dim with floating tears, that shot the sunset
In lightnings round me; and my name was borne
Upon her breath. Henceforth my name has been
A hallowed memory like the names of old,
A centred, glory-circled memory,
And a peculiar treasure, brooking not
Exchange or currency: and in that hour
A hope flowed round me, like a golden mist
Charmed amid eddies of melodious airs,
A moment, ere the onward whirlwind shatter it,
Wavered and floated–which was less than Hope,
Because it lacked the power of perfect Hope;
But which was more and higher than all Hope,
Because all other Hope had lower aim;
Even that this name to which her gracious lips
Did lend such gentle utterance, this one name,

i *416. most*] chiefest *1832.*

i *424. Shorn of its strength*: cp. *PL* ix 1062.

i *425. out to*] into *1832.*

i *429–30.* Cp. Milton, *Nativity Ode* 28: 'toucht with hallow'd fire'; based on *Isaiah* vi 6–7.

i *436.* Incorporated verbatim from *Timbuctoo* 21.

i *445. had*] hath *1832.*

i *446. gracious*] seraph *1832*

In some obscure hereafter, might inwreathe
(How lovelier, nobler then!) her life, her love,
With my life, love, soul, spirit, and heart and strength.
'Brother,' she said, 'let this be called henceforth
The Hill of Hope;' and I replied, 'O sister,
My will is one with thine; the Hill of Hope.'
Nevertheless, we did not change the name.

I did not speak: I could not speak my love.
Love lieth deep: Love dwells not in lip-depths.
Love wraps his wings on either side the heart,
Constraining it with kisses close and warm,
Absorbing all the incense of sweet thoughts
So that they pass not to the shrine of sound.
Else had the life of that delighted hour
Drunk in the largeness of the utterance
Of Love; but how should Earthly measure mete
The Heavenly-unmeasured or unlimited Love,
Who scarce can tune his high majestic sense
Unto the thundersong that wheels the spheres,
Scarce living in the Æolian harmony,
And flowing odour of the spacious air,
Scarce housed within the circle of this Earth,
Be cabined up in words and syllables,
Which pass with that which breathes them? Sooner Earth
Might go round Heaven, and the strait girth of Time
Inswathe the fulness of Eternity,
Than language grasp the infinite of Love.

O day which did enwomb that happy hour,
Thou art blessèd in the years, divinest day!
O Genius of that hour which dost uphold
Thy coronal of glory like a God,
Amid thy melancholy mates far-seen,
Who walk before thee, ever turning round
To gaze upon thee till their eyes are dim

i *455*] *Not 1832.*
i *462.* Keats, *Hyperion* i 51: 'that large utterance'.
i *465. Who*] Which *1832.*
i *469. within*] in *1832.*
i *471*] Which waste with the breath that made 'em. Sooner Earth *1832.*
i *478.* Cp. *Timbuctoo* 52: 'coronals and glories'.
i *480–82*] . . . thee, and whose eyes are dim / With gazing on the light . . . *1832. 1832* is the germ of *The Lotos-Eaters* 132: 'And eyes grown dim with gazing on the pilot-stars'.

With dwelling on the light and depth of thine,
Thy name is ever worshipped among hours!
Had I died then, I had not seemed to die,
For bliss stood round me like the light of Heaven,–
Had I died then, I had not known the death;
Yea had the Power from whose right hand the light
Of Life issueth, and from whose left hand floweth
The Shadow of Death, perennial effluences,
Whereof to all that draw the wholesome air,
Somewhile the one must overflow the other;
Then had he stemmed my day with night, and driven
My current to the fountain whence it sprang,–
Even his own abiding excellence–
On me, methinks, that shock of gloom had fallen
Unfelt, and in this glory I had merged
The other, like the sun I gazed upon,
Which seeming for the moment due to death,
And dipping his head low beneath the verge,
Yet bearing round about him his own day,
In confidence of unabated strength,
Steppeth from Heaven to Heaven, from light to light,
And holdeth his undimmèd forehead far
Into a clearer zenith, pure of cloud.

We trod the shadow of the downward hill;
We past from light to dark. On the other side
Is scooped a cavern and a mountain hall,

i *485. light*] lights *1832.*
i *485 ∧ 6*] That cannot fade, they are so burning bright. *1832.*
i *486 ∧ 7*] Planting my feet against this mound of Time
I 'ad thrown me on the vast, and from this impulse
Continuing and gathering ever, ever,
Agglomerated swiftness, I had lived
That intense moment through eternity. *1832*
i *487. Yea*] Oh *1832.*
i *487–9.* Cp. Arthur Hallam, *Meditative Fragments* iii, 1829 (Motter, p. 33): 'the effluence of thy holy calm. / Thou too art changed; and that perennial light . . .'
i *496–7*] Unfelt, and like the sun I gazed upon *1832 but corrected by T. in BM copy with* I gazed upon] *on which I gazed.*
i *498*] Which, lapt in seeming dissolution, *1832.*
i *504 ∧ 5*] So bearing on through Being limitless
The triumph of this foretaste, I had merged
Glory in glory, without sense of change. *1832,*
*deleted by T. in BM copy*

Which none have fathomed. If you go far in
(The country people rumour) you may hear
The moaning of the woman and the child,
Shut in the secret chambers of the rock.
I too have heard a sound–perchance of streams
Running far on within its inmost halls,
The home of darkness; but the cavern-mouth,
Half overtrailèd with a wanton weed,
Gives birth to a brawling brook, that passing lightly
Adown a natural stair of tangled roots,
Is presently received in a sweet grave
Of eglantines, a place of burial
Far lovelier than its cradle; for unseen,
But taken with the sweetness of the place,
It makes a constant bubbling melody
That drowns the nearer echoes. Lower down
Spreads out a little lake, that, flooding, leaves
Low banks of yellow sand; and from the woods
That belt it rise three dark, tall cypresses,–
Three cypresses, symbols of mortal woe,
That men plant over graves.

Hither we came,
And sitting down upon the golden moss,
Held converse sweet and low–low converse sweet,
In which our voices bore least part. The wind
Told a lovetale beside us, how he wooed
The waters, and the waters answering lisped
To kisses of the wind, that, sick with love,
Fainted at intervals, and grew again
To utterance of passion. Ye cannot shape
Fancy so fair as is this memory.
Methought all excellence that ever was
Had drawn herself from many thousand years,

i *511. chambers of the rock*: traditional diction since Pope, as in Wordsworth. Cp. also Thomson, *Winter* 168: 'Into the secret chambers of the deep'. T. had imitated Thomson in *The Devil and the Lady*, I 193: 'The stilly chambers of the mighty deep'.

i *516. brook, that passing*] stream, that stepping *1832*.

i *522*] It giveth out a constant melody *1832*.

i *524. leaves*] makes *1832*.

i *525. Low banks*] Cushions *1832*.

i *529. golden moss*: as in the lover's bower in Keats, *Endymion* ii 671.

i *533. waters answering*] crispèd waters *1832*.

i *534. To*] The *1832*.

And all the separate Edens of this earth,
To centre in this place and time. I listened,
And her words stole with most prevailing sweetness
Into my heart, as thronging fancies come
To boys and girls when summer days are new,
And soul and heart and body are all at ease:
What marvel my Camilla told me all?
It was so happy an hour, so sweet a place,
And I was as the brother of her blood,
And by that name I moved upon her breath;
Dear name, which had too much of nearness in it
And heralded the distance of this time!
At first her voice was very sweet and low,
As if she were afraid of utterance;
But in the onward current of her speech,
(As echoes of the hollow-bankèd brooks
Are fashioned by the channel which they keep),
Her words did of their meaning borrow sound,
Her cheek did catch the colour of her words.
I heard and trembled, yet I could but hear;
My heart paused–my raised eyelids would not fall,
But still I kept my eyes upon the sky.
I seemed the only part of Time stood still,
And saw the motion of all other things;
While her words, syllable by syllable,
Like water, drop by drop, upon my ear
Fell; and I wished, yet wished her not to speak;
But she spake on, for I did name no wish.
What marvel my Camilla told me all
Her maiden dignities of Hope and Love–

i *543. thronging*] throngèd *1832.*

i *544–5*] All unawares, into the poet's brain;
Or as the dewdrops on the petal hung,
When summer winds break their soft sleep with sighs,
Creep down into the bottom of the flower.
Her words were like a crownal of wild blooms
Strung in the very negligence of Art,
Or in the art of Nature, where each rose
Doth faint upon the bosom of the other,
Flooding its angry cheek with odorous tears:
So each with each inwoven lived in each,
And were in union more than double-sweet. *1832*

i *549. I . . . breath*] was wont to live in her speech, *1832.*

i *553. if*] though *1832.* *afraid*] afeard *1832.*

i *557. Her*] His *1832.*

'Perchance,' she said, 'returned.' Even then the stars
Did tremble in their stations as I gazed;
But she spake on, for I did name no wish,
No wish–no hope. Hope was not wholly dead,
But breathing hard at the approach of Death,–
Camilla, my Camilla, who was mine
No longer in the dearest sense of mine–
For all the secret of her inmost heart,
And all the maiden empire of her mind,
Lay like a map before me, and I saw
There, where I hoped myself to reign as king,
There, where that day I crowned myself as king,
There in my realm and even on my throne,
*Another!* then it seemed as though a link
Of some tight chain within my inmost frame
Was riven in twain: that life I heeded not
Flowed from me, and the darkness of the grave,
The darkness of the grave and utter night,
Did swallow up my vision; at her feet,
Even the feet of her I loved, I fell,
Smit with exceeding sorrow unto Death.

Then had the earth beneath me yawning cloven
With such a sound as when an iceberg splits
From cope to base–had Heaven from all her doors,
With all her golden thresholds clashing, rolled

i *574* ∧ *5*] Updrawn in expectation of her change – *1832 which has* charge *corrected by T. in BM copy.*
i *576. sense*] use *1832.*
i *577–83*] The written secrets of her inmost soul
Lay like an open scroll before my view,
And my eyes read, they read aright, her heart
Was Lionel's: then . . . *1832*
i *584. tight*] light *1832 but corrected by T. in BM copy.* *my inmost frame*: *Memory* [*Ay me*!] 3.
i *590. Matthew* xxvi 38, 'My soul is exceeding sorrowful, even unto death.'
i *591. cloven*] given *1832.*
i *592–4*] Sign of convulsion, and through horrid rifts
Sent up the moaning of unhappy Spirits
Imprisoned in her centre, with the heat
Of their infolding element; had the Angels,
The watchers at Heaven's gate, pushed them apart,
And from the golden threshold had downrolled *1832*
In the first line, 'horrid rifts' is from *Paradise Regained* iv 411.

Her heaviest thunder–I had lain as dead,
Mute, blind and motionless as then I lay;
Dead, for henceforth there was no life for me!
Mute, for henceforth what use were words to me!
Blind, for the day was as the night to me!
The night to me was kinder than the day;
The night in pity took away my day,
Because my grief as yet was newly born
Of eyes too weak to look upon the light;
And through the hasty notice of the ear
Frail Life was startled from the tender love
Of him she brooded over. Would I had lain
Until the plaited ivy-tress had wound
Round my worn limbs, and the wild brier had driven
Its knotted thorns through my unpaining brows,
Leaning its roses on my faded eyes.
The wind had blown above me, and the rain
Had fallen upon me, and the gilded snake
Had nestled in this bosom-throne of Love,
But I had been at rest for evermore.

Long time entrancement held me. All too soon
Life (like a wanton too-officious friend,
Who will not *hear* denial, vain and rude
With proffer of unwished-for services)
Entering all the avenues of sense
Past through into his citadel, the brain,

i 595. *Her*] Their *1832*. *dead*] still *1832*.
i 596. *Mute,*] And *1832*.
i 597–600] White as quenched ashes, cold as were the hopes
Of my lorn love! What happy air shall woo
The withered leaf fallen in the woods, or blasted
Upon the bough? a lightningstroke had come
Even from that Heaven in whose light I bloomed,
And taken away the greenness of my life,
The blossom and the fragrance. Who was curst
But I? who miserable but I? even Misery
Forgot herself in that extreme distress,
And with the overdoing of her part
Did fall away into oblivion. *1832*
i 603. *eyes too weak*] too weak eyes *1832*.
i 604. *through*] with *1832*.
i 607. *plaited*] pleachèd *1832*.
i 609. Cp. *Pierced through with knotted thorns of barren pain* (p. 472).
i 617. Cp. *Lycidas* 18: 'denial vain'.

With hated warmth of apprehensiveness.
And first the chillness of the sprinkled brook
Smote on my brows, and then I seemed to hear
Its murmur, as the drowning seaman hears,
Who with his head below the surface dropt
Listens the muffled booming indistinct
Of the confusèd floods, and dimly knows
His head shall rise no more: and then came in
The white light of the weary moon above,
Diffused and molten into flaky cloud.
Was my sight drunk that it did shape to me
Him who should own that name? Were it not well
If so be that the echo of that name

i *622. sprinkled brook*] mountain stream *1832.*
i *623. brows*] brow *1832.*
i *626. muffled booming*] dreadful murmur *1832.*
i *627. floods*] seas *1832.* *dimly knows*] knoweth not *1832.*
i *628. His . . . more*] Beyond the sound he lists *1832.*
i *629*] O'erhead the white light of the weary moon, *1832.* *weary moon*: traditional diction, as twice in Shelley.
i *632–45*] . . . name? or had my fancy
So lethargised discernment in the sense,
That she did act the stepdame to mine eyes,
Warping their nature, till they ministered
Unto her swift conceits? 'twere better thus,
If so be that the memory of that sound,
With mighty evocation, had updrawn
The fashion and the phantasm of the form
It should attach to. There was no such thing–
It was the man she loved, even Lionel,
The lover Lionel, the happy Lionel,
The lowvoiced, tenderspirited Lionel,
All joy; who drew the happy atmosphere
Of my unhappy sighs, fed with my tears,
To him the honeydews of orient hope.
O! rather had some lothly ghastful brow,
Half-bursten from the shroud, in cerecloth bound,
The dead skin withering on the fretted bone,
The very Spirit of Paleness made still paler
By the shuddering moonlight, fixed his eyes on mine,
Horrible with the anger and the heat
Of the remorseful soul alive within,
And damned unto his loathèd tenement,
Methinks I could have sooner met that gaze! *1832*

T. made the following corrections to *1832* in *BM* copy: l. [2] *lethargised*]

Ringing within the fancy had updrawn
A fashion and a phantasm of the form
It should attach to? Phantom!–had the ghastliest
That ever lusted for a body, sucking
The foul steam of the grave to thicken by it,
There in the shuddering moonlight brought its face
And what it has for eyes as close to mine
As he did–better that than his, than he
The friend, the neighbour, Lionel, the beloved,
The loved, the lover, the happy Lionel,
The low-voiced, tender-spirited Lionel,
All joy, to whom my agony was a joy.
O how her choice did leap forth from his eyes!
O how her love did clothe itself in smiles
About his lips! and–not one moment's grace–
Then when the effect weighed seas upon my head
To come my way! to twit me with the cause!

Was not the land as free through all her ways
To him as me? Was not his wont to walk
Between the going light and growing night?
Had I not learnt my loss before he came?
Could that be more because he came my way?
Why should he not come my way if he would?
And yet tonight, tonight–when all my wealth
Flashed from me in a moment and I fell

palsied all l. [6] *memory*] echo l. [7] Ringing within the spirit, had updrawn l. [8] *The . . . the*] A . . . a l. [9] *There . . . thing*] *deleted.*

i *648*] About his lips! This was the very archmock
And insolence of uncontrollèd Fate, *1832*

i *649. Then when*] When *1832.*

i *650–9*] To twit me with the cause.
Why how was this?
Could he not walk what paths he chose, nor breathe
What airs he pleased? Was not the wide world free,
With all her interchange of hill and plain,
To him as well as me? I know not, 'faith:
But Misery, like a fretful wayward child,
Refused to look his author in the face.
Must he come my way too? was not the South,
The East, the West all open, if he had fallen
In love in twilight? why should he come my way, *1832*

T. corrected the last line in *BM* copy of *1832*: *in twilight*] with twilight. Cp. the fourth line with *PL* ix 115–16: 'interchange / Of Hill and Vallie, Rivers, Woods and Plaines'.

Beggared for ever–why *should* he come my way
Robed in those robes of light I must not wear,
With that great crown of beams about his brows–
Come like an angel to a damnèd soul,
To tell him of the bliss he had with God–
Come like a careless and a greedy heir
That scarce can wait the reading of the will
Before he takes possession? Was mine a mood
To be invaded rudely, and not rather
A sacred, secret, unapproachèd woe,
Unspeakable? I was shut up with Grief;
She took the body of my past delight,
Narded and swathed and balmed it for herself,
And laid it in a sepulchre of rock
Never to rise again. I was led mute
Into her temple like a sacrifice;
I was the High Priest in her holiest place,
Not to be loudly broken in upon.

Oh friend, thoughts deep and heavy as these well-nigh
O'erbore the limits of my brain: but he
Bent o'er me, and my neck his arm upstayed.
I thought it was an adder's fold, and once
I strove to disengage myself, but failed,
Being so feeble: she bent above me, too;
Wan was her cheek; for whatsoe'er of blight
Lives in the dewy touch of pity had made
The red rose there a pale one–and her eyes–

i *670–3. John* xix 40–1.
i *672–3*] . . . in a new-hewn sepulchre / Where man had never lain. I . . . *1832*.
i *673*. Cp. *Isaiah* liii 7: 'He is brought as a lamb to the slaughter, and as a sheep before her shearers is dumb, so he openeth not his mouth.'
i *679–86*] . . . upstayed
From earth. I thought it was an adder's fold
And once I strove to disengage myself,
But failed, I was so feeble. She was there too;
She bent above me too: her cheek was pale,
Oh! very fair and pale: rare pity had stolen
The living bloom away, as though a red rose
Should change into a white one suddenly.
Her eyes, I saw, were full of tears in the moon, *1832*
In *BM* copy, T. added to *1832* the word 'I' in the third line, and in the last line corrected *morn*] moon.

I saw the moonlight glitter on their tears—
And some few drops of that distressful rain
Fell on my face, and her long ringlets moved,
Drooping and beaten by the breeze, and brushed
My fallen forehead in their to and fro,
For in the sudden anguish of her heart
Loosed from their simple thrall they had flowed abroad,
And floated on and parted round her neck,
Mantling her form halfway. She, when I woke,
Something she asked, I know not what, and asked,
Unanswered, since I spake not; for the sound
Of that dear voice so musically low,
And now first heard with any sense of pain,
As it had taken life away before,
Choked all the syllables, that strove to rise
From my full heart.

The blissful lover, too,
From his great hoard of happiness distilled
Some drops of solace; like a vain rich man,
That, having always prospered in the world,
Folding his hands, deals comfortable words
To hearts wounded for ever; yet, in truth,
Fair speech was his and delicate of phrase,
Falling in whispers on the sense, addressed
More to the inward than the outward ear,
As rain of the midsummer midnight soft,
Scarce-heard, recalling fragrance and the green

i *688*] Being wafted on the wind, drove in my sight,
And being there they did break forth afresh
In a new birth, immingled with my own,
And still bewept my grief, keeping unchanged
The purport of their coinage. Her long ringlets, *1832*

i *689. by . . . brushed*] with the plaining wind, *1832*.

i *690. My fallen*] Did brush my *1832*.

i *693*] And onward floating in a full dark wave,
Parted on either side her argent neck, *1832*

i *695*] After my refluent health made tender quest, *1832*.

i *696. since*] for *1832*.

i *700–01*] . . . that in my throat
Strove to uprise, laden with mournful thanks,
From my full heart: and ever since that hour,
My voice hath somewhat faltered—and what wonder
That when hope died, part of her eloquence
Died with her? He, the blissful lover, too, *1832*

Of the dead spring: but mine was wholly dead,
No bud, no leaf, no flower, no fruit for me.
Yet who had done, or who had suffered wrong?
And why was I to darken their pure love,
If, as I found, they two did love each other,
Because my own was darkened? Why was I
To cross between their happy star and them?
To stand a shadow by their shining doors,
And vex them with my darkness? Did I love her?
Ye know that I did love her; to this present
My full-orbed love has waned not. Did I love her,
And could I look upon her tearful eyes?
What had *she* done to weep? Why should *she* weep?
O innocent of spirit–let my heart
Break rather–whom the gentlest airs of Heaven
Should kiss with an unwonted gentleness.
Her love did murder mine? What then? She deemed
I wore a brother's mind: she called me brother:
She told me all her love: she shall not weep.

The brightness of a burning thought, awhile
In battle with the glooms of my dark will,
Moonlike emerged, and to itself lit up
There on the depth of an unfathomed woe
Reflex of action. Starting up at once,
As from a dismal dream of my own death,

i *712–4*] . . . spring–such as in other minds
Had filmed the margents of the recent wound. *1832*

i *716. found*] knew *1832.*

i *718–20*] To stand within the level of their hopes,
Because my hope was widowed, like the cur
In the child's adage? Did I love Cadrilla? *1832*

i *722. has*] hath *1832.*

i *723 ∧ 4*] Tears wept for me! for me–weep at my grief? *1832.*

i *732. In battle*] Battailing *1832.*

i *733. and . . . up*] lit up unto itself, *1832.*

i *734. There on*] Upon *1832.*

i *736–43*] As men do from a vague and horrid dream,
And throwing by all consciousness of self,
In eager haste I shook him by the hand;
Then flinging myself down upon my knees,
Even where the grass was warm where I had lain,
I prayed aloud to God that he would hold
The hand of blessing over Lionel,
And her whom he would make his wedded wife–

I, for I loved her, lost my love in Love;
I, for I loved her, graspt the hand she loved,
And laid it in her own, and sent my cry
Through the blank night to Him who loving made
The happy and the unhappy love, that He
Would hold the hand of blessing over them,
Lionel, the happy, and her, and her, his bride!
Let them so love that men and boys may say,
'Lo! how they love each other!' till their love
Shall ripen to a proverb, unto all
Known, when their faces are forgot in the land–
One golden dream of love, from which may death
Awake them with heaven's music in a life
More living to some happier happiness,
Swallowing its precedent in victory.
And as for me, Camilla, as for me,–
The dew of tears is an unwholesome dew,
They will but sicken the sick plant the more.
Deem that I love thee but as brothers do,
So shalt thou love me still as sisters do;
Or if thou dream aught farther, dream but how
I could have loved thee, had there been none else
To love as lovers, loved again by thee.

Or this, or somewhat like to this, I spake,
When I beheld her weep so ruefully;
For sure my love should ne'er indue the front

Cadrilla! May their days be golden days,
And their long life a dream of linkèd love,
From which may rude Death never startle them,
But grow upon them like a glorious vision
Of unconceived and awful happiness,
Solemn but splendid, full of shapes and sounds,
Swallowing its precedent in victory. *1832*

The last line became l. 751.

i *748–51*] *Not 1832*. See preceding note.

i *752 ∧ 3*] Think not thy tears will make my name grow green; *1832*.

i *753 ∧ 4*] The course of Hope is dried–the life o' the plant– *1832*.

i *754. plant*] *1832 but corrected by T. in BM copy to* heart.

i *755. that*] than *1832* (*error*).

i *757. dream*] dreamest *1832*.

i *761. beheld*] did see *1832*.

i *762. indue*] induce *1832, corrected by T. in fragment of proofs* (*10 Nov. 1832*) *at Lincoln.*

And mask of Hate, who lives on others' moans.
Shall Love pledge Hatred in her bitter draughts,
And batten on her poisons? Love forbid!
Love passeth not the threshold of cold Hate,
And Hate is strange beneath the roof of Love.
O Love, if thou be'st Love, dry up these tears
Shed for the love of Love; for though mine image,
The subject of thy power, be cold in her,
Yet, like cold snow, it melteth in the source
Of these sad tears, and feeds their downward flow.
So Love, arraigned to judgment and to death,
Received unto himself a part of blame,
Being guiltless, as an innocent prisoner,
Who, when the woful sentence hath been past,
And all the clearness of his fame hath gone
Beneath the shadow of the curse of man,
First falls asleep in swoon, wherefrom awaked,
And looking round upon his tearful friends,
Forthwith and in his agony conceives
A shameful sense as of a cleaving crime–
For whence without some guilt should such grief be?

So died that hour, and fell into the abysm
Of forms outworn, but not to me outworn,
Who never hailed another–was there one?
There might be one–one other, worth the life
That made it sensible. So that hour died
Like odour rapt into the wingèd wind
Borne into alien lands and far away.

There be some hearts so airily built, that they,
They–when their love is wrecked–if Love can wreck–
On that sharp ridge of utmost doom ride highly
Above the perilous seas of Change and Chance;
Nay, more, hold out the lights of cheerfulness;
As the tall ship, that many a dreary year

*763*] And mask of Hate, whom woeful aliments
Of unavailing tears and heartdeep moans
Feed and envenom, as the milky blood
Of hateful herbs a subtlefangèd snake. *1832*

i *764. her*] his *1832.*
i *765. her*] his *1832.*
i *786–7*] Who never hailed another worth the life *1832.*
i *788. that hour died*] died that hour *1832.*
i *791. airily . . . they*] airy-fashionèd *1832.*
i *792*] That in the death of Love, if e'er they loved, *1832.*

Knit to some dismal sandbank far at sea,
All through the livelong hours of utter dark,
Showers slanting light upon the dolorous wave.
For me–what light, what gleam on those black ways
Where Love could walk with banished Hope no more?

It was ill-done to part you, Sisters fair;
Love's arms were wreathed about the neck of Hope,
And Hope kissed Love, and Love drew in her breath
In that close kiss, and drank her whispered tales.
They said that Love would die when Hope was gone,
And Love mourned long, and sorrowed after Hope;
At last she sought out Memory, and they trod
The same old paths where Love had walked with Hope,
And Memory fed the soul of Love with tears.

## II

From that time forth I would not see her more;
But many weary moons I lived alone–
Alone, and in the heart of the great forest.
Sometimes upon the hills beside the sea
All day I watched the floating isles of shade,
And sometimes on the shore, upon the sands
Insensibly I drew her name, until
The meaning of the letters shot into
My brain; anon the wanton billow washed
Them over, till they faded like my love.
The hollow caverns heard me–the black brooks
Of the midforest heard me–the soft winds,
Laden with thistledown and seeds of flowers,
Paused in their course to hear me, for my voice
Was all of thee: the merry linnet knew me,
The squirrel knew me, and the dragonfly
Shot by me like a flash of purple fire.
The rough brier tore my bleeding palms; the hemlock,
Brow-high, did strike my forehead as I past;
Yet trod I not the wildflower in my path,

i *800–1*] For me all other Hopes did sway from that
Which hung the frailest: falling, they fell too,
Crushed link on link into the beaten earth,
And Love did walk with banished Hope no more. *1832*

i *803*. See l. 103–11*n*. Cp. Byron's *Lines Written Beneath a Picture* 5–8: ''Tis said with Sorrow Time can cope; / But this I feel can ne'er be true: / For by the death-blow of my Hope / My Memory immortal grew.'

Nor bruised the wildbird's egg.
Was this the end?
Why grew we then together in one plot?
Why fed we from one fountain? drew one sun?
Why were our mothers' branches of one stem?
Why were we one in all things, save in that
Where to have been one had been the cope and crown
Of all I hoped and feared?–if that same nearness
Were father to this distance, and that *one*
Vauntcourier to this *double*? if Affection
Living slew Love, and Sympathy hewed out
The bosom-sepulchre of Sympathy?

Chiefly I sought the cavern and the hill
Where last we roamed together, for the sound
Of the loud stream was pleasant, and the wind
Came wooingly with woodbine smells. Sometimes
All day I sat within the cavern-mouth,
Fixing my eyes on those three cypress-cones
That spired above the wood; and with mad hand
Tearing the bright leaves of the ivy-screen,
I cast them in the noisy brook beneath,
And watched them till they vanished from my sight
Beneath the bower of wreathèd eglantines:
And all the fragments of the living rock
(Huge blocks, which some old trembling of the world
Had loosened from the mountain, till they fell
Half-digging their own graves) these in my agony
Did I make bare of all the golden moss,
Wherewith the dashing runnel in the spring
Had liveried them all over. In my brain

ii *22. in one*] i' the same *1832.*
ii *23. from one . . . one*] the same . . . the same *1832.*
ii *26. cope*] roof *1832.*
ii *29. to*] *Not 1832 but added by T. in BM copy.* Cp. *Lear* III ii 5: 'vauntcouriers of oak-cleaving thunderbolts'.
ii *35. woodbine*] violet *1832.*
ii *38. That*] Which *1832.*
ii *44–6*] (Huge splinters, which the sap of earliest showers,
Or moisture of the vapour, left in clinging,
When the shrill stormblast feeds it from behind,
And scatters it before, had shattered from
The mountain, till they fell, and with the shock
Half-dug their own graves,) in mine agony *1832*
ii *47. golden*] deep rich *1832.*

The spirit seemed to flag from thought to thought,
As moonlight wandering through a mist: my blood
Crept like marsh drains through all my languid limbs;
The motions of my heart seemed far within me,
Unfrequent, low, as though it told its pulses;
And yet it shook me, that my frame would shudder,
As if 'twere drawn asunder by the rack.
But over the deep graves of Hope and Fear,
And all the broken palaces of the Past,
Brooded one master-passion evermore,
Like to a low-hung and a fiery sky
Above some fair metropolis, earth-shocked,–
Hung round with ragged rims and burning folds,–
Embathing all with wild and woful hues,
Great hills of ruins, and collapsèd masses
Of thundershaken columns indistinct,
And fused together in the tyrannous light–
Ruins, the ruin of all my life and me!

Sometimes I thought Camilla was no more,
Some one had told me she was dead, and asked
If I would see her burial: then I seemed
To rise, and through the forest-shadow borne
With more than mortal swiftness, I ran down
The steepy sea-bank, till I came upon

ii *51. As*] Like *1832*.

ii *52*] Crept like the drains of a marsh through all my body; *1832 but corrected by T., retaining* body. *languid limbs*: as twice in Shelley.

ii *55. would*] did *1832*.

ii *56. if 'twere*] it were *1832*.

ii *58*] The wrecks of ruined life and shattered thought, *1832*.

ii *61. fair*] great *1832*.

ii *62. ragged rims and*] raggedrimmèd *1832*.

ii *67*]

So gazed I on the ruins of that thought
Which was the playmate of my youth–for which
I lived and breathed: the dew, the sun, the rain,
Unto the growth of body and of mind;
The blood, the breath, the feeling, and the motion,
The slope unto the current of my years,
Which drove them onward–made them sensible;
The precious jewel of my honoured life,
Erewhile close couched in golden happiness,
Now provèd counterfeit, was shaken out,
And, trampled on, left to its own decay. *1832*

ii *69*] *1832*; . . . told she was dead, and asked me *1879* (*error*).

The rear of a procession, curving round
The silver-sheeted bay: in front of which
Six stately virgins, all in white, upbare
A broad earth-sweeping pall of whitest lawn,
Wreathed round the bier with garlands: in the distance,
From out the yellow woods upon the hill
Looked forth the summit and the pinnacles
Of a gray steeple–thence at intervals
A low bell tolling. All the pageantry,
Save those six virgins which upheld the bier,
Were stoled from head to foot in flowing black;
One walked abreast with me, and veiled his brow,
And he was loud in weeping and in praise
Of her, we followed: a strong sympathy
Shook all my soul: I flung myself upon him
In tears and cries: I told him all my love,
How I had loved her from the first; whereat
He shrank and howled, and from his brow drew back
His hand to push me from him; and the face,
The very face and form of Lionel
Flashed through my eyes into my innermost brain,
And at his feet I seemed to faint and fall,
To fall and die away. I could not rise
Albeit I strove to follow. They past on,
The lordly Phantasms! in their floating folds
They past and were no more: but I had fallen
Prone by the dashing runnel on the grass.

Alway the inaudible invisible thought,
Artificer and subject, lord and slave,
Shaped by the audible and visible,
Moulded the audible and visible;
All crispèd sounds of wave and leaf and wind,
Flattered the fancy of my fading brain;
The cloud-pavilioned element, the wood,
The mountain, the three cypresses, the cave,
Storm, sunset, glows and glories of the moon

ii *81–2*] Of a gray steeple. All the pageantry, *1832*.
ii *87. her, we followed*] the departed *1832*.
ii *91. shrank*] shrunk *1832*.
ii *97. to*] *Not 1832 but added by T. in BM copy.*
ii *107. cloud-*] storm- *1832*.
ii *109–11*] *Not 1832*. T. supplied them from *Who is it comes hither* 13–16: 'like the glow / Of the unrisen moon below / Dark firs, when creeping winds by night / Lay the long mist in streaks and bars.'

Below black firs, when silent-creeping winds
Laid the long night in silver streaks and bars,
Were wrought into the tissue of my dream:
The moanings in the forest, the loud brook,
Cries of the partridge like a rusty key
Turned in a lock, owl-whoop and dorhawk-whirr
Awoke me not, but were a part of sleep,
And voices in the distance calling to me
And in my vision bidding me dream on,
Like sounds without the twilight realm of dreams,
Which wander round the bases of the hills,
And murmur at the low-dropt eaves of sleep,
Half-entering the portals. Oftentimes
The vision had fair prelude, in the end
Opening on darkness, stately vestibules
To caves and shows of Death: whether the mind,
With some revenge–even to itself unknown,–
Made strange division of its suffering
With her, whom to have suffering viewed had been
Extremest pain; or that the clear-eyed Spirit,
Being blunted in the Present, grew at length
Prophetical and prescient of whate'er
The Future had in store: or that which most
Enchains belief, the sorrow of my spirit
Was of so wide a compass it took in
All I had loved, and my dull agony,
Ideally to her transferred, became
Anguish intolerable.

The day waned;
Alone I sat with her: about my brow
Her warm breath floated in the utterance
Of silver-chorded tones: her lips were sundered
With smiles of tranquil bliss, which broke in light
Like morning from her eyes–her eloquent eyes,
(As I have seen them many a hundred times)

ii *113. brook*] stream *1832.*
ii *114–15*] *Not 1832.*
ii *119. without*] within *1832.* *realm*] realms *1832.*
ii *121. at*] in *1832.*
ii *122. Half-entering*] But faint within *1832.*
ii *125. caves*] cares *1832 but corrected by T. in BM copy.*
ii *126. some*] a *1832 but corrected by T. in BM copy.*
ii *130. blunted*] blasted *1832 but corrected by T. in BM copy.*
ii *143. a*] *Not 1832.*

Filled all with pure clear fire, through mine down rained
Their spirit-searching splendours. As a vision
Unto a haggard prisoner, iron-stayed
In damp and dismal dungeons underground,
Confined on points of faith, when strength is shocked
With torment, and expectancy of worse
Upon the morrow, through the ragged walls,
All unawares before his half-shut eyes,
Comes in upon him in the dead of night,
And with the excess of sweetness and of awe,
Makes the heart tremble, and the sight run over
Upon his steely gyves; so those fair eyes
Shone on my darkness, forms which ever stood
Within the magic cirque of memory,
Invisible but deathless, waiting still
The edict of the will to reassume
The semblance of those rare realities
Of which they were the mirrors. Now the light
Which was their life, burst through the cloud of thought
Keen, irrepressible.

It was a room
Within the summer-house of which I spake,
Hung round with paintings of the sea, and one
A vessel in mid-ocean, her heaved prow
Clambering, the mast bent and the ravin wind
In her sail roaring. From the outer day,
Betwixt the close-set ivies came a broad
And solid beam of isolated light,
Crowded with driving atomies, and fell
Slanting upon that picture, from prime youth
Well-known well-loved. She drew it long ago
Forthgazing on the waste and open sea,
One morning when the upblown billow ran
Shoreward beneath red clouds, and I had poured

ii *154. sight*] eyes *1832*.

ii *162–3*. Cp. *Sense and Conscience* 54: 'irrepressible fire of his keen eyes'; see i 344–9*n*. Also Arthur Hallam, *Alas, that sometimes* (1831): 'irrepressible thoughts' (Motter, p. 98).

ii *167. ravin*] revin *1832 but corrected by T. in BM copy*. An archaic or Shakespearean form of 'ravening'.

ii *169. close-set*] closest *1832 but corrected by T. in BM copy*.

ii *176–89*. Cp. *Locksley Hall Sixty Years After* 13–16, lines which were originally part of *Locksley Hall*: 'In the hall there hangs a painting–Amy's

Into the shadowing pencil's naked forms
Colour and life: it was a bond and seal
Of friendship, spoken of with tearful smiles;
A monument of childhood and of love;
The poesy of childhood; my lost love
Symbolled in storm. We gazed on it together
In mute and glad remembrance, and each heart
Grew closer to the other, and the eye
Was riveted and charm-bound, gazing like
The Indian on a still-eyed snake, low-couched–
A beauty which is death; when all at once
That painted vessel, as with inner life,
Began to heave upon that painted sea;
An earthquake, my loud heart-beats, made the ground
Reel under us, and all at once, soul, life
And breath and motion, past and flowed away
To those unreal billows: round and round
A whirlwind caught and bore us; mighty gyres
Rapid and vast, of hissing spray wind-driven
Far through the dizzy dark. Aloud she shrieked;
My heart was cloven with pain; I wound my arms
About her: we whirled giddily; the wind
Sung; but I clasped her without fear: her weight
Shrank in my grasp, and over my dim eyes,
And parted lips which drank her breath, down-hung

arms about my neck– / Happy children in a sunbeam sitting on the ribs of wreck. // In my life there was a picture, she that clasped my neck had flown; / I was left within the shadow sitting on the wreck alone.'

ii *185–7.* Cp. *Love* [*Thou, from the first*] iii: 'And now–methinks I gaze upon thee now, / As on a serpent in his agonies / Awestricken Indians; what time laid low . . . / And in his writhings awful hues begin / To wander down his sable-sheeny sides . . .'

ii *186. low-couched*] low-crouched *1832 but corrected by T. in BM copy.*

ii *189. Began to*] 'Gan rock and *1832.*

ii *191. Reel*] Roll *1832 but corrected by T. in BM copy.*

ii *194–205.* The drowning vision anticipates Ida's rescue in *The Princess,* as Paden says (p. 91); and cp. the Prince's seizures. T. is influenced by Cary's translation of Dante, *Inferno* xxvi, which he used for *Ulysses,* and of which there was a copy at Somersby (*Lincoln*). Ulysses's last voyage ends: 'From the new land / A whirlwind sprung, and at her foremost side / Did strike the vessel. Thrice it whirl'd her round / With all the waves, the fourth time lifted up / The poop, and sank the prow: so fate decreed: / And over us the booming billow clos'd.'

ii *194. gyres*] gyves *1832 but corrected by T. in BM copy.*

ii *199. Sung*] *1832 but corrected by T. in BM copy to* Sang.

The jaws of Death: I, groaning, from me flung
Her empty phantom: all the sway and whirl
Of the storm dropt to windless calm, and I
Down weltered through the dark ever and ever.

III

I came one day and sat among the stones
Strewn in the entry of the moaning cave;
A morning air, sweet after rain, ran over
The rippling levels of the lake, and blew
Coolness and moisture and all smells of bud
And foliage from the dark and dripping woods
Upon my fevered brows that shook and throbbed
From temple unto temple. To what height
The day had grown I know not. Then came on me
The hollow tolling of the bell, and all
The vision of the bier. As heretofore
I walked behind with one who veiled his brow.
Methought by slow degrees the sullen bell
Tolled quicker, and the breakers on the shore
Sloped into louder surf: those that went with me,
And those that held the bier before my face,
Moved with one spirit round about the bay,
Trod swifter steps; and while I walked with these
In marvel at that gradual change, I thought
Four bells instead of one began to ring,
Four merry bells, four merry marriage-bells,
In clanging cadence jangling peal on peal–
A long loud clash of rapid marriage-bells.
Then those who led the van, and those in rear,
Rushed into dance, and like wild Bacchanals
Fled onward to the steeple in the woods:

ii *202. groaning*] screaming *1832*.
ii *203. Her*] The *1832*.
ii *203–4*. Cp. Shelley, *Prometheus Unbound* I 241–2: 'Driven me, a frail and empty phantom, hither / On direst storms'. *windless calm*: *Armageddon* i 111; Shelley, *Scenes from Calderon* ii 97.

iii *4. levels*: Latin *aequora*; cp. *Morte d'Arthur* 51: 'the shining levels of the lake'.
iii *13*. Shakespeare, *Sonnet 71*: 'No longer mourn for me when I am dead, Than you shall hear the surly sullen bell.'
iii *14. shore*] sand *1868*.
iii *18. these*] them *1868*.

I, too, was borne along and felt the blast
Beat on my heated eyelids: all at once
The front rank made a sudden halt; the bells
Lapsed into frightful stillness; the surge fell
From thunder into whispers; those six maids
With shrieks and ringing laughter on the sand
Threw down the bier; the woods upon the hill
Waved with a sudden gust that sweeping down
Took the edges of the pall, and blew it far
Until it hung, a little silver cloud
Over the sounding seas: I turned: my heart
Shrank in me, like a snowflake in the hand,
Waiting to see the settled countenance
Of her I loved, adorned with fading flowers.
But she from out her death-like chrysalis,
She from her bier, as into fresher life,
My sister, and my cousin, and my love,
Leapt lightly clad in bridal white–her hair
Studded with one rich Provence rose–a light
Of smiling welcome round her lips–her eyes
And cheeks as bright as when she climbed the hill.
One hand she reached to those that came behind,
And while I mused nor yet endured to take
So rich a prize, the man who stood with me
Stept gaily forward, throwing down his robes,
And claspt her hand in his: again the bells
Jangled and clanged: again the stormy surf
Crashed in the shingle: and the whirling rout
Led by those two rushed into dance, and fled
Wind-footed to the steeple in the woods,
Till they were swallowed in the leafy bowers,
And I stood sole beside the vacant bier.

There, there, my latest vision–then the event!

IV

## THE GOLDEN SUPPER

*Another speaks*

He flies the event: he leaves the event to me:

iii *27–8.* Cp. *Sonnet* [*Shall the hag Evil*] 10–11: 'slake / With points of blast-borne hail their heated eyne!'
iii *30–1*] Lapsed into frightful stillness; those six maids *1868.*
iii *48. reached*] stretched *1868.*
iii *53. stormy surf*] yeasty surge *1868.* T. had 'yeasty surges' in *The Sailor Boy* 9; and cp. *Timbuctoo* 15: 'yeasty waves'; from *Macbeth* IV i 53.
iii *54. Crashed in*] Splashed on *1868.*

Poor Julian–how he rushed away; the bells,
Those marriage-bells, echoing in ear and heart–
But cast a parting glance at me, you saw,
As who should say 'Continue'. Well he had
One golden hour–of triumph shall I say?
Solace at least–before he left his home.

Would you had seen him in that hour of his!
He moved through all of it majestically–
Restrained himself quite to the close–but now–

Whether they *were* his lady's marriage-bells,
Or prophets of them in his fantasy,
I never asked: but Lionel and the girl
Were wedded, and our Julian came again
Back to his mother's house among the pines.
But these, their gloom, the mountains and the Bay,
The whole land weighed him down as Ætna does
The Giant of Mythology: he would go,
Would leave the land for ever, and had gone
Surely, but for a whisper, 'Go not yet,'
Some warning–sent divinely–as it seemed
By that which followed–but of this I deem
As of the visions that he told–the event
Glanced back upon them in his after life,
And partly made them–though he knew it not.

And thus he stayed and would not look at her–
No not for months: but, when the eleventh moon
After their marriage lit the lover's Bay,
Heard yet once more the tolling bell, and said,
Would you could toll me out of life, but found–
All softly as his mother broke it to him–
A crueller reason than a crazy ear,
For that low knell tolling his lady dead–
Dead–and had lain three days without a pulse:
All that looked on her had pronounced her dead.
And so they bore her (for in Julian's land
They never nail a dumb head up in elm),
Bore her free-faced to the free airs of heaven,
And laid her in the vault of her own kin.

iv *16*] But they, their gloom, the Lover's Bay, the hills
And chiefly what they call the Hill of Woe– *1868*

iv *21. sent*] *1879*; and *1869–78*.

iv *36–7*. See headnote on Boccaccio.

iv *36. so*] *Not 1868*.

iv *39. her own kin*] Lionel's race *1868*.

What did he then? not die: he is here and hale–
Not plunge headforemost from the mountain there,
And leave the name of Lover's Leap: not he:
He knew the meaning of the whisper now,
Thought that he knew it. 'This, I stayed for this;
O love, I have not seen you for so long.
Now, now, will I go down into the grave,
I will be all alone with all I love,
And kiss her on the lips. She is his no more:
The dead returns to me, and I go down
To kiss the dead.'

The fancy stirred him so
He rose and went, and entering the dim vault,
And, making there a sudden light, beheld
All round about him that which all will be.
The light was but a flash, and went again.
Then at the far end of the vault he saw
His lady with the moonlight on her face;
Her breast as in a shadow-prison, bars
Of black and bands of silver, which the moon
Struck from an open grating overhead
High in the wall, and all the rest of her
Drowned in the gloom and horror of the vault.

'It was my wish,' he said, 'to pass, to sleep,
To rest, to be with her–till the great day
Pealed on us with that music which rights all,
And raised us hand in hand.' And kneeling there
Down in the dreadful dust that once was man,
Dust, as he said, that once was loving hearts,
Hearts that had beat with such a love as mine–
Not such as mine, no, nor for such as her–
He softly put his arm about her neck
And kissed her more than once, till helpless death
And silence made him bold–nay, but I wrong him,
He reverenced his dear lady even in death;

iv *41. the mountain there*] the Hill of Woe *1868.*
iv *42. leave . . . of*] change . . . to *1868.*
iv *52. making*] striking *1868.*
iv *54. went*] went away *1868.*
iv *62–3*] . . . said, 'that night to die, / Die by her, and lie by her, till . . . *1868.*
iv *65. raised*] raises *1868.* *there*] then *1868.*
iv *73.* See headnote on Boccaccio.

But, placing his true hand upon her heart,
'O, you warm heart,' he moaned, 'not even death
Can chill you all at once:' then starting, thought
His dreams had come again. 'Do I wake or sleep?
Or am I made immortal, or my love
Mortal once more?' It beat–the heart–it beat:
Faint–but it beat: at which his own began
To pulse with such a vehemence that it drowned
The feebler motion underneath his hand.
But when at last his doubts were satisfied,
He raised her softly from the sepulchre,
And, wrapping her all over with the cloak
He came in, and now striding fast, and now
Sitting awhile to rest, but evermore
Holding his golden burthen in his arms,
So bore her through the solitary land
Back to the mother's house where she was born.

There the good mother's kindly ministering,
With half a night's appliances, recalled
Her fluttering life: she raised an eye that asked
'Where?' till the things familiar to her youth
Had made a silent answer: then she spoke
'Here! and how came I here?' and learning it
(They told her somewhat rashly as I think)
At once began to wander and to wail,
'Ay, but you know that you must give me back:
Send! bid him come;' but Lionel was away–
Stung by his loss had vanished, none knew where.
'He casts me out,' she wept, 'and goes'–a wail
That seeming something, yet was nothing, born
Not from believing mind, but shattered nerve,
Yet haunting Julian, as her own reproof
At some precipitance in her burial.
Then, when her own true spirit had returned,
'Oh yes, and you,' she said, 'and none but you?
For you have given me life and love again,
And none but you yourself shall tell him of it,
And you shall give me back when he returns.'
'Stay then a little,' answered Julian, 'here,
And keep yourself, none knowing, to yourself;
And I will do your will. I may not stay,
No, not an hour; but send me notice of him
When he returns, and then will I return,

iv *74. heart*] breast *1868*.
iv *77. Do I wake or sleep?*: Keats, *Ode to a Nightingale* 80.

And I will make a solemn offering of you
To him you love.' And faintly she replied,
'And I will do *your* will, and none shall know.'

Not know? with such a secret to be known.
But all their house was old and loved them both,
And all the house had known the loves of both;
Had died almost to serve them any way,
And all the land was waste and solitary:
And then he rode away; but after this,
An hour or two, Camilla's travail came
Upon her, and that day a boy was born,
Heir of his face and land, to Lionel.

And thus our lonely lover rode away,
And pausing at a hostel in a marsh,
There fever seized upon him: myself was then
Travelling that land, and meant to rest an hour;
And sitting down to such a base repast,
It makes me angry yet to speak of it–
I heard a groaning overhead, and climbed
The mouldered stairs (for everything was vile)
And in a loft, with none to wait on him,
Found, as it seemed, a skeleton alone,
Raving of dead men's dust and beating hearts.

A dismal hostel in a dismal land,
A flat malarian world of reed and rush!
But there from fever and my care of him
Sprang up a friendship that may help us yet.
For while we roamed along the dreary coast,
And waited for her message, piece by piece
I learnt the drearier story of his life;
And, though he loved and honoured Lionel,
Found that the sudden wail his lady made
Dwelt in his fancy: did he know her worth,
Her beauty even? should he not be taught,
Even by the price that others set upon it,
The value of that jewel he had to guard?

iv *127. that . . . born*] she bore a noble boy *1868*.
iv *141*] A world of reed and rush, and far away
The phantom circle of a moaning sea. *1868*
T. incorporated the second line as *The Passing of Arthur* 87 (1869); it was originally the concluding line, all but verbatim, of *Lines* [*Mablethorpe*] (1833, p. 499), the *T.MS* of which may not be quoted.

Suddenly came her notice and we past,
I with our lover to his native Bay.

This love is of the brain, the mind, the soul:
*That* makes the sequel pure; though some of us
Beginning at the sequel know no more.
Not such am I: and yet I say the bird
That will not hear my call, however sweet,
But if my neighbour whistle answers him–
What matter? there are others in the wood.
Yet when I saw her (and I thought him crazed,
Though not with such a craziness as needs
A cell and keeper), those dark eyes of hers–
Oh! such dark eyes! and not her eyes alone,
But all from these to where she touched on earth,
For such a craziness as Julian's looked
No less than one divine apology.

So sweetly and so modestly she came
To greet us, her young hero in her arms!
'Kiss him,' she said. 'You gave me life again.
He, but for you, had never seen it once.
His other father you! Kiss him, and then
Forgive him, if his name be Julian too.'

Talk of lost hopes and broken heart! his own
Sent such a flame into his face, I knew
Some sudden vivid pleasure hit him there.

But he was all the more resolved to go,
And sent at once to Lionel, praying him
By that great love they both had borne the dead,
To come and revel for one hour with him
Before he left the land for evermore;
And then to friends–they were not many–who lived
Scatteringly about that lonely land of his,
And bad them to a banquet of farewells.

And Julian made a solemn feast: I never
Sat at a costlier; for all round his hall
From column on to column, as in a wood,
Not such as here–an equatorial one,
Great garlands swung and blossomed; and beneath,

iv *154. native Bay*] 'Lover's Bay' *1868.*
iv *163. Though*] But *1868.*
iv *167. looked*] *1872*; seemed *1869.*

Heirlooms, and ancient miracles of Art,
Chalice and salver, wines that, Heaven knows when,
Had sucked the fire of some forgotten sun,
And kept it through a hundred years of gloom,
Yet glowing in a heart of ruby-cups
Where nymph and god ran ever round in gold–
Others of glass as costly–some with gems
Moveable and resettable at will,
And trebling all the rest in value–Ah heavens!
Why need I tell you all?–suffice to say
That whatsoever such a house as his,
And his was old, has in it rare or fair
Was brought before the guest: and they, the guests,
Wondered at some strange light in Julian's eyes
(I told you that he had his golden hour),
And such a feast, ill-suited as it seemed
To such a time, to Lionel's loss and his
And that resolved self-exile from a land
He never would revisit, such a feast
So rich, so strange, and stranger even than rich,
But rich as for the nuptials of a king.

And stranger yet, at one end of the hall
Two great funereal curtains, looping down,
Parted a little ere they met the floor,
About a picture of his lady, taken
Some years before, and falling hid the frame.
And just above the parting was a lamp:
So the sweet figure folded round with night
Seemed stepping out of darkness with a smile.

Well then–our solemn feast–we ate and drank,
And might–the wines being of such nobleness–
Have jested also, but for Julian's eyes,
And something weird and wild about it all:
What was it? for our lover seldom spoke,
Scarce touched the meats; but ever and anon
A priceless goblet with a priceless wine
Arising, showed he drank beyond his use;
And when the feast was near an end, he said:

iv *191–3*. Cp. *The Palace of Art* 181–3, *1832* text: 'Sunchanged, when sea-winds sleep. // With graceful chalices of curious wine, / Wonders of art–and costly jars, / And bossèd salvers.'
iv *210*. *stranger even*] even more strange *1868*.
iv *218*. *So*] And *1868*.

'There is a custom in the Orient, friends–
I read of it in Persia–when a man
Will honour those who feast with him, he brings
And shows them whatsoever he accounts
Of all his treasures the most beautiful,
Gold, jewels, arms, whatever it may be.
This custom–'

Pausing here a moment, all
The guests broke in upon him with meeting hands
And cries about the banquet–'Beautiful!
Who could desire more beauty at a feast?'

The lover answered, 'There is more than one
Here sitting who desires it. Laud me not
Before my time, but hear me to the close.
This custom steps yet further when the guest
Is loved and honoured to the uttermost.
For after he hath shown him gems or gold,
He brings and sets before him in rich guise
That which is thrice as beautiful as these,
The beauty that is dearest to his heart–
"O my heart's lord, would I could show you," he says,
"Even my heart too." And I propose tonight
To show you what is dearest to my heart,
And my heart too.

'But solve me first a doubt.
I knew a man, nor many years ago;
He had a faithful servant, one who loved
His master more than all on earth beside.
He falling sick, and seeming close on death,
His master would not wait until he died,
But bad his menials bear him from the door,
And leave him in the public way to die.
I knew another, not so long ago,
Who found the dying servant, took him home,
And fed, and cherished him, and saved his life.
I ask you now, should this first master claim
His service, whom does it belong to? him
Who thrust him out, or him who saved his life?'

This question, so flung down before the guests,
And balanced either way by each, at length

iv *234–5*] . . . be / Most beautiful. This custom–' . . . *1868*.
iv *244. hath*] *1872*; has *1869*.
iv *266*] And handled differently by each, at last *1868*.

When some were doubtful how the law would hold,
Was handed over by consent of all
To one who had not spoken, Lionel.

Fair speech was his, and delicate of phrase.
And he beginning languidly–his loss
Weighed on him yet–but warming as he went,
Glanced at the point of law, to pass it by,
Affirming that as long as either lived,
By all the laws of love and gratefulness,
The service of the one so saved was due
All to the saver–adding, with a smile,
The first for many weeks–a semi-smile
As at a strong conclusion–'body and soul
And life and limbs, all his to work his will'.

Then Julian made a secret sign to me
To bring Camilla down before them all.
And crossing her own picture as she came,
And looking as much lovelier as herself
Is lovelier than all others–on her head
A diamond circlet, and from under this
A veil, that seemed no more than gilded air,
Flying by each fine ear, an Eastern gauze
With seeds of gold–so, with that grace of hers,
Slow-moving as a wave against the wind,
That flings a mist behind it in the sun–
And bearing high in arms the mighty babe,
The younger Julian, who himself was crowned
With roses, none so rosy as himself–
And over all her babe and her the jewels
Of many generations of his house
Sparkled and flashed, for he had decked them out
As for a solemn sacrifice of love–
So she came in:–I am long in telling it,
I never yet beheld a thing so strange,
Sad, sweet, and strange together–floated in–
While all the guests in mute amazement rose–
And slowly pacing to the middle hall,
Before the board, there paused and stood, her breast
Hard-heaving, and her eyes upon her feet,
Not daring yet to glance at Lionel.

iv *273. to pass*] but past *1868*.

iv *276–7*] The one so saved–his service was all due
To him who saved him–adding, with a smile, *1868*

iv *289. so*] she so *1868*.

But him she carried, him nor lights nor feast
Dazed or amazed, nor eyes of men; who cared
Only to use his own, and staring wide
And hungering for the gilt and jewelled world
About him, looked, as he is like to prove,
When Julian goes, the lord of all he saw.

'My guests,' said Julian: 'you are honoured now
Even to the uttermost: in her behold
Of all my treasures the most beautiful,
Of all things upon earth the dearest to me.'
Then waving us a sign to seat ourselves,
Led his dear lady to a chair of state.
And I, by Lionel sitting, saw his face
Fire, and dead ashes and all fire again
Thrice in a second, felt him tremble too,
And heard him muttering, 'So like, so like;
She never had a sister. I knew none.
Some cousin of his and hers–O God, so like!'
And then he suddenly asked her if she were.
She shook, and cast her eyes down, and was dumb.
And then some other questioned if she came
From foreign lands, and still she did not speak.
Another, if the boy were hers: but she
To all their queries answered not a word,
Which made the amazement more, till one of them
Said, shuddering, 'Her spectre!' But his friend
Replied, in half a whisper, 'Not at least
The spectre that will speak if spoken to.
Terrible pity, if one so beautiful
Prove, as I almost dread to find her, dumb!'

But Julian, sitting by her, answered all:
'She is but dumb, because in her you see
That faithful servant whom we spoke about,
Obedient to her second master now;
Which will not last. I have here tonight a guest
So bound to me by common love and loss–
What! shall I bind him more? in his behalf,
Shall I exceed the Persian, giving him
That which of all things is the dearest to me,
Not only showing? and he himself pronounced
That my rich gift is wholly mine to give.

'Now all be dumb, and promise all of you
Not to break in on what I say by word

iv *322. So . . . like*] Like, so like, so like *1868*.

Or whisper, while I show you all my heart.'
And then began the story of his love
As here today, but not so wordily–
The passionate moment would not suffer that–
Past through his visions to the burial; thence
Down to this last strange hour in his own hall;
And then rose up, and with him all his guests
Once more as by enchantment; all but he,
Lionel, who fain had risen, but fell again,
And sat as if in chains–to whom he said:

'Take my free gift, my cousin, for your wife;
And were it only for the giver's sake,
And though she seem so like the one you lost,
Yet cast her not away so suddenly,
Lest there be none left here to bring her back:
I leave this land for ever.' Here he ceased.

Then taking his dear lady by one hand,
And bearing on one arm the noble babe,
He slowly brought them both to Lionel.
And there the widower husband and dead wife
Rushed each at each with a cry, that rather seemed
For some new death than for a life renewed;
Whereat the very babe began to wail;
At once they turned, and caught and brought him in
To their charmed circle, and, half killing him
With kisses, round him closed and claspt again.
But Lionel, when at last he freed himself
From wife and child, and lifted up a face
All over glowing with the sun of life,
And love, and boundless thanks–the sight of this
So frighted our good friend, that turning to me
And saying, 'It is over: let us go'–
There were our horses ready at the doors–
We bad them no farewell, but mounting these
He past for ever from his native land;
And I with him, my Julian, back to mine.

iv *362. the one you lost*] your other wife *1868*.
iv *363. Yet*] O *1868*.
iv *372. Whereat*] *1872*; At this *1869*.
iv *384–5*. Unlike in Boccaccio (see headnote); but a trial edition of *1869* (see headnote) added concluding lines. They are also in *1868*, with the 'I's and 'You's reversed. *1869* trial edition has them spoken by 'Constantine' to 'Vincent' (the narrator of *The Golden Supper*):

# 154 'Mine be the strength of spirit, full and free'

Published *1832* as the volume's prefatory sonnet; not reprinted till restored in *1872* as 'Juvenilia', 'Early Sonnets III'. It was effectively ridiculed by J. W. Croker in *QR*, April 1833. Probably influenced by Washington Irving's *Life of Columbus* (1828), the source of *Anacaona* (1830): 'the great quantity of fresh water that sweetened the neighbouring sea'; it 'rushes with such force into the ocean . . . it must be some mighty river which had wandered through a great extent of country, collecting all its streams, and pouring them in one vast current into the ocean . . . the continuation of which now bears the name of the Gulf Stream' (X iii–iv).

Mine be the strength of spirit, full and free,
Like some broad river rushing down alone,
With the selfsame impulse wherewith he was thrown
From his loud fount upon the echoing lea:–
Which with increasing might doth forward flee
By town, and tower, and hill, and cape, and isle,
And in the middle of the green salt sea
Keeps his blue waters fresh for many a mile.

---

Ever? *is* it an ever? You bade me here,
My friend, to meet him in these woods today,
His lonely haunt, that if he could be brought
At last to tell his story, I might hear
Both for the strangeness of it, and my mind
Upon it, after: and I ask you now,
Whether his not unwillingness to tell it–
Although he ran and left the event to you–
His heat and his diffuseness–since for years
He scarce would touch upon it, even to you–
And all his tropes and figures may not prove
The pain of this day, not the pain of that,
But changed and loosening. If you think with me,
The time is nearly come for his return:
Then may you take him to this land of love,
Where he shall see his lady once again;
Break from his dream, and play with all her boys.

¶ 154.*1. full*] *1872*; fierce *1832*.
*4. loud*] fresh *Allen MS.*

Mine be the power which ever to its sway
Will win the wise at once, and by degrees
May into uncongenial spirits flow;
Even as the warm gulf-stream of Florida
Floats far away into the Northern seas
The lavish growths of southern Mexico.

# 155 'My life is full of weary days'

Published *1832*, as *To–*, when it was not in two sections and had two more stanzas. It was not reprinted until restored in *1865*, which omitted section ii; restored in full, *1872*, 'Juvenilia'. It was mercilessly ridiculed by J. W. Croker in *QR*, April 1833. Written 1830–2. *Heath MS* and *Allen MS* have i, dated 1830; Spedding quoted i, 1 April 1832 (F. M. Brookfield, *The Cambridge 'Apostles'*, 1906, p. 258). Spedding says it was addressed to Arthur Hallam; H.T. remarks that it was 'originally two poems'. Cp. *To–*[*As when with downcast eyes*] (p. 459). The unusual stanza is that of *On a Mourner*, which is also about Hallam (p. 557). T. violated the scheme of the first stanza in revision; J. F. A. Pyre points out that this is 'absolutely the sole example in which a later version of a revised poem is less consistent in its rhymed structure than was the original' (*The Formation of Tennyson's Style*, 1921, p. 39). T. effected many of the later changes, including the division into two sections and the deletion of stanza vi of section ii, in the copy of *1832* which he gave to the Lushingtons, 21 Dec. 1832 (G. O. Marshall, *Library Chronicle of Texas*, Spring 1959). It cost T. a great deal of trouble, as is clear from this corrected copy of *1832* and from the one given to J. M. Heath (*Fitzwilliam Museum*); *H.Nbk 4* shows that T. was uncertain about the order of lines and stanzas.

I

My life is full of weary days,
  But good things have not kept aloof,
Nor wandered into other ways:
  I have not lacked thy mild reproof,
Nor golden largess of thy praise.

*12. warm*] *1872*; great *1832*. *Florida*: the rhyme is a traditional license; Shelley rhymes 'pray / America / betray', and Browning rhymes 'say / pray / Africa'.

¶ 155.*1–5*] *1865*; *1832 had the order of lines: 2* (All good . . .), *3, 4, 5, 1* (But life . . .).

And now shake hands across the brink
 Of that deep grave to which I go:
Shake hands once more: I cannot sink
 So far – far down, but I shall know
Thy voice, and answer from below.

II

When in the darkness over me
 The four-handed mole shall scrape,
Plant thou no dusky cypress-tree,
 Nor wreathe thy cap with doleful crape,
 But pledge me in the flowing grape.

And when the sappy field and wood
 Grow green beneath the showery gray,
And rugged barks begin to bud,
 And through damp holts new-flushed with may,
 Ring sudden scritches of the jay,

Then let wise Nature work her will,
 And on my clay her darnel grow;
Come only, when the days are still,
 And at my headstone whisper low,
 And tell me if the woodbines blow.

6. *And . . . hands*] *1865*; Shake hands, my friend, *1832*.
13. *dusky*] darkspired *H.MS intermediate reading*.
20. *scritches*] *1872*; laughters *1832*; clamours *1832 revised for Lushington*; scritchings *1832 revised for Heath*.
21–2] Let broadleaved docks and nettles grow
 And let wise Nature work her will; *H.MS*
22. *darnel*] *1872*; darnels *1832*.
25] *1832 continues:*

VI

If thou art blest, my mother's smile
 Undimmed, if bees are on the wing:
Then cease, my friend, a little while,
 That I may hear the throstle sing
 His bridal song, the boast of spring.

VII

Sweet as the noise in parchèd plains
 Of bubbling wells that fret the stones,
(If any sense in me remains)
 Thy words will be; thy cheerful tones
 As welcome to my crumbling bones.

These lines had been ridiculed by J. W. Croker, *QR*, April 1833: 'We take upon ourselves to reassure Mr Tennyson, that, even after he shall be dead and buried, as much "*sense*" will still remain as he has now the good fortune to possess'.

# 156 Buonaparte

Published *1832*; not reprinted till restored in *1872* as 'Juvenilia', 'Early Sonnets V'. Probably written 1832; Arthur Hallam apparently saw it for the first time in the proofs, Oct. (*Mem.* i 89–90). In *T.Nbk 19* (which may not be quoted) is a long poem on Napoleon's retreat from Moscow; 'among historical events the doings of Wellington and Napoleon were the themes of story and verse' (*Mem.* i 5).

He thought to quell the stubborn hearts of oak,
Madman!–to chain with chains, and bind with bands
That island queen who sways the floods and lands
From Ind to Ind, but in fair daylight woke,
When from her wooden walls,–lit by sure hands,–
With thunders, and with lightnings, and with smoke,–
Peal after peal, the British battle broke,
Lulling the brine against the Coptic sands.
We taught him lowlier moods, when Elsinore
Heard the war moan along the distant sea,
Rocking with shattered spars, with sudden fires
Flamed over: at Trafalgar yet once more
We taught him: late he learned humility
Perforce, like those whom Gideon schooled with briers.

# 157 *Sonnet [O beauty, passing beauty! sweetest Sweet!]

Published *1832*, not reprinted. An irregular sonnet, like most of T.'s early ones.

O beauty, passing beauty! sweetest Sweet!
    How canst thou let me waste my youth in sighs?
I only ask to sit beside thy feet.
    Thou knowest I dare not look into thine eyes.
Might I but kiss thy hand! I dare not fold
    My arms about thee–scarcely dare to speak.

¶ 156.*8*. The Battle of the Nile, 1798. *lulling*: the notion that gunfire stills the waves.
*9*. The defeat of the Danish fleet at Copenhagen, 1801, which thwarted Napoleon's plans.
*14*. *Judges* viii 16: 'And he took the elders of the city, and thorns of the wilderness and briers, and with them he taught the men of Succoth.'

And nothing seems to me so wild and bold,
As with one kiss to touch thy blessèd cheek.
Methinks if I should kiss thee, no control
Within the thrilling brain could keep afloat
The subtle spirit. Even while I spoke,
The bare word KISS hath made my inner soul
To tremble like a lutestring, ere the note
Hath melted in the silence that it broke.

## 158 'If I were loved, as I desire to be'

Published *1832*; not reprinted till restored in *1872* as 'Juvenilia', 'Early Sonnets X'. Presumably to Arthur Hallam; it anticipates the mood and thought of *In Memoriam*, and the image of the bowman (ll. 5–6) recurs there in lxxxvii 25–30 as praise of Hallam; note also the reference to geology, and 'hand-in-hand'. Cp. *To–*[*As when with downcast eyes*] (p. 459), another sonnet probably to Hallam.

If I were loved, as I desire to be,
What is there in the great sphere of the earth,
And range of evil between death and birth,
That I should fear,–if I were loved by thee?
All the inner, all the outer world of pain
Clear Love would pierce and cleave, if thou wert mine.
As I have heard that, somewhere in the main,
Fresh-water springs come up through bitter brine.
'Twere joy, not fear, claspt hand-in-hand with thee,
To wait for death–mute–careless of all ills,
Apart upon a mountain, though the surge
Of some new deluge from a thousand hills
Flung leagues of roaring foam into the gorge
Below us, as far on as eye could see.

¶ 158.*1. If I were*] *1872*; But were I *1832*; Were I so *Allen MS.*

*2. great sphere*] circle *Allen MS.*

*7–8.* Possibly suggested by a description in Washington Irving's *Columbus* (1828), the source of *Anacaona* (Paden, p. 141).

*8. come up through*] jet through the *Allen MS.*

*12. some new deluge*: the geological theory of catastrophism; possibly remembering Marvell's 'And Earth some new Convulsion tear', in another poem on 'two perfect Loves', *The Definition of Love*.

*13.* Cp. *Home* 4: 'Leagues of sounding foam'.

# 159 The Lady of Shalott

Published *1832*, much revised *1842*. Written by *c.* May 1832 (FitzGerald's *Letters*, ed. W. A. Wright, 1889, i 8). T. says it was 'taken from an Italian novelette, *Donna di Scalotta*'. The source is quoted in Italian, *Mat.* iv 461: 'The following is the Italian novella on which *The Lady of Shalott* was founded: Novella LXXXI *Quì conta come la Damigella di Scalot morì per amore di Lancialotto de Lac.* From the *Cento Novelle Antiche*, dated conjecturally before 1321. Text from the Milan edn, ed. G. Ferrario, 1804.' The source had been mentioned by F. T. Palgrave and by John Churton Collins, and was investigated by L. S. Potwin, *MLN* xvii (1902) 473–7, and by D. L. Chambers, *MLN* xviii (1903) 227–8. But the story is very different; it has no Arthur, Queen, mirror, weaving, curse, song, river, or island. Apart from the Lady's death, the main links are that Camelot is the end of the funeral voyage, and is–unusually–on the sea-shore, and that there is an astonished crowd about the body. The *1832* text is slightly closer in some details, e.g. her death-letter. F. J. Furnivall quotes T. in Jan. 1868: 'I met the story first in some Italian *novelle*: but the web, mirror, island, etc., were my own. Indeed, I doubt whether I should ever have put it in that shape if I had been then aware of the Maid of Astolat in *Mort Arthur*' (*Rossetti Papers 1862–1870*, ed. W. M. Rossetti, 1903, p. 341). T. may have seen Thomas Roscoe's translation (1825), where she is 'the Lady', not 'Damsel'. T. says: 'The Lady of Shalott is evidently the Elaine of the *Morte d'Arthur* [cp. *Lancelot and Elaine*, p. 1621], but I do not think that I had ever heard of the latter when I wrote the former. Shalott was a softer sound than "Scalott".' See Malory xviii. Paden (pp. 156–7) notes the general influence of T. C. Croker's *Fairy Legends* (1825–8) and of Thomas Keightley's *Fairy Mythology* (1828), both of which T. knew. He also argues for the influence of G. S. Faber's religious mythologizing: 'It may be suggested that she is one of those nymphs, occupied in weaving, whom Porphyry explained as human souls about to be born into the world'; Faber claimed them as symbols for the epoptae of the mysteries. 'Bishop Percy had affirmed, in a note at the end of the ballad on the death of Arthur, that "*Ladies* was the word our old English writers used for *Nymphs*". In a very Tennysonian revision of Faber, the birth of a soul is identified with the coming of love, and love brings with it the doom of God.' Two books by Faber were at Somersby (*Lincoln*): *Horae Mosaicae* (1818 edn), and *The Difficulties of Infidelity* (2nd edn, 1833). L. Stevenson (*Critical Essays on Tennyson*, ed. Killham, pp. 129–30) suggests the influence of Shelley's *Witch of Atlas*, for an onlooker who weaves, and who has a magic boat: ''Tis said in after times her spirit free / Knew what love was, and felt itself alone.' T. comments (*Mem.* i 117): 'The new-born love for something, for some one in the wide world from which she has been so long secluded, takes her out of the region of shadows into that of realities.' H.T. comments: 'The key to this tale of magic symbolism is of deep human significance and is to be found in the lines [69–72].' Cp. the companion poem, *Life of the Life* (p. 504).

PART I

On either side the river lie
Long fields of barley and of rye,
That clothe the wold and meet the sky;
And through the field the road runs by
    To many-towered Camelot;
And up and down the people go,
Gazing where the lilies blow
Round an island there below,
    The island of Shalott.

Willows whiten, aspens quiver,
Little breezes dusk and shiver
Through the wave that runs for ever
By the island in the river
    Flowing down to Camelot.
Four gray walls, and four gray towers,
Overlook a space of flowers,
And the silent isle imbowers
    The Lady of Shalott.

By the margin, willow-veiled,
Slide the heavy barges trailed
By slow horses; and unhailed
The shallop flitteth silken-sailed
    Skimming down to Camelot:

¶ 159.5. *many-towered*: followed by 'lilies', this suggests *Ilion, Ilion* (p. 259).
*6–9*] *1842*; The yellowleavèd waterlily,
    The greensheathèd daffodilly,
    Tremble in the water chilly,
      Round about Shalott. *1832*
T. altered J. M. Heath's copy of *1832* (*Fitzwilliam Museum*) to 'The yellow globe o' the waterlily'. Cp. *Anacreontics* 2–3 (1830): 'And drooping daffodilly, / And silverleavèd lily.'
*10. quiver*] *1842*; shiver *1832*.
*11–12*] *1842*; The sunbeam-showers break and quiver
    In the stream that runneth ever *1832*
*19–27, 28–36*] *1842*; *transposed 1832*.
*19–21*] *1842*; The little isle is all inrailed
    With a rose-fence, and overtrailed
    With roses: by the marge unhailed *1832*

But who hath seen her wave her hand?
Or at the casement seen her stand?
Or is she known in all the land,
The Lady of Shalott?

Only reapers, reaping early
In among the bearded barley,
Hear a song that echoes cheerly
From the river winding clearly,
Down to towered Camelot:
And by the moon the reaper weary,
Piling sheaves in uplands airy,
Listening, whispers ''Tis the fairy
Lady of Shalott.'

PART II

There she weaves by night and day
A magic web with colours gay.
She has heard a whisper say,
A curse is on her if she stay
To look down to Camelot.
She knows not what the curse may be,
And so she weaveth steadily,

*24–6*] *1842*; A pearlgarland winds her head:
She leaneth on a velvet bed,
Full royally apparellèd, *1832*

*27. Shalott?*] *1842*; Shalott. *1832*.

*28–34*] *1842*; Underneath the bearded barley,
The reaper, reaping late and early,
Hears her ever chanting cheerly,
Like an angel, singing clearly,
O'er the stream of Camelot.
Piling the sheaves in furrows airy,
Beneath the moon, the reaper weary *1832*

*30. cheerly*: T. compares *Richard II* I iii 66: 'But lusty, young, and cheerly drawing breath'.

*34.* Thomas Warton has 'airy uplands' in his *Sonnet ii*, 'When late the trees' (1777).

*37–40*] *1842*; No time hath she to sport and play:
A charmèd web she weaves alway.
A curse is on her, if she stay
Her weaving, either night or day, *1832*

*43. And so*] *1842*; Therefore *1832*.

And little other care hath she,
    The Lady of Shalott.

And moving through a mirror clear
That hangs before her all the year,
Shadows of the world appear.
There she sees the highway near
    Winding down to Camelot:
There the river eddy whirls,
And there the surly village-churls,
And the red cloaks of market girls,
    Pass onward from Shalott.

Sometimes a troop of damsels glad,
An abbot on an ambling pad,
Sometimes a curly shepherd-lad,
Or long-haired page in crimson clad,
    Goes by to towered Camelot;
And sometimes through the mirror blue
The knights come riding two and two:
She hath no loyal knight and true,
    The Lady of Shalott.

But in her web she still delights
To weave the mirror's magic sights,
For often through the silent nights
A funeral, with plumes and lights
    And music, went to Camelot:

*44. And little*] *1842*; Therefore no *1832*.
*46–51*] *1842*; She lives with little joy or fear.
    Over the water, running near,
    The sheepbell tinkles in her ear.
    Before her hangs a mirror clear,
      Reflecting towered Camelot.
    And, as the mazy web she whirls, *1832*

*46*. The mirror is not there simply for the fairy-tale; it was set behind the tapestry so that the worker could see the effect from the right side. This was slightly clearer in the sequence of lines in *1832*. T. was much influenced by Spenser's *Faerie Queene* III ii, on Britomart and Artegall: 'The wondrous myrrhour, by which she in love with him did fall'. Spenser mentions 'the Towre, / Wherein th' Ægyptian *Phao* long did lurke / From all mens vew, that none might her discoure, / Yet she might all men vew out of her bowre.' Britomart looks in the mirror: 'Eftsoones there was presented to her eye / A comely knight, all arm'd in complet wize.' She is then languishing: 'Till death make one end of my dayes and miserie'.

*52. And there*] *1842*; She sees *1832*.

*68. went to*] *1842;* came from *1832*.

Or when the moon was overhead,
Came two young lovers lately wed;
'I am half sick of shadows,' said
The Lady of Shalott.

PART III

A bow-shot from her bower-eaves,
He rode between the barley-sheaves,
The sun came dazzling through the leaves,
And flamed upon the brazen greaves
Of bold Sir Lancelot.
A red-cross knight for ever kneeled
To a lady in his shield,
That sparkled on the yellow field,
Beside remote Shalott.

The gemmy bridle glittered free,
Like to some branch of stars we see
Hung in the golden Galaxy.
The bridle bells rang merrily
As he rode down to Camelot:
And from his blazoned baldric slung
A mighty silver bugle hung,
And as he rode his armour rung,
Beside remote Shalott.

All in the blue unclouded weather
Thick-jewelled shone the saddle-leather,
The helmet and the helmet-feather
Burned like one burning flame together,
As he rode down to Camelot.
As often through the purple night,
Below the starry clusters bright,
Some bearded meteor, trailing light,
Moves over still Shalott.

His broad clear brow in sunlight glowed;
On burnished hooves his war-horse trode;
From underneath his helmet flowed
His coal-black curls as on he rode,
As he rode down to Camelot.

*78. red-cross knight*: for the Spenserian influence, see l. 46*n*.
*82ff.* For the knight's appearance, T. takes up details from *Faerie Queene* I vii st. 29 ff.
*86. to*] *1842*; from *1832*. Likewise in ll. 95, 104.
*99. still*] *1842*; green *1832*.

From the bank and from the river
He flashed into the crystal mirror,
'Tirra lirra,' by the river
Sang Sir Lancelot.

She left the web, she left the loom,
She made three paces through the room,
She saw the water-lily bloom,
She saw the helmet and the plume,
She looked down to Camelot.
Out flew the web and floated wide;
The mirror cracked from side to side;
'The curse is come upon me,' cried
The Lady of Shalott.

PART IV

In the stormy east-wind straining,
The pale yellow woods were waning,
The broad stream in his banks complaining.
Heavily the low sky raining
Over towered Camelot;
Down she came and found a boat
Beneath a willow left afloat,
And round about the prow she wrote
*The Lady of Shalott.*

And down the river's dim expanse
Like some bold seër in a trance,
Seeing all his own mischance–

*107*] *1842*; 'Tirra lirra, tirra lirra,' *1832*. From *Winter's Tale* IV iii 9.
*111. water-lily*] *1842*; waterflower *1832*.
*123*] *1842*; Outside the isle a shallow boat *1832*.
*124. left*] *1842*; lay *1832*.
*126. And . . . prow*] *1842*; Below the carven stern *1832*.
*126 ∧ 7*]
A cloudwhite crown of pearl she dight.
All raimented in snowy white
That loosely flew, (her zone in sight,
Clasped with one blinding diamond bright,)
Her wide eyes fixed on Camelot,
Though the squally eastwind keenly
Blew, with folded arms serenely
By the water stood the queenly
Lady of Shalott. *1832*

Cp. l. 136.
*127*] *1842*; With a steady, stony glance – *1832*.
*129. Seeing*] *1842*; Beholding *1832*.

With a glassy countenance
Did she look to Camelot.
And at the closing of the day
She loosed the chain, and down she lay;
The broad stream bore her far away,
The Lady of Shalott.

Lying, robed in snowy white
That loosely flew to left and right–
The leaves upon her falling light–
Through the noises of the night
She floated down to Camelot:
And as the boat-head wound along
The willowy hills and fields among,
They heard her singing her last song,
The Lady of Shalott.

Heard a carol, mournful, holy,
Chanted loudly, chanted lowly,
Till her blood was frozen slowly,
And her eyes were darkened wholly,
Turned to towered Camelot.
For ere she reached upon the tide
The first house by the water-side,
Singing in her song she died,
The Lady of Shalott.

Under tower and balcony,
By garden-wall and gallery,

*130. With*] *1842*; Mute, with *1832*.
*131. Did she look*] *1842*; She looked down *1832*.
*132. And at*] *1842*; It was *1832*.
*136–41*] *1842*; As when to sailors while they roam,
By creeks and outfalls far from home,
Rising and dropping with the foam,
From dying swans wild warblings come,
Blown shoreward; so to Camelot
Still as . . . *1832*
*143. singing her last song*] *1842*; chanting her deathsong *1832*. With this stanza, especially *1832*, cp. *The Dying Swan* (p. 231), and *Morte d'Arthur* 266–9 (p. 596).
*145. Heard a*] *1842*; A longdrawn *1832*.
*146. Chanted*] *1842*; She chanted *1832*.
*147, 148*] *1842*; *transposed 1832* (Till her eyes . . .).
*148*] *1842*; And her smooth face sharpened slowly *1832*. T. records that George Eliot liked my first [version] the best'.

A gleaming shape she floated by,
Dead-pale between the houses high,
    Silent into Camelot.
Out upon the wharfs they came,
Knight and burgher, lord and dame,
And round the prow they read her name,
    *The Lady of Shalott.*

Who is this? and what is here?
And in the lighted palace near
Died the sound of royal cheer;
And they crossed themselves for fear,
    All the knights at Camelot:
But Lancelot mused a little space;
He said, 'She has a lovely face;
God in his mercy lend her grace,
    The Lady of Shalott.'

# 160 Mariana in the South

Published *1832*; 'Juvenilia'. It was considerably rewritten for *1842*; T. began such revision very soon after *1832* (*Mem.* i 141, 145). It was written 1830–31: 'the idea of this came into my head between Narbonne and Perpignan' (T.), during his tour of the Pyrenees with Arthur Hallam, summer 1830. Hallam enclosed it, spring 1831 (*Mat.* iv 453–5), referring to it as *A*

*156. gleaming shape*] *1842*; pale, pale corpse *1832*.
*157. Dead-pale*] *1855*; Deadcold *1832*; A corse *1842–53*.
*158*] *1842*; Dead into towered Camelot. *1832*.
*159, 160*] *1842*; *transposed 1832*.
*159*] *1842*; To the plankèd wharfage came: *1832*.
*161. And ... prow*] *1842*; Below the stern *1832*. As E. F. Shannon points out, *Tennyson and the Reviewers* (1952), p. 41, J. W. Croker 'had noted with derision that the name, *The Lady of Shalott*, was "below the stern" of the boat'.
*163–71*] *1842*; They crossed themselves, their stars they blest,
    Knight, minstrel, abbot, squire and guest.
    There lay a parchment on her breast,
    That puzzled more than all the rest,
        The wellfed wits at Camelot.
    '*The web was woven curiously*
    *The charm is broken utterly,*
    *Draw near and fear not–this is I,*
        *The Lady of Shalott.*' *1832*
John Stuart Mill objected to the *1832* stanza, *London Review*, July 1835.

*Southern Mariana*, the title in *H.Lpr 142*. Hallam wrote to W. B. Donne in 1831, apparently Feb. (*Mem.* i 500–1): 'It is intended, you will perceive, as a kind of pendant to his former poem of *Mariana* [p. 187], the idea of both being the expression of desolate loneliness, but with this distinctive variety in the second, that it paints the forlorn feeling as it would exist under the influence of different impressions of sense. When we were journeying together this summer through the South of France we came upon a range of country just corresponding to his preconceived thought of a barrenness, so as in the South, and the portraiture of the scenery in this poem is most faithful. You will, I think, agree with me that the essential and distinguishing character of the conception requires in the *Southern Mariana* a greater lingering on the outward circumstances, and a less palpable transition of the poet into Mariana's feelings, than was the case in the former poem.'

The reviewer of *1832* in *The True Sun* (19 Jan. 1833), probably John Forster, spoke of T.'s heroine as 'exceedingly lovely in her desertion, with the scenery around in keeping with her heart' (E. F. Shannon, *Tennyson and the Reviewers*, 1952, p. 18). The poem was influenced by Sappho's *Fragment 111*: *Δέδυκε μὲν ἀ σελάννα / καὶ Πληιάδες, μέσαι δὲ / νύκτες, παρὰ δ'ἔρχετ' ὤρα, / ἔγω δὲ μόνα κατεύδω.* ('The Moon is gone / And the Pleiads set, / Midnight is nigh; / Time passes on, / And passes; yet / Alone I lie.') Hallam referred to 'the fragments of Sappho, in which I see much congeniality to Alfred's peculiar power', when enclosing the poem.
*Revision*: In *1832* the first stanza violated the scheme by having twelve lines plus refrain; the last stanza likewise, and with a false rhyme. *T.Nbk 23* (which may not be quoted) shows that an earlier stage of the poem consisted of stanzas of sixteen lines plus refrain, i.e. joining two of the final stanzas. J. F. A. Pyre (*The Formation of Tennyson's Style*, 1921, pp. 59–60) shows that the *1842* revisions make for regularity of rhythm, which is apt to the persistent monotony.

With one black shadow at its feet,
  The house through all the level shines,
Close-latticed to the brooding heat,
  And silent in its dusty vines:

¶ 160. *Title*: *1832* note: 'See *Poems, chiefly Lyrical*'.
*1–12*] *1842*; Behind the barren hill upsprung
  With pointed rocks against the light,
The crag sharpshadowed overhung
  Each glaring creek and inlet bright.
Far, far, one lightblue ridge was seen,
  Looming like baseless fairyland;
  Eastward a slip of burning sand,
Dark-rimmed with sea, and bare of green.
Down in the dry salt-marshes stood

A faint-blue ridge upon the right,
An empty river-bed before,
And shallows on a distant shore,
In glaring sand and inlets bright.
But 'Ave Mary,' made she moan,
And 'Ave Mary,' night and morn,
And 'Ah,' she sang, 'to be all alone,
To live forgotten, and love forlorn.'

She, as her carol sadder grew,
From brow and bosom slowly down
Through rosy taper fingers drew
Her streaming curls of deepest brown
To left and right, and made appear
Still-lighted in a secret shrine,
Her melancholy eyes divine,
The home of woe without a tear.
And 'Ave Mary,' was her moan,
'Madonna, sad is night and morn,'
And 'Ah,' she sang, 'to be all alone,
To live forgotten, and love forlorn.'

Till all the crimson changed, and past
Into deep orange o'er the sea,
Low on her knees herself she cast,
Before Our Lady murmured she;

That house darklatticed. Not a breath
Swayed the sick vineyard underneath,
Or moved the dusty southernwood.
'Madonna,' with melodious moan
Sang Mariana, night and morn,
'Madonna! lo! I am all alone,
Love-forgotten and love-forlorn.' *1832*

*H.Lpr 141* has an intermediate revision of ll. 1–28, close to *1842* but with e.g. l. 1 'The beams on all the level beat'; l. 3 'Dark-latticed'; l. 4 'the blighted vines'; l. 5 'The flats are far to left and right'.

*9–11.* Cp. *Song* [*I' the glooming light*] 12–17 (p. 215): 'Death standeth by; / She will not die; / With glazèd eye / She looks at her grave: she cannot sleep; / Ever alone / She maketh her moan.'

*14*] *1842*; From her warm brow and bosom down *1832*.

*15. taper fingers*: Keats, *I stood tip-toe* 59, as in T.'s *Madeline* 44.

*17. To . . . right*] *1842*; On either side *1832*.

*21–4*] *1842*; *1832 has the refrain as in its first stanza.*

*25. Till . . . crimson*] *1842*; When the dawncrimson *1832*.

*28. Before . . . murmured*] *1842*; Unto . . . prayèd *1832*.

Complaining, 'Mother, give me grace
To help me of my weary load.'
And on the liquid mirror glowed
The clear perfection of her face.
'Is this the form,' she made her moan,
'That won his praises night and morn?'
And 'Ah,' she said, 'but I wake alone,
I sleep forgotten, I wake forlorn.'

Nor bird would sing, nor lamb would bleat,
Nor any cloud would cross the vault,

*29–36*] *1842*; She moved her lips, she prayed alone,
She praying disarrayed and warm
From slumber, deep her wavy form
In the darklustrous mirror shone.
'Madonna,' in a low clear tone
Said Mariana, night and morn,
Low she mourned, 'I am all alone,
Love-forgotten, and love-forlorn.' *1832*

*29*] 'Madonna Mary lend me grace *Lincoln revision of 1832*.

*31. liquid mirror*: as in Shelley, *Alastor* 462, where it has the more common application to water.

*32*] Her bounteous form and beauteous face. *Lincoln rev., 1st reading.*

*33. form', she made her*] beauty,' she made *Lincoln rev., 1st reading.*

*35*] Yet mother look I wake alone, *Lincoln rev., 1st reading.*

*37–48*] *1842*; At noon she slumbered. All along
The silvery field, the large leaves talked
With one another, as among
The spikèd maize in dreams she walked.
The lizard leapt: the sunlight played:
She heard the callow nestling lisp,
And brimful meadow-runnels crisp,
In the full-leavèd platan-shade.
In sleep she breathed in a lower tone,
Múrmuring as at night and morn,
'Madonna! lo! I am all alone,
Love-forgotten and love-forlorn.' *1832*

Cp. *Claribel* 17–19: 'The callow throstle lispeth . . . / The babbling runnel crispeth.' *Lincoln rev. of 1832* has an intermediate version of ll. 37–40:

And Day moved on with steps of Death
And Silence added heat to heat
In fields of drought without a breath
That never felt the shadow fleet.

*37. lamb*] herd *Lincoln rev., 2nd reading.*

But day increased from heat to heat,
On stony drought and steaming salt;
Till now at noon she slept again,
And seemed knee-deep in mountain grass,
And heard her native breezes pass,
And runlets babbling down the glen.
She breathed in sleep a lower moan,
And murmuring, as at night and morn,
She thought, 'My spirit is here alone,
Walks forgotten, and is forlorn.'

Dreaming, she knew it was a dream:
She felt he was and was not there.
She woke: the babble of the stream
Fell, and, without, the steady glare
Shrank one sick willow sere and small.
The river-bed was dusty-white;
And all the furnace of the light
Struck up against the blinding wall.
She whispered, with a stifled moan
More inward than at night or morn,
'Sweet Mother, let me not here alone
Live forgotten and die forlorn.'

And, rising, from her bosom drew
Old letters, breathing of her worth,
For 'Love,' they said, 'must needs be true,
To what is loveliest upon earth.'
An image seemed to pass the door,
To look at her with slight, and say
'But now thy beauty flows away,
So be alone for evermore.'
'O cruel heart,' she changed her tone,
'And cruel love, whose end is scorn,

*42. knee-deep in*] to walk on *Lincoln rev., 1st reading.*
*44. runlets babbling*] runnels crisping *Lincoln rev., 1st reading.*
*49–50. dream: / She felt he*] *1842*; dream / Most false: *he 1832.*
*53. one*] *1850*; the *1832–48.* *willow*] *1853*; olive *1832–51.*
*55–6*] *1842*; From the bald rock the blinding light
Beat ever on the sunwhite wall. *1832*
*59–60*] *1842*; 'Madonna, leave me not all alone,
To die forgotten and live forlorn.' *1832*
*61–84*] *1842*; *not 1832.* Possibly precipitated by the death of Hallam; cp. the 'letters' ('love', 'worth') with *In Memoriam* xcv; the 'image' which speaks makes use of the *In Memoriam* stanza in ll. 65–8.

Is this the end to be left alone,
To live forgotten, and die forlorn?'

But sometimes in the falling day
An image seemed to pass the door,
To look into her eyes and say,
'But thou shalt be alone no more.'
And flaming downward over all
From heat to heat the day decreased,
And slowly rounded to the east
The one black shadow from the wall.
'The day to night,' she made her moan,
'The day to night, the night to morn,
And day and night I am left alone
To live forgotten, and love forlorn.'

At eve a dry cicala sung,
There came a sound as of the sea;
Backward the lattice-blind she flung,
And leaned upon the balcony.
There all in spaces rosy-bright
Large Hesper glittered on her tears,

*85–6*] *1842*; One dry cicala's summer song
At night filled all the gallery, *1832*

T. says that the MS of l. 85 read: 'At fall of eve a cricket sung'.

*89–91*. Cp. the opening of Beattie's *Retirement* (1758): 'When in the crimson cloud of even / The lingering light decays, / And Hesper on the front of heaven / His glittering gem displays; / Deep in the silent vale...' There was a copy of Beattie's *Minstrel* at Somersby (*Lincoln*).

*89–96*] *1842*; Ever the low wave seemed to roll
Up to the coast: far on, alone
In the East, large Hesper overshone
The mourning gulf, and on her soul
Poured divine solace, or the rise
Of moonlight from the margin gleamed,
Volcano-like, afar, and streamed
On her white arm, and heavenward eyes.
Not all alone she made her moan,
Yet ever sang she, night and morn,
'Madonna, lo! I am all alone,
Love-forgotten and love-forlorn.' *1832*

*90*. Cp. *The Lover's Tale* i 248: 'I saw the moonlight glitter on their tears'. A reminiscence of Keats, *Hyperion* ii 5–6: 'light / Could glimmer on their tears'. Cp. Thomson, *Autumn* 200–1, where Lavinia's eyes 'like the dewy star / Of evening, shone in tears'.

*90–2*. *tears... night*: this had been part of the third stanza of *The Voyage* (p. 654), in *T.Nbk 21*.

And deepening through the silent spheres
Heaven over Heaven rose the night.
And weeping then she made her moan,
'The night comes on that knows not morn,
When I shall cease to be all alone,
To live forgotten, and love forlorn.'

# 161 Eleänore

Published *1832*; 'Juvenilia'.

I

Thy dark eyes opened not,
Nor first revealed themselves to English air,
For there is nothing here,
Which, from the outward to the inward brought,
Moulded thy baby thought.
Far off from human neighbourhood,
Thou wert born, on a summer morn,
A mile beneath the cedar-wood.
Thy bounteous forehead was not fanned
With breezes from our oaken glades,
But thou wert nursed in some delicious land
Of lavish lights, and floating shades:
And flattering thy childish thought
The oriental fairy brought,
At the moment of thy birth,
From old well-heads of haunted rills,
And the hearts of purple hills,
And shadowed coves on a sunny shore,
The choicest wealth of all the earth,
Jewel or shell, or starry ore,
To deck thy cradle, Eleänore.

II

Or the yellow-banded bees,
Through half-open lattices
Coming in the scented breeze,
Fed thee, a child, lying alone,

¶ 161.*12*. *lavish light*: to be found in Arthur Hallam's *To Two Sisters* 20 (Motter, p. 95), a poem to T.'s sister Emily, Feb. 1831, after their engagement. *floating shades*: as in Shelley, *Alastor* 124. Cp. *Shall the hag Evil* 14: 'Nor blot with floating shades the solar light'.

With whitest honey in fairy gardens culled–
A glorious child, dreaming alone,
In silk-soft folds, upon yielding down,
With the hum of swarming bees
Into dreamful slumber lulled.

III

Who may minister to thee?
Summer herself should minister
To thee, with fruitage golden-rinded
On golden salvers, or it may be,
Youngest Autumn, in a bower
Grape-thickened from the light, and blinded
With many a deep-hued bell-like flower
Of fragrant trailers, when the air
Sleepeth over all the heaven,
And the crag that fronts the Even,
All along the shadowing shore,
Crimsons over an inland mere,
Eleänore!

IV

How may full-sailed verse express,
How may measured words adore
The full-flowing harmony
Of thy swan-like stateliness,
Eleänore?
The luxuriant symmetry
Of thy floating gracefulness,
Eleänore?
Every turn and glance of thine,
Every lineament divine,
Eleänore,
And the steady sunset glow,
That stays upon thee? For in thee
Is nothing sudden, nothing single;
Like two streams of incense free
From one censer in one shrine,
Thought and motion mingle,
Mingle ever. Motions flow
To one another, even as though
They were modulated so
To an unheard melody,

*44.* Shakespeare, *Sonnet 86*: 'the proud full sail of his great verse'.
*53.* Cp. the 'lineaments divine' of Milton's bird-like angel, *PL* v 278.
*64.* Cp. Keats, *Grecian Urn* 11–12: 'Heard melodies are sweet, but those unheard / Are sweeter'.

Which lives about thee, and a sweep
Of richest pauses, evermore
Drawn from each other mellow-deep;
Who may express thee, Eleänore?

V

I stand before thee, Eleänore;
I see thy beauty gradually unfold,
Daily and hourly, more and more.
I muse, as in a trance, the while
Slowly, as from a cloud of gold,
Comes out thy deep ambrosial smile.
I muse, as in a trance, whene'er
The languors of thy love-deep eyes
Float on to me. I would I were
So tranced, so rapt in ecstasies,
To stand apart, and to adore,
Gazing on thee for evermore,
Serene, imperial Eleänore!

VI

Sometimes, with most intensity
Gazing, I seem to see
Thought folded over thought, smiling asleep,
Slowly awakened, grow so full and deep
In thy large eyes, that, overpowered quite,
I cannot veil, or droop my sight,
But am as nothing in its light:
As though a star, in inmost heaven set,
Even while we gaze on it,
Should slowly round his orb, and slowly grow
To a full face, there like a sun remain
Fixed–then as slowly fade again,
And draw itself to what it was before;
So full, so deep, so slow,
Thought seems to come and go
In thy large eyes, imperial Eleänore.

VII

As thunder-clouds that, hung on high,
Roofed the world with doubt and fear,
Floating through an evening atmosphere,
Grow golden all about the sky;

*78.* Cp. *Love* [*Almighty Love!*] 14: 'So full, so great thine ecstacy'.

*99. Roofed the world*] *1842*; Did roof noonday *1832*. Adapted in *The Sisters* [*They have left*] 17: 'the cloud that roofs our noon with night'.

In thee all passion becomes passionless,
Touched by thy spirit's mellowness,
Losing his fire and active might
In a silent meditation,
Falling into a still delight,
And luxury of contemplation:
As waves that up a quiet cove
Rolling slide, and lying still
Shadow forth the banks at will:
Or sometimes they swell and move,
Pressing up against the land,
With motions of the outer sea:
And the self-same influence
Controlleth all the soul and sense
Of Passion gazing upon thee.
His bow-string slackened, languid Love,
Leaning his cheek upon his hand,
Droops both his wings, regarding thee,
And so would languish evermore,
Serene, imperial Eleänore.

VIII

But when I see thee roam, with tresses unconfined,
While the amorous, odorous wind

*108–9*] *1842*; As waves that from the outer deep
Roll into a quiet cove,
There fall away, and lying still,
Having glorious dreams in sleep, *1832*

E. F. Shannon observes that a reviewer in the *Literary Gazette* had objected to the last line (*Tennyson and the Reviewers*, 1952, p. 42).

*117. languid Love*: as twice in Shelley. Cupid is with *remisso arcu*, instead of *intento arcu*, Horace's *Odes* III xxvii 67–8. Alongside John Churton Collins's note on this (*Cornhill*, Jan. 1880), T. wrote: 'possibly' (*Lincoln*). Cp. *The Burial of Love* 5, where Love has 'His bow unstrung'.

*122–3.* Cp. Byron, *Maid of Athens* 7–8: 'By those tresses unconfined, / Wooed by each Aegean wind.' *odorous wind*: as four times in Shelley.

*122–44.* T. compares Sappho, *Fragment 2*: φαίνεταί μοι κῆνος ἴσος θεοῖσιν/ ἔμμεν ὤνηρ, ὄστις ἐναντίος τοι / ἰζάνει, καὶ πλασίον ἆδυ φωνεύ- / σας ὑπακούει // καὶ γελαίσας ἰμερόεν, τό μοι μὰν / καρδίαν ἐν στήθεσιν ἐπτόασεν· / ὡς γὰρ εἰς σ' ἴδω βραχέως με φώνας / οὐδὲν ἔτ' εἴκει· // ἀλλὰ καμ μὲν γλῶσσα ἔαγε λέπτον δ' / αὔτικα χρῶ πῦρ ὑπαδεδρόμακεν, / ὀππάτεσσι δ' οὐδὲν ὄρημ', ἐπιρρόμ- / βεισι δ' ἄκουαι // ἀ δέ μ' ἴδρως κακχέεται, τρόμος δὲ / πᾶσαν ἄγρει· χλωροτέρα δὲ ποίας / ἔμμι· τεθνάκην δ' ὀλίγω 'πιδεύης / φαίνομαι ἄλλα / ἀλλὰ πὰν τόλ-

Breathes low between the sunset and the moon;
Or, in a shadowy saloon,
On silken cushions half reclined;
I watch thy grace; and in its place
My heart a charmèd slumber keeps,
While I muse upon thy face;
And a languid fire creeps
Through my veins to all my frame,
Dissolvingly and slowly: soon
From thy rose-red lips MY name
Floweth; and then, as in a swoon,
With dinning sound my ears are rife,
My tremulous tongue faltereth,
I lose my colour, I lose my breath,
I drink the cup of a costly death,
Brimmed with delirious draughts of warmest life.
I die with my delight, before
I hear what I would hear from thee;
Yet tell my name again to me,
I *would* be dying evermore,
So dying ever, Eleänore.

## 162 The Miller's Daughter

Published *1832*, much revised *1842*. Written by April 1832 (F. M. Brookfield, *The Cambridge 'Apostles'*, 1906, p. 259). It was influenced by Mary Russell Mitford's idyll, *The Queen of the Meadow* (1827; reprinted in *Our Village*, 1828), a story which also suggested details in *The Brook*. T. may

---

*ματον, ἐπεὶ καὶ πένητα.* ('It is to be a God, methinks, to sit before you and listen close by to the sweet accents and winning laughter which have made the heart in my breast beat fast, I warrant you. When I look on you, Brocheo, my speech comes short or fails me quite, I am tongue-tied; in a moment a delicate fire has overrun my flesh, my eyes grow dim and my ears sing, the sweat runs down me and a trembling takes me altogether, till I am as green and pale as the grass, and death itself seems not very far away;–but now that I am poor, I must fain be content.') This was also a source for *Fatima* (p. 382), of which see ll. 15–19.

*127*] *1842*; I gaze on thee the cloudless noon
Of mortal beauty: in its place *1832*

*134*] *1845*; Floweth; then I faint, I swoon *1832*; Floweth; then, as in a swoon *1842–3*.

*143–4*. Cp. *Fatima* 39, 42: 'I *will* possess him or will die . . . / Die, dying clasped in his embrace.'

have remembered Robert Bloomfield's *The Miller's Maid*, about an adopted daughter, in *Rural Tales* (1801), of which a copy was at Somersby (*Lincoln*). T. had thought of a series of 'Daughter' poems; cp. *The Gardener's Daughter* (p. 507), and *The Doctor's Daughter* (p. 283). An intended *Innkeeper's Daughter* is mentioned by Arthur Hallam in a letter to R. Monteith (22 June [1832], *Bodleian Library*). T. says: 'No particular mill, but if I thought at all of any mill it was that of Trumpington, near Cambridge.'

I see the wealthy miller yet,
  His double chin, his portly size,
And who that knew him could forget
  The busy wrinkles round his eyes?
The slow wise smile that, round about
  His dusty forehead drily curled,
Seemed half-within and half-without,
  And full of dealings with the world?

In yonder chair I see him sit,
  Three fingers round the old silver cup–
I see his gray eyes twinkle yet
  At his own jest–gray eyes lit up
With summer lightnings of a soul
  So full of summer warmth, so glad,
So healthy, sound, and clear and whole,
  His memory scarce can make me sad.

Yet fill my glass: give me one kiss:
  My own sweet Alice, we must die.

¶ 162.*1*] *1832 (but not 1842) preceded this with the stanza:*

I met in all the close green ways,
  While walking with my line and rod,
The wealthy miller's mealy face,
  Like the moon in an ivytod.
He looked so jolly and so good–
  While fishing in the milldam-water,
I laughed to see him as he stood,
  And dreamt not of the miller's daughter.

T. revised this before and after publication (*Mem.* i 117), including:

. . . my rod and line,
The miller with his mealy face,
  And longed to take his hand in mine . . .

FitzGerald, *More Letters* (1901), p. 154, says that this was 'by way of getting out of Christopher North's objections to "Line and Rod" instead of "Rod and Line", as also the rather ludicrous Ivy-tod Owl that rhymed to it.'

*13. lightnings of a soul*: cp. Shelley, *Epipsychidion* 89.

*16. can make*] *1842*; makes *1832*.

*18. own sweet*] *1842*; darling *1832*.

There's somewhat in this world amiss
　Shall be unriddled by and by.
There's somewhat flows to us in life,
　But more is taken quite away.
Pray, Alice, pray, my darling wife,
　That we may die the self-same day.

Have I not found a happy earth?
　I least should breathe a thought of pain.
Would God renew me from my birth
　I'd almost live my life again.
So sweet it seems with thee to walk,
　And once again to woo thee mine–
It seems in after-dinner talk
　Across the walnuts and the wine–

To be the long and listless boy
　Late-left an orphan of the squire,
Where this old mansion mounted high
　Looks down upon the village spire:
For even here, where I and you
　Have lived and loved alone so long,
Each morn my sleep was broken through
　By some wild skylark's matin song.

And oft I heard the tender dove
　In firry woodlands making moan;
But ere I saw your eyes, my love,
　I had no motion of my own.
For scarce my life with fancy played
　Before I dreamed that pleasant dream–
Still hither thither idly swayed
　Like those long mosses in the stream.

*23. darling*] *1842*; own sweet *1832*.
*25–32*] *1842; not 1832*.
*33–7*] *1842*; My father's mansion, mounted high,
　Looked down upon the village-spire.
I was a long and listless boy,
　And son and heir unto the squire.
In these dear walls, where . . . *1832*
*41*] *1842*; I often heard the cooing dove *1832*.
*42. making moan*] *1842*; mourn alone *1832*.
*48. those*] *1842*; the *1832*.
*48 ∧ 9*] Sometimes I whistled in the wind,
　Sometimes I angled, thought and deed
Torpid, as swallows left behind
　That winter 'neath the floating weed:

Or from the bridge I leaned to hear
  The milldam rushing down with noise,
And see the minnows everywhere
  In crystal eddies glance and poise,
The tall flag-flowers when they sprung
  Below the range of stepping-stones,
Or those three chestnuts near, that hung
  In masses thick with milky cones.

But, Alice, what an hour was that,
  When after roving in the woods
('Twas April then), I came and sat
  Below the chestnuts, when their buds

---

At will to wander everyway
  From brook to brook my sole delight,
As lithe eels over meadows gray
  Oft shift their glimmering pool by night. *1832*

*1832* followed these lines with its text of ll. 97–104. T.'s revised copy of *1832* (*Lincoln*) had, ll. 48 ^ 9:

So knew I every rill that danced,
  The netted beam on sandy shelves;
The foambell into eddies glanced,
  The wanton ripples chased themselves–
Here flickering through a chain of stars,
  Here slow through margins widely swerved,
Here babbling over shingly bars,
  Here round some cressy islet curved.

T. adapted these lines to form *The Brook* 176–82 (p. 1030). The third line was adapted as l. 52. Cp. the fourth with 'the seeming-wanton ripple', *In Memoriam* xlix 11; and the last line with 'cressy islets', *Geraint and Enid* 475.

*49–56*] *1842* (*but see ll. 53, 55n*);

I loved from off the bridge to hear
  The rushing sound the water made,
And see the fish that everywhere
  In the backcurrent glanced and played;
Low down the tall flagflower that sprung
  Beside the noisy steppingstones,
And the massed chestnutboughs that hung
  Thickstudded over with white cones. *1832*

*53. when*] *1853*; where *1842–51*.

*55. Or*] *1853*; And *1842–51*.

*57*] *1842*; Remember you that pleasant day *1832*.

*59. sat*] *1842*; lay *1832*.

*60–3*] *1842*; Beneath those gummy chestnutbuds
  That glistened in the April blue.
  Upon the slope so smooth and cool,
  I lay and never thought of *you*, *1832*

Were glistening to the breezy blue;
And on the slope, an absent fool,
I cast me down, nor thought of you,
But angled in the higher pool.

A love-song I had somewhere read,
An echo from a measured strain,
Beat time to nothing in my head
From some odd corner of the brain.
It haunted me, the morning long,
With weary sameness in the rhymes,
The phantom of a silent song,
That went and came a thousand times.

Then leapt a trout. In lazy mood
I watched the little circles die;
They past into the level flood,
And there a vision caught my eye;
The reflex of a beauteous form,
A glowing arm, a gleaming neck,
As when a sunbeam wavers warm
Within the dark and dimpled beck.

For you remember, you had set,
That morning, on the casement-edge
A long green box of mignonette,
And you were leaning from the ledge:
And when I raised my eyes, above
They met with two so full and bright–
Such eyes! I swear to you, my love,
That these have never lost their light.

*64. higher pool*] *1842*; deep millpool *1832*.
*65–72*] *1842; not 1832*.
*73–80*] *1842*; A water-rat from off the bank
Plunged in the stream. With idle care,
Downlooking through the sedges rank,
I saw your troubled image there.
Upon the dark and dimpled beck
It wandered like a floating light,
A full fair form, a warm white neck,
And two white arms–how rosy white! *1832*
*81. For*] *1842*; If *1832*.
*82. That . . . the*] *1842*; Upon the narrow *1832*.
*85*] *1842*; I raised my eyes at once: above *1832*.
*86. with . . . full*] *1842*; two eyes so blue *1832*.
*88. these*] *1842*; they *1832*.

I loved, and love dispelled the fear
That I should die an early death:
For love possessed the atmosphere,
And filled the breast with purer breath.
My mother thought, What ails the boy?
For I was altered, and began
To move about the house with joy,
And with the certain step of man.

I loved the brimming wave that swam
Through quiet meadows round the mill,
The sleepy pool above the dam,
The pool beneath it never still,
The meal-sacks on the whitened floor,
The dark round of the dripping wheel,
The very air about the door
Made misty with the floating meal.

And oft in ramblings on the wold,
When April nights began to blow,
And April's crescent glimmered cold,
I saw the village lights below;
I knew your taper far away,
And full at heart of trembling hope,

*89–96*] *1842*; That slope beneath the chestnut tall
Is wooed with choicest breaths of air:
Methinks that I could tell you all
The cowslips and the kingcups there.
Each coltsfoot down the grassy bent,
Whose round leaves hold the gathered shower,
Each quaintly-folded cuckoopint,
And silver-paly cuckooflower. *1832*

*91–2*. Cp. Shelley, *To Jane – The Recollection* 51–4: 'One fair form that filled with love / The lifeless atmosphere', continuing in the manner of T.'s poem: 'We paused beside the pools that lie / Under the forest bough'.

*97–9*] *1842*; How dear to me in youth, my love,
Was every thing about the mill,
The black and silent pool above, *1832*

For the placing of ll. 97–104 in *1832*, see ll. 48 ∧ 9*n*.

*100. it never*] *1842*; that ne'er stood *1832*.

*105–8*] *1842*; In rambling on the eastern wold,
When through the showery April nights
Their hueless crescent glimmered cold,
From all the other village-lights *1832*

*110. And . . . heart*] *1842*; My heart was full *1832*.

From off the wold I came, and lay
  Upon the freshly-flowered slope.

The deep brook groaned beneath the mill;
  And 'by that lamp,' I thought, 'she sits!'
The white chalk-quarry from the hill
  Gleamed to the flying moon by fits.
'O that I were beside her now!
  O will she answer if I call?
O would she give me vow for vow,
  Sweet Alice, if I told her all?'

Sometimes I saw you sit and spin;
  And, in the pauses of the wind,
Sometimes I heard you sing within;
  Sometimes your shadow crossed the blind.
At last you rose and moved the light,
  And the long shadow of the chair
Flitted across into the night,
  And all the casement darkened there.

But when at last I dared to speak,
  The lanes, you know, were white with may,
Your ripe lips moved not, but your cheek
  Flushed like the coming of the day;
And so it was–half-sly, half-shy,
  You would, and would not, little one!
Although I pleaded tenderly,
  And you and I were all alone.

And slowly was my mother brought
  To yield consent to my desire:

111. *From off*] *1842*; Down from *1832*.
112. *freshly-flowered*] *1842*; dewyswarded *1832*.
113–20] *1842*; The white chalkquarry from the hill
    Upon the broken ripple gleamed,
  I murmured lowly, sitting still
    While round my feet the eddy streamed:
  'Oh! that I were the wreath she wreathes,
    The mirror where her sight she feeds,
  The song she sings, the air she breathes,
    The letters of the book she reads.' *1832*
129. *But . . . last*] *1842*; I loved, but when *1832*.
130. *The . . . know,*] *1842*; My love, the lanes *1832*.
133. *And so it was–*] *1842*; Rosecheekt, roselipt, *1832*.
137–60] *1842*; Remember you the clear moonlight,
    That whitened all the eastern ridge,

She wished me happy, but she thought
 I might have looked a little higher;
And I was young—too young to wed:
 'Yet must I love her for your sake;
Go fetch your Alice here,' she said:
 Her eyelid quivered as she spake.

And down I went to fetch my bride:
 But, Alice, you were ill at ease;
This dress and that by turns you tried,
 Too fearful that you should not please.
I loved you better for your fears,
 I knew you could not look but well;
And dews, that would have fallen in tears,
 I kissed away before they fell.

---

When o'er the water, dancing white,
 I stepped upon the old millbridge.
I heard you whisper from above
 A lutetoned whisper, 'I am here;'
I murmured, 'Speak again, my love,
 The stream is loud: I cannot hear.'

I heard, as I have seemed to hear,
 When all the under-air was still,
The low voice of the glad new year
 Call to the freshly-flowered hill.
I heard, as I have often heard
 The nightingale in leavy woods
Call to its mate, when nothing stirred
 To left or right but falling floods. *1832*

*H.Nbk 9* (fragmentary MS) begins with:

O then beneath a lover's moon
 I led you homeward down the ridge;
I left you and returning soon
 I stept once more upon the bridge . . .

These lines in *H.MS* were placed ll. 160 ^ 61, and were followed by a stanza which T. adopted almost verbatim as *The Letters* 41–8 (p. 1094):

Then parted. Lightly dipt the stars,
 Soft shone the vapor-braided blue,
Soft breezes brusht the belfry-bars,
 As homeward by the church I drew.
The very graves appeared to smile,
 So fresh they rose in shadowed swells;
'Dark porch!' I said, 'and silent aisle,
 There comes a sound of marriage-bells.'

I watched the little flutterings,
    The doubt my mother would not see;
She spoke at large of many things,
    And at the last she spoke of me;
And turning looked upon your face,
    As near this door you sat apart,
And rose, and, with a silent grace
    Approaching, pressed you heart to heart.

Ah, well–but sing the foolish song
    I gave you, Alice, on the day
When, arm in arm, we went along,
    A pensive pair, and you were gay
With bridal flowers–that I may seem,
    As in the nights of old, to lie
Beside the mill-wheel in the stream,
    While those full chestnuts whisper by.

It is the miller's daughter,
    And she is grown so dear, so dear,
That I would be the jewel
    That trembles in her ear:
For hid in ringlets day and night,
I'd touch her neck so warm and white.

---

*161*] *1842*; Come, Alice, sing to me the song *1832*.
*162*] *1843*; I made you on our marriageday, *1832*; I gave you on the joyful day *1842*.
*164. A pensive pair*] *1842*; Half-tearfully *1832*.
*165–8*] *1842*; With brooch and ring: for I shall seem,
    The while you sing that song, to hear
The millwheel turning in the stream,
    And the green chestnut whisper near. *1832*
*169–86*] *1842* (*but see l. 172n*);

SONG

I wish I were her earring,
    Ambushed in auburn ringlets sleek,
(So might my shadow tremble
    Over her downy cheek,)
        Hid in her hair, all day and night,
        Touching her neck so warm and white.

I wish I were the girdle
    Buckled about her dainty waist,
That her heart might beat against me,
    In sorrow and in rest.
        I should know well if it beat right,
        I'd clasp it round so close and tight.

And I would be the girdle
  About her dainty dainty waist,
And her heart would beat against me,
  In sorrow and in rest:
And I should know if it beat right,
I'd clasp it round so close and tight.

And I would be the necklace,
  And all day long to fall and rise
Upon her balmy bosom,
  With her laughter or her sighs,
And I would lie so light, so light,
I scarce should be unclasped at night.

A trifle, sweet! which true love spells–
  True love interprets—right alone.
His light upon the letter dwells,
  For all the spirit is his own.
So, if I waste words now, in truth
  You must blame Love. His early rage
Had force to make me rhyme in youth,
  And makes me talk too much in age.

---

I wish I were her necklace,
  So might I ever fall and rise
Upon her balmy bosom
  With her laughter, or her sighs.
    I would lie round so warm and light
    I would not be unclasped at night. *1832*

The lover's wishes in these songs are traditional. Cp. in particular Anacreon, *Ode* xxii; Thomas Moore's translation (1800) may have influenced T.'s *Anacreontics.*

*172. in*] *1870*; at *1842–69.*

*189–98*] *1842*; For o'er each letter broods and dwells,
  (Like light from running waters thrown
On flowery swaths) the blissful flame
  Of his sweet eyes, that, day and night,
With pulses thrilling through his frame
  Do inly tremble, starrybright.

How I waste language – yet in truth
  You must blame love, whose early rage
Made me a rhymster in my youth,
  And over-garrulous in age. *1832*

T.'s revised copy of *1832* (*Lincoln*) substituted for the last eight lines:

Yet heightened angel-ears receive
  Each morn his praises from the lark;
Yet their gold beaks the blackbirds cleave,
  Hymning to love from dawn to dark.

And now those vivid hours are gone,
　Like mine own life to me thou art,
Where Past and Present, wound in one,
　Do make a garland for the heart:
So sing that other song I made,
　Half-angered with my happy lot,
The day, when in the chestnut shade
　I found the blue Forget-me-not.

Love that hath us in the net,
Can we pass, and we forget?
Many suns arise and set.
Many a chance the years beget.
Love the gift is Love the debt.
　Even so.
Love is hurt with jar and fret.
Love is made a vague regret.
Eyes with idle tears are wet.
Idle habit links us yet.
What is love? for we forget:
　Ah, no! no!

Look through mine eyes with thine. True wife,
　Round my true heart thine arms entwine

---

Shall not my voice be mixt with theirs?
　Bless Love, for blest are all his ways–
The fluttering doubt, the jealous cares,
　Transparent veils that drink his rays.

*199. So sing*] *1842*; Sing me *1832*.
*201*] *1842*; When in the breezy limewood-shade, *1832*.
*203–14*] *1842*;

SONG

All yesternight you met me not.
My ladylove, forget me not.
When I am gone, regret me not,
But, here or there, forget me not.
With your arched eyebrow threat me not,
　And tremulous eyes, like April skies,
　　That seem to say, 'forget me not.'
　　I pray you, love, forget me not.

In idle sorrow set me not;
Regret me not: forget me not:
Oh! leave me not; oh, let me not
Wear quite away;–forget me not.
With roguish laughter fret me not
　From dewy eyes, like April skies,
　　That ever *look*, 'forget me not,'
　　Blue as the blue forget-me-not. *1832*

My other dearer life in life,
Look through my very soul with thine!
Untouched with any shade of years,
May those kind eyes for ever dwell!
They have not shed a many tears,
Dear eyes, since first I knew them well.

Yet tears they shed: they had their part
Of sorrow: for when time was ripe,
The still affection of the heart
Became an outward breathing type,
That into stillness past again,
And left a want unknown before;
Although the loss had brought us pain,
That loss but made us love the more,

With farther lookings on. The kiss,
The woven arms, seem but to be
Weak symbols of the settled bliss,
The comfort, I have found in thee:
But that God bless thee, dear–who wrought
Two spirits to one equal mind–
With blessings beyond hope or thought,
With blessings which no words can find.

Arise, and let us wander forth,
To yon old mill across the wolds;
For look, the sunset, south and north,
Winds all the vale in rosy folds,
And fires your narrow casement glass,
Touching the sullen pool below:
On the chalk-hill the bearded grass
Is dry and dewless. Let us go.

## 163 Fatima

Published *1832*, with no title, but an epigraph from Sappho's *Fragment 2*: *φαίνεταί μοι κῆνος ἴσος θέοισιν / ἔμμεν ὤνηρ*. Especially in ll. 15–19, it closely imitates Sappho, the same poem adapted in *Eleänore* (p. 370). Paden (p. 39) observes that Sappho merges with the story of Jemily from C.-E.

*223–38*] *1842* (*but see l. 229n*); *not 1832*.
*229. had*] *1884*; that *1842–83*.
*239*] *1842*; I've half a mind to walk, my love, *1832*.
*240. yon*] *1842*; the *1832*.
*241. south and north*] *1842*; from above *1832*.

Savary's *Letters on Egypt* (the acknowledged source of *Egypt*; T. used the 1799 translation, *Lincoln*). She waits for her lover who dare not come because of her husband: 'extending herself on the ground, [she] rolled among and crushed the tender flowers' (ll. 11–12). Though this stanza did not appear till *1842*, Paden (p. 132) points out that: 'It is not safe to assume that the added stanza was written after 1832, for Tennyson often returned from the published to the manuscript version of a poem.' The name 'Fatima' occurs in the poem of the *Moâllakât* which inspired *Locksley Hall*; in Savary; and in the *Arabian Nights*. For the scheme of rhyme and metre, cp. *The Lady of Shalott*, which simply adds rhyming refrains.

O Love, Love, Love! O withering might!
O sun, that from thy noonday height
Shudderest when I strain my sight,
Throbbing through all thy heat and light,
  Lo, falling from my constant mind,
  Lo, parched and withered, deaf and blind,
  I whirl like leaves in roaring wind.

Last night I wasted hateful hours
Below the city's eastern towers:
I thirsted for the brooks, the showers:
I rolled among the tender flowers:
  I crushed them on my breast, my mouth;
  I looked athwart the burning drouth
  Of that long desert to the south.

Last night, when some one spoke his name,
From my swift blood that went and came
A thousand little shafts of flame
Were shivered in my narrow frame.
  O Love, O fire! once he drew
  With one long kiss my whole soul through
  My lips, as sunlight drinketh dew.

¶ 163. *Title*] *1842; not 1832.*
*2. from*] *1842*; at *1832.*
*8–14*] *1842; not 1832.*
*11–12.* Cp., in addition to Savary (headnote), *Sense and Conscience* 57–8: 'crushed and massed / The pleasurable flowers'.
*13.* Adapted from *A Fragment* 17: 'Looking athwart the burning flats'; and cp. *Mariana* 20: 'And glanced athwart the glooming flats'.
*15–19.* Cp., in addition to Sappho (headnote), *Eleänore* 122 ff.
*19–21.* A traditional notion, as in *Locksley Hall* 38. Cp. Marlowe's *Dr Faustus* 1331: 'Her lips sucke forth my soule'; and Donne's *The Expiration*: 'So, so, breake off this last lamenting kisse, / Which sucks two soules, and vapors both awav.'

Before he mounts the hill, I know
He cometh quickly: from below
Sweet gales, as from deep gardens, blow
Before him, striking on my brow.
In my dry brain my spirit soon,
Down-deepening from swoon to swoon,
Faints like a dazzled morning moon.

The wind sounds like a silver wire,
And from beyond the noon a fire
Is poured upon the hills, and nigher
The skies stoop down in their desire;
And, isled in sudden seas of light,
My heart, pierced through with fierce delight,
Bursts into blossom in his sight.

My whole soul waiting silently,
All naked in a sultry sky,
Droops blinded with his shining eye:
I *will* possess him or will die.
I will grow round him in his place,
Grow, live, die looking on his face,
Die, dying clasped in his embrace.

# 164 Œnone

Published *1832*, much revised for *1842*. The changes are well discussed by P. F. Baum (*Tennyson Sixty Years After*, 1948, pp. 75–82). T. began such changes soon after *1832*, as is clear from the copy presented to J. M. Heath (*Fitzwilliam Museum*), which has various intermediate alterations to the opening lines and elsewhere. T. wrote to Spedding in 1835 of 'my old poems, most of which I have so corrected (particularly *Œnone*) as to make them much less imperfect' (*Mem.* i 145). It was written 1830–32; the scenery was suggested by the Pyrenees, where according to T. part of it was written, summer 1830. T.'s note observes that Œnone was 'married to Paris, and afterwards deserted by him for Helen. The sequel of the tale is poorly given in Quintus Calaber' (which T. was to adapt in *The Death of Œnone*, p. 1427). The sources and classical allusions–in particular Ovid's *Heroides* and Theocritus–have been comprehensively discussed by P. Turner *JEGP* lxi (1962) 57–72), who subsumes previous commentators and on whom the following notes draw extensively. D. Bush (*Mythology and the*

*39–42*. Cp. the end of *Eleänore*: 'I *would* be dying evermore, / So dying ever, Eleänore.'

*Romantic Tradition*, 1937, p. 204) describes the poem as an epyllion, or minor epic, in the manner of Theocritus. Some variants are selected from *Huntington MS* (HM 19501), ll. 54–124. The early version in *T.Nbk 23* (1830; it may not be quoted) is much briefer, and omits e.g. ll. 52–84. T. says: 'I had an idiotic hatred of hyphens in those days, but though I printed such words as "glénríver," "téndriltwíne" I always gave them in reading their full two accents. Coleridge thought because of these hyphened words that I could not scan.'

There lies a vale in Ida, lovelier
Than all the valleys of Ionian hills.
The swimming vapour slopes athwart the glen,
Puts forth an arm, and creeps from pine to pine,
And loiters, slowly drawn. On either hand
The lawns and meadow-ledges midway down
Hang rich in flowers, and far below them roars
The long brook falling through the cloven ravine
In cataract after cataract to the sea.
Behind the valley topmost Gargarus
Stands up and takes the morning: but in front
The gorges, opening wide apart, reveal
Troas and Ilion's columned citadel,
The crown of Troas.
                                        Hither came at noon
Mournful Œnone, wandering forlorn

¶ 164.*1–14*] *1842;* There is a dale in Ida, lovelier
Than any in old Ionia, beautiful
With emerald slopes of sunny sward, that lean
Above the loud glenriver, which hath worn
A path through steepdown granite walls below
Mantled with flowering tendriltwine. In front
The cedarshadowy valleys open wide.
Far-seen, high over all the Godbuilt wall
And many a snowycolumned range divine,
Mounted with awful sculptures–men and Gods,
The work of Gods–bright on the darkblue sky
The windy citadel of Ilion
Shone, like the crown of Troas. Hither came *1832*

*1. Ida*: the mountain on the south of the Troas. Paris describes the scene of the Judgment: *Est locus in mediis nemorosae vallibus Idae* . . . (Ovid, *Heroides* xvi 53–8). T.'s opening paragraphs follow the pastoral love-lament: hopeless lover, loved one, setting.

*10. Gargarus*: 'the highest part of Mount Ida'; T. compares Virgil's *Georgics* i 103: *Ipsa suas mirantur Gargara messes.*

Of Paris, once her playmate on the hills.
Her cheek had lost the rose, and round her neck
Floated her hair or seemed to float in rest.
She, leaning on a fragment twined with vine,
Sang to the stillness, till the mountain-shade
Sloped downward to her seat from the upper cliff.

'O mother Ida, many-fountained Ida,
Dear mother Ida, harken ere I die.
For now the noonday quiet holds the hill:
The grasshopper is silent in the grass:
The lizard, with his shadow on the stone,
Rests like a shadow, and the winds are dead.

*16–17*] *1842*; . . . playmate. Round her neck, / Her neck all marblewhite and marblecold, *1832*. *forlorn of*: Spenserian and Miltonic.
*17–18*. P. Turner suggests that this associates Œnone ominously with Cassandra: *diffusis comis* (*Heroides* v 114); and with Dido: *aut videt aut vidisse putat* (*Aeneid* vi 454).
*19*. *fragment . . . vine*] *1842*; vine-entwinèd stone *1832*.
*20*. *-shade*] *1842*; -shadow *1832*.
*20–1*. As in Virgil's *Eclogues* i 83: *maioresque cadunt altis de montibus umbrae*.
*22*. T. remarks that 'this sort of refrain is found in Theocritus'. *mother*: because of Theocritus ix 15; in the source of 'many-fountained' (*Iliad* xiv 283), Ida is 'mother of wild beasts'; hence the pard and panther later. *ere I die*: a traditional feature of the pastoral love-poem.
*24*] *1842; not 1832*. In *Eversley*, T. quotes Callimachus, *Lavacrum Palladis* 72: μεσαμβρινὴ δ' εἶχ' ὄρος ἡσυχία ('and noontide quiet held all the hill'). And yet when John Churton Collins originally suggested this, T. wrote in the margin: 'not known to me' (*Cornhill*, Jan. 1880, *Lincoln*).
*25–9*. Based on Virgil's *Eclogues* ii 8–13, where *cicadis* suggested the cicala of *1832*. The antithesis, *rests/awake*, is from Theocritus ii 38–9; and the lizard, from vii 21–3. Alongside John Churton Collins's suggestion of Theocritus, T. wrote: 'from nature in the south of France' (*Cornhill*, Jan. 1880, *Lincoln*).
*27*] *1883*; Sleeps like a shadow, and the scarletwinged
Cicala in the noonday leapeth not
Along the water-rounded granite-rock. *1832*;
Rests like a shadow, and the cicala sleeps *1842–82*. T. says: 'In these lines describing a perfect stillness, I did not like the jump, "Rests like a shadow –and the cicala sleeps". Moreover, in the heat of noon the cicala is generally at its loudest, though I have read that, in extreme heat, it is silent. Some one (I forget who) found them silent at noon on the slopes of Etna.' *1832* note: 'In the Pyrenees, where part of this poem was written, I saw a very beautiful species of Cicala, which had scarlet wings spotted with black.

The purple flower droops: the golden bee
Is lily-cradled: I alone awake.
My eyes are full of tears, my heart of love,
My heart is breaking, and my eyes are dim,
And I am all aweary of my life.

'O mother Ida, many-fountained Ida,
Dear mother Ida, harken ere I die.
Hear me, O Earth, hear me, O Hills, O Caves
That house the cold crowned snake! O mountain brooks,
I am the daughter of a River-God,
Hear me, for I will speak, and build up all
My sorrow with my song, as yonder walls
Rose slowly to a music slowly breathed,
A cloud that gathered shape: for it may be
That, while I speak of it, a little while
My heart may wander from its deeper woe.

'O mother Ida, many-fountained Ida,
Dear mother Ida, harken ere I die.
I waited underneath the dawning hills,
Aloft the mountain lawn was dewy-dark,
And dewy dark aloft the mountain pine:
Beautiful Paris, evil-hearted Paris,
Leading a jet-black goat white-horned, white-hooved,
Came up from reedy Simois all alone.

Probably nothing of the kind exists in Mount Ida.' T. emended J. M. Heath's copy of *1832* (*Fitzwilliam Museum*) to:

. . . and the garrulous
Cicala ceaseth now to burst the brake
With thick dry clamour chafed from griding wings.

*28. flower droops*] *1832, 1883*; flowers droop *1842–82* (*'misprint', T.*).

*30.* T. denied the influence of *2 Henry VI* II iii 17: 'Mine eyes are full of tears, my heart of grief'.

*35–8.* Echoing Aeschylus, *Prometheus Vinctus* 88–91; and Shelley, *Prometheus Unbound* I 25–9.

*37.* The claim made by Ovid's Œnone, *Heroides* v 9–10.

*38–41.* Suggested by Ovid's Œnone, who boasts that Apollo was her first lover (as in T.; ll. 61–2, *1832* text) – Apollo, *Troiae munitor* (*Heroides* v 139). For the building of Troy, cp. *Tithonus* 62–3: 'Like that strange song I heard Apollo sing, / While Ilion like a mist rose into towers.' Also *Ilion, Ilion* (p. 258) throughout. H.T. compares *Heroides* xvi 182.

*46*] *1842; not 1832.* *the dawning hills*: *Paradise Lost* vi 528.

*50.* With the apple of l. 65, the traditional rustic gifts of the pastoral; a goat, Theocritus iii 34–6.

*51. Simois*: one of the two rivers of the plain of Troy.

'O mother Ida, harken ere I die.
Far-off the torrent called me from the cleft:
Far up the solitary morning smote
The streaks of virgin snow. With down-dropt eyes
I sat alone: white-breasted like a star
Fronting the dawn he moved; a leopard skin
Drooped from his shoulder, but his sunny hair
Clustered about his temples like a God's:
And his cheek brightened as the foam-bow brightens
When the wind blows the foam, and all my heart
Went forth to embrace him coming ere he came.

'Dear mother Ida, harken ere I die.
He smiled, and opening out his milk-white palm
Disclosed a fruit of pure Hesperian gold,

*53–6*] *1842*; I sate alone: the goldensandalled morn
Rosehued the scornful hills: I sate alone
With downdropt eyes: whitebreasted . . . *1832*.
T. emended ll. 53–4 in J. M. Heath's copy of *1832*:
I sate alone: the torrent in the cleft
Called me: far up, far on the rosy glows
O'er trackless woods smote all the snowy streaks,
Smote all the scarrèd spurs. I sat alone
*Huntington MS* of ll. 54–6 shows T.'s uncertainty:
Far up the lonely morning lit the streaks
Of virgin snow; with downdropt eyes I sat:
I heard a voice: white-breasted . . .
*56.* Cp. the Homeric *Hymn to Aphrodite* 89–90; and Theocritus ii 79. T. uses details from Theocritus and Virgil, but changes from the first meeting to the last.
*57. moved*] *1842*; came *1832*. The leopard skin is from *Iliad* iii 17.
*58*] *1842*; From his white shoulder drooped: his sunny hair *1832*.
*59–62.* Based on Catullus lxiv 270–8, the arrival of the gods (cp. below) at a wedding.
*60. foam-bow*: 'the rainbow in the cataract' (T.).
*61–2*] *1842*; . . . and I called out,
'Welcome Apollo, welcome home Apollo,
Apollo, my Apollo, loved Apollo.' *1832*
*62.* Cp. Venus, in *Who is it* 12–13 (see ll. 213–15*n* below): 'Whose coming ere she comes doth strike / On expectation.' Also *PL* vi 768: 'He onward came, farr off his coming shon'.
*64. smiled . . . out*] *1842*; mildly smiling, in *1832*.
*65.* A pastoral gift, as in Theocritus iii 10–11 (see l. 50*n*), but here the apple of Discord. For the Hesperian apples, see *The Hesperides* (p. 423).
*65–7*] *1842*; Close-held a golden apple, lightningbright
With changeful flashes, dropt with dew of Heaven

That smelt ambrosially, and while I looked
And listened, the full-flowing river of speech
Came down upon my heart.
'"My own Œnone,
Beautiful-browed Œnone, my own soul,
Behold this fruit, whose gleaming rind ingraven
'For the most fair,' would seem to award it thine,
As lovelier than whatever Oread haunt
The knolls of Ida, loveliest in all grace
Of movement, and the charm of married brows."

'Dear mother Ida, harken ere I die.
He prest the blossom of his lips to mine,
And added "This was cast upon the board,
When all the full-faced presence of the Gods

Ambrosially smelling. From his lip,
Curved crimson, the fullflowing . . . *1832*

*69. my*] *1842*; mine *1832*. For the meeting eyebrows (as in l. 74), T. compares Theocritus viii 72–3, of a beautiful girl watching from a cave (cp. l. 85).

*71–87*] *1842*; 'For the most fair,' in aftertime may breed
Deep evilwilledness of heaven and sere
Heartburning toward hallowèd Ilion;
And all the colour of my afterlife
Will be the shadow of today. Today
Here [Herè] and Pallas and the floating grace
Of laughterloving Aphrodite meet
In manyfolded Ida to receive
This meed of beauty, she to whom my hand
Award the palm. Within the green hillside,
Under yon whispering tuft of oldest pine,
Is an ingoing grotto, strown with spar
And ivymatted at the mouth, wherein
Thou unbeholden mayst behold, unheard *1832*

*Hn MS* shows T.'s efforts; ll. 71–83:
. . . fair, hath bred dispute in Heaven
For Hermes brought it, telling that today
To me, chosen arbiter, would Herè come *1st reading*;
. . . fair, perplexes Heaven with feud
For Hermes brought it, telling that today
(So much they do me honour) unto me
Selected arbiter, would Herè come *2nd reading*

*72. Oread*: mountain-nymph.

*76.* Ominously recalling Bion's *Lament for Adonis* 11–12: 'The rose departs from his lip, and the kiss that Cypris shall never have so again, that kiss dies upon it and is gone.' Cp. l. 17 above.

Ranged in the halls of Peleus; whereupon
Rose feud, with question unto whom 'twere due:
But light-foot Iris brought it yester-eve,
Delivering, that to me, by common voice
Elected umpire, Herè comes today,
Pallas and Aphroditè, claiming each
This meed of fairest. Thou, within the cave
Behind yon whispering tuft of oldest pine,
Mayst well behold them unbeheld, unheard
Hear all, and see thy Paris judge of Gods."

'Dear mother Ida, harken ere I die.
It was the deep midnoon: one silvery cloud
Had lost his way between the piney sides
Of this long glen. Then to the bower they came,
Naked they came to that smooth-swarded bower,
And at their feet the crocus brake like fire,
Violet, amaracus, and asphodel,
Lotos and lilies: and a wind arose,

*81. Iris*: the messenger of the gods. T. translated *Iliad* xviii 202 as 'light-foot Iris', *Achilles* 1.

*86. whispering . . . oldest*] sobbing growth of twisted *Hn MS, to which T. reverted in emending J. M. Heath's copy of 1832.* *whispering*: Theocritus i 1.

*91. sides*] *1842*; hills *1832*. Cp. Thomson, *Summer* 1303–4: 'Paris on the piny top / Of Ida'.

*92*] *1842*; They came–all three–the Olympian goddesses: *1832*.

*93. that*] *1842*; the *1832*. The setting is from *Iliad* xiv 346–51, where the cloud dropping dew (cp. ll. 103–4) envelops Herè (Hera) and not her peacock. Cp. *PL* iv 700–702, the bower of Adam and Eve: 'underfoot the Violet, / Crocus, and Hyacinth with rich inlay / Broiderd the ground.'

*94–7*] *1842*; Lustrous with lilyflower, violeteyed
Both white and blue, with lotetree-fruit thickset,
Shadowed with singing pine; and all the while,
Above, the overwandering ivy and vine *1832*

T. emended J. M. Heath's copy of *1832*: 'Lustrous with lily and myrtle – myriad-eyed / With violet-hues.' *Hn MS* of ll. 94–5 included a further allusion to Milton:

That darkened all with violets underneath
Through which like fire the sudden crocus came,
Amaracus, immortal asphodel,

*like fire*: T. spoke of the 'flame-like petal . . . not only the colour'. This note was written alongside John Churton Collins's remark that the comparison was not 'original' (*Cornhill*, Jan. 1880, *Lincoln*). Cp. 'The ground-flame of the crocus', *The Progress of Spring* 1 and *n* (p. 476). H.T. compares *Oedipus Coloneus* 685.

And overhead the wandering ivy and vine,
This way and that, in many a wild festoon
Ran riot, garlanding the gnarlèd boughs
With bunch and berry and flower through and through.

'O mother Ida, harken ere I die.
On the tree-tops a crested peacock lit,
And o'er him flowed a golden cloud, and leaned
Upon him, slowly dropping fragrant dew.
Then first I heard the voice of her, to whom
Coming through Heaven, like a light that grows
Larger and clearer, with one mind the Gods
Rise up for reverence. She to Paris made
Proffer of royal power, ample rule
Unquestioned, overflowing revenue
Wherewith to embellish state, "from many a vale
And river-sundered champaign clothed with corn,
Or laboured mine undrainable of ore.
Honour," she said, "and homage, tax and toll,
From many an inland town and haven large,

*97–9.* Cp. Leigh Hunt, *Rimini* ii 137–8: 'And still from tree to tree the early vines / Hung garlanding the way.' T. jotted down phrases from *Rimini* in *H.Nbk 4*.

*101–8*] *1842*; On the treetops a golden glorious cloud
Leaned, slowly dropping down ambrosial dew.
How beautiful they were, too beautiful
To look upon! but Paris was to me
More lovelier than all the world beside.
'O mother Ida, hearken ere I die.
First spake the imperial Olympian
With archèd eyebrow smiling sovranly,
Fulleyèd Here. She to Paris made *1832*

*102. peacock*: 'sacred to Herè' (T.).

*108. Rise up*: as in *Iliad* xv 86.

*113*] *1882*; ... mines ... *1842–81*; Or upland glebe wealthy in oil and wine – *1832*.

*114*] *1842*; Honour and homage, tribute, tax and toll, *1832*.

In *1832*, ll. 113–4 bring out more clearly the debt to *Paradise Regained* iii 257–60, noted by D. Bush (*Major British Writers* (1959) ii 387): 'Fair Champain with less rivers interveind, / Then meeting joyn'd thir tribute to the Sea: / Fertil of corn the glebe, of oyl and wine, / With herds the pastures throng'd . . .'. The reminiscence is due to the similar situation, of tempting offers being made. Cp. *The Palace of Art* 79: 'upland, prodigal in oil'; *Hn MS* of *Œnone* 113 has 'Or upland prodigal of oil and wine'.

Mast-thronged beneath her shadowing citadel
In glassy bays among her tallest towers."

'O mother Ida, harken ere I die.
Still she spake on and still she spake of power,
"Which in all action is the end of all;
Power fitted to the season; wisdom-bred
And throned of wisdom–from all neighbour crowns
Alliance and allegiance, till thy hand
Fail from the sceptre-staff. Such boon from me,
From me, Heaven's Queen, Paris, to thee king-born,
A shepherd all thy life but yet king-born,
Should come most welcome, seeing men, in power
Only, are likest gods, who have attained
Rest in a happy place and quiet seats
Above the thunder, with undying bliss
In knowledge of their own supremacy."

'Dear mother Ida, harken ere I die.
She ceased, and Paris held the costly fruit
Out at arm's-length, so much the thought of power
Flattered his spirit; but Pallas where she stood
Somewhat apart, her clear and bared limbs
O'erthwarted with the brazen-headed spear
Upon her pearly shoulder leaning cold,
The while, above, her full and earnest eye
Over her snow-cold breast and angry cheek
Kept watch, waiting decision, made reply.

'"Self-reverence, self-knowledge, self-control,
These three alone lead life to sovereign power.

*116. beneath*] *1842*; below *1832*.
*121*] *1842*; . . . season, measured by / The height of the general feeling, wisdomborn *1832*.
*123–5*] *1842*; . . . allegiance evermore. / Such boon from me Heaven's Queen to thee kingborn, *1832*.
*126. but*] *1842*; and *1832*.
*127. power*] *1842*; this *1832*.
*127–31.* Based, as T. says, on Lucretius's account of the Epicurean gods, iii 18–24; and on *Aeneid* iv 379–80. With a reminiscence of *PL* vi 301: 'Of Godlike Power: for likest Gods they seemd'.
*131 ∧ 2*] The changeless calm of undisputed right,
The highest height and topmost strength of power.' *1832*
*135. spirit*] *1842*; heart *1832*.
*137. O'erthwarted*: T. says it was founded on the Chaucerian word 'overthwart', across, *Troilus and Criseyde* iii 685.
*143*] *1842*; Are the three hinges of the gates of Life,
That open into power, everyway
Without horizon, bound or shadow or cloud. *1832*

Yet not for power (power of herself
Would come uncalled for) but to live by law,
Acting the law we live by without fear;
And, because right is right, to follow right
Were wisdom in the scorn of consequence."

'Dear mother Ida, harken ere I die.
Again she said: "I woo thee not with gifts.
Sequel of guerdon could not alter me
To fairer. Judge thou me by what I am,
So shalt thou find me fairest.
                                        Yet, indeed,
If gazing on divinity disrobed
Thy mortal eyes are frail to judge of fair,
Unbiased by self-profit, oh! rest thee sure
That I shall love thee well and cleave to thee,
So that my vigour, wedded to thy blood,
Shall strike within thy pulses, like a God's,

*145. Would*] *1842*; Will *1832*.

*148.* Traditionally Pallas had offered Paris success in war, until (as D. Bush noted, *Mythology and the Romantic Tradition*, 1937, p. 206) the fifth–sixth-century writer Fulgentius made the offer that of wisdom.

*150–64*] *1842*;

Not as men value gold because it tricks
And blazons outward Life with ornament,
But rather as the miser, for itself.
Good for selfgood doth half destroy selfgood.
The means and end, like two coiled snakes, infect
Each other, bound in one with hateful love.
So both into the fountain and the stream
A drop of poison falls. Come hearken to me,
And look upon me and consider me,
So shalt thou find me fairest, so endurance,
Like to an athlete's arm, shall still become
Sinewed with motion, till thine active will
(As the dark body of the Sun robed round
With his own ever-emanating lights)
Be flooded o'er with her own effluences,
And thereby grow to freedom.' *1832*

There is an intermediate version of l. 163 in J. M. Heath's copy of *1832*, which T. emended:

Circled through all experience, narrowing up
From orb to orb, still nigher rest, remain
A polestar fixt in truth and so made one
With effort, wholly one herself, pure law,

*151. Sequel of guerdon*: 'addition of reward' (T.).

To push thee forward through a life of shocks,
Dangers, and deeds, until endurance grow
Sinewed with action, and the full-grown will,
Circled through all experiences, pure law,
Commeasure perfect freedom."
'Here she ceased,
And Paris pondered, and I cried, "O Paris,
Give it to Pallas!" but he heard me not,
Or hearing would not hear me, woe is me!

'O mother Ida, many-fountained Ida,
Dear mother Ida, harken ere I die.
Idalian Aphroditè beautiful,
Fresh as the foam, new-bathed in Paphian wells,
With rosy slender fingers backward drew
From her warm brows and bosom her deep hair
Ambrosial, golden round her lucid throat
And shoulder: from the violets her light foot
Shone rosy-white, and o'er her rounded form
Between the shadows of the vine-bunches
Floated the glowing sunlights, as she moved.

*160–64.* Paraphrasing Horace's definition of a Stoic, *Satires* II vii 83–6.
*162. 2 Henry IV* IV i 172: 'Insinewed to this action'.
*165. and I cried*] *1842*; I cried out *1832*.
*166–7.* The antithesis, *heard/hear*, is from Aeschylus, *Prometheus Vinctus* 448; Turner observes that it 'carries the implication that Paris is in the same state of primitive animalism as the human race before Prometheus began to civilize it'.
*170. beautiful*] *1842*; oceanborn *1832*.
*170–1.* 'Idalium and Paphos in Cyprus are sacred to Aphrodite' (T.), who was born from the sea-foam.
*172. backward*] *1842*; upward *1832*.
*173. brows . . . deep*] *1842*; brow . . . dark *1832*. Adapted from *Mariana in the South* 14, *1832* text: 'From her warm brow and bosom down'.
*174–6*] *1842*; Fragrant and thick, and on her head upbound
In a purple band: below her lucid neck
Shone ivorylike, and from the ground her foot
Gleamed rosywhite . . . *1832*
T. emended ll. 174–5 in J. M. Heath's copy of *1832*:
Deep, fragrant. Dimpled was her chin–her throat
Shone pure, and from the all-flowering ground her foot
*176–8.* Cp. the Oread in *Lucretius* 188–90: 'how the sun delights / To glance and shift about her slippery sides, / And rosy knees and supple roundedness.'

'Dear mother Ida, harken ere I die.
She with a subtle smile in her mild eyes,
The herald of her triumph, drawing nigh
Half-whispered in his ear, "I promise thee
The fairest and most loving wife in Greece,"
She spoke and laughed: I shut my sight for fear:
But when I looked, Paris had raised his arm,
And I beheld great Herè's angry eyes,
As she withdrew into the golden cloud,
And I was left alone within the bower;
And from that time to this I am alone,
And I shall be alone until I die.

'Yet, mother Ida, harken ere I die.
Fairest–why fairest wife? am I not fair?
My love hath told me so a thousand times.
Methinks I must be fair, for yesterday,
When I past by, a wild and wanton pard,
Eyed like the evening star, with playful tail
Crouched fawning in the weed. Most loving is she?
Ah me, my mountain shepherd, that my arms
Were wound about thee, and my hot lips prest
Close, close to thine in that quick-falling dew
Of fruitful kisses, thick as Autumn rains
Flash in the pools of whirling Simois.

'O mother, hear me yet before I die.
They came, they cut away my tallest pines,
My tall dark pines, that plumed the craggy ledge
High over the blue gorge, and all between
The snowy peak and snow-white cataract

*184*] *1842; not 1832.*
*185–6*] *1842*; I only saw my Paris raise his arm: / I only saw great . . . *1832*.
*192–4*. Using the pastoral convention of Theocritus vi 34–6 and Virgil's *Eclogues* ii 25–6.
*195–7*. Based on Horace's *Odes* I xx 9–12. Cp. Keats, *Lamia* i 49–50: 'freckled like a pard, / Eyed like a peacock'. Turner remarks this as 'bringing with it associations of illusory and evanescent love'.
*203*] *1842*; 'Dear mother Ida, hearken ere I die. *1832*.
*204–5*. Suggested by *Heroides* v 41–2; but there, as Turner says, 'Œnone's only objection to the felling of the pines is that it provides transport for Paris and Helen'.
*205. tall dark*] *1884*; dark tall *1832–83*.
*206*] *1843*; . . . gorge, or lower down / Filling greengulphèd Ida, all between *1832–42*.

Fostered the callow eaglet–from beneath
Whose thick mysterious boughs in the dark morn
The panther's roar came muffled, while I sat
Low in the valley. Never, never more
Shall lone Œnone see the morning mist
Sweep through them; never see them overlaid
With narrow moon-lit slips of silver cloud,
Between the loud stream and the trembling stars.

'O mother, hear me yet before I die.
I wish that somewhere in the ruined folds,
Among the fragments tumbled from the glens,
Or the dry thickets, I could meet with her
The Abominable, that uninvited came
Into the fair Peleïan banquet-hall,
And cast the golden fruit upon the board,
And bred this change; that I might speak my mind,
And tell her to her face how much I hate
Her presence, hated both of Gods and men.

'O mother, hear me yet before I die.
Hath he not sworn his love a thousand times,
In this green valley, under this green hill,
Even on this hand, and sitting on this stone?
Sealed it with kisses? watered it with tears?
O happy tears, and how unlike to these!
O happy Heaven, how canst thou see my face?
O happy earth, how canst thou bear my weight?
O death, death, death, thou ever-floating cloud,
There are enough unhappy on this earth,
Pass by the happy souls, that love to live:
I pray thee, pass before my light of life,
And shadow all my soul, that I may die.
Thou weighest heavy on the heart within,
Weigh heavy on my eyelids: let me die.

*213–5.* Adapted from *Amy* 54–6: 'Like streaks of cloud by night / That overlay the stars in January / But cannot hide their light.' Also from *Who is it* 14–16 (see l. 62*n* above): 'the unrisen moon below / Dark firs, when creeping winds by night / Lay the long mist in streaks and bars.'

*216–25*] *1842; not 1832.*

*220.* Eris, 'the goddess of strife' (T.).

*225.* Cp. Aeschylus, *Eumenides* 644: ὦ παντομισῆ κνώδαλα, στύγη θεῶν,

*226*] *1842*; 'Oh! mother Ida, hearken ere I die. *1832.*

*233.* A classical commonplace; cp. *Odyssey* xx 379.

'O mother, hear me yet before I die.
I will not die alone, for fiery thoughts
Do shape themselves within me, more and more,
Whereof I catch the issue, as I hear
Dead sounds at night come from the inmost hills,
Like footsteps upon wool. I dimly see
My far-off doubtful purpose, as a mother
Conjectures of the features of her child
Ere it is born: her child!–a shudder comes
Across me: never child be born of me,
Unblest, to vex me with his father's eyes!

'O mother, hear me yet before I die.
Hear me, O earth. I will not die alone,
Lest their shrill happy laughter come to me
Walking the cold and starless road of Death
Uncomforted, leaving my ancient love
With the Greek woman. I will rise and go
Down into Troy, and ere the stars come forth
Talk with the wild Cassandra, for she says
A fire dances before her, and a sound
Rings ever in her ears of armèd men.
What this may be I know not, but I know

*241*] *1842*; 'Yet, mother Ida, hear me ere I die. *1832*.
*246*. The simile is from Theocritus v 50–1.
*249–51*] *1842*; Ere it is born. I will not die alone. *1832*.
*252*] *1842*; 'Dear mother Ida, hearken ere I die. *1832*.
*253–6*. The association of Œnone and Dido (cp. l. 18) was, as Turner says, 'inevitable, considering the similarity of their histories (both being deserted by Trojan lovers, and both committing suicide on funeral pyres)'. The image here is from Dido's dream, *Aeneid* iv 465–8.
*257*. *the Greek woman*: *Heroides* v 117 etc.
*259*. Turner points out that 'Ovid's Œnone refers to Cassandra's prophecy that Helen will be the ruin of Troy, but she is also perfectly aware . . . that the rape of Helen is going to cause a major war'; T. gives Œnone 'some of Cassandra's vague prophetic power . . . depriving her of any accurate knowledge'.
*260*. T. compares Aeschylus, *Agamemnon* 1256: *παπαῖ, οἷον τὸ π·ρῦ ἐπέρχεται δέ μοι* ('Oh, oh! What fire! It comes upon me').
*260–64*. Turner links *fire* as a traditional metaphor for love, with it as magic for bringing back the faithless lover (Theocritus ii 23–4 etc.); with Hecuba's dream before the birth of Paris (*Heroides* xvi 43–50); and with the fires of Dido, including her funeral pyre (*Aeneid* iv 604–5, 661–2, 669–71).

That, wheresoe'er I am by night and day,
All earth and air seem only burning fire.'

# 165 The Sisters [We were two daughters of one race]

Published *1832*. Written by 15 July 1831 (*Mem.* i 80). It was influenced by Scott's *Minstrelsy of the Scottish Border* (from which T. knew ballads by heart), e.g. *The Cruel Sister.*

We were two daughters of one race:
She was the fairest in the face:
   The wind is blowing in turret and tree.
They were together, and she fell;
Therefore revenge became me well.
   O the Earl was fair to see!

She died: she went to burning flame:
She mixed her ancient blood with shame.
   The wind is howling in turret and tree.
Whole weeks and months, and early and late,
To win his love I lay in wait:
   O the Earl was fair to see!

I made a feast; I bad him come;
I won his love, I brought him home.
   The wind is roaring in turret and tree.
And after supper, on a bed,
Upon my lap he laid his head:
   O the Earl was fair to see!

I kissed his eyelids into rest:
His ruddy cheek upon my breast.
   The wind is raging in turret and tree.
I hated him with the hate of hell,
But I loved his beauty passing well.
   O the Earl was fair to see!

*264.* John Churton Collins compared Webster, *Duchess of Malfi* IV ii 25–6: 'Th' heaven o'er my head seems made of molten brass, / The earth of flaming sulphur.' Alongside this, T. wrote: 'Nonsense' (*Cornhill*, Jan. 1880, *Lincoln*).

¶ 165.*19–20*. Cp. Byron, *The Bride of Abydos* 301–2: 'Come, lay thy head upon my breast, / And I will kiss thee into rest.'

I rose up in the silent night:
I made my dagger sharp and bright.
  The wind is raving in turret and tree.
As half-asleep his breath he drew,
Three times I stabbed him through and through.
  O the Earl was fair to see!

I curled and combed his comely head,
He looked so grand when he was dead.
  The wind is blowing in turret and tree.
I wrapt his body in the sheet,
And laid him at his mother's feet.
  O the Earl was fair to see!

# 166 To – . With the Following Poem [The Palace of Art]

Published *1832*. It is addressed to R. C. Trench (*Tennyson and His Friends*, p. 79), a remark by whom prompted *The Palace of Art* (p. 400). It proclaims the view of poetry (morally opposed to aestheticism) which was strongly held by the Cambridge 'Apostles'.

I send you here a sort of allegory,
(For you will understand it) of a soul,
A sinful soul possessed of many gifts,
A spacious garden full of flowering weeds,
A glorious Devil, large in heart and brain,
That did love Beauty only, (Beauty seen
In all varieties of mould and mind)
And Knowledge for its beauty; or if Good,
Good only for its beauty, seeing not
That Beauty, Good, and Knowledge, are three sisters
That doat upon each other, friends to man,
Living together under the same roof,
And never can be sundered without tears.
And he that shuts Love out, in turn shall be

¶ 166.*1. here*] *1842*;, Friend, *1832*.
*2*] *1842*; (You are an artist and will understand
Its many lesser meanings) of a soul, *1832*
*7*. Cp. 'variety', 'moulds of mind', in *The constant spirit* (p. 291).
*10*. Cp. *Fragment: We have a rumour* 4 (p. 1788): 'If beauty, then true knowledge. Sisters fair'.

Shut out from Love, and on her threshold lie
Howling in outer darkness. Not for this
Was common clay ta'en from the common earth
Moulded by God, and tempered with the tears
Of angels to the perfect shape of man.

# 167 The Palace of Art

Published *1832*, much revised *1842*. Written by April 1832 (*Mem.* i 85). It was probably not begun before Oct. 1831, the date of Arthur Hallam's *Theodicaea Novissima* (see l. 223*n*). T. reports: R. C. Trench 'said, when we were at Trinity (Cambridge) together, "Tennyson, we cannot live in Art". This poem is the embodiment of my own belief that the Godlike life is with man and for man.' See the introductory poem, *To*–(p. 399), which is to Trench. T. had many sources or analogues. *Ecclesiastes* ii 1–17, 'I said in mine heart, Go to now, I will prove thee with mirth, therefore enjoy pleasure. . . . I made me great works; I builded me houses. . . . I gathered me also silver and gold, and the peculiar treasure of kings. . . . And whatsoever mine eyes desired I kept not from them, I withheld not my heart from any joy. . . . Then I looked on all the works that my hands had wrought, and on the labour that I had laboured to do: and, behold, all was vanity and vexation of spirit, and there was no profit under the sun. . . . Therefore I hated life.' *Luke* xii 19–20, 'And I will say to my soul, Soul, thou hast much goods laid up for many years; take thine ease, eat, drink, and be merry. But God said unto him, Thou fool, this night thy soul shall be required of thee.' Herbert, *The World*: '*Love* built a stately house . . . / Then *Pleasure* came, who, liking not the fashion, / Began to make *Balcones*, *Terraces*, / Till she had weakned all by alteration . . . / But *Love* and *Grace* took *Glorie* by the hand, / And built a braver Palace than before.' Shelley, *Queen Mab* ii 56–64: the Fairy 'pointed to the gorgeous dome, / "This is a wondrous sight / And mocks all human grandeur; / But, were it virtue's only meed,

*15–16.* Cp. *Hamlet* V i 234–6: 'I tell thee, churlish priest, / A minist'ring angel shall my sister be, / When thou liest howling.' Hence 'he that shuts Love out' suggests the priest's 'She should in ground unsanctified have lodged'. *Matthew* viii 12, 'But the children of the kingdom shall be cast out into outer darkness: there shall be weeping and gnashing of teeth'.
*18–19.* Cp. *Genesis* ii 7. But T. uses Sir William Jones's translation of the *Khelassut ul Akhbar* of Khondemeer. At the creation of Adam, Gabriel and the other angels were 'compassionating the earth's distress' when the earth feared it might be involved in any 'offence' caused by man; 'In the space of forty days, the clay was kneaded into form by the hands of the angels'. Jones's *Works* were at Somersby (*Lincoln*). It is T. who links the tears and the actual making of man.

to dwell / In a celestial palace, all resigned / To pleasurable impulses, immured / Within the prison of itself, the will / Of changeless Nature would be unfulfilled. / Learn to make others happy".' (Noted by H. N. Fairchild, *TLS*, 11 Jan. 1947.) L. Stevenson (*Critical Essays on Tennyson*, ed. Killham, pp. 131–2) cites more examples from Shelley: the Elysian temple in *The Revolt of Islam* I li–liii, and the setting in *The Witch of Atlas* xviii–xxi. T. was probably influenced by Sir William Jones, a favourite of his when young. Jones's works were at Somersby (*Lincoln*); his *The Palace of Fortune* has similar disillusionments. A few touches suggest the futile splendours of Milton's Pandæmonium, *PL* i 710–30. There are also affinities with George Sandys's account of Egyptian 'Palaces' in his *Travels* (the 1658 edition was at Somersby, *Lincoln*). Sandys moralizes the labyrinth: 'The first entrance was of white marble, within thorowout adorned with marble columns, and diversity of figures. By this defigured they the perplexed life of man, combred and intangled with manifold mischiefs, one succeeding another' (p. 88). The stanza was independently developed (T. approached it in *The Poet*, and cp. *A Dream of Fair Women*), but it is that of Vaughan's *They are all gone into the world of light*.

I built my soul a lordly pleasure-house,
    Wherein at ease for aye to dwell.
I said, 'O Soul, make merry and carouse,
    Dear soul, for all is well.'

A huge crag-platform, smooth as burnished brass
    I chose. The rangèd ramparts bright
From level meadow-bases of deep grass
    Suddenly scaled the light.

Thereon I built it firm. Of ledge or shelf
    The rock rose clear, or winding stair.
My soul would live alone unto herself
    In her high palace there.

And 'while the world runs round and round,' I said,
    'Reign thou apart, a quiet king,
Still as, while Saturn whirls, his stedfast shade
    Sleeps on his luminous ring.'

¶ 167.*6. The*] *1842*; whose *1832*.
*7. level*] *1842*; great broad *1832*.
*13. And* '*while the*] *1842*; 'While the great *1832*.
*15–16.* H.T. comments: 'The shadow of Saturn thrown on the luminous ring, though the planet revolves in ten and a half hours, appears to be motionless.'
*16 ∧ 17*] 'And richly feast within thy palacehall,
    Like to the dainty bird that sups,
Lodged in the lustrous crown-imperial,
    Draining the honeycups.' *1832*

To which my soul made answer readily:
'Trust me, in bliss I shall abide
In this great mansion, that is built for me,
So royal-rich and wide.'

* * * *
* * * *

Four courts I made, East, West and South and
North,
In each a squarèd lawn, wherefrom
The golden gorge of dragons spouted forth
A flood of fountain-foam.

And round the cool green courts there ran a row
Of cloisters, branched like mighty woods,
Echoing all night to that sonorous flow
Of spouted fountain-floods.

And round the roofs a gilded gallery
That lent broad verge to distant lands,
Far as the wild swan wings, to where the sky
Dipt down to sea and sands.

From those four jets four currents in one swell
Across the mountain streamed below
In misty folds, that floating as they fell
Lit up a torrent-bow.

*21–52*] *1842*; *preceding l. 129 in 1832.*
*21*] *1842*; Four ample courts there were, East, West, South, North, *1832.*
*23. The . . . dragons*] *1842*; A golden-gorgèd dragon *1832.*
*24*] *1842*; The fountain's diamond foam. *1832.* D. Bush (*MLR*, liv, 1959, 423) compares H. J. Weber's *Tales of the East* (1812), i 115: 'Four large gilded dragons adorned the angles of the bason, which was of a square form; and these dragons spouted out water clearer than rock crystal.'
*25. And*] *1842*; All *1832.*
*29–32, 33–6*] *1842*; *transposed 1832.*
*29. a gilded gallery*] *1842*; ran gilded galleries *1832.*
*30. lent broad verge*] *1842*; gave large view *1832. broad verge*: 'a broad horizon' (T.).
*31–2*] *1842*; Tall towns and mounds, and close beneath the skies
Long lines of amber sands. *1832*
*34. Across the mountain*] *1842*; Over the black rock *1832.*
*35. misty*] *1842*; steamy *1832.*

And high on every peak a statue seemed
    To hang on tiptoe, tossing up
A cloud of incense of all odour steamed
        From out a golden cup.

So that she thought, 'And who shall gaze upon
    My palace with unblinded eyes,
While this great bow will waver in the sun,
        And that sweet incense rise?'

For that sweet incense rose and never failed,
    And, while day sank or mounted higher,
The light aërial gallery, golden-railed,
        Burnt like a fringe of fire.

Likewise the deep-set windows, stained and traced,
    Would seem slow-flaming crimson fires
From shadowed grots of arches interlaced,
        And tipt with frost-like spires.

* * * *

* * * *

Full of long-sounding corridors it was,
    That over-vaulted grateful gloom,
Through which the livelong day my soul did pass,
    Well-pleased, from room to room.

*37–47*] *1842*; Huge incense-urns along the balustrade,
    Hollowed of solid amethyst,
Each with a different odour fuming, made
        The air a silver mist.

Far-off 'twas wonderful to look upon
    Those sumptuous towers between the gleam
Of that great foambow trembling in the sun,
        And the argent incense-steam;

And round the terraces and round the walls,
    While day sank lower or rose higher,
To see those rails with all their knobs and balls, *1832*

*48. Burnt*] *1842*; Burn *1832*.

*50. Would seem*] *1842*; Burned, like *1832*.

*52. tipt*] *1842*; topped *1832*.

*54. gloom*] *1842*; glooms *1832*. Cp. *Inverlee* 15: 'vaulted glooms'.

*55–6*] *1842*; Roofed with thick plates of green and orange glass
        Ending in stately rooms. *1832*

Full of great rooms and small the palace stood,
All various, each a perfect whole
From living Nature, fit for every mood
And change of my still soul.

For some were hung with arras green and blue,
Showing a gaudy summer-morn,
Where with puffed cheek the belted hunter blew
His wreathèd bugle-horn.

One seemed all dark and red – a tract of sand,
And some one pacing there alone,
Who paced for ever in a glimmering land,
Lit with a low large moon.

One showed an iron coast and angry waves.
You seemed to hear them climb and fall
And roar rock-thwarted under bellowing caves,
Beneath the windy wall.

And one, a full-fed river winding slow
By herds upon an endless plain,

*58. each . . . whole*] *1842*; all beautiful *1832*.
*59. From . . . for*] *1842*; Looking all ways, fitted to *1832*.
*61ff.* Cp. the scenes depicted in Thomson's *Castle of Indolence* I xxxvi ff, where 'the rooms with costly tapestry were hung'.
*64 ∧ 5*] *1832 had its version of ll. 85–8.* In *Heath MS*, there are four 'Stanzas omitted or altered in *The Palace of Art*'; the first is marked 'x', and if this refers to *1832* numbering, then it belongs here:

One seemed a place of mart. The seller held
The buyer's hand, and winked and smiled,
And pointed to his wares. The teeming field
On stalls lay stored and piled.

*65–8*] *1842*; Some were all dark and red, a glimmering land
Lit with a low round moon,
Among brown rocks a man upon the sand
Went weeping all alone. *1832*

*68 ∧ 9*] *1832 had its version of ll. 81–4. Heath MS* has a stanza 'XII':

One shewed deep floods with dusky shadows gloomed,
A blissful island high and bright
With three white peaks mythic Trinacria loomed
Far off in gleaming light.

*Trinacria*: Sicily.
*69–80*] *1842*; Some showed far-off thick woods mounted with towers,
Nearer, a flood of mild sunshine
Poured on long walks and lawns and beds and bowers
Trellised with bunchy vine. *1832*

The ragged rims of thunder brooding low,
With shadow-streaks of rain.

And one, the reapers at their sultry toil.
In front they bound the sheaves. Behind
Were realms of upland, prodigal in oil,
And hoary to the wind.

And one a foreground black with stones and slags,
Beyond, a line of heights, and higher
All barred with long white cloud the scornful crags,
And highest, snow and fire.

And one, an English home–gray twilight poured
On dewy pastures, dewy trees,
Softer than sleep–all things in order stored,
A haunt of ancient Peace.

Nor these alone, but every landscape fair,
As fit for every mood of mind,
Or gay, or grave, or sweet, or stern, was there
Not less than truth designed.

* * * *

* * * *

Or the maid-mother by a crucifix,

*75.* Cp. *The Lover's Tale* ii 59–63 (p. 332): 'palaces', 'brooded', 'Like to a low-hung and a fiery sky . . . / Hung round with ragged rims'.
*79–80.* Cp. Wordsworth, *Descriptive Sketches* 8 (1793): 'Or moonlight Upland lifts her hoary breast'. See *Œnone* 113, *1832* text (p. 391).
*80.* 'The underside of the olive leaf is white' (T.).
*81–4*] *See ll. 68 ‸ 9n.*
*81. And one*] *1842*; One seemed *1832*.
*82*] *1842*; Below sunsmitten icy spires *1832*.
*83. All barred*] *1842*; Rose striped *1832*. Cp. *1842* with Keats, *To Autumn* 25: 'barred clouds'.
*84*] *1842*; Deeptrenched with thunderfires. *1832*.
*85–8*] *See ll. 64 ‸ 5n.*
*85. And one,*] *1842*; One showed *1832*.
*86–7.* J. H. Buckley (p. 264) compares *Ode: O Bosky Brook* 56: 'Close pastures soft as dewy sleep'. Virgil, *Eclogues* vii 45: *somno mollior herba.*
*89–92*] *1842*; *not 1832.*
*93*] *1832 note*: 'When I first conceived the plan of the Palace of Art, I intended to have introduced both sculptures and paintings into it; but it is the most difficult of all things to *devise* a statue in verse. Judge whether I have succeeded in the statues of Elijah and Olympias.

In tracts of pasture sunny-warm,
Beneath branch-work of costly sardonyx
Sat smiling, babe in arm.

Or in a clear-walled city on the sea,
Near gilded organ-pipes, her hair
Wound with white roses, slept St Cecily;
An angel looked at her.

---

One was the Tishbite whom the raven fed,
As when he stood on Carmel-steeps,
With one arm stretched out bare, and mocked and said,
'Come cry aloud–he sleeps.'

Tall, eager, lean and strong, his cloak windborne
Behind, his forehead heavenly-bright
From the clear marble pouring glorious scorn,
Lit as with inner light.

One was Olympias: the floating snake
Rolled round her ancles, round her waist
Knotted, and folded once about her neck,
Her perfect lips to taste

Round by the shoulder moved: she seeming blythe
Declined her head: on every side
The dragon's curves melted and mingled with
The woman's youthful pride

Of rounded limbs.'

*1842* dropped this. Elijah, *1 Kings* xviii 27; 'Olympias was the mother of Alexander the Great, and devoted to the Orphic rites' (T.). T. altered the thirteenth line to 'Down from the shoulder . . .' (*Eversley*).

94. *tracts of pasture*] *1842*; yellow pastures *1832*.

95. T. comments: 'The Parisian jewellers apply graduated degrees of heat to the sardonyx, by which the original colour is changed to various colours. They imitate thus, among other things, bunches of grapes with green tendrils.'

*96 ^ 7*] Or Venus in a snowy shell alone,
Deepshadowed in the glassy brine,
Moonlike glowed double on the blue, and shone
A naked shape divine. *1832*

*Heath MS* has stanzas following the 'maid-mother' stanza:
Behind her rose blue hills, and at her feet
The star-led Kings of old Cologne
Laid myrrh, laid gold, laid precious oils, and sweet
Incense before her throne.

Or thronging all one porch of Paradise
 A group of Houris bowed to see
The dying Islamite, with hands and eyes
 That said, We wait for thee.

Or mythic Uther's deeply-wounded son
 In some fair space of sloping greens
Lay, dozing in the vale of Avalon,
 And watched by weeping queens.

Or hollowing one hand against his ear,
 To list a foot-fall, ere he saw
The wood-nymph, stayed the Ausonian king to hear
 Of wisdom and of law.

Or over hills with peaky tops engrailed,
 And many a tract of palm and rice,

Or shamed Tarpeia mused with head-decline,
 As one whom her own soul condemns,
In caverns of the dark Capitoline,
 Hung round with baleful gems.

Arthur Hallam wrote to T., 10 Oct. 1832 (*Mem.* i 90): 'I hear Tennant has written to dissuade you from publishing "Kriemhild," "Tarpeia" (in the *Fair Women*). Don't be humbugged, they are very good.' See ll. 109–116*n.*

*101–4*] *1842* (*see l. 103n*); *not 1832.*

*103. hands*] *1843*; heads *1842*.

*105–8*] *1842*; Or that deepwounded child of Pendragon
 Mid misty woods on sloping greens
Dozed in the valley of Avilion,
 Tended by crownèd queens. *1832*

Cp. *Morte d'Arthur* (p. 585).

*109–16*] *1842* (*see ll. 110, 111n*);
Or blue-eyed Kriemhilt from a craggy hold,
 Athwart the lightgreen rows of vine,
Poured blazing hoards of Nibelungen gold,
 Down to the gulfy Rhine. *1832*

See ll. 96 ∧ 7*n*.

*110. list*] *1843*; listen for *1842*.

*111. Ausonian*] *1850*; Tuscan *1842–8*. The nymph is 'Egeria, who gave the laws to Numa Pompilius' (T.). The story is told in Rollin's *Ancient History*, of which a copy was at Somersby (*Lincoln*).

*113. engrailed*: 'heraldic term for serrated' (H.T.). Cp. *Pierced through* 40: 'With semblance of the peaky wave engrailed'. T.'s is the earliest use of *peaky* in *OED*.

The throne of Indian Cama slowly sailed
 A summer fanned with spice.

Or sweet Europa's mantle blew unclasped,
 From off her shoulder backward borne:
From one hand drooped a crocus: one hand grasped
 The mild bull's golden horn.

Or else flushed Ganymede, his rosy thigh
 Half-buried in the Eagle's down,
Sole as a flying star shot through the sky
 Above the pillared town.

Nor these alone: but every legend fair
 Which the supreme Caucasian mind
Carved out of Nature for itself, was there,
 Not less than life, designed.

* * * *

* * * *

*115. Cama*: T. comments: 'The Hindu God of young love, son of Brahma'. For Cama, or Camdeo, and his 'wingèd throne', see *Love* (p. 244), and *Love* (p. 146) where T. quotes Sir William Jones's *Hymn to Camdeo*.

*117*] *1842*; Europa's scarf blew in an arch, unclasped, *1832*.

*118. off her*] *1842*; her bare *1832*.

*120 ∧ 21*] He through the streaming crystal swam, and rolled
 Ambrosial breaths that seemed to float
In lightwreathed curls. She from the ripple cold
 Updrew her sandalled foot. *1832*

*124. Above*] *1842*; Over *1832*.

*125*] *1842*; Not these alone: but many a legend fair, *1832*.

*126. Caucasian*: Indo-European (an early nineteenth-century sense).

*128*] *1842*; Broidered in screen and blind. *1832*. After this line, *1832* had:

So that my soul beholding in her pride
 All these, from room to room did pass;
And all things that she saw, she multiplied,
 A manyfacèd glass;

And, being both the sower and the seed,
 Remaining in herself became
All that she saw, Madonna, Ganymede,
  Or the Asiatic dame–

Still changing, as a lighthouse in the night
 Changeth athwart the gleaming main,
From red to yellow, yellow to pale white,
 Then back to red again.

Then in the towers I placed great bells that swung,
  Moved of themselves, with silver sound;
And with choice paintings of wise men I hung
    The royal dais round.

For there was Milton like a seraph strong,
  Beside him Shakespeare bland and mild;
And there the world-worn Dante grasped his song,
    And somewhat grimly smiled.

And there the Ionian father of the rest;
  A million wrinkles carved his skin;

'From change to change four times within the womb
  The brain is moulded,' she began,
'So through all phases of all thought I come
    Into the perfect man.

'All nature widens upward: evermore
  The simpler essence lower lies.
More complex is more perfect, owning more
    Discourse, more widely wise.

'I take possession of men's minds and deeds.
  I live in all things great and small.
I dwell apart, holding no forms of creeds,
    But contemplating all.'

T. made the following revisions (*Eversley*): l. [13] 'From shape to shape at first within the womb'. l. [15] *So*] And. l. [16] *Into*] Unto. Lines [21–4] became ll. 209–12; and ll. [13–20] became ll. 193–204 (until revised in *1851*). *H.Lpr 182* includes another version of ll. [10–12]:

From hue to hue, from glow to glow;
O'er gleaming seas the pilot knows the light
  And all the death below.

The scientific ideas in ll. [13–20] are well discussed by J. Killham (*Tennyson and 'The Princess'*, 1958, pp. 234–41). 'The discovery of the fourfold resemblances of the foetal human brain to the brains of other vertebrates was made by Friedrich Tiedemann.' Tennyson 'sought to exorcise those [doubts] raised by Tiedemann's theory by making the erring Soul foolishly base its own hubristic confidence upon it'.

*129*] *See ll. 21–52n.* *Then*] *1842*; Up *1832*.

*133–4. For . . . him*] *1842*; There deephaired Milton like an angel tall
  Stood limnèd, *1832*

*135–6*] *1842*; Grim Dante pressed his lips, and from the wall
  The bald blind Homer smiled. *1832*

*137–64*] *1842*; And underneath freshcarved in cedarwood,
  Somewhat alike in form and face,
The Genii of every climate stood,
  All brothers of one race:

A hundred winters snowed upon his breast,
From cheek and throat and chin.

Above, the fair hall-ceiling stately-set
Many an arch high up did lift,
And angels rising and descending met
With interchange of gift.

Below was all mosaic choicely planned
With cycles of the human tale
Of this wide world, the times of every land
So wrought, they will not fail.

The people here, a beast of burden slow,
Toiled onward, pricked with goads and stings;
Here played, a tiger, rolling to and fro
The heads and crowns of kings;

Here rose, an athlete, strong to break or bind
All force in bonds that might endure,
And here once more like some sick man declined,
And trusted any cure.

But over these she trod: and those great bells
Began to chime. She took her throne:
She sat betwixt the shining Oriels,
To sing her songs alone.

---

Angels who sway the seasons by their art,
And mould all shapes in earth and sea;
And with great effort build the human heart
From earliest infancy.

And in the sunpierced Oriel's coloured flame
Immortal Michael Angelo
Looked down, bold Luther, largebrowed Verulam,
The king of those who know.

Cervantes, the bright face of Calderon,
Robed David touching holy strings,
The Halicarnasseän, and alone,
Alfred the flower of kings,

Isaïah with fierce Ezekiel,
Swarth Moses by the Coptic sea,
Plato, Petrarca, Livy, and Raphaël,
And eastern Confutzee: *1832*

A fragment in *H.Nbk 5* shows that T. thought also of including Pyrrho, Averröes, Virgil, and Cicero.

*137–40.* Cp. the statue of Homer in Pope's *Temple of Fame* 185: 'His Silver Beard wav'd gently o'er his Breast'.

And through the topmost Oriels' coloured flame
Two godlike faces gazed below;
Plato the wise, and large-browed Verulam,
The first of those who know.

And all those names, that in their motion were
Full-welling fountain-heads of change,
Betwixt the slender shafts were blazoned fair
In diverse raiment strange:

Through which the lights, rose, amber, emerald, blue,
Flushed in her temples and her eyes,
And from her lips, as morn from Memnon, drew
Rivers of melodies.

No nightingale delighteth to prolong
Her low preamble all alone,
More than my soul to hear her echoed song
Throb through the ribbèd stone;

Singing and murmuring in her feastful mirth,
Joying to feel herself alive,
Lord over Nature, Lord of the visible earth,
Lord of the senses five;

Communing with herself: 'All these are mine,
And let the world have peace or wars,
'Tis one to me.' She–when young night divine
Crowned dying day with stars,

*161–4*] *See ll. 137–64n for the placing in 1832.*
*164. 1832* note: '*Il maëstro di color chi sanno*–Dante, *Inferno* iii'. T. remarks that this praise of Francis Bacon (Lord Verulam) was Dante's praise of Aristotle. (*Inferno* iv 131.)
*165*] *1842*; And many more, that in their lifetime were *1832*.
*167. Betwixt . . . were*] *1842*; Between the stone shafts glimmered, *1832*.
*171. Memnon*: the statue that made music when touched by the sun. Cp. *A Fragment* 16 (p. 290).
*173–4.* Adapted from *Sonnet* [*Check every outflash*] 9: 'The nightingale, with long and low preamble'.
*181–3*] *1842*; As some rich tropic mountain, that infolds
All change, from flats of scattered palms
Sloping through five great zones of climate, holds
His head in snows and calms –

Full of her own delight and nothing else,
My vainglorious, gorgeous soul
Sat throned between the shining oriels,
In pomp beyond control;

Making sweet close of his delicious toils–
Lit light in wreaths and anadems,
And pure quintessences of precious oils
In hollowed moons of gems,

To mimic heaven; and clapt her hands and cried,
'I marvel if my still delight
In this great house so royal-rich, and wide,
Be flattered to the height.

With piles of flavorous fruits in basket-twine
Of gold, upheapèd, crushing down
Muskscented blooms–all taste–grape, gourd or pine–
In bunch, or singlegrown–

Our growths, and such as brooding Indian heats
Make out of crimson blossoms deep,
Ambrosial pulps and juices, sweets from sweets
Sunchanged, when seawinds sleep.

With graceful chalices of curious wine,
Wonders of art–and costly jars,
And bossèd salvers. Ere young night divine *1832*

*186. anadems*: 'crowns' (T.). H.T. compares Shelley, *Adonais* 94: 'the wreath upon him, like an anadem'.

*186–92*] *1842*; She lit white streams of dazzling gas,
And soft and fragrant flames of precious oils
In moons of purple glass

Ranged on the fretted woodwork to the ground.
Thus her intense untold delight,
In deep or vivid colour, smell and sound,
Was flattered day and night. *1832*

*1832* continued with a note (omitted in *1842*): 'If the Poem were not already too long, I should have inserted in the text the following stanzas, expressive of the joy wherewith the soul contemplated the results of astronomical experiment. In the centre of the four quadrangles rose an immense tower.

Hither, when all the deep unsounded skies
Shuddered with silent stars, she clomb,
And as with optic glasses her keen eyes
Pierced through the mystic dome,

Regions of lucid matter taking forms,
Brushes of fire, hazy gleams,
Clusters and beds of worlds, and bee-like swarms
Of suns, and starry streams.

She saw the snowy poles of moonless Mars,
That marvellous round of milky light
Below Orion, and those double stars
Whereof the one more bright

Is circled by the other, &c.'

(J. W. Croker, *QR*, April 1833, as in l. 93, ridiculed T.'s 'ingenious device . . . for reconciling the rigour of criticism with the indulgence of parental partiality'.) H.T. quotes T.'s revision of the last stanza, necessitated by astronomical discovery in 1877:

She saw the snowy poles and moons of Mars,
That mystic field of drifted light
In mid Orion and the married stars . . .

T. made this revision in a copy of W. J. Rolfe's edition of *Select Poems* (Boston, 1885, at *Lincoln*). The allusion is to the theory of the nebulous matter diffused throughout the universe; 'lucid', 'matter', and 'forms' are all scientific terms. Cp. *The Princess* ii 101–4 (p. 762). *H.Lpr 182* has deleted stanzas leading up to those on astronomy:

Yet saw she shadowed in her vast abode
The secret entities of Faith,
Those ethnic instincts of Eternal God
And epic dreams of Death.

She saw them blind and vague in form and face,
Not yet mixt up with human deeds,
But always waiting in a dusky place
To clothe themselves in creeds.

And likewise many a fair philosophy
From Plato to the German, wrought
In mystic groups as far as this might be
That served the central thought.

Yet saw she Earth laid open. Furthermore
How the strong Ages had their will,
A range of Giants breaking down the shore
And heaving up the hill.

And likewise every life that Nature made,
What yet is left and what is gone
To where the classes vanish, shade by shade,
Life and half-life, to none.

And likewise every Science fair displayed
By which men work with Nature's power.
And in the centre of the courts I made
With toil a wondrous tower,

To which, when all the deep unsounded skies . . .

The fourth stanza was adapted to form *Ode on Wellington* 259–61:

'O all things fair to sate my various eyes!
O shapes and hues that please me well!
O silent faces of the Great and Wise,
My Gods, with whom I dwell!

'O God-like isolation which art mine,
I can but count thee perfect gain,
What time I watch the darkening droves of swine
That range on yonder plain.

'In filthy sloughs they roll a prurient skin,
They graze and wallow, breed and sleep;
And oft some brainless devil enters in,
And drives them to the deep.'

Then of the moral instinct would she prate
And of the rising from the dead,
As hers by right of full-accomplished Fate;
And at the last she said:

'I take possession of man's mind and deed.
I care not what the sects may brawl.
I sit as God holding no form of creed,
But contemplating all.'

* * * *
* * * *

For though the Giant Ages heave the hill
And break the shore, and evermore
Make and break, and work their will.

With the fifth stanza, cp. *In Memoriam* lv (p. 910). *H.Nbk 4* has a further astronomical stanza between the second and third of *1832*:

Bright points the centre of a hazy shroud,
Cold Uranus, cold Jupiter,
Girthed eight times round with slowly streaming cloud
And through his red-brown air

Sparkled the snowy poles . . .

*188.* 'Gems hollowed out for lamps' (H.T.).

*193–204*] *1851; not 1832; 1842–50 had the revised text of ll.* [*13–20*] *of the lines from 1832 quoted at l. 128n* (*retaining* Into, *and with* moulded] *modelled*)

*205–8*] *1842; not 1832.*

*209–12*] *1850; not 1832* (*see l. 128n*);

'I take possession of men's minds and deeds.
I live in all things great and small.
I sit apart, holding no forms of creeds,
But contemplating all.' *1842–8*

Full oft the riddle of the painful earth
  Flashed through her as she sat alone,
Yet not the less held she her solemn mirth,
  And intellectual throne.

And so she throve and prospered: so three years
  She prospered: on the fourth she fell,
Like Herod, when the shout was in his ears,
  Struck through with pangs of hell.

Lest she should fail and perish utterly,
  God, before whom ever lie bare
The abysmal deeps of Personality,
  Plagued her with sore despair.

When she would think, where'er she turned her sight
  The airy hand confusion wrought,
Wrote, 'Mene, mene,' and divided quite
  The kingdom of her thought.

Deep dread and loathing of her solitude
  Fell on her, from which mood was born
Scorn of herself; again, from out that mood
  Laughter at her self-scorn.

*213. Full oft*] *1842*; Sometimes *1832.*
*216–7*] *1850*; . . . throne / Of fullsphered contemplation. So three years *1832–48.*
*218. prospered:*] *1850*; throve, but *1832–48.*
*219–20. Acts* xii 21–3: 'And upon a set day Herod, arrayed in royal apparel, sat upon his throne, and made an oration unto them. And the people gave a shout, saying, It is the voice of a god, and not of a man. And immediately the angel of the Lord smote him, because he gave not God the glory: and he was eaten of worms, and gave up the ghost.'
*223.* T. points out that this was from Arthur Hallam's *Theodicaea Novissima*: 'God's election, with whom alone rest the abysmal secrets of personality' (Motter, pp. 210–11). Cp. *Psalm* cxxxix 1–4: 'O Lord, thou hast searched me and known me . . .'
*227.* As at the feast of Belshazzar, *Daniel* v 23–7: who 'hast praised the gods of silver, and gold, of brass, iron, wood, and stone, which see not, nor hear, nor know: and the God in whose hand thy breath is, and whose are all thy ways, hast thou not glorified . . . This is the interpretation of the thing: MENE; God hath numbered thy kingdom, and finished it. TEKEL; Thou art weighed in the balances, and art found wanting. PERES; Thy kingdom is divided . . .'
*232 ∧ 3*] 'Who hath drawn dry the fountains of delight,
  That from my deep heart everywhere
Moved in my blood and dwelt, as power and might
  Abode in Sampson's hair? *1832*

'What! is not this my place of strength,' she said,
'My spacious mansion built for me,
Whereof the strong foundation-stones were laid
Since my first memory?'

But in dark corners of her palace stood
Uncertain shapes; and unawares
On white-eyed phantasms weeping tears of blood,
And horrible nightmares,

And hollow shades enclosing hearts of flame,
And, with dim fretted foreheads all,
On corpses three-months-old at noon she came,
That stood against the wall.

A spot of dull stagnation, without light
Or power of movement, seemed my soul,
'Mid onward-sloping motions infinite
Making for one sure goal.

A still salt pool, locked in with bars of sand,
Left on the shore; that hears all night
The plunging seas draw backward from the land
Their moon-led waters white.

A star that with the choral starry dance
Joined not, but stood, and standing saw
The hollow orb of moving Circumstance
Rolled round by one fixed law.

*239.* Cp. another guilty soul, that of Faustus, in Marlowe's *Dr Faustus* 1386–8: 'I would weep, but the devil draws in my tears. Gush forth blood, instead of tears.' Also Shelley, *Prologue to Hellas* 88: 'Whose pores wept tears of blood'.

*241.* Beckford's *Vathek*, which has a palace, mentions spirits with hearts like Soliman, 'discerned through his bosom, which was as transparent as crystal, his heart enveloped in flames' (A. C. Howell, *SP* xxxiii (1936) 517). But when Arthur Coleridge suggested this influence to Tennyson, he replied: 'No, merely spectral visions' (*Tennyson and His Friends*, p. 264). On possible echoes of *Vathek* see A. A. Mendilow, 'Tennyson's Palace of the Sinful Muse', *Scripta Hierosolymitana* xvii (1966) 164–5.

*242. fretted*: 'worm-fretted' (T.).

*247. onward-*] *1842*; downward- *1832*.

*255.* T. comments: 'Some old writer calls the Heavens "the Circumstance" .... Here it is more or less a play on the word.' Cp. Milton's astronomy: 'the hollow Universal Orb', *PL* vii 257.

Back on herself her serpent pride had curled.
'No voice,' she shrieked in that lone hall,
'No voice breaks through the stillness of this world:
One deep, deep silence all!'

She, mouldering with the dull earth's mouldering sod,
Inwrapt tenfold in slothful shame,
Lay there exilèd from eternal God,
Lost to her place and name;

And death and life she hated equally,
And nothing saw, for her despair,
But dreadful time, dreadful eternity,
No comfort anywhere;

Remaining utterly confused with fears,
And ever worse with growing time,
And ever unrelieved by dismal tears,
And all alone in crime:

Shut up as in a crumbling tomb, girt round
With blackness as a solid wall,
Far off she seemed to hear the dully sound
Of human footsteps fall.

As in strange lands a traveller walking slow,
In doubt and great perplexity,
A little before moon-rise hears the low
Moan of an unknown sea;

And knows not if it be thunder, or a sound
Of rocks thrown down, or one deep cry

*257.* Probably referring to the scorpion's stinging itself to death. T. calls a scorpion a 'serpent' of the mind in *The Passions* 16. Cp. Byron, *The Giaour* 422–3: 'The Mind, that broods o'er guilty woes, / Is like the Scorpion girt by fire.'

*277–84.* Cp. a fragment of the poem in *H.Nbk 4*:

And as a lated man that makes all night
For some warm town, [but?] dazzled and cold,
Finds but a wreath of straw that ploughmen light
Upon a windy wold
To scorch the glebe and he has far to go–
Even so she seemèd to have strayed from love,
The central [?] light of knowledge; [even so?]
She had no strength to move.

*281. a*] *1842*; the *1832*.

*282. rocks*] *1850*; stones *1832–48*.

Of great wild beasts; then thinketh, 'I have found
A new land, but I die.'

She howled aloud, 'I am on fire within.
There comes no murmur of reply.
What is it that will take away my sin,
And save me lest I die?'

So when four years were wholly finishèd,
She threw her royal robes away.
'Make me a cottage in the vale,' she said,
'Where I may mourn and pray.

'Yet pull not down my palace towers, that are
So lightly, beautifully built:
Perchance I may return with others there
When I have purged my guilt.'

# 168 The May Queen

Published *1832*, the *Conclusion* being added *1842*. 'An early poem first written in Lincolnshire' (H.T.). Arthur Hallam's poem to T., *Those Gothic windows* (*Mem.* i 66), may allude to *New-Year's Eve* 26; cp. 'Beauty lurk'd for thee in the long gray fields'. If so, T.'s poem was probably written by 1830.

You must wake and call me early, call me early, mother dear;
Tomorrow 'ill be the happiest time of all the glad New-year;
Of all the glad New-year, mother, the maddest merriest day;
For I'm to be Queen o' the May, mother, I'm to be Queen o' the
May.

There's many a black black eye, they say, but none so bright as mine;
There's Margaret and Mary, there's Kate and Caroline:
But none so fair as little Alice in all the land they say,
So I'm to be Queen o' the May, mother, I'm to be Queen o' the
May.

I sleep so sound all night, mother, that I shall never wake,
If you do not call me loud when the day begins to break:
But I must gather knots of flowers, and buds and garlands gay,
For I'm to be Queen o' the May, mother, I'm to be Queen o' the
May.

288. *And . . . lest*] *1842*; Dying the death *1832*.
¶ 168.*2*. *glad*] *1842*; blythe *1832*.
*10*. *you*] *1842*; ye *1832*.

As I came up the valley whom think ye should I see,
But Robin leaning on the bridge beneath the hazel-tree?
He thought of that sharp look, mother, I gave him yesterday,
But I'm to be Queen o' the May, mother, I'm to be Queen o' the May.

He thought I was a ghost, mother, for I was all in white,
And I ran by him without speaking, like a flash of light.
They call me cruel-hearted, but I care not what they say,
For I'm to be Queen o' the May, mother, I'm to be Queen o' the May.

They say he's dying all for love, but that can never be:
They say his heart is breaking, mother–what is that to me?
There's many a bolder lad 'ill woo me any summer day,
And I'm to be Queen o' the May, mother, I'm to be Queen o' the May.

Little Effie shall go with me tomorrow to the green,
And you'll be there, too, mother, to see me made the Queen;
For the shepherd lads on every side 'ill come from far away,
And I'm to be Queen o' the May, mother, I'm to be Queen o' the May.

The honeysuckle round the porch has woven its wavy bowers,
And by the meadow-trenches blow the faint sweet cuckoo-flowers;
And the wild marsh-marigold shines like fire in swamps and hollows gray,
And I'm to be Queen o' the May, mother, I'm to be Queen o' the May.

The night-winds come and go, mother, upon the meadow-grass,
And the happy stars above them seem to brighten as they pass;
There will not be a drop of rain the whole of the livelong day,
And I'm to be Queen o' the May, mother, I'm to be Queen o' the May.

All the valley, mother, 'ill be fresh and green and still,
And the cowslip and the crowfoot are over all the hill,
And the rivulet in the flowery dale 'ill merrily glance and play,
For I'm to be Queen o' the May, mother, I'm to be Queen o' the May.

So you must wake and call me early, call me early, mother dear,
Tomorrow 'ill be the happiest time of all the glad New-year:
Tomorrow 'ill be of all the year the maddest merriest day,
For I'm to be Queen o' the May, mother, I'm to be Queen o' the May.

### NEW-YEAR'S EVE

If you're waking call me early, call me early, mother dear,
For I would see the sun rise upon the glad New-year.

*30.* A separate jotting in *H.Nbk 3*: 'And by the meadow runnel blows the faint sweet cuckooflower'.

It is the last New-year that I shall ever see,
Then you may lay me low i' the mould and think no more of me.

Tonight I saw the sun set: he set and left behind
The good old year, the dear old time, and all my peace of mind;
And the New-year's coming up, mother, but I shall never see
The blossom on the blackthorn, the leaf upon the tree.

Last May we made a crown of flowers: we had a merry day;
Beneath the hawthorn on the green they made me Queen of May;
And we danced about the may-pole and in the hazel copse,
Till Charles's Wain came out above the tall white chimney-tops.

There's not a flower on all the hills: the frost is on the pane:
I only wish to live till the snowdrops come again:
I wish the snow would melt and the sun come out on high:
I long to see a flower so before the day I die.

The building rook 'll caw from the windy tall elm-tree,
And the tufted plover pipe along the fallow lea,
And the swallow 'ill come back again with summer o'er the wave,
But I shall lie alone, mother, within the mouldering grave.

Upon the chancel-casement, and upon that grave of mine,
In the early early morning the summer sun 'ill shine,
Before the red cock crows from the farm upon the hill,
When you are warm-asleep, mother, and all the world is still.

When the flowers come again, mother, beneath the waning light
You'll never see me more in the long gray fields at night;
When from the dry dark wold the summer airs blow cool
On the oat-grass and the sword-grass, and the bulrush in the pool.

You'll bury me, my mother, just beneath the hawthorn shade,
And you'll come sometimes and see me where I am lowly laid.
I shall not forget you, mother, I shall hear you when you pass,
With your feet above my head in the long and pleasant grass.

I have been wild and wayward, but you'll forgive me now;
You'll kiss me, my own mother, and forgive me ere I go;
Nay, nay, you must not weep, nor let your grief be wild,
You should not fret for me, mother, you have another child.

If I can I'll come again, mother, from out my resting-place;
Though you'll not see me, mother, I shall look upon your face;
Though I cannot speak a word, I shall harken what you say,
And be often, often with you when you think I'm far away.

Goodnight, goodnight, when I have said goodnight for evermore,
And you see me carried out from the threshold of the door;

*New-Year's Eve*

*4. you*] *1842*; ye *1832 passim except in ll. 24, 44, 52.*

*8. blossom on*] *1842*; may upon *1832*. T. comments: 'How did this reading get into the original text? The May was so late that there was only blackthorn in May.'

*34. and . . . go*] *1850*; upon my cheek and brow *1832–48*.

Don't let Effie come to see me till my grave be growing green:
She'll be a better child to you than ever I have been.

She'll find my garden-tools upon the granary floor:
Let her take 'em: they are hers: I shall never garden more:
But tell her, when I'm gone, to train the rosebush that I set
About the parlour-window and the box of mignonette.

Goodnight, sweet mother: call me before the day is born.
All night I lie awake, but I fall asleep at morn;
But I would see the sun rise upon the glad New-year,
So, if you're waking, call me, call me early, mother dear.

### CONCLUSION

I thought to pass away before, and yet alive I am;
And in the fields all round I hear the bleating of the lamb.
How sadly, I remember, rose the morning of the year!
To die before the snowdrop came, and now the violet's here.

O sweet is the new violet, that comes beneath the skies,
And sweeter is the young lamb's voice to me that cannot rise,
And sweet is all the land about, and all the flowers that blow,
And sweeter far is death than life to me that long to go.

It seemed so hard at first, mother, to leave the blessèd sun,
And now it seems as hard to stay, and yet His will be done!
But still I think it can't be long before I find release;
And that good man, the clergyman, has told me words of peace.

O blessings on his kindly voice and on his silver hair!
And blessings on his whole life long, until he meet me there!
O blessings on his kindly heart and on his silver head!
A thousand times I blest him, as he knelt beside my bed.

He taught me all the mercy, for he showed me all the sin.
Now, though my lamp was lighted late, there's One will let me in:
Nor would I now be well, mother, again if that could be,
For my desire is but to pass to Him that died for me.

I did not hear the dog howl, mother, or the death-watch beat,
There came a sweeter token when the night and morning meet:
But sit beside my bed, mother, and put your hand in mine,
And Effie on the other side, and I will tell the sign.

49. *before . . . born*] *1842*; when it begins to dawn *1832*.

*Conclusion*

11. *I . . . long*] *1843*; it can't be long, mother, *1842*.
12. *has told me*] *1843*; he preaches *1842*.
17. *taught . . . showed*] *1850*; *transposed 1842–48*.
18. The foolish virgins, *Matthew* XXV 1–13.
21. *death-watch*: 'a beetle . . . whose ticking is supposed to forebode death' (T.).

All in the wild March-morning I heard the angels call;
It was when the moon was setting, and the dark was over all;
The trees began to whisper, and the wind began to roll,
And in the wild March-morning I heard them call my soul.

For lying broad awake I thought of you and Effie dear;
I saw you sitting in the house, and I no longer here;
With all my strength I prayed for both, and so I felt resigned,
And up the valley came a swell of music on the wind.

I thought that it was fancy, and I listened in my bed,
And then did something speak to me–I know not what was said;
For great delight and shuddering took hold of all my mind,
And up the valley came again the music on the wind.

But you were sleeping; and I said, 'It's not for them: it's mine.'
And if it come three times, I thought, I take it for a sign.
And once again it came, and close beside the window-bars,
Then seemed to go right up to Heaven and die among the stars.

So now I think my time is near. I trust it is. I know
The blessèd music went that way my soul will have to go.
And for myself, indeed, I care not if I go today.
But, Effie, you must comfort *her* when I am past away.

And say to Robin a kind word, and tell him not to fret;
There's many a worthier than I, would make him happy yet.
If I had lived–I cannot tell–I might have been his wife;
But all these things have ceased to be, with my desire of life.

O look! the sun begins to rise, the heavens are in a glow;
He shines upon a hundred fields, and all of them I know.
And there I move no longer now, and there his light may shine–
Wild flowers in the valley for other hands than mine.

O sweet and strange it seems to me, that ere this day is done
The voice, that now is speaking, may be beyond the sun–
For ever and for ever with those just souls and true–
And what is life, that we should moan? why make we such ado?

For ever and for ever, all in a blessèd home–
And there to wait a little while till you and Effie come–
To lie within the light of God, as I lie upon your breast–
And the wicked cease from troubling, and the weary are at rest.

*38. come*] *1884*; comes *1842–83*.
*39. window-bars*: 'Looks as if brought in for the rhyme. I was thinking of our old house, where all the upper windows had iron bars' (T.).
*46. a*] *1870; not 1842–69*.
*60. Job* iii 17: 'There the wicked cease from troubling; and there the weary be at rest.' Contrast the context of Christian acceptance with that of Job's bitter wish that he had died at birth.

# 169 *The Hesperides

Published *1832*, not reprinted. It was harshly criticized by reviewers, especially by J. W. Croker, in *QR*, April 1833. Also over-complication of metre and rhyme scheme influenced T. in suppressing many of his early poems. H.T. printed it, *Mem.* i 61–5 and in the *Eversley* notes, with revised punctuation and heavy capitalization; the text below is *1832*, with variants from H.T. noted. It was reprinted 'in consequence of a talk that I had with him, in which he regretted that he had done away with it from among his "Juvenilia".' *Heath MS* (all variants are below) includes it 'in the shape in which originally written'. It was recited Oct. 1830 (H. Alford, *Life*, 1873, p. 61), and is in *T.Nbk 23* (1830). The daughters of Hesperus, who lived in the west where the sun sets, guarded the golden apples given by Earth to Hera; Hercules slew the guardian dragon and stole the apples. On the symbolism, see Paden (pp. 154–5). He argues that T. was influenced by the religious mythologizing of G. S. Faber (see l. 28*n*), 'writing a mystic and allusive song for a hierophant: "All things are not told to all".' The apples would be associated with Eden (Hesperean fruit is mentioned in *Paradise Lost*); and the guarding dragon was an antithetical type of the Satanic serpent. The theft by Hercules may be linked with Christ; cp. the comparison of Christ to Hercules in *Paradise Regained* iv 565, and l. 69: 'Lest the old wound of the world be healèd'. Paden sums up: 'Among so many competing symbols, it would not be strange if Tennyson became slightly unintelligible.' There was a copy at Somersby (*Lincoln*) of Faber's *Horae Mosaicae* (1818 edn). It refers to 'the garden of the Hesperides, an evident tradition of the Mosaical Paradise', and it quotes Ralegh–'the prophecies, that Christ should break the serpent's head, and conquer the power of hell, occasioned the fables of Hercules killing the serpent of the Hesperides, and descending into hell' (i 81). Douglas Bush, *Major British Writers* (1959) ii 382, observes: 'Tennyson may have seen the curious book by Edward Davies, *Celtic Researches* (1804), which says (p. 193): "These apples were metaphorical, and pointed at science, discipline, or mystery".' T. later owned Davies's *Mythology of the British Druids* (*Lincoln*). T.'s prologue is based on the Periplus of the Carthaginian Hanno, who navigated the west coast of Africa in the fifth century B.C. Bush points out T.'s source: he 'presumably used *The Voyage of Hanno*, translated T. Falconer (1797); Falconer has, with much else, remarks on the island of the Hesperides'. To Bush's excellent notes may be added that the map in Falconer actually marks *olim Hesperides Insulae*, and that Falconer may have influenced a basic notion of the Song, that the fruit can be guarded only by ceaseless singing. T. may here owe something to Falconer's gloss (from Bruce's *Travels*) on Hanno's hearing music: 'Dancing, singing, and music, at once exhilarate the mind, and contribute, by alarming the beasts of prey, to keep their flocks in safety.' Diodorus Siculus iv 26 had discussed in some detail the belief that the golden apples were really valuable flocks to be guarded. The

*English Encyclopaedia* (1802), of which a copy was at Somersby (*Lincoln*), says: 'Pliny and Solinus will have the dragon to be no other than an arm of the sea, wherewith the garden was encompassed, and which defended the entrance thereof; and Varro supposes, that the golden apples were nothing but sheep.' See also G. R. Stange's argument that the poem is 'a symbolic statement of the situation of the artist' (*PMLA* 1952, reprinted in *Critical Essays on Tennyson*, ed. J. Killham, 1960).

Hesperus and his daughters three,
That sing about the golden tree.
*Comus* [982–3]

The Northwind fallen, in the newstarrèd night
Zidonian Hanno, voyaging beyond
The hoary promontory of Soloë
Past Thymiaterion, in calmèd bays,
Between the southern and the western Horn,
Heard neither warbling of the nightingale,
Nor melody o' the Lybian lotusflute
Blown seaward from the shore; but from a slope
That ran bloombright into the Atlantic blue,
Beneath a highland leaning down a weight
Of cliffs, and zoned below with cedarshade,
Came voices, like the voices in a dream,
Continuous, till he reached the outer sea.

SONG

I

The golden apple, the golden apple, the hallowed
fruit,

¶ 169.*1. newstarrèd*] thickstarrèd *Heath MS.*
*2. voyaging beyond*] wandering beyond *Mem.*; wandering about *MS.*
*3. hoary*] heavy *Heath MS, Allen MS* (*presumably a slip*). Bush quotes Falconer: 'Soloeis, a promontory of Libya'; modern Cape Cantin in Morocco. T. derived the form 'Soloe' from the map in Falconer.
*4. in calmèd bays*] on the calmèd bay *MS. Thymiaterion*: Bush remarks that this was the name in Falconer's Greek text (Thymiaterium in his translation); modern Mehedia.
5] *Not MS.* Bush notes that the Horns are named in Falconer; modern Sherbro Sound and Bissagos Bay.
*8–11*] Blown seaward from the shore; but all night long
Among the wooded inland hills, upstood
Pillars of still white fire; and from a slope
Leafthick which flourished forth against the West
Under a purple highland, cedardark
Running bloombright into the Atlantic blue, *MS*
*13 ∧ 14*] Song of the Three Sisters *Mem.*

Guard it well, guard it warily,
Singing airily,
Standing about the charmèd root.
Round about all is mute,
As the snowfield on the mountain-peaks,
As the sandfield at the mountain-foot.
Crocodiles in briny creeks
Sleep and stir not: all is mute.
If ye sing not, if ye make false measure,
We shall lose eternal pleasure,
Worth eternal want of rest.
Laugh not loudly: watch the treasure
Of the wisdom of the west.
In a corner wisdom whispers. Five and three
(Let it not be preached abroad) make an awful
    mystery.
For the blossom unto threefold music bloweth;
Evermore it is born anew;

*19–30*] Save the summer westwind breathing
While we sing to left and right;
All is mute,
But the bloomful buds unsheathing
[5] In the middle of the night.
In the stillness the leaf gloometh,
The bough buddeth, the bud bloometh,
Bloom is changèd evermore into fruit,
Goldbright,
[*10*] The sunset yelloweth it in the light,
The rich dew melloweth it all the night,
The starbeam quickeneth,
The wind bloweth, *MS*

Cp. *The Lotos-Eaters* 70–9 (noting l. [7] above): 'Lo! in the middle of the wood, / The folded leaf is wooed from out the bud / With winds upon the branch, and there / Grows green and broad, and takes no care, / Sun-steeped at noon, and in the moon / Nightly dew-fed; and turning yellow / Falls, and floats adown the air. / Lo! sweetened with the summer light, / The full-juiced apple, waxing over-mellow, / Drops in a silent autumn night.' Cp. ll. 99–103 below, which presumably caused T. to drop the *MS* passage.

*21.* Suggested, as Bush says, by Falconer: 'another river . . . full of crocodiles'.

*28. Five and three*: making 8, the sacred ogdoad of the Faberian mysteries (Paden). The number is discussed in Jacob Bryant's *New System of Ancient Mythology* (1807 edn, iv 11–14), of which there was a copy at Somersby (*Lincoln*).

And the sap to threefold music floweth,
From the root
Drawn in the dark,
Up to the fruit,
Creeping under the fragrant bark,
Liquid gold, honeysweet, through and through.
Keen-eyed Sisters, singing airily,
Looking warily
Every way,
Guard the apple night and day,
Lest one from the East come and take it away.

II

Father Hesper, Father Hesper, watch, watch, ever
and aye,
Looking under silver hair with a silver eye.
Father, twinkle not thy stedfast sight;
Kingdoms lapse, and climates change, and races die;
Honour comes with mystery;
Hoarded wisdom brings delight.
Number, tell them over and number
How many the mystic fruittree holds,
Lest the redcombed dragon slumber
Rolled together in purple folds.
Look to him, father, lest he wink, and the golden
apple be stolen away,
For his ancient heart is drunk with overwatchings
night and day,

*32*] The bough thickneth,
The sap floweth, *MS*

*37*. T. accented this for H.T.: 'Líquid góld, hóneyswéet thró' and thró'' adding the note 'slow movement'.

*37 ∧ 8*] Westward hangeth the burnished fruit,
Eastward runneth the fangèd root,
'Tis fathomdeep, and deepens still
Far down: and the mighty boughs are upheld
From underneath the hollow hill
Cedarshadowy, purpledelled. *MS*

Cp. the second line with *The Devil and the Lady* III ii 41: 'the lowest fang o' the root.'

*44*. Hesperus as the evening star.

*45–8*] *Not MS.*

*50*. *mystic*] charmèd *MS*.

Round about the hallowed fruittree curled–
Sing away, sing aloud evermore in the wind, without stop,
Lest his scalèd eyelid drop,
For he is older than the world.
If he waken, we waken,
Rapidly levelling eager eyes.
If he sleep, we sleep,
Dropping the eyelid over the eyes.
If the golden apple be taken
The world will be overwise.
Five links, a golden chain, are we,
Hesper, the dragon, and sisters three,
Bound about the golden tree.

III

Father Hesper, Father Hesper, watch, watch, night and day,
Lest the old wound of the world be healèd,
The glory unsealèd,
The golden apple stolen away,
And the ancient secret revealèd.
Look from west to east along:
Father, old Himala weakens, Caucasus is bold and strong.
Wandering waters unto wandering waters call;
Let them clash together, foam and fall.
Out of watchings, out of wiles,
Comes the bliss of secret smiles.
All things are not told to all.
Half-round the mantling night is drawn,
Purplefringèd with even and dawn.
Hesper hateth Phosphor, evening hateth morn.

55. *hallowed*] golden *MS.*
56. T. accented this: 'Sing awáy, sing alóud evermóre in the wínd without stóp', adding the note 'Anapaest'.
59. T. accented 'hé . . . wé', and in l. 61.
62. *the eyes*] our eyes *MS.*
67. *Bound*] Round *MS.*
69. Cp. *Revelation* xiii 3 (a chapter which includes a dragon): 'and his deadly wound was healed: and all the world wondered after the beast'.
73–9] *Not MS.*
79–82] *1832 punctuation*; *Mem. has:* 'to all, / . . . is drawn. / . . . and dawn / . . . morn.'
82 ∧ 3] *MS omits* 'IV'.

IV

Every flower and every fruit the redolent breath
Of this warm seawind ripeneth,
Arching the billow in his sleep;
But the landwind wandereth,
Broken by the highland-steep,
Two streams upon the violet deep:
For the western sun and the western star,
And the low west wind, breathing afar,
The end of day and beginning of night
Make the apple holy and bright;
Holy and bright, round and full, bright and blest,
Mellowed in a land of rest;
Watch it warily day and night;
All good things are in the west.
Till midnoon the cool east light
Is shut out by the round of the tall hillbrow;
But when the fullfaced sunset yellowly
Stays on the flowering arch of the bough,
The luscious fruitage clustereth mellowly,
Goldenkernelled, goldencored,
Sunset-ripened above on the tree.
The world is wasted with fire and sword,
But the apple of gold hangs over the sea.
Five links, a golden chain, are we,
Hesper, the dragon, and sisters three,
Daughters three,
Bound about
All round about
The gnarlèd bole of the charmèd tree.

*84. this*] the *Mem.*

*88. upon the violet*] into the purple *MS.*

*92. Make*] Keep *MS.*

*96.* Cp. *Leonine Elegiacs* 13: 'The ancient poetess singeth, that Hesperus all things bringeth', i.e. Sappho (see p. 185). Also *Locksley Hall Sixty Years After* 185: 'Hesper, whom the poet called the Bringer home of all good things'.

*100. flowering*] flowerful *MS.*

*104–5.* Cp. Marvell, *Upon Appleton House* 323–8, on England's '*Paradise* of four Seas': 'But, to exclude the World, did guard / With watry if not flaming Sword; / What luckless Apple did we taste, / To make us Mortal, and thee waste?'

*109. Bound*] Round *MS.*

*111. bole of the charmèd*] golden *MS.*

The golden apple, the golden apple, the hallowed
 fruit,
Guard it well, guard it warily,
Watch it warily,
Singing airily,
Standing about the charmèd root.

# 170 The Lotos-Eaters

Published *1832*. The important revisions in *1842* were the addition of ll. 114–32 and the rewriting of ll. 150–73. Written 1830–32 (*Mem.* i 86); T. dated ll. 8, 11, 42, as 1830. The main source was *Odyssey* ix 82–104: 'We set foot on the land of the Lotus-eaters, who eat a flowery food. . . . So they went straightway and mingled with the Lotus-eaters, and the Lotus-eaters did not plan death for my comrades, but gave them of the lotus to taste. And whosoever of them ate of the honey-sweet fruit of the lotus, had no longer any wish to bring back word or to return, but there they were fain to abide among the Lotus-eaters, feeding on the lotus, and forgetful of their homeward way. These men, therefore, I brought back perforce to the ships, weeping.' T. jotted in *H.Nbk 4* (1831–2): 'Alzerbe's isle / Where dwelt the folk that lotos eat erewhile.' From Fairfax's translation of Tasso, *Jerusalem Delivered* XV xviii. T. was influenced by Washington Irving's *Columbus* (1828), the source of *Anacaona* (p. 283); Irving describes the idyllic life on Haiti. For T.'s interest in Islands of the Blest, see Paden (pp. 141–3). Cp. *The Hesperides* (p. 423), which mentions the 'lotus-flute'; and *The Sea-Fairies* (p. 254). Spenser was the major influence on the style and tone; note in particular the cave of Morpheus, *Faerie Queene* I i st. 41; the blandishments of Despair, I ix st. 40; the 'Idle lake' and its enervating island, II vi st. 10; and the mermaids and the Bower of Bliss, II xii st. 32. There are a few touches from James Thomson's Spenserian imitation, *The Castle of Indolence* I v–vi: 'And up the hills, on either side, a wood / Of blackening pines, ay waving to and fro, / Sent forth a sleepy horror through the blood; / And where this valley winded out, below, / The murmuring main was heard, and scarcely heard, to flow. // A pleasing land of drowsyhed it was: / Of dreams that wave before the half-shut eye; / And of gay castles in the clouds that pass, / For ever flushing round a summer sky: / There eke the soft delights, that witchingly / Instil a wanton sweetness through the breast, / And the calm pleasures always hovered nigh; / But whate'er smacked of noyance, or unrest, / Was far far off expelled from this delicious nest.' The earliest MS is *H.Nbk 3*, which breaks off at l. 98 (all variants are below, *A*). *H.Lpr 131* (*B*) is likewise not in T.'s hand. There is a copy in Arthur Hallam's hand at the *University of Hawaii*.

*112. the hallowed*] and hallowed *MS*.

'Courage!' he said, and pointed toward the land,
'This mounting wave will roll us shoreward soon.'
In the afternoon they came unto a land
In which it seemèd always afternoon.
All round the coast the languid air did swoon,
Breathing like one that hath a weary dream.
Full-faced above the valley stood the moon;
And like a downward smoke, the slender stream
Along the cliff to fall and pause and fall did seem.

A land of streams! some, like a downward smoke,
Slow-dropping veils of thinnest lawn, did go;
And some through wavering lights and shadows broke,
Rolling a slumbrous sheet of foam below.
They saw the gleaming river seaward flow
From the inner land: far off, three mountain-tops,
Three silent pinnacles of agèd snow,
Stood sunset-flushed: and, dewed with showery drops,
Up-clomb the shadowy pine above the woven copse.

The charmèd sunset lingered low adown
In the red West: through mountain clefts the dale
Was seen far inland, and the yellow down
Bordered with palm, and many a winding vale

¶ 170.*3*. T. says: '"The strand" was, I think, my first reading, but the no rhyme of "land" and "land" was lazier.'
*4. seemèd always*] always seemèd *A*.
*7*] *1842 and A*; Above the valley burned the golden moon; *1832*. J. M. Kemble wrote to W. B. Donne, 22 June 1833: 'Some d—— friend or other told him that the full moon was never seen while the sunset lingered in the West; which is a lie, for I have seen it in Spain, and in the Lotos Land too!' *W. B. Donne*, ed. C. B. Johnson (1905) p. 16. Cp. *The Hesperides* 99: 'the fullfaced sunset'.
*8*. T. says: 'Taken from the waterfall at Gavarnie, in the Pyrenees, when I was 20 or 21', as was l. 11.
*10–18*] *Not A*.
*11*. 'When I printed this, a critic informed me that "lawn" was the material used in theatres to imitate a waterfall, and graciously added, "Mr T. should not go to the boards of a theatre but to Nature herself for his suggestions." And I *had* gone to Nature herself' (*Mem*. i 259). Cp. Herrick, *Upon Julia's Washing Herself in the River* 5–6: 'As in the River Julia did, / Halfe with a Lawne of water hid.'
*14. river*] *1842*; river's *1832*.
*16*] *1842*; Three thundercloven thrones of oldest snow, *1832*.
*20. red*] flushed *A*.

And meadow, set with slender galingale;
A land where all things always seemed the same!
And round about the keel with faces pale,
Dark faces pale against that rosy flame,
The mild-eyed melancholy Lotos-eaters came.

Branches they bore of that enchanted stem,
Laden with flower and fruit, whereof they gave
To each, but whoso did receive of them,
And taste, to him the gushing of the wave
Far far away did seem to mourn and rave
On alien shores; and if his fellow spake,
His voice was thin, as voices from the grave;
And deep-asleep he seemed, yet all awake,
And music in his ears his beating heart did make.

They sat them down upon the yellow sand,
Between the sun and moon upon the shore;
And sweet it was to dream of Fatherland,
Of child, and wife, and slave; but evermore
Most weary seemed the sea, weary the oar,
Weary the wandering fields of barren foam.
Then some one said, 'We will return no more;'
And all at once they sang, 'Our island home
Is far beyond the wave; we will no longer roam.'

## CHORIC SONG

### I

There is sweet music here that softer falls
Than petals from blown roses on the grass,
Or night-dews on still waters between walls
Of shadowy granite, in a gleaming pass;
Music that gentlier on the spirit lies,
Than tired eyelids upon tired eyes;

*23*] Thickset with lavender and galingale–*A*.
*24*. Lucretius iii 945: *eadem sunt omnia semper*. See l. 155*n*.
*26*] Pale in the steady sunset's rosy flame, *A*.
*34*. *His*] The *A*. Cp. the ghosts, *Aeneid* vi 492: *pars tollere vocem exiguam*.
*40*. *but*] that *A*.
*41–2*. Cp. *Home* 3–4: 'the weary sea, / Leagues of sounding foam'.
*42*. T. comments: 'Made by me on a voyage from Bordeaux to Dublin (1830)'.
*48*. *still*] smooth *A*.
*51*. *tired eyelids*] heavy eyelids *A*. T. comments: 'tiërd'; but also adds 'making the word neither monosyllabic nor disyllabic, but a dreamy child of the two'.

Music that brings sweet sleep down from the blissful skies.
Here are cool mosses deep,
And through the moss the ivies creep,
And in the stream the long-leaved flowers weep,
And from the craggy ledge the poppy hangs in sleep.

II

Why are we weighed upon with heaviness,
And utterly consumed with sharp distress,
While all things else have rest from weariness?
All things have rest: why should we toil alone,
We only toil, who are the first of things,
And make perpetual moan,
Still from one sorrow to another thrown:
Nor ever fold our wings,
And cease from wanderings,
Nor steep our brows in slumber's holy balm;
Nor harken what the inner spirit sings,
'There is no joy but calm!'
Why should we only toil, the roof and crown of things?

III

Lo! in the middle of the wood,
The folded leaf is wooed from out the bud

*52. down from the*] from the dark *A*.
*53–4*] Here are cool springs and mosses deep, *A*.
*53–6.* The effect of the rhymes, and the subject-matter, suggest the end of Marvell's *Thyrsis and Dorinda*, which–after 44 lines of couplets–concludes: 'Then let us give Carillo charge o' th Sheep, / And thou and I'le pick poppies and them steep / In wine, and drink on't even till we weep, / So shall we smoothly pass away in sleep.'
*60–9.* Cp. *Faerie Queene* II vi st. 17, on the relaxing island: 'Why then dost thou, O man, that of them all / Art Lord, and eke of nature Soveraine, / Wilfully make thy selfe a wretched thrall, / And wast thy joyous houres in needlesse paine, / Seeking for daunger and adventures vaine?'
*62. moan*] moaning *A* (*slip?*).
*65*] *Not A*; [wings] Of thought from wanderings, *B*.
*70. Lo!*] For *A*.
*70–83.* For Nature's effortlessness, cp. *Faerie Queene* (again the island, II vi st. 15): 'Behold, O man, that toilesome paines doest take, / The flowres, the fields, and all that pleasant growes . . . / They spring, they bud, they blossome fresh and faire . . . / Yet no man for them taketh paines or care, / Yet no man to them can his carefull paines compare.'

With winds upon the branch, and there
Grows green and broad, and takes no care,
Sun-steeped at noon, and in the moon
Nightly dew-fed; and turning yellow
Falls, and floats adown the air.
Lo! sweetened with the summer light,
The full-juiced apple, waxing over-mellow,
Drops in a silent autumn night.
All its allotted length of days,
The flower ripens in its place,
Ripens and fades, and falls, and hath no toil,
Fast-rooted in the fruitful soil.

IV

Hateful is the dark-blue sky,
Vaulted o'er the dark-blue sea.
Death is the end of life; ah, why
Should life all labour be?
Let us alone. Time driveth onward fast,
And in a little while our lips are dumb.
Let us alone. What is it that will last?
All things are taken from us, and become
Portions and parcels of the dreadful Past.
Let us alone. What pleasure can we have
To war with evil? Is there any peace
In ever climbing up the climbing wave?
All things have rest, and ripen toward the grave
In silence; ripen, fall and cease:
Give us long rest or death, dark death, or dreamful
ease.

72. *winds . . . branch*] dalliance of sweet winds *A*.
74–5] Nightly dew-steeped; and turning yellow *A*.
75–8. The rhyme *yellow/mellow* and the account of the apple recall *The Hesperides* 99–101 (p. 428).
76. *adown*] upon *A*.
80. Cp. *Psalm* xxi 4: 'He asked life of thee, and thou gavest it him, even length of days for ever and ever.'
84–5. Cp. *Aeneid* iv 451: *taedet caeli convexa tueri.*
85. *Vaulted o'er*] Wearisome *A*.
86. A commonplace, but note the context of Spenser's 'Death is the end of woes': Despair's easeful seductions, I ix st. 47; ll. 96–8 below are tinged with Spenser's stanza 40: 'Sleepe after toyle, port after stormie seas, / Ease after warre, death after life does greatly please.'
88–92] *Not A.*
94] In warring with mischances, or what peace *A*.
98] *A breaks off here.*

V

How sweet it were, hearing the downward stream,
With half-shut eyes ever to seem
Falling asleep in a half-dream!
To dream and dream, like yonder amber light,
Which will not leave the myrrh-bush on the height;
To hear each other's whispered speech;
Eating the Lotos day by day,
To watch the crisping ripples on the beach,
And tender curving lines of creamy spray;
To lend our hearts and spirits wholly
To the influence of mild-minded melancholy;
To muse and brood and live again in memory,
With those old faces of our infancy
Heaped over with a mound of grass,
Two handfuls of white dust, shut in an urn of brass!

VI

Dear is the memory of our wedded lives,
And dear the last embraces of our wives
And their warm tears: but all hath suffered change:
For surely now our household hearths are cold:
Our sons inherit us: our looks are strange:
And we should come like ghosts to trouble joy.
Or else the island princes over-bold
Have eat our substance, and the minstrel sings
Before them of the ten years' war in Troy,
And our great deeds, as half-forgotten things.
Is there confusion in the little isle?
Let what is broken so remain.
The Gods are hard to reconcile:
'Tis hard to settle order once again.
There *is* confusion worse than death,
Trouble on trouble, pain on pain,
Long labour unto agèd breath,

*100–101.* Cp. Thomson (headnote).
*108–9.* Adapted from 'give up wholly / Thy spirit to mild-minded Melancholy', *Sonnet* [*Check every outflash*], as is perhaps 'dark and holy', l. 136.
*111. those*] *1842*; the *1832*.
*114–32*] *1842; not 1832.*
*116–9.* A preoccupation of T.'s; cp. *The Coach of Death* 65–8 (p. 77), *In Memoriam* xc (p. 942), and the story of *Enoch Arden*.
*120–21.* Cp. *Odyssey* xi 115, the wooing of Penelope in Ithaca: 'proud men that devour thy livelihood'.

Sore task to hearts worn out by many wars
And eyes grown dim with gazing on the pilot-stars.

VII

But, propt on beds of amaranth and moly,
How sweet (while warm airs lull us, blowing lowly)
With half-dropt eyelid still,
Beneath a heaven dark and holy,
To watch the long bright river drawing slowly
His waters from the purple hill–
To hear the dewy echoes calling
From cave to cave through the thick-twinèd vine–
To watch the emerald-coloured water falling
Through many a woven acanthus-wreath divine!
Only to hear and see the far-off sparkling brine,
Only to hear were sweet, stretched out beneath the
pine.

VIII

The Lotos blooms below the barren peak:
The Lotos blows by every winding creek:
All day the wind breathes low with mellower tone:
Through every hollow cave and alley lone
Round and round the spicy downs the yellow
Lotos-dust is blown.
We have had enough of action, and of motion we,
Rolled to starboard, rolled to larboard, when the
surge was seething free,
Where the wallowing monster spouted his foam-
fountains in the sea.

*131. by*] *1865*; with *1842–64*.
*132.* Cp. *The Lover's Tale* i 480–82, *1832* text: 'whose eyes are dim / With gazing on the light'.
*133. But, propt on*] *1842*; Or, propt on lavish *1832*. *amaranth*: 'the immortal flower of legend' (T.), as in Milton's Heaven, *Paradise Lost* iii *352*; *moly*: 'the sacred herb of mystical power, used as a charm by Odysseus against Circe' mentioned in *Comus 636*.
*134*] *Not B.*
*135. half-dropt eyelid*] *1872*; half-dropt eyelids *1832–70*; half-shut eyelids *B*.
*137. long bright*] *lacuna in B and Hawaii MS.*
*141. watch*] *1851*; hear *1832–50*.
*145. barren*] *1851*; flowery *1832–50*.
*149. yellow*] *Not B.*
*150–73*] We have had enough of motion,
Weariness and wild alarm,
Tossing on the tossing ocean,
Where the tuskèd seahorse walloweth

In a stripe of grassgreen calm,
At noon tide beneath the lee;
And the monstrous narwhale swalloweth
His foamfountains in the sea.
Long enough the winedark wave our weary bark did carry.
This is lovelier and sweeter,
Men of Ithaca, this is meeter,
In the hollow rosy vale to tarry,
Like a dreamy Lotos-eater, a delirious Lotos-eater!
We will eat the Lotos, sweet
As the yellow honeycomb,
In the valley some, and some
On the ancient heights divine;
And no more roam,
On the loud hoar foam,
To the melancholy home
At the limit of the brine,
The little isle of Ithaca, beneath the day's decline.
We'll lift no more the shattered oar,
No more unfurl the straining sail;
With the blissful Lotoseaters pale
We will abide in the golden vale
Of the Lotos-land, till the Lotos fail;
We will not wander more.
Hark! how sweet the horned ewes bleat
On the solitary steeps,
And the merry lizard leaps,
And the foamwhite waters pour;
And the dark pine weeps,
And the lithe vine creeps,
And the heavy melon sleeps
On the level of the shore:
Oh! islanders of Ithaca, we will not wander more.
Surely, surely slumber is more sweet than toil, the shore
Than labour in the ocean, and rowing with the oar.
Oh! islanders of Ithaca, we will return no more. *1832*

*B* has the following variants: l. [4] *tuskèd*] broadmaned. l. [9] *winedark*] weary. l. [12] *rosy*] golden. l. [16] Where the briar never clomb. l. [21] *limit*] limits. l. [28] We will return no more. l. [31] *merry*] rapid. l. [37] *not wander*] return no. l. [39] *and*] or. J. M. Kemble wrote (see l. 7*n*): 'Then again what think you of the "tusked sea-horse" for the "broad-maned sea-horse"? Here also some *stumpf* told him that the Walrus or sea-horse had no mane; as if he and you and I do not know very well that he never meant the Walrus or any such Northern Brute, but a good mythological, Neptunian charger! But Ælfred piques himself upon Natural History, for which may a sound rope's end be his portion.'

Let us swear an oath, and keep it with an equal mind,
In the hollow Lotos-land to live and lie reclined
On the hills like Gods together, careless of mankind.
For they lie beside their nectar, and the bolts are hurled
Far below them in the valleys, and the clouds are lightly curled
Round their golden houses, girdled with the gleaming world:
Where they smile in secret, looking over wasted lands,
Blight and famine, plague and earthquake, roaring deeps and fiery sands,
Clanging fights, and flaming towns, and sinking ships, and praying hands.
But they smile, they find a music centred in a doleful song
Steaming up, a lamentation and an ancient tale of wrong,
Like a tale of little meaning though the words are strong;
Chanted from an ill-used race of men that cleave the soil,
Sow the seed, and reap the harvest with enduring toil,
Storing yearly little dues of wheat, and wine and oil;
Till they perish and they suffer–some, 'tis whispered–down in hell
Suffer endless anguish, others in Elysian valleys dwell,
Resting weary limbs at last on beds of asphodel.
Surely, surely, slumber is more sweet than toil, the shore

*155–70.* The Gods are based on Lucretius's account of Epicureanism. H.T. compares *deos securum agere aevom* v 82; and iii 18–22: *apparet divum numen sedesque quietae / quas neque concutiunt venti nec nubila nimbis / aspergunt neque nix acri concreta pruina / cana cadens violat semperque innubilus aether / integit, et large diffuso lumine ridet.* ('Before me appear the gods in their majesty, and their peaceful abodes, which no winds ever shake nor clouds besprinkle with rain, which no snow congealed by the bitter frost mars with its white fall, but the air ever cloudless encompasses them and laughs with its light spread wide abroad'.) Cp. T.'s *Lucretius* 109–10: 'Nor sound of human sorrow mounts to mar / Their sacred everlasting calm!'

Than labour in the deep mid-ocean, wind and wave and oar;
Oh rest ye, brother mariners, we will not wander more.

# 171 Rosalind

Published *1832*; not reprinted until restored *1884*, 'Juvenilia'. Written by July 1831 (*Mem.* i 80–1). See also *My Rosalind* (below), which was originally part of *Rosalind*. Cp. Skelton's *To Margaret Hussey*, who also is likened to falcon and hawk. There are a few touches suggesting the Rosalind of *As You Like It* III ii.

I

My Rosalind, my Rosalind,
My frolic falcon, with bright eyes,
Whose free delight, from any height of rapid flight,
Stoops at all game that wing the skies,
My Rosalind, my Rosalind,
My bright-eyed, wild-eyed falcon, whither,
Careless both of wind and weather,
Whither fly ye, what game spy ye,
Up or down the streaming wind?

II

The quick lark's closest-carolled strains,
The shadow rushing up the sea,
The lightning flash atween the rains,
The sunlight driving down the lea,
The leaping stream, the very wind,
That will not stay, upon his way,
To stoop the cowslip to the plains,
Is not so clear and bold and free
As you, my falcon Rosalind.
You care not for another's pains,
Because you are the soul of joy,
Bright metal all without alloy.
Life shoots and glances through your veins,
And flashes off a thousand ways,
Through lips and eyes in subtle rays.
Your hawk-eyes are keen and bright,
Keen with triumph, watching still

¶ 171. 2. *frolic falcon*] tassel gentil *Heath MS.*

To pierce me through with pointed light;
But oftentimes they flash and glitter
Like sunshine on a dancing rill,
And your words are seeming-bitter,
Sharp and few, but seeming-bitter
From excess of swift delight.

III

Come down, come home, my Rosalind,
My gay young hawk, my Rosalind:
Too long you keep the upper skies;
Too long you roam and wheel at will;
But we must hood your random eyes,
That care not whom they kill,
And your cheek, whose brilliant hue
Is so sparkling-fresh to view,
Some red heath-flower in the dew,
Touched with sunrise. We must bind
And keep you fast, my Rosalind,
Fast, fast, my wild-eyed Rosalind,
And clip your wings, and make you love:
When we have lured you from above,
And that delight of frolic flight, by day or night,
From North to South,
We'll bind you fast in silken cords,
And kiss away the bitter words
From off your rosy mouth.

# 172 *'My Rosalind, my Rosalind'

Published *1832* at the end of *Rosalind* (above), with the note: 'Perhaps the following lines may be allowed to stand as a separate poem; originally they made part of the text, where they were manifestly superfluous'. Not reprinted. *Heath MS* includes it as 'stanzas rejected from *Rosalind*'. Written by July 1831 (*Mem.* i 80–81). *T.Nbk 16* (which may not be quoted) has a longer note of explanation, indicating T.'s dissatisfaction with the rhythms.

My Rosalind, my Rosalind,
Bold, subtle, careless Rosalind,
Is one of those who know no strife
Of inward woe or outward fear;

*36 ∧ 7*] Round and round the flowery hill: *Heath MS.*
*49. bind*] knit *Heath MS.*

To whom the slope and stream of life,
The life before, the life behind,
In the ear, from far and near,
Chimeth musically clear.
My falconhearted Rosalind,
Fullsailed before a vigorous wind,
Is one of those, who cannot weep
For others' woes, but overleap
All the petty shocks and fears
That trouble life in early years,
With a flash of frolic scorn
And keen delight, that never falls
Away from freshness, self-upborne
With such gladness as, whenever
The freshflushing springtime calls
To the flooding waters cool,
Young fishes, on an April morn,
Up and down a rapid river,
Leap the little waterfalls
That sing into the pebbled pool.
My happy falcon, Rosalind,
Hath daring fancies of her own,
Fresh as the dawn before the day,
Fresh as the early seasmell blown
Through vineyards from an inland bay.
My Rosalind, my Rosalind,
Because no shadow on you falls
Think you hearts are tennisballs,
To play with, wanton Rosalind?

# 173 A Dream of Fair Women

Published *1832*, revised subsequently. Written 1831–2. In *Allen MS*, it is entitled *The Legend of Fair Women*; all variants are below. T. comments on l. 3: 'Chaucer, the first great English poet, wrote the *Legend of Good Women*. From among these Cleopatra alone appears in my poem.' J. F. A. Pyre points out that T.'s stanza form is used in Vaughan's *Psalm 104* (*The Formation of Tennyson's Style*, 1921, p. 44). Cp. the stanza of *The Poet* (p. 222), and of *The Palace of Art* (p. 400).

¶ 173. *Opening*] *1832 preceded l. 1 with four stanzas:*

As when a man, that sails in a balloon,
  Downlooking sees the solid shining ground
Stream from beneath him in the broad blue noon,–
  Tilth, hamlet, mead and mound:

I read, before my eyelids dropt their shade,
  '*The Legend of Good Women*', long ago
Sung by the morning star of song, who made
  His music heard below;

Dan Chaucer, the first warbler, whose sweet breath
  Preluded those melodious bursts that fill
The spacious times of great Elizabeth
  With sounds that echo still.

And, for a while, the knowledge of his art
  Held me above the subject, as strong gales
Hold swollen clouds from raining, though my heart,
  Brimful of those wild tales,

And takes his flags and waves them to the mob,
  That shout below, all faces turned to where
Glows rubylike the far-up crimson globe,
  Filled with a finer air:

So, lifted high, the Poet at his will
  Lets the great world flit from him, seeing all,
Higher through secret splendours mounting still,
  Selfpoised, nor fears to fall,

Hearing apart the echoes of his fame.
  While I spoke thus, the seedsman, memory,
Sowed my deepfurrowed thought with many a name,
  Whose glory will not die.

E. F. Shannon (*PQ* xxxi (1952) 441–5) suggests that T.'s source was probably the participation of his friend Richard Monckton Milnes in a flight from Cambridge, 19 May 1829. T. may also have remembered the plates (under 'Aerostation') in the *English Encyclopaedia* (1802), of which there was a copy at Somersby (*Lincoln*). It has two balloon ascents, plus 'A View from a Balloon above the Clouds'. Cp. the seventh line with Keats, *Imitation of Spenser* 13: 'Cast upward, through the waves, a ruby glow'. Instead of these stanzas, *Allen MS* has:

The poet's steadfast soul, poured out in songs,
  Unmoved moves all things with exceeding might,
Fixed as between his wings the Eagle's lungs
  Unshook of his wide flight.

*1. my . . . their*] I dropt my eyelids' *H.Nbk 4*.
*3.* Arthur Hallam had called Chaucer 'our beautiful morning star', in *The Influence of Italian upon English Literature* (1831; Motter, p. 227). He was echoing Denham, *On Cowley* 1: 'Old Chaucer, like the morning Star'.
*5.* H.T. compares *Faerie Queene* IV ii st. 32: 'Dan Chaucer, well of English undefyled'.
*9–10.* Cp. Marvell, *On Paradise Lost* 5–6: 'the Argument / Held me a while misdoubting his Intent.' There 'argument' means 'subject'.

Charged both mine eyes with tears. In every land
   I saw, wherever light illumineth,
Beauty and anguish walking hand in hand
   The downward slope to death.

Those far-renownèd brides of ancient song
   Peopled the hollow dark, like burning stars,
And I heard sounds of insult, shame, and wrong,
   And trumpets blown for wars;

And clattering flints battered with clanging hoofs;
   And I saw crowds in columned sanctuaries;
And forms that passed at windows and on roofs
   Of marble palaces;

Corpses across the threshold; heroes tall
   Dislodging pinnacle and parapet
Upon the tortoise creeping to the wall;
   Lances in ambush set;

And high shrine-doors burst through with heated
      blasts
   That run before the fluttering tongues of fire;
White surf wind-scattered over sails and masts,
   And ever climbing higher;

Squadrons and squares of men in brazen plates,
   Scaffolds, still sheets of water, divers woes,

*16 ∧ 17*] In every land I thought that, more or less,
   The stronger sterner nature overbore
The softer, uncontrolled by gentleness
   And selfish evermore:

And whether there were any means whereby,
   In some far aftertime, the gentler [gentle *Allen MS*] mind
Might reassume its just and full degree
   Of rule among mankind. *1832*

These lines anticipate the concerns of *The Princess* (1847).

*18. the hollow dark*: *In deep and solemn dreams* 59. The phrase occurs in Keats, *The Fall of Hyperion* i 455 (not published, though, till 1856), which suggests the status of romantic poetic diction.

*21–32*] *Not H.MS.*

*23. passed*] *1842*; screamed *1832*.

*25–8*] *Not Allen MS.*

*27. tortoise*: 'the "testudo" of ancient war. Warriors with shields upheld on their heads' (T.).

*29.* Cp. *Semele* 3: 'The blast of Godhead bursts the doors'.

*33. Squadrons and squares*] And I saw files *Allen MS 1st reading.*

Ranges of glimmering vaults with iron grates,
And hushed seraglios.

So shape chased shape as swift as, when to land
Bluster the winds and tides the self-same way,
Crisp foam-flakes scud along the level sand,
Torn from the fringe of spray.

I started once, or seemed to start in pain,
Resolved on noble things, and strove to speak,
As when a great thought strikes along the brain,
And flushes all the cheek.

And once my arm was lifted to hew down
A cavalier from off his saddle-bow,
That bore a lady from a leaguered town;
And then, I know not how,

All those sharp fancies, by down-lapsing thought
Streamed onward, lost their edges, and did creep
Rolled on each other, rounded, smoothed, and brought
Into the gulfs of sleep.

At last methought that I had wandered far
In an old wood: fresh-washed in coolest dew
The maiden splendours of the morning star
Shook in the stedfast blue.

*35. grates*] rails *Allen MS* (*error*). *iron grates*: T. said of 'Thorough the iron gates of life', *To His Coy Mistress* 44: 'he could fancy *grates* would have intensified Marvell's image' (*Mem.* ii 501).

*36. seraglios*: Paden (p. 136) remarks the influence, here and in other details, of C.-E. Savary's *Letters on Egypt* (T. used the 1799 translation, *Lincoln*, for *Fatima* and other poems).

*36 ∧ 7*] And as a dog goes round and round again
And eyes his place of rest before he sleep,
So my s. s[l]. [? sad slumber] with a continual pain
Flowed eddylike and deep,
Returning on itself *H.MS*.

*37–40*] *Added in H.MS, but beginning* So thought chased thought . . .

*45–52*] *Not H.MS; ll. 45–8 deleted in Allen MS.*

*52.* Cp. Shelley, *Queen Mab* ix 175: 'the transient gulf-dream of a startling sleep'.

*53–6, 69–72*] *Added in H.MS, which does not have ll. 57–68.*

*54.* T. says: 'The wood is the Past', and ll. 83–4, 'i.e. time backward'.

*56. Shook . . . stedfast*] Throbbed . . . deepening *H.MS*.

Enormous elm-tree-boles did stoop and lean
Upon the dusky brushwood underneath
Their broad curved branches, fledged with clearest green,
New from its silken sheath.

The dim red morn had died, her journey done,
And with dead lips smiled at the twilight plain,
Half-fallen across the threshold of the sun,
Never to rise again.

There was no motion in the dumb dead air,
Not any song of bird or sound of rill;
Gross darkness of the inner sepulchre
Is not so deadly still

As that wide forest. Growths of jasmine turned
Their humid arms festooning tree to tree,
And at the root through lush green grasses burned
The red anemone.

I knew the flowers, I knew the leaves, I knew
The tearful glimmer of the languid dawn
On those long, rank, dark wood-walks drenched in dew,
Leading from lawn to lawn.

*61–4.* T. comments: 'Refers to the early past. How magnificently old Turner would have painted it'.

*62. twilight*] languid *Allen MS.*

*67.* Cp. *Ode: O Bosky Brook* 108–10: 'With stillness like the stillness of the tomb / And grossest gloom, / As it were of the inner sepulchre.' The sepulchre, as Paden says (p. 136), derives from Savary's *Letters on Egypt*, the interior of the great pyramid. Cp. *Isaiah* lx 2: 'The darkness shall cover the earth, and gross darkness the people.'

*69. As . . . of*] Black ivy, and star-flowered *H.MS.* *Growths of*] *1842*; Clasping *1832*.

*70. Their humid*] *1842*; Its twinèd *1832*.

*73–92*] *Not H.MS (missing sheet?).*

*77–80.* Cp. *Song*, which immediately followed this poem in *1832*:

Who can say
Why Today
Tomorrow will be yesterday?
Who can tell
Why to smell
The violet, recalls the dewy prime
Of youth and buried time?
The cause is nowhere found in rhyme.

The smell of violets, hidden in the green,
Poured back into my empty soul and frame
The times when I remember to have been
Joyful and free from blame.

And from within me a clear under-tone
Thrilled through mine ears in that unblissful clime,
'Pass freely through: the wood is all thine own,
Until the end of time.'

At length I saw a lady within call,
Stiller than chiselled marble, standing there;
A daughter of the gods, divinely tall,
And most divinely fair.

Her loveliness with shame and with surprise
Froze my swift speech: she turning on my face
The star-like sorrows of immortal eyes,
Spoke slowly in her place.

'I had great beauty: ask thou not my name:
No one can be more wise than destiny.
Many drew swords and died. Where'er I came
I brought calamity.'

'No marvel, sovereign lady: in fair field
Myself for such a face had boldly died,'
I answered free; and turning I appealed
To one that stood beside.

But she, with sick and scornful looks averse,
To her full height her stately stature draws;
'My youth,' she said, 'was blasted with a curse:
This woman was the cause.

82. *mine . . . unblissful*] my . . . unjoyful *Allen MS.*

83. Paden (pp. 36, 52) contrasts the wood in Savary's *Letters on Egypt*: 'Thus abandoned to the delights of contemplation, and indulging those delicious sensations the time and place inspired, I incautiously proceeded towards the thickest part of the wood; when a terrifying voice suddenly exclaimed–where are you going? Stand, or you are dead.–It was a slave who guarded the entrance of the grove, that no rash curiosity might disturb the females who reposed upon the verdant banks.'

87. Cp. *The Mystic* 26: 'Daughters of time, divinely tall'. Helen, 'daughter of Zeus and Leda' (T.).

100. 'Iphigenia, who was sacrificed by Agamemnon to Artemis' (T.).

101. *sick . . . looks*] sad . . . eyes *Allen MS 1st reading.*

'I was cut off from hope in that sad place,
Which men called Aulis in those iron years:
My father held his hand upon his face;
I, blinded with my tears,

'Still strove to speak: my voice was thick with sighs
As in a dream. Dimly I could descry
The stern black-bearded kings with wolfish eyes,
Waiting to see me die.

'The high masts flickered as they lay afloat;
The crowds, the temples, wavered, and the shore;
The bright death quivered at the victim's throat;
Touched; and I knew no more.'

Whereto the other with a downward brow:
'I would the white cold heavy-plunging foam,
Whirled by the wind, had rolled me deep below,
Then when I left my home.'

Her slow full words sank through the silence drear,
As thunder-drops fall on a sleeping sea:
Sudden I heard a voice that cried, 'Come here,
That I may look on thee.'

*106*] *1883*; Which yet to name my spirit loathes and fears: *1832–82*. T. says that the revised 'line (as far as I recollect) is almost synchronous with the old reading; but the inversion there . . . displeased me'.

*107*. H.T. comments: 'No doubt my father had in his mind the famous picture by Timanthes, *The Sacrifice of Iphigeneia* (described by Valerius Maximus, VIII ii 6), of which there is a Pompeiian wall-painting. Also the passage in Lucretius, i 84 foll.'

*113–16*] *1853*; 'The tall masts quivered as they lay afloat,
The temples and the people and the shore.
One drew a sharp knife through my tender throat
Slowly,–and nothing more.' *1832–51*

'I thought [it] too ghastly realistic' (T.). It had been ridiculed by J. W. Croker, *QR*, April 1833: 'what touching simplicity–what pathetic resignation–he cut my throat–"*nothing more!*" One might indeed ask, "*What more*" she would have?'

*117–20*. Cp. Helen, *Iliad* vi 345ff: 'I would that on the day when first my mother gave me birth an evil storm-wind had borne me away to some mountain or to the wave of the loud-resounding sea, where the wave might have swept me away or ever these things came to pass.'

*120*] *H.MS breaks off here.*

I turning saw, throned on a flowery rise,
One sitting on a crimson scarf unrolled;
A queen, with swarthy cheeks and bold black eyes,
Brow-bound with burning gold.

She, flashing forth a haughty smile, began:
'I governed men by change, and so I swayed
All moods. 'Tis long since I have seen a man.
Once, like the moon, I made

'The ever-shifting currents of the blood
According to my humour ebb and flow.
I have no men to govern in this wood:
That makes my only woe.

'Nay–yet it chafes me that I could not bend
One will; nor tame and tutor with mine eye
That dull cold-blooded Cæsar. Prythee, friend,
Where is Mark Antony?

'The man, my lover, with whom I rode sublime
On Fortune's neck: we sat as God by God:
The Nilus would have risen before his time
And flooded at our nod.

*127.* T. comments: 'I was thinking of Shakespeare's Cleopatra: "Think of me / That am with Phoebus' amorous pinches black" (*Antony and Cleopatra* I v 28). Millais has made a mulatto of her in his illustration. I know perfectly well that she was a Greek. "Swarthy" merely means sunburnt. I should not have spoken of her breast as "polished silver" if I had not known her as a white woman. Read "sunburnt" if you like it better.' Cp. *Antony to Cleopatra* (p. 91).

*128. Coriolanus* II ii 96: 'Brow-bound with the oak'.

*129. haughty*] subtle *Allen MS.*

*132–4.* John Churton Collins compared John Ford's *Witch of Edmonton* II ii: 'You are the powerful moon of my blood's sea, / To make it ebb or flow.' Alongside Collins's note (*Cornhill*, Jan. 1880), T. wrote: 'Not known to me' (*Lincoln*).

*139. dull*] proud *Allen MS.*

*141–4*] *1843*; 'By him great [Beside him *Allen MS 1st reading*] Pompey dwarfs and suffers pain,
A mortal man before immortal Mars;
The glories of great Julius lapse and wane,
And shrink from suns to stars. *1832–42*

'We drank the Libyan Sun to sleep, and lit
Lamps which out-burned Canopus. O my life
In Egypt! O the dalliance and the wit,
The flattery and the strife,

'And the wild kiss, when fresh from war's alarms,
My Hercules, my Roman Antony,
My mailèd Bacchus leapt into my arms,
Contented there to die!

'And there he died: and when I heard my name
Sighed forth with life I would not brook my fear
Of the other: with a worm I balked his fame.
What else was left? look here!'

(With that she tore her robe apart, and half
The polished argent of her breast to sight

*145–8*] *1845*; 'That man, of all the men I ever knew,
Most touched my fancy. O! what days and nights
We had in Egypt, ever reaping new
Harvest [Harvests *Allen MS*] of ripe delights,

'Realmdraining revels! Life was one long feast.
What wit! what words! what sweet words, only made
Less sweet by the kiss that broke 'em, liking best
To be so richly stayed! *1832–42*;

What nights we had in Egypt! I could hit
His humours while I crossed them: O the life
I led him, and the dalliance . . . *1843*

*146. Canopus*: 'in the constellation of Argo' (T.). Moore's *Lalla Rookh: The Fire-Worshippers* had a footnote to 'the Star of Egypt': 'The brilliant Canopus, unseen in European climates.' The index to Charles Rollin's *Ancient History* has 'Canopus: a city of the Lower Egypt, remarkable for lewdness'; there was a copy of Rollin (1789 translation) at Somersby (*Lincoln*).

*149. And . . . kiss*] *1843*; What dainty strifes *1832–42*. Cp. these lines with *Antony and Cleopatra* IV viii 14–16: 'Chain mine armed neck; leap thou, attire and all, / Through proof of harness to my heart, and there / Ride on the pants triumphing!'

*150. Roman*] *1843*; gallant *1832–42*.

*151. Bacchus*] *1843*; captain *1832–42*.

*153. there . . . when*] *1843*; in those arms he died: *1832–42*.

*154. life . . . my*] *1845*; life: then I shook off all *1832–42*; life: I had no further *1843*. *Allen MS has fragmentary line*: In his last sigh.

*155*] *1845*; Oh what a little snake [worm *1843*] stole Caesar's fame! *1832–42*.

Laid bare. Thereto she pointed with a laugh,
Showing the aspick's bite.)

'I died a Queen. The Roman soldier found
Me lying dead, my crown about my brows,
A name for ever!–lying robed and crowned,
Worthy a Roman spouse.'

Her warbling voice, a lyre of widest range
Struck by all passion, did fall down and glance
From tone to tone, and glided through all change
Of liveliest utterance.

When she made pause I knew not for delight;
Because with sudden motion from the ground
She raised her piercing orbs, and filled with light
The interval of sound.

Still with their fires Love tipt his keenest darts;
As once they drew into two burning rings
All beams of Love, melting the mighty hearts
Of captains and of kings.

Slowly my sense undazzled. Then I heard
A noise of some one coming through the lawn,
And singing clearer than the crested bird
That claps his wings at dawn.

'The torrent brooks of hallowed Israel
From craggy hollows pouring, late and soon,
Sound all night long, in falling through the dell,
Far-heard beneath the moon.

*160. aspick's*] aspic- *Allen MS, which breaks off with l. 160 (end of sheet), and then has on following sheet ll. 249–56 only.*

*161–4.* T. compares *non humilis mulier*, Horace's *Odes* I xxxvii 32, on the death of Cleopatra.

*166. Struck*] *1843*; Touched *1832–42.*

*178. A noise*] The sound *H.MS extra sheet.*

*179. singing*] chanting *H.MS extra sheet.*

*181–4, 216–20.* Adapted from *Margaret* 35 ∧ 6, MS (p. 455):

Or when the Gileadite returned,
Whether Jephtha's daughter mourned
Two moons beside the heavy flow
Of torrent brooks in purple glens
Of Judah, leaving far below,
Leaving the fruitful olive plains,
Leaving the hope of her bride bower
In royal Mizpeh's battled tower.

'The balmy moon of blessèd Israel
Floods all the deep-blue gloom with beams divine:
All night the splintered crags that wall the dell
With spires of silver shine.'

As one that museth where broad sunshine laves
The lawn by some cathedral, through the door
Hearing the holy organ rolling waves
Of sound on roof and floor

Within, and anthem sung, is charmed and tied
To where he stands, – so stood I, when that flow
Of music left the lips of her that died
To save her father's vow;

The daughter of the warrior Gileadite,
A maiden pure; as when she went along
From Mizpeh's towered gate with welcome light,
With timbrel and with song.

My words leapt forth: 'Heaven heads the count of crimes
With that wild oath.' She rendered answer high:
'Not so, nor once alone; a thousand times
I would be born and die.

'Single I grew, like some green plant, whose root
Creeps to the garden water-pipes beneath,
Feeding the flower; but ere my flower to fruit
Changed, I was ripe for death.

'My God, my land, my father – these did move
Me from my bliss of life, that Nature gave,
Lowered softly with a threefold cord of love
Down to a silent grave.

'And I went mourning, "No fair Hebrew boy
Shall smile away my maiden blame among
The Hebrew mothers" – emptied of all joy,
Leaving the dance and song,

Jephtha's daughter was sacrificed by him because of his vow to God: 'If thou shalt without fail deliver the children of Ammon into mine hands, Then it shall be, that whatsoever cometh forth of the doors of my house to meet me, when I return in peace from the children of Ammon, shall surely be the Lord's, and I will offer it up for a burnt offering' (*Judges* xi 30–1). She appears in Percy's *Reliques* (*Jephtha, Judge of Israel*), as do Rosamond and Eleanor, ll. 250–6 (*Fair Rosamond*).

*211. cord*] *1842*; chord *1832*.

'Leaving the olive-gardens far below,
    Leaving the promise of my bridal bower,
The valleys of grape-loaded vines that glow
    Beneath the battled tower.

'The light white cloud swam over us. Anon
    We heard the lion roaring from his den;
We saw the large white stars rise one by one,
    Or, from the darkened glen,

'Saw God divide the night with flying flame,
    And thunder on the everlasting hills.
I heard Him, for He spake, and grief became
    A solemn scorn of ills.

'When the next moon was rolled into the sky,
    Strength came to me that equalled my desire.
How beautiful a thing it was to die
    For God and for my sire!

'It comforts me in this one thought to dwell,
    That I subdued me to my father's will;
Because the kiss he gave me, ere I fell,
    Sweetens the spirit still.

'Moreover it is written that my race
    Hewed Ammon, hip and thigh, from Aroer
On Arnon unto Minneth.' Here her face
    Glowed, as I looked at her.

She locked her lips: she left me where I stood:
    'Glory to God,' she sang, and past afar,
Thridding the sombre boskage of the wood,
    Toward the morning-star.

Losing her carol I stood pensively,
    As one that from a casement leans his head,
When midnight bells cease ringing suddenly,
    And the old year is dead.

*222. from*] *1853*; in *1832–51*.
*225.* H.T. compares Horace, *Odes* I xxxiv 5–6: *Diespiter / igni corusco nubila dividens.*
*242–4.* Cp. *Job* xxxviii 7: 'When the morning stars sang together, and all the sons of God shouted for joy'.
*243.* T. compares *Comus* 313: 'every bosky bourn'.

'Alas! alas!' a low voice, full of care,
Murmured beside me: 'Turn and look on me:
I am that Rosamond, whom men call fair,
If what I was I be.

'Would I had been some maiden coarse and poor!
O me, that I should ever see the light!
Those dragon eyes of angered Eleanor
Do hunt me, day and night.'

She ceased in tears, fallen from hope and trust:
To whom the Egyptian: 'O, you tamely died!
You should have clung to Fulvia's waist, and thrust
The dagger through her side.'

With that sharp sound the white dawn's creeping beams,
Stolen to my brain, dissolved the mystery
Of folded sleep. The captain of my dreams
Ruled in the eastern sky.

Morn broadened on the borders of the dark,
Ere I saw her, who clasped in her last trance
Her murdered father's head, or Joan of Arc,
A light of ancient France;

Or her who knew that Love can vanquish Death,
Who kneeling, with one arm about her king,

*251.* Rosamond de Clifford, the mistress of Henry II, was said to have been poisoned by Queen Eleanor. Cp. *Rosamund's Bower* (p. 735). She appears in T.'s play *Becket*. T. may have read of her in the *English Encyclopaedia* (1802), of which there was a copy at Somersby (*Lincoln*).

*253. poor*] fair *Allen MS.*

*259. Fulvia*: 'wife of Antony, named by Cleopatra as a parallel to Eleanor' (T.).

*263. The captain*: 'Venus, the star of morning' (T.).

*266.* T. comments: 'Margaret Roper, daughter of Sir Thomas More, who is said to have transferred his headless corpse from the Tower to Chelsea Church. Sir Thomas More's head had remained for fourteen days on London Bridge after his execution, and was about to be thrown into the Thames to make room for others, when she claimed and bought it. . . . [Her] vault was opened, and it is stated that she was found in her coffin, clasping the small leaden box which inclosed her father's head.'

*266–7. who . . . head*] *1842*; that in her latest trance / Clasped her dead father's heart *1832*.

*269–72.* T. comments: 'Eleanor, wife of Edward I, went with him to the Holy Land (1269), where he was stabbed at Acre with a poisoned dagger. She sucked the poison from the wound.'

Drew forth the poison with her balmy breath,
Sweet as new buds in Spring.

No memory labours longer from the deep
Gold-mines of thought to lift the hidden ore
That glimpses, moving up, than I from sleep
To gather and tell o'er

Each little sound and sight. With what dull pain
Compassed, how eagerly I sought to strike
Into that wondrous track of dreams again!
But no two dreams are like.

As when a soul laments, which hath been blest,
Desiring what is mingled with past years,
In yearnings that can never be exprest
By signs or groans or tears;

Because all words, though culled with choicest art,
Failing to give the bitter of the sweet,
Wither beneath the palate, and the heart
Faints, faded by its heat.

# 174 *Song [Who can say]

Published *1832*, not reprinted. It appears with other poems of *1832* in *T.Nbk 16*. *Nbk 20* (1833), also not to be quoted, makes it clear that T. then thought of incorporating it into a passage of blank-verse dialogue. The pattern of the resulting poem resembles *The Ancient Sage*. The first question (ll. 1–3) is answered by six lines of blank verse invoking the sweeping movement of the earth; the second question (ll. 4–7) is answered by invoking the marriage bond between all the senses and the analogy that one art when it excels includes elements of all. T. was to quarry this blank verse for, e.g., *The Princess*. The violets and memory of youth suggest *A Dream of Fair Women* 77–80 (p. 445) which immediately preceded this *Song* in *1832*. Cp. *The 'How' and the 'Why'* (p. 186).

Who can say
Why Today
Tomorrow will be yesterday?
Who can tell
Why to smell
The violet, recalls the dewy prime
Of youth and buried time?
The cause is nowhere found in rhyme.

# 175 Margaret

Published *1832*; 'Juvenilia'. A companion poem to *Adeline* (p. 216); see l. 48.

I

O sweet pale Margaret,
O rare pale Margaret,
What lit your eyes with tearful power,
Like moonlight on a falling shower?
Who lent you, love, your mortal dower
Of pensive thought and aspect pale,
Your melancholy sweet and frail
As perfume of the cuckoo-flower?
From the westward-winding flood,
From the evening-lighted wood,
From all things outward you have won
A tearful grace, as though you stood
Between the rainbow and the sun.
The very smile before you speak,
That dimples your transparent cheek,
Encircles all the heart, and feedeth
The senses with a still delight
Of dainty sorrow without sound,
Like the tender amber round,
Which the moon about her spreadeth,
Moving through a fleecy night.

II

You love, remaining peacefully,
To hear the murmur of the strife,
But enter not the toil of life.
Your spirit is the calmèd sea,
Laid by the tumult of the fight.
You are the evening star, alway
Remaining betwixt dark and bright:
Lulled echoes of laborious day
Come to you, gleams of mellow light
Float by you on the verge of night.

¶ 175.*7–8*. *H.Nbk 3* has as a separate jotting:
A melancholy frail and sweet
As perfume of the cuckooflower.
See ll. 49–51*n*.
*21*. Milton, *Il Penseroso* 72: 'stooping through a fleecy cloud'.
*25–6*. The notion that gunfire stills the waves.

III

What can it matter, Margaret,
 What songs below the waning stars
The lion-heart, Plantagenet,
 Sang looking through his prison bars?
  Exquisite Margaret, who can tell
The last wild thought of Chatelet,
 Just ere the falling axe did part
 The burning brain from the true heart,
  Even in her sight he loved so well?

IV

A fairy shield your Genius made
 And gave you on your natal day.
Your sorrow, only sorrow's shade,
 Keeps real sorrow far away.
You move not in such solitudes,
 You are not less divine,
But more human in your moods,
 Than your twin-sister, Adeline.
Your hair is darker, and your eyes
 Touched with a somewhat darker hue,
 And less aërially blue,
 But ever trembling through the dew
Of dainty-woeful sympathies.

34. *lion-heart*] *1842*; lionsouled *1832*. Richard I, a troubadour and hero of troubadours, was imprisoned in Dürenstein on the Danube, in 1192–3.

35 ∧ 6]
 Or when the Gileadite returned,
 Whether Jephtha's daughter mourned
 Two moons beside the heavy flow
 Of torrent brooks in purple glens
 Of Judah, leaving far below,
 Leaving the fruitful olive plains,
 Leaving the hope of her bride bower
 In royal Mizpeh's battled tower. *Heath MS*

These lines are in *Heath MS* as 'Conclusion of *Margaret*, transferred to the *Dream of Fair Women*'. In one MS draft, these lines stood, as here, following l. 35 (*Walford's Antiquarian* xii (1887) 81–2, quoting from a copy of *1832*). They were adapted for *A Dream of Fair Women* 181 ff. (p. 449).

37. *Chatelet*: for Chastelard, executed in 1563 for importuning Mary Queen of Scots.

48. *1832* note: '*Poems chiefly Lyrical*'.

49–51. *H.Nbk 3* has a separate jotting: 'with eyes aerially blue'. See ll. 7–8*n*.

51. *less*] *1842*; more *1832*.

52. *But*] *1842*; And *1832*.

V

O sweet pale Margaret,
O rare pale Margaret,
Come down, come down, and hear me speak:
Tie up the ringlets on your cheek:
The sun is just about to set,
The arching limes are tall and shady,
And faint, rainy lights are seen,
Moving in the leavy beech.
Rise from the feast of sorrow, lady,
Where all day long you sit between
Joy and woe, and whisper each.
Or only look across the lawn,
Look out below your bower-eaves,
Look down, and let your blue eyes dawn
Upon me through the jasmine-leaves.

# 176 *Kate

Published *1832*; not reprinted, though H.T. restored it in 1895, People's Edition. J. Killham points out that this fierce feminist suggests the heroine of *The Princess* (*Tennyson and 'The Princess'*, 1958, p. 193). Ida's will has an 'axelike edge' (cp. ll. 11–12); and cp. the tournament (ll. 21–8).

I know her by her angry air,
Her brightblack eyes, her brightblack hair,
Her rapid laughters wild and shrill,
As laughters of the woodpecker
From the bosom of a hill.
'Tis Kate–she sayeth what she will:
For Kate hath an unbridled tongue,
Clear as the twanging of a harp.
Her heart is like a throbbing star.
Kate hath a spirit ever strung
Like a new bow, and bright and sharp
As edges of the scymetar.

*61. leavy*: T. compares *Much Ado* II iii 72: 'Since summer first was leavy'.
¶ 176.*2*. Cp. *Sense and Conscience* 67: 'Lovely with bright black eyes and long black hair'.
*4*. Cp. *My life is full* 20, *1832* text: 'laughters of the jay'.
*7*. Cp. *The Tempest* II ii 51–2: 'But none of us cared for Kate, / For she had a tongue with a tang.'
*9. like a throbbing star*: Keats, *Eve of St Agnes* 318.

Whence shall she take a fitting mate?
For Kate no common love will feel;
My woman-soldier, gallant Kate,
As pure and true as blades of steel.

Kate saith 'the world is void of might.'
Kate saith 'the men are gilded flies.'
Kate snaps her fingers at my vows;
Kate will not hear of lover's sighs.
I would I were an armèd knight,
Farfamed for wellwon enterprise,
And wearing on my swarthy brows
The garland of new-wreathed emprise;
For in a moment I would pierce
The blackest files of clanging fight,
And strongly strike to left and right,
In dreaming of my lady's eyes.
Oh! Kate loves well the bold and fierce;
But none are bold enough for Kate,
She cannot find a fitting mate.

# 177 *Sonnet

## Written on hearing of the outbreak of the Polish Insurrection

Published *1832*, not reprinted. The Poles rose against Russia in Nov. 1830; the war lasted from Jan. to Sept. 1831. See *Poland* and its headnote (p. 458), and *Hail Briton* 190–6 (p. 489). There are two drafts in *H.Nbk 5*.

Blow ye the trumpet, gather from afar
The hosts to battle: be not bought and sold.
Arise, brave Poles, the boldest of the bold;
Break through your iron shackles–fling them far.
O for those days of Piast, ere the Czar
Grew to this strength among his deserts cold;
When even to Moscow's cupolas were rolled

¶ 177.*1–4*] *H.Nbk 5, 1st draft, had the lines in the order 3, 4, 1, 2, with l. 4:* Break ye your iron gyves and fling . .
5] O for those days in Fame's great chart enrolled
Of Piast and Jagiello ere the Czar *first draft, fragmentary*
*Piast*: founder of the dynasty who ruled Poland till 1370. *Jagiello*, or Wladislaus II, King of Poland.
*7. cúpolas*: domes.

The growing murmurs of the Polish war!
Now must your noble anger blaze out more
Than when from Sobieski, clan by clan,
The Moslem myriads fell, and fled before–
Than when Zamoysky smote the Tatar Khan;
Than earlier, when on the Baltic shore
Boleslas drove the Pomeranian.

# 178 Poland

Published *1832*, as *Sonnet: On the Result of the Late Russian Invasion of Poland*; not reprinted till restored in *1872* as 'Juvenilia', 'Early Sonnets vi'. The Poles rose against Russia in Nov. 1830; the war lasted from Jan. to Sept. 1831. Probably written 1831. Cp. *Sonnet written on hearing of the outbreak of the Polish Insurrection* (above), and *Hail Briton* 191–204 (p. 489). Poland was evidently important to the young T. He told William Allingham, 'When I was 22 I wrote a beautiful poem on Poland, hundreds of lines long, and the housemaid lit the fire with it' (*Diary*, 1907, p. 303). Cp. Milton's *On the late Massacre in Piemont.*

How long, O God, shall men be ridden down,
And trampled under by the last and least
Of men? The heart of Poland hath not ceased
To quiver, though her sacred blood doth drown
The fields, and out of every smouldering town
Cries to Thee, lest brute Power be increased,
Till that o'ergrown Barbarian in the East
Transgress his ample bound to some new crown:–
Cries to Thee, 'Lord, how long shall these
things be?
How long this icy-hearted Muscovite

9] *Second draft, variously*: (i) Ye must put forth your native valour more (ii) Indue, great Poles, your native valour more (iii) Now let your native valour sparkle more.

*10. Sobieski*: later John III of Poland, who defeated the Turks in 1673–5.

*12. Zamoysky*: sixteenth-century Polish statesman who resisted the Tatars (Tartars). *Tatar* is the legitimate spelling in *1832* and *MS.*

*14.* Boleslaw I gained a sea-board in 996 by seizing Pomerania.

¶ 178.*1. Revelation* vi 10: 'How long, O Lord, holy and true, dost thou not judge and avenge our blood on them that dwell on the earth?'

*7.* Tsar Nicholas I.

*10. this*] *1872*; shall the *1832*. *icy-*] iron- *H.Nbk 5 1st reading.*

Oppress the region?' Us, O Just and Good,
Forgive, who smiled when she was torn in three;
Us, who stand now, when we should aid the right–
A matter to be wept with tears of blood!

# 179 To–[As when with downcast eyes]

Published *1832*, as *Sonnet*; not reprinted till restored in *1872* as 'Juvenilia', 'Early Sonnets I'. Presumably to Arthur Hallam, whom T. met early in 1829. Cp. *If I were loved* (p. 353), another early sonnet to Hallam. All variants from *H.Lpr 2* are below.

As when with downcast eyes we muse and brood,
And ebb into a former life, or seem
To lapse far back in some confusèd dream
To states of mystical similitude;
If one but speaks or hems or stirs his chair,
Ever the wonder waxeth more and more,
So that we say, 'All this hath been before,
All this hath been, I know not when or where.'
So, friend, when first I looked upon your face,
Our thought gave answer each to each, so true–
Opposèd mirrors each reflecting each–
That though I knew not in what time or place,
Methought that I had often met with you,
And either lived in either's heart and speech.

*12.* The partition of Poland, effected by treaties 1793–7.
*14.* Cp. Shelley's Christ 'whose pores wept tears of blood', *Prologue to Hellas* 88, a poem comparable in its political impulse ('Russia desires to possess, not to liberate Greece', Shelley). Also *The Palace of Art* 239: 'weeping tears of blood'.

¶ 179.*3. lapse far*] wander *H.MS.* *some*] *1872*; a *1832*. *confused*] mysterious *MS 1st reading*.
*5. If one but*] And if one *MS*.
*6. waxeth*] groweth *MS*.
*9*] So dearest friend when first I saw thy face, *MS 1st reading*.
*12. That though*] *1872*; Although *1832*.
*14*] *1872*; And each [both *MS*] had lived in the other's mind and speech. *1832*.

# 180 *O Darling Room

Published *1832*, not reprinted (it was ridiculed by J. W. Croker, *QR*, April 1833). Written 1832; T. toured the Rhine with Arthur Hallam in July. Cp. Byron's song about the Rhine, *Childe Harold* III lv following.

I

O darling room, my heart's delight,
Dear room, the apple of my sight,
With thy two couches soft and white,
There is no room so exquisite,
No little room so warm and bright,
Wherein to read, wherein to write.

II

For I the Nonnenwerth have seen,
And Oberwinter's vineyards green,
Musical Lurlei; and between
The hills to Bingen have I been,
Bingen in Darmstadt, where the Rhene
Curves toward Mentz, a woody scene.

III

Yet never did there meet my sight,
In any town, to left or right,
A little room so exquisite,
With two such couches, soft and white;
Not any room so warm and bright,
Wherein to read, wherein to write.

# 181 *To Christopher North

Published *1832*, not reprinted. Written Oct. 1832 (*Mem.* i 88, 95). 'Christopher North' (John Wilson) wrote in *Blackwood's Magazine*, Feb. 1832: "'I have good hopes of Alfred Tennyson. But the cockneys are doing what they may to spoil him . . . . He has a fine ear for melody and harmony too–and rare and rich glimpses of imagination. He has–*genius*.' [First speaker:] 'Affectations.' [Second speaker:] 'Too many. But I admire

¶ 180.*2*. This line, ridiculed by Croker, had already been deleted by T. in a presentation copy of *1832*, 21 Dec. 1832 (G. O. Marshall, *Library Chronicle of Texas*, Spring 1959). T. added, ll. 3 ∧ 4, 'Thy books and pictures ranged aright'.

*9. Lurlei*: Lorelei, the echoing rock in the Rhine, with its legendary siren.

Alfred–and hope–nay trust–that one day he will prove himself a poet. If he do not–then am I no prophet.'" Wilson's review of *1830* in *Blackwood's* (May 1832) expanded this, pouring scorn on those who overpraised T., including Arthur Hallam. Hallam wrote to reassure T. (*Mem.* i 84), and hinted that T. should not publish the epigram: 'I have scruples whether you should publish it. Perhaps he may like the lines and you the better for them; but . . .' (*Mem.* i 88). T. certainly regretted having published it (cp. *Literary Squabbles*, p. 739); in a letter to Wilson, he wrote: 'though I may have done, written, said foolish things, not excepting a silly squib to Christopher North . . .' (*Mem.* i 95). For further details, see A. L. Strout, *RES* xiv (1938) 428–39. The rhyming is natural to indignation, so that the often-quoted lines are merely analogues: 'ould rustie, dustie, mustie, fustie, crustie firebran' (*The Comedy of Mucedorus*, 1598, III v); 'rusty–musty–crusty–fusty–dusty old dotard' (Randolph's *Hey for Honesty* II i). But T. used John Walker's *Rhyming Dictionary*, 1801 (*Lincoln*), which gives: Dusty, Fusty, Gusty, Musty, Rusty, Crusty, Trusty (ii 286). A copy of *1832* (in the possession of Mr W. S. G. Macmillan) shows that T.'s original refrain throughout was 'Tipsy Kit'; his note reads: 'One of my sisters when I showed them this version persuaded me that Tipsy Kit was too sharp: so Crusty Xopher took his place.'

You did late review my lays,
   Crusty Christopher;
You did mingle blame and praise,
   Rusty Christopher.
When I learnt from whom it came,
I forgave you all the blame,
   Musty Christopher;
I could *not* forgive the praise,
   Fusty Christopher.

# 182 The Death of the Old Year

Published *1832*. Cp. *New Year's Eve* 5 (p. 675): 'Now the year is almost gone . . .'

Full knee-deep lies the winter snow,
   And the winter winds are wearily sighing:
Toll ye the church-bell sad and slow,
And tread softly and speak low,
For the old year lies a-dying.

¶ 181.*8*] How could I forgive the praise? *presentation copy of 1832, Virginia.*

¶ 182.*1. winter*] *Not H.Nbk 4.*

*2. wearily*] *Not MS.*

Old year, you must not die;
You came to us so readily,
You lived with us so steadily,
Old year, you shall not die.

He lieth still: he doth not move:
He will not see the dawn of day.
He hath no other life above.
He gave me a friend, and a true true-love,
And the New-year will take 'em away.
Old year, you must not go;
So long as you have been with us,
Such joy as you have seen with us,
Old year, you shall not go.

He frothed his bumpers to the brim;
A jollier year we shall not see.
But though his eyes are waxing dim,
And though his foes speak ill of him,
He was a friend to me.
Old year, you shall not die;
We did so laugh and cry with you,
I've half a mind to die with you,
Old year, if you must die.

He was full of joke and jest,
But all his merry quips are o'er.
To see him die, across the waste
His son and heir doth ride post-haste,
But he'll be dead before.
Every one for his own.
The night is starry and cold, my friend,
And the New-year blithe and bold, my friend,
Comes up to take his own.

How hard he breathes! over the snow
I heard just now the crowing cock.
The shadows flicker to and fro:
The cricket chirps: the light burns low:
'Tis nearly twelve o'clock.

*12*] He was tender and proud as a turtledove. *MS.*

*21. waxing*] glazed and *MS.*

*33*] You may hear him on his way. *MS.*

*36*] Is heard upon his way. *MS.*

*38. just now*] *Not MS.*

*41. twelve*] *1842*; one *1832*.

Shake hands, before you die.
Old year, we'll dearly rue for you:
What is it we can do for you?
Speak out before you die.

His face is growing sharp and thin.
Alack! our friend is gone.
Close up his eyes: tie up his chin:
Step from the corpse, and let him in
That standeth there alone,
And waiteth at the door.
There's a new foot on the floor, my friend,
And a new face at the door, my friend,
A new face at the door.

# 183 To J.S.

Published *1832*. T. noted: 'Addressed to James Spedding, the biographer of Bacon. His brother was Edward Spedding, a friend of mine, who died in his youth.' Edward died 24 Aug. 1832. Arthur Hallam wrote to T. in Oct.: 'The lines to J.S. are perfect. James, I am sure, will be most grateful' *Mem.* i 88). T. may have remembered Hallam's praise when he came to write *In Memoriam*, which is comparable in style and gravity. The belief that the dead 'sleep sweetly' is discussed in *In Memoriam* xliii (p. 900): 'If Sleep and Death be truly one'. For the opening of *To J.S.* T. adapted the opening (all he had written) of part ii of a poem which he had already sent to James Spedding; *Dear friend* (p. 1786) was quoted by Spedding in a letter to his brother Edward, 9 March 1831 (copy at *Lincoln*), and so will have been particularly appropriate.

The wind, that beats the mountain, blows
More softly round the open wold,
And gently comes the world to those
That are cast in gentle mould.

49. *Step . . . corpse*] Open the door *MS.*
54] *MS ends with a fragmentary stanza:*
We loved you well while you were here,
We loved you dear, merry old year,
We'll not forget now you're dead
For you were a gentleman born and bred,
Merry old year, merry old year.

¶ 183.*1–4*. Adapted from *Dear friend* (see headnote): 'The wind that beats the mountain cold / All night in early April blows / Softly on the open wold, / And gently comes the world to those / That are of gentle mould,

And me this knowledge bolder made,
Or else I had not dared to flow
In these words toward you, and invade
Even with a verse your holy woe.

'Tis strange that those we lean on most,
Those in whose laps our limbs are nursed,
Fall into shadow, soonest lost:
Those we love first are taken first.

God gives us love. Something to love
He lends us; but, when love is grown
To ripeness, that on which it throve
Falls off, and love is left alone.

This is the curse of time. Alas!
In grief I am not all unlearned;
Once through mine own doors Death did pass;
One went, who never hath returned.

He will not smile–not speak to me
Once more. Two years his chair is seen
Empty before us. That was he
Without whose life I had not been.

Your loss is rarer; for this star
Rose with you through a little arc
Of heaven, nor having wandered far
Shot on the sudden into dark.

I knew your brother: his mute dust
I honour and his living worth:
A man more pure and bold and just
Was never born into the earth.

I have not looked upon you nigh,
Since that dear soul hath fallen asleep.
Great Nature is more wise than I:
I will not tell you not to weep.

And though mine own eyes fill with dew,
Drawn from the spirit through the brain,

*5. And me*] *1842*; My heart *1832*.
*6. I*] *1842*; it *1832*.
*19–24*. T. comments: 'The death of my father', in March 1831.
*31. bold*] *1842*; mild *1832*.
*37–44*. Cp. *The Gardener's Daughter* 193: 'A thought would fill my eyes with happy dew'. Cp. Gray's Alcaic fragment (which provided an epi-

I will not even preach to you,
  'Weep, weeping dulls the inward pain.'

Let Grief be her own mistress still.
  She loveth her own anguish deep
More than much pleasure. Let her will
  Be done–to weep or not to weep.

I will not say, 'God's ordinance
  Of Death is blown in every wind;'
For that is not a common chance
  That takes away a noble mind.

His memory long will live alone
  In all our hearts, as mournful light
That broods above the fallen sun,
  And dwells in heaven half the night.

Vain solace! Memory standing near
  Cast down her eyes, and in her throat
Her voice seemed distant, and a tear
  Dropt on the letters as I wrote.

I wrote I know not what. In truth,
  How *should* I soothe you anyway,
Who miss the brother of your youth?
  Yet something I did wish to say:

graph for a poem by T.'s brother Charles in *1827*, p. 11): *O lachrymarum Fons, tenero sacros / Ducentium ortus ex animo; quater / Felix! in imo qui scatentem / Pectore te, pia Nympha, sensit!* ('O fountain of tears which have their sacred sources in the sensitive soul! Four times blessed he who has felt thee, holy Nymph, bubbling up from the depths of his heart!') Yet alongside John Churton Collins's suggestion of this (*Cornhill*, Jan. 1880, *Lincoln*), T. wrote 'no!'. Cp. *Fragment: Why are my moments* (p. 1790).

*45–8.* Cp. *In Memoriam* vi 1–4: 'One writes, that "Other friends remain," / That "Loss is common to the race"– / And common is the commonplace, / And vacant chaff well meant for grain.'

*49–52.* Cp. Vaughan's poem on the same theme, *They are all gone into the world of light*: 'Their very memory is fair and bright . . . / Or those faint beams in which this hill is drest, / After the Sun's remove.' John Churton Collins said that this stanza by T. 'may have been distilled from two lines in Dryden's noble tragedy of *Don Sebastian*, act I scene 1': 'If I fall, / I shall be like myself; a setting sun / Should leave a track of glory in the skies.' Alongside this suggestion, T. wrote: 'Nonsense' (*Cornhill*, Jan. 1880, *Lincoln*).

*51. fallen*] *1842*; sunken *1832*.

*56. the letters*] *1845*; my tablets *1832–43*.

For he too was a friend to me:
    Both are my friends, and my true breast
Bleedeth for both; yet it may be
    That only silence suiteth best.

Words weaker than your grief would make
    Grief more. 'Twere better I should cease
Although myself could almost take
    The place of him that sleeps in peace.

Sleep sweetly, tender heart, in peace:
    Sleep, holy spirit, blessèd soul,
While the stars burn, the moons increase,
    And the great ages onward roll.

Sleep till the end, true soul and sweet.
    Nothing comes to thee new or strange.
Sleep full of rest from head to feet;
    Lie still, dry dust, secure of change.

## 184 *‘From the East of life joybeams did strike’

*Mat.* i 35–6 printed ll. 13–24: ‘As a boy he would reel off hundreds of lines such as these’. *Mem.* i 18 printed ll. 21–4 only. The MS of ll. 1–20 is in *H.Nbk 12*, *c.* 1832; ll. 21–4, only, are in *Nbk 11*. The subject and the tone suggest *Youth* (1833, p. 577); see l. 14*n* below.

From the East of life joybeams did strike
On my young brows. Joy rose up like
White Venus, whiter than all stars–
Then uprose trouble, red like Mars.
Joy set: he stayed: as Mars in heaven
Burns by the lonely sisters seven

*64. only*] *1842*; holy *1832*.
*67*] *1842*; Although to calm you I would take *1832*. The original hyperbole aroused FitzGerald's scepticism; he wrote in a copy of *1842* (*Trinity College*): ‘I used to ask if this was not *un peu trop fort*. I think it's altered or omitted in future Editions. It is all rather affected.’
*76*. Cp. *Paradise Lost* iv 791: ‘asleep secure of harme’.
¶ 184.*3*. Incorporated as *Who is it comes hither* 11, and see ll. 5–8*n* below. Cp. Keats, *On leaving some friends* 3: ‘Whiter than a star’.
*4*. Cp. *The Devil and the Lady* II vi 63: ‘Mars with front as red as fire’.
*5–8*. Cp. *The Lover's Tale* i 52–61, MS: ‘Mars, glaring by the lonely

When Venus having measured all
The arch in western mist doth fall.

When I was young and full of love
I took my fancies from above,
But as I wander from my birth
My fancies savour of the earth.

My earthy spirit grieves alone
Housed like the caddisworm in stone,
Pent in a gleaming chrysalis,
Which an eternal prison is.

The brownringed serpent sloughs–so do
The water-efts that bite in two
The red earthworm in weedy swamps.
The dragonfly is born from damps.

The quickwinged gnat doth make a boat
Of his old husk wherewith to float
To a new life: all low things range
To higher but I cannot change.

# 185 *Sonnet [Alas! how weary are my human eyes]

Printed by Sir Charles Tennyson, *Nineteenth Century* cix (1931) 506; then *1931*, p. 59, from *H.Lpr 2* where it accompanies *As when with downcast eyes* (*1832* sonnet). Cp. *My life is full of weary days*, written 1830–32 (p. 350).

sisters seven / Followed white Venus, whiter than all stars, / Down to the quiet limit of the world.'
*13. earthy*] earthly *Mat.*
*14.* Verbatim in MS stanza introducing *Youth*:

Though what I sought I knew not well,
I was not made to live alone,
My heart was never meant to dwell
Housed like the caddisworm in stone.

The larva of the Mayfly lives in water, making for itself a cylinder of small stones. T.'s line also appears in a poem on authorship in *T.Nbk 26*, which may not be quoted.
*16. Which*] Mine *Mat.*
*19. weedy*] reedy *Mat.*
*20–24.* Cp. the significance given to the dragonfly's change, *The Two Voices* 8–15 (p. 523).

Alas! how weary are my human eyes
With all the thousand tears of human scorn.
Alas! how like the dazzled moon at morn
My waning spirit after darkness sighs.
Through kindling buds hale March will yearly blow
On hollow winds his gusty showerdrops,
And many an April sprinkle the blue copse
With snowy sloethorn-flowers when I am low,
And brown September laughing cheerily
Bruise his gold grain upon his threshing-floor,
And all the infinite variety
Of the dear world will vary evermore.
Close weary eyes, breathe out my weary breath,
One only thought I have, and that is death.

# 186 *The Christian Penitent

Unpublished. It is the original version of *Doubt and Prayer* (p. 1454); T. printed it in a trial edition of *1892* (*Lincoln*) and then revised. For ll. 8–14, the text is that in *H.Nbk 3*, where the sonnet is with poems of *1832*, the date of many of T.'s sonnets; all variants from the printed trial edition are given. Unfortunately ll. 1–7 have been cut off from the *H.MS*, so it is possible, but unlikely, that those lines had already undergone some slight revision before the trial edition. The sonnet is more regular than those of *1830*.

We sin and so we suffer, and alas
We see not we are chastened with the rod;
From sin through sorrow into God we pass
By the same path our true forefathers trod;
Seal not mine eyes with night, nor let the sod
Feed from my mouldering frame Thy flowers and grass
Before I know Thy Love which is and was,

¶ 185.*2. tears*] shades *H.MS 1st reading.*
*3. dazzled*] *MS, Nineteenth Century*; dappled *1931*. Cp. *Paradise Lost* iv 798: 'Daz'ling the Moon', and Keats, *Otho* III ii 228: 'To dazzle the soft moon'.
*5. kindling buds*: Shelley, *Adonais* 137. Cp. *In Memoriam* xxxix 11: 'Thy gloom is kindled at the tips'.
*10. Bruise*: *OED* 4, to grind. Cp. *In Memoriam* xxxv 23: 'Had bruised the herb and crushed the grape'.
*13. weary eyes*] my wan eyes *MS 1st reading.*

My Father, and my Brother, and my God!
Touch me with sorrow! soften me with grief!
Blow thou the trumpet strongly night and day,
Until this battled wall of unbelief
Built round my warring spirit fall away!
Then take me to Thyself–a full-eared sheaf
Ripe for the harvest on an autumn day.

# 187 Alexander

Published *1872*, 'Juvenilia', 'Early Sonnets IV', 'although written much earlier' (H.T.). It is in *H.Nbk 5*, together with sonnets of *1832*. Alexander visited the temple of Zeus Ammon and was told that he was indeed the favoured son of Zeus. T.'s main source was Charles Rollin's *Ancient History* (Paden, p. 126), of which the 1789 translation was at Somersby (*Lincoln*). Possibly it was influenced by G. S. Faber's *Horae Mosaicae* (1801), of which T.'s father had a copy (*Lincoln*); Faber compares Eden and this sacred spot, 'shaded from the sun . . . watered by the meandering streams of numerous fountains' (i 83). Cp. *Persia* (p. 102), and *The High Priest to Alexander* (p. 138).

Warrior of God, whose strong right arm debased
The throne of Persia, when her Satrap bled
At Issus by the Syrian gates, or fled
Beyond the Memmian naphtha-pits, disgraced
For ever–thee (thy pathway sand-erased)
Gliding with equal crowns two serpents led
Joyful to that palm-planted fountain-fed

¶ 186.*10. the*] *H.MS*; thy *Lincoln trial edition.*
*10–12.* The fall of Jericho, *Joshua* vi.
*13–14*] *MS*; Then bring thou to my leaguered soul relief
And strike Thy glory through my darkened day! *trial edition*
¶ 187.*1. debased*] displaced *H.MS 1st reading.*
*2–3.* Paden points out that Darius (the 'Satrap', viceroy) was not wounded at Issus, though Alexander was.
*3. the Syrian gates*: as in *Persia* 61.
*4. Memmian*: should be Memnian (cp. Milton's 'Memnonian', *Paradise Lost* x 308), the place being Memnis. But it was at Babylon that Alexander admired the naphtha-pits; T.'s confusion is due to Rollin's haste (Paden).
*5*] Then when thy track the blowing sands erased *MS 1st reading*; For ever, thee, thy track by sands erased *MS.*

Ammonian Oasis in the waste.
There in a silent shade of laurel brown
Apart the Chamian Oracle divine
Sheltered his unapproachèd mysteries:
High things were spoken there, unhanded down;
Only they saw thee from the secret shrine
Returning with hot cheek and kindled eyes.

# 188 *Sonnet [The Wise, the Pure, the lights of our dull clime]

Printed by Sir Charles Tennyson, *Nineteenth Century* cix (1931) 506; then *1931*, p. 61, from *H.Nbk 5* (inscribed 'Somersby' and including several sonnets of *1832*). Cp. *Sonnet [Woe to the double-tongued]* (p. 471).

The Wise, the Pure, the lights of our dull clime,
Fall from the age, and we shall roam the gloom,
Wild hearts, whom their own rage and heat consume,
Weak wings, that every sophister can lime.
They will not hear the loud lies of the time
To come, the shallow fret and frothy fume
Of brass-mouthed demagogues, O'Connell, Hume,
And the others whom the sacred Muse of rhyme
Disdains to name. O that true Liberty
Would ride upon the singing winds, and blow
Her silver trumpet clear from sky to sky,
That we might see, who love her all in all
For her fair self, and of a surety know
Those men that to the golden idol fall.

*8–11.* Tinged by reminiscences of Milton: the serpent 'to which transformd / Ammonian Jove' (*PL* ix 507–8); 'old Cham, / Whom Gentiles Ammon call' (iv 276–7); and the Miltonic 'unapproachèd' (God in 'unapproached light', iii 4).
*9. silent*] glittering *MS 1st reading*; secret *MS*.
*13. secret*] inmost *MS*.
*14. hot . . . kindled*] flushed . . . brightened *MS*.
¶ 118.*3–4.* Adapted as *Love thou thy Land* 11–12: 'The herd, wild hearts and feeble wings / That every sophister can lime.' *Love thou* 69 takes up the 'idol' from l. 14. *lime*: catch a bird with quicklime.
*7.* Daniel O'Connell (1775–1847) and Joseph Hume (1777–1855), Irish and British politicians. They are disparaged in *An Idle Rhyme* 34 (p. 663). On

# 189 *Sonnet [Woe to the double-tongued]

Printed by Sir Charles Tennyson, *Nineteenth Century* cix (1931) 507; then *1931*, p. 62, from *H.Nbk 5* (inscribed 'Somersby' and including several sonnets of *1832*). Cp. *Sonnet [The Wise, the Pure]* (p. 470).

Woe to the double-tongued, the land's disease,
   Lords of the hustings, whose mob-rhetoric rends
   The ears of Truth! How shall they make amends,
Those that would shatter England's ancient ease
Built on broad bases and the solid peace
   Wherein she prospered?–Woe to those false friends
   That mouth great things and for their own vile
      ends
Make swarm with brazen clang the humming bees;
   Those that would turn the ploughshares into swords,
   Those that inflame themselves with idle words
In every market-place. Their doom is signed,
   Though they shall cause confusion and the storms
   Of civil blood–moths, cankers, palmer-worms
That gnaw the bud, blind leaders of the blind.

10 March 1833, T. described O'Connell as 'as double-dyed a rascal as ever was dipped in the Styx of political villainy'; H.T. comments: 'He softened this opinion when he came to know more about O'Connell.' *brass-mouthed*: cp. 'Brass mouths and iron lungs', *Freedom* 40 (which had orignally been part of *Love thou thy land*; p. 613).

¶ 189.*2. mob-*] loud *H.MS 1st reading.*

*4–5.* Cp. *To the Queen* 35: 'Broad-based upon her people's will'.

*5. Built . . . bases*] Which was her glory *MS 1st reading.*

*7. things*] words *MS 1st reading.*

*8.* Bees swarm in response to the sound.

*13. blood–moths*] contest–*MS 1st reading.* *palmer-worms*: caterpillars destructive to vegetation. *OED* quotes Geneva Bible, *Joel* i 4: 'That which is left of the palmer worme, hathe the grashopper eaten'; and Topsell (1608): 'a very apt name amongst us Englishmen, to be called Palmer-worms, by reason of their wandering and roguish life, (for they never stay in one place, but are ever wandering)'.

# 190 *'Pierced through with knotted thorns of barren pain'

Unpublished, *H.Nbk 4*. Written *c.* 1832. It shares several lines with *Perdidi Diem* (p. 269): ll. 17–18, 22–4. This confirms that T.'s moods of despondency preceded the death of Arthur Hallam. Lines 30–41 had earlier been part of *Armageddon* (p. 65) in *T.Nbk 18*, which may not be quoted. *Armageddon* was patched up as *Timbuctoo* (p. 170), so it is natural that these dozen lines embody a vision similar to the latter. A version of these lines appears in *The Coach of Death* (p. 82). The description of the volcano probably owes something to the lavish descriptions in a book which T. used for many poems of *1827*: *The Hundred Wonders of the World* by 'C. C. Clarke' (1818).

Pierced through with knotted thorns of barren pain,
Deep in forethought of dark calamities,
Sick of the coming time and coming woe,
As one that tramples some volcanic plain
And through the yawning rifts and chasms hears
The scummy sulphur seething far below
And dares not to advance or to retire
But with a wan discoloured countenance
Remaining still, lamenteth bitterly
For fear the hidden wells of scorching fire
Should spout between the clefts and shower flame
And flicker round his body that he die:
E'en so I lay upon my bed at night:
All my delight was gone: my hope was fresh
No longer: and I lay with sobbing breath,
Walled round, shut up, imbarred, moaning for light,
A carcase in the coffin of this flesh,
Pierced through with loathly worms of utter death.

¶ 190.*1*. *knotted thorns*: *The Lover's Tale* i 609. In connection with l. 29 below, suggesting *In Memoriam* lxix: 'I took the thorns to bind my brows . . . / He reached the glory of a hand, / That seemed to touch it into leaf.'
*10*. Cp. Shelley, *Prometheus Unbound* IV 284: 'Wells of unfathomed fire'.
*17–24*. *Perdidi Diem* 7–12 (p. 269): 'A carcase in the coffin of this flesh, / Pierced through with loathly worms of utter Death. / My soul is but the eternal mystic lamp, / Lighting that charnel damp, / Wounding with dreadful rays that solid gloom, / And shadowing forth the unutterable tomb.'
*17*. Cp. *Vastness* 33: 'in being our own corpse-coffins at last'.
*18*. Cp. the scene as in Hell, *The Vision of Sin* 209: 'Below were men and horses pierced with worms'. *loathly worms*: Shelley, *Prometheus Unbound* III iv 36.

And in that spiritual charnel low and damp
All my past thoughts and actions I did mark
Thick-thronging to and fro amid the gloom.
My soul was but the eternal mystic lamp
Wounding with dreadful rays the solid dark
And shadowing out the unutterable tomb.
I closed my eyes and so I kept them tight
And strove to mutter over ancient prayers
And would not look on the phantasmal night
.......................................
....................my eyelids unawares
Were touched and opened by a finger bright.

* * * *

Thereon I looked on every living thing,
Mammoth and Mastodonte in my dream,
Which the wide-weltering sea somewhere enwombs,
And toward the sloping roof on equal wing
Mystic Iönah wandered and the gleam
Of Heaven's first arch was on her amber plumes.
On the Eastern wall in a clear light revealed
Stood kingly Dionys, prime worship hailed,
The bunchy vine down-dangled to his heel.
And close behind him on a carven field
With semblance of the peaky wave engrailed
Laboured an immeasurable keel.

*19.* Cp. the relation of 'charnel' to 'spiritual' in *To–[Thou mayst remember]* (p. 282).
*27–8] Lacuna thus in H.MS.*
*30–41.* See headnote.
*31. Mastodonte*: the French form, used by Cuvier in 1806. The earliest *OED* example of 'mastodon' is 1813.
*34. Iönah*: from a book that was at Somersby (*Lincoln*), Jacob Bryant's *New System of Ancient Mythology* (1807 edn, iii 117). The prophetic bird Iönah was the dove sent forth from the Ark. Hence l. 35 on God's rainbow. T. recalls a memorable plate in Bryant (v 286), showing the Ark, the Dove, and the Rainbow. The lines are possibly influenced by Shelley's Ione in *Prometheus Unbound*; she uses the words 'mystic' (III iii 70) and 'plumes' (I 320), and she has 'plumes', like Panthea (I 439).
*36–8.* The link between Dionysus and the Ark is Bryant iv 249: 'The Cuthites worshipped the Patriarch Noah under the name of Nusos, and Dio-nusos.' Cp. the description of Bacchus (Dionys) in *Semele* (p. 574).
*37. prime*: primitive.
*38. bunchy vine*: *The Palace of Art* 69–80, *1832* text.
*40.* Adapted as *The Palace of Art* 113: 'Or over hills with peaky tops

# 191 *Inscription by a Brook

Printed *Mem.* i 55, as *By a Brook*, dated 1828. *Heath MS*, entitled *Inscription by a Brook* (as in *H.MS*), is dated 1833, and occurs later in the commonplace book than the 1828 poems. The later date is supported by *H.Nbk 13*; possibly T. revised an earlier version. It belongs to a popular and classical genre, and closely resembles Akenside's blank-verse *Inscriptions*, e.g. iii: 'Whoe'er thou art whose path in summer lies / Through yonder village, turn thee . . .'. Akenside's *Inscriptions* were among the poems at Somersby (*Lincoln*). Cp. also Samuel Rogers's *Inscription in the Crimea* (1812), which includes a character called Fatima, and which begins: 'Shepherd, or Huntsman, or worn Mariner, Whate'er thou art, who wouldst allay thy thirst, / Drink and be glad.'

Townsmen, or of the hamlet, young or old,
Whithersoever you may wander now,
Where'er you roam from, would you waste an hour,
Or sleep through one brief dream upon the grass,–
Pause here. The murmurs of the rivulet,
Rippling by cressy isles or bars of sand,
Are pleasant from the early Spring to when,
Full fields of barley shifting tearful lights
On growing spears, by fits the lady ash
With twinkling finger sweeps her yellow keys.

# 192 *The Ruined Kiln

Printed by Sir Charles Tennyson, *Nineteenth Century* cix (1931) 503–4; then *1931*, p. 71: 'These lines occur in a small pocket-book, which is dated in Hallam Tennyson's handwriting 1831–3, and I have found a slightly different version written by Tennyson in ink in a proof copy of the volume of 1832.' The pocket-book, *H.Nbk 16* (*A* below), is watermarked 1833 and includes poems written in that year. The *1832* volume (*B* below) is at *Lincoln*. All variants are below.

engrailed'. *peaky*: T.'s is the earliest example in *OED*. Cp. Shelley, *Prince Athanase* 188: 'peakèd wave'.

¶ 191.*2. may . . . now*] are wandering *H.MS 1st reading.*

5 ∧ 6] That wins a way through dimpled curves and bays *H.MS, deleted.*

*6. or*] *Mem.*; and *Heath MS, H.MS.*

*7. Spring*] May *Heath MS, H.MS.*

*9. growing*] grainy *H.MS.*

I

A million gossamers in field and fold
Were twinkling into green and gold,
Then basked the filmy stubbles warm and bare,
While thousands in a silent air
Of dappled cloudlets roofed the day,
And sparrows in a jangling throng
Chirped all in one–a storm of song–
As by the ruined kiln I lay.

II

All else like me, one peaceful presence kept,
On his bound sheaf October slept,
Through crumbling bricks the woolly thistle grew;
Yet in the round kiln slept the dew
And, over harrowed glebe, was seen
Hard by one waning elm, the farm
In tempered sunshine white and warm,
Where Lucy lived the village-queen.

# 193 The Progress of Spring

Published *1889.* Written 'in early youth' (H.T.). The opening is in *H.Nbk 17* (all variants are below, *A*), and there is a draft in *T.Nbk 17* (which may not be quoted). Both of these are 1833, which is the date that T. mentioned for l. 56. T. revised it for *1889* (*H.Nbk 55*; all variants are

¶ 192.*1. A million*] The *B.*
*2. green and*] threads of *B.* These two lines were adapted as *In Memoriam* xi 7–8: 'And all the silvery gossamers / That twinkle into green and gold.'
*3*] The stubbles basking warm and bare, B. *filmy*] *added to A.*
*4. thousands in*] millions, o'er *B.*
*5. cloudlets*: four times in Keats.
*6. And*] The *B.*
*8. by*] in *B.*
*9*] All else was placid as my happy love. *A 1st reading*; All else was still as happy love. *B.*
*10*] Earth dreaming, Heaven dreamed above. *A 1st reading, B.*
*11, 12*] *Transposed B.*
*11. woolly*] *added to A*; *not B.*
*12. round*] *added to A*; *not B. slept*] lay *A 1st reading*; yet lay *B.*
*13. over . . . glebe*] closed in crowded ricks *A 1st reading*; o'er a stubble-slope *B.*
*15. tempered*] steady *A 1st reading*; glowing *B.*
*16. lived*] lives *B.*

below, *B*). The trial edition of *1889* (*Trinity College*) shows that T. undertook the revision at this stage; his ink corrections bring it virtually to the final form. It was entitled *Ode on the Progress of Spring*, which suggests T.'s mingling of two familiar eighteenth-century kinds; cp. Gray's *Ode on the Spring* and *The Progress of Poesy*. For the concluding political lines, cp. the other political poems of 1832–3, and their fear that reform may become revolution. See *To Mary Boyle* (p. 1402).

I

The groundflame of the crocus breaks the mould,
  Fair Spring slides hither o'er the Southern sea,
Wavers on her thin stem the snowdrop cold
  That trembles not to kisses of the bee:
Come Spring, for now from all the dripping eaves
  The spear of ice has wept itself away,
And hour by hour unfolding woodbine leaves
  O'er his uncertain shadow droops the day.
She comes! The loosened rivulets run;
  The frost-bead melts upon her golden hair;
Her mantle, slowly greening in the Sun,
  Now wraps her close, now arching leaves her bare
  To breaths of balmier air;

¶ 193.*1*. Cp. T.'s letter to W. H. Brookfield in 1832–3: 'The Spring is burgeoning fast about us, and the crocus pierces through the dark moist moulds like a tongue of flame' (F. M. Brookfield, *The Cambridge 'Apostles'*, 1906, p. 28). Cp. *Œnone* 94: 'And at their feet the crocus brake like fire'.

*4 ∧ 5*] *A–B have ll. 7–8:*

Now hour by hour unbinding woodbine leaves *A–B*
  O'er his vague shadow stoops the day. *A*; *B as 1889*

*5*] For little spears of ice from dripping eaves *A–B*.

*6*] Have wept themselves away *A*; And jutting beams have wept themselves away *B*.

*8. uncertain shadow*: Arthur Hallam, *Written in View of Ben Lomond* 20 (1829; Motter, p. 52). The phrase appears in *T.MS* of *Tithon* 40 ∧ 41*n* (p. 567), on the death of Hallam.

*9*] Come Spring! she comes! the frost is done, *A–B*.

*10*] *Not A.* *frost-bead*] ice-bead *B*.

*11*] Her pale cheeks gather colour in the sun, *A–B*.

*12. Now . . . now*] And her green mantle *B*.

*12–13*] In warmer air the laurels twinkle
  While violets spring beneath the tree,
And jewel spheres of trembling dewdrops sprinkle
  The soft anemone. *A*

*13. breaths*] draughts *B*. Cp. *Sir Launcelot* 9.

II

Up leaps the lark, gone wild to welcome her,
About her glance the tits, and shriek the jays,
Before her skims the jubilant woodpecker,
The linnet's bosom blushes at her gaze,
While round her brows a woodland culver flits,
Watching her large light eyes and gracious looks,
And in her open palm a halcyon sits
Patient–the secret splendour of the brooks.
Come Spring! She comes on waste and wood,
On farm and field: but enter also here,
Diffuse thyself at will through all my blood,
And, though thy violet sicken into sere,
Lodge with me all the year!

III

Once more a downy drift against the brakes,
Self-darkened in the sky, descending slow!
But gladly see I through the wavering flakes
Yon blanching apricot like snow in snow.
These will thine eyes not brook in forest-paths,
On their perpetual pine, nor round the beech;
They fuse themselves to little spicy baths,
Solved in the tender blushes of the peach;
They lose themselves and die
On that new life that gems the hawthorn line;
Thy gay lent-lilies wave and put them by,
And out once more in varnished glory shine
Thy stars of celandine.

IV

She floats across the hamlet. Heaven lours,
But in the tearful splendour of her smiles

*14*] Up shouts the merry lark to welcome her, *B*.
*18. While round her*] Round her wide *B*.
*21. secret splendours*: *A Dream of Fair Women*, opening, *1832* text.
*23*] Leave waste and wood, O Spring, and enter here! *B*.
*27. Once more*] Lo yet *B*.
*29. But*] Yet *B*.
*33*. Cp. (with l. 30) *The Two Voices* 60, *Heath MS*: 'In spicy tufts of vernal snow'.
*36. gems*: buds (Miltonic).
*37. Thy*] Her *B*.
*39. Thy*] Her *B*.
*40–41*] Over the town she passes. Heaven lours,
But broad lights sweep beneath her when she smiles. *B*

I see the slowly-thickening chestnut towers
   Fill out the spaces by the barren tiles.
Now past her feet the swallow circling flies,
   A clamorous cuckoo stoops to meet her hand;
Her light makes rainbows in my closing eyes,
   I hear a charm of song through all the land.
Come, Spring! She comes, and Earth is glad
   To roll her North below thy deepening dome,
But ere thy maiden birk be wholly clad,
   And these low bushes dip their twigs in foam,
   Make all true hearths thy home.

V

Across my garden! and the thicket stirs,
   The fountain pulses high in sunnier jets,
The blackcap warbles, and the turtle purrs,
   The starling claps his tiny castanets.
Still round her forehead wheels the woodland dove,
   And scatters on her throat the sparks of dew,
The kingcup fills her footprint, and above
   Broaden the glowing isles of vernal blue.
Hail ample presence of a Queen,
   Bountiful, beautiful, apparelled gay,
Whose mantle, every shade of glancing green,
   Flies back in fragrant breezes to display
   A tunic white as May!

VI

She whispers, 'From the South I bring you balm,
   For on a tropic mountain was I born,
While some dark dweller by the coco-palm
   Watched my far meadow zoned with airy morn;

42. *I see*] She sees *B*.
43 ∧ 4] *B at first had ll. 53–6 here.*
44] About her steps the circling swallow flies, *B*.
45. *A*] The *B*.
47. *song*] songs *B*. *charm*: imitating Milton's use of the word 'charm', bird-song, *Paradise Lost* iv 642.
49. *deepening*] brightening *B*.
54. *pulses high*] shoots to heaven *B*. See ll. 43 ∧ 4*n*.
57. *woodland*] burnished *B*. T. incorporated 'the burnished dove' in *Locksley Hall* 19.
58] And shakes about her throat the sparkling dew *B*. *sparks of dew*: *In Memoriam*: *Epilogue* 118, *Lincoln MS*.
67. *tropic mountain*: *The Palace of Art* 181, *1832* text.

From under rose a muffled moan of floods;
I sat beneath a solitude of snow;
There no one came, the turf was fresh, the woods
Plunged gulf on gulf through all their vales below.
I saw beyond their silent tops
The steaming marshes of the scarlet cranes,
The slant seas leaning on the mangrove copse,
And summer basking in the sultry plains
About a land of canes;

VII

'Then from my vapour-girdle soaring forth
I scaled the buoyant highway of the birds,
And drank the dews and drizzle of the North,
That I might mix with men, and hear their words
On pathwayed plains; for–while my hand exults
Within the bloodless heart of lowly flowers
To work old laws of Love to fresh results,
Through manifold effect of simple powers–
I too would teach the man
Beyond the darker hour to see the bright,
That his fresh life may close as it began,
The still-fulfilling promise of a light
Narrowing the bounds of night.'

VIII

So wed thee with my soul, that I may mark
The coming year's great good and varied ills,
And new developments, whatever spark
Be struck from out the clash of warring wills;
Or whether, since our nature cannot rest,
The smoke of war's volcano burst again
From hoary deeps that belt the changeful West,
Old Empires, dwellings of the kings of men;

75. Paden (pp. 140–1) observes that the scarlet cranes are from Washington Irving's *Columbus* (1828), as in *Anacaona* 31.
79. *Then*] And *B*.
80. *I scaled*] Rose o'er *B*.
81. *dews . . . the*] drizzle of the fragile *B*.
85. Cp. *The constant spirit* 4: 'Old principles still working new results'.
92. *thee*] thou *B*.
97. *smoke . . . volcano*] smoky swathes of battle *B*.
98. *hoary*] umber *B*. *changeful*] thoughtful *B*. Cp. ll. 97–8 with Milton's Hell, *PL* ii 888–91: 'like a Furnace mouth / Cast forth redounding smoak and ruddy flame. / Before thir eyes in sudden view appear / The secrets of the hoarie deep.'

Or should those fail, that hold the helm,
While the long day of knowledge grows and warms,
And in the heart of this most ancient realm
A hateful voice be uttered, and alarms
Sounding 'To arms! to arms!'

IX

A simpler, saner lesson might he learn
Who reads thy gradual process, Holy Spring.
Thy leaves possess the season in their turn,
And in their time thy warblers rise on wing.
How surely glidest thou from March to May,
And changest, breathing it, the sullen wind,
Thy scope of operation, day by day,
Larger and fuller, like the human mind!
Thy warmths from bud to bud
Accomplish that blind model in the seed,
And men have hopes, which race the restless blood,
That after many changes may succeed
Life, which is Life indeed.

# 194 *'Hail Briton!'

Printed by M. J. Donahue, *PMLA* lxiv (1949) 385–99. Written 1831–33, judging from its position in the *Heath MS*, its references to the Polish war, and the atmosphere of the Reform Bill (1832). There are various drafts among *H.MSS*, making it clear that later T. thought of adapting and publishing parts of it. *H.Nbk 11* [*A*], *c.* 1833, is a complete text, close to *Heath MS*, though more confused with additions and deletions. *H.Nbk 15* [*B*], *c.* 1833–4, reduces the poem to about a quarter of its length, and has variants throughout. *H.Nbk 17* [*C*], *c.* 1833–4, reduces the poem to about half its length, and has variants throughout. *H.Nbk 46* [*D*], 1883, is a transcript in H.T.'s hand, selecting a few stanzas and headed: 'In Memory of Tel el Kebir 1883', changed to: 'Retrospect 1883'. (See *The Charge of the Heavy Brigade: Prologue*, p. 1304.) *H.Lpr 74* [*E*], 1886, is in the hand of T.'s

*107. Thy*] Whose *B.*
*108. time thy*] times whose *B.*
*109. surely*] softly *B.*
*114.* Cp., with the political application, *I loving Freedom* 17–20 (1832–4): 'The state within herself contains / A vital strength as in the seed, / The model of her future form, / And liberty indeed.'
*115. And men*] We too *B.*
*117. Life,*] That *B.*

wife Emily; it was printed by Sir Charles Tennyson (*Nineteenth Century* cix (1931) 625; *1931*, p. 73). This consists of ll. 1–12 (with slight variants), followed by:

But that in righteousness thy power
  Doth stand, thine empire on thy word–
  In thee no traitor voice be heard
Whatever danger threats the hour!

God keep thee strong as thou art free,
  Free in the freedom of His law,
  And brave all wrong to overawe,
Strong in the strength of unity!

*1931* did not print a final deleted stanza:

Symbol of loyal brotherhood!
  Lo, brother-hands shall raise the walls
  Of these their own Imperial Halls
And toil within for brothers' good.
    God bless our work!
    God save our Empress-Queen!

H.T. printed stanzas of the poem, *Mat.* i 128–30, *Mem.* i 110–11.

The text below is from *Heath MS* because that is the version which T. made available at the original time of composition; T.'s corrections are given. *H.MS A* does not differ much; from it, the footnotes give all but a few trivial variants, plus a few of the variants from *MS C.* Miss Donahue's transcription of *Heath MS* has errors and omissions (C. Ricks, *RES*, n.s. xv (1964) 53–5). For its importance to T.'s politics, see Miss Donahue's commentary, and cp. in particular the other political poems of this date that use the *In Memoriam* stanza: *You ask me, why* (p. 489); *Of old sat Freedom* (p. 617); and *Love thou thy land* (p. 613). Its greatest importance (see footnotes) was as a quarry for T.'s later poems, a point made by Sir Charles Tennyson (*1931*, p. 74) and by Miss Donahue.

Hail Briton! in whatever zone
  Binds the broad earth beneath the blue,
  In ancient seasons or in new,
No bolder front than thine is shown:

Not for the wide sail-wandered tides
  That ever round thee come and go–
  The many ships of war that blow
The battle from their oaken sides–

¶ 194.*2. Binds*: because of the secondary meaning 'girdle' for 'zone'.
*7–8.* Adapted for *Britons, Guard Your Own* 37–8 (1852): 'Call home your ships across Biscayan tides, / To blow the battle from their oaken sides.' T. had thought of adapting the lines for *To the Queen* (1851); MS, *The Greyfriar*, Dec. 1921 (Appendix A, p. 1778).

Not for a power, that knows not check,
To spread and float an ermined pall
Of Empire, from the ruined wall
Of royal Delhi to Quebec–

But thou mayst speak thy mind aloud,
And in the streets, or sitting still
Art free to blame or praise at will
The throne, the senate, and the crowd.

Yet fear that passion may convulse
Thy judgment: fear the neighbourhood
Of that unstable Celtic blood
That never keeps an equal pulse.

For Britain had an hour of rest;
But now her steps are swift and rash;
She moving, at her girdle clash
The golden keys of East and West.

A stiller time thy fathers saw
When each man by his hearth could sit,
And lightly round his will were knit
The cords of order and of law.

But in the land diseases grew
From want of motion which is meet,
And power that still should change and fleet
Had festered in the hands of few.

And they that took it thence began
To stir too quickly for the health
Of such an agèd commonwealth,
And spread a fear from man to man

Lest this great people, chafed in mind,
Should slight the things that went before:
This people that hath finisht more
Than any other for mankind–

*11–12.* The wars against the Marathas in 1803–4, when Delhi came under British administration.

*19.* Cp. *In Memoriam* cix 16: 'The blind hysterics of the Celt'.

*21–4.* Adapted, as Sir Charles Tennyson observes (*1931*, p. 74), for *To the Marquis of Dufferin* 1–4 (*1889*): 'At times our Britain cannot rest, / At times her steps are swift and rash; / She moving, at her girdle clash / The golden keys of East and West.'

And lest the strength of common sense
That saved us many times should fail,
And love of novel forms avail
To quench the light of Reverence.

For babbling voices vex the days
We live in, teaching hate of laws,
And teaching lose their own applause
To win a shallow journal's praise–

Men loud against all forms of power,
Unfurnisht foreheads, iron lungs,
And voluble with windy tongues
To compass all things in an hour.

Still changing, whom no change can please,
Despotic hearts reviling kings,
They deal with names and know not things
And handle types of emptiness.

Not such was Hampden when he broke
Indignant from a silent life,
A single voice before the strife
That, as it were a people, spoke:

45. Cp. *I loving Freedom* 7–8 (*c.* 1833), on 'the cuckoo-tongue [-voice *Mem.* i 41] that loves / To babble its own name'.

47. *own*] self *Heath MS 1st reading.*

49–52. Adapted, as Sir Charles Tennyson observes (p. 476), for *Freedom* 37–40 (1884): 'Men loud against all forms of power – / Unfurnished brows, tempestuous tongues– / Expecting all things in an hour– / Brass mouths and iron lungs!' But these lines had also been part of the early draft of *Freedom* (1833–4). *Unfurnisht*: a traditional epithet; cp. Cowper, *The Task* iv 209: 'To fill the void of an unfurnished brain'.

53] More proud than peers, they canker peace [cankers of peace *1st reading*], *MS A.*

56 ∧ 7]
Not such are they that Freedom claims
As patriot-martyrs of her creed,
They were not slaves that names mislead
Nor traitors that mislead by names. *MS A, deleted*

*MS C* shuffled the lines. This stanza appears *Mem.* ii 382, under 1890: 'He also wrote this stanza for an American lady, who had asked for an autograph'.

57–64. Cp. *England and America* 19 (written 1832–4): 'that deep chord which Hampden smote'. John Hampden, who refused to pay ship-money to Charles I, was fatally wounded during the Civil War, on Chalgrove Field, 1643.

In whom the spirit of law prevailed
To war with edicts, and increased
By losing, but the mission ceased
In Chalgrove, and the glory failed.

Not such who made old custom swerve
Too roughly, when they shook the trust
Of all prerogative to dust,
But men of Saxon pith of nerve.

Who lit on times from which our own
Look diverse, when the court grew vast
And public rights were wholly cast
In shadow from the growing throne.

They gave their bodies to the death.
They lived for haughtier aims than this–
To be the light ephemeris
That flutters in the popular breath.

Not such the venerable names
That led the nation when it sprung,
Pricked by the Papal spurs, and flung
The burthen of the second James.

They wrought a work which time reveres,
A precedent to all the lands,
And an example reaching hands
For ever into coming years.

*65–7.* T.'s horror of the French Revolution.

*71*] And public privileges past *Heath MS 1st reading.*

*75. ephemeris*: Cp. *The Devil and the Lady* II i 16: 'This lone ephemeris of one small hour'. Following Shelley's use of the word for 'ephemera', Mayfly. Also with the journalistic associations, as in Johnson's 'These papers of a day, the Ephemerae of learning', *Rambler 145*.

*79–80.* Adapted for *The Third of February, 1852* 27–8: 'Pricked by the Papal spur, we reared, / We flung the burthen of the second James.' James's Declaration of Indulgence to Roman Catholics led to the landing of William of Orange, 1688.

*81–4*] *Added in the margin of Heath MS, with alternative version of 82–3*:

A great example to the lands
Further and further reaching hands

This stanza is also in *MS A*. Cp. *In Memoriam* lxxx 15–16: 'Unused example from the grave / Reach out dead hands to comfort me.' Also *Tiresias* 122–3: 'their examples reach a hand / Far through all years'.

*84 ∧ 5*] For where is he, the citizen
Deephearted, moderate, firm, who sees
His path before him? not with these,
Shadows of statesmen, clever men. *MS A*

They worshipt Freedom for her sake:
We faint unless the wanton ear
Be tickled with the loud 'hear hear'
To which the slight-built hustings shake.

One pants for place: one seeks relief
From life's monotony: one runs
For any goal: another shuns
The pressure of a private grief.

Uncertain of ourselves we chase
The clap of hands: we jar like boys:
And in the hurry and the noise
Great spirits grow akin to base.

An evil sound in ancient states
When Genius clamours, far from Good,
A pandar to the lust for blood,
And talent without wisdom prates!–

A sound of words that change to blows!
A sound of blows on armèd breasts,
And individual interests
Becoming bands of armèd foes!

85. Cp. the sentiment of *I loving Freedom for herself.*
88. Cp. *Maud* i 243: 'when the rotten hustings shake'.
96 ∧ 7]
And licensed boldness gathers force
Becoming when the time has birth
A lever to uplift the earth
And roll it in another course

With many shocks that come and go,
With agonies, with energies,
With overthrowings and with cries
And undulations to and fro. *MS A*

These lines became *In Memoriam* cxiii 13–20, an important later borrowing. In *MS B*, these lines were introduced by:

The visionary gleam of good,
The forethought of a working brain,
The dream of love which bred disdain
And which the days misunderstood,

In secret grows and gathers force . . .

Cp. *Love thou thy land* 89, and *Merlin and Vivien* 228.
103. *individual*: inseparable.

A noise of hands that disarrange
The social engine! fears that waste
The strength of men lest overhaste
Should fire the many wheels of change!

Ill fares a people passion-wrought,
A land of many days that cleaves
In two great halves, when each one leaves
The middle road of sober thought.

The prudent man must wear perforce
The badge of party–must arise
Alike the madman and the wise,
And gird his brand and leap his horse.

The land is filled with crying wrongs,
The bonds are snapt that bound our hearts,
Law speaks unheeded, and the Arts
Hush all their many-varied songs;

For who may frame his thought at ease
Mid sights that civil contest yields–
The blood of men in quiet fields
And sprinkled on the sheaves of peace.

How loathsome are the works of rage.
Shall this old tale again be told?
Are we not wiser being old?
Or fretted with the ills of age?

We should be wiser: on our heads
Such burthens of example weigh:
We should be wiser day by day
Did wisdom spread as knowledge spreads.

Who loves not knowledge? who shall rail
Against her beauty? may she mix
With men and prosper! who shall fix
Her pillars? let her work prevail.

*109–10.* Cp. Goldsmith, *The Deserted Village* 51: 'Ill fares the land, to hastening [l. 107] ills a prey'.
*123–4.* Incorporated as *Ode on Wellington* 170 ^ 1, *1852* text, verbatim from 'yields . . .' (E. F. Shannon, *Studies in Bibliography* xiii (1960) 176).
*125*] What, shall reform be merged in rage? *Heath MS 1st reading. MS A changed the final Heath MS reading to* Disgraceful are . . .
*133–6*] *Added in margin of Heath MS.* Incorporated verbatim, as Sir Charles Tennyson points out (*1931*, p. 74), as *In Memoriam* cxiv 1–4.
*136. Proverbs* ix 1, 'Wisdom hath builded her house, she hath hewn out her seven pillars'.

But they that know not oft are wise,
  And wisdom oft is latest-born
  Of knowledge, and an evil scorn
Has seared the careless lip with lies.

So that good maxims are forgot
  And men but darkly understand
  Who loves at heart his fatherland
And buys the name of patriot.

Not he that breaks the dams but he
  That through the channels of the state
  Convoys the people's wish, is great:
His course is pure, his name is free.

He cares, if ancient usage fade,
  To shape, to settle, to repair
  With seasonable changes fair
And innovation grade by grade.

Or if the sense of most require
  A precedent of larger scope,
  Not deals in threats, but works with hope
And lights at length on his desire.

He reads this time and what is gone:
  And like a father loves his race,
  The people and the populace
Whom knowledge yearns to mix in one.

*140*] Has filled the lips of men with lies. *Heath MS 1st reading.*
*142. men*] we *Heath MS 1st reading.*
*143. at heart*] in truth *Heath MS 1st reading. Who*: who it is who.
*145–8.* T. published this stanza in a charity volume, *Shakspearean Show-Book* (1884), as Miss Donahue notes. Cp. *You ask me, why* 23: 'Though every channel of the State'.
*148 ∧ 9*]
He slights not checks of government
  Nor slaves his soul to ages gone
  But wills that freedom broaden on
From precedent to precedent. *MS C*

Cp. *You ask me, why* 11–12 (rhyming with 'government'): 'Where Freedom slowly broadens down / From precedent to precedent.'
*152.* Cp. T.'s quotation from Bacon, in his *Eversley* note to *Freedom*: 'It were good that men in their innovations should follow the example of Time itself, which indeed innovateth greatly but quietly, and by degrees, scarce to be perceived.'
*160.* Cp. *Love thou thy land* 55–6: 'The Spirit of the years to come / Yearning to mix himself with Life.'

He feels those laws are just alone
That contemplate a mighty plan:
The frame, the mind, the soul of man
Like one that cultivates his own.

He seeing far an end sublime,
Contends, despising party-rage,
To hold the spirit of the Age
Against the spirit of the Time–

O civic Muse, for such a name,
Deep-minded Muse, for ages long
Preserve a broad approach of song
And ringing avenues of fame.

He shall not moulder with the dead:
The child whose little limbs are set
Upon his mother's lap ere yet
God shuts the doors within his head–

The germ that liveth blind and dumb,
A thread within the house of birth,
Shall reach completion, learn his worth,
And preach it in the years to come.

But he that or by deed or word,
And in an ancient land and free
Where none may plead necessity,
Would make unsheathed the civil sword:

*161–4, 165–8*] *Transposed at first in Heath MS (then marked in margin by T.).*
*161. He feels*] Knowing *Heath MS 1st reading.*
*168.* T. was to incorporate this line in an early draft of *To the Duke of Argyll* (1881), *T.Nbk 21.*
*169–72.* Adapted, as Sir Charles Tennyson says (*1931*, p. 74), for *Ode on Wellington* 75–9: 'O civic muse, to such a name, / To such a name for ages long, / To such a name, / Preserve a broad approach of fame, / And ever-ringing [*1852*] avenues of song.'
*169. for*] to *MSS A, C*; *T.MS* of the *Ode on Wellington* has verbatim *Hail Briton* 172.
*173–6*] *Bracketed in Heath MS, T.'s tentative sign for deletion.*
*176.* Adapted, as Sir Charles Tennyson points out, for *In Memoriam* xliv 3–4: 'But he forgets the days before / God shut the doorways of his head.' 'Closing of the skull after babyhood' (T.).
*177. liveth*] lieth *MS C.* Cp. T.'s stillborn child, *Little bosom* 11: 'thou liest blind and mute'.

For that he strove to kindle storm
From quiet, sought without respect
To soil the work of intellect,
And forge confusion from reform–

He will do well to hide his eyes,
Lest we should count him lower than
The Cossack curst of God and man
To whom the Polish virgin cries.

She cries unheard. So just a war,
So pure a hope is rendered vain
Till God rise up and break in twain
The iron sceptre of the Czar–

Who rules a savage land where meet
The coarse extremes of Power and Fear–
A land where knowledge dreads to hear
Her footsteps falling in the street–

Who bides his time and quiet lies
Though step by step his power grows
And gathers like the silent snows
And binds in fetters like the ice.

## 195 'You ask me, why, though ill at ease'

Published *1842*. Written *c.* 1833 (H.T.); it is one of the six poems added in vol. i, *1842*, 'which, with one exception, were written in 1833' (*1842* note). Cp. the other political poems of this date, also in the *In Memoriam* stanza: *Hail Briton* (p. 480), *Love thou thy land* (p. 613), and *Of old sat Freedom* (p. 617). T. sent the latter two poems to his Cambridge friend James Spedding (possibly the 'You' of this poem) shortly after 9 Sept. 1834 (*Mem.* i 140–2). T. feared the results of the political agitation which had led to the Reform Bill, 1832. *1865* gave the title *Britain*.

*191–204.* The Poles rose against Russia in Nov. 1830; the war lasted from Jan. to Sept. 1831. It was of great concern to the young T. See *Poland* (p. 458), and *Sonnet on hearing of the outbreak of the Polish Insurrection* (p. 457).
*200. footsteps*] footstep *MS A*.

You ask me, why, though ill at ease,
  Within this region I subsist,
  Whose spirits falter in the mist,
And languish for the purple seas.

It is the land that freemen till,
  That sober-suited Freedom chose,
  The land, where girt with friends or foes
A man may speak the thing he will;

A land of settled government,
  A land of just and old renown,
  Where Freedom slowly broadens down
From precedent to precedent:

Where faction seldom gathers head,
  But by degrees to fulness wrought,
  The strength of some diffusive thought
Hath time and space to work and spread.

Should banded unions persecute
  Opinion, and induce a time
  When single thought is civil crime,
And individual freedom mute;

Though Power should make from land to land
  The name of Britain trebly great–
  Though every channel of the State
Should fill and choke with golden sand–

Yet waft me from the harbour-mouth,
  Wild wind! I seek a warmer sky,
  And I will see before I die
The palms and temples of the South.

¶ 195.*3. falter in*] *1845*; fail within *1842–3*.
*4.* 'The purple sea', *On Sublimity* 4.
*6. sober-suited*: probably from *Romeo and Juliet* III ii 11.
*11. slowly broadens*] *1882*; broadens slowly *1842–81* ('misprint', H.T.). Corrected by T. in a copy of *Works*, 1881 (Lincoln).
*11–12.* Cp. *Hail Briton* 148 ^ 9, *MS C*:

He slights not checks of government
  Nor slaves his soul to ages gone
  But wills that freedom broaden on
From precedent to precedent.

*23.* Cp. *Hail Briton* 145–7: 'Not he that breaks the dams but he / That through the channels of the state / Convoys the people's wish, is great.'
*24. fill and*] *1865*; almost *1842–63*.
*26–8.* Cp. *Sonnet* [*I lingered yet*] 2: 'that far South, for which my spirits ache'.

# 196 The Goose

Published *1842*. Written 1833 (*H.Nbk 13*); it is one of the six poems added in vol. i of *1842* 'which, with one exception, were written in 1833'. It is probably an attack on radicalism and the Reform Bill agitation (1832); cp. *I loving Freedom* (p. 619). J. H. Buckley (p. 81) follows W. J. Fox (1845): 'a warning, perhaps, to the Tories that their Corn Laws are killing commerce'; but this seems unlikely, and does not very well fit the date of composition. The political fable has an eighteenth-century air; cp. Thomas Yalden's *The Blind Woman and Her Doctors* (1702): 'Like a stuck pig the woman stared, / And up and down she run: / With naked house and walls quite scared, / She found herself undone.'

I knew an old wife lean and poor,
  Her rags scarce held together;
There strode a stranger to the door,
  And it was windy weather.

He held a goose upon his arm,
  He uttered rhyme and reason,
'Here, take the goose, and keep you warm,
  It is a stormy season.'

She caught the white goose by the leg,
  A goose–'twas no great matter.
The goose let fall a golden egg
  With cackle and with clatter.

She dropt the goose, and caught the pelf,
  And ran to tell her neighbours;
And blessed herself, and cursed herself,
  And rested from her labours.

¶ 196.*3*. *stranger*] pedlar *H.MS.*
*6*] Was fat beyond all reason *MS.*
*13–24*]
Then got she fowl, then bought she flesh,
  Her [*lacuna*] blood to nourish
And planted orchards green and fresh
  Of all the fruits that flourish.

Her new cap flared from withered brows,
  She set it at the village:
And built two stories to her house
  And purchased glebe and tillage.

In stuffs and silks and thick brocade
  She rustled and she crackled,
But ah! the more the white goose laid
  The more it clackt and cackled.

And feeding high, and living soft,
  Grew plump and able-bodied;
Until the grave churchwarden doffed,
  The parson smirked and nodded.

So sitting, served by man and maid,
  She felt her heart grow prouder:
But ah! the more the white goose laid
  It clacked and cackled louder.

It cluttered here, it chuckled there;
  It stirred the old wife's mettle:
She shifted in her elbow-chair,
  And hurled the pan and kettle.

'A quinsy choke thy cursèd note!'
  Then waxed her anger stronger.
'Go, take the goose, and wring her throat,
  I will not bear it longer.'

Then yelped the cur, and yawled the cat;
  Ran Gaffer, stumbled Gammer.
The goose flew this way and flew that,
  And filled the house with clamour.

As head and heels upon the floor
  They floundered all together,
There strode a stranger to the door,
  And it was windy weather:

He took the goose upon his arm,
  He uttered words of scorning;
'So keep you cold, or keep you warm,
  It is a stormy morning.'

The wild wind rang from park and plain,
  And round the attics rumbled,
Till all the tables danced again,
  And half the chimneys tumbled.

The glass blew in, the fire blew out,
  The blast was hard and harder.
Her cap blew off, her gown blew up,
  And a whirlwind cleared the larder:

She crammed her crazy ears with wool
  And heapt her chests and closets,
Sat sipping flip and nogg and mull–
  All kinds of creamy possets. *MS*

And while on all sides breaking loose
Her household fled the danger,
Quoth she, 'The Devil take the goose,
And God forget the stranger!'

## 197 Mechanophilus

(In the Time of the First Railways)

Published *1892*. Written *c.* 1833, as is clear from *H.Nbk 17* and *T.Nbk 17*. It is one of T.'s many political poems of this date. The *H.MS* (all variants are below) is entitled *Æonophilus*, the lover of the age, and has four extra stanzas; *T.MS* (which may not be quoted) differs only slightly from *H.MS*, except that at some points it ordered the stanzas differently. The poem is not in the first trial edition of *1892* (*Lincoln*).

Now first we stand and understand,
And sunder false from true,
And handle boldly with the hand,
And see and shape and do.

Dash back that ocean with a pier,
Strow yonder mountain flat,
A railway there, a tunnel here,
Mix me this Zone with that!

Bring me my horse–my horse? my wings
That I may soar the sky,
For Thought into the outward springs,
I find her with the eye.

¶ 197.*4. see*] act *H.MS.*
4 ∧ 5] Away with shadows! render all
Plain, palpable and bold,
Then give the crude material
That we may carve and mould.

All other times were but the shade–
The preface unto this.
Now knowledge comes, a mortal maid,
Whom we may clasp and kiss: *MS*

*5–8*] *MS has these lines following l. 16.*
*5. that ocean*] those breakers *MS.*
*7. railway*] railroad *MS.*
*8. Zone*] realm *MS.*
*9*] Bring me my horse–bring me my wings *MS.*
*12. find*] see *MS.*

O will she, moonlike, sway the main,
And bring or chase the storm,
Who was a shadow in the brain,
And is a living form?

Far as the Future vaults her skies,
From this my vantage ground
To those still-working energies
I spy nor term nor bound.

As we surpass our father's skill,
Our sons will shame our own;
A thousand things are hidden still
And not a hundred known.

And had some prophet spoken true
Of all we shall achieve,
The wonders were so wildly new,
That no man would believe.

*13–14*] Soon moonlike will she rule the main
And puff the cloud and storm. *MS*

*15. Who*] She *MS.*

*16. And*] She *MS.*

*16 $_\wedge$ 17*] *MS here (i.e. ll. 8 $_\wedge$ 17) inserts in the margin three stanzas:*

[i] *ll. 33–6, in the order 35–6, 33–4* (Yet what . . .)

[ii] Till thick grass clothe the craggy way,
Thick corn the barest glen,
And by his hearth the cotter weigh
The thoughts of mighty men.

[iii] Till in his office none be mute,
But equal to the hour,
To add, to prune, to substitute
By gradual scales of power.

*18. my*] high *MS.*

*20*] I see no term or bound. *MS.*

*21–4.* T. signed and inscribed these lines (l. 24: *Scarce a . . .*), 25 June 1884, in a volume given to Sir Henry Parkes, prime minister of Australia for most of the 1870s and 1880s (*Mitchell Library, Sydney*).

*25–8*] But if what will be once achieved
Had prophets speaking true,
The wonder would not be believed,
It were so strange and new. *MS*

Meanwhile, my brothers, work, and
wield
The forces of today,
And plow the Present like a field,
And garner all you may!

You, what the cultured surface grows,
Dispense with careful hands:
Deep under deep for ever goes,
Heaven over heaven expands.

# 198 *Stanzas

Published Nov.–Dec. 1850 in *The Keepsake* for 1851; not reprinted. Written 1833 (*T.Nbk 17*). The triplets are those of *The Two Voices* (p. 522) and *The Eagle* (below).

What time I wasted youthful hours,
One of the shining wingèd powers
Showed me vast cliffs, with crowns of towers.

As towards that gracious light I bowed,
They seemed high palaces and proud,
Hid now and then with sliding cloud.

He said, 'The labour is not small;
Yet winds the pathway free to all: –
Take care thou dost not fear to fall!'

# 199 The Eagle

Fragment

Published *1851*. The envelope of the *Widener MS* (Harvard) is dated 2 Oct. 1849. T. entered it in Dora Wordsworth's album when in the Lake District in summer 1850 (*CT*, p. 205, mistakenly suggests that this was in 1845, following F. V. Morley, *Dora Wordsworth: Her Book*, 1924, p. 164). T. entered too on this page of the album *The Two Voices* 436–8, also in triplets. T. probably had *The Eagle* in mind before 1849; its placing in *Eversley*

*29–30*] Meantime, push forward, work and wield.
Let man be really man *MS*

*31. And*] To *MS.*

*32. you may!*] he can. *MS, which had at first ended here, but see ll. 16 ^ 17n.*

¶ 198.*3*. Incorporated in a blank verse fragment in *T.Nbk 22* (1833), which may not be quoted.

suggests composition before 1842, and its triplets are those of *The Two Voices* and *Stanzas* (both 1833).

He clasps the crag with crookèd hands;
Close to the sun in lonely lands,
Ringed with the azure world, he stands.

The wrinkled sea beneath him crawls;
He watches from his mountain walls,
And like a thunderbolt he falls.

# 200 *Early Spring [1833]

Printed inaccurately by T. J. Wise, *Bibliography of Tennyson* (1908), i 267–9; then printed by Sir Charles Tennyson, *Cornhill* cliii (1936) 441–3. The text below is from Heath MS, *c.* 1833. It is an early version of *Early Spring* [*1883*] (p 1314.); T. was to add four stanzas, omit stanzas II, IV, VI, VIII, IX, and revise and rearrange the others. A draft of 1833 in *T.Nbk 17* (which may not be quoted) approximates to *Heath MS*, but has two extra stanzas, deleted: one, ll. 7–12 of *1883*; the other, describing the birds. The shorter draft in *H.Nbk 13* (1833) is in four-line stanzas, e.g. the first stanza consists of ll. 3–6; for its lines additional to *Heath MS*, see l. 6 ∧ 7*n.*

Once more the Heavenly Power
　Makes all things new,
Bows over red-plowed hills
　The loving blue;
The blackbirds have their wills,
　The throstles too.

¶ 199.*1. crookèd*] *1865*; hookèd *1851–63*. The original reading is even closer to *Aeneid* vi 360: *prensantemque uncis manibus capita aspera montis* ('I caught with bent fingers at the rugged cliff-peaks').
*4. The wrinkled sea*: occurs in *Two Visits to a Grave*, by T.'s friend Richard Monckton Milnes, *Athenaeum*, 4 March 1829. (Noted by Joyce Green, *The Development of the Poetic Image in Tennyson*, Cambridge thesis, 1954, p. 178.) Shelley had 'the wrinkled ocean', *Hellas* 139.
*6.* Cp. *Samson Agonistes* 1695–6: 'as an Eagle / His cloudless thunder bolted on thir heads'.
¶ 200.*6* ∧ *7*]　From hidden woodland ways
　The airs move
In gushes sweet as praise
　From those we love.

Gay looks the girlish year
From winter's foil,
I watch all buds that joy
To burst the soil,
Earnest as redbreasts eye
The delver's toil.

My leaping blood obeys
The season's lure!
My heart looks down and up
Serene, secure,
Warm as the crocus cup,
Like snowdrops, pure!

From her good works the Spring
Her welcome earns:
With air she fills my bones:
My quick ear learns
Her millions of half tones
That trill by turns.

Hearing thy chuckled note,
O twinkling bird,
My tricksy fancies range,
And, lightly stirred,
Ring little bells of change
From word to word.

Ah! lightest words are lead,
Gross to make plain
Myriads of hints of things
That orb and wane,
Before a gnat's quick wings
Beat once again.

The winding dales unroll
Their carpets bright,
Like a dove's neck my soul
Reflects the light. *H.Nbk 13*

At this point, *T.MS* has, deleted, ll. 7–12 of *Early Spring* [*1883*].
*11–12*. Adapted, as Sir Charles Tennyson notes, for *Marriage of Geraint* 774: 'As careful robins eye the delver's toil'. G. G. Loane compares the line from *Geraint* with Pope: 'In vain the observer eyes the builder's toil' (*Echoes in Tennyson*, 1928, p. 11).
*27*. *tricksy*: playful; cp. (with l. 30) 'a tricksy word', *Merchant of Venice* III v 63.

Past, Future sparkle linkt
By some light spell,
Charms, touches, mysteries
Words may not tell,
Faint, fragile sympathies
In sound and smell!

O fullness of the worlds!
O termless field,
Relation, difference,
Not all concealed,
Fair feast of every sense
In part revealed.

O soul reflecting forms
Of this wide beach,
Comparing at thy will
Each form with each,
Let tears of wonder fill
Thy void of speech.

## 201 *'This Earth is wondrous, change on change'

Unpublished, except that *Mem.* i 40 printed ll. 21–8, as *The Moon*. Text from *H.Nbk 16*, which indicates composition in 1833.

This Earth is wondrous, change on change,
All coloured, beautiful and bright,
Almost almighty to fulfil
All comprehension of delight,

And yet because free space is left
And spreads and rounds her everywhere,
My freakish fancy sometimes fumes
And flits and leaves her hung in air,

And in a twinkle flashing up
Through fifty miles of atmosphere
I hit my head against the moon,
Turn on my legs and walk the sphere.

44. *termless*: boundless.
47] Great banquet of the sense *Heath MS 1st reading*.

Quicker than Dan O'Rourke I fly,
  Or Jack that up the beanstalk borne
Grasping the large pods one by one
  Crept up and clutching caught her horn.

Jack lied: for horns the moon hath none:
  Nor could I find from North to South,
That old one by his bunch of sticks,
  Who with peas-porridge burnt his mouth.

But glens I found and sunless gulfs
  Set round with many a toppling spire
And monstrous rocks from craggy snouts
  Disploding globes of roaring fire.

Large as a human eye, the Sun
  Drew down the West his feeble light,
And then a night, all moons, confused
  The shadows from the icy heights.

## 202 *Lines

Published *Manchester Athenaeum Album*, 1850; not reprinted. In *Mem.* i 161 it is entitled *Mablethorpe*, where the Tennysons stayed: 'A fragment of a poem about Mablethorpe he wrote then', i.e. 1837. But *T.Nbk 17* includes it along with poems all of 1833; T. was very frequently at Mablethorpe, including in March 1833 (*Mem.* i 100). This draft (which may not be

¶201.*13*. Daniel O'Rourke flew to the moon on an eagle. The legend is in a book T. certainly knew and was to own in the 1834 edn (*Lincoln*): T. C. Croker's *Fairy Legends* (1825), which links the other men in the moon with O'Rourke.

*21. But*] *H.MS*; Deep *Mem.*   *sunless gulfs*: *Prefatory Sonnet* 14.

*23*. Cp. Shelley, *Faust* ii 49: 'the giant-snouted crags'.

*24. Disploding*: Milton's 'displode' (*Paradise Lost* vi 605) is the earliest example in *OED*.

*24 ∧ 5*]
It were not worth a wise man's while
  To till it, for I saw the whole,
'Tis nothing but one ashy calx,
  One cinder all from pole to pole. *MS, deleted*

*26. light*] *MS*; lights *Mem.*

*27. a night, all moons*: 'means that when seen from the airless moon all the principal stars and planets would be very large and bright in the black heavens, and strike the eye there as the moon strikes the eye here' (*Mem.* i 40).

quoted) has a second stanza describing T.'s love of and delight in the scene, and it ends with a version, all but verbatim, of the famous line, 'The phantom circle of a moaning sea', *The Passing of Arthur* 87.

Here often, when a child, I lay reclined,
  I took delight in this locality.
Here stood the infant Ilion of the mind,
  And here the Grecian ships did seem to be.
And here again I come, and only find
  The drain-cut levels of the marshy lea,–
Gray sandbanks, and pale sunsets,–dreary wind,
  Dim shores, dense rains, and heavy-clouded sea!

# 203 *What Thor Said to the Bard Before Dinner

Printed *Mat.* i 116–17: 'he defies the malignant censures of his critics in this sort of way'. Text and title from *T.Nbk 23* (1832–3), where the poem is preceded by an introductory couplet. *Mem.* i 97 printed the first stanza under 1832, but as E. F. Shannon says (*Tennyson and the Reviewers*, 1952, p. 197), 'the context in which it occurs is after the *Quarterly* review of April 1833'. The poem was then printed in *1931*, pp. 75–6. It is in *H.Nbk 4* with poems of *1830* and *1832*. Cp. the unadopted stanza of *The New Timon, Part II* (p. 738): 'And mobs no doubt will often make / The judgement private taste abhors; / We shall not wonder if they take / Your penny-hammer, Sir, for Thor's.'

  Wherever evil customs thicken
Break through with the hammer of iron rhyme,
  Till priest-craft and king-craft sicken,
But pap-meat-pamper not the time
  With the flock of the thunder-stricken.

¶ 202.*2. locality*] fair strand and free *Mem.*
*4. did seem*] all seemed *Mem.*
*6. levels*] level *Mem.*
¶ 203.*3. priest-craft*: in this sense, coined by Dryden, *Absalom and Achitophel* 1.
*4.* Cp. *Love thou thy land* 9: 'But pamper not a hasty time'.
*5. flock*] *Mat.*, *1931*; race *H.MS.* 'Flock' and 'thunderstricken' suggest *Paradise Lost* vi 854–7. Cp. *The pallid thunderstricken sigh for gain* (p. 243).

If the world caterwaul, lay harder upon her
Till she clapperclaw no longer,
Bang thy stithy stronger and stronger,
Thy rhyme-hammer *shall* have honour.

Be not fairspoken neither stammer,
Nail her, knuckle her, thou swinge-buckler!
Spare not: ribroast gaffer and gammer,
Be no shuffler, wear no muffler,
But on thine anvil hammer and hammer!
If she call out lay harder upon her,
This way and that, nail
Tagrag and bobtail,
Thy rhyme-hammer *shall* have honour.

On squire and parson, broker and banker,
Down let fall thine iron spanker,
Spare not king or duke or critic,
Dealing out cross-buttock and flanker
With thy clanging analytic!
If she call out lay harder upon her,
Stun her, stagger her,
Care not for swaggerer,
Thy rhyme-hammer *shall* have honour.

# 204 Poets and Critics

Published *1892*. Written 1833–4, referring to the reviews of *1832*. All variants from *H.Nbk 17*, of this early date, are given below.

This thing, that thing is the rage,
Helter-skelter runs the age;
Minds on this round earth of ours
Vary like the leaves and flowers,

6. *caterwaul*] *Mat.*, *1931*; call out *MS.*
7. *clapperclaw*: to scratch, revile.
11. *swinge-buckler*: swashbuckler (*2 Henry IV* III ii 23).
12. *ribroast*: to cudgel.
13. *muffler*: boxing-glove (*OED* 2 a).
16. *that, nail*] that nail *MS*, *1931*; that way nail *Mat.*
20. *spanker*: a blow.
21. *or duke or*] *MS*, *1931*; nor dupe, nor *Mat.*
22. *cross-buttock*: a wrestling throw. *flanker*: a blow from the side.

Fashioned after certain laws;
Sing thou low or loud or sweet,
All at all points thou canst not meet,
Some will pass and some will pause.

What is true at last will tell:
Few at first will place thee well;
Some too low would have thee shine,
Some too high – no fault of thine –
Hold thine own, and work thy will!
Year will graze the heel of year,
But seldom comes the poet here,
And the Critic's rarer still.

# 205 Sir Launcelot and Queen Guinevere

## A Fragment

Published *1842*. 'Partly if not wholly written in 1830' (*Mem.* ii 122); but both *Heath MS* (all variants are below) and *T.Nbk 15* make it clear that T. was still working on it in 1833. *T.MS*, which may not be quoted, explains T.'s subtitle *A Fragment*; it describes the meeting of Launcelot and Guinevere with Merlin, and their journey. T. later quarried these lines, e.g. for *The Princess* v 250–3. See *Life of the Life* (p. 504), which was a song within *Sir Launcelot* and which was quoted in a letter from J. M. Kemble to W. B. Donne, 22 June 1833 (now in the possession of Mrs C. B. Johnson):

'A companion to *The Lady of Shalott* is in Progress, called the *Ballad of Sir Lancelot*; a most triumphant matter whereof I will give you a sketch; in the Spring, Queen Guinevere and Sir Lancelot ride through the forest green, fayre and amorous: And such a queen! such a knight! Merlin with spindle shanks, vast brows and beard and a forehead like a mundane egg, over a face wrinkled with ten thousand crow-feet meets them, and tells Sir L. that he's doing well for his fame to be riding about with a light o' love &c. Whereupon the knight, nowise backward in retort, tells him it is a shame such an old scandal to antiquity should be talking, since his own propensities are no secret, and since he very well knows what will become of him in the valley of Avilion some day. Merlin, who tropically is

¶ 204.*10. place*] weigh *H.MS.*
*13. Hold thine own*] Strike thy harp *MS.*
*14. will*] doth *MS.*
*15. But*] And *MS.*
*16. And*] But *MS.*

Worldly Prudence, is of course miserably floored. So are the representatives of Worldly Force, who in the shape of three knights, sheathed, Sir, in trap from toe to toe, run at Sir L. and are most unceremoniously shot from their saddles like stones from a sling. But the Garde Joyeuse is now in sight; the knight I confess is singing but a loose song, when his own son Sir Galahad (the type of Chastity) passes by; he knows his father but does not speak to him, *blushes and rides on his way!* Voila tout. Much of this is written and stupendous; I regret bitterly that I had not opportunity to take down what there is of it; as it is I can only offer you Sir L.'s song.'

*T.MS* does not cover all of this, since it has only four extra stanzas. Cp. *Sir Galahad* (p. 610). The affinities with *The Lady of Shalott* (p. 354) are emphasised by the use of the same stanza, except that here the fifth and ninth lines are not refrains. Cp. the ride of Launcelot and the Queen in *Guinevere* 377–97 (p. 1734).

Like souls that balance joy and pain,
With tears and smiles from heaven again
The maiden Spring upon the plain
Came in a sun-lit fall of rain.
    In crystal vapour everywhere
Blue isles of heaven laughed between,
And far, in forest-deeps unseen,
The topmost elm-tree gathered green
    From draughts of balmy air.

Sometimes the linnet piped his song:
Sometimes the throstle whistled strong:
Sometimes the sparhawk, wheeled along,
Hushed all the groves from fear of wrong:
    By grassy capes with fuller sound
In curves the yellowing river ran,
And drooping chestnut-buds began
To spread into the perfect fan,
    Above the teeming ground.

Then, in the boyhood of the year,
Sir Launcelot and Queen Guinevere
Rode through the coverts of the deer,
With blissful treble ringing clear.
    She seemed a part of joyous Spring:
A gown of grass-green silk she wore,
Buckled with golden clasps before;
A light-green tuft of plumes she bore
    Closed in a golden ring.

¶ 205.*4. fall*] shower *Heath MS.*
*8. elm-tree*] *1853*; linden *1842–51.*

Now on some twisted ivy-net,
Now by some tinkling rivulet,
In mosses mixt with violet
Her cream-white mule his pastern set:
    And fleeter now she skimmed the plains
Than she whose elfin prancer springs
By night to eery warblings,
When all the glimmering moorland rings
    With jingling bridle-reins.

As fast she fled through sun and shade,
The happy winds upon her played,
Blowing the ringlet from the braid:
She looked so lovely, as she swayed
    The rein with dainty finger-tips,
A man had given all other bliss,
And all his worldly worth for this,
To waste his whole heart in one kiss
    Upon her perfect lips.

# 206 *'Life of the Life within my blood'

Printed *Mem.* i 59: 'Some verses of *Sir Launcelot and Queen Guinevere* were handed about at Cambridge among my father's contemporaries. The following unpublished lines were among them, and kept by Edward FitzGerald.' FitzGerald's annotated copy of *1842* (*Trinity College*) does in fact

*27 ∧ 8*]
Each clasp, a point of brightest light
Was made, a Lady and a Knight:
And when the clasp was buckled tight
The Lady seemed to fold the Knight *Heath MS*

A space was left after these lines. They are in *T.MS.*

*30. In*] *1851*; On *1842–50. mixt*] *1853*; thick *1842–51*; black *Heath MS.*

*32. fleeter now*] *1853*; now more fleet *1842–51.*

*33. she*] her *Heath MS.*

*33–6.* Paden (p. 157) cites a book which T. certainly knew, and later owned, T. C. Croker's *Fairy Legends* (1825): 'the sound of bridles ringing through the air accompanies the whirlwind which marks the progress of a fairy journey'. D. L. Chambers (*MLN*, xviii, 1903, 231) suggests Carlyle's *Essay on Goethe's Helena* (1828): 'these fine warblings and trippings on the light fantastic toe . . . as perhaps of elfin-bells when the Queen of Faery rides by moonlight'.

*37. fast she fled*] *1890*; she fled fast *1842–89.*

include ll. 5–6 ('I prithee stay . . .'), but ll. 5–8 were first printed by Sir Charles Tennyson, *Cornhill* cliii (1936) 447, from *Heath MS.* J. M. Kemble wrote to W. B. Donne, 22 June 1833: 'a companion to the *Lady of Shalott* is in Progress, called the *Ballad of Sir Lancelot*. . . . I regret bitterly that I had not opportunity to take down what there is of it; as it is I can only offer you Sir L.'s song, though for the sake of my future clerical views and Ælfred's and Sir L.'s character, I must request that it be kept as quiet as possible'. Kemble then quotes *Life of the Life.* For more of the letter, see *Sir Launcelot* (p. 502).

Life of the Life within my blood,
  Light of the Light within mine eyes,
The May begins to breathe and bud,
  And softly blow the balmy skies;
Draw nigh me; stay not to be wooed,
  It is not glorious to be wise.
Come feed my lip with costly food,
  My ear with low replies;

Bathe with me in the fiery flood,
  And mingle kisses, tears, and sighs,
Life of the Life within my blood,
  Light of the Light within mine eyes.

# 207 *The Ante-Chamber

Printed *Mem.* i 199–200: 'originally intended as a prologue to *The Gardener's Daughter* . . . My father wished it never to be printed in front of *The Gardener's Daughter* because this is already full enough. It is however too good to be lost. The portrait in *The Ante-Chamber* might be himself at the period,–so his friends say,–but that was by no means his intention.' T. J.

¶ 206.*1.* Cp. *The Gardener's Daughter* 75–80, MS: 'my heart / Beat in my bosom, like a Life in Life'. 'Life of life' occurs four times in Shelley, and T. later referred to Shelley's lyric *Life of Life* (*Prometheus Unbound* II v) as 'one of those flights in which the poet "seemed to go up, and burst"' (*Mem.* ii 500).
*3. breathe*] bloom *Heath MS.*
*4. softly*] warmly *Heath MS.*
*6*] 'Tis choicer to be mad than wise. *Heath MS 1st reading.*
*9.* Paden (p. 157) compares *Measure for Measure* III i 120–21: 'And the delighted spirit / To bathe in fiery floods'. Shelley has 'fiery flood', *Mont Blanc* 87.
*10. tears*] words *Heath MS.*

Wise privately printed it in 1906, from a MS dated 15 Oct. 1834; *Heath MS* says it is 'part of *The Gardener's Daughter*'. It describes T.'s friendship with Arthur Hallam; see ll. 10–14.

That is his portrait painted by himself.
Look on those manly curls so glossy dark,
Those thoughtful furrows in the swarthy cheek;
Admire that stalwart shape, those ample brows,
And that large table of the breast dispread,
Between low shoulders; how demure a smile,
How full of wisest humour and of love,
With some half-consciousness of inward power,
Sleeps round those quiet lips; not quite a smile;
And look you what an arch the brain has built
Above the ear! and what a settled mind,
Mature, harboured from change, contemplative,
Tempers the peaceful light of hazel eyes,
Observing all things. This is he I loved,
This is the man of whom you heard me speak.
My fancy was the more luxurious,
But his was minted in a deeper mould,
And took in more of Nature than mine own:
Nor proved I such delight as he, to mark
The humours of the polling and the wake,
The hubbub of the market and the booths:
How this one smiled, that other waved his arms,
These careful and those candid brows, how each–
Down to his slightest turns and attitudes–
Was something that another could not be,
How every brake and flower spread and rose,
Distinct in individualities,
A various world! which he compelled once more
Through his own nature, with well mingled hues,

¶ 207.*10–14*. T. thought of incorporating these lines in *The Epic* (p. 582), where they describe the poet Everard Hall, who to some extent stands for T. himself:

I marvelled what an arch the brain had built
Above his ear and what a settled mind
Tempered the peaceful light of hazel eyes
Observing all things. *H.Lpr 53*

*18* ^ *19*] In its wide circle closing half of mine: *Heath MS.*
*20* ^ *21*] The meally clown, the puppet on the planks, *Heath MS added by T.*
*27*] *Heath MS*; *not Mem.* H.T. included this line when first printing the poem in *Mat.* i 243; presumably he dropped it after noticing that T. had transferred it verbatim to *The Princess* vii 275.

Into another shape, born of the first,
As beautiful, but yet another world.
  All this so stirred him in his hour of joy,
Mixed with the phantom of his coming fame,
That once he spake: 'I lift the eyes of thought,
I look through all my glimmering life, I see
At the end, as 'twere athwart a coloured cloud,
O'er the bowed shoulder of a bland old Age,
The face of placid Death.' Long, Eustace, long
May my strong wish, transgressing the low bound
Of mortal hope, act on Eternity
To keep thee here amongst us! Yet he lives;
His and my friendship have not suffered loss,
His fame is equal to his years: his praise
Is neither overdealt, nor idly won.
  Step through these doors, and I will show to you
Another countenance, one yet more dear,
More dear, for what is lost is made more dear;
'More dear' I will not say, but rather bless
The All-perfect Framer, Him, who made the heart,
Forethinking its twinfold necessity,
Through one whole life an overflowing urn,
Capacious both of Friendship and of Love.

# 208 The Gardener's Daughter

## Or, The Pictures

Published *1842*; among 'English Idyls'. Written 1833–4 (*Mem.* i 103, and *Heath MS*). The transcript in *H.Lpr 67* is dated 1833, and T. J. Wise privately printed the poem in 1906 from a MS dated 15 Oct. 1834. (Most of Wise's variants from *Heath MS* are trivial, and many are plainly errors.) It appears in *T.Nbks 15* and *17* of this date. T. says that he had written it at Cambridge. Arthur Hallam wrote, 31 July 1833: 'I trust you finished *The Gardener's Daughter*' (*Mem.* i 103). The poem brings together T.'s friendship for Hallam (the narrator's for Eustace) and Hallam's love for T.'s sister Emily (Eustace's for Juliet). See the prologue, *The Ante-Chamber* (p. 505). T. had thought of a series of 'Daughter' poems; cp. *The Miller's Daughter* (p. 371) and *The Doctor's Daughter* (p. 283). A letter by Hallam

*38. face of placid*] *Mem.*, *1906*; placid face of *Heath MS*. Cp. Shelley, *The Cenci* V i 14–15: 'the placid death / Which she prepares for overwearied age'.

*40. hope*] *Mem.*, *1906*; hopes *Heath MS*.

mentions a projected *Innkeeper's Daughter* (22 June [1832], *Bodleian Library*). Like T.'s other 'English Idyls', it is indebted to Theocritus, especially the 7th Idyll. It shares with *The Lover's Tale* (p. 299) a romantically expansive style; T. says: 'The centre of the poem, that passage describing the girl [ll. 124–40], must be full and rich. The poem is so, to a fault, especially the descriptions of nature, for the lover is an artist, but, this being so, the central picture must hold its place.' Aubrey de Vere recorded of the poem (*Mem.* i 508–9): 'The poet had corrected it as carefully as he had originally composed it in his head, where he was in the habit of keeping more than one poem at a time before he wrote down any of them. I found him one day in James Spedding's rooms. He shewed me the MS and said, "The corrections jostled each other, and the poem seemed out of gear. Spedding has just now remarked that it wants nothing but that this passage, forty lines, should be omitted. He is right." It was omitted.' As this suggests, the poem in its earlier drafts had been considerably longer. All the variants and unadopted passages in the *Heath MS* are given below; some were printed by Sir Charles Tennyson (*Cornhill* cliii (1936) 439–41). Some revision had been carried out by 1833–4, since *Heath MS* gave the poem 'in its original form'. The version in *T.Nbk 17* may not be quoted; it has many more such unadopted passages. It begins with about twenty lines of apologetic preamble, and it has about thirty lines on a death in the family which takes Eustace away to the funeral but which leaves the narrator strangely untroubled. Eustace mildly rebukes him for being too happy. A passage expanding l.252 suggests T.'s difficulties in courting Rosa Baring, and there are also about twenty lines on the various disguises which the narrator had to adopt in order to have access to Rose. This *T.MS* makes even more clear than does *Heath MS* that the unused lines were later a very important quarry for T. *Edwin Morris* (p. 708) in particular incorporates many of these lines; written as it was when T. had become disillusioned with Rosa, it could criticize his earlier self and earlier poetry by direct quotation.

This morning is the morning of the day,
When I and Eustace from the city went
To see the Gardener's Daughter; I and he,
Brothers in Art; a friendship so complete
Portioned in halves between us, that we grew
The fable of the city where we dwelt.

¶ 208.*1–3*] Eustace and I were painters in one house, *Heath MS, immediately following The Ante-Chamber.*

*4. a . . . complete*] with such a perfect love *MS.*

*5. grew*] were *MS.*

*6.* Horace, *Epodes* xi 7–8: *per urbem . . . fabula quanta fui.*

*6 ∧ 7*] For we were bound in straiter amity
Than are two playful foals – whose limbs have grown

My Eustace might have sat for Hercules;
So muscular he spread, so broad of breast.
He, by some law that holds in love, and draws
The greater to the lesser, long desired
A certain miracle of symmetry,
A miniature of loveliness, all grace
Summed up and closed in little;–Juliet, she
So light of foot, so light of spirit–oh, she
To me myself, for some three careless moons,
The summer pilot of an empty heart
Unto the shores of nothing! Know you not
Such touches are but embassies of love,
To tamper with the feelings, ere he found
Empire for life? but Eustace painted her,
And said to me, she sitting with us then,
'When will *you* paint like this?' and I replied,
(My words were half in earnest, half in jest,)
''Tis not your work, but Love's. Love, unperceived,
A more ideal Artist he than all,
Came, drew your pencil from you, made those eyes
Darker than darkest pansies, and that hair
More black than ashbuds in the front of March.'

Betwixt the same green hedges – that sometimes
Race round the pasture, sometimes idly stand
Musing together in the shade, and each
Sleeking for love the shoulder of his mate. *MS*

Probably suggested by *The Winter's Tale* I ii 67, the friendship of Leontes and Polixenes: 'We were as twinned lambs that did frisk i' the sun'.

*8. spread*] was *MS.*

*9. some*] a *MS.*

*10. long desired*] languished for *MS.*

*13*] . . . in little. She was meant
By nature for a fairy, but her heart
Had made her human – childlike Juliet *MS*

*14*] . . . light of heart, and such
A winsome shape to fondle and to fold. *MS*

Shakespeare's Juliet has 'so light a foot', *Romeo and Juliet* II vi 16.

*15–21*] Eustace had drawn her, and would often say *MS.*

*22. and I replied*] I answered him *MS.*

*23*] *Not MS.*

*25*] *Not MS.*

*26. Came, drew*] Drawing *MS.*

*28. March*] May *MS.*

And Juliet answered laughing, 'Go and see
The Gardener's daughter: trust me, after that,
You scarce can fail to match his masterpiece.'
And up we rose, and on the spur we went.

Not wholly in the busy world, nor quite
Beyond it, blooms the garden that I love.
News from the humming city comes to it
In sound of funeral or of marriage bells;
And, sitting muffled in dark leaves, you hear
The windy clanging of the minster clock;
Although between it and the garden lies
A league of grass, washed by a slow broad stream,
That, stirred with languid pulses of the oar,
Waves all its lazy lilies, and creeps on,
Barge-laden, to three arches of a bridge
Crowned with the minster-towers.
The fields between
Are dewy-fresh, browsed by deep-uddered kine,
And all about the large lime feathers low,
The lime a summer home of murmurous wings.

*29–31*] That pretty background may be mine or yours,
I might have painted it' (for space was left
On either side the figure where one caught
A glimpse of landskip crisp with shining woods
And summer holts that tufted wavy wolds)
'But would you know' said I 'what scope my shaft
Of art can fly to, wait till I have seen
The Gardener's daughter: trust me, from that hour
I shall not doubt to match your masterpiece.' *MS*

T. adapted ll. [4–5] for 'A summer crisp with shining woods', *The Day-Dream*: *Prologue* 8, and at one stage he adapted them for *Edwin Morris* (*T.Nbk 26*). Line [5] was also part of *Margaret* (*T.Nbk 23*).

*32*] *Not MS.*

*46*] Half pasture closely cropt, half meadow-ground
Whose graceful undulations, rounding, die
Each into each – with tall green hawthorn closed
In flowery squares – knee-deep in mallowtufts –
Hoary with seeded grasses, into which,
With every gale that sighs itself to death,
From bramble wreaths the balmy dewdrop melts –
From bramble wreaths, with woodbine, arching high
To bind the lower branches of the lime, *MS*

*47. murmurous*] humming *MS*. Cp. Keats, *Ode to a Nightingale* 50: 'The murmurous haunt of flies on summer eves'. Arthur Hallam had written of 'murmurous wings', *Sonnet* [*Oh, ye spring hours*] (Motter, p. 44).

In that still place she, hoarded in herself,
Grew, seldom seen; not less among us lived
Her fame from lip to lip. Who had not heard
Of Rose, the Gardener's daughter? Where was he,
So blunt in memory, so old at heart,
At such a distance from his youth in grief,
That, having seen, forgot? The common mouth,
So gross to express delight, in praise of her
Grew oratory. Such a lord is Love,
And Beauty such a mistress of the world.

And if I said that Fancy, led by Love,
Would play with flying forms and images,
Yet this is also true, that, long before
I looked upon her, when I heard her name
My heart was like a prophet to my heart,
And told me I should love. A crowd of hopes,
That sought to sow themselves like wingèd seeds,
Born out of everything I heard and saw,
Fluttered about my senses and my soul;
And vague desires, like fitful blasts of balm
To one that travels quickly, made the air
Of Life delicious, and all kinds of thought,
That verged upon them, sweeter than the dream
Dreamed by a happy man, when the dark East,
Unseen, is brightening to his bridal morn.

And sure this orbit of the memory folds
For ever in itself the day we went

*48–9*] Though, like a mellowing strawberry, beneath
Its own leaf-shade, she grew, among us lived *MS*

*55–6*] Despite of nature, in her praise became
A full-celled honeycomb of eloquence
Stored from all flowers. Love is such a King *MS*

T. incorporated these lines in *Edwin Morris* 25–7: 'was he not / A full-celled honeycomb of eloquence / Stored from all flowers?'

*58–60*] *Not MS.*

*61. I looked upon*] Long ere I saw *MS.*

*66 ∧ 7*] And blissful palpitations in the blood
Stirring a sudden transport, rose and fell: *MS*

T. incorporated these lines as *The Princess* iv 10–11.

*67–9.* Suggesting *Paradise Lost* ii 400–02: balm, air, delicious. *fitful blast*: as twice in Shelley, and in *The Voyage* (MS).

*73*] The orbit of the memory will fold *MS.*

*74. the . . . went*] that joyful day *MS.*

To see her. All the land in flowery squares,
Beneath a broad and equal-blowing wind,
Smelt of the coming summer, as one large cloud
Drew downward: but all else of heaven was pure
Up to the Sun, and May from verge to verge,
And May with me from head to heel. And now,
As though 'twere yesterday, as though it were
The hour just flown, that morn with all its sound,
(For those old Mays had thrice the life of these,)
Rings in mine ears. The steer forgot to graze,
And, where the hedge-row cuts the pathway, stood,
Leaning his horns into the neighbour field,
And lowing to his fellows. From the woods
Came voices of the well-contented doves.

*75–80*] When I and Eustace from the city stole
To see the Gardener's daughter. All the land
Smelt of the coming summer. One large cloud –
One only (all the other Heaven was pure
Up to the sun) below the minster-towers
Drew slowly down his rounded crystal piles,
Before a broad and equal-blowing wind;
But, in the world below it, little airs
Sang of the blossoms they were born in, o'er
The wrinkled glasses of the reedy creeks
Made by the river. If you moved, you crushed
A hundred daisies: budding thistle-tops
Had spiked their purple cushions in the field,
And the wild cherry in untrodden groves
Grew green from being hoary. 'Twas the time
When my smooth lip whitened with early down
Soft as the silk that lined the tender leaf
Of the young quince-tree, but the wanton growth
Of my long tresses, run in sunny rings,
Divided shining streams of girlish curls
Upon transparent temples clear of care.
My heart was filled with sunshine without shade,
For I was vain, and young, and felt my blood
How pure it swept the veins, and how my heart
Beat in my bosom, like a Life in Life. *MS*

Cp. the final lines with *Life of the Life within my blood* (p. 504).

*77*. Cp. Theocritus vii 143: *πάντ᾽ ὦσδεν θέρεος μάλα πίονος, ὦσδε δ᾽ὀπώρας*. ('All nature smelt of the opulent summer-time, smelt of the season of fruit.')

*83*] *Not MS.*

*88*. *well-*] self- *MS.*

The lark could scarce get out his notes for joy,
But shook his song together as he neared
His happy home, the ground. To left and right,
The cuckoo told his name to all the hills;
The mellow ouzel fluted in the elm;
The redcap whistled; and the nightingale
Sang loud, as though he were the bird of day.

And Eustace turned, and smiling said to me,
'Hear how the bushes echo! by my life,
These birds have joyful thoughts. Think you they sing
Like poets, from the vanity of song?
Or have they any sense of why they sing?
And would they praise the heavens for what they have?'
And I made answer, 'Were there nothing else
For which to praise the heavens but only love,
That only love were cause enough for praise.'

Lightly he laughed, as one that read my thought,
And on we went; but ere an hour had passed,
We reached a meadow slanting to the North;
Down which a well-worn pathway courted us
To one green wicket in a privet hedge;
This, yielding, gave into a grassy walk
Through crowded lilac-ambush trimly pruned;
And one warm gust, full-fed with perfume, blew
Beyond us, as we entered in the cool.
The garden stretches southward. In the midst
A cedar spread his dark-green layers of shade.

*89–90*] That ever bowing cooed and cooing bowed,
And to themselves were all in all. The lark –
His baptism of earthly dew new-dried
On fluttering wings, – dropt from the doors of Heaven,
Crowded his notes together as he neared *MS*

The MS adapts *Sense and Conscience* 49–51: 'doves, / Which ever bowing cooed and cooing bowed / Unto each other as they could not cease.'

*93–4*. Thomson, *Spring* 604–5: 'The blackbird whistles from the thorny brake, / The mellow bullfinch answers from the grove.' G. G. Loane (*Echoes in Tennyson*, 1928, p. 6) cites James Hurdis, *The Favourite Village* iv: 'And ouzel fluting with melodious pipe'.

*93. in the elm*] and aloft *MS*.

*94. redcap whistled*] starling chittered *MS*.

*96–105*] *Not MS*.

*106–7*] An hour had past when I and Eustace came
To a still meadow . . . *MS*

The garden-glasses glanced, and momently
The twinkling laurel scattered silver lights.

'Eustace,' I said, 'this wonder keeps the house.'
He nodded, but a moment afterwards
He cried, 'Look! look!' Before he ceased I turned,
And, ere a star can wink, beheld her there.

For up the porch there grew an Eastern rose,
That, flowering high, the last night's gale had caught,
And blown across the walk. One arm aloft–
Gowned in pure white, that fitted to the shape–
Holding the bush, to fix it back, she stood,
A single stream of all her soft brown hair
Poured on one side: the shadow of the flowers
Stole all the golden gloss, and, wavering
Lovingly lower, trembled on her waist–
Ah, happy shade–and still went wavering down,
But, ere it touched a foot, that might have danced
The greensward into greener circles, dipt,
And mixed with shadows of the common ground!
But the full day dwelt on her brows, and sunned
Her violet eyes, and all her Hebe bloom,

*116. glanced*] *1891*; shone *1842–90*. *garden-glasses*: bell-glasses over plants.

*121*] And, ere a frosty star can twinkle, saw
The substance of the shadow in my thought. *MS*

*122–3*] There grew a china-rose, that budding high
Above the tiles, the last-night gale had caught, *MS*

*125. that*] close- *MS*.

*126. bush . . . back*] branch, half-turned to us *MS*.

*128. flowers*] branch *MS*.

*130. her*] a *MS*.

*131–2*] That, falling gently inward, made all round
A bed for Love's own arms – Ah happy shade
That still went wavering down, and ere it touched
A foot and ankle light as those which beat *MS*

*133. dipt*] fell *MS*. Like a fairy.

*135–9*] An unforgotten vision! The clear heat
Bathing the ripe anemones, that kissed
Each other in her lips, deepened the blush
Below her violet eyes and underneath
Glowed on one polished shoulder, – basking warm
Between the halfseen swell of maiden breasts,
Moulded in smoothest curves. Half-light, half-shade, *MS*

*136. Hebe*: goddess of youth.

And doubled his own warmth against her lips,
And on the bounteous wave of such a breast
As never pencil drew. Half light, half shade,
She stood, a sight to make an old man young.

So rapt, we neared the house; but she, a Rose
In roses, mingled with her fragrant toil,
Nor heard us come, nor from her tendance turned
Into the world without; till close at hand,
And almost ere I knew mine own intent,
This murmur broke the stillness of that air
Which brooded round about her:
'Ah, one rose,
One rose, but one, by those fair fingers culled,
Were worth a hundred kisses pressed on lips
Less exquisite than thine.'
She looked: but all
Suffused with blushes–neither self-possessed
Nor startled, but betwixt this mood and that,
Divided in a graceful quiet–paused,
And dropt the branch she held, and turning, wound
Her looser hair in braid, and stirred her lips
For some sweet answer, though no answer came,
Nor yet refused the rose, but granted it,
And moved away, and left me, statue-like,
In act to render thanks.
I, that whole day,
Saw her no more, although I lingered there
Till every daisy slept, and Love's white star
Beamed through the thickened cedar in the dusk.

*140. man*] heart *MS.*

*141. So . . . house*] On to the house we crept *MS.*

*141–3.* Suggesting Eve in Eden (cp. l. 187) among the roses: 'Her self, though fairest unsupported Flow'r', *Paradise Lost* ix 432. The flowers 'toucht by her fair tendance gladlier grew', viii 47. For 'Rose/In roses', cp. *June on many a flower* 4, to Rosa Baring.

*143*] Nor heard, nor from her blissful tendance gazed *MS.*

*144. world without*] colder world *MS.*

*145. And almost ere*] Almost before *MS.*

*146*] This murmur smote the chaste and silent air *MS.*

*147. Which*] That MS.

*150. all*] filled *MS.*

*150 ^ 51*] With virgin pride, and bashful majesty *MS.* Again suggesting 'the Virgin Majestie of *Eve*', *PL* ix 270.

So home we went, and all the livelong way
With solemn gibe did Eustace banter me.
'Now,' said he, 'will you climb the top of Art.
You cannot fail but work in hues to dim
The Titianic Flora. Will you match
My Juliet? you, not you,—the Master, Love,
A more ideal Artist he than all.'

So home I went, but could not sleep for joy,
Reading her perfect features in the gloom,
Kissing the rose she gave me o'er and o'er,
And shaping faithful record of the glance
That graced the giving—such a noise of life
Swarmed in the golden present, such a voice
Called to me from the years to come, and such
A length of bright horizon rimmed the dark.
And all that night I heard the watchman peal
The sliding season: all that night I heard
The heavy clocks knolling the drowsy hours.
The drowsy hours, dispensers of all good,
O'er the mute city stole with folded wings,
Distilling odours on me as they went
To greet their fairer sisters of the East.

Love at first sight, first-born, and heir to all,
Made this night thus. Henceforward squall nor storm

*163. home we went*] we went thence *MS.*
*164. solemn*] laughing *MS.*
*166–9*]
Call for your pallet: happy impulses
Untaken, waste, and running dry, become
Occasion lost: yet now I prophesy
That you will paint to startle Titian
And ancient Leonardo – it may be
To match my little Juliet: then, I'll swear,
(Right tit for tat) the painter was true Love.' *MS*
*167.* Titian's painting in Florence.
*171 ∧ 2*] Kissing the very pillow for her cheek, *MS.*
*174–5.* Cp. *The Talking Oak* 213: 'the swarming sound of life'.
*178. watchman*] *1863*; watchmen *1842–62.*
*181.* Cp. *Love and Duty* 56: 'The slow sweet hours that bring us all things good'; based on Theocritus xv 104.
*183. odours*] incense *MS.* *went*] past *MS.*
*185–208*] *MS has two versions:*
(i) Yet might you swear that neither squall nor shower
Could keep me from the garden, in those days.
'Twas sweet even to sleep – to wake. How sweet

Was either twilight and the day between,
Sweeter than all, the moments that I spent
In watching how her pure and virgin soul,
(That hoarded all its odour in itself,
Deep blooming fold in fold by slow degrees)
Opened before me, till she read and knew
The meaning of my glances; even until
Mutely, with drooping eyelids yielded she
Her bosom to the transport of mine arms
Or [And *1st reading*] trembled without speaking, as the storm
Of my first welcome [transport *1st reading*], pouring kiss on kiss
Incessantly, like flashes of soft light [Like . . . light, incessantly *1st reading*]
Melted from lip to lip, and from my heart
Sank, fused in hers now growing one with mine.
My love of [for *1st reading*] Nature and my love for her,
Of different ages, like twinsisters throve.
Her beauty with the growing season grew
Or seemed to grow, till drawn in narrowing arcs
The southing Autumn touched with sallower gleams
The granges on the fallows.
At that time
Tired of the noisy town I wandered there,
The bell tolled four by the time I reached
The wicket gate, I found her by herself,
I took her hand, I led her, we sat down,

(ii) From that time forth as in a dream I walked
Threading the fervent market place alone.
Nor could the famous beauties of the place,
The graceful city damsels, woo mine ear
To their light footfalls on the flags. Nor turned
Mine eyes, although on hollowed tubes in range
Purselipped the swarthy piper moved his beard.

* * * *

Nor would you find me in the city walk,
Nor in the ruin on the castle hill,
Nor yet, with Eustace, on the bustling quay
At eve, when, new-arrived, the packet stilled
Her splashing paddle wheels, and overhead
The snoring funnel whizzed with silver steam.
You may be sure that neither squall or shower
Could keep me from the garden: there I came
Both when the currant hid with vinelike leaf
Its half-ripe growths, and when the swath-rake cleared

Could keep me from that Eden where she dwelt.
Light pretexts drew me; sometimes a Dutch love
For tulips; then for roses, moss or musk,
To grace my city rooms; or fruits and cream
Served in the weeping elm; and more and more
A word could bring the colour to my cheek;
A thought would fill my eyes with happy dew;
Love trebled life within me, and with each
The year increased.
The daughters of the year,
One after one, through that still garden passed;
Each garlanded with her peculiar flower
Danced into light, and died into the shade;
And each in passing touched with some new grace
Or seemed to touch her, so that day by day,
Like one that never can be wholly known,
Her beauty grew; till Autumn brought an hour
For Eustace, when I heard his deep 'I will,'
Breathed, like the covenant of a God, to hold

The short green eddish. With the summer grew,
Or seemed to grow her beauty: with it grew
My bliss and throve, till drawn in narrowing arcs
Descending daylight touched with sallower gleams
The granges in the fallows: there I came
Last when the sleepy Autumn nodding rode
Brushing the linden on the pilèd wain.
The bell tolled four &c.

T. incorporated lines from (i) for *Edwin Morris* 31–40:

My love for Nature and my love for her,
Of different ages, like twin-sisters grew . . .
And either twilight and the day between;
For daily hope fulfilled, to rise again
Revolving toward fulfilment, made it sweet
To walk, to sit, to sleep, to wake, to breathe.

The lines on the lovers' embraces, immediately preceding these, were also incorporated by T. at one stage of *Edwin Morris* (*T. Nbk 26*). *T.MS* of *The Gardener's Daughter* includes more lines of *Edwin Morris*. H.T. quoted the lines about the autumn landscape: 'I remember my father's telling me that FitzGerald had guessed rightly that the autumn landscape . . . was taken from the background of a Titian (Lord Ellesmere's *Ages of Man*). My father said that perhaps in consequence they had been omitted.' T. at one stage incorporated ll. [7, 13] of (ii) into *Audley Court*.

*187.* Rader (p. 31) suggests that 'garden of Eden' hinted at Rosa Baring, since her home was that of her stepfather Arthur Eden.

*196. that still garden*: *In Memoriam* xliii 10.

From thence through all the worlds: but I rose up
Full of his bliss, and following her dark eyes
Felt earth as air beneath me, till I reached
The wicket-gate, and found her standing there.

There sat we down upon a garden mound,
Two mutually enfolded; Love, the third,
Between us, in the circle of his arms
Enwound us both; and over many a range
Of waning lime the gray cathedral towers,
Across a hazy glimmer of the west,
Revealed their shining windows: from them clashed
The bells; we listened; with the time we played,
We spoke of other things; we coursed about
The subject most at heart, more near and near,
Like doves about a dovecote, wheeling round
The central wish, until we settled there.

Then, in that time and place, I spoke to her,
Requiring, though I knew it was mine own,
Yet for the pleasure that I took to hear,
Requiring at her hand the greatest gift,
A woman's heart, the heart of her I loved;
And in that time and place she answered me,

*209*] We two sat down upon one thymy mound, *MS.*

*212–4*] Enwound us both – while over waning woods
And meads newmown the blue cathedral towers,
Soft through a hazy glimmer in the sun *MS*

*215. clashed*] rang *MS.*

*216–20*] A peal of marriage-bells; but nigh at hand,
Hot on the snow-white wall the waxen plum
Pampered his luscious cheek: tall hollyoaks
Clustered their largest roses in the glow.
The wind was fitful: every musky gust
Tumbled the mellow pear: the apple boughs
O'erburdened bowed, loaded with rosy globes
Brushing the fat black mould: and at our feet
Through two round stones, two cushions of dark moss,
Bubbled a pebbly runlet frosty-cool. *MS*

Sir Charles Tennyson, *Cornhill* cliii (1936) 441, observes that the fifth and sixth lines were adapted for *In Memoriam* lxxxix 19–20: 'The gust that round the garden flew, / And tumbled half the mellowing pears!' The *MS* passage was at one stage incorporated as *Audley Court* 73–7.

*221*] In that same place and time I spake to her, *MS.*

*226. time and place*] place and time *MS.*

And in the compass of three little words,
More musical than ever came in one,
The silver fragments of a broken voice,
Made me most happy, faltering, 'I am thine.'

Shall I cease here? Is this enough to say
That my desire, like all strongest hopes,
By its own energy fulfilled itself,
Merged in completion? Would you learn at full
How passion rose through circumstantial grades
Beyond all grades developed? and indeed
I had not stayed so long to tell you all,
But while I mused came Memory with sad eyes,
Holding the folded annals of my youth;
And while I mused, Love with knit brows went by,
And with a flying finger swept my lips,
And spake, 'Be wise: not easily forgiven
Are those, who setting wide the doors that bar
The secret bridal-chambers of the heart,
Let in the day.' Here, then, my words have end.

Yet might I tell of meetings, of farewells–
Of that which came between, more sweet than each,

230. *faltering*] *1851*; lisping *1842–50*.

234–9]
Drowned in completion? Would you rather learn
Amplier detailed how these spring shoots of love
Through circumstantial changes, prosperously
Accomplishing all grades of increase, rose
Beyond a mellower growth mature in ear?
And I in truth had freely told you how, *MS*

240. *And*] But *MS*.

243. *those*] they *MS 1st reading. doors*] valves *MS*. *bar*] close *MS 1st reading.*

244. Hallam had written of 'my heart's chambers', *Lines Written in Great Depression of Mind* (Motter, p. 34).

246–9]
Yet might I tell of meetings in the dark,
Of meetings – of farewells – of that which came
Between, more sweet than either; I might tell
Until the shadow, sweeping from the sun,
Married with night – of whispers and of sighs *MS*

A later version in *MS* takes up the third line:

I might tell
Of kisses and of whispers and of sighs –
Of kisses paid with kisses which again

In whispers, like the whispers of the leaves
That tremble round a nightingale—in sighs
Which perfect Joy, perplexed for utterance,
Stole from her sister Sorrow. Might I not tell
Of difference, reconcilement, pledges given,
And vows, where there was never need of vows,
And kisses, where the heart on one wild leap
Hung tranced from all pulsation, as above
The heavens between their fairy fleeces pale
Sowed all their mystic gulfs with fleeting stars;
Or while the balmy glooming, crescent-lit,
Spread the light haze along the river-shores,
And in the hollows; or as once we met
Unheedful, though beneath a whispering rain
Night slid down one long stream of sighing wind,
And in her bosom bore the baby, Sleep.

But this whole hour your eyes have been intent
On that veiled picture–veiled, for what it holds
May not be dwelt on by the common day.
This prelude has prepared thee. Raise thy soul;
Make thine heart ready with thine eyes: the time
Is come to raise the veil.
Behold her there,
As I beheld her ere she knew my heart,
My first, last love; the idol of my youth,
The darling of my manhood, and, alas!
Now the most blessèd memory of mine age.

Bore flower of kisses blossoming on lips
The softest lips that ever learned to kiss –

concluding with ll.248–9 (*Of* . . . *of* . . .).

251. *Might I not*] I might *MS*.

252. *T.MS* has a passage expanding this, suggesting T.'s difficulties with Rosa.

252–5] Even yet of close embraces or the warm
Love-pressure of half-yielded hands, what time *MS*

258. *while*] when *MS*.

261. *rain*] shower *MS*.

263. Shelley has 'the baby Sleep', *Queen Mab* i 40.

264. *But this whole hour*] This whole half-hour *MS*.

265. *holds*] hides *MS*.

266. *day*] light *MS*.

267. *has*] hath *MS*.

269. *come to raise*] ripe, to lift *MS*.

# 209 The Two Voices

Published *1842*, dated '1833'. H.T. describes it as 'begun under the cloud of his overwhelming sorrow after the death of Arthur Hallam', news of which reached T. on 1 October 1833. This statement has not hitherto been disputed, but that T. had begun it before Hallam's death is clear from a letter by J. M. Kemble to W. B. Donne (MS belonging to Mrs C. B. Johnson). The latter is dated 'Saturday 22 June', and from internal evidence (it refers to the British Association meeting in Cambridge), it indubitably belongs to June 1833: 'Next Sir are some superb meditations on Selfdestruction called *Thoughts of a Suicide* wherein he argues the point with his soul and is thoroughly floored. These are amazingly fine and deep, and show a mighty stride in intellect since the *Second-Rate Sensitive Mind*.' Clearly a version of *The Two Voices* was already in existence. In its origin, as Kemble points out, it is a poem like *Supposed Confessions* (*1830*, p. 197), and the earlier *Remorse* (*1827*, p. 87). But T.'s writing of it may well have been affected by the death of Hallam. Both *Heath MS* (all variants are below) and *H.Lpr 254* (virtually identical with *Heath MS*) stop after l. 309 with three lines added. This would be a feasible ending, and conceivably a better one. The published ending was developed later; Edmund Lushington says that T. 'left it for some time unfinished.... The termination ... I first heard him read' in 1837 or early 1838 (*Mat.* i 246). Miss M. J. Donahue quotes FitzGerald's note on l. 453: 'Composed as he walked about the Dulwich meadows'; she remarks that T. was there in 1835 (*Studies in the 10 Years' Silence*, Yale thesis, 1946, p. 142). *T.Nbk 15*, which may not be quoted, includes two drafts (*T.MS*); the first ends with l.96, and the second runs from l.229–321. (But sheets are missing from this notebook.) *T.Nbk 26* (*T.MS B*) has a fragment beginning at l.298, and breaking off with l.393. The *Hn MS* (HM 1320) ends with l.174; all its variants that differ from *Heath MS* are given below.

H.T. says that the poem, 'describing the conflict in a soul between Faith and Scepticism, was begun under the cloud of his overwhelming sorrow after the death of Arthur Hallam, which, as my father told me, for a while blotted out all joy from his life, and made him long for death'. *Thoughts of a Suicide* is the title in *Heath MS*, as in Kemble's letter. T.'s later title may owe something, as Miss Donahue suggests, to Wordsworth's sonnet *Two voices are there*, which T. read in spring 1835 (*Mem.* i 151). In his handling of the theme, T. was indebted to Lucretius's discussion of death (iii 830–1094); to the solicitations of Despair in *Faerie Queene* I ix; and to Hamlet's 'To be or not to be ...' T.'s tone was influenced by *Job*, as Carlyle suggested in 1842 (*Mem.* i 213), *Psalms*, and *Ecclesiastes*. There are many similarities, in idea and phrasing, to *In Memoriam*, especially xliii–xlvii: and to *On a Mourner*, on Hallam's death (p. 557). The triplet had been used by T.'s brother Charles in *1827* in *Ode on the Death of Lord Byron*. T. used it in *Stanzas* (1833, p. 495), and *The Eagle* (p. 495).

A still small voice spake unto me,
'Thou art so full of misery,
Were it not better not to be?'

Then to the still small voice I said;
'Let me not cast in endless shade
What is so wonderfully made.'

To which the voice did urge reply;
'Today I saw the dragon-fly
Come from the wells where he did lie.

'An inner impulse rent the veil
Of his old husk: from head to tail
Came out clear plates of sapphire mail.

¶ 209.*1*. Contrast *1 Kings* xix 12, where the 'still small voice' is the Lord's.
*2–3*. Cp. *Remorse* 42–4: 'yet I cling / To life, whose every hour to me / Hath been increase of misery.'
*5*] I will not die and cast in shade *Heath MS 1st reading*.
*5–6*. *Psalm* cxxxix 11–14: 'If I say, Surely the darkness shall cover me; even the night shall be light about me . . . . I will praise thee; for I am fearfully and wonderfully made.'
*8–15*. T. adapts a traditional emblem, found in Jacob Bryant's *New System of Ancient Mythology* (1807 edn iii 247–8). Bryant's work was at Somersby (*Lincoln*). His Plate xx is of 'The Chrysalis . . . and other emblems relating to the renewal of life, and the immortality of the soul'. Bryant: 'The Aurelia, after its first stage as an Eruca, or worm, lies for a season in a manner dead; and is inclosed in a sort of a coffin. In this state of darkness it remains all the winter: but at the return of spring it bursts its bonds, and comes out with new life, and in the most beautiful attire. The Egyptians thought this a very proper picture of the soul of man, and of the immortality, to which it aspired.' Cp. Olinthus Gregory, *On the Evidences of the Christian Religion* (1811, often reprinted): 'On the Resurrection of the Body' uses the example of the dragonfly (described in detail) to support the likelihood of resurrection. Cp. *Timbuctoo* 146–54 (p. 177), where the change from worm to dragonfly is T.'s simile for the lifting of his thoughts from the earthly to the infinite. Also *From the East of life* 20–24 (p. 467): 'The dragonfly is born from damps. // The quickwinged gnat doth make a boat / Of his old husk wherewith to float / To a new life: all low things range / To higher but I cannot change.'
*9*. *Come*] Rise *Heath MS 1st reading*.
*12*] Burst blazing plates of crimson mail. *Heath MS*; Burst burnisht plates of sapphire mail. *Hn MS*.

'He dried his wings: like gauze they grew;
Through crofts and pastures wet with dew
A living flash of light he flew.'

I said, 'When first the world began,
Young Nature through five cycles ran,
And in the sixth she moulded man.

'She gave him mind, the lordliest
Proportion, and, above the rest,
Dominion in the head and breast.'

Thereto the silent voice replied;
'Self-blinded are you by your pride:
Look up through night: the world is wide.

'This truth within thy mind rehearse,
That in a boundless universe
Is boundless better, boundless worse.

'Think you this mould of hopes and fears
Could find no statelier than his peers
In yonder hundred million spheres?'

It spake, moreover, in my mind:
'Though thou wert scattered to the wind,
Yet is there plenty of the kind.'

Then did my response clearer fall:
'No compound of this earthly ball
Is like another, all in all.'

To which he answered scoffingly;
'Good soul! suppose I grant it thee,
Who'll weep for thy deficiency?

*14. crofts*] holts *Heath MS.*

*16–18.* Invoking science as well as religion, 'the "creative eras" which Buffon and his English followers equated with the 6 creative days of Genesis'. M. Millhauser, *PMLA* lxix (1954) 337.

*19–21*] *Added in margin T.MS.*

*21. head*] heart *Heath MS. Psalm* viii 6: 'Thou madest him to have dominion over the works of thy hands.'

*23. by*] with *Heath MS.*

*24. up through*] through the *Heath MS 1st reading.*

*32–3.* Cp. *In Memoriam* lv–lvi (p. 910).

*39. thy deficiency*: 'the want of thee' (T.).

'Or will one beam be less intense,
When thy peculiar difference
Is cancelled in the world of sense?'

I would have said, 'Thou canst not know,'
But my full heart, that worked below,
Rained through my sight its overflow.

Again the voice spake unto me:
'Thou art so steeped in misery,
Surely 'twere better not to be.

'Thine anguish will not let thee sleep,
Nor any train of reason keep:
Thou canst not think, but thou wilt weep.'

I said, 'The years with change advance:
If I make dark my countenance,
I shut my life from happier chance.

'Some turn this sickness yet might take,
Even yet.' But he: 'What drug can make
A withered palsy cease to shake?'

I wept, 'Though I should die, I know
That all about the thorn will blow
In tufts of rosy-tinted snow;

'And men, through novel spheres of thought
Still moving after truth long sought,
Will learn new things when I am not.'

'Yet,' said the secret voice, 'some time,
Sooner or later, will gray prime
Make thy grass hoar with early rime.

'Not less swift souls that yearn for light,
Rapt after heaven's starry flight,
Would sweep the tracts of day and night.

*40–42*] *Added in margin T.MS.*

*45.* Cp. *The Lover's Tale* i 23, *1832* text: 'for fear the mind / Rain through my sight'.

*50. Nor*] Or *Heath MS.*

*52–7*] *Not T.MS, Heath MS; added in margin Hn MS. T.MS has, deleted, ll. 229–31.*

*52–3.* Cp. *Job* xiv 20: 'Thou prevailest for ever against him, and he passeth: thou changest his countenance, and sendest him away.'

*59–60*] That through green lanes the thorn will blow
In spicy tufts of vernal snow; *Heath MS*

*67–9*] *Transposed with ll. 70–72 in T.MS, Heath MS; emended Hn MS.*

*67. that*] would *Hn MS 1st reading.*

'Not less the bee would range her cells,
The furzy prickle fire the dells,
The foxglove cluster dappled bells.'

I said that 'all the years invent;
Each month is various to present
The world with some development.

'Were this not well, to bide mine hour,
Though watching from a ruined tower
How grows the day of human power?'

'The highest-mounted mind,' he said,
'Still sees the sacred morning spread
The silent summit overhead.

'Will thirty seasons render plain
Those lonely lights that still remain,
Just breaking over land and main?

'Or make that morn, from his cold crown
And crystal silence creeping down,
Flood with full daylight glebe and town?

'Forerun thy peers, thy time, and let
Thy feet, millennium hence, be set
In midst of knowledge, dreamed not yet.

'Thou hast not gained a real height,
Nor art thou nearer to the light,
Because the scale is infinite.

*73–5] Not T.MS, Heath MS;*

I said that every month invents
And every various year presents
The world with new developments. *Hn MS*

*76–8]* I murmured 'Through the space between
New knowledge, shooting beams serene,
Might curve new boughs of haler green.' *Heath MS 1st reading*

T. revised l. [1] 'Yet' said I 'On the . . . l. [2] *shooting beams*] dropping dew l. [3] *curve new boughs*] feed fresh shoots. He then further revised l. 76 '*Were this not*] I said 'twere l. 78 *grows the day*] creep the tides

*80. sees*] views *Heath MS.*

*82–4] T.MS formed these from nine lines on Time.*

*83.* 'lonely light', *The Outcast* 14.

*88–93] Not T.MS (which has three lines on climbing); not Heath MS; added in margin Hn MS.*

‘’Twere better not to breathe or speak,
Than cry for strength, remaining weak,
And seem to find, but still to seek.

‘Moreover, but to seem to find
Asks what thou lackest, thought resigned,
A healthy frame, a quiet mind.’

I said, ‘When I am gone away,
“He dared not tarry,” men will say,
Doing dishonour to my clay.’

‘This is more vile,’ he made reply,
‘To breathe and loathe, to live and sigh,
Than once from dread of pain to die.

‘Sick art thou–a divided will
Still heaping on the fear of ill
The fear of men, a coward still.

‘Do men love thee? Art thou so bound
To men, that how thy name may sound
Will vex thee lying underground?

‘The memory of the withered leaf
In endless time is scarce more brief
Than of the garnered Autumn-sheaf.

‘Go, vexèd Spirit, sleep in trust;
The right ear, that is filled with dust,
Hears little of the false or just.’

‘Hard task, to pluck resolve,’ I cried,
‘From emptiness and the waste wide
Of that abyss, or scornful pride!

*97*] To enjoy the found, or seem to find *Heath MS.*

*99*] Strength, tempered will, a quiet mind. *Heath MS.*

*107. the*] thee *Heath MS.*

*110. may*] will *Heath MS 1st reading.*

*111 ^ 2*]
Thou shrinkest from the probe of blame,
Yet out of all that owns a name
The vainest form is human fame. *Heath MS, deleted*

*113. more*] less *Heath MS 1st reading.*

*118–20*] *Added in Heath MS.*

*119–20.* Note the Miltonic ‘abyss’, and ‘waste wide Anarchie’, *PL* x 282–3.

'Nay–rather yet that I could raise
One hope that warmed me in the days
While still I yearned for human praise.

'When, wide in soul and bold of tongue,
Among the tents I paused and sung,
The distant battle flashed and rung.

'I sung the joyful Pæan clear,
And, sitting, burnished without fear
The brand, the buckler, and the spear–

'Waiting to strive a happy strife,
To war with falsehood to the knife,
And not to lose the good of life–

'Some hidden principle to move,
To put together, part and prove,
And mete the bounds of hate and love–

'As far as might be, to carve out
Free space for every human doubt,
That the whole mind might orb about–

'To search through all I felt or saw,
The springs of life, the depths of awe,
And reach the law within the law:

'At least, not rotting like a weed,
But, having sown some generous seed,
Fruitful of further thought and deed,

*121. Nay – rather yet*] I groaned. 'Yet oh *Heath MS 1st reading*; Oh – rather yet *Hn MS 1st reading*.
*122. One hope*] Those hopes *Heath MS 1st reading*. *warmed me*] flourished *Heath MS*.
*124–45*] *Missing from Hn MS*.
*124–56*. On the moral certainties of battle, cp. *Locksley Hall* 103–4; *Thy voice is heard* (*The Princess* iv ^ v); and the conclusion of *Maud*.
*126. distant*] swaying *Heath MS*.
*133–41*] *Not Heath MS, which has, deleted:*

My purposed thought, at full to weave,
Then dying well all round to leave
The sunset of a splendid eve.

*138*. Cp. *In Memoriam* xxiv 15: 'And orb into the perfect star'.
*142*] Not rotting like an idle weed, *Heath MS*. Cp. *Hamlet* I v 32–3: 'Duller shouldst thou be than the fat weed / That rots itself in ease on Lethe wharf.' See l. 280.

'To pass, when Life her light withdraws,
Not void of righteous self-applause,
Nor in a merely selfish cause–

'In some good cause, not in mine own,
To perish, wept for, honoured, known,
And like a warrior overthrown;

'Whose eyes are dim with glorious tears,
When, soiled with noble dust, he hears
His country's war-song thrill his ears:

'Then dying of a mortal stroke,
What time the foeman's line is broke,
And all the war is rolled in smoke.'

'Yea!' said the voice, 'thy dream was good,
While thou abodest in the bud.
It was the stirring of the blood.

'If Nature put not forth her power
About the opening of the flower,
Who is it that could live an hour?

'Then comes the check, the change, the fall,
Pain rises up, old pleasures pall.
There is one remedy for all.

'Yet hadst thou, through enduring pain,
Linked month to month with such a chain
Of knitted purport, all were vain.

'Thou hadst not between death and birth
Dissolved the riddle of the earth.
So were thy labour little-worth.

'That men with knowledge merely played,
I told thee–hardly nigher made,
Though scaling slow from grade to grade;

*145–7*] *Not Heath MS.*
*148. good*] great *Heath MS.*
*151. with glorious tears*] through glorious fears *Heath MS.*
*152.* Horace's *Odes* II i 22: *non indecoro pulvere sordidos*, which T. had quoted as a note to 'Your brows with noble dust defiled', *The Vale of Bones* 88.
*170. The Palace of Art* 213: 'The riddle of the painful earth'.
*172–3*] I told thee, men, like children, played / With science – hardly ... *Heath MS.*

'Much less this dreamer, deaf and blind,
Named man, may hope some truth to find,
That bears relation to the mind.

'For every worm beneath the moon
Draws different threads, and late and soon
Spins, toiling out his own cocoon.

'Cry, faint not: either Truth is born
Beyond the polar gleam forlorn,
Or in the gateways of the morn.

'Cry, faint not, climb: the summits slope
Beyond the furthest flights of hope,
Wrapt in dense cloud from base to cope.

'Sometimes a little corner shines,
As over rainy mist inclines
A gleaming crag with belts of pines.

'I will go forward, sayest thou,
I shall not fail to find her now.
Look up, the fold is on her brow.

'If straight thy track, or if oblique,
Thou know'st not. Shadows thou dost strike,
Embracing cloud, Ixion-like;

'And owning but a little more
Than beasts, abidest lame and poor,
Calling thyself a little lower

*187–9.* Cp. *The Vale of Bones* 7–8: 'At times her partial splendour shines / Upon the grove of deep-black pines.'

*192. fold*: 'cloud' (T.).

*193.* T. comments 'I pronounce "oblique" *oblīque*', on the analogy of '*obleege*'/*oblige*. Wordsworth rhymed *strike*/*oblique* in the MS of *An Evening Walk*.

*194. Shadows*] Phantoms *H.Lpr 254*.

*195.* 'Ixion embraced a cloud, hoping to embrace a goddess' (T.).

*196–9.* Combining *Ecclesiastes* iii 19, 'For that which befalleth the sons of men befalleth beasts; even one thing befalleth them: as the one dieth, so dieth the other'; with *Psalm* viii 4–5, 'What is man, that thou art mindful of him? and the son of man, that thou visitest him? For thou hast made him a little lower than the angels.'

'Than angels. Cease to wail and brawl!
Why inch by inch to darkness crawl?
There is one remedy for all.'

'O dull, one-sided voice,' said I,
'Wilt thou make everything a lie,
To flatter me that I may die?

'I know that age to age succeeds,
Blowing a noise of tongues and deeds,
A dust of systems and of creeds.

'I cannot hide that some have striven,
Achieving calm, to whom was given
The joy that mixes man with Heaven:

'Who, rowing hard against the stream,
Saw distant gates of Eden gleam,
And did not dream it was a dream;

'But heard, by secret transport led,
Even in the charnels of the dead,
The murmur of the fountain-head–

'Which did accomplish their desire,
Bore and forbore, and did not tire,
Like Stephen, an unquenchèd fire.

'He heeded not reviling tones,
Nor sold his heart to idle moans,
Though cursed and scorned, and bruised with stones:

'But looking upward, full of grace,
He prayed, and from a happy place
God's glory smote him on the face.'

199. *Cease to wail*] Why complain *Heath MS.*
200. *Why*] And *Heath MS.*
205–7] *Not Heath MS.* Cp. the two deleted stanzas of *The Vision of Sin* 103–6, 114 ∧ 5, beginning 'Systems! . . .' and 'Creeds! . . .' (p. 721).
210. Horace's *Odes* I i 30: *dis miscent superis.*
211. *Who, rowing*] Which did row *Heath MS 1st reading*; Which rowing *Heath MS.*
212–3] Making to one great light, nor seem / Even to dream . . . *Heath MS 1st reading.*
215. *Even*] Deep *Heath MS.*
222–5. *Acts* vii 55, 'But he, being full of the Holy Ghost, looked up stedfastly into heaven, and saw the glory of God.'

The sullen answer slid betwixt:
'Not that the grounds of hope were fixed,
The elements were kindlier mixed.'

I said, 'I toil beneath the curse,
But, knowing not the universe,
I fear to slide from bad to worse.

'And that, in seeking to undo
One riddle, and to find the true,
I knit a hundred others new:

'Or that this anguish fleeting hence,
Unmanacled from bonds of sense,
Be fixed and frozen to permanence:

'For I go, weak from suffering here:
Naked I go, and void of cheer:
What is it that I may not fear?'

'Consider well,' the voice replied,
'His face, that two hours since hath died;
Wilt thou find passion, pain or pride?

'Will he obey when one commands?
Or answer should one press his hands?
He answers not, nor understands.

'His palms are folded on his breast:
There is no other thing expressed
But long disquiet merged in rest.

*228. Julius Caesar* V v 73–5: 'The elements / So mixed in him that Nature might stand up / And say to all the world "This was a man!"' T. comments 'Some have happier dispositions.'

*228 ∧ 9*]
For these two shadows stand afar –
One, cloakt with night, and looking war,
The other wears the morning star.

One urn they hold; o'er land and sea
They shake it, and disorderly
The lots leap out to thee and me'. *Heath MS*

*232–40*] *Not T.MS, Heath MS.*

*236–7.* The rhyme *sense/permanence* and 'fixed' recall Arthur Hallam's sonnet *On the Picture of the Three Fates*, 1827 (Motter, p. 3).

*239. Ecclesiastes* v 15: 'naked shall he return to go as he came'.

*243. passion*] pleasure *Heath MS*. Cp. Pope, *Epistle to Oxford* 24: 'Above all Pain, all Passion, and all Pride'.

*244–6*] *Transposed with ll.247–9 T.MS.*

*247. A Dirge* 2: 'Fold thy palms across thy breast'.

'His lips are very mild and meek:
Though one should smite him on the cheek,
And on the mouth, he will not speak.

'His little daughter, whose sweet face
He kissed, taking his last embrace,
Becomes dishonour to her race–

'His sons grow up that bear his name,
Some grow to honour, some to shame,–
But he is chill to praise or blame.

'He will not hear the north-wind rave,
Nor, moaning, household shelter crave
From winter rains that beat his grave.

'High up the vapours fold and swim:
About him broods the twilight dim:
The place he knew forgetteth him.'

'If all be dark, vague voice,' I said,
'These things are wrapt in doubt and dread,
Nor canst thou show the dead are dead.

'The sap dries up: the plant declines.
A deeper tale my heart divines.
Know I not Death? the outward signs?

'I found him when my years were few;
A shadow on the graves I knew,
And darkness in the village yew.

*251.* As in *Come hither* (p. 152).
*253–8*] *Added in margin T.MS.*
*256–7. Job* xiv 21, on the dead man: 'His sons come to honour, and he knoweth it not; and they are brought low, but he perceiveth it not of them.'
*259–61*] *Transposed with ll. 262–4 T.MS.*
*264. Psalm* ciii 16, 'the place thereof shall know it no more'–man as a dead flower.
*264 ∧ 5*] *T.MS. has nine lines on eliciting from the dead a vow to return after death.*
*267. Nor canst thou*] Thou canst not *Heath MS.*
*268–318*] *Not T.MS, which has nine lines on primeval times.*
*271–3*] He stands among the graves, the floods
Speak of him – and the winds: the woods
Whisper his name among the buds. *Heath MS*

'From grave to grave the shadow crept:
In her still place the morning wept:
Touched by his feet the daisy slept.

'The simple senses crowned his head:
"Omega! thou art Lord," they said,
"We find no motion in the dead."

'Why, if man rot in dreamless ease,
Should that plain fact, as taught by these,
Not make him sure that he shall cease?

'Who forged that other influence,
That heat of inward evidence,
By which he doubts against the sense?

'He owns the fatal gift of eyes,
That read his spirit blindly wise,
Not simple as a thing that dies.

'Here sits he shaping wings to fly:
His heart forebodes a mystery:
He names the name Eternity.

'That type of Perfect in his mind
In Nature can he nowhere find.
He sows himself on every wind.

'He seems to hear a Heavenly Friend,
And through thick veils to apprehend
A labour working to an end.

274] He rises from unsounded deeps: *Heath MS.*
275. *wept*] weeps *Heath MS.*
276. *slept*] sleeps *Heath MS.*
277–9] *Not Heath MS.* 'The simple senses made death a king' (T.). Contrast *Revelation* i 8: 'I am Alpha and Omega, the beginning and the ending, saith the Lord.'
280–2] Yet if man find unconscious ease
Why should that glassy frame of peace
Fail to persuade him he shall cease? *Heath MS*
280. *Hamlet* I v 32–3: 'the fat weed / That rots itself in ease'; see l. 142.
283. *other*] mightier *Heath MS.*
284. *That heat*] What heats *Heath MS.* Cp. *In Memoriam* cxxiv 13–14: 'A warmth within the breast would melt / The freezing reason's colder part.'
285. *By which he doubts*] That makes him doubt *Heath MS.*
292–4] *Not Heath MS.*
297. To be found verbatim in *Youth* 60; cp. *In Memoriam* cxxviii 24: 'toil cöoperant to an end'.

'The end and the beginning vex
His reason: many things perplex,
With motions, checks, and counterchecks.

'He knows a baseness in his blood
At such strange war with something good,
He may not do the thing he would.

'Heaven opens inward, chasms yawn,
Vast images in glimmering dawn,
Half shown, are broken and withdrawn.

'Ah! sure within him and without,
Could his dark wisdom find it out,
There must be answer to his doubt,

'But thou canst answer not again.
With thine own weapon art thou slain,
Or thou wilt answer but in vain.

'The doubt would rest, I dare not solve.
In the same circle we revolve.
Assurance only breeds resolve.'

*300.* A version of this line is to be found in *Who can say*, *T.Nbk 20*.

*301–3*] His faith, his fear in secret hours
Shock like the isles of ice – he cowers
Before uncomprehended powers. *Heath MS*

Cp. *Morte d'Arthur* 140 (also on Hallam's death): 'where the moving isles of winter shock'.

*301–3.* Combining *Romans* vii 18–19: 'For I know that in me (that is, in my flesh), dwelleth no good thing'; with *Galatians* v 17: 'For the flesh lusteth against the Spirit, and the Spirit against the flesh: and these are contrary the one to the other: so that ye cannot do the things that ye would.'

*304*] Stars shake – Heaven rolls in – chasms yawn, *Heath MS.*

*305–6.* Cp. *Paradise Lost* ii 1035–9: 'from the walls of Heav'n / Shoots farr into the bosom of dim Night / A glimmering dawn' – making Chaos a 'brok'n foe'. Cp. the end of *The Vision of Sin*: 'And on the glimmering limit far withdrawn / God made Himself an awful rose of dawn.'

*307. him*] *Heath MS, revised to* me.

*308. his*] *Heath MS, revised to* my.

*309. must be*] is an *Heath MS 1st reading.* *his*] the *Heath MS.*

*309 ∧ 10*] And every soul whatever wine
Of thought fermenteth, coarse or fine,
Infolds the elements of mine. *Added to Heath MS which then ends.*

*313.* Cp. *Youth* 50: 'Unvext by doubts I cannot solve'.

As when a billow, blown against,
Falls back, the voice with which I fenced
A little ceased, but recommenced.

'Where wert thou when thy father played
In his free field, and pastime made,
A merry boy in sun and shade?

'A merry boy they called him then,
He sat upon the knees of men
In days that never come again.

'Before the little ducts began
To feed thy bones with lime, and ran
Their course, till thou wert also man:

'Who took a wife, who reared his race,
Whose wrinkles gathered on his face,
Whose troubles number with his days:

'A life of nothings, nothing-worth,
From that first nothing ere his birth
To that last nothing under earth!'

'These words,' I said, 'are like the rest:
No certain clearness, but at best
A vague suspicion of the breast:

'But if I grant, thou mightst defend
The thesis which thy words intend–
That to begin implies to end;

'Yet how should I for certain hold,
Because my memory is so cold,
That I first was in human mould?

'I cannot make this matter plain,
But I would shoot, howe'er in vain,
A random arrow from the brain.

'It may be that no life is found,
Which only to one engine bound
Falls off, but cycles always round.

*321*] *T.MS follows this with three lines on the mother, and then ends.*
*333 ∧ 4*] From when his baby pulses beat
To when his hands in their last heat
Pick at the death-mote on the sheet. *MS, Eversley* (*T.MS B, deleted*) H.T. says these were 'omitted . . . as too dismal' (*Mem.* i 109).
*334–9*] *Added to T.MS B.*
*347–9*] *H.Nbk 11* has these lines as the centre of an important unadopted

passage of forty-five lines, of which ll. [28–9] became *In Memoriam* lxxxv 21–2:

The voice was something low and weak,
Replying 'dost thou answer seek,
Put one thing clear that I may speak.'

And as a man that choosing draws
One thing from many, but because
He must choose one, I broke the pause.

'That individual unity
Which each calls I, may never flee
To many parts and cease to be.'

'Were this self-evident as seems,'
He answered, 'who had flown to schemes
Of revelations and of dreams?'

Again he said in crafty words
'And wilt thou grant it to the herds,
The fishes and the tribe of birds?'

'Perchance' I said 'no life is found
That only to one engine bound
Falls off, but cycles always round.'

'And things' he said 'which thou mayst cleave
To many parts that each receive
Another life, dost thou believe

They feel thus one? So Nature spins
A various web and knowledge wins
No surety where this sense begins.

Nor whereabouts to fainter fades
Through tints and neutral tints and shades
Life and half-life, a million grades.

And those Intelligences fair,
That range above thy state, declare
If thou canst fathom what they are.'

'This knowledge' said I thereupon,
'As self-inorbed and perfect, one
Derives not from comparison.'

He said 'it should be always clear
And still the same, not but as mere
Result of parts made whole appear.

Yet step by step it grows, for can
The retrospection of the man
Remember when the child began?'

'As old mythologies relate,
Some draught of Lethe might await
The slipping through from state to state.

'As here we find in trances, men
Forget the dream that happens then,
Until they fall in trance again.

'So might we, if our state were such
As one before, remember much,
For those two likes might meet and touch.

'But, if I lapsed from nobler place,
Some legend of a fallen race
Alone might hint of my disgrace;

'Some vague emotion of delight
In gazing up an Alpine height,
Some yearning toward the lamps of night;

'Or if through lower lives I came–
Though all experience past became
Consolidate in mind and frame–

'I might forget my weaker lot;
For is not our first year forgot?
The haunts of memory echo not.

'And step by step I cease to keep
My consciousness' I said 'and creep
In the long gradual cloud of sleep.

It fadeth likewise when I swoon,
It dips and darkens as the moon
And comes again

*349.* Pythagoras's metempsychosis, and Plato's myth of Er (*Republic* x).
*351.* Cp. *In Memoriam* lxxxii 6: 'From state to state the spirit walks'.
*355–7] Added to T.MS B.*
*364.* G. R. Potter (*PQ* xvi (1937) 335–6) argues that T. 'is writing about the transmigration of souls, and the lines refer not so much to material as to spiritual progress – a sort of semi-evolutionary idea that appears more than once in the writings of eighteenth-century thinkers'. The word *frame* 'injects the idea of physical change into these speculations concerning the soul. But from the lines themselves we cannot be at all sure whether Tennyson was thinking of changes in species, or of the same idea that he reflects in his Cambridge discussion, that the human body in its embryonic stages has resemblances to lower organisms.'
*366 ∧ 7] T.MS B has a deleted stanza on memory.*

'And men, whose reason long was blind,
From cells of madness unconfined,
Oft lose whole years of darker mind.

'Much more, if first I floated free,
As naked essence, must I be
Incompetent of memory:

'For memory dealing but with time,
And he with matter, could she climb
Beyond her own material prime?

'Moreover, something is or seems,
That touches me with mystic gleams,
Like glimpses of forgotten dreams–

'Of something felt, like something here;
Of something done, I know not where;
Such as no language may declare.'

The still voice laughed. 'I talk,' said he,
'Not with thy dreams. Suffice it thee
Thy pain is a reality.'

'But thou,' said I, 'hast missed thy mark,
Who sought'st to wreck my mortal ark,
By making all the horizon dark.

'Why not set forth, if I should do
This rashness, that which might ensue
With this old soul in organs new?

'Whatever crazy sorrow saith,
No life that breathes with human breath
Has ever truly longed for death.

''Tis life, whereof our nerves are scant,
Oh life, not death, for which we pant;
More life, and fuller, that I want.'

*373–9] Added to T.MS B, with a (deleted) stanza on reasoning.*
*378.* Arthur Hallam spoke of 'the material prime', *Written in View of Ben Lomond* 14, 1829 (Motter, p. 52).
*395–6. Job* iii 20–1, 'Wherefore is light given to him that is in misery, and life unto the bitter in soul; Which long for death but it cometh not.'
*397–9.* Cp. *Life* [*Why suffers human life so soon eclipse?*] 5: 'Would I could pile fresh life on life'; and *Ulysses* 24–5: 'Life piled on life / Were all too little'.
*399. John* x 10, 'I am come that they might have life, and that they might have it more abundantly.'

I ceased, and sat as one forlorn.
Then said the voice, in quiet scorn,
'Behold, it is the Sabbath morn.'

And I arose, and I released
The casement, and the light increased
With freshness in the dawning east.

Like softened airs that blowing steal,
When meres begin to uncongeal,
The sweet church bells began to peal.

On to God's house the people prest:
Passing the place where each must rest,
Each entered like a welcome guest.

One walked between his wife and child,
With measured footfall firm and mild,
And now and then he gravely smiled.

The prudent partner of his blood
Leaned on him, faithful, gentle, good,
Wearing the rose of womanhood.

And in their double love secure,
The little maiden walked demure,
Pacing with downward eyelids pure.

These three made unity so sweet,
My frozen heart began to beat,
Remembering its ancient heat.

I blest them, and they wandered on:
I spoke, but answer came there none:
The dull and bitter voice was gone.

A second voice was at mine ear,
A little whisper silver-clear,
A murmur, 'Be of better cheer'.

As from some blissful neighbourhood,
A notice faintly understood,
'I see the end, and know the good'.

A little hint to solace woe,
A hint, a whisper breathing low,
'I may not speak of what I know'.

*424.* Cp. the Ancient Mariner's release from guilt when he 'blessed them unaware. / The self-same moment I could pray' (ll. 287–8).

Like an Æolian harp that wakes
No certain air, but overtakes
Far thought with music that it makes:

Such seemed the whisper at my side:
'What is it thou knowest, sweet voice?' I cried.
'A hidden hope,' the voice replied:

So heavenly-toned, that in that hour
From out my sullen heart a power
Broke, like the rainbow from the shower,

To feel, although no tongue can prove,
That every cloud, that spreads above
And veileth love, itself is love.

And forth into the fields I went,
And Nature's living motion lent
The pulse of hope to discontent.

I wondered at the bounteous hours,
The slow result of winter showers:
You scarce could see the grass for flowers.

I wondered, while I paced along:
The woods were filled so full with song,
There seemed no room for sense of wrong;

And all so variously wrought,
I marvelled how the mind was brought
To anchor by one gloomy thought;

And wherefore rather I made choice
To commune with that barren voice,
Than him that said, 'Rejoice! Rejoice!'

*447.* Cp. the unadopted lines for *The Miller's Daughter* 189–98*n*: 'Bless Love, for blest are all his ways – / The fluttering doubt, the jealous cares, / Transparent veils that drink his rays.'

*453.* John Churton Collins compared George Peele's *The Arraignment of Paris*: 'Ye may ne see for peeping flowers the grass'. Alongside this suggestion, T. wrote: 'No – close as it seems. Made in the fields' (*Cornhill*, Jan. 1880, *Lincoln*). FitzGerald says: 'Composed as he walked about the Dulwich meadows.'

*457*] *1884*; So variously seemed all things wrought, *1842–83*.

*462.* Cp. *In Memoriam* cxxx 5–16, MS: 'I walk the meadows and rejoice / And prosper, compassed by thy voice.' *Philippians* iv 4: 'Rejoice in the

# 210 St Simeon Stylites

Published *1842*. Written 1833 (dated, *Heath MS*), by Nov. (*Mem.* i 130). It is unlikely to have been written in Oct., the month when T. heard of Hallam's death. The important MSS are: *H.Nbk 13:19*, an early much-corrected draft of ll. 1–68 (*A*); revised as *H.Nbk 13:13* (*B*); and *Heath MS*. Simeon was the first and most famous of the pillar-hermits (*Stylites*, from Greek στῦλος, pillar). H.T. gives as the sources William Hone's *Every-Day Book* (1825), which supplied almost all the details (under 'January 5'), and Gibbon's *Decline and Fall of the Roman Empire*, Chapter 37. FitzGerald says that 'this is one of the Poems A.T. would read with grotesque Grimness, especially at such passages as "Coughs, Aches, Stitches, etc." [ll. 13–16], laughing aloud at times'. H.T. describes *St Telemachus* (p. 1431) as its 'pendant'. Cp. *St Agnes' Eve* (p. 552), and *St Lawrence* (p. 298). J. H. Buckley (p. 26) suggests that it was influenced by contempt for Charles Simeon, a notoriously exclamatory and influential preacher at Cambridge. In his review of *1842* in the *Church of England Quarterly Review* (Oct. 1842), Leigh Hunt called it 'a powerfully graphic, and in some respects appalling satire on the pseudo-aspirations of egotistical asceticism and superstition .... We do not recollect to have met with a more startling picture of the sordid and the aspiring – the selfish and the self-sacrificing – the wretched, weak body and mind and resolute soul – the abject, the dominant, the stupid, the imaginative – and, alas, the misgiving ... all mixed up in the poor phantom-like person of the almost incredible Saint of the Pillar – the almost solitary Christian counterpart of the Yogees of the Hindoos, who let birds build in their hair, and the nails of their fingers grow through the palms of their hands. We say Christian, out of Christian charity; for though real Christianity is a quintessence of good sense, both in its human and angelical aspirations, as the flower of it in due time will make manifest, yet these and other dark absurdities have, no doubt, lurked about its roots, and for a time, with equal absurdity, been confounded with the flower.'

---

Lord alway: and again I say, Rejoice'; *Ecclesiastes* xi 9: 'Rejoice, O young man, in thy youth.' Cp. Keats, *Sleep and Poetry* 37–9: 'Sometimes it gives a glory to the voice, / And from the heart up-springs "Rejoice! rejoice!" / Sounds which will reach the Framer of all things.' Also 'Barry Cornwall' (B. W. Procter), *The Little Voice* (*English Songs*, 1832): 'Once there was a little Voice, / Merry as the month of May, / That did cry "*Rejoice! Rejoice!*" / Now 'tis flown away! // Sweet it was, and very clear, / Chasing every thought of pain ...' In *Friendship's Offering* for 1833, to which T. contributed, there is R. F. Housman's *Away to the Greenwood*: 'And at every pause, the lute-like voice / Of the cuckoo sings – "Rejoice! rejoice!"' Edmund Blunden points out in his selection (1960) from T that Coleridge's *Dejection* ends with the word 'rejoice'.

Although I be the basest of mankind,
From scalp to sole one slough and crust of sin,
Unfit for earth, unfit for heaven, scarce meet
For troops of devils, mad with blasphemy,
I will not cease to grasp the hope I hold
Of saintdom, and to clamour, mourn and sob,
Battering the gates of heaven with storms of prayer,
Have mercy, Lord, and take away my sin.

Let this avail, just, dreadful, mighty God,
This not be all in vain, that thrice ten years,
Thrice multiplied by superhuman pangs,
In hungers and in thirsts, fevers and cold,
In coughs, aches, stitches, ulcerous throes and cramps,
A sign betwixt the meadow and the cloud,
Patient on this tall pillar I have borne
Rain, wind, frost, heat, hail, damp, and sleet, and
snow;

¶ 210.2] *Several drafts:*
(i) Plunged to the throat in crime – polluted, blurred,
Blained, rank, corrupt, one crust of noisome filth – *A*
(ii) Plunged to the throat in slough of crime – pollute,
Blained, blurred, corrupt – one crust of noisome filth – *Heath MS 1st reading*
(iii) Sloughed to the throat in crime – from scalp to sole
Blood, bone, breath, sinew, pulse and motion, sin – *Heath MS*

Based on *Deuteronomy* xxviii 35: 'The Lord shall smite thee in the knees, and in the legs, with a sore botch that cannot be healed, from the sole of thy foot unto the top of thy head.' *Job* ii 7: 'and smote Job with sore boils from the sole of his foot unto his crown.' *Isaiah* i 6: 'From the sole of the foot even unto the head there is no soundness in it; but wounds, and bruises, and putrifying sores.'

*4. mad with*] loud in *A*.

*5–6*] I will not cease to clamour, day and night *A–B*.

*7*] *Not A. gates*] ears *Heath MS correction by T.*

*9–10*] Let this avail, O God, that thrice ten years *A*.

*11*] *Not A–B.*

*12–13*] *Transposed at first in A:*
. . . thirsts, hour after hour,
In aches and stitches, cramps and ulcerous pangs,

A reminiscence of Prospero to Caliban: 'tonight thou shalt have cramps, / Side-stitches . . . I'll rack thee with old cramps, / Fill all thy bones with aches', *The Tempest* I ii 326–7, 370–1. See ll. 170–75*n*.

*14*] *Not A–B. betwixt*] between *Heath MS*.

*15. on . . . pillar*] *A*; upon tall pillars *B*.

And I had hoped that ere this period closed
Thou wouldst have caught me up into thy rest,
Denying not these weather-beaten limbs
The meed of saints, the white robe and the palm.

O take the meaning, Lord: I do not breathe,
Not whisper, any murmur of complaint.
Pain heaped ten-hundred-fold to this, were still
Less burthen, by ten-hundred-fold, to bear,
Than were those lead-like tons of sin that crushed
My spirit flat before thee.
O Lord, Lord,
Thou knowest I bore this better at the first,
For I was strong and hale of body then;
And though my teeth, which now are dropt away,
Would chatter with the cold, and all my beard
Was tagged with icy fringes in the moon,
I drowned the whoopings of the owl with sound
Of pious hymns and psalms, and sometimes saw
An angel stand and watch me, as I sang.
Now am I feeble grown; my end draws nigh;
I hope my end draws nigh: half deaf I am,
So that I scarce can hear the people hum
About the column's base, and almost blind,
And scarce can recognise the fields I know;

17. *closed*] *Not A–B.*
18] Into thy rest thou wouldst have caught me up *A*.
20. *Revelation* vii 9, 'clothed with white robes, and palms in their hands'.
21. *O . . . Lord*] Mistake me not, my God. *A–B*; My God, mistake me not: *Heath MS.*
23–4] *Several drafts:*
(i) *A is confused, but works towards (ii)*
(ii) Pain summed tenfold to this – ten-hundredfold
Heaped on to that – beyond all form and mode
Of tolerance – were less ten-hundredfold
Than I deserve; and heavier to endure,
If not a little by thy finger stayed, *B*
(iii) Pain summed tenfold to this – tenhundredfold
Heaped on to that – beyond all agonies,
All energies of tolerance – were less
Tenhundredfold less burthensome to bear *Heath MS*
25] These weights – these leadlike tons of sin that crush *B*.
29. *dropt away*] fallen out *A–B*.
37–9] *Added in A, which is very confused at this point.*

And both my thighs are rotted with the dew;
Yet cease I not to clamour and to cry,
While my stiff spine can hold my weary head,
Till all my limbs drop piecemeal from the stone,
Have mercy, mercy: take away my sin.

O Jesus, if thou wilt not save my soul,
Who may be saved? who is it may be saved?
Who may be made a saint, if I fail here?
Show me the man hath suffered more than I.
For did not all thy martyrs die one death?
For either they were stoned, or crucified,
Or burned in fire, or boiled in oil, or sawn
In twain beneath the ribs; but I die here
Today, and whole years long, a life of death.
Bear witness, if I could have found a way
(And heedfully I sifted all my thought)
More slowly-painful to subdue this home
Of sin, my flesh, which I despise and hate,
I had not stinted practice, O my God.

For not alone this pillar-punishment,
Not this alone I bore: but while I lived
In the white convent down the valley there,
For many weeks about my loins I wore
The rope that haled the buckets from the well,
Twisted as tight as I could knot the noose;

*40.* 'One of his thighs rotted a whole year, during which time he stood on one leg only' (Hone).

*42*] *Added in A.*

*46.* *Matthew* xix 25: 'When his disciples heard it, they were exceedingly amazed, saying, Who then can be saved?'

*47*] *Not A; preceding l. 45, B.*

*48*] *Added in A.*

*49–53*] *Not A; added to margin of B* (*l.52:* In sunder by the ribs . . .).

*52. In twain*] Atwain *Heath MS.*

*55 ∧ 6*] Devising every means and mode of ill *A–B, Heath MS.*

*56. slowly-painful*] painful-slow *A–B, Heath MS 1st reading.* *subdue*] mortify *A–B, Heath MS 1st reading.* *this home*] my flesh *A first reading, which then added l. 57.*

Based on *Romans* vii 17–18: 'sin that dwelleth in me. For I know that in me (that is, in my flesh) dwelleth no good thing.'

*60. lived*] dwelt *A.*

*61.* Where according to Hone he was thought over-austere.

*62. wore*] bore *A.*

*64*] *Added in A, where it appeared ll. 62 ∧ 3.*

And spake not of it to a single soul,
Until the ulcer, eating through my skin,
Betrayed my secret penance, so that all
My brethren marvelled greatly. More than this
I bore, whereof, O God, thou knowest all.

Three winters, that my soul might grow to thee,
I lived up there on yonder mountain side.
My right leg chained into the crag, I lay
Pent in a roofless close of ragged stones;
Inswathed sometimes in wandering mist, and twice
Blacked with thy branding thunder, and sometimes
Sucking the damps for drink, and eating not,
Except the spare chance-gift of those that came
To touch my body and be healed, and live:
And they say then that I worked miracles,
Whereof my fame is loud amongst mankind,
Cured lameness, palsies, cancers. Thou, O God,
Knowest alone whether this was or no.
Have mercy, mercy! cover all my sin.

Then, that I might be more alone with thee,
Three years I lived upon a pillar, high
Six cubits, and three years on one of twelve;
And twice three years I crouched on one that rose
Twenty by measure; last of all, I grew
Twice ten long weary weary years to this,
That numbers forty cubits from the soil.

I think that I have borne as much as this–
Or else I dream–and for so long a time,

65] And told it not unto a single soul *A*.

67. *so that all*] by the scent *A–B, Heath MS 1st reading.*

68] So that my brethren marvelled. More than this *A–B, Heath MS 1st reading*; My brethren marvelled. More, much more than this *Heath MS. A* breaks off here.

70–71] . . . thee / More nigh, I lived on yonder mountain-top – *B*.

72. *crag, I lay*] solid crag *B first reading*.

74–5] Inswathed sometimes in wandering mist, sometimes *B*.

80. *amongst*] *B, Heath MS*.

81. *Acts* viii 7, 'Many taken with palsies, and that were lame, were healed'.

82. *this was*] I did *B, Heath MS*.

83. *Psalm* lxxxv 2, 'Thou hast forgiven the iniquity of thy people, thou hast covered all their sin.'

86. *cubit*: about 18 inches.

91–102] *Not B; added on later page of Heath MS.*

If I may measure time by yon slow light,
And this high dial, which my sorrow crowns –
So much – even so.
And yet I know not well,
For that the evil ones come here, and say,
'Fall down, O Simeon: thou hast suffered long
For ages and for ages!' then they prate
Of penances I cannot have gone through,
Perplexing me with lies; and oft I fall,
Maybe for months, in such blind lethargies
That Heaven, and Earth, and Time are
choked.
But yet
Bethink thee, Lord, while thou and all the saints
Enjoy themselves in heaven, and men on earth
House in the shade of comfortable roofs,
Sit with their wives by fires, eat wholesome food,
And wear warm clothes, and even beasts have stalls,
I, 'tween the spring and downfall of the light,
Bow down one thousand and two hundred times,
To Christ, the Virgin Mother, and the saints;
Or in the night, after a little sleep,
I wake: the chill stars sparkle; I am wet
With drenching dews, or stiff with crackling frost.
I wear an undressed goatskin on my back;
A grazing iron collar grinds my neck;
And in my weak, lean arms I lift the cross,

*93. light*] fire *Heath MS 1st reading.* Simeon thinks of the pillar as a sundial.
*96. For that*] Because *Heath MS.*
*98. then*] and *Heath MS.*
*106*] *Not B.*
*107.* Simeon likens himself to Christ, *Matthew* viii 20: 'The foxes have holes, and the birds of the air have nests; but the Son of man hath not where to lay his head.'
*109.* According to Hone and Gibbon, one thousand two hundred and forty four.
*111–3*] *Not B.*
*112. chill*] still *Heath MS.*
*113.* Cp. Gray, *The Descent of Odin* 31–3: 'Long on these mould'ring bones have beat / The winter's snow, the summer's heat, / The drenching dews, and driving rain!'
*114. on my back*] hard and stiff *B.*
*115*] I wear an iron collar round my neck *B.*
*116. weak, lean*] withered *B.* As shown in the illustration to Hone.

And strive and wrestle with thee till I die:
O mercy, mercy! wash away my sin.

O Lord, thou knowest what a man I am;
A sinful man, conceived and born in sin:
'Tis their own doing; this is none of mine;
Lay it not to me. Am I to blame for this,
That here come those that worship me? Ha! ha!
They think that I am somewhat. What am I?
The silly people take me for a saint,
And bring me offerings of fruit and flowers:
And I, in truth (thou wilt bear witness here)
Have all in all endured as much, and more
Than many just and holy men, whose names
Are registered and calendared for saints.

Good people, you do ill to kneel to me.
What is it I can have done to merit this?
I am a sinner viler than you all.
It may be I have wrought some miracles,
And cured some halt and maimed; but what of that?
It may be, no one, even among the saints,
May match his pains with mine; but what of that?
Yet do not rise; for you may look on me,
And in your looking you may kneel to God.
Speak! is there any of you halt or maimed?
I think you know I have some power with Heaven
From my long penance: let him speak his wish.

*117. And . . . wrestle*] Wrestling and striving *B. Genesis* xxxii 24, 'And Jacob was left alone; and there wrestled a man with him until the breaking of the day.'

*118. Acts* xxii 16: 'Arise, and be baptized, and wash away thy sins.'

*120. Psalm* li 5: 'I was shapen in iniquity; and in sin did my mother conceive me.'

*122.* Contrast the martyrdom of Stephen, *Acts* vii 60: 'And he kneeled down, and cried with a loud voice, Lord, lay not this sin to their charge'.

*124. somewhat . . . I?*] somewhat on the earth. *B.*

*126. of*] and *B 1st reading.*

*131. kneel to*] worship *B.*

*132. can*] *Not B.*

*133*] *Not B, where it appears later; see ll. 166–82n.*

*134. wrought*] worked *B.*

*136–9*] *Not B.*

*143–7*] Hearken, my brethren, for the power of God
Is strong in me to preach and save your souls. *B*

See ll. 157 ^ 8*n.*

Yes, I can heal him. Power goes forth from me.
They say that they are healed. Ah, hark! they shout
'St Simeon Stylites.' Why, if so,
God reaps a harvest in me. O my soul,
God reaps a harvest in thee. If this be,
Can I work miracles and not be saved?
This is not told of any. They were saints.
It cannot be but that I shall be saved;
Yea, crowned a saint. They shout, 'Behold a saint!'
And lower voices saint me from above.
Courage, St Simeon! This dull chrysalis
Cracks into shining wings, and hope ere death
Spreads more and more and more, that God hath now
Sponged and made blank of crimeful record all
My mortal archives.
O my sons, my sons,
I, Simeon of the pillar, by surname
Stylites, among men; I, Simeon,
The watcher on the column till the end;
I, Simeon, whose brain the sunshine bakes;
I, whose bald brows in silent hours become
Unnaturally hoar with rime, do now
From my high nest of penance here proclaim
That Pontius and Iscariot by my side
Showed like fair seraphs. On the coals I lay,
A vessel full of sin: all hell beneath
Made me boil over. Devils plucked my sleeve,
Abaddon and Asmodeus caught at me.

*146–7.* Suggesting *Leviticus* xxiii 10–11: 'reap the harvest thereof.... And he shall wave the sheaf before the Lord, to be accepted for you.'
*156. of*] the *Heath MS 1st reading.*
*157 ‸ 8*] God's grace is strong through me to preach and save. *Heath MS.* See ll. 143–7*n*.
*160 ‸ 61*] Whom the lark passeth in her road to Heaven –
To whose chill ears bats hook their leathern wings, *B*
*Heath MS* has only the second line.
*161. I . . . whose*] Even I, whose withered *B*.
*166–82*] Show like fair Seraphs. O my sons, my sons
I am a sinner viler than you all,
The last and least of men. Give God the praise: *B*
See l. 133*n*.
*168.* Cp. Bunyan's *Grace Abounding*: 'I have in my bed been greatly afflicted, while asleep, with the apprehensions of Devils, and wicked spirits.'
*169. Revelation* ix 11: 'The angel of the bottomless pit, whose name in the Hebrew tongue is Abaddon.' *Tobit* iii 8: 'Asmodeus the evil spirit'.

I smote them with the cross; they swarmed again.
In bed like monstrous apes they crushed my chest:
They flapped my light out as I read: I saw
Their faces grow between me and my book;
With colt-like whinny and with hoggish whine
They burst my prayer. Yet this way was left,
And by this way I 'scaped them. Mortify
Your flesh, like me, with scourges and with thorns;
Smite, shrink not, spare not. If it may be, fast
Whole Lents, and pray. I hardly, with slow steps,
With slow, faint steps, and much exceeding pain,
Have scrambled past those pits of fire, that still
Sing in mine ears. But yield not me the praise:
God only through his bounty hath thought fit,
Among the powers and princes of this world,
To make me an example to mankind,
Which few can reach to. Yet I do not say
But that a time may come–yea, even now,
Now, now, his footsteps smite the threshold stairs
Of life–I say, that time is at the doors
When you may worship me without reproach;
For I will leave my relics in your land,
And you may carve a shrine about my dust,
And burn a fragrant lamp before my bones,
When I am gathered to the glorious saints.

While I spake then, a sting of shrewdest pain
Ran shrivelling through me, and a cloudlike change,
In passing, with a grosser film made thick
These heavy, horny eyes. The end! the end!
Surely the end! What's here? a shape, a shade,

*170–5.* Cp. Caliban, on Prospero's 'spirits', *The Tempest* II ii 8–10: 'For every trifle are they set upon me – / Sometime like apes, that mow and chatter at me, / And after bite me.' See ll. 12–13*n*.
*178. Isaiah* lviii 1: 'Cry aloud, spare not, lift up thy voice like a trumpet, and shew my people their transgression, and the house of Jacob their sins.'
*179. Whole Lents*: as Simeon did in Hone.
*183. God . . . his*] God in his grace and *B*; 'Tis God who in his *Heath MS.*
*184*] *Not B.*
*187. yea*] and *B.*
*191–3*] I leave my bones, my relicks in your land *B.*
*197–200.* Cp. Keats, *Endymion* ii 323–4: 'Before mine eyes thick films and shadows float – / O let me 'noint them with the heaven's light!'
*198. heavy, horny eyes*] globes of arid horn *B.*
*199. shape . . . shade*] shade . . . shape *B.*

A flash of light. Is that the angel there
That holds a crown? Come, blessèd brother, come.
I know thy glittering face. I waited long;
My brows are ready. What! deny it now?
Nay, draw, draw, draw nigh. So I clutch it. Christ!
'Tis gone: 'tis here again; the crown! the crown!
So now 'tis fitted on and grows to me,
And from it melt the dews of Paradise,
Sweet! sweet! spikenard, and balm, and frankincense.
Ah! let me not be fooled, sweet saints: I trust
That I am whole, and clean, and meet for Heaven.

Speak, if there be a priest, a man of God,
Among you there, and let him presently
Approach, and lean a ladder on the shaft,
And climbing up into my airy home,
Deliver me the blessèd sacrament;
For by the warning of the Holy Ghost,
I prophesy that I shall die tonight,
A quarter before twelve.
But thou, O Lord,
Aid all this foolish people; let them take
Example, pattern: lead them to thy light.

*200. the*] an *B*, *Heath MS*. The angel is mentioned in Hone.
202] *Not B*.
*204. So . . . Christ!*] is it? is it not? *B*; So I have it – God! *Heath MS*.
*205. the crown! the crown!*] Give me the crown. *B*. Based on *Revelation* ii 7–10: 'To him that overcometh will I give to eat of the tree of life . . . and I will give thee a crown of life.'
*208.* 'When Simeon died, Anthony smelt a precious odour emanating from his body' (Hone).
209] O Holy, Holy, Holy now I know *B*, *Heath MS*.
*210. whole*] white *B*. *Heaven*] thee *Heath MS*.
*214. my*] *1846*; mine *1842–5*.
*217.* The prophecy is not in Gibbon or Hone. See *Bede*, ed. A. Hamilton Thompson (1935), pp. 211–3: 'Sometimes the day was prophesied by the appearance of angels in a vision . . . . This particular form of prophecy is of course a commonplace in the lives of the saints from the Life of St. Antony onwards . . . . The idea underlying this widespread tradition was that the saint was thus granted time to prepare himself for the great change and to be fortified by receiving the Communion.'
*218–9. Psalm* lxxiv 18: 'O Lord, and that the foolish people have blasphemed thy name.' *Jeremiah* v 21: 'Hear now this, O foolish people'.
*220. Example, pattern:*] Pattern from me – so *Heath MS*.

## 211 The Beggar Maid

Published *1842*. Written Sept. 1833 (dated, *Heath MS*). J. M. Kemble sent a MS with the title *How King Cophetua wooed the beggar-maid* to W. B. Donne, March–April 1834. T. gives the reference to *Romeo and Juliet* II i 13-4: '*Young* Adam Cupid, he that shot so trim, / When King Cophetua loved the beggar-maid.' T. would have met the ballad in Percy's *Reliques*.

Her arms across her breast she laid;
She was more fair than words can say:
Bare-footed came the beggar maid
Before the king Cophetua.
In robe and crown the king stept down,
To meet and greet her on her way;
'It is no wonder,' said the lords,
'She is more beautiful than day.'

As shines the moon in clouded skies,
She in her poor attire was seen:
One praised her ancles, one her eyes,
One her dark hair and lovesome mien.
So sweet a face, such angel grace,
In all that land had never been:
Cophetua sware a royal oath:
'This beggar maid shall be my queen!'

## 212 St Agnes' Eve

Published Nov. 1836, in *The Keepsake* for 1837, as *St Agnes*; then *1842*. The title was expanded in 1855. It was written Sept. 1833 (dated, *Heath MS*). The draft in *H.Nbk 16:4* (*A* below) consists of ll. 1–12 only, divided into three stanzas and underlined at the end as completed. The slightly later draft in *Nbk 16:14* (*B*) is full-length, as is the *Heath MS*. St Agnes was a martyr at thirteen; her refusal to marry caused her to be violated before execution, but by a miracle she remained a virgin. A maiden who fasted on her Eve might see a vision of her destined lover. T. says: 'Here the legend is told by a nun' (*Eversley* draft, British Museum). T. had written of her in *Amy* 13–17: 'St Agnes on St Agnes' Eve, who leadeth / Over the

¶ 211.*2. can*] may *Kemble MS*.
*9. in*] through *MS*.
*11. One. . . one*] Some . . . some *MS*.
*12. One*] Some *MS*. *hair*] locks *MS*. *lovesome*] winsom *H.Nbk 16 1st reading*.

snowy hill / Her snowwhite lambs and with hushed footstep treadeth, / Is not so chaste and still / In the cold moon.'

As W. C. DeVane suggests in his selection (1940), T.'s source was William Hone's *Every-Day Book* (1825, under 'January 21'), the acknowledged source of *St Simeon Stylites* (p. 542). Hone quoted from Keats, *Eve of St Agnes*. T. says the poem is a 'pendant to *Sir Galahad*' (p. 610). Cp. also *St Lawrence* (p. 298).

Deep on the convent-roof the snows
  Are sparkling to the moon:
My breath to heaven like vapour goes:
  May my soul follow soon!
The shadows of the convent-towers
  Slant down the snowy sward,
Still creeping with the creeping hours
  That lead me to my Lord:
Make Thou my spirit pure and clear
  As are the frosty skies,
Or this first snowdrop of the year
  That in my bosom lies.

As these white robes are soiled and dark,
  To yonder shining ground;
As this pale taper's earthly spark,
  To yonder argent round;
So shows my soul before the Lamb,
  My spirit before Thee;
So in mine earthly house I am,
  To that I hope to be.
Break up the heavens, O Lord! and far,
  Through all yon starlight keen,
Draw me, thy bride, a glittering star,
  In raiment white and clean.

He lifts me to the golden doors;
  The flashes come and go;
All heaven bursts her starry floors,
  And strows her lights below,

¶ 212.*1.* -roof] *1842*; roofs *1836*.
*2. sparkling to*] glittering in *A*.
*9. spirit*] soul as *Heath MS*, *B*. *pure*] chaste *A*.
*10*] As yonder frosty ray *A*.
*12*] Which I have pluckt today. *A*. *in*] *1842*; on *1836*.
*19. earthly house*: *2 Corinthians* v 1.
*22. all yon*] all your *1836* (*misprint*); yonder *Heath MS*.
*25*] The moon draws nigh the golden doors; *B 1st reading*.
*28. strows*] *1842*; strews *1836*.

And deepens on and up! the gates
Roll back, and far within
For me the Heavenly Bridegroom waits,
To make me pure of sin.
The sabbaths of Eternity,
One sabbath deep and wide–
A light upon the shining sea–
The Bridegroom with his bride!

## 213 *'From sorrow sorrow yet is born'

*Mem.* i 123 printed ll. 3–4; Sir Charles Tennyson, *Cornhill* cliii (1936) 447–448, printed ll. 3–8 (both with 'Teach me . . .', l. 4); Joyce Green, *PMLA* lxvi (1951) 670, printed ll. 1–2 only. *Heath MS* is dated Sept. 1833, as is *Y.MS.* The news of Arthur Hallam's death did not in fact reach T. till 1 Oct., but the poem appears among Harvard transcripts (*Nbk 21*) with sections of *In Memoriam*, the tone and style of which it anticipates, and with *On a Mourner* (p. 557), which was written on Hallam's death and which, like *From sorrow*, invokes the consoling touch of Nature. The likelihood is therefore strong that H.T. was right to quote the poem in the context of T.'s 'utter prostration from grief'; the date Sept. may be read as that of the tragedy and not of composition, though it is also possible that T. wished slightly to veil the personal grief of the poem; cp. the veiling of *On a Mourner* for publication. On the other hand, the fact that *The Two Voices* antedates Hallam's death makes it by no means out of the question that *From sorrow* does too.

From sorrow sorrow yet is born,
Hopes flow like water through a sieve,
But leave not thou thy son forlorn;
Touch me, great Nature, make me live.

*29. on and up*] in and on *Heath MS.*
*29–30*] The Heavens are broken up! the gates
Are broken: far within *B 1st reading*
*31. Revelation* xxi 9, 'I will shew thee the Bride, the Lamb's wife'.
*32. make . . . of*] *1842*; wash . . . from *1836*.
*33. Hebrews* iv 9–11, 'There remaineth therefore a rest ['or, keeping of a Sabbath'] to the people of God. . . . Let us labour therefore to enter into that rest.'
*35. the shining sea*: *Revelation* xv 2.

As when thy sunlights, a mild heat,
  Touch some dun mere that sleepeth still;
As when thy moonlights, dim and sweet,
  Touch some gray ruin on the hill.

## 214 *'Hark! the dogs howl!'

Unpublished, *H.Nbk 16*; except that *Mem.* i 107 printed ll. 7–8, 10–11, 18–21, 26: 'On the evening of one of these sad winter days [late 1833] my father had already noted down in his scrap-book some fragmentary lines, which proved to be the germ of *In Memoriam*.' The news of Arthur Hallam's death reached T. on 1 Oct. 1833.

Hark! the dogs howl! the sleetwinds blow,
The church-clocks knoll: the hours haste,
I leave the dreaming world below.
Blown o'er frore heads of hills I go,
Long narrowing friths and stripes of snow–
Time bears my soul into the waste.
I seek the voice I loved–ah where
Is that dear hand that I should press,
Those honoured brows that I would kiss?
Lo! the broad Heavens cold and bare,
The stars that know not my distress.
My sighs are wasted in the air,
My tears are dropt into the abyss.
Now riseth up a little cloud–
Divideth like a broken wave–
Shows Death a drooping youth pale-browed
And crowned with daisies of the grave.
The vapour labours up the sky,
Uncertain forms are darkly moved,
Larger than human passes by
The shadow of the man I loved.

¶ 214.*3*. Cp. the visionary flight in *In Memoriam* xii 6: 'I leave this mortal ark behind'.

*4–5*. Cp. *In Memoriam: Epilogue* 114–5: 'And catch at every mountain head / And o'er the friths that branch and spread.'

*7–9, 10–11*] *Transposed at first in MS. Mem. omits l. 9.*

*7. I seek*] *MS*; Where is *MS 1st reading, Mem.*

*8. Is that*] *MS, Mem.*; The dear *MS 1st reading. should*] *MS*; would *Mem.*

*20*. Cp. *Morte d'Arthur* 183: 'Larger than human on the frozen hills'; also inspired by the death of Hallam. The ghost of Romulus in Ovid's *Fasti*, ii

I wind my arms for one embrace–
Can this be he? is that his face?
In my strait throat expires the cry.
He bends his eyes reproachfully
And clasps his hands, as one that prays.

[1833. *In Memoriam* – see p. 853]

# 215 *Whispers

Printed *Mem.* i 145, omitting ll. 13–16 though they were in an early draft of *Mem.* (*Lincoln*); they are now supplied from *Heath MS*, where the poem has no title. T. included it (dated 1833) among the poems sent to Julia Heath, 29 Oct. 1833, of which all but *St Agnes* seem directly concerned with the recent death of Arthur Hallam. For the influence of Nature, cp. *On a Mourner* (p. 557) and *From sorrow sorrow yet is born* (p. 554), both of which were sent with this poem; and cp. the sentiment of ll. 6–8 with *In Memoriam* v 3–4: 'For words, like Nature, half reveal / And half conceal the Soul within.' The second half of each stanza is in the *In Memoriam* stanza.

'Tis not alone the warbling woods,
 The starred abysses of the sky,
The silent hills, the stormy floods,
 The green that fills the eye–
These only do not move the breast;
 Like some wise artist, Nature gives,
 Through all her works, to each that lives
A hint of somewhat unexprest.

Whate'er I see, where'er I move,
 These whispers rise, and fall away,
Something of pain–of bliss–of Love,
 But what, were hard to say.

503, was *humano maior*. Cp. T.'s projected essay on Ghosts for the 'Apostles': 'Forth issue from the inmost gloom the colossal Presences of the Past majores humano, some as they lived, seemingly pale with exhaustion and faintly smiling; some as they died in a still agony . . .' (*H.Nbk* 7, quoted by J. H. Buckley, p. 33). Also *In Memoriam* ciii 41–3: 'The man we loved was there on deck, / But thrice as large as man he bent / To greet us.'

¶ 215. 2. *The abysses of the sky*: Shelley's *Prometheus Unbound* III iv 99. Macaulay has 'abyss of sky', *Evening* 60. T. may well have read Macaulay's poem (which won the Chancellor's Medal at Cambridge in 1821) when working on his prize poem *Timbuctoo*.

I could not tell it: if I could
Yet every form of mind is made
To vary in some light or shade
So were my tale misunderstood.

# 216 On a Mourner

Published *1865*. Written Oct. 1833 (*Y.MS*), immediately after T. heard of the death of Arthur Hallam. T. probably delayed publication because it was too directly personal. In revising it for *1865*, he veiled and objectified the poem by adding the title; by addressing it to another, changing 'my' to 'thy'; and by omitting two explicit stanzas, ll. 15 ^ 16. All variants from *Heath MS* are below. The beautiful but ineffective consolations of Nature form a recurring theme of *In Memoriam*, with sections of which this poem appears in *Yale* and *Harvard MSS*. T. had used the same unusual stanza for *My life is full* (p. 350), a comparable poem on death and Nature addressed to Hallam in his lifetime.

I

Nature, so far as in her lies,
Imitates God, and turns her face
To every land beneath the skies,
Counts nothing that she meets with base,
But lives and loves in every place;

II

Fills out the homely quickset-screens,
And makes the purple lilac ripe,
Steps from her airy hill, and greens
The swamp, where hummed the dropping snipe,
With moss and braided marish-pipe;

*13–16*] *Heath MS, H.Nbk 16*; *not Mem.*

¶ *216.6. homely*] edging *Heath MS*. The quickset (whitethorn) appears twice in *In Memoriam*, in lxxxviii 2 and in the consolation of spring in cxv: 'Now fades the last long streak of snow, / Now burgeons every maze of quick . . . / . . . and in my breast / Spring wakens too; and my regret / Becomes an April violet, / And buds and blossoms like the rest.'

*9. hummed*] *1889, MS*; hums *1865–88*. The snipe's humming is caused by its vibrating tail-feathers.

*10*] And shoots the fringèd paddock-pipe – *MS*.

III

And on thy heart a finger lays,
Saying, 'Beat quicker, for the time
Is pleasant, and the woods and ways
Are pleasant, and the beech and lime
Put forth and feel a gladder clime.'

IV

And murmurs of a deeper voice,
Going before to some far shrine,
Teach that sick heart the stronger choice,
Till all thy life one way incline
With one wide Will that closes thine.

V

And when the zoning eve has died
Where yon dark valleys wind forlorn,

*11. thy*] my *MS.* The touch of Nature (who 'imitates God', l. 2) gives man life as did the finger of Michelangelo's God at the Creation. Cp. *From sorrow* 4: 'Touch me, great Nature, make me live' (on Hallam's death). Contrast *In Memoriam* lxxxv 20: 'God's finger touched him, and he slept'.
*12. quicker, for*], mournful heart! *MS.*
*14. beech*] elm *MS.*
*15 ^ 16*] 'Come, beat a little quicker now,
When all things own my quickening breath:
Thy friend is mute: his brows are low:
But I am with thee till thy death.'
Some such kind words to me she saith.

Yet is she mortal even as I,
Or as that friend I loved in vain:
She only whispering [Did she but whisper *1st reading*] low or high,
Through this vast cloud of grief and pain
I had not found my peace again. *MS*

Cp. *In Memoriam* xxxiv, where 'this round of green' would in itself, for all its beauty, be as nothing: ''Twere hardly worth my while to choose / Of things all mortal'.
*16. And . . . deeper*] Deep . . . holier *MS.*
*18*] Are learning me the purer choice, *MS.*
*19–20*] Till all my soul concentric shine
With that wide will that closes mine. *MS*

Cp. 'A will concentric with all fate', in the unpublished section of *In Memoriam*, *Young is the grief* 15.
*21*] For when the fringing eve hath died *MS.* *zoning*: striping, as in *The*

Come Hope and Memory, spouse and bride,
From out the borders of the morn,
With that fair child betwixt them born.

VI

And when no mortal motion jars
The blackness round the tombing sod,
Through silence and the trembling stars
Comes Faith from tracts no feet have trod,
And Virtue, like a household god

VII

Promising empire; such as those
Once heard at dead of night to greet
Troy's wandering prince, so that he rose
With sacrifice, while all the fleet
Had rest by stony hills of Crete.

*Progress of Spring* 69; it suggests the elegiac and speculative context of Keats, *Fall of Hyperion* i 310–12: 'No stir of life / Was in this shrouded vale, not so much air / As in the zoning of a summer's day . . .' Moneta had just been addressed as 'Shade of Memory'. *The Fall of Hyperion* was published posthumously in 1856, and so may have affected T.'s revision of 'fringing' into 'zoning'. Yet later T. objected specifically to Keats's lines (*Mem.* ii 286).
*24. out*] forth *MS.*
*25. betwixt*] between *MS.* *child*: presumably Love; cp. *The Lover's Tale* i 802–10 (p. 330).
*26. mortal motion*] human murmur *MS.*
*27. blackness*] darkness *MS.*
*28. silence and the*] silences of *MS.*
*29. Comes*] Slides *MS.* As in l. 28, T. disliked the sibilants.
*32*] *1884*; That once at dead of night did greet *1865–83*; Which in the hush of night did greet *MS.* Cp. the elegiac 'dead calm', *In Memoriam* xi 19.
*32–5. Aeneid* iii 147–78: Aeneas's cares were dispelled by the voices which promised him empire and success, after which he offered gifts to the gods: *tum sic adfari et curas his demere dictis . . . / idem venturos tollemus in astra nepotes / imperiumque urbi dabimus . . . / surge age et haec laetus longaevo dicta parenti / haud dubitanda refer.* ('Then thus they spake to me and with these words dispelled my cares . . . . We too shall exalt to heaven thy sons that are to be, and give empire to their city . . . . Come, arise, and with good cheer bear to thine aged parent these certain tidings.') For T., this would be apt not only as divine assurance of certainty (*haud dubitanda*), but also because *tollemus in astra nepotes* hinted at immortality.
*35. Had rest by*] Moored under *MS.*

# 217 Ulysses

Published *1842*. Written 20 Oct. 1833 (dated, *Heath MS*), soon after T. heard the news of Arthur Hallam's death. T. made two slightly different comments. First, 'The poem was written soon after Arthur Hallam's death, and it gives the feeling [gave my feeling *Mem.* i 196] about the need of going forward and braving the struggle of life perhaps more simply than anything in *In Memoriam*' (*Eversley*). Second, comparing *In Memoriam*, 'There is more about myself in *Ulysses*, which was written under the sense of loss and that all had gone by, but that still life must be fought out to the end. It was more written with the feeling of his loss upon me than many poems in *In Memoriam*' (to James Knowles, *Nineteenth Century* xxxiii (1893) 182). For T.'s other attempts at this date to find solace and understanding in a classical figure, see *Tithonus* (p. 1112), which he said was intended as a 'pendant' to *Ulysses*, and *Tiresias* (p. 568).

The text in *Heath MS* is virtually that of *1842*; *H.Nbk 16* is earlier. All variants from *Heath MS* and *H.MS* are below. *T.Nbk 22* is later than both. J. M. Kemble sent it to W. B. Donne (the poem dated 20 Oct. 1833) in March–April 1834, with the comment: 'I will fill up my paper with a grand thing of Alfred's, unfinished though it be.' Kemble's text is that of *Heath MS*, except for two slips.

*Sources*. T. specifies *Odyssey* xi 100–137, and Dante's *Inferno* xxvi 90 ff. Tiresias speaks, *Odyssey* xi 112–37: 'Late shalt thou come home and in evil case, after losing all thy comrades, in a ship that is another's, and thou shalt find woes in thy house – proud men that devour thy livelihood, wooing thy godlike wife, and offering wooers' gifts. Yet verily on their violent deeds shalt thou take vengeance when thou comest. But when thou hast slain the wooers in thy halls, whether by guile or openly with the sharp sword, then do thou go forth, taking a shapely oar, until thou comest to men that know naught of . . . ships . . . . And death shall come to thee thyself far from the sea [possibly 'from out of the sea'], a death so gentle, that shall lay thee low when thou art overcome with sleek old age, and thy people shall dwell in prosperity around thee.' On this 'mysterious voyage', H.T. comments: 'This is elaborated by the author of the *Telegoneia*. My father, like Eugammon, takes up the story of further wanderings at the end of the *Odyssey*. Ulysses has lived in Ithaca for a long while before the craving for fresh travel seizes him. The comrades he addresses are of the same heroic mould as his old comrades.' The last sentence is meant to meet the objection that Ulysses' companions were dead. In a note H.T. added: 'Perhaps the *Odyssey* has not been strictly adhered to, and some of the old comrades may be still left.'

Dante is the more important source. T. probably used H. F. Cary's translation (1805); there is a copy at *Lincoln*. (There is also a copy of Henry Boyd's translation.) Ulysses speaks, xxvi 90–124 (Cary):

When I escap'd
From Circe, who beyond a circling year
Had held me near Caieta, by her charms,
Ere thus Eneas yet had nam'd the shore,
Nor fondness for my son, nor reverence
Of my old father, nor return of love,
That should have crown'd Penelope with joy,
Could overcome in me the zeal I had
T' explore the world, and search the ways of life,
Man's evil and his virtue. Forth I sail'd
Into the deep illimitable main,
With but one bark, and the small faithful band
That yet cleav'd to me. As Iberia far,
Far as Marocco either shore I saw,
And the Sardinian and each isle beside
Which round that ocean bathes. Tardy with age
Were I and my companions, when we came
To the strait pass, where Hercules ordain'd
The bound'ries not to be o'erstepp'd by man.
The walls of Seville to my right I left,
On the' other hand already Ceuta past.
'O brothers!' I began, 'who to the west
'Through perils without number now have reach'd,
'To this the short remaining watch, that yet
'Our senses have to wake, refuse not proof
'Of the unpeopled world, following the track
'Of Phoebus. Call to mind from whence ye sprang:
'Ye were not form'd to live the life of brutes,
'But virtue to pursue and knowledge high.'
With these few words I sharpen'd for the voyage
The mind of my associates, that I then
Could scarcely have withheld them. To the dawn
Our poop we turn'd . . .

Ulysses then describes the last and fatal voyage. It has been much discussed whether or not we are to find T.'s Ulysses altogether noble; the most scrupulous account of the arguments is by J. Pettigrew, *Victorian Poetry* i (1963) 27–45.

It little profits that an idle king,
By this still hearth, among these barren crags,
Matched with an agèd wife, I mete and dole
Unequal laws unto a savage race,

¶ 217.2. *still*] dull *H.MS 1st reading.*
*4. Unequal*: not 'unjust', but 'not affecting all in the same manner or degree', a primitive state of law consequent upon the Ithacans' being 'a savage race'.

That hoard, and sleep, and feed, and know not me.

I cannot rest from travel: I will drink
Life to the lees: all times I have enjoyed
Greatly, have suffered greatly, both with those
That loved me, and alone; on shore, and when
Through scudding drifts the rainy Hyades
Vext the dim sea: I am become a name;
For always roaming with a hungry heart
Much have I seen and known; cities of men
And manners, climates, councils, governments,
Myself not least, but honoured of them all;
And drunk delight of battle with my peers,
Far on the ringing plains of windy Troy.

5. *not me*] me not *H.MS.* Cp. *Hamlet* IV iv 33–9, which not only echoes 'sleep and feed', but is also apt to the theme of the poem: 'What is a man, / If his chief good and market of his time / Be but to sleep and feed? a beast, no more: / Sure he that made us with such large discourse, / Looking before and after, gave us not / That capability and god-like reason / To fust in us unused.'
6–9] Much have I suffered both on shore and when *H.MS.*
6–7. J. Pettigrew (see headnote) compares *Macbeth* II iii 94–5: 'The wine of life is drawn, and the mere lees / Is left this vault to brag of'.
10. *scudding drifts*: *Pleiadum choro / scindente nubes* (Horace, *Odes* IV xiv 21–2). T. quotes *pluviasque Hyadas* (*Aeneid* i 744); the rising of these stars was thought to bring storm.
10–11. Cp. Shelley, *Revolt of Islam* III xxxii 3–4: 'the starry giant dips / His zone in the dim sea'.
11. *Vext*: cp. *The Tempest* I ii 229: 'the still-vexed Bermoothes'; *Paradise Lost* i 305–6: 'with fierce Winds *Orion* arm'd / Hath vext the Red-Sea Coast'; and Pope's *Iliad* iii 5–6: 'When inclement Winters vex the plain / With piercing frosts, or thick-descending rain.' This sense is common in Shelley.
12] *Not H.MS, Heath MS, T.MS.* J. C. Maxwell (private communication) suggests the influence of *avido . . . pectore* in Cicero's free version of the song of the Sirens, *De Finibus* V xviii 49.
13. *and*], much *H.MS.*
13–14. *Odyssey* i 3–5: *πολλῶν δ' ἀνθρώπων ἴδεν ἄστεα καὶ νόον ἔγνω, / πολλὰ δ' ὅ γ' ἐν πόντῳ πάθεν ἄλγεα ὃν κατὰ θυμόν.* ('Many were the men whose cities he saw and whose mind he learned, aye, and many the woes he suffered in his heart upon the sea'.) Hence Horace on Ulysses, *Epistles* I ii 19–20: *qui . . . multorum providus urbes / et mores hominum inspexit.*
17. *windy Troy*: Homer's *προτὶ Ἴλιον ἠνεμόεσσαν.*

I am a part of all that I have met;
Yet all experience is an arch wherethrough
Gleams that untravelled world, whose margin fades
For ever and for ever when I move.
How dull it is to pause, to make an end,
To rust unburnished, not to shine in use!
As though to breathe were life. Life piled on life
Were all too little, and of one to me
Little remains: but every hour is saved
From that eternal silence, something more,
A bringer of new things; and vile it were
For some three suns to store and hoard myself,
And this gray spirit yearning in desire

*18*] *Not H.MS.* T. cites Aeneas's account of his experiences, *Aeneid* ii 5–6: *quaeque ipse miserrima vidi / et quorum pars magna fui.* Cp. Byron, *Childe Harold* III lxxii 1–2: 'I live not in myself, but I become / Portion of that around me'. Byron's passage has lines relevant to *Ulysses* (lxx 6–9, lxxv 1–2): 'on the sea / The boldest steer but where their ports invite – / But there are wanderers o'er Eternity, / Whose bark drives on and on, and anchored ne'er shall be . . . / Are not the mountains, waves, and skies, a part / Of me and of my Soul.'

*19. wherethrough*] through which *H.MS, Heath MS.*

*19–21.* Matthew Arnold, *On Translating Homer* (1861) iii, commented on these lines: 'It is no blame to their rhythm, which belongs to another order of movement than Homer's, but it is true that these three lines by themselves take up nearly as much time as a whole book of the *Iliad*'.

*20–22*] Gleams the untravelled world: how dull it is *H.MS.* J. Pettigrew compares 'the unpeopled world', Cary's Dante, *Inf.* xxvi 117.

*23.* Cp. Ulysses's words, *Troilus and Cressida* III iii 150–53: 'Perseverance, dear my lord, / Keeps honour bright: to have done, is to hang / Quite out of fashion, like a rusty mail / In monumental mockery.' T. later cited this speech as one of 'the noblest things' in Shakespeare (*Tennyson and His Friends*, p. 265). D. Bush, *MLR* xxxviii (1943) 38, compares *Hamlet* IV iv 39 (see l. 5*n*).

*24*] As though to live were all the end of life. *H.MS 1st reading*; As though to live were life. Little of life *H.MS.* J. H. Buckley (p. 267) quotes 'Would I could pile fresh life on life', in *Life*, a poem on mortality beginning 'Why suffers human life so soon eclipse' (p. 296).

*25*] *Not H.MS*; Were all too little. Of one life to me *Heath MS.*

*26*] Little of life *H.MS 1st reading, deleted*; Remains, but every hour is something more *H.MS.*

*27*] *Not H.MS.*

*28. vile it were*] this were vile *H.MS.*

*29. store and hoard*] hoard and save *H.MS.*

*30. gray spirit*] old heart yet *H.MS, Heath MS 1st reading.* F. J. Rowe and

To follow knowledge like a sinking star,
Beyond the utmost bound of human thought.

This is my son, mine own Telemachus,
To whom I leave the sceptre and the isle–
Well-loved of me, discerning to fulfil
This labour, by slow prudence to make mild
A rugged people, and through soft degrees
Subdue them to the useful and the good.
Most blameless is he, centred in the sphere
Of common duties, decent not to fail
In offices of tenderness, and pay
Meet adoration to my household gods,
When I am gone. He works his work, I mine.

There lies the port; the vessel puffs her sail:
There gloom the dark broad seas. My mariners,
Souls that have toiled, and wrought, and thought with me–
That ever with a frolic welcome took
The thunder and the sunshine, and opposed
Free hearts, free foreheads–you and I are old;
Old age hath yet his honour and his toil;
Death closes all: but something ere the end,

W. T. Webb, in their *Selections* (1888), described the syntax as 'absolute case'; T. wrote: 'No. The accusative after *store* etc.' (*Lincoln*). (H. T. confusingly notes: 'accusative absolute'.)

*31–2.* To be found verbatim in a draft (1833) of *Tiresias*, where they formed part of the opening lines (*T.Nbk 15*). Cp. *The Lover's Tale* i 50 ∧ 51: 'O'er long loud waters, like a sinking star'. Cary's Dante has 'following the track / Of Phoebus', and 'virtue to pursue and knowledge high' (see headnote).

*33–42*] *Added to H.MS.*

*33. mine own*] my child *H.MS.*

*39–40*] Decent and blameless is he, not to fail *H.MS deleted but without the revision.* *decent*: having a sense of what is fitting.

*42. Meet*] Just *H.MS.*

*43*] *Not H.MS.* In *T.MS* (which may not be quoted), the first version of this line included an approving comment on Telemachus which made it clear that Ulysses was not here scornful of him.

*44. the vessel*] yon vessel *H.MS 1st reading.*

*45. :There gloom*] Beyond *H.MS.*

*47–9*] My mariners, though I and you are old *H.MS.*

*48–9*] The thunder and the sunshine – we are old; *Heath MS.*

*51 ∧ 2*] Not all unworthy of heroic souls *added as H.MS 1st reading*; [l. 53] *H.MS.*

Some work of noble note, may yet be done,
Not unbecoming men that strove with Gods.
The lights begin to twinkle from the rocks:
The long day wanes: the slow moon climbs: the deep
Moans round with many voices. Come, my friends,
'Tis not too late to seek a newer world.
Push off, and sitting well in order smite
The sounding furrows; for my purpose holds
To sail beyond the sunset, and the baths
Of all the western stars, until I die.
It may be that the gulfs will wash us down:
It may be we shall touch the Happy Isles,
And see the great Achilles, whom we knew.
Though much is taken, much abides; and though
We are not now that strength which in old days

53] *See previous note.*

54–7] *Not H.MS.*

55. D. Bush, *Major British Writers* (1959) ii 396, remarks that 'Homeric voyages commonly begin in the evening; here the accent is on the evening of life.' Contrast Cary's Dante: 'To the dawn / Our poop we turn'd', where Ulysses' account of his fatal voyage goes on to mention the moon and the stars.

*58–9.* Translating, as T. noted, a Homeric commonplace: ἑξῆς δ'ἑζόμενοι πολιὴν ἅλα τύπτον ἐρετμοῖς (*Odyssey* iv 580 etc.).

*59. my . . . holds*] I purpose now *H.MS 1st reading.*

*60–61.* Adapting *Odyssey* v 270–5:

αὐτὰρ ὁ πηδαλίῳ ἰθύνετο τεχνηέντως / ἥμενος, οὐδέ οἱ ὕπνος ἐπὶ βλεφάροισιν ἔπιπτεν / Πληιάδας τ' ἐσορῶντι καὶ ὀψὲ δύοντα Βοώτην / Ἄρκτον θ', ἣν καὶ Ἄμαξαν ἐπίκλησιν καλέουσιν. / ἥ τ' αὐτοῦ στρέφεται καί τ' Ὠρίωνα δοκεύει, / οἴη δ' ἄμμορός ἐστι λοετρῶν Ὠκεανοῖο·

(Odysseus 'watched the Pleiads, and late-setting Bootes, and the Bear, which men also call the Wain, which ever circles where it is and watches Orion, and alone has no part in the baths of Ocean.')

*62–5*] *Not H.MS.*

*63.* The Isles of the Blest were thought to lie beyond the Pillars of Hercules (Gibraltar), and it is beyond the Pillars that Dante's Ulysses urges his companions to sail with him.

*66. that . . . days*] the men that in one night *H.MS 1st reading*; that strength that [which *Heath MS*] in one night *H.MS, Heath MS.*

*66–9.* Recalling Hallam's *To J.M.G.* [James Milnes Gaskell], written May 1829 and printed 1830 (Motter, p. 47): 'We are not as we were . . . / We are not as we were: our silent tombs / Shall have us not, till we have drunk our fill / Of a new glorious joy, restoring heart and will!' Cp. ll. 6–7 above.

Moved earth and heaven; that which we are, we are;
One equal temper of heroic hearts,
Made weak by time and fate, but strong in will
To strive, to seek, to find, and not to yield.

# 218 *Tithon

Printed from *Heath MS* by M. J. Donahue, *PMLA* lxiv (1949) 401–2. Written 1833, it is an early, shorter version of *Tithonus* (1860, p. 1112). The major revisions are noted below, and the details under *Tithonus*. There are earlier drafts in *T.Nbks 20–21* (1833). T.'s revisions are interestingly discussed by Miss Donahue. T. remarks that Tithonus was 'beloved by Aurora, who gave him eternal life but not eternal youth. He grew old and infirm, and as he could not die, according to the legend, was turned into a grasshopper.' Cp. *The Grasshopper* 5, 28 (*1830*): 'No Tithon thou as poets feign . . . / No withered immortality.' Written after the shock of Arthur Hallam's death, the poem is a companion to *Ulysses*, which was begun at the same time (*Mem.* ii 9). The theme may have been influenced by the grief of T.'s sister Emily (Hallam's betrothed); she wrote to T., 12 July 1834, 'What is life to me! If I die (which the Tennysons never do)' (*Mem.* 135, cited by Miss Donahue).

Ay me! ay me! the woods decay and fall,
The vapours weep their substance to the ground,
Man comes and tills the earth and lies beneath,
And after many summers dies the rose.
Me only fatal immortality
Consumes: I wither slowly in thine arms,
Here at the quiet limit of the world,
A white-haired shadow roaming like a dream
The ever-silent spaces of the East,
Far-folded mists, and gleaming halls of morn.
  Ay me! ay me! what everlasting pain,
Being immortal with a mortal heart,
To live confronted with eternal youth:
To look on what is beautiful nor know
Enjoyment save through memory. Can thy love,
Thy beauty, make amends, though even now,
Close over us, the silver star, thy guide,
Shines in those tremulous eyes that fill with tears?

*67. Moved . . . heaven*] Swathed Troy with flame *H.MS, Heath MS.*
*68*] *Not H.MS.*
¶ 218.*11–15*] *Expanded in 1860.*

Release me: let me go: take back thy gift:
Why should a man desire in any shape
To vary from his kind, or beat the roads
Of life, beyond the goal of ordinance
Where all should pause, as is most meet for all?
Or let me call thy ministers, the hours,
To take me up, to wind me in their arms,
To shoot the sunny interval of day,
And lap me deep within the lonely west.
  A soft air fans the cloud apart; there comes
A glimpse of that dark world where I was born.
Once more the old mysterious glimmer steals
From thy pure brows, and from thy shoulders pure,
And bosom throbbing with a fresher heart.
Thy cheek begins to bloom a fuller red,
Thy sweet eyes brighten slowly close to mine,
Ere yet they blind the stars, and thy wild team,
Spreading a rapid glow with loosened manes,
Fly, trampling twilight into flakes of fire.
  'Tis ever thus: thou growest more beautiful,
Thou partest: when a little warmth returns
Thou partest, and thy tears are on my cheek.
  Ay me! ay me! with what another heart,
By thy divine embraces circumfused,
Thy black curls burning into sunny rings,
With thy change changed, I felt this wondrous glow
That, gradually blooming, flushes all
Thy pale fair limbs: what time my mortal frame
Molten in thine immortal, I lay wooed,
Lips, forehead, eyelids, growing dewy-warm
With kisses balmier than opening buds;
Anon the lips that dealt them moved themselves
In wild and airy whisperings more sweet
Than that strange song I heard Apollo sing,

24–7] *Not 1860.*
29–32] *Not T.MS 1st draft.*
35–7] *Not T.MS 1st draft.*
35 ∧ 6] *1860 added a line.*
40 ∧ 41] *1860 added four lines. T.MS 1st draft*, from here to the end, differs considerably from *Heath MS.* It has eight lines, threatening Aurora that he will call up Death; then a shorter version of the closing lines, ending with l. 63 but incorporating a description of Aurora's horses (different from *Heath MS*). *T.MS 2nd draft* has the eight lines on Death following l. 53, and then breaks off.
42] *Expanded in 1860.*

While Ilion like a mist rose into towers.
Ah! keep me not for ever in the East:
How can my nature longer mix with thine?
Coldly thy rosy shadows bathe me, cold
Are all thy lights, and cold my wrinkled feet
Upon these glimmering thresholds, when the steam
Floats up from those still fields that dream below.
Release me! so restore me to the ground;
Thou seest all things, thou wilt see my grave:
Thou wilt renew thy beauty with the morn;
I earth in earth forget these empty courts,
And thee returning on thy silver wheels.

# 219 Tiresias

Published *1885*. H.T. says that it was 'partly written at the same time' as *Ulysses*, i.e. 1833. See the dedicatory poem, *To FitzGerald* (p. 1317). There is a draft in *T.Nbk 20* (1833–4); this may not be quoted, and there are sheets missing, but it seems to have contained the whole central section, ll. 82–145. Lines 160 to the end are in T.'s late hand. Since *T.Nbk 15* includes the opening of the poem, it is probable that the poem is substantially of 1833. It was revised in 1883; T.'s wife Emily wrote to Edward Lear, 14 Aug. (*Lincoln*): 'Ally has been finishing one of his old world poems begun about the *Ulysses* period and discarded as what Carlyle called "a dead dog" but Ally has come to think that the world will receive lessons thus when it discards them in modern garb.' It was recited 25 Aug. 1883 (F. T. Palgrave's *Journals*, 1899, p. 178). There are drafts of the late text in *H.Nbks 46–7* and *Lpr 251*. Of the sources, the most important is Euripides, *Phoenissae*. Something of the battle-setting was from Aeschylus, *Septem Contra Thebas*. 'Before he had left Somersby for Cambridge, he had written in Greek hexameters an Homeric book on the Seven against Thebes' (*Mem.* i 40). The sources are discussed by D. Bush, *Mythology and the Romantic Tradition* (1937), pp. 216–9. Rivalry between brothers has made imminent the destruction of Thebes in Boeotia. Tiresias, the blind seer, is asked by Creon how Thebes can be saved, and he replies that the battle is inevitable; he is reluctant to say more till at last he declares that the only remedy is the sacrifice of Menœceus, Creon's son and a descendant of Cadmus. It was Cadmus who had offended the god Ares. *Phoenissae* 931–5: 'In that den where the earth-born dragon lay / Watching the streams of Dirce, must he yield, / Slaughtered, a blood-oblation to the earth; / For Ares, nursing wrath 'gainst Cadmus long, / Now would avenge his earth-born dragon's death.' Creon urges silence and presses Menœceus to flee; Menœceus pretends he will do so, but sacrifices himself. T. changes this to a direct meeting

*59 ∧ 60] 1860 added two lines.*

of Tiresias and Menœceus, and removes the prophet's hesitation. The fact that Creon is not mentioned, and that Tiresias throughout calls Menœceus 'my son', suggests (like *Demeter and Persephone*, p. 1373) that the pagans 'yearn / For larger glimpses of that more than man' (ll. 19–20), and are aspiring towards Christianity. Tenuously adumbrated here is the sacrifice of God and His Son. The poem's origins in 1833 suggest that T., after Arthur Hallam's death, looked to a classical story for an insight into mortality. Where *Ulysses* (p. 560) was written from a feeling of the need for the courage of life, and *Tithonus* (p. 1112) from a feeling that immortality was not in itself a blessing, *Tiresias* finds strength and consolation in deliberate self-sacrifice, 'fearing not to plunge / Thy torch of life in darkness' (ll. 153–4). T.'s political pessimism (ll. 63–75) had deepened by 1883, but he had hardly been a political optimist in 1833.

I wish I were as in the years of old,
While yet the blessèd daylight made itself
Ruddy through both the roofs of sight, and woke
These eyes, now dull, but then so keen to seek
The meanings ambushed under all they saw,
The flight of birds, the flame of sacrifice,
What omens may foreshadow fate to man
And woman, and the secret of the Gods.
    My son, the Gods, despite of human prayer,
Are slower to forgive than human kings.
The great God, Arês, burns in anger still
Against the guiltless heirs of him from Tyre,
Our Cadmus, out of whom thou art, who found
Beside the springs of Dircê, smote, and stilled
Through all its folds the multitudinous beast,
The dragon, which our trembling fathers called
The God's own son.
                        A tale, that told to me,
When but thine age, by age as winter-white
As mine is now, amazed, but made me yearn
For larger glimpses of that more than man
Which rolls the heavens, and lifts, and lays the deep,
Yet loves and hates with mortal hates and loves,
And moves unseen among the ways of men.
    Then, in my wanderings all the lands that lie

¶ 219.5–6. Suggested by Tiresias's speech when he enters, *Phoenissae* 838–40, speaking to his daughter: 'Guard in thy maiden hand the augury-lots / Which, when I marked the bodings of the birds, / In the holy seat I took, where I divine.' Also Callimachus's *Fifth Hymn* 123–4 (see l. 33*n*), where Athene says: 'He shall know the birds – which is of good omen among all the countless birds that fly and what birds are of ill-omened flight.'

Subjected to the Heliconian ridge
Have heard this footstep fall, although my wont
Was more to scale the highest of the heights
With some strange hope to see the nearer God.
One naked peak – the sister of the sun
Would climb from out the dark, and linger there
To silver all the valleys with her shafts –
There once, but long ago, five-fold thy term
Of years, I lay; the winds were dead for heat;
The noonday crag made the hand burn; and sick
For shadow – not one bush was near – I rose
Following a torrent till its myriad falls
Found silence in the hollows underneath.
There in a secret olive-glade I saw
Pallas Athene climbing from the bath
In anger; yet one glittering foot disturbed
The lucid well; one snowy knee was prest
Against the margin flowers; a dreadful light
Came from her golden hair, her golden helm
And all her golden armour on the grass,
And from her virgin breast, and virgin eyes
Remaining fixt on mine, till mine grew dark
For ever, and I heard a voice that said
'Henceforth be blind, for thou hast seen too much,
And speak the truth that no man may believe.'
Son, in the hidden world of sight, that lives
Behind this darkness, I behold her still,
Beyond all work of those who carve the stone,
Beyond all dreams of Godlike womanhood,
Ineffable beauty, out of whom, at a glance,
And as it were, perforce, upon me flashed
The power of prophesying – but to me

25. *Subjected*: cp. *Paradise Lost* xii 640: 'the subjected Plaine'; *subiectos Orientis orae*, Horace, *Odes* I xii 55.

33–40. The surprising of Pallas Athene is based on Callimachus's *Fifth Hymn* 73–81, as D. Bush says: 'Noontide quiet held all the hill. Those two were bathing and it was the noontide hour and a great quiet held that hill. Only Tiresias, on whose cheek the down was just darkening, still ranged with his hounds the holy place. And, athirst beyond telling, he came unto the flowing fountain, wretched man! and unwillingly saw that which is not lawful to be seen. And Athena was angered, yet said to him: "What god, O son of Everes, led thee on this grievous way? hence shalt thou never more take back thine eyes!".' In Callimachus, Athene is accompanied by the mother of Tiresias; it is for her sake that Athene gives him the power of prophecy. T. altered what would have been a distraction.

No power–so chained and coupled with the curse
Of blindness and their unbelief, who heard
And heard not, when I spake of famine, plague,
Shrine-shattering earthquake, fire, flood, thunderbolt,
And angers of the Gods for evil done
And expiation lacked–no power on Fate,
Theirs, or mine own! for when the crowd would roar
For blood, for war, whose issue was their doom,
To cast wise words among the multitude
Was flinging fruit to lions; nor, in hours
Of civil outbreak, when I knew the twain
Would each waste each, and bring on both the yoke
Of stronger states, was mine the voice to curb
The madness of our cities and their kings.
  Who ever turned upon his heel to hear
My warning that the tyranny of one
Was prelude to the tyranny of all?
My counsel that the tyranny of all
Led backward to the tyranny of one?
  This power hath worked no good to aught that lives,
And these blind hands were useless in their wars.
O therefore that the unfulfilled desire,
The grief for ever born from griefs to be,
The boundless yearning of the Prophet's heart–
Could *that* stand forth, and like a statue, reared
To some great citizen, win all praise from all
Who past it, saying, 'That was he!'
                                                  In vain!
Virtue must shape itself in deed, and those
Whom weakness or necessity have cramped
Within themselves, immerging, each, his urn
In his own well, draw solace as he may.
  Menœceus, thou hast eyes, and I can hear
Too plainly what full tides of onset sap
Our seven high gates, and what a weight of war
Rides on those ringing axles! jingle of bits,

*57–9. Phoenissae* 878–9: 'What did I not? What warnings spake I not? – / And had for guerdon hate of Oedipus' sons.' Cp. *Comus* 519: 'unbelief is blind'.

*73.* Cp. *I loving Freedom* 35–6: 'The tyranny of all begins / The tyranny of one.' Cp. the unadopted political passage in *To FitzGerald* (p. 1320).

*91–3.* Cp. *Aeneid* vi 590–1, which T. used to quote 'for descriptive beauty and fine sound' (*Mem.* ii 13): *demens, qui nimbos et non imitabile fulmen / aere et cornipedum pulsu simularet equorum.* ('Madman! to mimic the stormclouds and inimitable thunder with brass and the tramp of horn-footed horses.')

Shouts, arrows, tramp of the hornfooted horse
That grind the glebe to powder! Stony showers
Of that ear-stunning hail of Arês crash
Along the sounding walls. Above, below,
Shock after shock, the song-built towers and gates
Reel, bruised and butted with the shuddering
War-thunder of iron rams; and from within
The city comes a murmur void of joy,
Lest she be taken captive–maidens, wives,
And mothers with their babblers of the dawn,
And oldest age in shadow from the night,
Falling about their shrines before their Gods,
And wailing 'Save us.'
                                        And they wail to thee!
These eyeless eyes, that cannot see thine own,
See this, that only in thy virtue lies
The saving of our Thebes; for, yesternight,
To me, the great God Arês, whose one bliss
Is war, and human sacrifice–himself
Blood-red from battle, spear and helmet tipt
With stormy light as on a mast at sea,
Stood out before a darkness, crying 'Thebes,
Thy Thebes shall fall and perish, for I loathe
The seed of Cadmus–yet if one of these
By his own hand–if one of these–'
                                                    My son,
No sound is breathed so potent to coerce,
And to conciliate, as their names who dare
For that sweet mother land which gave them birth
Nobly to do, nobly to die. Their names,
Graven on memorial columns, are a song
Heard in the future; few, but more than wall
And rampart, their examples reach a hand

93. *Stony showers*: Cowley has 'stony shower' in his imitation of Pindar, *The Plagues of Egypt*, stanza xi. (There was a copy of Cowley at Somersby, *Lincoln.*) Gray's translation of a phrase of Statius (*Thebaid* vi 656–7: *moenia saxis frangere*) uses the same metaphor, and is on the same subject as T.'s line: 'And batter Cadmus' walls with stony showers' (this translation, though, was not published till 1853).

96. *song-built*: Thebes was built to the music of Amphion.

122–3. In view of the link between *Tiresias* and Hallam's death, cp. *In Memoriam* i 5–8: 'But who shall so forecast the years / And find in loss a gain to match? / Or reach a hand through time to catch / The far-off interest of tears?' This was based on *Hail Briton* 81–4, the patriotic mood of which is close to *Tiresias*: 'They wrought a work which time reveres, /

Far through all years, and everywhere they meet
And kindle generous purpose, and the strength
To mould it into action pure as theirs.
    Fairer thy fate than mine, if life's best end
Be to end well! and thou refusing this,
Unvenerable will thy memory be
While men shall move the lips: but if thou dare–
Thou, one of these, the race of Cadmus–then
No stone is fitted in yon marble girth
Whose echo shall not tongue thy glorious doom,
Nor in this pavement but shall ring thy name
To every hoof that clangs it, and the springs
Of Dircê laving yonder battle-plain,
Heard from the roofs by night, will murmur thee
To thine own Thebes, while Thebes through thee
        shall stand
Firm-based with all her Gods.
                                        The Dragon's cave
Half hid, they tell me, now in flowing vines–
Where once he dwelt and whence he rolled himself
At dead of night–thou knowest, and that smooth rock
Before it, altar-fashioned, where of late
The woman-breasted Sphinx, with wings drawn back,
Folded her lion paws, and looked to Thebes.
There blanch the bones of whom she slew, and these
Mixt with her own, because the fierce beast found
A wiser than herself, and dashed herself
Dead in her rage: but thou art wise enough,
Though young, to love thy wiser, blunt the curse
Of Pallas, hear, and though I speak the truth
Believe I speak it, let thine own hand strike
Thy youthful pulses into rest and quench
The red God's anger, fearing not to plunge
Thy torch of life in darkness, rather–thou
Rejoicing that the sun, the moon, the stars
Send no such light upon the ways of men
As one great deed.
                                Thither, my son, and there
Thou, that hast never known the embrace of love,
Offer thy maiden life.
                                    This useless hand!
I felt one warm tear fall upon it. Gone!

A precedent to all the lands, / And an example reaching hands / For ever into coming years.'

*143.* The story of the Sphinx is from *Phoenissae.*

He will achieve his greatness.
But for me,
I would that I were gathered to my rest,
And mingled with the famous kings of old,
On whom about their ocean-islets flash
The faces of the Gods – the wise man's word,
Here trampled by the populace underfoot,
There crowned with worship – and these eyes will find
The men I knew, and watch the chariot whirl
About the goal again, and hunters race
The shadowy lion, and the warrior-kings,
In height and prowess more than human, strive
Again for glory, while the golden lyre
Is ever sounding in heroic ears
Heroic hymns, and every way the vales
Wind, clouded with the grateful incense-fume
Of those who mix all odour to the Gods
On one far height in one far-shining fire.

## 220 *Semele

Printed by H.T. *1913* (p. xxiv), as a fragment written *c.* 1835. But it is in *T.Nbk 20* (which may not be quoted) with poems of 1833. H.T. combines two drafts. T. apparently took a few hints from it for *The Vision of Sin* (p. 718). Semele insisted on Zeus's appearing in his majesty as god of lightning, and was burnt to death; but her child Bacchus (Dionysus) was saved from the flames and later born from Zeus. Cp. the description of Dionysus in *Pierced through* (p. 473), which formed part too of *The Coach of Death* and *Armageddon*. The free verse is very unusual for T.

I wished to see Him. Who may feel
His light and live? He comes.
The blast of Godhead bursts the doors,

*164. -islets*] *1888*; islands *1885*.
*168–77.* T. compares Pindar's *Dirge on Elysium*. ('For them the sun shineth in his strength, in the world below, while here 'tis night; and, in meadows red with roses, the space before their city is shaded by the incense-tree, and is laden with golden fruits . . . . Some of them delight themselves with horses and with wrestling; others with draughts, and with lyres; while beside them bloometh the fair flower of perfect bliss. And o'er that lovely land fragrance is ever shed, while they mingle all manner of incense with the far-shining fire on the altars of the gods.') T. liked to quote the closing lines of *Tiresias* as a 'sample' of his blank verse (*Mem.* ii 318).
¶ *220.2. live*] love *1913*.

His mighty hands are twined
About the triple forks, and when He speaks
The crown of sunlight shudders round
Ambrosial temples, and aloft,
Fluttering through Elysian air,
His green and azure mantles float in wavy
Foldings, and melodious thunder
Wheels in circles.
But thou, my son, who shalt be born
When I am ashes, to delight the world–
Now with measured cymbal-clash
Moving on to victory;
Now on music-rolling orbs,
A sliding throne, voluptuously
Panther-drawn,
To throbbings of the thunderous gong,
And melody o' the merrily-blowing flute;
Now with troops of clamorous revellers,
Merrily, merrily,
Rapidly, giddily,
Rioting, triumphing
Bacchanalians,
Rushing in cadence,
All in order,
Plunging down the viney valleys–

## 221 *The Mother's Ghost

Printed *Mem.* i 124–5, as written 1833–4. It is in *T.Nbk 15* with poems of late 1833.

Not a whisper stirs the gloom,
    It will be the dawning soon,
We may glide from room to room,
    In the glimmer of the moon:
Every heart is laid to rest,

5. Zeus's thunderbolts, as in *Of old sat Freedom* 15: 'Who, God-like, grasps the triple forks.'

*10. melodious thunder*: as in a fragment in *T.Nbk 22*, and in *The Princess* ii 452.

*16–23.* T. drew on these lines for the similar scene in *The Vision of Sin* 17ff (p. 719).

*18.* The panther traditionally accompanied Bacchus.

*25. Bacchanalians*: worshippers of Bacchus.

¶ 221.5. *laid*] *Lincoln MS* (*H.T.'s copy from T.MS*); lain *Mem.*

All the house is fast in sleep,
Were I not a spirit blest,
Sisters, I could almost weep.

In that cradle sleeps my child,
She whose birth brought on my bliss:
On her forehead undefiled
I will print an airy kiss:
See, she dreameth happy dreams,
Her hands are folded quietly,
Like to one of us she seems,
One of us my child will be.

## 222 *'Over the dark world flies the wind'

Printed by Sir Charles Tennyson, *Nineteenth Century* cix (1931) 504; also in F. M. Brookfield's *The Cambridge 'Apostles'* (1906), pp. 326–7; W. H. Brookfield had quoted it from memory, 15 Oct. 1868. Then *1931*, p. 72: 'This is from the same little pocket-book as the preceding lines [*The Ruined Kiln*, in *H.Nbk 16*, watermarked 1833 and including part of *In Memoriam* and poems written in that year]. It is characteristic of Tennyson's nature poetry during the early *In Memoriam* period. MS evidence suggests that many sections of that poem were founded on brief mood pictures like this, written in various metres.'

Over the dark world flies the wind
And clatters in the sapless trees,
From cloud to cloud through darkness blind
Quick stars scud o'er the sounding seas:
I look: the showery skirts unbind:
Mars by the lonely Pleiades
Burns overhead: with brows declined
I muse: I wander from my peace,
And still divide the rapid mind
This way and that in search of ease.

¶222.4. *Quick*] *H.MS*; Swift *Brookfield, Leeds MS. o'er the*] *H.MS*; over *Brookfield, Leeds MS.* *sounding seas*: *Lycidas* 154.
6–7. Cp. *From the East of life* 5–6 (p. 466): 'Joy set: he stayed: as Mars in heaven / Burns by the lonely sisters seven.'
9. *And still divide*] *H.MS*; Dividing still *Brookfield, Leeds MS*. Cp. *Morte d'Arthur* 60: 'This way and that dividing the swift mind'; for which T. cited *Aeneid* iv 285: *atque animum nunc huc celerem, nunc dividit illuc.* ('And now hither, now thither he swiftly throws his mind.')

# 223 *Youth

Printed *Mem.* i 112–5, dated 1833. There are MSS (without a title) in: *H.Nbk 12* (the opening only, along with early drafts of *In Memoriam* including *abab* stanzas), *A* below; *H.Nbk 16* which includes *Ulysses*, *B* below; and *H.Nbk 17*, which includes part of *In Memoriam*, *C* below. The probability is therefore very strong that *Youth* was affected by the death of Arthur Hallam (15 Sept. 1833), though it should be remembered that earlier poems like *In deep and solemn dreams* (p. 277) already show much of the mood of *In Memoriam*. Cp. the unpublished section from *In Memoriam*, *The path by which I walked alone* (p. 1772). Cp. the different use of the idea of two voices in *The Two Voices* (p. 522).

I

Youth, lapsing through fair solitudes,
 Poured by long glades and meadowy mounds,
Crowned with soft shade her deepening floods
 That washed her shores with blissful sounds:

Her silver eddies in their play
 Drove into lines and studs of light
The image of the sun by day,
 The image of the moon by night.

The months, ere they began to rise,
 Sent through my blood a prophet voice
Before the first white butterflies,
 And where the secret streams rejoice.

I heard Spring laugh in hidden rills,
 Summer through all her sleepy leaves
Murmured: a voice ran round the hills
 When corny Lammas browned the sheaves:

¶ 223.*1*. *Youth*] Life *A*. This MS precedes the opening line with two stanzas:

Though what I sought I knew not well,
 I was not made to live alone,
My heart was never meant to dwell
 Housed like the caddisworm in stone.

2

I had one true friend, to whose light
 My soul her early tendrils curled,
For whom my love was infinite
 Who is the mother of the world.

The fourth line was incorporated as *From the East of life* 14 (p. 467).

*2. long*] *Mem.*, *C*; thick *B*.

*10. prophet*] *Mem.*, *C*; warning *B*.

*16. browned*] *B–C*; bound *Mem. Lammas*: the harvest festival, 1 August.

A voice, when night had crept on high,
  To snowy crofts and winding scars,
Rang like a trumpet clear and dry,
  And shook the frosty winter stars.

When I was somewhat older grown
  These voices did not cease to cry,
Only they took a sweeter tone,
  But did not sound so joyfully:

Lower and deeper evermore
  They grew, and they began at last
To speak of what had gone before,
  And how all things become the past.

Life, to this wind, turned all her vanes,
  Moaned in her chimneys and her eaves;
I grieved as woods in dripping rains
  Sigh over all their fallen leaves;

Beside my door at morning stood
  The tearful spirit of the time;
He moaned, 'I wander from my good!'
  He chanted some old doleful rhyme.

So lived I without aim or choice,
  Still humming snatches of old song,
Till suddenly a sharper voice
  Cried in the future 'Come along'.

When to this sound my face I turned,
  Intent to follow on the track,
Again the low sweet voices mourned
  In distant fields, 'Come back, come back'.

*17–20*] *Mem.*; *not B; added in margin of C.*
*31. grieved*] *Mem.*, *C*; mourned *B.*
*32 ∧ 3*]
Yet, by a rule of contraries,
  My spirit in that doleful clime
Shot herself down beneath the skies
  In rapid rills of merry rhyme.

I was like purple glass, that glows
  Most rich and warm, but if more nigh
You look through it, it only shows
  A frosted land, a chilly sky. *B, which ends*

*33–6*] *Added in margin of C* (*reading* doors).
*36. old*] *Mem.*; *not C.*
*43. the*] *Mem.*; those *C.*

Confused, and ceasing from my quest,
  I loitered in the middle way,
So pausing 'twixt the East and West,
  I found the present where I stay:

Now idly in my natal bowers,
  Unvext by doubts I cannot solve,
I sit among the scentless flowers
  And see and hear the world revolve:

Yet well I know that nothing stays,
  And I must traverse yonder plain:
Sooner or later from the haze
  The second voice will peal again.

II

A rumour of a mystery,
  A noise of winds that meet and blend,
An energy, an agony,
  A labour working to an end.

Now shall I rest or shall I rise?
  It is the early morning, Hark!
A voice like many voices cries,
  Comes hither throbbing through the dark;

Now one faint line of light doth glow,
  I follow to the morning sun,
Behind yon hill the trumpets blow,
  And there is something greatly done:

45. *Confused, and*] I loitered *C 1st reading.*
46] Confused like Francis in the play, *C 1st reading.* A reference to the successful play *Francis I*, by Frances Ann Kemble (Fanny Kemble, a friend of T.'s), published in 1832, first performed 15 March. Through a deception, Francis loses the one he loves. *Mem.* i 83 discusses the play, and quotes Arthur Hallam's praise of it.
49. *idly*] standing *C 1st reading.*
53. *Yet*] Full *C 1st reading.*
59. Cp. *In Memoriam* cxiii 18: 'With agonies, with energies'; *St Simeon Stylites* 23–4, *Heath MS*: 'All agonies, / All energies'. Arthur Hallam had joined the two, in his *Timbuctoo* 74–6 (Motter, p. 40): 'the energies / Of Guilt, and desolate the poor man's sleep. / Yet not alone for torturing agonies . . .'
60. Incorporated as *The Two Voices* 297. Cp. *In Memoriam* cxxviii 24: 'toil cöoperant to an end'.
63–4] *Completed in C in H.T.'s hand.* Cp. the vision in *The Ring* 40–1: 'the Voices of the day / Are heard across the Voices of the dark'.

The voice cries 'Come'. Upon the brink
A solitary fortress burns,
And shadows strike and shadows sink,
And Heaven is dark and bright by turns.

'Come' and I come, the wind is strong:
Hush! there floats upward from the gulf
A murmur of heroic song,
A howling of the mountain wolf;

A tempest strikes the craggy walls,
Faint shouts are heard across the glen,
A moan of many waterfalls,
And in the pauses groans of men.

'Come' and I come, no more I sleep:
The thunder cannot make thee dumb;
'Come' and I come, the vale is deep,
My heart is dark, but yet I come.

Up hither have I found my way,
The latest thunder-peal hath pealed,
Down from the summit sweeps the day
And rushes o'er a boundless field.

Out bursts a rainbow in the sky–
Away with shadows! on they move!
Beneath those double arches lie
Fair with green fields the realms of Love.

The whole land glitters after rain,
Through wooded isles the river shines,
The casements sparkle on the plain,
The towers gleam among the vines;

'Come' and I come, and all comes back
Which in that early voice was sweet,
Yet am I dizzy in the track,
A light wind wafts me from my feet.

*72. Heaven*] all *C 1st reading.*
*77–80.* Cp. Collins, *Ode to Fear* 50–52: 'Or in some hollow'd Seat, / 'Gainst which the big Waves beat, / Hear drowning Sea-men's Cries in Tempests brought!'
*90*] *Mem.; not C.*
*96. gleam*] stand *C 1st reading.*

* * * *

Now quicker and quicker giddily
Till all the plain confused and dim
Streams backward like a moving sea.

Warm beats my blood, my spirit thirsts;
Fast by me flash the cloudy streaks,
And from the golden vapour bursts
A mountain bright with triple peaks:

With all his groves he bows, he nods,
The clouds unswathe them from the height,
And there sit figures as of Gods
Rayed round with beams of living light.

## 224 *'Love's latest hour is this'

Unpublished. From a letter, March–April 1834, from J. M. Kemble to W. B. Donne (now belonging to Mrs C. B. Johnson). At the end, Kemble comments: 'Wouldn't verses like these make one half believe that Ælfred has had nothing to think about all his life, but illicit loves?' A torn sheet, giving only the opening lines, is in *H.Nbk 16* (late 1833), along with a version beginning 'Ah Love! what world is this' and consisting of four-line stanzas: ll. 1–2, 5–6; 7–8, 11–12; 19–20, 23–4; 27, 26, 29–30 (with trivial variants). There are a few affinities with *Oh! that 'twere possible* (p. 598).

Love's latest hour is this,
True love from love must part,

*101–3*] *C*; *not Mem.* The MS has a lacuna for the first line of the stanza. H.T. at first printed the lines, *Mat.* i 134.
*106. golden vapour*: in the unpublished section of *In Memoriam*, *The path by which I walked alone* 7 (p. 1772).
*107.* Discussing *The Lotos-Eaters* 16 ('Three silent pinnacles of agèd snow'), Paden (p. 157) refers to the religious mythologizing of G. S. Faber: 'the three mountain-peaks that, according to Faber, were characteristic of all holy mountains and hence of all legendary Lands of the Blest.' A. A. Mendilow quotes Arthur Hallam on the 'three sinuous hills' (Motter, pp. 44–5), and comments: 'The peaks high above the plateau of the Muses sometimes . . . take the form of a trinity of summits.' *Scripta Hierosolymitana* xvii (1966) 163–6.
*111. living light*: *Macbeth* II iv 10; *Timbuctoo* 74; *Love* [*Thou, from the first*] iii 15.
¶ 224.*1. latest hour*: of death, as in Dryden and Keats.

Yet ere I lose my bliss,
Sweet! let me feel thine heart.
One Kiss! one Kiss! One Kiss!
Cling, clasp me heart to heart!

One Kiss! I scarce can speak,
And thy lips tremble now.
Yet let me kiss thy cheek,
Ah! let me kiss thy brow!
One on thy neck, thy cheek,
Another on thy brow!

I go: the day steals on.
Henceforth I hate the skies.
I go: my hope is gone.
Yet let me kiss thine eyes!
I go: not yet! yet one,
One Kiss between thine eyes!

How sweet to stand embraced
Till I grow stiff and cold
In folding thy dear waist
Which I no more shall fold;
Dear lips! Dear eyes! Dear waist!
Which I no more shall fold.

The world is nothing worth,
Here let me fall and lie;
What is there else on earth?
'Twere better far to die!
Lay lip to lip! Pluck forth
My heart that I may die!

# 225 The Epic [Morte d'Arthur]

Published *1842*; among 'English Idyls'. Written after 1835 (FitzGerald), probably 1837–8, judging by the references to skating and geology (*Mem.* i 150, 162 – noted by W. C. DeVane). The draft in *H.Lpr 53* is watermarked 1838. This frame for *Morte d'Arthur* (both introduction and conclusion – see p. 597) did not accompany the poem in T.'s trial-edition of *1842* (T. J. Wise, *Bibliography of Tennyson*, i 77). For Leigh Hunt's strictures on T.'s framing, see *Godiva* (p. 731). FitzGerald says that it was added to *Morte d'Arthur* 'to anticipate or excuse the "faint Homeric echoes"', and 'to give a reason for telling an old-world [Fairy-] tale'; he compares the framework of *The Day-Dream* (p. 624). It hints at T.'s ambitions for an epic on Arthur, though the *Morte* was to be the last, not the penultimate, book

(l. 41). The germ of such an introduction was probably *Morte d'Arthur* 225, *Fitzwilliam MS* (p. 595): 'Before the eyes of ladies thrice as fair / As those that win the love of modern men.' T. says: 'Mrs Browning wanted me to continue this: she has put my answer in *Aurora Leigh*.'

At Francis Allen's on the Christmas-eve,–
The game of forfeits done–the girls all kissed
Beneath the sacred bush and past away–
The parson Holmes, the poet Everard Hall,
The host, and I sat round the wassail-bowl,
Then half-way ebbed: and there we held a talk,
How all the old honour had from Christmas gone,
Or gone, or dwindled down to some odd games
In some odd nooks like this; till I, tired out
With cutting eights that day upon the pond,
Where, three times slipping from the outer edge,
I bumped the ice into three several stars,
Fell in a doze; and half-awake I heard
The parson taking wide and wider sweeps,
Now harping on the church-commissioners,
Now hawking at Geology and schism;
Until I woke, and found him settled down
Upon the general decay of faith
Right through the world, 'at home was little left,
And none abroad: there was no anchor, none,
To hold by.' Francis, laughing, clapt his hand
On Everard's shoulder, with 'I hold by him.'
'And I,' quoth Everard, 'by the wassail-bowl.'
'Why yes,' I said, 'we knew your gift that way
At college: but another which you had,
I mean of verse (for so we held it then),
What came of that?' 'You know,' said Frank, 'he burnt
His epic, his King Arthur, some twelve books'–
And then to me demanding why? 'Oh, sir,
He thought that nothing new was said, or else
Something so said 'twas nothing–that a truth
Looks freshest in the fashion of the day:

¶ 225.1] *H. Lpr 53 begins with its draft of ll. 35–8 (see below), and then returns to the opening.*
*15.* An inquiry was set up in 1835; the Ecclesiastical Commissioners Act was passed in 1836, and revised in 1840–1.
*27–8*] *1850*; . . . he flung / His epic of King Arthur in the fire!' *1842–8.*
*32 ∧ 3*] Old things are gone: we are wiser than our Sires. *MS.* Incorporated in *Love thou 72*: 'That we are wiser than our sires'.

God knows: he has a mint of reasons: ask.
It pleased *me* well enough.' 'Nay, nay,' said Hall,
'Why take the style of those heroic times?
For nature brings not back the Mastodon,
Nor we those times; and why should any man
Remodel models? these twelve books of mine
Were faint Homeric echoes, nothing-worth,
Mere chaff and draff, much better burnt.' 'But I,'
Said Francis, 'picked the eleventh from this hearth
And have it: keep a thing, its use will come.
I hoard it as a sugar-plum for Holmes.'
He laughed, and I, though sleepy, like a horse
That hears the corn-bin open, pricked my ears;
For I remembered Everard's college fame
When we were Freshmen: then at my request
He brought it; and the poet little urged,
But with some prelude of disparagement,
Read, mouthing out his hollow oes and aes,
Deep-chested music, and to this result.

*35–8*] *MS has two drafts. The first was intended to open the poem*:

Why, what you ask–if any writer now
May take the style of some heroic age
Gone like the mastodon–nay, why should he
Remodel models rather than the life?
Yet this belief was lately half-unhinged
At Edward Allen's–on the Christmas Eve . . .

*The second draft follows l. 34*:

You scarce have hit the nail upon the head.
Nor yet had I. No doubt some modern lights,
Indeed the rising suns of their own times,
Have touched the distance into fresh results.
I had not done it. Those twelve books of mine

*38*] *1845*; Remodel models rather than the life?
And these twelve books of mine (to speak the truth) *1842–3*

*45*] *MS adds*:

For having lately met with Everard Hall,
I marvelled what an arch the brain had built
Above his ear and what a settled mind
Tempered the peaceful light of hazel eyes
Observing all things.

T. incorporated these lines as *The Ante-Chamber* 10–14 (p. 506), where they almost certainly describe Arthur Hallam.

*50*. 'This is something as A.T. read' (FitzGerald).

# 226 Morte d'Arthur

Published *1842*. Written 1833–4 (*Mem.* i 129, 138, and *Heath MS*), under the shock of Arthur Hallam's death, the news of which reached T. on 1 Oct. 1833. Cp. *Merlin and the Gleam* 77–80: 'Arthur had vanished / I knew not whither, / The king who loved me, / And cannot die.'

*Text.* There are fragments and drafts in *T.Nbk 17* (which may not be quoted). In *Fitzwilliam Museum*, there is an early MS, not in T.'s hand, which is apparently earlier than *Heath MS*, itself earlier than *Hn MS* (HM 1320) which breaks off at l. 180. All variants from *Heath MS* are given below, plus all the significant variants from *Fitzwilliam* and *Huntington*. The poem is T.'s first major Arthurian work, later incorporated in full into the *Idylls of the King* as *The Passing of Arthur* (1869), when it was preceded by 169 lines and followed by 29 lines. Cp. *The Palace of Art* 105–8, *1832* text: 'Or that deepwounded child of Pendragon / Mid misty woods on sloping greens / Dozed in the valley of Avilion, / Tended by crownèd queens.' It is based closely on Malory's *Morte d'Arthur* xxi 4–5. T. seems to have used the 3 vol. edition of 1816 (*Lincoln*), which is quoted throughout below, with Caxton's numbering added in square brackets. T.'s note refers also to Geoffrey of Monmouth and Walter Map. See R. S. Loomis, *The Development of Arthurian Romance* (1963). Paden (pp. 80–88) argues that 'the narrative of Malory was suffused with and heightened by connotations drawn' from G. S. Faber's *Origin of Pagan Idolatry* (1816). Faber's account of Helio-Arkite mythology implied 'that the legend of Arthur's death is a veiled but unmistakable account of a death of the transmigrating Great Father'. Paden's internal evidence alone is not decisive. But two other books by Faber were at Somersby (*Lincoln*): *Horae Mosaicae* (1818 edn), and *The Difficulties of Infidelity* (2nd edn, 1833). Paden links details of setting and imagery; e.g. the change from Malory's death in summer to winter; 'the mighty bones of ancient men' (l. 47), suggesting the tribe of Cush who brought the Helio-Arkite mysteries to Britain; the symbolism of the Round Table (l. 234); and the dying swan (l. 266). All of these have Faberian associations. The poem is introduced in *The Epic* as including 'Homeric echoes'. Among these may be noted: set epithets, and set lines introducing and closing speeches; the words of one speaker being quoted by another; repetition of words and lines; and soliloquies.

*Criticism.* John Sterling's adverse comments on *Morte d'Arthur* in *QR* discouraged T. from continuing with his epic (E. F. Shannon, *Tennyson and the Reviewers*, 1952, p. 91). Sterling said that the poem's 'inferiority' was not compensated for 'by any stronger human interest'; 'the miraculous legend of "Excalibur" does not come very near to us, and as reproduced by any modern writer must be a mere ingenious exercise of fancy'. Shannon (p. 95) also quotes Leigh Hunt's criticisms in the *Church of England Quarterly Review*: 'It treats the modes and feelings of one generation in the style of another, always a fatal thing, unless it be reconciled with something of self-banter in the course of the poem itself, or the mixture of light with grave.'

So all day long the noise of battle rolled
Among the mountains by the winter sea;
Until King Arthur's table, man by man,
Had fallen in Lyonnesse about their Lord,
King Arthur: then, because his wound was deep,
The bold Sir Bedivere uplifted him,
Sir Bedivere, the last of all his knights,
And bore him to a chapel nigh the field,
A broken chancel with a broken cross,
That stood on a dark strait of barren land.
On one side lay the Ocean, and on one
Lay a great water, and the moon was full.

Then spake King Arthur to Sir Bedivere:
'The sequel of today unsolders all

¶ *226.1–5*] After that battle, where King Arthur lost
The flower of all the Earth, his knights, which made
'The table round', because his wound was deep, *Heath MS*

*1.* One of the 'Homeric echoes' mentioned in *The Epic* 39: *Iliad* vi 1, xvii 384. Cp. T.'s translation: 'All day the men contend in grievous war', *Achilles* 9.

*4. Lyonnesse*: 'the country of legend that lay between Cornwall and the Scilly Islands' (T.), described in *The Passing of Arthur* (p. 1744).

*5–12.* Malory III clxvi [xxi]: 'And the noble King Arthur fell in a swoon to the earth. And there he swooned often times. And Sir Lucan and Sir Bedivere oftentimes heaved him up, and so weakly they led him between them both unto a little chapel not far from the sea side.'

*13 ∧ 14*] 'Well said old Merlin ere his time was come,
"Experience never closes all-in-all
But there is always something to be learnt
Even in the gate of death". So clear a dream–
Which I neglected with my waking mind–
Came yesternight–Sir Gawain as he lived–
Most like Sir Gawain in his eyes and hair.
Bare-headed, circled with a gracious light,
Seven ladies, like the seven rainy stars,
For whom he fought and whom he saved from shame–
Beautiful, tearful: and he spoke and said
"Go thou not forth tomorrow to the fight"–
But I went forth, and fought it, and lie here.'
*Heath MS, Fitzwilliam MS*

The MSS have these lines in brackets, T.'s tentative sign for deletion. This draft of the dream of Gawain's ghost is based on Malory xxi; T. was to adapt it for *The Passing of Arthur* (p. 1743).

*14–17.* Malory III cl [xx 9]: 'For I have now lost the fairest fellowship of noble knights that ever held christian King together.'

The goodliest fellowship of famous knights
Whereof this world holds record. Such a sleep
They sleep—the men I loved. I think that we
Shall never more, at any future time,
Delight our souls with talk of knightly deeds,
Walking about the gardens and the halls
Of Camelot, as in the days that were.
I perish by this people which I made,—
Though Merlin sware that I should come again
To rule once more—but let what will be, be,
I am so deeply smitten through the helm
That without help I cannot last till morn.
Thou therefore take my brand Excalibur,
Which was my pride: for thou rememberest how
In those old days, one summer noon, an arm
Rose up from out the bosom of the lake,
Clothed in white samite, mystic, wonderful,
Holding the sword—and how I rowed across
And took it, and have worn it, like a king:
And, wheresoever I am sung or told
In aftertime, this also shall be known:
But now delay not: take Excalibur,

*16. this*] the *Heath MS.*
*20. about*] among *Heath MS.*
*22–4*] *Not Heath MS; added in Huntington MS, which had as first reading*:

And I that taught this people all I know
Have overlived myself, and overlived
The grateful heart, and perish by their hands.

*23.* Malory III clxx [xxi 7]: 'Some men yet say in many parts of England that King Arthur is not dead, but by the will of our Lord in another place. And men say that he will come again.'
*28–33.* Malory I xxiii [i 25]: 'So they rode till they came to a lake, which was a fair water, and abroad [a broad], and in the midst of the lake King Arthur was ware of an arm, clothed in white samite, that held a fair sword in the hand.'
*29–30*] In the old days, one summer noon, there rose / An arm from . . . *Heath MS.*
*36–44.* Malory III clxvii [xxi] (subsequent quotations from Malory, unless noted otherwise, run on consecutively without omissions): '"Therefore take you Excalibur, my good sword, and go with it unto yonder water side, and when thou comest there, I charge thee throw my sword into that water, and come again and tell me what thou shalt see there." "My lord," said Sir Bedivere, "your command shall be done, and lightly bring you word again."'

And fling him far into the middle mere:
Watch what thou seëst, and lightly bring me word.'

To him replied the bold Sir Bedivere:
'It is not meet, Sir King, to leave thee thus,
Aidless, alone, and smitten through the helm.
A little thing may harm a wounded man.
Yet I thy hest will all perform at full,
Watch what I see, and lightly bring thee word.'

So saying, from the ruined shrine he stept
And in the moon athwart the place of tombs,
Where lay the mighty bones of ancient men,
Old knights, and over them the sea-wind sang
Shrill, chill, with flakes of foam. He, stepping down
By zig-zag paths, and juts of pointed rock,
Came on the shining levels of the lake.

There drew he forth the brand Excalibur,
And o'er him, drawing it, the winter moon,
Brightening the skirts of a long cloud, ran forth
And sparkled keen with frost against the hilt:
For all the haft twinkled with diamond sparks,
Myriads of topaz-lights, and jacinth-work
Of subtlest jewellery. He gazed so long
That both his eyes were dazzled, as he stood,
This way and that dividing the swift mind,
In act to throw: but at the last it seemed
Better to leave Excalibur concealed

*44. thee*] the *Heath MS*; thee *Fitzwilliam MS, Huntington MS.*
*45–65.* Malory: 'And so Sir Bedivere departed, and by the way he beheld that noble sword, where the pomel and the haft were all of precious stones, and then he said to himself: "If I throw this rich sword into the water, thereof shall never come good, but harm and loss." And then Sir Bedivere hid Excalibur under a tree, and as soon as he might he came again unto King Arthur, and said he had been at the water, and had thrown the sword into the water.'
*45. stept*] went *Heath MS.*
*51. levels*: cp. *The Lover's Tale* iii 4: 'the rippling levels of the lake'.
*52. There*] Then *Heath MS.*
*56. sparks*] *1855*; studs *1842–53.*
*60.* T. compares *Aeneid* iv 285: *atque animum nunc huc celerem, nunc dividit illuc* ('And now hither, now thither, he swiftly throws his mind'). From *Iliad* i 188: ἐν δέ οἱ ἦτορ . . . . διάνδιχα μερμήριξεν ('and within his shaggy breast his heart was divided in counsel').
*61.* G. G. Loane compares Pope's *Iliad* iv 570: 'In act to throw; but cautious, looked around' (*Echoes in Tennyson*, 1928, p. 6).

There in the many-knotted waterflags,
That whistled stiff and dry about the marge.
So strode he back slow to the wounded King.

Then spake King Arthur to Sir Bedivere:
'Hast thou performed my mission which I gave?
What is it thou hast seen? or what hast heard?'

And answer made the bold Sir Bedivere:
'I heard the ripple washing in the reeds,
And the wild water lapping on the crag.'

To whom replied King Arthur, faint and pale:
'Thou hast betrayed thy nature and thy name,
Not rendering true answer, as beseemed
Thy fëalty, nor like a noble knight:
For surer sign had followed, either hand,
Or voice, or else a motion of the mere.
This is a shameful thing for men to lie.
Yet now, I charge thee, quickly go again
As thou art lief and dear, and do the thing
I bad thee, watch, and lightly bring me word'.

Then went Sir Bedivere the second time
Across the ridge, and paced beside the mere,
Counting the dewy pebbles, fixed in thought;
But when he saw the wonder of the hilt,
How curiously and strangely chased, he smote
His palms together, and he cried aloud,

'And if indeed I cast the brand away,
Surely a precious thing, one worthy note,

*66–81.* Malory: '"What sawest thou there?" said the King. "Sir," said he, "I saw nothing but waves and wind." "That is untruly said of thee," said King Arthur, "therefore go thou lightly and do my command, as thou art to me life [lief] and dear, spare not but throw it in."'

*66. spake*] spoke *Heath MS.*

*71. lapping*] wapping *Heath MS.* The archaic word is from Malory; see ll. 113–32*n*.

*82–112.* Malory: 'Then Sir Bedivere returned again, and took the sword in his hand; and then he thought it sin and shame to throw away that noble sword. And so after he hid the sword, and returned again, and told to the King that he had been at the water, and done his command.'

*82. the*] a *Heath MS.*

*83*] *1853; not 1842–51.*

*88. 'And if indeed*] 'Ay me! and should *Heath MS.*

Should thus be lost for ever from the earth,
Which might have pleased the eyes of many men.
What good should follow this, if this were done?
What harm, undone? deep harm to disobey,
Seeing obedience is the bond of rule.
Were it well to obey then, if a king demand
An act unprofitable, against himself?
The King is sick, and knows not what he does.
What record, or what relic of my lord
Should be to aftertime, but empty breath
And rumours of a doubt? but were this kept,
Stored in some treasure-house of mighty kings,
Some one might show it at a joust of arms,
Saying, "King Arthur's sword, Excalibur,
Wrought by the lonely maiden of the Lake.
Nine years she wrought it, sitting in the deeps
Upon the hidden bases of the hills."
So might some old man speak in the aftertime
To all the people, winning reverence.
But now much honour and much fame were lost.'

So spake he, clouded with his own conceit,
And hid Excalibur the second time,
And so strode back slow to the wounded King.

Then spoke King Arthur, breathing heavily:
'What is it thou hast seen? or what hast heard?'

*94. Seeing*] Because *Heath MS.*
*97*] A question to be answered without fear. *Heath MS.*
*100. but were this*] Say this were *Heath MS.*
*104. lonely maiden*] prudent Lady *Heath MS.* The friendly sorceress of Malory I xxiii [i 25, out of the sequence]: '"That is the *Lady of the Lake*," said Merlin, "and within that lake is a rock, and therein is as fair a place [palace] as any is on earth, and richly beseen."'
*105–6.* Cp. Pope's *Iliad* xviii 468–72, where Vulcan is about to make the shield of Achilles: 'Chains, bracelets, pendants, all their toys I wrought. / Nine years kept secret in the dark abode, / Secure I lay concealed from man and God. / Deep in a caverned rock my days were led; / The rushing ocean murmured o'er my head.'
*106. bases of the hills*: incorporated from *The Lover's Tale* ii 120. Instead of this line, *Trinity MS* has *The Lover's Tale* i 511.
*110. conceit*: fancy.
*113. breathing heavily*] drawing thicker breath *Heath MS.*
*113–32.* Malory: '"What saw ye there," said the King. "Sir," said he, "I saw nothing but the water wap and the waves wan." "Ah traitor, untrue," said King Arthur, "now hast thou betrayed me two times, who would

And answer made the bold Sir Bedivere:
'I heard the water lapping on the crag,
And the long ripple washing in the reeds.'

To whom replied King Arthur, much in wrath:
'Ah, miserable and unkind, untrue,
Unknightly, traitor-hearted! Woe is me!
Authority forgets a dying king,
Laid widowed of the power in his eye
That bowed the will. I see thee what thou art,
For thou, the latest-left of all my knights,
In whom should meet the offices of all,
Thou wouldst betray me for the precious hilt;
Either from lust of gold, or like a girl
Valuing the giddy pleasure of the eyes.
Yet, for a man may fail in duty twice,
And the third time may prosper, get thee hence:
But, if thou spare to fling Excalibur,
I will arise and slay thee with my hands.'

Then quickly rose Sir Bedivere, and ran,
And, leaping down the ridges lightly, plunged
Among the bulrush-beds, and clutched the sword,
And strongly wheeled and threw it. The great brand
Made lightnings in the splendour of the moon,
And flashing round and round, and whirled in an
arch,

have wend [weened] that thou hast been unto me so self [lief] and dear, and thou art named a noble Knight, and wouldest betray me for the rich sword. But now, go again lightly, for thy long tarrying putteth me in great jeopardy of my life, for I have taken cold. And but if thou do as I command thee, and if ever I may see thee, I shall slay thee with mine own hands, for thou wouldest for my rich sword see me dead."'

*116. lapping*] wapping *Heath MS.*

*118. much in wrath*] filled with scorn *Heath MS.*

*128.* Cp. Horace, *Epistles* II i 188: *oculos et gaudia vana.*

*133–66.* Malory: 'Then Sir Bedivere departed, and went to the sword, and lightly took it up, and went to the water side, and there he bound the girdle about the hilt. And then he threw the sword into the water as far as he might, and there came an arm and an hand above the water, and met it and caught it, and so shook it thrice and brandished. And then the hand vanished away with the sword in the water. So Sir Bedivere came again to the King and told him what he had seen. "Alas," said the King, "help me from hence, for I dread me I have tarried over long."'

Shot like a streamer of the northern morn,
Seen where the moving isles of winter shock
By night, with noises of the northern sea.
So flashed and fell the brand Excalibur:
But ere he dipt the surface, rose an arm
Clothed in white samite, mystic, wonderful,
And caught him by the hilt, and brandished him
Three times, and drew him under in the mere.
And lightly went the other to the King.

Then spoke King Arthur, drawing thicker breath:
'Now see I by thine eyes that this is done.
Speak out: what is it thou hast heard, or seen?'

And answer made the bold Sir Bedivere:
'Sir King, I closed mine eyelids, lest the gems
Should blind my purpose, for I never saw,
Nor shall see, here or elsewhere, till I die,
Not though I live three lives of mortal men,
So great a miracle as yonder hilt.
Then with both hands I flung him, wheeling him;
But when I looked again, behold an arm,
Clothed in white samite, mystic, wonderful,
That caught him by the hilt, and brandished him
Three times, and drew him under in the mere.'

And answer made King Arthur, breathing hard:
'My end draws nigh; 'tis time that I were gone.
Make broad thy shoulders to receive my weight,
And bear me to the margin; yet I fear
My wound hath taken cold, and I shall die.'

*139.* Cp. this simile with Scott's *Lay of the Last Minstrel* II viii (of which there was a copy at Somersby, *Lincoln*): 'And red and bright the streamers light / Were dancing in the glowing north. / So had he seen, in fair Castile, / The youth in glittering squadrons start, / Sudden the flying jennet wheel, / And hurl the unexpected dart. / He knew, by the streamers that shot so bright, / That spirits were riding the northern light.'

*140. isles*] thrones *Heath MS.* Cp. Thomas Gisborne, on the Arctic: 'With shock of floating isles', *Walks in a Forest* (1794). There was a copy of Gisborne at Somersby (*Lincoln*).

*148*] Then spoke the wounded Arthur faint and pale: *Heath MS.*

*150*] What is it thou hast seen? or what hast heard? *Heath MS.*

*151. And answer made*] To whom replied *Heath MS.*

*155.* T. compares *Odyssey* iii 245, *τρὶς γὰρ δή μίν φασιν ἀνάξασθαι γένε' ἀνδρῶν.* ('For thrice, men say, has he been King for a generation of men.')

So saying, from the pavement he half rose,
Slowly, with pain, reclining on his arm,
And looking wistfully with wide blue eyes
As in a picture. Him Sir Bedivere
Remorsefully regarded through his tears,
And would have spoken, but he found not words,
Then took with care, and kneeling on one knee,
O'er both his shoulders drew the languid hands,
And rising bore him through the place of tombs.

But, as he walked, King Arthur panted hard,
Like one that feels a nightmare on his bed
When all the house is mute. So sighed the King,
Muttering and murmuring at his ear, 'Quick, quick!
I fear it is too late, and I shall die.'
But the other swiftly strode from ridge to ridge,
Clothed with his breath, and looking, as he walked,
Larger than human on the frozen hills.
He heard the deep behind him, and a cry
Before. His own thought drove him, like a goad.
Dry clashed his harness in the icy caves
And barren chasms, and all to left and right
The bare black cliff clanged round him, as he based
His feet on juts of slippery crag that rang
Sharp-smitten with the dint of armèd heels–
And on a sudden, lo! the level lake,
And the long glories of the winter moon.

*167–203.* Malory: 'Then Sir Bedivere took King Arthur upon his back, and so went with him to the water's side. And when they were at the water's side, even fast by the bank, hoved a little barge, with many fair ladies in it, and among them all was a Queen, and all they had black hoods, and they wept and shrieked when they saw King Arthur.'
*172*] *Added to Heath MS by T.*
*177*] Like one on whom a dusky nightmare leaps *Fitzwilliam MS.*
*183. Larger than human*: *humano maior*, like the ghost of Romulus in Ovid, *Fasti* ii 503. Cp. *Hark! the dogs howl* 20–21, which is also on the death of Hallam: 'Larger than human passes by / The shadow of the man I loved.' Also T.'s projected essay on Ghosts for the Cambridge 'Apostles', quoted by J. H. Buckley (p. 33): 'Forth issue from the inmost gloom the colossal Presences of the Past majores humano, some as they lived, seemingly pale with exhaustion and faintly smiling; some as they died in a still agony . . .' (*H.Nbk 7*).
*192.* Betty Miller, *Twentieth Century* clxvii (1960) 526, compares Dryden, *Aeneis* i 10: 'And the long Glories of Majestick *Rome*'. Henry Boyd quoted Dryden's line prominently in his translation of Dante (1802), of which a copy was at Somersby (*Lincoln*); Boyd also mentions 'the long glories of his line' (i 97, 102).

Then saw they how there hove a dusky barge,
Dark as a funeral scarf from stem to stern,
Beneath them; and descending they were ware
That all the decks were dense with stately forms
Black-stoled, black-hooded, like a dream–by these
Three Queens with crowns of gold–and from them rose
A cry that shivered to the tingling stars,
And, as it were one voice, an agony
Of lamentation, like a wind, that shrills
All night in a waste land, where no one comes,
Or hath come, since the making of the world.

Then murmured Arthur, 'Place me in the barge,'
And to the barge they came. There those three Queens
Put forth their hands, and took the King, and wept.
But she, that rose the tallest of them all
And fairest, laid his head upon her lap,
And loosed the shattered casque, and chafed his hands,
And called him by his name, complaining loud,
And dropping bitter tears against his brow
Striped with dark blood: for all his face was white
And colourless, and like the withered moon
Smote by the fresh beam of the springing east;
And all his greaves and cuisses dashed with drops
Of onset; and the light and lustrous curls–
That made his forehead like a rising sun

*204–25.* Malory: '"Now put me into the barge," said the King. And so he did softly, and there received him three Queens with great mourning, and so these three Queens set him down, and in one of their laps King Arthur laid his head. And then that Queen said: "Ah, dear brother, why have ye tarried so long from me. Alas, this wound on your head hath taken over much cold."'

*205–6*] And those three Queens received him, weeping wild. *Heath MS.* G. G. Loane (*Echoes in Tennyson*, 1928, p. 5) compares Wordsworth, the death of *Lucy Gray*: 'And to the bridge they came'. Malory III clxix [xxi 6, out of the sequence]: 'Thus was he led away in a barge wherein were three Queens. That one was King Arthur's sister Morgan le Fay; the other was the Queen of Northgalis; and the third was the Queen of the Waste Lands.' T. commented: 'Some say that the three Queens are Faith, Hope, and Charity. . . . They are three of the noblest of women. They are also those three Graces, but they are much more.'

*215. greaves and cuisses*: armour for shin and thigh.

*217. That*] Which *Heath MS.*

High from the daïs-throne–were parched with dust;
Or, clotted into points and hanging loose,
Mixed with the knightly growth that fringed his lips.
So like a shattered column lay the King;
Not like that Arthur who, with lance in rest,
From spur to plume a star of tournament,
Shot through the lists at Camelot, and charged
Before the eyes of ladies and of kings.

Then loudly cried the bold Sir Bedivere,
'Ah! my Lord Arthur, whither shall I go?
Where shall I hide my forehead and my eyes?
For now I see the true old times are dead,
When every morning brought a noble chance,
And every chance brought out a noble knight.
Such times have been not since the light that led
The holy Elders with the gift of myrrh.
But now the whole ROUND TABLE is dissolved
Which was an image of the mighty world;
And I, the last, go forth companionless,
And the days darken round me, and the years,
Among new men, strange faces, other minds.'

And slowly answered Arthur from the barge:
'The old order changeth, yielding place to new,
And God fulfils Himself in many ways,
Lest one good custom should corrupt the world.

*220. knightly*] stubborn *Heath MS.*
*223*] *Not Fitzwilliam MS.*
*224*] Rapidly galloping at Camelot charged *Heath MS*; Rapidly galloping in the list, went by *Fitzwilliam MS.*
*225*] Before the eyes of ladies thrice as fair
As those that win the love of modern men. *Fitzwilliam MS*
The germ of *The Epic.*
*226–38.* Malory: 'And so then they rowed from the land. And Sir Bedivere beheld all these ladies go from him, then Sir Bedivere cried: "Ah, my lord Arthur, what shall become of me now ye go from me, and leave me here alone among mine enemies."'
*234–5.* Malory III 1 [xiv 2, out of the sequence]: 'Also Merlin made the *Round Table* in token of the roundness of the world. For by the *Round Table* is the world signified by right.'
*239–64.* Malory: '"Comfort thyself," said King Arthur, "and do as well as thou mayest, for in me is no trust for to trust in, for I will into the vale of Avilion, for to heal me of my grievous wound. And if thou never hear more of me, pray for my soul."'
*242.* '*e.g.* chivalry, by formalism of habit or by any other means' (T.).

Comfort thyself: what comfort is in me?
I have lived my life, and that which I have done
May He within Himself make pure! but thou,
If thou shouldst never see my face again,
Pray for my soul. More things are wrought by prayer
Than this world dreams of. Wherefore, let thy voice
Rise like a fountain for me night and day.
For what are men better than sheep or goats
That nourish a blind life within the brain,
If, knowing God, they lift not hands of prayer
Both for themselves and those who call them friend?
For so the whole round earth is every way
Bound by gold chains about the feet of God.
But now farewell. I am going a long way
With these thou seëst–if indeed I go–
(For all my mind is clouded with a doubt)
To the island-valley of Avilion;
Where falls not hail, or rain, or any snow,
Nor ever wind blows loudly; but it lies
Deep-meadowed, happy, fair with orchard-lawns
And bowery hollows crowned with summer sea,
Where I will heal me of my grievous wound.'

So said he, and the barge with oar and sail
Moved from the brink, like some full-breasted swan
That, fluting a wild carol ere her death,
Ruffles her pure cold plume, and takes the flood

*249. like*] as *Heath MS.*

*255.* A commonplace found variously in Homer, Plato, Chaucer, Spenser, Milton–though none exactly parallels T.'s use. 'My father said that this passage was not, as has been said, suggested by *Iliad* viii 19 or by Plato, *Theaetetus* 153' (H.T.).

*259.* 'From which he will some day return–the Isle of the Blest' (T.).

*260–3.* T. compares *Odyssey* iv 566ff, and Lucretius iii 18ff; adapted again as *Lucretius* 104–10 (p. 1210).

*262. Deep-meadowed*: T. compared Pindar, *Pythian Odes* x 23, and *Iliad* ix 151.

*263.* T. compares *Odyssey* x 195, *νῆσον, τὴν πέρι πόντος ἀπείριτος ἐστεφάνωται* ('the island, about which is set as a crown the boundless deep').

*265–72.* Malory: 'But evermore the Queens and the ladies wept and shrieked, that it was pity for to hear them. And as soon as Sir Bedivere had lost sight of the barge, he wept and wailed, and so took the forest, and so he went all the night.'

*267. fluting*] piping *Heath MS.*

*268. plume*] plumes *Heath MS.*

With swarthy webs. Long stood Sir Bedivere
Revolving many memories, till the hull
Looked one black dot against the verge of dawn,
And on the mere the wailing died away.

[THE EPIC]

Here ended Hall, and our last light, that long
Had winked and threatened darkness, flared and fell:
At which the Parson, sent to sleep with sound,
And waked with silence, grunted 'Good!' but we
Sat rapt: it was the tone with which he read–
Perhaps some modern touches here and there
Redeemed it from the charge of nothingness–
Or else we loved the man, and prized his work;
I know not: but we sitting, as I said,
The cock crew loud; as at that time of year
The lusty bird takes every hour for dawn:
Then Francis, muttering, like a man ill-used,
'There now–that's nothing!' drew a little back,
And drove his heel into the smouldered log,
That sent a blast of sparkles up the flue:
And so to bed; where yet in sleep I seemed
To sail with Arthur under looming shores,
Point after point; till on to dawn, when dreams
Begin to feel the truth and stir of day,
To me, methought, who waited with a crowd,
There came a bark that, blowing forward, bore
King Arthur, like a modern gentleman
Of stateliest port; and all the people cried,

*270. Revolving*: Miltonic, cp. 'much revolving', *Paradise Lost* iv 31; deriving from *Aeneid* i 305: *per noctem plurima volvens.*

[*The Epic*]

*282–3. Hamlet* I i 157–60: 'It faded on the crowing of the cock. / Some say that ever 'gainst that season comes / Wherein our Saviour's birth is celebrated / This bird of dawning singeth all night long.' This passage was quoted in Thomas Keightley's *Fairy Mythology* (1828; 2nd edn, 1833, ii 137), which T. used when working on *Morte d'Arthur* in 1833 (*Mem.* i 129), and later owned (*Lincoln*).

*286–7.* John Churton Collins compared Dante's *Paradiso* xviii 100–1: '*Poi come nel percuoter de' ciocchi arsi / surgono innumerabili faville.*' ('Then, as when burning logs are struck rise innumerable sparks.') Alongside this, T. wrote '!!!' (*Cornhill*, Jan. 1880, *Lincoln*).

*290–1.* A traditional belief; cp. Shelley, *Hellas* 122: 'The truth of day lightens upon my dream'.

*294.* Anticipating the *Dedication* and *Epilogue* of the *Idylls*; cp. l. 225*n*.

'Arthur is come again: he cannot die.'
Then those that stood upon the hills behind
Repeated–'Come again, and thrice as fair;'
And, further inland, voices echoed–'Come
With all good things, and war shall be no more.'
At this a hundred bells began to peal,
That with the sound I woke, and heard indeed
The clear church-bells ring in the Christmas-morn.

## 227 *'Oh! that 'twere possible'

Published, as *Stanzas*, in *The Tribute* (ed. Lord Northampton), Sept. 1837. T. created it by adding to a poem he had written after the death of Arthur Hallam, 1833–4; this exists in two drafts in *Heath MS* (*A*, *B*). Later T. took it as the 'germ' of *Maud* (1855), where *Oh! that 'twere possible* falls into place (p. 1082). A decision where to place it chronologically is difficult; there seem to be the least disadvantages if the poem is given under 1833–4, but in the text which T. published, that of *1837*. All the variants between the later version in *Heath* (*B*) and *1837* are given below, and the concluding stanzas added in *1837* are placed within square brackets. A full collation of *Heath A* and *B*, *1837*, and *1855* is given under *Maud*, together with other notes. G. O. Marshall discusses the changes in *PMLA* lxxviii (1963) 225–9.

In its original form of 1833–4, the poem is plainly precipitated by the death of Hallam, and it has many links with *In Memoriam*. *Heath A* is 'an incomplete fragment', dated 1833, consisting of 41 lines (6 stanzas). *Heath B* has 68 lines (10 stanzas). On 19 Sept. 1834 Spedding acknowledged to T., 'I have also the alterations of *Oh that 'twere possible*, improvements I must admit, tho' I own I did not think that could have been' (*Mem.* i 139). Then in Dec. 1836, T. angered Richard Monckton Milnes by refusing to contribute to *The Tribute* (*Mem.* i 157–60). T. relented, and later wrote: 'I have *not* been forgetful; these two poems have been causing me infinite bother to get them into shape; one I cannot send: it is too raw, but as I have made the other double its former size, I hope it will do' (J. Pope-Hennessy, *Monckton Milnes*: *The Years of Promise*, 1949, p. 93). R. W. Rader (p. 6) comments: 'Tennyson finished and published his poem in 1837 against his will, cobbling up an ending for it under pressure because he wished to pacify Milnes and had no other poem to do it with. But that he continued to think of his poem as incomplete (the 1834 version ended unsatisfactorily with "And weep / My whole soul out to thee") is suggested by the existence of a fair copy, dated April, 1838, in which it has been returned to its pre-1837 form; and by the fact that he did not reprint this lovely lyric in the *1842* volumes or in any other collection before *Maud*'. Reviewing *The Tribute*, the *Edinburgh Review* said: 'We do not profess perfectly to understand the somewhat mysterious contribution of Mr Alfred Tennyson, entitled *Stanzas*' (E. F. Shannon, *Tennyson and the Reviewers*, 1952, p. 29). T. later assented to Jowett's opinion that these were his most touching lines (*Mem.* ii 466).

Oh! that 'twere possible,
After long grief and pain,
To find the arms of my true-love
Round me once again!

When I was wont to meet her
In the silent woody places
Of the land that gave me birth,
We stood tranced in long embraces,
Mixt with kisses sweeter, sweeter,
Than any thing on earth.

A shadow flits before me–
Not thou, but like to thee.
Ah God! that it were possible
For one short hour to see
The souls we loved, that they might tell us
What and where they be.

It leads me forth at Evening,
It lightly winds and steals
In a cold white robe before me,
When all my spirit reels
At the shouts, the leagues of lights,
And the roaring of the wheels.

Half the night I waste in sighs,
In a wakeful doze I sorrow
For the hand, the lips, the eyes–
For the meeting of tomorrow,
The delight of happy laughter,
The delight of low replies.

¶ *227.13. God*] Christ *Heath B, 1855.*
*17–22*] *Not Heath A.*
*18. It*] And *Heath B.*
*24*] Half, in dreams I sorrow after *Heath B, 1855.*
*25. For*] *Not Heath B.*
*26*] *Not Heath B.*
*27*] The winsome laughter. *Heath B.*
*28*] *Not Heath B.*

Do I hear the pleasant ditty,
  That I heard her chant of old?
    But I wake–my dream is fled.
Without knowledge, without pity–
  In the shuddering dawn behold,
    By the curtains of my bed,
  That abiding phantom cold.

Then I rise: the eave-drops fall
  And the yellow-vapours choke
    The great city sounding wide;
The day comes–a dull red ball,
  Wrapt in drifts of lurid smoke,
    On the misty river-tide.

Through the hubbub of the market
  I steal, a wasted frame;
It crosseth here, it crosseth there–
Through all that crowd, confused and loud,
  The shadow still the same;
And on my heavy eyelids
    My anguish hangs like shame.

Alas for her that met me,
  That heard me softly call–
Came glimmering through the laurels
  At the quiet even-fall,
In the garden by the turrets
  Of the old Manorial Hall.

Then the broad light glares and beats,
  And the sunk eye flits and fleets,
And will not let me be.
  I loathe the squares and streets,
And the faces that one meets,
  Hearts with no love for me;

*29. Do*] And *Heath B.*
*30. old?*] old; *Heath B.*
*33. dawn*] grey *Heath B.*
*35. abiding*] dreadful *Heath B.*
*35 ∧ 6*] *Heath B, like 1855, had ll. 65–70 here (they are not in Heath A).*
*36–41*] *Not Heath A.*
*39. The*] And *Heath B.*
*40. Wrapt in drifts*] In a drift *Heath B.*
*49–57*] *Not Heath A.*
*55. Then*] *Not Heath B.*

Always I long to creep
To some still cavern deep,
And to weep, and weep and weep
My whole soul out to thee.

Get thee hence, nor come again,
Pass and cease to move about–
Pass, thou death-like type of pain,
Mix not memory with doubt.
'Tis the blot upon the brain
That *will* show itself without.

[Would the happy Spirit descend
In the chamber or the street
As she looks among the blest;
Should I fear to greet my friend,
Or to ask her, 'Take me, sweet,
To the region of thy rest.'

But she tarries in her place,
And I paint the beauteous face
Of the maiden, that I lost,
In my inner eyes again,
Lest my heart be overborne
By the thing I hold in scorn,
By a dull mechanic ghost
And a juggle of the brain.

I can shadow forth my bride
As I knew her fair and kind,
As I wooed her for my wife;
She is lovely by my side
In the silence of my life–
'Tis a phantom of the mind.
'Tis a phantom fair and good;
I can call it to my side,
So to guard my life from ill,
Though its ghastly sister glide
And be moved around me still
With the moving of the blood,
That is moved not of the will.

*65–70*] *See ll. 35 ∧ 6n.*
*66, 68*] *Transposed in Heath B* (Mixing . . .).
*71–6*] *Not Heath B.* In *1855* these lines were incorporated (ll. 54 ∧ 5).
*77–110*] *Not Heath B.* These lines of *1837* found no place in *1855*, except that ll. 83–4 became *Maud* ii 82, 90.

Let it pass, the dreary brow,
Let the dismal face go by.
Will it lead me to the grave?
Then I lose it: it will fly:
Can it overlast the nerves?
Can it overlive the eye?
But the other, like a star,
Through the channel windeth far
Till it fade and fail and die,
To its Archetype that waits,
Clad in light by golden gates–
Clad in light the Spirit waits
To embrace me in the sky.]

## 228 'Break, break, break'

Published *1842*. Written in Lincolnshire one spring (*Mem.* i 190), so presumably before early 1837, when the Tennysons left Somersby, and after Sept. 1833, since it is on the death of Arthur Hallam. Probably spring 1834. Cecilia Tennyson recited it on 16 March 1839 (*Blackwood's* clv (1894) 609). Cp. *In Memoriam*, especially for ll. 11–12; and also the lines which H.T. gave as the germ of *In Memoriam*: 'Where is the voice I loved? ah where / Is that dear hand that I would press? / Lo! the broad heavens cold and bare, / The stars that know not my distress!' For these lines (*Mem.* i 107), see *Hark! the dogs howl* (p. 555).

Break, break, break,
On thy cold gray stones, O Sea!
And I would that my tongue could utter
The thoughts that arise in me.

O well for the fisherman's boy,
That he shouts with his sister at play!
O well for the sailor lad,
That he sings in his boat on the bay!

And the stately ships go on
To their haven under the hill;
But O for the touch of a vanished hand,
And the sound of a voice that is still!

Break, break, break,
At the foot of thy crags, O Sea!
But the tender grace of a day that is dead
Will never come back to me.

# 229 The Lord of Burleigh

Published *1842*. Written 1833–4 (*Heath MS* and *T.Nbk 17*). It is based, as T. observes, on the true story of Sarah Hoggins, who married in 1791 and died 1797. Hazlitt told the story in *New Monthly Magazine* (April 1822), reprinted in *The Picture Galleries in England* (1824), of which T. had a copy (*Lincoln*). Thomas Moore had versified the story, changing the names and giving it a happy ending, in *You remember Ellen* (*Irish Melodies*, collected 1820). FitzGerald says: 'When this poem was read from MS in 1835 I remember the Author doubting if it were not too familiar with its "Let us see the handsome houses, etc.," for public Taste. But a Sister, he said, had liked it: *we* never got it out of our heads from the first hearing; and now is there a greater favourite where English is spoken?'

In her ear he whispers gaily,
    'If my heart by signs can tell,
Maiden, I have watched thee daily,
    And I think thou lov'st me well.'
She replies, in accents fainter,
    'There is none I love like thee.'
He is but a landscape-painter,
    And a village maiden she.
He to lips, that fondly falter,
    Presses his without reproof:
Leads her to the village altar,
    And they leave her father's roof.
'I can make no marriage present:
    Little can I give my wife.
Love will make our cottage pleasant,
    And I love thee more than life.'
They by parks and lodges going
    See the lordly castles stand:
Summer woods, about them blowing,
    Made a murmur in the land.
From deep thought himself he rouses,
    Says to her that loves him well,
'Let us see these handsome houses
    Where the wealthy nobles dwell.'
So she goes by him attended,
    Hears him lovingly converse,
Sees whatever fair and splendid
    Lay betwixt his home and hers;
Parks with oak and chestnut shady,
    Parks and ordered gardens great,
Ancient homes of lord and lady,
    Built for pleasure and for state.

All he shows her makes him dearer:
   Evermore she seems to gaze
On that cottage growing nearer,
   Where they twain will spend their days.
O but she will love him truly!
   He shall have a cheerful home;
She will order all things duly,
   When beneath his roof they come.
Thus her heart rejoices greatly,
   Till a gateway she discerns
With armorial bearings stately,
   And beneath the gate she turns;
Sees a mansion more majestic
   Than all those she saw before:
Many a gallant gay domestic
   Bows before him at the door.
And they speak in gentle murmur,
   When they answer to his call,
While he treads with footstep firmer,
   Leading on from hall to hall.
And, while now she wonders blindly,
   Nor the meaning can divine,
Proudly turns he round and kindly,
   'All of this is mine and thine.'
Here he lives in state and bounty,
   Lord of Burleigh, fair and free,
Not a lord in all the county
   Is so great a lord as he.
All at once the colour flushes
   Her sweet face from brow to chin:
As it were with shame she blushes,
   And her spirit changed within.
Then her countenance all over
   Pale again as death did prove:
But he clasped her like a lover,
   And he cheered her soul with love.
So she strove against her weakness,
   Though at times her spirit sank:
Shaped her heart with woman's meekness
   To all duties of her rank:
And a gentle consort made he,
   And her gentle mind was such

¶ 229.*63–4*. T. comments: 'The mood changes from happiness to unhappiness, and the present tense changes to the past.'
*70. spirit*] *1865*; spirits *1842–63*.

That she grew a noble lady,
  And the people loved her much.
But a trouble weighed upon her,
  And perplexed her, night and morn,
With the burthen of an honour
  Unto which she was not born.
Faint she grew, and ever fainter,
  And she murmured, 'Oh, that he
Were once more that landscape-painter,
  Which did win my heart from me!'
So she drooped and drooped before him,
  Fading slowly from his side:
Three fair children first she bore him,
  Then before her time she died.
Weeping, weeping late and early,
  Walking up and pacing down,
Deeply mourned the Lord of Burleigh,
  Burleigh-house by Stamford-town.
And he came to look upon her,
  And he looked at her and said,
'Bring the dress and put it on her,
  That she wore when she was wed.'
Then her people, softly treading,
  Bore to earth her body, drest
In the dress that she was wed in,
  That her spirit might have rest.

## 230 The Captain

### A Legend of the Navy

Published *1865*. Probably written in its original form 1833–4. *H.Nbk 14* (*A* below) is in eight-line stanzas, with only the closing line of each stanza (instead of alternate lines) having 5 syllables. *H.Nbk 21* (watermarked 1836, *B* below, not in T.'s hand) is in four-line stanzas. All variants from *A* and *B* are below. T. says it was 'possibly suggested by the story told of the ship *Hermione* (1797)', though that was an ordinary mutiny. The details are in I. Schomberg, *Naval Chronology* (1802).

He that only rules by terror
  Doeth grievous wrong.
Deep as Hell I count his error.
  Let him hear my song.

*82. And*] *1865*; As *1842–63*.
¶ 230.*1–4*] *Not A*.
*3*] Would he learn how deep his error *B*.

Brave the Captain was: the seamen
Made a gallant crew,
Gallant sons of English freemen,
Sailors bold and true.
But they hated his oppression,
Stern he was and rash;
So for every light transgression
Doomed them to the lash.
Day by day more harsh and cruel
Seemed the Captain's mood.
Secret wrath like smothered fuel
Burnt in each man's blood.
Yet he hoped to purchase glory,
Hoped to make the name
Of his vessel great in story,
Wheresoe'er he came.
So they past by capes and islands,
Many a harbour-mouth,
Sailing under palmy highlands
Far within the South.
On a day when they were going
O'er the lone expanse,
In the north, her canvas flowing,
Rose a ship of France.
Then the Captain's colour heightened,
Joyful came his speech:

*6*] Were a gallant-minded crew, *A*.
*7*] They were sons . . . *A*; Worthy to be sons of freemen, *B*.
*8*] Firm in battle, sailors true. *A*; English sailors true. *B*.
*10. Stern he was*] Rigid was his mood *A*.
*11. So*] He, *A*; And *B*.
*14*] Did he seem in act and speech. *A*.
*16*] Burnt within the breast of each. *A*.
*17. Yet*] But *A*.
*18. Hoped*] Always hoped *A*.
*21. capes and*] many *A–B*.
*22. Many*] And by many *A*.
*24–7*]
In the waters of the South.
In the waters lightly going,
As the vessel did advance,
All her snowy canvas blowing, *A*
*26. lone*] smooth *B*.
*28. Rose*] Came *A*.
*29. Then the Captain's*] Glad he was: his *A*.
*30*] To their guns his men he sent. *A*.

But a cloudy gladness lightened
In the eyes of each.
'Chase,' he said: the ship flew forward,
And the wind did blow;
Stately, lightly, went she Norward,
Till she neared the foe.
Then they looked at him they hated,
Had what they desired:
Mute with folded arms they waited–
Not a gun was fired.
But they heard the foeman's thunder
Roaring out their doom;
All the air was torn in sunder,
Crashing went the boom,
Spars were splintered, decks were shattered,
Bullets fell like rain;
Over mast and deck were scattered
Blood and brains of men.
Spars were splintered; decks were broken:
Every mother's son–
Down they dropt–no word was spoken–
Each beside his gun.

*32*] In their faces as they went. *A*.
*33–6*] *Not A*.
*33*. *said*] cried *B*.
*35*. *Stately*] Lightly *B*.
*37–9*] Sorrows had they suffered many:
This was what their souls desired:
Not an arm was raised by any: *A*
See ll. 45–50*n*.
*41*. *But*] And *A*.
*42*] Rend the cannons' iron wombs; *A*; Bellow sounding doom; *B*. The transcriber of *B* underlined 'doom' and 'bomb' (l. 44), to draw attention to the imperfect rhyme.
*43*. *torn*] split *B*. *in sunder*] asunder *A*.
*44*] With the singing of the bombs. *A*; With the sounding bomb. *B*.
*45–50*] 'Shall we fight for him we hated?
Let him perish with the rest.'
So with folded arms they waited
And with lips compress.
And their silence was not broken:
Man by man, each mother's son, *A*
*46*. *rain*] *underlined in B* (*the imperfect rhyme with* 'men', *l. 48, is underlined*).
*47*. *scattered*] spattered *B*.
*48*. *and*] with *B*.
*51*. *Down they dropt*] Down they fell *A*; Man by man *B*.
*52*. *Each*] Each man dropt *A*; Dropt *B*.

On the decks as they were lying,
Were their faces grim.
In their blood, as they lay dying,
Did they smile on him.
Those, in whom he had reliance
For his noble name,
With one smile of still defiance
Sold him unto shame.
Shame and wrath his heart confounded,
Pale he turned and red,
Till himself was deadly wounded
Falling on the dead.
Dismal error! fearful slaughter!
Years have wandered by,
Side by side beneath the water
Crew and Captain lie;
There the sunlit ocean tosses
O'er them mouldering,
And the lonely seabird crosses
With one waft of the wing.

## 231 *Mine Host

Printed *Mem.* i 134–5, omitting ll. 5–8. Text from *H.Nbk 16*, noting all variants. Written July 1834, when visiting John Heath.

Yon huddled cloud his motion shifts,
Where, by the tavern on the dale,
The thirsty horseman, nodding, lifts
The creaming horn of corny ale.

54. *faces*] countenances *A*.
57. *had*] placed *A*. *A breaks off with this line.*
59. *one*] a *B*.
65. *Dismal*] Fatal *B*.
69–72]
Rest their angry hearts and never
Hear the winds increase–
Peace be with them now and ever!
May they wake in peace! *B*

*B* underlined the feeble second line.
¶ 231.*1*] *H.MS begins with a fragment*:
The Southwind soughs in gusty fits,
By burning turf the Shepherd sits.

2. *on*] in *Mem.*

Mellowing, like some old cucumber
 That curves and fattens on its bed,
From his own vats, right jolly fare,
 Full thirty suns mine host hath fed.

His tavern is our chief resort,
 For he, whose cellar is his pride,
Gives stouter ale and riper port
 Than any in the countryside.

Mine host is fat, and gray, and wise,
 He strokes his beard before he speaks;
And when he laughs, his little eyes
 Are swallowed in his pampered cheeks.

He brims his beaker to the top,
 With jokes you never heard before,
And sometimes with a twinkling drop
 For those who will not taste it more.

## 232 *The Little Maid

Printed *Mem.* i 146, without ll. 5–8. It was written by Sept. 1834 (*Mem.* i 139), and it appears in two drafts (*A, B*) in *H.Nbk 16* (watermarked 1833) with poems of 1834. None of the MSS quoted below has a title.

Along this glimmering gallery
 A child, she loved to play;
This chamber she was born in. See
 The cradle where she lay.

This was her study, these her books.
 Here lived she all her life.
She touched this mute guitar, and here
 I wooed her for my wife.

*5–8*] *MS*; *not Mem.*
*9. His . . . our*] This . . . their *Mem.*
*20. For*] To *Mem.*
¶ 232.*1. glimmering*] echoing *Hn MS* (*HM 19484*). *gallery*] corridor *B.*
*3*] In this room she was [was she *B*] born; this is *Heath MS.*
*5–8*] *Heath MS, B*; *not Mem*;

She painted this: she broidered that:
 She touched this mute guitar.
This was her Bible: here she sat
 And watched yon evening star. *Hn MS*;

That little garden was her pride,
With yellow groundsel grown.
Those holly-thickets only hide
Her grave–a simple stone.

## 233 *'Fair is that cottage in its place'

Unpublished, *Heath MS*. An early version of *Requiescat* (p. 1185), which was to adapt slightly ll. 1–4 and to replace ll. 5–8, the stanza-form too being modified. Written by Sept. 1834 (*Mem.* i 139).

Fair is that cottage in its place,
Where yon broad water glides,
That sees itself from thatch to base
Dream in the sliding tides.

The dimpling eddies kiss the shore
And in the shingle crisp;
The ripples wrinkle to the door
And round the threshold lisp.

## 234 Sir Galahad

Published *1842*. Written by Sept. 1834 (*Heath MS*, *Mem.* i 139). T. says it was 'intended for something of a male counterpart to *St Agnes*' (*Mem.* i 142; p. 552). See J. M. Kemble's letter, *Sir Launcelot* (p. 502). Cp. *The Holy Grail* (p. 1661).

My good blade carves the casques of men,
My tough lance thrusteth sure,
My strength is as the strength of ten,
Because my heart is pure.

This was her Bible [study *1st reading*]: here she sat:
She touched this silent fife,
This mute guitar: she broidered that:
Here lived she all her life. *A*

*9*] This is her little flower-plot *Heath MS, B.*
*11*] Step by that holly – you will see *Heath MS, B.*

The shattering trumpet shrilleth high,
    The hard brands shiver on the steel,
The splintered spear-shafts crack and fly,
    The horse and rider reel:
They reel, they roll in clanging lists,
    And when the tide of combat stands,
Perfume and flowers fall in showers,
    That lightly rain from ladies' hands.

How sweet are looks that ladies bend
    On whom their favours fall!
For them I battle till the end,
    To save from shame and thrall:
But all my heart is drawn above,
    My knees are bowed in crypt and shrine:
I never felt the kiss of love,
    Nor maiden's hand in mine.
More bounteous aspects on me beam,
    Me mightier transports move and thrill;
So keep I fair through faith and prayer
    A virgin heart in work and will.

When down the stormy crescent goes,
    A light before me swims,
Between dark stems the forest glows,
    I hear a noise of hymns:
Then by some secret shrine I ride;
    I hear a voice but none are there;
The stalls are void, the doors are wide,
    The tapers burning fair.
Fair gleams the snowy altar-cloth,
    The silver vessels sparkle clean,
The shrill bell rings, the censer swings,
    And solemn chaunts resound between.

Sometimes on lonely mountain-meres
    I find a magic bark;
I leap on board: no helmsman steers:
    I float till all is dark.
A gentle sound, an awful light!
    Three angels bear the holy Grail:
With folded feet, in stoles of white,
    On sleeping wings they sail.
Ah, blessèd vision! blood of God!
    My spirit beats her mortal bars,
As down dark tides the glory slides,
    And star-like mingles with the stars.

When on my goodly charger borne
  Through dreaming towns I go,
The cock crows ere the Christmas morn,
  The streets are dumb with snow.
The tempest crackles on the leads,
  And, ringing, springs from brand and mail;
But o'er the dark a glory spreads,
  And gilds the driving hail.
I leave the plain, I climb the height;
  No branchy thicket shelter yields;
But blessèd forms in whistling storms
  Fly o'er waste fens and windy fields.

A maiden knight – to me is given
  Such hope, I know not fear;
I yearn to breathe the airs of heaven
  That often meet me here.
I muse on joy that will not cease,
  Pure spaces clothed in living beams,
Pure lilies of eternal peace,
  Whose odours haunt my dreams;

¶ 234.*50. dreaming*] sleeping *Heath MS 1st reading.* Here and below all variants in *Heath MS* were altered in T.'s hand to *1842*. The variants are discussed by M. J. Donahue, *PQ* xxviii (1949) 326–9.

*53–4*] The frostwind in my helmet hums,
  The tempest crackles on my mail, *Heath MS*

Corrected by T. to *1842* except for 'spinning, rings' in l. 54.

*54. springs*] *1862*; spins *1842–60*.

*55*] Upon the dark a glory comes *Heath MS*.

*56. And*] That *Heath MS*.

*60 ^ 61*] Oh power outsoaring human ken!
  Oh Knighthood chaste and true!
With God, with Angels, and with men
  What is it I may not do?
Not only in the tourney-field
  The unpure are beaten from the fray,
Not only evil customs yield,
  The very stars give way.
Lo! those bright stars which thou hast made,
  They tremble fanned on by thy breath:
Yea Lord! they shine, those lamps of thine
  In Heaven and in the gulphs of Death. *Heath MS*

T. wrote to James Spedding in 1834: 'I dare say you are right about the stanza in *Sir Galahad*' (*Mem.* i 142). There is an earlier draft of this stanza in *T.Nbk 20*, which may not be quoted.

*61–72*] *Transposed with the final stanza in H.Nbk 15.*

And, stricken by an angel's hand,
This mortal armour that I wear,
This weight and size, this heart and eyes,
Are touched, are turned to finest air.

The clouds are broken in the sky,
And through the mountain-walls
A rolling organ-harmony
Swells up, and shakes and falls.
Then move the trees, the copses nod,
Wings flutter, voices hover clear:
'O just and faithful knight of God!
Ride on! the prize is near.'
So pass I hostel, hall, and grange;
By bridge and ford, by park and pale,
All-armed I ride, whate'er betide,
Until I find the holy Grail.

## 235 'Love thou thy land, with love far-brought'

Published *1842*. Written, according to *Mat.* i 173, in 1832, but more probably 1833–4, judging by its place in *Heath MS* and in *T.Nbk 17*. T. sent it to James Spedding in Sept. 1834, including corrections and variants (*Lincoln*). Cp. the many political poems of 1831–4, especially those also in the *In Memoriam* stanza, including *Hail Briton* (p. 480). There are three drafts in the *T.Nbk* (which may not be quoted), the earliest of which is half the length of *1842*, being for example without ll. 69–92. This version included l. 40 of *Freedom*, a poem which it stood next to in the Notebook.

Love thou thy land, with love far-brought
From out the storied Past, and used
Within the Present, but transfused
Through future time by power of thought.

True love turned round on fixèd poles,
Love, that endures not sordid ends,
For English natures, freemen, friends,
Thy brothers and immortal souls.

But pamper not a hasty time,
Nor feed with crude imaginings
The herd, wild hearts and feeble wings
That every sophister can lime.

Deliver not the tasks of might
To weakness, neither hide the ray
From those, not blind, who wait for day,
Though sitting girt with doubtful light.

Make knowledge circle with the winds;
But let her herald, Reverence, fly
Before her to whatever sky
Bear seed of men and growth of minds.

Watch what main-currents draw the years:
Cut Prejudice against the grain:
But gentle words are always gain:
Regard the weakness of thy peers:

Nor toil for title, place, or touch
Of pension, neither count on praise:
It grows to guerdon after-days:
Nor deal in watch-words overmuch:

Not clinging to some ancient saw;
Not mastered by some modern term;
Not swift nor slow to change, but firm:
And in its season bring the law;

That from Discussion's lip may fall
With Life, that, working strongly, binds–
Set in all lights by many minds,
To close the interests of all.

For Nature also, cold and warm,
And moist and dry, devising long,

¶ 235.*9*. Cp. *What Thor Said* 4: 'But pap-meat-pamper not the time'.
*11–12*. Adapted from *Sonnet* [*The Wise, the Pure*] 3–4: 'Wild hearts, whom their own rage and heat consume, / Weak wings, that every sophister can lime.' This sonnet also has 'idol' (cp. l. 69). *lime*: catch a bird with quicklime.
*17–18*. Adapted for *In Memoriam*: *Prologue* 25–6: 'Let knowledge grow from more to more, / But more of reverence in us dwell.'
*20. and*] *1843*; or *1842*.
*27. guerdon*: to reward.
*33. That*: i.e. the law.
*37–40*. G. R. Potter, *PQ* xvi (1937) 334–5, warns against taking this as

Through many agents making strong,
Matures the individual form.

Meet is it changes should control
Our being, lest we rust in ease.
We all are changed by still degrees,
All but the basis of the soul.

So let the change which comes be free
To ingroove itself with that which flies,
And work, a joint of state, that plies
Its office, moved with sympathy.

A saying, hard to shape in act;
For all the past of Time reveals
A bridal dawn of thunder-peals,
Wherever Thought hath wedded Fact.

Even now we hear with inward strife
A motion toiling in the gloom–
The Spirit of the years to come
Yearning to mix himself with Life.

A slow-developed strength awaits
Completion in a painful school;
Phantoms of other forms of rule,
New Majesties of mighty States–

The warders of the growing hour,
But vague in vapour, hard to mark;
And round them sea and air are dark
With great contrivances of Power.

Darwinian evolution, since there is no suggestion that one develops from the other.
*40. individual*: indivisible.
*41–4.* Cp. *I loving Freedom* 21–4: 'A mightier change may come to pass, / Than ever yet their fathers saw / To those that change by just degrees / With reason and with law.'
*49–51*] Hard words to render into Act!
All Time a cloudy dawn reveals
That rises rolling thunder-peals *Heath MS*
T.'s letter to Spedding (*Lincoln*) deplores this stanza, noting that it was originally 'in a different metre', *abab*.
*53. inward strife*: *Ode: O Bosky Brook* 89.
*56.* Cp. *Hail Briton* 160: 'yearns to mix in one'.
*61–2*] They heighten tower after tower / Deep in the vapour . . . *Heath MS 1st reading*.

Of many changes, aptly joined,
Is bodied forth the second whole.
Regard gradation, lest the soul
Of Discord race the rising wind;

A wind to puff your idol-fires,
And heap their ashes on the head;
To shame the boast so often made,
That we are wiser than our sires.

Oh yet, if Nature's evil star
Drive men in manhood, as in youth,
To follow flying steps of Truth
Across the brazen bridge of war–

If New and Old, disastrous feud,
Must ever shock, like armèd foes,
And this be true, till Time shall close,
That Principles are rained in blood;

Not yet the wise of heart would cease
To hold his hope through shame and guilt,
But with his hand against the hilt,
Would pace the troubled land, like Peace;

Not less, though dogs of Faction bay,
Would serve his kind in deed and word,
Certain, if knowledge bring the sword,
That knowledge takes the sword away–

Would love the gleams of good that broke
From either side, nor veil his eyes:
And if some dreadful need should rise
Would strike, and firmly, and one stroke:

Tomorrow yet would reap today,
As we bear blossom of the dead;
Earn well the thrifty months, nor wed
Raw Haste, half-sister to Delay.

68. *the rising wind*: 'of revolutionary change' (H.T.).
71. *boast . . . made*] *1843*; boasting words, we said *1842*; boast of Diomed *Heath MS*.
72. Cp. *The Epic* 32 ∧ 3, MS: 'Old things are gone: we are wiser than our Sires'.
76. The path between battle-lines, *Iliad* viii 553; so translated in T.'s *Specimen of a Translation* 9.
89. Cp. *Hail Briton* 96 ∧ 7, MS B (p. 485): 'The visionary gleam of good'.
95. *Earn*: glean (Yorkshire dialect).

# 236 'Of old sat Freedom on the heights'

Published *1842*. Written *c.* 1833, according to H.T. The note in vol. i of *1842* spoke of the six poems 'which, with one exception, were written in 1833'. The placing in *Heath MS* suggests possibly 1834; T. quoted ll. 13–20 to James Spedding in Sept. 1834 (*Mem.* i 141–2). T. at one stage incorporated those eight lines in *Freedom*, an early draft of which (*c.* 1833) is in *T.Nbk 17*. T. was to give the temporary title *Freedom* to *Of old* in *1865*. Cp. the other political poems of 1832–4. T. draws on the traditional association of freedom and the mountains, as in Milton's 'Mountain-Nymph, sweet Liberty', *L'Allegro* 36; Coleridge's 'the bloodless freedom of the mountaineer', *France* 77; and Wordsworth's sonnet 'Advance–come forth from thy Tyrolean ground, / Dear Liberty!' Cp. *Montenegro* (p. 1239).

Of old sat Freedom on the heights,
  The thunders breaking at her feet:
Above her shook the starry lights:
  She heard the torrents meet.

There in her place she did rejoice,
  Self-gathered in her prophet-mind,
But fragments of her mighty voice
  Came rolling on the wind.

Then stept she down through town and field
  To mingle with the human race,
And part by part to men revealed
  The fulness of her face–

Grave mother of majestic works,
  From her isle-altar gazing down,
Who, God-like, grasps the triple forks,
  And, King-like, wears the crown:

¶ 236.5. *There in her place*] *1851*; Within her place *1842–50*; Among the rocks *Heath MS 1st reading.*

7. Cp. *The Gardener's Daughter* 229: 'the silver fragments of a broken voice'.

15. T. comments: 'Like Zeus with his *trisulca fulmina*, the thunderbolts'. As in *Semele* 4–5: 'His mighty hands are twined / About the triple forks'.

Her open eyes desire the truth.
The wisdom of a thousand years
Is in them. May perpetual youth
Keep dry their light from tears;

That her fair form may stand and shine,
Make bright our days and light our dreams,
Turning to scorn with lips divine
The falsehood of extremes!

# 237 England and America in 1782

Published *New York Ledger*, 6 Jan. 1872; then 1874, Cabinet Edition. T. 'had been offered £1000 by the *New York Ledger* for any poem of 3 stanzas' (*Mat.* iii 177). This version was sent 10 Nov. 1871 (*Mem.* ii 110), but T. was adapting a poem originally written in 1832–4. The early version is at *Harvard* (*MS Eng. 952.6*), along with *I loving Freedom* (p. 619) and *O mother Britain* (p. 622); there it has no title. All variants from this MS are below. *H.Lpr 50* is entitled *Thoughts of a liberal Englishman anno 17–*; see ll. 10 ∧ 11*n*. T. had thought of incorporating ll. 16–20 in *Ode on Wellington* (1852), *T.Nbk 25*. *1782*: the end of the War of Independence. Cp. the appeal to America for aid, in *Hands All Round!* [*1852*] (p. 1002).

O thou, that sendest out the man
To rule by land and sea,
Strong mother of a Lion-line,
Be proud of those strong sons of thine
Who wrenched their rights from thee!

*18.* Edmund Blunden's selection (1960) suggests that this hints at King Alfred. Cp. *Ode on Wellington* 188: 'Truth-teller was our England's Alfred named'.

*21. That . . . may*] Hail Titan-statue! *Heath MS.*

¶ 237.*1–5*] O! thou, the centre of the world,
That sendest out the ships,
Give welcome when they come from far,
The freemen of the western star –
Be friendly with thy lips. *H.MS Eng.*

What wonder, if in noble heat
 Those men thine arms withstood,
Retaught the lesson thou hadst taught,
And in thy spirit with thee fought–
 Who sprang from English blood!

But Thou rejoice with liberal joy,
 Lift up thy rocky face,
And shatter, when the storms are black,
In many a streaming torrent back,
 The seas that shock thy base!

Whatever harmonies of law
 The growing world assume,
Thy work is thine–The single note
From that deep chord which Hampden smote
 Will vibrate to the doom.

# 238 *'I loving Freedom for herself'

Unpublished, except ll. 1–8, *Mem.* i 41. Text from *H.MS Eng. 952.6*, giving below all variants from *H.Nbk 16*. Written 1832–4. Cp. the other political poems of this time (the Reform Bill, 1832), especially *Hail Briton* (p. 480), and for T.'s politics see *Mem.* i 41–2. For T.'s adaptation of phrases for later poems, see footnotes. The marking of the MS suggests that it originally ended after l. 48, and then after l. 52.

*7. Those*] These *MS.Eng.*
*10*] For they were British blood? *MS.Eng.*
*10 ^ 11*] Their speech is thine, their vigour thine,
 Another Thou begun.
 Behold, were Europe lost in night,
 The stars of freedom, there a light
 Beyond our darkened sun. *H.Lpr 50*
*11–15*] *Not MS.Eng.*
*16–20.* See headnote.
*17. growing*] future *MS.Eng.*
*18. single*] warning *MS.Eng.*
*19*] The single [On that strong *1st reading*] chord that Hampden smote *MS Eng.* John Hampden refused to pay ship-money to Charles I; cp. *Hail Briton* 57–60: 'Not such was Hampden when he broke / Indignant from a silent life, / A single voice before the strife / That, as it were a people, spoke.'

I loving Freedom for herself,
And much of that which is her form,
Wed to no faction in the state,
A voice before the storm–

I mourn in spirit, when I think
The year that comes may come with shame
Lured by the cuckoo-tongue that loves
To babble its own name–

That brings us tales across the sea
Of newer lands, a fresher sky:
But that which prospers in the green
May perish in the dry.

I trust the leaders of the land
May well surmount the coming shock
By climbing steps their fathers carved
Within the living rock.

The state within herself concludes
The power to change, as in the seed,
The model of her future form,
And liberty indeed.

A mightier change may come to pass,
Than ever yet their fathers saw

¶ 238.1] *H.Nbk 16 precedes the opening with the fragment*:

I would this people were to me
As is a single friend.

*1–4*. Cp. Shelley, *Prologue to Hellas* 108–9: 'Upon the name of Freedom; from the storm / Of faction'.

*7. tongue*] voice *MS*. Cp. *Hail Briton* 45–6: 'For babbling voices vex the days / We live in'.

*9–12*] *Not MS.*

*11–12*. Cp. *In Memoriam* lxxv 13: 'Thy leaf has perished in the green'.

*13*] I trust the spirits of the time *MS*.

*13–16*. Cp. *In Memoriam* cxxxi 1–4: 'living will . . . suffer shock . . . spiritual rock.'

*14. well*] yet *MS*.

*17–20*. Cp. the political parable in *The Progress of Spring* 113–5, written *c.* 1833: 'Thy warmths from bud to bud / Accomplish that blind model in the seed, / And men have hopes . . .'

*17. concludes*] contains *MS*.

*18. The . . . change*] A vital strength *MS*.

To those that change by just degrees
With reason and with law.

What nobler than an ancient land
That passing an august decree
Makes wider in a settled peace
The lists of liberty?

What baser than a land that falls
From freedom crying on her name
Through cycles of disastrous change
To forge the links of shame?

The full-drawn circle meets itself–
The waves are laid, the winds are gone:
The tyranny of all begins
The tyranny of one.

Clean temple of the Memory,
Save thou for ever, carved in gold,
The name that such a patriot wears
Who dares be wise and bold,

To pluck us backward from a time,
When only to be bold shall be
The whole of wisdom and the last
Resource of liberty.

*23.* Cp. *Love thou thy land* 43: 'We all are changed by still degrees'; another political poem of this date.

*24 ∧ 5*]
I trust that England may be saved
On this her ancient eminence
By that which saved her many times,
The strength of common sense. *MS*

*25–8.* Cp. *To the Queen* 31–3: 'and make / The bounds of freedom wider yet // By shaping some august decree.'

*30. crying on her*] blushing freedom's *MS.*

*32. To forge the*] Still forging her own *MS.*

*34*] Our hearts are tired – our vigour gone: *MS.*

*35–6.* Adapted for *Tiresias* 74–5, begun at this date: 'My counsel that the tyranny of all / Led backward to the tyranny of one.' T.'s following lines therefore suggest *Tiresias* 116–20: 'No sound is breathed so potent to coerce, / And to conciliate, as their names who dare / For that sweet mother land which gave them birth / Nobly to do, nobly to die. Their names, / Graven on memorial columns, are a song . . .'

*37–44*] *Not MS.*

But though the worst should find the worst,
    The world would earn her second youth.
Confusion, Order, Peace and War
    Are ministers of Truth.

Cold comfort since to human will
    There seems a blessing and a curse,
Two paths to every human end,
    A better and a worse.

Cold comfort unto thee and me
    But yet a comfort, proving still
There lives a power to shape our ends
    Rough-hew them as we will!

## 239 *'O mother Britain lift thou up'

Unpublished, *H.MS Eng. 952.6.* Written 1832–4; cp. the other patriotic poems of this date, especially *England and America in 1782* (p. 618), and *Love thou thy land* (p. 613).

O mother Britain lift thou up,
    Lift up a joyful brow,
There lies not in the circled seas
    A land so great as thou.

O let the far-off shores be glad,
    The isles break out in song,
For thou didst buy them with a price
    To ransom them from wrong.

A time may come: this world of men
    Shall roll in broader light,
But never shall this world forget
    Who taught the peoples right.

45–6] If this should happen, not the less
    The world will have another youth. *MS*

49–56] *Not MS.*

55–6. *Hamlet* V ii 10–11: 'There's a divinity that shapes our ends, / Rough-hew them how we will.'

O let the hills of canes rejoice,
The palmy valleys ring!
What other people old or young
Had done so just a thing?

A time may come. Forgotten Thames
May curve his dreary rounds
By ruined hearths and heaps of brick
And Babylonian mounds.

But thy good deed shall never die,
It spreads from shore to shore,
And with the sun and moon renews
Its light for evermore.

[1833. *Freedom* – see p. 1339]

# 240 The Blackbird

Published *1842*. Written about 1833 (H.T.). It is one of the six poems added in vol. i of *1842*, 'which, with one exception, were written in 1833'. T. sent it to James Spedding in Sept. 1834 (*Lincoln*). The stanza-form is that of *In Memoriam*, and of the poem which accompanied *The Blackbird* in the letter to Spedding, *Love thou thy land*.

O blackbird! sing me something well:
While all the neighbours shoot thee round,
I keep smooth plats of fruitful ground,
Where thou mayst warble, eat and dwell.

The espaliers and the standards all
Are thine; the range of lawn and park:
The unnetted black-hearts ripen dark,
All thine, against the garden wall.

Yet, though I spared thee all the spring,
Thy sole delight is, sitting still,
With that gold dagger of thy bill
To fret the summer jenneting.

¶ 239.*21–4*. Cp. *The Princess* iii 237–9: 'great deeds cannot die; / They with the sun and moon renew their light / For ever.'

¶ 240.*5*. *espaliers*: trees trained on lattices. *standards*: erect trees.

*7*. *black-hearts*: cultivated cherries.

*9*. *all the spring*] *1853*; kith and kin *1842–51*.

*12*. *jenneting*] *1853*; jennetin *1842–51*. An early apple.

A golden bill! the silver tongue,
    Cold February loved, is dry:
    Plenty corrupts the melody
That made thee famous once, when young:

And in the sultry garden-squares,
    Now thy flute-notes are changed to coarse,
    I hear thee not at all, or hoarse
As when a hawker hawks his wares.

Take warning! he that will not sing
    While yon sun prospers in the blue,
    Shall sing for want, ere leaves are new,
Caught in the frozen palms of Spring.

## 241 The Day-Dream

One section, *The Sleeping Beauty*, was published *1830*; the whole sequence was published *1842*. It was completed by *c.* June 1834 (*Mem.* i 134), except for the *Prologue* and *Epilogue*, which were 'added after 1835 (when the poem was written), for the same reason that caused the Prologue of the *Morte d'Arthur*, giving an excuse for telling an old-world [Fairy-] tale' (FitzGerald). This resemblance to *The Epic* might suggest 1837–8 for the *Prologue* and *Epilogue*. Perhaps it became tinged with T.'s feelings for Rosa Baring in 1833–4. The whole sequence is in *T.Nbk 26* (which may not be quoted), where *Moral* was at first called *Epilogue*, and where *L'Envoi* at one stage concluded the sequence.

### PROLOGUE

O Lady Flora, let me speak:
    A pleasant hour has passed away
While, dreaming on your damask cheek,
    The dewy sister-eyelids lay.
As by the lattice you reclined,
    I went through many wayward moods
To see you dreaming–and, behind,
    A summer crisp with shining woods.

*17*] *1843*; I better brook the drawling stares, *1842*. That is, starlings.

*18–19*. Cp. *Paradise Lost* vii 24–5: 'unchang'd / To hoarse'.

*19*. *I . . . not*] *1843*; Not hearing thee *1842*.

¶ 241. *Prologue*

*4*. *dewy sister-eyelids*: *To Rosa* ii 10 (1836).

*8*. Adapted from *The Gardener's Daughter* 29–31, MS: 'crisp with shining woods / And summer holts'. At one stage T. thought of using this in *Edwin Morris* (*T.Nbk 26*).

And I too dreamed, until at last
Across my fancy, brooding warm,
The reflex of a legend past,
And loosely settled into form.
And would you have the thought I had,
And see the vision that I saw,
Then take the broidery-frame, and add
A crimson to the quaint Macaw,
And I will tell it. Turn your face,
Nor look with that too-earnest eye—
The rhymes are dazzled from their place,
And ordered words asunder fly.

## THE SLEEPING PALACE

I

The varying year with blade and sheaf
Clothes and reclothes the happy plains,
Here rests the sap within the leaf,
Here stays the blood along the veins.
Faint shadows, vapours lightly curled,
Faint murmurs from the meadows come,
Like hints and echoes of the world
To spirits folded in the womb.

II

Soft lustre bathes the range of urns
On every slanting terrace-lawn.
The fountain to his place returns
Deep in the garden lake withdrawn.
Here droops the banner on the tower,
On the hall-hearths the festal fires,
The peacock in his laurel bower,
The parrot in his gilded wires.

15. *Then*] *1853*; So *1842–51*.

*The Sleeping Palace*
3. *rests*] stays *H.Nbk 15 1st reading*.
4. *stays*] sleeps *MS 1st reading*.
8. *folded*] dreaming *MS 1st reading*.
9. Cp. Shelley, *Rosalind* 832: 'lustre bright and soft', a passage which might have come to T.'s mind because it describes how 'Sudden sleep would seize him oft / Like death, so calm'.
13. *droops*] rests *MS 1st reading*.

III

Roof-haunting martins warm their eggs:
In these, in those the life is stayed.
The mantles from the golden pegs
Droop sleepily: no sound is made,
Not even of a gnat that sings.
More like a picture seemeth all
Than those old portraits of old kings,
That watch the sleepers from the wall.

IV

Here sits the Butler with a flask
Between his knees, half-drained; and there
The wrinkled steward at his task,
The maid-of-honour blooming fair;
The page has caught her hand in his:
Her lips are severed as to speak:
His own are pouted to a kiss:
The blush is fixed upon her cheek.

V

Till all the hundred summers pass,
The beams, that through the Oriel shine,
Make prisms in every carven glass,
And beaker brimmed with noble wine.
Each baron at the banquet sleeps,
Grave faces gathered in a ring.
His state the king reposing keeps.
He must have been a jovial king.

*17*] He heard the ringdoves warm their eggs: *MS 1st reading*. Cp. *Macbeth* I vi 4: 'temple-haunting martlet'.

*21. gnat*] midge *MS*.

*26. and there*] by him *MS revision*.

*28*] The waiting woman tight and trim *MS*; The waiting woman spruce and fair *MS 1st reading*. With *MS*, cp. *Edwin Morris* 46–7: 'a dame in-doors, that trims us up, / And keeps us tight'.

*33. Till all*] When will *MS 1st reading*.

*34. through the Oriel*] o'er the dais *MS 1st reading*.

*36. noble*] glowing *MS revision*.

*37. baron*] noble *MS*.

*37–40*]
The guests are strown on couch and floor,
His state the king reposing keeps.
They neither nod, or dream, or snore,
The mind, the heart, the breathing sleeps. *MS 1st reading*

Line 38 was inserted subsequently.

*40. jovial*] *1853*; jolly *1842–51*.

VI

All round a hedge upshoots, and shows
At distance like a little wood;
Thorns, ivies, woodbine, mistletoes,
And grapes with bunches red as blood;
All creeping plants, a wall of green
Close-matted, bur and brake and briar,
And glimpsing over these, just seen,
High up, the topmost palace spire.

VII

When will the hundred summers die,
And thought and time be born again,
And newer knowledge, drawing nigh,
Bring truth that sways the soul of men?
Here all things in their place remain,
As all were ordered, ages since.
Come, Care and Pleasure, Hope and Pain,
And bring the fated fairy Prince.

## THE SLEEPING BEAUTY

I

Year after year unto her feet,
She lying on her couch alone,
Across the purple coverlet,
The maiden's jet-black hair has grown,
On either side her trancèd form
Forth streaming from a braid of pearl:
The slumbrous light is rich and warm,
And moves not on the rounded curl.

II

The silk star-broidered coverlid
Unto her limbs itself doth mould
Languidly ever; and, amid
Her full black ringlets downward rolled,
Glows forth each softly-shadowed arm
With bracelets of the diamond bright:
Her constant beauty doth inform
Stillness with love, and day with light.

*46. bur and*] tendril *MS.*
*54. were*] was *MS 1st reading.*

*The Sleeping Beauty*
*2*] *1842*; The while she slumbereth alone, *1830.*
*3. Across*] *1842*; Over *1830.* *purple*] *1884*; purpled *1830–83.*
*4. has*] *1842*; hath *1830.*
*9. star-broidered*] *1842*; starbraided *1830.*

III

She sleeps: her breathings are not heard
 In palace chambers far apart.
The fragrant tresses are not stirred
 That lie upon her charmèd heart.
She sleeps: on either hand upswells
 The gold-fringed pillow lightly prest:
She sleeps, nor dreams, but ever dwells
 A perfect form in perfect rest.

### THE ARRIVAL

I

All precious things, discovered late,
 To those that seek them issue forth;
For love in sequel works with fate,
 And draws the veil from hidden worth.
He travels far from other skies–
 His mantle glitters on the rocks–
A fairy Prince, with joyful eyes,
 And lighter-footed than the fox.

II

The bodies and the bones of those
 That strove in other days to pass,
Are withered in the thorny close,
 Or scattered blanching on the grass.
He gazes on the silent dead:
 'They perished in their daring deeds.'
This proverb flashes through his head,
 'The many fail: the one succeeds.'

III

He comes, scarce knowing what he seeks:
 He breaks the hedge: he enters there:
The colour flies into his cheeks:
 He trusts to light on something fair;

*21. hand*] *1842*; side *1830*.

*The Arrival*
*4. veil*] cloud *MS.*
*6*] And lighter-footed than the pard, *MS.*
*8*] In azure samite silver starred. *MS.*
*9–16*] *Not MS.*
*12. on*] *1853*; in *1842–51*.
*18. he*] and *MS.*
*19. flies*] comes *MS.*

For all his life the charm did talk
About his path, and hover near
With words of promise in his walk,
And whispered voices at his ear.

IV

More close and close his footsteps wind:
The Magic Music in his heart
Beats quick and quicker, till he find
The quiet chamber far apart.
His spirit flutters like a lark,
He stoops–to kiss her–on his knee.
'Love, if thy tresses be so dark,
How dark those hidden eyes must be!'

### THE REVIVAL

I

A touch, a kiss! the charm was snapt.
There rose a noise of striking clocks,
And feet that ran, and doors that clapt,
And barking dogs, and crowing cocks;
A fuller light illumined all,
A breeze through all the garden swept,
A sudden hubbub shook the hall,
And sixty feet the fountain leapt.

II

The hedge broke in, the banner blew,
The butler drank, the steward scrawled,
The fire shot up, the martin flew,
The parrot screamed, the peacock squalled,
The maid and page renewed their strife,
The palace banged, and buzzed and clackt,
And all the long-pent stream of life
Dashed downward in a cataract.

21. *talk*] keep *MS.*
22. *his . . . and*] him and did *MS.*
23. *walk*] sleep *MS.*
24. *at*] *1851*; in *1842–50.*
25. *close and close*] near and near *MS.*
26. Cp. 'magic music' as a Christmas game, *The Princess*: *Prologue* 192. The music is loud and fast when the seeker is 'warm'; soft and slow when he is 'cold'.
27. *Beats quick*] Plays quicker *MS.*

III

And last with these the king awoke,
  And in his chair himself upreared,
And yawned, and rubbed his face, and spoke,
  'By holy rood, a royal beard!
How say you? we have slept, my lords.
  My beard has grown into my lap.'
The barons swore, with many words,
  'Twas but an after-dinner's nap.

IV

'Pardy,' returned the king, 'but still
  My joints are somewhat stiff or so.
My lord, and shall we pass the bill
  I mentioned half an hour ago?'
The chancellor, sedate and vain,
  In courteous words returned reply:
But dallied with his golden chain,
  And, smiling, put the question by.

THE DEPARTURE

I

And on her lover's arm she leant,
  And round her waist she felt it fold,
And far across the hills they went
  In that new world which is the old:
Across the hills, and far away
  Beyond their utmost purple rim,
And deep into the dying day
  The happy princess followed him.

II

'I'd sleep another hundred years,
  O love, for such another kiss;'
'O wake for ever, love,' she hears,
  'O love, 'twas such as this and this.'
And o'er them many a sliding star,
  And many a merry wind was borne,
And, streamed through many a golden bar,
  The twilight melted into morn.

*The Revival*

17. *with these*] *1853*; of all *1842–51*.

26. *somewhat*] *1862*; something *1842–60*.

*The Departure*

4. 'The world of Love' (T.).

13. *sliding*: traditional diction in such a context. Cp. Dryden, *Palamon*

III

'O eyes long laid in happy sleep!'
'O happy sleep, that lightly fled!'
'O happy kiss, that woke thy sleep!'
'O love, thy kiss would wake the dead!'
And o'er them many a flowing range
Of vapour buoyed the crescent-bark,
And, rapt through many a rosy change,
The twilight died into the dark.

IV

'A hundred summers! can it be?
And whither goest thou, tell me where?'
'O seek my father's court with me,
For there are greater wonders there.'
And o'er the hills, and far away
Beyond their utmost purple rim,
Beyond the night, across the day,
Through all the world she followed him.

MORAL

I

So, Lady Flora, take my lay,
And if you find no moral there,
Go, look in any glass and say,
What moral is in being fair.
Oh, to what uses shall we put
The wildweed-flower that simply blows?
And is there any moral shut
Within the bosom of the rose?

II

But any man that walks the mead,
In bud or blade, or bloom, may find,
According as his humours lead,
A meaning suited to his mind.
And liberal applications lie
In Art like Nature, dearest friend;
So 'twere to cramp its use, if I
Should hook it to some useful end.

*and Arcite* iii 129–33: 'Creator Venus, genial power of love, / The bliss of men below and gods above! / Beneath the sliding sun thou runn'st thy race, / Dost fairest shine, and best become thy place; / For thee the winds their eastern blasts forbear . . .'

## L'ENVOI

I

You shake your head. A random string
  Your finer female sense offends.
Well–were it not a pleasant thing
  To fall asleep with all one's friends;
To pass with all our social ties
  To silence from the paths of men;
And every hundred years to rise
  And learn the world, and sleep again;
To sleep through terms of mighty wars,
  And wake on science grown to more,
On secrets of the brain, the stars,
  As wild as aught of fairy lore;
And all that else the years will show,
  The Poet-forms of stronger hours,
The vast Republics that may grow,
  The Federations and the Powers;
Titanic forces taking birth
  In divers seasons, divers climes;
For we are Ancients of the earth,
  And in the morning of the times.

II

So sleeping, so aroused from sleep
  Through sunny decads new and strange,
Or gay quinquenniads would we reap
  The flower and quintessence of change.

III

Ah, yet would I–and would I might!
  So much your eyes my fancy take–
Be still the first to leap to light
  That I might kiss those eyes awake!
For, am I right, or am I wrong,
  To choose your own you did not care;
You'd have *my* moral from the song,
  And I will take my pleasure there:

*L'Envoi*

*10–12.* Cp. *Locksley Hall* 12: 'With the fairy tales of science, and the long result of Time'.

*16.* Cp. *Locksley Hall* 128: 'the Parliament of man, the Federation of the world'.

*24.* Cp. *In Memoriam* lxi 4, MS: 'The flower and quintessence of Time'.

And, am I right or am I wrong,
My fancy, ranging through and through,
To search a meaning for the song,
Perforce will still revert to you;
Nor finds a closer truth than this
All-graceful head, so richly curled,
And evermore a costly kiss
The prelude to some brighter world.

IV

For since the time when Adam first
Embraced his Eve in happy hour,
And every bird of Eden burst
In carol, every bud to flower,
What eyes, like thine, have wakened hopes,
What lips, like thine, so sweetly joined?
Where on the double rosebud droops
The fulness of the pensive mind;
Which all too dearly self-involved,
Yet sleeps a dreamless sleep to me;
A sleep by kisses undissolved,
That lets thee neither hear nor see:
But break it. In the name of wife,
And in the rights that name may give,
Are clasped the moral of thy life,
And that for which I care to live.

EPILOGUE

So, Lady Flora, take my lay,
And, if you find a meaning there,
O whisper to your glass, and say,
'What wonder, if he thinks me fair?'
What wonder I was all unwise,
To shape the song for your delight
Like long-tailed birds of Paradise
That float through Heaven, and cannot light?
Or old-world trains, upheld at court
By Cupid-boys of blooming hue–
But take it–earnest wed with sport,
And either sacred unto you.

47. 'A recollection of the bust of Clyte' (T.). Clyte watches Apollo leaving her; T. had a bust of her at High Beech (*Mem.* i 151).
49. *Which . . . dearly*] *1843*; The pensive mind that *1842*.
52. *That*] *1843*; Which *1842*.

*Epilogue*
*7–8*. In legend they do not alight.

# 242 *'Thy rosy lips are soft and sweet'

Printed by H. D. Rawnsley, *Memories of the Tennysons* (1900), p. 63. It is the first of T.'s verses to Rosa Baring, a beautiful and rich girl who lived two miles from Somersby. He was disillusioned by the end of 1836. She married in 1838. See *Early Verses of Compliment* (below), and *To Rosa* (p. 648). The most important of those poems that relate to T.'s disillusionment with her and with 'marriage-hindering Mammon' are *Locksley Hall*, *Edwin Morris*, and *Maud*. The present poem was written for Rosa's birthday, 23 Sept. 1834 (Rader, p. 130).

Thy rosy lips are soft and sweet,
Thy fairy form is so complete,
Thy motions are so airy free,
Love lays his armour at thy feet
And yields his bow to thee;
Take any dart from out his quiver
And pierce what heart thou wilt for ever.

# 243 *Early Verses of Compliment to Miss Rose Baring

Printed by K. W. Gransden, *The Book Collector* iv (1955) 160–1. Stanzas had been quoted by M. Luce, *Tennyson* (1901), pp. 155–6. The text is in F. T. Palgrave's hand in the British Museum; T. recited it to him at Farringford in 1854. For T.'s love-affair with Rosa Baring, see *Thy rosy lips* (above). Written *c.* 1834.

June on many a flower reposes,
Many a blossom May discloses,
  But in Autumn unto me
Blooms a rose, the rose of roses.

Rose of roses, bliss of blisses,
Rosebud-lips for honey-kisses;
  East and West and North and South
Bear not such a rose as this is.

¶ 243.*5–6*. Keatsian; cp. 'honey-feel of bliss', 'One kiss brings honey-dew', *Endymion* i 903, ii 7.

Perfect world of winning graces,
Music-made for Love's embraces,
Many a face I see, but thine
Sweeter than all human faces.

Rose of roses, bliss of blisses,
What care I for others' kisses?
When a thousand years are dead
Comes there no such rose as this is.

Love and fancy shape caresses,
Twenty million tendernesses;
All my life and heart and soul
Tangle in her shining tresses.

Rose of roses, bliss of blisses,
Were not thine the kiss of kisses?
Ah! for such a kiss as that!
Ah! for such a rose as this is!

# 244 *The Rosebud

Published in E. V. Boyle's *Ros Rosarum* (1885), as 'Unpublished fragment'; not reprinted. The title is from *Mem.* ii 311. Written *c.* 1834, on Rosa Baring; see *Thy rosy lips* (p. 634). Rader (p. 136) quotes W. D. Paden's remarks on the likeness to Rosa's Harrington Hall; and T.'s words are close to those of H. D. Rawnsley: the Hall 'faced westward, and smiled a rosy welcome across the level meadows to all who came from the direction of Somersby' (*Memories of the Tennysons*, 1900, p. 15). It is in *T.Nbk 21* (which may not be quoted), where there is an extra line opening the poem (on kneeling in the flowers), and also an extra line, ll. 3 ∧ 4 (describing Love). Cp. *Maud* i 857, 882: 'And the planet of Love is on high', 'And the soul of the rose went into my blood'.

The night with sudden odour reeled,
The southern stars a music pealed,
Warm beams across the meadow stole;
For Love flew over grove and field,
Said, 'Open, Rosebud, open, yield
Thy fragrant soul.'

*13–14.* Maud (whose story is based on T.'s love of Rosa) was 'rose of the rosebud garden'; and the hero asked 'What care I' (i 902, 639).
*16.* Cp. *The Princess* vii 229: 'When comes another such?'
*21. bliss of blisses*: rhyming with 'kisses', this is from *Hero to Leander* 10–12 (p. 228).

## 245 *'Sweet, ask me not why I am sad'

Printed by H. D. Rawnsley, *Memories of the Tennysons* (1900), p. 64: 'Another of the Lincolnshire girls in the Somersby neighbourhood who knew him well in his boyhood's day was my aunt, Sophy Rawnsley. She was a special favourite .... It was in mind of her he wrote–at least that was an article of faith in our family–"Airy, fairy Lilian," [p. 182] and that he was much attached to her in his days of calf-love, cannot, I think, well be doubted. In 1834 he wrote to her the following graceful sextette.' Sophy was a friend of Rosa Baring. Cp. *To thee, with whom my best affections dwell* (p. 649), also to Sophy.

Sweet, ask me not why I am sad,
But, when sad thoughts arise,
Look on me, make my spirit glad
To gaze upon thine eyes.
For how can sorrow dwell in mine
If they might always gaze on thine?

## 246 Lady Clara Vere de Vere

Published *1842*, but 'written early' (H.T.). Probably *c.* 1835 like *Lady Clare*, since it is not in the *Heath MS*, but later than *The Lord of Burleigh*. It is probably the exception of which T. spoke when adding six poems in vol. i of *1842*: 'which, with one exception, were written in 1833'. 'A dramatic poem drawn from no particular character' (T.).

Lady Clara Vere de Vere,
  Of me you shall not win renown:
You thought to break a country heart
  For pastime, ere you went to town.
At me you smiled, but unbeguiled
  I saw the snare, and I retired:
The daughter of a hundred Earls,
  You are not one to be desired.

Lady Clara Vere de Vere,
  I know you proud to bear your name,
Your pride is yet no mate for mine,
  Too proud to care from whence I came.

Nor would I break for your sweet sake
A heart that doats on truer charms.
A simple maiden in her flower
Is worth a hundred coats-of-arms.

Lady Clara Vere de Vere,
Some meeker pupil you must find,
For were you queen of all that is,
I could not stoop to such a mind.
You sought to prove how I could love,
And my disdain is my reply.
The lion on your old stone gates
Is not more cold to you than I.

Lady Clara Vere de Vere,
You put strange memories in my head.
Not thrice your branching limes have blown
Since I beheld young Laurence dead.
Oh your sweet eyes, your low replies:
A great enchantress you may be;
But there was that across his throat
Which you had hardly cared to see.

Lady Clara Vere de Vere,
When thus he met his mother's view,
She had the passions of her kind,
She spake some certain truths of you.
Indeed I heard one bitter word
That scarce is fit for you to hear;
Her manners had not that repose
Which stamps the caste of Vere de Vere.

Lady Clara Vere de Vere,
There stands a spectre in your hall:
The guilt of blood is at your door:
You changed a wholesome heart to gall.
You held your course without remorse,
To make him trust his modest worth,
And, last, you fixed a vacant stare,
And slew him with your noble birth.

Trust me, Clara Vere de Vere,
From yon blue heavens above us bent
The gardener Adam and his wife
Smile at the claims of long descent.

¶ 246.51. *The gardener Adam*] The grand old gardener *MS quoted in Eversley*. 'Altered . . . because of the frequent letters from friends asking me for explanation' (T.).

Howe'er it be, it seems to me,
'Tis only noble to be good.
Kind hearts are more than coronets,
And simple faith than Norman blood.

I know you, Clara Vere de Vere,
You pine among your halls and towers:
The languid light of your proud eyes
Is wearied of the rolling hours.
In glowing health, with boundless wealth,
But sickening of a vague disease,
You know so ill to deal with time,
You needs must play such pranks as these.

Clara, Clara Vere de Vere,
If time be heavy on your hands,
Are there no beggars at your gate,
Nor any poor about your lands?
Oh! teach the orphan-boy to read,
Or teach the orphan-girl to sew,
Pray Heaven for a human heart,
And let the foolish yeoman go.

# 247 Lady Clare

Published *1842*. T. says it was founded on Susan Ferrier's novel *The Inheritance* (1824), where the substituted baby becomes an heiress; T. alters the fact that the lover spurns Miss St Clair on discovering the secret of her birth. Arthur Hallam was reading the novel in July 1831 (*Mem.* i 81), and it is the edition of 1831 which T. owned (*Lincoln*). But the poem is presumably later, since it is not in *Heath MS*. Probably it was written *c.* 1835, like *Lady Clara Vere de Vere*, and following *The Lord of Burleigh*.

It was the time when lilies blow,
And clouds are highest up in air,
Lord Ronald brought a lily-white doe
To give his cousin, Lady Clare.

I trow they did not part in scorn:
Lovers long-betrothed were they:
They two will wed the morrow morn:
God's blessing on the day!

¶ 247.*1–4*] *1851*; Lord Ronald courted Lady Clare, *1842–50*.
*6*] *1851*; Lord Ronald, her cousin, courted her, *1842–50*.
*7. They two*] *1851*; And they *1842–50*.
*8*] *1851; not 1842–50.*

'He does not love me for my birth,
 Nor for my lands so broad and fair;
He loves me for my own true worth,
 And that is well,' said Lady Clare.

In there came old Alice the nurse,
 Said, 'Who was this that went from thee?'
'It was my cousin,' said Lady Clare,
 'Tomorrow he weds with me.'

'O God be thanked!' said Alice the nurse,
 'That all comes round so just and fair:
Lord Ronald is heir of all your lands,
 And you are *not* the Lady Clare.'

'Are ye out of your mind, my nurse, my nurse?'
 Said Lady Clare, 'that ye speak so wild?'
'As God's above,' said Alice the nurse,
 'I speak the truth: you are my child.

'The old Earl's daughter died at my breast;
 I speak the truth, as I live by bread!
I buried her like my own sweet child,
 And put my child in her stead.'

'Falsely, falsely have ye done,
 O mother,' she said, 'if this be true,
To keep the best man under the sun
 So many years from his due.'

'Nay now, my child,' said Alice the nurse,
 'But keep the secret for your life,
And all you have will be Lord Ronald's,
 When you are man and wife.'

'If I'm a beggar born,' she said,
 'I will speak out, for I dare not lie.
Pull off, pull off, the brooch of gold,
 And fling the diamond necklace by.'

'Nay now, my child,' said Alice the nurse,
 'But keep the secret all ye can.'
She said, 'Not so: but I will know
 If there be any faith in man.'

'Nay now, what faith?' said Alice the nurse,
 'The man will cleave unto his right.'
'And he shall have it,' the lady replied,
 'Though I should die tonight.'

'Yet give one kiss to your mother dear!
  Alas, my child, I sinned for thee.'
'O mother, mother, mother,' she said,
  'So strange it seems to me.

'Yet here's a kiss for my mother dear,
  My mother dear, if this be so,
And lay your hand upon my head,
  And bless me, mother, ere I go.'

She clad herself in a russet gown,
  She was no longer Lady Clare:
She went by dale, and she went by down,
  With a single rose in her hair.

The lily-white doe Lord Ronald had brought
  Leapt up from where she lay,
Dropt her head in the maiden's hand,
  And followed her all the way.

Down stept Lord Ronald from his tower:
  'O Lady Clare, you shame your worth!
Why come you drest like a village maid,
  That are the flower of the earth?'

'If I come drest like a village maid,
  I am but as my fortunes are:
I am a beggar born,' she said,
  'And not the Lady Clare.'

'Play me no tricks,' said Lord Ronald,
  'For I am yours in word and in deed.
Play me no tricks,' said Lord Ronald,
  'Your riddle is hard to read.'

O and proudly stood she up!
  Her heart within her did not fail:
She looked into Lord Ronald's eyes,
  And told him all her nurse's tale.

He laughed a laugh of merry scorn:
  He turned and kissed her where she stood:
'If you are not the heiress born,
  And I,' said he, 'the next in blood–

'If you are not the heiress born,
  And I,' said he, 'the lawful heir,
We two will wed tomorrow morn,
  And you shall still be Lady Clare.'

61–4] *1851*; *not 1842–3*; A lily-white . . . *1845–50*.

# 248 Dora

Published *1842*; among 'English Idyls'. Written by 1835 (*Mem.* i 151), and unlikely to be earlier because it is not in the *Heath MS*. T. remarks that it was partly suggested by Mary Russell Mitford's story *Dora Creswell* (*Our Village*, iii, 1828), 'which is cheerful in tone, whereas this is sad'. From l. 72 to the end, 'I have not followed Miss Mitford'; but this note is misleading, since the scene with the wreath of flowers is in Mitford; after the dialogue, she cuts to the same place next day when the farmer is playing with the child, watched by Dora and Mary, all now being well. T. attempts a Wordsworthian simplicity, such as that of *Michael*, which T. read to FitzGerald in 1835 (*Mem.* i 151); the best comparison of *Dora* and Wordsworth is by Arnold, *On Translating Homer: Last Words*. '*Dora*, being the tale of a nobly simple country girl, had to be told in the simplest possible poetical language, and therefore was one of the poems which gave most trouble' (T., *Mem.* i 196). Half the MS (ll. 1–94) is in the *Huntington*; the other half at *Yale*.

With farmer Allan at the farm abode
William and Dora. William was his son,
And she his niece. He often looked at them,
And often thought, 'I'll make them man and wife.'
Now Dora felt her uncle's will in all,
And yearned toward William; but the youth, because
He had been always with her in the house,
Thought not of Dora.
                                Then there came a day
When Allan called his son, and said, 'My son:
I married late, but I would wish to see
My grandchild on my knees before I die:
And I have set my heart upon a match.
Now therefore look to Dora; she is well
To look to; thrifty too beyond her age.
She is my brother's daughter: he and I
Had once hard words, and parted, and he died
In foreign lands; but for his sake I bred

¶ 248.*1*. *Allan*] Anson *HnMS 1st reading passim*.
*6*. *toward*] *1890*; towards *1842–89*.
*8–14*. H. A. Mason (*Delta*, Summer 1963, p. 14) points out the Biblical phrasing: 'There came a day when'; 'called his son and said . . . before I die . . . now therefore', cp. *Genesis* xxvii 1–4. 'Well to look to', cp. *1 Samuel* xvi 12: 'goodly to look to'.
*12*] *Transferred in MS from where it followed l. 18*.
*16–17*. 'This quarrel is not in Miss Mitford' (T.).

His daughter Dora: take her for your wife;
For I have wished this marriage, night and day,
For many years.' But William answered short;
'I cannot marry Dora; by my life,
I will not marry Dora.' Then the old man
Was wroth, and doubled up his hands, and said:
'You will not, boy! you dare to answer thus!
But in my time a father's word was law,
And so it shall be now for me. Look to it;
Consider, William: take a month to think,
And let me have an answer to my wish;
Or, by the Lord that made me, you shall pack,
And never more darken my doors again.'
But William answered madly; bit his lips,
And broke away. The more he looked at her
The less he liked her; and his ways were harsh;
But Dora bore them meekly. Then before
The month was out he left his father's house,
And hired himself to work within the fields;
And half in love, half spite, he wooed and wed
A labourer's daughter, Mary Morrison.

Then, when the bells were ringing, Allan called
His niece and said: 'My girl, I love you well;
But if you speak with him that was my son,
Or change a word with her he calls his wife,
My home is none of yours. My will is law.'
And Dora promised, being meek. She thought,
'It cannot be: my uncle's mind will change!'

*18–19*] His daughter up. And take her: she is yours,
For I have set my heart upon this match *MS 1st reading*

*22–4*] . . . Dora.' Thus he made
His father wroth who raised his voice and cried
'You will not marry Dora! you will *not*! *MS 1st reading*

*27–31*] *1843*; Consider: take a month to think, and give
An answer to my wish; or by the Lord
That made me, you shall pack, and nevermore
Darken my doors again.' And William heard,
And answered something madly . . . *1842*

T.'s alteration of the line-endings suggests an arbitrariness in the rhythms of *Dora*.

*42. change a word*] ever speak *MS 1st reading*.

*43. will*] word *MS 1st reading*.

*44. meek. She*] meek and *MS 1st reading*.

And days went on, and there was born a boy
To William; then distresses came on him;
And day by day he passed his father's gate,
Heart-broken, and his father helped him not.
But Dora stored what little she could save,
And sent it them by stealth, nor did they know
Who sent it; till at last a fever seized
On William, and in harvest time he died.

Then Dora went to Mary. Mary sat
And looked with tears upon her boy, and thought
Hard things of Dora. Dora came and said:

'I have obeyed my uncle until now,
And I have sinned, for it was all through me
This evil came on William at the first.
But, Mary, for the sake of him that's gone,
And for your sake, the woman that he chose,
And for this orphan, I am come to you:
You know there has not been for these five years
So full a harvest: let me take the boy,
And I will set him in my uncle's eye
Among the wheat; that when his heart is glad
Of the full harvest, he may see the boy,
And bless him for the sake of him that's gone.'

And Dora took the child, and went her way
Across the wheat, and sat upon a mound
That was unsown, where many poppies grew.
Far off the farmer came into the field
And spied her not; for none of all his men
Dare tell him Dora waited with the child;
And Dora would have risen and gone to him,
But her heart failed her; and the reapers reaped,
And the sun fell, and all the land was dark.

*54–6*] Then Dora rose and went to Mary's house
Where Mary sat and lookt upon her boy
And thought of Dora: 'Dora shall have all,
My boy may starve'; and Dora came and said *MS 1st reading*

*61. chose*] loved *MS 1st reading.*

*68*] And taken, bless him for his father's sake.' *MS 1st reading.*

*70. Across the wheat*] Into the field *MS 1st reading.*

*73. spied*] saw *MS 1st reading.*

*77.* T. compares, as l. 107, *Odyssey, passim*: δύσετό τ' ἠέλιος, σκιόωντό τε πᾶσαι ἀγυιαί.

But when the morrow came, she rose and took
The child once more, and sat upon the mound;
And made a little wreath of all the flowers
That grew about, and tied it round his hat
To make him pleasing in her uncle's eye.
Then when the farmer passed into the field
He spied her, and he left his men at work,
And came and said: 'Where were you yesterday?
Whose child is that? What are you doing here?'
So Dora cast her eyes upon the ground,
And answered softly, 'This is William's child!'
'And did I not,' said Allan, 'did I not
Forbid you, Dora?' Dora said again:
'Do with me as you will, but take the child,
And bless him for the sake of him that's gone!'
And Allan said, 'I see it is a trick
Got up betwixt you and the woman there.
I must be taught my duty, and by you!
You knew my word was law, and yet you dared
To slight it. Well–for I will take the boy;
But go you hence, and never see me more.'

So saying, he took the boy that cried aloud
And struggled hard. The wreath of flowers fell
At Dora's feet. She bowed upon her hands,
And the boy's cry came to her from the field,
More and more distant. She bowed down her head,
Remembering the day when first she came,
And all the things that had been. She bowed down
And wept in secret; and the reapers reaped,
And the sun fell, and all the land was dark.

Then Dora went to Mary's house, and stood
Upon the threshold. Mary saw the boy

*78ff.* Cp. the setting and story in *Ruth*, e.g. ii 5, 'Then said Boaz unto his servant that was set over the reapers, Whose damsel is this?' Thomas Carlyle suggested the likeness in 1842 (*Mem.* i 213).
*81. grew about*] grow in corn *MS 1st reading.*
*82. pleasing*] gracious *MS 1st reading.*
*84–5*] He saw her where she sat and came to her.
'How now!' he said . . . *MS 1st reading.*
*90. Dora said*] Then she said *MS 1st reading.*
*91. will*] please *MS 1st reading.*
*93. is a*] all, a *MS 1st reading.*
*100. flowers*] cornflowers *Y.MS 1st reading.*
*108 11*] Then Dora rose and went to Mary's house
And Mary ran to meet her and they met

Was not with Dora. She broke out in praise
To God, that helped her in her widowhood.
And Dora said, 'My uncle took the boy;
But, Mary, let me live and work with you:
He says that he will never see me more.'
Then answered Mary, 'This shall never be,
That thou shouldst take my trouble on thyself:
And, now I think, he shall not have the boy,
For he will teach him hardness, and to slight
His mother; therefore thou and I will go,
And I will have my boy, and bring him home;
And I will beg of him to take thee back:
But if he will not take thee back again,
Then thou and I will live within one house,
And work for William's child, until he grows
Of age to help us.'
So the women kissed
Each other, and set out, and reached the farm.
The door was off the latch: they peeped, and saw
The boy set up betwixt his grandsire's knees,
Who thrust him in the hollows of his arm,
And clapt him on the hands and on the cheeks,
Like one that loved him: and the lad stretched out
And babbled for the golden seal, that hung
From Allan's watch, and sparkled by the fire.
Then they came in: but when the boy beheld
His mother, he cried out to come to her:
And Allan set him down, and Mary said:

'O Father!–if you let me call you so–
I never came a-begging for myself,
Or William, or this child; but now I come
For Dora: take her back; she loves you well.
O Sir, when William died, he died at peace
With all men; for I asked him, and he said,

Upon the threshold. Then she saw the boy
Was not with Dora so she spoke and praised
The Lord that helped . . . *MS 1st reading*

*114*] Because he said, 'go hence nor see me more.' *MS 1st reading.*

*117. the*] my *MS 1st reading.*

*119–20*] His mother; and I could not see him there
–So let us go: for I will fetch the boy, *MS 1st reading*

*127–30*] The door was open, and they lookt and saw
The old man with the boy betwixt his knees.
He clapt him on the legs and on the cheeks, *MS 1st reading*

*140 ∧ 1*] Indeed she does. What harm has Dora done? *MS 1st reading*

He could not ever rue his marrying me–
I had been a patient wife: but, Sir, he said
That he was wrong to cross his father thus:
"God bless him!" he said, "and may he never know
The troubles I have gone through!" Then he turned
His face and passed–unhappy that I am!
But now, Sir, let me have my boy, for you
Will make him hard, and he will learnt to slight
His father's memory; and take Dora back,
And let all this be as it was before.'

So Mary said, and Dora hid her face
By Mary. There was silence in the room;
And all at once the old man burst in sobs:–

'I have been to blame–to blame. I have killed my son.
I have killed him–but I loved him–my dear son.
May God forgive me!–I have been to blame.
Kiss me, my children.'
Then they clung about
The old man's neck, and kissed him many times.
And all the man was broken with remorse;
And all his love came back a hundredfold;
And for three hours he sobbed o'er William's child
Thinking of William.
So those four abode
Within one house together; and as years
Went forward, Mary took another mate;
But Dora lived unmarried till her death.

# 249 *Sonnet [I lingered yet awhile to bend my way]

Printed by Sir Charles Tennyson, *Nineteenth Century* cix (1931) 505; then *1931*, p. 64: 'Tennyson in his youth had a great longing to go and live in some Mediterranean country, as his eldest brother, Frederick, did soon after leaving Cambridge. The sonnet is rather obscure, but I think the

*144. patient*] faithful *MS 1st reading.*
*153–4*] . . . and Dora clung to her / In silence; and the child cried out and ceased. *MS 1st reading.*
*156–7.* Cp. the story of *Aylmer's Field* (p. 1159).
*161–2*] *Added in MS.*
*163. for three hours*] half the night *MS 1st reading.*

"Jewel" was human and feminine.' She was Rosa Baring, as R. W. Rader shows (*Tennyson's Maud*, 1963); see *Sonnet [Ah, fade not yet]* and headnote (below). *1931* printed from *H.Lpr 93* (which is watermarked 1836 and includes *How thought you*, p. 652, also to Rosa). This Loosepaper is *A* below. There are also drafts in *H.Nbk 8* (*B* below), and *H.Lpr 20* (watermarked 1835, *C* below) where the poem is on the same page as *Caressed or chidden* (p. 651, also probably to Rosa Baring). All variants are below. The imagery of the icy jewel (a rich and aloof beauty) reappears in *Maud*, which is T.'s most important handling of his experience with Rosa: 'my jewel', 'precious stone', 'a cold and clear-cut face . . . icily regular' (i 352, 498, 79, 82).

I lingered yet awhile to bend my way
    To that far South, for which my spirits ache,
For under rainy hills a jewel lay
    And this dark land was precious for its sake,
    A rosy-coloured jewel, fit to make
An emperor's signet-ring, to save or slay
    Whole peoples, such as some great King might take
To clasp his mantle on a festal day:
But yet a jewel only made to shine,
    And icy-cold although 'tis rosy-clear–
        Why did I linger? I myself condemn,
For ah! 'tis far too costly to be mine,
    And Nature never dropt a human tear
        In those chill dews whereof she froze the gem.

# 250 *Sonnet [Ah, fade not yet from out the green arcades]

Printed by Sir Charles Tennyson, *Nineteenth Century* cix (1931) 507; then *1931*, p. 63, from *H.Lpr 1*: 'The last line suggests that the lament is for the departure of some human rose from the Somersby district.' The human

¶ 249.*1. bend*] *A–B*; take *C 1st reading.*
2. Cp. *You ask me, why* 26–8.
4. *this*] *A, C*; the *B*.
5. *rosy-coloured*] *A–B*; jewel, rosy-tinted *C*. *fit to*] *A, B, C*; that might *C 1st reading.*
6. *signet-ring*] *A–B*; signet, so *C*.
7] *A–B*; Or such as some imperial hand might take *C*.
8. *his mantle on*] *A–B*; the purple of *C*.
9. *But*] *A–B*; Ah *C*; And *1931*.
11. *Why . . . linger?*] *A*; And for this weakness *B*; And if I lingered, *C*.
12. *ah! 'tis*] *A*; it is *B*; this is *C*.

rose has been identified by R. W. Rader (*Tennyson's Maud*, 1963) as Rosa Baring, with whom T. fell in love. See *Thy rosy lips* (p. 634). Cp. *Sonnet* [*I lingered yet awhile*] (p. 646). Rader (pp. 34–5) shows that both sonnets belong to the period 1835–6, and that *Ah, fade not yet* 'seems to have been written during a rainy Lincolnshire fall (in 1835 or 1836) when Rosa was going up to London for the season with her family'. Variants below are from *H.Lpr 57*, the recto of *How thought you* (p. 652, probably also to Rosa).

Ah, fade not yet from out the green arcades,
 Fade not, sweet Rose, for hark the woodland shrills!
A lamentation grows in all the shades,
 And grief in copses where the linnet trills:
 The sweet Rose fades from all the winding rills
And waning arches of the golden glades:
 From all the circuit of the purple hills
The sweet Rose fades, alas, how soon it fades.
It does not fade, but from the land it goes,
 And leaves the land to winter. I remain,
 To waste alone the slowly-narrowing days.
It fades to me: for they transplant the Rose,
 And further South the Rose will bloom again
 Like a mere Rose that only cares for praise.

# 251 *To Rosa

Printed by H. D. Rawnsley, *Memories of the Tennysons* (1900), pp. 66–7. Dated 1836 (perhaps written 1835; Rader, p. 131). On T.'s love-affair with Rosa Baring, see *Thy rosy lips* (p. 634). This poem, on their lovers'-quarrel at a ball, points towards the deepening disillusionment of the later sonnets *Ah, fade not yet, I lingered yet awhile, How thought you that this thing*, and the *Three Sonnets to a Coquette*. The sonnet-form here is very irregular, as is usual in T.'s early sonnets.

¶ 250.*1*] Fade not, sweet Rose! our songs and serenades *H.Lpr 57*.
*2. Fade . . . for*] Were sung to thee and *MS*.
*3. A*] With *MS*. *grows in all*] running through *MS*.
*4. grief in*] hollow *MS*.
*10. And . . . winter.*] It cannot fade or fall but *MS*.
*11. waste*] weep *MS*. *the slowly-*] through all the *MS*.
*14*. Cp. *Three Sonnets to a Coquette* ii 14: 'She still would take the praise, and care no more'. (These sonnets are probably to Rosa.)

I

Sole rose of beauty, loveliness complete,
If those few words were bitter or unjust,
Yet is thy gentle nature so discreet
That they will pass thee like an idle gust.
Henceforward, fancy shall not force distrust,
But all my blood in time to thine shall beat,
Henceforth I lay my pride within the dust
And my whole heart is vassal at thy feet.
Blow, summer rose, thy beauty makes me shamed
That I could blame thee! Heaven's dewdrop pure
Bathe, with my tears, thy maiden blossom sweet:
Blow, summer rose, nor fall; and, oh, be sure
That if I had not loved, I had not blamed;
For my whole heart is vassal at thy feet.

II

By all my grief for that which I did say,
By all the life of love that never dies,
By all that Paradise for which we pray
And all the Paradise that round thee lies,
By thoughts of thee that like the Heavens rise,
Star after star, within me, day by day,
And night by night, in musing on thine eyes,
Which look me through when thou art far away,
By that madonna grace of parted hair
And dewy sister eyelids drooping chaste,
By each dear foot, so light on field, or floor,
By thy full form and slender moulded waist,
And that all perfect smile of thine, I swear,
That these rash lips shall blame thee, Rose, no more.

## 252 *'To thee, with whom my best affections dwell'

Printed *Mem.* i 161–2, as written 'at the end of 1837 or the beginning of 1838'. H. D. Rawnsley printed it (*Memories of the Tennysons*, 1900, p. 65) as *To Sophy, 1836*, noting that it was written after a quarrel with Sophy Rawnsley at the Spilsby ball. Rawnsley's date is probably right; the poem is dated '1836' in *H.Lpr 239*. Cp. *Sweet, ask me not* (p. 636), also to Sophy, and *To Rosa*, 1836 (above).

¶ 251.ii *9–10*. Cp. the chaste *Isabel* (line 6) with her hair 'Madonna-wise'.

To thee, with whom my best affections dwell,
That I was harsh to thee, let no one know;
It were, O Heaven! a stranger tale to tell
Than if the vine had borne the bitter sloe:
Though I was harsh, my nature is not so:
A momentary cloud upon me fell:
My coldness was mistimed like summer-snow;
Cold words I spoke, yet loved thee warm and well.
Was I so harsh? Ah, dear, it could not be.
Seemed I so cold? What madness moved my blood
To make me thus belie my constant heart
That watch't with love thine earliest infancy,
Slow-ripening to the grace of womanhood,
Through every change that made thee what thou art.

## 253 *'Thy natal day awakens bright'

Printed by H. D. Rawnsley, *Memories of the Tennysons* (1900), p. 64. For Rosa Baring's birthday, 23 Sept. 1836. See *Thy rosy lips* (p. 634), for T.'s love-affair with her.

Thy natal day awakens bright,
Once more that happy morn doth rise
Whereon thine eyes first saw the light
And light grew lighter for thine eyes.
So let the varying moments flee,
And, passing, change us less or more,
Whilst Time himself, in love with thee,
But makes thee lovelier than before.

## 254 Three Sonnets to a Coquette

Published *Selection* 1865 with this title; subsequently as 'Juvenilia', 'Early Sonnets VII–IX'. 'Written in early life' (H.T.). They express T.'s disillusionment with Rosa Baring, so were written probably *c.* 1836 (the first of the three is in *H.Lpr 20*, watermarked 1835); for this love affair, see

¶ 252.*1. best*] *Rawnsley*; true *Mem.*
¶ 253.*1. awakens*] *1900*; arises *W. F. Rawnsley*. W. F. Rawnsley quotes a text with a few variants in *Nineteenth Century* xcvii (1925) 193.
*3. Whereon*] *W. F. Rawnsley*; Wherein *1900*.

*Thy rosy lips* (p. 634). Cp. T.'s other sonnets on Rosa: *Ah, fade not yet* (p. 647); *I lingered yet awhile* (p. 646); and *How thought you that this thing* (p. 652). For the theme of the second sonnet (*The form . . .*), cp. *To Rosa* (p. 648), written after a lovers'-quarrel at a ball, and also the dance in *Maud*.

I

Caressed or chidden by the slender hand,
And singing airy trifles this or that,
Light Hope at Beauty's call would perch and stand,
And run through every change of sharp and flat;
And Fancy came and at her pillow sat,
When Sleep had bound her in his rosy band,
And chased away the still-recurring gnat,
And woke her with a lay from fairy land.
But now they live with Beauty less and less,
For Hope is other Hope and wanders far,
Nor cares to lisp in love's delicious creeds;
And Fancy watches in the wilderness,
Poor Fancy sadder than a single star,
That sets at twilight in a land of reeds.

II

The form, the form alone is eloquent!
A nobler yearning never broke her rest
Than but to dance and sing, be gaily drest,
And win all eyes with all accomplishment:
Yet in the whirling dances as we went,
My fancy made me for a moment blest
To find my heart so near the beauteous breast
That once had power to rob it of content.
A moment came the tenderness of tears,
The phantom of a wish that once could move,
A ghost of passion that no smiles restore–
For ah! the slight coquette, she cannot love,
And if you kissed her feet a thousand years,
She still would take the praise, and care no more.

¶ 254. i *1. slender*] *1872*; dainty *1865–70*.
i *3*] Light Hope on Beauty's shoulder percht would stand, *H.Lpr 20*.
i *6*] She lying bound in Slumber's dewy band, *MS*.

ii *1*. Cp. *How thought you* 12: 'An angel's form–a waiting-woman's heart'.
ii *5. whirling dances*] *1872*; waltzing-circle *1865–70*.
ii *12–14*. Contrast the aspiration of *Early Verses to Rose Baring* 14–16: 'What care I for others' kisses? / When a thousand years are dead / Comes there no such rose as this is.'
ii *14*. Cp. *Ah, fade not yet* 14: 'Like a mere Rose that only cares for praise'.

III

Wan Sculptor, weepest thou to take the cast
Of those dead lineaments that near thee lie?
O sorrowest thou, pale Painter, for the past,
In painting some dead friend from memory?
Weep on: beyond his object Love can last:
His object lives: more cause to weep have I:
My tears, no tears of love, are flowing fast,
No tears of love, but tears that Love can die.
I pledge her not in any cheerful cup,
Nor care to sit beside her where she sits–
Ah pity–hint it not in human tones,
But breathe it into earth and close it up
With secret death for ever, in the pits
Which some green Christmas crams with weary bones.

# 255 *Sonnet [How thought you that this thing could captivate?]

Printed by Sir Charles Tennyson, *Nineteenth Century* cix (1931) 508; then *1931*, p. 77: 'This sonnet is written on an old sheet of notepaper [*H.Lpr 93*] which contains also an early version of the "Bridesmaid" sonnet [p. 661]. This was written in 1836, so that the sonnet here printed evidently belongs to that date'. This Loosepaper is watermarked 1836. There is another draft in *H.Lpr 94* (all variants are below). A further draft, omitting ll. 3–8, is in *H.Lpr 57* together with *Ah, fade not yet* (p. 647), suggesting that this sonnet expresses T.'s disillusionment with Rosa Baring. See *Thy rosy lips* (p. 634); and cp. *Three Sonnets to a Coquette* (p. 650). Sir Charles Tennyson believes that these poems are too harsh to be directly concerned with Rosa.

How thought you that this thing could captivate?
  What are those graces that could make her dear,
  Who is not worth the notice of a sneer
To rouse the vapid devil of her hate?
A speech conventional, so void of weight
  That after it has buzzed about one's ear,
  'Twere rich refreshment for a week to hear
The dentist babble or the barber prate;

iii *14.* Proverb: 'a green Yule makes a fat churchyard'.

¶ 255.*3–5*]   A silver speech that, if the tones be clear,
The vapid devil of a vulgar hate
  Makes so conventionally void of weight *H.Lpr 94*

*6. about one's*] in either *MS.*

*7. rich . . . week*] like iced hock in fevered throats *MS.*

A hand displayed with many a little art;
An eye that glances on her neighbour's dress;
A foot too often shown for my regard;
An angel's form – a waiting-woman's heart;
A perfect-featured face, expressionless,
Insipid, as the Queen upon a card.

## 256 *'Woman of noble form and noble mind!'

Printed *Mem.* i 147, with the note: 'To a friend, Mrs [Mary Langton] Neville, who had lately lost her husband (written between 1830 and 1840)'. It seems from *CT* (pp. 165, 173) that she had lost him in that he was sent back from Australia for forgery; T.'s lines were written when she and her family emigrated to America, apparently in 1836.

Woman of noble form and noble mind!
Whithersoever through the wilderness
Thou bearest from the threshold of thy friends
The sacred sorrows of as pure a heart
As e'er beat time to Nature, take with thee
Our warmest wishes, silent Guardians
But true till Death; and let them go in hope,
Like birds of passage, to return with thee
Some happy Summer morning, when the winds
Are fallen or changed; and, watered by thy tears,
The two fair lilies growing at thy side
Have slowly prospered into stately flowers.

## 257 The Voyage

Published *1864*. It is in *T.Nbk 21*, with *The Flight*, which suggests composition *c.* 1836. It was written by 29 Dec. 1863 (*Mat.* ii 383). T. comments:

*10. that glances*] still-glancing *MS.*
*12.* Cp. *Three Sonnets to a Coquette* ii 1: 'The form, the form alone is eloquent'.
*13.* Cp. *Maud* i 80–3 (which also has links with Rosa Baring): 'Perfectly beautiful: let it be granted her: where is the fault? . . . / Faultily faultless, icily regular, splendidly null, / Dead perfection, no more.'
*14.* Incorporated, as Sir Charles Tennyson remarks, as *Aylmer's Field* 28 (1864).

'Life is the search after the ideal'. Cp. *Ulysses* (p. 560), and *Merlin and the Gleam* (p. 1412).

I

We left behind the painted buoy
That tosses at the harbour-mouth;
And madly danced our hearts with joy,
As fast we fleeted to the South:
How fresh was every sight and sound
On open main or winding shore!
We knew the merry world was round,
And we might sail for evermore.

II

Warm broke the breeze against the brow,
Dry sang the tackle, sang the sail:
The Lady's-head upon the prow
Caught the shrill salt, and sheered the gale.
The broad seas swelled to meet the keel,
And swept behind; so quick the run,
We felt the good ship shake and reel,
We seemed to sail into the Sun!

III

How oft we saw the Sun retire,
And burn the threshold of the night,
Fall from his Ocean-lane of fire,
And sleep beneath his pillared light!
How oft the purple-skirted robe
Of twilight slowly downward drawn,
As through the slumber of the globe
Again we dashed into the dawn!

IV

New stars all night above the brim
Of waters lightened into view;
They climbed as quickly, for the rim
Changed every moment as we flew.
Far ran the naked moon across
The houseless ocean's heaving field,
Or flying shone, the silver boss
Of her own halo's dusky shield;

¶ 257.*18. the threshold of the night*: *In Memoriam* xxix 6. This stanza in *T.MS* includes a version of *Mariana in the South* 90–92 (p. 366), and, broken into two lines, *Locksley Hall* 183: 'Through the shadow of the globe we sweep into the younger day'.

*29–32.* Sir Charles Tennyson (*1931*, p. 25) points out the adaptation of

V

The peaky islet shifted shapes,
High towns on hills were dimly seen,
We past long lines of Northern capes
And dewy Northern meadows green.
We came to warmer waves, and deep
Across the boundless east we drove,
Where those long swells of breaker sweep
The nutmeg rocks and isles of clove.

VI

By peaks that flamed, or, all in shade,
Gloomed the low coast and quivering brine
With ashy rains, that spreading made
Fantastic plume or sable pine;
By sands and steaming flats, and floods
Of mighty mouth, we scudded fast,
And hills and scarlet-mingled woods
Glowed for a moment as we past.

VII

O hundred shores of happy climes,
How swiftly streamed ye by the bark!
At times the whole sea burned, at times
With wakes of fire we tore the dark;
At times a carven craft would shoot
From havens hid in fairy bowers,
With naked limbs and flowers and fruit,
But we nor paused for fruit nor flowers.

VIII

For one fair Vision ever fled
Down the waste waters day and night,
And still we followed where she led,
In hope to gain upon her flight.
Her face was evermore unseen,
And fixt upon the far sea-line;
But each man murmured, 'O my Queen,
I follow till I make thee mine.'

*Ode: O Bosky Brook* 61–4: 'the bright boss / Of thine own Halo's dusky shield', rhyming with 'field' (i.e. sea).
51. *burned*: 'with phosphorescence' (T.). This stanza in *T.MS* shared some phrasing with *In Memoriam* xii 9–12 (p. 875).
57–65. Cp. *Merlin and the Gleam* (p. 1412).

IX

And now we lost her, now she gleamed
  Like Fancy made of golden air,
Now nearer to the prow she seemed
  Like Virtue firm, like Knowledge fair,
Now high on waves that idly burst
  Like Heavenly Hope she crowned the sea,
And now, the bloodless point reversed,
  She bore the blade of Liberty.

X

And only one among us–him
  We pleased not–he was seldom pleased:
He saw not far: his eyes were dim:
  But ours he swore were all diseased.
'A ship of fools,' he shrieked in spite,
  'A ship of fools,' he sneered and wept.
And overboard one stormy night
  He cast his body, and on we swept.

XI

And never sail of ours was furled,
  Nor anchor dropt at eve or morn;
We loved the glories of the world,
  But laws of nature were our scorn.
For blasts would rise and rave and cease,
  But whence were those that drove the sail
Across the whirlwind's heart of peace,
  And to and through the counter gale?

XII

Again to colder climes we came,
  For still we followed where she led:
Now mate is blind and captain lame,
  And half the crew are sick or dead,
But, blind or lame or sick or sound,
  We follow that which flies before:
We know the merry world is round,
  And we may sail for evermore.

*77. ship of fools*: Sebastian Brant's *Narrenschiff* (1494) set this fashion, followed later by Alexander Barclay's *Ship of Fools* (1509) and many others.
*87.* Cp. Wordsworth, *Excursion* iv 1146–7: 'And central peace, subsisting at the heart / Of endless agitation'.

# 258 *The Skipping-Rope

Published *1842*; reprinted *1843–50*, and not subsequently. T. wrote it at the end of John Walker's *Rhyming Dictionary* (1800, *Lincoln*), which includes in the index, under "ope", all of T.'s rhymes. 'Did he ever use a rhyming dictionary? He had tried it in earlier days, but found it of little use: "There was no natural congruity between the rhymes thus alphabetically grouped together"' (*Mem.* ii 496). Written *c.* 1836, judging from *H.Lpr 226;* cp. the other jocular poems of *c.* 1837. *Loosepapers 224–5* are earlier drafts, more clearly in the form of dialogue; the former begins 'While Annie whirled the skipping-rope, / Said Harry standing by...' The latter has four lines from 'He' and four from 'She'.

Sure never yet was Antelope
Could skip so lightly by.
Stand off, or else my skipping-rope
Will hit you in the eye.
How lightly whirls the skipping-rope!
How fairy-like you fly!
Go, get you gone, you muse and mope–
I hate that silly sigh.
Nay, dearest, teach me how to hope,
Or tell me how to die.
There, take it, take my skipping-rope,
And hang yourself thereby.

# 259 The Flight

Published *1885*. T. said it was 'a very early poem', and he told William Allingham on 6 Nov. 1885: 'This was written fifty years ago' (*Diary*, 1907, p. 344). It is in *T.Nbk 21*, along with *The Voyage* (*c.* 1836?). This MS does not have stanzas vi–vii, x–xi, xv, xx; and it has some of the other stanzas differently placed. Written *c.* 1836(?); revised 1885. It appears in *H.Nbk 52* with other poems of *1885*; there its original title was *The Betrothed*, and it is in H.T.'s hand, revised by T. It does not appear in the first of the three trial editions of *1885* in the British Museum. The theme of mercenary marriage suggests T.'s anxieties in 1836–7, and the poems precipitated by his loss of Rosa Baring (see *Thy rosy lips*, p. 634). In particular, *Locksley Hall* and *Edwin Morris*. (The lover in *The Flight* is called Edwin.) There are affinities too with *Maud*.

I

Are you sleeping? have you forgotten? do not sleep, my sister dear!
How *can* you sleep? the morning brings the day I hate and fear;
The cock has crowed already once, he crows before his time;
Awake! the creeping glimmer steals, the hills are white with rime.

II

Ah, clasp me in your arms, sister, ah, fold me to your breast!
Ah, let me weep my fill once more, and cry myself to rest!
To rest? to rest and wake no more were better rest for me,
Than to waken every morning to that face I loathe to see:

III

I envied your sweet slumber, all night so calm you lay,
The night was calm, the morn is calm, and like another day;
But I could wish yon moaning sea would rise and burst the shore,
And such a whirlwind blow these woods, as never blew before.

IV

For, one by one, the stars went down across the gleaming pane,
And project after project rose, and all of them were vain;
The blackthorn-blossom fades and falls and leaves the bitter sloe,
The hope I catch at vanishes and youth is turned to woe.

V

Come, speak a little comfort! all night I prayed with tears,
And yet no comfort came to me, and now the morn appears,
When he will tear me from your side, who bought me for his slave:
This father pays his debt with me, and weds me to my grave.

VI

What father, this or mine, was he, who, on that summer day
When I had fallen from off the crag we clambered up in play,
Found, feared me dead, and groaned, and took and kissed me, and again
He kissed me; and I loved him then; he *was* my father then.

VII

No father now, the tyrant vassal of a tyrant vice!
The Godless Jephtha vows his child . . . to one cast of the dice.
These ancient woods, this Hall at last will go–perhaps have gone,
Except his own meek daughter yield her life, heart, soul to one–

VIII

To one who knows I scorn him. O the formal mocking bow,
The cruel smile, the courtly phrase that masks his malice now–
But often in the sidelong eyes a gleam of all things ill–
It is not Love but Hate that weds a bride against her will;

IX

Hate, that would pluck from this true breast the locket that I wear,
The precious crystal into which I braided Edwin's hair!

¶ 259.26. Jephtha sacrificed his daughter (*Judges* xi 30–31): 'And Jephtha vowed a vow unto the Lord, and said, If thou shalt without fail deliver the children of Ammon into mine hands, Then it shall be, that whatsoever cometh forth of the doors of my house to meet me, when I return in peace from the children of Ammon, shall surely be the Lord's, and I will offer it up for a burnt offering.' Cp. the similar use of the allusion–a father sacrificing his daughter to 'marriage-hindering Mammon'–in *Aylmer's Field* 280.

The love that keeps this heart alive beats on it night and day–
One golden curl, his golden gift, before he past away.

X

He left us weeping in the woods; his boat was on the sand;
How slowly down the rocks he went, how loth to quit the land!
And all my life was darkened, as I saw the white sail run,
And darken, up that lane of light into the setting sun.

XI

How often have we watched the sun fade from us through the West,
And follow Edwin to those isles, those islands of the Blest!
Is *he* not there? would I were there, the friend, the bride, the wife,
With him, where summer never dies, with Love, the Sun of life!

XII

O would I were in Edwin's arms–once more–to feel his breath
Upon my cheek–on Edwin's ship, with Edwin, even in death,
Though all about the shuddering wreck the death-white sea should rave,
Or if lip were laid to lip on the pillows of the wave.

XIII

Shall I take *him*? I kneel with *him*? I swear and swear forsworn
To love him most, whom most I loathe, to honour whom I scorn?
The Fiend would yell, the grave would yawn, my mother's ghost would rise–
To lie, to lie–in God's own house–the blackest of all lies!

XIV

Why–rather than that hand in mine, though every pulse would freeze,
I'd sooner fold an icy corpse dead of some foul disease:
Wed him? I will not wed him, let them spurn me from the doors,
And I will wander till I die about the barren moors.

XV

The dear, mad bride who stabbed her bridegroom on her bridal night–
If mad, then I am mad, but sane, if she were in the right.
My father's madness makes me mad–but words are only words!
I am not mad, not yet, not quite–There! listen how the birds

XVI

Begin to warble yonder in the budding orchard trees!
The lark has past from earth to Heaven upon the morning breeze!
How gladly, were I one of those, how early would I wake!
And yet the sorrow that I bear is sorrow for *his* sake.

XVII

They love their mates, to whom they sing; or else their songs, that meet
The morning with such music, would never be so sweet!
And though these fathers will not hear, the blessèd Heavens are just,
And Love is fire, and burns the feet would trample it to dust.

51. The mother is dead as in *Maud*.

57. The climax of Scott's *The Bride of Lammermoor*, which T. versified in *The Bridal* (p. 164), and which influenced *Maud*.

XVIII

A door was opened in the house–who? who? my father sleeps!
A stealthy foot upon the stair! he–some one–this way creeps!
If he? yes, he . . . lurks, listens, fears his victim may have fled–
He! where is some sharp-pointed thing? he comes, and finds me dead.

XIX

Not he, not yet! and time to act–but how my temples burn!
And idle fancies flutter me, I know not where to turn;
Speak to me, sister; counsel me; this marriage must not be.
You only know the love that makes the world a world to me!

XX

Our gentle mother, had *she* lived–but we were left alone:
That other left us to ourselves; he cared not for his own;
So all the summer long we roamed in these wild woods of ours,
My Edwin loved to call us then 'His two wild woodland flowers.'

XXI

Wild flowers blowing side by side in God's free light and air,
Wild flowers of the secret woods, when Edwin found us there,
Wild woods in which we roved with him, and heard his passionate vow,
Wild woods in which we rove no more, if we be parted now!

XXII

You will not leave me thus in grief to wander forth forlorn;
We never changed a bitter word, not once since we were born;
Our dying mother joined our hands; she knew this father well;
She bad us love, like souls in Heaven, and now I fly from Hell,

XXIII

And you with me; and we shall light upon some lonely shore,
Some lodge within the waste sea-dunes, and hear the waters roar,
And see the ships from out the West go dipping through the foam,
And sunshine on that sail at last which brings our Edwin home.

XXIV

But look, the morning grows apace, and lights the old church-tower,
And lights the clock! the hand points five–O me–it strikes the hour–
I bide no more, I meet my fate, whatever ills betide!
Arise, my own true sister, come forth! the world is wide.

XXV

And yet my heart is ill at ease, my eyes are dim with dew,
I seem to see a new-dug grave up yonder by the yew!
If we should never more return, but wander hand in hand
With breaking hearts, without a friend, and in a distant land.

XXVI

O sweet, they tell me that the world is hard, and harsh of mind,
But can it be so hard, so harsh, as those that should be kind?
That matters not: let come what will; at last the end is sure,
And every heart that loves with truth is equal to endure.

77–8. Cp. *Maud*.

# 260 The Bridesmaid

Published *1872*, 'Juvenilia', 'Early Sonnets XI'. Written 1836–7, judging from *H.Nbk 21* where the poem appears 'Copied June [? Jan.] 1837'; from *Loosepaper 93*; and from the fact that on 24 May 1836 T.'s brother Charles married Louisa Sellwood. Her sister Emily, who was to marry T. in 1850 (the engagement being recognized in 1838), was a bridesmaid.

O Bridesmaid, ere the happy knot was tied,
Thine eyes so wept that they could hardly see;
Thy sister smiled and said, 'No tears for me!
A happy bridesmaid makes a happy bride.'
And then, the couple standing side by side,
Love lighted down between them full of glee,
And over his left shoulder laughed at thee,
'O happy bridesmaid, make a happy bride.'
And all at once a pleasant truth I learned,
For while the tender service made thee weep,
I loved thee for the tear thou couldst not hide,
And prest thy hand, and knew the press returned,
And thought, 'My life is sick of single sleep:
O happy bridesmaid, make a happy bride!'

# 261 'Move eastward, happy earth, and leave'

Published *1842*. It is an epithalamium; cp. *The Bridesmaid* (above), and perhaps it too dates from the marriage of T.'s brother Charles in May 1836. Alternatively, T.'s engagement to Emily Sellwood was recognized early in 1838 (*CT*, p. 177).

Move eastward, happy earth, and leave
    Yon orange sunset waning slow:
From fringes of the faded eve,
    O, happy planet, eastward go;
Till over thy dark shoulder glow
    Thy silver sister-world, and rise
    To glass herself in dewy eyes
That watch me from the glen below.

¶ 261.*1*. *happy earth*: Arthur Hallam's *Sonnet to a Lady on Her Marriage* (Motter, p. 77).
*3*. Cp. *On a Mourner* 21, MS: 'the fringing eve'.
*6*. *sister-world*: 'the moon' (T.). Perhaps hinting at Emily Sellwood, with whom Tennyson fell in love at the wedding of Charles to her sister.

Ah, bear me with thee, smoothly borne,
Dip forward under starry light,
And move me to my marriage-morn,
And round again to happy night.

## 262 *An Idle Rhyme

Printed by Sir Charles Tennyson, *Nineteenth Century* cix (1931) 626–7; then *1931*, pp. 79–80: 'Style and mood suggest that this poem was written at about the same date as *The Talking Oak* and *Will Waterproof*, both of which were published in 1842'. The latter poems were written *c.* 1837. The MS is split into *H.Lpr 270* and *H.Lpr 20* (watermarked 1835), where *An Idle Rhyme* is with *Caressed or chidden* (written *c.* 1836). It has many affinities with *In Memoriam* lxxxix (p. 940).

Oh, what care I how many a fluke
Sticks in the liver of the time?
I cannot prate against the Duke,
I love to have an idle rhyme.

The muse would stumble from the tune,
If I should ask her 'Plump my purse,
Be for some popular forenoon
The leading article in verse.'

So gross a whisper in her ear
Would make her dull as Davy's sow,
And with a sudden mildew sear
The rathe fruitblossom on her brow.

For, though she has her hopes and fears,
She dwells not on a single page,
But thrids the annals of the years,
And runs her eye from age to age.

9. *smoothly*] *1853*; lightly *1842–53*. Cp. *Paradise Lost* viii 166, where the earth, advancing from the west, 'beares thee soft with the smooth Air along'.

¶ 262.1. *fluke*: a worm which attacks the liver of sheep.

3. *the Duke*: Wellington.

9. *whisper*] *H.MS*; murmur *1931*.

10. *Davy's sow*: the proverb, 'as drunk as David's sow'.

12. *rathe*: early.

What's near is large to modern eyes,
  But disproportions fade away
Lowered in the sleepy pits where lies
  The dropsied Epos of the day–

The day that rose like ours sublime
  In dreaming dreams and planning plans,
That thought herself the crown of time
  And took her many geese for swans.

Oh, so, when modern things are thrust
  By death below the coffin lid,
Our liberal sons will spurn our dust
  And wonder what it was we did–

However, you have spoken well,
  But, now the summer sun descends,
Unbroach that flask of cool Moselle
  And let us drink to all our friends.

But if you prate of 'In' and 'Out',
  And Dan and Joe, whoe'er they be,
Then '*οἱη φυλλων*' will I spout,
  '*οἱη περ φυλλων γενεη*'.

As stretched beside the river clear
  That's round this glassy foreland curled,
I cool my face in flowers, and hear
  The deep pulsations of the world.

# 263 *'The tenth of April! is it not?'

Printed by M. J. Donahue, *Notes and Queries*, 27 Nov. 1948 (from *HnMS*: HM 19504). Written at High Beech, 10 April 1837, shortly after the family move; this was when T. read (l. 3) Charles Lyell's *Principles of Geology*

*20. Epos*: epic poem or epic event (*OED*'s examples postdate T.).
*34. Joe*] Hume *MS 1st reading*. Referring, as Sir Charles Tennyson says, to Daniel O'Connell and Joseph Hume, Irish and British politicians. See *Sonnet* [*The Wise, the Pure*] and note (p. 470).
*35–6. Iliad* vi 146 ('Even as are the generations of leaves, such are those also of men'). Sir Charles Tennyson comments: 'It is interesting to see how, in the few words of Greek, the poet follows English accent and not Greek quantity.' Possibly T. intended, by mis-scanning, to give the effect of a threadbare tag.
*40.* Incorporated as *In Memoriam* xcv 40.

(*Mem.* i 162), which discusses 'the extreme of cold, or what may be termed the winter of the "great year"' (1835 edn, i 181). *Gentleman's Magazine* records snow on 10 April.

The tenth of April! is it not?
Yet Nature wears her frozen robe.
How deep, Charles Lyell, are we got
In that great winter of the globe?
For now so bleakly shrill the squalls,
So frosty-hard the pavements sound,
One almost thinks the dome of Paul's
Should keep his snow the whole year round.

## 264 *'Black Bull of Aldgate'

Printed by M. J. Donahue, *Notes and Queries*, 27 Nov. 1948 (from *HnMS*: HM 19488). Written at High Beech, Epping Forest, where the Tennysons had moved early in 1837. H.T. mentions T.'s 'evening journeys between London and High Beech' (*Mem.* i 150).

Black Bull of Aldgate, may thy horns rot from the sockets!
For, jingling threepence, porter's pay, in hungry pockets,
And thirty times at least beneath thy doorway stepping
I've waited for this lousy coach that runs to Epping.
Ill luck befall thee, that hast made me so splenetic,
Through all thy holes and closets up from tap to attic,
Through all thy boys and bootses, chambermaids, and waiters,
And yonder booking-office-clerk in fustian gaiters.
Black Bull of Aldgate! mayst thou more miscarry
Than ever hasty Clement's did with bloated Harry!

¶ 264.*3*. thy] *HnMS*; your *1948*.
*6*. *tap*: tap-room.
*10*. Clement VII, 'Pope, memorable for his refusing to divorce Catherine of Arragon from Henry VIII; and for the bull he published upon the king's marriage with Anne Boleyn; which, according to the Romish authors, lost him England' (*English Encyclopaedia*, Supplement, 1802, of which there was a copy at Somersby, *Lincoln*).

# 265 A Farewell

Published *1842*. It is to the brook at Somersby (H.T.), so it was presumably written in early 1837 when the family left. R. J. Tennant wrote to T.'s mother, 2 May 1837: 'I am grieved to think how deserted Somersby will soon be' (*Brotherton Collection*). It is probably not later than 1837, since it is in *H.Nbk 21* (watermarked 1836). Cp. *In Memoriam* ci 9–10, on the same parting (p. 954): 'Unloved, by many a sandy bar, / The brook shall babble down the plain.'

Flow down, cold rivulet, to the sea,
  Thy tribute wave deliver:
No more by thee my steps shall be,
  For ever and for ever.

Flow, softly flow, by lawn and lea,
  A rivulet then a river:
No where by thee my steps shall be,
  For ever and for ever.

But here will sigh thine alder tree,
  And here thine aspen shiver;
And here by thee will hum the bee,
  For ever and for ever.

A thousand suns will stream on thee,
  A thousand moons will quiver;
But not by thee my steps shall be,
  For ever and for ever.

[1837. *Oh! that 'twere possible*–see p. 598]

# 266 *The Queen of the Isles

Printed by E. F. Shannon and W. H. Bond, *Harvard Library Bulletin* x (1956) 261–2 (with trivial first readings). *Mem.* i 161 printed ll. 17–20. It was written 1837, for Queen Victoria's accession (20 June), and forwarded to James Spedding to be sent to *The Times* 'or some paper with a circulation'–'It is little more than newspaper verse, but it might have an effect if good music went along with it'. Cp. *To the Queen* (p. 990).

¶ 265.*10*. Leaving Somersby, T. may have remembered a book (*Lincoln*) in the library there: Thomas Gisborne's *Walks in a Forest: Spring* (1794): 'And rustling aspens shiver by the brook'.
*13. thousand*] *1843*; hundred *1842*.

My friends since you wish for a health from the host,
Come fill up your glasses: I'll give you a toast.
Let us drink to the health that we value the most–
To the health of the Queen of the Isles.

The reigns of her fathers were long or were short,
They plagued us in anger or vext us in sport.
Let them sleep in their good or their evil report–
But a health to the Queen of the Isles.

May those in her council that have the chief voice
Be true hearts of oak that the land may rejoice
And her people may love her the more for her choice–
So a health to the Queen of the Isles.

No slaves of a party, straightforward and clear,
Let them speak out like men without bias or fear
That the voice of her people may reach to her ear
With a health to the Queen of the Isles–

That the voice of a satisfied people may keep
A sound in her ear like the sound of the deep,
Like the voice of the sea when the wind is asleep
And a health to the Queen of the Isles.

Let her flag as [of old be] the first on the seas,
That the good [of the] land and the world may increase
And Power may balance the nations in Peace
With a health to the Queen of the Isles.

But if despots and fools must be taught with the rod,
Let her soldier tread firm as his fathers have trod
And her cannon roar out like the judgement of God
With a health to the Queen of the Isles.

My brothers and friends! may the days that commence
Be so fruitful in genius, in worth and in sense
That a man's eye shall glisten, a thousand years hence,
When he reads of the Queen of the Isles!

And since Time never pauses but Change must ensue,
Let us wish that old things may fit well with the new,
For the blessing of promise is on her like dew–
So a health to the Queen of the Isles.

¶ 266.21–2] *Lacunae 1956; readings now guessed.*

God bless her! and long may she hold the command
Till the hair of the boy shall be gray in the land
And the ball and the sceptre shall pass from her hand
To the race of the Queen of the Isles.

So fill up your glasses and hold them on high,
Were the health fathoms-deep I would drink it or die,
And send out your voices and join in the cry
To the health of the Queen of the Isles.

# 267 Will Waterproof's Lyrical Monologue

## Made at The Cock

Published *1842*. Written *c.* 1837, ten years after the death of Canning (ll. 101–4). *HnMS* (HM 1320) is watermarked 1835. Cp. the similar poems of this date, *Amphion* (p. 685) and *The Talking Oak* (p. 675). A draft of ll. 1–20 is in Edward FitzGerald's copy of *1842* (*Trinity College*), as part of a letter from T. 'Thus far had I got in writing out a poem to you, when I made a blot and grew disgusted with the MSS.' (T.'s friendship with FitzGerald dated from 1835.) The Cock Tavern, Fleet Street, had long been a favourite resort for men of letters.

O plump head-waiter at The Cock,
To which I most resort,
How goes the time? 'Tis five o'clock.
Go fetch a pint of port:
But let it not be such as that
You set before chance-comers,
But such whose father-grape grew fat
On Lusitanian summers.

No vain libation to the Muse,
But may she still be kind,
And whisper lovely words, and use
Her influence on the mind,
To make me write my random rhymes,
Ere they be half-forgotten;
Nor add and alter, many times,
Till all be ripe and rotten.

I pledge her, and she comes and dips
Her laurel in the wine,
And lays it thrice upon my lips,
These favoured lips of mine;

Until the charm have power to make
  New lifeblood warm the bosom,
And barren commonplaces break
  In full and kindly blossom.

I pledge her silent at the board;
  Her gradual fingers steal
And touch upon the master-chord
  Of all I felt and feel.
Old wishes, ghosts of broken plans,
  And phantom hopes assemble;
And that child's heart within the man's
  Begins to move and tremble.

Through many an hour of summer suns,
  By many pleasant ways,
Against its fountain upward runs
  The current of my days:
I kiss the lips I once have kissed;
  The gas-light wavers dimmer;
And softly, through a vinous mist,
  My college friendships glimmer.

I grow in worth, and wit, and sense,
  Unboding critic-pen,
Or that eternal want of pence,
  Which vexes public men,
Who hold their hands to all, and cry
  For that which all deny them–
Who sweep the crossings, wet or dry,
  And all the world go by them.

Ah yet, though all the world forsake,
  Though fortune clip my wings,
I will not cramp my heart, nor take
  Half-views of men and things.

¶ *267.24. In*] *1853*; To *1842–51*.
*27. master-chord*: cp. *Henry VIII* III ii 105–6: 'the string, / The master-cord on's heart'.
*35*] *1853*; Like Hezekiah's, backward runs *1842–51*.
*36. current*] *1853*; shadow *1842–51*. *2 Kings* xx 11, where the sign of the Lord to Hezekiah was that 'he brought the shadow ten degrees backward'. Cp. the revised version with *The Lover's Tale* i 492–3: 'and driven / My current to the fountain whence it sprang'.
*38. gas-light*] gas-lamp *HnMS*.
*42. Unboding*: without forebodings as to (*OED*, 'bode' 5).

Let Whig and Tory stir their blood;
There must be stormy weather;
But for some true result of good
All parties work together.

Let there be thistles, there are grapes;
If old things, there are new;
Ten thousand broken lights and shapes,
Yet glimpses of the true.
Let raffs be rife in prose and rhyme,
We lack not rhymes and reasons,
As on this whirligig of Time
We circle with the seasons.

This earth is rich in man and maid;
With fair horizons bound:
This whole wide earth of light and shade
Comes out a perfect round.
High over roaring Temple-bar,
And set in Heaven's third story,
I look at all things as they are,
But through a kind of glory.

---

Head-waiter, honoured by the guest
Half-mused, or reeling ripe,
The pint, you brought me, was the best
That ever came from pipe.
But though the port surpasses praise,
My nerves have dealt with stiffer.
Is there some magic in the place?
Or do my peptics differ?

For since I came to live and learn,
No pint of white or red
Had ever half the power to turn
This wheel within my head,

*55–6. Romans* viii 28, 'And we know that all things work together for good'.
*59. broken lights: In Memoriam: Prologue* 19.
*61. raffs*: 'scraps' (T.).
*63.* The 'whirligig of Time' is from *Twelfth Night* V i 376.
*76. came*] buzzed *MS 1st reading.*
*78. stiffer*: stronger, as in 'stiff port' (surviving as 'a stiff drink').
*80. peptics*: digestive organs (the first such sense in *OED*).
*81. came to*] first could *MS 1st reading.*

Which bears a seasoned brain about,
Unsubject to confusion,
Though soaked and saturate, out and out,
Through every convolution.

For I am of a numerous house,
With many kinsmen gay,
Where long and largely we carouse
As who shall say me nay:
Each month, a birth-day coming on,
We drink defying trouble,
Or sometimes two would meet in one,
And then we drank it double;

Whether the vintage, yet unkept,
Had relish fiery-new,
Or elbow-deep in sawdust, slept,
As old as Waterloo;
Or stowed, when classic Canning died,
In musty bins and chambers,
Had cast upon its crusty side
The gloom of ten Decembers.

The Muse, the jolly Muse, it is!
She answered to my call,
She changes with that mood or this,
Is all-in-all to all:
She lit the spark within my throat,
To make my blood run quicker,
Used all her fiery will, and smote
Her life into the liquor.

*100.* 1815. Such dating was a classical commonplace; cp. Horace, *Odes* III xiv 18: *cadum Marsi memorem duelli* ('a jar that remembers the Marsian War').

*101.* George Canning, famous for his oratory, died in 1827. Cp. Horace, *Odes* III xxi 1: *O nata mecum consule Manlio . . . pia testa* ('Thou faithful jar, born with me in Manlius' consulship').

*105–9*]
Can sipping solitary wet
Affect one so much more,
Than drinking when good fellows set
The banquet in a roar?
Oh sure the Muse slipt down my throat *MS 1st reading*

*111*] And with a full volition smote *MS 1st reading.*

*111–2.* Cp. *The Holy Grail* 467: 'smote itself into the bread'.

And hence this halo lives about
The waiter's hands, that reach
To each his perfect pint of stout,
His proper chop to each.
He looks not like the common breed
That with the napkin dally;
I think he came like Ganymede,
From some delightful valley.

The Cock was of a larger egg
Than modern poultry drop,
Stept forward on a firmer leg,
And crammed a plumper crop;
Upon an ampler dunghill trod,
Crowed lustier late and early,
Sipt wine from silver, praising God,
And raked in golden barley.

A private life was all his joy,
Till in a court he saw
A something-pottle-bodied boy
That knuckled at the taw:
He stooped and clutched him, fair and good,
Flew over roof and casement:
His brothers of the weather stood
Stock-still for sheer amazement.

But he, by farmstead, thorpe and spire,
And followed with acclaims,
A sign to many a staring shire
Came crowing over Thames.
Right down by smoky Paul's they bore,
Till, where the street grows straiter,
One fixed for ever at the door,
And one became head-waiter.

---

*119. Ganymede*: snatched up by the eagle to be Jove's cupbearer.
*127.* T. comments: 'As the bird drinks he holds up his neck. There is accordingly an old English saying about the cock "praising God" when he drinks.'
*131. pottle-bodied*: pot-bellied.
*132.* 'The game of marbles' (T.).
*142*] *1845*; With motion less or greater; *1842–3*.

But whither would my fancy go?
How out of place she makes
The violet of a legend blow
Among the chops and steaks!
'Tis but a steward of the can,
One shade more plump than common;
As just and mere a serving-man
As any born of woman.

I ranged too high: what draws me down
Into the common day?
Is it the weight of that half-crown,
Which I shall have to pay?
For, something duller than at first,
Nor wholly comfortable,
I sit, my empty glass reversed,
And thrumming on the table:

Half fearful that, with self at strife,
I take myself to task;
Lest of the fulness of my life
I leave an empty flask:
For I had hope, by something rare,
To prove myself a poet:
But, while I plan and plan, my hair
Is gray before I know it.

So fares it since the years began,
Till they be gathered up;
The truth, that flies the flowing can,
Will haunt the vacant cup:
And others' follies teach us not,
Nor much their wisdom teaches;
And most, of sterling worth, is what
Our own experience preaches.

Ah, let the rusty theme alone!
We know not what we know.
But for my pleasant hour, 'tis gone;
'Tis gone, and let it go.
'Tis gone: a thousand such have slipt
Away from my embraces,

*145–52*] *Not MS.*
*177–8*] And I am sitting here alone
A little mused or so: *MS 1st reading*
*179. But for my*] I had a *MS 1st reading.*

And fallen into the dusty crypt
Of darkened forms and faces.

Go, therefore, thou! thy betters went
Long since, and came no more;
With peals of genial clamour sent
From many a tavern-door,
With twisted quirks and happy hits,
From misty men of letters;
The tavern-hours of mighty wits–
Thine elders and thy betters.

Hours, when the Poet's words and looks
Had yet their native glow:
Nor yet the fear of little books
Had made him talk for show;
But, all his vast heart sherris-warmed,
He flashed his random speeches,
Ere days, that deal in ana, swarmed
His literary leeches.

So mix for ever with the past,
Like all good things on earth!
For should I prize thee, couldst thou last,
At half thy real worth?
I hold it good, good things should pass:
With time I will not quarrel:
It is but yonder empty glass
That makes me maudlin-moral.

---

Head-waiter of the chop-house here,
To which I most resort,
I too must part: I hold thee dear
For this good pint of port.
For this, thou shalt from all things suck
Marrow of mirth and laughter;
And wheresoe'er thou move, good luck
Shall fling her old shoe after.

*183. dusty*] dusky *MS 1st reading*. Cp. *In Memoriam* lxxxix 12 and *n* (p. 940).
*195. Nor*] *1853*; Not *1842–53*.
*197.* Invoking the full-blooded magnanimity and wit of Falstaff: 'The second property of your excellent sherris is the warming of the blood . . .' (*2 Henry IV* IV iii 99–101).
*199. ana*: as in 'Shakespeariana' (T.). *swarmed*: bred a swarm of (the only such sense in *OED*).
*200*] *MS ends.*

But thou wilt never move from hence,
　The sphere thy fate allots:
Thy latter days increased with pence
　Go down among the pots:
Thou battenest by the greasy gleam
　In haunts of hungry sinners,
Old boxes, larded with the steam
　Of thirty thousand dinners.

We fret, we fume, would shift our skins,
　Would quarrel with our lot;
Thy care is, under polished tins,
　To serve the hot-and-hot;
To come and go, and come again,
　Returning like the pewit,
And watched by silent gentlemen,
　That trifle with the cruet.

Live long, ere from thy topmost head
　The thick-set hazel dies;
Long, ere the hateful crow shall tread
　The corners of thine eyes:
Live long, nor feel in head or chest
　Our changeful equinoxes,
Till mellow Death, like some late guest,
　Shall call thee from the boxes.

But when he calls, and thou shalt cease
　To pace the gritted floor,
And, laying down an unctuous lease
　Of life, shalt earn no more;
No carved cross-bones, the types of Death,
　Shall show thee past to Heaven:
But carved cross-pipes, and, underneath,
　A pint-pot neatly graven.

## 268 *New Year's Eve

Printed by Sir Charles Tennyson, *Nineteenth Century* cix (1931) 626; then *1931*, p. 78: 'Cf. "The mellow lin-lan-lone of evening bells" in *Far-Far-Away*–published 1889' (p. 1405). From *H.Lpr 125* (watermarked 183[ ]),

*219–20.* 'Latter days', 'increased', 'go down': all Biblical in mock-seriousness.
*223. boxes*: 'the pews where the diners sit' (T.).
*230. pewit*: with the common pronunciation 'piū· it'.
*243. unctuous*: here both spiritual and greasy.

on the other side of *Will Waterproof* (written *c.* 1837). Cp. *The Death of the Old Year* (*1832*, p. 461).

Listen! bells in yonder town,
  Lin, lan, lone,
Over dale and over down,
  Lin, lan, lone,
Now the year is almost gone,
  Lin, lan, lone,
Dying, dying, almost gone,
  Lin, lan, lone,
Almost, almost, almost gone.

Listen how the bells begin, what a merry din,
  With a lin, lan, lin,
For the old year out and the new year in,
  With a lin-lan-lan and a lan-lan-lin,
And the old year out and the new year in,
  With a clash and a lin-lan-lin.

Put out the lights and let us go to bed,
The baby year is born, his father dead,
And, settling back after that storm of sound,
From all the starry circle overhead
Hard silence drops upon the stony ground.

# 269 The Talking Oak

Published *1842*. Written by 1837 or early 1838 (*Mat.* i 246); cp. the other jocular poems of this date, *Will Waterproof* (p. 667) and *Amphion* (p. 685). *HnMS* (HM 1320) is watermarked 1835. T. calls it 'an experiment meant to test the degree in which it was in [his] power as a poet to humanise external nature'. It was influenced by *As You Like It* III ii 1–10ff: 'O Rosalind! these trees shall be my books, / And in their barks my thoughts I'll character . . . / Run, run, Orlando, carve on every tree / The fair, the chaste and unexpressive she.' T.'s MS jotting 'P.V. 832' refers to Aeschylus, *Prometheus Vinctus* 832 ('that marvel passing all belief, the talking oaks, by which thou clearly, and in no riddling terms, wast saluted as the renowed spouse of Zeus that was to be'). There is a letter from T. to FitzGerald in the latter's copy of *1842* (*Trinity College*); in it, T. speaks of a

¶ 268.*10. what . . . din*] *H.MS; not 1931.*
*17. father*] *MS*; father's *1931.*
*18. storm of sound*: Shelley, *Prometheus Unbound* II ii 59, and his *Woodman* 36–7.

production based on Pope's *Rape of the Lock* at the Olympic Theatre. (It was by J. Oxenford, produced 27 March 1837; A. Nicoll, *History of English Drama* iv (1955) 367.) FitzGerald connects this with ll. 61–4, about Queen Anne.

Once more the gate behind me falls;
  Once more before my face
I see the mouldered Abbey-walls,
  That stand within the chace.

Beyond the lodge the city lies,
  Beneath its drift of smoke;
And ah! with what delighted eyes
  I turn to yonder oak.

For when my passion first began,
  Ere that, which in me burned,
The love, that makes me thrice a man,
  Could hope itself returned;

To yonder oak within the field
  I spoke without restraint,
And with a larger faith appealed
  Than Papist unto Saint.

For oft I talked with him apart,
  And told him of my choice,
Until he plagiarised a heart,
  And answered with a voice.

Though what he whispered under Heaven
  None else could understand;
I found him garrulously given,
  A babbler in the land.

But since I heard him make reply
  Is many a weary hour;
'Twere well to question him, and try
  If yet he keeps the power.

Hail, hidden to the knees in fern,
  Broad Oak of Sumner-chace,
Whose topmost branches can discern
  The roofs of Sumner-place!

Say thou, whereon I carved her name,
  If ever maid or spouse,
As fair as my Olivia, came
  To rest beneath thy boughs.–

¶ *269.30. Broad*] Tall *HnMS.*

'O Walter, I have sheltered here
Whatever maiden grace
The good old Summers, year by year
Made ripe in Sumner-chace:

'Old Summers, when the monk was fat,
And, issuing shorn and sleek,
Would twist his girdle tight, and pat
The girls upon the cheek,

'Ere yet, in scorn of Peter's-pence,
And numbered bead, and shrift,
Bluff Harry broke into the spence
And turned the cowls adrift:

'And I have seen some score of those
Fresh faces, that would thrive
When his man-minded offset rose
To chase the deer at five;

'And all that from the town would stroll,
Till that wild wind made work
In which the gloomy brewer's soul
Went by me, like a stork:

'The slight she-slips of loyal blood,
And others, passing praise,
Strait-laced, but all-too-full in bud
For puritanic stays:

45. *Peter's-pence*: tax paid to the Pope, abolished just before Henry VIII's dissolution of the monasteries, the subject of ll. 47–8.
47. *spence*: 'the monks' buttery' (T.).
51. *offset*: 'the young shoots that spring from the roots of plants' (*English Encyclopaedia*, 1802, of which a copy was at Somersby, *Lincoln*). Here, Queen Elizabeth.
52. *chase the deer*] ribs of beef *MS 1st reading*; hunt the deer *MS 2nd reading, then 1842.*
54–6. 'That old Tory the oak calls him a brewer, as the old Cavaliers did' (T.). T. points out that 'The stork, a republican bird, is said to have gone out of England with the Commonwealth. And though the Commonwealth did not expire till some months after the death of Oliver, it practically went out with him. The night when he died was a night of storm.' The superstition about the stork is in Browne's *Vulgar Errors* (of which there was a copy at Somersby, *Lincoln*); Byron has a note on the stormy night, in *Elegy on Newstead Abbey*. William Collins refers to the stork and liberty in his *Ode to Liberty* 57 and *n.*

'And I have shadowed many a group
Of beauties, that were born
In teacup-times of hood and hoop,
Or while the patch was worn;

'And, leg and arm with love-knots gay,
About me leaped and laughed
The modish Cupid of the day,
And shrilled his tinsel shaft.

'I swear (and else may insects prick
Each leaf into a gall)
This girl, for whom your heart is sick,
Is three times worth them all;

'For those and theirs, by Nature's law,
Have faded long ago;
But in these latter springs I saw
Your own Olivia blow,

'From when she gambolled on the greens
A baby-germ, to when
The maiden blossoms of her teens
Could number five from ten.

'I swear, by leaf, and wind, and rain,
(And hear me with thine ears,)
That, though I circle in the grain
Five hundred rings of years–

'Yet, since I first could cast a shade,
Did never creature pass
So slightly, musically made,
So light upon the grass:

'For as to fairies, that will flit
To make the greensward fresh,
I hold them exquisitely knit,
But far too spare of flesh.'

Oh, hide thy knotted knees in fern,
And overlook the chace;
And from thy topmost branch discern
The roofs of Sumner-place.

*63*. 'Queen Anne's times' (T.).
*66. About*] Within *MS 1st reading*.
*96 ∧ 7*]
Indeed I willingly convince
My judgement and believe
That no such maid has flourisht, since
My furthest mother, Eve. *MS, deleted*

But thou, whereon I carved her name,
   That oft hast heard my vows,
Declare when last Olivia came
   To sport beneath thy boughs.

'O yesterday, you know, the fair
   Was holden at the town;
Her father left his good arm-chair,
   And rode his hunter down.

'And with him Albert came on his.
   I looked at him with joy:
As cowslip unto oxlip is,
   So seems she to the boy.

'An hour had past–and, sitting straight
   Within the low-wheeled chaise,
Her mother trundled to the gate
   Behind the dappled grays.

'But as for her, she stayed at home,
   And on the roof she went,
And down the way you use to come,
   She looked with discontent.

'She left the novel half-uncut
   Upon the rosewood shelf;
She left the new piano shut:
   She could not please herself.

'Then ran she, gamesome as the colt,
   And livelier than a lark
She sent her voice through all the holt
   Before her, and the park.

'A light wind chased her on the wing,
   And in the chase grew wild,
As close as might be would he cling
   About the darling child:

'But light as any wind that blows
   So fleetly did she stir,
The flower, she touched on, dipt and rose,
   And turned to look at her.

'And here she came, and round me played,
   And sang to me the whole
Of those three stanzas that you made
   About my "giant bole";

'And in a fit of frolic mirth
  She strove to span my waist:
Alas, I was so broad of girth,
  I could not be embraced.

'I wished myself the fair young beech
  That here beside me stands,
That round me, clasping each in each,
  She might have locked her hands.

'Yet seemed the pressure thrice as sweet
  As woodbine's fragile hold,
Or when I feel about my feet
  The berried briony fold.'

O muffle round thy knees with fern,
  And shadow Sumner-chace!
Long may thy topmost branch discern
  The roofs of Sumner-place!

But tell me, did she read the name
  I carved with many vows
When last with throbbing heart I came
  To rest beneath thy boughs?

'O yes, she wandered round and round
  These knotted knees of mine,
And found, and kissed the name she found,
  And sweetly murmured thine.

'A teardrop trembled from its source,
  And down my surface crept.
My sense of touch is something coarse,
  But I believe she wept.

'Then flushed her cheek with rosy light,
  She glanced across the plain;
But not a creature was in sight:
  She kissed me once again.

*168 ∧ 9]* The woodpecker is kindly bred,
  Has often tapt and clung,
And hammered with his garnet head,
  And kist me with his tongue.
*MS, bracketed for tentative deletion*

'Her kisses were so close and kind,
That, trust me on my word,
Hard wood I am, and wrinkled rind,
But yet my sap was stirred:

'And even into my inmost ring
A pleasure I discerned,
Like those blind motions of the Spring,
That show the year is turned.

'Thrice-happy he that may caress
The ringlet's waving balm–
The cushions of whose touch may press
The maiden's tender palm.

'I, rooted here among the groves
But languidly adjust
My vapid vegetable loves
With anthers and with dust:

'For ah! my friend, the days were brief
Whereof the poets talk,
When that, which breathes within the leaf,
Could slip its bark and walk.

'But could I, as in times foregone,
From spray, and branch, and stem,
Have sucked and gathered into one
The life that spreads in them,

'She had not found me so remiss;
But lightly issuing through,
I would have paid her kiss for kiss,
With usury thereto.'

*169*] Yet never seemed his kiss so kind *MS.*
*170. That*] And *MS.*
*175.* Horace's *Odes* III xxvii 21–2: *caecos / sentiant motus* ('May they feel the blind onset').
*183.* 'Vegetable Love', Marvell's *To His Coy Mistress* 11.
*185. my friend, the days*] *1851*; the Dryad-days *1842–50.*
*196* ∧ *7*]
Ah! bring her often, let me greet
The maid with sounds and calls,
As when I rouse myself to meet
The sunlight ere it falls.

When toward me, after sudden showers,
The sweeping beam declines,
And underneath yon two grey towers
The leaded minster shines.

O flourish high, with leafy towers,
And overlook the lea,
Pursue thy loves among the bowers
But leave thou mine to me.

O flourish, hidden deep in fern,
Old oak, I love thee well;
A thousand thanks for what I learn
And what remains to tell.

''Tis little more: the day was warm;
At last, tired out with play,
She sank her head upon her arm
And at my feet she lay.

'Her eyelids dropped their silken eaves.
I breathed upon her eyes
Through all the summer of my leaves
A welcome mixed with sighs.

'I took the swarming sound of life–
The music from the town–
The murmurs of the drum and fife
And lulled them in my own.

'Sometimes I let a sunbeam slip,
To light her shaded eye;
A second fluttered round her lip
Like a golden butterfly;

'A third would glimmer on her neck
To make the necklace shine;
Another slid, a sunny fleck,
From head to ancle fine,

'Then close and dark my arms I spread,
And shadowed all her rest–
Dropt dews upon her golden head,
An acorn in her breast.

These lines were printed in *The Academy* (27 Jan. 1894), from a copy of *Poems* (*1849, South Kensington*), where they were written in at the end of the poem. They are spoken by the oak, and one can only guess where T. would have placed them.

*199. bowers*] flowers *MS.*

*215. murmurs*] whispers *MS.*

*224 ∧ 5*]
Another flickered through the shade
To dance upon her lap.
The sixth a little glory made
All round the muslin cap. *MS, deleted*

'But in a pet she started up,
And plucked it out, and drew
My little oakling from the cup,
And flung him in the dew.

'And yet it was a graceful gift–
I felt a pang within
As when I see the woodman lift
His axe to slay my kin.

'I shook him down because he was
The finest on the tree.
He lies beside thee on the grass.
O kiss him once for me.

'O kiss him twice and thrice for me,
That have no lips to kiss,
For never yet was oak on lea
Shall grow so fair as this.'

Step deeper yet in herb and fern,
Look further through the chace,
Spread upward till thy boughs discern
The front of Sumner-place.

This fruit of thine by Love is blest,
That but a moment lay
Where fairer fruit of Love may rest
Some happy future day.

I kiss it twice, I kiss it thrice,
The warmth it thence shall win
To riper life may magnetise
The baby-oak within.

But thou, while kingdoms overset,
Or lapse from hand to hand,
Thy leaf shall never fail, nor yet
Thine acorn in the land.

May never saw dismember thee,
Nor wielded axe disjoint,
That art the fairest-spoken tree
From here to Lizard-point.

O rock upon thy towery-top
All throats that gurgle sweet!
All starry culmination drop
Balm-dews to bathe thy feet!

267. *culmination*: reaching the meridian.

All grass of silky feather grow–
 And while he sinks or swells
The full south-breeze around thee blow
 The sound of minster bells.

The fat earth feed thy branchy root,
 That under deeply strikes!
The northern morning o'er thee shoot,
 High up, in silver spikes!

Nor ever lightning char thy grain,
 But, rolling as in sleep,
Low thunders bring the mellow rain,
 That makes thee broad and deep!

And hear me swear a solemn oath,
 That only by thy side
Will I to Olive plight my troth,
 And gain her for my bride.

And when my marriage morn may fall,
 She, Dryad-like, shall wear
Alternate leaf and acorn-ball
 In wreath about her hair.

And I will work in prose and rhyme,
 And praise thee more in both
Than bard has honoured beech or lime,
 Or that Thessalian growth,

In which the swarthy ringdove sat,
 And mystic sentence spoke;
And more than England honours that,
 Thy famous brother-oak,

Wherein the younger Charles abode
 Till all the paths were dim,
And far below the Roundhead rode,
 And hummed a surly hymn.

*273. fat*] *MS, revised to* deep.
*274. deeply*] *MS, revised to* strongly.
*275*] *MS, revised to* The pale North-West above thee shoot.
*276. High up*] Far up *MS, revised to* All night.
*292–4.* The oaks at Dodona, where the dove 'pronounced that in this place should be set up an oracle of Zeus' (T.).

# 270 Amphion

Published *1842*. Probably written *c.*1837–8, like the similar poems *The Talking Oak* and *Will Waterproof*. Amphion was the musician to whose lyre the stones moved to build Thebes; here, a type of the poet, the moral being that 'Genius must not deem itself exempt from work' (T.'s wife Emily). For this theme, cp. *The Flower* (p. 1185). T. was probably influenced by a song and picture of dancing fishes in a book he certainly knew (and owned; the 1834 edn is at *Lincoln*): T. C. Croker's *Fairy Legends* ii (1828) 71–6. Croker connects the fishes' dance with Amphion. T. may have merged Amphion with Orpheus, but in Skelton's *Garland of Laurel* Amphion too made the trees dance.

My father left a park to me,
  But it is wild and barren,
A garden too with scarce a tree,
  And waster than a warren:
Yet say the neighbours when they call,
  It is not bad but good land,
And in it is the germ of all
  That grows within the woodland.

O had I lived when song was great
  In days of old Amphion,
And ta'en my fiddle to the gate,
  Nor cared for seed or scion!
And had I lived when song was great,
  And legs of trees were limber,
And ta'en my fiddle to the gate,
  And fiddled in the timber!

'Tis said he had a tuneful tongue,
  Such happy intonation,
Wherever he sat down and sung
  He left a small plantation;
Wherever in a lonely grove
  He set up his forlorn pipes,
The gouty oak began to move,
  And flounder into hornpipes.

The mountain stirred its bushy crown,
  And, as tradition teaches,
Young ashes pirouetted down
  Coquetting with young beeches;

And briony-vine and ivy-wreath
Ran forward to his rhyming,
And from the valleys underneath
Came little copses climbing.

The linden broke her ranks and rent
The woodbine wreaths that bind her,
And down the middle, buzz! she went
With all her bees behind her;
The poplars, in long order due,
With cypress promenaded,
The shock-head willows two and two
By rivers gallopaded.

Came wet-shod alder from the wave,
Came yews, a dismal coterie;
Each plucked his one foot from the grave,
Poussetting with a sloe-tree:
Old elms came breaking from the vine,
The vine streamed out to follow,
And, sweating rosin, plumped the pine
From many a cloudy hollow.

And wasn't it a sight to see,
When, ere his song was ended,
Like some great landslip, tree by tree,
The country-side descended;
And shepherds from the mountain-eaves
Looked down, half-pleased, half-frightened,
As dashed about the drunken leaves
The random sunshine lightened!

Oh, nature first was fresh to men,
And wanton without measure;
So youthful and so flexile then,
You moved her at your pleasure.

¶ 270.*33–6*] *1855*; The birch-tree swang her fragrant hair,
The bramble cast her berry,
The gin within the juniper
Began to make him merry. *1842–53*

*37. long order*: T. mocks its usual solemnity; cp. Gray, *Ode for Music* 37–8: 'High Potentates and Dames of royal birth / And mitred Fathers in long order go.'

*40. gallopade*: a dance of Hungarian origin (the earliest *OED* example is 1831).

*44. Poussetting*: country dancing (not a country word, but from the French; the earliest *OED* example is 1812).

Twang out, my fiddle! shake the twigs!
And make her dance attendance;
Blow, flute, and stir the stiff-set sprigs,
And scirrhous roots and tendons.

'Tis vain! in such a brassy age
I could not move a thistle;
The very sparrows in the hedge
Scarce answer to my whistle;
Or at the most, when three-parts-sick
With strumming and with scraping,
A jackass heehaws from the rick,
The passive oxen gaping.

But what is that I hear? a sound
Like sleepy counsel pleading;
O Lord!–'tis in my neighbour's ground,
The modern Muses reading.
They read Botanic Treatises,
And Works on Gardening through there,
And Methods of transplanting trees
To look as if they grew there.

The withered Misses! how they prose
O'er books of travelled seamen,
And show you slips of all that grows
From England to Van Diemen.
They read in arbours clipt and cut,
And alleys, faded places,
By squares of tropic summer shut
And warmed in crystal cases.

But these, though fed with careful dirt,
Are neither green nor sappy;
Half-conscious of the garden-squirt,
The spindlings look unhappy.
Better to me the meanest weed
That blows upon its mountain,
The vilest herb that runs to seed
Beside its native fountain.

64. *scirrhous*: hard with cancer.
84. *Van Diemen*: Tasmania.
92. *spindlings*] *1851*; poor things *1842–50*.
93–4. Cp. Wordsworth, *Immortality Ode* 206: 'to me the meanest flower that blows'. Echoing Gray, *Ode on Vicissitude* 49: 'The meanest flowret of the vale'.

And I must work through months of toil,
  And years of cultivation,
Upon my proper patch of soil
  To grow my own plantation.
I'll take the showers as they fall,
  I will not vex my bosom:
Enough if at the end of all
  A little garden blossom.

# 271 Locksley Hall

Published *1842*. Written 1837–8; so Rader (pp. 41–2) argues convincingly. (i) Edmund Lushington thought he remembered that it was read to him in 1837 or early 1838 (*Mat.* i 246). (ii) It relates to T.'s disillusionment with Rosa Baring, and was probably influenced by the talk in 1837 of her engagement, and her marriage in Oct. 1838. (iii) T. read T. Pringle (the source of ll. 135–6) in 1837 (*Mem.* i 162), and l. 114 was written at High Beech where the Tennysons lived from 1837–40 (*Mem.* i 150). (iv) *Y.MS* is watermarked '1835' and is not likely to be very much later. (Rader (p. 41) mistakenly calls this 'the sole MS of the poem'; in fact the poem appears with the *1842* poems in *HnMS* (HM 1320), which at this point is watermarked 1838.) Rader adds, for those who wish to associate it with Lincolnshire, that T. was there in the spring of 1838. Furthermore Walter White says that it 'was written at High Beech' (*Journals*, 1898, pp. 151–2), and he corroborates Lushington in that much of it was seen and heard at Mitre Court Buildings, The Temple. W. D. Templeman's preference for 1840–1 is supported by J. H. Buckley (writing before Rader, however), who believes it refers to T.'s breaking off his engagement with Emily in 1840; Rader's discoveries make this unnecessary, as is Templeman's suggestion that T. was adapting the unhappy love affair in Carlyle's *Sartor Resartus* (*Booker Memorial Studies*, 1950). All variants from *Y.MS* are given below. *Biography*. The main source from T.'s life is his unhappy love affair with Rosa; see *Thy rosy lips* (p. 634) and *To Rosa* (p. 648). T.'s experience of 'marriage-hindering Mammon' precipitated, among other poems, *Locksley Hall*, *Edwin Morris* and *Maud*. Rader points out that hers was an arranged marriage (cp. ll. 59–62), and that the Hall was suggested by her Harrington Hall (and see ll. 25–6*n*). Sir Charles Tennyson notes that the story of 'family estrangement owes much of its form and atmosphere to the feud between Somersby and Bayons' (p. 194), the latter being the home of Charles Tennyson-d'Eyncourt, in whose favour T.'s father had virtually been disinherited; also that the heroes of *Locksley Hall* and *Maud* 'have more than a little reference to Frederick', T.'s brother (again, Rader's discoveries suggest that this might be modified). T., as so often, maintained

that it was 'an imaginary place and imaginary hero': 'The whole poem represents young life, its good side, its deficiencies, and its yearnings.' *Sources.* 'Sir William Jones's prose translation of the Moâllakát, the seven Arabic poems ... hanging up in the temple of Mecca, gave the idea of the poem' (H.T.). Jones summarized the first Poem, of Amriolkais: 'The poet ... supposes himself attended on a journey by a company of friends; and, as they pass near a place, where his mistress had lately dwelled ... he desires them to stop awhile, that he might indulge the painful pleasure of weeping over the deserted remains of her tent. They comply with his request, but exhort him to show more strength of mind, and urge two topicks of consolation; namely, that he had before been equally unhappy, and that he had enjoyed his full share of pleasures: thus by the recollection of his passed delight his imagination is kindled, and his grief suspended.' Then follows an account of Amriolkais's amours (among them 'Fathima'; cp. *Fatima*); the poem ends, as does T.'s poem, with a violent storm. See below ll. 9–10*n*, 75–6*n*, 89–90*n*, 122*n*. E. F. Shannon (*Note and Queries*, June 1959) suggests that 'Locksley' is from Scott's *Ivanhoe*, where it is Robin Hood's pseudonym (from his birthplace): 'Locksley is the pseudonym of a man alienated from society ... indict[ing] the corruption and self-seeking of his day.' He mentions the bugle-horn (ll. 2, 145) with its insistent association with Scott's Locksley; and see l. 50*n*. T. had earlier written of *Amy*: 'I love thee, Amy, / And woo thee for my wife'. Reminiscences of *Hamlet* were apt to an attack on a corrupt society, dealing with an unhappy love-affair; see ll. 43–4*n*, 69*n*, 133*n*, and cp. T.'s description of *Maud*, a poem similar in many ways to *Locksley Hall*, as 'a little *Hamlet*'.
*Metre.* 'Mr Hallam [Henry Hallam] said to me that the English people liked verse in trochaics, so I wrote the poem in this metre' (T.). J. F. A. Pyre, *The Formation of Tennyson's Style* (1921), pp. 110–12, points out that T. used this 8-stress trochaic line in sporadic couplets in the revised *1842* ending of *The Lotos-Eaters*, and that he came very near such a metre in a trochaic ballad like *The Lord of Burleigh*. Edmund Blunden in his selection (1960) points out that it was used in *Sabbation* (1838) by T.'s friend R. C. Trench. The spur to its use may well have been the fact that, in the poem of Amriolkais, Jones's prose fell naturally into it: 'Thus I spoke, when my companions stopped their course[r]s by my side.' Jones has approximations like 'Thy condition, they replied, is not more painful than when thou ...'; and half-lines like 'On that day I killed my camel', 'On that happy day I entered'. T.'s acute receptiveness to rhythms is famous (see the headnote to *The Charge of the Light Brigade*, p. 1034), and Jones's prose probably ran in his head (C. Ricks, *Notes and Queries*, Aug. 1965). Cp. *Locksley Hall Sixty Years After* (p. 1359).

Comrades, leave me here a little, while as yet 'tis early morn:
Leave me here, and when you want me, sound upon the bugle-horn.

¶ 271.*1. while ... morn*] 'tis the place where I was born *Y.MS.*
*2. Leave ... and*] Comrades leave me: *MS.*

'Tis the place, and all around it, as of old, the curlews call,
Dreary gleams about the moorland flying over Locksley Hall;

Locksley Hall, that in the distance overlooks the sandy tracts,
And the hollow ocean-ridges roaring into cataracts.

Many a night from yonder ivied casement, ere I went to rest,
Did I look on great Orion sloping slowly to the West.

Many a night I saw the Pleiads, rising through the mellow shade,
Glitter like a swarm of fire-flies tangled in a silver braid.

Here about the beach I wandered, nourishing a youth sublime
With the fairy tales of science, and the long result of Time;

When the centuries behind me like a fruitful land reposed;
When I clung to all the present for the promise that it closed:

When I dipt into the future far as human eye could see;
Saw the Vision of the world, and all the wonder that would be.—

In the Spring a fuller crimson comes upon the robin's breast;
In the Spring the wanton lapwing gets himself another crest;

*3. 'Tis . . . it*] *1843*; 'Tis the place, and round the gables *1842*; Round the gable, round the turret *MS*.
*3–4.* T. says that this means '*while* dreary gleams', not in apposition to 'curlews'. Marian Bradley, in her diary (11 Jan. 1870, British Museum), reports: 'He wishes he had used "sweeping"–instead of "flying"–it would have been more explicit' (quoted *Mem.* ii 93). G. G. Loane, *Echoes in Tennyson* (1928), p. 6, compares John Leyden: 'But formless shadows seemed to fly / Along the muir-land dun . . . / And round did float, with clamorous note / And scream, the hoarse curlew.' Leyden's *The Cout of Keeldar* is in Scott's *Minstrelsy of the Scottish Border*, which T. certainly knew.
*5. that . . . overlooks*] before me and behind *MS*.
*6.* Adapted from *The Lover's Tale* i 52–61, MS: 'The roaring ridges into cataracts' (pointed out by Sir Charles Tennyson, *Cornhill* cliii (1936) 445).
*8.* Horace, *Odes* III xxvii 18: *pronus Orion.*
*9–10.* From the *Moâllakát* (see headnote): 'It was the hour, when the Pleiads appeared in the firmament, like the folds of a silken sash variously decked with gems.'
*11–16*] *Not at first in MS.* T. had simply the one visionary passage beginning at l. 119. He then revised that passage, and moved the vision (ll. 11–16, 121–30, as one) to this early point. For publication, he split the vision into two, and repeated ll. 15–16 as ll. 119–20.
*12. long*] great *MS*. The Miltonic 'great result' (*PL* ii 515) must have seemed unapt. *the long result*: *In Memoriam* i 14. Cp. *The Day-Dream*: *L'Envoi* 10–12: 'science . . . / As wild as aught of fairy lore.'
*13–14.* See ll. 117–18*n*.
*18. another*] a novel *MS intermediate reading.*

In the Spring a livelier iris changes on the burnished dove;
In the Spring a young man's fancy lightly turns to thoughts of love.

Then her cheek was pale and thinner than should be for one so young,
And her eyes on all my motions with a mute observance hung.

And I said, 'My cousin Amy, speak, and speak the truth to me,
Trust me, cousin, all the current of my being sets to thee.'

On her pallid cheek and forehead came a colour and a light,
As I have seen the rosy red flushing in the northern night.

And she turned–her bosom shaken with a sudden storm of sighs–
All the spirit deeply dawning in the dark of hazel eyes–

Saying, 'I have hid my feelings, fearing they should do me wrong;'
Saying, 'Dost thou love me, cousin?' weeping, 'I have loved thee long.'

Love took up the glass of Time, and turned it in his glowing hands;
Every moment, lightly shaken, ran itself in golden sands.

Love took up the harp of Life, and smote on all the chords with might;
Smote the chord of Self, that, trembling, passed in music out of sight.

Many a morning on the moorland did we hear the copses ring,
And her whisper thronged my pulses with the fulness of the Spring.

Many an evening by the waters did we watch the stately ships,
And our spirits rushed together at the touching of the lips.

O my cousin, shallow-hearted! O my Amy, mine no more!
O the dreary, dreary moorland! O the barren, barren shore!

*19–20.* Recalling the effect of spring in Thomson's *Spring* 786–8: 'the cooing dove / Flies thick in amorous chase, and wanton rolls / The glancing eye, and turns the changeful neck.'
*22. motions*] movements *MS*.
*25–6.* Rader (p. 45) refers to Rosa's blush, remembered years after in *The Roses on the Terrace* (p. 1423).
*31. glowing hands*: traditional; cp. Keats, *Eve of St Agnes* 271: 'These delicates he heaped with glowing hand / On golden dishes'. T. had used it, again with personification, in *Time* 59: 'Bright Fame, with glowing hand'; and *Mithridates* 10: 'The glowing hands of Honour'.
*37. the stately ships*: *Break, break, break* 9.
*38.* A traditional notion; cp. *Fatima* 19–21 and *n*: 'he drew / With one long kiss my whole soul through / My lips' (p. 383).
*38 ∧ 9*] In the hall there hangs a painting, Amy's arms are round my neck,
Happy children in a sunbeam, sitting on the ribs of wreck.

In my life there is a picture: she that claspt my neck is flown.
I am left within the shadow, sitting on the wreck alone. *HnMS*

T. deleted these lines from the proofs of *1842* (*Lincoln*); they became the nucleus, ll. 13–16, of *Locksley Hall Sixty Years After*.

Falser than all fancy fathoms, falser than all songs have sung,
Puppet to a father's threat, and servile to a shrewish tongue!

Is it well to wish thee happy?–having known me–to decline
On a range of lower feelings and a narrower heart than mine!

Yet it shall be: thou shalt lower to his level day by day,
What is fine within thee growing coarse to sympathise with clay.

As the husband is, the wife is: thou art mated with a clown,
And the grossness of his nature will have weight to drag thee down.

He will hold thee, when his passion shall have spent its novel force,
Something better than his dog, a little dearer than his horse.

What is this? his eyes are heavy: think not they are glazed with wine.
Go to him: it is thy duty: kiss him: take his hand in thine.

It may be my lord is weary, that his brain is overwrought:
Soothe him with thy finer fancies, touch him with thy lighter thought.

He will answer to the purpose, easy things to understand–
Better thou wert dead before me, though I slew thee with my hand!

Better thou and I were lying, hidden from the heart's disgrace,
Rolled in one another's arms, and silent in a last embrace.

Cursèd be the social wants that sin against the strength of youth!
Cursèd be the social lies that warp us from the living truth!

Cursèd be the sickly forms that err from honest Nature's rule!
Cursèd be the gold that gilds the straitened forehead of the fool!

Well–'tis well that I should bluster!–Hadst thou less unworthy proved–
Would to God–for I had loved thee more than ever wife was loved.

Am I mad, that I should cherish that which bears but bitter fruit?
I will pluck it from my bosom, though my heart be at the root.

Never, though my mortal summers to such length of years should come
As the many-wintered crow that leads the clanging rookery home.

43. *having . . . to*] now that thou hast dared *Y.MS 1st reading.*
44. *On*] To *MS 1st reading.* *narrower*] lesser *MS.* Cp. these lines with *Hamlet* I v 50–52: 'To decline / Upon a wretch whose natural gifts were poor / To those of mine'.
48. *will*] shall *MS.*
50. A common indictment; E. F. Shannon compares *Ivanhoe*, Chapter 29: 'His war-horse–his hunting hound are dearer to him than the despised Jewess!'
63. *Well . . . bluster!*] Cursèd–No I curse not thee. O *MS 1st reading*; No–I curse not thee, my cousin *MS.*
68. Cp. the 'treble dated Crow' in Shakespeare's *The Phoenix and Turtle*; Horace, *Odes* III xvii 13, *annosa cornix*. T. comments: 'Rooks are called crows in the Northern counties.'

Where is comfort? in division of the records of the mind?
Can I part her from herself, and love her, as I knew her, kind?

I remember one that perished: sweetly did she speak and move:
Such a one do I remember, whom to look at was to love.

Can I think of her as dead, and love her for the love she bore?
No–she never loved me truly: love is love for evermore.

Comfort? comfort scorned of devils! this is truth the poet sings,
That a sorrow's crown of sorrow is remembering happier things.

Drug thy memories, lest thou learn it, lest thy heart be put to proof,
In the dead unhappy night, and when the rain is on the roof.

Like a dog, he hunts in dreams, and thou art staring at the wall,
Where the dying night-lamp flickers, and the shadows rise and fall.

Then a hand shall pass before thee, pointing to his drunken sleep,
To thy widowed marriage-pillows, to the tears that thou wilt weep.

Thou shalt hear the 'Never, never,' whispered by the phantom years,
And a song from out the distance in the ringing of thine ears;

And an eye shall vex thee, looking ancient kindness on thy pain.
Turn thee, turn thee on thy pillow: get thee to thy rest again.

Nay, but Nature brings thee solace; for a tender voice will cry.
'Tis a purer life than thine; a lip to drain thy trouble dry.

Baby lips will laugh me down: my latest rival brings thee rest.
Baby fingers, waxen touches, press me from the mother's breast.

*69.* Cp. *Hamlet* I v 98–9: 'From the table of my memory / I'll wipe away all trivial fond records'.

*70*] Can I hate her falsehood now and love the days when she was kind? *MS 1st reading.*

*74. No*] Nay *MS.*

*75. Comfort . . . devils*] Hollow, hollow, hollow comfort *MS 1st reading.*

*75–6. the poet*: Dante. T.'s note quotes *Nessun maggior dolore, / Che ricordarsi del tempo felice / Nella miseria* (*Inferno* v 121–3). At the age of twelve, he had quoted this, via Byron's *Corsair* (*Mem.* i 8). These lines are in effect a retort to the *Moâllakât*'s 'consolation': 'that he had enjoyed his full share of pleasures: thus by the recollection of his passed delight his imagination is kindled, and his grief suspended.'

*77. Drug . . . it*] Thou shalt know it: drug thy memories *MS.*

*79.* The dreaming dog is from Lucretius; see *Lucretius* 44–6*n* (p. 1208).

*81–2*] Every tear that slowly gathers but a ghastly jest shall seem.
Then a hand shall pass before thee pointing to his drunken dream.
*MS 1st reading*

*87. Nay . . . thee*] Rise–there is a little *MS 1st reading.*

*89–90*] *Added to MS.* The baby as 'rival' should be contrasted with the *Moâllakât*'s very different tone: 'Many a lovely mother have I diverted from the care of her yearling infant . . . When the suckling behind her

O, the child too clothes the father with a dearness not his due.
Half is thine and half is his: it will be worthy of the two.

O, I see thee old and formal, fitted to thy petty part,
With a little hoard of maxims preaching down a daughter's heart.

'They were dangerous guides the feelings–she herself was not exempt–
Truly, she herself had suffered'–Perish in thy self-contempt!

Overlive it–lower yet–be happy! wherefore should I care?
I myself must mix with action, lest I wither by despair.

What is that which I should turn to, lighting upon days like these?
Every door is barred with gold, and opens but to golden keys.

Every gate is thronged with suitors, all the markets overflow.
I have but an angry fancy: what is that which I should do?

I had been content to perish, falling on the foeman's ground,
When the ranks are rolled in vapour, and the winds are laid with sound.

But the jingling of the guinea helps the hurt that Honour feels,
And the nations do but murmur, snarling at each other's heels.

Can I but relive in sadness? I will turn that earlier page.
Hide me from my deep emotion, O thou wondrous Mother-Age!

Make me feel the wild pulsation that I felt before the strife,
When I heard my days before me, and the tumult of my life;

Yearning for the large excitement that the coming years would yield,
Eager-hearted as a boy when first he leaves his father's field,

cried, she turned round to him with half her body; but half of it, pressed beneath my embrace, was not turned from me.'

92. *it will be*] God send it *MS 1st reading*.

93. *fitted . . . part*] verse't in many a vulgar art *MS 1st reading*.

96. *Truly . . . suffered*] She could speak from sad experience *MS 1st reading*. T. had used 'sad experience' in l. 144.

97. *lower . . . happy*!] which is basest! wherefore, *MS*.

98. The theme developed in *Maud*, especially the closing section.

102. *an angry*] a wandering *MS*.

103–4. Cp. the aspiration, contrasted with despair, in *The Two Voices* 149–56: 'To perish . . . like a warrior overthrown' (also 'foeman', 'smoke'). *laid*: the notion that gunfire stills the waves.

105. *jingling . . . hurt*] tightness of the purse-string salves the sore *MS*. ('tightness', because of the weight of the money.)

107. *that earlier*] the former *MS*.

107–8] . . . sadness? Shall I not arise and fling / Fancy back a little further through the freshness of the spring? *MS 1st reading*.

109] When I felt the wild pulsation that is prophet to the strife, *MS 1st reading*. *the wild pulsation*: *In Memoriam* xii 4.

111. *years*] age *MS*.

And at night along the dusky highway near and nearer drawn,
Sees in heaven the light of London flaring like a dreary dawn;

And his spirit leaps within him to be gone before him then,
Underneath the light he looks at, in among the throngs of men:

Men, my brothers, men the workers, ever reaping something new:
That which they have done but earnest of the things that they shall do:

For I dipt into the future, far as human eye could see,
Saw the Vision of the world, and all the wonder that would be;

Saw the heavens fill with commerce, argosies of magic sails,
Pilots of the purple twilight, dropping down with costly bales;

Heard the heavens fill with shouting, and there rained a ghastly dew
From the nations' airy navies grappling in the central blue;

*117–40*] *Deleted in MS, then revised.* See ll. 11–16*n* for the change of plan as to the visions.
*117–18*] *Appearing in MS ll. 174 ∧ 5. MS* at first had instead ll.13–14 ('Then . . .').
*119. For*] Then *MS 1st reading.*
*120. Saw . . . wonder*] I had visions in my head of all the wonders *MS 1st reading.*
*121*] When a man shall range the spaces, using unimagined sails, *MS 1st reading.* *fill*] throng *MS.*
*122. Pilots . . . twilight*] Merchants in a rosy sunset *MS 1st reading*; Argosies that roam the twilight *MS 2nd reading.* T.'s final version, since it omits 'merchants', is not quite so clearly related to the *Moâllakát.* T. translates into prophetic fact the *Moâllakát*'s beautiful simile for rain: 'The cloud unloads its freight on the desert of Ghabeit, like a merchant of Yemen alighting with his bales of rich apparel.' Cp. also *The Mermaid* 44: 'the purple twilights under the sea'. After l. 122, *MS* had at first:

When the pilot of the whirlwind flying by the northern star
Showers through [along *1st reading*] the polar hollow, meteors of aërial war.

*123. Heard . . . and*] Saw [When *1st reading*] the heavens fill with battle, when *MS. rained*] rains *MS 1st reading.* Cp. the blood from the battle in *The Vale of Bones* 77: 'the red dew o'er thee rained'. *The Oak of the North* (*1827*), by T.'s brother Frederick, calls blood 'that deadly dew'. Also Shelley, *Mask of Anarchy* 192: 'Blood is on the grass like dew'; and Byron, *Childe Harold* IV cxxvi: 'The skies which rain their plagues on men like dew'.
*123–4, 125–6*] *Transposed in MS 1st reading; ll. 125–6 then deleted.*
*124.* E. F. Shannon, *PQ* xxxi (1952) 441–5, compares the 'balloon' stanzas that originally began *A Dream of Fair Women*, and argues that T. was thinking mainly of balloons here.

Far along the world-wide whisper of the south-wind rushing warm,
With the standards of the peoples plunging through the thunder-storm;

Till the war-drum throbbed no longer, and the battle-flags were furled
In the Parliament of man, the Federation of the world.

There the common sense of most shall hold a fretful realm in awe,
And the kindly earth shall slumber, lapt in universal law.

So I triumphed ere my passion sweeping through me left me dry,
Left me with the palsied heart, and left me with the jaundiced eye;

Eye, to which all order festers, all things here are out of joint:
Science moves, but slowly slowly, creeping on from point to point:

Slowly comes a hungry people, as a lion creeping nigher,
Glares at one that nods and winks behind a slowly-dying fire.

Yet I doubt not through the ages one increasing purpose runs,
And the thoughts of men are widened with the process of the suns.

What is that to him that reaps not harvest of his youthful joys,
Though the deep heart of existence beat for ever like a boy's?

126. *standards of the*] standard of his *MS 1st reading.*
127] Saw the peoples brother-minded laying battle-standards furled *MS.* *throbbed . . . were*] throb . . . are *MS 1st reading.*
129. *There*] Where *MS.*
131. *triumphed ere*] dreamed before *MS 1st reading.*
133. *Eye, to which all*] Nothing pleases, *MS 1st reading.* Cp. *Hamlet* I v 188–9: 'The time is out of joint, O cursèd spite, / That ever I was born to set it right.'
134. *Science . . . creeping*] Little moves but Science creeping slowly *MS 1st reading.*
135] Or the crowd that stumbling forward in their hunger drawing near,
With a lingering will divided by their famine and their fear,

As a lion in his hunger and his anger creeping nigher, *MS 1st reading*

The lion is from Thomas Pringle's *Travels,* which T. read in 1837 (*Mem.* i 162). Miss M. J. Donahue notes that H.T. confused Pringle's *Travels* and his *Poetical Works* when quoting T.'s letter of 1837 (*Mat.* i 200); but this need not invalidate the statement in *Mem.* that T. read the *Travels* then.
136 ∧ 7] Yet I doubt not that a glory waits upon some later morn–
Every moment dies a man and every moment one is born.
*MS 1st reading*

The second line became *The Vision of Sin* 97–8: 'Every moment dies a man, / Every moment one is born.'
137. *Yet . . . ages*] And through all the generations *MS 1st reading*; Yet I know through all the ages *MS.*
139. *youthful*] natural *MS 1st reading.*

Knowledge comes, but wisdom lingers, and I linger on the shore,
And the individual withers, and the world is more and more.

Knowledge comes, but wisdom lingers, and he bears a laden breast,
Full of sad experience, moving toward the stillness of his rest.

Hark, my merry comrades call me, sounding on the bugle-horn,
They to whom my foolish passion were a target for their scorn:

Shall it not be scorn to me to harp on such a mouldered string?
I am shamed through all my nature to have loved so slight a thing.

Weakness to be wroth with weakness! woman's pleasure, woman's pain–
Nature made them blinder motions bounded in a shallower brain:

Woman is the lesser man, and all thy passions, matched with mine,
Are as moonlight unto sunlight, and as water unto wine–

Here at least, where nature sickens, nothing. Ah, for some retreat
Deep in yonder shining Orient, where my life began to beat;

Where in wild Mahratta-battle fell my father evil-starred;–
I was left a trampled orphan, and a selfish uncle's ward.

Or to burst all links of habit–there to wander far away,
On from island unto island at the gateways of the day.

Larger constellations burning, mellow moons and happy skies,
Breadths of tropic shade and palms in cluster, knots of Paradise.

Never comes the trader, never floats an European flag,
Slides the bird o'er lustrous woodland, swings the trailer from the crag;

*141. and . . . shore*] like a beggar at the door *MS alternative.* 'Knowledge comes', exclaims the lover of the age, Æonophilus; see *Mechanophilus* 4 ^ 5*n* (p. 493).
*144. toward*] towards *MS.*
*149–50*] Woman is the lesser being: all her pleasure and her pain
Is a feebler blinder motion bounded by a shallower brain. *MS*
*153–6*] *Not MS.*
*155. Mahratta*: soldiers of Bombay who were conquered in 1818.
*156. orphan*: cp. the story of *Maud.*
*157. Or . . . to*] I will burst the links of habit–I will *MS.*
*158. On from island unto island*] Roaming Oriental islands *MS.*
*160 ^ 1*] All about a summer ocean, leagues on leagues of golden calm,
And within melodious waters rolling round the knolls of palm.
H.T. quotes these lines from the 'original MS'; they are not in *Y.MS.* 'In the first unpublished edition . . . omitted lest the description should be too long' (*Mem.* i 195).
*162. swings*] *1851*; droops *1842–50.* *trailer*] garland *MS.* Adapted from *Anacaona* 39–40, the 'birds . . . in the lustrous woodland', another poem that shows T.'s lifelong interest in island paradises (see Paden, pp. 141–3).

Droops the heavy-blossomed bower, hangs the heavy-fruited tree–
Summer isles of Eden lying in dark-purple spheres of sea.

There methinks would be enjoyment more than in this march of mind,
In the steamship, in the railway, in the thoughts that shake mankind.

There the passions cramped no longer shall have scope and breathing
    space;
I will take some savage woman, she shall rear my dusky race.

Iron jointed, supple-sinewed, they shall dive, and they shall run,
Catch the wild goat by the hair, and hurl their lances in the sun;

Whistle back the parrot's call, and leap the rainbows of the brooks,
Not with blinded eyesight poring over miserable books–

Fool, again the dream, the fancy! but I *know* my words are wild,
But I count the gray barbarian lower than the Christian child.

I, to herd with narrow foreheads, vacant of our glorious gains,
Like a beast with lower pleasures, like a beast with lower pains!

Mated with a squalid savage–what to me were sun or clime?
I the heir of all the ages, in the foremost files of time–

*163. heavy-blossomed bower*] crimson-blossomed trailer *MS*.
*167*] There my heart should find expression and my passions breathing space; *MS 1st reading. the*] my *MS*.
*168–9*. Cp. Beaumont's *Philaster* IV i: 'Oh, that I had been nourished in these woods /. . . and not known / The right of Crowns, nor the dissembling Trains / Of Women's looks . . . / And then had taken me some Mountain Girl /. . . and have borne at her big breasts / My large coarse issue. This had been a life / Free from vexation.' Alongside John Churton Collins's note on this (*Cornhill*, Jan. 1880), T. wrote 'possibly' (*Lincoln*). The works of Beaumont and Fletcher were at Somersby (*Lincoln*).
*169. dive*] ride *MS 1st reading*.
*171. Whistle . . . leap*] Shouting in the gorges, leaping through *MS 1st reading*.
*173. Fool . . . but*] What is this I utter? madness. Well *MS*.
*174. But*] Well *MS*.
*174 ∧ 5*] Were there any good in living if we reapt not something new?
That which we have done is earnest of the things that we shall do. *MS*
These became ll. 117–18.
*175*] Could I live with narrow foreheads! herd with these about the plains, *MS*.
*176. lower pains*] lesser pains *MS*.
*177–8*] Could I wed a savage woman steept perhaps in monstrous crime?
Am I not a modern man, a leader of the files of Time? *MS*.

I that rather held it better men should perish one by one,
Than that earth should stand at gaze like Joshua's moon in Ajalon!

Not in vain the distance beacons. Forward, forward let us range,
Let the great world spin for ever down the ringing grooves of change.

Through the shadow of the globe we sweep into the younger day:
Better fifty years of Europe than a cycle of Cathay.

Mother-Age (for mine I knew not) help me as when life begun:
Rift the hills, and roll the waters, flash the lightnings, weigh the Sun.

O, I see the crescent promise of my spirit hath not set.
Ancient founts of inspiration well through all my fancy yet.

Howsoever these things be, a long farewell to Locksley Hall!
Now for me the woods may wither, now for me the roof-tree fall.

Comes a vapour from the margin, blackening over heath and holt,
Cramming all the blast before it, in its breast a thunderbolt.

Let it fall on Locksley Hall, with rain or hail, or fire or snow;
For the mighty wind arises, roaring seaward, and I go.

# 272 'Come not, when I am dead'

Published Nov.–Dec. 1850 as *Stanzas*, in *The Keepsake* for 1851; then *Poems*, 7th edn (1851), where its placing, as in *Eversley*, suggests it belongs with *1842*. The MS (now belonging to W. P. Jeffcock) was given by T. to J. M. Gully in 1847; all variants are below, and see ll. 6 ∧ 7*n* (C. Ricks, *MP* lxii (1964) 139). Probably, as Rader suggests (p. 132), it reflects T.'s disillusionment with Rosa Baring; on the love affair, see *Thy rosy lips* (p. 634). If

*179. I . . . it*] It were better, ten times *MS*.
*180. Joshua* x 12.
*182. great world*] *1843*, *MS*; peoples *1842*. T. comments: 'When I went by the first train from Liverpool to Manchester (1830) I thought that the wheels ran in a groove. It was a black night, and there was such a vast crowd round the train at the station that we could not see the wheels. Then I made this line.'
*183. globe*] *1843*, *MS*; world *1842*. This line stood originally as two lines of *The Voyage* (*T.Nbk 21*). *shadow . . . sweep*] shadows . . . rush *MS*.
*184. Cathay*: China.
*185–6*] *Not MS*.
*186 ∧ 7*] Life is battle, let me fight it: win or lose it? lose it, nay!
Block my paths with toil and danger, I will find or force a way!
Added to a copy belonging to James Knowles (*Nineteenth Century* xxxiii (1893) 168).
*190. roof-tree*: the main beam; T.'s hero may include the meaning 'the whole family, the house'.

so, it was perhaps written *c.*1838, when she married; cp. l. 9 with the theme of *Locksley Hall*, *Edwin Morris* and *Maud*.

Come not, when I am dead,
To drop thy foolish tears upon my grave,
To trample round my fallen head,
And vex the unhappy dust thou wouldst not save.
There let the wind sweep and the plover cry;
But thou, go by.

Child, if it were thine error or thy crime
I care no longer, being all unblest:
Wed whom thou wilt, but I am sick of Time,
And I desire to rest.
Pass on, weak heart, and leave me where I lie:
Go by, go by.

# 273 Walking to the Mail

Published *1842*; among 'English Idyls'. Written 1837–8 (?); see *Audley Court* (p. 704), and ll. 63–8*n* below. Cp. Theocritus, 4th Idyll. The poltergeist story (ll. 27–38) is widespread; T. probably derived it from T. C. Croker's *Fairy Legends* (1825; 1834 edn *Lincoln*), the word 'flitting' being suggested by the words of the Scandinavian Nis, 'See, idag flytter vi' ('see, today we're moving').

¶ 272.5] Pass on and leave me under sun and sky, *Jeffcock MS.*
6] But go thou by. *Keepsake*; Go by, Go by. *Jeffcock MS.* T. said that the *Keepsake* reading was a printer's error, and he is supported by *H.Lpr 27.*
6 ∧ 7] Lone as the cromlech or the mountain cairn
Let my grave be upon the dreary heath,
By swamps and pools, waste places of the hern
And solitudes of death.
There let the wind sweep and the plover cry,
Go by, go by. *MS*

. tightened the poem by cutting this stanza, salvaging the fifth line to replace his original l. 5. His third line he salvaged for *Geraint and Enid* 31 (1859): 'Gray swamps and pools, waste places of the hern'. Cp. 'mountain', 'cairn', 'cromlech', in *Idylls: To the Queen* 40–1 (1873). F. T. Palgrave noted, apparently in 1863 (T.'s *Poems* 1853, British Museum): 'Lone as a cromlech (verse left out). He had forgotten the rest. A.T.'
7. *Child*] Now *MS.*

*John.* I'm glad I walked. How fresh the meadows look
Above the river, and, but a month ago,
The whole hill-side was redder than a fox.
Is yon plantation where this byway joins
The turnpike?
*James.* Yes.
*John.* And when does this come by?
*James.* The mail? At one o'clock.
*John.* What is it now?
*James.* A quarter to.
*John.* Whose house is that I see?
No, not the County Member's with the vane:
Up higher with the yew-tree by it, and half
A score of gables.
*James.* That? Sir Edward Head's:
But he's abroad: the place is to be sold.
*John.* Oh, his. He was not broken.
*James.* No, sir, he,
Vexed with a morbid devil in his blood
That veiled the world with jaundice, hid his face
From all men, and commercing with himself,
He lost the sense that handles daily life–
That keeps us all in order more or less–
And sick of home went overseas for change.
*John.* And whither?
*James.* Nay, who knows? he's here and there.
But let him go; his devil goes with him,
As well as with his tenant, Jocky Dawes.
*John.* What's that?

¶ 273.*1–3*] I'm glad I walked. The savour of the briars
Goes through me to the kernel of my brain–*HnMS* (*HM 1320*)

*1. meadows look*] *1843*; country looks! *1842*.

*2–3*] *1843*; *not 1842*.

*4. yon plantation*] *1843*; yonder planting *1842*.

*7–10*] *1851*; ... Whose house is that I see
Beyond the watermills?
*James.* Sir Edward Head's: *1842–50*

*12. broken*: bankrupt.

*15*. Cp. Milton's Melancholy, 'commercing with the skies', *Il Penseroso 39*.

*16–17*. Incorporated from a MS of *The Gardener's Daughter, T.Nbk 17*.

*21–9*] As chanced to one that lived at Audley Grange. *HnMS 1st reading*. Cp. the name *Audley Court*.

*22–30*] *1853*; ... You saw the man but yesterday:
He picked the pebble from your horse's foot.

*James.* You saw the man—on Monday, was it?—
There by the humpbacked willow; half stands up
And bristles; half has fallen and made a bridge;
And there he caught the younker tickling trout—
Caught *in flagrante*—what's the Latin word?—
*Delicto:* but his house, for so they say,
Was haunted with a jolly ghost, that shook
The curtains, whined in lobbies, tapt at doors,
And rummaged like a rat: no servant stayed:
The farmer vext packs up his beds and chairs,
And all his household stuff; and with his boy
Betwixt his knees, his wife upon the tilt,
Sets out, and meets a friend who hails him, 'What!
You're flitting!' 'Yes, we're flitting,' says the ghost
(For they had packed the thing among the beds,)
'Oh well,' says he, 'you flitting with us too—
Jack, turn the horses' heads and home again.'
*John.* *He* left *his* wife behind; for so I heard.
*James.* He left her, yes. I met my lady once:
A woman like a butt, and harsh as crabs.
*John.* Oh yet but I remember, ten years back—
'Tis now at least ten years—and then she was—
You could not light upon a sweeter thing:
A body slight and round, and like a pear
In growing, modest eyes, a hand, a foot

His house was haunted by a jolly ghost
That rummaged like a rat: no servant stayed:
*1842–51*;

... You saw the man—on Monday, was it?—
There by the humpbacked willow; half stands up
Shock-headed; half has fallen and made a bridge;
He caught the miller's younker tickling trout—
Caught *in flagrante*—what's the Latin word?—
*Delicto*. One was flouncing out his life
Among the kingcups when we past: but he—
Where was I? O his house—the Grange they call it,
His house was haunted with a jolly ghost
That whisked the curtains, pattered down the stairs,
Grunted in lobbies, knocked three times at doors
And rummaged like a rat &c. *H.Nbk 26*

*25. younker*: youngsters.
*33. tilt*: the waggon's awning or cover.
*34. out*] *1853*; forth *1842–51*.
*41*] A woman like a fungus bloated white—
And harsh as verjuice, harsh to me, to all. *HnMS 1st reading*.

Lessening in perfect cadence, and a skin
As clean and white as privet when it flowers.
*James.* Ay, ay, the blossom fades, and they that loved
At first like dove and dove were cat and dog.
She was the daughter of a cottager,
Out of her sphere. What betwixt shame and pride,
New things and old, himself and her, she soured
To what she is: a nature never kind!
Like men, like manners: like breeds like, they say:
Kind nature is the best: those manners next
That fit us like a nature second-hand;
Which are indeed the manners of the great.
*John.* But I had heard it was this bill that past,
And fear of change at home, that drove him hence.
*James.* That was the last drop in the cup of gall.
I once was near him, when his bailiff brought
A Chartist pike. You should have seen him wince
As from a venomous thing: he thought himself
A mark for all, and shuddered, lest a cry
Should break his sleep by night, and his nice eyes
Should see the raw mechanic's bloody thumbs
Sweat on his blazoned chairs; but, sir, you know
That these two parties still divide the world–
Of those that want, and those that have: and still
The same old sore breaks out from age to age
With much the same result. Now I myself,
A Tory to the quick, was as a boy
Destructive, when I had not what I would.
I was at school–a college in the South:
There lived a flayflint near; we stole his fruit,
His hens, his eggs; but there was law for *us*;
We paid in person. He had a sow, sir. She,
With meditative grunts of much content,
Lay great with pig, wallowing in sun and mud.
By night we dragged her to the college tower
From her warm bed, and up the corkscrew stair

*59.* The Reform Bill of 1832.

*63–8.* Recalling the French Revolution. Carlyle has a section 'The Feast of Pikes' in *The French Revolution* (1837). M. J. Donahue refers to the Chartist agitations in 1838 (*Studies in the 10 Years' Silence*, Yale thesis, 1946).

*72. myself,*] *1845*; , that am *1842–3*.

*75–92.* 'This is an Eton story' (H.T.).

*78*] *1843*; We paid in person, scored upon the part
Which cherubs want. He had a sow, sir. She, *1842*

With hand and rope we haled the groaning sow,
And on the leads we kept her till she pigged.
Large range of prospect had the mother sow,
And but for daily loss of one she loved
As one by one we took them–but for this–
As never sow was higher in this world–
Might have been happy: but what lot is pure?
We took them all, till she was left alone
Upon her tower, the Niobe of swine,
And so returned unfarrowed to her sty.
*John.* They found you out?
*James.* Not they.
*John.* Well–after all–
What know we of the secret of a man?
His nerves were wrong. What ails us, who are sound,
That we should mimic this raw fool the world,
Which charts us all in its coarse blacks or whites,
As ruthless as a baby with a worm,
As cruel as a schoolboy ere he grows
To Pity–more from ignorance than will.

But put your best foot forward, or I fear
That we shall miss the mail: and here it comes
With five at top: as quaint a four-in-hand
As you shall see–three pyebalds and a roan.

[1838. *The Epic*–see p. 582
*The Day-Dream*–see p. 624]

# 274 Audley Court

Published *1842*; among 'English Idyls'. It was written autumn 1838 at Torquay (*Mem.* i 165), 'partially suggested by Abbey Park at Torquay in the old time' (T.). In *T.Nbk 26*, it opens with a description of Francis's arrival by boat; T. incorporated, from the MS of *The Gardener's Daughter*, 'The snoring funnel whizzed with silver steam'. There is an early draft in the *FitzGerald MS* at *Trinity*. In form and mood, the poem is based on Theocritus's 7th Idyll, where Simichidas's song (ll. 96–127) resembles Francis's. Cp. the setting of *The Princess* with its picnic and songs, especially the swallow-song (iv).

'The Bull, the Fleece are crammed, and not a room
For love or money. Let us picnic there

*91.* All Niobe's children were killed by the gods.
95] *HnMS ends.*

At Audley Court.'
I spoke, while Audley feast
Hummed like a hive all round the narrow quay,
To Francis, with a basket on his arm,
To Francis just alighted from the boat,
And breathing of the sea. 'With all my heart,'
Said Francis. Then we shouldered through the swarm,
And rounded by the stillness of the beach
To where the bay runs up its latest horn.

We left the dying ebb that faintly lipped
The flat red granite; so by many a sweep
Of meadow smooth from aftermath we reached
The griffin-guarded gates, and passed through all
The pillared dusk of sounding sycamores,
And crossed the garden to the gardener's lodge,
With all its casements bedded, and its walls
And chimneys muffled in the leafy vine.

There, on a slope of orchard, Francis laid
A damask napkin wrought with horse and hound,
Brought out a dusky loaf that smelt of home,
And, half-cut-down, a pasty costly-made,
Where quail and pigeon, lark and leveret lay,
Like fossils of the rock, with golden yolks
Imbedded and injellied; last, with these,
A flask of cider from his father's vats,
Prime, which I knew; and so we sat and eat
And talked old matters over; who was dead,
Who married, who was like to be, and how
The races went, and who would rent the hall:
Then touched upon the game, how scarce it was
This season; glancing thence, discussed the farm,

¶ 274.*3. Audley Court*] Oxley-Hall *FitzGerald MS.*
4] Hummed like a hive, and over hollowed tubes
Purse-lipt the swarthy piper moved his beard. *MS*
The last line and a half were incorporated from *The Gardener's Daughter* 185–208, MS.
*10. runs . . . horn*] scoops out its latest curve *MS.*
*13. aftermath*: after-mowing.
*15.* Cp. *Paradise Lost* ix 1106: 'Pillard shade'.
*18. leafy vine*: traditional, as in Shelley.
*19*] We found a slope of thyme where Francis laid *MS.*
*28–9. over . . . Who*], who was dead, and who / Was *MS.*

The four-field system, and the price of grain;
And struck upon the corn-laws, where we split,
And came again together on the king
With heated faces; till he laughed aloud;
And, while the blackbird on the pippin hung
To hear him, clapt his hand in mine and sang–

'Oh! who would fight and march and countermarch,
Be shot for sixpence in a battle-field,
And shovelled up into some bloody trench
Where no one knows? but let me live my life.
'Oh! who would cast and balance at a desk,
Perched like a crow upon a three-legged stool,
Till all his juice is dried, and all his joints
Are full of chalk? but let me live my life.
'Who'd serve the state? for if I carved my name
Upon the cliffs that guard my native land,
I might as well have traced it in the sands;
The sea wastes all: but let me live my life.
'Oh! who would love? I wooed a woman once,
But she was sharper than an eastern wind,
And all my heart turned from her, as a thorn
Turns from the sea; but let me live my life.'

He sang his song, and I replied with mine:
I found it in a volume, all of songs,
Knocked down to me, when old Sir Robert's pride,
His books–the more the pity, so I said–
Came to the hammer here in March–and this–
I set the words, and added names I knew.

'Sleep, Ellen Aubrey, sleep, and dream of me:
Sleep, Ellen, folded in thy sister's arm,
And sleeping, haply dream her arm is mine.
'Sleep, Ellen, folded in Emilia's arm;
Emilia, fairer than all else but thou,
For thou art fairer than all else that is.

*34–5.* There was Corn-Law agitation in 1837, the year in which William IV was gravely ill for a month and then died.

*37–8*] He clapt his hand in mine: he cleared his pipes
And while the blackbird on the rennet hung
To hear him, sang me out a random song. *MS*

*41. some*] *1872*; a *1842–70*.

*47. carved*] wrote *MS*.

*51. love*] wed *MS*.

*56–60*] *Not MS*.

'Sleep, breathing health and peace upon her breast:
Sleep, breathing love and trust against her lip:
I go tonight: I come tomorrow morn.
'I go, but I return: I would I were
The pilot of the darkness and the dream.
Sleep, Ellen Aubrey, love, and dream of me.'

So sang we each to either, Francis Hale,
The farmer's son, who lived across the bay,
My friend; and I, that having wherewithal,
And in the fallow leisure of my life
A rolling stone of here and everywhere,
Did what I would; but ere the night we rose
And sauntered home beneath a moon, that, just
In crescent, dimly rained about the leaf
Twilights of airy silver, till we reached
The limit of the hills; and as we sank
From rock to rock upon the glooming quay,
The town was hushed beneath us: lower down
The bay was oily calm; the harbour-buoy,
Sole star of phosphorescence in the calm,
With one green sparkle ever and anon
Dipt by itself, and we were glad at heart.

*73–7*]
So sang we couch't in thyme while overhead
The large peach fattened and the waxen plum
Pampered his luscious cheek: tall hollyoaks
Clustered their largest roses: orchard boughs
Dragged earthward overburdened: every gust
Tumbled the mellowing pear and at our feet
Through two round stones, two cushions of dark moss,
A pebbly runlet bubbled from the mound. *MS*

This adapts *The Gardener's Daughter* 216–20, MS.

*77*] *1855; not 1842–53.*

*78–80*]
There sat we till night fell, and rose at last
Returning home beneath a quarter-moon
That dimly rained about the lisping leaf *MS*

*81. airy*] showery *MS.*

*82–3*]
The latest limit of the seaward hill.
Then as we stept down toward the glooming quay *MS*

*86*] *1869; not 1842–68.* 'The little buoy appearing and disappearing in the dark sea' (T.).

*88.* Cp. the image of moon and stars ending *Iliad* viii, as in T.'s *Specimen of a Translation*: 'and the Shepherd gladdens in his heart'.

# 275 Edwin Morris

## or, The Lake

Published 1851, *Poems*, 7th edn; among 'English Idyls'. Written 1839 (*Mem.* i 174), which is the date of the *FitzGerald MS* at Trinity. All variants from this, and from *H.Nbk 26*, are below. The *FitzGerald MS* begins (at the top of a page) with the closing lines of Edwin's speech (ll. 62–70), in this version adapting further lines from *The Gardener's Daughter*; see ll. 26–40*n*. The poem was inspired by T.'s disillusionment with Rosa Baring; on this love affair, see *Thy rosy lips* (p. 634). She married Robert Duncombe Shafto. The complaint, here treated more lightly ('the rentroll Cupid'), is treated tragically as 'marriage-hindering Mammon' in *Aylmer's Field*, *Locksley Hall*, and *Maud*. T. criticizes his earlier manner in the poet Edwin Morris, most of whose lines are from the MS version (e.g. *T.Nbk 17*) of *The Gardener's Daughter*, another poem inspired by Rosa, of which the speaker is again a landscape painter. Edward Bull's views on women were to be more fully presented by the King in *The Princess*. The earliest draft in *T.Nbk 26* is much briefer, and the conversation different. There is no character Edward Bull; and Morris tells of an episode, suggesting *Maud*, in which his lover's cousin jealously lies in wait for him with a cudgel, unsuccessfully. This MS may not be quoted, nor may the later *Trinity* draft in which the poem begins with l. 13. The important revision is that which eliminates too harsh a resentment against Rosa, cutting out 'O facile nose of wax!', and 'the doll' (ll. 122–5*n*).

O me, my pleasant rambles by the lake,
My sweet, wild, fresh three quarters of a year,
My one Oasis in the dust and drouth
Of city life! I was a sketcher then:
See here, my doing: curves of mountain, bridge,
Boat, island, ruins of a castle, built
When men knew how to build, upon a rock
With turrets lichen-gilded like a rock:
And here, new-comers in an ancient hold,
New-comers from the Mersey, millionaires,
Here lived the Hills – a Tudor-chimnied bulk
Of mellow brickwork on an isle of bowers.

O me, my pleasant rambles by the lake
With Edwin Morris and with Edward Bull
The curate; he was fatter than his cure.

¶ 275. *2–4*] A dilettante sketcher I was then: *H.MS.*
5. *doing*] drawings *H.MS.*
*13*] *Later Trinity draft begins here.*

But Edwin Morris, he that knew the names,
Long learnèd names of agaric, moss and fern,
Who forged a thousand theories of the rocks,
Who taught me how to skate, to row, to swim,
Who read me rhymes elaborately good,
His own – I called him Crichton, for he seemed
All-perfect, finished to the finger nail.

And once I asked him of his early life,
And his first passion; and he answered me;
And well his words became him: was he not
A full-celled honeycomb of eloquence
Stored from all flowers? Poet-like he spoke.

'My love for Nature is as old as I;
But thirty moons, one honeymoon to that,
And three rich sennights more, my love for her.
My love for Nature and my love for her,
Of different ages, like twin-sisters grew,
Twin-sisters differently beautiful.
To some full music rose and sank the sun,
And some full music seemed to move and change
With all the varied changes of the dark,
And either twilight and the day between;
For daily hope fulfilled, to rise again
Revolving toward fulfilment, made it sweet
To walk, to sit, to sleep, to wake, to breathe.'

*17. agaric*: a fungus.
*18*] *Added in H.MS.*
*19. skate . . . swim*] to sketch, to skate, to row, *H.MS.*
*21.* James (the Admirable) Crichton was a sixteenth-century Scottish prodigy; P. F. Tytler's life of him was published 1819.
*22.* Horace, *Satires* I v 32–3: *ad unguem factus homo.*
*26–40.* These lines were incorporated, with only minor modifications, from MSS of *The Gardener's Daughter* (see headnote); some are in *Heath MS* version, others in *T.MS* drafts (which may not be quoted). T. apparently added ll. 28–30, 33. At one stage in the composition of *Edwin Morris* (*T.Nbk 26*), T. further incorporated in Edwin's second speech (ending at l. 70) the dozen lines immediately preceding these in *The Gardener's Daughter* MS, describing the lovers' embraces (p. 517). Likewise in *FitzGerald MS.*
*27. Poet-like*] like to this *H.MS.*
*28. for*] of *H.MS 1st reading.*
*32. grew*] *1853*; throve *1851.*
*40. to wake, to breathe*] *1853; transposed 1851–3.*

Or this or something like to this he spoke.
Then said the fat-faced curate Edward Bull,

'I take it, God made the woman for the man,
And for the good and increase of the world.
A pretty face is well, and this is well,
To have a dame indoors, that trims us up,
And keeps us tight; but these unreal ways
Seem but the theme of writers, and indeed
Worn threadbare. Man is made of solid stuff.
I say, God made the woman for the man,
And for the good and increase of the world.'

'Parson,' said I, 'you pitch the pipe too low:
But I have sudden touches, and can run
My faith beyond my practice into his:
Though if, in dancing after Letty Hill,
I do not hear the bells upon my cap,
I scarce have other music: yet say on.
What should one give to light on such a dream?'
I asked him half-sardonically.
'Give?
Give all thou art,' he answered, and a light
Of laughter dimpled in his swarthy cheek;
'I would have hid her needle in my heart,
To save her little finger from a scratch
No deeper than the skin: my ears could hear
Her lightest breath; her least remark was worth
The experience of the wise. I went and came;
Her voice fled always through the summer land;
I spoke her name alone. Thrice-happy days!
The flower of each, those moments when we met,
The crown of all, we met to part no more.'

Were not his words delicious, I a beast
To take them as I did? but something jarred;

*41*] *Not H.MS.*

*47. tight*: neat.

*52. Parson*] O sir *H.MS 1st reading.*

*55. Letty*] Emma *H.MS.*

*57. have*] *1869*; hear *1851–68.*

*59*] *Not H.MS.*

*62–70.* Adapted from MSS of *The Gardener's Daughter*; see headnote and ll. *26–40n.*

*65. breath*] *1872*; breaths *1851–70.*

*71–5.* Implicit criticism by T. of his earlier poetic manner; see ll. *62–70n.* The name 'Edwin' for such a poet may have been suggested by the hero of

Whether he spoke too largely; that there seemed
A touch of something false, some self-conceit,
Or over-smoothness: howsoe'er it was,
He scarcely hit my humour, and I said:

'Friend Edwin, do not think yourself alone
Of all men happy. Shall not Love to me,
As in the Latin song I learnt at school,
Sneeze out a full God-bless-you right and left?
But you can talk: yours is a kindly vein:
I have, I think,–Heaven knows–as much within;
Have, or should have, but for a thought or two,
That like a purple beech among the greens
Looks out of place: 'tis from no want in her:
It is my shyness, or my self-distrust,
Or something of a wayward modern mind
Dissecting passion. Time will set me right.'

So spoke I knowing not the things that were.
Then said the fat-faced curate, Edward Bull:
'God made the woman for the use of man,
And for the good and increase of the world.'
And I and Edwin laughed; and now we paused
About the windings of the marge to hear

Beattie's *Minstrel* (ii 524–6), which provided an epigraph for *1827* (p. 61), of which there was a copy at Somersby (*Lincoln*) and of which T.'s mother was fond (H. D. Rawnsley, *Memories of the Tennysons*, 1900, pp. 225–6): 'Of late, with cumbersome, though pompous show, / Edwin would oft his flowery rhyme deface, / Through ardour to adorn.' Cp. l. 27 above.

*74. some*] or *FitzGerald MS.*

*75–6*] I know not what: a screw was loose: I said: *H.MS*, *FitzGerald MS.*

*79*] *Not H.MS*, *FitzGerald MS.*

*80.* H.T. compares Catullus xlv 8–9: *hoc ut dixit, Amor, sinistra, ut ante / dextra, sternuit approbationem.* ('As he said this, Love on the left, as before on the right, sneezed goodwill.')

*81. yours is*] you have *FitzGerald MS.* *kindly vein*: Horace, *Odes* II xviii 10: *benigna vena.*

*82–3*] I have, I think, as much within–I have / Or I should . . . *H.MS*, *FitzGerald MS.* Cp. *Hamlet* I ii 85: 'But I have that within which passes show.'

*84. purple*] *1853*; copper *1851.*

*85. from*] for *FitzGerald MS.*

*87–8. Or . . . passion*: originally in the MS of *The Gardener's Daughter* (*T.Nbk 17*); see ll. 62–70*n*.

The soft wind blowing over meadowy holms
And alders, garden-isles; and now we left
The clerk behind us, I and he, and ran
By ripply shallows of the lisping lake,
Delighted with the freshness and the sound.

But, when the bracken rusted on their crags,
My suit had withered, nipt to death by him
That was a God, and is a lawyer's clerk,
The rentroll Cupid of our rainy isles.
'Tis true, we met; one hour I had, no more:
She sent a note, the seal an *Elle vous suit*,
The close, 'Your Letty, only yours;' and this
Thrice underscored. The friendly mist of morn
Clung to the lake. I boated over, ran
My craft aground, and heard with beating heart
The Sweet-Gale rustle round the shelving keel;
And out I stept, and up I crept: she moved,
Like Proserpine in Enna, gathering flowers:
Then low and sweet I whistled thrice; and she,
She turned, we closed, we kissed, swore faith, I breathed
In some new planet: a silent cousin stole

95. *over . . . holms*] in the osiered aits *H.MS*, *FitzGerald MS*. (As in *To the Vicar of Shiplake* 30.)
96. *left*] *1853*; ran *1851*.
97] *1853*; *not 1851*.
100] But ere November [December *FitzGerald MS*] came, my own suit failed, *H.MS*.
101–2] Nipt by the true magician of the ring, *FitzGerald MS*.
101–3] Nipt by the rentroll Cupid of the realms. *H.MS*.
103. *our*] *1853*; the *1851*.
104–14] 'Tis true, we met: we kisst: swore faith: I breathed *FitzGerald MS*.
105–8] She sent a note: I boated over, ran *H.MS*.
105. Byron, *Don Juan* I cxcviii: 'The seal a sunflower: "*Elle vous suit partout*"', a moment in Don Juan's 'earliest scrape'.
111] And out I leapt and hid myself. She walked *H.MS*.
112. Eve in Paradise, *Paradise Lost* iv 269, with suggestions of precariousness. T. had praised Rosa with the allusion in *The Gardener's Daughter* 187.
114. *we closed*] she came *H.MS*.
115. *cousin*] brother *FitzGerald MS*, *H.MS 1st reading*. An interesting parallel with the situation in *Maud*, where the brother steals upon the lovers.
115–20] . . . silent brother came
Upon us: ere a man could clap his hands,
The cat was in the creampot. Out they came, *FitzGerald MS*

Upon us and departed: 'Leave,' she cried,
'O leave me!' 'Never, dearest, never: here
I brave the worst:' and while we stood like fools
Embracing, all at once a score of pugs
And poodles yelled within, and out they came
Trustees and Aunts and Uncles. 'What, with him!
Go' (shrilled the cotton-spinning chorus); 'him!'
I choked. Again they shrieked the burthen–'Him!'
Again with hands of wild rejection 'Go!–
Girl, get you in!' She went–and in one month
They wedded her to sixty thousand pounds,
To lands in Kent and messuages in York,
And slight Sir Robert with his watery smile
And educated whisker. But for me,
They set an ancient creditor to work:
It seems I broke a close with force and arms:
There came a mystic token from the king
To greet the sheriff, needless courtesy!
I read, and fled by night, and flying turned:
Her taper glimmered in the lake below:
I turned once more, close-buttoned to the storm;

*116–8. 'Leave . . . worst:'*] 'O', she said,
'O leave me, leave me.' 'Never, let us brave
The worst at once' *H.MS*
*122*] *1853; not 1851. cotton-spinning*: possibly this refers to one of Rosa's uncles (Rader, p. 135); 'cotton' is used with contempt in *Maud* i 370, and 'cotton-spinners' in *The Third of February, 1852*, but there in dislike of the peace-loving politics of Manchester. Rader also remarks that 'trustees' (l. 121) is unexplained in Letty's case, but that Rosa's rich father had died.
*122–5*] 'Go, Sir' and 'collar him' and 'get you in'
And 'let him go.' O facile nose of wax! *FitzGerald MS*;
They clamoured, and again in chorus, 'him!',
'Go, Sir' and 'collar him' and 'let him go'
And 'get *you* in'–the doll–and in one month *H.MS*
*123. I choked.*] *1853*; 'Go Sir!' *1851*.
*125. She went*] *1853*; to her *1851*.
*127*] *Not FitzGerald MS.*
*128. And . . . watery*] To . . . vapid *FitzGerald MS. H.MS* ends with l. 128 at the bottom of a page, so a page is probably missing).
*131–6*] *Not FitzGerald MS.*
*132.* 'Writ from the old Court of Common Pleas' (T.).
*134*] *1853*; I read and wished to crush the race of man,
And fled by night; turned once upon the hills; *1851*
*135. below*] *1853*; and then *1851*.
*136*] *1853; not 1851.*

So left the place, left Edwin, nor have seen
Him since, nor heard of her, nor cared to hear.

Nor cared to hear? perhaps: yet long ago
I have pardoned little Letty; not indeed,
It may be, for her own dear sake but this,
She seems a part of those fresh days to me;
For in the dust and drouth of London life
She moves among my visions of the lake,
While the prime swallow dips his wing, or then
While the gold-lily blows, and overhead
The light cloud smoulders on the summer crag.

# 276 The Golden Year

Published *1846*. Sir Charles Tennyson (p. 211) says that, like *Edwin Morris*, it was written at Llanberis in summer 1845. But it was almost certainly written on the visit there in 1839. It is in *T.Nbk 26*; *Edwin Morris* is to be dated 1839; the song in *The Golden Year* (ll. 22–51), which is the core of the poem, is to be found on a sheet of the *Y.MS* of *Locksley Hall* (1837–8); and the discussion of free trade resembles, as does the poem in general, *Audley Court* (1838) and *Walking to the Mail* (1837–8). See also the reference to Charles Babbage (1837), ll. 59–64*n*. The incorporated song suggests Theocritus, especially vi. Cp. *Audley Court* (p. 704). The idea of the golden year is based on the classical conception of the great new era, as in Virgil, *Eclogue* iv. In the earlier draft (*H.Lpr 72*), Leonard too had doubts about progress; see ll. 59–64*n*.

Well, you shall have that song which Leonard wrote:
It was last summer on a tour in Wales:
Old James was with me: we that day had been
Up Snowdon; and I wished for Leonard there,
And found him in Llanberis: then we crost
Between the lakes, and clambered half way up
The counter side; and that same song of his
He told me; for I bantered him, and swore
They said he lived shut up within himself,

*137. So*] *1853*; I *1851*.
*139–43*] *Not FitzGerald MS.*
*144*] Yet comes at times a vision of the lake, *FitzGerald MS.*
*145. While*] When *FitzGerald MS.*
¶ *276.2–7*] *Not T.MS*; I came with James upon him while he sat
Beside the mere; and that same song of his *H.MS*
*5–7*] *1851*; And found him in Llanberis; and that same song *1846–50*.

A tongue-tied Poet in the feverous days,
That, setting the *how much* before the *how*,
Cry, like the daughters of the horseleech, 'Give,
Cram us with all,' but count not me the herd!

To which 'They call me what they will,' he said:
'But I was born too late: the fair new forms,
That float about the threshold of an age,
Like truths of Science waiting to be caught–
Catch me who can, and make the catcher crowned–
Are taken by the forelock. Let it be.
But if you care indeed to listen, hear
These measured words, my work of yestermorn.

'We sleep and wake and sleep, but all things move;
The Sun flies forward to his brother Sun;
The dark Earth follows wheeled in her ellipse;
And human things returning on themselves
Move onward, leading up the golden year.
'Ah, though the times, when some new thought can bud,
Are but as poets' seasons when they flower,
Yet oceans daily gaining on the land,
Have ebb and flow conditioning their march,
And slow and sure comes up the golden year.
'When wealth no more shall rest in mounded heaps,
But smit with freër light shall slowly melt
In many streams to fatten lower lands,
And light shall spread, and man be liker man
Through all the season of the golden year.
'Shall eagles not be eagles? wrens be wrens?
If all the world were falcons, what of that?
The wonder of the eagle were the less,

*12. Proverbs* xxx 15: 'The horse-leech hath two daughters, crying, Give, give.'

*29*] *1890*; Yet seas that daily gain upon the shore *1846–89*. Shakespeare, *Sonnet 64*: 'the hungry ocean gain / Advantage on the kingdom of the shore'.

*32–33*. Cp. a fragment in *H.Lpr 210*, from 'an old idyll never published' (William Allingham, *Diary*, 1907, p. 303): 'The rich shall wed the rich, the poor the poor, / So shall this mound of wealth be higher still, / So shall this gulf of want be deeper still, / Until this mountain melt into this gulf / With all confusion.'

*37*. The antithesis *wrens / eagles* suggests *Richard III* I iii 71.

But he not less the eagle. Happy days
Roll onward, leading up the golden year.
 'Fly, happy happy sails, and bear the Press;
Fly happy with the mission of the Cross;
Knit land to land, and blowing havenward
With silks, and fruits, and spices, clear of toll,
Enrich the markets of the golden year.
 'But we grow old. Ah! when shall all men's good
Be each man's rule, and universal Peace
Lie like a shaft of light across the land,
And like a lane of beams athwart the sea,
Through all the circle of the golden year?'

 Thus far he flowed, and ended; whereupon
'Ah, folly!' in mimic cadence answered James–
'Ah, folly! for it lies so far away,
Not in our time, nor in our children's time,
'Tis like the second world to us that live;
'Twere all as one to fix our hopes on Heaven
As on this vision of the golden year.'

 With that he struck his staff against the rocks
And broke it,–James,–you know him,–old, but full

*42.* Cp. Washington Irving's *Columbus* (1828) I vi, on the new uniting forces in the world: 'light . . . would still shine on, dispensed to happier parts of the world, by the diffusive powers of the press.' T. used the book for *Anacaona* and *Columbus*.

*48–52.* Cp. Shelley, *Queen Mab* viii 53–7: 'O human Spirit! spur thee to the goal / Where virtue fixes universal peace, / And midst the ebb and flow of human things, / Shew somewhat stable, somewhat certain still, / A lighthouse o'er the wild of dreary waves.' Cp. also l. 30.

*53*] Right in his rhythm and cadence answered James. *H.MS.* James speaks as a Carlylean, as W. C. DeVane observes.

*59–64*]
He said; and having business in the town
Departed, leaving Leonard, who began
To ponder: 'will it come or, being come,
Be felt as gain? this age of ours is gold
To much before it; yet no happier we,
Nor may our sons be happier than ourselves.
O grand old sires, who wagged their beards in hall
And laughed and let the earth go round, nor knew
The noiseless ether curdling into worlds
And complicated clockwork of the suns.
Motion: why motion? were it not as well

Of force and choler, and firm upon his feet,
And like an oaken stock in winter woods,
O'erflourished with the hoary clematis:
Then added, all in heat:
'What stuff is this!
Old writers pushed the happy season back, –
The more fools they, – we forward: dreamers both:
You most, that in an age, when every hour
Must sweat her sixty minutes to the death,
Live on, God love us, as if the seedsman, rapt
Upon the teeming harvest, should not plunge
His hand into the bag: but well I know
That unto him who works, and feels he works,
This same grand year is ever at the doors.'

He spoke; and, high above, I heard them blast
The steep slate-quarry, and the great echo flap
And buffet round the hills, from bluff to bluff.

---

To fix a point, to rest? again, it seems
Most adverse to the nature of a man
To rest if there be any more to gain.
And there is all but what he is: no rest:
Why then, to be resolved into the all.
That will not do, being to lose myself.
What else?' – And here, methought he seemed to grasp
A pair of shadowy compasses, with these
To plant a centre and about it round
A wide and wider circle: and while he mused
Came James, his business ended, and resumed: *H.MS*

An important passage in *MS*, because of its close correspondence with T.'s thinking. For the astronomy, cp. Babbage, *The Ninth Bridgewater Treatise* (1837, p. 91), of which T. had a copy (*Lincoln*); of the heavens, Babbage says 'nebulous light is just curdling, as it were, into separate systems'. T.'s 'complicated clockwork' may owe something to the fact that Babbage passes on to his clockwork 'calculating engine'.

*63.* Cp. *Twelfth Night* III iv 368: 'empty trunks o'erflourished'.

*70. plunge*] *1865 Selection*; dip *1846–65*.

*72 ∧ 3*] Howe'er it be, by some true art of Life, *H.MS*.

*74. above*] *1851*; above us *1846–50*; o'erhead *Eversley 'original reading'*.

*76.* T. comments: 'Onomatopoeic. "Bluff to bluff" gives the echo of the blasting as I heard it from the mountain on the counter side, opposite to Snowdon.' Cp. *The Princess* vii 229–30, MS: 'Till the last fire shall catch and flap from peak / To peak across the world.'

# 277 The Vision of Sin

Published *1842*. *HnMS* (HM 1320) is watermarked 1835. Not completed till after 1839. The fountain (ll. 8–32) was 'partly suggested by Turner's "Fountain of Fallacy"' (F. T. Palgrave's note from T.; see C. Ricks, *MP* lxii (1964) 139–40). This was exhibited in 1839, and J. M. W. Turner's verse-fragment in the catalogue spoke of 'its rainbow-dew' (cp. ll. 32, 42). T. comments: 'This describes the soul of a youth who has given himself up to pleasure and Epicureanism. He at length is worn out and wrapt in the mists of satiety. Afterwards he grows into a cynical old man afflicted with the "curse of nature", and joining in the Feast of Death. Then we see the landscape which symbolizes God, Law and the future life.' In a letter (*Brotherton Collection*), T. described it as 'one of my poems, which I confess has always been a favourite with myself'. FitzGerald remarks that 'Johnson's "Long-expected one-and-twenty" has the swing, and something of the spirit of the old sinner's lyric.' Cp. section iv with the drinking-song at the end of Burns's *The Jolly Beggars*: 'What is title? what is treasure? / What is reputation's care? / If we lead a life of pleasure, / 'Tis no matter, how or where!' J. H. Buckley (p. 72) tentatively compares Keats's *Lamia* ii, 'purple-lined palace of sweet sin'. A few details suggest Shelley's *The Triumph of Life*. All variants from *HnMS* (HM 1320) are given below. The use of the heroic couplet is very unusual for T.

I

I had a vision when the night was late:
A youth came riding toward a palace-gate.
He rode a horse with wings, that would have flown,
But that his heavy rider kept him down.
And from the palace came a child of sin,
And took him by the curls, and led him in,
Where sat a company with heated eyes,
Expecting when a fountain should arise:
A sleepy light upon their brows and lips–
As when the sun, a crescent of eclipse,

¶ 277.*1*. *vision . . . was*] dream when night was wearing *HnMS 1st reading*.
*6*. A. A. Mendilow suggests that this ironically adapts the angel of *Ezekiel* viii 3, 'And he put forth the form of a hand, and took me by a lock of mine head; and the spirit lifted me up between the earth and the heaven, and brought me in the visions of God to Jerusalem', *Scripta Hierosolymitana* xvii (1966) 177.
*9*] A glooming trance of light on brows and lips–*MS 1st reading*.

Dreams over lake and lawn, and isles and capes–
Suffused them, sitting, lying, languid shapes,
By heaps of gourds, and skins of wine, and piles of
grapes.

II

Then methought I heard a mellow sound,
Gathering up from all the lower ground;
Narrowing in to where they sat assembled
Low voluptuous music winding trembled,
Woven in circles: they that heard it sighed,
Panted hand-in-hand with faces pale,
Swung themselves, and in low tones replied;
Till the fountain spouted, showering wide
Sleet of diamond-drift and pearly hail;
Then the music touched the gates and died;
Rose again from where it seemed to fail,
Stormed in orbs of song, a growing gale;
Till thronging in and in, to where they waited,
As 'twere a hundred-throated nightingale,
The strong tempestuous treble throbbed and palpitated;
Ran into its giddiest whirl of sound,
Caught the sparkles, and in circles,
Purple gauzes, golden hazes, liquid mazes,
Flung the torrent rainbow round:
Then they started from their places,
Moved with violence, changed in hue,
Caught each other with wild grimaces,
Half-invisible to the view,
Wheeling with precipitate paces
To the melody, till they flew,
Hair, and eyes, and limbs, and faces,
Twisted hard in fierce embraces,
Like to Furies, like to Graces,
Dashed together in blinding dew:

*12. Suffused*] Rained round *MS 1st reading.*

*14. mellow sound*: rhyming with 'ground', in Keats, *Endymion* i 146.

*17–45.* Cp. the Bacchantes in *Semele* (*c.*1833, p. 574): 'voluptuous', 'throbbed', 'melody', 'giddiest'. 'Music-rolling orbs' suggests l. 25, 'orbs of song'.

*30–2.* Cp. *Those worldly goods* (*1827*), by T.'s brother Charles: 'As torrent-rainbows, which appear / Still dwindling as we still draw near; / And yet contracting on the eye, / Till the bright circling colours die.'

*31. liquid*] lucid *MS 1st reading.*

*35–6*] *Added in MS.*

*40 ∧ 1*] Fierce embraces, wild grimaces, *MS, deleted.*

Till, killed with some luxurious agony,
The nerve-dissolving melody
Fluttered headlong from the sky.

III

And then I looked up toward a mountain-tract,
That girt the region with high cliff and lawn:
I saw that every morning, far withdrawn
Beyond the darkness and the cataract,
God made Himself an awful rose of dawn,
Unheeded: and detaching, fold by fold,
From those still heights, and, slowly drawing near,
A vapour heavy, hueless, formless, cold,
Came floating on for many a month and year,
Unheeded: and I thought I would have spoken,
And warned that madman ere it grew too late:
But, as in dreams, I could not. Mine was broken,
When that cold vapour touched the palace gate,
And linked again. I saw within my head
A gray and gap-toothed man as lean as death,
Who slowly rode across a withered heath,
And lighted at a ruined inn, and said:

IV

'Wrinkled ostler, grim and thin!
Here is custom come your way;
Take my brute, and lead him in,
Stuff his ribs with mouldy hay.

'Bitter barmaid, waning fast!
See that sheets are on my bed;
What! the flower of life is past:
It is long before you wed.

'Slip-shod waiter, lank and sour,
At the Dragon on the heath!
Let us have a quiet hour,
Let us hob-and-nob with Death.

'I am old, but let me drink;
Bring me spices, bring me wine;
I remember, when I think,
That my youth was half divine.

52] The brooding burthen of a nameless fear, *MS 1st reading.*
58. *touched*] swam *MS.*
75–8] *MS has, faintly, a half-worked version as well.*

'Wine is good for shrivelled lips,
When a blanket wraps the day,
When the rotten woodland drips,
And the leaf is stamped in clay.

'Sit thee down, and have no shame,
Cheek by jowl, and knee by knee:
What care I for any name?
What for order or degree?

'Let me screw thee up a peg:
Let me loose thy tongue with wine:
Callest thou that thing a leg?
Which is thinnest? thine or mine?

'Thou shalt not be saved by works:
Thou hast been a sinner too:
Ruined trunks on withered forks,
Empty scarecrows, I and you!

'Fill the cup, and fill the can:
Have a rouse before the morn:
Every moment dies a man,
Every moment one is born.

'We are men of ruined blood;
Therefore comes it we are wise.
Fish are we that love the mud,
Rising to no fancy-flies.

'Name and fame! to fly sublime
Through the courts, the camps, the schools,
Is to be the ball of Time,
Bandied by the hands of fools.

*87–8*] Screw thy fancies up a peg,
Neither take my moods amiss. *MS alternative fragment*

*91. Galatians* ii 16.

*97 and 98. moment*] *1851*; minute *1842–50*. *Locksley Hall* 136 ^ 7, MS (p. 696), included the line: 'Every moment dies a man and every moment one is born.'

*103–6*] Systems! we whose bones are chalk
Hear to these when made complete
As to odds and ends of talk
Heard in passing through the street. *MS 1st reading*

Together with the MS stanza, ll. 114 ^ 5, cp. *The Two Voices* 207: 'A dust of systems and of creeds'.

*106. by*] *1855*; in *1842–53*.

'Friendship!–to be two in one–
Let the canting liar pack!
Well I know, when I am gone,
How she mouths behind my back.

'Virtue!–to be good and just–
Every heart, when sifted well,
Is a clot of warmer dust,
Mixed with cunning sparks of hell.

'O! we two as well can look
Whited thought and cleanly life
As the priest, above his book
Leering at his neighbour's wife.

'Fill the cup, and fill the can:
Have a rouse before the morn:
Every moment dies a man,
Every moment one is born.

'Drink, and let the parties rave:
They are filled with idle spleen;
Rising, falling, like a wave,
For they know not what they mean.

'He that roars for liberty
Faster binds a tyrant's power;
And the tyrant's cruel glee
Forces on the freer hour.

'Fill the can, and fill the cup:
All the windy ways of men
Are but dust that rises up,
And is lightly laid again.

'Greet her with applausive breath,
Freedom, gaily doth she tread;
In her right a civic wreath,
In her left a human head.

*114 ∧ 5]* Creeds! go up: make straight the hair,
Give the chapter and the verse,
Whine the text and drawl the prayer–
Flee, belovèd, from the curse. *MS, deleted*

*117. his*] the *MS 1st reading.*
*121 and 122. moment*] *1851*; minute *1842–50.*
*128. a*] *1845*; the *1842–3.*

'No, I love not what is new;
She is of an ancient house:
And I think we know the hue
Of that cap upon her brows.

'Let her go! her thirst she slakes
Where the bloody conduit runs,
Then her sweetest meal she makes
On the first-born of her sons.

'Drink to lofty hopes that cool–
Visions of a perfect State:
Drink we, last, the public fool,
Frantic love and frantic hate.

'Chant me now some wicked stave,
Till thy drooping courage rise,
And the glow-worm of the grave
Glimmer in thy rheumy eyes.

'Fear not thou to loose thy tongue;
Set thy hoary fancies free;
What is loathsome to the young
Savours well to thee and me.

'Change, reverting to the years,
When thy nerves could understand
What there is in loving tears,
And the warmth of hand in hand.

'Tell me tales of thy first love–
April hopes, the fools of chance;
Till the graves begin to move,
And the dead begin to dance.

'Fill the can, and fill the cup:
All the windy ways of men
Are but dust that rises up,
And is lightly laid again.

'Trooping from their mouldy dens
The chap-fallen circle spreads:
Welcome, fellow-citizens,
Hollow hearts and empty heads!

'You are bones, and what of that?
Every face, however full,
Padded round with flesh and fat,
Is but modelled on a skull.

*175–8, 179–82*] *Transposed at first in MS.*

'Death is king, and Vivat Rex!
Tread a measure on the stones,
Madam–if I know your sex,
From the fashion of your bones.

'No, I cannot praise the fire
In your eye–nor yet your lip:
All the more do I admire
Joints of cunning workmanship.

'Lo! God's likeness–the ground-plan–
Neither modelled, glazed, nor framed:
Buss me, thou rough sketch of man,
Far too naked to be shamed!

'Drink to Fortune, drink to Chance,
While we keep a little breath!
Drink to heavy Ignorance!
Hob-and-nob with brother Death!

'Thou art mazed, the night is long,
And the longer night is near:
What! I am not all as wrong
As a bitter jest is dear.

'Youthful hopes, by scores, to all,
When the locks are crisp and curled;
Unto me my maudlin gall
And my mockeries of the world.

'Fill the cup, and fill the can:
Mingle madness, mingle scorn!
Dregs of life, and lees of man:
Yet we will not die forlorn.'

V

The voice grew faint: there came a further change:
Once more uprose the mystic mountain-range:

*188. nor*] *1874*; or *1842–72.*

*190* ∧ *1*] Death is king, and Vivat Rex!
Dance with me, ideal men–
Vivat Rex and Curat Lex,
Hands across and back again. *MS, deleted*

Alluding to the saying, *De minimis non curat lex.*

*193. heavy Ignorance*: Shakespeare, *Sonnet 78.*

*197–8*] Drink! I know that I am wrong / But . . . *MS 1st reading*; What! I reck not I am wrong . . . *MS 2nd reading, then 1842.*

*199.* , *by scores,*] are free *MS 1st reading.*

*208. Once more uprose*] *1851*; Again arose *1842–50.*

Below were men and horses pierced with worms,
And slowly quickening into lower forms;
By shards and scurf of salt, and scum of dross,
Old plash of rains, and refuse patched with moss.
Then some one spake: 'Behold! it was a crime
Of sense avenged by sense that wore with time.'
Another said: 'The crime of sense became
The crime of malice, and is equal blame.'
And one: 'He had not wholly quenched his power;
A little grain of conscience made him sour.'
At last I heard a voice upon the slope
Cry to the summit, 'Is there any hope?'
To which an answer pealed from that high land,
But in a tongue no man could understand;
And on the glimmering limit far withdrawn
God made Himself an awful rose of dawn.

*209–10*] Methought the men and horse with other forms
Lay under, slowly quickening [*from* festering] into worms;
*MS 1st reading*

*209.* Cp. *Perdidi Diem* 8: 'Pierced through with loathly worms of utter Death'. This line is also in *Pierced through* (p. 472).

*211.* Cp. the landscape of Milton's Hell, *Paradise Lost* i 672, 704: 'shon with a glossie scurff', 'scum'd the Bullion dross'.

*213. spake*] *1843*; said *1842.*

*214*] Of sense and it was well avenged by time.' *MS 1st reading.*

*213–4.* 'The sensualist becomes worn out by his senses' (T.).

*214 ∧ 5*] Another answered 'But a crime of sense?
Give him new nerves with old experience.' *1865 Selection*

These lines are in *HnMS*; F. T. Palgrave reports T. as saying they were 'omitted from fear of overlength' (C. Ricks, *MP* lxii (1964) 140). Since this was at Christmas 1863, it was presumably Palgrave who persuaded T. to include them in *1865*.

*215. Another said*] A third rejoined *MS 1st reading.*

*219*] At last a voice called upward from the slope *MS 1st reading.* *voice*] trumpet voice *MS jotting.* *upon*] from off *MS 2nd reading.*

*220. Cry to*] Unto *MS 1st reading.*

*220–4.* H.T. relates this to *In Memoriam* lv 20: 'When he speaks of "faintly trusting the larger hope", he means by "the larger hope" that the whole human race would through, perhaps, ages of suffering be at length purified and saved, even those who "better not with time"; so at the end of this Vision we read: "God made Himself an awful rose of dawn".' G. G. Loane (*Echoes in Tennyson*, 1928, p. 7) compares Keats, *Hyperion* i 203–12: 'Hyperion, leaving twilight in the rear, / Came slope upon the threshold of the west; / Then, as was wont, his palace-door flew ope . . . / And like a

# 278 Edward Gray

Published *1842*. Sent to Emily Sellwood (later T.'s wife) in 1840, as 'a virgin-ballad never yet written down . . . simple enough at any rate' (*Mem.* i 176). A ballad of the type of *Barbara Allen's Cruelty*, which is in Percy's *Reliques*: 'When he was dead, and laid in grave, / Her heart was struck with sorrow . . . / And sore repented of the day, / That she did ere deny him.' The name is commonplace, but T. may have taken it from Mary Russell Mitford's *The Queen of the Meadow* (1827; in *Our Village*, 1828), which he used for both *The Miller's Daughter* and *The Brook*.

Sweet Emma Moreland of yonder town
  Met me walking on yonder way,
'And have you lost your heart?' she said;
  'And are you married yet, Edward Gray?'

Sweet Emma Moreland spoke to me:
  Bitterly weeping I turned away:
'Sweet Emma Moreland, love no more
  Can touch the heart of Edward Gray.

'Ellen Adair she loved me well,
  Against her father's and mother's will:
Today I sat for an hour and wept,
  By Ellen's grave, on the windy hill.

'Shy she was, and I thought her cold;
  Thought her proud, and fled over the sea;
Filled I was with folly and spite,
  When Ellen Adair was dying for me.

'Cruel, cruel the words I said!
  Cruelly came they back today:
"You're too slight and fickle," I said,
  "To trouble the heart of Edward Gray."

rose in vermeil tint and shape, / In fragrance soft, and coolness to the eye, / That inlet to severe magnificence / Stood full blown, for the God to enter in.' Cp. also *The Two Voices* 304–6: 'Heaven opens inward, chasms yawn, / Vast images in glimmering dawn, / Half shown, are broken and withdrawn.' The 'voice' is a traditional folk-motif; cp. *The Voyage of Maildun* (trans. in P. W. Joyce's *Old Celtic Romances*, 1879, p. 151): 'After this they heard some one speaking on the top of the pillar, in a loud, clear, glad voice; but they knew neither what he said, nor in what language he spoke.'

'There I put my face in the grass–
Whispered, "Listen to my despair:
I repent me of all I did:
Speak a little, Ellen Adair!"

'Then I took a pencil, and wrote
On the mossy stone, as I lay,
"Here lies the body of Ellen Adair;
And here the heart of Edward Gray!"

'Love may come, and love may go,
And fly, like a bird, from tree to tree:
But I will love no more, no more,
Till Ellen Adair come back to me.

'Bitterly wept I over the stone:
Bitterly weeping I turned away:
There lies the body of Ellen Adair!
And there the heart of Edward Gray!'

## 279 Love and Duty

Published *1842*. Written *c.*1840. At this time T. broke off his engagement to Emily Sellwood (whom he did not marry till 1850); the difficulties were partly financial, but Rader (pp. 70–5) brings evidence to show that T. 'chose to leave Emily because her family was opposed to him, because this fact caused pain to Emily, and because he himself was not sure that he was worthy of her plighted love'. The poem resembles T.'s letter to Emily, Dec. 1839: 'How should this dependence on thy state coexist with my flying from thee? ask not. Believe that it does. 'Tis true, I fly thee for my good, perhaps for thine, at any rate for thine if mine is thine. If thou knewest why I fly thee there is nothing thou would'st more wish for than that I should fly thee. Sayest thou "are we to meet no more?" I answer I know not the word nor will know it. I neither know it nor believe it. The immortality of man disdains and rejects it–the immortality of man to which the cycles and the Aeons are as hours and as days' (*CT*, p. 181). T.'s brother Charles 'added that the love between your father and mother continued unshaken, and that but for an overstrained, morbid scrupulousness as to what was conceived to be duty, they might have been contented to wait (an engaged couple) and so both might have been spared much suffering' (*Mat.* ii 38). Rader suggests that the final meeting in summer (l. 71) must have been in 1840; he notes that T. published the poem in *1842*, 'rather more quickly than he was wont to publish personal poems, perhaps because he wanted Emily to see it there' (p. 139). The draft in *T.Nbk 26* (which may not be quoted) includes a deleted passage, an early version of ll. 45–50, on the legend of the ring that is placed on the finger of a statue, causing a phantom to come between bride and groom. T. will have read this legend in Thomas Moore's poem, *The Ring* (1801). A letter from James Spedding to W. H. Thompson, 14 Oct. 1840, is at *Trinity College* (quoted in *Tennyson and His Friends*, p. 408); it seems to fit *Love and Duty* more closely than any other of T.'s poems, but unfortunately the transcript mentioned is not with the letter: 'I send you a copy of a poem which I think he once repeated to you and me, and which we neither of us much entered into. Reading it again the other day, I was surprised with the power and beauty of it, and I now think it wants nothing but a better name, or, I should rather say, a historical foundation. I would have it put into the mouth of some noted man (among the many such that must have been) involved in [forced into *deleted*] a marriage which he does not like, in violation of a pre-existing attachment.'

Of love that never found his earthly close,
What sequel? Streaming eyes and breaking hearts?
Or all the same as if he had not been?

Not so. Shall Error in the round of time
Still father Truth? O shall the braggart shout
For some blind glimpse of freedom work itself
Through madness, hated by the wise, to law
System and empire? Sin itself be found
The cloudy porch oft opening on the Sun?
And only he, this wonder, dead, become
Mere highway dust? or year by year alone
Sit brooding in the ruins of a life,
Nightmare of youth, the spectre of himself?

If this were thus, if this, indeed, were all,
Better the narrow brain, the stony heart,
The staring eye glazed o'er with sapless days,
The long mechanic pacings to and fro,
The set gray life, and apathetic end.
But am I not the nobler through thy love?
O three times less unworthy! likewise thou
Art more through Love, and greater than thy years,
The Sun will run his orbit, and the Moon
Her circle. Wait, and Love himself will bring
The drooping flower of knowledge changed to fruit
Of wisdom. Wait: my faith is large in Time,
And that which shapes it to some perfect end.

¶ *279.5. shout*: a noun.

*15–18.* The mentally ill whom T. saw at this time in Dr Matthew Allen's asylum at Fairmead, near High Beech.

Will some one say, Then why not ill for good?
Why took ye not your pastime? To that man
My work shall answer, since I knew the right
And did it; for a man is not as God,
But then most Godlike being most a man.
– So let me think 'tis well for thee and me –
Ill-fated that I am, what lot is mine
Whose foresight preaches peace, my heart so slow
To feel it! For how hard it seemed to me,
When eyes, love-languid through half tears would dwell
One earnest, earnest moment upon mine,
Then not to dare to see! when thy low voice,
Faltering, would break its syllables, to keep
My own full-tuned, – hold passion in a leash,
And not leap forth and fall about thy neck,
And on thy bosom (deep desired relief!)
Rain out the heavy mist of tears, that weighed
Upon my brain, my senses and my soul!

For Love himself took part against himself
To warn us off, and Duty loved of Love–
O this world's curse, –beloved but hated–came
Like Death betwixt thy dear embrace and mine,
And crying, 'Who is this? behold thy bride,'
She pushed me from thee.
If the sense is hard
To alien ears, I did not speak to these–
No, not to thee, but to thyself in me:
Hard is my doom and thine: thou knowest it all.

Could Love part thus? was it not well to speak,
To have spoken once? It could not but be well.
The slow sweet hours that bring us all things good,
The slow sad hours that bring us all things ill,
And all good things from evil, brought the night
In which we sat together and alone,
And to the want, that hollowed all the heart,
Gave utterance by the yearning of an eye,

*27–32*] *Not T.MS 1st reading.*
*28. took . . . pastime*: this has erotic connotations for T.; as in *Love* [*Almighty Love*!] 27–8.
*56–7.* T. compares Theocritus xv 104–5: *βάρδισται μακάρων Ὧραι φίλαι ἀλλὰ ποθειναὶ ἔρχονται πάντεσσι βροτοῖς αἰεί τι φέρουσαι.* ('The Seasons, the Seasons, full slow they go and come, / But some sweet thing for all they bring, and so they are welcome home'.) Alongside John Churton Collins's note on this (*Cornhill*, Jan. 1880), T. wrote 'possibly' (*Lincoln*).

That burned upon its object through such tears
As flow but once a life.
The trance gave way
To those caresses, when a hundred times
In that last kiss, which never was the last,
Farewell, like endless welcome, lived and died.
Then followed counsel, comfort, and the words
That make a man feel strong in speaking truth;
Till now the dark was worn, and overhead
The lights of sunset and of sunrise mixed
In that brief night; the summer night, that paused
Among her stars to hear us; stars that hung
Love-charmed to listen: all the wheels of Time
Spun round in station, but the end had come.

O then like those, who clench their nerves to rush
Upon their dissolution, we two rose,
There–closing like an individual life–
In one blind cry of passion and of pain,
Like bitter accusation even to death,
Caught up the whole of love and uttered it,
And bade adieu for ever.
Live–yet live–
Shall sharpest pathos blight us, knowing all
Life needs for life is possible to will–
Live happy; tend thy flowers; be tended by
My blessing! Should my Shadow cross thy thoughts
Too sadly for their peace, remand it thou

*71–4.* Cp. Wordsworth, *Vaudracour and Julia* 97–101: 'meanwhile the galaxy displayed / Her fires, that like mysterious pulses beat / Aloft; momentous but uneasy bliss! / To their full hearts the universe seemed hung / On that brief meeting's slender filament.' T. (*Lincoln*) underlined John Churton Collins's reference in the *Cornhill* to Wordsworth as his 'model' here, and wrote 'nonsense'.

*73–4.* G. G. Loane (*Echoes in Tennyson*, 1928, p. 7) compares Chapman, *Bussy D'Ambois* II ii 157–65: 'Now all ye peaceful regents of the night / . . . this charm'd hour / Fix like the Centre; make the violent wheels / Of Time and Fortune stand.' Also Keats, *Hyperion* i 72–4: 'As when, upon a tranced summer-night / . . . branch-charmed by the earnest stars.'

*75. who*] *1846*; that *1842–5*.

*77. individual*: indivisible.

*82. pathos*: suffering, 'used in opposition to *apathetic*' in l. 18 (T.).

*84.* Cp. *Paradise Lost* viii 633: 'Live happie and love'; where l. 631 is 'Beyond the Earth's green Cape and verdant Isles'–cp. l. 98 below.

*86. remand it thou*] *1851*; so put it back *1842–50*.

For calmer hours to Memory's darkest hold,
If not to be forgotten–not at once–
Not all forgotten. Should it cross thy dreams,
O might it come like one that looks content,
With quiet eyes unfaithful to the truth,
And point thee forward to a distant light,
Or seem to lift a burthen from thy heart
And leave thee freër, till thou wake refreshed
Then when the first low matin-chirp hath grown
Full quire, and morning driven her plow of pearl
Far furrowing into light the mounded rack,
Beyond the fair green field and eastern sea.

## 280 Godiva

Published *1842*. Written after a visit to Coventry that took place in June 1840 (*Mem.* i 176). At Yale, there is a copy of a letter to T. from T. Lord, Nottingham, 23 Jan. [1841 ?]: 'In reply to your letter of the 21st inst. I beg to state that the celebrated Lady Godiva was a reality and no myth.' Lord sent detailed historical information for this famous eleventh-century story. In his notes, T. quotes William Dugdale's *Antiquities of Warwickshire* (1656). The poem is a short epyllion in the manner of Theocritus; cp. T.'s opening with that of the 13th Idyll (on Hylas), a poem which T. much admired (*Mem.* ii 495): 'From what God soever sprung, Nicias, Love was not, as we seem to think, born for us alone; nor first unto us of mortal flesh that cannot see the morrow, look things of beauty beautiful.' The *HnMS* (HM 1320) breaks off at l. 70. T.'s trial edition of *1842* did not have the four introductory lines (T. J. Wise, *Bibliography of Tennyson* i 78). *T.Nbk 26* (which may not be quoted) has eight concluding lines about the train departing, instead of the four introductory ones. In his review of *1842* in the *Church of England Quarterly Review* (Oct. 1842), Leigh Hunt wrote perceptively about T.'s framing of *Godiva* and *Morte d'Arthur* (p. 582): 'a

*87. to*] *1851*; in *1842–50*.
*88*] *1851*; *not 1842–50*.
*89. Not all forgotten.*] *1851*; If unforgotten! *1842–50*.
*90. O*] *1851*; So *1842–50*.
*97. rack*: floating cloud, as in Shakespeare, *Sonnet 33*: 'Full many a glorious morning have I seen / Flatter the mountain tops with sovereign eye, / Kissing with golden face the meadows green . . . / Anon permit the basest clouds to ride / With ugly rack on his celestial face.' Cp. Leigh Hunt, *The Nymphs* ii 95: 'rounded rack'; and Shelley, *Witch of Atlas* 482: 'the crudded rack'. Also *The Princess* iii 1–2: 'Morn in the white wake of the morning star / Came furrowing all the orient into gold.'

certain air of literary dandyism, or fine-gentlemanism, or fastidiousness, or whatever he may *not* be pleased to call it, which leads him to usher in his compositions with such exordiums as those to *Morte d'Arthur*, and *Godiva*; in the former of which he gives us to understand that he should have burnt his poem but for the "request of friends"; and, in the latter, that he "shaped" it while he was waiting "for the train at Coventry," and hanging on the bridge "with grooms and porters." Really this is little better than the rhyming fine-ladyism of Miss Seward, who said that she used to translate an ode of Horace "while her hair was curling".... This kind of mixed tone of contempt and nonchalance, or, at best, of fine-life phrases with better fellowship, looks a little instructive, and is, at all events, a little perilous.... We suspect that these poems of *Morte d'Arthur* and *Godiva* are among those which Mr. Tennyson thinks his best, and is most anxious that others should regard as he does; and therefore it is that he would affect to make trifles of them. The reader's opinion is at once to be of great importance to him, and yet none at all. There is a boyishness in this which we shall be happy to see Mr. Tennyson, who is no longer a boy, outgrow.'

*I waited for the train at Coventry;*
*I hung with grooms and porters on the bridge,*
*To watch the three tall spires; and there I shaped*
*The city's ancient legend into this:–*

Not only we, the latest seed of Time,
New men, that in the flying of a wheel
Cry down the past, not only we, that prate
Of rights and wrongs, have loved the people well,
And loathed to see them overtaxed; but she
Did more, and underwent, and overcame,
The woman of a thousand summers back,
Godiva, wife to that grim Earl, who ruled
In Coventry: for when he laid a tax

¶ 280.*2. grooms and porters*] broadbacked strangers *HnMS 1st reading.*
5. *seed*] heirs *MS 2nd reading.*
*6–8*] Who in the flight and fervor of a wheel
Cry down the past, have loved the people well, *MS 1st reading*
8. *rights and*] public *MS 2nd reading.*
9. *she*] one *MS 2nd reading.*
*10–11*] *MS had at first no l. 11; the next version had ll. 10–11, but transposed, beginning* A woman . . .
*13–14*] A thousand summers back, in Coventry.
For when he laid a gabel on the town
Beyond their power, and all the mothers brought *MS 1st reading*
*gabel*: tax. T. may have learnt the word from the *English Encyclopaedia* (1802), of which there was a copy at Somersby (*Lincoln*).

Upon his town, and all the mothers brought
Their children, clamouring, 'If we pay, we starve!'
She sought her lord, and found him, where he strode
About the hall, among his dogs, alone,
His beard a foot before him, and his hair
A yard behind. She told him of their tears,
And prayed him, 'If they pay this tax, they starve.'
Whereat he stared, replying, half-amazed,
'You would not let your little finger ache
For such as *these?*'–'But I would die,' said she.
He laughed, and swore by Peter and by Paul:
Then filliped at the diamond in her ear;
'Oh ay, ay, ay, you talk!'–'Alas!' she said,
'But prove me what it is I would not do.'
And from a heart as rough as Esau's hand,
He answered, 'Ride you naked through the town,
And I repeal it;' and nodding, as in scorn,
He parted, with great strides among his dogs.

So left alone, the passions of her mind,
As winds from all the compass shift and blow,
Made war upon each other for an hour,
Till pity won. She sent a herald forth,
And bade him cry, with sound of trumpet, all
The hard condition; but that she would loose
The people: therefore, as they loved her well,
From then till noon no foot should pace the street,
No eye look down, she passing; but that all
Should keep within, door shut, and window barred.

Then fled she to her inmost bower, and there
Unclasped the wedded eagles of her belt,
The grim Earl's gift; but ever at a breath

15. *clamouring*] weeping *MS*.
17. *among . . . alone*] alone among his dogs *MS 1st reading*.
20. '*If . . . tax*] saying 'If they pay *MS 1st reading*.
20 ‸ 21] Whereat he sware the tax was none of hers.
'The shame,' she answered, 'being yours is mine'. *MS 1st reading*
21. *Whereat he stared*] He raised his eyes *MS 1st reading*.
25. *filliped at*] filliping the *MS 1st reading*.
26–7] *Added in MS, beginning* O ay, quoth he, you . . .; *but cp. l.* 29.
28. *Genesis* xxvii 23.
29. *He answered,*] 'O ay but *MS 1st reading*.
39. *From . . . noon*] At such an hour *MS 1st reading*.

She lingered, looking like a summer moon
Half-dipt in cloud: anon she shook her head,
And showered the rippled ringlets to her knee;
Unclad herself in haste; adown the stair
Stole on; and, like a creeping sunbeam, slid
From pillar unto pillar, until she reached
The gateway; there she found her palfrey trapt
In purple blazoned with armorial gold.

Then she rode forth, clothed on with chastity:
The deep air listened round her as she rode,
And all the low wind hardly breathed for fear.
The little wide-mouthed heads upon the spout
Had cunning eyes to see: the barking cur
Made her cheek flame: her palfrey's footfall shot
Light horrors through her pulses: the blind walls
Were full of chinks and holes; and overhead
Fantastic gables, crowding, stared: but she
Not less through all bore up, till, last, she saw
The white-flowered elder-thicket from the field
Gleam through the Gothic archway in the wall.

Then she rode back, clothed on with chastity:
And one low churl, compact of thankless earth,
The fatal byword of all years to come,
Boring a little auger-hole in fear,
Peeped – but his eyes, before they had their will,
Were shrivelled into darkness in his head,
And dropt before him. So the Powers, who wait
On noble deeds, cancelled a sense misused;

*45–9.* Reminiscent of a poem by 'G.M.', *Godiva*, which was quoted from *The Etonian* in *QR* xxv (1821) 107, *QR* (copies were at Somersby, *Lincoln*) being a source for several of T.'s early poems: 'And let the traces of her raven hair / Flow down in wavy lightness to the ground, / Till half they veiled her limbs and bosom fair, / In dark and shadowy beauty floating round, / As clouds, in the still firmament of June, / Shade the pale splendours of the midnight moon.'

*47. showered*] loosed *MS 1st reading.*

*51. gateway; there*] gates by which *MS 1st reading.*

*53.* Adapting 'Clothed on with immortality', *Supposed Confessions* 39 ∧ 40, *1830* text.

*57. barking cur*] yelping hound *MS 1st reading.*

*64. archway*] *1874*; archways *1842–72.*

*66–9*]
And one (for so the rumour runs) a churl
Compact of thankless earth, the worse for him
Peept . . . *MS 1st reading*

*72.* Cp. *The Two Voices* 42: 'Is cancelled in the world of sense'.

And she, that knew not, passed: and all at once,
With twelve great shocks of sound, the shameless noon
Was clashed and hammered from a hundred towers,
One after one: but even then she gained
Her bower; whence reissuing, robed and crowned,
To meet her lord, she took the tax away
And built herself an everlasting name.

## 281 *Rosamund's Bower

Printed *Mem.* ii 197, under *Becket*: 'The story of Henry and Rosamund had long ago attracted him, and the germ of the play is to be found in a little song written before 1842.' MS: *H.Lpr 271.* Rosamond, the mistress of Henry II, was said to have been poisoned by Queen Eleanor; Henry, in legend, was guided by a clue through the labyrinth to her bower. She appears in *A Dream of Fair Women* (p. 452). The legend is told in the *English Encyclopaedia* (1802), of which there was a copy at Somersby (*Lincoln*).

*Rosamund loquitur*

What rustles hither in the dark?
A step? a footfall? What is that I hear?
The night is black and still; the deer
Bleat as with human voices in the park.
Is it the king? is it my love
Coming along the secret ways?
The man that round me wove
Inextricable brickwork maze in maze?
Maze in maze he wound me round
With love. Methought I heard a sound.
It is not he; far off from England's shore,
He comes no more.
An idle hope was in my breast,
My hope is false, my terror's true!
I shudder in my lonely nest,
And think a cunning hand has found the clue–
God be gracious to my soul!

[1842. *The May Queen*–see p. 418]

¶ 281. *9–10*] *H.MS*; Maze in maze he wound me in
With shame, with error and with sin. *1st reading*; *not Mem.*
*15. lonely*] guilty *MS 1st reading.*

# 282 The Poet's Song

Published as the last poem of volume ii in *1842*.

The rain had fallen, the Poet arose,
  He passed by the town and out of the street,
A light wind blew from the gates of the sun,
  And waves of shadow went over the wheat,
And he sat him down in a lonely place,
  And chanted a melody loud and sweet,
That made the wild-swan pause in her cloud,
  And the lark drop down at his feet.

The swallow stopt as he hunted the fly,
  The snake slipt under a spray,
The wild hawk stood with the down on his beak,
  And stared, with his foot on the prey,
And the nightingale thought, 'I have sung many songs,
  But never a one so gay,
For he sings of what the world will be
  When the years have died away.'

# 283 *The New Timon, and the Poets

## [PART I]

Published *Punch*, 28 Feb. 1846, signed 'Alcibiades' (who, in Shakespeare, reads the epitaph on Timon); not reprinted. It was a retort to Edward Bulwer-Lytton, whose *The New Timon* (anonymous; Part ii, Jan. 1846) had attacked T. and his pension (awarded in 1845): 'Let School-Miss Alfred vent her chaste delight / On "darling little rooms so warm and bright!" / Chaunt, "I'm aweary," in infectious strain, / And catch her "blue fly singing i' the pane."' Lytton had a note on T. 'in the prime of life, belonging to a wealthy family, without, I believe, wife or children', and now 'quartered on the public purse'. Moreover, T. suspected that Lytton had adversely reviewed *1832* (E. F. Shannon, *Tennyson and the Reviewers*, 1952, p. 17, thinks Lytton probably had); and T. was aggrieved at Lytton's having just stayed with the Tennyson-d'Eyncourts. It was John Forster, not T., who sent the lines to *Punch* (*Mem.* i 244–5), and T. published his regret–see *Literary Squabbles* (p. 739). Lytton dropped the offending passage. For further details, see Sir Charles Tennyson, *Nineteenth Century* cix (1931) 756–64; and Part ii, which follows below (p. 738).

¶ 282.*9. fly*] *1888*; bee *1842–86*. William Allingham's *Diary*, 21 Aug. 1881 (1907, p. 312), makes it clear that T. spoke of flies as bees.

We know him, out of Shakspeare's art,
And those fine curses which he spoke;
The old Timon, with his noble heart,
That, strongly loathing, greatly broke.

So died the Old: here comes the New.
Regard him: a familiar face:
I *thought* we knew him: What, it's you,
The padded man–that wears the stays–

Who killed the girls and thrilled the boys,
With dandy pathos when you wrote,
A Lion, you, that made a noise,
And shook a mane en papillotes.

And once you tried the Muses too;
You failed, Sir: therefore now you turn,
You fall on those who are to you,
As Captain is to Subaltern.

But men of long-enduring hopes,
And careless what this hour may bring,
Can pardon little would-be Popes
And Brummels, when they try to sting.

An artist, Sir, should rest in Art,
And waive a little of his claim;
To have the deep Poetic heart
Is more than all poetic fame.

But you, Sir, you are hard to please;
You never look but half content:
Nor like a gentleman at ease,
With moral breadth of temperament.

And what with spites and what with fears,
You cannot let a body be:
It's always ringing in your ears,
'They call this man as good as *me*.'

¶ 283.*11*. Perhaps an allusion to Lytton's *The Lady of Lyons* (1838).
*12*. *papillotes*: curl-papers.
*19*. Precipitated not only by Lytton's couplets, but also by his praise of Pope in contrast to T.; cp. Pope's 'Timon', *Moral Essays* iv.
*21–4*. Lytton: 'If to my verse denied the Poet's fame, / This merit, rare to verse that wins, I claim.'
*27*. Lytton's *Pelham* (1828) was subtitled 'The Adventures of a Gentleman'. Carlyle attacked it and Lytton in 'The Dandiacal Body', *Sartor Resartus* (1836); cp. l. 10.

What profits now to understand
The merits of a spotless shirt–
A dapper boot–a little hand–
If half the little soul is dirt?

*You* talk of tinsel! why we see
The old mark of rouge upon your cheeks.
*You* prate of Nature! you are he
That spilt his life about the cliques.

A Timon you! Nay, nay, for shame:
It looks too arrogant a jest–
The fierce old man–to take *his* name
You bandbox. Off, and let him rest.

# 284 *The New Timon, and the Poets

## [PART II]

Printed by Sir Charles Tennyson, *Nineteenth Century* cix (1931) 762–3, from *H.Lpr 160*. *Mem.* ii 165 printed ll. 25–32 as *Fame*. Written 1846; see headnote to *The New Timon* (p. 736). Sir Charles's papers record a version of Part ii, which includes stanzas from *The New Timon* plus the following, which suggests *What Thor Said* (p. 500): 'And mobs no doubt will often make / The judgement private taste abhors; / We shall not wonder if they take / Your penny-hammer, Sir, for Thor's.'

Will no one make this man secure
That all his paper boats will swim?
Fair Countess, keep him always sure
That all men always talk of him!

O tell him of his own great name,
That is to stare when mine shall die,
Through every marketplace of Fame
In every butterwoman's eye–

*35*. T. spoke of Lytton's vanity to Mrs Bradley (*Bodleian MS*): 'three inches of cork put in his heels,' 'shoes with pink chamois tips to them'.
*37*. Lytton: 'Than patch with frippery every tinsel line'.
¶ 284.*1*. *Will no one*] O some one *H.Lpr 161*.
*3*. Sir Charles Tennyson shows that this refers to the literary salon of Lytton's friend Lady Blessington.
*6*. *mine*] ours *H.Lpr 161*.
*8*. Suggesting Touchstone's contempt for 'the very false gallop of verses' as 'the right butterwomen's rank to market', *As You Like It* III ii 97.
*8* ∧ *9*] And hold before him still displayed
Whatever puff in seasons flown

If that would keep his bile in bounds,
 And help him not to rail and carp
At one poor poet's hundred pounds,
 His bit of laurel and his harp–

Who hates the byways of Disdain,
 Where one must trample things unsweet,
And would much rather of the twain
 Chaff some broad porter of the street,

And bandy slang, and heat his blood,
 And make him long to bruise and mall,
And if he threshed me well and good,
 And if he couldn't, good and well.

And then we two would make regale,
 And smoke the pipe of peace again
By some deep quart of stalwart ale,
 And call each other honest men.

For as to Fame who strides the earth
 With that long horn she loves to blow,
I know a little of her worth,
 And I will tell you what I know.

This London once was middle sea,
 Those hills were plains within the past,
They will be plains again–and we,
 Poor devils, babble, we shall last.

# 285 Literary Squabbles

Published *Punch*, 7 March 1846, as *After-Thought*, signed 'Alcibiades' (who reads the epitaph on Timon at the end of *Timon of Athens*). Then 1870, Miniature Edition. T. had now come to regret *The New Timon, and the Poets*, his retort to Lytton (p. 736). On this quarrel, see Sir Charles Tennyson, *Nineteenth Century* cix (1931) 756–64; he prints a differing draft (all variants are below), entitled *The Next Morning*, which begins:

Too harsh! I loathe it and retract,
 Yet see, sir, spite of spite is born,
And men turn vermin in the fact
 Of paying aught of scorn with scorn.

---

Himself upon himself has made,
 And sate him, sate him with his own. *H.Lpr 161*

*11.* T.'s pension was in fact £200 p.a.

Ah God! the petty fools of rhyme
    That shriek and sweat in pigmy wars
Before the stony face of Time,
    And looked at by the silent stars:

Who hate each other for a song,
    And do their little best to bite
And pinch their brethren in the throng,
    And scratch the very dead for spite:

And strain to make an inch of room
    For their sweet selves, and cannot hear
The sullen Lethe rolling doom
    On them and theirs and all things here:

When one small touch of Charity
    Could lift them nearer God-like state
Than if the crowded Orb should cry
    Like those who cried Diana great:

And I too, talk, and lose the touch
    I talk of. Surely, after all,
The noblest answer unto such
    Is perfect stillness when they brawl.

¶ 285.*1. the*] we *1931.*

*5–8*] *Not 1931.*

*5. Who*] *1870*; That *1846.*

*7. And . . . brethren*] *1870*; That . . . brothers *1846.*

*9. an*] one *1931.*

*10. their*] our *1931.*

*11.* Cp. Shelley, *Revolt of Islam* X xvii 9: 'Lethe's sullen water'.

*11–12.* For the association of Lethe with the geological processes of Time, T. may have remembered Bacon's *Essay on the Vicissitude of Things*: 'The river of Lethe runneth as well above ground as below'; Charles Lyell had quoted this sentence *à propos* the works of man, which 'must eventually perish', in *Principles of Geology* (1835 edn, iii 280). T. read Lyell in 1837 (*Mem.* i 162).

*12. them and theirs*] us and ours *1931.*

*14–15*] Would lift us more to Godlike state,
    Than if ten years the crowd should cry *1931*

*16. who cried*] *1870*; that cried *1846*; which called *1931.*

*17–20*] *Not 1931.*

*20. perfect stillness*] *1870*; kindly silence *1846.*

# 286 The Princess

## A Medley

Published 25 Dec. 1847.

*Composition.* 'He talked over the plan of the poem with my mother in 1839' (*Mem.* i 248): 'The plan of *The Princess* may have suggested itself when the project of a Women's College was in my father's mind (1839) [was in the air *Mem.*], or it may have arisen in its mock-heroic form from a Cambridge joke, such as he commemorated in the lines, *The Doctor's Daughter*' (p. 283). Sir Charles Tennyson, *Cornhill* cliii (1936) 673, deduces from *H.Nbk 22* that T. 'began work on *The Princess* certainly not later than 1839 . . . and it may be several years earlier'. This MS has the title *The New University*. Aubrey de Vere 'listened to the *University of Women*' on 18 April 1845 (W. Ward, *Aubrey de Vere*, 1904, p. 71). In the summer of 1845, Edmund Lushington reports that T. 'was engaged on *The Princess*, of which I had heard nothing before. He read or showed me the first part, beyond which it had then hardly advanced' (*Mem.* i 203). On 31 Jan. 1846, Elizabeth Barrett wrote to Browning (*Letters* (1899) i 444) that T. was ill: 'Which does not prevent his writing a new poem–he has finished the second book of it–and it is in blank verse and a fairy tale, and called the *University*, the university-members being all females. . . . I don't know what to think–it makes me open my eyes. Now isn't the world too old and fond of steam, for blank verse poems, in ever so many books, to be written on the fairies?' T. was 'putting the last touches' to it in 1847 (*Mat.* i 319). It is unfortunate that the MSS at University Library, Cambridge, may not be quoted. *H.Nbks 22–5* have lengthy sections; *H.Lprs 191–7* have a few scraps and some of the songs. See Sir Charles Tennyson, *Nineteenth Century* cix (1931) 632–6, and *Cornhill* cliii (1936) 672–80.

*Revisions after publication.* These were more extensive than with any other of T.'s long poems; see E. F. Shannon, *Tennyson and the Reviewers* (1952), pp. 97–140. Since only a month or two elapsed between the 1st edition (Dec. 1847) and the 2nd (Jan.–Feb. 1848, dedicated to Henry Lushington), T. was able to make little more than stylistic changes–but he had already started on removing those extra syllables which now seemed to have become something of a mannerism in the blank verse. For the 3rd edition (1850), T. revised considerably; on 2 April 1849 he had read to Palgrave 'certain songs which he thought he might do well to place between the sections' (*Mem.* ii 486). These six songs have been since *1850* placed between the sections of the poem (not to be confused with the blank-verse lyrics, like *Tears, idle tears*, which have been since *1847* part of the body of the narrative). T. comments: 'The child is the link through the parts, as shown in the Songs (inserted 1850), which are the best interpreters of the poem. . . . Before the first edition came out, I deliberated with myself whether I should put songs between the separate divisions of the poem;

again I thought that the poem would explain itself, but the public did not see the drift.' For alternative songs drafted by T. see Appendix A (pp. 1768–1772). In the 4th edition (1851), T. made the major additions due to the 'weird seizures' of the Prince, with their stress on a world of 'shadows'; this revision has been often deplored. T. says that 'the words "dream, shadow", "were and were not" doubtless refer to the anachronisms and improbabilities of the story'. The proofs for P. M. Wallace's edition of *The Princess* (1891, *Lincoln*) were seen by T. Wallace had said: 'It must be clearly shown that it was not the glamour of [the Prince's] physical or moral brilliance that won his lady from her isolation. His too emotional temperament and susceptibility to cataleptic seizures, added for the first time in the fourth Edition of the Poem, was no doubt intended partly to emphasise this point.' T. changed 'no doubt' to 'probably,' and deleted 'partly'. Cp. the fainting in *The Lover's Tale* i 586 and ii 205 (pp. 321, 337). For the 5th edition (1853), T. enlarged the *Prologue*, and the poem reached virtually its final form. Shannon mentions the 'remarkable extent' to which T. was affected by his reviewers in these changes.

*Sources*. T. had long anticipated many of the concerns of *The Princess*. In his definitive study of *Tennyson and 'The Princess': Reflections of an Age* (1958), John Killham draws attention to lines in the *1832* text of *A Dream of Fair Women* (p. 442, dropped in *1842*): 'In every land I thought that, more or less, / The stronger sterner nature overbore / The softer, uncontrolled by gentleness / And selfish evermore: // And whether there were any means whereby, / In some far aftertime, the gentler mind / Might reassume its just and full degree / Of rule among mankind.' Killham (pp. 179–84) also shows the relevance of *Recollections of the Arabian Nights*. The blunt views of the King in *The Princess* had been those of Edward Bull the curate in *Edwin Morris* (p. 708). As a spur to T.'s writing, Herbert Grierson suggested (in his selection, 1907) that T. may have been influenced by the reviewer of *1830* in *Westminster Review*, Jan. 1831, who spoke warmly on female education. It should be added that Hannah More's *Female Education* (1799) is at *Lincoln*, and that *English Encyclopaedia* (1802), which was at Somersby (*Lincoln*), includes a lengthy discussion 'Of the Education of Females', under both 'Education' and 'Sex'.

Killham studies in detail the relation between the poem and the feminism of the age. 'Whether the marriage-relationship could survive the fulfilment of women's aspirations is the real point at issue' (p. 65). Hence T.'s stress on the child, both in the narrative (Aglaïa) and in the intercalated songs. On Arthur Hallam and 'Feminism at Cambridge', see Killham's Chapter iv.

Killham is sceptical about the sources suggested for the story (as distinct from the topical theme), and he singles out Wallace's edition, which 'mentioned that some had traced it to a passage in *Rasselas* wherein Nekayah, herself a Princess, contemplates founding a College for women. He also mentioned Defoe's Project for an Academy for Women, and the Duchess of Newcastle's play *The Female Academy* (1662). For good measure he threw in *Love's Labour's Lost*' (p. 16). But Killham is a little severe; the proofs of Wallace's edition now show that T. did not try to delete Wallace's paragraphs (as he did elsewhere). T.'s final suggestion for the wording was: 'Most likely Tennyson did not derive the idea of his College from any one of these [Johnson, Defoe, Newcastle]. But perhaps it was suggested to him by [the obverse side of the matter that forms the plot of Shakespeare's *Love's Labour's Lost*, in which, though there it is a strictly male Academy that is invaded by a band of ladies . . .].' Killham points to the importance of eastern tales (pp. 198–230).

*A medley*. T. comments: 'In the Prologue the "Tale from mouth to mouth" was a game which I have more than once played when I was at Trinity College, Cambridge, with my brother-undergraduates. Of course, if he "that inherited the tale" had not attended very carefully to his predecessors, there were contradictions; and if the story were historical, occasional anachronisms.

'In defence of what some have called the too poetical passages, it should be recollected that the poet of the party was requested to "dress the tale up poetically," and he was full of the "gallant and heroic chronicle." A parable is perhaps the teacher that can most surely enter in at all doors. . . .

'It may be remarked that there is scarcely anything in the story which is not prophetically glanced at in the Prologue.' T.'s letter to S. E. Dawson, his Canadian editor, is given in *Eversley*: 'You have seen amongst other things that if women ever were to play such freaks, the burlesque and the tragic might go hand in hand.' Frederick Locker-Lampson records in 1869 (*Mem*. ii 70–1): 'He talked of *The Princess* with something of regret, of its fine blank verse, and the many good things in it: "but," said he, "though truly original, it is, after all, only a medley." He added that it was very difficult in blank verse to give descriptions, such as [*Prologue* 79–138], and at the same time to retain poetical elevation. Tennyson insisted that the employment of rhyme would have made it much easier.'

## PROLOGUE

Sir Walter Vivian all a summer's day
Gave his broad lawns until the set of sun
Up to the people: thither flocked at noon
His tenants, wife and child, and thither half

¶ 286. *Prologue*
'The Prologue was written about a feast of the Mechanics' Institute held in the Lushingtons' grounds at Park House, near Maidstone, 6th July 1842' (T.). Killham (pp. 61–2) quotes from the *Maidstone and Kentish Advertiser*, 12 July 1842, which is very close to T.'s description of the occasion. Cp. T.'s 'English Idyls', especially *Audley Court* (p. 704).

*1*. Cp. *Paradise Lost* i 449: 'In amorous dittyes all a Summers day'–from a passage which T. 'would repeatedly chant out with the deepest admiration, as the finest of all', *Nineteenth Century* xxxiii (1893) 172.

The neighbouring borough with their Institute
Of which he was the patron. I was there
From college, visiting the son, – the son
A Walter too, – with others of our set,
Five others: we were seven at Vivian-place.

And me that morning Walter showed the house,
Greek, set with busts: from vases in the hall
Flowers of all heavens, and lovelier than their names,
Grew side by side; and on the pavement lay
Carved stones of the Abbey-ruin in the park,
Huge Ammonites, and the first bones of Time;
And on the tables every clime and age
Jumbled together; celts and calumets,
Claymore and snowshoe, toys in lava, fans
Of sandal, amber, ancient rosaries,
Laborious orient ivory sphere in sphere,
The cursed Malayan crease, and battle-clubs
From the isles of palm: and higher on the walls,
Betwixt the monstrous horns of elk and deer,
His own forefathers' arms and armour hung.

And 'this' he said 'was Hugh's at Agincourt;
And that was old Sir Ralph's at Ascalon:
A good knight he! we keep a chronicle
With all about him' – which he brought, and I
Dived in a hoard of tales that dealt with knights,
Half-legend, half-historic, counts and kings
Who laid about them at their wills and died;
And mixt with these, a lady, one that armed
Her own fair head, and sallying through the gate,
Had beat her foes with slaughter from her walls.

'O miracle of women,' said the book,
'O noble heart who, being strait-besieged

9] *1850; not 1847–8.*
15. *Ammonites*: whorled fossil-stones.
17. *celts*: stone or bronze hatchets. *calumets*: 'Longfellow sent me one of these pipes of peace, which belonged to a Red Indian chief' (T.).
19. *sandal*: a scented wood.
21. *crease*: kris, Malayan dagger.
26. *Ascalon*: Richard I's victory over the Saracens in 1192.
35–49] *1853; not 1847–51.* Cp. *Faerie Queene* III iv st. 1: 'Where is the Antique glory now become, / That whilome wont in women to appeare? / Where be the brave atchievements doen by some? / Where be the battels, where the shield and speare, / And all the conquests, which them high did

By this wild king to force her to his wish,
Nor bent, nor broke, nor shunned a soldier's death,
But now when all was lost or seemed as lost–
Her stature more than mortal in the burst
Of sunrise, her arm lifted, eyes on fire–
Brake with a blast of trumpets from the gate,
And, falling on them like a thunderbolt,
She trampled some beneath her horses' heels,
And some were whelmed with missiles of the wall,
And some were pushed with lances from the rock,
And part were drowned within the whirling brook:
O miracle of noble womanhood!'
  So sang the gallant glorious chronicle;
And, I all rapt in this, 'Come out,' he said,
'To the Abbey: there is Aunt Elizabeth
And sister Lilia with the rest.' We went
(I kept the book and had my finger in it)
Down through the park: strange was the sight to me;
For all the sloping pasture murmured, sown
With happy faces and with holiday.
There moved the multitude, a thousand heads:
The patient leaders of their Institute
Taught them with facts. One reared a font of stone
And drew, from butts of water on the slope,
The fountain of the moment, playing, now
A twisted snake, and now a rain of pearls,
Or steep-up spout whereon the gilded ball
Danced like a wisp: and somewhat lower down
A man with knobs and wires and vials fired
A cannon: Echo answered in her sleep
From hollow fields: and here were telescopes
For azure views; and there a group of girls
In circle waited, whom the electric shock
Dislinked with shrieks and laughter: round the lake
A little clock-work steamer paddling plied
And shook the lilies: perched about the knolls
A dozen angry models jetted steam:
A petty railway ran: a fire-balloon
Rose gem-like up before the dusky groves

reare, / That matter made for famous Poets verse, / And boastfull men so oft abasht to heare? / Bene they all dead, and laid in dolefull herse? / Or doen they onely sleepe, and shall againe reverse?'

63. *steep-up*: cp. Shakespeare, *Sonnet 7*: 'And having climbed the steep-up heavenly hill . . . / Attending on his golden pilgrimage.'

74. *fire-balloon*: raised by heated air, not gas.

And dropt a fairy parachute and past:
And there through twenty posts of telegraph
They flashed a saucy message to and fro
Between the mimic stations; so that sport
Went hand in hand with Science; otherwhere
Pure sport: a herd of boys with clamour bowled
And stumped the wicket; babies rolled about
Like tumbled fruit in grass; and men and maids
Arranged a country dance, and flew through light
And shadow, while the twangling violin
Struck up with Soldier-laddie, and overhead
The broad ambrosial aisles of lofty lime
Made noise with bees and breeze from end to end.

Strange was the sight and smacking of the time;
And long we gazed, but satiated at length
Came to the ruins. High-arched and ivy-claspt,
Of finest Gothic lighter than a fire,
Through one wide chasm of time and frost they gave
The park, the crowd, the house; but all within
The sward was trim as any garden lawn:
And here we lit on Aunt Elizabeth,
And Lilia with the rest, and lady friends
From neighbour seats: and there was Ralph himself,
A broken statue propt against the wall,
As gay as any. Lilia, wild with sport,
Half child half woman as she was, had wound
A scarf of orange round the stony helm,
And robed the shoulders in a rosy silk,
That made the old warrior from his ivied nook
Glow like a sunbeam: near his tomb a feast
Shone, silver-set; about it lay the guests,
And there we joined them: then the maiden Aunt
Took this fair day for text, and from it preached
An universal culture for the crowd,
And all things great; but we, unworthier, told
Of college: he had climbed across the spikes,
And he had squeezed himself betwixt the bars,
And he had breathed the Proctor's dogs; and one
Discussed his tutor, rough to common men,
But honeying at the whisper of a lord;
And one the Master, as a rogue in grain
Veneered with sanctimonious theory.

*80. Went . . . Science*] *1853*; With Science hand in hand went *1847–51*.
*97–8*] *1850*; And Lilia with the rest, and Ralph himself, *1847–8*.
*113*. 'Made the proctor's attendants out of breath' (T.).

But while they talked, above their heads I saw
The feudal warrior lady-clad; which brought
My book to mind: and opening this I read
Of old Sir Ralph a page or two that rang
With tilt and tourney; then the tale of her
That drove her foes with slaughter from her walls,
And much I praised her nobleness, and 'Where,'
Asked Walter, patting Lilia's head (she lay
Beside him) 'lives there such a woman now?'

Quick answered Lilia 'There are thousands now
Such women, but convention beats them down:
It is but bringing up; no more than that:
You men have done it: how I hate you all!
Ah, were I something great! I wish I were
Some mighty poetess, I would shame you then,
That love to keep us children! O I wish
That I were some great princess, I would build
Far off from men a college like a man's,
And I would teach them all that men are taught;
We are twice as quick!' And here she shook aside
The hand that played the patron with her curls.

And one said smiling 'Pretty were the sight
If our old halls could change their sex, and flaunt
With prudes for proctors, dowagers for deans,
And sweet girl-graduates in their golden hair.
I think they should not wear our rusty gowns,
But move as rich as Emperor-moths, or Ralph
Who shines so in the corner; yet I fear,
If there were many Lilias in the brood,
However deep you might embower the nest,
Some boy would spy it.'
At this upon the sward
She tapt her tiny silken-sandaled foot:
'That's your light way; but I would make it death
For any male thing but to peep at us.'

*125–6. patting . . . him)*] *1850; not 1847–8.*
*131–3*] *1850; not 1847–8.*
*134. That I were*] *1850*; O were I *1847–8.*
*135. like a man's*] *1850*; of my own *1847–8.*
*136. that . . . taught*] *1850*; things: you should see.' *1847–8.*
*137–8*] *1850; not 1847–8.*
*142.* Cp. Keats, *Lamia* i 197–8: 'As though in Cupid's college she had spent / Sweet days a lovely graduate'.

Petulant she spoke, and at herself she laughed;
A rosebud set with little wilful thorns,
And sweet as English air could make her, she:
But Walter hailed a score of names upon her,
And 'petty Ogress', and 'ungrateful Puss',
And swore he longed at college, only longed,
All else was well, for she-society.
They boated and they cricketed; they talked
At wine, in clubs, of art, of politics;
They lost their weeks; they vext the souls of deans;
They rode; they betted; made a hundred friends,
And caught the blossom of the flying terms,
But missed the mignonette of Vivian-place,
The little hearth-flower Lilia. Thus he spoke,
Part banter, part affection.
'True,' she said,
'We doubt not that. O yes, you missed us much.
I'll stake my ruby ring upon it you did.'

She held it out; and as a parrot turns
Up through gilt wires a crafty loving eye,
And takes a lady's finger with all care,
And bites it for true heart and not for harm,
So he with Lilia's. Daintily she shrieked
And wrung it. 'Doubt my word again!' he said.
'Come, listen! here is proof that you were missed:
We seven stayed at Christmas up to read;
And there we took one tutor as to read:
The hard-grained Muses of the cube and square
Were out of season: never man, I think,
So mouldered in a sinecure as he:
For while our cloisters echoed frosty feet,
And our long walks were stript as bare as brooms,
We did but talk you over, pledge you all
In wassail; often, like as many girls–
Sick for the hollies and the yews of home–
As many little trifling Lilias–played
Charades and riddles as at Christmas here,
And *what's my thought* and *when* and *where* and *how*,

*161. weeks*: of required attendance.
*177–9*] *1850*; We seven took one tutor. Never man *1847–8*.
*179*] No churchman deep in some neglected fen *H.Nbk 24*.
*181. frosty*] studious *H.MS*. T. disliked the echo of *Il Penseroso* 155–6: 'But let my due feet never fail, / To walk the studious Cloysters pale.'
*182. were stript*] stuck up *H.MS*.

And often told a tale from mouth to mouth
As here at Christmas.'
She remembered that:
A pleasant game, she thought: she liked it more
Than magic music, forfeits, all the rest.
But these–what kind of tales did men tell men,
She wondered, by themselves?
A half-disdain
Perched on the pouted blossom of her lips:
And Walter nodded at me; '*He* began,
The rest would follow, each in turn; and so
We forged a sevenfold story. Kind? what kind?
Chimeras, crotchets, Christmas solecisms,
Seven-headed monsters only made to kill
Time by the fire in winter.'
'Kill him now,
The tyrant! kill him in the summer too,'
Said Lilia; 'Why not now?' the maiden Aunt.
'Why not a summer's as a winter's tale?
A tale for summer as befits the time,
And something it should be to suit the place,
Heroic, for a hero lies beneath,
Grave, solemn!'
Walter warped his mouth at this
To something so mock-solemn, that I laughed
And Lilia woke with sudden-thrilling mirth

*190. She remembered*] *1850*; 'I remember *1847–8*.
*191. , she thought: she*] *1850*; ,'she said; 'I *1847–8*.
*192. magic music*: a game like hunt the thimble, with music played fast and loud when the seeker is 'warm', and slow and soft when he is 'cold'. Cp. *The Day-Dream: Arrival* 26 (p. 629).
*193. did*] *1850*; do *1847–8*.
*194. She wondered*] *1850*; I wonder *1847–8*.
*197. , each . . . so*] *1850*; ; so we tost the ball: *1847–8*.
*198–200*] *1850*; What kind of tales? why, such as served to kill *1847–8*. Shannon (p. 125) observes that the change is to escape accusations of oddity or inconsistency.
*202–3*] *1850*; Tell one' she said 'kill him in summer too,'
And 'tell one' cried the solemn maiden aunt. *1847–8*
*204–5*. Cp. *Winter's Tale* II i 25: 'A sad tale's best for winter'. See l. 231.
*207–8*] *1850*; Grave, moral, solemn, like the mouldering walls / About us.' *1847–8*. Shannon (p. 127) observes that this is to meet the objection by reviewers that the poem was pitched too unheroically at the beginning.
*210–11*. Cp. *Kate* 3–4: 'Her rapid laughters wild and shrill, / As laughters of the woodpecker.'

An echo like a ghostly woodpecker,
Hid in the ruins; till the maiden Aunt
(A little sense of wrong had touched her face
With colour) turned to me with 'As you will;
Heroic if you will, or what you will,
Or be yourself your hero if you will.'

'Take Lilia, then, for heroine' clamoured he,
'And make her some great Princess, six feet high,
Grand, epic, homicidal; and be you
The Prince to win her!'
'Then follow me, the Prince,'
I answered, 'each be hero in his turn!
Seven and yet one, like shadows in a dream.–
Heroic seems our Princess as required–
But something made to suit with Time and place,
A Gothic ruin and a Grecian house,
A talk of college and of ladies' rights,
A feudal knight in silken masquerade,
And, yonder, shrieks and strange experiments
For which the good Sir Ralph had burnt them all–
This *were* a medley! we should have him back
Who told the "Winter's tale" to do it for us.
No matter: we will say whatever comes.

*211. a ghostly*] *1853*; an April *1848–51*.

*214–39*] *1850 (except ll. 222, 229–30)*;

With colour) turned to me: 'Well–as you will–
Just as you will,' she said; 'be, if you will,
Yourself your hero.'
'Look then' added he
'Since Lilia would be princess, that you stoop
No lower than a prince.'
To which I said,
'Take care then that my tale be followed out
By all the lieges in my royal vein:
But one that really suited time and place
Were such a medley, we should . . . [*ll. 230–1, 225–9*
(*reading* yonder] *there with l. 228*)]
The nineteenth century gambols on the grass.
[*l. 232*]
Here are we seven: if each man take his turn
We make a sevenfold story:' then began. *1847–8*

*222*] *1851; not 1850.*

*229*] *1851, 1847–8; not 1850.*

*230. This were*] *1851*; Were such *1847–50*.

And let the ladies sing us, if they will,
From time to time, some ballad or a song
To give us breathing-space.'
So I began,
And the rest followed: and the women sang
Between the rougher voices of the men,
Like linnets in the pauses of the wind:
And here I give the story and the songs.

## I

A prince I was, blue-eyed, and fair in face,
Of temper amorous, as the first of May,
With lengths of yellow ringlet, like a girl,
For on my cradle shone the Northern star.

There lived an ancient legend in our house.
Some sorcerer, whom a far-off grandsire burnt
Because he cast no shadow, had foretold,
Dying, that none of all our blood should know
The shadow from the substance, and that one
Should come to fight with shadows and to fall.
For so, my mother said, the story ran.
And, truly, waking dreams were, more or less,
An old and strange affection of the house.
Myself too had weird seizures, Heaven knows what:
On a sudden in the midst of men and day,
And while I walked and talked as heretofore,
I seemed to move among a world of ghosts,
And feel myself the shadow of a dream.
Our great court-Galen poised his gilt-head cane,
And pawed his beard, and muttered 'catalepsy'.
My mother pitying made a thousand prayers;
My mother was as mild as any saint,
Half-canonized by all that looked on her,
So gracious was her tact and tenderness:
But my good father thought a king a king;
He cared not for the affection of the house;

*238.* Cp. *The Miller's Daughter* 122: 'And, in the pauses of the wind'.
*239.* See Appendix A (p. 1768), for the earlier introductory fragments.

i *2*] *1850; not 1847–8.*
i *5–21*] *1851 (except l. 20); not 1847–50.*
i *19. Galen*: 'the great doctor of Pergamus, 131 to 200 A.D.' (T.).
i *20. muttered*] *1853*; called it *1851*.
i *23*] *1850*; And nearly canonized by all she knew, *1847–8*.
i *26*] *1851; not 1847–50.*

He held his sceptre like a pedant's wand
To lash offence, and with long arms and hands
Reached out, and picked offenders from the mass
For judgment.
Now it chanced that I had been,
While life was yet in bud and blade, betrothed
To one, a neighbouring Princess: she to me
Was proxy-wedded with a bootless calf
At eight years old; and still from time to time
Came murmurs of her beauty from the South,
And of her brethren, youths of puissance;
And still I wore her picture by my heart,
And one dark tress; and all around them both
Sweet thoughts would swarm as bees about their queen.

But when the days drew nigh that I should wed,
My father sent ambassadors with furs
And jewels, gifts, to fetch her: these brought back
A present, a great labour of the loom;
And therewithal an answer vague as wind:
Besides, they saw the king; he took the gifts;
He said there was a compact; that was true:
But then she had a will; was he to blame?
And maiden fancies; loved to live alone
Among her women; certain, would not wed.

That morning in the presence room I stood
With Cyril and with Florian, my two friends:
The first, a gentleman of broken means
(His father's fault) but given to starts and bursts
Of revel; and the last, my other heart,
And almost my half-self, for still we moved
Together, twinned as horse's ear and eye.

i *27*. *pedant*: schoolmaster.
i *33*. 'The proxy of the king used to place his bare leg under the coverlet of the king's betrothed' (T.); H.T. adds: 'Bacon in his *Henry VII* writes of the proxy marriage of Maximilian, the king of the Romans, with Anne of Brittany, 1489: "For she was not only publicly contracted, but stated as a bride, and solemnly bedded; and after she was laid, there came in Maximilian's ambassador, with letters of procuration, and in the presence of sundry noble personages, men and women, put his leg, stript naked to the knee, between the espousal sheets; to the end that the ceremony might be thought to amount to a consummation and actual knowledge."'
i *36*. *youths*] *1850*; knights *1847–8*.
i *55*. *And almost*] *1851*; My shadow, *1847–50*.
i *56*. *twinned*] *1851*; kin *1847–50*.

Now, while they spake, I saw my father's face
Grow long and troubled like a rising moon,
Inflamed with wrath: he started on his feet,
Tore the king's letter, snowed it down, and rent
The wonder of the loom through warp and woof
From skirt to skirt; and at the last he sware
That he would send a hundred thousand men,
And bring her in a whirlwind: then he chewed
The thrice-turned cud of wrath, and cooked his spleen,
Communing with his captains of the war.

At last I spoke. 'My father, let me go.
It cannot be but some gross error lies
In this report, this answer of a king,
Whom all men rate as kind and hospitable:
Or, maybe, I myself, my bride once seen,
Whate'er my grief to find her less than fame,
May rue the bargain made.' And Florian said:
'I have a sister at the foreign court,
Who moves about the Princess; she, you know,
Who wedded with a nobleman from thence:
He, dying lately, left her, as I hear,
The lady of three castles in that land:
Through her this matter might be sifted clean.'
And Cyril whispered: 'Take me with you too.'
Then laughing 'what, if these weird seizures come
Upon you in those lands, and no one near
To point you out the shadow from the truth!
Take me: I'll serve you better in a strait;
I grate on rusty hinges here:' but 'No!'
Roared the rough king, 'you shall not; we ourself
Will crush her pretty maiden fancies dead
In iron gauntlets: break the council up.'

But when the council broke, I rose and past
Through the wild woods that hung about the town;
Found a still place, and plucked her likeness out;
Laid it on flowers, and watched it lying bathed

i 65. *cooked his spleen*: *Iliad* iv 513: ἐπὶ νηυσὶ χόλον θυμαλγέα πέσσει.
i 72. Horace, *Epistles* I xi 3: *maiora minorave fama* ('whether above or below their fame').
i 80. *And . . . whispered*] *1851*; Then whispered Cyril *1847–50*.
i 81–3] *1851; not 1847–50*.
i 84. *Take*] *1851*; Trust *1847–50*.
i 86] *1850*; Replied the king, 'you shall not; I myself *1847–8*.
i 87. *her*] *1851*; these *1847–50*.

In the green gleam of dewy-tasselled trees:
What were those fancies? wherefore break her troth?
Proud looked the lips: but while I meditated
A wind arose and rushed upon the South,
And shook the songs, the whispers, and the shrieks
Of the wild woods together; and a Voice
Went with it, 'Follow, follow, thou shalt win.'

Then, ere the silver sickle of that month
Became her golden shield, I stole from court
With Cyril and with Florian, unperceived,
Cat-footed through the town and half in dread
To hear my father's clamour at our backs
With Ho! from some bay-window shake the night;
But all was quiet: from the bastioned walls
Like threaded spiders, one by one, we dropt,
And flying reached the frontier: then we crost
To a livelier land; and so by tilth and grange,
And vines, and blowing bosks of wilderness,
We gained the mother-city thick with towers,
And in the imperial palace found the king.

i *93. dewy-tasselled*: with catkins; cp. *In Memoriam* lxxxvi 6.
i *96–9.* Cp. *Prometheus Unbound* II i 156–9: 'A wind arose among the pines; it shook / The clinging music from their boughs, and then / Low, sweet, faint sounds, like the farewell of ghosts, / Were heard: "O, follow, follow, follow me!"' T. wrote to S. E. Dawson (*Eversley*, p. 240): 'I believe the resemblance which you note is just a chance one. Shelley's lines are not familiar to me, though of course, if they occur in the *Prometheus*, I must have read them.' T. wished P. M. Wallace to delete a reference to this parallel passage from his edition of *The Princess* (proofs, 1891, *Lincoln*).
i *103–5*] *1851; not 1847–50.*
i *106–7*] *1851*; Down from the bastioned walls we dropt by night, *1847–8*;

Down from the bastioned wall, suspense by night,
Like threaded spiders from a balk, we dropt, *1850*

i *109. tilth and grange*] *1850*; town and thorpe *1847–8.*
i *110. vines*] *1850*; tilth *1847–8.* *blowing bosks*: 'blossoming thickets' (T.).
i *111–2*] We crost into a land where mile-high towers
Pufft out a night of smoke that drowsed the sun;
Huge pistons rose and fell, and everywhere
We heard the clank of chains, the creak of cranes,
Ringing of blocks and throb of hammers mixt
With water split and split on groaning wheels,
Until we reacht the court. *H.Nbk 22*

His name was Gama; cracked and small his voice,
But bland the smile that like a wrinkling wind
On glassy water drove his cheek in lines;
A little dry old man, without a star,
Not like a king: three days he feasted us,
And on the fourth I spake of why we came,
And my betrothed. 'You do us, Prince,' he said,
Airing a snowy hand and signet gem,
'All honour. We remember love ourselves
In our sweet youth: there did a compact pass
Long summers back, a kind of ceremony–
I think the year in which our olives failed.
I would you had her, Prince, with all my heart,
With my full heart: but there were widows here,
Two widows, Lady Psyche, Lady Blanche;
They fed her theories, in and out of place
Maintaining that with equal husbandry
The woman were an equal to the man.
They harped on this; with this our banquets rang;
Our dances broke and buzzed in knots of talk;
Nothing but this; my very ears were hot
To hear them: knowledge, so my daughter held,
Was all in all: they had but been, she thought,
As children; they must lose the child, assume
The woman: then, Sir, awful odes she wrote,
Too awful, sure, for what they treated of,
But all she is and does is awful; odes
About this losing of the child; and rhymes
And dismal lyrics, prophesying change
Beyond all reason: these the women sang;
And they that know such things–I sought but peace;
No critic I–would call them masterpieces:
They mastered *me*. At last she begged a boon,

i *114–5*] *1851; not 1847–8;* But bland the smile that puckered up his cheeks; *1850*. Cp. *Paradise Lost* xi 842–4: 'Drivn by a keen North-winde, that blowing drie / Wrinkl'd the face of Deluge, as decai'd; / And the cleer Sun on his wide watrie Glass . . .'

i *120*. Cp. Juvenal, *Satires* i 28–9: *ventilet aestivum digitis sudantibus aurum, / nec sufferre queat maioris pondera gemmae* ('whilst on his sweating finger he airs a summer ring of gold, unable to endure the weight of a heavier gem').

i *122*. Horace, *Odes* I xvi 23: *in dulci iuventa.*

i *134–45*] *1850 (except ll. 138–9)*; To hear them. Last, my daughter begged a boon, *1847–8.*

i *138–9*] *1851; not 1850.*

A certain summer-palace which I have
Hard by your father's frontier: I said no,
Yet being an easy man, gave it: and there,
All wild to found an University
For maidens, on the spur she fled; and more
We know not,–only this: they see no men,
Not even her brother Arac, nor the twins
Her brethren, though they love her, look upon her
As on a kind of paragon; and I
(Pardon me saying it) were much loth to breed
Dispute betwixt myself and mine: but since
(And I confess with right) you think me bound
In some sort, I can give you letters to her;
And yet, to speak the truth, I rate your chance
Almost at naked nothing.'
Thus the king;
And I, though nettled that he seemed to slur
With garrulous ease and oily courtesies
Our formal compact, yet, not less (all frets
But chafing me on fire to find my bride)
Went forth again with both my friends. We rode
Many a long league back to the North. At last
From hills, that looked across a land of hope,
We dropt with evening on a rustic town
Set in a gleaming river's crescent-curve,
Close at the boundary of the liberties;
There, entered an old hostel, called mine host
To council, plied him with his richest wines,
And showed the late-writ letters of the king.

He with a long low sibilation, stared
As blank as death in marble; then exclaimed

i *151. only this*] *1850*; have not been *1847–8.*
i *152. Arac*] Eric *H.MS.*
i *153. her brethren*: 'accusative after "see"' (T.).
i *165*] *1851*; Set out once more with those two gallant boys; *1847–50.*
i *165* ∧ *6*] Then pushing onward under sun and stars *1847–8.*
i *166. At last*] *1851*; we came *1847–8*; we past *1850.*
i *167*] *1851*; When the first fern-owl whirred about the copse, *1847–8*; And came (the fern-owl whirring in the copse) *1850.*
i *168–9*] *1851*; Upon a little town within a wood *1847–50.*
i *170.* H.T. comments: 'Blackstone in his *Commentaries,* ii 37, defines a "liberty" as a "Royal privilege or branch of the King's prerogative, subsisting in the hands of a subject." The term "liberties" is here applied to the estate over which the privilege can be exercised.'
i *171. entered an old*] *1850*; entering in an *1847–8.*

Averring it was clear against all rules
For any man to go: but as his brain
Began to mellow, 'If the king,' he said,
'Had given us letters, was he bound to speak?
The king would bear him out;' and at the last–
The summer of the vine in all his veins–
'No doubt that we might make it worth his while.
She once had past that way; he heard her speak;
She scared him; life! he never saw the like;
She looked as grand as doomsday and as grave:
And he, he reverenced his liege-lady there;
He always made a point to post with mares;
His daughter and his housemaid were the boys:
The land, he understood, for miles about
Was tilled by women; all the swine were sows,
And all the dogs'–
But while he jested thus,
A thought flashed through me which I clothed in act,
Remembering how we three presented Maid
Or Nymph, or Goddess, at high tide of feast,
In masque or pageant at my father's court.
We sent mine host to purchase female gear;
He brought it, and himself, a sight to shake
The midriff of despair with laughter, holp
To lace us up, till, each, in maiden plumes
We rustled: him we gave a costly bribe
To guerdon silence, mounted our good steeds,
And boldly ventured on the liberties.

We followed up the river as we rode,
And rode till midnight when the college lights
Began to glitter firefly-like in copse
And linden alley: then we past an arch,

i *183*] *1850; not 1847–8.*
i *184*] *1851; not 1847–50.*
i *185*] *1850; not 1847–8.*
i *186. And he*] *1850*; For him *1847–8.*
i *188. boys*: postilions.
i *197–200*] *1850*; Which brought and clapt upon us, we tweezered out
What slender blossom lived on lip or cheek
Of manhood, gave mine host a costly bribe *1847–8*
Shannon (p. 118) points out that *QR* had ridiculed this.
i *201. guerdon*: to reward.
i *203*] *1851; not 1847–50.*
i *204. And*] *1851*; We *1847–50.*
i *206. then*] *1850*; and then *1847–8.*

Whereon a woman-statue rose with wings
From four winged horses dark against the stars;
And some inscription ran along the front,
But deep in shadow: further on we gained
A little street half garden and half house;
But scarce could hear each other speak for noise
Of clocks and chimes, like silver hammers falling
On silver anvils, and the splash and stir
Of fountains spouted up and showering down
In meshes of the jasmine and the rose:
And all about us pealed the nightingale,
Rapt in her song, and careless of the snare.

There stood a bust of Pallas for a sign,
By two sphere lamps blazoned like Heaven and Earth
With constellation and with continent,
Above an entry: riding in, we called;
A plump-armed Ostleress and a stable wench
Came running at the call, and helped us down.
Then stept a buxom hostess forth, and sailed,
Full-blown, before us into rooms which gave
Upon a pillared porch, the bases lost
In laurel: her we asked of that and this,
And who were tutors. 'Lady Blanche' she said,
'And Lady Psyche.' 'Which was prettiest,
Best-natured?' 'Lady Psyche.' 'Hers are we,'
One voice, we cried; and I sat down and wrote,
In such a hand as when a field of corn
Bows all its ears before the roaring East;

'Three ladies of the Northern empire pray
Your Highness would enroll them with your own,
As Lady Psyche's pupils.'
This I sealed:
The seal was Cupid bent above a scroll,
And o'er his head Uranian Venus hung,

i *207–10*] *1850*; Inscribed too dark for legible, and gained *1847–8*. Shannon (p. 119) points out that the reviewers had objected.

i *212. scarce could*] *1850*; could not *1847–8*.

i *222. entry*] *1850*; archway *1847–8*.

i *227. a pillared porch*: Keats, *Lamia* i 379.

i *231. Hers are*] *1850*; Her pupils *1847–8*.

i *238–41*] *1850 (except l. 239)*; (A Cupid reading) to be sent with dawn; *1847–8*.

i *239. o'er his head*] *1851*; over him *1850*. *Uranian*: the higher love of Plato's *Symposium*.

And raised the blinding bandage from his eyes:
I gave the letter to be sent with dawn;
And then to bed, where half in doze I seemed
To float about a glimmering night, and watch
A full sea glazed with muffled moonlight, swell
On some dark shore just seen that it was rich.

[I ∧ II]

As through the land at eve we went,
And plucked the ripened ears,
We fell out, my wife and I,
O we fell out I know not why,
And kissed again with tears.
And blessings on the falling out
That all the more endears,
When we fall out with those we love
And kiss again with tears!
For when we came where lies the child
We lost in other years,
There above the little grave,
O there above the little grave,
We kissed again with tears.

## II

At break of day the College Portress came:
She brought us Academic silks, in hue
The lilac, with a silken hood to each,
And zoned with gold; and now when these were on,
And we as rich as moths from dusk cocoons,
She, curtseying her obeisance, let us know
The Princess Ida waited: out we paced,
I first, and following through the porch that sang
All round with laurel, issued in a court
Compact of lucid marbles, bossed with lengths
Of classic frieze, with ample awnings gay
Betwixt the pillars, and with great urns of flowers.
The Muses and the Graces, grouped in threes,
Enringed a billowing fountain in the midst;
And here and there on lattice edges lay
Or book or lute; but hastily we past,
And up a flight of stairs into the hall.

i ∧ ii Like the other songs between Parts of the poem, it was written 1849, added *1850*. Cp. *The Miller's Daughter* 228–30 (p. 382).

i ∧ ii *4, 13*] *1851; not 1850.*

i ∧ ii *6–9*] *1850, 1862; not 1851–61.* These lines, which he had temporarily discarded, T. thought of using in *Maud*; see p. 1071.

There at a board by tome and paper sat,
With two tame leopards couched beside her throne,
All beauty compassed in a female form,
The Princess; liker to the inhabitant
Of some clear planet close upon the Sun,
Than our man's earth; such eyes were in her head,
And so much grace and power, breathing down
From over her arched brows, with every turn
Lived through her to the tips of her long hands,
And to her feet. She rose her height, and said:

'We give you welcome: not without redound
Of use and glory to yourselves ye come,
The first-fruits of the stranger: aftertime,
And that full voice which circles round the grave,
Will rank you nobly, mingled up with me.
What! are the ladies of your land so tall?'
'We of the court' said Cyril. 'From the court'
She answered, 'then ye know the Prince?' and he:
'The climax of his age! as though there were
One rose in all the world, your Highness that,
He worships your ideal:' she replied:
'We scarcely thought in our own hall to hear
This barren verbiage, current among men,
Light coin, the tinsel clink of compliment.
Your flight from out your bookless wilds would seem
As arguing love of knowledge and of power;
Your language proves you still the child. Indeed,
We dream not of him: when we set our hand
To this great work, we purposed with ourself
Never to wed. You likewise will do well,
Ladies, in entering here, to cast and fling
The tricks, which make us toys of men, that so,
Some future time, if so indeed you will,
You may with those self-styled our lords ally
Your fortunes, justlier balanced, scale with scale.'

At those high words, we conscious of ourselves,
Perused the matting; then an officer

ii *29. use and glory to*] *1850*; fame and profit unto *1847–8.*
ii *38. she*] *1850*; and she *1847–8.*
ii *39. scarcely thought*] *1850*; did not think *1847–8.*
ii *42–4*] *1850 (except l. 44); not 1847–8.*
ii *44. Indeed*] *1851*; For us *1850.*
ii *45. dream*] *1850*; think *1847–8.*
ii *46. ourself*] *1862*; ourselves *1847–61.*

Rose up, and read the statutes, such as these:
Not for three years to correspond with home;
Not for three years to cross the liberties;
Not for three years to speak with any men;
And many more, which hastily subscribed,
We entered on the boards: and 'Now,' she cried,
'Ye are green wood, see ye warp not. Look, our hall!
Our statues! – not of those that men desire,
Sleek Odalisques, or oracles of mode,
Nor stunted squaws of West or East; but she
That taught the Sabine how to rule, and she
The foundress of the Babylonian wall,
The Carian Artemisia strong in war,
The Rhodope, that built the pyramid,
Clelia, Cornelia, with the Palmyrene
That fought Aurelian, and the Roman brows
Of Agrippina. Dwell with these, and lose
Convention, since to look on noble forms
Makes noble through the sensuous organism
That which is higher. O lift your natures up:
Embrace our aims: work out your freedom. Girls,
Knowledge is now no more a fountain sealed:

ii *55–8.* Cp. the decrees in *Love's Labour's Lost* I i, among them not to see a woman.
ii *60. boards*: the college register.
ii *63. Odalisques*: 'female slaves of the harem' (T.).
ii *64–5.* 'The wood-nymph Egeria, who was said to have given the laws to Numa Pompilius' (T.). Cp. *The Palace of Art* 109–12.
ii *66.* 'Semiramis' (T.).
ii *67.* 'She who fought so bravely for Xerxes at Salamis that he said that his women had become men and his men women' (T.).
ii *68.* 'A celebrated Greek courtesan of Thracian origin, who was said to have built a pyramid near Memphis' (T.). T. cites *1 Henry VI* I vi 21–2: 'A statelier pyramis to her I'll rear / Than Rhodope's of Memphis ever was.'
ii *69. Clelia*: 'who swam the Tiber in escaping from Porsenna's camp (Livy ii 13)' (T.). *Cornelia*: 'mother of the Gracchi' (T.). *Palmyrene*: 'Zenobia, Queen of Palmyra' (T.); H.T. refers to Gibbon, Chapter xi, A.D. 272.
ii *71. Agrippina*: 'grand-daughter of Augustus, married to Germanicus' (T.).
ii *71–4. Dwell . . . higher*] *1850; not 1847–8.*
ii *74–80. O . . . noble*] *1851; not 1847–50.*
ii *76.* Cp. *Song of Solomon* iv 12: 'A garden inclosed is my sister, my spouse; a spring shut up, a fountain sealed.'

Drink deep, until the habits of the slave,
The sins of emptiness, gossip and spite
And slander, die. Better not be at all
Than not be noble. Leave us: you may go:
Today the Lady Psyche will harangue
The fresh arrivals of the week before;
For they press in from all the provinces,
And fill the hive.'
She spoke, and bowing waved
Dismissal: back again we crost the court
To Lady Psyche's: as we entered in,
There sat along the forms, like morning doves
That sun their milky bosoms on the thatch,
A patient range of pupils; she herself
Erect behind a desk of satin-wood,
A quick brunette, well-moulded, falcon-eyed,
And on the hither side, or so she looked,
Of twenty summers. At her left, a child,
In shining draperies, headed like a star,
Her maiden babe, a double April old,
Aglaïa slept. We sat: the Lady glanced:
Then Florian, but no livelier than the dame
That whispered 'Asses' ears', among the sedge,
'My sister.' 'Comely, too, by all that's fair,'
Said Cyril. 'O hush, hush!' and she began.

'This world was once a fluid haze of light,
Till toward the centre set the starry tides,
And eddied into suns, that wheeling cast
The planets: then the monster, then the man;
Tattooed or woaded, winter-clad in skins,
Raw from the prime, and crushing down his mate;
As yet we find in barbarous isles, and here
Among the lowest.'
Thereupon she took
A bird's-eye-view of all the ungracious past;

ii *84. She . . . bowing*] *1850*; So saying, she bowed and *1847–8*.
ii *94. headed like a star*: 'with bright golden hair' (T.); H.T. compares *Iliad* vi 401, the description of Astyanax.
ii *96. Aglaïa*: Brightness, the name of one of the Graces.
ii *97–8*. 'Midas in *The Wyf of Bathe's Tale* confides the secret of his hairy asses' ears only to his wife' (T.).
ii *101*. 'The nebular theory as formulated by Laplace' (T.). H.T. compares *In Memoriam* cxviii 9–12, and lxxxix 45–8. Cp. *The Palace of Art* 186–92*n* (p. 412).

Glanced at the legendary Amazon
As emblematic of a nobler age;
Appraised the Lycian custom, spoke of those
That lay at wine with Lar and Lucumo;
Ran down the Persian, Grecian, Roman lines
Of empire, and the woman's state in each,
How far from just; till warming with her theme
She fulmined out her scorn of laws Salique
And little-footed China, touched on Mahomet
With much contempt, and came to chivalry:
When some respect, however slight, was paid
To woman, superstition all awry:
However then commenced the dawn: a beam
Had slanted forward, falling in a land
Of promise; fruit would follow. Deep, indeed,
Their debt of thanks to her who first had dared
To leap the rotten pales of prejudice,
Disyoke their necks from custom, and assert
None lordlier than themselves but that which made
Woman and man. She had founded; they must build.
Here might they learn whatever men were taught:
Let them not fear: some said their heads were less:
Some men's were small; not they the least of men;
For often fineness compensated size:
Besides the brain was like the hand, and grew
With using; thence the man's, if more was more;
He took advantage of his strength to be
First in the field: some ages had been lost;
But woman ripened earlier, and her life
Was longer; and albeit their glorious names
Were fewer, scattered stars, yet since in truth
The highest is the measure of the man,
And not the Kaffir, Hottentot, Malay,

ii *112*. 'Herodotus (i 73) says that the Lycians took their names from their mothers instead of their fathers' (T.).

ii *113*. *Lar*: 'noble' (H.T.). *Lucumo*: 'an Etruscan prince or priest' (T.).

ii *117*. *fulmined*: cp. *Paradise Regained* iv 268–70, on the orators 'whose resistless eloquence / Wielded at will that fierce Democratie, / Shook the Arsenal and fulmin'd over Greece.' *Salique*: 'the laws of the Salian Franks forbad inheritance by women' (T.).

ii *118*. *little-footed*: the custom of deforming the feet.

ii *118–9*. 'Had she heard that, according to the Mohammedan doctrine, hell was chiefly occupied by women?' (T.).

ii *123–4*. *land of promise*: *Hebrews* xi 9.

ii *135*. *more was more*: 'greater in size meant greater in power.' (T.).

Nor those horn-handed breakers of the glebe,
But Homer, Plato, Verulam; even so
With woman: and in arts of government
Elizabeth and others; arts of war
The peasant Joan and others; arts of grace
Sappho and others vied with any man:
And, last not least, she who had left her place,
And bowed her state to them, that they might grow
To use and power on this Oasis, lapt
In the arms of leisure, sacred from the blight
Of ancient influence and scorn.
At last
She rose upon a wind of prophecy
Dilating on the future; 'everywhere
Two heads in council, two beside the hearth,
Two in the tangled business of the world,
Two in the liberal offices of life,
Two plummets dropt for one to sound the abyss
Of science, and the secrets of the mind:
Musician, painter, sculptor, critic, more:
And everywhere the broad and bounteous Earth
Should bear a double growth of those rare souls,
Poets, whose thoughts enrich the blood of the world.'

She ended here, and beckoned us: the rest
Parted; and, glowing full-faced welcome, she
Began to address us, and was moving on
In gratulation, till as when a boat
Tacks, and the slackened sail flaps, all her voice
Faltering and fluttering in her throat, she cried
'My brother!' 'Well, my sister.' 'O,' she said,
'What do you here? and in this dress? and these?
Why who are these? a wolf within the fold!
A pack of wolves! the Lord be gracious to me!
A plot, a plot, a plot, to ruin all!'
'No plot, no plot,' he answered. 'Wretched boy,
How saw you not the inscription on the gate,
LET NO MAN ENTER IN ON PAIN OF DEATH?'
'And if I had,' he answered, 'who could think
The softer Adams of your Academe,
O sister, Sirens though they be, were such
As chanted on the blanching bones of men?'
'But you will find it otherwise' she said.

i *144*. Cp. *The Palace of Art* 163 (p. 411).
i *149*. , *last . . . she*] *1850*; she, though last not least, *1847–8*.

'You jest: ill jesting with edge-tools! my vow
Binds me to speak, and O that iron will,
That axelike edge unturnable, our Head,
The Princess.' 'Well then, Psyche, take my life,
And nail me like a weasel on a grange
For warning: bury me beside the gate,
And cut this epitaph above my bones;
*Here lies a brother by a sister slain,*
*All for the common good of womankind.*'
'Let me die too,' said Cyril, 'having seen
And heard the Lady Psyche.'
I struck in:
'Albeit so masked, Madam, I love the truth;
Receive it; and in me behold the Prince
Your countryman, affianced years ago
To the Lady Ida: here, for here she was,
And thus (what other way was left) I came.'
'O Sir, O Prince, I have no country; none;
If any, this; but none. Whate'er I was
Disrooted, what I am is grafted here.
Affianced, Sir? love-whispers may not breathe
Within this vestal limit, and how should I,
Who am not mine, say, live: the thunderbolt
Hangs silent; but prepare: I speak; it falls.'
'Yet pause,' I said: 'for that inscription there,
I think no more of deadly lurks therein,
Than in a clapper clapping in a garth,
To scare the fowl from fruit: if more there be,
If more and acted on, what follows? war;
Your own work marred: for this your Academe,
Whichever side be Victor, in the halloo
Will topple to the trumpet down, and pass
With all fair theories only made to gild
A stormless summer.' 'Let the Princess judge
Of that' she said: 'farewell, Sir–and to you.
I shudder at the sequel, but I go.'

'Are you that Lady Psyche,' I rejoined,
'The fifth in line from that old Florian,
Yet hangs his portrait in my father's hall
(The gaunt old Baron with his beetle brow

ii *184–5. my . . . that*] *1850*; I am bound / To tell her. O, she has an *1847–8*.
ii *186. That*] *1850*; An *1847–8*.
ii *209. garth*: enclosed ground.

Sun-shaded in the heat of dusty fights)
As he bestrode my Grandsire, when he fell,
And all else fled? we point to it, and we say,
The loyal warmth of Florian is not cold,
But branches current yet in kindred veins.'
'Are you that Psyche,' Florian added; 'she
With whom I sang about the morning hills,
Flung ball, flew kite, and raced the purple fly,
And snared the squirrel of the glen? are you
That Psyche, wont to bind my throbbing brow,
To smoothe my pillow, mix the foaming draught
Of fever, tell me pleasant tales, and read
My sickness down to happy dreams? are you
That brother-sister Psyche, both in one?
You were that Psyche, but what are you now?'
'You are that Psyche,' Cyril said, 'for whom
I would be that for ever which I seem,
Woman, if I might sit beside your feet,
And glean your scattered sapience.'
Then once more,
'Are you that Lady Psyche,' I began,
'That on her bridal morn before she past
From all her old companions, when the king
Kissed her pale cheek, declared that ancient ties
Would still be dear beyond the southern hills;
That were there any of our people there
In want or peril, there was one to hear
And help them? look! for such are these and I.'
'Are you that Psyche,' Florian asked, 'to whom,
In gentler days, your arrow-wounded fawn
Came flying while you sat beside the well?
The creature laid his muzzle on your lap,
And sobbed, and you sobbed with it, and the blood
Was sprinkled on your kirtle, and you wept.
That was fawn's blood, not brother's, yet you wept.
O by the bright head of my little niece,
You were that Psyche, and what are you now?'
'You are that Psyche,' Cyril said again,
'The mother of the sweetest little maid,

ii *224. bestrode*: 'in defence' (T.). H.T. compares *1 Henry IV* V i 122, and *Comedy of Errors* V i 192: 'When I bestrid thee in the wars'.

ii *240. Woman*] *1850*; A woman *1847–8*.

ii *251–6.* J. Killham, *Critical Essays on Tennyson*, pp. 229–30, compares Marvell's *Nymph Complaining for the Death of her Faun*. Cp. also Silvia's wounded stag, *Aeneid* vii 500–4.

That ever crowed for kisses.'
                                        'Out upon it!'
She answered, 'peace! and why should I not play
The Spartan Mother with emotion, be
The Lucius Junius Brutus of my kind?
Him you call great: he for the common weal,
The fading politics of mortal Rome,
As I might slay this child, if good need were,
Slew both his sons: and I, shall I, on whom
The secular emancipation turns
Of half this world, be swerved from right to save
A prince, a brother? a little will I yield.
Best so, perchance, for us, and well for you.
O hard, when love and duty clash! I fear
My conscience will not count me fleckless; yet–
Hear my conditions: promise (otherwise
You perish) as you came, to slip away
Today, tomorrow, soon: it shall be said,
These women were too barbarous, would not learn;
They fled, who might have shamed us: promise, all.'

What could we else, we promised each; and she,
Like some wild creature newly-caged, commenced
A to-and-fro, so pacing till she paused
By Florian; holding out her lily arms
Took both his hands, and smiling faintly said:
'I knew you at the first: though you have grown
You scarce have altered: I am sad and glad
To see you, Florian. *I* give thee to death
My brother! it was duty spoke, not I.
My needful seeming harshness, pardon it.
Our mother, is she well?'
                                        With that she kissed
His forehead, then, a moment after, clung
About him, and betwixt them blossomed up
From out a common vein of memory
Sweet household talk, and phrases of the hearth,
And far allusion, till the gracious dews
Began to glisten and to fall: and while

ii *264*. 'Who condemned his sons to death for conspiracy against the city (Livy, ii 5)' (T.).

ii *269*. *secular*: lasting through ages.

ii *285–6*] *1850*; You are grown, and yet I knew you at the first.
I am very glad, and I am very vext *1847–8*

ii *291*. *then*,] *1850*; and *1847–8*.

They stood, so rapt, we gazing, came a voice,
'I brought a message here from Lady Blanche.'
Back started she, and turning round we saw
The Lady Blanche's daughter where she stood,
Melissa, with her hand upon the lock,
A rosy blonde, and in a college gown,
That clad her like an April daffodilly
(Her mother's colour) with her lips apart,
And all her thoughts as fair within her eyes,
As bottom agates seen to wave and float
In crystal currents of clear morning seas.

So stood that same fair creature at the door.
Then Lady Psyche, 'Ah–Melissa–you!
You heard us?' and Melissa, 'O pardon me
I heard, I could not help it, did not wish:
But, dearest Lady, pray you fear me not,
Nor think I bear that heart within my breast,
To give three gallant gentlemen to death.'
'I trust you,' said the other, 'for we two
Were always friends, none closer, elm and vine:
But yet your mother's jealous temperament–
Let not your prudence, dearest, drowse, or prove
The Danaïd of a leaky vase, for fear
This whole foundation ruin, and I lose
My honour, these their lives.' 'Ah, fear me not'
Replied Melissa; 'no–I would not tell,
No, not for all Aspasia's cleverness,
No, not to answer, Madam, all those hard things
That Sheba came to ask of Solomon.'
'Be it so' the other, 'that we still may lead

ii *304. colour*: that worn by her pupils, her 'side'.
ii *306. seen*] *1850*; seem *1847–8*.
ii *306–7*. 'It has been said that I took this simile partly from Beaumont and Fletcher, partly from Shakespeare, whereas I made it while I was bathing in Wales' (T.).
ii *311. wish*] *1850*; mean *1847–8*.
ii *312. pray*] *1850*; I pray *1847–8*.
ii *319*. The Danaids, who murdered their husbands, were punished in Hades by having to carry water in sieves.
ii *323. Aspasia*: hostess to the finest literary and philosophical minds in Athens.
ii *325. 1 Kings* x 1: 'And when the queen of Sheba heard of the fame of Solomon concerning the name of the Lord, she came to prove him with hard questions.'
ii *326. still may*] *1850*; may live to *1847–8*.

The new light up, and culminate in peace,
For Solomon may come to Sheba yet.'
Said Cyril, 'Madam, he the wisest man
Feasted the woman wisest then, in halls
Of Lebanonian cedar: nor should you
(Though, Madam, *you* should answer, *we* would ask)
Less welcome find among us, if you came
Among us, debtors for our lives to you,
Myself for something more.' He said not what,
But 'Thanks,' she answered 'Go: we have been too long
Together: keep your hoods about the face;
They do so that affect abstraction here.
Speak little; mix not with the rest; and hold
Your promise: all, I trust, may yet be well.'

We turned to go, but Cyril took the child,
And held her round the knees against his waist,
And blew the swollen cheek of a trumpeter,
While Psyche watched them, smiling, and the child
Pushed her flat hand against his face and laughed;
And thus our conference closed.
And then we strolled
For half the day through stately theatres
Benched crescent-wise. In each we sat, we heard
The grave Professor. On the lecture slate
The circle rounded under female hands
With flawless demonstration: followed then
A classic lecture, rich in sentiment,
With scraps of thundrous Epic lilted out
By violet-hooded Doctors, elegies
And quoted odes, and jewels five-words-long
That on the stretched forefinger of all Time
Sparkle for ever: then we dipt in all
That treats of whatsoever is, the state,
The total chronicles of man, the mind,
The morals, something of the frame, the rock,
The star, the bird, the fish, the shell, the flower,

ii *331*. Cp. T.'s letter to James Spedding, 15 Feb. 1835 (*Mem.* i 143–4): 'I will come to you as Sheba came to Solomon. "She travelled far from Indian streams, / And he a royal welcome made / In ample chambers overlaid / With Lebanonian cedar-beams." I forget where I read this.' Apparently T. had made up the lines.

ii *333*. *if*] *1850*; if e'er *1847–8*.

ii *347*] *1850; not 1847–8.*

ii *348*. *Benched crescent-wise*] *1850*; From room to room *1847–8*.

ii *360*. *something of the frame*: physiology.

Electric, chemic laws, and all the rest,
And whatsoever can be taught and known;
Till like three horses that have broken fence,
And glutted all night long breast-deep in corn,
We issued gorged with knowledge, and I spoke:
'Why, Sirs, they do all this as well as we.'
'They hunt old trails' said Cyril 'very well;
But when did woman ever yet invent?'
'Ungracious!' answered Florian; 'have you learnt
No more from Psyche's lecture, you that talked
The trash that made me sick, and almost sad?'
'O trash' he said, 'but with a kernel in it.
Should I not call her wise, who made me wise?
And learnt? I learnt more from her in a flash,
Than if my brainpan were an empty hull,
And every Muse tumbled a science in.
A thousand hearts lie fallow in these halls,
And round these halls a thousand baby loves
Fly twanging headless arrows at the hearts,
Whence follows many a vacant pang; but O
With me, Sir, entered in the bigger boy,
The Head of all the golden-shafted firm,
The long-limbed lad that had a Psyche too;
He cleft me through the stomacher; and now
What think you of it, Florian? do I chase
The substance or the shadow? will it hold?
I have no sorcerer's malison on me,
No ghostly hauntings like his Highness. I
Flatter myself that always everywhere
I know the substance when I see it. Well,
Are castles shadows? Three of them? Is she
The sweet proprietress a shadow? If not,
Shall those three castles patch my tattered coat?
For dear are those three castles to my wants,

ii *384*. The legend of Cupid and Psyche.
ii *386–7*] *1851*; What think you of it, Florian? will it hold? *1847–50*.
ii *388–93*] *1851; not 1847–50*.
ii *394 ∧ 5*] 'Oh but,' he answered, 'women's fancies hook
On rusty props. Remember her we called
The 'Star of midnight", how she used to hang
On that flat-headed and bush-cheeked baboon,
Lost to all else and peering up to find
Her God within that blur he called his eye,
The greasy casement of a vacant house.' *MS*
Quoted by Sir Charles Tennyson, *Nineteenth Century* cix (1931) 632.

And dear is sister Psyche to my heart,
And two dear things are one of double worth,
And much I might have said, but that my zone
Unmanned me: then the Doctors! O to hear
The Doctors! O to watch the thirsty plants
Imbibing! once or twice I thought to roar,
To break my chain, to shake my mane: but thou,
Modulate me, Soul of mincing mimicry!
Make liquid treble of that bassoon, my throat;
Abase those eyes that ever loved to meet
Star-sisters answering under crescent brows;
Abate the stride, which speaks of man, and loose
A flying charm of blushes o'er this cheek,
Where they like swallows coming out of time
Will wonder why they came: but hark the bell
For dinner, let us go!'
And in we streamed
Among the columns, pacing staid and still
By twos and threes, till all from end to end
With beauties every shade of brown and fair
In colours gayer than the morning mist,
The long hall glittered like a bed of flowers.
How might a man not wander from his wits
Pierced through with eyes, but that I kept mine own
Intent on her, who rapt in glorious dreams,
The second-sight of some Astræan age,
Sat compassed with professors: they, the while,
Discussed a doubt and tost it to and fro:
A clamour thickened, mixt with inmost terms
Of art and science: Lady Blanche alone
Of faded form and haughtiest lineaments,

ii *398. zone*: girdle.

ii *402. thou*] *1850*; come *1847–8*.

ii *416*. 'Lady Psyche's "side" (pupils) wore lilac robes, and Lady Blanche's robes of daffodil colour' (T.).

ii *419*] *1851*; Intent upon the Princess, where she sat *1847–8*; Intent on her, who rapt in awful dreams, *1850*.

ii *420–23*] *1850*; Among her grave Professors, scattering gems *1847–8*. Aubrey de Vere had objected to the impression of lordliness given by the original (Shannon, p. 136).

ii *420. Astræan*: 'Astræa, daughter of Zeus and Themis, is to come back first of the celestials on the return of the Golden Age' (T.).

ii *424. Lady Blanche alone*] *1850*; only Lady Blanche, *1847–8*.

ii *425*] *1850*; A double-rouged and treble-wrinkled Dame, *1847–8*.

With all her autumn tresses falsely brown,
Shot sidelong daggers at us, a tiger-cat
In act to spring.
At last a solemn grace
Concluded, and we sought the gardens: there
One walked reciting by herself, and one
In this hand held a volume as to read,
And smoothed a petted peacock down with that:
Some to a low song oared a shallop by,
Or under arches of the marble bridge
Hung, shadowed from the heat: some hid and sought
In the orange thickets: others tost a ball
Above the fountain-jets, and back again
With laughter: others lay about the lawns,
Of the older sort, and murmured that their May
Was passing: what was learning unto them?
They wished to marry; they could rule a house;
Men hated learned women: but we three
Sat muffled like the Fates; and often came
Melissa hitting all we saw with shafts
Of gentle satire, kin to charity,
That harmed not: then day droopt; the chapel bells
Called us: we left the walks; we mixt with those
Six hundred maidens clad in purest white,
Before two streams of light from wall to wall,
While the great organ almost burst his pipes,
Groaning for power, and rolling through the court
A long melodious thunder to the sound
Of solemn psalms, and silver litanies,
The work of Ida, to call down from Heaven
A blessing on her labours for the world.

[II ‸ III]

Sweet and low, sweet and low,
Wind of the western sea,

ii *426. autumn tresses*] *1850*; faded Autumns *1847–8*.

ii *442–3*] *1850*; Men hated learned women: and to us came *1847–8*.

ii *446. then . . . bells*] *1850*; so we sat; and now when day *1847–8*.

ii *447. Called . . . mixt*] *1850*; Drooped, and the chapel tinkled, mixt *1847–8*.

ii *452*. Cp. *The Poet's Mind* 27: 'a low melodious thunder'. Also *Semele* 10.

ii ‸ iii Written 1849, added *1850*. Cp. the lullaby in Theocritus xxiv 7–9. For alternative versions, see Appendix A (p. 1769).

ii ‸ iii *1*. Cp. *Hero to Leander* 33: 'Thy voice is sweet and low' (contrasted with the sea). Also *The Lover's Tale* i 530: 'Held converse sweet and low–low converse sweet'; i 552: 'her voice was very sweet and low'.

Low, low, breathe and blow,
  Wind of the western sea!
Over the rolling waters go,
Come from the dying moon, and blow,
  Blow him again to me;
While my little one, while my pretty one, sleeps.

Sleep and rest, sleep and rest,
  Father will come to thee soon;
Rest, rest, on mother's breast,
  Father will come to thee soon;
Father will come to his babe in the nest,
Silver sails all out of the west
  Under the silver moon:
Sleep, my little one, sleep, my pretty one, sleep.

## III

Morn in the white wake of the morning star
Came furrowing all the orient into gold.
We rose, and each by other drest with care
Descended to the court that lay three parts
In shadow, but the Muses' heads were touched
Above the darkness from their native East.

  There while we stood beside the fount, and watched
Or seemed to watch the dancing bubble, approached
Melissa, tinged with wan from lack of sleep,
Or grief, and glowing round her dewy eyes
The circled Iris of a night of tears;
'And fly,' she cried, 'O fly, while yet you may!
My mother knows:' and when I asked her 'how,'
'My fault' she wept 'my fault! and yet not mine;
Yet mine in part. O hear me, pardon me.
My mother, 'tis her wont from night to night
To rail at Lady Psyche and her side.
She says the Princess should have been the Head,
Herself and Lady Psyche the two arms;

ii iii *6. dying*] *1851*; dropping *1850*.

iii *1–2*. Cp. the end of *Love and Duty*: '. . . and morning driven her plow of pearl / Far furrowing into light the mounded rack, / Beyond the fair green field and eastern sea.'

iii *7. There*] *1850*; And *1847–8*.

iii *10. grief*] *1850*; sorrow *1847–8*.

iii *11. Iris*: rainbow. Cp. *All's Well* I iii 147–50: 'What's the matter, / That this distempered messenger of wet, / The many-coloured Iris, rounds thine eye? / Why? that you are my daughter?'

iii *13. when I asked her*] *1850*; we demanding *1847–8*.

And so it was agreed when first they came;
But Lady Psyche was the right hand now,
And she the left, or not, or seldom used;
Hers more than half the students, all the love.
And so last night she fell to canvass you:
*Her* countrywomen! she did not envy her.
"Who ever saw such wild barbarians?
Girls?–more like men!" and at these words the snake,
My secret, seemed to stir within my breast;
And oh, Sirs, could I help it, but my cheek
Began to burn and burn, and her lynx eye
To fix and make me hotter, till she laughed:
"O marvellously modest maiden, you!
Men! girls, like men! why, if they had been men
You need not set your thoughts in rubric thus
For wholesale comment." Pardon, I am shamed
That I must needs repeat for my excuse
What looks so little graceful: "men" (for still
My mother went revolving on the word)
"And so they are,–very like men indeed–
And with that woman closeted for hours!"
Then came these dreadful words out one by one,
"Why–these–*are*–men:" I shuddered: "and you know it."
"O ask me nothing," I said: "And she knows too,
And she conceals it." So my mother clutched
The truth at once, but with no word from me;
And now thus early risen she goes to inform
The Princess: Lady Psyche will be crushed;
But you may yet be saved, and therefore fly;
But heal me with your pardon ere you go.'

'What pardon, sweet Melissa, for a blush?'
Said Cyril: 'Pale one, blush again: than wear
Those lilies, better blush our lives away.
Yet let us breathe for one hour more in Heaven'
He added, 'lest some classic Angel speak
In scorn of us, "They mounted, Ganymedes,
To tumble, Vulcans, on the second morn."

iii *34. rubric*: red letters.
iii *34–8*] *1850*; And in their fulsome fashion wooed you, child,
You need not take so deep a rouge: like men–*1847–8*
iii *40*] *1850*; And closeted with her for hours. Aha!' *1847–8*.
iii *55–6*. Ganymede, snatched up to heaven; Vulcan, hurled from it.

But I will melt this marble into wax
To yield us farther furlough:' and he went.

Melissa shook her doubtful curls, and thought
He scarce would prosper. 'Tell us,' Florian asked,
'How grew this feud betwixt the right and left.'
'O long ago,' she said, 'betwixt these two
Division smoulders hidden; 'tis my mother,
Too jealous, often fretful as the wind
Pent in a crevice: much I bear with her:
I never knew my father, but she says
(God help her) she was wedded to a fool;
And still she railed against the state of things.
She had the care of Lady Ida's youth,
And from the Queen's decease she brought her up.
But when your sister came she won the heart
Of Ida: they were still together, grew
(For so they said themselves) inosculated;
Consonant chords that shiver to one note;
One mind in all things: yet my mother still
Affirms your Psyche thieved her theories,
And angled with them for her pupil's love:
She calls her plagiarist; I know not what:
But I must go: I dare not tarry,' and light,
As flies the shadow of a bird, she fled.

Then murmured Florian gazing after her,
'An open-hearted maiden, true and pure.
If I could love, why this were she: how pretty
Her blushing was, and how she blushed again,
As if to close with Cyril's random wish:
Not like your Princess crammed with erring pride,
Nor like poor Psyche whom she drags in tow.'

'The crane,' I said, 'may chatter of the crane,
The dove may murmur of the dove, but I

iii *58. furlough*: leave of absence, here permission in general.
iii *67. help*] *1850*; pardon *1847–8*.
iii *71. heart*] *1850*; love *1847–8*.
iii *72. Ida*] *1850*; the Princess *1847–8*.
iii *73. inosculated*: intertwined, kissing.
iii *74*. 'If two stringed instruments are together, and a note is struck on one, the other will vibrate with the same harmony' (T.).
iii *75. yet . . . still*] *1850*; only Lady Blanche *1847–8*.
iii *77. her pupil's love*] *1850*; the Royal heart *1847–8*.
iii *88–90*. Cp. Theocritus ix 31–2: 'O cricket is to cricket dear, and ant for ant doth long, / The hawk's the darling of his fere, and o' me the Muse

An eagle clang an eagle to the sphere.
My princess, O my princess! true she errs,
But in her own grand way: being herself
Three times more noble than three score of men,
She sees herself in every woman else,
And so she wears her error like a crown
To blind the truth and me: for her, and her,
Hebes are they to hand ambrosia, mix
The nectar; but–ah she–whene'er she moves
The Samian Herè rises and she speaks
A Memnon smitten with the morning Sun.'

So saying from the court we paced, and gained
The terrace ranged along the Northern front,
And leaning there on those balusters, high
Above the empurpled champaign, drank the gale
That blown about the foliage underneath,
And sated with the innumerable rose,
Beat balm upon our eyelids. Hither came
Cyril, and yawning 'O hard task,' he cried;
'No fighting shadows here! I forced a way
Through solid opposition crabbed and gnarled.
Better to clear prime forests, heave and thump
A league of street in summer solstice down,
Than hammer at this reverend gentlewoman.
I knocked and, bidden, entered; found her there
At point to move, and settled in her eyes
The green malignant light of coming storm.
Sir, I was courteous, every phrase well-oiled,
As man's could be; yet maiden-meek I prayed

and her song.' Also *Isaiah* xxxviii 14: 'Like a crane or a swallow, so did I chatter: I did mourn as a dove: mine eyes fail with looking upward.'

iii *90. clang*: cp. Leigh Hunt, *Hero and Leander* 201–2: 'The crane / Began to clang against the coming rain.'

iii *92*] *1850*; For being, and wise in knowing that she is, *1847–8*.

iii *97. Hebes are they*] *1850*; They are Hebes meet *1847–8*.

iii *99*. 'The Greek Herè, whose favourite abode was Samos' (T.).

iii *100*. 'The statue in Egypt which gave forth a musical note when "smitten with the morning sun"' (T.).

iii *101. from*] *1850*; from out *1847–8*.

iii *109–10*] *1851; not 1847–50*.

iii *111. prime*: primeval.

iii *114. entered;*] *1850*; went in: I *1847–8*.

iii *115. move*] *1850*; sally *1847–8*.

iii *116. malignant light*: *Perdidi Diem* 22.

iii *118. man's*] *1851*; man *1847–50*.

Concealment: she demanded who we were,
And why we came? I fabled nothing fair,
But, your example pilot, told her all.
Up went the hushed amaze of hand and eye.
But when I dwelt upon your old affiance,
She answered sharply that I talked astray.
I urged the fierce inscription on the gate,
And our three lives. True–we had limed ourselves
With open eyes, and we must take the chance.
But such extremes, I told her, well might harm
The woman's cause. "Not more than now," she said,
"So puddled as it is with favouritism."
I tried the mother's heart. Shame might befall
Melissa, knowing, saying not she knew:
Her answer was "Leave me to deal with that."
I spoke of war to come and many deaths,
And she replied, her duty was to speak,
And duty duty, clear of consequences.
I grew discouraged, Sir; but since I knew
No rock so hard but that a little wave
May beat admission in a thousand years,
I recommenced; "Decide not ere you pause.
I find you here but in the second place,
Some say the third–the authentic foundress you.
I offer boldly: we will seat you highest:
Wink at our advent: help my prince to gain
His rightful bride, and here I promise you
Some palace in our land, where you shall reign
The head and heart of all our fair she-world,
And your great name flow on with broadening time
For ever." Well, she balanced this a little,
And told me she would answer us today,
Meantime be mute: thus much, nor more I gained.'

He ceasing, came a message from the Head.
'That afternoon the Princess rode to take
The dip of certain strata to the North.
Would we go with her? we should find the land
Worth seeing; and the river made a fall
Out yonder:' then she pointed on to where

iii *120. fabled . . . fair*] *1850*; minted . . . false *1847–8*. A review had objected (Shannon, p. 119).
iii *126. True–*] *1850*; She said *1847–8*. *limed*: ensnared.
iii *146. Some palace in our*] *1850*; A palace in our own *1847–8*.
iii *153. That*] *1850*; In the *1847–8*.

A double hill ran up his furrowy forks
Beyond the thick-leaved platans of the vale.

Agreed to, this, the day fled on through all
Its range of duties to the appointed hour.
Then summoned to the porch we went. She stood
Among her maidens, higher by the head,
Her back against a pillar, her foot on one
Of those tame leopards. Kittenlike he rolled
And pawed about her sandal. I drew near;
I gazed. On a sudden my strange seizure came
Upon me, the weird vision of our house:
The Princess Ida seemed a hollow show,
Her gay-furred cats a painted fantasy,
Her college and her maidens, empty masks,
And I myself the shadow of a dream,
For all things were and were not. Yet I felt
My heart beat thick with passion and with awe;
Then from my breast the involuntary sigh
Brake, as she smote me with the light of eyes
That lent my knee desire to kneel, and shook
My pulses, till to horse we got, and so
Went forth in long retinue following up
The river as it narrowed to the hills.

I rode beside her and to me she said:
'O friend, we trust that you esteemed us not
Too harsh to your companion yestermorn;
Unwillingly we spake.' 'No–not to her,'
I answered, 'but to one of whom we spake
Your Highness might have seemed the thing you say.'
'Again?' she cried, 'are you ambassadresses
From him to me? we give you, being strange,
A license: speak, and let the topic die.'

I stammered that I knew him–could have wished–
'Our king expects–was there no precontract?
There is no truer-hearted–ah, you seem
All he prefigured, and he could not see
The bird of passage flying south but longed

iii *158. furrowy*] *1851*; dark-blue *1847–50.*
iii *159. thick-*] *1851*; full- *1847–50.* Adapted from *Mariana in the South* 44, *1832* text: 'the full-leavèd platan-shade'.
iii *167–73*] *1851; not 1847–50.*
iii *175. Then*] *1850*; And *1847–8.*
iii *178. got*] *1851*; clomb *1847–50.*

To follow: surely, if your Highness keep
Your purport, you will shock him even to death,
Or baser courses, children of despair.'

'Poor boy,' she said, 'can he not read–no books?
Quoit, tennis, ball–no games? nor deals in that
Which men delight in, martial exercise?
To nurse a blind ideal like a girl,
Methinks he seems no better than a girl;
As girls were once, as we ourself have been:
We had our dreams; perhaps he mixt with them:
We touch on our dead self, nor shun to do it,
Being other–since we learnt our meaning here,
To lift the woman's fallen divinity
Upon an even pedestal with man.'

She paused, and added with a haughtier smile
'And as to precontracts, we move, my friend,
At no man's beck, but know ourself and thee,
O Vashti, noble Vashti! Summoned out
She kept her state, and left the drunken king
To brawl at Shushan underneath the palms.'

'Alas your Highness breathes full East,' I said,
'On that which leans to you. I know the Prince,
I prize his truth: and then how vast a work
To assail this gray preëminence of man!
You grant me license; might I use it? think;
Ere half be done perchance your life may fail;
Then comes the feebler heiress of your plan,
And takes and ruins all; and thus your pains
May only make that footprint upon sand
Which old-recurring waves of prejudice
Resmooth to nothing: might I dread that you,
With only Fame for spouse and your great deeds
For issue, yet may live in vain, and miss,
Meanwhile, what every woman counts her due,
Love, children, happiness?'
And she exclaimed,

iii *199*. *tennis*: the earlier game, played in a walled court.
iii *200*. *exercise*] *1851*; exercises *1847–50*.
iii *203*. *ourself*] *1864*; ourselves *1847–62*.
iii *207*. *lift*] *1850*; uplift *1847–8*.
iii *211*. *ourself*] *1864*; ourselves *1847–62*.
iii *212–4*. *Esther* i 11–12.
iii *215*. 'A playful reference to the cold manner of an Eastern queen and the east wind' (T.).

'Peace, you young savage of the Northern wild!
What! though your Prince's love were like a God's,
Have we not made ourself the sacrifice?
You are bold indeed: we are not talked to thus:
Yet will we say for children, would they grew
Like field-flowers everywhere! we like them well:
But children die; and let me tell you, girl,
Howe'er you babble, great deeds cannot die;
They with the sun and moon renew their light
For ever, blessing those that look on them.
Children–that men may pluck them from our hearts,
Kill us with pity, break us with ourselves–
O–children–there is nothing upon earth
More miserable than she that has a son
And sees him err: nor would we work for fame;
Though she perhaps might reap the applause of Great,
Who learns the one POU STO whence after-hands
May move the world, though she herself effect
But little: wherefore up and act, nor shrink
For fear our solid aim be dissipated
By frail successors. Would, indeed, we had been,
In lieu of many mortal flies, a race
Of giants living, each, a thousand years,
That we might see our own work out, and watch
The sandy footprint harden into stone.'

I answered nothing, doubtful in myself
If that strange Poet-princess with her grand
Imaginations might at all be won.
And she broke out interpreting my thoughts:

'No doubt we seem a kind of monster to you;
We are used to that: for women, up till this
Cramped under worse than South-sea-isle taboo,
Dwarfs of the gynæceum, fail so far

iii *232. ourself*] *1850*; ourselves *1847–8*.
iii *237–9*. Cp. *O mother Britain* 21–4: 'But thy good deed shall never die, / It spreads from shore to shore, / And with the sun and moon renews / Its light for evermore.'
iii *242–4*. *Proverbs* x 1, 'A wise son maketh a glad father: but a foolish son is the heaviness of his mother.'
iii *246*. 'δὸς ποῦ στῶ καὶ κόσμον κινήσω ('Give me where I may stand and I will move the world'), an often-quoted saying of Archimedes' (T.).
iii *250. By*] *1851*; Of *1847–50*.
iii *256–7*] *1851*; If that strange maiden could at all be won. *1847–50*.
iii *262. gynæceum*: 'women's quarters in a Greek house' (T.).

In high desire, they know not, cannot guess
How much their welfare is a passion to us.
If we could give them surer, quicker proof–
Oh if our end were less achievable
By slow approaches, than by single act
Of immolation, any phase of death,
We were as prompt to spring against the pikes,
Or down the fiery gulf as talk of it,
To compass our dear sisters' liberties.'

She bowed as if to veil a noble tear;
And up we came to where the river sloped
To plunge in cataract, shattering on black blocks
A breadth of thunder. O'er it shook the woods,
And danced the colour, and, below, stuck out
The bones of some vast bulk that lived and roared
Before man was. She gazed awhile and said,
'As these rude bones to us, are we to her
That will be.' 'Dare we dream of that,' I asked,
'Which wrought us, as the workman and his work,
That practice betters?' 'How,' she cried, 'you love
The metaphysics! read and earn our prize,
A golden brooch: beneath an emerald plane
Sits Diotima, teaching him that died
Of hemlock; our device; wrought to the life;
She rapt upon her subject, he on her:
For there are schools for all.' 'And yet' I said
'Methinks I have not found among them all
One anatomic.' 'Nay, we thought of that,'
She answered, 'but it pleased us not: in truth
We shudder but to dream our maids should ape
Those monstrous males that carve the living hound,
And cram him with the fragments of the grave,
Or in the dark dissolving human heart,
And holy secrets of this microcosm,
Dabbling a shameless hand with shameful jest,
Encarnalize their spirits: yet we know
Knowledge is knowledge, and this matter hangs:

iii *269–70.* The acts of self-sacrifice by Publius Decius Mus and by Marcus Curtius.
iii *285. Diotima*: 'Said to have been an instructress of Socrates. She was a priestess of Mantinea. (Cf. Plato's *Symposium*.)' (T.).
iii *293–4.* 'See Hogarth's picture in the "Stages of Cruelty". It was asserted that they used to give dogs the remnants of the dissecting-room' (T.).

Howbeit ourself, foreseeing casualty,
Nor willing men should come among us, learnt,
For many weary moons before we came,
This craft of healing. Were you sick, ourself
Would tend upon you. To your question now,
Which touches on the workman and his work.
Let there be light and there was light: 'tis so:
For was, and is, and will be, are but is;
And all creation is one act at once,
The birth of light: but we that are not all,
As parts, can see but parts, now this, now that,
And live, perforce, from thought to thought, and make
One act a phantom of succession: thus
Our weakness somehow shapes the shadow, Time;
But in the shadow will we work, and mould
The woman to the fuller day.'
She spake
With kindled eyes; we rode a league beyond,
And, o'er a bridge of pinewood crossing, came
On flowery levels underneath the crag,
Full of all beauty. 'O how sweet' I said
(For I was half-oblivious of my mask)
'To linger here with one that loved us.' 'Yea,'
She answered, 'or with fair philosophies
That lift the fancy; for indeed these fields
Are lovely, lovelier not the Elysian lawns,
Where paced the Demigods of old, and saw
The soft white vapour streak the crownèd towers
Built to the Sun:' then, turning to her maids,
'Pitch our pavilion here upon the sward;
Lay out the viands.' At the word, they raised
A tent of satin, elaborately wrought
With fair Corinna's triumph; here she stood,

iii *300. ourself*] *1850*; ourselves *1847–8*. Likewise in l. 303.

iii *305. Ephesians* ii 10: 'For we are his workmanship, created in Christ Jesus unto good works.'

iii *316. league beyond*] *1850*; little higher *1847–8*.

iii *317*] *1850*; To cross the flood by a narrow bridge, and came *1847–8*. A review had objected to the rhythm (Shannon, p. 120).

iii *318*. Cp. Akenside's *Pleasures of Imagination* (*Lincoln*) ii: 'flowery level', which occurs in *Ilion, Ilion 6*.

iii *319*. . 'O] *1848*; ; and 'O *1847*.

iii *331*. *Corinna*: 'She is the Boeotian poetess who is said to have triumphed over Pindar in poetical competition (Pausanias, ix 22). The Princess probably exaggerates' (T.).

Engirt with many a florid maiden-cheek,
The woman-conqueror; woman-conquered there
The bearded Victor of ten-thousand hymns,
And all the men mourned at his side: but we
Set forth to climb; then, climbing, Cyril kept
With Psyche, with Melissa Florian, I
With mine affianced. Many a little hand
Glanced like a touch of sunshine on the rocks,
Many a light foot shone like a jewel set
In the dark crag: and then we turned, we wound
About the cliffs, the copses, out and in,
Hammering and clinking, chattering stony names
Of shale and hornblende, rag and trap and tuff,
Amygdaloid and trachyte, till the Sun
Grew broader toward his death and fell, and all
The rosy heights came out above the lawns.

[III ^ IV]

The splendour falls on castle walls
And snowy summits old in story:
The long light shakes across the lakes,
And the wild cataract leaps in glory.
Blow, bugle, blow, set the wild echoes flying,
Blow, bugle; answer, echoes, dying, dying, dying.

O hark, O hear! how thin and clear,
And thinner, clearer, farther going!
O sweet and far from cliff and scar
The horns of Elfland faintly blowing!
Blow, let us hear the purple glens replying:
Blow, bugle; answer, echoes, dying, dying, dying.

O love, they die in yon rich sky,
They faint on hill or field or river:
Our echoes roll from soul to soul,
And grow for ever and for ever.
Blow, bugle, blow, set the wild echoes flying,
And answer, echoes, answer, dying, dying, dying.

iii *337. with Melissa Florian,*] *1850*; Florian with the other, and *1847–8*.

iii *344–5*. The glossary to vol. i of Lyell's *Principles of Geology* (4th edn, 1835), which T. read in 1837, gives: *shale*: 'indurated slaty clay'. *hornblende*: 'a simple mineral of a dark green or black colour'. *trap*: 'volcanic rocks'. *tuff*: 'a variety of volcanic rock of an earthy texture'. *amygdaloid*: 'one of the forms of the trap-rocks'. *trachyte*: 'a variety of lava'. To these, add *rag*: a hard coarse kind of stone.

iii ^ iv Added *1850*. 'Written after hearing the echoes at Killarney in 1848. When I was there I heard a bugle blown beneath the "Eagle's Nest," and eight distinct echoes' (T.). Cp. *The Vale of Bones* 3–7 (p. 97).

## IV

'There sinks the nebulous star we call the Sun,
If that hypothesis of theirs be sound'
Said Ida; 'let us down and rest;' and we
Down from the lean and wrinkled precipices,
By every coppice-feathered chasm and cleft,
Dropt through the ambrosial gloom to where below
No bigger than a glow-worm shone the tent
Lamp-lit from the inner. Once she leaned on me,
Descending; once or twice she lent her hand,
And blissful palpitations in the blood,
Stirring a sudden transport rose and fell.

But when we planted level feet, and dipt
Beneath the satin dome and entered in,
There leaning deep in broidered down we sank
Our elbows: on a tripod in the midst
A fragrant flame rose, and before us glowed
Fruit, blossom, viand, amber wine, and gold.

Then she, 'Let some one sing to us: lightlier move
The minutes fledged with music:' and a maid,
Of those beside her, smote her harp, and sang.

'Tears, idle tears, I know not what they mean,
Tears from the depth of some divine despair
Rise in the heart, and gather to the eyes,
In looking on the happy Autumn-fields,
And thinking of the days that are no more.

---

iv *1–2*. 'Norman Lockyer says that this is a true description of the sun' (T.). The second line was added at the suggestion of G. S. Venables (F. M. Brookfield, *The Cambridge 'Apostles'*, 1906, p. 349). On Laplace's cosmogony and the nebular hypothesis, see E. A. Mooney, *MLN* lxiv (1949) 98–102, and M. Millhauser, *PMLA* lxix (1954) 337–43.

iv *6*. *ambrosial gloom*: cp. the fragment of an early play (*Mem.* i 24), 'In your high pomp of shade, and make beneath / Ambrosial gloom'.

iv *10–11*. Incorporated verbatim from *The Gardener's Daughter* 66 ∧ 7, MS (p. 511).

iv *16*. *fragrant flame*: *The Palace of Art* 187, *1832* text.

iv *17*. *blossom, viand,*] *1850*; viand, blossom, and *1847–8*.

iv *21*. *Tears, idle*] Ah foolish *MS in Eversley 1st reading*. Cp. the song in *The Miller's Daughter* 210–11: 'Love is made a vague regret. / Eyes with idle tears are wet'; and Virgil, *Aeneid* iv 449, x 465: *lacrimae inanes*.

iv *21–40*. On *Tears, idle tears*, T. remarks: 'This song came to me on the yellowing autumn-tide at Tintern Abbey, full for me of its bygone memories. It is the sense of the abiding in the transient.' Among the memories (Douglas Bush suggests, *Major British Writers*, 1959) may have

'Fresh as the first beam glittering on a sail,
That brings our friends up from the underworld,
Sad as the last which reddens over one
That sinks with all we love below the verge;
So sad, so fresh, the days that are no more.

'Ah, sad and strange as in dark summer dawns
The earliest pipe of half-awakened birds
To dying ears, when unto dying eyes
The casement slowly grows a glimmering square;
So sad, so strange, the days that are no more.

'Dear as remembered kisses after death,
And sweet as those by hopeless fancy feigned
On lips that are for others; deep as love,

been that Arthur Hallam is buried near Tintern; cp. *In Memoriam* xix (p. 881). Frederick Locker-Lampson reports (*Mem.* ii 73): 'He told me that he was moved to write *Tears, idle tears* at Tintern Abbey; and that it was not real woe, as some people might suppose; "it was rather the yearning that young people occasionally experience for that which seems to have passed away from them for ever." That in him it was strongest when he was quite a youth.' To James Knowles, T. said: 'It is in a way like St Paul's "groanings which cannot be uttered." . . . It is what I have always felt even from a boy, and what as a boy I called the "passion of the past." And it is so always with me now; it is the distance that charms me in the landscape, the picture and the past, and not the immediate to-day in which I move', *Nineteenth Century* xxxiii (1893) 170. Cp. *No More* (1826, p. 161): 'Oh sad *No More!* Oh sweet *No More!* / Oh strange *No More!*' On the diction, see *Tithonus* 59*n* (p. 1117). Southey's *Remembrance* has 'The days that are no more' as the concluding line of the first and last stanzas; its epigraph is 'The remembrance of Youth is a sigh', and it ends: 'Its idle hopes are o'er, / Yet age remembers with a sigh / The days that are no more.' Cp. Hallam's poem (Motter, p. 108), *Scene at Rome* 41, 45, 53, which was probably written on the Rhine journey taken with T. It describes remembered thoughts as friends, 'Borne to the silent things that are no more . . . / There they lie dead, and here I'd weep for them . . . / These friends once harboured with me, now departed.' John Sparrow, *RES* n.s. xiv (1963) 59, compares Gray's Alcaic fragment, *O lachrymarum Fons*; this had provided an epigraph in *1827*.

iv *26*. Cp. *Egypt* 13: 'But the first glitter of his rising beam'.

iv *34*. Cp. Leigh Hunt, *Hero and Leander* 284–5: 'And when the casement, at the dawn of light, / Began to show a square of ghastly white.' Hero is about to kill herself.

iv *35*. *so*] and *MS Eversley 1st reading*. Cp. *The Lover's Tale* iv 301: 'Sad, sweet, and strange together'.

iv *36*. Cp. Moschus, *Lament for Bion* 68–9 ('and Cypris, she's fainer far of you than the kiss she gave Adonis when he died the other day').

Deep as first love, and wild with all regret;
O Death in Life, the days that are no more.'

She ended with such passion that the tear,
She sang of, shook and fell, an erring pearl
Lost in her bosom: but with some disdain
Answered the Princess, 'If indeed there haunt
About the mouldered lodges of the Past
So sweet a voice and vague, fatal to men,
Well needs it we should cram our ears with wool
And so pace by: but thine are fancies hatched
In silken-folded idleness; nor is it
Wiser to weep a true occasion lost,
But trim our sails, and let old bygones be,
While down the streams that float us each and all
To the issue, goes, like glittering bergs of ice,
Throne after throne, and molten on the waste
Becomes a cloud: for all things serve their time
Toward that great year of equal mights and rights,
Nor would I fight with iron laws, in the end
Found golden: let the past be past; let be
Their cancelled Babels: though the rough kex break
The starred mosaic, and the beard-blown goat
Hang on the shaft, and the wild figtree split
Their monstrous idols, care not while we hear
A trumpet in the distance pealing news
Of better, and Hope, a poising eagle, burns

iv *47–8.* Odysseus stopped the ears of his crew with wax so that they could not hear the song of the Sirens.

iv *50. lost*] *1850*; gone *1847–8.*

iv *51. old bygones be*] *1850*; the old proverb serve *1847–8.*

iv *52. float . . . all*] *1850*; buoy each separate craft *1847–8.*

iv *53–4.* Cp. *In Memoriam* cxxvii 9–13: 'But ill for him that wears a crown, / And him, the lazar, in his rags: / They tremble, the sustaining crags; / The spires of ice are toppled down, // And molten up, and roar in flood.'

iv *59. kex*: 'hemlock' (T.).

iv *60. beard-blown goat*] *1860*; wild goat hang *1847–58.*

iv *61. Hang on the shaft*] *1860*; Upon the pillar *1847–8*; Upon the shaft *1850–58.* 'The wind blew his beard on the height of the ruined pillar' (T.). Cp. Samuel Rogers, *Pleasures of Memory* ii: 'High hung in air the hoary goat reclined, / His streaming beard the sport of every wind.' *figtree split*: H.T. compares Juvenal, *Satires* x 145: *discutienda valent sterilis mala robora fici* ('. . . stones which may be rent asunder by the rude strength of the barren fig-tree').

Above the unrisen morrow:' then to me;
'Know you no song of your own land,' she said,
'Not such as moans about the retrospect,
But deals with the other distance and the hues
Of promise; not a death's-head at the wine.'

Then I remembered one myself had made,
What time I watched the swallow winging south
From mine own land, part made long since, and part
Now while I sang, and maidenlike as far
As I could ape their treble, did I sing.

'O Swallow, Swallow, flying, flying South,
Fly to her, and fall upon her gilded eaves,
And tell her, tell her, what I tell to thee.

'O tell her, Swallow, thou that knowest each,
That bright and fierce and fickle is the South,
And dark and true and tender is the North.

'O Swallow, Swallow, if I could follow, and light
Upon her lattice, I would pipe and trill,
And cheep and twitter twenty million loves.

'O were I thou that she might take me in,
And lay me on her bosom, and her heart
Would rock the snowy cradle till I died.

'Why lingereth she to clothe her heart with love,
Delaying as the tender ash delays
To clothe herself, when all the woods are green?

'O tell her, Swallow, that thy brood is flown:
Say to her, I do but wanton in the South,
But in the North long since my nest is made.

'O tell her, brief is life but love is long,
And brief the sun of summer in the North,
And brief the moon of beauty in the South.

'O Swallow, flying from the golden woods,
Fly to her, and pipe and woo her, and make her mine,
And tell her, tell her, that I follow thee.'

iv *65. then*] *1848*; and then *1847*.
iv *75–98.* This song was 'first composed in rhyme' (*Mem.* ii 74). Cp. the isometric songs in Theocritus iii and xi.
iv *85–6.* Cp. *Venus and Adonis* 1185–6: 'Lo, in this hollow cradle take thy rest; / My throbbing heart shall rock thee day and night.'

I ceased, and all the ladies, each at each,
Like the Ithacensian suitors in old time,
Stared with great eyes, and laughed with alien lips,
And knew not what they meant; for still my voice
Rang false: but smiling 'Not for thee,' she said,
'O Bulbul, any rose of Gulistan
Shall burst her veil: marsh-divers, rather, maid,
Shall croak thee sister, or the meadow-crake
Grate her harsh kindred in the grass: and this
A mere love-poem! O for such, my friend,
We hold them slight: they mind us of the time
When we made bricks in Egypt. Knaves are men,
That lute and flute fantastic tenderness,
And dress the victim to the offering up,
And paint the gates of Hell with Paradise,
And play the slave to gain the tyranny.
Poor soul! I had a maid of honour once;
She wept her true eyes blind for such a one,
A rogue of canzonets and serenades.
I loved her. Peace be with her. She is dead.
So they blaspheme the muse! But great is song
Used to great ends: ourself have often tried
Valkyrian hymns, or into rhythm have dashed
The passion of the prophetess; for song
Is duer unto freedom, force and growth
Of spirit than to junketing and love.
Love is it? Would this same mock-love, and this
Mock-Hymen were laid up like winter bats,
Till all men grew to rate us at our worth,
Not vassals to be beat, nor pretty babes
To be dandled, no, but living wills, and sphered

iv *100–101*. Alluding, as H.T. says, to *Odyssey* xx 347 (οἱ δ' ἤδη γναθμοῖσι γελώων ἀλλοτρίοισιν), 'And now they laughed with alien lips'–there too introducing a critical moment for the suitors.
iv *104*. *Bulbul*: nightingale. *Gulistan*: rose-garden. Both Persian.
iv *106*. *meadow-crake*: 'corn-crake or landrail' (T.).
iv *109*. *hold*] *1850*; prize *1847–8*.
iv *115–24*] *1850; not 1847–8*.
iv *121*. 'Like those sung by the Valkyrian maidens, "the choosers of the slain," in the Northern mythology' (H.T.).
iv *122*. *Exodus* xv 20, 'And Miriam the prophetess, the sister of Aaron, took a timbrel in her hand; and all the women went out after her with timbrels and with dances.' See v 500.
iv *125*. *Would*] *1850*; I would *1847–8*.
iv *129*. Cp. *In Memoriam* cxxxi: 'O living will'.

Whole in ourselves and owed to none. Enough!
But now to leaven play with profit, you,
Know you no song, the true growth of your soil,
That gives the manners of your country-women?'

She spoke and turned her sumptuous head with eyes
Of shining expectation fixt on mine.
Then while I dragged my brains for such a song,
Cyril, with whom the bell-mouthed glass had wrought,
Or mastered by the sense of sport, began
To troll a careless, careless tavern-catch
Of Moll and Meg, and strange experiences
Unmeet for ladies. Florian nodded at him,
I frowning; Psyche flushed and wanned and shook;
The lilylike Melissa drooped her brows;
'Forbear,' the Princess cried; 'Forbear, Sir' I;
And heated through and through with wrath and love,
I smote him on the breast; he started up;
There rose a shriek as of a city sacked;
Melissa clamoured 'Flee the death;' 'To horse'
Said Ida; 'home! to horse!' and fled, as flies
A troop of snowy doves athwart the dusk,
When some one batters at the dovecote-doors,
Disorderly the women. Alone I stood
With Florian, cursing Cyril, vext at heart,
In the pavilion: there like parting hopes
I heard them passing from me: hoof by hoof,
And every hoof a knell to my desires,
Clanged on the bridge; and then another shriek,
'The Head, the Head, the Princess, O the Head!'
For blind with rage she missed the plank, and rolled
In the river. Out I sprang from glow to gloom:
There whirled her white robe like a blossomed branch
Rapt to the horrible fall: a glance I gave,
No more; but woman-vested as I was
Plunged; and the flood drew; yet I caught her; then
Oaring one arm, and bearing in my left
The weight of all the hopes of half the world,

iv *137*. *Cyril*] *1850*; Did Cyril *1847–8*. *glass*] *1862*; flask *1847–61*.
iv *138*. *began*] *1850*; begin *1847–8*.
iv *149*] *1850*; Said Lady Ida; and fled at once, as flies *1847–8*.
iv *164*. Cp. the drowning in *The Lover's Tale* ii 194–205 (p. 336).

Strove to buffet to land in vain. A tree
Was half-disrooted from his place and stooped
To drench his dark locks in the gurgling wave
Mid-channel. Right on this we drove and caught,
And grasping down the boughs I gained the shore.

There stood her maidens glimmeringly grouped
In the hollow bank. One reaching forward drew
My burthen from mine arms; they cried 'she lives:'
They bore her back into the tent: but I,
So much a kind of shame within me wrought,
Not yet endured to meet her opening eyes,
Nor found my friends; but pushed alone on foot
(For since her horse was lost I left her mine)
Across the woods, and less from Indian craft
Than beelike instinct hiveward, found at length
The garden portals. Two great statues, Art
And Science, Caryatids, lifted up
A weight of emblem, and betwixt were valves
Of open-work in which the hunter rued
His rash intrusion, manlike, but his brows
Had sprouted, and the branches thereupon
Spread out at top, and grimly spiked the gates.

A little space was left between the horns,
Through which I clambered o'er at top with pain,
Dropt on the sward, and up the linden walks,
And, tost on thoughts that changed from hue to hue,
Now poring on the glowworm, now the star,
I paced the terrace, till the Bear had wheeled
Through a great arc his seven slow suns.
A step
Of lightest echo, then a loftier form
Than female, moving through the uncertain gloom,
Disturbed me with the doubt 'if this were she,'

iv *174. ; they cried*] *1850*; , and crying *1847–8*.
iv *180. woods*] *1848*; thicket *1847*.
iv *182. garden portals*] *1850*; gates of the garden *1847–8*.
iv *183. Caryatids*: '"female figures used as bearing shafts" (Vitruvius i), e.g. the maidens supporting the light entablature of the portico of the Erechtheum at Athens' (T.).
iv *184. valves*: gates.
iv *185. open-work*] *1848*; open metal *1847*. *hunter*] *1848*; old hunter *1847*.
iv *185–6*. 'Actaeon turned into a stag for looking on Diana bathing' (T.).
iv *196. then*] *1848*; and then *1847*.

But it was Florian. 'Hist O Hist,' he said,
'They seek us: out so late is out of rules.
Moreover "seize the strangers" is the cry.
How came you here?' I told him: 'I' said he,
'Last of the train, a moral leper, I,
To whom none spake, half-sick at heart, returned.
Arriving all confused among the rest
With hooded brows I crept into the hall,
And, couched behind a Judith, underneath
The head of Holofernes peeped and saw.
Girl after girl was called to trial: each
Disclaimed all knowledge of us: last of all,
Melissa: trust me, Sir, I pitied her.
She, questioned if she knew us men, at first
Was silent; closer prest, denied it not:
And then, demanded if her mother knew,
Or Psyche, she affirmed not, or denied:
From whence the Royal mind, familiar with her,
Easily gathered either guilt. She sent
For Psyche, but she was not there; she called
For Psyche's child to cast it from the doors;
She sent for Blanche to accuse her face to face;
And I slipt out: but whither will you now?
And where are Psyche, Cyril? both are fled:
What, if together? that were not so well.
Would rather we had never come! I dread
His wildness, and the chances of the dark.'

'And yet,' I said, 'you wrong him more than I
That struck him: this is proper to the clown,
Though smocked, or furred and purpled, still the clown,
To harm the thing that trusts him, and to shame
That which he says he loves: for Cyril, howe'er
He deal in frolic, as tonight–the song
Might have been worse and sinned in grosser lips
Beyond all pardon–as it is, I hold
These flashes on the surface are not he.
He has a solid base of temperament:
But as the waterlily starts and slides

iv *202*] *1850*; I found the key in the doors: how came you here? *1847–8*.
iv *207–8*. *Judith* xiii.
iv *215*. *Psyche, she*] *1850*; Lady Psyche, *1847–8*.
iv *236–8*. 'Water-lilies in my own pond, seen on a gusty day with my own eyes', said T., denying the influence of Wordsworth's *Excursion* v 567–9:

Upon the level in little puffs of wind,
Though anchored to the bottom, such is he.'

Scarce had I ceased when from a tamarisk near
Two Proctors leapt upon us, crying, 'Names:'
He, standing still, was clutched; but I began
To thrid the musky-circled mazes, wind
And double in and out the boles, and race
By all the fountains: fleet I was of foot:
Before me showered the rose in flakes; behind
I heard the puffed pursuer; at mine ear
Bubbled the nightingale and heeded not,
And secret laughter tickled all my soul.
At last I hooked my ankle in a vine,
That claspt the feet of a Mnemosyne,
And falling on my face was caught and known.

They haled us to the Princess where she sat
High in the hall: above her drooped a lamp,
And made the single jewel on her brow
Burn like the mystic fire on a mast-head,
Prophet of storm: a handmaid on each side
Bowed toward her, combing out her long black hair
Damp from the river; and close behind her stood
Eight daughters of the plough, stronger than men,
Huge women blowzed with health, and wind, and rain,
And labour. Each was like a Druid rock;
Or like a spire of land that stands apart
Cleft from the main, and wailed about with mews.

Then, as we came, the crowd dividing clove
An advent to the throne: and therebeside,

'And, like the water-lily, lives and thrives, / Whose root is fixed in stable earth, whose head / Floats on the tossing waves.'

iv *242. the musky-circled*] *1850*; through all the musky *1847–8*. Cp. *Rape of the Lock* ii 139: 'Some thrid the mazy Ringlets of her Hair'. Also Shelley, *The Triumph of Life* 347: 'and threaded all the forest's maze'.

iv *249. hooked*] *1850*; took *1847–8*.

iv *250. Mnemosyne*: 'goddess of memory, mother of the Muses' (T.).

iv *255. fire*: 'St Elmo's fire' (T.). H.T. adds: 'St Elmo's phosphorescent light flickers on the tops of masts when a storm is brewing', and compares *The Tempest* I ii 199.

iv *260. blowzed*: 'blown-red' (T.).

iv *263. wailed*] *1851*; clanged *1847–50*. Cp. *Paradise Lost* xi 835: 'Sea-mews clang'.

Half-naked as if caught at once from bed
And tumbled on the purple footcloth, lay
The lily-shining child; and on the left,
Bowed on her palms and folded up from wrong,
Her round white shoulder shaken with her sobs,
Melissa knelt; but Lady Blanche erect
Stood up and spake, an affluent orator.

'It was not thus, O Princess, in old days:
You prized my counsel, lived upon my lips:
I led you then to all the Castalies;
I fed you with the milk of every Muse;
I loved you like this kneeler, and you me
Your second mother: those were gracious times.
Then came your new friend: you began to change–
I saw it and grieved–to slacken and to cool;
Till taken with her seeming openness
You turned your warmer currents all to her,
To me you froze: this was my meed for all.
Yet I bore up in part from ancient love,
And partly that I hoped to win you back,
And partly conscious of my own deserts,
And partly that you were my civil head,
And chiefly you were born for something great,
In which I might your fellow-worker be,
When time should serve; and thus a noble scheme
Grew up from seed we two long since had sown;
In us true growth, in her a Jonah's gourd,
Up in one night and due to sudden sun:
We took this palace; but even from the first
You stood in your own light and darkened mine.
What student came but that you planed her path
To Lady Psyche, younger, not so wise,
A foreigner, and I your countrywoman,
I your old friend and tried, she new in all?
But still her lists were swelled and mine were lean;
Yet I bore up in hope she would be known:
Then came these wolves: *they* knew her: *they* endured,
Long-closeted with her the yestermorn,
To tell her what they were, and she to hear:

iv *273. old*] *1850*; the old *1847–8*.
iv *275*. Castaly, a fountain on Parnassus sacred to the Muses.
iv *283. To . . . froze*] *1850*; You froze to me *1847–8*.
iv *292. Jonah* iv 6–10, the gourd 'which came up in a night, and perished in a night'.

And me none told: not less to an eye like mine
A lidless watcher of the public weal,
Last night, their mask was patent, and my foot
Was to you: but I thought again: I feared
To meet a cold "We thank you, we shall hear of it
From Lady Psyche:" you had gone to her,
She told, perforce; and winning easy grace,
No doubt, for slight delay, remained among us
In our young nursery still unknown, the stem
Less grain than touchwood, while my honest heat
Were all miscounted as malignant haste
To push my rival out of place and power.
But public use required she should be known;
And since my oath was ta'en for public use,
I broke the letter of it to keep the sense.
I spoke not then at first, but watched them well,
Saw that they kept apart, no mischief done;
And yet this day (though you should hate me for it)
I came to tell you; found that you had gone,
Ridden to the hills, she likewise: now, I thought,
That surely she will speak; if not, then I:
Did she? These monsters blazoned what they were,
According to the coarseness of their kind,
For thus I hear; and known at last (my work)
And full of cowardice and guilty shame,
I grant in her some sense of shame, she flies;
And I remain on whom to wreak your rage,
I, that have lent my life to build up yours,
I that have wasted here health, wealth, and time,
And talent, I–you know it–I will not boast:
Dismiss me, and I prophesy your plan,
Divorced from my experience, will be chaff
For every gust of chance, and men will say
We did not know the real light, but chased
The wisp that flickers where no foot can tread.'

She ceased: the Princess answered coldly, 'Good:
Your oath is broken: we dismiss you: go.

iv *306*. *lidless*: 'wakeful, wide-eyed' (T.). In this sense, *OED* quotes only Coleridge and Shelley before T.

iv *319*. *2 Corinthians* iii 6, 'Not of the letter, but of the spirit: for the letter killeth, but the spirit giveth life'.

iv *323*. *came . . . that*] *1850*; judged it best to speak; but *1847–8*.

iv *325*. *speak*] *1850*; tell you *1847–8*.

iv *330*. *some sense*] *1850*; the merit *1847–8*.

For this lost lamb (she pointed to the child)
Our mind is changed: we take it to ourself.'

Thereat the Lady stretched a vulture throat,
And shot from crooked lips a haggard smile.
'The plan was mine. I built the nest' she said
'To hatch the cuckoo. Rise!' and stooped to updrag
Melissa: she, half on her mother propt,
Half-drooping from her, turned her face, and cast
A liquid look on Ida, full of prayer,
Which melted Florian's fancy as she hung,
A Niobëan daughter, one arm out,
Appealing to the bolts of Heaven; and while
We gazed upon her came a little stir
About the doors, and on a sudden rushed
Among us, out of breath, as one pursued,
A woman-post in flying raiment. Fear
Stared in her eyes, and chalked her face, and winged
Her transit to the throne, whereby she fell
Delivering sealed dispatches which the Head
Took half-amazed, and in her lion's mood
Tore open, silent we with blind surmise
Regarding, while she read, till over brow
And cheek and bosom brake the wrathful bloom
As of some fire against a stormy cloud,
When the wild peasant rights himself, the rick
Flames, and his anger reddens in the heavens;
For anger most it seemed, while now her breast,
Beaten with some great passion at her heart,
Palpitated, her hand shook, and we heard
In the dead hush the papers that she held
Rustle: at once the lost lamb at her feet
Sent out a bitter bleating for its dam;
The plaintive cry jarred on her ire; she crushed
The scrolls together, made a sudden turn
As if to speak, but, utterance failing her,

iv *343. take*] *1850*; assume *1847–8*. *ourself*] *1864*; ourselves *1847–62*.
iv *352*. 'Niobe was proud of her twelve children, and in consequence boasted herself as superior to Leto, mother of Apollo and Artemis, who in revenge shot them all dead' (T.).
iv *355. rushed*] *1848*; ran in *1847*.
iv *356*] *1850*; Among us, all out of breath, as pursued, *1847–8*. A review had objected to the rhythm (Shannon, p. 120).
iv *366. the rick*] *1850*; and the rick *1847–8*. 'I remember seeing thirty ricks burning near Cambridge, and I helped to pass the bucket from the well to help to quench the fire' (T.).

She whirled them on to me, as who should say
'Read,' and I read–two letters–one her sire's.

'Fair daughter, when we sent the Prince your way
We knew not your ungracious laws, which learnt,
We, conscious of what temper you are built,
Came all in haste to hinder wrong, but fell
Into his father's hands, who has this night,
You lying close upon his territory,
Slipt round and in the dark invested you,
And here he keeps me hostage for his son.'

The second was my father's running thus:
'You have our son: touch not a hair of his head:
Render him up unscathed: give him your hand:
Cleave to your contract: though indeed we hear
You hold the woman is the better man;
A rampant heresy, such as if it spread
Would make all women kick against their Lords
Through all the world, and which might well deserve
That we this night should pluck your palace down;
And we will do it, unless you send us back
Our son, on the instant, whole.'
So far I read;
And then stood up and spoke impetuously.

'O not to pry and peer on your reserve,
But led by golden wishes, and a hope
The child of regal compact, did I break
Your precinct; not a scorner of your sex
But venerator, zealous it should be
All that it might be: hear me, for I bear,
Though man, yet human, whatsoe'er your wrongs,
From the flaxen curl to the gray lock a life
Less mine than yours: my nurse would tell me of you;
I babbled for you, as babies for the moon,
Vague brightness; when a boy, you stooped to me
From all high places, lived in all fair lights,
Came in long breezes rapt from inmost south
And blown to inmost north; at eve and dawn
With Ida, Ida, Ida, rang the woods;

iv *389. Render*] *1850*; Deliver *1847–8.*
iv *411. inmost*] *1850*; the inmost *1847–8.* Likewise in l. 412.

The leader wildswan in among the stars
Would clang it, and lapt in wreaths of glowworm light
The mellow breaker murmured Ida. Now,
Because I would have reached you, had you been
Sphered up with Cassiopëia, or the enthroned
Persephonè in Hades, now at length,
Those winters of abeyance all worn out,
A man I came to see you: but, indeed,
Not in this frequence can I lend full tongue,
O noble Ida, to those thoughts that wait
On you, their centre: let me say but this,
That many a famous man and woman, town
And landskip, have I heard of, after seen
The dwarfs of presage: though when known, there grew
Another kind of beauty in detail
Made them worth knowing; but in you I found
My boyish dream involved and dazzled down
And mastered, while that after-beauty makes
Such head from act to act, from hour to hour,
Within me, that except you slay me here,
According to your bitter statute-book,
I cannot cease to follow you, as they say
The seal does music; who desire you more
Than growing boys their manhood; dying lips,
With many thousand matters left to do,
The breath of life; O more than poor men wealth,
Than sick men health–yours, yours, not mine–but half
Without you; with you, whole; and of those halves
You worthiest; and howe'er you block and bar
Your heart with system out from mine, I hold
That it becomes no man to nurse despair,
But in the teeth of clenched antagonisms
To follow up the worthiest till he die:
Yet that I came not all unauthorized
Behold your father's letter.'
                                        On one knee

iv *417. had you*] *1850*; though you had *1847–8*.
iv *418. Cassiopëia*: a mythical Queen of Ethiopia, subsequently a constellation.
iv *422. Paradise Regained* i 128–9: 'in full frequence bright / Of Angels'.
iv *427. dwarfs of presage*: 'afterwards seen to be far short of expectation' (H.T.).
iv *430. My boyish dream*] *1850*; Mine old ideal *1847–8*.

Kneeling, I gave it, which she caught, and dashed
Unopened at her feet: a tide of fierce
Invective seemed to wait behind her lips,
As waits a river level with the dam
Ready to burst and flood the world with foam:
And so she would have spoken, but there rose
A hubbub in the court of half the maids
Gathered together: from the illumined hall
Long lanes of splendour slanted o'er a press
Of snowy shoulders, thick as herded ewes,
And rainbow robes, and gems and gemlike eyes,
And gold and golden heads; they to and fro
Fluctuated, as flowers in storm, some red, some pale,
All open-mouthed, all gazing to the light,
Some crying there was an army in the land,
And some that men were in the very walls,
And some they cared not; till a clamour grew
As of a new-world Babel, woman-built,
And worse-confounded: high above them stood
The placid marble Muses, looking peace.

Not peace she looked, the Head: but rising up
Robed in the long night of her deep hair, so
To the open window moved, remaining there
Fixt like a beacon-tower above the waves
Of tempest, when the crimson-rolling eye
Glares ruin, and the wild birds on the light
Dash themselves dead. She stretched her arms and called
Across the tumult and the tumult fell.

'What fear ye, brawlers? am not I your Head?
On me, me, me, the storm first breaks: *I* dare
All these male thunderbolts: what is it ye fear?
Peace! there are those to avenge us and they come:
If not,–myself were like enough, O girls,
To unfurl the maiden banner of our rights,
And clad in iron burst the ranks of war,

iv *450. at her feet*] *1850*; on the marble *1847–8*.

iv *468. looking peace*: P. M. Wallace's edition, of which T. saw the proofs (1891, *Lincoln*), remarks: 'half "looking peacefully", half "shedding peace"'.

iv *472–5*. H.T. compares *Enoch Arden* 724–6: 'Allured him, as the beacon-blaze allures / The bird of passage, till he madly strikes / Against it, and beats out his weary life.'

iv *474. birds*] *1848*; sea-birds *1847*.

Or, falling, protomartyr of our cause,
Die: yet I blame you not so much for fear:
Six thousand years of fear have made you that
From which I would redeem you: but for those
That stir this hubbub–you and you–I know
Your faces there in the crowd–tomorrow morn
We hold a great convention: then shall they
That love their voices more than duty, learn
With whom they deal, dismissed in shame to live
No wiser than their mothers, household stuff,
Live chattels, mincers of each other's fame,
Full of weak poison, turnspits for the clown,
The drunkard's football, laughing-stocks of Time,
Whose brains are in their hands and in their heels,
But fit to flaunt, to dress, to dance, to thrum,
To tramp, to scream, to burnish, and to scour,
For ever slaves at home and fools abroad.'

She, ending, waved her hands: thereat the crowd
Muttering, dissolved: then with a smile, that looked
A stroke of cruel sunshine on the cliff,
When all the glens are drowned in azure gloom
Of thunder-shower, she floated to us and said:

'You have done well and like a gentleman,
And like a prince: you have our thanks for all:
And you look well too in your woman's dress:
Well have you done and like a gentleman.
You saved our life: we owe you bitter thanks:
Better have died and spilt our bones in the flood–
Then men had said–but now–What hinders me
To take such bloody vengeance on you both?–
Yet since our father–Wasps in our good hive,
You would-be quenchers of the light to be,
Barbarians, grosser than your native bears–
O would I had his sceptre for one hour!
You that have dared to break our bound, and gulled

iv 485. *you*] *1862*; ye *1847–61*. Likewise in ll. 486, 487.

iv 486. Lionel Stevenson (*Darwin among the Poets*, 1932, p. 73) points out that Ida's grasp of evolution is not consistently maintained, since 6,000 years is the chronology of Archbishop Ussher.

v 490. *hold . . . convention*] *1850*; meet to elect new tutors *1847–8*.

v 506. *You*] *1848*; Ye *1847*.

v 510. *saved*] *1850*; have saved *1847–8*.

v 514. *our good*] *1850*; the wholesome *1847–8*.

Our servants, wronged and lied and thwarted us–
*I* wed with thee! *I* bound by precontract
Your bride, your bondslave! not though all the gold
That veins the world were packed to make your crown,
And every spoken tongue should lord you. Sir,
Your falsehood and yourself are hateful to us:
I trample on your offers and on you:
Begone: we will not look upon you more.
Here, push them out at gates.'
In wrath she spake.
Then those eight mighty daughters of the plough
Bent their broad faces toward us and addressed
Their motion: twice I sought to plead my cause,
But on my shoulder hung their heavy hands,
The weight of destiny: so from her face
They pushed us, down the steps, and through the court,
And with grim laughter thrust us out at gates.

We crossed the street and gained a petty mound
Beyond it, whence we saw the lights and heard
The voices murmuring. While I listened, came
On a sudden the weird seizure and the doubt:
I seemed to move among a world of ghosts;
The Princess with her monstrous woman-guard,
The jest and earnest working side by side,
The cataract and the tumult and the kings
Were shadows; and the long fantastic night
With all its doings had and had not been,
And all things were and were not.
This went by
As strangely as it came, and on my spirits
Settled a gentle cloud of melancholy;
Not long; I shook it off; for spite of doubts
And sudden ghostly shadowings I was one
To whom the touch of all mischance but came
As night to him that sitting on a hill

iv *519. servants*] *1850*; tutors *1847–8.*
iv *524. yourself are hateful*] *1851*; your face are loathsome *1847–50.*
iv *537–46. While . . . came,*] *1851; not 1847–50.*
iv *546. and on*] *1851*; till upon *1847–50.*
iv *548*] *1851*; Which I shook off, for I was young, and one *1847–8*; Which I shook off, for I was ever one *1850.*
iv *549*] *1851; not 1847–50.*
iv *550. touch*] *1851*; shadow *1847–50.*

Sees the midsummer, midnight, Norway sun
Set into sunrise; then we moved away.

[IV ∧ V]

Thy voice is heard through rolling drums,
That beat to battle where he stands;
Thy face across his fancy comes,
And gives the battle to his hands:
A moment, while the trumpets blow,
He sees his brood about thy knee;
The next, like fire he meets the foe,
And strikes him dead for thine and thee.

So Lilia sang: we thought her half-possessed,
She struck such warbling fury through the words;
And, after, feigning pique at what she called
The raillery, or grotesque, or false sublime–
Like one that wishes at a dance to change
The music–clapt her hands and cried for war,
Or some grand fight to kill and make an end:
And he that next inherited the tale
Half turning to the broken statue, said,
'Sir Ralph has got your colours: if I prove
Your knight, and fight your battle, what for me?'
It chanced, her empty glove upon the tomb
Lay by her like a model of her hand.
She took it and she flung it. 'Fight' she said,
'And make us all we would be, great and good.'
He knightlike in his cap instead of casque,
A cap of Tyrol borrowed from the hall,
Arranged the favour, and assumed the Prince.

V

Now, scarce three paces measured from the mound,
We stumbled on a stationary voice,
And 'Stand, who goes?' 'Two from the palace' I.
'The second two: they wait,' he said, 'pass on;

iv ∧ v The 26 lines of song and interlude were added *1850*. For alternative versions of the song, see Appendix A (p. 1770), and *The Tourney* (p. 850). On the nobility of a just war, cp. *The Two Voices* 124–56 (p. 528), and the conclusion of *Maud*.

iv ∧ v *1–2*] *1851*; When all among the thundering drums
Thy soldier in the battle stands, *1850*

iv ∧ v *8. And strikes*] *1851*; Strikes *1850*. *thine*] *1851*; them *1850*. *1850* follows this line with 'Tara ta tantara!'

v *2. stationary*: pertaining to a military post (*OED* 4b).

His Highness wakes:' and one, that clashed in arms,
By glimmering lanes and walls of canvas led
Threading the soldier-city, till we heard
The drowsy folds of our great ensign shake
From blazoned lions o'er the imperial tent
Whispers of war.
Entering, the sudden light
Dazed me half-blind: I stood and seemed to hear,
As in a poplar grove when a light wind wakes
A lisping of the innumerous leaf and dies,
Each hissing in his neighbour's ear; and then
A strangled titter, out of which there brake
On all sides, clamouring etiquette to death,
Unmeasured mirth; while now the two old kings
Began to wag their baldness up and down,
The fresh young captains flashed their glittering teeth,
The huge bush-bearded Barons heaved and blew,
And slain with laughter rolled the gilded Squire.

At length my Sire, his rough cheek wet with tears,
Panted from weary sides 'King, you are free!
We did but keep you surety for our son,
If this be he,–or a draggled mawkin, thou,
That tends her bristled grunters in the sludge:'
For I was drenched with ooze, and torn with briers,
More crumpled than a poppy from the sheath,
And all one rag, disprinced from head to heel.
Then some one sent beneath his vaulted palm
A whispered jest to some one near him, 'Look,
He has been among his shadows.' 'Satan take
The old women and their shadows! (thus the King
Roared) make yourself a man to fight with men.
Go: Cyril told us all.'
As boys that slink
From ferule and the trespass-chiding eye,
Away we stole, and transient in a trice

v *6. glimmering lanes*: 'the lines of tents just visible in the darkness' (T.).
v *7. till*] *1850*; until *1847–8*.
v *12–13*. Cp. Keats, *To Autumn* 29: 'as the light wind lives or dies'. Milton describes boughs as 'innumerous', *Comus* 349.
v *15. there brake*] *1850*; outbrake *1847–8*.
v *23. King . . . free*] *1850*; You are free, O King! *1847–8*.
v *25. mawkin*: kitchen-wench. H.T. compares *Coriolanus* II i 205.
v *30–34*] *1851*; 'But hence' he said 'indue yourselves like men. *1847–50*.
v *35. Go:*] *1851*; Your *1847–50*.
v *36. ferule*: cane.

From what was left of faded woman-slough
To sheathing splendours and the golden scale
Of harness, issued in the sun, that now
Leapt from the dewy shoulders of the Earth,
And hit the Northern hills. Here Cyril met us.
A little shy at first, but by and by
We twain, with mutual pardon asked and given
For stroke and song, resoldered peace, whereon
Followed his tale. Amazed he fled away
Through the dark land, and later in the night
Had come on Psyche weeping: 'then we fell
Into your father's hand, and there she lies,
But will not speak, nor stir.'
He showed a tent
A stone-shot off: we entered in, and there
Among piled arms and rough accoutrements,
Pitiful sight, wrapped in a soldier's cloak,
Like some sweet sculpture draped from head to foot,
And pushed by rude hands from its pedestal,
All her fair length upon the ground she lay:
And at her head a follower of the camp,
A charred and wrinkled piece of womanhood,
Sat watching like a watcher by the dead.

Then Florian knelt, and 'Come' he whispered to her,
'Lift up your head, sweet sister: lie not thus.
What have you done but right? you could not slay
Me, nor your prince: look up: be comforted:
Sweet is it to have done the thing one ought,
When fallen in darker ways.' And likewise I:
'Be comforted: have I not lost her too,
In whose least act abides the nameless charm
That none has else for me?' She heard, she moved,
She moaned, a folded voice; and up she sat,
And raised the cloak from brows as pale and smooth
As those that mourn half-shrouded over death
In deathless marble. 'Her,' she said, 'my friend–
Parted from her–betrayed her cause and mine–
Where shall I breathe? why kept ye not your faith?
O base and bad! what comfort? none for me!'
To whom remorseful Cyril, 'Yet I pray
Take comfort: live, dear lady, for your child!'
At which she lifted up her voice and cried.

v 37. *transient*: 'passing from one thing or person to another. Now *rare*' (*OED* 3).

'Ah me, my babe, my blossom, ah, my child,
My one sweet child, whom I shall see no more!
For now will cruel Ida keep her back;
And either she will die from want of care,
Or sicken with ill-usage, when they say
The child is hers–for every little fault,
The child is hers; and they will beat my girl
Remembering her mother: O my flower!
Or they will take her, they will make her hard,
And she will pass me by in after-life
With some cold reverence worse than were she dead.
Ill mother that I was to leave her there,
To lag behind, scared by the cry they made,
The horror of the shame among them all:
But I will go and sit beside the doors,
And make a wild petition night and day,
Until they hate to hear me like a wind
Wailing for ever, till they open to me,
And lay my little blossom at my feet,
My babe, my sweet Aglaïa, my one child:
And I will take her up and go my way,
And satisfy my soul with kissing her:
Ah! what might that man not deserve of me
Who gave me back my child?' 'Be comforted,'
Said Cyril, 'you shall have it:' but again
She veiled her brows, and prone she sank, and so
Like tender things that being caught feign death,
Spoke not, nor stirred.
By this a murmur ran
Through all the camp and inward raced the scouts
With rumour of Prince Arac hard at hand.
We left her by the woman, and without
Found the gray kings at parle: and 'Look you' cried
My father 'that our compact be fulfilled:
You have spoilt this child; she laughs at you and man:
She wrongs herself, her sex, and me, and him:
But red-faced war has rods of steel and fire;
She yields, or war.'
Then Gama turned to me:

v *110. you*] *1850*; to it *1847–8.*
v *111. be fulfilled*] *1850*; is performed *1847–8.*
v *112. child*] *1850*; girl *1847–8.*
v *113*] *1850*; She shall not legislate for Nature, king, *1847–8.*
v *114*] *1850; not 1847–8.*
v *115. She*] *1850*; But *1847–8.*

'We fear, indeed, you spent a stormy time
With our strange girl: and yet they say that still
You love her. Give us, then, your mind at large:
How say you, war or not?'
'Not war, if possible,
O king,' I said, 'lest from the abuse of war,
The desecrated shrine, the trampled year,
The smouldering homestead, and the household flower
Torn from the lintel–all the common wrong–
A smoke go up through which I loom to her
Three times a monster: now she lightens scorn
At him that mars her plan, but then would hate
(And every voice she talked with ratify it,
And every face she looked on justify it)
The general foe. More soluble is this knot,
By gentleness than war. I want her love.
What were I nigher this although we dashed
Your cities into shards with catapults,
She would not love;–or brought her chained, a slave,
The lifting of whose eyelash is my lord,
Not ever would she love; but brooding turn
The book of scorn, till all my flitting chance
Were caught within the record of her wrongs,
And crushed to death: and rather, Sire, than this
I would the old God of war himself were dead,
Forgotten, rusting on his iron hills,
Rotting on some wild shore with ribs of wreck,
Or like an old-world mammoth bulked in ice,
Not to be molten out.'
And roughly spake

v *117. girl*] *1850*; child *1847–8.*
v *121. year*: crop.
v *126. him that mars*] *1850*; the enemy of *1847–8.*
v *129* ∧ *30*] Like almost all the rest if men were wise, *1847–8.*
v *132. shards*: fragments. Cp. Cowley (whose works were at Somersby, *Lincoln*), *Davideis* ii 714–5: 'And scarce ought now of that vast Citie's found / But shards and rubbish'.
v *132* ∧ *3*] And dusted down your domes with mangonels; *1847–8.*
v *136. flitting*] *1870*; little *1847–68.*
v *140.* Cp. *In Memoriam* lvi 20: 'Or sealed within the iron hills'.
v *142.* 'Bulky mammoth buried in ice' (T.). Lyell's *Principles of Geology* (4th edn, 1835), i 147, mentions that 'The entire carcass of a mammoth was obtained in 1803. . . . It fell from a mass of ice, in which it had been encased, on the banks of the Lena.'

My father, 'Tut, you know them not, the girls.
Boy, when I hear you prate I almost think
That idiot legend credible. Look you, Sir!
Man is the hunter; woman is his game:
The sleek and shining creatures of the chase,
We hunt them for the beauty of their skins;
They love us for it, and we ride them down.
Wheedling and siding with them! Out! for shame!
Boy, there's no rose that's half so dear to them
As he that does the thing they dare not do,
Breathing and sounding beauteous battle, comes
With the air of the trumpet round him, and leaps in
Among the women, snares them by the score
Flattered and flustered, wins, though dashed with death
He reddens what he kisses: thus I won
Your mother, a good mother, a good wife,
Worth winning; but this firebrand–gentleness
To such as her! if Cyril spake her true,
To catch a dragon in a cherry net,
To trip a tigress with a gossamer,
Were wisdom to it.'
'Yea but Sire,' I cried,
'Wild natures need wise curbs. The soldier? No:
What dares not Ida do that she should prize
The soldier? I beheld her, when she rose
The yesternight, and storming in extremes,
Stood for her cause, and flung defiance down
Gagelike to man, and had not shunned the death,
No, not the soldier's: yet I hold her, king,
True woman: but you clash them all in one,
That have as many differences as we.
The violet varies from the lily as far
As oak from elm: one loves the soldier, one
The silken priest of peace, one this, one that,
And some unworthily; their sinless faith,
A maiden moon that sparkles on a sty,
Glorifying clown and satyr; whence they need
More breadth of culture: is not Ida right?
They worth it? truer to the law within?
Severer in the logic of a life?
Twice as magnetic to sweet influences

v *145–51*] *1850 (except ll. 145–6)*; They prize hard knocks and to be won by force. *1847–8.*

v *145–6*] *1851; not 1850.*

Of earth and heaven? and she of whom you speak,
My mother, looks as whole as some serene
Creation minted in the golden moods
Of sovereign artists; not a thought, a touch,
But pure as lines of green that streak the white
Of the first snowdrop's inner leaves; I say,
Not like the piebald miscellany, man,
Bursts of great heart and slips in sensual mire,
But whole and one: and take them all-in-all,
Were we ourselves but half as good, as kind,
As truthful, much that Ida claims as right
Had ne'er been mooted, but as frankly theirs
As dues of Nature. To our point: not war:
Lest I lose all.'
'Nay, nay, you spake but sense'
Said Gama. 'We remember love ourself
In our sweet youth; we did not rate him then
This red-hot iron to be shaped with blows.
You talk almost like Ida: *she* can talk;
And there is something in it as you say:
But you talk kindlier: we esteem you for it.–
He seems a gracious and a gallant Prince,
I would he had our daughter: for the rest,
Our own detention, why, the causes weighed,
Fatherly fears–you used us courteously–
We would do much to gratify your Prince–
We pardon it; and for your ingress here
Upon the skirt and fringe of our fair land,
You did but come as goblins in the night,
Nor in the furrow broke the ploughman's head,
Nor burnt the grange, nor bussed the milking-maid,
Nor robbed the farmer of his bowl of cream:
But let your Prince (our royal word upon it,
He comes back safe) ride with us to our lines,
And speak with Arac: Arac's word is thrice
As ours with Ida: something may be done–
I know not what–and ours shall see us friends.
You, likewise, our late guests, if so you will,
Follow us: who knows? we four may build some plan

v *190–91*] *1850*; Not like strong bursts of sample among men, *1847–8*.
v *192. whole and one*] *1850*; all one piece *1847–8*.
v *195. frankly*] *1850*; easily *1847–8*.
v *198. ourself*] *1864*; ourselves *1847–62*.
v *211–4*. Cp. *L'Allegro*, including ll. 105–6: 'Tells how the drudging Goblin swet, / To ern his Cream-bowle duly set.'

Foursquare to opposition.'
Here he reached
White hands of farewell to my sire, who growled
An answer which, half-muffled in his beard,
Let so much out as gave us leave to go.

Then rode we with the old king across the lawns
Beneath huge trees, a thousand rings of Spring
In every bole, a song on every spray
Of birds that piped their Valentines, and woke
Desire in me to infuse my tale of love
In the old king's ears, who promised help, and oozed
All o'er with honeyed answer as we rode
And blossom-fragrant slipt the heavy dews
Gathered by night and peace, with each light air
On our mailed heads: but other thoughts than
Peace
Burnt in us, when we saw the embattled squares,
And squadrons of the Prince, trampling the flowers
With clamour: for among them rose a cry
As if to greet the king; they made a halt;
The horses yelled; they clashed their arms; the drum
Beat; merrily-blowing shrilled the martial fife;
And in the blast and bray of the long horn
And serpent-throated bugle, undulated
The banner: anon to meet us lightly pranced
There captains out; nor ever had I seen
Such thews of men: the midmost and the highest
Was Arac: all about his motion clung
The shadow of his sister, as the beam
Of the East, that played upon them, made them
glance
Like those three stars of the airy Giant's zone,
That glitter burnished by the frosty dark;
And as the fiery Sirius alters hue,
And bickers into red and emerald, shone
Their morions, washed with morning, as they came.

v *231–2*. Cp. *Sea Dreams* 150–1: 'And then began to bloat himself, and ooze / All over with the fat affectionate smile . . .'

v *241*. Cp. *Semele* 20: 'And melody o' the merrily-blowing flute'.

v *250*. 'The stars in the belt of Orion' (T.).

v *251*. *burnished by the frosty dark*: incorporated from an extra stanza of *Sir Launcelot and Queen Guinevere* (*T.MS*).

v *252–3*. Cp. *The Lover's Tale* i 52–61*n*, MS: 'The bickering Dog-star danced in sparkles'. The comparison of armour to starlight suggests *Iliad* v 5.

v *254*. *morions*: 'steel helmets' (H.T.). Cp. Dryden, *Palamon and Arcite* iii

And I that prated peace, when first I heard
War-music, felt the blind wildbeast of force,
Whose home is in the sinews of a man,
Stir in me as to strike: then took the king
His three broad sons; with now a wandering hand
And now a pointed finger, told them all:
A common light of smiles at our disguise
Broke from their lips, and, ere the windy jest
Had laboured down within his ample lungs,
The genial giant, Arac, rolled himself
Thrice in the saddle, then burst out in words.

'Our land invaded, 'sdeath! and he himself
Your captive, yet my father wills not war:
And, 'sdeath! myself, what care I, war or no?
But then this question of your troth remains:
And there's a downright honest meaning in her;
She flies too high, she flies too high! and yet
She asked but space and fairplay for her scheme;
She prest and prest it on me–I myself,
What know I of these things? but, life and soul!
I thought her half-right talking of her wrongs;
I say she flies too high, 'sdeath! what of that?
I take her for the flower of womankind,
And so I often told her, right or wrong,
And, Prince, she can be sweet to those she loves,
And, right or wrong, I care not: this is all,
I stand upon her side: she made me swear it–
'Sdeath–and with solemn rites by candle-light–

450–52: 'glittring Arms, too dazling to behold; / And polish'd Steel that cast the View aside, / And Crested Morions, with their Plumy Pride.'

v *262–5. , ere . . . words.*] *1850*; Arac turning said; *1847–8*.

v *266. 'sdeath! and he*] *1851*; life and soul! *1847–50*.

v *268*] *1851; not 1847–8*; And, life! myself I care not, war or no: *1850*.

v *269. then this*] *1850*; , Prince, the *1847–8*.

v *271*] *1850; not 1847–8*.

v *273. I myself,*] *1850*; life! I felt *1847–8*.

v *274*] *1850; not 1847–8*.

v *275. I thought her*] *1850*; That she was *1847–8*.

v *276–88*] *1850 (except ll. 276–9, 280, 282, 288)*;

And I'll stand by her. Waive your claim, or else
Decide it here: why not? we are three to three.' *1847–8*

See l. 300*n*.

v *276–9*] *1851; not 1850*.

v *280. And*] *1851*; Yet *1850*.

v *282. 'Sdeath*] *1851*; Life *1850*. Likewise in l. 288.

Swear by St something – I forget her name –
Her that talked down the fifty wisest men;
*She* was a princess too; and so I swore.
Come, this is all; she will not: waive your claim:
If not, the foughten field, what else, at once
Decides it, 'sdeath! against my father's will.'

I lagged in answer loth to render up
My precontract, and loth by brainless war
To cleave the rift of difference deeper yet;
Till one of those two brothers, half aside
And fingering at the hair about his lip,
To prick us on to combat 'Like to like!
The woman's garment hid the woman's heart.'
A taunt that clenched his purpose like a blow!
For fiery-short was Cyril's counter-scoff,
And sharp I answered, touched upon the point
Where idle boys are cowards to their shame,
'Decide it here: why not? we are three to three.'

Then spake the third 'But three to three? no more?
No more, and in our noble sister's cause?
More, more, for honour: every captain waits
Hungry for honour, angry for his king.
More, more, some fifty on a side, that each
May breathe himself, and quick! by overthrow
Of these or those, the question settled die.'

'Yea,' answered I, 'for this wild wreath of air,
This flake of rainbow flying on the highest
Foam of men's deeds – this honour, if ye will.
It needs must be for honour if at all:

v *284*. 'St Catherine of Alexandria, niece of Constantine the Great' (T.). H.T. adds: 'The Emperor Maxentius during his persecution is related to have sent fifty of his wisest men to convert her from Christianity, but she combated and confuted them all.'

v *289. render up*] *1850*; strike her kin, *1847–8*.

v *290*] *1850; not 1847–8*.

v *291. To*] *1850*; And *1847–8*.

v *294. Like to like!*] *1850*; Three to three? *1847–8*.

v *295*] *1850*; But such a three to three were three to one.' *1847–8*.

v *296. taunt*] *1850*; boast *1847–8*.

v *298. point*] *1850*; sense *1847–8*.

v *300*] *1850*; And tipt with sportive malice to and fro
Like pointed arrows leapt the taunts and hit. *1847–8*

See ll. 276–88*n*.

Since, what decision? if we fail, we fail,
And if we win, we fail: she would not keep
Her compact.' ''Sdeath! but we will send to her,'
Said Arac, 'worthy reasons why she should
Bide by this issue: let our missive through,
And you shall have her answer by the word.'

'Boys!' shrieked the old king, but vainlier than a hen
To her false daughters in the pool; for none
Regarded; neither seemed there more to say:
Back rode we to my father's camp, and found
He thrice had sent a herald to the gates,
To learn if Ida yet would cede our claim,
Or by denial flush her babbling wells
With her own people's life: three times he went:
The first, he blew and blew, but none appeared:
He battered at the doors; none came: the next,
An awful voice within had warned him thence:
The third, and those eight daughters of the plough
Came sallying through the gates, and caught his hair,
And so belaboured him on rib and cheek
They made him wild: not less one glance he caught
Through open doors of Ida stationed there
Unshaken, clinging to her purpose, firm
Though compassed by two armies and the noise
Of arms; and standing like a stately Pine
Set in a cataract on an island-crag,
When storm is on the heights, and right and left
Sucked from the dark heart of the long hills roll
The torrents, dashed to the vale: and yet her will
Bred will in me to overcome it or fall.

But when I told the king that I was pledged
To fight in tourney for my bride, he clashed
His iron palms together with a cry;
Himself would tilt it out among the lads:
But overborne by all his bearded lords
With reasons drawn from age and state, perforce
He yielded, wroth and red, with fierce demur:

v *314*. *'Sdeath ... her,'*] *1851*; 'We will send to her' Arac said, *1847–8*; Life! but we will send to her,' *1850*.

v *315*. *Said Arac,'*] *1850*; 'A score of *1847–8*.

v *333*. *open*] *1850*; the open *1847–8*.

v *336–7*. 'Taken from a torrent above Cauteretz' (T.).

And many a bold knight started up in heat,
And sware to combat for my claim till death.

All on this side the palace ran the field
Flat to the garden-wall: and likewise here,
Above the garden's glowing blossom-belts,
A columned entry shone and marble stairs,
And great bronze valves, embossed with Tomyris
And what she did to Cyrus after fight,
But now fast barred: so here upon the flat
All that long morn the lists were hammered up,
And all that morn the heralds to and fro,
With message and defiance, went and came;
Last, Ida's answer, in a royal hand,
But shaken here and there, and rolling words
Oration-like. I kissed it and I read.

'O brother, you have known the pangs we felt,
What heats of indignation when we heard
Of those that iron-cramped their women's feet;
Of lands in which at the altar the poor bride
Gives her harsh groom for bridal-gift a scourge;
Of living hearts that crack within the fire
Where smoulder their dead despots; and of those, –
Mothers, – that, all prophetic pity, fling
Their pretty maids in the running flood, and swoops
The vulture, beak and talon, at the heart
Made for all noble motion: and I saw
That equal baseness lived in sleeker times
With smoother men: the old leaven leavened all:
Millions of throats would bawl for civil rights,
No woman named: therefore I set my face
Against all men, and lived but for mine own.

v *355*. *Tomyris*: 'queen of the Massagetæ, who cut off the head of Cyrus the Great after defeating him, and dipped it in a skin which she had filled with blood and bade him, as he was insatiate of blood, to drink his fill, gorge himself with blood' (T.). H.T. adds the reference to Herodotus i 212.
v *364*. 'O . . . *known*] *1850*; 'You have known, O brother, all *1847–8*.
v *365*. *indignation*] *1850*; moral anger *1847–8*.
v *368*. 'An old Russian custom' (T.). H.T. adds: 'See Hakluyt's *Navigations*, 1599–1600'.
v *369*. 'Suttee in India' (T.).
v *372*. *flood*: 'Ganges' (T.).
v *375*] *1850*; That it was little better in better times *1847–8*.
v *376*. *1 Corinthians* v 6–7, 'Know ye not that a little leaven leaveneth the whole lump. Purge out therefore the old leaven.'

Far off from men I built a fold for them:
I stored it full of rich memorial:
I fenced it round with gallant institutes,
And biting laws to scare the beasts of prey
And prospered; till a rout of saucy boys
Brake on us at our books, and marred our peace,
Masked like our maids, blustering I know not what
Of insolence and love, some pretext held
Of baby troth, invalid, since my will
Sealed not the bond–the striplings!–for their sport!–
I tamed my leopards: shall I not tame these?
Or you? or I? for since you think me touched
In honour–what, I would not aught of false–
Is not our cause pure? and whereas I know
Your prowess, Arac, and what mother's blood
You draw from, fight; you failing, I abide
What end soever: fail you will not. Still
Take not his life: he risked it for my own;
His mother lives: yet whatsoe'er you do,
Fight and fight well; strike and strike home. O dear
Brothers, the woman's Angel guards you, you
The sole men to be mingled with our cause,
The sole men we shall prize in the after-time,
Your very armour hallowed, and your statues
Reared, sung to, when, this gad-fly brushed aside,
We plant a solid foot into the Time,
And mould a generation strong to move

v *380. I*] *1850*; we *1847–8*. Likewise in ll. 381, 382, 386.
v *382. institutes*: laws.
v *383*. Cp. *Measure for Measure* I iii 19–23: 'We have strict statutes and most biting laws, / The needful bits and curbs for headstrong wills, / Which for these fourteen years we have let sleep, / Even like an o'ergrown lion in a cave, / That goes not out to prey.'
v *384. rout*] *1850*; set *1847–8*.
v *388. baby troth*] *1850*; old affiance *1847–8*. *my*] *1850*; our *1847–8*.
v *390. I . . . I*] *1850*; We have tamed our leopards: shall we *1847–8*.
v *391. I*] *1850*; we *1847–8*. *me*] *1850*; we are *1847–8*.
v *392. what, I*] *1850*; nay, we *1847–8*.
v *393. I*] *1850*; we *1847–8*.
v *395. you . . . abide*] *1850*; we abide what end soe'er *1847–8*.
v *396. What . . . fail*] *1851*; You failing: but we know *1847–8*; What end soever: but *1850*.
v *397*] *1850*; You must not slay him: he risked his life for ours, *1847–8*.

With claim on claim from right to right, till she
Whose name is yoked with children's, know herself;
And Knowledge in our own land make her free,
And, ever following those two crownèd twins,
Commerce and conquest, shower the fiery grain
Of freedom broadcast over all that orbs
Between the Northern and the Southern morn.'

Then came a postscript dashed across the rest.
'See that there be no traitors in your camp:
We seem a nest of traitors–none to trust
Since our arms failed–this Egypt-plague of men!
Almost our maids were better at their homes,
Than thus man-girdled here: indeed I think
Our chiefest comfort is the little child
Of one unworthy mother; which she left:
She shall not have it back: the child shall grow
To prize the authentic mother of her mind.
I took it for an hour in mine own bed
This morning: there the tender orphan hands
Felt at my heart, and seemed to charm from thence
The wrath I nursed against the world: farewell.'

I ceased; he said, 'Stubborn, but she may sit
Upon a king's right hand in thunder-storms,
And breed up warriors! See now, though yourself
Be dazzled by the wildfire Love to sloughs
That swallow common sense, the spindling king,
This Gama swamped in lazy tolerance.
When the man wants weight, the woman takes it up,
And topples down the scales; but this is fixt
As are the roots of earth and base of all;
Man for the field and woman for the hearth:

v *407* ∧ *8*] The woman-phantom, she that seemed no more
Than the man's shadow in a glass, her name *1847–50*.
v *408*. *Whose . . . yoked*] *1851*; Yoked in his mouth *1847–50*.
v *409*. *in . . . free*] *1850*; liberate her, nor only here *1847–8*.
v *410*. *And*] *1850*; But *1847–8*.
v *419*. *I*] *1850*; we *1847–8*.
v *424*. *I*] *1850*; We *1847–8*. *in . . . bed*] *1850*; this morning to us, *1847–8*.
v *425*. *This . . . there*] *1850*; In our own bed: *1847–8*.
v *426*. *my*] *1850*; our *1847–8*.
v *427*. *I*] *1850*; we *1847–8*.

Man for the sword and for the needle she:
Man with the head and woman with the heart:
Man to command and woman to obey;
All else confusion. Look you! the gray mare
Is ill to live with, when her whinny shrills
From tile to scullery, and her small goodman
Shrinks in his arm-chair while the fires of Hell
Mix with his hearth: but you–she's yet a colt–
Take, break her: strongly groomed and straitly
curbed
She might not rank with those detestable
That let the bantling scald at home, and brawl
Their rights or wrongs like potherbs in the street.
They say she's comely; there's the fairer chance:
*I* like her none the less for rating at her!
Besides, the woman wed is not as we,
But suffers change of frame. A lusty brace
Of twins may weed her of her folly. Boy,
The bearing and the training of a child
Is woman's wisdom.'
Thus the hard old king:
I took my leave, for it was nearly noon:
I pored upon her letter which I held,
And on the little clause 'take not his life:'
I mused on that wild morning in the woods,
And on the 'Follow, follow, thou shalt win:'
I thought on all the wrathful king had said,
And how the strange betrothment was to end:
Then I remembered that burnt sorcerer's curse
That one should fight with shadows and should
fall;
And like a flash the weird affection came:
King, camp and college turned to hollow shows;
I seemed to move in old memorial tilts,
And doing battle with forgotten ghosts,
To dream myself the shadow of a dream:
And ere I woke it was the point of noon,
The lists were ready. Empanoplied and plumed

v *441. you!*] *1850*; to it: *1847–8*. The proverb, 'the grey mare is the better horse', said of the domineering wife.

v *445. you . . . colt–*] *1850*; take and break her, you! *1847–8*.

v *446*] *1850*; She's yet a colt. Well groomed and strongly curbed *1847–8*.

v *448. let . . . home*] *1850*; to the hireling leave their babe *1847–8*.

v *457–71. for . . . woke*] *1851; not 1847–50*.

v *472ff*. Killham (pp. 272–4) discusses the Eglinton tournament, Sept.

We entered in, and waited, fifty there
Opposed to fifty, till the trumpet blared
At the barrier like a wild horn in a land
Of echoes, and a moment, and once more
The trumpet, and again: at which the storm
Of galloping hoofs bare on the ridge of spears
And riders front to front, until they closed
In conflict with the crash of shivering points,
And thunder. Yet it seemed a dream, I dreamed
Of fighting. On his haunches rose the steed,
And into fiery splinters leapt the lance,
And out of stricken helmets sprang the fire.
Part sat like rocks: part reeled but kept their
seats:
Part rolled on the earth and rose again and drew:
Part stumbled mixt with floundering horses. Down
From those two bulks at Arac's side, and down
From Arac's arm, as from a giant's flail,
The large blows rained, as here and everywhere
He rode the mellay, lord of the ringing lists,
And all the plain,–brand, mace, and shaft, and
shield–
Shocked, like an iron-clanging anvil banged
With hammers; till I thought, can this be he
From Gama's dwarfish loins? if this be so,
The mother makes us most–and in my dream
I glanced aside, and saw the palace-front
Alive with fluttering scarfs and ladies' eyes,
And highest, among the statues, statuelike,
Between a cymballed Miriam and a Jael,
With Psyche's babe, was Ida watching us,

1839, which took place in armour and was widely reported: 'to one considering the position of women in a changing world the interest provoked in 1839 by the Eglinton tournament, especially among women, would have seemed bizarre in the extreme'.

v *474*] *1850*; To fifty, till the terrible trumpet blared *1847–8*. A review had objected to the rhythm (Shannon, p. 121).

v *475–6. like . . . echoes*] *1851; not 1847–50*.

v *476. and a*] *1851*; yet a *1847–50*.

v *480. conflict*] *1850*; the middle *1847–8*.

v *481–2. Yet . . . fighting*] *1851; not 1847–50*.

v *496. in my dream*] *1851*; thinking thus *1847–50*.

v *497. aside*] *1850*; to the left *1847–8*.

v *500. Exodus* xv 20 (see iv 122*n*); *Judges* iv 21 (Jael slays Sisera with the nail).

A single band of gold about her hair,
Like a Saint's glory up in heaven: but she
No saint–inexorable–no tenderness–
Too hard, too cruel: yet she sees me fight,
Yea, let her see me fall! with that I drave
Among the thickest and bore down a Prince,
And Cyril, one. Yea, let me make my dream
All that I would. But that large-moulded man,
His visage all agrin as at a wake,
Made at me through the press, and, staggering back
With stroke on stroke the horse and horseman, came
As comes a pillar of electric cloud,
Flaying the roofs and sucking up the drains,
And shadowing down the champaign till it strikes
On a wood, and takes, and breaks, and cracks, and splits,
And twists the grain with such a roar that Earth
Reels, and the herdsmen cry; for everything
Gave way before him: only Florian, he
That loved me closer than his own right eye,
Thrust in between; but Arac rode him down:
And Cyril seeing it, pushed against the Prince,
With Psyche's colour round his helmet, tough,
Strong, supple, sinew-corded, apt at arms;
But tougher, heavier, stronger, he that smote
And threw him: last I spurred; I felt my veins
Stretch with fierce heat; a moment hand to hand,
And sword to sword, and horse to horse we hung,
Till I struck out and shouted; the blade glanced,
I did but shear a feather, and dream and truth
Flowed from me; darkness closed me; and I fell.

[v ∧ vi]

Home they brought her warrior dead:
She nor swooned, nor uttered cry:

v *506. fall!*] *1851*; die. *1847–50.*

v *508–9. Yea . . . would.*] *1851; not 1847–50.*

v *510*] *1850; not 1847–8.*

v *514. Flaying*] *1850*; Flaying off *1847–8.* A review had objected to the rhythm, and in l. 517 (Shannon, p. 121).

v *517. Earth*] *1850*; the Earth *1847–8.*

v *525. heavier*] *1850*; suppler *1847–8.*

v *530. dream and truth*] *1851*; life and love *1847–50.*

All her maidens, watching, said,
'She must weep or she will die.'

Then they praised him, soft and low,
Called him worthy to be loved,
Truest friend and noblest foe;
Yet she neither spoke nor moved.

Stole a maiden from her place,
Lightly to the warrior stept,
Took the face-cloth from the face;
Yet she neither moved nor wept.

Rose a nurse of ninety years,
Set his child upon her knee–
Like summer tempest came her tears–
'Sweet my child, I live for thee.'

## VI

My dream had never died or lived again.
As in some mystic middle state I lay;
Seeing I saw not, hearing not I heard:
Though, if I saw not, yet they told me all
So often that I speak as having seen.

For so it seemed, or so they said to me,
That all things grew more tragic and more strange;
That when our side was vanquished and my cause
For ever lost, there went up a great cry,
The Prince is slain. My father heard and ran
In on the lists, and there unlaced my casque
And grovelled on my body, and after him
Came Psyche, sorrowing for Aglaïa.

v ∧ vi Written 1849, added *1850*. For an alternative version, see Appendix A (p. 1771). Both versions resemble Scott's *Lay of the Last Minstrel* I ix: 'In sorrow o'er Lord Walter's bier / The warlike foresters had bent; / And many a flower and many a tear / Old Teviot's maids and matrons lent: / But o'er her warrior's bloody bier / The Ladye dropp'd nor flower nor tear! / Vengeance, deep-brooding o'er the slain, / Had lock'd the source of softer woe; / And burning pride and high disdain / Forbade the rising tear to flow; / Until, amid his sorrowing clan, / Her son lisp'd from the nurse's knee– / "And if I live to be a man, / My father's death reveng'd shall be!" / Then fast the mother's tears did seek / To dew the infant's kindling cheek.' T.'s song is also close to the Icelandic *Guþrunarkviþa I*, which J. S. Conybeare translated in *Illustrations of Anglo-Saxon Poetry* (1826); see R. M. Lumiansky, *Notes and Queries* clxxix (1940) 23–4.

vi *1–4*] *1851*; What followed, though I saw not, yet I heard *1847–50*.
vi *6–7*] *1851*; *not 1847–50*.
vi *8. That*] *1850*; For *1847–8*.

But high upon the palace Ida stood
With Psyche's babe in arm: there on the roofs
Like that great dame of Lapidoth she sang.

'Our enemies have fallen, have fallen: the seed,
The little seed they laughed at in the dark,
Has risen and cleft the soil, and grown a bulk
Of spanless girth, that lays on every side
A thousand arms and rushes to the Sun.

'Our enemies have fallen, have fallen: they came;
The leaves were wet with women's tears: they heard
A noise of songs they would not understand:
They marked it with the red cross to the fall,
And would have strown it, and are fallen themselves.

'Our enemies have fallen, have fallen: they came,
The woodmen with their axes: lo the tree!
But we will make it faggots for the hearth,
And shape it plank and beam for roof and floor,
And boats and bridges for the use of men.

'Our enemies have fallen, have fallen: they struck;
With their own blows they hurt themselves, nor knew
There dwelt an iron nature in the grain:
The glittering axe was broken in their arms,
Their arms were shattered to the shoulder blade.

'Our enemies have fallen, but this shall grow
A night of Summer from the heat, a breadth
Of Autumn, dropping fruits of power: and rolled
With music in the growing breeze of Time,
The tops shall strike from star to star, the fangs
Shall move the stony bases of the world.

'And now, O maids, behold our sanctuary
Is violate, our laws broken: fear we not

vi *16. Judges* iv 4, 'And Deborah, a prophetess, the wife of Lapidoth, she judged Israel at that time.' v 1–2, 'Then sang Deborah and Barak the son of Abinoam on that day, saying, Praise ye the Lord for the avenging of Israel.' Ida's song may also recall v 14, 'Out of Ephraim was there a root of them against Amalek'; and v 31, 'So let all thine enemies perish, O Lord.'

vi *17. Isaiah* xxi 9, 'Babylon is fallen, is fallen'; also *Revelation* xviii 2, xiv 8. The song's theme of the seed is linked by Killham (p. 118) with Anna Jameson's *Woman's Mission and Woman's Position* (in *Memoirs and Essays*, 1846), which is prefaced with the story of Donna Maria d'Escobar, who planted a few grains of wheat in her garden at Lima, and thence produced all the wheat in Peru.

vi *40. growing*] *1850*; Æonian *1847–8*.

vi *41.* Cp. *The Hesperides* 37 ∧ 8, MS: 'the fangèd root',

To break them more in their behoof, whose arms
Championed our cause and won it with a day
Blanched in our annals, and perpetual feast,
When dames and heroines of the golden year
Shall strip a hundred hollows bare of Spring,
To rain an April of ovation round
Their statues, borne aloft, the three: but come,
We will be liberal, since our rights are won.
Let them not lie in the tents with coarse mankind,
Ill nurses; but descend, and proffer these
The brethren of our blood and cause, that there
Lie bruised and maimed, the tender ministries
Of female hands and hospitality.'

She spoke, and with the babe yet in her arms,
Descending, burst the great bronze valves, and led
A hundred maids in train across the Park.
Some cowled, and some bare-headed, on they came,
Their feet in flowers, her loveliest: by them went
The enamoured air sighing, and on their curls
From the high tree the blossom wavering fell,
And over them the tremulous isles of light
Slided, they moving under shade: but Blanche
At distance followed: so they came: anon
Through open field into the lists they wound
Timorously; and as the leader of the herd
That holds a stately fretwork to the Sun,
And followed up by a hundred airy does,
Steps with a tender foot, light as on air,
The lovely, lordly creature floated on
To where her wounded brethren lay; there
stayed;
Knelt on one knee,—the child on one,—and prest
Their hands, and called them dear deliverers,
And happy warriors, and immortal names,

vi *47. Blanched*: marked in white chalk as propitious days.
vi *48.* Cp. *The Golden Year* (p. 714).
vi *59. valves*: leaves of a door.
vi *65–6.* 'Spots of sunshine coming through the leaves, and seeming to slide from one to the other, as the procession of girls "moves under shade"' (T.). *isles of light*: as in Thomas Gisborne's *Walks in a Forest* ('Summer.–Moonlight'), which was at Somersby (*Lincoln*). Shelley has 'slide / Tremulous . . . isle' in *A Vision of the Sea* 131–3.
vi *68. open*] *1850*; the open *1847–8*.
vi *77.* Cp. Wordsworth's *Who is the happy Warrior?*

And said 'You shall not lie in the tents but here,
And nursed by those for whom you fought, and served
With female hands and hospitality.'

Then, whether moved by this, or was it chance,
She past my way. Up started from my side
The old lion, glaring with his whelpless eye,
Silent; but when she saw me lying stark,
Dishelmed and mute, and motionlessly pale,
Cold even to her, she sighed; and when she saw
The haggard father's face and reverend beard
Of grisly twine, all dabbled with the blood
Of his own son, shuddered, a twitch of pain
Tortured her mouth, and o'er her forehead past
A shadow, and her hue changed, and she said:
'He saved my life: my brother slew him for it.'
No more: at which the king in bitter scorn
Drew from my neck the painting and the tress,
And held them up: she saw them, and a day
Rose from the distance on her memory,
When the good Queen, her mother, shore the tress
With kisses, ere the days of Lady Blanche:
And then once more she looked at my pale face:
Till understanding all the foolish work
Of Fancy, and the bitter close of all,
Her iron will was broken in her mind;
Her noble heart was molten in her breast;
She bowed, she set the child on the earth; she laid
A feeling finger on my brows, and presently
'O Sire,' she said, 'he lives: he is not dead:
O let me have him with my brethren here
In our own palace: we will tend on him
Like one of these; if so, by any means,
To lighten this great clog of thanks, that make
Our progress falter to the woman's goal.'

She said: but at the happy word 'he lives'
My father stooped, re-fathered o'er my wounds.
So those two foes above my fallen life,
With brow to brow like night and evening mixt
Their dark and gray, while Psyche ever stole
A little nearer, till the babe that by us,

vi *91. her*] *1848*; all her *1847*.
vi *110. make*] *1850*; makes *1847–8*.

Half-lapt in glowing gauze and golden brede,
Lay like a new-fallen meteor on the grass,
Uncared for, spied its mother and began
A blind and babbling laughter, and to dance
Its body, and reach its fatling innocent arms
And lazy lingering fingers. She the appeal
Brooked not, but clamouring out 'Mine–mine–
not yours,
It is not yours, but mine: give me the child'
Ceased all on tremble: piteous was the cry:
So stood the unhappy mother open-mouthed,
And turned each face her way: wan was her cheek
With hollow watch, her blooming mantle torn,
Red grief and mother's hunger in her eye,
And down dead-heavy sank her curls, and half
The sacred mother's bosom, panting, burst
The laces toward her babe; but she nor cared
Nor knew it, clamouring on, till Ida heard,
Looked up, and rising slowly from me, stood
Erect and silent, striking with her glance
The mother, me, the child; but he that lay
Beside us, Cyril, battered as he was,
Trailed himself up on one knee: then he drew
Her robe to meet his lips, and down she looked
At the armed man sideways, pitying as it seemed,
Or self-involved; but when she learnt his face,
Remembering his ill-omened song, arose
Once more through all her height, and o'er him
grew
Tall as a figure lengthened on the sand
When the tide ebbs in sunshine, and he said:

'O fair and strong and terrible! Lioness
That with your long locks play the Lion's mane!
But Love and Nature, these are two more terrible
And stronger. See, your foot is on our necks,
We vanquished, you the Victor of your will.
What would you more? give her the child! remain
Orbed in your isolation: he is dead,
Or all as dead: henceforth we let you be:
Win you the hearts of women; and beware

vi *118–9. brede*: 'embroidery' (T.). Cp. Keats, *Lamia* i 157–60: 'And, as the lava ravishes the mead, / Spoilt all her silver mail, and golden brede . . . / Eclips'd her crescents, and lick'd up her stars.'
vi *137. he that*] *1850*; Cyril, who *1847–8*.
vi *138*] *1850*; Bruised, where he fell, not far off, much in pain, *1847–8*.

Lest, where you seek the common love of these,
The common hate with the revolving wheel
Should drag you down, and some great Nemesis
Break from a darkened future, crowned with fire,
And tread you out for ever: but howsoe'er
Fixed in yourself, never in your own arms
To hold your own, deny not hers to her,
Give her the child! O if, I say, you keep
One pulse that beats true woman, if you loved
The breast that fed or arm that dandled you,
Or own one port of sense not flint to prayer,
Give her the child! or if you scorn to lay it,
Yourself, in hands so lately claspt with yours,
Or speak to her, your dearest, her one fault
The tenderness, not yours, that could not kill,
Give *me* it: *I* will give it her.'
He said:
At first her eye with slow dilation rolled
Dry flame, she listening; after sank and sank
And, into mournful twilight mellowing, dwelt
Full on the child; she took it: 'Pretty bud!
Lily of the vale! half opened bell of the woods!
Sole comfort of my dark hour, when a world
Of traitorous friend and broken system made
No purple in the distance, mystery,
Pledge of a love not to be mine, farewell;
These men are hard upon us as of old,
We two must part: and yet how fain was I
To dream thy cause embraced in mine, to think
I might be something to thee, when I felt
Thy helpless warmth about my barren breast
In the dead prime: but may thy mother prove
As true to thee as false, false, false to me!

vi *159*. Cp. *Ode on Wellington* 170 ‸ 71, *1852* text: 'a darkening future'.
vi *165*. *arm*] *1850*; the arm *1847–8*.
vi *166*. *port*] *1880*; part *1847–78*. T. says this was a misprint, and glosses *port* as 'haven'. Cp. *2 Henry IV* IV v 24: 'That keep'st the ports of slumber open wide', where the meaning is 'portals'.
vi *168*. Cp. *In Memoriam* x 19: 'And hands so often clasped in mine'.
vi *171*. *I*] *1850*; and I *1847–8*.
vi *178*. *broken system*] broken purpose *H.MS*. As in the song, vii 199.
vi *179*. Cp. *In Memoriam* xxxviii 3: 'The purple from the distance dies'.
vi *185*. *helpless . . . barren*] *1851*; waxen . . . milkless *1847–50*. *barren breast*: *L'Allegro* 73.
vi *186*. *dead prime*: 'earliest dawn' (T.).

And, if thou needs must bear the yoke, I wish it
Gentle as freedom'–here she kissed it: then–
'All good go with thee! take it Sir,' and so
Laid the soft babe in his hard-mailèd hands,
Who turned half-round to Psyche as she sprang
To meet it, with an eye that swum in thanks;
Then felt it sound and whole from head to foot,
And hugged and never hugged it close enough,
And in her hunger mouthed and mumbled it,
And hid her bosom with it; after that
Put on more calm and added suppliantly:

'We two were friends: I go to mine own land
For ever: find some other: as for me
I scarce am fit for your great plans: yet speak to me,
Say one soft word and let me part forgiven.'

But Ida spoke not, rapt upon the child.
Then Arac. 'Ida–'sdeath! you blame the man;
You wrong yourselves–the woman is so hard
Upon the woman. Come, a grace to me!
I am your warrior: I and mine have fought
Your battle: kiss her; take her hand, she weeps:
'Sdeath! I would sooner fight thrice o'er than see it.'

But Ida spoke not, gazing on the ground,
And reddening in the furrows of his chin,
And moved beyond his custom, Gama said:

'I've heard that there is iron in the blood,
And I believe it. Not one word? not one?
Whence drew you this steel temper? not from me,
Not from your mother, now a saint with saints.
She said you had a heart–I heard her say it–
"Our Ida has a heart"–just ere she died–
"But see that some one with authority
Be near her still" and I–I sought for one–
All people said she had authority–
The Lady Blanche: much profit! Not one word;
No! though your father sues: see how you stand
Stiff as Lot's wife, and all the good knights
maimed,

vi *193*. *meet*] *1850*; embrace *1847–8*.
vi *204*. *Ida–'sdeath*] *1851*; Soul and life! *1847–50*.
vi *206* ^ *7*] I am your brother; I advise you well: *1847–8*.
vi *209*. *'Sdeath*] *1851*; Life *1847–50*.

I trust that there is no one hurt to death,
For your wild whim: and was it then for this,
Was it for this we gave our palace up,
Where we withdrew from summer heats and state,
And had our wine and chess beneath the planes,
And many a pleasant hour with her that's gone,
Ere you were born to vex us? Is it kind?
Speak to her I say: is this not she of whom,
When first she came, all flushed you said to me
Now had you got a friend of your own age,
Now could you share your thought; now should men see
Two women faster welded in one love
Than pairs of wedlock; she you walked with, she
You talked with, whole nights long, up in the tower,
Of sine and arc, spheroïd and azimuth,
And right ascension, Heaven knows what; and now
A word, but one, one little kindly word,
Not one to spare her: out upon you, flint!
You love nor her, nor me, nor any; nay,
You shame your mother's judgment too. Not one?
You will not? well–no heart have you, or such
As fancies like the vermin in a nut
Have fretted all to dust and bitterness.'
So said the small king moved beyond his wont.

But Ida stood nor spoke, drained of her force
By many a varying influence and so long.
Down through her limbs a drooping languor wept:
Her head a little bent; and on her mouth
A doubtful smile dwelt like a clouded moon
In a still water: then brake out my sire,
Lifting his grim head from my wounds. 'O you,
Woman, whom we thought woman even now,
And were half fooled to let you tend our son,
Because he might have wished it–but we see
The accomplice of your madness unforgiven,

vi *225*] *1850; not 1847–8.* T. wrote to Aubrey de Vere (*Mem.* i 282), who had reviewed the poem in the *Edinburgh Review*, Oct. 1849: 'Now I certainly did not mean to kill anyone, and therefore I put this new line into the old king's mouth, "I trust that there is no one hurt to death", and in the old tourneys it really did happen now and then that there was only a certain amount of bruises and bangs and no death.'

vi *239*. 'The azimuth of any point on a horizontal plane is the angle between a line drawn to that point, and a fixed line in the horizontal plane, usually chosen to be a line drawn due North' (H.T.).

And think that you might mix his draught with death,
When your skies change again: the rougher hand
Is safer: on to the tents: take up the Prince.'

He rose, and while each ear was pricked to attend
A tempest, through the cloud that dimmed her broke
A genial warmth and light once more, and shone
Through glittering drops on her sad friend.
'Come hither.
O Psyche,' she cried out, 'embrace me, come,
Quick while I melt; make reconcilement sure
With one that cannot keep her mind an hour:
Come to the hollow heart they slander so!
Kiss and be friends, like children being chid!
*I* seem no more: *I* want forgiveness too:
I should have had to do with none but maids,
That have no links with men. Ah false but dear,
Dear traitor, too much loved, why?–why?–
Yet see,
Before these kings we embrace you yet once more
With all forgiveness, all oblivion,
And trust, not love, you less.
And now, O sire,
Grant me your son, to nurse, to wait upon him,
Like mine own brother. For my debt to him,
This nightmare weight of gratitude, I know it;
Taunt me no more: yourself and yours shall have
Free adit; we will scatter all our maids
Till happier times each to her proper hearth:
What use to keep them here–now? grant my
prayer.
Help, father, brother, help; speak to the king:
Thaw this male nature to some touch of that
Which kills me with myself, and drags me down
From my fixt height to mob me up with all
The soft and milky rabble of womankind,
Poor weakling even as they are.'
Passionate tears
Followed: the king replied not: Cyril said:
'Your brother, Lady,–Florian,–ask for him
Of your great head–for he is wounded too–
That you may tend upon him with the prince.'
'Ay so,' said Ida with a bitter smile,
'Our laws are broken: let him enter too.'

vi *283. adit*: access (T.'s is the earliest example in *OED* in precisely this sense).

Then Violet, she that sang the mournful song,
And had a cousin tumbled on the plain,
Petitioned too for him. 'Ay so,' she said,
'I stagger in the stream: I cannot keep
My heart an eddy from the brawling hour:
We break our laws with ease, but let it be.'
'Ay so?' said Blanche: 'Amazed am I to hear
Your Highness: but your Highness breaks with
    ease
The law your Highness did not make: 'twas I.
I had been wedded wife, I knew mankind,
And blocked them out; but these men came to woo
Your Highness–verily I think to win.'

So she, and turned askance a wintry eye:
But Ida with a voice, that like a bell
Tolled by an earthquake in a trembling tower,
Rang ruin, answered full of grief and scorn.

'Fling our doors wide! all, all, not one, but all,
Not only he, but by my mother's soul,
Whatever man lies wounded, friend or foe,
Shall enter, if he will. Let our girls flit,
Till the storm die! but had you stood by us,
The roar that breaks the Pharos from his base
Had left us rock. She fain would sting us too,
But shall not. Pass, and mingle with your likes.
We brook no further insult but are gone.'

vi *304. Amazed am I*] *1850*; I am all amaze *1847–8*.

vi *313* ∧ *4*] 'What! in our time of glory when the cause
Now stands up, first, a trophied pillar–now
So clipt, so stinted in our triumph–barred
Even from our free heart-thanks, and every way
Thwarted and vext, and lastly catechised
By our own creature! one that made our laws!
Our great she-Solon! her that built the nest
To hatch the cuckoo! whom we called our friend!
But we will crush the lie that glances at us
As cloaking in the larger charities
Some baby predilection: all amazed!
We must amaze this legislator more. *1847–8*

vi *321* ∧ *2*] Go, help the half-brained dwarf, Society,
To find low motives unto noble deeds,
To fix all doubt upon the darker side;
Go, fitter thou for narrowest neighbourhoods,
Old talker, haunt where gossip breeds and seethes

She turned; the very nape of her white neck
Was rosed with indignation: but the Prince
Her brother came; the king her father charmed
Her wounded soul with words: nor did mine own
Refuse her proffer, lastly gave his hand.

Then us they lifted up, dead weights, and bare
Straight to the doors: to them the doors gave way
Groaning, and in the Vestal entry shrieked
The virgin marble under iron heels:
And on they moved and gained the hall, and there
Rested: but great the crush was, and each base,
To left and right, of those tall columns drowned
In silken fluctuation and the swarm
Of female whisperers: at the further end
Was Ida by the throne, the two great cats
Close by her, like supporters on a shield,
Bow-backed with fear: but in the centre stood
The common men with rolling eyes; amazed
They glared upon the women, and aghast
The women stared at these, all silent, save
When armour clashed or jingled, while the day,
Descending, struck athwart the hall, and shot
A flying splendour out of brass and steel,
That o'er the statues leapt from head to head,
Now fired an angry Pallas on the helm,
Now set a wrathful Dian's moon on flame,
And now and then an echo started up,
And shuddering fled from room to room, and died
Of fright in far apartments.
Then the voice
Of Ida sounded, issuing ordinance:
And me they bore up the broad stairs, and through
The long-laid galleries past a hundred doors
To one deep chamber shut from sound, and due

And festers in provincial sloth: and, you,
That think we sought to practise on a life
Risked for our own and trusted to our hands,
What say you, Sir? you hear us: deem ye not
'Tis all too like that even now we scheme,
In one broad death confounding friend and foe,
To drug them all? revolve it: you are man,
And therefore no doubt wise; but after this *1847–8*

Cp. *In Memoriam* xxi 8 $_\wedge$ 9, MS: 'to find / Low motives for a noble deed.'
vi *332. on they moved*] *1850*; they moved on *1847–8*.

To languid limbs and sickness; left me in it;
And others otherwhere they laid; and all
That afternoon a sound arose of hoof
And chariot, many a maiden passing home
Till happier times; but some were left of those
Held sagest, and the great lords out and in,
From those two hosts that lay beside the walls,
Walked at their will, and everything was changed.

[VI ∧ VII]

Ask me no more: the moon may draw the sea;
The cloud may stoop from heaven and take the shape
With fold to fold, of mountain or of cape;
But O too fond, when have I answered thee?
Ask me no more.

Ask me no more: what answer should I give?
I love not hollow cheek or faded eye:
Yet, O my friend, I will not have thee die!
Ask me no more, lest I should bid thee live;
Ask me no more.

Ask me no more: thy fate and mine are sealed:
I strove against the stream and all in vain:
Let the great river take me to the main:
No more, dear love, for at a touch I yield;
Ask me no more.

VII

So was their sanctuary violated,
So their fair college turned to hospital;

vi ∧ vii Written 1849, added *1850*. Cp. Thomas Carew's *Song*, of which each stanza begins 'Aske me no more': 'Aske me no more where Jove bestowes, / When June is past, the fading rose: / For in your beauties orient deepe, / These flowers as in their causes, sleepe. . . .'

vi ∧ vii *2. cloud . . . and*] chill gray cloud may stoop to *HnMS* (*HM 19486*).

vi ∧ vii *5 ∧ 6*] Ask me no more: it is not that I hate,
But I, shall I that cared not for thy bloom
Be captive to thy paleness and thy gloom?
Ask me no more or thou wilt seal thy fate;
Ask me no more. *HnMS*

vi ∧ vii *7–8*] It cannot be that I would have thee die.
My life were all too short for my reply. *HnMS*

vi ∧ vii *11. Ask . . . more*] What use to ask? *HnMS*.

vi ∧ vii *12. all*] strove *HnMS*. Cp. *Venus and Adonis* 772: 'And all in vain you strive against the stream'.

vi ∧ vii *13. take*] bear *HnMS*.

vi ∧ vii *14. No . . . love,*] But ask no more *HnMS*.

At first with all confusion: by and by
Sweet order lived again with other laws:
A kindlier influence reigned; and everywhere
Low voices with the ministering hand
Hung round the sick: the maidens came, they talked,
They sang, they read: till she not fair began
To gather light, and she that was, became
Her former beauty treble; and to and fro
With books, with flowers, with Angel offices,
Like creatures native unto gracious act,
And in their own clear element, they moved.

But sadness on the soul of Ida fell,
And hatred of her weakness, blent with shame.
Old studies failed; seldom she spoke: but oft
Clomb to the roofs, and gazed alone for hours
On that disastrous leaguer, swarms of men
Darkening her female field: void was her use,
And she as one that climbs a peak to gaze
O'er land and main, and sees a great black cloud
Drag inward from the deeps, a wall of night,
Blot out the slope of sea from verge to shore,
And suck the blinding splendour from the sand,
And quenching lake by lake and tarn by tarn
Expunge the world: so fared she gazing there;
So blackened all her world in secret, blank
And waste it seemed and vain; till down she came,
And found fair peace once more among the sick.

And twilight dawned; and morn by morn the lark
Shot up and shrilled in flickering gyres, but I
Lay silent in the muffled cage of life:
And twilight gloomed; and broader-grown the bowers
Drew the great night into themselves, and Heaven,
Star after star, arose and fell; but I,
Deeper than those weird doubts could reach me, lay
Quite sundered from the moving Universe,
Nor knew what eye was on me, nor the hand
That nursed me, more than infants in their sleep.

vii *19. void was her use*: her usual occupations neglected.
vii *36*] *1851; not 1847–50.*
vii *37. Quite*] *1851*; Lay *1847–50.*

But Psyche tended Florian: with her oft,
Melissa came; for Blanche had gone, but left
Her child among us, willing she should keep
Court-favour: here and there the small bright head,
A light of healing, glanced about the couch,
Or through the parted silks the tender face
Peeped, shining in upon the wounded man
With blush and smile, a medicine in themselves
To wile the length from languorous hours, and draw
The sting from pain; nor seemed it strange that soon
He rose up whole, and those fair charities
Joined at her side; nor stranger seemed that hearts
So gentle, so employed, should close in love,
Than when two dewdrops on the petal shake
To the same sweet air, and tremble deeper down,
And slip at once all-fragrant into one.

Less prosperously the second suit obtained
At first with Psyche. Not though Blanche had sworn
That after that dark night among the fields
She needs must wed him for her own good name;
Not though he built upon the babe restored;
Nor though she liked him, yielded she, but feared
To incense the Head once more; till on a day
When Cyril pleaded, Ida came behind
Seen but of Psyche: on her foot she hung
A moment, and she heard, at which her face
A little flushed, and she past on; but each
Assumed from thence a half-consent involved
In stillness, plighted troth, and were at peace.

Nor only these: Love in the sacred halls
Held carnival at will, and flying struck
With showers of random sweet on maid and man.
Nor did her father cease to press my claim,
Nor did mine own, now reconciled; nor yet
Did those twin-brothers, risen again and whole;
Nor Arac, satiate with his victory.

But I lay still, and with me oft she sat:
Then came a change; for sometimes I would catch

vii *56. obtained*: 'prevailed' (T.).
vii *60. upon the babe restored*] *1850*; on what she said of the child *1847–8*. Cp. T.'s Latinism with *Comus* 48: 'After the Tuscan Mariners transform'd'.
vii *61. yielded she*] *1850*; would she yield *1847–8*.

Her hand in wild delirium, gripe it hard,
And fling it like a viper off, and shriek
'You are not Ida;' clasp it once again,
And call her Ida, though I knew her not,
And call her sweet, as if in irony,
And call her hard and cold which seemed a truth:
And still she feared that I should lose my mind,
And often she believed that I should die:
Till out of long frustration of her care,
And pensive tendance in the all-weary noons,
And watches in the dead, the dark, when clocks
Throbbed thunder through the palace floors, or called
On flying Time from all their silver tongues–
And out of memories of her kindlier days,
And sidelong glances at my father's grief,
And at the happy lovers heart in heart–
And out of hauntings of my spoken love,
And lonely listenings to my muttered dream,
And often feeling of the helpless hands,
And wordless broodings on the wasted cheek–
From all a closer interest flourished up,
Tenderness touch by touch, and last, to these,
Love, like an Alpine harebell hung with tears
By some cold morning glacier; frail at first
And feeble, all unconscious of itself,
But such as gathered colour day by day.

Last I woke sane, but well-nigh close to death
For weakness: it was evening: silent light
Slept on the painted walls, wherein were wrought
Two grand designs; for on one side arose
The women up in wild revolt, and stormed
At the Oppian law. Titanic shapes, they crammed
The forum, and half-crushed among the rest
A dwarf-like Cato cowered. On the other side

vii *89.* Cp. *Semele* 19: 'To throbbings of the thunderous gong'.

vii *90.* Cp. *Amy* 5: 'The silver tongues of featherfooted rumour'.

vii *109.* 'When Hannibal was nearing Rome a law was carried by C. Oppius, Trib. Pleb., B.C. 215, forbidding women to wear more than half an ounce of gold, or brilliant dresses, and no woman was to come within a mile of Rome or of any town save on account of public sacrifices in a conveyance drawn by horses' (T.). H.T. adds: 'In B.C. 195 the Oppian Law was, in spite of Cato's protests, repealed. Livy xxxiv 8.'

vii *111. dwarf-like*] *1850*; little *1847–8*.

Hortensia spoke against the tax; behind,
A train of dames: by axe and eagle sat,
With all their foreheads drawn in Roman scowls,
And half the wolf's-milk curdled in their veins,
The fierce triumvirs; and before them paused
Hortensia pleading: angry was her face.

I saw the forms: I knew not where I was:
They did but look like hollow shows; nor more
Sweet Ida: palm to palm she sat: the dew
Dwelt in her eyes, and softer all her shape
And rounder seemed: I moved: I sighed: a touch
Came round my wrist, and tears upon my hand:
Then all for languor and self-pity ran
Mine down my face, and with what life I had,
And like a flower that cannot all unfold,
So drenched it is with tempest, to the sun,
Yet, as it may, turns toward him, I on her
Fixt my faint eyes, and uttered whisperingly:

'If you be, what I think you, some sweet dream,
I would but ask you to fulfil yourself:
But if you be that Ida whom I knew,
I ask you nothing: only, if a dream,
Sweet dream, be perfect. I shall die tonight.
Stoop down and seem to kiss me ere I die.'

I could no more, but lay like one in trance,
That hears his burial talked of by his friends,
And cannot speak, nor move, nor make one sign,
But lies and dreads his doom. She turned; she paused;
She stooped; and out of languor leapt a cry;
Leapt fiery Passion from the brinks of death;

vii *112. Hortensia*: 'she pleaded against the proposed tax on Roman matrons after the assassination of Julius Caesar which was to be raised in order to pay for the expenses of the war against Brutus and Cassius' (H.T.).
vii *119*] *1854*; Sad [Strange *1850*] phantoms conjured out of circumstance,
Ghosts of the fading brain, they seemed; nor more *1847–50*;
They did but seem as hollow shows; nor more *1851–3*.
vii *122. seemed*] *1854*; showed *1847–53*.
vii *140*] *1850*; She stooped; and with a great shock of the heart
Our mouths met: out of languor leapt a cry, *1847–8*
vii *141*] *1850*; Crowned [Leapt *1848*] Passion from the brinks of death and up *1847–8*. A review had objected to the rhythm (Shannon, p. 120).

And I believed that in the living world
My spirit closed with Ida's at the lips;
Till back I fell, and from mine arms she rose
Glowing all over noble shame; and all
Her falser self slipt from her like a robe,
And left her woman, lovelier in her mood
Than in her mould that other, when she came
From barren deeps to conquer all with love;
And down the streaming crystal dropt; and she
Far-fleeted by the purple island-sides,
Naked, a double light in air and wave,
To meet her Graces, where they decked her out
For worship without end; nor end of mine,
Stateliest, for thee! but mute she glided forth,
Nor glanced behind her, and I sank and slept,
Filled through and through with Love, a happy
        sleep.

  Deep in the night I woke: she, near me, held
A volume of the Poets of her land:
There to herself, all in low tones, she read.

  'Now sleeps the crimson petal, now the white;
Nor waves the cypress in the palace walk;
Nor winks the gold fin in the porphyry font:
The fire-fly wakens: waken thou with me.

  Now droops the milkwhite peacock like a ghost,
And like a ghost she glimmers on to me.

---

vii *142*] *1851; not 1847–50.*

vii *143*] *1850*; Along the shuddering senses struck the soul,
And closed on fire with Ida's at the lips; *1847–8*

vii *147–8*. 'Aphrodite passed before his brain, drowsy with weakness' (T.). The lines that follow refer to Aphrodite's rising from the sea.

vii *150*. *the streaming crystal*: *The Palace of Art* 120 ∧ 21, *1832* text.

vii *161–74*. This song draws on eastern sources; the best summary is by Killham (pp. 219–20). The form is that of a ghazal–'the requisite number of couplets, the repetition of a single final word at short intervals to produce what is tantamount to rhyme, and . . . the standard images and ornaments of the Persian love poem, roses, lilies, peacocks, the stars, the cypress'. T. probably learnt of the ghazal from the works of Sir William Jones (*Lincoln*). On the controversy as to how much Persian T. knew (listed in Killham), there should be added T.'s own jotting: 'I don't read Persian' (C. Ricks, *ELN* iv (1966) 46– ).

vii *165*. Cp. *The Day-Dream: The Sleeping Palace* 15, where droops 'The

Now lies the Earth all Danaë to the stars,
And all thy heart lies open unto me.

Now slides the silent meteor on, and leaves
A shining furrow, as thy thoughts in me.

Now folds the lily all her sweetness up,
And slips into the bosom of the lake:
So fold thyself, my dearest, thou, and slip
Into my bosom and be lost in me.'

I heard her turn the page; she found a small
Sweet Idyl, and once more, as low, she read:

'Come down, O maid, from yonder mountain height:
What pleasure lives in height (the shepherd sang)
In height and cold, the splendour of the hills?
But cease to move so near the Heavens, and cease
To glide a sunbeam by the blasted Pine,
To sit a star upon the sparkling spire;
And come, for Love is of the valley, come,
For Love is of the valley, come thou down
And find him; by the happy threshold, he,
Or hand in hand with Plenty in the maize,
Or red with spirted purple of the vats,
Or foxlike in the vine; nor cares to walk

---

peacock in his laurel bower', the setting that of the urns and the lake. There too a prince enters to rescue a princess.

vii *167*. 'Zeus came down to Danaë when shut up in the tower in a shower of golden stars' (T.). J. H. Buckley (p. 269) suggests that T. may have been inspired by a memory of Arthur Hallam's last letter to him, 6 Sept. 1833 (*Mem.* i 104): 'and oh Alfred such Titians! by Heaven, that man could paint! I wish you could see his Danaë. Do you just write as perfect a Danaë!'

vii *170*. Cp. *A Dream of Fair Women, 1832* opening: 'my deepfurrowed thought'.

vii *177–207*. '*Come down, O maid* is said to be taken from Theocritus, but there is no real likeness except perhaps in the Greek Idyllic feeling' (T.). H.T. adds: 'For simple rhythm and vowel music my father considered this Idyllic song, written in Switzerland–chiefly at Lauterbrunnen and Grindelwald–and descriptive of the waste Alpine heights and gorges and of the sweet rich valleys below, as among his most successful work.'

vii *188*. *Song of Solomon* ii 15, 'Take us the foxes, the little foxes, that spoil the vines; for our vines have tender grapes.' *walk*: H.T. compares *Hamlet* I i 166–7: 'But look, the morn in russet mantle clad / Walks o'er the dew of yon high eastward hill.'

With Death and Morning on the silver horns,
Nor wilt thou snare him in the white ravine,
Nor find him dropt upon the firths of ice,
That huddling slant in furrow-cloven falls
To roll the torrent out of dusky doors:
But follow; let the torrent dance thee down
To find him in the valley; let the wild
Lean-headed Eagles yelp alone, and leave
The monstrous ledges there to slope, and spill
Their thousand wreaths of dangling water-smoke,
That like a broken purpose waste in air:
So waste not thou; but come; for all the vales
Await thee; azure pillars of the hearth
Arise to thee; the children call, and I
Thy shepherd pipe, and sweet is every sound,
Sweeter thy voice, but every sound is sweet;
Myriads of rivulets hurrying through the lawn,
The moan of doves in immemorial elms,
And murmuring of innumerable bees.'

So she low-toned; while with shut eyes I lay
Listening; then looked. Pale was the perfect face;

vii *189. silver horns*] *1854*; Silver Horns *1847–53*. A letter by T. (of which H.T. was sent a copy in 1920) says: 'simply the snowy peaks–you know there is a Silbernhorn in Switzerland so called from its beautifully shaped snow peak'. John Churton Collins had noticed this, and pointed to a suggestion of Diana's crescent. 'Death is the lifelessness on the high snow peaks' (T.).

vii *192.* Cp. *Comus* 495: 'the huddling brook'.

vii *193.* 'The opening of the gorge is called dusky as a contrast with the snows all about' (T.).

vii *196–7.* Cp. Theocritus xi, the apostrophe of Polyphemus to Galatea–e.g. l. 42: 'O leave it be, the blue blue sea, to gasp an't will o' the shore'.

vii *199.* Cp. John Armstrong's *Art of Preserving Health* (1744, *Lincoln*) ii 427–8: 'The virgin stream / In boiling wastes its finer soul in air'. Also Sir William Jones (whose works, too, are at *Lincoln*), *The Palace of Fortune*: 'To catch each rising wish, each ardent prayer, / And some to grant, and some to waste in air.' *broken purpose*: see vi 178*n*.

vii *201.* Cp. Ovid, *Pontic Epistles* I iii 33–4, on Ulysses: *non dubia est Ithaci prudentia, sed tamen optat / fumum de patriis posse videre focis.* ('None doubt the Ithacan's wisdom, but yet he prays that he may see the smoke from his native hearth.')

vii *205–7.* Cp. *Sense and Conscience* 46–9: 'hum of murmurous bees . . . moan of waterfalls . . . voice of doves'.

vii *207.* T. compares Virgil, *Eclogues* i 58: *nec gemere aëria cessabit turtur ab ulmo.*

The bosom with long sighs laboured; and meek
Seemed the full lips, and mild the luminous eyes,
And the voice trembled and the hand. She said
Brokenly, that she knew it, she had failed
In sweet humility; had failed in all;
That all her labour was but as a block
Left in the quarry; but she still were loth,
She still were loth to yield herself to one
That wholly scorned to help their equal rights
Against the sons of men, and barbarous laws.
She prayed me not to judge their cause from her
That wronged it, sought far less for truth than power
In knowledge: something wild within her breast,
A greater than all knowledge, beat her down.
And she had nursed me there from week to week:
Much had she learnt in little time. In part
It was ill counsel had misled the girl
To vex true hearts: yet was she but a girl–
'Ah fool, and made myself a Queen of farce!
When comes another such? never, I think,
Till the Sun drop, dead, from the signs.'
Her voice
Choked, and her forehead sank upon her hands,
And her great heart through all the faultful Past
Went sorrowing in a pause I dared not break;
Till notice of a change in the dark world
Was lispt about the acacias, and a bird,
That early woke to feed her little ones,
Sent from a dewy breast a cry for light:
She moved, and at her feet the volume fell.

'Blame not thyself too much,' I said, 'nor blame
Too much the sons of men and barbarous laws;
These were the rough ways of the world till now.
Henceforth thou hast a helper, me, that know
The woman's cause is man's: they rise or sink

vii *229–30*] To lapse so far from sweet humility
The mother of all virtues, to desire
Knowledge for power, power more than truth!
When comes another such? Never I think
Till the last fire shall catch and flap from peak
To peak across the world, and the sun hang
Dead in the signs. *H.Nbk 25*

Together, dwarfed or godlike, bond or free:
For she that out of Lethe scales with man
The shining steps of Nature, shares with man
His nights, his days, moves with him to one goal,
Stays all the fair young planet in her hands–
If she be small, slight-natured, miserable,
How shall men grow? but work no more alone!
Our place is much: as far as in us lies
We two will serve them both in aiding her–
Will clear away the parasitic forms
That seem to keep her up but drag her down–
Will leave her space to burgeon out of all
Within her–let her make herself her own
To give or keep, to live and learn and be
All that not harms distinctive womanhood.
For woman is not undevelopt man,
But diverse: could we make her as the man,
Sweet Love were slain: his dearest bond is this,
Not like to like, but like in difference.
Yet in the long years liker must they grow;
The man be more of woman, she of man;

vii *244.* Cp. *1 Corinthians* xii 13, 'whether we be Jews or Gentiles, whether we be bond or free'.

vii *249–50.* Killham (pp. 262–5) quotes from Robert Chambers's *Vestiges of Creation* 'two passages . . . which have a direct bearing upon feminism. The first discusses in general terms the evils present in keeping classes of societies in an unjust subordination; the other takes this much further by stating as an indisputable fact that if women suffer weak health or misery, they may fail to transmit acquired characteristics to their children, and the whole society will in time revert to a lower condition.'

vii *250–3*] *1850*; How shall men grow? We two will serve them both
In aiding her, strip off, as in us lies,
(Our place is much) the parasitic forms *1847–8*

vii *255. space . . . all*] *1850*; field to burgeon and to bloom *1847–8.*

vii *256*] *1850*; From all within her, make herself her own *1847–8.*

vii *261. : his*] *1850*; , whose *1847–8.*

vii *264.* Cp. a draft by T.

And if aught be comprising in itself
The man, the woman, let it sit [apart]
Godlike, alone, or only rapt on heaven–
What need for such to wed? or if there be
Men-women, let them wed with women-men
And make a proper marriage. *H.Nbk 25*

Quoted by Sir Charles Tennyson, *Nineteenth Century* cix (1931) 633. Cp. *On One who Affected an Effeminate Manner* (p. 1424), and *Locksley Hall Sixty Years After* 48*n* (p. 1361).

He gain in sweetness and in moral height,
Nor lose the wrestling thews that throw the world;
She mental breadth, nor fail in childward care,
Nor lose the childlike in the larger mind;
Till at the last she set herself to man,
Like perfect music unto noble words;
And so these twain, upon the skirts of Time,
Sit side by side, full-summed in all their powers,
Dispensing harvest, sowing the To-be,
Self-reverent each and reverencing each,
Distinct in individualities,
But like each other even as those who love.
Then comes the statelier Eden back to men:
Then reign the world's great bridals, chaste and calm:
Then springs the crowning race of humankind.
May these things be!'
Sighing she spoke 'I fear
They will not.'
'Dear, but let us type them now
In our own lives, and this proud watchword rest
Of equal; seeing either sex alone
Is half itself, and in true marriage lies
Nor equal, nor unequal: each fulfils
Defect in each, and always thought in thought,
Purpose in purpose, will in will, they grow,
The single pure and perfect animal,
The two-celled heart beating, with one full stroke,
Life.'
And again sighing she spoke: 'A dream
That once was mine! what woman taught you this?'

'Alone,' I said, 'from earlier than I know,
Immersed in rich foreshadowings of the world,
I loved the woman: he, that doth not, lives
A drowning life, besotted in sweet self,
Or pines in sad experience worse than death,

vii *268*] *1850*; More as the double-natured Poet each: *1847–8*.
vii *272*. Cp. *Paradise Regained* i 14–15: 'With prosperous wing full summ'd to tell of deeds / Above Heroic'.
vii *275*. Killham (p. 260) points out that this line was originally written as *The Ante-Chamber* 27 in *Heath MS*, but that H.T. dropped it in *Mem*. i 199. (*Mat*. i 243 had included it.)
vii *282*. *rest*: be no more mentioned (H.T. in Wallace's edition, 1891, *Lincoln*).

Or keeps his winged affections clipt with crime:
Yet was there one through whom I loved her, one
Not learnèd, save in gracious household ways,
Not perfect, nay, but full of tender wants,
No Angel, but a dearer being, all dipt
In Angel instincts, breathing Paradise,
Interpreter between the Gods and men,
Who looked all native to her place, and yet
On tiptoe seemed to touch upon a sphere
Too gross to tread, and all male minds perforce
Swayed to her from their orbits as they moved,
And girdled her with music. Happy he
With such a mother! faith in womankind
Beats with his blood, and trust in all things high
Comes easy to him, and though he trip and fall
He shall not blind his soul with clay.'

'But I,'
Said Ida, tremulously, 'so all unlike–
It seems you love to cheat yourself with words:
This mother is your model. I have heard
Of your strange doubts: they well might be: I seem
A mockery to my own self. Never, Prince;
You cannot love me.'

'Nay but thee' I said
'From yearlong poring on thy pictured eyes,
Ere seen I loved, and loved thee seen, and saw
Thee woman through the crust of iron moods
That masked thee from men's reverence up, and forced
Sweet love on pranks of saucy boyhood: now,
Given back to life, to life indeed, through thee,
Indeed I love: the new day comes, the light
Dearer for night, as dearer thou for faults
Lived over: lift thine eyes; my doubts are dead,
My haunting sense of hollow shows: the change,
This truthful change in thee has killed it. Dear,
Look up, and let thy nature strike on mine,
Like yonder morning on the blind half-world;
Approach and fear not; breathe upon my brows;
In that fine air I tremble, all the past

vii *313. tremulously,'*] *1850*; 'so unlike, *1847–8.*
vii *315–7. I . . . self*] *1851; not 1847–50.*
vii *319* ^ *20*] Or some mysterious or magnetic touch, *1847–8.*
vii *327–9. my . . . Dear*] *1851*; doubt me no more *1847–50.* 'You have become a real woman to me' (T.).

Melts mist-like into this bright hour, and this
Is morn to more, and all the rich to-come
Reels, as the golden Autumn woodland reels
Athwart the smoke of burning weeds. Forgive me,
I waste my heart in signs: let be. My bride,
My wife, my life. O we will walk this world,
Yoked in all exercise of noble end,
And so through those dark gates across the wild
That no man knows. Indeed I love thee: come,
Yield thyself up: my hopes and thine are one:
Accomplish thou my manhood and thyself;
Lay thy sweet hands in mine and trust to me.'

## CONCLUSION

So closed our tale, of which I give you all
The random scheme as wildly as it rose:
The words are mostly mine; for when we ceased
There came a minute's pause, and Walter said,
'I wish she had not yielded!' then to me,
'What, if you drest it up poetically?'
So prayed the men, the women: I gave assent:
Yet how to bind the scattered scheme of seven
Together in one sheaf? What style could suit?
The men required that I should give throughout
The sort of mock-heroic gigantesque,
With which we bantered little Lilia first:

vii *335. Is . . . more*] *1851*; I scarce believe *1847–50*.
vii *335–7*. Adapted from *In Memoriam: Epilogue* 96 ∧ 7, MS (p. 985).
vii *337. weeds*] *1851*; flowers *1847–8*; leaves *1850*.

*Conclusion*
*c 1–35*] *1850*; Here closed our compound story which at first
Had only [Perhaps, but *1848*] meant to banter little maids
With mock-heroics and with parody:
But slipt in some strange way, crost with burlesque,
From mock to earnest, even into tones
Of tragic, and with less and less of jest
To such a serious end that Lilia fixt
A showery glance upon her Aunt and said
'You–tell us what we are;' who there began
A treatise, growing with it, and might have flowed
In axiom worthier to be graven on rock,
Than all that lasts of old-world hieroglyph,
Or lichen-fretted Rune and arrowhead; *1847–8*

The women–and perhaps they felt their power,
For something in the ballads which they sang,
Or in their silent influence as they sat,
Had ever seemed to wrestle with burlesque,
And drove us, last, to quite a solemn close–
They hated banter, wished for something real,
A gallant fight, a noble princess–why
Not make her true-heroic–true-sublime?
Or all, they said, as earnest as the close?
Which yet with such a framework scarce could be.
Then rose a little feud betwixt the two,
Betwixt the mockers and the realists:
And I, betwixt them both, to please them both,
And yet to give the story as it rose,
I moved as in a strange diagonal,
And maybe neither pleased myself nor them.

But Lilia pleased me, for she took no part
In our dispute: the sequel of the tale
Had touched her; and she sat, she plucked the grass,
She flung it from her, thinking: last, she fixt
A showery glance upon her aunt, and said,
'You–tell us what we are' who might have told,
For she was crammed with theories out of books,
But that there rose a shout: the gates were closed
At sunset, and the crowd were swarming now,
To take their leave, about the garden rails.

So I and some went out to these: we climbed
The slope to Vivian-place, and turning saw
The happy valleys, half in light, and half
Far-shadowing from the west, a land of peace;
Gray halls alone among their massive groves;
Trim hamlets; here and there a rustic tower
Half-lost in belts of hop and breadths of wheat;
The shimmering glimpses of a stream; the seas;
A red sail, or a white; and far beyond,
Imagined more than seen, the skirts of France.

*c 27.* In the proofs of Wallace's edition (1891, *Lincoln*), T. deleted 'perhaps' in the note: 'The expression was perhaps suggested by the principle of the Parallelogram of Forces.'

*c 37. sunset*] *1850*; sundown *1847–8*.

*c 39*] *1850*; And I and some went out, and mingled with them. *1847–8*.

*c 40–80*] *1850* (*except l. 65*); *not 1847–8*. 'Written just after the disturbances in France, February 1848, when Louis Philippe was compelled to abdicate' (T.).

'Look there, a garden!' said my college friend,
The Tory member's elder son, 'and there!
God bless the narrow sea which keeps her off,
And keeps our Britain, whole within herself,
A nation yet, the rulers and the ruled–
Some sense of duty, something of a faith,
Some reverence for the laws ourselves have made,
Some patient force to change them when we will,
Some civic manhood firm against the crowd–
But yonder, whiff! there comes a sudden heat,
The gravest citizen seems to lose his head,
The king is scared, the soldier will not fight,
The little boys begin to shoot and stab,
A kingdom topples over with a shriek
Like an old woman, and down rolls the world
In mock heroics stranger than our own;
Revolts, republics, revolutions, most
No graver than a schoolboys' barring out;
Too comic for the solemn things they are,
Too solemn for the comic touches in them,
Like our wild Princess with as wise a dream
As some of theirs–God bless the narrow seas!
I wish they were a whole Atlantic broad.'

'Have patience,' I replied, 'ourselves are full
Of social wrong; and maybe wildest dreams
Are but the needful preludes of the truth:
For me, the genial day, the happy crowd,
The sport half-science, fill me with a faith.
This fine old world of ours is but a child
Yet in the go-cart. Patience! Give it time
To learn its limbs: there is a hand that guides.'

In such discourse we gained the garden rails,
And there we saw Sir Walter where he stood,
Before a tower of crimson holly-hoaks,
Among six boys, head under head, and looked
No little lily-handed Baronet he,
A great broad-shouldered genial Englishman,
A lord of fat prize-oxen and of sheep,
A raiser of huge melons and of pine,
A patron of some thirty charities,

*c 65. most*] *1853*; all *1850–51*.
*c 84.* 'An imaginary character' (T.).
*c 87. pine*: 'pine-apple' (T.).

A pamphleteer on guano and on grain,
A quarter-sessions chairman, abler none;
Fair-haired and redder than a windy morn;
Now shaking hands with him, now him, of those
That stood the nearest–now addressed to speech–
Who spoke few words and pithy, such as closed
Welcome, farewell, and welcome for the year
To follow: a shout rose again, and made
The long line of the approaching rookery swerve
From the elms, and shook the branches of the deer
From slope to slope through distant ferns, and rang
Beyond the bourn of sunset; O, a shout
More joyful than the city-roar that hails
Premier or king! Why should not these great Sirs
Give up their parks some dozen times a year
To let the people breathe? So thrice they cried,
I likewise, and in groups they streamed away.

But we went back to the Abbey, and sat on,
So much the gathering darkness charmed: we sat
But spoke not, rapt in nameless reverie,
Perchance upon the future man: the walls
Blackened about us, bats wheeled, and owls whooped,
And gradually the powers of the night,
That range above the region of the wind,
Deepening the courts of twilight broke them up
Through all the silent spaces of the worlds,
Beyond all thought into the Heaven of Heavens.

Last little Lilia, rising quietly,
Disrobed the glimmering statue of Sir Ralph
From those rich silks, and home well-pleased we went.

c 96. *rose*] *1850*; arose *1847–8*.
c 102. *should not*] *1850*; don't *1847–8*. *great*] *1850*; acred *1847–8*.
c 103. *Give*] *1850*; Throw *1847–8*.
c 104. *To*] *1850*; And *1847–8*.
c 108. *But spoke not*] *1850*; Saying little *1847–8*.
c 111–5. Incorporated verbatim from *The Lover's Tale* i 52–61*n*, MS (p. 303).
c 115. *the Heaven of Heavens*: *Nehemiah* ix 6.
c 116. *quietly*] *1850*; without sound *1847–8*.

# 287 *'Because she bore the iron name'

Printed *Daily News*, 27 Jan. 1890; then in the Edition de Luxe (1898–9) of *Mem.* ii 19, as 'a *jeu d'esprit*'. It was for Katherine Bradshaw; T. sent it to her mother, in a letter from the Crown Hotel, Lyndhurst (a copy is at *Trinity College*). The letter apologizes for his depression, which perhaps confirms the date 1847 suggested by H.T.'s placing of the poem.

Because she bore the iron name
Of him who doomed the king to die,
I deemed her one of stately frame
And looks to awe the standers by,
But found a maiden tender, shy,
With fair blue eyes and winning sweet,
And longed to kiss her hand and lie
A thousand summers at her feet.

# 288 The Wanderer

Published *1892*. It is not in an early trial edition (*Lincoln*) of *1892*. T. sent the poem to Mrs Bradshaw, in a letter (?1847) of which there is a copy at *Trinity College*, together with *Because she bore* (above). The present poem, without a title, is introduced: 'I send you the lines which should have gone into the Album. I cannot say that I like them much myself: they are too morbid but as I promised them here they are'. Below the poem, T. added: 'These are lines I made at your picnic when I seemed so sulky'. All variants are below. Cp. *The Dying Man to His Friend* (*1827*, p. 153).

The gleam of household sunshine ends,
And here no longer can I rest;
Farewell!–You will not speak, my friends,
Unfriendly of your parted guest.

¶ 287.*1–2*. Her ancestor was John Bradshaw, president of the court which condemned Charles I.

*2. the*] his *1890*.
*3. stately*] harsher *1890*.
*4. to . . . by*] that awe the passer-by *1890*.
*6. winning*] passing *1890*.
*7. hand*] hands *1890*.

¶ 288.*1–4*] Farewell, true hearts, with whom I felt
That mine might have one hour of rest!
Farewell, dear maids, whose eyes have dwelt
With kindness on the passing guest! *T.MS*

O well for him that finds a friend,
Or makes a friend where'er he come,
And loves the world from end to end,
And wanders on from home to home!

O happy he, and fit to live,
On whom a happy home has power
To make him trust his life, and give
His fealty to the halcyon hour!

I count you kind, I hold you true;
But what may follow who can tell?
Give me a hand–and you–and you–
And deem me grateful, and farewell!

# 289 To —, After Reading a Life and Letters

Published *The Examiner*, 24 March 1849, as *Stanzas To–*; then *Poems*, 6th edn (1850). The epigraph appeared in 1850; the final title in 1853. H.T. says: 'My father was indignant that Keats' wild love-letters should have been published; but he said he did not wish the public to think that this poem had been written with any particular reference to *Letters and Literary Remains of Keats* (published in 1848), by Lord Houghton.' Since Houghton (Richard Monckton Milnes) was a friend of his, T. wished to veil the poem; it seems very likely that Houghton's publication (Aug. 1848) precipitated the poem. But W. M. Rossetti reports T. as saying it was 'written in a fit of intense disgust after reading Medwin's book about Byron' (*Rossetti Papers*, 1903, p. 239). Since Thomas Medwin's *Journal of the Conversations of Byron* was published in 1824, and is not strictly a Life and Letters, it would not have been more than one of the books that T. had in mind. All his life T. profoundly disliked inquisitive biography: 'What business has the public to want to know all about Byron's wildnesses?' (*Mem.* ii 165). Cp. *Come hither* (p. 152) and *The Dead Prophet* (p. 1322). Many guesses have

5. *well for him*] happy he *MS.*
7. *And*] Who *MS.*
*9–12*]
But such sweet days are mine no more;
A sailor in a stormy sky,
I see the peaceful light on shore,
And the wild tempest whirls me by. *MS*
*Y.MS includes these MS lines followed by the published ll. 9–12.*
*13–14*]
Not less, I count you kind and true;
I prize you more than I can tell. *MS*
*16*] And once again–and so farewell. *MS.*

been made as to the identity of the person addressed: Charles Tennyson Turner (according to T. J. Wise); John Sterling (F. M. Brookfield, *The Cambridge 'Apostles'*, 1906, p. 300); James Spedding (Una Taylor, *Guests and Memories*, 1924, p. 195). T. told F. T. Palgrave that it was to 'an ideal Friend' (note in *Poems*, 1853, *British Museum*).

'Cursed be he that moves my bones.'
*Shakespeare's Epitaph*

You might have won the Poet's name,
If such be worth the winning now,
And gained a laurel for your brow
Of sounder leaf than I can claim;

But you have made the wiser choice,
A life that moves to gracious ends
Through troops of unrecording friends,
A deedful life, a silent voice:

And you have missed the irreverent doom
Of those that wear the Poet's crown:
Hereafter, neither knave nor clown
Shall hold their orgies at your tomb.

For now the Poet cannot die,
Nor leave his music as of old,
But round him ere he scarce be cold
Begins the scandal and the cry:

'Proclaim the faults he would not show:
Break lock and seal: betray the trust:
Keep nothing sacred: 'tis but just
The many-headed beast should know.'

Ah shameless! for he did but sing
A song that pleased us from its worth;
No public life was his on earth,
No blazoned statesman he, nor king.

He gave the people of his best:
His worst he kept, his best he gave.
My Shakespeare's curse on clown and knave
Who will not let his ashes rest!

¶ 289. *6.* 'gracious end', Pope, *Essay on Man* i 141.
*17. Proclaim*] *1850*; Give out *1849*.
*20. many-headed beast*: Pope, *Imitations of Horace: Epistles* I i 121 (a commonplace after Horace).
*27. My . . . on*] *1853*; My curse upon the *1849–51*.

Who make it seem more sweet to be
The little life of bank and brier,
The bird that pipes his lone desire
And dies unheard within his tree,

Than he that warbles long and loud
And drops at Glory's temple-gates,
For whom the carrion vulture waits
To tear his heart before the crowd!

## 290 *The Losing of the Child

Printed *Eversley* iv 242–3, as one of the (unadopted) songs to be added to *The Princess*. (*Mem.* i 255 printed ll. 1–9 only.) T. wrote them in April 1849, for the 3rd edition, 1850 (*Mem.* ii 486). Others that he did not use are *Child-Songs* (p. 852), *The Tourney* (p. 850), *The Baby Boy* (p. 851), and *The Little Lady* (p. 851). 'The first song I wrote was named *The Losing of the Child*. The child is sitting on the bank of the river and playing with flowers; a flood comes down; a dam has been broken through–the child is borne down by the flood; the whole village distracted; after a time the flood has subsided; the child is thrown safe and sound again upon the bank; and there is a chorus of jubilant women.' These songs were to emphasize the importance of the child in *The Princess*.

The child was sitting on the bank
Upon a stormy day.
He loved the river's roaring sound;
The river rose and burst his bound,
Flooded fifty leagues around,
Took the child from off the ground,
And bore the child away.
O the child so meek and wise,
Who made us wise and mild!
All was strife at home about him,
Nothing could be done without him;
Father, mother, sister, brother,
All accusing one another;
O to lose the child!

*29. seem more sweet*] *1850*; sweeter seem *1849*.

*30–2.* The dying birds in Pope's *Windsor Forest* 134 'leave their little Lives in Air'.

*35–6.* The germ of *The Dead Prophet*: 'Then glided a vulturous Beldam forth . . .'

The river left the child unhurt,
But far within the wild.
Then we brought him home again,
Peace and order come again,
The river sought his bound again,
The child was lost and found again,
And we will keep the child.

# 291 The Sailor Boy

Published in Adelaide Anne Procter's and E. Faithfull's *The Victoria Regia* (1861); then *1864*. It was written by April 1849, when T. thought of using it as one of the intercalated songs in *The Princess* (MS, *University Library, Cambridge*). A. A. Procter had requested a contribution, and she asked, via Julia Cameron, for a title: 'I do not like to put "Lines" only' (*Lincoln*).

He rose at dawn and, fired with hope,
Shot o'er the seething harbour-bar,
And reached the ship and caught the rope,
And whistled to the morning star.

And while he whistled long and loud
He heard a fierce mermaiden cry,
'O boy, though thou art young and proud,
I see the place where thou wilt lie.

'The sands and yeasty surges mix
In caves about the dreary bay,
And on thy ribs the limpet sticks,
And in thy heart the scrawl shall play.'

¶ 291.*1*] He rose and flushed with fiery hope *HnMS 1st reading, then as 1864*. *fired*] *1864*; flushed *1861*.
*2*] Past the foaming harbour-bar, *MS 1st reading*.
*3. And reached*] Reached *MS 1st reading*.
*5*] And suddenly as he whistled loud *MS 1st reading*. *he . . . and*] *1864*; on deck he whistled *1861*.
*6. He heard*] Heard *MS 1st reading*.
*7. O*] *1864; not 1861*.
*9. yeasty surges*: *The Lover's Tale* iii 53, *1868* text, had 'yeasty surge'. Cp. *Timbuctoo* 15: 'yeasty waves', and *The Devil and the Lady* I i 73: 'yeasty wave'; from *Macbeth* IV i 53.
*12. scrawl*: T. says 'the young of the dog-crab', apparently quoting from J. O. Halliwell's *Dictionary of Archaic and Provincial Words* (1847).

'Fool,' he answered, 'death is sure
To those that stay and those that roam,
But I will nevermore endure
To sit with empty hands at home.

'My mother clings about my neck,
My sisters crying, "Stay for shame;"
My father raves of death and wreck,
They are all to blame, they are all to blame.

'God help me! save I take my part
Of danger on the roaring sea,
A devil rises in my heart,
Far worse than any death to me.'

# 292 The Tourney

Published *1892*. 'Rejected from the songs of *The Princess*' (H.T.). Written 1849; drafts of it are in the MS in *University Library, Cambridge* (which may not be quoted). *Eversley* makes it clear that *The Tourney* was replaced by *Thy voice is heard through rolling drums*, *The Princess*, interlude iv ^ v. Sir Ralph is the ancestor whose statue appears in the Prologue and in this interlude.

Ralph would fight in Edith's sight,
For Ralph was Edith's lover,
Ralph went down like a fire to the fight,
Struck to the left and struck to the right,
Rolled them over and over.
'Gallant Sir Ralph,' said the king.

Casques were cracked and hauberks hacked,
Lances snapt in sunder,
Rang the stroke, and sprang the blood,
Knights were thwacked and riven, and hewed
Like broad oaks with thunder.
'O what an arm,' said the king.

*13. 'Fool,' he answered*] Bold his answer *MS 1st reading*; He answered fiercely *MS 2nd reading, then 1864*.

*17–20*] 'My mother weeps beside the fire,
My sisters still would clasp my neck;
Fiercely raves my agèd Sire,
Dreads the storm and fears the wreck. *MS 1st reading*

*18. crying*] *1864*; clamour *1861*.

Edith bowed her stately head,
Saw them lie confounded,
Edith Montfort bowed her head,
Crowned her knight's, and flushed as red
As poppies when she crowned it.
'Take her Sir Ralph,' said the king.

## 293 *The Baby Boy

Printed *Mat.* i 331, as one of the (unadopted) songs to be added to *The Princess.* T. wrote them in April 1849, for the 3rd edn, 1850. Others that he did not use are *Child-Songs* (p. 852), *The Tourney* (above), *The Losing of the Child* (p. 848), and *The Little Lady* (below). The added songs were to emphasize the importance of the child in *The Princess.*

Bless thy full cheeks my noble boy!
God bless thee, thou art all my joy!
May all thy way of life be blest!
Another kiss, and rest thee, rest.
Mayst thou grow to manly prime,
And wed a bride in the primrose time.
Go little moth to my boy's bride,
Seek her out wherever she hide,
Dress her in satin all white and neat,
With a pair of silver bells at her feet!
Set her upon thy silver wings,
Over the shining seas and the springs,
Under the stars and over the corn,
And they'll be here with the peep of morn!

## 294 *The Little Lady

Printed *Mat.* i 332, as one of the (unadopted) songs to be added to *The Princess.* T. wrote them in April 1849, for the 3rd edn, 1850. Others that he did not use are *Child-Songs* (p. 852), *The Tourney* (above), *The Losing of the Child* (p. 848), and *The Baby Boy* (above). The added songs were to emphasize the importance of the child in *The Princess.* Cp. *Song: The Owl* (p. 204).

The night is fair and the wind is dead,
'Sleep little lady,' the white owl said,
With his 'I know who, I know who.'
And who was he that flung the ball
Over the top of the garden wall?
'And I know who and I know who.'

And who was he that left for me
The little note in the rosemary tree?
'And I know who and I know who.'
And who will give me honey to eat
And dress me in spangles from head to feet?
'And I know who and I know who.'

# 295 Child-Songs

Published *St Nicholas* (New York), Feb. 1880; then 1884, New Collected Edition. Both were 'rejected from *The Princess*' (T.); the intercalated songs were written April 1849 (*Mem.* ii 486), for the 3rd edn, 1850. T. incorporated *The City Child* in *Sea Dreams* 281–96 (1860), but then substituted the present 'Cradle Song'.

## I
## THE CITY CHILD

Dainty little maiden, whither would you wander?
  Whither from this pretty home, the home where mother dwells?
'Far and far away,' said the dainty little maiden,
'All among the gardens, auriculas, anemones,
  Roses and lilies and Canterbury-bells.'

Dainty little maiden, whither would you wander?
  Whither from this pretty house, this city-house of ours?
'Far and far away,' said the dainty little maiden,
'All among the meadows, the clover and the clematis,
  Daisies and kingcups and honeysuckle-flowers.'

## II
## MINNIE AND WINNIE

Minnie and Winnie
  Slept in a shell.
Sleep, little ladies!
  And they slept well.

¶ 295.i *1.* Cp. 'Goosey goosey gander, / Whither shall I wander?'
ii *17–20.* Based on part of another fragmentary song for *The Princess* (MS at *University Library, Cambridge*, which may not be quoted).

Pink was the shell within,
  Silver without;
Sounds of the great sea
  Wandered about.

Sleep, little ladies!
  Wake not soon!
Echo on echo
  Dies to the moon.

Two bright stars
  Peeped into the shell.
'What are they dreaming of?
  Who can tell?'

Started a green linnet
  Out of the croft;
Wake, little ladies,
  The sun is aloft!

# 296 In Memoriam A. H. H.

## OBIIT MDCCCXXXIII

Published, anonymously, *1850*.

*Arthur Hallam*. On 15 Sept. 1833, T.'s friend Arthur Henry Hallam died at Vienna. On 1 Oct. T. received the news: 'It has pleased God to remove him from this, his first scene of existence, to that better world for which he was created. He died at Vienna, on his return from Buda, by apoplexy, and I believe his remains come by sea from Trieste' (*Mem*. i 105). He was buried at Clevedon, Somerset, 3 Jan. 1834. No event in T.'s life was of greater importance. Arthur Hallam was born 1 Feb. 1811, and so was eighteen months younger than T. They met soon after Hallam came up to Trinity College, Cambridge, in Oct. 1828. 'Alfred was already a prominent figure in the College by that time and Hallam's passion for poetry must almost certainly have brought the two together before long' (*CT*, p. 66). Hallam's background was sufficiently different from T.'s for T. to find in him not only a lovable person but a largeness of aspiration and moneyed culture. The son of Henry Hallam the historian, he had been at Eton, where he made the friendship of Gladstone and J. Milnes Gaskell; since leaving Eton in 1827, he had spent some months in Italy and had become a proficient scholar and even poet in the language. But, as Sir Charles Tennyson notes in his excellent account of the friendship, Hallam had need of friends at Cambridge (Gladstone and Gaskell had gone to Oxford), and 'Alfred's need of a friend was even greater. The early months of 1829 were a time of peculiar distress for him, owing to the disastrous effect on Dr Tennyson of Frederick's rustication and the misery which the Doctor's condition was causing at Somersby.' Later in 1829, Hallam wrote a poem to T., and also praised him warmly in a poem to R. J. Tennant of Trinity College (*CT*, p. 77). At Christmas 1829 Hallam met T.'s sister Emily, to whom he wrote a sonnet before the end of the year and with whom he was soon in love. In 1830 he went on a trip to the Pyrenees with T., which T. was to remember in detail for the rest of his life. Hallam's love for Emily, however, ran into difficulties; Henry Hallam tried to discourage the match (Arthur had already been rapturously in love elsewhere) by insisting that Hallam should not see Emily or correspond with her till after his 21st birthday. In Aug. 1831 Hallam wrote a eulogistic but perceptive review of T.'s *1830* volume in the *Englishman's Magazine*, 'On Some of the Characteristics of Modern Poetry and on the Lyrical Poetry of Alfred Tennyson'. The influence upon T. of Hallam's writings was not limited to this. His *Theodicæa Novissima* (1831) was a considerable influence on the religious thinking of *In Memoriam*, though in general terms. It was to be at T.'s request that the *Theodicæa* was included in Hallam's *Remains* (1834). Hallam and T. spent July 1832 in a tour of the Rhine country. In 1833 Hallam's engagement to Emily was recognised. During all this period, the background to T.'s friendship for Hallam was one of dark family troubles and hostile reviews (both for *1830* and *1832*) which wounded T. deeply. On 15 Sept. 1833 Hallam died–'a blood-vessel near the brain had suddenly burst' (*Mem.* i 105). The news reached T. on 1 Oct.

In the words of Sir Charles Tennyson (p. 145):

'The shock to all Arthur's friends was terrible. The Cambridge circle had for so long regarded him as their centre. With his vivacity, unselfishness and breadth of interests he touched all their lives at so many points, that they seemed almost to have lost a part of themselves. The letters which passed between them as the news reached one after another, and the references in memoirs and poems written years afterwards by Gladstone, Alford, Trench, Milnes and others, all show their deep affection for him as a friend and their profound admiration for his intellectual powers.

'To both Alfred and Emily the blow was overwhelming. On Arthur's betrothed it fell at a moment when, after years of trial and disappointment, there seemed good prospect that their hopes would at last be crowned with marriage. For Alfred, a sudden and brutal stroke had annihilated in a moment a love "passing the love of women". The prop, round which his own growth had twined itself for four fruitful years, was suddenly removed. A lifelong prospect, founded on his own friendship and Emily's hoped-for union with his friend, was blotted out instantly and for ever.'

And, as Sir Charles adds (p. 146), 'The wretched state of poor Edward, the fears about Charles and Septimus [T.'s brothers] and the disastrous reception of his own work added to his misery.' Yet the misery spurred him almost immediately into writing some of his greatest work, much of it not explicitly about Hallam. (But see *On a Mourner*, p. 557.)

The very high estimate which T. had of Hallam's gifts was fully shared by the other friends. John Kemble wrote to his sister (*Mem.* i 106):

'This is a loss which will most assuredly be felt by this age, for if ever man was born for great things he was. Never was a more powerful intellect joined to a purer and holier heart; and the whole illuminated with the richest imagination, with the most sparkling yet the kindest wit.'

Gladstone wrote at the time (*Mem.* i 108): 'When much time has elapsed, when most bereavements will be forgotten, he will still be remembered, and his place, I fear, will be felt to be still vacant, singularly as his mind was calculated by its native tendencies to work powerfully and for good, in an age full of import to the nature and destinies of man.' Gladstone later reiterated this praise when writing of *In Memoriam* (*Mem.* i 299).

*The growth of the poem.* It is clear from the MSS that T. set about some sections of *In Memoriam* in Oct. 1833. He will have been affected by the plans to publish Hallam's works. R. J. Tennant wrote to him, 26 Nov. 1833 (*Mem.* i 498):

'It appears to be a universal wish among them, that whatever writings Arthur has left should be collected and published; that there may be some memorial of him among us, which, tho' it will fall very far short of what was hoped and expected of him, will yet be highly gratifying to his friends.'

Henry Hallam wrote to T. about the *Remains* (*Mem.* i 108):

'It will be necessary to prefix a short memoir. I must rely on his contemporaries and most intimate friends to furnish me with part of my materials; and I should wish to have anything that may be thought most worthy of being mentioned, communicated to me by letter. Perhaps you would do something. I should desire to have the character of his mind, his favourite studies and pursuits, his habits and views delineated'.

T.'s reply to this (14 Feb. 1834, *Eversley* iii 258) makes clear his long-term project:

'I attempted to draw up a memoir of his life and character, but I failed to do him justice. I failed even to please myself. I could scarcely have pleased you. I hope to be able at a future period to concentrate whatever powers I may possess on the construction of some tribute to those high speculative endowments and comprehensive sympathies which I ever loved to contemplate; but at present, though somewhat ashamed at my own weakness, I find the object yet is too near me to permit of any very accurate delineation. You, with your clear insight into human nature, may perhaps not wonder that in the dearest service I could have been employed in, I should be found most deficient.'

On T.'s state of mind immediately after Hallam's death, see R. W. Rader (pp. 11–21). Also *Hark! the dogs howl* (p. 555), which H.T. described as 'the germ of *In Memoriam*'. (Details of the MSS are in the next section.)

Of a visit to T. at Christmas 1841 (*Mem.* i 202), Edmund Lushington wrote: 'In the meantime [since 1840?] the number of the memorial poems had rapidly increased since I had seen the poet, his book containing many that were new to me. Some I heard him repeat before I had seen them in writing, others I learnt to know first from the book itself which he kindly allowed me to look through without stint.' On 17 April 1842, Aubrey de Vere records that T. 'read me some beautiful Elegies' (Wilfrid Ward, *Aubrey de Vere*, 1904, p. 71). On 29 Jan. 1845, FitzGerald reported that Spedding was putting pressure on T. to publish the elegies (letter to W. B. Donne, FitzGerald's *Letters and Literary Remains*, 1889, i 149): 'A.T. has near a volume of poems–elegiac–in memory of Arthur Hallam. Don't you think the world wants other notes than elegiac now? *Lycidas* is the utmost length an elegiac should reach. But Spedding praises: and I suppose the elegiacs will see daylight, public daylight, one day.' Of the summer of 1845, Lushington reported: 'He had then completed many of the cantos in *In Memoriam* .... He said to me, "I have brought in your marriage at the end of *In Memoriam*," and then showed me those poems of *In Memoriam* which were finished and which were a perfectly novel surprise to me' (*Mem.* i 203). In 1847 T. wrote to Aunt Russell (*Mem.* i 243): 'With respect to the non-publication of those poems which you mention, it is partly occasioned by the considerations you speak of, and partly by my sense of their present imperfectness; perhaps they will not see the light till I have ceased to be. I cannot tell but I have no wish to send them out yet.' Before 24 Jan. 1849, T. had promised de Vere 'to *print* at least his exquisite Elegies, and let his friends have a few copies'. Under 18 Aug. 1849, William Allingham's *Diary* records that Patmore showed him the MS of *In Memoriam*: 'Mrs Patmore had copied it out for the press, and Tennyson gave her the original.' W. D. Paden, in his important study of the final stages of *In Memoriam* (*The Library*, 5th ser. viii (1953) 259–73) shows that T.'s letter to de Vere (*Mem.* i 282) was written soon after 13 Nov. 1849:

'With respect to the "Elegies", I cannot say that I have turned my attention to them lately. I do not know whether I have done anything new in that quarter since you saw them, but I believe I am going to print them, and then I need not tell you that you will be perfectly welcome to a copy, on the condition that when the book is published, this avant-courier of it shall be either sent back to me, or die the death by fire in Curragh Chase. I shall print about twenty-five copies, and let them out among friends under the same condition of either return or cremation.'

This private issue, or trial edition, seems to have been printed in March 1850 (W. M. Rossetti, *PræRaphaelite Diaries*, 1900, p. 267; *Mem.* i 297 says 'May' in error). Patmore wrote to Allingham, 17 April 1850: 'His elegies are printed. I have one of the *only* half dozen copies at present in existence. He talks of publishing them next Christmas' (B. Champneys, *Memoir of Patmore*, 1900, ii 173). Very few copies are in existence: Professor Paden used one belonging to C. B. Tinker; there is one in the Bodleian Library, and one in the Tennyson Research Centre at Lincoln. All variants are given below. Mrs E. B. Mattes was the first to comment critically on the significance of the differences between the trial edition and *1850*; she remarks that the additions seem mainly meant to qualify an over-assurance, e.g. T. added lvi (the most openly sceptical) and xcvi on doubt (*In Memoriam: The Way of a Soul*, 1951). It has been said (*CT*, p. 241) that the trial edition was entitled *Fragments of an Elegy*; though T. certainly considered this title (*Mem.* i 293), it does not appear on the surviving copies. T. sometimes called it *The Way of the Soul* (*Mem.* i 393). The title *In Memoriam* was suggested by Emily Sellwood, whom T. married in June 1850 (*CT*, p. 350). The poem was published at the end of May 1850. W. D. Paden notes that though the poem was anonymous, the first commercial announcement, by an error (a helpful error), gave T. as the author (*Publishers' Circular*, 1 June). The 2nd edition appeared in the latter half of July; the 3rd, end of August; the 4th, Jan. 1851.

*Manuscripts*. Many sections can be dated, but we lack evidence for much more than that. The earliest group is in *T.Nbk 17* (*T.Nbk 17* in footnotes below), which belongs to 1833 and has: xxx, ix, xvii (headed 'II'), xviii (headed 'III'), xxxi–xxxii (a version), lxxxv, and xxviii. H.T. evidently intended to reproduce this list as that of the 'first written sections', but there are discrepancies between the three such lists which he gave (*Mat.* i 127–8, *Mem.* i 109, and *Eversley*). Nevertheless, ix, xxxi, and xxviii appear in all three lists; and lxxxv in both *Mem.* and *Eversley*. (*Mem.* has also xxx, correctly; *Eversley* has also xvii–xviii, correctly. *Mat.*, which was H.T.'s first attempt at a list, errs in listing i and ii, a mistake probably due to the numbering in *T.Nbk 17*; *Mat.*'s listing xxvi is inexplicable.)

*Heath MS* (compiled 1833–4) has: ix, xvii–xix, xxx–xxxi, and lxxxv. Of these, only xix is not in *T.Nbk 17*, and is therefore probably of 1834.

Both the later, full-scale *Trinity MS* (*T.MS* in footnotes below) and the similar *Lincoln MS* (*L.MS* in footnotes below) deserve to be described in some detail, but neither is of much help in dating, because of the time-span which they cover. Both these MSS are dated Nov. 1842; the significance is uncertain, but it may indicate that it was then that *Lincoln MS* took over from *Trinity MS*. Any assurance based on discrepancies between these MSS is weakened by the existence of *Huntington MS* (which is part of a MS now lost).

*T.MS* is watermarked 1834, and dated Nov. 1842. It is a working, not a fair, copy, and often has more than one section on a page. It includes some of the earliest sections (e.g. xxx), but there are sheets missing at the beginning of the notebook. (We know from *T.Nbk 17* that ix, xvii–xviii were in existence.) From such evidence as we have, the latest written section included in *T.MS* appears to be li, apparently written Christmas 1841 (*Mem.* i 202–3). It includes cii, which refers to the move from Somersby in 1837, but not ci and ciii on the same subject; nor does it have civ–cv about residence from 1837 at High Beech, or lxxxvi (probably 1839). The likelihood is that *T.MS* mainly represents sections written between 1833 and 1837, but that T. kept it by him at least till 1841. Its sections are not in the published order. The sections it does *not* have are: *Prologue*, ii–xii, xiv–xxii, xxvi–xxvii, xxxix, xlvii, l, lv–lvi, lviii–lix, lxiv, lxix–lxx, lxxii, lxxxiv, lxxxvi–lxxxvii, lxxxix–xc, xcv–ci, ciii, cvi–cvii, cix–cx, cxiii–cxvi, cxviii–cxxii, cxxiv, cxxvii, cxxix–cxxxi, *Epilogue.*

*Lincoln MS* sets out as virtually a fair copy, with minor corrections and with one section only on the recto of each leaf. But this gradually breaks down, and soon the MS has become altogether less neat and finished. Its first 42 pages are watermarked 1814. The sections are not precisely in the published order. The notebook is dated 3–4–5 Nov. 1842. It adds to *T.MS* many sections which cannot be pre-1837 (on leaving Somersby, on High Beech); it also adds such sections on Evolution as cxxiii. T. read Lyell's *Principles of Geology* in 1837 (*Mem.* i 162), and these sections were written 'some years before the publication of [Chambers's] *Vestiges of Creation* in 1844' (*Mem.* i 223). The *Lincoln MS* therefore adds to *T.MS* sections from *c.* 1837, but the MS itself may well have been compiled in 1842 (as dated). Its latest written section is even harder to pinpoint. It includes a draft of the *Epilogue*, on the marriage of T.'s sister Cecilia to Edmund Lushington, 10 Oct. 1842. Lushington says, of the summer of 1845: 'He had then completed many of the cantos in *In Memoriam* . . . . He said to me, "I have brought in your marriage at the end of *In Memoriam*, and then showed me those poems of *In Memoriam* which were finished and which were a perfectly novel surprise to me' (*Mem.* i 203). The similarities to Chambers's *Vestiges*, though by no means decisive, suggest that T. may not have written the *Epilogue* till 1844–5, shortly before showing it to Lushington. But since the draft of the *Epilogue* is an early one, the MS may belong to the month after the wedding. (Mrs Mattes–who used only a description of the MS–mistakenly says the *Lincoln MS* does not include the *Epilogue*, by which she dates all that it does include as pre-1845.) As for the date of the earliest of those sections *not* in *Lincoln MS*, which might provide a *terminus ad quem*, the following are *not* in *Lincoln MS*: *Prologue* (dated '1849'); vii–viii; xxxix (published 1869); lix (published 1851); lxxxviii (but in *T.MS*); xci (but in *T.MS*); xcvi–xcvii; cvi; cxiv; cxvi; cxix–cxxi; cxxv (but in *T.MS*); cxxviii (but in *T.MS*); cxxix. Of these, vii–viii, xcvi–xcvii, and cxix–cxxi are not in the trial edition of 1850 either, and so may well not have been written till 1850. Of the remaining sections not in *Lincoln MS*, only cvi can be even tentatively dated; it may belong to *c.* 1845–6. In view of the date of the *Epilogue*, the likelihood is therefore that *Lincoln MS* adds to *T.MS* many of the sections which were written between 1837 and 1845–6. Possibly it was originally compiled in 1842, and it may carry through till 1850.

The other MSS are more fragmentary. There are sections in *Harvard Notebooks* and *Loosepapers* in the Huntington Library, and in the possession of John Sparrow and of Richard Purdy. All variants from the trial edition and MSS are given below.

T. left unpublished eight drafted sections of the poem; since they might distract a reader from the sequence of the poem, they are printed in Appendix A (pp. 1772–7).

*The stanza*. T. says: 'As for the metre of *In Memoriam* I had no notion till 1880 that Lord Herbert of Cherbury had written his occasional verses in the same metre. I believed myself the originator of the metre, until after *In Memoriam* came out, when some one told me that Ben Jonson and Sir Philip Sidney had used it.' The year 1880 refers to John Churton Collins's article in *The Cornhill* (Jan.); T. wrote alongside Collins's reference to Lord Herbert 'I had no notion till I saw it here that such a poem existed' (*Lincoln*). Before *In Memoriam*, T. had used the stanza for many political poems of *c*. 1832, including *Hail Briton*. Early fragments of *In Memoriam* use the *abab* stanza. On T.'s predecessors in using the stanza, and on T.'s approaches to it in his earlier poems, see A. C. Bradley, *A Commentary on In Memoriam* (3rd edn, 1910, pp. 67–70).

*The structure*. The best discussion is still that in Bradley's *Commentary*, to which should be added T. S. Eliot's essay (*Essays Ancient and Modern*, 1936, and reprinted in J. Killham's collection). See also the chapter on the poem in *Mem*., which reports T. as saying (i 304–5):

'It must be remembered that this is a poem, *not* an actual biography. It is founded on our friendship, on the engagement of Arthur Hallam to my sister, on his sudden death at Vienna, just before the time fixed for their marriage, and on his burial at Clevedon Church. The poem concludes with the marriage of my youngest sister Cecilia. It was meant to be a kind of *Divina Commedia*, ending with happiness. The sections were written at many different places, and as the phases of our intercourse came to my memory and suggested them. I did not write them with any view of weaving them into a whole, or for publication, until I found that I had written so many. The different moods of sorrow as in a drama are dramatically given, and my conviction that fear, doubts, and suffering will find answer and relief only through Faith in a God of Love. "I" is not always the author speaking of himself, but the voice of the human race speaking through him. After the Death of A.H.H., the divisions of the poem are made by First Xmas Eve (Section xxviii), Second Xmas (lxxviii), Third Xmas Eve (civ and cv etc.).'

To James Knowles, when reading the poem, T. said (*Nineteenth Century* xxxiii (1893) 182):

'It is rather the cry of the whole human race than mine. In the poem altogether private grief swells out into thought of, and hope for, the whole world. It begins with a funeral and ends with a marriage–begins with death and ends in promise of a new life–a sort of Divine Comedy, cheerful at the close. It is a very impersonal poem as well as personal. There is more about myself in *Ulysses*, which was written under the sense of loss and that all had gone by, but that still life must be fought out to the end. It was more written with the feeling of his loss upon me than many poems in *In Memoriam* . . . [*sic*] It's too hopeful, this poem, more than I am myself . . . [*sic*] The general way of its being written was so queer that if there were a blank space I would put in a poem ... [*sic*] I think of adding another to it, a speculative one, bringing out the thoughts of *The Higher Pantheism*, and showing that all the arguments are about as good on one side as the other, and thus throw man back more on the primitive impulses and feelings.'

T. explained to Knowles that there were nine natural groups or divisions in the poem, as follows: i–viii, ix–xx, xx–xxvii, xxviii–xlix, l–lviii, lix–lxxi, lxxii–xcviii, xcix–ciii, civ–cxxxi. On the time-sequence in the poem, see *CT* (p. 177). It is worth noting that T. permitted F. T. Palgrave to print a selection from the poem in his *Lyrical Poems* from T. (1885), with the sections in a different order. Palgrave reports that the selections 'from *In Memoriam* (peculiarly difficult to frame, from the reasons which I have noted above in regard to Shakespeare's Sonnets) follow a list which he gave me' (*Mem.* ii 503).

*Shakespeare's Sonnets.* Important both as a source and as an analogue. Benjamin Jowett records (*Mat.* iv 460):

'Once again, perhaps in his weaker moments, he had thought of Shakespeare as happier in having the power to draw himself for his fellow men, and used to think Shakespeare greater in his sonnets than in his plays. But he soon returned to the thought which is indeed the thought of all the world. He would have seemed to me to be reverting for a moment to the great sorrow of his own mind. It would not have been manly or natural to have lived in it always. But in that peculiar phase of mind he found the sonnets a deeper expression of the never to be forgotten love which he felt more than any of the many moods of many minds which appear among his dramas. The love of the sonnets which he so strikingly expressed was a sort of sympathy with Hellenism.'

Fearing a homosexual misconstruction, H.T. cut this for *Mem.*, removing the last sentence and that which begins 'It would not have been manly ...' Arthur Hallam's own love for the *Sonnets* will also have played its part; he had written in his *Influence of Italian Upon English Literature* (1831; Motter, p. 229):

'It would have been strange, however, if, in the most universal mind that ever existed, there had been no express recognition of that mode of sentiment, which had first asserted the character, and designated the direction, of modern literature. I cannot help considering the Sonnets of Shakspeare as a sort of homage to that Genius of Christian Europe, necessarily exacted, although voluntarily paid, before he was allowed to take in hand the sceptre of his endless dominion.'

It seems likely that Arthur's father, Henry Hallam, was remembering the opinions of Arthur and of T. when he gave his very influential opinion of the *Sonnets* in 1839, between the death of Arthur and the publication of *In Memoriam*. Henry Hallam wrote in his *Introduction to the Literature of Europe*, iii 501–4:

'Perhaps there is now a tendency, especially among young men of poetical tempers, to exaggerate the beauties of these remarkable productions. . . . An attachment to some female, which seems to have touched neither his heart nor his fancy very sensibly, was overpowered, without entirely ceasing, by one to a friend; and this last is of such an enthusiastic character, and so extravagant in the phrases that the author uses, as to have thrown an unaccountable mystery over the whole work. It is true that in the poetry as well as in the fictions of early ages, we find a more ardent tone of affection in the language of friendship than has since been usual; and yet no instance has been adduced of such rapturous devotedness, such an idolatry of admiring love, as the greatest being whom nature ever produced in the human form pours forth to some unknown youth in the majority of these sonnets. . . . Notwithstanding the frequent beauties of these sonnets, the pleasure of their perusal is greatly diminished by these circumstances; and it is impossible not to wish that Shakspeare had never written them. There is a weakness and folly in all excessive and mis-placed affection, which is not redeemed by the touches of nobler sentiments that abound in this long series of sonnets.'

H.T. records T. as saying of the *Sonnets*: 'Henry Hallam made a great mistake about them: they are noble' (*Mem.* ii 289).

*Theology and Evolution.* 'They are always speaking of me', T. remarked, 'as if I were a writer of philosophical treatises' (*Mat.* ii 17). For his relationship to the thought of his day, see: G. R. Potter, 'Tennyson and the biological theory of mutability in species', *PQ* xvi (1937) 321–43; W. R. Rutland, 'Tennyson and the theory of evolution', *E & S* xxvi (1940) 7–29; G. Hough, 'The Natural Theology of *In Memoriam*', *RES* xxxiii (1947) 244–56; E. B. Mattes, *In Memoriam: The Way of a Soul* (1951); and J. Killham, *Tennyson and 'The Princess'* (1958). Of his poetic predecessors, the most important is James Thomson, whose *Autumn* includes a long passage on geology (ll. 743–833). The footnotes below give the more important of the sources and analogues from Lyell's *Principles of Geology* and Chambers's *Vestiges of Creation*.

## [PROLOGUE]

Strong Son of God, immortal Love,
    Whom we, that have not seen thy face,
    By faith, and faith alone, embrace,
Believing where we cannot prove;

Thine are these orbs of light and shade;
    Thou madest Life in man and brute;
    Thou madest Death; and lo, thy foot
Is on the skull which thou hast made.

Thou wilt not leave us in the dust:
Thou madest man, he knows not why,
He thinks he was not made to die;
And thou hast made him: thou art just.

Thou seemest human and divine,
The highest, holiest manhood, thou:
Our wills are ours, we know not how;
Our wills are ours, to make them thine.

¶ *296*. [*Prologue*] Dated '1849' from *1850*. Not *T.MS* and *L.MS*. The present edition follows A. C. Bradley in referring to this as the *Prologue*, though T. gave it no title. Mrs E. B. Mattes suggests a general indebtedness to the religious teaching of F. D. Maurice, and describes the *Prologue* as 'a conclusion more truly than an opening to *In Memoriam*. Insofar as it is a prologue, it is one not so much to the poems it precedes as to the new way of life Tennyson was about to enter.' She notes that the trial edition had the *Prologue* before, and not after, the title *In Memoriam A.H.H. Obiit MDCCCXXXIII*, which made a considerable break and gave a more accurate impression of the relationship of the *Prologue* to the succeeding poems (*In Memoriam: The Way of a Soul*, 1951, p. 98).

*P 1. immortal Love*: 'This might be taken in a St John sense' (T.); H.T. refers to *1 John* iv and v.

*P 1–12*. John Churton Collins called T.'s *Prologue* 'obviously a transfusion' from verses by George Herbert. Alongside this suggestion (*Cornhill*, Jan. 1880, *Lincoln*), T. wrote 'No'. Collins compared l. 12 with Herbert, *The Discharge* 55: 'My God hath promis'd; he is just'; T. wrote: 'No, close as it seems.' Cp. also T.'s opening with Herbert's *Love* [*I*] 1–4: 'Immortall Love, authour of this great frame, / Sprung from that beautie which can never fade; / How hath man parcel'd out thy glorious name, / And thrown it on that dust which thou hast made.' Also T.'s ll. 9, 12, with Herbert's *The Temper* [*I*] 25–6: 'Whether I flie with angels, fall with dust, / Thy hands made both.' Coventry Patmore, reviewing *In Memoriam*, said that it contained 'the best religious poetry that has ever been written in our language–if we except a very few of the lovely and too seldom appreciated effusions of George Herbert' (E. F. Shannon, *Tennyson and the Reviewers*, 1952, p. 145).

*P 2–3. 1 Peter* i 8: 'Whom having not seen, ye love; in whom, though now ye see him not, yet believing.'

*P 5. orbs*: 'sun and moon' (T.).

*P 7–8*. E. B. Mattes (p. 97) refers to Christ's victory over death as symbolized in medieval paintings of the Crucifixion in which his feet rest on a skull.

*P 9*. Cp. *Psalm* xvi 10: 'Thou wilt not leave my soul in hell'.

*P 9 12*. The rhymes suggest *Why should we weep for those who die?* 1–4 (*1827*, p. 86): die, dust, eternally, just.

Our little systems have their day;
They have their day and cease to be:
They are but broken lights of thee,
And thou, O Lord, art more than they.

We have but faith: we cannot know;
For knowledge is of things we see;
And yet we trust it comes from thee,
A beam in darkness: let it grow.

Let knowledge grow from more to more,
But more of reverence in us dwell;
That mind and soul, according well,
May make one music as before,

But vaster. We are fools and slight;
We mock thee when we do not fear:
But help thy foolish ones to bear;
Help thy vain worlds to bear thy light.

Forgive what seemed my sin in me;
What seemed my worth since I began;
For merit lives from man to man,
And not from man, O Lord, to thee.

*P 14–16*] Thou madest man, without, within,
But who shall say thou madest sin?
For who shall say, 'It is not mine'? *MS quoted in Eversley*

*P 15*. Cp. Sir Thomas Browne, *Religio Medici* i 36: 'Thus we are men, and we know not how'.

*P 17*. Cp. *The Two Voices* 207: 'dust of systems'.

*P 19. broken lights: Will Waterproof* 59. Arthur Hallam has 'broken light', *On Free Submission to God's Will* 4 (Motter, p. 67).

*P 22–4*. Cp. Charles Lyell on 'doubt and perplexity' in relation to geological knowledge: 'It has been justly said, that the greater the circle of light, the greater the boundary of darkness by which it is surrounded' (*Principles of Geology*, 4th edn, 1835, ii 291). T. read Lyell in 1837 (*Mem.* i 162).

*P 25–6*. Cp. *Love thou thy land* 17–18: 'Make knowledge circle with the winds; / But let her herald, Reverence, fly . . .' The antithesis is a commonplace, but T. may have been affected by Robert Chambers's use of it in speaking specifically of geological knowledge: 'The acquisition of this knowledge is consequently an available means of our growing in a genuine reverence for him [God]' (*Vestiges of Creation*, 1844, p. 233).

Forgive my grief for one removed,
  Thy creature, whom I found so fair.
  I trust he lives in thee, and there
I find him worthier to be loved.

Forgive these wild and wandering cries,
  Confusions of a wasted youth;
  Forgive them where they fail in truth,
And in thy wisdom make me wise.

1849

I

I held it truth, with him who sings
  To one clear harp in divers tones,
  That men may rise on stepping-stones
Of their dead selves to higher things.

But who shall so forecast the years
  And find in loss a gain to match?
  Or reach a hand through time to catch
The far-off interest of tears?

*P 36. Psalm* cxliii 2: 'in thy sight shall no man living be justified'.

*P 41. wild and wandering*: *Troilus and Cressida* I i 104. Cp. *A Dirge* 43: 'Wild words wander here and there'.

i Probably not completed till after 1846. *Mat.* i 127–8 listed it as one of the earliest sections, apparently in error (p. 857).

i *1–4*] *T. and L.MSS have only this stanza.* T. says: 'I alluded to Goethe's creed. Among his last words were . . . "from changes to higher changes"'. *divers tones*: 'Goethe is consummate in so many different styles' (T.). G. G. Loane (*Echoes in Tennyson*, 1928, p. 9) compares Byron, *Siege of Corinth* 239–41: 'Or pave the path with many a corse, / O'er which the following brave may rise, / Their stepping-stone–the last who dies!' Cp. *Timbuctoo* 194: 'And step by step to scale that mighty stair'. Also *To–[Thou mayst remember]* 3–6, 10–11: 'From the tomb / And charnel-place of purpose dead, / Through spiritual death we come / Into the light of spiritual life. . . . / Thy thought did scale a purer range / Of prospect up to self-control.'

i *4. their dead selves*: to be found in R. C. Trench's poem *To W. B. Donne* (both were Cambridge friends of T.), written 18 Oct. 1829 and in *Heath MS* alongside poems by T.

i *5–8.* Cp. *Tiresias* 122–3 (begun on the death of Hallam): 'their examples reach a hand / Far through all years'. Based on *Hail Briton* 81–4: 'They wrought a work which time reveres, / A precedent to all the lands, / And an example reaching hands / For ever into coming years.'

i *7–8.* Three apparent reminiscences of Shakespeare. *Sonnet 31* 5–7:

Let Love clasp Grief lest both be drowned,
Let darkness keep her raven gloss:
Ah, sweeter to be drunk with loss,
To dance with death, to beat the ground,

Than that the victor Hours should scorn
The long result of love, and boast,
'Behold the man that loved and lost,
But all he was is overworn.'

## II

Old Yew, which graspest at the stones
That name the under-lying dead,
Thy fibres net the dreamless head,
Thy roots are wrapt about the bones.

The seasons bring the flower again,
And bring the firstling to the flock;
And in the dusk of thee, the clock
Beats out the little lives of men.

O not for thee the glow, the bloom,
Who changest not in any gale,
Nor branding summer suns avail
To touch thy thousand years of gloom:

'How many a holy and obsequious tear / Hath dear religious love stolen from mine eye, / As interest of the dead.' *Rape of Lucrece* 1796–8: 'do not take away / My sorrow's interest; let no mourner say / He weeps for her.' *Richard III* IV iv 322–4: 'The liquid drops of tears that you have shed / Shall come again, transformed to orient pearl, / Advantaging their loan with interest.'

i *10. Comus* 251–2: 'Raven doune / Of darkness'.

i *12.* Cp. *Comus* 143: 'Come, knit hands, and beat the ground', and Horace, *Odes* I xxxvii 1–2, *pulsanda tellus.* Cp. 'beat the floor', cv 17.

i *13. the victor Hours*: as in the unpublished section, *Are these the far-famed Victor Hours?* (p. 1776).

i *14.* Cp. *Locksley Hall* 12: 'the long result of Time'.

*16. was*] loves *trial edition.*

ii Not *T.MS. Mat.* i 127–8 listed it as one of the earliest sections, apparently in error (p. 857).

ii *3.* T. compares: *Νεκύων ἀμενηνὰ κάρηνα* (*Odyssey* x 521 etc., 'the powerless heads of the dead').

ii *4. Job* viii 17: 'His roots are wrapped about the heap, and seeth the place of stones.'

ii *12.* Cp. *The Lover's Tale* iv 194: 'a hundred years of gloom'.

And gazing on thee, sullen tree,
Sick for thy stubborn hardihood,
I seem to fail from out my blood
And grow incorporate into thee.

III

O Sorrow, cruel fellowship,
O Priestess in the vaults of Death,
O sweet and bitter in a breath,
What whispers from thy lying lip?

'The stars,' she whispers, 'blindly run;
A web is woven across the sky;
From out waste places comes a cry,
And murmurs from the dying sun:

'And all the phantom, Nature, stands–
With all the music in her tone,
A hollow echo of my own,–
A hollow form with empty hands.'

ii *13. thee,*] *1851*; the *trial edition, 1850*; thy *corrected to* the *L.MS.*
ii *15. fail from out*: die away from (A. C. Bradley); cp. 'fail from thy desire', iv 6; 'Thy spirit should fail from off the globe', lxxxiv 36.

iii Not *T.MS.* The germ of it is in *H.Nbk 17* (1833).
iii *5–6.* Cp. Shelley, *Adonais* 482: 'Which through the web of being blindly wove', on Love versus mortality.
iii *5–8*] *H.Nbk 17* has an early fragment, rhyming *abab*:

A cloud was drawn across the sky,
The stars their courses blindly run.
Out of waste places came a cry
And murmurs from the dying sun.

In every form the sense receives
A something hitherto unmet,
In every motion of the leaves
The shadow of a vain regret.

The whole house shaken to its fall,
This travelled mind a foreign land,
Love mixt with all–love lord of all,
Thought drifting like the hills of sand.

The ninth line was echoed in 'And travelled men from foreign lands', x 6. Cp. the *1850* text with *Armageddon* i 36–7: 'Spirits of discord seemed to weave across / His fiery disk a web of bloody haze.'
iii *9. And all*] Because *H.Lpr 100.*
iii *10. the*] *1851 (5th), L.MS*; her *1850–51 (4th).*
iii *11.* Cp. Spenser: *Shepherd's Calendar*: *August* 160: 'The hollow Echo of my carefull cryes'.

And shall I take a thing so blind,
  Embrace her as my natural good;
  Or crush her, like a vice of blood,
Upon the threshold of the mind?

## IV

To Sleep I give my powers away;
  My will is bondsman to the dark;
  I sit within a helmless bark,
And with my heart I muse and say:

O heart, how fares it with thee now,
  That thou should'st fail from thy desire,
  Who scarcely darest to inquire,
'What is it makes me beat so low?'

Something it is which thou hast lost,
  Some pleasure from thine early years.
  Break, thou deep vase of chilling tears,
That grief hath shaken into frost!

Such clouds of nameless trouble cross
  All night below the darkened eyes;
  With morning wakes the will, and cries,
'Thou shalt not be the fool of loss.'

iii *14–15*. Cp. Shelley, *Queen Mab* iv 115–20, which mentions 'blood', 'vice', and 'Stifling with rudest grasp all natural good'; 'natural good' recurs in Shelley five lines later.
iii *15*. Cp. *Othello* I iii 123: 'I do confess the vices of my blood'.
iii *16*] *H.Lpr 100* has a further stanza, deleted:

But Sorrow cares not for my frown,
  And Sorrow says, 'We must not part,
  For if I die upon thy heart,
Then my dead weight will draw thee down.'

iv Not *T.MS*.
iv *11–12*. T. comments: 'Water can be brought below freezing-point and not turn into ice–if it be kept still; but if it be moved suddenly it turns into ice and may break the vase.' An important source has been noted by Elaine Jordan: Goethe's *Dichtung und Wahrheit*. 'While my thoughts were thus employed, the death of young Jerusalem took place. The most minute and circumstantial details of the event were immediately circulated. The plan of *Werther* was instantly conceived. The elements of that composition seemed now to amalgamate, to form a whole, just as water, on the point of freezing in a vase, receives from the slightest concussion the form of a compact piece of ice' (*Memoirs*, 1824 tr., ii 44–5).

## V

I sometimes hold it half a sin
To put in words the grief I feel;
For words, like Nature, half reveal
And half conceal the Soul within.

But, for the unquiet heart and brain,
A use in measured language lies;
The sad mechanic exercise,
Like dull narcotics, numbing pain.

In words, like weeds, I'll wrap me o'er,
Like coarsest clothes against the cold:
But that large grief which these enfold
Is given in outline and no more.

## VI

One writes, that 'Other friends remain,'
That 'Loss is common to the race'–
And common is the commonplace,
And vacant chaff well meant for grain.

That loss is common would not make
My own less bitter, rather more:
Too common! Never morning wore
To evening, but some heart did break.

v Not *T.MS.*
v *7. sad*] set *L.MS.*
v *9. weeds*: garments, with a suggestion of mourning (widow's weeds).

vi Not *T.MS.* The poem is mentioned by E. Lushington, as if it were one of the many new sections written between summer 1840 and Christmas 1841 (*Mem.* i 201–2).
vi *1–8.* T. compares Lucretius ii 578–80: *nec nox ulla diem neque noctem aurora secutast / quae non audierit mixtos vagitibus aegris / ploratus mortis comites et funeris atri.* ('No night ever followed day, or dawn followed night, but has heard mingled with their sickly wailings the lamentations that attend upon death and the black funeral.') Cp. *Hamlet* I ii 72: 'Thou know'st 'tis common, all that lives must die'. Also T.'s earlier elegiac poem, *To J. S.* 45–8: 'I will not say, "God's ordinance / Of Death is blown in every wind;" / For that is not a common chance / That takes away a noble mind.' Cp. *Why should we weep for those who die?* 12 (*1827*): 'They die the common death of man'.

O father, wheresoe'er thou be,
Who pledgest now thy gallant son;
A shot, ere half thy draught be done,
Hath stilled the life that beat from thee.

O mother, praying God will save
Thy sailor, – while thy head is bowed,
His heavy-shotted hammock-shroud
Drops in his vast and wandering grave.

Ye know no more than I who wrought
At that last hour to please him well;
Who mused on all I had to tell,
And something written, something thought;

Expecting still his advent home;
And ever met him on his way
With wishes, thinking, 'here today,'
Or 'here tomorrow will he come.'

O somewhere, meek, unconscious dove,
That sittest ranging golden hair;
And glad to find thyself so fair,
Poor child, that waitest for thy love!

vi *9–12*. Cp. *Aeneid* xi 49–52: *et nunc ille quidem spe multum captus inani / fors et vota facit cumulatque altaria donis; / nos iuvenem exanimum et nil iam caelestibus ullis / debentem vano maesti comitamur honore.* ('And now he, much beguiled by idle hope, perchance is offering vows and heaping the altars high with gifts; we, in sorrow, attend with bootless rites the lifeless son, who no more owes aught to any gods of heaven.')

vi *10*. *Who*] *1855*; that *1850–51*.

vi *16*. Cp. Clarence's dream of drowning, 'To find the empty, vast, and wand'ring air', *Richard III* I iv 39.

vi *19*. H.T. records that T. 'was writing to Arthur Hallam in the hour he died'.

vi *21–40*. Cp. Juvenal, *Satires* iii 261–5: *domus interea secura patellas / iam lavat et bucca foculum excitat et sonat unctis / striglibus et pleno componit lintea guto. / haec inter pueros varie properantur, at ille / iam sedet in ripa taetrumque novicius horret.* ('At home meanwhile the folk, unwitting, are washing the dishes, blowing up the fire with distended cheek, clattering over the greasy flesh-scrapers, filling the oil-flasks and laying out the towels. And while each of them is thus busy over his own task, their master is already sitting, a new arrival, upon the bank, and shuddering at the grim ferryman.')

For now her father's chimney glows
In expectation of a guest;
And thinking 'this will please him best,'
She takes a riband or a rose;

For he will see them on tonight;
And with the thought her colour burns;
And, having left the glass, she turns
Once more to set a ringlet right;

And, even when she turned, the curse
Had fallen, and her future Lord
Was drowned in passing through the ford,
Or killed in falling from his horse.

O what to her shall be the end?
And what to me remains of good?
To her, perpetual maidenhood,
And unto me no second friend.

## VII

Dark house, by which once more I stand
Here in the long unlovely street,
Doors, where my heart was used to beat
So quickly, waiting for a hand,

vi *32*. A friend described T.'s sister Emily, 'the first day since her loss that she had been able to meet anyone, and she came at last, dressed in deep mourning, a shadow of her former self, but with one white rose in her black hair as her Arthur loved to see her' (*Mem.* i 109).
vi *37–40*. T.'s friend W. F. Rawnsley said that 'all his early life Tennyson had heard "horse" in Lincolnshire pronounced "hurse"', *Nineteenth Century* xcvii (1925) 190. But *Hail Briton* 113–6 rhymes 'perforce' / 'horse'.

vii Not *T.MS, L.MS, trial edition*. Cp. *The Deserted House* 9–12 (*1830*, p. 238), in which the house is a corpse and which falls into something resembling the *In Memoriam* stanza: 'Close the door, the shutters close, / Or through the windows we shall see / The nakedness and vacancy / Of the dark deserted house.' J. H. Buckley (p. 111) quotes R. M. Milnes's poem on the death of Hallam (1844), which has interesting similarities.
vii *1*. T. comments: '67 Wimpole Street', Henry Hallam's house at this time.
vii *3*. *Doors*] Door *H.Lpr 104*.
vii *4*] In expectation of his hand, *H.MS 1st reading*; So quickly, waiting for the hand, *H.MS*. The first reading was probably rejected as too like 'In

A hand that can be clasped no more–
Behold me, for I cannot sleep,
And like a guilty thing I creep
At earliest morning to the door.

He is not here; but far away
The noise of life begins again,
And ghastly through the drizzling rain
On the bald street breaks the blank day.

## VIII

A happy lover who has come
To look on her that loves him well,
Who 'lights and rings the gateway bell,
And learns her gone and far from home;

He saddens, all the magic light
Dies off at once from bower and hall,
And all the place is dark, and all
The chambers emptied of delight:

So find I every pleasant spot
In which we two were wont to meet,
The field, the chamber and the street,
For all is dark where thou art not.

expectation of a guest', l. 30 of the preceding section. Cp. *Break, break, break* 11: 'But O for the touch of a vanished hand'.

vii *5*. Cp. *If I were loved* 9 (*1832*, probably to Hallam): 'Clasp hand-in-hand with thee'. Also *The Princess* vi 168: 'In hands so lately claspt with yours'.

vii *7*. *And*] But *H.MS*. Cp. the ghost in *Hamlet* I i 148: 'And then it started like a guilty thing'. Also Wordsworth's *Immortality Ode* 148–51 (note the subject, and 'blank'): 'Blank misgivings of a Creature / Moving about in worlds not realised, / High instincts before which our mortal Nature / Did tremble like a guilty Thing surprised.'

vii *9*. J. D. Rosenberg, *JEGP* lviii (1959) 230, suggests an allusion to *Luke* xxiv 6, with the angel before the empty sepulchre: 'He is not here, but is risen'.

vii *11*. *drizzling*] dripping *H.MS*.

viii Not *T.MS*, *L.MS*, *trial edition*. Written 1850 (?).

viii *12*. Cp. Arthur Hallam, *To Two Sisters* (to T.'s sisters Mary and Emily; Motter, p. 90) i 42–4: 'Sick and lone, / Roaming the weary desert of my doom, / Where thou art not.'

Yet as that other, wandering there
 In those deserted walks, may find
 A flower beat with rain and wind,
Which once she fostered up with care;

So seems it in my deep regret,
 O my forsaken heart, with thee
 And this poor flower of poesy
Which little cared for fades not yet.

But since it pleased a vanished eye,
 I go to plant it on his tomb,
 That if it can it there may bloom,
Or dying, there at least may die.

## IX

Fair ship, that from the Italian shore
 Sailest the placid ocean-plains
 With my lost Arthur's loved remains,
Spread thy full wings, and waft him o'er.

So draw him home to those that mourn
 In vain; a favourable speed
 Ruffle thy mirrored mast, and lead
Through prosperous floods his holy urn.

ix Not *T.MS* (missing sheets). Dated '6 Oct. 1833' in *Heath MS* and *Y.MS. H.Nbk 16* (1833) has an earlier draft than *Heath MS*. The poem is in *T.Nbk 17* (1833).

Cp. Horace, *Odes* I iii, with its prayer for a safe crossing for the ship carrying his poet friend Virgil: *Sic te diva potens Cypri, / sic fratres Helenae, lucida sidera, / ventorumque regat pater / obstrictis aliis praeter Iapyga, / navis . . .* ('May the goddess who rules over Cyprus, may Helen's brothers, gleaming fires, and the father of the winds, confining all but Iapyx, guide thee so, O ship . . .'). Theocritus vii 52–62 also implores fair weather for a crossing to Mitylene.

ix *2. placid*] glassy *H.MS 1st reading*. Cp. *Aeneid* x 103: *placida aequora*.

ix *5. So . . . home*] Convoy thy charge *H.MS 1st reading*; Draw thy dear freight *Heath MS 1st reading, H.MS 2nd reading*. Cp. 'thy dark freight', l. 8 of the following section.

ix *6. ; a favourable*] for him. A happy *H.MS 1st reading*.

ix 7] All day strain all thy cords, and lead *H.MS 1st reading*. T. also jotted down 'cords are tight'. *thy mirrored*] *H.MS, 1850*; the mirrored *trial edition*. *Ruffle*: cp. Shelley, *Queen Mab* viii 65 (see too l. 2 above): 'Ruffle the placid ocean-deep'.

ix *8. prosperous*: used similarly by Shelley, of the wind, *Rosalind* 817.

All night no ruder air perplex
Thy sliding keel, till Phosphor, bright
As our pure love, through early light
Shall glimmer on the dewy decks.

Sphere all your lights around, above;
Sleep, gentle heavens, before the prow;
Sleep, gentle winds, as he sleeps now,
My friend, the brother of my love;

My Arthur, whom I shall not see
Till all my widowed race be run;
Dear as the mother to the son,
More than my brothers are to me.

X

I hear the noise about thy keel;
I hear the bell struck in the night:
I see the cabin-window bright;
I see the sailor at the wheel.

Thou bring'st the sailor to his wife,
And travelled men from foreign lands;
And letters unto trembling hands;
And, thy dark freight, a vanished life.

So bring him: we have idle dreams:
This look of quiet flatters thus
Our home-bred fancies: O to us,
The fools of habit, sweeter seems

To rest beneath the clover sod,
That takes the sunshine and the rains,
Or where the kneeling hamlet drains
The chalice of the grapes of God;

ix *10. Phosphor*: T. comments 'star of dawn'.

ix *13. lights*] light *H.MS*. Cp. *Enoch Arden* 593: 'Then the great stars that globed themselves in Heaven'; and Virgil, *Georgics* iv 79: *magnum mixtae glomerantur in orbem*.

ix *15. winds*] waves *H.MS, Heath MS*.

x Not *T.MS*.

x *6*. Cp. 'This travelled mind a foreign land', iii 5–8*n*, MS.

x *8. thy dark freight*] dearer yet *L.MS 1st reading*. See ix 5*n*.

x *11. :O*] that *MS 1st reading*. *home-bred fancies*: 'the wish to rest in the churchyard or in the chancel' (H.T.).

x *12–20*. Cp. Ovid, *Tristia* I ii 53–4: *est aliquid, fatove suo ferrove cadentem / in solida moriens ponere corpus humo*. ("Tis something worth if falling by fate or by the steel one rests in death upon the solid ground'–this then

Than if with thee the roaring wells
  Should gulf him fathom-deep in brine;
  And hands so often clasped in mine,
Should toss with tangle and with shells.

## XI

Calm is the morn without a sound,
  Calm as to suit a calmer grief,
  And only through the faded leaf
The chestnut pattering to the ground:

Calm and deep peace on this high wold,
  And on these dews that drench the furze,
  And all the silvery gossamers
That twinkle into green and gold:

Calm and still light on yon great plain
  That sweeps with all its autumn bowers,
  And crowded farms and lessening towers,
To mingle with the bounding main:

Calm and deep peace in this wide air,
  These leaves that redden to the fall;
  And in my heart, if calm at all,
If any calm, a calm despair:

Calm on the seas, and silver sleep,
  And waves that sway themselves in rest,
  And dead calm in that noble breast
Which heaves but with the heaving deep.

## XII

Lo, as a dove when up she springs
  To bear through Heaven a tale of woe,
  Some dolorous message knit below
The wild pulsation of her wings;

contrasted with being lost at sea.) The passage is also echoed in xviii 1–4.
x *19.* Cp. *The Princess* vi 168: 'hands so lately claspt with yours'.
x *20. tangle:* 'oar-weed' (T.).

xi Not *T.MS.*
xi *6. these*] the *L.MS 1st reading.*
xi *7–8.* Adapted from *The Ruined Kiln* 1–2: 'A million gossamers in field and fold / Were twinkling into green and gold.'
xi *11.* Cp. Samuel Rogers, *The Sailor* (1786): 'The Sailor sighs as sinks his native shore, / As all its lessening turrets bluely fade'.
xi *20.* Cp. Byron, *Bride of Abydos* 1088: 'His head heaves with the heaving billow'.

xii Not *T.MS.* Suggested by *Genesis* viii 8–9, 'Also he sent forth a dove

Like her I go; I cannot stay;
I leave this mortal ark behind,
A weight of nerves without a mind,
And leave the cliffs, and haste away

O'er ocean-mirrors rounded large,
And reach the glow of southern skies,
And see the sails at distance rise,
And linger weeping on the marge,

And saying; 'Comes he thus, my friend?
Is this the end of all my care?'
And circle moaning in the air:
'Is this the end? Is this the end?'

And forward dart again, and play
About the prow, and back return
To where the body sits, and learn
That I have been an hour away.

## XIII

Tears of the widower, when he sees
A late-lost form that sleep reveals,
And moves his doubtful arms, and feels
Her place is empty, fall like these;

Which weep a loss for ever new,
A void where heart on heart reposed;
And, where warm hands have prest and closed,
Silence, till I be silent too.

from him, to see if the waters were abated from off the face of the ground; but the dove found no rest for the sole of her foot, and she returned unto him into the ark, for the waters were on the face of the whole earth.'

xii *6. ark*] arc *L.MS 1st reading.* *mortal ark*: *The Two Voices* 389. T. comments: 'My spirit flies from out my material self.' Cp. the visionary journey ('I leave the dreaming world below') in *Hark! the dogs howl!* (1833, p. 555), the germ of *In Memoriam.*

xii *9.* Incorporated from an early draft of *The Voyage* (*T.Nbk 20*, which may not be quoted).

xiii *3–4.* Cp. Milton's *Sonnet 19*, 'Methought I saw my late espoused Saint', which ends: 'But O as to embrace me she enclin'd / I wak'd, she fled, and day brought back my night.' Also Ovid, *Heroides* x 9–12, Ariadne reaching out for the phantom of Theseus.

Which weep the comrade of my choice,
An awful thought, a life removed,
The human-hearted man I loved,
A Spirit, not a breathing voice.

Come Time, and teach me, many years,
I do not suffer in a dream;
For now so strange do these things seem,
Mine eyes have leisure for their tears;

My fancies time to rise on wing,
And glance about the approaching sails,
As though they brought but merchants' bales,
And not the burthen that they bring.

## XIV

If one should bring me this report,
That thou hadst touched the land today,
And I went down unto the quay,
And found thee lying in the port;

And standing, muffled round with woe,
Should see thy passengers in rank
Come stepping lightly down the plank,
And beckoning unto those they know;

And if along with these should come
The man I held as half-divine;
Should strike a sudden hand in mine,
And ask a thousand things of home;

And I should tell him all my pain,
And how my life had drooped of late,
And he should sorrow o'er my state
And marvel what possessed my brain;

And I perceived no touch of change,
No hint of death in all his frame,
But found him all in all the same,
I should not feel it to be strange.

xiii *17–20*] *Not T.MS.*

xiii *18–19*. Cp. *Locksley Hall* 121–2, MS: 'unimagined sails, / Merchants in a rosy sunset, dropping down with costly bales.'

xiv Not *T.MS.*

xiv *2–3*. *OED* shows that Swift rhymed 'quay' and 'day', *Stella at Wood-Park* 46.

## XV

Tonight the winds begin to rise
  And roar from yonder dropping day:
  The last red leaf is whirled away,
The rooks are blown about the skies;

The forest cracked, the waters curled,
  The cattle huddled on the lea;
  And wildly dashed on tower and tree
The sunbeam strikes along the world:

And but for fancies, which aver
  That all thy motions gently pass
  Athwart a plane of molten glass,
I scarce could brook the strain and stir

That makes the barren branches loud;
  And but for fear it is not so,
  The wild unrest that lives in woe
Would dote and pore on yonder cloud

That rises upward always higher,
  And onward drags a labouring breast,
  And topples round the dreary west,
A looming bastion fringed with fire.

xv Not *T.MS.* Henry Hallam wrote to T., 30 Dec. 1833: 'You may have been apprehensive for the safety of the vessel'. There are many small similarities to *On Sublimity* (*1827*, p. 115): 'to pore'; 'the labouring vessel'; 'doats on solitude'; 'wild'; 'While the black clouds in strange and uncouth forms, / Come hurrying onward'; the winds at midnight; 'roar'; 'whirling'.

xv *1. begin*] *1855*, *L.MS*; began *1850–51*.

xv *3*. Cp. Coleridge, *Christabel* 48–9: 'There is not wind enough to twirl / The one red leaf, the last of its clan.'

xv *11. plane*: 'a calm sea' (T.). Cp. *Job* xxxvii 18: the sky 'as a molten looking glass'; *Revelation* iv 6: 'a sea of glass like unto crystal'. Cp. ix 2, MS: 'the glassy ocean-plains.'

xv *14–16*. 'The stormy night, except it were for my fear for the "sacred bark", would be in sympathy with me' (H.T.). *it is not so*: T. glossed this 'all is not peace with thee' (University of London Library, *Works*, 1884).

xv *15. wild unrest*: *Timbuctoo* 127.

xv *15–20*. Cp. Arthur Hallam, *The Garden Trees* 10–11 (Motter, p. 98): 'The wild gray light that fronts yon massive cloud, / Or the half bow, rising like pillared fire.'

xv *18*. Cp. *L'Allegro* 73–4: 'Mountains on whose barren brest / The labouring clouds do often rest.' Keats, *Hyperion* i 39–41: clouds and 'stored

## XVI

What words are these have fallen from me?
  Can calm despair and wild unrest
  Be tenants of a single breast,
Or sorrow such a changeling be?

Or doth she only seem to take
  The touch of change in calm or storm;
  But knows no more of transient form
In her deep self, than some dead lake

That holds the shadow of a lark
  Hung in the shadow of a heaven?
  Or has the shock, so harshly given,
Confused me like the unhappy bark

That strikes by night a craggy shelf,
  And staggers blindly ere she sink?
  And stunned me from my power to think
And all my knowledge of myself;

And made me that delirious man
  Whose fancy fuses old and new,
  And flashes into false and true,
And mingles all without a plan?

thunder labouring up'. Cp. 'The vapour labours up the sky', *Hark! the dogs howl!* 18, a poem which is the germ of *In Memoriam* (p. 555). Sir William Jones's translation of the *Moâllakát* (the acknowledged source of *Locksley Hall*), Amriolkais's poem, tells how night seemed 'to drag on her unwieldy length, and to advance slowly with her breast'.
xv *19–20.* Cp. *The Palace of Art* 48: 'Burnt like a fringe of fire'. Also *Armageddon* i 133–5: 'the livid West . . . melancholy red that fringed the sky'.

xvi Not *T.MS.*
xvi *13–16.* Cp. Herbert, *Miserie* 76–7: 'A sick toss'd vessel, dashing on each thing; / Nay, his own shelf.' John Churton Collins wrote: 'For this graphic touch see Napier, *History of the Peninsular War* (Battle of Albuera): "The Fusileer battalions, struck by the iron tempest, *reeled and staggered like a sinking ship.*"' Alongside this suggestion, T. wrote: '! ! !' (*Cornhill*, Jan. 1880, *Lincoln*).
xvi *20. And mingles all*] In all his words *L.MS 1st reading.*

## XVII

Thou comest, much wept for: such a breeze
 Compelled thy canvas, and my prayer
 Was as the whisper of an air
To breathe thee over lonely seas.

For I in spirit saw thee move
 Through circles of the bounding sky,
 Week after week: the days go by:
Come quick, thou bringest all I love.

Henceforth, wherever thou mayst roam,
 My blessing, like a line of light,
 Is on the waters day and night,
And like a beacon guards thee home.

So may whatever tempest mars
 Mid-ocean, spare thee, sacred bark;
 And balmy drops in summer dark
Slide from the bosom of the stars.

xvii Not *T.MS*. Written 1833. The chronology of the MSS is *H.Nbk 17* (1833), *Heath MS*, *Purdy MS*. Henry Hallam wrote to T., 30 Dec. 1833: 'You may have been apprehensive for the safety of the vessel'.

xvii *2–3*] Was on thee, hollowing all the sail.
 My prayer was, likewise, as a gale *H.MS*, *Heath MS 1st reading*

*H.MS* then changed 'likewise, as' to 'also like'. *thy canvas*] the canvas *Heath MS*, *Purdy MS*.

xvii *9–12*. Cp. Thomas Moore, *How dear to me the hour* 5–8: 'And, as I watch the line of light, that plays / Along the smooth wave t'ward the burning west, / I long to tread that golden path of rays, / And think 'twould lead to some bright isle of rest.'

xvii *10. like*] as *H.MS 1st reading*.

xvii *12. guards*] leads *MSS*.

xvii *13–16*] May never adverse wind incline,
 Thee moving swift thy burnisht sides
 From port to port in glassy tides
 Whose loudest motion comes from thine. *H.MS*

Cp. ciii 37–40 on the 'great ship' and her 'shining sides'; also the thought in xv 9–13. With the *1850* text, cp. Horace, *Odes* I iii (which influenced ix above); Shelley, *Queen Mab* i 114–7: 'Stars! your balmiest influence shed! / Elements! your wrath suspend! / Sleep, Ocean, in the rocky bounds / That circle thy domain!' Also *The Talking Oak* 267–8: 'All starry culmination drop / Balm-dews'.

So kind an office hath been done,
  Such precious relics brought by thee;
  The dust of him I shall not see
Till all my widowed race be run.

## XVIII

'Tis well; 'tis something; we may stand
  Where he in English earth is laid,
  And from his ashes may be made
The violet of his native land.

'Tis little; but it looks in truth
  As if the quiet bones were blest
  Among familiar names to rest
And in the places of his youth.

Come then, pure hands, and bear the head
  That sleeps or wears the mask of sleep,
  And come, whatever loves to weep,
And hear the ritual of the dead.

xvii *19*] More than my brothers are to me, *H.MS*, *Purdy MS*; Dear as a brother is to me, *Heath MS*.
xvii *20*] Dear as the mother to the son. *MSS*. Echoing the end of ix.

xviii Not *T.MS*. *H.Nbk 10* (1832–4) lacks ll. 1–12 (though see l. 20*n*) but numbers ll. 13–16 as stanza 'v', which means that there was an extra stanza. Written 1834, since it refers to Hallam's burial (3 Jan.).
xviii *1–4*. Cp. Ovid, *Tristia* I ii 53–4: *est aliquid, fatove suo ferrove cadentem / in solida moriens ponere corpus humo*. (''Tis something worth if falling by fate or by the steel one rests in death upon the solid ground'.)
xviii *2–4*. T. compares *Hamlet* V i 232–4: 'Lay her i' the earth, / And from her fair and unpolluted flesh / May violets spring!' Arthur Hallam had quoted, in praise of T. (*Englishman's Magazine*, Aug. 1831), Persius's *Satires* i 39–40: *Nunc non e ntumulo fortunataque favilla / ascentur violae*. 'When this Poet dies, will not the Graces and the Loves mourn over him?' Cp. *Aylmer's Field* 845*n* (p. 1183).
xviii *7*. *familiar names*: those of the Eltons, his mother's family. Arthur Hallam's *Remains* (1834, p. xxxv) spoke of the place of burial, Clevedon, as having been selected 'not only from the connexion of kindred' (Hallam's maternal grandmother). The wording of Henry Hallam (*Mem.* i 107) is close to T.: 'brought him home to rest among his kindred and in his own country'.
xviii *10*. *mask*] *MSS*, *1850*; mark *trial edition* (*error*).

Ah yet, even yet, if this might be,
  I, falling on his faithful heart,
  Would breathing through his lips impart
The life that almost dies in me;

That dies not, but endures with pain,
  And slowly forms the firmer mind,
  Treasuring the look it cannot find,
The words that are not heard again.

## XIX

The Danube to the Severn gave
  The darkened heart that beat no more;
  They laid him by the pleasant shore,
And in the hearing of the wave.

There twice a day the Severn fills;
  The salt sea-water passes by,
  And hushes half the babbling Wye,
And makes a silence in the hills.

The Wye is hushed nor moved along,
  And hushed my deepest grief of all,
  When filled with tears that cannot fall,
I brim with sorrow drowning song.

xviii *13*] Oh yet that–though it cannot be–*H.MS.* *might*] may *Purdy MS, Sparrow MS.*
xviii *13–16.* Cp. *2 Kings* iv 34, Elisha's miracle: 'And he went up, and lay upon the child, and put his mouth upon his mouth . . . and the flesh of the child waxed warm.'
xviii *15. Would*] Could *H.MS.*
xviii *20. that*] which *Purdy MS, Sparrow MS, Heath MS, H.MS. H.MS* concludes by then repeating ll. 1–4 (as stanza 'VII'), beginning 'And yet 'tis something here to stand'.

xix Not *T.MS.* 'Written at Tintern Abbey' (H.T.). See the unpublished section, *I keep no more a lone distress* (p. 1775). xix is the only section in *Heath MS* but not in *T.Nbk 17*; it refers to Hallam's burial (3 Jan. 1834), so was written 1834.
xix *1.* 'He died at Vienna and was brought to Clevedon to be buried' (T.).
xix *5–8.* 'Taken from my own observation–the rapids of the Wye are stilled by the incoming sea' (T.).
xix *12. sorrow*] sorrows *Heath MS.*

The tide flows down, the wave again
  Is vocal in its wooded walls;
  My deeper anguish also falls,
And I can speak a little then.

## XX

The lesser griefs that may be said,
  That breathe a thousand tender vows,
  Are but as servants in a house
Where lies the master newly dead;

Who speak their feeling as it is,
  And weep the fulness from the mind:
  'It will be hard,' they say, 'to find
Another service such as this.'

My lighter moods are like to these,
  That out of words a comfort win;
  But there are other griefs within,
And tears that at their fountain freeze;

For by the hearth the children sit
  Cold in that atmosphere of Death,
  And scarce endure to draw the breath.
Or like to noiseless phantoms flit:

But open converse is there none,
  So much the vital spirits sink
  To see the vacant chair, and think,
'How good! how kind! and he is gone.'

## XXI

I sing to him that rests below,
  And, since the grasses round me wave,
  I take the grasses of the grave,
And make them pipes whereon to blow.

xx Not *T.MS.*

xx *12*. Cp. Byron, *There's not a joy* 11: 'That heavy chill has frozen o'er the fountain of our tears'.

xxi Not *T.MS.*

The traveller hears me now and then,
And sometimes harshly will he speak:
'This fellow would make weakness weak,
And melt the waxen hearts of men.'

Another answers, 'Let him be,
He loves to make parade of pain,
That with his piping he may gain
The praise that comes to constancy.'

A third is wroth: 'Is this an hour
For private sorrow's barren song,
When more and more the people throng
The chairs and thrones of civil power?

'A time to sicken and to swoon,
When Science reaches forth her arms
To feel from world to world, and charms
Her secret from the latest moon?'

Behold, ye speak an idle thing:
Ye never knew the sacred dust:
I do but sing because I must,
And pipe but as the linnets sing:

xxi *6. sometimes*] pausing *Purdy MS.*
xxi *8 ‸ 9*] Yet I as soon would preach a creed
Whose baseness levels humankind
Or help an old man's vice to find
Low motives for a noble deed. *H.Lpr 103, deleted*
*Purdy MS* ends at this point with these lines for ll. 9–12, with variants: *preach*] use; *baseness*] hatred; *an old man's vice*] a cankered heart. Cp. *The Princess* vi 321 ‸ 2, *1847–8* text: 'To find low motives unto noble deeds'.
xxi *15–16.* Probably alluding to Chartism and, as so often in T., to the French Revolution. Carlyle in *The French Revolution* (1837, ii V xii), for example, told of the Procession of the Black Breeches, describing how 'Blind lake of Sansculottism welters stagnant through the King's Château, for the space of three hours'.
xxi *18–20.* Quoted à propos the spectroscope, *Mem.* ii 336. But it is not clear whether T. or H.T. made the application, and still less clear as to whether or not the lines are *referring* to the spectroscope. No specific astronomical allusion seems needed; for example J. Jacobs's suggestion of the discovery of Neptune (Sept. 1846) seems unfoundedly late for this section.

And one is glad; her note is gay,
  For now her little ones have ranged;
  And one is sad: her note is changed,
Because her brood is stolen away.

## XXII

The path by which we twain did go,
  Which led by tracts that pleased us well,
  Through four sweet years arose and fell,
From flower to flower, from snow to snow:

And we with singing cheered the way,
  And, crowned with all the season lent,
  From April on to April went,
And glad at heart from May to May:

But where the path we walked began
  To slant the fifth autumnal slope,
  As we descended following Hope,
There sat the Shadow feared of man;

Who broke our fair companionship,
  And spread his mantle dark and cold,
  And wrapt thee formless in the fold,
And dulled the murmur on thy lip,

xxi *25. one is glad;*] *1855*; unto one *1850–51*.
xxi *27. one is sad;*] *1855*; unto one *1850–51*.

xxii Not *T.MS*. See the unpublished section on the same page of *H.MS*: *The path by which I walked alone* (p. 1772). Possibly influenced by Petrarch's 47th Sonnet.
xxii *3. four*] three *H.Lpr 103*, *L.MS*. H.T. comments '1828–32'.
xxii *4* ∧ *5*] *H.MS* has xxiii 21–4, deleted.
xxii *6. lent*] sent *H.MS*.
xxii *8. glad at heart*] gaily stept *H.MS*.
xxii *10. To . . . fifth*] Its fourth and long *H.MS*; Its fourth long *L.MS*. *autumnal*: Hallam died 15 Sept. 1833.
xxii *11*] And we came down it high in hope, *H.MS*.
xxii *12*. Adapted from a line of *Tithon* 40 ∧ 41 (p. 567), *T.MS*. Suggesting 'the valley of the shadow of death', *Psalm* xxiii 4.
xxii *13. our*] the *H.MS*.
xxii *14–15*. Cp. *Supposed Confessions* 121–2: 'I am void, / Dark, formless, utterly destroyed'. Also *On Sublimity* 70: 'formless and still and dark'.
xxii *15. the*] its *H.MS*.

And bore thee where I could not see
  Nor follow, though I walk in haste,
  And think, that somewhere in the waste
The Shadow sits and waits for me.

## XXIII

Now, sometimes in my sorrow shut,
  Or breaking into song by fits,
  Alone, alone, to where he sits,
The Shadow cloaked from head to foot,

Who keeps the keys of all the creeds,
  I wander, often falling lame,
  And looking back to whence I came,
Or on to where the pathway leads;

And crying, How changed from where it ran
  Through lands where not a leaf was dumb;
  But all the lavish hills would hum
The murmur of a happy Pan:

When each by turns was guide to each,
  And Fancy light from Fancy caught,
  And Thought leapt out to wed with Thought
Ere Thought could wed itself with Speech;

And all we met was fair and good,
  And all was good that Time could bring,
  And all the secret of the Spring
Moved in the chambers of the blood;

And many an old philosophy
  On Argive heights divinely sang,
  And round us all the thicket rang
To many a flute of Arcady.

xxiii See the unpublished section, *H.MS: The path by which I walked alone* (p. 1772).

xxiii 5. John Churton Collins noted: 'Milton has described Death as the "keeper of the keys of all creeds."' Alongside this suggestion, T. wrote: 'Not known to me' (*Cornhill*, Jan. 1880, *Lincoln*).

xxiii *21–4*. See xxii 4 ∧ 5*n*.

## XXIV

And was the day of my delight
   As pure and perfect as I say?
   The very source and fount of Day
Is dashed with wandering isles of night.

If all was good and fair we met,
   This earth had been the Paradise
   It never looked to human eyes
Since our first Sun arose and set.

And is it that the haze of grief
   Makes former gladness loom so great?
   The lowness of the present state,
That sets the past in this relief?

Or that the past will always win
   A glory from its being far;
   And orb into the perfect star
We saw not, when we moved therein?

## XXV

I know that this was Life,–the track
   Whereon with equal feet we fared;
   And then, as now, the day prepared
The daily burden for the back.

But this it was that made me move
   As light as carrier-birds in air;
   I loved the weight I had to bear,
Because it needed help of Love:

Nor could I weary, heart or limb,
   When mighty Love would cleave in twain
   The lading of a single pain,
And part it, giving half to him.

xxiv *3. The . . . fount*] We know the very Lord *trial edition.*
xxiv *4. wandering isles*: Shelley, *Prologue to Hellas* 18, *Witch of Atlas* 474. Here, 'sun-spots' (T.).
xxiv *8*] *1875*; Since Adam left his garden yet. *1850–72.*
xxiv *10*] *1851*; Hath stretched my former joy so great? *1850.*
xxiv *12. in*] *L.MS*; on *trial edition* (*error*).
xxiv *15–16.* H.T. compares *Locksley Hall Sixty Years After* 187–8:

   Hesper–Venus–were we native to that splendour or in Mars,
   We should see the Globe we groan in, fairest of their evening stars.

xxv *1. Life*: 'chequered, but the burden was shared' (T.).
xxv *2. with equal feet*: *Aeneid* ii 724, *non passibus aequis.*

## XXVI

Still onward winds the dreary way;
  I with it; for I long to prove
  No lapse of moons can canker Love,
Whatever fickle tongues may say.

And if that eye which watches guilt
  And goodness, and hath power to see
  Within the green the mouldered tree,
And towers fallen as soon as built–

Oh, if indeed that eye foresee
  Or see (in Him is no before)
  In more of life true life no more
And Love the indifference to be,

Then might I find, ere yet the morn
  Breaks hither over Indian seas,
  That Shadow waiting with the keys,
To shroud me from my proper scorn.

## XXVII

I envy not in any moods
  The captive void of noble rage,
  The linnet born within the cage,
That never knew the summer woods:

xxvi Not *T.MS. Mat.* i 127–8 listed it as one of the earliest sections, apparently in error (p. 857).
xxvi 5. *which*] that *L.MS.*
xxvi *9–10.* Cp. Marston, *Sophonisba* II i 134–5: 'Gods naught foresee, but see, for to their eyes / Naught is to come or past'.
xxvi *11*] In Being that it is no more, *L.MS 1st reading.*
xxvi *12. And*] In *L.MS 1st reading.*
xxvi *13. Then*] *1855*; So *1850–51.*
xxvi *14. Indian*] Eastern *trial edition.* H.T. compares *Comus* 139: 'The nice Morn on th' *Indian* steep'.
xxvi *16. shroud*] *1855*; cloak *1850–51.* Probably altered because of an objection by *The Times,* 28 Nov. 1851 (E. F. Shannon, *Tennyson and the Reviewers,* 1952, p. 162). *proper*: 'scorn of myself' (T.).

xxvii Not *T.MS.*
xxvii *2–3.* Cp. Gray, *Elegy* 51: 'Chill Penury repress'd their noble rage' (note the context); and Scott, *Lady of the Lake* VI xxii (a funeral lament): 'The captive thrush may brook the cage, / The prison'd eagle dies for rage.'

I envy not the beast that takes
His license in the field of time,
Unfettered by the sense of crime,
To whom a conscience never wakes;

Nor, what may count itself as blest,
The heart that never plighted troth
But stagnates in the weeds of sloth;
Nor any want-begotten rest.

I hold it true, whate'er befall;
I feel it, when I sorrow most;
'Tis better to have loved and lost
Than never to have loved at all.

## XXVIII

The time draws near the birth of Christ:
The moon is hid; the night is still;
The Christmas bells from hill to hill
Answer each other in the mist.

Four voices of four hamlets round,
From far and near, on mead and moor,
Swell out and fail, as if a door
Were shut between me and the sound:

Each voice four changes on the wind,
That now dilate, and now decrease,
Peace and goodwill, goodwill and peace,
Peace and goodwill, to all mankind.

This year I slept and woke with pain,
I almost wished no more to wake,
And that my hold on life would break
Before I heard those bells again:

But they my troubled spirit rule,
For they controlled me when a boy;
They bring me sorrow touched with joy,
The merry merry bells of Yule.

xxvii *11*. Cp. *Sonnet* [*Conrad!*] 14: 'This sloth-sprung weed'.

xxvii *15–16*. Many analogues have been found, among them Congreve: ''Tis better to be left, than never to have been lov'd', *Way of the World* II i; and Thomas Campbell's *The Jilted Nymph* 19–20: 'Better be courted and jilted / Than never be courted at all.'

xxviii One of the earliest sections, begun 1833 (*Mem.* i 109, substantiated by the fact that xxviii is one of the seven sections in *T.Nbk 17*, 1833).

## XXIX

With such compelling cause to grieve
  As daily vexes household peace,
  And chains regret to his decease,
How dare we keep our Christmas-eve;

Which brings no more a welcome guest
  To enrich the threshold of the night
  With showered largess of delight
In dance and song and game and jest?

Yet go, and while the holly boughs
  Entwine the cold baptismal font,
  Make one wreath more for Use and Wont,
That guard the portals of the house;

Old sisters of a day gone by,
  Gray nurses, loving nothing new;
  Why should they miss their yearly due
Before their time? They too will die.

## XXX

With trembling fingers did we weave
  The holly round the Christmas hearth;
  A rainy cloud possessed the earth,
And sadly fell our Christmas-eve.

At our old pastimes in the hall
  We gambolled, making vain pretence
  Of gladness, with an awful sense
Of one mute Shadow watching all.

xxix *2*] As that which drains our days of peace, *MS quoted in Eversley*. *household peace*: *Paradise Lost* x 908.
xxix *3*. *chains regret*] fetters thought *MS Eversley*.
xxix *6*. *the threshold of the night: The Voyage* 18.
xxix *8* ∧ *9*] But this–to keep it like the last,
    To keep it even for his sake;
    Lest one more link should seem to break,
  And Death sweep all into the Past. *MS Eversley*
xxix *11*. *Use and Wont*: Alfred Gatty quotes the motto to Scott's *Pirate*, Chapter 14: 'What religion . . . / Save the good use and wont that carries them / To worship how and where their fathers worshipp'd?'

xxx In *T.Nbk 17* (1833), and therefore one of the earliest sections; also in *T.MS*. Entitled in *Heath MS* 'Christmas Eve. 1833'.

We paused: the winds were in the beech:
  We heard them sweep the winter land;
  And in a circle hand-in-hand
Sat silent, looking each at each.

Then echo-like our voices rang;
  We sung, though every eye was dim,
  A merry song we sang with him
Last year: impetuously we sang:

We ceased: a gentler feeling crept
  Upon us: surely rest is meet:
  'They rest,' we said, 'their sleep is sweet,'
And silence followed, and we wept.

Our voices took a higher range;
  Once more we sang: 'They do not die
  Nor lose their mortal sympathy,
Nor change to us, although they change;

'Rapt from the fickle and the frail
  With gathered power, yet the same,
  Pierces the keen seraphic flame
From orb to orb, from veil to veil.'

Rise, happy morn, rise, holy morn,
  Draw forth the cheerful day from night:
  O Father, touch the east, and light
The light that shone when Hope was born.

xxx *9. paused*] ceased *Heath MS.*
xxx *17. ceased*] paused *Heath MS.*
xxx *19. rest . . . sleep*] sleep . . . rest *Heath MS 1st reading.*
xxx *20. And . . . followed*] We kissed each other *Heath MS, H.Lpr 101, L.MS 1st reading.*
xxx *22. Once more*] Again *Heath MS 1st reading.*
xxx *26. yet*] still *Heath MS 1st reading.*
xxx *27. Pierces*] Pierceth *Heath MS.* Cp. Shelley, *Revolt of Islam* xii 45: 'Pierce like reposing flames the tremulous atmosphere'.
xxx *28. From orb to orb*: *Œnone* 163–4, MS.
xxx *28–32.* Cp. the last lines of Shelley's *Adonais* (noting the elegiac context): 'Whilst, burning through the inmost veil of Heaven, / The soul of Adonais, like a star, / Beacons from the abode where the Eternal are.'
xxx *32. T.MS* has ll. 1–13 of an unpublished section, taking up this last line of xxx, in which his Muse speaks of hope.

## XXXI

When Lazarus left his charnel-cave,
And home to Mary's house returned,
Was this demanded–if he yearned
To hear her weeping by his grave?

'Where wert thou, brother, those four days?'
There lives no record of reply,
Which telling what it is to die
Had surely added praise to praise.

From every house the neighbours met,
The streets were filled with joyful sound,
A solemn gladness even crowned
The purple brows of Olivet.

Behold a man raised up by Christ!
The rest remaineth unrevealed;
He told it not; or something sealed
The lips of that Evangelist.

## XXXII

Her eyes are homes of silent prayer,
Nor other thought her mind admits
But, he was dead, and there he sits,
And he that brought him back is there.

Then one deep love doth supersede
All other, when her ardent gaze
Roves from the living brother's face,
And rests upon the Life indeed.

xxxi One of the earliest sections (*Mem.* i 109, substantiated by *T.Nbk 17*), written in 1833. It is in *Heath MS. T.Nbk 17* shows that xxxi and xxxii were originally envisaged as one section; this draft at first consisted of xxxi 1–8 plus xxxii 5–16, and was then revised to xxxi 1–8 plus xxxii 1–12. Cp. *Thou mayst remember* (p. 282), which in *T.Nbk 23* has a concluding stanza on the joy of Mary at the resurrection of Lazarus, the stanza deleted apparently by H.T. T. quotes: 'She goeth unto the grave to weep there', *John* xi 31.

xxxi *1. his*] the *H.Lpr 106, H.Nbk 21, Heath MS.*

xxxi *4. by*] at *MSS.*

xxxi *7. is*] was *H.Lpr 106.*

xxxi *9. every house*] all the lands *H.Nbk 21.*

xxxi *10. filled*] lined *H.Lpr 101.*

xxxi *13. raised up*] upraised *H.Lpr 106, H.Nbk 21, Heath MS.*

xxxi *13–16.* Cp. Pope, *Eloisa to Abelard* 9–10: 'rest ever unreveal'd, / Nor pass these lips in holy silence seal'd.'

xxxii Begun 1833; see xxxi *n.*

All subtle thought, all curious fears,
Borne down by gladness so complete,
She bows, she bathes the Saviour's feet
With costly spikenard and with tears.

Thrice blest whose lives are faithful prayers,
Whose loves in higher love endure;
What souls possess themselves so pure,
Or is there blessedness like theirs?

## XXXIII

O thou that after toil and storm
Mayst seem to have reached a purer air,
Whose faith has centre everywhere,
Nor cares to fix itself to form,

Leave thou thy sister when she prays,
Her early Heaven, her happy views;
Nor thou with shadowed hint confuse
A life that leads melodious days.

Her faith through form is pure as thine,
Her hands are quicker unto good:
Oh, sacred be the flesh and blood
To which she links a truth divine!

See thou, that countest reason ripe
In holding by the law within,
Thou fail not in a world of sin,
And even for want of such a type.

## XXXIV

My own dim life should teach me this,
That life shall live for evermore,
Else earth is darkness at the core,
And dust and ashes all that is;

xxxii *11. , she*] and *H.Lpr 101.*
xxxii *11–12. John* xii 3.

xxxiii *6. early*] local *trial edition.*
xxxiii *8.* T. compares Statius, *Silvae* I iii 22–3: *ceu* [*placidi*] *veritus turbare Vopisci / Pieriosque dies et habentes carmina somnos.* ('As if afraid to disturb the Pierian days and music-haunted slumbers of tranquil Vopiscus.')
xxxiii *10*] Nor could thy vision bring her good: *H.Lpr 101, L.MS.*
xxxiii *11. Oh,*] So *MSS.*

xxxiv *1. dim life*] dark heart *H.Lpr 101.* *should*] can *trial edition.*

This round of green, this orb of flame,
  Fantastic beauty; such as lurks
  In some wild Poet, when he works
Without a conscience or an aim.

What then were God to such as I?
  'Twere hardly worth my while to choose
  Of things all mortal, or to use
A little patience ere I die;

'Twere best at once to sink to peace,
  Like birds the charming serpent draws,
  To drop head-foremost in the jaws
Of vacant darkness and to cease.

## XXXV

Yet if some voice that man could trust
  Should murmur from the narrow house,
  'The cheeks drop in; the body bows;
Man dies: nor is there hope in dust:'

Might I not say? 'Yet even here,
  But for one hour, O Love, I strive
  To keep so sweet a thing alive:'
But I should turn mine ears and hear

The moanings of the homeless sea,
  The sound of streams that swift or slow
  Draw down Æonian hills, and sow
The dust of continents to be;

xxxiv *5–8.* On the same subject but in a different mood, cp. *On a Mourner* 15 ∧ 16 (p. 558), on Hallam's death, which says how slight the comforts of Nature are: 'Yet is she mortal even as I, / Or as that friend I loved in vain: / She only whispering low or high, / Through this vast cloud of grief and pain / I had not found my peace again.'
xxxiv *14.* Cp. Shelley, *Revolt of Islam* ii 414: 'as the charmed bird that haunts the serpent's den'.

xxxv *9. the homeless sea*: Shelley, *The Cyclops* 709. Cp. *Alastor* 566 (noting l. 10): 'The thunder and the hiss of homeless streams'. John Churton Collins suggested that T.'s line was 'partly from Horace, *Odes* II xx: *Visam gementis litora Bospori*'. Alongside this suggestion, T. wrote: 'Nonsense' (*Cornhill*, Jan. 1880, *Lincoln*).
xxxv *9–12.* T. commented to J. Knowles, *Nineteenth Century* xxxiii (1893) 182: 'The vastness of the future–the enormity of the ages to come after your little life would act against that love.'
xxxv *10–11.* Cp. *The Ring* 41: 'Æonian Evolution, swift or slow'.

And Love would answer with a sigh,
  'The sound of that forgetful shore
  Will change my sweetness more and more,
Half-dead to know that I shall die.'

O me, what profits it to put
  An idle case? If Death were seen
  At first as Death, Love had not been,
Or been in narrowest working shut,

Mere fellowship of sluggish moods,
  Or in his coarsest Satyr-shape
  Had bruised the herb and crushed the grape,
And basked and battened in the woods.

## XXXVI

Though truths in manhood darkly join,
  Deep-seated in our mystic frame,
  We yield all blessing to the name
Of Him that made them current coin;

For Wisdom dealt with mortal powers,
  Where truth in closest words shall fail,
  When truth embodied in a tale
Shall enter in at lowly doors.

And so the Word had breath, and wrought
  With human hands the creed of creeds
  In loveliness of perfect deeds,
More strong than all poetic thought;

xxxv *13–16*] *Added to T.MS in margin.*
xxxv *14. that forgetful shore*: T. comments: 'the land where all things are forgotten'. Cp. *Paradise Lost* ii 74: 'that forgetful Lake'.
xxxv *23–4.* Cp. *Sonnet* [*Alas! how weary*] 9–10: 'laughing cheerily / Bruise his gold grain upon his threshing-floor'. Also *PL* v 344–5: 'For drink the Grape / She crushes'; and *Comus* 46–7.

xxxvi *1. manhood*] Nature *trial edition.*
xxxvi *2. our*] her *trial edition.*
xxxvi *5*] Oh wisdom of eternal Powers! *H.Lpr 101.*
xxxvi *5–8.* T. comments: 'For divine Wisdom had to deal with the limited powers of humanity, to which truth logically argued out would be ineffectual, whereas truth coming in the story of the Gospel can influence the poorest.'
xxxvi *6. Where truth*] Truth chased *MS.*
xxxvi *9. Word had breath*] Logos breathed *MS.*
xxxvi *11. In*] Pure *MS.*

Which he may read that binds the sheaf,
Or builds the house, or digs the grave,
And those wild eyes that watch the wave
In roarings round the coral reef.

## XXXVII

Urania speaks with darkened brow:
'Thou pratest here where thou art least;
This faith has many a purer priest,
And many an abler voice than thou.

'Go down beside thy native rill,
On thy Parnassus set thy feet,
And hear thy laurel whisper sweet
About the ledges of the hill.'

And my Melpomene replies,
A touch of shame upon her cheek:
'I am not worthy even to speak
Of thy prevailing mysteries;

'For I am but an earthly Muse,
And owning but a little art
To lull with song an aching heart,
And render human love his dues;

xxxvi *15. wild eyes*: 'the Pacific Islanders' (T.).

xxxvii Arthur Hallam had remarked in his *Essay on the Philosophical Writings of Cicero* (1831; Motter, pp. 150–51): 'Poetry, indeed, is seductive by exciting in us that mood of feeling which conjoins all mental states that pass in review before it, according to congruity of sentiment, not agreement of conceptions; and it is with justice, therefore, that the Muses are condemned by the genius of a profound philosophy. But though poetry encourages a wrong condition of feeling with respect to the discovery of truth, its enchantments tend to keep the mind within that circle of contemplative enjoyment, which is not less indispensably necessary to the exertions of a philosophic spirit. We may be led wrong by the sorcery; but that wrong is contiguous to the right.'

xxxvii *9. Melpomene*: the Muse of Tragedy, here of Elegy, as in *Shepherd's Calendar: November* 53–4: 'Up then *Melpomene* thou mournefulst Muse of nyne, / Such cause of mourning never hadst afore.' As in Horace, *Odes* I xxiv 2–3, on the death of a friend: *praecipe lugubres / cantus, Melpomene* ('Teach me a song of mourning, O Melpomene').

xxxvii *11. even*] ev'n *1855*; but *1850–51*.

xxxvii *12. prevailing*: probably in the sense of the Latin *praevalens*, 'very strong', since there is no reason why Urania should prevail over Melpomene.

'But brooding on the dear one dead,
And all he said of things divine,
(And dear to me as sacred wine
To dying lips is all he said),

'I murmured, as I came along,
Of comfort clasped in truth revealed;
And loitered in the master's field,
And darkened sanctities with song.'

## XXXVIII

With weary steps I loiter on,
Though always under altered skies
The purple from the distance dies,
My prospect and horizon gone.

No joy the blowing season gives,
The herald melodies of spring,
But in the songs I love to sing
A doubtful gleam of solace lives.

If any care for what is here
Survive in spirits rendered free,
Then are these songs I sing of thee
Not all ungrateful to thine ear.

xxxvii *19. to me as sacred*] *1855*; as sacramental *1850–51*. Probably altered because of an objection in *The Times*, 28 Nov. 1851 (E. F. Shannon, *Tennyson and the Reviewers*, 1952, p. 161).
xxxvii *23. master's field*: T. comments: 'God's acre' (*Works, 1884*, University of London Lib.).
xxxvii *24.* Cp. Horace, *Odes* III iii 69: *non hoc iocosae conveniet lyrae* ('But this will not befit the sportive lyre').

xxxviii *3.* Cp. *The Princess* vi 179: 'No purple in the distance'.
xxxviii *5. blowing*: 'blossoming' (T.).
xxxviii *6.* Cp. Shakespeare, *Sonnet 1*: 'Herald to the gaudy spring'.
xxxviii *9–12.* H.T. (*1913*) compares *Aeneid* iv 34: *id cinerem aut manis credis curare sepultos?* ('Thinkest thou that dust or buried shades give heed to that?') Cp. Catullus xcvi 1–2: *Si quicquam mutis gratum acceptumve sepulcris / accidere a nostro, Calve, dolore potest.* ('If the silent grave can receive any pleasure, or sweetness at all from our grief, Calvus'.) The theme is that of *My life is full* (p. 350).

## XXXIX

Old warder of these buried bones,
And answering now my random stroke
With fruitful cloud and living smoke,
Dark yew, that graspest at the stones

And dippest toward the dreamless head,
To thee too comes the golden hour
When flower is feeling after flower;
But Sorrow – fixt upon the dead,

And darkening the dark graves of men, –
What whispered from her lying lips?
Thy gloom is kindled at the tips,
And passes into gloom again.

## XL

Could we forget the widowed hour
And look on Spirits breathed away,
As on a maiden in the day
When first she wears her orange-flower!

xxxix Written 1 April 1868 (*Mem.* ii 53), and so not in *T.MS* and *L.MS.* Published 1869, as a pendant to ii.

xxxix *3*. T. comments: 'The yew, when flowering, in a wind or if struck sends up its pollen like smoke'; H.T. compares *The Holy Grail* 13–15: 'Beneath a world-old yew-tree, darkening half / The cloisters, on a gustful April morn / That puffed the swaying branches into smoke.' The yew figures in Lyell's *Principles of Geology* (4th edn, 1835, iii 8): 'How often, during the heat of a summer's day, do we see the males of diœcious plants, such as the yew-tree, standing separate from the females, and sending off into the air, upon the slightest breath of wind, clouds of buoyant pollen.'

xxxix *7*. H.T. remarks: 'The yew is diœcious' (having the unisexual male and female flowers on separate plants).

xxxix *11*. This is more likely to refer to the shoots than to the flowers of the yew. ii 11–12 is about foliage. Cp. *Sonnet* [*Alas! how weary*] 5: 'kindling buds', a phrase used by Shelley, *Adonais* 137. Cp. Shelley's *Triumph of Life* 309–10: 'When all the forest-tips began to burn / With kindling green'. In 1838 T. spoke of 'the tops of the elms . . . beginning to kindle into green' (*Mem.* i 167). But 'kindling buds' might point to flowers; the section speaks of flowers; and tips would imply that the green tips of the yew are conspicuous while the yew blooms, which is not so.

When crownèd with blessing she doth rise
  To take her latest leave of home,
  And hopes and light regrets that come
Make April of her tender eyes;

And doubtful joys the father move,
  And tears are on the mother's face,
  As parting with a long embrace
She enters other realms of love;

Her office there to rear, to teach,
  Becoming as is meet and fit
  A link among the days, to knit
The generations each with each;

And, doubtless, unto thee is given
  A life that bears immortal fruit
  In those great offices that suit
The full-grown energies of heaven.

Ay me, the difference I discern!
  How often shall her old fireside
  Be cheered with tidings of the bride,
How often she herself return,

And tell them all they would have told,
  And bring her babe, and make her boast,
  Till even those that missed her most
Shall count new things as dear as old:

But thou and I have shaken hands,
  Till growing winters lay me low;
  My paths are in the fields I know,
And thine in undiscovered lands.

xl *7–8. Antony and Cleopatra* III ii 43: 'The April's in her eyes'. Cp. Arthur Hallam's poem to Emily Tennyson, *Oh best and fairest of the things that seem*: 'light of tender eyes' (*Victorian Poetry*, Supplement to vol. iii, 1965).
xl *12. other*] novel *trial edition.*
xl *19. those . . . that*] *1877*; such . . . as *1850–75*
xl *21–32*] *T.MS* ends with one stanza which was revised to form these three.
xl *25. would have told*: would desire to be told (H.T.).
xl *32.* Cp. Shelley, *Alastor* 77: 'To seek strange truths in undiscovered lands'. Also *Hamlet* III i 79–80: 'The undiscovered country, from whose bourn / No traveller returns'.

## XLI

Thy spirit ere our fatal loss
  Did ever rise from high to higher;
  As mounts the heavenward altar-fire,
As flies the lighter through the gross.

But thou art turned to something strange,
  And I have lost the links that bound
  Thy changes; here upon the ground,
No more partaker of thy change.

Deep folly! yet that this could be –
  That I could wing my will with might
  To leap the grades of life and light,
And flash at once, my friend, to thee.

For though my nature rarely yields
  To that vague fear implied in death;
  Nor shudders at the gulfs beneath,
The howlings from forgotten fields;

Yet oft when sundown skirts the moor
  An inner trouble I behold,
  A spectral doubt which makes me cold,
That I shall be thy mate no more,

xli *3. Judges* xiii 20: 'For it came to pass, when the flame went up toward heaven from off the altar, that the angel of the Lord ascended in the flame of the altar.'

xli *4. flies*] goes *HnMS.*

xli 5. Cp. *The Tempest* I ii 405: 'something rich and strange'.

xli *8 ∧ 9*]
        How far, how far gone upward now?
          Too far for me to catch the while
          The sweetness of thy proper smile
        Through those new splendours of thy brow! *HnMS deleted*

Cp. the third line with 'Thy sweetness from its proper place', lxxxiii 6.

xli *10. I could*] God would *HnMS 1st reading.*

xli *11.* Cp. *The Two Voices* 347–9, MS (p. 536): 'Life and half-life, a million grades'.

xli *16.* 'The eternal miseries of the Inferno' (T.). H.T. comments: 'forgotten, and consigned to everlasting nothingness', referring to *Inferno* iii 25–51. Cp. *Measure for Measure* III i 126–7: 'those that lawless and incertain thoughts / Imagine howling'; and *Hamlet* V i 235–6: 'A minist'ring angel shall my sister be, / When thou liest howling.' Also *To–with* [*The Palace of Art*] 15–16: 'Lie / Howling in outer darkness.'

xli *19. which*] that *HnMS.*

Though following with an upward mind
The wonders that have come to thee,
Through all the secular to-be,
But evermore a life behind.

## XLII

I vex my heart with fancies dim:
He still outstript me in the race;
It was but unity of place
That made me dream I ranked with him.

And so may Place retain us still,
And he the much-beloved again,
A lord of large experience, train
To riper growth the mind and will:

And what delights can equal those
That stir the spirit's inner deeps,
When one that loves but knows not, reaps
A truth from one that loves and knows?

## XLIII

If Sleep and Death be truly one,
And every spirit's folded bloom
Through all its intervital gloom
In some long trance should slumber on;

xli *23. secular to-be*: 'æons of the future' (T.).

xlii *10. spirit's inner*] spirit through its *HnMS.*

xliii *T.MS* and *L.MS* show that this originally consisted of ll. 1–8 plus a version of the last stanza (below). On the arguments during the Renaissance as to whether or not the dead 'sleep', see Helen Gardner, *Donne's Divine Poems* (1952), pp. xliii–xlvi. There was ample scriptural authority for the belief, e.g. *1 Thessalonians* iv 13–15. But it still excited controversy, e.g. O. Gregory's *On the Evidences of the Christian Religion* (1811; 3rd edn, 1815): 'There are some who contend that the soul *sleeps*, utterly void of sense, consciousness, and activity, from the time of death till the day of judgment' (p. 269). Gregory attacked this view, and the 'still more dangerous error' of not believing in eternal punishment. Cp. *To J.S.* (p. 463).
xliii *3. intervital*: the first usage in *OED*.

Unconscious of the sliding hour,
Bare of the body, might it last,
And silent traces of the past
Be all the colour of the flower:

So then were nothing lost to man;
So that still garden of the souls
In many a figured leaf enrolls
The total world since life began;

And love will last as pure and whole
As when he loved me here in Time,
And at the spiritual prime
Rewaken with the dawning soul.

## XLIV

How fares it with the happy dead?
For here the man is more and more;
But he forgets the days before
God shut the doorways of his head.

xliii *5. sliding*: a traditional epithet, as in Dryden's 'the sliding Sun', *Palamon and Arcite* iii 131; and 'the sliding year', Virgil's *Pastorals* iii 62.

xliii *7. silent traces*] only memories *trial edition.*

xliii *8. all . . . of*] scent and colour to *trial edition.*

xliii *9–12*] *Not T.MS, not originally L.MS.*

xliii *10. So*] *1851 (5th)*; But *1850–51 (4th). that still garden: The Gardener's Daughter* 196; cp. *The Lover's Tale* i 263: 'A man in some still garden'.

xliii *10–12.* Behind T.'s choice of this metaphor for xliii may be Lyell's remark on the bones of men: 'Even if the more solid parts of our species had disappeared, the impression of their form would have remained engraven on the rocks, as have the traces [l. 7] of the tenderest leaves of plants' (*Principles of Geology*, 4th edn, 1835, i 241).

xliii *13–16*] And thus our love, for ever new,
Would last through all; and pure and whole,
Within the centre of the soul
Lie lapt till dawn like golden dew. *trial edition*

*L.MS* likewise, but beginning 'And therefore that our love was true'. Cp. *Richard III* IV i 84: 'the golden dew of sleep'.

xliii *13. will*] *1851 (5th)*; would *1850–51 (4th).*

xliii *15. prime*: daybreak. Cp. *The Two Voices* 378: 'material prime'.

xliv *1.* John Sparrow, *London Mercury* xxi (1930) 429, compares James Thomson's *Song*: 'Tell me, thou soul of her I love, / Ah! tell me, whither art thou fled; / To what delightful world above, / Appointed for the happy dead?'

xliv *2.* Cp. *Locksley Hall* 142: 'The world is more and more'.

xliv *4. doorways of*] doors within *HnMS, H.Lpr 101.* Incorporated from

The days have vanished, tone and tint,
And yet perhaps the hoarding sense
Gives out at times (he knows not whence)
A little flash, a mystic hint;

And in the long harmonious years
(If Death so taste Lethean springs),
May some dim touch of earthly things
Surprise thee ranging with thy peers.

If such a dreamy touch should fall,
O turn thee round, resolve the doubt;
My guardian angel will speak out
In that high place, and tell thee all.

## XLV

The baby new to earth and sky,
What time his tender palm is prest
Against the circle of the breast,
Has never thought that 'this is I:'

But as he grows he gathers much,
And learns the use of 'I', and 'me',
And finds 'I am not what I see,
And other than the things I touch.'

*Hail Briton* 175–6, as Sir Charles Tennyson notes: 'ere yet / God shuts the doors within his head.' T. remarks: 'Closing of the skull after babyhood. The dead after this life may have no remembrance of life, like the living babe who forgets the time before the sutures of the skull are closed, yet the living babe grows in knowledge, and though the remembrance of his earliest days has vanished, yet with his increasing knowledge there comes a dreamy vision of what has been.' Cp. *The Two Voices* 368: 'For is not our first year forgot?' Also Wordsworth, *Immortality Ode* 58: 'Our birth is but a sleep and a forgetting'.

xliv *5. have vanished*] of many a *HnMS.*

xliv *6*] Have ceased to haunt the hoarding sense. *HnMS*; Yet send from out the hoarding sense. *H.MS.*

xliv *7*] Yet comes [At times *H.MS*], he hardly knows from whence *HnMS.*

xliv *8. little flash*] flash from these *HnMS.*

xliv *10.* Shelley, *Rosalind* 409: 'Lethean spring'. Cp. *The Two Voices* 350: 'Some draught of Lethe'.

xliv *15.* The 'guardian angel' is to be distinguished from Hallam.

xlv *8. And*] But *HnMS.*

So rounds he to a separate mind
From whence clear memory may begin,
As through the frame that binds him in
His isolation grows defined.

This use may lie in blood and breath,
Which else were fruitless of their due,
Had man to learn himself anew
Beyond the second birth of Death.

## XLVI

We ranging down this lower track,
The path we came by, thorn and flower,
Is shadowed by the growing hour,
Lest life should fail in looking back.

So be it: there no shade can last
In that deep dawn behind the tomb,
But clear from marge to marge shall bloom
The eternal landscape of the past;

xlv *10. From . . . clear*] And thence his *MS.*
xlv *12. grows*] is *MS.*
xlv *14*] And Life were pilfered of her due, *MS.*
xlv *15. man . . . himself*] men . . . themselves *MS.*
xlv *16.* Incorporated from lix 8 ‸ 9, MS:

Use other means than sobbing breath,
And other charms than misted eyes,
And broodings on the change that lies
Shut in the second birth of death.

xlvi *1–4*] In travelling through this lower clime,
With reason our memorial power
Is shadowed by the growing hour,
Lest this should be too much for time. *MS quoted in Eversley, H.Lpr 101, L.MS 1st reading*

xlvi *1.* Cp. Spenser, *Muiopotmos* 42: 'this lower tract'.
xlvi *2.* Cp. Arthur Hallam, *On My Sister's Birthday* 41–4 (Motter, p. 60): 'My own dear sister, thy career / Is all before thee, thorn and flower: / Scarce hast thou known by joy or fear / The still heart-pride of Friendship's hour.'
xlvi *3. shadowed*: cp. Shelley, *Hellas* 805: 'The coming age is shadowed on the Past'. *the growing hour: Love thou thy land 61.*
xlvi *5. So be it:*] Yet surely *H.MS, L.MS 1st reading.*

A lifelong tract of time revealed;
The fruitful hours of still increase;
Days ordered in a wealthy peace,
And those five years its richest field.

O Love, thy province were not large,
A bounded field, nor stretching far;
Look also, Love, a brooding star,
A rosy warmth from marge to marge.

## XLVII

That each, who seems a separate whole,
Should move his rounds, and fusing all
The skirts of self again, should fall
Remerging in the general Soul,

Is faith as vague as all unsweet:
Eternal form shall still divide
The eternal soul from all beside;
And I shall know him when we meet:

And we shall sit at endless feast,
Enjoying each the other's good:
What vaster dream can hit the mood
Of Love on earth? He seeks at least

xlvi *9. tract*] *L.MS, 1850*; track *trial edition* (error). *tract of time: Paradise Lost* v 498.

xlvi *12. five*] four *H.MS, L.MS 1st reading.*

xlvi *13. O Love, thy*] O me, Love's *H.MS, L.MS 1st reading* (the 'original reading', T.).

xlvi *15.* T. comments: 'As if Lord of the whole life', H.T. adding: 'not merely of those five years of friendship'. H.T. (*1913*) compares 'looks a flower', *A Dedication* 13.

xlvii Not *T.MS.* T. comments: 'The individuality lasts after death, and we are not utterly absorbed into the Godhead. If we are to be finally merged in the Universal Soul, Love asks to have at least one more parting before we lose ourselves.'

xlvii *1. who*] which *L.MS 1st reading.*

xlvii *2. his*] its *MS 1st reading.*

xlvii *5. Is faith . . . as*] Such faith as vague and *MS 1st reading.*

xlvii *11. vaster*] dimmer *MS 1st reading.*

Upon the last and sharpest height,
 Before the spirits fade away,
 Some landing-place, to clasp and say,
'Farewell! We lose ourselves in light.'

## XLVIII

If these brief lays, of Sorrow born,
 Were taken to be such as closed
 Grave doubts and answers here proposed,
Then these were such as men might scorn:

Her care is not to part and prove;
 She takes, when harsher moods remit,
 What slender shade of doubt may flit,
And makes it vassal unto love:

And hence, indeed, she sports with words,
 But better serves a wholesome law,
 And holds it sin and shame to draw
The deepest measure from the chords:

Nor dare she trust a larger lay,
 But rather loosens from the lip
 Short swallow-flights of song, that dip
Their wings in tears, and skim away.

xlvii *14*. T. noted for James Knowles: 'into the Universal Spirit–but at least one last parting! and always would want it again–of course' (*Nineteenth Century* xxxiii (1893) 183).

xlvii *15–16*. Cp. *Timbuctoo* 194–6: 'And step by step to scale that mighty stair / Whose landing-place is wrapt about with clouds / Of glory' of heaven. With earliest light of Spring . . .' T.'s use of 'landing-place' in a religious context may owe something to Coleridge's use of it prominently in *The Friend* (of which the 1844 edition is at *Lincoln*).

xlviii *1*. *brief*] light *H.Lpr 101*.

xlviii *5*. *part and prove: The Two Voices* 134.

xlviii *7*. *slender shade*] random ghost *MS*.

xlviii *8*. Cp. 'Lord of my love, to whom in vassalage', Shakespeare's *Sonnet 26*, a poem similar in its self-depreciation.

xlviii *15–16*. Adapted from *Dear friend* 19–22, which falls into something resembling the *In Memoriam* stanza: 'By thy placid scorns that play / Round the surfaces of things / And like swallows dip their wings / Evermore, and skim away.' Lines from *Dear friend* were also adapted for another elegiac poem, *To J.S.*

## XLIX

From art, from nature, from the schools,
  Let random influences glance,
  Like light in many a shivered lance
That breaks about the dappled pools:

The lightest wave of thought shall lisp,
  The fancy's tenderest eddy wreathe,
  The slightest air of song shall breathe
To make the sullen surface crisp.

And look thy look, and go thy way,
  But blame not thou the winds that make
  The seeming-wanton ripple break,
The tender-pencilled shadow play.

Beneath all fancied hopes and fears
  Ay me, the sorrow deepens down,
  Whose muffled motions blindly drown
The bases of my life in tears.

## L

Be near me when my light is low,
  When the blood creeps, and the nerves prick
  And tingle; and the heart is sick,
And all the wheels of Being slow.

xlix *6. tenderest*] lightest *L.MS 1st reading.*

xlix *11. seeming-wanton ripple*: 'wanton ripples', *The Miller's Daughter* 48 ^ 9, MS.

xlix *12. tender-pencilled*: cp. *The Daisy* 67: 'shadowy-pencilled'.

l Not *T.MS*. Cp. Arthur Hallam, *Meditative Fragments* vi 128–32 (Motter, pp. 73–4): 'But when our feelings coil upon themselves / At time's rude pressure; when the heart grows dry, / And burning with immedicable thirst / As though a plague-spot seared it, while the brain / Fevers with cogitations void of love.'

l *1. my light*] the pulse *L.MS 1st reading.*

l *2–3*. Cp. Shelley, *The Cenci* IV i 163–5: 'My blood is running up and down my veins; / A fearful pleasure makes it prick and tingle: / I feel a giddy sickness of strange awe.'

l *4. the wheels of Being*: Shelley, *Queen Mab* ix 151–2: 'urge / The restless wheels of being on their way', noted by J. D. Jump, *Notes and Queries* cxcvi (1951) 540–41.

Be near me when the sensuous frame
Is racked with pangs that conquer trust;
And Time, a maniac scattering dust,
And Life, a Fury slinging flame.

Be near me when my faith is dry,
And men the flies of latter spring,
That lay their eggs, and sting and sing
And weave their petty cells and die.

Be near me when I fade away,
To point the term of human strife,
And on the low dark verge of life
The twilight of eternal day.

## LI

Do we indeed desire the dead
Should still be near us at our side?
Is there no baseness we would hide?
No inner vileness that we dread?

Shall he for whose applause I strove,
I had such reverence for his blame,
See with clear eye some hidden shame
And I be lessened in his love?

I wrong the grave with fears untrue:
Shall love be blamed for want of faith?
There must be wisdom with great Death:
The dead shall look me through and through.

Be near us when we climb or fall:
Ye watch, like God, the rolling hours
With larger other eyes than ours,
To make allowance for us all.

l *5–6*. Cp. *Suggested by Reading* 56: 'the social frame is racked'.
l *8*. The Furies carried torches.

li It had just been composed at Christmas 1841, according to E. Lushington (*Mem.* i 202–3): 'On one other occasion he came and showed me a poem he had just composed, saying he liked it better than most he had done lately'.
li *7*. *eye . . . hidden*] sight my secret *H.Lpr 101*.
li *10*. Cp. *Gareth and Lynette* 293: 'Let love be blamed for it, not she, nor I'.

## LII

I cannot love thee as I ought,
For love reflects the thing beloved;
My words are only words, and moved
Upon the topmost froth of thought.

'Yet blame not thou thy plaintive song,'
The Spirit of true love replied;
'Thou canst not move me from thy side,
Nor human frailty do me wrong.

'What keeps a spirit wholly true
To that ideal which he bears?
What record? not the sinless years
That breathed beneath the Syrian blue:

'So fret not, like an idle girl,
That life is dashed with flecks of sin.
Abide: thy wealth is gathered in,
When Time hath sundered shell from pearl.'

## LIII

How many a father have I seen,
A sober man, among his boys,
Whose youth was full of foolish noise,
Who wears his manhood hale and green:

And dare we to this fancy give,
That had the wild oat not been sown,
The soil, left barren, scarce had grown
The grain by which a man may live?

Or, if we held the doctrine sound
For life outliving heats of youth,
Yet who would preach it as a truth
To those that eddy round and round?

lii *4.* John Churton Collins compared Persius, *Satires* i 104–5: *Summa delumbe saliva / hoc natat in labris.* ('Floating and spluttering on the lips, on the top of the spittle.') (This satire is apparently alluded to in xviii 3–4.) But T. wrote 'Nonsense' at this point on his copy of Collins's article, *Cornhill*, Jan. 1880 (*Lincoln*).

lii *15. Abide*: 'wait without wearying' (T.).

lii *16. Time hath sundered*] years have rotted *trial edition.*

liii *5. fancy*] *1850* (*3rd*); doctrine *1850* (*1st–2nd*).

liii *7. scarce had*] *1850* (*3rd*); had not *1850* (*1st–2nd*).

liii *9. Or,*] *1882*; Oh! *1850–81* (T. made this change in a copy of *Works*, 1881, *Lincoln*).

liii *12. those*] lives *trial edition.*

Hold thou the good: define it well:
For fear divine Philosophy
Should push beyond her mark, and be
Procuress to the Lords of Hell.

## LIV

Oh yet we trust that somehow good
Will be the final goal of ill,
To pangs of nature, sins of will,
Defects of doubt, and taints of blood;

That nothing walks with aimless feet;
That not one life shall be destroyed,
Or cast as rubbish to the void,
When God hath made the pile complete;

That not a worm is cloven in vain;
That not a moth with vain desire
Is shrivelled in a fruitless fire,
Or but subserves another's gain.

Behold, we know not anything;
I can but trust that good shall fall
At last–far off–at last, to all,
And every winter change to spring.

So runs my dream: but what am I?
An infant crying in the night:
An infant crying for the light:
And with no language but a cry.

liii *14. divine Philosophy: Comus* 476. Cp. *Colossians* ii 8: 'Beware lest any man spoil you through philosophy and vain deceit, after the tradition of men, after the rudiments of the world, and not after Christ.'
liii *16. Procuress*] A pandar *L.MS.*

liv *12* ∧ *13*] *T.MS* has four lines saying that there has not been such a revelation of after-life to man; deleted presumably for religious reasons.
liv *18. infant: infans,* unable to speak. Cp. *Jeremiah* i 6: 'Then said I, Ah, Lord God! behold, I cannot speak: for I am a child.'

## LV

The wish, that of the living whole
  No life may fail beyond the grave,
  Derives it not from what we have
The likest God within the soul?

Are God and Nature then at strife,
  That Nature lends such evil dreams?
  So careful of the type she seems,
So careless of the single life;

That I, considering everywhere
  Her secret meaning in her deeds,
  And finding that of fifty seeds
She often brings but one to bear,

I falter where I firmly trod,
  And falling with my weight of cares
  Upon the great world's altar-stairs
That slope through darkness up to God,

I stretch lame hands of faith, and grope,
  And gather dust and chaff, and call
  To what I feel is Lord of all,
And faintly trust the larger hope.

lv Not *T.MS.* The sections about evolution were written 'some years' before the publication of Robert Chambers's *Vestiges of Creation* in 1844 (*Mem.* i 223). The use of 'type' and 'life' suggests the influence of Charles Lyell's *Principles of Geology*, which T. read in 1837 (*Mem.* i 162, noted by J. Killham, *Tennyson and 'The Princess'*, 1958, p. 248). Cp. the MS of *The Palace of Art* 186–92*n* (p. 413): 'And likewise every life that Nature made, / What yet is left and what is gone / To where the classes vanish, shade by shade, / Life and half-life, to none.' Also *The Two Voices* 32–3: 'Though thou wert scattered to the wind, / Yet is there plenty of the kind.'

lv *7–8.* Cp. Chambers (p. 377): 'It is clear, moreover, from the whole scope of the natural laws, that the individual, as far as the present sphere of being is concerned, is to the Author of Nature a consideration of inferior moment. Everywhere we see the arrangements for the species perfect; the individual is left, as it were, to take his chance amidst the *mêlée* of the various laws affecting him. If he be found inferiorly endowed, or ill befalls him, there was at least no partiality against him. The system has the fairness of a lottery, in which every one has the like chance of drawing the prize.'

lv *11.* '"Fifty" should be "myriad"' (T.).

lv *20.* See *The Vision of Sin* 220–4*n* (p. 725).

## LVI

'So careful of the type?' but no.
From scarpèd cliff and quarried stone
She cries, 'A thousand types are gone:
I care for nothing, all shall go.

'Thou makest thine appeal to me:
I bring to life, I bring to death:
The spirit does but mean the breath:
I know no more.' And he, shall he,

Man, her last work, who seemed so fair,
Such splendid purpose in his eyes,
Who rolled the psalm to wintry skies,
Who built him fanes of fruitless prayer,

lvi Not *T.MS* and *trial edition*. *Mem.* i 223 says that the sections about evolution existed some years before the publication of Chambers's *Vestiges of Creation* in 1844. E. B. Mattes (*In Memoriam: The Way of a Soul*, 1951, p. 58) remarks: 'It was almost certainly his reading in the *Principles of Geology* that led Tennyson to write lvi. Lyell's second volume has this disconcerting quotation on its title-page: "The inhabitants of the globe, like all the other parts of it, are subject to change. It is not only the individual that perishes, but whole species".' Lyell also says: 'Species cannot be immortal, but must perish, one after the other, like the individuals which compose them' (4th edn, 1835, iii 155). 'And even when they have been included in rocky strata, . . . they must nevertheless eventually perish; for every year some portion of the earth's crust is shattered by earthquakes or melted by volcanic fire, or ground to dust by the moving waters on the surface' (iii 280). T. read Lyell in 1837 (*Mem.* i 162), which was also the date of publication of C. Babbage's *Ninth Bridgewater Treatise* (*Lincoln*). Babbage praised God's foreseeing 'that the extinction of every race should be as certain as the death of each individual; and the advent of new genera be as inevitable as the destruction of their predecessors' (p. 46).
lvi *1. but no*] not so *L.MS 1st reading*.
lvi *5–8*] *Added to L.MS in margin*.
lvi *8–16*. Cp. Thomson's *Spring* 349–58: 'But man, whom Nature formed of milder clay, / With every kind emotion in his heart, / And taught alone to weep . . . shall he, fair form! / Who wears sweet smiles, and looks erect on Heaven, / E'er stoop to mingle with the prowling herd, / And dip his tongue in gore? The beast of prey, / Blood-stained, deserves to bleed.'
lvi *9*] Shall he that seemed so grand and fair, *L.MS 1st reading*.
lvi *11. wintry*] Sabbath *L.MS*. Cp. T.'s childhood translation of Horace (*Lincoln*): 'roll away / Along yon wintry skies'.
lvi *12. fruitless*] praise and *L.MS*.

Who trusted God was love indeed
And love Creation's final law–
Though Nature, red in tooth and claw
With ravine, shrieked against his creed–

Who loved, who suffered countless ills,
Who battled for the True, the Just,
Be blown about the desert dust,
Or sealed within the iron hills?

No more? A monster then, a dream,
A discord. Dragons of the prime,
That tare each other in their slime,
Were mellow music matched with him.

O life as futile, then, as frail!
O for thy voice to soothe and bless!
What hope of answer, or redress?
Behind the veil, behind the veil.

## LVII

Peace; come away: the song of woe
Is after all an earthly song:
Peace; come away: we do him wrong
To sing so wildly: let us go.

lvi *15. in*] with *L.MS.*

lvi *16. With . . . shrieked*] And . . . cried *L.MS.*

lvi *18*] Who yearned for True and Good and Just, *L.MS.*

lvi *20. iron hills: The Princess* v 140.

lvi *23. tare*] tore *L.MS.*

lvi *28.* The 'veil' has attracted much commentary. E. B. Mattes (pp. 62–3) suggests that T. probably 'had in mind the myth of the veiled statue of Truth at Sais, which one might unveil only at the cost of one's life'; Arthur Hallam had alluded to this in a sonnet to Emily Tennyson (Motter, p. 83): 'Who in my Sais-temple wast a light / Behind all veils of thought.' T. may have learned of it from William Heckford's *Succinct Account of All the Religions* (1791), of which a copy was at Somersby (*Lincoln*): 'on whose temple at Sais was the following remarkable inscription: "I am all that hath been, is, and shall be, and my veil hath no mortal yet uncovered"' (p. 5). Cp. also *Hebrews* vi 19: 'Which hope we have as an anchor of the soul, both sure and stedfast, and which entereth into that within the veil.' The word was a favourite of Shelley's.

lvii *L.MS* introduces this with an unpublished section, *O Sorrower for the faded leaf* (p. 1773).

Come; let us go: your cheeks are pale;
But half my life I leave behind:
Methinks my friend is richly shrined;
But I shall pass; my work will fail.

Yet in these ears, till hearing dies,
One set slow bell will seem to toll
The passing of the sweetest soul
That ever looked with human eyes.

I hear it now, and o'er and o'er,
Eternal greetings to the dead;
And 'Ave, Ave, Ave,' said,
'Adieu, adieu' for evermore.

## LVIII

In those sad words I took farewell:
Like echoes in sepulchral halls,
As drop by drop the water falls
In vaults and catacombs, they fell;

And, falling, idly broke the peace
Of hearts that beat from day to day,
Half-conscious of their dying clay,
And those cold crypts where they shall cease.

The high Muse answered: 'Wherefore grieve
Thy brethren with a fruitless tear?
Abide a little longer here,
And thou shalt take a nobler leave.'

lvii *8*. T. comments: 'The poet speaks of these poems. Methinks I have built a rich shrine to my friend, but it will not last.'
lvii *8 ^ 9*] *T.MS* has 4 lines depreciating his verse.
lvii *15–16*. T. compares Catullus ci, 'these terribly pathetic lines': *Accipe fraterno multum manantia fletu, / atque in perpetuum, frater, ave atque vale*. ('Take them, wet with many tears of a brother, and for ever, O my brother, hail and farewell!') T. added: 'Nor can any modern elegy, so long as men retain the least hope in the after-life of those whom they loved, equal in pathos the desolation of that everlasting farewell.' Cp. *Frater Ave Atque Vale* (p. 1284).

lviii Not *T.MS*.
lviii *9–12*] The grave Muse answered: 'Go not yet.
A speechless child can move the heart,
But thine, my friend, is nobler Art.
I lent thee force, and pay the debt.

Why wouldst thou make thy brethren grieve?
Depart not with an idle tear
But wait: there comes a stronger year
When thou shalt take a nobler leave.' *L.MS 1st reading*

## LIX

O Sorrow, wilt thou live with me
No casual mistress, but a wife,
My bosom-friend and half of life;
As I confess it needs must be;

O Sorrow, wilt thou rule my blood,
Be sometimes lovely like a bride,
And put thy harsher moods aside,
If thou wilt have me wise and good.

My centred passion cannot move,
Nor will it lessen from today;
But I'll have leave at times to play
As with the creature of my love;

lix Not published till *1851* (*4th*), 'as a pendant to iii' (H.T.). Not *T.MS*, *L.MS*. *H.Lpr 99* antedates *Sparrow MS* (which has no variants).
lix *1*. *wilt*] would'st *H.MS*.
lix *1–2*. Cp. *Richard II* V i 93–4: 'Come, come, in wooing sorrow let's be brief, / Since, wedding it, there is such length in grief.'
lix *4* ∧ *5*] I cannot put thee forth again,
Nor lose thee in the cloud of change,
The times that grow to something strange,
The faces and the minds of men. *H.MS*
These became lxxi 10–11: 'Of men and minds, the dust of change, / The days that grow to something strange.' Cp. *Morte d'Arthur* 238: 'Among new men, strange faces, other minds'.
lix *6*. *like*] as *H.MS*.
lix *7*. *harsher*] deeper *H.MS*.
lix *8*. *wilt*] would'st *H.MS*.
lix *8* ∧ *9*] Use other means than sobbing breath,
And other charms than misted eyes,
And broodings on the change that lies
Shut in the second birth of death.
Nor shalt thou only wear the rue,
But there are daisies on the grave,
And sweeter blooms which thou shalt have,
Not dipt with tears but dasht with dew. *H.MS*
l. [8] *dipt*] dasht *H.MS 1st reading*, suggesting that 'with tears' was inadvertently left for 'in tears'. l. [3] was adapted as 'But brooding on the dear one dead', xxxvii 17. l. [4] was adapted as 'Beyond the second birth of Death', xlv 16. l. [8] was adapted as 'Deep tulips dashed with fiery dew', lxxxiii 11. For the daisy, dew, and grave, cp. the unpublished section, *I keep no more a lone distress* (p. 1775).
lix *9*. *centred*] deepset *H.MS*.
lix *10*] Be less tomorrow than today; *H.MS*.

And set thee forth, for thou art mine,
With so much hope for years to come,
That, howsoe'er I know thee, some
Could hardly tell what name were thine.

## LX

He past; a soul of nobler tone:
My spirit loved and loves him yet,
Like some poor girl whose heart is set
On one whose rank exceeds her own.

He mixing with his proper sphere,
She finds the baseness of her lot,
Half jealous of she knows not what,
And envying all that meet him there.

The little village looks forlorn;
She sighs amid her narrow days,
Moving about the household ways,
In that dark house where she was born.

The foolish neighbours come and go,
And tease her till the day draws by:
At night she weeps, 'How vain am I!
How should he love a thing so low?'

## LXI

If, in thy second state sublime,
Thy ransomed reason change replies
With all the circle of the wise,
The perfect flower of human time;

And if thou cast thine eyes below,
How dimly charactered and slight,
How dwarfed a growth of cold and night,
How blanched with darkness must I grow!

Yet turn thee to the doubtful shore,
Where thy first form was made a man;
I loved thee, Spirit, and love, nor can
The soul of Shakspeare love thee more.

lix *13*] And set thee forth so trim and fine, *H.MS.*
lix *15*] That though I know thee well yet some *H.MS.*

lxi *1. state sublime*: Gray, *Ode for Music* 25.
lxi *4*] The flower and quintessence of Time; *HnMS.* The MS line is *The Day Dream: L'Envoi* 24, which suggests that lxi was written *c.* 1833–4.
lxi *12.* Arthur Hallam speaks of Shakespeare in a context of Heaven and

## LXII

Though if an eye that's downward cast
  Could make thee somewhat blench or fail,
  Then be my love an idle tale,
And fading legend of the past;

And thou, as one that once declined,
  When he was little more than boy,
  On some unworthy heart with joy,
But lives to wed an equal mind;

And breathes a novel world, the while
  His other passion wholly dies,
  Or in the light of deeper eyes
Is matter for a flying smile.

## LXIII

Yet pity for a horse o'er-driven,
  And love in which my hound has part,
  Can hang no weight upon my heart
In its assumptions up to heaven;

And I am so much more than these,
  As thou, perchance, art more than I,
  And yet I spare them sympathy,
And I would set their pains at ease.

friendship, in a poem with many affinities to *In Memoriam: To One Early Loved*, stanza xiii (Motter, p. 82): 'Brave spirits are, whom I will have to friend . . . / . . . to whom th'approach is free / Of unbarred Heaven, and the full mystery / Unfolded to the penetrative mind. / Such is the mighty Florentine, and He / Who saw the solar angel, nor was blind; / Such the deep, simple Shakespeare, greatest of mankind.' Hallam also spoke of Shakespeare as 'the most universal mind that ever existed' in praising the *Sonnets* (*The Influence of Italian upon English Literature*, 1831; Motter, p. 229). For *In Memoriam* and the *Sonnets*, see headnote (p. 860).

lxii *3. Then*] *1851*; So *1850*.

lxii *5–7*. Cp. *Locksley Hall* 43–4: 'Having known me—to decline / On a range of lower feelings and a narrower heart than mine'. Based on *Hamlet* I v 50–52: 'to decline / Upon a wretch whose natural gifts were poor / To those of mine.'

lxiii *4. assumptions*: including the theological suggestion as in the Virgin Mary's reception into heaven.

So mayst thou watch me where I weep,
As, unto vaster motions bound,
The circuits of thine orbit round
A higher height, a deeper deep.

## LXIV

Dost thou look back on what hath been,
As some divinely gifted man,
Whose life in low estate began
And on a simple village green;

Who breaks his birth's invidious bar,
And grasps the skirts of happy chance,
And breasts the blows of circumstance,
And grapples with his evil star;

Who makes by force his merit known
And lives to clutch the golden keys,
To mould a mighty state's decrees,
And shape the whisper of the throne;

And moving up from high to higher,
Becomes on Fortune's crowning slope
The pillar of a people's hope,
The centre of a world's desire;

Yet feels, as in a pensive dream,
When all his active powers are still,
A distant dearness in the hill,
A secret sweetness in the stream,

The limit of his narrower fate,
While yet beside its vocal springs
He played at counsellors and kings,
With one that was his earliest mate;

Who ploughs with pain his native lea
And reaps the labour of his hands,
Or in the furrow musing stands;
'Does my old friend remember me?'

lxiv Not *T.MS.* 'Composed by my father when he was walking up and down the Strand and Fleet Street' (H.T.).
lxiv *6. skirts*] skirt *L.MS.*
lxiv *21. limit*] limits *MS 1st reading.*
lxiv *22. its vocal*] his native *MS 1st reading. Chorus* 15 has 'vocal spring'.

## LXV

Sweet soul, do with me as thou wilt;
I lull a fancy trouble-tost
With 'Love's too precious to be lost,
A little grain shall not be spilt.'

And in that solace can I sing,
Till out of painful phases wrought
There flutters up a happy thought,
Self-balanced on a lightsome wing:

Since we deserved the name of friends,
And thine effect so lives in me,
A part of mine may live in thee
And move thee on to noble ends.

## LXVI

You thought my heart too far diseased;
You wonder when my fancies play
To find me gay among the gay,
Like one with any trifle pleased.

The shade by which my life was crost,
Which makes a desert in the mind,
Has made me kindly with my kind,
And like to him whose sight is lost;

Whose feet are guided through the land,
Whose jest among his friends is free,
Who takes the children on his knee,
And winds their curls about his hand:

He plays with threads, he beats his chair
For pastime, dreaming of the sky;
His inner day can never die,
His night of loss is always there.

## LXVII

When on my bed the moonlight falls,
I know that in thy place of rest
By that broad water of the west,
There comes a glory on the walls;

lxvi *9*] Like one gone blind within the land, *HnMS*, *L.MS 1st reading*.

lzvii has a general likeness to *On the Moon-Light Shining upon a Friend's Grave* (*1827*, p. 1808). Cp. also *Inverlee* (p. 160), with its chancel, church, moonlight, coffin and dusk.

lxvii *3*. *water*] river *L.MS*. 'The Severn' (T.).

Thy marble bright in dark appears,
As slowly steals a silver flame
Along the letters of thy name,
And o'er the number of thy years.

The mystic glory swims away;
From off my bed the moonlight dies;
And closing eaves of wearied eyes
I sleep till dusk is dipt in gray:

And then I know the mist is drawn
A lucid veil from coast to coast,
And in the dark church like a ghost
Thy tablet glimmers to the dawn.

## LXVIII

When in the down I sink my head,
Sleep, Death's twin-brother, times my breath;
Sleep, Death's twin-brother, knows not Death,
Nor can I dream of thee as dead:

I walk as ere I walked forlorn,
When all our path was fresh with dew,
And all the bugle breezes blew
Reveillée to the breaking morn.

lxvii *5*. Cp. Shakespeare, *Sonnet 43*: 'And darkly bright are bright in dark directed'.
lxvii *9*. *The*] *L.MS*; Thy *trial edition* (*error*).
lxvii *14*. *lucid veil*: as in Thomson's *Autumn* 962, and Thomas Moore, *Odes of Anacreon* (1800), xvi. Also Thomas Gisborne, *Walks in a Forest: Autumn*: 'The rime / Floats thin diffused in air . . . / Twinkling in the sun its lucid veil'. The 4th edn is at *Lincoln*, having belonged to T.'s mother. A.C. Bradley (pp. 247–8) noted that Wordsworth speaks of 'a lucid veil' in *Poems During a Tour of 1833* xxxv (1835). But the earlier instances preclude using this to date lxvii.
lxvii *15*. *dark church*] *1855*; chancel *1850–51*. T. remarks: 'I myself did not see Clevedon till years after the burial of A.H.H. (January 3, 1834), and then in later editions . . . I altered the word "chancel" (which was the word used by Mr Hallam in his *Memoir* [1834]) to "dark church"'. Cp. *The Walk at Midnight* 38: 'The chancel's lettered stone above'.
lxvii *15–16*. Cp. *The Princess* vii 165–6: 'Now droops the milkwhite peacock like a ghost, / And like a ghost she glimmers on to me.' Also *To the Queen*, MS (p. 1777): 'And glimmers to the Northern morn'.

lxviii *2*. T. compares *Aeneid* vi 278: *Consanguineus Leti Sopor*.
lxviii *5–8*] *Not HnMS, T.MS 1st reading*.
lxviii *5*. Cp. *Mariana* 30: 'In sleep she seemed to walk forlorn'.

But what is this? I turn about,
I find a trouble in thine eye,
Which makes me sad I know not why,
Nor can my dream resolve the doubt:

But ere the lark hath left the lea
I wake, and I discern the truth;
It is the trouble of my youth
That foolish sleep transfers to thee.

## LXIX

I dreamed there would be Spring no more,
That Nature's ancient power was lost:
The streets were black with smoke and frost,
They chattered trifles at the door:

I wandered from the noisy town,
I found a wood with thorny boughs:
I took the thorns to bind my brows,
I wore them like a civic crown:

I met with scoffs, I met with scorns
From youth and babe and hoary hairs:
They called me in the public squares
The fool that wears a crown of thorns:

They called me fool, they called me child:
I found an angel of the night;
The voice was low, the look was bright;
He looked upon my crown and smiled:

lxviii *9*] Again with thee I wander out *HnMS*.
lxviii *10. I find a*] But there is *HnMS*.
lxviii *13*] But when the bird is in the tree *HnMS*.
lxviii *15. trouble*] sorrow *HnMS*.

lxix Not *T.MS* and *trial edition*, but this section is in *L.MS* where it comes between lxvi and lxvii.

lxix *2. That . . . ancient*] I dreamed that Nature's *L.MS*. For the darkness this causes, cp. *The Two Voices* 160–62: 'If Nature put not forth her power / About the opening of the flower, / Who is it that could live an hour?'

lxix *5*. Cp. *The Gardener's Daughter* 185–208*n* (p. 517): 'Tired of the noisy town I wandered there'.

lxix *10. youth and babe*] babe and youth *MS*.

lxix *12*. T. comments: 'To write poems about death and grief is "to wear a crown of thorns," which the people say ought to be laid aside.' Cp. *Pierced through with knotted thorns of barren pain* (p. 472).

lxix *14. I . . . angel*] There came a Vision *MS*. T. comments: 'But the Divine Thing in the gloom brought comfort.'

lxix *15. look was*] eyes were *MS*.

He reached the glory of a hand,
 That seemed to touch it into leaf:
 The voice was not the voice of grief,
The words were hard to understand.

## LXX

I cannot see the features right,
 When on the gloom I strive to paint
 The face I know; the hues are faint
And mix with hollow masks of night;

Cloud-towers by ghostly masons wrought,
 A gulf that ever shuts and gapes,
 A hand that points, and pallèd shapes
In shadowy thoroughfares of thought;

And crowds that stream from yawning doors,
 And shoals of puckered faces drive;
 Dark bulks that tumble half alive,
And lazy lengths on boundless shores;

lxx Not *T.MS.* *L.MS* has two drafts (*A*, *B* below).

lxx *1. see*] get *A*. *the*] *A–B*; thy *trial edition* (*error*).

lxx *1–4.* Cp. *Ah! yes, the lip may faintly smile* 7–9, on 'the rainbow of the night': 'But seldom seen, it dares to bloom / Upon the bosom of the gloom. / Its tints are sad and coldly pale.' Also Arthur Hallam, *Sonnets to Emily Tennyson* i 6: 'And paint upon the gloom thy mimic form' (Motter, p. 87).

lxx *5. Cloud-towers*] A fort *B*. Cp. this nightmare scene with Carlyle on the taking of Fort L'Eguillette, *The French Revolution* (1837), iii V iii: 'Toulon sees fusillading, grapeshotting in mass, as Lyons saw; and "death is poured out in great floods, *vomie à grands flots*"; and Twelve-thousand Masons are requisitioned from the neighbouring country, to raze Toulon from the face of the Earth. . . . There in black death-cloud we must leave it.' See l. 10*n*.

lxx *7. hand . . . and*] long long train of *A*.

lxx *8. In shadowy*] That sweep the *A*. John Churton Collins said that this line 'was obviously inspired by that weird line in Sophocles [*Oedipus Rex* 67], so infinite in its suggestiveness–πολλὰς δ᾽ ὁδοὺς ἐλθόντα φροντίδος πλάνοις ['And threaded many a maze of weary thought']–on which Shelley has written an admirable commentary' [Note on *Prometheus Unbound*]. Alongside this suggestion, T. wrote: 'Nonsense' (*Cornhill*, Jan. 1880, *Lincoln*).

lxx *8* ∧ *9*]
  Revolving spheres and weltering waves,
   And gusts of sand and foam and snow
   That down a dreary margin go,
  And lamps that wink at yawning graves; *B*

lxx *9*] High shadows crossing dreary moors, *A*; *lacuna B*.

lxx *10.* Cp. Carlyle: 'the victims tumble confusedly . . . ravens darken the river', *The French Revolution* iii V iii, alluded to in *Aylmer's Field* 765–8.

lxx *11. bulk*: a word with evolutionary suggestions for T.; 'The bones of

Till all at once beyond the will
I hear a wizard music roll,
And through a lattice on the soul
Looks thy fair face and makes it still.

## LXXI

Sleep, kinsman thou to death and trance
And madness, thou hast forged at last
A night-long Present of the Past
In which we went through summer France.

Hadst thou such credit with the soul?
Then bring an opiate trebly strong,
Drug down the blindfold sense of wrong
That so my pleasure may be whole;

While now we talk as once we talked
Of men and minds, the dust of change,
The days that grow to something strange,
In walking as of old we walked

Beside the river's wooded reach,
The fortress, and the mountain ridge,
The cataract flashing from the bridge,
The breaker breaking on the beach.

some vast bulk that lived and roared / Before man was', *The Princess* iii 277–8; and 'an old-world mammoth bulked in ice', *ibid* v 142.

lxx *13–16*. Cp. the end of cxxvii and *n* (p. 977), which seems to allude to the French Revolution: 'And compassed by the fires of Hell; / While thou, dear spirit, happy star, / O'erlook'st the tumult from afar, / And smilest, knowing all is well.'

lxx *16*] Look thy fair eyes and make it still. *B.*

lxxi *1–2*] Kinsman of madness, waking trance
And death, O Sleep! hast forged at last *trial edition*;
Old things are clear in waking trance,
And thou, O Sleep, hast made at last *MS quoted in Eversley*

lxxi *4. went*] paced *trial edition.* Alluding to T.'s tour in the south of France with Arthur Hallam in 1830; see *In the Valley of Cauteretz* (p. 1123).

lxxi *6. Then*] *1851 (5th)*; So *1850–51 (4th)*. *trebly strong*] *1855*; treble strong *1850–51*.

lxxi *8. so . . . may*] *1851*; thus . . . might *1850*.

lxxi *10–11*. Adapted from lix 4 ∧ 5, MS:
Nor lose thee in the cloud of change,
The times that grow to something strange,

lxxi *13. Beside*] Besides *L.MS.*

lxxi *14*] The meadow set with summer flags, *MS Eversley.*

lxxi *15. flashing . . . bridge*] clashing . . . crags *MS Eversley.*

## LXXII

Risest thou thus, dim dawn, again,
And howlest, issuing out of night,
With blasts that blow the poplar white,
And lash with storm the streaming pane?

Day, when my crowned estate begun
To pine in that reverse of doom,
Which sickened every living bloom,
And blurred the splendour of the sun;

Who usherest in the dolorous hour
With thy quick tears that make the rose
Pull sideways, and the daisy close
Her crimson fringes to the shower;

Who might'st have heaved a windless flame
Up the deep East, or, whispering, played
A chequer-work of beam and shade
Along the hills, yet looked the same.

As wan, as chill, as wild as now;
Day, marked as with some hideous crime,
When the dark hand struck down through time,
And cancelled nature's best: but thou,

Lift as thou mayst thy burthened brows
Through clouds that drench the morning star,
And whirl the ungarnered sheaf afar,
And sow the sky with flying boughs,

And up thy vault with roaring sound
Climb thy thick noon, disastrous day;
Touch thy dull goal of joyless gray,
And hide thy shame beneath the ground.

lxxii Not *T.MS.*
lxxii *8. blurred*] sucked *L.MS 1st reading.* *of*] from *L.MS.*
lxxii *10. quick tears*: Shelley, *Rosalind* 366.
lxxii *15. L'Allegro* 96: 'Chequer'd shade'.
lxxii *16. Along the hills*] *1855*; From hill to hill *1850–51.* *yet*] and *L.MS.*
lxxii *26.* Cp. *Armageddon* iii 13–14: 'A day / Of darkness riseth on ye, a thick day'. Also T.'s *Sonnet*: 'Though Night hath climbed her peak of highest noon, / And bitter blasts the screaming autumn whirl.'
lxxii *28.* Cp. Shakespeare's *Sonnet 33*, on the sun: 'And from the forlorn world his visage hide / Stealing unseen to west with this disgrace.'

## LXXIII

So many worlds, so much to do,
So little done, such things to be,
How know I what had need of thee,
For thou wert strong as thou wert true?

The fame is quenched that I foresaw,
The head hath missed an earthly wreath:
I curse not nature, no, nor death;
For nothing is that errs from law.

We pass; the path that each man trod
Is dim, or will be dim, with weeds:
What fame is left for human deeds
In endless age? It rests with God.

O hollow wraith of dying fame,
Fade wholly, while the soul exults,
And self-infolds the large results
Of force that would have forged a name.

## LXXIV

As sometimes in a dead man's face,
To those that watch it more and more,
A likeness, hardly seen before,
Comes out—to some one of his race:

So, dearest, now thy brows are cold,
I see thee what thou art, and know
Thy likeness to the wise below,
Thy kindred with the great of old.

But there is more than I can see,
And what I see I leave unsaid,
Nor speak it, knowing Death has made
His darkness beautiful with thee.

lxxiii *6. hath*] has *H.Lpr 101.*
lxxiii *8.* 'Zoroaster's saying, "Nought errs from law"' (T.).

lxxiv *3.* , *hardly*] comes, scarce *HnMS.*
lxxiv *4. Comes . . . one*] Unto some other *HnMS.*
lxxiv *6. art*] wert *HnMS.*
lxxiv *9. But*] And *HnMS.*
lxxiv *11. knowing*] seeing *HnMS.*

## LXXV

I leave thy praises unexpressed
In verse that brings myself relief,
And by the measure of my grief
I leave thy greatness to be guessed;

What practice howsoe'er expert
In fitting aptest words to things,
Or voice the richest-toned that sings,
Hath power to give thee as thou wert?

I care not in these fading days
To raise a cry that lasts not long,
And round thee with the breeze of song
To stir a little dust of praise.

Thy leaf has perished in the green,
And, while we breathe beneath the sun,
The world which credits what is done
Is cold to all that might have been.

So here shall silence guard thy fame;
But somewhere, out of human view,
Whate'er thy hands are set to do
Is wrought with tumult of acclaim.

## LXXVI

Take wings of fancy, and ascend,
And in a moment set thy face
Where all the starry heavens of space
Are sharpened to a needle's end;

lxxv *9. these*] our *HnMS*.
lxxv *11*] And with the breeze of lyric song *HnMS 1st reading*.
lxxv *13*. Cp. *I loving Freedom* 11–12: 'But that which prospers in the green / May perish in the dry.'
lxxv *17. So here*] *HnMS 1st reading*; Here then *HnMS*.
lxxv *20. tumult of acclaim*: a phrase from *To Poesy* 8, written by Hallam and T. Cp. 'The tumult of their acclaim', *The Dying Swan* 33; and *Ode on Wellington* 142–6 (p. 1012).

lxxvi *1*. John Churton Collins compared Petrarch, *Sonnet 82*; T. wrote alongside this suggestion, '!!! nonsense' (*Cornhill*, Jan. 1880, *Lincoln*).
lxxvi *3. starry heavens*] milky girths *L.MS*.
lxxvi *3–4*. Cp. *Cymbeline* I iii 18–19: 'Till the diminution / Of space had pointed him sharp as my needle'.

Take wings of foresight; lighten through
The secular abyss to come,
And lo, thy deepest lays are dumb
Before the mouldering of a yew;

And if the matin songs, that woke
The darkness of our planet, last,
Thine own shall wither in the vast,
Ere half the lifetime of an oak.

Ere these have clothed their branchy bowers
With fifty Mays, thy songs are vain;
And what are they when these remain
The ruined shells of hollow towers?

## LXXVII

What hope is here for modern rhyme
To him, who turns a musing eye
On songs, and deeds, and lives, that lie
Foreshortened in the tract of time?

These mortal lullabies of pain
May bind a book, may line a box,
May serve to curl a maiden's locks;
Or when a thousand moons shall wane

A man upon a stall may find,
And, passing, turn the page that tells
A grief, then changed to something else,
Sung by a long-forgotten mind.

But what of that? My darkened ways
Shall ring with music all the same;
To breathe my loss is more than fame,
To utter love more sweet than praise.

lxxvi *8. Before*] Ere half *L.MS 1st reading.*
lxxvi *9. matin songs*: 'the great early poets' (T.).
lxxvi *11.* Cp. *Epilogue to The Charge of the Heavy Brigade* 39: 'But Song will vanish in the Vast'.
lxxvi *14. With fifty*] A hundred *L.MS.*

lxxvii *2. musing eye*: Arthur Hallam's *To Two Sisters* i 13 (to T.'s sisters Emily and Mary; Motter, p. 89).
lxxvii *4.* Cp. Marvell, *First Anniversary* 139: 'Fore-shortned Time its useless Course would stay'; also *Paradise Lost* v 498: 'tract of time'.
lxxvii *6. may*] or *trial edition.*
lxxvii *7. May*] Or *trial edition.*
lxxvii *8. a thousand moons*: *A Farewell* 14, a poem resembling *In Memoriam.*

## LXXVIII

Again at Christmas did we weave
The holly round the Christmas hearth;
The silent snow possessed the earth,
And calmly fell our Christmas-eve:

The yule-clog sparkled keen with frost,
No wing of wind the region swept,
But over all things brooding slept
The quiet sense of something lost.

As in the winters left behind,
Again our ancient games had place,
The mimic picture's breathing grace,
And dance and song and hoodman-blind.

Who showed a token of distress?
No single tear, no mark of pain:
O sorrow, then can sorrow wane?
O grief, can grief be changed to less?

O last regret, regret can die!
No–mixt with all this mystic frame,
Her deep relations are the same,
But with long use her tears are dry.

## LXXIX

'More than my brothers are to me,'–
Let this not vex thee, noble heart!
I know thee of what force thou art
To hold the costliest love in fee.

lxxviii *5*. The Yule-Clog (log) was placed on the fire on Christmas Eve. T. may have recalled J. Brand's *Popular Antiquities* (1810, *Lincoln*), which spoke of 'its being burnt as an Emblem of the returning Sun' (p. 174).
lxxviii *11*. 'Tableaux vivants' (T.).
lxxviii *12*. *hoodman-blind*: blind man's buff (T.). H.T. compares *Hamlet* III iv 76–7: 'What devil was't / That thus hath cozened you at hoodman-blind?'.
lxxviii *14*. *mark*] *1855*; type *1850–51*. *tear*] *MSS*; tears *trial edition* (*error*).
lxxviii *16*. *be changed to*] become the *HnMS, L.MS 1st reading*; decline to *L.MS 2nd reading*.
lxxviii *17–20*] *Not HnMS*.
lxxix 'Addressed to my brother Charles (Tennyson Turner)' (T.). Cp. *Prefatory Poem to My Brother's Sonnets* (p. 1260).
lxxix *1*. ix 20.

But thou and I are one in kind,
As moulded like in Nature's mint;
And hill and wood and field did print
The same sweet forms in either mind.

For us the same cold streamlet curled
Through all his eddying coves; the same
All winds that roam the twilight came
In whispers of the beauteous world.

At one dear knee we proffered vows,
One lesson from one book we learned,
Ere childhood's flaxen ringlet turned
To black and brown on kindred brows.

And so my wealth resembles thine,
But he was rich where I was poor,
And he supplied my want the more
As his unlikeness fitted mine.

## LXXX

If any vague desire should rise,
That holy Death ere Arthur died
Had moved me kindly from his side,
And dropt the dust on tearless eyes;

Then fancy shapes, as fancy can,
The grief my loss in him had wrought,
A grief as deep as life or thought,
But stayed in peace with God and man.

I make a picture in the brain;
I hear the sentence that he speaks;
He bears the burthen of the weeks
But turns his burthen into gain.

His credit thus shall set me free;
And, influence-rich to soothe and save,
Unused example from the grave
Reach out dead hands to comfort me.

lxxix *9.* Cp. Crabbe, *Delay Has Danger* 707: 'And the cold stream curl'd onward'.

lxxix *11. that roam the twilight*: incorporated from *Locksley Hall* 122, MS.

lxxix *16. kindred*] brother *trial edition.*

lxxx *15–16.* Adapted from *Hail Briton* 81–4: 'They wrought a work which time reveres, / A precedent to all the lands, / And an example reaching hands / For ever into coming years.' Cp. *Tiresias* 122–23: 'their examples reach a hand / Far through all years'.

## LXXXI

Could I have said while he was here,
'My love shall now no further range;
There cannot come a mellower change,
For now is love mature in ear.'

Love, then, had hope of richer store:
What end is here to my complaint?
This haunting whisper makes me faint,
'More years had made me love thee more.'

But Death returns an answer sweet:
'My sudden frost was sudden gain,
And gave all ripeness to the grain,
It might have drawn from after-heat.'

## LXXXII

I wage not any feud with Death
For changes wrought on form and face;
No lower life that earth's embrace
May breed with him, can fright my faith.

Eternal process moving on,
From state to state the spirit walks;
And these are but the shattered stalks,
Or ruined chrysalis of one.

Nor blame I Death, because he bare
The use of virtue out of earth:
I know transplanted human worth
Will bloom to profit, otherwhere.

For this alone on Death I wreak
The wrath that garners in my heart;
He put our lives so far apart
We cannot hear each other speak.

lxxxi *1. Could I have said*: 'Would that I could have said' (T.).
lxxxi *3–4.* Adapted from *The Gardener's Daughter* 234–9*n*, MS: 'Beyond a mellower growth mature in ear'.
lxxxi *4. ear.*] H.T. reports: 'he told me, as far as I remember, that a note of exclamation had been omitted by accident after "ear" (thus, "ear!")'. But H.T. did not change the text.
lxxxi *8* ∧ *9*] *T.MS* has 4 lines on his suffering.

lxxxii *6. From state to state*: *The Two Voices* 351 (a similar context), and *Demeter and Persephone* 7.
lxxxii *10. out of*] from the *L.MS.*
lxxxii *14. Othello* IV ii 58: 'where I have garner'd up my heart'.

## LXXXIII

Dip down upon the northern shore,
O sweet new-year delaying long;
Thou doest expectant nature wrong;
Delaying long, delay no more.

What stays thee from the clouded noons,
Thy sweetness from its proper place?
Can trouble live with April days,
Or sadness in the summer moons?

Bring orchis, bring the foxglove spire,
The little speedwell's darling blue,
Deep tulips dashed with fiery dew,
Laburnums, dropping-wells of fire.

O thou, new-year, delaying long,
Delayest the sorrow in my blood,
That longs to burst a frozen bud
And flood a fresher throat with song.

## LXXXIV

When I contemplate all alone
The life that had been thine below,
And fix my thoughts on all the glow
To which thy crescent would have grown;

I see thee sitting crowned with good,
A central warmth diffusing bliss
In glance and smile, and clasp and kiss,
On all the branches of thy blood;

lxxxiii *2*. Cp. Shelley, *Prometheus Unbound* II i 15: 'Too long desired, too long delaying, come'.
lxxxiii *5–8*, *9–12*] *Transposed T.MS.*
lxxxiii *6*. Adapted from 'The sweetness of thy proper smile', xli 8 ∧ 9, MS (p. 899).
lxxxiii *9–12*. Cp. (noting the context) the flower-passage, *Lycidas* 142–51: 'Bring the rathe Primrose that forsaken dies . . .'
lxxxiii *11*. See lix 8 ∧ *9n*.
lxxxiii *11*, *15*. From Shelley, *Epipsychidion* 110–111: 'Beyond the sense, like fiery dews that melt / Into the bosom of a frozen bud.'
lxxxiii *16*. *The Dying Swan* 42: 'Were flooded over with eddying song'.
lxxxiv Not *T.MS* (but there are leaves missing).
lxxxiv *1*. *contémplate*: as cxviii 1.

Thy blood, my friend, and partly mine;
For now the day was drawing on,
When thou shouldst link thy life with one
Of mine own house, and boys of thine

Had babbled 'Uncle' on my knee;
But that remorseless iron hour
Made cypress of her orange flower,
Despair of Hope, and earth of thee.

I seem to meet their least desire,
To clap their cheeks, to call them mine.
I see their unborn faces shine
Beside the never-lighted fire.

I see myself an honoured guest,
Thy partner in the flowery walk
Of letters, genial table-talk,
Or deep dispute, and graceful jest;

While now thy prosperous labour fills
The lips of men with honest praise,
And sun by sun the happy days
Descend below the golden hills

With promise of a morn as fair;
And all the train of bounteous hours
Conduct by paths of growing powers,
To reverence and the silver hair;

Till slowly worn her earthly robe,
Her lavish mission richly wrought,
Leaving great legacies of thought,
Thy spirit should fail from off the globe;

What time mine own might also flee,
As linked with thine in love and fate,
And, hovering o'er the dolorous strait
To the other shore, involved in thee,

lxxxiv *25–6*. Cp. *Hail Briton* 139–40, MS: 'An evil scorn / Has filled the lips of men with lies'.

lxxxiv *37–44*. Cp. Horace, *Odes* II xvii 5–8: *a, te meae si partem animae rapit / maturior vis, quid moror altera, / nec carus aeque nec superstes / integer?* ('Alas, if some untimely blow snatches thee, the half of my own life, away, why do I, the other half, still linger on, neither so dear as before nor surviving whole?'). Cp. lxxxv 63–4.

Arrive at last the blessèd goal,
And He that died in Holy Land
Would reach us out the shining hand,
And take us as a single soul.

What reed was that on which I leant?
Ah, backward fancy, wherefore wake
The old bitterness again, and break
The low beginnings of content.

## LXXXV

This truth came borne with bier and pall,
I felt it, when I sorrowed most,
'Tis better to have loved and lost,
Than never to have loved at all—

O true in word, and tried in deed,
Demanding, so to bring relief
To this which is our common grief,
What kind of life is that I lead;

And whether trust in things above
Be dimmed of sorrow, or sustained;
And whether love for him have drained
My capabilities of love;

lxxxiv *41*. Cp. *Paradise Lost* ii 409–10: 'Ere he arrive / The happy Ile'.
lxxxiv *43*. Cp. *Maud* i 382–8, MS: 'Reached me a shining hand of help'.
lxxxiv *45*. *Isaiah* xxxvi 6: 'Lo, thou trustest in the staff of this broken reed, on Egypt; whereon if a man lean, it will go into his hand, and pierce it.'
lxxxiv *47*. *break*] shake *L.MS 1st reading*.

lxxxv The version in *T.Nbk 17* (1833) has only 44 lines; that in *Heath MS* and *H.Lpr 106* has 48 lines. For a study of the *Heath* version, see M. J. Ellmann, *MLN* lxv (1950) 22–30. *T.MS* has leaves missing and begins at l. 93. *L.MS* has the final version, and so is not included in references to *MSS* below. In *Eversley*, H.T. notes: 'addressed to Edmund Lushington'; but he dropped this note in *1913*, possibly because he came across the 1833 version. Mrs Ellmann (without pointing out that H.T. dropped his note) suggests 1841 as a probable date for the revision, since T.'s friendship with Lushington was then strong. H.T. added a note in *1913* on ll. 115–6: 'refers to his "bride to be", Emily Sellwood'; this suggests that the revision of the poem will have been later than 1838, when they became engaged.
lxxxv *5–40*] *Not H.MS, Heath MS, T.Nbk 17.*

Your words have virtue such as draws
  A faithful answer from the breast,
  Through light reproaches, half exprest,
And loyal unto kindly laws.

My blood an even tenor kept,
  Till on mine ear this message falls,
  That in Vienna's fatal walls
God's finger touched him, and he slept.

The great Intelligences fair
  That range above our mortal state,
  In circle round the blessèd gate,
Received and gave him welcome there;

And led him through the blissful climes,
  And showed him in the fountain fresh
  All knowledge that the sons of flesh
Shall gather in the cycled times.

But I remained, whose hopes were dim,
  Whose life, whose thoughts were little worth,
  To wander on a darkened earth,
Where all things round me breathed of him.

O friendship, equal-poised control,
  O heart, with kindliest motion warm,
  O sacred essence, other form,
O solemn ghost, O crownèd soul!

Yet none could better know than I,
  How much of act at human hands
  The sense of human will demands
By which we dare to live or die.

lxxxv *20*. J. H. Buckley (p. 114) observes: 'an image reversing Michelangelo's view of the Creation'. Cp. *On a Mourner* 11 (on Hallam's death): 'And on thy heart a finger lays'.

lxxxv *21–4*. Adapted from a passage unadopted in *The Two Voices* (p. 537): 'And those Intelligences fair, / That range above thy state, declare / If thou canst fathom what they are'. Cp. Arthur Hallam, *On the Madonna* 1–3 (Motter, p. 3): 'Not with a glory of stars, a throne inwrought / With elemental splendors, and a host / Of rare intelligences'. The words 'intelligences fair' occur in Spenser, *Tears of the Muses* 509–10: 'The Spirites and Intelligences fayre, / And Angels waighting on th'Almighties chayre.' With the account here of Hallam's reception in Heaven, T. compares *Lycidas* 178–82.

lxxxv *40*. Cp. Pope, *Essay on Man* iv 4: 'For which we bear to live, or dare to die'.

Whatever way my days decline,
I felt and feel, though left alone,
His being working in mine own,
The footsteps of his life in mine;

A life that all the Muses decked
With gifts of grace, that might express
All-comprehensive tenderness,
All-subtilising intellect:

And so my passion hath not swerved
To works of weakness, but I find
An image comforting the mind,
And in my grief a strength reserved.

Likewise the imaginative woe,
That loved to handle spiritual strife,
Diffused the shock through all my life,
But in the present broke the blow.

My pulses therefore beat again
For other friends that once I met;
Nor can it suit me to forget
The mighty hopes that make us men.

I woo your love: I count it crime
To mourn for any overmuch;
I, the divided half of such
A friendship as had mastered Time;

Which masters Time indeed, and is
Eternal, separate from fears:
The all-assuming months and years
Can take no part away from this:

lxxxv *41–4*] *Not T.Nbk 17.*
lxxxv *41. days decline*] life incline *H.MS, Heath MS.*
lxxxv *45–8*] *Not MSS.*
lxxxv *51. the*] my *MSS.*
lxxxv *53–6*] *Not MSS.*
lxxxv *57. My . . . therefore*] These mortal pulses *MSS.*
lxxxv *58. that*] whom *H.MS.*
lxxxv *59. can*] doth *MSS.*
lxxxv *60. mighty hopes*: Shelley, *Revolt of Islam* iv 127.
lxxxv *63–4.* See Horace's *Odes* II xvii 5–8 (quoted under lxxxiv 37–44*n*).

But Summer on the steaming floods,
And Spring that swells the narrow brooks,
And Autumn, with a noise of rooks,
That gather in the waning woods,

And every pulse of wind and wave
Recalls, in change of light or gloom,
My old affection of the tomb,
And my prime passion in the grave:

My old affection of the tomb,
A part of stillness, yearns to speak:
'Arise, and get thee forth and seek
A friendship for the years to come.

'I watch thee from the quiet shore;
Thy spirit up to mine can reach;
But in dear words of human speech
We two communicate no more.'

And I, 'Can clouds of nature stain
The starry clearness of the free?
How is it? Canst thou feel for me
Some painless sympathy with pain?'

And lightly does the whisper fall;
''Tis hard for thee to fathom this;
I triumph in conclusive bliss,
And that serene result of all.'

So hold I commerce with the dead;
Or so methinks the dead would say;
Or so shall grief with symbols play
And pining life be fancy-fed.

lxxxv *72*. Cp. *The Lady of Shalott* 119: 'The pale yellow woods were waning'.
lxxxv *74*. *or*] and *MSS*.
lxxxv *77–96*] *Not MSS*.
lxxxv *95*. Cp. *Song* [*Every day*] 25–6: 'Grief and Sadness steal / Symbols of each other'.

Now looking to some settled end,
That these things pass, and I shall prove
A meeting somewhere, love with love,
I crave your pardon, O my friend;

If not so fresh, with love as true,
I, clasping brother-hands, aver
I could not, if I would, transfer
The whole I felt for him to you.

For which be they that hold apart
The promise of the golden hours?
First love, first friendship, equal powers,
That marry with the virgin heart.

Still mine, that cannot but deplore,
That beats within a lonely place,
That yet remembers his embrace,
But at his footstep leaps no more,

My heart, though widowed, may not rest
Quite in the love of what is gone,
But seeks to beat in time with one
That warms another living breast.

Ah, take the imperfect gift I bring,
Knowing the primrose yet is dear,
The primrose of the later year,
As not unlike to that of Spring.

lxxxv *97. Now . . . some*] Yet . . . a *MSS.*
lxxxv *98. I*] we *H.MS.*
lxxxv *104. whole*] all *MSS.*
lxxxv *105. which be they*] who are those *MSS.*
lxxxv *109–20*] But yet I love you–count it crime
To mourn for any overmuch;
I, the divided half of such
A friendship as had mastered time. *MSS*

Repeating ll. 61–4. *T.Nbk 17* had originally placed this repetition as ll. 104 ∧ 5.

lxxxv *113*. R. W. Rader (p. 16) quotes Rashdall's diary, 14 Jan. 1834, speaking of T.: 'Hallam seems to have left his heart a widowed one.' Rader notes that if we did not know that this particular stanza was probably not composed till much later, the similarity might lead us to think that during his visit Tennyson had read Rashdall this very early elegy.

lxxxv *115–6*. See general note above.

## LXXXVI

Sweet after showers, ambrosial air,
  That rollest from the gorgeous gloom
  Of evening over brake and bloom
And meadow, slowly breathing bare

The round of space, and rapt below
  Through all the dewy-tasselled wood,
  And shadowing down the hornèd flood
In ripples, fan my brows and blow

The fever from my cheek, and sigh
  The full new life that feeds thy breath
  Throughout my frame, till Doubt and Death,
Ill brethren, let the fancy fly

From belt to belt of crimson seas
  On leagues of odour streaming far,
  To where in yonder orient star
A hundred spirits whisper 'Peace.'

## LXXXVII

I past beside the reverend walls
  In which of old I wore the gown;
  I roved at random through the town,
And saw the tumult of the halls;

lxxxvi Not *T.MS.* 'Written at Barmouth' (T.). He was there in 1839, and apparently not previously (*Mem.* i 173). Knowles reported T. as saying 'Bournemouth', but this was presumably misheard (*Nineteenth Century* xxxiii (1893) 185). Cp. *The Lover's Tale* iii 3 (p. 337): 'A morning air, sweet after rain . . .'.
lxxxvi *1. ambrosial*] delicious *L.MS 1st reading.* Cp. 'Ambrosial gloom', fragment of a play (*Mem.* i 24); and *The Princess* iv 6.
lxxxvi *6.* Cp. *The Princess* i 93: 'dewy-tasselled trees'.
lxxxvi *7. the hornèd flood*: 'between two promontories' (T.). As in *Paradise Lost* xi 827.
lxxxvi *11. Throughout*] Through all *L.MS 1st reading.*
lxxxvi *13–16.* T. remarked to Knowles: 'The west wind rolling to the Eastern seas till it meets the evening star'. Cp. *Milton* 13–16: 'Where some refulgent sunset of India / Streams o'er a rich ambrosial ocean isle, / And crimson-hued the stately palm-woods / Whisper in odorous heights of even.'

lxxxvii Not *T.MS.*

And heard once more in college fanes
The storm their high-built organs make,
And thunder-music, rolling, shake
The prophet blazoned on the panes;

And caught once more the distant shout,
The measured pulse of racing oars
Among the willows; paced the shores
And many a bridge, and all about

The same gray flats again, and felt
The same, but not the same; and last
Up that long walk of limes I past
To see the rooms in which he dwelt.

Another name was on the door:
I lingered; all within was noise
Of songs, and clapping hands, and boys
That crashed the glass and beat the floor;

Where once we held debate, a band
Of youthful friends, on mind and art,
And labour, and the changing mart,
And all the framework of the land;

When one would aim an arrow fair,
But send it slackly from the string;
And one would pierce an outer ring,
And one an inner, here and there;

And last the master-bowman, he,
Would cleave the mark. A willing ear
We lent him. Who, but hung to hear
The rapt oration flowing free

lxxxvii *6–7*] The silver anthem trilling wake
And that melodious thunder shake *L.MS 1st reading*

lxxxvii *8. prophet*] *1884*; prophets *1850–83*.

lxxxvii *15*. The limes at Trinity College; 'that walk of limes', *To the Rev. W. H. Brookfield* 6.

lxxxvii *20. beat*] smote *trial edition*.

lxxxvii *21–4*. T. said to James Knowles: 'The "Water Club," because there was no wine. They used to make speeches–I never did'. *Nineteenth Century* xxxiii (1893) 185.

lxxxvii *25. When*] And *MS 1st reading*.

lxxxvii *25–30*. The same metaphor is used in another poem to Arthur Hallam, *If I were loved 5–6*:

All the inner, all the outer world of pain
Clear Love would pierce and cleave, if thou wert mine.

From point to point, with power and grace
And music in the bounds of law,
To those conclusions when we saw
The God within him light his face,

And seem to lift the form, and glow
In azure orbits heavenly-wise;
And over those ethereal eyes
The bar of Michael Angelo.

## LXXXVIII

Wild bird, whose warble, liquid sweet,
Rings Eden through the budded quicks,
O tell me where the senses mix,
O tell me where the passions meet,

Whence radiate: fierce extremes employ
Thy spirits in the darkening leaf,
And in the midmost heart of grief
Thy passion clasps a secret joy:

And I – my harp would prelude woe –
I cannot all command the strings;
The glory of the sum of things
Will flash along the chords and go.

lxxxvii *36.* Motter (p. 43) compares Arthur Hallam's *Timbuctoo* 190: 'God triumphed in her face'.
lxxxvii *39. ethereal*] seraphic *L.MS.*
lxxxvii *40.* T. comments: 'the broad bar of frontal bone over the eyes of Michael Angelo.' 'These lines I wrote from what Arthur Hallam said after reading of the prominent ridge of bone over the eyes of Michael Angelo: "Alfred, look over my eyes; surely I have the bar of Michael Angelo!"' (*Mem.* i 38). On the significance of such a bar, cp. Coleridge: 'A few whose eyes were bright, and either piercing or steady, and whose ample foreheads, with the weighty bar, ridge-like, above the eyebrows, bespoke observation followed by meditative thought' (*A Lay Sermon*, 1817, 'Allegoric Vision').

lxxxviii Not *L.MS* but in *T.MS.*
lxxxviii *1. Wild bird*: 'To the Nightingale' (T.).
lxxxviii *2. Eden*: 'a paradisal song' (T., copy of *Works, 1884*, Univ. of London Library). *quicks*: quickset thorn (H.T.). Cp. 'Fills out the homely quickset-screens', *On a Mourner* 6 (on the death of Hallam).
lxxxviii *5. fierce extremes*: *King John* V vii 13; *Paradise Lost* ii 599, vii 272 (note 'Eden', l. 2); Wordsworth, *Ecclesiastical Sonnets* III xi 12.
lxxxviii *6. darkening*] *1855*; dusking *1850–51.*
lxxxviii *11. the sum of things*: *Paradise Lost* vi 673.

## LXXXIX

Witch-elms that counterchange the floor
Of this flat lawn with dusk and bright;
And thou, with all thy breadth and height
Of foliage, towering sycamore;

How often, hither wandering down,
My Arthur found your shadows fair,
And shook to all the liberal air
The dust and din and steam of town:

He brought an eye for all he saw;
He mixt in all our simple sports;
They pleased him, fresh from brawling courts
And dusty purlieus of the law.

O joy to him in this retreat,
Immantled in ambrosial dark,
To drink the cooler air, and mark
The landscape winking through the heat:

O sound to rout the brood of cares,
The sweep of scythe in morning dew,
The gust that round the garden flew,
And tumbled half the mellowing pears!

lxxxix Not *T.MS.* It has many affinities, both in phrasing and in mood, with *An Idle Rhyme* (p. 662).
lxxxix *1. counterchange*: chequer (heraldic). J. H. Buckley (p. 264) compares *Ode: O Bosky Brook* 58–9: 'woods, whose counterchanged embroidery / Of light and darkness chequered the old moss'. Also *Recollections of the Arabian Nights* 84–6: 'counterchanged / The level lake with diamond-plots / Of dark and bright'.
lxxxix *2.* Cp. *Marion* 48, MS: 'stealing shadows dusk and bright'.
lxxxix *7. shook*] flung *L.MS 1st reading.* *the liberal air*: Byron, *Manfred* I ii 50.
lxxxix *8.* Cp. *Playfellow Winds* 7: 'With steam of this dull town'; and *To the Rev. F. D. Maurice* 13: 'Where, far from noise and smoke of town'. From Horace, *Odes* III xxix 12: *fumum et opes strepitumque Romae* ('The smoke, the riches, and the din of Rome').
lxxxix *12. dusty*] *1855, trial edition, L.MS*; dusky *1850–51.* Cp. *Will Waterproof* 183, where 'dusty crypt' had originally been 'dusky crypt'.
lxxxix *15. To . . . air*] With me to suck the cool *L.MS.*
lxxxix *19–20.* Adapted from the MS of *The Gardener's Daughter* 216–20n (Sir Charles Tennyson, *Cornhill* cliii (1936) 441): 'The wind was fitful: every musky gust / Tumbled the mellow pear'.

O bliss, when all in circle drawn
  About him, heart and ear were fed
  To hear him, as he lay and read
The Tuscan poets on the lawn:

Or in the all-golden afternoon
  A guest, or happy sister, sung,
  Or here she brought the harp and flung
A ballad to the brightening moon:

Nor less it pleased in livelier moods,
  Beyond the bounding hill to stray,
  And break the livelong summer day
With banquet in the distant woods;

Whereat we glanced from theme to theme,
  Discussed the books to love or hate,
  Or touched the changes of the state,
Or threaded some Socratic dream;

But if I praised the busy town,
  He loved to rail against it still,
  For 'ground in yonder social mill
We rub each other's angles down,

'And merge' he said 'in form and gloss
  The picturesque of man and man.'
  We talked: the stream beneath us ran,
The wine-flask lying couched in moss,

Or cooled within the glooming wave;
  And last, returning from afar,
  Before the crimson-circled star
Had fallen into her father's grave,

And brushing ankle-deep in flowers,
  We heard behind the woodbine veil
  The milk that bubbled in the pail,
And buzzings of the honied hours.

lxxxix 25. *all-golden*] golden *L.MS 1st reading.*
lxxxix *31–2.* Horace, *Odes* II vii 6–7: *cum quo morantem saepe diem mero / fregi* ('with whom I many a time have beguiled the lagging day with wine').
lxxxix *35. touched*] grazed *L.MS 1st reading.*
lxxxix *36. threaded ... Socratic*] handled ... Platonic *L.MS 1st reading.*
lxxxix *47–8.* T. comments: 'Before Venus, the evening star, had dipt into the sunset. The planets, according to Laplace, were evolved from the sun.'
lxxxix *48. Had*] *L.MS*; Has *trial edition (error).*

## XC

He tasted love with half his mind,
Nor ever drank the inviolate spring
Where nighest heaven, who first could fling
This bitter seed among mankind;

That could the dead, whose dying eyes
Were closed with wail, resume their life,
They would but find in child and wife
An iron welcome when they rise:

'Twas well, indeed, when warm with wine,
To pledge them with a kindly tear,
To talk them o'er, to wish them here,
To count their memories half divine;

But if they came who past away,
Behold their brides in other hands;
The hard heir strides about their lands,
And will not yield them for a day.

Yea, though their sons were none of these,
Not less the yet-loved sire would make
Confusion worse than death, and shake
The pillars of domestic peace.

Ah dear, but come thou back to me:
Whatever change the years have wrought,
I find not yet one lonely thought
That cries against my wish for thee.

xc Not *T.MS.*

xc *13–20.* A recurrent theme in T. Cp. *The Lotos-Eaters* 114–9: 'Dear is the memory of our wedded lives, / And dear the last embraces of our wives / And their warm tears: but all hath suffered change: / For surely now our household hearths are cold: / Our sons inherit us: our looks are strange: / And we should come like ghosts to trouble joy.' 'Confusion worse than death' (l. 19) is incorporated from *The Lotos-Eaters* 128. The theme is also that of *Enoch Arden.*

xc *21–4*] Alas–but could I gaze on him
Reclothed with human life from dust,
My friend should share my latest crust,
Though famine tore me limb from limb. *L.MS 1st reading*

## XCI

When rosy plumelets tuft the larch,
And rarely pipes the mounted thrush;
Or underneath the barren bush
Flits by the sea-blue bird of March;

Come, wear the form by which I know
Thy spirit in time among thy peers;
The hope of unaccomplished years
Be large and lucid round thy brow.

When summer's hourly-mellowing change
May breathe, with many roses sweet,
Upon the thousand waves of wheat,
That ripple round the lonely grange;

Come: not in watches of the night,
But where the sunbeam broodeth warm,
Come, beauteous in thine after form,
And like a finer light in light.

## XCII

If any vision should reveal
Thy likeness, I might count it vain
As but the canker of the brain;
Yea, though it spake and made appeal

To chances where our lots were cast
Together in the days behind,
I might but say, I hear a wind
Of memory murmuring the past.

Yea, though it spake and bared to view
A fact within the coming year;
And though the months, revolving near,
Should prove the phantom-warning true,

xci Not *L.MS* but in *T.MS*.

xci *4*. T. comments: '"Darts the sea-shining bird of March" would best suit the Kingfisher. I used to see him in our brook first in March . . . ἁλιπόρφυρος εἴαρος ὄρνις ["sea-flashing bird of spring"] (Alcman)'.

xci *7–8*. The nimbus of Iulus, *Aeneid* ii 681–4.

xci *12*. Cp. 'the lonely moated grange' of *Mariana*.

xcii *1*. *If any*] Yet if a *L.MS 1st reading*.

xcii *3*. Cp. *Maud* ii 200: 'the blot upon the brain'.

They might not seem thy prophecies,
But spiritual presentiments,
And such refraction of events
As often rises ere they rise.

## XCIII

I shall not see thee. Dare I say
No spirit ever brake the band
That stays him from the native land
Where first he walked when claspt in clay?

No visual shade of some one lost,
But he, the Spirit himself, may come
Where all the nerve of sense is numb;
Spirit to Spirit, Ghost to Ghost.

O, therefore from thy sightless range
With gods in unconjectured bliss,
O, from the distance of the abyss
Of tenfold-complicated change,

Descend, and touch, and enter; hear
The wish too strong for words to name;
That in this blindness of the frame
My Ghost may feel that thine is near.

## XCIV

How pure at heart and sound in head,
With what divine affections bold
Should be the man whose thought would hold
An hour's communion with the dead.

xcii *13–16*. Cp. Coleridge, *Death of Wallenstein* (1800) V i 98–102: 'As the sun, / Ere it is risen, sometimes paints its image / In the atmosphere, so often do the spirits / Of great events stride on before the events, / And in to-day already walks to-morrow.'

xciii *9–12*. H.T. comments: 'the ten heavens of Dante. Cf. *Paradiso* xxviii 15 ff.' *sightless*: invisible, as cxv 8.

xciii *13*] Stoop soul and touch me: wed me: hear *L.MS 1st reading*.

xciv John Churton Collins said that 'The whole of this piece is little else than a translation of the noble passage about the mood in which man is fitted for communion with his God in Jeremy Taylor's Fifth Golden Grove Sermon.' Alongside this suggestion, T. wrote: 'Not known to me' (*Cornhill*, Jan. 1880, *Lincoln*).

xciv *3*. *thought*] thoughts *L.MS*.

xciv *3–4*. Cp. Arthur Hallam, *Who has not dreamt* 3–4 (Motter, p. 5):

In vain shalt thou, or any, call
The spirits from their golden day,
Except, like them, thou too canst say,
My spirit is at peace with all.

They haunt the silence of the breast,
Imaginations calm and fair,
The memory like a cloudless air,
The conscience as a sea at rest:

But when the heart is full of din,
And doubt beside the portal waits,
They can but listen at the gates,
And hear the household jar within.

## XCV

By night we lingered on the lawn,
For underfoot the herb was dry;
And genial warmth; and o'er the sky
The silvery haze of summer drawn;

And calm that let the tapers burn
Unwavering: not a cricket chirred:
The brook alone far-off was heard,
And on the board the fluttering urn:

'Spirits that but seem / To hold communion with the dead'. Cp. *On Sublimity* 67: 'For thou dost hold communion with the dead'. G. G. Loane, *Notes and Queries* clxxix (1940) 275, compares *Duchess of Malfi* IV ii 20–21: 'O that it were possible we might / But hold some two days' conference with the dead.'

xciv *6*. Cp. Young, *Night Thoughts* iv 144: 'The spirit of the golden day'.

xciv *9–12*. T. said to Knowles: 'I figure myself in this rather' (*Nineteenth Century* xxxiii (1893) 185).

xciv *14–16*. The metaphor suggests Herbert's *The Family*.

xcv Not *T.MS*. Possibly written 1841–2, since Dean Stanley 'was greatly struck by his describing to us on one singularly still starlit evening, how he and his friends had once sat out far into the night having tea at a table on the lawn beneath the stars, and that the candles had burned with steady upright flame, disturbed from time to time by the inrush of a moth or cockchafer, as tho' in a closed room. I do not know whether he had already written, or was perhaps even then shaping, the lines in *In Memoriam*, which so many years afterwards brought back to me the incident' (*Mem.* i 205). See *Mariana in the South* 61–84*n* (p. 365).

And bats went round in fragrant skies,
 And wheeled or lit the filmy shapes
 That haunt the dusk, with ermine capes
And woolly breasts and beaded eyes;

While now we sang old songs that pealed
 From knoll to knoll, where, couched at ease,
 The white kine glimmered, and the trees
Laid their dark arms about the field.

But when those others, one by one,
 Withdrew themselves from me and night,
 And in the house light after light
Went out, and I was all alone,

A hunger seized my heart; I read
 Of that glad year which once had been,
 In those fallen leaves which kept their green,
The noble letters of the dead:

And strangely on the silence broke
 The silent-speaking words, and strange
 Was love's dumb cry defying change
To test his worth; and strangely spoke

The faith, the vigour, bold to dwell
 On doubts that drive the coward back,
 And keen through wordy snares to track
Suggestion to her inmost cell.

So word by word, and line by line,
 The dead man touched me from the past,
 And all at once it seemed at last
The living soul was flashed on mine,

xcv *10*. 'Moths' (T.). *lit*: alighted (H.T.). From Shelley, *Unfinished Drama* 236–8: 'And on it little quaint and filmy shapes, / With dizzy motion, wheel and rise and fall, / Like clouds of gnats with perfect lineaments.'

xcv *18*. The setting and mood suggest Gray's *Elegy* 1–4: '. . . And leaves the world to darkness and to me.'

xcv *32*. *inmost cell*: as in Gray's translation from Tasso; Shelley, *The Cenci* V ii 163, and *Epipsychidion* 569.

xcv *33*. *Isaiah* xxviii 13: 'But the word of the Lord was unto them precept upon precept, precept upon precept; line upon line, line upon line.'

xcv *36*. *The*] *1872*; His *1850–70*. T. comments: 'The Deity, maybe. The first reading . . . troubled me, as perhaps giving a wrong impression.' H.T. quotes T., 'The greater Soul may include the less', and 'I have often had

And mine in this was wound, and whirled
About empyreal heights of thought,
And came on that which is, and caught
The deep pulsations of the world,

Æonian music measuring out
The steps of Time – the shocks of Chance –
The blows of Death. At length my trance
Was cancelled, stricken through with doubt.

Vague words! but ah, how hard to frame
In matter-moulded forms of speech,
Or even for intellect to reach
Through memory that which I became:

Till now the doubtful dusk revealed
The knolls once more where, couched at ease,
The white kine glimmered, and the trees
Laid their dark arms about the field:

And sucked from out the distant gloom
A breeze began to tremble o'er
The large leaves of the sycamore,
And fluctuate all the still perfume,

And gathering freshlier overhead,
Rocked the full-foliaged elms, and swung
The heavy-folded rose, and flung
The lilies to and fro, and said

'The dawn, the dawn,' and died away;
And East and West, without a breath,
Mixt their dim lights, like life and death,
To broaden into boundless day.

that feeling of being whirled up and rapt into the Great Soul.' Cp. *The Ancient Sage* (p. 1349).
xcv *37. this*] *1872*; his *1850–70.*
xcv *38. heights*] heigths [ ?heighths] *L.MS.*
xcv *40.* Incorporated from *An Idle Rhyme* 40 (p. 663). Cp. *Armageddon* iv 29–31: 'An indefinable pulsation / Inaudible to outward sense, but felt / Through the deep heart of every living thing.'
xcv *42–3.* Cp. Milton, *On Time* 22: 'Triumphing over Death, and Chance, and thee O Time'.
xcv *54–5.* Adapted, as Sir Charles Tennyson observes, from *In deep and solemn dreams* 47–8 (p. 279): 'And the sweet winds tremble o'er / The large leaves of the sycamore.'
xcv *63.* Cp. Pope, *Elegy to the Memory of an Unfortunate Lady* 19: 'Dim lights of life'.

## XCVI

You say, but with no touch of scorn,
  Sweet-hearted, you, whose light-blue eyes
  Are tender over drowning flies,
You tell me, doubt is Devil-born.

I know not: one indeed I knew
  In many a subtle question versed,
  Who touched a jarring lyre at first,
But ever strove to make it true:

Perplext in faith, but pure in deeds,
  At last he beat his music out.
  There lives more faith in honest doubt,
Believe me, than in half the creeds.

He fought his doubts and gathered strength,
  He would not make his judgment blind,
  He faced the spectres of the mind
And laid them: thus he came at length

To find a stronger faith his own;
  And Power was with him in the night,
  Which makes the darkness and the light,
And dwells not in the light alone,

xcvi Not *T.MS, L.MS, trial edition.*

xcvi *1. You say, but*] Dear Lady *H.Nbk 19 1st reading.* This variant and that in l. 2 show that, in so far as a particular person is addressed, it is more likely to be Emily Sellwood (whose religious scruples about T. had been one factor in delaying their marriage; H. D. Rawnsley, *Memories of the Tennysons*, 1900, p. 71), and not T.'s mother.

xcvi *2. , you,*] maid *MS 1st reading.*

xcvi *4. tell me,*] say that *MS.*

xcvi *5. one*: Arthur Hallam, as T. says. Cp. *He was too good* 2–4: 'in his hour / Of darkest doubt, and in his power, / To fling his doubts into the street.' T. refers, as Motter says (p. 92), to Hallam's sonnet, *Then what is Life*, which wrestles with his doubts and ends: 'Those who know and feel that it is Night'.

xcvi *10. At last he*] Till he had *MS 1st reading.*

xcvi *11–12.* In his copy of P. J. Bailey's *Festus* (2nd edn, 1845; *Lincoln*), T. marked in the margin the line 'Who never doubted never half believed' (p. 63).

xcvi *15. faced*] met *MS 1st reading.*

xcvi *17. find*] make *MS 1st reading.*

xcvi *19. makes*] made *MS 1st reading.*

But in the darkness and the cloud,
As over Sinaï's peaks of old,
While Israel made their gods of gold,
Although the trumpet blew so loud.

## XCVII

My love has talked with rocks and trees;
He finds on misty mountain-ground
His own vast shadow glory-crowned;
He sees himself in all he sees.

Two partners of a married life–
I looked on these and thought of thee
In vastness and in mystery,
And of my spirit as of a wife.

These two–they dwelt with eye on eye,
Their hearts of old have beat in tune,
Their meetings made December June,
Their every parting was to die.

xcvi *21–4*. T. compares *Exodus* xix 16, 'And it came to pass on the third day in the morning, that there were thunders and lightnings, and a thick cloud upon the mount, and the voice of the trumpet exceeding loud.'

xcvii Not *T.MS*, *L.MS*, *trial edition*. There are two drafts in *H.Nbk 19* (*A*, *B* below). *A* opens with the isolated line: 'Long married souls, dear friend, are we,' and has the lines–with variants–in the order: 9–12; 33, 18–20; 13–16; 21–24; 29, 31, 30, 32; 25–28; 33–36. *B* omits ll. 1–4 but follows the line-order of *1850*. T. says: 'The relation of one on earth to one in the other and higher world. Not my relation to him here. He looked up to me as I looked up to him.

'The spirit yet in the flesh but united in love with the spirit out of the flesh resembles the wife of a great man of science. She looks up to him–but what he knows is a mystery to her' (*1913*).

xcvii *1–4*] *Not A–B.*

xcvii *3*. 'Like the spectre of the Brocken' (T.).

xcvii *5–8*] *Not A.*

xcvii *5*. *married*] common *B*.

xcvii *6*. *looked . . . and*] saw them and I *B*.

xcvii *8*. *spirit as of a*] soul as of thy *B*.

xcvii *9–12*] They madly drank each other's breath
With breast to breast in early years.
They met with passion and with tears,
Their every parting was a death. *A*

*B* likewise, with *They madly drank*] These two have drunk.

Their love has never past away;
The days she never can forget
Are earnest that he loves her yet,
Whate'er the faithless people say.

Her life is lone, he sits apart,
He loves her yet, she will not weep,
Though rapt in matters dark and deep
He seems to slight her simple heart.

He thrids the labyrinth of the mind,
He reads the secret of the star,
He seems so near and yet so far,
He looks so cold: she thinks him kind.

She keeps the gift of years before,
A withered violet is her bliss:
She knows not what his greatness is,
For that, for all, she loves him more.

For him she plays, to him she sings
Of early faith and plighted vows;
She knows but matters of the house,
And he, he knows a thousand things.

Her faith is fixt and cannot move,
She darkly feels him great and wise,
She dwells on him with faithful eyes,
'I cannot understand: I love.'

xcvii *13. Their*] His *A.* *past*] died *A–B.*
xcvii *17*] Her faith is fixt and cannot move, *A–B* (l. 33).
xcvii *20. heart*] love *A–B.*
xcvii *24. she . . . him*] knows so *A*; and is so *A 1st reading.*
xcvii *25. keeps . . . of*] dwells upon the *A.*
xcvii *26*] To think he loves her is his bliss, *A* (his, *error for* hers).
xcvii *27. knows*] knowing *A.*
xcvii *28. For . . . all,*] And yet for that *A.*
xcvii *30–31*] *Transposed A.*
xcvii *30*] She looks upon his ample brows, *A.*
xcvii *32. And he,*] And thinks *A.*
xcvii *33*] His thoughts in vaster orbits move, *B 1st reading.* Cp. 'orbits', lxxxvii 38.
xcvii *34. darkly feels him*] feels him, darkly *A.* The MS is even closer to Pope's 'A being darkly wise, and rudely great', *Essay on Man* ii 4.

## XCVIII

You leave us: you will see the Rhine,
And those fair hills I sailed below,
When I was there with him; and go
By summer belts of wheat and vine

To where he breathed his latest breath,
That City. All her splendour seems
No livelier than the wisp that gleams
On Lethe in the eyes of Death.

Let her great Danube rolling fair
Enwind her isles, unmarked of me:
I have not seen, I will not see
Vienna; rather dream that there,

A treble darkness, Evil haunts
The birth, the bridal; friend from friend
Is oftener parted, fathers bend
Above more graves, a thousand wants

Gnarr at the heels of men, and prey
By each cold hearth, and sadness flings
Her shadow on the blaze of kings:
And yet myself have heard him say,

That not in any mother town
With statelier progress to and fro
The double tides of chariots flow
By park and suburb under brown

xcviii Not *T.MS.*
xcviii *1.* '"You" is imaginary' (T.). But *Mem.* i 148 says that it alludes to the honeymoon of T.'s brother Charles, on the Rhine in 1836.
xcviii *2*] And watch the impetuous current flow *L.MS 1st reading.*
xcviii *3. When . . . there*] That once I watched *MS 1st reading.*
xcviii *12. rather dream*] but methinks *MS 1st reading.*
xcviii *13. A . . . darkness*] In tenfold frequence *MS 1st reading.*
xcviii *14. birth, the bridal*] threshold, oftener *MS 1st reading.*
xcviii *15. oftener . . . fathers*] plucked asunder, parents *MS 1st reading.*
xcviii *16. more graves*] their dead *MS 1st reading.*
xcviii *17. Gnarr*: 'snarl' (T.).
xcviii *20*] And Pain [Death *1st reading*] is lord; albeit they say *MS.*
xcviii *21. mother town*: 'metropolis' (T.).

Of lustier leaves; nor more content,
He told me, lives in any crowd,
When all is gay with lamps, and loud
With sport and song, in booth and tent,

Imperial halls, or open plain;
And wheels the circled dance, and breaks
The rocket molten into flakes
Of crimson or in emerald rain.

## XCIX

Risest thou thus, dim dawn, again,
So loud with voices of the birds,
So thick with lowings of the herds,
Day, when I lost the flower of men;

Who tremblest through thy darkling red
On yon swollen brook that bubbles fast
By meadows breathing of the past,
And woodlands holy to the dead;

Who murmurest in the foliaged eaves
A song that slights the coming care,
And Autumn laying here and there
A fiery finger on the leaves;

xcviii *26. He . . . any*] Sits on the foreheads of the *MS 1st reading*; They tell me, lives in any *MS.*
xcviii *28. and tent*] or tent *MS.*
xcviii *30. And*] As *MS 1st reading*; While *MS.* The MS originally ended as *1850*, but another stanza was added:

As once I watched them at his side
And heard him breathe a broken line
From that stronghearted Florentine:
'*O vana gloria!*', thus he cried.

Hallam had spoken of the influence of 'the mighty Florentine' upon himself, in the last paragraph of *The Influence of Italian upon English Literature* (Motter, p. 234). *Purgatorio* xi 91: *oh vana gloria dell'umane posse!* ('O empty glory of human powers!').

xcix Not *T.MS. L.MS* has a first draft (*A*, below), deleted, between lxxxv and lxxxvi; a later draft (*B*) in its final position.
xcix *5–8*] *Not A.*
xcix *6. swollen*] wild *B.*
xcix *9. foliaged eaves*: cp. Shelley, *Alastor* 464: 'foliaged attice'.
xcix *9–10*] Who risest not as one that grieves
In silence for a world of care, *A*

Who wakenest with thy balmy breath
  To myriads on the genial earth,
  Memories of bridal, or of birth,
And unto myriads more, of death.

O wheresoever those may be,
  Betwixt the slumber of the poles,
  Today they count as kindred souls;
They know me not, but mourn with me.

## C

I climb the hill: from end to end
  Of all the landscape underneath,
  I find no place that does not breathe
Some gracious memory of my friend;

No gray old grange, or lonely fold,
  Or low morass and whispering reed,
  Or simple stile from mead to mead,
Or sheepwalk up the windy wold;

Nor hoary knoll of ash and haw
  That hears the latest linnet trill,
  Nor quarry trenched along the hill
And haunted by the wrangling daw;

Nor runlet tinkling from the rock;
  Nor pastoral rivulet that swerves
  To left and right through meadowy curves,
That feed the mothers of the flock;

But each has pleased a kindred eye,
  And each reflects a kindlier day;
  And, leaving these, to pass away,
I think once more he seems to die.

xcix *13. balmy breath*: *Othello* V ii 16 (a context both of bridal and of death).
xcix *19. they count as*] I count them *A*.

c Not *T.MS.* c–ciii allude to the Tennysons' move from Somersby in 1837, as T. observes.
c *1. climb the hill*] *1855*; wake, I rise *1850–51*.
c *8. the windy wold*: *Who claps the gate* 3 (*The Princess* ii ^ iii, p. 1769).
c *12. wrangling*] jangling *L.MS.*
c *13. runlet tinkling*] fountain sparkling *MS.*

## CI

Unwatched, the garden bough shall sway,
The tender blossom flutter down,
Unloved, that beech will gather brown,
This maple burn itself away;

Unloved, the sun-flower, shining fair,
Ray round with flames her disk of seed,
And many a rose-carnation feed
With summer spice the humming air;

Unloved, by many a sandy bar,
The brook shall babble down the plain,
At noon or when the lesser wain
Is twisting round the polar star;

Uncared for, gird the windy grove,
And flood the haunts of hern and crake;
Or into silver arrows break
The sailing moon in creek and cove;

Till from the garden and the wild
A fresh association blow,
And year by year the landscape grow
Familiar to the stranger's child;

As year by year the labourer tills
His wonted glebe, or lops the glades;
And year by year our memory fades
From all the circle of the hills.

## CII

We leave the well-belovèd place
Where first we gazed upon the sky;
The roofs, that heard our earliest cry,
Will shelter one of stranger race.

ci Not *T.MS.* c–ciii allude to the Tennysons' move from Somersby in 1837, as T. observes. Cp. *A Farewell* (p. 665), on the same theme.
ci *3. that beech*] those elms *L.MS 1st reading*. The MS is even closer to *Sir Launcelot and Queen Guinevere* 8, 'The topmost elm-tree gathered green'.
ci *8*. Cp. Arthur Hallam, *A Scene in Summer* 20–21 (Motter, p. 99): 'humming things that summer loves, / Through the warm air'.
ci *14*. Cp. *The Brook* 23: 'I come from haunts of coot and hern'.
ci *19*] And all the landskip slowly grow *MS 1st reading*.

We go, but ere we go from home,
As down the garden-walks I move,
Two spirits of a diverse love
Contend for loving masterdom.

One whispers, 'Here thy boyhood sung
Long since its matin song, and heard
The low love-language of the bird
In native hazels tassel-hung.'

The other answers, 'Yea, but here
Thy feet have strayed in after hours
With thy lost friend among the bowers,
And this hath made them trebly dear.'

These two have striven half the day,
And each prefers his separate claim,
Poor rivals in a losing game,
That will not yield each other way.

I turn to go: my feet are set
To leave the pleasant fields and farms;
They mix in one another's arms
To one pure image of regret.

## CIII

On that last night before we went
From out the doors where I was bred,
I dreamed a vision of the dead,
Which left my after-morn content.

Methought I dwelt within a hall,
And maidens with me: distant hills
From hidden summits fed with rills
A river sliding by the wall.

cii *7–8*. T. comments: 'First, the love of the native place; second, this enhanced by the memory of A. H. H.' The phrasing suggests Shakespeare's *Sonnet 144*: 'Two loves I have of comfort and despair, / Which like two spirits do suggest me still.'
cii *19*. Cp. Shelley, *Queen Mab* iii 172–3: 'mutual foes, forever play / A losing game into each other's hands'.
cii *22*. Cp. *Paradise Lost* ix 448: 'the pleasant Villages and Farmes'.

ciii Not *T.MS*. c–ciii allude to the Tennysons' move from Somersby in 1837, as T. observes.
ciii *6*. *maidens*: 'They are the Muses, poetry, arts–all that made life beautiful here, which we hope will pass with us beyond the grave' (T.).
ciii *7*. *summits*: 'the divine' (T.).
ciii *8*. *river*: 'life' (T.).

The hall with harp and carol rang.
They sang of what is wise and good
And graceful. In the centre stood
A statue veiled, to which they sang;

And which, though veiled, was known to me,
The shape of him I loved, and love
For ever: then flew in a dove
And brought a summons from the sea:

And when they learnt that I must go
They wept and wailed, but led the way
To where a little shallop lay
At anchor in the flood below;

And on by many a level mead,
And shadowing bluff that made the banks,
We glided winding under ranks
Of iris, and the golden reed;

And still as vaster grew the shore
And rolled the floods in grander space,
The maidens gathered strength and grace
And presence, lordlier than before;

And I myself, who sat apart
And watched them, waxed in every limb;
I felt the thews of Anakim,
The pulses of a Titan's heart;

As one would sing the death of war,
And one would chant the history
Of that great race, which is to be,
And one the shaping of a star;

Until the forward-creeping tides
Began to foam, and we to draw
From deep to deep, to where we saw
A great ship lift her shining sides.

ciii *16. sea*: 'eternity' (T.).
ciii *25–8.* 'The progress of the Age' (T.).
ciii *31. Anakim*: the giants of *Deuteronomy* ii 10. Cp. *A Fragment* 20: 'the strong and sunborn Anakim'.
ciii *33–6.* 'The great hopes of humanity and science' (T.).
ciii *37.* Cp. *Recollections of the Arabian Nights* 4: 'The forward-flowing tide of time'.
ciii *40.* Cp. Arthur Hallam, of a ship: 'Did not the sides wear brilliance', *Lines Written at Brighton* 21 (Motter, p. 49).

The man we loved was there on deck,
    But thrice as large as man he bent
    To greet us. Up the side I went,
And fell in silence on his neck:

Whereat those maidens with one mind
    Bewailed their lot; I did them wrong:
    'We served thee here,' they said, 'so long,
And wilt thou leave us now behind?'

So rapt I was, they could not win
    An answer from my lips, but he
    Replying, 'Enter likewise ye
And go with us:' they entered in.

And while the wind began to sweep
    A music out of sheet and shroud,
    We steered her toward a crimson cloud
That landlike slept along the deep.

## CIV

The time draws near the birth of Christ;
    The moon is hid, the night is still;
    A single church below the hill
Is pealing, folded in the mist.

A single peal of bells below,
    That wakens at this hour of rest
    A single murmur in the breast,
That these are not the bells I know.

Like strangers' voices here they sound,
    In lands where not a memory strays,
    Nor landmark breathes of other days,
But all is new unhallowed ground.

ciii *41. there on*] on the *L.MS 1st reading.*

ciii *45–8.* T. commented to James Knowles: 'He was wrong to drop his earthly hopes and powers–they will be still of use to him', *Nineteenth Century* xxxiii (1893) 187.

civ *3. church*: 'Waltham Abbey church' (T.).

civ *10. lands*] fields *L.MS 1st reading.*

civ *12.* 'High Beech, Epping Forest (where we were living)' (T.).

## CV

Tonight ungathered let us leave
 This laurel, let this holly stand:
 We live within the stranger's land,
And strangely falls our Christmas-eve.

Our father's dust is left alone
 And silent under other snows:
 There in due time the woodbine blows,
The violet comes, but we are gone.

No more shall wayward grief abuse
 The genial hour with mask and mime;
 For change of place, like growth of time,
Has broke the bond of dying use.

Let cares that petty shadows cast,
 By which our lives are chiefly proved,
 A little spare the night I loved,
And hold it solemn to the past.

But let no footstep beat the floor,
 Nor bowl of wassail mantle warm;
 For who would keep an ancient form
Through which the spirit breathes no more?

Be neither song, nor game, nor feast;
 Nor harp be touched, nor flute be blown;
 No dance, no motion, save alone
What lightens in the lucid east

Of rising worlds by yonder wood.
 Long sleeps the summer in the seed;
 Run out your measured arcs, and lead
The closing cycle rich in good.

## CVI

Ring out, wild bells, to the wild sky,
 The flying cloud, the frosty light:
 The year is dying in the night;
Ring out, wild bells, and let him die.

cv Referring to Christmas 1837, at High Beech, Epping Forest.
cv *1–2*] *1863*; This holly by the cottage-eave,
 To night, ungathered, shall it stand: *1850–62*
(*This*] The *H.Lpr 101.*)

cvi Not *T.MS*, *L.MS*. This was the only section of *In Memoriam* included

Ring out the old, ring in the new,
  Ring, happy bells, across the snow:
  The year is going, let him go;
Ring out the false, ring in the true.

Ring out the grief that saps the mind,
  For those that here we see no more;
  Ring out the feud of rich and poor,
Ring in redress to all mankind.

Ring out a slowly dying cause,
  And ancient forms of party strife;
  Ring in the nobler modes of life,
With sweeter manners, purer laws.

Ring out the want, the care, the sin,
  The faithless coldness of the times;
  Ring out, ring out my mournful rhymes,
But ring the fuller minstrel in.

Ring out false pride in place and blood,
  The civic slander and the spite;
  Ring in the love of truth and right,
Ring in the common love of good.

Ring out old shapes of foul disease;
  Ring out the narrowing lust of gold;
  Ring out the thousand wars of old,
Ring in the thousand years of peace.

Ring in the valiant man and free,
  The larger heart, the kindlier hand;
  Ring out the darkness of the land,
Ring in the Christ that is to be.

in *Songs* (1872). H. N. Fairchild, *MLN* lxiv (1949) 256–8, observes the general similarity to a passage in P. J. Bailey's *Festus*. This would suggest composition *c.* 1845–6, since there is a copy of the 2nd edition of *Festus* (1845) at *Lincoln*, with T.'s marginal markings; T. urged FitzGerald to read *Festus* on 12 Nov. 1846 (*Mem.* i 234).

cvi *15. modes of life*: *Lisette* 30.

cvi *28. Revelation* xx 2–4 tells of the binding of Satan for 'a thousand years'.

cvi *32.* 'The broader Christianity of the future' (T.).

## CVII

It is the day when he was born,
A bitter day that early sank
Behind a purple-frosty bank
Of vapour, leaving night forlorn.

The time admits not flowers or leaves
To deck the banquet. Fiercely flies
The blast of North and East, and ice
Makes daggers at the sharpened eaves,

And bristles all the brakes and thorns
To yon hard crescent, as she hangs
Above the wood which grides and clangs
Its leafless ribs and iron horns

Together, in the drifts that pass
To darken on the rolling brine
That breaks the coast. But fetch the wine,
Arrange the board and brim the glass;

Bring in great logs and let them lie,
To make a solid core of heat;
Be cheerful-minded, talk and treat
Of all things even as he were by;

We keep the day. With festal cheer,
With books and music, surely we
Will drink to him, whate'er he be,
And sing the songs he loved to hear.

cvii Not *T.MS. L.MS* has it between lxxxiii and lxxxiv. A. C. Bradley compares Horace, *Odes* I ix, for the setting, and Alcaeus's *Fragment 34* on which the Ode was based.
cvii *1*. 'February 1, 1811' (T.).
cvii *11*. Cp. *Chorus* 13 (*1830*): 'The heavy thunder's griding might'. In *H.Nbk 4* (1830), T.'s glossary includes 'griding – rubbing', noting 'Sax. Chr.' (Saxon Chronicle). The sense of grating, rather than piercing, suggests *Prometheus Unbound* III i 47–8: 'the thunder of the fiery wheels / Griding the winds'. The word 'iron' suggests Wordsworth, *Guilt and Sorrow* 492–3, where however the sense follows that in Milton, 'piercing': 'Through his brain / At once the griding iron passage found'. T. had used it of sound in *Œnone* 27, MS, where the 'cicala ceaseth now to burst the brake / With thick dry clamour chafed from griding wings' (note 'brake').
cvii *13*. 'Fine snow which passes in squalls to fall into the breaker, and darkens before melting in the sea' (H.T.).

## CVIII

I will not shut me from my kind,
And, lest I stiffen into stone,
I will not eat my heart alone,
Nor feed with sighs a passing wind:

What profit lies in barren faith,
And vacant yearning, though with might
To scale the heaven's highest height,
Or dive below the wells of Death?

What find I in the highest place,
But mine own phantom chanting hymns?
And on the depths of death there swims
The reflex of a human face.

I'll rather take what fruit may be
Of sorrow under human skies:
'Tis held that sorrow makes us wise,
Whatever wisdom sleep with thee.

## CIX

Heart-affluence in discursive talk
From household fountains never dry;
The critic clearness of an eye,
That saw through all the Muses' walk;

Seraphic intellect and force
To seize and throw the doubts of man;
Impassioned logic, which outran
The hearer in its fiery course;

cviii *3*. *OED* 6c: '*To eat one's own heart*: to suffer from silent grief or vexation'. Most commonly, of envy or jealousy, as in *Faerie Queene* I ii st. 6, where the Red Cross Knight 'could not rest, but did his stout heart eat'.
cviii *4*. *Nor*] And *L.MS.*
cviii *5–8*. Cp. *Romans* x 6–7: 'But the righteousness which is of faith speaketh on this wise, Say not in thine heart, Who shall ascend into heaven? (that is, to bring Christ down from above:) or, Who shall descend into the deep? (that is, to bring up Christ again from the dead)'.
cviii *7*. *highest height: Œnone* 131 ∧ 2, *1832* text, on the gods' calm.
cviii *16*] Yet how much wisdom sleeps with thee. *MS quoted in Eversley.*

cix Not *T.MS.*
cix *1*. *Heart-affluence*] Heart-effluence *L.MS.*
cix *6*. Cp. xcvi 5 and *n*.

High nature amorous of the good,
  But touched with no ascetic gloom;
  And passion pure in snowy bloom
Through all the years of April blood;

A love of freedom rarely felt,
  Of freedom in her regal seat
  Of England; not the schoolboy heat,
The blind hysterics of the Celt;

And manhood fused with female grace
  In such a sort, the child would twine
  A trustful hand, unasked, in thine,
And find his comfort in thy face;

All these have been, and thee mine eyes
  Have looked on: if they looked in vain,
  My shame is greater who remain,
Nor let thy wisdom make me wise.

## CX

Thy converse drew us with delight,
  The men of rathe and riper years:
  The feeble soul, a haunt of fears,
Forgot his weakness in thy sight.

On thee the loyal-hearted hung,
  The proud was half disarmed of pride,
  Nor cared the serpent at thy side
To flicker with his double tongue.

cix *15–16*. Cp. *The Princess: Conclusion* 66, on revolutions in France: 'No graver than a schoolboys' barring out'. Also *Hail Briton* 19: 'that unstable Celtic blood'.

cix *17*. Cp. *Locksley Hall Sixty Years After* 48 and *n*. T. spoke of 'what he called the "man-woman" in Christ, the union of tenderness and strength' (*Mem*. i 326).

cix *21*. *been, and thee*] vanished from *L.MS 1st reading*.

cix *22*] All these have been, and if in vain *L.MS 1st reading*.

cix *24*. *Nor*: 'If I do not . . .' (T.).

cx Not *T.MS*.

cx *2*. *rathe*: early.

cx *7*. *cared*] loved *L.MS*.

cx *8*. *double*] *1855*; treble *1850–51*. *Aeneid* ii 475: *linguis trisulcis*.

The stern were mild when thou wert by,
The flippant put himself to school
And heard thee, and the brazen fool
Was softened, and he knew not why;

While I, thy nearest, sat apart,
And felt thy triumph was as mine;
And loved them more, that they were thine,
The graceful tact, the Christian art;

Nor mine the sweetness or the skill,
But mine the love that will not tire,
And, born of love, the vague desire
That spurs an imitative will.

## CXI

The churl in spirit, up or down
Along the scale of ranks, through all,
To him who grasps a golden ball,
By blood a king, at heart a clown;

The churl in spirit, howe'er he veil
His want in forms for fashion's sake,
Will let his coltish nature break
At seasons through the gilded pale:

For who can always act? but he,
To whom a thousand memories call,
Not being less but more than all
The gentleness he seemed to be,

Best seemed the thing he was, and joined
Each office of the social hour
To noble manners, as the flower
And native growth of noble mind;

cx *13. nearest*] *1875*; dearest *1850–72.*

cx *16. art*] heart *MS 1st reading.*

cx *17. Nor*] *1864*; Not *1850–63.*

cx *20.* Adapted from 'She spurs an imitative will', *Young is the grief* 6, an unpublished section of *In Memoriam.*

cxi *2. scale*] scales *L.MS 1st reading.*

cxi *3. him who grasps*] *1855*; who may grasp *1850–51.*

cxi *13. Best . . . was*] *1855*; So wore his outward best *1850–51.*

cxi *15–16.* Cp. *Guinevere* 333–4: 'For manners are not idle, but the fruit / Of loyal nature, and of noble mind'.

Nor ever narrowness or spite,
Or villain fancy fleeting by,
Drew in the expression of an eye,
Where God and Nature met in light;

And thus he bore without abuse
The grand old name of gentleman,
Defamed by every charlatan,
And soiled with all ignoble use.

## CXII

High wisdom holds my wisdom less,
That I, who gaze with temperate eyes
On glorious insufficiencies,
Set light by narrower perfectness.

But thou, that fillest all the room
Of all my love, art reason why
I seem to cast a careless eye
On souls, the lesser lords of doom.

For what wert thou? some novel power
Sprang up for ever at a touch,
And hope could never hope too much,
In watching thee from hour to hour,

cxi *23. charlatan*: T. observes: 'From Ital. *ciarlatano*, a mountebank; hence the accent on the last syllable.' T. may have learnt this from the *English Encyclopaedia* (1802), of which a copy was at Somersby (*Lincoln*).

cxii *1–4.* H.T. comments: '*High wisdom* is ironical. "High wisdom" has been twitting the poet that although he gazes with calm and indulgent eyes on unaccomplished greatness, yet he makes light of narrower natures more perfect in their own small way.'

cxii *3. glorious insufficiencies*: 'unaccomplished greatness such as Arthur Hallam's' (T.).

cxii *4. set light by*: 'make light of' (T.). Hallam had written of 'Reason's perfectness, / To our deject and most imbased eye', his *Timbuctoo* 117–8 (Motter, p. 41).

cxii *5–8*] For souls, the lesser lords of doom,
Are worth all praise from young and old,
Though those are quick to judge that hold
Completion in a little room. *H. Lpr 101*

(Echoing Marlowe: 'Infinite riches in a little room', *The Jew of Malta* I i 37.)

cxii *8.* 'Those that have free-will, but less intellect' (T.).

cxii *9. For . . . thou?*] Such wert not thou: *MS.* *novel power*: cp. Hallam: 'What novel power is mine that makes me bold?', *How is it that*

Large elements in order brought,
And tracts of calm from tempest made,
And world-wide fluctuation swayed
In vassal tides that followed thought.

## CXIII

'Tis held that sorrow makes us wise;
Yet how much wisdom sleeps with thee
Which not alone had guided me,
But served the seasons that may rise;

For can I doubt, who knew thee keen
In intellect, with force and skill
To strive, to fashion, to fulfil–
I doubt not what thou wouldst have been:

A life in civic action warm,
A soul on highest mission sent,
A potent voice of Parliament,
A pillar steadfast in the storm,

Should licensed boldness gather force,
Becoming, when the time has birth,
A lever to uplift the earth
And roll it in another course,

With thousand shocks that come and go,
With agonies, with energies,
With overthrowings, and with cries,
And undulations to and fro.

*I look toward the swell*, which uses nautical imagery to describe fear (*Victorian Poetry*, Supplement to Vol. iii, 1965).

cxii *14*. Hallam had described himself as one who 'faced / Himself the tempest, and can prize the calm', *Lines for Ellen Hallam* 11–12 (Motter, p. 103).

cxii *16*. Cp. Shelley, *Daemon* ii 46: 'The mighty tide of thought'.

cxiii Not *T.MS*.

cxiii *11*. *potent voice: Paradise Lost* vii 100.

cxiii *13–20*. Incorporated from *Hail Briton* 96 ∧ 7 (p. 485), a very important borrowing.

cxiii *17*. *thousand*] *1855*; many *1850–51*. The final version suggests 'The thousand natural shocks / That flesh is heir to', *Hamlet* III i 62–3.

cxiii *18*. Cp. *Youth* 59: 'An energy, an agony'; *St Simeon Stylites* 23–4, MS: 'All agonies, / All energies'. Hallam had joined the two, his *Timbuctoo* 74–6 (Motter, p. 40): 'the energies / Of Guilt, and desolate the poor man's sleep. / Yet not alone for torturing agonies . . .'

## CXIV

Who loves not Knowledge? Who shall rail
Against her beauty? May she mix
With men and prosper! Who shall fix
Her pillars? Let her work prevail.

But on her forehead sits a fire:
She sets her forward countenance
And leaps into the future chance,
Submitting all things to desire.

Half-grown as yet, a child, and vain–
She cannot fight the fear of death.
What is she, cut from love and faith,
But some wild Pallas from the brain

Of Demons? fiery-hot to burst
All barriers in her onward race
For power. Let her know her place;
She is the second, not the first.

A higher hand must make her mild,
If all be not in vain; and guide
Her footsteps, moving side by side
With wisdom, like the younger child:

For she is earthly of the mind,
But Wisdom heavenly of the soul.
O, friend, who camest to thy goal
So early, leaving me behind,

I would the great world grew like thee,
Who grewest not alone in power
And knowledge, but by year and hour
In reverence and in charity.

cxiv Not *T.MS, L.MS.*
cxiv *1–4.* Incorporated verbatim from *Hail Briton* 133–6, as Sir Charles Tennyson notes. T. compares *Proverbs* ix 1: 'Wisdom hath builded her house, she hath hewn out her seven pillars.' On 'knowledge' and 'Reverence', cp. *Love thou thy land* 17–20.
cxiv *27. by year and*] *1855*; from hour to *1850–51.*

## CXV

Now fades the last long streak of snow,
  Now burgeons every maze of quick
  About the flowering squares, and thick
By ashen roots the violets blow.

Now rings the woodland loud and long,
  The distance takes a lovelier hue,
  And drowned in yonder living blue
The lark becomes a sightless song.

Now dance the lights on lawn and lea,
  The flocks are whiter down the vale,
  And milkier every milky sail
On winding stream or distant sea;

Where now the seamew pipes, or dives
  In yonder greening gleam, and fly
  The happy birds, that change their sky
To build and brood; that live their lives

From land to land; and in my breast
  Spring wakens too; and my regret
  Becomes an April violet,
And buds and blossoms like the rest.

## CXVI

Is it, then, regret for buried time
  That keenlier in sweet April wakes,
  And meets the year, and gives and takes
The colours of the crescent prime?

Not all: the songs, the stirring air,
  The life re-orient out of dust,
  Cry through the sense to hearten trust
In that which made the world so fair.

cxv Not *T.MS*. Cp. *On a Mourner* (p. 557).
cxv 2. *quick*: quickset thorn (T.).
cxv 3. *flowering*] greening *L.MS 1st reading*. Cp. *The Gardener's Daughter* 75: 'flowery squares'.
cxv 15. Horace's *caelum . . . mutant* (*Epistles* I xi 27).
cxv 16. *that*] and *L.MS 1st reading*.

cxvi Not *T.MS, L.MS*. But see the unpublished section from *L.MS*, *Let Death and Memory* (p. 1775).
cxvi 4. *crescent prime*: 'growing spring' (T.).

Not all regret: the face will shine
Upon me, while I muse alone;
And that dear voice, I once have known,
Still speak to me of me and mine:

Yet less of sorrow lives in me
For days of happy commune dead;
Less yearning for the friendship fled,
Than some strong bond which is to be.

## CXVII

O days and hours, your work is this
To hold me from my proper place,
A little while from his embrace,
For fuller gain of after bliss:

That out of distance might ensue
Desire of nearness doubly sweet;
And unto meeting when we meet,
Delight a hundredfold accrue,

For every grain of sand that runs,
And every span of shade that steals,
And every kiss of toothèd wheels,
And all the courses of the suns.

## CXVIII

Contemplate all this work of Time,
The giant labouring in his youth;
Nor dream of human love and truth,
As dying Nature's earth and lime;

cxvi *11*] *1855*; The dear, dear voice that I have known, *1850–51*.
cxvi *12*. *Still*] *1855*; Will *1850–51*. This line is adapted from *Let Death and Memory* 8.

cxvii *10*. 'The sun-dial' (T.). Cp. Shakespeare, *Sonnet 77*: 'thy dial's shady stealth'.
cxvii *12*. Cp. Shakespeare, *Sonnet 59*: 'five hundred courses of the sun'.

cxviii Not *T.MS*. 'The sections of *In Memoriam* about Evolution had been read by his friends some years before the publication of [Robert Chambers's] *Vestiges of Creation* in 1844' (*Mem.* i 223). T. read Charles Lyell's *Principles of Geology* in 1837 (*Mem.* i 162).
cxviii *1*. *all*] thou *L.MS 1st reading*.

But trust that those we call the dead
Are breathers of an ampler day
For ever nobler ends. They say,
The solid earth whereon we tread

In tracts of fluent heat began,
And grew to seeming-random forms,
The seeming prey of cyclic storms,
Till at the last arose the man;

Who throve and branched from clime to clime,
The herald of a higher race,
And of himself in higher place,
If so he type this work of time

Within himself, from more to more;
Or, crowned with attributes of woe
Like glories, move his course, and show
That life is not as idle ore,

But iron dug from central gloom,
And heated hot with burning fears,
And dipt in baths of hissing tears,
And battered with the shocks of doom

cxviii *9. tracts of fluent*] fields of fluid *L.MS 1st reading.* *heat*] fire *L.MS.*
cxviii *9–11.* As W. R. Rutland, *Essays and Studies* xxvi (1940) 13, shows, this refers to Cuvier's cataclysmic theory. J. Killham (*Tennyson and 'The Princess'*, 1958, p. 246) remarks that 'the resemblances between the anatomical structures of present-day animals and fossils of extinct species were to be explained by the occurrence of fresh creations after each of a series of cataclysms, of which the Flood was perhaps one'. This theory, as Killham says, is incompatible with others that T. mentions, e.g. marine erosion.
cxviii *12–17.* G. R. Potter, *PQ* xvi (1937) 337, shows that though this is close to a theory of mutability of species, the concept is still of 'an evolving Nature'. 'Branched' means divided into different races, but still as man. There is no clear-cut belief in mutability of species here. T.'s wording resembles Chambers, *Vestiges of Creation* (despite T.'s denial—see above): 'It may only have been when a varied climate arose, that the originally few species branched off into the present extensive variety' (p. 262).
cxviii *18. Or*] *1850* (*2nd*); And *1850* (*1st*).
cxviii *21–3.* Cp. *Chorus from The Devil and the Lady*, printed *Cornhill* cliii (1936) 443–4: 'And our frequent tears / Hiss into drought on the burning cheek'. Also *Sense and Conscience* 119–22: 'Which would not fall because his burning eyes / Did hiss them into drought. Aloud he wept, / Loud did he weep, for now the iron had come / Into his soul.'

To shape and use. Arise and fly
The reeling Faun, the sensual feast;
Move upward, working out the beast,
And let the ape and tiger die.

## CXIX

Doors, where my heart was used to beat
So quickly, not as one that weeps
I come once more; the city sleeps;
I smell the meadow in the street;

I hear a chirp of birds; I see
Betwixt the black fronts long-withdrawn
A light-blue lane of early dawn,
And think of early days and thee,

And bless thee, for thy lips are bland,
And bright the friendship of thine eye;
And in my thoughts with scarce a sigh
I take the pressure of thine hand.

## CXX

I trust I have not wasted breath:
I think we are not wholly brain,
Magnetic mockeries; not in vain,
Like Paul with beasts, I fought with Death;

Not only cunning casts in clay:
Let Science prove we are, and then
What matters Science unto men,
At least to me? I would not stay.

cxviii *26. sensual feast*: Shakespeare, *Sonnet 141*.

cxix Not *T.MS, L.MS, trial edition*. But based on an unpublished section from *L.MS, Let Death and Memory* (p. 1775). A pendant to vii.
cxix *9–12*. Adapted from *Let Death and Memory* 9–12 (p. 1775).

cxx Not *T.MS, L.MS, trial edition*.
cxx *3*. J. Killham compares Robert Chambers's account of the seemingly electrical nature of nervous and cerebral action, mentioning magnetism (*Vestiges of Creation*, 1844, p. 333).
cxx *4*. T. compares *1 Corinthians* xv 32: 'If after the manner of men I have fought with beasts at Ephesus, what advantageth it me?'

Let him, the wiser man who springs
Hereafter, up from childhood shape
His action like the greater ape,
But I was *born* to other things.

## CXXI

Sad Hesper o'er the buried sun
And ready, thou, to die with him,
Thou watchest all things ever dim
And dimmer, and a glory done:

The team is loosened from the wain,
The boat is drawn upon the shore;
Thou listenest to the closing door,
And life is darkened in the brain.

Bright Phosphor, fresher for the night,
By thee the world's great work is heard
Beginning, and the wakeful bird;
Behind thee comes the greater light:

The market boat is on the stream,
And voices hail it from the brink;
Thou hear'st the village hammer clink,
And see'st the moving of the team.

cxx *9–11.* 'Spoken ironically against mere materialism, not against evolution' (T.).
cxx *12. born*] [ital.] *1872*; born [*rom.*] *1850–70*.

cxxi Not *T.MS*, *L.MS*, *trial edition*. In H. D. Rawnsley's *Memories of the Tennysons* (1900), p. 121, W. F. Rawnsley reports: 'My earliest remembrance of him is of his visiting my parents at Shiplake, before 1850, when I was turned out of my little room in order that he might have a place of his own to smoke in. He was then still working on *In Memoriam*, and it was in this little room of mine that he wrote the "Hesper Phosphor" canto.' Cp. Shelley's translation of an epigram attributed to Plato: 'Thou wert the morning star among the living, / Ere thy fair light had fled;– / Now, having died, thou art as Hesperus, giving / New splendour to the dead.' And Horace, *Odes* II ix 10–12: *nec tibi Vespero / surgente decedunt amores / nec rapidum fugiente solem.* ('Nor do thy words of love cease either when Vesper comes out at evening, or when he flies before the swiftly coursing sun.')
cxxi *11. the wakeful bird*: *Paradise Lost* iii 38.
cxxi *12.* Cp. *Genesis* i 16, 'The greater light to rule the day'.

Sweet Hesper-Phosphor, double name
For what is one, the first, the last,
Thou, like my present and my past,
Thy place is changed; thou art the same.

## CXXII

Oh, wast thou with me, dearest, then,
While I rose up against my doom,
And yearned to burst the folded gloom,
To bare the eternal Heavens again,

To feel once more, in placid awe,
The strong imagination roll
A sphere of stars about my soul,
In all her motion one with law;

If thou wert with me, and the grave
Divide us not, be with me now,
And enter in at breast and brow,
Till all my blood, a fuller wave,

Be quickened with a livelier breath,
And like an inconsiderate boy,
As in the former flash of joy,
I slip the thoughts of life and death;

And all the breeze of Fancy blows,
And every dew-drop paints a bow,
The wizard lightnings deeply glow,
And every thought breaks out a rose.

cxxi *18. Revelation* i 11, 'Alpha and Omega, the first and the last'.

cxxii Not *T.MS.*

cxxii *1.* T. said to James Knowles: 'If anybody thinks I ever called him "dearest" in his life they are much mistaken, for I never even called him "dear"', *Nineteenth Century* xxxiii (1893) 187.

cxxii *2. doom*: 'that of grief' (T.).

cxxii *3. yearned*] *1850 (2nd)*; strove *1850 (1st)*.

cxxii *10–12.* Cp. Arthur Hallam: 'Tho' innumerable waves divide us now', *To One Early Loved* 2, a poem similar in theme to *In Memoriam* (Motter, p. 78).

cxxii *17. breeze*] storm *L.MS 1st reading.*

cxxii *18.* 'Every dew-drop turns into a miniature rainbow' (T.).

## CXXIII

There rolls the deep where grew the tree.
O earth, what changes hast thou seen!
There where the long street roars, hath been
The stillness of the central sea.

The hills are shadows, and they flow
From form to form, and nothing stands;
They melt like mist, the solid lands,
Like clouds they shape themselves and go.

But in my spirit will I dwell,
And dream my dream, and hold it true;
For though my lips may breathe adieu,
I cannot think the thing farewell.

## CXXIV

That which we dare invoke to bless;
Our dearest faith; our ghastliest doubt;
He, They, One, All; within, without;
The Power in darkness whom we guess;

cxxiii The sections on Evolution were written 'some years' before the publication of Chambers's *Vestiges of Creation* in 1844 (*Mem.* i 223). T. read Charles Lyell's *Principles of Geology* in 1837 (*Mem.* i 162); E. B. Mattes (p. 61) compares Lyell: 'many flourishing inland towns, and a still greater number of ports, now stand where the sea rolled its waves' (4th edn, 1835, i 375–the concluding paragraph of vol. i).

cxxiii *4 ∧ 5*] Like days and hours the cycles fleet,
The deep seas pass away like steam,
But Love hath such a real dream
It cannot pass, it is so sweet.

These lines (*T.MS*, deleted) are in H.T.'s hand in a copy of *Works* (1884, *Lincoln*), as 'Unpublished verse (your epitaph)'. In the second line, T. changed 'roll' to 'pass'.

cxxiii *8*. Cp. Wordsworth, *White Doe* 969–70: 'A thousand, thousand rings of light / That shape themselves and disappear'.

cxxiii *8 ∧ 9*] But in my love will I rejoice,
Nor should my song of love be mute,
Though Earth should shake beneath my foot,
And Heaven's axle break with noise. *MS*

These lines (*T.MS*, deleted) are from proofs of H.T.'s edition of *In Memoriam* (1905) at *Lincoln*.

cxxiv Not *T.MS*. The poem originally began at l. 9, as is clear from *H.Lpr 102*, *L.MS*, and *trial edition*.

cxxiv *1–8*] *Not trial edition*. T. rejected Paley's arguments for the existence of God, based on design in the natural world. Paley (whose *Natural Theology* was at Somersby, *Lincoln*) wrote: 'we have made choice of the eye as

I found Him not in world or sun,
Or eagle's wing, or insect's eye;
Nor through the questions men may try,
The petty cobwebs we have spun:

If e'er when faith had fallen asleep,
I heard a voice 'believe no more'
And heard an ever-breaking shore
That tumbled in the Godless deep;

A warmth within the breast would melt
The freezing reason's colder part,
And like a man in wrath the heart
Stood up and answered 'I have felt.'

No, like a child in doubt and fear:
But that blind clamour made me wise;
Then was I as a child that cries,
But, crying, knows his father near;

And what I am beheld again
What is, and no man understands;
And out of darkness came the hands
That reach through nature, moulding men.

an instance upon which to rest the argument of this chapter' (1803 edn, p. 44). At a meeting of the 'Apostles' at Cambridge, T. had voted 'No' to the question 'Is an intelligible First Cause deducible from the phenomena of the Universe?' (*Mem.* i 44).

cxxiv *9. had*] *L.MS*; hath *trial edition* (*error*).

cxxiv *10. I . . . voice*] And doubt began *L.MS 1st reading.*

cxxiv *11*] I heard upon the crumbling shore *L.MS 1st reading.*

cxxiv *12. That . . . in*] The long roll of *L.MS 1st reading.*

cxxiv *13–14*. Cp. 'That heat of inward evidence', *The Two Voices* 284.

cxxiv *17–20*] *Not trial edition.* E. B. Mattes notes the bearing of this on Henry Sidgwick's praise of this section: 'At this point, if the stanzas had stopped here ["I have felt"], we should have shaken our heads and said, "Feeling must not usurp the function of Reason. Feeling is not knowing. It is the duty of a rational being to follow truth wherever it leads." But the poet's instinct knows this; he knows that this usurpation by Feeling of the function of Reason is too bold and confident; accordingly in the next stanza he gives the turn to humility in the protest of Feeling which is required (I think) to win the assent of the "man in men" at this stage of human thought' (*Mem.* i 303).

cxxiv *21. am*] *1859*; seem *1850–56*. *what I am*] the inner eye *trial edition.*

cxxiv *22–3*] The form which no one understands,
And glimpses of the shadowy hands, *trial edition*

## CXXV

Whatever I have said or sung,
  Some bitter notes my harp would give,
  Yea, though there often seemed to live
A contradiction on the tongue,

Yet Hope had never lost her youth;
  She did but look through dimmer eyes;
  Or Love but played with gracious lies,
Because he felt so fixed in truth:

And if the song were full of care,
  He breathed the spirit of the song;
  And if the words were sweet and strong
He set his royal signet there;

Abiding with me till I sail
  To seek thee on the mystic deeps,
  And this electric force, that keeps
A thousand pulses dancing, fail.

## CXXVI

Love is and was my Lord and King,
  And in his presence I attend
  To hear the tidings of my friend,
Which every hour his couriers bring.

Love is and was my King and Lord,
  And will be, though as yet I keep
  Within his court on earth, and sleep
Encompassed by his faithful guard,

And hear at times a sentinel
  Who moves about from place to place,
  And whispers to the worlds of space,
In the deep night, that all is well.

cxxv Not *L.MS* but in *T.MS*.

cxxvi *L.MS* has the opening words only, but this section is in *T.MS*.

cxxvi *2–3*. Cp. Herbert, *The Holy Communion* 23–4: 'While those to spirits refin'd, at doore attend / Dispatches from their friend.'

cxxvi *5–8*] Love is my king, nor here alone,
  But where I see the distance loom,
  For in the field behind the tomb
There rests the shadow of his throne. *MS quoted in Eversley*

cxxvi *10. Who*] *1855*; That *1850–51*.

cxxvi *11. worlds*] *1855*; vast *1850–51*.

cxxvi *12. In ... night*] *1855*; Among the worlds *1850–51*.

## CXXVII

And all is well, though faith and form
Be sundered in the night of fear;
Well roars the storm to those that hear
A deeper voice across the storm,

cxxvii Not *T.MS.* There is no specific reference to any particular revolution, but Arthur Hallam's words in his *Influence of Italian upon English Literature* (1831; Motter, p. 233) have obvious affinities:

'Looking, then, to the lurid presages of the times that are coming; believing that amidst the awful commotions of society, which few of us do not expect, – the disruption, it may be, of those common bands which hold together our social existence, necessarily followed by an occurrence on a larger scale of the same things that were witnessed in France forty years ago . . . that, in such a desolation, nothing possibly can be found to support men but a true spiritual Christianity, I am not entirely without hope, that round such an element of vital light, constrained once more to put forth its illuminating energies for protection and deliverance to its children, may gather once again the scattered rays of human knowledge.'

The close of the poem also suggests Hallam's *A Farewell to the South* 679–83 (Motter, p. 26): 'as when mountains fling / Their central fire aloft, strugglings and rout, /Which uproar all our being's harmony, / And yoke our very consciousness to doubt. /Who smiles on such a scene? Yes, poesy!'

Such sentiments as Hallam's and T.'s may now sound complacent but they were in line with serious geological study. In *Principles of Geology* (4th edn, 1835, ii 290–1), Lyell insists that 'the general tendency of subterranean movements, when their effects are considered for a sufficient lapse of ages, is eminently beneficial, and that they constitute an essential part of that mechanism by which the integrity of the habitable surface is preserved, and the very existence and perpetuation of dry land secured. Why the working of this same machinery should be attended with so much evil, is a mystery far beyond the reach of our philosophy, and must probably remain so until we are permitted to investigate, not our planet alone and its inhabitants, but other parts of the moral and material universe with which they may be connected.' Another paragraph by Lyell (ii 403) suggests the geological-political analogy: 'Causes acting in the interior of the earth; which, although so often the source of death and terror to the inhabitants of the globe – visiting, in succession, every zone, and filling the earth with monuments of ruin and disorder – are, nevertheless, the agents of a conservative principle above all others essential to the stability of the system.'

cxxvii 4. Cp. *Revelation* xvi 17–18: 'And the seventh angel poured out his vial into the air; and there came a great voice out of the temple of heaven, from the throne, saying, It is done. And there were voices, and thunders,

Proclaiming social truth shall spread,
And justice, even though thrice again
The red fool-fury of the Seine
Should pile her barricades with dead.

But ill for him that wears a crown,
And him, the lazar, in his rags:
They tremble, the sustaining crags;
The spires of ice are toppled down,

And molten up, and roar in flood;
The fortress crashes from on high,
The brute earth lightens to the sky,
And the great Æon sinks in blood,

And compassed by the fires of Hell;
While thou, dear spirit, happy star,
O'erlook'st the tumult from afar,
And smilest, knowing all is well.

and lightnings; and there was a great earthquake, such as was not since men were upon the earth.'
cxxvii *6. even*] yea *L.MS 1st reading.* *thrice*] once *trial edition.*
cxxvii *7. red fool-fury*] red-capt harlot *L.MS*. Cp. *Switzerland* 28–9 (Appendix C, p. 1810): 'And bid the Seine / Be choked with slain.' Cp. *Beautiful City* (p. 1422).
cxxvii *9. But . . . him*] *1850 (2nd)*; Woe to the head *L.MS 1st reading*; But woe to him *1850 (1st)*. Cp. *2 Henry IV* III i 31: 'Uneasy lies the head that wears a crown.'
cxxvii *12.* Cp. 'icy spires', *The Palace of Art* 82, *1832* text. Cp. (noting ll. 10–17) *This Earth is wondrous* 22–4: 'Set round with many a toppling spire / And monstrous rocks from craggy snouts / Disploding globes of roaring fire.' Also Shelley, *Prometheus Unbound* II iii 28–30: 'mountains / From icy spires of sun-like radiance fling / The dawn'; Shelley then applies this to revolution: 'and the nations echo round, / Shaken to their roots, as do the mountains now.' The revolutionary situation recurs in *The Princess* iv 53–4: 'Like glittering bergs of ice, / Throne after throne, and molten on the waste.'
cxxvii *14. fortress*] mountain *L.MS.*
cxxvii *15. Comus* 797–9: 'And the brute Earth would lend her nerves, and shake, / Till all thy magick structures rear'd so high, /Were shatter'd into heaps.'
cxxvii *16. great*] *1851*; vast *1850*.
cxxvii *18. happy star*] from afar *trial edition.*
cxxvii *19. O'erlook'st*] Look'st o'er *L.MS.* *from afar*] like a star *trial edition.*

## CXXVIII

The love that rose on stronger wings,
Unpalsied when he met with Death,
Is comrade of the lesser faith
That sees the course of human things.

No doubt vast eddies in the flood
Of onward time shall yet be made,
And thronèd races may degrade;
Yet O ye mysteries of good,

Wild Hours that fly with Hope and Fear,
If all your office had to do
With old results that look like new;
If this were all your mission here,

To draw, to sheathe a useless sword,
To fool the crowd with glorious lies,
To cleave a creed in sects and cries,
To change the bearing of a word,

To shift an arbitrary power,
To cramp the student at his desk,
To make old bareness picturesque
And tuft with grass a feudal tower;

Why then my scorn might well descend
On you and yours. I see in part
That all, as in some piece of art,
Is toil cöoperant to an end.

cxxviii Not *L.MS*, *trial edition*. *T.MS* begins at l. 9; *H.Lpr 102* at l. 5.
cxxviii *1–4*] *Not T.MS, H.MS.*
cxxviii *5–8*] *Not T.MS.*
cxxviii *8. mysteries*] *1850* (*2nd*); ministers *1850* (*1st*).
cxxviii *11.* Cp. *The constant spirit* 4: 'Old principles still working new results'.
cxxviii *14*] To choke a creed with mythic lies, *H.MS.* *glorious lies*: Horace's *splendide mendax* (*Odes* III xi 35). John Churton Collins said that 'glorious lies' 'is probably a mistranslation of Plato's θεῖα ψευδῆ'. Alongside this suggestion, T. wrote: '!!' (*Cornhill*, Jan. 1880, *Lincoln*).
cxxviii *15. To . . . in*] Or cleave it into *H.MS.*
cxxviii *16. To*] Or *H.MS.*
cxxviii *19. bareness*] *1850* (*2nd*); baseness *1850* (*1st*), *T.MS*, *H.MS*. Cp. 'She finds the baseness of her lot', i.e. lowliness, lx 6.
cxxviii *24.* Cp. *Youth* 60: 'A labour working to an end', which was incorporated as *The Two Voices* 297.

## CXXIX

Dear friend, far off, my lost desire,
So far, so near in woe and weal;
O loved the most, when most I feel
There is a lower and a higher;

Known and unknown; human, divine;
Sweet human hand and lips and eye;
Dear heavenly friend that canst not die,
Mine, mine, for ever, ever mine;

Strange friend, past, present, and to be;
Loved deeplier, darklier understood;
Behold, I dream a dream of good,
And mingle all the world with thee.

## CXXX

Thy voice is on the rolling air;
I hear thee where the waters run;
Thou standest in the rising sun,
And in the setting thou art fair.

cxxix Not *T.MS*, *L.MS*. Transposed with cxxx in *trial edition.*
cxxix *2. So far*] Sweet friend *trial edition.*
cxxix *3. O loved the*] Dear friend, loved *trial edition.*
cxxix *6. hand and lips*] voice, and hand *trial edition*. Cp. 'Dear lips, loved eyes, ye fade, ye fly', from *In deep and solemn dreams* 57, a poem with many affinities with *In Memoriam.*
cxxix *8. Mine, mine*] My friend *trial edition.*
cxxix *11–12*] Let me not lose my faith in good
Lest I make less my love for thee. *trial edition*

cxxx Not *T.MS*. Transposed with cxxix in *trial edition.*
cxxx *1. on*] in *L.MS 1st reading*. Cp. Arthur Hallam's poem to T.'s sister Emily, *Lady, I bid thee* 6 (Motter, p. 97): 'Old Dante's voice encircles all the air'. Also Shelley, *Adonais* 370–87, beginning: 'He is made one with Nature: there is heard / His voice in all her music'.
cxxx *3.* Cp. *Revelation* xix 17, 'And I saw an angel standing in the sun; and he cried with a loud voice'. Hallam himself had alluded to this verse, in speaking of friendship and Heaven, *To One Early Loved* stanza xiii (Motter, p. 82): 'Brave spirits are, whom I will have to friend . . . / . . . to whom th' approach is free / Of unbarred Heaven, and the full mystery / Unfolded to the penetrative mind. / Such is the mighty Florentine, and He / Who saw the solar angel, nor was blind; / Such the deep, simple Shakespeare, greatest of mankind.' Hallam's note to the penultimate line: 'St John, *Revelations*, Chap. x'.
cxxx *4. setting*] flowers *L.MS 1st reading.*

What art thou then? I cannot guess;
But though I seem in star and flower
To feel thee some diffusive power,
I do not therefore love thee less:

My love involves the love before;
My love is vaster passion now;
Though mixed with God and Nature thou,
I seem to love thee more and more.

Far off thou art, but ever nigh;
I have thee still, and I rejoice;
I prosper, circled with thy voice;
I shall not lose thee though I die.

## CXXXI

O living will that shalt endure
When all that seems shall suffer shock,
Rise in the spiritual rock,
Flow through our deeds and make them pure,

cxxx *5–16*] No more I yearn, no longer grieve:
I walk the meadows and rejoice
And prosper, compassed by thy voice
For ever. Strange that I should live

To say such wondrous things of thee!
I know the beauty which thou wast,
Thy single sweetness in the Past,
Yet art thou oft as God to me. *L.MS 1st reading, deleted*

Cp. the end of *The Two Voices* (p. 541).
cxxx *13. Far . . . art*] O thou far off *L.MS.*
cxxx *15. circled*] compassed *L.MS.*

cxxxi Not *T.MS.*
cxxxi *1.* 'That which we know as Free-will in man' (T.).
cxxxi *1–4. I loving Freedom* 14–16: 'May well surmount the coming shock / By climbing steps their fathers carved / Within the living rock.'
cxxxi *2*] When mountains [*lacuna*] shock *H.Nbk 18.*
cxxxi *3. 1 Corinthians* x 4: 'for they drank of that spiritual Rock that followed them: and that Rock was Christ.'

That we may lift from out of dust
    A voice as unto him that hears,
    A cry above the conquered years
To one that with us works, and trust,

With faith that comes of self-control,
    The truths that never can be proved
    Until we close with all we loved,
And all we flow from, soul in soul.

---

## [EPILOGUE]

O true and tried, so well and long,
    Demand not thou a marriage lay;
    In that it is thy marriage day
Is music more than any song.

cxxxi *5. lift*] speak *H.MS.* *of*] *1850 (2nd)*; the *1850 (1st)*.
cxxxi *5–6. Isaiah* xxix 4: 'And thou shalt be brought down, and shalt speak out of the ground, and thy speech shall be low out of the dust, and thy voice shall be, as of one that hath a familiar spirit, out of the ground, and thy speech shall whisper out of the dust.'
cxxxi *6*] As unto one that hears and sees *H.MS.* *him*] one *L.MS 1st reading*.
cxxxi *7*] Some little of the vast to be *H.MS.*
cxxxi *8*] [*lacuna*] trust *H.MS.*
cxxxi *8. Mark* xvi 20: 'And they went forth, and preached every where, the Lord working with them, and confirming the word with signs following' (the concluding verse of the Gospel).
cxxxi *9*] With ever more of [ever-growing *1st reading*] strength and grace, *H.MS.* Cp. 'The maidens gathered strength and grace', ciii 27.
cxxxi *11–12*] And come to look on those we loved
And That which made us, face to face. *H.MS*
Cp. *Crossing the Bar* 15: 'I hope to see my Pilot face to face'. From *1 Corinthians* xiii 12: 'For now we see through a glass, darkly; but then face to face: now I know in part; but then shall I know even as also I am known.'

[*Epilogue*] Not *T.MS.* The present edition follows A. C. Bradley in referring to this as the Epilogue, though T. gave it no title. It describes the marriage of T.'s sister Cecilia to his friend Edmund Lushington, 10 Oct. 1842. The version in *L.MS* could belong to 1842 (see ll. 9–10), but the similarities to Chambers's *Vestiges of Creation* (1844) in the conclusion, though not decisive, suggest that T. did not write it till 1844–5. Lushington says, of the summer of 1845: 'He had then completed many of the cantos in *In Memoriam*. . . . He said to me, "I have brought in your marriage at the end of *In Memoriam*," and then showed me those poems of *In Memoriam* which were finished and which were a perfectly novel surprise to me' (*Mem.* i 203).
*E 2. Demand not thou*] Why ask of me *L.MS 1st reading*.

Nor have I felt so much of bliss
Since first he told me that he loved
A daughter of our house; nor proved
Since that dark day a day like this;

Though I since then have numbered o'er
Some thrice three years: they went and came,
Remade the blood and changed the frame,
And yet is love not less, but more;

No longer caring to embalm
In dying songs a dead regret,
But like a statue solid-set,
And moulded in colossal calm.

Regret is dead, but love is more
Than in the summers that are flown,
For I myself with these have grown
To something greater than before;

Which makes appear the songs I made
As echoes out of weaker times,
As half but idle brawling rhymes,
The sport of random sun and shade.

But where is she, the bridal flower,
That must be made a wife ere noon?
She enters, glowing like the moon
Of Eden on its bridal bower:

On me she bends her blissful eyes
And then on thee; they meet thy look
And brighten like the star that shook
Betwixt the palms of paradise.

O when her life was yet in bud,
He too foretold the perfect rose.
For thee she grew, for thee she grows
For ever, and as fair as good.

*E 7*] Her elder sister: no, nor proved *MS 1st reading.*
*E 10. they . . . came*] have seen them go *MS 1st reading.*
*E 11*] With change of blossom, fruit and snow; *MS 1st reading.*
*E 21. appear*] me deem *MS 1st reading.*
*E 24 ∧ 5*] For if the wisest rule, to rest
In Him, is wisest; all are His;
And so we leave whatever is
To Him the Wisest and the Best; *MS deleted*
*E 31–2.* The stars shook when Zeus nodded approval of the marriage of Peleus and Thetis, Catullus lxiv (DeVane's selection, 1947).

And thou art worthy; full of power;
As gentle; liberal-minded, great,
Consistent; wearing all that weight
Of learning lightly like a flower.

But now set out: the noon is near,
And I must give away the bride;
She fears not, or with thee beside
And me behind her, will not fear.

For I that danced her on my knee,
That watched her on her nurse's arm,
That shielded all her life from harm
At last must part with her to thee;

Now waiting to be made a wife,
Her feet, my darling, on the dead;
Their pensive tablets round her head,
And the most living words of life

Breathed in her ear. The ring is on,
The 'wilt thou' answered, and again
The 'wilt thou' asked, till out of twain
Her sweet 'I will' has made you one.

Now sign your names, which shall be read,
Mute symbols of a joyful morn,
By village eyes as yet unborn;
The names are signed, and overhead

Begins the clash and clang that tells
The joy to every wandering breeze;
The blind wall rocks, and on the trees
The dead leaf trembles to the bells.

O happy hour, and happier hours
Await them. Many a merry face
Salutes them–maidens of the place,
That pelt us in the porch with flowers.

E 39. *Consistent*: in the sense of having qualities that 'stand well' together.
E 41. *now set out*] we must go *MS 1st reading.*
E 56. *you*] *1872*; ye *1850–70*
E 58. *joyful*] blissful *MS.*
E 65] Come out: a day of happy hours *MS 1st reading.*
E 66. *Await them*] Awaits you *MS 1st reading.*
E 67. *Salutes them*] Will greet you *MS 1st reading.*
E 68. *That*] They *MS 1st reading.*

O happy hour, behold the bride
  With him to whom her hand I gave.
  They leave the porch, they pass the grave
That has today its sunny side.

Today the grave is bright for me,
  For them the light of life increased,
  Who stay to share the morning feast,
Who rest tonight beside the sea.

Let all my genial spirits advance
  To meet and greet a whiter sun;
  My drooping memory will not shun
The foaming grape of eastern France.

It circles round, and fancy plays,
  And hearts are warmed and faces bloom,
  As drinking health to bride and groom
We wish them store of happy days.

Nor count me all to blame if I
  Conjecture of a stiller guest,
  Perchance, perchance, among the rest,
And, though in silence, wishing joy.

*E 69*] Return with him: return a bride *MS 1st reading.*
*E 70. her*] thy *MS 1st reading.*
*E 71*] Step lightly by the sunny grave, *MS 1st reading.*
*E 72. That*] It *MS 1st reading.*
*E 73–6*]
For all is light and life increased
  For you and so for us today,
  Albeit you leave us here: but stay
A little: share the morning feast. *MS 1st reading*

See ll. 88 ‸ 9*n*.
*E 77–9. Samson Agonistes* 594: 'my genial spirits droop'.
*E 78. whiter sun*: *candidi soles*, Catullus viii 3.
*E 81. and*] the *MS 1st reading.*
*E 82. And . . . and*] The . . . the *MS 1st reading.*
*E 86. a stiller*] another *MS 1st reading.*
*E 87. Perchance, perchance*] As here unseen *MS 1st reading.*
*E 88 ‸ 9*]
A passing fancy, let it be:
  However wished, their joy will grow
  Beyond the wish: but they must go:
They rest tonight beside the sea. *MS deleted*

The last line became l. 76.

But they must go, the time draws on,
   And those white-favoured horses wait;
   They rise, but linger; it is late;
Farewell, we kiss, and they are gone.

A shade falls on us like the dark
   From little cloudlets on the grass,
   But sweeps away as out we pass
To range the woods, to roam the park,

Discussing how their courtship grew,
   And talk of others that are wed,
   And how she looked, and what he said,
And back we come at fall of dew.

Again the feast, the speech, the glee,
   The shade of passing thought, the wealth
   Of words and wit, the double health,
The crowning cup, the three-times-three,

And last the dance;–till I retire:
   Dumb is that tower which spake so loud,
   And high in heaven the streaming cloud,
And on the downs a rising fire:

And rise, O moon, from yonder down,
   Till over down and over dale
   All night the shining vapour sail
And pass the silent-lighted town,

*E 89*] Farewell–and yet they linger on: *MS 1st reading.*
*E 91. linger*] go not *MS 1st reading.*
*E 94. grass*] sun *MS 1st reading.*
*E 95–6*] But out we go, we walk, we run,
We loiter in and out the park: *MS 1st reading*
*E 96 ∧ 7*] We pace the stubble bare of sheaves,
We watch the brimming river steal
And half the golden woodland reel
Athwart the smoke of burning leaves. *MS deleted*
Adapted as *The Princess* vii 335–7: 'all the rich to-come / Reels, as the golden Autumn woodland reels / Athwart the smoke of burning weeds' [*1851*; leaves *1850*].
*E 97. Discussing*] We talk of *MS 1st reading.*
*E 98. And talk*] We speak *MS 1st reading.*
*E 102–3. the wealth of words*: *Œnone* 105, MS.
*E 104. The . . . cup*] And close on that *MS 1st reading.*
*E 109. down*] downs *MS 1st reading.*
*E 109–20.* There are many affinities with *The Vale of Bones* 1–10 (*1827*, p. 97).
*E 110*] And over tower and grove and vale *MS 1st reading.*
*E 112. pass*] cross *MS alternative.* *town*] towns *MS 1st reading.*

The white-faced halls, the glancing rills,
  And catch at every mountain head,
  And o'er the friths that branch and spread
Their sleeping silver through the hills;

And touch with shade the bridal doors,
  With tender gloom the roof, the wall;
  And breaking let the splendour fall
To spangle all the happy shores

By which they rest, and ocean sounds,
  And, star and system rolling past,
  A soul shall draw from out the vast
And strike his being into bounds,

And, moved through life of lower phase,
  Result in man, be born and think,
  And act and love, a closer link
Betwixt us and the crowning race

E 113. *The . . . halls,*] And cross with gloom *MS 1st reading.*
E 114. *catch*] touch *MS 1st reading.*
E 114–5. Cp. the visionary flight in the 'germ' of *In Memoriam, Hark! the dogs howl* (p. 555).
E 117. *touch with shade the*] o'er the blessèd *MS 1st reading.*
E 118] And pausing fall in sparks of dew, *MS 1st reading.* *sparks of dew*: *The Progress of Spring* 58. *tender gloom*: Thomson's *Castle of Indolence* i 507.
E 119. *fall*] through *MS 1st reading.*
E 121. *they rest*] Love rests *MS 1st reading.*
E 122] And night delays, until at last *MS 1st reading.* Cp. *1850* with *God and the Universe* 3: 'Rush of Suns, and roll of systems'; also *The Devil and the Lady* II i 40: 'Suns and spheres and stars and belts and systems'.
E 123–4. Cp. *Crossing the Bar* 7: 'When that which drew from out the boundless deep'.
E 124. *strike*] smite *MS 1st reading.*
E 125. *And,*] Who *MS 1st reading.* *life*] lives *MS.* G. R. Potter, *PQ* xvi (1937) 339, notes that in these concluding lines there is no certain implication of change of species, and that 'life of lower phase' refers to Von Baer's (and Tiedemann's) theory that the embryo reproduces the stages of the different forms of life. See also J. Killham, *Tennyson and 'The Princess'* (1958), pp. 234–40. The phrase 'the crowning race' in l. 128 also occurs in *The Princess* vii 279. W. R. Rutland, *Essays and Studies* xxvi (1940) 22, suggested the influence of Robert Chambers's *Vestiges of Creation*, for which T. asked Moxon in 1844 (*Mem.* i 222); he noted Chambers's question, 'Is our race but the initial of the grand crowning type?'. Killham observes that this, with other relevant passages, was

Of those that, eye to eye, shall look
On knowledge; under whose command
Is Earth and Earth's, and in their hand
Is Nature like an open book;

No longer half-akin to brute,
For all we thought and loved and did,
And hoped, and suffered, is but seed
Of what in them is flower and fruit;

quoted in a review in *The Examiner*, 9 Nov. 1844. Killham (p. 257) remarks the association of Tiedemann's foetal theory with evolutionary hypotheses, and quotes Chambers: 'There may then be occasion for a nobler type of humanity.' *The Examiner* 'specially emphasized that the operation of the law of development depended entirely upon the "generative system". It is in consequence of this, I suggest, that a marriage concludes *In Memoriam*; in marriage we come closest to participating in the cosmic purpose, though we must continually seek to "type" the qualities we desire to make permanent in man.' T.'s *Epilogue* has a clear link with Chambers's insistence (p. 71) on the 'parity of law affecting the progress of general creation, and the progress of an individual foetus of one of the more perfect animals', and also on the 'parity, or rather identity, of laws presiding over the development of the animated tribes on the face of the earth, and that of the individual in embryo' (p. 202). The *Epilogue* may well have been suggested by such remarks of Chambers as: 'The production of new forms . . . has never been anything more than a new stage of progress in gestation, an event as simply natural, and attended as little by any circumstances of a wonderful or startling kind, as the silent advance of an ordinary mother from one week to another of her pregnancy' (pp. 222–3). See also E. B. Mattes (pp. 84–5).

*E 126. Result*] Shall end *MS 1st reading.*

*E 128–30.* Cp. Chambers's *Vestiges of Creation*, p. 6: 'A time may come when we shall be much more in the thick of the stars of our astral system than we are now, and have of course much more brilliant nocturnal skies; but it may be countless ages before the eyes which are to see this added resplendence shall exist.'

*E 129. Of those*] The men *MS 1st reading.* Cp. Shakespeare, *Sonnet 81*: 'Your monument shall be my gentle verse, / Which eyes not yet created shall o'er-read.'

*E 130. whose*] their *MS 1st reading.*

*E 132.* This traditional metaphor was invigorated by its geological aptness. Chambers (p. 57) speaks of fossils and 'the leaves of the *Stone Book*', just as he speaks often of 'the Divine Author'. Lyell (*Principles of Geology*, 4th edn, 1835, i 27) writes: 'The ancient history of the globe was to them a sealed book . . . although written in characters of the most striking and imposing kind'; and he mentions 'the alphabet and grammar of geology' (iii 332).

Whereof the man, that with me trod
This planet, was a noble type
Appearing ere the times were ripe,
That friend of mine who lives in God,

That God, which ever lives and loves,
One God, one law, one element,
And one far-off divine event,
To which the whole creation moves.

## 297 *To the Vicar of Shiplake

Printed *Mem.* i 330–1, and then (adding ll. 11–20) in the notes to *Eversley* (the text below). It was written on T.'s wedding-day, 13 June 1850, and sent in a letter to T.'s friend Drummond Rawnsley who had officiated. 'Dear Drummond,–I send you my poem, made for the most part in your own carriage, between Shiplake and Reading. *Keep it to yourself* as I should have kept it to *my*self if Kate had not asked for it, *i.e.* keep it till I give you leave to make it public' (H. D. Rawnsley, *Memories of the Tennysons*, 1900, pp. 73–4). The text accompanying this letter (*Harvard Rawnsley 12*) has the six stanzas; there are drafts in *H.Nbk 27* (four stanzas, one of them deleted); in *H.Lpr 247* (four stanzas); and at *Lincoln* (three stanzas). 'On his revisiting Shiplake in December he added two stanzas to the four which he wrote on the wedding day'. W. F. Rawnsley, *Nineteenth Century* xcvii (1925) 4.

Vicar of that pleasant spot,
Where it was my chance to marry,
Happy, happy be your lot
In the Vicarage by the quarry:
You were he that knit the knot.

*E 137–8*] In them whereof the friend that trod
This Earth with me was once a type *MS 1st reading*

*E 140. who*] *MS*; that *trial edition.* *lives in*] walks with *MS 1st reading.*

*E 141–4.* Cp. Arthur Hallam's *On the Picture of the Three Fates* 12–13 (Motter, p. 3): 'The Love / Toward which all being solemnly doth move'. Also *Revelation* x 6–7: 'And sware by him that liveth for ever and ever, who created heaven, and the things that therein are, and the earth, and the things that therein are, and the sea, and the things which are therein, that there should be time no longer: But in the days of the voice of the seventh angel, when he shall begin to sound, the mystery of God should be finished.' As Mrs Mattes observes, T. much admired these verses (*Mem.* i 279).

¶297. *1. that*] this *Mem.*

Sweetly, smoothly flow your life.
  Never parish feud perplex you,
Tithe unpaid, or party strife.
  All things please you, nothing vex you;
You have given me such a wife.

Have I seen in one so near
  Aught but sweetness aye prevailing?
Or, through more than half a year,
  Half the fraction of a failing?
Therefore bless you, Drummond dear.

Good she is, and pure and just.
  Being conquered by her sweetness
I shall come through her, I trust,
  Into fuller-orbed completeness;
Though but made of erring dust.

You, meanwhile, shall day by day
  Watch your standard roses blowing,
And your three young things at play
  And your triple terrace growing
Green and greener every May.

Smoothly flow your life with Kate's,
  Glancing off from all things evil,
Smooth as Thames below your gates,
  Thames along the silent level
Streaming through his osiered aits.

*7–8. parish feud . . . Tithe unpaid*] *transposed Mem.*
*11–20*] *Not Mem.*
*21. You . . . shall*] Live and prosper! *Mem.*
*26. Smoothly*] Sweetly *Mem.* *Kate*: Mrs Drummond Rawnsley.
*27. H.Lpr 247* has a note by T. '"Undisturbed by tedious Greville" would be a better rhyme but I do not love to be personal. The poem would be more perfect without the third stanza [ll. 21–5]: but I do not think you would like to miss it. Cut off this tailpiece if Kate wishes to insert the poem in her Album'.
*30. osiered aits*: as in *Edwin Morris* 95, MS; i.e. willowed islets. Osiers and aits form a traditional pairing; cp. Richard Hodges: 'The Ait where the Osiers grew' (cited by *OED*, 'ait'). Cp. Collins, *Ode on Popular Superstitions* 136: 'The ozier'd shore'.

# 298 To W. C. Macready

1851

Printed *The Times*, 3 March 1851; *The Athenaeum*, 8 March, etc. Macready (1793–1875) was an actor-manager, famous like Garrick and John Philip Kemble (l. 7) for his Shakespearean roles. The poem was quoted in the reports of the farewell banquet given to Macready on 7 March, where it was read by John Forster. Published, *Works* (1891). T. had intended to include it in *1889* (*Virginia* trial edition). The long delay in publication was influenced by its unfavourable reception in 1851: '... which we give in honour rather of the occasion than of any particular merit of its own' (*Athenaeum*).

Farewell, Macready, since tonight we part;
Full-handed thunders often have confessed
Thy power, well-used to move the public breast.
We thank thee with our voice, and from the heart.
Farewell, Macready, since this night we part,
Go, take thine honours home; rank with the best,
Garrick and statelier Kemble, and the rest
Who made a nation purer through their art.
Thine is it that our drama did not die,
Nor flicker down to brainless pantomime,
And those gilt gauds men-children swarm to see.
Farewell, Macready; moral, grave, sublime;
Our Shakespeare's bland and universal eye
Dwells pleased, through twice a hundred years, on thee.

# 299 To the Queen

Published as dedication of *Poems*, 7th edn (1851). Dated 'March 1851', it was T.'s first publication as Poet Laureate. The revisions and the many drafts (see Appendix A, p. 1777) show that the poem cost T. much difficulty. T.'s friendship and respect for Queen Victoria are traced in *Mem.* and in *CT*. It is apt that the poem uses the *In Memoriam* stanza since T. 'was appointed Poet Laureate, owing chiefly to Prince Albert's admiration for *In Memoriam*' (*Mem.* i 334). Moreover T. had long used it for major patriotic poems, e.g. *Hail Briton*.

¶298. *4. our*] *Athenaeum, 1891*; one *Times*.

Revered, beloved–O you that hold
  A nobler office upon earth
  Than arms, or power of brain, or birth
Could give the warrior kings of old,

Victoria,–since your Royal grace
  To one of less desert allows
  This laurel greener from the brows
Of him that uttered nothing base;

And should your greatness, and the care
  That yokes with empire, yield you time
  To make demand of modern rhyme
If aught of ancient worth be there;

Then–while a sweeter music wakes,
  And through wild March the throstle calls,
  Where all about your palace-walls
The sun-lit almond-blossom shakes–

Take, Madam, this poor book of song;
  For though the faults were thick as dust
  In vacant chambers, I could trust
Your kindness. May you rule us long,

And leave us rulers of your blood
  As noble till the latest day!
  May children of our children say,
'She wrought her people lasting good;

'Her court was pure; her life serene;
  God gave her peace; her land reposed;
  A thousand claims to reverence closed
In her as Mother, Wife, and Queen;

¶299. *1.* , *beloved–O*] *1853*; Victoria, *1851*.
*5. Victoria,–since*] *1853*; I thank you that *1851*.
*8. him*: Wordsworth, T.'s predecessor as Poet Laureate.
*9–12*] Nor should I dare to flatter state,
    Nor such a lay would you receive,
    Were I to shape it, who believe
  Your nature true as you are great. *proof quoted in Eversley*
*11. modern rhyme*: *In Memoriam* lxxvii 1.
*13–16*] *1853*; *not 1851*.
*20. kindness*] *1853*; sweetness *1851*.
*28‸9*] 'She brought a vast design to pass,
    When Europe and the scattered ends
    Of our fierce world were mixt as friends
  And brethren in her halls of glass; *1851*
The topical allusion to the Great Exhibition in the Crystal Palace (1851) had lost its point by 1853.

'And statesmen at her council met
Who knew the seasons when to take
Occasion by the hand, and make
The bounds of freedom wider yet

'By shaping some august decree,
Which kept her throne unshaken still,
Broad-based upon her people's will,
And compassed by the inviolate sea.'

*March* 1851

## 300 *'Little bosom not yet cold'

Unpublished, *H.Nbk 26.* T.'s first child, a boy, was stillborn, 20 April 1851: 'dear little nameless one that hast lived tho' thou hast never breathed' (*Mem.* i 340). T. wrote to Mrs Patmore: 'He looked, I thought, as if he had had a battle for his life' (*Boston College MS*). Cp. *The Grandmother* 62–8, where T. is remembering his own child: 'There lay the sweet little body that never had drawn a breath . . . / But I wept like a child that day, for the babe had fought for his life . . . / But I wept like a child for the child that was dead before he was born . . .'. Cp. *De Profundis*, on the birth of H.T. (p. 1281).

Little bosom not yet cold,
Noble forehead made for thought,
Little hands of mighty mould
Clenched as in the fight which they had fought.
He had done battle to be born,
But some brute force of Nature had prevailed
And the little warrior failed.

*32. wider*] *1853*; broader *1851*.

*32–3.* Cp. *I loving Freedom* 25–8:

What nobler than an ancient land
That passing an august decree
Makes wider in a settled peace
The lists of liberty?

*35.* Cp. *Sonnet* [*Woe to the double-tongued*] 4–5: 'England's ancient ease / Built on broad bases'.

¶300. *7.* After the birth of Lionel in 1854, T. looked back to his dead child: 'He lay like a little warrior, having fought the fight, and failed, with his hands clenched, and a frown on his brow' (*Mem.* i 375).

Whate'er thou wert, whate'er thou art,
Whose life was ended ere thy breath begun,
Thou nine-months neighbour of my dear one's heart,
And howsoe'er thou liest blind and mute,
Thou lookest bold and resolute,
God bless thee dearest son.

## 301 To E.L., on His Travels in Greece

Published *Poems*, 8th edn (1853). In praise of Edward Lear's *Journals of a Landscape Painter in Albania and Illyria* (1851). It was written 1851–2 (*H.Nbk 26* has two drafts, the first of which is quoted below). T.'s friend Lear is now best known for his nonsense verse, but he had a considerable reputation as a traveller and as a painter, especially of landscapes. (*Poems by Tennyson Illustrated by Lear*, 1889, is still of some interest.) T. was to use the *In Memoriam* stanza to congratulate another author on his travel-book, in *To Ulysses* (p. 1396).

Illyrian woodlands, echoing falls
Of water, sheets of summer glass,
The long divine Peneïan pass,
The vast Akrokeraunian walls,

Tomohrit, Athos, all things fair,
With such a pencil, such a pen,
You shadow forth to distant men,
I read and felt that I was there:

*11.* Cp. the embryo, 'The germ that lieth blind and dumb', *Hail Briton* 177, *MS C.*

¶301. *1. woodlands*] olives *H.MS.* *echoing*] foaming *MS 1st reading.*
*2. sheets*] lakes *MS.*
*3.* Illustrated by Lear (facing p. 410).
*4.* From Horace, *Odes* I iii 20: *scopulos Acroceraunia.* Lear spoke of 'the Acroceraunian range' (p. 210).
*6*] So well with pencil and with pen, *MS.* T. courteously repudiates Lear's self-depreciation: 'No pen or pencil can do justice to the scenery of Metéora' (p. 397).
*8*] I could but feel that I was there. *MS.*

And trust me while I turned the page,
And tracked you still on classic ground,
I grew in gladness till I found
My spirits in the golden age.

For me the torrent ever poured
And glistened – here and there alone
The broad-limbed Gods at random thrown
By fountain-urns; – and Naiads oared

A glimmering shoulder under gloom
Of cavern pillars; on the swell
The silver lily heaved and fell;
And many a slope was rich in bloom

From him that on the mountain lea
By dancing rivulets fed his flocks
To him who sat upon the rocks,
And fluted to the morning sea.

## 302 *The Penny-Wise

Published *Morning Chronicle*, 24 Jan. 1852, with a superscription to the Editor:

Sir – If you please, insert the inclosed. My name is known well enough in the literary world, though I have rather chosen to subscribe myself,

A Scorner of the Penny-Wise.

The same text appeared in the *Evening Journal*, 24–26 Jan.; a text entitled *Arm, Arm, Arm!*, with trivial variants (see C. Ricks, *MP* lxii (1964) 140–1),

---

9] And while [as *1st reading*] I turned the [your *1st reading*] storied page, *MS*.
*10. tracked you still*] mapped your course *MS*. *classic ground*: a classic phrase; cp. Addison's *Letter from Italy* 11–12 (written 1701): 'Poetic fields encompass me around, / And still I seem to tread on Classic ground.'
*11. grew . . . till*] grew so joyful that *MS 1st reading*; waxt in gladness till *MS*.
*13*] Through sacred clefts the torrent poured *MS*.
*14. glistened*] glittered *MS*.
*15. broad-limbed*] broad-browed *MS*.
*16. urns*] heads *MS*.
*18. cavern pillars;*] columned caves, as *MS*.
*19. lily*] lilies *MS*.
*20*] And all the region burst in bloom *MS*.
*22. dancing*] leaping *MS*.
*23. who*] that *MS*.

was in *The Leader*, 24 Jan. It is one of T.'s many political poems of 1852, dealing with the threat of invasion from France; for some reason, it has not been mentioned with the other poems. Cp. in particular *For the Penny-Wise* (p. 999). T. did not reprint it, but it was reprinted in *The Critic*, N.Y. (1884–5), p. 268. *Mat.* ii 56–7 gave the title *Arm!*, and reduced the poem to four stanzas by omitting ll. 28–31, substituting ll. 37–40, and then omitting ll. 41–5. These changes made the poem less violent, especially in the removal of: 'And bastard Christianity'. A version in three stanzas was printed in *Tennyson's Patriotic Poems* (1914). (Also *The Spectator*, 3 Oct. 1914.)

O where is he, the simple fool,
  Who says that wars are over?
What bloody portent flashes there
  Across the straits of Dover?
Four hundred thousand slaves in arms
  May seek to bring us under:
Are we ready, Britons all,
  To answer them with thunder?
    Arm, arm, arm!

You–sleepy Lords of Admiralty,
  Your errors are too grievous;
See that your work be workmanlike,
  Or else go out and leave us.
O shame on selfish patronage,
  It is the country's ruin;
Come, put the right man in his place,
  And up, now, and be doing.
    Arm, arm, arm!

And you – ye brawlers penny-wise,
  Through you the land is cheated,
Till by barbarians better-armed
  Our greatness is defeated.
The cheapest things are not the best,
  The best things are the cheapest;
But wake, arise! O noble blood
  Of England, how thou creepest!
    Arm, arm, arm!

¶302. *3*] The bloody meteor looms again *H.Nbk 26*.

*21. barbarians*] monkey Kaffirs *MS*. There were severe British losses in the Caffre wars in the Cape Colony, still continuing in 1852. Cp. *For the Penny-Wise* 7–8: 'But the Kaffirs knocked us over, /With the last inventions.'

*25–6*] O filthy worm of Mammon, how
  O'er council boards thou creepest! *MS*

The allusion to Mammon brings out how close the mood of the poem is

O gather, gallant volunteers,
In every British village!
Or have the tigers of Algiers
Your licence here to pillage?
O babbling Peace Societies,
Where many a dreamer trifles!
Is this a time to cry for peace,
When we should shriek for rifles?
Arm, arm, arm!

O big-limbed yeomen, leave awhile
The fattening of your cattle;
And if indeed ye long for peace,
Make ready to do battle–
To fight the battle of the world,
Of progress and humanity,
Spite of his eight million lies
And bastard Christianity.
Arm, arm, arm!

## 303 *Rifle Clubs!!!

Printed by C. Ricks, *RES* n.s. xv (1964) 401–4, from the MS at *Boston College*, together with the accompanying letter from T.'s wife Emily to Coventry Patmore, 28 Jan. 1852. It is one of T.'s many political poems of early 1852, after Louis Napoleon's *coup d'état* (Dec. 1851) had made war imminent. Cp. *Britons, Guard Your Own* 13–14: 'Peace-lovers we–sweet Peace we all desire– / Peace-lovers we–but who can trust a liar?' The references to 'peace', 'olive', 'tradesmen', and 'gain', all anticipate the mood of *Maud*. The title refers to Patmore's 'institution of the first volunteer rifle-club' (his note); his letter to *The Times* appeared 22 Jan. 1852. Patmore has also added the note: 'Another sketch by A.T. of a Rifle-Club song. Same date as other'; see *Riflemen Form!* (p. 1110). À propos a poem by Herrick about Charon, J. B. Leishman remarks: 'Dialogues between Charon and either a mourner or the soul of the departed would seem to have become common enough to invite parody, for Lovelace has *A Mock Charon*, satirising a Parliamentary sequestrator' (*The Art of Marvell's Poetry*, 1965, p. 112*n*).

to that of *Maud*; cp. the attack on Peace Societies with *Maud* i 366–81 (p. 1059).

*33. many a dreamer*] Bright or Cobden *MS*. John Bright and Richard Cobden were the most important opponents of war (against France, and in the Crimea) during the 1850s.

Peace is thirty-seven years old,
Sweet Peace can no man blame,
But Peace of sloth or of avarice born,
Her olive is her shame;
And I dreamt of Charon alone in my bed–
His boat was crammed and he rose and said
'I carry the dead, the dead, the dead,
Killed in the *Coup d'État*'.

Half a million of men in arms,
Yet peace we all require.
Half a million of men in arms,
And the head of them all a liar.
'They wronged him not', the ferryman said,
'Yet look at his bullets in heart and head–
So I carry the dead, the dead, the dead,
Killed in the *Coup d'État*'.

Some love Peace for her own dear sake,
Tradesmen love her for gain,
But in France the rifle is all-in-all,
And the crimson trousers reign–
'Children and women–their wounds are red,
And I wait for Louis', the ferryman said,
'To follow the dead, the dead, the dead,
Killed in the *Coup d'État*'.

# 304 *Britons, Guard Your Own

Published, unsigned, in *The Examiner*, 31 Jan. 1852; not reprinted, though a version was published with music by Emily Tennyson (*Mem.* i 344), omitting ll. 7–36, 49–54, and for 3–4, substituting the inoffensive ll. 9–10. It is one of the 'National Songs' with which T. responded to the *coup d'état*, Dec. 1851, of Louis Napoleon (Napoleon III) and the rejection by the House of Lords of the Bill to organize a militia. Cp. *Hands All Round!* (p. 1002) and the other political poems of 1852; also the attack on Napoleon

¶303. *1. Peace*] Sweet Peace *Boston MS 1st reading.* It was thirty-seven years since Waterloo (1815).

*2. Sweet*] *MS 1st reading; the revision is illegible*: 'Meek'?–cp. Milton's 'meek-eyd Peace', *Nativity Ode* 46. 'Kind'?–cp. 'kind Peace', *The Third of February, 1852* 9.

*6. he rose and*] the ferryman *MS 1st reading.*

*21*] 'They harmed him not but his wounds are red, *MS 1st reading.*

*22. And*] So *MS 1st reading.*

III in the *Ode on Wellington* 171 (MS, not finally incorporated), urging 'Guard guard guard your coasts'.

Rise, Britons, rise, if manhood be not dead;
The world's last tempest darkens overhead;
The Pope has blessed him;
The Church caressed him;
He triumphs; may be, we shall stand alone:
Britons, guard your own.

His ruthless host is bought with plundered gold,
By lying priests the peasant's vote controlled;
All freedom vanished,
The true men banished,
He triumphs: may be, we shall stand alone:
Britons, guard your own.

Peace-lovers we–sweet Peace we all desire–
Peace-lovers we–but who can trust a liar?–
Peace-lovers, haters
Of shameless traitors,
We hate not France, but this man's heart of stone.
Britons, guard your own.

We hate not France, but France has lost her voice,
This man is France, the man they call her choice.
By tricks and spying,
And craft and lying,
And murder, was her freedom overthrown.
Britons, guard your own.

'Vive l'Empereur' may follow by and bye;
'God save the Queen' is here a truer cry,
God save the nation,
The toleration,
And the free speech that makes a Briton known.
Britons, guard your own.

Rome's dearest daughter now is captive France,
The Jesuit laughs, and reckoning on his chance
Would unrelenting
Kill all dissenting,
Till we were left to fight for truth alone.
Britons, guard your own.

¶304. *37–8*. Adapted from *Hail Briton* 7–8: 'The many ships of war that blow / The battle from their oaken sides.' T. had thought of using these lines in *To the Queen*, 1851 (MS, *The Greyfriar*, Dec. 1921).

Call home your ships across Biscayan tides,
To blow the battle from their oaken sides.
Why waste they yonder
Their idle thunder?
Why stand they there to guard a foreign throne?
Seamen, guard your own.

We were the best of marksmen long ago,
We won old battles with our strength, the bow.
Now practise, yeomen,
Like those bowmen,
Till your balls fly as their true shafts have flown.
Yeomen, guard your own.

His soldier-ridden Highness might incline
To shake Sardinia, Belgium, or the Rhine:
Shall we stand idle,
Nor seek to bridle
His vile aggressions till we stand alone?–
Make their cause your own!

Should he land here, and for one hour prevail,
There must no man go back to bear the tale:
No man to bear it,–
Swear it! We swear it!
Although we fought the banded world alone,
We swear to guard our own.

# 305 *For the Penny-Wise

Published *Fraser's Magazine*, Feb. 1852, unsigned; not reprinted. MSS: *H.Lprs 268–9*. It combines T.'s fear of an invasion by Louis Napoleon (Napoleon III), as in *Britons, Guard Your Own* (above), with his dismay at the British losses in the Caffre wars in the Cape Colony, still continuing in 1852. A letter in *The Times*, 3 Jan. 1852, argued that our arms were out of date and that we needed Minié rifles; an editorial, 6 Jan., said: 'we are only contending with savages, and yet those savages so excel us in the equipments desirable for campaigning that they maintain themselves against numerical odds'.

*Title*. Cp. *O where is he*, which T. signed 'A Scorner of the Penny-Wise', and in one printing entitled *The Penny-Wise* (p. 994).

*37–41*. The British navy at Lisbon. *The Times* said on 17 Jan. 1852: 'What is our fleet doing in the South when it should do us service in the North? Why are we leaving the British Channel comparatively defenceless, in order to exhibit our flag at the mouth of the Tagus?'

We used to fight the French,
And beat them, says the story;
But now the cry 're-trench'
Has a little docked our glory.

We meant to beat the Kaffirs,
We had the best intentions;
But the Kaffirs knocked us over,
With the last inventions.

Poor little people, we,
And in the world belated!
Our musket, as it seems,
Is superannuated.

Friends! the soldier still
Is worthy of his calling,
But who are they that want
A little over-hauling?

## 306 The Third of February, 1852

Published *The Examiner*, 7 Feb. 1852, signed 'Merlin'; then *1872*. In *H.Lpr 234* it has the title *Are these our Peers?* Written 'when the House of Lords seemed to condone Louis Napoleon's *coup d'état* in Dec. 1851, and rejected the Bill for the organization of the Militia when he was expected to attack England' (H.T.). On 3 Feb., Derby in the House of Lords was applauded after his attack on the British press for antagonizing Napoleon while lamenting our weak army ('feeble hosts', l. 38). T. apparently revised an earlier (Jan.) attack on the Lords (*Mem.* i 347). Cp. the other patriotic poems of these months. FitzGerald comments: 'The Authorship was kept secret, because of the Poet being Laureate to the Queen, then being, and wishing to be, on good Terms with Napoleon.'

My Lords, we heard you speak: you told us all
That England's honest censure went too far;
That our free press should cease to brawl,
Not sting the fiery Frenchman into war.
It was our ancient privilege, my Lords,
To fling whate'er we felt, not fearing, into words.

We love not this French God, the child of Hell,
Wild War, who breaks the converse of the wise;
But though we love kind Peace so well,
We dare not even by silence sanction lies.
It might be safe our censures to withdraw;
And yet, my Lords, not well: there is a higher law.

As long as we remain, we must speak free,
  Though all the storm of Europe on us break;
No little German state are we,
  But the one voice in Europe: we *must* speak;
That if tonight our greatness were struck dead,
There might be left some record of the things we said.

If you be fearful, then must we be bold.
  Our Britain cannot salve a tyrant o'er.
Better the waste Atlantic rolled
  On her and us and ours for evermore.
What! have we fought for Freedom from our prime,
At last to dodge and palter with a public crime?

Shall we fear *him?* our own we never feared.
  From our first Charles by force we wrung our claims.
Pricked by the Papal spur, we reared,
  We flung the burthen of the second James.
I say, we *never* feared! and as for these,
We broke them on the land, we drove them on the
    seas.

And you, my Lords, you make the people muse
  In doubt if you be of our Barons' breed–
Were those your sires who fought at Lewes?
  Is this the manly strain of Runnymede?
O fallen nobility, that, overawed,
Would lisp in honeyed whispers of this monstrous
    fraud!

*We* feel, at least, that silence here were sin,
  Not ours the fault if we have feeble hosts–
If easy patrons of their kin
  Have left the last free race with naked coasts!
They knew the precious things they had to guard:
For us, we will not spare the tyrant one hard word.

¶306. *24.* Note the military context in *Antony and Cleopatra* III xi 61–3: 'Now I must / To the young man send humble treaties, dodge / And palter in the shifts of lowness.' T., while attacking Louis Napoleon, contrasted Wellington (*Ode on Wellington* 171, MS): was he 'A man to dodge and shuffle with the Truth / And palter'?
*27–8.* Adapted from *Hail Briton* 79–80: 'Pricked by the Papal spurs, and flung / The burthen of the second James.' James's Declaration of Indulgence to Roman Catholics led to the landing of William of Orange, 1688.
*36.* Keats, *Endymion* i 955–6: 'send honey-whispers / Round every leaf, that all those gentle lispers'.

Though niggard throats of Manchester may bawl,
What England was, shall her true sons forget?
We are not cotton-spinners all,
But some love England and her honour yet.
And these in our Thermopylæ shall stand,
And hold against the world this honour of the land.

## 307 *Hands All Round! [1852]

Published *The Examiner*, 7 Feb. 1852, signed 'Merlin'; not reprinted. It was later altogether recast, retaining only stanza 1; see *Hands All Round [1882]* (p. 1310). It was one of T.'s many poems on the threat from Louis Napoleon (Napoleon III); see *Britons, Guard Your Own* (p. 997).

First drink a health, this solemn night,
A health to England, every guest;
That man's the best cosmopolite,
Who loves his native country best.
May Freedom's oak for ever live
With stronger life from day to day;
That man's the true Conservative,
Who lops the mouldered branch away.
Hands all round!
God the tyrant's hope confound!
To this great cause of freedom drink, my friends,
And the great name of England round and round.

A health to Europe's honest men!
Heaven guard them from her tyrants' jails!
From wronged Poerio's noisome den,
From ironed limbs and tortured nails!

*3. niggard throats of*] Bright and niggard *H.Nbk 28 1st reading*. T. attacked Bright and Cobden (of the 'Manchester Peace-at-any-Price School') in *The Penny-Wise* 33, MS, written at this time (p. 996). Cp. ll. 43–5 with *Maud* i 371–2, the pacifist 'Whose ear is crammed with his cotton, and rings / Even in dreams to the chink of his pence.'

¶307. *15. 1852* note: 'See Gladstone's Letter.' The case of Carlo Poerio was particularly stressed by Gladstone in *A Letter to the Earl of Aberdeen* (1851), his exposure of the horrors of the Neapolitan dungeons. *noisome den*: as in Wordsworth's political sonnet *To Toussaint L'Ouverture* (1815 text).

*16.* Gladstone described the 'double irons' and 'torture' by 'thrusting of sharp instruments under the finger-nails'.

We curse the crimes of southern kings,
The Russian whips and Austrian rods–
We, likewise, have our evil things;
Too much we make our Ledgers, Gods.
Yet hands all round!
God the tyrant's cause confound!
To Europe's better health we drink, my friends,
And the great name of England round and round.

What health to France, if France be she,
Whom martial prowess only charms?
Yet tell her–Better to be free
Than vanquish all the world in arms.
Her frantic city's flashing heats
But fire, to blast, the hopes of men.
Why change the titles of your streets?
You fools, you'll want them all again.
Yet hands all round!
God the tyrant's cause confound!
To France, the wiser France, we drink, my friends,
And the great name of England round and round.

Gigantic daughter of the West,
We drink to thee across the flood,
We know thee most, we love thee best,
For art thou not of British blood?
Should war's mad blast again be blown,
Permit not thou the tyrant powers
To fight thy mother here alone,
But let thy broadsides roar with ours.
Hands all round!
God the tyrant's cause confound!
To our great kinsmen of the West, my friends,
And the great name of England round and round.

O rise, our strong Atlantic sons,
When war against our freedom springs!

*18. Russian*: of Nicholas I; cp. *Poland* (p. 458) and *Hail Briton* 192–204 (p. 489). *Austrian*: following Napoleon's *coup d'état* in Dec. 1851, the Emperor Francis Joseph reasserted his absolutism; General Haynau brutally suppressed the Italians in 1848 and the Hungarians in 1849. Cp. *Maud* i 147–8: 'Shall I weep if a Poland fall? shall I shriek if a Hungary fail? / Or an infant civilisation be ruled with rod or with knout?'
*20.* Cp. *Maud* i 35: 'When only the ledger lives'.
*29–30.* Cp. *Beautiful City* (p. 1422).
*37–60.* Cp. the unpublished stanza of *England and America in 1782* (p. 619).

O speak to Europe through your guns!
They *can* be understood by kings.
You must not mix our Queen with those
That wish to keep their people fools;
Our freedom's foemen are her foes,
She comprehends the race she rules.
Hands all round!
God the tyrant's cause confound!
To our dear kinsmen of the West, my friends,
And the great cause of freedom round and round.

## 308 *Suggested by Reading an Article in a Newspaper

Published *The Examiner*, 14 Feb. 1852; not reprinted. T. praises himself ('Merlin') for *The Third of February, 1852* and *Hands All Round!*: '*Sir*,–I have read with much interest the poems by *Merlin*. The enclosed is longer than either of those, and certainly not so good; yet as I flatter myself that it has a smack of Merlin's style in it, and as I feel that it expresses forcibly enough some of the feelings of our time, perhaps you may be induced to admit it. *Taliessin*'
T.'s authorship is made certain by *H. Lpr 90* in his hand, and by *Mat.* ii 61. He expected an invasion by Napoleon III. The indictment of 'our commercial mire' was soon followed by *Maud*.

How much I love this writer's manly style!
By such men led, our press had ever been
The public conscience of our noble isle,
Severe and quick to feel a civic sin,
To raise the people and chastise the times
With such a heat as lives in great creative rhymes.

O you, the Press! what good from you might spring!
What power is yours to blast a cause or bless!
I fear for you, as for some youthful king,
Lest you go wrong from power in excess.
Take heed of your wide privileges! we,
The thinking men of England, loathe a tyranny.

¶308. 7. Contrast the optimism of *The Golden Year* 42: 'Fly, happy happy sails, and bear the Press'.

A freeman is, I doubt not, freest here;
The single voice may speak his mind aloud;
An honest isolation need not fear
The court, the church, the Parliament, the crowd,
No, nor the Press! and look you well to that–
We must not dread in you the nameless Autocrat.

And you, dark Senate of the public pen,
You may not, like yon tyrant, deal in spies.
Yours are the public acts of public men,
But yours are not their household privacies.
I grant you one of the Great Powers on earth,
But be not you the blatant traitors of the hearth.

You hide the hand that writes: it must be so,
For better so you fight for public ends;
But some you strike can scarce return the blow;
You should be all the nobler, O my friends.
Be noble, you! nor work with faction's tools
To charm a lower sphere of fulminating fools.

But, knowing all your power to heat or cool,
To soothe a civic wound, or keep it raw,
Be loyal, if you wish for wholesome rule:
Our ancient boast is this–we reverence law.
We still were loyal in our wildest fights,
Or, loyally disloyal, battled for our rights.

O Grief and Shame if while I preach of laws
Whereby to guard our freedom from offence–
And trust an ancient manhood and the cause
Of England and her health of common sense–
There hang within the heavens a dark disgrace,
Some vast Assyrian doom to burst upon our race.

I feel the thousand cankers of our state,
I fain would shake their triple-folded ease,
The hogs, who can believe in nothing great,
Sneering bedridden in the down of Peace,

*13–16.* Cp. *Hail Briton* 13–16: 'But thou mayst speak thy mind aloud, / And in the streets, or sitting still / Art free to blame or praise at will / The throne, the senate, and the crowd.'

*20. tyrant*: Napoleon III.

*42. Assyrian doom*: to supplant Britain as the Assyrians supplanted Babylonia and then Egypt.

*43.* Cp. (with l. 46) *Maud* iii 50: 'For the long, long canker of peace is over and done', *1855* text.

Over their scrips and shares, their meats and wine,
With stony smirks at all things human and divine!

I honour much, I say, this man's appeal.
We drag so deep in our commercial mire,
We move so far from greatness, that I feel
Exception to be charactered in fire.
Who looks for Godlike Greatness here shall see
The British Goddess, sleek Respectability.

Alas for her and all her small delights!
She feels not how the social frame is racked.
She loves a little scandal which excites;
A little feeling is a want of tact.
For her there lie in wait millions of foes,
And yet the 'Not too much' is all the rule she knows.

Poor soul! behold her: what decorous calm!–
She, with her weekday worldliness sufficed,
Stands in her pew and hums her decent psalm,
With decent dippings at the name of Christ!
And she has moved on that smooth way so long,
She hardly can believe that she shall suffer wrong.

Alas, our Church! alas, her growing ills,
And those who tolerate not her tolerance,
But needs must sell the burthen of their wills
To that half-pagan harlot kept by France!
Free subjects of the kindliest of all thrones,
Headlong they plunge their doubts among old rags and bones.

Alas, church-writers, altercating tribes–
The vessel of your church may sink in storms;
Christ cried, Woe, woe, to Pharisees and scribes;
Like them, you bicker less for truth than forms.
I sorrow when I read the things you write,
What unheroic pertness! what unchristian spite!

Alas, our youth, so clever yet so small,
Thin dilettanti deep in nature's plan,
Who make the emphatic One, by whom is all,
An essence less concentred than a man!–
Better wild Mahmoud's war-cry once again!
O fools, we want a manlike God and Godlike men.

*83*] Better grim Cromwell's rule, ay once again! *Mat.* ii 63. *Mahmoud*: Mohammed.

*84*. *God and Godlike men*: incorporated in *Ode on Wellington* 266.

Go, frightful omens. Yet once more I turn
   To you that mould men's thoughts, I call on you
To make opinion warlike, lest we learn
   A sharper lesson than we ever knew.
I hear a thunder though the skies are fair,
But shrill you, loud and long, the warning note–
      Prepare.

[1852. *De Profundis* — see p. 1281.]

# 309 Ode on the Death of the Duke of Wellington

Published in 1852

Published 16 Nov. 1852; 2nd edn, Feb.–March 1853 (it is twenty-nine lines longer and has many changes); then *1855*. It was T.'s first separate publication since becoming Poet Laureate. (While T. was still a child at Somersby, 'the doings of Wellington and Napoleon were the themes of story and verse', *Mem.* i 5.) On the MSS, textual changes, background, reception, etc., see E. F. Shannon, *Studies in Bibliography* xiii (1960) 149–77. The Duke of Wellington died 14 Sept. 1852; the funeral was on 18 Nov. Shannon connects ll. 8–9 with the protracted discussion of 'when, where, and with what state . . . the great Duke of Wellington shall be buried' (*Illustrated London News*). He quotes the Prime Minister's letter of 20 Sept. that the Duke would be buried in St Paul's, 'there to rest by the side of Nelson–the greatest military by the side of the greatest naval chief who ever reflected lustre upon the annals of England'; cp. ll. 80–4. Shannon also relates the poem to T.'s many patriotic verses of 1852; see l. 171*n*. He notes that T. had been pressed for time for the 1st edition, and that it was to be an advantage to him to commemorate rather than anticipate the funeral. Many of the reviews were hostile; T. seems to have paid little attention to specific complaints (except perhaps for the opening lines), but he paid some attention to general suggestions. He also intensified the religious note. The early draft in *T.Nbk 25* (which may not be quoted) is not mentioned by Shannon; this draft includes, deleted, the final stanza of *England and America in 1782* (written 1832–4; published 1872). Immediately following it, is *Will* 10–20 (p. 1017), which has clear affinities with the *Ode* and which T. may well have considered incorporating.

I

Bury the Great Duke
   With an empire's lamentation,
Let us bury the Great Duke
   To the noise of the mourning of a mighty nation,

¶309. *1. Bury*] *1855*; Let us bury *1852–3*.

Mourning when their leaders fall,
Warriors carry the warrior's pall,
And sorrow darkens hamlet and hall.

II

Where shall we lay the man whom we deplore?
Here, in streaming London's central roar.
Let the sound of those he wrought for,
And the feet of those he fought for,
Echo round his bones for evermore.

III

Lead out the pageant: sad and slow,
As fits an universal woe,
Let the long long procession go,
And let the sorrowing crowd about it grow,
And let the mournful martial music blow;
The last great Englishman is low.

IV

Mourn, for to us he seems the last,
Remembering all his greatness in the Past.
No more in soldier fashion will he greet
With lifted hand the gazer in the street.
O friends, our chief state-oracle is mute:
Mourn for the man of long-enduring blood,
The statesman-warrior, moderate, resolute,
Whole in himself, a common good.
Mourn for the man of amplest influence,
Yet clearest of ambitious crime,
Our greatest yet with least pretence,
Great in council and great in war,
Foremost captain of his time,
Rich in saving common-sense,
And, as the greatest only are,
In his simplicity sublime.

5] *1853*; When laurel-garlanded leaders fall, *1852*.
*6. Warriors*] *1853*; And warriors *1852*.
*7.* Cp. the conclusion of *The Sea-Fairies*, *1830* text: 'sorrow shall darken ye . . . no more'.
*8–12*] *Not T.MS.*
*8 ∧ 9*] He died on Walmer's lonely shore, *1853*.
*9*] *1855*; *not 1852*; But here . . . *1853*.
*20*] *1853*; Our sorrow draws but on the golden Past. *1852*.
*21–22*] *1853*; *not 1852*.
*26.* Horace, *Satires* II vii 86: *in se ipso totus.*
*27. amplest*] *1853*; largest *1852*.
*28. clearest of*] *1853*; freëst from *1852*.

O good gray head which all men knew,
O voice from which their omens all men drew,
O iron nerve to true occasion true,
O fallen at length that tower of strength
Which stood four-square to all the winds that blew!
Such was he whom we deplore.
The long self-sacrifice of life is o'er.
The great World-victor's victor will be seen no more.

V

All is over and done:
Render thanks to the Giver,
England, for thy son.
Let the bell be tolled.
Render thanks to the Giver,
And render him to the mould.
Under the cross of gold
That shines over city and river,
There he shall rest for ever
Among the wise and the bold.
Let the bell be tolled:
And a reverent people behold
The towering car, the sable steeds:
Bright let it be with its blazoned deeds,
Dark in its funeral fold.
Let the bell be tolled:
And a deeper knell in the heart be knolled;

*35.* Claudian, *Venerandus apex et cognita cunctis canities*, was quoted in a speech by Disraeli on Wellington's death. But in a copy of F. J. Rowe and W. T. Webb's *Selections* from his poems (1888, *Lincoln*), T. commented: 'never heard of Claudian's line!'

*38–9.* Adapted from *Young is the grief* 16: 'A life four-square to all the winds'. For the epithet, T. compares Simonides (τετράγωνος), 'though I did not think of this parallel when I wrote it'. Cp. Dante's *Purgatorio* v 14–15: *sta come torre ferma, che non crolla / già mai la cima per soffiar de' venti.* ('Stand like a firm tower that never shakes its top for blast of wind.')

*42. World-victor*: Napoleon.

*46.* A special honour, since the Great Bell was tolled only for the Royal Family, the Bishop, the Dean, and the Lord Mayor.

*56. its*] *1859*; his *1852–6*.

*59*] *1855*; *not 1852*; A deeper . . . *1853*. Cp. the praise of the brave dead, 'God's soldier', *Macbeth* V viii 50–51: '"And so his knell is knolled." "He's worth more sorrow, / And that I'll spend for him."' T. probably recalled Shelley's lines *On the Death of Napoleon* 11, 22 (1821): 'Is not *his* death-knell knolled? . . . / All my sons when their knell is knolled.'

And the sound of the sorrowing anthem rolled
Through the dome of the golden cross;
And the volleying cannon thunder his loss;
He knew their voices of old.
For many a time in many a clime
His captain's-ear has heard them boom
Bellowing victory, bellowing doom:
When he with those deep voices wrought,
Guarding realms and kings from shame;
With those deep voices our dead captain taught
The tyrant, and asserts his claim
In that dread sound to the great name,
Which he has worn so pure of blame,
In praise and in dispraise the same,
A man of well-attempered frame.
O civic muse, to such a name,
To such a name for ages long,
To such a name,
Preserve a broad approach of fame,
And ever-echoing avenues of song.

VI

Who is he that cometh, like an honoured guest,
With banner and with music, with soldier and with
    priest,
With a nation weeping, and breaking on my rest?
Mighty Seaman, this is he
Was great by land as thou by sea.
Thine island loves thee well, thou famous man,
The greatest sailor since our world began.
Now, to the roll of muffled drums,
To thee the greatest soldier comes;
For this is he
Was great by land as thou by sea;
His foes were thine; he kept us free;
O give him welcome, this is he
Worthy of our gorgeous rites,
And worthy to be laid by thee;

*75–9.* Adapted, as Sir Charles Tennyson observes (*1931*, p. 74), from *Hail Briton* 169–72: 'O civic Muse, for such a name, / Deep-minded Muse, for ages long / Preserve a broad approach of song / And ringing avenues of fame.' In *T.MS*, the last line is exactly as in *Hail Briton*.

*79. ever-echoing*] *1865*; ever-ringing *1852–64*.

*80–83.* Nelson speaks.

*91*] *1853*; His martial wisdom kept us free; *1852*.

*92. give . . . welcome*] *1853*; warrior-seaman *1852*.

For this is England's greatest son,
He that gained a hundred fights,
Nor ever lost an English gun;
This is he that far away
Against the myriads of Assaye
Clashed with his fiery few and won;
And underneath another sun,
Warring on a later day,
Round affrighted Lisbon drew
The treble works, the vast designs
Of his laboured rampart-lines,
Where he greatly stood at bay,
Whence he issued forth anew,
And ever great and greater grew,
Beating from the wasted vines
Back to France her banded swarms,
Back to France with countless blows,
Till o'er the hills her eagles flew
Beyond the Pyrenean pines,
Followed up in valley and glen
With blare of bugle, clamour of men,
Roll of cannon and clash of arms,
And England pouring on her foes.
Such a war had such a close.
Again their ravening eagle rose
In anger, wheeled on Europe-shadowing wings,
And barking for the thrones of kings;
Till one that sought but Duty's iron crown
On that loud sabbath shook the spoiler down;

*95*] *1852 has this line ll. 92 ∧ 3, beginning* This . . . .
*97. Nor ever*] *1853*; And never *1852*. Disraeli's speech on Wellington also mentions that he 'captured 3,000 cannon from the enemy, and never lost a single gun'.
*98*] *1853*; He that in his earlier day *1852*.
*99*. Hindustan, 1803.
*101*. The Latin *alio sole*.
*102*] *1853*; Made the soldier, led him on, *1852*.
*103–7*] *1853*; *not 1852*.
*105*. Torres Vedras, 1810.
*110*] *1853*; All their marshals' bandit swarms, *1852*.
*112*] *1853*; Till their host of eagles flew *1852*. *eagles*: Napoleon's ensigns.
*113. Beyond*] *1864*; Past *1852–62*.
*118 ∧ 9*] He withdrew to brief repose. *1852–3*.
*121. barking*: as in *Boädicea* 13.
*123*. Waterloo, Sunday 18 June 1815.

A day of onsets of despair!
Dashed on every rocky square
Their surging charges foamed themselves away;
Last, the Prussian trumpet blew;
Through the long-tormented air
Heaven flashed a sudden jubilant ray,
And down we swept and charged and overthrew.
So great a soldier taught us there,
What long-enduring hearts could do
In that world-earthquake, Waterloo!
Mighty Seaman, tender and true,
And pure as he from taint of craven guile,
O saviour of the silver-coasted isle,
O shaker of the Baltic and the Nile,
If aught of things that here befall
Touch a spirit among things divine,
If love of country move thee there at all,
Be glad, because his bones are laid by thine!
And through the centuries let a people's voice
In full acclaim,
A people's voice,
The proof and echo of all human fame,
A people's voice, when they rejoice
At civic revel and pomp and game,
Attest their great commander's claim
With honour, honour, honour, honour to him,
Eternal honour to his name.

VII

A people's voice! we are a people yet.
Though all men else their nobler dreams forget,
Confused by brainless mobs and lawless Powers;
Thank Him who isled us here, and roughly set

*129.* 'The setting sun glanced on this last charge of the English and Prussians' (T.).

*133. world-earthquake*] *1872*; world's-earthquake *1852–70*.

*137.* The defeat of the Danish fleet (1801), and of Napoleon at Aboukir (1798).

*139.* T. says: 'Dwell upon the word "touch" and make it as long as "can touch."'

*142–6.* Cp. the 'death-hymn' in *The Dying Swan* 31–3: 'As when a mighty people rejoice . . . / And the tumult of their acclaim is rolled.' Cp. l. 4 above.

*154–5*] *1853*; *not 1852*.

His Briton in blown seas and storming showers,
We have a voice, with which to pay the debt
Of boundless love and reverence and regret
To those great men who fought, and kept it ours.
And keep it ours, O God, from brute control;
O Statesmen, guard us, guard the eye, the soul
Of Europe, keep our noble England whole,
And save the one true seed of freedom sown
Betwixt a people and their ancient throne,
That sober freedom out of which there springs
Our loyal passion for our temperate kings;
For, saving that, ye help to save mankind
Till public wrong be crumbled into dust,
And drill the raw world for the march of mind,
Till crowds at length be sane and crowns be just.
But wink no more in slothful overtrust.
Remember him who led your hosts;

*155. Briton*] *1864*; Saxon *1853–62*.
*157. Of boundless love and*] *1855*; Of most unbounded *1852*; Of boundless *1853*.
*159*] *1853*; *not 1852*.
*166. help to*] *1853*; *not 1852*.
*168*] *1853*; And help the march of human mind *1852*.
*169. at length*] *1855*; *not 1852–3*.
*170 ∧ 1*]
Perchance our greatness will increase;
Perchance a darkening future yields
Some reverse from worse to worse,
The blood of men in quiet fields,
And sprinkled on the sheaves of peace. *1852*

These lines are adapted, as Shannon remarks, from *Hail Briton* 121–4: 'For who may frame his thought at ease / Mid sights that civil contest yields– / The blood of men in quiet fields / And sprinkled on the sheaves of peace.'
*171. Remember*] *1853*; And O remember *1852*. Shannon prints from *Pierpont Morgan MS* an attack on Napoleon III which links with ll. 171, 185–6. Emily T.'s note added: 'This might perhaps have been altered had it been intended for publication–made stronger I mean.' The lines are in *T.MS*.

But O remember him who led your hosts
And take his counsel ere too late.
There sits a silent man beyond the strait–
Guard guard guard your coasts.
His are all the powers of the state,
His are all the passions of the rabble–
A man of silence in a world of babble.
Sudden blows are strokes of fate,

He bad you guard the sacred coasts.
Your cannons moulder on the seaward wall;
His voice is silent in your council-hall
For ever; and whatever tempests lour
For ever silent; even if they broke
In thunder, silent; yet remember all
He spoke among you, and the Man who spoke;
Who never sold the truth to serve the hour,
Nor paltered with Eternal God for power;
Who let the turbid streams of rumour flow
Through either babbling world of high and low;
Whose life was work, whose language rife
With rugged maxims hewn from life;
Who never spoke against a foe;
Whose eighty winters freeze with one rebuke
All great self-seekers trampling on the right:
Truth-teller was our England's Alfred named;
Truth-lover was our English Duke;
Whatever record leap to light
He never shall be shamed.

Yet to be true is more than half of great.
By the hollow blatant cry,
Half-godded underneath a scornful sky
Their great Napoleons live and die
With rolling echoes by the nations heard.
But shall we count them Gods who break their word?
The word is God: thou shalt not lie.
Was our great Chief (his life is bare from youth
To all men's comment till his latest hour)
A man to dodge and shuffle with the Truth
And palter with Eternal God for power?
His eighty winters &c.

Walter White observed, 5 Nov. 1852, that it 'contains a grand invective against Louis Napoleon of France which will be omitted' (*Journals*, 1898, p. 147). Cp. T.'s patriotic poems of 1852, especially *Britons, Guard Your Own* (p. 997).

*172*] *1855*; Respect his sacred warning; guard your coasts. *1852*; Revere his warning; guard your sacred coasts. *1853*.

*173*] *1853*; *not 1852.*

*181–2*] *1855*; *not 1852–3.*

*183–4*] *1853*; *not 1852.*

*185*] *1855*; *not 1852–3.*

*186. Whose*] *1853*; His *1852*.

VIII

Lo, the leader in these glorious wars
Now to glorious burial slowly borne,
Followed by the brave of other lands,
He, on whom from both her open hands
Lavish Honour showered all her stars,
And affluent Fortune emptied all her horn.
Yea, let all good things await
Him who cares not to be great,
But as he saves or serves the state.
Not once or twice in our rough island-story,
The path of duty was the way to glory:
He that walks it, only thirsting
For the right, and learns to deaden
Love of self, before his journey closes,
He shall find the stubborn thistle bursting
Into glossy purples, which outredden
All voluptuous garden-roses.
Not once or twice in our fair island-story,
The path of duty was the way to glory:
He, that ever following her commands,
On with toil of heart and knees and hands,
Through the long gorge to the far light has won
His path upward, and prevailed,
Shall find the toppling crags of Duty scaled
Are close upon the shining table-lands
To which our God Himself is moon and sun.
Such was he: his work is done.
But while the races of mankind endure,
Let his great example stand
Colossal, seen of every land,
And keep the soldier firm, the statesman pure:
Till in all lands and through all human story
The path of duty be the way to glory:
And let the land whose hearths he saved from shame

*195–7.* 'These are full-vowelled lines to describe Fortune emptying her Cornucopia' (T.).

*202.* Cp. Gray's *Elegy* 36: 'The paths of glory lead but to the grave.'

*209–15.* Based on the 15th fragment of Simonides, an influence suggested by H. G. Dakyns (tutor to T.'s sons), in *Tennyson and His Friends*, p. 200.

*217. Revelation* xxi 23: 'And the city had no need of the sun, neither of the moon, to shine in it: for the glory of God did lighten it.'

*218*] *1853*; He has not failed: he hath prevailed: *1852*.

*219–24*] *1853*; *not 1852*.

*225. And*] *1853*; So *1852*. *land*] *1853*; men *1852*.

For many and many an age proclaim
At civic revel and pomp and game,
And when the long-illumined cities flame,
Their ever-loyal iron leader's fame,
With honour, honour, honour, honour to him,
Eternal honour to his name.

IX

Peace, his triumph will be sung
By some yet unmoulded tongue
Far on in summers that we shall not see:
Peace, it is a day of pain
For one about whose patriarchal knee
Late the little children clung:
O peace, it is a day of pain
For one, upon whose hand and heart and brain
Once the weight and fate of Europe hung.
Ours the pain, be his the gain!
More than is of man's degree
Must be with us, watching here
At this, our great solemnity.
Whom we see not we revere;
We revere, and we refrain
From talk of battles loud and vain,
And brawling memories all too free
For such a wise humility
As befits a solemn fane:
We revere, and while we hear
The tides of Music's golden sea
Setting toward eternity,
Uplifted high in heart and hope are we,
Until we doubt not that for one so true
There must be other nobler work to do
Than when he fought at Waterloo,
And Victor he must ever be.
For though the Giant Ages heave the hill

*226. For*] *1853*; Through *1852*.
*241*] *1853*; *not 1852*.
*251–3*] *1853*; *not 1852*.
*254*] *1855*; For solemn, too, this day are we, *1852*; Lifted up in heart are we, *1853*.
*255. Until*] *1853*; O friends, *1852*.
*259–61*] *1853*; *not 1852*. The lines are adapted from a cancelled stanza of *The Palace of Art* (*H. Lpr 182*):

Yet saw she Earth laid open. Furthermore
How the strong Ages had their will,

And break the shore, and evermore
Make and break, and work their will;
Though world on world in myriad myriads roll
Round us, each with different powers,
And other forms of life than ours,
What know we greater than the soul?
On God and Godlike men we build our trust.
Hush, the Dead March wails in the people's ears:
The dark crowd moves, and there are sobs and tears:
The black earth yawns: the mortal disappears;
Ashes to ashes, dust to dust;
He is gone who seemed so great.–
Gone; but nothing can bereave him
Of the force he made his own
Being here, and we believe him
Something far advanced in State,
And that he wears a truer crown
Than any wreath that man can weave him.
Speak no more of his renown,
Lay your earthly fancies down,
And in the vast cathedral leave him.
God accept him, Christ receive him.

1852

# 310 Will

Published *1855*. There are two drafts of the second stanza in *T.Nbk 25* (which may not be quoted), immediately following the MS of the *Ode on Wellington* (1852); T. probably considered using these lines as part of the *Ode*, with which the first stanza too has affinities. A MS of the second stanza only is at the *University of Sydney* (all variants are below). H.T.

---

A range of Giants breaking down the shore
And heaving up the hill.

*262. world on world*] *1856*; worlds on worlds *1852–5*.

*266–70*] *1853*; *not 1852*. 'God and Godlike men', from *Suggested by Reading* 84, as Sir Charles Tennyson says (p. 266). Cp. *Love and Duty* 31: 'But then most Godlike being most a man'. Also *Paradise Regained* iv 348: 'Where God is prais'd aright, and Godlike men'; and Byron, *Childe Harold* II lxxxv 2: 'Gods and godlike men'.

*267. wails*] *1855*; sounds *1853*.

*271. He*] *1853*; The man *1852*.

*278. Speak*] *1864*; But speak *1852–62*.

*281. Romans* xiv 3: 'God hath received him.'

relates the second stanza to T.'s religious thinking, especially that of *The Vision of Sin* (*Mem.* i 322).

I

O well for him whose will is strong!
He suffers, but he will not suffer long;
He suffers, but he cannot suffer wrong:
For him nor moves the loud world's random mock,
Nor all Calamity's hugest waves confound,
Who seems a promontory of rock,
That, compassed round with turbulent sound,
In middle ocean meets the surging shock,
Tempest-buffeted, citadel-crowned.

II

But ill for him who, bettering not with time,
Corrupts the strength of heaven-descended Will,
And ever weaker grows through acted crime,
Or seeming-genial venial fault,
Recurring and suggesting still!

¶310. *1–9.* Cp. Horace, *Odes* III iii 1–8: *Iustum et tenacem propositi virum / non civium ardor prava iubentium, / non vultus instantis tyranni / mente quatit solida neque Auster, // dux inquieti turbidus Hadriae, / nec fulminantis magna manus Iovis; / si fractus inlabatur orbis, / impavidum ferient ruinae.* ('The man tenacious of his purpose in a righteous cause is not shaken from his firm resolve by the frenzy of his fellow-citizens bidding what is wrong, not by the face of threatening tyrant, not by Auster, stormy master of the restless Adriatic, not by the mighty hand of thundering Jove. Were the vault of heaven to break and fall upon him, its ruins would smite him undismayed.')
*4. mock*: mockery, with an archaic ring by this date. Cp. Shelley, *The Cenci* IV i 156–7: 'the clamorous scoffs / Of the loud world'.
*5–9.* Cp. *Aeneid* x 693–6: *ille velut rupes, vastum quae prodit in aequor, / obvia ventorum furiis expostaque ponto, / vim cunctam atque minas perfert caelique marisque, / ipsa immota manens.* ('Even as a cliff that juts into the vast deep, exposed to the raving winds and braving the main, that endures all the stress, all the menace of sky and sea, itself fixed unshaken.')
*8–9.* Sir Charles Tennyson remarks the adaptation of *Ode: O Bosky Brook* 76, 79: 'Citadel-crowned and tempest-buffeted . . . / And in the middle ocean meets the surging shock.'
*10. But ill*] Alas *Sydney MS.*
*11. strength of heaven-descended*] God-given force of his own *MS.*
*12. And*] Which *MS.* *acted*] some vile *MS.*
*13. seeming-genial venial*] only seeming-venial *MS.*
*14. suggesting*: tempting. Cp. Shakespeare, *Sonnet 144*: 'Which like two spirits do suggest me still.'

He seems as one whose footsteps halt,
Toiling in immeasurable sand,
And o'er a weary sultry land,
Far beneath a blazing vault,
Sown in a wrinkle of the monstrous hill,
The city sparkles like a grain of salt.

# 311 The Daisy

## Written at Edinburgh

Published *1855*. Written Aug. 1853 (*Mem.* i 364; *Mat.* ii 85). T. says it was written to his wife Emily, remembering their Italian tour of 1851: 'In a metre which I invented, representing in some measure the grandest of metres, the Horatian Alcaic.' T. was to modify the stanza for other epistolary poems, *To the Rev. F. D. Maurice* (p. 1022) and *To Prof. Jebb* (p. 1326), and still further for *To the Master of Balliol* (p. 1426).

O love, what hours were thine and mine,
In lands of palm and southern pine;
    In lands of palm, of orange-blossom,
Of olive, aloe, and maize and vine.

What Roman strength Turbia showed
In ruin, by the mountain road;
    How like a gem, beneath, the city
Of little Monaco, basking, glowed.

How richly down the rocky dell
The torrent vineyard streaming fell
    To meet the sun and sunny waters,
That only heaved with a summer swell.

What slender campanili grew
By bays, the peacock's neck in hue;
    Where, here and there, on sandy beaches
A milky-belled amaryllis blew.

*15. halt*] ever halt *MS.*
*16.* Cp. Shelley, *Queen Mab* viii 70: 'Those deserts of immeasurable sand'.
*17. And*] While *MS.* *sultry*] weary *MS.*
*18. Far*] Far on *MS.*
*20.* Perhaps suggested by 'the city of salt', *Joshua* xv 62.
¶311. *8. Mónaco.*
*13. campanili*: bell-towers.
*14.* T. in Cornwall, 8 June 1848: 'sea purple and green like a peacock's neck' (*Mem.* i 275).

How young Columbus seemed to rove,
Yet present in his natal grove,
Now watching high on mountain cornice,
And steering, now, from a purple cove,

Now pacing mute by ocean's rim;
Till, in a narrow street and dim,
I stayed the wheels at Cogoletto,
And drank, and loyally drank to him.

Nor knew we well what pleased us most,
Not the clipt palm of which they boast;
But distant colour, happy hamlet,
A mouldered citadel on the coast,

Or tower, or high hill-convent, seen
A light amid its olives green;
Or olive-hoary cape in ocean;
Or rosy blossom in hot ravine,

Where oleanders flushed the bed
Of silent torrents, gravel-spread;
And, crossing, oft we saw the glisten
Of ice, far up on a mountain head.

We loved that hall, though white and cold,
Those nichèd shapes of noble mould,
A princely people's awful princes,
The grave, severe Genovese of old.

At Florence too what golden hours,
In those long galleries, were ours;
What drives about the fresh Cascinè,
Or walks in Boboli's ducal bowers.

In bright vignettes, and each complete,
Of tower or duomo, sunny-sweet,
Or palace, how the city glittered,
Through cypress avenues, at our feet.

But when we crost the Lombard plain
Remember what a plague of rain;
Of rain at Reggio, rain at Parma;
At Lodi, rain, Piacenza, rain.

36. *up*] *1856*; off *1855*.
37. 'The Palazzo Ducale' (T.).
43. 'The Park of Florence' (T.).
51. *Reggio, rain*] *1856*; Reggio *1855*.

And stern and sad (so rare the smiles
Of sunlight) looked the Lombard piles;
Porch-pillars on the lion resting,
And sombre, old, colonnaded aisles.

O Milan, O the chanting quires,
The giant windows' blazoned fires,
The height, the space, the gloom, the glory!
A mount of marble, a hundred spires!

I climbed the roofs at break of day;
Sun-smitten Alps before me lay.
I stood among the silent statues,
And statued pinnacles, mute as they.

How faintly-flushed, how phantom-fair,
Was Monte Rosa, hanging there
A thousand shadowy-pencilled valleys
And snowy dells in a golden air.

Remember how we came at last
To Como; shower and storm and blast
Had blown the lake beyond his limit,
And all was flooded; and how we past

From Como, when the light was gray,
And in my head, for half the day,
The rich Virgilian rustic measure
Of Lari Maxume, all the way,

Like ballad-burthen music, kept,
As on The Lariano crept
To that fair port below the castle
Of Queen Theodolind, where we slept;

Or hardly slept, but watched awake
A cypress in the moonlight shake,
The moonlight touching o'er a terrace
One tall Agavè above the lake.

57. *Milan.*
60–62. Cp. *The Palace of Art* 82, *1832* text: 'Below sunsmitten icy spires'.
75–6. Virgil, *Georgics* ii 159–60: *Anne lacus tantos? te, Lari maxime, teque / fluctibus et fremitu adsurgens, Benace, marino?* ('Or of our mighty lakes? Of thee, Larius, our greatest; and thee, Benacus, with the roaring, surging swell of the sea?') Lake Como was the Lacus Larius of the Romans.
79. 'Varenna' (T.).
80. *Theodolind*: wife of a sixth-century king of the Lombards.
84. *Agavè*: a handsome tropical plant.

What more? we took our last adieu,
And up the snowy Splugen drew,
But ere we reached the highest summit
I plucked a daisy, I gave it you.

It told of England then to me,
And now it tells of Italy.
O love, we two shall go no longer
To lands of summer across the sea;

So dear a life your arms enfold
Whose crying is a cry for gold:
Yet here tonight in this dark city,
When ill and weary, alone and cold,

I found, though crushed to hard and dry,
This nurseling of another sky
Still in the little book you lent me,
And where you tenderly laid it by:

And I forgot the clouded Forth,
The gloom that saddens Heaven and Earth,
The bitter east, the misty summer
And gray metropolis of the North.

Perchance, to lull the throbs of pain,
Perchance, to charm a vacant brain,
Perchance, to dream you still beside me,
My fancy fled to the South again.

# 312 To the Rev. F. D. Maurice

Published *1855*, dated 'January, 1854'. *H. Lpr 245* shows T. changing the order of the stanzas. H.T. says of this 'invitation to Farringford' that 'Mr Maurice had been ejected from his professorship at King's College for non-orthodoxy. He had especially alarmed some of the "weaker brethren" by pointing out that the word "eternal" in "eternal punishment" (*αἰώνιος*), strictly translated, referred to the quality not the duration of the punishment.' Maurice (1805–72) had argued in *Theological Essays* (1853) that the popular belief in the endlessness of future punishment was superstitious; in Oct. 1853 a council of King's College, London, forced his resignation. T. abhorred the belief in eternal punishment (*Despair* 26, *Faith* 7–8). Maurice had agreed to be godfather of H.T. in Aug. 1852, the month of birth. Apparently he did not see the poem till it was published in *1855*, to judge from his letter of 27 July 1855 (*Mat.* ii 147–8). Cp. Horace's

*93*. H.T. was born Aug. 1852.
*98*. Shelley, *The Cloud* 74: 'the nursling of the Sky'.

*Epistle* I v, and, e.g., Ben Jonson's *Inviting a Friend to Supper*. Cp. the stanza form of *The Daisy* (p. 1019), and *To Professor Jebb* (p. 1372).

Come, when no graver cares employ,
Godfather, come and see your boy:
  Your presence will be sun in winter,
Making the little one leap for joy.

For, being of that honest few,
Who give the Fiend himself his due,
  Should eighty-thousand college-councils
Thunder 'Anathema,' friend, at you;

Should all our churchmen foam in spite
At you, so careful of the right,
  Yet one lay-hearth would give you welcome
(Take it and come) to the Isle of Wight;

Where, far from noise and smoke of town,
I watch the twilight falling brown
  All round a careless-ordered garden
Close to the ridge of a noble down.

You'll have no scandal while you dine,
But honest talk and wholesome wine,
  And only hear the magpie gossip
Garrulous under a roof of pine:

¶312. *1. when*] if *H.MS. T.Nbk 36* (which may not be quoted) opens with four lines attacking Hell and Calvinism.
*3. sun in winter*] light among us *MS.*
*8. Anathema*: the curse of the church, denouncing a doctrine as damnable. (Ironic, in view of Maurice's doctrine.)
*9–10*] The bigot needs must bear a spite
To priests so faithful to the light, *MS*
*11. Yet one lay-hearth*] But there is one *MS.*
*12. (Take . . . the*] Here in the sweet little *MS.*
*13*] Far off from hum and noise of town, *MS.* Horace's *fumum et opes strepitumque Romae* (*Odes* III xxix 12), as in *In Memoriam* lxxxix 8: 'The dust and din and steam of town'.
*14. falling*] mellowing *MS.*
*15. All round*] About *MS.*
*17. You'll . . . you*] We'll . . . we *MS.*
*18. wholesome*] an honest *MS.*
*19. only*] sitting *MS.*
*20 ∧ 21*] For these are frequent here with me ·
O not ill-omened may they be.

For groves of pine on either hand,
To break the blast of winter, stand;
  And further on, the hoary Channel
Tumbles a billow on chalk and sand;

Where, if below the milky steep
Some ship of battle slowly creep,
  And on through zones of light and shadow
Glimmer away to the lonely deep,

We might discuss the Northern sin
Which made a selfish war begin;
  Dispute the claims, arrange the chances;
Emperor, Ottoman, which shall win:

Or whether war's avenging rod
Shall lash all Europe into blood;
  Till you should turn to dearer matters,
Dear to the man that is dear to God;

How best to help the slender store,
How mend the dwellings, of the poor;
  How gain in life, as life advances,
Valour and charity more and more.

Here comes the fieldfare, here the starling,
Mixt with a clangorous bird of sea. *MS*

This stanza appears on its own; it was presumably intended to follow the magpie, but would have disrupted the sequence in ll. 20–1.

24. *billow*] *1872*; breaker *1855–70*.

25. *Where,*] Or *MS.*

27] And bearing on her towers of silver *MS.*

28. *lonely*] silent *MS.*

29–32]
We would not scruple to discuss
The claims that shake the Bosporus,
  Nor Oltenitza, nor Sinope,
Ottoman, Emperor, Turk and Russ. *MS*

The Russo–Turkish war began in Oct. 1853; l. [3] mentions two battles. It was Russia's destruction of the Turkish ships in Nov. that shocked British opinion; by the end of March 1854 England was to find herself at war with Russia in the Crimea.

33–6] Nor how the chance of war may fall *MS with lacuna.*

37. *best to help*] to eke out *MS.*

Come, Maurice, come: the lawn as yet
Is hoar with rime, or spongy-wet;
But when the wreath of March has blossomed,
Crocus, anemone, violet,

Or later, pay one visit here,
For those are few we hold as dear;
Nor pay but one, but come for many,
Many and many a happy year.

*January*, 1854

# 313 The Brook

Published *1855*, with the subtitle 'An Idyl'. Fragments are in *H.Nbk 20* (1854?). Cp. *The Miller's Daughter* (p. 371), and 'English Idyls' such as *The Gardener's Daughter* (p. 507). It was influenced, as was *The Miller's Daughter*, by Mary Russell Mitford's *The Queen of the Meadow* (1827; reprinted in *Our Village*, 1828); the heroine of the idyl is Katy, and see ll. 71–2*n*. 'Not the brook near Somersby' (T.).

Here, by this brook, we parted; I to the East
And he for Italy—too late—too late:
One whom the strong sons of the world despise;
For lucky rhymes to him were scrip and share,
And mellow metres more than cent for cent;
Nor could he understand how money breeds,
Thought it a dead thing; yet himself could make
The thing that is not as the thing that is.

*41–5*. Recalling Horace's invitation to enjoy the springtime (*Odes* I iv), and also Milton's *Sonnet 17* (which makes use of Horace): 'Now that the Fields are dank, and ways are mire, / Where shall we sometimes meet, and by the fire / Help wast a sullen day; what may be won / From the hard Season gaining: time will run / On smoother, till *Favonius* re-inspire / The frozen earth; and cloth in fresh attire / The Lillie and Rose, that neither sow'd nor spun. / What neat repast shall feast us . . .'

*41. lawn*] park *MS.*

*42. spongy-wet*] dank with wet *MS.*

*43. wreath*] pride *MS.*

*46. as*] so *MS.*

*47. pay but*] only *MS.*

¶313. *6*. Shylock says of money: 'I make it breed as fast', *Merchant of Venice* I iii 93.

O had he lived! In our schoolbooks we say,
Of those that held their heads above the crowd,
They flourished then or then; but life in him
Could scarce be said to flourish, only touched
On such a time as goes before the leaf,
When all the wood stands in a mist of green,
And nothing perfect: yet the brook he loved,
For which, in branding summers of Bengal,
Or even the sweet half-English Neilgherry air
I panted, seems, as I re-listen to it,
Prattling the primrose fancies of the boy,
To me that loved him; for 'O brook,' he says,
'O babbling brook,' says Edmund in his rhyme,
'Whence come you?' and the brook, why not? replies.

I come from haunts of coot and hern,
  I make a sudden sally,
And sparkle out among the fern,
  To bicker down a valley.

By thirty hills I hurry down,
  Or slip between the ridges,
By twenty thorps, a little town,
  And half a hundred bridges.

Till last by Philip's farm I flow
  To join the brimming river,
For men may come and men may go,
  But I go on for ever.

'Poor lad, he died at Florence, quite worn out,
Travelling to Naples. There is Darnley bridge,
It has more ivy; there the river; and there
Stands Philip's farm where brook and river meet.

I chatter over stony ways,
  In little sharps and trebles,
I bubble into eddying bays,
  I babble on the pebbles.

With many a curve my banks I fret
  By many a field and fallow,
And many a fairy foreland set
  With willow-weed and mallow.

I chatter, chatter, as I flow
  To join the brimming river,
For men may come and men may go,
  But I go on for ever.

13–14. A separate jotting of description (*Mem.* i 466).
17. *Neilgherry*: mountains of Madras.

'But Philip chattered more than brook or bird;
Old Philip; all about the fields you caught
His weary daylong chirping, like the dry
High-elbowed grigs that leap in summer grass.

I wind about, and in and out,
With here a blossom sailing,
And here and there a lusty trout,
And here and there a grayling,

And here and there a foamy flake
Upon me, as I travel
With many a silvery waterbreak
Above the golden gravel,

And draw them all along, and flow
To join the brimming river,
For men may come and men may go,
But I go on for ever.

'O darling Katie Willows, his one child!
A maiden of our century, yet most meek;
A daughter of our meadows, yet not coarse;
Straight, but as lissome as a hazel wand;
Her eyes a bashful azure, and her hair
In gloss and hue the chestnut, when the shell
Divides threefold to show the fruit within.

'Sweet Katie, once I did her a good turn,
Her and her far-off cousin and betrothed,
James Willows, of one name and heart with her.
For here I came, twenty years back—the week
Before I parted with poor Edmund; crost
By that old bridge which, half in ruins then,
Still makes a hoary eyebrow for the gleam
Beyond it, where the waters marry—crost,
Whistling a random bar of Bonny Doon,
And pushed at Philip's garden-gate. The gate,
Half-parted from a weak and scolding hinge,
Stuck; and he clamoured from a casement, "Run"
To Katie somewhere in the walks below,
"Run, Katie!" Katie never ran: she moved
To meet me, winding under woodbine bowers,

54. *grigs*: 'crickets' (T.). Cp. *Iliad* iii 150, the old men who 'In summer days, like grasshoppers rejoice' (Pope).

*59–61*. Cp. Wordsworth, *To May* 75: 'Gurgling in foamy water-break'.

*71–2*. Miss Mitford's Katy had 'hair of the very hue of the glossy rind of the horse chesnut'.

A little fluttered, with her eyelids down,
Fresh apple-blossom, blushing for a boon.

'What was it? less of sentiment than sense
Had Katie; not illiterate; nor of those
Who dabbling in the fount of fictive tears,
And nursed by mealy-mouthed philanthropies,
Divorce the Feeling from her mate the Deed.

'She told me. She and James had quarrelled. Why?
What cause of quarrel? None, she said, no cause;
James had no cause: but when I prest the cause,
I learnt that James had flickering jealousies
Which angered her. Who angered James? I said.
But Katie snatched her eyes at once from mine,
And sketching with her slender pointed foot
Some figure like a wizard pentagram
On garden gravel, let my query pass
Unclaimed, in flushing silence, till I asked
If James were coming. "Coming every day,"
She answered, "ever longing to explain,
But evermore her father came across
With some long-winded tale, and broke him short;
And James departed vext with him and her."
How could I help her? "Would I—was it wrong?"
(Claspt hands and that petitionary grace
Of sweet seventeen subdued me ere she spoke)
"O would I take her father for one hour,
For one half-hour, and let him talk to me!"
And even while she spoke, I saw where James
Made toward us, like a wader in the surf,
Beyond the brook, waist-deep in meadow-sweet.

'O Katie, what I suffered for your sake!
For in I went, and called old Philip out
To show the farm: full willingly he rose:
He led me through the short sweet-smelling lanes
Of his wheat-suburb, babbling as he went.
He praised his land, his horses, his machines;
He praised his ploughs, his cows, his hogs, his dogs;
He praised his hens, his geese, his guinea-hens;
His pigeons, who in session on their roofs
Approved him, bowing at their own deserts:
Then from the plaintive mother's teat he took
Her blind and shuddering puppies, naming each,

*92. nor of those*] *1859*; neither one *1855–6*.
*103. wizard*] *1872*; wizard's *1855–70*.

And naming those, his friends, for whom they were:
Then crost the common into Darnley chase
To show Sir Arthur's deer. In copse and fern
Twinkled the innumerable ear and tail.
Then, seated on a serpent-rooted beech,
He pointed out a pasturing colt, and said:
"That was the four-year-old I sold the Squire."
And there he told a long long-winded tale
Of how the Squire had seen the colt at grass,
And how it was the thing his daughter wished,
And how he sent the bailiff to the farm
To learn the price, and what the price he asked,
And how the bailiff swore that he was mad,
But he stood firm; and so the matter hung;
He gave them line: and five days after that
He met the bailiff at the Golden Fleece,
Who then and there had offered something more,
But he stood firm; and so the matter hung;
He knew the man; the colt would fetch its price;
He gave them line: and how by chance at last
(It might be May or April, he forgot,
The last of April or the first of May)
He found the bailiff riding by the farm,
And, talking from the point, he drew him in,
And there he mellowed all his heart with ale,
Until they closed a bargain, hand in hand.

'Then, while I breathed in sight of haven, he,
Poor fellow, could he help it? recommenced,
And ran through all the coltish chronicle,
Wild Will, Black Bess, Tantivy, Tallyho,
Reform, White Rose, Bellerophon, the Jilt,
Arbaces, and Phenomenon, and the rest,
Till, not to die a listener, I arose,
And with me Philip, talking still; and so
We turned our foreheads from the falling sun,
And following our own shadows thrice as long
As when they followed us from Philip's door,
Arrived, and found the sun of sweet content
Re-risen in Katie's eyes, and all things well.

I steal by lawns and grassy plots,
I slide by hazel covers;

*134.* Cp. Wordsworth, *An Evening Walk* 63–4 (1793 text): 'the troubled deer / Shook the still-twinkling tail and glancing ear'. 'This line made in the New Forest' (T.).

I move the sweet forget-me-nots
That grow for happy lovers.

I slip, I slide, I gloom, I glance,
Among my skimming swallows;
I make the netted sunbeam dance
Against my sandy shallows.

I murmur under moon and stars
In brambly wildernesses;
I linger by my shingly bars;
I loiter round my cresses;

And out again I curve and flow
To join the brimming river,
For men may come and men may go,
But I go on for ever.

Yes, men may come and go; and these are gone,
All gone. My dearest brother, Edmund, sleeps,
Not by the well-known stream and rustic spire,
But unfamiliar Arno, and the dome
Of Brunelleschi; sleeps in peace: and he,
Poor Philip, of all his lavish waste of words
Remains the lean P. W. on his tomb:
I scraped the lichen from it: Katie walks
By the long wash of Australasian seas
Far off, and holds her head to other stars,
And breathes in April-autumns. All are gone.'

So Lawrence Aylmer, seated on a stile
In the long hedge, and rolling in his mind
Old waifs of rhyme, and bowing o'er the brook
A tonsured head in middle age forlorn,

*176–82.* Adapting a stanza which T. inserted in a copy of *1832* (*Lincoln*), part of *The Miller's Daughter*:

So knew I every rill that danced,
The netted beam on sandy shelves;
The foambell into eddies glanced,
The wanton ripples chased themselves–
Here flickering through a chain of stars,
Here slow through margins widely swerved,
Here babbling over shingly bars,
Here round some cressy islet curved.

*189–90. dome of Brunelleschi*: the cathedral at Florence, the work of Brunelleschi.

*196. April-autumns*] *1889*; converse seasons *1855–86*; April-Autumn *1888*. The earlier version 'was too sibilant in sound' (T.).

*197. Aylmer*: cp. *Aylmer's Field* (p. 1159).

Mused, and was mute. On a sudden a low breath
Of tender air made tremble in the hedge
The fragile bindweed-bells and briony rings;
And he looked up. There stood a maiden near,
Waiting to pass. In much amaze he stared
On eyes a bashful azure, and on hair
In gloss and hue the chestnut, when the shell
Divides threefold to show the fruit within:
Then, wondering, asked her 'Are you from the farm?'
'Yes' answered she. 'Pray stay a little: pardon me;
What do they call you?' 'Katie.' 'That were strange.
What surname?' 'Willows.' 'No!' 'That is my name.'
'Indeed!' and here he looked so self-perplext,
That Katie laughed, and laughing blushed, till he
Laughed also, but as one before he wakes,
Who feels a glimmering strangeness in his dream.
Then looking at her; 'Too happy, fresh and fair,
Too fresh and fair in our sad world's best bloom,
To be the ghost of one who bore your name
About these meadows, twenty years ago.'

'Have you not heard?' said Katie, 'we came back.
We bought the farm we tenanted before.
Am I so like her? so they said on board.
Sir, if you knew her in her English days,
My mother, as it seems you did, the days
That most she loves to talk of, come with me.
My brother James is in the harvest-field:
But she—you will be welcome—O, come in!'

# 314 Forlorn

Published *1889*. 'An early poem' (H.T.). It appears, in several drafts that culminate in virtually its final form, in *H.Nbk 20*, with *The Brook* and a fragment of *Maud*, which suggests it was written *c.* 1854. It was revised slightly (*H.Nbk 55*) for *1889*, where it was followed by *Happy* as a pendent. The melodramatic theme of seduction, and the refrain, suggest *The Sisters* [*We were two daughters*] (p. 398).

I

'He is fled—I wish him dead—
He that wrought my ruin—
O the flattery and the craft
Which were my undoing . . .

*228.* 'The Father is dead' (T.).

In the night, in the night,
When the storms are blowing.

II

'Who was witness of the crime?
Who shall now reveal it?
He is fled, or he is dead,
Marriage will conceal it . . .
In the night, in the night,
While the gloom is growing.'

III

Catherine, Catherine, in the night,
What is this you're dreaming?
There is laughter down in Hell
At your simple scheming . . .
In the night, in the night,
When the ghosts are fleeting.

IV

You to place a hand in his
Like an honest woman's,
You that lie with wasted lungs
Waiting for your summons . . .
In the night, O the night!
O the deathwatch beating!

V

There will come a witness soon
Hard to be confuted,
All the world will hear a voice
Scream you are polluted . . .
In the night! O the night,
When the owls are wailing!

VI

Shame and marriage, Shame and marriage,
Fright and foul dissembling,
Bantering bridesman, reddening priest,
Tower and altar trembling . . .
In the night, O the night,
When the mind is failing!

VII

Mother, dare you kill your child?
How your hand is shaking!
Daughter of the seed of Cain,
What is this you're taking? . . .
In the night, O the night,
While the house is sleeping.

VIII

Dreadful! has it come to this,
O unhappy creature?
You that would not tread on a worm
For your gentle nature . . .
In the night, O the night,
O the night of weeping!

IX

Murder would not veil your sin,
Marriage will not hide it,
Earth and Hell will brand your name,
Wretch you must abide it . . .
In the night, O the night,
Long before the dawning.

X

Up, get up, and tell him all,
Tell him you were lying!
Do not die with a lie in your mouth,
You that know you're dying . . .
In the night, O the night,
While the grave is yawning.

XI

No—you will not die before,
Though you'll ne'er be stronger;
You will live till *that* is born,
Then a little longer . . .
In the night, O the night,
While the Fiend is prowling.

XII

Death and marriage, Death and marriage!
Funeral hearses rolling!
Black with bridal favours mixt!
Bridal bells with tolling! . . .
In the night, O the night,
When the wolves are howling.

XIII

Up, get up, the time is short,
Tell him now or never!
Tell him all before you die,
Lest you die for ever . . .
In the night, O the night,
Where there's no forgetting.

XIV

Up she got, and wrote him all,
  All her tale of sadness,
Blistered every word with tears,
  And eased her heart of madness . . .
  In the night, and nigh the dawn,
  And while the moon was setting.

# 315 The Charge of the Light Brigade

Published *The Examiner*, 9 Dec. 1854, signed 'A.T.'; then *1855*. The Crimean charge took place 25 Oct. 1854; cp. *The Charge of the Heavy Brigade* (p. 1305). Written 2 Dec. 1854, 'in a few minutes, after reading . . . *The Times* in which occurred the phrase "some one had blundered", and this was the origin of the metre of his poem' (*Mem.* i 381). The editorial (13 Nov.) in fact spoke of 'some hideous blunder'. T. also drew on the report (14 Nov.), where – as he says –'only 607 sabres are mentioned'. T. wrote to Forster, 6 Dec.: 'six is much better than seven hundred (as I think) metrically so keep it' (*Lincoln*).
*Text*: T. soon deplored his *1855* revision, which omitted ll. 5–12 ('Some one had blundered') and closed feebly. He reverted in *1856* to earlier readings. 'Not a poem on which I pique myself' (*Mem.* i 409–10); at one stage he intended to omit it from the 3rd edition of *Maud and Other Poems* (*Virginia*).
*Sources*: Drayton's *Ballad of Agincourt* was suggested at least as early as 1872; T. said it 'was not in my mind; my poem is dactyllic'. Chatterton's *Song to Ælla* is similar in rhythm, form, and theme, e.g., 'Down to the depth of hell/Thousands of Dacyanns went . . .'. T. may have remembered it unconsciously.

I

Half a league, half a league,
  Half a league onward,
All in the valley of Death
  Rode the six hundred.
'Forward, the Light Brigade!
Charge for the guns!' he said:
Into the valley of Death
  Rode the six hundred.

¶315. *3. the valley of Death*: as the soldiers called it (*The Times*).
*5–8*] *1856*; Into the valley of Death
  Rode the six hundred,

II

'Forward, the Light Brigade!'
Was there a man dismayed?
Not though the soldier knew
  Some one had blundered:
Their's not to make reply,
Their's not to reason why,
Their's but to do and die:
Into the valley of Death
  Rode the six hundred.

III

Cannon to right of them,
Cannon to left of them,
Cannon in front of them
  Volleyed and thundered;
Stormed at with shot and shell,
Boldly they rode and well,
Into the jaws of Death,
Into the mouth of Hell
  Rode the six hundred.

IV

Flashed all their sabres bare,
Flashed as they turned in air
Sabring the gunners there,
Charging an army, while
  All the world wondered:
Plunged in the battery-smoke
Right through the line they broke;

For up came an order which
  Some one had blundered.
'Forward, the Light Brigade!
Take the guns,' Nolan said:
Into the valley of Death
  Rode the six hundred. *1854 as separate stanza*;
'Charge,' was the captain's cry; *1855*.

*9–12*] *1856*; . . . / No man was there dismayed, / . . . *1854*; *not 1855*.

*13–14*] *Transposed 1855*.

*17. hundred*: pronounced 'hunderd' in Lincolnshire, according to T.'s friend W. F. Rawnsley.

*27–32*. 'Through the clouds of smoke we could see their sabres flashing' (*The Times*).

*28. as they turned*] *1856*; all at once *1854–5*.

*33*] *1856*; With many a desperate stroke *1854*; Fiercely the line . . . *1855*.

Cossack and Russian
Reeled from the sabre-stroke
    Shattered and sundered.
Then they rode back, but not
    Not the six hundred.

V

Cannon to right of them,
Cannon to left of them,
Cannon behind them
    Volleyed and thundered;
Stormed at with shot and shell,
While horse and hero fell,
They that had fought so well
Came through the jaws of Death,
Back from the mouth of Hell,
All that was left of them,
    Left of six hundred.

VI

When can their glory fade?
O the wild charge they made!
    All the world wondered.
Honour the charge they made!
Honour the Light Brigade,
    Noble six hundred!

34] *1856*; The Russian line they broke; *1854*; Strong was the sabre-stroke; *1855*.

35–6] *1856*; *not 1854*; Making an army reel
Shaken and sundered. *1855*

44] *1854*, *1856*; *not 1855*.

45. *fought*] *1854*, *1856*; struck *1855*.

46. *Came*] *1854*, *1856*; Rode *1855*. *through*] *1855*; from *1854*.

46 ^ 7] Half a league back again, *1855*.

47. *Back*] *1854*, *1856*; Up *1855*.

49. 'Only 195 returned' (T.).

50–55] *1854*, *1856*; Honour the brave and bold!
Long shall the tale be told,
Yea, when our babes are old–
How they rode onward. *1855*

T. J. Wise (*Bibliography of Tennyson* i 148) says that *The Examiner* proofs had a fifth line, cancelled by T., 'No man was there afraid'.

# 316 Maud
## A MONODRAMA

Published *1855*.

*Composition.* T. worked on *Maud*, 'morning and evening', in 1854 (*Mem.* i 377). On 10 Jan. 1855, he had 'finished, and read out, several lyrics of *Maud*' (*Mem.* i 382); in Feb. 1855, 'he made the mad scene in *Maud* in twenty minutes' (*Mat.* ii 108). On 25 April 1855, he 'copied out *Maud* for the press', and put 'the last touch' to it on 7 July (*Mem.* i 384–5). On the trial edition see T. J. Wise, *Bibliography* i 126–31. The germ of *Maud* was the early lyric *Oh! that 'twere possible* (p. 598; now *Maud* ii 141–238), which T. had written in 1833–4 soon after the death of Arthur Hallam. There are two drafts of this in *Heath MS* and T. published an expansion in *The Tribute*, Sept. 1837 (for details, see p. 1082), apparently with reluctance. R. W. Rader (p. 6) comments: 'Tennyson finished and published his poem in 1837 against his will, cobbling up an ending for it under pressure because he wished to pacify Milnes and had no other poem to do it with. But that he continued to think of his poem as incomplete (the 1834 version ended unsatisfactorily with "And weep / My whole soul out to thee") is suggested by the existence of a fair copy, dated April, 1838, in which it has been returned to its pre-1837 form; and by the fact that he did not reprint this lovely lyric in the *1842* volumes or in any other collection before *Maud*.' In *Eversley*, T. records: 'Sir John Simeon years after begged me to weave a story round this poem, and so *Maud* came into being.' Aubrey de Vere's account in *Mem.* i 379 differs slightly: 'Its origin and composition were, as he described them, singular. He had accidentally lighted upon a poem of his own which begins, "O that 'twere possible", and which had long before been published in a selected volume got up by Lord Northampton for the aid of a sick clergyman. It had struck him, in consequence, I think, of a suggestion made by Sir John Simeon, that, to render the poem fully intelligible, a preceding one was necessary. He wrote it; the second poem too required a predecessor: and thus the whole poem was written, as it were, *backwards*.' But in H.T.'s notes (*Lincoln*) for the early version in *Mat.* the phrase 'in consequence . . . Simeon' does not appear. Rader argues, persuasively, that though Simeon's remark may well have spurred T. on, it would be wrong to give it too much weight, since T. must have long thought of doing something more with *Oh! that 'twere possible*. 'Tennyson plainly intended to do something with the piece eight months before his friendship with Simeon began', since in Oct. 1853 his father-in-law, Henry Sellwood, sent by request to Emily T. a copy of the poem from *The Tribute*. See Rader, pp. 1–11. In *1913*, H.T. records: 'My father told [Simeon] that the poem had appeared years before in *The Tribute*, but that it was really intended to be part of a dramatic poem' (p. xxxix). The lyric beginning 'See what a lovely shell' (II ii) had also been written in the 1830s and laid aside (*CT*, p. 281; the authority is the memory of D. D.

Heath in 1894, quoting Spedding); and 'Go not happy day' (I xvii) had originally been intended as a song for *The Princess* (MS, *University Library, Cambridge*). The fierce social criticism of his society was begun in T.'s political poems of 1852. The original title was *Maud or the Madness* (*Mem.* i 402); T. 'intended to revert to the original title, as the words "or the Madness" are added in his hand in the present copy' (1855, *Virginia*). E. F. Shannon notes that the addition of 'A Monodrama' to the title in 1875 was probably suggested by R. J. Mann's calling it a monodrama in 1856 (*Maud Vindicated*), a term echoed by Alexander Macmillan in 1859 ('The Critical Reception of *Maud*', *PMLA* lxviii (1953) 397–417). Shannon shows that the reception was on the whole unfavourable, though there were more favourable reviews than is usually said. By Oct. 1855, more than 8,000 copies had been sold. Only one of the passages castigated was altered in the 2nd edition (1856), namely, iii 50. On the other hand, as Shannon says, the additions in *1856* improved the logic of the poem; T. added three stanzas to the opening section; mitigated the attack on the peace-party in I x; and added a stanza at the very close of the poem. He also added I xix (on the mother's death-bed), and II iii (on Maud's death). The division into Parts I and II was made in *1859*; the further division into a Part III was made in *1865*. It is unfortunate that the most important MS, in *T.Nbk 36*, may not be quoted. There are fragments in Harvard (Notebooks 13, 20–21, 27, 29–31; Loosepapers 145–9, 274); the Huntington Library (HM 19495–6); and the Berg Collection.

*Sources*. J. H. Buckley observes that *Maud* 'in form, theme, and substance recalled the more ambitious efforts of Alexander Smith and Sydney Dobell', the so-called 'Spasmodics' (*The Victorian Temper*, 1952, p. 63). Smith published *A Life Drama* in 1852, and Dobell published *Balder* in 1853. T. owned the editions of 1853 and 1854 respectively (*Lincoln*), and he spoke of Smith as 'a poet of considerable promise' (*Mem.* ii 73, i 468) and pointed out 'the real merits of *Balder*' (*Mem.* ii 506). The plot of *Maud* Edward FitzGerald spoke of as 'leaving something of a Bride of Lammermoor Gloom on one' (16 July 1856, *Lincoln*). Andrew Lang later stressed the similarity to Scott's novel (which T. alludes to in *The Flight* 57): the hero 'is merely The Master of Ravenswood in modern costume, and without Lady Ashton. Her part is taken by Maud's brother. The situations are nearly identical'–ruin; dawdling by a lost ancestral home; love; and duelling (*Alfred Tennyson*, 1901, p. 89). T. P. Harrison, '*Maud* and Shakspere', *Shakespeare Association Bulletin* xvii (1942) 80–5, points out that only Part I has much affinity with *Hamlet* (which T. invoked), and that the erotic theme is from *Romeo and Juliet*–feud, dance, duel, and flight, with the brother similar to Tybalt. G. O. Marshall, *Georgia Review* xvi (1962) 463–4, remarks on a ballad which appeared in *The Tribute* (along with *Oh! that 'twere possible*) in 1837: 'For the name "Maud" if not for part of his story he was possibly indebted to one of the contributions, an anonymous ballad entitled *The Wicked Nephew*, in which the Lady Maud waits for her lover .... There are several elements common to both poems:

murder for material gain, overseas flight after a murder, madness caused by having committed a murder, presence of ghost, and death after a fall.' The importance of another literary source, Charles Kingsley's *Alton Locke* (1850), was suggested by Sir Charles Tennyson: 'Alfred and Emily both read *Alton Locke*, and the story of the tailor poet particularly moved Alfred' (p. 260). Sir Charles suggests that the social denunciations in *Maud* 'sprang from his long talks with Charles Kingsley and F. D. Maurice about the terrible conditions in the rapidly growing industrial cities' (p. 281). The detailed resemblances to *Alton Locke* are described by J. B. Steane, *Tennyson* (1966) pp. 93–4, 111–2. T.'s attitudes are close to those of the political poems of 1852, and he was also influenced by 'Peace and War: A Dialogue', in *Blackwood's* lxxvi (Nov. 1854) 589–98. R. C. Schweik, *Notes and Queries* ccv (1960) 457–8, points out the parallels, including the mention of 'civil war'; the adulteration of food; and the Quaker. See also C. Ricks, *Notes and Queries* ccvii (1962) 230. The attack on Mammonism clearly owes something to Carlyle as well as to Kingsley (G. O. Marshall, *Notes and Queries* cciv (1959) 77–8).
*Biographical relevance*. See R. W. Rader, *Tennyson's 'Maud'* (1963), *passim*; he shows that T. here draws together all the strands of his early life–the hero's father and his rage, the lonely mother, the old man ('of the wolds'), the politician son, and above all the love for Rosa Baring–though Maud herself blends Rosa, Sophy Rawnsley, and T.'s wife Emily (everything about Maud in the last part of the poem recalls Emily rather than Rosa). The story of a love thwarted by Mammonism resembles that of *Edwin Morris*, *Aylmer's Field*, *Locksley Hall*, and *The Flight*; and there are many likenesses to the poems about Rosa, such as *The Rosebud*, *Three Sonnets to a Coquette*, and *To Rosa*, 1836. Sir Charles Tennyson observes that the mad scenes are based on T.'s recollections of Dr Matthew Allen's asylum at High Beech (p. 286); furthermore T. owned a copy of Allen's *Essay on the Classification of the Insane* (1837, Lincoln). H.T. records:

'My father liked reading aloud this poem, a "Drama of the Soul", set in a landscape glorified by Love, and, according to Lowell, "The antiphonal voice to *In Memoriam*", which is the "Way of the Soul" . . . . My father said, "This poem of *Maud or the Madness* is a little *Hamlet*, the history of a morbid, poetic soul, under the blighting influence of a recklessly speculative age. He is the heir of madness, an egoist with the makings of a cynic, raised to a pure and holy love which elevates his whole nature, passing from the height of triumph to the lowest depth of misery, driven into madness by the loss of her whom he has loved, and, when he has at length passed through the fiery furnace, and has recovered his reason, giving himself up to work for the good of mankind through the unselfishness born of a great passion. The peculiarity of this poem is that different phases of passion in one person take the place of different characters.'

W. E. Gladstone modified in *Gleanings of Past Years* (1879, ii 146–7; quoted in *Mem.* i 398–9) his earlier criticisms of *Maud* (*QR*, Oct. 1859):

'I can now see, and I at once confess, that a feeling, which had reference to the growth of the war-spirit in the outer world at the date of this article, dislocated my frame of mind, and disabled me from dealing even tolerably with the work as a work of imagination. Whether it is to be desired that a poem should require from common men a good deal of effort in order to comprehend it; whether all that is put into the mouth of the Soliloquist in *Maud* is within the lines of poetical verisimilitude, whether this poem has the full moral equilibrium which is so marked a characteristic of the sister-works; are questions open, perhaps, to discussion. But I have neither done justice in the text to its rich and copious beauties of detail, nor to its great lyrical and metrical power. And what is worse, I have failed to comprehend rightly the relation between particular passages in the poem and its general scope. This is, I conceive, not to set forth any coherent strain, but to use for poetical ends all the moods and phases allowable under the laws of the art, in a special form of character, which is impassioned, fluctuating, and ill-grounded. The design, which seems to resemble that of the Ecclesiastes in another sphere, is arduous; but Mr Tennyson's power of execution is probably nowhere greater. Even as regards the passages devoted to war-frenzy, equity should have reminded me of the fine lines in the *latter* portion of X iii (Part I), and of the emphatic words [ii 332–3]: "I swear to you, lawful and lawless war / Are scarcely even akin."'

See also J. Killham, in his *Critical Essays on the Poetry of Tennyson.*

## PART I

### I

i

I hate the dreadful hollow behind the little wood,
Its lips in the field above are dabbled with blood-red
    heath,
The red-ribbed ledges drip with a silent horror of
    blood,
And Echo there, whatever is asked her, answers
    'Death.'

ii

For there in the ghastly pit long since a body was
    found,
His who had given me life – O father! O God! was it
    well?–

¶ 316. i *1–3.* 'My father would say that in calling heath "blood"-red the hero showed his extravagant fancy, which is already on the road to madness' (H.T.). Cp. *The Vale of Bones* 81–2, where the flowers 'Blush with the big and purple drops, / That dribbled from the leafy copse.' Also *The Lover's Tale* i 388–9: 'heath and hill, / And hollow lined and wooded to the lips'.

Mangled, and flattened, and crushed, and dinted into the ground:
There yet lies the rock that fell with him when he fell.

III

Did he fling himself down? who knows? for a vast speculation had failed,
And ever he muttered and maddened, and ever wanned with despair,
And out he walked when the wind like a broken worldling wailed,
And the flying gold of the ruined woodlands drove through the air.

IV

I remember the time, for the roots of my hair were stirred
By a shuffled step, by a dead weight trailed, by a whispered fright,
And my pulses closed their gates with a shock on my heart as I heard
The shrill-edged shriek of a mother divide the shuddering night.

V

Villainy somewhere! whose? One says, we are villains all.
Not he: his honest fame should at least by me be maintained:
But that old man, now lord of the broad estate and the Hall,
Dropt off gorged from a scheme that had left us flaccid and drained.

VI

Why do they prate of the blessings of Peace? we have made them a curse,
Pickpockets, each hand lusting for all that is not its own;

i *9. vast*] *1856*; great *1855*. *fling himself down*] slay [kill *alternative*] himself *HnMS*.

i *21–8*. Valerie Pitt (*Tennyson Laureate*, 1962, p. 175) compares Carlyle, *Past and Present* (1843), IV i: '"Violence", "war", "disorder": well, what is war, and death itself, to such a perpetual life-in-death, and "peace, peace, where there is no peace!"' In his edition (1896) of *Sartor Resartus*,

And lust of gain, in the spirit of Cain, is it better or worse
Than the heart of the citizen hissing in war on his own hearthstone?

VII

But these are the days of advance, the works of the men of mind,
When who but a fool would have faith in a tradesman's ware or his word?
Is it peace or war? Civil war, as I think, and that of a kind
The viler, as underhand, not openly bearing the sword.

VIII

Sooner or later I too may passively take the print
Of the golden age – why not? I have neither hope nor trust;
May make my heart as a millstone, set my face as a flint,
Cheat and be cheated, and die: who knows? we are ashes and dust.

IX

Peace sitting under her olive, and slurring the days gone by,
When the poor are hovelled and hustled together, each sex, like swine,
When only the ledger lives, and when only not all men lie;
Peace in her vineyard – yes! – but a company forges the wine.

A. MacMechan had compared III v: 'Where each, isolated, regardless of his neighbour, turned against his neighbour, clutches what he can get, and cries "Mine!" and calls it Peace, because, in the cut-purse and cut-throat Scramble, no steel knives, but only a far cunninger sort, can be employed?'

i *31*. *Job* xli 24: 'His heart is as firm as a stone: yea, as hard as a piece of the nether millstone.' *Isaiah* l 7: 'Therefore have I set my face like a flint, and I know that I shall not be ashamed.'

i *33*, *36*. *Micah* iv 3–4: 'Neither shall they learn war any more. But they shall sit every man under his vine and under his fig tree; and none shall make them afraid.'

i *35*. Cp. *Hands All Round!* 20: 'Too much we make our Ledgers, Gods'. *Psalm* cxvi 11: 'I said in my haste, All men are liars.'

X

And the vitriol madness flushes up in the ruffian's head,
Till the filthy by-lane rings to the yell of the trampled wife,
And chalk and alum and plaster are sold to the poor for bread,
And the spirit of murder works in the very means of life,

XI

And Sleep must lie down armed, for the villainous centre-bits
Grind on the wakeful ear in the hush of the moonless nights,
While another is cheating the sick of a few last gasps, as he sits
To pestle a poisoned poison behind his crimson lights.

XII

When a Mammonite mother kills her babe for a burial fee,
And Timour-Mammon grins on a pile of children's bones,

i *39. And*] *1865*; While *1855–64*. A notorious scandal. E. F. Shannon refers to A. H. Hassall's articles (*The Lancet*, 1851–4) on the adulteration of food, published as a book in 1855. J. B. Steane compares *Alton Locke*: 'Bread full o' alum and bones, and sic filth.'

i *41. centre-bits*: 'An instrument used for making cylindrical holes. (Noted as a burglar's tool.)', *OED*, which quotes *Oliver Twist*: '"None", said Sikes. "'Cept a centre-bit and a boy."'

i *43*] While the chemist cheats the sick of his last poor sleep, and sits *HnMS 1st reading.*

i *44. poison*: the drug wantonly dispensed.

i *45*. W. C. DeVane's selection (1947) points out that T.'s use of Mammonite derives from Carlyle; G. O. Marshall adds from *Past and Present*, I i, how in 1841, 'a Mother and a Father are arraigned and found guilty of poisoning three of their children, to defraud a "burial-society" of some £3.8s. due on the death of each child: they are arraigned, found guilty; and the official authorities, it is whispered, hint that perhaps the case is not solitary, that perhaps you had better not probe farther into that department of things'. Marshall's suggestion is supported by the variant: *kills*] poisons *HnMS 1st reading.*

i *46. grins*] sits *HnMS 1st reading.* *Timour*: or Tamerlane the conqueror credited with atrocities in such works as M. G. Lewis's *Timour* (1811).

Is it peace or war? better, war! loud war by land and by sea,
War with a thousand battles, and shaking a hundred thrones.

XIII

For I trust if an enemy's fleet came yonder round by the hill,
And the rushing battle-bolt sang from the three-decker out of the foam,
That the smooth-faced snubnosed rogue would leap from his counter and till,
And strike, if he could, were it but with his cheating yardwand, home.—

XIV

What! am I raging alone as my father raged in his mood?
Must *I* too creep to the hollow and dash myself down and die
Rather than hold by the law that I made, nevermore to brood
On a horror of shattered limbs and a wretched swindler's lie?

XV

Would there be sorrow for *me?* there was *love* in the passionate shriek,
Love for the silent thing that had made false haste to the grave–
Wrapt in a cloak, as I saw him, and thought he would rise and speak
And rave at the lie and the liar, ah God, as he used to rave.

i *53–64*] *1856*; *not 1855*.
i *53*. *What!*] O God *H.Lpr 149*. *raging . . . raged*] raving . . . raved *H.Lpr*.
i *54*. *hollow*] pit *H.Lpr*.
i *60* ∧ *61*]

So that I hardly believed there was nothing further to dread
From the furious moods of the man and his ever restless eye,
But over and over again these words flasht into my head:
The work of the lie–the work of the lie–the work of the lie. *H.Lpr*

XVI

I am sick of the Hall and the hill, I am sick of the
 moor and the main.
Why should I stay? can a sweeter chance ever come to
 me here?
O, having the nerves of motion as well as the nerves
 of pain,
Were it not wise if I fled from the place and the pit
 and the fear?

XVII

Workmen up at the Hall!–they are coming back from
 abroad;
The dark old place will be gilt by the touch of a
 millionaire:
I have heard, I know not whence, of the singular
 beauty of Maud;
I played with the girl when a child; she promised then
 to be fair.

XVIII

Maud with her venturous climbings and tumbles and
 childish escapes,
Maud the delight of the village, the ringing joy of the
 Hall,
Maud with her sweet purse-mouth when my father
 dangled the grapes,
Maud the beloved of my mother, the moon-faced
 darling of all,–

XIX

What is she now? My dreams are bad. She may bring
 me a curse.
No, there is fatter game on the moor; she will let me
 alone.

i *61–2*]
Why should I stay? is it habit, but habit, that makes me remain?
That, or a dream of a better chance that may come to me here? *H.Lpr*

i *65. Workmen*] *1862*; There are workmen *1855–61.*

i *69. childish*] pretty *HnMS.*

i *70. the . . . village,*] in her aftersummers *HnMS.*

i *72. beloved*] delight *HnMS.*

i *73–6*] *Not HnMS.* But T. selected these four lines from two expanded

Thanks, for the fiend best knows whether woman or man be the worse.
I will bury myself in myself, and the Devil may pipe to his own.

II

Long have I sighed for a calm: God grant I may find it at last!
It will never be broken by Maud, she has neither savour nor salt,

versions which are in this MS. Both follow Section II instead of preceding it–that is, they take place after and not before the hero has seen Maud.

(*a*) Comes she not out of a race that my wrongs have made me despise?
I to be taken with Maud! it would only have turned to a curse.
Now am I proof, heartproof to her unseen beautiful eyes,
Proof for a hundred summers to whatsoever is hers.
Not to be dragged in her shining wake as a rustic prize,
Not to be trapt in her tresses however redundantly curled,
Proof to it all, thank God; so in time I may hope to be wise.
I will bury myself in my books and the Devil may dance through his world.

The second version is vituperative; T.'s indignation after losing Rosa Baring could not find a true place in *Maud*, but the lines have a fierce impulse:

(*b*) What is she now that to see her a moment provokes me to spite?
One of the monkeys who mimic wisdom, whom nothing can shake?
One whom earthquake and deluge would touch with a feeble delight?
One who can hate so sweetly with mannerly polish, and make
Pointed with 'love' and 'my dearest' a sweet innuendo bite?
One who has travelled, is knowing? a beauty and ruined with praise?
Well, I was half-afraid but I shall not die for her sake,
Not be her 'savage' and 'O the monster'! their delicate ways!
Their finical interlarding of French and the giggle and shrug!
Taken with Maud–not so–for what could she prove but a curse.
Being so hard, she has hardly a decent regard for her pug.
Thanks! there is fatter game on the moor; she will let me alone;
Thanks, for the Devil best knows whether woman or man be the worse.
I will bury myself in my books and the Devil may pipe to his own.

Eyes, what care I for her eyes, those eyes that I did not behold.
Can they be more whether black or blue, fullrolling or small,
More than the beldam-tutored Demos commonplace eyes,
Lying a splendid whoredom to full-fed heirs at the Ball,
'Buy me, O buy me and have me, for I am here to be sold'.

i *76. in myself*] *1865*; in my books *1855–64*.

i *78. Matthew* v 13: 'But if the salt have lost his savour, wherewith shall it be salted?'

But a cold and clear-cut face, as I found when her carriage past,
Perfectly beautiful: let it be granted her: where is the fault?
All that I saw (for her eyes were downcast, not to be seen)
Faultily faultless, icily regular, splendidly null,
Dead perfection, no more; nothing more, if it had not been
For a chance of travel, a paleness, an hour's defect of the rose,
Or an underlip, you may call it a little too ripe, too full,
Or the least little delicate aquiline curve in a sensitive nose,
From which I escaped heart-free, with the least little touch of spleen.

## III

Cold and clear-cut face, why come you so cruelly meek,
Breaking a slumber in which all spleenful folly was drowned,
Pale with the golden beam of an eyelash dead on the cheek,
Passionless, pale, cold face, star-sweet on a gloom profound;
Womanlike, taking revenge too deep for a transient wrong
Done but in thought to your beauty, and ever as pale as before
Growing and fading and growing upon me without a sound,

i *79.* The ensuing description of Maud recalls the Rosa Baring of the early poems. *Sonnet* [*I lingered yet awhile*]: 'And yet a jewel only made to shine, / And icy-cold although 'tis rosy-clear – / Why did I linger? I myself condemn, / For ah! 'tis far too costly to be mine, / And Nature never dropt a human tear / In those chill dews whereof she froze the gem.' *Sonnet* [*How thought you*] 13: 'A perfect-featured face, expressionless.'

i *80*] Perfectly beautiful – that, no doubt; but there is the fault. *HnMS 1st reading.*

i *81. downcast,*] down and could *HnMS 1st reading.*

i *84. an hour's*] a slight *HnMS 1st reading.*

i *84 ∧ 5*] That will blossom again to the surface as bright, with an hour's repose, *HnMS deleted.*

Luminous, gemlike, ghostlike, deathlike, half the night long
Growing and fading and growing, till I could bear it no more,
But arose, and all by myself in my own dark garden ground,
Listening now to the tide in its broad-flung shipwrecking roar,
Now to the scream of a maddened beach dragged down by the wave,
Walked in a wintry wind by a ghastly glimmer, and found
The shining daffodil dead, and Orion low in his grave.

IV

I

A million emeralds break from the ruby-budded lime
In the little grove where I sit–ah, wherefore cannot I be
Like things of the season gay, like the bountiful season bland,
When the far-off sail is blown by the breeze of a softer clime,
Half-lost in the liquid azure bloom of a crescent of sea,
The silent sapphire-spangled marriage ring of the land?

II

Below me, there, is the village, and looks how quiet and small!
And yet bubbles o'er like a city, with gossip, scandal, and spite;
And Jack on his ale-house bench has as many lies as a Czar;
And here on the landward side, by a red rock, glimmers the Hall;
And up in the high Hall-garden I see her pass like a light;
But sorrow seize me if ever that light be my leading star!

i *99–101.* Cp. *Oh! ye wild winds* 22–4: 'The shrilly wailings of the grave! / And mingle with the maddened skies, / The rush of wind, and roar of wave.'
i *101. shining daffodil*] sweet Narcissus *trial edition.* (T. J. Wise, *Bibliography* i 126–31, derived this and other variants from R. H. Shepherd.)
i *110. Czar*: Nicholas I and the Crimean war.

III

When have I bowed to her father, the wrinkled head of the race?
I met her today with her brother, but not to her brother I bowed:
I bowed to his lady-sister as she rode by on the moor;
But the fire of a foolish pride flashed over her beautiful face.
O child, you wrong your beauty, believe it, in being so proud;
Your father has wealth well-gotten, and I am nameless and poor.

IV

I keep but a man and a maid, ever ready to slander and steal;
I know it, and smile a hard-set smile, like a stoic, or like
A wiser epicurean, and let the world have its way:
For nature is one with rapine, a harm no preacher can heal;
The Mayfly is torn by the swallow, the sparrow speared by the shrike,
And the whole little wood where I sit is a world of plunder and prey.

V

We are puppets, Man in his pride, and Beauty fair in her flower;
Do we move ourselves, or are moved by an unseen hand at a game

i *115. today*] *1856*; abroad *1855*.

i *120*] I keep but one little maid readyripe to plunder and steal *H.MS*.

i *124. torn . . . swallow*] rent by the robin *H.MS*. The MS reading suggests Keats, *To Reynolds* 93–105 (published 1848): 'I saw / Too far into the sea; where every maw / The greater on the less feeds evermore:– / But I saw too distinct into the core / Of an eternal fierce destruction, / And so from Happiness I far was gone. / Still am I sick of it: and though today / I've gathered young spring-leaves, and flowers gay / Of Periwinkle and wild strawberry, / Still do I that most fierce destruction see, / The Shark at savage prey–the hawk at pounce, / The gentle Robin, like a pard or ounce, / Ravening a worm.'

i *127. Do . . . moved*] We do not play but are played *H.Nbk 29*.

i *127–8*. John Churton Collins thought T. owed these lines to FitzGerald's *Rubáiyát*, stanza xlix; but T. wrote in the margin: 'I don't read Persian and F.'s translation was not published when this was written' (*Cornhill*, Jan. 1880, *Lincoln*). FitzGerald published in 1859.

That pushes us off from the board, and others ever succeed?
Ah yet, we cannot be kind to each other here for an hour;
We whisper, and hint, and chuckle, and grin at a brother's shame;
However we brave it out, we men are a little breed.

VI

A monstrous eft was of old the Lord and Master of Earth,
For him did his high sun flame, and his river billowing ran,
And he felt himself in his force to be Nature's crowning race.
As nine months go to the shaping an infant ripe for his birth,
So many a million of ages have gone to the making of man:
He now is first, but is he the last? is he not too base?

VII

The man of science himself is fonder of glory, and vain,
An eye well-practised in nature, a spirit bounded and poor;
The passionate heart of the poet is whirled into folly and vice.
I would not marvel at either, but keep a temperate brain;

i *132.* 'The great old lizards of geology' (T.).

i *132–7.* W. R. Rutland, *Essays and Studies* xxvi (1940) 23, suggests the influence of Chambers's *Vestiges of Creation*: 'Are there yet to be species superior to us in organization, purer in feeling, more powerful in device and act, and who shall take a rule over us?' J. Killham adds from Chambers: 'The gestation of a single organism is the work of but a few days, weeks or months; but the gestation, so to speak, of a whole creation is a matter probably involving enormous spaces of time' (*Tennyson and 'The Princess'*, p. 258).

i *138. himself . . . glory*] is greedy of glory and selfish *H.MS.*

i *139. spirit bounded*] soul that is narrow *H.MS.*

For not to desire or admire, if a man could learn it, were more
Than to walk all day like the sultan of old in a garden of spice.

VIII

For the drift of the Maker is dark, an Isis hid by the veil.
Who knows the ways of the world, how God will bring them about?
Our planet is one, the suns are many, the world is wide.
Shall I weep if a Poland fall? shall I shriek if a Hungary fail?
Or an infant civilisation be ruled with rod or with knout?
*I* have not made the world, and He that made it will guide.

IX

Be mine a philosopher's life in the quiet woodland ways,
Where if I cannot be gay let a passionless peace be my lot,
Far-off from the clamour of liars belied in the hubbub of lies;
From the long-necked geese of the world that are ever hissing dispraise
Because their natures are little, and, whether he heed it or not,
Where each man walks with his head in a cloud of poisonous flies.

i *142.* Horace's *Nil admirari* (*Epistles* I vi 1).

i *143.* Cp. *Song of Solomon* iv 16: 'Blow upon my garden, that the spices thereof may flow out. Let my beloved come into his garden, and eat his pleasant fruits.'

i *144.* 'The great Goddess of the Egyptians' (T.).

i *146*] We are not first, our planet is one, and the worlds are wide. *H.MS.*

i *147–8.* Referring to the Russian and Austrian occupation of Cracow in 1846, and the defeat of the Hungarians in 1849. Cp. *Hands All Round!* 18*n* (p. 1003): 'The Russian whips and Austrian rods.'

i *150–52*]

O green little wood, O quiet of winding woodland ways,
If I cannot be merry yet here shall peace be my lot,
I shall hear no more the liar belied in the hubbub of lies; *H.MS*

X

And most of all would I flee from the cruel madness of love,
The honey of poison-flowers and all the measureless ill.
Ah Maud, you milkwhite fawn, you are all unmeet for a wife.
Your mother is mute in her grave as her image in marble above;
Your father is ever in London, you wander about at your will;
You have but fed on the roses and lain in the lilies of life.

## V

I

A voice by the cedar tree
In the meadow under the Hall!
She is singing an air that is known to me,
A passionate ballad gallant and gay,
A martial song like a trumpet's call!
Singing alone in the morning of life,
In the happy morning of life and of May,
Singing of men that in battle array,
Ready in heart and ready in hand,
March with banner and bugle and fife
To the death, for their native land.

II

Maud with her exquisite face,
And wild voice pealing up to the sunny sky,
And feet like sunny gems on an English green,
Maud in the light of her youth and her grace,
Singing of Death, and of Honour that cannot die,
Till I well could weep for a time so sordid and mean,
And myself so languid and base.

III

Silence, beautiful voice!
Be still, for you only trouble the mind
With a joy in which I cannot rejoice,
A glory I shall not find.
Still! I will hear you no more,
For your sweetness hardly leaves me a choice

But to move to the meadow and fall before
Her feet on the meadow grass, and adore,
Not her, who is neither courtly nor kind,
Not her, not her, but a voice.

VI

I

Morning arises stormy and pale,
No sun, but a wannish glare
In fold upon fold of hueless cloud,
And the budded peaks of the wood are bowed
Caught and cuffed by the gale:
I had fancied it would be fair.

II

Whom but Maud should I meet
Last night, when the sunset burned
On the blossomed gable-ends
At the head of the village street,
Whom but Maud should I meet?
And she touched my hand with a smile so sweet,
She made me divine amends
For a courtesy not returned.

III

And thus a delicate spark
Of glowing and growing light
Through the livelong hours of the dark
Kept itself warm in the heart of my dreams,
Ready to burst in a coloured flame;
Till at last when the morning came
In a cloud, it faded, and seems
But an ashen-gray delight.

IV

What if with her sunny hair
And smile as sunny as cold,
She meant to weave me a snare
Of some coquettish deceit,
Cleopatra-like as of old
To entangle me when we met,
To have her lion roll in a silken net
And fawn at a victor's feet.

i *191*. Cp. Keats, *Lamia* i 57: 'wannish fire'.

i *206*. Cp. *The Lover's Tale* i 798: 'All through the livelong hours of utter dark'.

V

Ah, what shall I be at fifty
Should Nature keep me alive,
If I find the world so bitter
When I am but twenty-five?
Yet, if she were not a cheat,
If Maud were all that she seemed,
And her smile were all that I dreamed,
Then the world were not so bitter
But a smile could make it sweet.

VI

What if though her eye seemed full
Of a kind intent to me,
What if that dandy-despot, he,
That jewelled mass of millinery,
That oiled and curled Assyrian Bull
Smelling of musk and of insolence,
Her brother, from whom I keep aloof,
Who wants the finer politic sense
To mask, though but in his own behoof,
With a glassy smile his brutal scorn–
What if he had told her yestermorn
How prettily for his own sweet sake
A face of tenderness might be feigned,
And a moist mirage in desert eyes,
That so, when the rotten hustings shake
In another month to his brazen lies,
A wretched vote may be gained.

VII

For a raven ever croaks, at my side,
Keep watch and ward, keep watch and ward,
Or thou wilt prove their tool.
Yea, too, myself from myself I guard,
For often a man's own angry pride
Is cap and bells for a fool.

i *233*. 'With hair curled like that of the bulls on Assyrian sculpture' (T.). T. had read Layard's *Nineveh* in 1852 (*Mem.* i 356).

i *234*. The zeugma suggests *Paradise Lost* i 501–2: 'the Sons / Of Belial, flown with insolence and wine'.

i *243*. Cp. *Hail Briton* 88: 'To which the slight-built hustings shake'.

VIII

Perhaps the smile and tender tone
Came out of her pitying womanhood,
For am I not, am I not, here alone
So many a summer since she died,
My mother, who was so gentle and good?
Living alone in an empty house,
Here half-hid in the gleaming wood,
Where I hear the dead at midday moan,
And the shrieking rush of the wainscot mouse,
And my own sad name in corners cried,
When the shiver of dancing leaves is thrown
About its echoing chambers wide,
Till a morbid-hate and horror have grown
Of a world in which I have hardly mixt,
And a morbid eating lichen fixt
On a heart half-turned to stone.

IX

O heart of stone, are you flesh, and caught
By that you swore to withstand?
For what was it else within me wrought
But, I fear, the new strong wine of love,
That made my tongue so stammer and trip
When I saw the treasured splendour, her hand,
Come sliding out of her sacred glove,
And the sunlight broke from her lip?

X

I have played with her when a child;
She remembers it now we meet.
Ah well, well, well, I *may* be beguiled
By some coquettish deceit.
Yet, if she were not a cheat,
If Maud were all that she seemed,
And her smile had all that I dreamed,
Then the world were not so bitter
But a smile could make it sweet.

## VII

I

Did I hear it half in a doze
    Long since, I know not where?

i *260*. Cp. *Mariana* 63–4: 'the mouse / Behind the mouldering wainscot shrieked'.

i *285–300*. 'He remembers his father and her father talking just before the

Did I dream it an hour ago,
When asleep in this arm-chair?

II

Men were drinking together,
Drinking and talking of me;
'Well, if it prove a girl, the boy
Will have plenty: so let it be.'

III

Is it an echo of something
Read with a boy's delight,
Viziers nodding together
In some Arabian night?

IV

Strange, that I hear two men,
Somewhere, talking of me;
'Well, if it prove a girl, my boy
Will have plenty: so let it be.'

## VIII

She came to the village church,
And sat by a pillar alone;
An angel watching an urn
Wept over her, carved in stone;
And once, but once, she lifted her eyes,
And suddenly, sweetly, strangely blushed
To find they were met by my own;
And suddenly, sweetly, my heart beat stronger
And thicker, until I heard no longer

birth of Maud' (T.). W. D. Paden (pp. 93, 161) points out that the reference in ll. 293–6 is to *The Story of Nourredin Ali and Bedreddin Hassan*, in Galland's translation of the *Arabian Nights*; the brothers agree to pair their children if of opposite sexes; they quarrel, but the children finally marry. 'The hero vaguely remembers, or believes that he remembers, from his childhood that his father and Maud's father betrothed them, over the wine, when Maud was born .... The betrothal, as a matter of fact, had taken place. Maud had been told of the compact by her dying mother, for whose sake she now desires to be reconciled to the man that her father had wronged.'

The snowy-banded, dilettante,
Delicate-handed priest intone;
And thought, is it pride, and mused and sighed
'No surely, now it cannot be pride.'

## IX

I was walking a mile,
More than a mile from the shore,
The sun looked out with a smile
Betwixt the cloud and the moor,
And riding at set of day
Over the dark moor land,
Rapidly riding far away,
She waved to me with her hand.
There were two at her side,
Something flashed in the sun,
Down by the hill I saw them ride,
In a moment they were gone:
Like a sudden spark
Struck vainly in the night,
Then returns the dark
With no more hope of light.

## X

### I

Sick, am I sick of a jealous dread?
Was not one of the two at her side
This new-made lord, whose splendour plucks
The slavish hat from the villager's head?
Whose old grandfather has lately died,
Gone to a blacker pit, for whom
Grimy nakedness dragging his trucks
And laying his trams in a poisoned gloom
Wrought, till he crept from a gutted mine
Master of half a servile shire,
And left his coal all turned into gold
To a grandson, first of his noble line,
Rich in the grace all women desire,
Strong in the power that all men adore,
And simper and set their voices lower,

i *313*. 'It cannot be pride that she did not return his bow', T.–alluding to i 116–7.

i *328*. *Then*] *1865*; And back *1855–64*.

And soften as if to a girl, and hold
Awe-stricken breaths at a work divine,
Seeing his gewgaw castle shine,
New as his title, built last year,
There amid perky larches and pine,
And over the sullen-purple moor
(Look at it) pricking a cockney ear.

II

What, has he found my jewel out?
For one of the two that rode at her side
Bound for the Hall, I am sure was he:
Bound for the Hall, and I think for a bride.
Blithe would her brother's acceptance be.
Maud could be gracious too, no doubt
To a lord, a captain, a padded shape,
A bought commission, a waxen face,
A rabbit mouth that is ever agape–
Bought? what is it he cannot buy?
And therefore splenetic, personal, base,
A wounded thing with a rancorous cry,
At war with myself and a wretched race,
Sick, sick to the heart of life, am I.

i *347–8*. Probably a memory of the rebuilding of Bayons Manor in 1835 by T.'s favoured uncle, Charles Tennyson-d'Eyncourt (J. H. Buckley, p. 69).

i *353–4*] This babe-faced lord, I am sure it was he, *trial edition* (supported by *Berg MS* – abbreviated hereafter to *B.MS*).

i *358–60*]
To the dawdling drawl of the tender ape,
His bought commission and padded shape,
His one half-grain of sense, and his three
Straw-coloured hairs upon either side
Of a rabbit mouth . . . *trial edition*

i *363–4*] *1856; not 1855.*

i *365 ∧ 6*]
Now are they serf-like, horribly bland,
To this lord-captain up at the Hall:
Will she smile if he presses her hand?
Captain! he to hold a command!
He can hold a cue, he can pocket a ball;
And sure not a bantam cockerel lives
With a weaker crow upon English land,
Whether he boast of a horse that gains,
Or cackle his own applause, when he gives
A filthy story at second-hand,
Where the point is missed, and the filth remains.

III

Last week came one to the county town,
To preach our poor little army down,
And play the game of the despot kings,
Though the state has done it and thrice as well:
This broad-brimmed hawker of holy things,
Whose ear is crammed with his cotton, and rings
Even in dreams to the chink of his pence,
This huckster put down war! can he tell
Whether war be a cause or a consequence?
Put down the passions that make earth Hell!
Down with ambition, avarice, pride,
Jealousy, down! cut off from the mind
The bitter springs of anger and fear;
Down too, down at your own fireside,
With the evil tongue and the evil ear,
For each is at war with mankind.

IV

I wish I could hear again
The chivalrous battle-song

---

Bought commission! can such as he
Be wholesome guards for an English throne,
When if France but make a lunge, why she,
God knows, might prick us to the backbone?

What use for a single mouth to rage
At the rotten creak of the old machine;
Though it makes friends weep and enemies smile,
That here in the face of a watchful age,
The sons of a gray-beard-ridden isle
Should dance in a round of an old routine,
And a few great families lead the reels,
While pauper manhood lies in the dirt,
And Favour and Wealth with gilded heels
Trample service and tried desert. *trial edition*

T. quotes ll. [2–9], [16–21], in the *Eversley* notes; the only variant of interest is his change in l. [17] to 'State-machine'. *Mat.* ii 131 prints ll. [12–15].

i *366–73*. 'The *Westminster Review* said this was an attack on John Bright. I did not even know at the time that he was a Quaker' (T.). See *The Third of February* 43, MS (p. 1002), and *The Penny-Wise* 33, MS (p. 996). T. probably took over the Quaker, as the type of peace-at-any-price, from *Blackwood's* (see headnote).

i *371. crammed*] *1859*; stuffed *1855–6*.

i *382–8*] *1856*; *not 1855*;

And Maud, who when I had languished long,
Reached me a shining hand of help

That she warbled alone in her joy!
I might persuade myself then
She would not do herself this great wrong,
To take a wanton dissolute boy
For a man and leader of men.

V

Ah God, for a man with heart, head, hand,
Like some of the simple great ones gone
For ever and ever by,
One still strong man in a blatant land,
Whatever they call him, what care I,
Aristocrat, democrat, autocrat–one
Who can rule and dare not lie.

VI

And ah for a man to arise in me,
That the man I am may cease to be!

## XI

I

O let the solid ground
Not fail beneath my feet
Before my life has found
What some have found so sweet;
Then let come what come may,
What matter if I go mad,
I shall have had my day.

To arouse me, that May morning, when
She chanted a chivalrous battle-song,
Maud, can she do herself so much wrong
As to take this waxen effeminate whelp
For a man and leader of men. *trial edition*

(supported by *B.MS*). The second MS line will have seemed too close to *In Memoriam* lxxxiv 43: 'Would reach us out the shining hand'.

i *394. Aristocrat*, the usual nineteenth-century pronunciation.

i *396–7*] *1856; not 1855.*

i *398*] Let not the sound earth fail *British Museum first draft* (*as below throughout*); Let not the solid ground *MS in Eversley*.

i *399*] And open under my feet *BM MS.* *Not fail*] Fail *MS Eversley*.

i *400. has found*] finds out *BM MS.*

i *401. some*] others *BM MS.*

i *402–4.* Cp. *Macbeth* I iii 146–7: 'Come what come may, / Time and the hour runs through the roughest day.'

i *403*] To a life that has been so sad, *BM MS.*

II

Let the sweet heavens endure,
Not close and darken above me
Before I am quite quite sure
That there is one to love me;
Then let come what come may
To a life that has been so sad,
I shall have had my day.

## XII

I

Birds in the high Hall-garden
When twilight was falling,
Maud, Maud, Maud, Maud,
They were crying and calling.

II

Where was Maud? in our wood;
And I, who else, was with her,
Gathering woodland lilies,
Myriads blow together.

III

Birds in our wood sang
Ringing through the valleys,
Maud is here, here, here
In among the lilies.

IV

I kissed her slender hand,
She took the kiss sedately;
Maud is not seventeen,
But she is tall and stately.

V

I to cry out on pride
Who have won her favour!
O Maud were sure of Heaven
If lowliness could save her.

i *405*] Let not the sweet Heaven fail, *BM MS*. Cp. *Lear* I v 45–6: 'O, let me not be mad, not mad, sweet heaven! / Keep me in temper; I would not be mad!'

i *406. Not close*] Close *BM MS*.

i *408*] That Maud *does* love me; *BM MS*.

i *410*] What matter if I go mad, *BM MS*.

i *411. had*] lived *BM MS, MS Eversley*.

VI

I know the way she went
Home with her maiden posy,
For her feet have touched the meadows
And left the daisies rosy.

VII

Birds in the high Hall-garden
Were crying and calling to her,
Where is Maud, Maud, Maud?
One is come to woo her.

VIII

Look, a horse at the door,
And little King Charley snarling,
Go back, my lord, across the moor,
You are not her darling.

## XIII

I

Scorned, to be scorned by one that I scorn,
Is that a matter to make me fret?
That a calamity hard to be borne?
Well, he may live to hate me yet.
Fool that I am to be vext with his pride!
I past him, I was crossing his lands;
He stood on the path a little aside;
His face, as I grant, in spite of spite,
Has a broad-blown comeliness, red and white,
And six feet two, as I think, he stands;
But his essences turned the live air sick,
And barbarous opulence jewel-thick
Sunned itself on his breast and his hands.

i *435*. 'Because if you tread on the daisy, it turns up a rosy underside' (T.).
i *441*. *Charley*] *1864*; Charles is *1855–62*. A spaniel.
i *454*] But a gust of his essences made me sick *B.MS*; For his essences made the morning sick *trial edition*.
i *455*] And those fat fingers foolishly thick *B.MS*.
i *456*] With jewels, stunted obstinate hands. *B.MS*; Flashed on his obstinate-fingered hands. *trial edition*.

II

Who shall call me ungentle, unfair,
I longed so heartily then and there
To give him the grasp of fellowship;
But while I past he was humming an air,
Stopt, and then with a riding-whip
Leisurely tapping a glossy boot,
And curving a contumelious lip,
Gorgonised me from head to foot
With a stony British stare.

III

Why sits he here in his father's chair?
That old man never comes to his place:
Shall I believe him ashamed to be seen?
For only once, in the village street,
Last year, I caught a glimpse of his face,
A gray old wolf and a lean.
Scarcely, now, would I call him a cheat;
For then, perhaps, as a child of deceit,
She might by a true descent be untrue;
And Maud is as true as Maud is sweet:
Though I fancy her sweetness only due
To the sweeter blood by the other side;
Her mother has been a thing complete,
However she came to be so allied.
And fair without, faithful within,
Maud to him is nothing akin:
Some peculiar mystic grace
Made her only the child of her mother,
And heaped the whole inherited sin
On the huge scapegoat of the race,
All, all upon the brother.

IV

Peace, angry spirit, and let him be!
Has not his sister smiled on me?

i *458. heartily*] *1856*; earnestly *1855*.
i *464–5*. T. (in 1849?) 'made a line on the Oxford "masher's" general reception of a stranger: "With one Oxonian stare from heel to head"' (*Mem.* ii 485).
i *470. Last year*] Long since *trial edition*.
i *482*. Cp. *PL* iii 183: 'peculiar grace'; v 15: 'peculiar Graces'.

## XIV

I

Maud has a garden of roses
And lilies fair on a lawn;
There she walks in her state
And tends upon bed and bower,
And thither I climbed at dawn
And stood by her garden-gate;
A lion ramps at the top,
He is claspt by a passion-flower.

II

Maud's own little oak-room
(Which Maud, like a precious stone
Set in the heart of the carven gloom,
Lights with herself, when alone
She sits by her music and books
And her brother lingers late
With a roystering company) looks
Upon Maud's own garden-gate:
And I thought as I stood, if a hand, as white
As ocean-foam in the moon, were laid
On the hasp of the window, and my Delight
Had a sudden desire, like a glorious ghost, to glide,
Like a beam of the seventh Heaven, down to my side,
There were but a step to be made.

III

The fancy flattered my mind,
And again seemed overbold;
Now I thought that she cared for me,
Now I thought she was kind
Only because she was cold.

IV

I heard no sound where I stood
But the rivulet on from the lawn
Running down to my own dark wood;
Or the voice of the long sea-wave as it swelled
Now and then in the dim-gray dawn;
But I looked, and round, all round the house I beheld
The death-white curtain drawn;

i 495. *PL* iv 343: 'Sporting the Lion rampd'.
i 508. *like . . . ghost*] *Not BM MS.*

Felt a horror over me creep,
Prickle my skin and catch my breath,
Knew that the death-white curtain meant but sleep,
Yet I shuddered and thought like a fool of the sleep
of death.

## XV

So dark a mind within me dwells,
And I make myself such evil cheer,
That if *I* be dear to some one else,
Then some one else may have much to fear;
But if *I* be dear to some one else,
Then I should be to myself more dear.
Shall I not take care of all that I think,
Yea even of wretched meat and drink,
If I be dear,
If I be dear to some one else.

## XVI

### I

This lump of earth has left his estate
The lighter by the loss of his weight;
And so that he find what he went to seek,
And fulsome Pleasure clog him, and drown
His heart in the gross mud-honey of town,
He may stay for a year who has gone for a week:
But this is the day when I must speak,
And I see my Oread coming down,
O this is the day!
O beautiful creature, what am I
That I dare to look her way;
Think that I may hold dominion sweet,
Lord of the pulse that is lord of her breast,
And dream of her beauty with tender dread,
From the delicate Arab arch of her feet
To the grace that, bright and light as the crest
Of a peacock, sits on her shining head,
And she knows it not: O, if she knew it,
To know her beauty might half undo it.
I know it the one bright thing to save
My yet young life in the wilds of Time,
Perhaps from madness, perhaps from crime,
Perhaps from a selfish grave.

i *551*. Like the arched neck of an Arab horse.

II

What, if she be fastened to this fool lord,
Dare I bid her abide by her word?
Should I love her so well if she
Had given her word to a thing so low?
Shall I love her as well if she
Can break her word were it even for me?
I trust that it is not so.

III

Catch not my breath, O clamorous heart,
Let not my tongue be a thrall to my eye,
For I must tell her before we part,
I must tell her, or die.

## XVII

Go not, happy day,
  From the shining fields,
Go not, happy day,
  Till the maiden yields.
Rosy is the West,
  Rosy is the South,
Roses are her cheeks,
  And a rose her mouth
When the happy Yes
  Falters from her lips,
Pass and blush the news
  Over glowing ships;
Over blowing seas,
  Over seas at rest,
Pass the happy news,
  Blush it through the West;
Till the red man dance
  By his red cedar-tree,
And the red man's babe
  Leap, beyond the sea.

i *571–98.* This appears with the songs written in 1849 for the 3rd edition of *The Princess* (1850) in the MS at *University Library, Cambridge.* T. recited this poem, 'which found a place in *Maud*', to Palgrave in 1853 (*Mem.* ii 504). In the 1865 *Selection*, T. placed this song, not with *Come into the garden, Maud,* but immediately after *Three Sonnets to a Coquette* (which are about Rosa Baring). It is relevant that this lyric in *Maud* was much ridiculed by the critics. Cp. *Early Verses* (p. 634) to Rosa.

i *582. Over glowing*] *1865 Selection*; O'er the blowing *1855–65*. E. F. Shannon points out that a reviewer had objected to 'blowing'.

Blush from West to East,
Blush from East to West,
Till the West is East,
Blush it through the West.
Rosy is the West,
Rosy is the South,
Roses are her cheeks,
And a rose her mouth.

## XVIII

I

I have led her home, my love, my only friend.
There is none like her, none.
And never yet so warmly ran my blood
And sweetly, on and on
Calming itself to the long-wished-for end,
Full to the banks, close on the promised good.

II

None like her, none.
Just now the dry-tongued laurels' pattering talk
Seemed her light foot along the garden walk,
And shook my heart to think she comes once more;
But even then I heard her close the door,
The gates of Heaven are closed, and she is gone.

III

There is none like her, none.
Nor will be when our summers have deceased.
O, art thou sighing for Lebanon
In the long breeze that streams to thy delicious East,
Sighing for Lebanon,
Dark cedar, though thy limbs have here increased,
Upon a pastoral slope as fair,
And looking to the South, and fed
With honeyed rain and delicate air,
And haunted by the starry head

i *599. led*] brought *H.Nbk 30.*

i *601. warmly*] sweetly *H.MS.*

i *602*] So like a sunwarm river on and on *H.MS.*

i *607. Seemed*] Like *H.MS.* *foot*] feet *H.MS.*

i *608. And . . . heart*] Made my heart shake *H.MS.*

i *615. Psalm* civ 16: 'The trees of the Lord are full of sap; the cedars of Lebanon, which he hath planted.'

i *619. rain and delicate*] showers and tender *H.MS. The Brook* 202 speaks of 'tender air'.

Of her whose gentle will has changed my fate,
And made my life a perfumed altar-flame;
And over whom thy darkness must have spread
With such delight as theirs of old, thy great
Forefathers of the thornless garden, there
Shadowing the snow-limbed Eve from whom she
came.

IV

Here will I lie, while these long branches sway,
And you fair stars that crown a happy day
Go in and out as if at merry play,
Who am no more so all forlorn,
As when it seemed far better to be born
To labour and the mattock-hardened hand,
Than nursed at ease and brought to understand
A sad astrology, the boundless plan
That makes you tyrants in your iron skies,
Innumerable, pitiless, passionless eyes,
Cold fires, yet with power to burn and brand
His nothingness into man.

V

But now shine on, and what care I,
Who in this stormy gulf have found a pearl
The countercharm of space and hollow sky,
And do accept my madness, and would die
To save from some slight shame one simple girl.

i *628. you fair*] watch the *H.MS.*

i *632. mattock*: farm tool.

i *634. A sad astrology,*] Some cheerless fragment of *H.MS.* T. comments: 'The *sad astrology* is modern astronomy, for of old astrology was thought to sympathise with and rule man's fate. The stars are "cold fires", for though they emit light of the highest intensity, no perceptible warmth reaches us. His newer astrology describes them [l. 677] as "soft splendours."' Cp. *Time* 52–6: 'All human grandeur fades away / Before their flashing, fiery, hollow eyes; / Beneath the terrible control / Of those vast armèd orbs, which roll / Oblivion on the creatures of a day.'

i *635. That . . . in*] Which is the despot of *H.MS.*

i *636–7. PL* vii 87–8: Heaven 'with moving Fires adornd / Innumerable'.

i *640. stormy*] *Not H.MS.*

i *641. hollow*] *Not H.MS.*

VI

Would die; for sullen-seeming Death may give
More life to Love than is or ever was
In our low world, where yet 'tis sweet to live.
Let no one ask me how it came to pass;
It seems that I am happy, that to me
A livelier emerald twinkles in the grass,
A purer sapphire melts into the sea.

VII

Not die; but live a life of truest breath,
And teach true life to fight with mortal wrongs.
O, why should Love, like men in drinking-songs,
Spice his fair banquet with the dust of death?
Make answer, Maud my bliss,
Maud made my Maud by that long loving kiss,
Life of my life, wilt thou not answer this?
'The dusky strand of Death inwoven here
With dear Love's tie, makes Love himself more dear.'

VIII

Is that enchanted moan only the swell
Of the long waves that roll in yonder bay?
And hark the clock within, the silver knell
Of twelve sweet hours that past in bridal white,
And died to live, long as my pulses play;
But now by this my love has closed her sight
And given false death her hand, and stolen away
To dreamful wastes where footless fancies dwell
Among the fragments of the golden day.
May nothing there her maiden grace affright!
Dear heart, I feel with thee the drowsy spell.
My bride to be, my evermore delight,
My own heart's heart, my ownest own, farewell;
It is but for a little space I go:

i *644–6*] *Not H.MS.*
i *651–61*] *Not H.MS.*
i *656. loving*] *1882*; lover's *1855–81.*
i *657.* Cp. *Life of the Life* (p. 504).
i *662. And . . . within*] The clock within strikes twelve *H.MS.*
i *663. that . . . bridal*] for ever marked with *H.MS.*
i *664*] And yet I scarce have heart to break the spell *H.MS.*
i *669. grace*] heart *H.MS.*
i *670*] *Not H.MS.*
i *672. own . . . heart*] life's own life *H.MS.* *my*] *1872*; and *1855–70.*

And ye meanwhile far over moor and fell
Beat to the noiseless music of the night!
Has our whole earth gone nearer to the glow
Of your soft splendours that you look so bright?
*I* have climbed nearer out of lonely Hell.
Beat, happy stars, timing with things below,
Beat with my heart more blest than heart can tell,
Blest, but for some dark undercurrent woe
That seems to draw–but it shall not be so:
Let all be well, be well.

## XIX

I

Her brother is coming back tonight,
Breaking up my dream of delight.

II

My dream? do I dream of bliss?
I have walked awake with Truth.
O when did a morning shine
So rich in atonement as this
For my dark-dawning youth,
Darkened watching a mother decline
And that dead man at her heart and mine:
For who was left to watch her but I?
Yet so did I let my freshness die.

III

I trust that I did not talk
To gentle Maud in our walk
(For often in lonely wanderings
I have cursed him even to lifeless things)
But I trust that I did not talk,
Not touch on her father's sin:
I am sure I did but speak
Of my mother's faded cheek
When it slowly grew so thin,
That I felt she was slowly dying
Vext with lawyers and harassed with debt:
For how often I caught her with eyes all wet,

i *674. moor*] fold *H.MS.*
i *677. you look*] they stream *H.MS.*
i *679. Beat, happy*] Beat on, true *H.MS.*
i *681–2*] But for some strange and unconjectured woe,
Some undercurrent–may it not be so: *H.MS*
i *684–786*] *1856; not 1855.*

Shaking her head at her son and sighing
A world of trouble within!

IV

And Maud too, Maud was moved
To speak of the mother she loved
As one scarce less forlorn,
Dying abroad and it seems apart
From him who had ceased to share her heart,
And ever mourning over the feud,
The household Fury sprinkled with blood
By which our houses are torn:
How strange was what she said,
When only Maud and the brother
Hung over her dying bed–
That Maud's dark father and mine
Had bound us one to the other,
Betrothed us over their wine,
On the day when Maud was born;
Sealed her mine from her first sweet breath.
Mine, mine by a right, from birth till death.
Mine, mine–our fathers have sworn.

V

But the true blood spilt had in it a heat
To dissolve the precious seal on a bond,

i *726* ∧ *7*] 'My blessing on the falling out
That all the more endears,
When we fall out with those we love
And kiss again with tears'
That is the song: I have heard it before:
Boy, I love not songs at the door:
*She* told you to sing at the house below?
*She* told you to sing me this!
Well, there is money: take it: go:
O God what a riddle it is. *H.MS*

An example of T.'s self-borrowing, since the song is from *The Princess*, i ∧ ii (p. 759). These four lines were part of the song in *The Princess* in *1850*; T. then dropped them from *1851* to *1861*, but restored them in *1862*. The present *Harvard* draft for *Maud* was considerably revised; it follows these lines with ll. 760–7 and then precedes l. 727 with:

Was he not bound the more
After the horrible end
Of the man that he called his friend,
By the promise sworn-to before?

That, if left uncancelled, had been so sweet;
And none of us thought of a something beyond,
A desire that awoke in the heart of the child,
As it were a duty done to the tomb,
To be friends for her sake, to be reconciled;
And I was cursing them and my doom,
And letting a dangerous thought run wild
While often abroad in the fragrant gloom
Of foreign churches–I see her there,
Bright English lily, breathing a prayer
To be friends, to be reconciled!

VI

But then what a flint is he!
Abroad, at Florence, at Rome,
I find whenever she touched on me
This brother had laughed her down,
And at last, when each came home,
He had darkened into a frown,
Chid her, and forbid her to speak
To me, her friend of the years before;
And this was what had reddened her cheek
When I bowed to her on the moor.

VII

Yet Maud, although not blind
To the faults of his heart and mind,
I see she cannot but love him,
And says he is rough but kind,
And wishes me to approve him,
And tells me, when she lay
Sick once, with a fear of worse,
That he left his wine and horses and play,
Sat with her, read to her, night and day,
And tended her like a nurse.

VIII

Kind? but the deathbed desire
Spurned by this heir of the liar–
Rough but kind? yet I know
He has plotted against me in this,
That he plots against me still.
Kind to Maud? that were not amiss.
Well, rough but kind; why let it be so:
For shall not Maud have her will?

IX

For, Maud, so tender and true,
As long as my life endures
I feel I shall owe you a debt,
That I never can hope to pay;
And if ever I should forget
That I owe this debt to you
And for your sweet sake to yours;
O then, what then shall I say?–
If ever I *should* forget,
May God make me more wretched
Than ever I have been yet!

X

So now I have sworn to bury
All this dead body of hate,
I feel so free and so clear
By the loss of that dead weight,
That I should grow light-headed, I fear,
Fantastically merry;
But that her brother comes, like a blight
On my fresh hope, to the Hall tonight.

## XX

I

Strange, that I felt so gay,
Strange, that *I* tried today
To beguile her melancholy;
The Sultan, as we name him,–
She did not wish to blame him–
But he vext her and perplext her
With his worldly talk and folly:
Was it gentle to reprove her
For stealing out of view
From a little lazy lover
Who but claims her as his due?
Or for chilling his caresses
By the coldness of her manners,
Nay, the plainness of her dresses?
Now I know her but in two,
Nor can pronounce upon it

i *790–91*] Because the lubber dandy *H.MS.*
i *792. But he*] Had *H.MS.*
i *794. Was it gentle*] Ah booby *H.MS.*

If one should ask me whether
The habit, hat, and feather,
Or the frock and gipsy bonnet
Be the neater and completer;
For nothing can be sweeter
Than maiden Maud in either.

II

But tomorrow, if we live,
Our ponderous squire will give
A grand political dinner
To half the squirelings near;
And Maud will wear her jewels,
And the bird of prey will hover,
And the titmouse hope to win her
With his chirrup at her ear.

III

A grand political dinner
To the men of many acres,
A gathering of the Tory,
A dinner and then a dance
For the maids and marriage-makers,
And every eye but mine will glance
At Maud in all her glory.

IV

For I am not invited,
But, with the Sultan's pardon,
I am all as well delighted,
For I know her own rose-garden,
And mean to linger in it
Till the dancing will be over;
And then, oh then, come out to me
For a minute, but for a minute,
Come out to your own true lover,
That your true lover may see
Your glory also, and render
All homage to his own darling,
Queen Maud in all her splendour.

## XXI

Rivulet crossing my ground,
And bringing me down from the Hall
This garden-rose that I found,

Forgetful of Maud and me,
And lost in trouble and moving round
Here at the head of a tinkling fall,
And trying to pass to the sea;
O Rivulet, born at the Hall,
My Maud has sent it by thee
(If I read her sweet will right)
On a blushing mission to me,
Saying in odour and colour, 'Ah, be
Among the roses tonight.'

## XXII

I

Come into the garden, Maud,
  For the black bat, night, has flown,
Come into the garden, Maud,
  I am here at the gate alone;
And the woodbine spices are wafted abroad,
  And the musk of the rose is blown.

II

For a breeze of morning moves,
  And the planet of Love is on high,
Beginning to faint in the light that she loves
  On a bed of daffodil sky,
To faint in the light of the sun she loves,
  To faint in his light, and to die.

III

All night have the roses heard
  The flute, violin, bassoon;

i *850–923.* The stanzaic and rhythmical likeness to Dryden was pointed out as long ago as 1873 (*Notes and Queries*, 4th series, xi 105); see his Song for *The Pilgrim*: 'Song of a Scholar and his Mistress, who being Cross'd by their Friends, fell Mad for one another; and now first meet in Bedlam'. Phyllis sings: 'Shall I Marry the Man I love? / And shall I conclude my Pains? / Now blest be the Powers above, / I feel the Blood bound in my Veins . . .' Phyllis has said 'For, like him, there is none'; cp. i 600, etc. Cp. *The Rosebud* (p. 635).

i *855. rose is*] *1872*; roses *1855–70.*

i *859.* Cp. 'One dark heron flew over the sea, backed by a daffodil sky' (Nov. 1853; *Mem.* i 365).

i *861. to*] *Not HnMS.*

All night has the casement jessamine stirred
To the dancers dancing in tune;
Till a silence fell with the waking bird,
And a hush with the setting moon.

IV

I said to the lily, 'There is but one
With whom she has heart to be gay.
When will the dancers leave her alone?
She is weary of dance and play.'
Now half to the setting moon are gone,
And half to the rising day;
Low on the sand and loud on the stone
The last wheel echoes away.

V

I said to the rose, 'The brief night goes
In babble and revel and wine.
O young lord-lover, what sighs are those,
For one that will never be thine?
But mine, but mine,' so I sware to the rose,
'For ever and ever, mine.'

VI

And the soul of the rose went into my blood,
As the music clashed in the hall;
And long by the garden lake I stood,
For I heard your rivulet fall
From the lake to the meadow and on to the wood,
Our wood, that is dearer than all;

VII

From the meadow your walks have left so sweet
That whenever a March-wind sighs

i *866. fell . . . waking*] came . . . morning *HnMS 1st reading* (*as below throughout*).
i *870*] O dancers leave my darling alone, *HnMS*.
i *873. rising*] breaking *HnMS*.
i *874. sand*] grass *HnMS*.
i *876–7*] 'O leave her a little to sweet repose.
You are merry with feast and wine. *HnMS*
i *878. sighs*] looks *HnMS*.
i *879. one*] a heart *HnMS*.
i *880. so I sware*] I said *HnMS*.
i *888. your . . . left*] you pace and have made *HnMS*.
i *889. whenever*] it sets when *HnMS*.

He sets the jewel-print of your feet
  In violets blue as your eyes,
To the woody hollows in which we meet
  And the valleys of Paradise.

VIII

The slender acacia would not shake
  One long milk-bloom on the tree;
The white lake-blossom fell into the lake
  As the pimpernel dozed on the lea;
But the rose was awake all night for your sake,
  Knowing your promise to me;
The lilies and roses were all awake,
  They sighed for the dawn and thee.

IX

Queen rose of the rosebud garden of girls,
  Come hither, the dances are done,
In gloss of satin and glimmer of pearls,
  Queen lily and rose in one;
Shine out, little head, sunning over with curls,
  To the flowers, and be their sun.

X

There has fallen a splendid tear
  From the passion-flower at the gate.
She is coming, my dove, my dear;
  She is coming, my life, my fate;
The red rose cries, 'She is near, she is near;'
  And the white rose weeps, 'She is late;'
The larkspur listens, 'I hear, I hear;'
  And the lily whispers, 'I wait.'

XI

She is coming, my own, my sweet;
  Were it ever so airy a tread,

i *890. He sets the*] The dewy *HnMS.*
i *896. white lake-*] water *HnMS.*
i *897. As the pimpernel*] The daisy *HnMS.*
i *898. all . . . your*] for thy sweet *HnMS.*
i *899. Knowing your*] And felt thy *HnMS.*
i *901. sighed for the*] waited for *HnMS.*
i *902. rosebud*] muskrose *HnMS.*
i *906. out,*] sweet *HnMS.*
i *916–23.* Cp. *To Rosa* i 6–8: 'But all my blood in time to thine shall

My heart would hear her and beat,
  Were it earth in an earthy bed;
My dust would hear her and beat,
  Had I lain for a century dead;
Would start and tremble under her feet,
  And blossom in purple and red.

## PART II

### I

I

'The fault was mine, the fault was mine'–
Why am I sitting here so stunned and still,
Plucking the harmless wild-flower on the hill?–
It is this guilty hand!–
And there rises ever a passionate cry
From underneath in the darkening land–
What is it, that has been done?
O dawn of Eden bright over earth and sky,
The fires of Hell brake out of thy rising sun,
The fires of Hell and of Hate;
For she, sweet soul, had hardly spoken a word,
When her brother ran in his rage to the gate,
He came with the babe-faced lord;
Heaped on her terms of disgrace,
And while she wept, and I strove to be cool,
He fiercely gave me the lie,
Till I with as fierce an anger spoke,
And he struck me, madman, over the face,
Struck me before the languid fool,
Who was gaping and grinning by:
Struck for himself an evil stroke;
Wrought for his house an irredeemable woe;
For front to front in an hour we stood,
And a million horrible bellowing echoes broke

beat, / Henceforth I lay my pride within the dust / And my whole heart is vassal at thy feet.' Cp. *My life is full* 8–10 (p. 351), and *The May Queen: New-Year's Eve* 31–2 (p. 420). The romantic prophecy in *Maud* is ironically answered in ii 239–58.

i *918. her*] it *HnMS.*

i *919. earth*] hushed *HnMS.* Cp. St Paul on the resurrection of the dead, *1 Corinthians* xv 47, 'The first man is of the earth, earthy: the second man is the Lord from heaven.'

i *920. her*] it *HnMS.*

ii *12.* Cp. *Edwin Morris* (p. 708).

From the red-ribbed hollow behind the wood,
And thundered up into Heaven the Christless code,
That must have life for a blow.
Ever and ever afresh they seemed to grow.
Was it he lay there with a fading eye?
'The fault was mine,' he whispered, 'fly!'
Then glided out of the joyous wood
The ghastly Wraith of one that I know;
And there rang on a sudden a passionate cry,
A cry for a brother's blood:
It will ring in my heart and my ears, till I die, till I die.

II

Is it gone? my pulses beat–
What was it? a lying trick of the brain?
Yet I thought I saw her stand,
A shadow there at my feet,
High over the shadowy land.
It is gone; and the heavens fall in a gentle rain,
When they should burst and drown with deluging storms
The feeble vassals of wine and anger and lust,
The little hearts that know not how to forgive:
Arise, my God, and strike, for we hold Thee just,
Strike dead the whole weak race of venomous worms,
That sting each other here in the dust;
We are not worthy to live.

## II

I

See what a lovely shell,
Small and pure as a pearl,
Lying close to my foot,
Frail, but a work divine,
Made so fairily well
With delicate spire and whorl,
How exquisitely minute,
A miracle of design!

II

What is it? a learned man
Could give it a clumsy name.

ii *49*. 'In Brittany. The shell undestroyed amid the storm perhaps symbolises to him his own first and highest nature preserved amid the storms of passion' (T.). This lyric had been written in the 1830s (see headnote).

Let him name it who can,
The beauty would be the same.

III

The tiny cell is forlorn,
Void of the little living will
That made it stir on the shore.
Did he stand at the diamond door
Of his house in a rainbow frill?
Did he push, when he was uncurled,
A golden foot or a fairy horn
Through his dim water-world?

IV

Slight, to be crushed with a tap
Of my finger-nail on the sand,
Small, but a work divine,
Frail, but of force to withstand,
Year upon year, the shock
Of cataract seas that snap
The three decker's oaken spine
Athwart the ledges of rock,
Here on the Breton strand!

V

Breton, not Briton; here
Like a shipwrecked man on a coast
Of ancient fable and fear–
Plagued with a flitting to and fro,
A disease, a hard mechanic ghost
That never came from on high
Nor ever arose from below,
But only moves with the moving eye,
Flying along the land and the main–
Why should it look like Maud?
Am I to be overawed
By what I cannot but know
Is a juggle born of the brain?

ii *67–8*. Cp. Keats, *Endymion* iii 101–3: 'A moon-beam to the deep, deep water-world, / To find Endymion. On gold sand impearl'd / With lily shells, and pebbles milky white . . .'.
ii *82, 90*. Adapted from *Oh! that 'twere possible* 83–4 (1837): 'By a dull mechanic ghost / And a juggle of the brain.' See l. 141*n*.

VI

Back from the Breton coast,
Sick of a nameless fear,
Back to the dark sea-line
Looking, thinking of all I have lost;
An old song vexes my ear;
But that of Lamech is mine.

VII

For years, a measureless ill,
For years, for ever, to part–
But she, she would love me still;
And as long, O God, as she
Have a grain of love for me,
So long, no doubt, no doubt,
Shall I nurse in my dark heart,
However weary, a spark of will
Not to be trampled out.

VIII

Strange, that the mind, when fraught
With a passion so intense
One would think that it well
Might drown all life in the eye,–
That it should, by being so overwrought,
Suddenly strike on a sharper sense
For a shell, or a flower, little things
Which else would have been past by!
And now I remember, I,
When he lay dying there,
I noticed one of his many rings
(For he had many, poor worm) and thought
It is his mother's hair.

IX

Who knows if he be dead?
Whether I need have fled?
Am I guilty of blood?
However this may be,
Comfort her, comfort her, all things good,
While I am over the sea!

ii *92. nameless fear*: *The Vision of Sin* 52, MS.
ii *96.* T. cites *Genesis* iv 23, 'I have slain a man to my wounding, and a young man to my hurt.'

Let me and my passionate love go by,
But speak to her all things holy and high,
Whatever happen to me!
Me and my harmful love go by;
But come to her waking, find her asleep,
Powers of the height, Powers of the deep,
And comfort her though I die.

## III

Courage, poor heart of stone!
I will not ask thee why
Thou canst not understand
That thou art left for ever alone:
Courage, poor stupid heart of stone.–
Or if I ask thee why,
Care not thou to reply:
She is but dead, and the time is at hand
When thou shalt more than die.

## IV

### I

O that 'twere possible
After long grief and pain
To find the arms of my true love
Round me once again!

### II

When I was wont to meet her
In the silent woody places
By the home that gave me birth,

ii *132–40*] *1856*; *not 1855*. T.'s wife Emily told Edward Lear that this ('the saddest possible little poem') was written on 30 Aug. 1855 (*Lincoln*). But the sadness is tempered by *Ezekiel* xi 19: 'And I will give them one heart, and I will put a new spirit within you; and I will take the stony heart out of their flesh, and will give them an heart of flesh.' Cp. i 268.
i *141–238*. This section, 'O that 'twere possible', was written 1833–4, and published 1837 (see p. 598). All variants from *Heath MS* (two drafts, *A*, *B*) and from *1837* are given below. (Unless differentiated, *1837* subsumes *Heath MS A-B* in the following notes.) The links with *In Memoriam* have often been noticed; see G. O. Marshall, *PMLA* lxxviii (1963) 225–9. The opening resembles the famous early sixteenth-century lyric: 'Westron winde, when wilt thou blow, / The smalle raine downe can raine? / Christ if my love were in my armes, / And I in my bed againe.'
ii *147*. *By the home*] *1856*; Of the land *1837*, *1855*.

We stood tranced in long embraces
Mixt with kisses sweeter sweeter
Than anything on earth.

III

A shadow flits before me,
Not thou, but like to thee:
Ah Christ, that it were possible
For one short hour to see
The souls we loved, that they might tell us
What and where they be.

IV

It leads me forth at evening,
It lightly winds and steals
In a cold white robe before me,
When all my spirit reels
At the shouts, the leagues of lights,
And the roaring of the wheels.

V

Half the night I waste in sighs,
Half in dreams I sorrow after
The delight of early skies;
In a wakeful doze I sorrow
For the hand, the lips, the eyes,
For the meeting of the morrow,
The delight of happy laughter,
The delight of low replies.

ii *151.* Shelley, *Hellas* 716–7: 'What shadow flits / Before?'

ii *153. Christ*] *Heath A-B*; God *1837*. In 'Tennyson and Musset' (1881), Swinburne compared these lines with Webster's *Duchess of Malfi* IV ii 20–24: 'O that it were possible we might / But hold some two days' conference with the dead, / From them I should learn somewhat, I am sure / I never shall know here:–I'll tell thee a miracle– / I am not mad yet, to my cause of sorrow.'

ii *157–62*] *Not Heath A.*

ii *158. It*] And *Heath B.*

ii *164*] *Heath A-B*; *not 1837*. *Half*] Or *Heath A 1st reading.*

ii *165*] Her hands, her lips, her eyes, *Heath A*; The hand, the lips, the eyes, *Heath B*; *not 1837*.

ii *166–7*] *Not Heath A-B (see l. 165n).*

ii *168*] *Not Heath A-B.* *the morrow*] tomorrow *1837*.

ii *169*] The [Her *Heath A*] winsome laughter. *Heath B.*

ii *170*] *Not Heath A-B.* *low replies*: *Life of the Life* 8.

VI

'Tis a morning pure and sweet,
And a dewy splendour falls
On the little flower that clings
To the turrets and the walls;
'Tis a morning pure and sweet,
And the light and shadow fleet;
She is walking in the meadow,
And the woodland echo rings;
In a moment we shall meet;
She is singing in the meadow
And the rivulet at her feet
Ripples on in light and shadow
To the ballad that she sings.

VII

Do I hear her sing as of old,
My bird with the shining head,
My own dove with the tender eye?
But there rings on a sudden a passionate cry,
There is some one dying or dead,
And a sullen thunder is rolled;
For a tumult shakes the city,
And I wake, my dream is fled;
In the shuddering dawn, behold,
Without knowledge, without pity,
By the curtains of my bed
That abiding phantom cold.

ii *171–83*] *Not 1837.*
ii *172. a dewy splendour*: Shelley, *Witch of Atlas* 78, which goes on to describe 'A lovely lady garmented in light'.
ii *176.* Cp. *Mariana in the South* 40, MS: 'That never felt the shadow fleet'.
ii *184–90*] Do [And *Heath A-B*] I hear the pleasant ditty,
That I heard her [She was wont to *Heath A*] chant of old?
*1837*

*I hear*] the sound of *Heath A 1st reading.*
ii *189. sullen thunder*: Shelley, *Revolt of Islam* VI xlv 5.
ii *191. And*] But *1837.*
ii *192. shuddering*] glimmering *Heath A.* *dawn*] grey *Heath A-B. 1837* transposes ll. 192, 193; the original order in *Heath MS* was: 191, 192, 194, 193, 195.
ii *195. abiding*] dreadful *Heath A-B.*

VIII

Get thee hence, nor come again,
Mix not memory with doubt,
Pass, thou deathlike type of pain,
Pass and cease to move about!
'Tis the blot upon the brain
That *will* show itself without.

IX

Then I rise, the eavedrops fall,
And the yellow vapours choke
The great city sounding wide;
The day comes, a dull red ball
Wrapt in drifts of lurid smoke
On the misty river-tide.

X

Through the hubbub of the market
I steal, a wasted frame,
It crosses here, it crosses there,
Through all that crowd confused and loud,
The shadow still the same;
And on my heavy eyelids
My anguish hangs like shame.

XI

Alas for her that met me,
That heard me softly call,
Came glimmering through the laurels
At the quiet evenfall,
In the garden by the turrets
Of the old manorial hall.

ii *196–207*] *Not Heath A. 1837* (unlike *Heath B*) places ll. 196–201 after l.238.
ii *197, 199*] *Transposed in 1837* (*unlike Heath B*).
ii *197. Mix not*] Mixing *Heath B.*
ii *198.* Cp. *In Memoriam* lxxviii 14 (*1850* reading): 'type of pain'.
ii *200.* Cp. *In Memoriam* xcii 1–3: 'If any vision should reveal / Thy likeness, I might count it vain / As but the canker of the brain.'
ii *205. The*] And *Heath B.*
ii *206. Wrapt in drifts*] In a drift *Heath B.* *lurid smoke*: Shelley, *Prometheus Unbound* II iv 151.
ii *208. the hubbub of the market*: *The Ante-Chamber* 21.
ii *210. crosses . . . crosses*] crosseth . . . crosseth *1837.*
ii *215–20*] *Not Heath A.*

XII

Would the happy spirit descend,
From the realms of light and song,
In the chamber or the street,
As she looks among the blest,
Should I fear to greet my friend
Or to say 'Forgive the wrong,'
Or to ask her, 'Take me, sweet,
To the regions of thy rest'?

XIII

But the broad light glares and beats,
And the shadow flits and fleets
And will not let me be;
And I loathe the squares and streets,
And the faces that one meets,
Hearts with no love for me:
Always I long to creep
Into some still cavern deep,
There to weep, and weep, and weep
My whole soul out to thee.

## V

I

Dead, long dead,
Long dead!
And my heart is a handful of dust,
And the wheels go over my head,

ii *221–8*] *Not Heath A–B*; *1837* after l. 220 runs: 229–38, 196–201, 221–8 (but omitting 222 and 226); it then adds a further thirty-four lines (see p. 601).
ii *228. regions*] region *1837*.
ii *229–31*] *Not Heath A*.
ii *229. But the*] The *Heath B*; Then the *1837*.
ii *230. shadow*] sunk eye *1837*.
ii *232. And*] *Not 1837*.
ii *236. Into*] To *1837*.
ii *237. There to*] And *Heath A–B*; And to *1837*.
ii *238*. Cp. *Song* [*A spirit haunts*] 16: 'My very heart faints and my whole soul grieves'.
ii *239 ff.* 'About the mad-scene one of the best-known doctors for the insane wrote that it was "the most faithful representation of madness since

And my bones are shaken with pain,
For into a shallow grave they are thrust,
Only a yard beneath the street,
And the hoofs of the horses beat, beat,
The hoofs of the horses beat,
Beat into my scalp and my brain,
With never an end to the stream of passing feet,
Driving, hurrying, marrying, burying,
Clamour and rumble, and ringing and clatter,
And here beneath it is all as bad,
For I thought the dead had peace, but it is not so;
To have no peace in the grave, is that not sad?
But up and down and to and fro,
Ever about me the dead men go;
And then to hear a dead man chatter
Is enough to drive one mad.

II

Wretchedest age, since Time began,
They cannot even bury a man;
And though we paid our tithes in the days that are gone,
Not a bell was rung, not a prayer was read;
It is that which makes us loud in the world of the dead;
There is none that does his work, not one;
A touch of their office might have sufficed,
But the churchmen fain would kill their church,
As the churches have killed their Christ.

Shakespeare' (*Mem.* i 398). Campbell's *The Death-Boat of Heligoland* (written 1828) begins: 'Can restlessness reach the cold sepulchred head?– / Ay, the quick have their sleep-walkers, so have the dead. / There are brains, though they moulder, that dream in the tomb, / And that maddening forehear the last trumpet of doom.' The eleventh line of Campbell's poem says: 'The foam of the Baltic had sparkled like fire'; cp. iii 51. J. C. Maxwell compares *The Old Curiosity Shop*, chapter I: 'That constant pacing to and fro, that never-ending restlessness, that incessant tread of feet wearing the rough stones smooth and glossy–is it not a wonder how the dwellers in narrow ways can bear to hear it! Think of a sick man . . . think of the hum and noise being always present to his senses, and of the stream of life that will not stop, pouring on, on, on, through all his restless dreams, as if he were condemned to lie, dead but conscious, in a noisy churchyard, and had no hope of rest for centuries to come!'

ii *241*. Cp. *The Lotos-Eaters* 113: 'Two handfuls of white dust, shut in an urn of brass'.

ii *257*. Cp. *The Coach of Death* 95: 'The chattering of the fleshless jaws'.

III

See, there is one of us sobbing,
No limit to his distress;
And another, a lord of all things, praying
To his own great self, as I guess;
And another, a statesman there, betraying
His party-secret, fool, to the press;
And yonder a vile physician, blabbing
The case of his patient–all for what?
To tickle the maggot born in an empty head,
And wheedle a world that loves him not,
For it is but a world of the dead.

IV

Nothing but idiot gabble!
For the prophecy given of old
And then not understood,
Has come to pass as foretold;
Not let any man think for the public good,
But babble, merely for babble.
For I never whispered a private affair
Within the hearing of cat or mouse,
No, not to myself in the closet alone,
But I heard it shouted at once from the top of the house;
Everything came to be known.
Who told *him* we were there?

V

Not that gray old wolf, for he came not back
From the wilderness, full of wolves, where he used to lie;
He has gathered the bones for his o'ergrown whelp to
    crack;
Crack them now for yourself, and howl, and die.

ii *274–5*. Possibly recalling Dr Allen; in Allen's *Essay on the Classification of the Insane* (*Lincoln*, 1837), Case No. 22 is one 'whose mind was instantly wrecked by the female of his heart unexpectedly marrying another the very day previous to that on which she had promised to be made his own for ever'.

ii *287–8*. *Luke* xii 3: 'Therefore whatsoever ye have spoken in darkness shall be heard in the light; and that which ye have spoken in the ear in closets shall be proclaimed upon the house-tops.'

ii *291*. See i 471.

ii *294*. 'For his son is, he thinks, dead' (T.).

VI

Prophet, curse me the blabbing lip,
And curse me the British vermin, the rat;
I know not whether he came in the Hanover ship,
But I know that he lies and listens mute
In an ancient mansion's crannies and holes:
Arsenic, arsenic, sure, would do it,
Except that now we poison our babes, poor souls!
It is all used up for that.

VII

Tell him now: she is standing here at my head;
Not beautiful now, not even kind;
He may take her now; for she never speaks her mind,
But is ever the one thing silent here.
She is not *of* us, as I divine;
She comes from another stiller world of the dead,
Stiller, not fairer than mine.

VIII

But I know where a garden grows,
Fairer than aught in the world beside,
All made up of the lily and rose
That blow by night, when the season is good,
To the sound of dancing music and flutes:
It is only flowers, they had no fruits,
And I almost fear they are not roses, but blood;
For the keeper was one, so full of pride,
He linkt a dead man there to a spectral bride;
For he, if he had not been a Sultan of brutes,
Would he have that hole in his side?

IX

But what will the old man say?
He laid a cruel snare in a pit

ii *296–7.* 'The Norwegian rat has driven out the old English rat' (T.). H.T. adds: 'The Jacobites asserted that the brown Norwegian rat came to England with the House of Hanover, 1714, and hence called it "the Hanover rat".'

ii *300. sure*] *1856*; sir *1855*. Cp. *Lear* IV vi 89–90: 'Peace, peace; this piece of toasted cheese will do it'.

ii *301. babes*] wives *trial edition*.

ii *318. dead man*: 'himself in his fancy' (T.).

ii *319. a Sultan*] the prince *trial edition*.

To catch a friend of mine one stormy day;
Yet now I could even weep to think of it;
For what will the old man say
When he comes to the second corpse in the pit?

X

Friend, to be struck by the public foe,
Then to strike him and lay him low,
That were a public merit, far,
Whatever the Quaker holds, from sin;
But the red life spilt for a private blow–
I swear to you, lawful and lawless war
Are scarcely even akin.

XI

O me, why have they not buried me deep enough?
Is it kind to have made me a grave so rough,
Me, that was never a quiet sleeper?
Maybe still I am but half-dead;
Then I cannot be wholly dumb;
I will cry to the steps above my head
And somebody, surely, some kind heart will come
To bury me, bury me
Deeper, ever so little deeper.

## PART III

### VI

I

My life has crept so long on a broken wing
Through cells of madness, haunts of horror and fear,
That I come to be grateful at last for a little thing:
My mood is changed, for it fell at a time of year
When the face of night is fair on the dewy downs,

ii *334–42*. See i *916–23n*.

iii 'Sane, but shattered. Written when the cannon was heard booming from the battleships in the Solent before the Crimean War' (T.). When T. made the division for Part III in *1865*, he did not start again with the numbering of sections, as he had with Part II; this may have been an omission, but it has the effect of linking Parts II and III more closely than I and II.

iii *2. cells of madness*: *The Two Voices* 371.

And the shining daffodil dies, and the Charioteer
And starry Gemini hang like glorious crowns
Over Orion's grave low down in the west,
That like a silent lightning under the stars
She seemed to divide in a dream from a band of the blest,
And spoke of a hope for the world in the coming wars–
'And in that hope, dear soul, let trouble have rest,
Knowing I tarry for thee,' and pointed to Mars
As he glowed like a ruddy shield on the Lion's breast.

II

And it was but a dream, yet it yielded a dear delight
To have looked, though but in a dream, upon eyes so fair,
That had been in a weary world my one thing bright;
And it was but a dream, yet it lightened my despair
When I thought that a war would arise in defence of the right,
That an iron tyranny now should bend or cease,
The glory of manhood stand on his ancient height,
Nor Britain's one sole God be the millionaire:
No more shall commerce be all in all, and Peace
Pipe on her pastoral hillock a languid note,
And watch her harvest ripen, her herd increase,
Nor the cannon-bullet rust on a slothful shore,
And the cobweb woven across the cannon's throat
Shall shake its threaded tears in the wind no more.

III

And as months ran on and rumour of battle grew,
'It is time, it is time, O passionate heart,' said I
(For I cleaved to a cause that I felt to be pure and true),
'It is time, O passionate heart and morbid eye,
That old hysterical mock-disease should die.'

iii *6. shining daffodil*] sweet Narcissus *trial edition.*

iii *13–14.* T. wrote, 17 March 1854 (*Trinity College*): 'A boy was born last night–a stout little fellow. Mars was culminating in the Lion–does that mean soldiership?' The Lion represents Britain.

iii *19 ff.* For war in a just cause as contrasted with despairing self-absorption, cp. *The Two Voices* 124–56 (p. 528).

And I stood on a giant deck and mixed my breath
With a loyal people shouting a battle cry,
Till I saw the dreary phantom arise and fly
Far into the North, and battle, and seas of death.

IV

Let it go or stay, so I wake to the higher aims
Of a land that has lost for a little her lust of gold,
And love of a peace that was full of wrongs and shames,
Horrible, hateful, monstrous, not to be told;
And hail once more to the banner of battle unrolled!
Though many a light shall darken, and many shall weep
For those that are crushed in the clash of jarring claims,
Yet God's just wrath shall be wreaked on a giant liar;
And many a darkness into the light shall leap,
And shine in the sudden making of splendid names,
And noble thought be freër under the sun,
And the heart of a people beat with one desire;
For the peace, that I deemed no peace, is over and done,
And now by the side of the Black and the Baltic deep,
And deathful-grinning mouths of the fortress, flames
The blood-red blossom of war with a heart of fire.

V

Let it flame or fade, and the war roll down like a wind,
We have proved we have hearts in a cause, we are noble still,

iii *36*. As G. O. Marshall points out, Maud's ghost takes a dual form; the 'ghastly Wraith' of ii 32, 82, 90, and the blessed spirit of iii 10.

iii *45*. *wrath*] *1856*; doom *1855*.

iii *50*. *peace . . . no*] *1856*; long, long canker of *1855*. The original reading had been deplored by *Tait's Edinburgh Magazine*, Sept. 1855: 'If any man comes forward to say or sing that the slaughter of 30,000 Englishmen in the Crimea tends to prevent women poisoning their babies, for the sake of the burial fees, in Birmingham, he is bound to show cause, and not bewilder our notions of morals and of lexicography by calling thirty years of intermitted war (absolute peace we have *not* had during the interval) a "long, long *canker* of peace".'

iii *54–59*] *1856*; *not 1855*. A British Museum copy of *1855* (first American edition) has cancelled drafts of this last stanza, which show T. attempting to relate the war to the love for Maud:

Let it go or stay, so I walk henceforth resigned
By the light of a love not lost, with a purer mind
And rejoice in my native land, and am one with my kind.

Also: 'And I rise from a life half-lost with a better mind . . .'

And myself have awaked, as it seems, to the better
    mind;
It is better to fight for the good than to rail at the ill;
I have felt with my native land, I am one with my
    kind,
I embrace the purpose of God, and the doom assigned.

# 317 The Letters

Published *1855*. The last stanza, probably the germ of the poem, had originally been part of *The Miller's Daughter* (*1832*; see p. 378). Expanded 1853–5, judging from *H.Nbk 27* and from *Mat.* ii 133–4, where it was inadvertently printed as an unpublished poem, *Marriage Bells*. This omitted ll. 17–24, 29–36, and so had no mention of 'The Letters'. Rader (p. 132) links the poem with T.'s break with Rosa Baring in 1836–7, which may perhaps be supported by its appearing in *Mat.* in the chapter on *Maud*, a poem certainly linked with Rosa.

I

Still on the tower stood the vane,
    A black yew gloomed the stagnant air,
I peered athwart the chancel pane
    And saw the altar cold and bare.
A clog of lead was round my feet,
    A band of pain across my brow;
'Cold altar, Heaven and earth shall meet
    Before you hear my marriage vow.'

II

I turned and hummed a bitter song
    That mocked the wholesome human heart,
And then we met in wrath and wrong,
    We met, but only meant to part.
Full cold my greeting was and dry;
    She faintly smiled, she hardly moved;
I saw with half-unconscious eye
    She wore the colours I approved.

III

She took the little ivory chest,
    With half a sigh she turned the key,
Then raised her head with lips comprest,
    And gave my letters back to me.

¶317. 2. *the stagnant air*: Shelley, *Revolt of Islam* IX xxxii 7.

And gave the trinkets and the rings,
My gifts, when gifts of mine could please;
As looks a father on the things
Of his dead son, I looked on these.

IV

She told me all her friends had said;
I raged against the public liar;
She talked as if her love were dead,
But in my words were seeds of fire.
'No more of love; your sex is known:
I never will be twice deceived.
Henceforth I trust the man alone,
The woman cannot be believed.

V

'Through slander, meanest spawn of Hell—
And women's slander is the worst,
And you, whom once I loved so well,
Through you, my life will be accurst.'
I spoke with heart, and heat and force,
I shook her breast with vague alarms—
Like torrents from a mountain source
We rushed into each other's arms.

VI

We parted: sweetly gleamed the stars,
And sweet the vapour-braided blue,
Low breezes fanned the belfry bars,
As homeward by the church I drew.
The very graves appeared to smile,
So fresh they rose in shadowed swells;
'Dark porch,' I said, 'and silent aisle,
There comes a sound of marriage bells.'

## 318 *'Harp, harp, the voice of Cymry'

Unpublished. From *H.Lpr 85*, where it appears with lines from *Geraint and Enid*, suggesting 1856: 'In July and August my father and mother took us children to Wales, and here *Enid* was all but finished' (*Mem.* i 415). T. climbed Cader Idris: 'I heard the roar of waters, streams and cataracts' (cp. ll. 9–11), his wife noted.

Harp, harp, the voice of Cymry,
Voice, whose music yet prevails,
Honour to the Head of Britain,
Honour to our Queen of Wales.
Speak, speak, thou land of Aedd,
Land of stream and mountain peak,
Land of Arthur and Taliessin,
Land of old Aneurin, speak.
Speak, speak ye mountain voices,
Cataracts breaking down the vales,
Caer Eryri, Cader Idris,
Honour to our Queen of Wales!
Hers, hers the men of Cymry,
High on hill or low on plain,
Praying God to guard and guide her,
Guide and guard her long to reign.
Red, red the blood of Cymry
Flows through all her mountain-dales,
Red with life and rich in loyalty
Runs the noble blood of Wales.

[1857. *The Marriage of Geraint*, *Geraint and Enid*, and *Merlin and Vivien* – see pp. 1525, 1551, 1593]

# 319 Sea Dreams

Published *Macmillan's Magazine*, Jan. 1860, with the subtitle *An Idyll*; then *1864*. Written Dec. 1857 (*Mat.* ii 191), probably revised 1858 (*Mem.* i 429). Walter White referred to it as *The Three Clerks*, 11 Nov. 1859 (*Journals*, 1898, p. 150). It is based on T.'s disastrous investing in 1840 of his whole fortune of £3,000 (*CT*, p. 186), in a wood-carving scheme floated by Dr Matthew Allen. By 1843 it was all lost, which precipitated T.'s intense

¶318. *1. Cymry*: ancient name of Wales; the harp, the hereditary instrument of the Bards.

*5. Aedd*: Edward Davies, *Mythology of the British Druids* (1809), pp. 243–4, refers to '*Aedd the Great*, a mystical personage'. T. was given a copy of Davies in 1846 (*Lincoln*).

*7. Taliessin*: sixth-century Bard; used by T. as a pseudonym when publishing *Suggested by Reading*.

*8. Aneurin*: sixth-century Bard.

*11. Caer Eryri*: Snowdon, where the babe Arthur was found (*Gareth and Lynette* 490). *Cader Idris*: one of the highest mountains in N. Wales, frequently mentioned in literature and legend.

depression. In 1845 Allen, whose life had been insured in T.'s favour, died of heart disease. The recurring religious concern derives from T.'s indignation that Allen should have been the author of *On the Temper and Spirit of the Christian Religion* (1820; 2nd edn, 1831, *On the Graces of the Christian Character ... and Christian Forbearance*); see ll. 184–93. There are many similarities to Theocritus xxi, on poverty and dreams. Two people wake from sleep at night beside the sea. One, who is troubled by poverty, tells a dream about catching a golden fish. He is advised by the other to 'Go seek the fish of flesh and blood, or you will die of hunger and golden visions.' Theocritus's poem begins: 'There is but one stirrer-up of the crafts, Diophantus, and her name is Poverty. She is the true teacher of labour; for a man of toil may not so much as sleep for the disquietude of his heart. Nay, if he nod ever so little o'nights, then is his slumber broke suddenly short by the cares that beset him.' T.'s original subtitle, *An Idyll*, would suggest Theocritus. His note on *Sea Dreams* was: 'The glorification of honest labour, whether of head or hand, no hasting to be rich, no bowing down to any idol'.

A city clerk, but gently born and bred;
His wife, an unknown artist's orphan child—
One babe was theirs, a Margaret, three years old:
They, thinking that her clear germander eye
Droopt in the giant-factoried city-gloom,
Came, with a month's leave given them, to the sea:
For which his gains were docked, however small:
Small were his gains, and hard his work; besides,
Their slender household fortunes (for the man
Had risked his little) like the little thrift,
Trembled in perilous places o'er a deep:
And oft, when sitting all alone, his face
Would darken, as he cursed his credulousness,
And that one unctuous mouth which lured him, rogue,
To buy strange shares in some Peruvian mine.
Now seaward-bound for health they gained a coast,
All sand and cliff and deep-inrunning cave,
At close of day; slept, woke, and went the next,
The Sabbath, pious variers from the church,
To chapel; where a heated pulpiteer,

¶319. *4. germander*: blue speedwell (T.).

*8. Small . . . gains*] *1864*; His gains were small *1860*.

*10. thrift*: a plant whose native home is on the grassy tops of cliffs. Here it is punningly apt, though originally this simile was jotted down at Torquay (*Mem.* i 465); cp. ll. 55–6*n*.

*15. strange*] *1864*; wild *1860*.

*20–31.* J. H. Buckley (p. 139) shows that T. was probably thinking of the

Not preaching simple Christ to simple men,
Announced the coming doom, and fulminated
Against the scarlet woman and her creed;
For sideways up he swung his arms, and shrieked
'Thus, thus with violence,' even as if he held
The Apocalyptic millstone, and himself
Were that great Angel; 'Thus with violence
Shall Babylon be cast into the sea;
Then comes the close.' The gentle-hearted wife
Sat shuddering at the ruin of a world;
He at his own: but when the wordy storm
Had ended, forth they came and paced the shore,
Ran in and out the long sea-framing caves,
Drank the large air, and saw, but scarce believed
(The sootflake of so many a summer still
Clung to their fancies) that they saw, the sea.
So now on sand they walked, and now on cliff,
Lingering about the thymy promontories,
Till all the sails were darkened in the west,
And rosed in the east: then homeward and to bed:
Where she, who kept a tender Christian hope,
Haunting a holy text, and still to that
Returning, as the bird returns, at night,
'Let not the sun go down upon your wrath,'
Said, 'Love, forgive him:' but he did not speak;
And silenced by that silence lay the wife,
Remembering her dear Lord who died for all,
And musing on the little lives of men,
And how they mar this little by their feuds.

But while the two were sleeping, a full tide
Rose with ground-swell, which, on the foremost rocks
Touching, upjetted in spirts of wild sea-smoke,

influential anti-Romanist preacher John Cumming, whom George Eliot had attacked as 'Boanerges' (l. 243) for his denunciations of 'the scarlet whore'. She contrasted the charity of *In Memoriam* (*Westminster Review*, Oct. 1855). T. used to ridicule Cumming (*Mem.* i 265). With this passage, cp. the religious violence in *Despair* (p. 1299).

*25–6. Revelation* xviii 21.

*32. came*] *1864*; moved *1860*. *shore*] *1864*; sand *1860*.

*34. large air*: T. cites *Aeneid* vi 640: *largior . . . aether*.

*38.* Cp. Shelley's seascape, *Revolt of Islam* VII xl 2: 'Which round some thymy cape will lag'.

*39. Till all*] *1864*; Until *1860*.

*44. Ephesians* iv 26.

*47. her*] *1864*; our *1860*.

And scaled in sheets of wasteful foam, and fell
In vast sea-cataracts—ever and anon
Dead claps of thunder from within the cliffs
Heard through the living roar. At this the babe,
Their Margaret cradled near them, wailed and woke
The mother, and the father suddenly cried,
'A wreck, a wreck!' then turned, and groaning said,

'Forgive! How many will say, "forgive," and find
A sort of absolution in the sound
To hate a little longer! No; the sin
That neither God nor man can well forgive,
Hypocrisy, I saw it in him at once.
Is it so true that second thoughts are best?
Not first, and third, which are a riper first?
Too ripe, too late! they come too late for use.
Ah love, there surely lives in man and beast
Something divine to warn them of their foes:
And such a sense, when first I fronted him,
Said, "Trust him not;" but after, when I came
To know him more, I lost it, knew him less;
Fought with what seemed my own uncharity;
Sat at his table; drank his costly wines;
Made more and more allowance for his talk;
Went further, fool! and trusted him with all,
All my poor scrapings from a dozen years
Of dust and deskwork: there is no such mine,
None; but a gulf of ruin, swallowing gold,
Not making. Ruined! ruined! the sea roars
Ruin: a fearful night!'
'Not fearful; fair,'
Said the good wife, 'if every star in heaven
Can make it fair: you do but hear the tide.
Had you ill dreams?'
'O yes,' he said, 'I dreamed
Of such a tide swelling toward the land,
And I from out the boundless outer deep
Swept with it to the shore, and entered one
Of those dark caves that run beneath the cliffs.

55–6. *claps . . . roar*: a separate jotting observed at Valencia (*Mem.* i 466); cp. l. 10*n*.

65–6] *1864*; It is not true that second thoughts are best,
But first, and third, which are a riper first; *1860*

70. *fronted*] *1864*; lighted on *1860*.

85–6. T. was to recast these phrases for *Crossing the Bar* (p. 1458).

I thought the motion of the boundless deep
Bore through the cave, and I was heaved upon it
In darkness: then I saw one lovely star
Larger and larger. "What a world," I thought,
"To live in!" but in moving on I found
Only the landward exit of the cave,
Bright with the sun upon the stream beyond:
And near the light a giant woman sat,
All over earthy, like a piece of earth,
A pickaxe in her hand: then out I slipt
Into a land all sun and blossom, trees
As high as heaven, and every bird that sings:
And here the night-light flickering in my eyes
Awoke me.'
'That was then your dream,' she said,
'Not sad, but sweet.'
'So sweet, I lay,' said he,
'And mused upon it, drifting up the stream
In fancy, till I slept again, and pieced
The broken vision; for I dreamed that still
The motion of the great deep bore me on,
And that the woman walked upon the brink:
I wondered at her strength, and asked her of it:
"It came," she said, "by working in the mines:"
O then to ask her of my shares, I thought;
And asked; but not a word; she shook her head.
And then the motion of the current ceased,
And there was rolling thunder; and we reached
A mountain, like a wall of burs and thorns;
But she with her strong feet up the steep hill
Trod out a path: I followed; and at top
She pointed seaward: there a fleet of glass,
That seemed a fleet of jewels under me,
Sailing along before a gloomy cloud
That not one moment ceased to thunder, past
In sunshine: right across its track there lay,
Down in the water, a long reef of gold,
Or what seemed gold: and I was glad at first
To think that in our often-ransacked world
Still so much gold was left; and then I feared
Lest the gay navy there should splinter on it,
And fearing waved my arm to warn them off;
An idle signal, for the brittle fleet

*97. 1 Corinthians* xv 47, 'The first man is of the earth, earthy'.
*127. the*] *1864*; that *1860*.

(I thought I could have died to save it) neared,
Touched, clinked, and clashed, and vanished, and I woke,
I heard the clash so clearly. Now I see
My dream was Life; the woman honest Work;
And my poor venture but a fleet of glass
Wrecked on a reef of visionary gold.'

'Nay,' said the kindly wife to comfort him,
'You raised your arm, you tumbled down and broke
The glass with little Margaret's medicine in it;
And, breaking that, you made and broke your dream:
A trifle makes a dream, a trifle breaks.'

'No trifle,' groaned the husband; 'yesterday
I met him suddenly in the street, and asked
That which I asked the woman in my dream.
Like her, he shook his head. "Show me the books!"
He dodged me with a long and loose account.
"The books, the books!" but he, he could not wait,
Bound on a matter he of life and death:
When the great Books (see Daniel seven and ten)
Were opened, I should find he meant me well;
And then began to bloat himself, and ooze
All over with the fat affectionate smile
That makes the widow lean. "My dearest friend,
Have faith, have faith! We live by faith," said he;
"And all things work together for the good
Of those"—it makes me sick to quote him—last
Gript my hand hard, and with God-bless-you went.
I stood like one that had received a blow:
I found a hard friend in his loose accounts,
A loose one in the hard grip of his hand,
A curse in his God-bless-you: then my eyes
Pursued him down the street, and far away,
Among the honest shoulders of the crowd,

*148. seven and ten*] *1864*; seven, the tenth *1860*. *Daniel* vii 10: 'the judgment was set, and the books were opened.' The religious phrases relate the rogue to the preacher, and were apt to Allen (see headnote); cp. ll. 184–93.

*150–1.* Like Gama in *The Princess* v 231–2, who 'oozed / All o'er with honeyed answer'.

*152.* Christ attacked those 'which devour widows' houses, and for a pretence make long prayers', *Mark* xii 40.

*153. Romans* i 17: 'The just shall live by faith'.

*154. Romans* viii 28: 'And we know that all things work together for good, to them that love God.'

Read rascal in the motions of his back,
And scoundrel in the supple-sliding knee.'
'Was he so bound, poor soul?' said the good wife;
'So are we all: but do not call him, love,
Before you prove him, rogue, and proved, forgive.
His gain is loss; for he that wrongs his friend
Wrongs himself more, and ever bears about
A silent court of justice in his breast,
Himself the judge and jury, and himself
The prisoner at the bar, ever condemned:
And that drags down his life: then comes what comes
Hereafter: and he meant, he said he meant,
Perhaps he meant, or partly meant, you well.'

'"With all his conscience and one eye askew"—
Love, let me quote these lines, that you may learn
A man is likewise counsel for himself,
Too often, in that silent court of yours—
"With all his conscience and one eye askew,
So false, he partly took himself for true;
Whose pious talk, when most his heart was dry,
Made wet the crafty crowsfoot round his eye;
Who, never naming God except for gain,
So never took that useful name in vain,
Made Him his catspaw and the Cross his tool,
And Christ the bait to trap his dupe and fool;
Nor deeds of gift, but gifts of grace he forged,
And snake-like slimed his victim ere he gorged;
And oft at Bible meetings, o'er the rest
Arising, did his holy oily best,
Dropping the too rough H in Hell and Heaven,
To spread the Word by which himself had thriven."
How like you this old satire?'

'Nay,' she said,

*165. bound*: 'Bound on a matter he of life and death', l. 147.
*184.* In *Absalom and Achitophel* 587–8, Dryden's Shimei 'Did wisely from Expensive Sins refrain, / And never broke the Sabbath, but for Gain.' T. aims here to suggest Augustan satire (see l. 194).
*186–7] 1864; not 1860.*
*188.* Cp. Pope, *Epilogue to the Satires* ii 190: 'Because the Deed he forged was not my own'.
*192.* Pope's Dean 'never mentions Hell to ears polite', *Epistle to Burlington* 150.

'I loathe it: he had never kindly heart,
Nor ever cared to better his own kind,
Who first wrote satire, with no pity in it.
But will you hear *my* dream, for I had one
That altogether went to music? Still
It awed me.'
Then she told it, having dreamed
Of that same coast.
—But round the North, a light,
A belt, it seemed, of luminous vapour, lay,
And ever in it a low musical note
Swelled up and died; and, as it swelled, a ridge
Of breaker issued from the belt, and still
Grew with the growing note, and when the note
Had reached a thunderous fulness, on those cliffs
Broke, mixt with awful light (the same as that
Living within the belt) whereby she saw
That all those lines of cliffs were cliffs no more,
But huge cathedral fronts of every age,
Grave, florid, stern, as far as eye could see,
One after one: and then the great ridge drew,
Lessening to the lessening music, back,
And past into the belt and swelled again

*200–1*] *1864*; It awed me. Well–I dreamed that round the north *1860*. This was in fact a dream of T.'s (*Mat.* ii 191).
*202. belt . . . seemed*] *1864*; light, a belt *1860*.
*205. issued from*] *1864*; came from out *1860*.
*207. those*] *1864*; these *1860*.
*207–17.* The link between the cliffs and the cathedral (the destructive work of time) is a section in Charles Lyell's *Principles of Geology* (1835 edn, ii 33, 37, 48), a book which T. read in 1837 (*Mem.* i 162). Lyell speaks of a formation called 'the "Church Cliffs"', and he has a picture of Reculver Church, which by 1834 stood on the edge of the cliffs: 'Gardner's description of the cemeteries laid open by the waves reminds us of the scene which has been so well depicted by Bewick [*History of British Birds*, 1821 edn, ii 220], and of which numerous points on the same coast might have suggested the idea. On the verge of a cliff, which the sea has undermined, are represented the unshaken tower and western end of an abbey. The eastern aisle is gone, and the pillars of the cloister are soon to follow. The waves have almost isolated the promontory, and invaded the cemetery, where they have made sport with the mortal relics, and thrown up a skull upon the beach.' As a child T. had been fascinated by Bewick (*Mem.* i 17).
*209*] *1864*; Which lived within the belt) by which I saw *1860*.
*210. those*] *1864*; these *1860*. 'The ages that go on with their illumination breaking down everything' (T.).

Slowly to music: ever when it broke
The statues, king or saint, or founder fell;
Then from the gaps and chasms of ruin left
Came men and women in dark clusters round,
Some crying, 'Set them up! they shall not fall!'
And others, 'Let them lie, for they have fallen.'
And still they strove and wrangled: and she grieved
In her strange dream, she knew not why, to find
Their wildest wailings never out of tune
With that sweet note; and ever as their shrieks
Ran highest up the gamut, that great wave
Returning, while none marked it, on the crowd
Broke, mixt with awful light, and showed their eyes
Glaring, and passionate looks, and swept away
The men of flesh and blood, and men of stone,
To the waste deeps together.
'Then I fixt
My wistful eyes on two fair images,
Both crowned with stars and high among the stars,—
The Virgin Mother standing with her child
High up on one of those dark minster-fronts—
Till she began to totter, and the child
Clung to the mother, and sent out a cry
Which mixt with little Margaret's, and I woke,
And my dream awed me:—well—but what are dreams?
Yours came but from the breaking of a glass,
And mine but from the crying of a child.'

'Child? No!' said he, 'but this tide's roar, and his,
Our Boanerges with his threats of doom,
And loud-lung'd Antibabylonianisms
(Although I grant but little music there)
Went both to make your dream: but if there were

*216*] *1864*; To music: ever when it broke I saw *1860*.
*217*] *1864*; The statues, saint or king, or founder fall; *1860*.
*218*] *1864*; Then from the gaps of ruin which it left *1860*.
*222. she*] *1864*; I *1860*.
*223. her . . . she*] *1864*; my . . . I *1860*.
*225. as*] *1864*; when *1860*. *that sweet note*: 'the great music of the World' (T.).
*227. while*] *1864*; though *1860*.
*231. Then*] *1864*; and *1860*.
*243. Mark* iii 17: 'He surnamed them Boanerges, which is, The sons of thunder.' See l. 20*n*.
*244.* Apocalyptic attacks on Rome as Babylon.
*246. if there were*] *1864*; were there such *1860*.

A music harmonizing our wild cries,
Sphere-music such as that you dreamed about,
Why, that would make our passions far too like
The discords dear to the musician. No—
One shriek of hate would jar all the hymns of heaven:
True Devils with no ear, they howl in tune
With nothing but the Devil!'
'"True" indeed!
One of our town, but later by an hour
Here than ourselves, spoke with me on the shore;
While you were running down the sands, and made
The dimpled flounce of the sea-furbelow flap,
Good man, to please the child. She brought strange news.
Why were you silent when I spoke tonight?
I had set my heart on your forgiving him
Before you knew. We *must* forgive the dead.'

'Dead! who is dead?
'The man your eye pursued.
A little after you had parted with him,
He suddenly dropt dead of heart-disease.'

'Dead? he? of heart-disease? what heart had he
To die of? dead!'
'Ah, dearest, if there be
A devil in man, there is an angel too,
And if he did that wrong you charge him with,
His angel broke his heart. But your rough voice
(You spoke so loud) has roused the child again.
Sleep, little birdie, sleep! will she not sleep
Without her "little birdie"? well then, sleep,
And I will sing you "birdie."'

Saying this,
The woman half turned round from him she loved,
Left him one hand, and reaching through the night
Her other, found (for it was close beside)
And half-embraced the basket cradle-head
With one soft arm, which, like the pliant bough
That moving moves the nest and nestling, swayed
The cradle, while she sang this baby song.

*248.* The ancient notion of the divine music made by the spheres.
*257. sea-furbelow*: 'sea-weed' (T.).
*259–61*] *1864*; I would not tell you then to spoil your day,
But he, at whom you rail so much is dead.' *1860*

What does little birdie say
In her nest at peep of day?
Let me fly, says little birdie,
Mother, let me fly away.
Birdie, rest a little longer,
Till the little wings are stronger.
So she rests a little longer,
Then she flies away.

What does little baby say,
In her bed at peep of day?
Baby says, like little birdie,
Let me rise and fly away.
Baby, sleep a little longer,
Till the little limbs are stronger.
If she sleeps a little longer,
Baby too shall fly away.

'She sleeps: let us too, let all evil, sleep.
He also sleeps—another sleep than ours.
He can do no more wrong: forgive him, dear,
And I shall sleep the sounder!'
Then the man,
'His deeds yet live, the worst is yet to come.
Yet let your sleep for this one night be sound:
I do forgive him!'
'Thanks, my love,' she said,
'Your own will be the sweeter,' and they slept.

# 320 *Havelock

## NOV. 25th, 1857

Printed *Mem.* i 423–4. General Sir Henry Havelock was the hero of the relief of Lucknow during the Indian Mutiny; news of his death (given as 25 Nov. 1857) reached England on 7 Jan. 1858. 'When this sad news came, my father wrote the following lines.' Cp. *The Defence of Lucknow* (p. 1251).

Bold Havelock marched,
Many a mile went he,
Every mile a battle,
Every battle a victory.

*281–96.* T. included this, as *Cradle Song*, in *1865 Selection. T.Nbk 28* had at first, instead of this song, *Child-Songs* i (written 1849, published 1880, p. 852).

Bold Havelock marched,
Charged with his gallant few,
Ten men fought a thousand,
Slew them and overthrew.

Bold Havelock marched,
Wrought with his hand and his head,
Marched and thought and fought,
Marched and fought himself dead.

Bold Havelock died,
Tender and great and good,
And every man in Britain
Says 'I am of Havelock's blood!'

## 321 The Grandmother

Published *Once a Week*, 16 July 1859, as *The Grandmother's Apology*; then *1864*. Jowett wrote, Dec. 1858: 'An old lady once said to me quite simply, "The spirits of my children always seem to hover about me." Might not something of the kind be expressed in verse?' (*Mem.* i 432). H.T. adds: 'My father had heard this saying before, and it was the germ of *The Grandmother*.' T. wrote to his wife Emily, 22 June 1859: 'Evans has offered me £100 for the Old Woman to put in his new paper' (*Lincoln*). T. may have remembered a passage from Scott's *The Antiquary* which had been singled out in *QR* xv (1816) 136–7; T. knew *QR* well. It describes a funeral:

'But the figure of the old grandmother was the most remarkable of the sorrowing group. Seated on her accustomed chair, with her usual air of apathy, and want of interest in what surrounded her . . . But she spoke not a word, neither had she shed a tear; nor did one of the family understand, either from look or expression, to what extent she comprehended the uncommon bustle around her. So she sat among the funeral assembly like a connecting link between the surviving mourners and the dead corpse which they bewailed–a being in whom the light of existence was already obscured by the encroaching shadows of death.'

I

And Willy, my eldest-born, is gone, you say, little Anne?
Ruddy and white, and strong on his legs, he looks like a man.
And Willy's wife has written: she never was over-wise,
Never the wife for Willy: he wouldn't take my advice.

II

For, Annie, you see, her father was not the man to save,
Hadn't a head to manage, and drank himself into his grave.
Pretty enough, very pretty! but I was against it for one.
Eh!–but he wouldn't hear me–and Willy, you say, is gone.

III

Willy, my beauty, my eldest-born, the flower of the flock;
Never a man could fling him: for Willy stood like a rock.
'Here's a leg for a babe of a week!' says doctor; and he would be bound,
There was not his like that year in twenty parishes round.

IV

Strong of his hands, and strong on his legs, but still of his tongue!
I ought to have gone before him: I wonder he went so young.
I cannot cry for him, Annie: I have not long to stay;
Perhaps I shall see him the sooner, for he lived far away.

V

Why do you look at me, Annie? you think I am hard and cold;
But all my children have gone before me, I am so old:
I cannot weep for Willy, nor can I weep for the rest;
Only at your age, Annie, I could have wept with the best.

VI

For I remember a quarrel I had with your father, my dear,
All for a slanderous story, that cost me many a tear.
I mean your grandfather, Annie: it cost me a world of woe,
Seventy years ago, my darling, seventy years ago.

VII

For Jenny, my cousin, had come to the place, and I knew right well
That Jenny had tript in her time: I knew, but I would not tell.
And she to be coming and slandering me, the base little liar!
But the tongue is a fire as you know, my dear, the tongue is a fire.

VIII

And the parson made it his text that week, and he said likewise,
That a lie which is half a truth is ever the blackest of lies,
That a lie which is all a lie may be met and fought with outright,
But a lie which is part a truth is a harder matter to fight.

IX

And Willy had not been down to the farm for a week and a day;
And all things looked half-dead, though it was the middle of May.
Jenny, to slander me, who knew what Jenny had been!
But soiling another, Annie, will never make oneself clean.

X

And I cried myself well-nigh blind, and all of an evening late
I climbed to the top of the garth, and stood by the road at the gate.

¶321. *9. eldest-born*] *1864*; eldest boy *1859*.
*11–12.* Said, apparently, at T.'s birth (*Mem.* i 2).
*28. James* iii 6.

The moon like a rick on fire was rising over the dale,
And whit, whit, whit, in the bush beside me chirrupt the nightingale.

XI

All of a sudden he stopt: there past by the gate of the farm,
Willy,–he didn't see me,–and Jenny hung on his arm.
Out into the road I started, and spoke I scarce knew how;
Ah, there's no fool like the old one–it makes me angry now.

XII

Willy stood up like a man, and looked the thing that he meant;
Jenny, the viper, made me a mocking curtsey and went.
And I said, 'Let us part: in a hundred years it'll all be the same,
You cannot love me at all, if you love not my good name.'

XIII

And he turned, and I saw his eyes all wet, in the sweet moonshine:
'Sweetheart, I love you so well that your good name is mine.
And what do I care for Jane, let her speak of you well or ill;
But marry me out of hand: we two shall be happy still.'

XIV

'Marry you, Willy!' said I, 'but I needs must speak my mind,
And I fear you'll listen to tales, be jealous and hard and unkind.'
But he turned and claspt me in his arms, and answered, 'No, love, no;'
Seventy years ago, my darling, seventy years ago.

XV

So Willy and I were wedded: I wore a lilac gown;
And the ringers rang with a will, and he gave the ringers a crown.
But the first that ever I bare was dead before he was born,
Shadow and shine is life, little Annie, flower and thorn.

XVI

That was the first time, too, that ever I thought of death.
There lay the sweet little body that never had drawn a breath.
I had not wept, little Anne, not since I had been a wife;
But I wept like a child that day, for the babe had fought for his life.

XVII

His dear little face was troubled, as if with anger or pain:

54. *And I fear you'll*] *1864*; I fear you will *1859*.
62–8. T. seems to be thinking of his still-born boy (1851). Cp. the poem on that event, *Little bosom not yet cold* (p. 992): 'Clenched as in the fight which they had fought. / He had done battle to be born . . .'. T. wrote of his 'dear little nameless one that hast lived tho' thou hast never breathed' (*Mem.* i 340); 'he looked, I thought, as if he had had a battle for his life' (*Boston College MS*, letter to Mrs Patmore).
64] Foam on his lips, and his hands were clenched, he had fought for his life. *Ashley Library MS 1st reading.*
65] His dear little forehead was wrinkled with anger or trouble or pain: *Ashley MS 1st reading.*

For Willy I cannot weep, I shall see him another morn:
But I wept like a child for the child that was dead before he was born.

XVIII

But he cheered me, my good man, for he seldom said me nay:
Kind, like a man, was he; like a man, too, would have his way:
Never jealous–not he: we had many a happy year;
And he died, and I could not weep–my own time seemed so near.

XIX

But I wished it had been God's will that I, too, then could have died:
I began to be tired a little, and fain had slept at his side.
And that was ten years back, or more, if I don't forget:
But as to the children, Annie, they're all about me yet.

XX

Pattering over the boards, my Annie who left me at two,
Patter she goes, my own little Annie, an Annie like you:
Pattering over the boards, she comes and goes at her will,
While Harry is in the five-acre and Charlie ploughing the hill.

XXI

And Harry and Charlie, I hear them too–they sing to their team:
Often they come to the door in a pleasant kind of a dream.
They come and sit by my chair, they hover about my bed–
I am not always certain if they be alive or dead.

XXII

And yet I know for a truth, there's none of them left alive;
For Harry went at sixty, your father at sixty-five:
And Willy, my eldest-born, at nigh threescore and ten;
I knew them all as babies, and now they're elderly men.

XXIII

For mine is a time of peace, it is not often I grieve;
I am oftener sitting at home in my father's farm at eve:
And the neighbours come and laugh and gossip, and so do I;
I find myself often laughing at things that have long gone by.

XXIV

To be sure the preacher says, our sins should make us sad:
But mine is a time of peace, and there is Grace to be had;
And God, not man, is the Judge of us all when life shall cease;
And in this Book, little Annie, the message is one of Peace.

XXV

And age is a time of peace, so it be free from pain,
And happy has been my life; but I would not live it again.
I seem to be tired a little, that's all, and long for rest;
Only at your age, Annie, I could have wept with the best.
I looked at the still little body–his trouble had all been in vain.

95. *Romans* xiv 3–4, 'God hath received him. Who art thou that judgest another man's servant?'

XXVI

So Willy has gone, my beauty, my eldest-born, my flower;
But how can I weep for Willy, he has but gone for an hour,–
Gone for a minute, my son, from this room into the next;
I, too, shall go in a minute. What time have I to be vext?

XXVII

And Willy's wife has written, she never was over-wise.
Get me my glasses, Annie: thank God that I keep my eyes.
There is but a trifle left you, when I shall have past away.
But stay with the old woman now: you cannot have long to stay.

[1859. *Lancelot and Elaine* and *Guinevere*—see pp. 1621, 1724]

# 322 Riflemen Form!

Published *The Times*, 9 May 1859, as *The War*, signed 'T.' Not reprinted till restored in *1892*: 'I have been asked to republish this old poem, which was first published in *The Times*, May 9, 1859, before the Volunteer movement began.' It was written on the outbreak of the Franco-Austrian war; see *Jack Tar* (p. 1111). But T. was adapting a poem which he had originally written when invasion from France seemed imminent in Jan. 1852. On that occasion he wrote two songs called *Rifle-Clubs!!!*; for one, see p. 996; for the other, which is the original version of *Riflemen Form!*, see Appendix A (p. 1778). Its first stanza begins 'Riflemen form', and ends: 'Ready, be ready to meet the storm! / Riflemen, form! Riflemen, form! / Riflemen, riflemen, riflemen form!' For the dating, see C. Ricks, *RES* n.s. xv (1964) 401–4. The limited edition of *Rifle-Clubs!!!* (1899) remarks that T.'s friend Alfred Gatty received *Riflemen Form!* on 5 May 1859, and that this MS included a stanza which was deleted before publication:

Form, for France is dumb in her chains;
Form, for yours is the one free land;
Yours is the one free voice that remains.
Save the voice, and practise the hand.

There is a sound of thunder afar,
Storm in the South that darkens the day!
Storm of battle and thunder of war!
Well if it do not roll our way.
Storm, Storm, Riflemen form!
Ready, be ready against the storm!
Riflemen, Riflemen, Riflemen form!

¶322. *6. against*] *1892*; to meet *1859*.

Be not deaf to the sound that warns,
Be not gulled by a despot's plea!
Are figs of thistles? or grapes of thorns?
How can a despot feel with the Free?
Form, Form, Riflemen Form!
Ready, be ready to meet the storm!
Riflemen, Riflemen, Riflemen form!

Let your reforms for a moment go!
Look to your butts, and take good aims!
Better a rotten borough or so
Than a rotten fleet and a city in flames!
Storm, Storm, Riflemen form!
Ready, be ready against the storm!
Riflemen, Riflemen, Riflemen form!

Form, be ready to do or die!
Form in Freedom's name and the Queen's!
True we have got – *such* a faithful ally
That only the Devil can tell what he means.
Form, Form, Riflemen Form!
Ready, be ready to meet the storm!
Riflemen, Riflemen, Riflemen form!

## 323 *Jack Tar

Printed *Mem.* i 437–8. *Y.MS* is another draft. On 14 May 1859, 'Mr Peel took up *Jack Tar* to London; but A.T. decided not to publish it' (*Mat.* ii 217). It is a naval counterpart to *Riflemen Form!* (above) anticipating war with France. The Franco–Austrian war had begun on 26 April; the news of the treaty between Russia and France was in *The Times*, 27 April: 'France and Russia have declared that alliance which has long been suspected, and which has always been a probability in every European embroilment.'

They say some foreign powers have laid their heads together
To break the pride of Britain, and bring her on her knees,
There's a treaty, so they tell us, of some dishonest fellows
To break the noble pride of the Mistress of the Seas.

*11. can . . . the*] *1892*; should a despot set men *1859*.
*18. and*] *1892*; or *1859*.
*19. Storm, Storm,*] *1892*; Form! form! *1859*.
*20. against*] *1892*; to meet *1859*.
*24. we . . . such*] *1892*; , that we have *1859*.
*25. That . . . tell*] *1892*; But only the Devil knows *1859*.
¶*323. 3. some*] two *Y.MS*.

Up, Jack Tars, and save us!
The whole world shall not brave us!
Up and save the pride of the Mistress of the Seas!

We quarrel here at home, and they plot against us yonder,
They will not let an honest Briton sit at home at ease:
Up, Jack Tars, my hearties! and the d---l take the parties!
Up and save the pride of the Mistress of the Seas!
Up, Jack Tars, and save us!
The whole world shall not brave us!
Up and save the pride of the Mistress of the Seas!

The lasses and the little ones, Jack Tars, they look to you!
The despots over yonder, let 'em do whate'er they please!
God bless the little isle where a man may still be true!
God bless the noble isle that is Mistress of the Seas!
Up, Jack Tars, and save us!
The whole world shall not brave us!
If *you* will save the pride of the Mistress of the Seas.

# 324 Tithonus

Published *Cornhill Magazine*, Feb. 1860; then *1864*.
In 1859 Thackeray importuned T. for a poem to be published in his *Cornhill* (first number, Jan. 1860; *Letters*, ed. G. N. Ray, iv (1946) 168). T. says: 'My friend Thackeray and his publishers had been so urgent with me to send them something, that I ferreted among my old books and found this *Tithonus*, written upwards of a quarter of a century ago. . . . It was originally a pendent to the *Ulysses* in my former volumes, and I wanted Smith to insert a letter, not of mine, to the editor stating this, and how long ago it had been written, but he thought it would lower the value of the contribution in the public eye' (*Mem.* i 459). At the end of a proof of *1860*, T. added the date '1833' and then deleted it (*Lincoln*). The poem was originally written in a shorter form, *Tithon*, in 1833 (p. 566); all the revisions from the *Heath MS* are below. There is an interesting discussion of them by M. J. Donahue, *PMLA* lxiv (1949) 400–16, where *Tithon* was first printed. There are earlier drafts (which may not be quoted) in *T.Nbks 20–21* (1833). T. revised it in Nov.–Dec. 1859 (*Mem.* i 443, *Mat.* ii 240), which suggests that T.'s mind may have been turned to the poem by a

6] Shall France and Russia brave us? *MS.*
8. *We . . . home*] The parties quarrel here *MS.*
15] Are they coming, are they coming to avenge their *Vaterloo*? *MS.*
21] *MS has a deleted stanza:*

Are they coming in their might? we will meet them in the fight,
With the flag of England flying all gaily in the breeze,
With the muzzle to the left, and the muzzle to the right,
And redcoats on the land, and blue-jackets on the seas [*etc.*]

letter, 10 April 1859, from Jowett who had just visited the grave of Arthur Hallam: 'It is a strange feeling about those who are taken young that while we are getting old and dusty they are as they were' (*Lincoln*). For the delay in publication, cp. *On a Mourner* (p. 557), which is also on the death of Hallam, written 1833 but not published till *1865*.

Written after the shock of Hallam's death, the poem is a companion to *Ulysses* (p. 560) and *Tiresias* (p. 568), begun at the same time. T. turned to a classical story for an insight into mortality, and here explores the possibility that immortality would not simply in itself be a blessing. Cp. *Ulysses* (the need for the courage of life), and *Tiresias* (the courage of self-sacrifice). The theme may have been influenced by the grief of T.'s sister Emily (Hallam's betrothed); she wrote to T., 12 July 1834: 'What is life to me! if I die (which the Tennysons never do)' (*Mem.* i 135, cited by Miss Donahue). As Miss Donahue says, 'It is not that anything so obvious and simple as the identification of Eos [Aurora] with Hallam is possible or that the emotional relationship between Tennyson and Hallam is wholly clarified by *Tithonus*. But it is clear that, in choosing the mask of Tithonus, Tennyson reached out to two of the most basic symbols, those of love between man and woman and the frustration of love by age, to express the peculiar and individual nature of his own emotional injury.' Moreover Tithonus is as much a fear as to the *nature* of Hallam's immortality (a fear which recurs in *In Memoriam*) as a mask for T.

Tithonus, as T. remarks, was 'beloved by Aurora [goddess of the dawn], who gave him eternal life but not eternal youth. He grew old and infirm, and as he could not die, according to the legend, was turned into a grasshopper.' Cp. *The Grasshopper* 5, 28 (*1830*): 'No Tithon thou as poets feign . . . / No withered immortality.' The story is told in the Homeric *Hymn to Aphrodite* where it ends (l. 239 ff.) with words that are apt to T.'s feelings: 'I would not have you be deathless among the deathless gods and live continually after such sort. Yet if you could live on such as now you are in look and in form, and be called my husband, sorrow would not then enfold my careful heart.' Also apt to T.'s feelings were two appearances of Tithonus in Horace's *Odes*. I xxviii is on the universality of death, apparently the dramatic monologue of a ghost: *nec quicquam tibi prodest // aërias temptasse domos animoque rotundum / percurrisse polum morituro. / occidit et Pelopis genitor, conviva deorum, / Tithonusque remotus in auras . . . // sed omnes una manet nox, / et calcanda semel via leti.* ('Nor doth it aught avail thee that thou didst once explore the gods' ethereal homes and didst traverse in thought the circling vault of heaven. For thou wast born to die! Death befell also Pelops' sire, though once he sat at the table of the gods; Tithonus, too, translated to the skies . . . . But a common night awaiteth every man, and Death's path must be trodden once for all.') II xvi is on patience in adversity: *nihil est ab omni / parte beatum. // abstulit clarum cita mors Achillem, / longa Tithonum minuit senectus; / et mihi forsan, tibi quod negarit, / porriget hora.* ('Nothing is happy altogether. Achilles for all his glory was snatched away by an early death; Tithonus, though granted a long old age, wasted to a shadow; and to me mayhap the passing hour will grant what it denies to thee.') T.'s translations of some of the *Odes*, written at school, are at *Lincoln*. For the theme of the danger of loving a deity, cp. *Semele*, written *c.* 1833 (p. 574).

The woods decay, the woods decay and fall,
The vapours weep their burthen to the ground,
Man comes and tills the field and lies beneath,
And after many a summer dies the swan.
Me only cruel immortality
Consumes: I wither slowly in thine arms,
Here at the quiet limit of the world,
A white-haired shadow roaming like a dream
The ever-silent spaces of the East,
Far-folded mists, and gleaming halls of morn.

Alas! for this gray shadow, once a man –
So glorious in his beauty and thy choice,
Who madest him thy chosen, that he seemed
To his great heart none other than a God!

¶324. *1. The woods decay,*] *1864*; Ay me! ay me! *1860*. The revision suggests the influence of one of T.'s favourite passages of Wordsworth (*Mem.* i 151), the account of the Simplon Pass, *The Prelude* vi 624–5 (published 1845): 'The immeasurable height / Of woods decaying, never to be decayed'. This is apt to Tithonus's immortal decay.
*1 ∧ 2*] *Trinity first draft has a line on the stars.*
*2. burthen*] substance *Tithon.*
*3. field*] *1864*; earth *1860*.
*4*] And after many summers dies the rose. *Tithon. Trinity drafts* show that the 'rose' is not, as Sir Charles Tennyson has suggested, an error in *Heath MS*. The swan was noted for its longevity, and was taken as a type of white-haired age (F. L. Lucas, *Tennyson*, 1957, p. 27). Its singing too is suggested; cp. *The Dying Swan* (p. 231).
*5. cruel*] fatal *Tithon.*
*7.* Adapted from a fragment of *The Lover's Tale*, *Heath MS* (p. 303): 'Down to the quiet limit of the world'. Cp. the *Hymn to Aphrodite* 225–7: 'He lived rapturously with golden-throned Eos, the early-born, by the streams of Ocean, at the ends of the earth.'
*8.* Euripides, *Phoenissae* 1543–5: 'A white-haired shape, like a phantom that fades / On the sight, or a ghost from the underworld shades, / Or a dream that hath wings.'
*11–23*] Ay me! ay me! what everlasting pain,
Being immortal with a mortal heart,
To live confronted with eternal youth:
To look on what is beautiful nor know
Enjoyment save through memory. Can thy love, *Tithon*

I asked thee, 'Give me immortality.'
Then didst thou grant mine asking with a smile,
Like wealthy men who care not how they give.
But thy strong Hours indignant worked their wills,
And beat me down and marred and wasted me,
And though they could not end me, left me maimed
To dwell in presence of immortal youth,
Immortal age beside immortal youth,
And all I was, in ashes. Can thy love,
Thy beauty, make amends, though even now,
Close over us, the silver star, thy guide,
Shines in those tremulous eyes that fill with tears
To hear me? Let me go: take back thy gift:
Why should a man desire in any way
To vary from the kindly race of men,
Or pass beyond the goal of ordinance
Where all should pause, as is most meet for all?

A soft air fans the cloud apart; there comes
A glimpse of that dark world where I was born.

*21.* Cp. Shelley, *Prometheus Unbound* III iii 88–9: 'And through my withered, old, and icy frame / The warmth of an immortal youth shoots down.'

*23.* The image was suggested by the comparable tragedy in *Semele*: 'When I am ashes'.

*25. star*: 'Venus' (T.).

*26. tears*] tears? *Tithon.* *tremulous eyes*: as in the song in *The Miller's Daughter* (*1832* text, p. 381), which perhaps suggested 'dewy', l. 58 (the *Trinity first draft* supports this). Cp. Keats, *I stood tip-toe* 146–7, on Cupid and Psyche: 'And how they kist each other's tremulous eyes: / The silver lamp,–'. Also Shelley, *Revolt of Islam* XII xiv 1–2: 'The warm tears burst in spite of faith and fear / From many a tremulous eye'. The phrase occurs in Keble's best-seller, *The Christian Year* (1827), xviii; T.'s copy is at *Lincoln.*

*26–7. that . . . go*] *Not Trinity 1st draft.*

*27. To hear me?*] Release me: *Tithon.*

*28. way*] shape *Tithon.*

*29*] To vary from his kind, or beat the roads *Tithon.*

*30. Or pass*] Of life, *Tithon.* *goal of ordinance*: 'appointed limit' (T.). Cp. *Cymbeline* IV ii 145–6: 'Let ordinance / Come as the gods fore-say it'.

*31 ∧ 2*]
Or let me call thy ministers, the hours,
To take me up, to wind me in their arms,
To shoot the sunny interval of day,
And lap me deep within the lonely west. *Tithon*

*33–6*] *Not Trinity 1st draft.*

Once more the old mysterious glimmer steals
From thy pure brows, and from thy shoulders pure,
And bosom beating with a heart renewed.
Thy cheek begins to redden through the gloom,
Thy sweet eyes brighten slowly close to mine,
Ere yet they blind the stars, and the wild team
Which love thee, yearning for thy yoke, arise,
And shake the darkness from their loosened manes,
And beat the twilight into flakes of fire.

Lo! ever thus thou growest beautiful
In silence, then before thine answer given
Departest, and thy tears are on my cheek.

Why wilt thou ever scare me with thy tears,
And make me tremble lest a saying learnt,
In days far-off, on that dark earth, be true?
'The Gods themselves cannot recall their gifts.'

*36*] And bosom throbbing with a fresher heart. *Tithon.*

*37. redden . . . gloom*] to bloom a fuller red *Tithon.*

*39. the wild*] *1864*; that wild *1860*; thy wild *Tithon.*

*39–42. and . . . fire*] *Not Trinity 1st draft.*

*40*] *Not Tithon, Trinity 1st and 2nd drafts.*

*41*] Spreading a rapid glow with loosened manes, *Tithon.*

*42. And beat the*] Fly, trampling *Tithon.* Traditional for the dawn; cp. a poem which T. used for *Boädicea*, Catullus lxiii 41: *pepulitque noctis umbras vegetis sonipedibus.* Also *The Coach of Death* 128: 'They broke the ground with hoofs of fire.' Apparently also a reminiscence of Marston's *Antonio's Revenge* I ii 120, i 107–8; 'flakes of fire', 'coursers of the morn / Beat up the light with their bright silver hooves' (noted by C. R. Forker, *Notes and Queries*, Dec. 1959).

*43–4*] 'Tis ever thus: thou growest more beautiful,
Thou partest: when a little warmth returns *Tithon*

*45. Departest*] Thou partest *Tithon.*

*45 ∧ 6*] *Trinity 1st draft*, from here to the end, differs considerably from *Tithon*. It has eight lines, threatening Aurora that he will call up Death; then a shorter version of the closing lines, ending with l. 75 but incorporating a description of Aurora's horses (different from *Tithon*). *Trinity 2nd draft* has the eight lines on Death following l. 63, and then breaks off.

*46–9*] *Not Tithon, Trinity 1st and 2nd drafts.*

*49. Paradise Lost* ix 926–7: 'But past who can recall, or don undoe? / Not God Omnipotent, nor Fate.' John Churton Collins said that T.'s line 'is, of course, from Agathon, as quoted by Aristotle (*Eth.N.* vi 2)'. Alongside this suggestion, T. wrote: 'not known to me' (*Cornhill*, Jan. 1880, *Lincoln*).

Ay me! ay me! with what another heart
In days far-off, and with what other eyes
I used to watch – if I be he that watched –
The lucid outline forming round thee; saw
The dim curls kindle into sunny rings;
Changed with thy mystic change, and felt my blood
Glow with the glow that slowly crimsoned all
Thy presence and thy portals, while I lay,
Mouth, forehead, eyelids, growing dewy-warm
With kisses balmier than half-opening buds
Of April, and could hear the lips that kissed
Whispering I knew not what of wild and sweet,
Like that strange song I heard Apollo sing,
While Ilion like a mist rose into towers.

Yet hold me not for ever in thine East:
How can my nature longer mix with thine?

*51–3*] By thy divine embraces circumfused, *Tithon*.

*53. forming*] growing *1860 proof* (*Lincoln, but altered by T.*).

*54. The . . . kindle*] Thy black curls burning *Tithon*. Cp. the final version with 'My long tresses, run in sunny rings', *The Gardener's Daughter* 75–80, *Heath MS*.

*55–7*] With thy change changed, I felt this wondrous glow
That, gradually blooming, flushes all
Thy pale fair limbs: what time my mortal frame
Molten in thine immortal, I lay wooed, *Tithon*

*58. Mouth*] Lips *Tithon*.

*59. half-opening buds*] opening buds; *Tithon*. The change in this erotic image suggests the similarity in sound of the 'half-awakened birds' in *Tears, idle tears* – a poem which, as F. L. Gwynn says (*PMLA* lxvii (1952) 572–5), employs to a remarkable extent the same vocabulary as *Tithon* and *Tithonus*.

*60–1*] Anon the lips that dealt them moved themselves
In wild and airy whisperings more sweet *Tithon*

*62. Like*] Than *Tithon*. Cp. ll. 61–2 with Shelley, *To Constantia, Singing* 12: 'Wild, sweet, but uncommunicably strange'.

*63.* Troy was built by the music of Apollo; see *Ilion, Ilion* (p. 258), where it is 'melody born'. Cp. Milton's Pandaemonium, *PL* i 711–2: 'Rose like an Exhalation, with the sound / Of Dulcet Symphonies and voices sweet.' The mythologist Jacob Bryant wrote of 'towers' in his *New System of Ancient Mythology* (1807 edn, ii 127–8): 'Tithonus, whose longevity is so much celebrated, was nothing more than one of these structures, a Pharos, sacred to the sun, as the name plainly shews.' There was a copy of Bryant at Somersby (*Lincoln*), and he influenced *A Fragment* (p. 289) and *Pierced through* (p. 472).

*64*] Ah! keep me not for ever in the East: *Tithon*.

Coldly thy rosy shadows bathe me, cold
Are all thy lights, and cold my wrinkled feet
Upon thy glimmering thresholds, when the steam
Floats up from those dim fields about the homes
Of happy men that have the power to die,
And grassy barrows of the happier dead.
Release me, and restore me to the ground;
Thou seëst all things, thou wilt see my grave:
Thou wilt renew thy beauty morn by morn;
I earth in earth forget these empty courts,
And thee returning on thy silver wheels.

## 325 Boädicea

Published *1864*, among 'Experiments' because of its metre. Written Feb. 1859, probably revised till April 1860 (*Mat.* ii 213, 303). It was precipitated by an engraving of Thomas Stothard's Boadicea haranguing the Britons (1812), which Thomas Woolner sent to T., 12 Feb. 1859; it has most of T.'s pictorial details. The historical source was Tacitus, *Annals* XIV xxix–xxxv: while the Roman Governor was destroying the Druids' groves in Anglesey, the Iceni rebelled after Boadicea was flogged, her daughters raped, and the land plundered. They attacked the veterans' settlement at Camulodunum, already in terror from omens. T. takes little from the actual paragraph in which Tacitus tells of Boadicea's battle speech; for dramatic and patriotic effect, he moves it from its place in Tacitus, immediately preceding her defeat, and makes it the prelude to the successful risings. The literary source is Cowper's *Boadicea* (Cowper's poems were at Somersby, *Lincoln*), and hence Gray's *The Bard*, both of which are built on prophetic denunciations of the invader–a genre of which T. had long been fond (cp. *Lamentation of the Peruvians*, p. 131, one of many in *1827*).
*Metre.* "'Yélled and shríeked betwéen her daúghters o'er a wíld con-

*68. thy*] these *Tithon.*
*69. dim . . . homes*] still fields that dream below. *Tithon.*
*70–1*] *Not Tithon.*
*72. , and*] ! so *Tithon.*
*74. morn by*] with the *Tithon.*
*75*] *Trinity 1st draft ended with this line*; see ll. 45 ∧ 6*n*. T. quotes '*terra in terra* (Dante)'. He wrote this alongside John Churton Collins's observation that: 'This happy Hellenism is in Stephen Hawes' *Pastime of Pleasure*, capit. xlv.: "When *earth in earth* hath ta'en his corrupt taste"' (*Cornhill*, Jan. 1880, *Lincoln*). T.'s reference is to *Paradiso* xxv 124–6: *In terra terra è'l mio corpo, e saràgli / tanto con li altri, che'l numero nostro / con l'etterno proposito s'agguagli.* ('My body is earth in the earth, and it will be there with the rest till our number tallies with the eternal purpose.')

féderacy" is accented as I mark the accents. Let it be read straight like prose and it will come all right'. Yet in 1861 he wrote: '*Boädicea*, no, I cannot publish her yet, perhaps never, for who can read her except myself?' (*Mem.* i 477). The metre is 'a far-off echo of the *Attis* of Catullus' (T.); 'the distinctive character of the [galliambic] metre gives the effect of tumultuous and breathless speed' (C. J. Fordyce, *Catullus*, 1961, p. 263): *Super alta vectus Attis celeri rate maria.* Catullus's Poem lxiii would have come to T.'s mind because of comparable subject matter; Fordyce says that 'the contrast between civilization and savage nature . . . is at the heart of the poem'. Like *Boädicea*, it deals with frenzy and madness: *alios age incitatos, alios age rabidos.* As leader, Attis incites the others to follow, and they yell and clash their cymbals (ll. 74–9 below); and it too has its passionate patriotism: *Patria o mei creatrix, patria o mea genetrix.*

*Manuscripts.* There is a late draft among *Hn MSS* (HM 19489). Readings below are from this, except where stated. *H.Nbks 28* and *62* have many early fragments, one of which has a male speaker ('There he smote his hands together, there he wept in his agony'), and an Irish setting: 'On the solemn hills of Tara when the kings were inaugurated'. Another fragment shows that T. at one stage intended a poem in this metre on contemporary politics:

Half a home of clashing systems, half of refluent barbarism,
While the peoples foamed together, multitudinous anarchy,
While the Russian glacier creeping down from desolate wildernesses
Armed with million battling ices crept to beautiful Hungary,
Sloping down to summer Europe
God avert the shameful augury, God avert the horrible doom.

Such a denunciation suggests *Locksley Hall Sixty Years After* (p. 1359). T. would have seen *Boädicea* in its final form as apt to the 'refluent barbarism' around him.

While about the shore of Mona those Neronian legionaries
Burnt and broke the grove and altar of the Druid and Druidess,
Far in the East Boädicéa, standing loftily charioted,
Mad and maddening all that heard her in her fierce volubility,
Girt by half the tribes of Britain, near the colony Cámulodúne,
Yelled and shrieked between her daughters o'er a wild confederacy.

'They that scorn the tribes and call us Britain's barbarous populaces,
Did they hear me, would they listen, did they pity me supplicating?

¶325. *1–2.* Cp. *The Druid's Prophecies* (p. 104, from the same section of Tacitus: 'Mona! with flame thine oaks are streaming.') Gosse reports T. as saying in 1877: 'He mentioned that he would have given his ears to end the first line with "emissaries" instead of "legionaries", but he found it would not do' (*Victorian Studies*, viii, 1965, 341).

*5.* Colchester.

*8 ∧ 9*] For my daughters, O my dear ones, in the grasp of a violator? *HnMS 1st reading.*

Shall I heed them in their anguish? shall I brook to be supplicated?
Hear Icenian, Catieuchlanian, hear Coritanian, Trinobant!
Must their ever-ravening eagle's beak and talon annihilate us?
Tear the noble heart of Britain, leave it gorily quivering?
Bark an answer, Britain's raven! bark and blacken innumerable,
Blacken round the Roman carrion, make the carcase a skeleton,
Kite and kestrel, wolf and wolfkin, from the wilderness, wallow in it,
Till the face of Bel be brightened, Taranis be propitiated.
Lo their colony half-defended! lo their colony, Cámulodúne!
There the horde of Roman robbers mock at a barbarous adversary.
There the hive of Roman liars worship an emperor-idiot.
Such is Rome, and this her deity: hear it, Spirit of Cássivëlaún!

'Hear it, Gods! the Gods have heard it, O Icenian, O Coritanian!
Doubt not ye the Gods have answered, Catieuchlanian, Trinobant.
These have told us all their anger in miraculous utterances,

*9. anguish*] agony *MS 1st reading.*
*10.* Of these tribes, Tacitus mentions only the first and last.
*11.* Cp. *Ode on Wellington* 119–21: 'their ravening eagle . . . barking'.
*12. gorily quivering*] bloodily palpitating *MS 1st reading.*
*13–15.* For the tradition, cp. *Battle of Brunanburh* 105–10: carcase, carrion, eagle, raven, war-hawk, wolf of the weald (p. 1238).
*16.* Celtic gods, not mentioned by Tacitus. T. would have heard of Belinus ('shining') and Taranis, the Apollo and the Thunderer of the Druids, long ago in Christopher Wordsworth's *The Druids*, which won the Gold Medal at Cambridge in 1827, two years before T. did. Edward Davies's *Mythology of the British Druids* (1809), of which T. was given a copy in 1846 (*Lincoln*), says that Belinus was 'expressly identified with Apollo' (p. 116). Boadicea's hint here of human sacrifice is based on Dion Cassius (*Historia Romana* LXII vi–vii), which says that during the war she offered Roman women in sacrifice.
*17–19.* Tacitus: 'Driving the natives from their homes, ejecting them from their lands–they styled them "captives" and "slaves" . . . More than this, the temple raised to the deified Claudius continually met the view, like the citadel of an eternal tyranny.'
*18*] *Added to MS.*
*19. an*] *1890*; a gluttonous *1864–89.*
*20. Cassivelaun*: the British chief who opposed Julius Caesar.
*22–30.* Tacitus: 'Meanwhile, for no apparent reason, the statue of Victory at Camulodunum fell, with its back turned as if in retreat from the enemy. Women, converted into maniacs by excitement, cried that destruction was at hand and that alien cries had been heard in the invaders' senate-house: the theatre had rung with shrieks, and in the estuary of the Thames had been seen a vision of the ruined colony. Again, that the ocean had appeared blood-red and that the ebbing tide had left behind it what looked to be human corpses, were indications read by the Britons with hope and by the veterans with corresponding alarm.'

Thunder, a flying fire in heaven, a murmur heard aërially,
Phantom sound of blows descending, moan of an enemy massacred,
Phantom wail of women and children, multitudinous agonies.
Bloodily flowed the Tamesa rolling phantom bodies of horses and men;
Then a phantom colony smouldered on the refluent estuary;
Lastly yonder yester-even, suddenly giddily tottering–
There was one who watched and told me–down their statue of Victory fell.
Lo their precious Roman bantling, lo the colony Cámulodúne,
Shall we teach it a Roman lesson? shall we care to be pitiful?
Shall we deal with it as an infant? shall we dandle it amorously?

'Hear Icenian, Catieuchlanian, hear Coritanian, Trinobant!
While I roved about the forest, long and bitterly meditating,
There I heard them in the darkness, at the mystical ceremony,
Loosely robed in flying raiment, sang the terrible prophetesses,
"Fear not, isle of blowing woodland, isle of silvery parapets!
Though the Roman eagle shadow thee, though the gathering enemy narrow thee,
Thou shalt wax and he shall dwindle, thou shalt be the mighty one yet!
Thine the liberty, thine the glory, thine the deeds to be celebrated,
Thine the myriad-rolling ocean, light and shadow illimitable,
Thine the lands of lasting summer, many-blossoming Paradises,
Thine the North and thine the South and thine the battle-thunder of God,"
So they chanted: how shall Britain light upon auguries happier?
So they chanted in the darkness, and there cometh a victory now.

'Hear Icenian, Catieuchlanian, hear Coritanian, Trinobant!
Me the wife of rich Prasútagus, me the lover of liberty,
Me they seized and me they tortured, me they lashed and humiliated,
Me the sport of ribald Veterans, mine of ruffian violators!
See they sit, they hide their faces, miserable in ignominy!
Wherefore in me burns an anger, not by blood to be satiated.
Lo the palaces and the temple, lo the colony Cámulodúne!
There they ruled, and thence they wasted all the flourishing territory,
Thither at their will they haled the yellow-ringleted Britoness–
Bloodily, bloodily fall the battle-axe, unexhausted, inexorable.

*24*] Thunder, and flying fires in heaven, and voices heard aerially, *MS.*
*29–30. suddenly . . . me*] *Added to MS, but beginning* hastily.
*36–46.* In Cowper's *Boadicea*, the Druid prophesies that the British 'Shall a wider world command. // Regions Caesar never knew / Thy posterity shall sway, / Where his eagles never flew.'
*38. parapets*] promontories *MS 1st reading.*
*45*] *Added to MS.*
*50.* Cowper's Boadicea calls the Romans 'ruffians'. *mine*: her daughters (ll. 8 ∧ 9*n*).
*51.* T. remarks: '*miserable in ignominy* is metrically equivalent to Catullus', for I put a tribrach where Catullus has a trochee'.
*53*] Lo the colony, lo the colony, lo the colony Camulodune! *MS.*

Shout Icenian, Catieuchlanian, shout Coritanian, Trinobant,
Till the victim hear within and yearn to hurry precipitously
Like the leaf in a roaring whirlwind, like the smoke in a hurricane whirled.
Lo the colony, there they rioted in the city of Cúnobelíne!
There they drank in cups of emerald, there at tables of ebony lay,
Rolling on their purple couches in their tender effeminacy.
There they dwelt and there they rioted; there–there–they dwell no more.
Burst the gates, and burn the palaces, break the works of the statuary,
Take the hoary Roman head and shatter it, hold it abominable,
Cut the Roman boy to pieces in his lust and voluptuousness,
Lash the maiden into swooning, me they lashed and humiliated,
Chop the breasts from off the mother, dash the brains of the little one out,
Up my Britons, on my chariot, on my chargers, trample them under us.'

So the Queen Boädicéa, standing loftily charioted,
Brandishing in her hand a dart and rolling glances lioness-like,
Yelled and shrieked between her daughters in her fierce volubility.
Till her people all around the royal chariot agitated,
Madly dashed the darts together, writhing barbarous lineäments,
Made the noise of frosty woodlands, when they shiver in January,
Roared as when the roaring breakers boom and blanch on the precipices,
Yelled as when the winds of winter tear an oak on a promontory.
So the silent colony hearing her tumultuous adversaries
Clash the darts and on the buckler beat with rapid unanimous hand,
Thought on all her evil tyrannies, all her pitiless avarice,
Till she felt the heart within her fall and flutter tremulously,
Then her pulses at the clamouring of her enemy fainted away.

*56.* As Latin *inexórabilis*, unlike Shakespeare, Dryden, and Thomson.

*58. victim*] doomed one *MS 1st reading.*

*60.* Before the Romans, Cunobelinus was ruler at Verulamium, St Albans.

*62*] *HMS includes the fragmentary phrase* Lo the brothels.

*67. humiliated*] they lacerated *H.MS 1st reading.*

*68. breasts*] paps *H.MS.* Cp. Lady Macbeth's murderous violence after she has unsexed herself, and would have 'dashed the brains out' of her baby (I vii 54–8).

*72*] *HnMS 1st reading repeats l. 6.*

*74*] Danced and dashed the darts together, writhing barbarous countenances, *MS.*

*76. roaring*] *1882*; rolling *1864–81.* Corrected by T. in his copy of *Works*, 1881 (*Lincoln*).

*76–82*] *Added to MS on a separate sheet beginning* Then the tender colony . . . .

*81–2*] Till her spirit failed within her, and her pulses fainted away. *MS 1st reading*; Till the heart within her breast began to flutter tremulously / And her pulses . . . *MS.*

Out of evil evil flourishes, out of tyranny tyranny buds.
Ran the land with Roman slaughter, multitudinous agonies.
Perished many a maid and matron, many a valorous legionary,
Fell the colony, city, and citadel, London, Verulam, Cámulodúne.

# 326 In the Valley of Cauteretz

Published *1864*. Written 7 Aug. 1861, on visiting 'a valley in the Pyrenees, where I had been with Arthur Hallam' (T.) in 1830. 'After hearing the voice of the torrent seemingly sound deeper as the night grew' (T., *Mem.* i 474–5). T. said in 1863: 'Altogether I like the little piece as well as anything I have written' (*Mem.* i 492). Cp. the elegy *In the Garden at Swainston* (p. 1219). All variants from *H.Lpr 113* are below.

All along the valley, stream that flashest white,
Deepening thy voice with the deepening of the night,
All along the valley, where thy waters flow,
I walked with one I loved two and thirty years ago.
All along the valley, while I walked today,
The two and thirty years were a mist that rolls away;
For all along the valley, down thy rocky bed,
Thy living voice to me was as the voice of the dead,
And all along the valley, by rock and cave and tree,
The voice of the dead was a living voice to me.

# 327 Northern Farmer

## OLD STYLE

Published *1864*, without the subtitle. Written Feb. 1861 (*Mem.* i 471), and completed by Oct. 1861 (F. T. Palgrave, *Journals*, 1899, p. 64). T. says

*83. flourishes*] blossometh *MS 1st reading.*
*86. city, and citadel*] fell the city *MS 1st reading.*
¶326. *1*] Brook that runnest madly, brook that flashest white, *H.MS.*
*3. waters flow*] mad waters go *MS.*
*4. one I loved*] Arthur Hallam *MS.* 'My father was vexed that he had written "two and thirty years ago" . . . instead of "one and thirty years ago," and as late as 1892 wished to alter it since he hated inaccuracy. I persuaded him to let his first reading stand, for the public had learnt to love the poem in its present form: and besides "two and thirty" was more melodious' (*Mem.* i 475).
*5–7*] All along the valley thou ravest down thy bed, *MS.*
*8. was*] is *MS, as in l. 10.*
*9. And all*] All *MS.*

it was 'founded on the dying words of a farm-bailiff, as reported . . . by my old great-uncle . . . "God A'mighty little knows what He's about a-taking me. An' Squire will be so mad an' all".' Cp. *Northern Farmer, New Style* (p. 1189). All glossarial notes below are by T.

I

Wheer 'asta beän saw long and meä liggin' 'ere aloän?
Noorse? thourt nowt o' a noorse: whoy, Doctor's abeän an' agoän:
Says that I moänt 'a naw moor aäle: but I beänt a fool:
Git ma my aäle, fur I beänt a-gawin' to breäk my rule.

II

Doctors, they knaws nowt, fur a says what's nawways true:
Naw soort o' koind o' use to saäy the things that a do.
I've 'ed my point o' aäle ivry noight sin' I beän 'ere,
An' I've 'ed my quart ivry market-noight for foorty year.

III

Parson's a beän loikewoise, an' a sittin' 'ere o' my bed.
'The amoighty's a taäkin o' you to 'issén, my friend,' a said,
An' a towd ma my sins, an's toithe were due, an' I gied it in hond;
I done moy duty boy 'um, as I 'a done boy the lond.

IV

Larned a ma' beä. I reckons I 'annot sa mooch to larn.
But a cast oop, thot a did, 'bout Bessy Marris's barne.
Thaw a knaws I hallus voäted wi' Squoire an' choorch an' staäte,
An' i' the woost o' toimes I wur niver agin the raäte.

V

An' I hallus coomed to 's chooch afoor moy Sally wur deäd,
An' 'eärd 'um a bummin' awaäy loike a buzzard-clock ower my 'eäd,
An' I niver knawed whot a meäned but I thowt a 'ad summat to saäy,
An' I thowt a said whot a owt to 'a said an' I coomed awaäy.

VI

Bessy Marris's barne! tha knaws she laäid it to meä.
Mowt a beän, mayhap, for she wur a bad un, sheä.
'Siver, I kep 'um, I kep 'um, my lass, tha mun understond;
I done moy duty boy 'um as I 'a done boy the lond.

VII

But Parson a cooms an' a goäs, an' a says it eäsy an' freeä
'The amoighty's a taäkin o' you to 'issén, my friend,' says 'eä.
I weänt saäy men be loiars, thaw summun said it in 'aäste:
But 'e reäds wonn sarmin a weeäk, an' I 'a stubbed Thurnaby waäste.

VIII

D'ya moind the waäste, my lass? naw, naw, tha was not born then;
Theer wur a boggle in it, I often 'eärd 'um mysen;

¶327. *10. you*: ou as in hour.
*18. buzzard-clock*: cockchafer.
*27. Psalm* cxvi 11, 'I said in my haste, All men are liars.'

Moäst loike a butter-bump, fur I 'eärd 'um about an' about,
But I stubbed 'um oop wi' the lot, an' raäved an' rembled 'um out.

IX

Keäper's it wur; fo' they fun 'um theer a-laäid of 'is faäce
Down i' the woild 'enemies afoor I coomed to the plaäce.
Noäks or Thimbleby–toäner 'ed shot 'um as deäd as a naäil.
Noäks wur 'anged for it oop at 'soize–but git ma my aäle.

X

Dubbut looök at the waäste: theer warn't not feeäd for a cow;
Nowt at all but bracken an' fuzz, an' looök at it now–
Warnt worth nowt a haäcre, an' now theer's lots o' feeäd,
Fourscoor yows upon it an' some on it down i' seeäd.

XI

Nobbut a bit on it's left, an' I meäned to 'a stubbed it at fall,
Done it ta-year I meäned, an' runned plow thruff it an' all,
If godamoighty an' parson 'ud nobbut let ma aloän,
Meä, wi' haäte hoonderd haäcre o' Squoire's, an' lond o' my oän.

XII

Do godamoighty knaw what a's doing a-taäkin' o' meä?
I beänt wonn as saws 'ere a beän an' yonder a peä;
An' Squoire 'ull be sa mad an' all–a' dear a' dear!
And I 'a managed for Squoire coom Michaelmas thutty year.

XIII

A mowt 'a taäen owd Joänes, as 'ant not a 'aäpoth o' sense,
Or a mowt 'a taäen young Robins–a niver mended a fence:
But godamoighty a moost taäke meä an' taäke ma now
Wi' aäf the cows to cauve an' Thurnaby hoälms to plow!

XIV

Loook 'ow quoloty smoiles when they seeäs ma a passin' boy,
Says to thessén naw doubt 'what a man a beä sewer-loy!'
Fur they knaws what I beän to Squoire sin fust a coomed to the 'All;
I done moy duty by Squoire an' I done moy duty boy hall.

XV

Squoire's i' Lunnon, an' summun I reckons 'ull 'a to wroite,
For whoä's to howd the lond ater meä thot muddles ma quoit;
Sartin-sewer I beä, thot a weänt niver give it to Joänes,
Naw, nor a moänt to Robins–a niver rembles the stoäns.

31. *butter-bump*: bittern.
33–6] *Added in trial edition of 1864* (*Univ. of London Lib.*).
34. *'enemies*: anemones.
35. *toaner*: one or other.
40. *Fourscoor*: ou as in hour. *seead*: clover.
49. *taäen owd*] *1870*; *taäken 1864–9*.
50. *taäen young*] *1870*; *taäken 1864–9*.
60. *Naw, nor*] *1870*; Noither *1864–9*.

XVI

But summun 'ull come ater meä mayhap wi' 'is kittle o' steäm
Huzzin' an' maäzin' the blessèd feälds wi' the Divil's oän teäm.
Sin' I mun doy I mun doy, thaw loife they says is sweet,
But sin' I mun doy I mun doy, for I couldn abeär to see it.

XVII

What atta stannin' theer fur, an' doesn bring ma the aäle?
Doctor's a 'toättler, lass, an a's hallus i' the owd taäle;
I weänt breäk rules fur Doctor, a knaws naw moor nor a floy;
Git ma my aäle I tell tha, an' if I mun doy I mun doy.

# 328 Helen's Tower

Privately printed 1861; published *Good Words*, Jan. 1884, then *1885*. 'Written at the request of my friend, Lord Dufferin' (*1885*). Written Sept.–Oct. 1861 (*Mat.* ii 337), for the tower which Lord Dufferin had built and named after his mother: 'In it I have placed on a golden tablet the birthday verses which my mother wrote to me on the day I came of age.' Dufferin acknowledged the different versions, 8 Oct. 1861 (*Lincoln*). T. wrote, 23 Jan. 1862: 'Ask him [Dufferin] how he had decided as to the Helen's-tower inscription. I hope he has not made a medley of the three separate forms which I sent him' (*Lincoln*). Browning was among those who later provided a poem.

Helen's Tower, here I stand,
Dominant over sea and land.
Son's love built me, and I hold
Mother's love in lettered gold.
Love is in and out of time,
I am mortal stone and lime.
Would my granite girth were strong
As either love, to last as long!
I should wear my crown entire
To and through the Doomsday fire,
And be found of angel eyes
In earth's recurring Paradise.

*63. thaw*] *1872*; an' *1864–70*.
*68. if*] *1870*; gin *1864–9*.
¶328. *4. in lettered*] *1888*; engraved in *1861–84*; engrav'n in *1885*.
*5–6*] *1884*; *not 1861*.
*12.* 'The fancy of some poets and theologians that Paradise is to be the renovated earth' (T.). Possibly recalling a letter by T.'s brother Frederick, 5 Nov. 1852: 'The Paradise of Man will be this earth on which we live renewed and adapted' (*Mat.* ii 280).

# 329 Ode Sung at the Opening of the International Exhibition

Published with music by W. S. Bennett, 12 April 1862; *The Times*, 24 April (with errors); *Fraser's Magazine*, June; then *1872*. It was written by request and for a choir of thousands, 21 Oct. 1861 (*Mat.* ii 339). Mrs Marian Bradley's diary, Dec. 1861 (*British Museum*) says: 'He explained to me that the rhythm and composition was hampered by the necessity of its being arranged for the choir of 4000 voices.' The Duke of Argyll praised it to T., 17 Nov. 1861 (*Lincoln*). 'The lines [7–10] on the death of the Prince Consort had to be put in after the first draft' (*Mem.* i 480); Albert died 14 Dec. 1861. Emily T.'s copy (*British Museum*) is dated 1 Jan. 1862. T. remarks that 'the Prince Consort originated International Exhibitions'.

I

Uplift a thousand voices full and sweet,
In this wide hall with earth's invention stored,
And praise the invisible universal Lord,
Who lets once more in peace the nations meet,
Where Science, Art, and Labour have outpoured
Their myriad horns of plenty at our feet.

II

O silent father of our Kings to be
Mourned in this golden hour of jubilee,
For this, for all, we weep our thanks to thee!

III

The world-compelling plan was thine, –
And, lo! the long laborious miles
Of Palace; lo! the giant aisles,
Rich in model and design;
Harvest-tool and husbandry,
Loom and wheel and enginery,
Secrets of the sullen mine,
Steel and gold, and corn and wine,
Fabric rough, or fairy-fine,
Sunny tokens of the Line,
Polar marvels, and a feast
Of wonder, out of West and East,
And shapes and hues of Art divine!

¶329. *10. -compelling*: 'This word he explained as being used in the old sense of gathering together' (Mrs Bradley).

All of beauty, all of use,
That one fair planet can produce,
  Brought from under every star,
Blown from over every main,
And mixt, as life is mixt with pain,
  The works of peace with works of war.

IV

Is the goal so far away?
Far, how far no tongue can say,
Let us dream our dream today.

V

O ye, the wise who think, the wise who reign,
From growing commerce loose her latest chain,
And let the fair white-winged peacemaker fly
To happy havens under all the sky,
And mix the seasons and the golden hours;
Till each man find his own in all men's good,
And all men work in noble brotherhood,
Breaking their mailèd fleets and armèd towers,
And ruling by obeying Nature's powers,
And gathering all the fruits of earth and crowned
  with all her flowers.

*28 ∧ 9*]  War himself must make alliance
  With rough Labour and fine Science,
  Else he would but strike in vain. *Fraser's*

These 'three lines which have been omitted' (*Fraser's*) are deleted in Emily T.'s copy.

*29–31*] *1862*, *1874*; *not 1872*. T.'s uncertainty about these lines is confirmed by the Duke of Argyll's letter, 17 Nov. 1861 (*Lincoln*): 'The 3 lines you speak doubtfully of are beautiful–But in some respects "Hope" would be better than "dream"; which implies that the "goal" besides being "far away" is altogether visionary.'

*29. Is*] *1874*; And is *1862*.

*30. tongue*] *1874*; man *1862*.

*31. us dream*] *1874*; us have *1862*. *our dream*] *1862*; our dreams *1874*, *corrected by Errata from* 'no dreams'.

*34–7*. Tinged with *The Golden Year* 43–7: fly, happy, golden, all men's good.

*35 ∧ 6*]  And leave or take a gift at every door,
  And comfort the waste places and the poor;
*Added by T. in Emily's copy*

*41. earth*] *1872*; Peace *1862*.

# 330 Enoch Arden

Published *1864*. Written Nov. 1861–April 1862 (A. Woolner, *Thomas Woolner*, 1917, p. 208; *Mat.* ii 351). T. wrote to his wife Emily, 26 April 1862: 'Spedding is coming to hear me read the Fisherman' (*Lincoln*). Walter White, 13 Feb. 1864, reports T. as saying that 'he had had a proof more than a year, could not yet make up his mind to publish' (*Journals*, 1898, p. 155). At one stage the poem was to be called simply *Enoch* (early mock-up, *Lincoln*). The many biblical echoes in the poem suggest also *Genesis* v 24: 'And Enoch walked with God: and he was not; for God took him.' Like *Aylmer's Field* (p. 1159), it was based on a prose sketch sent by T.'s friend Thomas Woolner (pp. 208–12), who had read the story in 1854 and had since told it to T. (For a faint doubt as to Amy Woolner's text, see P. G. Scott, *Notes and Queries*, May 1968.) T. took the outline and many details from Woolner's *The Fisherman's Story*, but in Woolner there were no names; no episode with Philip seeing Enoch and Annie in love (ll. 61–78); and none of the pressures on Enoch to make the voyage (ll. 101–10). The 'sickly' babe (l. 229) was deduced from Woolner's reference to its death; Woolner gave no details of the parting, or of Philip's courtship; no praying for a sign (ll. 485–504); no details of life on the tropical island; and no details of the journey home. Woolner's ending was much expanded by T., who omitted Woolner's detail of 'no news . . . beyond the fact that the ship . . . was wrecked, . . . and all hands lost'.

T. applied to FitzGerald in order to authenticate the seafaring details (*Mem.* i 515–16). The poem was also influenced by Crabbe's verse tale *The Parting Hour* (*Tales*, 1812); T. read it in 1859 and again in 1862 (*Mat.* ii 212, 341); in Crabbe, the rival is also called Philip. Mrs Gaskell's tale *Sylvia's Lovers* (1863) has a somewhat similar story, and seems to have suggested, presumably as an inserted detail, the ship's name *Good Fortune* (l. 524); her tale had an epigraph from T. on the title-page. Mrs Marian Bradley commented in her diary, 4 Jan. 1864, after hearing T. read *Enoch the Fisherman*: 'A great resemblance in the story to *Sylvia's Lovers* – singular' (*British Museum*). Adelaide Anne Procter's poem *Homeward Bound* (*Legends and Lyrics*, 1858) is an interesting analogue. There is a copy at *Lincoln*, but H.T. has a note (*Mem.* ii 1): 'Adelaide Procter wrote a poem on a similar subject, but this my father did not know until after *Enoch Arden* had been published.' T. also had a presentation copy of *The Morning Watch* (N.Y., 1850): 'the scene is in a tropic land'; see l. 131*n* below.

The poem brings to a climax a lifelong preoccupation of T.'s; cp. the ghosts in *The Coach of Death* 65–8: 'They see the light of their blest firesides, / They hear each household voice: / The whispered love of the fair young wives; / And the laugh of their rose-lipped boys.' The Lotos-Eaters (ll. 117–9) knew it would be better not to return to Ithaca: 'For surely now our household hearths are cold: / Our sons inherit us: our looks are strange: / And we should come like ghosts to trouble joy.' Again, *In Memoriam* xc 13–20: 'But if they came who past away, / Behold their brides in other hands; / The hard heir strides about their lands, / And will not yield them for a day. // Yea, though their sons were none of these, / Not less the yet-loved sire would make / Confusion worse than death, and shake / The pillars of domestic peace.'

Long lines of cliff breaking have left a chasm;
And in the chasm are foam and yellow sands;
Beyond, red roofs about a narrow wharf
In cluster; then a mouldered church; and higher
A long street climbs to one tall-towered mill;
And high in heaven behind it a gray down
With Danish barrows; and a hazelwood,
By autumn nutters haunted, flourishes
Green in a cuplike hollow of the down.

Here on this beach a hundred years ago,
Three children of three houses, Annie Lee,
The prettiest little damsel in the port,
And Philip Ray the miller's only son,
And Enoch Arden, a rough sailor's lad
Made orphan by a winter shipwreck, played
Among the waste and lumber of the shore,
Hard coils of cordage, swarthy fishing-nets,
Anchors of rusty fluke, and boats updrawn;
And built their castles of dissolving sand
To watch them overflowed, or following up
And flying the white breaker, daily left
The little footprint daily washed away.

A narrow cave ran in beneath the cliff:
In this the children played at keeping house.
Enoch was host one day, Philip the next,
While Annie still was mistress; but at times
Enoch would hold possession for a week:
'This is my house and this my little wife.'
'Mine too' said Philip 'turn and turn about:'
When, if they quarrelled, Enoch stronger-made
Was master: then would Philip, his blue eyes
All flooded with the helpless wrath of tears,
Shriek out 'I hate you, Enoch,' and at this
The little wife would weep for company,
And pray them not to quarrel for her sake,
And say she would be little wife to both.

But when the dawn of rosy childhood past,
And the new warmth of life's ascending sun
Was felt by either, either fixt his heart
On that one girl; and Enoch spoke his love,
But Philip loved in silence; and the girl
Seemed kinder unto Philip than to him;
But she loved Enoch; though she knew it not,
And would if asked deny it. Enoch set
A purpose evermore before his eyes,
To hoard all savings to the uttermost,
To purchase his own boat, and make a home
For Annie: and so prospered that at last
A luckier or a bolder fisherman,
A carefuller in peril, did not breathe
For leagues along that breaker-beaten coast
Than Enoch. Likewise had he served a year
On board a merchantman, and made himself
Full sailor; and he thrice had plucked a life
From the dread sweep of the down-streaming seas:
And all men looked upon him favourably:
And ere he touched his one-and-twentieth May
He purchased his own boat, and made a home
For Annie, neat and nestlike, halfway up
The narrow street that clambered toward the mill.

Then, on a golden autumn eventide,
The younger people making holiday,
With bag and sack and basket, great and small,
Went nutting to the hazels. Philip stayed
(His father lying sick and needing him)
An hour behind; but as he climbed the hill,
Just where the prone edge of the wood began
To feather toward the hollow, saw the pair,
Enoch and Annie, sitting hand-in-hand,
His large gray eyes and weather-beaten face
All-kindled by a still and sacred fire,
That burned as on an altar. Philip looked,
And in their eyes and faces read his doom;
Then, as their faces drew together, groaned,
And slipt aside, and like a wounded life
Crept down into the hollows of the wood;
There, while the rest were loud in merrymaking,
Had his dark hour unseen, and rose and past
Bearing a lifelong hunger in his heart.

So these were wed, and merrily rang the bells,
And merrily ran the years, seven happy years,

Seven happy years of health and competence,
And mutual love and honourable toil;
With children; first a daughter. In him woke,
With his first babe's first cry, the noble wish
To save all earnings to the uttermost,
And give his child a better bringing-up
Than his had been, or hers; a wish renewed,
When two years after came a boy to be
The rosy idol of her solitudes,
While Enoch was abroad on wrathful seas,
Or often journeying landward; for in truth
Enoch's white horse, and Enoch's ocean-spoil
In ocean-smelling osier, and his face,
Rough-reddened with a thousand winter gales,
Not only to the market-cross were known,
But in the leafy lanes behind the down,
Far as the portal-warding lion-whelp,
And peacock-yewtree of the lonely Hall,
Whose Friday fare was Enoch's ministering.

Then came a change, as all things human change.
Ten miles to northward of the narrow port
Opened a larger haven: thither used
Enoch at times to go by land or sea;
And once when there, and clambering on a mast
In harbour, by mischance he slipt and fell:
A limb was broken when they lifted him;
And while he lay recovering there, his wife
Bore him another son, a sickly one:
Another hand crept too across his trade
Taking her bread and theirs: and on him fell,
Although a grave and staid God-fearing man,
Yet lying thus inactive, doubt and gloom.
He seemed, as in a nightmare of the night,
To see his children leading evermore
Low miserable lives of hand-to-mouth,
And her, he loved, a beggar: then he prayed
'Save them from this, whatever comes to me.'
And while he prayed, the master of that ship
Enoch had served in, hearing his mischance,
Came, for he knew the man and valued him,
Reporting of his vessel China-bound,
And wanting yet a boatswain. Would he go?
There yet were many weeks before she sailed,
Sailed from this port. Would Enoch have the place?
And Enoch all at once assented to it,
Rejoicing at that answer to his prayer.

So now that shadow of mischance appeared
No graver than as when some little cloud
Cuts off the fiery highway of the sun,
And isles a light in the offing: yet the wife –
When he was gone – the children – what to do?
Then Enoch lay long-pondering on his plans;
To sell the boat – and yet he loved her well –
How many a rough sea had he weathered in her!
He knew her, as a horseman knows his horse –
And yet to sell her – then with what she brought
Buy goods and stores – set Annie forth in trade
With all that seamen needed or their wives –
So might she keep the house while he was gone.
Should he not trade himself out yonder? go
This voyage more than once? yea twice or thrice –
As oft as needed – last, returning rich,
Become the master of a larger craft,
With fuller profits lead an easier life,
Have all his pretty young ones educated,
And pass his days in peace among his own.

Thus Enoch in his heart determined all:
Then moving homeward came on Annie pale,
Nursing the sickly babe, her latest-born.
Forward she started with a happy cry,
And laid the feeble infant in his arms;
Whom Enoch took, and handled all his limbs,
Appraised his weight and fondled fatherlike,
But had no heart to break his purposes
To Annie, till the morrow, when he spoke.

Then first since Enoch's golden ring had girt
Her finger, Annie fought against his will:
Yet not with brawling opposition she,
But manifold entreaties, many a tear,
Many a sad kiss by day by night renewed
(Sure that all evil would come out of it)
Besought him, supplicating, if he cared
For her or his dear children, not to go.

¶330. *131.* Makes 'islands of light on the sea' (T.). *offing*: 'in the sea-language, that part of the sea, a good distance from shore, where there is deep water, and no need of a pilot to conduct the ship' (*English Encyclopaedia*, 1802, of which there was a copy at Somersby, *Lincoln*). Cp. *The Morning Watch* (see headnote): 'A small white cloud is seen in the offing.' From 'as when' to 'offing' had at first been a separate nature jotting by T. (*H.Nbk 18*).

He not for his own self caring but her,
Her and her children, let her plead in vain;
So grieving held his will, and bore it through.

For Enoch parted with his old sea-friend,
Bought Annie goods and stores, and set his hand
To fit their little streetward sitting-room
With shelf and corner for the goods and stores.
So all day long till Enoch's last at home,
Shaking their pretty cabin, hammer and axe,
Auger and saw, while Annie seemed to hear
Her own death-scaffold raising, shrilled and rang,
Till this was ended, and his careful hand, –
The space was narrow, – having ordered all
Almost as neat and close as Nature packs
Her blossom or her seedling, paused; and he,
Who needs would work for Annie to the last,
Ascending tired, heavily slept till morn.

And Enoch faced this morning of farewell
Brightly and boldly. All his Annie's fears,
Save, as his Annie's, were a laughter to him.
Yet Enoch as a brave God-fearing man
Bowed himself down, and in that mystery
Where God-in-man is one with man-in-God,
Prayed for a blessing on his wife and babes
Whatever came to him: and then he said
'Annie, this voyage by the grace of God
Will bring fair weather yet to all of us.
Keep a clean hearth and a clear fire for me,
For I'll be back, my girl, before you know it.'
Then lightly rocking baby's cradle 'and he,
This pretty, puny, weakly little one, –
Nay – for I love him all the better for it –
God bless him, he shall sit upon my knees
And I will tell him tales of foreign parts,
And make him merry, when I come home again.
Come, Annie, come, cheer up before I go.'

Him running on thus hopefully she heard,
And almost hoped herself; but when he turned
The current of his talk to graver things
In sailor fashion roughly sermonizing
On providence and trust in Heaven, she heard,
Heard and not heard him; as the village girl,
Who sets her pitcher underneath the spring,
Musing on him that used to fill it for her,
Hears and not hears, and lets it overflow.

At length she spoke 'O Enoch, you are wise;
And yet for all your wisdom well know I
That I shall look upon your face no more.'

'Well then,' said Enoch, 'I shall look on yours.
Annie, the ship I sail in passes here
(He named the day) get you a seaman's glass,
Spy out my face, and laugh at all your fears.'

But when the last of those last moments came,
'Annie, my girl, cheer up, be comforted,
Look to the babes, and till I come again
Keep everything shipshape, for I must go.
And fear no more for me; or if you fear
Cast all your cares on God; that anchor holds.
Is He not yonder in those uttermost
Parts of the morning? if I flee to these
Can I go from Him? and the sea is His,
The sea is His: He made it.'
Enoch rose,
Cast his strong arms about his drooping wife,
And kissed his wonder-stricken little ones;
But for the third, the sickly one, who slept
After a night of feverous wakefulness,
When Annie would have raised him Enoch said
'Wake him not; let him sleep; how should the child
Remember this?' and kissed him in his cot.
But Annie from her baby's forehead clipt
A tiny curl, and gave it: this he kept
Through all his future; but now hastily caught
His bundle, waved his hand, and went his way.

She when the day, that Enoch mentioned, came,
Borrowed a glass, but all in vain: perhaps
She could not fix the glass to suit her eye;

*212.* Cp. *Acts* xx 38: 'Sorrowing most of all for the words which he spake, that they should see his face no more. And they accompanied him unto the ship.'

*222–6. 1 Peter* v 7: 'Casting all your care upon him, for he careth for you'; *Hebrews* vi 19: 'Which hope we have as an anchor of the soul both sure and stedfast'; *Psalm* cxxxix 9: 'If I take the wings of the morning, and dwell in the uttermost parts of the sea'; *Psalm* xcv 5: 'The sea is his, and he made it'.

*228.* Cp. Shelley, *Revolt of Islam* V xliii 5: 'Which now the wonder-stricken breezes kissed'.

Perhaps her eye was dim, hand tremulous;
She saw him not: and while he stood on deck
Waving, the moment and the vessel past.

Even to the last dip of the vanishing sail
She watched it, and departed weeping for him;
Then, though she mourned his absence as his grave,
Set her sad will no less to chime with his,
But throve not in her trade, not being bred
To barter, nor compensating the want
By shrewdness, neither capable of lies,
Nor asking overmuch and taking less,
And still foreboding 'what would Enoch say?'
For more than once, in days of difficulty
And pressure, had she sold her wares for less
Than what she gave in buying what she sold:
She failed and saddened knowing it; and thus,
Expectant of that news which never came,
Gained for her own a scanty sustenance,
And lived a life of silent melancholy.

Now the third child was sickly-born and grew
Yet sicklier, though the mother cared for it
With all a mother's care: nevertheless,
Whether her business often called her from it,
Or through the want of what it needed most,
Or means to pay the voice who best could tell
What most it needed – howsoe'er it was,
After a lingering, – ere she was aware, –
Like the caged bird escaping suddenly,
The little innocent soul flitted away.

In that same week when Annie buried it,
Philip's true heart, which hungered for her peace
(Since Enoch left he had not looked upon her),
Smote him, as having kept aloof so long.
'Surely,' said Philip, 'I may see her now,
May be some little comfort;' therefore went,
Past through the solitary room in front,
Paused for a moment at an inner door,
Then struck it thrice, and, no one opening,
Entered; but Annie, seated with her grief,
Fresh from the burial of her little one,

*246.* 'She mourned as if his absence were his grave' (Woolner).

*248–9.* 'Not having been bred to barter' (Woolner).

*249. compénsating*: apparently the usual pronunciation till the mid-nineteenth century.

Cared not to look on any human face,
But turned her own toward the wall and wept.
Then Philip standing up said falteringly
'Annie, I came to ask a favour of you.'

He spoke; the passion in her moaned reply
'Favour from one so sad and so forlorn
As I am!' half abashed him; yet unasked,
His bashfulness and tenderness at war,
He set himself beside her, saying to her:

'I came to speak to you of what he wished,
Enoch, your husband: I have ever said
You chose the best among us – a strong man:
For where he fixt his heart he set his hand
To do the thing he willed, and bore it through.
And wherefore did he go this weary way,
And leave you lonely? not to see the world –
For pleasure? – nay, but for the wherewithal
To give his babes a better bringing-up
Than his had been, or yours: that was his wish.
And if he come again, vext will he be
To find the precious morning hours were lost.
And it would vex him even in his grave,
If he could know his babes were running wild
Like colts about the waste. So, Annie, now –
Have we not known each other all our lives?
I do beseech you by the love you bear
Him and his children not to say me nay –
For, if you will, when Enoch comes again
Why then he shall repay me – if you will,
Annie – for I am rich and well-to-do.
Now let me put the boy and girl to school:
This is the favour that I came to ask.'

Then Annie with her brows against the wall
Answered 'I cannot look you in the face;
I seem so foolish and so broken down.
When you came in my sorrow broke me down;
And now I think your kindness breaks me down;
But Enoch lives; that is borne in on me:
He will repay you: money can be repaid;
Not kindness such as yours.'
And Philip asked
'Then you will let me, Annie?'
There she turned,
She rose, and fixt her swimming eyes upon him,

And dwelt a moment on his kindly face,
Then calling down a blessing on his head
Caught at his hand, and wrung it passionately,
And past into the little garth beyond.
So lifted up in spirit he moved away.

Then Philip put the boy and girl to school,
And bought them needful books, and everyway,
Like one who does his duty by his own,
Made himself theirs; and though for Annie's sake,
Fearing the lazy gossip of the port,
He oft denied his heart his dearest wish,
And seldom crost her threshold, yet he sent
Gifts by the children, garden-herbs and fruit,
The late and early roses from his wall,
Or conies from the down, and now and then,
With some pretext of fineness in the meal
To save the offence of charitable, flour
From his tall mill that whistled on the waste.

But Philip did not fathom Annie's mind:
Scarce could the woman when he came upon her,
Out of full heart and boundless gratitude
Light on a broken word to thank him with.
But Philip was her children's all-in-all;
From distant corners of the street they ran
To greet his hearty welcome heartily;
Lords of his house and of his mill were they;
Worried his passive ear with petty wrongs
Or pleasures, hung upon him, played with him
And called him Father Philip. Philip gained
As Enoch lost; for Enoch seemed to them
Uncertain as a vision or a dream,
Faint as a figure seen in early dawn
Down at the far end of an avenue,
Going we know not where: and so ten years,
Since Enoch left his hearth and native land,
Fled forward, and no news of Enoch came.

It chanced one evening Annie's children longed
To go with others, nutting to the wood,
And Annie would go with them; then they begged
For Father Philip (as they called him) too:
Him, like the working bee in blossom-dust,
Blanched with his mill, they found; and saying to him
'Come with us Father Philip' he denied;
But when the children plucked at him to go,

He laughed, and yielded readily to their wish,
For was not Annie with them? and they went.

But after scaling half the weary down,
Just where the prone edge of the wood began
To feather toward the hollow, all her force
Failed her; and sighing, 'Let me rest' she said:
So Philip rested with her well-content;
While all the younger ones with jubilant cries
Broke from their elders, and tumultuously
Down through the whitening hazels made a plunge
To the bottom, and dispersed, and bent or broke
The lithe reluctant boughs to tear away
Their tawny clusters, crying to each other
And calling, here and there, about the wood.

But Philip sitting at her side forgot
Her presence, and remembered one dark hour
Here in this wood, when like a wounded life
He crept into the shadow: at last he said,
Lifting his honest forehead, 'Listen, Annie,
How merry they are down yonder in the wood.
Tired, Annie?' for she did not speak a word.
'Tired?' but her face had fallen upon her hands;
At which, as with a kind of anger in him,
'The ship was lost,' he said, 'the ship was lost!
No more of that! why should you kill yourself
And make them orphans quite?' And Annie said
'I thought not of it: but – I know not why –
Their voices make me feel so solitary.'

Then Philip coming somewhat closer spoke.
'Annie, there is a thing upon my mind,
And it has been upon my mind so long,
That though I know not when it first came there,
I know that it will out at last. O Annie,
It is beyond all hope, against all chance,
That he who left you ten long years ago
Should still be living; well then – let me speak:
I grieve to see you poor and wanting help:
I cannot help you as I wish to do
Unless – they say that women are so quick –
Perhaps you know what I would have you know –
I wish you for my wife. I fain would prove
A father to your children: I do think
They love me as a father: I am sure
That I love them as if they were mine own;

And I believe, if you were fast my wife,
That after all these sad uncertain years,
We might be still as happy as God grants
To any of his creatures. Think upon it:
For I am well-to-do – no kin, no care,
No burthen, save my care for you and yours:
And we have known each other all our lives,
And I have loved you longer than you know.'

Then answered Annie; tenderly she spoke:
'You have been as God's good angel in our house.
God bless you for it, God reward you for it,
Philip, with something happier than myself.
Can one love twice? can you be ever loved
As Enoch was? what is it that you ask?'
'I am content' he answered 'to be loved
A little after Enoch.' 'O' she cried,
Scared as it were, 'dear Philip, wait a while:
If Enoch comes – but Enoch will not come –
Yet wait a year, a year is not so long:
Surely I shall be wiser in a year:
O wait a little!' Philip sadly said
'Annie, as I have waited all my life
I well may wait a little.' 'Nay' she cried
'I am bound: you have my promise – in a year:
Will you not bide your year as I bide mine?'
And Philip answered 'I will bide my year.'

Here both were mute, till Philip glancing up
Beheld the dead flame of the fallen day
Pass from the Danish barrow overhead;
Then fearing night and chill for Annie, rose
And sent his voice beneath him through the wood.
Up came the children laden with their spoil;
Then all descended to the port, and there
At Annie's door he paused and gave his hand,
Saying gently 'Annie, when I spoke to you,
That was your hour of weakness. I was wrong,
I am always bound to you, but you are free.'
Then Annie weeping answered 'I am bound.'

She spoke; and in one moment as it were,
While yet she went about her household ways,
Even as she dwelt upon his latest words,
That he had loved her longer than she knew,
That autumn into autumn flashed again,
And there he stood once more before her face,

Claiming her promise. 'Is it a year?' she asked.
'Yes, if the nuts' he said 'be ripe again:
Come out and see.' But she – she put him off –
So much to look to – such a change – a month –
Give her a month – she knew that she was bound –
A month – no more. Then Philip with his eyes
Full of that lifelong hunger, and his voice
Shaking a little like a drunkard's hand,
'Take your own time, Annie, take your own time.'
And Annie could have wept for pity of him;
And yet she held him on delayingly
With many a scarce-believable excuse,
Trying his truth and his long-sufferance,
Till half-another year had slipt away.

By this the lazy gossips of the port,
Abhorrent of a calculation crost,
Began to chafe as at a personal wrong.
Some thought that Philip did but trifle with her;
Some that she but held off to draw him on;
And others laughed at her and Philip too,
As simple folk that knew not their own minds,
And one, in whom all evil fancies clung
Like serpent eggs together, laughingly
Would hint at worse in either. Her own son
Was silent, though he often looked his wish;
But evermore the daughter prest upon her
To wed the man so dear to all of them
And lift the household out of poverty;
And Philip's rosy face contracting grew
Careworn and wan; and all these things fell on her
Sharp as reproach.

At last one night it chanced
That Annie could not sleep, but earnestly
Prayed for a sign 'my Enoch is he gone?'
Then compassed round by the blind wall of night
Brooked not the expectant terror of her heart,
Started from bed, and struck herself a light,
Then desperately seized the holy Book,
Suddenly set it wide to find a sign,
Suddenly put her finger on the text,
'Under the palm-tree.' That was nothing to her:

*487–96.* Cp. *Judges* vi 17: 'If now I have found grace in thy sight, then show me a sign'.

*494. the*] *1870*; a *1864–9*. Misquoting *Judges* iv 5: 'And she dwelt under the palm tree of Deborah'.

No meaning there: she closed the Book and slept:
When lo! her Enoch sitting on a height,
Under a palm-tree, over him the Sun:
'He is gone,' she thought, 'he is happy, he is singing
Hosanna in the highest: yonder shines
The Sun of Righteousness, and these be palms
Whereof the happy people strowing cried
"Hosanna in the highest!"' Here she woke,
Resolved, sent for him and said wildly to him
'There is no reason why we should not wed.'
'Then for God's sake,' he answered, 'both our sakes,
So you will wed me, let it be at once.'

So these were wed and merrily rang the bells,
Merrily rang the bells and they were wed.
But never merrily beat Annie's heart.
A footstep seemed to fall beside her path,
She knew not whence; a whisper on her ear,
She knew not what; nor loved she to be left
Alone at home, nor ventured out alone.
What ailed her then, that ere she entered, often
Her hand dwelt lingeringly on the latch,
Fearing to enter: Philip thought he knew:
Such doubts and fears were common to her state,
Being with child: but when her child was born,
Then her new child was as herself renewed,
Then the new mother came about her heart,
Then her good Philip was her all-in-all,
And that mysterious instinct wholly died.

And where was Enoch? prosperously sailed
The ship 'Good Fortune', though at setting forth
The Biscay, roughly ridging eastward, shook
And almost overwhelmed her, yet unvext
She slipt across the summer of the world,
Then after a long tumble about the Cape
And frequent interchange of foul and fair,
She passing through the summer world again,
The breath of heaven came continually
And sent her sweetly by the golden isles,
Till silent in her oriental haven.

There Enoch traded for himself, and bought
Quaint monsters for the market of those times,
A gilded dragon, also, for the babes.

500. *The Sun of Righteousness*: *Malachi* iv 2. *palms*: *John* xii 13.
527. 'The Equator' (T.).

Less lucky her home-voyage: at first indeed
Through many a fair sea-circle, day by day,
Scarce-rocking, her full-busted figure-head
Stared o'er the ripple feathering from her bows:
Then followed calms, and then winds variable,
Then baffling, a long course of them; and last
Storm, such as drove her under moonless heavens
Till hard upon the cry of 'breakers' came
The crash of ruin, and the loss of all
But Enoch and two others. Half the night,
Buoyed upon floating tackle and broken spars,
These drifted, stranding on an isle at morn
Rich, but the loneliest in a lonely sea.

No want was there of human sustenance,
Soft fruitage, mighty nuts, and nourishing roots;
Nor save for pity was it hard to take
The helpless life so wild that it was tame.
There in a seaward-gazing mountain-gorge
They built, and thatched with leaves of palm, a hut,
Half hut, half native cavern. So the three,
Set in this Eden of all plenteousness,
Dwelt with eternal summer, ill-content.

For one, the youngest, hardly more than boy,
Hurt in that night of sudden ruin and wreck,
Lay lingering out a five-years' death-in-life.
They could not leave him. After he was gone,
The two remaining found a fallen stem;
And Enoch's comrade, careless of himself,
Fire-hollowing this in Indian fashion, fell
Sun-stricken, and that other lived alone.
In those two deaths he read God's warning 'wait'.

The mountain wooded to the peak, the lawns
And winding glades high up like ways to Heaven,
The slender coco's drooping crown of plumes,
The lightning flash of insect and of bird,
The lustre of the long convolvuluses
That coiled around the stately stems, and ran
Even to the limit of the land, the glows

*542.* 'Having met a long course of baffling winds' (Woolner).

*561. five-*] *1869*; three- *1864–7*.

*570.* The coco-palm appears in *The Progress of Spring* 68.

*574–5.* Cp. *The Deity* 12 (by T.'s brother Charles, *1827*): 'the broad glow of glory'; and *The Lover's Tale* i 392, ii 109: 'glory of broad waters', 'glows and glories of the moon'.

And glories of the broad belt of the world,
All these he saw; but what he fain had seen
He could not see, the kindly human face,
Nor ever hear a kindly voice, but heard
The myriad shriek of wheeling ocean-fowl,
The league-long roller thundering on the reef,
The moving whisper of huge trees that branched
And blossomed in the zenith, or the sweep
Of some precipitous rivulet to the wave,
As down the shore he ranged, or all day long
Sat often in the seaward-gazing gorge,
A shipwrecked sailor, waiting for a sail:
No sail from day to day, but every day
The sunrise broken into scarlet shafts
Among the palms and ferns and precipices;
The blaze upon the waters to the east;
The blaze upon his island overhead;
The blaze upon the waters to the west;
Then the great stars that globed themselves in Heaven,
The hollower-bellowing ocean, and again
The scarlet shafts of sunrise–but no sail.

There often as he watched or seemed to watch,
So still, the golden lizard on him paused,
A phantom made of many phantoms moved
Before him haunting him, or he himself
Moved haunting people, things and places, known
Far in a darker isle beyond the line;
The babes, their babble, Annie, the small house,
The climbing street, the mill, the leafy lanes,
The peacock-yewtree and the lonely Hall,
The horse he drove, the boat he sold, the chill
November dawns and dewy-glooming downs,
The gentle shower, the smell of dying leaves,
And the low moan of leaden-coloured seas.

Once likewise, in the ringing of his ears,
Though faintly, merrily–far and far away–
He heard the pealing of his parish bells;
Then, though he knew not wherefore, started up
Shuddering, and when the beauteous hateful isle
Returned upon him, had not his poor heart

*606–8.* Shelley's *Alastor* 555–7 has 'seas', 'gloom', 'leaden-coloured'.
*611.* T. says 'Kinglake told me that he had heard his own parish bells in the midst of an Eastern desert'; and refers to *Eothen*, chapter xvii.
*613.* The theme of *The Islet* (p. 1186).

Spoken with That, which being everywhere
Lets none, who speaks with Him, seem all alone,
Surely the man had died of solitude.

Thus over Enoch's early-silvering head
The sunny and rainy seasons came and went
Year after year. His hopes to see his own,
And pace the sacred old familiar fields,
Not yet had perished, when his lonely doom
Came suddenly to an end. Another ship
(She wanted water) blown by baffling winds,
Like the Good Fortune, from her destined course,
Stayed by this isle, not knowing where she lay:
For since the mate had seen at early dawn
Across a break on the mist-wreathen isle
The silent water slipping from the hills,
They sent a crew that landing burst away
In search of stream or fount, and filled the shores
With clamour. Downward from his mountain gorge
Stept the long-haired long-bearded solitary,
Brown, looking hardly human, strangely clad,
Muttering and mumbling, idiotlike it seemed,
With inarticulate rage, and making signs
They knew not what: and yet he led the way
To where the rivulets of sweet water ran;
And ever as he mingled with the crew,
And heard them talking, his long-bounden tongue
Was loosened, till he made them understand;
Whom, when their casks were filled they took aboard:
And there the tale he uttered brokenly,
Scarce-credited at first but more and more,
Amazed and melted all who listened to it:
And clothes they gave him and free passage home;
But oft he worked among the rest and shook
His isolation from him. None of these
Came from his country, or could answer him,
If questioned, aught of what he cared to know.
And dull the voyage was with long delays,
The vessel scarce sea-worthy; but evermore
His fancy fled before the lazy wind
Returning, till beneath a clouded moon

*638.* T. compares *Aeneid* i 167: *intus aquae dulces vivoque sedilia saxo* ('within are fresh waters and seats in the living stone').

*640–1.* Cp. *Luke* i 64: 'And his mouth was opened immediately, and his tongue loosed, and he spake, and praised God.'

*649. country*] *1875*; county *1864–72*.

He like a lover down through all his blood
Drew in the dewy meadowy morning-breath
Of England, blown across her ghostly wall:
And that same morning officers and men
Levied a kindly tax upon themselves,
Pitying the lonely man, and gave him it:
Then moving up the coast they landed him,
Even in that harbour whence he sailed before.

There Enoch spoke no word to any one,
But homeward–home–what home? had he a home?
His home, he walked. Bright was that afternoon,
Sunny but chill; till drawn through either chasm,
Where either haven opened on the deeps,
Rolled a sea-haze and whelmed the world in gray;
Cut off the length of highway on before,
And left but narrow breadth to left and right
Of withered holt or tilth or pasturage.
On the nigh-naked tree the robin piped
Disconsolate, and through the dripping haze
The dead weight of the dead leaf bore it down:
Thicker the drizzle grew, deeper the gloom;
Last, as it seemed, a great mist-blotted light
Flared on him, and he came upon the place.

Then down the long street having slowly stolen,
His heart foreshadowing all calamity,
His eyes upon the stones, he reached the home
Where Annie lived and loved him, and his babes
In those far-off seven happy years were born;
But finding neither light nor murmur there
(A bill of sale gleamed through the drizzle) crept
Still downward thinking 'dead or dead to me!'

Down to the pool and narrow wharf he went,
Seeking a tavern which of old he knew,
A front of timber-crost antiquity,
So propt, worm-eaten, ruinously old,
He thought it must have gone; but he was gone
Who kept it; and his widow Miriam Lane,
With daily-dwindling profits held the house;
A haunt of brawling seamen once, but now
Stiller, with yet a bed for wandering men.
There Enoch rested silent many days.

But Miriam Lane was good and garrulous,
Nor let him be, but often breaking in,
Told him, with other annals of the port,

Not knowing–Enoch was so brown, so bowed,
So broken–all the story of his house.
His baby's death, her growing poverty,
How Philip put her little ones to school,
And kept them in it, his long wooing her,
Her slow consent, and marriage, and the birth
Of Philip's child: and o'er his countenance
No shadow past, nor motion: any one,
Regarding, well had deemed he felt the tale
Less than the teller: only when she closed
'Enoch, poor man, was cast away and lost'
He, shaking his gray head pathetically,
Repeated muttering 'cast away and lost;'
Again in deeper inward whispers 'lost!'

But Enoch yearned to see her face again;
'If I might look on her sweet face again
And know that she is happy.' So the thought
Haunted and harassed him, and drove him forth,
At evening when the dull November day
Was growing duller twilight, to the hill.
There he sat down gazing on all below;
There did a thousand memories roll upon him,
Unspeakable for sadness. By and by
The ruddy square of comfortable light,
Far-blazing from the rear of Philip's house,
Allured him, as the beacon-blaze allures
The bird of passage, till he madly strikes
Against it, and beats out his weary life.

For Philip's dwelling fronted on the street,
The latest house to landward; but behind,
With one small gate that opened on the waste,
Flourished a little garden square and walled:
And in it throve an ancient evergreen,
A yewtree, and all round it ran a walk
Of shingle, and a walk divided it:
But Enoch shunned the middle walk and stole
Up by the wall, behind the yew; and thence
That which he better might have shunned, if griefs
Like his have worse or better, Enoch saw.

For cups and silver on the burnished board
Sparkled and shone; so genial was the hearth:
And on the right hand of the hearth he saw
Philip, the slighted suitor of old times,

Stout, rosy, with his babe across his knees;
And o'er her second father stoopt a girl,
A later but a loftier Annie Lee,
Fair-haired and tall, and from her lifted hand
Dangled a length of ribbon and a ring
To tempt the babe, who reared his creasy arms,
Caught at and ever missed it, and they laughed;
And on the left hand of the hearth he saw
The mother glancing often toward her babe,
But turning now and then to speak with him,
Her son, who stood beside her tall and strong,
And saying that which pleased him, for he smiled.

Now when the dead man come to life beheld
His wife his wife no more, and saw the babe
Hers, yet not his, upon the father's knee,
And all the warmth, the peace, the happiness,
And his own children tall and beautiful,
And him, that other, reigning in his place,
Lord of his rights and of his children's love,–
Then he, though Miriam Lane had told him all,
Because things seen are mightier than things heard,
Staggered and shook, holding the branch, and feared
To send abroad a shrill and terrible cry,
Which in one moment, like the blast of doom,
Would shatter all the happiness of the hearth.

He therefore turning softly like a thief,
Lest the harsh shingle should grate underfoot,
And feeling all along the garden-wall,
Lest he should swoon and tumble and be found,
Crept to the gate, and opened it, and closed,
As lightly as a sick man's chamber-door,
Behind him, and came out upon the waste.

And there he would have knelt, but that his knees
Were feeble, so that falling prone he dug
His fingers into the wet earth, and prayed.

'Too hard to bear! why did they take me thence?
O God Almighty, blessèd Saviour, Thou
That didst uphold me on my lonely isle,
Uphold me, Father, in my loneliness
A little longer! aid me, give me strength

*742.* 'He saw the miller, stout rosy and happy, with a two years old child on his knee' (Woolner).

*780.* *Psalm* cxlv 14: 'The Lord upholdeth all that fall'.

Not to tell her, never to let her know.
Help me not to break in upon her peace.
My children too! must I not speak to these?
They know me not. I should betray myself.
Never: No father's kiss for me–the girl
So like her mother, and the boy, my son.'

There speech and thought and nature failed a little,
And he lay tranced; but when he rose and paced
Back toward his solitary home again,
All down the long and narrow street he went
Beating it in upon his weary brain,
As though it were the burthen of a song,
'Not to tell her, never to let her know.'

He was not all unhappy. His resolve
Upbore him, and firm faith, and evermore
Prayer from a living source within the will,
And beating up through all the bitter world,
Like fountains of sweet water in the sea,
Kept him a living soul. 'This miller's wife'
He said to Miriam 'that you spoke about,
Has she no fear that her first husband lives?'
'Ay, ay, poor soul' said Miriam, 'fear enow!
If you could tell her you had seen him dead,
Why, that would be her comfort;' and he thought
'After the Lord has called me she shall know,
I wait His time,' and Enoch set himself,
Scorning an alms, to work whereby to live.
Almost to all things could he turn his hand.
Cooper he was and carpenter, and wrought
To make the boatmen fishing-nets, or helped
At lading and unlading the tall barks,
That brought the stinted commerce of those days;
Thus earned a scanty living for himself:
Yet since he did but labour for himself,
Work without hope, there was not life in it
Whereby the man could live; and as the year
Rolled itself round again to meet the day
When Enoch had returned, a languor came
Upon him, gentle sickness, gradually
Weakening the man, till he could do no more,
But kept the house, his chair, and last his bed.

*801. spoke about*] *1872*; told me of *1864–70*.

*816.* Cp. Coleridge, *Work without Hope* 13–14: 'Work without Hope draws nectar in a sieve, / And Hope without an object cannot live.'

And Enoch bore his weakness cheerfully.
For sure no gladlier does the stranded wreck
See through the gray skirts of a lifting squall
The boat that bears the hope of life approach
To save the life despaired of, than he saw
Death dawning on him, and the close of all.

For through that dawning gleamed a kindlier hope
On Enoch thinking 'after I am gone,
Then may she learn I loved her to the last.'
He called aloud for Miriam Lane and said
'Woman, I have a secret–only swear,
Before I tell you–swear upon the book
Not to reveal it, till you see me dead.'
'Dead,' clamoured the good woman, 'hear him talk!
I warrant, man, that we shall bring you round.'
'Swear,' added Enoch sternly 'on the book.'
And on the book, half-frighted, Miriam swore.
Then Enoch rolling his gray eyes upon her,
'Did you know Enoch Arden of this town?'
'Know him?' she said 'I knew him far away.
Ay, ay, I mind him coming down the street;
Held his head high, and cared for no man, he.'
Slowly and sadly Enoch answered her;
'His head is low, and no man cares for him.
I think I have not three days more to live;
I am the man.' At which the woman gave
A half-incredulous, half-hysterical cry.
'You Arden, you! nay,–sure he was a foot
Higher than you be.' Enoch said again
'My God has bowed me down to what I am;
My grief and solitude have broken me;
Nevertheless, know you that I am he
Who married–but that name has twice been changed–
I married her who married Philip Ray.
Sit, listen.' Then he told her of his voyage,
His wreck, his lonely life, his coming back,
His gazing in on Annie, his resolve,
And how he kept it. As the woman heard,
Fast flowed the current of her easy tears,
While in her heart she yearned incessantly
To rush abroad all round the little haven,
Proclaiming Enoch Arden and his woes;
But awed and promise-bounden she forbore,
Saying only 'See your bairns before you go!
Eh, let me fetch 'em, Arden,' and arose

Eager to bring them down, for Enoch hung
A moment on her words, but then replied:
'Woman, disturb me not now at the last,
But let me hold my purpose till I die.
Sit down again; mark me and understand,
While I have power to speak. I charge you now,
When you shall see her, tell her that I died
Blessing her, praying for her, loving her;
Save for the bar between us, loving her
As when she laid her head beside my own.
And tell my daughter Annie, whom I saw
So like her mother, that my latest breath
Was spent in blessing her and praying for her.
And tell my son that I died blessing him.
And say to Philip that I blest him too;
He never meant us any thing but good.
But if my children care to see me dead,
Who hardly knew me living, let them come,
I am their father; but she must not come,
For my dead face would vex her after-life.
And now there is but one of all my blood
Who will embrace me in the world-to-be:
This hair is his: she cut it off and gave it,
And I have borne it with me all these years,
And thought to bear it with me to my grave;
But now my mind is changed, for I shall see him,
My babe in bliss: wherefore when I am gone,
Take, give her this, for it may comfort her:
It will moreover be a token to her,
That I am he.'
He ceased; and Miriam Lane
Made such a voluble answer promising all,
That once again he rolled his eyes upon her
Repeating all he wished, and once again
She promised.
Then the third night after this,
While Enoch slumbered motionless and pale,
And Miriam watched and dozed at intervals,
There came so loud a calling of the sea,

891. *years,*] *1864*; years. *Eversley*.
904. *calling*: 'a ground swell' (T.). Cp. the death in 'Barry Cornwall', *A Sicilian Story* (1820): 'The seas / Did rise and fall, and then that fearful swell / Came silently which seamen know so well; / And all was like an Omen.' T. gave 'calling of the sea' as an example of the difficulty of translation: 'a clear night with a sea-sound on the shore in calm. A German

That all the houses in the haven rang.
He woke, he rose, he spread his arms abroad
Crying with a loud voice 'A sail! a sail!
I am saved;' and so fell back and spoke no more.

So past the strong heroic soul away.
And when they buried him the little port
Had seldom seen a costlier funeral.

[1862. *Dedication* to *Idylls of the King*–see p. 1467]

# 331 A Welcome to Alexandra

## MARCH 7, 1863

Published *The Times*, 10 March 1863; then *1864*. Princess Alexandra of Denmark landed on 7 March and married, on 10 March, Albert Edward, Prince of Wales, later Edward VII. Cp. *A Welcome to Alexandrovna* (p. 1223). T. described it in March 1863 as 'a little lyrical flash, an impromptu which I sent to the Queen and for which she returned me Her warmest thanks' (letter to the Duke and Duchess of Argyll, *Lincoln*).

Sea-kings' daughter from over the sea,
Alexandra!
Saxon and Norman and Dane are we,
But all of us Danes in our welcome of thee,
Alexandra!
Welcome her, thunders of fort and of fleet!
Welcome her, thundering cheer of the street!
Welcome her, all things youthful and sweet,
Scatter the blossom under her feet!
Break, happy land, into earlier flowers!
Make music, O bird, in the new-budded bowers!
Blazon your mottoes of blessing and prayer!
Welcome her, welcome her, all that is ours!
Warble, O bugle, and trumpet, blare!

translator rendered it "Geschrei," which suggested storm, etc., wrongly. He meant a big voice of the sea, but coming through the calm' (1865; J. A. Symonds, *Letters and Papers*, 1923, p. 10).

*911.* T. replied to criticism of this line: 'The costly funeral is all that poor Annie could do for him after he was gone. This is entirely introduced for her sake, and, in my opinion, quite necessary to the perfection of the Poem and the simplicity of the narrative.'

¶331. *12*] *1864*; *not 1863*.

Flags, flutter out upon turrets and towers!
Flames, on the windy headland flare!
Utter your jubilee, steeple and spire!
Clash, ye bells, in the merry March air!
Flash, ye cities, in rivers of fire!
Rush to the roof, sudden rocket, and higher
Melt into stars for the land's desire!
Roll and rejoice, jubilant voice,
Roll as a ground-swell dashed on the strand,
Roar as the sea when he welcomes the land,
And welcome her, welcome the land's desire,
The sea-kings' daughter as happy as fair,
Blissful bride of a blissful heir,
Bride of the heir of the kings of the sea–
O joy to the people and joy to the throne,
Come to us, love us and make us your own:
For Saxon or Dane or Norman we,
Teuton or Celt, or whatever we be,
We are each all Dane in our welcome of thee,
Alexandra!

# 332 On Translations of Homer

## HEXAMETERS AND PENTAMETERS

Published *Cornhill*, Dec. 1863, among 'Attempts at Classic Metres in Quantity'; then *1872*, among 'Experiments in Quantity'. Written 1863. T. comments: 'Some, and among these one at least of our best and greatest (Sir John Herschel), have endeavoured to give us the *Iliad* in English hexameters, and by what appears to me their failure, have gone far to prove the impossibility of the task.' Herschel had published his lines in *Cornhill*, May 1862, being spurred on by Arnold's experiments in *On Translating Homer* (1861). Arnold took T.'s epigram as referring to himself (R. H. Super, *TLS*, 28 Oct. 1960); cp. *Specimen of a Translation* (p. 1156). The other

*20–24*] *1864*; *not 1863*.
*25. And*] *1864*; *not 1863*.
*25 ∧ 6*] Alexandra! *1863*.
*26. The*] *1864*; *not 1863*.
*31–3*. John Churton Collins said: 'The Laureate has been anticipated in his exquisite adulation by Martial *De Spectaculis* (Epig. iii.), enumerating the various nations which welcome Caesar home. He concludes–

*Vox diversa sonat populorum, est vox tamen una*
*Cum verus patriae diceris esse pater.*'

Alongside this suggestion (*Cornhill*, Jan. 1880, *Lincoln*), T. wrote '!!'.

'Experiments' were reprinted in *1864*; Herschel had died by 1872, as Super observes. T. wrote to the Duchess of Argyll, 26 Dec. 1863: 'my feeling is against writing in Magazines. "Why then did you"–I know the argument against me. But what I put into the *Cornhill* were things *sui generis*, experiments which I wished to try with the public' (*Lincoln*). Cp. Coleridge's 'experiments in metre', written 1799, published 1834; T. quotes one of them with disapproval in *Eversley*.

These lame hexameters the strong-winged music of Homer!
No– but a most burlesque barbarous experiment.
When was a harsher sound ever heard, ye Muses, in England?
When did a frog coarser croak upon our Helicon?
Hexameters no worse than daring Germany gave us,
Barbarous experiment, barbarous hexameters.

# 333 Milton
## ALCAICS

Published *Cornhill*, Dec. 1863, among 'Attempts at Classic Metres in Quantity'; then *1864*, 'Experiments in Quantity'. Written 16 Nov. 1863 (*Mat.* ii 381). T. says it was 'not intended for Horatian Alcaics . . . the Greek Alcaic, if we may judge from the two or three specimens left, had a much freer and lighter movement'. All variants from *HnMS* (HM 19497) are below.

O mighty-mouthed inventor of harmonies,
O skilled to sing of Time or Eternity,
God-gifted organ-voice of England,
Milton, a name to resound for ages;
Whose Titan angels, Gabriel, Abdiel,
Starred from Jehovah's gorgeous armouries,
Tower, as the deep-domed empyrëan
Rings to the roar of an angel onset–
Me rather all that bowery loneliness,
The brooks of Eden mazily murmuring,
And bloom profuse and cedar arches

¶332. *5.* J. H. Voss's translations of the *Odyssey* (1781) and the *Iliad* (1793); Arnold's first lecture had referred to Voss.

¶333. *6. from Jehovah's*] out of Heaven's own *HnMS*. *Starred*: adorned; cp. Pope, *Iliad* i 326: 'His Sceptre starr'd with golden Studs around.'

*10. The*] Those *MS.*

*11. bloom*] blooms *MS.*

Charm, as a wanderer out in ocean,
Where some refulgent sunset of India
Streams o'er a rich ambrosial ocean isle,
And crimson-hued the stately palm-woods
Whisper in odorous heights of even.

# 334 Hendecasyllabics

Published *Cornhill*, Dec. 1863, as the third of 'Attempts at Classic Metres in Quantity'; then *1864*, among 'Experiments in Quantity'. Written autumn 1863 (*CT*, p. 346). All variants from *HnMS* (HM 19498) are below. 'These must be read with the English accent' (T.). He used the metre again for an attack on a critic, *The Gentle Life* (p. 1230). Cp. Campion's epigrams in his *Observations in the Art of English Poesy* (1602).

O you chorus of indolent reviewers,
Irresponsible, indolent reviewers,
Look, I come to the test, a tiny poem
All composed in a metre of Catullus,
All in quantity, careful of my motion,
Like the skater on ice that hardly bears him,
Lest I fall unawares before the people,
Waking laughter in indolent reviewers.
Should I flounder awhile without a tumble
Through this metrification of Catullus,
They should speak to me not without a welcome,
All that chorus of indolent reviewers.
Hard, hard, hard is it, only not to tumble,
So fantastical is the dainty metre.
Wherefore slight me not wholly, nor believe me
Too presumptuous, indolent reviewers.

*12*] Captivate even as one who gazes *MS.*
*13. Where*] While *MS.*
*14. Streams*] Dies *MS.*
*14–16.* The picture and many of the words recall *In Memoriam* lxxxvi (p. 937).
¶334. *2*] *Not HnMS.*
*3. Look, I*] Here I *MS.*
*4.* 'The Phalaecian hendecasyllable, the metre in which all but seventeen of the short poems 1–60 are written' (C. J. Fordyce, *Catullus*, 1961, p. 83).
*10. metrification*] versification *MS.*
*14. fantastical*] tyrannical *MS.*
*15. slight*] scorn *MS.*

O blatant Magazines, regard me rather–
Since I blush to belaud myself a moment–
As some rare little rose, a piece of inmost
Horticultural art, or half coquette-like
Maiden, not to be greeted unbenignly.

## 335 Specimen of a Translation of the Iliad in Blank Verse

Published *Cornhill*, Dec. 1863, with 'Attempts at Classic Metres in Quantity'; then *1864*, among 'Experiments'. Written summer 1863 (*Mem.* i 493). *1863* headnote: 'Some, and among these one at least of our best and greatest [Sir John Herschel; see *On Translations of Homer*, p. 1153], have endeavoured to give us the *Iliad* in English hexameters, and by what appears to me their failure, have gone far to prove the impossibility of the task. I have long held by our blank verse in this matter, and now after having spoken so disrespectfully here of these hexameters, I venture, or rather feel bound, to subjoin a specimen, however brief and with whatever demerits, of a blank-verse translation.' Arnold, in *On Translating Homer* iii (1861), had said: 'If blank verse is used in translating Homer . . . it must not be Mr Tennyson's blank verse'; in *Last Words* (1862), he defended the remark, specified this passage from Book viii, and himself translated a few lines. T. translated several passages of Homer; see *Achilles Over the Trench* (p. 1157); *Nor lingered Paris*, and *And when they came together* (Appendix A, p. 1779).

So Hector spake; the Trojans roared applause;
Then loosed their sweating horses from the yoke,
And each beside his chariot bound his own;
And oxen from the city, and goodly sheep

*17. blatant*] loud-lung'd *MS.*
*19. rare little*] *1864*; exquisite *1863*. Presumably changed because of the doubt as to *éxquisite* or *exquísite*.
*19–20*] As some exquisite rose, or half-coquettish *MS.*
*19–21.* Cp. Catullus lxii 39–45: *ut flos in saeptis secretus nascitur hortis . . . / sic virgo dum intacta manet, dum cara suis est.* ('As a flower springs up secretly in a fenced garden . . . so a maiden, whilst she remains untouched, so long is she dear to her own.')
*21. greeted*] treated *MS.*
¶335. *1*] *1872*; He ceased, and sea-like roared the Trojan host, *1863*; So Hector said, and sea-like roared his host; *1864–70*.
2. *Then*] *1864*; And *1863*.

In haste they drove, and honey-hearted wine
And bread from out the houses brought, and heaped
Their firewood, and the winds from off the plain
Rolled the rich vapour far into the heaven.
And these all night upon the bridge of war
Sat glorying; many a fire before them blazed:
As when in heaven the stars about the moon
Look beautiful, when all the winds are laid,
And every height comes out, and jutting peak
And valley, and the immeasurable heavens
Break open to their highest, and all the stars
Shine, and the Shepherd gladdens in his heart:
So many a fire between the ships and stream
Of Xanthus blazed before the towers of Troy,
A thousand on the plain; and close by each
Sat fifty in the blaze of burning fire;
And eating hoary grain and pulse the steeds,
Fixt by their cars, waited the golden dawn.

*Iliad* viii 542–561.

# 336 Achilles Over the Trench

## Iliad xviii 202

Published *Nineteenth Century*, Aug. 1877; then *1880*, among 'Translations'. Written probably 1863–4; it was recited 28 Dec. 1864 (*Mat.* ii 408), and again 8 Dec. 1865: 'No, I shan't read it. It's only a little thing. Must be judged by comparison with the Greek. Can only be appreciated by the difficulties overcome' (J. A. Symonds, quoting T.; *Letters and Papers*, 1923, pp. 5–10). Symonds describes the talk between T. and Gladstone on

5. *honey-hearted*: *1863* note: 'Or, "wine sweet to the mind," but I use this epithet simply as a synonym of "sweet."'
9. *upon*] *1864*; sat on *1863*. *bridge*: *1864* note: 'Or, ridge'.
10. *Sat glorying*] *1864*; Triumphant *1863*.
16. *Shepherd gladdens*] *1864*; hind rejoices *1863*.
21–2] *1872*; And champing golden grain, their horses stood
Hard by the chariots, waiting for the dawn. *1863*;
*1864–70 as 1863*, except for *the* horses and *their* chariots. *1863 note*: 'Or, if something like the spondaic close of the line be required, "And waited–by their chariots–the fair dawn." Or more literally,
"And, champing the white barley and spelt, their steeds
Stood by the cars, waiting the thronèd morn."'
*1864* note: 'Or more literally–
And eating hoary grain and pulse the steeds
Stood by their cars, waiting the thronèd morn.'

translating Homer; in a few respects T. seems to have altered his text at Gladstone's suggestion: 'Gladstone would object, "But you will say Jove and Greeks: can't we have Zeus and Achæans?" "But the sound of Jove! Jove is much softer than Zeus– Zeus– Zeus." "Well, Mr Worsley gives us Achæans." "Mr Worsley has chosen a convenient long metre; he can give you Achæans, and a great deal else."' See ll. 24, 29*n*. For T. and the general argument about translating Homer, see *Specimen of a Translation of the Iliad* (p. 1156). The *Pierpont Morgan MS* of *Achilles* continues for 8 more lines (see below), and is accompanied by two more translations from Homer: *Nor lingered Paris in the lofty house*; and *And when they came together in one place* (see Appendix A, p. 1779).

So saying, light-foot Iris passed away.
Then rose Achilles dear to Zeus; and round
The warrior's puissant shoulders Pallas flung
Her fringèd ægis, and around his head
The glorious goddess wreathed a golden cloud,
And from it lighted an all-shining flame.
As when a smoke from a city goes to heaven
Far off from out an island girt by foes,
All day the men contend in grievous war
From their own city, but with set of sun
Their fires flame thickly, and aloft the glare
Flies streaming, if perchance the neighbours round
May see, and sail to help them in the war;
So from his head the splendour went to heaven.
From wall to dyke he stept, he stood, nor joined
The Achæans–honouring his wise mother's word–
There standing, shouted, and Pallas far away
Called; and a boundless panic shook the foe.
For like the clear voice when a trumpet shrills,
Blown by the fierce beleaguerers of a town,
So rang the clear voice of Æakidês;
And when the brazen cry of Æakidês
Was heard among the Trojans, all their hearts
Were troubled, and the full-maned horses whirled

¶336. 7. Cp. *Joshua* viii 20: 'And behold, the smoke of the city ascended up to heaven.'

*17. and*] *1880; not 1877.*

*21. Æakides*: Achilles was one of the descendants of Æacus.

*24.* T. 'translated "beauteous horses." He thought it meant sleek, etc.; might have said "fair-headed," but wanted same quality of sound which "beauteous" had. Gladstone said ... that καλλίτριχες was meant as a picturesque epithet, to describe the flowing mane of the horses as they stopped suddenly and turned, affrighted by the shout of Achilles' (Symonds, pp. 8–9).

The chariots backward, knowing griefs at hand;
And sheer-astounded were the charioteers
To see the dread, unweariable fire
That always o'er the great Peleion's head
Burned, for the bright-eyed goddess made it burn.
Thrice from the dyke he sent his mighty shout,
Thrice backward reeled the Trojans and allies;
And there and then twelve of their noblest died
Among their spears and chariots.

# 337 Aylmer's Field

## 1793

Published *1864*. Written July 1862–Dec. 1863 (A. Woolner, *Thomas Woolner*, 1917, p. 218; *Mat.* ii 383). Seven pages telling this 'Suffolk story' were sent to T. (as was the story of *Enoch Arden*) by his friend Woolner, who had heard it in childhood. (For a faint doubt as to Amy Woolner's text, see P. G. Scott, *Notes and Queries*, May 1968.) T. took from Woolner (pp. 218–25) most of his story. But he supplied: the names, the French Revolution dating, their being orphans, the cousin from India with his gift of the dagger, the early jilting of Averill and of the other man (ll. 388–91), the hidden letters (in Woolner, all letters were destroyed), the mystical

*27. Peleion*: Achilles was son of Peleus.
*29. Γλαυκῶπις*: T. 'translated this "grey-eyed," in the Shakespearean meaning of "blue-eyed". Gladstone said it ought to be "bright-eyed" (Symonds, p. 8).
*33*] *Pierpont Morgan MS has 2 versions of succeeding lines*:

(i) Among their spears and chariots; but the Greeks
Drew out Patroclus from beneath the darts
And placed him on the litter, and his friends
Wept round him and with these Achilles went
Pouring warm tears to see his best-beloved
Laid on the bier and gashed with cruel brass;
Him, whom he sent with horse and chariot out
To battle, nor again received him whole.

(ii) Among their spears and chariots; with joy
The Achaeans drew Patroclus from the fight,
And laid him on a litter, where his friends
Mourned round him, and with these Achilles followed
Weeping warm tears to see his best-beloved
Stretched on the bier, gashed into gaping wounds,
Him whom he sped with steeds and chariot forth
To battle, nor had welcomed his return.

intuition that Edith is dead (in Woolner, there is the letter), and the return of the lover (ll. 545–51). The sermon is almost entirely T.'s, and he supplied its text, which was perhaps suggested by Woolner's reference to 'desolation'. Nor had Woolner any equivalent to T.'s closing lines. T. at first took over Woolner's title, *The Sermon*. In her diary, 30 Dec. 1863, Mrs Marian Bradley reports that T. referred to the poem as *Edith*: 'He said as he read, from time to time, how incalculably difficult the story was to tell, the dry facts of it so prosaic in themselves' (*British Museum*). 'He often pointed out how hard he had found such and such a passage, how much work and thought it had cost him; for instance, the lawyer at work in chambers; the pompous old Aylmer in his wrath; the suicide. He liked his own descriptions of English landscape, and of cottages covered with creepers; and especially the passage about the Traveller's Joy' (*Mem.* i 495). The date '1793' was a late addition to a trial edition of *1864* (*Trinity College*); it is to invoke the French Revolution (ll. 265, 464, 763–8), which was relevant to T.'s theme of social injustice: 'Was this a time for these to flaunt their pride?' (l. 770). In 'an old idyll never published' (William Allingham's *Diary*, 1907, p. 303: 21 Oct. 1880), T. had written:

The rich shall wed the rich, the poor the poor,
So shall this mound of wealth be higher still,
So shall this gulf of want be deeper still,
Until this mountain melt into this gulf
With all confusion. *H.Lpr 210*

T. felt very strongly about 'this filthy marriage-hindering Mammon' (l. 374), partly because of his rejection by Rosa Baring (see l. 28*n*). The poem 'describes the Nemesis which fell upon Sir Aylmer Aylmer in his pride of wealth. My father always felt a prophet's righteous wrath against this form of selfishness; and no one can read his terrible denunciations of such pride trampling on a holy human love, without being aware that the poet's heart burnt within him while at work on this tale of wrong' (*Mem.* ii 9). Cp., among other poems, *Locksley Hall*, *Edwin Morris*, and *Maud*. The name 'Aylmer' may unconsciously have been suggested by Landor's famous *Rose* Aylmer (1846 text), though there is a Lawrence Aylmer in *The Brook*. Leolin is cognate with Lionel, the hero of *The Lover's Tale*, which T. quarried here. Sir Charles Tennyson (p. 351) believes that there are 'undoubted glimpses' of Arthur Hallam in Averill. In conception and manner the poem is influenced by the verse tales of Crabbe, whom T. was reading in 1862 (*Mat.* ii 341).

Dust are our frames; and, gilded dust, our pride
Looks only for a moment whole and sound;
Like that long-buried body of the king,

¶337. 3–6. T. comments: 'This happened on opening an Etruscan tomb at the city of Tarquinii in Italy.' His source for this incident at Tarquinia was

Found lying with his urns and ornaments,
Which at a touch of light, an air of heaven,
Slipt into ashes, and was found no more.

Here is a story which in rougher shape
Came from a grizzled cripple, whom I saw
Sunning himself in a waste field alone–
Old, and a mine of memories–who had served,
Long since, a bygone Rector of the place,
And been himself a part of what he told.

Sir Aylmer Aylmer, that almighty man,
The county God–in whose capacious hall,
Hung with a hundred shields, the family tree
Sprang from the midriff of a prostrate king–
Whose blazing wyvern weathercocked the spire,
Stood from his walls and winged his entry-gates
And swang besides on many a windy sign–
Whose eyes from under a pyramidal head
Saw from his windows nothing save his own–
What lovelier of his own had he than her,
His only child, his Edith, whom he loved
As heiress and not heir regretfully?
But 'he that marries her marries her name'
This fiat somewhat soothed himself and wife,
His wife a faded beauty of the Baths,
Insipid as the Queen upon a card;
Her all of thought and bearing hardly more
Than his own shadow in a sickly sun.

A land of hops and poppy-mingled corn,
Little about it stirring save a brook!
A sleepy land, where under the same wheel
The same old rut would deepen year by year;
Where almost all the village had one name;

Mrs Hamilton Gray's *Tour of Etruria* (1840; 1843 edn, *Lincoln*), pp. 206–7. Cp. *The Etrurian King* (1842) by T.'s friend R. C. Trench, based on Mrs Gray's book: 'A few short moments,–and a shrunken heap / Of common dust survived, of all that pride.'

*12. Aeneid* ii 6: *quorum pars magnum fui*.

*17. wyvern*: heraldic dragon.

*19.* Cp. *Locksley Hall Sixty Years After* 247: 'There is one old Hostel left us where they swing the Locksley shield.'

*28.* Verbatim from *How thought you that this thing* (p. 652), which is very probably on Rosa Baring.

*30.* Cp. Crabbe, *Delay Has Danger* 720: 'And slowly blackened in the sickly sun'.

Where Aylmer followed Aylmer at the Hall
And Averill Averill at the Rectory
Thrice over; so that Rectory and Hall,
Bound in an immemorial intimacy,
Were open to each other; though to dream
That Love could bind them closer well had made
The hoar hair of the Baronet bristle up
With horror, worse than had he heard his priest
Preach an inverted scripture, sons of men
Daughters of God; so sleepy was the land.

And might not Averill, had he willed it so,
Somewhere beneath his own low range of roofs,
Have also set his many-shielded tree?
There was an Aylmer-Averill marriage once,
When the red rose was redder than itself,
And York's white rose as red as Lancaster's,
With wounded peace which each had pricked to death.
'Not proven' Averill said, or laughingly
'Some other race of Averills'–proven or no,
What cared he? what, if other or the same?
He leaned not on his fathers but himself.
But Leolin, his brother, living oft
With Averill, and a year or two before
Called to the bar, but ever called away
By one low voice to one dear neighbourhood,
Would often, in his walks with Edith, claim
A distant kinship to the gracious blood
That shook the heart of Edith hearing him.

Sanguine he was: a but less vivid hue
Than of that islet in the chestnut-bloom
Flamed in his cheek; and eager eyes, that still
Took joyful note of all things joyful, beamed,
Beneath a manelike mass of rolling gold,
Their best and brightest, when they dwelt on hers,
Edith, whose pensive beauty, perfect else,
But subject to the season or the mood,
Shone like a mystic star between the less
And greater glory varying to and fro,
We know not wherefore; bounteously made,

*44–5. Genesis* vi 2: 'The sons of God saw the daughters of men that they were fair; and they took them wives of all which they chose.'

*49. once,*] *1864*; once. *Eversley*.

*72–3.* 'The variable star of astronomy with its maximums and minimums of brightness' (T.).

And yet so finely, that a troublous touch
Thinned, or would seem to thin her in a day,
A joyous to dilate, as toward the light.
And these had been together from the first.
Leolin's first nurse was, five years after, hers:
So much the boy foreran; but when his date
Doubled her own, for want of playmates, he
(Since Averill was a decad and a half
His elder, and their parents underground)
Had tost his ball and flown his kite, and rolled
His hoop to pleasure Edith, with her dipt
Against the rush of the air in the prone swing,
Made blossom-ball or daisy-chain, arranged
Her garden, sowed her name and kept it green
In living letters, told her fairy-tales,
Showed her the fairy footings on the grass,
The little dells of cowslips, fairy palms,
The petty marestail forest, fairy pines,
Or from the tiny pitted target blew
What looked a flight of fairy arrows aimed
All at one mark, all hitting: make-believes
For Edith and himself: or else he forged,
But that was later, boyish histories
Of battle, bold adventure, dungeon, wreck,
Flights, terrors, sudden rescues, and true love
Crowned after trial; sketches rude and faint,
But where a passion yet unborn perhaps
Lay hidden as the music of the moon
Sleeps in the plain eggs of the nightingale.
And thus together, save for college-times
Or Temple-eaten terms, a couple, fair
As ever painter painted, poet sang,
Or Heaven in lavish bounty moulded, grew.
And more and more, the maiden woman-grown,
He wasted hours with Averill; there, when first
The tented winter-field was broken up
Into that phalanx of the summer spears
That soon should wear the garland; there again
When burr and bine were gathered; lastly there

*92. marestail*: a marsh plant.

*105.* As a student in the Temple he had to eat a number of dinners to keep terms.

*110.* 'The way in which the hop poles are stacked in winter' (T.).

*113. burr and bine*: 'refer to the hop-plant. "Burr", the rough cone; "bine", the climbing stem' (T.).

At Christmas; ever welcome at the Hall,
On whose dull sameness his full tide of youth
Broke with a phosphorescence charming even
My lady; and the Baronet yet had laid
No bar between them: dull and self-involved,
Tall and erect, but bending from his height
With half-allowing smiles for all the world,
And mighty courteous in the main–his pride
Lay deeper than to wear it as his ring–
He, like an Aylmer in his Aylmerism,
Would care no more for Leolin's walking with her
Than for his old Newfoundland's, when they ran
To loose him at the stables, for he rose
Twofooted at the limit of his chain,
Roaring to make a third: and how should Love,
Whom the cross-lightnings of four chance-met eyes
Flash into fiery life from nothing, follow
Such dear familiarities of dawn?
Seldom, but when he does, Master of all.

So these young hearts not knowing that they loved,
Not she at least, nor conscious of a bar
Between them, nor by plight or broken ring
Bound, but an immemorial intimacy,
Wandered at will, and oft accompanied
By Averill: his, a brother's love, that hung
With wings of brooding shelter o'er her peace,
Might have been other, save for Leolin's–
Who knows? but so they wandered, hour by hour
Gathered the blossom that rebloomed, and drank
The magic cup that filled itself anew.

A whisper half revealed her to herself.
For out beyond her lodges, where the brook
Vocal, with here and there a silence, ran
By sallowy rims, arose the labourers' homes,
A frequent haunt of Edith, on low knolls

*116. charming*] *1872*; cheering *1864–70*.
*123. Aylmerism*: like 'babyisms' (l. 539), this suggests the stylistic influence of Carlyle in a denunciatory mood. *Past and Present* (1843) is full of *isms*, and its tone and subject matter were apt to T.'s poem. The French Revolution setting, too, will have brought Carlyle to mind. Cp. ll. 374*n*, 765–8*n*.
*135. broken*: in troth between lovers.
*136. immemorial intimacy*: Woolner's phrase.
*137. and*] *1872*; but *1864–70*.
*147. sallowy*: willowy.

That dimpling died into each other, huts
At random scattered, each a nest in bloom.
Her art, her hand, her counsel all had wrought
About them: here was one that, summer-blanched,
Was parcel-bearded with the traveller's-joy
In Autumn, parcel ivy-clad; and here
The warm-blue breathings of a hidden hearth
Broke from a bower of vine and honeysuckle:
One looked all rosetree, and another wore
A close-set robe of jasmine sown with stars:
This had a rosy sea of gillyflowers
About it; this, a milky-way on earth,
Like visions in the Northern dreamer's heavens,
A lily-avenue climbing to the doors;
One, almost to the martin-haunted eaves
A summer burial deep in hollyhocks;
Each, its own charm; and Edith's everywhere;
And Edith ever visitant with him,
He but less loved than Edith, of her poor:
For she–so lowly-lovely and so loving,
Queenly responsive when the loyal hand
Rose from the clay it worked in as she past,
Not sowing hedgerow texts and passing by,
Nor dealing goodly counsel from a height
That makes the lowest hate it, but a voice
Of comfort and an open hand of help,
A splendid presence flattering the poor roofs
Revered as theirs, but kindlier than themselves
To ailing wife or wailing infancy
Or old bedridden palsy,–was adored;
He, loved for her and for himself. A grasp
Having the warmth and muscle of the heart,
A childly way with children, and a laugh
Ringing like proven golden coinage true,
Were no false passport to that easy realm,
Where once with Leolin at her side the girl,

*153. parcel-*: T. glosses this 'partly-', and compares 'parcel-gilt', *2 Henry IV* II i *87*.

*161.* Swedenborg and the spiritual world. There were translations of Swedenborg at Somersby (*Lincoln*).

*163–4. Macbeth* I vi 3–4: 'This guest of summer, / The temple-haunting martlet'.

*175.* Cp. *Recollections of the Arabian Nights 76*: 'flattering the golden prime'; from Shakespeare, *Sonnet 33*: 'Full many a glorious morning have I seen, / Flatter the mountain tops with sovereign eye'.

Nursing a child, and turning to the warmth
The tender pink five-beaded baby-soles,
Heard the good mother softly whisper 'Bless,
God bless 'em: marriages are made in Heaven.'

A flash of semi-jealousy cleared it to her.
My lady's Indian kinsman unannounced
With half a score of swarthy faces came.
His own, though keen and bold and soldierly,
Seared by the close ecliptic, was not fair;
Fairer his talk, a tongue that ruled the hour,
Though seeming boastful: so when first he dashed
Into the chronicle of a deedful day,
Sir Aylmer half forgot his lazy smile
Of patron 'Good! my lady's kinsman! good!'
My lady with her fingers interlocked,
And rotatory thumbs on silken knees,
Called all her vital spirits into each ear
To listen: unawares they flitted off,
Busying themselves about the flowerage
That stood from out a stiff brocade in which,
The meteor of a splendid season, she,
Once with this kinsman, ah so long ago,
Stept through the stately minuet of those days:
But Edith's eager fancy hurried with him
Snatched through the perilous passes of his life:
Till Leolin ever watchful of her eye,
Hated him with a momentary hate.
Wife-hunting, as the rumour ran, was he:
I know not, for he spoke not, only showered
His oriental gifts on everyone
And most on Edith: like a storm he came,
And shook the house, and like a storm he went.

Among the gifts he left her (possibly
He flowed and ebbed uncertain, to return
When others had been tested) there was one,
A dagger, in rich sheath with jewels on it
Sprinkled about in gold that branched itself
Fine as ice-ferns on January panes
Made by a breath. I know not whence at first,
Nor of what race, the work; but as he told
The story, storming a hill-fort of thieves
He got it; for their captain after fight,
His comrades having fought their last below,

193. *ecliptic*: path of the 'sun of tropics' (T.).

Was climbing up the valley; at whom he shot:
Down from the beetling crag to which he clung
Tumbled the tawny rascal at his feet,
This dagger with him, which when now admired
By Edith whom his pleasure was to please,
At once the costly Sahib yielded to her.

And Leolin, coming after he was gone,
Tost over all her presents petulantly:
And when she showed the wealthy scabbard, saying
'Look what a lovely piece of workmanship!'
Slight was his answer 'Well–I care not for it:'
Then playing with the blade he pricked his hand,
'A gracious gift to give a lady, this!'
'But would it be more gracious' asked the girl
'Were I to give this gift of his to one
That is no lady?' 'Gracious? No' said he.
'Me?–but I cared not for it. O pardon me,
I seem to be ungraciousness itself.'
'Take it' she added sweetly, 'though his gift;
For I am more ungracious even than you,
I care not for it either;' and he said
'Why then I love it:' but Sir Aylmer past,
And neither loved nor liked the thing he heard.

The next day came a neighbour. Blues and reds
They talked of: blues were sure of it, he thought:
Then of the latest fox–where started–killed
In such a bottom: 'Peter had the brush,
My Peter, first:' and did Sir Aylmer know
That great pock-pitten fellow had been caught?
Then made his pleasure echo, hand to hand,
And rolling as it were the substance of it
Between his palms a moment up and down–
'The birds were warm, the birds were warm upon him;
We have him now:' and had Sir Aylmer heard–
Nay, but he must–the land was ringing of it–
This blacksmith border-marriage–one they knew–
Raw from the nursery–who could trust a child?
That cursèd France with her egalities!
And did Sir Aylmer (deferentially

*233. costly*: lavish, as in Dryden and Goldsmith.

*251–2. blues and reds*: conservatives and republicans.

*263.* At Gretna Green a blacksmith married runaway couples.

*265.* The date is '1793'.

With nearing chair and lowered accent) think–
For people talked–that it was wholly wise
To let that handsome fellow Averill walk
So freely with his daughter? people talked–
The boy might get a notion into him;
The girl might be entangled ere she knew.
Sir Aylmer Aylmer slowly stiffening spoke:
'The girl and boy, Sir, know their differences!'
'Good,' said his friend, 'but watch!' and he, 'Enough,
More than enough, Sir! I can guard my own.'
They parted, and Sir Aylmer Aylmer watched.

Pale, for on her the thunders of the house
Had fallen first, was Edith that same night;
Pale as the Jephtha's daughter, a rough piece
Of early rigid colour, under which
Withdrawing by the counter door to that
Which Leolin opened, she cast back upon him
A piteous glance, and vanished. He, as one
Caught in a burst of unexpected storm,
And pelted with outrageous epithets,
Turning beheld the Powers of the House
On either side the hearth, indignant; her,
Cooling her false cheek with a featherfan,
Him, glaring, by his own stale devil spurred,
And, like a beast hard-ridden, breathing hard.
'Ungenerous, dishonourable, base,
Presumptuous! trusted as he was with her,
The sole succeeder to their wealth, their lands,
The last remaining pillar of their house,
The one transmitter of their ancient name,
Their child.' 'Our child!' 'Our heiress!' 'Ours!' for still,
Like echoes from beyond a hollow, came
Her sicklier iteration. Last he said,
'Boy, mark me! for your fortunes are to make.

*272.* 'Neighbours to hint that it was dangerous . . . as her feelings might become entangled' (Woolner).

*280.* Because of his vow, Jephtha sacrificed his virgin daughter to his God (*Judges* xi), as does Sir Aylmer. She is prominent in *A Dream of Fair Women* (p. 449). It is not evident that T. alludes to a specific work of art, but it is possible that he remembered Lebrun's painting in the Uffizi (which he visited in 1851–the 'long galleries' of *The Daisy* 41–2).

*280–1.* Cp. Arthur Hallam, *On the Picture of the Three Fates at Florence* (Motter, p. 3): 'None but a Tuscan hand could fix ye here / In rigidness of sober coloring. / Pale are ye . . .'

I swear you shall not make them out of mine.
Now inasmuch as you have practised on her,
Perplext her, made her half forget herself,
Swerve from her duty to herself and us–
Things in an Aylmer deemed impossible,
Far as we track ourselves–I say that this–
Else I withdraw favour and countenance
From you and yours for ever–shall you do.
Sir, when you see her–but you shall not see her–
No, you shall write, and not to her, but me:
And you shall say that having spoken with me,
And after looked into yourself, you find
That you meant nothing–as indeed you know
That you meant nothing. Such a match as this!
Impossible, prodigious!' These were words,
As meted by his measure of himself,
Arguing boundless forbearance: after which,
And Leolin's horror-stricken answer, 'I
So foul a traitor to myself and her,
Never oh never,' for about as long
As the wind-hover hangs in balance, paused
Sir Aylmer reddening from the storm within,
Then broke all bonds of courtesy, and crying
'Boy, should I find you by my doors again,
My men shall lash you from them like a dog;
Hence!' with a sudden execration drove
The footstool from before him, and arose;
So, stammering 'scoundrel' out of teeth that ground
As in a dreadful dream, while Leolin still
Retreated half-aghast, the fierce old man
Followed, and under his own lintel stood
Storming with lifted hands, a hoary face
Meet for the reverence of the hearth, but now,
Beneath a pale and unimpassioned moon,
Vext with unworthy madness, and deformed.

Slowly and conscious of the rageful eye
That watched him, till he heard the ponderous door
Close, crashing with long echoes through the land,
Went Leolin; then, his passions all in flood
And masters of his motion, furiously
Down through the bright lawns to his brother's ran,
And foamed away his heart at Averill's ear:
Whom Averill solaced as he might, amazed:

*302–4.* Another outraged father, Brabantio, speaks of Othello's 'practices' by which he 'wrought upon' Desdemona (I iii 102–6).

The man was his, had been his father's, friend:
He must have seen, himself had seen it long;
He must have known, himself had known: besides,
He never yet had set his daughter forth
Here in the woman-markets of the west,
Where our Caucasians let themselves be sold.
Some one, he thought, had slandered Leolin to him.
'Brother, for I have loved you more as son
Than brother, let me tell you: I myself–
What is their pretty saying? jilted, is it?
Jilted I was: I say it for your peace.
Pained, and, as bearing in myself the shame
The woman should have borne, humiliated,
I lived for years a stunted sunless life;
Till after our good parents past away
Watching your growth, I seemed again to grow.
Leolin, I almost sin in envying you:
The very whitest lamb in all my fold
Loves you: I know her: the worst thought she has
Is whiter even than her pretty hand:
She must prove true: for, brother, where two fight
The strongest wins, and truth and love are strength,
And you are happy: let her parents be.'

But Leolin cried out the more upon them–
Insolent, brainless, heartless! heiress, wealth,
Their wealth, their heiress! wealth enough was theirs
For twenty matches. Were he lord of this,
Why twenty boys and girls should marry on it,
And forty blest ones bless him, and himself
Be wealthy still, ay wealthier. He believed
This filthy marriage-hindering Mammon made
The harlot of the cities: nature crost
Was mother of the foul adulteries
That saturate soul with body. Name, too! name,
Their ancient name! they *might* be proud; its worth
Was being Edith's. Ah how pale she had looked
Darling, tonight! they must have rated her
Beyond all tolerance. These old pheasant-lords,
These partridge-breeders of a thousand years,
Who had mildewed in their thousands, doing nothing
Since Egbert–why, the greater their disgrace!

374. This attack on Mammon suggests Carlyle, whose *Past and Present* contains a chapter on 'The Gospel of Mammonism' as well as innumerable references to it.

Fall back upon a name! rest, rot in that!
Not *keep* it noble, make it nobler? fools,
With such a vantage-ground for nobleness!
He had known a man, a quintessence of man,
The life of all–who madly loved–and he,
Thwarted by one of these old father-fools,
Had rioted his life out, and made an end.
He would not do it! her sweet face and faith
Held him from that: but he had powers, he knew it:
Back would he to his studies, make a name,
Name, fortune too: the world should ring of him
To shame these mouldy Aylmers in their graves:
Chancellor, or what is greatest would he be–
'O brother, I am grieved to learn your grief–
Give me my fling, and let me say my say.'

At which, like one that sees his own excess,
And easily forgives it as his own,
He laughed; and then was mute; but presently
Wept like a storm: and honest Averill seeing
How low his brother's mood had fallen, fetched
His richest beeswing from a binn reserved
For banquets, praised the waning red, and told
The vintage–when *this* Aylmer came of age–
Then drank and past it; till at length the two,
Though Leolin flamed and fell again, agreed
That much allowance must be made for men.
After an angry dream this kindlier glow
Faded with morning, but his purpose held.

Yet once by night again the lovers met,
A perilous meeting under the tall pines
That darkened all the northward of her Hall.
Him, to her meek and modest bosom prest
In agony, she promised that no force,
Persuasion, no, nor death could alter her:
He, passionately hopefuller, would go,
Labour for his own Edith, and return
In such a sunlight of prosperity
He should not be rejected. 'Write to me!
They loved me, and because I love their child
They hate me: there is war between us, dear,
Which breaks all bonds but ours; we must remain
Sacred to one another.' So they talked,
Poor children, for their comfort: the wind blew;

406. *the waning red*: port maturing becomes less red.

The rain of heaven, and their own bitter tears,
Tears, and the careless rain of heaven, mixt
Upon their faces, as they kissed each other
In darkness, and above them roared the pine.

So Leolin went; and as we task ourselves
To learn a language known but smatteringly
In phrases here and there at random, toiled
Mastering the lawless science of our law,
That codeless myriad of precedent,
That wilderness of single instances,
Through which a few, by wit or fortune led,
May beat a pathway out to wealth and fame.
The jests, that flashed about the pleader's room,
Lightning of the hour, the pun, the scurrilous tale,–
Old scandals buried now seven decads deep
In other scandals that have lived and died,
And left the living scandal that shall die–
Were dead to him already; bent as he was
To make disproof of scorn, and strong in hopes,
And prodigal of all brain-labour he,
Charier of sleep, and wine, and exercise,
Except when for a breathing-while at eve,
Some niggard fraction of an hour, he ran
Beside the river-bank: and then indeed
Harder the times were, and the hands of power
Were bloodier, and the according hearts of men
Seemed harder too; but the soft river-breeze,
Which fanned the gardens of that rival rose
Yet fragrant in a heart remembering
His former talks with Edith, on him breathed
Far purelier in his rushings to and fro,
After his books, to flush his blood with air,
Then to his books again. My lady's cousin,
Half-sickening of his pensioned afternoon,
Drove in upon the student once or twice,
Ran a Malayan amuck against the times,
Had golden hopes for France and all mankind,
Answered all queries touching those at home
With a heaved shoulder and a saucy smile,

455. T. says: 'The Temple garden where Somerset picked the red, Plantaganet the white roses', as in *1 Henry VI* II iv.

463. *amuck*] *1884*; muck *1864–83*.

464. Cp. Wordsworth on revolutionary hopes, *The Prelude* vi 340: 'France standing on the top of golden hours'.

And fain had haled him out into the world,
And aired him there: his nearer friend would say
'Screw not the chord too sharply lest it snap.'
Then left alone he plucked her dagger forth
From where his worldless heart had kept it warm,
Kissing his vows upon it like a knight.
And wrinkled benchers often talked of him
Approvingly, and prophesied his rise:
For heart, I think, helped head: her letters too,
Though far between, and coming fitfully
Like broken music, written as she found
Or made occasion, being strictly watched,
Charmed him through every labyrinth till he saw
An end, a hope, a light breaking upon him.

But they that cast her spirit into flesh,
Her worldly-wise begetters, plagued themselves
To sell her, those good parents, for her good.
Whatever eldest-born of rank or wealth
Might lie within their compass, him they lured
Into their net made pleasant by the baits
Of gold and beauty, wooing him to woo.
So month by month the noise about their doors,
And distant blaze of those dull banquets, made
The nightly wirer of their innocent hare
Falter before he took it. All in vain.
Sullen, defiant, pitying, wroth, returned
Leolin's rejected rivals from their suit
So often, that the folly taking wings
Slipt o'er those lazy limits down the wind
With rumour, and became in other fields
A mockery to the yeomen over ale,
And laughter to their lords: but those at home,
As hunters round a hunted creature draw
The cordon close and closer toward the death,
Narrowed her goings out and comings in;
Forbad her first the house of Averill,
Then closed her access to the wealthier farms,
Last from her own home-circle of the poor
They barred her: yet she bore it: yet her cheek
Kept colour: wondrous! but, O mystery!

*469.* 'His reason snapt like the overdrawn cord of a bow' on the news of her death (Woolner).

*479–80.* 'He himself almost began to see something like light breaking through the difficult ways' (Woolner).

What amulet drew her down to that old oak,
So old, that twenty years before, a part
Falling had let appear the brand of John–
Once grovelike, each huge arm a tree, but now
The broken base of a black tower, a cave
Of touchwood, with a single flourishing spray.
There the manorial lord too curiously
Raking in that millennial touchwood-dust
Found for himself a bitter treasure-trove;
Burst his own wyvern on the seal, and read
Writhing a letter from his child, for which
Came at the moment Leolin's emissary,
A crippled lad, and coming turned to fly,
But scared with threats of jail and halter gave
To him that flustered his poor parish wits
The letter which he brought, and swore besides
To play their go-between as heretofore
Nor let them know themselves betrayed; and then,
Soul-stricken at their kindness to him, went
Hating his own lean heart and miserable.

Thenceforward oft from out a despot dream
The father panting woke, and oft, as dawn
Aroused the black republic on his elms,
Sweeping the frothfly from the fescue brushed
Through the dim meadow toward his treasure-trove,
Seized it, took home, and to my lady,–who made
A downward crescent of her minion mouth,
Listless in all despondence,–read; and tore,
As if the living passion symbolled there
Were living nerves to feel the rent; and burnt,
Now chafing at his own great self defied,
Now striking on huge stumbling-blocks of scorn
In babyisms, and dear diminutives
Scattered all over the vocabulary
Of such a love as like a chidden child,
After much wailing, hushed itself at last
Hopeless of answer: then though Averill wrote
And bad him with good heart sustain himself–

*509.* T. comments: 'In cutting down trees in Sherwood Forest, letters have been found in the heart of the trees, showing the brands of particular reigns–those of James I, William and Mary, and one of King John. King John's was eighteen inches within the bark.'
*529.* Obliquely alluding to the French Revolution.
*530. frothfly from the fescue*: T. comments: 'The fly that lives in the cuckoo spit on the meadow fescue, a kind of grass, *Festuca pratensis*.'

All would be well–the lover heeded not,
But passionately restless came and went,
And rustling once at night about the place,
There by a keeper shot at, slightly hurt,
Raging returned: nor was it well for her
Kept to the garden now, and grove of pines,
Watched even there; and one was set to watch
The watcher, and Sir Aylmer watched them all,
Yet bitterer from his readings: once indeed,
Warmed with his wines, or taking pride in her,
She looked so sweet, he kissed her tenderly
Not knowing what possessed him: that one kiss
Was Leolin's one strong rival upon earth;
Seconded, for my lady followed suit,
Seemed hope's returning rose: and then ensued
A Martin's summer of his faded love,
Or ordeal by kindness; after this
He seldom crost his child without a sneer;
The mother flowed in shallower acrimonies:
Never one kindly smile, one kindly word:
So that the gentle creature shut from all
Her charitable use, and face to face
With twenty months of silence, slowly lost
Nor greatly cared to lose, her hold on life.
Last, some low fever ranging round to spy
The weakness of a people or a house,
Like flies that haunt a wound, or deer, or men,
Or almost all that is, hurting the hurt–
Save Christ as we believe him–found the girl
And flung her down upon a couch of fire,
Where careless of the household faces near,
And crying upon the name of Leolin,
She, and with her the race of Aylmer, past.

Star to star vibrates light: may soul to soul
Strike through a finer element of her own?
So,–from afar,–touch as at once? or why
That night, that moment, when she named his name,
Did the keen shriek 'Yes love, yes, Edith, yes,'
Shrill, till the comrade of his chambers woke,
And came upon him half-arisen from sleep,
With a weird bright eye, sweating and trembling,
His hair as it were crackling into flames,
His body half flung forward in pursuit,
And his long arms stretched as to grasp a flyer:
Nor knew he wherefore he had made the cry;

And being much befooled and idioted
By the rough amity of the other, sank
As into sleep again. The second day,
My lady's Indian kinsman rushing in,
A breaker of the bitter news from home,
Found a dead man, a letter edged with death
Beside him, and the dagger which himself
Gave Edith, reddened with no bandit's blood:
'From Edith' was engraven on the blade.

Then Averill went and gazed upon his death.
And when he came again, his flock believed–
Beholding how the years which are not Time's
Had blasted him–that many thousand days
Were clipt by horror from his term of life.
Yet the sad mother, for the second death
Scarce touched her through that nearness of the first,
And being used to find her pastor texts,
Sent to the harrowed brother, praying him
To speak before the people of her child,
And fixt the Sabbath. Darkly that day rose:
Autumn's mock sunshine of the faded woods
Was all the life of it; for hard on these,
A breathless burthen of low-folded heavens
Stifled and chilled at once; but every roof
Sent out a listener: many too had known
Edith among the hamlets round, and since
The parents' harshness and the hapless loves
And double death were widely murmured, left
Their own gray tower, or plain-faced tabernacle,
To hear him; all in mourning these, and those
With blots of it about them, ribbon, glove
Or kerchief; while the church,–one night, except
For greenish glimmerings through the lancets,–made
Still paler the pale head of him, who towered
Above them, with his hopes in either grave.

Long o'er his bent brows lingered Averill,
His face magnetic to the hand from which
Livid he plucked it forth, and laboured through
His brief prayer-prelude, gave the verse 'Behold,
Your house is left unto you desolate!'

*606.* 'She had given Averill the text upon which he preached' (T.).
*622–3.* Cp. *The Lover's Tale* i 632–45, *1832* text: 'Spirit of Paleness made still paler'.
*629.* From *Luke* xiii 35; Jesus's lament over Jerusalem to the Pharisees.

But lapsed into so long a pause again
As half amazed half frighted all his flock:
Then from his height and loneliness of grief
Bore down in flood, and dashed his angry heart
Against the desolations of the world.

Never since our bad earth became one sea,
Which rolling o'er the palaces of the proud,
And all but those who knew the living God–
Eight that were left to make a purer world–
When since had flood, fire, earthquake, thunder, wrought
Such waste and havock as the idolatries,
Which from the low light of mortality
Shot up their shadows to the Heaven of Heavens,
And worshipt their own darkness in the Highest?
'Gash thyself, priest, and honour thy brute Baäl,
And to thy worst self sacrifice thyself,
For with thy worst self hast thou clothed thy God.
Then came a Lord in no wise like to Baäl.
The babe shall lead the lion. Surely now
The wilderness shall blossom as the rose.
Crown thyself, worm, and worship thine own lusts!–
No coarse and blockish God of acreage
Stands at thy gate for thee to grovel to–
Thy God is far diffused in noble groves
And princely halls, and farms, and flowing lawns,
And heaps of living gold that daily grow,
And title-scrolls and gorgeous heraldries.
In such a shape dost thou behold thy God.
Thou wilt not gash thy flesh for *him*; for thine
Fares richly, in fine linen, not a hair
Ruffled upon the scarfskin, even while
The deathless ruler of thy dying house
Is wounded to the death that cannot die;
And though thou numberest with the followers

643. *in*] *1884 New Collected*; as *1864–84*.
644. The priests of Baal gashed themselves, *1 Kings* xviii 28.
649. *Isaiah* xxxv 1: 'The wilderness and the solitary place shall be glad for them; and the desert shall rejoice and blossom as the rose.'
651. 'The Roman god Terminus, who presided over the boundaries of private properties' (T.).
659. The 'fine linen' of Dives, who 'fared sumptuously', *Luke* xvi 19.
660. *scarfskin*: outer skin.
661. *ruler*: 'the soul' (T.).

Of One who cried, "Leave all and follow me."
Thee therefore with His light about thy feet,
Thee with His message ringing in thine ears,
Thee shall thy brother man, the Lord from Heaven,
Born of a village girl, carpenter's son,
Wonderful, Prince of peace, the Mighty God,
Count the more base idolater of the two;
Crueller: as not passing through the fire
Bodies, but souls–thy children's–through the smoke,
The blight of low desires–darkening thine own
To thine own likeness; or if one of these,
Thy better born unhappily from thee,
Should, as by miracle, grow straight and fair–
Friends, I was bid to speak of such a one
By those who most have cause to sorrow for her–
Fairer than Rachel by the palmy well,
Fairer than Ruth among the fields of corn,
Fair as the Angel that said "Hail!" she seemed,
Who entering filled the house with sudden light.
For so mine own was brightened: where indeed
The roof so lowly but that beam of Heaven
Dawned sometime through the doorway? whose the babe
Too ragged to be fondled on her lap,
Warmed at her bosom? The poor child of shame
The common care whom no one cared for, leapt
To greet her, wasting his forgotten heart,
As with the mother he had never known,
In gambols; for her fresh and innocent eyes
Had such a star of morning in their blue,
That all neglected places of the field
Broke into nature's music when they saw her.
Low was her voice, but won mysterious way
Through the sealed ear to which a louder one
Was all but silence–free of alms her hand–
The hand that robed your cottage-walls with flowers
Has often toiled to clothe your little ones;

*669.* From *Isaiah* ix 6.

*671–2.* The Lord to Moses: 'And thou shalt not let any of thy seed pass through the fire to Molech' (in sacrifice), *Leviticus* xviii 21. Also *Colossians* iii 5: 'Covetousness, which is idolatry.'

*679. Genesis* xxix 10.

*680. Ruth* ii.

*681. Luke* i 28.

*689. wasting* ...: 'lavishing his neglected feelings of love' (T.).

How often placed upon the sick man's brow
Cooled it, or laid his feverous pillow smooth!
Had you one sorrow and she shared it not?
One burthen and she would not lighten it?
One spiritual doubt she did not soothe?
Or when some heat of difference sparkled out,
How sweetly would she glide between your wraths,
And steal you from each other! for she walked
Wearing the light yoke of that Lord of love,
Who stilled the rolling wave of Galilee!
And one–of him I was not bid to speak–
Was always with her, whom you also knew.
Him too you loved, for he was worthy love.
And these had been together from the first;
They might have been together till the last.
Friends, this frail bark of ours, when sorely tried,
May wreck itself without the pilot's guilt,
Without the captain's knowledge: hope with me.
Whose shame is that, if he went hence with shame?
Nor mine the fault, if losing both of these
I cry to vacant chairs and widowed walls,
"My house is left unto me desolate."'

While thus he spoke, his hearers wept; but some,
Sons of the glebe, with other frowns than those
That knit themselves for summer shadow, scowled
At their great lord. He, when it seemed he saw
No pale sheet-lightnings from afar, but forked
Of the near storm, and aiming at his head,
Sat anger-charmed from sorrow, soldierlike,
Erect: but when the preacher's cadence flowed
Softening through all the gentle attributes
Of his lost child, the wife, who watched his face,
Paled at a sudden twitch of his iron mouth;
And 'O pray God that he hold up' she thought
'Or surely I shall shame myself and him.'

'Nor yours the blame–for who beside your hearths
Can take her place–if echoing me you cry
"Our house is left unto us desolate"?
But thou, O thou that killest, hadst thou known,

715. *frail bark*: three times in Shelley, e.g. *Rosalind* 815.

738–9. 'O Jerusalem, Jerusalem, which killest the prophets, and stonest them that are sent unto thee', *Luke* xiii 34, the verse preceding Averill's text.

O thou that stonest, hadst thou understood
The things belonging to thy peace and ours!
Is there no prophet but the voice that calls
Doom upon kings, or in the waste "Repent"?
Is not our own child on the narrow way,
Who down to those that saunter in the broad
Cries "Come up hither," as a prophet to us?
Is there no stoning save with flint and rock?
Yes, as the dead we weep for testify–
No desolation but by sword and fire?
Yes, as your moanings witness, and myself
Am lonelier, darker, earthlier for my loss.
Give me your prayers, for he is past your prayers,
Not past the living fount of pity in Heaven.
But I that thought myself long-suffering, meek,
Exceeding "poor in spirit"–how the words
Have twisted back upon themselves, and mean
Vileness, we are grown so proud–I wished my voice
A rushing tempest of the wrath of God
To blow these sacrifices through the world–
Sent like the twelve-divided concubine
To inflame the tribes: but there–out yonder–earth
Lightens from her own central Hell–O there
The red fruit of an old idolatry–
The heads of chiefs and princes fall so fast,
They cling together in the ghastly sack–
The land all shambles–naked marriages

*739–40. Luke* xix 42; Jesus weeping over Jerusalem: 'If thou hadst known, even thou, at least in this thy day, the things which belong unto thy peace! but now they are hid from thine eyes.'

*745. Matthew* vii 14, 'Strait is the gate, and narrow is the way, which leadeth unto life.' *Revelation* xi 12, 'And they heard a great voice from heaven saying unto them, Come up hither. And they ascended up to heaven in a cloud.'

*759–60. Judges* xix 29. The Levite's concubine was raped to death by men of Gibeah, so he sent parts of her body to all the tribes of Israel to stir them to revenge.

*760. out yonder*: in France.

*764.* T. comments: 'He alludes to the report, horrible and hardly credible, that when the heads were taken out of the sack, two were sometimes found clinging together, one having bitten into the other in the momentary convulsion that followed decapitation.'

*765–8.* From Carlyle's *French Revolution* iii V iii: 'women and men are tied together, feet and feet, hands and hands; and flung in: this they call *Mariage Républicain*, Republican Marriage ... the victims tumble con-

Flash from the bridge, and ever-murdered France,
By shores that darken with the gathering wolf,
Runs in a river of blood to the sick sea.
Is this a time to madden madness then?
Was this a time for these to flaunt their pride?
May Pharaoh's darkness, folds as dense as those
Which hid the Holiest from the people's eyes
Ere the great death, shroud this great sin from all!
Doubtless our narrow world must canvass it:
O rather pray for those and pity them,
Who, through their own desire accomplished, bring
Their own gray hairs with sorrow to the grave–
Who broke the bond which they desired to break,
Which else had linked their race with times to come–
Who wove coarse webs to snare her purity,
Grossly contriving their dear daughter's good–
Poor souls, and knew not what they did, but sat
Ignorant, devising their own daughter's death!
May not that earthly chastisement suffice?
Have not our love and reverence left them bare?
Will not another take their heritage?
Will there be children's laughter in their hall
For ever and for ever, or one stone
Left on another, or is it a light thing
That I, their guest, their host, their ancient friend,
I made by these the last of all my race,
Must cry to these the last of theirs, as cried
Christ ere His agony to those that swore
Not by the temple but the gold, and made
Their own traditions God, and slew the Lord,

fusedly seaward along the Loire stream; the tide rolling them back: clouds of ravens darken the River; wolves prowl on the shoal-places.'

*771.* *Exodus* x 21.

*777.* Jacob said of Benjamin: 'if mischief befall him by the way in the which ye go, then shall ye bring down my gray hairs with sorrow to the grave', *Genesis* xlii 38.

*786.* Of Judas: 'Let his habitation be desolate, and let no man dwell therein: and his bishoprick let another take', *Acts* i 20.

*788–9.* Jesus, on the Temple: 'There shall not be left one stone upon another', *Mark* xiii 2.

*793–4.* *Matthew* xxiii 16, 'Woe unto you, ye blind guides, which say, Whosoever shall swear by the temple, it is nothing; but whosoever shall swear by the gold of the temple, he is a debtor!'

*795.* *Matthew* xv 6, Jesus to the Pharisees, on honouring one's father and mother: 'Thus have ye made the commandment of God of none effect by your tradition.'

And left their memories a world's curse–"Behold,
Your house is left unto you desolate"?'

Ended he had not, but she brooked no more:
Long since her heart had beat remorselessly,
Her crampt-up sorrow pained her, and a sense
Of meanness in her unresisting life.
Then their eyes vext her; for on entering
He had cast the curtains of their seat aside–
Black velvet of the costliest–she herself
Had seen to that: fain had she closed them now,
Yet dared not stir to do it, only neared
Her husband inch by inch, but when she laid,
Wife-like, her hand in one of his, he veiled
His face with the other, and at once, as falls
A creeper when the prop is broken, fell
The woman shrieking at his feet, and swooned.
Then her own people bore along the nave
Her pendant hands, and narrow meagre face
Seamed with the shallow cares of fifty years:
And her the Lord of all the landscape round
Even to its last horizon, and of all
Who peered at him so keenly, followed out
Tall and erect, but in the middle aisle
Reeled, as a footsore ox in crowded ways
Stumbling across the market to his death,
Unpitied; for he groped as blind, and seemed
Always about to fall, grasping the pews
And oaken finials till he touched the door;
Yet to the lychgate where his chariot stood,
Strode from the porch, tall and erect again.

But nevermore did either pass the gate
Save under pall with bearers. In one month,
Through weary and yet ever wearier hours,
The childless mother went to seek her child;
And when he felt the silence of his house
About him, and the change and not the change,
And those fixt eyes of painted ancestors
Staring for ever from their gilded walls
On him their last descendant, his own head
Began to droop, to fall; the man became
Imbecile; his one word was 'desolate;'
Dead for two years before his death was he;
But when the second Christmas came, escaped
His keepers, and the silence which he felt,
To find a deeper in the narrow gloom

By wife and child; nor wanted at his end
The dark retinue reverencing death
At golden thresholds; nor from tender hearts,
And those who sorrowed o'er a vanished race,
Pity, the violet on the tyrant's grave.
Then the great Hall was wholly broken down,
And the broad woodland parcelled into farms;
And where the two contrived their daughter's good,
Lies the hawk's cast, the mole has made his run,
The hedgehog underneath the plantain bores,
The rabbit fondles his own harmless face,
The slow-worm creeps, and the thin weasel there
Follows the mouse, and all is open field.

# 338 *‘Long as the heart beats life within her breast’

Printed *Court Journal*, 19 March 1864; and *Mem.* ii 17: ‘The Queen having asked for some lines to be inscribed on the Duchess of Kent's statue in the Mausoleum at Frogmore’. Victoria's mother, she had died 1861; the Mausoleum was erected 1862–70. The Dean of Windsor on 18 Jan. 1864 sent the Queen's request for ‘four lines . . . to be placed beneath the statue of the

842. *retínue*: ‘Shakespeare and Milton accented this word in the same way’ (T.).
843. The ‘golden thresholds’ of Heaven, as in *The Lover's Tale* i 594.
845. *the tyrant*: Nero. Cp. Byron on Nero's death, *Don Juan* III cix: ‘Some hands unseen strewed flowers upon his tomb: / Perhaps the weakness of a heart not void / Of feeling for some kindness done.’ Byron's note refers to Suetonius. The draft of *Eversley* (*British Museum*) acknowledged Byron as T.'s source here, but mistakenly said *Childe Harold*. Cp. also Persius, *Satires* i 39–40: *nunc non e tumulo fortunataque favilla / nascentur violae?* (‘Will not violets now spring up from the tomb and its thrice-blessed ashes?’) T. says this was ‘a chance parallel’, but Arthur Hallam had quoted these lines in praise of T.; cp. *In Memoriam* xviii 3–4 (p. 880).
848–53. Cp. *Acts* i 20, quoted l. 786*n*. Also *Isaiah* xiii 20–2: ‘It shall never be inhabited, neither shall it be dwelt in from generation to generation . . . . But wild beasts of the desert shall lie there; and their houses shall be full of doleful creatures . . . . And the wild beasts of the islands shall cry in their desolate houses.’ T. had versified this in *Babylon* 41–4, where he retained ‘desolate houses’–which here is linked with the text of the sermon: ‘Your house is left unto you desolate.’
852–3] There the thin weasel, with faint hunting cry / Follows his game . . . *Eversley* ‘*original reading*’.

Duchess of Kent . . . as soon as possible' (*Lincoln*). T.'s lines were acknowledged 27 Jan. 1864 (*Mat.* ii 391–2), T. having sent three versions from which Victoria chose this. Epigraph: *Proverbs* xxxi 28, on the 'virtuous woman'.

*Her children rise up and call her blessed*

Long as the heart beats life within her breast,
Thy child will bless thee, guardian-mother mild,
And far away thy memory will be blessed
By children of the children of thy child.

# 339 A Dedication

Published *1864*. It is to T.'s wife Emily, as is the dedication *June Bracken and Heather* (p. 1440). T. mentioned it on 23 June 1864 (*Mat.* ii 399). It cost him great difficulty, judging by the MS (*British Museum*) and a trial edition *Virginia*).

Dear, near and true–no truer Time himself
Can prove you, though he make you evermore
Dearer and nearer, as the rapid of life
Shoots to the fall–take this and pray that he
Who wrote it, honouring your sweet faith in him,
May trust himself; and after praise and scorn,
As one who feels the immeasurable world,
Attain the wise indifference of the wise;
And after Autumn past–if left to pass
His autumn into seeming-leafless days–
Draw toward the long frost and longest night,
Wearing his wisdom lightly, like the fruit
Which in our winter woodland looks a flower.

¶338. *2. guardian-mother*] *T. added the hyphen on his cutting of 1864 (H.Nbk 64).*

*4.* T. echoes *To the Queen 23*: 'children of our children'.

¶339. *5–6*]

Who wrote it, for his own sake, as for theirs,
May grow less careful of his brother fools, *trial edition 1st reading*;

Who wrote it, self reliant when assailed, *trial edition*

*6. after*] *1872*; spite of *1864–70*.

*11*] May draw toward the longest night in peace, *British Museum MS, deleted.*

*13. 1864* note: 'The fruit of the Spindle-tree (*Euonymus Europæus*)'.

# 340 The Flower

Published *1864*. Mrs Richard Ward reports: 'The lines of *The Flower* were the result of an investigation of the "love-in-idleness" growing at Farringford. He made them nearly all on the spot, and said them to me (as they are) next day' (*Eversley*). T. said: 'This does not refer to my poetry. It was written as a universal apologue, and the people do not as yet call my flower a weed.' But H.T. deleted the word 'alone' after 'my poetry' (*Lincoln*). R. Preyer, *MP* lv (1958) 249, suggests the influence of Blake's *Poison Tree*. T.'s friend William Allingham was very interested in Blake (*Diary*, 1907, pp. 349–50).

Once in a golden hour
  I cast to earth a seed.
Up there came a flower,
  The people said, a weed.

To and fro they went
  Through my garden-bower,
And muttering discontent
  Cursed me and my flower.

Then it grew so tall
  It wore a crown of light,
But thieves from o'er the wall
  Stole the seed by night.

Sowed it far and wide
  By every town and tower,
Till all the people cried,
  'Splendid is the flower.'

Read my little fable:
  He that runs may read.
Most can raise the flowers now,
  For all have got the seed.

And some are pretty enough,
  And some are poor indeed;
And now again the people
  Call it but a weed.

# 341 Requiescat

Published *1864*. It is a reworking of *Fair is that cottage* (*c.* 1834, p. 610), of which it adapts ll. 1–4 and replaces ll. 5–8, at the same time modifying the stanza form. An intermediate revision was undertaken *c.* 1851 (*H.Nbk 26*).

But T. made further revision in a trial edition of *1864* (*Univ. of London Lib.*).

Fair is her cottage in its place,
  Where yon broad water sweetly slowly glides.
It sees itself from thatch to base
  Dream in the sliding tides.

And fairer she, but ah how soon to die!
  Her quiet dream of life this hour may cease.
Her peaceful being slowly passes by
  To some more perfect peace.

# 342 The Islet

Published *1864*. T. says that ll. 15–23 were 'a fragment, the nucleus of the poem, and perhaps it would have been better not to have expanded them'. This fragment is in *H.Nbk 31* (1855–8). The whole poem is in *Lpr 114*, with other poems of *1864*. Paden (p. 141) suggests the influence of Washington Irving's *Columbus* (1828), the source of *Anacaona*. Cp. *The Lotos-Eaters* (p. 429).

'Whither, O whither, love, shall we go,
For a score of sweet little summers or so?'
The sweet little wife of the singer said,
On the day that followed the day she was wed,
'Whither, O whither, love, shall we go?'
And the singer shaking his curly head
Turned as he sat, and struck the keys
There at his right with a sudden crash,
Singing, 'And shall it be over the seas
With a crew that is neither rude nor rash,
But a bevy of Eroses apple-cheeked,
In a shallop of crystal ivory-beaked,
With a satin sail of a ruby glow,
To a sweet little Eden on earth that I know,
A mountain islet pointed and peaked;

¶341. *2. sweetly slowly*] *Not 1834, H.MS.*
*2* ∧ *3*] *MS repeats l. 1.*
*5–8*]
And fairer she, who lies within,
  Whose dream of life will cease;
Whose dreams of deeper life begin;
She passes from this world of sin
  Into that world of peace. *MS*

¶342. *15. islet*] summit *H.Nbk 31.*

Waves on a diamond shingle dash,
Cataract brooks to the ocean run,
Fairily-delicate palaces shine
Mixt with myrtle and clad with vine,
And overstreamed and silvery-streaked
With many a rivulet high against the Sun
The facets of the glorious mountain flash
Above the valleys of palm and pine.'

'Thither, O thither, love, let us go.'

'No, no, no!
For in all that exquisite isle, my dear,
There is but one bird with a musical throat,
And his compass is but of a single note,
That it makes one weary to hear.'

'Mock me not! mock me not! love, let us go.'

'No, love, no.
For the bud ever breaks into bloom on the tree,
And a storm never wakes on the lonely sea,
And a worm is there in the lonely wood,
That pierces the liver and blackens the blood;
And makes it a sorrow to be.'

# 343 *The Ringlet

Published *1864*; not reprinted except in printings of *1864*. It is in *H.Lpr 114* with other poems of *1864*, and there is a draft in a trial edition of *1864* (*Univ. of London Library*).

I

'Your ringlets, your ringlets,
That look so golden-gay,

*25 ^ 6*] For love there is nothing to do but lie
In the hollow valleys and look at the sky,
At the sky above and the sea below.'
'Yet, thither, O thither, love, let us go.'
'No, no, no.' *trial edition 1864*

These lines were printed in the trial edition (*Univ. of London Lib.*); T. altered the first line to 'For what would it profit to wander and lie', and then deleted the lines.

*32*. Cp. *The Hesperides* (p. 425), another poem about an island-paradise: 'The bough buddeth, the bud bloometh, / Bloom is changèd evermore into fruit.' Also *The Lotos-Eaters* 70–74 (p. 432).

*34. a worm is there*] there lives a worm *1864 trial edition* (*Virginia*).

If you will give me one, but one,
To kiss it night and day,
Then never chilling touch of Time
Will turn it silver-gray;
And then shall I know it is all true gold
To flame and sparkle and stream as of old,
Till all the comets in heaven are cold,
And all her stars decay.'
'Then take it, love, and put it by;
This cannot change, nor yet can I.'

2

'My ringlet, my ringlet,
That art so golden-gay,
Now never chilling touch of Time
Can turn thee silver-gray;
And a lad may wink, and a girl may hint,
And a fool may say his say;
For my doubts and fears were all amiss,
And I swear henceforth by this and this,
That a doubt will only come for a kiss,
And a fear to be kissed away.'
'Then kiss it, love, and put it by:
If this can change, why so can I.'

II

O Ringlet, O Ringlet,
I kissed you night and day,
And Ringlet, O Ringlet,
You still are golden-gay,
But Ringlet, O Ringlet,
You should be silver-gray:
For what is this which now I'm told,
I that took you for true gold,
She that gave you's bought and sold,
Sold, sold.

2

O Ringlet, O Ringlet,
She blushed a rosy red,
When Ringlet, O Ringlet,
She clipt you from her head,
And Ringlet, O Ringlet,
She gave you me, and said,
'Come, kiss it, love, and put it by:
If this can change, why so can I.'
O fie, you golden nothing, fie
You golden lie.

3

O Ringlet, O Ringlet,
I count you much to blame,
For Ringlet, O Ringlet,
You put me much to shame,
So Ringlet, O Ringlet,
I doom you to the flame.
For what is this which now I learn,
Has given all my faith a turn?
Burn, you glossy heretic, burn,
Burn, burn.

# 344 Northern Farmer

## NEW STYLE

Published *1869* ('*1870*'). The Duke of Argyll wrote to T., 18 Feb. 1865: 'I hear you have got something new to match the *Lincolnshire Farmer*' (*Lincoln*). Walter White refers to it, 9 July 1865 (*Journals*, 1898, p. 160). T. says it was 'founded on a single sentence: "When I canters my 'erse along the ramper (highway) I 'ears 'proputty, proputty, proputty'".' Cp. *Northern Farmer, Old Style* (p. 1123). Contrast this comic treatment of 'marriage-hindering Mammon' with that in *Maud* and in the other poems connected with Rosa Baring. All glossarial notes below are by T.

I

Dosn't thou 'ear my 'erse's legs, as they canters awaäy?
Proputty, proputty, proputty–that's what I 'ears 'em saäy.
Proputty, proputty, proputty–Sam, thou's an ass for thy paaïns:
Theer's moor sense i' one o' 'is legs nor in all thy braaïns.

II

Woä–theer's a craw to pluck wi' tha, Sam: yon's parson's 'ouse–
Dosn't thou knaw that a man mun be eäther a man or a mouse?
Time to think on it then; for thou'll be twenty to weeäk.
Proputty, proputty–woä then woä–let ma 'ear mysén speäk.

III

Me an' thy muther, Sammy, 'as beän a-talkin' o' thee;
Thou's beän talkin' to muther, an' she beän a tellin' it me.
Thou'll not marry for munny–thou's sweet upo' parson's lass–
Noä–thou'll marry for luvv–an' we boäth on us thinks tha an ass.

¶344. 7. *to weeäk*: this week.

IV

Seeä'd her todaäy goä by–Saäint's-daäy–they was ringing the bells.
She's a beauty thou thinks–an' soä is scoors o' gells,
Them as 'as munny an' all–wot's a beauty?–the flower as blaws.
But proputty, proputty sticks, an' proputty, proputty graws.

V

Do'ant be stunt: taäke time: I knaws what maäkes tha sa mad.
Warn't I craäzed fur the lasses mysén when I wur a lad?
But I knawed a Quaäker feller as often 'as towd ma this:
'Doänt thou marry for munny, but goä wheer munny is!'

VI

An' I went wheer munny war: an' thy muther coom to 'and,
Wi' lots o' munny laaïd by, an' a nicetish bit o' land.
Maäybe she warn't a beauty:–I niver giv it a thowt–
But warn't she as good to cuddle an' kiss as a lass as 'ant nowt?

VII

Parson's lass 'ant nowt, an' she weänt 'a nowt when 'e's deäd,
Mun be a guvness, lad, or summut, and addle her breäd:
Why? fur 'e's nobbut a curate, an' weänt niver git hissen clear,
An' 'e maäde the bed as 'e ligs on afoor 'e coomed to the shere.

VIII

An' thin 'e coomed to the parish wi' lots o' Varsity debt,
Stook to his taaïl they did, an' 'e 'ant got shut on 'em yet.
An' 'e ligs on 'is back i' the grip, wi' noän to lend 'im a shuvv,
Woorse nor a far-weltered yowe: fur, Sammy, 'e married fur luvv.

IX

Luvv? what's luvv? thou can luvv thy lass an' 'er munny too,
Maakin' 'em goä togither as they've good right to do.
Could'n I luvv thy muther by cause o' 'er munny laaïd by?
Naäy–fur I luvved 'er a vast sight moor fur it: reäson why.

X

Ay an' thy muther says thou wants to marry the lass,
Cooms of a gentleman burn: an' we boäth on us think tha an ass.
Woä then, proputty, wiltha?–an ass as near as mays nowt–
Woä then, wiltha? dangtha!–the bees is as fell as owt.

17. *stunt*: obstinate.
26. *addle*: earn.
27. *hissen clear*] *1888*; naw 'igher *1869–86*.
32. *far-weltered*: or fow-weltered,–said of a sheep lying on its back.
39. *mays nowt*: makes nothing.
40. *the bees is as fell as owt*: the flies are as fierce as anything.

XI

Breäk me a bit o' the esh for his 'eäd lad, out o' the fence!
Gentleman burn! what's gentleman burn? is it shillins an' pence?
Proputty, proputty's ivrything 'ere, an', Sammy, I'm blest
If it isn't the saäme oop yonder, fur them as 'as it's the best.

XII

Tis'n them as 'as munny as breäks into 'ouses an' steäls,
Them as 'as coäts to their backs an' taäkes their regular meäls.
Noä, but it's them as niver knaws wheer a meäl's to be 'ad.
Taäke my word for it, Sammy, the poor in a loomp is bad.

XIII

Them or thir feythers, tha sees, mun 'a beän a laäzy lot,
Fur work mun 'a gone to the gittin' whiniver munny was got.
Feyther 'ad ammost nowt; leästways 'is munny was 'id.
But 'e tued an' moiled 'issén deäd, an 'e died a good un, 'e did.

XIV

Look thou theer wheer Wrigglesby beck cooms out by the 'ill!
Feyther run oop to the farm, an' I runs oop to the mill;
An' I'll run oop to the brig, an' that thou'll live to see;
And if thou marries a good un I'll leäve the land to thee.

XV

Thim's my noätions, Sammy, wheerby I means to stick;
But if thou marries a bad un, I'll leäve the land to Dick.–
Coom oop, proputty, proputty–that's what I 'ears 'im saäy–
Proputty, proputty, proputty–canter an' canter awaäy.

# 345 To Dante
## (WRITTEN AT REQUEST OF THE FLORENTINES)

Published *1880*, among 'Translations, Etc.' *Mem.* ii 22 has, under 7 May 1865: 'Last evening, in answer to a letter from Florence asking for lines on Dante, he made six and sent them off to-day in honour of Dante's six hundredth centenary.' T. wrote: 'You only asked for "duo versi" and I have taken you at your word and send you something like a Greek epigram' (*Lincoln*). The subsequent delay in publication seems to have been because T. entirely forgot the lines (*Mem.* ii 255–6). Cp. *To Virgil* (p. 1311).

King, that hast reigned six hundred years, and grown
In power, and ever growest, since thine own
Fair Florence honouring thy nativity,
Thy Florence now the crown of Italy,
Hath sought the tribute of a verse from me,

I, wearing but the garland of a day,
Cast at thy feet one flower that fades away.

# 346 *1865-1866

Published *Good Words*, March 1868; 'ruined by the absurd illustrations' (H.T., *1913*), and not reprinted. Written 31 Dec. 1865 (*Mem.* ii 33). Cp. *The Death of the Old Year* (p. 461).

I stood on a tower in the wet,
And New Year and Old Year met,
And winds were roaring and blowing;
And I said, 'O years, that meet in tears,
Have ye aught that is worth the knowing?
Science enough and exploring,
Wanderers coming and going,
Matter enough for deploring,
But aught that is worth the knowing?'
Seas at my feet were flowing,
Waves on the shingle pouring,
Old Year roaring and blowing,
And New Year blowing and roaring.

# 347 The Snowdrop

Published *1889*. Written 'about 1860' (H.T.); it is in *H.Nbk 37* (watermarked 1863), which includes *Lucretius* (written 1865–8). In this draft, and in the modification of it, T. had the lines in a different order. Cp. the MS of *Balin and Balan* 264ff: 'the firstlings of the snow – / Fair maids of February as we say' (*Cornhill* cliii (1936) 555).

Many, many welcomes
February fair-maid,
Ever as of old time,
Solitary firstling,
Coming in the cold time,
Prophet of the gay time,
Prophet of the May time,
Prophet of the roses,
Many, many welcomes
February fair-maid!

¶347. *6*] *Not H.MS, which has however*: Prophet of the crocus, / Prophet of the primrose.

# 348 A Voice Spake Out of the Skies

Published *1892*. It was apparently in T.'s mind on 8 Dec. 1865: 'I cannot but think moral good is the crown of man. But what is it without immortality? "Let us eat and drink, for to-morrow we die." If I knew the world were coming to an end in six hours, would I give my money to a starving beggar? No, if I did not believe myself immortal' (J. A. Symonds, *Letters and Papers*, 1923, p. 6). T. quoted it to Oscar Browning *c.* 1866 (*Memories*, 1923, p. 116), beginning 'The Lord spake', as in the *Fitzwilliam MS* and *H.Lpr 256*. One of T.'s letters at *Lincoln* shows that he offered 'God spake out of the skies' to *Macmillan's Magazine* to publish with *Wages* (Feb. 1868); it was printed in a *Lincoln* trial edition of *1869* ('*1870*'), with the title *The Minute*. It was a late addition, in pencil, to a trial edition of *1892* (*Lincoln*).

A Voice spake out of the skies
To a just man and a wise–
'The world and all within it
Will only last a minute!'
And a beggar began to cry
'Food, food or I die'!
Is it worth his while to eat,
Or mine to give him meat,
If the world and all within it
Were nothing the next minute?

# 349 'Flower in the crannied wall'

Published *1869* ('*1870*'). 'The flower was plucked out of a wall at "Waggoners Wells", near Haslemere' (T.).

Flower in the crannied wall,
I pluck you out of the crannies,
I hold you here, root and all, in my hand,
Little flower–but *if* I could understand
What you are, root and all, and all in all,
I should know what God and man is.

¶349. *3. I hold*] *1882*; Hold *1869–81*. Corrected by T. in his copy of *Works, 1881* (*Lincoln*).

# 350 The Victim

Published *Good Words*, 1 Jan. 1868; then *1869* ('*1870*'). It had been printed Nov. 1867 at Canford Manor (no variants from *1868*). It was written May 1866 (*Mem.* ii 35). *Eversley* reports T. as saying he took the story from Charlotte M. Yonge's *Book of Golden Deeds* (1864), as he did *Kapiolani*, adding he 'made it Scandinavian'. But where these last words are in T.'s hand, it is H.T.'s hand (*Lincoln*) that adds 'I read the original in "Golden Deeds".' Since the story is not in Yonge, H.T. may have confused it with *Kapiolani*. Possibly it was influenced by T.'s visit in Aug. 1864 (Brittany) to a chamber where 'human victims used to be bound before they were sacrificed' (*Mat.* ii 403).

I

A plague upon the people fell,
  A famine after laid them low,
Then thorpe and byre arose in fire,
  For on them brake the sudden foe;
So thick they died the people cried,
  'The Gods are moved against the land.'
The Priest in horror about his altar
  To Thor and Odin lifted a hand:
    'Help us from famine
    And plague and strife!
    What would you have of us?
    Human life?
    Were it our nearest,
    Were it our dearest,
    (Answer, O answer)
    We give you his life.'

II

But still the foeman spoiled and burned,
  And cattle died, and deer in wood,
And bird in air, and fishes turned
  And whitened all the rolling flood;
And dead men lay all over the way,
  Or down in a furrow scathed with flame:
And ever and aye the Priesthood moaned,
  Till at last it seemed that an answer came.

¶350. 22. *scathed*: by lightning. Cp. *The Devil and the Lady* I iv 143: 'the red bolt scathe thee'. From *Paradise Lost* i 613; Scott has 'scathed with flame', *Lady of the Lake* III x, and it is common in this sense in Shelley.

'The King is happy
In child and wife;
Take you his dearest,
Give us a life.'

III

The Priest went out by heath and hill;
The King was hunting in the wild;
They found the mother sitting still;
She cast her arms about the child.
The child was only eight summers old,
His beauty still with his years increased,
His face was ruddy, his hair was gold,
He seemed a victim due to the priest.
The Priest beheld him,
And cried with joy,
'The Gods have answered:
We give them the boy.'

IV

The King returned from out the wild,
He bore but little game in hand;
The mother said, 'They have taken the child
To spill his blood and heal the land:
The land is sick, the people diseased,
And blight and famine on all the lea:
The holy Gods, they must be appeased,
So I pray you tell the truth to me.
They have taken our son,
They will have his life.
Is *he* your dearest?
Or I, the wife?'

V

The King bent low, with hand on brow,
He stayed his arms upon his knee:
'O wife, what use to answer now?
For now the Priest has judged for me.'
The King was shaken with holy fear;
'The Gods,' he said, 'would have chosen well;

26 ∧ 7] Take you his nearest, *1868*.
*37. beheld him*] *1869*; exulted *1868*.
39] *1869*; 'Here is his nearest,
Here is his dearest, *1868*
*40. give them*] *1869*; take *1868*.
50 ∧ 1] Is *he* your nearest? *1868*.
51 ∧ 2] (Answer, O answer) *1868*.

Yet both are near, and both are dear,
And which the dearest I cannot tell!'
But the Priest was happy,
His victim won:
'We have his dearest,
His only son!'

VI

The rites prepared, the victim bared,
The knife uprising toward the blow
To the altar-stone she sprang alone,
'Me, not my darling, no!'
He caught her away with a sudden cry;
Suddenly from him brake his wife,
And shrieking '*I* am his dearest, I–
*I* am his dearest!' rushed on the knife.
And the Priest was happy,
'O, Father Odin,
We give you a life.
Which was his nearest?
Who was his dearest?
The Gods have answered;
We give them the wife!'

## 351 The Window
### or, The Song of the Wrens

Printed privately by Sir Ivor Guest, Nov. 1867 (Canford Manor), with the subtitle *The Loves of the Wrens*, and with the songs untitled. Published, with music by Arthur Sullivan, Dec. 1870 ('*1871*'); then *1874*. Written Oct. 1866–7 (*Mat.* iii 49–51, *Mem.* ii 44). On 5 Oct. 1866, George Grove wrote to T.:

'Mr Payne tells me he has communicated to you a little proposal of mine for a Book of Songs, and at his request I send you Heine's *Lieder* because I alluded to them in my letter as being often used by the German musicians to set to music. Those I was more particularly thinking of are the Songs I to VIII, p. 36–45, which Schumann has set as *Liederkreis*, and those beginning p. 106, out of which he has made a similar selection. [These references fit Heine's *Werke* i, 1857.] But why one should send you patterns of songs

62 ∧ 3] 'We have his nearest, *1868*.
*68.* '*Me, not*] *1869*; 'Me, me, not him, *1868*.
*70. his*] *1869*; the *1868*.
*77. Who*] *1869*; Which *1868*.

when your own "Little Birdie" . . . is a perfect model, I don't know. It was more because of the way the Germans have of connecting several songs together. If the idea of the first song could be brought back again in the last it would help the composer very much, for nothing is so charming in music as to wind off a composition in that way. Beethoven (as great in small things as in the greatest) has done it with masterly effect in a Liederkreis called "An die ferne Geliebte." If you like I will write that out for you with the greatest pleasure.'

H.T. noted (*Mem.* ii 40) that T. was fond of these songs. Grove's mention of 'Little Birdie' (from *Sea Dreams*, p. 1105), and the fact that Heine's Song iii is a conversation between the lover and the birds, suggested as the theme of this love poem 'The Song of the Wrens'. Grove's request was on behalf of Sullivan (who in 1866 was aged twenty-four), and it was suggested that Millais should illustrate the cycle (he completed one picture). T. was at first unwilling; Sullivan wrote: 'He read me all the songs (twelve in number), which are absolutely lovely, but I fear there will be a great difficulty in getting them from him. He thinks they are too light, and will damage his reputation etc.' (H. Sullivan and N. Flower, *Sir Arthur Sullivan*, 2nd edn, 1950, pp. 57–9). But agreement and collaboration followed, though clearly T. never much admired the songs. On 22 Nov. 1866 he read *The Window* to William Allingham (*Diary*, 1907, p. 146), 'prefacing it by the remark "They're quite silly!".' T. sent the poem to Guest at Canford Manor, Oct. 1867 (*Lincoln*): 'I don't suppose that half the songs will be published.' Yet despite this 1867 printing, T. was very reluctant to publish, and is said to have offered Sullivan £500 to cancel the arrangement. In Nov. 1870, T. wrote to his publisher Strahan:

'"He that sweareth to his neighbour and disappointeth him not"–so I must consent to the publication of the songs, however much against my inclination and my judgment, and that I may meet your wishes as to the time of publication, I must also consent to their being published this Xmas, however much more against my inclination and judgment–provided, as I stated yesterday that the fact of their having been written four years ago, and of their being published by yourself, be mentioned in the preface, also that no one but Millais shall illustrate them.'

See T.'s prefatory note below, of which the last sentence alludes to the Franco–Prussian war. Sullivan was hurt, but T. finally soothed him.

Four years ago Mr Sullivan requested me to write a little song-cycle, German fashion, for him to exercise his art upon. He had been very successful in setting such old songs as 'Orpheus with his lute,' and I drest up for him, partly in the old style, a puppet, whose almost only merit is, perhaps, that it can dance to Mr Sullivan's instrument. I am sorry that my four-year-old puppet should have to dance at all in the dark shadow of these days; but the music is now completed, and I am bound by my promise.

*December*, 1870. *A. Tennyson*

### ON THE HILL

The lights and shadows fly!
Yonder it brightens and darkens down on the plain.
A jewel, a jewel dear to a lover's eye!
Oh is it the brook, or a pool, or her window-pane,
When the winds are up in the morning?

Clouds that are racing above,
And winds and lights and shadows that cannot be still,
All running on one way to the home of my love,
You are all running on, and I stand on the slope of the hill,
And the winds are up in the morning!

Follow, follow the chase!
And my thoughts are as quick and as quick, ever on, on, on.
O lights, are you flying over her sweet little face?
And my heart is there before you are come, and gone,
When the winds are up in the morning!

Follow them down the slope!
And I follow them down to the window-pane of my dear,
And it brightens and darkens and brightens like my hope,
And it darkens and brightens and darkens like my fear,
And the winds are up in the morning.

### AT THE WINDOW

Vine, vine and eglantine,
Clasp her window, trail and twine!
Rose, rose and clematis,
Trail and twine and clasp and kiss,
Kiss, kiss; and make her a bower
All of flowers, and drop me a flower,
Drop me a flower.

Vine, vine and eglantine,
Cannot a flower, a flower, be mine?
Rose, rose and clematis,
Drop me a flower, a flower, to kiss,
Kiss, kiss–and out of her bower
All of flowers, a flower, a flower,
Dropt, a flower.

### GONE

Gone!
Gone, till the end of the year,
Gone, and the light gone with her, and left me in shadow
here!
Gone—flitted away,
Taken the stars from the night and the sun from the day!
Gone, and a cloud in my heart, and a storm in the air!
Flown to the east or the west, flitted I know not where!
Down in the south is a flash and a groan: she is there!
she is there!

### WINTER

The frost is here,
And fuel is dear,
And woods are sear,
And fires burn clear,
And frost is here
And has bitten the heel of the going year.

Bite, frost, bite!
You roll up away from the light
The blue wood-louse, and the plump dormouse,
And the bees are stilled, and the flies are killed,
And you bite far into the heart of the house,
But not into mine.

Bite, frost, bite!
The woods are all the searer,
The fuel is all the dearer,
The fires are all the clearer,
My spring is all the nearer,
You have bitten into the heart of the earth,
But not into mine.

### SPRING

Birds' love and birds' song
Flying here and there,
Birds' song and birds' love,
And you with gold for hair!

¶351. *35–42.* Perhaps a reminiscence of Rosa Baring's leaving Lincolnshire. Cp. l. 42 with *Ah, fade not yet* 13 (p. 648): 'And further South the Rose will bloom again'. *The Window* is in many respects an attenuated *Maud.*

Birds' song and birds' love,
Passing with the weather,
Men's song and men's love,
To love once and for ever.

Men's love and birds' love,
And women's love and men's!
And you my wren with a crown of gold,
You my queen of the wrens!
You the queen of the wrens–
We'll be birds of a feather,
I'll be King of the Queen of the wrens,
And all in a nest together.

THE LETTER

Where is another sweet as my sweet,
Fine of the fine, and shy of the shy?
Fine little hands, fine little feet–
Dewy blue eye.
Shall I write to her? shall I go?
Ask her to marry me by and by?
Somebody said that she'd say no;
Somebody knows that she'll say ay!

Ay or no, if asked to her face?
Ay or no, from shy of the shy?

*68. Men's song*] *1870*; Birds' love *1867*.

*69 ∧ 70*]
Birds' love and men's love,
Once and once for all;
And you so small and you so fair,
You so fair and small!
You so fair! am I so black?
Arn't we birds of a feather?
You so small! am I so tall?
Can't we come together? *1867*

*77. all in*] *1870*; we'll have *1867*.

*78–93.* This section cost T. much difficulty. *1870* note: 'The Music was composed to an earlier version.' T. altered it again in the proofs of *1870* (*Virginia*).

*79*] *1870*; Such another beneath the sky? *1867*.

*81*] *1870*; Fine little heart, and merry blue eye. *1867*.

*85. Somebody*] *1870*; But somebody *1867*.

*85 ∧ 6*] Ay ay, ay ay, ay ay, ay ay–
Ay ay, ay ay. *1867*

*86. Ay or no*] *1870*; Ah my lady *1867*.

*87*] *1870*; Might say no, for she is but shy: *1867*.

Go, little letter, apace, apace,
Fly;
Fly to the light in the valley below—
Tell my wish to her dewy blue eye:
Somebody said that she'd say no;
Somebody knows that she'll say ay!

NO ANSWER

The mist and the rain, the mist and the rain!
Is it ay or no? is it ay or no?
And never a glimpse of her window-pane!
And I may die but the grass will grow,
And the grass will grow when I am gone,
And the wet west wind and the world will go on.

Ay is the song of the wedded spheres,
No is trouble and cloud and storm,
Ay is life for a hundred years,
No will push me down to the worm,
And when I am there and dead and gone,
The wet west wind and the world will go on.

The wind and the wet, the wind and the wet!
Wet west wind how you blow, you blow!
And never a line from my lady yet!
Is it ay or no? is it ay or no?
Blow then, blow, and when I am gone,
The wet west wind and the world may go on.

NO ANSWER

Winds are loud and you are dumb,
Take my love, for love will come,
Love will come but once a life.
Winds are loud and winds will pass!
Spring is here with leaf and grass:
Take my love and be my wife.
After-loves of maids and men

*88. Go*] *1870*; Fly *1867*.
*89*] *1870*; Down to the light in the valley fly, *1867*.
*91. dewy*] *1870*; merry *1867*.
*92. Somebody*] *1870*; For somebody *1867*.
*93*] *1870*; And she won't say no, and I'll tell you why,
She *will* say ay, ay ay, ay ay—
Ay ay, ay ay. *1867*
*118–9*. T. said to William Allingham: 'That's very like Shakespeare' (*Diary*, 1907, p. 146).

Are but dainties drest again:
Love me now, you'll love me then:
  Love can love but once a life.

### THE ANSWER

Two little hands that meet,
Claspt on her seal, my sweet!
Must I take you and break you,
Two little hands that meet?
I must take you, and break you,
And loving hands must part–
Take, take–break, break–
Break–you may break my heart.
    Faint heart never won–
    Break, break, and all's done.

### AY

Be merry, all birds, today,
  Be merry on earth as you never were merry before,
Be merry in heaven, O larks, and far away,
  And merry for ever and ever, and one day more.
        Why?
    For it's easy to find a rhyme.

Look, look, how he flits,
  The fire-crowned king of the wrens, from out of the
    pine!
Look how they tumble the blossom, the mad little tits!
  'Cuck-oo! Cuck-oo!' was ever a May so fine?
        Why?
    For it's easy to find a rhyme.

O merry the linnet and dove,
  And swallow and sparrow and throstle, and have
    your desire!
O merry my heart, you have gotten the wings of love,
  And flit like the king of the wrens with a crown of fire.
        Why?
    For it's ay ay, ay ay.

*119. drest*] *1870*; cooked *1867*.
*132–49. 1870* note: 'This Song has not been set to Music'.
*149*] *1874*; For it's ay ay ay, ay ay. *1867–70*.

### WHEN

Sun comes, moon comes,
  Time slips away.
Sun sets, moon sets,
  Love, fix a day.

'A year hence, a year hence.'
  'We shall both be gray.'
'A month hence, a month hence.'
  'Far, far away.'

'A week hence, a week hence.'
  'Ah, the long delay.'
'Wait a little, wait a little,
  You shall fix a day.'

'Tomorrow, love, tomorrow,
  And that's an age away.'
Blaze upon her window, sun,
  And honour all the day.

### MARRIAGE MORNING

Light, so low upon earth,
  You send a flash to the sun.
Here is the golden close of love,
  All my wooing is done.
Oh, the woods and the meadows,
  Woods, where we hid from the wet,
Stiles where we stayed to be kind,
  Meadows in which we met!
Light, so low in the vale
  You flash and lighten afar,
For this is the golden morning of love,
  And you are his morning star.
Flash, I am coming, I come,
  By meadow and stile and wood,
Oh, lighten into my eyes and my heart,
  Into my heart and my blood!
Heart, are you great enough
  For a love that never tires?
O heart, are you great enough for love?
  I have heard of thorns and briers.
Over the thorns and briers,
  Over the meadows and stiles,
Over the world to the end of it
  Flash for a million miles.

165. *And . . . all*] *1870*; In . . . of *1867*.

# 352 *'Speak to the Lord: He is close at thy hand'

Unpublished, *HnMS* (HM 19503). In sentiment as well as in phrasing, it is clearly the germ of *The Higher Pantheism* (below), which was written Dec. 1867 (*Mem.* ii 48) and recited to the Metaphysical Society in 1869: 'Speak to Him thou for He hears, and Spirit with Spirit can meet – / Closer is He than breathing, and nearer than hands and feet.'

Speak to the Lord: He is close at thy hand,
He is closer than hand and knee:
Through the million of million decillions of worlds
He will hear, He will answer thee.

Speak to the Lord, as a Spirit who trusts
That a Spirit can hear and see:
Brute as thou art in thy hates and thy lusts,
Thou art His: He will answer thee.

O Spirit of Spirits, if I could speak,
With a power to speak to Thee,
Through the million of million decillions of worlds
As a flash, Thou wilt answer me.

# 353 The Higher Pantheism

Published *1869* ('*1870*'). Written Dec. 1867 (*Mem.* ii 48); it was read at the first formal meeting of the Metaphysical Society, 2 June 1869 (at the earnest request of R. H. Hutton, *Lincoln*). See *Speak to the Lord* (above), which is apparently an early version. For the Metaphysical Society, see *Mem.* ii 166–72, and A. W. Brown, *The Metaphysical Society* (1947). Cp. *Romans* i 20: 'For the invisible things of him from the creation of the world are clearly seen, being understood by the things that are made, even his eternal Power and Godhead.'

The sun, the moon, the stars, the seas, the hills and the plains–
Are not these, O Soul, the Vision of Him who reigns?

Is not the Vision He? though He be not that which He seems?
Dreams are true while they last, and do we not live in dreams?

¶352. *3. decillion*: 'The tenth power of a million; a number which would be denoted by 1 followed by 60 ciphers' (*OED*, whose only example before the date of T.'s is Hood in 1845).

¶353. *4.* Contrast 'All thoughts, all creeds, all dreams are true' (p. 257).

Earth, these solid stars, this weight of body and limb,
Are they not sign and symbol of thy division from Him?

Dark is the world to thee: thyself art the reason why;
For is He not all but that which has power to feel 'I am I'?

Glory about thee, without thee; and thou fulfillest thy doom,
Making Him broken gleams, and a stifled splendour and gloom.

Speak to Him thou for He hears, and Spirit with Spirit can meet–
Closer is He than breathing, and nearer than hands and feet.

God is law, say the wise; O Soul, and let us rejoice,
For if He thunder by law the thunder is yet His voice.

Law is God, say some: no God at all, says the fool;
For all we have power to see is a straight staff bent in a pool;

And the ear of man cannot hear, and the eye of man cannot see;
But if we could see and hear, this Vision–were it not He?

# 354 Wages

Published *Macmillan's Magazine*, Feb. 1868; then *1869* ('*1870*'). *Mem.* ii 49 mentions 'the MS of *Wages*, which he had perfected during the night', Dec. 1867. T. offered *A Voice Spake Out of the Skies* (p. 1193) to *Macmillan's*

*8. that which has*] *1891*; thou, that hast *1869–90*.
*10.* Cp. Shelley, *Adonais* III: 'Splendours, and Glooms, and glimmering Incarnations'.
*11.* Combining *Psalm* xvii 6: 'I have called upon thee, for thou wilt hear me, O God: incline thine ear unto me, and hear my speech'; with *Romans* viii 16: 'The Spirit itself beareth witness with our spirit, that we are the children of God.'
*11–12.* Cp. *Speak to the Lord* 1–6: 'Speak to the Lord: He is close at thy hand, / He is closer than hand and knee: / Through the million of million decillions of worlds / He will hear, He will answer thee. // Speak to the Lord, as a Spirit who trusts / That a Spirit can hear and see . . .' *Acts* xvii 27: 'That they should seek the Lord, if haply they might feel after him, and find him, though he be not far from every one of us'. Compare T.'s words after reading aloud *The Holy Grail*, reported in Mrs Marian Bradley's diary (*British Museum*), 2 Jan. 1869: 'Yes, it is true, there are moments when the flesh is nothing to me, when I feel and know the flesh to be the vision, God and the spiritual only the real and true–depend on it the spiritual is the real–it belongs to one more than this hand or foot' (quoted in *Mem.* ii 90).
*14.* *Psalm* lxxvii 18: 'The voice of thy thunder was in the heaven.'
*15.* *Psalm* xiv 1: 'The fool hath said in his heart, There is no God.'
*17.* *1 Corinthians* ii 9: 'But as it is written, Eye hath not seen, nor ear heard, neither have entered into the heart of man, the things which God hath prepared for them that love him' (invoking *Isaiah* lxiv 4).

at the same time. For the theme, cp. *Vastness* (p. 1346). *Romans* vi 23: 'For the wages of sin is death: but the gift of God is eternal life, through Jesus Christ our Lord.'

Glory of warrior, glory of orator, glory of song,
  Paid with a voice flying by to be lost on an endless sea–
Glory of Virtue, to fight, to struggle, to right the wrong–
  Nay, but she aimed not at glory, no lover of glory she:
Give her the glory of going on, and still to be.

The wages of sin is death: if the wages of Virtue be dust,
  Would she have heart to endure for the life of the worm and the fly?
She desires no isles of the blest, no quiet seats of the just,
  To rest in a golden grove, or to bask in a summer sky:
Give her the wages of going on, and not to die.

# 355 Lucretius

Published *Macmillan's Magazine*, May 1868, and *Every Saturday*, 2 May 1868; then *1869* ('*1870*'). Written Oct. 1865–Jan. 1868 (*Mem.* ii 28; George Grove's *Life*, 1903, p. 155). T.'s friend Hugh Munro published his full-scale edition of Lucretius in 1864; T.'s copy is at *Lincoln*. It was Munro who checked the poem: 'Munro said that everything was Lucretian through this poem, and that there was no suggestion which he could make. He, however, did suggest the alteration of "shepherds" to "neat-herds" [l. 88]' (T.). It is based on the legend of Lucretius's death in Jerome's addition to the Eusebian Chronicle: *Titus Lucretius poeta nascitur qui postea amatorio poculo in furorem versus, cum aliquot libros per intervalla insaniae conscripsisset, quos postea Cicero emendavit, propria se manu interfecit anno aetatis XLIV* (H.T.). For the origins of this legend, see D. L. Chambers, *MLN* xviii (1903) 231–2. T. could have read of the legend in the *English Encyclopaedia* (1802), of which there was a copy at Somersby (*Lincoln*). The poem is constructed by adapting passages from *De Rerum Natura*. For further parallel passages, see R. C. Jebb, *Macmillan's Magazine* xviii (1868) 97–103; K. Allen, *Poet-Lore* xi (1899) 529–48; W. P. Mustard, *Classical Echoes in Tennyson* (1904); and O. L. Wilner, *Classical Journal* xxv (1930) 347–66. For a detailed study of the textual changes, including the proofs and text for *Every Saturday*, see W. D. Paden, *The Library* 5th ser. viii (1953) 269–73 (also xx 63–4, C. Ricks).

Lucilia, wedded to Lucretius, found
Her master cold; for when the morning flush
Of passion and the first embrace had died
Between them, though he loved her none the less,
Yet often when the woman heard his foot

Return from pacings in the field, and ran
To greet him with a kiss, the master took
Small notice, or austerely, for–his mind
Half buried in some weightier argument,
Or fancy-borne perhaps upon the rise
And long roll of the Hexameter–he past
To turn and ponder those three hundred scrolls
Left by the Teacher, whom he held divine.
She brooked it not; but wrathful, petulant,
Dreaming some rival, sought and found a witch
Who brewed the philtre which had power, they said,
To lead an errant passion home again.
And this, at times, she mingled with his drink,
And this destroyed him; for the wicked broth
Confused the chemic labour of the blood,
And tickling the brute brain within the man's
Made havock among those tender cells, and checked
His power to shape: he loathed himself; and once
After a tempest woke upon a morn
That mocked him with returning calm, and cried:

'Storm in the night! for thrice I heard the rain
Rushing; and once the flash of a thunderbolt–
Methought I never saw so fierce a fork–
Struck out the streaming mountain-side, and showed
A riotous confluence of watercourses
Blanching and billowing in a hollow of it,
Where all but yester-eve was dusty-dry.

¶355. *13.* Epicurus; *deus ille fuit, deus,* Lucretius v 8.
*22.* Cp. John Armstrong's *The Art of Preserving Health* (1744), i 90–1: 'This caustick venom would perhaps corrode / Those tender cells that draw the vital air.' There was a copy at Somersby (*Lincoln*).
*26–32.* Lucretius vi 281–92: *inde ubi percaluit venti vis et gravis ignis / impetus incessit, maturum tum quasi fulmen / perscindit subito nubem, ferturque coruscis / omnia luminibus lustrans loca percitus ardor. / quem gravis insequitur sonitus, displosa repente / opprimere ut caeli videatur templa superne. / inde tremor terras graviter pertemptat et altum / murmura percurrunt caelum; nam tota fere tum / tempestas concussa tremit fremitusque moventur. / quo de concussu sequitur gravis imber et uber, / omnis uti videatur in imbrem vertier aether / atque ita praecipitans ad diluviem revocare.* ('Next, when the force of the wind has grown hot and the strong impulse of the fire has thrust in, then the thunderbolt, now as it were ripe, suddenly cleaves the cloud, and out flies the speeded flame, sweeping over all places with flashing lights. Next follows a loud crash, so that it seems suddenly to disrupt apart and

'Storm, and what dreams, ye holy Gods, what dreams!
For thrice I wakened after dreams. Perchance
We do but recollect the dreams that come
Just ere the waking: terrible! for it seemed
A void was made in Nature; all her bonds
Cracked; and I saw the flaring atom-streams
And torrents of her myriad universe,
Ruining along the illimitable inane,
Fly on to clash together again, and make
Another and another frame of things
For ever: that was mine, my dream, I knew it–
Of and belonging to me, as the dog
With inward yelp and restless forefoot plies
His function of the woodland: but the next!
I thought that all the blood by Sylla shed
Came driving rainlike down again on earth,
And where it dashed the reddening meadow, sprang
No dragon warriors from Cadmean teeth,
For these I thought my dream would show to me,
But girls, Hetairai, curious in their art,
Hired animalisms, vile as those that made
The mulberry-faced Dictator's orgies worse
Than aught they fable of the quiet Gods.
And hands they mixt, and yelled and round me drove
In narrowing circles till I yelled again
Half-suffocated, and sprang up, and saw–
Was it the first beam of my latest day?

to overwhelm the regions of the sky above. Then tremblings violently assail the earth, murmurs roll through the lofty sky, for then all the tempest together quivers with the shock and roarings are aroused. From this shock follows rain heavy and full, so that the whole ether seems to be turning into rain, and then tumbling violently down, again to make all a deluge.')
*38–43*. H.T. compares i 999ff, of which ll. 1102–3 are: *ne volucri ritu flammarum moenia mundi / diffugiant subito magnum per inane soluta*. ('Or else the walls of heaven would suddenly be dissolved and flee apart after the fashion of flying flames through the void.') Cp. also ii 1053–62, iii 16ff.
*44–6*. H.T. compares iv 991–2: *venantumque canes in molli saepe quiete / iactant crura*. ('Hunters' dogs often in soft sleep all at once jerk their legs.') Cp. *Locksley Hall* 79: 'Like a dog, he hunts in dreams'.
*50*. Cadmus sowed dragon's teeth which sprang up as warriors.
*52*. *Hetairai*: 'courtezans' (T.).
*54*. 'Sylla in his later life. Cp. Plutarch, *Sulla* ii 451' (H.T.).
*55*. *quiet*: at ease; cp. Horace's *Odes* III iii 35–6: *quietis ordinibus ... deorum*.

'Then, then, from utter gloom stood out the breasts,
The breasts of Helen, and hoveringly a sword
Now over and now under, now direct,
Pointed itself to pierce, but sank down shamed
At all that beauty; and as I stared, a fire,
The fire that left a roofless Ilion,
Shot out of them, and scorched me that I woke.

'Is this thy vengeance, holy Venus, thine,
Because I would not one of thine own doves,
Not even a rose, were offered to thee? thine,
Forgetful how my rich prooemion makes
Thy glory fly along the Italian field,
In lays that will outlast thy Deity?

'Deity? nay, thy worshippers. My tongue
Trips, or I speak profanely. Which of these
Angers thee most, or angers thee at all?
Not if thou be'st of those who, far aloof
From envy, hate and pity, and spite and scorn,
Live the great life which all our greatest fain
Would follow, centered in eternal calm.

'Nay, if thou canst, O Goddess, like ourselves
Touch, and be touched, then would I cry to thee

*60–6.* Cp. Lucretius i 473–5: *numquam Tyndaridis forma conflatus amoris / ignis, Alexandri Phrygio sub pectore gliscens, / clara accendisset saevi certamina belli.* ('No love's fire fanned to flame by the beauty of Tyndaris, and glowing beneath the breast of Phrygian Alexander, would ever have set alight blazing battles of savage war.') Adapted 'with a curious reversal', as Wilner observes.
*61.* D. Bush compares Euripides, *Andromache* 628–31 (*Major British Writers*, 1959, ii 451).
*67.* Suggested by vi 68ff.
*68.* H.T. compares v 1198ff.
*70.* H.T. compares i 1–4: *Aeneadum genetrix, hominum divomque voluptas, / alma Venus, caeli subter labentia signa / quae mare navigerum, quae terras frugiferentis / concelebras ....* ('Mother of Aeneas and his race, darling of men and gods, nurturing Venus, who beneath the smooth-moving heavenly signs fillest with thyself the sea full-laden with ships, the earth with her kindly fruits.')
*80–1.* Cp. i 304: *tangere enim et tangi, nisi corpus, nulla potest res.* ('For nothing can touch or be touched, save body.'); and v 152: *tangere enim non quit quod tangi non licet ipsum.* ('For that cannot touch which may not be touched itself.')

To kiss thy Mavors, roll thy tender arms
Round him, and keep him from the lust of blood
That makes a steaming slaughter-house of Rome.

'Ay, but I meant not thee; I meant not her,
Whom all the pines of Ida shook to see
Slide from that quiet heaven of hers, and tempt
The Trojan, while his neat-herds were abroad;
Nor her that o'er her wounded hunter wept
Her Deity false in human-amorous tears;
Nor whom her beardless apple-arbiter
Decided fairest. Rather, O ye Gods,
Poet-like, as the great Sicilian called
Calliope to grace his golden verse–
Ay, and this Kypris also–did I take
That popular name of thine to shadow forth
The all-generating powers and genial heat
Of Nature, when she strikes through the thick blood
Of cattle, and light is large, and lambs are glad
Nosing the mother's udder, and the bird
Makes his heart voice amid the blaze of flowers:
Which things appear the work of mighty Gods.

'The Gods! and if I go *my* work is left
Unfinished–*if* I go. The Gods, who haunt

*82.* T. compares i 29–30, the prayer to Venus to restrain Mars: *effice ut interea fera moenera militiai / per maria ac terras omnis sopita quiescant ....* ('Cause meanwhile the savage works of war to sleep and be still over every sea and land.')

*85–92.* Venus and her love of Endymion, Adonis, and Paris.

*93–5.* Empedocles; T. (*1913*) compares i 729–31: *nil tamen hoc habuisse viro praeclarius in se / nec sanctum magis et mirum carumque videtur.* ('Yet it seems to have in it nothing more illustrious than this man, nor more sacred and wonderful and dear.')

*94.* Empedocles's fragmentary invocation to Calliope, muse of epic poetry.

*95. Kypris*: Venus as Lady of Cyprus, where in Hesiod she first landed.

*96.* H.T. compares i 1ff; see l. 70*n*.

*97. genial heat*: traditional diction, *genial* meaning generative.

*97–101.* Combining i 7ff; ii 320, 370.

*99. large*: abounding, as in *large ... lumine*, iii 22, and *largus ... fons luminis*, v 281.

*102.* Cp. i 153–4: *quorum operum causas nulla ratione videre / possunt ac fieri divino numine rentur* ('Whose causes they can by no means see, and they think them to be done by divine power').

*104–10.* Cp. iii 18–24: *apparet divum numen sedesque quietae / quas neque concutiunt venti nec nubila nimbis / aspergunt neque nix acri concreta pruina /*

The lucid interspace of world and world,
Where never creeps a cloud, or moves a wind,
Nor ever falls the least white star of snow,
Nor ever lowest roll of thunder moans,
Nor sound of human sorrow mounts to mar
Their sacred everlasting calm! and such,
Not all so fine, nor so divine a calm,
Not such, nor all unlike it, man may gain
Letting his own life go. The Gods, the Gods!
If all be atoms, how then should the Gods
Being atomic not be dissoluble,
Not follow the great law? My master held
That Gods there are, for all men so believe.
I prest my footsteps into his, and meant
Surely to lead my Memmius in a train
Of flowery clauses onward to the proof
That Gods there are, and deathless. Meant? I meant?
I have forgotten what I meant: my mind
Stumbles, and all my faculties are lamed.

'Look where another of our Gods, the Sun,
Apollo, Delius, or of older use
All-seeing Hyperion–what you will–
Has mounted yonder; since he never sware,

*cana cadens violat semperque innubilus aether / integit, et large diffuso lumine ridet. / omnia suppeditat porro natura neque ulla / res animi pacem delibat tempore in ullo.* ('Before me appear the gods in their majesty, and their peaceful abodes, which no winds ever shake nor clouds besprinkle with rain, which no snow congealed by the bitter frost mars with its white fall, but the air ever cloudless encompasses them and laughs with its light spread wide abroad. There moreover nature supplies everything, and nothing at any time impairs their peace of mind.') T. observes that this was in imitation of *Odyssey* iv 566ff. Previously adapted in *Morte d'Arthur* 260–3 (p. 596).

*105.* Cp. Cicero, *De Natura Deorum* i 18: *tamquam modo ex deorum concilio et ex Epicuri intermundiis* ('from the assembly of the gods in the intermundane spaces of Epicurus').

*117.* H.T. compares v 146–94, 1161–1291. Lucretius agreed with Epicurus that this was the only ground for belief.

*118.* H.T. compares iii 3–4, *inque tuis nunc / ficta pedum pono pressis vestigia signis* ('and now on the marks thou hast left I plant my own footsteps firm').

*119.* Caius Memmius, to whom *De Rerum Natura* was dedicated.

*126.* D. Bush observes that this is accented correctly, *Hyperíon* (*Major British Writers*, 1959, ii 451).

Except his wrath were wreaked on wretched man,
That he would only shine among the dead
Hereafter; tales! for never yet on earth
Could dead flesh creep, or bits of roasting ox
Moan round the spit–nor knows he what he sees;
King of the East although he seem, and girt
With song and flame and fragrance, slowly lifts
His golden feet on those empurpled stairs
That climb into the windy halls of heaven:
And here he glances on an eye new-born,
And gets for greeting but a wail of pain;
And here he stays upon a freezing orb
That fain would gaze upon him to the last;
And here upon a yellow eyelid fallen
And closed by those who mourn a friend in vain,
Not thankful that his troubles are no more.
And me, although his fire is on my face
Blinding, he sees not, nor at all can tell
Whether I mean this day to end myself,
Or lend an ear to Plato where he says,
That men like soldiers may not quit the post
Allotted by the Gods: but he that holds
The Gods are careless, wherefore need he care
Greatly for them, nor rather plunge at once,
Being troubled, wholly out of sight, and sink
Past earthquake–ay, and gout and stone, that break
Body toward death, and palsy, death-in-life,
And wretched age–and worst disease of all,
These prodigies of myriad nakednesses,
And twisted shapes of lust, unspeakable,
Abominable, strangers at my hearth
Not welcome, harpies miring every dish,
The phantom husks of something foully done,

*29–32. Odyssey* xii 374–96, the Sun's wrath at the slaughter of his sacred oxen, whose flesh moved and moaned as Odysseus's companions prepared to eat it.

*136.* Adapted from *Ode: O Bosky Brook* 29: 'Heaven's windy Hall'. *The Lover's Tale* i 63, MS: 'Heaven's windy halls'.

*137–43.* The examples taken variously from Lucretius, e.g. ii 576ff, v 224–6, iii 900.

*147–9. Phaedo* vi (T.).

*150.* Cp. v 82: *deos securum agere aevom* ('the gods lead a life without care').

*157–8.* Cp. *Paradise Lost* ii 626: 'Abominable, inutterable'.

*159. Aeneid* iii 227.

*160. phantom husks*: Lucretius's *simulacra*, as in l. 165.

And fleeting through the boundless universe,
And blasting the long quiet of my breast
With animal heat and dire insanity?

'How should the mind, except it loved them, clasp
These idols to herself? or do they fly
Now thinner, and now thicker, like the flakes
In a fall of snow, and so press in, perforce
Of multitude, as crowds that in an hour
Of civic tumult jam the doors, and bear
The keepers down, and throng, their rags and they
The basest, far into that council-hall
Where sit the best and stateliest of the land?

'Can I not fling this horror off me again,
Seeing with how great ease Nature can smile,
Balmier and nobler from her bath of storm,
At random ravage? and how easily
The mountain there has cast his cloudy slough,
Now towering o'er him in serenest air,
A mountain o'er a mountain, – ay, and within
All hollow as the hopes and fears of men?

'But who was he, that in the garden snared
Picus and Faunus, rustic Gods? a tale
To laugh at – more to laugh at in myself –
For look! what is it? there? yon arbutus
Totters; a noiseless riot underneath
Strikes through the wood, sets all the tops quivering –
The mountain quickens into Nymph and Faun;
And here an Oread – how the sun delights

*165. idols*: the Epicurean doctrine that all surfaces are streaming images, Lucretius iv 30–2: *simulacra vocamus; / quae, quasi membranae summo de corpore rerum / dereptae, volitant ultroque citroque per auras* ('we call images; which, like films drawn from the outermost surface of things, flit about hither and thither through the air').

*168–72.* Cp. *In Memoriam* xxi 13–16: 'an hour . . . / When more and more the people throng / The chairs and thrones of civil power.' T. is once again probably thinking of the French Revolution, one such event of which Carlyle compared with the Goths bursting into the Roman Senate.

*176–80.* Based on vi 189–98.

*178. serenest air*: Shelley's *Prometheus Unbound* I 64, which describes mountains and whirlwinds.

*181–2.* Numa caught Picus and Faunus, and drew from them the secret of averting Jove's lightning (Ovid's *Fasti* iii 285ff).

*188–91*] And here an Oread, and this way she runs *Macmillan's*. W. E. Buckler (*RES* n.s. v, 1954, 269–71) uses a Macmillan letter to suggest that

To glance and shift about her slippery sides,
And rosy knees and supple roundedness,
And budded bosom-peaks–who this way runs
Before the rest–A satyr, a satyr, see,
Follows; but him I proved impossible;
Twy-natured is no nature: yet he draws
Nearer and nearer, and I scan him now
Beastlier than any phantom of his kind
That ever butted his rough brother-brute
For lust or lusty blood or provender:
I hate, abhor, spit, sicken at him; and she
Loathes him as well; such a precipitate heel,
Fledged as it were with Mercury's ankle-wing,
Whirls her to me: but will she fling herself,
Shameless upon me? Catch her, goat-foot: nay,
Hide, hide them, million-myrtled wilderness,
And cavern-shadowing laurels, hide! do I wish–
What?–that the bush were leafless? or to whelm
All of them in one massacre? O ye Gods,
I know you careless, yet, behold, to you
From childly wont and ancient use I call–
I thought I lived securely as yourselves–
No lewdness, narrowing envy, monkey-spite,
No madness of ambition, avarice, none:
No larger feast than under plane or pine
With neighbours laid along the grass, to take

their cut was critical as well as prudish. But T. wrote to the editor: 'With respect to the Oread please yourself, but send the full passage to America. They are not so squeamish as we are' (3 March 1868); again, 'My wife is copying *Lucretius* ... *She* says she does not think it will shock people' (A. T. Scheuer, N.Y., Catalogue 3, 1927). For the phrasing, cp. *The Kraken* 4–5: 'faintest sunlights flee / About his shadowy sides'. Cp. Horace, *Odes* I xix 8: *lubricus aspici* ('seductive to behold').

*193.* H.T. compares ii 700, v 837ff, 878ff.

*194.* Long a concern of T.'s; cp. *Amy* 73–6: 'Yet take blind Passion; give him eyes; and freeing / His spirit from his frame, / Make double-natured love lose half his being / In thy spiritual flame.'

*203. goat-foot*: *capripedes* iv 580.

*213–4.* H.T. compares ii 29–31: *cum tamen inter se prostrati in gramine molli / propter aquae rivum sub ramis arboris altae / non magnis opibus iucunde corpora curant.* ('When all the same stretched forth in groups upon the soft grass beside a rill of water under the branches of a tall tree men merrily refresh themselves at no great cost.') Cp. Horace, *Odes* II xi 13–4: *cur non sub alta vel platano vel hac / pinu iacentes* ... ('Why not reclining under this lofty plane or pine').

Only such cups as left us friendly-warm,
Affirming each his own philosophy–
Nothing to mar the sober majesties
Of settled, sweet, Epicurean life.
But now it seems some unseen monster lays
His vast and filthy hands upon my will,
Wrenching it backward into his; and spoils
My bliss in being; and it was not great;
For save when shutting reasons up in rhythm,
Or Heliconian honey in living words,
To make a truth less harsh, I often grew
Tired of so much within our little life,
Or of so little in our little life–
Poor little life that toddles half an hour
Crowned with a flower or two, and there an end–
And since the nobler pleasure seems to fade,
Why should I, beastlike as I find myself,
Not manlike end myself?–our privilege–
What beast has heart to do it? And what man,
What Roman would be dragged in triumph thus?
Not I; not he, who bears one name with her
Whose death-blow struck the dateless doom of kings,
When, brooking not the Tarquin in her veins,
She made her blood in sight of Collatine
And all his peers, flushing the guiltless air,
Spout from the maiden fountain in her heart.
And from it sprang the Commonwealth, which breaks
As I am breaking now!

*218.* H.T. compares iii 66: *semota ab dulci vita stabilique* ('far removed from sweetness and stability of life').
*224.* H.T. compares i 945–7, repeated iv 20–2: *volui tibi suaviloquenti / carmine Pierio rationem exponere nostram / et quasi musaeo dulci contingere melle.* ('I have chosen to set forth my doctrine to you in sweet-speaking Pierian song, and as it were to touch it with the Muses' delicious honey.')
*228.* Cp. iii 913–4: *et inumbrant ora coronis, / ex animo ut dicant* '*brevis hic est fructus homullis*' ('and shade their brows with garlands, that they often say from their hearts "Short enjoyment is given to poor mankind"').
*235. her*: 'Lucretia' (T.), i.e. Lucrece.
*242–8.* Cp. ii 874–80: *praeterea cunctas itidem res vertere sese. / vertunt se fluvii frondes et pabula laeta / in pecudes, vertunt pecudes in corpora nostra / naturam, et nostro de corpore saepe ferarum / augescunt vires et corpora pennipotentum. / ergo omnes natura cibos in corpora viva / vertit et hinc sensus animantum procreat omnes* ('and besides, you may see all things changing in the same way. Rivers, leaves, luxuriant pastures change into animals, animals change their substance into our bodies, often from our bodies

'And therefore now
Let her, that is the womb and tomb of all,
Great Nature, take, and forcing far apart
Those blind beginnings that have made me man,
Dash them anew together at her will
Through all her cycles–into man once more,
Or beast or bird or fish, or opulent flower:
But till this cosmic order everywhere
Shattered into one earthquake in one day
Cracks all to pieces,–and that hour perhaps
Is not so far when momentary man
Shall seem no more a something to himself,
But he, his hopes and hates, his homes and fanes,
And even his bones long laid within the grave,
The very sides of the grave itself shall pass,
Vanishing, atom and void, atom and void,
Into the unseen for ever,–till that hour,
My golden work in which I told a truth

those of wild beasts do increase their strength and those of birds strong-i'-the-wing. Therefore nature changes all foods into living bodies, and from them brings forth all the feelings of animals').

*243.* H.T. compares v 258: *omniparens eadem rerum commune sepulcrum.* Also *PL* ii 911: 'The Womb of nature and perhaps her Grave.'

*249–58.* H.T. compares v 92–6: *principio maria ac terras caelumque tuere; / quorum naturam triplicem, tria corpora, Memmi, / tris species tam dissimilis, tria talia texta, / una dies dabit exitio, multosque per annos / sustentata ruet moles et machina mundi.* ('Observe first of all sea and earth and sky: this threefold nature, these three masses, Memmius, these three forms so different, these three textures so interwoven, one day shall consign to destruction; the mighty and complex system of the universe, upheld through many years, shall crash into ruins.') Cp. v 105ff, 259; also Ovid, *Amores* I xv 23–4: *carmina sublimis tunc sunt peritura Lucreti, / exitio terras cum dabit una dies.* ('The verses of sublime Lucretius will perish only then when a single day shall give the earth to doom.')

*251–3.* Cp. Lucretius iii 878: *sed facit esse sui quiddam super inscius ipse* ('but unknown to himself he makes something of himself to survive').

*259.* H.T. compares iii 978–83, arguing that there is no world of the dead: *Atque ea nimirum quaecumque Acherunte profundo / prodita sunt esse, in vita sunt omnia nobis. / nec miser inpendens magnum timet aere saxum / Tantalus, ut famast, cassa formidine torpens; / sed magis in vita divom metus urget inanis / mortalis casumque timent quem cuique ferat fors.* ('And of a surety whatsoever things are fabled to exist in deep Acheron, these all exist for us in this life. There is no wretched Tantalus, as the story goes, fearing the great rock that hangs over him in the air and frozen with vain terror; rather it is in this

That stays the rolling Ixionian wheel,
And numbs the Fury's ringlet-snake, and plucks
The mortal soul from out immortal hell,
Shall stand: ay, surely: then it fails at last
And perishes as I must; for O Thou,
Passionless bride, divine Tranquillity,
Yearned after by the wisest of the wise,
Who fail to find thee, being as thou art
Without one pleasure and without one pain,
Howbeit I know thou surely must be mine
Or soon or late, yet out of season, thus
I woo thee roughly, for thou carest not
How roughly men may woo thee so they win–
Thus–thus: the soul flies out and dies in the air.'

With that he drove the knife into his side:
She heard him raging, heard him fall; ran in,
Beat breast, tore hair, cried out upon herself
As having failed in duty to him, shrieked
That she but meant to win him back, fell on him,
Clasped, kissed him, wailed: he answered, 'Care not thou!
Thy duty? What is duty? Fare thee well!'

life that the fear of gods oppresses mortals without cause, and the fall they fear is any that chance may bring.') Also iv 8ff.

*260.* Ixion tried to seduce Hera, and was punished in Tartarus by being bound to a fiery wheel.

*261. And*] *1868–94*; That *Eversley, presumably in error.*

*261–2.* Cp. iii 867–9: *nec miserum fieri qui non est posse neque hilum / differre anne ullo fuerit iam tempore natus, / mortalem vitam mors cum inmortalis ademit* ('that he who is not cannot be miserable, that it makes not one jot of difference whether he has ever been born at any time before, when death the immortal has taken away his mortal life'). Cp. *St Lawrence* 12: 'plucked me forth from Hell'. Also Virgil, *Georgics* iv 481–4.

*266.* Adapted from *The Devil and the Lady* III ii 176: 'passionless tranquillity' (D. Bush, *Mythology and the Romantic Tradition*, 1937, p. 214).

*273.* Cp. iii 543–4: *mortalem tamen esse animam fateare necesse, / nec refert utrum pereat dispersa per auras* ('yet you must needs confess the spirit to be mortal, for it matters not whether it pass away dispersed abroad through the air'); and iii 455–6: *ergo dissolui quoque convenit omnem animai / naturam, ceu fumus, in altas aeris auras* ('it follows therefore that the whole nature of the spirit is dissolved abroad like smoke into the high winds of the air').

*280*] What matters? All is over: Fare thee well!' *Macmillan's.*

# 356 The Spiteful Letter

Published *Once A Week*, 4 Jan. 1868, as *On a Spiteful Letter*; then *1872*. T. says: 'It is no particular letter that I meant. I have had dozens of them from one quarter and another.' 'For forty-two years my father had had among his various strange letters an anonymous abusive letter, evidently from the same writer, on the appearance of every new volume' (*Mem.* ii 398). The core of the poem, ll. 13–16, had been written as an epigram in *H.Nbk 37* (watermarked 1863), which includes many of T.'s epigrams.

Here, it is here, the close of the year,
 And with it a spiteful letter.
My name in song has done him much wrong,
 For himself has done much better.

O little bard, is your lot so hard,
 If men neglect your pages?
I think not much of yours or of mine,
 I hear the roll of the ages.

Rhymes and rhymes in the range of the times!
 Are mine for the moment stronger?
Yet hate me not, but abide your lot,
 I last but a moment longer.

This faded leaf, our names are as brief;
 What room is left for a hater?
Yet the yellow leaf hates the greener leaf,
 For it hangs one moment later.

¶356. *3. name*] *1872*; fame *1868*.
*5. little*] *1872*; foolish *1868*. *H.Nbk 32 includes two unadopted stanzas*:
 O little bard, is your lot so hard?
  Do they send you millions of verses?
 Send you millions of reams of rhyme?
  Have you my millions of curses?

 O little bard with your scoffs and scorns!
  Call *me* as wealthy as Crassus!
 You foolish fellow, the Devil's two horns
  Are the peaks of your Parnassus.
*9–10*] *1872*; This fallen leaf, isn't fame as brief?
  My rhymes may have been the stronger. *1868*
*13*] *1872*; O faded leaf, isn't fame as brief? *1868*.
*14. left*] *1872*; here *1868*.

Greater than I–is that your cry?
 And men will live to see it.
Well–if it be so–so it is, you know;
 And if it be so, so be it.

Brief, brief is a summer leaf,
 But this is the time of hollies.
O hollies and ivies and evergreens,
 How I hate the spites and the follies!

[1868. *The Lover's Tale*–see p. 299]

[1869. *The Coming of Arthur*, *The Holy Grail*, *Pelleas and Ettarre*, *The Passing of Arthur*–see pp. 1469, 1660, 1687, 1742]

# 357 In the Garden at Swainston

Published 1874, Cabinet Edition. Written 31 May 1870 (*Mem.* ii 97–8; see *CT*, p. 389), on the occasion of the funeral of T.'s friend and neighbour Sir John Simeon, who died 21 May at Fribourg. The 'three dead men' (l. 15) were Arthur Hallam, Henry Lushington and Simeon (T.). Cp. the elegy *In the Valley of Cauteretz* (p. 1123).

Nightingales warbled without,
 Within was weeping for thee:
Shadows of three dead men
 Walked in the walks with me,
 Shadows of three dead men and thou wast one
  of the three.

Nightingales sang in his woods:
 The Master was far away:
Nightingales warbled and sang
 Of a passion that lasts but a day;
 Still in the house in his coffin the Prince of
  courtesy lay.

*17. is*] *1872*; isn't *1868.*
*18. men will*] *1872*; I shall *1868.*
*21*] *1872*; O summer leaf, isn't life as brief? *1868.*
*23*] *1872*; And my heart, my heart is an evergreen: *1868.*
*24. How*] *1872*; *not 1868.*

Two dead men have I known
  In courtesy like to thee:
Two dead men have I loved
  With a love that ever will be:
  Three dead men have I loved and thou art last
    of the three.

## 358 *The Christ of Ammergau

Printed *Twentieth Century* clvii (1955) 2–3, with a note found among the papers of T.'s friend James Knowles: 'I read to him a newspaper paragraph saying that the man who took the character of Christ in the Ober Ammergau Passion Play had been carried off as a conscript to serve in the army. It was at the time of the Vatican Council and the definition of the Pope's infallibility, which was promulgated [18 July 1870] in a thunderstorm, and we had also been talking about that. Then, quite impromptu, as he lay upon his bed, he made and chanted in a great voice the following lines.' The MS in Knowles's hand at *Lincoln* shows, though, that T. undertook some revision; all variants are below. *The Times*, 23 July 1870: 'In the midst of thunder, lightning, and rain Pius IX pro-theosized himself, if I may be allowed to coin a word, and is now registered among the Dii Majores.' Cp. *Desolate, why, crowned city* (p. 1798).

They made the old Pope God–
  Which God, if He will, may pardon–
And Christ stepped down from the cross,
  Christ came out of the garden.

They made the old Pope God
  While God was rolling his thunder,
And Christ came out from Ammergau
  To massacre, burn, and plunder.

Christ came out from the Play–
  Children, love one another!–
In bitter earnest out he came
  To mash the skull of his brother.

¶358. *1*] It was when they made the Pope God – *L.MS 1st reading*. Pius IX was seventy-eight.

*2. He*] *MS*; he *1955*.

*5. the old Pope*] his holiness *MS 1st reading*.

*6*] All in a storm of thunder *MS 1st reading*.

Went to slay and be slain,
  Armed with his gun and his sabre,
To show the world he loved himself
  No better than his neighbour.

'Lebe der König!' 'Vive la guerre!'
  Let the brother mangle his brother,
For, O little children, we see by this
  What love ye bear one another.

[1871. *The Last Tournament*, and *England and America in 1782* – see p. 1705 and p. 618]

[1872. *Gareth and Lynette*, and *To the Queen: Idylls of the King* – see pp. 1484, 1755]

# 359 The Voice and the Peak

Published *1874*. T. began to write it, 4 Sept. 1873, in the Val d'Anzasca (*Mem.* ii 148). The draft in *H.Nbk 34* breaks off after l. 20; all variants are below.

I

The voice and the Peak
  Far over summit and lawn,
The lone glow and long roar
  Green-rushing from the rosy thrones of dawn!

II

All night have I heard the voice
  Rave over the rocky bar,
But thou wert silent in heaven,
  Above thee glided the star.

*13. slay ... slain*] kill ... killed *MS 1st reading.*
*14. gun and his*] musket and *MS 1st reading.*
*15. world*] world that *MS.*
*18*] Let brother mangle brother *MS, deleting* his.
¶359. *2*] Far into heaven withdrawn, *H.MS.*
*5–8*]
The silence and the height,
  Far up in heaven like a dream –
Why art thou silent O height?
  Why dost thou roar, O stream? *MS*

III

Hast thou no voice, O Peak,
That standest high above all?
'I am the voice of the Peak,
I roar and rave for I fall.

IV

'A thousand voices go
To North, South, East, and West;
They leave the heights and are troubled,
And moan and sink to their rest.

V

'The fields are fair beside them,
The chestnut towers in his bloom;
But they–they feel the desire of the deep–
Fall, and follow their doom.

VI

'The deep has power on the height,
And the height has power on the deep;
They are raised for ever and ever,
And sink again into sleep.'

VII

Not raised for ever and ever,
But when their cycle is o'er,
The valley, the voice, the peak, the star
Pass, and are found no more.

VIII

The Peak is high and flushed
At his highest with sunrise fire;
The Peak is high, and the stars are high,
And the thought of a man is higher.

10. *above*] over *MS*.
12. *I . . . for*] And I roar because *MS*.
13. *A thousand*] Many *MS 1st reading*.
15. *heights*] height *MS*.
16] They roar till they find a rest. *MS 1st reading*; And rave and moan to their rest. *MS*.
17] Sweep by the fair green fields, *MS*.
18. *towers in his*] towering in *MS*.
19] Down from the height–down to the deep–*MS*.

IX

A deep below the deep,
And a height beyond the height!
Our hearing is not hearing,
And our seeing is not sight.

X

The voice and the Peak
Far into heaven withdrawn,
The lone glow and long roar
Green-rushing from the rosy thrones of dawn!

# 360 A Welcome to Her Royal Highness Marie Alexandrovna, Duchess of Edinburgh

## MARCH 7, 1874

Published *The Times*, 7 March 1874; then 1874, Cabinet Edition. The Grand Duchess Marie Alexandrovna of Russia, and Alfred, Duke of Edinburgh, landed in England on 7 March; they had married on 23 Jan. at St Petersburg. Cp. *A Welcome to Alexandra* (p. 1152).

I

The Son of him with whom we strove for power–
Whose will is lord through all his world-domain–
Who made the serf a man, and burst his chain–
Has given our Prince his own imperial Flower,
Alexandrovna.
And welcome, Russian flower, a people's pride,
To Britain, when her flowers begin to blow!
From love to love, from home to home you go,
From mother unto mother, stately bride,
Marie Alexandrovna!

33. *deep . . . deep*] voice . . . voice *1874, corrected in Errata.*
35–6. Cp. *The Higher Pantheism* 17–18: 'And the ear of man cannot hear, and the eye of man cannot see; / But if we could see and hear, this Vision– were it not He?'
¶360. *1.* Tsar Alexander II, son of Nicholas I (Britain's enemy in the Crimean War).

II

The golden news along the steppes is blown,
And at thy name the Tartar tents are stirred;
Elburz and all the Caucasus have heard;
And all the sultry palms of India known,
Alexandrovna.
The voices of our universal sea
On capes of Afric as on cliffs of Kent,
The Maoris and that Isle of Continent,
And loyal pines of Canada murmur thee,
Marie Alexandrovna!

III

Fair empires branching, both, in lusty life!–
Yet Harold's England fell to Norman swords;
Yet thine own land has bowed to Tartar hordes
Since English Harold gave its throne a wife,
Alexandrovna!
For thrones and peoples are as waifs that swing,
And float or fall, in endless ebb and flow;
But who love best have best the grace to know
That Love by right divine is deathless king,
Marie Alexandrovna!

IV

And Love has led thee to the stranger land,
Where men are bold and strongly say their say;–
See, empire upon empire smiles today,
As thou with thy young lover hand in hand
Alexandrovna!
So now thy fuller life is in the west,
Whose hand at home was gracious to thy poor:
Thy name was blest within the narrow door;
Here also, Marie, shall thy name be blest,
Marie Alexandrovna!

V

Shall fears and jealous hatreds flame again?
Or at thy coming, Princess, everywhere,
The blue heaven break, and some diviner air
Breathe through the world and change the hearts of men,
Alexandrovna?

*19.* Cp. T. on Canadian loyalty in *Idylls: To the Queen* 14–18.
*43–4.* Cp. *The Sisters* [*They have left*] 13: 'Breathe, diviner Air!'

But hearts that change not, love that cannot cease,
And peace be yours, the peace of soul in soul!
And howsoever this wild world may roll,
Between your peoples truth and manful peace,
Alfred–Alexandrovna!

# 361 *Epigrams 1868–1874

i–vii were printed by Sir Charles Tennyson, *Nineteenth Century* cix (1931) 630–1. i–vi are from *H.Nbk 37*, where they are with poems of *c.* 1868; vii is from *H.Lpr 139*, and, as Sir Charles notes, its epigraph is from *Pilgrims* in *Songs before Sunrise* (1871).

I

What I most am shamed about,
That I least am blamed about;
What I least am loud about,
That I most am praised about.

II

Birth and circumstance are Fate,
Thence have we thief and whore.
Why therefore should we scorn and hate?
We feel there's something more.

III

You have spite enough–that is plain enough–
But you hide your name for fear of a lashing–
Out with it, skunk! are you vain enough
To think you are worth the thrashing?

IV

I ran upon life unknowing, without or science or art,
I found the first pretty maiden but she was a harlot at heart;
I wandered about the woodland after the melting of snow,
'Here is the first pretty snowdrop'–and it was the dung of a crow!

V

A variant of *By a Darwinian* (p. 1227), which is on the same page.

We come from monkeys–prove it who can–
But here is a clue to the vices of man.

¶361. i 1–2. *shamed . . . blamed*] *MS*; *transposed 1931*.
iv *3. of*] *MS*; of the *1931*.

## VI

Printed *Mat.* iii 87, as though written August 1868, 'after a sarcastic attack on his poems'–most probably that by Alfred Austin, *Temple Bar*, though it did not appear till May 1869; T. mentions this attack in a letter (p. 1229), and Austin called him a 'small poet'. The *1931* text is that of the MS 1st readings.

Somebody being a nobody,
Thinking to look like a somebody,
Said that he thought me a nobody:
Good little somebody-nobody,
Had you not known me a somebody,
Would you have called me a nobody?

## VII

*All men born are mortal but not man.*
(Swinburne)

Man is as mortal as men,
The cycle sweeps him away;
I am the worm of a minute,
The fly will last for a day;
Both in a minute are gone,
The day and the minute are one.

## VIII

Unpublished, *H.Nbk 37.*

For you and yours I have small respect;
You may save us or damn;
But I look to the greater Intellect
Who knows what I am–
Damn and save us and damn us again,
But if there be a God–why then
He needs must know what I am.

## IX

Printed by J. H. Buckley (p. 163). *H.Nbk 37.*

Home is home, though never so homely,
And a harlot a harlot, though never so comely.

vi 2. *look like a*] make himself *1931.*
vi 5. *known me a*] felt I was *1931.*

## X

Printed by J. H. Buckley (p. 163). *H.Nbk 37*.

What I've come to, you know well,
What I've gone through none can tell.

## XI

Unpublished, *H.Nbk 37*.

Yes, you prize him so dearly,
You spare him a gleam of your pity,
Give him a touch of your scorn too–
Doubtless you see him so clearly,
You know what the man was bound with
And all that the man was born to.
If you knew these two things when you wrote of him so and so,
I could worship you as a God, but you never can know!

## XII. Sadness

Printed *Mem.* ii 17, as written 1864. But it is from *T.Nbk 33* (1868), where, however, there is no epigraph.

*Eternal illimitable darkness is brother to eternal silence.*

Immeasurable sadness!
And I know it as a poet,
And I greet it, and I meet it,
Immeasurable sadness!
And the voice that apes a nation–
Let it cry an affectation,
Or a fancy or a madness,–
But I know it as a poet,
And I meet it, and I greet it,
And I say it, and repeat it,
Immeasurable sadness!

## XIII. By a Darwinian

Printed *Mem.* ii 58, as written *c.* 1868, apparently Oct. (*Mat.* iii 90). T. wrote several versions of it; it appears with other epigrams in *H.Nbk 37* and *HnMS* (HM 19505). The title seems to be H.T.'s. T. thought of publishing it in *1885*; the second of the *British Museum* trial editions (unlike the first and the third) prints it at the end of *The Dead Prophet*, with the title *Reversion*, ll. 4–6 being a reply by 'Evolutionist'. This trial edition makes clear that T. by this date had come to connect it, like *The Dead Prophet* (p. 1322), with his indignation at J. A. Froude's revelations about Carlyle. 'Tennyson's main trouble seemed to be that the bones of Carlyle should be flung about, and one evening he repeated to my wife and myself a quatrain he had composed about the delight of apes in seeing a man dragged down to their own apehood' (M. D. Conway, *Autobiography*, 1904, ii 192–3).

How is it that men have so little grace,
When a great man's found to be bad and base,
That they chuckle and chatter and mock?
We come from apes—and are far removed—
But rejoice when a bigger brother has proved
That he springs from the common stock.

## XIV. Darwin's Gemmule

Unpublished, *HnMS* (HM 19493). Probably written 1868; Darwin visited T. that year in August, and H.T. gives this as the date of the preceding epigram, *By a Darwinian*. It was in 1868 that Darwin proposed his 'Provisional Hypothesis of Pangenesis' in *The Variation of Animals and Plants*; a gemmule was thought to be thrown off from each cell, and transmitted from parents to offspring, thus being responsible for physical inheritance. Darwin mentioned 'inherited gout', which would be the result of 'modified gemmules'.

Curse you, you wandering gemmule,
And nail you fast in Hell!
You gave me gout and bandy legs,
You beast, you wanted a cell!
Gout, and gravel, and evil days—
(Theology speaks, shaking her head)
But there is One who knows your ways!

## XV

Printed *Mat.* ii 425–6, as *History* (*now-a-days*), among 'Epigrams of this period', 1864. But it appears in *T.Nbk 33* (1868).

The cursed will be blest,
And the blest will be cursed,
And great things turn into small things;
And the worst is the best
And the best is the worst,
And topsy-turvy go all things.

xiii 2. *bad*] lewd *H.MS 1st reading*.
xiii *3*] We chuckle; it gives us, our brother's disgrace, / Such a pleasant kind of a shock: *MS 1st reading*.

## XVI

Unpublished, *H.Lprs 3–4*. The accompanying letter describes how T. had seen 'that happy mixture of ass, rogue, and peacock the so-called Captain Bertrand Payne, who has lately bribed his bully to write me down in *Temple Bar*, by way of spiting me and spoiling Strahan's bargain'. The reference is to Alfred Austin's article, *Temple Bar*, May 1869. T. had broken away from his publishers, Moxon (managed by Payne), and had made an agreement with Alexander Strahan in Feb. 1869 (*Mem.* ii 63). Strahan's office was on Ludgate Hill, near St Paul's.

Ancient Pistol, peacock Payne,
Brute in manner, rogue in grain,
How you squeezed me, peacock Payne!
Scared was I and out I ran
And found by Paul's an honest man.
Peace be with you, peacock Payne,
I have left you, you remain
Ancient Pistol, sealskin Payne.

## XVII. Art for Art's sake (instead of Art for Art – and – Man's sake)

Printed *Mem.* ii 91–2: 'When certain adverse critics discovered that throughout all the new *Idylls of the King* [Dec. 1869] there was a great moral significance, he was attacked with the cry of "Art for Art's sake". After reading one of these attacks he reeled off this epigram.'

Art for Art's sake! Hail, truest Lord of Hell!
Hail Genius, blaster of the Moral Will!
'The filthiest of all paintings painted well
Is mightier than the purest painted ill!'
Yes, mightier than the purest painted well,
So prone are we toward that broad way to Hell.

## XVIII

Printed *Mem.* ii 74, under 1869. Frederick Locker-Lampson reports that T. 'spoke to me several times, almost with horror, of the way people who have won fame are likely to be maligned after their death. I have an old commonplace book, into which, with many other scraps of prose and verse, I had copied an epigram by Thomas Hood. It runs as follows:

"What is a modern poet's fate?
To write his thoughts upon a slate;
The critic spits on what is done,
*Gives it a wipe*–and all is gone."

T. HOOD

xvii *2. blaster*] *H.Lpr 6*; Master *Mem.*
xvii *6. that*] *MS*; the *Mem.*

This quatrain amused Tennyson, and he said: "It is a good joke, and now I'll write you a grave *truth*." Which he did as follows, adding the words "a joke" by the side of Hood's lines.'

A truth. While I live, the owls!
When I die, the GHOULS!!!

This version is in *H.Nbk 37* (1868), and in *HnMS* (HM 19506) which is watermarked 1870. H. D. Rawnsley, *Memories of the Tennysons* (1900), p. 113, reports that T. said to him in May 1890:

In my youth the growls!
In mine age the owls!
After death the ghouls!

## XIX. The Gentle Life

Printed by Sir Charles Tennyson (1949), p. 391, from *H.Lpr 70*; he had printed a milder version, on 'Buzz-well, Bizz-well', in *Nineteenth Century* cix (1931) 628–30 (*H.Nbk 45*). Written Oct.–Nov. 1870, when J. H. Friswell reissued his essays *The Gentle Life* and also published *Modern Men of Letters Honestly Criticised*–with an attack on T. both personal and literary. Friswell's poems in 1865 had been dedicated to T.; hence l. 3. In *Nbk 45*, the epigram is on the same page as *Somebody being a nobody* (p. 1226). T. uses the same metre as in his attack on reviewers, *Hendecasyllabics* (p. 1155).

*Gentle Life*–what a title! here's a subject
Calls aloud for a gentleman to handle!
Who has handled it? he, the would-be poet,
Friswell, Pisswell–a liar and a twaddler–
Pisswell, Friswell–a clown beyond redemption,
Brutal, personal, infinitely blackguard.

## XX

Unpublished, *H.Nbk 40* (1871–2).

Some pleasure and exceeding pain,
Then stench and putrefying brain,
And then a larger crop of grain,
And then the farmer says 'tis well.

xix *2. handle*] treat it *1931*.
xix *3. handled it? he*] treated it? Who? *1931*.
xix *4–5*] Buzz-well, Bizz-well–an ass beyond redemption.
Oust him, down with him, all the holy Muses!
Oust him, Muses, a liar and a twaddler, *1931*
xix *6. infinitely*] absolutely *1931*.

I swear by my small lesser [?] light,
My little [reason?] in the night,
I swear by God it is not right,
*Le jeu ne vaut pas la chandelle.*

## XXI. Popularity

Printed *Mem.* ii 157, as an impromptu made about April 1874.

Popular, Popular, Unpopular!
'You're no Poet'–the critics cried!
'Why?' said the Poet. 'You're unpopular!'
Then they cried at the turn of the tide–
'You're no Poet!' 'Why?'–'You're popular!'
Pop-gun, Popular and Unpopular!

## XXII

Unpublished, *H.Nbk 32.* Written *c.* 1874.

The Lord has grown as commonplace
As the peal of the parish bells:
The Lord has grown so popular He
That His popularity tells,
Tells against Him, but we are we
And beasts are beasts, and He is He.

The Lord has a face of man to man,
So to the Lord we call,
And a face of star-man toward the stars,
For the Lord is all-in-all,
Out of the clockwork of suns and years,
And other and other than He appears.

[1874. *Balin and Balan*–see p. 1576]

# 362 *Sonnet [Guess well, and that is well]

Printed by Sir Charles Tennyson, *Nineteenth Century* cix (1931) 628. It is from a notebook (*Harvard Nbk 32*) for *Queen Mary* and intended

xx *8*. T. in 1865: 'I would not say that the game is not worth the candle, but that the candle is too dear for me' (*Mem.* ii 20).

xxii *11*. Cp. *The Golden Year* 59–64, MS: 'complicated clockwork of the suns'.

to preface it. Written 1874–5. Cp. *Old ghosts* (p. 1342), the preface to *Becket*; and *Show-Day at Battle Abbey* (p. 1234), the preface to *Harold*. D. B. MacEachen (*Victorian Newsletter*, Fall 1958) shows that it is one of the only two late sonnets (the other, *Old ghosts*) which have an irregular rhyme-scheme; possibly that is why these two remained unpublished, since T.'s sonnets were now formalized.

Guess well, and that is well. Our age can find
The shower that fell a million years ago,
An ever-vanished ocean's ebb and flow
Rock-written; but no man can send his mind
Into man's past so well, that he can form
A perfect likeness of long-vanished souls,
Whate'er new lights be let on ancient scrolls
And secular perforations of the worm.
Courage, old Clio! we have read the rocks,
You see the past dilated through the fog
Of ages. Do your best, for that remains.
More will you do. We are more than goat or ox,
More than the long-descended horse and dog,
Whose one dumb record is their limbs and brains.

# 363 To the Rev. W. H. Brookfield

Published in Brookfield's *Sermons*, July 1875: 'Lastly, the Poet Laureate, who, as will have been noticed, was one of his most intimate associates at Cambridge, replied to our request, so to speak, "in character"' (p. xxxviii).

¶362. 5. *well . . . can*] wholly as to *H.Nbk 59, apparently a later revision.*
7. *lights*] light *Nbk 59.*
8. *secular*: continuing through long ages (a word which had become a technical term in geology).
9. *Clio*: Muse of history.
9–14]
Let him that writes our annals not abuse,
Far as he knows, the deeds that once have been:
The playwright hath more license to confuse
This date with that and make a living scene.
I do command the voices that I use,
And am not Froude or Freeman, Hook or Green.
*Nbk 32 1st reading, deleted.*
In the fourth line, *1931* reads 'busy scene'. The historians James Anthony Froude (1818–94), Edward Augustus Freeman (1823–92), Walter Farquhar Hook (1798–1875), and John Richard Green (1837–83).
10. *dilated*] *1931*; dilations *Nbk 32* (*probably a confusion with l. 8*); misshapen *Nbk 59.*

Then *1880*; it is not in the earlier *Lincoln* trial editions of *1880*. Brookfield had died 12 July 1874.

Brooks, for they called you so that knew you best,
Old Brooks, who loved so well to mouth my rhymes,
How oft we two have heard St Mary's chimes!
How oft the Cantab supper, host and guest,
Would echo helpless laughter to your jest!
How oft with him we paced that walk of limes,
Him, the lost light of those dawn-golden times,
Who loved you well! Now both are gone to rest.
You man of humorous-melancholy mark,
Dead of some inward agony–is it so?
Our kindlier, trustier Jaques, past away!
I cannot laud this life, it looks so dark:
*Σκιᾶς ὄναρ*–dream of a shadow, go–
God bless you. I shall join you in a day.

# 364 Sir John Franklin

## On the Cenotaph in Westminster Abbey

Published *1880*, among 'Translations, Etc.'. It had been printed in *The Times*, 31 July 1875, when the monument to Franklin was unveiled. A. P. Stanley requested it for the monument in July 1875, and acknowledged it, 25 July (*Lincoln*). Emily Tennyson's uncle, an Arctic explorer, Franklin sailed on his fatal expedition in 1845. T. thought this the best of his epitaphs (*Mem.* ii 273).

Not here! the white North has thy bones; and thou,
    Heroic sailor-soul,
Art passing on thine happier voyage now
    Toward no earthly pole.

¶363. *6. him*: Arthur Hallam. Cp. *In Memoriam* lxxxvii 15, on Trinity College: 'Up that long walk of limes I past'.
*10. inward agony*: *Claribel* 7 (*1830*, a poem from T.'s Cambridge days).
*11. Jaques*: the 'humorous-melancholy' character in *As You Like It*.
*13.* Pindar, *Pythian Odes* viii 95: 'Creatures of a day, what is any one? What is he not? Man is but a dream of a shadow.'
*14.* Brookfield's last words were 'Good-bye: God bless you!' (p. xlix).

# 365 Show-Day at Battle Abbey, 1876

Published as the prefatory sonnet to *Harold* in 1876 ('*1877*'). Written at Hastings, 9 May 1876 (dated, *H.Lpr 79*). A sonnet on the regular Italian model. Cp. *Old ghosts* (p. 1342), the prefatory sonnet to *Becket*; and *Sonnet* [*Guess well*] (p. 1231), the preface to *Queen Mary*.

A garden here–May breath and bloom of spring–
The cuckoo yonder from an English elm
Crying 'with my false egg I overwhelm
The native nest:' and fancy hears the ring
Of harness, and that deathful arrow sing,
And Saxon battleaxe clang on Norman helm.
Here rose the dragon-banner of our realm:
Here fought, here fell, our Norman-slandered king.
O Garden blossoming out of English blood!
O strange hate-healer Time! We stroll and stare
Where might made right eight hundred years ago;
Might, right? ay good, so all things make for good–
But he and he, if soul be soul, are where
Each stands full face with all he did below.

# 366 Battle of Brunanburh

Published *1880*; among 'Translations'. Probably written 1876–7. T. said: 'I have more or less availed myself of my son's [H.T.'s] prose translation of this poem in the *Contemporary Review* (Nov. 1876).' T. takes over much from H.T., e.g. ll. 23, 30, 'the bark's bosom' (49), 'on the fallow flood' (61), 99, 110; but it is clear that T. also studied the original. Like H.T., he used the text and translation in E. Guest's *History of English Rhythms* (1838); the copy at *Lincoln* has annotations by H.T. In *Harold*, written and published 1876, T. twice refers to 'that old song of Brunanburg / Where England conquered' (V i), and the verse (IV iii) breaks into such a style: 'Marked how the war-axe swang, / Heard how the war-horn sang, / Marked how the spear-head sprang, / Heard how the shield-wall rang, / Iron on iron clang, / Anvil on hammer bang–.' The tenth-century Old English poem is one of a group of panegyrics on royalty, using an earlier style both in metre and diction. T.'s is in general a close translation. His metre is unrhymed dactylics and trochaics: 'In rendering this Old English

¶365. *12. Romans* viii 28: 'all things work together for good, to them that love God.'

war-song into modern language and alliterative rhythm I have made free use of the dactylic beat. I suppose that the original was chanted to a slow, swinging recitative' (*Harold*, Eversley). T. wrote ten lines of a translation of *Beowulf*: 'The enemy's leader / His wordhoard unlocked . . .' *H.Nbk 4* (*c.* 1830–1). T.'s headnote: 'Constantinus, King of the Scots, after having sworn allegiance to Athelstan, allied himself with the Danes of Ireland under Anlaf, and invading England, was defeated by Athelstan and his brother Edmund with great slaughter at Brunanburh in the year 937.'

I

Athelstan King,
Lord among Earls,
Bracelet-bestower and
Baron of Barons,
He with his brother,
Edmund Atheling,
Gaining a lifelong
Glory in battle,
Slew with the sword-edge
There by Brunanburh,
Brake the shield-wall,
Hewed the lindenwood,
Hacked the battleshield,
Sons of Edward with hammered brands.

II

Theirs was a greatness
Got from their Grandsires–
Theirs that so often in
Strife with their enemies
Struck for their hoards and their hearths and their
homes.

III

Bowed the spoiler,
Bent the Scotsman,
Fell the shipcrews
Doomed to the death.
All the field with blood of the fighters
Flowed, from when first the great
Sun-star of morningtide,
Lamp of the Lord God
Lord everlasting,

¶366. *3–4*. T.'s expansion of *beorna beahgifa*, ring-giver of warriors.
*6. Atheling*: a member of an English royal family.
*12. 1880* note: 'Shields of lindenwood.'

Glode over earth till the glorious creature
Sank to his setting.

IV

There lay many a man
Marred by the javelin,
Men of the Northland
Shot over shield.
There was the Scotsman
Weary of war.

V

We the West-Saxons,
Long as the daylight
Lasted, in companies
Troubled the track of the host that we hated,
Grimly with swords that were sharp from the grindstone,
Fiercely we hacked at the flyers before us.

VI

Mighty the Mercian,
Hard was his hand-play,
Sparing not any of
Those that with Anlaf,
Warriors over the
Weltering waters
Borne in the bark's-bosom,
Drew to this island:
Doomed to the death.

VII

Five young kings put asleep by the sword-stroke,
Seven strong Earls of the army of Anlaf
Fell on the war-field, numberless numbers,
Shipmen and Scotsmen.

VIII

Then the Norse leader,
Dire was his need of it,

*29. Glode*: glided, suggested by the original's *glad* and probably by Shelley's usage, three times in *The Revolt of Islam* (M. L. Woods, *Poetry Review* xxxiii (1942) 277).

*30. Sank*] *1882*; Sunk *1880–81*. Corrected by T. in his copy of *Works*, 1881 (*Lincoln*).

*37. We*: added by T., as in l. 42.

*43. Mighty*: added by T.

*50. this island*: in the original simply 'land'.

Few were his following,
Fled to his warship:
Fleeted his vessel to sea with the king in it,
Saving his life on the fallow flood.

IX

Also the crafty one,
Constantinus,
Crept to his North again,
Hoar-headed hero!

X

Slender warrant had
*He* to be proud of
The welcome of war-knives–
He that was reft of his
Folk and his friends that had
Fallen in conflict,
Leaving his son too
Lost in the carnage,
Mangled to morsels,
A youngster in war!

XI

Slender reason had
*He* to be glad of
The clash of the war-glaive–
Traitor and trickster
And spurner of treaties–
He nor had Anlaf
With armies so broken
A reason for bragging
That they had the better
In perils of battle
On places of slaughter–
The struggle of standards,
The rush of the javelins,
The crash of the charges,

*61. fallow*: yellowish, *fealo*.

*66. warrant*] *1882*; reason *1880–81*. Corrected by T. in his copy of *Works*, 1881 (*Lincoln*).

*68. welcome of war-knives*: literally 'fellowship or meeting of . . .', a kenning for battle.

*79–80*. T. freely adapts the original, literally 'the grey-haired man, the old deceiver'.

*88. rush*: literally 'meeting'.

*89. 1880* note: 'Literally "the gathering of men"'.

The wielding of weapons–
The play that they played with
The children of Edward.

XII

Then with their nailed prows
Parted the Nórsemen, a
Blood-reddened relic of
Javelins over
The jarring breaker, the deep-sea billow,
Shaping their way toward Dyflen again,
Shamed in their souls.

XIII

Also the brethren,
King and Atheling,
Each in his glory,
Went to his own in his own West-Saxonland,
Glad of the war.

XIV

Many a carcase they left to be carrion,
Many a livid one, many a sallow-skin–
Left for the white tailed eagle to tear it, and
Left for the horny-nibbed raven to rend it, and
Gave to the garbaging war-hawk to gorge it, and
That gray beast, the wolf of the weald.

XV

Never had huger
Slaughter of heroes
Slain by the sword-edge–
Such as old writers
Have writ of in histories–
Hapt in this isle, since
Up from the East hither
Saxon and Angle from
Over the broad billow
Broke into Britain with

*96–7. over / The jarring breaker*: the original has *on Dingesmere*, probably the name of a part of the sea, but possibly from *dinnes*, noise.
*98. 1880* note: 'Dublin'.
*102.* The original has simply 'both together'.
*106.* The original is agreed to apply not to the corpses, but to the eagle (dun-coated) and the raven (dark-coated). Cp. *Boädicea* 11–15; eagle, raven, carrion, carcase, 'kite and kestrel, wolf and wolfkin, from the wilderness, wallow in it'.

Haughty war-workers who
Harried the Welshman, when
Earls that were lured by the
Hunger of glory gat
Hold of the land.

# 367 Prefatory Sonnet to the 'Nineteenth Century'

Published, without a title, in the first number of the *Nineteenth Century*, March 1877; then *1880*. James Knowles had been the editor of the *Contemporary Review*, 1870–77 (l. 3); he requested T. to write something, 20 Jan. 1877, and acknowledged it on 23 Jan. (*Lincoln*). Knowles, with T., was a founder of the Metaphysical Society (ll. 9–14; *Mem.* ii 166). T. has unconsciously recalled the prefatory sonnet to John Moultrie's *Poems* (1838, *Lincoln*); cp. T.'s l. 8 with Moultrie's 'And braves once more the doubtful sea and sky'. T. and Moultrie share the same extended metaphor, and the rhymes: *past / fast / mast.*

Those that of late had fleeted far and fast
To touch all shores, now leaving to the skill
Of others their old craft seaworthy still,
Have chartered this; where, mindful of the past,
Our true co-mates regather round the mast;
Of diverse tongue, but with a common will
Here, in this roaring moon of daffodil
And crocus, to put forth and brave the blast;
For some, descending from the sacred peak
Of hoar high-templed Faith, have leagued again
Their lot with ours to rove the world about;
And some are wilder comrades, sworn to seek
If any golden harbour be for men
In seas of Death and sunless gulfs of Doubt.

# 368 Montenegro

Published *Nineteenth Century*, May 1877; then *1880*. 'In March 1877 my father wrote *Montenegro*, which he always put first among his sonnets' (*Mem.* ii 217), 'after talking with Gladstone about the bravery of the Montenegrins' against the Turks. When published, it was followed by an

*123–4.* The original is agreed to mean simply 'glorious Earls'.

¶367. *14. sunless gulfs*: incorporated from *This Earth is wondrous* 21.

article on Montenegro by Gladstone, who wrote: 'I gladly accept the honour of having been invited to supply a commentary to his text.' D. B. MacEachen (*Victorian Newsletter*, Fall 1958) suggests that the mountain-people of Montenegro probably recalled another such people, the Waldenses, and Milton's sonnet *On the late Massacre in Piemont*.

They rose to where their sovran eagle sails,
They kept their faith, their freedom, on the height,
Chaste, frugal, savage, armed by day and night
Against the Turk; whose inroad nowhere scales
Their headlong passes, but his footstep fails,
And red with blood the Crescent reels from fight
Before their dauntless hundreds, in prone flight
By thousands down the crags and through the vales.
O smallest among peoples! rough rock-throne
Of Freedom! warriors beating back the swarm
Of Turkish Islam for five hundred years,
Great Tsernogora! never since thine own
Black ridges drew the cloud and brake the storm
Has breathed a race of mightier mountaineers.

# 369 To Victor Hugo

Published *Nineteenth Century*, June 1877; then *1880*. 'After my son Lionel's visit to him in Paris' (T.), which took place in 1877 (*1913*, p. xlviii).

Victor in Drama, Victor in Romance,
Cloud-weaver of phantasmal hopes and fears,
French of the French, and Lord of human tears;
Child-lover; Bard whose fame-lit laurels glance
Darkening the wreaths of all that would advance,
Beyond our strait, their claim to be thy peers;
Weird Titan by thy winter weight of years
As yet unbroken, Stormy voice of France!
Who dost not love our England–so they say;
I know not–England, France, all man to be
Will make one people ere man's race be run:
And I, desiring that diviner day,
Yield thee full thanks for thy full courtesy
To younger England in the boy my son.

¶368. *2.* The traditional notion expressed in *Of old sat Freedom on the heights*.

*12. Tsernogora*: the Slavonic name for Montenegro, 'black mountain' (T.).

¶369. *1. Drama*] *1880*; Poesy *1877*.

# 370 The Revenge

## A Ballad of the Fleet

Published *Nineteenth Century*, March 1878; then *1880*. T. had read J. A. Froude (1852: reprinted in *Short Studies*, 1867); and Edward Arber sent T. his 'English Reprint' on *The Revenge* (1591), published 15 Nov. 1871 (*TLS*, 21 Jan. 1932). Arber included the contemporary accounts by Ralegh, Gervase Markham, and J. H. Van Linschoten, which supplied T. with all the details of his poem. T.'s copy of Arber is in *Boston Public Library*. The author of *The Charge of the Light Brigade* might have been struck by Arber's description of *The Revenge*'s fight as 'the Balaclava charge of that Spanish War'. In March 1873, T. discussed Grenville with C. R. Markham, and then wrote his opening line (*T.Nbk 38*; *Mem.* ii 142). He rediscovered Arber's reprint early in 1877, and then worked at the poem (*CT*, pp. 402, 438). 'He set to work and finished the ballad at last all at once in a day or two' (H.T.). T. was possibly influenced by Browning's *Hervé Riel* (March 1871). For the spirit of his poem, cp. Thomas Campbell's *Battle of the Baltic* and Macaulay's *The Armada*.

I

At Flores in the Azores Sir Richard Grenville lay,
And a pinnace, like a fluttered bird, came flying from far
    away:
'Spanish ships of war at sea! we have sighted fifty-three!'
Then sware Lord Thomas Howard: ''Fore God I am
    no coward;
But I cannot meet them here, for my ships are out of gear,
And the half my men are sick. I must fly, but follow quick.
We are six ships of the line; can we fight with fifty-three?'

II

Then spake Sir Richard Grenville: 'I know you are
    no coward;
You fly them for a moment to fight with them again.
But I've ninety men and more that are lying sick ashore.
I should count myself the coward if I left them, my Lord
    Howard,
To these Inquisition dogs and the devildoms of Spain.'

III

So Lord Howard past away with five ships of war that day,
Till he melted like a cloud in the silent summer heaven;
But Sir Richard bore in hand all his sick men from the land
Very carefully and slow,

¶370. *17.* Grenville was from Bideford.

Men of Bideford in Devon,
And we laid them on the ballast down below;
For we brought them all aboard,
And they blest him in their pain, that they were not left to Spain,
To the thumbscrew and the stake, for the glory of the Lord.

IV

He had only a hundred seamen to work the ship and to fight,
And he sailed away from Flores till the Spaniard came in sight,
With his huge sea-castles heaving upon the weather bow.
'Shall we fight or shall we fly?
Good Sir Richard, tell us now,
For to fight is but to die!
There'll be little of us left by the time this sun be set.'
And Sir Richard said again: 'We be all good English men.
Let us bang these dogs of Seville, the children of the devil,
For I never turned my back upon Don or devil yet.'

V

Sir Richard spoke and he laughed, and we roared a hurrah, and so
The little Revenge ran on sheer into the heart of the foe,
With her hundred fighters on deck, and her ninety sick below;
For half of their fleet to the right and half to the left were seen,
And the little Revenge ran on through the long sea-lane between.

VI

Thousands of their soldiers looked down from their decks and laughed,
Thousands of their seamen made mock at the mad little craft
Running on and on, till delayed
By their mountain-like San Philip that, of fifteen hundred tons,
And up-shadowing high above us with her yawning tiers of guns,
Took the breath from our sails, and we stayed.

*26. tell us now*] *1880*; let us know *1878*.

VII

And while now the great San Philip hung above us like a cloud
Whence the thunderbolt will fall
Long and loud,
Four galleons drew away
From the Spanish fleet that day,
And two upon the larboard and two upon the starboard lay,
And the battle-thunder broke from them all.

VIII

But anon the great San Philip, she bethought herself and went
Having that within her womb that had left her ill content;
And the rest they came aboard us, and they fought us hand to hand,
For a dozen times they came with their pikes and musqueteers,
And a dozen times we shook 'em off as a dog that shakes his ears
When he leaps from the water to the land.

IX

And the sun went down, and the stars came out far over the summer sea,
But never a moment ceased the fight of the one and the fifty-three.
Ship after ship, the whole night long, their high-built galleons came,
Ship after ship, the whole night long, with her battle-thunder and flame;
Ship after ship, the whole night long, drew back with her dead and her shame.
For some were sunk and many were shattered, and so could fight us no more—
God of battles, was ever a battle like this in the world before?

X

For he said 'Fight on! fight on!'
Though his vessel was all but a wreck;
And it chanced that, when half of the short summer night was gone,
With a grisly wound to be drest he had left the deck,
But a bullet struck him that was dressing it suddenly dead,
And himself he was wounded again in the side and the head,
And he said 'Fight on! fight on!'

*65. short] 1880; not 1878.*

XI

And the night went down, and the sun smiled out far over
 the summer sea,
And the Spanish fleet with broken sides lay round us all
 in a ring;
But they dared not touch us again, for they feared that we
 still could sting,
So they watched what the end would be.
And we had not fought them in vain,
But in perilous plight were we,
Seeing forty of our poor hundred were slain,
And half of the rest of us maimed for life
In the crash of the cannonades and the desperate strife;
And the sick men down in the hold were most of them
 stark and cold,
And the pikes were all broken or bent, and the powder was
 all of it spent;
And the masts and the rigging were lying over the side;
But Sir Richard cried in his English pride,
'We have fought such a fight for a day and a night
As may never be fought again!
We have won great glory, my men!
And a day less or more
At sea or ashore,
We die—does it matter when?
Sink me the ship, Master Gunner—sink her, split her in
 twain!
Fall into the hands of God, not into the hands of Spain!'

XII

And the gunner said 'Ay, ay,' but the seamen made reply:
'We have children, we have wives,
And the Lord hath spared our lives.
We will make the Spaniard promise, if we yield, to let us go;
We shall live to fight again and to strike another blow.'
And the lion there lay dying, and they yielded to the foe.

XIII

And the stately Spanish men to their flagship bore him then,
Where they laid him by the mast, old Sir Richard caught at
 last,
And they praised him to his face with their courtly foreign
 grace;
But he rose upon their decks, and he cried:
'I have fought for Queen and Faith like a valiant man
 and true;

I have only done my duty as a man is bound to do:
With a joyful spirit I Sir Richard Grenville die!'
And he fell upon their decks, and he died.

XIV

And they stared at the dead that had been so valiant and true,
And had holden the power and glory of Spain so cheap
That he dared her with one little ship and his English few;
Was he devil or man? He was devil for aught they knew,
But they sank his body with honour down into the deep,
And they manned the Revenge with a swarthier alien crew,
And away she sailed with her loss and longed for her own;
When a wind from the lands they had ruined awoke from sleep,
And the water began to heave and the weather to moan,
And or ever that evening ended a great gale blew,
And a wave like the wave that is raised by an earthquake grew,
Till it smote on their hulls and their sails and their masts and their flags,
And the whole sea plunged and fell on the shot-shattered navy of Spain,
And the little Revenge herself went down by the island crags
To be lost evermore in the main.

# 371 Rizpah

17—

Published *1880*. Written 1878; it was recited, as *Bones*, 5 June 1879 (Mary Drew, née Gladstone, *Diaries*, 1930, p. 158). It is based on the story of a man executed in 1793; Mary Brotherton (*Mem*. ii 249) says:

'I told him the story one day at Farringford, knowing it would touch him, and he came up to see my husband and me next day, and asked me to tell it him again: on which I gave him the little penny magazine I found it in. It was an unpretentious account of "Old Brighton." Many months after he took me up to his library, after a walk, and read me what he called *Bones*. That was before it was called *Rizpah* and published.'

T. comments: 'founded on a fact which I read related in two or three lines in some *Leisure Hour*' (*Eversley* draft, *British Museum*). The issue is that of 8 Dec. 1877. The relevant paragraph, describing the mother's gathering and interring the bones, is quoted *Mem*. ii 250–1; it ends 'What a sad story

*112. the lands*: 'West Indies' (T.).

of a Brighton Rizpah!' (*Mem.* ii 249 mistakenly says that the name of the magazine–not of the article–was *Old Brighton.*) For the story of Rizpah, see *2 Samuel* xxi 8–10: 'But the king took the two sons of Rizpah .... And he delivered them into the hands of the Gibeonites, and they hanged them in the hill before the Lord .... And Rizpah the daughter of Aiah took sackcloth, and spread it for her upon the rock, from the beginning of harvest until water dropped upon them [the bones] out of heaven, and suffered neither the birds of the air to rest on them by day, nor the beasts of the field by night.' In a trial edition of *1880* (*Lincoln*), the title *The Mother* was added, preceding *Rizpah*, together with an introductory note on the story which ended: 'She is here represented on her deathbed with a lady visitor.'

I

Wailing, wailing, wailing, the wind over land and sea–
And Willy's voice in the wind, 'O mother, come out to me.'
Why should he call me tonight, when he knows that I cannot go?
For the downs are as bright as day, and the full moon stares at the snow.

II

We should be seen, my dear; they would spy us out of the town.
The loud black nights for us, and the storm rushing over the down,
When I cannot see my own hand, but am led by the creak of the chain,
And grovel and grope for my son till I find myself drenched with the rain.

III

Anything fallen again? nay–what was there left to fall?
I have taken them home, I have numbered the bones, I have hidden them all.
What am I saying? and what are *you?* do you come as a spy?
Falls? what falls? who knows? As the tree falls so must it lie.

IV

Who let her in? how long has she been? you–what have you heard?
Why did you sit so quiet? you never have spoken a word.
O–to pray with me–yes–a lady–none of their spies–
But the night has crept into my heart, and begun to darken my eyes.

V

Ah–you, that have lived so soft, what should *you* know of the night,
The blast and the burning shame and the bitter frost and the fright?
I have done it, while you were asleep–you were only made for the day.
I have gathered my baby together–and now you may go your way.

¶371. *12. Ecclesiastes* xi 3: 'In the place where the tree falleth, there it shall be.'

VI

Nay–for it's kind of you, Madam, to sit by an old dying wife.
But say nothing hard of my boy, I have only an hour of life.
I kissed my boy in the prison, before he went out to die.
'They dared me to do it,' he said, and he never has told me a lie.
I whipt him for robbing an orchard once when he was but a child–
'The farmer dared me to do it,' he said; he was always so wild–
And idle–and couldn't be idle–my Willy–he never could rest.
The King should have made him a soldier, he would have been one of his best.

VII

But he lived with a lot of wild mates, and they never would let him be good;
They swore that he dare not rob the mail, and he swore that he would;
And he took no life, but he took one purse, and when all was done
He flung it among his fellows–I'll none of it, said my son.

VIII

I came into court to the Judge and the lawyers. I told them my tale,
God's own truth–but they killed him, they killed him for robbing the mail.
They hanged him in chains for a show–we had always borne a good name–
To be hanged for a thief–and then put away–isn't that enough shame?
Dust to dust–low down–let us hide! but they set him so high
That all the ships of the world could stare at him, passing by.
God 'ill pardon the hell-black raven and horrible fowls of the air,
But not the black heart of the lawyer who killed him and hanged him there.

IX

And the jailer forced me away. I had bid him my last goodbye;
They had fastened the door of his cell. 'O mother!' I heard him cry.
I couldn't get back though I tried, he had something further to say,
And now I never shall know it. The jailer forced me away.

X

Then since I couldn't but hear that cry of my boy that was dead,
They seized me and shut me up: they fastened me down on my bed.
'Mother, O mother!'–he called in the dark to me year after year–
They beat me for that, they beat me–you know that I couldn't but hear;
And then at the last they found I had grown so stupid and still
They let me abroad again–but the creatures had worked their will.

XI

Flesh of my flesh was gone, but bone of my bone was left–
I stole them all from the lawyers–and you, will you call it a theft?–
My baby, the bones that had sucked me, the bones that had laughed and had cried–
Theirs? O no! they are mine–not theirs–they had moved in my side.

XII

Do you think I was scared by the bones? I kissed 'em, I buried 'em all–
I can't dig deep, I am old–in the night by the churchyard wall.
My Willy 'ill rise up whole when the trumpet of judgment 'ill sound,
But I charge you never to say that I laid him in holy ground.

XIII

They would scratch him up–they would hang him again on the cursèd tree.
Sin? O yes–we are sinners, I know–let all that be,
And read me a Bible verse of the Lord's good will toward men–
'Full of compassion and mercy, the Lord'–let me hear it again;
'Full of compassion and mercy–long-suffering.' Yes, O yes!
For the lawyer is born but to murder–the Saviour lives but to bless.
*He*'ll never put on the black cap except for the worst of the worst,
And the first may be last–I have heard it in church–and the last may be first.
Suffering–O long-suffering–yes, as the Lord must know,
Year after year in the mist and the wind and the shower and the snow.

XIV

Heard, have you? what? they have told you he never repented his sin.
How do they know it? are *they* his mother? are *you* of his kin?
Heard! have you ever heard, when the storm on the downs began,
The wind that 'ill wail like a child and the sea that 'ill moan like a man?

XV

Election, Election and Reprobation–it's all very well.
But I go tonight to my boy, and I shall not find him in Hell.

51. *Genesis* ii 23: 'And Adam said, This is now bone of my bones, and flesh of my flesh.'
63. *Psalm* lxxxvi 15: 'But thou, O Lord, art a God full of compassion, and gracious: long-suffering, and plenteous in mercy and truth.'
73. *Election and Reprobation*: the antitheses in the Calvinistic doctrine of predestination.

For I cared so much for my boy that the Lord has looked into my care,
And He means me I'm sure to be happy with Willy, I know not where.

XVI

And if *he* be lost–but to save *my* soul that is all your desire:
Do you think that I care for *my* soul if my boy be gone to the fire?
I have been with God in the dark–go, go, you may leave me alone–
You never have borne a child–you are just as hard as a stone.

XVII

Madam, I beg your pardon! I think that you mean to be kind,
But I cannot hear what you say for my Willy's voice in the wind–
The snow and the sky so bright–he used but to call in the dark,
And he calls to me now from the church and not from the gibbet–for hark!
Nay–you can hear it yourself–it is coming–shaking the walls–
Willy–the moon's in a cloud—Good-night. I am going. He calls.

# 372 *Cleopatra's Needle

Printed *Mem.* ii 232: 'When Cleopatra's Needle was brought to London, [Dean] Stanley asked my father to make some lines upon it; to be engraven on the base.' Stanley wrote to T., 28 July 1878: 'you should be asked to write 6, 8, or 10 lines, expressive of the sum total of what its history represents .... Pray undertake the task' (*Lincoln*). The obelisk was erected in Sept. 1878, but T.'s lines were not engraved.

Here, I that stood in On beside the flow
Of sacred Nile, three thousand years ago!–
A Pharaoh, kingliest of his kingly race,
First shaped, and carved, and set me in my place.
A Caesar of a punier dynasty
Thence haled me toward the Mediterranean sea,
Whence your own citizens, for their own renown,
Through strange seas drew me to your monster town.
I have seen the four great empires disappear.
I was when London was not. I am here.

¶372. *1. On*: the Biblical name for the ancient city of Heliopolis.
*5. a punier dynasty*] the smaller times of Rome *H.Nbk 62 1st reading.*
*6. toward*] to *MS. Mediterranean sea*] Alexandrian foam *MS 1st reading*; midland sea *MS.*
*8. monster*] monstrous *MS.*
*9.* The empires of Assyria, Persia, Greece, and Rome.

# 373 Dedicatory Poem to the Princess Alice

Published *Nineteenth Century*, April 1879, dedicating *The Defence of Lucknow*; then *1880*. Written March 1879 (*Mat.* iii 383). As was well known, on 14 Dec. 1878 Princess Alice 'died of kissing her child, who was ill with diphtheria' (T.). Lady Ely wrote: 'The Queen thinks it might be lightly mentioned but not dwelt upon. I hope you will forgive my having asked the question, as it is best to know exactly what the Queen thinks and wishes.' By marriage Alice was grand duchess of Hesse-Darmstadt (l. 8), but her deathbed request to her husband was that she should have an English flag on her coffin (ll. 15–17). This request was reported to Tennyson from the Queen, with the warning, 'Of course the exact words must not be made public' (*Mat.* iii 384). Hence (ll. 20–1) T.'s dedication to Alice of *The Defence of Lucknow*, whose refrain is 'And ever upon the topmost roof our banner of England blew'.

Dead Princess, living Power, if that, which lived
True life, live on–and if the fatal kiss,
Born of true life and love, divorce thee not
From earthly love and life–if what we call
The spirit flash not all at once from out
This shadow into Substance–then perhaps
The mellowed murmur of the people's praise
From thine own State, and all our breadth of realm,
Where Love and Longing dress thy deeds in light,
Ascends to thee; and this March morn that sees
Thy Soldier-brother's bridal orange-bloom
Break through the yews and cypress of thy grave,
And thine Imperial mother smile again,
May send one ray to thee! and who can tell–
Thou–England's England-loving daughter–thou
Dying so English thou wouldst have her flag
Borne on thy coffin–where is he can swear
But that some broken gleam from our poor earth
May touch thee, while remembering thee, I lay
At thy pale feet this ballad of the deeds
Of England, and her banner in the East?

¶373. *11.* Duke of Connaught, married 13 March 1879.
*13.* Queen Victoria.
*17–19.* The aspiration of *In Memoriam* lxxxv.
*18.* Cp. *The Higher Pantheism* 10: 'broken gleams'.

# 374 The Defence of Lucknow

Published *Nineteenth Century*, April 1879; then *1880*. Written March 1879 (*Mat.* iii 385); T. elicited information from the survivors. During the Indian Mutiny, Lucknow was relieved on 25 Sept. 1857. T. mentions 'Outram's account and Colonel Inglis's modest manly record'; Outram led the forces of relief, Inglis led the garrison. Inglis's detailed dispatch was given in *The Defence of Lucknow: By A Staff Officer* (1858), of which T. had a copy (*Lincoln*). Cp. *Havelock* (p. 1105).

I

Banner of England, not for a season, O banner of Britain, hast thou
Floated in conquering battle or flapt to the battle-cry!
Never with mightier glory than when we had reared thee on high
Flying at top of the roofs in the ghastly siege of Lucknow–
Shot through the staff or the halyard, but ever we raised thee anew,
And ever upon the topmost roof our banner of England blew.

II

Frail were the works that defended the hold that we held with our lives–
Women and children among us, God help them, our children and wives!
Hold it we might–and for fifteen days or for twenty at most.
'Never surrender, I charge you, but every man die at his post!'
Voice of the dead whom we loved, our Lawrence the best of the brave:
Cold were his brows when we kissed him–we laid him that night in his grave.
'Every man die at his post!' and there hailed on our houses and halls
Death from their rifle-bullets, and death from their cannon-balls,
Death in our innermost chamber, and death at our slight barricade,
Death while we stood with the musket, and death while we stoopt to the spade,
Death to the dying, and wounds to the wounded, for often there fell,
Striking the hospital wall, crashing through it, their shot and their shell,
Death–for their spies were among us, their marksmen were told of our best,
So that the brute bullet broke through the brain that could think for the rest;
Bullets would sing by our foreheads, and bullets would rain at our feet–
Fire from ten thousand at once of the rebels that girdled us round–
Death at the glimpse of a finger from over the breadth of a street,
Death from the heights of the mosque and the palace, and death in the ground!
Mine? yes, a mine! Countermine! down, down! and creep through the hole!
Keep the revolver in hand! you can hear him–the murderous mole!

¶374. *11.* Sir Henry Lawrence died 4 July 1857.

Quiet, ah! quiet–wait till the point of the pickaxe be through!
Click with the pick, coming nearer and nearer again than before–
Now let it speak, and you fire, and the dark pioneer is no more;
And ever upon the topmost roof our banner of England blew!

III

Ay, but the foe sprung his mine many times, and it chanced on a day
Soon as the blast of that underground thunderclap echoed away,
Dark through the smoke and the sulphur like so many fiends in their hell–
Cannon-shot, musket-shot, volley on volley, and yell upon yell–
Fiercely on all the defences our myriad enemy fell.
What have they done? where is it? Out yonder. Guard the Redan!
Storm at the Water-gate! storm at the Bailey-gate! storm, and it ran
Surging and swaying all round us, as ocean on every side
Plunges and heaves at a bank that is daily devoured by the tide–
So many thousands that if they be bold enough, who shall escape?
Kill or be killed, live or die, they shall know we are soldiers and men!
Ready! take aim at their leaders–their masses are gapped with our grape–
Backward they reel like the wave, like the wave flinging forward again,
Flying and foiled at the last by the handful they could not subdue;
And ever upon the topmost roof our banner of England blew.

IV

Handful of men as we were, we were English in heart and in limb,
Strong with the strength of the race to command, to obey, to endure,
Each of us fought as if hope for the garrison hung but on him;
Still–could we watch at all points? we were every day fewer and fewer.
There was a whisper among us, but only a whisper that past:
'Children and wives–if the tigers leap into the fold unawares–
Every man die at his post–and the foe may outlive us at last–
Better to fall by the hands that they love, than to fall into theirs!'
Roar upon roar in a moment two mines by the enemy sprung
Clove into perilous chasms our walls and our poor palisades.
Rifleman, true is your heart, but be sure that your hand be as true!
Sharp is the fire of assault, better aimed are your flank fusillades–
Twice do we hurl them to earth from the ladders to which they had clung,
Twice from the ditch where they shelter we drive them with hand-grenades;
And ever upon the topmost roof our banner of England blew.

V

Then on another wild morning another wild earthquake out-tore
Clean from our lines of defence ten or twelve good paces or more.
Rifleman, high on the roof, hidden there from the light of the sun–
One has leapt up on the breach, crying out: 'Follow me, follow me!'–
Mark him–he falls! then another, and *him* too, and down goes he.

*39. devoured*] *1890*; drowned *1879–89*.

Had they been bold enough then, who can tell but the traitors had
won?
Boardings and rafters and doors–an embrasure! make way for the gun!
Now double-charge it with grape! It is charged and we fire, and they
run.
Praise to our Indian brothers, and let the dark face have his due!
Thanks to the kindly dark faces who fought with us, faithful and few,
Fought with the bravest among us, and drove them, and smote them,
and slew,
That ever upon the topmost roof our banner in India blew.

VI

Men will forget what we suffer and not what we do. We can fight!
But to be soldier all day and be sentinel all through the night–
Ever the mine and assault, our sallies, their lying alarms,
Bugles and drums in the darkness, and shoutings and soundings to arms,
Ever the labour of fifty that had to be done by five,
Ever the marvel among us that one should be left alive,
Ever the day with its traitorous death from the loop-holes around,
Ever the night with its coffinless corpse to be laid in the ground,
Heat like the mouth of a hell, or a deluge of cataract skies,
Stench of old offal decaying, and infinite torment of flies,
Thoughts of the breezes of May blowing over an English field,
Cholera, scurvy, and fever, the wound that *would* not be healed,
Lopping away of the limb by the pitiful-pitiless knife,–
Torture and trouble in vain,–for it never could save us a life.
Valour of delicate women who tended the hospital bed,
Horror of women in travail among the dying and dead,
Grief for our perishing children, and never a moment for grief,
Toil and ineffable weariness, faltering hopes of relief,
Havelock baffled, or beaten, or butchered for all that we knew–
Then day and night, day and night, coming down on the still-shattered
walls
Millions of musket-bullets, and thousands of cannon-balls–
But ever upon the topmost roof our banner of England blew.

VII

Hark cannonade, fusillade! is it true what was told by the scout,
Outram and Havelock breaking their way through the fell mutineers?
Surely the pibroch of Europe is ringing again in our ears!
All on a sudden the garrison utter a jubilant shout,
Havelock's glorious Highlanders answer with conquering cheers,
Sick from the hospital echo them, women and children come out,
Blessing the wholesome white faces of Havelock's good fusileers,
Kissing the war-hardened hand of the Highlander wet with their tears!
Dance to the pibroch!–saved! we are saved!–is it you? is it you?
Saved by the valour of Havelock, saved by the blessing of Heaven!
'Hold it for fifteen days!' we have held it for eighty-seven!
And ever aloft on the palace roof the old banner of England blew.

*100. Sick . . . them,*] *1880*; Forth from their holes and their hidings our *1879*.

# 375 The First Quarrel
## (IN THE ISLE OF WIGHT)

Published *1880*. It was recited to Mary Gladstone, 5 June 1879 (*Diaries*, 1930, p. 158). T. said it was 'founded on facts told me by Dr Dabbs, who is the doctor'. G. H. R. Dabbs was in practice in the Isle of Wight from 1870. *Mem.* ii 249 shows that T.'s note of the facts does not mention the fatal letter; he may therefore have been influenced by Augustus Hare: 'When I went, in [Oct.] 1877, to visit A.T., he asked me to give him a subject for "A Domestic Village Tragedy"' (*The Story of My Life*, 1896, i 258). Hare's story turned on a love-letter. For a 'village tragedy', cp. T.'s play, *The Promise of May*.

I

'Wait a little,' you say, 'you are sure it'll all come right,'
But the boy was born i' trouble, an' looks so wan an' so white:
Wait! an' once I ha' waited–I hadn't to wait for long.
Now I wait, wait, wait for Harry.–No, no, you are doing me wrong!
Harry and I were married: the boy can hold up his head,
The boy was born in wedlock, but after my man was dead;
I ha' worked for him fifteen years, an' I work an' I wait to the end.
I am all alone in the world, an' you are my only friend.

II

Doctor, if *you* can wait, I'll tell you the tale o' my life.
When Harry an' I were children, he called me his own little wife;
I was happy when I was with him, an' sorry when he was away,
An' when we played together, I loved him better than play;
He workt me the daisy chain–he made me the cowslip ball,
He fought the boys that were rude, an' I loved him better than all.
Passionate girl though I was, an' often at home in disgrace,
I never could quarrel with Harry–I had but to look in his face.

III

There was a farmer in Dorset of Harry's kin, that had need
Of a good stout lad at his farm; he sent, an' the father agreed;
So Harry was bound to the Dorsetshire farm for years an' for years;
I walked with him down to the quay, poor lad, an' we parted in tears.
The boat was beginning to move, we heard them a-ringing the bell,
'I'll never love any but you, God bless you, my own little Nell.'

IV

I was a child, an' he was a child, an' he came to harm;
There was a girl, a hussy, that workt with him up at the farm,
One had deceived her an' left her alone with her sin an' her shame,
And so she was wicked with Harry; the girl was the most to blame.

V

And years went over till I that was little had grown so tall,
The men would say of the maids, 'Our Nelly's the flower of 'em all.'
I didn't take heed o' *them*, but I taught myself all I could
To make a good wife for Harry, when Harry came home for good.

VI

Often I seemed unhappy, and often as happy too,
For I heard it abroad in the fields 'I'll never love any but you;'
'I'll never love any but you' the morning song of the lark,
'I'll never love any but you' the nightingale's hymn in the dark.

VII

And Harry came home at last, but he looked at me sidelong and shy,
Vext me a bit, till he told me that so many years had gone by,
I had grown so handsome and tall – that I might ha' forgot him somehow –
For he thought – there were other lads – he was feared to look at me now.

VIII

Hard was the frost in the field, we were married o' Christmas day,
Married among the red berries, an' all as merry as May –
Those were the pleasant times, my house an' my man were my pride,
We seemed like ships i' the Channel a-sailing with wind an' tide.

IX

But work was scant in the Isle, though he tried the villages round,
So Harry went over the Solent to see if work could be found;
An' he wrote 'I ha' six weeks' work, little wife, so far as I know;
I'll come for an hour tomorrow, an' kiss you before I go.'

X

So I set to righting the house, for wasn't he coming that day?
An' I hit on an old deal-box that was pushed in a corner away,
It was full of old odds an' ends, an' a letter along wi' the rest,
I had better ha' put my naked hand in a hornets' nest.

XI

'Sweetheart' – this was the letter – this was the letter I read –
'You promised to find me work near you, an' I wish I was dead –
Didn't you kiss me an' promise? you haven't done it, my lad,
An' I almost died o' your going away, an' I wish that I had.'

XII

I too wish that I had – in the pleasant times that had past,
Before I quarrelled with Harry – *my* quarrel – the first an' the last.

XIII

For Harry came in, an' I flung him the letter that drove me wild,
An' he told it me all at once, as simple as any child,
'What can it matter, my lass, what I did wi' my single life?
I ha' been as true to you as ever a man to his wife;
An' *she* wasn't one o' the worst.' 'Then,' I said, 'I'm none o' the best.'
An' he smiled at me, 'Ain't you, my love? Come, come, little wife, let it rest!
The man isn't like the woman, no need to make such a stir.'
But he angered me all the more, an' I said 'You were keeping with her,
When I was a-loving you all along an' the same as before.'
An' he didn't speak for a while, an' he angered me more and more.
Then he patted my hand in his gentle way, 'Let bygones be!'
'Bygones! you kept yours hushed,' I said, 'when you married me!

By-gones ma' be come-agains; an' *she*–in her shame an' her sin–
You'll have her to nurse my child, if I die o' my lying in!
You'll make her its second mother! I hate her–an' I hate you!'
Ah, Harry, my man, you had better ha' beaten me black an' blue
Than ha' spoken as kind as you did, when I were so crazy wi' spite,
'Wait a little, my lass, I am sure it 'ill all come right.'

XIV

An' he took three turns in the rain, an' I watched him, an' when he came in
I felt that my heart was hard, he was all wet through to the skin,
An' I never said 'off wi' the wet,' I never said 'on wi' the dry,'
So I knew my heart was hard, when he came to bid me goodbye.
'You said that you hated me, Ellen, but that isn't true, you know;
I am going to leave you a bit–you'll kiss me before I go?'

XV

'Going! you're going to her–kiss her–if you will,' I said,–
I was near my time wi' the boy, I must ha' been light i' my head–
'I had sooner be cursed than kissed!'–I didn't know well what I meant,
But I turned my face from *him*, an' he turned *his* face an' he went.

XVI

And then he sent me a letter, 'I've gotten my work to do;
You wouldn't kiss me, my lass, an' I never loved any but you;
I am sorry for all the quarrel an' sorry for what she wrote,
I ha' six weeks' work in Jersey an' go tonight by the boat.'

XVII

An' the wind began to rise, an' I thought of him out at sea,
An' I felt I had been to blame; he was always kind to me.
'Wait a little, my lass, I am sure it 'ill all come right'–
An' the boat went down that night–the boat went down that night.

# 376 The Northern Cobbler

Published *1880*. It was being written in Feb. 1879 (*Mat.* iii 381); it was recited on 6 June 1879 to Mary Gladstone (*Diaries*, 1930, p. 159). 'Founded on a fact that I heard in early youth' (T.). The anecdote is a familiar temperance one; cp. l. 74 with 'Facing an Enemy' in E. P. Hood's *World of Moral and Religious Anecdote* (1870), where a cobbler puts the bottle in the window; and with R. Crompton's ballad *Facing the Inimy* (1875). All the notes except that in l. 13 are by T.

I

Waäit till our Sally cooms in, fur thou mun a' sights to tell.
Eh, but I be maäin glad to seeä tha sa 'arty an' well.

¶376. *1. sights*: *1880* note: 'The vowels *aï*, pronounced separately though in the closest conjunction, best render the sound of the long *i* and *y* in this

'Cast awaäy on a disolut land wi' a vartical soon!'
Strange fur to goä fur to think what saäilors a' seëan an' a' doon;
'Summat to drink–sa' 'ot?' I 'a nowt but Adam's wine:
What's the 'eät o' this little 'ill-side to the 'eät o' the line?

II

'What's i' tha bottle a-stanning theer?' I'll tell tha. Gin.
But if thou wants thy grog, tha mun goä fur it down to the inn.
Naay–fur I be maäin-glad, but thaw tha was iver sa dry,
Thou gits naw gin fro' the bottle theer, an' I'll tell tha why.

III

Meä an' thy sister was married, when wur it? back-end o' June,
Ten years sin', and wa 'greed as well as a fiddle i' tune:
I could fettle and clump owd booöts and shoes wi' the best on 'em all,
As fer as fro' Thursby thurn hup to Harmsby and Hutterby Hall.
We was busy as beeäs i' the bloom an' as 'appy as 'art could think,
An' then the babby wur burn, and then I taäkes to the drink.

IV

An' I weänt gaäinsaäy it, my lad, thaw I be hafe shaämed on it now,
We could sing a good song at the Plow, we could sing a good song at the Plow;
Thaw once of a frosty night I slithered an' hurted my huck,
An' I coomed neck-an-crop soomtimes slaäpe down i' the squad an' the muck:
An' once I fowt wi' the Taäilor–not hafe ov a man, my lad–
Fur he scrawmed an' scratted my faäce like a cat, an' it maäde 'er sa mad
That Sally she turned a tongue-banger, an' raäted ma, 'Sottin' thy braäins
Guzzlin' an' soäkin' an' smoäkin' an' hawmin' about i' the laänes,
Soä sow-droonk that tha doesn not touch thy 'at to the Squire;'
An' I looöked cock-eyed at my noäse an' I seeäd 'im a-gittin' o' fire;
But sin' I wur hallus i' liquor an' hallus as droonk as a king,
Foälks' coostom flitted awaäy like a kite wi' a brokken string.

V

An' Sally she weshed foälks' cloäths to keep the wolf fro' the door,
Eh but the moor she riled me, she druv me to drink the moor,
Fur I fun', when 'er back wur turned, wheer Sally's owd stockin' wur 'id,
An' I grabbed the munny she maäde, and I weäred it o' liquor, I did.

dialect. But since such words as *craïin'*, *daïin'*, *whaï*, *aï* (I), etc., look awkward except in a page of express phonetics, I have thought it better to leave the simple *i* and *y*, and to trust that my readers will give them the broader pronunciation.'

3. *soon*: the *oo* short, as in 'wood'.
13. *fettle and clump*: to mend and sole (H.T.).
19. *huck*: hip.
23. *tongue-banger*: scold.
24. *hawmin'*: lounging.

VI

An' one night I cooms 'oäm like a bull gotten loose at a faäir,
An' she wur a-waäitin' fo'mma, an' cryin' and teärin' 'er 'aäir,
An' I tummled athurt the craädle an' sweäred as I'd breäk ivry stick
O' furnitur 'ere i' the 'ouse, an' I gied our Sally a kick,
An' I mashed the taäbles an' chairs, an' she an' the babby beäled,
Fur I knawed naw moor what I did nor a mortal beäst o' the feäld.

VII

An' when I waäked i' the murnin' I seeäd that our Sally went laämed
Cos' o' the kick as I gied 'er, an' I wur dreädful ashaämed;
An' Sally wur sloomy an' draggle taäiled in an owd turn gown,
An' the babby's faäce wurn't weshed an' the 'ole 'ouse hupside down.

VIII

An' then I minded our Sally sa pratty an' neät an' sweeät,
Straät as a pole an' cleän as a flower fro' 'eäd to feeät:
An' then I minded the fust kiss I gied 'er by Thursby thurn;
Theer wur a lark a-singin' 'is best of a Sunday at murn,
Couldn't see 'im, we 'eärd 'im a-mountin' oop 'igher an' 'igher,
An' then 'e turned to the sun, an' 'e shined like a sparkle o' fire.
'Doesn't tha see 'im,' she axes, 'fur I can see 'im?' an' I
Seeäd nobbut the smile o' the sun as danced in 'er pratty blue eye;
An' I says 'I mun gie tha a kiss,' an' Sally says 'Noä, thou moänt,'
But I gied 'er a kiss, an' then anoother, an' Sally says 'doänt!'

IX

An' when we coomed into Meeätin', at fust she wur all in a tew,
But, arter, we singed the 'ymn togither like birds on a beugh;
An' Muggins 'e preäched o' Hell-fire an' the loov o' God fur men,
An' then upo' coomin' awaäy Sally gied me a kiss ov 'ersen.

X

Heer wur a fall fro' a kiss to a kick like Saätan as fell
Down out o' heaven i' Hell-fire – thaw theer's naw drinkin' i' Hell;
Meä fur to kick our Sally as kep the wolf fro' the door,
All along o' the drink, fur I looved 'er as well as afoor.

XI

Sa like a greät num-cumpus I blubbered awaäy o' the bed –
'Weänt niver do it naw moor;' an' Sally looökt up an' she said,
'I'll upowd it tha weänt; thou'rt like the rest o' the men,
Thou'll goä sniffin' about the tap till tha does it agëan.
Theer's thy hennemy, man, an' I knaws, as knaws tha sa well,
That, if tha seeäs 'im an' smells 'im tha'll foller 'im slick into Hell.'

XII

'Naäy,' says I, 'fur I weänt goä sniffin' about the tap.'
'Weänt tha?' she says, an' mysen I thowt i' mysen 'mayhap.'
'Noä:' an' I started awaäy like a shot, an' down to the Hinn,
An' I browt what tha seeäs stannin' theer, yon big black bottle o' gin.

37. *beäled*: bellowed, cried out.
41. *sloomy*: sluggish, out of spirits.
63. *upowd*: uphold.

XIII

'That caps owt,' says Sally, an' saw she begins to cry,
But I puts it inter 'er 'ands an' I says to 'er, 'Sally,' says I,
'Stan' 'im theer i' the naäme o' the Lord an' the power ov 'is Graäce,
Stan' 'im theer, fur I'll looök my hennemy straït i' the faäce,
Stan' 'im theer i' the winder, an' let ma looök at 'im then,
'E seeäms naw moor nor watter, an' 'e's the Divil's oän sen.'

XIV

An' I wur down i' tha mouth, couldn't do naw work an' all,
Nasty an' snaggy an' shaäky, an' poonched my 'and wi' the hawl,
But she wur a power o' coomfut, an' sattled 'ersen o' my knee,
An' coäxd an' coodled me oop till ageän I feeled mysen free.

XV

An' Sally she telled it about, an' foälk stood a-gawmin' in,
As thaw it wur summat bewitched istead of a quart o' gin;
An' some on 'em said it wur watter–an' I wur chousin' the wife,
Fur I couldn't 'owd 'ands off gin, wur it nobbut to saäve my life;
An' blacksmith 'e strips me the thick ov 'is airm, an' 'e shaws it to me,
'Feëal thou this! thou can't graw this upo' watter!' says he.
An' Doctor 'e calls o' Sunday an' just as candles was lit,
'Thou moänt do it,' he says, 'tha mun breäk 'im off bit by bit.'
'Thou'rt but a Methody-man,' says Parson, and laäys down 'is 'at,
An' 'e points to the bottle o' gin, 'but I respecks tha fur that;'
An' Squire, his oän very sen, walks down fro' the 'All to see,
An' 'e spanks 'is 'and into mine, 'fur I respecks tha,' says 'e;
An' coostom ageän drawed in like a wind fro' far an' wide,
And browt me the booöts to be cobbled fro' hafe the coontryside.

XVI

An' theer 'e stans an' theer 'e shall stan to my dying daäy;
I 'a gotten to loov 'im ageän in anoother kind of a waäy,
Proud on 'im, like, my lad, an' I keeäps 'im cleän an' bright,
Loovs 'im, an' roobs 'im, an' doosts 'im, an' puts 'im back i' the light.

XVII

Wouldn't a pint a' sarved as well as a quart? Naw doubt:
But I liked a bigger feller to fight wi' an' fowt it out.
Fine an' meller 'e mun be by this, if I cared to taäste,
But I moänt, my lad, and I weänt, fur I'd feäl mysen cleän disgraäced.

XVIII

An' once I said to the Missis, 'My lass, when I cooms to die,
Smash the bottle to smithers, the Divil's in 'im,' said I.
But arter I chaänged my mind, an' if Sally be left aloän,
I'll hev 'im a-buried wi'mma an' taäke 'im afoor the Throän.

XIX

Coom thou 'eer–yon laädy a-steppin' along the streeät,
Doesn't tha knaw 'er–sa pratty, an' feät, an' neät, an' sweeät?

71. *That caps owt*: That's beyond everything.
81. *a-gawmin'*: staring vacantly.

Look at the cloäths on 'er back, thebbe ammost spick-span-new,
An' Tommy's faäce be as fresh as a codlin weshed i' the dew.

XX

'Ere be our Sally an' Tommy, an' we be a-goin to dine,
Baäcon an' taätes, an' a beslings-puddin' an' Adam's wine;
But if tha wants ony grog tha mun goä fur it down to the Hinn,
Fur I weänt shed a drop on 'is blood, noä, not fur Sally's oän kin.

# 377 Prefatory Poem to My Brother's Sonnets

## Midnight, June 30, 1879

Published 1880, with Charles Tennyson Turner's *Collected Sonnets*; then *1885*. In 1880 it has the subtitle only, which provides the date of composition; Charles died 25 April 1879. There are drafts in *H.Nbk 33* (*A* below) and *Lpr 186* (*B*). Cp. '*Frater Ave atque Vale*' (p. 1284).

I

Midnight–in no midsummer tune
The breakers lash the shores:
The cuckoo of a joyless June
Is calling out of doors:

And thou hast vanished from thine own
To that which looks like rest,
True brother, only to be known
By those who love thee best.

II

Midnight–and joyless June gone by,
And from the deluged park
The cuckoo of a worse July
Is calling through the dark:

But thou art silent underground,
And o'er thee streams the rain,
True poet, surely to be found
When Truth is found again.

*110. be*] *1884*; is *1880–83*. *weshed*] *1884*; 'at's weshed *1880–83*.
*111. 'Ere be*] *1884*; 'Ere's *1880–83*.
*112. beslings-puddin'*: a pudding made with the first milk of the cow after calving.

III

And, now to these unsummered skies
The summer bird is still,
Far off a phantom cuckoo cries
From out a phantom hill;
And through this midnight breaks the sun
Of sixty years away,
The light of days when life begun,
The days that seem today,
When all my griefs were shared with thee,
As all my hopes were thine–
As all thou wert was one with me,
May all thou art be mine!

# 378 In the Children's Hospital

## EMMIE

Published *1880*. 'A true story told me by Mary Gladstone' (T.); for the paragraph from her letter, simply telling the story, see *Mem.* ii 253–4. Written 1879–80; her friendship with the Tennysons was established summer 1879. It does not appear in the earlier trial editions of *1880* (*Lincoln*). The story, *Alice's Christmas Day*, was in *St Cyprian's Banner*, Dec. 1872; D. L. Chambers (*MLN* xviii, 1903, 232–3) points out that it was reprinted in *New and Old* (1875), and suggests that T. must have read it, since he seems to include elements not derived from Mary Gladstone, e.g. that the story is told by the nurse. Chambers adds that in the story the child was not an orphan, and that it was the coarse doctor who made the fatal remark (l. 42). The poem was attacked; hence T.'s note: 'The doctors and hospital are unknown to me. The two children are the only characters

¶377. *17–20*] *Not A.*
*17*] Midnight. The ceaseless shower falls, *B.*
*18. summer*] sunless *B.*
*19*] Flown! But [At last *1st reading*] a phantom cuckoo calls [falls *1st reading*] *B.*
*23*] The days when life had just begun, *A.*
*24 ∧ 25*]
Our brother-days that will not die–
And, now thou art withdrawn
So far I cannot follow, I cry
To that first light of dawn *B*
*26. As*] *1885*; And *1880.*
*27 ∧ 28*] So, brother, whatsoe'er thou be. *A.*

taken from life in this little dramatic poem, in which the hospital nurse and not the poet is speaking throughout.'

I

Our doctor had called in another, I never had seen him before,
But he sent a chill to my heart when I saw him come in at the door,
Fresh from the surgery-schools of France and of other lands–
Harsh red hair, big voice, big chest, big merciless hands!
Wonderful cures he had done, O yes, but they said too of him
He was happier using the knife than in trying to save the limb,
And that I can well believe, for he looked so coarse and so red,
I could think he was one of those who would break their jests on the dead,
And mangle the living dog that had loved him and fawned at his knee–
Drenched with the hellish oorali–that ever such things should be!

II

Here was a boy–I am sure that some of our children would die
But for the voice of Love, and the smile, and the comforting eye–
Here was a boy in the ward, every bone seemed out of its place–
Caught in a mill and crushed–it was all but a hopeless case:
And he handled him gently enough; but his voice and his face were not kind,
And it was but a hopeless case, he had seen it and made up his mind,
And he said to me roughly 'The lad will need little more of your care.'
'All the more need,' I told him, 'to seek the Lord Jesus in prayer;
They are all his children here, and I pray for them all as my own:'
But he turned to me, 'Ay, good woman, can prayer set a broken bone?'
Then he muttered half to himself, but I know that I heard him say
'All very well–but the good Lord Jesus has had his day.'

III

Had? has it come? It has only dawned. It will come by and by.
O how could I serve in the wards if the hope of the world were a lie?
How could I bear with the sights and the loathsome smells of disease
But that He said 'Ye do it to me, when ye do it to these'?

IV

So he went. And we past to this ward where the younger children are laid:
Here is the cot of our orphan, our darling, our meek little maid;
Empty you see just now! We have lost her who loved her so much–
Patient of pain though as quick as a sensitive plant to the touch;
Hers was the prettiest prattle, it often moved me to tears,
Hers was the gratefullest heart I have found in a child of her years–

¶378. *10. oorali*: 'curari, which paralyses the nerves while still the victim feels' (T.).
*26. Matthew* xxv 40: 'Inasmuch as ye have done it unto one of the least of these my brethren, ye have done it unto me.'

Nay you remember our Emmie; you used to send her the flowers;
How she would smile at 'em, play with 'em, talk to 'em hours after hours!
They that can wander at will where the works of the Lord are revealed
Little guess what joy can be got from a cowslip out of the field;
Flowers to these 'spirits in prison' are all they can know of the spring,
They freshen and sweeten the wards like the waft of an Angel's wing;
And she lay with a flower in one hand and her thin hands crost on her breast–
Wan, but as pretty as heart can desire, and we thought her at rest,
Quietly sleeping–so quiet, our doctor said 'Poor little dear,
Nurse, I must do it tomorrow; she'll never live through it, I fear.'

V

I walked with our kindly old doctor as far as the head of the stair,
Then I returned to the ward; the child didn't see I was there.

VI

Never since I was nurse, had I been so grieved and so vext!
Emmie had heard him. Softly she called from her cot to the next,
'He says I shall never live through it, O Annie, what shall I do?'
Annie considered. 'If I,' said the wise little Annie, 'was you,
I should cry to the dear Lord Jesus to help me, for, Emmie, you see,
It's all in the picture there: "Little children should come to me."'
(Meaning the print that you gave us, I find that it always can please
Our children, the dear Lord Jesus with children about his knees.)
'Yes, and I will,' said Emmie, 'but then if I call to the Lord,
How should he know that it's me? such a lot of beds in the ward!'
That was a puzzle for Annie. Again she considered and said:
'Emmie, you put out your arms, and you leave 'em outside on the bed–
The Lord has so *much* to see to! but, Emmie, you tell it him plain,
It's the little girl with her arms lying out on the counterpane.'

VII

I had sat three nights by the child–I could not watch her for four–
My brain had begun to reel–I felt I could do it no more.
That was my sleeping-night, but I thought that it never would pass.
There was a thunderclap once, and a clatter of hail on the glass,
And there was a phantom cry that I heard as I tost about,
The motherless bleat of a lamb in the storm and the darkness without;
My sleep was broken besides with dreams of the dreadful knife
And fears for our delicate Emmie who scarce would escape with her life;
Then in the gray of the morning it seemed she stood by me and smiled,
And the doctor came at his hour, and we went to see to the child.

VIII

He had brought his ghastly tools: we believed her asleep again–
Her dear, long, lean, little arms lying out on the counterpane;
Say that His day is done! Ah why should we care what they say?
The Lord of the children had heard her, and Emmie had past away.

37. *1 Peter* iii 19: 'By which also he went and preached unto the spirits in prison.'
50. *Mark* x 14: 'Suffer the little children to come unto me.'

# 379 Columbus

Published *1880*. Written 1879–80, since it is in *H.Nbks 44–45*. It does not appear in the earlier trial editions of *1880* (*Lincoln*). 'Written after repeated entreaties from certain prominent Americans that he would commemorate the discovery of America in verse' (*Mem.* ii 255). T. acknowledged as his source Washington Irving's *Life of Columbus* (1828), which he had used for *Anacaona*; it tells how Columbus preserved the chains in which he was sent back to Spain, 'as relics and memorials of the reward of my services' (XIII iv). All T.'s details are from Irving.

Chains, my good lord: in your raised brows I read
Some wonder at our chamber ornaments.
We brought this iron from our isles of gold.

Does the king know you deign to visit him
Whom once he rose from off his throne to greet
Before his people, like his brother king?
I saw your face that morning in the crowd.

At Barcelona–though you were not then
So bearded. Yes. The city decked herself
To meet me, roared my name; the king, the queen
Bad me be seated, speak, and tell them all
The story of my voyage, and while I spoke
The crowd's roar fell as at the 'Peace, be still!'
And when I ceased to speak, the king, the queen,
Sank from their thrones, and melted into tears,
And knelt, and lifted hand and heart and voice
In praise to God who led me through the waste.
And then the great 'Laudamus' rose to heaven.

¶379. *5–6.* 'As Columbus approached, the sovereigns rose, as if receiving a person of the highest rank' (Irving V vi).
*6–18.* Suggested by Irving XVIII iii: 'He, who but a few years before had entered the city of Barcelona in triumph . . .'.
*10–11.* 'They ordered him to seat himself in their presence; a rare honour in this proud and punctilious court' (Irving V vi).
*13.* Jesus stilling the waters, *Mark* iv 39.
*14–17.* 'When he had finished, they sank on their knees, and, raising their clasped hands to heaven, their eyes filled with tears of joy and gratitude, they poured forth thanks and praises to God' (Irving V vi).
*18.* 'The anthem of *Te Deum Laudamus* . . . rose up from the midst in a full body of sacred harmony; bearing up, as it were, the feelings and thoughts of the auditors to heaven' (Irving V vi).

Chains for the Admiral of the Ocean! chains
For him who gave a new heaven, a new earth,
As holy John had prophesied of me,
Gave glory and more empire to the kings
Of Spain than all their battles! chains for him
Who pushed his prows into the setting sun,
And made West East, and sailed the Dragon's
mouth,
And came upon the Mountain of the World,
And saw the rivers roll from Paradise!

Chains! we are Admirals of the Ocean, we,
We and our sons for ever. Ferdinand
Hath signed it and our Holy Catholic queen–
Of the Ocean–of the Indies–Admirals we–
Our title, which we never mean to yield,
Our guerdon not alone for what we did,
But our amends for all we might have done–
The vast occasion of our stronger life–
Eighteen long years of waste, seven in your Spain,
Lost, showing courts and kings a truth the babe
Will suck in with his milk hereafter–earth
A sphere.
Were *you* at Salamanca? No.
We fronted there the learning of all Spain,
All their cosmogonies, their astronomies:
Guess-work *they* guessed it, but the golden guess
Is morning-star to the full round of truth.
No guess-work! I was certain of my goal;
Some thought it heresy, but that would not hold.
King David called the heavens a hide, a tent

*20–21.* 'He read, as he supposed, his contemplated discovery foretold in Holy Writ, and shadowed forth darkly in the mystic revelations of the prophets' (Irving I v).

*21. Revelation* xxi 1.

*25.* Bocca del Drago, the channel, named by Columbus, between Trinidad and S. America.

*27.* The Vale of Paradise, in Hayti (Irving IV vii).

*28–31.* The document is in Irving II viii.

*29–31.* His heirs were 'never to use any other title than simply "The Admiral"' (Irving IX iii).

*39–54.* The council of Salamanca, at which Columbus put his case to the university (Irving II iv).

*46ff.* The *Psalms* of David (civ 2), the detailed ridicule by Lactantius (the fourth-century Christian apologist) and Augustine are all mentioned by Irving.

Spread over earth, and so this earth was flat:
Some cited old Lactantius: could it be
That trees grew downward, rain fell upward, men
Walked like the fly on ceilings? and besides,
The great Augustine wrote that none could breathe
Within the zone of heat; so might there be
Two Adams, two mankinds, and that was clean
Against God's word: thus was I beaten back,
And chiefly to my sorrow by the Church,
And thought to turn my face from Spain, appeal
Once more to France or England; but our Queen
Recalled me, for at last their Highnesses
Were half-assured this earth might be a sphere.

All glory to the all-blessèd Trinity,
All glory to the mother of our Lord,
And Holy Church, from whom I never swerved
Not even by one hair's-breadth of heresy,
I have accomplished what I came to do.

Not yet–not all–last night a dream–I sailed
On my first voyage, harassed by the frights
Of my first crew, their curses and their groans.
The great flame-banner borne by Teneriffe,
The compass, like an old friend false at last
In our most need, appalled them, and the wind
Still westward, and the weedy seas–at length
The landbird, and the branch with berries on it,

*51–3.* 'The insupportable heat of the torrid zone' would make crossing it impossible; hence 'to assert that there were inhabited lands on the opposite side of the globe, would be to maintain that there were nations not descended from Adam . . . [and] to discredit the bible' (Irving, paraphrasing Augustine).
*65ff.* The details of the first voyage are from Irving III i ff. 'Teneriffe . . . sending out volumes of flames and smoke. The crew were terrified at sight of this eruption.'
*69–70.* 'The variation of the needle . . . filled them with consternation' (Irving).
*70–1.* 'They began to imagine that the wind, in these seas, always prevailed from the east, and if so, would never permit them to return to Spain' (Irving).
*71.* 'This weedy sea' (Irving).
*72.* 'A branch of thorn with berries on it, and recently separated from the tree, floated by them; then they picked up a reed, a small board, and, above all, a staff artificially carved' (Irving).

The carven staff–and last the light, the light
On Guanahani! but I changed the name;
San Salvador I called it; and the light
Grew as I gazed, and brought out a broad sky
Of dawning over–not those alien palms,
The marvel of that fair new nature–not
That Indian isle, but our most ancient East
Moriah with Jerusalem; and I saw
The glory of the Lord flash up, and beat
Through all the homely town from jasper, sapphire,
Chalcedony, emerald, sardonyx, sardius,
Chrysolite, beryl, topaz, chrysoprase,
Jacynth, and amethyst–and those twelve gates,
Pearl–and I woke, and thought–death–I shall die–
I am written in the Lamb's own Book of Life
To walk within the glory of the Lord
Sunless and moonless, utter light–but no!
The Lord had sent this bright, strange dream to me
To mind me of the secret vow I made
When Spain was waging war against the Moor–
I strove myself with Spain against the Moor.
There came two voices from the Sepulchre,

*73.* 'Suddenly, about ten o'clock, he thought he beheld a light glimmering at a great distance' (Irving).

*74.* The native name of the first island discovered by Columbus.

*80–9.* Based on *Revelation* xxi (see ll. 20–1*n*), the new Jerusalem with its precious stones and its twelve gates of pearl, for those who 'are written in the Lamb's book of life'. 'And the city had no need of the sun, neither of the moon, to shine in it; for the glory of God did lighten it.' Moriah is the location of the Temple in Palestine.

*94ff.* 'During this siege [Malaga], a circumstance took place, which appears to have made a deep impression on the devout and enthusiastic spirit of Columbus. Two reverend friars arrived at the Spanish camp, employed in the holy sepulchre at Jerusalem. They brought a message from the Grand Soldan of Egypt, threatening to put to death all the Christians in his dominions, and to destroy the sepulchre, if the sovereigns did not desist from the war against Grenada.' Hence Columbus 'determined to devote the profits arising from his contemplated discovery, to a holy enterprise to rescue the holy sepulchre from the power of the infidels'. 'It is essential to a full comprehension of the character and motives of Columbus, that this wild and visionary project should be borne in recollection. It will be found to have entwined itself in his mind with his enterprise of discovery, and that a holy crusade was to be the consummation of those divine purposes, for which he considered himself selected by heaven as an agent' (Irving II v, V vi).

Two friars crying that if Spain should oust
The Moslem from her limit, he, the fierce
Soldan of Egypt, would break down and raze
The blessèd tomb of Christ; whereon I vowed
That, if our Princes harkened to my prayer,
Whatever wealth I brought from that new world
Should, in this old, be consecrate to lead
A new crusade against the Saracen,
And free the Holy Sepulchre from thrall.

Gold? I had brought your Princes gold enough
If left alone! Being but a Genovese,
I am handled worse than had I been a Moor,
And breached the belting wall of Cambalu,
And given the Great Khan's palaces to the Moor,
Or clutched the sacred crown of Prester John,
And cast it to the Moor: but *had* I brought
From Solomon's now-recovered Ophir all
The gold that Solomon's navies carried home,
Would that have gilded *me*? Blue blood of Spain,
Though quartering your own royal arms of Spain,
I have not: blue blood and black blood of Spain,
The noble and the convict of Castile,
Howled me from Hispaniola; for you know
The flies at home, that ever swarm about
And cloud the highest heads, and murmur down
Truth in the distance–these outbuzzed me so
That even our prudent king, our righteous queen–
I prayed them being so calumniated
They would commission one of weight and worth
To judge between my slandered self and me–
Fonseca my main enemy at their court,
They sent me out *his* tool, Bovadilla, one
As ignorant and impolitic as a beast–
Blockish irreverence, brainless greed–who sacked
My dwelling, seized upon my papers, loosed
My captives, feed the rebels of the crown,
Sold the crown-farms for all but nothing, gave
All but free leave for all to work the mines,
Drove me and my good brothers home in chains,
And gathering ruthless gold–a single piece

*107.* H.T. refers to *Paradise Lost* xi 388: 'Cambalu, seat of Cathaian Can'.
*109.* *Prester John*: the legendary medieval Christian monarch of Asia.
*117.* Columbus's name for Hayti. The incident is from Irving XIII iv.
*130.* *feed*: fee'd, bribed.

Weighed nigh four thousand Castillanos–so
They tell me–weighed him down into the abysm–
The hurricane of the latitude on him fell,
The seas of our discovering over-roll
Him and his gold; the frailer caravel,
With what was mine, came happily to the shore.
*There* was a glimmering of God's hand.
And God
Hath more than glimmered on me. O my lord,
I swear to you I heard his voice between
The thunders in the black Veragua nights,
'O soul of little faith, slow to believe!
Have I not been about thee from thy birth?
Given thee the keys of the great Ocean-sea?
Set thee in light till time shall be no more?
Is it I who have deceived thee or the world?
Endure! thou hast done so well for men, that men
Cry out against thee: was it otherwise
With mine own Son?'
And more than once in days
Of doubt and cloud and storm, when drowning hope
Sank all but out of sight, I heard his voice,
'Be not cast down. I lead thee by the hand,
Fear not.' And I shall hear his voice again–
I know that he has led me all my life,
I am not yet too old to work his will–
His voice again.
Still for all that, my lord,
I lying here bedridden and alone,
Cast off, put by, scouted by court and king–
The first discoverer starves–his followers, all
Flower into fortune–our world's way–and I,

*137–41.* 'When Columbus learnt the signal destruction that had overwhelmed his enemies, almost before his eyes, he was deeply impressed with awe, and considered his own preservation as little less than miraculous' (Irving XV i).
*144. Veragua*: Spanish province of New Granada, S. America.
*146–7.* 'He had been chosen by heaven . . . in his tender years, he had been guided by a divine impulse to embrace the profession of the sea' (Irving XIV iv).
*156.* Cp. *Deuteronomy* xxxi 8: 'And the Lord, he it is that doth go before thee, he will be with thee, he will not fail thee, neither forsake thee: fear not, neither be dismayed.'

Without a roof that I can call mine own,
With scarce a coin to buy a meal withal,
And seeing what a door for scoundrel scum
I opened to the West, through which the lust,
Villany, violence, avarice, of your Spain
Poured in on all those happy naked isles –
Their kindly native princes slain or slaved,
Their wives and children Spanish concubines,
Their innocent hospitalities quenched in blood,
Some dead of hunger, some beneath the scourge,
Some over-laboured, some by their own hands, –
Yea, the dear mothers, crazing Nature, kill
Their babies at the breast for hate of Spain –
Ah God, the harmless people whom we found
In Hispaniola's island-Paradise!
Who took us for the very Gods from Heaven,
And we have sent them very fiends from Hell;
And I myself, myself not blameless, I
Could sometimes wish I had never led the way.

Only the ghost of our great Catholic Queen
Smiles on me, saying 'Be thou comforted!
This creedless people will be brought to Christ
And own the holy governance of Rome.'

But who could dream that we, who bore the Cross
Thither, were excommunicated there,
For curbing crimes that scandalised the Cross,
By him, the Catalonian Minorite,
Rome's Vicar in our Indies? who believe
These hard memorials of our truth to Spain
Clung closer to us for a longer term
Than any friend of ours at Court? and yet
Pardon – too harsh, unjust. I am racked with pains.

You see that I have hung them by my bed,
And I will have them buried in my grave.

*164–5.* 'I do not own a roof in Spain. If I desire to eat or sleep, I have no resort but an inn; and, for the most times, have not wherewithal to pay my bill' (Irving XVIII ii).
*177–80.* Cp. *Anacaona* (p. 283).
*190.* Bernard Buil, a Benedictine monk, was sent by the Pope to the West Indies in June 1493 as Apostolic Vicar; he continually tried to thwart Columbus.
*197.* 'He requested that when he died they [the chains] might be buried with him' (Irving XIII iv, quoted in a note by T.).

Sir, in that flight of ages which are God's
Own voice to justify the dead—perchance
Spain once the most chivalric race on earth,
Spain then the mightiest, wealthiest realm on earth,
So made by me, may seek to unbury me,
To lay me in some shrine of this old Spain,
Or in that vaster Spain I leave to Spain.
Then some one standing by my grave will say,
'Behold the bones of Christopher Colòn'—
'Ay, but the chains, what do *they* mean—the chains?'—
I sorrow for that kindly child of Spain
Who then will have to answer, 'These same chains
Bound these same bones back through the Atlantic
sea,
Which he unchained for all the world to come.'

O Queen of Heaven who seest the souls in Hell
And purgatory, I suffer all as much
As they do—for the moment. Stay, my son
Is here anon: my son will speak for me
Ablier than I can in these spasms that grind
Bone against bone. You will not. One last word.

You move about the Court, I pray you tell
King Ferdinand who plays with me, that one,
Whose life has been no play with him and his
Hidalgos—shipwrecks, famines, fevers, fights,
Mutinies, treacheries—winked at, and condoned—
That I am loyal to him till the death,
And ready—though our Holy Catholic Queen,
Who fain had pledged her jewels on my first voyage,
Whose hope was mine to spread the Catholic faith,
Who wept with me when I returned in chains,
Who sits beside the blessèd Virgin now,
To whom I send my prayer by night and day—
She is gone—but you will tell the King, that I,
Racked as I am with gout, and wrenched with pains
Gained in the service of His Highness, yet
Am ready to sail forth on one last voyage,

*202–4.* Columbus's body was taken afterwards to Seville, then later to Hayti, thence to Cuba.
*221.* *Hidalgos*: noblemen.
*225.* 'Isabella exclaimed, "I . . . will pledge my private jewels to raise the necessary funds"' (Irving II vii).
*227.* As told in Irving XIV i.
*233.* Cp. *Ulysses* (p. 560), as also l. 158 above.

And readier, if the King would hear, to lead
One last crusade against the Saracen,
And save the Holy Sepulchre from thrall.

Going? I am old and slighted: you have dared
Somewhat perhaps in coming? my poor thanks!
I am but an alien and a Genovese.

# 380 The Village Wife

## OR, THE ENTAIL

Published *1880*. Probably written 1879–80 (it is in *H.Nbk 48*). 'The village wife herself is the only portrait that is drawn from life in the Lincolnshire poems' (T.).

I

'Ouse-keeper sent tha my lass, fur New Squire coomed last night.
Butter an' heggs–yis–yis. I'll goä wi' tha back: all right;
Butter I warrants be prime, an' I warrants the heggs be as well,
Hafe a pint o' milk runs out when ya breäks the shell.

II

Sit thysen down fur a bit: hev a glass o' cowslip wine!
I liked the owd Squire an' 'is gells as thaw they was gells o' mine,
Fur then we was all es one, the Squire an' 'is darters an' me,
Hall but Miss Annie, the heldest, I niver not took to she:
But Nelly, the last of the cletch, I liked 'er the fust on 'em all,
Fur hoffens we talkt o' my darter es died o' the fever at fall:
An' I thowt 'twur the will o' the Lord, but Miss Annie she said it wur draäins,
Fur she hedn't naw coomfut in 'er, an' arned naw thanks fur 'er paäins.
Eh! thebbe all wi' the Lord my childer, I han't gotten none!
Sa new Squire's coomed wi' 'is taäil in 'is 'and, an' owd Squire's gone.

III

Fur 'staäte be i' taäil, my lass: tha dosn' knaw what that be?
But I knaws the law, I does, for the lawyer ha towd it me.
'When theer's naw 'eäd to a 'Ouse by the fault o' that ere maäle–
The gells they counts fur nowt, and the next un he taäkes the taäil.'

IV

What be the next un like? can tha tell ony harm on 'im lass?–
Naay sit down–naw 'urry–sa cowd!–hev another glass!
Straänge an' cowd fur the time! we may happen a fall o' snaw–
Not es I cares fur to hear ony harm, but I likes to knaw.

¶380. *9. cletch*: 'a brood of chickens' (T.).
*17.* 'By default of the heir male' (T.).

An' I 'oäps es 'e beänt boooklarned: but 'e dosn' not coom fro' the shere;
We'd anew o' that wi' the Squire, an' we haätes boooklarnin' ere.

V

Fur Squire wur a Varsity scholard, an' niver lookt arter the land–
Whoäts or tonups or taätes–'e 'ed hallus a booök i' 'is 'and,
Hallus aloän wi' 'is booöks, thaw nigh upo' seventy year.
An' booöks, what's booöks? thou knaws thebbe naither 'ere nor theer.

VI

An' the gells, they hedn't naw taäils, an' the lawyer he towd it me
That 'is taäil were soä tied up es he couldn't cut down a tree!
'Drat the trees,' says I, to be sewer I haätes 'em, my lass,
Fur we puts the muck o' the land an' they sucks the muck fro' the grass.

VII

An' Squire wur hallus a-smilin', an' gied to the tramps goin' by–
An' all o' the wust i' the parish–wi' hoffens a drop in 'is eye.
An' ivry darter o' Squire's hed her awn ridin-erse to 'ersen,
An' they rampaged about wi' their grooms, an' was 'untin' arter the men,
An' hallus a-dallackt an' dizened out, an' a-buyin' new cloäthes,
While 'e sit like a graät glimmer-gowk wi' 'is glasses athurt 'is noäse,
An' 'is noäse sa grufted wi' snuff es it couldn't be scroobed awaäy,
Fur atween 'is reädin' an' writin' 'e snifft up a box in a daäy,
An' 'e niver runned arter the fox, nor arter the birds wi' 'is gun,
An' 'e niver not shot one 'are, but 'e leäved it to Charlie 'is son,
An' 'e niver not fished 'is awn ponds, but Charlie 'e cotched the pike,
For 'e warn't not burn to the land, an' 'e didn't take kind to it like;
But I eärs es 'e'd gie fur a howry owd book thutty pound an' moor,
An' 'e'd wrote an owd book, his awn sen, sa I knawed es 'e'd coom to be poor;
An' 'e gied–I be feared fur to tell tha 'ow much–fur an own scratted stoän,
An' 'e digged up a loomp i' the land an' 'e got a brown pot an' a boän,
An' 'e bowt owd money, es wouldn't goä, wi' good gowd o' the Queen,
An' 'e bowt little statues all-naäkt an' which was a shaame to be seen;
But 'e niver looökt ower a bill, nor 'e niver not seed to owt,
An' 'e niver knawd nowt but booöks, an' booöks, as thou knaws, beänt nowt.

VIII

But owd Squire's laädy es long es she lived she kep 'em all clear,
Thaw es long es she lived I niver hed none of 'er darters 'ere;
But arter she died we was all es one, the childer an' me,
An' sarvints runned in an' out, an' offens we hed 'em to tea.
Lawk! 'ow I laughed when the lasses 'ud talk o' their Missis's waäys,
An' the Missis talked o' the lasses.–I'll tell tha some o' these daäys.

37. *a-dallackt*: 'overdrest in gay colours' (T.).
38. *glimmer-gowk*: 'owl' (T.).
45. *howry*: 'filthy' (T.).

Hoänly Miss Annie were saw stuck oop, like 'er mother afoor–
'Er an' 'er blessèd darter–they niver derkened my door.

IX

An' Squire 'e smiled an' 'e smiled till 'e'd gotten a fright at last,
An' 'e calls fur 'is son, fur the 'turney's letters they follered sa fast;
But Squire wur afeared o' 'is son, an' 'e says to 'im, meek as a mouse,
'Lad, thou mun cut off thy taäil, or the gells 'ull goä to the 'Ouse,
Fur I finds es I be that i' debt, es I 'oäps es thou'll 'elp me a bit,
An' if thou'll 'gree to cut off thy taäil I may saäve mysen yit.'

X

But Charlie 'e sets back 'is ears, an' 'e sweärs, an' 'e says to 'im 'Noa.
I've gotten the 'staäte by the taäil an' be danged if I iver let goa!
Coom! coom! feyther,' 'e says, 'why shouldn't thy booöks be sowd?
I hears es soom o' thy booöks mebbe worth their weight i' gowd.'

XI

Heäps an' heäps o' booöks, I ha' see'd 'em, belonged to the Squire,
But the lasses 'ed teärd out leäves i' the middle to kindle the fire;
Sa moäst on 'is owd big booöks fetched nigh to nowt at the saäle,
And Squire were at Charlie ageän to git 'im to cut off 'is taäil.

XII

Ya wouldn't find Charlie's likes–'e were that outdacious at 'oäm,
Not thaw ya went fur to raäke out Hell wi' a small-tooth coämb–
Droonk wi' the Quoloty's wine, an' droonk wi' the farmer's aäle,
Mad wi' the lasses an' all–an' 'e wouldn't cut off the taäil.

XIII

Thou's coomed oop by the beck; and a thurn be a-grawin' theer,
I niver ha see'd it sa white wi' the Maäy es I see'd it to-year–
Theerabouts Charlie joompt–and it gied me a scare tother night,
Fur I thowt it wur Charlie's ghoäst i' the derk, fur it looökt sa white.
'Billy,' says 'e, 'hev a joomp!'–thaw the banks o' the beck be sa high,
Fur he ca'd 'is 'erse Billy-rough-un, thaw niver a hair wur awry;
But Billy fell bakkuds o' Charlie, an' Charlie 'e brok 'is neck,
Sa theer wur a hend o' the taäil, fur 'e lost 'is taäil i' the beck.

XIV

Sa 'is taäil wur lost an' 'is booöks wur gone an' 'is boy wur deäd,
An' Squire 'e smiled an' 'e smiled, but 'e niver not lift oop 'is 'eäd:
Hallus a soft un Squire! an' 'e smiled, fur 'e hedn't naw friend,
Sa feyther an' son was buried togither, an' this wur the hend.

*64*. *'Ouse*: 'workhouse' (H.T.).
*71–3*. T. comments: 'This really happened to some of the most valuable books in the great library formed by Johnson's friend, Bennet Langton.' T.'s father bought many of his books at the sale of Langton's library (*CT*, p. 12).
*76*. A phrase from the cook when T. was a child (*Mem.* i 15).

XV

An' Parson as hesn't the call, nor the mooney, but hes the pride,
'E reäds of a sewer an' sartan 'oäp o' the tother side;
But I beänt that sewer es the Lord, howsiver they praäyed an' praäyed,
Lets them inter 'eaven eäsy es leäves their debts to be paäid.
Siver the mou'ds rattled down upo' poor owd Squire i' the wood,
An' I cried along wi' the gells, fur they weänt niver coom to naw good.

XVI

Fur Molly the long un she walkt awaäy wi' a hofficer lad,
An' nawbody 'eärd on 'er sin, sa o' coorse she be gone to the bad!
An' Lucy wur laäme o' one leg, sweet'arts she niver 'ed none–
Straänge an' unheppen Miss Lucy! we naämed her 'Dot an' gaw one!'
An' Hetty wur weak i' the hattics, wi'out ony harm i' the legs,
An' the fever 'ed baäked Jinny's 'eäd as bald as one o' them heggs,
An' Nelly wur up fro' the craädle as big i' the mouth as a cow,
An' saw she mun hammergrate, lass, or she weänt git a maäte onyhow!
An' es for Miss Annie es called me afoor my awn foälks to my faäce
'A hignorant village wife as 'ud hev to be larned her awn plaäce,'
Hes fur Miss Hannie the heldest hes now be a-grawin' sa howd,
I knaws that mooch o' sheä, es it beänt not fit to be towd!

XVII

Sa I didn't not taäke it kindly ov owd Miss Annie to saäy
Es I should be talking ageän 'em, es soon es they went awaäy,
Fur, lawks! 'ow I cried when they went, an' our Nelly she gied me 'er 'and,
Fur I'd ha done owt for the Squire an' 'is gells es belonged to the land;
Boooks, es I said afoor, thebbe neyther 'ere nor theer!
But I sarved 'em wi' butter an' heggs fur huppuds o' twenty year.

XVIII

An' they hallus paäid what I haxed, sa I hallus dealed wi' the Hall,
An' they knawed what butter wur, an' they knawed what a hegg wur an' all;
Hugger-mugger they lived, but they wasn't that eäsy to pleäse,
Till I gied 'em Hinjian curn, an' they laäid big heggs es tha seeas;
An' I niver puts saäme i' *my* butter, they does it at Willis's farm,
Taäste another drop o' the wine–tweänt do tha naw harm.

XIX

Sa new Squire's coomed wi' 'is taäil in 'is 'and, an' owd Squire's gone;
I heard 'im a roomlin' by, but arter my nightcap wur on;

*95.* H.T.: 'However, the earth rattled down on poor old Squire's coffin.'
*97. long un*] *1881*; youngest *1880*.
**100.** ***unheppen***: 'ungainly, awkward' (T.).
**104.** ***hammergrate***: 'emigrate' (T.).
**119.** ***saäme***: 'lard' (T.).
**122.** ***roomlin'***: 'rumbling' (H.T.).

Sa I han't clapt eyes on 'im yit, fur he coomed last night sa laäte–
Pluksh! ! ! the hens i' the peäs! why didn't tha hesp the gaäte?

# 381 The Voyage of Maeldune

## (Founded on an Irish Legend. A.D. 700)

Published *1880*. Written Dec. 1879–1880. It is not in a *Lincoln* trial edition of *1880*. T. comments: 'The oldest form of Maeldune is in *The Book of the Dun Cow* (1160 A.D.). I read the legend in Joyce's *Old Celtic Romances*, but most of the details are mine.' T. was sent a copy of P. W. Joyce's book on publication, Dec. 1879, by A. P. Graves, whom in 1878 he had asked to suggest 'a suitable subject' for 'an Irish poem' (Graves, *Irish Studies*, 1913, p. 8). The date A.D. 700 is from Joyce, who discussed the '*Imrama* or voluntary sea expeditions', the best known of which is the Voyage of St Brendan; cp. the classical wanderings of Jason, Ulysses and Aeneas. T. took the outline of the fabulous voyage, ending in Maeldune's meeting the murderer without taking revenge. T. supplied the details. For each pair of islands, Joyce was the source of one; T. elaborated, and provided an antithesis. Thus Joyce suggested the Isle of Shouting, but not the Silent Isle; the Isle of Fruits, but not the Isle of Flowers; the Isle under water, but not the Isle of Fire. T.'s most important change was the addition of the travellers' sufferings and perpetual disillusion, and in particular their brawling and killing. (The original is much less sombre.) T. said, 21 Oct. 1880: 'At first I made half the men kill the other half in every fray, and Maildun himself return *alone*' (William Allingham's *Diary*, 1907, p. 304). 'By this story my father intended to represent, in his own original way, the Celtic genius' (H.T.). The MS at the *University of London Library* has many variants, but of little interest.

I

I was the chief of the race–he had stricken my father dead–
But I gathered my fellows together, I swore I would strike off his head.
Each of them looked like a king, and was noble in birth as in worth,
And each of them boasted he sprang from the oldest race upon earth.
Each was as brave in the fight as the bravest hero of song,
And each of them liefer had died than have done one another a wrong.
*He* lived on an isle in the ocean–we sailed on a Friday morn–
He that had slain my father the day before I was born.

124. *Pluksh*: 'a cry accompanied by a clapping of hands to scare trespassing fowl' (T.).

¶381. 7. Joyce: 'The druid . . . told him the exact day on which he was to set out.'

II

And we came to the isle in the ocean, and there on the shore was he.
But a sudden blast blew us out and away through a boundless sea.

III

And we came to the Silent Isle that we never had touched at before,
Where a silent ocean always broke on a silent shore,
And the brooks glittered on in the light without sound, and the long waterfalls
Poured in a thunderless plunge to the base of the mountain walls,
And the poplar and cypress unshaken by storm flourished up beyond sight,
And the pine shot aloft from the crag to an unbelievable height,
And high in the heaven above it there flickered a songless lark,
And the cock couldn't crow, and the bull couldn't low, and the dog couldn't bark.
And round it we went, and through it, but never a murmur, a breath–
It was all of it fair as life, it was all of it quiet as death,
And we hated the beautiful Isle, for whenever we strove to speak
Our voices were thinner and fainter than any flittermouse-shriek;
And the men that were mighty of tongue and could raise such a battle-cry
That a hundred who heard it would rush on a thousand lances and die–
O they to be dumbed by the charm!–so flustered with anger were they
They almost fell on each other; but after we sailed away.

IV

And we came to the Isle of Shouting, we landed, a score of wild birds
Cried from the topmost summit with human voices and words;
Once in an hour they cried, and whenever their voices pealed
The steer fell down at the plow and the harvest died from the field,
And the men dropt dead in the valleys and half of the cattle went lame,
And the roof sank in on the hearth, and the dwelling broke into flame;
And the shouting of these wild birds ran into the hearts of my crew,
Till they shouted along with the shouting and seized one another and slew;
But I drew them the one from the other; I saw that we could not stay,
And we left the dead to the birds and we sailed with our wounded away.

*9–10.* As in Joyce.
*20–1.* Cp. *The Islet* (p. 1186).
*22.* Cp. *The Lotos-Eaters* 34: 'His voice was thin, as voices from the grave'. *Aeneid* vi 492, the ghosts: *tollere vocem exiguam.* *flittermouse*: 'bat' (T.).
*27–8.* Joyce: 'The Isle of Speaking Birds . . . who were all shouting and speaking with human voices'–but without the violent consequence that T. presents. There are beneficent birds with human voices in 'The Island of the Birds' (St Brendan), in P. Kennedy's *Fictions of the Irish Celts* (1866, *Lincoln*).

V

And we came to the Isle of Flowers: their breath met us out on the seas,
For the Spring and the middle Summer sat each on the lap of the breeze;
And the red passion-flower to the cliffs, and the dark-blue clematis, clung,
And starred with a myriad blossom the long convolvulus hung;
And the topmost spire of the mountain was lilies in lieu of snow,
And the lilies like glaciers winded down, running out below
Through the fire of the tulip and poppy, the blaze of gorse, and the blush
Of millions of roses that sprang without leaf or a thorn from the bush;
And the whole isle-side flashing down from the peak without ever a tree
Swept like a torrent of gems from the sky to the blue of the sea;
And we rolled upon capes of crocus and vaunted our kith and our kin,
And we wallowed in beds of lilies, and chanted the triumph of Finn,
Till each like a golden image was pollened from head to feet
And each was as dry as a cricket, with thirst in the middle-day heat.
Blossom and blossom, and promise of blossom, but never a fruit!
And we hated the Flowering Isle, as we hated the isle that was mute,
And we tore up the flowers by the million and flung them in bight and bay,
And we left but a naked rock, and in anger we sailed away.

VI

And we came to the Isle of Fruits: all round from the cliffs and the capes,
Purple or amber, dangled a hundred fathom of grapes,
And the warm melon lay like a little sun on the tawny sand,
And the fig ran up from the beach and rioted over the land,
And the mountain arose like a jewelled throne through the fragrant air,
Glowing with all-coloured plums and with golden masses of pear,
And the crimson and scarlet of berries that flamed upon bine and vine,
But in every berry and fruit was the poisonous pleasure of wine;
And the peak of the mountain was apples, the hugest that ever were seen,
And they prest, as they grew, on each other, with hardly a leaflet between,
And all of them redder than rosiest health or than utterest shame,
And setting, when Even descended, the very sunset aflame;
And we stayed three days, and we gorged and we maddened, till every one drew
His sword on his fellow to slay him, and ever they struck and they slew;
And myself, I had eaten but sparely, and fought till I sundered the fray,
Then I bad them remember my father's death, and we sailed away.

*40.* Cp. *The Poet's Mind* 7 ∧ II, *1830* text (p. 224): 'a blossomstarrèd shore'. Also Shelley, *Alastor* 440: 'Starred with ten thousand blossoms'.
*48.* *Finn*: 'the most famous of old Irish leaders' (T.).
*55.* Suggested by 'The Isle of Intoxicating Wine-Fruits' in Joyce.

VII

And we came to the Isle of Fire: we were lured by the light from afar,
For the peak sent up one league of fire to the Northern Star;
Lured by the glare and the blare, but scarcely could stand upright,
For the whole isle shuddered and shook like a man in a mortal affright;
We were giddy besides with the fruits we had gorged, and so crazed that at last
There were some leaped into the fire; and away we sailed, and we past
Over that undersea isle, where the water is clearer than air:
Down we looked: what a garden! O bliss, what a Paradise there!
Towers of a happier time, low down in a rainbow deep
Silent palaces, quiet fields of eternal sleep!
And three of the gentlest and best of my people, whate'er I could say,
Plunged head down in the sea, and the Paradise trembled away.

VIII

And we came to the Bounteous Isle, where the heavens lean low on the land,
And ever at dawn from the cloud glittered o'er us a sunbright hand,
Then it opened and dropt at the side of each man, as he rose from his rest,
Bread enough for his need till the labourless day dipt under the West;
And we wandered about it and through it. O never was time so good!
And we sang of the triumphs of Finn, and the boast of our ancient blood,
And we gazed at the wandering wave as we sat by the gurgle of springs,
And we chanted the songs of the Bards and the glories of fairy kings;
But at length we began to be weary, to sigh, and to stretch and yawn,
Till we hated the Bounteous Isle and the sunbright hand of the dawn,
For there was not an enemy near, but the whole green Isle was our own,
And we took to playing at ball, and we took to throwing the stone,
And we took to playing at battle, but that was a perilous play,
For the passion of battle was in us, we slew and we sailed away.

IX

And we past to the Isle of Witches and heard their musical cry–
'Come to us, O come, come' in the stormy red of a sky
Dashing the fires and the shadows of dawn on the beautiful shapes,
For a wild witch naked as heaven stood on each of the loftiest capes,
And a hundred ranged on the rock like white sea-birds in a row,
And a hundred gambolled and pranced on the wrecks in the sand below,

*77–82.* Suggested by Joyce: 'looking down, they could see, beneath the clear water, a beautiful country, with many mansions surrounded by groves and woods'. T. adds the suicidal delusion of the calenture, often mentioned in seventeenth-century verse.

*83–6.* Combining Joyce's 'Isle of the Blest', and his 'Aged Hermit': 'every morning the angels bring me half a cake'.

*97–104.* Cp. *The Sea-Fairies* (p. 254), and the sirens of the *Odyssey* xii 185–205. Joyce described the seductions of the 'Island Queen'.

And a hundred splashed from the ledges, and bosomed the burst of the spray,
But I knew we should fall on each other, and hastily sailed away.

X

And we came in an evil time to the Isle of the Double Towers,
One was of smooth-cut stone, one carved all over with flowers,
But an earthquake always moved in the hollows under the dells,
And they shocked on each other and butted each other with clashing of bells,
And the daws flew out of the Towers and jangled and wrangled in vain,
And the clash and boom of the bells rang into the heart and the brain,
Till the passion of battle was on us, and all took sides with the Towers,
There were some for the clean-cut stone, there were more for the carven flowers,
And the wrathful thunder of God pealed over us all the day,
For the one half slew the other, and after we sailed away.

XI

And we came to the Isle of a Saint who had sailed with St Brendan of yore,
He had lived ever since on the Isle and his winters were fifteen score,
And his voice was low as from other worlds, and his eyes were sweet,
And his white hair sank to his heels and his white beard fell to his feet,
And he spake to me, 'O Maeldune, let be this purpose of thine!
Remember the words of the Lord when he told us "Vengeance is mine!"
His fathers have slain thy fathers in war or in single strife,
Thy fathers have slain his fathers, each taken a life for a life,
Thy father had slain his father, how long shall the murder last?
Go back to the Isle of Finn and suffer the Past to be Past.'
And we kissed the fringe of his beard and we prayed as we heard him pray,
And the Holy man he assoiled us, and sadly we sailed away.

XII

And we came to the Isle we were blown from, and there on the shore was he,
The man that had slain my father. I saw him and let him be.
O weary was I of the travel, the trouble, the strife and the sin,
When I landed again, with a tithe of my men, on the Isle of Finn.

*105.* Suggested by Joyce's 'Isle of the Four Precious Walls' and 'The Silver Pillar'. H.T. comments: 'Symbolical of the contest between Roman Catholics and Protestants.'

*115.* Combining the pilgrim who sailed after St Brendan, and the hermit who urges Maeldune to abandon revenge (Joyce). T. comments: 'St Brendan sailed on his voyage some time in the sixth century from Kerry, and some say he visited America.' Many of Brendan's adventures were borrowed from the story of Maeldune, which mentions him.

*127–8.* As in Joyce.

# 382 To Princess Frederica on Her Marriage

Published *1880*, among 'Translations, Etc.'. H.T. says: 'Written on the marriage of Princess Frederica, daughter of George V, the blind King of Hanover, with Baron von Pawel-Rammingen at Windsor, 24 April 1880.'

O you that were eyes and light to the King till he past away
  From the darkness of life–
He saw not his daughter–he blest her: the blind King sees
    you today,
  He blesses the wife.

# 383 De Profundis

Published *Nineteenth Century*, May 1880; then *1880*. Begun at H.T.'s birth, 11 Aug. 1852 (H.T.). It was apparently completed in 1880, to judge by *T.Nbk 38*. There the title (which may not be quoted) refers to spiritualism. Cp. *Little bosom* (p. 992), on T.'s stillborn child. The title invokes *Psalm* cxxx 1: 'Out of the depths have I cried unto thee, O Lord.' For T.'s discussion of the metaphysics of the poem, see Wilfrid Ward in *Problems and Persons* (1903). Cp. *The Ancient Sage* (p. 1349). It was probably influenced by T.'s membership of the Metaphysical Society (1869–80). For the image in *The Two Greetings*, cp. *The Passing of Arthur* 445: 'From the great deep to the great deep he goes'; and *Crossing the Bar* (p. 1458). The poem is tinged with Wordsworth's *Immortality Ode*, in its vision of the baby 'that, deaf and silent, read'st the eternal deep', and 'that immortal sea / Which brought us hither'. The concluding hymn, *The Human Cry*, does not appear in *T.MS*; in a *Lincoln* trial edition of *1880*, its title is *His Human Cry*. 'Jowett asked him to write an anthem about God for Balliol Chapel and he wrote *The Human Cry*' (*Mem.* i 312).

## THE TWO GREETINGS

### I

Out of the deep, my child, out of the deep,
Where all that was to be, in all that was,

¶383. *1–12.* In the spirit of the celebration of birth in *In Memoriam: Epilogue* 123–5: 'A soul shall draw from out the vast / And strike his being into bounds, // And, moved through life of lower phase . . .', with which cp. l. 7. Cp. l. 12 with this *Epilogue* 137–9: 'Whereof the man, that with me trod / This planet, was a noble type / Appearing ere the times were ripe.'

Whirled for a million æons through the vast
Waste dawn of multitudinous-eddying light–
Out of the deep, my child, out of the deep,
Through all this changing world of changeless law,
And every phase of ever-heightening life,
And nine long months of antenatal gloom,
With this last moon, this crescent–her dark orb
Touched with earth's light–thou comest, darling
boy;
Our own; a babe in lineament and limb
Perfect, and prophet of the perfect man;
Whose face and form are hers and mine in one,
Indissolubly married like our love;
Live, and be happy in thyself, and serve
This mortal race thy kin so well, that men
May bless thee as we bless thee, O young life
Breaking with laughter from the dark; and may
The fated channel where thy motion lives
Be prosperously shaped, and sway thy course
Along the years of haste and random youth
Unshattered; then full-current through full man;
And last in kindly curves, with gentlest fall,
By quiet fields, a slowly-dying power,
To that last deep where we and thou are still.

II

I

Out of the deep, my child, out of the deep,
From that great deep, before our world begins,
Whereon the Spirit of God moves as he will–
Out of the deep, my child, out of the deep,
From that true world within the world we see,
Whereof our world is but the bounding shore–
Out of the deep, Spirit, out of the deep,
With this ninth moon, that sends the hidden sun
Down yon dark sea, thou comest, darling boy.

II

For in the world, which is not ours, They said
'Let us make man' and that which should be man,
From that one light no man can look upon,
Drew to this shore lit by the suns and moons
And all the shadows. O dear Spirit half-lost
In thine own shadow and this fleshly sign

28. *Genesis* i 2: 'And the Spirit of God moved upon the face of the waters.'

That thou art thou–who wailest being born
And banished into mystery, and the pain
Of this divisible-indivisible world
Among the numerable-innumerable
Sun, sun, and sun, through finite-infinite space
In finite-infinite Time–our mortal veil
And shattered phantom of that infinite One,
Who made thee unconceivably Thyself
Out of His whole World-self and all in all–
Live thou! and of the grain and husk, the grape
And ivyberry, choose; and still depart
From death to death through life and life, and find
Nearer and ever nearer Him, who wrought
Not Matter, nor the finite-infinite,
But this main-miracle, that thou art thou,
With power on thine own act and on the world.

### THE HUMAN CRY

I

Hallowed be Thy name–Halleluiah!–
  Infinite Ideality!
  Immeasurable Reality!
  Infinite Personality!
Hallowed be Thy name–Halleluiah!

II

We feel we are nothing–for all is Thou and in Thee;
We feel we are something–*that* also has come from
    Thee;
We know we are nothing–but Thou wilt help us to be.
Hallowed be Thy name–Halleluiah!

## 384 To Alfred Tennyson My Grandson

Published as the dedication of *1880*. It was added by pen to a *Lincoln* trial edition of *1880*. T.'s grandson was born 20 Nov. 1878, so this poem was written *c.* May 1880 (l. 3). Cp. *Little Aubrey* (p. 1802).

*62–3.* Cp. *The 'How' and the 'Why'* 23–4: 'I feel there is something; but how and what? / I know there is somewhat . . .'. Also *The Higher Pantheism* (p. 1204).

*64. know . . . nothing*] are nothing, O Thou *Nineteenth Century*.

Golden-haired Ally whose name is one with mine,
Crazy with laughter and babble and earth's new wine,
Now that the flower of a year and a half is thine,
O little blossom, O mine, and mine of mine,
Glorious poet who never hast written a line,
Laugh, for the name at the head of my verse is thine.
Mayst thou never be wronged by the name that is mine!

## 385 'Frater Ave atque Vale'

Published *Nineteenth Century*, March 1883; then *1885*. Written on a visit to Sirmio, June 1880 (*Mem.* ii 247). It alludes to T.'s brother Charles, who had died in 1879 (cp. *Prefatory Poem to My Brother's Sonnets*, p. 1260). The beauty of Sirmio is the subject of Catullus's *Poem* xxxi, which begins *Paene insularum, Sirmio, insularumque / ocelle* (T.'s 'all-but-island'); exclaims *o venusta Sirmio* (T.'s l. 2); and ends *o Lydiae lacus undae*: / *ridete, quicquid est domi cachinnorum* (T.'s l. 8). T. characteristically combines this poem of joy (*o quid solutis est beatius curis*) with the sadness of Catullus's *Poem* ci, an elegy for his dead brother, beginning *Multas per gentes et multa per aequora vectus* (apt to T.'s travels), and ending *atque in perpetuum, frater, ave atque vale*. The mingling of the two moods resembles *Tears, idle tears*: '. . . gather to the eyes, / In looking on the happy Autumn-fields'.

Row us out from Desenzano, to your Sirmione row!
So they rowed, and there we landed–'O venusta
Sirmio!'
There to me through all the groves of olive in the summer
glow,
There beneath the Roman ruin where the purple flowers
grow,
Came that 'Ave atque Vale' of the Poet's hopeless woe,
Tenderest of Roman poets nineteen-hundred years ago,
'Frater Ave atque Vale'–as we wandered to and fro
Gazing at the Lydian laughter of the Garda Lake below
Sweet Catullus's all-but-island, olive-silvery Sirmio!

¶385. *3. through all*] among *H.Nbk 47 1st reading.*
*6.* T. had apparently called Catullus 'tenderest of Roman poets' in 1846–7 (*Mem.* i 266).
*8. laughter*] laughters *MS.* D. Bush, *Major British Writers* (1959) ii 463, observes that the ancient Etruscans of this region were said to be descended from the Lydians of Asia Minor.

# 386 Sir John Oldcastle, Lord Cobham

(In Wales)

Published *1880*. In May 1858, T.'s wife Emily reports: 'A.T. read to me about Oldcastle in Sharon Turner and would like to write a poem about him but Sir John Simeon has dissuaded him for the present because the subject is too contentious and anti-Catholic' (*Mat.* ii 198). For evidence that T. may have contemplated some such poem as early as *c.* 1852, see l. 26*n*. There are fragments in *T.Nbk 36* (? *c.* 1855); the main composition was 1880 (*H.Nbk 64*, and a MS at *Univ. of London Lib.*). It was 4 Nov. 1880 that T.'s friend Knowles supplied the Welsh 'Dim Saesneg', l. 21 (*Lincoln*). T. took over several lines from his early poem on martyrdom by fire, *St Lawrence* (1833, p. 298); see ll. 176–81*n*. Turner's *History of England*, ii (1815) 306–7, gave the outline. Oldcastle was persecuted under Henry V as a follower of Wycliffe; he escaped from the Tower, was captured after being betrayed, and martyred. The details are from Thomas Gaspey's *The Good Lord Cobham* (1843, *Lincoln*); T. closely follows Gaspey (who derives from Bale and from Foxe's *Book of Martyrs*) in his account of the interrogation, ll. 127–60. T. had read Foxe while writing his play *Queen Mary* in 1874–5 (*Mem.* ii 176).

My friend should meet me somewhere hereabout
To take me to that hiding in the hills.

I have broke their cage, no gilded one, I trow–
I read no more the prisoner's mute wail
Scribbled or carved upon the pitiless stone;
I find hard rocks, hard life, hard cheer, or none,
For I am emptier than a friar's brains;
But God is with me in this wilderness,
These wet black passes and foam-churning chasms–
And God's free air, and hope of better things.

I would I knew their speech; not now to glean,
Not now–I hope to do it–some scattered ears,
Some ears for Christ in this wild field of Wales–
But, bread, merely for bread. This tongue that wagged
They said with such heretical arrogance
Against the proud archbishop Arundel–
So much God's cause was fluent in it–is here
But as a Latin Bible to the crowd;
'Bara!'–what use? The Shepherd, when I speak,

¶386. *19*. *'Bara!'*: Welsh for bread.

Vailing a sudden eyelid with his hard
'Dim Saesneg' passes, wroth at things of old–
No fault of mine. Had he God's word in Welsh
He might be kindlier: happily come the day!

Not least art thou, thou little Bethlehem
In Judah, for in thee the Lord was born;
Nor thou in Britain, little Lutterworth,
Least, for in thee the word was born again.

Heaven-sweet Evangel, ever-living word,
Who whilome spakest to the South in Greek
About the soft Mediterranean shores,
And then in Latin to the Latin crowd,
As good need was–thou hast come to talk our isle.
Hereafter thou, fulfilling Pentecost,
Must learn to use the tongues of all the world.
Yet art thou thine own witness that thou bringest
Not peace, a sword, a fire.
What did he say,
My frighted Wiclif-preacher whom I crost
In flying hither? that one night a crowd
Thronged the waste field about the city gates:
The king was on them suddenly with a host.
Why there? they came to hear their preacher. Then
Some cried on Cobham, on the good Lord Cobham;
Ay, for they love me! but the king–nor voice
Nor finger raised against him–took and hanged,
Took, hanged and burnt–how many–thirty-nine–
Called it rebellion–hanged, poor friends, as rebels
And burned alive as heretics! for your Priest
Labels–to take the king along with him–
All heresy, treason: but to call men traitors
May make men traitors.
Rose of Lancaster,
Red in thy birth, redder with household war,
Now reddest with the blood of holy men,

20. *sudden*] *1884*; sullen *1880–83*. *Vailing*: casting down.

21. '*Dim Saesneg*': Welsh for 'No English' (T.).

24–5. *Matthew* ii 6: 'And thou Bethlehem, in the land of Juda, art not the least among the princes of Juda, for out of thee shall come a Governor.' An echo of *Micah* v 2, where Bethlehem has the epithet 'little'.

26. *Lutterworth*: Wycliffe's principal rectory. Adapting a jotting in *H.Nbk 28* (*c.* 1852): 'O little star low-shining in the dark, / Low morning-star of homely Lutterworth.'

36. *Matthew* x 34: 'I came not to send peace, but a sword.'

Redder to be, red rose of Lancaster–
If somewhere in the North, as Rumour sang
Fluttering the hawks of this crown-lusting line–
By firth and loch thy silver sister grow,
That were my rose, there my allegiance due.
Self-starved, they say–nay, murdered, doubtless dead.
So to this king I cleaved: my friend was he,
Once my fast friend: I would have given my life
To help his own from scathe, a thousand lives
To save his soul. He might have come to learn
Our Wiclif's learning: but the worldly Priests
Who fear the king's hard common-sense should find
What rotten piles uphold their mason-work,
Urge him to foreign war. O had he willed
I might have stricken a lusty stroke for him,
But he would not; far liever led my friend
Back to the pure and universal church,
But he would not: whether that heirless flaw
In his throne's title make him feel so frail,
He leans on Antichrist; or that his mind,
So quick, so capable in soldiership,
In matters of the faith, alas the while!
More worth than all the kingdoms of this world,
Runs in the rut, a coward to the Priest.

Burnt–good Roger Acton, my dear friend!
Burnt too, my faithful preacher, Beverley!
Lord give thou power to thy two witnesses!
Lest the false faith make merry over them!
Two–nay but thirty-nine have risen and stand,
Dark with the smoke of human sacrifice,
Before thy light, and cry continually–
Cry–against whom?
Him, who should bear the sword
Of Justice–what! the kingly, kindly boy;

*56. 1880* note: 'Richard II.'

*70–2.* Cp. Turner: 'or from his father [Henry IV] having founded his dynasty on the policy of supporting the papal hierarchy in England'.

*78.* John of Beverley, burnt in 1414 (T.).

*79. Revelation* xi 3, 'And I will give power unto my two witnesses, and they shall prophesy.'

*83–4.* Cp. *Deuteronomy* xv 9: 'and he cry unto the Lord against thee'; also xxiv 15.

*85–7.* Henry V as Prince Hal, alluding, as T. says, to the story that Oldcastle was the original of Falstaff. Gaspey discusses it.

Who took the world so easily heretofore,
My boon companion, tavern-fellow–him
Who gibed and japed–in many a merry tale
That shook our sides–at Pardoners, Summoners,
Friars, absolution-sellers, monkeries
And nunneries, when the wild hour and the wine
Had set the wits aflame.
                                        Harry of Monmouth,
Or Amurath of the East?
                                        Better to sink
Thy fleurs-de-lys in slime again, and fling
Thy royalty back into the riotous fits
Of wine and harlotry–thy shame, and mine,
Thy comrade–than to persecute the Lord,
And play the Saul that never will be Paul.

Burnt, burnt! and while this mitred Arundel
Dooms our unlicensed preacher to the flame,
The mitre-sanctioned harlot draws his clerks
Into the suburb–their hard celibacy,
Sworn to be veriest ice of pureness, molten
Into adulterous living, or such crimes
As holy Paul–a shame to speak of them–
Among the heathen–
                                        Sanctuary granted
To bandit, thief, assassin–yea to him
Who hacks his mother's throat–denied to him,
Who finds the Saviour in his mother tongue.
The Gospel, the Priest's pearl, flung down to swine–
The swine, lay-men, lay-women, who will come,
God willing, to outlearn the filthy friar.
Ah rather, Lord, than that thy Gospel, meant
To course and range through all the world, should be
Tethered to these dead pillars of the Church–
Rather than so, if thou wilt have it so,

*92–3.* Henry V, when newly crowned, told men not to fear: 'Not Amurath an Amurath succeeds, / But Harry, Harry' (*2 Henry IV* V ii 48–9).
*97. Acts* ix 4: 'Saul, Saul, why persecutest thou me?'
*100.* The Lollards were persecuted for 'setting them up to preach whom the bishops had not licensed' (Foxe).
*102–4. suburb*: as used for the brothel-districts in *Measure for Measure*; T. associates the priests with the lustful hypocrisy of Angelo, 'whose blood / Is very snow-broth', I iv 57–8.
*105–6. Ephesians* v 12: 'For it is a shame even to speak of those things which are done of them in secret.'

Burst vein, snap sinew, and crack heart, and life
Pass in the fire of Babylon! but how long,
O Lord, how long!
My friend should meet me here.
Here is the copse, the fountain and–a Cross!
To thee, dead wood, I bow not head nor knees.
Rather to thee, green boscage, work of God,
Black holly, and white-flowered wayfaring-tree!
Rather to thee, thou living water, drawn
By this good Wiclif mountain down from heaven,
And speaking clearly in thy native tongue–
No Latin–He that thirsteth, come and drink!

Eh! how I angered Arundel asking me
To worship Holy Cross! I spread mine arms,
God's work, I said, a cross of flesh and blood
And holier. That was heresy. (My good friend
By this time should be with me.) 'Images?'
'Bury them as God's truer images
Are daily buried.' 'Heresy.–Penance?' 'Fast,
Hairshirt and scourge–nay, let a man repent,
Do penance in his heart, God hears him.' 'Heresy–
Not shriven, not saved?' 'What profits an ill Priest
Between me and my God? I would not spurn
Good counsel of good friends, but shrive myself
No, not to an Apostle.' 'Heresy.'
(My friend is long in coming.) 'Pilgrimages?'
'Drink, bagpipes, revelling, devil's-dances, vice.
The poor man's money gone to fat the friar.
Who reads of begging saints in Scripture?'–'Heresy'–
(Hath he been here–not found me–gone again?
Have I mislearnt our place of meeting?) 'Bread–
Bread left after the blessing?' how they stared,
That was their main test-question–glared at me!
'He veiled Himself in flesh, and now He veils
His flesh in bread, body and bread together.'

*118.* See ll. 167–170.

*119.* *Revelation* vi 10: 'How long, O Lord, holy and true, dost thou not judge and avenge our blood on them that dwell on the earth?'

*127.* *Isaiah* lv 1: 'Every one that thirsteth, come ye to the waters'; *John* vii 37: 'if any man thirst, let him come unto me'; *John* iv 10: 'He would have given thee living water' (cp. l. 124).

*133.* Gaspey i 226: 'bury them fair in the ground, as is done by aged people whom we know well to be God's images'; a paraphrase of Foxe: 'as ye do other aged people . . .'.

Then rose the howl of all the cassocked wolves,
'No bread, no bread. God's body!' Archbishop,
Bishop,
Priors, Canons, Friars, bellringers, Parish-clerks –
'No bread, no bread!' – 'Authority of the Church,
Power of the keys!' – Then I, God help me, I
So mocked, so spurned, so baited two whole days –
I lost myself and fell from evenness,
And railed at all the Popes, that ever since
Sylvester shed the venom of world-wealth
Into the church, had only proven themselves
Poisoners, murderers. Well – God pardon all –
Me, them, and all the world – yea, that proud Priest,
That mock-meek mouth of utter Antichrist,
That traitor to King Richard and the truth,
Who rose and doomed me to the fire.
Amen!
Nay, I can burn, so that the Lord of life
Be by me in my death.
Those three! the fourth
Was like the Son of God! Not burnt were they.
On *them* the smell of burning had not past.
That was a miracle to convert the king.
These Pharisees, this Caiaphas-Arundel
What miracle could turn? *He* here again,
*He* thwarting their traditions of Himself,
*He* would be found a heretic to Himself,
And doomed to burn alive.
So, caught, I burn.
Burn? heathen men have borne as much as this,
For freedom, or the sake of those they loved,
Or some less cause, some cause far less than mine;
For every other cause is less than mine.
The moth will singe her wings, and singed return,
Her love of light quenching her fear of pain –
How now, my soul, we do not heed the fire?

*159. Sylvester*: the fourth-century Pope who was granted temporal dominion by the supposed Donation of Constantine.

*166.* Cp. *St Lawrence* 6: 'I cannot argue, I can burn.'

*167–70.* The three in Nebuchadnezzar's fiery furnace, *Daniel* iii 25, 27: 'Lo, I see four men loose, walking in the midst of the fire, and they have no hurt; and the . . . fourth is like the Son of God. . . . Nor the smell of fire had passed on them.' This is the 'fire of Babylon' (*Daniel* iii 6) of l. 118.

*176–81.* Taken almost verbatim from *St Lawrence* (1833), of which the MS in *T.Nbk 15* may not be quoted.

Faint-hearted? tut!–faint-stomached! faint as I am,
God willing, I will burn for Him.
Who comes?
A thousand marks are set upon my head.
Friend?–foe perhaps–a tussle for it then!
Nay, but my friend. Thou art so well disguised,
I knew thee not. Hast thou brought bread with thee?
I have not broken bread for fifty hours.
None? I am damned already by the Priest
For holding there was bread where bread was none–
No bread. My friends await me yonder? Yes.
Lead on then. *Up* the mountain? Is it far?
Not far. Climb first and reach me down thy hand.
I am not like to die for lack of bread,
For I must live to testify by fire.

# 387 The Sisters

## [THEY HAVE LEFT THE DOORS AJAR]

Published *1880*. It is in *H.Nbk 48* with *The Village Wife* (*1880*) and *Becket* (trial edition, 1879). 'Partly founded on a story, known to my father, of a girl who consented to be bridesmaid to her sister, although she secretly loved the bridegroom. The night after the wedding the poor bridesmaid ran away from home. They searched for her high and low, and at last she was found, knocking at the church door, in the "pitiless rush of autumn rain", her wits gone' (H.T.). For the story of two sisters in love with the same man, cp. the cousins in *The Ring* (p. 1383).

They have left the doors ajar; and by their clash,
And prelude on the keys, I know the song,
Their favourite–which I call 'The Tables Turned.'
Evelyn begins it 'O diviner Air.'

EVELYN

O diviner Air,
Through the heat, the drowth, the dust, the glare,
Far from out the west in shadowing showers,

*185–6.* Oldcastle in Wales was betrayed, under the guise of friendship, for a large reward.

*196. 1880* note: 'He was burnt on Christmas Day, 1417.'

¶387. *5. diviner Air*: *A Welcome to Alexandrovna* 43.

Over all the meadow baked and bare,
Making fresh and fair
All the bowers and the flowers,
Fainting flowers, faded bowers,
Over all this weary world of ours,
Breathe, diviner Air!

A sweet voice that–you scarce could better that.
Now follows Edith echoing Evelyn.

EDITH

O diviner light,
Through the cloud that roofs our noon with night,
Through the blotting mist, the blinding showers,
Far from out a sky for ever bright,
Over all the woodland's flooded bowers,
Over all the meadow's drowning flowers,
Over all this ruined world of ours,
Break, diviner light!

Marvellously like, their voices–and themselves!
Though one is somewhat deeper than the other,
As one is somewhat graver than the other–
Edith than Evelyn. Your good Uncle, whom
You count the father of your fortune, longs
For this alliance: let me ask you then,
Which voice most takes you? for I do not doubt
Being a watchful parent, you are taken
With one or other: though sometimes I fear
You may be flickering, fluttering in a doubt
Between the two–which must not be–which might
Be death to one: they both are beautiful:
Evelyn is gayer, wittier, prettier, says
The common voice, if one may trust it: she?
No! but the paler and the graver, Edith.
Woo her and gain her then: no wavering, boy!
The graver is perhaps the one for you
Who jest and laugh so easily and so well.
For love will go by contrast, as by likes.

No sisters ever prized each other more.
Not so: their mother and her sister loved
More passionately still.
But that my best
And oldest friend, your Uncle, wishes it,
And that I know you worthy everyway
To be my son, I might, perchance, be loath

To part them, or part from them: and yet one
Should marry, or all the broad lands in your view
From this bay window–which our house has held
Three hundred years–will pass collaterally.

My father with a child on either knee,
A hand upon the head of either child,
Smoothing their locks, as golden as his own
Were silver, 'get them wedded' would he say.
And once my prattling Edith asked him 'why?'
Ay, why? said he, 'for why should I go lame?'
Then told them of his wars, and of his wound.
For see–this wine–the grape from whence it flowed
Was blackening on the slopes of Portugal,
When that brave soldier, down the terrible ridge
Plunged in the last fierce charge at Waterloo,
And caught the laming bullet. He left me this,
Which yet retains a memory of its youth,
As I of mine, and my first passion. Come!
Here's to your happy union with my child!

Yet must you change your name: no fault of mine!
You say that you can do it as willingly
As birds make ready for their bridal-time
By change of feather: for all that, my boy,
Some birds are sick and sullen when they moult.
An old and worthy name! but mine that stirred
Among our civil wars and earlier too
Among the Roses, the more venerable.
*I* care not for a name–no fault of mine.
Once more–a happier marriage than my own!

You see yon Lombard poplar on the plain.
The highway running by it leaves a breadth
Of sward to left and right, where, long ago,
One bright May morning in a world of song,
I lay at leisure, watching overhead
The aërial poplar wave, an amber spire.

I dozed; I woke. An open landaulet
Whirled by, which, after it had past me, showed
Turning my way, the loveliest face on earth.
The face of one there sitting opposite,
On whom I brought a strange unhappiness,

*68–76.* Cp. the (Tennyson) d'Eyncourts and the (Tennyson) Turners.

*83.* Virgil's *Eclogues* i 58: *nec gemere aëria cessabit turtur ab ulmo* ('and the turtle-dove shall cease not their moaning from the skyey elm').

That time I did not see.
Love at first sight
May seem – with goodly rhyme and reason for it –
Possible – at first glimpse, and for a face
Gone in a moment – strange. Yet once, when first
I came on lake Llanberris in the dark,
A moonless night with storm – one lightning-fork
Flashed out the lake; and though I loitered there
The full day after, yet in retrospect
That less than momentary thunder-sketch
Of lake and mountain conquers all the day.

The sun himself has limned the face for me.
Not quite so quickly, no, nor half as well.
For look you here – the shadows are too deep,
And like the critic's blurring comment make
The veriest beauties of the work appear
The darkest faults: the sweet eyes frown: the lips
Seem but a gash. My sole memorial
Of Edith – no, the other, – both indeed.

So that bright face was flashed through sense and soul
And by the poplar vanished – to be found
Long after, as it seemed, beneath the tall
Tree-bowers, and those long-sweeping beechen boughs
Of our New Forest. I was there alone:
The phantom of the whirling landaulet
For ever past me by: when one quick peal
Of laughter drew me through the glimmering glades
Down to the snowlike sparkle of a cloth
On fern and foxglove. Lo, the face again,
My Rosalind in this Arden – Edith – all
One bloom of youth, health, beauty, happiness,
And moved to merriment at a passing jest.

There one of those about her knowing me
Called me to join them; so with these I spent
What seemed my crowning hour, my day of days.

I wooed her then, nor unsuccessfully,

*93–5.* 'What I saw myself at Llanberis' (T.).
*114. glimmering glades:* Samuel Rogers, *Italy: Meillerie* 2. 'Rogers used often to read to him passages of his writings, and to consult him about the notes to his *Italy*' (*Mem.* ii 72). Cp. *Il Penseroso* 27: 'glimmering Bowres, and glades'.
*115.* 'A personal experience in the New Forest' (H.T.).

The worse for her, for me! was I content?
Ay–no, not quite; for now and then I thought
Laziness, vague love-longings, the bright May,
Had made a heated haze to magnify
The charm of Edith–that a man's ideal
Is high in Heaven, and lodged with Plato's God,
Not findable here–content, and not content,
In some such fashion as a man may be
That having had the portrait of his friend
Drawn by an artist, looks at it, and says,
'Good! very like! not altogether he.'

As yet I had not bound myself by words,
Only, believing I loved Edith, made
Edith love *me*. Then came the day when I,
Flattering myself that all my doubts were fools
Born of the fool this Age that doubts of all–
Not I that day of Edith's love or mine–
Had braced my purpose to declare myself:
I stood upon the stairs of Paradise.
The golden gates would open at a word.
I spoke it–told her of my passion, seen
And lost and found again, had got so far,
Had caught her hand, her eyelids fell–I heard
Wheels, and a noise of welcome at the doors–
On a sudden after two Italian years
Had set the blossom of her health again,
The younger sister, Evelyn, entered–there,
There was the face, and altogether she.
The mother fell about the daughter's neck,
The sisters closed in one another's arms,
Their people thronged about them from the hall,
And in the thick of question and reply
I fled the house, driven by one angel face,
And all the Furies.

I was bound to her;
I could not free myself in honour–bound
Not by the sounded letter of the word,
But counterpressures of the yielded hand
That timorously and faintly echoed mine,
Quick blushes, the sweet dwelling of her eyes
Upon me when she thought I did not see–
Were these not bonds? nay, nay, but could I wed her
Loving the other? do her that great wrong?
Had I not dreamed I loved her yestermorn?

129. *Republic* 509 D.

Had I not known where Love, at first a fear,
Grew after marriage to full height and form?
Yet after marriage, that mock-sister there–
Brother-in-law–the fiery nearness of it–
Unlawful and disloyal brotherhood–
What end but darkness could ensue from this
For all the three? So Love and Honour jarred
Though Love and Honour joined to raise the full
High-tide of doubt that swayed me up and down
Advancing nor retreating.
                                        Edith wrote:
'My mother bids me ask' (I did not tell you–
A widow with less guile than many a child.
God help the wrinkled children that are Christ's
As well as the plump cheek–she wrought us harm,
Poor soul, not knowing) 'are you ill?' (so ran
The letter) 'you have not been here of late.
You will not find me here. At last I go
On that long-promised visit to the North.
I told your wayside story to my mother
And Evelyn. She remembers you. Farewell.
Pray come and see my mother. Almost blind
With ever-growing cataract, yet she thinks
She sees you when she hears. Again farewell.'

Cold words from one I had hoped to warm so far
That I could stamp my image on her heart!
'Pray come and see my mother, and farewell.'
Cold, but as welcome as free airs of heaven
After a dungeon's closeness. Selfish, strange!
What dwarfs are men! my strangled vanity
Uttered a stifled cry–to have vext myself
And all in vain for her–cold heart or none–
No bride for me. Yet so my path was clear
To win the sister.
                                        Whom I wooed and won.
For Evelyn knew not of my former suit,
Because the simple mother worked upon
By Edith prayed me not to whisper of it.
And Edith would be bridesmaid on the day.
But on that day, not being all at ease,
I from the altar glancing back upon her,
Before the first 'I will' was uttered, saw
The bridesmaid pale, statuelike, passionless–
'No harm, no harm' I turned again, and placed
My ring upon the finger of my bride.

So, when we parted, Edith spoke no word,
She wept no tear, but round my Evelyn clung
In utter silence for so long, I thought
'What, will she never set her sister free?'

We left her, happy each in each, and then,
As though the happiness of each in each
Were not enough, must fain have torrents, lakes,
Hills, the great things of Nature and the fair,
To lift us as it were from commonplace,
And help us to our joy. Better have sent
Our Edith through the glories of the earth,
To change with her horizon, if true Love
Were not his own imperial all-in-all.

Far off we went. My God, I would not live
Save that I think this gross hard-seeming world
Is our misshaping vision of the Powers
Behind the world, that make our griefs our gains.

For on the dark night of our marriage-day
The great Tragedian, that had quenched herself
In that assumption of the bridesmaid – she
That loved me – our true Edith – her brain broke
With over-acting, till she rose and fled
Beneath a pitiless rush of Autumn rain
To the deaf church – to be let in – to pray
Before *that* altar – so I think; and there
They found her beating the hard Protestant doors.
She died and she was buried ere we knew.

I learnt it first. I had to speak. At once
The bright quick smile of Evelyn, that had sunned
The morning of our marriage, past away:
And on our home-return the daily want
Of Edith in the house, the garden, still
Haunted us like her ghost; and by and by,
Either from that necessity for talk
Which lives with blindness, or plain innocence
Of nature, or desire that her lost child
Should earn from both the praise of heroism,
The mother broke her promise to the dead,
And told the living daughter with what love
Edith had welcomed my brief wooing of her,
And all her sweet self-sacrifice and death.

Henceforth that mystic bond betwixt the twins –
Did I not tell you they were twins? – prevailed

So far that no caress could win my wife
Back to that passionate answer of full heart
I had from her at first. Not that her love,
Though scarce as great as Edith's power of love,
Had lessened, but the mother's garrulous wail
For ever woke the unhappy Past again,
Till that dead bridesmaid, meant to be my bride,
Put forth cold hands between us, and I feared
The very fountains of her life were chilled;
So took her thence, and brought her here, and here
She bore a child, whom reverently we called
Edith; and in the second year was born
A second–this I named from her own self,
Evelyn; then two weeks–no more–she joined,
In and beyond the grave, that one she loved.
Now in this quiet of declining life,
Through dreams by night and trances of the day,
The sisters glide about me hand in hand,
Both beautiful alike, nor can I tell
One from the other, no, nor care to tell
One from the other, only know they come,
They smile upon me, till, remembering all
The love they both have borne me, and the love
I bore them both–divided as I am
From either by the stillness of the grave–
I know not which of these I love the best.

But *you* love Edith; and her own true eyes
Are traitors to her; our quick Evelyn–
The merrier, prettier, wittier, as they talk,
And not without good reason, my good son–
Is yet untouched: and I that hold them both
Dearest of all things–well, I am not sure–
But if there lie a preference eitherway,
And in the rich vocabulary of Love
'Most dearest' be a true superlative–
I think *I* likewise love your Edith most.

# 388 To the Duke of Argyll

Published *1885*. It is not in the first two *British Museum* trial editions, but is in the third; it was added by pen to a *Lincoln* trial edition. H.T. says: 'Written when the Duke resigned the office of Privy Seal [April 1881] on account of his vehement opposition to Gladstone's Irish Bill.' The eighth Duke (1823–1900) had been a friend of T.'s for more than twenty years.

O Patriot Statesman, be thou wise to know
The limits of resistance, and the bounds
Determining concession; still be bold
Not only to slight praise but suffer scorn;
And be thy heart a fortress to maintain
The day against the moment, and the year
Against the day; thy voice, a music heard
Through all the yells and counter-yells of feud
And faction, and thy will, a power to make
This ever-changing world of circumstance,
In changing, chime with never-changing Law.

# 389 Despair

Published *Nineteenth Century*, Nov. 1881, with subtitle *A Dramatic Monologue*; then *1885*. It is dated 9 June 1881 in *H.Lpr 48*. A letter from T. to Knowles, editor of the *Nineteenth Century*, in 1882, replied to his protest at the publication of *The Charge of the Heavy Brigade* in *Macmillan's*: 'You distinctly refused it and accepted *Despair* which at that time I scarcely wished to publish without its pendent poem of *Hope* or *Faith*. However you prevailed upon me to let you have it' (*Lincoln*). In *1892*, T. published *Faith* (p. 1455). The subject was suggested by Mary Gladstone; herparagraph was expanded to provide the headnote (*Mem.* ii 264). T.'s early headnote (*H.Nbk 48*) had said that 'the subject of this poem was taken from a newspaper', and had elaborated: 'A man and his wife the other day flung themselves into a river with the intention of committing suicide. The man was rescued, the woman drowned. I have substituted the sea for the river and hypothesized the feelings of a would-be-suicide in this latter half of our nineteenth century.' Horror at a Godless universe and at a belief in eternal torment were lifelong preoccupations of T. Possibly he was influenced by James Thomson's *The City of Dreadful Night* (1870–4; in volume form, 1880); it tells of those 'whose faith and hope are dead, and who would die': 'when the tide / Swept up to her there kneeling by my side, / She clasped that corpse-like me, and they were borne / Away.'

A man and his wife having lost faith in a God, and hope of a life to come, and being utterly miserable in this, resolve to end themselves by drowning. The woman is drowned, but the man rescued by a minister of the sect he had abandoned.

I

Is it you, that preached in the chapel there looking over the sand?
Followed us too that night, and dogged us, and drew me to land?

¶388. *6–7*. An early draft in *T.Nbk 21* had incorporated *Hail Briton* 168: 'Against the spirit of the Time' (p. 488).

II

What did I feel that night? You are curious. How should I tell?
Does it matter so much what I felt? You rescued me–yet–was it well
That you came unwished for, uncalled, between me and the deep and
 my doom,
Three days since, three more dark days of the Godless gloom
Of a life without sun, without health, without hope, without any delight
In anything here upon earth? but ah God, that night, that night
When the rolling eyes of the lighthouse there on the fatal neck
Of land running out into rock–they had saved many hundreds from
 wreck–
Glared on our way toward death, I remember I thought, as we past,
Does it matter how many they saved? we are all of us wrecked at last–
'Do you fear?' and there came through the roar of the breaker a
 whisper, a breath,
'Fear? am I not with you? I am frighted at life not death.'

III

And the suns of the limitless Universe sparkled and shone in the sky,
Flashing with fires as of God, but we knew that their light was a lie–
Bright as with deathless hope–but, however they sparkled and shone,
The dark little worlds running round them were worlds of woe like
 our own–
No soul in the heaven above, no soul on the earth below,
A fiery scroll written over with lamentation and woe.

IV

See, we were nursed in the drear night-fold of your fatalist creed,
And we turned to the growing dawn, we had hoped for a dawn indeed,
When the light of a Sun that was coming would scatter the ghosts of the
 Past,
And the cramping creeds that had maddened the peoples would vanish
 at last,
And we broke away from the Christ, our human brother and friend,
For He spoke, or it seemed that He spoke, of a Hell without help,
 without end.

V

Hoped for a dawn and it came, but the promise had faded away;
We had past from a cheerless night to the glare of a drearier day;
He is only a cloud and a smoke who was once a pillar of fire,
The guess of a worm in the dust and the shadow of its desire–

¶389. *13. fear?*] *1894*; fear, *Eversley*, *1881–5*.
*20. Ezekiel* ii 9–10: 'A roll of a book ... and there was written therein lamentations, and mourning, and woe.'
*21. drear*] *1885*; dark *1881*.
*29. Exodus* xiii 21.
*30–32.* Cp. *Job* xxv 6: 'How much less man, that is a worm: and the son of man, which is a worm.'

Of a worm as it writhes in a world of the weak trodden down by the strong,
Of a dying worm in a world, all massacre, murder, and wrong.

VI

O we poor orphans of nothing–alone on that lonely shore–
Born of the brainless Nature who knew not that which she bore!
Trusting no longer that earthly flower would be heavenly fruit–
Come from the brute, poor souls–no souls–and to die with the brute–

VII

Nay, but I am not claiming your pity: I know you of old–
Small pity for those that have ranged from the narrow warmth of your fold,
Where you bawled the dark side of your faith and a God of eternal rage,
Till you flung us back on ourselves, and the human heart, and the Age.

VIII

But pity–the Pagan held it a vice–was in her and in me,
Helpless, taking the place of the pitying God that should be!
Pity for all that aches in the grasp of an idiot power,
And pity for our own selves on an earth that bore not a flower;
Pity for all that suffers on land or in air or the deep,
And pity for our own selves till we longed for eternal sleep.

IX

'Lightly step over the sands! the waters–you hear them call!
Life with its anguish, and horrors, and errors–away with it all!'
And she laid her hand in my own–she was always loyal and sweet–
Till the points of the foam in the dusk came playing about our feet.
*There* was a strong sea-current would sweep us out to the main.
'Ah God' though I felt as I spoke I was taking the name in vain–
'Ah God' and we turned to each other, we kissed, we embraced, she and I,
Knowing the Love we were used to believe everlasting would die:
We had read their know-nothing books and we leaned to the darker side–
Ah God, should we find Him, perhaps, perhaps, if we died, if we died;
We never had found Him on earth, this earth is a fatherless Hell–
'Dear Love, for ever and ever, for ever and ever farewell,'
Never a cry so desolate, not since the world began,
Never a kiss so sad, no, not since the coming of man!

X

But the blind wave cast me ashore, and you saved me, a valueless life.
Not a grain of gratitude mine! You have parted the man from the wife.

35. Cp. the hope of *In Memoriam: Epilogue* 132–6: 'Nature like an open book'; 'all we thought ... is but seed / Of what in them is flower and fruit' (p. 987).
55. *know-nothing*: 'agnostic' was a topical word apparently put in circulation by Huxley in 1869; cp. l. 94.
61. *blind wave*: *Merlin and Vivien* 230.

I am left alone on the land, she is all alone in the sea;
If a curse meant aught, I would curse you for not having let me be.

XI

Visions of youth–for my brain was drunk with the water, it seems;
I had past into perfect quiet at length out of pleasant dreams,
And the transient trouble of drowning–what was it when matched with the pains
Of the hellish heat of a wretched life rushing back through the veins?

XII

Why should I live? one son had forged on his father and fled,
And if I believed in a God, I would thank him, the other is dead,
And there was a baby-girl, that had never looked on the light:
Happiest she of us all, for she past from the night to the night.

XIII

But the crime, if a crime, of her eldest-born, her glory, her boast,
Struck hard at the tender heart of the mother, and broke it almost;
Though, glory and shame dying out for ever in endless time,
Does it matter so much whether crowned for a virtue, or hanged for a crime?

XIV

And ruined by *him*, by *him*, I stood there, naked, amazed
In a world of arrogant opulence, feared myself turning crazed,
And I would not be mocked in a madhouse! and she, the delicate wife,
With a grief that could only be cured, if cured, by the surgeon's knife,–

XV

Why should we bear with an hour of torture, a moment of pain,
If every man die for ever, if all his griefs are in vain,
And the homeless planet at length will be wheeled through the silence of space,
Motherless evermore of an ever-vanishing race,
When the worm shall have writhed its last, and its last brother-worm will have fled
From the dead fossil skull that is left in the rocks of an earth that is dead?

XVI

Have I crazed myself over their horrible infidel writings? O yes,
For these are the new dark ages, you see, of the popular press,
When the bat comes out of his cave, and the owls are whooping at noon,
And Doubt is the lord of this dunghill and crows to the sun and the moon,

*75. glory*] *1885*; name *1881*.
*77–9.* All the details here suggest *Maud*, as do ll. 30–2.
*88–9.* Adapted from a poem on the pains of authorship which is in *T.Nbk 26* (1839) and may not be quoted. Cp. *Locksley Hall Sixty* 137: 'Bring the old dark ages back without the faith, without the hope'.

Till the Sun and the Moon of our science are both of them turned into blood,
And Hope will have broken her heart, running after a shadow of good;
For their knowing and know-nothing books are scattered from hand to hand–
*We* have knelt in your know-all chapel too looking over the sand.

XVII

What! I should call on that Infinite Love that has served us so well?
Infinite cruelty rather that made everlasting Hell,
Made us, foreknew us, foredoomed us, and does what he will with his own;
Better our dead brute mother who never has heard us groan!

XVIII

Hell? if the souls of men were immortal, as men have been told,
The lecher would cleave to his lusts, and the miser would yearn for his gold,
And so there were Hell for ever! but were there a God as you say,
His Love would have power over Hell till it utterly vanished away.

XIX

Ah yet–I have had some glimmer, at times, in my gloomiest woe,
Of a God behind all–after all–the great God for aught that I know;
But the God of Love and of Hell together–they cannot be thought,
If there be such a God, may the Great God curse him and bring him to nought!

XX

Blasphemy! whose is the fault? is it mine? for why would you save
A madman to vex you with wretched words, who is best in his grave?
Blasphemy! ay, why not, being damned beyond hope of grace?
O would I were yonder with her, and away from your faith and your face!
Blasphemy! true! I have scared you pale with my scandalous talk,
But the blasphemy to *my* mind lies all in the way that you walk.

XXI

Hence! she is gone! can I stay? can I breathe divorced from the Past?
You needs must have good lynx-eyes if I do not escape you at last.
Our orthodox coroner doubtless will find it a felo-de-se,
And the stake and the cross-road, fool, if you will, does it matter to me?

91. *Joel* ii 31, 'The sun shall be turned into darkness, and the moon into blood, before the great and the terrible day of the Lord come.'
96. *cruelty*] *1885*; wickedness *1881*.
97. Combining *Romans* viii 29: 'For whom he did foreknow, he also did predestinate'; and *Matthew* xx 15: 'Is it not lawful for me to do what I will with mine own?'
115–6. The suicide was traditionally buried at the crossroads with a stake in his heart.

# 390 Prologue to General Hamley

[The Charge of the Heavy Brigade]

Published *1885*. Written Nov. 1883 (dated, *H.Nbk 46*). Edward Hamley, who had earlier served with distinction in the Crimea, was later widely regarded as having been given too little credit for the victory at Tel-el-Kebir. T.'s earlier draft (ll. 30–1*n*) did not mention General Wolseley. T. had thought of adapting *Hail Briton* (p. 480) for a poem on Tel-el-Kebir.

Our birches yellowing and from each
 The light leaf falling fast,
While squirrels from our fiery beech
 Were bearing off the mast,
You came, and looked and loved the view
 Long-known and loved by me,
Green Sussex fading into blue
 With one gray glimpse of sea;
And, gazing from this height alone,
 We spoke of what had been
Most marvellous in the wars your own
 Crimean eyes had seen;
And now–like old-world inns that take
 Some warrior for a sign
That therewithin a guest may make
 True cheer with honest wine–
Because you heard the lines I read
 Nor uttered word of blame,
I dare without your leave to head
 These rhymings with your name,
Who know you but as one of those
 I fain would meet again,
Yet know you, as your England knows
 That you and all your men
Were soldiers to her heart's desire,
 When, in the vanished year,
You saw the league-long rampart-fire
 Flare from Tel-el-Kebir
Through darkness, and the foe was driven,

¶390. *2. light leaf*] round leaves *H.Nbk 46.*
*3. fiery*] flaming *MS.*
*4. mast*: the fruit of the beech.
*8*] Far off on down and sea; *MS.*
*11*] Great deeds of battle which your own *MS 1st reading.*
*27. rampart-fire*] stream of fire *MS.*
*28. Flare*] Flash *MS.* Wolseley's defeat of Arabi Pasha, 13 Sept. 1882.

And Wolseley overthrew
Arâbi, and the stars in heaven
Paled, and the glory grew.

# 391 The Charge of the Heavy Brigade at Balaclava

October 25, 1854

Published *Macmillan's Magazine*, March 1882; then *1885*, when the *Prologue* and *Epilogue* were added. It was begun March 1881, when A. W. Kinglake mentions it (*Lincoln*); Emily T.'s Journal notes it as written Feb. 1882. T. says that it was written at the request of Kinglake, author of *The Invasion of the Crimea* (1863). He sent T. a memorandum (H.T.). T. probably drew on *The Times*, 14 Nov. 1854, as for *The Charge of the Light Brigade* (p. 1034); he seems to have had the poem in mind since then (*Mem.* i 380). *1882* note: 'The "three hundred" of the "Heavy Brigade" who made this famous charge were the Scots Greys and the 2nd squadron of Inniskillings; the remainder of the "Heavy Brigade" subsequently dashing up to their support. The "three" were Scarlett's aide-de-camp, Elliot, and the trumpeter and Shegog the orderly, who had been close behind him.'

I

The charge of the gallant three hundred, the Heavy Brigade!
Down the hill, down the hill, thousands of Russians,
Thousands of horsemen, drew to the valley–and stayed;
For Scarlett and Scarlett's three hundred were riding by
When the points of the Russian lances arose in the sky;
And he called 'Left wheel into line!' and they wheeled and obeyed.
Then he looked at the host that had halted he knew not why,
And he turned half round, and he bad his trumpeter sound
To the charge, and he rode on ahead, as he waved his blade

*30–1*] Arâbi's tawny crew,
Before us, as the stars in heaven *MS*

¶391. *5. arose in*] *1885*; broke in on *1882*.

To the gallant three hundred whose glory will never
die–
'Follow,' and up the hill, up the hill, up the hill,
Followed the Heavy Brigade.

II

The trumpet, the gallop, the charge, and the might
of the fight!
Thousands of horsemen had gathered there on the
height,
With a wing pushed out to the left, and a wing to the
right,
And who shall escape if they close? but he dashed up
alone
Through the great gray slope of men,
Swayed his sabre, and held his own
Like an Englishman there and then;
All in a moment followed with force
Three that were next in their fiery course,
Wedged themselves in between horse and horse,
Fought for their lives in the narrow gap they had made–
Four amid thousands! and up the hill, up the hill,
Gallopt the gallant three hundred, the Heavy Brigade.

III

Fell like a cannonshot,
Burst like a thunderbolt,
Crashed like a hurricane,
Broke through the mass from below,
Drove through the midst of the foe,
Plunged up and down, to and fro,
Rode flashing blow upon blow,
Brave Inniskillens and Greys
Whirling their sabres in circles of light!
And some of us, all in amaze,
Who were held for a while from the fight,
And were only standing at gaze,
When the dark-muffled Russian crowd
Folded its wings from the left and the right,

*14*] *1885*; Down the hill, slowly, thousands of Russians
Drew to the valley, and halted at last on the height, *1882*

*16. And . . . but*] *1885*; But Scarlett was far on ahead, and *1882*.

*18*] *1885*; And he wheeled his sabre, he held his own *1882*.

*20–1*] *1885*; And the three that were nearest him followed with force, *1882*.

And rolled them around like a cloud,–
O mad for the charge and the battle were we,
When our own good redcoats sank from sight,
Like drops of blood in a dark-gray sea,
And we turned to each other, whispering, all dismayed,
'Lost are the gallant three hundred of Scarlett's
Brigade!'

IV

'Lost one and all' were the words
Muttered in our dismay;
But they rode like Victors and Lords
Through the forest of lances and swords
In the heart of the Russian hordes,
They rode, or they stood at bay–
Struck with the sword-hand and slew,
Down with the bridle-hand drew
The foe from the saddle and threw
Underfoot there in the fray–
Ranged like a storm or stood like a rock
In the wave of a stormy day;
Till suddenly shock upon shock
Staggered the mass from without,
Drove it in wild disarray,
For our men gallopt up with a cheer and a shout,
And the foeman surged, and wavered, and reeled
Up the hill, up the hill, up the hill, out of the field,
And over the brow and away.

V

Glory to each and to all, and the charge that they made!
Glory to all the three hundred, and all the Brigade!

## 392 Epilogue

[The Charge of the Heavy Brigade]

Published *1885*. Written after Sept. 1883, based on a conversation with Laura Tennant (*Mem.* ii 319). The subtitle *To a Young Lady* appears in *H.Nbk 47*. For the name Irene (the Greek for Peace), cp. the dialogue on

44. *whispering*] *1885*; muttering *1882*.
45. *of Scarlett's Brigade*] *1885*; the Heavy Brigade *1882*.
46–7] *1885*; *not 1882*.
60] *1885*; *not 1882*.
62. *foeman*] *1885*; Russian *1882*.
66. *and all the Brigade*] *1885*; the Heavy Brigade *1882*.

the morality of war, between Irenæus and Tlepolemus in *Blackwood's*, Nov. 1854; T. used it for *Maud*.

IRENE

Not this way will you set your name
A star among the stars.

POET

What way?

IRENE

You praise when you should blame
The barbarism of wars.
A juster epoch has begun.

POET

Yet though this cheek be gray,
And that bright hair the modern sun,
Those eyes the blue today,
You wrong me, passionate little friend.
I would that wars should cease,
I would the globe from end to end
Might sow and reap in peace,
And some new Spirit o'erbear the old,
Or Trade re-frain the Powers
From war with kindly links of gold,
Or Love with wreaths of flowers.
Slav, Teuton, Kelt, I count them all
My friends and brother souls,
With all the peoples, great and small,
That wheel between the poles.
But since, our mortal shadow, Ill
To waste this earth began–
Perchance from some abuse of Will
In worlds before the man
Involving ours–he needs must fight
To make true peace his own,
He needs must combat might with might,
Or Might would rule alone;
And who loves War for War's own sake
Is fool, or crazed, or worse;
But let the patriot-soldier take
His meed of fame in verse;

¶392. *1–2.* Horace's *stellis inserere* (*Odes* III xxv 6).
*14.* *re-frain*: stressing the derivation, to bridle.

Nay–though that realm were in the wrong
For which her warriors bleed,
It still were right to crown with song
The warrior's noble deed–
A crown the Singer hopes may last,
For so the deed endures;
But Song will vanish in the Vast;
And that large phrase of yours
'A Star among the stars,' my dear,
Is girlish talk at best;
For dare we dally with the sphere
As he did half in jest,
Old Horace? 'I will strike' said he
'The stars with head sublime,'
But scarce could see, as now we see,
The man in Space and Time,
So drew perchance a happier lot
Than ours, who rhyme today.
The fires that arch this dusky dot–
Yon myriad-worlded way–
The vast sun-clusters' gathered blaze,
World-isles in lonely skies,
Whole heavens within themselves, amaze
Our brief humanities;
And so does Earth; for Homer's fame,
Though carved in harder stone–
The falling drop will make his name
As mortal as my own.

IRENE

No!

POET

Let it live then–ay, till when?
Earth passes, all is lost
In what they prophesy, our wise men,
Sun-flame or sunless frost,
And deed and song alike are swept
Away, and all in vain
As far as man can see, except
The man himself remain;

*39–60.* Cp. *Parnassus* (p. 1410).

*45–6. Odes* I i 35–6: *quodsi me lyricis vatibus inseris, / sublimi feriam sidera vertice.* ('But if you rank me among lyric bards, I shall touch the stars with my exalted head.')

*59.* Cp. *Job* xiv 19: 'The waters wear the stones, thou washest away the things which grow out of the dust of the earth, and thou destroyest the hope of man.'

And though, in this lean age forlorn,
  Too many a voice may cry
That man can have no after-morn,
  Not yet of these am I.
The man remains, and whatsoe'er
  He wrought of good or brave
Will mould him through the cycle-year
  That dawns behind the grave.

---

And here the Singer for his Art
  Not all in vain may plead
'The song that nerves a nation's heart,
  Is in itself a deed.'

## 393 Hands All Round [1882]

Published with music by T.'s wife Emily, for Queen Victoria's birthday, 15 March 1882 (*Tennyson and His Friends*, pp. 481–4); then *1885*. It does not appear in the first of the *British Museum* trial editions of *1885*. It is a drastic recasting of *Hands All Round!* [*1852*] (p. 1002), retaining only stanza 1, with trivial changes, from the original attack on Louis Napoleon (Napoleon III).

First pledge our Queen this solemn night,
  Then drink to England, every guest;
That man's the best Cosmopolite
  Who loves his native country best.
May freedom's oak for ever live
  With stronger life from day to day;
That man's the true Conservative
  Who lops the mouldered branch away.
    Hands all round!
  God the traitor's hope confound!

¶393. *1–2. this . . . drink*] *1885*; my friends, and then / A health *1882*.
*3*] *1885*; He best will serve the race of men, *1882*. This change from the poem of 1852 was deplored in *St. James's Gazette*, 16 March 1882, as was the change in l. 7. T. returned to his earlier readings.
*5. live*] *1885*; last *1882*.
*6. stronger*] *1885*; larger *1882*.
*7*] *1888*; He loves the present and the past, *1882*; That man's the best Conservative *1885*.
*11. this*] *1885*; the *1882, as in ll. 23, 35*.

To this great cause of Freedom drink, my friends,
And the great name of England, round and round.

To all the loyal hearts who long
To keep our English Empire whole!
To all our noble sons, the strong
New England of the Southern Pole!
To England under Indian skies,
To those dark millions of her realm!
To Canada whom we love and prize,
Whatever statesman hold the helm.
Hands all round!
God the traitor's hope confound!
To this great name of England drink, my friends,
And all her glorious empire, round and round.

To all our statesmen so they be
True leaders of the land's desire!
To both our Houses, may they see
Beyond the borough and the shire!
We sailed wherever ship could sail,
We founded many a mighty state;
Pray God our greatness may not fail
Through craven fears of being great.
Hands all round!
God the traitor's hope confound!
To this great cause of Freedom drink, my friends,
And the great name of England, round and round.

# 394 To Virgil

## Written at the Request of the Mantuans for the Nineteenth Centenary of Virgil's Death

Published *Nineteenth Century*, Sept. 1882; then *1885*. The letter of request from the Vergilian Academy of Mantua was dated 23 June 1882: 'One verse of yours, one writing however small, that could be published in the Vergilian Album will be agreeable, not only to us . . .' (*Mat.* iv 26–7). The poem was acknowledged 10 Sept. Cp. *To Dante* (p. 1191). D. Bush points out that the 'rolling trochaic lines suggest something of the sound of the Virgilian hexameter' (*Major British Writers*, 1959, ii 463).

*19–20.* Alluding to the controversy about the value and loyalty of Canada in 1872; cp. *Idylls: To the Queen* 14–17*n* (p. 1755).
*23–4*] *1885*; *as ll. 11–12, 1882.*

I

Roman Virgil, thou that singest
Ilion's lofty temples robed in fire,
Ilion falling, Rome arising,
wars, and filial faith, and Dido's pyre;

II

Landscape-lover, lord of language
more than he that sang the Works and Days,
All the chosen coin of fancy
flashing out from many a golden phrase;

III

Thou that singest wheat and woodland,
tilth and vineyard, hive and horse and herd;
All the charm of all the Muses
often flowering in a lonely word;

IV

Poet of the happy Tityrus
piping underneath his beechen bowers;
Poet of the poet-satyr
whom the laughing shepherd bound with flowers;

V

Chanter of the Pollio, glorying
in the blissful years again to be,
Summers of the snakeless meadow,
unlaborious earth and oarless sea;

¶394. *1–2. Aeneid*: 'temples', Book ii; Dido, iv; 'faith', vi.
*3. he*: Hesiod, Virgil's predecessor in writing of rural life.
*5. Georgics*, as summarized at i 1–5: *Quid faciat laetas segetes, quo sidere terram . . . .*
*7. Eclogue* i 1: *Tityre, tu patulae recubans sub tegmine fagi.* ('You, Tityrus, lie under your spreading beech's covert.')
*8.* Silenus, seized in *Eclogue* vi 19: *iniciunt ipsis ex vincula sertis.* ('They cast him into fetters made from his own garlands.')
*9. Eclogue* iv, prophetic of a golden age, often taken as anticipating the birth of Christ.
*10. Eclogue* iv: *occidet et serpens* (24); *At tibi prima, puer, mullo munuscula cultu / errantis hederas passim cum baccare tellus . . .* (18–19: 'But for thee, child, shall the earth untilled pour forth, as her first pretty gifts, straggling ivy with foxglove everywhere'); *cedet et ipse mari vector* (38: 'even the trader shall quit the sea').

VI

Thou that seëst Universal
Nature moved by Universal Mind;
Thou majestic in thy sadness
at the doubtful doom of human kind;

VII

Light among the vanished ages;
star that gildest yet this phantom shore;
Golden branch amid the shadows,
kings and realms that pass to rise no more;

VIII

Now thy Forum roars no longer,
fallen every purple Cæsar's dome–
Though thine ocean-roll of rhythm
sound for ever of Imperial Rome–

IX

Now the Rome of slaves hath perished,
and the Rome of freemen holds her place,
I, from out the Northern Island
sundered once from all the human race,

X

I salute thee, Mantovano,
I that loved thee since my day began,
Wielder of the stateliest measure
ever moulded by the lips of man.

# 395 The Throstle

Published *New Review*, Oct. 1889; then *1889*. H.T. says that *NR* 'misprinted' it; T.'s letter to the editor (*Lincoln*) says that Gosse, who 'asked me to let him have a poem for' *NR*, was responsible for the errors. This

*11. Aeneid* vi 727: *mens agitat molem* ('mind sways the mass').
*12. Aeneid* i 462: *sunt lacrimae rerum et mentem mortalia tangunt* ('there are tears for misfortune and mortal sorrows touch the heart').
*14.* Praising Virgil as himself the golden bough that gives mysterious access to the underworld, *Aeneid* vi 208.
*15. purple Cæsar*: Horace's *Odes* I xxxv 12: *purpurei tyranni.*
*18.* H.T. cited *Eclogue* i 66: *et penitus toto divisos orbe Britannos* ('and the Britons, wholly sundered from all the world').
*19. Mantovano:* Mantuan. H.T. cited Dante, *Purgatorio* vi 74: *Mantovano,* which allows T. to join Dante in venerating Virgil.

is supported by T.'s pamphlet issue of May 1889. Composition: 'toward the end of Feb. [1889] ... finishing his song ..., which had been begun in the same garden years ago' (H.T.). H.T.'s transcript, *H.Nbk 66*, ends: 'From St James Nov 23/'82'.

'Summer is coming, summer is coming.
I know it, I know it, I know it.
Light again, leaf again, life again, love again,'
Yes, my wild little Poet.

Sing the new year in under the blue.
Last year you sang it as gladly.
'New, new, new, new'! Is it then *so* new
That you should carol so madly?

'Love again, song again, nest again, young again,'
Never a prophet so crazy!
And hardly a daisy as yet, little friend,
See, there is hardly a daisy.

'Here again, here, here, here, happy year'!
O warble unchidden, unbidden!
Summer is coming, is coming, my dear,
And all the winters are hidden.

# 396 Early Spring [1883]

Published *Youth's Companion* (Boston), 13 Dec. 1883; then *1885*. 'An early poem, slightly altered' (H.T.). For the 1833 version, see p. 496. T. now omitted five stanzas, added stanzas ii–iv, viii, and revised and re-arranged the others. The letter sending the poem to Boston is dated 12 March 1883. There is a draft in T.'s late hand in the *University of London Library*; all variants are below. The late version is entitled *February* in *H.Lpr 227*.

I

Once more the Heavenly Power
Makes all things new,
And domes the red-plowed hills
With loving blue;

¶395. *8. should*] *Not NR* (*see headnote*).
*13. here,*] *Not NR* (*see headnote*).
¶396. *3. And domes the*] Bows over *1833*.
*4. With*] The *1833*.

The blackbirds have their wills,
The throstles too.

II

Opens a door in Heaven;
From skies of glass
A Jacob's ladder falls
On greening grass,
And o'er the mountain-walls
Young angels pass.

III

Before them fleets the shower,
And burst the buds,
And shine the level lands,
And flash the floods;
The stars are from their hands
Flung through the woods,

IV

The woods with living airs
How softly fanned,
Light airs from where the deep,
All down the sand,
Is breathing in his sleep,
Heard by the land.

V

O follow, leaping blood,
The season's lure!
O heart, look down and up
Serene, secure,
Warm as the crocus cup,
Like snowdrops, pure!

VI

Past, Future glimpse and fade
Through some slight spell,

7–24] *Not 1833; but ll. 7–12 are deleted in the draft in T.Nbk 17 (1833).*
9–10, 11–12] *Transposed London MS, with l. 11* Athwart . . . .
13–18] *Not London MS.*
19. *The*] O *London MS. with*] *1885*; by *1883*.
20. *softly*] *1885*; freshly *1883*; gently *London MS.*
25] My leaping blood obeys *1833*.
27. *O heart, look*] My heart looks *1833*.
31. *glimpse and fade*] sparkle linkt *1833*.
32. *Through some slight*] By some light *1833*.

A gleam from yonder vale,
    Some far blue fell,
And sympathies, how frail,
    In sound and smell!

VII

Till at thy chuckled note,
    Thou twinkling bird,
The fairy fancies range,
    And, lightly stirred,
Ring little bells of change
    From word to word.

VIII

For now the Heavenly Power
    Makes all things new,
And thaws the cold, and fills
    The flower with dew;
The blackbirds have their wills,
    The poets too.

## 397 Epitaph on Caxton

### IN ST MARGARET'S, WESTMINSTER

Published *1885*. Written for a painted window at the request of F. W. Farrar, who suggested that it should turn on *Fiat Lux* (*Life of Farrar*, 1904, p. 226). Farrar wrote to H.T., 7 May 1883: 'I hardly ventured to hope that he would be able to give thought to so difficult a matter as a quatrain on Caxton. I am delighted with [it]' (*Lincoln*). William Caxton was the first English printer. 'With the exception of that on Sir John Franklin . . . he thought this the best of his epitaphs' (H.T.). Cp. *2 Peter* i 19: 'We have also a more sure word of prophecy . . . as unto a light that shineth in a dark place, until the day dawn, and the day star arise in your hearts.'

*33. A*] *1885*; Some *1883*, *London MS*.
*33–5*] Charms, touches, mysteries
    Words may not tell,
Faint, fragile sympathies *1833*
*37. Till at*] Hearing *1833*.
*38. Thou*] O *1833*.
*39. The fairy*] My tricksy *1833*.
*43. For now*] Once more *London MS 1st reading*.
*43–8*] *Not 1833*.
*45. thaws the cold*] melts the rime *London MS*.

*Fiat Lux* (*his motto*).

Thy prayer was 'Light–more Light–while Time
shall last!'
Thou sawest a glory growing on the night,
But not the shadows which that light would cast,
Till shadows vanish in the Light of Light.

## 398 To E. FitzGerald

Published *1885*, introducing *Tiresias* (p. 568). Written *c.* June 1883; Edward FitzGerald died 14 June, and T. wrote to Frederick Pollock: 'I had written a poem to him the last week, which he will never see' (A. M. Terhune, *Life of FitzGerald*, 1947, p. 344). T. therefore concluded *Tiresias* by returning to FitzGerald and mourning his death (below). The poem, one of the finest of T.'s epistles, recalls the last visit by T. and H.T. to FitzGerald in Sept. 1876, as H.T. points out. For T.'s change of conception, see ll. 50–6*n* (*H.Nbk 46*).

Old Fitz, who from your suburb grange,
Where once I tarried for a while,
Glance at the wheeling Orb of change,
And greet it with a kindly smile;
Whom yet I see as there you sit
Beneath your sheltering garden-tree,
And while your doves about you flit,
And plant on shoulder, hand and knee,
Or on your head their rosy feet,
As if they knew your diet spares
Whatever moved in that full sheet
Let down to Peter at his prayers;
Who live on milk and meal and grass;
And once for ten long weeks I tried
Your table of Pythagoras,
And seemed at first 'a thing enskied'

¶397. *2.* Cp. *The Making of Man 6*: 'a glory slowly gaining on the shade'.

¶398. *1. grange*: FitzGerald's home, Little Grange, Woodbridge, Suffolk.

*3. the wheeling Orb*: as in *On golden evenings* (*1827*), by T.'s brother Charles.

*11–12. Acts* x 11–13: 'And a certain vessel descending unto him, as it had been a great sheet knit at the four corners, and let down to the earth: Wherein were all manner of four-footed beasts of the earth, and wild beasts, and creeping things, and fowls of the air. And there came a voice to him, Rise, Peter: kill, and eat.'

*15.* Pythagoras's vegetarianism is connected with the belief that the transmigration of souls included animals.

(As Shakespeare has it) airy-light
    To float above the ways of men,
Then fell from that half-spiritual height
    Chilled, till I tasted flesh again
One night when earth was winter-black,
    And all the heavens flashed in frost;
And on me, half-asleep, came back
    That wholesome heat the blood had lost,
And set me climbing icy capes
    And glaciers, over which there rolled
To meet me long-armed vines with grapes
    Of Eshcol hugeness; for the cold
Without, and warmth within me, wrought
    To mould the dream; but none can say
That Lenten fare makes Lenten thought,
    Who reads your golden Eastern lay,
Than which I know no version done
    In English more divinely well;
A planet equal to the sun
    Which cast it, that large infidel
Your Omar; and your Omar drew
    Full-handed plaudits from our best
In modern letters, and from two,
    Old friends outvaluing all the rest,
Two voices heard on earth no more;
    But we old friends are still alive,
And I am nearing seventy-four,
    While you have touched at seventy-five,

*16. Measure for Measure* I iv 34–5: 'I hold you as a thing enskied and sainted / By your renouncement–an immortal spirit.' 'Renouncement' (Isabella's nunhood) calls out the allusion, which leads into ll. 18–19.
*23–8.* 'One of the most wonderful experiences I ever had was this. I had gone without meat for six weeks, living only on vegetables; and at the end of the time, when I came to eat a mutton-chop, I shall never forget the sensation. I never felt such joy in my blood. When I went to sleep, I dreamt that I saw the vines of the South, with huge Eschol branches, trailing over the glaciers of the North' (*Mem.* ii 317).
*28. Numbers* xiii 23: 'And they came unto the brook of Eshcol, and cut down from thence a branch with one cluster of grapes, and they bare it between two upon a staff' (Eshcol, meaning 'a cluster of grapes').
*32. The Rubáiyát of Omar Khayyám*, published 1859 and subsequently revised.
*41.* James Spedding, died 1881; and W. H. Brookfield, died 1874.
*43–5.* A Horatian touch; cp. *Epistles* I xx 27: *me quater undenos sciat implevisse Decembris* ('let him know that I completed my forty-fourth

And so I send a birthday line
Of greeting; and my son, who dipt
In some forgotten book of mine
With sallow scraps of manuscript,
And dating many a year ago,
Has hit on this, which you will take
My Fitz, and welcome, as I know
Less for its own than for the sake
Of one recalling gracious times,

December in . . .'). T. would be 74 on 6 Aug. 1883; since FitzGerald was born 31 March 1809 and died 14 June 1883, he never 'touched at seventy-five', nor are these two ages compatible. Probably T. thought that FitzGerald was 75 in March 1883, and his 'birthday greeting' was going to be a month or two late. The confusion is unimportant except in its possible bearing on the date of the poem. T.'s lines resemble Peacock's *Letter to Lord Broughton*, a copy of which is among T.'s papers (*Lincoln*): 'Old friend, whose rhymes so kindly mix / Thoughts grave and gay with seventy-six, / I hope it may to you be given / To do the same at seventy-seven; / Whence your still living friends may date / A new good wish for seventy-eight; / And thence again extend the line, / Until it passes seventy-nine.'

*45–6*]
At seventy-five! I asked a friend
What I should send you on the day
When you were born. He answered, 'Send
Bound in the sumptuousest way
Your books'–'He knows them line by line'–
'Well then, send this', for he had dipt
*H.Nbk 46 1st draft*

*49. many a*] forty *MS 1st reading.*
*50. this: Tiresias.*
*50–6*] *There are many fragmentary drafts in MS:*

(i)
And found these lines, which you will take,
Old Fitz, and value, as I know,
Less for their own than for my sake,
Who love you,
Yours

(ii) *includes as ll. 53–4:*
Of me remembering gracious times,
Who keep the love of older days.

(iii)
Has hit on this, which you will take,
My Fitz, and welcome, as I know,
Less for its own, than for my sake,
Who love you always.
Ah if I

When, in our younger London days,
You found some merit in my rhymes,
And I more pleasure in your praise.

---

'One height and one far-shining fire'
And while I fancied that my friend
For this brief idyll would require
A less diffuse and opulent end,
And would defend his judgment well,
If I should deem it over nice–
The tolling of his funeral bell
Broke on my Pagan Paradise,

---

Should play Tiresias to the times,
I fear I might but prophesy
Of faded faiths, and civic crimes,
And fierce Transition's blood-red morn,
And years with lawless voices loud,
Old vessels from their moorings torn,
And cataclysm and thundercloud,
And one lean hope, that at the last
Perchance–if this small world endures–
Our heirs may find the stormy Past
Has left their Present purer.
Yours

*An earlier draft of the last four lines reads*:
And yet if our poor earth should last,
And evolution still endures,
Our heirs may find that stormy Past
True mother of their Present.
Yours

T. and FitzGerald had been friends since about 1835. Cp. FitzGerald's letter of 1862: 'You can't remember this: in old Charlotte Street, ages ago' (*Tennyson and His Friends*, p. 130). The passage of political prophecy in (iii) links the dedication and *Tiresias* itself (cp. *Tiresias* 71–5), but T. must have decided that its fierceness and lack of connection with FitzGerald would obtrude.

57. From the closing line of *Tiresias* (p. 574), which followed l. 56 in *1885*.

64 ^ 5] And drove the shadows far apart
With echoes of our College hall–
Old voices. Hushed the loyal heart,
The wit, truth, delicate humour, all. *MS, deleted*

This *MS* also has a deleted passage that continues from l. 80:

And mixt the dreams of classic times,
  And all the phantoms of the dream,
With present grief, and made the rhymes,
  That missed his living welcome, seem
Like would-be guests an hour too late,
  Who down the highway moving on
With easy laughter find the gate
  Is bolted, and the master gone.
Gone into darkness, that full light
  Of friendship! past, in sleep, away
By night, into the deeper night!
  The deeper night? A clearer day
Than our poor twilight dawn on earth–
  If night, what barren toil to be!
What life, so maimed by night, were worth
  Our living out? Not mine to me
Remembering all the golden hours
  Now silent, and so many dead,
And him the last; and laying flowers,
  This wreath, above his honoured head,
And praying that, when I from hence
  Shall fade with him into the unknown,
My close of earth's experience
  May prove as peaceful as his own.

[1883. *Prologue* and *Epilogue* to *The Charge of the Heavy Brigade*– see pp. 1304–1307]

# 399 Poets and their Bibliographies

Published *1885*. The title was added in 1888. T. ran through many titles: *Book-making* (*Lincoln* trial edition of *1885*); *Old Poets*; *On publishing every discarded scrap of a Poet*; *Poets and Bibliophils* (another *Lincoln* trial edition). A matter that often irritated T., but he may have thought in particular of R. H. Shepherd, who tried to reprint T.'s early poems, and whose *Tennysoniana* (2nd edn, 1879) caused T. reluctantly to print, in 1884, *Lines on Cambridge*. The present poem immediately precedes those *Lines* in *H.Nbk 47*, apparently dating from *c.* 1883 at this point. William Allingham: 'Put last now (it was first) is a Sonnet against raking together and publishing the fragments of a deceased Poet' (*Diary*, 1907, p. 344; 6 Nov. 1885).

Who, sorrowing, send you, to be laid
  Upon your coffin, flowers, a sign
You flower in me and will not fade
  While my few years on earth are mine.

The poem is the first in the *British Museum* trial edition. It cost T. some difficulty, as is clear from the MS, from this trial edition, and from one at *Lincoln*.

Old poets fostered under friendlier skies,
Old Virgil who would write ten lines, they say,
At dawn, and lavish all the golden day
To make them wealthier in his readers' eyes;
And you, old popular Horace, you the wise
Adviser of the nine-years-pondered lay,
And you, that wear a wreath of sweeter bay,
Catullus, whose dead songster never dies;
If, glancing downward on the kindly sphere
That once had rolled you round and round the Sun,
You see your Art still shrined in human shelves,
You should be jubilant that you flourished here
Before the Love of Letters, overdone,
Had swampt the sacred poets with themselves.

# 400 The Dead Prophet

182–

Published *1885*. Written 1882–4, judging from MSS in *H.Nbks 52* and *68*, and from its probably being occasioned by J. A. Froude's frank revelations about Carlyle's private life (1882–4). T. said it was 'about no particular prophet', but H.T.'s note goes on: 'At this time he said of Mr and Mrs Carlyle: "I am sure that Froude is wrong. I saw a great deal of them. They were always 'chaffing' one another, and they could not have done that if they had got on so 'badly together' as Froude thinks."' Froude's Preface (1882) had spoken of Carlyle as a 'teacher and a prophet in the Jewish sense of the word', and in 1884 his introductory note described Carlyle as 'a man who could thus take on himself the character of a prophet'. Cp. the beldam's argument in ll. 44–56 with Froude:

'When a man has exercised a large influence on the minds of his contemporaries, the world requires to know whether his own actions have corresponded with his teaching, and whether his moral and personal character entitles him to confidence. This is not idle curiosity; it is a legitimate demand. In proportion to a man's greatness is the scrutiny to which his conduct is submitted.'

¶399. *5–6. Ars Poetica* 386–90.
*8.* Catullus iii, on Lesbia's sparrow.

Froude's introductory note spoke too of vague biographies as leaving great men 'a prey to be torn in pieces'. Moreover M. D. Conway (who himself had preceded Froude with a study of Carlyle) wrote of this controversy: 'Tennyson's main trouble seemed to be that the bones of Carlyle should be flung about' (*Autobiography*, 1904, ii 192)–note the metaphor. Froude protested, 20 March 1882, at T.'s having said Froude 'had sold [his] Master for thirty pieces of silver'; H.T. placated him, denying the rumour since T. had said no more than that 'it would have been better if you had omitted 3 or 4 pages' (*Lincoln*).

The poem does not appear in No. 1 of the *British Museum* trial editions of *1885*. No. 2 followed the poem with *By a Darwinian* (p. 1227), entitled *Reversion*, which is on the same subject. The fact that *Reversion* was, in this trial edition, on the same page is probably due to the printer; in the earlier trial edition (*Lincoln*), *Reversion* is in MS on the verso of the last page of the MS of *The Dead Prophet*. No. 3 added the note: 'It may be as well to state that this allegory is not in any way personal. The speaker in it is as imaginary as the prophet'. The false date '182–' does not appear in the *BM* trial editions; when T. first added a date to a *Lincoln* trial edition, he put '17—'. (Like *Aylmer's Field*, '1793', this suggests the French Revolution.) Cp. the veiling of *To ——, After Reading a Life and Letters* (p. 846), which is on the same theme of the intrusive biography, and which includes the germ of *The Dead Prophet*: 'For whom the carrion vulture waits / To tear his heart before the crowd!' Since this was about Keats, '182–' may have been suggested by Keats's death (1821). Cp. also T.'s poem of *1827*, *Come hither* (p. 152), on the mocked corpse of Henri IV: 'There came a woman from the crowd and smote / The corpse upon the cheek.' (See l. 25*n*.) Since *Come hither* is about the French Revolution, by 1882 it might have come to suggest Carlyle. T.'s source for *Come hither* (*Quarterly Review* xxi (1819) 376) included: 'When the King is dead, his body was placed upon a carriage in such a position that the head hung down to the ground and the hair dragged upon the ground; a woman followed and with a besom threw dust upon the head of the corpse. At the same time, a cryer proclaimed, with a loud voice, O men! behold your King! he was your master yesterday, but the empire which he possessed is passed away.' Cp. also the MS versions of *Locksley Hall Sixty* 134: 'Pillory the dead face ...', 'Pillory the dumb corpse ...' A *Lincoln* trial edition added as epigraph (slightly misquoted) *Henry V* IV i 229–31: 'O hard condition, / Twin-born with greatness, subject to the breath / Of every fool.'

I

Dead!
And the Muses cried with a stormy cry
'Send them no more, for evermore.
Let the people die.'

¶400. *1*] There lay a prophet [dead man *1st reading*] on the heath, *H.Nbk 68.*

II

Dead!
 'Is it *he* then brought so low?'
And a careless people flocked from the fields
 With a purse to pay for the show.

III

Dead, who had served his time,
 Was one of the people's kings,
Had laboured in lifting them out of slime,
 And showing them, souls have wings!

IV

Dumb on the winter heath he lay.
 His friends had stript him bare,
And rolled his nakedness everyway
 That all the crowd might stare.

V

A storm-worn signpost not to be read,
 And a tree with a mouldered nest
On its barkless bones, stood stark by the dead;
 And behind him, low in the West,

VI

With shifting ladders of shadow and light,
 And blurred in colour and form,
The sun hung over the gates of Night,
 And glared at a coming storm.

VII

Then glided a vulturous Beldam forth,
 That on dumb death had thriven;
They called her 'Reverence' here upon earth,
 And 'The Curse of the Prophet' in Heaven.

VIII

She knelt—'We worship him'—all but wept—
 'So great so noble was he!'

5–12] A prophet dead upon the heath *MS*.
*14. friends had*] best friend *MS*. The MS points to Froude.
15] Tore all the decent coverings off *MS*.
*17–24*] *Not MS*.
25] There came a beldam from the crowd *MS*. Cp. 'There came a woman from the crowd', *Come hither* 21. See headnote.
*26. dumb death*] dead flesh *MS*.
*27. here*] *Not MS*.
*29–68*] *Not MS*.

She cleared her sight, she arose, she swept
  The dust of earth from her knee.

IX

'Great! for he spoke and the people heard,
  And his eloquence caught like a flame
From zone to zone of the world, till his Word
  Had won him a noble name.

X

Noble! he sung, and the sweet sound ran
  Through palace and cottage door,
For he touched on the whole sad planet of man,
  The kings and the rich and the poor;

XI

And he sung not alone of an old sun set,
  But a sun coming up in his youth!
Great and noble–O yes–but yet–
  For man is a lover of Truth,

XII

And bound to follow, wherever she go
  Stark-naked, and up or down,
Through her high hill-passes of stainless snow,
  Or the foulest sewer of the town–

XIII

Noble and great–O ay–but then,
  Though a prophet should have his due,
Was he noblier-fashioned than other men?
  Shall we see to it, I and you?

XIV

For since he would sit on a Prophet's seat,
  As a lord of the Human soul,
We needs must scan him from head to feet
  Were it but for a wart or a mole?'

54] And preached of a deathless soul *H.Nbk 52 1st reading*. This MS has pages missing, and consists only of ll. 49–56, plus:

He found his truth in an old shadow-land,
  In a ghost-tale told us afresh.
We prize a truth that is closer at hand,
  The truth, my friends, in the flesh.'

And one of the people arose with a frown,
  'Will you help the people to be
By pulling the people's leaders down
  To the people's level?' but she,

XV

His wife and his child stood by him in tears,
But she–she pushed them aside.
'Though a name may last for a thousand years,
Yet a truth is a truth,' she cried.

XVI

And she that had haunted his pathway still,
Had often truckled and cowered
When he rose in his wrath, and had yielded her will
To the master, as overpowered,

XVII

She tumbled his helpless corpse about.
'Small blemish upon the skin!
But I think we know what is fair without
Is often as foul within.'

XVIII

She crouched, she tore him part from part,
And out of his body she drew
The red 'Blood-eagle' of liver and heart;
She held them up to the view;

XIX

She gabbled, as she groped in the dead,
And all the people were pleased;
'See, what a little heart,' she said,
'And the liver is half-diseased!'

XX

She tore the Prophet after death,
And the people paid her well.
Lightnings flickered along the heath;
One shrieked 'The fires of Hell!'

*69*] She tore the Prophet's hidden part *Nbk 68.*

*71. Blood-eagle*: *1885* note: 'Old Viking term for lungs, liver, etc., when torn by the conqueror out of the body of the conquered.'

*73*] Her talons raked into the dead *MS.*

*76 ^ 7*] 'The People! the People!' a thin ghost-cry
Fled over the blasted tree,
Far away to be lost in a stormy sky,
'I had lifted them up:' but she, *BM trial edition 2*

*80*] They were the fires of Hell. *MS.* Perhaps suggested by Froude's introductory note: 'The fire in his soul burnt red to the end, and sparks flew from it which fell hot on those about him.'

# 401 The Spinster's Sweet-Arts

Published *1885*. Written by 18 Jan. 1884 (E. Rawnsley, *Canon Rawnsley*, 1923, p. 93). It is in *H.Nbk 50*, which suggests 1882–4. The subject, an old woman talking to her cats, was suggested by H.T. (W. F. Rawnsley, *Nineteenth Century* xcvii (1925) 9). Cp. the other Lincolnshire poems.

I

Milk for my sweet-arts, Bess! fur it mun be the time about now
When Molly cooms in fro' the far-end close wi' her paäils fro' the cow.
Eh! tha be new to the plaäce–thou'rt gaäpin'–doesn't tha see
I calls 'em arter the fellers es once was sweet upo' me?

II

Naäy to be sewer it be past 'er time. What maäkes 'er sa laäte?
Goä to the laäne at the back, an' looök thruf Maddison's gaäte!

III

Sweet-arts! Molly belike may 'a lighted tonight upo' one.
Sweet-arts! thanks to the Lord that I niver not listened to noän!
So I sits i' my oän armchair wi' my oän kettle theere o' the hob,
An' Tommy the fust, an' Tommy the second, an' Steevie an' Rob.

IV

Rob, coom oop 'ere o' my knee. Thou sees that i' spite o' the men
I 'a kep' thruf thick an' thin my two 'oonderd a-year to mysen;
Yis! thaw tha called me es pretty es ony lass i' the Shere;
An' thou be es pretty a Tabby, but Robby I seed thruf ya theere.

V

Feyther 'ud saäy I wur ugly es sin, an' I beänt not vaäin,
But I niver wur downright hugly, thaw soom 'ud 'a thowt ma plaäin,
An' I wasn't sa plaäin i' pink ribbons, ye said I wur pretty i' pinks,
An' I liked to 'ear it I did, but I beänt sich a fool as ye thinks;
Ye was stroäkin ma down wi' the 'air, as I be a-stroäkin o' you,
But whiniver I looöked i' the glass I wur sewer that it couldn't be true;
Niver wur pretty, not I, but ye knawed it wur pleasant to 'ear,
Thaw it warn't not me es wur pretty, but my two 'oonderd a-year.

VI

D'ya mind the murnin' when we was a-walkin' togither, an' stood
By the claäyed-oop pond, that the foälk be sa scared at, i' Gigglesby
    wood,
Wheer the poor wench drowndid hersen, black Sal, es 'ed been
    disgraäced?
An' I feeled thy arm es I stood wur a-creeäpin about my waäist;
An' me es wur allus afeared of a man's gittin' ower fond,
I sidled awaäy an' awaäy till I plumpt foot fust i' the pond;

¶401. *6*. George Maddison was a family friend in Lincolnshire (*Tennyson and His Friends*, p. 22).

And, Robby, I niver 'a liked tha sa well, as I did that daäy,
Fur tha joompt in thysen, an' tha hoickt my feet wi' a flop fro' the claäy.
Ay, stick oop thy back, an' set oop thy taäil, tha may gie ma a kiss,
Fur I walked wi' tha all the way hoam an' wur niver sa nigh saäyin' Yis.
But wa boäth was i' sich a clat we was shaämed to cross Gigglesby Greeän,
Fur a cat may looök at a king thou knaws but the cat mun be cleän.
Sa we boäth on us kep out o' sight o' the winders o' Gigglesby Hinn–
Naäy, but the claws o' tha! quiet! they pricks cleän thruf to the skin–
An' wa boäth slinkt 'oäm by the brokken shed i' the laäne at the back,
Wheer the poodle runned at tha once, an' thou runned oop o' the thack;
An' tha squeedged my 'and i' the shed, fur theere we was forced to 'ide,
Fur I seed that Steevie wur coomin', and one o' the Tommies beside.

VII

Theere now, what art'a mewin at, Steevie? for owt I can tell–
Robby wur fust to be sewer, or I mowt 'a liked tha as well.

VIII

But, Robby, I thowt o' tha all the while I wur chaängin' my gown,
An' I thowt shall I chaänge my staäte? but, O Lord, upo' coomin' down–
My bran-new carpet es fresh es a midder o' flowers i' Maäy–
Why 'edn't tha wiped thy shoes? it wur clatted all ower wi' claäy.
An' I could 'a cried ammost, fur I seed that it couldn't be,
An' Robby I gied tha a raätin that sattled thy coortin o' me.
An' Molly an' me was agreed, as we was a-cleänin' the floor,
That a man be a durty thing an' a trouble an' plague wi' indoor.
But I rued it arter a bit, fur I stuck to tha moor na the rest,
But I couldn't 'a lived wi' a man an' I knaws it be all fur the best.

IX

Naäy–let ma stroäk tha down till I maäkes tha es smooth es silk,
But if I 'ed married tha, Robby, thou'd not 'a been worth thy milk,
Thou'd niver 'a cotched ony mice but 'a left me the work to do,
And 'a taäen to the bottle beside, so es all that I 'ears be true;
But I loovs tha to maäke thysen 'appy, an' soa purr awaäy, my dear,
Thou 'ed wellnigh purred ma awaäy fro' my oän two 'oonderd a-year.

X

Sweärin agean, you Toms, as ye used to do twelve year sin'!
Ye niver 'eärd Steevie sweär 'cep' it wur at a dog coomin' in,
An' boath o' ye mun be fools to be hallus a-shawin' your claws,
Fur I niver cared nothink for neither–an' one o' ye deäd ye knaws!
Coom give hoäver then, weant ye? I warrant ye soom fine daäy–
Theere, lig down–I shall hev to gie one or tother awaäy.
Can't ye taäke pattern by Steevie? ye shant hev a drop fro' the paäil.
Steevie be right good manners bang thruf to the tip o' the taäil.

XI

Robby, git down wi'tha, wilt tha? let Steevie coom oop o' my knee.
Steevie, my lad, thou 'ed very nigh been the Steevie fur me!
Robby wur fust to be sewer, 'e wur burn an' bred i' the 'ouse,
But thou be es 'ansom a tabby es iver patted a mouse.

XII

An' I beänt not vaäin, but I knaws I 'ed led tha a quieter life
Nor her wi' the hepitaph yonder! 'A faäithful an' loovin' wife!'
An' 'cos o' thy farm by the beck, an' thy windmill oop o' the croft,
Tha thowt tha would marry ma, did tha? but that wur a bit ower soft,
Thaw thou was es soäber es daäy, wi' a niced red faäce, an' es cleän
Es a shillin' fresh fro' the mint wi' a bran-new 'eäd o' the Queeän,
An' thy farmin' es cleän es thysen, fur, Steevie, tha kep' it sa neät
That I niver not spied sa much es a poppy along wi' the wheät,
An' the wool of a thistle a-flyin' an' seeädin' tha haäted to see;
'Twur es bad es a battle-twig 'ere i' my oän blue chaumber to me.
Ay, roob thy whiskers ageän ma, fur I could 'a taäen to tha well,
But fur thy bairns, poor Steevie, a bouncin' boy an' a gell.

XIII

An' thou was es fond o' thy bairns es I be mysen o' my cats,
But I niver not wished fur childer, I hevn't naw likin' fur brats;
Pretty anew when ya dresses 'em oop, an' they goäs fur a walk,
Or sits wi' their 'ands afoor 'em, an' doesn't not 'inder the talk!
But their bottles o' pap, an' their mucky bibs, an' the clats an' the clouts,
An' their mashin' their toys to pieäces an' maäkin' ma deäf wi' their shouts,
An' hallus a-joompin' about ma as if they was set upo' springs,
An' a haxin' ma hawkard questions, an' saäyin' ondecent things,
An' a-callin' ma 'hugly' mayhap to my faäce, or a teärin' my gown –
Dear! dear! dear! I mun part them Tommies – Steevie git down.

XIV

Ye be wuss nor the men-tommies, you. I telled ya, na moor o' that!
Tom, lig theere o' the cushion, an' tother Tom 'ere o' the mat.

XV

Theere! I ha' mastered *them*! Hed I married the Tommies – O Lord,
To loove an' obaäy the Tommies! I couldn't 'a stuck by my word.
To be hordered about, an' waäked, when Molly 'd put out the light,
By a man coomin' in wi' a hiccup at ony hour o' the night!
An' the taäble staäined wi' 'is aäle, an' the mud o' 'is boots o' the stairs,
An' the stink o' 'is pipe i' the 'ouse, an' the mark o' 'is 'eäd o' the chairs!
An' noän o' my four sweet-arts 'ud 'a let me 'a hed my oän waäy,
Sa I likes 'em best wi' taäils when they 'evn't a word to saäy.

XVI

An' I sits i' my oän little parlour, an' sarved by my oän little lass,
Wi' my oän little garden outside, an' my oän bed o' sparrow-grass,

80. *battle-twig*: 'earwig' (T.).

An' my oän door-poorch wi' the woodbine an' jessmine a-dressin' it greeän,
An' my oän fine Jackman i' purple a roäbin' the 'ouse like a Queeän.

XVII

An' the little gells bobs to ma hoffens es I be abroad i' the laänes,
When I goäs fur to coomfut the poor es be down wi' their haäches an' their paäins:
An' a haäf-pot o' jam, or a mossel o' meät when it beänt too dear,
They maäkes ma a graäter Laädy nor 'er i' the mansion theer,
Hes 'es hallus to hax of a man how much to spare or to spend;
An' a spinster I be an' I will be, if soä pleäse God, to the hend.

XVIII

Mew! mew!–Bess wi' the milk! what ha maäde our Molly sa laäte?
It should 'a been 'ere by seven, an' theere–it be strikin' height–
'Cushie wur craäzed fur 'er cauf' well–I 'eärd 'er a maäkin' 'er moän,
An' I thowt to mysen 'thank God that I hevn't naw cauf o' my oän.'
Theere!
Set it down!
Now Robby!
You Tommies shall waäit tonight
Till Robby an' Steevie 'es 'ed their lap–an' it sarves ye right.

# 402 *Prince Leopold

## An Epitaph

Printed *Mem.* ii 437. Written March 1884, at the death of the Duke of Albany, and sent to Queen Victoria.

Early-wise, and pure, and true,
Prince, whose Father lived in you,
If you could speak, would you not say:
'I seem, but am not, far away;
Wherefore should your eyes be dim?
I am here again with him.
O Mother-Queen, and weeping Wife,
The Death for which you mourn is Life.'

# 403 Epitaph on Lord Stratford de Redcliffe

## In Westminster Abbey

Published *1885*. Written spring 1884; the statue to Stratford Canning, Ambassador at Constantinople (died 1880), was unveiled 24 May 1884.

*106. Jackman*: 'clematis Jackmanni' (T., *1913*).
¶402. *2. Father*: Prince Albert.

It does not appear in a trial edition of *1885* (*British Museum*). Working on it in spring 1884, T. said to H. D. Rawnsley: 'I hate doing this kind of thing ... but they bother one out of one's life if one refuses.' Rawnsley *Memories of the Tennysons*, 1900, pp. 94–6) says: 'He read me three alternatives for the epitaph he was engaged upon, and it was very interesting to hear him speak of the *pros* and *cons* of the word arrangements. The first began:

'De Redcliffe, now thy long day's work hath ceased,
Stand here among our noblest and our best.'

The second was like it [but transposing the lines]. And he was in doubt as to whether he should, in the second couplet, write:

'Silent, in this great minster of the West,
*Who wast* the voice of England in the East.'

or, 'Silent ... *But once* the voice ...'. He was not satisfied–the rhymes of the quatrain were too nearly akin; but he wished to emphasize the difference between West and East, and he risked the assonance.'

Thou third great Canning, stand among our best
And noblest, now thy long day's work hath ceased,
Here silent in our Minster of the West
Who wert the voice of England in the East.

# 404 Tomorrow

Published *1885*. It is with other poems of *1885* in *T.Nbk 32*, with the title *Molly Magee*. Written by July 1884, and subsequently revised (William Allingham's *Diary*, 1907, p. 324). T. told Allingham: '"I've done an Irish poem and I want you to help me with the brogue." ... Then he produced the MS of *Molly Maghee* (I asked him to strike out the "h"), and we spent about an hour over it. ... Aubrey de Vere gave him the subject, as a fact. ... The same incident is told of a Cornish miner, and I published a prose story upon it in Leigh Hunt's Journal' (on 18 Jan. 1851). The main source is undoubtedly de Vere, who 'had told him this story: "The body of a young man was laid out on the grass by the door of a Chapel in the West of Ireland, and an old woman came, and recognized it as that of her young lover, who had been lost in a peat bog many years before: the peat having kept him fresh and fair as when she last saw him"' (*Mem.* ii 319). On 18 Sept. 1883, T. and H.T. 'saw in their oak coffins ... human bodies which had been dug up out of the peat-bogs in Jutland' (*Mem.* ii 283). T. 'corrected his Irish from Carleton's admirable *Traits of the Irish*

¶403. *1.* George Canning (1770–1827), statesman; and Charles Canning (1812–62), Governor-General of India.
*2.* Cp. *A Dirge* 1: 'Now is done thy long day's work'.

*Peasantry'*. There is a copy of the second series (1877) at *Lincoln*. Cp. the poems in Lincolnshire dialect.

I

Her, that yer Honour was spakin' to? Whin, yer Honour? last year—
Standin' here be the bridge, when last yer Honour was here?
An' yer Honour ye gev her the top of the mornin', 'Tomorra' says she.
What did they call her, yer Honour? They called her Molly Magee.
An' yer Honour's the thrue ould blood that always manes to be kind,
But there's rason in all things, yer Honour, for Molly was out of her mind.

II

Shure, an' meself remimbers wan night comin' down be the sthrame,
An' it seems to me now like a bit of yisther-day in a dhrame—
Here where yer Honour seen her—there was but a slip of a moon,
But I hard thim—Molly Magee wid her batchelor, Danny O'Roon—
'You've been takin' a dhrop o' the crathur' an' Danny says 'Troth an' I been
Dhrinkin' yer health wid Shamus O'Shea at Katty's shebeen;
But I must be lavin' ye soon.' 'Ochone are ye goin' away?'
'Goin' to cut the Sassenach whate' he says 'over the say'—
'An' whin will ye meet me agin?' an' I hard him 'Molly asthore,
I'll meet you agin tomorra,' says he, 'be the chapel-door.'
'An' whin are ye goin' to lave me?' 'O' Monday mornin'' says he;
'An' shure thin ye'll meet me tomorra?' 'Tomorra, tomorra, Machree!'
Thin Molly's ould mother, yer Honour, that had no likin' for Dan,
Called from her cabin an' tould her to come away from the man,
An' Molly Magee kem flyin' acrass me, as light as a lark,
An' Dan stood there for a minute, and thin wint into the dark.
But wirrah! the storm that night—the tundher, an' rain that fell,
An' the sthrames runnin' down at the back o' the glin 'ud 'a dhrownded Hell.

III

But airth was at pace nixt mornin', an' Hiven in its glory smiled,
As the Holy Mother o' Glory that smiles at her sleepin' child—
Ethen—she stept an the chapel-green, an' she turned herself roun'
Wid a diamond dhrop in her eye, for Danny was not to be foun',
An' many's the time that I watched her at mass lettin' down the tear,
For the Divil a Danny was there, yer Honour, for forty year.

IV

Och, Molly Magee, wid the red o' the rose an' the white o' the May,
An' yer hair as black as the night, an' yer eyes as bright as the day!

¶404. *11. crathur*: liquor, especially whisky (Irish).
*12. shebeen*: *1885* note: 'Grog-shop'.
*14.* T. heard from Gladstone in 1883 about Irish labourers who 'crossed to the northern English counties to cut the "Sassenach's wheat"' (*Mem.* ii 274).
*15a. sthore*: dear.

Achora, yer laste little whishper was sweet as the lilt of a bird!
Acushla, ye set me heart batin' to music wid ivery word!
An' sorra the Queen wid her sceptre in sich an illigant han',
An' the fall of yer foot in the dance was as light as snow an the lan',
An' the sun kem out of a cloud whiniver ye walkt in the shtreet,
An' Shamus O'Shea was yer shadda, an' laid himself undher yer feet,
An' I loved ye meself wid a heart and a half, me darlin', and he
'Ud 'a shot his own sowl dead for a kiss of ye, Molly Magee.

V

But shure we wor betther frinds whin I cracked his skull for her sake,
An' he ped me back wid the best he could give at ould Donovan's wake–
For the boys wor about her agin whin Dan didn't come to the fore,
An' Shamus along wid the rest, but she put thim all to the door.
An', afther, I thried her meself av the bird 'ud come to me call,
But Molly, begorrah, 'ud listhen to naither at all, at all.

VI

An' her nabours an frinds 'ud consowl an' condowl wid her, airly and late,
'Your Danny,' they says, 'niver crasst over say to the Sassenach whate;
He's gone to the States, aroon, an' he's married another wife,
An' ye'll niver set eyes an the face of the thraithur agin in life!
An' to dhrame of a married man, death alive, is a mortial sin.'
But Molly says 'I'd his hand-promise, an' shure he'll meet me agin.'

VII

An' afther her paärints had intered glory, an' both in wan day,
She began to spake to herself, the crathur, an' whishper, an' say
'Tomorra, Tomorra!' an' Father Molowny he tuk her in han',
'Molly, you're manin',' he says, 'me dear, av I undherstan',
That ye'll meet your paärints agin an' yer Danny O'Roon afore God
Wid his blessèd Marthyrs an' Saints;' an' she gev him a frindly nod,
'Tomorra, Tomorra,' she says, an' she didn't intind to desave,
But her wits wor dead, an' her hair was as white as the snow an a grave.

VIII

Arrah now, here last month they wor diggin' the bog, an' they foun'
Dhrownded in black bog-wather a corp lyin' undher groun'.

IX

Yer Honour's own agint, he says to me wanst, at Katty's shebeen,
'The Divil take all the black lan', for a blessin' 'ud come wid the green!'
An' where 'ud the poor man, thin, cut his bit o' turf for the fire?
But och! bad scran to the bogs whin they swallies the man intire!
An' sorra the bog that's in Hiven wid all the light an' the glow,
An' there's hate enough, shure, widout *thim* in the Divil's kitchen below.

66. *scran*: luck.

X

Thim ould blind nagers in Agypt, I hard his Riverence say,
Could keep their haithen kings in the flesh for the Jidgemint day,
An', faix, be the piper o' Moses, they kep the cat an' the dog,
But it 'ud 'a been aisier work av they lived be an Irish bog.

XI

How-an-iver they laid this body they foun' an the grass
Be the chapel-door, an' the people 'ud see it that wint in to mass–
But a frish gineration had riz, an' most of the ould was few,
An' I didn't know him meself, an' nōne of the parish knew.

XII

But Molly kem limpin' up wid her stick, she was lamed iv a knee,
Thin a slip of a gossoon called, 'Div ye know him, Molly Magee?'
An' she stood up strait as the Queen of the world–she lifted her head–
'He said he would meet me tomorra!' an' dhropt down dead an the dead.

XIII

Och, Molly, we thought, machree, ye would start back agin into life,
Whin we laid yez, aich be aich, at yer wake like husban' an' wife.
Sorra the dhry eye thin but was wet for the frinds that was gone!
Sorra the silent throat but we hard it cryin' 'Ochone!'
An' Shamus O'Shea that has now ten childer, hansome an' tall,
Him an' his childer wor keenin' as if he had lost thim all.

XIV

Thin his Riverence buried thim both in wan grave be the dead boor-tree,
The young man Danny O'Roon wid his ould woman, Molly Magee.

XV

May all the flowers o' Jeroosilim blossom an' spring from the grass,
Imbrashin' an' kissin' aich other–as ye did–over yer Crass!
An' the lark fly out o' the flowers wid his song to the Sun an' the Moon,
An' tell thim in Hiven about Molly Magee an' her Danny O'Roon,
Till Holy St Pether gets up wid his kays an' opens the gate!
An' shure, be the Crass, that's betther nor cuttin' the Sassenach whate
To be there wid the Blessèd Mother, an' Saints an' Marthyrs galore,
An' singin' yer 'Aves' an' 'Pathers' for iver an' ivermore.

XVI

An' now that I tould yer Honour whativer I hard an' seen,
Yer Honour 'ill give me a thrifle to dhrink yer health in potheen.

# 405 The Wreck

Published *1885*. H.T. comments: 'The catastrophe which happened to an Italian vessel, named the *Rosina*, bound from Catania for New York, was the nucleus of the poem.' T. read of this in the *Pall Mall Gazette*, 8 Dec.

*87. boor-tree*: *1885* note: 'Elder-tree'.

1881 (*Mat.* iv 93); it provided no more than the fatal surge (l. 109) and the rescue (l. 121). Written 1883–4, judging from *H.Nbk 46* and *47* (where there is a long prose version of the poem). On 6 Nov. 1884, T. read a few lines from the MS (ll. 71–4) to the naturalist A. R. Wallace, questioning him about the accuracy of the tropical description (William Allingham's *Diary*, 1907, p. 334). Of ll. 81–2, T. says: 'This happened in the *Pembroke Castle* on our voyage to Copenhagen in [Sept.] 1883.' It is another of T.'s poems on the wickedness of the arranged marriage; cp., among others, *Aylmer's Field* (p. 1159), and *The Flight* (p. 657). T. never forgot Rosa Baring.

I

Hide me, Mother! my Fathers belonged to the church of old,
I am driven by storm and sin and death to the ancient fold,
I cling to the Catholic Cross once more, to the Faith that saves,
My brain is full of the crash of wrecks, and the roar of waves,
My life itself is a wreck, I have sullied a noble name,
I am flung from the rushing tide of the world as a waif of shame,
I am roused by the wail of a child, and awake to a livid light,
And a ghastlier face than ever has haunted a grave by night,
I would hide from the storm without, I would flee from the storm within,
I would make my life one prayer for a soul that died in his sin,
I was the tempter, Mother, and mine was the deeper fall;
I will sit at your feet, I will hide my face, I will tell you all.

II

He that they gave me to, Mother, a heedless and innocent bride–
I never have wronged his heart, I have only wounded his pride–
Spain in his blood and the Jew–dark-visaged, stately and tall–
A princelier-looking man never stept through a Prince's hall.
And who, when his anger was kindled, would venture to give him the nay?
And a man men fear is a man to be loved by the women they say.
And I could have loved him too, if the blossom can doat on the blight,
Or the young green leaf rejoice in the frost that sears it at night;
He would open the books that I prized, and toss them away with a yawn,
Repelled by the magnet of Art to the which my nature was drawn,
The word of the Poet by whom the deeps of the world are stirred,
The music that robes it in language beneath and beyond the word!

¶405. *7.* Cp. Henry Boyd's translation of Dante (1802, i 155): 'The waves roll pale beneath the livid light'. A copy of Boyd was at Somersby (*Lincoln*). In 1880, T. admired a painting of 'a shipwreck off the coast of Essex, lit up by a weird light' (*Mem.* ii 245).
*23.* The high notion of poetry which T. had shared with F. D. Maurice and the Cambridge 'Apostles'. Cp. Arthur Hallam, *Then what is Life* (Motter, p. 92): 'From his rent deeps / Of soul the Poet cast that burning word'. T. alluded to these lines in *In Memoriam* xcvi.

My Shelley would fall from my hands when he cast a contemptuous glance
From where he was poring over his Tables of Trade and Finance;
My hands, when I heard him coming would drop from the chords or the keys,
But ever I failed to please him, however I strove to please–
All day long far-off in the cloud of the city, and there
Lost, head and heart, in the chances of dividend, consol, and share–
And at home if I sought for a kindly caress, being woman and weak,
His formal kiss fell chill as a flake of snow on the cheek:
And so, when I bore him a girl, when I held it aloft in my joy,
He looked at it coldly, and said to me 'Pity it isn't a boy.'
The one thing given me, to love and to live for, glanced at in scorn!
The child that I felt I could die for–as if she were basely born!
I had lived a wild-flower life, I was planted now in a tomb;
The daisy will shut to the shadow, I closed my heart to the gloom;
I threw myself all abroad–I would play my part with the young
By the low foot-lights of the world–and I caught the wreath that was flung.

III

Mother, I have not–however their tongues may have babbled of me–
Sinned through an animal vileness, for all but a dwarf was he,
And all but a hunchback too; and I looked at him, first, askance,
With pity–not he the knight for an amorous girl's romance!
Though wealthy enough to have basked in the light of a dowerless smile,
Having lands at home and abroad in a rich West-Indian isle;
But I came on him once at a ball, the heart of a listening crowd–
Why, what a brow was there! he was seated–speaking aloud
To women, the flower of the time, and men at the helm of state–
Flowing with easy greatness and touching on all things great,
Science, philosophy, song–till I felt myself ready to weep
For I knew not what, when I heard that voice,–as mellow and deep
As a psalm by a mighty master and pealed from an organ,–roll
Rising and falling–for, Mother, the voice was the voice of the soul;
And the sun of the soul made day in the dark of his wonderful eyes.
Here was the hand that would help me, would heal me–the heart that was wise!
And he, poor man, when he learnt that I hated the ring I wore,
He helpt me with death, and he healed me with sorrow for evermore.

IV

For I broke the bond. That day my nurse had brought me the child.
The small sweet face was flushed, but it cooed to the Mother and smiled.
'Anything ailing,' I asked her, 'with baby?' She shook her head,
And the Motherless Mother kissed it, and turned in her haste and fled.

V

Low warm winds had gently breathed us away from the land–
Ten long sweet summer days upon deck, sitting hand in hand–

When he clothed a naked mind with the wisdom and wealth of his own,
And I bowed myself down as a slave to his intellectual throne,
When he coined into English gold some treasure of classical song,
When he flouted a statesman's error, or flamed at a public wrong,
When he rose as it were on the wings of an eagle beyond me, and past
Over the range and the change of the world from the first to the last,
When he spoke of his tropical home in the canes by the purple tide,
And the high star-crowns of his palms on the deep-wooded mountain-side,
And cliffs all robed in lianas that dropt to the brink of his bay,
And trees like the towers of a minster, the sons of a winterless day.
'Paradise there!' so he said, but I seemed in Paradise then
With the first great love I had felt for the first and greatest of men;
Ten long days of summer and sin–if it must be so–
But days of a larger light than I ever again shall know–
Days that will glimmer, I fear, through life to my latest breath;
'No frost there,' so he said, 'as in truest Love no Death.'

VI

Mother, one morning a bird with a warble plaintively sweet
Perched on the shrouds, and then fell fluttering down at my feet;
I took it, he made it a cage, we fondled it, Stephen and I,
But it died, and I thought of the child for a moment, I scarce know why.

VII

But if sin be sin, not inherited fate, as many will say,
My sin to my desolate little one found me at sea on a day,
When her orphan wail came borne in the shriek of a growing wind,
And a voice rang out in the thunders of Ocean and Heaven 'Thou hast sinned.'
And down in the cabin were we, for the towering crest of the tides
Plunged on the vessel and swept in a cataract off from her sides,
And ever the great storm grew with a howl and a hoot of the blast
In the rigging, voices of hell–then came the crash of the mast.
'The wages of sin is death,' and there I began to weep,
'I am the Jonah, the crew should cast me into the deep,
For ah God, what a heart was mine to forsake her even for you.'
'Never the heart among women,' he said, 'more tender and true.'
'The heart! not a mother's heart, when I left my darling alone.'
'Comfort yourself, for the heart of the father will care for his own.'
'The heart of the father will spurn her,' I cried, 'for the sin of the wife,
The cloud of the mother's shame will enfold her and darken her life.'
Then his pale face twitched; 'O Stephen, I love you, I love you, and yet'–
As I leaned away from his arms–'would God, we had never met!'

66. *intellectual throne*: associated with disillusion, as it had been in *The Palace of Art* 213–6: 'Full oft the riddle of the painful earth / Flashed through her as she sat alone, / Yet not the less held she her solemn mirth, / And intellectual throne.'

93. *there*] *1888*; then *1885*.

And he spoke not–only the storm; till after a little, I yearned
For his voice again, and he called to me 'Kiss me!' and there–as I turned–
'The heart, the heart!' I kissed him, I clung to the sinking form,
And the storm went roaring above us, and he–was out of the storm.

VIII

And then, then, Mother, the ship staggered under a thunderous shock,
That shook us asunder, as if she had struck and crashed on a rock;
For a huge sea smote every soul from the decks of The Falcon but one;
All of them, all but the man that was lashed to the helm had gone;
And I fell–and the storm and the days went by, but I knew no more–
Lost myself–lay like the dead by the dead on the cabin floor,
Dead to the death beside me, and lost to the loss that was mine,
With a dim dream, now and then, of a hand giving bread and wine,
Till I woke from the trance, and the ship stood still, and the skies were blue,
But the face I had known, O Mother, was not the face that I knew.

IX

The strange misfeaturing mask that I saw so amazed me, that I
Stumbled on deck, half mad. I would fling myself over and die!
But one–he was waving a flag–the one man left on the wreck–
'Woman'–he graspt at my arm–'stay there'–I crouched upon deck–
'We are sinking, and yet there's hope: look yonder,' he cried, 'a sail'
In a tone so rough that I broke into passionate tears, and the wail
Of a beaten babe, till I saw that a boat was nearing us–then
All on a sudden I thought, I shall look on the child again.

X

They lowered me down the side, and there in the boat I lay
With sad eyes fixt on the lost sea-home, as we glided away,
And I sighed, as the low dark hull dipt under the smiling main,
'Had I stayed with *him*, I had now–with *him*–been out of my pain.'

XI

They took us aboard: the crew were gentle, the captain kind;
But *I* was the lonely slave of an often-wandering mind;
For whenever a rougher gust might tumble a stormier wave,
'O Stephen,' I moaned, 'I am coming to thee in thine Ocean-grave.'
And again, when a balmier breeze curled over a peacefuller sea,
I found myself moaning again 'O child, I am coming to thee.'

XII

The broad white brow of the Isle–that bay with the coloured sand–
Rich was the rose of sunset there, as we drew to the land;
All so quiet the ripple would hardly blanch into spray
At the feet of the cliff; and I prayed–'my child'–for I still could pray–

*120. upon*] *1888*; on the *1885*.
*135.* 'Alum Bay in the Isle of Wight' (T.).

'May her life be as blissfully calm, be never gloomed by the curse
Of a sin, not hers!'
Was it well with the child?
I wrote to the nurse
Who had borne my flower on her hireling heart; and an answer came
Not from the nurse–nor yet to the wife–to her maiden name!
I shook as I opened the letter–I knew that hand too well–
And from it a scrap, clipt out of the 'deaths' in a paper, fell.
'Ten long sweet summer days' of fever, and want of care!
And gone–that day of the storm–O Mother, she came to me there.

# 406 *Compromise

Printed (apparently unauthorized) in *St James's Gazette*, 29 Oct. 1884, beginning 'Statesman . . .'; not reprinted, except *Mem.* ii 308. T. J. Wise's *Bibliography of Tennyson* (1908), i 337, gives publication as *Pall Mall Gazette* (15 Nov., signed John York Adams), but it does not appear there. It was addressed to Gladstone, at the height of the agitation about the Franchise Bill, and received by his daughter Mary, 5 Nov. (letter, *British Museum*). The phrase 'The Compromise' had appeared as the theme of countless editorials and arguments. For similar exhortations to Gladstone, cp. *Politics* (p. 1343) and *Captain, Guide* (p. 1803).

Steersman, be not precipitate in thine act
Of steering, for the river here, my friend,
Parts in two channels, moving to one end–
This goes straight forward to the cataract:
That streams about the bend;
But though the cataract seem the nearer way,
Whate'er the crowd on either bank may say,
Take thou the 'bend,' 'twill save thee many a day.

# 407 Freedom

Published *Macmillan's Magazine*, Dec. 1884, where it was dated '1884'; then *1885*. T.'s 'first political utterance as a peer' (*Mem.* ii 305); he took his seat in March. An early version (1833–4), of twenty lines, stands next to *Love thou thy land* in *T.Nbk 17* (which may not be quoted); this began with stanzas i–ii and ended with x, and it incorporated *Of old sat Freedom* 13–20.

¶406. *6.* T. 'said it was a cataract like those on the Nile (not precipitous)' (25 Nov. 1884; William Allingham's *Diary*, 1907, p. 336).

I

O thou so fair in summers gone,
While yet thy fresh and virgin soul
Informed the pillared Parthenon,
The glittering Capitol;

II

So fair in southern sunshine bathed,
But scarce of such majestic mien
As here with forehead vapour-swathed
In meadows ever green;

III

For thou – when Athens reigned and Rome,
Thy glorious eyes were dimmed with pain
To mark in many a freeman's home
The slave, the scourge, the chain;

IV

O follower of the Vision, still
In motion to the distant gleam,
Howe'er blind force and brainless will
May jar thy golden dream

V

Of Knowledge fusing class with class,
Of civic Hate no more to be,

¶407. *3. pillared*] *1885*; columned *1884* (*'misprinted'*, *T.*).
*13–14.* Cp. *Merlin and the Gleam* (p. 1412).
*17–20*] *1885*; *not 1884*;

Of more than Poet ever sung,
Of equal day from pole to pole,
A warless world, a single tongue,
One body, thou the soul; *Lincoln trial edition 1885*

These lines were added by hand in the trial edition, and then revised, adding ll. 17–20:

Of Knowledge fusing class with class,
Of civic Hatred stricken dumb,
Of Love that leavens all the mass,
Of all that vague To-come,
On Earth so old, but yet so young,
Of equal . . .

T. adapted these for *Locksley Hall Sixty* 165–6: 'Earth at last a warless world, a single race, a single tongue – / I have seen her far away – for is not Earth as yet so young? –'

Of Love to leaven all the mass,
Till every Soul be free;

VI

Who yet, like Nature, wouldst not mar
By changes all too fierce and fast
This order of Her Human Star,
This heritage of the past;

VII

O scorner of the party cry
That wanders from the public good,
Thou–when the nations rear on high
Their idol smeared with blood,

VIII

And when they roll their idol down–
Of saner worship sanely proud;
Thou loather of the lawless crown
As of the lawless crowd;

IX

How long thine ever-growing mind
Hath stilled the blast and strown the wave,
Though some of late would raise a wind
To sing thee to thy grave,

*21–4*] And knowest all the scrolls of Time,
And willest all good things to all,
But oft has seen that those who climb
A rungless ladder fall;

And fearest, halfway up the height
To lapse once more into the abysm,
When flickering party seems the light
Of sunlike patriotism. *trial edition*

These lines were added by hand to the trial edition, and the first stanza then revised to:

Who see'st so often that to climb
A rungless ladder is to fall;
And, from that slope of terraced Time
Attained to, watching all,

T. was to adapt this for the MS version of *Locksley Hall Sixty Years After* 130: 'I can tell them that to scale a rungless ladder is to fall' *H.Nbk 51*.
*21. Who yet, like*] *1885*; Who, like great *1884*; Like mighty *trial edition*.
*23. Her*] *1885*; our *1884*.

X

Men loud against all forms of power –
Unfurnished brows, tempestuous tongues –
Expecting all things in an hour –
Brass mouths and iron lungs!

# 408 *'Old ghosts whose day was done ere mine began'

Printed *Mem.* i xi. 'Written originally as a preface to *Becket*', which was printed 1879, published 1884, and produced 1893. Written 1884(?), since it is not in the trial edition of *Becket* (*Lincoln*). Cp. the prefatory sonnet for *Harold: Show-Day at Battle Abbey 1876* (p. 1234); and that for *Queen Mary: Guess well* (p. 1231). D. B. MacEachen (*Victorian Newsletter*, Fall 1958) observes that this is one of the only two of T.'s late sonnets (*Guess well* being the other) that have an irregular rhyme scheme; possibly that is why these two remained unpublished.

Old ghosts whose day was done ere mine began,
If earth be seen from your conjectured heaven,
Ye know that History is half-dream – ay even
The man's life in the letters of the man.
There lies the letter, but it is not he
As he retires into himself and is:
Sender and sent-to go to make up this,
Their offspring of this union. And on me
Frown not, old ghosts, if I be one of those
Who make you utter things you did not say,
And mould you all awry and mar your worth;
For whatsoever knows us truly, knows
That none can truly write his single day,
And none can write it for him upon earth.

*37–40.* Adapted, as Sir Charles Tennyson remarks (p. 476), from *Hail Briton* 49–52 (1831–3): 'Men loud against all forms of power, / Unfurnisht foreheads, iron lungs, / And voluble with windy tongues / To compass all things in an hour.' But see headnote above on *T.Nbk*; and l. 40 of *Freedom* had been part of *Love thou thy land* in this Notebook. The 'Brass mouths' suggest the 'brass-mouthed demagogues' of *Sonnet* [*The Wise, the Pure*] (*c.* 1831), which also provided the 'idol' of ll. 28–9 above.

# 409 Politics

Published *1889*. 'Addressed to Gladstone' (H.T.). Gladstone had difficulties with the Franchise (1884) and with Irish Home Rule (1885). Cp. *Compromise* (p. 1339), and *Captain, Guide* (p. 1803), both to Gladstone. The version in the *Virginia* trial edition of *1889* has only eight lines; T. deleted this in the *Trinity* trial edition, and rephrased the epigram on a later page.

We move, the wheel must always move,
  Nor always on the plain,
And if we move to such a goal
  As Wisdom hopes to gain,
Then you that drive, and know your Craft,
  Will firmly hold the rein,
Nor lend an ear to random cries,
  Or you may drive in vain,
For some cry 'Quick' and some cry 'Slow,'
  But, while the hills remain,
Up hill 'Too-slow' will need the whip,
  Down hill 'Too-quick,' the chain.

# 410 The Fleet

Published *The Times*, 23 April 1885, with the subtitle *On its reported insufficiency*; then *1886*. In a trial edition of *1886* (*British Museum*), the title is *On the Reported Inefficiencies of the Fleet*. 'In April [1885] the *Pall Mall Gazette* had some articles on the weakness of our navy, which roused my father to write' (*Mem.* ii 314). In *1886*, T. added as a note a long extract from a speech by Sir Graham Berry (delivered subsequent to T.'s writing), 9 Nov. 1886.

I

You, you, *if* you shall fail to understand
  What England is, and what her all-in-all,
On you will come the curse of all the land,
  Should this old England fall
    Which Nelson left so great.

¶409. *12.* 'Too-quick,'] *1890*; 'Too-quick' *1889*, *Eversley*.

¶410. *1. shall fail*] *1886*; have failed *1885*.

*2*] *1886*; The Fleet of England is her all-in-all, *1885*.

*4. Should this*] *1886*; If that *1885*.

II

His isle, the mightiest Ocean-power on earth,
Our own fair isle, the lord of every sea–
Her fuller franchise–what would that be worth–
Her ancient fame of Free–
Were she . . . a fallen state?

III

Her dauntless army scattered, and so small,
Her island-myriads fed from alien lands–
The fleet of England is her all-in-all;
Her fleet is in your hands,
And in her fleet her Fate.

IV

You, you, that have the ordering of her fleet,
*If* you should only compass her disgrace,
When all men starve, the wild mob's million feet
Will kick you from your place,
But then too late, too late.

# 411 Epitaph on General Gordon

## In the Gordon Boys' National Memorial Home near Woking

Published *The Times*, 7 May 1885; then *1885*. It does not appear in a trial edition of *1885* (*British Museum*). The news of Gordon's death at Khartoum reached England on 5 Feb.; in March, J. G. Whittier requested that T. write an epitaph (Whittier's *Life*, 1895, ii 706). The letter enclosing the poem is dated 4 May (*Pierpont Morgan Library*).

*6. His*] *1886*; This *1885*. *Ocean-*] *1886*; naval *1885*.
*7. Our own fair*] *1886*; This one small *1885*.
*8–10*] *1886*; Poor England, what would all these votes be worth,
And what avail thine ancient fame of 'Free,'
Wert thou . . . a fallen state? *1885*
*11–15*] *1886*; *not 1885*.
*16. that have*] *1886*; who had *1885*.
*17. should only compass*] *1886*; have only compassed *1885*.

Warrior of God, man's friend, and tyrant's foe,
Now somewhere dead far in the waste Soudan,
Thou livest in all hearts, for all men know
This earth has never borne a nobler man.

# 412 To H.R.H. Princess Beatrice

Published *The Times*, 23 July 1885; then *1885*. In honour of the Princess's marriage with Prince Henry of Battenberg. T. wrote to Queen Victoria, 9 July: 'Should the poem, which I send, be approved of by your Majesty and the Princess, shall I have some copies printed?' (*Mem.* ii 442). On 20 July: 'I am glad that Your Majesty and Your dear Princess approve it' (*Lincoln*).

Two Suns of Love make day of human life,
Which else with all its pains, and griefs, and deaths,
Were utter darkness–one, the Sun of dawn
That brightens through the Mother's tender eyes,
And warms the child's awakening world–and one
The later-rising Sun of spousal Love,
Which from her household orbit draws the child
To move in other spheres. The Mother weeps
At that white funeral of the single life,
Her maiden daughter's marriage; and her tears
Are half of pleasure, half of pain–the child
Is happy–even in leaving *her!* but Thou,
True daughter, whose all-faithful, filial eyes
Have seen the loneliness of earthly thrones,
Wilt neither quit the widowed Crown, nor let
This later light of Love have risen in vain,
But moving through the Mother's home, between
The two that love thee, lead a summer life,
Swayed by each Love, and swaying to each Love,
Like some conjectured planet in mid heaven
Between two Suns, and drawing down from both
The light and genial warmth of double day.

¶411. *1. and tyrant's foe*] *1890*; not laid [here *Times*] below *1885–9*. Perhaps changed because of an objection in *Punch*, 16 May 1885.
*2. Now*] *1890*; But *Times*, *1885–9*.
*4*] *1890*; This earth has [hath *Times*] borne no simpler, nobler man. *1885–9*.

# 413 Vastness

Published *Macmillan's Magazine*, Nov. 1885; then *1889*. J. H. Buckley (pp. 231–2) discusses the draft in *H.Nbk 52* (with poems of *1885*), noting that the poem originally consisted of stanzas i–iii, xviii. It is on one of T.'s recurring themes; cp. *Despair* (p. 1299). 'His MS note is, "What matters anything in this world without full faith in the Immortality of the Soul and of Love?"' (*Mem.* ii 343).

I

Many a hearth upon our dark globe sighs after many
a vanished face,
Many a planet by many a sun may roll with the dust
of a vanished race.

II

Raving politics, never at rest–as this poor earth's
pale history runs,–
What is it all but a trouble of ants in the gleam
of a million million of suns?

III

Lies upon this side, lies upon that side, truthless violence
mourned by the Wise,
Thousands of voices drowning his own in a popular
torrent of lies upon lies;

IV

Stately purposes, valour in battle, glorious annals of army
and fleet,
Death for the right cause, death for the wrong cause,
trumpets of victory, groans of defeat;

V

Innocence seethed in her mother's milk, and Charity
setting the martyr aflame;
Thraldom who walks with the banner of Freedom,
and recks not to ruin a realm in her name.

VI

Faith at her zenith, or all but lost in the gloom of doubts
that darken the schools;
Craft with a bunch of all-heal in her hand,
followed up by her vassal legion of fools;

¶413. *9. Exodus* xxxiv 26: 'Thou shalt not seethe a kid in his mother's milk.'

VII

Trade flying over a thousand seas with her spice
    and her vintage, her silk and her corn;
Desolate offing, sailorless harbours, famishing populace,
    wharves forlorn;

VIII

Star of the morning, Hope in the sunrise;
    gloom of the evening, Life at a close;
Pleasure who flaunts on her wide down-way
    with her flying robe and her poisoned rose;

IX

Pain, that has crawled from the corpse of Pleasure,
    a worm which writhes all day, and at night
Stirs up again in the heart of the sleeper, and stings him
    back to the curse of the light;

X

Wealth with his wines and his wedded harlots;
    honest Poverty, bare to the bone;
Opulent Avarice, lean as Poverty; Flattery gilding
    the rift in a throne;

XI

Fame blowing out from her golden trumpet
    a jubilant challenge to Time and to Fate;
Slander, her shadow, sowing the nettle on all the laurelled
    graves of the Great;

XII

Love for the maiden, crowned with marriage,
    no regrets for aught that has been,
Household happinesss, gracious children,
    debtless competence, golden mean;

*13–16*] *1889*; *not 1885*. A draft of ll. 15–16 was inserted by T. between l. 6 and l. 7 in the offprint of *1885* he sent to Gladstone (*British Museum*).
*14. offing*: the sea seen from the shore.
*19.* Cp. *By an Evolutionist* 8: 'Youth and Health, and birth and wealth, and choice of women and of wines'.
*19–20*] *1889*; *the second half of the lines transposed with each other in 1885*.
*20. in*] *1889*; of *1885*.
*21–2*] *1889*; *not 1885*.

XIII

National hatreds of whole generations, and pigmy spites
of the village spire;
Vows that will last to the last death-ruckle, and vows
that are snapt in a moment of fire;

XIV

He that has lived for the lust of the minute,
and died in the doing it, flesh without mind;
He that has nailed all flesh to the Cross,
till Self died out in the love of his kind;

XV

Spring and Summer and Autumn and Winter,
and all these old revolutions of earth;
All new-old revolutions of Empire–change of the tide–
what is all of it worth?

XVI

What the philosophies, all the sciences, poesy,
varying voices of prayer?
All that is noblest, all that is basest, all that is filthy
with all that is fair?

XVII

What is it all, if we all of us end but in being our own
corpse-coffins at last,
Swallowed in Vastness, lost in Silence, drowned
in the deeps of a meaningless Past?

XVIII

What but a murmur of gnats in the gloom,
or a moment's anger of bees in their hive?–

* * * *

Peace, let it be! for I loved him, and love him for ever:
the dead are not dead but alive.

25. *spites . . . spire*] hates of the litterateur *H.MS.*
33. Cp. *Pierced through* 17: 'A carcase in the coffin of this flesh'.
36] Save for a hope that we shall not be lost in the Vastness,
a dream that the dead are alive? *MS 1st reading*
Peace, for I hold that I shall not be lost in the darkness,
the dead are not dead but alive. *MS 2nd reading*
Nay, for I knew thee, O brother, and loved thee,
and I hold thee as one not dead but alive. *MS 3rd reading*
The end is usually taken as referring to Arthur Hallam, but J. H. Buckley suggests that T. may have been thinking of his brother Charles, who died

# 414 In Memoriam
## W. G. WARD

Published in Wilfrid Ward's *W. G. Ward and the Oxford Movement*, May 1889; then *1889*. It had been printed in *The Athenaeum*, 11 May 1889. W. G. Ward, the Roman Catholic theologian, was a neighbour of T.'s at Freshwater; he had died 6 July 1882. Wilfrid Ward wrote to H.T., 8 Dec. 1885: 'Thank you most warmly for saying "the word in season" about the epitaph. I have written to your father . . . to express my gratitude. I suppose it will come with the others in the new book. I cannot say how much I value it' (*Lincoln*). The date 1885 is supported by *H.Lpr 37*, where the poem is on the back of a late draft of *The Dead Prophet* (*1885*), and begins 'Old Ward gone too!' It is not in the *Virginia* trial edition of *1889*.

Farewell, whose living like I shall not find,
  Whose Faith and Work were bells of full accord,
My friend, the most unworldly of mankind,
  Most generous of all Ultramontanes, Ward,
How subtle at tierce and quart of mind with mind,
  How loyal in the following of thy Lord!

# 415 The Ancient Sage

Written and published *1885*. The subject was suggested by Jowett, who wrote to Emily T., 6 July 1885: 'I hope *Laotsee* has prospered. I shall consider myself fortunate if I have succeeded in finding a subject for Alfred' (*Lincoln*). 'What the Ancient Sage says is not the philosophy of the

---

in 1879. But Hallam seems more likely; for the word 'brother', cp. *In Memoriam* ix 16, 20: 'My friend, the brother of my love . . . / More than my brothers are to me.' Also ciii 14–15: 'him I loved, and love / For ever'. Wilfrid Ward wrote of T. and this poem: it 'had, as he first read it to me, two distinct voices – the last line being placed in the mouth of a separate speaker who answers the rest of the poem' (*New Review* xv (1896) 84).

¶414. *1. living like*] *1895*; like on earth *1889–93*.
*3. the*] *1889*; thou *Ath.*, *Ward* (*'misprint', T. noted in his copy of Ward at Lincoln*).
*4. generous*] liberal *original reading*. It was in the copy sent to Ward's relations (F. M. Brookfield, *The Cambridge 'Apostles'*, 1906, p. 327). *Ultramontanes*: strong supporters of Papal authority.
*5. tierce and quart*: parries in fencing.

Chinese philosopher Laot-ze, but it was written after reading his life and maxims' (T.). Again, 'The whole poem is very personal. The passages about "Faith" and the "Passion of the Past" were more especially my own personal feelings' (*Mem.* ii 319). H.T. says: 'My father considered this as one of his best later poems.' Again, '"What I might have believed," my father said, "about the deeper problems of life 'A thousand summers ere the birth of Christ'."' T. discarded several titles: *Laotzee*, *The Way of Life*, *The Venerable Master* (*H.Nbk 51*); *The Ancient Mystic*, *The Old Seer* (trial editions of *1885*, *British Museum*). In *The Speculations of Lau-Tsze* (1868), John Chalmers noted that the name probably means 'The old Philosopher', and he referred to 'the ancient sages'. Cp. *The Mystic* (p. 229) and *De Profundis* (p. 1281); and for its comparative religion, *Akbar's Dream* (p. 1441). Arnold's *Empedocles on Etna* (1852) may have suggested the interweaving of faith and disillusionment, of blank verse and songs, as the old man leaves the city followed by a young singer. But in T. the roles are reversed and the sage is altogether wise.

A thousand summers ere the time of Christ
From out his ancient city came a Seer
Whom one that loved, and honoured him, and yet
Was no disciple, richly garbed, but worn
From wasteful living, followed–in his hand
A scroll of verse–till that old man before
A cavern whence an affluent fountain poured
From darkness into daylight, turned and spoke.

This wealth of waters might but seem to draw
From yon dark cave, but, son, the source is higher,
Yon summit half-a-league in air–and higher,
The cloud that hides it–higher still, the heavens
Whereby the cloud was moulded, and whereout
The cloud descended. Force is from the heights.
I am wearied of our city, son, and go
To spend my one last year among the hills.
What hast thou there? Some deathsong for the Ghouls
To make their banquet relish? let me read.

'How far through all the bloom and brake
That nightingale is heard!
What power but the bird's could make
This music in the bird?
How summer-bright are yonder skies,
And earth as fair in hue!
And yet what sign of aught that lies
Behind the green and blue?

But man today is fancy's fool
 As man hath ever been.
The nameless Power, or Powers, that rule
 Were never heard or seen.'

If thou would'st hear the Nameless, and wilt dive
Into the Temple-cave of thine own self,
There, brooding by the central altar, thou
Mayst haply learn the Nameless hath a voice,
By which thou wilt abide, if thou be wise,
As if thou knewest, though thou canst not know;
For Knowledge is the swallow on the lake
That sees and stirs the surface-shadow there
But never yet hath dipt into the abysm,
The Abysm of all Abysms, beneath, within
The blue of sky and sea, the green of earth,
And in the million-millionth of a grain
Which cleft and cleft again for evermore,
And ever vanishing, never vanishes,
To me, my son, more mystic than myself,
Or even than the Nameless is to me.
 And when thou sendest thy free soul through heaven,
Nor understandest bound nor boundlessness,
Thou seest the Nameless of the hundred names.
 And if the Nameless should withdraw from all
Thy frailty counts most real, all thy world
Might vanish like thy shadow in the dark.

 'And since–from when this earth began–
 The nameless never came
 Among us, never spake with man,
 And never named the Name'–

Thou canst not prove the Nameless, O my son,
Nor canst thou prove the world thou movest in,
Thou canst not prove that thou art body alone,
Nor canst thou prove that thou art spirit alone,
Nor canst thou prove that thou art both in one:
Thou canst not prove thou art immortal, no
Nor yet that thou art mortal–nay my son,
Thou canst not prove that I, who speak with thee,
Am not thyself in converse with thyself,
For nothing worthy proving can be proven,
Nor yet disproven: wherefore thou be wise,

¶415. *40.* Laotze spoke of 'the abyss of abysses' (Chalmers's translation).

Cleave ever to the sunnier side of doubt,
And cling to Faith beyond the forms of Faith!
She reels not in the storm of warring words,
She brightens at the clash of 'Yes' and 'No,'
She sees the Best that glimmers through the Worst,
She feels the Sun is hid but for a night,
She spies the summer through the winter bud,
She tastes the fruit before the blossom falls,
She hears the lark within the songless egg,
She finds the fountain where they wailed 'Mirage'!

'What Power? aught akin to Mind,
The mind in me and you?
Or power as of the Gods gone blind
Who see not what they do?'

But some in yonder city hold, my son,
That none but Gods could build this house of ours,
So beautiful, vast, various, so beyond
All work of man, yet, like all work of man,
A beauty with defect–till That which knows,
And is not known, but felt through what we feel
Within ourselves is highest, shall descend
On this half-deed, and shape it at the last
According to the Highest in the Highest.

'What Power but the Years that make
And break the vase of clay,
And stir the sleeping earth, and wake
The bloom that fades away?
What rulers but the Days and Hours
That cancel weal with woe,
And wind the front of youth with flowers,
And cap our age with snow?'

The days and hours are ever glancing by,
And seem to flicker past through sun and shade,
Or short, or long, as Pleasure leads, or Pain;
But with the Nameless is nor Day nor Hour;
Though we, thin minds, who creep from thought to thought
Break into 'Thens' and 'Whens' the Eternal Now:

*68.* J. H. Buckley (p. 13) cites *The Devil and the Lady* I iv 97: 'Who would not cleave to the sunny side o' the wall?'

*84.* The world 'so various, so beautiful', in Arnold's *Dover Beach* 32.

*104. Eternal Now*: Cowley's *Davideis* i: 'Nothing is there *To come*, and nothing *Past*, / But an *Eternal Now* does always last.' Cp. *The 'How' and the 'Why'* 22: 'But what is the meaning of *then* and *now*'.

This double seeming of the single world!–
My words are like the babblings in a dream
Of nightmare, when the babblings break the dream.
But thou be wise in this dream-world of ours,
Nor take thy dial for thy deity,
But make the passing shadow serve thy will.

'The years that made the stripling wise
Undo their work again,
And leave him, blind of heart and eyes,
The last and least of men;
Who clings to earth, and once would dare
Hell-heat or Arctic cold,
And now one breath of cooler air
Would loose him from his hold;
His winter chills him to the root,
He withers marrow and mind;
The kernel of the shrivelled fruit
Is jutting through the rind;
The tiger spasms tear his chest,
The palsy wags his head;
The wife, the sons, who love him best
Would fain that he were dead;
The griefs by which he once was wrung
Were never worth the while'–

Who knows? or whether this earth-narrow life
Be yet but yolk, and forming in the shell?

'The shaft of scorn that once had stung
But wakes a dotard smile.'

The placid gleam of sunset after storm!

'The statesman's brain that swayed the past
Is feebler than his knees;
The passive sailor wrecks at last
In ever-silent seas;
The warrior hath forgot his arms,
The Learnèd all his lore;
The changing market frets or charms
The merchant's hope no more;
The prophet's beacon burned in vain,
And now is lost in cloud;
The plowman passes, bent with pain,
To mix with what he plowed;
The poet whom his Age would quote

144–5. Cp. *Tithonus* 3: 'Man comes and tills the field and lies beneath.'

As heir of endless fame–
He knows not even the book he wrote,
Not even his own name.
For man has overlived his day,
And, darkening in the light,
Scarce feels the senses break away
To mix with ancient Night.'

The shell must break before the bird can fly.

'The years that when my Youth began
Had set the lily and rose
By all my ways where'er they ran,
Have ended mortal foes;
My rose of love for ever gone,
My lily of truth and trust–
They made her lily and rose in one,
And changed her into dust.
O rosetree planted in my grief,
And growing, on her tomb,
Her dust is greening in your leaf,
Her blood is in your bloom.
O slender lily waving there,
And laughing back the light,
In vain you tell me "Earth is fair"
When all is dark as night.'

My son, the world is dark with griefs and graves,
So dark that men cry out against the Heavens.
Who knows but that the darkness is in man?
The doors of Night may be the gates of Light;
For wert thou born or blind or deaf, and then
Suddenly healed, how would'st thou glory in all
The splendours and the voices of the world!
And we, the poor earth's dying race, and yet
No phantoms, watching from a phantom shore
Await the last and largest sense to make
The phantom walls of this illusion fade,
And show us that the world is wholly fair.

'But vain the tears for darkened years
As laughter over wine,
And vain the laughter as the tears,
O brother, mine or thine,
For all that laugh, and all that weep,
And all that breathe are one
Slight ripple on the boundless deep
That moves, and all is gone.'

But that one ripple on the boundless deep
Feels that the deep is boundless, and itself
For ever changing form, but evermore
One with the boundless motion of the deep.

'Yet wine and laughter friends! and set
The lamps alight, and call
For golden music, and forget
The darkness of the pall.'

If utter darkness closed the day, my son–
But earth's dark forehead flings athwart the heavens
Her shadow crowned with stars–and yonder–out
To northward–some that never set, but pass
From sight and night to lose themselves in day.
I hate the black negation of the bier,
And wish the dead, as happier than ourselves
And higher, having climbed one step beyond
Our village miseries, might be borne in white
To burial or to burning, hymned from hence
With songs in praise of death, and crowned with flowers!

'O worms and maggots of today
Without their hope of wings!'

But louder than thy rhyme the silent Word
Of that world-prophet in the heart of man.

'Though some have gleams or so they say
Of more than mortal things.'

Today? but what of yesterday? for oft
On me, when boy, there came what then I called,
Who knew no books and no philosophies,
In my boy-phrase 'The Passion of the Past.'
The first gray streak of earliest summer-dawn,
The last long stripe of waning crimson gloom,
As if the late and early were but one–
A height, a broken grange, a grove, a flower
Had murmurs 'Lost and gone and lost and gone!'
A breath, a whisper–some divine farewell–
Desolate sweetness–far and far away–

*204–9*. T. said on his mother's death in 1865: 'We all of us hate the pompous funeral we have to join in, black plumes, black coaches and nonsense. We should like all to go in white and gold rather' (*Mem.* ii 18–19).

*219–27*. Cp. *Tears, idle tears* (p. 784). 'This Passion of the Past I used to feel when a boy' (T.). H.T. compares *Far–Far–Away* (p. 1405).

What had he loved, what had he lost, the boy?
I know not and I speak of what has been.
  And more, my son! for more than once when I
Sat all alone, revolving in myself
The word that is the symbol of myself,
The mortal limit of the Self was loosed,
And past into the Nameless, as a cloud
Melts into Heaven. I touched my limbs, the limbs
Were strange not mine–and yet no shade of doubt,
But utter clearness, and through loss of Self
The gain of such large life as matched with ours
Were Sun to spark–unshadowable in words,
Themselves but shadows of a shadow-world.

  'And idle gleams will come and go,
    But still the clouds remain;'

The clouds themselves are children of the Sun.

  'And Night and Shadow rule below
    When only Day should reign.'

And Day and Night are children of the Sun,
And idle gleams to thee are light to me.
Some say, the Light was father of the Night,
And some, the Night was father of the Light.
No night no day!–I touch thy world again–
No ill no good! such counter-terms, my son,
Are border-races, holding, each its own
By endless war: but night enough is there
In yon dark city: get thee back: and since
The key to that weird casket, which for thee
But holds a skull, is neither thine nor mine,
But in the hand of what is more than man,
Or in man's hand when man is more than man,
Let be thy wail and help thy fellow men,
And make thy gold thy vassal not thy king,
And fling free alms into the beggar's bowl,
And send the day into the darkened heart;

*229–39.* 'This is also a personal experience which I have had more than once' (T.). He describes 'a kind of waking trance I have frequently had, quite up from boyhood, when I have been all alone. This has generally come upon me through repeating my own name two or three times to myself silently . . . and this not a confused state, but the clearest of the clearest' (*Mem.* i 320).

*254–5.* Cp. the caskets in *The Merchant of Venice* II vii; the one with the skull held a cynical 'scroll' (l. 6 above).

Nor list for guerdon in the voice of men,
A dying echo from a falling wall;
Nor care–for Hunger hath the Evil eye–
To vex the noon with fiery gems, or fold
Thy presence in the silk of sumptuous looms;
Nor roll thy viands on a luscious tongue,
Nor drown thyself with flies in honied wine;
Nor thou be rageful, like a handled bee,
And lose thy life by usage of thy sting;
Nor harm an adder through the lust for harm,
Nor make a snail's horn shrink for wantonness;
And more–think well! Do-well will follow thought,
And in the fatal sequence of this world
An evil thought may soil thy children's blood;
But curb the beast would cast thee in the mire,
And leave the hot swamp of voluptuousness
A cloud between the Nameless and thyself,
And lay thine uphill shoulder to the wheel,
And climb the Mount of Blessing, whence, if thou
Look higher, then–perchance–thou mayest–beyond
A hundred ever-rising mountain lines,
And past the range of Night and Shadow–see
The high-heaven dawn of more than mortal day
Strike on the Mount of Vision!
So, farewell.

# 416 Opening of the Indian and Colonial Exhibition by the Queen

Written at the Request of the Prince of Wales

Published *1886*; the Exhibition opened 4 May. The secretary to the Prince of Wales acknowledged the proofs, 22 April (*Lincoln*). Cp. *Ode Sung at the Opening of the International Exhibition* (p. 1127). For the refrain, cp. *Britons, Guard Your Own*. T. had thought of adapting *Hail Briton* for this occasion (see p. 481).

I

Welcome, welcome with one voice!
In your welfare we rejoice,
Sons and brothers that have sent,
From isle and cape and continent,

*285*. Cp. *2 Peter* i 18–19: 'the holy mount . . . as unto a light that shineth in a dark place.'

Produce of your field and flood,
Mount and mine, and primal wood;
Works of subtle brain and hand,
And splendours of the morning land,
Gifts from every British zone;
Britons, hold your own!

II

May we find, as ages run,
The mother featured in the son;
And may yours for ever be
That old strength and constancy
Which has made your fathers great
In our ancient island State,
And wherever her flag fly,
Glorying between sea and sky,
Makes the might of Britain known;
Britons, hold your own!

III

Britain fought her sons of yore–
Britain failed; and never more,
Careless of our growing kin,
Shall we sin our fathers' sin,
Men that in a narrower day–
Unprophetic rulers they–
Drove from out the mother's nest
That young eagle of the West
To forage for herself alone;
Britons, hold your own!

IV

Sharers of our glorious past,
Brothers, must we part at last?
Shall we not through good and ill
Cleave to one another still?
Britain's myriad voices call,
'Sons, be welded each and all,
Into one imperial whole,
One with Britain, heart and soul!
One life, one flag, one fleet, one Throne!'
Britons, hold your own!

¶416. *21–30.* Cp. *England and America in 1782* (p. 618).

# 417 Locksley Hall Sixty Years After

Published *1886*. Written 1886, recited 27 Oct. (*Mem.* ii 324, 506). The title in the trial edition of *1886* (*British Museum*) is *Locksley Hall 1886*. See *Locksley Hall* and headnote (p. 668). *H.Nbks 51, 53* (1885–6) and *Lpr 128* contain many drafts; some of the more important variants are given below, but without distinguishing in general between first and final readings. J. H. Buckley (p. 234) points out that T. 'strove through heavy revision of several early drafts to control the invective . . . late in the composition of the poem he added several lines' [151–4] of retreat, as he did in *Maud*. 'The nucleus of the poem' (T.) was ll. 13–15, which had been dropped from *Locksley Hall*. The idea of a sequel probably owed something to a comment by A. H. Japp in 1865 (*Three Great Teachers*, p. 132):

'The poet has here carried the poem to the strict limit of his experience at the time it was written. It closes, but does not cease. It abounds with suggestions as to a higher result in prospect. It points to a region of lofty possibility. In one respect, however, it was unsafe for the poet to leave his hero here; that is, when viewed simply from the formally moral standpoint, which requires that a direct lesson be drawn from everything. If, however, the poet ever again wrote on a kindred theme, it would test at once his insight and fuller experience,–whether he would conduct his hero to a more worthy goal.'

Possibly T. was again influenced by the *Moâllakát*, the acknowledged source of *Locksley Hall*; Amriolkais says, 'O how oft have I rejected the admonitions of a morose adviser, vehement in censuring my passion for thee; nor have I been moved by his reproaches!' For an important reply to T.'s onslaught on the age, see W. E. Gladstone, *Nineteenth Century*, Jan. 1887. On the biographical level, Rader (p. 58) suggests that T. was reappraising Rosa Baring and her husband (ll. 239–40). 'Edith' is T.'s wife Emily ('very woman of very woman,' l. 51, is applied to her, *Mem.* i 331), to whom the volume was dedicated. Sir Charles Tennyson (p. 493) stresses the reconciliation with the other branch of T.'s family at Bayons (e.g. ll. 43–4). For the death of T.'s son Lionel, see l. 55*n*. T. said that it was 'a dramatic poem, and the Dramatis Personae are imaginary'. 'My father said that the old man in the second *Locksley Hall* had a stronger faith in God and in human goodness than he had had in his youth; but he had also endeavoured to give the moods of despondency which are caused by the decreased energy of life.' T. said: 'There is not one touch of biography in it from beginning to end' (*Mem.* ii 329–31).

Late, my grandson! half the morning have I paced these sandy tracts,
Watched again the hollow ridges roaring into cataracts,

Wandered back to living boyhood while I heard the curlews call,
I myself so close on death, and death itself in Locksley Hall.

So–your happy suit was blasted–she the faultless, the divine;
And you liken–boyish babble–this boy-love of yours with mine.

I myself have often babbled doubtless of a foolish past;
Babble, babble; our old England may go down in babble at last.

'Curse him!' curse your fellow-victim? call him dotard in your rage?
Eyes that lured a doting boyhood well might fool a dotard's age.

Jilted for a wealthier! wealthier? yet perhaps she was not wise;
I remember how you kissed the miniature with those sweet eyes.

In the hall there hangs a painting–Amy's arms about my neck–
Happy children in a sunbeam sitting on the ribs of wreck.

In my life there was a picture, she that clasped my neck had flown;
I was left within the shadow sitting on the wreck alone.

Yours has been a slighter ailment, will you sicken for her sake?
You, not you! your modern amourist is of easier, earthlier make.

Amy loved me, Amy failed me, Amy was a timid child;
But your Judith–but your worldling–*she* had never driven me wild.

She that holds the diamond necklace dearer than the golden ring,
She that finds a winter sunset fairer than a morn of Spring.

She that in her heart is brooding on his briefer lease of life,
While she vows 'till death shall part us,' she the would-be-widow wife.

She the worldling born of worldlings–father, mother–be content,
Even the homely farm can teach us there is something in descent.

Yonder in that chapel, slowly sinking now into the ground,
Lies the warrior, my forefather, with his feet upon the hound.

Crossed! for once he sailed the sea to crush the Moslem in his pride;
Dead the warrior, dead his glory, dead the cause in which he died.

Yet how often I and Amy in the mouldering aisle have stood,
Gazing for one pensive moment on that founder of our blood.

There again I stood today, and where of old we knelt in prayer,
Close beneath the casement crimson with the shield of Locksley–there,

All in white Italian marble, looking still as if she smiled,
Lies my Amy dead in child-birth, dead the mother, dead the child.

Dead–and sixty years ago, and dead her agèd husband now–
I this old white-headed dreamer stoopt and kissed her marble brow.

¶417. *9–10*] Curse the old goat, you say? poor goat, that through the desert bears the curse.
Should be yours! the would-be widow thinks he bears the longer purse. *H.MS*

*13–16.* The nucleus of the poem, deleted in proof from *Locksley Hall.* Cp. the painting in *The Lover's Tale* ii 165ff.

Gone the fires of youth, the follies, furies, curses, passionate tears,
Gone like fires and floods and earthquakes of the planet's dawning years.

Fires that shook me once, but now to silent ashes fallen away.
Cold upon the dead volcano sleeps the gleam of dying day.

Gone the tyrant of my youth, and mute below the chancel stones,
All his virtues–I forgive them–black in white above his bones.

Gone the comrades of my bivouac, some in fight against the foe,
Some through age and slow diseases, gone as all on earth will go.

Gone with whom for forty years my life in golden sequence ran,
She with all the charm of woman, she with all the breadth of man,

Strong in will and rich in wisdom, Edith, yet so lowly-sweet,
Woman to her inmost heart, and woman to her tender feet,

Very woman of very woman, nurse of ailing body and mind,
She that linked again the broken chain that bound me to my kind.

Here today was Amy with me, while I wandered down the coast,
Near us Edith's holy shadow, smiling at the slighter ghost.

Gone our sailor son thy father, Leonard early lost at sea;
Thou alone, my boy, of Amy's kin and mine art left to me.

Gone thy tender-natured mother, wearying to be left alone,
Pining for the stronger heart that once had beat beside her own.

Truth, for Truth is Truth, he worshipt, being true as he was brave;
Good, for Good is Good, he followed, yet he looked beyond the grave,

Wiser there than you, that crowning barren Death as lord of all,
Deem this over-tragic drama's closing curtain is the pall!

42. Cp. *Mariana in the South* 89–96*n*, *1832* text: 'gleamed, volcano-like'. Here influenced by T.'s memories of 'the still more magnificent view of the dead volcanoes' in 1861 (*Mem.* i 476). 'My father always quoted this line as the most imaginative in the poem' (H.T.).

*48*] As our greatest is man-woman, so was she the woman-man. *MS*. 'What he called "the man-woman" in Christ, the union of tenderness and strength' (*Mem.* i 326). A recurring aspiration of T.'s; cp. *The Princess*, and contrast *On One Who Affected an Effeminate Manner* (p. 1424).

*49. yet so lowly-sweet*] *1888*; loyal, lowly, sweet *1886*.

*50. Woman . . . woman*] *1888*; Feminine . . . feminine *1886*.

*55.* Suggested by the death of T.'s son Lionel (a name cognate with Leonard) at sea, on his return from India in April 1886; ll. 59–60, 71–2, 'were written immediately after the death of my brother, and described his chief characteristics' (*Mem.* ii 329).

*59–60*] She in him was wise and truthful, she in him was good and brave.
Love your father. She had taught him not to shudder at the grave.
*MS*

*61–2.* Cp. *The Play* (p. 1423).

Beautiful was death in him, who saw the death, but kept the deck,
Saving women and their babes, and sinking with the sinking wreck,
Gone for ever! Ever? no–for since our dying race began,
Ever, ever, and for ever was the leading light of man.

Those that in barbarian burials killed the slave, and slew the wife,
Felt within themselves the sacred passion of the second life.

Indian warriors dream of ampler hunting grounds beyond the night;
Even the black Australian dying hopes he shall return, a white.

Truth for truth, and good for good! The Good, the True, the Pure, the Just–
Take the charm 'For ever' from them, and they crumble into dust.

Gone the cry of 'Forward, Forward,' lost within a growing gloom;
Lost, or only heard in silence from the silence of a tomb.

Half the marvels of my morning, triumphs over time and space,
Staled by frequence, shrunk by usage into commonest commonplace!

'Forward' rang the voices then, and of the many mine was one.
Let us hush this cry of 'Forward' till ten thousand years have gone.

Far among the vanished races, old Assyrian kings would flay
Captives whom they caught in battle–iron-hearted victors they.

Ages after, while in Asia, he that led the wild Moguls,
Timur built his ghastly tower of eighty thousand human skulls,

Then, and here in Edward's time, an age of noblest English names,
Christian conquerors took and flung the conquered Christian into flames.

Love your enemy, bless your haters, said the Greatest of the great;
Christian love among the Churches looked the twin of heathen hate.

From the golden alms of Blessing man had coined himself a curse:
Rome of Cæsar, Rome of Peter, which was crueller? which was worse?

France had shown a light to all men, preached a Gospel, all men's good;
Celtic Demos rose a Demon, shrieked and slaked the light with blood.

*66* ∧ *7*] Prove that all the race will perish wholly, worst and best,
Give me chloroform, set me free of it–without pain–and let me rest. *MS*

*Mem.* ii 35 tells of a man chloroforming himself: '"That's what I should do," my father said, "if I thought there was no future life".'

*70.* 'Some Negros, who believe the Resurrection, think that they shall rise white', Thomas Browne's *Christian Morals* ii 6 (where it derives from the traveller Mandelslo).

*72* ∧ *3*] So at least it seems to me, that man can never wholly die *MS.*

*74–5*] *Transposed in the earlier MS.*

Hope was ever on her mountain, watching till the day begun–
Crowned with sunlight–over darkness–from the still unrisen sun.

Have we grown at last beyond the passions of the primal clan?
'Kill your enemy, for you hate him,' still, 'your enemy' was a man.

Have we sunk below them? peasants maim the helpless horse, and drive
Innocent cattle under thatch, and burn the kindlier brutes alive.

Brutes, the brutes are not your wrongers–burnt at midnight, found at morn,
Twisted hard in mortal agony with their offspring, born-unborn,

Clinging to the silent mother! Are we devils? are we men?
Sweet St Francis of Assisi, would that he were here again,

He that in his Catholic wholeness used to call the very flowers
Sisters, brothers–and the beasts–whose pains are hardly less than ours!

Chaos, Cosmos! Cosmos, Chaos! who can tell how all will end?
Read the wide world's annals, you, and take their wisdom for your friend.

Hope the best, but hold the Present fatal daughter of the Past,
Shape your heart to front the hour, but dream not that the hour will last.

Ay, if dynamite and revolver leave you courage to be wise:
When was age so crammed with menace? madness? written, spoken lies?

Envy wears the mask of Love, and, laughing sober fact to scorn,
Cries to Weakest as to Strongest, 'Ye are equals, equal-born.'

Equal-born? O yes, if yonder hill be level with the flat.
Charm us, Orator, till the Lion look no larger than the Cat,

Till the Cat through that mirage of overheated language loom
Larger than the Lion,–Demos end in working its own doom.

Russia bursts our Indian barrier, shall we fight her? shall we yield?
Pause! before you sound the trumpet, hear the voices from the field.

Those three hundred millions under one Imperial sceptre now,
Shall we hold them? shall we loose them? take the suffrage of the plow.

Nay, but these would feel and follow Truth if only you and you,
Rivals of realm-ruining party, when you speak were wholly true.

*95–8.* 'The modern Irish cruelties' (T.); he had deplored them in 1883 (*Mem.* ii 457).
*97. wrongers*] landlord *MS.*
*99*] Falling from their roasted bowels ...; Jutting from the silent mother ... *MSS.*
*110 ∧ 1*] Nature, Caesar, and Napoleon give your equal men the lie. *MS.*
*115. Indian*] Afghan *MS.* Russia attacked Penjdeh, 30 March 1885, and for some weeks war seemed imminent.
*116. Pause . . . trumpet*] What is Afghan? wars are taxes *MS.*
*118*] Subject to the voice of one who sees one yard beyond his plow. *MS.*

Plowmen, Shepherds, have I found, and more than once, and still could find,
Sons of God, and kings of men in utter nobleness of mind,

Truthful, trustful, looking upward to the practised hustings-liar;
So the Higher wields the Lower, while the Lower is the Higher.

Here and there a cotter's babe is royal-born by right divine;
Here and there my lord is lower than his oxen or his swine.

Chaos, Cosmos! Cosmos, Chaos! once again the sickening game;
Freedom, free to slay herself, and dying while they shout her name.

Step by step we gained a freedom known to Europe, known to all;
Step by step we rose to greatness,–through the tonguesters we may fall.

You that woo the Voices–tell them 'old experience is a fool,'
Teach your flattered kings that only those who cannot read can rule.

Pluck the mighty from their seat, but set no meek ones in their place;
Pillory Wisdom in your markets, pelt your offal at her face.

Tumble Nature heel o'er head, and, yelling with the yelling street,
Set the feet above the brain and swear the brain is in the feet.

Bring the old dark ages back without the faith, without the hope,
Break the State, the Church, the Throne, and roll their ruins down the slope.

Authors–essayist, atheist, novelist, realist, rhymester, play your part,
Paint the mortal shame of nature with the living hues of Art.

*122.* Cp. *John* i 12–13: 'But as many as received him, to them gave he power to become the sons of God, even to them that believe on his Name: Which were born, not of blood, nor of the will of the flesh, nor of the will of man, but of God.'
*130.* See *Freedom* 21–4*n* (p. 1341).
*131.* Suggesting (with l. 134) *Coriolanus* II iii, where Coriolanus solicits votes.
*133.* *Luke* i 52.
*134*] Pillory the dead face . . .; Pillory the dumb corpse . . . *MSS.* These suggest that T. is remembering the indignities inflicted by the mob in the French Revolution; he had written about such in *Come hither* (p. 152). Cp. *The Dead Prophet* (p. 1322).
*137.* Cp. *Despair* 88: 'For these are the new dark ages'.
*139. essayist, atheist*] *1888*; *transposed 1886.*
*139–40*] Wild young Poet, glancing forward, drag us backward, play your part,
Crown the dying filths of Nature with the living flowers of Art.
Dying are they? No, nor will, and would that I myself were dead
Ere the living body of Britain die beneath her dying head. *MS*
*140.* Cp. *Art for Art's sake* (p. 1229). *living hues*: as in Shelley, *West Wind* 12.

Rip your brothers' vices open, strip your own foul passions bare;
Down with Reticence, down with Reverence–forward–naked–
let them stare.

Feed the budding rose of boyhood with the drainage of your sewer;
Send the drain into the fountain, lest the stream should issue pure.

Set the maiden fancies wallowing in the troughs of Zolaism,–
Forward, forward, ay and backward, downward too into the abysm.

Do your best to charm the worst, to lower the rising race of men;
Have we risen from out the beast, then back into the beast again?

Only 'dust to dust' for me that sicken at your lawless din,
Dust in wholesome old-world dust before the newer world begin.

Heated am I? you–you wonder–well, it scarce becomes mine age–
Patience! let the dying actor mouth his last upon the stage.

Cries of unprogressive dotage ere the dotard fall asleep?
Noises of a current narrowing, not the music of a deep?

Ay, for doubtless I am old, and think gray thoughts, for I am gray:
After all the stormy changes shall we find a changeless May?

After madness, after massacre, Jacobinism and Jacquerie,
Some diviner force to guide us through the days I shall not see?

When the schemes and all the systems, Kingdoms and Republics fall,
Something kindlier, higher, holier–all for each and each for all?

All the full-brain, half-brain races, led by Justice, Love, and Truth;
All the millions one at length with all the visions of my youth?

All diseases quenched by Science, no man halt, or deaf or blind;
Stronger ever born of weaker, lustier body, larger mind?

*145*] Till the delicate lady wallow in the sewer of Zolaism, *MS*.
*148*. Cp. *Passing of Arthur* 25–6: 'All my realm / Reels back into the beast'.
*149–50*] Only this worldweary being, sick of senseless rage and sin
Fain would lie below the surface ere this newer world begin. *MS*
*152 ∧ 3*] Who'd have thought of so much blood–to quote our Lady of Macbeth–
'So much blood in the old man' yet, who stumbles down the steps of death. *MS*
*153–4*] *Added later to MS*.
*156*] Earth may come to iceless winters, Earth may find a deathless May. *MS*.
*157*. *Jacquerie*: 'Originally a revolt in 1358 against the Picardy nobles; and afterwards applied to insurrections of the mob' (T.).
*159*] Light on some new form of Power, after Europe's rulers fall, *MS*.

Earth at last a warless world, a single race, a single tongue–
I have seen her far away–for is not Earth as yet so young?–

Every tiger madness muzzled, every serpent passion killed,
Every grim ravine a garden, every blazing desert tilled,

Robed in universal harvest up to either pole she smiles,
Universal ocean softly washing all her warless Isles.

Warless? when her tens are thousands, and her thousands millions, then–
All her harvest all too narrow–who can fancy warless men?

Warless? war will die out late then. Will it ever? late or soon?
Can it, till this outworn earth be dead as yon dead world the moon?

Dead the new astronomy calls her. . . . On this day and at this hour,
In this gap between the sandhills, whence you see the Locksley tower,

Here we met, our latest meeting–Amy–sixty years ago–
She and I–the moon was falling greenish through a rosy glow,

Just above the gateway tower, and even where you see her now–
Here we stood and claspt each other, swore the seeming-deathless vow. . . .

Dead, but how her living glory lights the hall, the dune, the grass!
Yet the moonlight is the sunlight, and the sun himself will pass.

Venus near her! smiling downward at this earthlier earth of ours,
Closer on the Sun, perhaps a world of never fading flowers.

Hesper, whom the poet called the Bringer home of all good things.
All good things may move in Hesper, perfect peoples, perfect kings.

Hesper–Venus–were we native to that splendour or in Mars,
We should see the Globe we groan in, fairest of their evening stars.

*165.* Cp. *Isaiah* ii 4: 'Neither shall they learn war any more'.
*165–6.* T. adapts an unadopted stanza of *Freedom*:

On Earth so old, but yet so young,
Of equal day from pole to pole,
A warless world, a single tongue . . .

*166 ∧ 7*] When the great elastick name will flash through all from end to end,
Make, as in the simple body, every member friend with friend.
*MS*

*178.* The tints at twilight were due to the eruption of Krakatoa in Aug. 1883; cp. the opening of *St Telemachus* (p. 1431).
*185–6.* T. compares Sappho (as in *Leonine Elegiacs* 13): *ϝέσπερε, πάντα φέρεις, ὅσα φαίνολις ἐσκέδασ᾽ αὔως, φέρεις ὄϊν, φέρεις ᾶιγα, φέρεις ματέρι παῖδα.* ('Evening Star that bringest back all that lightsome Dawn hath scattered afar, thou bringest the sheep, thou bringest the goat, thou bringest her child home to the mother'.)

Could we dream of wars and carnage, craft and madness, lust and spite,
Roaring London, raving Paris, in that point of peaceful light?

Might we not in glancing heavenward on a star so silver-fair,
Yearn, and clasp the hands and murmur, 'Would to God that
we were there'?

Forward, backward, backward, forward, in the immeasurable sea,
Swayed by vaster ebbs and flows than can be known to you or me.

All the suns–are these but symbols of innumerable man,
Man or Mind that sees a shadow of the planner or the plan?

Is there evil but on earth? or pain in every peopled sphere?
Well be grateful for the sounding watchword, 'Evolution' here,

Evolution ever climbing after some ideal good,
And Reversion ever dragging Evolution in the mud.

What are men that He should heed us? cried the king of sacred song;
Insects of an hour, that hourly work their brother insect wrong,

While the silent Heavens roll, and Suns along their fiery way,
All their planets whirling round them, flash a million miles a day.

Many an Æon moulded earth before her highest, man, was born,
Many an Æon too may pass when earth is manless and forlorn,

Earth so huge, and yet so bounded–pools of salt, and plots of land–
Shallow skin of green and azure–chains of mountain, grains of sand!

Only That which made us, meant us to be mightier by and by,
Set the sphere of all the boundless Heavens within the human eye,

Sent the shadow of Himself, the boundless, through the human soul;
Boundless inward, in the atom, boundless outward, in the Whole.

* * * *

Here is Locksley Hall, my grandson, here the lion-guarded gate.
Not tonight in Locksley Hall–tomorrow–you, you come so late.

Wrecked—your train–or all but wrecked? a shattered wheel? a vicious
boy!
Good, this forward, you that preach it, is it well to wish you joy?

Is it well that while we range with Science, glorying in the Time,
City children soak and blacken soul and sense in city slime?

There among the glooming alleys Progress halts on palsied feet,
Crime and hunger cast our maidens by the thousand on the street.

193. *the immeasurable sea*: Shelley, *Daemon of the World* i 190.
201. *Psalm* viii 4.
204. Cp. *The Window: Marriage Morning*: 'Flash for a million miles'.
217–24] *Added later on separate sheet of MS.*
217] Well that while we range with Science glorying through the field of Time, *MS.*
219. *glooming*] squalid *MS.*

There the Master scrimps his haggard sempstress of her daily bread,
There a single sordid attic holds the living and the dead.

There the smouldering fire of fever creeps across the rotted floor,
And the crowded couch of incest in the warrens of the poor.

Nay, your pardon, cry your 'forward,' yours are hope and youth, but I–
Eighty winters leave the dog too lame to follow with the cry,

Lame and old, and past his time, and passing now into the night;
Yet I would the rising race were half as eager for the light.

Light the fading gleam of Even? light the glimmer of the dawn?
Agèd eyes may take the growing glimmer for the gleam withdrawn.

Far away beyond her myriad coming changes earth will be
Something other than the wildest modern guess of you and me.

Earth may reach her earthly-worst, or if she gain her earthly-best,
Would she find her human offspring this ideal man at rest?

Forward then, but still remember how the course of Time will swerve,
Crook and turn upon itself in many a backward streaming curve.

Not the Hall tonight, my grandson! Death and Silence hold their own.
Leave the Master in the first dark hour of his last sleep alone.

Worthier soul was he than I am, sound and honest, rustic Squire,
Kindly landlord, boon companion–youthful jealousy is a liar.

Cast the poison from your bosom, oust the madness from your brain.
Let the trampled serpent show you that you have not lived in vain.

Youthful! youth and age are scholars yet but in the lower school,
Nor is he the wisest man who never proved himself a fool.

Yonder lies our young sea-village–Art and Grace are less and less:
Science grows and Beauty dwindles–roofs of slated hideousness!

There is one old Hostel left us where they swing the Locksley shield,
Till the peasant cow shall butt the 'Lion passant' from his field.

Poor old Heraldry, poor old History, poor old Poetry, passing hence,
In the common deluge drowning old political common-sense!

Poor old voice of eighty crying after voices that have fled!
All I loved are vanished voices, all my steps are on the dead.

All the world is ghost to me, and as the phantom disappears,
Forward far and far from here is all the hope of eighty years.

* * * *

In this Hostel–I remember–I repent it o'er his grave–
Like a clown–by chance he met me–I refused the hand he gave.

*222*] There among his living orphans lies the still-unburied dead. *MS.*

*236 ∧ 7*] Like our earthly streams that lapse into the level from the steep,
Time is not a still canal that moves still forward to the deep. *MS*

*250.* Cp. *Far shines that land* (*H.Lpr 60*): 'to drown in deluge all the old.'

From that casement where the trailer mantles all the mouldering bricks–
I was then in early boyhood, Edith but a child of six–

While I sheltered in this archway from a day of driving showers–
Peept the winsome face of Edith like a flower among the flowers.

Here tonight! the Hall tomorrow, when they toll the Chapel bell!
Shall I hear in one dark room a wailing, 'I have loved thee well.'

Then a peal that shakes the portal–one has come to claim his bride,
Her that shrank, and put me from her, shrieked, and started from my side–

Silent echoes! You, my Leonard, use and not abuse your day,
Move among your people, know them, follow him who led the way,

Strove for sixty widowed years to help his homelier brother men,
Served the poor, and built the cottage, raised the school, and drained the fen.

Hears he now the Voice that wronged him? who shall swear it cannot be?
Earth would never touch her worst, were one in fifty such as he.

Ere she gain her Heavenly-best, a God must mingle with the game:
Nay, there may be those about us whom we neither see nor name,

Felt within us as ourselves, the Powers of Good, the Powers of Ill,
Strowing balm, or shedding poison in the fountains of the Will.

Follow you the Star that lights a desert pathway, yours or mine.
Forward, till you see the highest Human Nature is divine.

Follow Light, and do the Right–for man can half-control his doom–
Till you find the deathless Angel seated in the vacant tomb.

Forward, let the stormy moment fly and mingle with the Past.
I that loathed, have come to love him. Love will conquer at the last.

Gone at eighty, mine own age, and I and you will bear the pall;
Then I leave thee Lord and Master, latest Lord of Locksley Hall.

# 418 On the Jubilee of Queen Victoria

Published *Macmillan's Magazine*, April 1887, as *Carmen Saeculare. An Ode In Honour of the Jubilee . . .*; then *1889*. The Jubilee was the fiftieth anniversary of the Coronation, June 1887. Written Dec. 1886–Feb. 1887 (*Tennyson*

*267–8*] I that never turned away the truthful pauper from my door,
I that being poor myself have ever striven to raise the poor! *MS*

*269–76, 279–80*] *Added later on separate sheet of MS.*

*and His Friends*, p. 212; *Mem.* ii 335). 'It was at the Queen's suggestion that he added the final lines', said C. V. Stanford, who wrote the music at T.'s request (*Pages from an Unwritten Diary*, 1914, p. 233). T. says of Catullus: '*Collis o Heliconii* is in a beautiful metre. I wrote a great part of my "Jubilee Ode" in it' (*Mem.* ii 400)–i.e. ii, iv, etc. Horace's *Carmen Saeculare* is a similar celebratory prayer.

I

Fifty times the rose has flowered and faded,
Fifty times the golden harvest fallen,
Since our Queen assumed the globe, the sceptre.

II

She beloved for a kindliness
Rare in Fable or History,
Queen, and Empress of India,
Crowned so long with a diadem
Never worn by a worthier,
Now with prosperous auguries
Comes at last to the bounteous
Crowning year of her Jubilee.

III

Nothing of the lawless, of the Despot,
Nothing of the vulgar, or vainglorious,
All is gracious, gentle, great and Queenly.

IV

You then joyfully, all of you,
Set the mountain aflame tonight,
Shoot your stars to the firmament,
Deck your houses, illuminate
All your towns for a festival,
And in each let a multitude
Loyal, each, to the heart of it,
One full voice of allegiance,
Hail the fair Ceremonial
Of this year of her Jubilee.

V

Queen, as true to womanhood as Queenhood,
Glorying in the glories of her people,
Sorrowing with the sorrows of the lowest!

¶418. *15. joyfully*] *1889*; loyally *1887*.
*16–17*] *1889*; *not 1887*.
*23. fair*] *1889*; great *1887*.

VI

You, that wanton in affluence,
Spare not now to be bountiful,
Call your poor to regale with you,
All the lowly, the destitute,
Make their neighbourhood healthfuller,
Give your gold to the Hospital,
Let the weary be comforted,
Let the needy be banqueted,
Let the maimed in his heart rejoice
At this glad Ceremonial,
And this year of her Jubilee.

VII

Henry's fifty years are all in shadow,
Gray with distance Edward's fifty summers,
Even her Grandsire's fifty half forgotten.

VIII

You, the Patriot Architect,
You that shape for Eternity,
Raise a stately memorial,
Make it regally gorgeous,
Some Imperial Institute,
Rich in symbol, in ornament,
Which may speak to the centuries,
All the centuries after us,
Of this great Ceremonial,
And this year of her Jubilee.

IX

Fifty years of ever-broadening Commerce!
Fifty years of ever-brightening Science!
Fifty years of ever-widening Empire!

X

You, the Mighty, the Fortunate,
You, the Lord-territorial,
You, the Lord-manufacturer,

*31*] *1889*; *not 1887*.
*37*] *1889*; *not 1887*.
*38*. *And*] *1889*; At *1887*.
*39–41*. The long reigns of Henry III, Edward III, and George III.
*43*] *1889*; *not 1887*.
*44*. *Raise*] *1889*; Shape *1887*.
*50*] *1889*; *not 1887*.
*51*. *And*] *1889*; Of *1887*.

You, the hardy, laborious,
Patient children of Albion,
You, Canadian, Indian,
Australasian, African,
All your hearts be in harmony,
All your voices in unison,
Singing 'Hail to the glorious
Golden year of her Jubilee!'

XI

Are there thunders moaning in the distance?
Are there spectres moving in the darkness?
Trust the Hand of Light will lead her people,
Till the thunders pass, the spectres vanish,
And the Light is Victor, and the darkness
Dawns into the Jubilee of the Ages.

# 419 To Professor Jebb, with the Following Poem

[Demeter and Persephone]

Published *1889*, introducing *Demeter and Persephone* (p. 1373). It is not in the *Virginia* trial edition of *1889*, but is added by pen to a *Lincoln* trial edition. R. C. Jebb (1841–1905), classical scholar and an acquaintance of T.'s, had written an Ode in Greek for the 800th anniversary of the University of Bologna, June 1888. Jebb sent T. a copy on 26 June (*Lincoln*). He had assisted T. with the sources of *Demeter and Persephone*. T.'s dedication is mentioned by Jebb during a visit to T., 5 Oct. 1889 (*Life and Letters*, ed. C. Jebb, 1907, p. 274).

Fair things are slow to fade away,
Bear witness you, that yesterday
    From out the Ghost of Pindar in you
Rolled an Olympian; and they say

*68. Hand . . . will lead*] *1889*; Lord . . . to guide *1887*.

¶419. *2. 1889* note: 'In Bologna'.

*4.* Pindar's Olympian Odes were in honour of victors at the games. *Rolled*: cp. (noting the subject) Cowley's *Praise of Pindar* 12–13: 'So Pindar does new Words and Figures roul / Down his impetuous Dithyrambique Tide'. There was a copy of Cowley at Somersby (*Lincoln*). *1889* note: 'They say, for the fact is doubtful'.

That here the torpid mummy wheat
Of Egypt bore a grain as sweet
    As that which gilds the glebe of England,
Sunned with a summer of milder heat.

So may this legend for awhile,
If greeted by your classic smile,
    Though dead in its Trinacrian Enna,
Blossom again on a colder isle.

# 420 Demeter and Persephone

(In Enna)

Published *1889*. R. C. Jebb (see above) directed H.T. to the *Homeric Hymn to Demeter*, 19 Aug. 1886 (*Lincoln*); the poem was finished May 1887 (*Mem.* ii 335). The title is *Demeter* in a trial edition (*Lincoln*). 'The poem was written at my request, because I knew that my father considered Demeter one of the most beautiful types of womanhood. He said: "I will write it, but when I write an antique like this I must put it into a frame–something modern about it. It is no use giving a mere *réchauffé* of old legends." He would give as an example of the frame [ll. 126–36]' (H.T.). C. Dahl (*VS* i, 1958, 356–62) argues that T.'s 'frame' may be not only the Christian application, but also a reply to Swinburne's *Hymn to Proserpine*. J. Kissane (*VS* vi, 1962, 25–8) relates it to Victorian attitudes to mythology, and suggests affinities with Pater's essay *The Myth of Demeter and Persephone*. H.T. gives as sources the *Homeric Hymn to Demeter*; Ovid, *Metamorphoses* v 341–571, and *Fasti* iv 419–618; all three of which provide the outline of the legend and many details. D. Bush adds Claudian's *Proserpine*, which T. had translated in his youth (p. 3), for such details as those of the Fates and of Hell (*Mythology and the Romantic Tradition*, 1937, p. 220). The concluding prophecy of Christianity may owe something to comparable effects in Browning, as in *Cleon*.

Faint as a climate-changing bird that flies
All night across the darkness, and at dawn
Falls on the threshold of her native land,
And can no more, thou camest, O my child,

5. *mummy wheat*: a variety grown in Egypt and said to come from grains found in mummy-cases. Martin Tupper claimed to have 'resuscitated mummy-wheat', and he exhibited it in the library of the Royal Institution (*Literary Gazette*, 18 June 1842).
11. *Trinacrian*: Sicilian. Enna is the location of *Demeter and Persephone*.

Led upward by the God of ghosts and dreams,
Who laid thee at Eleusis, dazed and dumb
With passing through at once from state to state,
Until I brought thee hither, that the day,
When here thy hands let fall the gathered flower,
Might break through clouded memories once again
On thy lost self. A sudden nightingale
Saw thee, and flashed into a frolic of song
And welcome; and a gleam as of the moon,
When first she peers along the tremulous deep,
Fled wavering o'er thy face, and chased away
That shadow of a likeness to the king
Of shadows, thy dark mate. Persephone!
Queen of the dead no more – my child! Thine eyes
Again were human-godlike, and the Sun
Burst from a swimming fleece of winter gray,
And robed thee in his day from head to feet –
'Mother!' and I was folded in thine arms.

¶420. *5–6.* Hermes or Mercury brought Persephone back from Hades to Eleusis where Demeter awaited her; as in the *Homeric Hymn.*
*8–11*] *H.Nbk 53* has three stages:

(*a*) I brought thee hither that a glance
At thy last sight on earth, the flowery gleam
Of Enna, might have power to disentrance
Thy senses.

(*b*) I brought thee hither, to the fields
Where thou and thy sea-nymphs were used to roam
And thy scared hands let fall the gathered flower,
For here thy last bright day beneath the sun
Might float across thy memory and unfold
The sleeping sense.

(*c*) I brought thee hither, where thy hands
Let fall the gathered flowers, that here again
Thy last bright hours of sunshine upon earth
Might break on darkened memories.

J. H. Buckley (pp. 245–6) quotes and discusses these stages in composition. G. R. Stange notes the echo of *Paradise Lost* iv 268–71 (Killham, *Critical Essays on Tennyson*, p. 145).

*13–20.* Cp. Ovid's *Metamorphoses* v 569–71: *nam modo quae poterat Diti quoque maesta videri, / laeta deae frons est, ut sol, qui tectus aquosis / nubibus ante fuit, victis e nubibus exit.* ('For she who but lately even to Dis seemed sad, now wears a joyful countenance; like the sun which, long concealed behind dark and misty clouds, disperses the clouds and reveals his face.')

Child, those imperial disimpassioned eyes
Awed even me at first, thy mother–eyes
That oft had seen the serpent-wanded power
Draw downward into Hades with his drift
Of flickering spectres, lighted from below
By the red race of fiery Phlegethon;
But when before have Gods or men beheld
The Life that had descended re-arise,
And lighted from above him by the Sun?
So mighty was the mother's childless cry,
A cry that rang through Hades, Earth, and Heaven!

So in this pleasant vale we stand again,
The field of Enna, now once more ablaze
With flowers that brighten as thy footstep falls,
All flowers–but for one black blur of earth
Left by that closing chasm, through which the car
Of dark Aïdoneus rising rapt thee hence.
And here, my child, though folded in thine arms,
I feel the deathless heart of motherhood
Within me shudder, lest the naked glebe
Should yawn once more into the gulf, and thence
The shrilly whinnyings of the team of Hell,
Ascending, pierce the glad and songful air,
And all at once their arched necks, midnight-maned,
Jet upward through the mid-day blossom. No!
For, see, thy foot has touched it; all the space
Of blank earth-baldness clothes itself afresh,
And breaks into the crocus-purple hour
That saw thee vanish.
Child, when thou wert gone,
I envied human wives, and nested birds,
Yea, the cubbed lioness; went in search of thee
Through many a palace, many a cot, and gave
Thy breast to ailing infants in the night,
And set the mother waking in amaze
To find her sick one whole; and forth again

25. *serpent-wanded*: Mercury's *caduceus*, his staff entwined with serpents.
28. *race*: strong current.
39. *Aidoneus*: Pluto or Dis.
44. Cp. *Oh! ye wild winds* 22: 'the shrilly wailings'.
53*ff*. The fullest account of Demeter's wanderings was in *Fasti* iv.
57. In the *Homeric Hymn*, Demeter nurses the baby Demophoon; in *Fasti* iv 537–44, she cures a child.

Among the wail of midnight winds, and cried,
'Where is my loved one? Wherefore do ye wail?'
And out from all the night an answer shrilled,
'We know not, and we know not why we wail.'
I climbed on all the cliffs of all the seas,
And asked the waves that moan about the world
'Where? do ye make your moaning for my child?'
And round from all the world the voices came
'We know not, and we know not why we moan.'
'Where'? and I stared from every eagle-peak,
I thridded the black heart of all the woods,
I peered through tomb and cave, and in the storms
Of Autumn swept across the city, and heard
The murmur of their temples chanting me,
Me, me, the desolate Mother! 'Where'? – and turned,
And fled by many a waste, forlorn of man,
And grieved for man through all my grief for thee, –
The jungle rooted in his shattered hearth,
The serpent coiled about his broken shaft,
The scorpion crawling over naked skulls; –
I saw the tiger in the ruined fane
Spring from his fallen God, but trace of thee
I saw not; and far on, and, following out
A league of labyrinthine darkness, came
On three gray heads beneath a gleaming rift.
'Where'? and I heard one voice from all the three
'We know not, for we spin the lives of men,
And not of Gods, and know not why we spin!
There is a Fate beyond us.' Nothing knew.

Last as the likeness of a dying man,
Without his knowledge, from him flits to warn

*62–3.* Based on the *Homeric Hymn* and Ovid, but cp. *Lycidas* 91–3: 'He ask'd the Waves, and ask'd the Fellon winds, / What hard mishap hath doom'd this gentle swain? / And question'd every gust of rugged wings.'
*67.* 'stared', 'eagle', 'peak' suggest Keats, *On First Looking into Chapman's Homer.*
*72. desolate Mother*: *mater dolorosa.*
*83–6.* T. compares Virgil, *Ecloques* iv 46–7: '*Talia saecla*', *suis dixerunt* '*currite*' *fusis / concordes stabili fatorum numine Parcae.* ('"Ages such as these, glide on!" cried to their spindles the Fates, voicing in unison the fixed will of Destiny!')
*87.* Cp. Lucretius iv 37–8, 760–61: *ne forte animas Acherunte reamur / effugere aut umbras inter vivos volitare . . . / certe ut videamur cernere eum*

A far-off friendship that he comes no more,
So he, the God of dreams, who heard my cry,
Drew from thyself the likeness of thyself
Without thy knowledge, and thy shadow past
Before me, crying 'The Bright one in the highest
Is brother of the Dark one in the lowest,
And Bright and Dark have sworn that I, the child
Of thee, the great Earth-Mother, thee, the Power
That lifts her buried life from gloom to bloom,
Should be for ever and for evermore
The Bride of Darkness.'
So the Shadow wailed.
Then I, Earth-Goddess, cursed the Gods of Heaven.
I would not mingle with their feasts; to me
Their nectar smacked of hemlock on the lips,
Their rich ambrosia tasted aconite.
The man, that only lives and loves an hour,
Seemed nobler than their hard Eternities.
My quick tears killed the flower, my ravings hushed
The bird, and lost in utter grief I failed
To send my life through olive-yard and vine
And golden grain, my gift to helpless man.
Rain-rotten died the wheat, the barley-spears
Were hollow-husked, the leaf fell, and the sun,
Pale at my grief, drew down before his time
Sickening, and Ætna kept her winter snow.
Then He, the brother of this Darkness, He
Who still is highest, glancing from his height
On earth a fruitless fallow, when he missed
The wonted steam of sacrifice, the praise
And prayer of men, decreed that thou should'st dwell
For nine white moons of each whole year with me,
Three dark ones in the shadow with thy King.

*quem / rellicta vita.* ('Lest by chance we should think that spirits escape from Acheron or ghosts flit about amongst the living . . . that we seem verily to see him who has left his life').

*93–4.* Zeus was brother of Aidoneus; these lines were suggested by the *Homeric Hymn.*

*101.* Based on *Homeric Hymn* 49–50.

*110.* *Rain-rotten*: a detail from *Metamorphoses* v 483.

*119–20.* In the *Homeric Hymn*, 8 months to 4; in Ovid, 6 to 6. A last-minute correction by T. from 'eight . . . Four' (trial edition of *1889*, *Lincoln*).

Once more the reaper in the gleam of dawn
Will see me by the landmark far away,
Blessing his field, or seated in the dusk
Of even, by the lonely threshing-floor,
Rejoicing in the harvest and the grange.
Yet I, Earth-Goddess, am but ill-content
With them, who still are highest. Those gray heads,
What meant they by their 'Fate beyond the Fates'
But younger kindlier Gods to bear us down,
As we bore down the Gods before us? Gods,
To quench, not hurl the thunderbolt, to stay,
Not spread the plague, the famine; Gods indeed,
To send the noon into the night and break
The sunless halls of Hades into Heaven?
Till thy dark lord accept and love the Sun,
And all the Shadow die into the Light,
When thou shalt dwell the whole bright year with me,
And souls of men, who grew beyond their race,
And made themselves as Gods against the fear
Of Death and Hell; and thou that hast from men,
As Queen of Death, that worship which is Fear,
Henceforth, as having risen from out the dead,
Shalt ever send thy life along with mine
From buried grain through springing blade, and bless
Their garnered Autumn also, reap with me,
Earth-mother, in the harvest hymns of Earth
The worship which is Love, and see no more
The Stone, the Wheel, the dimly-glimmering lawns
Of that Elysium, all the hateful fires
Of torment, and the shadowy warrior glide
Along the silent field of Asphodel.

*121–5.* Recalling Keats, *To Autumn*.

*129.* H.T. compares the prophecy of the downfall of Zeus, Aeschylus's *Prometheus Bound* 907ff. The reference to 'younger gods' suggests Aeschylus's *Eumenides* 808, and also (as D. Bush says) Keats's *Hyperion* ii 71, the theme of which might be summed up by T.'s ll. 129–30.

*139–47*] *Added by pen to Trinity College trial edition of 1889* ('against . . . Love').

*150–1.* Cp. *Odyssey* xi 538–9: *Ὣς ᾿εφάμην, ψυχὴ δὲ ποδώκεος Αἰακίδαο φοίτα μακρὰ βιβᾶσα κατ᾽ ἀσφοδελὸν λειμῶνα.* ('So I spoke, and the spirit of the son of Aeacus departed with long strides over the field of asphodel.').

# 421 Owd Roä

Published *1889*. Written and ready for the press, 15 Dec. 1887 (*Mem.* ii 343), though 'still open to correction' in Aug. 1889 (H. D. Rawnsley, *Memories of the Tennysons*, 1900, p. 134). T. says: 'I read in one of the daily papers of a child saved by a black retriever from a burning house. The details in this story are, of course, mine.' All glossarial notes below are by T. in *1889*.

Naäy, noä mander o' use to be callin' 'im Roä, Roä, Roä,
Fur the dog's stoän-deäf, an' 'e's blind, 'e can naither stan' nor goä.

But I meäns fur to maäke 'is owd aäge as 'appy as iver I can,
Fur I owäs owd Roäver moor nor I iver owäd mottal man.

Thou's rode of 'is back when a babby, afoor thou was gotten too owd,
Fur 'e'd fetch an' carry like owt, 'e was allus as good as gowd.

Eh, but 'e'd fight wi' a will *when* 'e fowt; 'e could howd 'is oan,
An' Roä was the dog as knawed when an' wheere to bury his boane.

An' 'e kep his heäd hoop like a king, an' 'e'd niver not down wi' is taäil,
Fur 'e'd niver done nowt to be shaämed on, when we was i' Howlaby Daäle.

An' 'e sarved me sa well when 'e lived, that, Dick, when 'e cooms to be deäd,
I thinks as I'd like fur to hev soom soort of a sarvice reäd.

Fur 'e's moor good sense na the Parliament man 'at stans fur us 'ere,
An' I'd voät fur 'im, my oän sen, if 'e could but stan fur the Shere.

'Faäithful an' True'–them words be i' Scriptur–an' Faäithful an' True
Ull be fun' upo' four short legs ten times fur one upo' two.

An' maäybe they'll walk upo' two but I knaws they runs upo' four,–
Bedtime, Dicky! but waäit till tha 'eärs it be strikin' the hour.

Fur I wants to tell tha o' Roä when we lived i' Howlaby Daäle,
Ten year sin–Naäy–naäy! tha mun nobbut hev' one glass of aäle.

Straänge an' owd-farraned the 'ouse, an' belt long afoor my daäy
Wi' haäfe o' the chimleys a-twizzened an' twined like a band o' haäy.

¶421. *Title*: Old Rover.
*1. mander*: manner.
*7. howd*: hold.
*15. Revelation* xix 11, 'a white horse, and he that sat upon him was called faithful and true'.
*16. fun'*: found.
*17. four*: 'ou' as in 'house'.
*21. owd-farraned*: old-fashioned. *belt*: built.
*22. a-twizzened*: twisted.

The fellers as maäkes them picturs, 'ud coom at the fall o' the year,
An' sattle their ends upo' stools to pictur the door-poorch theere,

An' the Heagle 'as hed two heäds stannin' theere o' the brokken stick;
An' they niver 'ed seed sich ivin' as grawed hall ower the brick;

An' theere i' the 'ouse one night–but it's down, an' all on it now
Goan into mangles an' tonups, an' raäved slick thruf by the plow–

Theere, when the 'ouse wur a house, one night I wur sittin' aloän,
Wi' Roäver athurt my feeät, an' sleeäpin still as a stoän,

Of a Christmas Eäve, an' as cowd as this, an' the midders as white,
An' the fences all on 'em bolstered oop wi' the windle that night;

An' the cat wur a-sleeäpin alongside Roäver, but I wur awaäke,
An' smoäkin' an' thinkin' o' things–Doänt maäke thysen sick wi' the caäke.

Fur the men ater supper 'ed sung their songs an' 'ed 'ed their beer,
An' 'ed goän their waäys; ther was nobbut three, an' noän on 'em theere.

They was all on 'em feared o' the Ghoäst an' dussn't not sleeäp i' the 'ouse,
But Dicky, the Ghoäst moästlins was nobbut a rat or a mouse.

An' I looökt out wonst at the night, an' the daäle was all of a thaw,
Fur I seed the beck coomin' down like a long black snaäke i' the snaw,

An' I heärd greät heäps o' the snaw slushin' down fro' the bank to the beck,
An' then as I stood i' the doorwaäy, I feeäld it drip o' my neck.

Saw I turned in ageän, an' I thowt o' the good owd times 'at was goan,
An' the munney they maäde by the war, an' the times 'at was coomin' on;

Fur I thowt if the Staäte was a gawin' to let in furriners' wheät,
Howiver was British farmers to stan' ageän o' their feeät.

Howiver was I fur to find my rent an' to paäy my men?
An' all along o' the feller as turned 'is back of hissen.

Thou slep i' the chaumber above us, we couldn't ha' 'eärd tha call,
Sa Moother 'ed telled ma to bring tha down, an' thy craädle an' all;

25. 'On a staff *ragulé*' (T.), i.e., with stumps like those from branches cut off near the stem.
26. *ivin'*: ivy.
28. *mangles an' tonups*: mangolds and turnips.
31. *midders*: meadows.
32. *windle*: drifted snow.
38. *moästlins*: for the most part, generally.
39. *wonst*: once.
48. *the feller*: Peel (T.), referring to the Corn Laws.

Fur the gell o' the farm 'at slep wi' tha then 'ed gotten wer leäve,
Fur to goä that night to 'er foälk by cause o' the Christmas Eäve;

But I cleän forgot tha, my lad, when Moother 'ed gotten to bed,
An' I slep i' my chair hup-on-end, an' the Freeä Traäde runned 'i my 'ead,

Till I dreämed 'at Squire walkt in, an' I says to him 'Squire, ya're laäte,'
Then I seed at 'is faäce wur as red as the Yule-block theer i' the graäte.

An' 'e says 'can ya paäy me the rent tonight?' an' I says to 'im 'Noä,'
An' 'e cotched howd hard o' my hairm, 'Then hout tonight tha shall goä.'

'Tha'll niver,' says I, 'be a-turnin ma hout upo' Christmas Eäve?'
Then I waäked an' I fun it was Roäver a-tuggin' an' teärin' my slieäve.

An' I thowt as 'e'd goän cleän-wud, fur I noäwaäys knawed 'is intent;
An' I says 'Git awaäy, ya beäst,' an' I fetcht 'im a kick an' 'e went.

Then 'e tummled up stairs, fur I 'eard 'im, as if 'e'd 'a brokken 'is neck,
An' I'd cleär forgot, little Dicky, thy chaumber door wouldn't sneck;

An' I slep' i' my chair ageän wi' my hairm hingin' down to the floor,
An' I thowt it was Roäver a-tuggin' an' teärin' me wuss nor afoor,

An' I thowt 'at I kicked 'im ageän, but I kicked thy Moother istead.
'What arta snorin' theere fur? the house is afire,' she said.

Thy Moother 'ed beän a-naggin' about the gell o' the farm,
She offens 'ud spy summut wrong when there warn't not a mossel o' harm;

An' she didn't not solidly meän I wur gawin' that waäy to the bad,
Fur the gell was as howry a trollope as iver traäpesed i' the squad.

But Moother was free of 'er tongue, as I offens 'ev telled 'er mysen,
Sa I kep i' my chair, fur I thowt she was nobbut a-rilin' ma then.

An' I says 'I'd be good to tha, Bess, if tha'd onywaäys let ma be good,'
But she skelpt ma haäfe ower i' the chair, an' screeäd like a Howl gone wud–

'Ya mun run fur the lether. Git oop, if ya're onywaäys good for owt.'
And I says 'If I beänt noäwaäys–not nowadaäys–good fur nowt–

*58. hairm*: arm.
*61. -wud*: mad.
*64. sneck*: latch.
*72.* 'The girl was as dirty a slut as ever trudged in the mud, but there is a sense of slatternliness in "traäpesed" which is not expressed in "trudged"' (T.).
*76.* 'She half overturned me and shrieked like an owl gone mad' (T.).
*77. lether*: ladder.

Yit I beänt sich a Nowt of all Nowts as 'ull hallus do as 'e's bid.'
'But the stairs is afire,' she said; then I seed 'er a-cryin', I did.

An' she beäld 'Ya mun saäve little Dick, an' be sharp about it an' all,'
Sa I runs to the yard fur a lether, an' sets 'im ageän the wall,

An' I claums an' I mashes the winder hin, when I gits to the top,
But the heät druv hout i' my heyes till I feäld mysen ready to drop.

Thy Moother was howdin' the lether, an' tellin' me not to be skeärd,
An' I wasn't afeärd, or I thinks leästwaäys as I wasn't afeärd;

But I couldn't see fur the smoäke wheere thou was a-liggin, my lad,
An' Roäver was theere i' the chaumber a-yowlin' an' yaupin' like mad;

An' thou was a-beälin' likewise, an' a-squeälin', as if tha was bit,
An' it wasn't a bite but a burn, fur the merk's o' thy shou'der yit;

Then I called out Roä, Roä, Roä, thaw I didn't haäfe think as 'e'd 'ear,
*But 'e coomed thruf the fire wi' my bairn i' 'is mouth to the winder theere!*

He coomed like a Hangel o' marcy as soon as 'e 'eärd 'is naäme,
Or like tother Hangel i' Scriptur 'at summun seed i' the flaäme,

When summun 'ed haxed fur a son, an' 'e promised a son to she,
An' Roä was as good as the Hangel i' saävin' a son fur me.

Sa I browt tha down, an' I says 'I mun gaw up ageän fur Roä.'
'Gaw up ageän fur the varmint?' I telled 'er 'Yeäs I mun goä.'

An' I claumbed up ageän to the winder, an' clemmed owd Roä by the 'eäd,
An 'is 'air coomed off i' my 'ands an' I taäked 'im at fust fur deäd;

Fur 'e smelled like a herse a-singein', an' seeämed as blind as a poop,
An' haäfe on 'im bare as a bublin'. I cauldn't wakken 'im oop,

But I browt 'im down, an' we got to the barn, fur the barn wouldn't burn
Wi' the wind blawin' hard tother waäy, an' the wind wasn't like to turn.

An' *I* kep a-callin' o' Roä till 'e waggled 'is taäil fur a bit,
But the cocks kep a-crawin' an' crawin' all night, an' I 'ears 'em yit;

An' the dogs was a-yowlin' all round, and thou was a-squeälin' thysen,
An' Moother was naggin' an' groänin' an' moänin' an' naggin' ageän;

An' I 'eärd the bricks an' the baulks rummle down when the roof gev waäy,
Fur the fire was a-raägin' an' raävin' an' roarin' like judgment daäy.

79. *Nowt*: 'a thoroughly insignificant or worthless person' (T.).
90. *merk*: mark.
94. T. cites *Judges* xiii 20, 'the Angel of the Lord ascended in the flame of the altar'.
99. *clemmed*: clutched.
102. *bublin'*: a young unfledged bird.
109. *baulks*: beams.

Warm enew theere sewer-ly, but the barn was as cowd as owt,
An' we cuddled and huddled togither, an' happt wersens oop as we mowt.

An' I browt Roä round, but Moother 'ed beän sa soäked wi' the thaw
'At she cotched 'er death o' cowd that night, poor soul, i' the straw.

Haäfe o' the parish runned oop when the rigtree was tummlin' in–
Too laäte–but it's all ower now–hall hower–an' ten year sin;

Too laäte, tha mun git tha to bed, but I'll coom an' I'll squench the light,
Fur we moänt 'ev naw moor fires–and soa little Dick, good-night.

# 422 The Ring

## Dedicated to the Hon. J. Russell Lowell

Published *1889*. T. says: 'Mr Lowell told me this legend, or something like it, of a house near where he had once lived.' Written by autumn 1887 (*CT*, pp. 499–500). Lowell answered a letter about the legend, 3 Aug. 1887 (*Lincoln*; the letter is not dated in *Mem.* ii 365, and is misdated '1889' in *Mat.* iv 231). The poem is in *H.Nbk 53* (in H.T.'s hand, revised by T.), of 1887–9; and it is partly in prose in *Nbk 54*. Lowell pointed out that he had told the legend to Henry James, who had used it for *The Romance of Certain Old Clothes* (1868), which deals with the same rivalry between two sisters and the supernatural vengeance taken by the one who dies. (See Miriam Allott, *RES* n.s. vi, 1955, 399–401.) In James, the lover permits his second wife to have the key that guards the relics; in T. she steals it from him. Sir Charles Tennyson suggests that ll. 32–7 were influenced by T.'s meeting with his brother Frederick, who was a spiritualist, in Aug. 1887. In the *Virginia* trial edition of *1889* the poem begins at l. 32; in the *Lincoln* trial edition, ll. 1–31 are added by hand, with many corrections. T. had originally written the opening song in 1833; it is in *T.Nbk 17*, which may not be quoted. In about 1834 (?) (*H.Nbk 18*), he had jotted down: 'He that takes off a ring and feels the phantom of it still pressing his finger.' Cp. the story of *The Sisters* [*They have left the doors ajar*] (p. 1291).

MIRIAM AND HER FATHER

*Miriam* (*singing*)

Mellow moon of heaven,
Bright in blue,
Moon of married hearts,
Hear me, you!

*112. happt wersens*: wrapt ourselves.
*115. rigtree*: the beam that runs along the roof of the house just beneath the ridge.

Twelve times in the year
Bring me bliss,
Globing Honey Moons
Bright as this.

Moon, you fade at times
From the night.
Young again you grow
Out of sight.

Silver crescent-curve,
Coming soon,
Globe again, and make
Honey Moon.

Shall not *my* love last,
Moon, with you,
For ten thousand years
Old and new?

*Father*

And who was he with such love-drunken eyes
They made a thousand honey moons of one?

*Miriam*

The prophet of his own, my Hubert–his
The words, and mine the setting. 'Air and Words,'
Said Hubert, when I sang the song, 'are bride
And bridegroom.' Does it please you?

*Father*

Mainly, child,
Because I hear your Mother's voice in yours.
She—, why, you shiver though the wind is west
With all the warmth of summer.

*Miriam*

Well, I felt
On a sudden I know not what, a breath that past
With all the cold of winter.

*Father (muttering to himself)*

Even so.
The Ghost in Man, the Ghost that once was Man,
But cannot wholly free itself from Man,
Are calling to each other through a dawn
Stranger than earth has ever seen; the veil
Is rending, and the Voices of the day
Are heard across the Voices of the dark.
No sudden heaven, nor sudden hell, for man,
But through the Will of One who knows and rules–

And utter knowledge is but utter love–
Æonian Evolution, swift or slow,
Through all the Spheres–an ever opening height,
An ever lessening earth–and she perhaps,
My Miriam, breaks her latest earthly link
With me today.

*Miriam*

You speak so low, what is it?
Your 'Miriam breaks'–is making a new link
Breaking an old one?

*Father*

No, for we, my child,
Have been till now each other's all-in-all.

*Miriam*

And you the lifelong guardian of the child.

*Father*

I, and one other whom you have not known.

*Miriam*

And who? what other?

*Father*

Whither are you bound?
For Naples which we only left in May?

*Miriam*

No! father, Spain, but Hubert brings me home
With April and the swallow. Wish me joy!

*Father*

What need to wish when Hubert weds in you
The heart of Love, and you the soul of Truth
In Hubert?

*Miriam*

Though you used to call me once
The lonely maiden-Princess of the wood,
Who meant to sleep her hundred summers out
Before a kiss should wake her.

*Father*

Ay, but now
Your fairy Prince has found you, take this ring.

*Miriam*

'Io t'amo'–and these diamonds–beautiful!
'From Walter,' and for me from you then?

*Father*

Well,
One way for Miriam.

*Miriam*

Miriam am I not?

*Father*

This ring bequeathed you by your mother, child,
Was to be given you–such her dying wish–
Given on the morning when you came of age
Or on the day you married. Both the days
Now close in one. The ring is doubly yours.
Why do you look so gravely at the tower?

*Miriam*

I never saw it yet so all ablaze
With creepers crimsoning to the pinnacles,
As if perpetual sunset lingered there,
And all ablaze too in the lake below!
And how the birds that circle round the tower
Are cheeping to each other of their flight
To summer lands!

*Father*

And that has made you grave?
Fly–care not. Birds and brides must leave the nest.
Child, I am happier in your happiness
Than in mine own.

*Miriam*

It is not that!

*Father*

What else?

*Miriam*

That chamber in the tower.

*Father*

What chamber, child?
Your nurse is here?

*Miriam*

My Mother's nurse and mine.
She comes to dress me in my bridal veil.

*Father*

What did she say?

*Miriam*

She said, that you and I
Had been abroad for my poor health so long
She feared I had forgotten her, and I asked
About my Mother, and she said, 'Thy hair
Is golden like thy Mother's, not so fine.'

*Father*

What then? what more?

*Miriam*

She said–perhaps indeed

¶422. *88. Mother's] 1889–94*; Mother *Eversley*.

She wandered, having wandered now so far
Beyond the common date of death–that you,
When I was smaller than the statuette
Of my dear Mother on your bracket here–
You took me to that chamber in the tower,
The topmost–a chest there, by which you knelt–
And there were books and dresses–left to me,
A ring too which you kissed, and I, she said,
I babbled, Mother, Mother–as I used
To prattle to her picture–stretched my hands
As if I saw her; then a woman came
And caught me from my nurse. I hear her yet–
A sound of anger like a distant storm.

*Father*

Garrulous old crone.

*Miriam*

Poor nurse!

*Father*

I bad her keep,
Like a sealed book, all mention of the ring,
For I myself would tell you all today.

*Miriam*

'She too might speak today,' she mumbled. Still,
I scarce have learnt the title of your book,
But you will turn the pages.

*Father*

Ay, today!
I brought you to that chamber on your third
September birthday with your nurse, and felt
An icy breath play on me, while I stoopt
To take and kiss the ring.

*Miriam*

This very ring
Io t'amo?

*Father*

Yes, for some wild hope was mine
That, in the misery of my married life,
Miriam your Mother might appear to me.
She came to you, not me. The storm, you hear
Far-off, is Muriel–your step-mother's voice.

*Miriam*

Vext, that you thought my Mother came to me?
Or at my crying 'Mother'? or to find
My Mother's diamonds hidden from her there,
Like worldly beauties in the Cell, not shown
To dazzle all that see them?

*Father*

Wait a while.
Your mother and step-mother–Miriam Erne
And Muriel Erne–the two were cousins–lived
With Muriel's mother on the down, that sees
A thousand squares of corn and meadow, far
As the gray deep, a landscape which your eyes
Have many a time ranged over when a babe.

*Miriam*

I climbed the hill with Hubert yesterday,
And from the thousand squares, one silent voice
Came on the wind, and seemed to say 'Again.'
We saw far off an old forsaken house,
Then home, and past the ruined mill.

*Father*

And there
I found these cousins often by the brook,
For Miriam sketched and Muriel threw the fly;
The girls of equal age, but one was fair,
And one was dark, and both were beautiful.
No voice for either spoke within my heart
Then, for the surface eye, that only doats
On outward beauty, glancing from the one
To the other, knew not that which pleased it most,
The raven ringlet or the gold; but both
Were dowerless, and myself, I used to walk
This Terrace–morbid, melancholy; mine
And yet not mine the hall, the farm, the field;
For all that ample woodland whispered 'debt,'
The brook that feeds this lakelet murmured 'debt,'
And in yon arching avenue of old elms,
Though mine, not mine, I heard the sober rook
And carrion crow cry 'Mortgage.'

*Miriam*

Father's fault
Visited on the children!

*Father*

Ay, but then
A kinsman, dying, summoned me to Rome–
He left me wealth–and while I journeyed hence,
And saw the world fly by me like a dream,
And while I communed with my truest self,
I woke to all of truest in myself,
Till, in the gleam of those mid-summer dawns,
The form of Muriel faded, and the face

Of Miriam grew upon me, till I knew;
And past and future mixed in Heaven and made
The rosy twilight of a perfect day.

*Miriam*

So glad? no tear for him, who left you wealth,
Your kinsman?

*Father*

I had seen the man but once;
He loved my name not me; and then I passed
Home, and through Venice, where a jeweller,
So far gone down, or so far up in life,
That he was nearing his own hundred, sold
This ring to me, then laughed 'the ring is weird.'
And weird and worn and wizard-like was he.
'Why weird?' I asked him; and he said 'The souls
Of two repentant Lovers guard the ring;'
Then with a ribald twinkle in his bleak eyes–
'And if you give the ring to any maid,
They still remember what it cost them here,
And bind the maid to love you by the ring;
And if the ring were stolen from the maid,
The theft were death or madness to the thief,
So sacred those Ghost Lovers hold the gift.'
And then he told their legend:

'Long ago
Two lovers parted by a scurrilous tale
Had quarrelled, till the man repenting sent
This ring "Io t'amo" to his best beloved,
And sent it on her birthday. She in wrath
Returned it on her birthday, and that day
His death-day, when, half-frenzied by the ring,
He wildly fought a rival suitor, him
The causer of that scandal, fought and fell;
And she that came to part them all too late,
And found a corpse and silence, drew the ring
From his dead finger, wore it till her death,
Shrined him within the temple of her heart,
Made every moment of her after life
A virgin victim to his memory,
And dying rose, and reared her arms, and cried
"I see him, Io t'amo, Io t'amo."'

*Miriam*

Legend or true? so tender should be true!
Did *he* believe it? did you ask him?

*Father*

Ay!

But that half skeleton, like a barren ghost
From out the fleshless world of spirits, laughed:
A hollow laughter!

*Miriam*

Vile, so near the ghost
Himself, to laugh at love in death! But you?

*Father*

Well, as the bygone lover through this ring
Had sent his cry for her forgiveness, I
Would call through this 'Io t'amo' to the heart
Of Miriam; then I bad the man engrave
'From Walter' on the ring, and send it–wrote
Name, surname, all as clear as noon, but he–
Some younger hand must have engraven the ring–
His fingers were so stiffened by the frost
Of seven and ninety winters, that he scrawled
A 'Miriam' that might seem a 'Muriel';
And Muriel claimed and opened what I meant
For Miriam, took the ring, and flaunted it
Before that other whom I loved and love.
A mountain stayed me here, a minster there,
A galleried palace, or a battlefield,
Where stood the sheaf of Peace: but–coming home–
And on your Mother's birthday–all but yours–
A week betwixt–and when the tower as now
Was all ablaze with crimson to the roof,
And all ablaze too plunging in the lake
Head-foremost–who were those that stood between
The tower and that rich phantom of the tower?
Muriel and Miriam, each in white, and like
May-blossoms in mid autumn–was it they?
A light shot upward on them from the lake.
What sparkled there? whose hand was that? they stood
So close together. I am not keen of sight,
But coming nearer–Muriel had the ring–
'O Miriam! have you given your ring to her?
O Miriam!' Miriam reddened, Muriel clenched
The hand that wore it, till I cried again:
'O Miriam, if you love me take the ring!'
She glanced at me, at Muriel, and was mute.
'Nay, if you cannot love me, let it be.'
Then–Muriel standing ever statue-like–
She turned, and in her soft imperial way
And saying gently: 'Muriel, by your leave,'
Unclosed the hand, and from it drew the ring,

And gave it me, who passed it down her own,
'Io t'amo, all is well then.' Muriel fled.

*Miriam*

Poor Muriel!

*Father*

Ay, poor Muriel when you hear
What follows! Miriam loved me from the first,
Not through the ring; but on her marriage-morn
This birthday, death-day, and betrothal ring,
Laid on her table overnight, was gone;
And after hours of search and doubt and threats,
And hubbub, Muriel entered with it, 'See!–
Found in a chink of that old mouldered floor!'
My Miriam nodded with a pitying smile,
As who should say 'that those who lose can find.'
Then I and she were married for a year,
One year without a storm, or even a cloud;
And you my Miriam born within the year;
And she my Miriam dead within the year.
I sat beside her dying, and she gaspt:
'The books, the miniature, the lace are hers,
My ring too when she comes of age, or when
She marries; you–you loved me, kept your word.
You love me still "Io t'amo."–Muriel–no–
She cannot love; she loves her own hard self,
Her firm will, her fixed purpose. Promise me,
Miriam not Muriel–she shall have the ring.'
And there the light of other life, which lives
Beyond our burial and our buried eyes,
Gleamed for a moment in her own on earth.
I swore the vow, then with my latest kiss
Upon them, closed her eyes, which would not close,
But kept their watch upon the ring and you.
Your birthday was her death-day.

*Miriam*

O poor Mother!
And you, poor desolate Father, and poor me,
The little senseless, worthless, wordless babe,
Saved when your life was wrecked!

*Father*

Desolate? yes!
Desolate as that sailor, whom the storm
Had parted from his comrade in the boat,
And dashed half dead on barren sands, was I.
Nay, you were my one solace; only–you
Were always ailing. Muriel's mother sent,

And sure am I, by Muriel, one day came
And saw you, shook her head, and patted yours,
And smiled, and making with a kindly pinch
Each poor pale cheek a momentary rose–
'*That* should be fixed,' she said; 'your pretty bud,
So blighted here, would flower into full health
Among our heath and bracken. Let her come!
And we will feed her with our mountain air,
And send her home to you rejoicing.' No–
We could not part. And once, when you my girl
Rode on my shoulder home–the tiny fist
Had graspt a daisy from your Mother's grave–
By the lych-gate was Muriel. 'Ay,' she said,
'Among the tombs in this damp vale of yours!
You scorn my Mother's warning, but the child
Is paler than before. We often walk
In open sun, and see beneath our feet
The mist of autumn gather from your lake,
And shroud the tower; and once we only saw
Your gilded vane, a light above the mist'–
(Our old bright bird that still is veering there
Above his four gold letters) 'and the light,'
She said, 'was like that light'–and there she paused,
And long; till I believing that the girl's
Lean fancy, groping for it, could not find
One likeness, laughed a little and found her two–
'A warrior's crest above the cloud of war'–
'A fiery phœnix rising from the smoke,
The pyre he burnt in.'–'Nay,' she said, 'the light
That glimmers on the marsh and on the grave.'
And spoke no more, but turned and passed away.
Miriam, I am not surely one of those
Caught by the flower that closes on the fly,
But after ten slow weeks her fixed intent,
In aiming at an all but hopeless mark
To strike it, struck; I took, I left you there;
I came, I went, was happier day by day;
For Muriel nursed you with a mother's care;
Till on that clear and heather-scented height
The rounder cheek had brightened into bloom.
She always came to meet me carrying you,
And all her talk was of the babe she loved;
So, following her old pastime of the brook,
She threw the fly for me; but oftener left
That angling to the mother. 'Muriel's health
Had weakened, nursing little Miriam. Strange!

She used to shun the wailing babe, and doats
On this of yours.' But when the matron saw
That hinted love was only wasted bait,
Not risen to, she was bolder. 'Ever since
You sent the fatal ring'–I told her 'sent
To Miriam,' 'Doubtless–ay, but ever since
In all the world my dear one sees but you–
In your sweet babe she finds but you–she makes
Her heart a mirror that reflects but you.'
And then the tear fell, the voice broke. *Her* heart!
I gazed into the mirror, as a man
Who sees his face in water, and a stone,
That glances from the bottom of the pool,
Strike upward through the shadow; yet at last,
Gratitude–loneliness–desire to keep
So skilled a nurse about you always–nay!
Some half remorseful kind of pity too–
Well! well, you know I married Muriel Erne.
'I take thee Muriel for my wedded wife'–
I had forgotten it was your birthday, child–
When all at once with some electric thrill
A cold air passed between us, and the hands
Fell from each other, and were joined again.
No second cloudless honeymoon was mine.
For by and by she sickened of the farce,
She dropt the gracious mask of motherhood,
She came no more to meet me, carrying you,
Nor ever cared to set you on her knee,
Nor ever let you gambol in her sight,
Nor ever cheered you with a kindly smile,
Nor ever ceased to clamour for the ring;
Why had I sent the ring at first to her?
Why had I made her love me through the ring,
And then had changed? so fickle are men–the best!
Not she–but now my love was hers again,
The ring by right, she said, was hers again.
At times too shrilling in her angrier moods,
'That weak and watery nature love you? No!
"*Io* t'amo, *Io* t'amo"!' flung herself
Against my heart, but often while her lips
Were warm upon my cheek, an icy breath,
As from the grating of a sepulchre,
Past over both. I told her of my vow,
No pliable idiot I to break my vow;
But still she made her outcry for the ring;

For one monotonous fancy maddened her,
Till I myself was maddened with her cry,
And even that 'Io t'amo,' those three sweet
Italian words, became a weariness.
My people too were scared with eerie sounds,
A footstep, a low throbbing in the walls,
A noise of falling weights that never fell,
Weird whispers, bells that rang without a hand,
Door-handles turned when none was at the door,
And bolted doors that opened of themselves:
And one betwixt the dark and light had seen
*Her*, bending by the cradle of her babe.

*Miriam*

And I remember once that being waked
By noises in the house–and no one near–
I cried for nurse, and felt a gentle hand
Fall on my forehead, and a sudden face
Looked in upon me like a gleam and passed,
And I was quieted, and slept again.
Or is it some half memory of a dream?

*Father*

Your fifth September birthday.

*Miriam*

And the face,
The hand,–my Mother.

*Father*

Miriam, on that day
Two lovers parted by no scurrilous tale–
Mere want of gold–and still for twenty years
Bound by the golden cord of their first love–
Had asked us to their marriage, and to share
Their marriage-banquet. Muriel, paler then
Than ever you were in your cradle, moaned,
'I am fitter for my bed, or for my grave,
I cannot go, go you.' And then she rose,
She clung to me with such a hard embrace,
So lingeringly long, that half-amazed
I parted from her, and I went alone.
And when the bridegroom murmured, 'With this ring,'
I felt for what I could not find, the key,
The guardian of her relics, of *her* ring.
I kept it as a sacred amulet
About me,–gone! and gone in that embrace!
Then, hurrying home, I found her not in house
Or garden–up the tower–an icy air

Fled by me.–There, the chest was open–all
The sacred relics tost about the floor–
Among them Muriel lying on her face–
I raised her, called her 'Muriel, Muriel wake!'
The fatal ring lay near her; the glazed eye
Glared at me as in horror. Dead! I took
And chafed the freezing hand. A red mark ran
All round one finger pointed straight, the rest
Were crumpled inwards. Dead!–and maybe stung
With some remorse, had stolen, worn the ring–
Then torn it from her finger, or as if–
For never had I seen her show remorse–
As if–

*Miriam*

–those two Ghost lovers–

*Father*

Lovers yet–

*Miriam*

Yes, yes!

*Father*

–but dead so long, gone up so far,
That now their ever-rising life has dwarfed
Or lost the moment of their past on earth,
As we forget our wail at being born.
As if–

*Miriam*

a dearer ghost had–

*Father*

–wrenched it away.

*Miriam*

Had floated in with sad reproachful eyes,
Till from her own hand she had torn the ring
In fright, and fallen dead. And I myself
Am half afraid to wear it.

*Father*

Well, no more!
No bridal music this! but fear not you!
You have the ring she guarded; that poor link
With earth is broken, and has left her free,
Except that, still drawn downward for an hour,
Her spirit hovering by the church, where she
Was married too, may linger, till she sees
Her maiden coming like a Queen, who leaves
Some colder province in the North to gain
Her capital city, where the loyal bells
Clash welcome–linger, till her own, the babe

She leaned to from her Spiritual sphere,
Her lonely maiden-Princess, crowned with flowers,
Has entered on the larger woman-world
Of wives and mothers.
But the bridal veil–
Your nurse is waiting. Kiss me child and go.

# 423 To Ulysses

Published *1889*. Written early 1888 (ll. 6–8), and read to F. T. Palgrave in Nov. (*Mem.* ii 507). T. comments that *Ulysses* was 'the title of a number of essays by W. G. Palgrave. He died at Monte Video before seeing my poem'. Palgrave was the brother of F. T. Palgrave (friend of T., and editor of *The Golden Treasury*); T. had met him many times since 1860. His *Ulysses* was published in Nov. 1887, and T. was presented with a copy; he died 30 Sept. 1888 (*Mem.* ii 507). T. uses the *In Memoriam* stanza to praise the book, as in *To E.L.* (p. 993).

I

Ulysses, much-experienced man,
Whose eyes have known this globe of ours,
Her tribes of men, and trees, and flowers,
From Corrientes to Japan,

II

To you that bask below the Line,
I soaking here in winter wet–
The century's three strong eights have met
To drag me down to seventy-nine

III

In summer if I reach my day–
To you, yet young, who breathe the balm
Of summer-winters by the palm
And orange grove of Paraguay,

¶423. *1–3.* Palgrave's epigraph (in explanation of his title) had been *Qui multorum hominum mores et vidit et urbes*, i.e. Horace's *Epistles* I ii 19–20: *qui . . . multorum providus urbes / et mores hominum inspexit*, from *Odyssey* i 3. Cp. *Ulysses* 13: 'Much have I seen and known; cities of men . . .'.
*4. Corrientes*: in Argentina.
*10–11.* Cp. *The Brook* 196: 'breathes in April–autumns'.
*11. summer-winters*] sunnier summers *H.Nbk 55*.

IV

I tolerant of the colder time,
Who love the winter woods, to trace
On paler heavens the branching grace
Of leafless elm, or naked lime,

V

And see my cedar green, and there
My giant ilex keeping leaf
When frost is keen and days are brief–
Or marvel how in English air

VI

My yucca, which no winter quells,
Although the months have scarce begun,
Has pushed toward our faintest sun
A spike of half-accomplished bells–

VII

Or watch the waving pine which here
The warrior of Caprera set,
A name that earth will not forget
Till earth has rolled her latest year–

VIII

I, once half-crazed for larger light
On broader zones beyond the foam,
But chaining fancy now at home
Among the quarried downs of Wight,

14. *the winter woods,*] with careful [patient *1st reading*] eye *MS.*
17. *And*] Who *MS.*
20. *Or . . . how*] While yonder out *MS 1st reading.*
21. *My*] One *MS 1st reading.*
23. *our faintest*] the hazy *MS 1st reading*; our feeblest *MS 2nd reading.*
25. *Or*] Who *MS 1st reading.* *waving pine*] slim pine wave *MS 1st reading.*
26. *1889* note: 'Garibaldi said to me, alluding to his barren island, "I wish I had your trees."' T. noted that Garibaldi planted a Wellingtonia at Farringford, April 1864. *Caprera*: Garibaldi's home, an island off Sardinia.
29. *once half-crazed*] yearning once *MS 1st reading*; once half-mad *MS 2nd reading.* Cp. *You ask me, why* 26–8: 'I seek a warmer sky, / And I will see before I die / The palms and temples of the South.' Recalled perhaps because it uses the *In Memoriam* stanza.
31. *chaining fancy now*] now with fancy chained *MS 1st reading.*

IX

Not less would yield full thanks to you
For your rich gift, your tale of lands
I know not, your Arabian sands;
Your cane, your palm, tree-fern, bamboo,

X

The wealth of tropic bower and brake;
Your Oriental Eden-isles,
Where man, nor only Nature smiles;
Your wonder of the boiling lake;

XI

Phra-Chai, the Shadow of the Best,
Phra-bat the step; your Pontic coast;
Crag-cloister; Anatolian Ghost;
Hong-Kong, Karnac, and all the rest.

XII

Through which I followed line by line
Your leading hand, and came, my friend,
To prize your various book, and send
A gift of slenderer value, mine.

33. *Not less*] I yet *MS 1st reading*.
34. *1889* note: 'The tale of Nejd' (in Arabia).
38. *1889* note: 'The Philippines'. Cp. *Locksley Hall* 164: 'summer isles of Eden'. Palgrave may have been thinking of this (he was certainly thinking of *The Lotos-Eaters*) when he called the Philippines 'isles of Eden, lotus-lands' (p. 113). T., as it were, returns the compliment.
40. *wonder*] marvel *MS 1st reading*. *1889* note: 'In Dominica' (West Indies).
40–44. The listing of the natural wonders suggests *On Sublimity* 81–100 (p. 118).
41. *1889* note: 'The Shadow of the Lord. Certain obscure markings on a rock in Siam, which express the image of Buddha to the Buddhist more or less distinctly according to his faith and his moral worth.'
42. *Phra-bat*: *1889* note: 'The footstep of the Lord on another rock.'
43. *1889* notes: 'The monastery of Sumelas', and 'Anatolian Spectre stories'.
44. *Hong-Kong*: *1889* note: 'The Three Cities' (the title of Palgrave's chapter on Hong-Kong). *Karnac*: *1889* note: 'Travels in Egypt'.

# 424 Happy

## The Leper's Bride

Published *1889*. Written Feb.–April 1888 (*Mem.* ii 345). A note shows that it was suggested by an article mentioning the churches' attitude to lepers' marriages, 4 Feb. 1888, by E. Boucher-James in the *Isle of Wight County Press*: 'with a love stronger than this living death, lepers were followed into banishment from the haunts of men by their faithful wives'. T. learnt here of the ceremony of quasi-burial (ll. 48–56); his stress on the crusades was suggested by Boucher-James's remarking that leprosy 'was supposed to be a legacy' of them. T.'s emphases on marriage, religion, and morality, suggest that he may have thought of it as a contrast to the morbid necrophily of Swinburne's *The Leper* (1866). Cp. T.'s ending 'In the name / Of the everlasting God, I will live and die with you', with Swinburne's stress on 'God hateth us' and his ending 'Will not God do right?' The poem is a companion to *Forlorn* (p. 1031), which it followed in *1889*.

I

Why wail you, pretty plover? and what is it that you fear?
  Is he sick your mate like mine? have you lost him, is he fled?
And there – the heron rises from his watch beside the mere,
  And flies above the leper's hut, where lives the living-dead.

II

Come back, nor let me know it! would he live and die alone?
  And has he not forgiven me yet, his over-jealous bride,
Who am, and was, and will be his, his own and only own,
  To share his living death with him, die with him side by side?

III

Is that the leper's hut on the solitary moor,
  Where noble Ulric dwells forlorn, and wears the leper's weed?
The door is open. He! is he standing at the door,
  My soldier of the Cross? it is he and he indeed!

IV

My roses – will he take them *now* – mine, his – from off the tree
  We planted both together, happy in our marriage morn?
O God, I could blaspheme, for he fought Thy fight for Thee,
  And Thou hast made him leper to compass him with scorn –

V

Hast spared the flesh of thousands, the coward and the base,
  And set a crueller mark than Cain's on him, the good and brave!
He sees me, waves me from him. I will front him face to face.
  You need not wave me from you. I would leap into your grave.

* * * *

VI

My warrior of the Holy Cross and of the conquering sword,
The roses that you cast aside–once more I bring you these.
No nearer? do you scorn me when you tell me, O my lord,
You would not mar the beauty of your bride with your disease.

VII

You say your body is so foul–then here I stand apart,
Who yearn to lay my loving head upon your leprous breast.
The leper plague may scale my skin but never taint my heart;
Your body is not foul to me, and body is foul at best.

VIII

I loved you first when young and fair, but now I love you most;
The fairest flesh at last is filth on which the worm will feast;
This poor rib-grated dungeon of the holy human ghost,
This house with all its hateful needs no cleaner than the beast,

IX

This coarse diseaseful creature which in Eden was divine,
This Satan-haunted ruin, this little city of sewers,
This wall of solid flesh that comes between your soul and mine,
Will vanish and give place to the beauty that endures,

X

The beauty that endures on the Spiritual height,
When we shall stand transfigured, like Christ on Hermon hill,
And moving each to music, soul in soul and light in light,
Shall flash through one another in a moment as we will.

XI

Foul! foul! the word was yours not mine, I worship that right hand
Which felled the foes before you as the woodman fells the wood,
And swayed the sword that lightened back the sun of Holy land,
And clove the Moslem crescent moon, and changed it into blood.

XII

And once I worshipt all too well this creature of decay,
For Age will chink the face, and Death will freeze the supplest limbs–
Yet you in your mid manhood–O the grief when yesterday
They bore the Cross before you to the chant of funeral hymns.

XIII

'Libera me, Domine!' you sang the Psalm, and when
The Priest pronounced you dead, and flung the mould upon your feet,
A beauty came upon your face, not that of living men,
But seen upon the silent brow when life has ceased to beat.

¶424. *32.* Cp. *By an Evolutionist* 1: 'The Lord let the house of a brute to the soul of a man.'
*38. Matthew* xvii 2.
*39. soul in soul*: *In Memoriam* cxxxi 12. *light in light*: xci 16. Cp. ll. 39–40 with xcv 36: 'The living soul was flashed on mine.'
*46.* Cp. *The Lover's Tale* i 126–7: 'the clear brow . . . chinked as you see'.

XIV

'Libera *nos*, Domine'–you knew not one was there
Who saw you kneel beside your bier, and weeping scarce could see;
May I come a little nearer, I that heard, and changed the prayer
And sang the married 'nos' for the solitary 'me'.

XV

*My* beauty marred by you? by you! so be it. All is well
If I lose it and myself in the higher beauty, yours.
*My* beauty lured that falcon from his eyry on the fell,
Who never caught one gleam of the beauty which endures–

XVI

The Count who sought to snap the bond that linked us life to life,
Who whispered me 'your Ulric loves'–a little nearer still–
He hissed, 'Let us revenge ourselves, your Ulric woos my wife'–
A lie by which he thought he could subdue me to his will.

XVII

I knew that you were near me when I let him kiss my brow;
*Did* he touch me on the lips? I was jealous, angered, vain,
And I meant to make *you* jealous. Are you jealous of me now?
Your pardon, O my love, if I ever gave you pain.

XVIII

You never once accused me, but I wept alone, and sighed
In the winter of the Present for the summer of the Past;
That icy winter silence–how it froze you from your bride,
Though I made one barren effort to break it at the last.

XIX

I brought you, you remember, these roses, when I knew
You were parting for the war, and you took them though you frowned;
You frowned and yet you kissed them. All at once the trumpet blew,
And you spurred your fiery horse, and you hurled them to the ground.

XX

You parted for the Holy War without a word to me,
And clear myself unasked–not I. My nature was too proud.
And him I saw but once again, and far away was he,
When I was praying in a storm–the crash was long and loud–

*64* ∧ *5*] And she, the wife, they told me she boasted she would make
Your noble heart the villain vassal of her wanton smile.
I never glanced at her full bust but wished myself the snake
That bit the harlot bosom of that heathen by the Nile.
*H.Nbk 55, deleted*

These are presumably the lines referred to in W. F. Rawnsley's report of T.'s reading of *Happy*: 'My wife and son won't let me put those in; I don't see why: I see no harm in them' (*Nineteenth Century* xcvii (1925) 195).

*66. Did . . . lips?*] *1890*; Well, he kissed me on the lips, *1889*.

XXI

That God would ever slant His bolt from falling on your head–
Then I lifted up my eyes, he was coming down the fell–
I clapt my hands. The sudden fire from Heaven had dashed him dead,
And sent him charred and blasted to the deathless fire of Hell.

XXII

See, I sinned but for a moment. I repented and repent,
And trust myself forgiven by the God to whom I kneel.
A little nearer? Yes. I shall hardly be content
Till I be leper like yourself, my love, from head to heel.

XXIII

O foolish dreams, that you, that I, would slight our marriage oath:
I held you at that moment even dearer than before;
Now God has made you leper in His loving care for both,
That we might cling together, never doubt each other more.

XXIV

The Priest, who joined you to the dead, has joined our hands of old;
If man and wife be but one flesh, let mine be leprous too,
As dead from all the human race as if beneath the mould;
If you be dead, then I am dead, who only live for you.

XXV

Would Earth though hid in cloud not be followed by the Moon?
The leech forsake the dying bed for terror of his life?
The shadow leave the Substance in the brooding light of noon?
Or if *I* had been the leper would you have left the wife?

XXVI

Not take them? Still you wave me off–poor roses–must I go–
I have worn them year by year–from the bush we both had set–
What? fling them to you?–well–that were hardly gracious. No!
Your plague but passes by the touch. A little nearer yet!

XXVII

There, there! he buried you, the Priest; the Priest is not to blame,
He joins us once again, to his either office true:
I thank him. I am happy, happy. Kiss me. In the name
Of the everlasting God, I will live and die with you.

# 425 To Mary Boyle

## With the Following Poem

## [The Progress of Spring]

Published *1889*, introducing *The Progress of Spring* (p. 475). Written spring 1888 (l. 13*n*, and l. 45), it is not in the *Virginia* trial edition of *1889*. H.T. says: 'Mary Boyle was an aunt of my wife's (Audrey Tennyson, *née* Boyle)'; T. first met her in 1882 (*Mem.* ii 294).

I

'Spring-flowers'! While you still delay to take
Your leave of Town,
Our elmtree's ruddy-hearted blossom-flake
Is fluttering down.

II

Be truer to your promise. There! I heard
Our cuckoo call.
Be needle to the magnet of your word,
Nor wait, till all

III

Our vernal bloom from every vale and plain
And garden pass,
And all the gold from each laburnum chain
Drop to the grass.

IV

Is memory with your Marian gone to rest,
Dead with the dead?
For ere she left us, when we met, you prest
My hand, and said

V

'I come with your spring-flowers.' You came not, friend;
My birds would sing,
You heard not. Take then this spring-flower I send,
This song of spring,

VI

Found yesterday–forgotten mine own rhyme
By mine old self,
As I shall be forgotten by old Time,
Laid on the shelf–

VII

A rhyme that flowered betwixt the whitening sloe
And kingcup blaze,
And more than half a hundred years ago,
In rick-fire days,

¶425. *13.* 'Lady Marian Alford' (T.). She died 9 Feb. 1888.
*27–37. The Progress of Spring* was begun in the early 1830s, in the days of political upheaval and Reform agitation; see *Mem.* i 41, and T.'s recurring memory of rick-burning in *The Princess* iv 366, and *The Grandmother* 39. T. says that the 'homestead' was near Cambridge, 1830.

VIII

When Dives loathed the times, and paced his land
In fear of worse,
And sanguine Lazarus felt a vacant hand
Fill with *his* purse.

IX

For lowly minds were maddened to the height
By tonguester tricks,
And once–I well remember that red night
When thirty ricks,

X

All flaming, made an English homestead Hell–
These hands of mine
Have helpt to pass a bucket from the well
Along the line,

XI

When this bare dome had not begun to gleam
Through youthful curls,
And you were then a lover's fairy dream,
His girl of girls;

XII

And you, that now are lonely, and with Grief
Sit face to face,
Might find a flickering glimmer of relief
In change of place.

XIII

What use to brood? this life of mingled pains
And joys to me,
Despite of every Faith and Creed, remains
The Mystery.

XIV

Let golden youth bewail the friend, the wife,
For ever gone.
He dreams of that long walk through desert life
Without the one.

XV

The silver year should cease to mourn and sigh–
Not long to wait–
So close are we, dear Mary, you and I
To that dim gate.

XVI

Take, read! and be the faults your Poet makes
Or many or few,
He rests content, if his young music wakes
A wish in you

XVII

To change our dark Queen-city, all her realm
Of sound and smoke,
For his clear heaven, and these few lanes of elm
And whispering oak.

# 426 Far–Far–Away

(For Music)

Published *1889*. Recited Aug. 1888 (*Mem.* ii 346), though H.T. also says that it was written after T.'s severe illness, which began Sept. 1888. T. presumably revised it. 'The words "far, far away" had always a strange charm for me' (T. on his early childhood). He made many changes to the drafts in *H.Nbks 54* and *87* (*A* and *B* below), including the change from 'I' to 'he' throughout. He altered the sequence of lines and stanzas, and the poem cost him great difficulty. Stanzas that found no place in *1889* are given below, l. 18*n*. A trial edition of *1889* (*Virginia*) has only four stanzas.

What sight so lured him through the fields he knew
As where earth's green stole into heaven's own hue,
Far–far–away?

What sound was dearest in his native dells?
The mellow lin-lan-lone of evening bells
Far–far–away.

What vague world-whisper, mystic pain or joy,
Through those three words would haunt him when a boy,
Far–far–away?

¶426. *1*] What field so witched him in the land he knew *Harvard B 1st reading*.
*2. hue*] blue *Harvard B 1st reading*.
5. Sir Charles Tennyson (*1931*, p. 78) compares 'lin, lan, lone', *New Year's Eve*, from *c*. 1837.
*7–8*] That strange world-whisper came to me, a boy,
A haunting notice, neither grief, nor joy, *Harvard A*

A whisper from his dawn of life? a breath
From some fair dawn beyond the doors of death
Far–far–away?

Far, far, how far? from o'er the gates of Birth,
The faint horizons, all the bounds of earth,
Far–far–away?

What charm in words, a charm no words could give?
O dying words, can Music make you live
Far–far–away?

# 427 To the Marquis of Dufferin and Ava

Published *1889*. It is not in the *Virginia* trial edition of *1889*. Its subject is the death in April 1886 of T.'s son Lionel (born 1854) in the Red Sea when returning from India where he had caught fever. His host had been Lord Dufferin (1826–1902), the Governor-General of India (1884–8) and an old friend of T.'s. Dufferin took care of Lionel for the months of his illness before the fatal journey. Since the poem acts as the introduction to *1889* (see ll. 15–16), it was probably written in that year or in 1888 (supported by its placing in *H.Nbk 55*). T. would have had it in mind since 1886. He uses the *In Memoriam* stanza.

I

At times our Britain cannot rest,
At times her steps are swift and rash;
She moving, at her girdle clash
The golden keys of East and West.

*14*] And all the faint horizons of the earth, *Harvard A*; Beyond the faint horizons of his earth, *Harvard B 1st reading.*
*17. dying*] poor dead *Harvard B 1st reading.*
*18*] *The following stanzas appear in the MSS* (*the sequences of which are quite different from 1889*):
(i) That weird soul-phrase of something half-divine,
In earliest youth, in latest age is mine,
Far – far – away. *Harvard A*
(ii) Ghost, do the men that walk this planet seem
[Ghost, can you see us, hear us? do we seem *1st reading*]
Far, far away, a truth and yet a dream,
Far – far – away? *Harvard B*

¶427. *1–4.* Sir Charles Tennyson (*1931*, p. 74) points out that these lines had been *Hail Briton* 21–4: 'For Britain had an hour of rest; / But now her steps' etc., *verbatim* (p. 482).

II

Not swift or rash, when late she lent
The sceptres of her West, her East,
To one, that ruling has increased
Her greatness and her self-content.

III

Your rule has made the people love
Their ruler. Your viceregal days
Have added fulness to the phrase
Of 'Gauntlet in the velvet glove.'

IV

But since your name will grow with Time,
Not all, as honouring your fair fame
Of Statesman, have I made the name
A golden portal to my rhyme:

V

But more, that you and yours may know
From me and mine, how dear a debt
We owed you, and are owing yet
To you and yours, and still would owe.

VI

For he–your India was his Fate,
And drew him over sea to you–
He fain had ranged her through and
through,
To serve her myriads and the State,–

VII

A soul that, watched from earliest youth,
And on through many a brightening year,
Had never swerved for craft or fear,
By one side-path, from simple truth;

*6.* Dufferin had been Governor-General of Canada, 1872–8.

*7–8.* Cp. *Ode on Wellington* 170 ^ 71: 'Perchance our greatness will increase'.

*10–12.* Dufferin's rule in India was characterized by a strengthening of the army and by many military operations.

*21–4.* Lionel's work in the India Office, including a Blue Book, had been very successful (*Mem.* ii 322–3).

*25–8.* Cp. the similar praise of the dead Lionel in *Locksley Hall Sixty Years After* 59–60 (p. 1361).

VIII

Who might have chased and clasp't Renown
And caught her chaplet here–and there
In haunts of jungle-poisoned air
The flame of life went wavering down;

IX

But ere he left your fatal shore,
And lay on that funereal boat,
Dying, 'Unspeakable' he wrote
'Their kindness,' and he wrote no more;

X

And sacred is the latest word;
And now the Was, the Might-have-been,
And those lone rites I have not seen,
And one drear sound I have not heard,

XI

Are dreams that scarce will let me be,
Not there to bid my boy farewell,
When That within the coffin fell,
Fell–and flashed into the Red Sea,

XII

Beneath a hard Arabian moon
And alien stars. To question, why
The sons before the fathers die,
Not mine! and I may meet him soon;

XIII

But while my life's late eve endures,
Nor settles into hueless gray,
My memories of his briefer day
Will mix with love for you and yours.

# 428 By an Evolutionist

Published *1889*. Written Feb. 1889 (*Mem.* ii 353), between attacks of a severe illness. T. created it from separate epigrams. W. Boyd Carpenter said T. quoted the poem in July 1887 (*Some Pages*, 1911, p. 257), but this will probably have been ll. 1–4, which appear as an epigram in *H.Nbk 55*. In the enlarged poem, l. 11 is very likely to be precise. The poem is not in the *Virginia* trial edition of *1889*; in a *Lincoln* trial edition, it consists of ll. 1–8, 13–16 only. In another *Lincoln* trial edition, ll. 9–12 are added by hand, apparently as a separate epigram, 'Old Man' to 'Old Age'. It will be these lines to which *Mem.* ii 348 refers: 'At the crisis of his illness [end of 1888] he made an epigram about himself, and on the pain killing the devil that was born in him eighty years back.'

The Lord let the house of a brute to the soul of a man,
And the man said 'Am I your debtor?'
And the Lord–'Not yet: but make it as clean as you can,
And then I will let you a better.'

I

If my body come from brutes, my soul uncertain, or a fable,
Why not bask amid the senses while the sun of morning shines,
I, the finer brute rejoicing in my hounds, and in my stable,
Youth and Health, and birth and wealth, and choice of women and of wines?

II

What hast thou done for me, grim Old Age, save breaking my bones on the rack?
Would I had past in the morning that looks so bright from afar!

OLD AGE

Done for thee? starved the wild beast that was linkt with thee eighty years back.
Less weight now for the ladder-of-heaven that hangs on a star.

I

If my body come from brutes, though somewhat finer than their own,
I am heir, and this my kingdom. Shall the royal voice be mute?
No, but if the rebel subject seek to drag me from the throne,
Hold the sceptre, Human Soul, and rule thy Province of the brute.

II

I have climbed to the snows of Age, and I gaze at a field in the Past,
Where I sank with the body at times in the sloughs of a low desire,
But I hear no yelp of the beast, and the Man is quiet at last
As he stands on the heights of his life with a glimpse of a height that is higher.

# 429 *Cephalis

Printed by Sir Charles Tennyson, *Nineteenth Century* cix (1931) 631, as 'a very rough draft, apparently of the early 'seventies'. But it appears with poems of *1889* in *H.Nbk 55*, where it follows *By an Evolutionist* 1–4 (above), with which it has obvious affinities: 'The Lord let the house of a brute to the soul of a man.' The title is from the Greek for the head.

¶428. *1.* Cp. *Happy* 32: 'This house with all its hateful needs no cleaner than the beast'.
*8.* Cp. *Vastness* 19: 'Wealth with his wines and his wedded harlots'.

I have got two wives, both fair, and they dwell with me under a dome
With a couple of windows, and there they both of them have their home.
One lives in a room to the left and one in a room to the right,
And I sit between them and hear them call to me day and night.
'Come' said the left, 'I can teach you the older and truer way'–
'Come' said the right, 'She's a beast, I can teach you the newer way'–
And they wrangle and babble so often I know not if I be I,
But I hope to be cleared of the crime of this bigamy–When? When I die.

# 430 Parnassus

Published *1889*, written 26 May (*Mat.* iv 214). *H.Nbk 55* has an epigrammatic version, a draft of ll. 9–12, 15–16. As *Fame*, it is in a *Lincoln* trial edition of *1889*, where it consisted of ll. 1–4, 7–8. But other *Harvard* drafts suggest an earlier date. *Lpr 165* (*A* below) is on the back of part of *Becket* (printed 1879) and *The Northern Cobbler* (*1880*); and *Lpr 45* (*B*) is on the back of *De Profundis* (*1880*). Both these versions consist of section II only; T. extended and revised this in 1889, as is clear from another *Lincoln* trial edition of *1889*, where ll. 5–8 had the title *Fame* and where furthermore section III is shown to be a late addition. The poem's theme is common in T.; cp. the *Epilogue* to *The Charge of the Heavy Brigade* (p. 1309): 'Old Horace . . . Earth passes, all is lost . . . The man remains'. Also *Little Aubrey* (p. 1802). Jowett wrote to T., Dec. 1858, suggesting topics for poems: 'Have not many sciences such as Astronomy or Geology a side of feeling which is poetry?' (*Mem.* i 433). Herbert Warren (*Tennyson and His Friends*, pp. 136–8) compares a letter by FitzGerald to E. B. Cowell in 1847, and remarks on the 'extraordinarily close' parallel. Since this letter was published in July 1889 in FitzGerald's *Letters and Literary Remains* (ed. W. A. Wright, i 181–2), it may have influenced T. in his final drafting of the poem:

'Yet, as I often think, it is not the poetical imagination, but bare Science that every day more and more unrolls a greater Epic than the Iliad; the history of the World, the infinitudes of Space and Time! I never take up a book of Geology or Astronomy but this strikes me. And when we think that Man must go on to discover in the same plodding way, one fancies that the Poet of to-day may as well fold his hands, or turn them to dig and delve, considering how soon the march of discovery will distance all his imaginations, [and] dissolve the language in which they are uttered . . . . It is not only that this vision of Time must wither the Poet's hope of immortality; but it is in itself more wonderful than all the conceptions of Dante and Milton.'

¶429. *7. often*] *MS*; that *1931*, *MS 1st reading*.

Epigraph: Horace prophesies his work's immortality, epilogue to *Odes* iii ('I have finished a monument . . . that the countless chain of years and the ages' flight cannot destroy').

*Exegi monumentum . . .*
*Quod non . . .*
*Possit diruere . . .*
*. . . innumerabilis*
*Annorum series et fuga temporum.*
HORACE

I

What be those crowned forms high over the sacred fountain?
Bards, that the mighty Muses have raised to the heights of the mountain,
And over the flight of the Ages! O Goddesses, help me up thither!
Lightning may shrivel the laurel of Cæsar, but mine would not wither.
Steep is the mountain, but you, you will help me to overcome it,
And stand with my head in the zenith, and roll my voice from the summit,
Sounding for ever and ever through Earth and her listening nations,
And mixt with the great Sphere-music of stars and of constellations.

II

What be those two shapes high over the sacred fountain,
Taller than all the Muses, and huger than all the mountain?
On those two known peaks they stand ever spreading and heightening;
Poet, that evergreen laurel is blasted by more than lightning!
Look, in their deep double shadow the crowned ones all disappearing!
Sing like a bird and be happy, nor hope for a deathless hearing!
'Sounding for ever and ever?' pass on! the sight confuses–
These are Astronomy and Geology, terrible Muses!

¶430. *1.* The Castalian fountain on Mount Parnassus, sacred to the Muses.
*4.* The superstition that laurels are proof against lightning; cp. Marvell, *Horatian Ode* 23–4: 'And *Caesars* head at last / Did through his Laurels blast.'

*Section II] A begins:*
O little poet who fain would be fussy, and bristle, and rave
Of the glory implied in the slander that even follows the grave–
O little poet, of all little poets the least and the latest,
One little solace is thine, that thou wilt die with the greatest.

*9. those two*] the two vast *A*; the two great *B*.
*11. On those*] There on the *A–B*.
*12. Poet . . . is*] Look, little poet, thy laurels are *A–B*.
*13–14] Not A, Notebook 45; B has here the third and fourth of the introductory lines in A (see Section IIn).*
*15. 'Sounding . . . ever?'*] Look no more, little poet! *A–B*.

III

If the lips were touched with fire from off a pure Pierian altar,
Though their music here be mortal need the singer greatly care?
Other songs for other worlds! the fire within him would not falter;
Let the golden Iliad vanish, Homer here is Homer there.

# 431 Merlin and the Gleam

Published *1889*, written Aug. (*Mem.* ii 366). It is not in the *Virginia* and *Trinity* trial editions of *1889*, but is added by hand to a *Lincoln* trial edition, with many corrections and variants. T. says: 'In the story of *Merlin and Nimuë* I have read that Nimuë means the "Gleam", which signifies in my poem the higher poetic imagination.' The Vivien (in the equating of Nimuë and Vivien) is not the Vivien of the *Idylls*; G. S. Haight, *SP* xliv (1947) 559, shows that T.'s source was W. F. Skene's *The Four Ancient Books of Wales* (1868, *Lincoln*)–'which my father often quoted' (H.T.). J. Killham (*Notes and Queries*, Dec. 1958) endorses M. W. MacCallum's point that T. was influenced by John Veitch, who had recently identified Merlin's early love with 'The Gleam', in his poem *Merlin* (April 1889). T. was possibly also influenced by Robert Buchanan's *Book of Orm* (1870), which is metrically comparable; it tells of a quest to see 'the Face', and refers to 'the Master'. T.'s metre has the rhythms of Old Welsh poetry, and is also intended to give something of the effect of Anglo-Saxon verse; cp. *Battle of Brunanburh* (p. 1234), which is likewise mainly trochaics and dactylics in 2-stress lines. T. had used the pseudonym 'Merlin' when publishing *The Third of February* (1852). As Haight observes, Wordsworth had juxtaposed 'gleam' with poetic imagination in a poem that was one of T.'s favourites (*Mem.* i 151), *Elegiac Stanzas suggested by a Picture of Peele Castle* 14–16: 'add the gleam, / The light that never was, on sea or land, / The consecration, and the Poet's dream.' T. had long used it for the idealist's vision: 'Gleams that untravelled world, whose margin fades' (*Ulysses* 20); 'For one fair Vision ever fled . . . now she gleamed' (*The Voyage* 57, 65); 'O follower of the Vision, still / In motion to the distant gleam' (*Freedom* 13–14).
*Biographical allegory*. 'For those who cared to know about his literary history he wrote *Merlin and the Gleam*' (H.T.). But it presents difficulties. H.T. gives 'the reading of the poet's riddle as he gave it to me'. Section i, 'From his boyhood he had felt the magic of Merlin–that spirit of poetry'.

17. *Pieria*: a haunt of the Muses. Cp. Milton, *Nativity Ode* 28: 'From out his secret Altar toucht with hallow'd fire'. Hence Pope, *Messiah* 6: 'Who touch'd *Isaiah's* hallow'd Lips with Fire!' Based on the seraph, *Isaiah* vi 6–7. The link with the mountain may be a reminiscence of *The Lover's Tale* i 315–7: 'and touched far-off / His mountain-altars, his high hills, with flame / Milder and purer.'

ii, the poetry of T.'s youth. iii, 'the harsh voice of those who were unsympathetic'. iv, renewed inspiration from romantic fancy and nature, or 'the early imagination' (T.). v, Eclogues and English Idyls, or 'the Pastorals' (T.). vi, 'human love and human heroism', and he 'began what he had already devised, his Epic of king Arthur'. vii, the death of Arthur Hallam 'made him almost fail in this purpose'. viii, finding 'a stronger faith his own'. ix, 'Up to the end he faced death with the same earnest and unfailing courage that he had always shown, but with an added sense of the awe and the mystery of the Infinite'. But is the poem meant to be chronological, and if so should not Hallam's death come much earlier? Unless iii refers, not to the reviewers of *1832*, but, as Sir Charles Tennyson suggests (p. 517), to the family troubles which followed Dr Tennyson's death in 1831, and the attempts made by T.'s grandfather to divert him from poetry. In which case iii–vi would be the development during T.'s friendship with Hallam. Yet H.T. took iii as the reviewers: 'the "Raven croaked" ominously in the shape of the *Quarterly*. This Review and the death of Arthur Hallam almost "deadened the melody"' (*Mat.* i 141). These sentences were dropped for *Mem.*, but there is no telling whether simply as one of many cuts or because H.T. thought them mistaken. Haight argues that the poem is not a systematic account of the published volumes, but of the various inspirations, so that iv becomes 'early imagination' and the supernatural; v, common life spurred on by Wordsworth; vi, Arthurian matter beginning with *The Lady of Shalott.* A summary conclusion might be that T. did not mind its being enigmatic, a 'riddle' (H.T.), but that it was meant to be chronological; what thwarted this was the gap of seventeen years between Hallam's death and the publication of *In Memoriam.* T. had to present these events in consecutive stanzas, since otherwise the poem might seem casual about both Hallam's death and the 'stronger faith', but in doing so T. was forced to obscure the chronology.

I

O young Mariner,
You from the haven
Under the sea-cliff,
You that are watching
The gray Magician
With eyes of wonder,
*I* am Merlin,
And *I* am dying,
*I* am Merlin
Who follow The Gleam.

II

Mighty the Wizard
Who found me at sunrise

¶431. *11*] A mighty Master *Lincoln trial edition 1st reading*; Mighty the

Sleeping, and woke me
And learned me Magic!
Great the Master,
And sweet the Magic,
When over the valley,
In early summers,
Over the mountain,
On human faces,
And all around me,
Moving to melody,
Floated The Gleam.

III

Once at the croak of a Raven
who crost it,
A barbarous people,
Blind to the magic,
And deaf to the melody,
Snarled at and cursed me.
A demon vext me,
The light retreated,
The landskip darkened,
The melody deadened,
The Master whispered
'Follow The Gleam.'

Master *trial edition*. Haight suggests a reference to the Wizard of the North, Walter Scott, who was a major influence on the young T. (*Mem.* i 12).
*24–34.* Reviewers or family or both? See headnote. Haight, like T. O. Mabbott (*Notes and Queries*, 10 Jan. 1948), takes 'croak' as suggesting J. W. Croker, who reviewed *1832* in *QR*; and H.T. might seem to support this. But Veitch's *Merlin* had spoken of 'the croak of the raven brood', and T. used the word elsewhere of ravens. J. H. Buckley (p. 287) prefers Christopher North, whose journalist's familiar was a raven, 'since the raven was associated with North and since [T.] believed that North had not only attacked in his own review but had also instigated Croker's'. Mabbott adds that the transition from 'raven' to 'barbarous' suggests the Danes and their standard (apt to the Anglo-Saxon tone of the poem); he compares *Guinevere* 132–4: 'The Raven, flying high, / Croaked . . . / For now the Heathen of the Northern Sea . . .'.
*24*] *Added in trial edition.*
*26*] Who hated Magic, *trial edition 1st reading.*
*27*] *Added in trial edition.*
*28. Snarled*] Railed *trial edition.*
*32*] *Added in trial edition.*
*33*] I heard a whisper *trial edition 1st reading.*

IV

Then to the melody,
Over a wilderness
Gliding, and glancing at
Elf of the woodland,
Gnome of the cavern,
Griffin and Giant,
And dancing of Fairies
In desolate hollows,
And wraiths of the mountain,
And rolling of dragons
By warble of water,
Or cataract music
Of falling torrents,
Flitted The Gleam.

V

Down from the mountain
And over the level,
And streaming and shining on
Silent river,
Silvery willow,
Pasture and plowland,
Innocent maidens,
Garrulous children,
Homestead and harvest,
Reaper and gleaner,
And rough-ruddy faces
Of lowly labour,
Slided The Gleam–

VI

Then, with a melody
Stronger and statelier,
Led me at length
To the city and palace
Of Arthur the king;
Touched at the golden
Cross of the churches,
Flashed on the Tournament,
Flickered and bickered
From helmet to helmet,
And last on the forehead
Of Arthur the blameless
Rested The Gleam.

54 ∧ 5] Horses and oxen, *1889*.

VII

Clouds and darkness
Closed upon Camelot;
Arthur had vanished
I knew not whither,
The king who loved me,
And cannot die;
For out of the darkness
Silent and slowly
The Gleam, that had waned
to a wintry glimmer
On icy fallow
And faded forest,
Drew to the valley
Named of the shadow,
And slowly brightening
Out of the glimmer,
And slowly moving again to a
melody
Yearningly tender,
Fell on the shadow,
No longer a shadow,
But clothed with The Gleam.

VIII

And broader and brighter
The Gleam flying onward,
Wed to the melody,
Sang through the world;
And slower and fainter,
Old and weary,
But eager to follow,
I saw, whenever
In passing it glanced upon
Hamlet or city,
That under the Crosses
The dead man's garden,

*75–80.* Cp. *Morte d'Arthur* (p. 585).
*79*] *Trial edition has more explicit drafts*:
(*a*) The friend who loved me,
And heard my counsel,
(*b*) He that I leaned on,
Arthur, who loved me,
The king who prized me,
And heard my counsel,

The mortal hillock,
Would break into blossom;
And so to the land's
Last limit I came–
And can no longer,
But die rejoicing,
For through the Magic
Of Him the Mighty,
Who taught me in childhood,
There on the border
Of boundless Ocean,
And all but in Heaven
Hovers The Gleam.

IX

Not of the sunlight,
Not of the moonlight,
Not of the starlight!
O young Mariner,
Down to the haven,
Call your companions,
Launch your vessel,
And crowd your canvas,
And, ere it vanishes
Over the margin,
After it, follow it,
Follow The Gleam.

## 432 Romney's Remorse

Published *1889*. Written 1889; it was apparently suggested by a letter of FitzGerald's (published July 1889)–see T.'s headnote. It is in *H.Nbk 54*, following *Merlin and the Gleam* (*1889*); it is not in the *Virginia* trial edition of *1889*. T. drew on lives of the artist George Romney (1734–1802) by William Hayley (1809) and by John Romney (1830). But he invented many details. His choice of the deathbed setting was influenced by FitzGerald's letter, but probably owes something to the fact, given by Hayley, that Romney had originally married Mary Abbot after she nursed him compassionately during a severe illness. Of the 'remorse', T. said: 'I don't know whether he did feel it, so I put him under the influence of the opiate, and if you take an opiate without needing it, it acts on your feelings' (H. D. Rawnsley, *Memories of the Tennysons*, 1900, p. 132). Cp. Browning's dramatic monologues, especially *Andrea del Sarto* (1855).

'I read Hayley's Life of Romney the other day–Romney wanted but education and reading to make him a very fine painter; but his ideal was not high nor fixed. How touching is the close of his life! He married at nineteen, and because Sir Joshua and others had said that "marriage spoilt an artist" almost immediately left his wife in the North and scarce saw her till the end of his life; when old, nearly mad and quite desolate, he went back to her and she received him and nursed him till he died. This quiet act of hers is worth all Romney's pictures! even as a matter of Art, I am sure.' (*Letters and Literary Remains of Edward FitzGerald*, vol. i.) [1889, p. 102]

'Beat, little heart–I give you this and this'
  Who are you? What! the Lady Hamilton?
Good, I am never weary painting you.
To sit once more? Cassandra, Hebe, Joan,
Or spinning at your wheel beside the vine–
Bacchante, what you will; and if I fail
To conjure and concentrate into form
And colour all you are, the fault is less
In me than Art. What Artist ever yet
Could make pure light live on the canvas? Art!
Why should I so disrelish that short word?
  Where am I? snow on all the hills! so hot,
So fevered! never colt would more delight
To roll himself in meadow grass than I
To wallow in that winter of the hills.
  Nurse, were you hired? or came of your own will
To wait on one so broken, so forlorn?
Have I not met you somewhere long ago?
I am all but sure I have–in Kendal church–
O yes! I hired you for a season there,
And then we parted; but you look so kind
That you will not deny my sultry throat
One draught of icy water. There–you spill
The drops upon my forehead. Your hand shakes.
I am ashamed. I am a trouble to you,
Could kneel for your forgiveness. Are they tears?
For me–they do me too much grace–for me?

¶432. *2–5.* Lady Hamilton often modelled for Romney in such roles. *Hebe* is listed by John Romney among Romney's work, but is not of Lady Hamilton. *Joan*: Joan of Arc. John Romney lists 'The Spinstress'.
*26.* The reconciliation suggests that of Lear and Cordelia, the subject of one of Romney's earliest paintings in which Mrs Romney was the model for Cordelia (John Romney): the slow recognition, and 'Be your tears wet?' (IV vii 71); and 'I'll kneel down / And ask of thee forgiveness' (V iii 10–11). He painted often from *Lear*.

O Mary, Mary!
Vexing you with words!
Words only, born of fever, or the fumes
Of that dark opiate dose you gave me,–words,
Wild babble. I have stumbled back again
Into the common day, the sounder self.
God stay me there, if only for your sake,
The truest, kindliest, noblest-hearted wife
That ever wore a Christian marriage-ring.
My curse upon the Master's apothegm,
That wife and children drag an Artist down!
This seemed my lodestar in the Heaven of Art,
And lured me from the household fire on earth.
To you my days have been a life-long lie,
Grafted on half a truth; and though you say
'Take comfort you have won the Painter's fame,'
The best in me that sees the worst in me,
And groans to see it, finds no comfort there.
What fame? I am not Raphaël, Titian–no
Nor even a Sir Joshua, some will cry.
Wrong there! The painter's fame? but mine, that grew
Blown into glittering by the popular breath,
May float awhile beneath the sun, may roll
The rainbow hues of heaven about it–
There!
The coloured bubble bursts above the abyss
Of Darkness, utter Lethe.
Is it so?
Her sad eyes plead for my own fame with me
To make it dearer.
Look, the sun has risen
To flame along another dreary day.
Your hand. How bright you keep your marriage-ring!
Raise me. I thank you.
Has your opiate then
Bred this black mood? or am I conscious, more
Than other Masters, of the chasm between
Work and Ideal? Or does the gloom of Age
And suffering cloud the height I stand upon
Even from myself? stand? stood . . . no more.
And yet

50. Combining 'rainbow hues' and 'hues of heaven', Shelley's *Alastor* 334, 197.

The world would lose, if such a wife as you
Should vanish unrecorded. Might I crave
One favour? I am bankrupt of all claim
On your obedience, and my strongest wish
Falls flat before your least unwillingness.
Still would you–if it please you–sit to me?
  I dreamed last night of that clear summer noon,
When seated on a rock, and foot to foot
With your own shadow in the placid lake,
You claspt our infant daughter, heart to heart.
I had been among the hills, and brought you down
A length of staghorn-moss, and this you twined
About her cap. I see the picture yet,
Mother and child. A sound from far away,
No louder than a bee among the flowers,
A fall of water lulled the noon asleep.
You stilled it for the moment with a song
Which often echoed in me, while I stood
Before the great Madonna-masterpieces
Of ancient Art in Paris, or in Rome.
  Mary, my crayons! if I can, I will.
You should have been–I might have made you once,
Had I but known you as I know you now–
The true Alcestis of the time. Your song–
Sit, listen! I remember it, a proof
That I–even I–at times remembered *you*.

  'Beat upon mine, little heart! beat, beat!
  Beat upon mine! you are mine, my sweet!
  All mine from your pretty blue eyes to your feet,
          My sweet.'

Less profile! turn to me–three-quarter face.

  'Sleep, little blossom, my honey, my bliss!

*69–78.* John Romney describes an early landscape with figures, a lake scene; Mrs Romney often spoke of this excursion to Windermere, with the mountain 'involved in its own shadow', and the 'inverted picture'; two of the figures were the artist and his wife.

*83.* John Romney says of the artist's last years, 'He still, however, could take likenesses with great accuracy; but not having any oil colours with him, his attempts were only in crayons.'

*86.* In the tragedy by Euripides, Alcestis consented to die in place of her husband, and was afterwards rescued by Hercules.

For I give you this, and I give you this!
And I blind your pretty blue eyes with a kiss!
Sleep!'

Too early blinded by the kiss of death–
'Father and Mother will watch you grow'–
You watched not I, she did not grow, she died.

'Father and Mother will watch you grow,
And gather the roses whenever they blow,
And find the white heather wherever you go,
My sweet.'

Ah, my white heather only blooms in heaven
With Milton's amaranth. There, there, there! a child
Had shamed me at it–Down, you idle tools,
Stampt into dust–tremulous, all awry,
Blurred like a landskip in a ruffled pool,–
Not one stroke firm. This Art, that harlot-like
Seduced me from you, leaves me harlot-like,
Who love her still, and whimper, impotent
To win her back before I die–and then–
Then, in the loud world's bastard judgment-day,
One truth will damn me with the mindless mob,
Who feel no touch of my temptation, more
Than all the myriad lies, that blacken round
The corpse of every man that gains a name;
'This model husband, this fine Artist'! Fool,
What matters? Six foot deep of burial mould
Will dull their comments! Ay, but when the shout
Of His descending peals from Heaven, and throbs
Through earth, and all her graves, if *He* should ask
'Why left you wife and children? for my sake,
According to my word?' and I replied

*100.* The daughter who died is mentioned by Hayley and John Romney.

*105. blooms*] *1890*; grows *1889*.

*106. Paradise Lost* iii 353. Milton was the subject of one of Romney's most famous pictures.

*117. Than*] More than *1889 corrected in Errata*.

*117–8.* Cp. *Boädicea* 14: 'Blacken round the Roman carrion'.

*121. 1 Thessalonians* iv 16: 'For the Lord himself shall descend from heaven with a shout, with the voice of the Archangel, and with the trump of God: and the dead in Christ shall rise first.'

'Nay, Lord, for *Art,*' why, that would sound so mean
That all the dead, who wait the doom of Hell
For bolder sins than mine, adulteries,
Wife-murders, – nay, the ruthless Mussulman
Who flings his bowstrung Harem in the sea,
Would turn, and glare at me, and point and jeer,
And gibber at the worm, who, living, made
The wife of wives a widow-bride, and lost
Salvation for a sketch.
I am wild again!
The coals of fire you heap upon my head
Have crazed me. Someone knocking there without?
No! Will my Indian brother come? to find
Me or my coffin? Should I know the man?
This worn-out Reason dying in her house
May leave the windows blinded, and if so,
Bid him farewell for me, and tell him –
Hope!
I hear a death-bed Angel whisper 'Hope.'
"The miserable have no medicine
But only Hope!" He said it . . . in the play.
His crime was of the senses; of the mind
Mine; worse, cold, calculated.
Tell my son –
O let me lean my head upon your breast.
'Beat little heart' on this fool brain of mine.
I once had friends – and many – none like you.
I love you more than when we married. Hope!
O yes, I hope, or fancy that, perhaps,
Human forgiveness touches heaven, and thence –
For you forgive me, you are sure of that –
Reflected, sends a light on the forgiven.

[1889. *Crossing the Bar* — see p. 1458
*To Professor Jebb* — see p. 1372]

# 433 Beautiful City

Published *1889*. 'Paris' (T.). On the French Revolution, cp. *Aylmer's Field* 763–8, and *In Memoriam* cxxvii 8. T. is thinking too of the revolution

*137*. T. comments: 'When his brother arrived from India, Romney did not know him.' The detail is from Hayley.

*143–4*. Claudio in *Measure for Measure* III i 2–3. Romney painted many Shakespearean subjects.

of 1848 and the Paris Commune of 1871. It was written in T.'s eightieth year (H.T., note with MS, *Nat. Lib. of Australia*), presumably 1889. It is not in the *Virginia* and *Trinity College* trial editions of *1889*; there are two drafts by hand in a *Lincoln* trial edition. T. may well have sympathized with Boulanger, who in April 1889 fled to England and was arraigned in France. A late notebook of T. (*Lincoln*) has the jotting: 'Revolution–to speak epigrammatically–is just Evolution.' In 1884 (apparently), he said that 'evolution has often come through revolution' (*Mem.* ii 303).

Beautiful city, the centre and crater of European confusion,
O you with your passionate shriek for the rights of an equal
  humanity,
How often your Re-volution has proven but E-volution
Rolled again back on itself in the tides of a civic insanity!

# 434 The Roses on the Terrace

Published *1889*. It is not in the *Virginia* trial edition of *1889*. As a late addition to a *Lincoln* trial edition, it had the title *The Rose*. Written into an earlier *Lincoln* trial edition, it consisted only of four lines which told how the memory 'warms my heart today'. It is to Rosa Baring (see *Thy rosy lips*, p. 634). Rader (p. 33) remarks that it may have been written in the spring–or summer–of 1889 after Tennyson heard the news of Rosa's husband's death in March, or perhaps at some time during the previous few years. T. combines the terrace at Aldworth with the terraced garden of Rosa's Harrington Hall. Cp. the blush in *Locksley Hall* 25–6.

Rose, on this terrace fifty years ago,
  When I was in my June, you in your May,
Two words, '*My* Rose' set all your face aglow,
  And now that I am white, and you are gray,
That blush of fifty years ago, my dear,
  Blooms in the Past, but close to me today
As this red rose, which on our terrace here
  Glows in the blue of fifty miles away.

# 435 The Play

Published *1889*. T. rewrote it, after having it printed in a *Lincoln* trial edition of *1889* as:

First Act! you hiss it, all but rise to go–
  More pain than pleasure in the shifting scenes!
Be still, and trust the grand Play-wright will show
  In his fifth Act what our wild Drama means!

Written after 1887 (it is in *H.Nbk 53*). Cp. *Locksley Hall Sixty Years After* 61–2 (1886): 'Wiser there than you, that crowning barren Death as lord of all, / Deem this over-tragic drama's closing curtain is the pall!' Francis Quarles, *Emblems* I xv: 'My soul, sit thou a patient looker on; / Judge not the Play before the Play is done: / Her Plot has many changes: Every day / Speaks a new Scene; the last act crowns the Play.' T.'s friend William Allingham had a copy of Quarles's *Emblems*, which he showed to Browning (Allingham's *Diary*, 1907, p. 249).

Act first, this Earth, a stage so gloomed with woe
You all but sicken at the shifting scenes.
And yet be patient. Our Playwright may show
In some fifth Act what this wild Drama means.

# 436 On One Who Affected an Effeminate Manner

Published *1889*. It is not in the *Virginia* trial edition; it is added by hand to a *Lincoln* trial edition, with the title *To one who affected effeminacy*. Cp. T.'s praise of 'manhood fused with female grace', *In Memoriam* cix 17; also 'She with all the charm of woman, she with all the breadth of man', *Locksley Hall Sixty Years After* 48, which was even stronger in MS: 'As our greatest is man-woman, so was she the woman-man', alluding to Christ (*Mem.* i 326). Cp. *The Princess*. A late notebook of T. (*Lincoln*) has the jotting, 'Men should be androgynous and women gynandrous, but men should not be gynandrous nor women androgynous.'

While man and woman still are incomplete,
I prize that soul where man and woman meet,
Which types all Nature's male and female plan,
But, friend, man-woman is not woman-man.

# 437 To One Who Ran Down the English

Published *1889*. It is not in the *Virginia* trial edition, but is added by pen to a *Lincoln* trial edition. In *The Princess* vi 159, T. had spoken of 'a darkened future'; cp. *Ode on Wellington* 170 ^ 71: 'Perchance a darkening future yields / Some reverse from worse to worse.'

You make our faults too gross, and thence maintain
Our darker future. May your fears be vain!
At times the small black fly upon the pane
May seem the black ox of the distant plain.

## 438 *'A quotable snatch of Ovidian song'

Unpublished. It is printed in a *Lincoln* trial edition of *1889* on the same page as *To One Who Ran Down the English*, but was dropped from later trial editions. Cp. the other epigrams of *1889*. The epigraph is from *Metamorphoses* vii 20–1: 'I see the better and approve it, but I follow the worse.' Cowper had used this as the epigraph to *Pity for Poor Africans* (published 1800).

*Video meliora, proboque,*
*Deteriora sequor.*
(OVID)

A quotable snatch of Ovidian song
And a saying true to the letter,
Yet–if we follow the worse too long
We may cease to believe in the Better.

## 439 The Oak

Published *1889*. Probably written 1889 (it is in *H.Nbk 54*). 'My father called this poem "clean-cut like a Greek epigram." The allusion is to the gold of the young oak leaves in spring, and to the autumnal gold of the fading leaves (at Aldworth)' (H.T.).

Live thy Life,
Young and old,
Like yon oak,
Bright in spring,
Living gold;

Summer-rich
Then; and then
Autumn-changed,
Soberer-hued
Gold again.

¶439. *1*] Be your life, *H.MS.*
*4*] All your Spring *MS.*
*6*] Summer-green *MS.*
*8–9*] *Transposed MS.*

All his leaves
  Fallen at length,
Look, he stands,
  Trunk and bough,
  Naked strength.

[1889. *The Progress of Spring*–see p. 475]

# 440 To the Master of Balliol

Published *1892*, introducing *The Death of Œnone* (below), which T. completed July 1890. It was written by April 1891 (*Mem.* ii 386), presumably during the winter 1890–1 (l. 9). Benjamin Jowett (1817–93) had long been a close friend of T.

I

Dear Master in our classic town,
You, loved by all the younger gown
  There at Balliol,
Lay your Plato for one minute down,

II

And read a Grecian tale re-told,
Which, cast in later Grecian mould,
  Quintus Calaber
Somewhat lazily handled of old;

III

And on this white midwinter day–
For have the far-off hymns of May,
  All her melodies,
All her harmonies echoed away?–

IV

Today, before you turn again
To thoughts that lift the soul of men,
  Hear my cataract's
Downward thunder in hollow and glen,

*13*] There he stands, *MS*; Stand, like him, *MS alternative*.

¶440. *4.* Jowett was at work revising his *Plato* (1871) for its third edition (1892). Cp. Milton's *Sonnet 18* ('Cyriack . . .'), with its cordial invitation and injunction: 'Let *Euclid* rest and *Archimedes* pause'. Milton and T. recall Horace, *Odes* II xi 1–6.

*6–7.* T.'s source for *The Death of Œnone*, Quintus Smyrnaeus's *The Fall of Troy*.

V

Till, led by dream and vague desire,
The woman, gliding toward the pyre,
Find her warrior
Stark and dark in his funeral fire.

# 441 The Death of Œnone

Published *1892*, as a sequel to *Œnone* (p. 384). It was written Aug. 1889–July 1890 (*Mem.* ii 359, 509). T. said that 'he considered it even more strictly classical in form and language than the old *Œnone*' (*Mem.* ii 386). Source: Quintus Smyrnaeus, *The Fall of Troy* (post-Homeric, 4th century A.D.); T. adapts about 200 lines of Book x. See *To the Master of Balliol* (above). H.T. says that the information was supplied by R. C. Jebb. W. P. Mustard (*Classical Echoes in Tennyson*, 1904, pp. 45–51) compares T. and Quintus, noting that almost all T.'s details were supplied or suggested. He points out that Quintus had stressed the marriage bond between Œnone and Paris.

Œnone sat within the cave from out
Whose ivy-matted mouth she used to gaze
Down at the Troad; but the goodly view
Was now one blank, and all the serpent vines
Which on the touch of heavenly feet had risen,
And gliding through the branches overbowered
The naked Three, were withered long ago,
And through the sunless winter morning-mist
In silence wept upon the flowerless earth.
And while she stared at those dead cords that ran
Dark through the mist, and linking tree to tree,
But once were gayer than a dawning sky
With many a pendent bell and fragrant star,
Her Past became her Present, and she saw
Him, climbing toward her with the golden fruit,
Him, happy to be chosen Judge of Gods,
Her husband in the flush of youth and dawn,
Paris, himself as beauteous as a God.
Anon from out the long ravine below,
She heard a wailing cry, that seemed at first

¶441. *2.* Adapted from *Œnone* 71–87, *1832* text: 'ivymatted at the mouth'.
*3. Troad*: the district about Troy.
*7. Three*: the goddesses at the Judgment of Paris.

Thin as the batlike shrillings of the Dead
When driven to Hades, but, in coming near,
Across the downward thunder of the brook
Sounded 'Œnone'; and on a sudden he,
Paris, no longer beauteous as a God,
Struck by a poisoned arrow in the fight,
Lame, crookèd, reeling, livid, through the mist
Rose, like the wraith of his dead self, and moaned
'Œnone, *my* Œnone, while we dwelt
Together in this valley–happy then–
Too happy had I died within thine arms,
Before the feud of Gods had marred our peace,
And sundered each from each. I am dying now
Pierced by a poisoned dart. Save me. Thou knowest,
Taught by some God, whatever herb or balm
May clear the blood from poison, and thy fame
Is blown through all the Troad, and to thee
The shepherd brings his adder-bitten lamb,
The wounded warrior climbs from Troy to thee.
My life and death are in thy hand. The Gods
Avenge on stony hearts a fruitless prayer
For pity. Let me owe my life to thee.
I wrought thee bitter wrong, but thou forgive,
Forget it. Man is but the slave of Fate.
Œnone, by thy love which once was mine,
Help, heal me. I am poisoned to the heart.'
'And I to mine' she said 'Adulterer,
Go back to thine adulteress and die!'
He groaned, he turned, and in the mist at once
Became a shadow, sank and disappeared,
But, ere the mountain rolls into the plain,
Fell headlong dead; and of the shepherds one
Their oldest, and the same who first had found
Paris, a naked babe, among the woods
Of Ida, following lighted on him there,

*21. Odyssey* xxiv 6: *ὡς δ' ὅτε νυκτερίδες μυχῷ ἄντρου θεσπεσίοιο τρίζουσαι ποτέονται.* ('And as in the innermost recess of a wondrous cave bats flit about gibbering'.)

*29–46.* Paris's plea is based closely on Quintus.

*35. herb or balm*: based on Ovid's *Heroides* v 147–9, Œnone to Paris: *quaecumque herba potens ad opem radixque medendo / utilio in toto nascitur orbe, mea est. / me miseram, quod amor non est medicabilis herbis!* ('Whatever herb potent for aid, whatever root that is used for healing grows in all the world, is mine. Alas, wretched me, that love may not be healed by herbs!')

And shouted, and the shepherds heard and came.
  One raised the Prince, one sleeked the squalid hair,
One kissed his hand, another closed his eyes,
And then, remembering the gay playmate reared
Among them, and forgetful of the man,
Whose crime had half unpeopled Ilion, these
All that day long laboured, hewing the pines,
And built their shepherd-prince a funeral pile;
And, while the star of eve was drawing light
From the dead sun, kindled the pyre, and all
Stood round it, hushed, or calling on his name.
  But when the white fog vanished like a ghost
Before the day, and every topmost pine
Spired into bluest heaven, still in her cave,
Amazed, and ever seeming stared upon
By ghastlier than the Gorgon head, a face,–
*His* face deformed by lurid blotch and blain–
There, like a creature frozen to the heart
Beyond all hope of warmth, Œnone sat
Not moving, till in front of that ravine
Which drowsed in gloom, self-darkened from the west,
The sunset blazed along the wall of Troy.
  Then her head sank, she slept, and through her dream
A ghostly murmur floated, 'Come to me,
Œnone! I can wrong thee now no more,
Œnone, my Œnone,' and the dream
Wailed in her, when she woke beneath the stars.
  What star could burn so low? not Ilion yet.
What light was there? She rose and slowly down,
By the long torrent's ever-deepened roar,
Paced, following, as in trance, the silent cry.
She waked a bird of prey that screamed and past;

72. Combining 'Botches and blaines' (*Paradise Lost* xii 180) and Shelley's 'lurid blains', *Revolt of Islam* X xxi 8. Shelley's stanza describes those who (like T.'s Paris) 'came, / Seeking to quench the agony of the flame, / Which raged like poison through their bursting veins.' Shelley's next stanza offers parallels to T., including the theme of suicide: 'Many saw / Their own lean image everywhere, it went / A ghastlier self beside them, till the awe / Of that dread sight to self-destruction sent / Those shrieking victims.'

She roused a snake that hissing writhed away;
A panther sprang across her path, she heard
The shriek of some lost life among the pines,
But when she gained the broader vale, and saw
The ring of faces reddened by the flames
Enfolding that dark body which had lain
Of old in her embrace, paused–and then asked
Falteringly, 'Who lies on yonder pyre?'
But every man was mute for reverence.
Then moving quickly forward till the heat
Smote on her brow, she lifted up a voice
Of shrill command, 'Who burns upon the pyre?'
Whereon their oldest and their boldest said,
'He, whom thou wouldst not heal!' and all at once
The morning light of happy marriage broke
Through all the clouded years of widowhood,
And muffling up her comely head, and crying
'Husband!' she leapt upon the funeral pile,
And mixt herself with *him* and past in fire.

# 442 *'Remembering him who waits thee far away'

Printed *Mem.* ii 452. An inscription for the prayer-book presented to Queen Victoria by her children on the fiftieth anniversary of her wedding, 10 Feb. 1890. It had been requested by Princess Beatrice (*Mat.* iv 416).

Remembering him who waits thee far away,
And with thee, Mother, taught us first to pray,
Accept on this your golden bridal day
The Book of Prayer.

# 443 St Telemachus

Published *1892*. Composition was begun Aug. 1890 (*Mem.* ii 381), after F. W. Farrar had told T. the story. Farrar (as he says in *Saturday Magazine*, March 1893) then sent T. the extract which T. used as a concluding note:

'For Honorius, who succeeded to the sovereignty over Europe, suppresst the gladiatorial combats practised of old in Rome, on occasion of the

*104–6.* Based closely on Quintus.

following event. There was one Telemachus, embracing the ascetic mode of life, who setting out from the East and arriving at Rome for this very purpose, while that accursed spectacle was being performed, entered himself the circus, and descending into the arena, attempted to hold back those who wielded deadly weapons against each other. The spectators of the murderous fray, possest with the drunken glee of the demon who delights in such bloodshed, stoned to death the preacher of peace. The admirable Emperor learning this put a stop to that evil exhibition.– Theodoret's *Ecclesiastical History* [Book V, Chapter xxvi].'

T. may have had some such poem in mind earlier. H.T. calls it a 'pendant' to *St Simeon Stylites* (p. 542), and Jowett suggested topics in 1858: 'A representative from one of the Monastic orders similar in idea to St Simeon Stylites and to be called St Francis of Assisi, more Christian and less barbarous, would perhaps be possible' (*Mem.* i 433). T. would have met the story of St Telemachus in Charlotte M. Yonge's *Book of Golden Deeds* (1864), the acknowledged source of *Kapiolani*. 'My father thought of also writing the story of St Perpetua in verse as a companion poem' (H.T.).

Had the fierce ashes of some fiery peak
Been hurled so high they ranged about the globe?
For day by day, through many a blood-red eve,
In that four-hundredth summer after Christ,
The wrathful sunset glared against a cross
Reared on the tumbled ruins of an old fane
No longer sacred to the Sun, and flamed
On one huge slope beyond, where in his cave
The man, whose pious hand had built the cross,
A man who never changed a word with men,
Fasted and prayed, Telemachus the Saint.
  Eve after eve that haggard anchorite
Would haunt the desolated fane, and there
Gaze at the ruin, often mutter low
'Vicisti Galilæe'; louder again,
Spurning a shattered fragment of the God,
'Vicisti Galilæe!' but–when now
Bathed in that lurid crimson–asked 'Is earth

¶443. *1–5.* 'Suggested by the memory of the eruption of Krakatoa' (T.). This eruption in the Dutch East Indies, Aug. 1883, caused coloured twilights in England in Nov. and Dec.; cp. *Locksley Hall Sixty Years After* 178.

*15.* The dying words of Julian the Apostate. T. here may intend a covert retort to Swinburne, who had used the words in his *Hymn to Proserpine*, as the epigraph, and as: 'Thou hast conquered, O pale Galilean; the world has grown grey from thy breath' (*Songs and Ballads*, 1866).

On fire to the West? or is the Demon-god
Wroth at his fall?' and heard an answer 'Wake
Thou deedless dreamer, lazying out a life
Of self-suppression, not of selfless love.'
And once a flight of shadowy fighters crost
The disk, and once, he thought, a shape with wings
Came sweeping by him, and pointed to the West,
And at his ear he heard a whisper 'Rome'
And in his heart he cried 'The call of God!'
And called arose, and, slowly plunging down
Through that disastrous glory, set his face
By waste and field and town of alien tongue,
Following a hundred sunsets, and the sphere
Of westward-wheeling stars; and every dawn
Struck from him his own shadow on to Rome.
Foot-sore, way-worn, at length he touched his goal,
The Christian city. All her splendour failed
To lure those eyes that only yearned to see,
Fleeting betwixt her columned palace-walls,
The shape with wings. Anon there past a crowd
With shameless laughter, Pagan oath, and jest,
Hard Romans brawling of their monstrous games;
He, all but deaf through age and weariness,
And muttering to himself 'The call of God'
And borne along by that full stream of men,
Like some old wreck on some indrawing sea,
Gained their huge Colosseum. The caged beast
Yelled, as he yelled of yore for Christian blood.
Three slaves were trailing a dead lion away,
One, a dead man. He stumbled in, and sat
Blinded; but when the momentary gloom,
Made by the noonday blaze without, had left
His agèd eyes, he raised them, and beheld
A blood-red awning waver overhead,
The dust send up a steam of human blood,
The gladiators moving toward their fight,
And eighty thousand Christian faces watch
Man murder man. A sudden strength from heaven,
As some great shock may wake a palsied limb,

35. Charlotte M. Yonge said of gladiatorial combat: 'It went on for full a hundred years after Rome had, in name, become a Christian city.' The point was also stressed by Farrar. Cp. l. 55.

52. *awning*: the velarium, shading the spectators; it is mentioned by Yonge.

Turned him again to boy, for up he sprang,
And glided lightly down the stairs, and o'er
The barrier that divided beast from man
Slipt, and ran on, and flung himself between
The gladiatorial swords, and called 'Forbear
In the great name of Him who died for men,
Christ Jesus!' For one moment afterward
A silence followed as of death, and then
A hiss as from a wilderness of snakes,
Then one deep roar as of a breaking sea,
And then a shower of stones that stoned him dead,
And then once more a silence as of death.
His dream became a deed that woke the world,
For while the frantic rabble in half-amaze
Stared at him dead, through all the nobler hearts
In that vast Oval ran a shudder of shame.
The Baths, the Forum gabbled of his death,
And preachers lingered o'er his dying words,
Which would not die, but echoed on to reach
Honorius, till he heard them, and decreed
That Rome no more should wallow in this old lust
Of Paganism, and make her festal hour
Dark with the blood of man who murdered man.

# 444 The Church-Warden and the Curate

Published *1892*. Written 1890 (H.T.), 'founded on two sayings which Canon Rawnsley told him [May 1890]. One of a "Lincolnshire Church-warden" [ll. 49–50]. The other, that of a Lincolnshire farmer [ll. 15–16]'. The latter is told of a farmer's wife, not specifically in Lincolnshire, in *A Memoir of C. M. Young* by J. C. Young (1871, ii 265); she says of Baptists to the clergyman, 'I aint no idea of their coming and leaving all their nasty sins behind them in my water.' *1892* note: 'This is written in the dialect which was current in my youth at Spilsby and in the country about it.' All notes below are T.'s.

I

Eh? good daäy! good daäy! thaw it bean't not mooch of a daäy,
Nasty, casselty weather! an' mea haäfe down wi' my haäy!

¶444. 2. *casselty*: 'casualty, chance weather.' *haäfe down wi' my haäy*: 'while my grass is only half-mown.'

II

How be the farm gittin on? noäways. Gittin on i'deeäd!
Why, tonups was haäfe on 'em fingers an' toäs, an' the mare brokken-kneeäd,
An' pigs didn't sell at fall, an' wa lost wer Haldeny cow,
An' it beäts ma to knaw wot she died on, but wool's looking oop ony how.

III

An' soä they've maäde tha a parson, an' thou'll git along, niver fear,
Fur I beän chuch-warden mysen i' the parish fur fifteen year.
Well–sin ther beä chuch-wardens, ther mun be parsons an' all,
An' if t'ōne stick alongside t'uther the chuch weänt happen a fall.

IV

Fur I wur a Baptis wonst, an' ageän the toithe an' the raäte,
Till I fun that it warn't not the gaäinist waäy to the narra Gaäte.
An' I can't abeär 'em, I can't, fur a lot on 'em coomed ta-year–
I wur down wi' the rheumatis then–to *my* pond to wesh thessens theere–
Sa I sticks like the ivin as long as I lives to the owd chuch now,
Fur they weshed their sins i' *my* pond, an' I doubts they poisoned the cow.

V

Ay, an' ya seed the Bishop. They says 'at he coomed fra nowt–
Burn i' traäde. Sa I warrants 'e niver said haafe wot 'e thowt,
But 'e creeäpt an' 'e crawled along, till 'e feeäld 'e could howd 'is oän,
Then 'e married a greät Yerl's darter, an' sits o' the Bishop's throän.

VI

Now I'll gie tha a bit o' my mind an' tha weant be taakin' offence,
Fur thou be a big scholard now wi' a hoonderd haäcre o' sense–
But sich an obstropulous lad–naay, naay–fur I minds tha sa well,
Tha'd niver not hopple thy tongue, an' the tongue's sit afire o' Hell,
As I says to my missis todaay, when she hurled a plaäte at the cat
An' anoother ageän my noäse. Ya was niver sa bad as that.

VII

But I minds when i' Howlaby beck won daäy ya was ticklin' o' trout,
An' keeäper 'e seed ya an rooned, an' 'e bealed to ya 'Lad coom hout'

4. *fingers an' toäs*: 'a disease in turnips.'
5. *fall*: 'autumn.'
10. *if t'ōne stick alongside t'uther*: 'if the one hold by the other. "Ōne" is pronounced like "own".'
12. *fun*: 'found.' *gaäinist*: 'nearest.'
13. *ta-year*: 'this year.'
15. *ivin*: 'ivy.'
23. *obstropulous*: 'obstreperous–here the Curate makes a sign of deprecation.'
24. *hopple*: 'or "hobble", to tie the legs of a skittish cow when she is being milked.'
28. *bealed*: 'bellowed.'

An' ya stood oop naäkt i' the beck, an' ya telled 'im to knaw his awn plaäce
An' ya called 'im a clown, ya did, an' ya thrawed the fish i' 'is faäce,
An' 'e torned as red as a stag-tuckey's wattles, but theer an' then
I coämbed 'im down, fur I promised ya'd niver not do it ageän.

VIII

An' I cotched tha wonst i' my garden, when thou was a height-year-howd,
An' I fun thy pockets as full o' my pippins as iver they'd 'owd,
An' thou was as peärky as owt, an' tha maäde me as mad as mad,
But I says to tha 'keeap 'em, an' welcome' fur thou was the Parson's lad.

IX

An' Parson 'e 'ears on it all, an' then taäkes kindly to me,
An' then I wur chose chuch-warden an' coomed to the top o' the tree,
Fur Quoloty's hall my friends, an' they maäkes ma a help to the poor,
When I gits the plaäte fuller o' Soondays nor ony chuch-warden afoor,
Fur if iver thy feyther 'ed riled me I kep' mysen meeäk as a lamb,
An' saw by the Graäce o' the Lord, Mr Harry, I ham wot I ham.

X

But Parson 'e *will* speäk out, saw, now 'e be sixty-seven,
He'll niver swap Owlby an' Scratby fur owt but the Kingdom o' Heaven;
An' thou'll be 'is Curate 'ere, but, if iver tha meäns to git 'igher,
Tha mun tackle the sins o' the Wo'ld, an' not the faults o' the Squire.
An' I reckons tha'll light of a livin' somewheers i' the Wowd or the Fen,
If tha cottons down to thy betters, an' keeäps thysen to thysen.
But niver not speäk plaain out, if tha wants to git forrards a bit,
But creeäp along the hedge-bottoms, an' thou'll be a Bishop yit.

XI

Naäy, but tha *mun* speäk hout to the Baptises here i' the town,
Fur moäst on 'em talks ageän tithe, an' I'd like tha to preäch 'em down,
Fur *they*'ve bin a-preächin' *mea* down, they heve, an' I haätes 'em now,
Fur they leäved their nasty sins i' *my* pond, an' it poisoned the cow.

31. *torned*: 'in such words as "torned" (turned), "hurled", the *r* is hardly audible.' *stag-tuckey*: 'turkey-cock.'
33. *height-year-howd*: 'eight-year-old.'
34. *'owd*: 'hold.'
35. *peärky*: 'pert.'
46. *Wo'ld*: 'the world. Short *o*.'
47. *Wowd*: 'wold.'

# 445 Charity

Published *1892*. 'Founded on a true story' (H.T.). In *H.Nbk 56* (*c.* 1890), it is in another hand, revised by T., which perhaps suggests that it was written somewhat earlier.

I

What am I doing, you say to me, 'wasting the sweet summer hours'?
Haven't you eyes? I am dressing the grave of a woman with flowers.

II

For a woman ruined the world, as God's own scriptures tell,
And a man ruined mine, but a woman, God bless her, kept me from Hell.

III

Love me? O yes, no doubt–how long–till you threw me aside!
Dresses and laces and jewels and never a ring for the bride.

IV

All very well just now to be calling me darling and sweet,
And after a while would it matter so much if I came on the street?

V

You when I met you first–when *he* brought you!–I turned away
And the hard blue eyes have it still, that stare of a beast of prey.

VI

*You* were his friend–you–you–when he promised to make me his bride,
And you knew that he meant to betray me–you knew–you knew that he lied.

VII

He married an heiress, an orphan with half a shire of estate,–
I sent him a desolate wail and a curse, when I learned my fate.

VIII

For I used to play with the knife, creep down to the river-shore,
Moan to myself 'one plunge–then quiet for evermore.'

IX

Would the man have a touch of remorse when he heard what an end was mine?
Or brag to his fellow rakes of his conquest over their wine?

X

Money–my hire–*his* money–I sent him back what he gave,–
Will you move a little that way? your shadow falls on the grave.

XI

Two trains clashed: then and there he was crushed in a moment and died,
But the new-wedded wife was unharmed, though sitting close at his side.

¶445. *13.* Cp. the story of *Locksley Hall*, *Maud* and the other marriage poems.

XII

She found my letter upon him, my wail of reproach and scorn;
I had cursed the woman he married, and him, and the day I was born.

XIII

They put him aside for ever, and after a week–no more–
A stranger as welcome as Satan–a widow came to my door:

XIV

So I turned my face to the wall, I was mad, I was raving-wild,
I was close on that hour of dishonour, the birth of a baseborn child.

XV

O you that can flatter your victims, and juggle, and lie and cajole,
Man, can you even guess at the love of a soul for a soul?

XVI

I had cursed her as woman and wife, and in wife and woman I found
The tenderest Christ-like creature that ever stept on the ground.

XVII

She watched me, she nursed me, she fed me, she sat day and night by
my bed,
Till the joyless birthday came of a boy born happily dead.

XVIII

And her name? what was it? I asked her. She said with a sudden glow
On her patient face 'My dear, I will tell you before I go.'

XIX

And I when I learnt it at last, I shrieked, I sprang from my seat,
I wept, and I kissed her hands, I flung myself down at her feet,

XX

And we prayed together for *him*, for *him* who had given her the name.
She has left me enough to live on. I need no wages of shame.

XXI

She died of a fever caught when a nurse in a hospital ward.
She is high in the Heaven of Heavens, she is face to face with her Lord,

XXII

And He sees not her like anywhere in this pitiless world of ours!
I have told you my tale. Get you gone. I am dressing her grave with
flowers.

# 446 *Author and Critics

Unpublished. It is added by hand in a *Lincoln* trial edition of *1889*. Cp. the other epigrams of *1889*. T. glosses the last line 'Lockyer's hypothesis', which dates the poem 1890, when J. N. Lockyer published *The Meteoritic Hypothesis*. T. read it in proof in 1890 (*Tennyson and His Friends*, p. 287).

Some used to call you 'The coming Light,'
Some swore you would never emerge from night;
They struck at each other, left and right;
    And so your Day has begun.
The clash of so many a meteorite
    Has made your Name a Sun.

# 447 *'We lost you—for how long a time'

Published at the head of I. Gollancz's edition of the fourteenth-century poem *Pearl* (1891); not reprinted. It was written after a request in a letter of 18 Nov. 1890 (*Lincoln*). T. thought of including it in *1892*, but deleted it from the trial edition (*Lincoln*). He rephrased it in *T.Nbk 37*.

We lost you–for how long a time–
True Pearl of our poetic prime!
We found you, and you gleam re-set
In Britain's lyric coronet.

[1891. *To the Master of Balliol* — see p. 1426]

# 448 The Bandit's Death

Published *1892*. T. was working at it in Feb. 1891 (*Mem.* ii 384). But he apparently had it in mind in 1884–5, since the dedication to Scott appears among poems of *1885* in *H.Nbk 47*. *1892* note: 'I have adopted Sir Walter Scott's version of the following story as given in his last journal (Death of Il Bizarro)–but I have taken the liberty of making some slight alterations.' The last volume of Scott's *Journal* was edited in 1890; T. marked the story in his copy (*Lincoln*), and he quoted it in a trial edition of *1892* (*Lincoln*). But T. would already have known the entry on Il Bizarro (1832), since it had been quoted by J. G. Lockhart in his *Memoirs of Scott* (1837). T. added the name Piero and the dagger as the instrument of both the killings.

TO SIR WALTER SCOTT

*O great and gallant Scott,*
*True gentleman, heart, blood and bone,*
*I would it had been my lot*
*To have seen thee, and heard thee, and known.*

¶446. 5. Cp. *God and the Universe* 3: 'your fiery clash of meteorites'.

Sir, do you see this dagger? nay, why do you start aside?
I was not going to stab you, though I *am* the Bandit's bride.

You have set a price on his head: I may claim it without a lie.
What have I here in the cloth? I will show it you by-and-by.

Sir, I was once a wife. I had one brief summer of bliss.
But the Bandit had wooed me in vain, and he stabbed my Piero with this.

And he dragged me up there to his cave in the mountain, and there one day
He had left his dagger behind him. I found it. I hid it away.

For he reeked with the blood of Piero; his kisses were red with his crime,
And I cried to the Saints to avenge me. They heard, they bided their time.

In a while I bore him a son, and he loved to dandle the child,
And that was a link between us; but I–to be reconciled?–

No, by the Mother of God, though I think I hated him less,
And–well, if I sinned last night, I will find the Priest and confess.

Listen! we three were alone in the dell at the close of the day.
I was lilting a song to the babe, and it laughed like a dawn in May.

Then on a sudden we saw your soldiers crossing the ridge,
And he caught my little one from me; we dipt down under the bridge

By the great dead pine–you know it–and heard as we crouched below,
The clatter of arms, and voices, and men passing to and fro.

Black was the night when we crept away–not a star in the sky–
Hushed as the heart of the grave, till the little one uttered a cry.
I whispered 'give it to me,' but he would not answer me–then
He gript it so hard by the throat that the boy never cried again.

We returned to his cave–the link was broken–he sobbed and he wept,
And cursed himself; then he yawned, for the wretch *could* sleep, and he slept

Ay, till dawn stole into the cave, and a ray red as blood
Glanced on the strangled face–I could make Sleep Death, if I would–

Glared on at the murdered son, and the murderous father at rest, . . .
I drove the blade that had slain my husband thrice through his breast.

He was loved at least by his dog: it was chained, but its horrible yell
'She has killed him, has killed him, has killed him' rang out all down through the dell,

Till I felt I could end myself too with the dagger–so deafened and dazed–
Take it, and save me from it! I fled. I was all but crazed

With the grief that gnawed at my heart, and the weight that dragged at my hand;
But thanks to the Blessèd Saints that I came on none of his band;
And the band will be scattered now their gallant captain is dead,
For I with this dagger of his–do you doubt me? Here is his head!

## 449 *'Take, Lady, what your loyal nurses give'

Printed *The Times*, 27 June 1891. *Mem.* ii 383: 'Inscribed by my father in a copy of his works to be presented by the Royal Guild of Nurses of England to Princess Louise Augusta of Schleswig-Holstein on her marriage.' The presentation was decided on, 6 Feb. 1891 (*The Times*, 9 Feb.).

Take, Lady, what your loyal nurses give,
    Their full God-bless-you with this book of song,
And may the life, which, heart in heart, you live
    With him you love, be cloudless and be long!

## 450 June Bracken and Heather

TO –

Published *1892*. A dedication to T.'s wife Emily (as was *A Dedication*, p. 1184), it was written June 1891. The date is deduced from l. 6 (Emily was born 9 July 1813), and confirmed by *T.Nbk 37*.

There on the top of the down,
The wild heather round me and over me June's high blue,
When I looked at the bracken so bright and the heather so brown,
I thought to myself I would offer this book to you,
This, and my love together,
To you that are seventy-seven,
With a faith as clear as the heights of the June-blue heaven,
And a fancy as summer-new
As the green of the bracken amid the gloom of the heather.

# 451 Akbar's Dream

Published *1892*. Written 1891–2. As with *The Ancient Sage* (p. 1350), the subject was suggested by Jowett, who wrote to H.T. in Dec. 1890: 'I send books relating to Akbar. . . . I rely on your making a study of the books and presenting some of the contents of them in a form which will be available to your Father' (*Lincoln*). The books were from Balliol College Library and the orientalist Sir William Hunter (who sent details via Jowett). They are listed also in *Mem.* ii 388, and include: Abul-Fazl's *Ain-i-Akbari*, tr. Blochmann (1872–7); W. Hunter, *Asiatic Quarterly*, July 1890; H. Elliot's *History of India* (1867–77, vol. vi); M. Elphinstone's *History of India* (1874 edn); and A. Lyall's *Asiatic Studies* (1882). It was Jowett 'who first suggested an Indian subject, saying to me: "Your father appreciates the East."' Jowett wrote to H.T., 31 March 1891: 'I am delighted to hear that Akbar makes progress'; and on 17 April 1891 he sent a long letter on the significance of Akbar (*Lincoln*). For Jowett the poem was the culmination of many years during which he had encouraged T. to write a visionary religious poem. He 'urged him to write on . . . the idea that "All religions are one," or on "The religions of all good men"' (*Mem.* ii 372). The concluding Hymn was written June 1891 (*Mat.* iv 274); the poem as a whole was finished in 1892 (*Mem.* ii 398). The Hymn is in the same stanza as *Faith* (p. 1455), and *The Making of Man* (p. 1454): '"I should like," he said, "to write a long poem in the metre of 'Akbar's Hymn,' it is a magnificent metre".' T.'s 'own spirit of toleration' is manifest in the poem: 'In *Akbar* he thought that the language of theology had to be interchanged with that of philosophy, and that the highest good of Akbar's code of morals was, as far as he could make it out, quite within the Christian ideal' (*Mem.* ii 388). Cp. the sketch for a poem, *Ormuzd and Ahriman*, 1885 (*Mem.* ii 321). T.'s note reads:

'The great Mogul Emperor Akbar was born October 14, 1542, and died 1605. At 13 he succeeded his father Humayun; at 18 he himself assumed the sole charge of government. He subdued and ruled over fifteen large provinces; his empire included all India north of the Vindhya Mountains–in the south of India he was not so successful. His tolerance of religions and his abhorrence of religious persecution put our Tudors to shame. He invented a new eclectic religion by which he hoped to unite all creeds, castes, and peoples: and his legislation was remarkable for vigour, justice, and humanity.'

AN INSCRIPTION BY ABUL FAZL FOR A TEMPLE IN KASHMIR (Blochmann xxxii)

O God in every temple I see people that see thee, and in every language I hear spoken, people praise thee.
Polytheism and Islám feel after thee.
Each religion says, 'Thou art one, without equal.'

If it be a mosque people murmur the holy prayer, and if it be a Christian Church, people ring the bell from love to Thee.

Sometimes I frequent the Christian cloister, and sometimes the mosque.

But it is thou whom I search from temple to temple.

Thy elect have no dealings with either heresy or orthodoxy; for neither of them stands behind the screen of thy truth.

Heresy to the heretic, and religion to the orthodox,

But the dust of the rose-petal belongs to the heart of the perfume seller.

AKBAR *and* ABUL FAZL *before the palace at Futehpur-Sikri at night.*

'Light of the nations' asked his Chronicler
Of Akbar 'what has darkened thee tonight?'
Then, after one quick glance upon the stars,
And turning slowly toward him, Akbar said
'The shadow of a dream—an idle one
It may be. Still I raised my heart to heaven,
I prayed against the dream. To pray, to do–
To pray, to do according to the prayer,
Are, both, to worship Alla, but the prayers,
That have no successor in deed, are faint
And pale in Alla's eyes, fair mothers they
Dying in childbirth of dead sons. I vowed
Whate'er my dreams, I still would do the right
Through all the vast dominion which a sword,
That only conquers men to conquer peace,
Has won me. Alla be my guide!
But come,
My noble friend, my faithful counsellor,
Sit by my side. While thou art one with me,
I seem no longer like a lonely man
In the king's garden, gathering here and there
From each fair plant the blossom choicest-grown
To wreathe a crown not only for the king
But in due time for every Mussulmân,
Brahmin, and Buddhist, Christian, and Parsee,
Through all the warring world of Hindustan.
Well spake thy brother in his hymn to heaven
"Thy glory baffles wisdom. All the tracks

¶451. *25. 1892* note: 'Akbar's rapid conquests and the good government of his fifteen provinces with their complete military, civil and political systems make him conspicuous among the great kings of history.'

*27. 1892* note: 'The Emperor quotes from a hymn to the Deity by Faizi, brother of Abul Fazl, Akbar's chief friend and minister, who wrote the *Ain i Akbari* (Annals of Akbar). His influence on his age was immense. It may be that he and his brother Faizi led Akbar's mind away from Islám

Of science making toward Thy Perfectness
Are blinding desert sand; we scarce can spell
The Alif of Thine alphabet of Love."
He knows Himself, men nor themselves nor Him,
For every splintered fraction of a sect
Will clamour "*I* am on the Perfect Way,

and the Prophet–this charge is brought against him by every Muhammadan writer; but Abul Fazl also led his sovereign to a true appreciation of his duties, and from the moment that he entered Court, the problem of successfully ruling over mixed races, which Islám in few other countries had to solve, was carefully considered, and the policy of toleration was the result (Blochmann xxix.).

'*Abul Fazl* thus gives an account of himself: "The advice of my Father with difficulty kept me back from acts of folly; my mind had no rest and my heart felt itself drawn to the sages of Mongolia or to the hermits on Lebanon. I longed for interviews with the Llamás of Tibet or with the padres of Portugal, and I would gladly sit with the priests of the Parsis and the learned of the Zendavesta. I was sick of the learned of my own land."

'He became the intimate friend and adviser of Akbar, and helped him in his tolerant system of government. Professor Blochmann writes: "Impressed with a favourable idea of the value of his Hindu subjects, he (Akbar) had resolved when pensively sitting in the evenings on the solitary stone at Futehpur-Sikri to rule with an even hand all men in his dominions; but as the extreme views of the learned and the lawyers continually urged him to persecute instead of to heal, he instituted discussions, because, believing himself to be in error, he thought it his duty as ruler to inquire." "These discussions took place every Thursday night in the Ibadat-khana, a building at Futehpur-Sikri, erected for the purpose" (Malleson).

'In these discussions Abul Fazl became a great power, and he induced the chief of the disputants to draw up a document defining the "divine Faith" as it was called, and assigning to Akbar the rank of a Mujahid, or supreme khalifah, the vicegerent of the one true God.

'Abul Fazl was finally murdered at the instigation of Akbar's son Salim, who in his Memoirs declares that it was Abul Fazl who had perverted his father's mind so that he denied the divine mission of Mahomet, and turned away his love from his son.

'*Faizi*. When Akbar conquered the North-West Provinces of India, Faizi, then 20, began his life as a poet, and earned his living as a physician. He is reported to have been very generous and to have treated the poor for nothing. His fame reached Akbar's ears, who commanded him to come to the camp at Chitor. Akbar was delighted with his varied knowledge and scholarship and made the poet teacher to his sons. Faizi at 33 was appointed Chief Poet (1588). He collected a fine library of 4300 MSS. and died at the age of 40 (1595) when Akbar incorporated his collection of rare books in the Imperial Library.'

All else is to perdition."
Shall the rose
Cry to the lotus "No flower thou"? the palm
Call to the cypress "I alone am fair"?
The mango spurn the melon at his foot?
"Mine is the one fruit Alla made for man."
Look how the living pulse of Alla beats
Through all His world. If every single star
Should shriek its claim "I only am in heaven"
Why that were such sphere-music as the Greek
Had hardly dreamed of. There is light in all,
And light, with more or less of shade, in all
Man-modes of worship; but our Ulama,
Who "sitting on green sofas contemplate
The torment of the damned" already, these
Are like wild brutes new-caged–the narrower
The cage, the more their fury. Me they front
With sullen brows. What wonder! I decreed
That even the dog was clean, that men may taste
Swine-flesh, drink wine; they know too that whene'er
In our free Hall, where each philosophy
And mood of faith may hold its own, they blurt
Their furious formalisms, I but hear
The clash of tides that meet in narrow seas,–
Not the Great Voice not the true Deep.
To drive
A people from their ancient fold of Faith,
And wall them up perforce in mine–unwise,
Unkinglike;–and the morning of my reign
Was reddened by that cloud of shame when I . . .
I hate the rancour of their castes and creeds,
I let men worship as they will, I reap
No revenue from the field of unbelief.
I cull from every faith and race the best
And bravest soul for counsellor and friend.

*45. Ulama*: or ulema, the trained body of Mohammedan divines.

*57–8. 1892* note: 'Malleson says: "This must have happened because Akbar states it, but of the forced conversions I have found no record. This must have taken place whilst he was still a minor, and whilst the chief authority was wielded by Bairam".'

*64. 1892* note: 'The Hindus are fond of pilgrimages and Akbar removed a remunerative tax raised by his predecessors on pilgrimages. He also abolished the fezza or capitation tax on those who differed from the Mahomedan faith. He discouraged all *excessive* prayers, fasts and pilgrimages.'

I loathe the very name of infidel.
I stagger at the Korân and the sword.
I shudder at the Christian and the stake;
Yet "Alla," says their sacred book, "is Love,"
And when the Goan Padre quoting Him,
Issa Ben Mariam, his own prophet, cried
"Love one another little ones" and "bless"
Whom? even "your persecutors"! there methought
The cloud was rifted by a purer gleam
Than glances from the sun of our Islâm.
And thou rememberest what a fury shook
Those pillars of a mouldered faith, when he,
That other, prophet of their fall, proclaimed
His Master as "the Sun of Righteousness,"
Yea, Alla here on earth, who caught and held
His people by the bridle-rein of Truth.
What art thou saying? "And was not Alla called
In old Irân the Sun of Love? and Love
The net of truth?"
A voice from old Irân!
Nay, but I know it–*his*, the hoary Sheik,
On whom the women shrieking "Atheist" flung
Filth from the roof, the mystic melodist
Who all but lost himself in Alla, him
Abû Saîd—
–a sun but dimly seen

*71. 1892* note: 'Abul Fazl relates that "one night the Ibadat-khana was brightened by the presence of Padre Rodolpho, who for intelligence and wisdom was unrivalled among Christian doctors. Several carping and bigoted men attacked him, and this afforded an opportunity for the display of the calm judgment and justice of the assembly. These men brought forward the old received assertions, and did not attempt to arrive at truth by reasoning. Their statements were torn to pieces, and they were nearly put to shame, when they began to attack the contradictions of the Gospel, but they could not prove their assertions. With perfect calmness, and earnest conviction of the truth he replied to their arguments".'

*90. 1892* note: '"Love is the net of Truth, Love is the noose of God" is a quotation from the great Sufee poet Abû Sa'îd–born A.D. 968, died at the age of 83. He is a mystical poet, and some of his expressions have been compared to our George Herbert. Of Shaikh Abû Sa'îd it is recorded that he said, "when my affairs had reacht a certain pitch I buried under the dust my books and opened a shop on my own account (*i.e.* began to teach with authority), and verily men represented me as that which I was not, until it came to this, that they went to the Qâdhî and testified against me of

Here, till the mortal morning mists of earth
Fade in the noon of heaven, when creed and race
Shall bear false witness, each of each, no more,
But find their limits by that larger light,
And overstep them, moving easily
Through after-ages in the love of Truth,
The truth of Love.
                    The sun, the sun! they rail
At me the Zoroastrian. Let the Sun,
Who heats our earth to yield us grain and fruit,
And laughs upon thy field as well as mine,
And warms the blood of Shiah and Sunnee,
Symbol the Eternal! Yea and may not kings
Express Him also by their warmth of love
For all they rule–by equal law for all?
By deeds a light to men?
                    But no such light
Glanced from our Presence on the face of one,
Who breaking in upon us yestermorn,
With all the Hells a-glare in either eye,
Yelled "hast *thou* brought us down a new Korân
From heaven? art *thou* the Prophet? canst *thou* work
Miracles?" and the wild horse, anger, plunged
To fling me, and failed. Miracles! no, not I
Nor he, nor any. I can but lift the torch
Of Reason in the dusky cave of Life,

unbelieverhood; and women got upon the roofs and cast unclean things upon me." (*Vide* reprint from article in *National Review*, March 1891, by C. J. Pickering.)'

*101. Shiah and Sunnee*: two Mohammedan sects.

*106–7. 1892* note: 'I am not aware that there is any record of such intrusion upon the king's privacy, but the expressions in the text occur in a letter sent by Akbar's foster-brother Aziz, who refused to come to court when summoned and threw up his government, and "after writing an insolent and reproachful letter to Akbar in which he asked him if he had received a book from heaven, or if he could work miracles like Mahomet that he presumed to introduce a new religion, warned him that he was on the way to eternal perdition, and concluded with a prayer to God to bring him back into the path of salvation" (Elphinstone).

'The Koran, the Old and New Testament, and the Psalms of David are called *books* by way of excellence, and their followers "People of the Book" (Elphinstone).

'*Akbar* according to Abdel Kadir had his son Murad instructed in the Gospel, and used to make him begin his lessons "In the name of Christ" instead of in the usual way "In the name of God".'

And gaze on this great miracle, the World,
Adoring That who made, and makes, and is,
And is not, what I gaze on–all else Form,
Ritual, varying with the tribes of men.
Ay but, my friend, thou knowest I hold that forms
Are needful: only let the hand that rules,
With politic care, with utter gentleness,
Mould them for all his people.
And what are forms?
Fair garments, plain or rich, and fitting close
Or flying looselier, warmed but by the heart
Within them, moved but by the living limb,
And cast aside, when old, for newer,–Forms!
The Spiritual in Nature's market-place–
The silent Alphabet-of-heaven-in-man
Made vocal–banners blazoning a Power
That is not seen and rules from far away–
A silken cord let down from Paradise,
When fine Philosophies would fail, to draw
The crowd from wallowing in the mire of earth,
And all the more, when these behold their Lord,
Who shaped the forms, obey them, and himself
Here on this bank in *some* way live the life
Beyond the bridge, and serve that Infinite
Within us, as without, that All-in-all,
And over all, the never-changing One
And ever-changing Many, in praise of Whom
The Christian bell, the cry from off the mosque,
And vaguer voices of Polytheism
Make but one music, harmonising "Pray."
There westward–under yon slow-falling star,
The Christians own a Spiritual Head;
And following thy true counsel, by thine aid,
Myself am such in our Islâm, for no
Mirage of glory, but for power to fuse
My myriads into union under one;
To hunt the tiger of oppression out
From office; and to spread the Divine Faith

*151. 1892* note: 'The Divine Faith slowly passed away under the immediate successors of Akbar. An idea of what the Divine Faith was may be gathered from the inscription at the head of the poem. The document referred to, Abul Fazl says, "brought about excellent results (1) the Court became a gathering-place of the sages and learned of all creeds; the good doctrines of all religious systems were recognized, and their defects were not allowed to obscure their good features; (2) perfect toleration or peace with all was

Like calming oil on all their stormy creeds,
And fill the hollows between wave and wave;
To nurse my children on the milk of Truth,
And alchemise old hates into the gold
Of Love, and make it current; and beat back
The menacing poison of intolerant priests,
Those cobras ever setting up their hoods–
One Alla! one Kalifa!
Still–at times
A doubt, a fear,–and yester afternoon
I dreamed,–thou knowest how deep a well of love
My heart is for my son, Saleem, mine heir,–
And yet so wild and wayward that my dream–
He glares askance at thee as one of those
Who mix the wines of heresy in the cup
Of counsel–so–I pray thee–
Well, I dreamed
That stone by stone I reared a sacred fane,
A temple, neither Pagod, Mosque, nor Church,
But loftier, simpler, always open-doored
To every breath from heaven, and Truth and Peace
And Love and Justice came and dwelt therein;
But while we stood rejoicing, I and thou,
I heard a mocking laugh "the new Korân!"
And on the sudden, and with a cry "Saleem"
Thou, thou–I saw thee fall before me, and then
Me too the black-winged Azrael overcame,
But Death had ears and eyes; I watched my son,
And those that followed, loosen, stone from stone,
All my fair work; and from the ruin arose
The shriek and curse of trampled millions, even
As in the time before; but while I groaned,
From out the sunset poured an alien race,
Who fitted stone to stone again, and Truth,
Peace, Love and Justice came and dwelt therein,
Nor in the field without were seen or heard
Fires of Súttee, nor wail of baby-wife,

established; and (3) the perverse and evil-minded were covered with shame on seeing the disinterested motives of His Majesty, and these stood in the pillory of disgrace". Dated September 1579–Ragab 987 (Blochmann xiv).'

*159. Kalifa*: civil and religious leader.

*176. Azrael*: Mohammedan angel of death.

*186–7. 1892* note: 'Akbar decreed that every widow who showed the least desire not to be burnt on her husband's funeral pyre, should be let go free and unharmed. He forbad marriage before the age of puberty. Akbar ordained that remarriage was lawful.'

Or Indian widow; and in sleep I said
"All praise to Alla by whatever hands
My mission be accomplished!" but we hear
Music: our palace is awake, and morn
Has lifted the dark eyelash of the Night
From off the rosy cheek of waking Day.
Our hymn to the sun. They sing it. Let us go.'

HYMN

I

Once again thou flamest heavenward, once again we see thee rise.
Every morning is thy birthday gladdening human hearts and eyes.
Every morning here we greet it, bowing lowly down before thee,
Thee the Godlike, thee the changeless in thine ever-changing skies.

II

Shadow-maker, shadow-slayer, arrowing light from clime to clime,
Hear thy myriad laureates hail thee monarch in their woodland rhyme.
Warble bird, and open flower, and, men, below the dome of azure
Kneel adoring Him the Timeless in the flame that measures Time!

## 452 *'I weeded my garden for hours and hours'

Printed by L. Magnus, *Herbert Warren* (1932), p. 231. It is in *T.Nbk 34* (1892), and refers to one of the many American editions which reprinted poems that T. had suppressed.

I weeded my garden for hours and hours,
To make it a pleasure for women and men;
But a Yankee planted the weeds again,
Little he cared for the flowers.

*190. 1892* note: '"About a watch before daybreak," says Abul Fazl, the musicians played to the king in the palace. "His Majesty had such a knowledge of the science of music as trained musicians do not possess".'

# 453 The Death of the Duke of Clarence and Avondale

### To the Mourners

Published *Nineteenth Century*, Feb. 1892; then *1892*. Written Jan., it is not in the first trial edition of *1892* (*Lincoln*). The first draft consisted of ll. 5–11 (H. D. Rawnsley, *Memories of the Tennysons*, 1900, p. 145). The Duke, Queen Victoria's grandson, had died 14 Jan., aged 28; in Dec. 1891 he had become engaged to Princess Victoria of Teck. T. had not written a poem when the Duke came of age, so 'he was anxious, although unwell at the time, to speak some words of comfort for the poor mother [the Princess of Wales], when the Duke died. He wrote his poem in two days' (*Mem.* ii 395).

The bridal garland falls upon the bier,
The shadow of a crown, that o'er him hung,
Has vanished in the shadow cast by Death.
So princely, tender, truthful, reverent, pure–
Mourn! That a world-wide Empire mourns with you,
That all the Thrones are clouded by your loss,
Were slender solace. Yet be comforted;
For if this earth be ruled by Perfect Love,
Then, after his brief range of blameless days,
The toll of funeral in an Angel ear
Sounds happier than the merriest marriage-bell.
The face of Death is toward the Sun of Life,
His shadow darkens earth: his truer name
Is 'Onward,' no discordance in the roll
And march of that Eternal Harmony
Whereto the worlds beat time, though faintly heard
Until the great Hereafter. Mourn in hope!

# 454 Kapiolani

Written and published *1892* (*Mem.* ii 398). It is not in the first trial edition of *1892* (*Lincoln*). The story, of which the action occurred in 1825, was from Charlotte Yonge's *Book of Golden Deeds* (1864), H.T. says. But T. will have been reminded of Kapiolani by a full account of her by Edward Clifford, *Nineteenth Century* xxv (1889) 871. Clifford sent T. a copy of his collected articles (*Father Damien*, 1889), which T. acknowledged by saying

¶453. *12–13.* Cp. *Love and Death* 10–11: 'Thou art the shadow of life, and as the tree / Stands in the sun and shadows all beneath . . .'

that he had read them in the *Nineteenth Century* (*Lincoln*). Sir Charles Tennyson (p. 523) connects it and its rhythms with the visit to T. of Queen Emma of the Sandwich Islands in 1865. For the mood, and attitude to priestcraft, cp. *The Victim* (p. 1194), also said to be from *Golden Deeds*.

Kapiolani was a great chieftainess who lived in the Sandwich Islands at the beginning of this century. She won the cause of Christianity by openly defying the priests of the terrible goddess Peelè. In spite of their threats of vengeance she ascended the volcano Mauna-Loa, then clambered down over a bank of cinders 400 feet high to the great lake of fire (nine miles round) – Kilauēä – the home and haunt of the goddess, and flung into the boiling lava the consecrated berries which it was sacrilege for a woman to handle.

I

When from the terrors of Nature a people have
  fashioned and worship a Spirit of Evil,
Blest be the Voice of the Teacher who calls to them
'Set yourselves free!'

II

Noble the Saxon who hurled at his Idol a valorous
  weapon in olden England!
Great and greater, and greatest of women, island
  heroine, Kapiolani
Clomb the mountain, and flung the berries, and dared
  the Goddess, and freed the people
Of Hawa-i-ee!

III

A people believing that Peelè the Goddess would
  wallow in fiery riot and revel
On Kilauēä,
Dance in a fountain of flame with her devils, or shake
  with her thunders and shatter her island,
Rolling her anger
Through blasted valley and flaring forest in blood-red
  cataracts down to the sea!

IV

Long as the lava-light
Glares from the lava-lake

¶454. *8*. 'There the fiery goddess still revelled in her fearful gambols' (Yonge).

*9–12*. 'I rode up to Kilauea . . . . Two years ago there was a most terrific earthquake here, and the lava flowed down to the sea in a river' (Clifford, who also speaks of 'these fire fountains').

Dazing the starlight,
Long as the silvery vapour in daylight
Over the mountain
Floats, will the glory of Kapiolani be mingled with either on Hawa-i-ee.

V

What said her Priesthood?
'Woe to this island if ever a woman should handle or gather the berries of Peelè!
Accursèd were she!
And woe to this island if ever a woman should climb to the dwelling of Peelè the Goddess!
Accursèd were she!'

VI

One from the Sunrise
Dawned on His people, and slowly before him
Vanished shadow-like
Gods and Goddesses,
None but the terrible Peelè remaining as Kapiolani ascended her mountain,
Baffled her priesthood,
Broke the Taboo,
Dipt to the crater,
Called on the Power adored by the Christian, and crying 'I dare her, let Peelè avenge herself'!
Into the flame-billow dashed the berries, and drove the demon from Hawa-i-ee.

# 455 The Dawn

Published *1892*, 'written at the end of his life' (H.T.). It is in *H.Nbk 56* with other poems of *1892*.

*Epigraph*: T. applies to his purposes Plato's *Timaeus* 22: 'Whereupon one of the priests, a prodigiously old man, said, "O Solon, Solon, you Greeks are always children: there is not such a thing as an old Greek." And on hearing this he asked, "What mean you by this saying?" And the priest replied, "You are young in soul, every one of you. For therein you possess not a single belief that is ancient and derived from old tradition, nor yet one science that is hoary with age. And this is the cause thereof: There have

*16–18*. 'Formed by the action of the air upon the vapour . . . like cobwebs of spun glass' (Yonge). 'All round the lake is a deposit of "Pele's hair," a dun-coloured glassy thread' (Clifford).

been and there will be many and divers destructions of mankind, of which the greatest are by fire and water, and lesser ones by countless other means".'

*You are but children.*
EGYPTIAN PRIEST TO SOLON

I

Red of the Dawn!
Screams of a babe in the red-hot palms of a Moloch of Tyre,
Man with his brotherless dinner on man in the tropical wood,
Priests in the name of the Lord passing souls through fire to the fire,
Head-hunters and boats of Dahomey that float upon human blood!

II

Red of the Dawn!
Godless fury of peoples, and Christless frolic of kings,
And the bolt of war dashing down upon cities and blazing farms,
For Babylon was a child new-born, and Rome was a babe in arms,
And London and Paris and all the rest are as yet but in leading-strings.

III

Dawn not Day,
While scandal is mouthing a bloodless name at *her* cannibal feast,
And rake-ruined bodies and souls go down in a common wreck,
And the press of a thousand cities is prized for it smells of the beast,
Or easily violates virgin Truth for a coin or a cheque.

IV

Dawn not Day!
Is it Shame, so few should have climbed from the dens in the level below,
Men, with a heart and a soul, no slaves of a four-footed will?
But if twenty million of summers are stored in the sunlight still,
We are far from the noon of man, there is time for the race to grow.

V

Red of the Dawn!
Is it turning a fainter red? so be it, but when shall we lay
The Ghost of the Brute that is walking and haunting us yet, and be free?
In a hundred, a thousand winters? Ah, what will *our* children be,
The men of a hundred thousand, a million summers away?

¶455. 5. T. said in conversation, *c.* 1869–70: 'On the accession of a king in Dahomey [W. Africa] enough women victims are killed to float a small canoe (with their blood)' (Sir Charles Tennyson, *Twentieth Century* clxv (1959) 37). T. owned a copy (*Lincoln*) of Sir Richard Burton's *A Mission to Gelele, King of Dahome* (1864), which discusses sceptically the 'report that the king floated a canoe and paddled himself in a tank full of human blood' (i 344).
*19.* As estimated by scientists like William Thomson.

# 456 The Making of Man

Published *1892*, 'written at the end of his life' (H.T.). It is not in the first trial edition of *1892* (*Lincoln*); in the later one, the title is *It is Finished.* Cp. *Maud* i 136: 'So many a million of ages have gone to the making of man'.

Where is one that, born of woman, altogether can escape
From the lower world within him, moods of tiger, or of ape?
  Man as yet is being made, and ere the crowning Age of ages,
Shall not æon after æon pass and touch him into shape?

All about him shadow still, but, while the races flower and fade,
Prophet-eyes may catch a glory slowly gaining on the shade,
  Till the peoples all are one, and all their voices blend in choric
Hallelujah to the Maker 'It is finished. Man is made.'

# 457 Doubt and Prayer

Published *1892*. 'An early sonnet, altered' (H.T.). The early version, *The Christian Penitent* (1832, p. 468), was printed in a trial edition of *1892* (*Lincoln*) and then revised. All variants are below.

Though Sin too oft, when smitten by Thy rod,
Rail at 'Blind Fate' with many a vain 'Alas!'
From sin through sorrow into Thee we pass
By that same path our true forefathers trod;
And let not Reason fail me, nor the sod
Draw from my death Thy living flower and grass,
Before I learn that Love, which is, and was
My Father, and my Brother, and my God!

¶456. *1. Job* xiv 1: 'Man that is born of a woman is of few days, and full of trouble.'

*8. John* xix 30: 'It is finished.'

¶457. *1–2*] We sin and so we suffer, and alas
We see not we are chastened with the rod; *1832*

*3. Thee*] God *1832*.

*4. that*] the *1832*.

*5–6*] Seal not mine eyes with night, nor let the sod
Feed from my mouldering frame Thy flowers and grass *1832*

*7. learn that*] know Thy *1832*.

Steel me with patience! soften me with grief!
Let blow the trumpet strongly while I pray,
Till this embattled wall of unbelief
My prison, not my fortress, fall away!
Then, if Thou willest, let my day be brief,
So Thou wilt strike Thy glory through the day.

# 458 Faith

Published *1892*, 'written at the end of his life' (H.T.). It is not in the first trial edition of *1892* (*Lincoln*). Apparently it is the long-delayed 'pendent' to *Despair* (see headnote, p. 1299).

I

Doubt no longer that the Highest is the wisest and the best,
Let not all that saddens Nature blight thy hope or break thy rest,
  Quail not at the fiery mountain, at the shipwreck, or the rolling
Thunder, or the rending earthquake, or the famine, or the pest!

II

Neither mourn if human creeds be lower than the heart's desire!
Through the gates that bar the distance comes a gleam of what is higher.
  Wait till Death has flung them open, when the man will make the Maker
Dark no more with human hatreds in the glare of deathless fire!

*9. Steel . . . patience*] Touch me with sorrow *1832*.
*10*] Blow thou the [thy *trial edition 1892*] trumpet strongly night and day, *1832*.
*10–12*. The fall of Jericho, *Joshua* vi.
*11. Till this embattled*] Until this battled *1832*.
*12*] Built round my warring spirit fall away! *1832*.
*13. Thou*] *1892*; thou *Eversley*.
*13–14*] Then take me to Thyself–a full-eared sheaf
Ripe for the harvest on an autumn day. *1832*;
Then bring thou to my leaguered soul relief
And strike Thy glory through my darkened day!
*trial edition 1892*
¶458. *6–7*. Cp. *God and the Universe* 6: 'the silent Opener of the Gate'.
*7–8*. T. persistently refused to believe in 'the deathless fire of Hell', *Happy* 84; cp. the theme of *Despair*.

# 459 The Silent Voices

Published *1892*. 'Written at the end of his life' (H.T.). It is in *H.Nbk 56* with other poems of *1892*. Cp. H.T.'s observation that in 1880, 'after my uncle Charles' death my father was very unwell, suffering from a liver attack, and hearing perpetual ghostly voices' (*Mem.* ii 244).

When the dumb Hour, clothed in black,
Brings the Dreams about my bed,
Call me not so often back,
Silent Voices of the dead,
Toward the lowland ways behind me,
And the sunlight that is gone!
Call me rather, silent voices,
Forward to the starry track
Glimmering up the heights beyond me
On, and always on!

# 460 God and the Universe

Written and published *1892* (*Mem.* ii 398). The title in a trial edition of *1892* (*Lincoln*) had been *God and the World.*

I

Will my tiny spark of being wholly vanish in your deeps and heights?
Must my day be dark by reason, O ye Heavens, of your boundless nights,
Rush of Suns, and roll of systems, and your fiery clash of meteorites?

II

'Spirit, nearing yon dark portal at the limit of thy human state,
Fear not thou the hidden purpose of that Power which alone is great,
Nor the myriad world, His shadow, nor the silent Opener of the Gate.'

# 461 The Dreamer

Written and published *1892*, 'the last poem he finished' (*Mem.* ii 419). Apparently T. first wrote the song (ll. 17–32), *T.Nbk 34*. The poem is not in the first trial edition of *1892* (*Lincoln*).

¶460. *3.* Cp. *In Memoriam*: *Epilogue* 122: 'star and system rolling past'; and *Author and Critics* 5: 'The clash of so many a meteorite', deriving from J. N. Lockyer's *The Meteoritic Hypothesis* (1890).
*6.* Cp. the open gates in *Faith* 6–7.

On a midnight in midwinter when all but the winds
were dead,
'The meek shall inherit the earth' was a Scripture that
rang through his head,
Till he dreamed that a Voice of the Earth went
wailingly past him and said:

'I am losing the light of my Youth
And the Vision that led me of old,
And I clash with an iron Truth,
When I make for an Age of gold,
And I would that my race were run,
For teeming with liars, and madmen, and knaves,
And wearied of Autocrats, Anarchs, and Slaves,
And darkened with doubts of a Faith that saves,
And crimson with battles, and hollow with graves,
To the wail of my winds, and the moan of my waves
I whirl, and I follow the Sun.'

Was it only the wind of the Night shrilling out
Desolation and wrong
Through a dream of the dark? Yet he thought that he
answered her wail with a song–

Moaning your losses, O Earth,
Heart-weary and overdone!
But all's well that ends well,
Whirl, and follow the Sun!

He is racing from heaven to heaven
And less will be lost than won,
For all's well that ends well,
Whirl, and follow the Sun!

The Reign of the Meek upon earth,
O weary one, has it begun?
But all's well that ends well,
Whirl, and follow the Sun!

For moans will have grown sphere-music
Or ever your race be run!
And all's well that ends well,
Whirl, and follow the Sun!

¶461. 2. *Psalm* xxxvii 11.
18. *overdone*: exhausted.
29. The celestial music traditionally made by the spheres.

# 462 Crossing the Bar

Published *1889*. It is not in the *Virginia* trial edition of *1889*. Written Oct. 1889 while crossing the Solent: 'When he repeated it to me in the evening, I said, "That is the crown of your life's work." He answered, "It came in a moment"' (H.T.). T. said to W. F. Rawnsley that he 'began and finished it in twenty minutes' (*Nineteenth Century* xcvii (1925) 195). It had been in T.'s mind since April or May 1889, when his nurse suggested he write a hymn after his recovery from a serious illness (J. Tennyson, *The Times*, 5 Nov. 1936). For the image, cp. *De Profundis* (p. 1281), and *The Passing of Arthur* 445: 'From the great deep to the great deep he goes.' The 'bar' is the sandbank across the harbour-mouth. All variants from *H.Nbk 54* are below. The poem is here printed out of sequence because of T.'s wish: 'Mind you put my *Crossing the Bar* at the end of all editions of my poems.'

Sunset and evening star,
  And one clear call for me!
And may there be no moaning of the bar,
  When I put out to sea,

But such a tide as moving seems asleep,
  Too full for sound and foam,
When that which drew from out the boundless deep
  Turns again home.

Twilight and evening bell,
  And after that the dark!
And may there be no sadness of farewell,
  When I embark;

¶462. *2. And*] But *H.MS*. The 'call' is a marine term, a summons to duty, here suggesting that of God; but it is ominous too. Cp. the death of Enoch Arden, when 'There came so loud a calling of the sea' (p. 1151 and *n*).
*3.* Cp. Charles Kingsley's *The Three Fishers*, a poem on death: 'And the harbour bar be moaning'. T. had a copy (*Lincoln*) of *Andromeda and Other Poems* (1858), in which this poem appeared.
*7. drew*] came *MS*. 'The boundless deep' recurs often in T., with something of the same mood and theme in *The Ancient Sage* 189–94; and cp. *Sea Dreams* 85–6: 'such a tide', 'from out the boundless outer deep'. Cp. *In Memoriam*: *Epilogue* 123–4: 'A soul shall draw from out the vast / And strike his being into bounds.'
*10. after that*] then *MS 1st reading*.
*11. And*] But *MS*.

For though from out our bourne of Time and Place
　　The flood may bear me far,
I hope to see my Pilot face to face
　　When I have crost the bar.

*13. For . . . our*] Alone from out the *MS.* *bourne*: suggested by Hamlet on death, 'from whose bourn / No traveller returns', III i 79–80.
*13–16.* J. H. Buckley (p. 287) compares H. F. Lyte's famous hymn: 'Praise, my soul, the King of Heaven . . . / Ye behold him face to face . . . / Dwellers all in time and space.' Also *1 Corinthians* xiii 12: 'For now we see through a glass, darkly; but then face to face.' As so often, T.'s mind may have gone back to Arthur Hallam, to *In Memoriam* cxxxi: 'And come to look on those we loved / And that which made us, face to face' *H.MS.*
*14*] Alone I sail, and far, *MS.*
*15. I*] But *MS.* 'The pilot has been on board all the while, but in the dark I have not seen him' (T.). 'He explained the Pilot as "that Divine and Unseen Who is always guiding us"' (H.T.). T. J. Assad discusses the objections to the image, *Tulane Studies in English* viii (1958) 153–63.

# 463–476 Idylls of the King

H.T. introduces the *Idylls* as follows:

'With the publication of *Gareth and Lynette* in 1872 my father thought that he had completed the cycle of the *Idylls*; but later he felt that some further introduction to *Merlin and Vivien* was necessary, and so wrote *Balin and Balan.*

'From his earliest years he had written out in prose various histories of Arthur. His prefatory MS note about the historical Arthur is: "He lived about 500 A.D. and defeated his enemies in a pitched battle in the Welsh kingdom of Strathclyde: and the earliest allusions to him are to be found in the Welsh bards of the seventh century. In the twelfth century Geoffrey of Monmouth collected the legends about him as an European conqueror in his *History of the Britons*: and translated them from Celtic into Latin. [*note*: Wace translated them into French and added the story of the Round Table.] The *Morte d'Arthur* by Sir Thomas Malory was printed by Caxton in 1485." On Malory, on Layamon's *Brut*, on Lady Charlotte Guest's translation of the *Mabinogion*, on the old Chronicles, on old French Romance, on Celtic folklore, and largely on his own imagination, my father founded his epic; he has made the old legends his own, restored the idealism, and infused into them a spirit of modern thought and an ethical significance, setting his characters in a rich and varied landscape; as indeed otherwise these archaic stories, "loosely strung together without art," would not have appealed to the modern world.

'In 1832 appeared the first of the Arthurian poems in the form of a lyric, *The Lady of Shalott* (another version of the story of Lancelot and Elaine), and this was followed in 1842 by the other lyrics, *Sir Launcelot and Queen Guinevere* (partly if not wholly written in 1830) and *Sir Galahad.*

'The 1842 volume also contained the *Morte d' Arthur*, which now forms part of the *Passing of Arthur.*

'The earliest fragment of an epic [*note*: My father told me he was prevented from doing his Arthur Epic, in twelve books, by John Sterling's review in the *Quarterly* [Sept. 1842]. "I had it all in my mind, could have done it without any trouble. But then I thought that a small vessel, built on fine lines, is likely to float further down the stream of Time than a big raft."] that I can find among my father's MSS in my possession was probably written about 1833, and is a sketch in prose. I give it as it stands.'

*King Arthur*

On the latest limit of the West in the land of Lyonnesse, where, save the rocky Isles of Scilly, all is now wild sea, rose the sacred Mount of Camelot. It rose from the deeps with gardens and bowers and palaces, and at the top of the Mount was King Arthur's hall, and the holy Minster with the Cross of gold. Here dwelt the King in glory apart, while the Saxons whom he had overthrown in twelve battles ravaged the land, and ever came nearer and nearer.

The Mount was the most beautiful in the world, sometimes green and fresh in the beam of morning, sometimes all one splendour, folded in the golden mists of the West. But all underneath it was hollow, and the mountain trembled, when the seas rushed bellowing through the porphyry caves; and there ran a prophecy that the mountain and the city on some wild morning would topple into the abyss and be no more.

It was night. The King sat in his Hall. Beside him sat the sumptuous Guinevere and about him were all his lords and knights of the Table Round. There they feasted, and when the feast was over the Bards sang to the King's glory.

---

'The following memorandum was presented by my father to Sir James Knowles at Aldworth on October 1, 1869, who told him that it was between thirty and forty years old. It was probably written at the same time as the fragment which I have just quoted. However, the allegorical drift here marked out was fundamentally changed in the later scheme of the *Idylls*.

From an original MS, about 1833:

K.A. Religious Faith

King Arthur's three Guineveres.

The Lady of the Lake?

Two Guineveres. The first prim. Christianity. 2d Roman Catholicism. The first is put away and dwells apart. 2d Guinevere flies. Arthur takes to the first again but finds her changed by lapse of Time.

Modred, the sceptical understanding. He pulls Guinevere, Arthur's latest wife, from the throne.

Merlin Emrys, the enchanter. Science. Marries his daughter to Modred.

Excalibur, war.

The sea, the people.<br>The Saxons, the people. } The S. are a sea-people and it is theirs and a type of them.

The Round Table: liberal institutions.

Battle of Camlan.

2d Guinevere with the enchanted book and cup.

---

'Before 1840 it is evident that my father wavered between casting the Arthurian legends into the form of an epic or into that of a musical masque; for in one of his 1833–1840 MS books there is the following first rough draft of a scenario, into which the Lancelot and Elaine scenes were afterwards introduced.'

*First Act*

Sir Mordred and his party. Mordred inveighs against the King and the Round Table. The knights, and the quest. Mordred scoffs at the Ladies of the Lake, doubts whether they are supernatural beings, etc. Mordred's cringing interview with Guinevere. Mordred and the Lady of the Lake. Arthur lands in Albyn.

*Second Act*

Lancelot's embassy and Guinevere. The Lady of the Lake meets Arthur and endeavours to persuade him not to fight with Sir Mordred. Arthur will not be moved from his purpose. Lamentation of the Lady of the Lake. Elaine. Marriage of Arthur.

*Third Act*

Oak tomb of Merlin. The song of Nimuë. Sir Mordred comes to consult Merlin. Coming away meets Arthur. Their fierce dialogue. Arthur consults Sir L. and Sir Bedivere. Arthur weeps over Merlin and is reproved by Nimuë, who inveighs against Merlin. Arthur asks Merlin the issue of the battle. Merlin will not enlighten him. Nimuë requests Arthur to question Merlin again. Merlin tells him he shall bear rule again, but that the Ladies of the Lake can return no more. Guinevere throws away the diamonds into the river. The Court and the dead Elaine.

*Fourth Act*

Discovery by Mordred and Nimuë of Lancelot and Guinevere. Arthur and Guinevere's meeting and parting.

*Fifth Act*

The battle. Chorus of the Ladies of the Lake. The throwing away of Excalibur and departure of Arthur.

---

'After this my father began to study the epical King Arthur in earnest. He had travelled in Wales, and meditated a tour in Cornwall. He thought, read, talked about King Arthur. He made a poem on Lancelot's quest of the San Graal; "in as good verse," he said, "as I ever wrote–no, I did not write, I made it in my head, and it has altogether slipt out of memory." [*note*: Letter from my father to the Duke of Argyll, 1859.] What he called "the greatest of all poetical subjects" perpetually haunted him. But it was not till 1855 that he determined upon the final shape of the poem, and not until 1859 that he published the first instalment, *Enid, Vivien, Elaine, Guinevere*. In spite of the public applause he did not rush headlong into the other *Idylls of the King*, although he had carried a more or less perfected scheme of them in his head over thirty years. For one thing, he did not consider that the time was ripe. In addition to this, he did not find himself in the proper mood to write them, and he never could work except at what his heart impelled him to do.–Then, however, he devoted himself with all his energies and with infinite enthusiasm to that work alone.

'He also gave some other reasons for pausing in the production of the *Idylls*. "One," he wrote, "is because I could hardly light upon a finer close than that ghostlike passing away of the king" (in *Guinevere*), although the *Morte d'Arthur* was the natural close. The second was that he was not sure he could keep up to the same high level throughout the remaining *Idylls*. "I have thought about it," he writes in 1862, "and arranged all the intervening *Idylls*, but I dare not set to work for fear of a failure, and time lost." The third was, to give it in his own words, '"I doubt whether such a subject as the San Graal could be handled in these days without incurring a charge of irreverence. It would be too much like playing with sacred things." *The Holy Grail*, however, later on seemed to come suddenly, as if by a breath of inspiration; and that volume was given to the world in 1869, containing *The Coming of Arthur*, *The Holy Grail*, *Pelleas and Ettarre*, and *The Passing of Arthur*.

'In 1871 *The Last Tournament* was privately printed, and then published in the *Contemporary Review*: re-published with *Gareth and Lynette* in 1872. These with *Balin and Balan* (published in 1885) make up the "twelve books," – the number mentioned in the Introduction to the *Morte d'Arthur*.

'In 1870 an article on the *Idylls* by Dean Alford, the old college friend of Arthur Hallam and of my father, came out in the *Contemporary*: an able letter also by J. T. Knowles appeared in the *Spectator*. [*note*: See *Contemporary Review*, May 1873.] These reviews my father considered the best. But in later years he often said, "They have taken my hobby, and ridden it too hard, and have explained some things too allegorically, although there is an allegorical or perhaps rather a parabolic drift in the poem." "Of course Camelot for instance, a city of shadowy palaces, is everywhere symbolic of the gradual growth of human beliefs and institutions, and of the spiritual development of man. Yet there is no single fact or incident in the *Idylls*, however seemingly mystical, which cannot be explained as without any mystery or allegory whatever." The Bishop of Ripon (Boyd Carpenter) once asked him whether they were right who interpreted the three Queens, who accompanied King Arthur on his last voyage, as Faith, Hope and Charity. He answered: "They are right, and they are not right. They mean that and they do not. They are three of the noblest of women. They are also those three Graces, but they are much more. I hate to be tied down to say, '*This* means *that*,' because the thought within the image is much more than any one interpretation."

'As for the many meanings of the poem my father would affirm, "Poetry is like shot-silk with many glancing colours. Every reader must find his own interpretation according to his ability, and according to his sympathy with the poet." The general drift of the *Idylls* is clear enough. "The whole," he said, "is the dream of man coming into practical life and ruined by one sin. Birth is a mystery and death is a mystery, and in the midst lies the tableland of life, and its struggles and performances. It is not the history of one man or of one generation but of a whole cycle of generations." . . . My father said on his eightieth birthday: "My meaning in the *Idylls of the King* was spiritual. I took the legendary stories of the

Round Table as illustrations. I intended Arthur to represent the Ideal Soul of Man coming into contact with the warring elements of the flesh." . . .

'"The vision of an ideal Arthur as I have drawn him," my father said, "had come upon me when, little more than a boy, I first lighted upon Malory" [*note*: My father's MS]; and it dwelt with him to the end; and we may perhaps say that now the completed poem, regarded as a whole, gives his innermost being more fully, though not more truly, than *In Memoriam*. He felt himself justified in having always pictured Arthur as the Ideal man by such passages as this from Joseph of Exeter: "The old world knows not his peer, nor will the future show us his equal: he alone towers over other kings, better than the past ones and greater than those that are to be." So this from Alberic:

"Hic jacet Arturus, flos regum, gloria regni,
Quem probitas morum commendat laude perenni."

'. . . On the other hand, having this vision of Arthur, my father thought that perhaps he had not made the real humanity of the King sufficiently clear in his epilogue; so he inserted in 1891, as his last correction, "Ideal manhood closed in real man," before the lines:

Rather than that gray king, whose name, a ghost,
Streams like a cloud, man-shaped, from mountain peak,
And cleaves to cairn and cromlech still.

'. . . To sum up: if Epic unity is looked for in the *Idylls*, we find it not in the wrath of an Achilles, nor in the wanderings of an Ulysses, but in the unending war of humanity in all ages,–the world-wide war of Sense and Soul, typified in individuals, with the subtle interaction of character upon character, the central dominant figure being the pure, generous, tender, brave, human-hearted Arthur–so that the links (with here and there symbolic accessories) which bind the *Idylls* into an artistic whole, are perhaps somewhat intricate. . . .'

In her important detailed study of 'Tennyson's Serial Poem' (*Mid-Victorian Studies*, 1965, pp. 80–109), Kathleen Tillotson points out that one of T.'s difficulties was 'that his matter was new. In 1842, Arthurian story was still strange to the ordinary reader, and even felt to be unacceptable as a subject for poetry; and this was undoubtedly one reason for the first long interval of seventeen years between the serial appearances.' John Sterling's criticisms in *QR* (Sept. 1842) bring this home, and T. explicitly referred to Sterling when talking to Allingham in 1867: 'I had it all in my mind, could have done it without any trouble. The King is the complete man, the Knights are the passions' (W. Allingham, *Diary*, 1907, p. 150). T. said to Knowles: 'When I was twenty-four I meant to write a whole great poem on it, and began it in the *Morte d'Arthur*. I said I should do it in twenty years; but the Reviews stopped me . . . By King Arthur I always meant the soul, and by the Round Table the passions and capacities of a man. There is no grander subject in the world than King Arthur'

(*Nineteenth Century* xxxiii (1893) 181–2). 'By 1855 Tennyson had planned the final shape of his long poem; but the two items that he chose to write first were as distant as possible from the *Morte d'Arthur*: in order of writing they were *Nimuë* (afterwards *Vivien*), and *Enid*, from the *Mabinogion*, partly written during two months in Wales, exploring Welsh manuscripts and studying the language' (K. Tillotson).

In May 1857, there was set up *Enid and Nimuë: the True and the False* (*Mat.* ii 180). The British Museum copy, which includes corrections by T., has a note by F. T. Palgrave: 'These two Idylls it was A.T.'s original intention to publish by themselves. Six copies were struck off, but owing to a remark upon *Nimuë* which reached him, he at once recalled the copies out: giving me leave, however, to retain the present.' (An edition was printed from this copy in 1902.)

In spring 1859, he prepared the four *Idylls* for publication (*Mem.* i 436); on 8 March 1859, he wrote to the Duke of Argyll: 'I could be well content to be silent for ever: however the Poems–there are four of them (your Grace heard two) are finished' (*Lincoln*). For trial editions of *1859*, see Richard Jones, *The Growth of the Idylls of the King* (1895), and *Virginia*.

In a letter of 23 Feb. 1862, the Duke of Argyll said that the Princess Royal 'is very anxious that you should make the *Morte d'Arthur* the ending of the Idylls–adding only something to connect it with the ending of *Guinevere*' (*Lincoln*). T. replied: 'As to joining these with the *Morte d'Arthur*, there are two objections,–one that I could scarcely light upon a finer close than that ghostlike passing away of the king, and the other that the *Morte* is older in style. I have thought about it and arranged all the intervening Idylls, but I dare not set to work for fear of a failure, and time lost' (*Mem.* i 482–3). (A note to this letter quotes T.: '*The Coming* and *The Passing of Arthur* are simpler and more severe in style, as dealing with the awfulness of Birth and Death'.) But the Duke persisted: 'I wonder whether you are right about the Idylls–I don't see any incongruity between them and the *Morte*' (26 Feb., *Lincoln*). Sir Charles Tennyson (p. 403) points out that T.'s later changes of *1859* archaized the text, and brought it closer to the style of *Morte d'Arthur*. When *The Passing of Arthur*, expanding *1842*, was published in *1869* ('*1870*'), a note read: 'This last, the earliest written of the Poems, is here connected with the rest in accordance with an early project of the author's.' In Dec. 1868, T. had said of *The Holy Grail*: 'I shall write three or four more of the *Idylls*, and link them together as well as I may' (*Mem.* ii 62). It was in *1869* ('*1870*') that T. provided the collective title *The Round Table*, and gave a note on the ordering of the series. In April 1873, R. H. Hutton warned T. not to add or alter, and T. said, 'with a grim smile, "I must have two more Idylls at the least to make *Vivien* come later into the Poem, as it comes in far too soon as it stands"' (*Diary of Alfred Domett*, 1953, p. 79). In fact, the only major modification was T.'s addition of *Balin and Balan*, which he wrote in 1872–4, but did not publish till 1885, 'whether for the sake of purchasers or because he had not decided whether to make it into one or two' (K. Tillotson).

*Sources.* See John Churton Collins, *Illustrations of Tennyson* (1891). Some of the school and university editions of individual poems, by F. J. Rowe, W. T. Webb and G. C. Macaulay, were submitted to T. and H.T. for approval (*Lincoln*); T. suggested changes, and H.T. draws heavily on their notes for *Eversley*. See also A. Hamann, *An Essay on Tennyson's Idylls of the King* (1887); H. Littledale, *Essays on Tennyson's Idylls of the King* (1893); and Richard Jones, *The Growth of the Idylls of the King* (1895). T. owned both the 1816 reprints of Malory (the Wilks and the Walker editions, *Lincoln*); all quotations from Malory below are from the Walker edition, preceded by Caxton's numbering for convenience. This Walker edition was given to T. by Leigh Hunt in 1835, and was 'much used' by T. (*Mem.* i 156). It is clear that T. also knew Southey's edition (1817) and Thomas Wright's (1858). On his knowledge of Geoffrey of Monmouth, see J. M. Gray, *Notes and Queries* (Feb. 1967). See also Tom Peete Cross, 'Tennyson as a Celticist', *MP* xviii (1921) 149–56; and W. D. Paden.

On the MSS, see Sir Charles Tennyson, *Cornhill* cliii (1936) 534–57, reprinted in *Six Tennyson Essays* (1954). Also Wise, *Bibliography*, passim. On T.'s textual changes, Richard Jones, *The Growth of the Idylls of the King* (1895), is instructive. For T.'s prose drafts, see *Mem.* ii 134–41, *Eversley* v 425–32.

Of modern criticism of the *Idylls*, the most important items are F. E. L. Priestley (*University of Toronto Quarterly*, xxiii, 1949), and J. H. Buckley (*Tennyson: the Growth of a Poet*, 1960).

# Idylls of the King

## IN TWELVE BOOKS

*Flos Regum Arthurus* (JOSEPH OF EXETER)

# 463 Dedication

Published 1862. 'To the Prince Consort' (T.), who had died on 14 Dec. 1861. It was written by about Christmas 1861 (*Tennyson and His Friends*, p. 208).

These to His Memory–since he held them dear,
Perchance as finding there unconsciously
Some image of himself–I dedicate,
I dedicate, I consecrate with tears–
These Idylls.
And indeed He seems to me
Scarce other than my king's ideal knight,
'Who reverenced his conscience as his king;
Whose glory was, redressing human wrong;
Who spake no slander, no, nor listened to it;
Who loved one only and who clave to her–'
Her–over all whose realms to their last isle,
Commingled with the gloom of imminent war,
The shadow of His loss drew like eclipse,
Darkening the world. We have lost him: he is gone:
We know him now: all narrow jealousies

¶463. *1.* Prince Albert had asked T. to inscribe a copy of the *Idylls*, 17 May 1860 (*Mem.* i 455).

*4.* Cp. Catullus, *Fragmenta* 2: *tibi dedico consecroque.*

*5. Idylls*: 'Regarding the Greek derivation, I spelt my Idylls with two *l*'s mainly to divide them from the ordinary pastoral idyls usually spelt with one *l*. These idylls group themselves round one central figure' (T.). T. pronounced the word with an I as in 'idle'.

*6. king's*] *1882*; own *1862–81*. 'The first reading ... was altered because Leslie Stephen and others called King Arthur a portrait of the Prince Consort' (H.T.).

*12.* 'Owing to the *Trent* affair [1861], when two Southern Commissioners accredited to Great Britain and France by the Confederate States were taken off a British steamship, the *Trent*, by the captain of the Federal man-of-war *San Jacinto*. The Queen and the Prince Consort were said to have averted war by their modification of a dispatch' (T.).

*13. drew*] *1863*; moved *1862*.

*15* ∧ *16*. The MS had included a reference to 'The fume and babble of a petulant hour'. The Duke and Duchess of Argyll (to whom T. sent the *Dedication* in Jan. 1862; *Lincoln*) criticised this, and other lines: 'Worthy the sacred name of gentleman', and l. 25. The Duke thought it 'expedient to omit all ... allusion to *Jealousies* of the Prince ... I do not advise the insertion of the line "The sudden little petulance of an hour" ... Let it [petulance] be forgotten, if possible.'

Are silent; and we see him as he moved,
How modest, kindly, all-accomplished, wise,
With what sublime repression of himself,
And in what limits, and how tenderly;
Not swaying to this faction or to that;
Not making his high place the lawless perch
Of winged ambitions, nor a vantage-ground
For pleasure; but through all this tract of years
Wearing the white flower of a blameless life,
Before a thousand peering littlenesses,
In that fierce light which beats upon a throne,
And blackens every blot: for where is he,
Who dares foreshadow for an only son
A lovelier life, a more unstained, than his?
Or how should England dreaming of *his* sons
Hope more for these than some inheritance
Of such a life, a heart, a mind as thine,
Thou noble Father of her Kings to be,
Laborious for her people and her poor–
Voice in the rich dawn of an ampler day–
Far-sighted summoner of War and Waste
To fruitful strifes and rivalries of peace–
Sweet nature gilded by the gracious gleam
Of letters, dear to Science, dear to Art,
Dear to thy land and ours, a Prince indeed,
Beyond all titles, and a household name,
Hereafter, through all times, Albert the Good.

Break not, O woman's-heart, but still endure;
Break not, for thou art Royal, but endure,
Remembering all the beauty of that star
Which shone so close beside Thee that ye made
One light together, but has past and leaves
The Crown a lonely splendour.

May all love,
His love, unseen but felt, o'ershadow Thee,
The love of all Thy sons encompass Thee,
The love of all Thy daughters cherish Thee,
The love of all Thy people comfort Thee,
Till God's love set Thee at his side again!

*36–7.* 'The Prince Consort's work in the planning of the International Exhibitions of 1851 and 1862' (H.T.).

*40. thy land*: 'Saxe-Coburg Gotha' (T.).

*47. leaves*] *1863*; left *1862*.

*49. o'ershadow*: *OED* 2, to protect.

# 464 The Coming of Arthur

Published *1869* (‘*1870*’). T.’s wife records that on 13 Feb. 1869 T. ‘read what he had done of the birth and marriage of Arthur’; the poem was finished ‘before the end of Feb.’ (*Mem.* ii 63–4). The title in the trial edition was *The Birth of Arthur* (Wise, *Bibliography* i 197–201). Based on Malory i. ‘In this Idyll the poet lays bare the main lines of his story and of his parable’ (H.T.). T. comments:

‘How much of history we have in the story of Arthur is doubtful. Let not my readers press too hardly on details whether for history or for allegory. Some think that King Arthur may be taken to typify conscience. He is anyhow meant to be a man who spent himself in the cause of honour, duty and self-sacrifice, who felt and aspired with his nobler knights, though with a stronger and a clearer conscience than any of them, “reverencing his conscience as his king.” “In short, God has not made since Adam was, the man more perfect than Arthur,” as an old writer says. “Major praeteritis majorque futuris Regibus.” The vision of Arthur as I have drawn him came upon me when, little more than a boy, I first lighted upon Malory.

þe time cō þe wes icoren:
þa wes Arður iboren.
Sone swa he com an eorðe:
aluen hine iuengen.
heo bigolen þat child:
mid galdere swiðe stronge.
heo ȝeuē him mihte:
to beon bezst alre cnihten.
heo ȝeuen him an oðer þing:
þat he scolde beon riche king.
heo ȝiuen hī þat þridde:
þat he scolde longe libben.
heo ȝifen him þat kine-bern:
custen swiðe gode.
þat he wes mete-custi:
of alle quikemonnen.
þis þe alue him ȝef:
And al swa þat child iþæh.

Layamon’s *Brut*, Madden, vol. ii 384.

‘(The time came that was chosen, then was Arthur born. So soon as he came on earth, elves took him; they enchanted the child with magic most strong, they gave him might to be the best of all knights; they gave him another thing, that he should be a rich king; they gave him the third, that he should live long; they gave to him, the child, virtues most good, so that he was *most* generous of all men alive: This the elves gave him, and thus the child thrived.)

'The Coming of Arthur is on the night of the New Year; when he is wedded "the world is white with May"; on a summer night the vision of the Holy Grail appears; and the "Last Tournament" is in the "yellowing autumn-tide." Guinevere flees through the mists of autumn, and Arthur's death takes place at midnight in mid-winter. The form of the *Coming of Arthur* and of the *Passing* is purposely more archaic than that of the other Idylls. The blank verse throughout each of the twelve Idylls varies according to the subject.'

Leodogran, the King of Cameliard,
Had one fair daughter, and none other child;
And she was fairest of all flesh on earth,
Guinevere, and in her his one delight.
　For many a petty king ere Arthur came
Ruled in this isle, and ever waging war
Each upon other, wasted all the land;
And still from time to time the heathen host
Swarmed overseas, and harried what was left.
And so there grew great tracts of wilderness,
Wherein the beast was ever more and more,
But man was less and less, till Arthur came.
For first Aurelius lived and fought and died,
And after him King Uther fought and died,
But either failed to make the kingdom one.
And after these King Arthur for a space,
And through the puissance of his Table Round,
Drew all their petty princedoms under him,
Their king and head, and made a realm, and reigned.

　And thus the land of Cameliard was waste,
Thick with wet woods, and many a beast therein,
And none or few to scare or chase the beast;
So that wild dog, and wolf and boar and bear

¶464. *5.* 'This explains the existence of Leodogran, one of the petty princes. "Cameliard is apparently", according to Wright, "the district called Carmelide in the English metrical romance of *Merlin*, on the border of which was a town called 'Breckenho' (Brecknock)"–T. Wright's edition of the *Mort d'Arthure*' (T.).

*13.* 'Aurelius (Emrys) Ambrosius was brother of King Uther' (T.). H.T. adds: 'For the histories of Aurelius and Uther see Geoffrey of Monmouth's *Chronicle*, Bks v and vi.'

*17.* 'A table called King Arthur's is kept at Winchester. It was supposed to symbolise the world, being flat and round' (T.).

*18.* 'The several petty princedoms were under one head, the "pendragon"' (T.).

Came night and day, and rooted in the fields,
And wallowed in the gardens of the King.
And ever and anon the wolf would steal
The children and devour, but now and then,
Her own brood lost or dead, lent her fierce teat
To human sucklings; and the children, housed
In her foul den, there at their meat would growl,
And mock their foster-mother on four feet,
Till, straightened, they grew up to wolf-like men,
Worse than the wolves. And King Leodogran
Groaned for the Roman legions here again,
And Cæsar's eagle: then his brother king,
Urien, assailed him: last a heathen horde,
Reddening the sun with smoke and earth with blood,
And on the spike that split the mother's heart
Spitting the child, brake on him, till, amazed,
He knew not whither he should turn for aid.

But–for he heard of Arthur newly crowned,
Though not without an uproar made by those
Who cried, 'He is not Uther's son'–the King
Sent to him, saying, 'Arise, and help us thou!
For here between the man and beast we die.'

And Arthur yet had done no deed of arms,
But heard the call, and came: and Guinevere
Stood by the castle walls to watch him pass;
But since he neither wore on helm or shield
The golden symbol of his kinglihood,
But rode a simple knight among his knights,
And many of these in richer arms than he,
She saw him not, or marked not, if she saw,
One among many, though his face was bare.
But Arthur, looking downward as he past,
Felt the light of her eyes into his life
Smite on the sudden, yet rode on, and pitched
His tents beside the forest. Then he drave

*31.* 'Imitate the wolf by going on four feet' (T.).

*32.* 'Compare what is told of in some parts of India (*Journal of Anthropological Society of Bombay*, vol. i) and of the loup-garous and were-wolves of France and Germany' (T.).

*34.* 'Cf. *Groans of the Britons*, by Gildas' (T.).

*36. Urien*] *1873*; Rience *1869–70*. 'King of North Wales' (T.).

*50.* 'The golden dragon' (T.).

*58. Then*] *1873*; And *1869–70*.

The heathen; after, slew the beast, and felled
The forest, letting in the sun, and made
Broad pathways for the hunter and the knight
And so returned.

For while he lingered there,
A doubt that ever smouldered in the hearts
Of those great Lords and Barons of his realm
Flashed forth and into war: for most of these,
Colleaguing with a score of petty kings,
Made head against him, crying, 'Who is he
That he should rule us? who hath proven him
King Uther's son? for lo! we look at him,
And find nor face nor bearing, limbs nor voice,
Are like to those of Uther whom we knew.
This is the son of Gorloïs, not the King;
This is the son of Anton, not the King.'

And Arthur, passing thence to battle, felt
Travail, and throes and agonies of the life,
Desiring to be joined with Guinevere;
And thinking as he rode, 'Her father said
That there between the man and beast they die.
Shall I not lift her from this land of beasts
Up to my throne, and side by side with me?
What happiness to reign a lonely king,
Vext–O ye stars that shudder over me,
O earth that soundest hollow under me,
Vext with waste dreams? for saving I be joined
To her that is the fairest under heaven,
I seem as nothing in the mighty world,
And cannot will my will, nor work my work
Wholly, nor make myself in mine own realm
Victor and lord. But were I joined with her,
Then might we live together as one life,
And reigning with one will in everything
Have power on this dark land to lighten it,
And power on this dead world to make it live.'

Thereafter–as he speaks who tells the tale–
When Arthur reached a field-of-battle bright

59. *;after*] *1873*; ,and he *1869–70*. *heathen*: 'Angles, Jutes, and Saxons' (T.).

60. *letting*] *1873*; and let *1869–70*.

*66*] *1873*; *not 1869–70*.

*94–133*] *1873*; *not 1869–70*.

With pitched pavilions of his foe, the world
Was all so clear about him, that he saw
The smallest rock far on the faintest hill,
And even in high day the morning star.
So when the King had set his banner broad,
At once from either side, with trumpet-blast,
And shouts, and clarions shrilling unto blood,
The long-lanced battle let their horses run.
And now the Barons and the kings prevailed,
And now the King, as here and there that war
Went swaying; but the Powers who walk the world
Made lightnings and great thunders over him,
And dazed all eyes, till Arthur by main might,
And mightier of his hands with every blow,
And leading all his knighthood threw the kings
Carádos, Urien, Cradlemont of Wales,
Claudias, and Clariance of Northumberland,
The King Brandagoras of Latangor,
With Anguisant of Erin, Morganore,
And Lot of Orkney. Then, before a voice
As dreadful as the shout of one who sees
To one who sins, and deems himself alone
And all the world asleep, they swerved and brake
Flying, and Arthur called to stay the brands
That hacked among the flyers, 'Ho! they yield!'
So like a painted battle the war stood
Silenced, the living quiet as the dead,
And in the heart of Arthur joy was lord.
He laughed upon his warrior whom he loved
And honoured most. 'Thou dost not doubt me King,
So well thine arm hath wrought for me today.'
'Sir and my liege,' he cried, 'the fire of God
Descends upon thee in the battle-field:
I know thee for my King!' Whereat the two,
For each had warded either in the fight,
Sware on the field of death a deathless love.
And Arthur said, 'Man's word is God in man:
Let chance what will, I trust thee to the death.'

Then quickly from the foughten field he sent
Ulfius, and Brastias, and Bedivere,
His new-made knights, to King Leodogran,
Saying, 'If I in aught have served thee well,
Give me thy daughter Guinevere to wife.'

134] *1873*; And Arthur from the field of battle sent *1869–70*.

Whom when he heard, Leodogran in heart
Debating–'How should I that am a king,
However much he holp me at my need,
Give my one daughter saving to a king,
And a king's son?'–lifted his voice, and called
A hoary man, his chamberlain, to whom
He trusted all things, and of him required
His counsel: 'Knowest thou aught of Arthur's birth?'

Then spake the hoary chamberlain and said,
'Sir King, there be but two old men that know:
And each is twice as old as I; and one
Is Merlin, the wise man that ever served
King Uther through his magic art; and one
Is Merlin's master (so they call him) Bleys,
Who taught him magic; but the scholar ran
Before the master, and so far, that Bleys
Laid magic by, and sat him down, and wrote
All things and whatsoever Merlin did
In one great annal-book, where after-years
Will learn the secret of our Arthur's birth.'

To whom the King Leodogran replied,
'O friend, had I been holpen half as well
By this King Arthur as by thee today,
Then beast and man had had their share of me:
But summon here before us yet once more
Ulfius, and Brastias, and Bedivere.'

Then, when they came before him, the King said,
'I have seen the cuckoo chased by lesser fowl,
And reason in the chase: but wherefore now
Do these your lords stir up the heat of war,
Some calling Arthur born of Gorloïs,
Others of Anton? Tell me, ye yourselves,
Hold ye this Arthur for King Uther's son?'

And Ulfius and Brastias answered, 'Ay.'
Then Bedivere, the first of all his knights
Knighted by Arthur at his crowning, spake–
For bold in heart and act and word was he,
Whenever slander breathed against the King–

'Sir, there be many rumours on this head:
For there be those who hate him in their hearts,
Call him baseborn, and since his ways are sweet,
And theirs are bestial, hold him less than man:
And there be those who deem him more than man,

And dream he dropt from heaven: but my belief
In all this matter–so ye care to learn–
Sir, for ye know that in King Uther's time
The prince and warrior Gorloïs, he that held
Tintagil castle by the Cornish sea,
Was wedded with a winsome wife, Ygerne:
And daughters had she borne him,–one whereof,
Lot's wife, the Queen of Orkney, Bellicent,
Hath ever like a loyal sister cleaved
To Arthur,–but a son she had not borne.
And Uther cast upon her eyes of love:
But she, a stainless wife to Gorloïs,
So loathed the bright dishonour of his love,
That Gorloïs and King Uther went to war:
And overthrown was Gorloïs and slain.
Then Uther in his wrath and heat besieged
Ygerne within Tintagil, where her men,
Seeing the mighty swarm about their walls,
Left her and fled, and Uther entered in,
And there was none to call to but himself.
So, compassed by the power of the King,
Enforced she was to wed him in her tears,
And with a shameful swiftness: afterward,
Not many moons, King Uther died himself,
Moaning and wailing for an heir to rule
After him, lest the realm should go to wrack.
And that same night, the night of the new year,
By reason of the bitterness and grief
That vext his mother, all before his time
Was Arthur born, and all as soon as born
Delivered at a secret postern-gate
To Merlin, to be holden far apart
Until his hour should come; because the lords
Of that fierce day were as the lords of this,
Wild beasts, and surely would have torn the child
Piecemeal among them, had they known; for each
But sought to rule for his own self and hand,
And many hated Uther for the sake
Of Gorloïs. Wherefore Merlin took the child,
And gave him to Sir Anton, an old knight
And ancient friend of Uther; and his wife
Nursed the young prince, and reared him with her own;

*185–222.* See Malory i 1–5, which T. modifies considerably.

*189.* 'The kingdom of Orkney and Lothian composed the North and East of Scotland' (T.).

And no man knew. And ever since the lords
Have foughten like wild beasts among themselves,
So that the realm has gone to wrack: but now,
This year, when Merlin (for his hour had come)
Brought Arthur forth, and set him in the hall,
Proclaiming, "Here is Uther's heir, your king,"
A hundred voices cried, "Away with him!
No king of ours! a son of Gorloïs he,
Or else the child of Anton, and no king,
Or else baseborn." Yet Merlin through his craft,
And while the people clamoured for a king,
Had Arthur crowned; but after, the great lords
Banded, and so brake out in open war.'

Then while the King debated with himself
If Arthur were the child of shamefulness,
Or born the son of Gorloïs, after death,
Or Uther's son, and born before his time,
Or whether there were truth in anything
Said by these three, there came to Cameliard,
With Gawain and young Modred, her two sons,
Lot's wife, the Queen of Orkney, Bellicent;
Whom as he could, not as he would, the King
Made feast for, saying, as they sat at meat,

'A doubtful throne is ice on summer seas.
Ye come from Arthur's court. Victor his men
Report him! Yea, but ye–think ye this king–
So many those that hate him, and so strong,
So few his knights, however brave they be–
Hath body enow to hold his foemen down?'

'O King,' she cried, 'and I will tell thee: few,
Few, but all brave, all of one mind with him;
For I was near him when the savage yells
Of Uther's peerage died, and Arthur sat
Crowned on the daïs, and his warriors cried,
"Be thou the king, and we will work thy will
Who love thee." Then the King in low deep tones,
And simple words of great authority,
Bound them by so strait vows to his own self,

*234*. T. quotes Malory i 7: 'Wherefore all the commons cried at once, "We will have Arthur unto our king".'

*248–9*] *1873*; Ye come from Arthur's court: think ye this king–*1869–70*.

*250*] *1873*; *not 1869–70*.

*252. hold*] *1873*; beat *1869–70*. *body enow*: 'strength' (T.).

That when they rose, knighted from kneeling, some
Were pale as at the passing of a ghost,
Some flushed, and others dazed, as one who wakes
Half-blinded at the coming of a light.

'But when he spake and cheered his Table Round
With large, divine, and comfortable words,
Beyond my tongue to tell thee – I beheld
From eye to eye through all their Order flash
A momentary likeness of the King:
And ere it left their faces, through the cross
And those around it and the Crucified,
Down from the casement over Arthur, smote
Flame-colour, vert and azure, in three rays,
One falling upon each of three fair queens,
Who stood in silence near his throne, the friends
Of Arthur, gazing on him, tall, with bright
Sweet faces, who will help him at his need.

'And there I saw mage Merlin, whose vast wit
And hundred winters are but as the hands
Of loyal vassals toiling for their liege.

'And near him stood the Lady of the Lake,
Who knows a subtler magic than his own –
Clothed in white samite, mystic, wonderful.
She gave the King his huge cross-hilted sword,
Whereby to drive the heathen out: a mist
Of incense curled about her, and her face
Wellnigh was hidden in the minster gloom;
But there was heard among the holy hymns
A voice as of the waters, for she dwells
Down in a deep; calm, whatsoever storms
May shake the world, and when the surface rolls,
Hath power to walk the waters like our Lord.

'There likewise I beheld Excalibur
Before him at his crowning borne, the sword
That rose from out the bosom of the lake,
And Arthur rowed across and took it – rich

*282.* 'The Lady of the Lake in the old legends is the Church' (T.).
*290.* T. compares *Revelation* xiv 2: 'I heard a voice from heaven, as the voice of many waters.'
*294. Excalibur*: 'Said to mean "cut-steel". In the Romance of *Merlin* the sword bore the following inscription: "Ich am y-hote Escalabore / Unto a king a fair tresore", and it is added: "On Inglis is this writing / Kerve steel and yren and al thing"' (T.).

With jewels, elfin Urim, on the hilt,
Bewildering heart and eye–the blade so bright
That men are blinded by it–on one side,
Graven in the oldest tongue of all this world,
"Take me," but turn the blade and ye shall see,
And written in the speech ye speak yourself,
"Cast me away!" And sad was Arthur's face
Taking it, but old Merlin counselled him,
"Take thou and strike! the time to cast away
Is yet far-off." So this great brand the king
Took, and by this will beat his foemen down.'

Thereat Leodogran rejoiced, but thought
To sift his doubtings to the last, and asked,
Fixing full eyes of question on her face,
'The swallow and the swift are near akin,
But thou art closer to this noble prince,
Being his own dear sister;' and she said,
'Daughter of Gorloïs and Ygerne am I;'
'And therefore Arthur's sister?' asked the King.
She answered, 'These be secret things,' and signed
To those two sons to pass, and let them be.
And Gawain went, and breaking into song
Sprang out, and followed by his flying hair
Ran like a colt, and leapt at all he saw:
But Modred laid his ear beside the doors,
And there half-heard; the same that afterward
Struck for the throne, and striking found his doom.

And then the Queen made answer, 'What know I?
For dark my mother was in eyes and hair,
And dark in hair and eyes am I; and dark
Was Gorloïs, yea and dark was Uther too,
Wellnigh to blackness; but this King is fair
Beyond the race of Britons and of men.
Moreover, always in my mind I hear
A cry from out the dawning of my life,
A mother weeping, and I hear her say,
"O that ye had some brother, pretty one,
To guard thee on the rough ways of the world."'

*298. Urim*: *Exodus* xxviii 30: 'And thou shalt put in the breastplate of judgment the Urim and the Thummim' (oraculous gems).

*302. ye*] *1873*; you *1869–70*.

*306–7. Ecclesiastes* iii 6: 'A time to get, and a time to lose; a time to keep, and a time to cast away.'

'Ay,' said the King, 'and hear ye such a cry?
But when did Arthur chance upon thee first?'

'O King!' she cried, 'and I will tell thee true:
He found me first when yet a little maid:
Beaten I had been for a little fault
Whereof I was not guilty; and out I ran
And flung myself down on a bank of heath,
And hated this fair world and all therein,
And wept, and wished that I were dead; and he–
I know not whether of himself he came,
Or brought by Merlin, who, they say, can walk
Unseen at pleasure–he was at my side,
And spake sweet words, and comforted my heart,
And dried my tears, being a child with me.
And many a time he came, and evermore
As I grew greater grew with me; and sad
At times he seemed, and sad with him was I,
Stern too at times, and then I loved him not,
But sweet again, and then I loved him well.
And now of late I see him less and less,
But those first days had golden hours for me,
For then I surely thought he would be king.

'But let me tell thee now another tale:
For Bleys, our Merlin's master, as they say,
Died but of late, and sent his cry to me,
To hear him speak before he left his life.
Shrunk like a fairy changeling lay the mage;
And when I entered told me that himself
And Merlin ever served about the King,
Uther, before he died; and on the night
When Uther in Tintagil past away
Moaning and wailing for an heir, the two
Left the still King, and passing forth to breathe,
Then from the castle gateway by the chasm
Descending through the dismal night–a night
In which the bounds of heaven and earth were lost–
Beheld, so high upon the dreary deeps
It seemed in heaven, a ship, the shape thereof
A dragon winged, and all from stem to stern
Bright with a shining people on the decks,
And gone as soon as seen. And then the two
Dropt to the cove, and watched the great sea fall,
Wave after wave, each mightier than the last,

Till last, a ninth one, gathering half the deep
And full of voices, slowly rose and plunged
Roaring, and all the wave was in a flame:
And down the wave and in the flame was borne
A naked babe, and rode to Merlin's feet,
Who stoopt and caught the babe, and cried "The King!
Here is an heir for Uther!" And the fringe
Of that great breaker, sweeping up the strand,
Lashed at the wizard as he spake the word,
And all at once all round him rose in fire,
So that the child and he were clothed in fire.
And presently thereafter followed calm,
Free sky and stars: "And this same child," he said,
"Is he who reigns; nor could I part in peace
Till this were told." And saying this the seer
Went through the strait and dreadful pass of death,
Not ever to be questioned any more
Save on the further side; but when I met
Merlin, and asked him if these things were truth–
The shining dragon and the naked child
Descending in the glory of the seas–
He laughed as is his wont, and answered me
In riddling triplets of old time, and said:

'"Rain, rain, and sun! a rainbow in the sky!
A young man will be wiser by and by;
An old man's wit may wander ere he die.
Rain, rain, and sun! a rainbow on the lea!
And truth is this to me, and that to thee;
And truth or clothed or naked let it be.
Rain, sun, and rain! and the free blossom blows:
Sun, rain, and sun! and where is he who knows?
From the great deep to the great deep he goes."

'So Merlin riddling angered me; but thou
Fear not to give this King thine only child,
Guinevere: so great bards of him will sing
Hereafter; and dark sayings from of old

*379*. 'Every ninth wave is supposed by the Welsh bards to be larger than those that go before' (H.T.).

*402*. 'The truth appears in different guise to divers persons. The one fact is that man comes from the great deep and returns to it. This is an echo of the triads of the Welsh bards' (T.). O. L. Jiriczek (*Anglia, Beiblatt*, 1926, p. 120) quotes a triad's reference to 'the Great Deep or Lowest Point of Existence', and suggests that T. was indebted to the notes to Southey's *Madoc*. H.T. compares *Gareth and Lynette* 280–2.

Ranging and ringing through the minds of men,
And echoed by old folk beside their fires
For comfort after their wage-work is done,
Speak of the King; and Merlin in our time
Hath spoken also, not in jest, and sworn
Though men may wound him that he will not die,
But pass, again to come; and then or now
Utterly smite the heathen underfoot,
Till these and all men hail him for their king.'

She spake and King Leodogran rejoiced,
But musing 'Shall I answer yea or nay?'
Doubted, and drowsed, nodded and slept, and saw,
Dreaming, a slope of land that ever grew,
Field after field, up to a height, the peak
Haze-hidden, and thereon a phantom king,
Now looming, and now lost; and on the slope
The sword rose, the hind fell, the herd was driven,
Fire glimpsed; and all the land from roof and rick,
In drifts of smoke before a rolling wind,
Streamed to the peak, and mingled with the haze
And made it thicker; while the phantom king
Sent out at times a voice; and here or there
Stood one who pointed toward the voice, the rest
Slew on and burnt, crying, 'No king of ours,
No son of Uther, and no king of ours;'
Till with a wink his dream was changed, the haze
Descended, and the solid earth became
As nothing, but the King stood out in heaven,
Crowned. And Leodogran awoke, and sent
Ulfius, and Brastias and Bedivere,
Back to the court of Arthur answering yea.

Then Arthur charged his warrior whom he loved
And honoured most, Sir Lancelot, to ride forth
And bring the Queen;–and watched him from the gates:
And Lancelot past away among the flowers,
(For then was latter April) and returned
Among the flowers, in May, with Guinevere.

*420.* Malory xxi 7: 'Some men yet say, in many parts of England, that king Arthur is not dead; but, by the will of our Lord Jesu Christ, into another place: and men say, that he will come again, and he shall win the holy cross.'

*442. but*] *1873*; and *1869–70*.

*451.* Cp. the May scene in Malory xx 1.

To whom arrived, by Dubric the high saint,
Chief of the church in Britain, and before
The stateliest of her altar-shrines, the King
That morn was married, while in stainless white,
The fair beginners of a nobler time,
And glorying in their vows and him, his knights
Stood round him, and rejoicing in his joy.
Far shone the fields of May through open door,
The sacred altar blossomed white with May,
The Sun of May descended on their King,
They gazed on all earth's beauty in their Queen,
Rolled incense, and there past along the hymns
A voice as of the waters, while the two
Sware at the shrine of Christ a deathless love:
And Arthur said, 'Behold, thy doom is mine.
Let chance what will, I love thee to the death!'
To whom the Queen replied with drooping eyes,
'King and my lord, I love thee to the death!'
And holy Dubric spread his hands and spake,
'Reign ye, and live and love, and make the world
Other, and may thy Queen be one with thee,
And all this Order of thy Table Round
Fulfil the boundless purpose of their king!'

So Dubric said; but when they left the shrine
Great Lords from Rome before the portal stood,
In scornful stillness gazing as they past;
Then while they paced a city all on fire
With sun and cloth of gold, the trumpets blew,
And Arthur's knighthood sang before the King:–

'Blow trumpet, for the world is white with May;
Blow trumpet, the long night hath rolled away!
Blow through the living world–"Let the King reign."

452. *Dubric*: 'Archbishop of Caerleon. His crozier is said to be at St David's' (T.).
454. 'According to Malory, the Church of St Stephen at Camelot' (T.).
*459–69*] *1873*; *not 1869–70*.
*475–502*] *1873*; *not 1869–70*. 'My father wrote to my mother that this Viking song, a pendant to Merlin's song, "rings like a grand music". This and Leodogran's dream give the drift and grip of the poem, which describes the aspirations and ambitions of Arthur and his knights, doomed to downfall–the hints of coming doom being heard throughout' (H.T.). T. wrote the song in Nov. 1872 (*Mem.* ii 117).
*476–7*. 'Because Rome had been the Lord of Britain' (T.).

'Shall Rome or Heathen rule in Arthur's realm?
Flash brand and lance, fall battleaxe upon helm,
Fall battleaxe, and flash brand! Let the King reign.

'Strike for the King and live! his knights have heard
That God hath told the King a secret word.
Fall battleaxe, and flash brand! Let the King reign.

'Blow trumpet! he will lift us from the dust.
Blow trumpet! live the strength and die the lust!
Clang battleaxe, and clash brand! Let the King reign.

'Strike for the King and die! and if thou diest,
The King is King, and ever wills the highest.
Clang battleaxe, and clash brand! Let the King reign.

'Blow, for our Sun is mighty in his May!
Blow, for our Sun is mightier day by day!
Clang battleaxe, and clash brand! Let the King reign.

'The King will follow Christ, and we the King
In whom high God hath breathed a secret thing.
Fall battleaxe, and flash brand! Let the King reign.'

So sang the knighthood, moving to their hall.
There at the banquet those great Lords from Rome,
The slowly-fading mistress of the world,
Strode in, and claimed their tribute as of yore.
But Arthur spake, 'Behold, for these have sworn
To wage my wars, and worship me their King;
The old order changeth, yielding place to new;
And we that fight for our fair father Christ,
Seeing that ye be grown too weak and old
To drive the heathen from your Roman wall,
No tribute will we pay:' so those great lords
Drew back in wrath, and Arthur strove with Rome.

And Arthur and his knighthood for a space
Were all one will, and through that strength the King
Drew in the petty princedoms under him,
Fought, and in twelve great battles overcame
The heathen hordes, and made a realm and reigned.

*499.* *1 Corinthians* xi 1: 'Be ye followers of me, even as I also am of Christ.'

*503*] *1873*; Then at the marriage feast came in from Rome, *1869–70*.

*505.* *Strode in, and*] *1873*; Great lords, who *1869–70*.

*506.* Based on Malory v 2.

*507.* *wage*] *1873*; fight *1869–70*.

*511.* 'A line of forts built by Agricola betwixt the Firth of Forth and the Clyde, forty miles long' (T.).

# 465 Gareth and Lynette

Published *1872*. In Feb. 1861, T. 'read of Sir Gareth in the *Morte d'Arthur*' (*Mem.* i 471). T.'s wife records, 7 Oct. 1869: 'He gave me his beginning of Beaumains . . . (the golden time of Arthur's Court) to read (written, as was said jokingly, "to describe a pattern youth for his boys").' T. set it aside for a while. On 5 April 1872, he wrote to Knowles (*Mem.* ii 113*n*): '*Gareth* is not finished yet. I left him off once altogether, finding him more difficult to deal with than anything excepting perhaps *Aylmer's Field*. If I were at liberty, which I think I am not, to print the names of the speakers 'Gareth' 'Linette' over the short snip-snap of their talk, and so avoid the perpetual 'said' and its varieties, the work would be much easier. I have made out the plan however, and perhaps some day it will be completed; and it will be then to consider whether or no it should go into the *Contemporary* or elsewhere.' T. sent it to press, 9 July 1872. Based on Malory vii; T.'s lines 1–430 have no counterpart in Malory. For the MSS and trial edition, see Wise, *Bibliography* i 216–21; E. F. Shannon, *Bibliographical Society of America* xli (1947) 321–40; and J. E. Hartman, *Harvard Library Bulletin* xiii (1959) 239–41. There is also a MS in the Bodleian Library.

The last tall son of Lot and Bellicent,
And tallest, Gareth, in a showerful spring
Stared at the spate. A slender-shafted Pine
Lost footing, fell, and so was whirled away.
'How he went down,' said Gareth, 'as a false knight
Or evil king before my lance if lance
Were mine to use–O senseless cataract,
Bearing all down in thy precipitancy–
And yet thou art but swollen with cold snows
And mine is living blood; thou dost His will,
The Maker's, and not knowest, and I that know,
Have strength and wit, in my good mother's hall
Linger with vacillating obedience,
Prisoned, and kept and coaxed and whistled to–
Since the good mother holds me still a child!
Good mother is bad mother unto me!
A worse were better; yet no worse would I.
Heaven yield her for it, but in me put force
To weary her ears with one continuous prayer,
Until she let me fly discaged to sweep

¶465. *3. the spate*: 'the river in flood' (T.).
*18.* H.T. compares *Antony and Cleopatra* IV ii 33: 'And the gods yield you for't.'

In ever-highering eagle-circles up
To the great Sun of Glory, and thence swoop
Down upon all things base, and dash them dead,
A knight of Arthur, working out his will,
To cleanse the world. Why, Gawain, when he came
With Modred hither in the summertime,
Asked me to tilt with him, the proven knight.
Modred for want of worthier was the judge.
Then I so shook him in the saddle, he said,
"Thou hast half prevailed against me," said so–he–
Though Modred biting his thin lips was mute,
For he is alway sullen: what care I?'

And Gareth went, and hovering round her chair
Asked, 'Mother, though ye count me still the child,
Sweet mother, do ye love the child?' She laughed,
'Thou art but a wild-goose to question it.'
'Then, mother, an ye love the child,' he said,
'Being a goose and rather tame than wild,
Hear the child's story.' 'Yea, my well-beloved,
An 'twere but of the goose and golden eggs.'

And Gareth answered her with kindling eyes,
'Nay, nay, good mother, but this egg of mine
Was finer gold than any goose can lay;
For this an Eagle, a royal Eagle, laid
Almost beyond eye-reach, on such a palm
As glitters gilded in thy Book of Hours.
And there was ever haunting round the palm
A lusty youth, but poor, who often saw
The splendour sparkling from aloft, and thought
"An I could climb and lay my hand upon it,
Then were I wealthier than a leash of kings."
But ever when he reached a hand to climb,
One, that had loved him from his childhood, caught
And stayed him, "Climb not lest thou break thy neck,
I charge thee by my love," and so the boy,
Sweet mother, neither clomb, nor brake his neck,

*21.* 'He invents a verb in his youthful exuberance' (T.).
*25.* 'Gawain and Modred, brothers of Gareth' (T.).
*51.* 'Three kings. Cf. a leash of dogs' (T.).

But brake his very heart in pining for it,
And past away.'
To whom the mother said,
'True love, sweet son, had risked himself and climbed,
And handed down the golden treasure to him.'

And Gareth answered her with kindling eyes,
'Gold? said I gold?–ay then, why he, or she,
Or whosoe'er it was, or half the world
Had ventured–*had* the thing I spake of been
Mere gold–but this was all of that true steel,
Whereof they forged the brand Excalibur,
And lightnings played about it in the storm,
And all the little fowl were flurried at it,
And there were cries and clashings in the nest,
That sent him from his senses: let me go.'

Then Bellicent bemoaned herself and said,
'Hast thou no pity upon my loneliness?
Lo, where thy father Lot beside the hearth
Lies like a log, and all but smouldered out!
For ever since when traitor to the King
He fought against him in the Barons' war,
And Arthur gave him back his territory,
His age hath slowly droopt, and now lies there
A yet-warm corpse, and yet unburiable,
No more; nor sees, nor hears, nor speaks, nor knows.
And both thy brethren are in Arthur's hall,
Albeit neither loved with that full love
I feel for thee, nor worthy such a love:
Stay therefore thou; red berries charm the bird,
And thee, mine innocent, the jousts, the wars,
Who never knewest finger-ache, nor pang
Of wrenched or broken limb–an often chance
In those brain-stunning shocks, and tourney-falls,
Frights to my heart; but stay: follow the deer
By these tall firs and our fast-falling burns;
So make thy manhood mightier day by day;
Sweet is the chase: and I will seek thee out
Some comfortable bride and fair, to grace
Thy climbing life, and cherish my prone year,
Till falling into Lot's forgetfulness
I know not thee, myself, nor anything.
Stay, my best son! ye are yet more boy than man.'

Then Gareth, 'An ye hold me yet for child,
Hear yet once more the story of the child.
For, mother, there was once a King, like ours.
The prince his heir, when tall and marriageable,
Asked for a bride; and thereupon the King
Set two before him. One was fair, strong, armed–
But to be won by force–and many men
Desired her; one, good lack, no man desired.
And these were the conditions of the King:
That save he won the first by force, he needs
Must wed that other, whom no man desired,
A red-faced bride who knew herself so vile,
That evermore she longed to hide herself,
Nor fronted man or woman, eye to eye–
Yea–some she cleaved to, but they died of her.
And one–they called her Fame; and one,–
O Mother,
How can ye keep me tethered to you–Shame.
Man am I grown, a man's work must I do.
Follow the deer? follow the Christ, the King,
Live pure, speak true, right wrong, follow the King–
Else, wherefore born?'

To whom the mother said,
'Sweet son, for there be many who deem him not,
Or will not deem him, wholly proven King–
Albeit in mine own heart I knew him King,
When I was frequent with him in my youth,
And heard him Kingly speak, and doubted him
No more than he, himself; but felt him mine,
Of closest kin to me: yet–wilt thou leave
Thine easeful biding here, and risk thine all,
Life, limbs, for one that is not proven King?
Stay, till the cloud that settles round his birth
Hath lifted but a little. Stay, sweet son.'

And Gareth answered quickly, 'Not an hour,
So that ye yield me–I will walk through fire,
Mother, to gain it–your full leave to go.
Not proven, who swept the dust of ruined Rome
From off the threshold of the realm, and crushed
The Idolaters, and made the people free?
Who should be King save him who makes us free?'

So when the Queen, who long had sought in vain
To break him from the intent to which he grew,
Found her son's will unwaveringly one,

She answered craftily, 'Will ye walk through fire?
Who walks through fire will hardly heed the smoke.
Ay, go then, an ye must: only one proof,
Before thou ask the King to make thee knight,
Of thine obedience and thy love to me,
Thy mother, – I demand.'

And Gareth cried,
'A hard one, or a hundred, so I go.
Nay – quick! the proof to prove me to the quick!'

But slowly spake the mother looking at him,
'Prince, thou shalt go disguised to Arthur's hall,
And hire thyself to serve for meats and drinks
Among the scullions and the kitchen-knaves,
And those that hand the dish across the bar.
Nor shalt thou tell thy name to anyone.
And thou shalt serve a twelvemonth and a day.'

For so the Queen believed that when her son
Beheld his only way to glory lead
Low down through villain kitchen-vassalage,
Her own true Gareth was too princely-proud
To pass thereby; so should he rest with her,
Closed in her castle from the sound of arms.

Silent awhile was Gareth, then replied,
'The thrall in person may be free in soul,
And I shall see the jousts. Thy son am I,
And since thou art my mother, must obey.
I therefore yield me freely to thy will;
For hence will I, disguised, and hire myself
To serve with scullions and with kitchen-knaves;
Nor tell my name to any – no, not the King.'

Gareth awhile lingered. The mother's eye
Full of the wistful fear that he would go,
And turning toward him wheresoe'er he turned,
Perplext his outward purpose, till an hour,
When wakened by the wind which with full voice
Swept bellowing through the darkness on to dawn,
He rose, and out of slumber calling two
That still had tended on him from his birth,
Before the wakeful mother heard him, went.

The three were clad like tillers of the soil.
Southward they set their faces. The birds made

172. *outward purpose*: 'purpose to go' (T.).

Melody on branch, and melody in mid air.
The damp hill-slopes were quickened into green,
And the live green had kindled into flowers,
For it was past the time of Easterday.

So, when their feet were planted on the plain
That broadened toward the base of Camelot,
Far off they saw the silver-misty morn
Rolling her smoke about the Royal mount,
That rose between the forest and the field.
At times the summit of the high city flashed;
At times the spires and turrets half-way down
Pricked through the mist; at times the great gate shone
Only, that opened on the field below:
Anon, the whole fair city had disappeared.

Then those who went with Gareth were amazed,
One crying, 'Let us go no further, lord.
Here is a city of Enchanters, built
By fairy Kings.' The second echoed him,
'Lord, we have heard from our wise man at home
To Northward, that this King is not the King,
But only changeling out of Fairyland,
Who drave the heathen hence by sorcery
And Merlin's glamour.' Then the first again,
'Lord, there is no such city anywhere,
But all a vision.'

Gareth answered them
With laughter, swearing he had glamour enow
In his own blood, his princedom, youth and hopes,
To plunge old Merlin in the Arabian sea;
So pushed them all unwilling toward the gate.
And there was no gate like it under heaven.
For barefoot on the keystone, which was lined
And rippled like an ever-fleeting wave,
The Lady of the Lake stood: all her dress
Wept from her sides as water flowing away;
But like the cross her great and goodly arms
Stretched under all the cornice and upheld:
And drops of water fell from either hand;

*182.* Cp. *In Memoriam* xxxix 11 and *n* (p. 897).

*198. man*] *1875*; men *1872–4*.

*212.* 'The Lady of the Lake in the old romances of Lancelot instructs him in the mysteries of the Christian faith' (T.).

And down from one a sword was hung, from one
A censer, either worn with wind and storm;
And o'er her breast floated the sacred fish;
And in the space to left of her, and right,
Were Arthur's wars in weird devices done,
New things and old co-twisted, as if Time
Were nothing, so inveterately, that men
Were giddy gazing there; and over all
High on the top were those three Queens, the
friends
Of Arthur, who should help him at his need.

Then those with Gareth for so long a space
Stared at the figures, that at last it seemed
The dragon-boughts and elvish emblemings
Began to move, seethe, twine and curl: they called
To Gareth, 'Lord, the gateway is alive.'

And Gareth likewise on them fixt his eyes
So long, that even to him they seemed to move.
Out of the city a blast of music pealed.
Back from the gate started the three, to whom
From out thereunder came an ancient man,
Long-bearded, saying, 'Who be ye, my sons?'

Then Gareth, 'We be tillers of the soil,
Who leaving share in furrow come to see
The glories of our King: but these, my men,
(Your city moved so weirdly in the mist)
Doubt if the King be King at all, or come
From Fairyland; and whether this be built
By magic, and by fairy Kings and Queens;
Or whether there be any city at all,
Or all a vision: and this music now
Hath scared them both, but tell thou these the
truth.'

Then that old Seer made answer playing on him
And saying, 'Son, I have seen the good ship sail

*219. fish*: ancient symbol of Christianity.

*229. dragon-boughts*: 'folds of the dragons' tails' (T.). H.T. compares *Faerie Queene* I xi stanza 11: 'His huge long tayle wound up in hundred foldes, / Does overspred his long bras-scaly backe, / Whose wreathed boughts when ever he unfoldes, / Bespotted as with shields of red and blacke . . .'.

*236*. 'Merlin' (T.).

*249*. 'Refraction by mirage' (T.).

Keel upward, and mast downward, in the heavens,
And solid turrets topsy-turvy in air:
And here is truth; but an it please thee not,
Take thou the truth as thou hast told it me.
For truly as thou sayest, a Fairy King
And Fairy Queens have built the city, son;
They came from out a sacred mountain-cleft
Toward the sunrise, each with harp in hand,
And built it to the music of their harps.
And, as thou sayest, it is enchanted, son,
For there is nothing in it as it seems
Saving the King; though some there be that hold
The King a shadow, and the city real:
Yet take thou heed of him, for, so thou pass
Beneath this archway, then wilt thou become
A thrall to his enchantments, for the King
Will bind thee by such vows, as is a shame
A man should not be bound by, yet the which
No man can keep; but, so thou dread to swear,
Pass not beneath this gateway, but abide
Without, among the cattle of the field.
For an ye heard a music, like enow
They are building still, seeing the city is built
To music, therefore never built at all,
And therefore built for ever.'

Gareth spake
Angered, 'Old Master, reverence thine own beard
That looks as white as utter truth, and seems
Wellnigh as long as thou art statured tall!
Why mockest thou the stranger that hath been
To thee fair-spoken?'

But the Seer replied,
'Know ye not then the Riddling of the Bards?
"Confusion, and illusion, and relation,
Elusion, and occasion, and evasion"?
I mock thee not but as thou mockest me,
And all that see thee, for thou art not who
Thou seemest, but I know thee who thou art.

*253.* 'Ironical' (T.).
*257.* 'The religions and the arts that came from the East' (T.).
*269–70.* 'Be a mere beast' (T.).
*272–3.* 'By the Muses' (T.).
*285.* *Luke* iv 34: 'I know thee who thou art; the Holy One of God.'

And now thou goest up to mock the King,
Who cannot brook the shadow of any lie.'

Unmockingly the mocker ending here
Turned to the right, and past along the plain;
Whom Gareth looking after said, 'My men,
Our one white lie sits like a little ghost
Here on the threshold of our enterprise.
Let love be blamed for it, not she, nor I:
Well, we will make amends.'

With all good cheer
He spake and laughed, then entered with his twain
Camelot, a city of shadowy palaces
And stately, rich in emblem and the work
Of ancient kings who did their days in stone;
Which Merlin's hand, the Mage at Arthur's court,
Knowing all arts, had touched, and everywhere
At Arthur's ordinance, tipt with lessening peak
And pinnacle, and had made it spire to heaven.
And ever and anon a knight would pass
Outward, or inward to the hall: his arms
Clashed; and the sound was good to Gareth's ear.
And out of bower and casement shyly glanced
Eyes of pure women, wholesome stars of love;
And all about a healthful people stept
As in the presence of a gracious king.

Then into hall Gareth ascending heard
A voice, the voice of Arthur, and beheld
Far over heads in that long-vaulted hall
The splendour of the presence of the King
Throned, and delivering doom–and looked no more–
But felt his young heart hammering in his ears,
And thought, 'For this half-shadow of a lie
The truthful King will doom me when I speak.'
Yet pressing on, though all in fear to find
Sir Gawain or Sir Modred, saw nor one
Nor other, but in all the listening eyes
Of those tall knights, that ranged about the throne,
Clear honour shining like the dewy star
Of dawn, and faith in their great King, with pure
Affection, and the light of victory,
And glory gained, and evermore to gain.

302. 'Symbolizing the divine' (T.).

Then came a widow crying to the King,
'A boon, Sir King! Thy father, Uther, reft
From my dead lord a field with violence:
For howsoe'er at first he proffered gold,
Yet, for the field was pleasant in our eyes,
We yielded not; and then he reft us of it
Perforce, and left us neither gold nor field.'

Said Arthur, 'Whether would ye? gold or field?'
To whom the woman weeping, 'Nay, my lord,
The field was pleasant in my husband's eye.'

And Arthur, 'Have thy pleasant field again,
And thrice the gold for Uther's use thereof,
According to the years. No boon is here,
But justice, so thy say be proven true.
Accursed, who from the wrongs his father did
Would shape himself a right!'

And while she past,
Came yet another widow crying to him,
'A boon, Sir King! Thine enemy, King, am I.
With thine own hand thou slewest my dear lord,
A knight of Uther in the Barons' war,
When Lot and many another rose and fought
Against thee, saying thou wert basely born.
I held with these, and loathe to ask thee aught.
Yet lo! my husband's brother had my son
Thralled in his castle, and hath starved him dead;
And standeth seized of that inheritance
Which thou that slewest the sire hast left the son.
So though I scarce can ask it thee for hate,
Grant me some knight to do the battle for me,
Kill the foul thief, and wreak me for my son.'

Then strode a good knight forward, crying to him,
'A boon, Sir King! I am her kinsman, I.
Give me to right her wrong, and slay the man.'

Then came Sir Kay, the seneschal, and cried,
'A boon, Sir King! even that thou grant her none,
This railer, that hath mocked thee in full hall–
None; or the wholesome boon of gyve and gag.'

359. 'In the *Roman de la Rose* Sir Kay is given as a pattern of rough discourtesy' (T.).

But Arthur, 'We sit King, to help the wronged
Through all our realm. The woman loves her lord.
Peace to thee, woman, with thy loves and hates!
The kings of old had doomed thee to the flames,
Aurelius Emrys would have scourged thee dead,
And Uther slit thy tongue: but get thee hence—
Lest that rough humour of the kings of old
Return upon me! Thou that art her kin,
Go likewise; lay him low and slay him not,
But bring him here, that I may judge the right,
According to the justice of the King:
Then, be he guilty, by that deathless King
Who lived and died for men, the man shall die.'

Then came in hall the messenger of Mark,
A name of evil savour in the land,
The Cornish king. In either hand he bore
What dazzled all, and shone far-off as shines
A field of charlock in the sudden sun
Between two showers, a cloth of palest gold,
Which down he laid before the throne, and knelt,
Delivering, that his lord, the vassal king,
Was even upon his way to Camelot;
For having heard that Arthur of his grace
Had made his goodly cousin, Tristram, knight,
And, for himself was of the greater state,
Being a king, he trusted his liege-lord
Would yield him this large honour all the more;
So prayed him well to accept this cloth of gold,
In token of true heart and feälty.

Then Arthur cried to rend the cloth, to rend
In pieces, and so cast it on the hearth.
An oak-tree smouldered there. 'The goodly knight!
What! shall the shield of Mark stand among these?'
For, midway down the side of that long hall
A stately pile, – whereof along the front,
Some blazoned, some but carven, and some blank,
There ran a treble range of stony shields, –
Rose, and high-arching overbrowed the hearth.
And under every shield a knight was named:
For this was Arthur's custom in his hall;
When some good knight had done one noble deed,
His arms were carven only; but if twain
His arms were blazoned also; but if none,

*367.* Uther's brother, who preceded him as king.

The shield was blank and bare without a sign
Saving the name beneath; and Gareth saw
The shield of Gawain blazoned rich and bright,
And Modred's blank as death; and Arthur cried
To rend the cloth and cast it on the hearth.

'More like are we to reave him of his crown
Than make him knight because men call him king.
The kings we found, ye know we stayed their hands
From war among themselves, but left them kings;
Of whom were any bounteous, merciful,
Truth-speaking, brave, good livers, them we enrolled
Among us, and they sit within our hall.
But Mark hath tarnished the great name of king,
As Mark would sully the low state of churl:
And, seeing he hath sent us cloth of gold,
Return, and meet, and hold him from our eyes,
Lest we should lap him up in cloth of lead,
Silenced for ever–craven–a man of plots,
Craft, poisonous counsels, wayside ambushings–
No fault of thine: let Kay the seneschal
Look to thy wants, and send thee satisfied–
Accursed, who strikes nor lets the hand be seen!'

And many another suppliant crying came
With noise of ravage wrought by beast and man,
And evermore a knight would ride away.

Last, Gareth leaning both hands heavily
Down on the shoulders of the twain, his men,
Approached between them toward the King, and asked,
'A boon, Sir King (his voice was all ashamed),
For see ye not how weak and hungerworn
I seem–leaning on these? grant me to serve

*422.* Cp. *The Passionate Pilgrim, As it fell upon a day* 23–4: 'King Pandion he is dead; / All thy friends are lapped in lead.'

*431–6.* Malory vii 1: 'Right so came into the hall two men, well beseen and richly, and upon their shoulders there leaned the goodliest young man, and the fairest that ever they saw, and he was large, long and broad in the shoulders, and well visaged, and the fairest and the largest hands that ever man saw; but he fared as though he might not go, nor bear himself, but if he leaned upon their shoulders.'

*436–40.* Malory vii 1: '"Now, sir," said he, "this is my petition for this feast, that ye will give me meat and drink sufficiently for these twelvemonths; and at that day I will ask mine other two gifts."–"My fair son,"

For meat and drink among thy kitchen-knaves
A twelvemonth and a day, nor seek my name.
Hereafter I will fight.'
To him the King,
'A goodly youth and worth a goodlier boon!
But so thou wilt no goodlier, then must Kay,
The master of the meats and drinks, be thine.'

He rose and past; then Kay, a man of mien
Wan-sallow as the plant that feels itself
Root-bitten by white lichen,
'Lo ye now!
This fellow hath broken from some Abbey, where,
God wot, he had not beef and brewis enow,
However that might chance! but an he work,
Like any pigeon will I cram his crop,
And sleeker shall he shine than any hog.'

Then Lancelot standing near, 'Sir Seneschal,
Sleuth-hound thou knowest, and gray, and all the hounds;
A horse thou knowest, a man thou dost not know:
Broad brows and fair, a fluent hair and fine,
High nose, a nostril large and fine, and hands
Large, fair and fine!–Some young lad's mystery–

said king Arthur, "ask better, I counsel thee, for this is but a simple asking; for my heart giveth me to thee greatly that thou art come of men of worship . . . Ye shall have meat and drink enough; I never offended none, neither my friend nor foe. But what is thy name? I would fain know."–"I cannot tell you," said he. "That have I marvel of thee," said the king, "that thou knowest not thine own name, and thou art one of the goodliest young men that ever I saw."'

*441. so*] *1873*; an *1872*.

*441–2.* Malory vii 1: 'Then the noble king Arthur betook him unto the steward, sir Kaye, and charged him that he should give him of all manner of meats and drinks of the best; and, also, that he have all manner of finding, as though he were a lord's son.'

*446–50.* Malory vii 1–2: '"Pain of my life he was brought up and fostered in some abbey; and howsomever it was they failed of meat and drink, and so hither he is come for sustenance . . . And into the kitchen I shall bring him, and there he shall have fat brewis every day, that he shall be as fat by twelvemonth's end as a pork hog."' *brewis*: 'broth' (T.).

*451–9.* Malory vii 2 includes: 'And especially sir Launcelot, for he bid sir Kaye leave his mocking, "for I dare lay my head he shall prove a man of great worship".'

But, or from sheepcot or king's hall, the boy
Is noble-natured. Treat him with all grace,
Lest he should come to shame thy judging of him.'

Then Kay, 'What murmurest thou of mystery?
Think ye this fellow will poison the King's dish?
Nay, for he spake too fool-like: mystery!
Tut, an the lad were noble, he had asked
For horse and armour: fair and fine, forsooth!
Sir Fine-face, Sir Fair-hands? but see thou to it
That thine own fineness, Lancelot, some fine day
Undo thee not–and leave my man to me.'

So Gareth all for glory underwent
The sooty yoke of kitchen-vassalage;
Ate with young lads his portion by the door,
And couched at night with grimy kitchen-knaves.
And Lancelot ever spake him pleasantly,
But Kay the seneschal, who loved him not,
Would hustle and harry him, and labour him
Beyond his comrade of the hearth, and set
To turn the broach, draw water, or hew wood,
Or grosser tasks; and Gareth bowed himself
With all obedience to the King, and wrought
All kind of service with a noble ease
That graced the lowliest act in doing it.
And when the thralls had talk among themselves,
And one would praise the love that linkt the King
And Lancelot–how the King had saved his life
In battle twice, and Lancelot once the King's–
For Lancelot was the first in Tournament,
But Arthur mightiest on the battle-field–
Gareth was glad. Or if some other told,
How once the wandering forester at dawn,
Far over the blue tarns and hazy seas,

*463–5.* Malory vii 1: '"That shall little need," said sir Kaye, "to do such cost upon him, for I dare well undertake that he is a villain born, and never will make man; for and he had been come of a gentleman, he would have asked of you horse and harness, but such as he is he hath asked. And sithence he hath no name, I shall give him a name, that shall be Beaumains; that is to say fair hands."'

*470–2.* Malory vii 2: 'And so sir Kaye had got him a place, and sat down to eat. So Beaumains went to the hall door, and sat him down among boys and lads, and there he eat sadly.'

*476. broach*: 'spit' (T.).

On Caer-Eryri's highest found the King,
A naked babe, of whom the Prophet spake,
'He passes to the Isle Avilion,
He passes and is healed and cannot die'–
Gareth was glad. But if their talk were foul,
Then would he whistle rapid as any lark,
Or carol some old roundelay, and so loud
That first they mocked, but, after, reverenced him.
Or Gareth telling some prodigious tale
Of knights, who sliced a red life-bubbling way
Through twenty folds of twisted dragon, held
All in a gap-mouthed circle his good mates
Lying or sitting round him, idle hands,
Charmed; till Sir Kay, the seneschal, would come
Blustering upon them, like a sudden wind
Among dead leaves, and drive them all apart.
Or when the thralls had sport among themselves,
So there were any trial of mastery,
He, by two yards in casting bar or stone
Was counted best; and if there chanced a joust,
So that Sir Kay nodded him leave to go,
Would hurry thither, and when he saw the knights
Clash like the coming and retiring wave,
And the spear spring, and good horse reel, the boy
Was half beyond himself for ecstasy.

So for a month he wrought among the thralls;
But in the weeks that followed, the good Queen,
Repentant of the word she made him swear,
And saddening in her childless castle, sent,
Between the in-crescent and de-crescent moon,
Arms for her son, and loosed him from his vow.

This, Gareth hearing from a squire of Lot
With whom he used to play at tourney once,
When both were children, and in lonely haunts
Would scratch a ragged oval on the sand,
And each at either dash from either end–
Shame never made girl redder than Gareth joy.

*490*. 'Snowdon' (T.).

*506–14*. Malory vii 2: 'But ever when he knew of any jousting of knights, that would he see and he might . . . And whereas were any masteries done, there would he be, and there might none cast the bar or stone to him by two yards.'

*515–72*. Added to Malory.

He laughed; he sprang. 'Out of the smoke, at once
I leap from Satan's foot to Peter's knee–
These news be mine, none other's–nay, the King's–
Descend into the city:' whereon he sought
The King alone, and found, and told him all.

'I have staggered thy strong Gawain in a tilt
For pastime; yea, he said it: joust can I.
Make me thy knight–in secret! let my name
Be hidden, and give me the first quest, I spring
Like flame from ashes.'

Here the King's calm eye
Fell on, and checked, and made him flush, and bow
Lowly, to kiss his hand, who answered him,
'Son, the good mother let me know thee here,
And sent her wish that I would yield thee thine.
Make thee my knight? my knights are sworn to vows
Of utter hardihood, utter gentleness,
And, loving, utter faithfulness in love,
And uttermost obedience to the King.'

Then Gareth, lightly springing from his knees,
'My King, for hardihood I can promise thee.
For uttermost obedience make demand
Of whom ye gave me to, the Seneschal,
No mellow master of the meats and drinks!
And as for love, God wot, I love not yet,
But love I shall, God willing.'

And the King–
'Make thee my knight in secret? yea, but he,
Our noblest brother, and our truest man,
And one with me in all, he needs must know.'

'Let Lancelot know, my King, let Lancelot know,
Thy noblest and thy truest!'

And the King–
'But wherefore would ye men should wonder at you?
Nay, rather for the sake of me, their King,
And the deed's sake my knighthood do the deed,
Than to be noised of.'

Merrily Gareth asked,
'Have I not earned my cake in baking of it?
Let be my name until I make my name!

My deeds will speak: it is but for a day.'
So with a kindly hand on Gareth's arm
Smiled the great King, and half-unwillingly
Loving his lusty youthhood yielded to him.
Then, after summoning Lancelot privily,
'I have given him the first quest: he is not proven.
Look therefore when he calls for this in hall,
Thou get to horse and follow him far away.
Cover the lions on thy shield, and see
Far as thou mayest, he be nor ta'en nor slain.'

Then that same day there past into the hall
A damsel of high lineage, and a brow
May-blossom, and a cheek of apple-blossom,
Hawk-eyes; and lightly was her slender nose
Tip-tilted like the petal of a flower;
She into hall past with her page and cried,

'O King, for thou hast driven the foe without,
See to the foe within! bridge, ford, beset
By bandits, everyone that owns a tower
The Lord for half a league. Why sit ye there?
Rest would I not, Sir King, an I were king,
Till even the lonest hold were all as free
From cursèd bloodshed, as thine altar-cloth
From that best blood it is a sin to spill.'

'Comfort thyself,' said Arthur, 'I nor mine
Rest: so my knighthood keep the vows they swore,
The wastest moorland of our realm shall be

*573–96.* Malory vii 2: 'Right so there came in a damsel and saluted the king, and prayed him for succour. "For whom?" said the king: "what is the adventure?"–"Sir," said she, "I have a lady of great worship and renown, and she is besieged with a tyrant, so that she may not go out of her castle; and, because that here in your court are called the noblest knights of the world, I come unto you and pray you for succour."–"What call ye your lady? where dwelleth she? and what is his name that hath besieged her?"–"Sir king," said she, "as for my lady's name, that shall not be known for me as at this time; but I let you wit she is a lady of great worship, and of great lands: and, as for the tyrant that besiegeth her, and destroyeth her land, he is called the red knight of the red lands."–"I know him not," said the king . . . "there be knights here that would do their power to rescue your lady, but because ye will not tell her name, nor where she dwelleth; therefore, none of my knights that be here now shall go with you by my will."–"Then must I speak [seek] further," said the damsel.'

Safe, damsel, as the centre of this hall.
What is thy name? thy need?'

'My name?' she said–
'Lynette my name; noble; my need, a knight
To combat for my sister, Lyonors,
A lady of high lineage, of great lands,
And comely, yea, and comelier than myself.
She lives in Castle Perilous: a river
Runs in three loops about her living-place;
And o'er it are three passings, and three knights
Defend the passings, brethren, and a fourth
And of that four the mightiest, holds her stayed
In her own castle, and so besieges her
To break her will, and make her wed with him:
And but delays his purport till thou send
To do the battle with him, thy chief man
Sir Lancelot whom he trusts to overthrow,
Then wed, with glory: but she will not wed
Save whom she loveth, or a holy life.
Now therefore have I come for Lancelot.'

Then Arthur mindful of Sir Gareth asked,
'Damsel, ye know this Order lives to crush
All wrongers of the Realm. But say, these four,
Who be they? What the fashion of the men?'

'They be of foolish fashion, O Sir King,
The fashion of that old knight-errantry
Who ride abroad, and do but what they will;
Courteous or bestial from the moment, such
As have nor law nor king; and three of these
Proud in their fantasy call themselves the Day,
Morning-Star, and Noon-Sun, and Evening-Star,
Being strong fools; and never a whit more wise
The fourth, who alway rideth armed in black,
A huge man-beast of boundless savagery.
He names himself the Night and oftener Death,
And wears a helmet mounted with a skull,
And bears a skeleton figured on his arms,
To show that who may slay or scape the three,
Slain by himself, shall enter endless night.
And all these four be fools, but mighty men,
And therefore am I come for Lancelot.'

624. Cp. Maleger, *Faerie Queene* II xi st. 22.

Hereat Sir Gareth called from where he rose,
A head with kindling eyes above the throng,
'A boon, Sir King–this quest!' then–for he marked
Kay near him groaning like a wounded bull–
'Yea, King, thou knowest thy kitchen-knave am I,
And mighty through thy meats and drinks am I,
And I can topple over a hundred such.
Thy promise, King,' and Arthur glancing at him,
Brought down a momentary brow. 'Rough, sudden,
And pardonable, worthy to be knight–
Go therefore,' and all hearers were amazed.

But on the damsel's forehead shame, pride, wrath
Slew the May-white: she lifted either arm,
'Fie on thee, King! I asked for thy chief knight,
And thou hast given me but a kitchen-knave.'
Then ere a man in hall could stay her, turned,
Fled down the lane of access to the King,
Took horse, descended the slope street, and past
The weird white gate, and paused without, beside
The field of tourney, murmuring 'kitchen-knave.'

Now two great entries opened from the hall,
At one end one, that gave upon a range
Of level pavement where the King would pace
At sunrise, gazing over plain and wood;
And down from this a lordly stairway sloped
Till lost in blowing trees and tops of towers;
And out by this main doorway past the King.
But one was counter to the hearth, and rose
High that the highest-crested helm could ride
Therethrough nor graze: and by this entry fled
The damsel in her wrath, and on to this

*630–49*. Malory vii 3: 'Then with these words came before the king Beaumains, while the damsel was there, and thus he said: "Sir king, God thank you, I have been these twelvemonths in your kitchen, and have had my full sustenance; and now I will ask my two gifts that be behind."–"Ask upon my peril," said the king. "Sir, these shall be my two gifts: first, that ye will grant me to have this adventure of the damsel, for it belongeth to me."–"Thou shalt have it," said the king; "I grant it thee."–"Then, sir, this is now the other gift: that ye shall bid sir Launcelot du Lake to make me a knight, for of him I will be made knight, or else of none. And when I am past, I pray you let him ride after me, and make me knight when I require him."–"All this shall be done," said the king.–"Fie on thee," said the damsel; "shall I have none but one that is your kitchen page." Then was she wrath, and took her horse and departed.'

Sir Gareth strode, and saw without the door
King Arthur's gift, the worth of half a town,
A warhorse of the best, and near it stood
The two that out of north had followed him:
This bare a maiden shield, a casque; that held
The horse, the spear; whereat Sir Gareth loosed
A cloak that dropt from collar-bone to heel,
A cloth of roughest web, and cast it down,
And from it like a fuel-smothered fire,
That lookt half-dead, brake bright, and flashed as those
Dull-coated things, that making slide apart
Their dusk wing-cases, all beneath there burns
A jewelled harness, ere they pass and fly.
So Gareth ere he parted flashed in arms.
Then as he donned the helm, and took the shield
And mounted horse and graspt a spear, of grain
Storm-strengthened on a windy site, and tipt
With trenchant steel, around him slowly prest
The people, while from out of kitchen came
The thralls in throng, and seeing who had worked
Lustier than any, and whom they could but love,
Mounted in arms, threw up their caps and cried,
'God bless the King, and all his fellowship!'
And on through lanes of shouting Gareth rode
Down the slope street, and past without the gate.

So Gareth past with joy; but as the cur
Pluckt from the cur he fights with, ere his cause
Be cooled by fighting, follows, being named,
His owner, but remembers all, and growls

*665–85.* Malory vii 3–4: 'And with that there came one to Beaumains, and told him that his horse and armour was come for him, and there was a dwarf come with all things that him needeth, in the richest manner; thereat, all the court had much marvel from whence came all that jeer [gear]. So when he was armed, there was none but few so goodly a man as he was. And right so he came into the hall and took his leave of king Arthur, and of sir Gawaine, and of sir Launcelot, and prayed him that he would hie after him; and so departed and rode after the damsel. But there went many after to behold how well he was horsed and trapped in cloth of gold, but he had neither shield nor spear.'

*671–2.* 'Certain insects which have brilliant bodies underneath dull wing-cases' (T.). H.T. compares *The Two Voices* 8–15.

*675. as*] *1873*; while *1872*.

*679. while*] *1873*; and *1872*.

Remembering, so Sir Kay beside the door
Muttered in scorn of Gareth whom he used
To harry and hustle.
'Bound upon a quest
With horse and arms–the King hath past his time–
My scullion knave! Thralls to your work again,
For an your fire be low ye kindle mine!
Will there be dawn in West and eve in East?
Begone!–my knave!–belike and like enow
Some old head-blow not heeded in his youth
So shook his wits they wander in his prime–
Crazed! How the villain lifted up his voice,
Nor shamed to bawl himself a kitchen-knave.
Tut: he was tame and meek enow with me,
Till peacocked up with Lancelot's noticing.
Well—I will after my loud knave, and learn
Whether he know me for his master yet.
Out of the smoke he came, and so my lance
Hold, by God's grace, he shall into the mire–
Thence, if the King awaken from his craze,
Into the smoke again.'
But Lancelot said,
'Kay, wherefore wilt thou go against the King,
For that did never he whereon ye rail,
But ever meekly served the King in thee?
Abide: take counsel; for this lad is great
And lusty, and knowing both of lance and sword.'
'Tut, tell not me,' said Kay, 'ye are overfine
To mar stout knaves with foolish courtesies:'
Then mounted, on through silent faces rode
Down the slope city, and out beyond the gate.

But by the field of tourney lingering yet
Muttered the damsel, 'Wherefore did the King
Scorn me? for, were Sir Lancelot lackt, at least
He might have yielded to me one of those
Who tilt for lady's love and glory here,
Rather than–O sweet heaven! O fie upon him–
His kitchen-knave.'

*690–718.* Malory vii 4: 'Then sir Kaye said openly in the hall, "I will ride after my boy of the kitchen, for to wit whether he will know me for his better." Sir Launcelot and sir Gawaine said, "Yet abide at home." So sir Kaye made him ready, and took his horse and his spear, and rode after him.'

*710. wilt thou*] *1873*; will ye *1872*. Likewise l. 813.

To whom Sir Gareth drew
(And there were none but few goodlier than he)
Shining in arms, 'Damsel, the quest is mine.
Lead, and I follow.' She thereat, as one
That smells a foul-fleshed agaric in the holt,
And deems it carrion of some woodland thing,
Or shrew, or weasel, nipt her slender nose
With petulant thumb and finger, shrilling, 'Hence!
Avoid, thou smellest all of kitchen-grease.
And look who comes behind,' for there was Kay.
'Knowest thou not me? thy master? I am Kay.
We lack thee by the hearth.'
And Gareth to him,
'Master no more! too well I know thee, ay–
The most ungentle knight in Arthur's hall.'
'Have at thee then,' said Kay: they shocked, and Kay
Fell shoulder-slipt, and Gareth cried again,
'Lead, and I follow,' and fast away she fled.

But after sod and shingle ceased to fly
Behind her, and the heart of her good horse
Was nigh to burst with violence of the beat,
Perforce she stayed, and overtaken spoke.

'What dost thou, scullion, in my fellowship?
Deem'st thou that I accept thee aught the more

*729.* 'An evil-smelling fungus of the wood common at Aldworth' (T.).

*733.* Malory vii 5: 'What dost thou here? thou stinkest all of the kitchen, thy clothes be all bawdy of the grease and tallow.'

*735–40.* Malory vii 4: 'And right as Beaumains overtook the damsel, right so came sir Kaye and said, "What, sir Beaumains, know ye not me?" Then he turned his horse, and knew that it was sir Kaye, which had done him all the despite that ye have heard afore. "Ye?" said sir Beaumains, "I know you for an ungentle knight of the court, and therefore beware of me." Therewith sir Kaye put his spear in the rest, and ran upon him with his sword in his hand; and so he put away the spear with his sword, and with a foin thrust him through the side, that sir Kaye fell down as though he had been dead; and he alighted down and took sir Kaye's shield and his spear, and started upon his own horse, and rode his way.'

*746–52.* Malory vii 5: '"Weenest thou," said she, "that I allow thee for yonder knight that thou hast slain? nay, truly, for thou slewest him unhappily and cowardly; therefore, return again bawdy kitchen page. I know thee well; for sir Kaye named thee Beaumains: what art thou but a lusk and turner of broaches, and a washer of dishes?"'

Or love thee better, that by some device
Full cowardly, or by mere unhappiness,
Thou hast overthrown and slain thy master–thou!–
Dish-washer and broach-turner, loon!–to me
Thou smellest all of kitchen as before.'

'Damsel,' Sir Gareth answered gently, 'say
Whate'er ye will, but whatsoe'er ye say,
I leave not till I finish this fair quest,
Or die therefore.'

'Ay, wilt thou finish it?
Sweet lord, how like a noble knight he talks!
The listening rogue hath caught the manner of it.
But, knave, anon thou shalt be met with, knave,
And then by such a one that thou for all
The kitchen brewis that was ever supt
Shalt not once dare to look him in the face.'

'I shall assay,' said Gareth with a smile
That maddened her, and away she flashed again
Down the long avenues of a boundless wood,
And Gareth following was again beknaved.

'Sir Kitchen-knave, I have missed the only way
Where Arthur's men are set along the wood;
The wood is nigh as full of thieves as leaves:
If both be slain, I am rid of thee; but yet,
Sir Scullion, canst thou use that spit of thine?
Fight, an thou canst: I have missed the only way.'

So till the dusk that followed evensong
Rode on the two, reviler and reviled;
Then after one long slope was mounted, saw,
Bowl-shaped, through tops of many thousand pines
A gloomy-gladed hollow slowly sink
To westward—in the deeps whereof a mere,
Round as the red eye of an Eagle-owl,
Under the half-dead sunset glared; and shouts

*753–6.* Malory vii 5: '"Damsel," said sir Beaumains, "say to me what ye list, I will not go from you whatsoever ye say; for I have undertaken of king Arthur for to achieve your adventure, and I shall finish it to the end, or I shall die therefore."'

*756–62.* Malory vii 5: 'Fie on thee, kitchen knave, wilt thou finish mine adventure? thou shalt anon be met withal, that thou wouldest not, for all the broth that ever thou suppest, once look him in the face.'

*763.* Malory vii 5: '"I shall assay," said Beaumains.'

Ascended, and there brake a servingman
Flying from out of the black wood, and crying,
'They have bound my lord to cast him in the mere.'
Then Gareth, 'Bound am I to right the wronged,
But straitlier bound am I to bide with thee.'
And when the damsel spake contemptuously,
'Lead, and I follow,' Gareth cried again,
'Follow, I lead!' so down among the pines
He plunged; and there, blackshadowed nigh the mere,
And mid-thigh-deep in bulrushes and reed,
Saw six tall men haling a seventh along,
A stone about his neck to drown him in it.
Three with good blows he quieted, but three
Fled through the pines; and Gareth loosed the stone
From off his neck, then in the mere beside
Tumbled it; oilily bubbled up the mere.
Last, Gareth loosed his bonds and on free feet
Set him, a stalwart Baron, Arthur's friend.

'Well that ye came, or else these caitiff rogues
Had wreaked themselves on me; good cause is theirs
To hate me, for my wont hath ever been
To catch my thief, and then like vermin here
Drown him, and with a stone about his neck;
And under this wan water many of them
Lie rotting, but at night let go the stone,
And rise, and flickering in a grimly light
Dance on the mere. Good now, ye have saved a life
Worth somewhat as the cleanser of this wood.
And fain would I reward thee worshipfully.
What guerdon will ye?'

*781–3.* Malory vii 5: 'So, as they thus rode in the wood, there came a knight flying all that he might. "Whether [Whither] wilt thou", said Beaumains. "O Lord!" said he, "help me; for hereby in a sludge [slade] are six thieves, which have taken my lord and bound him, and I am afraid lest they will slay him."' T.'s ll. 789–96 were presumably suggested by 'sludge'.

*791–6.* Malory vii 5: 'And so they rode together, till they came there as the knight was bound, and then he rode unto the thieves, and struck one at the first stroke to death, and then another; and, at the third stroke, he slew the third thief: and then the other three fled, and he rode after and overtook them; and then those three thieves turned again, and hard assailed sir Beaumains; but, at the last, he slew them, and then returned and unbound the knight.'

*809–23.* Malory vii 5: '"Sir," said sir Beaumains, "I will no reward have:

Gareth sharply spake,
'None! for the deed's sake have I done the deed,
In uttermost obedience to the King.
But wilt thou yield this damsel harbourage?'

Whereat the Baron saying, 'I well believe
You be of Arthur's Table,' a light laugh
Broke from Lynette, 'Ay, truly of a truth,
And in a sort, being Arthur's kitchen-knave!–
But deem not I accept thee aught the more,
Scullion, for running sharply with thy spit
Down on a rout of craven foresters.
A thresher with his flail had scattered them.
Nay–for thou smellest of the kitchen still.
But an this lord will yield us harbourage,
Well.'

So she spake. A league beyond the wood,
All in a full-fair manor and a rich,
His towers where that day a feast had been
Held in high hall, and many a viand left,
And many a costly cate, received the three.
And there they placed a peacock in his pride
Before the damsel, and the Baron set
Gareth beside her, but at once she rose.

'Meseems, that here is much discourtesy,
Setting this knave, Lord Baron, at my side.
Hear me–this morn I stood in Arthur's hall,
And prayed the King would grant me Lancelot
To fight the brotherhood of Day and Night–

I was this day made knight of the noble sir Launcelot; and, therefore, I will have no reward, but God reward me: and, also, I must follow this damsel." And when he came nigher, she bid him ride from her, "for thou smellest all of the kitchen. Weenest thou that I have joy of thee? for all this deed that thou hast done is but mishappened thee: but thou shalt see a sight that shall make thee to turn again, and that lightly."'

*815. You*] *1873*; Ye *1872*. Likewise ll. 996, 1142, 1143, 1145, 1227, 1266, 1296.

*824–46.* Malory vii 5: 'Then the same knight, which was rescued of the thieves, rode after the damsel, and prayed her to lodge with him all that night; and, because it was near night, the damsel rode with him to his castle, and there they had great cheer. And, at supper, the knight set sir Beaumains before the damsel. "Fie, fie," said she, "sir knight, ye are uncourteous for to set a kitchen page before me: him beseemeth better to stick a swine, than to sit before a damsel of high parentage."'

The last a monster unsubduable
Of any save of him for whom I called –
Suddenly bawls this frontless kitchen-knave,
"The quest is mine; thy kitchen-knave am I,
And mighty through thy meats and drinks am I."
Then Arthur all at once gone mad replies,
"Go therefore," and so gives the quest to him –
Him – here – a villain fitter to stick swine
Than ride abroad redressing women's wrong,
Or sit beside a noble gentlewoman.'

Then half-ashamed and part-amazed, the lord
Now looked at one and now at other, left
The damsel by the peacock in his pride,
And, seating Gareth at another board,
Sat down beside him, ate and then began.

'Friend, whether thou be kitchen-knave, or not,
Or whether it be the maiden's fantasy,
And whether she be mad, or else the King,
Or both or neither, or thyself be mad,
I ask not: but thou strikest a strong stroke,
For strong thou art and goodly therewithal,
And saver of my life; and therefore now,
For here be mighty men to joust with, weigh
Whether thou wilt not with thy damsel back
To crave again Sir Lancelot of the King.
Thy pardon; I but speak for thine avail,
The saver of my life.'
And Gareth said,
'Full pardon, but I follow up the quest,
Despite of Day and Night and Death and Hell.'

So when, next morn, the lord whose life he saved
Had, some brief space, conveyed them on their way

*839. frontless*: 'shameless' (T.).
*847–51.* Malory vii 5: 'Then the knight was ashamed of her words, and took him up and sat before him at a sideboard, and set himself before him: and so all that night they had good and merry rest.'
*849.* 'Brought in on the trencher with his tail-feathers left' (T.). H.T. quotes Edward Stanley's *History of Birds*: when it was served, 'all the guests, male and female, took a solemn vow; the knights vowing bravery, and the ladies engaging to be loving and faithful.'
*852. thou*] *1873*; ye *1872*.
*862.* Malory vii 6: 'I say it for thine avail.'

And left them with God-speed, Sir Gareth spake,
'Lead, and I follow.' Haughtily she replied.
'I fly no more: I allow thee for an hour.
Lion and stoat have isled together, knave,
In time of flood. Nay, furthermore, methinks
Some ruth is mine for thee. Back wilt thou, fool?
For hard by here is one will overthrow
And slay thee: then will I to court again,
And shame the King for only yielding me
My champion from the ashes of his hearth.'

To whom Sir Gareth answered courteously,
'Say thou thy say, and I will do my deed.
Allow me for mine hour, and thou wilt find
My fortunes all as fair as hers who lay
Among the ashes and wedded the King's son.'

Then to the shore of one of those long loops
Wherethrough the serpent river coiled, they came.
Rough-thicketed were the banks and steep; the stream
Full, narrow; this a bridge of single arc
Took at a leap; and on the further side
Arose a silk pavilion, gay with gold
In streaks and rays, and all Lent-lily in hue,
Save that the dome was purple, and above,
Crimson, a slender banneret fluttering.
And therebefore the lawless warrior paced
Unarmed, and calling, 'Damsel, is this he,
The champion thou hast brought from Arthur's hall?
For whom we let thee pass.' 'Nay, nay,' she said,
'Sir Morning-Star. The King in utter scorn

*881–2.* 'Cinderella's' (T.).

*883.* 'The three loops of the river typify the three ages of life; and the guardians at the crossing the temptations of these ages' (T., *1913*).

*886–7.* Cp. *The Coach of Death* 147–8: 'It takes the ocean at a leap / And in its leap is fixed.'

*889. Lent-lily*: 'daffodil' (T.).

*893–900.* Malory vii 7: 'With that the black knight came to the damsel and said, "Fair damsel, have ye brought this knight from king Arthur's court to be your champion?"–"Nay, fair knight," said she, "this is but a kitchen knave, that hath been fed in king Arthur's kitchen for alms."'

*894. thou hast*] *1873*; ye have *1872*.

*896.* In Malory, there is a succession of knights, among them the Black Knight, the Green Knight, and the Red Knight.

Of thee and thy much folly hath sent thee here
His kitchen-knave: and look thou to thyself:
See that he fall not on thee suddenly,
And slay thee unarmed: he is not knight but knave.'

Then at his call, 'O daughters of the Dawn,
And servants of the Morning-Star, approach,
Arm me,' from out the silken curtain-folds
Bare-footed and bare-headed three fair girls
In gilt and rosy raiment came: their feet
In dewy grasses glistened; and the hair
All over glanced with dewdrop or with gem
Like sparkles in the stone Avanturine.
These armed him in blue arms, and gave a shield
Blue also, and thereon the morning star.
And Gareth silent gazed upon the knight,
Who stood a moment, ere his horse was brought,
Glorying; and in the stream beneath him, shone
Immingled with Heaven's azure waveringly,
The gay pavilion and the naked feet,
His arms, the rosy raiment, and the star.

Then she that watched him, 'Wherefore stare ye so?
Thou shakest in thy fear: there yet is time:
Flee down the valley before he get to horse.
Who will cry shame? Thou art not knight but knave.'

Said Gareth, 'Damsel, whether knave or knight,
Far liefer had I fight a score of times
Than hear thee so missay me and revile.
Fair words were best for him who fights for thee;
But truly foul are better, for they send
That strength of anger through mine arms, I know
That I shall overthrow him.'

*904.* Malory vii 8: 'And there he blew three deadly notes, and there came three damsels that lightly armed him.'

*908. Avanturine*: 'sometimes called the Panther-stone–a kind of gray-green or brown quartz with sparkles in it' (T.). H.T. quotes the first reading: 'Like stars within the stone Avanturine'.

*918–20.* Malory vii 7: 'When the damsel saw the black knight she bade sir Beaumains flee down the valley; for his horse was not saddled. "I thank you," said sir Beaumains; "for always ye will have me a coward."'

*921–4.* Malory vii 11: '"Damsel," said sir Beaumains, "ye are to blame so to rebuke me; for I had rather to do five battles than be so rebuked: let him come, and then let him do his worst ... All the missaying that ye missayed furthered me in my battles."'

And he that bore
The star, when mounted, cried from o'er the bridge,
'A kitchen-knave, and sent in scorn of me!
Such fight not I, but answer scorn with scorn.
For this were shame to do him further wrong
Than set him on his feet, and take his horse
And arms, and so return him to the King.
Come, therefore, leave thy lady lightly, knave.
Avoid: for it beseemeth not a knave
To ride with such a lady.'

'Dog, thou liest.
I spring from loftier lineage than thine own.'
He spake; and all at fiery speed the two
Shocked on the central bridge, and either spear
Bent but not brake, and either knight at once,
Hurled as a stone from out of a catapult
Beyond his horse's crupper and the bridge,
Fell, as if dead; but quickly rose and drew,
And Gareth lashed so fiercely with his brand
He drave his enemy backward down the bridge,
The damsel crying, 'Well-stricken, kitchen-knave!'
Till Gareth's shield was cloven; but one stroke
Laid him that clove it grovelling on the ground.

Then cried the fallen, 'Take not my life: I yield.'
And Gareth, 'So this damsel ask it of me
Good–I accord it easily as a grace.'
She reddening, 'Insolent scullion: I of thee?

*928. when*] *1886*; being *1872–84*.
*929–36.* Malory vii 7: '"Wherefore cometh he in such array?" said the knight: "it is a great shame that he beareth your company . . . I shall put him down upon his feet, and his horse and his armour he shall leave with me; for it were shame for me to do him any more harm . . . For it beseemeth not a kitchen knave to ride with such a lady."'
*936–48.* Malory vii 7: '"Thou liest," said sir Beaumains: "I am a gentleman born, and of more high lineage than thou art, and that I will prove upon thy body." Then in great wrath they departed with their horses, and came together as it had been thunder: and the black knight's spear broke; and sir Beaumains thrust him through both his sides, and therewith his spear brake, and the truncheon stuck still in his side; but, nevertheless, the black knight drew his sword, and smote many eager strokes and of great might, and hurt sir Beaumains full sore. But at the last the black knight, within an hour and a half, fell down from his horse in a swoon, and there died forthwith.'
*949–59.* Based on Malory vii 8.

I bound to thee for any favour asked!'
'Then shall he die.' And Gareth there unlaced
His helmet as to slay him, but she shrieked,
'Be not so hardy, scullion, as to slay
One nobler than thyself.' 'Damsel, thy charge
Is an abounding pleasure to me. Knight,
Thy life is thine at her command. Arise
And quickly pass to Arthur's hall, and say
His kitchen-knave hath sent thee. See thou crave
His pardon for thy breaking of his laws.
Myself, when I return, will plead for thee.
Thy shield is mine–farewell; and, damsel, thou,
Lead, and I follow.'
And fast away she fled.
Then when he came upon her, spake, 'Methought,
Knave, when I watched thee striking on the bridge
The savour of thy kitchen came upon me
A little faintlier: but the wind hath changed:
I scent it twenty-fold.' And then she sang,
'"O morning star" (not that tall felon there
Whom thou by sorcery or unhappiness
Or some device, hast foully overthrown),
"O morning star that smilest in the blue,
O star, my morning dream hath proven true,
Smile sweetly, thou! my love hath smiled on me."

'But thou begone, take counsel, and away,
For hard by here is one that guards a ford–
The second brother in their fool's parable–
Will pay thee all thy wages, and to boot.
Care not for shame: thou art not knight but knave.'

To whom Sir Gareth answered, laughingly,
'Parables? Hear a parable of the knave.
When I was kitchen-knave among the rest
Fierce was the hearth, and one of my co-mates
Owned a rough dog, to whom he cast his coat,
"Guard it," and there was none to meddle with it.

*967–9.* Malory vii 7: '"Away, kitchen knave! go out of the wind; for the smell of thy bawdy clothes grieveth me."'

*972.* Malory vii 7: '"Alas! that ever such a knight as thou art should, by mishap, slay so good a knight as thou hast slain."'

*980.* Malory vii 7: '"But hereby is a knight that shall pay thee all thy payment."'

And such a coat art thou, and thee the King
Gave me to guard, and such a dog am I,
To worry, and not to flee–and–knight or knave–
The knave that doth thee service as full knight
Is all as good, meseems, as any knight
Toward thy sister's freeing.'

'Ay, Sir Knave!
Ay, knave, because thou strikest as a knight,
Being but knave, I hate thee all the more.'

'Fair damsel, you should worship me the more,
That, being but knave, I throw thine enemies.'

'Ay, ay,' she said, 'but thou shalt meet thy match.'

So when they touched the second river-loop,
Huge on a huge red horse, and all in mail
Burnished to blinding, shone the Noonday Sun
Beyond a raging shallow. As if the flower,
That blows a globe of after arrowlets,
Ten thousand-fold had grown, flashed the fierce
shield,
All sun; and Gareth's eyes had flying blots
Before them when he turned from watching him.
He from beyond the roaring shallow roared,
'What doest thou, brother, in my marches here?'
And she athwart the shallow shrilled again,
'Here is a kitchen-knave from Arthur's hall
Hath overthrown thy brother, and hath his arms.'
'Ugh!' cried the Sun, and vizoring up a red
And cipher face of rounded foolishness,
Pushed horse across the foamings of the ford,
Whom Gareth met midstream: no room was there

*1002.* 'The dandelion' (T.).

*1008–11.* Malory vii 8: '"Is that my brother, the black knight, that ye have brought with you?"–"Nay, nay," said she, "this unhappy kitchen knave hath slain your brother through unhappiness."'

*1015–31.* Malory vii 6: 'And therewith he rushed into the water, and in the midst of the water either broke their spears to their hands, and then they drew their swords, and smote at each other eagerly: and, at the last, sir Beaumains smote the other upon the helm, that his head was stunned, and therewith he fell down into the water, and there was drowned . . . "Alas," said she, "that ever kitchen page should have the fortune to destroy two such doughty knights: thou weenest thou hast done doughtily, and that is not so; for the first knight's horse stumbled, and there he was drowned in

For lance or tourney-skill: four strokes they struck
With sword, and these were mighty; the new knight
Had fear he might be shamed; but as the Sun
Heaved up a ponderous arm to strike the fifth,
The hoof of his horse slipt in the stream, the stream
Descended, and the Sun was washed away.

Then Gareth laid his lance athwart the ford;
So drew him home; but he that fought no more,
As being all bone-battered on the rock,
Yielded; and Gareth sent him to the King.
'Myself when I return will plead for thee.'
'Lead, and I follow.' Quietly she led.
'Hath not the good wind, damsel, changed again?'
'Nay, not a point: nor art thou victor here.
There lies a ridge of slate across the ford;
His horse thereon stumbled–ay, for I saw it.

'"O Sun" (not this strong fool whom thou, Sir Knave,
Hast overthrown through mere unhappiness),
"O Sun, that wakenest all to bliss or pain,
O moon, that layest all to sleep again,
Shine sweetly: twice my love hath smiled on me."

'What knowest thou of lovesong or of love?
Nay, nay, God wot, so thou wert nobly born,
Thou hast a pleasant presence. Yea, perchance,–

'"O dewy flowers that open to the sun,
O dewy flowers that close when day is done,
Blow sweetly: twice my love hath smiled on me."

the water, and never it was by thy force and might: and the last knight, by mishap thou camest behind him, and shamefully thou slewest him."'

*1032–51.* Cp. *Be merry*, an unpublished song by T. in the *Hn MSS* (HM 19487):

Be merry, be merry: the woods begin to blow;
Be merry the lark aloft, the thrush below;
Be merry my heart, as merry as heart can be.

Be merry, be merry: the world begins to love;
Be merry the jay, the tit, the pink, the dove;
Be merry my heart, for love has smiled on me.

Be merry my little heart as lambs at play,
And merry as birds are merry among the may;
Be merry my heart, as ever a heart can be.

*1033. unhappiness*: 'mischance' (T.).

'What knowest thou of flowers, except, belike,
To garnish meats with? hath not our good King
Who lent me thee, the flower of kitchendom,
A foolish love for flowers? what stick ye round
The pasty? wherewithal deck the boar's head?
Flowers? nay, the boar hath rosemaries and bay.

'"O birds, that warble to the morning sky,
O birds that warble as the day goes by,
Sing sweetly: twice my love hath smiled on me."

'What knowest thou of birds, lark, mavis, merle,
Linnet? what dream ye when they utter forth
May-music growing with the growing light,
Their sweet sun-worship? these be for the snare
(So runs thy fancy) these be for the spit,
Larding and basting. See thou have not now
Larded thy last, except thou turn and fly.
There stands the third fool of their allegory.'

For there beyond a bridge of treble bow,
All in a rose-red from the west, and all
Naked it seemed, and glowing in the broad
Deep-dimpled current underneath, the knight,
That named himself the Star of Evening, stood.

And Gareth, 'Wherefore waits the madman there
Naked in open dayshine?' 'Nay,' she cried,
'Not naked, only wrapt in hardened skins
That fit him like his own; and so ye cleave
His armour off him, these will turn the blade.'

Then the third brother shouted o'er the bridge,
'O brother-star, why shine ye here so low?
Thy ward is higher up: but have ye slain
The damsel's champion?' and the damsel cried,

'No star of thine, but shot from Arthur's heaven
With all disaster unto thine and thee!
For both thy younger brethren have gone down
Before this youth; and so wilt thou, Sir Star;
Art thou not old?'

*1051.* 'Because of his having overthrown two knights. A light has broken on her. Her morning dream has twice proved true, that she should find a worthy champion' (H.T.).
*1067.* 'Allegory of habit' (T.).
*1071.* 'Gareth has taken the shield of the Morning-Star' (H.T.).

'Old, damsel, old and hard,
Old, with the might and breath of twenty boys.'
Said Gareth, 'Old, and over-bold in brag!
But that same strength which threw the Morning Star
Can throw the Evening.'
Then that other blew
A hard and deadly note upon the horn.
'Approach and arm me!' With slow steps from out
An old storm-beaten, russet, many-stained
Pavilion, forth a grizzled damsel came,
And armed him in old arms, and brought a helm
With but a drying evergreen for crest,
And gave a shield whereon the Star of Even
Half-tarnished and half-bright, his emblem, shone.
But when it glittered o'er the saddle-bow,
They madly hurled together on the bridge;
And Gareth overthrew him, lighted, drew,
There met him drawn, and overthrew him again,
But up like fire he started: and as oft
As Gareth brought him grovelling on his knees,
So many a time he vaulted up again;
Till Gareth panted hard, and his great heart,
Foredooming all his trouble was in vain,
Laboured within him, for he seemed as one
That all in later, sadder age begins
To war against ill uses of a life,
But these from all his life arise, and cry,
'Thou hast made us lords, and canst not put us down!'
He half despairs; so Gareth seemed to strike
Vainly, the damsel clamouring all the while,
'Well done, knave-knight, well stricken, O good knight-knave–
O knave, as noble as any of all the knights–
Shame me not, shame me not. I have prophesied–
Strike, thou art worthy of the Table Round–
His arms are old, he trusts the hardened skin–
Strike–strike–the wind will never change again.'
And Gareth hearing ever stronglier smote,
And hewed great pieces of his armour off him,
But lashed in vain against the hardened skin,
And could not wholly bring him under, more
Than loud Southwesterns, rolling ridge on ridge,

*1092ff.* Cp. the fight with Maleger, *Faerie Queene* II xi sts 20–46.

The buoy that rides at sea, and dips and springs
For ever; till at length Sir Gareth's brand
Clashed his, and brake it utterly to the hilt.
'I have thee now;' but forth that other sprang,
And, all unknightlike, writhed his wiry arms
Around him, till he felt, despite his mail,
Strangled, but straining even his uttermost
Cast, and so hurled him headlong o'er the bridge
Down to the river, sink or swim, and cried,
'Lead, and I follow.'

But the damsel said,
'I lead no longer; ride thou at my side;
Thou art the kingliest of all kitchen-knaves.

'"O trefoil, sparkling on the rainy plain,
O rainbow with three colours after rain,
Shine sweetly: thrice my love hath smiled on me."

'Sir,—and, good faith, I fain had added—Knight,
But that I heard thee call thyself a knave,—
Shamed am I that I so rebuked, reviled,
Missaid thee; noble I am; and thought the King
Scorned me and mine; and now thy pardon, friend,
For thou hast ever answered courteously,
And wholly bold thou art, and meek withal
As any of Arthur's best, but, being knave,
Hast mazed my wit: I marvel what thou art.'

'Damsel,' he said, 'you be not all to blame,
Saving that you mistrusted our good King
Would handle scorn, or yield you, asking, one
Not fit to cope your quest. You said your say;
Mine answer was my deed. Good sooth! I hold
He scarce is knight, yea but half-man, nor meet
To fight for gentle damsel, he, who lets
His heart be stirred with any foolish heat
At any gentle damsel's waywardness.
Shamed? care not! thy foul sayings fought for me:
And seeing now thy words are fair, methinks
There rides no knight, not Lancelot, his great self,
Hath force to quell me.'

*1135–6.* Malory vii 11: '"Alas!" said she, "fair sir Beaumains forgive me all that I have missayed and misdone against you."'
*1144. you*] *1873*; thee *1872*.
*1145. your quest*] *1873*; thy quest *1872*.

Nigh upon that hour
When the lone hern forgets his melancholy,
Lets down his other leg, and stretching, dreams
Of goodly supper in the distant pool,
Then turned the noble damsel smiling at him,
And told him of a cavern hard at hand,
Where bread and baken meats and good red wine
Of Southland, which the Lady Lyonors
Had sent her coming champion, waited him.

Anon they past a narrow comb wherein
Were slabs of rock with figures, knights on horse
Sculptured, and deckt in slowly-waning hues.
'Sir Knave, my knight, a hermit once was here,
Whose holy hand hath fashioned on the rock
The war of Time against the soul of man.
And yon four fools have sucked their allegory
From these damp walls, and taken but the form.
Know ye not these?' and Gareth lookt and read–
In letters like to those the vexillary
Hath left crag-carven o'er the streaming Gelt–
'Phosphorus,' then 'Meridies'–'Hesperus'–
'Nox'–'Mors,' beneath five figures, armèd men,
Slab after slab, their faccs forward all,
And running down the Soul, a Shape that fled
With broken wings, torn raiment and loose hair,
For help and shelter to the hermit's cave.
'Follow the faces, and we find it. Look,
Who comes behind?'

For one–delayed at first
Through helping back the dislocated Kay
To Camelot, then by what thereafter chanced,
The damsel's headlong error through the wood–
Sir Lancelot, having swum the river-loops–
His blue shield-lions covered–softly drew
Behind the twain, and when he saw the star

*1172–5*. T. comments: 'Years ago when I was visiting the Howards at Naworth Castle, I drove over to the little river Gelt to see the inscription carved upon the crags. It seemed to me very pathetic, this sole record of the vexillary or standard-bearer of the sacred Legion (Augusta). This is the inscription: VEX.LLEG.II AVG. ON. AP. APRO E MAXIMO CONSULIBUS SUB AGRICOLA OP. OFICINA MERCATI.' Of the 'figures', H.T. says: 'Symbolical of the temptations of youth, of middle-age, of later life, and of death overcome by the youthful and joyous Gareth.'

*1185–93*. Suggested by Gareth's jousting with Lancelot, Malory vii 4.

Gleam, on Sir Gareth's turning to him, cried,
'Stay, felon knight, I avenge me for my friend.'
And Gareth crying pricked against the cry;
But when they closed–in a moment–at one touch
Of that skilled spear, the wonder of the world–
Went sliding down so easily, and fell,
That when he found the grass within his hands
He laughed; the laughter jarred upon Lynette:
Harshly she asked him, 'Shamed and overthrown,
And tumbled back into the kitchen-knave,
Why laugh ye? that ye blew your boast in vain?'
'Nay, noble damsel, but that I, the son
Of old King Lot and good Queen Bellicent,
And victor of the bridges and the ford,
And knight of Arthur, here lie thrown by whom
I know not, all through mere unhappiness–
Device and sorcery and unhappiness–
Out, sword; we are thrown!' And Lancelot answered, 'Prince,
O Gareth–through the mere unhappiness
Of one who came to help thee, not to harm,
Lancelot, and all as glad to find thee whole,
As on the day when Arthur knighted him.'

Then Gareth, 'Thou–Lancelot!–thine the hand
That threw me? An some chance to mar the boast
Thy brethren of thee make–which could not chance–
Had sent thee down before a lesser spear,
Shamed had I been, and sad–O Lancelot–thou!'

Whereat the maiden, petulant, 'Lancelot,
Why came ye not, when called? and wherefore now
Come ye, not called? I gloried in my knave,
Who being still rebuked, would answer still
Courteous as any knight–but now, if knight,
The marvel dies, and leaves me fooled and tricked,
And only wondering wherefore played upon:
And doubtful whether I and mine be scorned.
Where should be truth if not in Arthur's hall,
In Arthur's presence? Knight, knave, prince and fool,
I hate thee and for ever.'

*1198.* Malory vii 11: '"Fie, fie!" said the damsel, "that ever such a stinking knave should blow such a boast."'

And Lancelot said,
'Blessèd be thou, Sir Gareth! knight art thou
To the King's best wish. O damsel, be you wise
To call him shamed, who is but overthrown?
Thrown have I been, nor once, but many a time.
Victor from vanquished issues at the last,
And overthrower from being overthrown.
With sword we have not striven; and thy good horse
And thou are weary; yet not less I felt
Thy manhood through that wearied lance of thine.
Well hast thou done; for all the stream is freed,
And thou hast wreaked his justice on his foes,
And when reviled, hast answered graciously,
And makest merry when overthrown. Prince, Knight,
Hail, Knight and Prince, and of our Table Round!'

And then when turning to Lynette he told
The tale of Gareth, petulantly she said,
'Ay well–ay well–for worse than being fooled
Of others, is to fool one's self. A cave,
Sir Lancelot, is hard by, with meats and drinks
And forage for the horse, and flint for fire.
But all about it flies a honeysuckle.
Seek, till we find.' And when they sought and found,
Sir Gareth drank and ate, and all his life
Past into sleep; on whom the maiden gazed.
'Sound sleep be thine! sound cause to sleep hast thou.
Wake lusty! Seem I not as tender to him
As any mother? Ay, but such a one
As all day long hath rated at her child,
And vext his day, but blesses him asleep–
Good lord, how sweetly smells the honeysuckle
In the hushed night, as if the world were one
Of utter peace, and love, and gentleness!
O Lancelot, Lancelot'–and she clapt her hands–
'Full merry am I to find my goodly knave
Is knight and noble. See now, sworn have I,
Else yon black felon had not let me pass,
To bring thee back to do the battle with him.
Thus an thou goest, he will fight thee first;
Who doubts thee victor? so will my knight-knave
Miss the full flower of this accomplishment.'

Said Lancelot, 'Peradventure he, you name,
May know my shield. Let Gareth, an he will,

Change his for mine, and take my charger, fresh,
Not to be spurred, loving the battle as well
As he that rides him.' 'Lancelot-like,' she said,
'Courteous in this, Lord Lancelot, as in all.'

And Gareth, wakening, fiercely clutched the shield;
'Ramp ye lance-splintering lions, on whom all spears
Are rotten sticks! ye seem agape to roar!
Yea, ramp and roar at leaving of your lord!–
Care not, good beasts, so well I care for you.
O noble Lancelot, from my hold on these
Streams virtue–fire–through one that will not shame
Even the shadow of Lancelot under shield.
Hence: let us go.'

Silent the silent field
They traversed. Arthur's harp though summer-wan,
In counter motion to the clouds, allured
The glance of Gareth dreaming on his liege.
A star shot: 'Lo,' said Gareth, 'the foe falls!'
An owl whoopt: 'Hark the victor pealing there!'
Suddenly she that rode upon his left
Clung to the shield that Lancelot lent him, crying,
'Yield, yield him this again: 'tis he must fight:
I curse the tongue that all through yesterday
Reviled thee, and hath wrought on Lancelot now
To lend thee horse and shield: wonders ye have done;
Miracles ye cannot: here is glory enow
In having flung the three: I see thee maimed,
Mangled: I swear thou canst not fling the fourth.'

'And wherefore, damsel? tell me all ye know.
You cannot scare me; nor rough face, or voice,
Brute bulk of limb, or boundless savagery
Appal me from the quest.'

'Nay, Prince,' she cried,
'God wot, I never looked upon the face,
Seeing he never rides abroad by day;
But watched him have I like a phantom pass
Chilling the night: nor have I heard the voice.
Always he made his mouthpiece of a page
Who came and went, and still reported him

*1281.* 'Lyra' (T.).

As closing in himself the strength of ten,
And when his anger tare him, massacring
Man, woman, lad and girl–yea, the soft babe!
Some hold that he hath swallowed infant flesh,
Monster! O Prince, I went for Lancelot first,
The quest is Lancelot's: give him back the shield.'

Said Gareth laughing, 'An he fight for this,
Belike he wins it as the better man:
Thus–and not else!'

But Lancelot on him urged
All the devisings of their chivalry
When one might meet a mightier than himself;
How best to manage horse, lance, sword and shield,
And so fill up the gap where force might fail
With skill and fineness. Instant were his words.

Then Gareth, 'Here be rules. I know but one–
To dash against mine enemy and to win.
Yet have I watched thee victor in the joust,
And seen thy way.' 'Heaven help thee,' sighed
Lynette.

Then for a space, and under cloud that grew
To thunder-gloom palling all stars, they rode
In converse till she made her palfrey halt,
Lifted an arm, and softly whispered, 'There.'
And all the three were silent seeing, pitched
Beside the Castle Perilous on flat field,
A huge pavilion like a mountain peak
Sunder the glooming crimson on the marge,
Black, with black banner, and a long black horn
Beside it hanging; which Sir Gareth graspt,
And so, before the two could hinder him,
Sent all his heart and breath through all the horn.
Echoed the walls; a light twinkled; anon
Came lights and lights, and once again he blew;
Whereon were hollow tramplings up and down

*1315. When*] *1873*; Where *1872*.

*1330. crimson*: 'sunrise' (T.).

*1331*. Malory vii 6 (where this encounter takes place earlier): 'And then they came to a black land, and there was a black hawthorn, and thereon hung a black banner; and on the other side there hung a black shield, and by it stood a black spear and a long, and a great black horse covered with silk, and black stone fast by it. There sat a knight all armed in black harness, and his name was the knight of the black lands.'

And muffled voices heard, and shadows past;
Till high above him, circled with her maids,
The Lady Lyonors at a window stood,
Beautiful among lights, and waving to him
White hands, and courtesy; but when the Prince
Three times had blown–after long hush–at last–
The huge pavilion slowly yielded up,
Through those black foldings, that which housed therein.
High on a nightblack horse, in nightblack arms,
With white breast-bone, and barren ribs of Death,
And crowned with fleshless laughter–some ten steps–
In the half-light–through the dim dawn–advanced
The monster, and then paused, and spake no word.

But Gareth spake and all indignantly,
'Fool, for thou hast, men say, the strength of ten,
Canst thou not trust the limbs thy God hath given,
But must, to make the terror of thee more,
Trick thyself out in ghastly imageries
Of that which Life hath done with, and the clod,
Less dull than thou, will hide with mantling flowers
As if for pity?' But he spake no word;
Which set the horror higher: a maiden swooned;
The Lady Lyonors wrung her hands and wept,
As doomed to be the bride of Night and Death;
Sir Gareth's head prickled beneath his helm;
And even Sir Lancelot through his warm blood felt
Ice strike, and all that marked him were aghast.

At once Sir Lancelot's charger fiercely neighed,
And Death's dark war-horse bounded forward with him.
Then those that did not blink the terror, saw

*1340.* Malory vii 16: '"Sir," said the damsel, Linet, unto sir Beaumains, "look that ye be merry and light, for yonder is your deadly enemy, and at yonder window is my lady, my sister, dame Lyons."–"Where?" said sir Beaumains. "Yonder," said the damsel, and pointed with her finger. "That is sooth," said sir Beaumains, "she seemeth a far the fairest lady that ever I looked upon; and truly," said he, "I ask no better quarrel, than now to do battle: for truly she shall be my lady, and for her will I fight."'

*1348.* 'With a grinning skull' (T.).

*1366. And . . . war-*] *1873*; At once the black *1872*.

That Death was cast to ground, and slowly rose.
But with one stroke Sir Gareth split the skull.
Half fell to right and half to left and lay.
Then with a stronger buffet he clove the helm
As throughly as the skull; and out from this
Issued the bright face of a blooming boy
Fresh as a flower new-born, and crying, 'Knight,
Slay me not: my three brethren bad me do it,
To make a horror all about the house,
And stay the world from Lady Lyonors.
They never dreamed the passes would be past.'
Answered Sir Gareth graciously to one
Not many a moon his younger, 'My fair child,
What madness made thee challenge the chief knight
Of Arthur's hall?' 'Fair Sir, they bad me do it.
They hate the King, and Lancelot, the King's friend,
They hoped to slay him somewhere on the stream,
They never dreamed the passes could be past.'

Then sprang the happier day from underground;
And Lady Lyonors and her house, with dance
And revel and song, made merry over Death,
As being after all their foolish fears
And horrors only proven a blooming boy.
So large mirth lived and Gareth won the quest.

And he that told the tale in older times
Says that Sir Gareth wedded Lyonors,
But he, that told it later, says Lynette.

# 466 The Marriage of Geraint

Printed privately in 1857 at Canford Manor, as *Enid, an Idyll*, along with Lady Charlotte Guest's *Geraint*, translated from the *Mabinogion*. Published *1859*, the first half of *Enid*. The title *Enid* was expanded to *Geraint and Enid* in *1870* ('*1869*'); the poem was divided into two parts in *1873*; and the final titles given in *1886*. H.T. notes: 'In 1857 six copies of *Enid and Nimuë: the True and the False* were printed. This Idyll is founded on *Geraint, son of Erbin*, in the *Mabinogion*, translated by Lady Charlotte Guest [1840, collected 1849, vol. ii], and has "brought the story within compass". It was begun on 16 April 1856, and first published in 1859 in the *Idylls of the King*. My father had also read *Erec and Enid*, by Chrestien de Troyes. The

*1392–4*. H.T. glosses this: 'Malory' and 'my father'.

greater part of the Idylls contained in the volume of 1859 was written at Farringford. But the end of *Geraint and Enid* was written in July and August of 1856 in Wales, where he read, in the original, *Hanes Cymru* (Welsh history), the *Mabinogion*, and Llywarch Hen.' T. is very close in incidents and often in wording to the Guest translation; for a detailed comparison, see H. G. Wright, *Essays and Studies* xiv (1929) 80–103. G. C. Macaulay's edition (1892), pp. xxviii–xxx, lists T.'s possible debts to the French versions. For a detailed account of T.'s textual changes, see Richard Jones, *The Growth of the Idylls of the King* (1895), chapter ii. There is a copy of *Enid and Nimuë* (1857) in the British Museum; an edition was printed from this in 1902.

The brave Geraint, a knight of Arthur's court,
A tributary prince of Devon, one
Of that great Order of the Table Round,
Had married Enid, Yniol's only child,
And loved her, as he loved the light of Heaven.
And as the light of Heaven varies, now
At sunrise, now at sunset, now by night
With moon and trembling stars, so loved Geraint
To make her beauty vary day by day,
In crimsons and in purples and in gems.
And Enid, but to please her husband's eye,
Who first had found and loved her in a state
Of broken fortunes, daily fronted him
In some fresh splendour; and the Queen herself,
Grateful to Prince Geraint for service done,
Loved her, and often with her own white hands
Arrayed and decked her, as the loveliest,
Next after her own self, in all the court.
And Enid loved the Queen, and with true heart
Adored her, as the stateliest and the best
And loveliest of all women upon earth.
And seeing them so tender and so close,
Long in their common love rejoiced Geraint.
But when a rumour rose about the Queen,
Touching her guilty love for Lancelot,
Though yet there lived no proof, nor yet was heard
The world's loud whisper breaking into storm,
Not less Geraint believed it; and there fell

¶466. *4. married*] *1862*; wedded *1859–61*. 'He found out that the "E" in "Enid" was pronounced short (as if it were spelt "Ennid"), and so altered the phrase in the proofs "wedded Enid" to "married Enid"' (H.T.).
*24–9.* Added to *Mabinogion*, so that T. could link these two idylls with his main theme.

A horror on him, lest his gentle wife,
Through that great tenderness for Guinevere,
Had suffered, or should suffer any taint
In nature: wherefore going to the King,
He made this pretext, that his princedom lay
Close on the borders of a territory,
Wherein were bandit earls, and caitiff knights,
Assassins, and all flyers from the hand
Of Justice, and whatever loathes a law:
And therefore, till the King himself should please
To cleanse this common sewer of all his realm,
He craved a fair permission to depart,
And there defend his marches; and the King
Mused for a little on his plea, but, last,
Allowing it, the Prince and Enid rode,
And fifty knights rode with them, to the shores
Of Severn, and they past to their own land;
Where, thinking, that if ever yet was wife
True to her lord, mine shall be so to me,
He compassed her with sweet observances
And worship, never leaving her, and grew
Forgetful of his promise to the King,
Forgetful of the falcon and the hunt,
Forgetful of the tilt and tournament,
Forgetful of his glory and his name,
Forgetful of his princedom and its cares.

*33–41.* In *Mabinogion*, this is no pretext; Geraint needs 'to protect his dominions and his boundaries, seeing that his father was unable to do so'.
*45.* 'Geraint was at Caerleon, and would have to cross the Bristol Channel to go to Devon' (T.). 'I like the *t*–the strong perfect in verbs ending in *s*, *p*, and *x*–past, slipt, vext' (T.).
*46–68.* *Mabinogion*: 'He began to love ease and pleasure, for there was no one who was worth his opposing. And he loved his wife, and liked to continue in the palace, with minstrelsy and diversions. And for a long time he abode at home. And after that he began to shut himself up in the chamber of his wife, and he took no delight in anything besides, insomuch that he gave up the friendship of his nobles, together with his hunting and his amusements, and lost the hearts of all the host in his Court; and there was murmuring and scoffing concerning him among the inhabitants of the palace, on account of his relinquishing so completely their companionship for the love of his wife . . . "There is nothing more hateful to me than this." And she knew not what she should do, for, although it was hard for her to own this to Geraint, yet was it not more easy for her to listen to what she heard, without warning Geraint concerning it. And she was very sorrowful.'

And this forgetfulness was hateful to her.
And by and by the people, when they met
In twos and threes, or fuller companies,
Began to scoff and jeer and babble of him
As of a prince whose manhood was all gone,
And molten down in mere uxoriousness.
And this she gathered from the people's eyes:
This too the women who attired her head,
To please her, dwelling on his boundless love,
Told Enid, and they saddened her the more:
And day by day she thought to tell Geraint,
But could not out of bashful delicacy;
While he that watched her sadden, was the more
Suspicious that her nature had a taint.

At last, it chanced that on a summer morn
(They sleeping each by either) the new sun
Beat through the blindless casement of the room,
And heated the strong warrior in his dreams;
Who, moving, cast the coverlet aside,
And bared the knotted column of his throat,
The massive square of his heroic breast,
And arms on which the standing muscle sloped,
As slopes a wild brook o'er a little stone,
Running too vehemently to break upon it.
And Enid woke and sat beside the couch,
Admiring him, and thought within herself,

*69–108. Mabinogion*: 'And one morning in the summer time, they were upon their couch, and Geraint lay upon the edge of it. And Enid was without sleep in the apartment which had windows of glass. And the sun shone upon the couch. And the clothes had slipped from off his arms and his breast, and he was asleep. Then she gazed upon the marvellous beauty of his appearance, and she said, "Alas, and am I the cause that these arms and this breast have lost their glory and the warlike fame which they once so richly enjoyed!"' T. adds words capable of misconstruction.

*70. either*] *1870* ('*1869*'); other *1859–69*.

*77.* T. remarks: 'I made this simile from a stream, and it is different, though like Theocritus, *Idyll* xxii 48ff: ἐν δὲ μύες στερεοῖσι βραχίοσιν ἄκρον ὑπ' ὦμον ἕστασαν, ἠΰτε πέτροι ὀλοίτροχοι, οὕστε κυλίνδων χειμάρρους ποταμὸς μεγάλαις περιέξεσε δίναις.' ('Moreover, the sinews upon his brawny arms upstood beside the shoulder like the boulder-stones some torrent hath rolled and rounded in his swirling eddies.') H.T. adds: 'When some one objected that he had taken this simile from Theocritus, he answered: "It is quite different. Geraint's muscles are not compared to the rounded stones, but to the stream pouring vehemently over them."'

Was ever man so grandly made as he?
Then, like a shadow, past the people's talk
And accusation of uxoriousness
Across her mind, and bowing over him,
Low to her own heart piteously she said:

'O noble breast and all-puissant arms,
Am I the cause, I the poor cause that men
Reproach you, saying all your force is gone?
I *am* the cause, because I dare not speak
And tell him what I think and what they say.
And yet I hate that he should linger here;
I cannot love my lord and not his name.
Far liefer had I gird his harness on him,
And ride with him to battle and stand by,
And watch his mightful hand striking great blows
At caitiffs and at wrongers of the world.
Far better were I laid in the dark earth,
Not hearing any more his noble voice,
Not to be folded more in these dear arms,
And darkened from the high light in his eyes,
Than that my lord through me should suffer shame.
Am I so bold, and could I so stand by,
And see my dear lord wounded in the strife,
Or maybe pierced to death before mine eyes,
And yet not dare to tell him what I think,
And how men slur him, saying all his force
Is melted into mere effeminacy?
O me, I fear that I am no true wife.'

Half inwardly, half audibly she spoke,
And the strong passion in her made her weep
True tears upon his broad and naked breast,
And these awoke him, and by great mischance
He heard but fragments of her later words,
And that she feared she was not a true wife.
And then he thought, 'In spite of all my care,
For all my pains, poor man, for all my pains,
She is not faithful to me, and I see her
Weeping for some gay knight in Arthur's hall.'
Then though he loved and reverenced her too much

*109–18. Mabinogion*: 'And as she said this, the tears dropped from her eyes, and they fell upon his breast. And the tears she shed, and the words she had spoken, awoke him; and another thing contributed to awaken him, and that was the idea that it was not in thinking of him that she spoke thus, but that it was because she loved some other man more than him.'

To dream she could be guilty of foul act,
Right through his manful breast darted the pang
That makes a man, in the sweet face of her
Whom he loves most, lonely and miserable.
At this he hurled his huge limbs out of bed,
And shook his drowsy squire awake and cried,
'My charger and her palfrey;' then to her,
'I will ride forth into the wilderness;
For though it seems my spurs are yet to win,
I have not fallen so low as some would wish.
And thou, put on thy worst and meanest dress
And ride with me.' And Enid asked, amazed,
'If Enid errs, let Enid learn her fault.'
But he, 'I charge thee, ask not, but obey.'
Then she bethought her of a faded silk,
A faded mantle and a faded veil,
And moving toward a cedarn cabinet,
Wherein she kept them folded reverently
With sprigs of summer laid between the folds,
She took them, and arrayed herself therein,
Remembering when first he came on her
Drest in that dress, and how he loved her in it,
And all her foolish fears about the dress,
And all his journey to her, as himself
Had told her, and their coming to the court.

For Arthur on the Whitsuntide before
Held court at old Caerleon upon Usk.
There on a day, he sitting high in hall,
Before him came a forester of Dean,
Wet from the woods, with notice of a hart
Taller than all his fellows, milky-white,

*124–33. Mabinogion*: 'And thereupon Geraint was troubled in his mind, and he called his squire; and when he came to him, "Go quickly," said he, "and prepare my horse and my arms, and make them ready. And do thou arise," said he to Enid, "and apparel thyself; and cause thy horse to be accoutred, and clothe thee in the worst riding-dress that thou hast in thy possession." . . . So she arose, and clothed herself in her meanest garments. "I know nothing, Lord", said she, "of thy meaning". "Neither wilt thou know at this time", said he.'

*130. thou . . . thy*] *1873*; you . . . your *1859–70*.

*133. thee*] *1873*; you *1859–70*.

*138.* 'Lavender' (T.).

*146.* 'Arthur's capital, *castra Legionis*, is in Monmouthshire on the Usk, which flows into the Bristol Channel' (T.).

First seen that day: these things he told the King.
Then the good King gave order to let blow
His horns for hunting on the morrow morn.
And when the Queen petitioned for his leave
To see the hunt, allowed it easily.
So with the morning all the court were gone.
But Guinevere lay late into the morn,
Lost in sweet dreams, and dreaming of her love
For Lancelot, and forgetful of the hunt;
But rose at last, a single maiden with her,
Took horse, and forded Usk, and gained the wood;
There, on a little knoll beside it, stayed
Waiting to hear the hounds; but heard instead
A sudden sound of hoofs, for Prince Geraint,
Late also, wearing neither hunting-dress
Nor weapon, save a golden-hilted brand,
Came quickly flashing through the shallow ford
Behind them, and so galloped up the knoll.
A purple scarf, at either end whereof
There swung an apple of the purest gold,
Swayed round about him, as he galloped up
To join them, glancing like a dragon-fly
In summer suit and silks of holiday.
Low bowed the tributary Prince, and she,
Sweetly and statelily, and with all grace
Of womanhood and queenhood, answered him:
'Late, late, Sir Prince,' she said, 'later than we!'
'Yea, noble Queen,' he answered, 'and so late
That I but come like you to see the hunt,
Not join it.' 'Therefore wait with me,' she said;
'For on this little knoll, if anywhere,
There is good chance that we shall hear the hounds:
Here often they break covert at our feet.'

And while they listened for the distant hunt,
And chiefly for the baying of Cavall,
King Arthur's hound of deepest mouth, there rode
Full slowly by a knight, lady, and dwarf;
Whereof the dwarf lagged latest, and the knight

*157–9. Mabinogion*: 'And Arthur wondered that Gwenhwyvar did not awake, and did not move in her bed; and the attendants wished to awaken her. "Disturb her not", said Arthur, "for she had rather sleep than go to see the hunting."' T.'s addition stresses a theme of the *Idylls*.

*186.* T. compares *Midsummer Night's Dream* IV i 122: 'matched in mouth like bells'.

Had vizor up, and showed a youthful face,
Imperious, and of haughtiest lineaments.
And Guinevere, not mindful of his face
In the King's hall, desired his name, and sent
Her maiden to demand it of the dwarf;
Who being vicious, old and irritable,
And doubling all his master's vice of pride,
Made answer sharply that she should not know.
'Then will I ask it of himself,' she said.
'Nay, by my faith, thou shalt not,' cried the dwarf;
'Thou art not worthy even to speak of him;'
And when she put her horse toward the knight,
Struck at her with his whip, and she returned
Indignant to the Queen; whereat Geraint
Exclaiming, 'Surely I will learn the name,'
Made sharply to the dwarf, and asked it of him,
Who answered as before; and when the Prince
Had put his horse in motion toward the knight,
Struck at him with his whip, and cut his cheek.
The Prince's blood spirted upon the scarf,
Dyeing it; and his quick, instinctive hand
Caught at the hilt, as to abolish him:
But he, from his exceeding manfulness
And pure nobility of temperament,
Wroth to be wroth at such a worm, refrained
From even a word, and so returning said:

'I will avenge this insult, noble Queen,
Done in your maiden's person to yourself:
And I will track this vermin to their earths:
For though I ride unarmed, I do not doubt
To find, at some place I shall come at, arms
On loan, or else for pledge; and, being found,
Then will I fight him, and will break his pride,
And on the third day will again be here,
So that I be not fallen in fight. Farewell.'

*190. haughtiest lineaments*: *The Princess* ii 425.

*201. Mabinogion*: 'Then the maiden turned her horse's head towards the knight, upon which the dwarf struck her with the whip that was in his hand across the face and the eyes, until the blood flowed forth.'

*202. whereat*] *1870* ('*1869*'); at which *1859–69*.

*211–4. Mabinogion*: 'But he took counsel with himself, and considered that it would be no vengeance for him to slay the dwarf, and to be attacked unarmed by the armed knight, so he returned to where Gwenhwyvar was.'

'Farewell, fair Prince,' answered the stately Queen.
'Be prosperous in this journey, as in all;
And may you light on all things that you love,
And live to wed with her whom first you love:
But ere you wed with any, bring your bride,
And I, were she the daughter of a king,
Yea, though she were a beggar from the hedge,
Will clothe her for her bridals like the sun.'

And Prince Geraint, now thinking that he heard
The noble hart at bay, now the far horn,
A little vext at losing of the hunt,
A little at the vile occasion, rode,
By ups and downs, through many a grassy glade
And valley, with fixt eye following the three.
At last they issued from the world of wood,
And climbed upon a fair and even ridge,
And showed themselves against the sky, and sank.
And thither came Geraint, and underneath
Beheld the long street of a little town
In a long valley, on one side whereof,
White from the mason's hand, a fortress rose;
And on one side a castle in decay,
Beyond a bridge that spanned a dry ravine:
And out of town and valley came a noise
As of a broad brook o'er a shingly bed
Brawling, or like a clamour of the rooks
At distance, ere they settle for the night.

And onward to the fortress rode the three,
And entered, and were lost behind the walls.
'So,' thought Geraint, 'I have tracked him to his
earth.'
And down the long street riding wearily,
Found every hostel full, and everywhere
Was hammer laid to hoof, and the hot hiss

*226–31.* No equivalent in *Mabinogion*.
*239. Mabinogion*: 'And they went along a fair, and even, and lofty ridge of ground.'
*242–55.* Expanding *Mabinogion*.
*243. whereof*] *1870* ('*1869*'); of which *1859–69*.
*255–92. Mabinogion*: 'And every house he saw was full of men, and arms, and horses. And they were polishing shields, and burnishing swords, and washing armour, and shoeing horses.' In *Mabinogion*, Geraint's enemies (the knight, the lady and the dwarf) are warmly welcomed in the city.

And bustling whistle of the youth who scoured
His master's armour; and of such a one
He asked, 'What means the tumult in the town?'
Who told him, scouring still, 'The sparrow-hawk!'
Then riding close behind an ancient churl,
Who, smitten by the dusty sloping beam,
Went sweating underneath a sack of corn,
Asked yet once more what meant the hubbub here?
Who answered gruffly, 'Ugh! the sparrow-hawk.'
Then riding further past an armourer's,
Who, with back turned, and bowed above his work,
Sat riveting a helmet on his knee,
He put the self-same query, but the man
Not turning round, nor looking at him, said:
'Friend, he that labours for the sparrow-hawk
Has little time for idle questioners.'
Whereat Geraint flashed into sudden spleen:
'A thousand pips eat up your sparrow-hawk!
Tits, wrens, and all winged nothings peck him dead!
Ye think the rustic cackle of your bourg
The murmur of the world! What is it to me?
O wretched set of sparrows, one and all,
Who pipe of nothing but of sparrow-hawks!
Speak, if ye be not like the rest, hawk-mad,
Where can I get me harbourage for the night?
And arms, arms, arms to fight my enemy? Speak!'
Whereat the armourer turning all amazed
And seeing one so gay in purple silks,
Came forward with the helmet yet in hand
And answered, 'Pardon me, O stranger knight;
We hold a tourney here tomorrow morn,
And there is scantly time for half the work.
Arms? truth! I know not: all are wanted here.
Harbourage? truth, good truth, I know not, save,
It may be, at Earl Yniol's, o'er the bridge
Yonder.' He spoke and fell to work again.

*274. pips*: 'a bird-disease' (T.).

*280. ye*] *1870* ('*1869*'); you *1859–69*. Likewise ll. 304, 421, 684, 719, 726.

*283. Whereat*] *1873*; At this *1859–70*.

*290–7. Mabinogion*: 'At a little distance from the town he saw an old palace in ruins, wherein was a hall that was falling to decay. And as he knew not anyone in the town, he went towards the old palace; and when he came near to the palace, he saw but one chamber, and a bridge of marble-stone leading to it. And upon the bridge he saw sitting a hoary-headed man, upon whom were tattered garments.'

Then rode Geraint, a little spleenful yet,
Across the bridge that spanned the dry ravine.
There musing sat the hoary-headed Earl,
(His dress a suit of frayed magnificence,
Once fit for feasts of ceremony) and said:
'Whither, fair son?' to whom Geraint replied,
'O friend, I seek a harbourage for the night.'
Then Yniol, 'Enter therefore and partake
The slender entertainment of a house
Once rich, now poor, but ever open-doored.'
'Thanks, venerable friend,' replied Geraint;
'So that ye do not serve me sparrow-hawks
For supper, I will enter, I will eat
With all the passion of a twelve hours' fast.'
Then sighed and smiled the hoary-headed Earl,
And answered, 'Graver cause than yours is mine
To curse this hedgerow thief, the sparrow-hawk:
But in, go in; for save yourself desire it,
We will not touch upon him even in jest.'

Then rode Geraint into the castle court,
His charger trampling many a prickly star
Of sprouted thistle on the broken stones.
He looked and saw that all was ruinous.
Here stood a shattered archway plumed with fern;
And here had fallen a great part of a tower,
Whole, like a crag that tumbles from the cliff,
And like a crag was gay with wilding flowers:
And high above a piece of turret stair,
Worn by the feet that now were silent, wound
Bare to the sun, and monstrous ivy-stems
Clasp the gray walls with hairy-fibred arms,
And sucked the joining of the stones, and looked
A knot, beneath, of snakes, aloft, a grove.

And while he waited in the castle court,
The voice of Enid, Yniol's daughter, rang
Clear through the open casement of the hall,
Singing; and as the sweet voice of a bird,
Heard by the lander in a lonely isle,
Moves him to think what kind of bird it is

*298–311.* Expanding *Mabinogion.*
*319.* 'These lines were made at Middleham Castle' (T.) (*Mem.* i 487).
*322–3.* 'Tintern Abbey' (T.). These lines had originally been part of *The Princess: Prologue*, in MS.
*326–60.* Not in *Mabinogion.*

That sings so delicately clear, and make
Conjecture of the plumage and the form;
So the sweet voice of Enid moved Geraint;
And made him like a man abroad at morn
When first the liquid note beloved of men
Comes flying over many a windy wave
To Britain, and in April suddenly
Breaks from a coppice gemmed with green and red,
And he suspends his converse with a friend,
Or it may be the labour of his hands,
To think or say, 'There is the nightingale;'
So fared it with Geraint, who thought and said,
'Here, by God's grace, is the one voice for me.'

It chanced the song that Enid sang was one
Of Fortune and her wheel, and Enid sang:

'Turn, Fortune, turn thy wheel and lower the proud;

*347–58.* H.T. notes: 'This song of noble and enduring womanhood has its refrain in "Però giri Fortuna la sua ruota, / Come le piace"' (Dante, *Inferno* xv 95–6). But when John Churton Collins originally suggested this, T. wrote alongside '!!!' (*Cornhill*, Jan. 1880, *Lincoln*). Sir Charles Tennyson (*Cornhill* cliii (1936) 535) quotes from *H.MS* another version of the song:

Come in, the ford is roaring on the plain,
The distant hills are pale across the rain;
Come in, come in, for open is the gate.
Come in, poor man, and let the tempest blow.
Let Fortune frown and old possession go,
But health is wealth in high or low estate;
Though Fortune frown thou shalt not hear us rail,
The frown of Fortune never turned us pale,
For man is man and master of his fate.
Turn, Fortune, turn thy wheel with smile or frown,
With thy false wheel we go not up or down,
Our hoard is little but our hearts are great.
Smile and we smile, the lords of many lands,
Frown and we smile, the lords of our own hands,
For man is man and master of his fate.
The river ford will fall on yonder plain,
The flying rainbow chase the flying rain,
The sun at last will smile however late;
Come in, come in, whoever lingers there,
Nor scorn the ruined house and homely fare,
The house is poor but open is the gate.

Turn thy wild wheel through sunshine, storm, and cloud;
Thy wheel and thee we neither love nor hate.

'Turn, Fortune, turn thy wheel with smile or frown;
With that wild wheel we go not up or down;
Our hoard is little, but our hearts are great.

'Smile and we smile, the lords of many lands;
Frown and we smile, the lords of our own hands;
For man is man and master of his fate.

'Turn, turn thy wheel above the staring crowd;
Thy wheel and thou are shadows in the cloud;
Thy wheel and thee we neither love nor hate.'

'Hark, by the bird's song ye may learn the nest,'
Said Yniol; 'enter quickly.' Entering then,
Right o'er a mount of newly-fallen stones,
The dusky-raftered many-cobwebbed hall,
He found an ancient dame in dim brocade;
And near her, like a blossom vermeil-white,
That lightly breaks a faded flower-sheath,
Moved the fair Enid, all in faded silk,
Her daughter. In a moment thought Geraint,
'Here by God's rood is the one maid for me.'
But none spake word except the hoary Earl:
'Enid, the good knight's horse stands in the court;
Take him to stall, and give him corn, and then
Go to the town and buy us flesh and wine;
And we will make us merry as we may.
Our hoard is little, but our hearts are great.'

He spake: the Prince, as Enid past him, fain
To follow, strode a stride, but Yniol caught
His purple scarf, and held, and said, 'Forbear!
Rest! the good house, though ruined, O my son,

*359. ye*] *1873*; you *1859–70*. Likewise ll. 430, 698.

*360–8. Mabinogion*: 'And in the chamber he beheld an old decrepit woman, sitting on a cushion, with old, tattered garments of satin upon her; and it seemed to him that he had never seen a woman fairer than she must have been, when in the fulness of youth. And beside her was a maiden, upon whom were a vest and a veil, that were old, and beginning to be worn out. And truly, he never saw a maiden more full of comeliness, and grace, and beauty, than she.'

*368.* 'Rood (originally the same as "rod") is the old word for cross' (T.).

*375–81.* Not in *Mabinogion*.

Endures not that her guest should serve himself.'
And reverencing the custom of the house
Geraint, from utter courtesy, forbore.

So Enid took his charger to the stall;
And after went her way across the bridge,
And reached the town, and while the Prince and Earl
Yet spoke together, came again with one,
A youth, that following with a costrel bore
The means of goodly welcome, flesh and wine.
And Enid brought sweet cakes to make them cheer,
And in her veil enfolded, manchet bread.
And then, because their hall must also serve
For kitchen, boiled the flesh, and spread the board,
And stood behind, and waited on the three.
And seeing her so sweet and serviceable,
Geraint had longing in him evermore
To stoop and kiss the tender little thumb,
That crost the trencher as she laid it down:
But after all had eaten, then Geraint,
For now the wine made summer in his veins,
Let his eye rove in following, or rest
On Enid at her lowly handmaid-work,
Now here, now there, about the dusky hall;
Then suddenly addrest the hoary Earl:

'Fair Host and Earl, I pray your courtesy;
This sparrow-hawk, what is he? tell me of him.
His name? but no, good faith, I will not have it:
For if he be the knight whom late I saw
Ride into that new fortress by your town,
White from the mason's hand, then have I sworn
From his own lips to have it–I am Geraint
Of Devon–for this morning when the Queen
Sent her own maiden to demand the name,
His dwarf, a vicious under-shapen thing,
Struck at her with his whip, and she returned
Indignant to the Queen; and then I swore
That I would track this caitiff to his hold,

*386–9. Mabinogion*: 'And a youth with her, bearing on his back a costrel full of good purchased mead, and a quarter of a young bullock. And in the hands of the maiden was a quantity of white bread, and she had some manchet bread in her veil, and she came into the chamber.' *costrel*: 'a bottle with ear or ears, by which it could be hung from the waist (*costrer*, by the side), hence sometimes called "pilgrim's bottle"' (T.). *manchet bread*: 'little loaves or rolls made of fine wheat flour' (T.).

And fight and break his pride, and have it of him.
And all unarmed I rode, and thought to find
Arms in your town, where all the men are mad;
They take the rustic murmur of their bourg
For the great wave that echoes round the world;
They would not hear me speak: but if ye know
Where I can light on arms, or if yourself
Should have them, tell me, seeing I have sworn
That I will break his pride and learn his name,
Avenging this great insult done the Queen.'

Then cried Earl Yniol, 'Art thou he indeed,
Geraint, a name far-sounded among men
For noble deeds? and truly I, when first
I saw you moving by me on the bridge,
Felt ye were somewhat, yea, and by your state
And presence might have guessed you one of those
That eat in Arthur's hall at Camelot.
Nor speak I now from foolish flattery;
For this dear child hath often heard me praise
Your feats of arms, and often when I paused
Hath asked again, and ever loved to hear;
So grateful is the noise of noble deeds
To noble hearts who see but acts of wrong:
O never yet had woman such a pair
Of suitors as this maiden; first Limours,
A creature wholly given to brawls and wine,
Drunk even when he wooed; and be he dead
I know not, but he past to the wild land.
The second was your foe, the sparrow-hawk,
My curse, my nephew–I will not let his name
Slip from my lips if I can help it–he,
When I that knew him fierce and turbulent

*447ff.* H.T. comments: 'In the *Mabinogion* Earl Yniol is the wrong-doer, and has earned his reward; but the poet has made the story more interesting and more poetic by making the tale of wrong-doing a calumny on the part of the Earl's nephew.

'And when they had finished eating, Geraint talked with the hoary-headed man, and he asked him in the first place, to whom belonged the palace that he was in. "Truly", said he, "it was I that built it, and to me also belonged the city and the castle which thou sawest". "Alas!" said Geraint, "how is it that thou hast lost them now?" "I lost a great Earldom as well as these", said he, "and this is how I lost them. I had a nephew, the son of my brother, and I took his possessions to myself; and when he came to his

Refused her to him, then his pride awoke;
And since the proud man often is the mean,
He sowed a slander in the common ear,
Affirming that his father left him gold,
And in my charge, which was not rendered to him;
Bribed with large promises the men who served
About my person, the more easily
Because my means were somewhat broken into
Through open doors and hospitality;
Raised my own town against me in the night
Before my Enid's birthday, sacked my house;
From mine own earldom foully ousted me;
Built that new fort to overawe my friends,
For truly there are those who love me yet;
And keeps me in this ruinous castle here,
Where doubtless he would put me soon to death,
But that his pride too much despises me:
And I myself sometimes despise myself;
For I have let men be, and have their way;
Am much too gentle, have not used my power:
Nor know I whether I be very base
Or very manful, whether very wise
Or very foolish; only this I know,
That whatsoever evil happen to me,
I seem to suffer nothing heart or limb,
But can endure it all most patiently.'

'Well said, true heart,' replied Geraint, 'but arms,
That if the sparrow-hawk, this nephew, fight
In next day's tourney I may break his pride.'

And Yniol answered, 'Arms, indeed, but old
And rusty, old and rusty, Prince Geraint,
Are mine, and therefore at thine asking, thine.
But in this tournament can no man tilt,

strength, he demanded of me his property, but I withheld it from him. So he made war upon me, and wrested from me all that I possessed."'

In the Idyll, for the greater unity of the tale, the nephew and the knight of the Sparrow-hawk are one.'

*475*] *1870* ('*1869*'); That if, as I suppose, your nephew fights *1859–69*.

*479. thine . . . thine*] *1873*; your . . . yours *1859–70*.

*480–5. Mabinogion*: 'In the midst of a meadow which is here, two forks will be set up, and upon the two forks a silver rod, and upon the silver rod a Sparrow-Hawk . . . and no man can joust for the Sparrow-Hawk, except the lady he loves best be with him.'

Except the lady he loves best be there.
Two forks are fixt into the meadow ground,
And over these is placed a silver wand,
And over that a golden sparrow-hawk,
The prize of beauty for the fairest there.
And this, what knight soever be in field
Lays claim to for the lady at his side,
And tilts with my good nephew thereupon,
Who being apt at arms and big of bone
Has ever won it for the lady with him,
And toppling over all antagonism
Has earned himself the name of sparrow-hawk.
But thou, that hast no lady, canst not fight.'

To whom Geraint with eyes all bright replied,
Leaning a little toward him, 'Thy leave!
Let *me* lay lance in rest, O noble host,
For this dear child, because I never saw,
Though having seen all beauties of our time,
Nor can see elsewhere, anything so fair.
And if I fall her name will yet remain
Untarnished as before; but if I live,
So aid me Heaven when at mine uttermost,
As I will make her truly my true wife.'

Then, howsoever patient, Yniol's heart
Danced in his bosom, seeing better days.
And looking round he saw not Enid there,
(Who hearing her own name had stolen away)
But that old dame, to whom full tenderly
And folding all her hand in his he said,
'Mother, a maiden is a tender thing,
And best by her that bore her understood.
Go thou to rest, but ere thou go to rest
Tell her, and prove her heart toward the Prince.'

483. *placed*] *1873*; laid *1859–70*.
484. *a golden*] *1873*; is placed the *1859–70*.
493. *thou . . . hast . . . canst*] *1873*; you . . . have . . . cannot *1859–70*.
495. *Thy*] *1873*; Your *1859–70*. Likewise l. 780.
495–503. *Mabinogion*: 'And if . . . thou wilt permit me, Sir, to challenge for yonder maiden that is thy daughter, I will engage, if I escape from the tournament, to love the maiden as long as I live; and if I do not escape, she will remain unsullied as before.'
504–32. Not in *Mabinogion*.
507. *stolen*] *1873*; slipt *1859–70*.

So spake the kindly-hearted Earl, and she
With frequent smile and nod departing found,
Half disarrayed as to her rest, the girl;
Whom first she kissed on either cheek, and then
On either shining shoulder laid a hand,
And kept her off and gazed upon her face,
And told her all their converse in the hall,
Proving her heart: but never light and shade
Coursed one another more on open ground
Beneath a troubled heaven, than red and pale
Across the face of Enid hearing her;
While slowly falling as a scale that falls,
When weight is added only grain by grain,
Sank her sweet head upon her gentle breast;
Nor did she lift an eye nor speak a word,
Rapt in the fear and in the wonder of it;
So moving without answer to her rest
She found no rest, and ever failed to draw
The quiet night into her blood, but lay
Contemplating her own unworthiness;
And when the pale and bloodless east began
To quicken to the sun, arose, and raised
Her mother too, and hand in hand they moved
Down to the meadow where the jousts were held,
And waited there for Yniol and Geraint.

And thither came the twain, and when Geraint
Beheld her first in field, awaiting him,
He felt, were she the prize of bodily force,
Himself beyond the rest pushing could move
The chair of Idris. Yniol's rusted arms
Were on his princely person, but through these
Princelike his bearing shone; and errant knights
And ladies came, and by and by the town
Flowed in, and settling circled all the lists.
And there they fixt the forks into the ground,
And over these they placed the silver wand,
And over that the golden sparrow-hawk.
Then Yniol's nephew, after trumpet blown,

*531–2.* H.T. compares *Aeneid* iv 529–31: *neque umquam / solvitur in somnos, oculisve aut pectore noctem / accipit.* ('She never sinks to sleep, nor draws the night into eyes or heart.')

*543.* 'Idris was one of the three primitive Bards. Cader Idris, the noblest mountain next to Snowdon in N. Wales' (T.).

*549, 550. the*] *1873*; a *1859–70*.

Spake to the lady with him and proclaimed,
'Advance and take, as fairest of the fair,
What I these two years past have won for thee,
The prize of beauty.' Loudly spake the Prince,
'Forbear: there is a worthier,' and the knight
With some surprise and thrice as much disdain
Turned, and beheld the four, and all his face
Glowed like the heart of a great fire at Yule,
So burnt he was with passion, crying out,
'Do battle for it then,' no more; and thrice
They clashed together, and thrice they brake their spears.
Then each, dishorsed and drawing, lashed at each
So often and with such blows, that all the crowd
Wondered, and now and then from distant walls
There came a clapping as of phantom hands.
So twice they fought, and twice they breathed, and still
The dew of their great labour, and the blood
Of their strong bodies, flowing, drained their force.
But either's force was matched till Yniol's cry,
'Remember that great insult done the Queen,'
Increased Geraint's, who heaved his blade aloft,
And cracked the helmet through, and bit the bone,
And felled him, and set foot upon his breast,
And said, 'Thy name?' To whom the fallen man
Made answer, groaning, 'Edyrn, son of Nudd!
Ashamed am I that I should tell it thee.
My pride is broken: men have seen my fall.'
'Then, Edyrn, son of Nudd,' replied Geraint,
'These two things shalt thou do, or else thou diest.
First, thou thyself, with damsel and with dwarf,
Shalt ride to Arthur's court, and coming there,
Crave pardon for that insult done the Queen,
And shalt abide her judgment on it; next,
Thou shalt give back their earldom to thy kin.
These two things shalt thou do, or thou shalt die.'
And Edyrn answered, 'These things will I do,
For I have never yet been overthrown,

554. *What*] *1886*; For *1859–84*. *won*] *1886*; won it *1859–84*.
562–74. The combat is based closely on *Mabinogion*.
565–6. 'This is the echo of the sword-clash' (T.).
581. *with ... with*] *1873*; thy lady, and thy *1859–70*.
582. *coming*] *1873*; being *1859–70*.
584–5. This addition to *Mabinogion* was necessitated by T.'s changes.

And thou hast overthrown me, and my pride
Is broken down, for Enid sees my fall!'
And rising up, he rode to Arthur's court,
And there the Queen forgave him easily.
And being young, he changed and came to loathe
His crime of traitor, slowly drew himself
Bright from his old dark life, and fell at last
In the great battle fighting for the King.

But when the third day from the hunting-morn
Made a low splendour in the world, and wings
Moved in her ivy, Enid, for she lay
With her fair head in the dim-yellow light,
Among the dancing shadows of the birds,
Woke and bethought her of her promise given
No later than last eve to Prince Geraint–
So bent he seemed on going the third day,
He would not leave her, till her promise given–
To ride with him this morning to the court,
And there be made known to the stately Queen,
And there be wedded with all ceremony.
At this she cast her eyes upon her dress,
And thought it never yet had looked so mean.
For as a leaf in mid-November is
To what it was in mid-October, seemed
The dress that now she looked on to the dress
She looked on ere the coming of Geraint.
And still she looked, and still the terror grew
Of that strange bright and dreadful thing, a court,
All staring at her in her faded silk:
And softly to her own sweet heart she said:

*592–6. Mabinogion* later gives a detailed account of Edyrn's return to the court, which suggested T.'s handling of the close of *Geraint and Enid*.
*593. and . . . loathe*] *1870* ('*1869*'); himself, and grew *1859–69*.
*594–5*] *1870* ('*1869*');

To hate the sin that seemed so like his own
Of Modred, Arthur's nephew, and fell at last *1859–69*.

*609ff.* H.T. quotes *Mabinogion*: '"Where is the Earl Ynywl", said Geraint, "and his wife, and his daughter?". "They are in the chamber yonder", said the Earl's chamberlain, "arraying themselves in garments which the Earl has caused to be brought for them". "Let not the damsel array herself", said he, "except in her vest and her veil, until she come to the Court of Arthur, to be clad by Gwenhwyvar, in such garments as she may choose". So the maiden did not array herself.' From this point T. considerably expands, through to l. 826.

'This noble prince who won our earldom back,
So splendid in his acts and his attire,
Sweet heaven, how much I shall discredit him!
Would he could tarry with us here awhile,
But being so beholden to the Prince,
It were but little grace in any of us,
Bent as he seemed on going this third day,
To seek a second favour at his hands.
Yet if he could but tarry a day or two,
Myself would work eye dim, and finger lame,
Far liefer than so much discredit him.'

And Enid fell in longing for a dress
All branched and flowered with gold, a costly gift
Of her good mother, given her on the night
Before her birthday, three sad years ago,
That night of fire, when Edyrn sacked their house,
And scattered all they had to all the winds:
For while the mother showed it, and the two
Were turning and admiring it, the work
To both appeared so costly, rose a cry
That Edyrn's men were on them, and they fled
With little save the jewels they had on,
Which being sold and sold had bought them bread:
And Edyrn's men had caught them in their flight,
And placed them in this ruin; and she wished
The Prince had found her in her ancient home;
Then let her fancy flit across the past,
And roam the goodly places that she knew;
And last bethought her how she used to watch,
Near that old home, a pool of golden carp;
And one was patched and blurred and lustreless
Among his burnished brethren of the pool;
And half asleep she made comparison
Of that and these to her own faded self
And the gay court, and fell asleep again;
And dreamt herself was such a faded form
Among her burnished sisters of the pool;
But this was in the garden of a king;
And though she lay dark in the pool, she knew
That all was bright; that all about were birds
Of sunny plume in gilded trellis-work;
That all the turf was rich in plots that looked
Each like a garnet or a turkis in it;
And lords and ladies of the high court went
In silver tissue talking things of state;

And children of the King in cloth of gold
Glanced at the doors or gamboled down the walks;
And while she thought 'They will not see me,' came
A stately queen whose name was Guinevere,
And all the children in their cloth of gold
Ran to her, crying, 'If we have fish at all
Let them be gold; and charge the gardeners now
To pick the faded creature from the pool,
And cast it on the mixen that it die.'
And therewithal one came and seized on her,
And Enid started waking, with her heart
All overshadowed by the foolish dream,
And lo! it was her mother grasping her
To get her well awake; and in her hand
A suit of bright apparel, which she laid
Flat on the couch, and spoke exultingly:

'See here, my child, how fresh the colours look
How fast they hold like colours of a shell
That keeps the wear and polish of the wave.
Why not? It never yet was worn, I trow:
Look on it, child, and tell me if ye know it.'

And Enid looked, but all confused at first,
Could scarce divide it from her foolish dream:
Then suddenly she knew it and rejoiced,
And answered, 'Yea, I know it; your good gift,
So sadly lost on that unhappy night;
Your own good gift!' 'Yea, surely,' said the dame,
'And gladly given again this happy morn.
For when the jousts were ended yesterday,
Went Yniol through the town, and everywhere
He found the sack and plunder of our house
All scattered through the houses of the town;
And gave command that all which once was ours
Should now be ours again: and yester-eve,
While ye were talking sweetly with your Prince,
Came one with this and laid it in my hand,
For love or fear, or seeking favour of us,
Because we have our earldom back again.
And yester-eve I would not tell you of it,
But kept it for a sweet surprise at morn.
Yea, truly is it not a sweet surprise?
For I myself unwillingly have worn
My faded suit, as you, my child, have yours,

672. *mixen*: dung-hill.

And howsoever patient, Yniol his.
Ah, dear, he took me from a goodly house,
With store of rich apparel, sumptuous fare,
And page, and maid, and squire, and seneschal,
And pastime both of hawk and hound, and all
That appertains to noble maintenance.
Yea, and he brought me to a goodly house;
But since our fortune swerved from sun to shade,
And all through that young traitor, cruel need
Constrained us, but a better time has come;
So clothe yourself in this, that better fits
Our mended fortunes and a Prince's bride:
For though ye won the prize of fairest fair,
And though I heard him call you fairest fair,
Let never maiden think, however fair,
She is not fairer in new clothes than old.
And should some great court-lady say, the Prince
Hath picked a ragged-robin from the hedge,
And like a madman brought her to the court,
Then were ye shamed, and, worse, might shame the
Prince
To whom we are beholden; but I know,
When my dear child is set forth at her best,
That neither court nor country, though they sought
Through all the provinces like those of old
That lighted on Queen Esther, has her match.'

Here ceased the kindly mother out of breath;
And Enid listened brightening as she lay;
Then, as the white and glittering star of morn
Parts from a bank of snow, and by and by
Slips into golden cloud, the maiden rose,
And left her maiden couch, and robed herself,
Helped by the mother's careful hand and eye,
Without a mirror, in the gorgeous gown;
Who, after, turned her daughter round, and said,
She never yet had seen her half so fair;
And called her like that maiden in the tale,

*714. swerved*] *1882*; slipt *1859–81*.

*731. Esther* ii 3.

*742.* T. quotes from *Mabinogion*, 'The Tale of Math, son of Mathonwy': 'So they took the blossoms of the oak, and the blossoms of the broom, and the blossoms of the meadow-sweet, and produced from them a maiden, the fairest and most graceful that man ever saw. And they baptized her and gave her the name of Blodeuwedd' (flower-vision).

Whom Gwydion made by glamour out of flowers
And sweeter than the bride of Cassivelaun,
Flur, for whose love the Roman Cæsar first
Invaded Britain, 'But we beat him back,
As this great Prince invaded us, and we,
Not beat him back, but welcomed him with joy
And I can scarcely ride with you to court,
For old am I, and rough the ways and wild;
But Yniol goes, and I full oft shall dream
I see my princess as I see her now,
Clothed with my gift, and gay among the gay.'

But while the women thus rejoiced, Geraint
Woke where he slept in the high hall, and called
For Enid, and when Yniol made report
Of that good mother making Enid gay
In such apparel as might well beseem
His princess, or indeed the stately Queen,
He answered: 'Earl, entreat her by my love,
Albeit I give no reason but my wish,
That she ride with me in her faded silk.'
Yniol with that hard message went; it fell
Like flaws in summer laying lusty corn:
For Enid, all abashed she knew not why,
Dared not to glance at her good mother's face,
But silently, in all obedience,
Her mother silent too, nor helping her,
Laid from her limbs the costly-broidered gift,
And robed them in her ancient suit again,
And so descended. Never man rejoiced
More than Geraint to greet her thus attired;
And glancing all at once as keenly at her
As careful robins eye the delver's toil,
Made her cheek burn and either eyelid fall,
But rested with her sweet face satisfied;
Then seeing cloud upon the mother's brow,
Her by both hands he caught, and sweetly said,

*744*. H.T. comments: 'The love of a British maiden named Flur, who was betrothed to Cassivelaunus, according to the Welsh legend, led Caesar to invade Britain', from *Mabinogion*, 'Manawyddan the Son of Llyr'.
*764*. H.T. compares *Hamlet* V i 210: 'the winter's flaw'–gusts of wind.
*774*. Cp. *Early Spring* (1833) 11–12 (p. 497), which must modify H.T.'s note: 'This line was made one day while my father was digging . . . at Farringford.'

'O my new mother, be not wroth or grieved
At thy new son, for my petition to her.
When late I left Caerleon, our great Queen,
In words whose echo lasts, they were so sweet,
Made promise, that whatever bride I brought,
Herself would clothe her like the sun in Heaven.
Thereafter, when I reached this ruined hall,
Beholding one so bright in dark estate,
I vowed that could I gain her, our fair Queen,
No hand but hers, should make your Enid burst
Sunlike from cloud–and likewise thought perhaps,
That service done so graciously would bind
The two together; fain I would the two
Should love each other: how can Enid find
A nobler friend? Another thought was mine;
I came among you here so suddenly,
That though her gentle presence at the lists
Might well have served for proof that I was loved,
I doubted whether daughter's tenderness,
Or easy nature, might not let itself
Be moulded by your wishes for her weal;
Or whether some false sense in her own self
Of my contrasting brightness, overbore
Her fancy dwelling in this dusky hall;
And such a sense might make her long for court
And all its perilous glories: and I thought,
That could I someway prove such force in her
Linked with such love for me, that at a word
(No reason given her) she could cast aside
A splendour dear to women, new to her,
And therefore dearer; or if not so new,
Yet therefore tenfold dearer by the power
Of intermitted usage; then I felt
That I could rest, a rock in ebbs and flows,
Fixt on her faith. Now, therefore, I do rest,
A prophet certain of my prophecy,

785. *hall*] *1873*; hold *1859–70*.
787. *fair*] *1873*; kind *1859–70*.
791. *fain I would*] *1873*; for I wish *1859–70*.
792. *Should*] *1873*; To *1859–70*. *can*] *1873*; should *1859–70*.
793. *was mine*] *1873*; I had *1859–70*.
797. *daughter's*] *1873*; filial *1859–70*.
798. *might*] *1873*; did *1859–70*.
804. *perilous*] *1873*; dangerous *1859–70*.
811. *usage*] *1873*; custom *1859–70*.

That never shadow of mistrust can cross
Between us. Grant me pardon for my thoughts:
And for my strange petition I will make
Amends hereafter by some gaudy-day,
When your fair child shall wear your costly gift
Beside your own warm hearth, with, on her knees,
Who knows? another gift of the high God,
Which, maybe, shall have learned to lisp you thanks.'

He spoke: the mother smiled, but half in tears,
Then brought a mantle down and wrapt her in it,
And claspt and kissed her, and they rode away.

Now thrice that morning Guinevere had climbed
The giant tower, from whose high crest, they say,
Men saw the goodly hills of Somerset,
And white sails flying on the yellow sea;
But not to goodly hill or yellow sea
Looked the fair Queen, but up the vale of Usk,
By the flat meadow, till she saw them come;
And then descending met them at the gates,
Embraced her with all welcome as a friend,
And did her honour as the Prince's bride,
And clothed her for her bridals like the sun;
And all that week was old Caerleon gay,
For by the hands of Dubric, the high saint,
They twain were wedded with all ceremony.

And this was on the last year's Whitsuntide.
But Enid ever kept the faded silk,
Remembering how first he came on her,
Drest in that dress, and how he loved her in it,
And all her foolish fears about the dress,
And all his journey toward her, as himself
Had told her, and their coming to the court.

And now this morning when he said to her,
'Put on your worst and meanest dress,' she found
And took it, and arrayed herself therein.

*818. gaudy-day*: 'Holiday – now only used of special feast-days at the Universities' (H.T.).

*826.* In *Mabinogion*, Guinevere places a watch on the ramparts.

*836. Mabinogion*: 'And the choicest of all Gwenhwyvar's apparel was given to the maiden.'

# 467 Geraint and Enid

*Enid* was privately printed in 1857. Published *1859*, the second half of *Enid*. The title *Enid* was expanded to *Geraint and Enid* in *1870* ('*1869*'); the poem was divided into two parts in *1873*; and the final titles given in *1886*. See headnote to *The Marriage of Geraint* (p. 1525). 'The sin of Lancelot and Guinevere begins to breed, even among those who would "rather die than doubt", despair and want of trust in God and man' (H.T.).

O purblind race of miserable men,
How many among us at this very hour
Do forge a life-long trouble for ourselves,
By taking true for false, or false for true;
Here, through the feeble twilight of this world
Groping, how many, until we pass and reach
That other, where we see as we are seen!

So fared it with Geraint, who issuing forth
That morning, when they both had got to horse,
Perhaps because he loved her passionately,
And felt that tempest brooding round his heart,
Which, if he spoke at all, would break perforce
Upon a head so dear in thunder, said:
'Not at my side. I charge thee ride before,
Ever a good way on before; and this
I charge thee, on thy duty as a wife,
Whatever happens, not to speak to me,
No, not a word!' and Enid was aghast;
And forth they rode, but scarce three paces on,
When crying out, 'Effeminate as I am,

¶467. *1.* H.T. compares Lucretius ii 14: *O miseras hominum mentes, O pectora caeca.* ('O pitiable minds of men, O blind intelligences!') R. W. King, *RES* n.s. xiii (1962) 439, suggests that T.'s opening adapts that of *Paradiso* xi.

*7. 1 Corinthians* xiii 12: 'Now we see through a glass, darkly; but then face to face: now I know in part; but then shall I know even as also I am known.'

*14. thee*] *1873*; you *1859–70*. Likewise ll. 16, 230, 231, 347.

*14–18. Mabinogion*: 'And he desired Enid to mount her horse, and to ride forward, and to keep a long way before him. "And whatever thou mayest see, and whatever thou mayest hear concerning me", said he, "do thou not turn back. And unless I speak unto thee, say not thou one word either".'

*16. thy*] *1873*; your *1859–70*.

*20–6.* Not in *Mabinogion*.

I will not fight my way with gilded arms,
All shall be iron;' he loosed a mighty purse,
Hung at his belt, and hurled it toward the squire.
So the last sight that Enid had of home
Was all the marble threshold flashing, strown
With gold and scattered coinage, and the squire
Chafing his shoulder: then he cried again,
'To the wilds!' and Enid leading down the tracks
Through which he bad her lead him on, they past
The marches, and by bandit-haunted holds,
Gray swamps and pools, waste places of the hern,
And wildernesses, perilous paths, they rode:
Round was their pace at first, but slackened soon:
A stranger meeting them had surely thought
They rode so slowly and they looked so pale,
That each had suffered some exceeding wrong.
For he was ever saying to himself,
'O I that wasted time to tend upon her,
To compass her with sweet observances,
To dress her beautifully and keep her true'–
And there he broke the sentence in his heart
Abruptly, as a man upon his tongue
May break it, when his passion masters him.
And she was ever praying the sweet heavens
To save her dear lord whole from any wound.
And ever in her mind she cast about
For that unnoticed failing in herself,
Which made him look so cloudy and so cold;
Till the great plover's human whistle amazed
Her heart, and glancing round the waste she feared
In every wavering brake an ambuscade.
Then thought again, 'If there be such in me,
I might amend it by the grace of Heaven,
If he would only speak and tell me of it.'

But when the fourth part of the day was gone,
Then Enid was aware of three tall knights

*30. Mabinogion*: 'And he did not choose the pleasantest and most frequented road, but that which was the wildest and most beset by thieves.'

*31.* Adapted from an unpublished stanza of *Come not, when I am dead* (p. 700).

*35–54.* Not in *Mabinogion*.

*51.* Suggesting Juvenal x 19–21.

*55–100.* Based closely on *Mabinogion*, where however there are four attackers.

On horseback, wholly armed, behind a rock
In shadow, waiting for them, caitiffs all;
And heard one crying to his fellow, 'Look,
Here comes a laggard hanging down his head,
Who seems no bolder than a beaten hound;
Come, we will slay him and will have his horse
And armour, and his damsel shall be ours.'

Then Enid pondered in her heart, and said:
'I will go back a little to my lord,
And I will tell him all their caitiff talk;
For, be he wroth even to slaying me,
Far liefer by his dear hand had I die,
Than that my lord should suffer loss or shame.'

Then she went back some paces of return,
Met his full frown timidly firm, and said;
'My lord, I saw three bandits by the rock
Waiting to fall on you, and heard them boast
That they would slay you, and possess your horse
And armour, and your damsel should be theirs.'

He made a wrathful answer: 'Did I wish
Your warning or your silence? one command
I laid upon you, not to speak to me,
And thus ye keep it! Well then, look–for now,
Whether ye wish me victory or defeat,
Long for my life, or hunger for my death,
Yourself shall see my vigour is not lost.'

Then Enid waited pale and sorrowful,
And down upon him bare the bandit three.
And at the midmost charging, Prince Geraint
Drave the long spear a cubit through his breast
And out beyond; and then against his brace
Of comrades, each of whom had broken on him
A lance that splintered like an icicle,
Swung from his brand a windy buffet out
Once, twice, to right, to left, and stunned the twain
Or slew them, and dismounting like a man
That skins the wild beast after slaying him,
Stript from the three dead wolves of woman born
The three gay suits of armour which they wore,
And let the bodies lie, but bound the suits
Of armour on their horses, each on each,

77. *warning . . . silence*] *1862*; *transposed 1859–61.*
79, 80. *ye*] *1873*; you *1859–70*. Likewise ll. 310, 321, 339, 625.

And tied the bridle-reins of all the three
Together, and said to her, 'Drive them on
Before you;' and she drove them through the waste.

He followed nearer; ruth began to work
Against his anger in him, while he watched
The being he loved best in all the world,
With difficulty in mild obedience
Driving them on: he fain had spoken to her,
And loosed in words of sudden fire the wrath
And smouldered wrong that burnt him all within;
But evermore it seemed an easier thing
At once without remorse to strike her dead,
Than to cry 'Halt,' and to her own bright face
Accuse her of the least immodesty:
And thus tongue-tied, it made him wroth the more
That she *could* speak whom his own ear had heard
Call herself false: and suffering thus he made
Minutes an age: but in scarce longer time
Than at Caerleon the full-tided Usk,
Before he turn to fall seaward again,
Pauses, did Enid, keeping watch, behold
In the first shallow shade of a deep wood,
Before a gloom of stubborn-shafted oaks,
Three other horsemen waiting, wholly armed,
Whereof one seemed far larger than her lord,
And shook her pulses, crying, 'Look, a prize!
Three horses and three goodly suits of arms,
And all in charge of whom? a girl: set on.'
'Nay,' said the second, 'yonder comes a knight.'
The third, 'A craven; how he hangs his head.'
The giant answered merrily, 'Yea, but one?
Wait here, and when he passes fall upon him.'

And Enid pondered in her heart and said,
'I will abide the coming of my lord,
And I will tell him all their villainy.
My lord is weary with the fight before,
And they will fall upon him unawares.
I needs must disobey him for his good;
How should I dare obey him to his harm?
Needs must I speak, and though he kill me for it,
I save a life dearer to me than mine.'

*101–15.* Not in *Mabinogion.*
*118–45.* Based closely on *Mabinogion.*

And she abode his coming, and said to him
With timid firmness, 'Have I leave to speak?'
He said, 'Ye take it, speaking,' and she spoke.

'There lurk three villains yonder in the wood,
And each of them is wholly armed, and one
Is larger-limbed than you are, and they say
That they will fall upon you while ye pass.'

To which he flung a wrathful answer back:
'And if there were an hundred in the wood,
And every man were larger-limbed than I,
And all at once should sally out upon me,
I swear it would not ruffle me so much
As you that not obey me. Stand aside,
And if I fall, cleave to the better man.'

And Enid stood aside to wait the event,
Not dare to watch the combat, only breathe
Short fits of prayer, at every stroke a breath.
And he, she dreaded most, bare down upon him.
Aimed at the helm, his lance erred; but Geraint's,
A little in the late encounter strained,
Struck through the bulky bandit's corselet home,
And then brake short, and down his enemy rolled,
And there lay still; as he that tells the tale
Saw once a great piece of a promontory,
That had a sapling growing on it, slide
From the long shore-cliff's windy walls to the beach,
And there lie still, and yet the sapling grew:
So lay the man transfixt. His craven pair
Of comrades making slowlier at the Prince,
When now they saw their bulwark fallen, stood;
On whom the victor, to confound them more,
Spurred with his terrible war-cry; for as one,
That listens near a torrent mountain-brook,
All through the crash of the near cataract hears
The drumming thunder of the huger fall
At distance, were the soldiers wont to hear

*141. Ye*] *1870* ('*1869*'); You *1859–69*. Likewise in ll. 145, 221, 262, 412, 415, 417, 425, 445, 488, 547, 550, 670, 676, 681, 813, 887, 895, 896.
*146–52.* Not in *Mabinogion*.
*153–78.* Expanding *Mabinogion*.
*163. slide*] *1873*; slip *1859–70*.
*170–75.* 'A memory of what I heard near Festiniog, but the scenery imagined is vaster' (T.).

His voice in battle, and be kindled by it,
And foemen scared, like that false pair who turned
Flying, but, overtaken, died the death
Themselves had wrought on many an innocent.

Thereon Geraint, dismounting, picked the lance
That pleased him best, and drew from those dead wolves
Their three gay suits of armour, each from each,
And bound them on their horses, each on each,
And tied the bridle-reins of all the three
Together, and said to her, 'Drive them on
Before you,' and she drove them through the wood.

He followed nearer still: the pain she had
To keep them in the wild ways of the wood,
Two sets of three laden with jingling arms,
Together, served a little to disedge
The sharpness of that pain about her heart:
And they themselves, like creatures gently born
But into bad hands fallen, and now so long
By bandits groomed, pricked their light ears, and felt
Her low firm voice and tender government.

So through the green gloom of the wood they past,
And issuing under open heavens beheld
A little town with towers, upon a rock,
And close beneath, a meadow gemlike chased
In the brown wild, and mowers mowing in it:
And down a rocky pathway from the place
There came a fair-haired youth, that in his hand
Bare victual for the mowers: and Geraint
Had ruth again on Enid looking pale:
Then, moving downward to the meadow ground,
He, when the fair-haired youth came by him, said,
'Friend, let her eat; the damsel is so faint.'
'Yea, willingly,' replied the youth; 'and thou,

*186–94.* Not in *Mabinogion*, which has a further episode with five attackers, thus making Enid drive twelve horses in all.

*195–9. Mabinogion*: 'And early in the day they left the wood, and they came to an open country, with meadows on one hand, and mowers mowing the meadows.'

*198. chased*: set like a jewel.

*201–31.* Based on *Mabinogion.*

*207. thou*] *1873*; you *1859–70*. Likewise ll. 228, 491.

My lord, eat also, though the fare is coarse,
And only meet for mowers;' then set down
His basket, and dismounting on the sward
They let the horses graze, and ate themselves.
And Enid took a little delicately,
Less having stomach for it than desire
To close with her lord's pleasure; but Geraint
Ate all the mowers' victual unawares,
And when he found all empty, was amazed;
And 'Boy,' said he, 'I have eaten all, but take
A horse and arms for guerdon; choose the best.'
He, reddening in extremity of delight,
'My lord, you overpay me fifty-fold.'
'Ye will be all the wealthier,' cried the Prince.
'I take it as free gift, then,' said the boy,
'Not guerdon; for myself can easily,
While your good damsel rests, return, and fetch
Fresh victual for these mowers of our Earl;
For these are his, and all the field is his,
And I myself am his; and I will tell him
How great a man thou art: he loves to know
When men of mark are in his territory:
And he will have thee to his palace here,
And serve thee costlier than with mowers' fare.'

Then said Geraint, 'I wish no better fare:
I never ate with angrier appetite
Than when I left your mowers dinnerless.
And into no Earl's palace will I go.
I know, God knows, too much of palaces!
And if he want me, let him come to me.
But hire us some fair chamber for the night,
And stalling for the horses, and return
With victual for these men, and let us know.'

'Yea, my kind lord,' said the glad youth, and went,
Held his head high, and thought himself a knight,
And up the rocky pathway disappeared,
Leading the horse, and they were left alone.

But when the Prince had brought his errant eyes
Home from the rock, sideways he let them glance

*228. art*] *1873*; are *1859–70*.
*245–60*. Not in *Mabinogion*.

At Enid, where she droopt: his own false doom,
That shadow of mistrust should never cross
Betwixt them, came upon him, and he sighed;
Then with another humorous ruth remarked
The lusty mowers labouring dinnerless,
And watched the sun blaze on the turning scythe,
And after nodded sleepily in the heat.
But she, remembering her old ruined hall,
And all the windy clamour of the daws
About her hollow turret, plucked the grass
There growing longest by the meadow's edge,
And into many a listless annulet,
Now over, now beneath her marriage ring,
Wove and unwove it, till the boy returned
And told them of a chamber, and they went;
Where, after saying to her, 'If ye will,
Call for the woman of the house,' to which
She answered, 'Thanks, my lord;' the two remained
Apart by all the chamber's width, and mute
As creatures voiceless through the fault of birth,
Or two wild men supporters of a shield,
Painted, who stare at open space, nor glance
The one at other, parted by the shield.

On a sudden, many a voice along the street,
And heel against the pavement echoing, burst
Their drowse; and either started while the door,
Pushed from without, drave backward to the wall,
And midmost of a rout of roisterers,
Femininely fair and dissolutely pale,
Her suitor in old years before Geraint,
Entered, the wild lord of the place, Limours.
He moving up with pliant courtliness,
Greeted Geraint full face, but stealthily,
In the mid-warmth of welcome and graspt hand,
Found Enid with the corner of his eye,
And knew her sitting sad and solitary.
Then cried Geraint for wine and goodly cheer
To feed the sudden guest, and sumptuously
According to his fashion, bad the host

*247. doom*: 'judgment' (T.).
*276–7.* In *Mabinogion*, the Earl is not her previous suitor, though 'he set all his thoughts and his affections upon her'. G. C. Macaulay points out that T. transposes the names of Earl Limours and Earl Doorm; on a possibly intended Doorm / doom resonance, see J. M. Gray, *VP* iv (1966) 131–2.

Call in what men soever were his friends,
And feast with these in honour of their Earl;
'And care not for the cost; the cost is mine.'

And wine and food were brought, and Earl Limours
Drank till he jested with all ease, and told
Free tales, and took the word and played upon it,
And made it of two colours; for his talk,
When wine and free companions kindled him,
Was wont to glance and sparkle like a gem
Of fifty facets; thus he moved the Prince
To laughter and his comrades to applause.
Then, when the Prince was merry, asked Limours,
'Your leave, my lord, to cross the room, and speak
To your good damsel there who sits apart,
And seems so lonely?' 'My free leave,' he said;
'Get her to speak: she doth not speak to me.'
Then rose Limours, and looking at his feet,
Like him who tries the bridge he fears may fail,
Crost and came near, lifted adoring eyes,
Bowed at her side and uttered whisperingly:

'Enid, the pilot star of my lone life,
Enid, my early and my only love,
Enid, the loss of whom hath turned me wild–
What chance is this? how is it I see you here?
Ye are in my power at last, are in my power.
Yet fear me not: I call mine own self wild,
But keep a touch of sweet civility
Here in the heart of waste and wilderness.
I thought, but that your father came between,
In former days you saw me favourably.
And if it were so do not keep it back:
Make me a little happier: let me know it:
Owe you me nothing for a life half-lost?
Yea, yea, the whole dear debt of all you are.
And, Enid, you and he, I see with joy,
Ye sit apart, you do not speak to him,
You come with no attendance, page or maid,
To serve you–doth he love you as of old?
For, call it lovers' quarrels, yet I know

*306–47.* Expanding and modifying *Mabinogion*.
*308. hath*] *1873*; has *1859–70*.
*320. see*] *1873*; see it *1859–70*.
*323. doth*] *1873*; does *1859–70*.

Though men may bicker with the things they love,
They would not make them laughable in all eyes,
Not while they loved them; and your wretched dress,
A wretched insult on you, dumbly speaks
Your story, that this man loves you no more.
Your beauty is no beauty to him now:
A common chance–right well I know it–palled–
For I know men: nor will ye win him back,
For the man's love once gone never returns.
But here is one who loves you as of old;
With more exceeding passion than of old:
Good, speak the word: my followers ring him round:
He sits unarmed; I hold a finger up;
They understand: nay; I do not mean blood:
Nor need ye look so scared at what I say:
My malice is no deeper than a moat,
No stronger than a wall: there is the keep;
He shall not cross us more; speak but the word:
Or speak it not; but then by Him that made me
The one true lover whom you ever owned,
I will make use of all the power I have.
O pardon me! the madness of that hour,
When first I parted from thee, moves me yet.'

At this the tender sound of his own voice
And sweet self-pity, or the fancy of it,
Made his eye moist; but Enid feared his eyes,
Moist as they were, wine-heated from the feast;
And answered with such craft as women use,
Guilty or guiltless, to stave off a chance
That breaks upon them perilously, and said:

'Earl, if you love me as in former years,
And do not practise on me, come with morn,
And snatch me from him as by violence;
Leave me tonight: I am weary to the death.'

Low at leave-taking, with his brandished plume
Brushing his instep, bowed the all-amorous Earl,

332. *ye*] *1870*; you *1859–69*.
338. *nay*] *1873*; no *1859–70*.
344. *whom*] *1873*; which *1859–70*. *owned*] *1873*; had *1859–70*.
348–51. Not in *Mabinogion*.
352. *Mabinogion*: 'and she considered that it was advisable to encourage him in his request.'
359–64. Not in *Mabinogion*.

And the stout Prince bad him a loud good-night.
He moving homeward babbled to his men,
How Enid never loved a man but him,
Nor cared a broken egg-shell for her lord.

But Enid left alone with Prince Geraint,
Debating his command of silence given,
And that she now perforce must violate it,
Held commune with herself, and while she held
He fell asleep, and Enid had no heart
To wake him, but hung o'er him, wholly pleased
To find him yet unwounded after fight,
And hear him breathing low and equally.
Anon she rose, and stepping lightly, heaped
The pieces of his armour in one place,
All to be there against a sudden need;
Then dozed awhile herself, but overtoiled
By that day's grief and travel, evermore
Seemed catching at a rootless thorn, and then
Went slipping down horrible precipices,
And strongly striking out her limbs awoke;
Then thought she heard the wild Earl at the door,
With all his rout of random followers,
Sound on a dreadful trumpet, summoning her;
Which was the red cock shouting to the light,
As the gray dawn stole o'er the dewy world,
And glimmered on his armour in the room.
And once again she rose to look at it,
But touched it unawares: jangling, the casque
Fell, and he started up and stared at her.
Then breaking his command of silence given,
She told him all that Earl Limours had said,
Except the passage that he loved her not;
Nor left untold the craft herself had used;
But ended with apology so sweet,
Low-spoken, and of so few words, and seemed
So justified by that necessity,
That though he thought 'was it for him she wept
In Devon?' he but gave a wrathful groan,
Saying, 'Your sweet faces make good fellows fools
And traitors. Call the host and bid him bring
Charger and palfrey.' So she glided out
Among the heavy breathings of the house,

373–5. *Mabinogion*: 'At midnight she arose, and placed all Geraint's armour together, so that it might be ready to put on.' T.'s ll. 387–9 are his addition.

And like a household Spirit at the walls
Beat, till she woke the sleepers, and returned:
Then tending her rough lord, though all unasked,
In silence, did him service as a squire;
Till issuing armed he found the host and cried,
'Thy reckoning, friend?' and ere he learnt it, 'Take
Five horses and their armours;' and the host
Suddenly honest, answered in amaze,
'My lord, I scarce have spent the worth of one!'
'Ye will be all the wealthier,' said the Prince,
And then to Enid, 'Forward! and today
I charge you, Enid, more especially,
What thing soever ye may hear, or see,
Or fancy (though I count it of small use
To charge you) that ye speak not but obey.'

And Enid answered, 'Yea, my lord, I know
Your wish, and would obey; but riding first,
I hear the violent threats you do not hear,
I see the danger which you cannot see:
Then not to give you warning, that seems hard;
Almost beyond me: yet I would obey.'

'Yea so,' said he, 'do it: be not too wise;
Seeing that ye are wedded to a man,
Not all mismated with a yawning clown,
But one with arms to guard his head and yours,
With eyes to find you out however far,
And ears to hear you even in his dreams.'

With that he turned and looked as keenly at her
As careful robins eye the delver's toil;
And that within her, which a wanton fool,
Or hasty judger would have called her guilt,
Made her cheek burn and either eyelid fall.
And Geraint looked and was not satisfied.

Then forward by a way which, beaten broad,
Led from the territory of false Limours
To the waste earldom of another earl,
Doorm, whom his shaking vassals called the Bull,
Went Enid with her sullen follower on.
Once she looked back, and when she saw him ride
More near by many a rood than yestermorn,

*409.* In *Mabinogion*, the remaining eleven.
*418–35.* Not in *Mabinogion*.
*426. all*] *1873*; quite *1859–70*.

It wellnigh made her cheerful; till Geraint
Waving an angry hand as who should say
'Ye watch me,' saddened all her heart again.
But while the sun yet beat a dewy blade,
The sound of many a heavily-galloping hoof
Smote on her ear, and turning round she saw
Dust, and the points of lances bicker in it.
Then not to disobey her lord's behest,
And yet to give him warning, for he rode
As if he heard not, moving back she held
Her finger up, and pointed to the dust.
At which the warrior in his obstinacy,
Because she kept the letter of his word,
Was in a manner pleased, and turning, stood.
And in the moment after, wild Limours,
Borne on a black horse, like a thunder-cloud
Whose skirts are loosened by the breaking storm,
Half ridden off with by the thing he rode,
And all in passion uttering a dry shriek,
Dashed on Geraint, who closed with him, and bore
Down by the length of lance and arm beyond
The crupper, and so left him stunned or dead,
And overthrew the next that followed him,
And blindly rushed on all the rout behind.
But at the flash and motion of the man
They vanished panic-stricken, like a shoal
Of darting fish, that on a summer morn
Adown the crystal dykes at Camelot
Come slipping o'er their shadows on the sand,
But if a man who stands upon the brink
But lift a shining hand against the sun,
There is not left the twinkle of a fin
Betwixt the cressy islets white in flower;
So, scared but at the motion of the man,
Fled all the boon companions of the Earl,
And left him lying in the public way;
So vanish friendships only made in wine.

Then like a stormy sunlight smiled Geraint,
Who saw the chargers of the two that fell
Start from their fallen lords, and wildly fly,

*450–6*. In *Mabinogion*, Enid simply speaks.

*458*. 'The horse's mane is compared to the skirts of the rain-cloud' (T.).

*467–79*. Not in *Mabinogion*, where Geraint has hereafter various combats, is wounded, meets Arthur, rests and is healed.

*475*. T. had 'cressy islet' in a revision of *The Miller's Daughter* 48 ^ 9.

Mixt with the flyers. 'Horse and man,' he said,
'All of one mind and all right-honest friends!
Not a hoof left: and I methinks till now
Was honest–paid with horses and with arms;
I cannot steal or plunder, no nor beg:
And so what say ye, shall we strip him there
Your lover? has your palfrey heart enough
To bear his armour? shall we fast, or dine?
No?–then do thou, being right honest, pray
That we may meet the horsemen of Earl Doorm,
I too would still be honest.' Thus he said:
And sadly gazing on her bridle-reins,
And answering not one word, she led the way.

But as a man to whom a dreadful loss
Falls in a far land and he knows it not,
But coming back he learns it, and the loss
So pains him that he sickens nigh to death;
So fared it with Geraint, who being pricked
In combat with the follower of Limours,
Bled underneath his armour secretly,
And so rode on, nor told his gentle wife
What ailed him, hardly knowing it himself,
Till his eye darkened and his helmet wagged;
And at a sudden swerving of the road,
Though happily down on a bank of grass,
The Prince, without a word, from his horse fell.

And Enid heard the clashing of his fall,
Suddenly came, and at his side all pale
Dismounting, loosed the fastenings of his arms,
Nor let her true hand falter, nor blue eye
Moisten, till she had lighted on his wound,
And tearing off her veil of faded silk
Had bared her forehead to the blistering sun,
And swathed the hurt that drained her dear lord's life.
Then after all was done that hand could do,
She rested, and her desolation came
Upon her, and she wept beside the way.

*490.* 'Shall we go hungry, or shall we take his spoils and pay for our dinner with them?' (T.).

*491.* 'Enid shrinks from taking anything from her old lover' (T.).

*500.* In *Mabinogion*, Geraint is wounded by giants, and faints. Doorm (there named Limours) comes upon Enid who is with a damsel whose husband has been killed by the giants.

And many past, but none regarded her,
For in that realm of lawless turbulence,
A woman weeping for her murdered mate
Was cared as much for as a summer shower:
One took him for a victim of Earl Doorm,
Nor dared to waste a perilous pity on him:
Another hurrying past, a man-at-arms,
Rode on a mission to the bandit Earl;
Half whistling and half singing a coarse song,
He drove the dust against her veilless eyes:
Another, flying from the wrath of Doorm
Before an ever-fancied arrow, made
The long way smoke beneath him in his fear;
At which her palfrey whinnying lifted heel,
And scoured into the coppices and was lost,
While the great charger stood, grieved like a man.

But at the point of noon the huge Earl Doorm,
Broad-faced with under-fringe of russet beard,
Bound on a foray, rolling eyes of prey,
Came riding with a hundred lances up;
But ere he came, like one that hails a ship,
Cried out with a big voice, 'What, is he dead?'
'No, no, not dead!' she answered in all haste.
'Would some of your kind people take him up,
And bear him hence out of this cruel sun?
Most sure am I, quite sure, he is not dead.'

Then said Earl Doorm: 'Well, if he be not dead,
Why wail ye for him thus? ye seem a child.
And be he dead, I count you for a fool;
Your wailing will not quicken him: dead or not,
Ye mar a comely face with idiot tears.
Yet, since the face *is* comely–some of you,
Here, take him up, and bear him to our hall:
An if he live, we will have him of our band;
And if he die, why earth has earth enough
To hide him. See ye take the charger too,
A noble one.'
He spake, and past away,
But left two brawny spearmen, who advanced,
Each growling like a dog, when his good bone

*542.* In *Mabinogion*, Enid thought Geraint was dead, and it was the Earl who 'thought that there still remained some life in Geraint'.
*546–78.* Expanding *Mabinogion*.

Seems to be plucked at by the village boys
Who love to vex him eating, and he fears
To lose his bone, and lays his foot upon it,
Gnawing and growling: so the ruffians growled,
Fearing to lose, and all for a dead man,
Their chance of booty from the morning's raid,
Yet raised and laid him on a litter-bier,
Such as they brought upon their forays out
For those that might be wounded; laid him on it
All in the hollow of his shield, and took
And bore him to the naked hall of Doorm,
(His gentle charger following him unled)
And cast him and the bier in which he lay
Down on an oaken settle in the hall,
And then departed, hot in haste to join
Their luckier mates, but growling as before,
And cursing their lost time, and the dead man,
And their own Earl, and their own souls, and her.
They might as well have blest her: she was deaf
To blessing or to cursing save from one.

So for long hours sat Enid by her lord,
There in the naked hall, propping his head,
And chafing his pale hands, and calling to him.
Till at the last he wakened from his swoon,
And found his own dear bride propping his head,
And chafing his faint hands, and calling to him;
And felt the warm tears falling on his face;
And said to his own heart, 'She weeps for me:'
And yet lay still, and feigned himself as dead,
That he might prove her to the uttermost,
And say to his own heart, 'She weeps for me.'

But in the falling afternoon returned
The huge Earl Doorm with plunder to the hall.
His lusty spearmen followed him with noise:
Each hurling down a heap of things that rang
Against the pavement, cast his lance aside,
And doffed his helm: and then there fluttered in,
Half-bold, half-frighted, with dilated eyes,
A tribe of women, dressed in many hues,

568. *Mabinogion*: 'He had him carried with him in the hollow of his shield.'

579–607. Not in *Mabinogion*.

582. *Till*] *1873*; And *1859–70*.

And mingled with the spearmen: and Earl Doorm
Struck with a knife's haft hard against the board,
And called for flesh and wine to feed his spears.
And men brought in whole hogs and quarter beeves,
And all the hall was dim with steam of flesh:
And none spake word, but all sat down at once,
And ate with tumult in the naked hall,
Feeding like horses when you hear them feed;
Till Enid shrank far back into herself,
To shun the wild ways of the lawless tribe.
But when Earl Doorm had eaten all he would,
He rolled his eyes about the hall, and found
A damsel drooping in a corner of it.
Then he remembered her, and how she wept;
And out of her there came a power upon him;
And rising on the sudden he said, 'Eat!
I never yet beheld a thing so pale.
God's curse, it makes me mad to see you weep.
Eat! Look yourself. Good luck had your good man,
For were I dead who is it would weep for me?
Sweet lady, never since I first drew breath
Have I beheld a lily like yourself.
And so there lived some colour in your cheek,
There is not one among my gentlewomen
Were fit to wear your slipper for a glove.
But listen to me, and by me be ruled,
And I will do the thing I have not done,
For ye shall share my earldom with me, girl,
And we will live like two birds in one nest,
And I will fetch you forage from all fields,
For I compel all creatures to my will.'

He spoke: the brawny spearman let his cheek
Bulge with the unswallowed piece, and turning stared;
While some, whose souls the old serpent long had drawn
Down, as the worm draws in the withered leaf
And makes it earth, hissed each at other's ear
What shall not be recorded–women they,
Women, or what had been those gracious things,

*617–717.* T. greatly expands this, though the main events are in *Mabinogion* (the brief commands to eat, drink, and change apparel, and the blow).

*631. old serpent*: *Revelation* xii 9.

*632.* 'My father would quote this simile as good' (H.T.).

But now desired the humbling of their best,
Yea, would have helped him to it: and all at once
They hated her, who took no thought of them,
But answered in low voice, her meek head yet
Drooping, 'I pray you of your courtesy,
He being as he is, to let me be.'

She spake so low he hardly heard her speak,
But like a mighty patron, satisfied
With what himself had done so graciously,
Assumed that she had thanked him, adding, 'Yea,
Eat and be glad, for I account you mine.'

She answered meekly, 'How should I be glad
Henceforth in all the world at anything,
Until my lord arise and look upon me?'

Here the huge Earl cried out upon her talk,
As all but empty heart and weariness
And sickly nothing; suddenly seized on her,
And bare her by main violence to the board,
And thrust the dish before her, crying, 'Eat.'

'No, no,' said Enid, vext, 'I will not eat
Till yonder man upon the bier arise,
And eat with me.' 'Drink, then,' he answered. 'Here!'
(And filled a horn with wine and held it to her,)
'Lo! I, myself, when flushed with fight, or hot,
God's curse, with anger–often I myself,
Before I well have drunken, scarce can eat:
Drink therefore and the wine will change your will.'

'Not so,' she cried, 'by Heaven, I will not drink
Till my dear lord arise and bid me do it,
And drink with me; and if he rise no more,
I will not look at wine until I die.'

At this he turned all red and paced his hall,
Now gnawed his under, now his upper lip,
And coming up close to her, said at last:
'Girl, for I see ye scorn my courtesies,
Take warning: yonder man is surely dead;
And I compel all creatures to my will.
Not eat nor drink? And wherefore wail for one,
Who put your beauty to this flout and scorn
By dressing it in rags? Amazed am I,
Beholding how ye butt against my wish,

That I forbear you thus: cross me no more.
At least put off to please me this poor gown,
This silken rag, this beggar-woman's weed:
I love that beauty should go beautifully:
For see ye not my gentlewomen here,
How gay, how suited to the house of one
Who loves that beauty should go beautifully?
Rise therefore; robe yourself in this: obey.'

He spoke, and one among his gentlewomen
Displayed a splendid silk of foreign loom,
Where like a shoaling sea the lovely blue
Played into green, and thicker down the front
With jewels than the sward with drops of dew,
When all night long a cloud clings to the hill,
And with the dawn ascending lets the day
Strike where it clung: so thickly shone the gems.

But Enid answered, harder to be moved
Than hardest tyrants in their day of power,
With life-long injuries burning unavenged,
And now their hour has come; and Enid said:

'In this poor gown my dear lord found me first,
And loved me serving in my father's hall:
In this poor gown I rode with him to court,
And there the Queen arrayed me like the sun:
In this poor gown he bad me clothe myself,
When now we rode upon this fatal quest
Of honour, where no honour can be gained:
And this poor gown I will not cast aside
Until himself arise a living man,
And bid me cast it. I have griefs enough:
Pray you be gentle, pray you let me be:
I never loved, can never love but him:
Yea, God, I pray you of your gentleness,
He being as he is, to let me be.'

Then strode the brute Earl up and down his hall,
And took his russet beard between his teeth;
Last, coming up quite close, and in his mood
Crying, 'I count it of no more avail,

679. *weed*: 'garment' (T.).

688–9. 'I made these lines on the High Down one morning at Freshwater' (T.).

694. 'The worst tyrants are those who have long been tyrannised over, if they have tyrann ous natures' (T.).

Dame, to be gentle than ungentle with you;
Take my salute,' unknightly with flat hand,
However lightly, smote her on the cheek.

Then Enid, in her utter helplessness,
And since she thought, 'He had not dared to do it,
Except he surely knew my lord was dead,'
Sent forth a sudden sharp and bitter cry,
As of a wild thing taken in the trap,
Which sees the trapper coming through the wood.

This heard Geraint, and grasping at his sword,
(It lay beside him in the hollow shield),
Made but a single bound, and with a sweep of it
Shore through the swarthy neck, and like a ball
The russet-bearded head rolled on the floor.
So died Earl Doorm by him he counted dead.
And all the men and women in the hall
Rose when they saw the dead man rise, and fled
Yelling as from a spectre, and the two
Were left alone together, and he said:

'Enid, I have used you worse than that dead man;
Done you more wrong: we both have undergone
That trouble which has left me thrice your own;
Henceforward I will rather die than doubt.
And here I lay this penance on myself,
Not, though mine own ears heard you yestermorn–
You thought me sleeping, but I heard you say,
I heard you say, that you were no true wife:
I swear I will not ask your meaning in it:
I do believe yourself against yourself,
And will henceforward rather die than doubt.'

And Enid could not say one tender word,
She felt so blunt and stupid at the heart:
She only prayed him, 'Fly, they will return
And slay you; fly, your charger is without,
My palfrey lost.' 'Then, Enid, shall you ride
Behind me.' 'Yea,' said Enid, 'let us go.'
And moving out they found the stately horse,
Who now no more a vassal to the thief,

*718–21.* As in *Mabinogion*.

*727–8.* In *Mabinogion*, merely 'he clove him in twain'.

*734–44.* *Mabinogion*: 'He was grieved for two causes; one was, to see that Enid had lost her colour and her wonted aspect; and the other, to know that she was in the right.'

But free to stretch his limbs in lawful fight,
Neighed with all gladness as they came, and stooped
With a low whinny toward the pair: and she
Kissed the white star upon his noble front,
Glad also; then Geraint upon the horse
Mounted, and reached a hand, and on his foot
She set her own and climbed; he turned his face
And kissed her climbing, and she cast her arms
About him, and at once they rode away.

And never yet, since high in Paradise
O'er the four rivers the first roses blew,
Came purer pleasure unto mortal kind
Than lived through her, who in that perilous hour
Put hand to hand beneath her husband's heart,
And felt him hers again: she did not weep,
But o'er her meek eyes came a happy mist
Like that which kept the heart of Eden green
Before the useful trouble of the rain:
Yet not so misty were her meek blue eyes
As not to see before them on the path,
Right in the gateway of the bandit hold,
A knight of Arthur's court, who laid his lance
In rest, and made as if to fall upon him.
Then, fearing for his hurt and loss of blood,
She, with her mind all full of what had chanced,
Shrieked to the stranger 'Slay not a dead man!'
'The voice of Enid,' said the knight; but she,
Beholding it was Edyrn son of Nudd,
Was moved so much the more, and shrieked again,
'O cousin, slay not him who gave you life.'
And Edyrn moving frankly forward spake:
'My lord Geraint, I greet you with all love;
I took you for a bandit knight of Doorm;
And fear not, Enid, I should fall upon him,
Who love you, Prince, with something of the love
Wherewith we love the Heaven that chastens us.
For once, when I was up so high in pride
That I was halfway down the slope to Hell,
By overthrowing me you threw me higher.
Now, made a knight of Arthur's Table Round,
And since I knew this Earl, when I myself
Was half a bandit in my lawless hour,

*762ff.* In *Mabinogion* there are other adventures, but the rest of T.'s poem is his own.

I come the mouthpiece of our King to Doorm
(The King is close behind me) bidding him
Disband himself, and scatter all his powers,
Submit, and hear the judgment of the King.'

'He hears the judgment of the King of kings,'
Cried the wan Prince; 'and lo, the powers of Doorm
Are scattered,' and he pointed to the field,
Where, huddled here and there on mound and knoll,
Were men and women staring and aghast,
While some yet fled; and then he plainlier told
How the huge Earl lay slain within his hall.
But when the knight besought him, 'Follow me,
Prince, to the camp, and in the King's own ear
Speak what has chanced; ye surely have endured
Strange chances here alone;' that other flushed,
And hung his head, and halted in reply,
Fearing the mild face of the blameless King,
And after madness acted question asked:
Till Edyrn crying, 'If ye will not go
To Arthur, then will Arthur come to you,'
'Enough,' he said, 'I follow,' and they went.
But Enid in their going had two fears,
One from the bandit scattered in the field,
And one from Edyrn. Every now and then,
When Edyrn reined his charger at her side,
She shrank a little. In a hollow land,
From which old fires have broken, men may fear
Fresh fire and ruin. He, perceiving, said:

'Fair and dear cousin, you that most had cause
To fear me, fear no longer, I am changed.
Yourself were first the blameless cause to make
My nature's prideful sparkle in the blood
Break into furious flame; being repulsed
By Yniol and yourself, I schemed and wrought
Until I overturned him; then set up
(With one main purpose ever at my heart)
My haughty jousts, and took a paramour;
Did her mock-honour as the fairest fair,
And, toppling over all antagonism,
So waxed in pride, that I believed myself
Unconquerable, for I was wellnigh mad:
And, but for my main purpose in these jousts,
I should have slain your father, seized yourself.

I lived in hope that sometime you would come
To these my lists with him whom best you loved;
And there, poor cousin, with your meek blue eyes,
The truest eyes that ever answered Heaven,
Behold me overturn and trample on him.
Then, had you cried, or knelt, or prayed to me,
I should not less have killed him. And you came,–
But once you came,–and with your own true eyes
Beheld the man you loved (I speak as one
Speaks of a service done him) overthrow
My proud self, and my purpose three years old,
And set his foot upon me, and give me life.
There was I broken down; there was I saved:
Though thence I rode all-shamed, hating the life
He gave me, meaning to be rid of it.
And all the penance the Queen laid upon me
Was but to rest awhile within her court;
Where first as sullen as a beast new-caged,
And waiting to be treated like a wolf,
Because I knew my deeds were known, I found,
Instead of scornful pity or pure scorn,
Such fine reserve and noble reticence,
Manners so kind, yet stately, such a grace
Of tenderest courtesy, that I began
To glance behind me at my former life,
And find that it had been the wolf's indeed:
And oft I talked with Dubric, the high saint,
Who, with mild heat of holy oratory,
Subdued me somewhat to that gentleness,
Which, when it weds with manhood, makes a man.
And you were often there about the Queen,
But saw me not, or marked not if you saw;
Nor did I care or dare to speak with you,
But kept myself aloof till I was changed;
And fear not, cousin; I am changed indeed.'

He spoke, and Enid easily believed,
Like simple noble natures, credulous
Of what they long for, good in friend or foe,
There most in those who most have done them ill.
And when they reached the camp the King himself
Advanced to greet them, and beholding her
Though pale, yet happy, asked her not a word,
But went apart with Edyrn, whom he held
In converse for a little, and returned,
And, gravely smiling, lifted her from horse,

And kissed her with all pureness, brother-like,
And showed an empty tent allotted her,
And glancing for a minute, till he saw her
Pass into it, turned to the Prince, and said:

'Prince, when of late ye prayed me for my leave
To move to your own land, and there defend
Your marches, I was pricked with some reproof,
As one that let foul wrong stagnate and be,
By having looked too much through alien eyes,
And wrought too long with delegated hands,
Not used mine own: but now behold me come
To cleanse this common sewer of all my realm,
With Edyrn and with others: have ye looked
At Edyrn? have ye seen how nobly changed?
This work of his is great and wonderful.
His very face with change of heart is changed.
The world will not believe a man repents:
And this wise world of ours is mainly right.
Full seldom doth a man repent, or use
Both grace and will to pick the vicious quitch
Of blood and custom wholly out of him,
And make all clean, and plant himself afresh.
Edyrn has done it, weeding all his heart
As I will weed this land before I go.
I, therefore, made him of our Table Round,
Not rashly, but have proved him everyway
One of our noblest, our most valorous,
Sanest and most obedient: and indeed
This work of Edyrn wrought upon himself
After a life of violence, seems to me
A thousand-fold more great and wonderful
Than if some knight of mine, risking his life,
My subject with my subjects under him,
Should make an onslaught single on a realm
Of robbers, though he slew them one by one,
And were himself nigh wounded to the death.'

So spake the King; low bowed the Prince, and felt
His work was neither great nor wonderful,
And past to Enid's tent; and thither came
The King's own leech to look into his hurt;
And Enid tended on him there; and there
Her constant motion round him, and the breath

*901. doth*] *1873*; *does 1859–70.*

Of her sweet tendance hovering over him,
Filled all the genial courses of his blood
With deeper and with ever deeper love,
As the south-west that blowing Bala lake
Fills all the sacred Dee. So past the days.

But while Geraint lay healing of his hurt,
The blameless King went forth and cast his eyes
On each of all whom Uther left in charge
Long since, to guard the justice of the King:
He looked and found them wanting; and as now
Men weed the white horse on the Berkshire hills
To keep him bright and clean as heretofore,
He rooted out the slothful officer
Or guilty, which for bribe had winked at wrong,
And in their chairs set up a stronger race
With hearts and hands, and sent a thousand men
To till the wastes, and moving everywhere
Cleared the dark places and let in the law,
And broke the bandit holds and cleansed the land.

Then, when Geraint was whole again, they past
With Arthur to Caerleon upon Usk.
There the great Queen once more embraced her friend,
And clothed her in apparel like the day.
And though Geraint could never take again
That comfort from their converse which he took
Before the Queen's fair name was breathed upon,
He rested well content that all was well.
Thence after tarrying for a space they rode,
And fifty knights rode with them to the shores
Of Severn, and they past to their own land.
And there he kept the justice of the King
So vigorously yet mildly, that all hearts
Applauded, and the spiteful whisper died:
And being ever foremost in the chase,
And victor at the tilt and tournament,
They called him the great Prince and man of men.

*929.* T. compares *Lycidas* 55: 'Where Deva spreads her wisard stream'.

*932. each . . . whom*] *1870* ('*1869*'); whom his father *1859–69*.

*935.* 'The white horse near Wantage on the Berkshire hills which commemorates the victory at Ashdown of the English under Alfred over the Danes (871). The white horse was the emblem of the English or Saxons, as the raven was of the Danes, and as the dragon was of the Britons' (T.).

But Enid, whom her ladies loved to call
Enid the Fair, a grateful people named
Enid the Good; and in their halls arose
The cry of children, Enids and Geraints
Of times to be; nor did he doubt her more,
But rested in her fëalty, till he crowned
A happy life with a fair death, and fell
Against the heathen of the Northern Sea
In battle, fighting for the blameless King.

# 468 Balin and Balan

Published *1885*. H.T. comments: 'Partly founded on Book II of Malory, written mostly at Aldworth, soon after *Gareth and Lynette* [completed 1872] . . . The story of the poem is largely original. "Loyal natures are wrought to anger and madness against the world".' Written 1872–4 (according to *CT*, pp. 402, 484). Apart from the final fight between Balin and Balan, T. takes very little from Malory; the theme of Guinevere's guilt and the appearance by Vivien are additions. The poem was to lead into *Merlin and Vivien*; in *H.MS*, T. incorporated an account by Vivien at court (*Cornhill* cliii (1936) 552–3):

'I bring thee here a message from the dead'.
And therewithal shewing Sir Balan's hair,
'Know ye not this? not so, belike; but this
A most strange red, is easier known'. The Queen
Took the dead hair and slightly shuddering asked
'Sir Balin's? is he slain?' 'Yea, noble Queen,
Likewise his brother, Balan: for they fought,
Not knowing–some misprision of their shields–
I know not what. I found them side by side
And wounded to the death, unlaced their helms,
And gave them air and water, held their heads,
Wept with them; and thy Balin joyed my heart
Calling thee stainless wife and perfect Queen,
Heaven's white earth-angel; then they bade me clip
One tress from either head and bring it thee,
Proof that my message is not feigned; and prayed
King Arthur would despatch some holy man,
As these had lain together in one womb,
To give them burial in a single grave–

*967*. H.T. quotes, from the notes to *Mabinogion*, Llywarch Hen's elegy on Geraint's death in the battle of Llongborth. Mrs Patmore, by request, sent a copy of the elegy to T. in Nov. 1857 (Patmore, *Memoir* (1900) ii 308).

Sent their last blessings to their King and thee,
And therewithal their dying word, that thou,
For that good service I had done thy knights,
Wouldst yield me shelter for mine innocency'.
To whom the Queen made answer, 'We must hear
Thy story further; thou shalt bide the while.
I know no more of thee than that thy tale
Hath chilled me to the heart. Ghastly mischance,
Enough to make all childless motherhood
Fain so to bide for ever. Where do they lie?'
And Vivien's voice was broken answering her.
'Dead in a nameless corner of the woods,
Each locked in either's arms. I know the place,
But scarce can word it plain for thee to know'.
'And therefore damsel shalt thou ride at once
With Arthur's knights and guide them through the woods.
Thy wish, and these dead men's, if such were theirs,
Must bide mine answer till we meet again.'
After, when Vivien on returning came
To Guinevere and spake 'I saw the twain
Buried, and wept above their woodland grave.
But grant me now my wish and theirs', . . .

For T.'s prose draft from Malory, see *Eversley* v 425–32 (*Mem.* ii 134–41).

Pellam the King, who held and lost with Lot
In that first war, and had his realm restored
But rendered tributary, failed of late
To send his tribute; wherefore Arthur called
His treasurer, one of many years, and spake,
'Go thou with him and him and bring it to us,
Lest we should set one truer on his throne.
Man's word is God in man.'
His Baron said
'We go but harken: there be two strange knights
Who sit near Camelot at a fountain-side,
A mile beneath the forest, challenging
And overthrowing every knight who comes.
Wilt thou I undertake them as we pass,
And send them to thee?'
Arthur laughed upon him.
'Old friend, too old to be so young, depart,
Delay not thou for aught, but let them sit,
Until they find a lustier than themselves.'

So these departed. Early, one fair dawn,
The light-winged spirit of his youth returned

On Arthur's heart; he armed himself and went,
So coming to the fountain-side beheld
Balin and Balan sitting statuelike,
Brethren, to right and left the spring, that down,
From underneath a plume of lady-fern,
Sang, and the sand danced at the bottom of it.
And on the right of Balin Balin's horse
Was fast beside an alder, on the left
Of Balan Balan's near a poplartree.
'Fair Sirs,' said Arthur, 'wherefore sit ye here?'
Balin and Balan answered 'For the sake
Of glory; we be mightier men than all
In Arthur's court; that also have we proved;
For whatsoever knight against us came
Or I or he have easily overthrown.'
'I too,' said Arthur, 'am of Arthur's hall,
But rather proven in his Paynim wars
Than famous jousts; but see, or proven or not,
Whether me likewise ye can overthrow.'
And Arthur lightly smote the brethren down,
And lightly so returned, and no man knew.

Then Balin rose, and Balan, and beside
The carolling water set themselves again,
And spake no word until the shadow turned;
When from the fringe of coppice round them burst
A spangled pursuivant, and crying 'Sirs,
Rise, follow! ye be sent for by the King,'
They followed; whom when Arthur seeing asked
'Tell me your names; why sat ye by the well?'
Balin the stillness of a minute broke
Saying 'An unmelodious name to thee,
Balin, "the Savage"–that addition thine–
My brother and my better, this man here,
Balan. I smote upon the naked skull
A thrall of thine in open hall, my hand
Was gauntleted, half slew him; for I heard
He had spoken evil of me; thy just wrath
Sent me a three-years' exile from thine eyes.

¶468. *23–5.* Cp. Robert Bloomfield's *Rosy Hannah* (*Rural Tales*, 1801, *Lincoln*), which begins: 'A spring, o'erhung with many a flower, / The grey sand dancing in its bed.' Also Coleridge, *Inscription for a Fountain*: 'Nor ever cease / Yon tiny cone of sand its soundless dance, / Which at the bottom . . . dances still.' 'Suggested by a spring which rises near the house at Aldworth' (H.T.).

I have not lived my life delightsomely:
For I that did that violence to thy thrall,
Had often wrought some fury on myself,
Saving for Balan: those three kingless years
Have past–were wormwood-bitter to me. King,
Methought that if we sat beside the well,
And hurled to ground what knight soever spurred
Against us, thou would'st take me gladlier back,
And make, as ten-times worthier to be thine
Than twenty Balins, Balan knight. I have said.
Not so–not all. A man of thine today
Abashed us both, and brake my boast. Thy will?'
Said Arthur 'Thou hast ever spoken truth;
Thy too fierce manhood would not let thee lie.
Rise, my true knight. As children learn, be thou
Wiser for falling! walk with me, and move
To music with thine Order and the King.
Thy chair, a grief to all the brethren, stands
Vacant, but thou retake it, mine again!'

Thereafter, when Sir Balin entered hall,
The Lost one Found was greeted as in Heaven
With joy that blazed itself in woodland wealth
Of leaf, and gayest garlandage of flowers,
Along the walls and down the board; they sat,
And cup clashed cup; they drank and some one sang,
Sweet-voiced, a song of welcome, whereupon
Their common shout in chorus, mounting, made
Those banners of twelve battles overhead
Stir, as they stirred of old, when Arthur's host
Proclaimed him Victor, and the day was won.

Then Balan added to their Order lived
A wealthier life than heretofore with these
And Balin, till their embassage returned.

'Sir King' they brought report 'we hardly found,
So bushed about it is with gloom, the hall
Of him to whom ye sent us, Pellam, once
A Christless foe of thine as ever dashed
Horse against horse; but seeing that thy realm
Hath prospered in the name of Christ, the King
Took, as in rival heat, to holy things;
And finds himself descended from the Saint
Arimathæan Joseph; him who first
Brought the great faith to Britain over seas;
He boasts his life as purer than thine own;

Eats scarce enow to keep his pulse abeat;
Hath pushed aside his faithful wife, nor lets
Or dame or damsel enter at his gates
Lest he should be polluted. This gray King
Showed us a shrine wherein were wonders–yea–
Rich arks with priceless bones of martyrdom,
Thorns of the crown and shivers of the cross,
And therewithal (for thus he told us) brought
By holy Joseph hither, that same spear
Wherewith the Roman pierced the side of Christ.
He much amazed us; after, when we sought
The tribute, answered "I have quite foregone
All matters of this world: Garlon, mine heir,
Of him demand it," which this Garlon gave
With much ado, railing at thine and thee.

'But when we left, in those deep woods we found
A knight of thine spear-stricken from behind,
Dead, whom we buried; more than one of us
Cried out on Garlon, but a woodman there
Reported of some demon in the woods
Was once a man, who driven by evil tongues
From all his fellows, lived alone, and came
To learn black magic, and to hate his kind
With such a hate, that when he died, his soul
Became a Fiend, which, as the man in life
Was wounded by blind tongues he saw not whence,
Strikes from behind. This woodman showed the cave
From which he sallies, and wherein he dwelt.
We saw the hoof-print of a horse, no more.'

Then Arthur, 'Let who goes before me, see
He do not fall behind me: foully slain
And villainously! who will hunt for me
This demon of the woods?' Said Balan, 'I'!
So claimed the quest and rode away, but first,
Embracing Balin, 'Good my brother, hear!
Let not thy moods prevail, when I am gone
Who used to lay them! hold them outer fiends,
Who leap at thee to tear thee; shake them aside,
Dreams ruling when wit sleeps! yea, but to dream
That any of these would wrong thee, wrongs thyself.
Witness their flowery welcome. Bound are they
To speak no evil. Truly save for fears,

*126–8.* 'Symbolic of slander' (H.T.).

My fears for thee, so rich a fellowship
Would make me wholly blest: thou one of them,
Be one indeed: consider them, and all
Their bearing in their common bond of love,
No more of hatred than in Heaven itself,
No more of jealousy than in Paradise.'

So Balan warned, and went; Balin remained:
Who—for but three brief moons had glanced away
From being knighted till he smote the thrall,
And faded from the presence into years
Of exile—now would strictlier set himself
To learn what Arthur meant by courtesy,
Manhood, and knighthood; wherefore hovered round
Lancelot, but when he marked his high sweet smile
In passing, and a transitory word
Make knight or churl or child or damsel seem
From being smiled at happier in themselves—
Sighed, as a boy lame-born beneath a height,
That glooms his valley, sighs to see the peak
Sun-flushed, or touch at night the northern star;
For one from out his village lately climbed
And brought report of azure lands and fair,
Far seen to left and right; and he himself
Hath hardly scaled with help a hundred feet
Up from the base: so Balin marvelling oft
How far beyond him Lancelot seemed to move,
Groaned, and at times would mutter, 'These be gifts,
Born with the blood, not learnable, divine,
Beyond *my* reach. Well had I foughten—well—
In those fierce wars, struck hard—and had I crowned
With my slain self the heaps of whom I slew—
So—better!—But this worship of the Queen,
That honour too wherein she holds him—this,
This was the sunshine that hath given the man
A growth, a name that branches o'er the rest,
And strength against all odds, and what the King
So prizes—overprizes—gentleness.
Her likewise would I worship an I might.
I never can be close with her, as he
That brought her hither. Shall I pray the King
To let me bear some token of his Queen
Whereon to gaze, remembering her—forget
My heats and violences? live afresh?
What, if the Queen disdained to grant it! nay
Being so stately-gentle, would she make

My darkness blackness? and with how sweet grace
She greeted my return! Bold will I be–
Some goodly cognizance of Guinevere,
In lieu of this rough beast upon my shield,
Langued gules, and toothed with grinning savagery.'

And Arthur, when Sir Balin sought him, said
'What wilt thou bear?' Balin was bold, and asked
To bear her own crown-royal upon shield,
Whereat she smiled and turned her to the King,
Who answered 'Thou shalt put the crown to use.
The crown is but the shadow of the King,
And this a shadow's shadow, let him have it,
So this will help him of his violences!'
'No shadow' said Sir Balin 'O my Queen,
But light to me! no shadow, O my King,
But golden earnest of a gentler life!'

So Balin bare the crown, and all the knights
Approved him, and the Queen, and all the world
Made music, and he felt his being move
In music with his Order, and the King.

The nightingale, full-toned in middle May,
Hath ever and anon a note so thin
It seems another voice in other groves;
Thus, after some quick burst of sudden wrath,
The music in him seemed to change, and grow
Faint and far-off.
And once he saw the thrall
His passion half had gauntleted to death,
That causer of his banishment and shame,
Smile at him, as he deemed, presumptuously:
His arm half rose to strike again, but fell:
The memory of that cognizance on shield
Weighted it down, but in himself he moaned:

'Too high this mount of Camelot for me:
These high-set courtesies are not for me.
Shall I not rather prove the worse for these?
Fierier and stormier from restraining, break
Into some madness even before the Queen?'

Thus, as a hearth lit in a mountain home,
And glancing on the window, when the gloom

193. *Langued gules*: 'red-tongued – language of heraldry' (H.T.).
226–9. 'Suggested by what he often saw from his own study at Aldworth' (H.T.).

Of twilight deepens round it, seems a flame
That rages in the woodland far below,
So when his moods were darkened, court and King
And all the kindly warmth of Arthur's hall
Shadowed an angry distance: yet he strove
To learn the graces of their Table, fought
Hard with himself, and seemed at length in peace.

Then chanced, one morning, that Sir Balin sat
Close-bowered in that garden nigh the hall.
A walk of roses ran from door to door;
A walk of lilies crost it to the bower:
And down that range of roses the great Queen
Came with slow steps, the morning on her face;
And all in shadow from the counter door
Sir Lancelot as to meet her, then at once,
As if he saw not, glanced aside, and paced
The long white walk of lilies toward the bower.
Followed the Queen; Sir Balin heard her 'Prince,
Art thou so little loyal to thy Queen,
As pass without good morrow to thy Queen?'
To whom Sir Lancelot with his eyes on earth,
'Fain would I still be loyal to the Queen.'
'Yea so' she said 'but so to pass me by–
So loyal scarce is loyal to thyself,
Whom all men rate the king of courtesy.
Let be: ye stand, fair lord, as in a dream.'

Then Lancelot with his hand among the flowers
'Yea–for a dream. Last night methought I saw
That maiden Saint who stands with lily in hand
In yonder shrine. All round her prest the dark,
And all the light upon her silver face
Flowed from the spiritual lily that she held.
Lo! these her emblems drew mine eyes–away:
For see, how perfect-pure! As light a flush
As hardly tints the blossom of the quince
Would mar their charm of stainless maidenhood.'

'Sweeter to me' she said 'this garden rose
Deep-hued and many-folded! sweeter still
The wild-wood hyacinth and the bloom of May.
Prince, we have ridden before among the flowers
In those fair days–not all as cool as these,
Though season-earlier. Art thou sad? or sick?
Our noble King will send thee his own leech–
Sick? or for any matter angered at me?'

Then Lancelot lifted his large eyes; they dwelt
Deep-tranced on hers, and could not fall: her hue
Changed at his gaze: so turning side by side
They past, and Balin started from his bower.

'Queen? subject? but I see not what I see.
Damsel and lover? hear not what I hear.
My father hath begotten me in his wrath.
I suffer from the things before me, know,
Learn nothing; am not worthy to be knight;
A churl, a clown!' and in him gloom on gloom
Deepened: he sharply caught his lance and shield,
Nor stayed to crave permission of the King,
But, mad for strange adventure, dashed away.

He took the selfsame track as Balan, saw
The fountain where they sat together, sighed
'Was I not better there with him?' and rode
The skyless woods, but under open blue
Came on the hoarhead woodman at a bough
Wearily hewing. 'Churl, thine axe!' he cried,
Descended, and disjointed it at a blow:
To whom the woodman uttered wonderingly
'Lord, thou couldst lay the Devil of these woods
If arm of flesh could lay him.' Balin cried
'Him, or the viler devil who plays his part,
To lay that devil would lay the Devil in me.'
'Nay' said the churl, 'our devil is a truth,
I saw the flash of him but yestereven.
And some *do* say that our Sir Garlon too
Hath learned black magic, and to ride unseen.
Look to the cave.' But Balin answered him
'Old fabler, these be fancies of the churl,
Look to thy woodcraft,' and so leaving him,
Now with slack rein and careless of himself,
Now with dug spur and raving at himself,
Now with droopt brow down the long glades he rode;
So marked not on his right a cavern-chasm
Yawn over darkness, where, nor far within,
The whole day died, but, dying, gleamed on rocks
Roof-pendent, sharp; and others from the floor,
Tusklike, arising, made that mouth of night
Whereout the Demon issued up from Hell.
He marked not this, but blind and deaf to all
Save that chained rage, which ever yelpt within,
Past eastward from the falling sun. At once

He felt the hollow-beaten mosses thud
And tremble, and then the shadow of a spear,
Shot from behind him, ran along the ground.
Sideways he started from the path, and saw,
With pointed lance as if to pierce, a shape,
A light of armour by him flash, and pass
And vanish in the woods; and followed this,
But all so blind in rage that unawares
He burst his lance against a forest bough,
Dishorsed himself, and rose again, and fled
Far, till the castle of a King, the hall
Of Pellam, lichen-bearded, grayly draped
With streaming grass, appeared, low-built but strong;
The ruinous donjon as a knoll of moss,
The battlement overtopt with ivytods,
A home of bats, in every tower an owl.

Then spake the men of Pellam crying 'Lord,
Why wear ye this crown-royal upon shield?'
Said Balin 'For the fairest and the best
Of ladies living gave me this to bear.'
So stalled his horse, and strode across the court,
But found the greetings both of knight and King
Faint in the low dark hall of banquet: leaves
Laid their green faces flat against the panes,
Sprays grated, and the cankered boughs without
Whined in the wood; for all was hushed within,
Till when at feast Sir Garlon likewise asked
'Why wear ye that crown-royal?' Balin said
'The Queen we worship, Lancelot, I, and all,
As fairest, best and purest, granted me
To bear it!' Such a sound (for Arthur's knights
Were hated strangers in the hall) as makes
The white swan-mother, sitting, when she hears
A strange knee rustle through her secret reeds,
Made Garlon, hissing; then he sourly smiled.
'Fairest I grant her: I have seen; but best,
Best, purest? *thou* from Arthur's hall, and yet
So simple! hast thou eyes, or if, are these
So far besotted that they fail to see
This fair wife-worship cloaks a secret shame?
Truly, ye men of Arthur be but babes.'

A goblet on the board by Balin, bossed
With holy Joseph's legend, on his right

*357–62*. 'The goblet is embossed with scenes from the story of Joseph of

Stood, all of massiest bronze: one side had sea
And ship and sail and angels blowing on it:
And one was rough with wattling, and the walls
Of that low church he built at Glastonbury.
This Balin graspt, but while in act to hurl,
Through memory of that token on the shield
Relaxed his hold: 'I will be gentle' he thought
'And passing gentle' caught his hand away,
Then fiercely to Sir Garlon 'Eyes have I
That saw today the shadow of a spear,
Shot from behind me, run along the ground;
Eyes too that long have watched how Lancelot draws
From homage to the best and purest, might,
Name, manhood, and a grace, but scantly thine,
Who, sitting in thine own hall, canst endure
To mouth so huge a foulness–to thy guest,
Me, me of Arthur's Table. Felon talk!
Let be! no more!'
But not the less by night
The scorn of Garlon, poisoning all his rest,
Stung him in dreams. At length, and dim through leaves
Blinkt the white morn, sprays grated, and old boughs
Whined in the wood. He rose, descended, met
The scorner in the castle court, and fain,
For hate and loathing, would have past him by;
But when Sir Garlon uttered mocking-wise;
'What, wear ye still that same crown-scandalous?'
His countenance blackened, and his forehead veins
Bloated, and branched; and tearing out of sheath
The brand, Sir Balin with a fiery 'Ha!
So thou be shadow, here I make thee ghost,'
Hard upon helm smote him, and the blade flew
Splintering in six, and clinkt upon the stones.
Then Garlon, reeling slowly backward, fell,
And Balin by the banneret of his helm
Dragged him, and struck, but from the castle a cry

Arimathea, his voyage, and the wattle-built church he raised at Glastonbury. King Pellam represents the type of asceticism and superstition' (H.T.).

*361. wattling, and the walls*] *1886*; pole and scaffoldage *1885*.

*380–420.* Picked out by T. as 'a passage of rapid blank verse (where the pauses are light, and the accentuated syllables under the average – some being short in quantity, and the narrative brief and animated)'.

Sounded across the court, and–men-at-arms,
A score with pointed lances, making at him–
He dashed the pummel at the foremost face,
Beneath a low door dipt, and made his feet
Wings through a glimmering gallery, till he marked
The portal of King Pellam's chapel wide
And inward to the wall; he stept behind;
Thence in a moment heard them pass like wolves
Howling; but while he stared about the shrine,
In which he scarce could spy the Christ for Saints,
Beheld before a golden altar lie
The longest lance his eyes had ever seen,
Point-painted red; and seizing thereupon
Pushed through an open casement down, leaned on it,
Leapt in a semicircle, and lit on earth;
Then hand at ear, and harkening from what side
The blindfold rummage buried in the walls
Might echo, ran the counter path, and found
His charger, mounted on him and away.
An arrow whizzed to the right, one to the left,
One overhead; and Pellam's feeble cry
'Stay, stay him! he defileth heavenly things
With earthly uses'–made him quickly dive
Beneath the boughs, and race through many a mile
Of dense and open, till his goodly horse,
Arising wearily at a fallen oak,
Stumbled headlong, and cast him face to ground.

Half-wroth he had not ended, but all glad,

*402ff.* Altogether modifying Malory ii 15–16: 'And when Balin was weaponless, he came into a chamber for to seek some weapon, and so from chamber to chamber, and no weapon could he find; and always king Pellam followed him, and at the last he entered into a chamber that was marvellously well dight and richly, and a bed arrayed with cloth of gold, the richest that might be thought, and one lying therein, and thereby stood a table of clean gold, with four pillars of silver that bear up the table, and upon the table stood a marvellous spear, strangely wrought. And when Balin saw the spear, he gat it in his hand, and turned him to king Pellam, and smote him passingly sore with that spear, that king Pellam fell down in a swoon; and therewith the castle rove and walls break, and fell to the earth, and Balin fell down, so that he might not stir hand nor foot: and so the most part of the castle that was fallen down, through that dolorous stroke, lay upon king Pellam and Balin three days . . . And that was the same spear that Longius smote our Lord to the heart; and king Pellam was nigh of Joseph's kin.'

Knightlike, to find his charger yet unlamed,
Sir Balin drew the shield from off his neck,
Stared at the priceless cognizance, and thought
'I have shamed thee so that now thou shamest me,
Thee will I bear no more,' high on a branch
Hung it, and turned aside into the woods,
And there in gloom cast himself all along,
Moaning 'My violences, my violences!'

But now the wholesome music of the wood
Was dumbed by one from out the hall of Mark,
A damsel-errant, warbling, as she rode
The woodland alleys, Vivien, with her Squire.

'The fire of Heaven has killed the barren cold,
And kindled all the plain and all the wold.
The new leaf ever pushes off the old.
The fire of Heaven is not the flame of Hell.

'Old priest, who mumble worship in your quire–
Old monk and nun, ye scorn the world's desire,
Yet in your frosty cells ye feel the fire!
The fire of Heaven is not the flame of Hell.

'The fire of Heaven is on the dusty ways.
The wayside blossoms open to the blaze.
The whole wood-world is one full peal of praise.
The fire of Heaven is not the flame of Hell.

'The fire of Heaven is lord of all things good,
And starve not thou this fire within thy blood,
But follow Vivien through the fiery flood!
The fire of Heaven is not the flame of Hell!'

Then turning to her Squire 'This fire of Heaven,
This old sun-worship, boy, will rise again,
And beat the cross to earth, and break the King
And all his Table.'
Then they reached a glade,
Where under one long lane of cloudless air
Before another wood, the royal crown
Sparkled, and swaying upon a restless elm
Drew the vague glance of Vivien, and her Squire;
Amazed were these; 'Lo there' she cried–'a crown–
Borne by some high lord-prince of Arthur's hall,
And there a horse! the rider? where is he?
See, yonder lies one dead within the wood.
Not dead; he stirs!–but sleeping. I will speak.

Hail, royal knight, we break on thy sweet rest,
Not, doubtless, all unearned by noble deeds.
But bounden art thou, if from Arthur's hall,
To help the weak. Behold, I fly from shame,
A lustful King, who sought to win my love
Through evil ways: the knight, with whom I rode,
Hath suffered misadventure, and my squire
Hath in him small defence; but thou, Sir Prince,
Wilt surely guide me to the warrior King,
Arthur the blameless, pure as any maid,
To get me shelter for my maidenhood.
I charge thee by that crown upon thy shield,
And by the great Queen's name, arise and hence.'

And Balin rose, 'Thither no more! nor Prince
Nor knight am I, but one that hath defamed
The cognizance she gave me: here I dwell
Savage among the savage woods, here die–
Die: let the wolves' black maws ensepulchre
Their brother beast, whose anger was his lord.
O me, that such a name as Guinevere's,
Which our high Lancelot hath so lifted up,
And been thereby uplifted, should through me,
My violence, and my villainy, come to shame.'

Thereat she suddenly laughed and shrill, anon
Sighed all as suddenly. Said Balin to her
'Is this thy courtesy–to mock me, ha?
Hence, for I will not with thee.' Again she sighed
'Pardon, sweet lord! we maidens often laugh
When sick at heart, when rather we should weep.
I knew thee wronged. I brake upon thy rest,
And now full loth am I to break thy dream,
But thou art man, and canst abide a truth,
Though bitter. Hither, boy–and mark me well.
Dost thou remember at Caerleon once–
A year ago–nay, then I love thee not–
Ay, thou rememberest well–one summer dawn–
By the great tower–Caerleon upon Usk–
Nay, truly we were hidden: this fair lord,
The flower of all their vestal knighthood, knelt
In amorous homage–knelt–what else?–O ay
Knelt, and drew down from out his night-black hair
And mumbled that white hand whose ringed caress
Had wandered from her own King's golden head,
And lost itself in darkness, till she cried–

I thought the great tower would crash down on both–
"Rise, my sweet King, and kiss me on the lips,
Thou art my King." This lad, whose lightest word
Is mere white truth in simple nakedness,
Saw them embrace: he reddens, cannot speak,
So bashful, he! but all the maiden Saints,
The deathless mother-maidenhood of Heaven,
Cry out upon her. Up then, ride with me!
Talk not of shame! thou canst not, an thou would'st,
Do these more shame than these have done themselves.'

She lied with ease; but horror-stricken he,
Remembering that dark bower at Camelot,
Breathed in a dismal whisper 'It is truth.'

Sunnily she smiled 'And even in this lone wood,
Sweet lord, ye do right well to whisper this.
Fools prate, and perish traitors. Woods have tongues,
As walls have ears: but thou shalt go with me,
And we will speak at first exceeding low.
Meet is it the good King be not deceived.
See now, I set thee high on vantage ground,
From whence to watch the time, and eagle-like
Stoop at thy will on Lancelot and the Queen.'

She ceased; his evil spirit upon him leapt,
He ground his teeth together, sprang with a yell,
Tore from the branch, and cast on earth, the shield,
Drove his mailed heel athwart the royal crown,
Stampt all into defacement, hurled it from him
Among the forest weeds, and cursed the tale,
The told-of, and the teller.
That weird yell,
Unearthlier than all shriek of bird or beast,
Thrilled through the woods; and Balan lurking there
(His quest was unaccomplished) heard and thought
'The scream of that Wood-devil I came to quell!'
Then nearing 'Lo! he hath slain some brother-knight,
And tramples on the goodly shield to show
His loathing of our Order and the Queen.
My quest, meseems, is here. Or devil or man
Guard thou thine head.' Sir Balin spake not word,
But snatched a sudden buckler from the Squire,
And vaulted on his horse, and so they crashed
In onset, and King Pellam's holy spear,

547. Not so in Malory.

Reputed to be red with sinless blood,
Reddened at once with sinful, for the point
Across the maiden shield of Balan pricked
The hauberk to the flesh; and Balin's horse
Was wearied to the death, and, when they clashed,
Rolling back upon Balin, crushed the man
Inward, and either fell, and swooned away.

Then to her Squire muttered the damsel 'Fools!
This fellow hath wrought some foulness with his Queen:
Else never had he borne her crown, nor raved
And thus foamed over at a rival name:
But thou, Sir Chick, that scarce hast broken shell,
Art yet half-yolk, not even come to down–
Who never sawest Caerleon upon Usk–
And yet hast often pleaded for my love–
See what I see, be thou where I have been,
Or else Sir Chick–dismount and loose their casques
I fain would know what manner of men they be.'
And when the Squire had loosed them, 'Goodly!–look!
They might have cropt the myriad flower of May,
And butt each other here, like brainless bulls,
Dead for one heifer!'
Then the gentle Squire
'I hold them happy, so they died for love:
And, Vivien, though ye beat me like your dog,
I too could die, as now I live, for thee.'

'Live on, Sir Boy,' she cried. 'I better prize
The living dog than the dead lion: away!
I cannot brook to gaze upon the dead.'
Then leapt her palfrey o'er the fallen oak,
And bounding forward 'Leave them to the wolves.'

But when their foreheads felt the cooling air,
Balin first woke, and seeing that true face,

*578–620.* Malory ii 18: 'Then said Balin le Savage, "What knight art thou? for ere now I found never no knight that matched me".–"My name is", said he, "Balan, brother to the good knight Balin".–"Alas!" said Balin, "that ever I should see this day". And therewith he fell backward in a swoon. Then Balan went on all four, feet and hands, and put off the helm of his brother, and might not know him by the visage, it was so full hewn and bebled [be-bled]; but when he awoke, he said, "O Balan, my brother, thou hast slain me, and I thee, wherefore all the wide world shall speak of

Familiar up from cradle-time, so wan,
Crawled slowly with low moans to where he lay,
And on his dying brother cast himself
Dying; and *he* lifted faint eyes; he felt
One near him; all at once they found the world,
Staring wild-wide; then with a childlike wail,
And drawing down the dim disastrous brow
That o'er him hung, he kissed it, moaned and spake;

'O Balin, Balin, I that fain had died
To save thy life, have brought thee to thy death.
Why had ye not the shield I knew? and why
Trampled ye thus on that which bare the Crown?'

Then Balin told him brokenly, and in gasps,
All that had chanced, and Balan moaned again.

'Brother, I dwelt a day in Pellam's hall:
This Garlon mocked me, but I heeded not.
And one said "Eat in peace! a liar is he,
And hates thee for the tribute!" this good knight
Told me, that twice a wanton damsel came,
And sought for Garlon at the castle-gates,
Whom Pellam drove away with holy heat.
I well believe this damsel, and the one
Who stood beside thee even now, the same.
"She dwells among the woods" he said "and meets
And dallies with him in the Mouth of Hell."
Foul are their lives; foul are their lips; they lied.
Pure as our own true Mother is our Queen.'

'O brother' answered Balin 'woe is me!
My madness all thy life has been thy doom,
Thy curse, and darkened all thy day; and now
The night has come. I scarce can see thee now.

us both".–"Alas!" said Balin, "that ever I saw this day, that through mishap I might not know you; for I espied well your two swords, but because ye had another shield, I deemed you had been another knight".–"Alas!" said Balin, "all that made an unhappy knight in the castle, for he caused me to leave mine own shield to the destruction of us both; and if I might live I would destroy that castle for the ill customs"... "We came both out of one womb, that is to say, mother's belly, and so shall we lie both in one pit"... "Now", said Balin, "when we are buried in one tomb, and the mention made over us how two brethren slew each other, there will never good knight, nor good man, see our tomb, but they will pray for our souls".'

Goodnight! for we shall never bid again
Goodmorrow–Dark my doom was here, and dark
It will be there. I see thee now no more.
I would not mine again should darken thine,
Goodnight, true brother.'
Balan answered low
'Goodnight, true brother here! goodmorrow there!
We two were born together, and we die
Together by one doom:' and while he spoke
Closed his death-drowsing eyes, and slept the sleep
With Balin, either locked in either's arm.

# 469 Merlin and Vivien

Published *1859* as *Vivien* (the final title in *1870* ['*1869*']). 'Begun in Feb. and finished on March 31st, 1856' (H.T.). On 15 July 1856, James Spedding wrote to T. objecting to Merlin's seduction by Vivien (*Lincoln*). Sir Charles Tennyson says that in 1854 T. 'had already begun work on a poem about the enchantment of Merlin, but he laid this aside for *Maud*'. T.'s trial edition of *Enid and Nimuë: the True and the False* was set up in the summer of 1857; there is a copy in the British Museum (from which an edition was printed in 1902). For details of T.'s revisions, see Richard Jones, *The Growth of the Idylls of the King* (1895), Chapter ii; and Sir Charles Tennyson, *Cornhill* cliii (1936) 534–57. H.T. comments: 'My father created the character of Vivien with much care–as the evil genius of the Round Table [*note*: Even to the last. See *Guinevere* 97–8.]–who in her lustfulness of the flesh could not believe in anything either good or great. The story of the poem . . . is essentially original, and was founded on the following passage from Malory' [iv 1, slightly bowdlerized by H.T., here restored]:

'She was one of the damsels of the lake, which hight Nimue. But Merlin would let her have no rest, but always he would be with her in every place; and ever she made Merlin good cheer, till she had learned of him all manner of things that she desired, and he was so sore assotted upon her, that he might not be from her . . . And then he departed from king Arthur. And within a while the damsel of the lake departed, and Merlin went evermore with her wheresoever she went. And oftentimes Merlin would have had her privily away by his subtle crafts . . . And by the way as they went Merlin shewed her many wonders, and came into Cornwall. And always Merlin lay about the lady, for to have her maidenhead; and she was ever passing weary of him, and fain would have been delivered of him; for she was afraid of him, because he was a devil's son, and she could not put him away by any means. And so, upon a time, it happened that Merlin shewed to her in a rock where was a great wonder, and wrought by enchantment, which went under a stone. So, by her subtle craft and working, she made Merlin to go under that stone to let her wit of the marvels there; but she wrought so there for him, that he came never out, for all the craft that he could do: and so she departed, and left Merlin.'

'For the name of Vivien my father is indebted to the old *Romance of Merlin*' (H.T.). G. S. Haight (*SP* xliv (1947) 550–7) discusses the Vulgate *Merlin*, much of which is translated in Southey's edition of Malory (1817, pp. xliv–xlvi), where the relevant passage runs:

'When Merlin related all this to his master Blaise, who seems to have been his confessor as well as historiographer, Blaise was much troubled, and censured him greatly, and gave him good advice; but good advice was lost upon Merlin, who saw his own fate, and with all his wisdom was unable to avoid it. Accordingly one day the enchanter took leave of his old master, telling him "it was the last time he would ever see him, for from thenceforth he must abide with his mistress, and should never more have the power of leaving her, nor of going and coming at his pleasure. When Blaise heard this, he said to him full sorrowfully, Since then it is so that you will not be able to depart when once you shall have gone there, fair friend go not there at all, for you well know the thing that must happen to you. Certes, answered Merlin, I needs must go, for so I have covenanted and promised; and even if I had not covenanted, I am so taken with her love that I could not forbear going. All this have I done myself, for I have taught her great part of what I know, and she will still learn more from me, for I have no power to withhold myself. With that Merlin departed from Blaise his master, and travelled so long in few hours, that he came to Viviane his mistress." This was good travelling, for Blaise lived in Northumberland, and Viviane in France. They dwelt a long while together, and "she showed him greater semblance of love than she had ever done before, as one who knew so many enchantments that never other woman knew so much. So she devised within herself how she might detain him for ever more; but never could she compass nor achieve this: then was she full sorrowful and vexed, and cast about how she might discover it. Then began she to fawn and to flatter Merlin more than before; and she said to him, My sweet friend, I do not yet know one thing which I would fain know, I pray you teach me it. And Merlin, who well knew what it was, and to what she tended, said to her, Mistress, what is it? Sir, said Viviane, I would have you teach and show me how to inclose and imprison a man without a tower, without walls, without chains, but by enchantments alone, in such manner that he may never be able to go out, except by me. When Merlin heard her he shook his head, and began to sigh deeply; and Viviane, when she perceived it, asked of him wherefore he sighed thus. Dame, said Merlin, I will tell you. Well I know that you are devising how you may detain me; but I am so taken, that perforce will I or not, it behoves me to do your will. When Viviane heard this, for her great treason, and the better to delude and deceive him, she put her arms round his neck, and began to kiss him, saying, that he might well be hers, seeing that she was his: You well know, said she, that the great love which I have in you, has made me leave father and mother that I may have you in my arms day and night. All my desire and thought is in you; without you I have neither joy nor good. I have placed all my hope upon you, and I never look to have joy or good except from you. Seeing then that I love you, and you love me, is it not right that you should do my will and I yours? Certes, lady, yes, said Merlin, and I will do it; tell me what you would have. Sir, said she, I would that we should make a fair place and a suitable, so contrived by art and by cunning, that it might never be undone, and that you and I should be there in joy and in solace. My lady, said Merlin, I will perform all this. Sir, said she, I would not have you do it, but you shall teach me, and I will do it, and then it will be more to my will. I grant you this, said Merlin. Then he began to devise, and the damsel put it all in writing. And when he had devised the whole, then had the damsel full great joy, and showed him greater semblance of loving him than she had ever before made; and they sojourned together a long while. At length it fell out that as they were going one day hand in hand through the forest of Broceliande, they found a bush of white thorn which was laden with flowers; and they seated themselves under the shade of this white thorn upon the green grass, and they disported together and took their solace, and Merlin laid his head upon the damsel's lap, and then she began to feel if he were asleep. Then the damsel rose and made a ring with her wimple round the bush and round Merlin, and began her enchantments such as he himself had taught her; and nine times she made the ring, and nine times she made the enchantment; and then she went and sate down by him, and placed his head again upon her lap; and when he awoke and looked round him, it seemed to him that he was inclosed in the strongest tower in the world, and laid upon a fair bed; then said he to the dame, My lady, you have deceived me unless you abide with me, for no one hath power to unmake this tower, save you alone. Fair friend, she replied, I shall often be here, and you shall hold me in your arms, and I will hold you in mine. And in this she held her covenant to him, for afterwards there was never night nor day in which she was not there. And Merlin never went out of that tower where his mistress Viviane had inclosed him. But she entered and went out again when she listed; and often time she regretted what she had done, for she had thought that the thing which he taught her could not be true, and willingly would she have let him out if she could."

'The writer very properly remarks upon Merlin, for having taught his mistress so much, *quil en fut depuis, et est encore tenu pour fol.*'

Richard Jones had suggested that this version came to T. from the notes to Lady Charlotte Guest's *Mabinogion*. T. commented on the poem: 'Some even among the highest intellects become the slaves of the evil which is at first half disdained.'

A storm was coming, but the winds were still,
And in the wild woods of Broceliande,
Before an oak, so hollow, huge and old
It looked a tower of ivied masonwork,
At Merlin's feet the wily Vivien lay.

For he that always bare in bitter grudge
The slights of Arthur and his Table, Mark
The Cornish King, had heard a wandering voice,
A minstrel of Caerleon by strong storm
Blown into shelter at Tintagil, say
That out of naked knightlike purity
Sir Lancelot worshipt no unmarried girl
But the great Queen herself, fought in her name,
Sware by her–vows like theirs, that high in heaven
Love most, but neither marry, nor are given
In marriage, angels of our Lord's report.

He ceased, and then–for Vivien sweetly said
(She sat beside the banquet nearest Mark),
'And is the fair example followed, Sir,
In Arthur's household?'–answered innocently:

'Ay, by some few–ay, truly–youths that hold
It more beseems the perfect virgin knight
To worship woman as true wife beyond
All hopes of gaining, than as maiden girl.
They place their pride in Lancelot and the Queen.
So passionate for an utter purity
Beyond the limit of their bond, are these,
For Arthur bound them not to singleness.
Brave hearts and clean! and yet–God guide them–
young.'

Then Mark was half in heart to hurl his cup
Straight at the speaker, but forbore: he rose
To leave the hall, and, Vivien following him,
Turned to her: 'Here are snakes within the grass;
And you methinks, O Vivien, save ye fear

¶469. 2. *Broceliande*: 'The forest of Broceliand in Brittany near St Malo' (T.).

4. *ivied*] *1886*; ruined *1859–84*.

6–146] *1875*; *not 1859–73*. Until the final reading in *1886*, these added lines began: 'Whence came she? One that bare in bitter grudge / The scorn of Arthur. . . .'

14–16. *Matthew* xxii 30.

The monkish manhood, and the mask of pure
Worn by this court, can stir them till they sting.'

And Vivien answered, smiling scornfully,
'Why fear? because that fostered at *thy* court
I savour of thy–virtues? fear them? no.
As Love, if Love be perfect, casts out fear,
So Hate, if Hate be perfect, casts out fear.
My father died in battle against the King,
My mother on his corpse in open field;
She bore me there, for born from death was I
Among the dead and sown upon the wind–
And then on thee! and shown the truth betimes,
That old true filth, and bottom of the well,
Where Truth is hidden. Gracious lessons thine
And maxims of the mud! "This Arthur pure!
Great Nature through the flesh herself hath made
Gives him the lie! There is no being pure,
My cherub; saith not Holy Writ the same?"–
If I were Arthur, I would have thy blood.
Thy blessing, stainless King! I bring thee back,
When I have ferreted out their burrowings,
The hearts of all this Order in mine hand–
Ay–so that fate and craft and folly close,
Perchance, one curl of Arthur's golden beard.
To me this narrow grizzled fork of thine
Is cleaner-fashioned–Well, I loved thee first,
That warps the wit.'

Loud laughed the graceless Mark.
But Vivien, into Camelot stealing, lodged
Low in the city, and on a festal day
When Guinevere was crossing the great hall
Cast herself down, knelt to the Queen, and wailed.

'Why kneel ye there? What evil have ye wrought?
Rise!' and the damsel bidden rise arose
And stood with folded hands and downward eyes

*40.* *1 John* iv 18: 'perfect love casteth out fear.'

*47–8.* Sir Thomas Browne: 'Truth, which wise men say doth lye in a well' (Tilley's *Proverbs*, T582).

*51–2.* *Proverbs* xx 9: 'Who can say, I have made my heart clean, I am pure from my sin?'

*61*] Loud laughed the graceless king,
And like some long stilt-walker of the fens,
More wood than man, shambled away to bed. *H.MS*

Of glancing corner, and all meekly said,
'None wrought, but suffered much, an orphan maid!
My father died in battle for thy King,
My mother on his corpse–in open field,
The sad sea-sounding wastes of Lyonnesse–
Poor wretch–no friend!–and now by Mark the King
For that small charm of feature mine, pursued–
If any such be mine–I fly to thee.
Save, save me thou–Woman of women–thine
The wreath of beauty, thine the crown of power,
Be thine the balm of pity, O Heaven's own white
Earth-angel, stainless bride of stainless King–
Help, for he follows! take me to thyself!
O yield me shelter for mine innocency
Among thy maidens!'

Here her slow sweet eyes
Fear-tremulous, but humbly hopeful, rose
Fixt on her hearer's, while the Queen who stood
All glittering like May sunshine on May leaves
In green and gold, and plumed with green replied,
'Peace, child! of overpraise and overblame
We choose the last. Our noble Arthur, him
Ye scarce can overpraise, will hear and know.
Nay–we believe all evil of thy Mark–
Well, we shall test thee farther; but this hour
We ride a-hawking with Sir Lancelot.
He hath given us a fair falcon which he trained;
We go to prove it. Bide ye here the while.'

She past; and Vivien murmured after 'Go!
I bide the while.' Then through the portal-arch
Peering askance, and muttering broken-wise,
As one that labours with an evil dream,
Beheld the Queen and Lancelot get to horse.

'Is that the Lancelot? goodly–ay, but gaunt:
Courteous–amends for gauntness–takes her hand–
That glance of theirs, but for the street, had been
A clinging kiss–how hand lingers in hand!
Let go at last!–they ride away–to hawk
For waterfowl. Royaller game is mine.

*70–83.* Sir Charles Tennyson quotes from *H.MS* the first draft of Vivien's speech, in which she tells of the death of Balin and Balan (*Cornhill* cliii (1936) 552–3); see p. 1576.

*104 ∧ 5*] Bruise not the little fingers, courtesy! *MS.*

For such a supersensual sensual bond
As that gray cricket chirpt of at our hearth–
Touch flax with flame–a glance will serve–the
liars!
Ah little rat that borest in the dyke
Thy hole by night to let the boundless deep
Down upon far-off cities while they dance–
Or dream–of thee they dreamed not–nor of me
These–ay, but each of either: ride, and dream
The mortal dream that never yet was mine–
Ride, ride and dream until ye wake–to me!
Then, narrow court and lubber King, farewell!
For Lancelot will be gracious to the rat,
And our wise Queen, if knowing that I know,
Will hate, loathe, fear–but honour me the more.'

Yet while they rode together down the plain,
Their talk was all of training, terms of art,
Diet and seeling, jesses, leash and lure.
'She is too noble' he said 'to check at pies,
Nor will she rake: there is no baseness in her.'
Here when the Queen demanded as by chance
'Know ye the stranger woman?' 'Let her be,'
Said Lancelot and unhooded casting off
The goodly falcon free; she towered; her bells,
Tone under tone, shrilled; and they lifted up
Their eager faces, wondering at the strength,
Boldness and royal knighthood of the bird
Who pounced her quarry and slew it. Many a time
As once–of old–among the flowers–they rode.

But Vivien half-forgotten of the Queen
Among her damsels broidering sat, heard, watched
And whispered: through the peaceful court she crept

*107. supersensual sensual*] supersexual sexual *MS.*
*108* ∧ *9*] The heat and force of life all out of him, *MS.*
*109*] Touch flame with fire–a glance will do–no more.
Lies, lies! for which I hate the world–and him
That made me hate it, though he spake the truth–
Him least perchance–fool! for he wronged me most. *MS*
*116.* 'The only real bit of feeling, and the only pathetic line which Vivien speaks' (T.).
*123. seeling*: 'sewing up eyes of hawk' (H.T.). *jesses*: 'straps of leather fastened to legs' (H.T.).
*124. check at pies*: 'fly at magpies' (H.T.).
*125. Nor will she rake*: 'nor will she fly at other game' (H.T.).

And whispered: then as Arthur in the highest
Leavened the world, so Vivien in the lowest,
Arriving at a time of golden rest,
And sowing one ill hint from ear to ear,
While all the heathen lay at Arthur's feet,
And no quest came, but all was joust and play,
Leavened his hall. They heard and let her be.

Thereafter as an enemy that has left
Death in the living waters, and withdrawn,
The wily Vivien stole from Arthur's court.

She hated all the knights, and heard in thought
Their lavish comment when her name was named.
For once, when Arthur walking all alone,
Vext at a rumour issued from herself
Of some corruption crept among his knights,
Had met her, Vivien, being greeted fair,
Would fain have wrought upon his cloudy mood
With reverent eyes mock-loyal, shaken voice,
And fluttered adoration, and at last
With dark sweet hints of some who prized him more
Than who should prize him most; at which the King
Had gazed upon her blankly and gone by:
But one had watched, and had not held his peace:
It made the laughter of an afternoon
That Vivien should attempt the blameless King.
And after that, she set herself to gain
Him, the most famous man of all those times,
Merlin, who knew the range of all their arts,
Had built the King his havens, ships, and halls,
Was also Bard, and knew the starry heavens;
The people called him Wizard; whom at first
She played about with slight and sprightly talk,
And vivid smiles, and faintly-venomed points
Of slander, glancing here and grazing there;
And yielding to his kindlier moods, the Seer
Would watch her at her petulance, and play,
Even when they seemed unloveable, and laugh
As those that watch a kitten; thus he grew
Tolerant of what he half disdained, and she,
Perceiving that she was but half disdained,

*145–6.* 'Poisoned the wells' (T.).
*151. issued from herself*] *1873*; rife about the Queen, *1859–70*.
*152*] *1873*; *not 1859–70*.

Began to break her sports with graver fits,
Turn red or pale, would often when they met
Sigh fully, or all-silent gaze upon him
With such a fixt devotion, that the old man,
Though doubtful, felt the flattery, and at times
Would flatter his own wish in age for love,
And half believe her true: for thus at times
He wavered; but that other clung to him,
Fixt in her will, and so the seasons went.

Then fell on Merlin a great melancholy;
He walked with dreams and darkness, and he found
A doom that ever poised itself to fall,
An ever-moaning battle in the mist,
World-war of dying flesh against the life,
Death in all life and lying in all love,
The meanest having power upon the highest,
And the high purpose broken by the worm.

So leaving Arthur's court he gained the beach;
There found a little boat, and stept into it;
And Vivien followed, but he marked her not.
She took the helm and he the sail; the boat
Drave with a sudden wind across the deeps,
And touching Breton sands, they disembarked.
And then she followed Merlin all the way,
Even to the wild woods of Broceliande.
For Merlin once had told her of a charm,
The which if any wrought on anyone
With woven paces and with waving arms,
The man so wrought on ever seemed to lie
Closed in the four walls of a hollow tower,
From which was no escape for evermore;
And none could find that man for evermore,
Nor could he see but him who wrought the charm
Coming and going, and he lay as dead
And lost to life and use and name and fame.
And Vivien ever sought to work the charm
Upon the great Enchanter of the Time,
As fancying that her glory would be great
According to his greatness whom she quenched.

*187. on Merlin*] *1873*; upon him *1859–70.*
*188–94*] *1873*; *not 1859–70.*
*190.* 'The vision of the battle at the end' (T.).
*195. So*] *1873*; And *1859–70.*

There lay she all her length and kissed his feet,
As if in deepest reverence and in love.
A twist of gold was round her hair; a robe
Of samite without price, that more exprest
Than hid her, clung about her lissome limbs,
In colour like the satin-shining palm
On sallows in the windy gleams of March:
And while she kissed them, crying, 'Trample me,
Dear feet, that I have followed through the world,
And I will pay you worship; tread me down
And I will kiss you for it;' he was mute:
So dark a forethought rolled about his brain,
As on a dull day in an Ocean cave
The blind wave feeling round his long sea-hall
In silence: wherefore, when she lifted up
A face of sad appeal, and spake and said,
'O Merlin, do ye love me?' and again,
'O Merlin, do ye love me?' and once more,
'Great Master, do ye love me?' he was mute.
And lissome Vivien, holding by his heel,
Writhed toward him, slided up his knee and sat,
Behind his ankle twined her hollow feet
Together, curved an arm about his neck,
Clung like a snake; and letting her left hand
Droop from his mighty shoulder, as a leaf,
Made with her right a comb of pearl to part
The lists of such a beard as youth gone out
Had left in ashes: then he spoke and said,
Not looking at her, 'Who are wise in love
Love most, say least,' and Vivien answered quick,
'I saw the little elf-god eyeless once
In Arthur's arras hall at Camelot:
But neither eyes nor tongue–O stupid child!
Yet you are wise who say it; let me think
Silence is wisdom: I am silent then,
And ask no kiss;' then adding all at once,
'And lo, I clothe myself with wisdom,' drew
The vast and shaggy mantle of his beard

*228.* Cp. *Hail Briton* 96 ‸ 7, MS: 'The forethought of a working brain'.
*229–31.* 'This simile is taken from what I saw in the Caves of Ballybunion' (T.). This was in 1842 (*Mem.* i 218). In his copy of John Churton Collins's article (*Cornhill*, Jan. 1880, *Lincoln*), T. said that he had 'no thought of [Homer's] κῦμα κωφόν'.
*233. ye*] *1870* ('*1869*'); you *1859–69*. Likewise in ll. 234–5, 267, 313–14, 353, 358, 397, 442, 540, 551, 700–1.

Across her neck and bosom to her knee,
And called herself a gilded summer fly
Caught in a great old tyrant spider's web,
Who meant to eat her up in that wild wood
Without one word. So Vivien called herself,
But rather seemed a lovely baleful star
Veiled in gray vapour; till he sadly smiled:
'To what request for what strange boon,' he said,
'Are these your pretty tricks and fooleries,
O Vivien, the preamble? yet my thanks,
For these have broken up my melancholy.'

And Vivien answered smiling saucily,
'What, O my Master, have ye found your voice?
I bid the stranger welcome. Thanks at last!
But yesterday you never opened lip,
Except indeed to drink: no cup had we:
In mine own lady palms I culled the spring
That gathered trickling dropwise from the cleft,
And made a pretty cup of both my hands
And offered you it kneeling: then you drank
And knew no more, nor gave me one poor word;
O no more thanks than might a goat have given
With no more sign of reverence than a beard.
And when we halted at that other well,
And I was faint to swooning, and you lay
Foot-gilt with all the blossom-dust of those
Deep meadows we had traversed, did you know
That Vivien bathed your feet before her own?
And yet no thanks: and all through this wild wood
And all this morning when I fondled you:
Boon, ay, there was a boon, one not so strange–
How had I wronged you? surely ye are wise,
But such a silence is more wise than kind.'

And Merlin locked his hand in hers and said:
'O did ye never lie upon the shore,
And watch the curled white of the coming wave
Glassed in the slippery sand before it breaks?
Even such a wave, but not so pleasurable,
Dark in the glass of some presageful mood,
Had I for three days seen, ready to fall.
And then I rose and fled from Arthur's court

285. *ay*] *1873*; yes *1859–70*.
286. *ye*] *1873*; you *1859–70*. Likewise in ll. 289, 324, 334, 373, 381, 464, 466, 486, 514, 523, 547, 650, 686, 688, 770, 776.

To break the mood. You followed me unasked;
And when I looked, and saw you following still,
My mind involved yourself the nearest thing
In that mind-mist: for shall I tell you truth?
You seemed that wave about to break upon me
And sweep me from my hold upon the world,
My use and name and fame. Your pardon, child.
Your pretty sports have brightened all again.
And ask your boon, for boon I owe you thrice,
Once for wrong done you by confusion, next
For thanks it seems till now neglected, last
For these your dainty gambols: wherefore ask;
And take this boon so strange and not so strange.'

And Vivien answered smiling mournfully:
'O not so strange as my long asking it,
Not yet so strange as you yourself are strange,
Nor half so strange as that dark mood of yours.
I ever feared ye were not wholly mine;
And see, yourself have owned ye did me wrong.
The people call you prophet: let it be:
But not of those that can expound themselves.
Take Vivien for expounder; she will call
That three-days-long presageful gloom of yours
No presage, but the same mistrustful mood
That makes you seem less noble than yourself,
Whenever I have asked this very boon,
Now asked again: for see you not, dear love,
That such a mood as that, which lately gloomed
Your fancy when ye saw me following you,
Must make me fear still more you are not mine,
Must make me yearn still more to prove you mine,
And make me wish still more to learn this charm
Of woven paces and of waving hands,
As proof of trust. O Merlin, teach it me.
The charm so taught will charm us both to rest.
For, grant me some slight power upon your fate,
I, feeling that you felt me worthy trust,
Should rest and let you rest, knowing you mine.
And therefore be as great as ye are named,
Not muffled round with selfish reticence.
How hard you look and how denyingly!
O, if you think this wickedness in me,

*311. Not*] *1880*; Nor *1859–78*.

That I should prove it on you unawares,
That makes me passing wrathful; then our bond
Had best be loosed for ever: but think or not,
By Heaven that hears I tell you the clean truth,
As clean as blood of babes, as white as milk:
O Merlin, may this earth, if ever I,
If these unwitty wandering wits of mine,
Even in the jumbled rubbish of a dream,
Have tript on such conjectural treachery–
May this hard earth cleave to the Nadir hell
Down, down, and close again, and nip me flat,
If I be such a traitress. Yield my boon,
Till which I scarce can yield you all I am;
And grant my re-reiterated wish,
The great proof of your love: because I think,
However wise, ye hardly know me yet.'

And Merlin loosed his hand from hers and said,
'I never was less wise, however wise,
Too curious Vivien, though you talk of trust,
Than when I told you first of such a charm.
Yea, if ye talk of trust I tell you this,
Too much I trusted when I told you that,
And stirred this vice in you which ruined man
Through woman the first hour; for howsoe'er
In children a great curiousness be well,
Who have to learn themselves and all the world,
In you, that are no child, for still I find
Your face is practised when I spell the lines,
I call it,–well, I will not call it vice:
But since you name yourself the summer fly,
I well could wish a cobweb for the gnat,
That settles, beaten back, and beaten back
Settles, till one could yield for weariness:
But since I will not yield to give you power
Upon my life and use and name and fame,
Why will ye never ask some other boon?
Yea, by God's rood, I trusted you too much.'

And Vivien, like the tenderest-hearted maid
That ever bided tryst at village stile,
Made answer, either eyelid wet with tears:
'Nay, Master, be not wrathful with your maid;
Caress her: let her feel herself forgiven

338 ∧ 9] To make you lose your use and name and fame, *1859–70.*
339. *passing wrathful*] *1873*; most indignant *1859–70.*

Who feels no heart to ask another boon.
I think ye hardly know the tender rhyme
Of "trust me not at all or all in all."
I heard the great Sir Lancelot sing it once,
And it shall answer for me. Listen to it.

"In Love, if Love be Love, if Love be ours,
Faith and unfaith can ne'er be equal powers:
Unfaith in aught is want of faith in all.

"It is the little rift within the lute,
That by and by will make the music mute,
And ever widening slowly silence all.

"The little rift within the lover's lute
Or little pitted speck in garnered fruit,
That rotting inward slowly moulders all.

"It is not worth the keeping: let it go:
But shall it? answer, darling, answer, no.
And trust me not at all or all in all."

O Master, do ye love my tender rhyme?'

And Merlin looked and half believed her true,
So tender was her voice, so fair her face,
So sweetly gleamed her eyes behind her tears
Like sunlight on the plain behind a shower:
And yet he answered half indignantly:

'Far other was the song that once I heard
By this huge oak, sung nearly where we sit:
For here we met, some ten or twelve of us,
To chase a creature that was current then
In these wild woods, the hart with golden horns.
It was the time when first the question rose
About the founding of a Table Round,
That was to be, for love of God and men
And noble deeds, the flower of all the world.
And each incited each to noble deeds.
And while we waited, one, the youngest of us,
We could not keep him silent, out he flashed,
And into such a song, such fire for fame,
Such trumpet-blowings in it, coming down
To such a stern and iron-clashing close,
That when he stopt we longed to hurl together,
And should have done it; but the beauteous beast

403. 'The song about the clang of battle-axes, etc., in the *Coming of Arthur*' (T.).

Scared by the noise upstarted at our feet,
And like a silver shadow slipt away
Through the dim land; and all day long we rode
Through the dim land against a rushing wind,
That glorious roundel echoing in our ears,
And chased the flashes of his golden horns
Until they vanished by the fairy well
That laughs at iron–as our warriors did–
Where children cast their pins and nails, and cry,
"Laugh, little well!" but touch it with a sword,
It buzzes fiercely round the point; and there
We lost him: such a noble song was that.
But, Vivien, when you sang me that sweet rhyme,
I felt as though you knew this cursèd charm,
Were proving it on me, and that I lay
And felt them slowly ebbing, name and fame.'

And Vivien answered smiling mournfully:
'O mine have ebbed away for evermore,
And all through following you to this wild wood,
Because I saw you sad, to comfort you.
Lo now, what hearts have men! they never mount
As high as woman in her selfless mood.
And touching fame, howe'er ye scorn my song,
Take one verse more–the lady speaks it–this:

'"My name, once mine, now thine, is closelier mine,
For fame, could fame be mine, that fame were thine,
And shame, could shame be thine, that shame were mine.
So trust me not at all or all in all."

'Says she not well? and there is more–this rhyme
Is like the fair pearl-necklace of the Queen,
That burst in dancing, and the pearls were spilt;
Some lost, some stolen, some as relics kept.
But nevermore the same two sister pearls
Ran down the silken thread to kiss each other
On her white neck–so is it with this rhyme:
It lives dispersedly in many hands,
And every minstrel sings it differently;
Yet is there one true line, the pearl of pearls:
"Man dreams of Fame while woman wakes to love."

430. *fiercely*] *1873*; wildly *1859–70*.

Yea! Love, though Love were of the grossest, carves
A portion from the solid present, eats
And uses, careless of the rest; but Fame,
The Fame that follows death is nothing to us;
And what is Fame in life but half-disfame,
And counterchanged with darkness? ye yourself
Know well that Envy calls you Devil's son,
And since ye seem the Master of all Art,
They fain would make you Master of all vice.'

And Merlin locked his hand in hers and said,
'I once was looking for a magic weed,
And found a fair young squire who sat alone,
Had carved himself a knightly shield of wood,
And then was painting on it fancied arms,
Azure, an Eagle rising or, the Sun
In dexter chief; the scroll "I follow fame."
And speaking not, but leaning over him,
I took his brush and blotted out the bird,
And made a Gardener putting in a graff,
With this for motto, "Rather use than fame."
You should have seen him blush; but afterwards
He made a stalwart knight. O Vivien,
For you, methinks you think you love me well;
For me, I love you somewhat; rest: and Love
Should have some rest and pleasure in himself,
Not ever be too curious for a boon,
Too prurient for a proof against the grain
Of him ye say ye love: but Fame with men,
Being but ampler means to serve mankind,
Should have small rest or pleasure in herself,
But work as vassal to the larger love,
That dwarfs the petty love of one to one.
Use gave me Fame at first, and Fame again
Increasing gave me use. Lo, there my boon!
What other? for men sought to prove me vile,
Because I fain had given them greater wits:
And then did Envy call me Devil's son:
The sick weak beast seeking to help herself
By striking at her better, missed, and brought
Her own claw back, and wounded her own heart.
Sweet were the days when I was all unknown,
But when my name was lifted up, the storm

459. *Yea!*] *1873*; True: *1859–70*.
494. *fain . . . wits*] *1873*; wished to give them greater minds *1859–70*.

Brake on the mountain and I cared not for it.
Right well know I that Fame is half-disfame,
Yet needs must work my work. That other fame,
To one at least, who hath not children, vague,
The cackle of the unborn about the grave,
I cared not for it: a single misty star,
Which is the second in a line of stars
That seem a sword beneath a belt of three,
I never gazed upon it but I dreamt
Of some vast charm concluded in that star
To make fame nothing. Wherefore, if I fear,
Giving you power upon me through this charm,
That you might play me falsely, having power,
However well ye think ye love me now
(As sons of kings loving in pupilage
Have turned to tyrants when they came to power)
I rather dread the loss of use than fame;
If you–and not so much from wickedness,
As some wild turn of anger, or a mood
Of overstrained affection, it may be,
To keep me all to your own self,–or else
A sudden spurt of woman's jealousy,–
Should try this charm on whom ye say ye love.'

And Vivien answered smiling as in wrath:
'Have I not sworn? I am not trusted. Good!
Well, hide it, hide it; I shall find it out;
And being found take heed of Vivien.
A woman and not trusted, doubtless I
Might feel some sudden turn of anger born
Of your misfaith; and your fine epithet
Is accurate too, for this full love of mine
Without the full heart back may merit well
Your term of overstrained. So used as I,
My daily wonder is, I love at all.
And as to woman's jealousy, O why not?
O to what end, except a jealous one,
And one to make me jealous if I love,
Was this fair charm invented by yourself?

*501. Brake*] *1873*; Broke *1859–70*.

*506–8.* '$\theta$ Orionis–the nebula in which is imbedded the great multiple star. When this was written some astronomers fancied that this nebula in Orion was the vastest object in the Universe–a firmament of suns too far away to be resolved into stars by the telescope, and yet so huge as to be seen by the naked eye' (T.).

I well believe that all about this world
Ye cage a buxom captive here and there,
Closed in the four walls of a hollow tower
From which is no escape for evermore.'

Then the great Master merrily answered her:
'Full many a love in loving youth was mine;
I needed then no charm to keep them mine
But youth and love; and that full heart of yours
Whereof ye prattle, may now assure you mine;
So live uncharmed. For those who wrought it first,
The wrist is parted from the hand that waved,
The feet unmortised from their ankle-bones
Who paced it, ages back: but will ye hear
The legend as in guerdon for your rhyme?

'There lived a king in the most Eastern East,
Less old than I, yet older, for my blood
Hath earnest in it of far springs to be.
A tawny pirate anchored in his port,
Whose bark had plundered twenty nameless isles;
And passing one, at the high peep of dawn,
He saw two cities in a thousand boats
All fighting for a woman on the sea.
And pushing his black craft among them all,
He lightly scattered theirs and brought her off,
With loss of half his people arrow-slain;
A maid so smooth, so white, so wonderful,
They said a light came from her when she moved:
And since the pirate would not yield her up,
The King impaled him for his piracy;
Then made her Queen: but those isle-nurtured eyes
Waged such unwilling though successful war
On all the youth, they sickened; councils thinned,
And armies waned, for magnet-like she drew
The rustiest iron of old fighters' hearts;
And beasts themselves would worship; camels knelt
Unbidden, and the brutes of mountain back
That carry kings in castles, bowed black knees
Of homage, ringing with their serpent hands,
To make her smile, her golden ankle-bells.
What wonder, being jealous, that he sent

*553–97*. 'People have tried to discover this legend, but there is no legend of the kind that I know of' (T.).

*576. serpent hands*: *anguimanus*, as in Lucretius v 1303.

His horns of proclamation out through all
The hundred under-kingdoms that he swayed
To find a wizard who might teach the King
Some charm, which being wrought upon the Queen
Might keep her all his own: to such a one
He promised more than ever king has given,
A league of mountain full of golden mines,
A province with a hundred miles of coast,
A palace and a princess, all for him:
But on all those who tried and failed, the King
Pronounced a dismal sentence, meaning by it
To keep the list low and pretenders back,
Or like a king, not to be trifled with–
Their heads should moulder on the city gates.
And many tried and failed, because the charm
Of nature in her overbore their own:
And many a wizard brow bleached on the walls:
And many weeks a troop of carrion crows
Hung like a cloud above the gateway towers.'

And Vivien breaking in upon him, said:
'I sit and gather honey; yet, methinks,
Thy tongue has tript a little: ask thyself.
The lady never made *unwilling* war
With those fine eyes: she had her pleasure in it,
And made her good man jealous with good cause.
And lived there neither dame nor damsel then
Wroth at a lover's loss? were all as tame,
I mean, as noble, as the Queen was fair?
Not one to flirt a venom at her eyes,
Or pinch a murderous dust into her drink,
Or make her paler with a poisoned rose?
Well, those were not our days: but did they find
A wizard? Tell me, was he like to thee?'

She ceased, and made her lithe arm round his neck
Tighten, and then drew back, and let her eyes
Speak for her, glowing on him, like a bride's
On her new lord, her own, the first of men.

He answered laughing, 'Nay, not like to me.
At last they found–his foragers for charms–
A little glassy-headed hairless man,

600. *Thy . . . thyself*] *1873*; Your . . . yourself *1859–70*.
616–48. 'Nor is this a legend to be found' (T.).

Who lived alone in a great wild on grass;
Read but one book, and ever reading grew
So grated down and filed away with thought,
So lean his eyes were monstrous; while the skin
Clung but to crate and basket, ribs and spine.
And since he kept his mind on one sole aim,
Nor ever touched fierce wine, nor tasted flesh,
Nor owned a sensual wish, to him the wall
That sunders ghosts and shadow-casting men
Became a crystal, and he saw them through it,
And heard their voices talk behind the wall,
And learnt their elemental secrets, powers
And forces; often o'er the sun's bright eye
Drew the vast eyelid of an inky cloud,
And lashed it at the base with slanting storm;
Or in the noon of mist and driving rain,
When the lake whitened and the pinewood roared,
And the cairned mountain was a shadow, sunned
The world to peace again: here was the man.
And so by force they dragged him to the King.
And then he taught the King to charm the Queen
In such-wise, that no man could see her more,
Nor saw she save the King, who wrought the charm,
Coming and going, and she lay as dead,
And lost all use of life: but when the King
Made proffer of the league of golden mines,
The province with a hundred miles of coast,
The palace and the princess, that old man
Went back to his old wild, and lived on grass,
And vanished, and his book came down to me.'

And Vivien answered smiling saucily:
'Ye have the book: the charm is written in it:
Good: take my counsel: let me know it at once:
For keep it like a puzzle chest in chest,
With each chest locked and padlocked thirty-fold,
And whelm all this beneath as vast a mound
As after furious battle turfs the slain
On some wild down above the windy deep,
I yet should strike upon a sudden means
To dig, pick, open, find and read the charm:
Then, if I tried it, who should blame me then?'

633. *lashed*: 'like an eyelash' (T.).
634–6. A draft of these lines appears as a fragment in *H.Nbk 26*.

And smiling as a master smiles at one
That is not of his school, nor any school
But that where blind and naked Ignorance
Delivers brawling judgments, unashamed,
On all things all day long, he answered her:

'Thou read the book, my pretty Vivien!
O ay, it is but twenty pages long,
But every page having an ample marge,
And every marge enclosing in the midst
A square of text that looks a little blot,
The text no larger than the limbs of fleas;
And every square of text an awful charm,
Writ in a language that has long gone by.
So long, that mountains have arisen since
With cities on their flanks–thou read the book!
And every margin scribbled, crost, and crammed
With comment, densest condensation, hard
To mind and eye; but the long sleepless nights
Of my long life have made it easy to me.
And none can read the text, not even I;
And none can read the comment but myself;
And in the comment did I find the charm.
O, the results are simple; a mere child
Might use it to the harm of anyone,
And never could undo it: ask no more:
For though you should not prove it upon me,
But keep that oath ye sware, ye might, perchance,
Assay it on some one of the Table Round,
And all because ye dream they babble of you.'

And Vivien, frowning in true anger, said:
'What dare the full-fed liars say of me?
*They* ride abroad redressing human wrongs!
They sit with knife in meat and wine in horn!
*They* bound to holy vows of chastity!
Were I not woman, I could tell a tale.
But you are man, you well can understand
The shame that cannot be explained for shame.
Not one of all the drove should touch me: swine!'

*665. Thou*] *1873*; *You 1859–70.*

*674. thou*] *1873*; *you 1859–70.*

*686. sware*] *1873*; swore *1859–70.*

*690*] 'The filthy swine! what do they say of me? *MS.* Cp. the published text with the end of *The Lady of Shalott*, *1832* text: 'The wellfed wits at Camelot'.

Then answered Merlin careless of her words:
'You breathe but accusation vast and vague,
Spleen-born, I think, and proofless. If ye know,
Set up the charge ye know, to stand or fall!'

And Vivien answered frowning wrathfully:
'O ay, what say ye to Sir Valence, him
Whose kinsman left him watcher o'er his wife
And two fair babes, and went to distant lands;
Was one year gone, and on returning found
Not two but three? there lay the reckling, one
But one hour old! What said the happy sire?
A seven-months' babe had been a truer gift.
Those twelve sweet moons confused his fatherhood.'

Then answered Merlin, 'Nay, I know the tale.
Sir Valence wedded with an outland dame:
Some cause had kept him sundered from his wife:
One child they had: it lived with her: she died:
His kinsman travelling on his own affair
Was charged by Valence to bring home the child.
He brought, not found it therefore: take the truth.'

'O ay,' said Vivien, 'overtrue a tale.
What say ye then to sweet Sir Sagramore,
That ardent man? "to pluck the flower in season,"
So says the song, "I trow it is no treason."
O Master, shall we call him overquick
To crop his own sweet rose before the hour?'

And Merlin answered, 'Overquick art thou
To catch a loathly plume fallen from the wing
Of that foul bird of rapine whose whole prey
Is man's good name: he never wronged his bride.
I know the tale. An angry gust of wind
Puffed out his torch among the myriad-roomed
And many-corridored complexities
Of Arthur's palace: then he found a door,
And darkling felt the sculptured ornament
That wreathen round it made it seem his own;
And wearied out made for the couch and slept,
A stainless man beside a stainless maid;
And either slept, nor knew of other there;
Till the high dawn piercing the royal rose

707. *reckling*: 'the puny infant' (H.T.).
724. *art thou*] *1873*; are you *1859–70*.

In Arthur's casement glimmered chastely down,
Blushing upon them blushing, and at once
He rose without a word and parted from her:
But when the thing was blazed about the court,
The brute world howling forced them into bonds,
And as it chanced they are happy, being pure.'

'O ay,' said Vivien, 'that were likely too.
What say ye then to fair Sir Percivale
And of the horrid foulness that he wrought,
The saintly youth, the spotless lamb of Christ,
Or some black wether of St Satan's fold.
What, in the precincts of the chapel-yard,
Among the knightly brasses of the graves,
And by the cold Hic Jacets of the dead!'

And Merlin answered careless of her charge,
'A sober man is Percivale and pure;
But once in life was flustered with new wine,
Then paced for coolness in the chapel-yard;
Where one of Satan's shepherdesses caught
And meant to stamp him with her master's mark;
And that he sinned is not believable;
For, look upon his face!–but if he sinned,
The sin that practice burns into the blood,
And not the one dark hour which brings remorse,
Will brand us, after, of whose fold we be:
Or else were he, the holy king, whose hymns
Are chanted in the minster, worse than all.
But is your spleen frothed out, or have ye more?'

And Vivien answered frowning yet in wrath:
'O ay; what say ye to Sir Lancelot, friend
Traitor or true? that commerce with the Queen,
I ask you, is it clamoured by the child,
Or whispered in the corner? do ye know it?'

To which he answered sadly, 'Yea, I know it.
Sir Lancelot went ambassador, at first,
To fetch her, and she watched him from her walls.
A rumour runs, she took him for the King,
So fixt her fancy on him: let them be.

763. 'David' (T.).
773–4] *1873*; To fetch her, and she took him for the King; *1859–70.*
775. *them*] *1873*; him *1859–70.*

But have ye no one word of loyal praise
For Arthur, blameless King and stainless man?'

She answered with a low and chuckling laugh:
'Man! is he man at all, who knows and winks?
Sees what his fair bride is and does, and winks?
By which the good King means to blind himself,
And blinds himself and all the Table Round
To all the foulness that they work. Myself
Could call him (were it not for womanhood)
The pretty, popular name such manhood earns,
Could call him the main cause of all their crime;
Yea, were he not crowned King, coward, and fool.'

Then Merlin to his own heart, loathing, said:
'O true and tender! O my liege and King!
O selfless man and stainless gentleman,
Who wouldst against thine own eye-witness fain
Have all men true and leal, all women pure;
How, in the mouths of base interpreters,
From over-fineness not intelligible
To things with every sense as false and foul
As the poached filth that floods the middle street,
Is thy white blamelessness accounted blame!'

But Vivien, deeming Merlin overborne
By instance, recommenced, and let her tongue
Rage like a fire among the noblest names,
Polluting, and imputing her whole self,
Defaming and defacing, till she left
Not even Lancelot brave, nor Galahad clean.

Her words had issue other than she willed.
He dragged his eyebrow bushes down, and made
A snowy penthouse for his hollow eyes,
And muttered in himself, 'Tell *her* the charm!
So, if she had it, would she rail on me
To snare the next, and if she have it not
So will she rail. What did the wanton say?
"Not mount as high;" we scarce can sink as low:
For men at most differ as Heaven and earth,
But women, worst and best, as Heaven and Hell.

*779. Man!*] *1873*; Him? *1859–70*.
*796. poached*: trampled into mire.
*806*. Cp. Coleridge, *The Raven* 25: 'His brow, like a pent-house, hung over his eyes.'

I know the Table Round, my friends of old;
All brave, and many generous, and some chaste.
She cloaks the scar of some repulse with lies;
I well believe she tempted them and failed,
Being so bitter: for fine plots may fail,
Though harlots paint their talk as well as face
With colours of the heart that are not theirs.
I will not let her know: nine tithes of times
Face-flatterer and backbiter are the same.
And they, sweet soul, that most impute a crime
Are pronest to it, and impute themselves,
Wanting the mental range; or low desire
Not to feel lowest makes them level all;
Yea, they would pare the mountain to the plain,
To leave an equal baseness; and in this
Are harlots like the crowd, that if they find
Some stain or blemish in a name of note,
Not grieving that their greatest are so small,
Inflate themselves with some insane delight,
And judge all nature from her feet of clay,
Without the will to lift their eyes, and see
Her godlike head crowned with spiritual fire,
And touching other worlds. I am weary of her.'

He spoke in words part heard, in whispers part,
Half-suffocated in the hoary fell
And many-wintered fleece of throat and chin.
But Vivien, gathering somewhat of his mood,
And hearing 'harlot' muttered twice or thrice,
Leapt from her session on his lap, and stood
Stiff as a viper frozen; loathsome sight,
How from the rosy lips of life and love,
Flashed the bare-grinning skeleton of death!
White was her cheek; sharp breaths of anger puffed
Her fairy nostril out; her hand half-clenched
Went faltering sideways downward to her belt,
And feeling; had she found a dagger there
(For in a wink the false love turns to hate)
She would have stabbed him; but she found it not:
His eye was calm, and suddenly she took

*816*] *1873*; I think she cloaks the wounds of loss with lies; *1859–70*.
*817. well*] *1873*; do *1859–70*.
*818. Being*] *1873*; She is *1859–70*.
*822. Face-flatterer and backbiter*] *1873*; Face-flatterers and back-biters *1859–70*.

To bitter weeping like a beaten child,
A long, long weeping, not consolable.
Then her false voice made way, broken with sobs:

'O crueller than was ever told in tale,
Or sung in song! O vainly lavished love!
O cruel, there was nothing wild or strange,
Or seeming shameful–for what shame in love,
So love be true, and not as yours is–nothing
Poor Vivien had not done to win his trust
Who called her what he called her–all her crime,
All–all–the wish to prove him wholly hers.'

She mused a little, and then clapt her hands
Together with a wailing shriek, and said:
'Stabbed through the heart's affections to the heart!
Seethed like the kid in its own mother's milk!
Killed with a word worse than a life of blows!
I thought that he was gentle, being great:
O God, that I had loved a smaller man!
I should have found in him a greater heart.
O, I, that flattering my true passion, saw
The knights, the court, the King, dark in your light,
Who loved to make men darker than they are,
Because of that high pleasure which I had
To seat you sole upon my pedestal
Of worship–I am answered, and henceforth
The course of life that seemed so flowery to me
With you for guide and master, only you,
Becomes the sea-cliff pathway broken short,
And ending in a ruin–nothing left,
But into some low cave to crawl, and there,
If the wolf spare me, weep my life away,
Killed with inutterable unkindliness.'

She paused, she turned away, she hung her head,
The snake of gold slid from her hair, the braid
Slipt and uncoiled itself, she wept afresh,
And the dark wood grew darker toward the storm
In silence, while his anger slowly died
Within him, till he let his wisdom go
For ease of heart, and half believed her true:
Called her to shelter in the hollow oak,

867. *Exodus* xxiii 19: 'Thou shalt not seethe a kid in his mother's milk.'

'Come from the storm,' and having no reply,
Gazed at the heaving shoulder, and the face
Hand-hidden, as for utmost grief or shame;
Then thrice essayed, by tenderest-touching terms,
To sleek her ruffled peace of mind, in vain.
At last she let herself be conquered by him,
And as the cageling newly flown returns,
The seeming-injured simple-hearted thing
Came to her old perch back, and settled there.
There while she sat, half-falling from his knees,
Half-nestled at his heart, and since he saw
The slow tear creep from her closed eyelid yet,
About her, more in kindness than in love,
The gentle wizard cast a shielding arm.
But she dislinked herself at once and rose,
Her arms upon her breast across, and stood,
A virtuous gentlewoman deeply wronged,
Upright and flushed before him: then she said:

'There must be now no passages of love
Betwixt us twain henceforward evermore;
Since, if I be what I am grossly called,
What should be granted which your own gross heart
Would reckon worth the taking? I will go.
In truth, but one thing now–better have died
Thrice than have asked it once–could make me stay–
That proof of trust–so often asked in vain!
How justly, after that vile term of yours,
I find with grief! I might believe you then,
Who knows? once more. Lo! what was once to me
Mere matter of the fancy, now hath grown
The vast necessity of heart and life.
Farewell; think gently of me, for I fear
My fate or folly, passing gayer youth
For one so old, must be to love thee still.
But ere I leave thee let me swear once more
That if I schemed against thy peace in this,
May yon just heaven, that darkens o'er me, send

*921. Lo!*] *1873*; O, *1859–70*.
*922. hath*] *1873*; has *1859–70*.
*924. gently*] *1873*; kindly *1859–70*.
*925. folly, passing*] *1873*; fault, omitting *1859–70*.
*926, 927. thee*] *1873*; you *1859–70*.
*928. thy*] *1873*; your *1859–70*.

One flash, that, missing all things else, may make
My scheming brain a cinder, if I lie.'

Scarce had she ceased, when out of heaven a bolt
(For now the storm was close above them) struck,
Furrowing a giant oak, and javelining
With darted spikes and splinters of the wood
The dark earth round. He raised his eyes and saw
The tree that shone white-listed through the gloom.
But Vivien, fearing heaven had heard her oath,
And dazzled by the livid-flickering fork,
And deafened with the stammering cracks and claps
That followed, flying back and crying out,
'O Merlin, though you do not love me, save,
Yet save me!' clung to him and hugged him close;
And called him dear protector in her fright,
Nor yet forgot her practice in her fright,
But wrought upon his mood and hugged him close.
The pale blood of the wizard at her touch
Took gayer colours, like an opal warmed.
She blamed herself for telling hearsay tales:
She shook from fear, and for her fault she wept
Of petulancy; she called him lord and liege,
Her seer, her bard, her silver star of eve,
Her God, her Merlin, the one passionate love
Of her whole life; and ever overhead
Bellowed the tempest, and the rotten branch
Snapt in the rushing of the river-rain
Above them; and in change of glare and gloom
Her eyes and neck glittering went and came;
Till now the storm, its burst of passion spent,
Moaning and calling out of other lands,
Had left the ravaged woodland yet once more
To peace; and what should not have been had been,
For Merlin, overtalked and overworn,
Had yielded, told her all the charm, and slept.

Then, in one moment, she put forth the charm
Of woven paces and of waving hands,
And in the hollow oak he lay as dead,
And lost to life and use and name and fame.

Then crying 'I have made his glory mine,'
And shrieking out 'O fool!' the harlot leapt
Adown the forest, and the thicket closed
Behind her, and the forest echoed 'fool.'

937. *white-listed*: 'striped with white' (T.).

# 470 Lancelot and Elaine

Published *1859* as *Elaine* (the final title in *1870* ['*1869*']). 'Begun ... in July 1858' (H.T.). Thomas Woolner wrote to T.'s wife Emily, 7 June 1858: 'I most earnestly wish you could persuade him to do the *Maid of Astolat*' (A. Woolner, *Thomas Woolner*, 1917, p. 149). She wrote, 15 Feb. 1859 (p. 163): '*The Maid of Astolat* is quite finished now, all but last touches.' Cp. *The Lady of Shalott* (p. 354). 'The tenderest of all natures sinks under the blight, that which is of the highest in her working her doom' (T.). The source is Malory xviii 9–20, beginning: 'This old baron had a daughter at that time, that was called the fair maid of Astolat, and ever she beheld sir Launcelot wonderfully; and she cast such a love unto sir Launcelot, that she could not withdraw her love, wherefore she died; and her name was Elaine la Blaunch.'

Elaine the fair, Elaine the loveable,
Elaine, the lily maid of Astolat,
High in her chamber up a tower to the east
Guarded the sacred shield of Lancelot;
Which first she placed where morning's earliest ray
Might strike it, and awake her with the gleam;
Then fearing rust or soilure fashioned for it
A case of silk, and braided thereupon
All the devices blazoned on the shield
In their own tinct, and added, of her wit,
A border fantasy of branch and flower,
And yellow-throated nestling in the nest.
Nor rested thus content, but day by day,
Leaving her household and good father, climbed
That eastern tower, and entering barred her door,
Stript off the case, and read the naked shield,
Now guessed a hidden meaning in his arms,
Now made a pretty history to herself
Of every dint a sword had beaten in it,
And every scratch a lance had made upon it,
Conjecturing when and where: this cut is fresh;
That ten years back; this dealt him at Caerlyle;
That at Caerleon; this at Camelot:
And ah God's mercy, what a stroke was there!
And here a thrust that might have killed, but God
Broke the strong lance, and rolled his enemy down,
And saved him: so she lived in fantasy.

How came the lily maid by that good shield
Of Lancelot, she that knew not even his name?

He left it with her, when he rode to tilt
For the great diamond in the diamond jousts,
Which Arthur had ordained, and by that name
Had named them, since a diamond was the prize.

For Arthur, long before they crowned him King,
Roving the trackless realms of Lyonnesse,
Had found a glen, gray boulder and black tarn.
A horror lived about the tarn, and clave
Like its own mists to all the mountain side:
For here two brothers, one a king, had met
And fought together; but their names were lost;
And each had slain his brother at a blow;
And down they fell and made the glen abhorred:
And there they lay till all their bones were bleached,
And lichened into colour with the crags:
And he, that once was king, had on a crown
Of diamonds, one in front, and four aside.
And Arthur came, and labouring up the pass,
All in a misty moonshine, unawares
Had trodden that crowned skeleton, and the skull
Brake from the nape, and from the skull the crown
Rolled into light, and turning on its rims
Fled like a glittering rivulet to the tarn:
And down the shingly scaur he plunged, and caught,
And set it on his head, and in his heart
Heard murmurs, 'Lo, thou likewise shalt be King.'

Thereafter, when a King, he had the gems
Plucked from the crown, and showed them to his knights,
Saying, 'These jewels, whereupon I chanced
Divinely, are the kingdom's, not the King's–
For public use: henceforward let there be,
Once every year, a joust for one of these:
For so by nine years' proof we needs must learn
Which is our mightiest, and ourselves shall grow
In use of arms and manhood, till we drive

¶470. *34*] *1870* ('*1869*');

For Arthur when none knew from whence he came,
Long ere the people chose him for their king, *1859–69*

*35. Lyonnesse*: 'A land that is said to have stretched between Land's End and Scilly, and to have contained some of Cornwall as well' (T.).

*39–55.* This episode is not in Malory.

*45. he . . . was*] *1862*; one of these, the *1859–61*.

*53. scaur*: 'precipitous bank', variant of scar (*OED*, from 1805, Scott).

The heathen, who, some say, shall rule the land
Hereafter, which God hinder.' Thus he spoke:
And eight years past, eight jousts had been, and still
Had Lancelot won the diamond of the year,
With purpose to present them to the Queen,
When all were won; but meaning all at once
To snare her royal fancy with a boon
Worth half her realm, had never spoken word.

Now for the central diamond and the last
And largest, Arthur, holding then his court
Hard on the river nigh the place which now
Is this world's hugest, let proclaim a joust
At Camelot, and when the time drew nigh
Spake (for she had been sick) to Guinevere,
'Are you so sick, my Queen, you cannot move
To these fair jousts?' 'Yea, lord,' she said, 'ye know it.'
'Then will ye miss,' he answered, 'the great deeds
Of Lancelot, and his prowess in the lists,
A sight ye love to look on.' And the Queen
Lifted her eyes, and they dwelt languidly
On Lancelot, where he stood beside the King.
He thinking that he read her meaning there,
'Stay with me, I am sick; my love is more
Than many diamonds,' yielded; and a heart
Love-loyal to the least wish of the Queen
(However much he yearned to make complete
The tale of diamonds for his destined boon)
Urged him to speak against the truth, and say,
'Sir King, mine ancient wound is hardly whole,

*79–83*. Malory xviii 8: 'So king Arthur made him ready to depart to these jousts and would have had the queen with him, but at that time she would not go she said, for she was sick, and might not ride at that time. "Then me repenteth," said the king, "for these seven years ye saw not such a fellowship together, except at Whitsuntide, when sir Galahad departed from the court."–"Truly," said the queen unto the king, "ye must hold me excused, I may not be there, and that me repenteth." And many deemed that the queen would [not] be there, because of sir Launcelot du Lake, for sir Launcelot would not ride with the king, for he said that he was not whole of the wound, the which sir Mador had given him.'

*80. ye*] *1870* ('*1869*'); you *1859–69*. Likewise in ll. 81, 83, 98, 103–5, 135, 154, 197–8, 222, 227–8, 574, 657, 675–6, 711–12, 750, 763, 792, 910, 955, 1030, 1032–3, 1035, 1038, 1055, 1057, 1104, 1300, 1383.

*91. tale*: tally.

And lets me from the saddle;' and the King
Glanced first at him, then her, and went his way.
No sooner gone than suddenly she began:

'To blame, my lord Sir Lancelot, much to blame!
Why go ye not to these fair jousts? the knights
Are half of them our enemies, and the crowd
Will murmur, "Lo the shameless ones, who take
Their pastime now the trustful King is gone!"'
Then Lancelot vext at having lied in vain:
'Are ye so wise? ye were not once so wise,
My Queen, that summer, when ye loved me first.
Then of the crowd ye took no more account
Than of the myriad cricket of the mead,
When its own voice clings to each blade of grass,
And every voice is nothing. As to knights,
Them surely can I silence with all ease.
But now my loyal worship is allowed
Of all men: many a bard, without offence,
Has linked our names together in his lay,
Lancelot, the flower of bravery, Guinevere,
The pearl of beauty: and our knights at feast
Have pledged us in this union, while the King
Would listen smiling. How then? is there more?
Has Arthur spoken aught? or would yourself,
Now weary of my service and devoir,
Henceforth be truer to your faultless lord?'

She broke into a little scornful laugh:
'Arthur, my lord, Arthur, the faultless King,
That passionate perfection, my good lord–
But who can gaze upon the Sun in heaven?
He never spake word of reproach to me,
He never had a glimpse of mine untruth,
He cares not for me: only here today
There gleamed a vague suspicion in his eyes:
Some meddling rogue has tampered with him–else

*94. lets*: hinders.

*97–101.* Malory xviii 8: '"Sir Launcelot, ye are greatly to blame, thus to hold you behind my lord; what trow ye what your enemies and mine will say and deem? nought else but see how sir Launcelot holdeth him ever behind the king, and so doth the queen, for that they would have their pleasure together, and thus they will say," said the queen unto sir Launcelot.'

*103–4.* Malory xviii 9: '"Madam," said sir Launcelot to the queen, "I allow your wit, it is of late come sith ye were wise."'

Rapt in this fancy of his Table Round,
And swearing men to vows impossible,
To make them like himself: but, friend, to me
He is all fault who hath no fault at all:
For who loves me must have a touch of earth;
The low sun makes the colour: I am yours,
Not Arthur's, as ye know, save by the bond.
And therefore hear my words: go to the jousts:
The tiny-trumpeting gnat can break our dream
When sweetest; and the vermin voices here
May buzz so loud–we scorn them, but they sting.'

Then answered Lancelot, the chief of knights:
'And with what face, after my pretext made,
Shall I appear, O Queen, at Camelot, I
Before a King who honours his own word,
As if it were his God's?'

'Yea,' said the Queen,
'A moral child without the craft to rule,
Else had he not lost me: but listen to me,
If I must find you wit: we hear it said
That men go down before your spear at a touch,
But knowing you are Lancelot; your great name,
This conquers: hide it therefore; go unknown:
Win! by this kiss you will: and our true King
Will then allow your pretext, O my knight,
As all for glory; for to speak him true,
Ye know right well, how meek soe'er he seem,
No keener hunter after glory breathes.
He loves it in his knights more than himself:
They prove to him his work: win and return.'

Then got Sir Lancelot suddenly to horse,
Wroth at himself. Not willing to be known,
He left the barren-beaten thoroughfare,
Chose the green path that showed the rarer foot,
And there among the solitary downs,
Full often lost in fancy, lost his way;
Till as he traced a faintly-shadowed track,

*134.* The colours of sunrise and sunset.

*140–57.* Malory xviii 9: '"But, wit ye well," said sir Launcelot unto queen Guenever, "that at those jousts I will be against the king and all his fellowship."–"Ye may there do as ye list," said queen Guenever, "but by my counsel ye shall not be against your king and your fellowship, for therein are many hardy knights of your blood."'

That all in loops and links among the dales
Ran to the Castle of Astolat, he saw
Fired from the west, far on a hill, the towers.
Thither he made, and blew the gateway horn.
Then came an old, dumb, myriad-wrinkled man,
Who let him into lodging and disarmed.
And Lancelot marvelled at the wordless man;
And issuing found the Lord of Astolat
With two strong sons, Sir Torre and Sir Lavaine,
Moving to meet him in the castle court;
And close behind them stept the lily maid
Elaine, his daughter: mother of the house
There was not: some light jest among them rose
With laughter dying down as the great knight
Approached them: then the Lord of Astolat:
'Whence comest thou, my guest, and by what name
Livest between the lips? for by thy state
And presence I might guess thee chief of those,
After the King, who eat in Arthur's halls.
Him have I seen: the rest, his Table Round,
Known as they are, to me they are unknown.'

Then answered Lancelot, the chief of knights:
'Known am I, and of Arthur's hall, and known,
What I by mere mischance have brought, my shield.
But since I go to joust as one unknown
At Camelot for the diamond, ask me not,
Hereafter ye shall know me–and the shield–
I pray you lend me one, if such you have,
Blank, or at least with some device not mine.'

Then said the Lord of Astolat, 'Here is Torre's:
Hurt in his first tilt was my son, Sir Torre.
And so, God wot, his shield is blank enough.
His ye can have.' Then added plain Sir Torre,
'Yea, since I cannot use it, ye may have it.'
Here laughed the father saying, 'Fie, Sir Churl,
Is that an answer for a noble knight?
Allow him! but Lavaine, my younger here,
He is so full of lustihood, he will ride,
Joust for it, and win, and bring it in an hour,

*168. blew*] *1873*; wound *1859–70*.
*180–1.* An epic formula, as in *Aeneid* xii 235. Cp. *The Gardener's Daughter* 49–50: 'Among us lived / Her fame from lip to lip.'
*188.* The borrowing of the shield is in Malory.
*191. ye*] *1873*; you *1859–70*. Likewise in ll. 546, 665, 695, 766, 966.

And set it in this damsel's golden hair,
To make her thrice as wilful as before.'

'Nay, father, nay good father, shame me not
Before this noble knight,' said young Lavaine,
'For nothing. Surely I but played on Torre:
He seemed so sullen, vext he could not go:
A jest, no more! for, knight, the maiden dreamt
That some one put this diamond in her hand,
And that it was too slippery to be held,
And slipt and fell into some pool or stream,
The castle-well, belike; and then I said
That *if* I went and *if* I fought and won it
(But all was jest and joke among ourselves)
Then must she keep it safelier. All was jest.
But, father, give me leave, an if he will,
To ride to Camelot with this noble knight:
Win shall I not, but do my best to win:
Young as I am, yet would I do my best.'

'So ye will grace me,' answered Lancelot,
Smiling a moment, 'with your fellowship
O'er these waste downs whereon I lost myself,
Then were I glad of you as guide and friend:
And you shall win this diamond,–as I hear
It is a fair large diamond,–if ye may,
And yield it to this maiden, if ye will.'
'A fair large diamond,' added plain Sir Torre,
'Such be for queens, and not for simple maids.'
Then she, who held her eyes upon the ground,
Elaine, and heard her name so tost about,
Flushed slightly at the slight disparagement
Before the stranger knight, who, looking at her,
Full courtly, yet not falsely, thus returned:
'If what is fair be but for what is fair,
And only queens are to be counted so,
Rash were my judgment then, who deem this maid
Might wear as fair a jewel as is on earth,
Not violating the bond of like to like.'

He spoke and ceased: the lily maid Elaine,
Won by the mellow voice before she looked,
Lifted her eyes, and read his lineaments.
The great and guilty love he bare the Queen,

*210–13.* 'A vision prophetic of Guinevere hurling the diamonds into the Thames' (T.).

In battle with the love he bare his lord,
Had marred his face, and marked it ere his time.
Another sinning on such heights with one,
The flower of all the west and all the world,
Had been the sleeker for it: but in him
His mood was often like a fiend, and rose
And drove him into wastes and solitudes
For agony, who was yet a living soul.
Marred as he was, he seemed the goodliest man
That ever among ladies ate in hall,
And noblest, when she lifted up her eyes.
However marred, of more than twice her years,
Seamed with an ancient swordcut on the cheek,
And bruised and bronzed, she lifted up her eyes
And loved him, with that love which was her doom.

Then the great knight, the darling of the court,
Loved of the loveliest, into that rude hall
Stept with all grace, and not with half disdain
Hid under grace, as in a smaller time,
But kindly man moving among his kind:
Whom they with meats and vintage of their best
And talk and minstrel melody entertained.
And much they asked of court and Table Round,
And ever well and readily answered he:
But Lancelot, when they glanced at Guinevere,
Suddenly speaking of the wordless man,
Heard from the Baron that, ten years before,
The heathen caught and reft him of his tongue.
'He learnt and warned me of their fierce design
Against my house, and him they caught and maimed;
But I, my sons, and little daughter fled
From bonds or death, and dwelt among the woods
By the great river in a boatman's hut.
Dull days were those, till our good Arthur broke
The Pagan yet once more on Badon hill.'

'O there, great lord, doubtless,' Lavaine said, rapt
By all the sweet and sudden passion of youth
Toward greatness in its elder, 'you have fought.
O tell us–for we live apart–you know
Of Arthur's glorious wars.' And Lancelot spoke

*249–52.* Cp. *Luke* viii 29: 'For he had commanded the unclean spirit to come out of the man. For oftentimes it had caught him: and he was kept bound with chains and in fetters; and he brake the bands, and was driven of the devil into the wilderness.'

And answered him at full, as having been
With Arthur in the fight which all day long
Rang by the white mouth of the violent Glem;
And in the four loud battles by the shore
Of Duglas; that on Bassa; then the war
That thundered in and out the gloomy skirts
Of Celidon the forest; and again
By castle Gurnion, where the glorious King
Had on his cuirass worn our Lady's Head,
Carved of one emerald centered in a sun
Of silver rays, that lightened as he breathed;
And at Caerleon had he helped his lord,
When the strong neighings of the wild white Horse
Set every gilded parapet shuddering;
And up in Agned-Cathregonion too,
And down the waste sand-shores of Trath Treroit,
Where many a heathen fell; 'and on the mount
Of Badon I myself beheld the King
Charge at the head of all his Table Round,
And all his legions crying Christ and him,
And break them; and I saw him, after, stand
High on a heap of slain, from spur to plume
Red as the rising sun with heathen blood,
And seeing me, with a great voice he cried,
"They are broken, they are broken!" for the King,
However mild he seems at home, nor cares
For triumph in our mimic wars, the jousts–
For if his own knight cast him down, he laughs
Saying, his knights are better men than he–
Yet in this heathen war the fire of God
Fills him: I never saw his like: there lives
No greater leader.'

*286–302.* H.T. quotes from Nennius the account of these battles. On T.'s modifications, see J. M. Gray, *Notes and Queries* ccxi (1966) 341–2. (H.T., it should be added, was indebted to F. J. Rowe's edn of the poem in 1895, p. 57.)
*288. loud*] *1873*; wild *1859–70*.
*293.* In Nennius, the tradition was that Arthur bore the image of the Virgin Mary upon his shoulders (usually it was upon his shield). For the 'cuirass' (breastplate), cp. *Faerie Queene* I vii st.29–30: 'Athwart his brest a bauldrick brave he ware, / That shynd, like twinkling stars, with stons most pretious rare. // And in the midst thereof one pretious stone / Of wondrous worth, and eke of wondrous mights, / Shapt like a Ladies head, exceeding shone.'
*297.* The emblem of the Saxons was a white horse.

While he uttered this,
Low to her own heart said the lily maid,
'Save your great self, fair lord;' and when he fell
From talk of war to traits of pleasantry–
Being mirthful he, but in a stately kind–
She still took note that when the living smile
Died from his lips, across him came a cloud
Of melancholy severe, from which again,
Whenever in her hovering to and fro
The lily maid had striven to make him cheer,
There brake a sudden-beaming tenderness
Of manners and of nature: and she thought
That all was nature, all, perchance, for her.
And all night long his face before her lived,
As when a painter, poring on a face,
Divinely through all hindrance finds the man
Behind it, and so paints him that his face,
The shape and colour of a mind and life,
Lives for his children, ever at its best
And fullest; so the face before her lived,
Dark-splendid, speaking in the silence, full
Of noble things, and held her from her sleep.
Till rathe she rose, half-cheated in the thought
She needs must bid farewell to sweet Lavaine.
First as in fear, step after step, she stole
Down the long tower-stairs, hesitating:
Anon, she heard Sir Lancelot cry in the court,
'This shield, my friend, where is it?' and Lavaine
Past inward, as she came from out the tower.
There to his proud horse Lancelot turned, and smoothed
The glossy shoulder, humming to himself.
Half-envious of the flattering hand, she drew
Nearer and stood. He looked, and more amazed
Than if seven men had set upon him, saw
The maiden standing in the dewy light.
He had not dreamed she was so beautiful.
Then came on him a sort of sacred fear,
For silent, though he greeted her, she stood

*338. rathe*: 'early' (T.).

*341.* '"Stairs" is to be read as a monosyllable, with a pause after it' (T.). H.T. quotes James Spedding: 'The art with which A.T. has represented Elaine's action by the slow and lingering movement, the sudden arrest, and the hesitating advance of the metre, has been altogether lost on some critics.'

Rapt on his face as if it were a God's.
Suddenly flashed on her a wild desire,
That he should wear her favour at the tilt.
She braved a riotous heart in asking for it.
'Fair lord, whose name I know not–noble it is,
I well believe, the noblest–will you wear
My favour at this tourney?' 'Nay,' said he,
'Fair lady, since I never yet have worn
Favour of any lady in the lists.
Such is my wont, as those, who know me, know.'
'Yea, so,' she answered; 'then in wearing mine
Needs must be lesser likelihood, noble lord,
That those who know should know you.' And he turned
Her counsel up and down within his mind,
And found it true, and answered, 'True, my child.
Well, I will wear it: fetch it out to me:
What is it?' and she told him 'A red sleeve
Broidered with pearls,' and brought it: then he bound
Her token on his helmet, with a smile
Saying, 'I never yet have done so much
For any maiden living,' and the blood
Sprang to her face and filled her with delight;
But left her all the paler, when Lavaine
Returning brought the yet-unblazoned shield,
His brother's; which he gave to Lancelot,
Who parted with his own to fair Elaine:
'Do me this grace, my child, to have my shield
In keeping till I come.' 'A grace to me,'
She answered, 'twice today. I am your squire!'

*355–82.* Malory xviii 9: 'So thus as she came to and fro, she was so hot in her love, that she thought sir Launcelot should wear upon him at the jousts a token of her's. "Fair damsel," said sir Launcelot, "and if I grant you that, ye may say I do more for your love than ever I did for lady or damsel." Then he remembered him that he would ride unto the jousts disguised, and for because he had never before that time borne no manner of token of no damsel; then he bethought him that he would bear one of her's, that none of his blood thereby might know him. And then he said, "fair damsel, I will grant you to wear a token of yours upon my helmet; and, therefore, what it is, shew me."–"Sir," said she, "it is a red sleeve of mine of scarlet, well embroidered with great pearls"; and so she brought it him. So sir Launcelot received it and said, "Never or this time did I so much for no damsel." And then sir Launcelot betook the fair damsel his shield in keeping, and prayed her to keep it until he came again. And so that night he had merry rest and great cheer, for ever the fair damsel Elaine was about sir Launcelot all the while that she might be suffered.'

Whereat Lavaine said, laughing, 'Lily maid,
For fear our people call you lily maid
In earnest, let me bring your colour back;
Once, twice, and thrice: now get you hence to bed:'
So kissed her, and Sir Lancelot his own hand,
And thus they moved away: she stayed a minute,
Then made a sudden step to the gate, and there–
Her bright hair blown about the serious face
Yet rosy-kindled with her brother's kiss–
Paused by the gateway, standing near the shield
In silence, while she watched their arms far-off
Sparkle, until they dipt below the downs.
Then to her tower she climbed, and took the shield,
There kept it, and so lived in fantasy.

Meanwhile the new companions past away
Far o'er the long backs of the bushless downs,
To where Sir Lancelot knew there lived a knight
Not far from Camelot, now for forty years
A hermit, who had prayed, laboured and prayed,
And ever labouring had scooped himself
In the white rock a chapel and a hall
On massive columns, like a shorecliff cave,
And cells and chambers: all were fair and dry;
The green light from the meadows underneath
Struck up and lived along the milky roofs;
And in the meadows tremulous aspen-trees
And poplars made a noise of falling showers.
And thither wending there that night they bode.

But when the next day broke from underground,
And shot red fire and shadows through the cave,
They rose, heard mass, broke fast, and rode away:
Then Lancelot saying, 'Hear, but hold my name
Hidden, you ride with Lancelot of the Lake,'
Abashed Lavaine, whose instant reverence,
Dearer to true young hearts than their own praise,
But left him leave to stammer, 'Is it indeed?'
And after muttering 'The great Lancelot,'
At last he got his breath and answered, 'One,
One have I seen–that other, our liege lord,
The dread Pendragon, Britain's King of kings,
Of whom the people talk mysteriously,

*392. by ... near*] *1873*; in ... by *1859–70*.
*422.* Uther, Arthur's father.

He will be there – then were I stricken blind
That minute, I might say that I had seen.'

So spake Lavaine, and when they reached the lists
By Camelot in the meadow, let his eyes
Run through the peopled gallery which half round
Lay like a rainbow fallen upon the grass,
Until they found the clear-faced King, who sat
Robed in red samite, easily to be known,
Since to his crown the golden dragon clung,
And down his robe the dragon writhed in gold,
And from the carven-work behind him crept
Two dragons gilded, sloping down to make
Arms for his chair, while all the rest of them
Through knots and loops and folds innumerable
Fled ever through the woodwork, till they found
The new design wherein they lost themselves,
Yet with all ease, so tender was the work:
And, in the costly canopy o'er him set,
Blazed the last diamond of the nameless king.

Then Lancelot answered young Lavaine and said,
'Me you call great: mine is the firmer seat,
The truer lance: but there is many a youth
Now crescent, who will come to all I am
And overcome it; and in me there dwells
No greatness, save it be some far-off touch
Of greatness to know well I am not great:
There is the man.' And Lavaine gaped upon him
As on a thing miraculous, and anon
The trumpets blew; and then did either side,
They that assailed, and they that held the lists,
Set lance in rest, strike spur, suddenly move,
Meet in the midst, and there so furiously
Shock, that a man far-off might well perceive,
If any man that day were left afield,
The hard earth shake, and a low thunder of arms.
And Lancelot bode a little, till he saw
Which were the weaker; then he hurled into it
Against the stronger: little need to speak
Of Lancelot in his glory! King, duke, earl,
Count, baron – whom he smote, he overthrew.

*447–9.* T. said, 'When I wrote that, I was thinking of Wordsworth and myself' (*Tennyson and His Friends*, p. 210).

But in the field were Lancelot's kith and kin,
Ranged with the Table Round that held the lists,
Strong men, and wrathful that a stranger knight
Should do and almost overdo the deeds
Of Lancelot; and one said to the other, 'Lo!
What is he? I do not mean the force alone–
The grace and versatility of the man!
Is it not Lancelot?' 'When has Lancelot worn
Favour of any lady in the lists?
Not such his wont, as we, that know him, know.'
'How then? who then?' a fury seized them all,
A fiery family passion for the name
Of Lancelot, and a glory one with theirs.
They couched their spears and pricked their steeds, and thus,
Their plumes driven backward by the wind they made
In moving, all together down upon him
Bare, as a wild wave in the wide North-sea,
Green-glimmering toward the summit, bears, with all
Its stormy crests that smoke against the skies,
Down on a bark, and overbears the bark,
And him that helms it, so they overbore
Sir Lancelot and his charger, and a spear
Down-glancing lamed the charger, and a spear
Pricked sharply his own cuirass, and the head
Pierced through his side, and there snapt, and remained.

Then Sir Lavaine did well and worshipfully;
He bore a knight of old repute to the earth,

*468–74.* Malory xviii 11: '"O mercy, Jesu," said sir Gawaine, "what knight is that I see yonder, that doth so marvellous deeds of arms in the fields?"–"I wot well who is that," said king Arthur, "but all this time I will not name him."–"Sir," said sir Gawaine, "I would say it were sir Launcelot, by the riding, and by his buffets that I see him deal. But always me seemeth it should not be he, because he beareth the red sleeve upon the helm, for I wist him never yet bear token at no jousts of lady or gentlewoman."–"Let him be," said king Arthur, "for he will be better known, and do more, or he depart."'

*474. them all*] *1873*; on them *1859–70*.

*480–3.* 'Seen on a voyage of mine to Norway' (T.). H.T. quotes a letter by T., 24 July 1858: 'the green sea looking like a mountainous country, far-off waves with foam at the top looking like snowy mountains bounding the scene; one great wave, green-shining, past with all its crests smoking high up beside the vessel.'

And brought his horse to Lancelot where he lay.
He up the side, sweating with agony, got,
But thought to do while he might yet endure,
And being lustily holpen by the rest,
His party,–though it seemed half-miracle
To those he fought with,–drave his kith and kin,
And all the Table Round that held the lists,
Back to the barrier; then the trumpets blew
Proclaiming his the prize, who wore the sleeve
Of scarlet, and the pearls; and all the knights,
His party, cried 'Advance and take thy prize
The diamond;' but he answered, 'Diamond me
No diamonds! for God's love, a little air!
Prize me no prizes, for my prize is death!
Hence will I, and I charge you, follow me not.'

He spoke, and vanished suddenly from the field
With young Lavaine into the poplar grove.
There from his charger down he slid, and sat,
Gasping to Sir Lavaine, 'Draw the lance-head:'
'Ah my sweet lord Sir Lancelot,' said Lavaine,
'I dread me, if I draw it, you will die.'
But he, 'I die already with it: draw–
Draw,'–and Lavaine drew, and Sir Lancelot gave
A marvellous great shriek and ghastly groan,
And half his blood burst forth, and down he sank

*498. trumpets*] *1873*; heralds *1859–70*.
*501. thy*] *1873*; your *1859–70*. Likewise in l. 603.
*502–5.* Malory xviii 12, after Launcelot has been offered the prize: '"If I have deserved thanks, I have sore bought it, and that me repenteth, for I am like never to escape with my life; therefore, fair lords, I pray you that ye will suffer me to depart where me liketh, for I am sore hurt, I take no force of none honour; for I had lever to rest me, than to be lord of all the world."'
*509–16.* Malory xviii 12: '"O gentle knight, sir Lavaine, help me, that this truncheon were out of my side, for it sticketh so sore, that it almost slayeth me."–"O, mine own lord," said sir Lavaine, "I would fain help you, but it dreads me sore; and I draw out the truncheon, that ye shall be in peril of death."–"I charge you," said sir Launcelot, "as ye love me, draw it out." And therewith he descended from his horse, and so did sir Lavaine; and forthwith sir Lavaine drew the truncheon out of his side: and sir Launcelot gave a great shriek, and a marvellous ghastly groan, and his blood burst out nigh a pint at once, that at the last he sunk down upon his buttocks and swooned, pale and deadly.'
*513. Sir Lancelot*] *1873*; that other *1859–70*.

For the pure pain, and wholly swooned away.
Then came the hermit out and bare him in,
There stanched his wound; and there, in daily doubt
Whether to live or die, for many a week
Hid from the wide world's rumour by the grove
Of poplars with their noise of falling showers,
And ever-tremulous aspen-trees, he lay.

But on that day when Lancelot fled the lists,
His party, knights of utmost North and West,
Lords of waste marches, kings of desolate isles,
Came round their great Pendragon, saying to him,
'Lo, Sire, our knight, through whom we won the day,
Hath gone sore wounded, and hath left his prize
Untaken, crying that his prize is death.'
'Heaven hinder,' said the King, 'that such an one,
So great a knight as we have seen today–
He seemed to me another Lancelot–
Yea, twenty times I thought him Lancelot–
He must not pass uncared for. Wherefore, rise,
O Gawain, and ride forth and find the knight.
Wounded and wearied needs must he be near.
I charge you that you get at once to horse.
And, knights and kings, there breathes not one of you
Will deem this prize of ours is rashly given:
His prowess was too wondrous. We will do him
No customary honour: since the knight
Came not to us, of us to claim the prize,
Ourselves will send it after. Rise and take
This diamond, and deliver it, and return,
And bring us where he is, and how he fares,
And cease not from your quest until ye find.'

So saying, from the carven flower above,
To which it made a restless heart, he took,
And gave, the diamond: then from where he sat
At Arthur's right, with smiling face arose,
With smiling face and frowning heart, a Prince
In the mid might and flourish of his May,
Gawain, surnamed The Courteous, fair and strong,
And after Lancelot, Tristram, and Geraint

534. *Wherefore*] *1870* ('*1869*'); Gawain *1859–69*.
535. *O Gawain*] *1870* ('*1869*'); My nephew *1859–69*.
543. *Rise and*] *1870* ('*1869*'); Wherefore *1859–69*.
545. *where*] *1870* ('*1869*'); what *1859–69*.

And Gareth, a good knight, but therewithal
Sir Modred's brother, and the child of Lot,
Nor often loyal to his word, and now
Wroth that the King's command to sally forth
In quest of whom he knew not, made him leave
The banquet, and concourse of knights and kings.

So all in wrath he got to horse and went;
While Arthur to the banquet, dark in mood,
Past, thinking 'Is it Lancelot who hath come
Despite the wound he spake of, all for gain
Of glory, and hath added wound to wound,
And ridden away to die?' So feared the King,
And, after two days' tarriance there, returned.
Then when he saw the Queen, embracing asked,
'Love, are you yet so sick?' 'Nay, lord,' she said.
'And where is Lancelot?' Then the Queen amazed,
'Was he not with you? won he not your prize?'
'Nay, but one like him.' 'Why that like was he.'
And when the King demanded how she knew,
Said, 'Lord, no sooner had ye parted from us,
Than Lancelot told me of a common talk
That men went down before his spear at a touch,
But knowing he was Lancelot; his great name
Conquered; and therefore would he hide his name
From all men, even the King, and to this end
Had made the pretext of a hindering wound,
That he might joust unknown of all, and learn
If his old prowess were in aught decayed;
And added, "Our true Arthur, when he learns,
Will well allow my pretext, as for gain
Of purer glory."'
Then replied the King:
'Far lovelier in our Lancelot had it been,
In lieu of idly dallying with the truth,
To have trusted me as he hath trusted thee.
Surely his King and most familiar friend
Might well have kept his secret. True, indeed,
Albeit I know my knights fantastical,
So fine a fear in our large Lancelot
Must needs have moved my laughter: now remains

555. *Gareth*] *1873*; Lamorack *1859–70*.
556. *and . . . lot*] *1873*; of a crafty house *1859–70*.
563. *hath*] *1873*; has *1859–70*. Likewise in ll. 565, 588, 826.
588. *thee*] *1873*; you *1859–70*.

But little cause for laughter: his own kin–
Ill news, my Queen, for all who love him, this!–
His kith and kin, not knowing, set upon him;
So that he went sore wounded from the field:
Yet good news too: for goodly hopes are mine
That Lancelot is no more a lonely heart.
He wore, against his wont, upon his helm
A sleeve of scarlet, broidered with great pearls,
Some gentle maiden's gift.'
'Yea, lord,' she said,
'Thy hopes are mine,' and saying that, she choked,
And sharply turned about to hide her face,
Past to her chamber, and there flung herself
Down on the great King's couch, and writhed upon it,
And clenched her fingers till they bit the palm,
And shrieked out 'Traitor' to the unhearing wall,
Then flashed into wild tears, and rose again,
And moved about her palace, proud and pale.

Gawain the while through all the region round
Rode with his diamond, wearied of the quest,
Touched at all points, except the poplar grove,
And came at last, though late, to Astolat:
Whom glittering in enamelled arms the maid
Glanced at, and cried, 'What news from Camelot, lord?
What of the knight with the red sleeve?' 'He won.'
'I knew it,' she said. 'But parted from the jousts
Hurt in the side,' whereat she caught her breath;
Through her own side she felt the sharp lance go;
Thereon she smote her hand: wellnigh she swooned:
And, while he gazed wonderingly at her, came
The Lord of Astolat out, to whom the Prince
Reported who he was, and on what quest
Sent, that he bore the prize and could not find
The victor, but had ridden a random round
To seek him, and had wearied of the search.
To whom the Lord of Astolat, 'Bide with us,

*595. this*] *1873*; these *1859–70*.
*605. Past*] *1870* ('*1869*'); Moved *1859–69*.
*608.* Malory xviii 15: '"Ah! sir Bors, have ye heard say how falsely sir Launcelot hath betrayed me? . . . he is but a false, traitorous knight."'
*626. a random*] *1873*; wildly *1859–70*.
*627. had*] *1873*; was *1859–70*.

And ride no more at random, noble Prince!
Here was the knight, and here he left a shield;
This will he send or come for: furthermore
Our son is with him; we shall hear anon,
Needs must we hear.' To this the courteous Prince
Accorded with his wonted courtesy,
Courtesy with a touch of traitor in it,
And stayed; and cast his eyes on fair Elaine:
Where could be found face daintier? then her shape
From forehead down to foot, perfect–again
From foot to forehead exquisitely turned:
'Well–if I bide, lo! this wild flower for me!'
And oft they met among the garden yews,
And there he set himself to play upon her
With sallying wit, free flashes from a height
Above her, graces of the court, and songs,
Sighs, and slow smiles, and golden eloquence
And amorous adulation, till the maid
Rebelled against it, saying to him, 'Prince,
O loyal nephew of our noble King,
Why ask you not to see the shield he left,
Whence you might learn his name? Why slight
    your King,
And lose the quest he sent you on, and prove
No surer than our falcon yesterday,
Who lost the hern we slipt her at, and went
To all the winds?' 'Nay, by mine head,' said he,
'I lose it, as we lose the lark in heaven,
O damsel, in the light of your blue eyes;
But an ye will it let me see the shield.'
And when the shield was brought, and Gawain saw
Sir Lancelot's azure lions, crowned with gold,
Ramp in the field, he smote his thigh, and mocked:
'Right was the King! our Lancelot! that true man!'
'And right was I,' she answered merrily, 'I,
Who dreamed my knight the greatest knight of all.'
'And if *I* dreamed,' said Gawain, 'that you love
This greatest knight, your pardon! lo, ye know it!
Speak therefore: shall I waste myself in vain?'

*629. more at random*] *1873*; longer wildly *1859–70*.

*636.* As F. J. Rowe notes, in Malory Gawain appears as a loyal friend of Lancelot; these lines 'illustrate the increasing corruption of the Round Table'. T. departs from Malory throughout this episode.

*653. her*] *1882*; him *1859–81*.

*660. field*: surface of the shield.

Full simple was her answer, 'What know I?
My brethren have been all my fellowship;
And I, when often they have talked of love,
Wished it had been my mother, for they talked,
Meseemed, of what they knew not; so myself–
I know not if I know what true love is,
But if I know, then, if I love not him,
I know there is none other I can love.'
'Yea, by God's death,' said he, 'ye love him well,
But would not, knew ye what all others know,
And whom he loves.' 'So be it,' cried Elaine,
And lifted her fair face and moved away:
But he pursued her, calling, 'Stay a little!
One golden minute's grace! he wore your sleeve:
Would he break faith with one I may not name?
Must our true man change like a leaf at last?
Nay–like enow: why then, far be it from me
To cross our mighty Lancelot in his loves!
And, damsel, for I deem you know full well
Where your great knight is hidden, let me leave
My quest with you; the diamond also: here!
For if you love, it will be sweet to give it;
And if he love, it will be sweet to have it
From your own hand; and whether he love or not,
A diamond is a diamond. Fare you well
A thousand times!–a thousand times farewell!
Yet, if he love, and his love hold, we two
May meet at court hereafter: there, I think,
So ye will learn the courtesies of the court,
We two shall know each other.'

Then he gave,
And slightly kissed the hand to which he gave,
The diamond, and all wearied of the quest
Leapt on his horse, and carolling as he went
A true-love ballad, lightly rode away.

Thence to the court he past; there told the King
What the King knew, 'Sir Lancelot is the knight.'
And added, 'Sire, my liege, so much I learnt;

*674. I know*] *1873*; Methinks *1859–70*.
*683. Nay–like enow*] *1873*; May it be so? *1859–62*; Nay–like enough *1863–70*.
*686.* The leaving of the diamond and the king's anger with Gawain (ll. 710–13) are additions to Malory.

But failed to find him, though I rode all round
The region: but I lighted on the maid
Whose sleeve he wore; she loves him; and to her,
Deeming our courtesy is the truest law,
I gave the diamond: she will render it;
For by mine head she knows his hiding-place.'

The seldom-frowning King frowned, and replied,
'Too courteous truly! ye shall go no more
On quest of mine, seeing that ye forget
Obedience is the courtesy due to kings.'

He spake and parted. Wroth, but all in awe,
For twenty strokes of the blood, without a word,
Lingered that other, staring after him;
Then shook his hair, strode off, and buzzed abroad
About the maid of Astolat, and her love.
All ears were pricked at once, all tongues were loosed:
'The maid of Astolat loves Sir Lancelot,
Sir Lancelot loves the maid of Astolat.'
Some read the King's face, some the Queen's, and all
Had marvel what the maid might be, but most
Predoomed her as unworthy. One old dame
Came suddenly on the Queen with the sharp news.
She, that had heard the noise of it before,
But sorrowing Lancelot should have stooped so low,
Marred her friend's aim with pale tranquillity.
So ran the tale like fire about the court,
Fire in dry stubble a nine-days' wonder flared:
Till even the knights at banquet twice or thrice
Forgot to drink to Lancelot and the Queen,
And pledging Lancelot and the lily maid
Smiled at each other, while the Queen, who sat
With lips severely placid, felt the knot
Climb in her throat, and with her feet unseen
Crushed the wild passion out against the floor
Beneath the banquet, where the meats became
As wormwood, and she hated all who pledged.

But far away the maid in Astolat,
Her guiltless rival, she that ever kept
The one-day-seen Sir Lancelot in her heart,
Crept to her father, while he mused alone,
Sat on his knee, stroked his gray face and said,

728. *aim*] *1873*; point *1859–70*.

'Father, you call me wilful, and the fault
Is yours who let me have my will, and now,
Sweet father, will you let me lose my wits?'
'Nay,' said he, 'surely.' 'Wherefore, let me hence,'
She answered, 'and find out our dear Lavaine.'
'Ye will not lose your wits for dear Lavaine:
Bide,' answered he: 'we needs must hear anon
Of him, and of that other.' 'Ay,' she said,
'And of that other, for I needs must hence
And find that other, wheresoe'er he be,
And with mine own hand give his diamond to him,
Lest I be found as faithless in the quest
As yon proud Prince who left the quest to me.
Sweet father, I behold him in my dreams
Gaunt as it were the skeleton of himself,
Death-pale, for lack of gentle maiden's aid.
The gentler-born the maiden, the more bound,
My father, to be sweet and serviceable
To noble knights in sickness, as ye know
When these have worn their tokens: let me hence
I pray you.' Then her father nodding said,
'Ay, ay, the diamond: wit ye well, my child,
Right fain were I to learn this knight were whole,
Being our greatest: yea, and you must give it–
And sure I think this fruit is hung too high
For any mouth to gape for save a queen's–
Nay, I mean nothing: so then, get you gone,
Being so very wilful you must go.'

Lightly, her suit allowed, she slipt away,
And while she made her ready for her ride,
Her father's latest word hummed in her ear,
'Being so very wilful you must go,'
And changed itself and echoed in her heart,
'Being so very wilful you must die.'
But she was happy enough and shook it off,
As we shake off the bee that buzzes at us;
And in her heart she answered it and said,
'What matter, so I help him back to life?'
Then far away with good Sir Torre for guide
Rode o'er the long backs of the bushless downs
To Camelot, and before the city-gates
Came on her brother with a happy face

*786–92.* Malory xviii 15: 'By fortune sir Lavaine was ridden to play him and to enchase his horse. And anon as fair Elaine saw him, she knew him,

Making a roan horse caper and curvet
For pleasure all about a field of flowers:
Whom when she saw, 'Lavaine,' she cried, 'Lavaine,
How fares my lord Sir Lancelot?' He amazed,
'Torre and Elaine! why here? Sir Lancelot!
How know ye my lord's name is Lancelot?'
But when the maid had told him all her tale,
Then turned Sir Torre, and being in his moods
Left them, and under the strange-statued gate,
Where Arthur's wars were rendered mystically,
Past up the still rich city to his kin,
His own far blood, which dwelt at Camelot;
And her, Lavaine across the poplar grove
Led to the caves: there first she saw the casque
Of Lancelot on the wall: her scarlet sleeve,
Though carved and cut, and half the pearls away,
Streamed from it still; and in her heart she laughed,
Because he had not loosed it from his helm,
But meant once more perchance to tourney in it.
And when they gained the cell wherein he slept,
His battle-writhen arms and mighty hands
Lay naked on the wolfskin, and a dream
Of dragging down his enemy made them move.
Then she that saw him lying unsleek, unshorn,
Gaunt as it were the skeleton of himself,
Uttered a little tender dolorous cry.
The sound not wonted in a place so still
Woke the sick knight, and while he rolled his eyes
Yet blank from sleep, she started to him, saying,
'Your prize the diamond sent you by the King:'
His eyes glistened: she fancied 'Is it for me?'
And when the maid had told him all the tale
Of King and Prince, the diamond sent, the quest
Assigned to her not worthy of it, she knelt
Full lowly by the corners of his bed,
And laid the diamond in his open hand.
Her face was near, and as we kiss the child

and then she cried aloud unto him: and when he heard her, anon he came unto her, and then she asked her brother, "How fareth my lord, sir Launcelot?"–"Who told you, sister, that my lord's name was sir Launcelot!"'

*806. wherein*] *1873*; in which *1859–70*.

*807*. Cp. *Sense and Conscience* 57: 'battle-writhen sinews'.

That does the task assigned, he kissed her face.
At once she slipt like water to the floor.
'Alas,' he said, 'your ride hath wearied you.
Rest must you have.' 'No rest for me,' she said;
'Nay, for near you, fair lord, I am at rest.'
What might she mean by that? his large black eyes,
Yet larger through his leanness, dwelt upon her,
Till all her heart's sad secret blazed itself
In the heart's colours on her simple face;
And Lancelot looked and was perplext in mind,
And being weak in body said no more;
But did not love the colour; woman's love,
Save one, he not regarded, and so turned
Sighing, and feigned a sleep until he slept.

Then rose Elaine and glided through the fields,
And past beneath the weirdly-sculptured gates
Far up the dim rich city to her kin;
There bode the night: but woke with dawn, and past
Down through the dim rich city to the fields,
Thence to the cave: so day by day she past
In either twilight ghost-like to and fro
Gliding, and every day she tended him,
And likewise many a night: and Lancelot
Would, though he called his wound a little hurt
Whereof he should be quickly whole, at times
Brain-feverous in his heat and agony, seem
Uncourteous, even he: but the meek maid
Sweetly forbore him ever, being to him
Meeker than any child to a rough nurse,
Milder than any mother to a sick child,
And never woman yet, since man's first fall,
Did kindlier unto man, but her deep love
Upbore her; till the hermit, skilled in all
The simples and the science of that time,
Told him that her fine care had saved his life.
And the sick man forgot her simple blush,
Would call her friend and sister, sweet Elaine,
Would listen for her coming and regret

*839. weirdly-*] *1873*; wildly- *1859–70*.
*843–56.* Malory xviii 15: 'So this maid Elaine never went from sir Launcelot, but watched him day and night, and gave such attendance upon him, there was never woman did more kindlier for man than she did.'

Her parting step, and held her tenderly,
And loved her with all love except the love
Of man and woman when they love their best,
Closest and sweetest, and had died the death
In any knightly fashion for her sake.
And peradventure had he seen her first
She might have made this and that other world
Another world for the sick man; but now
The shackles of an old love straitened him,
His honour rooted in dishonour stood,
And faith unfaithful kept him falsely true.

Yet the great knight in his mid-sickness made
Full many a holy vow and pure resolve.
These, as but born of sickness, could not live:
For when the blood ran lustier in him again,
Full often the bright image of one face,
Making a treacherous quiet in his heart,
Dispersed his resolution like a cloud.
Then if the maiden, while that ghostly grace
Beamed on his fancy, spoke, he answered not,
Or short and coldly, and she knew right well
What the rough sickness meant, but what this meant
She knew not, and the sorrow dimmed her sight,
And drave her ere her time across the fields
Far into the rich city, where alone
She murmured, 'Vain, in vain: it cannot be.
He will not love me: how then? must I die?'
Then as a little helpless innocent bird,
That has but one plain passage of few notes,
Will sing the simple passage o'er and o'er
For all an April morning, till the ear
Wearies to hear it, so the simple maid
Went half the night repeating, 'Must I die?'
And now to right she turned, and now to left,
And found no ease in turning or in rest;
And 'Him or death,' she muttered, 'death or him,'
Again and like a burthen, 'Him or death.'

But when Sir Lancelot's deadly hurt was whole,
To Astolat returning rode the three.

*877. bright*] *1873*; sweet *1859–70.*
*880.* 'Vision of Guinevere' (T.).

There morn by morn, arraying her sweet self
In that wherein she deemed she looked her best,
She came before Sir Lancelot, for she thought
'If I be loved, these are my festal robes,
If not, the victim's flowers before he fall.'
And Lancelot ever prest upon the maid
That she should ask some goodly gift of him
For her own self or hers; 'and do not shun
To speak the wish most near to your true heart;
Such service have ye done me, that I make
My will of yours, and Prince and Lord am I
In mine own land, and what I will I can.'
Then like a ghost she lifted up her face,
But like a ghost without the power to speak.
And Lancelot saw that she withheld her wish,
And bode among them yet a little space
Till he should learn it; and one morn it chanced
He found her in among the garden yews,
And said, 'Delay no longer, speak your wish,
Seeing I go today:' then out she brake:
'Going? and we shall never see you more.
And I must die for want of one bold word.'
'Speak: that I live to hear,' he said, 'is yours.'
Then suddenly and passionately she spoke:
'I have gone mad. I love you: let me die.'
'Ah, sister,' answered Lancelot, 'what is this?'
And innocently extending her white arms,
'Your love,' she said, 'your love–to be your wife.'
And Lancelot answered, 'Had I chosen to wed,
I had been wedded earlier, sweet Elaine:
But now there never will be wife of mine.'
'No, no,' she cried, 'I care not to be wife,
But to be with you still, to see your face,

*920. go*] *1873*; must go *1859–70.*

*922–42.* Malory xviii 19: '"Have mercy upon me, and suffer me not to die for your love."–"What would you that I did?" said sir Launcelot. "I would have you unto my husband," said the maid Elaine. "Fair damsel, I thank you," said sir Launcelot; "but certainly," said he, "I cast me never to be married."–"Then, fair knight," said she, "will ye be my paramour?"–"Jesu defend me!" said sir Launcelot; "for then should I reward your father and your brother full evil for their great goodness."–"Alas!" said she, "then must I needs die for your love. . . . For but if ye will wed me, or else be my paramour at the least, wit ye well, sir Launcelot, my good days are done."'

To serve you, and to follow you through the world.'
And Lancelot answered, 'Nay, the world, the world,
All ear and eye, with such a stupid heart
To interpret ear and eye, and such a tongue
To blare its own interpretation–nay,
Full ill then should I quit your brother's love,
And your good father's kindness.' And she said,
'Not to be with you, not to see your face–
Alas for me then, my good days are done.'
'Nay, noble maid,' he answered, 'ten times nay!
This is not love: but love's first flash in youth,
Most common: yea, I know it of mine own self:
And you yourself will smile at your own self
Hereafter, when you yield your flower of life
To one more fitly yours, not thrice your age:
And then will I, for true you are and sweet
Beyond mine old belief in womanhood,
More specially should your good knight be poor,
Endow you with broad land and territory
Even to the half my realm beyond the seas,
So that would make you happy: furthermore,
Even to the death, as though ye were my blood,
In all your quarrels will I be your knight.
This will I do, dear damsel, for your sake,
And more than this I cannot.'
While he spoke
She neither blushed nor shook, but deathly-pale
Stood grasping what was nearest, then replied:
'Of all this will I nothing;' and so fell,
And thus they bore her swooning to her tower.

Then spake, to whom through those black walls of yew
Their talk had pierced, her father: 'Ay, a flash,
I fear me, that will strike my blossom dead.
Too courteous are ye, fair Lord Lancelot.
I pray you, use some rough discourtesy
To blunt or break her passion.'

*951–2.* Malory xviii 19: '"that wheresoever ye will set your heart upon some good knight that will wed you, I shall give you together a thousand pounds yearly to you and to your heirs."'
*966–9.* Added to Malory.

Lancelot said,
'That were against me: what I can I will;'
And there that day remained, and toward even
Sent for his shield: full meekly rose the maid,
Stript off the case, and gave the naked shield;
Then, when she heard his horse upon the stones,
Unclasping flung the casement back, and looked
Down on his helm, from which her sleeve had gone.
And Lancelot knew the little clinking sound;
And she by tact of love was well aware
That Lancelot knew that she was looking at him.
And yet he glanced not up, nor waved his hand,
Nor bad farewell, but sadly rode away.
This was the one discourtesy that he used.

So in her tower alone the maiden sat:
His very shield was gone; only the case,
Her own poor work, her empty labour, left.
But still she heard him, still his picture formed
And grew between her and the pictured wall.
Then came her father, saying in low tones,
'Have comfort,' whom she greeted quietly.
Then came her brethren saying, 'Peace to thee,
Sweet sister,' whom she answered with all calm.
But when they left her to herself again,
Death, like a friend's voice from a distant field
Approaching through the darkness, called; the owls
Wailing had power upon her, and she mixt
Her fancies with the sallow-rifted glooms
Of evening, and the moanings of the wind.

And in those days she made a little song,
And called her song 'The Song of Love and Death,'
And sang it: sweetly could she make and sing.

'Sweet is true love though given in vain, in vain;
And sweet is death who puts an end to pain:
I know not which is sweeter, no, not I.

'Love, art thou sweet? then bitter death must be:
Love, thou art bitter; sweet is death to me.
O Love, if death be sweeter, let me die.

*998.* The song takes the place of Elaine's religious meditation, Malory xviii 19.

'Sweet love, that seems not made to fade away,
Sweet death, that seems to make us loveless clay,
I know not which is sweeter, no, not I.

'I fain would follow love, if that could be;
I needs must follow death, who calls for me;
Call and I follow, I follow! let me die.'

High with the last line scaled her voice, and this,
All in a fiery dawning wild with wind
That shook her tower, the brothers heard, and thought
With shuddering, 'Hark the Phantom of the house
That ever shrieks before a death,' and called
The father, and all three in hurry and fear
Ran to her, and lo! the blood-red light of dawn
Flared on her face, she shrilling, 'Let me die!'

As when we dwell upon a word we know,
Repeating, till the word we know so well
Becomes a wonder, and we know not why,
So dwelt the father on her face, and thought
'Is this Elaine?' till back the maiden fell,
Then gave a languid hand to each, and lay,
Speaking a still good-morrow with her eyes.
At last she said, 'Sweet brothers, yesternight
I seemed a curious little maid again,
As happy as when we dwelt among the woods,
And when ye used to take me with the flood
Up the great river in the boatman's boat.
Only ye would not pass beyond the cape
That has the poplar on it: there ye fixt
Your limit, oft returning with the tide.
And yet I cried because ye would not pass
Beyond it, and far up the shining flood
Until we found the palace of the King.
And yet ye would not; but this night I dreamed
That I was all alone upon the flood,
And then I said, "Now shall I have my will:"
And there I woke, but still the wish remained.
So let me hence that I may pass at last
Beyond the poplar and far up the flood,
Until I find the palace of the King.
There will I enter in among them all,

*1015.* The Banshee, as described in J. Brand's *Popular Antiquities* (of which the 1810 edn is at *Lincoln*).

And no man there will dare to mock at me;
But there the fine Gawain will wonder at me,
And there the great Sir Lancelot muse at me;
Gawain, who bad a thousand farewells to me,
Lancelot, who coldly went, nor bad me one:
And there the King will know me and my love,
And there the Queen herself will pity me,
And all the gentle court will welcome me,
And after my long voyage I shall rest!'

'Peace,' said her father, 'O my child, ye seem
Light-headed, for what force is yours to go
So far, being sick? and wherefore would ye look
On this proud fellow again, who scorns us all?'

Then the rough Torre began to heave and move,
And bluster into stormy sobs and say,
'I never loved him: an I meet with him,
I care not howsoever great he be,
Then will I strike at him and strike him down,
Give me good fortune, I will strike him dead,
For this discomfort he hath done the house.'

To whom the gentle sister made reply,
'Fret not yourself, dear brother, nor be wroth,
Seeing it is no more Sir Lancelot's fault
Not to love me, than it is mine to love
Him of all men who seems to me the highest.'

'Highest?' the father answered, echoing 'highest?'
(He meant to break the passion in her) 'nay,
Daughter, I know not what you call the highest;
But this I know, for all the people know it,
He loves the Queen, and in an open shame:
And she returns his love in open shame;
If this be high, what is it to be low?'

Then spake the lily maid of Astolat:
'Sweet father, all too faint and sick am I
For anger: these are slanders: never yet
Was noble man but made ignoble talk.
He makes no friend who never made a foe.
But now it is my glory to have loved
One peerless, without stain: so let me pass,
My father, howsoe'er I seem to you,
Not all unhappy, having loved God's best
And greatest, though my love had no return:
Yet, seeing you desire your child to live,

Thanks, but you work against your own desire;
For if I could believe the things you say
I should but die the sooner; wherefore cease,
Sweet father, and bid call the ghostly man
Hither, and let me shrive me clean, and die.'

So when the ghostly man had come and gone,
She with a face, bright as for sin forgiven,
Besought Lavaine to write as she devised
A letter, word for word; and when he asked
'Is it for Lancelot, is it for my dear lord?
Then will I bear it gladly;' she replied,
'For Lancelot and the Queen and all the world,
But I myself must bear it.' Then he wrote
The letter she devised; which being writ
And folded, 'O sweet father, tender and true,
Deny me not,' she said–'ye never yet
Denied my fancies–this, however strange,
My latest: lay the letter in my hand
A little ere I die, and close the hand
Upon it; I shall guard it even in death.
And when the heat is gone from out my heart,
Then take the little bed on which I died
For Lancelot's love, and deck it like the Queen's
For richness, and me also like the Queen
In all I have of rich, and lay me on it.
And let there be prepared a chariot-bier
To take me to the river, and a barge
Be ready on the river, clothed in black.

*1092. ghostly man*: priest.

*1096–1129.* Malory xviii 19: 'And then she called her father, sir Bernard, and her brother, sir Tirre; and heartily she prayed her father, that her brother might write a letter like as she would indite it. And so her father granted it her. And, when the letter was written, word by word, as she had devised, then she prayed her father that she might be watched until she were dead. "And while my body is whole let this letter be put into my right hand, and my hand bound fast with the letter until that I be cold; and let me be put in a fair bed, with all the richest clothes that I have about me. And so let my bed, with all my rich clothes, be laid with me in a chariot to the next place whereas the Thames is; and there let me be put in a barge, and but one man with me, such as ye trust to steer me thither, and that my barge be covered with black samite over and over. Thus, father, I beseech you let be done." So her father granted her faithfully that all this thing should be done like as she had devised. Then her father and her brother made great dole; for, when this was done, anon she died.' See ll. 1239–47*n*.

I go in state to court, to meet the Queen.
There surely I shall speak for mine own self,
And none of you can speak for me so well.
And therefore let our dumb old man alone
Go with me, he can steer and row, and he
Will guide me to that palace, to the doors.'

She ceased: her father promised; whereupon
She grew so cheerful that they deemed her death
Was rather in the fantasy than the blood.
But ten slow mornings past, and on the eleventh
Her father laid the letter in her hand,
And closed the hand upon it, and she died.
So that day there was dole in Astolat.

But when the next sun brake from underground,
Then, those two brethren slowly with bent brows
Accompanying, the sad chariot-bier
Past like a shadow through the field, that shone
Full-summer, to that stream whereon the barge,
Palled all its length in blackest samite, lay.
There sat the lifelong creature of the house,
Loyal, the dumb old servitor, on deck,
Winking his eyes, and twisted all his face.
So those two brethren from the chariot took
And on the black decks laid her in her bed,
Set in her hand a lily, o'er her hung
The silken case with braided blazonings,
And kissed her quiet brows, and saying to her
'Sister, farewell for ever,' and again
'Farewell, sweet sister,' parted all in tears.
Then rose the dumb old servitor, and the dead,
Oared by the dumb, went upward with the flood–
In her right hand the lily, in her left
The letter–all her bright hair streaming down–
And all the coverlid was cloth of gold
Drawn to her waist, and she herself in white
All but her face, and that clear-featured face
Was lovely, for she did not seem as dead,
But fast asleep, and lay as though she smiled.

*1130–54.* Malory xviii 19: 'And so, when she was dead, the corpse and the bed, and all, were led the next way unto the Thames; and there a man, and the corpse and all, were put in a barge on the Thames: and so the man steered the barge to Westminster, and there he rode a great while to and fro, or any man discovered it.'
*1147. Oared*] *1870* ('*1869*'); Steered *1859–69*.

That day Sir Lancelot at the palace craved
Audience of Guinevere, to give at last
The price of half a realm, his costly gift,
Hard-won and hardly won with bruise and blow,
With deaths of others, and almost his own,
The nine-years-fought-for diamonds: for he saw
One of her house, and sent him to the Queen
Bearing his wish, whereto the Queen agreed
With such and so unmoved a majesty
She might have seemed her statue, but that he,
Low-drooping till he wellnigh kissed her feet
For loyal awe, saw with a sidelong eye
The shadow of some piece of pointed lace,
In the Queen's shadow, vibrate on the walls,
And parted, laughing in his courtly heart.

All in an oriel on the summer side,
Vine-clad, of Arthur's palace toward the stream,
They met, and Lancelot kneeling uttered, 'Queen,
Lady, my liege, in whom I have my joy,
Take, what I had not won except for you,
These jewels, and make me happy, making them
An armlet for the roundest arm on earth,
Or necklace for a neck to which the swan's
Is tawnier than her cygnet's: these are words:
Your beauty is your beauty, and I sin
In speaking, yet O grant my worship of it
Words, as we grant grief tears. Such sin in words
Perchance, we both can pardon: but, my Queen,
I hear of rumours flying through your court.
Our bond, as not the bond of man and wife,
Should have in it an absoluter trust
To make up that defect: let rumours be:
When did not rumours fly? these, as I trust
That you trust me in your own nobleness,
I may not well believe that you believe.'

While thus he spoke, half turned away, the Queen
Brake from the vast oriel-embowering vine
Leaf after leaf, and tore, and cast them off,
Till all the place whereon she stood was green;

*1167. some*] *1873*; a *1859–70.*

*1170–1235.* Malory xviii 20: 'So, by fortune, king Arthur and queen Guenever were speaking together at a window; and so as they looked into the Thames, they espied the black barge, and had marvel what it might mean. . . . And she lay as though she had smiled.'

Then, when he ceased, in one cold passive hand
Received at once and laid aside the gems
There on a table near her, and replied:
'It may be, I am quicker of belief
Than you believe me, Lancelot of the Lake.
Our bond is not the bond of man and wife.
This good is in it, whatsoe'er of ill,
It can be broken easier. I for you
This many a year have done despite and wrong
To one whom ever in my heart of hearts
I did acknowledge nobler. What are these?
Diamonds for me! they had been thrice their worth
Being your gift, had you not lost your own.
To loyal hearts the value of all gifts
Must vary as the giver's. Not for me!
For her! for your new fancy. Only this
Grant me, I pray you: have your joys apart.
I doubt not that however changed, you keep
So much of what is graceful: and myself
Would shun to break those bounds of courtesy
In which as Arthur's Queen I move and rule:
So cannot speak my mind. An end to this!
A strange one! yet I take it with Amen.
So pray you, add my diamonds to her pearls;
Deck her with these; tell her, she shines me down:
An armlet for an arm to which the Queen's
Is haggard, or a necklace for a neck
O as much fairer–as a faith once fair
Was richer than these diamonds–hers not mine–
Nay, by the mother of our Lord himself,
Or hers or mine, mine now to work my will–
She shall not have them.'

Saying which she seized,
And, through the casement standing wide for heat,
Flung them, and down they flashed, and smote the stream.
Then from the smitten surface flashed, as it were,
Diamonds to meet them, and they past away.
Then while Sir Lancelot leant, in half disdain
At love, life, all things, on the window ledge,
Close underneath his eyes, and right across

*1230. disdain*] *1873*; disgust *1859–70.*

Where these had fallen, slowly past the barge
Whereon the lily maid of Astolat
Lay smiling, like a star in blackest night.

But the wild Queen, who saw not, burst away
To weep and wail in secret; and the barge,
On to the palace-doorway sliding, paused.
There two stood armed, and kept the door; to whom,
All up the marble stair, tier over tier,
Were added mouths that gaped, and eyes that asked
'What is it?' but that oarsman's haggard face,
As hard and still as is the face that men
Shape to their fancy's eye from broken rocks
On some cliff-side, appalled them, and they said,
'He is enchanted, cannot speak – and she,
Look how she sleeps – the Fairy Queen, so fair!
Yea, but how pale! what are they? flesh and blood?
Or come to take the King to Fairyland?
For some do hold our Arthur cannot die,
But that he passes into Fairyland.'

While thus they babbled of the King, the King
Came girt with knights: then turned the tongueless man
From the half-face to the full eye, and rose
And pointed to the damsel, and the doors.
So Arthur bad the meek Sir Percivale
And pure Sir Galahad to uplift the maid;
And reverently they bore her into hall.
Then came the fine Gawain and wondered at her,
And Lancelot later came and mused at her,
And last the Queen herself, and pitied her:
But Arthur spied the letter in her hand,
Stoopt, took, brake seal, and read it; this was all:

'Most noble lord, Sir Lancelot of the Lake,
I, sometime called the maid of Astolat,

*1234–5.* G. H. Ford compares *Endymion* i 990–1: 'faint-smiling like a star / Through autumn mists' (*Keats and the Victorians*, 1944, p. 25*n*).
*1239–47.* Malory xviii 20: 'And there they found the fairest corpse, lying in a rich bed, that ever they saw, and a poor man sitting in the end of the barge, and no word would speak.'
*1262.* Malory xviii 20: 'Then the queen espied the letter in the right hand, and told the king thereof. Then the king took it in his hand.'
*1264–74.* Malory xviii 20: '"Most noble knight, my lord, sir Launcelot du

Come, for you left me taking no farewell,
Hither, to take my last farewell of you.
I loved you, and my love had no return,
And therefore my true love has been my death.
And therefore to our Lady Guinevere,
And to all other ladies, I make moan:
Pray for my soul, and yield me burial.
Pray for my soul thou too, Sir Lancelot,
As thou art a knight peerless.'
Thus he read;
And ever in the reading, lords and dames
Wept, looking often from his face who read
To hers which lay so silent, and at times,
So touched were they, half-thinking that her lips,
Who had devised the letter, moved again.

Then freely spoke Sir Lancelot to them all:
'My lord liege Arthur, and all ye that hear,
Know that for this most gentle maiden's death
Right heavy am I; for good she was and true,
But loved me with a love beyond all love
In women, whomsoever I have known.
Yet to be loved makes not to love again;
Not at my years, however it hold in youth.
I swear by truth and knighthood that I gave
No cause, not willingly, for such a love:
To this I call my friends in testimony,
Her brethren, and her father, who himself
Besought me to be plain and blunt, and use,
To break her passion, some discourtesy
Against my nature: what I could, I did.

Lake, now hath death made us two at debate for your love. I was your lover, that men called the Fair Maiden of Astolat; therefore unto all ladies I make my moan. Yet for my soul that ye pray, and bury me at the least, and offer me my mass penny. This is my last request: and a clean maid I died, I take God to my witness. Pray for my soul, sir Launcelot, as thou art a knight peerless."'

*1275–9.* Malory xviii 20: 'And when it was read, the queen and all the knights wept for pity of the doleful complaints.'

*1281–98.* Malory xviii 20: '"My lord, king Arthur, wit you well that I am right heavy of the death of this fair damsel. God knoweth I was never causer of her death by my will; and that I will report me unto her own brother here, he is sir Lavaine. I will not say nay", said sir Launcelot, "but that she was both fair and good; and much was I beholden unto her: but she loved me out of measure."'

I left her and I bad her no farewell;
Though, had I dreamt the damsel would have died,
I might have put my wits to some rough use,
And helped her from herself.'
Then said the Queen
(Sea was her wrath, yet working after storm)
'Ye might at least have done her so much grace,
Fair lord, as would have helped her from her death.'
He raised his head, their eyes met and hers fell,
He adding,
'Queen, she would not be content
Save that I wedded her, which could not be.
Then might she follow me through the world, she asked;
It could not be. I told her that her love
Was but the flash of youth, would darken down
To rise hereafter in a stiller flame
Toward one more worthy of her–then would I,
More specially were he, she wedded, poor,
Estate them with large land and territory
In mine own realm beyond the narrow seas,
To keep them in all joyance: more than this
I could not; this she would not, and she died.'

He pausing, Arthur answered, 'O my knight,
It will be to thy worship, as my knight,
And mine, as head of all our Table Round,
To see that she be buried worshipfully.'

So toward that shrine which then in all the realm
Was richest, Arthur leading, slowly went

*1298–301.* Malory xviii 20: '"Ye might have shewed her," said the queen, "some bounty and gentleness, that ye might have preserved her life."'

*1303–14.* Malory xviii 20: '"Madam," said sir Launcelot, "she would none other way be answered, but that she would be my wife, or else my paramour; and of these two I would not grant her; but I proffered her for her good love, which she shewed me, a thousand pounds yearly to her and her heirs, and to wed any manner of knight that she could find best to love in her heart. For, madam," said sir Launcelot, "I love not to be constrained to love; for love must arise of the heart, and not by constraint."'

*1315–8.* Malory xviii 20: 'Said the king unto sir Launcelot, "it will be your worship that ye oversee that she be buried worshipfully."'

*1316. thy*] *1870* ('*1869*'); your *1859–69*.

*1319–35.* Malory xviii 20: 'And so many knights went thither to behold the fair dead maid. And on the morrow she was richly buried, and sir

The marshalled Order of their Table Round,
And Lancelot sad beyond his wont, to see
The maiden buried, not as one unknown,
Nor meanly, but with gorgeous obsequies,
And mass, and rolling music, like a queen.
And when the knights had laid her comely head
Low in the dust of half-forgotten kings,
Then Arthur spake among them, 'Let her tomb
Be costly, and her image thereupon,
And let the shield of Lancelot at her feet
Be carven, and her lily in her hand.
And let the story of her dolorous voyage
For all true hearts be blazoned on her tomb
In letters gold and azure!' which was wrought
Thereafter; but when now the lords and dames
And people, from the high door streaming, brake
Disorderly, as homeward each, the Queen,
Who marked Sir Lancelot where he moved apart,
Drew near, and sighed in passing, 'Lancelot,
Forgive me; mine was jealousy in love.'
He answered with his eyes upon the ground,
'That is love's curse; pass on, my Queen, forgiven.'
But Arthur, who beheld his cloudy brows,
Approached him, and with full affection said,

'Lancelot, my Lancelot, thou in whom I have
Most joy and most affiance, for I know
What thou hast been in battle by my side,
And many a time have watched thee at the tilt
Strike down the lusty and long practised knight,
And let the younger and unskilled go by
To win his honour and to make his name,
And loved thy courtesies and thee, a man
Made to be loved; but now I would to God,

Launcelot offered her mass penny; and all the knights of the round table that were there, at that time, offered with sir Launcelot.' T. says of ll. 1319–27: 'This passage and the "tower-stair" passage [l. 341] are among the best blank verse in *Lancelot and Elaine*, I think' (T.).

*1337–42.* Malory xviii 20: 'Then the queen sent for sir Launcelot, and prayed him of mercy, for because she had been wrath with him causeless.– "This is not the first time", said sir Launcelot, "that ye have been displeased with my counsels [me causeless]; but, madam, ever I must suffer you, but what sorrow that I endure, ye take no force."'

*1344. said,]* *1873*; flung *1859–70.*

*1344 ∧ 5]* One arm about his neck, and spake and said. *1859–70.*

Seeing the homeless trouble in thine eyes,
Thou couldst have loved this maiden, shaped, it seems,
By God for thee alone, and from her face,
If one may judge the living by the dead,
Delicately pure and marvellously fair,
Who might have brought thee, now a lonely man
Wifeless and heirless, noble issue, sons
Born to the glory of thy name and fame,
My knight, the great Sir Lancelot of the Lake.'

Then answered Lancelot, 'Fair she was, my King,
Pure, as you ever wish your knights to be.
To doubt her fairness were to want an eye,
To doubt her pureness were to want a heart –
Yea, to be loved, if what is worthy love
Could bind him, but free love will not be bound.'

'Free love, so bound, were freëst,' said the King.
'Let love be free; free love is for the best:
And, after heaven, on our dull side of death,
What should be best, if not so pure a love
Clothed in so pure a loveliness? yet thee
She failed to bind, though being, as I think,
Unbound as yet, and gentle, as I know.'

And Lancelot answered nothing, but he went,
And at the inrunning of a little brook
Sat by the river in a cove, and watched
The high reed wave, and lifted up his eyes
And saw the barge that brought her moving down,
Far-off, a blot upon the stream, and said
Low in himself, 'Ah simple heart and sweet,
Ye loved me, damsel, surely with a love
Far tenderer than my Queen's. Pray for thy soul?
Ay, that will I. Farewell too – now at last –
Farewell, fair lily. "Jealousy in love?"
Not rather dead love's harsh heir, jealous pride?
Queen, if I grant the jealousy as of love,
May not your crescent fear for name and fame
Speak, as it waxes, of a love that wanes?
Why did the King dwell on my name to me?
Mine own name shames me, seeming a reproach,
Lancelot, whom the Lady of the Lake

1354] *1873*; For the wild people say wild things of thee, *1859–70*.

Caught from his mother's arms–the wondrous one
Who passes through the vision of the night–
She chanted snatches of mysterious hymns
Heard on the winding waters, eve and morn
She kissed me saying, "Thou art fair, my child,
As a king's son," and often in her arms
She bare me, pacing on the dusky mere.
Would she had drowned me in it, where'er it be!
For what am I? what profits me my name
Of greatest knight? I fought for it, and have it:
Pleasure to have it, none; to lose it, pain;
Now grown a part of me: but what use in it?
To make men worse by making my sin known?
Or sin seem less, the sinner seeming great?
Alas for Arthur's greatest knight, a man
Not after Arthur's heart! I needs must break
These bonds that so defame me: not without
She wills it: would I, if she willed it? nay,
Who knows? but if I would not, then may God,
I pray him, send a sudden Angel down
To seize me by the hair and bear me far,
And fling me deep in that forgotten mere,
Among the tumbled fragments of the hills.'

So groaned Sir Lancelot in remorseful pain,
Not knowing he should die a holy man.

# 471 The Holy Grail

Published *1869* (*'1870'*). H.T. quotes his mother's journal: '1868, *Sept. 9th.* A. read a bit of his *San Graal*, which he has just begun. *Sept. 14th.* He has almost finished the *San Graal*. It came like a breath of inspiration. *Sept. 23rd* . . . A. read the *San Graal* MS complete in the garden . . . I doubt whether the *San Graal* would have been written but for my endeavour, and the Queen's wish, and that of the Crown Princess. Thank God for it.

*1394–5*] *1873*; Stole from his mother–as the story runs–*1859–70*.
*1396. hymns*] *1873*; song *1859–70*.
*1418.* 'I asked my father why he did not write an Idyll "How Sir Lancelot came unto the hermitage, and how he took the habit unto him; how he went to Almesbury and found Queen Guinevere dead, whom they brought to Glastonbury; and how Sir Lancelot died a holy man"; and he answered, "Because it could not be done better than by Malory". My father loved his own great imaginative knight, the Lancelot of the *Idylls*' (H.T.).

He has had the subject in his mind for years, ever since he began to write about Arthur and his knights.' As long ago as 3 Oct. 1859, T. had written to the Duke of Argyll: 'As to Macaulay's suggestion of the Sangreal, I doubt whether such a subject could be handled in these days, without incurring a charge of irreverence' (*Mem.* i 456; *Mat.* ii 236). Emily wrote to Woolner, 24 Oct. 1863: 'I long for him to be at the *Sangreal*, feeling sure that is his work'; and again, 11 July 1864: 'I hope you think he has given your stories well. I wish he would give mine now and do the *Sangreal* for me' (A. Woolner, *Thomas Woolner*, 1917, pp. 240, 252). In April 1868 he wrote Ambrosius's speech (*Mem.* ii 53). Sir Charles Tennyson has pointed out the odd discrepancy between T.'s reluctance to tackle *The Holy Grail* and the statement in 1859 (*Eversley* v 440): 'He made a poem on Lancelot's quest of the San Graal; "in as good verse", he said, "as I ever wrote–no, I did not write, I made it in my head, and it has altogether slipt out of memory"'. Cp. *Sir Galahad* (p. 610).

The MS in *H.Nbk 38* includes a long prose draft, which 'carries the narrative to the close, but does not include Percival's meeting with Bors and his account of his meeting with Lancelot; and Percival's confession is evidently a later addition' (K. Tillotson, *Mid-Victorian Studies*, 1965, p. 98*n*). The beginning of the prose draft is quoted in *Mat.* iii 141–5. There is also a MS in *T.Nbk 29*. T.'s source was Malory xiii–xvii, which he modified very considerably. T. says of the poem: 'Faith declines, religion in many turns from practical goodness to the quest after the supernatural and marvellous and selfish religious excitement. Few are those for whom the quest is a source of spiritual strength. . . . *The Holy Grail* is one of the most imaginative of my poems. I have expressed there my strong feeling as to the Reality of the Unseen. The end, where the King speaks of his work and of his visions, is intended to be the summing up of all in the highest note by the highest of men.' 'My father looked on this description of Sir Galahad's quest, and on that of Sir Lancelot's, as among the best blank verse he had written. He pointed out the difference between the five visions of the Grail, as seen by the Holy Nun, Sir Galahad, Sir Percivale, Sir Lancelot, Sir Bors, according to their different, their own peculiar natures and circumstances, their selflessness, and the perfection or imperfection of their Christianity. He dwelt on the mystical treatment of every part of his subject, and said the key is to be found in a careful reading of Sir Percivale's visions. He would also call attention to the babbling homely utterances of the village priest Ambrosius as a contrast to the sweeping passages of blank verse that set forth the visions of spiritual enthusiasm' (H.T.).

From noiseful arms, and acts of prowess done
In tournament or tilt, Sir Percivale,
Whom Arthur and his knighthood called The Pure,

¶471. *2.* G. C. Macaulay points out that 'Sir Percivale was the original hero of the Grail legend, and always a most important person in it, though

Had passed into the silent life of prayer,
Praise, fast, and alms; and leaving for the cowl
The helmet in an abbey far away
From Camelot, there, and not long after, died.

And one, a fellow-monk among the rest,
Ambrosius, loved him much beyond the rest,
And honoured him, and wrought into his heart
A way by love that wakened love within,
To answer that which came: and as they sat
Beneath a world-old yew-tree, darkening half
The cloisters, on a gustful April morn
That puffed the swaying branches into smoke
Above them, ere the summer when he died,
The monk Ambrosius questioned Percivale:

'O brother, I have seen this yew-tree smoke,
Spring after spring, for half a hundred years:
For never have I known the world without,
Nor ever strayed beyond the pale: but thee,
When first thou camest–such a courtesy
Spake through the limbs and in the voice–I knew
For one of those who eat in Arthur's hall;
For good ye are and bad, and like to coins,
Some true, some light, but every one of you
Stamped with the image of the King; and now
Tell me, what drove thee from the Table Round,
My brother? was it earthly passion crost?'

'Nay,' said the knight; 'for no such passion mine.
But the sweet vision of the Holy Grail
Drove me from all vainglories, rivalries,
And earthly heats that spring and sparkle out
Among us in the jousts, while women watch
Who wins, who falls; and waste the spiritual
strength
Within us, better offered up to Heaven.'

To whom the monk: 'The Holy Grail!–I trust
We are green in Heaven's eyes; but here too much
We moulder–as to things without I mean–

his place was in the later form of the story partly taken by Galahad. Tennyson generally follows the later legend, but by making Percivale the narrator he has in fact given to him and to his adventures the chief degree of prominence.'

*18.* 'The pollen in Spring, which, blown abroad by the wind, looks like smoke' (T. compares *Mem.* ii 53, and *In Memoriam* xxxix).

Yet one of your own knights, a guest of ours,
Told us of this in our refectory,
But spake with such a sadness and so low
We heard not half of what he said. What is it?
The phantom of a cup that comes and goes?'

'Nay, monk! what phantom?' answered Percivale.
'The cup, the cup itself, from which our Lord
Drank at the last sad supper with his own.
This, from the blessèd land of Aromat–
After the day of darkness, when the dead
Went wandering o'er Moriah–the good saint
Arimathæan Joseph, journeying brought
To Glastonbury, where the winter thorn
Blossoms at Christmas, mindful of our Lord.
And there awhile it bode; and if a man
Could touch or see it, he was healed at once,
By faith, of all his ills. But then the times
Grew to such evil that the holy cup
Was caught away to Heaven, and disappeared.'

To whom the monk: 'From our old books I know
That Joseph came of old to Glastonbury,
And there the heathen Prince, Arviragus,
Gave him an isle of marsh whereon to build;
And there he built with wattles from the marsh
A little lonely church in days of yore,
For so they say, these books of ours, but seem
Mute of this miracle, far as I have read.
But who first saw the holy thing today?'

'A woman,' answered Percivale, 'a nun,
And one no further off in blood from me
Than sister; and if ever holy maid

48. *Aromat*: 'Used for Arimathea, the home of Joseph of Arimathea, who, according to the legend, received in the Grail the blood that flowed from our Lord's side' (T.).

49–50. *Matthew* xxvii 45 and 52–3: 'Now from the sixth hour there was darkness over all the land unto the ninth hour . . . And the graves were opened; and many bodies of the saints which slept arose, And came out of the graves after his resurrection, and went into the holy city, and appeared unto many.'

52–3. 'It was believed to have been grown from the staff of Joseph of Arimathea' (H.T.).

61. *Arviragus*: king of the Britons.

With knees of adoration wore the stone,
A holy maid; though never maiden glowed,
But that was in her earlier maidenhood,
With such a fervent flame of human love,
Which being rudely blunted, glanced and shot
Only to holy things; to prayer and praise
She gave herself, to fast and alms. And yet,
Nun as she was, the scandal of the Court,
Sin against Arthur and the Table Round,
And the strange sound of an adulterous race,
Across the iron grating of her cell
Beat, and she prayed and fasted all the more.

'And he to whom she told her sins, or what
Her all but utter whiteness held for sin,
A man wellnigh a hundred winters old,
Spake often with her of the Holy Grail,
A legend handed down through five or six,
And each of these a hundred winters old,
From our Lord's time. And when King Arthur made
His Table Round, and all men's hearts became
Clean for a season, surely he had thought
That now the Holy Grail would come again;
But sin broke out. Ah, Christ, that it would come,
And heal the world of all their wickedness!
"O Father!" asked the maiden, "might it come
To me by prayer and fasting?" "Nay," said he,
"I know not, for thy heart is pure as snow."
And so she prayed and fasted, till the sun
Shone, and the wind blew, through her, and I thought
She might have risen and floated when I saw her.

'For on a day she sent to speak with me.
And when she came to speak, behold her eyes
Beyond my knowing of them, beautiful,
Beyond all knowing of them, wonderful,
Beautiful in the light of holiness.
And "O my brother Percivale," she said,
"Sweet brother, I have seen the Holy Grail:
For, waked at dead of night, I heard a sound
As of a silver horn from o'er the hills
Blown, and I thought, 'It is not Arthur's use
To hunt by moonlight;' and the slender sound
As from a distance beyond distance grew
Coming upon me–O never harp nor horn,

Nor aught we blow with breath, or touch with
hand,
Was like that music as it came; and then
Streamed through my cell a cold and silver beam,
And down the long beam stole the Holy Grail,
Rose-red with beatings in it, as if alive,
Till all the white walls of my cell were dyed
With rosy colours leaping on the wall;
And then the music faded, and the Grail
Past, and the beam decayed, and from the walls
The rosy quiverings died into the night.
So now the Holy Thing is here again
Among us, brother, fast thou too and pray,
And tell thy brother knights to fast and pray,
That so perchance the vision may be seen
By thee and those, and all the world be healed."

'Then leaving the pale nun, I spake of this
To all men; and myself fasted and prayed
Always, and many among us many a week
Fasted and prayed even to the uttermost,
Expectant of the wonder that would be.

'And one there was among us, ever moved
Among us in white armour, Galahad.
"God make thee good as thou art beautiful,"
Said Arthur, when he dubbed him knight; and none,
In so young youth, was ever made a knight
Till Galahad; and this Galahad, when he heard
My sister's vision, filled me with amaze;
His eyes became so like her own, they seemed
Hers, and himself her brother more than I.

'Sister or brother none had he; but some
Called him a son of Lancelot, and some said
Begotten by enchantment–chatterers they,
Like birds of passage piping up and down,

*137.* Malory xiii 1: 'And on the morrow, at the hour of prime, at Galahad's desire, he [Lancelot] made him a knight, and said, "God make him a good man, for beauty faileth him not as any that liveth."'

*144–5.* Malory xi 2 tells of the enchantment by which Lancelot was made to sleep with Elaine (daughter of King Pelles), believing her to be Guinevere: 'and for this intent; the king knew well that sir Launcelot should get a child upon his daughter, the which should be named sir Galahad, the good knight, by whom all the foreign country should be brought out of danger, and by him the holy grail would be achieved.'

That gape for flies – we know not whence they come;
For when was Lancelot wanderingly lewd?

'But she, the wan sweet maiden, shore away
Clean from her forehead all that wealth of hair
Which made a silken mat-work for her feet;
And out of this she plaited broad and long
A strong sword-belt, and wove with silver thread
And crimson in the belt a strange device,
A crimson grail within a silver beam;
And saw the bright boy-knight, and bound it on him,
Saying, "My knight, my love, my knight of heaven,
O thou, my love, whose love is one with mine,
I, maiden, round thee, maiden, bind my belt.
Go forth, for thou shalt see what I have seen,
And break through all, till one will crown thee king
Far in the spiritual city:" and as she spake
She sent the deathless passion in her eyes
Through him, and made him hers, and laid her mind
On him, and he believed in her belief.

'Then came a year of miracle: O brother,
In our great hall there stood a vacant chair,
Fashioned by Merlin ere he past away,
And carven with strange figures; and in and out
The figures, like a serpent, ran a scroll
Of letters in a tongue no man could read.
And Merlin called it "The Siege perilous,"
Perilous for good and ill; "for there," he said,
"No man could sit but he should lose himself:"
And once by misadvertence Merlin sat

*149–60.* Malory xvii 7, in which Percival's sister speaks to Galahad: '"Lo! lords", said the gentlewoman, "here is a girdle that ought to be set about the sword; and wit ye well that the greatest part of this girdle was made of my hair, the which I loved full well while I was a woman of the world; but as soon as I wist that this adventure was ordained me, I clipped off my hair, and made this girdle . . . Now reck I not, though I die; for now I hold me [one of] the blessed maidens of the world, which hath made thee now the worthiest knights of the world."'
*151.* Cp. Keats, *Hyperion* i 82: 'A soft and silken mat for Saturn's feet.'
*162.* 'In the Grail legends "the spiritual city" is the city of Sarras, where Joseph of Arimathaea converted King Evelac' (G. C. Macaulay).
*172.* 'The perilous seat which stands for the spiritual imagination' (T.). See Malory xiii 4 for the empty seat at the Round Table, the letters on which came to read: 'This is the siege of sir Galahad the good knight.'

In his own chair, and so was lost; but he,
Galahad, when he heard of Merlin's doom,
Cried, "If I lose myself, I save myself!"

'Then on a summer night it came to pass,
While the great banquet lay along the hall,
That Galahad would sit down in Merlin's chair.

'And all at once, as there we sat, we heard
A cracking and a riving of the roofs,
And rending, and a blast, and overhead
Thunder, and in the thunder was a cry.
And in the blast there smote along the hall
A beam of light seven times more clear than day:
And down the long beam stole the Holy Grail

*178. Matthew* x 39: 'He that findeth his life shall lose it: and he that loseth his life for my sake shall find it.'
*182–202.* Malory xiii 7: 'Then anon they heard cracking and crying of thunder, that they thought the place should all to rive. In the midst of the blast entered a sun beam more clear by seven times than ever they saw day, and all they were alighted of the grace of the Holy Ghost. Then began every knight to behold other, and either saw other by their seeming fairer than ever they saw other, not for then there was no knight that might speak any word a great while; and so they looked every man on other as they had been dumb. Then they [there] entered into the hall, the holy grail covered with white samite, but there was none that might see it, nor who bear it, and there was all the hall fulfilled with great odours, and every knight had such meat and drink as he best loved in this world, and when the holy grail had been borne through the hall, then the holy vessel departed suddenly, that they wist not where it became. Then had they breath to speak, and then the king yielded thanks unto God of his grace that he had sent them. "Certainly," said king Arthur, "we ought greatly to thank our Lord, Jesus Christ, for that he hath shewed us this day at the reverence of this high feast of Pentecost".–"Now", said sir Gawaine, "we have been served this day of what meats and drinks we thought on, but one thing beguiled us, we might not see the holy grail, it was so preciously covered, wherefore I will make here a vow, that to-morrow, without any longer abiding, I shall labour in quest of the Sancgreal, that I shall hold me out a twelvemonth and a day, or more if need be, and never shall I return again unto the court till I have seen it more openly than it hath been seen here. And if I may not speed I shall return again, as he that may not be against the will of our Lord Jesus Christ". When they of the round table heard sir Gawaine say so, they arose the most part of them and avowed the same. And anon as king Arthur heard this, he was greatly displeased, for he wist well that they [he] might not again say [gainsay] their vows.'

All over covered with a luminous cloud,
And none might see who bare it, and it past.
But every knight beheld his fellow's face
As in a glory, and all the knights arose,
And staring each at other like dumb men
Stood, till I found a voice and sware a vow.

'I sware a vow before them all, that I,
Because I had not seen the Grail, would ride
A twelvemonth and a day in quest of it,
Until I found and saw it, as the nun
My sister saw it; and Galahad sware the vow,
And good Sir Bors, our Lancelot's cousin, sware,
And Lancelot sware, and many among the knights,
And Gawain sware, and louder than the rest.'

Then spake the monk Ambrosius, asking him,
'What said the King? Did Arthur take the vow?'

'Nay, for my lord,' said Percivale, 'the King,
Was not in hall: for early that same day,
Scaped through a cavern from a bandit hold,
An outraged maiden sprang into the hall
Crying on help: for all her shining hair
Was smeared with earth, and either milky arm
Red-rent with hooks of bramble, and all she wore
Torn as a sail that leaves the rope is torn
In tempest: so the King arose and went
To smoke the scandalous hive of those wild bees
That made such honey in his realm. Howbeit
Some little of this marvel he too saw,
Returning o'er the plain that then began
To darken under Camelot; whence the King
Looked up, calling aloud, "Lo, there! the roofs
Of our great hall are rolled in thunder-smoke!
Pray Heaven, they be not smitten by the bolt."
For dear to Arthur was that hall of ours,
As having there so oft with all his knights
Feasted, and as the stateliest under heaven.

'O brother, had you known our mighty hall,
Which Merlin built for Arthur long ago!
For all the sacred mount of Camelot,
And all the dim rich city, roof by roof,
Tower after tower, spire beyond spire,
By grove, and garden-lawn, and rushing brook,
Climbs to the mighty hall that Merlin built.

And four great zones of sculpture, set betwixt
With many a mystic symbol, gird the hall:
And in the lowest beasts are slaying men,
And in the second men are slaying beasts,
And on the third are warriors, perfect men,
And on the fourth are men with growing wings,
And over all one statue in the mould
Of Arthur, made by Merlin, with a crown,
And peaked wings pointed to the Northern Star.
And eastward fronts the statue, and the crown
And both the wings are made of gold, and flame
At sunrise till the people in far fields,
Wasted so often by the heathen hordes,
Behold it, crying, "We have still a King."

'And, brother, had you known our hall within,
Broader and higher than any in all the lands!
Where twelve great windows blazon Arthur's wars,
And all the light that falls upon the board
Streams through the twelve great battles of our King.
Nay, one there is, and at the eastern end,
Wealthy with wandering lines of mount and mere,
Where Arthur finds the brand Excalibur.
And also one to the west, and counter to it,
And blank: and who shall blazon it? when and how?–
O there, perchance, when all our wars are done,
The brand Excalibur will be cast away.

'So to this hall full quickly rode the King,
In horror lest the work by Merlin wrought,
Dreamlike, should on the sudden vanish, wrapt
In unremorseful folds of rolling fire.
And in he rode, and up I glanced, and saw
The golden dragon sparkling over all:
And many of those who burnt the hold, their arms
Hacked, and their foreheads grimed with smoke, and seared,
Followed, and in among bright faces, ours,
Full of the vision, prest: and then the King

*232–7.* 'The four zones represent human progress: the savage state of society; the state where man lords it over the beast; the full development of man; the progress toward spiritual ideals' (H.T.).
*261.* 'This line gives onomatopoeically the "unremorseful flames"' (T.).

Spake to me, being nearest, "Percivale,"
(Because the hall was all in tumult–some
Vowing, and some protesting), "what is this?"

'O brother, when I told him what had chanced,
My sister's vision, and the rest, his face
Darkened, as I have seen it more than once,
When some brave deed seemed to be done in vain,
Darken; and "Woe is me, my knights," he cried,
"Had I been here, ye had not sworn the vow."
Bold was mine answer, "Had thyself been here,
My King, thou wouldst have sworn." "Yea, yea," said he,
"Art thou so bold and hast not seen the Grail?"

'"Nay, lord, I heard the sound, I saw the light,
But since I did not see the Holy Thing,
I sware a vow to follow it till I saw."

'Then when he asked us, knight by knight, if any
Had seen it, all their answers were as one:
"Nay, lord, and therefore have we sworn our vows."

'"Lo now," said Arthur, "have ye seen a cloud?
What go ye into the wilderness to see?"

'Then Galahad on the sudden, and in a voice
Shrilling along the hall to Arthur, called,
"But I, Sir Arthur, saw the Holy Grail,
I saw the Holy Grail and heard a cry–
'O Galahad, and O Galahad, follow me.'"

'"Ah, Galahad, Galahad," said the King, "for such
As thou art is the vision, not for these.
Thy holy nun and thou have seen a sign–
Holier is none, my Percivale, than she–
A sign to maim this Order which I made.
But ye, that follow but the leader's bell"

*287.* Christ says of John the Baptist: 'What went ye out into the wilderness to see? A reed shaken with the wind?' (*Matthew* xi 7).

*290.* Sir Charles Tennyson suggests that Galahad is here Arthur's equal, since this is the only time he calls him 'Sir Arthur'.

*293–4.* 'The king thought that most men ought to do the duty that lies closest to them, and that to few only is given the true spiritual enthusiasm. Those who have it not ought not to affect it' (T.).

*298. ye*] *1873*; you *1869–70*. Likewise in ll. 319, 325.

(Brother, the King was hard upon his knights)
"Taliessin is our fullest throat of song,
And one hath sung and all the dumb will sing.
Lancelot is Lancelot, and hath overborne
Five knights at once, and every younger knight,
Unproven, holds himself as Lancelot,
Till overborne by one, he learns–and ye,
What are ye? Galahads?–no, nor Percivales"
(For thus it pleased the King to range me close
After Sir Galahad); "nay," said he, "but men
With strength and will to right the wronged, of power
To lay the sudden heads of violence flat,
Knights that in twelve great battles splashed and dyed
The strong White Horse in his own heathen blood–
But one hath seen, and all the blind will see.
Go, since your vows are sacred, being made:
Yet–for ye know the cries of all my realm
Pass through this hall–how often, O my knights,
Your places being vacant at my side,
This chance of noble deeds will come and go
Unchallenged, while ye follow wandering fires
Lost in the quagmire! Many of you, yea most,
Return no more: ye think I show myself
Too dark a prophet: come now, let us meet
The morrow morn once more in one full field
Of gracious pastime, that once more the King,
Before ye leave him for this Quest, may count
The yet-unbroken strength of all his knights,
Rejoicing in that Order which he made."

'So when the sun broke next from under ground,
All the great table of our Arthur closed
And clashed in such a tourney and so full,
So many lances broken–never yet

300. *Taliessin*: greatest of the ancient Welsh bards.

315–27. Malory xiii 7: '"Alas", said king Arthur unto sir Gawaine, "ye have nigh slain me with the vow and promise that ye have made, for through you ye have bereft me of the fairest fellowship, and the truest of knighthood, that ever were seen together in any realm of the world, for when they shall depart from hence I am sure that all shall never meet more in this world, for there shall many die in the quest, and so it forethinketh me a little, for I have loved them as well as my life; wherefore it shall grieve me right sore the separation of this fellowship, for I have had an old custom to have them in my fellowship."'

Had Camelot seen the like, since Arthur came;
And I myself and Galahad, for a strength
Was in us from the vision, overthrew
So many knights that all the people cried,
And almost burst the barriers in their heat,
Shouting, "Sir Galahad and Sir Percivale!"

'But when the next day brake from under ground–
O brother, had you known our Camelot,
Built by old kings, age after age, so old
The King himself had fears that it would fall,
So strange, and rich, and dim; for where the roofs
Tottered toward each other in the sky,
Met foreheads all along the street of those
Who watched us pass; and lower, and where the long
Rich galleries, lady-laden, weighed the necks
Of dragons clinging to the crazy walls,
Thicker than drops from thunder, showers of flowers
Fell as we past; and men and boys astride
On wyvern, lion, dragon, griffin, swan,
At all the corners, named us each by name,
Calling "God speed!" but in the ways below
The knights and ladies wept, and rich and poor
Wept, and the King himself could hardly speak
For grief, and all in middle street the Queen,
Who rode by Lancelot, wailed and shrieked aloud,
"This madness has come on us for our sins."
So to the Gate of the three Queens we came,
Where Arthur's wars are rendered mystically,
And thence departed every one his way.

'And I was lifted up in heart, and thought
Of all my late-shown prowess in the lists,
How my strong lance had beaten down the knights,
So many and famous names; and never yet
Had heaven appeared so blue, nor earth so green,

350. *wyvern*: 'two-legged dragon. Old French *wivre*, viper' (T.).
352. *ways*] *1873*; street *1869–70*.
353. Malory xiii 7: 'Then the queen departed into her chamber, so that no man should perceive her great sorrows . . . And there was weeping of the rich and poor, and the king returned [turned] away, and might not speak for weeping.'
355. *all in*] *1873*; in the *1869–70*.
358] *1873*; And then we reached the weirdly-sculptured gate, *1869–70*.
359. *are*] *1873*; were *1869–70*.

For all my blood danced in me, and I knew
That I should light upon the Holy Grail.

'Thereafter, the dark warning of our King,
That most of us would follow wandering fires,
Came like a driving gloom across my mind.
Then every evil word I had spoken once,
And every evil thought I had thought of old,
And every evil deed I ever did,
Awoke and cried, "This Quest is not for thee."
And lifting up mine eyes, I found myself
Alone, and in a land of sand and thorns,
And I was thirsty even unto death;
And I, too, cried, "This Quest is not for thee."

'And on I rode, and when I thought my thirst
Would slay me, saw deep lawns, and then a brook,
With one sharp rapid, where the crisping white
Played ever back upon the sloping wave,
And took both ear and eye; and o'er the brook
Were apple-trees, and apples by the brook
Fallen, and on the lawns. "I will rest here,"
I said, "I am not worthy of the Quest;"
But even while I drank the brook, and ate
The goodly apples, all these things at once
Fell into dust, and I was left alone,
And thirsting, in a land of sand and thorns.

'And then behold a woman at a door
Spinning; and fair the house whereby she sat,
And kind the woman's eyes and innocent,
And all her bearing gracious; and she rose
Opening her arms to meet me, as who should say,
"Rest here;" but when I touched her, lo! she, too,
Fell into dust and nothing, and the house
Became no better than a broken shed,
And in it a dead babe; and also this
Fell into dust, and I was left alone.

'And on I rode, and greater was my thirst.
Then flashed a yellow gleam across the world,
And where it smote the plowshare in the field,
The plowman left his plowing, and fell down

*387–90.* 'The gratification of sensual appetite brings Percivale no content' (T., who comments on the ensuing episodes: 'Nor does wifely love and the love of the family; nor does wealth, which is worshipt by labour; nor does glory; nor does Fame').

Before it; where it glittered on her pail,
The milkmaid left her milking, and fell down
Before it, and I knew not why, but thought
"The sun is rising," though the sun had risen.
Then was I ware of one that on me moved
In golden armour with a crown of gold
About a casque all jewels; and his horse
In golden armour jewelled everywhere:
And on the splendour came, flashing me blind;
And seemed to me the Lord of all the world,
Being so huge. But when I thought he meant
To crush me, moving on me, lo! he, too,
Opened his arms to embrace me as he came,
And up I went and touched him, and he, too,
Fell into dust, and I was left alone
And wearying in a land of sand and thorns.

'And I rode on and found a mighty hill,
And on the top, a city walled: the spires
Pricked with incredible pinnacles into heaven.
And by the gateway stirred a crowd; and these
Cried to me climbing, "Welcome, Percivale!
Thou mightiest and thou purest among men!"
And glad was I and clomb, but found at top
No man, nor any voice. And thence I past
Far through a ruinous city, and I saw
That man had once dwelt there; but there I found
Only one man of an exceeding age.
"Where is that goodly company," said I,
"That so cried out upon me?" and he had
Scarce any voice to answer, and yet gasped,
"Whence and what art thou?" and even as he spoke
Fell into dust, and disappeared, and I
Was left alone once more, and cried in grief,
"Lo, if I find the Holy Grail itself
And touch it, it will crumble into dust."

'And thence I dropt into a lowly vale,
Low as the hill was high, and where the vale
Was lowest, found a chapel, and thereby
A holy hermit in a hermitage,
To whom I told my phantoms, and he said:

'"O son, thou hast not true humility,
The highest virtue, mother of them all;
For when the Lord of all things made Himself
Naked of glory for His mortal change,
'Take thou my robe,' she said, 'for all is thine,'

And all her form shone forth with sudden light
So that the angels were amazed, and she
Followed Him down, and like a flying star
Led on the gray-haired wisdom of the east;
But her thou hast not known: for what is this
Thou thoughtest of thy prowess and thy sins?
Thou hast not lost thyself to save thyself
As Galahad." When the hermit made an end,
In silver armour suddenly Galahad shone
Before us, and against the chapel door
Laid lance, and entered, and we knelt in prayer.
And there the hermit slaked my burning thirst,
And at the sacring of the mass I saw
The holy elements alone; but he,
"Saw ye no more? I, Galahad, saw the Grail,
The Holy Grail, descend upon the shrine:
I saw the fiery face as of a child
That smote itself into the bread, and went;
And hither am I come; and never yet
Hath what thy sister taught me first to see,
This Holy Thing, failed from my side, nor come
Covered, but moving with me night and day,
Fainter by day, but always in the night
Blood-red, and sliding down the blackened marsh
Blood-red, and on the naked mountain top
Blood-red, and in the sleeping mere below
Blood-red. And in the strength of this I rode,
Shattering all evil customs everywhere,
And past through Pagan realms, and made them mine,
And clashed with Pagan hordes, and bore them down,
And broke through all, and in the strength of this
Come victor. But my time is hard at hand,
And hence I go; and one will crown me king
Far in the spiritual city; and come thou, too,
For thou shalt see the vision when I go."

'While thus he spake, his eye, dwelling on mine,
Drew me, with power upon me, till I grew

*453.* 'The Magi' (T.).
*462. sacring*: 'consecration' (T.).
*462–7.* Malory xvii 20: 'And then the bishop made semblance as though he would have gone to the sakering of the mass; and then he took a wafer, which was made in the likeness of bread, and at the lifting up there came a figure in the likeness of a child, and the visage was as red and as bright as any fire, and smote himself into that bread, so that they all saw that the bread was formed of a fleshly man.'

One with him, to believe as he believed.
Then, when the day began to wane, we went.

'There rose a hill that none but man could climb,
Scarred with a hundred wintry water-courses–
Storm at the top, and when we gained it, storm
Round us and death; for every moment glanced
His silver arms and gloomed: so quick and thick
The lightnings here and there to left and right
Struck, till the dry old trunks about us, dead,
Yea, rotten with a hundred years of death,
Sprang into fire: and at the base we found
On either hand, as far as eye could see,
A great black swamp and of an evil smell,
Part black, part whitened with the bones of men,
Not to be crost, save that some ancient king
Had built a way, where, linked with many a bridge,
A thousand piers ran into the great Sea.
And Galahad fled along them bridge by bridge,
And every bridge as quickly as he crost
Sprang into fire and vanished, though I yearned
To follow; and thrice above him all the heavens
Opened and blazed with thunder such as seemed
Shoutings of all the sons of God: and first
At once I saw him far on the great Sea,
In silver-shining armour starry-clear;
And o'er his head the Holy Vessel hung
Clothed in white samite or a luminous cloud.
And with exceeding swiftness ran the boat,
If boat it were–I saw not whence it came.
And when the heavens opened and blazed again
Roaring, I saw him like a silver star–
And had he set the sail, or had the boat
Become a living creature clad with wings?
And o'er his head the Holy Vessel hung
Redder than any rose, a joy to me,
For now I knew the veil had been withdrawn.
Then in a moment when they blazed again
Opening, I saw the least of little stars
Down on the waste, and straight beyond the star
I saw the spiritual city and all her spires

*491.* 'It was a time of storm when men could imagine miracles, and so storm is emphasized' (T.).

*509. Job* xxxviii 7: 'When the morning stars sang together, and all the sons of God shouted for joy.'

*526–7.* Cp. *Revelation* xxi.

And gateways in a glory like one pearl–
No larger, though the goal of all the saints–
Strike from the sea; and from the star there shot
A rose-red sparkle to the city, and there
Dwelt, and I knew it was the Holy Grail,
Which never eyes on earth again shall see.
Then fell the floods of heaven drowning the deep.
And how my feet recrost the deathful ridge
No memory in me lives; but that I touched
The chapel-doors at dawn I know; and thence
Taking my war-horse from the holy man,
Glad that no phantom vext me more, returned
To whence I came, the gate of Arthur's wars.'

'O brother,' asked Ambrosius,–'for in sooth
These ancient books–and they would win thee–teem,
Only I find not there this Holy Grail,
With miracles and marvels like to these,
Not all unlike; which oftentime I read,
Who read but on my breviary with ease,
Till my head swims; and then go forth and pass
Down to the little thorpe that lies so close,
And almost plastered like a martin's nest
To these old walls–and mingle with our folk;
And knowing every honest face of theirs
As well as ever shepherd knew his sheep,
And every homely secret in their hearts,
Delight myself with gossip and old wives,
And ills and aches, and teethings, lyings-in,
And mirthful sayings, children of the place,
That have no meaning half a league away:
Or lulling random squabbles when they rise,
Chafferings and chatterings at the market-cross,
Rejoice, small man, in this small world of mine,
Yea, even in their hens and in their eggs–
O brother, saving this Sir Galahad,
Came ye on none but phantoms in your quest,
No man, no woman?'

Then Sir Percivale:
'All men, to one so bound by such a vow,
And women were as phantoms. O, my brother,
Why wilt thou shame me to confess to thee
How far I faltered from my quest and vow?
For after I had lain so many nights,
A bedmate of the snail and eft and snake,
In grass and burdock, I was changed to wan

And meagre, and the vision had not come;
And then I chanced upon a goodly town
With one great dwelling in the middle of it;
Thither I made, and there was I disarmed
By maidens each as fair as any flower:
But when they led me into hall, behold,
The Princess of that castle was the one,
Brother, and that one only, who had ever
Made my heart leap; for when I moved of old
A slender page about her father's hall,
And she a slender maiden, all my heart
Went after her with longing: yet we twain
Had never kissed a kiss, or vowed a vow.
And now I came upon her once again,
And one had wedded her, and he was dead,
And all his land and wealth and state were hers.
And while I tarried, every day she set
A banquet richer than the day before
By me; for all her longing and her will
Was toward me as of old; till one fair morn,
I walking to and fro beside a stream
That flashed across her orchard underneath
Her castle-walls, she stole upon my walk,
And calling me the greatest of all knights,
Embraced me, and so kissed me the first time,
And gave herself and all her wealth to me.
Then I remembered Arthur's warning word,
That most of us would follow wandering fires,
And the Quest faded in my heart. Anon,
The heads of all her people drew to me,
With supplication both of knees and tongue:
"We have heard of thee: thou art our greatest knight,
Our Lady says it, and we well believe:
Wed thou our Lady, and rule over us,
And thou shalt be as Arthur in our land."
O me, my brother! but one night my vow
Burnt me within, so that I rose and fled,
But wailed and wept, and hated mine own self,
And even the Holy Quest, and all but her;
Then after I was joined with Galahad
Cared not for her, nor anything upon earth.'

Then said the monk, 'Poor men, when yule is cold,
Must be content to sit by little fires.

*575–605.* Based on the temptation of Percivale in Malory xiv 9.

And this am I, so that ye care for me
Ever so little; yea, and blest be Heaven
That brought thee here to this poor house of ours
Where all the brethren are so hard, to warm
My cold heart with a friend: but O the pity
To find thine own first love once more–to hold,
Hold her a wealthy bride within thine arms,
Or all but hold, and then–cast her aside,
Foregoing all her sweetness, like a weed.
For we that want the warmth of double life,
We that are plagued with dreams of something sweet
Beyond all sweetness in a life so rich,–
Ah, blessèd Lord, I speak too earthlywise,
Seeing I never strayed beyond the cell,
But live like an old badger in his earth,
With earth about him everywhere, despite
All fast and penance. Saw ye none beside,
None of your knights?'

'Yea so,' said Percivale:
'One night my pathway swerving east, I saw
The pelican on the casque of our Sir Bors
All in the middle of the rising moon:
And toward him spurred, and hailed him, and he me,
And each made joy of either; then he asked,
"Where is he? hast thou seen him–Lancelot?–Once,"
Said good Sir Bors, "he dashed across me–mad,
And maddening what he rode: and when I cried,
'Ridest thou then so hotly on a quest
So holy,' Lancelot shouted, 'Stay me not!
I have been the sluggard, and I ride apace,
For now there is a lion in the way.'
So vanished."

'Then Sir Bors had ridden on
Softly, and sorrowing for our Lancelot,
Because his former madness, once the talk
And scandal of our table, had returned;
For Lancelot's kith and kin so worship him
That ill to him is ill to them; to Bors
Beyond the rest: he well had been content
Not to have seen, so Lancelot might have seen,
The Holy Cup of healing; and, indeed,

*642–3. Proverb* xxvi 13: 'The slothful man saith, There is a lion in the way; a lion is in the streets.'
*646.* Malory xii 3–4, on Lancelot's madness and his cure by the Grail.

Being so clouded with his grief and love,
Small heart was his after the Holy Quest:
If God would send the vision, well: if not,
The Quest and he were in the hands of Heaven.

'And then, with small adventure met, Sir Bors
Rode to the lonest tract of all the realm,
And found a people there among their crags,
Our race and blood, a remnant that were left
Paynim amid their circles, and the stones
They pitch up straight to heaven: and their wise men
Were strong in that old magic which can trace
The wandering of the stars, and scoffed at him
And this high Quest as at a simple thing:
Told him he followed–almost Arthur's words–
A mocking fire: "what other fire than he,
Whereby the blood beats, and the blossom blows,
And the sea rolls, and all the world is warmed?"
And when his answer chafed them, the rough crowd,
Hearing he had a difference with their priests,
Seized him, and bound and plunged him into a cell
Of great piled stones; and lying bounden there
In darkness through innumerable hours
He heard the hollow-ringing heavens sweep
Over him till by miracle–what else?–
Heavy as it was, a great stone slipt and fell,
Such as no wind could move: and through the gap
Glimmered the streaming scud: then came a night
Still as the day was loud; and through the gap
The seven clear stars of Arthur's Table Round–
For, brother, so one night, because they roll
Through such a round in heaven, we named the stars,
Rejoicing in ourselves and in our King–
And these, like bright eyes of familiar friends,
In on him shone: "And then to me, to me,"
Said good Sir Bors, "beyond all hopes of mine,
Who scarce had prayed or asked it for myself–
Across the seven clear stars–O grace to me–
In colour like the fingers of a hand
Before a burning taper, the sweet Grail

*661–2.* 'The temples and upright stones of the Druidic religion' (T.).
*667.* 'The sun-worshippers that were said to dwell on Lyonnesse scoffed at Percivale' (T.).
*675. heavens*] *1869–94*; heaven *Eversley*.
*681.* 'The Great Bear' (T.).
*691–2.* 'It might have been a meteor' (T.).

Glided and past, and close upon it pealed
A sharp quick thunder." Afterwards, a maid,
Who kept our holy faith among her kin
In secret, entering, loosed and let him go.'

To whom the monk: 'And I remember now
That pelican on the casque: Sir Bors it was
Who spake so low and sadly at our board;
And mighty reverent at our grace was he:
A square-set man and honest; and his eyes,
An out-door sign of all the warmth within,
Smiled with his lips–a smile beneath a cloud,
But heaven had meant it for a sunny one:
Ay, ay, Sir Bors, who else? But when ye reached
The city, found ye all your knights returned,
Or was there sooth in Arthur's prophecy,
Tell me, and what said each, and what the King?'

Then answered Percivale: 'And that can I,
Brother, and truly; since the living words
Of so great men as Lancelot and our King
Pass not from door to door and out again,
But sit within the house. O, when we reached
The city, our horses stumbling as they trode
On heaps of ruin, hornless unicorns,
Cracked basilisks, and splintered cockatrices,
And shattered talbots, which had left the stones
Raw, that they fell from, brought us to the hall.

'And there sat Arthur on the daïs-throne,
And those that had gone out upon the Quest,
Wasted and worn, and but a tithe of them,
And those that had not, stood before the King,
Who, when he saw me, rose, and bad me hail,
Saying, "A welfare in thine eye reproves
Our fear of some disastrous chance for thee
On hill, or plain, at sea, or flooding ford.
So fierce a gale made havoc here of late
Among the strange devices of our kings;
Yea, shook this newer, stronger hall of ours,
And from the statue Merlin moulded for us
Half-wrenched a golden wing; but now–the Quest,
This vision–hast thou seen the Holy Cup,
That Joseph brought of old to Glastonbury?"

715. *basilisks*: 'the fabulous crowned serpent whose look killed' (T.). *cockatrices*: 'in heraldry, winged snakes' (T.).
716. *talbots*: 'heraldic dogs' (T.).

'So when I told him all thyself hast heard,
Ambrosius, and my fresh but fixt resolve
To pass away into the quiet life,
He answered not, but, sharply turning, asked
Of Gawain, "Gawain, was this Quest for thee?"

'"Nay, lord," said Gawain, "not for such as I.
Therefore I communed with a saintly man,
Who made me sure the Quest was not for me;
For I was much awearied of the Quest:
But found a silk pavilion in a field,
And merry maidens in it; and then this gale
Tore my pavilion from the tenting-pin,
And blew my merry maidens all about
With all discomfort; yea, and but for this,
My twelvemonth and a day were pleasant to me."

'He ceased; and Arthur turned to whom at first
He saw not, for Sir Bors, on entering, pushed
Athwart the throng to Lancelot, caught his hand,
Held it, and there, half-hidden by him, stood,
Until the King espied him, saying to him,
"Hail, Bors! if ever loyal man and true
Could see it, thou hast seen the Grail;" and Bors,
"Ask me not, for I may not speak of it:
I saw it;" and the tears were in his eyes.

'Then there remained but Lancelot, for the rest
Spake but of sundry perils in the storm;
Perhaps, like him of Cana in Holy Writ,
Our Arthur kept his best until the last;
"Thou, too, my Lancelot," asked the King, "my friend,
Our mightiest, hath this Quest availed for thee?"

'"Our mightiest!" answered Lancelot, with a groan;
"O King!"–and when he paused, methought I spied

*738.* Based on Malory xvi 5, though here and elsewhere T. worsened the character of Gawain. H.T. compares Malory xiii 19: 'And there he said, "My sin and my wretchedness hath brought me unto great dishonour: for when I sought worldly adventures, and worldly desires, I ever achieved them, and had the better in every place, and never was I discomfited in any quarrel, were it right or wrong; and now I take upon me the adventures of holy things: and now I see and understand that mine old sin hindereth me; and also shamed me, so that I had no power to stir, nor to speak, when the holy blood appeared before me." So thus he sorrowed till it was day, and heard the fowls of the air sing; then was he somewhat comforted.'
*758. John* ii 1–10.

A dying fire of madness in his eyes–
"O King, my friend, if friend of thine I be,
Happier are those that welter in their sin,
Swine in the mud, that cannot see for slime,
Slime of the ditch: but in me lived a sin
So strange, of such a kind, that all of pure,
Noble, and knightly in me twined and clung
Round that one sin, until the wholesome flower
And poisonous grew together, each as each,
Not to be plucked asunder; and when thy knights
Sware, I sware with them only in the hope
That could I touch or see the Holy Grail
They might be plucked asunder. Then I spake
To one most holy saint, who wept and said,
That save they could be plucked asunder, all
My quest were but in vain; to whom I vowed
That I would work according as he willed.
And forth I went, and while I yearned and strove
To tear the twain asunder in my heart,
My madness came upon me as of old,
And whipt me into waste fields far away;
There was I beaten down by little men,
Mean knights, to whom the moving of my sword
And shadow of my spear had been enow
To scare them from me once; and then I came
All in my folly to the naked shore,
Wide flats, where nothing but coarse grasses grew;
But such a blast, my King, began to blow,
So loud a blast along the shore and sea,
Ye could not hear the waters for the blast,
Though heapt in mounds and ridges all the sea
Drove like a cataract, and all the sand
Swept like a river, and the clouded heavens
Were shaken with the motion and the sound.
And blackening in the sea-foam swayed a boat,
Half-swallowed in it, anchored with a chain;
And in my madness to myself I said,
'I will embark and I will lose myself,
And in the great sea wash away my sin.'
I burst the chain, I sprang into the boat.
Seven days I drove along the dreary deep,
And with me drove the moon and all the stars;
And the wind fell, and on the seventh night

*777–9.* Based on Malory xiii 20, where the hermit refers specifically to Lancelot's love of Guinevere (which in T.'s context cannot be mentioned).

I heard the shingle grinding in the surge,
And felt the boat shock earth, and looking up,
Behold, the enchanted towers of Carbonek,
A castle like a rock upon a rock,
With chasm-like portals open to the sea,
And steps that met the breaker! there was none
Stood near it but a lion on each side
That kept the entry, and the moon was full.
Then from the boat I leapt, and up the stairs.
There drew my sword. With sudden-flaring manes
Those two great beasts rose upright like a man,
Each gript a shoulder, and I stood between;
And, when I would have smitten them, heard a voice,
'Doubt not, go forward; if thou doubt, the beasts
Will tear thee piecemeal.' Then with violence
The sword was dashed from out my hand, and fell.
And up into the sounding hall I past;
But nothing in the sounding hall I saw,
No bench nor table, painting on the wall
Or shield of knight; only the rounded moon
Through the tall oriel on the rolling sea.
But always in the quiet house I heard,
Clear as a lark, high o'er me as a lark,
A sweet voice singing in the topmost tower

*810.* The legendary home of the Grail.

*810–14.* Malory xvii 14: 'So it befel, upon a night, at midnight, he arrived afore a castle, on the back side, which was rich and fair; and there was a postern that opened toward the sea, and was open without any keeping, save two lions kept the entry; and the moon shined clear.'

*815–22.* Malory xvii 14: 'Then he ran to his arms, and armed him, and so he went unto the gate, and saw the two lions; then he set hands to his sword, and drew it. Then came there suddenly a dwarf, that smote him upon the arm so sore, that the sword fell out of his hand. Then he heard a voice, that said, "Oh, man of evil faith and poor belief, wherefore believest thou more in thy harness than in thy Maker; for he might more avail thee than thine armour, in whose service thou art set". Then said sir Launcelot, "Fair father, Jesu Christ, I thank thee, of thy great mercy, that thou reprovest me of my misdeed. Now see I well that thou holdest me for thy servant". Then took he again his sword, and put it upon his shield, and made a cross on his forehead, and came to the lions; and they made attempt to do him harm; notwithstanding, he passed by them without hurt, and entered into the castle, to the chief fortress.'

*827–8.* 'My father was fond of quoting these lines for the beauty of the sound. "The lark" in the tower toward the rising sun symbolizes Hope' (H.T.).

To the eastward: up I climbed a thousand steps
With pain: as in a dream I seemed to climb
For ever: at the last I reached a door,
A light was in the crannies, and I heard,
'Glory and joy and honour to our Lord
And to the Holy Vessel of the Grail.'
Then in my madness I essayed the door;
It gave; and through a stormy glare, a heat
As from a seventimes-heated furnace, I,
Blasted and burnt, and blinded as I was,
With such a fierceness that I swooned away–
O, yet methought I saw the Holy Grail,
All palled in crimson samite, and around
Great angels, awful shapes, and wings and eyes.
And but for all my madness and my sin,
And then my swooning, I had sworn I saw
That which I saw; but what I saw was veiled
And covered; and this Quest was not for me."

'So speaking, and here ceasing, Lancelot left
The hall long silent, till Sir Gawain–nay,
Brother, I need not tell thee foolish words,–
A reckless and irreverent knight was he,
Now boldened by the silence of his King,–

*833–6.* Malory xvii 15: 'Then he listened, and heard a voice, which sung so sweetly, that it seemed none earthly thing; and thought that the voice said, "Joy and honour be to the Father of heaven."'
*838–48.* Malory xvii 15: 'And with that he saw the chamber-door open, and with that there came out a great clearness, that the house was as bright as though all the torches of the world had been there. So came he to the chamber-door, and would have entered, and anon a voice said unto him, "Flee, sir Launcelot, and enter not, for thou oughtest not to do it; and, if thou enter, thou shalt forethink it". And he withdrew him back, and was right heavy in his mind. Then he looked up in the midst of the chamber, and saw a table of silver, and the holy vessel covered with red samite, and many angels about it, whereof one of them held a candle of wax burning, and the other held a cross, and the ornaments of the altar . . . Right so he entered into the chamber, and came toward the table of silver. And when he came nigh he felt a breath, that him thought was intermeddled with fire, which smote him so sore in the visage, that him thought it all to break his visage; and therewith he fell to the ground, and had no power to arise.'
*840. Daniel* iii 19, 'heat the furnace one seven times more than it was wont to be heated' (the story of Shadrach, Meshach, and Abednego).
*845. Ezekiel* x 12, 'And their whole body, and their backs, and their hands, and their wings, and the wheels, were full of eyes round about.'

Well, I will tell thee: "O King, my liege," he said,
"Hath Gawain failed in any quest of thine?
When have I stinted stroke in foughten field?
But as for thine, my good friend Percivale,
Thy holy nun and thou have driven men mad,
Yea, made our mightiest madder than our least.
But by mine eyes and by mine ears I swear,
I will be deafer than the blue-eyed cat,
And thrice as blind as any noonday owl,
To holy virgins in their ecstasies,
Henceforward."

"'Deafer,'' said the blameless King,
"Gawain, and blinder unto holy things
Hope not to make thyself by idle vows,
Being too blind to have desire to see.
But if indeed there came a sign from heaven,
Blessèd are Bors, Lancelot and Percivale,
For these have seen according to their sight.
For every fiery prophet in old times,
And all the sacred madness of the bard,
When God made music through them, could but speak
His music by the framework and the chord;
And as ye saw it ye have spoken truth.

"'Nay–but thou errest, Lancelot: never yet
Could all of true and noble in knight and man
Twine round one sin, whatever it might be,
With such a closeness, but apart there grew,
Save that he were the swine thou spakest of,
Some root of knighthood and pure nobleness;
Whereto see thou, that it may bear its flower.

"'And spake I not too truly, O my knights?
Was I too dark a prophet when I said
To those who went upon the Holy Quest,
That most of them would follow wandering fires,
Lost in the quagmire?–lost to me and gone,
And left me gazing at a barren board,
And a lean Order–scarce returned a tithe–
And out of those to whom the vision came
My greatest hardly will believe he saw;
Another hath beheld it afar off,

*862.* H.T. quotes the first chapter of Darwin's *Origin of Species*: 'Thus cats which are entirely white and have blue eyes are generally deaf; but it has lately been pointed out by Mr Tait that this is confined to the males.'

And leaving human wrongs to right themselves,
Cares but to pass into the silent life.
And one hath had the vision face to face,
And now his chair desires him here in vain,
However they may crown him otherwhere.

'"And some among you held, that if the King
Had seen the sight he would have sworn the vow:
Not easily, seeing that the King must guard
That which he rules, and is but as the hind
To whom a space of land is given to plow.
Who may not wander from the allotted field
Before his work be done; but, being done,
Let visions of the night or of the day
Come, as they will; and many a time they come,
Until this earth he walks on seems not earth,
This light that strikes his eyeball is not light,
This air that smites his forehead is not air
But vision–yea, his very hand and foot–
In moments when he feels he cannot die,
And knows himself no vision to himself,
Nor the high God a vision, nor that One
Who rose again: ye have seen what ye have seen."

'So spake the King: I knew not all he meant.'

# 472 Pelleas and Ettarre

Published *1869* ('*1870*'). On 28 June 1859, T. 'read *Sir Pelleas and Ettarre* [Malory iv 21–4] . . . with a view to a new poem' (*Mat.* ii 220). Written 1869 (*CT*, pp. 381–2). R. W. Rader (*Tennyson's 'Maud'*, 1963, pp. 54–5) argues that T. associated this poem 'consciously or unconsciously with memories of Rosa [Baring]', especially the rose-song (ll. 391–400). 'Almost the saddest of the Idylls. The breaking of the storm' (T.).

King Arthur made new knights to fill the gap
Left by the Holy Quest; and as he sat

*908.* 'Arthur suggests that all the material universe may be but vision' (T.).
*911–3.* H.T. compares *The Ancient Sage.*
*913–14.* 'My father said (I think) about this passage: "There is something miraculous in man, and there is more in Christianity than some people think. It is enough to look on Christ as Divine and Ideal without defining more. They will not easily beat the character of Christ, that union of man and woman, strength and sweetness"' (H.T.).

In hall at old Caerleon, the high doors
Were softly sundered, and through these a youth,
Pelleas, and the sweet smell of the fields
Past, and the sunshine came along with him.

'Make me thy knight, because I know, Sir King,
All that belongs to knighthood, and I love.'
Such was his cry: for having heard the King
Had let proclaim a tournament–the prize
A golden circlet and a knightly sword,
Full fain had Pelleas for his lady won
The golden circlet, for himself the sword:
And there were those who knew him near the King,
And promised for him: and Arthur made him knight.

And this new knight, Sir Pelleas of the isles–
But lately come to his inheritance,
And lord of many a barren isle was he–
Riding at noon, a day or twain before,
Across the forest called of Dean, to find
Caerleon and the King, had felt the sun
Beat like a strong knight on his helm, and reeled
Almost to falling from his horse; but saw
Near him a mound of even-sloping side,
Whereon a hundred stately beeches grew,
And here and there great hollies under them;
But for a mile all round was open space,
And fern and heath: and slowly Pelleas drew
To that dim day, then binding his good horse
To a tree, cast himself down; and as he lay
At random looking over the brown earth
Through that green-glooming twilight of the grove,
It seemed to Pelleas that the fern without
Burnt as a living fire of emeralds,
So that his eyes were dazzled looking at it.
Then o'er it crost the dimness of a cloud
Floating, and once the shadow of a bird
Flying, and then a fawn; and his eyes closed.
And since he loved all maidens, but no maid
In special, half-awake he whispered, 'Where?
O where? I love thee, though I know thee not.
For fair thou art and pure as Guinevere,

¶472. *10–11.* Malory iv 21: 'And who that proved him the best knight should have a passing good sword and a circlet of gold; and the circlet the knight should give it to the fairest lady that was at those jousts.'
*33–4.* 'Seen as I lay in the New Forest' (T.).

And I will make thee with my spear and sword
As famous–O my Queen, my Guinevere,
For I will be thine Arthur when we meet.'

Suddenly wakened with a sound of talk
And laughter at the limit of the wood,
And glancing through the hoary boles, he saw,
Strange as to some old prophet might have seemed
A vision hovering on a sea of fire,
Damsels in divers colours like the cloud
Of sunset and sunrise, and all of them
On horses, and the horses richly trapt
Breast-high in that bright line of bracken stood:
And all the damsels talked confusedly,
And one was pointing this way, and one that,
Because the way was lost.

And Pelleas rose,
And loosed his horse, and led him to the light.
There she that seemed the chief among them said,
'In happy time behold our pilot-star!
Youth, we are damsels-errant, and we ride,
Armed as ye see, to tilt against the knights
There at Caerleon, but have lost our way:
To right? to left? straight forward? back again?
Which? tell us quickly.'

Pelleas gazing thought,
'Is Guinevere herself so beautiful?'
For large her violet eyes looked, and her bloom
A rosy dawn kindled in stainless heavens,
And round her limbs, mature in womanhood;
And slender was her hand and small her shape;
And but for those large eyes, the haunts of scorn,
She might have seemed a toy to trifle with,
And pass and care no more. But while he gazed
The beauty of her flesh abashed the boy,
As though it were the beauty of her soul:
For as the base man, judging of the good,
Puts his own baseness in him by default
Of will and nature, so did Pelleas lend
All the young beauty of his own soul to hers,

*46–54*. Not in Malory. Cp. *Sir Orfeo*, long extracts from which are given in Thomas Keightley's *Fairy Mythology* (1833, i 82–6). Part of this from Keightley was copied out in *H.Nbk 7*. Orfeo sleeps under the trees, and then meets knights and ladies on fine horses.

Believing her; and when she spake to him,
Stammered, and could not make her a reply.
For out of the waste islands had he come,
Where saving his own sisters he had known
Scarce any but the women of his isles,
Rough wives, that laughed and screamed against the gulls,
Makers of nets, and living from the sea.

Then with a slow smile turned the lady round
And looked upon her people; and as when
A stone is flung into some sleeping tarn,
The circle widens till it lip the marge,
Spread the slow smile through all her company.
Three knights were thereamong; and they too smiled,
Scorning him; for the lady was Ettarre,
And she was a great lady in her land.

Again she said, 'O wild and of the woods,
Knowest thou not the fashion of our speech?
Or have the Heavens but given thee a fair face,
Lacking a tongue?'

'O damsel,' answered he,
'I woke from dreams; and coming out of gloom
Was dazzled by the sudden light, and crave
Pardon: but will ye to Caerleon? I
Go likewise: shall I lead you to the King?'

'Lead then,' she said; and through the woods they went.
And while they rode, the meaning in his eyes,
His tenderness of manner, and chaste awe,
His broken utterances and bashfulness,
Were all a burthen to her, and in her heart
She muttered, 'I have lighted on a fool,
Raw, yet so stale!' But since her mind was bent
On hearing, after trumpet blown, her name
And title, 'Queen of Beauty,' in the lists
Cried–and beholding him so strong, she thought
That peradventure he will fight for me,

*82–6.* Suggested by Malory iv 22: 'My name is sir Pelles, born in the isles, and of many isles I am lord, and never have I loved lady nor damsel till now.'

*94.* Malory iv 21: 'He loveth a great lady in this country, and her name is Ettarde.'

And win the circlet: therefore flattered him,
Being so gracious, that he wellnigh deemed
His wish by hers was echoed; and her knights
And all her damsels too were gracious to him,
For she was a great lady.
And when they reached
Caerleon, ere they past to lodging, she,
Taking his hand, 'O the strong hand,' she said,
'See! look at mine! but wilt thou fight for me,
And win me this fine circlet, Pelleas,
That I may love thee?'
Then his helpless heart
Leapt, and he cried, 'Ay! wilt thou if I win?'
'Ay, that will I,' she answered, and she laughed,
And straitly nipt the hand, and flung it from her;
Then glanced askew at those three knights of hers,
Till all her ladies laughed along with her.

'O happy world,' thought Pelleas, 'all, meseems,
Are happy; I the happiest of them all.'
Nor slept that night for pleasure in his blood,
And green wood-ways, and eyes among the leaves;
Then being on the morrow knighted, sware
To love one only. And as he came away,
The men who met him rounded on their heels
And wondered after him, because his face
Shone like the countenance of a priest of old
Against the flame about a sacrifice
Kindled by fire from heaven: so glad was he.

Then Arthur made vast banquets, and strange knights
From the four winds came in: and each one sat,
Though served with choice from air, land, stream, and sea,
Oft in mid-banquet measuring with his eyes
His neighbour's make and might: and Pelleas looked
Noble among the noble, for he dreamed
His lady loved him, and he knew himself
Loved of the King: and him his new-made knight
Worshipt, whose lightest whisper moved him more
Than all the rangèd reasons of the world.

Then blushed and brake the morning of the jousts,
And this was called 'The Tournament of Youth:'

*150–63.* Malory iv 21: 'And this knight, sir Pelles, was the best knight that

For Arthur, loving his young knight, withheld
His older and his mightier from the lists,
That Pelleas might obtain his lady's love,
According to her promise, and remain
Lord of the tourney. And Arthur had the jousts
Down in the flat field by the shore of Usk
Holden: the gilded parapets were crowned
With faces, and the great tower filled with eyes
Up to the summit, and the trumpets blew.
There all day long Sir Pelleas kept the field
With honour: so by that strong hand of his
The sword and golden circlet were achieved.

Then rang the shout his lady loved: the heat
Of pride and glory fired her face; her eye
Sparkled; she caught the circlet from his lance,
And there before the people crowned herself:
So for the last time she was gracious to him.

Then at Caerleon for a space–her look
Bright for all others, cloudier on her knight–
Lingered Ettarre: and seeing Pelleas droop,
Said Guinevere, 'We marvel at thee much,
O damsel, wearing this unsunny face
To him who won thee glory!' And she said,
'Had ye not held your Lancelot in your bower,
My Queen, he had not won.' Whereat the Queen,
As one whose foot is bitten by an ant,
Glanced down upon her, turned and went her way.

But after, when her damsels, and herself,
And those three knights all set their faces home,
Sir Pelleas followed. She that saw him cried,
'Damsels–and yet I should be shamed to say it–
I cannot bide Sir Baby. Keep him back
Among yourselves. Would rather that we had
Some rough old knight who knew the worldly way,
Albeit grizzlier than a bear, to ride
And jest with: take him to you, keep him off,

was there, and there five hundred knights; but there was never man that ever sir Pelles met withal, but that he struck him down, or else from his horse. And every day of the three days he struck down twenty knights; therefore, they gave him the prize.'

*182–3.* Malory iv 22: 'But she was so proud that she had scorn of him, and said, "That she would never love him, though he would die for her."'

And pamper him with papmeat, if ye will,
Old milky fables of the wolf and sheep,
Such as the wholesome mothers tell their boys.
Nay, should ye try him with a merry one
To find his mettle, good: and if he fly us,
Small matter! let him.' This her damsels heard,
And mindful of her small and cruel hand,
They, closing round him through the journey home,
Acted her hest, and always from her side
Restrained him with all manner of device,
So that he could not come to speech with her.
And when she gained her castle, upsprang the bridge,
Down rang the grate of iron through the groove,
And he was left alone in open field.

'These be the ways of ladies,' Pelleas thought,
'To those who love them, trials of our faith.
Yea, let her prove me to the uttermost,
For loyal to the uttermost am I.'
So made his moan; and, darkness falling, sought
A priory not far off, there lodged, but rose
With morning every day, and, moist or dry,
Full-armed upon his charger all day long
Sat by the walls, and no one opened to him.

And this persistence turned her scorn to wrath.
Then calling her three knights, she charged them, 'Out!
And drive him from the walls.' And out they came,
But Pelleas overthrew them as they dashed
Against him one by one; and these returned,
But still he kept his watch beneath the wall.

Thereon her wrath became a hate; and once,
A week beyond, while walking on the walls
With her three knights, she pointed downward, 'Look,
He haunts me–I cannot breathe–besieges me;
Down! strike him! put my hate into your strokes,
And drive him from my walls.' And down they went,

*188.* Cp. *What Thor Said* 4: 'But pap-meat-pamper not the time.'
*202–10.* Malory iv 22: 'And so this knight promised the lady Ettarde to follow her into this country, and never to leave her till she loved him; and thus he is here the most part nigh her, and lodged by a priory.'
*211–28.* Malory iv 22: 'And every week she sendeth knights to fight with him; and when he hath put them to the worst, then will he suffer them wilfully to take him prisoner, because he would have a sight of this lady.'

And Pelleas overthrew them one by one;
And from the tower above him cried Ettarre,
'Bind him, and bring him in.'
He heard her voice;
Then let the strong hand, which had overthrown
Her minion-knights, by those he overthrew
Be bounden straight, and so they brought him in.

Then when he came before Ettarre, the sight
Of her rich beauty made him at one glance
More bondsman in his heart than in his bonds.
Yet with good cheer he spake, 'Behold me, Lady,
A prisoner, and the vassal of thy will;
And if thou keep me in thy donjon here,
Content am I so that I see thy face
But once a day: for I have sworn my vows,
And thou hast given thy promise, and I know
That all these pains are trials of my faith,
And that thyself, when thou hast seen me strained
And sifted to the utmost, wilt at length
Yield me thy love and know me for thy knight.'

Then she began to rail so bitterly,
With all her damsels, he was stricken mute;
But when she mocked his vows and the great King,
Lighted on words: 'For pity of thine own self,
Peace, Lady, peace: is he not thine and mine?'
'Thou fool,' she said, 'I never heard his voice
But longed to break away. Unbind him now,
And thrust him out of doors; for save he be
Fool to the midmost marrow of his bones,
He will return no more.' And those, her three,
Laughed, and unbound, and thrust him from the gate.

And after this, a week beyond, again
She called them, saying, 'There he watches yet,
There like a dog before his master's door!
Kicked, he returns: do ye not hate him, ye?
Ye know yourselves: how can ye bide at peace,
Affronted with his fulsome innocence?
Are ye but creatures of the board and bed,
No men to strike? Fall on him all at once,
And if ye slay him I reck not: if ye fail,
Give ye the slave mine order to be bound,
Bind him as heretofore, and bring him in:
It may be ye shall slay him in his bonds.'

She spake; and at her will they couched their spears,
Three against one: and Gawain passing by,
Bound upon solitary adventure, saw
Low down beneath the shadow of those towers
A villainy, three to one: and through his heart
The fire of honour and all noble deeds
Flashed, and he called, 'I strike upon thy side–
The caitiffs!' 'Nay,' said Pelleas, 'but forbear;
He needs no aid who doth his lady's will.'

So Gawain, looking at the villainy done,
Forbore, but in his heat and eagerness
Trembled and quivered, as the dog, withheld
A moment from the vermin that he sees
Before him, shivers, ere he springs and kills.

And Pelleas overthrew them, one to three;
And they rose up, and bound, and brought him in.
Then first her anger, leaving Pelleas, burned
Full on her knights in many an evil name
Of craven, weakling, and thrice-beaten hound:
'Yet, take him, ye that scarce are fit to touch,
Far less to bind, your victor, and thrust him out,
And let who will release him from his bonds.
And if he comes again'–there she brake short;
And Pelleas answered, 'Lady, for indeed
I loved you and I deemed you beautiful,
I cannot brook to see your beauty marred
Through evil spite: and if ye love me not,
I cannot bear to dream you so forsworn:
I had liefer ye were worthy of my love,
Than to be loved again of you–farewell;
And though ye kill my hope, not yet my love,
Vex not yourself: ye will not see me more.'

While thus he spake, she gazed upon the man
Of princely bearing, though in bonds, and thought,
'Why have I pushed him from me? this man loves,
If love there be: yet him I loved not. Why?
I deemed him fool? yea, so? or that in him
A something–was it nobler than myself?–
Seemed my reproach? He is not of my kind.

*266.* In Malory, Gawain is told of Pelleas and seeks him out; Pelleas is not being attacked, and simply tells Gawain of Ettarde's treatment. The details are T.'s; in Malory, Pelleas says: 'When I am brought before her she rebuketh me in the foulest manner'.

He could not love me, did he know me well.
Nay, let him go–and quickly.' And her knights
Laughed not, but thrust him bounden out of door.

Forth sprang Gawain, and loosed him from his bonds,
And flung them o'er the walls; and afterward,
Shaking his hands, as from a lazar's rag,
'Faith of my body,' he said, 'and art thou not–
Yea thou art he, whom late our Arthur made
Knight of his table; yea and he that won
The circlet? wherefore hast thou so defamed
Thy brotherhood in me and all the rest,
As let these caitiffs on thee work their will?'

And Pelleas answered, 'O, their wills are hers
For whom I won the circlet; and mine, hers,
Thus to be bounden, so to see her face,
Marred though it be with spite and mockery now,
Other than when I found her in the woods;
And though she hath me bounden but in spite,
And all to flout me, when they bring me in,
Let me be bounden, I shall see her face;
Else must I die through mine unhappiness.'

And Gawain answered kindly though in scorn,
'Why, let my lady bind me if she will,
And let my lady beat me if she will:
But an she send her delegate to thrall
These fighting hands of mine–Christ kill me then
But I will slice him handless by the wrist,
And let my lady sear the stump for him,
Howl as he may. But hold me for your friend:
Come, ye know nothing: here I pledge my troth,
Yea, by the honour of the Table Round,
I will be leal to thee and work thy work,
And tame thy jailing princess to thine hand.
Lend me thine horse and arms, and I will say

*332–53.* Malory iv 22–3: '"Well", said sir Gawaine, "all this shall I amend, and ye will do as I shall devise: I will have your horse and your armour, and so will I ride to her castle, and tell her that I have slain you; and so shall I come within to her, to cause her to cherish me, and then shall I do my true part, that ye shall not fail to have her love". And therewithal sir Gawaine plight his troth unto sir Pelles to be true and faithful unto him. When they had plight their troth, the one to the other, they changed their horses and harness.'

That I have slain thee. She will let me in
To hear the manner of thy fight and fall;
Then, when I come within her counsels, then
From prime to vespers will I chant thy praise
As prowest knight and truest lover, more
Than any have sung thee living, till she long
To have thee back in lusty life again,
Not to be bound, save by white bonds and warm,
Dearer than freedom. Wherefore now thy horse
And armour: let me go: be comforted:
Give me three days to melt her fancy, and hope
The third night hence will bring thee news of gold.'

Then Pelleas lent his horse and all his arms,
Saving the goodly sword, his prize, and took
Gawain's, and said, 'Betray me not, but help–
Art thou not he whom men call light-of-love?'

'Ay,' said Gawain, 'for women be so light.'
Then bounded forward to the castle walls,
And raised a bugle hanging from his neck,
And winded it, and that so musically
That all the old echoes hidden in the wall
Rang out like hollow woods at hunting-tide.

Up ran a score of damsels to the tower;
'Avaunt,' they cried, 'our lady loves thee not.'
But Gawain lifting up his vizor said,
'Gawain am I, Gawain of Arthur's court,
And I have slain this Pelleas whom ye hate:

*342. prowest*: 'noblest' (T.).

*355–81.* Malory iv 23: 'And sir Gawaine departed and came to the castle, whereas stood the pavilions of this lady without the gate: and, as soon as Ettarde had espied sir Gawaine, she fled towards the castle. Then sir Gawaine spake on high and bid her abide, for he was not sir Pelles; "I am another knight, that hath slain sir Pelles". "Do off your helm", said the lady Ettarde, "that I may behold your visage". And when she saw it was not sir Pelles, she made him to alight, and led him unto her castle, and asked him faithfully whether he had slain sir Pelles? and he said yea. And then sir Gawaine told her that his name was sir Gawaine, and of the court of king Arthur, and his sister's son. "Truly", said she, "that is great pity, for he was a passing good knight of his body, but of all men on live I hated him most, for I never could be quiet for [quit of] him; and for that ye have slain him I shall be your woman, and do any thing that may please you". So she made sir Gawaine good cheer.'

Behold his horse and armour. Open gates,
And I will make you merry.'
And down they ran,
Her damsels, crying to their lady, 'Lo!
Pelleas is dead–he told us–he that hath
His horse and armour: will ye let him in?
He slew him! Gawain, Gawain of the court,
Sir Gawain–there he waits below the wall,
Blowing his bugle as who should say him nay.'

And so, leave given, straight on through open door
Rode Gawain, whom she greeted courteously.
'Dead, is it so?' she asked. 'Ay, ay,' said he,
'And oft in dying cried upon your name.'
'Pity on him,' she answered, 'a good knight,
But never let me bide one hour at peace.'
'Ay,' thought Gawain, 'and you be fair enow:
But I to your dead man have given my troth,
That whom ye loathe, him will I make you love.'

So those three days, aimless about the land,
Lost in a doubt, Pelleas wandering
Waited, until the third night brought a moon
With promise of large light on woods and ways.

Hot was the night and silent; but a sound
Of Gawain ever coming, and this lay–
Which Pelleas had heard sung before the Queen,
And seen her sadden listening–vext his heart,
And marred his rest–'A worm within the rose.'

'A rose, but one, none other rose had I,
A rose, one rose, and this was wondrous fair,
One rose, a rose that gladdened earth and sky,
One rose, my rose, that sweetened all mine air–
I cared not for the thorns; the thorns were there.

'One rose, a rose to gather by and by,
One rose, a rose, to gather and to wear,
No rose but one–what other rose had I?
One rose, my rose; a rose that will not die,–
He dies who loves it,–if the worm be there.'

365. *gates*] *1873*; gate *1869–70*.
386–403] *1873* (*see l. 397n*); The night was hot: he could not rest, but rode *1869–70*.
397. *a*] *1882*; one *1873–81*.

This tender rhyme, and evermore the doubt,
'Why lingers Gawain with his golden news?'
So shook him that he could not rest, but rode
Ere midnight to her walls, and bound his horse
Hard by the gates. Wide open were the gates,
And no watch kept; and in through these he past,
And heard but his own steps, and his own heart
Beating, for nothing moved but his own self,
And his own shadow. Then he crost the court,
And spied not any light in hall or bower,
But saw the postern portal also wide
Yawning; and up a slope of garden, all
Of roses white and red, and brambles mixt
And overgrowing them, went on, and found,
Here too, all hushed below the mellow moon,
Save that one rivulet from a tiny cave
Came lightening downward, and so spilt itself
Among the roses, and was lost again.

Then was he ware of three pavilions reared
Above the bushes, gilden-peakt: in one,
Red after revel, droned her lurdane knights

*410*] *1873*; *not 1869–70.*
*411. But*] *1873*; And *1869–70.*
*413. brambles*] *1873*; wild ones *1869–70.*
*419. of . . . reared*] *1873*; that white pavilions rose, *1869–70.*
*419–26.* Malory iv 23: 'And then it was in the month of May, that she and sir Gawaine went out of the castle and supped in a pavilion, and there was a bed made, and there sir Gawaine and the lady Ettarde went to bed together; and in another pavilion she laid her damsels; and in the third pavilion she laid part of her knights: for then she had no dread nor fear of sir Pelles. And there sir Gawaine lay with her, doing his pleasure in that pavilion, two days and two nights, against the faithful promise that he made to sir Pelles. And, on the third day, in the morning early, sir Pelles armed him, for he had not slept sith that sir Gawaine departed from him; for sir Gawaine had promised, by the faith of his body, to come unto him to his pavilion by the priory within the space of a day and a night. Then sir Pelles mounted on horseback, and came to the pavilions that stood without the castle, and found, in the first pavilion, three knights in their beds, and three squires lying at their feet; then went he to the second pavilion and found four gentlewomen lying in four beds: and then he went to the third pavilion, and found sir Gawaine lying in a bed with his lady Ettarde, and either clasping other in their arms.'
*420. Above*] *1873*; Three from *1869–70.*
*421. lurdane*: 'from Old French *lourdin*, heavy' (T.). H.T. compares Scott's *Abbot* iv: 'I found the careless lurdane feeding him with unwashed flesh'.

Slumbering, and their three squires across their feet:
In one, their malice on the placid lip
Frozen by sweet sleep, four of her damsels lay:
And in the third, the circlet of the jousts
Bound on her brow, were Gawain and Ettarre.

Back, as a hand that pushes through the leaf
To find a nest and feels a snake, he drew:
Back, as a coward slinks from what he fears
To cope with, or a traitor proven, or hound
Beaten, did Pelleas in an utter shame
Creep with his shadow through the court again,
Fingering at his sword-handle until he stood
There on the castle-bridge once more, and thought,
'I will go back, and slay them where they lie.'

And so went back, and seeing them yet in sleep
Said, 'Ye, that so dishallow the holy sleep,
Your sleep is death,' and drew the sword, and thought,
'What! slay a sleeping knight? the King hath bound
And sworn me to this brotherhood;' again,
'Alas that ever a knight should be so false.'
Then turned, and so returned, and groaning laid
The naked sword athwart their naked throats,
There left it, and them sleeping; and she lay,
The circlet of the tourney round her brows,
And the sword of the tourney across her throat.

And forth he past, and mounting on his horse
Stared at her towers that, larger than themselves

*427–46.* Malory iv 23: 'And when he saw that his heart almost burst for sorrow, and said, "Alas! that ever a knight should be found so false". And then he took his horse, and might no longer abide for sorrow. And when he had ridden nigh half a mile, he turned again, and thought to slay them both; and when he saw them both lie so fast sleeping, unneth he might hold him on horseback for sorrow, and said thus to himself: "Though he be never so false I will not slay him sleeping; for I will never destroy the high order of knighthood". And therewith he departed again, and left them sleeping. And or he had ridden half a mile he returned again, and thought then to slay them, making the greatest sorrow that any man might make; and when he came to the pavilions he tied his horse to a tree, and pulled out his sword, naked in his hand, and went straight to them whereas they lay together, and yet he thought that it were great shame for him to slay them sleeping, and laid the naked sword overthwart their throats, and then he took his horse and rode forth his way.'

*446.* 'The line gives the quiver of the sword across their throats' (T.).

In their own darkness, thronged into the moon.
Then crushed the saddle with his thighs, and clenched
His hands, and maddened with himself and moaned:

'Would they have risen against me in their blood
At the last day? I might have answered them
Even before high God. O towers so strong,
Huge, solid, would that even while I gaze
The crack of earthquake shivering to your base
Split you, and Hell burst up your harlot roofs
Bellowing, and charred you through and through within,
Black as the harlot's heart–hollow as a skull!
Let the fierce east scream through your eyelet-holes,
And whirl the dust of harlots round and round
In dung and nettles! hiss, snake–I saw him there–
Let the fox bark, let the wolf yell. Who yells
Here in the still sweet summer night, but I–
I, the poor Pelleas whom she called her fool?
Fool, beast–he, she, or I? myself most fool;
Beast too, as lacking human wit–disgraced,
Dishonoured all for trial of true love–
Love?–we be all alike: only the King
Hath made us fools and liars. O noble vows!
O great and sane and simple race of brutes
That own no lust because they have no law!
For why should I have loved her to my shame?
I loathe her, as I loved her to my shame.
I never loved her, I but lusted for her–
Away–'
He dashed the rowel into his horse,
And bounded forth and vanished through the night.

Then she, that felt the cold touch on her throat,
Awaking knew the sword, and turned herself
To Gawain: 'Liar, for thou hast not slain
This Pelleas! here he stood, and might have slain

*478–82.* Malory iv 23: 'Then sir Gawaine and the lady Ettarde awakened out of their sleep, and found the naked sword overthwart both their throats; then she knew well that it was sir Pelles' sword. "Alas!" said she to sir Gawaine, "ye have betrayed me and sir Pelles also; for ye told me that ye had slain him, and now I know well it is not so, he is alive: and if sir Pelles had been as courteous to you as you have been to him ye had been a dead knight, but ye have deceived me and betrayed me falsely, that all ladies and damsels may beware by you and me."'

Me and thyself.' And he that tells the tale
Says that her ever-veering fancy turned
To Pelleas, as the one true knight on earth,
And only lover; and through her love her life
Wasted and pined, desiring him in vain.

But he by wild and way, for half the night,
And over hard and soft, striking the sod
From out the soft, the spark from off the hard,
Rode till the star above the wakening sun,
Beside that tower where Percivale was cowled,
Glanced from the rosy forehead of the dawn.
For so the words were flashed into his heart
He knew not whence or wherefore: 'O sweet star,
Pure on the virgin forehead of the dawn!'
And there he would have wept, but felt his eyes
Harder and drier than a fountain bed
In summer: thither came the village girls
And lingered talking, and they come no more
Till the sweet heavens have filled it from the heights
Again with living waters in the change
Of seasons: hard his eyes; harder his heart
Seemed; but so weary were his limbs, that he,
Gasping, 'Of Arthur's hall am I, but here,
Here let me rest and die,' cast himself down,
And gulfed his griefs in inmost sleep; so lay,
Till shaken by a dream, that Gawain fired
The hall of Merlin, and the morning star
Reeled in the smoke, brake into flame, and fell.

He woke, and being ware of some one nigh,
Sent hands upon him, as to tear him, crying,
'False! and I held thee pure as Guinevere.'

But Percivale stood near him and replied,
'Am I but false as Guinevere is pure?
Or art thou mazed with dreams? or being one

*482–6.* Malory iv 23: 'The damsel of the Lake . . . cast such an enchantment upon her [Ettarde], that she loved him out of measure, that well nigh she was out of her mind. "Oh! Lord Jesus", said the lady Ettarde, "how is it befallen me that I now love him which I before most hated of all men living?"–"This is the right wise [righteous] judgment of God", said the lady of the lake'. Pelleas then spurns her. 'So the lady Ettarde died for sorrow, and the damsel of the lake rejoiced sir Pelles, and loved together during their lives.' T. completely changes this ending, and continues the tale of the bitter and violent sir Pelleas in *The Last Tournament.*

Of our free-spoken Table hast not heard
That Lancelot'–there he checked himself and paused.

Then fared it with Sir Pelleas as with one
Who gets a wound in battle, and the sword
That made it plunges through the wound again,
And pricks it deeper: and he shrank and wailed,
'Is the Queen false?' and Percivale was mute.
'Have any of our Round Table held their vows?'
And Percivale made answer not a word.
'Is the King true?' 'The King!' said Percivale.
'Why then let men couple at once with wolves.
What! art thou mad?'
But Pelleas, leaping up,
Ran through the doors and vaulted on his horse
And fled: small pity upon his horse had he,
Or on himself, or any, and when he met
A cripple, one that held a hand for alms–
Hunched as he was, and like an old dwarf-elm
That turns its back on the salt blast, the boy
Paused not, but overrode him, shouting, 'False,
And false with Gawain!' and so left him bruised
And battered, and fled on, and hill and wood
Went ever streaming by him till the gloom,
That follows on the turning of the world,
Darkened the common path: he twitched the reins,
And made his beast that better knew it, swerve
Now off it and now on; but when he saw
High up in heaven the hall that Merlin built,
Blackening against the dead-green stripes of even,
'Black nest of rats,' he groaned, 'ye build too high.'

Not long thereafter from the city gates
Issued Sir Lancelot riding airily,
Warm with a gracious parting from the Queen,
Peace at his heart, and gazing at a star
And marvelling what it was: on whom the boy,
Across the silent seeded meadow-grass
Borne, clashed: and Lancelot, saying, 'What name hast thou
That ridest here so blindly and so hard?'
'No name, no name,' he shouted, 'a scourge am I
To lash the treasons of the Table Round.'
'Yea, but thy name?' 'I have many names,' he cried:

550. *meadow-*] *1869–94*; *mellow- Eversley*.
553. *No name,*] *1890*; I have *1869–89*.

'I am wrath and shame and hate and evil fame,
And like a poisonous wind I pass to blast
And blaze the crime of Lancelot and the Queen.'
'First over me,' said Lancelot, 'shalt thou pass.'
'Fight therefore,' yelled the youth, and either knight
Drew back a space, and when they closed, at once
The weary steed of Pelleas floundering flung
His rider, who called out from the dark field,
'Thou art false as Hell: slay me: I have no sword.'
Then Lancelot, 'Yea, between thy lips–and sharp;
But here will I disedge it by thy death.'
'Slay then,' he shrieked, 'my will is to be slain,'
And Lancelot, with his heel upon the fallen,
Rolling his eyes, a moment stood, then spake:
'Rise, weakling; I am Lancelot; say thy say.'

And Lancelot slowly rode his warhorse back
To Camelot, and Sir Pelleas in brief while
Caught his unbroken limbs from the dark field,
And followed to the city. It chanced that both
Brake into hall together, worn and pale.
There with her knights and dames was Guinevere.
Full wonderingly she gazed on Lancelot
So soon returned, and then on Pelleas, him
Who had not greeted her, but cast himself
Down on a bench, hard-breathing. 'Have ye fought?'
She asked of Lancelot. 'Ay, my Queen,' he said.
'And thou hast overthrown him?' 'Ay, my Queen.'
Then she, turning to Pelleas, 'O young knight,
Hath the great heart of knighthood in thee failed
So far thou canst not bide, unfrowardly,
A fall from *him?*' Then, for he answered not,
'Or hast thou other griefs? If I, the Queen,
May help them, loose thy tongue, and let me know.'
But Pelleas lifted up an eye so fierce
She quailed; and he, hissing 'I have no sword,'
Sprang from the door into the dark. The Queen
Looked hard upon her lover, he on her;
And each foresaw the dolorous day to be:
And all talk died, as in a grove all song
Beneath the shadow of some bird of prey;
Then a long silence came upon the hall,
And Modred thought, 'The time is hard at hand.'

560. *youth*] *1886*; other *1869–84*.

565. H.T. compares *Cymbeline* III iv 33–4: 'No, 'tis slander, / Whose edge is sharper than the sword.'

# 473 The Last Tournament

Published *Contemporary Review*, Dec. 1871; then *1872*. T. thought of writing 'a poem on Tristram and Isolt' in 1859 (*Mat.* ii 218). Sir Charles Tennyson points out that the germ of it is in prose in the *H.MS* of *Gareth and Lynette*, written 1869–72. On 8 Nov. 1870, 'he repeated some of *The Last Tournament* which he had just written' (*Mem.* ii 100); the poem was completed by 21 May 1871 (*Mem.* ii 104). 'The bare outline of the story and of the vengeance of Mark is taken from Malory [viii–x]; my father often referred with pleasure to his creation of the half-humorous, half-pathetic fool Dagonet' (H.T.).

Dagonet, the fool, whom Gawain in his mood
Had made mock-knight of Arthur's Table Round,
At Camelot, high above the yellowing woods,
Danced like a withered leaf before the hall.
And toward him from the hall, with harp in hand,
And from the crown thereof a carcanet
Of ruby swaying to and fro, the prize
Of Tristram in the jousts of yesterday,
Came Tristram, saying, 'Why skip ye so, Sir Fool?'

For Arthur and Sir Lancelot riding once
Far down beneath a winding wall of rock
Heard a child wail. A stump of oak half-dead,
From roots like some black coil of carven snakes,
Clutched at the crag, and started through mid air
Bearing an eagle's nest: and through the tree
Rushed ever a rainy wind, and through the wind
Pierced ever a child's cry: and crag and tree
Scaling, Sir Lancelot from the perilous nest,
This ruby necklace thrice around her neck,
And all unscarred from beak or talon, brought
A maiden babe; which Arthur pitying took,
Then gave it to his Queen to rear: the Queen
But coldly acquiescing, in her white arms
Received, and after loved it tenderly,
And named it Nestling; so forgot herself
A moment, and her cares; till that young life

¶473. *1. mood*] *1872*; moods *1871*.

*10.* Kathleen Tillotson suggests as a source for the story of Nesting a legend of King Alfred told in Sharon Turner's *History* (*Mid-Victorian Studies*, 1965, p. 84*n*). *Mat.* provides evidence that T. read Turner.

*12–15.* These lines of description were written July 1866 (*Mem.* ii 39).

Being smitten in mid heaven with mortal cold
Past from her; and in time the carcanet
Vext her with plaintive memories of the child:
So she, delivering it to Arthur, said,
'Take thou the jewels of this dead innocence,
And make them, an thou wilt, a tourney-prize.'

To whom the King, 'Peace to thine eagle-borne
Dead nestling, and this honour after death,
Following thy will! but, O my Queen, I muse
Why ye not wear on arm, or neck, or zone
Those diamonds that I rescued from the tarn,
And Lancelot won, methought, for thee to wear.'

'Would rather you had let them fall,' she cried,
'Plunge and be lost–ill-fated as they were,
A bitterness to me!–ye look amazed,
Not knowing they were lost as soon as given–
Slid from my hands, when I was leaning out
Above the river–that unhappy child
Past in her barge: but rosier luck will go
With these rich jewels, seeing that they came
Not from the skeleton of a brother-slayer,
But the sweet body of a maiden babe.
Perchance–who knows?–the purest of thy knights
May win them for the purest of my maids.'

She ended, and the cry of a great jousts
With trumpet-blowings ran on all the ways
From Camelot in among the faded fields
To furthest towers; and everywhere the knights
Armed for a day of glory before the King.

But on the hither side of that loud morn
Into the hall staggered, his visage ribbed
From ear to ear with dogwhip-weals, his nose
Bridge-broken, one eye out, and one hand off,
And one with shattered fingers dangling lame,
A churl, to whom indignantly the King,

'My churl, for whom Christ died, what evil beast
Hath drawn his claws athwart thy face? or fiend?
Man was it who marred heaven's image in thee thus?'

Then, sputtering through the hedge of splintered
teeth,

*39. you*] *1873*; ye *1871–2*.

Yet strangers to the tongue, and with blunt stump
Pitch-blackened sawing the air, said the maimed churl,

'He took them and he drave them to his tower–
Some hold he was a table-knight of thine–
A hundred goodly ones–the Red Knight, he–
Lord, I was tending swine, and the Red Knight
Brake in upon me and drave them to his tower;
And when I called upon thy name as one
That doest right by gentle and by churl,
Maimed me and mauled, and would outright have slain,
Save that he sware me to a message, saying,
"Tell thou the King and all his liars, that I
Have founded my Round Table in the North,
And whatsoever his own knights have sworn
My knights have sworn the counter to it–and say
My tower is full of harlots, like his court,
But mine are worthier, seeing they profess
To be none other than themselves–and say
My knights are all adulterers like his own,
But mine are truer, seeing they profess
To be none other; and say his hour is come,
The heathen are upon him, his long lance
Broken, and his Excalibur a straw."'

Then Arthur turned to Kay the seneschal,
'Take thou my churl, and tend him curiously
Like a king's heir, till all his hurts be whole.
The heathen–but that ever-climbing wave,
Hurled back again so often in empty foam,
Hath lain for years at rest–and renegades,
Thieves, bandits, leavings of confusion, whom
The wholesome realm is purged of otherwhere,
Friends, through your manhood and your fëalty,–now
Make their last head like Satan in the North.
My younger knights, new-made, in whom your flower
Waits to be solid fruit of golden deeds,
Move with me toward their quelling, which achieved,
The loneliest ways are safe from shore to shore.
But thou, Sir Lancelot, sitting in my place
Enchaired tomorrow, arbitrate the field;
For wherefore shouldst thou care to mingle with it,

66. *strangers to the tongue*: 'rough' (T.). *blunt stump*: 'where the hand had been cut off and the stump had been pitched' (T.).
70. *the Red Knight*: 'Pelleas' (T.).
98. *Isaiah* xiv 13.

Only to yield my Queen her own again?
Speak, Lancelot, thou art silent: is it well?'

Thereto Sir Lancelot answered, 'It is well:
Yet better if the King abide, and leave
The leading of his younger knights to me.
Else, for the King has willed it, it is well.'

Then Arthur rose and Lancelot followed him,
And while they stood without the doors, the King
Turned to him saying, 'Is it then so well?
Or mine the blame that oft I seem as he
Of whom was written, "A sound is in his ears"?
The foot that loiters, bidden go,–the glance
That only seems half-loyal to command,–
A manner somewhat fallen from reverence–
Or have I dreamed the bearing of our knights
Tells of a manhood ever less and lower?
Or whence the fear lest this my realm, upreared,
By noble deeds at one with noble vows,
From flat confusion and brute violences,
Reel back into the beast, and be no more?'

He spoke, and taking all his younger knights,
Down the slope city rode, and sharply turned
North by the gate. In her high bower the Queen,
Working a tapestry, lifted up her head,
Watched her lord pass, and knew not that she sighed.
Then ran across her memory the strange rhyme
Of bygone Merlin, 'Where is he who knows?
From the great deep to the great deep he goes.'

But when the morning of a tournament,
By these in earnest those in mockery called
The Tournament of the Dead Innocence,
Brake with a wet wind blowing, Lancelot,
Round whose sick head all night, like birds of prey,
The words of Arthur flying shrieked, arose,
And down a streetway hung with folds of pure
White samite, and by fountains running wine,
Where children sat in white with cups of gold,
Moved to the lists, and there, with slow sad steps
Ascending, filled his double-dragoned chair.

116. *Job* xv 20–1: 'The wicked man travaileth with pain all his days, and the number of years is hidden to the oppressor. A dreadful sound is in his ears: in prosperity the destroyer shall come upon him.'

He glanced and saw the stately galleries,
Dame, damsel, each through worship of their Queen
White-robed in honour of the stainless child,
And some with scattered jewels, like a bank
Of maiden snow mingled with sparks of fire.
He looked but once, and vailed his eyes again.

The sudden trumpet sounded as in a dream
To ears but half-awaked, then one low roll
Of Autumn thunder, and the jousts began:
And ever the wind blew, and yellowing leaf
And gloom and gleam, and shower and shorn plume
Went down it. Sighing weariedly, as one
Who sits and gazes on a faded fire,
When all the goodlier guests are past away,
Sat their great umpire, looking o'er the lists.
He saw the laws that ruled the tournament
Broken, but spake not; once, a knight cast down
Before his throne of arbitration cursed
The dead babe and the follies of the King;
And once the laces of a helmet cracked,
And showed him, like a vermin in its hole,
Modred, a narrow face: anon he heard
The voice that billowed round the barriers roar
An ocean-sounding welcome to one knight,
But newly-entered, taller than the rest,
And armoured all in forest green, whereon
There tript a hundred tiny silver deer,
And wearing but a holly-spray for crest,
With ever-scattering berries, and on shield
A spear, a harp, a bugle–Tristram–late
From overseas in Brittany returned,
And marriage with a princess of that realm,
Isolt the White–Sir Tristram of the Woods–
Whom Lancelot knew, had held sometime with pain
His own against him, and now yearned to shake
The burthen off his heart in one full shock
With Tristram even to death: his strong hands gript
And dinted the gilt dragons right and left,
Until he groaned for wrath–so many of those,
That ware their ladies' colours on the casque,

*150. vailed*: 'drooped' (T.). H.T. compares *Hamlet* I ii 70–1: 'Do not ever with thy vailéd lids / Seek for thy noble father in the dust.'
*153.* 'The autumn of the Round Table' (T.).
*174–5.* 'He was a harper and a hunter' (T.). H.T. quotes Malory viii 3.

Drew from before Sir Tristram to the bounds,
And there with gibes and flickering mockeries
Stood, while he muttered, 'Craven crests! O shame!
What faith have these in whom they sware to love?
The glory of our Round Table is no more.'

So Tristram won, and Lancelot gave, the gems,
Not speaking other word than 'Hast thou won?
Art thou the purest, brother? See, the hand
Wherewith thou takest this, is red!' to whom
Tristram, half plagued by Lancelot's languorous mood,
Made answer, 'Ay, but wherefore toss me this
Like a dry bone cast to some hungry hound?
Let be thy fair Queen's fantasy. Strength of heart
And might of limb, but mainly use and skill,
Are winners in this pastime of our King.
My hand–belike the lance hath dript upon it–
No blood of mine, I trow; but O chief knight,
Right arm of Arthur in the battlefield,
Great brother, thou nor I have made the world;
Be happy in thy fair Queen as I in mine.'

And Tristram round the gallery made his horse
Caracole; then bowed his homage, bluntly saying,
'Fair damsels, each to him who worships each
Sole Queen of Beauty and of love, behold
This day my Queen of Beauty is not here.'
And most of these were mute, some angered, one
Murmuring, 'All courtesy is dead,' and one,
'The glory of our Round Table is no more.'

Then fell thick rain, plume droopt and mantle clung,
And pettish cries awoke, and the wan day
Went glooming down in wet and weariness:
But under her black brows a swarthy one
Laughed shrilly, crying, 'Praise the patient saints,
Our one white day of Innocence hath past,
Though somewhat draggled at the skirt. So be it.
The snowdrop only, flowering through the year,
Would make the world as blank as Winter-tide.

*192.* T. refers to ll. 49–50.
*205–12.* 'It was the law to give the prize to some lady on the field, but the laws are broken, and Tristram the courteous has lost his courtesy, for the great sin of Lancelot was sapping the Round Table' (T.).
*216. one*] *1872*; dame *1871*.
*220.* 'Because they were dressed in white' (T.).

Come–let us gladden their sad eyes, our Queen's
And Lancelot's, at this night's solemnity
With all the kindlier colours of the field.'

So dame and damsel glittered at the feast
Variously gay: for he that tells the tale
Likened them, saying, as when an hour of cold
Falls on the mountain in midsummer snows,
And all the purple slopes of mountain flowers
Pass under white, till the warm hour returns
With veer of wind, and all are flowers again;
So dame and damsel cast the simple white,
And glowing in all colours, the live grass,
Rose-campion, bluebell, kingcup, poppy, glanced
About the revels, and with mirth so loud
Beyond all use, that, half-amazed, the Queen,
And wroth at Tristram and the lawless jousts,
Brake up their sports, then slowly to her bower
Parted, and in her bosom pain was lord.

And little Dagonet on the morrow morn,
High over all the yellowing Autumn-tide,
Danced like a withered leaf before the hall.
Then Tristram saying, 'Why skip ye so, Sir Fool?'
Wheeled round on either heel, Dagonet replied,
'Belike for lack of wiser company;
Or being fool, and seeing too much wit
Makes the world rotten, why, belike I skip
To know myself the wisest knight of all.'
'Ay, fool,' said Tristram, 'but 'tis eating dry
To dance without a catch, a roundelay
To dance to.' Then he twangled on his harp,
And while he twangled little Dagonet stood
Quiet as any water-sodden log
Stayed in the wandering warble of a brook;
But when the twangling ended, skipt again;
And being asked, 'Why skipt ye not, Sir Fool?'
Made answer, 'I had liefer twenty years
Skip to the broken music of my brains
Than any broken music thou canst make.'
Then Tristram, waiting for the quip to come,
'Good now, what music have I broken, fool?'
And little Dagonet, skipping, 'Arthur, the King's;

222. *gladden*] *1872*; comfort *1871*.
227–8. 'Seen by me at Mürren in Switzerland' (T.).
259. *thou canst*] *1873*; ye can *1871–2*.

For when thou playest that air with Queen Isolt,
Thou makest broken music with thy bride,
Her daintier namesake down in Brittany–
And so thou breakest Arthur's music too.'
'Save for that broken music in thy brains,
Sir Fool,' said Tristram, 'I would break thy head.
Fool, I came late, the heathen wars were o'er,
The life had flown, we sware but by the shell–
I am but a fool to reason with a fool–
Come, thou art crabbed and sour: but lean me down,
Sir Dagonet, one of thy long asses' ears,
And harken if my music be not true.

'"Free love–free field–we love but while we may:
The woods are hushed, their music is no more:
The leaf is dead, the yearning past away:
New leaf, new life–the days of frost are o'er:
New life, new love, to suit the newer day:
New loves are sweet as those that went before:
Free love–free field–we love but while we may."

'Ye might have moved slow-measure to my tune,
Not stood stockstill. I made it in the woods,
And heard it ring as true as tested gold.'

But Dagonet with one foot poised in his hand,
'Friend, did ye mark that fountain yesterday
Made to run wine?–but this had run itself
All out like a long life to a sour end–
And them that round it sat with golden cups
To hand the wine to whosoever came–
The twelve small damosels white as Innocence,
In honour of poor Innocence the babe,
Who left the gems which Innocence the Queen
Lent to the King, and Innocence the King
Gave for a prize–and one of those white slips
Handed her cup and piped, the pretty one,
"Drink, drink, Sir Fool," and thereupon I drank,
Spat–pish–the cup was gold, the draught was mud.'

And Tristram, 'Was it muddier than thy gibes?
Is all the laughter gone dead out of thee?–
Not marking how the knighthood mock thee, fool–

*265*. 'Isolt of the white hands' (T.).
*270*. *shell*: 'husk' (T.).
*290*. *whosoever*] *1872*; whomsoever *1871*.

"Fear God: honour the King–his one true knight–
Sole follower of the vows"–for here be they
Who knew thee swine enow before I came,
Smuttier than blasted grain: but when the King
Had made thee fool, thy vanity so shot up
It frighted all free fool from out thy heart;
Which left thee less than fool, and less than swine,
A naked aught–yet swine I hold thee still,
For I have flung thee pearls and find thee swine.'

And little Dagonet mincing with his feet,
'Knight, an ye fling those rubies round my neck
In lieu of hers, I'll hold thou hast some touch
Of music, since I care not for thy pearls.
Swine? I have wallowed, I have washed–the world
Is flesh and shadow–I have had my day.
The dirty nurse, Experience, in her kind
Hath fouled me–an I wallowed, then I washed–
I have had my day and my philosophies–
And thank the Lord I am King Arthur's fool.
Swine, say ye? swine, goats, asses, rams and geese
Trooped round a Paynim harper once, who thrummed
On such a wire as musically as thou
Some such fine song–but never a king's fool.'

And Tristram, 'Then were swine, goats, asses, geese
The wiser fools, seeing thy Paynim bard
Had such a mastery of his mystery
That he could harp his wife up out of hell.'

Then Dagonet, turning on the ball of his foot,
'And whither harp'st thou thine? down! and thyself
Down! and two more: a helpful harper thou,
That harpest downward! Dost thou know the star
We call the harp of Arthur up in heaven?'

And Tristram, 'Ay, Sir Fool, for when our King
Was victor wellnigh day by day, the knights,
Glorying in each new glory, set his name
High on all hills, and in the signs of heaven.'

And Dagonet answered, 'Ay, and when the land
Was freed, and the Queen false, ye set yourself
To babble about him, all to show your wit–
And whether he were King by courtesy,

322. 'Orpheus' (T.). *Paynim*: pagan.
333. 'Lyra' (T.).

Or King by right–and so went harping down
The black king's highway, got so far, and grew
So witty that ye played at ducks and drakes
With Arthur's vows on the great lake of fire.
Tuwhoo! do ye see it? do ye see the star?'

'Nay, fool,' said Tristram, 'not in open day.'
And Dagonet, 'Nay, nor will: I see it and hear.
It makes a silent music up in heaven,
And I, and Arthur and the angels hear,
And then we skip.' 'Lo, fool,' he said, 'ye talk
Fool's treason: is the King thy brother fool?'
Then little Dagonet clapt his hands and shrilled,
'Ay, ay, my brother fool, the king of fools!
Conceits himself as God that he can make
Figs out of thistles, silk from bristles, milk
From burning spurge, honey from hornet-combs,
And men from beasts–Long live the king of fools!'

And down the city Dagonet danced away;
But through the slowly-mellowing avenues
And solitary passes of the wood
Rode Tristram toward Lyonnesse and the west.
Before him fled the face of Queen Isolt
With ruby-circled neck, but evermore
Past, as a rustle or twitter in the wood
Made dull his inner, keen his outer eye
For all that walked, or crept, or perched, or flew.
Anon the face, as, when a gust hath blown,
Unruffling waters re-collect the shape
Of one that in them sees himself, returned;
But at the slot or fewmets of a deer,
Or even a fallen feather, vanished again.

So on for all that day from lawn to lawn
Through many a league-long bower he rode. At length
A lodge of intertwisted beechen-boughs
Furze-crammed, and bracken-rooft, the which himself
Built for a summer day with Queen Isolt
Against a shower, dark in the golden grove
Appearing, sent his fancy back to where
She lived a moon in that low lodge with him:
Till Mark her lord had past, the Cornish King,

357. *burning spurge*: 'the juice of the common spurge' (T.).
366. *outer eye*: 'the hunter's eye' (T.).
371. *slot*: 'trail' (T.). *fewmets*: 'droppings' (T.).

With six or seven, when Tristram was away,
And snatched her thence; yet dreading worse than shame
Her warrior Tristram, spake not any word,
But bode his hour, devising wretchedness.

And now that desert lodge to Tristram lookt
So sweet, that halting, in he past, and sank
Down on a drift of foliage random-blown;
But could not rest for musing how to smoothe
And sleek his marriage over to the Queen.
Perchance in lone Tintagil far from all
The tonguesters of the court she had not heard.
But then what folly had sent him overseas
After she left him lonely here? a name?
Was it the name of one in Brittany,
Isolt, the daughter of the King? 'Isolt
Of the white hands' they called her: the sweet name
Allured him first, and then the maid herself,
Who served him well with those white hands of hers,
And loved him well, until himself had thought
He loved her also, wedded easily,
But left her all as easily, and returned.
The black-blue Irish hair and Irish eyes
Had drawn him home–what marvel? then he laid
His brows upon the drifted leaf and dreamed.

He seemed to pace the strand of Brittany
Between Isolt of Britain and his bride,
And showed them both the ruby-chain, and both
Began to struggle for it, till his Queen
Graspt it so hard, that all her hand was red.
Then cried the Breton, 'Look, her hand is red!
These be no rubies, this is frozen blood,
And melts within her hand–her hand is hot
With ill desires, but this I gave thee, look,
Is all as cool and white as any flower.'
Followed a rush of eagle's wings, and then
A whimpering of the spirit of the child,
Because the twain had spoiled her carcanet.

He dreamed; but Arthur with a hundred spears
Rode far, till o'er the illimitable reed,
And many a glancing plash and sallowy isle,
The wide-winged sunset of the misty marsh

421. *sallowy*: having willows.

Glared on a huge machicolated tower
That stood with open doors, whereout was rolled
A roar of riot, as from men secure
Amid their marshes, ruffians at their ease
Among their harlot-brides, an evil song.
'Lo there,' said one of Arthur's youth, for there,
High on a grim dead tree before the tower,
A goodly brother of the Table Round
Swung by the neck: and on the boughs a shield
Showing a shower of blood in a field noir,
And therebeside a horn, inflamed the knights
At that dishonour done the gilded spur,
Till each would clash the shield, and blow the horn.
But Arthur waved them back. Alone he rode.
Then at the dry harsh roar of the great horn,
That sent the face of all the marsh aloft
An ever upward-rushing storm and cloud
Of shriek and plume, the Red Knight heard, and all,
Even to tipmost lance and topmost helm,
In blood-red armour sallying, howled to the King,

'The teeth of Hell flay bare and gnash thee flat!–
Lo! art thou not that eunuch-hearted King
Who fain had clipt free manhood from the world–
The woman-worshipper? Yea, God's curse, and I!
Slain was the brother of my paramour
By a knight of thine, and I that heard her whine
And snivel, being eunuch-hearted too,
Sware by the scorpion-worm that twists in hell,
And stings itself to everlasting death,
To hang whatever knight of thine I fought
And tumbled. Art thou King?–Look to thy life!'

He ended: Arthur knew the voice; the face
Wellnigh was helmet-hidden, and the name
Went wandering somewhere darkling in his mind.
And Arthur deigned not use of word or sword,
But let the drunkard, as he stretched from horse
To strike him, overbalancing his bulk,

423. *machicolated*: machicolation, 'an opening between the corbels which support a projecting parapet, or in the vault of a portal, through which combustibles, molten lead, stones, etc., were dropped on the heads of the assailants' (*OED*).
439. Arthur Hallam had written of 'the upward rushing tempest' in a poem to T.'s sister Emily, *Oh save me* (*VP* iii (1965) Suppt.).
455. *the name*: 'Pelleas' (T.).

Down from the causeway heavily to the swamp
Fall, as the crest of some slow-arching wave,
Heard in dead night along that table-shore,
Drops flat, and after the great waters break
Whitening for half a league, and thin themselves,
Far over sands marbled with moon and cloud,
From less and less to nothing; thus he fell
Head-heavy; then the knights, who watched him, roared
And shouted and leapt down upon the fallen;
There trampled out his face from being known,
And sank his head in mire, and slimed themselves:
Nor heard the King for their own cries, but sprang
Through open doors, and swording right and left
Men, women, on their sodden faces, hurled
The tables over and the wines, and slew
Till all the rafters rang with woman-yells,
And all the pavement streamed with massacre:
Then, echoing yell with yell, they fired the tower,
Which half that autumn night, like the live North,
Red-pulsing up through Alioth and Alcor,
Made all above it, and a hundred meres
About it, as the water Moab saw
Come round by the East, and out beyond them flushed
The long low dune, and lazy-plunging sea.

So all the ways were safe from shore to shore,
But in the heart of Arthur pain was lord.

Then, out of Tristram waking, the red dream
Fled with a shout, and that low lodge returned,
Mid-forest, and the wind among the boughs.
He whistled his good warhorse left to graze
Among the forest greens, vaulted upon him,
And rode beneath an ever-showering leaf,
Till one lone woman, weeping near a cross,
Stayed him. 'Why weep ye?' 'Lord,' she said, 'my man
Hath left me or is dead;' whereon he thought–
'What, if she hate me now? I would not this.

*461–6.* 'As I have heard and seen the sea on the shore of Mablethorpe' (T.).

*467. ; then*] *1873*; , while *1871–2*.

*477. echoing . . . yell*] *1886*; yell with yell echoing *1871–84*.

*479. Alioth and Alcor*: 'two stars in the Great Bear' (T.).

*481. 2 Kings* iii 22: 'And the sun shone upon the water, and the Moabites saw the water on the other side as red as blood.'

*495, 496. if*] *1875*; an *1871–4*. *she*: 'his wife' (T.).

What, if she love me still? I would not that.
I know not what I would'–but said to her,
'Yet weep not thou, lest, if thy mate return,
He find thy favour changed and love thee not'–
Then pressing day by day through Lyonnesse
Last in a roky hollow, belling, heard
The hounds of Mark, and felt the goodly hounds
Yelp at his heart, but turning, past and gained
Tintagil, half in sea, and high on land,
A crown of towers.
                                Down in a casement sat,
A low sea-sunset glorying round her hair
And glossy-throated grace, Isolt the Queen.
And when she heard the feet of Tristram grind
The spiring stone that scaled about her tower,
Flushed, started, met him at the doors, and there
Belted his body with her white embrace,
Crying aloud, 'Not Mark–not Mark, my soul!
The footstep fluttered me at first: not he:
Catlike through his own castle steals my Mark,
But warrior-wise thou stridest through his halls
Who hates thee, as I him–even to the death.
My soul, I felt my hatred for my Mark
Quicken within me, and knew that thou wert nigh.'
To whom Sir Tristram smiling, 'I am here.
Let be thy Mark, seeing he is not thine.'

And drawing somewhat backward she replied,
'Can he be wronged who is not even his own,
But save for dread of thee had beaten me,
Scratched, bitten, blinded, marred me somehow–Mark?
What rights are his that dare not strike for them?
Not lift a hand–not, though he found me thus!
But harken! have ye met him? hence he went
Today for three days' hunting–as he said–
And so returns belike within an hour.
Mark's way, my soul!–but eat not thou with Mark,
Because he hates thee even more than fears;

501. *roky*: 'misty'; H.T. compares *Macbeth* III ii 51: 'th' rooky wood'. T. used the word in a fragment (p. 1796). *belling*: bellowing, with *OED* 2 specifically of deer.

509. 'Winding stone staircase' (T.).

530. *Mark*] *1872*; him *1871*.

Nor drink: and when thou passest any wood
Close vizor, lest an arrow from the bush
Should leave me all alone with Mark and hell.
My God, the measure of my hate for Mark
Is as the measure of my love for thee.'

So, plucked one way by hate and one by love,
Drained of her force, again she sat, and spake
To Tristram, as he knelt before her, saying,
'O hunter, and O blower of the horn,
Harper, and thou hast been a rover too,
For, ere I mated with my shambling king,
Ye twain had fallen out about the bride
Of one–his name is out of me–the prize,
If prize she were–(what marvel–she could see)–
Thine, friend; and ever since my craven seeks
To wreck thee villainously: but, O Sir Knight,
What dame or damsel have ye kneeled to last?'

And Tristram, 'Last to my Queen Paramount,
Here now to my Queen Paramount of love
And loveliness–ay, lovelier than when first
Her light feet fell on our rough Lyonnesse,
Sailing from Ireland.'

Softly laughed Isolt;
'Flatter me not, for hath not our great Queen
My dole of beauty trebled?' and he said,
'Her beauty is her beauty, and thine thine,
And thine is more to me–soft, gracious, kind–
Save when thy Mark is kindled on thy lips
Most gracious; but she, haughty, even to him,
Lancelot; for I have seen him wan enow
To make one doubt if ever the great Queen
Have yielded him her love.'

To whom Isolt,
'Ah then, false hunter and false harper, thou
Who brakest through the scruple of my bond,
Calling me thy white hind, and saying to me
That Guinevere had sinned against the highest,

542. *shambling*: Sir Charles Tennyson notices this detail in the MS of *Merlin and Vivien* (p. 1597).

553. 'Tristram had told his uncle Mark of the beauty of Isolt, when he saw her in Ireland, so Mark demanded her hand in marriage, which he obtained. Then Mark sent Tristram to fetch her as in my *Idylls* Arthur sent Lancelot for Guinevere' (T.).

And I–misyoked with such a want of man–
That I could hardly sin against the lowest.'

He answered, 'O my soul, be comforted!
If this be sweet, to sin in leading-strings,
If here be comfort, and if ours be sin,
Crowned warrant had we for the crowning sin
That made us happy: but how ye greet me–fear
And fault and doubt–no word of that fond tale–
Thy deep heart-yearnings, thy sweet memories
Of Tristram in that year he was away.'

And, saddening on the sudden, spake Isolt,
'I had forgotten all in my strong joy
To see thee–yearnings?–ay! for, hour by hour,
Here in the never-ended afternoon,
O sweeter than all memories of thee,
Deeper than any yearnings after thee
Seemed those far-rolling, westward-smiling seas,
Watched from this tower. Isolt of Britain dashed
Before Isolt of Brittany on the strand,
Would that have chilled her bride-kiss? Wedded her?
Fought in her father's battles? wounded there?
The King was all fulfilled with gratefulness,
And she, my namesake of the hands, that healed
Thy hurt and heart with unguent and caress–
Well–can I wish her any huger wrong
Than having known thee? her too hast thou left
To pine and waste in those sweet memories.
O were I not my Mark's, by whom all men
Are noble, I should hate thee more than love.'

And Tristram, fondling her light hands, replied,
'Grace, Queen, for being loved: she loved me well.
Did I love her? the name at least I loved.
Isolt?–I fought his battles, for Isolt!
The night was dark; the true star set. Isolt!
The name was ruler of the dark–Isolt?
Care not for her! patient, and prayerful, meek,
Pale-blooded, she will yield herself to God.'

And Isolt answered, 'Yea, and why not I?
Mine is the larger need, who am not meek,
Pale-blooded, prayerful. Let me tell thee now.
Here one black, mute midsummer night I sat,
Lonely, but musing on thee, wondering where,
Murmuring a light song I had heard thee sing,
And once or twice I spake thy name aloud.

Then flashed a levin-brand; and near me stood,
In fuming sulphur blue and green, a fiend–
Mark's way to steal behind one in the dark–
For there was Mark: "He has wedded her," he said,
Not said, but hissed it: then this crown of towers
So shook to such a roar of all the sky,
That here in utter dark I swooned away,
And woke again in utter dark, and cried,
"I will flee hence and give myself to God"–
And thou wert lying in thy new leman's arms.'

Then Tristram, ever dallying with her hand,
'May God be with thee, sweet, when old and gray,
And past desire!' a saying that angered her.
'"May God be with thee, sweet, when thou art old,
And sweet no more to me!" I need Him now.
For when had Lancelot uttered aught so gross
Even to the swineherd's malkin in the mast?
The greater man, the greater courtesy.
Far other was the Tristram, Arthur's knight!
But thou, through ever harrying thy wild beasts–
Save that to touch a harp, tilt with a lance
Becomes thee well–art grown wild beast thyself.
How darest thou, if lover, push me even
In fancy from thy side, and set me far
In the gray distance, half a life away,
Her to be loved no more? Unsay it, unswear!
Flatter me rather, seeing me so weak,
Broken with Mark and hate and solitude,
Thy marriage and mine own, that I should suck
Lies like sweet wines: lie to me: I believe.
Will ye not lie? not swear, as there ye kneel,
And solemnly as when ye sware to him,
The man of men, our King–My God, the power
Was once in vows when men believed the King!
They lied not then, who sware, and through their vows
The King prevailing made his realm:–I say,
Swear to me thou wilt love me even when old,
Gray-haired, and past desire, and in despair.'

Then Tristram, pacing moodily up and down,
'Vows! did you keep the vow you made to Mark
More than I mine? Lied, say ye? Nay, but learnt,

*627.* 'Slut among the beech nuts' (T.).
*629*] *1873*; *not 1871–2.*
*650. you . . . you*] *1873*; ye . . . ye *1871–2.*

The vow that binds too strictly snaps itself–
My knighthood taught me this–ay, being snapt–
We run more counter to the soul thereof
Than had we never sworn. I swear no more.
I swore to the great King, and am forsworn.
For once–even to the height–I honoured him.
"Man, is he man at all?" methought, when first
I rode from our rough Lyonnesse, and beheld
That victor of the Pagan throned in hall–
His hair, a sun that rayed from off a brow
Like hillsnow high in heaven, the steel-blue eyes,
The golden beard that clothed his lips with light–
Moreover, that weird legend of his birth,
With Merlin's mystic babble about his end
Amazed me; then, his foot was on a stool
Shaped as a dragon; he seemed to me no man,
But Michaël trampling Satan; so I sware,
Being amazed: but this went by–The vows!
O ay–the wholesome madness of an hour–
They served their use, their time; for every knight
Believed himself a greater than himself,
And every follower eyed him as a God;
Till he, being lifted up beyond himself,
Did mightier deeds than elsewise he had done,
And so the realm was made; but then their vows–
First mainly through that sullying of our Queen–
Began to gall the knighthood, asking whence
Had Arthur right to bind them to himself?
Dropt down from heaven? washed up from out the deep?
They failed to trace him through the flesh and blood
Of our old kings: whence then? a doubtful lord
To bind them by inviolable vows,
Which flesh and blood perforce would violate:
For feel this arm of mine–the tide within
Red with free chase and heather-scented air,
Pulsing full man; can Arthur make me pure
As any maiden child? lock up my tongue
From uttering freely what I freely hear?
Bind me to one? The wide world laughs at it.
And worldling of the world am I, and know
The ptarmigan that whitens ere his hour
Woos his own end; we are not angels here

*672.* 'When the man had an ideal before him' (T.).
*690.* *wide*] *1872*; great *1871*.
*692.* 'Seen by me in the Museum at Christiania in Norway' (T.).

Nor shall be: vows – I am woodman of the woods,
And hear the garnet-headed yaffingale
Mock them: my soul, we love but while we may;
And therefore is my love so large for thee,
Seeing it is not bounded save by love.'

Here ending, he moved toward her, and she said,
'Good: an I turned away my love for thee
To some one thrice as courteous as thyself –
For courtesy wins woman all as well
As valour may, but he that closes both
Is perfect, he is Lancelot – taller indeed,
Rosier and comelier, thou – but say I loved
This knightliest of all knights, and cast thee back
Thine own small saw, "We love but while we may,"
Well then, what answer?'

He that while she spake,
Mindful of what he brought to adorn her with,
The jewels, had let one finger lightly touch
The warm white apple of her throat, replied,
'Press this a little closer, sweet, until –
Come, I am hungered and half-angered – meat,
Wine, wine – and I will love thee to the death,
And out beyond into the dream to come.'

So then, when both were brought to full accord,
She rose, and set before him all he willed;
And after these had comforted the blood
With meats and wines, and satiated their hearts –
Now talking of their woodland paradise,
The deer, the dews, the fern, the founts, the lawns;
Now mocking at the much ungainliness,
And craven shifts, and long crane legs of Mark –
Then Tristram laughing caught the harp, and sang:

'Ay, ay, O ay – the winds that bend the brier!
A star in heaven, a star within the mere!
Ay, ay, O ay – a star was my desire,
And one was far apart, and one was near:
Ay, ay, O ay – the winds that bow the grass!
And one was water and one star was fire,

695. *yaffingale*: 'old word, and still provincial for the green wood-pecker (so called from its laughter). In Sussex "yaffel"' (T.).

725–32. 'Like an old Gaelic song – the two stars symbolic of the two Isolts' (T.).

And one will ever shine and one will pass.
Ay, ay, O ay – the winds that move the mere.'

Then in the light's last glimmer Tristram showed
And swung the ruby carcanet. She cried,
'The collar of some Order, which our King
Hath newly founded, all for thee, my soul,
For thee, to yield thee grace beyond thy peers.'

'Not so, my Queen,' he said, 'but the red fruit
Grown on a magic oak-tree in mid-heaven,
And won by Tristram as a tourney-prize,
And hither brought by Tristram for his last
Love-offering and peace-offering unto thee.'

He spoke, he turned, then, flinging round her neck,
Clasp it, and cried 'Thine Order, O my Queen!'
But, while he bowed to kiss the jewelled throat,
Out of the dark, just as the lips had touched,
Behind him rose a shadow and a shriek –
'Mark's way,' said Mark, and clove him through the brain.

That night came Arthur home, and while he climbed,
All in a death-dumb autumn-dripping gloom,
The stairway to the hall, and looked and saw
The great Queen's bower was dark, – about his feet
A voice clung sobbing till he questioned it,
'What art thou?' and the voice about his feet
Sent up an answer, sobbing, 'I am thy fool,
And I shall never make thee smile again.'

# 474 Guinevere

Published *1859*. H.T. records: '"Some one", writes my father, "asks how long it took to *write Guinevere*? About a fortnight" . . . My mother notes in her Journal: "*July 9th*, 1857. A. has brought me as a birthday present the

*743. spoke*] *1882*; rose *1871–81*. *then,*] *1872*; and *1871*.
*744–5*] *1872*; Clasp it; but while he bowed himself to lay
Warm kisses in the hollow of her throat, *1871*
Compare Malory xx 6: '"That is hard to do", said sir Launcelot; "for by sir Tristram I may have a warning: for when by means of the treaty sir Tristram brought again la beale Isoude unto king Marke, from Joyous Gard, look what fell on the end, how shamefully that false traitor (king Marke) slew that noble knight as he sat harping before his lady, la beale Isoude, with a sharp grounded glaive thrust him behind to the heart."'

first two lines that he has made of *Guinevere*, which might be the nucleus of a great poem. Arthur is parting from Guinevere, and says:

> But hither shall I never come again,
> Never lie by thy side; see thee no more–
> Farewell! [575–7]".'

T. does not seem to have proceeded till 1858; in Jan. '*The Parting of Arthur and Guinevere* was finished'; the song [166–77] was written on 8 March; and on 15 March *Guinevere* was 'finally completed' (*Mem.* i 424). The dates rule out G. S. Haight's suggestion that T. was concerned to counteract William Morris's *Defence of Guinevere* (pub. early March 1858). H.T. comments: 'This Idyll is largely original, being founded on the following passage from Malory [xxi 7, the beginning of the sentence being here added]':

'And when queen Guenever understood that her lord, king Arthur, was slain, and all the noble knights, sir Mordred and all the remnant, then she stole away, and five ladies with her: and so she went to Almesbury, and there she let make herself a nun, and wore white clothes and black: and great penance she took, as ever did sinful lady in this land, and never creature could make her merry, but lived in fastings, prayers, and alms-deeds, that all manner of people marvelled how virtuously she was changed. Now leave we queen Guenever in Almesbury, that was a nun in white clothes and in black, and there she was abbess and ruler as reason would.'

'Guinevere was called Gwenhwyvar (the white ghost) by the bards, and is said by Taliessin to have been "of a haughty disposition even in her youth". Malory calls her the daughter of Leodogran of the land of Camelyard' (H.T.). In Malory, the only interview at Almesbury is between Lancelot and Guinevere, since Guinevere does not go there till after hearing of the death of Arthur.

Queen Guinevere had fled the court, and sat
There in the holy house at Almesbury
Weeping, none with her save a little maid,
A novice: one low light betwixt them burned
Blurred by the creeping mist, for all abroad,
Beneath a moon unseen albeit at full,
The white mist, like a face-cloth to the face,
Clung to the dead earth, and the land was still.

For hither had she fled, her cause of flight
Sir Modred; he that like a subtle beast
Lay couchant with his eyes upon the throne,
Ready to spring, waiting a chance: for this
He chilled the popular praises of the King

¶474. *10*] *1870* ('*1869*'); Sir Modred; he the nearest to the King,
His nephew, ever like a subtle beast *1859–69*.

With silent smiles of slow disparagement;
And tampered with the Lords of the White Horse,
Heathen, the brood by Hengist left; and sought
To make disruption in the Table Round
Of Arthur, and to splinter it into feuds
Serving his traitorous end; and all his aims
Were sharpened by strong hate for Lancelot.

For thus it chanced one morn when all the court,
Green-suited, but with plumes that mocked the may,
Had been, their wont, a-maying and returned,
That Modred still in green, all ear and eye,
Climbed to the high top of the garden-wall
To spy some secret scandal if he might,
And saw the Queen who sat betwixt her best
Enid, and lissome Vivien, of her court
The wiliest and the worst; and more than this
He saw not, for Sir Lancelot passing by
Spied where he couched, and as the gardener's hand
Picks from the colewort a green caterpillar,
So from the high wall and the flowering grove
Of grasses Lancelot plucked him by the heel,
And cast him as a worm upon the way;
But when he knew the Prince though marred with dust,
He, reverencing king's blood in a bad man,
Made such excuses as he might, and these
Full knightly without scorn; for in those days
No knight of Arthur's noblest dealt in scorn;
But, if a man were halt or hunched, in him
By those whom God had made full-limbed and tall,
Scorn was allowed as part of his defect,
And he was answered softly by the King
And all his Table. So Sir Lancelot holp
To raise the Prince, who rising twice or thrice
Full sharply smote his knees, and smiled, and went:
But, ever after, the small violence done
Rankled in him and ruffled all his heart,
As the sharp wind that ruffles all day long
A little bitter pool about a stone
On the bare coast.

But when Sir Lancelot told
This matter to the Queen, at first she laughed
Lightly, to think of Modred's dusty fall,
Then shuddered, as the village wife who cries
'I shudder, some one steps across my grave;'
Then laughed again, but faintlier, for indeed

She half-foresaw that he, the subtle beast,
Would track her guilt until he found, and hers
Would be for evermore a name of scorn.
Henceforward rarely could she front in hall,
Or elsewhere, Modred's narrow foxy face,
Heart-hiding smile, and gray persistent eye:
Henceforward too, the Powers that tend the soul,
To help it from the death that cannot die,
And save it even in extremes, began
To vex and plague her. Many a time for hours,
Beside the placid breathings of the King,
In the dead night, grim faces came and went
Before her, or a vague spiritual fear–
Like to some doubtful noise of creaking doors,
Heard by the watcher in a haunted house,
That keeps the rust of murder on the walls–
Held her awake: or if she slept, she dreamed
An awful dream; for then she seemed to stand
On some vast plain before a setting sun,
And from the sun there swiftly made at her
A ghastly something, and its shadow flew
Before it, till it touched her, and she turned–
When lo! her own, that broadening from her feet,
And blackening, swallowed all the land, and in it
Far cities burnt, and with a cry she woke.
And all this trouble did not pass but grew;
Till even the clear face of the guileless King,
And trustful courtesies of household life,
Became her bane; and at the last she said,
'O Lancelot, get thee hence to thine own land,
For if thou tarry we shall meet again,
And if we meet again, some evil chance
Will make the smouldering scandal break and blaze
Before the people, and our lord the King.'
And Lancelot ever promised, but remained,
And still they met and met. Again she said,
'O Lancelot, if thou love me get thee hence.'
And then they were agreed upon a night
(When the good King should not be there) to meet
And part for ever. Vivien, lurking, heard.
She told Sir Modred. Passion-pale they met
And greeted. Hands in hands, and eye to eye,
Low on the border of her couch they sat
Stammering and staring. It was their last hour,

*97–8*] *1890*; And part for ever. Passion-pale they met *1859–89*.

A madness of farewells. And Modred brought
His creatures to the basement of the tower
For testimony; and crying with full voice
'Traitor, come out, ye are trapt at last,' aroused
Lancelot, who rushing outward lionlike
Leapt on him, and hurled him headlong, and he fell
Stunned, and his creatures took and bare him off,
And all was still: then she, 'The end is come,
And I am shamed for ever;' and he said,
'Mine be the shame; mine was the sin: but rise,
And fly to my strong castle overseas:
There will I hide thee, till my life shall end,
There hold thee with my life against the world.'
She answered, 'Lancelot, wilt thou hold me so?
Nay, friend, for we have taken our farewells.
Would God that thou couldst hide me from myself!
Mine is the shame, for I was wife, and thou
Unwedded: yet rise now, and let us fly,
For I will draw me into sanctuary,
And bide my doom.' So Lancelot got her horse,
Set her thereon, and mounted on his own,
And then they rode to the divided way,
There kissed, and parted weeping: for he past,
Love-loyal to the least wish of the Queen,
Back to his land; but she to Almesbury
Fled all night long by glimmering waste and weald,
And heard the Spirits of the waste and weald
Moan as she fled, or thought she heard them moan:
And in herself she moaned 'Too late, too late!'
Till in the cold wind that foreruns the morn,
A blot in heaven, the Raven, flying high,
Croaked, and she thought, 'He spies a field of death;
For now the Heathen of the Northern Sea,
Lured by the crimes and frailties of the court,
Begin to slay the folk, and spoil the land.'

And when she came to Almesbury she spake
There to the nuns, and said, 'Mine enemies
Pursue me, but, O peaceful Sisterhood,
Receive, and yield me sanctuary, nor ask
Her name to whom ye yield it, till her time
To tell you:' and her beauty, grace and power,
Wrought as a charm upon them, and they spared
To ask it.

*102–24.* Based on Malory xx 1–4.

So the stately Queen abode
For many a week, unknown, among the nuns;
Nor with them mixed, nor told her name, nor sought,
Wrapt in her grief, for housel or for shrift,
But communed only with the little maid,
Who pleased her with a babbling heedlessness
Which often lured her from herself; but now,
This night, a rumour wildly blown about
Came, that Sir Modred had usurped the realm,
And leagued him with the heathen, while the King
Was waging war on Lancelot: then she thought,
'With what a hate the people and the King
Must hate me,' and bowed down upon her hands
Silent, until the little maid, who brooked
No silence, brake it, uttering 'Late! so late!
What hour, I wonder, now?' and when she drew
No answer, by and by began to hum
An air the nuns had taught her; 'Late, so late!'
Which when she heard, the Queen looked up, and said,
'O maiden, if indeed ye list to sing,
Sing, and unbind my heart that I may weep.'
Whereat full willingly sang the little maid.

'Late, late, so late! and dark the night and chill!
Late, late, so late! but we can enter still.
Too late, too late! ye cannot enter now.

'No light had we: for that we do repent;
And learning this, the bridegroom will relent.
Too late, too late! ye cannot enter now.

'No light: so late! and dark and chill the night!
O let us in, that we may find the light!
Too late, too late: ye cannot enter now.

'Have we not heard the bridegroom is so sweet?
O let us in, though late, to kiss his feet!
No, no, too late! ye cannot enter now.'

So sang the novice, while full passionately,
Her head upon her hands, remembering
Her thought when first she came, wept the sad Queen.
Then said the little novice prattling to her,

*147. housel*: 'Anglo-Saxon *husel*, the Eucharist' (T.).
*163. ye*] *1870* ('*1869*'); you *1859–69*.
*166–77.* Based on *Matthew* xxv 1–13, the parable of the virgins.

'O pray you, noble lady, weep no more;
But let my words, the words of one so small,
Who knowing nothing knows but to obey,
And if I do not there is penance given–
Comfort your sorrows; for they do not flow
From evil done; right sure am I of that,
Who see your tender grace and stateliness.
But weigh your sorrows with our lord the King's,
And weighing find them less; for gone is he
To wage grim war against Sir Lancelot there,
Round that strong castle where he holds the Queen;
And Modred whom he left in charge of all,
The traitor–Ah sweet lady, the King's grief
For his own self, and his own Queen, and realm,
Must needs be thrice as great as any of ours.
For me, I thank the saints, I am not great.
For if there ever come a grief to me
I cry my cry in silence, and have done.
None knows it, and my tears have brought me good:
But even were the griefs of little ones
As great as those of great ones, yet this grief
Is added to the griefs the great must bear,
That howsoever much they may desire
Silence, they cannot weep behind a cloud:
As even here they talk at Almesbury
About the good King and his wicked Queen,
And were I such a King with such a Queen,
Well might I wish to veil her wickedness,
But were I such a King, it could not be.'

Then to her own sad heart muttered the Queen,
'Will the child kill me with her innocent talk?'
But openly she answered, 'Must not I,
If this false traitor have displaced his lord,
Grieve with the common grief of all the realm?'

'Yea,' said the maid, 'this is all woman's grief,
That *she* is woman, whose disloyal life
Hath wrought confusion in the Table Round
Which good King Arthur founded, years ago,
With signs and miracles and wonders, there
At Camelot, ere the coming of the Queen.'

Then thought the Queen within herself again,
'Will the child kill me with her foolish prate?'
But openly she spake and said to her,

'O little maid, shut in by nunnery walls,
What canst thou know of Kings and Tables Round,
Or what of signs and wonders, but the signs
And simple miracles of thy nunnery?'
  To whom the little novice garrulously,
'Yea, but I know: the land was full of signs
And wonders ere the coming of the Queen.
So said my father, and himself was knight
Of the great Table–at the founding of it;
And rode thereto from Lyonnesse, and he said
That as he rode, an hour or maybe twain
After the sunset, down the coast, he heard
Strange music, and he paused, and turning–there,
All down the lonely coast of Lyonnesse,
Each with a beacon-star upon his head,
And with a wild sea-light about his feet,
He saw them–headland after headland flame
Far on into the rich heart of the west:
And in the light the white mermaiden swam,
And strong man-breasted things stood from the sea,
And sent a deep sea-voice through all the land,
To which the little elves of chasm and cleft
Made answer, sounding like a distant horn.
So said my father–yea, and furthermore,
Next morning, while he past the dim-lit woods,
Himself beheld three spirits mad with joy
Come dashing down on a tall wayside flower,
That shook beneath them, as the thistle shakes
When three gray linnets wrangle for the seed:
And still at evenings on before his horse
The flickering fairy-cycle wheeled and broke
Flying, and linked again, and wheeled and broke
Flying, for all the land was full of life.
And when at last he came to Camelot,
A wreath of airy dancers hand-in-hand
Swung round the lighted lantern of the hall;
And in the hall itself was such a feast
As never man had dreamed; for every knight
Had whatsoever meat he longed for served
By hands unseen; and even as he said
Down in the cellars merry bloated things

*235–47.* On possible sources, see W. D. Paden (p. 158).
*262–3.* As happens when the Grail appears (*The Holy Grail* 182–202*n*, p. 1667).

Shouldered the spigot, straddling on the butts
While the wine ran: so glad were spirits and men
Before the coming of the sinful Queen.'

Then spake the Queen and somewhat bitterly,
'Were they so glad? ill prophets were they all,
Spirits and men: could none of them foresee,
Not even thy wise father with his signs
And wonders, what has fallen upon the realm?'

To whom the novice garrulously again,
'Yea, one, a bard; of whom my father said,
Full many a noble war-song had he sung,
Even in the presence of an enemy's fleet,
Between the steep cliff and the coming wave;
And many a mystic lay of life and death
Had chanted on the smoky mountain-tops,
When round him bent the spirits of the hills
With all their dewy hair blown back like flame:
So said my father—and that night the bard
Sang Arthur's glorious wars, and sang the King
As wellnigh more than man, and railed at those
Who called him the false son of Gorloïs:
For there was no man knew from whence he came;
But after tempest, when the long wave broke
All down the thundering shores of Bude and Bos,
There came a day as still as heaven, and then
They found a naked child upon the sands
Of dark Tintagil by the Cornish sea;
And that was Arthur; and they fostered him
Till he by miracle was approven King:
And that his grave should be a mystery
From all men, like his birth; and could he find
A woman in her womanhood as great
As he was in his manhood, then, he sang,
The twain together well might change the world.
But even in the middle of his song
He faltered, and his hand fell from the harp,

*266. spigot*: 'bung' (T.). Suggested by T. Crofton Croker's *Fairy Legends* (1834 edn, *Lincoln*, p. 82), 'The Haunted Cellar': 'and on advancing perceived a little figure, about six inches in height, seated astride upon the pipe of the oldest port in the place, and bearing a spigot upon his shoulder'.
*289. Bude and Bos*: 'north of Tintagil' (T.).
*292. dark Tintagil*] *1865 Selection*; wild Dundagil *1859–61*; dark Dundagil *1862–5*.

And pale he turned, and reeled, and would have fallen,
But that they stayed him up; nor would he tell
His vision; but what doubt that he foresaw
This evil work of Lancelot and the Queen?'

Then thought the Queen, 'Lo! they have set her on,
Our simple-seeming Abbess and her nuns,
To play upon me,' and bowed her head nor spake.
Whereat the novice crying, with clasped hands,
Shame on her own garrulity garrulously,
Said the good nuns would check her gadding tongue
Full often, 'and, sweet lady, if I seem
To vex an ear too sad to listen to me,
Unmannerly, with prattling and the tales
Which my good father told me, check me too
Nor let me shame my father's memory, one
Of noblest manners, though himself would say
Sir Lancelot had the noblest; and he died,
Killed in a tilt, come next, five summers back,
And left me; but of others who remain,
And of the two first-famed for courtesy–
And pray you check me if I ask amiss–
But pray you, which had noblest, while you moved
Among them, Lancelot or our lord the King?'

Then the pale Queen looked up and answered her,
'Sir Lancelot, as became a noble knight,
Was gracious to all ladies, and the same
In open battle or the tilting-field
Forbore his own advantage, and the King
In open battle or the tilting-field
Forbore his own advantage, and these two
Were the most nobly-mannered men of all;
For manners are not idle, but the fruit
Of loyal nature, and of noble mind.'

'Yea,' said the maid, 'be manners such fair fruit?
Then Lancelot's needs must be a thousand-fold
Less noble, being, as all rumour runs,
The most disloyal friend in all the world.'

To which a mournful answer made the Queen:
'O closed about by narrowing nunnery-walls,
What knowest thou of the world, and all its lights
And shadows, all the wealth and all the woe?
If ever Lancelot, that most noble knight,
Were for one hour less noble than himself,

Pray for him that he scape the doom of fire,
And weep for her who drew him to his doom.'

'Yea,' said the little novice, 'I pray for both;
But I should all as soon believe that his,
Sir Lancelot's, were as noble as the King's,
As I could think, sweet lady, yours would be
Such as they are, were you the sinful Queen.'

So she, like many another babbler, hurt
Whom she would soothe, and harmed where she would heal;
For here a sudden flush of wrathful heat
Fired all the pale face of the Queen, who cried,
'Such as thou art be never maiden more
For ever! thou their tool, set on to plague
And play upon, and harry me, petty spy
And traitress.' When that storm of anger brake
From Guinevere, aghast the maiden rose,
White as her veil, and stood before the Queen
As tremulously as foam upon the beach
Stands in a wind, ready to break and fly,
And when the Queen had added 'Get thee hence,'
Fled frighted. Then that other left alone
Sighed, and began to gather heart again,
Saying in herself, 'The simple, fearful child
Meant nothing, but my own too-fearful guilt,
Simpler than any child, betrays itself.
But help me, heaven, for surely I repent.
For what is true repentance but in thought–
Not even in inmost thought to think again
The sins that made the past so pleasant to us:
And I have sworn never to see him more,
To see him more.'

And even in saying this,
Her memory from old habit of the mind
Went slipping back upon the golden days
In which she saw him first, when Lancelot came,
Reputed the best knight and goodliest man,
Ambassador, to lead her to his lord
Arthur, and led her forth, and far ahead
Of his and her retinue moving, they,
Rapt in sweet talk or lively, all on love
And sport and tilts and pleasure, (for the time
Was maytime, and as yet no sin was dreamed,)
Rode under groves that looked a paradise

Of blossom, over sheets of hyacinth
That seemed the heavens upbreaking through the earth,
And on from hill to hill, and every day
Beheld at noon in some delicious dale
The silk pavilions of King Arthur raised
For brief repast or afternoon repose
By couriers gone before; and on again,
Till yet once more ere set of sun they saw
The Dragon of the great Pendragonship,
That crowned the state pavilion of the King,
Blaze by the rushing brook or silent well.

But when the Queen immersed in such a trance,
And moving through the past unconsciously,
Came to that point where first she saw the King
Ride toward her from the city, sighed to find
Her journey done, glanced at him, thought him cold,
High, self-contained, and passionless, not like him,
'Not like my Lancelot'–while she brooded thus
And grew half-guilty in her thoughts again,
There rode an armèd warrior to the doors.
A murmuring whisper through the nunnery ran,
Then on a sudden a cry, 'The King.' She sat
Stiff-stricken, listening; but when armèd feet
Through the long gallery from the outer doors
Rang coming, prone from off her seat she fell,
And grovelled with her face against the floor:
There with her milkwhite arms and shadowy hair
She made her face a darkness from the King:
And in the darkness heard his armèd feet
Pause by her; then came silence, then a voice,
Monotonous and hollow like a Ghost's
Denouncing judgment, but though changed, the King's:

'Liest thou here so low, the child of one
I honoured, happy, dead before thy shame?
Well is it that no child is born of thee.
The children born of thee are sword and fire,
Red ruin, and the breaking up of laws,
The craft of kindred and the Godless hosts
Of heathen swarming o'er the Northern Sea;
Whom I, while yet Sir Lancelot, my right arm,

*395.* 'The headship of the tribes who had confederated against the Lords of the White Horse. "Pendragon" not a dactyl as some make it, but Pén-drágon.'

*400. where*] *1870* ('*1869*'); when *1859–69.*

The mightiest of my knights, abode with me,
Have everywhere about this land of Christ
In twelve great battles ruining overthrown.
And knowest thou now from whence I come–from him,
From waging bitter war with him: and he,
That did not shun to smite me in worse way,
Had yet that grace of courtesy in him left,
He spared to lift his hand against the King
Who made him knight: but many a knight was slain;
And many more, and all his kith and kin
Clave to him, and abode in his own land.
And many more when Modred raised revolt,
Forgetful of their troth and fealty, clave
To Modred, and a remnant stays with me.
And of this remnant will I leave a part,
True men who love me still, for whom I live,
To guard thee in the wild hour coming on,
Lest but a hair of this low head be harmed.
Fear not: thou shalt be guarded till my death.
Howbeit I know, if ancient prophecies
Have erred not, that I march to meet my doom.
Thou hast not made my life so sweet to me,
That I the King should greatly care to live;
For thou hast spoilt the purpose of my life.
Bear with me for the last time while I show,
Even for thy sake, the sin which thou hast sinned.
For when the Roman left us, and their law
Relaxed its hold upon us, and the ways
Were filled with rapine, here and there a deed
Of prowess done redressed a random wrong.
But I was first of all the kings who drew
The knighthood-errant of this realm and all
The realms together under me, their Head,
In that fair Order of my Table Round,
A glorious company, the flower of men,
To serve as model for the mighty world,
And be the fair beginning of a time.
I made them lay their hands in mine and swear
To reverence the King, as if he were
Their conscience, and their conscience as their King,
To break the heathen and uphold the Christ,
To ride abroad redressing human wrongs,
To speak no slander, no, nor listen to it,
To honour his own word as if his God's,
To lead sweet lives in purest chastity,
To love one maiden only, cleave to her,

And worship her by years of noble deeds,
Until they won her; for indeed I knew
Of no more subtle master under heaven
Than is the maiden passion for a maid,
Not only to keep down the base in man,
But teach high thought, and amiable words
And courtliness, and the desire of fame,
And love of truth, and all that makes a man.
And all this throve before I wedded thee,
Believing, "lo mine helpmate, one to feel
My purpose and rejoicing in my joy."
Then came thy shameful sin with Lancelot;
Then came the sin of Tristram and Isolt;
Then others, following these my mightiest knights,
And drawing foul ensample from fair names,
Sinned also, till the loathsome opposite
Of all my heart had destined did obtain,
And all through thee! so that this life of mine
I guard as God's high gift from scathe and wrong,
Not greatly care to lose; but rather think
How sad it were for Arthur, should he live,
To sit once more within his lonely hall,
And miss the wonted number of my knights,
And miss to hear high talk of noble deeds
As in the golden days before thy sin.
For which of us, who might be left, could speak
Of the pure heart, nor seem to glance at thee?
And in thy bowers of Camelot or of Usk
Thy shadow still would glide from room to room,
And I should evermore be vext with thee
In hanging robe or vacant ornament,
Or ghostly footfall echoing on the stair.
For think not, though thou wouldst not love thy lord,
Thy lord has wholly lost his love for thee.
I am not made of so slight elements.
Yet must I leave thee, woman, to thy shame.
I hold that man the worst of public foes
Who either for his own or children's sake,
To save his blood from scandal, lets the wife
Whom he knows false, abide and rule the house:
For being through his cowardice allowed
Her station, taken everywhere for pure,
She like a new disease, unknown to men,
Creeps, no precaution used, among the crowd,

481. *before*] *1873*; until *1859–70*.

Makes wicked lightnings of her eyes, and saps
The fealty of our friends, and stirs the pulse
With devil's leaps, and poisons half the young.
Worst of the worst were that man he that reigns!
Better the King's waste hearth and aching heart
Than thou reseated in thy place of light,
The mockery of my people, and their bane.'

He paused, and in the pause she crept an inch
Nearer, and laid her hands about his feet.
Far off a solitary trumpet blew.
Then waiting by the doors the warhorse neighed
As at a friend's voice, and he spake again:

'Yet think not that I come to urge thy crimes,
I did not come to curse thee, Guinevere,
I, whose vast pity almost makes me die
To see thee, laying there thy golden head,
My pride in happier summers, at my feet.
The wrath which forced my thoughts on that fierce law,
The doom of treason and the flaming death,
(When first I learnt thee hidden here) is past.
The pang–which while I weighed thy heart with one
Too wholly true to dream untruth in thee,
Made my tears burn–is also past–in part.
And all is past, the sin is sinned, and I,
Lo! I forgive thee, as Eternal God
Forgives: do thou for thine own soul the rest.
But how to take last leave of all I loved?
O golden hair, with which I used to play
Not knowing! O imperial-moulded form,
And beauty such as never woman wore,
Until it came a kingdom's curse with thee–
I cannot touch thy lips, they are not mine,
But Lancelot's: nay, they never were the King's.
I cannot take thy hand; that too is flesh,
And in the flesh thou hast sinned; and mine own flesh,
Here looking down on thine polluted, cries
"I loathe thee:" yet not less, O Guinevere,
For I was ever virgin save for thee,
My love through flesh hath wrought into my life
So far, that my doom is, I love thee still.
Let no man dream but that I love thee still.

*534–6.* In Malory, Arthur condemned Guinevere to be burnt to death, and she was rescued by Lancelot.

Perchance, and so thou purify thy soul,
And so thou lean on our fair father Christ,
Hereafter in that world where all are pure
We two may meet before high God, and thou
Wilt spring to me, and claim me thine, and know
I am thine husband–not a smaller soul,
Nor Lancelot, nor another. Leave me that,
I charge thee, my last hope. Now must I hence.
Through the thick night I hear the trumpet blow:
They summon me their King to lead mine hosts
Far down to that great battle in the west,
Where I must strike against the man they call
My sister's son–no kin of mine, who leagues
With Lords of the White Horse, heathen, and knights,
Traitors–and strike him dead, and meet myself
Death, or I know not what mysterious doom.
And thou remaining here wilt learn the event;
But hither shall I never come again,
Never lie by thy side; see thee no more–
Farewell!'

And while she grovelled at his feet,
She felt the King's breath wander o'er her neck,
And in the darkness o'er her fallen head,
Perceived the waving of his hands that blest.

Then, listening till those armèd steps were gone,
Rose the pale Queen, and in her anguish found
The casement: 'peradventure,' so she thought,
'If I might see his face, and not be seen.'
And lo, he sat on horseback at the door!
And near him the sad nuns with each a light
Stood, and he gave them charge about the Queen,
To guard and foster her for evermore.
And while he spake to these his helm was lowered,
To which for crest the golden dragon clung
Of Britain; so she did not see the face,
Which then was as an angel's, but she saw,
Wet with the mists and smitten by the lights,
The Dragon of the great Pendragonship

*569–72*] *1870* ('*1869*');
Where I must strike against my sister's son,
Leagued with the lords of the White Horse and knights
Once mine, and strike him dead, and meet myself *1859–69*.

*591–2*. *Acts* vi 15, of Stephen: 'And all that sat in the council, looking stedfastly on him, saw his face as it had been the face of an angel.'

Blaze, making all the night a steam of fire.
And even then he turned; and more and more
The moony vapour rolling round the King,
Who seemed the phantom of a Giant in it,
Enwound him fold by fold, and made him gray
And grayer, till himself became as mist
Before her, moving ghostlike to his doom.

Then she stretched out her arms and cried aloud
'Oh Arthur!' there her voice brake suddenly,
Then–as a stream that spouting from a cliff
Fails in mid air, but gathering at the base
Re-makes itself, and flashes down the vale–
Went on in passionate utterance:

'Gone–my lord!
Gone through my sin to slay and to be slain!
And he forgave me, and I could not speak.
Farewell? I should have answered his farewell.
His mercy choked me. Gone, my lord the King,
My own true lord! how dare I call him mine?
The shadow of another cleaves to me,
And makes me one pollution: he, the King,
Called me polluted: shall I kill myself?
What help in that? I cannot kill my sin,
If soul be soul; nor can I kill my shame;
No, nor by living can I live it down.
The days will grow to weeks, the weeks to months,
The months will add themselves and make the years,
The years will roll into the centuries,
And mine will ever be a name of scorn.
I must not dwell on that defeat of fame.
Let the world be; that is but of the world.
What else? what hope? I think there was a hope,
Except he mocked me when he spake of hope;
His hope he called it; but he never mocks,
For mockery is the fume of little hearts.
And blessèd be the King, who hath forgiven
My wickedness to him, and left me hope
That in mine own heart I can live down sin
And be his mate hereafter in the heavens
Before high God. Ah great and gentle lord,
Who wast, as is the conscience of a saint
Among his warring senses, to thy knights–
To whom my false voluptuous pride, that took
Full easily all impressions from below,
Would not look up, or half-despised the height

To which I would not or I could not climb–
I thought I could not breathe in that fine air
That pure severity of perfect light–
I yearned for warmth and colour which I found
In Lancelot–now I see thee what thou art,
Thou art the highest and most human too,
Not Lancelot, nor another. Is there none
Will tell the King I love him though so late?
Now–ere he goes to the great Battle? none:
Myself must tell him in that purer life,
But now it were too daring. Ah my God,
What might I not have made of thy fair world,
Had I but loved thy highest creature here?
It was my duty to have loved the highest:
It surely was my profit had I known:
It would have been my pleasure had I seen.
We needs must love the highest when we see it,
Not Lancelot, nor another.'
Here her hand
Grasped, made her vail her eyes: she looked and saw
The novice, weeping, suppliant, and said to her,
'Yea, little maid, for am *I* not forgiven?'
Then glancing up beheld the holy nuns
All round her, weeping; and her heart was loosed
Within her, and she wept with these and said,

'Ye know me then, that wicked one, who broke
The vast design and purpose of the King.
O shut me round with narrowing nunnery-walls,
Meek maidens, from the voices crying "shame."
I must not scorn myself: he loves me still.
Let no one dream but that he loves me still.
So let me, if you do not shudder at me,
Nor shun to call me sister, dwell with you;
Wear black and white, and be a nun like you,
Fast with your fasts, not feasting with your feasts;
Grieve with your griefs, not grieving at your joys,
But not rejoicing; mingle with your rites;
Pray and be prayed for; lie before your shrines;
Do each low office of your holy house;
Walk your dim cloister, and distribute dole
To poor sick people, richer in His eyes
Who ransomed us, and haler too than I;
And treat their loathsome hurts and heal mine own;

642. *yearned for*] *1886*; wanted] *1859–84*. *Eversley* accidentally omits 'for'.

And so wear out in almsdeed and in prayer
The sombre close of that voluptuous day,
Which wrought the ruin of my lord the King.'

She said: they took her to themselves; and she
Still hoping, fearing 'is it yet too late?'
Dwelt with them, till in time their Abbess died.
Then she, for her good deeds and her pure life,
And for the power of ministration in her,
And likewise for the high rank she had borne,
Was chosen Abbess, there, an Abbess, lived
For three brief years, and there, an Abbess, past
To where beyond these voices there is peace.

# 475 The Passing of Arthur

Published *1869* ('*1870*'). Written 1869 (*CT*, p. 382). T. created it from his *Morte d'Arthur* (*1842*), which forms ll. 170–440 of *The Passing of Arthur*. (For the only changes in wording, see ll. 175 ^ 6*n*, and l. 373*n*.) For detailed notes to these lines, including the relevant passages from Malory, see *Morte d'Arthur* (p. 585). T. comments: 'The temporary triumph of evil, the confusion of moral order, closing in the Great Battle of the West.' The title had been *The Death of Arthur* in the trial edition (1869), for details of which see Wise, *Bibliography* i 197–209. Anne Ritchie, *Harper's Magazine* vii (1883) 31, reports: 'The first *Idyll* and the last, I have heard Mr Tennyson say, are intentionally more archaic than the others.'

That story which the bold Sir Bedivere,
First made and latest left of all the knights,
Told, when the man was no more than a voice
In the white winter of his age, to those
With whom he dwelt, new faces, other minds.

For on their march to westward, Bedivere,
Who slowly paced among the slumbering host,
Heard in his tent the moanings of the King:

'I found Him in the shining of the stars,
I marked Him in the flowering of His fields,
But in His ways with men I find Him not.
I waged His wars, and now I pass and die.
O me! for why is all around us here
As if some lesser god had made the world,

¶475. *6–28*] *1873*; *not 1869–70*.
*14*. 'Cf. the demiurge of Plato, and the gnostic belief that lesser Powers created the world' (T.).

But had not force to shape it as he would,
Till the High God behold it from beyond,
And enter it, and make it beautiful?
Or else as if the world were wholly fair,
But that these eyes of men are dense and dim,
And have not power to see it as it is:
Perchance, because we see not to the close;–
For I, being simple, thought to work His will,
And have but stricken with the sword in vain;
And all whereon I leaned in wife and friend
Is traitor to my peace, and all my realm
Reels back into the beast, and is no more.
My God, thou hast forgotten me in my death:
Nay–God my Christ–I pass but shall not die.'

Then, ere that last weird battle in the west,
There came on Arthur sleeping, Gawain killed
In Lancelot's war, the ghost of Gawain blown
Along a wandering wind, and past his ear
Went shrilling, 'Hollow, hollow all delight!
Hail, King! tomorrow thou shalt pass away.
Farewell! there is an isle of rest for thee.
And I am blown along a wandering wind,
And hollow, hollow, hollow all delight.'
And fainter onward, like wild birds that change
Their season in the night and wail their way
From cloud to cloud, down the long wind the dream
Shrilled; but in going mingled with dim cries
Far in the moonlit haze among the hills,
As of some lonely city sacked by night,
When all is lost, and wife and child with wail

*25–6.* Cp. *Locksley Hall Sixty Years After* 148: 'Then back into the beast again'.

*27. Psalm* xxii 1, and *Matthew* xxvii 46: 'My God, my God, why hast thou forsaken me?'

*29. Then, ere*] *1873*; Before *1869–70*.

*30–49.* For T.'s earlier version of the ghost of Gawain (a version closer to Malory xxi 3), see *Morte d'Arthur* 13 ∧ 14 (p. 586). In Malory xxi 4, the ghost of Gawain warned Arthur not to fight that day: 'How by misadventure of an adder the battle began'.

*36.* T. compares *Aeneid* vi 740–1, on the fate of the dead: *aliae panduntur inanes / suspensae ad ventos* ('Some are hung stretched out to the empty winds').

*37.* Cp. *Locksley Hall* 75, MS (p. 693): 'Hollow, hollow, hollow comfort'.

Pass to new lords; and Arthur woke and called,
'Who spake? A dream. O light upon the wind,
Thine, Gawain, was the voice–are these dim cries
Thine? or doth all that haunts the waste and wild
Mourn, knowing it will go along with me?'

This heard the bold Sir Bedivere and spake:
'O me, my King, let pass whatever will,
Elves, and the harmless glamour of the field;
But in their stead thy name and glory cling
To all high places like a golden cloud
For ever: but as yet thou shalt not pass.
Light was Gawain in life, and light in death
Is Gawain, for the ghost is as the man;
And care not thou for dreams from him, but rise–
I hear the steps of Modred in the west,
And with him many of thy people, and knights
Once thine, whom thou hast loved, but grosser grown
Than heathen, spitting at their vows and thee.
Right well in heart they know thee for the King.
Arise, go forth and conquer as of old.'

Then spake King Arthur to Sir Bedivere:
'Far other is this battle in the west
Whereto we move, than when we strove in youth,
And brake the petty kings, and fought with Rome,
Or thrust the heathen from the Roman wall,
And shook him through the north. Ill doom is mine
To war against my people and my knights.
The king who fights his people fights himself.
And they my knights, who loved me once, the stroke
That strikes them dead is as my death to me.
Yet let us hence, and find or feel a way
Through this blind haze, which ever since I saw
One lying in the dust at Almesbury,
Hath folded in the passes of the world.'

Then rose the King and moved his host by night,
And ever pushed Sir Modred, league by league,
Back to the sunset bound of Lyonnesse–
A land of old upheaven from the abyss

50–78] *Not trial edition (1869)*. See Wise, *Bibliography* i 207.
52. 'The legends which cluster round the King's name' (T.).
57. 'The spirit' (T.).
68] *1873; not 1869–70.*
69. Or] *1873*; And *1869–70*.

By fire, to sink into the abyss again;
Where fragments of forgotten peoples dwelt,
And the long mountains ended in a coast
Of ever-shifting sand, and far away
The phantom circle of a moaning sea.
There the pursuer could pursue no more,
And he that fled no further fly the King;
And there, that day when the great light of heaven
Burned at his lowest in the rolling year,
On the waste sand by the waste sea they closed.
Nor ever yet had Arthur fought a fight
Like this last, dim, weird battle of the west.
A deathwhite mist slept over sand and sea:
Whereof the chill, to him who breathed it, drew
Down with his blood, till all his heart was cold
With formless fear; and even on Arthur fell
Confusion, since he saw not whom he fought.
For friend and foe were shadows in the mist,
And friend slew friend not knowing whom he slew;
And some had visions out of golden youth,
And some beheld the faces of old ghosts
Look in upon the battle; and in the mist
Was many a noble deed, many a base,
And chance and craft and strength in single fights,
And ever and anon with host to host
Shocks, and the splintering spear, the hard mail hewn,
Shield-breakings, and the clash of brands, the crash
Of battleaxes on shattered helms, and shrieks
After the Christ, of those who falling down
Looked up for heaven, and only saw the mist;
And shouts of heathen and the traitor knights,
Oaths, insult, filth, and monstrous blasphemies,
Sweat, writhings, anguish, labouring of the lungs
In that close mist, and cryings for the light,
Moans of the dying, and voices of the dead.

*84.* 'Perhaps old Celts' (T.).
*87.* T. had thought of using this line in 1868 for *The Lover's Tale* iv 141: 'A world of reed and rush, and far away / The phantom circle of a moaning sea.' He had originally created the line as part of *Lines* [*How often*] (1833).
*91.* 'The winter solstice' (T.).
*93–4.* 'A Vision of Death' (T.).
*114.* T. compares *Revelation* xvi 21: 'and men blasphemed God', after the battle of Armageddon. 'This grim battle in the mist contrasts with Arthur's glorious battle in the *Coming of Arthur*, fought on a bright day when "he saw the smallest rock far on the faintest hill"' (T.). The landscape and the mist are additions to Malory.

Last, as by some one deathbed after wail
Of suffering, silence follows, or through death
Or deathlike swoon, thus over all that shore,
Save for some whisper of the seething seas,
A dead hush fell; but when the dolorous day
Grew drearier toward twilight falling, came
A bitter wind, clear from the North, and blew
The mist aside, and with that wind the tide
Rose, and the pale King glanced across the field
Of battle: but no man was moving there;
Nor any cry of Christian heard thereon,
Nor yet of heathen; only the wan wave
Brake in among dead faces, to and fro
Swaying the helpless hands, and up and down
Tumbling the hollow helmets of the fallen,
And shivered brands that once had fought with Rome,
And rolling far along the gloomy shores
The voice of days of old and days to be.

Then spake King Arthur to Sir Bedivere,
And whiter than the mist that all day long
Had held the field of battle was the King:

'Hearest thou this great voice that shakes the world,
And wastes the narrow realm whereon we move,
And beats upon the faces of the dead,
My dead, as though they had not died for me?–
O Bedivere, for on my heart hath fallen
Confusion, till I know not what I am,
Nor whence I am, nor whether I be King.
Behold, I seem but King among the dead.'

Then spake the bold Sir Bedivere: 'My King,
King everywhere! and so the dead have kings,
There also will I worship thee as King.
Yet still thy life is whole, and still I live
Who love thee; but who hates thee, he that brought
The heathen back among us, yonder stands,
Modred, unharmed, the traitor of thine house.'

Then spake the King: 'My house hath been my doom.
But call not thou this traitor of my house
Who hath but dwelt beneath one roof with me.
My house are rather they who sware my vows,
Yea, even while they brake them, owned me King.

And well for thee, saying in my dark hour,
When all the purport of my throne hath failed,
That quick or dead thou holdest me for King.
King am I, whatsoever be their cry;
And one last act of kinghood shalt thou see
Yet, ere I pass.' And uttering this the King
Made at the man: then Modred smote his liege
Hard on that helm which many a heathen sword
Had beaten thin; while Arthur at one blow,
Striking the last stroke with Excalibur,
Slew him, and all but slain himself, he fell.

So all day long the noise of battle rolled
Among the mountains by the winter sea;
Until King Arthur's Table, man by man,
Had fallen in Lyonnesse about their lord,
King Arthur. Then, because his wound was deep,
The bold Sir Bedivere uplifted him,
And bore him to a chapel nigh the field,
A broken chancel with a broken cross,
That stood on a dark strait of barren land:
On one side lay the Ocean, and on one
Lay a great water, and the moon was full.

Then spake King Arthur to Sir Bedivere:
'The sequel of today unsolders all
The goodliest fellowship of famous knights
Whereof this world holds record. Such a sleep
They sleep–the men I loved. I think that we
Shall never more, at any future time,
Delight our souls with talk of knightly deeds,
Walking about the gardens and the halls
Of Camelot, as in the days that were.
I perish by this people which I made,–
Though Merlin sware that I should come again
To rule once more; but, let what will be, be,
I am so deeply smitten through the helm
That without help I cannot last till morn.
Thou therefore take my brand Excalibur,
Which was my pride: for thou rememberest how
In those old days, one summer noon, an arm
Rose up from out the bosom of the lake,
Clothed in white samite, mystic, wonderful,
Holding the sword–and how I rowed across
And took it, and have worn it, like a king;

*175* ∧ *6*] Sir Bedivere, the last of all his knights, *Morte d'Arthur*.

And, wheresoever I am sung or told
In aftertime, this also shall be known:
But now delay not: take Excalibur,
And fling him far into the middle mere:
Watch what thou seëst, and lightly bring me word.'

To him replied the bold Sir Bedivere:
'It is not meet, Sir King, to leave thee thus,
Aidless, alone, and smitten through the helm–
A little thing may harm a wounded man;
Yet I thy hest will all perform at full,
Watch what I see, and lightly bring thee word.'

So saying, from the ruined shrine he stept,
And in the moon athwart the place of tombs,
Where lay the mighty bones of ancient men,
Old knights, and over them the sea-wind sang
Shrill, chill, with flakes of foam. He, stepping down
By zigzag paths, and juts of pointed rock,
Came on the shining levels of the lake.

There drew he forth the brand Excalibur,
And o'er him, drawing it, the winter moon,
Brightening the skirts of a long cloud, ran forth
And sparkled keen with frost against the hilt:
For all the haft twinkled with diamond sparks,
Myriads of topaz-lights, and jacinth-work
Of subtlest jewellery. He gazed so long
That both his eyes were dazzled as he stood,
This way and that dividing the swift mind,
In act to throw: but at the last it seemed
Better to leave Excalibur concealed
There in the many-knotted waterflags,
That whistled stiff and dry about the marge.
So strode he back slow to the wounded King.

Then spake King Arthur to Sir Bedivere:
'Hast thou performed my mission which I gave?
What is it thou hast seen? or what hast heard?'

And answer made the bold Sir Bedivere:
'I heard the ripple washing in the reeds,
And the wild water lapping on the crag.'

To whom replied King Arthur, faint and pale:
'Thou hast betrayed thy nature and thy name,
Not rendering true answer, as beseemed
Thy fëalty, nor like a noble knight:

For surer sign had followed, either hand,
Or voice, or else a motion of the mere.
This is a shameful thing for men to lie.
Yet now, I charge thee, quickly go again,
As thou art lief and dear, and do the thing
I bade thee, watch, and lightly bring me word.'

Then went Sir Bedivere the second time
Across the ridge, and paced beside the mere,
Counting the dewy pebbles, fixed in thought;
But when he saw the wonder of the hilt,
How curiously and strangely chased, he smote
His palms together, and he cried aloud:

'And if indeed I cast the brand away,
Surely a precious thing, one worthy note,
Should thus be lost for ever from the earth,
Which might have pleased the eyes of many men.
What good should follow this, if this were done?
What harm, undone? Deep harm to disobey,
Seeing obedience is the bond of rule.
Were it well to obey then, if a king demand
An act unprofitable, against himself?
The King is sick, and knows not what he does.
What record, or what relic of my lord
Should be to aftertime, but empty breath
And rumours of a doubt? But were this kept,
Stored in some treasure-house of mighty kings,
Some one might show it at a joust of arms,
Saying, "King Arthur's sword, Excalibur,
Wrought by the lonely maiden of the Lake.
Nine years she wrought it, sitting in the deeps
Upon the hidden bases of the hills."
So might some old man speak in the aftertime
To all the people, winning reverence.
But now much honour and much fame were lost.'

So spake he, clouded with his own conceit,
And hid Excalibur the second time,
And so strode back slow to the wounded King.

Then spoke King Arthur, breathing heavily:
'What is it thou hast seen? or what hast heard?'

And answer made the bold Sir Bedivere:
'I heard the water lapping on the crag,
And the long ripple washing in the reeds.'

To whom replied King Arthur, much in wrath:
'Ah, miserable and unkind, untrue,
Unknightly, traitor-hearted! Woe is me!
Authority forgets a dying king,
Laid widowed of the power in his eye
That bowed the will. I see thee what thou art,
For thou, the latest-left of all my knights,
In whom should meet the offices of all,
Thou wouldst betray me for the precious hilt;
Either from lust of gold, or like a girl
Valuing the giddy pleasure of the eyes.
Yet, for a man may fail in duty twice,
And the third time may prosper, get thee hence:
But, if thou spare to fling Excalibur,
I will arise and slay thee with my hands.'

Then quickly rose Sir Bedivere, and ran,
And, leaping down the ridges lightly, plunged
Among the bulrush beds, and clutched the sword,
And strongly wheeled and threw it. The great brand
Made lightnings in the splendour of the moon,
And flashing round and round, and whirled in an arch,
Shot like a streamer of the northern morn,
Seen where the moving isles of winter shock
By night, with noises of the Northern Sea.
So flashed and fell the brand Excalibur:
But ere he dipt the surface, rose an arm
Clothed in white samite, mystic, wonderful,
And caught him by the hilt, and brandished him
Three times, and drew him under in the mere.
And lightly went the other to the King.

Then spoke King Arthur, drawing thicker breath:
'Now see I by thine eyes that this is done.
Speak out: what is it thou hast heard, or seen?'

And answer made the bold Sir Bedivere:
'Sir King, I closed mine eyelids, lest the gems
Should blind my purpose, for I never saw,
Nor shall see, here or elsewhere, till I die,
Not though I live three lives of mortal men,
So great a miracle as yonder hilt.
Then with both hands I flung him, wheeling him;
But when I looked again, behold an arm,

*306.* 'The extra syllable gives the rush of the sword as it is whirled in parabolic curve' (T.).

Clothed in white samite, mystic, wonderful,
That caught him by the hilt, and brandished him
Three times, and drew him under in the mere.'

And answer made King Arthur, breathing hard:
'My end draws nigh; 'tis time that I were gone.
Make broad thy shoulders to receive my weight,
And bear me to the margin; yet I fear
My wound hath taken cold, and I shall die.'

So saying, from the pavement he half rose,
Slowly, with pain, reclining on his arm,
And looking wistfully with wide blue eyes
As in a picture. Him Sir Bedivere
Remorsefully regarded through his tears,
And would have spoken, but he found not words;
Then took with care, and kneeling on one knee,
O'er both his shoulders drew the languid hands,
And rising bore him through the place of tombs.

But, as he walked, King Arthur panted hard,
Like one that feels a nightmare on his bed
When all the house is mute. So sighed the King,
Muttering and murmuring at his ear, 'Quick, quick!
I fear it is too late, and I shall die.'
But the other swiftly strode from ridge to ridge,
Clothed with his breath, and looking, as he walked,
Larger than human on the frozen hills.
He heard the deep behind him, and a cry
Before. His own thought drove him like a goad.
Dry clashed his harness in the icy caves
And barren chasms, and all to left and right
The bare black cliff clanged round him, as he based
His feet on juts of slippery crag that rang
Sharp-smitten with the dint of armèd heels–
And on a sudden, lo! the level lake,
And the long glories of the winter moon.

Then saw they how there hove a dusky barge,
Dark as a funeral scarf from stem to stern,
Beneath them; and descending they were ware
That all the decks were dense with stately forms,
Black-stoled, black-hooded, like a dream–by these
Three Queens with crowns of gold: and from them rose
A cry that shivered to the tingling stars,
And, as it were one voice, an agony
Of lamentation, like a wind that shrills

All night in a waste land, where no one comes,
Or hath come, since the making of the world.

Then murmured Arthur, 'Place me in the barge.'
So to the barge they came. There those three Queens
Put forth their hands, and took the King, and wept.
But she, that rose the tallest of them all
And fairest, laid his head upon her lap,
And loosed the shattered casque, and chafed his hands,
And called him by his name, complaining loud,
And dropping bitter tears against a brow
Striped with dark blood: for all his face was white
And colourless, and like the withered moon
Smote by the fresh beam of the springing east;
And all his greaves and cuisses dashed with drops
Of onset; and the light and lustrous curls–
That made his forehead like a rising sun
High from the daïs-throne–were parched with dust;
Or, clotted into points and hanging loose,
Mixed with the knightly growth that fringed his lips.
So like a shattered column lay the King;
Not like that Arthur who, with lance in rest,
From spur to plume a star of tournament,
Shot through the lists at Camelot, and charged
Before the eyes of ladies and of kings.

Then loudly cried the bold Sir Bedivere:
'Ah! my Lord Arthur, whither shall I go?
Where shall I hide my forehead and my eyes?
For now I see the true old times are dead,
When every morning brought a noble chance,
And every chance brought out a noble knight.
Such times have been not since the light that led
The holy Elders with the gift of myrrh.
But now the whole Round Table is dissolved
Which was an image of the mighty world,
And I, the last, go forth companionless,
And the days darken round me, and the years,
Among new men, strange faces, other minds.'

And slowly answered Arthur from the barge:
'The old order changeth, yielding place to new,
And God fulfils himself in many ways,
Lest one good custom should corrupt the world.

*373. So*] And *Morte d'Arthur.*
*379. a*] *1873*; his *1869–70.*

Comfort thyself: what comfort is in me?
I have lived my life, and that which I have done
May He within himself make pure! but thou,
If thou shouldst never see my face again,
Pray for my soul. More things are wrought by prayer
Than this world dreams of. Wherefore, let thy voice
Rise like a fountain for me night and day.
For what are men better than sheep or goats
That nourish a blind life within the brain,
If, knowing God, they lift not hands of prayer
Both for themselves and those who call them friend?
For so the whole round earth is every way
Bound by gold chains about the feet of God.
But now farewell. I am going a long way
With these thou seëst–if indeed I go
(For all my mind is clouded with a doubt)–
To the island-valley of Avilion;
Where falls not hail, or rain, or any snow,
Nor ever wind blows loudly; but it lies
Deep-meadowed, happy, fair with orchard lawns
And bowery hollows crowned with summer sea,
Where I will heal me of my grievous wound.'

So said he, and the barge with oar and sail
Moved from the brink, like some full-breasted swan
That, fluting a wild carol ere her death,
Ruffles her pure cold plume, and takes the flood
With swarthy webs. Long stood Sir Bedivere
Revolving many memories, till the hull
Looked one black dot against the verge of dawn,
And on the mere the wailing died away.

But when that moan had past for evermore,
The stillness of the dead world's winter dawn
Amazed him, and he groaned, 'The King is gone.'
And therewithal came on him the weird rhyme,
'From the great deep to the great deep he goes.'

Whereat he slowly turned and slowly clomb
The last hard footstep of that iron crag;
Thence marked the black hull moving yet, and cried,

*441–5*] *1873; not 1869–70.*
*445.* 'Merlin's song when he was born' (T.). Cp. *De Profundis* (p. 1281).
*446*] *1873*; At length he groaned, and turning slowly clomb *1869–70.*

'He passes to be King among the dead,
And after healing of his grievous wound
He comes again; but–if he come no more–
O me, be yon dark Queens in yon black boat,
Who shrieked and wailed, the three whereat we gazed
On that high day, when, clothed with living light,
They stood before his throne in silence, friends
Of Arthur, who should help him at his need?'

Then from the dawn it seemed there came, but faint
As from beyond the limit of the world,
Like the last echo born of a great cry,
Sounds, as if some fair city were one voice
Around a king returning from his wars.

Thereat once more he moved about, and clomb
Even to the highest he could climb, and saw,
Straining his eyes beneath an arch of hand,
Or thought he saw, the speck that bare the King,
Down that long water opening on the deep
Somewhere far off, pass on and on, and go
From less to less and vanish into light.
And the new sun rose bringing the new year.

*457.* 'From (the dawn) the East, whence have sprung all the great religions of the world. A triumph of welcome is given to him who has proved himself "more than conqueror"' (T.).

*463. Even*] Ev'n *1873*; E'en *1869–70*.

*468.* 'The purpose of the individual man may fail for a time, but his work cannot die' (T.). T. compares Malory xxi 7: 'Some men yet say, in many parts of England, that king Arthur is not dead; but, by the will of our Lord Jesu Christ, into another place: and men say, that he will come again, and he shall win the holy cross.' T. adds: 'And cf. what Arthur says in Layamon's *Brut*, 28619, Madden's Edition iii 144: "And seothe ich cumen wulle / to mine kineriche, / and wunien mid Brutten, / mid muchelere wunne." (And afterwards I will come (again) to my kingdom, and dwell with the Britons with much joy).'

*469.* Wise, *Bibliography* i 207–8, quotes the trial edition (1869), which followed l. 467 with:

Then rose the new sun bringing the new year,
And on the heart of Bedivere returned
A rhyme of Merlin, 'Where is he who knows?
From the great deep to the great deep he goes'.

# 476 To the Queen

Published *1873*, Imperial Library Edition. T. had 'just written' it, 25 Dec. 1872 (*Mem.* ii 119). Cp. *To the Queen* (p. 990).

O loyal to the royal in thyself,
And loyal to thy land, as this to thee—
Bear witness, that rememberable day,
When, pale as yet, and fever-worn, the Prince
Who scarce had plucked his flickering life again
From halfway down the shadow of the grave,
Past with thee through thy people and their love,
And London rolled one tide of joy through all
Her trebled millions, and loud leagues of man
And welcome! witness, too, the silent cry,
The prayer of many a race and creed, and clime–
Thunderless lightnings striking under sea
From sunset and sunrise of all thy realm,
And that true North, whereof we lately heard
A strain to shame us 'keep you to yourselves;
So loyal is too costly! friends–your love
Is but a burthen: loose the bond, and go.'
Is this the tone of empire? here the faith
That made us rulers? this, indeed, her voice
And meaning, whom the roar of Hougoumont
Left mightiest of all peoples under heaven?
What shock has fooled her since, that she should speak
So feebly? wealthier–wealthier–hour by hour!
The voice of Britain, or a sinking land,
Some third-rate isle half-lost among her seas?
*There* rang her voice, when the full city pealed
Thee and thy Prince! The loyal to their crown
Are loyal to their own far sons, who love
Our ocean-empire with her boundless homes
For ever-broadening England, and her throne
In our vast Orient, and one isle, one isle,
That knows not her own greatness: if she knows
And dreads it we are fallen.—But thou, my Queen,

¶476. *3.* 'When the Queen and the Prince of Wales went to the thanksgiving at St Paul's (after the Prince's dangerous illness) in Feb. 1872' (T.).
*14–17.* 'Canada. A leading London journal had written advocating that Canada should sever her connection with Great Britain, as she was "too costly": hence these lines' (T.). Referring to *The Times*.
*20. Hougoumont*: 'Waterloo' (T.).

Not for itself, but through thy living love
For one to whom I made it o'er his grave
Sacred, accept this old imperfect tale,
New-old, and shadowing Sense at war with Soul,
Ideal manhood closed in real man,
Rather than that gray king, whose name, a ghost,
Streams like a cloud, man-shaped, from mountain peak,
And cleaves to cairn and cromlech still; or him
Of Geoffrey's book, or him of Malleor's, one
Touched by the adulterous finger of a time
That hovered between war and wantonness,
And crownings and dethronements: take withal
Thy poet's blessing, and his trust that Heaven
Will blow the tempest in the distance back
From thine and ours: for some are scared, who mark,
Or wisely or unwisely, signs of storm,
Waverings of every vane with every wind,
And wordy trucklings to the transient hour,
And fierce or careless looseners of the faith,
And Softness breeding scorn of simple life,
Or Cowardice, the child of lust for gold,
Or Labour, with a groan and not a voice,
Or Art with poisonous honey stolen from France,
And that which knows, but careful for itself,
And that which knows not, ruling that which knows
To its own harm: the goal of this great world
Lies beyond sight: yet–if our slowly-grown
And crowned Republic's crowning common-sense,
That saved her many times, not fail–their fears
Are morning shadows huger than the shapes
That cast them, not those gloomier which forego
The darkness of that battle in the West,
Where all of high and holy dies away.

*35*. See the *Dedication* to the Prince Consort (p. 1467).

*38*] *1899; not 1873–98.* See p. 1464.

*39*. 'The legendary Arthur from whom many mountains, hills, and cairns throughout Great Britain are named' (H.T.).

*42*. 'Geoffrey of Monmouth's', and 'Malory's name is given as Maleorye, Maleore, and Malleor' (T.).

*43*. Kathleen Tillotson points out that F. J. Furnivall in 1864 had drawn attention to Arthur's incest: 'It was perhaps because of such reference to the incest episode that Tennyson made the disclaimer' (*Mid-Victorian Studies*, 1965, p. 98).

# 477 Songs from the Plays

From *Queen Mary*, written 1874–5 (*Mem.* ii 176; *CT*, p. 414), published *1875*.

Shame upon you, Robin,
Shame upon you now!
Kiss me would you? with my hands
Milking the cow?
Daisies grow again,
Kingcups blow again,
And you came and kissed me milking the cow.

Robin came behind me,
Kissed me well I vow;
Cuff him could I? with my hands
Milking the cow?
Swallows fly again,
Cuckoos cry again,
And you came and kissed me milking the cow.

Come, Robin, Robin,
Come and kiss me now;
Help it can I? with my hands
Milking the cow?
Ringdoves coo again,
All things woo again.
Come behind and kiss me milking the cow!

(*Act III Scene v*)

Hapless doom of woman happy in betrothing!
Beauty passes like a breath and love is lost in loathing:
Low, my lute; speak low, my lute, but say the world is nothing–
Low, lute, low!
Love will hover round the flowers when they first awaken;
Love will fly the fallen leaf, and not be overtaken;
Low, my lute! oh low, my lute! we fade and are forsaken–
Low, dear lute, low!

(*Act V Scene ii*)

From *Harold*, written 1876 (*CT*, p. 432), published Dec. 1876 ('*1877*').

Love is come with a song and a smile,
Welcome Love with a smile and a song:
Love can stay but a little while.
Why cannot he stay? They call him away:
Ye do him wrong, ye do him wrong;
Love will stay for a whole life long.

(*Act I Scene ii*)

Two young lovers in winter weather,
None to guide them,
Walked at night on the misty heather;
Night, as black as a raven's feather;
Both were lost and found together,
None beside them.

Lost, lost, the light of day,
'I am beside thee.'
Lost, lost, we have lost the way.
'Love, I will guide thee.'
Whither, O whither? into the river,
Where we two may be lost together,
And lost for ever? 'Oh! never, oh! never,
Though we be lost and be found together.'

(*Act III Scene ii*)

From *Becket*, written 1876–9 (*Mem.* ii 193), published *1884*.

Over! the sweet summer closes,
The reign of the roses is done;
Over and gone with the roses,
And over and gone with the sun.

Over! the sweet summer closes,
And never a flower at the close;
Over and gone with the roses,
And winter again and the snows.

(*Prologue*)

DUET

1. Is it the wind of the dawn that I hear
in the pine overhead?
2. No; but the voice of the deep as it hollows
the cliffs of the land.
1. Is there a voice coming up with the
voice of the deep from the strand,
One coming up with a song in the
flush of the glimmering red?
2. Love that is born of the deep coming
up with the sun from the sea.
1. Love that can shape or can shatter a
life till the life shall have fled?
2. Nay, let us welcome him, Love that
can lift up a life from the dead.
1. Keep him away from the lone little isle.
Let us be, let us be.
2. Nay, let him make it his own, let him
reign in it–he, it is he,
Love that is born of the deep coming
up with the sun from the sea.

(*Act II Scene i*)

Babble in bower
Under the rose!
Bee mustn't buzz,
Whoop–but he knows.

Kiss me, little one,
Nobody near!
Grasshopper, grasshopper,
Whoop–you can hear.

Kiss in the bower,
Tit on the tree!
Bird mustn't tell,
Whoop–he can see.

(*Act III Scene i*)

Rainbow, stay,
Gleam upon gloom,
Bright as my dream,
Rainbow, stay!
But it passes away,
Gloom upon gleam,
Dark as my doom–
O rainbow stay.

(*Act III Scene i*)

From *The Cup*, written 1879–80 (*Mem.* ii 256), published *1884*. The lines to Artemis were not written till 1887 (*Mem.* ii 336), and were published in *1891*.

Moon on the field and the foam,
Moon on the waste and the wold,
Moon bring him home, bring him home
Safe from the dark and the cold,
Home, sweet moon, bring him home,
Home with the flock to the fold–
Safe from the wolf to the fold.

(*Act I Scene ii*)

Artemis, Artemis, hear us, O Mother, hear us, and bless us!
Artemis, thou that art life to the wind, to the wave, to the glebe, to the fire!
Hear thy people who praise thee! O help us from all that oppress us!
Hear thy priestesses hymn thy glory! O yield them all their desire!

(*Act II*)

From *The Falcon*, written 1879 (*Mem.* ii 256), published *1884*.

Dead mountain flowers, dead mountain-meadow flowers,
Dearer than when you made your mountain gay,
Sweeter than any violet of today,
Richer than all the wide world-wealth of May,
To me, though all your bloom has died away,
You bloom again, dead mountain-meadow flowers.
O mountain flowers!
Dead flowers!

From *The Promise of May*, written 1882 (*CT*, pp. 463–4), published *1886*.

The town lay still in the low sun-light,
The hen cluckt late by the white farm gate,
The maid to her dairy came in from the cow,
The stock-dove cooed at the fall of night,
The blossom had opened on every bough;
O joy for the promise of May, of May,
O joy for the promise of May.

But a red fire woke in the heart of the town,
And a fox from the glen ran away with the hen,
And a cat to the cream, and a rat to the cheese;
And the stock-dove cooed, till a kite dropt down,
And a salt wind burnt the blossoming trees;
O grief for the promise of May, of May,
O grief for the promise of May.

(*Act I*)

What did ye do, and what did ye saäy,
Wi' the wild white rose, an' the woodbine sa gaäy,
An' the midders all mowed, an' the sky sa blue–
What did ye saäy, and what did ye do,
When ye thowt there was nawbody watchin' o' you,
And you an' your Sally was forkin' the haäy,
At the end of the daäy,
For the last loäd hoäm?

What did we do, and what did we saäy,
Wi' the briar sa green, an' the willer sa graäy,
An' the midders all mowed, an' the sky sa blue–
Do ye think I be gawin' to tell it to you,
What we mowt saäy, and what we mowt do,
When me an' my Sally was forkin' the haäy,
At the end of the daäy,
For the last loäd hoäm?

But what did ye saäy, and what did ye do,
Wi' the butterflies out, and the swallers at plaäy,
An' the midders all mowed, an' the sky sa blue?
Why, coom then, owd feller, I'll tell it to you;
For me an' my Sally we sweäred to be true,
To be true to each other, let 'appen what maäy,
Till the end of the daäy
And the last loäd hoäm.

(*Act II*)

Gee oop! whoä! Gee oop! whoä!
Scizzars an' Pumpy was good uns to goä
Thruf slush an' squad
When roäds was bad,
But hallus ud stop at the Vine-an'-the-Hop,
Fur boäth on 'em knawed as well as mysen
That beer be as good fur 'erses as men.
Gee oop! whoä! Gee oop! whoä!
Scizzars an' Pumpy was good uns to goä.

(*Act II*)

O man, forgive thy mortal foe,
Nor ever strike him blow for blow;
For all the souls on earth that live
To be forgiven must forgive.
Forgive him seventy times and seven:
For all the blessèd souls in Heaven
Are both forgivers and forgiven.

(*Act III*)

O happy lark, that warblest high
  Above thy lowly nest,
O brook, that brawlest merrily by
  Through fields that once were blest,
O tower spiring to the sky,
  O graves in daisies drest,
O Love and Life, how weary am I,
  And how I long for rest.

(*Act III*)

From *The Foresters*, written 1881 (*CT*, p. 458), published *1892*. *Love flew in*: 'Before Christmas [1891] he had written . . . a new song "Love flew in at the window"' (*Mem.* ii 390). *To sleep*: published *New Review*, March 1891, as *A Song*; deleted from trial edition of *The Death of Œnone, 1892* (*Lincoln*). *There is no land*: adapted from *National Song* (*1830*, p. 252). *The bee buzzed*: deleted from trial edition of *The Death of Œnone, 1892*.

The warrior Earl of Allendale,
  He loved the Lady Anne;
The lady loved the master well,
  The maid she loved the man.
All in the castle garden,
  Or ever the day began,
The lady gave a rose to the Earl,
  The maid a rose to the man.

'I go to fight in Scotland
  With many a savage clan;'
The lady gave her hand to the Earl,
  The maid her hand to the man.

'Farewell, farewell, my warrior Earl!'
  And ever a tear down ran.
She gave a weeping kiss to the Earl,
  And the maid a kiss to the man.

(*Act I Scene i*)

Love flew in at the window
As Wealth walked in at the door.
'You have come for you saw Wealth coming,' said I.
But he fluttered his wings with a sweet little cry,
I'll cleave to you rich or poor.

Wealth dropt out of the window,
Poverty crept through the door.
'Well now you would fain follow Wealth,' said I,
But he fluttered his wings as he gave me the lie,
I cling to you all the more.

(*Act I Scene i*)

### DRINKING SONG

Long live Richard,
Robin and Richard!
Long live Richard!
Down with John!
Drink to the Lion-heart
Every one!
Pledge the Plantagenet,
Him that is gone.

Who knows whither?
God's good Angel
Help him back hither,
And down with John!
Long live Robin,
Robin and Richard!
Long live Robin,
And down with John!

(*Act I Scene ii*)

To sleep! to sleep! The long bright day is done,
And darkness rises from the fallen sun.
To sleep! to sleep!
Whate'er thy joys, they vanish with the day;
Whate'er thy griefs, in sleep they fade away.
To sleep! to sleep!
Sleep, mournful heart, and let the past be past!
Sleep, happy soul! all life will sleep at last.
To sleep! to sleep!

(*Act I Scene iii*)

There is no land like England
 Where'er the light of day be;
There are no hearts like English hearts
 Such hearts of oak as they be.
There is no land like England
 Where'er the light of day be;
There are no men like Englishmen
 So tall and bold as they be.

*Full Chorus*

And these will strike for England
 And man and maid be free
To foil and spoil the tyrant
 Beneath the greenwood tree.

There is no land like England
 Where'er the light of day be;
There are no wives like English wives
 So fair and chaste as they be.
There is no land like England
 Where'er the light of day be;
There are no maids like English maids
 So beautiful as they be.

*Full Chorus*

And these shall wed with freemen,
 And all their sons be free,
To sing the songs of England
 Beneath the greenwood tree.

(*Act II Scene i*)

Up with you, out of the forest and over the hills
 and away,
And over this Robin Hood's bay!
Up through the light of the seas by the moon's
 long-silvering ray!
To a land where the fay,
Not an eye to survey,
In the night, in the day,
Can have frolic and play.
Up with you, all of you, out of it! hear and obey.
Man, lying here alone,
Moody creature,

Of a nature
Stronger, sadder than my own,
Were I human, were I human,
I could love you like a woman.
Man, man,
You shall wed your Marian.
She is true, and you are true,
And you love her and she loves you;
Both be happy, and adieu for ever and for
evermore–adieu.

(*Act II Scene ii*)

By all the deer that spring
Through wood and lawn and ling,
When all the leaves are green;
By arrow and gray goosewing,
When horn and echo ring,
We care so much for a King;
We care not much for a Queen–
For a Queen, for a Queen o' the woods.

By all the leaves of spring,
And all the birds that sing
When all the leaves are green;
By arrow and by bowstring,
We care so much for a King
That we would die for a Queen–
For a Queen, for a Queen o' the woods.

(*Act III Scene i*)

The bee buzzed up in the heat.
'I am faint for your honey, my sweet.'
The flower said 'Take it, my dear,
For now is the spring of the year.
So come, come!'
'Hum!'
And the bee buzzed down from the heat.

And the bee buzzed up in the cold
When the flower was withered and old.
'Have you still any honey, my dear?'
She said 'It's the fall of the year,
But come, come!'
'Hum!'
And the bee buzzed off in the cold.

(*Act IV Scene i*)

Now the King is home again, and nevermore to
  roam again,
Now the King is home again, the King will have
  his own again,
Home again, home again, and each will have
  his own again,
All the birds in merry Sherwood sing and sing him
  home again.

(*Act IV Scene i*)

# Appendix A

## ★ALTERNATIVE DRAFTS

### ST LAWRENCE (p. 298)

The following are the three other versions printed by E. F. Shannon and W. H. Bond, *Harvard Library Bulletin* x (1956) 258–60.

(i) *Harvard Notebook 2, c. 1825*

No portion of my soul misgives.
Come, strip me: lay me on these bars.
Too slow–too slow: my spirits yearn
To float among the cold clear stars.
I know that my Redeemer lives.
I cannot argue–I can burn.
I am armed in Christ: all helmed and mailed
In Jesus unto victory.
Lord lead me to the battleplain,
For Love is mightier than pain,
Stronger than human agony–
Of power to blow me in fullsailed
Into the port of my desire.
The Lord that liveth over all–
My Lord–hath girdled Heaven with fire,
As he shut out from Paradise
(His garden on the mountain tall)
That Adam, with a living wall
Of fiery swords.

I will not mourn. I will not weep
Nor fail nor faint nor shrink nor tire
Though all my bones asunder leap
With the violence of fire.
Slowly comes on my painful death,
Slowly the iron heats beneath,
But yet my hope is clear and fresh.
Christ is my life, my blood, my breath,
And if God grant me grace and power
(God grant me power!), not even my flesh–
My frail flesh in the trying hour–
Shall tremble while I yield my breath.

(ii) *Harvard Notebook 3, c. 1831*

Slow fire! inch by inch to die,
And in the ebbing of the breath

To count each step that leads to death
And not to murmur–not to cry,
But to bear all–as is most fit.
The old Adam shrinks to fancy it–
But yet–God with us–we will try.

(iii) *Harvard Notebook 12, c. 1833*

Slow fire–inch by inch to die–to creep
Step by step down to death–and not to shriek,
Not to complain–but to bear all, as is
Most just, for him that hath borne all for me,
Knowing the eyes of God and man are set
To watch me, lest I fail.

THE PRINCESS (p. 741)

Sir Charles Tennyson has described the MSS in *Nineteenth Century* cix (1931) 632–6, and *Cornhill* cliii (1936) 672–80. He notes the Cambridge flavour of these fragments (*H.Nbk 23*) which sketch the layout. Arundel is 'in some degree a portrait of Tennyson himself'. See J. H. Buckley (p. 94).

[introducing ii]

I said my say; when Walter with a glance
At Lilia, meditating malice, took
The person of the Prince; but months have gone,
I can but give the substance not the words.

[iii]

The third that spoke, though steersman of our boat
At college, feared to steer the tale and cried
Against it–nothing could be done–but urged
By common voice, continued as he might.

[iv]

The next that spoke, a wild November fool,
Twice had he been convened and once had fought
A bargeman–he was Irish out of Clare.
For every prize he wrote and failed in all,
And many a song he made which no man knew–
The cleverest man in all our set was he,
And something like the Cyril in the tale.

[vi]

The next that spoke was Arthur Arundel
The Poet: rough his hair but fine to feel,

And dark his skin but softer than a babe's,
And large his hand as of the plastic kind,
And early furrows in his face he had:
Small were his themes–low builds the nightingale–
But promised more: and mellow was his voice,
He pitched it like a pipe to all he would;
And thus he brought our story back to life.

[vii]

The last that spoke was one we used to call
The lady: lady-like he read the parts
Of Viola, Beatrice, Hermione:
We thought he fancied Lilia: who could tell?
He coloured at the name of any girl.
He plucked a flower that like a moral grew
From *miserere* on the broken tomb
Beside us and he held it as he spoke.

[Conclusion]

Here closed our tale: I give it, not as told
But drest in words by Arthur Arundel
In aftertimes, a medley, which at first
Perhaps but meant &c.

ii ^ iii (p. 772)

Two alternative versions of *Sweet and low*. *Harvard Loosepaper 192* was printed by W. F. Rawnsley, *Nineteenth Century* xcvii (1925) 191:

Who claps the gate
So late, so late,
Who claps the gate on the windy wold?
O were it he
Come back from sea!
Sleep, sleep, my blossom; the night is cold–

Sleep, dearest dear!
The moon is clear
To light him back to my babe and me
And he'll come soon
All under the moon,
A thousand miles on the silver sea.

*Mem.* i 255: 'Two versions of *Sweet and low* were made, and were sent to my mother to choose which should be published. She chose the published one in preference to that which follows, because it seemed to her more song-like'. This version is dated 24 Nov. 1849 (*Lincoln*):

Bright is the moon on the deep,
Bright are the cliffs in her beam,
Sleep, my little one, sleep!
Look he smiles, and opens his hands,
He sees his father in distant lands,
And kisses him there in a dream,
Sleep, sleep.

Father is over the deep,
Father will come to thee soon,
Sleep, my pretty one, sleep!
Father will come to his babe in the nest,
Silver sails all out of the West,
Under the silver moon,
Sleep, sleep!

iv ^ v (p. 801)

Three alternative versions of *Thy voice is heard through rolling drums.* 'My first version of this song was published in *Selections*, 1865' (T.); he reprinted it in the Miniature Edition, 1870, only.

Lady, let the rolling drums
Beat to battle where thy warrior stands:
Now thy face across his fancy comes,
And gives the battle to his hands.

Lady, let the trumpets blow,
Clasp thy little babes about thy knee:
Now their warrior father meets the foe,
And strikes him dead for thine and thee.

Sir Charles Tennyson has printed two further versions, *Nineteenth Century* cix (1931) 635–6, describing them as probably the second and third versions. *H.Lpr 197*.

When all among the fifes and the thundering drums
Thy soldier in the battlefield, my Ada, stands,
Thy woman's face, believe it, across his fancy comes
And gives the battle, the battle to his hands.

Then though many a fatal bullet may whistle near,
And round him half his comrades may reel, may roll,
Thy whispers, O my life, will tremble at his ear,
Thy kisses, ah my darling, burn within his soul.

When the cannons roar and the trumpets, trumpets blow;
He will hear his young ones call him o'er the sea;
When the word is given, like a fire he meets the foe
And strikes a thousand dead for them and for thee.

---

When roars the fight to left and right
And on the field thy soldier stands,
When far and wide the cannon booms,
And shrill the fifes and beat the drums,
Thy face across his fancy comes
And gives the battle to his hands.

When roars the fight to left and right
And round him half his comrades roll,
Though many a bullet whistles near,
He fears not death, he knows not fear–
Thy whispers tremble at his ear,
Thy kisses burn within his soul.

When roars the fight to left and right,
He sees his young ones at thy knee.
The word is given; the trumpets blow;
The word is given, and on they go;
He heads the charge, he meets the foe
And strikes a thousand dead for thee.

v ∧ vi (p. 817)

An alternative version of *Home they brought her warrior dead* was published in *A Selection* (1865); it was reprinted in the Miniature Edition, 1870, and then only in *Songs* (1872).

Home they brought him slain with spears.
They brought him home at even-fall:
All alone she sits and hears
Echoes in his empty hall,
Sounding on the morrow.

The Sun peeped in from open field,
The boy began to leap and prance,
Rode upon his father's lance,
Beat upon his father's shield–
'O hush, my joy, my sorrow.'

IN MEMORIAM (p. 853)

The eight following sections which T. did not publish are printed in this Appendix, since they might distract from the final sequence of the poem. An unpublished fragment follows.

(i) 'SPEAK TO ME FROM THE STORMY SKY!'

Printed *Mem.* ii 517. In *H.Lpr 104* it is on the sheet facing vii (p. 870).

Speak to me from the stormy sky!
The wind is loud in holt and hill.
It is not kind to be so still.
Speak to me, dearest, lest I die.

Speak to me: let me hear or see!
Alas my life is frail and weak.
Seest thou my faults and wilt not speak?
They are not want of love for thee.

(ii) 'THE PATH BY WHICH I WALKED ALONE'

Unpublished, *H.Lpr 103*. It is on the same page as xxii (p. 884), with which it has obvious affinities. Cp. *Youth* (p. 577).

The path by which I walked alone
Ere yet thy motion caught mine eye
Was rich with many a prophecy
In every gale about me blown.

The blackbird warbled, 'Make thee whole
In spirit. Hear how glad I am.'
The lark on golden vapour swam
And chanted, 'Find a kindred soul.'

And yearning woke and was not stilled.
I could not find thee here or there,
I cried to all the breezes, 'Where?',
For all my want was unfulfilled.

ii 7. *golden vapour*: *Youth* 106.

But freshly did my feet advance
For twenty summers all but two
Till when the time was full I drew
To where I met thee as by chance.

### (iii) 'O SORROWER FOR THE FADED LEAF'

Unpublished, *Lincoln MS*, deleted. It follows lvi (p. 911), and acts as an introduction to lvii which is on the same page.

'O Sorrower for the faded leaf',
A dark and slothful spirit said,
'Why lingerest thou beside the dead?
Thy songs are fuel to thy grief.

They help not thee, and who will thank
Thy labour? What are these indeed
But sighings of the withered reed?
A little cry from off a plank

Of shipwreck, lost in shoreless seas,
A print in ever-shifting sands,
A spreading-out of feeble hands
To that which hears not?' Ill at ease

I faltered in my toil, and broke
The moulds that Fancy made; and turned
To that fair soul that with me mourned
About his tomb, and sighing spoke.

### (iv) THE PHILOSOPHER

Printed *Mat.* ii 274–5. *Mem.* i 457 omitted ll. 5–8, 13–16, and placed it as a poem of 1859. But it is in a MS of *The Princess* (mainly the songs–*University Library, Cambridge*), which shows that it belongs to *c.* 1849. It is presumably about Arthur Hallam and connected with *In Memoriam*; cp. in particular xcvi (p. 948).

He was too good and kind and sweet,
Even when I knew him in his hour
Of darkest doubt, and in his power,
To fling his doubts into the street.

Our modern authors young and vain
Must point and preach their doubts aloud,
And blurt to every passing crowd
Those indigestions of the brain.

Truth-seeking he and not afraid,
But questions that perplex us now–
What time (he thought) have loom or plough
To weigh them as they should be weighed?

But we that are not kind or just
We scatter seeds that spring or flame,
Or bear their fruit in London's shame–
The Sabbath journal mixt with lust.

We help the blatant voice abroad
To preach the freedom of despair,
And from the heart of all things fair
To pluck the sanction of a God.

### (v) 'YOUNG IS THE GRIEF I ENTERTAIN'

Printed *Mem.* i 306–7, from *T.MS* of *In Memoriam*, with the title *To A.H.H.* ('originally No. cviii'). In the MS it comes between cxi (p. 963) and *Are these the far-famed Victor Hours* (p. 1776).

Young is the grief I entertain,
And ever new the tale she tells,
And ever young the face that dwells
With reason cloistered in the brain:

Yet grief deserves a nobler name:
She spurs an imitative will;
'Tis shame to fail so far, and still
My failing shall be less my shame:

Considering what mine eyes have seen,
And all the sweetness which thou wast
And thy beginnings in the past,
And all the strength thou wouldst have been:

A master mind with master minds,
An orb repulsive of all hate,
A will concentric with all fate,
A life four-square to all the winds.

v *6.* Adapted as 'That spurs an imitative will', cx 20.
*11. And*] *Eversley*; In *Mem. Mem.* inaccurately transcribed *T.MS*. The correct reading was supplied by T. (*Eversley* proofs, *Lincoln*).
*15.* Cp. *On a Mourner* 19–20, MS (also on the death of Hallam, written Oct. 1833): 'Till all my soul concentric shine / With that wide will that closes mine.'
*16.* Adapted as 'Which stood four-square to all the winds that blew!', *Ode on Wellington* 39. For the epithet, T. compares Simonides, 'though I did not think of this parallel when I wrote it.'

*Plate 2* Tennyson aged about 22. Attributed to James Spedding

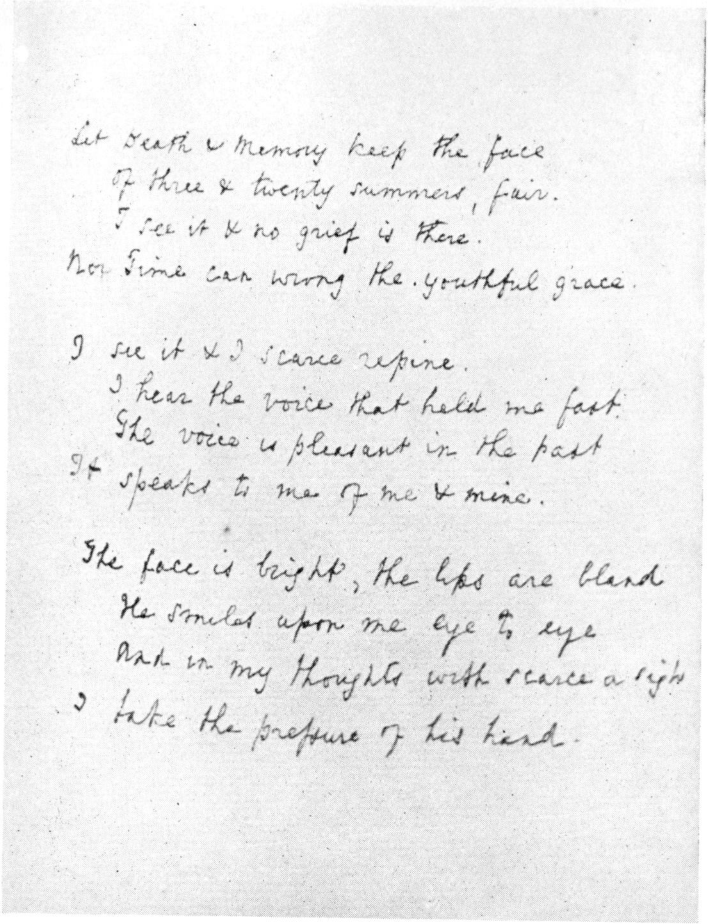

Let Death & Memory keep the face
Of three & twenty summers, fair.
I see it & no grief is there.
Nor Time can wrong the youthful grace.

I see it & I scarce repine.
I hear the voice that held me fast.
The voice is pleasant in the past
It speaks to me of me & mine.

The face is bright, the lips are bland
He smiles upon me eye to eye
And in my thoughts with scarce a sigh
I take the pressure of his hand.

*Plate 3* An unpublished section of *In Memoriam* from the Lincoln manuscript

### (vi) 'LET DEATH AND MEMORY KEEP THE FACE'

Printed, from *Lincoln MS* of *In Memoriam*, by Valerie Pitt, *Tennyson Laureate* (1962), p. 97. Miss Pitt's transcription has errors (noted below), and she states that this section comes in the MS between cxvii and cxviii, whereas it comes between cxvii (p. 968) and cxxii. The MS does not include cxvi (which incorporated a line from *Let Death*) or cxix (for which *Let Death* furnished the concluding stanza).

Let Death and Memory keep the face
Of three and twenty summers, fair.
I see it and no grief is there,
Nor Time can wrong the youthful grace.

I see it and I scarce repine.
I hear the voice that held me fast.
The voice is pleasant in the past,
It speaks to me of me and mine.

The face is bright, the lips are bland,
He smiles upon me eye to eye,
And in my thoughts with scarce a sigh
I take the pressure of his hand.

### (vii) 'I KEEP NO MORE A LONE DISTRESS'

Printed *Mem.* i 306, from *T.MS* of *In Memoriam*, with the title *The Grave* ('originally No. lvii'). In the MS it comes between cxxvi and cxxv (p. 975).

I keep no more a lone distress,
The crowd have come to see thy grave,
Small thanks or credit shall I have,
But these shall see it none the less.

vi *2. three*] thee *Pitt.* Arthur Hallam was twenty-three when he died.
*7. The*] Thy *Pitt.*
*8–9.* Adapted as cxvi 11–12: 'And that dear voice, I once have known, / Still speak to me of me and mine.'
*9–12.* Adapted as cxix 9–12: 'And bless thee, for thy lips are bland, / And bright the friendship of thine eye; / And in my thoughts with scarce a sigh / I take the pressure of thine hand.'
*10. smiles*] smiled *Pitt.*

The happy maiden's tears are free
And she will weep and give them way;
Yet one unschooled in want will say
'The dead are dead and let them be.'

Another whispers sick with loss:
'O let the simple slab remain!
The "Mercy Jesu" in the rain!
The "Miserere" in the moss!

I love the daisy weeping dew,
I hate the trim-set plots of art!'
My friend, thou speakest from the heart,
But look, for these are nature too.

(viii) 'ARE THESE THE FAR-FAMED VICTOR HOURS'

Printed *Mem.* i 307, from *T.MS* of *In Memoriam*, with the title *The Victor Hours* ('originally No. cxxvii'). In the MS it comes between *Young is the grief I entertain* (p. 1774) and cxxviii (p. 978).

Are these the far-famed Victor Hours
That ride to death the griefs of men?
I fear not; if I feared them, then
Is this blind flight the wingèd Powers.

Behold, ye cannot bring but good,
And see, ye dare not touch the truth,
Nor Sorrow beauteous in her youth,
Nor Love that holds a constant mood.

Ye must be wiser than your looks,
Or wise yourselves, or wisdom-led,
Else this wild whisper round my head
Were idler than a flight of rooks.

Go forward! crumble down a throne,
Dissolve a world, condense a star,
Unsocket all the joints of war,
And fuse the peoples into one.

vii *11–12.* 'As seen by me in Tintern Abbey' (T.); xix was 'written at Tintern Abbey', and is on the same theme of the relationship of the poems to T.'s sense of loss. Cp. *The Princess: Prologue*, MS (Appendix A, p. 1769): 'He plucked a flower that like a moral grew / From *miserere* on the broken tomb.'

viii *1. these*] *draft by H.T. at Lincoln*; those *Mem.*, *Eversley*. The Lincoln draft is supported by *T.MS*.

### *Fragment*

Unpublished, *H.Nbk 17*, where it follows ix (p. 872). Presumably from the earliest fragments, when *In Memoriam* was still in the *abab* stanza (cp. iii *n*, p. 866).

Time is not merely lapse of hours.
 This yearning is not idly given.
The hearts of angels ache for ours.
 Earth's laws are recognized in Heaven.

## TO THE QUEEN (p. 990)

In the Appendix to *The Growth of the Idylls of the King* (1895), Richard Jones printed 'a hitherto unpublished version' of *To the Queen* (1851), from the MS at the *Drexel Institute, Philadelphia.* (This MS was sold at the Parke-Bernet Galleries, Oct. 1944.) Lines that subsequently became part of the published poem are merely listed below, without their variants being given.

The noblest men are born and bred
 Among the Saxo-Norman race,
 And in this world the noblest place
Madam, is yours, our Queen and Head.

Your name is blown on every wind,
 Your flag through Austral ice is borne
 And glimmers to the Northern morn
And floats in either golden Ind.

The poets, they that often seem
 So wretched, touching mournful strings,
 They likewise are a kind of kings,
Nor is their empire all a dream.

Their words fly over land and main,
 Their warblings make the distance glad,
 Their voices heard hereafter add
A glory to a glorious reign.

A work not done by flattering state,
 Nor such a lay should kings receive,
 And kingly poets should believe
The king's heart true as he is great.

The taskwork ode has ever failed:
Not less the king in time to come
Will seem the greater under whom
The sacred poets have prevailed.

[ll. 5–8 of *1851*]

I would I were as those of old,
A mellow mouth of song to fill
Your reign with music which might still
Be music when my lips were cold.

That after-men might turn the page
And light on fancies true and sweet,
And kindle with a loyal heat
To fair Victoria's golden age.

But he your Laureate who succeeds,
A master such as all men quote,
Must feel as one of slender note
And piping low among the reeds.

[ll. 9–12, 17–20, 21–4, of *1851*]

As the dedication of *Mem.*, H.T. printed a draft of ll. 1–8 (*Drexel* text) plus a draft of ll. 17–20 (*1851*), as 'An Unpublished Version'. As the dedication of *Mat.*, he had printed a different draft, where the second stanza (ll. 5–8, *Drexel*) had run: 'Your power about the world is blown / From under icy Boreal moons, / Through our mid-planet's sweet lagoons / And downward to the central zone.' The MS in the *Charterhouse School Library* (*The Greyfriar*, Dec. 1921) consists of a draft of five stanzas, one of which praises the International Exhibition: 'A sight more noble on the tides / Of changing time, that forward flow, / Than all your ships of war that blow / The battle from their oaken sides!' These lines were adapted from *Hail Briton* 5–8, and the year after *To the Queen* they became *Britons, Guard Your Own* 37–8 (pp. 998–9). The above account makes no attempt to give all the variants in these drafts, but it quotes all such stanzas as did not appear in *1851*.

## RIFLE-CLUBS!!!

The original version of *Riflemen Form!* (p. 1110), and printed in a limited edition (1899), erroneously dated 1859 though in fact written 1852. See C. Ricks, *RES* n.s. xv (1964) 401–4. Also *Rifle Clubs!!!* (p. 996). Louis Napoleon had ominously alluded in public to Waterloo (l. 10), as was pointed out by a correspondent in *The Times*, 9 Jan. 1852. The engineers' strike (ll. 22–3) endangered all the iron trades in Jan. 1852. The accompanying letter to Coventry Patmore says: 'Very wild but I think too savage! Written in about 2 minutes! The authorship a most deep secret! mind, Mr P.! . . . really I think on writing it out it's enough to make a war of itself . . . My wife thinks it too insulting to the F. and too inflaming to the English.' The MS and letter are now in the *Berg Collection* (*N.Y. Public Library*).

Riflemen, form in town and in shire
  From John O'Groat's house to the wild Land's End!
Practise and fire, practise and fire–
  God, He knows what an hour may send.
    Ready, be ready to meet the storm!
    Riflemen, form! Riflemen, form!
    Riflemen, riflemen, riflemen form!

We thought them friends and we had them here,
  But now the traitor and tyrant rules:
And Waterloo from year to year
  Has rankled in the hearts of the fools.
    We love peace, but the French love storm, [*etc.*]

Ready, be ready! they mean no good:
  Ready, be ready! the times are wild!
Bearded monkeys of lust and blood
  Coming to violate woman and child!
    We love liberty: they love storm, [*etc.*]

Workmen, workmen, away with your strikes!
  Close with your masters! sound an alarm!
Get your weapons, muskets and pikes!
  Close with your masters and arm and arm–
    You love freedom: the French love storm: [*etc.*]

## TRANSLATIONS FROM HOMER

The *Pierpont Morgan MS* of *Achilles Over the Trench* (p. 1157; probably written 1863–4) includes other fragmentary translations by T. See also *Specimen of a Translation* (p. 1156). The more finished drafts have been chosen. For T.'s prose-translation of (ii), see *Mem.* ii 15–16 and *Eversley* vi 351–72.

(i) And when they came together in one place,
Then shocked the spears and bucklers and the strength
Of armèd warriors; then the bossy shields
Ground each on each, and huge uproar arose;

And then were heard the vaunts and groans of men
Slaying and being slain, and earth ran blood.
As winter torrents rolling from the hill
And flinging their fierce waters through the clefts
From mighty fountains downward to the gulf
Wherein they dash together; and far away
The shepherd on the mountain hears the sound,
Such the drear roar of battle when they mixt.

[*Iliad* iv 446–56]

(ii) Nor lingered Paris in the lofty house,
But armed himself and all in varied brass
Rushed through the city, glorying in his speed:
As when a horse at manger breaks his band
And riotously rushing down the plain–
Wont in the running river to wash himself
And riot, rears his head and all his mane
Flies back behind him glorying in himself
And galloping to the meadows of the mares–
So ran the son of Priam from the height
Of Ilion, Paris, sunlike all in arms
Glittering

[*Iliad* vi 503–14]

# Appendix B

## *FRAGMENTS

No attempt is made in the following pages to collect all of T.'s fragments, but the following are of some interest (sometimes biographical).

(i) Printed in *CT* (p. 316), 'four lines which he dreamed when ten years old':

May a cocksparrow
Write to a barrow?
I hope you'll excuse
My infantile Muse.

(ii) Printed *Mem.* i 23–5, as 'A scene, written at 14'. Cp. *The Devil and the Lady* (p. 7).

### ACT I, SCENE I (*in Spain*)

DRAMATIS PERSONÆ

Carlos (a spirited stripling with a spice of suspicion and a preponderance of pride).
Michael (his old attendant).

*Moonlight*

*Carl.* Hear you the sound of wheels?
*Mich.* No, faith, not I.
*Carl.* Methinks they tarry somewhat. What's the clock?
*Mich.* Half way toward midnight.
*Carl.* Why, they should be here.
*Mich.* 'Tis a clear night, they will be here anon.
*Carl.* Hist! what was that?
*Mich.* The night gale in those trees.
*Carl.* How beautifully looks the moonbeam through
The knotted boughs of this long avenue
Of thick dark oaks, that arch their arms above,
Coeval with the battlemented towers
Of my old ancestors!
I never look upon them but I glow
With an enthusiastic love of them.
Methinks an oak-tree never should be planted
But near the dwelling of some noble race;

For it were almost mockery to hang it
O'er the thatched cottage, or the snug brick box
Of some sleek citizen.
Ye proud aristocrats whose lordly shadows,
Chequered with moonlight's variation,
Richly and darkly girdle these gray walls, –
I and my son's sons and our offspring, all
Shall perish, and their monuments, with forms
Of the unfading marble carved upon them,
Which speak of us to other centuries,
Shall perish also, but ye still shall flourish
In your high pomp of shade, and make beneath
Ambrosial gloom. Thou dost remember, Michael,
How, when a boy, I joyed to place me on
The hollow-stemmed and well-nigh leafless oak
Which towers above the lake that ripples out
In the clear moonshine.
*Mich.* You were wont to call it
Your throne.
*Carl.* I was so, Michael.
*Mich.* You'd sit there
From dawn till sunset looking far away
On the blue mountains, and most joyful when
The wanton wind came singing lustily
Among the moss-grown branches, and threw back
Your floating hair.
*Carl.* Ha! Ha! Why even then
My Spanish blood ran proudly in my veins.
*Mich.* Ay, Ay, I warrant you, and when I came
And would have called you down to break your fast,
You would look down and knit your baby brows
Into your father's frown, and beckon me
Away.
*Carl.* Ha! Ha! 'twas laughable, and yet
It showed the seeds of innate dignity
That were within me; did it not, good Michael?
*Mich.* And when your age had somewhat riper grown,
And I was wont to dandle you upon
My knee, and ask you whether you would be
A great man in your time,
You'd weave your waxen fingers in these locks
(They are gray now) and tell me you were great
Already in your birth.
*Carl.* Ha! by St James
Mine was no vulgar mind in infancy,

Even then the force of nature and high birth
Had writ nobility upon my brow.
Hark! they are coming.

(iii) Printed *Mem.* i 18: 'As a boy he would reel off hundreds of lines such as these'.

When winds are east and violets blow,
And slowly stalks the parson crow.

(iv) Printed *Mem.* ii 399, recited by T. in 1892. 'I remember two early lines of mine' (*Eversley*):

Spurge with fairy crescent set,
Like the flower of Mahomet.

(v) Unpublished, *H.Nbk 1* (1824–7). Cp. *Time* (p. 119), and *The Coach of Death* (p. 74). Also 'the army of the dead' in *Oh! ye wild winds* (*1827*).

Who are ye, Who are ye that ride so fierce and fast
  Along the black profound of night,
That proudly bare your burning brows
    Unto the rushing blast,
  And shake your locks that flame with eldritch light?
    Why brandish in air the dubious gleam
      Of shadowy spears?
    Why down each burning visage stream
      Hot tears?
    Pass on. Trouble us not.

(vi) Printed by C. Ricks, *Victorian Poetry* iii (1965) 55–7 from *H.Lpr 185*, which attributes it to T. and is a copy of some poems of *1827* that were omitted 'for some forgotten reason'. H.T. printed four such poems in *1893*. It is in T.'s hand, deleted, in *T.MS*.

The wild-bee in the wide parterre
  Sips flowers of every hue,
The bright chamæleon feeds on air,
  The balm-cricket on dew.
But, black-eyed maid, one glance from thee,
One sigh, one smile, is food to me.

vi *1. wild-bee in*] bee within *H.MS 1st reading.*
*5. black-*] bright- *1st reading.*

(vii) Unpublished; dated 1826 in *Heath MS* (text below) and *Allen MS*. Almeida appears in *Love and Sorrow* (p. 239); the name was a favourite for tragic heroines in the late eighteenth century.

Almeida, love me, love me,
Swear that you love me, while I yet may hear
That Seraph voice above me
Murmur the thrilling accents to mine ear.
My brow is damp with death;
Swear that you love me, while I yet may feel
The warmth of that delicious breath
Along my clammy forehead steal.

(viii) Unpublished, *H.Nbk 2* (1827–9).

Night drew her shadowy sketch of waving hill
Around me and the undefinèd Moon
Half-melting into starless cloud stood still.

(ix) Unpublished, *H.Nbk 2* (1827–9).

Whither proud Spirit move thy daring wings?
To yon red wilderness, the end of things?
Is yon the indissoluble fiery bound
Which girds the World's impenetrable round?

(x) Unpublished, *H.Lpr 140* (1830–2?), where it is on the verso of *Margaret* (p. 454).

I cannot take that pleasure now
In early walks–but I want sleep,
My head aches and my hand is dry
And fevered strangely: I shall weep,
I know that I shall by and by
And that perhaps will make me we[ep? *MS torn*]
And if I like to weep I will,
For there is none to see me cry
And all the fields are dark and still.

(xi) Chorus from *The Devil and the Lady* (p. 7). Printed by Sir Charles Tennyson, from *Heath MS*, in *Cornhill* cliii (1936) 443–4: 'The "slender torrent" simile and the inclusion of the fragment in the *Commonplace Book* suggest that these lines were written after the Poet's visit to Spain in 1830, so that it would seem that he contemplated completing the play at this time.' Cp. *The Coach of Death* (p. 74).

*Vestibule of Hell on the borders of a black sea*
(*Divers Arch Devils*)

Our thrones in Heaven are cold
Where we sat long ago
In ineffable conclave;
The shining seats of old,
The everduring gold,
Round which the Angel raiment's vivid flow
Fell like a slender torrent's dissipated wave
Windshaken in its high descent
Fronting the amber East.

(*Voices within*)

For ever increased
The fuel, the feast,
Through infinite ages the same:
We are lost, we are burned,
We are tost, we are turned,
On the points of the pierceant flame.

(*Groom of the chambers within*)

Whist, whist, ye brawlers whist! ye sorry cinders,
Ye carbonate of man!
His Highness has just floored his salamanders,
And his burnt brandy, and would fain have sleep:
D'ye mark, ye marshless croakers, ye high leapers
Along the living flame? D'ye hear me?

(*Voices*)

They pass through us like spears
And our frequent tears
Hiss into drought on the burning cheek.

xi *1. thrones*] houses *Heath MS 1st reading.*
*16. Whist*: Hush!
*18. salamanders*: here a fiery drink or toast; T. antedates the first example (1868) given in *OED.*
*23–4.* Cp. *Sense and Conscience* 119–20: 'Which would not fall because his burning eyes / Did hiss them into drought.'

(*Groom of the chambers*)

A curse on your cracked voices! What the Devil,
I mean his Majesty, d'ye cackle there for
And crackle like so many laurel leaves
Thrusting your sharp black faces through the element
As though it were your first millennium!

(xii) Unpublished. It is quoted in a letter from James Spedding to his brother Edward, from Trinity College, 9 March 1831 (now in the possession of Lt. Col. J. E. Spedding). 'Both the Tennyson's have gone home suddenly; their Father is dead or dying. Alfred will probably not return to Cambridge; Chas. will take his degree next term; when he will make out his lessons reading with me. Alfred has, I believe, finished the ode you enquire about; but I have only seen the following fragments.' In the same state of incompleteness, the poem is in *T.Nbk 23*. T. adapted the opening of II for his poem to Spedding, *To J.S.* (p. 463), on the death of Edward. For another poem to a Cambridge friend which blends a landscape and a character study, see *Thy soul is like a landskip, friend* (p. 282).

I

Dear friend whom to have seen and known
Is ever to Life's fainting power
The gale before a coming shower–
Whose placid intellect has grown
Like little woods with glooming boughs
Where a fountain overflows
Cooling his marge alone;–
Mild-hearted friend, whose thoughts are boon
As summer air, whose liberal brows
Are ample as an harvest moon
The glory of an autumn night,
Full of promise, on the leaves
And vallies thick with pilèd sheaves,
A full orb of wealthy light;
Thou when fiery spirits fail
Overwearied in the strife,
By thy mildness shalt prevail
Looking through the dark of Life;

xii *9*. John Spedding has recently suggested (in a letter) that this may pun both on Spedding's political views and on his notoriously large forehead; FitzGerald wrote to Frederick Tennyson, 'they might sit together under the calm of Spedding's forehead'.

By thy placid scorns that play
Round the surfaces of things
And like swallows dip their wings
Evermore, and skim away;
Or like wildfires in woodland bowers
Round a river dancing ever,
Through the darkness of the river
Harming not its fringe of flowers.

II

The wind that beats the mountain cold
All night in early April blows
Softly on the open wold,
And gently comes the world to those
That are of gentle mould.

(xiii)

## LOVE AND FRIENDSHIP

### AN INDIAN TALE

Printed by Sir Charles Tennyson, *Cornhill* cliii (1936) 444–5, from *Heath MS*: 'reminiscent . . . of *The Lover's Tale* and no doubt composed at about the same time' (T. was revising this early work till 1832). The main source is Sappho, *Fragment 2*, which T. adapted in *Fatima* (*1832*) as: 'Last night, when some one spoke his name / From my swift blood that went and came / A thousand little shafts of flame / Were shivered in my narrow frame.' The subtitle points to an eighteenth-century genre of exotic love.

O Friend, dear Friend, I cannot speak of her,
I cannot think a moment of her face,
I cannot name her name thus passingly,
But my blood leaps and dances in my veins
Like a fire-fountain: 'tis a lava stream
Thrown on with fierce convulsions of the heart,
Which in its passage through me still shoots off
Small sparks and shafts of fire which tingle through me.
I am a wreath of flame lit on a hill
And the winds blow me fiercer: but for thee,

*19–22.* Adapted for *In Memoriam* xlviii 15–16: 'Short swallow-flights of song, that dip / Their wings in tears, and skim away.'
*23. wildfire*: will o' the wisp. Cp. *The Princess* v 431: 'Be dazzled by the wildfire Love'.
*27–31.* See *To J.S.* (p. 463).
xiii *9.* Cp. Shelley, *Queen Mab* vi 36–7: 'a wreath / Of ever-living flame'.

My sense, my tongue, mine eyes, my breath, my life,
Long since the fiery forethought of the wish
Had blotted out the wish and laid me here
Stiff in the creeping surf.

(xiv) Unpublished, *H.Nbk 3* (1832). The opening lines of the sonnet are cut from the MS, following the sonnet *Doubt and Prayer* (p. 1454) and preceding that beginning *Mine be the strength* (p. 349).

We have a rumour and a half-revealment
Of beauty everywhere in close concealment
Hid from us like the early life of Christ.
If beauty, then true knowledge. Sisters fair,
Although ye sit apart and seldom make
Unto our darker moods a clear reply,
We will live on: we never will despair.
We know ye *are* for we have heard ye speak
And in that knowledge would we live or die.

(xv) Unpublished, *H.Nbk 4* (1832).

Why, Mab, what, Mab–I'll not be fooled,
Have you no heart or one as cold
    As any marble slab?
I swear you must and shall be ruled,
    *I* care not for you, Mab.
I care not for your bold black eye,
Mad Mab: by all the saints on high
I swear I hate you heartily.
Nay–you may knit your brows at me,
    Kill me with frowning if you can.
So, so you're angered thoroughly–
    St Jude! she laughs. Was ever man
So plagued and crost as I?
    I'll tell you Mab: before I go
I'll make you swear you doat on me.
        Dear, dear, dear Mabel–give me hope,
    I know you love me. Sweet, say so,
        Or only hold your finger up

*14. surf*] *Allen MS; not Heath MS, 1936.*
xiv *4.* Cp. *To*–[*with The Palace of Art*] 10: 'Beauty, Good, and Knowledge, are three sisters.'

To show as much. What, what, you won't.
By Love's own arrow and his bow,
I'll kiss you soundly if you won't.
Mad Mabel 'tis not meet or fit
That you should ever prove
Quick of speech and quick of wit,
Light of heart and light of love,
Full of petulant abuse,
Taunts and quips and epithets,
As musically garrulous
As grasshoppers or rivulets.

(xvi) Unpublished, *H.Nbk 5* (1832). The MS is torn, but the lacuna in the first two lines of the sonnet is T.'s. Cp. Milton's *Sonnets 17* and *18*, imitating the Horatian invitation. 'James' is T.'s friend James Spedding (*To J.S.*, p. 463), whose 'liberal brows' are mentioned also in *Dear friend.*

What [
] and in what...
What garland cullest that may...
Thy thrice-refinèd tastes and liberal brow.
Gold seven-times-in-the-furnace-tried [art thou],
And this we know; and long our ardent love
Pants for thy presence here, ere winter move
On the short eddish flaws of...
So if thou canst resolve thee to be merry
And doff grave thought, nor, city-bred, despise
Our northern Pan's rude feast and rural fun,
James, we expect thee, now the elderberry
(Our huswife's vintage drunk with toast and spice)
Hath almost blackened in the harvest sun.

(xvii) Unpublished, *H.Nbk 7* (1832), where it appears, deleted, on the same page as *In deep and solemn dreams* (p. 277).

Hope journeyed with me as the Sun with one
Who treads a River's brink in clearest Noon–
In vacant thoughtlessness he hurries on,
Eyeing the vivid orb but ah! too soon
If rocky ledge invite the downward slope
Of the pure wave the gathered lustre shoots
Far scattered

xv *28–9.* Cp. *Œnone* 27, MS: 'the garrulous Cicala'.
xvi *8. eddish*: stubbly. *flaws*] drifts *MS 1st reading.*

(xviii) Unpublished, *H.Nbk 7* (1832). An incomplete sonnet.

Why are my moments wasted in this strife?
Oh! Melancholy hath a marvellous power!
See! in the moiety of one brief hour
As many as the days of my brief life,
Tears from mine eyes have stolen plenteously.
Why is the fount of sight the source of tears?
This surely hath some strange analogy.
For when the inward eye is dim with fears
And hopes which are another form of fear

(xix) Unpublished, *H.Nbk 8* (1832). The archaisms recall *The Lark* (1828, p. 168).

Strow lilies o'er me when I die,
White lilies full of early dew,
Ne asken me the reason why
My friends were false though I was true,
So wheresoe'er my cors may lie
Strow lilies o'er me when I die.

The lily is a flower I love,
The sweetest child of earth and air,
Whether it blow in vale or grove
I think that nothing is so fair.

(xx) Unpublished, *H.Nbk 8* (1832). The closing lines are only partly legible, the readings below being conjectural. Clarice Short associates this fragment with *The Lover's Tale* (p. 299), which follows it in *H.Nbk 8* (*PMLA* lxxxii, 1967, 78–84).

Fair face! fair form, sole [? sad? *deleted*] tenant of a brain
Peopled with griefs whose blackness cannot mar
Your lustre, when fatigued with things less fair
These eyes roll inward, gazing as they gazed
Upon the archetype in happier hours.
Beautiful permanence! indwelling light
Unvanishing! which never transient thought

xviii *6*. Cp. Gray's Alcaic stanza: *O lachrymarum Fons, tenero sacros / Ducentium ortus ex animo; quater / Felix! in imo qui scatentem / Pectore te, pia Nympha, sensit!* This provided the epigraph for a poem by T.'s brother Charles in *1827* (*Yes–there be some gay souls*). See *To J.S.* 37–44*n*.

Supplants or shades, for thou dost glow through all,
Intense Idea; though I close the lids
Of mental vision on thee thou dost burn
As sunlight, through them: Slumber is no veil
For thou art up and broad awake in dreams,
O deeply loved: yet like a cruel foe
Fast-centred in the heart thou hast undone
Which must exist for ever. Can it lose [love?]
Thy presence, when this head is low in dust?
And [?] unto thyself and sendest thence
Sharp arrows, from the fort which was mine own

(xxi) Unpublished, *H.Nbk 12* (1832–3). It is followed on the same page by a fragment relating it to *Margaret* (p. 454) and *Adeline* (p. 216):

Pale Marg[t] will sit for hours
* * * *
And like a gleam between two showers
The lightblue eyes of Adeline
Linger a moment there.

Who is it comes hither through the dew
With measured steps? What maiden fair
Walking across the breezy down,
With eyes of deepest violet hue,
Full of deep knowledge, and with hair
Of softest golden brown?
So starry-fair, so graceful tall–
Whose lucid eyelids when they fall,
Are like the cloud that holds moonlight–
With such soft-rounded temples, like
White Venus whiter than all stars–
Whose coming ere she comes doth strike
On expectation, like the glow
Of the unrisen moon below
Dark firs, when creeping winds by night
Lay the long mist in streaks and bars.

xxi *11*. Incorporated as *From the East of life* 3.
*12–13*. Cp. *Œnone* 62 and *n*: 'Went forth to embrace him coming ere he came.'
*13–16*. Adapted as *The Lover's Tale* ii 109–11: 'Storm, sunset, glows and glories of the moon / Below black firs, when silent-creeping winds / Laid the long night in silver streaks and bars.'

(xxii) Unpublished. The following four fragments (xxii–xxv) are from a notebook (1833 ?), now belonging to Mr W. Rayner Batty. A note with the notebook authenticates it as T.'s, as do the sketches in it, and the fragments (in pencil and illegible at some points) are apparently in T.'s hand.

Shout for thy sins are all forgiven,
And draw full deep thy breath,
For see the Angels stoop from Heaven,
To save thy soul from death.

(xxiii) I live through drink and through drink strive to speak,
And nature still alive this soul doth keep,
And in this sad life I can sweetly pray–
Nature thou humourest me in easy way.

Sin in thy body, sorrow in thine eyes,
Immortal-minded man with soul sublime,
The privilege of life thou canst not prize
But like myself abusest thy blest time.

## (xxiv) ON THE SYMPATHY OF NATURE

Have ye not found while hid in clouds of guilt
With what an awful sorrow nature teems,
And how through all her tender frame is felt
The silent sympathy with which she beams?

For when that great revolving light, man's mind,
Is darkened by perpetual deeds of sin,
Yet in that state great sympathy she finds–
The world is in the humour she is in.

And when the mind of man in fullest praise
Gazes on Heaven and for God she pines,
Mercy and truth come quickly from the skies.
Thus the unsullied love of glory shines.

Can he who doth abundantly shower down
His mercies on the just and unjust too
E'er look on sin with aught else but a frown,
Or give the sinner all the just man's due?

xxiv 16] *A concluding stanza is erased in MS.*

(xxv) Dearest Polly, when oh when
Shall I hear from thee again?
Or if I mistake not quite,
Thou didst never to me write–
I'm in melancholy plight,
Out of mind and out of sight.

Not so with Jill, Ciss, and Doll–
They have written before now,
But from thee my dearest Poll
Never have I heard I vow.
What a thing that is to say,
Dearest Polly lack-a-day.

For aught thou knowest Polly dear
I might to the moon be flying
Or in the lonely churchyard drear
With worms and things and cockroach lying–
Indolence in thee 't must be,
Write dear Polly unto me.

Mutually we are to blame,
So I cannot much blame thee–
We were always just the same
But let's now both better be,
And in being different, Polly,
Do away with all this folly.

Thou didst with defection teem
When Neville left thee in a hurry,
Now thy grand affections seem
Centered strong in Brackenbury–
For mankind no affection much.
I wish Jack Heath would soon thee clutch.

(xxvi) Printed by Sir Charles Tennyson, *Cornhill* cliii (1936) 446. From *Heath MS* (compiled 1833–4).

Glossy curl-clusters crowd and gather
On those smooth-rounded crescent temples white,
In fragrant shadow steep
And mantle all the light
Of eyes, twin baths of Love, that move together
Gleaming blandly, full of sleep.

(xxvii) Printed *Mem.* i 144, in a letter to James Spedding, 15 Feb. 1835: 'I will come to you as Sheba came to Solomon ... I forget where I read this.'

She travelled far from Indian streams,
And he a royal welcome made
In ample chambers overlaid
With Lebanonian cedar-beams.

(xxviii) Printed in William Allingham's *Diary* (1907), p. 303: 'Tennyson repeated some lines of his own from an old idyll never published' (21 Oct. 1880). Text from *H.Lpr 210*. It suggests T.'s disillusionment with Rosa Baring in 1836–7; cp. the 'confusion' that occurs in *Aylmer's Field* (p. 1159). Cp. *The Golden Year* 32–3: 'When wealth no more shall rest in mounded heaps, / But smit with freër light shall slowly melt ...'

The rich shall wed the rich, the poor the poor,
So shall this mound of wealth be higher still,
So shall this gulf of want be deeper still,
Until this mountain melt into this gulf
With all confusion.

(xxix) Printed in P. Norman's *London Signs and Inscriptions* (1893), p. 26, from a MS by T.; *Mem.* i 231, under 5 Aug. 1846, European tour. The legend was that the three kings of Cologne were the Magi; their bones are enshrined in the cathedral.

Gaspar and Melchior and Balthazar
Came to Cologne on the broad-breasted Rhine,
And founded there a temple which is yet
A fragment, but the wonder of the world.

(xxx) Unpublished, *H.Nbk 26* (1851).

There in a grove the fragile anemone blows.
Fade not, anemone, yet! but alas it fadeth already.
Lustier hours will arise, livelier harmony wake,
Many a blossom unroll to the breezes of May and of August.

(xxxi) Unpublished. It is in H.T.'s hand, in *Works* (1881, *Lincoln*). Cp. the political poems of 1852.

Wake middle classes, why so cold?
Are ye so sensual grown?
Arm, Mammon, arm and save your gold–
Awake! Arm! save your own!

(xxxii) Printed *Mem.* i 380: 'My father wrote the first stanza of a song entitled "The Alma River," which my mother finished and set to music' (10 Oct. 1854). Cp. *The Charge of the Light Brigade* (p. 1034).

Frenchman, a hand in thine!
  Our flags have waved together!
Let us drink to the health of thine and mine
  At the battle of Alma River.

(xxxiii) Printed *The Times*; 26 Jan. 1858; *Mem.* i 423. Written for the marriage of the Princess Royal to Prince Frederick William of Prussia. T. sent the stanzas as requested in Dec. 1857; on 9 Feb. 1858 he wrote to the Duchess of Argyll: 'As to my stanzas I do not pique myself upon them: they are neither much better nor worse than the rest of that loyal confection' (*Lincoln*).

God bless our Prince and Bride!
God keep their lands allied,
  God save the Queen!
Clothe them with righteousness,
Crown them with happiness,
Them with all blessings bless,
  God save the Queen.

Fair fall this hallowed hour,
Farewell our England's flower,
  God save the Queen!
Farewell, fair rose of May!
Let both the peoples say,
God bless thy marriage-day,
  God bless the Queen.

(xxxiv) Descriptive jottings. *a–f* were printed *Mem.* i 465–6, under 1860, from 'tours in Cornwall, Isle of Wight and Ireland'. Those incorporated in *The Brook* and *Sea Dreams* are here omitted. The corrected readings are from *H.Nbk 18.*

(*a*) (*Babbicombe*) Like serpent oils [coils *Mem.*] upon the deep.

(*b*) (*From the Old Red Sandstone*) As a stony spring
Blocks its own issue.

(*c*) (*The open sea*) Two great ships
That draw together in a calm.

(*d*) (*Isle of Wight*) As those that lie on happy shores and see
Through the near blossom slip the distant sail.

(*e*) (*Bray Head*)
O friend, the great deeps of Eternity
Roar only round the wasting isle [cliffs *Mem.*] of Time.

(*f*) (*The river Shannon, on the rapids*)
Ledges of battling water.

*g–h* were not printed by H.T. though in *H.Nbk 18.* (One incorporated in *Enoch Arden* is here omitted.)

(*g*) (*Mablethorpe*) –a ship on fire at sea,
Left by the crew, far off from any land,
Her light is on the water and the cloud
But none are there–

(*h*) (*Guernsey*) rolling up and down
A granite boulder in a granite trough.

*i–j* are from *H.Lpr 191*, unpublished (1847).

(*i*) Like Autumn blots upon the sycamore–

(*j*) –where age-crumbled Wales
Throngs heavenward with a hundred rugged heads
That drown their wrinkles in the roky West.

(xxxv) Printed *The Marlburian*, 20 Sept. 1871; *Mem.* ii 12. The 'comic end' of Alcaics which had been begun by H.T. Written 1864, after the other 'Experiments in Quantity'.

Thine early rising well repaid thee,
Munificently rewarded artist.

(xxxvi) Printed *Mem.* ii 82, 13 Sept. 1869, as part of a description of a storm.

With sullen thunders to and fro
That to a dreary distance go.

(xxxvii)

## RETICENCE

Printed *Mem.* ii 87–8, as an unfinished poem written 1869. From *T.Nbk 28.* 'The two *Her's* [ll. 13–14] coming together vexed him and he threw the poem aside–unfinished–and forgot all about it'; but cp. 'one of my father's later poems, and was by inadvertence never published by him' (*1913*).

Not to Silence would I build
A temple in her naked field;
Not to her would raise a shrine:
She no goddess is of mine;
But to one of finer sense,
Her half-sister, Reticence.

Latest of her worshippers,
I would shrine her in my verse!
Not like Silence shall she stand,
Finger-lipt, but with right hand
Moving toward her lips, and there
Hovering, thoughtful, poised in air.
Her garment slips, the left hand holds
Her up-gathered garment folds,
And veils a breast more fair to me
Than aught of Anadyomené!
Near the shrine, but half in sun,
I would have a river run,
Such as never overflows
With flush of rain, or molten snows,
Often shallow, pierced with light,
Often deep beyond the sight,
Here and there about the lawn
Wholly mute, but ever drawn
Under either grassy brink
In many a silver loop and link
Variously from its far spring,
With long tracts of murmuring,
Partly river, partly brook,
Which in one delicious nook,
Where the doubtful shadows play,
Lightly lisping, breaks away;
Thence, across the summit hurled,
Showers in a whisper o'er the world.

xxxvii *8–9*] I would raise her in my verse
Such a shrine and make her stand *L.MS alternative reading*

This MS, as in l. 11*n*, is H.T.'s copy from *T.Nbk 28*.

*11. lips*] *L.MS*; lip *Mem.*

*14–15*. Perhaps suggested by Shelley: 'Up-gathered into the bosom of rest', *Sensitive Plant* i 111.

*16. Anadyomené*: Venus.

(xxxviii) Unpublished. On verso of *L.MS* of *The Christ of Ammergau* (p. 1220), 1870, in James Knowles's hand.

I ruled the people well
And they have grown the stronger
And I swore before High God
That I would rule no longer.

(xxxix) Unpublished, *H.Lpr 47*. The occasion may have been Victor Emmanuel's entry into the Papal States in Sept. 1870, and their merging with Italy. Cp. T.'s poem on Papal Infallibility, July 1870, *The Christ of Ammergau* (p. 1220).

Desolate, why, crowned city of High God?
For art thou not immeasurably rich
In being loved, and giving back thy heart
To Him that loves thee? Woe, woe, woe to thee,
Thou too hast bowed thy heart to less than God.
O this strange riddle of the human heart,
Which made to know and free to love the best
And highest must fall down–I will not say
To wood and stone, things neither good nor ill,
But to the very spirit of evil itself.

(xl) Printed in *Tennyson and His Friends*, p. 226. Written *c.* 1872, about W. G. Ward's Jesuit chaplain: '"When Haythornthwaite dies," Tennyson once said, "I shall write as his epitaph"':

Here lies Peter Haythornthwaite,
Human by nature, Roman by fate!

(xli) Printed *Mat.* iii 220, Sept. 1873, on holiday at the Simplon Pass. The 'landlord brought his book to be written in, the following lines were penned':

Post Hotel good and nobody to tout,
Warm hearth within and mist and rain without,
Chamois superb, and very tasty trout.

xxxix *1*] Desolate, O crowned city of the High God *H.MS 1st reading.*
*2*] Wert not thou loved? *MS 1st reading.*
*6*] Strange human heart, *MS 1st reading.*

(xlii) *Eversley*, vol. ii, has an appendix of 'Experiments', with a note by H.T.:

'My father thought that quantitative English Hexameters were as a rule only fit for comic subjects, though he said: "Of course you might go on with perfect Hexameters of the following kind, but they would grow monotonous:

'High woods roaring above me, dark leaves falling about me.'"

Some of the Hexameters in two quantitative experiments, "Jack and the Beanstalk" and "Bluebeard," published by me anonymously in Miss Thackeray's *Bluebeard's Keys* [1874], were made or amended by him, and therefore I reprint them in this Appendix. Throughout the Hexameters, by his advice, quantity, except here and there for the sake of variety, coincides with accent.'

## JACK AND THE BEANSTALK

Jack was a poor widow's heir, but he lived as a drone in a beehive,
Hardly a handstir a day did he work. To squander her earnings
Seemed to the poor widow hard, who raved and scolded him always.
Nought in her house was left; not a cheese, not a loaf, not an onion;
Nought but a cow in her yard, and that must go to the market.
'Sell me the cow,' cried she; then he sold it, gad! for a handful–
Only to think!–of beans. She shied them out through the window,
Cursing him: hied to her bed, there slept, but awoke in amazement,
Seeing a huge beanstalk, many leaves, many pods, many flowers,
Rise to the clouds more tall than a tall California pine-tree;
High as a lark was Jack, scarce seen, and climbing away there.
'Nix Dolly Pals,' he shrilled; she beheld his boots disappearing;
Pod by pod Jack arose, till he came to a pod that alarmed him.
Bridge-like this long pod stretched out and touched on an island
Veiled in vapour. A shape from the island waved him a signal.
This was a shining maid, and Jack with an humble obeisance
Crawled to the maid. She exclaimed, 'I gave those beans to ye, darling.
I am a fairy, a friend to ye, Jack; see yonder a giant
Lives, who slew your own good father, see what a fortress!
Enter it, have no fear, since I, your fairy, protect you.'
Jack marched up to the gate, in a moment passed to the kitchen
Led by the savoury smell. This giant's wife with a ladle
Basted a young elephant (Jack's namesake shrieked and turned it).
Back Jack shrank in alarm: with fat cheeks peony-bulbous
Ladle in hand she stood, and spake in a tone of amusement:
'Oh! what a cramped-up, small, unsesquipedalian object!'
Then from afar came steps, heavy tramps, as a paviour hamm'ring;
Out of her huge moon-cheeks the redundant peony faded,
Jack's lank hair she grabbed, and, looking sad resolution,
Popped him aghast in among her saucepans' grimy recesses.
Then strode in, with a loud heavy-booted thunder of heel-taps,
He that had awed his wife–her giant, swarthy, colossal:

'I smell flesh of a man; yea, wife, though he prove but a morsel,
Man tastes good.' She replied, 'Sure thou be'est failing in eyesight;
'Tis but a young elephant, my sweetest lord, not a biped.'
Down he crooked his monstrous knees and rested his hip-bones,
Called for his hen, said 'Lay'; so she, with a chuck cock-a-doodle,
Dropped him an egg pure gold, a refulgent, luminous oval,
That was her use: then he pushed her aside, cried, 'Bring me the meat now,'
Gorged his enormous meal, fell prone, and lost recollection.
Jack from a saucepan watched his broad chest's monstrous upheavals:
'Now for it, hist!' says Jack–'coast clear, and none to behold me,'
Since to the chamber above the flush-faced dame had ascended.
So Jack jumped to the ground, and seized the plump, money-laying,
Priceless, mystical hen; ran forth, sped away to the beanstalk,
Sprang down pod by pod, with a bounding, grasshopper action,
Lighted on earth, whom she that bare him, fondly saluting,
Dropped a maternal tear, and dried that tear with her apron,
Seeing him home and safe; and after it, all was a hey-day,
Lots of loaves, and tons of cheeses, a barnful of onions;
Cows and calves, and creams, and gold eggs piled to the ceilings.
Ay! but he found in a while his life of laziness irksome.
'Climb me,' the beanstalk said with a whisper. Jack, reascending,
Swarmed to the wonderful isle once more, and high habitation,
Well-disguised; and marched to the fortress, passed to the kitchen
Unseen, hied him again to the saucepans' grimy recesses,
Peeped out into the room. The plump wife, peony-bulbous,
Toasted a great constrictor; he rolled in vast revolutions.
Then strode in, strong-booted again, with a roar, the colossus:
Called for his harp, said 'Play.' So this, with a sharp treble ting-tong,
Played him an air, a delightful, long-drawn, exquisite hymn-tune,
Played him an air untouched (the strings, by a mighty magician
Wrought, were alive). Then he shouted aloud, 'Wife, bring me the meat now,'
Gorged his elongate meal; the snake in warm revolutions,
Making his huge throat swell disappeared like Man's macaroni:
After, he yawned and snored, fell prone, and lost recollection.
So Jack seized the melodious harp, and bolted. A murmur
'Master, master, a rascal, a rascal!' rang through the harp-strings.
Jack to the beanpod sprang with a leap, and desperate hurled his
Limbs in a downward, furious, headlong precipitation,
Touched upon earth, up-glanced; his foeman's ponderous hob-nails
Shone from aloft: down crashed big pods, and bean avalanches.
'Haste mother, haste mother, oh! mother, haste, and bring me the hatchet!'
Cried little Jack. So at once she brought him an axe double-handed.
Jack cleft clean through the haulm; that giant desperate hurled his
Limbs in a crashing, roaring, thund'ring precipitation,
Fell to the ground stone-dead with a thump as a thump of a meal-sack.
'I'm your master now,' said Jack to the harp at his elbow;
'There's your old 'un! of him pray give your candid opinion!'
Sweetly the mystical harp responded, 'Master, a rascal!'

## BLUEBEARD

Bluebeard spake to his wife in tones of tender affection:
'Barbara, take these keys: thine husband goes on a journey;
Such a necessity drives me to go; unwilling I leave thee;
Be thou keeper of all while Bluebeard mourns in his absence:
All these household keys, one golden, key of a chamber
Into the which thou mayst not look, since evil awaits her,
Curious, who shall look. So, Barbara, leave it unopened.'
Bluebeard parted. At once her friends rushed all through the castle,
Into the chambers peered, tossed shawls and laces about them,
Saw great piles of gold, gold suits of wonderful armour,
Helmets, velvets, silks, gems, bracelets, necklaces ermine,
Gaudy brocades, and silver spears, and gorgeous hauberks.
Meanwhile that gold key grew warm in her ivory fingers;
Ah! what vast ill on earth is caused by curious wifehood!
Quickly she leapt as a hunted deer through gallery windings
Straight to the chamber door; unlocked it, saw through the doorway
Nine fair wives in a heap of helpless decapitation.
(These had Bluebeard slain for spying into the chamber.)
Seized with affright she shrieked; and, falling, fainted in horror;
Far from her hand in among those headless, beautiful Houris
Glided, alas! the glitt'ring key: but Barbara, bending,
Picked it in anguish up; ran forth, and carefully wiped it,
Stained as it was with a mark of murder, a horrible gore-spot,
Gore unwipeable, gore unwashable, not to be cleansèd.
Hearken! a noise in the hall, the strong portcullis ascending!
Bluebeard strode to his bride, and kissed his Barbara fiercely,
Thundering, 'Where's my key?' but waiting long for an answer
His blue beard grew dark, and writhed in an indigo blackness;
Barbara turned very pale, and all red again in an instant,
Handed him his strange key. He, roaring, 'Here is a gore-spot,
Gore unwipeable, gore unwashable, not to be cleansèd,
Gore o' my late wives' hearts. Die thou too, Barbara, join them,'
Straight strode out for a sword. She called upon Anna her sister,
'Anna, my sister, go up to the tower, and scream for assistance.'
'Come brothers; oh, come quick; bring swords, and smite, and avenge us!'
Anna returned with streaming eyes, and woefully sighing,
'Fie upon all that long, bare highway: no man approaches.'
So they wept and moaned, and groaned for a speedy deliv'rance.
Back to the tower once more clomb Anna, and screamed in a transport,
'Sister, I hear from afar rapid hoofs, as of horsemen approaching.'
'Come, brother Osman, come, brother Ali, come to the rescue.'
All in a wink those two, like wild cats, sprang through the casement,
Caught Bluebeard by the beard, and dyed it a raspberry crimson,
Making his head two halves. Then . . . Barbara dropt 'em a curtsey,
Clapt her white little hands with a laugh, and whirled pirouetting.

(xliii) Printed *Mem.* ii 386–7, under the year 1891: 'He talked of finishing the following little playful poem to Aubrey de Vere, and of alluding in a second verse to his [T.'s] youngest grandson, Alfred Aubrey [*b.* 1891]; but this second verse was never written.' The opening suggests the date May 1877, the month of publication of de Vere's *Antar and Zara, An Eastern Romance*; it is a song-sequence, dedicated to T., and T.'s copy is at *Lincoln*. (H.T. spoke of '*finishing* the following . . .', and *H.Lpr 127* ends with 'II', indicating that T. intended another stanza.)

Little Aubrey in the West! little Alfred in the East
Accepts the songs you gave, and he sends you his Salaam;
And he prays that you may live. But as Earth her orbit runs,
Little Homer, little Dante, little Shakespeare, can they last
In the vast
Of the rolling of the æons, and the changes of the suns?
Little poet, hear the little poet's epigram.

(xliv) Published in R. C. Jebb's *Greek Literature* (1877), p. 60. 'We asked him to make a Sapphic stanza in quantity, with the Greek cadence. He gave us this' (*Mem.* ii 231). Cp. the 'Experiments in Quantity' of 1863 (p. 1153). The stanza appears as the third of four, in a *Pierpont Morgan MS* in H.T.'s hand; R. C. Jebb's letter of 2 Jan. 1889 (*Lincoln*) confirms that the other stanzas were by H.T. *1913* (p. 940) refers to H.T.'s translation from Horace's *Persicos odi*, 'in which my father made the two lines: "Dream not of where some sunny rose may linger / Later in autumn!"'

Faded every violet, all the roses;
Gone the glorious promise, and the victim
Broken in this anger of Aphrodite
Yields to the victor.

(xlv) Printed *Mem.* ii 247, written 1880, in Venice. 'A fat little Armenian monk brought him a book to sign, whereupon he wrote, to the monk's satisfaction':

With all good wishes
And all good dishes
A.T.

xliii *2. Accepts . . . gave*] We have your songs you sent us *H.MS 1st reading*. *6. and*] *MS*; of *Mem.*

(xlvi) Printed *Mat.* iv 497, August 1881: 'The acceptance of Bacon's authorship of Shakespeare's dramas and the attack on Shakespeare's character made my father register his opinion thus.' Subsequently in *Tennyson and His Friends* (p. 496).

Not only with no sense of shame
On common-sense you tread,
Not only ride your hobby lame,
But make him kick the dead.

(xlvii) Printed in *Personal Papers of Lord Rendel* (1931), p. 61, on T.'s yacht trip to Denmark in 1883. 'To commemorate this, the party decided to present a piece of plate to Donald Currie, and Mr G. [Gladstone] asked Tennyson to write one or two lines for it. Tennyson brought the following and with much modesty asked Mr G. if they would do:

Grateful guests to gracious host
To and from the Danish coast.

The lines were by some thought paltry and bald, but Mr G. defended them as well-founded upon the Greek epigram, which aimed at swift terseness.'

(xlviii) ORLANDO GIBBONS

Unpublished. From a letter to C. V. Stanford, 1 June 1885 (Royal College of Music).

Thy voice, great Master, echoes through the soul,
While churches last, quires chant, and organs roll!

(xlix) 'CAPTAIN, GUIDE!'

Printed *Mem.* ii 339–40 (the title is from *Mat.* iv 167). It is in *H.Lpr 30* in T.'s hand, with 'To Gladstone' added by H.T. Cp. *Compromise* (p. 1339) and *Politics* (p. 1343), also to Gladstone. It probably refers to Gladstone's difficulties with the Franchise (1884) and with Irish Home Rule (1885). Of the three epigrams thus addressed to Gladstone, this perhaps best fits the acknowledgement made by Gladstone, 22 July 1885: 'I thank you very much for your Father's beautiful lines . . . Your Father's recommendation to me carries with it my whole heart' (*Lincoln*).

There be rocks old and new!
There a haven full in view!
Art thou wise? Art thou true?
Then, in change of wind and tide,
List no longer to the crew!
Captain, guide!

(l) Unpublished. It is in T.'s very late hand in his prayerbook (*Lincoln*), which has notes dated Oct. 1891 and Feb. 1892. Presumably it refers to Arthur Hallam.

Oh but alas for the smile of smiles that never but one face wore,
Oh for the voice that has flown away like a bird to an unseen shore,
Oh for the face the flower of flowers that blossoms on earth no more.

(li) Printed *Mem.* ii 399: 'lines he made on one of these walks' (1892). They are in H.T.'s hand, subscribed A.T., in a copy of Longfellow's *Poetical Works* (*Lincoln*).

Hold thou, my friend, no lesser life in scorn,
All Nature is the womb whence Man is born.

*Poems and fragments still unpublished*

There are many poems and fragments among the *Trinity MSS* which may not be quoted. Those of most interest are:

*Trinity Notebook 19* (1824–7). A poem (some sheets missing) of approximately one hundred lines, in heroic couplets, on Napoleon's retreat from Moscow. (A copy was in R. M. Milnes's volume of *Memorials*, which apparently is now lost; T. Wemyss Reid, *R. M. Milnes* (1890) i 82–3.)

*Trinity Notebook 22* (1833). A poem of forty-nine lines, in varied metres, on courting Selim (the décor is eastern).

*Trinity Notebook 24* (*c.* 1853). A six-line epigram on Fame, and a four-line epigram on being annoyed by a foolish book.

*Trinity Notebook 26* (1839). A poem of which there are two drafts (forty lines, and sixty-eight lines), in blank verse, on its not being worth publishing poetry.

*Trinity Notebook 28* (1859). An eight-line epigram on France's militarism.

Tennyson's schoolboy translations of some of Horace's *Odes* are at *Lincoln*. There are also scattered scraps throughout all the MSS, and the following fragments are too illegible to be printed:

*Harvard Notebook 7*: 'In early spring'.

*Harvard Loosepaper 60*: 'Far shines that land of promise'.

*Fragments previously printed but not included here*

Among Tennyson's trivia are: his modification of lines by Patmore (*Mem.* i 470). Jocular hexameters, nine lines, in which T. collaborated with H.T. (*Mem.* ii 109; see *Jack and the Beanstalk*, p. 1799). A fragment of fourteen lines 'cooked up by A.T., Peel and Whyte, 1846', quoted in F. M. Brookfield, *The Cambridge 'Apostles'* (1906), p. 325. Four comic lines attributed to T. in A. H. Sayce's *Reminiscences* (1923), p. 369. Twelve lines of nonsense-verse attributed to T. and Palgrave in E. M. Sellar, *Recollections and Impressions* (1907), pp. 54–6.

There are also dramatic fragments which belong with T.'s late plays: a six-line fragment, *c.* 1864, from *H.Nbk 28*, printed by Sir Charles Tennyson, *Nineteenth Century* cix (1931) 627–8; and an eight-line impromptu on Edgar of *The Promise of May* (*Mem.* ii 379).

# Appendix C

## DOUBTFUL POEMS: POEMS ATTRIBUTED TO TENNYSON

(i)

### *EGYPT

Published *1827*, not reprinted. See the Preface above (p. xxiv). *1893*: 'Begun C.T., finished A.T.' The Advertisement in *1827* said that the poems were written 'not conjointly, but individually'. In *T.MS*, the poem originally ended, underlined, at l. 20; the last two stanzas, only, were added in T.'s hand. The Haddelsey copy of *1827* attributes it to Charles; Charles's and the Russell copy make no attribution. The source was C.-E. Savary's *Letters on Egypt*, of which T. used the 1799 translation (*Lincoln*). Paden (pp. 129–30) quotes the passages versified, including 'Awful in their age, how often has the rising sun enlightened them, scorched their burning sides at noon, and gilded them as he set' (cp. l. 28*n*). Cp. *A Fragment* (p. 289). Epigraph: Thomas Moore's *Lalla Rookh: Paradise and the Peri* (1817), 151–2.

*Egypt's palmy groves,*
*Her grots, and sepulchres of kings.*
(MOORE'S *Lalla Rookh*)

The sombre pencil of the dim-grey dawn
  Draws a faint sketch of Egypt to mine eye,
As yet uncoloured by the brilliant morn,
  And her gay orb careering up the sky.

And see! at last he comes in radiant pride,
  Life in his eye, and glory in his ray;
No veiling mists his growing splendour hide,
  And hang their gloom around his golden way.

The flowery region brightens in his smile,
  Her lap of blossoms freights the passing gale,
That robs the odours of each balmy isle,
  Each fragrant field and aromatic vale.

But the first glitter of his rising beam
  Falls on the broad-based pyramids sublime,
As proud to show us with his earliest gleam,
  Those vast and hoary enemies of time.

i *13*. Cp. *Tears, idle tears* 6: 'Fresh as the first beam glittering on a sail'.
*14*. Cp. *A Fragment* 9–10: 'the great Pyramids / Broadbased'.

E'en History's self, whose certain scrutiny
  Few eras in the list of Time beguile,
Pauses, and scans them with astonished eye,
  As unfamiliar with their agèd pile.

Awful, august, magnificent, they tower
  Amid the waste of shifting sands around;
The lapse of year and month and day and hour,
  Alike unfelt, perform the unwearied round.

How often hath yon day-god's burning light,
  From the clear sapphire of his stainless heaven,
Bathed their high peaks in noontide brilliance
    bright,
  Gilded at morn, and purpled them at even!

(ii)

## *THE DEITY

Published *1827*, not reprinted. *1893*: 'A.T. or C.T.'; but all three marked copies of *1827* attribute it to Charles. W. J. Rolfe's edition (1898) cites H.T.: 'Lord Tennyson believes, as I do, that Charles wrote it.' It is in Charles's hand in *T.MS.*

*Immutable–immortal–infinite!*

MILTON [*PL* iii 373]

Where is the wonderful abode,
  The holy, secret, searchless shrine,
Where dwells the immaterial God,
  The all-pervading and benign?

O! that he were revealed to me,
  Fully and palpably displayed
In all the awful majesty
  Of heaven's consummate pomp arrayed–

How would the overwhelming light
  Of his tremendous presence beam!
And how insufferably bright
  Would the broad glow of glory stream!

What though this flesh would fade like grass,
  Before the intensity of day?
One glance at Him who always was,
  The fiercest pangs would well repay.

*28. 1827* note: 'See Savary's *Letters*'. See headnote.
ii *11. insufferably bright*: *Paradise Lost* ix 1084.
*12.* Cp. *Enoch Arden* 574–5: 'glows / And glories of the broad belt'.

When Moses on the mountain's brow
Had met the Eternal face to face,
While anxious Israel stood below,
Wondering and trembling at its base;

His visage, as he downward trod,
Shone starlike on the shrinking crowd,
With lustre borrowed from his God:
They could not brook it, and they bowed.

The mere reflection of the blaze
That lightened round creation's Lord,
Was too puissant for their gaze;
And he that caught it was adored.

Then how ineffably august,
How passing wondrous must He be,
Whose presence lent to earthly dust
Such permanence of brilliancy!

Throned in sequestered sanctity,
And with transcendant glories crowned;
With all his works beneath his eye,
And suns and systems burning round,–

How shall I hymn him? How aspire
His holy Name with song to blend,
And bid my rash and feeble lyre
To such an awless flight ascend?

(iii)

## *ON THE MOON-LIGHT SHINING UPON A FRIEND'S GRAVE

Published *1827*, not reprinted. *1893*: 'A.T.?'; but the text in *T.MS* appears to be in T.'s hand. However, all three marked copies of *1827* attribute it to Charles. Cp. *In Memoriam* lxvii (p. 918).

*17–28. Exodus* xxxiv 29ff.
*31–3.* Cp. Milton, *Upon the Circumcision* 19: 'High thron'd in secret bliss, for us frail dust'.
*34. transcendant glory*: *PL* ii 427.
*35. all his works*: repeatedly in *PL*, and cp. iii 58–9: 'bent down his eye, / His own works and their works at once to view: / About him all the Sanctities of Heaven . . .'. Cp. l. 33.
*36.* Cp. *God and the Universe* 3: 'Rush of Suns, and roll of systems'.

Show not, O Moon! with pure and liquid beam,
That mournful spot, where Memory fears to tread;
Glance on the grove, or quiver in the stream,
Or tip the hills–but shine not on the dead:
It wounds the lonely hearts that still survive,
And after buried friends are doomed to live.

(iv)

## *THE DYING CHRISTIAN

Published *1827*, not reprinted. *1893*: 'A.T. or C.T.' All three marked copies of *1827* attribute it to Charles; in *T.MS* it is in Charles's hand; and W. J. Rolfe's edition (1898) says: 'Quite certainly Charles's, as Lord Tennyson [H.T.] tells me that he also thinks.' The style more resembles that of Charles. But cp. *The Dying Man to His Friend* (p. 153), and *The Wanderer* (p. 845). Epigraph: *When coldness wraps this suffering clay* (1815).

*It cannot die, it cannot stay,*
*But leaves its darkened dust behind.*
(BYRON)

I die–my limbs with icy feeling
Bespeak that Death is near;
His frozen hand each pulse is stealing;
Yet still I do not fear!

There is a hope–not frail as that
Which rests on human things–
The hope of an immortal state,
And with the King of kings!

And ye may gaze upon my brow,
Which is not sad, though pale;
The hope-illumined features show
But little to bewail.

Death should not chase the wonted bloom
From off the Christian's face;
Ill prelude of the bliss to come,
Prepared by heavenly grace.

Lament no more–no longer weep
That I depart from men;
Brief is the intermediate sleep,
And bliss awaits me then!

iv *17–18*. Cp. Shakespeare, *Sonnet 71*: 'No longer mourn for me when I am dead / Than you shall hear the surly sullen bell.'

(v)

## *SWITZERLAND

Published *1827*, not reprinted. *1893*: 'A.T.?' All three marked copies of *1827* attribute it to Charles. It is in Charles's hand in *T.MS.* It describes the struggle against Napoleon from 1798. The epigraph is from the traditional Swiss song. Cp. *The Maid of Savoy* (p. 110).

*Tous les objets de mon amour,*
*Nos clairs ruisseaux,*
*Nos hameaux,*
*Nos coteaux,*
*Nos montagnes?*
(*Ranz des Vaches*)

With Memory's eye,
Thou land of joy!
I view thy cliffs once more;
And though thy plains
Red slaughter stains,
'Tis Freedom's blessèd gore.

Thy woody dells,
And shadowy fells,
Exceed a monarch's halls;
Thy pine-clad hills,
And gushing rills,
And foaming water-falls.

The Gallic foe
Has worked thee woe,
But trumpet never scared thee;
How could he think
That thou would'st shrink,
With all thy rocks to guard thee?

E'en now the Gaul,
That wrought thy fall,
At his own triumph wonders;
So long the strife
For death and life,
So loud our rival thunders!

O! when shall Time
Avenge the crime,
And to our rights restore us?
And bid the Seine
Be choked with slain,
And Paris quake before us?

(vi)

## *SONG [TO SIT BESIDE A CHRYSTAL SPRING]

Published *1827*, not reprinted. *1893* attributed it to T., but all three marked copies of *1827* attribute it to Charles. T. J. Wise's *Bibliography* (1908), i 11, refers to a facsimile of part of *T.MS* which includes this poem–in Charles's hand–from the 'under side of leaf fastened to end paper', and again–in T.'s hand–from the body of the MS. But this leaf is no longer with the MS, and in the body of the MS the hand is doubtful.

To sit beside a chrystal spring,
Cooled by the passing zephyr's wing,
And bend my every thought to thee,
Is life, is bliss, is ecstacy!

And as within that spring I trace
Each line, each feature of my face;
The faithful mirror tells me true–
It tells me that I think of *you!*

## POEMS ATTRIBUTED TO TENNYSON

*Lines on the death of Lord Houghton*, beginning 'Oh! Great Appreciator!'. Attributed to T. by Mrs W. P. Byrne, *Gossip of the Century* (1892), i 256.

*Lines on the christening of the infant daughter of the Duchess of Fife*, and *Lines to the memory of J. R. Lowell*. Attributed in Morton Luce's *Handbook* (1895), p. 430. The latter mistake is due to a misreading of *The Critic* (N.Y.), 22 Aug. 1891, which referred to the death of Lowell, mentioned T., and then quoted a poem by 'the venerable poet', i.e. Whittier.

*Has forgot Britain?*; *Lines on Bewick*; and *Hast thou ever in a travel*. T. J. Wise's *Bibliography* (1908), i 327, 359, 362, cites these attributions, but withdraws them at ii 208.

*Lines to the Picture of a Young Lady of Fashion*. Printed by Sir Charles Tennyson from *H.Lpr 274*. Sir Charles noted the similarity to a poem by W. M. Praed; it is in fact a second version by Praed (*Selected Poems*, ed. K. Allott, 1953, pp. 100–1).

In *Victorian Studies* iv (1961) 195–218, W. D. Paden printed eleven poems from *The Athenaeum*, 1829, which he attributed to T. One poem was subsequently proved to be by Horne (*VS* vi 299). Paden's attributions depend upon internal evidence, evidence which to the present editor and to Sir Charles Tennyson is quite unconvincing since it consists in commonplaces of poetic diction and imagery. A major factor in rejecting these attributions is that nothing from any of these poems appears to have survived in any of the innumerable Tennyson MSS. And as R. H. Super remarked, Paden 'asks us to believe that Tennyson published two poems in the *Athenaeum* in 1828 and nine (or eleven) more in 1829, but included none of these in his volume of 1830; at the same time he avoided sending to the *Athenaeum* any of the poems that did appear in that volume'. Professor Paden will shortly publish his inquiry into the poetry of *The Examiner*; he tentatively proposes for consideration two sonnets on the death of Czar Nicholas, in *The Examiner*, 17 March 1855, signed 'T.'. But again there is the lack of external or MS evidence, and in style the sonnets do not at all resemble T.'s political poems of the 1850s.

# Index of Titles and First Lines

This includes the sections of *In Memoriam*, and the songs from *The Princess*, *Idylls of the King* and elsewhere; it selects the more important material from the Appendices.